THE NEW INTERPRETER'S® BIBLE
ONE-VOLUME COMMENTARY

THE NEW INTERPRETER'S® BIBLE

ONE
VOLUME
COMMENTARY

Edited by

Beverly Roberts Gaventa and David Petersen

ABINGDON PRESS

Nashville

THE NEW INTERPRETER'S® BIBLE
ONE-VOLUME COMMENTARY

Copyright © 2010 by Abingdon Press

Library of Congress Cataloging-in-Publication Data

The New Interpreter's One-Volume Commentary on the Bible / editorial board, David L. Petersen, Beverly R. Gaventa.

    p. cm.
Includes index.
ISBN: 978-0-687-33411-7 (hardback : alk. paper)
1. Bible—Commentaries. I. Petersen, David L. II. Gaventa, Beverly Roberts.
BS491.3.N48 2010
220.7—dc22

2010008235

10 11 12 13 14—8 7 6 5 4 3 2 1
Manufactured in the United States of America

CONTRIBUTORS

PABLO R. ANDIÑACH
ISEDET, Instituto Universitario
ISEDET

DAVID L. BARTLETT
Columbia Theological Seminary

SHANE A. BERG
Princeton Theological Seminary

ADELE BERLIN
University of Maryland, College Park

MARK EDWARD BIDDLE
Baptist Theological Seminary
at Richmond

C. CLIFTON BLACK
Princeton Theological Seminary

M. EUGENE BORING
Brite Divinity School,
Texas Christian University

ALEJANDRO F. BOTTA
Boston University

NANCY R. BOWEN
Earlham School of Religion

JOHN T. CARROLL
Union Theological Seminary

M. DANIEL CARROLL R.
Denver Seminary

STEPHEN L. COOK
Virginia Theological Seminary

CHARLES B. COUSAR
Columbia Theological Seminary

SIDNIE WHITE CRAWFORD
University of Nebraska–Lincoln

JEROME F. D. CREACH
Pittsburgh Theological Seminary

KATHARINE J. DELL
University of Cambridge

FRED W. DOBBS-ALLSOPP
Princeton Theological Seminary

CAROL J. DEMPSEY
University of Portland

DAVID DOWNS
Fuller Theological Seminary

THOMAS B. DOZEMAN
United Theological Seminary

SUSAN GROVE EASTMAN
Duke University

CASEY ELLEDGE
Gustavus Adolphus College

JOHN T. FITZGERALD
University of Miami

STEPHEN E. FOWL
Loyola College in Maryland

SUSAN R. GARRETT
Louisville Presbyterian Theological
Seminary

BEVERLY ROBERTS GAVENTA
Princeton Theological Seminary

MATTHEW GOFF
Florida State University

CONTRIBUTORS

JOHN GOLDINGAY
Fuller Theological Seminary

BARBARA GREEN
Dominican School of Philosophy
and Theology

JOEL B. GREEN
Fuller Theological Seminary

DANIEL J. HARRINGTON
Weston Jesuit School of Theology

SUZANNE WATTS HENDERSON
Queens University

MATTHIAS HENZE
Rice University

RICHARD S. HESS
Denver Seminary

CAMERON BROWN RICHARDSON
HOWARD
The University of the South

JEREMY F. HULTIN
Yale University

ROLF JACOBSON
Luther Seminary

CRAIG S. KEENER
Palmer Theological Seminary of
Eastern University

JAMES M. KENNEDY
Baylor University

JUDITH L. KOVACS
University of Virginia

STEVEN KRAFTCHICK
Emory University

JACQUELINE E. LAPSLEY
Princeton Theological Seminary

DOROTHY ANN LEE
Trinity College Theological School

JOEL M. LeMON
Emory University

AMY-JILL LEVINE
Vanderbilt University

TOD LINAFELT
Georgetown University

THOMAS G. LONG
Emory University

BRUCE W. LONGENECKER
St. Mary's College, South Street,
University of St. Andrews

MARGARET Y. MacDONALD
St. Francis Xavier University

CARLEEN R. MANDOLFO
Colby College

STEVEN L. McKENZIE
Rhodes College

GORDON S. MIKOSKI
Princeton Theological Seminary

JOHN B. F. MILLER
McMurry University

CAROL NEWSOM
Emory University

JAMES NOGALSKI
Baylor University

DENNIS T. OLSON
Princeton Theological Seminary

GEORGE L. PARSENIOS
Princeton Theological Seminary

GLENN D. PEMBERTON
Abilene Christian University

DAVID L. PETERSEN
Emory University

EMERSON B. POWERY
Messiah College

IAIN W. PROVAN
Regent College

KATHARINE DOOB SAKENFELD
Princeton Theological Seminary

EILEEN M. SCHULLER
McMaster University

BARUCH J. SCHWARTZ
Hebrew University of Jerusalem

MATTHEW L. SKINNER
Luther Seminary

BRENT A. STRAWN
Emory University

LOREN STUCKENBRUCK
Princeton Theological Seminary

BETH LaNEEL TANNER
New Brunswick Theological Seminary

PATRICIA K. TULL
Louisville Presbyterian Theological Seminary

RICHARD VALANTASIS
Emory University

J. ROSS WAGNER
Princeton Theological Seminary

ROBERT WALTER WALL
Seattle Pacific University

SZE-KAR WAN
Perkins School of Theology

HAROLD C. WASHINGTON
Saint Paul School of Theology

JAMES W. WATTS
Syracuse University

STEPHEN WESTERHOLM
McMaster University

ROBERT R. WILSON
Yale University

WALTER T. WILSON
Emory University

BENJAMIN G. WRIGHT, III
Lehigh University

JACOB WRIGHT
Emory University

EDITORS' PREFACE

Study of the Bible has experienced a sea change since the *Interpreter's One-Volume Commentary on the Bible* was originally published in 1971. That is true in the arena of scholarly work, where the methods of study have exploded in recent decades, and in the range and number of scholarly interpreters. Alongside historical critical analysis, scholars now draw on literary analysis, social scientific work, postcolonial studies, and feminist criticism—to name only a few perspectives that inform contemporary biblical studies. Moreover, biblical scholars themselves are a more numerous and diverse group of people than was the case forty plus years ago.

What is sometimes overlooked is that the world of Bible study has also changed significantly for pastors and lay teachers of the Bible. In addition to the major shifts in the academy, serious readers of the Bible confront a vast array of resources, and sorting out the serious from the spurious is not always easy. Publications that purport to be exposés of various elements of early Christian history can muddy the waters, and some immensely popular works of fiction complicate matters further by raising questions about what actually is in the Bible and what is not.

Conscious of these developments, we offer this concise, one-volume commentary, confident that it provides both beginning and experienced readers of the Bible with reliable and accessible guidance. The contributors to this volume, who reflect the aforementioned diversity, were invited because of our confidence in both their scholarly competence and their abilities as communicators. No attempt is made to bring their various commentaries into a restrictive conformity, but we did ask all of them to avoid the jargon that too often mars scholarly work. In addition, we invited them to engage in theological reflection about the biblical literature they were addressing.

We also include articles that should make the commentary especially useful for pastors and teachers. In addition to overviews of specific kinds of literature (e.g., the prophetic literature or letters) and introductions to the cultural locations of biblical texts, this volume contains articles on preaching the Bible, teaching the Bible, the creation of the Bible, and the place of the Bible in the church.

As scholars and teachers of the Bible, we ourselves find it an endlessly fascinating book—surprising, challenging, sustaining. It is our hope that this volume will prove a genuinely valuable resource for others who join us in that study.

Beverly Roberts Gaventa
New Testament Editor

David L. Petersen
Old Testament Editor

ABBREVIATIONS AND EXPLANATIONS

BCE	Before the Common Era
CE	Common Era
c.	circa
cf.	compare
ch(s).	chapter(s)
d.	died
Dtr	Deuteronomistic historian
esp.	especially
fem.	feminine
Gk.	Greek
Heb.	Hebrew
l(l).	line(s)
LXX	Septuagint
MS(S)	manuscript(s)
MT	Masoretic Text
n.(n.)	note(s)
NT	New Testament
OL	Old Latin
OT	Old Testament
par.	parallel(s)
pl(s).	plate(s)
sing.	singular
v(v).	verse(s)
Vg	Vulgate

Names of Biblical Books (with the Apocrypha)

Gen	Isa	Pr Azar	John
Exod	Jer	Bel	Acts
Lev	Lam	Sg Three	Rom
Num	Ezek	Sus	1-2 Cor
Deut	Dan	1-2 Esd	Gal
Josh	Hos	Add Esth	Eph
Judg	Joel	Ep Jer	Phil
Ruth	Amos	Jdt	Col
1-2 Sam	Obad	1-2 Macc	1-2 Thess
1-2 Chr	Jonah	3-4 Macc	1-2 Tim
Ezra	Mic	Pr Man	Titus
Neh	Nah	Ps 151	Phlm
Esth	Hab	Sir	Heb
Job	Zeph	Tob	Jas
Ps/Pss	Hag	Wis	1-2 Pet
Prov	Zech	Matt	1-2-3 John
Eccl	Mal	Mark	Jude
Song	Bar	Luke	Rev

Names of Dead Sea Scrolls and Related Texts

Q	Qumran
1Q, 2Q, etc.	Numbered caves of Qumran, yielding written material; sometimes followed by abbreviation of biblical or apocryphal book
4Q385b	Fragmentary remains of Pseudo-Jeremiah which implies that Jeremiah went into Babylonian exile. Also known as *ApocJerc* or 4Q385 16.

Mishnah, Talmud, and Related Literature

m. B.Bat.	*Bava Batra* (Mishnah)
b. B.Bat.	*Bava Batra* (Babylonian Talmud)
y. Shevi'it	*Shevi'it* (Jerusalem Talmud)

Other Rabbinic Works

Song of Songs Rab.	Song of Songs Rabbah

Commonly Used Periodicals, Reference Works, and Serials

AB	Anchor Bible
ABD	Anchor Bible Dictionary
AfOB	Archiv für Orientforschung: Beiheft
ANET	*Ancient Near Eastern Texts Relating to the OT*
BAR	*Biblical Archaeology Review*
Bib	*Biblica*
BibOr	Biblica et orientalia
BKAT	Biblischer Kommentar, Altes Testament
BSac	*Bibliotheca Sacra*
BWANT	Beiträge zur Wissenschaft vom Alten (und Neuen) Testament
BZAW	Beihefte zur ZAW
CBQ	*Catholic Biblical Quarterly*
COS	*The Context of Scripture*
CRAI	Comptes rendus de l'Académie des inscriptions et belles-lettres
FOTL	Forms of Old Testament Literature
HAR	*Hebrew Annual Review*
HAT	Handbuch zum Alten Testament
HBC	Harper Bible Commentary
IB	Interpreter's Bible
IBC	Interpretation: A Bible Commentary for Teaching and Preaching
ICC	International Critical Commentary
Int	Interpretation
JBL	*Journal of Biblical Literature*
JNES	*Journal of Near Eastern Studies*
JNSL	*Journal of Northwest Semitic Languages*
JSOT	*Journal for the Study of the Old Testament*
JSOTSup	Journal for the Study of the Old Testament–Supplement Series
KAT	Kommentar zum Alten Testament
NIB	New Interpreter's Bible
NICOT	New International Commentary on the Old Testament
NIV	New International Version
NRSV	New Revised Standard Version
OTL	Old Testament Library
SBL	Society of Biblical Literature
SBLDS	SBL Dissertation Series
SBLMS	SBL Monograph Series
SBLRBS	Society of Biblical Literature Resources for Biblical Study
SBLSP	Society of Biblical Literature Seminar Papers
SBLSCS	SBL Septuagint and Cognate Studies
SBLSS	SBL Semeia Studies
SBLSymS	Society of Biblical Literature Symposium Series
SBT	Studies in Biblical Theology
TNK	Tanakh (Jewish Publication Society Version)
TSK	Theologische Studien und Kritiken
TZ	*Theologische Zeitschrift*
VT	*Vetus Testamentum*
VTSup	Vetus Testamentum, Supplements
WBC	Word Biblical Commentary
ZAW	*Zeitschrift für die alttestamentliche Wissenschaft*

CONTENTS

CONTENTS

CONTENTS

GENESIS

Dennis T. Olson

OVERVIEW

The book of Genesis brings together stories about the beginning of the world and humanity (Gen 1–11) with stories about the beginning of the particular people of Israel and their earliest ancestors (Gen 12–50). As such, Genesis is important in setting God's interaction and concern with God's specially chosen people, Israel, within the broader universal horizon of God's interaction and concern for all humanity and all creation.

Genesis 1–11 recount God's good creation of the heavens and the earth as well as repeated incidents of humans disobeying God, hurting fellow humans, and being discontent with what they are—human creatures tied to the earth. The several human rebellions are followed by devastating consequences, but also by God's continued blessing of humanity and divine acts of mercy and restraint. However, as the reader reaches the end of Gen 11, it is clear that the world and humanity have not been restored to the harmony and goodness that God had intended for God's creation in Gen 1. God's several attempts to deal with humanity as a whole prove less than fully successful. Thus, God moves to try a new strategy.

In Gen 12–50, God's new venture involves the selection of one special family within all the families of the earth who would become the vehicle of God's blessing of all the other "families of the earth" (Gen 12:3). God focuses on the family of Abraham and Sarah, the ancestors of the people of Israel. Genesis 12–50 is primarily a series of family stories involving Israel's ancestors and their interactions with other nations. The ancestors originate in Mesopotamia (modern-day Iraq), travel to Canaan (modern-day Israel/Palestine), and then move back and forth among the lands of Canaan, Egypt, and Mesopotamia.

Most modern scholars agree that the book of Genesis developed through several stages of collecting, writing, and editing over hundreds of years, sometime between the 8th and 5th centuries BCE. In this period, Israel was forced to reflect on its role as God's chosen nation as it interacted with the successive empires, cultures, and religions of Assyria, Babylon, and Persia as well as other neighboring nations. In particular, Israel's experience of forced migration from the promised land of Judah and the destruction of the holy city of Jerusalem by an army of the Babylonian empire in 587 BCE evoked a definitive reexamination of its core traditions and self-understanding as the people of God among the other nations of the world. The Babylonian exile, however, only solidified and sharpened what ancient Israel had learned earlier and continued to learn at various points throughout its history. God had chosen Israel from among the nations. God would stay committed to God's people, even though Israel was a young nation in comparison to the older and more powerful empires of the world. God would continue to bless Israel's ancestors, even though they often endured severe struggles, suffering, and near death, all of which appeared at the time to contradict God's promises to God's people. In the end, Genesis proclaims, God will be faithful.

OUTLINE

I. The Creation of the World and the Beginnings of Humankind (1:1–11:32)

    A. Two Stories of Creation (1:1–2:25)
        1:1–2:3. The First Creation Story—The Heavens and the Earth
        2:4–25. The Second Creation Story—The Garden of Eden

    B. Two Disobedience Stories (3:1–4:26)
        3:1–24. Adam and Eve—The First Act of Human Disobedience
        4:1–26. Cain Murders Abel—The Second Act of Human Disobedience

    C. Ten Generations from Adam and Eve to Noah (5:1–32)

    D. Breaking the Boundary Between Divine and Human—The Birth of Giants (6:1–4)

    E. The Flood Story (6:5–9:29)
        6:5–22. God Reveals to Noah the Plan for the Flood and the Ark

DETAILED ANALYSIS

I. The Creation of the World and the Beginnings of Humankind (1:1–11:32)

The opening chapters of Genesis describe God's continuing commitment to sustain and bless God's good creation and its inhabitants, including all human beings. God does so in spite of human disobedience and wrongdoing that leads to broken relationships between humans and God (Gen 3), humans and one another (Gen 4; 6), and also humans and non-human creation (3:15, 17–19;

9:1–5). The stories of Gen 1–11 contain elements that are mythic in character and not part of our normal human experience: a talking snake (3:1), human lifetimes that last nearly a thousand years (5:5), divine beings called "sons of God" who come to earth and procreate with humans (6:1–4), a catastrophic worldwide flood (7:17–24), and a time when all people of the world spoke only one language (11:1). Although some of these elements may seem strange and otherworldly, the stories of Gen 1–11 use these and other elements to explore profound and enduring truths about reality and the interactions of God, humans, and the world.

A. Two Stories of Creation (1:1–2:25)

The Bible begins by placing two different stories about the creation of the world side by side in Gen 1 and 2. These two versions arose at different times in Israel's history. Most scholars argue that the date of the composition of the creation story in Gen 2:4–24 is earlier than the composition of the creation story in Gen 1:1–2:3. Indeed, the earlier creation story reflects the first part of an extended tradition that weaves intermittently in and out of the book of Genesis. Some scholars understand this earlier tradition, sometimes termed by scholars as the Yahwist tradition (abbreviated as J from the German spelling *Jahweh*), as extending not only through Genesis but intermittently throughout much of the Pentateuch (the five books of Genesis-Deuteronomy). Other scholars would deny such a view, arguing instead that this earlier tradition exists only in Genesis. For our purposes, we will refer to this earlier set of traditions in Genesis as the "non-Priestly" tradition, differentiated from the later Priestly tradition which begins in Gen 1 and then extends into Exodus, Leviticus, and Numbers.

The later creation story in Gen 1:1–2:3, the Priestly version, likely came together in its present form at a later time than the Gen 2 creation account, probably during or after the Babylonian exile of the sixth century BCE. The key differences between the Priestly (P) creation story and the earlier non-Priestly creation story include the following: the divine name ("God" in P; "Lord God" in non-P); the state of the world before creation begins (watery chaos in P–1:2; dry desert in non-P–2:5–6); the order or sequence of what is created (six days with man and woman created together at the same time as the last of the creatures in P; the man created first, then the animals, and finally the woman in non-P); the mode of God's creating (by divine words of command in P–1:3, 6, 9; by God "forming," "planting," "making" in non-P–2:7, 8, 19, 22); the arena of creation (cosmic with the heavens and the earth in P; a smaller scale and localized garden of Eden in non-P); the portrayal of God (in full control, orderly, and transcendent in P; more intimate, hands-on, and experimental in non-P); and in literary style (a carefully ordered framework of seven days with a litany of repetitions in P; a more haphazard narrative of trial and error in non-P).

This pairing of two different creation stories at the beginning of Genesis illustrates a characteristic mode by which Genesis often renders truth. Genesis frequently sets up a dialogue among a variety of voices and stories that provide different but complementary angles of insight into a given event, theme, or relationship. Genesis thereby invites the reader to see a fuller truth by holding different but complementary viewpoints together at the same time.

1:1–2:3. The First Creation Story—The Heavens and the Earth. The first version of the creation story (Gen 1:1–2:3) begins with the world as a dark and formless void that hangs over primeval waters of chaos ("the deep"). God's "wind" (*ruakh*), which can also mean "spirit" or "breath," enters into this dark and empty chaos, joined with a divine word of command, "Let there be light" (v. 1). This "spirit/wind" coupled with God's command begins to create out of the earlier chaos an ordered, interdependent, and organic system that sustains life, goodness, and a balance of work and rest. Creation happens in Gen 1 within the framework and structure of a seven-day week. During the first three days of creation, God creates three broad regions into which God will later place their proper inhabitants: light/darkness, sky/sea, and dry land (1:3–13). God then creates the occupants of each region. The sun, moon, and stars inhabit and "rule over" the regions of light and dark (Day Four). Sea creatures (including "the great sea monsters") and birds inhabit the sea and sky (Day Five). Animals and humans occupy the dry land (1:14–31).

The creation story slows down and spends some time on the creation of the human, providing important insights into the nature and vocation of the human within God's creation. First of all, God commands, "Let us make humankind in our image, according to our likeness" (1:26). God is speaking here to other heavenly beings, reflecting the ancient motif of a heavenly community of divine beings (1 Kgs 22, Job 1, Ps 82, Isa 6). God's motivation for creation is not because God is lonely in the universe. Rather, creation involves God's desire for deepening and broadening the community of relationships that already exists in the divine realm. In creation, God's pre-existing experience of community spills over into a new arena and dimension, the realm of time (created by the alternation of light and dark, day and night) and space (the various ordered regions of sky, sea, and land).

Second, the human is created in God's "image" or "likeness" (1:26), reflecting a practice among ancient Near Eastern kings who erected stone statues or images of themselves throughout their realm as an extension and reminder of the king's dominion over the region. Given this background, humans are called to be living images or likenesses of God and extensions of God's dominion over all the earth. God entrusts humans with responsibility to exercise their dominion (1:28) in God's image of care and concern for all creation, including its most vulnerable members (see the model of a good Israelite king's "dominion" in Ps 72:8–14).

Third, humans are created together in community from the very beginning with both genders reflecting "the image of God": "in the image of God he created them, male and female he created them" (1:27). The image of God is neither exclusively male nor female but somehow encompasses both (cf. Deut 4:16).

Finally, the humans are the last in the series of created regions and creatures, all of which God evaluates as being "very good" (1:31). Although each part was pronounced "good" earlier (1:4, 12, 18, 21), it is only when the whole community of interdependent creatures and parts work together to foster life and blessing that God pronounces it all as "very good." Creation is "good," but it is not perfect or without continuing threats of chaos, disorder, and brokenness. The primeval waters of chaos were pushed by God's great dome (1:6–7) to the edges above and by the land below, but the threatening waters do not disappear. The waters of chaos remain as an element of the created order and will return later in the Genesis narrative in the flood narrative (Gen 7:11). God's world does not appear as a perfect paradise but rather as a "very good" creation (1:31).

After six days of work, God "rested on the seventh day" and "hallowed it" (2:2–3). This text is cited as the explanation for one of the Ten Commandments in Exod 20:8–11, mandating that the seventh day of every week be set aside as a day of rest and no work. The Sabbath in the Priestly tradition is anchored in creation so that the requirement of regular sabbath rest is built into every creature, both humans and animals, both Israelites and non-Israelites ("your son and daughter ... the alien resident in your town ... your livestock"–Exod 20:10). By resting on the Sabbath, God willingly enters into and becomes subject to the created framework of human time that God has just created. This becomes the first instance of God's gracious accommodation or self-limiting for the sake of God's creation. God's example also becomes a pedagogical model that promotes a healthy balance of work and rest, care of creation, and worship of the Creator.

2:4–25. The Second Creation Story—The Garden of Eden. Genesis 2:4 contains a recurring formulaic sentence that marks the beginning of new sections throughout Genesis: "These are the generations of" (sometimes translated as "these are the stories of" or "these are the descendants of": Gen 2:4; 6:9; 10:1; 11:27; 25:19; 37:2). Here it marks the beginning of a second creation story that has its own additional heading: "In the day that the LORD God made the earth and the heavens" (cf. Gen 1:1).

This second creation account begins with the image of a dry desert or wilderness. Like the waters of chaos that began the creation story in Gen 1, the wilderness is a frequent biblical image of a fearful place of chaos, evil, and death (Isa 21:1–3; 43:15–21). Two things are required to turn this dry desert into a flourishing garden of life: water and someone to till the ground. A stream appears and waters the ground (2:6). Meanwhile, the Lord God "forms" a man (*'adam*) from the dust of the ground (*'adamah*). The verb "forms" is a verb used of a potter who molds clay and portrays God's intimate involvement in the creative process. The Hebrew word play between "man" (*'adam*) and "ground" ('adamah) signifies the bond between the earth and the human earth creature who was created from the dust and who, in death, will return to dust (Gen 3:19). What distinguishes the human is that God breathes into the human lump of clay "the breath (ruakh) of life," and only then does the human become "a living being." Life is an intimately given divine gift with every human breath a reminder of the giftedness of life.

God's hands-on interaction continues in Gen 2:8–9 with God planting a lush garden of beauty and bounty in Eden. Two fruit trees stand at the center of the garden, the "tree of life" and the "tree of the knowledge of good and evil." These two trees will come into play later in the narrative (Gen 2:17; 3:1–7, 22–24). The garden of Eden is not a vacation resort for the human but a work-place in which the human exercises a vocation: to "till and keep" the garden (2:15). Alongside this vocational responsibility is also freedom ("you may freely eat of every tree"–2:16) mixed with one limiting prohibition ("but of the tree of the knowledge of good and evil you shall not eat, for in the day that you eat of it you shall [the Hebrew is emphatic—add 'surely'] die"–2:17). This combi-nation of positive responsibilities, negative limits, and wide freedoms sets the stage both for the exuberant joys as well as the deep tragedies of human existence, "the knowledge of good" and "the knowledge of evil."

The Lord God evaluates the garden and its human caretaker and realizes that something is lacking. "It is not good that the man should be alone." God recognizes that the human is an inherently social creature, in need of "a helper as his partner" (2:18). The Hebrew word for "helper" ('ezer) does not imply one of lower status or an inferior assistant. Rather, the "helper" in the Old Testament is often someone of an equal or higher status in comparison to the one being helped. God is often called a "helper" to those in need else-where in Scripture (Ps 10:14; 54:4).

God begins by creating all the animals and inviting the human to name them and thereby define their essence or character (2:18–20). God welcomes the human as a co-creator with God. However, the animals fail to address fully the human yearning for community. As a result, God tries another strategy. God puts the human to sleep, takes out one of the human's ribs, and forms

the rib into a second human being, a woman (2:21–22). Instantly, the man recognizes in the woman the fulfillment of the deep yearning for relationship as he joyfully proclaims: "This at last is bone of my bones and flesh of my flesh ... she shall be called Woman ('ishshah) because she was taken out of Man ('ish)" (2:23). Bound together in an intimate and trusting relationship, the two humans "become one flesh," naked, open, vulner-able, trusting, and "not ashamed" (2:24–25).

B. Two Disobedience Stories (3:1–4:26)

Without warning, the idyllic scene of human community and love in the lush garden of Eden at the end of Gen 2 is suddenly and irrevocably shattered in the two paired stories of disobedi-ence and murder that follow in Gen 3 and 4. The two chapters contain a number of verbal and thematic parallels that bind them together. Thus, for example, both stories in Gen 3 and 4 portray the lure of sin as a crafty animal (the shrewd serpent in 3:1–5; an animal lurking at the door in 4:7). The woman's "desire" for the man (Gen 3:16) parallels sin's "desire" for Cain (4:7). God asks the humans in both stories, "Where?" (3:9; 4:9). Phrases such as "cursed is/from the ground" 3:17; 4:11), "when you work the ground" (3:18; 4:12), and "east (of the garden) of Eden" (3:24; 4:16) are repeated in both narratives. The father (Adam) and son (Cain) share a number of simi-larities. Both give in to temptation and sin. Both seek to shift blame to someone else (the woman Eve, Abel). Both in the end try to blame God for their actions (Adam–"the woman whom you gave to be with me"–3:12; Cain–"Am I my brother's keeper?" [implying no, God is]–4:9). The key dif-ference between Adam and Cain is that Adam is overly passive and silent in Gen 3 while Cain is overly aggressive and violent in Gen 4.

3:1–24. Adam and Eve—The First Act of Human Disobedience. The story of the serpent's tempta-tion of Adam and Eve in Gen 3 does not so much explain the origins of sin and evil in the world as depict the enduring realities of the human con-dition. Genesis 3 explores the humans' yearning to go beyond the limits within which they were created, leading in a series of steps to temptation, transgression, and unforeseen consequences that flow out of such transgressions. All of this occurs within the context of the judgment of God but also the even stronger mercy of God.

The serpent in the garden is one of God's own creatures, excelling in being "more crafty" than any other wild animal (3:1). The serpent is not portrayed as Satan or an alien creature that has invaded the garden. The serpent simply asks questions and makes claims that appeal to the seeds of a yearning or suspicion that seem to be already present in the woman's mind. The serpent assures the woman that she would not die from eating the forbidden fruit. She would only gain knowledge, have her eyes opened, and would become "like God, knowing good and evil" (3:5). The woman is lured by the special fruit, its attraction as "good for food," its beauty as "a delight to the eyes," and its capacity "to make one wise" (3:6). She takes the fruit and then eats it (3:6).

What comes next is a bit of a surprise. She gives the fruit also to her husband "who was with her." The man was presumably present with her all along during the dialogue with the serpent. Without question or comment, the text simply says, "and he ate" (3:7). Here it is clear that the story does not intend to implicate the woman alone as uniquely at fault for the act of disobedience in the garden. Both the woman and the man were present with the serpent, and both are held accountable for their action and receive consequences for their transgression of the limits that God had set for their own good. By eating the fruit, their eyes were indeed opened, as the serpent had promised. However, their eyes were not opened to some glorious knowledge of a divine nature but rather to the mundane awareness that they were naked, ashamed, and now in need of clothing to hide behind.

The intimacy of God's presence in the garden (Gen 2) continues in Gen 3 as God appears, "walking in the garden at the time of the evening breeze" (3:8). For the first time, the humans hide from God. As God often does in the Bible, God comes looking for God's rebellious people. God interrogates the humans and discovers the transgression. The man refuses to accept responsibility, blaming instead the woman but also ultimately blaming God: "the woman whom you [God] gave to be with me, she gave me fruit" (3:12). The woman in turn blames the serpent. God then describes the consequences that will flow out of

transgression of human limits. The serpent loses his legs and becomes a creature repulsive to humans (3:14–15). The woman will experience increased pain in childbirth and inequality in her relationship with the man (3:16). The man will find his labor more difficult and his relationship with the land far more complicated (3:17–19).

God curses the serpent (3:14) and the ground (3:17) but not the humans themselves. God's mercy emerges as God exchanges the prickly fig-leaf clothing that the humans had made themselves (3:7) for softer garments of skins that God makes for them (3:21). Moreover, although God had said that the humans would "surely die" on the very day they ate of the forbidden fruit (2:17), God rescinds the immediate death penalty by allowing them to live. Eve becomes "the mother of all living" (3:20). At the same time, however, God imposes a limit on the length of human life by sending the humans forever out of the garden of Eden lest they eat of the other tree, the tree of life, and live forever (3:22–24). Adam and Eve will live long enough to have children in order that the human race may continue, but they themselves will not live forever. They will go back to the ground from which they came: "you are dust, and to dust you shall return" (3:19; see 2:7).

4:1–26. Cain Murders Abel—The Second Act of Human Disobedience. The phrase that begins the chapter, "now the man knew his wife Eve," signifies in this case the intimate knowledge of sexual union. Adam had earlier named Eve (3:20), and now Eve takes her turn and names a man, her son Cain whom she acknowledges as a gift from God (4:1). God continues to bless the humans in spite of their disobedience. Eve also gives birth to a second son, Abel.

Abel grows up as a sheep herder, and Cain is a farmer. They offer sacrifices to God, and God accepts Abel's animal offering but not Cain's grain offering. The text is not interested in explaining why God chose the sacrifice of Abel (the younger son) but not the sacrifice of Cain (the elder son). Rather, the text portrays the human reality that human envy, jealousy, and shame often lead to violence. Cain lures his brother Abel into the field and kills him. God appears and interrogates Cain about his brother's whereabouts. Cain claims not to know, asking God, "Am I my brother's keeper" (3:9). The question is a cynical one, implying that God bears the responsibility if anything has happened to Abel because God is traditionally supposed to be the one who "keeps" or "guards" God's people (Ps 121:5; Isa 27:3).

Abel's spilled blood cries out to God "from the ground" (3:10). Human and animal blood was understood in ancient Israel to contain the life force of an individual and thus was considered sacred. Thus, any spilling of blood was a matter that cried out for God's attention (Deut 12:23–24; Lev 17:10–14). The consequences for the farmer Cain are disastrous. The ground from which Abel's blood cried out will no longer produce food abundantly (4:11). Moreover, Cain will be forced to migrate from his land and be a fugitive and wanderer in foreign lands, rendering him vulnerable to attack, abuse and the possibility of blood revenge for his murder. However, in God's mercy, God places a protective mark on Cain that signifies that anyone who kills Cain will be avenged seven times over (3:15). God mercifully spares Cain from the death penalty for his murder, not enforcing the law of equal consequences found elsewhere in the Old Testament: "an eye for an eye, a life for a life" (Exod 21:24; Lev 24:20; Deut 19:21).

A new generation is born after Cain. Some humans begin to build cities (3:17), some herd sheep (4:20), some make music (4:21), and some become metal workers. The diversification of human culture and vocations is a sign of God's hidden activity of blessing. Lamech is a descendant of Cain who also exemplifies the continuing negative and violent side of the human condition as he boasts of initiating a spiral of violence by killing a man who had wounded him, promising to avenge anyone who tries to hurt him not just seven times (as with Cain) but seventy-seven times over. For him, violence and vengeance have no limits.

C. Ten Generations from Adam and Eve to Noah (5:1–32)

The listing of ten generations in Gen 5 provides a connecting bridge between the story of Adam and Eve (Gen 2–4) and the next major story of Noah and the flood (Gen 6–9). The genealogy in Gen 11:10–26 will trace the line from Noah's son Shem to Abraham. The family tree in Gen 46:8–27 lists in successive generations the descendants of Abraham's grandson Jacob. The listing of

generations illustrates the specific working out of God's blessing and human obedience of God's command to "be fruitful and multiply, and fill the earth" (Gen 1:28).

D. Breaking the Boundary Between Divine and Human—The Birth of Giants (6:1–4)

Thus far in Genesis, humans have tried to become "like God" (3:5), one human murdered a brother (4:8), and another human pledged an increasing spiral of violence and revenge against anyone who threatened him (4:23–24). The erosion and fracturing of God's "good" creation (1:31) steps up a notch with the short story about the transgression of the created boundary between heaven and earth. Divine beings called "the sons of God" come down to earth and engage in sexual unions with "daughters of humans," creating a super race of giant legendary warriors called "Nephilim" (Heb.: "Fallen Ones"). Later in Israel's story, Israelite spies will claim to have spotted the giant Nephilim warriors fighting for the Canaanites in the land of Canaan (Num 13:32–33). Some later Jewish and Christians interpreters of the Bible expanded on the story of the Nephilim, associating them with the origin of Satan or the devil as a rebellious "fallen angel" who waged war against God's people. In the present text, however, this breach of a boundary between heaven and earth is a sign of cosmic rupture and another threat to God's created order.

This breach of the divine-human boundary causes God to limit the life spans of humans even further, from an average of 800–900 years in Gen 5 to a maximum limit of 120 years in Gen 6:3. Later biblical tradition will speak of a normal limit of 70–80 years (Ps 90:10). The spread of sin and violence in creation correlates with the advancing power of death and mortality in human lives.

E. The Flood Story (6:5–9:29)

The increasing violence, corruption, and breakdown among humans result in God's decision to try a new strategy. God decides to start over with a remnant of all the species of non-human creation along with a man named Noah and his family. Noah will build an ark in which his family and pairs of all creatures will be spared while the rest of humanity and all other land creatures will be destroyed in a worldwide flood.

A number of variations, doublets, and other tensions in the story of Noah have suggested to many scholars that two originally distinct versions of the great flood story in Gen 6–9 have been woven together to form the present combined narrative. The style and elements of these two versions seem to correspond to the Priestly tradition that is evident in Gen 1, on one hand, and to the non-Priestly version that appears in the Gen 2 creation story, on the other. Unlike Gen 1–2 where the P and non-P accounts are juxtaposed and separate, the non-P and P accounts in Gen 6–9 are interwoven. The combination of the two versions of the flood (Priestly and non-Priestly) into one narrative provides a way of preserving the richness of divergent traditions about the flood while also maintaining a single story line, albeit with some tensions. Ancient Israelite writers likely borrowed and adapted some elements of the biblical flood story from an earlier epic tradition of a great primeval flood that had roots in Mesopotamia where major destructive floods actually occurred in ancient times. Archaeologists have uncovered multiple older Mesopotamian versions of an ancient flood story, e.g., in the Atrahasis myth and the epic of Gilgamesh, which contain numerous elements similar to the biblical account of Noah and the flood.

6:5–22. God Reveals to Noah the Plan for the Flood and the Ark.

Two separate introductions to the flood story stand side by side, one Priestly version in 6:9–22 and a non-Priestly version in 6:5–8 and 7:1–5. The non-Priestly version emphasizes the "wickedness of humankind" and the "thoughts of their hearts" as "only evil continually" (6:5). Wickedness for the non-P version focused on the inclinations of the human heart. The non-Priestly portrait of "the LORD" is also highly interior, emotive, and regretful: "The LORD was sorry" for creating humankind "and it grieved him to his heart" (6:7).

The Priestly version emphasizes a broader cosmic corruption including "all flesh" and the whole earth: "Now the earth was corrupt in God's sight, and the earth was filled with violence ... all flesh had corrupted its ways upon the earth" (11:13). God resolves to destroy "all flesh ... along with the earth" (6:13). Corruption for P infects the whole creation—"everything that is on the earth" (6:17). Corruption is seen not so much in

the interior life of humans but in outward acts of "violence" (6:11, 13). In the Priestly portrait of God, there is no mention of God's emotional life. God seems more resolved and in control: "I have determined to make an end of all flesh" (6:13).

God establishes a covenant in which God promises Noah, his family, and all the ark's creatures that God will "keep them alive" (6:18–19). Noah's obligations in this covenant is to build the ark and to collect two of every kind of animal, male and female, onto the ark. The content of the covenant will be expanded in more detail after the conclusion of the flood in 9:8–17.

7:1–8:19. The Great Flood.

Two versions of the great flood are combined with one another. In the non-Priestly version in 7:12, the flood is the result of a forty-day rain. In the Priestly version in 7:11, the flood results from the fountains of the deep from under the earth gushing forth from below and "the windows of the heavens" being opened from above, letting in the waters of chaos that God had earlier pushed up and back with the dome that formed the sky in the Priestly creation story (Gen 1:6–7). In the Priestly version, this swelling up of the waters of chaos lasts 150 days (7:24).

The most important verse in the whole flood story occurs in 8:1: "But God remembered Noah" and all the animals that were with him. This divine remembering involves recalling the covenant promise that God had made earlier in 6:18, a promise to save their lives and through them to establish and populate a new creation. The image of God making a "wind" (ruakh, "wind/breath/spirit") blow over the flood waters recalls God's "wind" blowing over the primeval waters of chaos in the Priestly creation story in Gen 1:2. As the waters recede, Noah sends out a series of birds until one bird does not return, indicating that the bird has found dry land; the flood is over. God then commands Noah and all his passengers to disembark from the ark in order to "be fruitful and multiply on the earth," a reassertion of God's original command in the Priestly creation story in Gen 1:28. A new creation has emerged.

8:20–9:17. God's Promise and Covenant with Noah.

The flood story concludes with two accounts of God's promise to Noah: a non-Priestly version (8:20–22) and an expanded Priestly version of God's covenant (9:1–17). In the non-

Priestly promise, Noah builds an altar and offers burnt offerings to God of every clean animal and bird that was on the ark. The Lord smells "the pleasing odor" of the sacrifices and responds with a promise to "never again curse the ground because of humankind." The Lord had earlier "cursed the ground" because of Adam (Gen 3:17) and Cain (Gen 4:11). Moreover, God promises never again to "destroy every living creature as I have done" (8:21). God resolves to preserve the life-giving rhythms of seedtime and harvest, summer and winter, day and night that sustain food production and life. God has learned that "the inclination of the human heart is evil from youth" (8:21), and not even a drastic purification of humanity through a flood could erase this evil inclination. God will need to learn how to work with humans whose inner inclinations are "evil from youth," since God has also committed to keep the human experiment alive and to continue to bless it.

The Priestly version of God's promise and covenant at the end of the flood story in 9:1–17 repeats the life-affirming divine command in the Priestly creation account in Gen 1:28: "be fruitful and multiply, and fill the earth" (9:1). But this "new creation" after the flood in Gen 9 also bears a shadow side. In the Priestly creation story, humans were granted an exclusively vegetarian diet (Gen 1:29). In Gen 9, humans are allowed to eat the meat of animals and birds ("just as I gave you green plants, I give you everything"–9:3). However, humans are not to eat any flesh with its blood because the blood of a creature is understood to contain the essence of its life (9:4). Thus, later laws will prescribe that the blood of any animal slaughtered for meat must be drained from the animal into the ground before the flesh is eaten as a sign that all life, human and animal, belongs ultimately to God and should be returned to God (Deut 12:23–25). The taking of life, and especially the taking of a human life, is a serious threat to the sanctity of life and the purity of a community "for in his own image God made humankind" (9:6). Thus, the taking of any life is a matter of sacred and divine concern. This idea is related to the Priestly concern for the "violence" of humankind at the beginning of the flood story (6:11, 13). God in effect concedes that humans will continue to be violent and to shed the blood of others even in this new post-flood world.

In spite of this prospect of continuing human violence, God pledges to renew the covenant first made with Noah at the beginning of the flood (6:18). Never again will God destroy the earth with a flood (9:8–12). God places the rainbow in the sky as a sign of this covenantal promise, a visual aid by which God will remember this covenant that God had made "between me and all flesh that is on the earth" (9:17). In this way, God enters into a covenant relationship with all creatures of the earth, marked by the visual sign of the rainbow. Just as human life is precious because humans are made in the image of God, so the life of all the earth's creatures is precious because God is in a covenant relationship with them.

9:18–10:32. The Descendants of Noah. Noah has three sons and from them "the whole earth was peopled" (9:18). Shem is pictured as the ancestor of the Semitic people who will come to include the people of Israel (see 10:21–31). Ham is the ancestor of the Hamitic peoples, including Egypt and other territories under Egypt's control, which included Canaan at some points in its history. Thus, Ham is portrayed as having a son named Canaan (see 10:6–20). Japheth is associated with the peoples who were north and west of Canaan in Asia Minor, Greece, and the coastland of the Mediterranean (see 10:2–5).

There is immediate evidence that the flood was not a successful strategy for eradicating human corruption. Just as the flood story had begun with an enigmatic and brief story about sexual irregularity with sons of God transgressing creational boundaries with daughters of humankind (Gen 6:1–4), so the flood story ends with another enigmatic and brief story about sexual impropriety with Noah and his sons. Noah makes wine, becomes intoxicated, lies naked in his tent, and his son Ham (father of Canaan) sees "the nakedness of his father" (9:22). "Seeing the nakedness" of another person may suggest some form of incest or other sexual taboo (Lev 18:6–8, 24–30). When Noah discovers what Ham had done, Noah curses Ham indirectly by cursing Ham's son Canaan and condemning him and his descendants to become slaves to Shem, an allusion to Israel's eventual conquest of the Canaanites in the book of Joshua. The curse of slavery imposed on the Egyptian/African Ham and Canaan has tragically and wrongly been used by some in the history of biblical interpretation as justification and warrant for American slavery of African Americans and for the oppression of other colonized peoples.

The segmented genealogy in Gen 10:1–32 lists the three sons of Noah and all their children, grandchildren and great grandchildren who represent diverse nations and peoples of the ancient Near East. These segmented genealogies serve throughout the book of Genesis to keep the larger family of all humankind in view as part of God's continuing concern and care even as the narrative will increasingly focus its attention on one particular family line of Abraham and Sarah and their descendants who will become God's specially chosen people, Israel.

One name in Gen 10 deserves special mention. Genesis 10:8–12 describes a legendary warrior named Nimrod of the "land of Shinar," which is another name for the land of Babylon or Babel, the empire responsible for the destruction of the city of Jerusalem and the exile of much of its population in 587 BCE (10:10). Nimrod is also credited with building "the great city" of Nineveh, the capital of the Assyrian empire, which conquered the northern kingdom in 722 BCE (10:11–12; see Mic 5:5–6 where Assyria is described as "the land of Nimrod"). Thus, Nimrod is an ancient figure who represents in Israel's cultural memory the military might of the two highly militarized and oppressive empires under which Israel suffered as a nation, both Babylon and Assyria. This imperial allusion will form important background to the story of the tower of Babel, which is set in Nimrod's "land of Shinar" (11:2).

F. The Tower of Babel and the Confusion of Human Language (11:1–9)

The listing of the spread of nations among the various lands of the known world in Gen 10 sets the stage for the story of the tower of Babel in Gen 11. The opening verse pictures an idyllic scenario: the peoples of all the earth communicated with ease, all speaking the same language (11:1). All the earth's people migrate together and settle "in the land of Shinar," another name for the land of Babylon (10:10). This is the land associated with the first mighty and legendary warrior Nimrod, an icon of imperial militarism (10:8–12). The world community decides to build a great brick city and "a tower with its top in the heavens" and thereby

"make a name for ourselves" (11:4). In a Babylonian context, the tower to the heavens may allude to tall, pyramid-like structures called ziggurats, which ancient Babylonian priests would ascend to offer sacrifices to their gods. In this story, however, the humans do not seek to praise the name of their gods but to make a name for themselves. They fear being "scattered abroad upon the face of the whole earth" (11:4); however, what they fear is precisely what will happen to them at the end of the story (11:9).

Ironically, the Lord must "come down" from the heavens to see the supposedly enormous building project that the humans believe reaches to the heavens (11:4–5). The Lord notes that they are all one people with one language, a unified world community, and now nothing they wish to do "will be impossible for them" (11:6). The larger literary context of Gen 1–11 suggests that God does not feel threatened or jealous of the humans' city and tower building. Rather, God's concern is what humans, unbridled by necessary restraints on human inclinations and power, will do to one another. The disobedience of Adam and Eve and their desire to move beyond their human limits "to be like God" (Gen 3:5) led to the next generation's horror of sibling murder as Cain killed his own brother Abel (4:8). The violence spiraled in Lamech's boast of unrestrained violence against anyone who hurt him (4:23–24). The chaotic breaking of boundaries between heaven and earth in the Nephilim story (Gen 6:1–4) created a super race of giants and military warriors, legendary purveyors of violence. God's desire to limit the violence of humans against other humans was a key reason for God's sending of the flood to try to start over with a new world (6:11, 13). In Gen 10, the land of Shinar is the "land of Nimrod," the legendary warrior and fighter associated with the imperial powers of Assyria and Babylon in ancient Israel's past.

Thus in the tower of Babel story, God sees humanity again pushing against its limits toward an imperial consolidation of power. There is nothing inherently wrong with humans wanting to have a name for themselves. God will grant a great name as a gift to Abram in the very next chapter (12:2). However, God knows from long experience with humans that the human yearning and inclination to be something other than human, to be like God, to leave earth and transgress the boundary of the divine, leads inevitably to suffering, abuse of power, violence, and oppression. The land of Shinar, the land of Nimrod, Babylon, and Assyria all represent the potential horrors of unrestrained empires that drain their client states of wealth, dignity, people, and spirit. This is what God fears in Gen 11: with the consolidation of military and political power in one empire, "nothing that they propose to do will now be impossible for them" (11:6). Their imperial unity will only result in the exponential growth of suffering, oppression, and violence.

In response, the Lord proposes to other heavenly beings in the divine council ("let us go down," see Gen 1:26) that they confuse the humans' language and scatter the humans abroad across the face of the earth (11:7–8). Divided now by language, culture, and territory, the humans abandon the building of their great unified city and tower. The place is called "Babel" which in the Babylonian language originally meant "Gate of God." However, the biblical storyteller associates the name "Babel" with a Hebrew verb meaning "to confuse" (*balal*), "because there the LORD confused the language of all the earth" (11:9). Ancient Israel's long and tortured history with many different empires (Egypt, Assyria, Babylon, Persia, Greece) demonstrated the truth of the tower of Babel story. Empires would rise and seek to unify diverse nations and peoples under one purpose and power. However, God would ensure that every empire would eventually fall to ruin as God judged and limited the inevitable tendency of empires to abuse their power, oppress their citizens, and overextend themselves with unbridled military violence.

G. The Family Line from Shem to Abraham (11:10–32)

The genealogy in Gen 11:10–32 begins with Noah's son, Shem, and extends for ten generations (the same number as in Gen 5), ending with Abram and his wife, Sarai. Abram and Sarai will become the originating ancestors of the people of Israel (later called Abraham and Sarah; 17:5, 15). Thus, the genealogy in Gen 11 represents the transition from stories involving all humanity (Gen 1–11) to stories focused on the one family line of Abraham and Sarah and their descendants, who will become the nation of Israel (Gen 12–50).

The genealogy includes notes about two very difficult family circumstances that will continue to haunt the family line of Abraham and Sarah across their generations. In 11:28, a parent (Terah) experiences the death of a son (Haran). The premature death or threat of the death of a son in the line of Abraham and Sarah will reappear at several points in Gen 12–50 (22:2; 27:41; 37:29–36; 38:6–11). The second genealogical note is that Abram's wife, Sarai, "was barren; she had no child" (11:30). Sarai's barrenness will be another major theme and source of suspense throughout the Abraham-Sarah stories in seeming contradiction to God's promise that Abraham would be the father of a "great nation" of innumerable descendants (12:2; 17:6). The motif of the barren wife will reappear with Rebekah (25:21) and Rachel (29:31). These two family tragedies—death of a child and barrenness or infertility—exemplify obstacles through which God must work to remain faithful to the promises that God has made for this family line. These challenges also serve as metaphors for the ongoing struggles and tragedies of the people of Israel throughout its history. National tragedies like the split of the northern and southern kingdoms (1 Kgs 12), the Assyrian conquest and exile of the northern kingdom and many of its people (2 Kgs 17), the Assyrian destruction of many of the villages and cities of southern Judah (2 Kgs 18–19), or the Babylonian destruction of Jerusalem and its Temple and the exile of many of its people (2 Kgs 24–25) often seemed to contradict God's promises of blessing, life, and becoming a great nation, all promises that God will make to Abraham and Sarah and their descendants (Gen 12:1–3).

II. The Family Stories of Israel's Ancestors (12:1–50:26)

Genesis 1–11 related the primeval history of God's interactions with all humanity and all creation, stretching from the beginnings of the heavens and the earth (Gen 1:1) to humanity's failed attempt to unify itself in the tower of Babel story (Gen 11:1–9). In order to protect humanity against itself, God ensures that humanity remains divided into different cultures and language groups with their power and capacity to do harm limited and restrained by being scattered among many different nations and peoples. Beginning in Gen 12, however, God embarks on a new and more positive strategy. God focuses divine efforts to bless humanity by concentrating on one chosen family line, the family of Abraham and Sarah. God will work in and through this one family with the ultimate aim of blessing this family and also thereby blessing "all the families of the earth" (Gen 12:3). The interactions between the family of Abraham and Sarah and the other nations will be mixed, sometimes positive and sometimes quite negative and tragic. But along the way, Genesis will provide glimpses of blessing, peace-making, reconciliation, generosity, and forgiveness between families and nations that hold out the hope and promise of a longer range trajectory toward which God seeks to bring humanity and the whole of creation (Gen 13:1–18;18:16–33; 21:22–34; 33:1–11; 50:15–21; see Isa 2:1–4; 11:1–9; 19:23–25; 56:1–8; 65:17–25).

A. The Family Stories of Abraham and Sarah and Their Son Isaac (12:1–25:18)

Two complementary themes weave and in out of the diverse stories that make up the Abraham-Sarah cycle of family stories in Gen 12–25. One theme is the promise that Abraham would become a great nation with a promised land and many descendants, more than the stars of the heavens (12:1–3, 4–9; 13:15–17; 15:5–7, 18–21; 17:1–8; 22:15–18; 23:1–20). A second recurring theme is the alternation between blessing and curse in the many interactions between the family of Abraham and other nations and peoples. The interactions are often positive (12:3; 13:1–18; 14:17–24; 18:16–33; 21:22–34; 23:1–20; 24:1–67), but they are also often tinged with judgment, conflict, or suffering (12:10–20; 14:1–16; 15:12–14; 16:1–6; 19:1–29; 20:1–18; 21:8–21; 23:1–20).

It should be noted that Abram's name will eventually be changed to Abraham, and Sarai's name will be changed to Sarah (17:5, 15).

12:1–9. God Calls Abram with a Promise of Blessing. Abram's father Terah lived in the city of Ur in southern Mesopotamia and had intended to migrate to the faraway land of Canaan with his family. Terah, however, had only reached the city of Haran in northern Mesopotamia when he died (11:31–32). In 12:1–9, God commands Terah's son Abram to "go from your country and your kindred and your father's house" in Mesopotamia and migrate "to the land that I will show you." In effect, God instructs Abram to fulfill his father Terah's failed plan to travel and settle in Canaan. If Abram obeys, God promises to make Abram "a great nation," to "bless" Abram, and to make his name great. Ironically, a great name was what the Babel tower builders had wanted to make for themselves (11:4). In 12:2, God promises to make Abram's name great as Abram responds to God's command and leaves behind his homeland and extended family. God promises to bless other peoples and nations that bless Abram, and God will curse other nations that curse him. These promises to Abram are not only for the benefit of Abram, but they are part of God's plan for the benefit of all humanity with whom God has been working in Gen 1–11: "in you all the families of the earth shall be blessed" (12:3). Abram immediately obeys God's command and travels to Canaan, lured by the promise of great blessing (12:4).

12:10–20. Abram and Sarai in Egypt: The First Wife-Sister Story. Abram and Sarai migrate from Canaan to Egypt in search of food in order to escape the famine in the land of Canaan. Generations later, Abraham's descendants will do the same thing when Jacob's sons go down to Egypt because of the famine in Canaan (41:53–42:3). Abram and Sarai are "aliens" in Egypt and thus do not have the same legal or social protections as natives (12:10). As a result, Abram worries that when the Egyptians see that Sarai is "a woman beautiful in appearance," they will take her as a wife and kill Abram. A fearful Abram instructs Sarai to deceive the Egyptians and tell them she is Abram's sister and not his wife. Abram is willing to endanger his own wife "so that it may go well with me" and "that my life may be spared" (12:11–13). Abram had just received God's promise that God would bless Abram and make him a "great nation" (12:2–3), but Abram seems not to trust fully in God's blessing and protection in this instance.

As Abram had feared, the Egyptian Pharaoh sees Sarai's beauty and takes her into his house. As a result, the Lord afflicts Pharaoh's house with "great plagues," causing Pharaoh to send Sarai out of Egypt after discovering she was Abram's wife (12:17–20). The plagues and flight out of Egypt prefigure the plagues and God's rescue of Israel in the exodus out of Egypt in the time of Moses (Exod 11:1). A similar "wife-sister story" will occur again with Abraham and Sarah in 20:1–17 and with Isaac and Rebekah in 26:6–11.

13:1–14:24. Abram's Generosity and Care for His Nephew Lot. Abram had just endangered his wife, Sarai, as well as Pharaoh and the other Egyptians by telling the Egyptians that Sarai was not his wife (12:10–20). This problematic story about Abram's interaction with another nation is paired with a more positive portrait of Abram and the nations in Gen 13–14. Lot, Abram's nephew, will become the ancestor of the nations of Moab and Ammon; these nations will become neighbors to the Israelites on their eastern border (19:30–38). Thus, Abram's generosity to Lot, Abram's rescue of Lot when he was kidnapped by the kings of Shinar, and the blessing of the Canaanite king-priest named Melchizedek in Gen 13–14, become examples of Abram being a blessing to "all the families of the earth" (12:3). This close pairing of different kinds of encounters with other nations and cultures, some positive and some negative, will be a recurring literary motif throughout the book of Genesis.

The Lord reaffirms the promise that the land of Canaan in all directions (north, south, east, and west) will belong to Abram and his descendants (13:14–15). The Lord also confirms the earlier promise of many descendants to Abram, specifying that they will be as many as the innumerable grains of dust on the earth (13:16). God will repeat the promise later, using the stars of heaven as the visual aid of the promise of innumerable descendants (15:5).

15:1–21. God's Covenant with Abram: Descendants and Land. The phrase that begins Gen 15, "After these things," occurs in two other places in Genesis, one at the beginning and one at the end of Gen 22 (22:1; 22:20). The two texts of Gen 15 and Gen 22 form a dramatic theological pair within the Abraham cycle of stories. On one hand, Gen 15 emphasizes God's willingness to lay God's future on the line to fulfill the promise of land and descendants to Abraham. On the other hand, Gen 22 emphasizes Abraham's willingness to lay his own life and future on the line in obeying God's command to offer up Isaac, his only son.

The Lord appears to Abram in a vision and reassures Abram that his "reward will be very great" (15:1). The elderly Abram complains that the Lord's earlier and more specific promise of many descendants (12:2; 13:16) has yet to be fulfilled. The Lord reassures Abram that he himself will have a child of his own. The Lord takes Abram outside and invites him to count the stars of the heavens, adding the wry comment, "if you are able to count them" (15:5). The Lord promises that Abram's descendants will be as innumerable as the stars of the nighttime sky.

The scene concludes with a theologically freighted assessment that falls into two parts. Part one affirms that "he [Abram] believed the Lord" (15:6a). This affirmation supports the traditional portrait of Abraham as a person of great trust in God's promises (Gal 3:6–9). The second part is rendered in the NRSV as "and the Lord reckoned it to him as righteousness" (15:6b). This is one possible way of translating the Hebrew text, and reflects the way in which the apostle Paul used this text in his argument that trusting or believing in the promise of God is what makes a person "righteous" rather than works of the law (Rom 4:1–15; Gal 3:6–18). However, the Hebrew of Gen 15:6 is somewhat more ambiguous and reads literally, "he [Abram] believed the Lord; and he [either "the Lord" or "Abram"] reckoned it to him [or "to himself"] as righteousness." In other words, it is possible to understand the verse as affirming that Abram believed the Lord, and that Abram was convinced ("reckoned to himself") that the Lord had acted rightly with him by promising him many descendants.

Although Abram may be satisfied with God's assurance that he will indeed have a child and heir, Abram immediately raises doubts about the Lord's second promise that Abram would be given the land of Canaan. (15:8–9). Abram remains a person of doubt and skepticism, demanding an additional sign of assurance from God. In response, the Lord performs an ancient ceremony of covenant-making, demonstrating how far God is willing to go to fulfill the promise of land to Abram. The Lord instructs Abram to slaughter a number of animals, cut them in half, and lay each half of the animals opposite to the other with a pathway between them. After a terrifying vision of Abraham's future descendants being in slavery for 400 years and the Lord returning them to the land of Canaan, the covenant-making ceremony proceeds with a "smoking fire pot" and "a flaming torch" moving down the pathway between the split animal carcasses (15:17–21). Fire frequently represents the presence of God in the Bible as it does here (Exod 3:2; 13:21; 19:18). The fire and smoke passing between the animals signifies God's oath to Abram that if God does not fulfill the promise of giving the land to his descendants, then God will be split in two like these animals (see Jer 34:18). God lays God's own future on the line as assurance that God's promise will be fulfilled. Whatever act of faith and obedience that Abraham may do in the future (Gen 22:1–19) will be grounded in this prior promise of God, guaranteed by God's dramatic pledge to Abram in Gen 15.

16:1–17:27. The Promise: From Abram-Hagar-Ishmael to Abraham-Sarah-Isaac. Abram had been assured by God in Gen 15 that Abram himself would be the father of a child and that his descendants would one day possess the land of Canaan. In Gen 16–17, the narrative lens widens to determine who will be the mother of this child. Abram's wife, Sarai, continues to be barren (11:30; 16:1). An ancient custom allowed a barren wife like Sarai to choose one of her women servants as a surrogate through whom her husband could have a child to be the couple's heir. Sarai has an "Egyptian slave-girl" named Hagar whom Sarai gives to Abram "as a wife" (16:3). Hagar becomes pregnant and begins to "look with contempt" on Sarai. As Abram had earlier complained to God (15:2, 8), now Sarai complains to Abram about Hagar's lack of respect for her. Abram gives Sarai permission to do to Hagar as she wishes, and so Sarai "dealt harshly" with her. The verb "to oppress" or "deal harshly with" ('anah–16:6) is the same verb that is used for what the Egyptians will eventually do to the Israelites as slaves in Egypt (Gen 15:13; Exod 1:11–12). The story acknowledges, in effect, that God's people are capable of unjustly oppressing an Egyptian slave as the Egyptians will unjustly oppress the Israelite slaves. This is part of the mixed picture of the relationship of Israel's ancestors and other nations, at times positive and at other times less so.

Hagar the Egyptian runs away out of Canaan into the wilderness, as the Israelites will run away into the wilderness in their exodus out of Egypt (Exod 13:3). In this case, however, the angel of the Lord urges Hagar to return from her exodus into the wilderness back to Abram and Sarai. The divine command to return to an oppressive relationship is troubling. However, the Lord gives to Hagar a promise that she will have so many descendants "that they cannot be counted." It is the same promise that God had given to Abram (13:16; 15:5). The Lord promises that she will bear a son whom she will name "Ishmael" (Heb.: "God Hears") because "the LORD has given heed to your affliction" (16:11). Adherents of Islam trace their spiritual lineage back to Abraham through Hagar and Ishmael as the chosen people of their deity, Allah, based on their holy book, the Qur'an. Even though Israel's Scripture is different from the Qur'an in eventually tracing the promised line through Abraham and Sarah and their son Isaac, Gen 16 acknowledges that Israel's God has also made a covenant and similar promise to Hagar and Ishmael. Israel's Scripture affirms that God is at work among other peoples and nations apart from Israel, even though their story may appear only briefly on the pages of the Scripture.

Hagar responds to God's promise by naming the LORD "El-roi" (Heb.: "God Who Sees"). Remarkably, this is the one example in all of Scripture in which a human names God; in all other cases, it is God who reveals God's name to humans (e.g., Gen 17:1; Exod 3:13–15). Hagar thus affirms through her son's name (Ishmael, "God Hears") and through God's name (El-roi, "God Who Sees") that God has both seen and heard her suffering and responded graciously to her plight (16:13). This combination of God hearing the cries of the oppressed and seeing the suffering of the enslaved is repeated again when God "hears" and "sees" the suffering of the Israelite slaves in Egypt (Exod 2:23–25; 3:7). God is concerned for all who suffer, whether Israelite or non-Israelite. God immediately makes good on the promise as Hagar bears a son to an eighty-six year old Abram who names his son Ishmael, as God had commanded Hagar (16:15).

As Gen 17 begins, the Lord appears again to Abram when he is ninety-nine years old. It has been thirteen years since Hagar gave birth to Ishmael (16:16–Abram is eighty-six). Abram has apparently assumed for those thirteen years that

Ishmael represents the fulfillment of the Lord's previous promises of a great nation and many descendants (12:3; 13:16; 15:5). Everything in the Hagar story in Gen 16 points to Ishmael as God's appointed child of promise for Abram. Although Abram and Sarai are the ones who conceive the plan to have a child through Hagar, it is God who insists that Hagar should return to Abram and Sarai in order that Ishmael will be raised as the son of Abram. God's own actions thus far suggest that Ishmael is the one Abram has been waiting for all along.

The Lord appears to the ninety-nine-year-old patriarch and reveals a new divine name, "I am God Almighty" (*'el shadday*, 17:1). God also gives "Abram" (with the Heb. meaning of "Exalted Ancestor") a new name, "Abraham" (understood here to mean in Heb. "Ancestor of a Multitude") (17:1, 5). The new names of "God Almighty" and "Abraham" mark this moment as an important transition point or milestone in God's relationship with Abraham. God confirms again the covenantal promise to Abraham that he would have a multitude of descendants (17:2) and then adds a new element. In 12:2, God had promised Abram that God would make of him "a great nation" (singular). Here in 17:3–7, God promises Abram for the first time that he will be the ancestor of not just one nation but "a multitude of nations." He will be the father of the wilderness nation of the Ishmaelites through Ishmael (25:12–18), the father of the Israelites through Isaac and Jacob, the father of the Midianites through his second wife Keturah (25:1–6), and the father of the Edomites through his grandson Esau (36:1–43).

God also confirms the promise of the land to Abraham and adds to it a new element involving time; God's covenant shall be an "everlasting covenant," and the land will be a "perpetual holding" (17:8). The covenant with Noah and all living creatures in Gen 9:16 was also an "everlasting covenant" as was God's covenant with King David and his dynasty (2 Sam 23:5; Isa 55:3). Alongside the promises of descendants, nations, and the land, God also promises an enduring relationship with Abraham and his family: "I will be their God" (17:8).

God introduces a new sign of this everlasting covenant with Abraham. As the rainbow was a physical sign of the "everlasting covenant" with

all creatures after the flood (Gen 9:12–17), so circumcision or the cutting off of the foreskin of the penis will be the physical sign upon the body of every male that they are part of the covenant people of God (17:9–14). Slaves and foreigners who live with Abraham's family also needed to be circumcised. The ritual of circumcisions was practiced by some of Israel's neighbors where it could function (e.g., Egypt) as a puberty rite (cf. Exod 4:24–26). Here circumcision involves a rite of initiation, intended for eight-day-old babies or new adult members of the community (17:12, 23–27). Jews and Muslims continue to practice the ritual of circumcision. Jews normally perform the ritual on eight-day-old babies. Muslims circumcise thirteen-year-old boys because Ishmael was circumcised at that age (17:25). The role of circumcision may be compared with the practice of baptism as an initiatory rite within Christian communities (Col 2:11–12).

God has one more surprise for Abraham. His wife "Sarai" also receives a new name, "Sarah," to signal God's initiative to provide Abraham a son through her. She will become the mother of "nations" and "kings" (17:15–16). The elderly Abraham falls on his face and "he laughs" as he thinks to himself about a man who is a hundred and a wife who is ninety having a baby together. The Hebrew verb "he laughs" (*yitskhaq*) is a word play on the name "Isaac" (*yits'aq*), the eventual name of Sarah's newborn son (17:17, 19; 18:12–15; 21:6–7). Abraham begs God to continue to consider his thirteen-year-old son Ishmael, the son of Hagar, as the primary child of the "everlasting covenant" rather than to transfer the promise to what seems an unlikely outcome, that Abraham and Sarah will have another son at their extremely advanced age. God says "no" to Abraham, insisting that Sarah will indeed have a son who will be named Isaac and who will become the child of the "everlasting covenant" (17:18–19). God reassures the disappointed Abraham that God will richly "bless" Ishmael, make him "exceedingly numerous" and "a great nation," all elements of the promise made originally to Abraham (Gen 12:1–3; 13:16; 15:5). Nonetheless, Ishmael is not given the promise of the land of Canaan and the promise of an "everlasting covenant." Ishmael will become a wilderness dweller (21:20–21). The line of promise and "everlasting covenant" will be established through Sarah with Isaac alone (17:21).

God's choosing of Isaac over Ishmael is the first instance of what will be a recurring theme in the stories of Abraham's descendants: the supplanting of the elder brother through the exalting and favoring of the younger brother (see 25:29–34; 27:30–40; 37:1–11; 48:8–22). In ancient traditional cultures, the eldest son was often the favored one who received the greatest inheritance and carried the greatest authority. God seems to work throughout Genesis in ways contrary to these human expectations, repeatedly choosing the unlikely person as the chosen agent of God's blessing and saving activity. Throughout their history, Israel as a people often saw themselves in this way. The Israelites were the weaker, younger, or more unlikely candidate among the nations, and yet they were God's favored and chosen people as opposed to the seemingly stronger empires, older cultures, and more exalted civilizations of Egypt, Assyria, Babylon, and Persia. Ancient Israel believed itself to be God's specially chosen and favored nation (Exod 19:6), even though it was "the fewest of all peoples" (Deut 7:7). Throughout Scripture, God often seems to favor and choose the younger, weaker, or more unlikely ones to be leaders or agents of God's work in the world (Exod 3:9–12; Judg 6:14–16; 1 Sam 2:1–10; 1 Sam 9:15–17, 21; 1 Sam 16:1–13; Jer 1:4–10; 1 Cor 1:26–31).

18:1–19:38. God's Promise Repeated, God's Justice Demonstrated. The Lord appears to Abraham and Sarah at "the oaks of Mamre," a tree shrine and holy place at Hebron where they reside as aliens in the land. It is also the place where Abraham and Sarah will eventually be buried (23:19; 25:9) along with their son Isaac (35:27), and their grandson Jacob (50:13). Abraham sees "three men" standing near him, and he invites them to stop, rest, and wait for "a little water" and "a little bread." The "bread and water" turns into a lavish four-course gourmet feast of tender meat, cakes of flour, curds, and milk for the three visitors who have not yet been identified (18:6–8). Abraham and Sarah welcome these strangers with lavish hospitality (cf. Heb 13:2).

As they eat, one of the three men tells Abraham that when he returns, Sarah will have a son. Sarah overhears the comment from within the tent and "laughs" to herself at the thought of her giving birth at her age, just as Abraham had done when he fell down and laughed when God told him that his elderly wife Sarah would give birth to a son (17:17). Suddenly the text discloses that it is "the LORD" (as one among the three men) who asks Abraham why Sarah laughed. Sarah denies having laughed at what seemed to her an impossible dream, not wanting to provoke God's anger (18:15). The Lord concludes, one might imagine with a good chuckle in the context of this lavish feast, "Oh yes, you did laugh" (18:15). The whole scene is based on the word play between the name of the newborn which will be "Isaac" (*yitskhaq*–17:19) and the Hebrew verb, "she laughed" (*titskhaq*–18:12).

The narrative mood quickly turns from light-hearted feasting to somber contemplation of a future death and judgment on the sinful cities of Sodom and Gomorrah. The "three men" set out toward Sodom along with Abraham, who shows them the way (18:16). Somehow the Lord is identical with or somehow associated with the "three men." The Lord reports to Abraham that "the outcry" of suffering from Sodom and Gomorrah has been "great," and so the Lord must "go down" and see if the situation is as grave as it sounds (18:20–21). The "outcry" that stirs God's response is reminiscent of the cry of Abel blood from the ground (4:10) or Hagar's cry of affliction (16:11). God's "going down" to investigate Sodom and Gomorrah reminds the reader of the tower of Babel story when God "came down" to investigate human wrongdoing (11:5).

The "men" turn and go toward Sodom, but "the LORD" remains with Abraham and engages in an extended philosophical discussion about God and justice. Would God forgive the wicked people of Sodom and not destroy the city if God could find a remnant of righteous people among them? "Shall not the Judge of all the earth do what is just?" Abraham asks (18:23–25). God's response is that if there are fifty righteous people, God would forgive the whole city. The principle is established: the righteousness of a few can redeem the whole.

Abraham's probing questions uncover what seems to be God's operative assumption in choosing the one family of Abraham and Sarah to be God's righteous and chosen people in order to bless and redeem "all the families of the earth" (12:3). A remnant of a few righteous people can redeem the whole. But how far can this be pushed? If there were only forty-five, would God still forgive? Yes! How about forty? Yes! Thirty-five? Yes! Thirty? Twenty? Ten? Yes, yes, yes! God would forgive the whole if only ten righteous people could be found (18:23–33). Abraham is engaging in persistent ancient Near Eastern bargaining with God (see 23:1–20). God appears open to being pushed and persuaded toward mercy and forgiveness, especially by the prayers and advocacy of the righteous on behalf of others who are outside the community. This divine readiness to hear and consider the pleas for mercy and deliverance stands behind the long and rich Jewish and Christian traditions of intercessory prayer on behalf of others in need. Abraham is fulfilling his role as an agent of blessing and advocacy on behalf of "the families of the earth" (12:3).

There are limits, however. Ten righteous people must be found in Sodom in order to save the city. God is gracious and merciful, forgiving and slow to anger, but God also does not simply "clear the guilty" without some consequences for their sin (Exod 34:6–7) or, as here in Gen 18, without some few righteous ones who will redeem the whole. Unfortunately, God will not be able to find ten righteous people in Sodom, and so the destruction of the city will eventually go forward (19:24–25).

The "three men" who visited Abraham and Sarah (18:2) and somehow included "the Lord" (18:1, 13) could also be distinguished from "the Lord" (18:22). Thus, the "three men" become "two angels" in 19:1. The "men" enter the city gate of Sodom, and Lot (the nephew of Abraham) offers them gracious hospitality, including a lavish feast (19:1–3; see 18:2–8). The obligation to extend generous hospitality to vulnerable strangers is deeply rooted in Israelite law (Exod 22:21; 23:9; Lev 19:33; 23:22; Deut 10:19; 24:17–21) and in ancient Near Eastern custom more generally.

The tranquil scene of generosity and kindness is suddenly interrupted by an angry mob of the citizens in Sodom, "all the people to the last man" who surround Lot's house with the two visitors inside. The men demand that Lot send the two men (angels) out to them so that "we may know them." The phrase is a euphemism for sexual intercourse and signals their intention to commit the violent act of male rape, a technique of humiliation and torture of vulnerable people (both men

and women) common even today in contexts of prisons or war. (See Judg 5:28–30.) The wickedness of Sodom here is not homosexuality. Sodom's sin is the lack of hospitality and the threatened violence by heterosexual men against vulnerable people in the community, those the community considers "aliens" and "strangers" in their midst.

The two men or angels intervene to rescue Lot and his family from the enraged throng. The angels strike everyone outside the house with a disabling blindness, allowing Lot's immediate family to escape and leave the city (19:10–23). Then the Lord rains down "sulfur and fire" upon the cities of Sodom and Gomorrah and all the surrounding territory. Lot's wife famously looks back as the destruction occurs and turns into "a pillar of salt" (19:24–26), likely reflecting a tradition about the origins of a crystalline formation in the region. The area associated with Sodom and Gomorrah is located southeast of the Dead Sea and remains to this day an arid desert with extensive sulfur and other mineral deposits.

The story of Lot concludes with an unflattering tale of drunkenness and incest in which the two daughters of Lot lie with their father, become pregnant and bear two sons, Moab and Ben-ammi. The two sons become the ancestors of the nations of Moab and Ammon, which lie on the eastern border of Israel in the Transjordan area (19:30–38). Israel's relationship with its neighbors Moab and Ammon was mixed over its history. Although a few positive or charitable texts concerning Moab and Ammon appear in Deut 2:9, 18 and Ruth 1–4, negative or hostile views of Moab and Ammon predominate in the Old Testament (Num 25:1–5; Deut 23:3; Judg 3:12–13; Judg 11:4; 1 Sam 11–12; 2 Sam 8; 10; 2 Kgs 3; 2 Kgs 24:2; Isa 15:1–16:13; Jer 48:1–49:6; Ezek 25:2–9; Amos 1:13–2:3; Zeph 2:8–9). This story about the origins of Ammon and Moab reflects this more negative view and also echoes the enigmatic tale at the end of the story of Noah and the flood, which includes a number of similarities to the Sodom and Gomorrah story (Gen 6–9; see 9:18–27).

20:1–18. Abraham and Sarah in Canaan: The Second Wife-Sister Story. As the reader comes to Gen 20, Sarah is scheduled to become pregnant with her son, Isaac, very soon in accord with God's promises (17:15–16; 18:10). Thus, Abraham's willingness to expose his wife Sarah to another man's sexual advances (the Canaanite king Abimelech) in this second episode of the wife-sister story (see 12:10–20) is an even more problematic and serious lapse in judgment because so much is at stake. As Abraham had feared, King Abimelech takes Sarah into his household. God quickly intervenes through a dream and warns the Canaanite ruler Abimelech that he is about to die because he has taken a married woman into his harem. Abraham has endangered not only his wife Sarah but also the Canaanite Abimelech. Once again, Abraham's record in being a blessing to others (12:3) is mixed, sometimes good and sometimes not. The narrator assures the reader that "Abimelech had not approached" Sarah. Thus, there is no possibility that Abimelech could be the father of Sarah's imminent pregnancy (20:4; see 21:1).

Abimelech confronts Abraham the next morning, and Abraham offers a weak defense of his actions. He argues that he was afraid there was "no fear of God at all in this place," but Abimelech's actions demonstrate more integrity and fear of God in his obedience than does Abraham. Abraham adds that, technically, Sarah is his half-sister so he was not entirely deceptive in saying Sarah was his sister (20:12). Telling this half-truth, however, had endangered the wellbeing of both Abimelech and Sarah.

21:1–21. The Arrival of Isaac and the Sending Away of Hagar-Ishmael.
The story of Abraham and Sarah builds to a climax with the hope and expectation of the birth of a son to Sarah. That hope began with God's promises to Abraham that he would be the father of a "great nation" (12:2) and innumerable descendants (13:16,15:5). Later, God promised that the formerly barren Sarah would become the mother of the one promised child of the "everlasting covenant" (17:15–22; 18:10, 14). Now after much waiting and many obstacles, a one-hundred-year-old Abraham and a ninety-year-old Sarah become parents of their promised son, Isaac (21:1–5). Sarah affirms that God has brought "laughter" to her in her old age and everyone who hears this story will "laugh" with her (21:6; cf. 17:17; 18:12). The references to "laughing" are puns on the name Isaac, which means "he laughs" (yitz'aq).

During a feast celebrating the weaning of young Isaac around the age of three, Sarah sees the teenage "son of Hagar the Egyptian," named Ishmael, "playing" with her three-year-old son Isaac. Sarah reacts by wishing to cast Ishmael and Hagar out of their household. The verb "playing" (metza'eq) is another word play on the name Isaac (yitz'aq). The verb can mean "laugh," "play" or "mock/insult." Thus, one could read this scene in two quite different ways. Sarah might have seen the teenage Ishmael playing by himself or in a kindly way with his young brother, but Sarah was spiteful and jealous of this other son of Abraham and his mother Hagar. On the other hand, if the teenage Ishmael were "mocking" or "insulting" the three-year-old Isaac, then Sarah's anger would be more justifiable as protecting little Isaac from a potentially abusive older brother.

Abraham is "greatly distressed" by Sarah's request to cast out Hagar and Ishmael since he remains attached to his first-born son. God, however, instructs Abraham to do as Sarah wishes, and God reassures Abraham that Isaac will have many offspring and that God will also make a nation of Ishmael (21:13). Abraham rises "early in the morning" to send away his son Ishmael (21:14); Abraham will do the same once again in Gen 22 when God commands him to give up his only remaining son, Isaac (22:3). Abraham gives Hagar and Ishmael bread and a skin of water and sends them into the wilderness where they soon exhaust their supply of water. Hagar leaves her son, Ishmael, under a bush and goes away to cry and lament over her dying child (21:15–16). God "hears the voice of the boy" who apparently was also crying in thirst and pain, and assures the mother Hagar that God has heard and God will make "a great nation" of Ishmael, just as God had earlier promised to Abraham (12:3) and to her (16:10). Moreover, God "opened the eyes" of Hagar, enabling her to see a well of water that provided life-giving water to them. God continued to be "with the boy," giving blessing and protection as he grew up and "lived in the wilderness" (21:20–21). The story of Hagar and Ishmael continues off the pages of Scripture as the book of Genesis will concentrate from this point forward on the story of Abraham, Sarah, Isaac, and their descendants. However, Hagar and Ishmael will not be forgotten and will continue as part of God's often hidden story of interaction with all humanity and all creation.

21:22–34. Abraham Reconciles with the Canaanite King Abimelech. Abraham encounters the Canaanite ruler Abimelech a second time (see 20:1–18) and enters into a covenant of peace with him, agreeing not to "deal falsely" but loyally with Abimelech and his descendants (21:22–24). Abimelech again demonstrates that he fears God, affirming that he knows that Abraham's "God is with you in all that you do" (21:22). Sometime later, Abraham has a dispute with Abimelech's servants over a well that Abraham had dug but that had been seized by Abimelech's servants. The dispute is resolved between Abraham and Abimelech, offering an example of negotiated reconciliation rather than conflict and violence.

22:1–24. God Commands Abraham to Sacrifice His Son Isaac. Few stories in the Bible are as haunting, distressing, and challenging as this story of Abraham's near-sacrifice of Isaac. The phrase, "after these things," comes at the beginning and end of Gen 22 (vv. 1, 20) and occurs only one other place in Genesis at the beginning of ch. 15 (v. 1). Gen 15 and Gen 22 are linked by this phrase and by the dramatic content that the two chapters share in relating the willingness of one party to lay their whole future on the line in fulfilling the covenant relationship with another party. In Gen 15, it is God who lays God's future on the line for the sake of the promise to Abraham (see the commentary there). In Gen 22, it will be Abraham who will be asked to lay his future on the line in the form of his one remaining son, Isaac.

The narrator begins the story by informing the reader (but not Abraham) that God is "testing" Abraham (22:1). Abraham's trust in God's protection and faithfulness in fulfilling the promises of God has wavered from time to time in the past, most recently in 20:1–18. God commands Abraham to take his only remaining son, Isaac, whom he loves and go to the land of Moriah and "offer him there as a burnt offering" on one of its mountains (22:2). Later in the Old Testament, this "Moriah" is associated with Mount Zion, Jerusalem, and the Temple with its sacrifices there (2 Chron 3:1). As Abraham, Isaac, and the servants approach the mountain on the third day of the journey to Moriah, Abraham looks up and "sees the place far away" (22:4). This is the first instance of a series of references to

"seeing" throughout the story, the word acting as a keyword in the narrative. Abraham instructs the servants to remain back with the donkey while Abraham and Isaac go up to worship. Abraham reassures the servants that "we will come back to you" (22:5). The story is told in such a way that we do not know what Abraham is actually thinking as he utters these words. Does he believe that he and Isaac will indeed "come back," believing that God would not allow him actually to carry out the sacrifice? Or does Abraham simply not want to frighten Isaac or the servants by telling them what is truly supposed to happen, that is, Isaac will be offered up as a sacrifice and only Abraham will "come back"? The story does not tell the reader what is in Abraham's mind.

Ironically, Abraham gives Isaac the wood to carry, but Abraham himself takes the dangerous implements of the torch and the knife lest Isaac be harmed in any way. Then the narrative reports for the first time what it will repeat again in v. 8: "the two of them walked on together" (22:6). Isaac asks a challenging question as they walk up toward the place of sacrifice. They have the fire and the wood, "but where is the lamb for a burnt offering?" Abraham responds, "God himself will provide the lamb for a burnt offering, my son" (22:8). The Hebrew for the verb "provide" plays on the verb "to see"; in effect, Abraham responds that God will "provide/see to" the lamb for the sacrifice. Again, the reader does not know for sure what Abraham is thinking. Does Abraham believe God will indeed provide a substitute animal to replace his son as the sacrifice? Or is Abraham thinking that God has already "seen to" the lamb, and that lamb is Isaac, although Abraham is reluctant to reveal that horrific news to his son? In any case, the narrative repeats again the phrase, "the two of them walked together" (22:8). Abraham and Isaac are joined together as one, parent and child, walking together and exchanging terms of endearment—"father," "my son" (22:7–8). The life and future of one is bound up together with the other.

The narrative's action slows to a crawl as the story reaches its climax. Abraham builds the altar, stacks the wood, and then "binds" (*ya'aqodh*) Isaac and lays him on the altar (22:9). In Jewish tradition, this story is called the "Binding of Isaac" or simply the "Binding" (the *Akedah*). Among many elements that are left unspecified in this story is the age of Isaac. We know Isaac is old enough to speak, to carry wood, and to know that sacrifices require animals. But is he very young so that the elderly Abraham could still have the strength to bind the boy if he were to resist? Or is Isaac a young adult, strong and mature, who must have willingly gone through with the sacrifice, since the older Abraham could not overpower him if he struggled and tried to escape? Some early Jewish and Christian post-biblical interpretations assumed that Isaac was older and thus was a willing victim or martyr. In its present form, however, Gen 22 is focused on Abraham and the "testing" of Abraham's faith and obedience, even in the face of a commanded action that seems to contradict all the promises and plans of God.

As Abraham raises the knife to kill his son, an "angel of the LORD" calls out from heaven, "Abraham! Abraham!" At the beginning of the story, God had called Abraham's name once (22:1), but now at this urgent juncture Abraham hears his name twice (22:11). The angel instructs Abraham not to harm the boy because "now I know that you fear God" (22:12). God has apparently gained new knowledge about Abraham: Abraham fears God, trusts in God's promises, and obeys God's voice, even to the extraordinary extent of being willing to sacrifice his only remaining son, his one remaining link to his ongoing life and future through his descendants. Abraham next raises his eyes and "sees" a ram caught in a bush by its horns, which Abraham retrieves and offers as a sacrifice instead of his son. Abraham names the place "The LORD Will Provide" or "The LORD Will See to It," a name that continues in a saying that "on the mount of the LORD it shall be provided/seen to" which can also be translated in Hebrew, "on the mount, the LORD will be seen" (22:14). The Hebrew verb "to see" (*ra'ah*) may also be related as a word play on the name "Moriah" (Heb.: *moriyyah*; 22:2).

Gen 22:15–18 is likely an editorial addition to the story as the angel speaks "a second time." The angel's second speech explicitly links this dramatic story of Abraham's obedience to all of the Genesis promises of blessing (12:1–3) innumerable descendants (13:16; 15:5), and Abraham's vocation as an agent of blessing for all the nations of the earth (12:3): "Because you have done this ... I will indeed bless you ... because you have obeyed my voice" (22:16, 18). The theological emphasis in this second speech focuses on Abraham's obedience as an essential element in the blessings that God will give to Abraham and his descendants. The theological emphasis of the whole story in the larger narrative setting of the Abraham cycle as a whole emphasizes Abraham's trust that God will fulfill the promises that God has repeatedly made. Most important was God's promise to stake God's self and future on the line back in Gen 15:7–20 when God promised that God would be split in two like the animal carcasses that had been slaughtered if God did not fulfill the promises of land and descendants that God had made to Abraham. Abraham takes that memory and assurance with him as he obeys God's command to offer his own life and future back to God by sacrificing his only and beloved son in obedience to God's command.

23:1–20. Abraham Buys an Expensive Piece of the Promised Land. At the conclusion of Gen 22, God had reaffirmed the promises of many descendants to Abraham and Sarah. The story of Gen 23 focuses on the other major part of God's repeated promises, the promise that the land of Canaan would one day belong to Abraham's offspring (12:7; 13:14–17; 15:7–21; 17:8). Abraham's wife Sarah dies at the age of 127, and Abraham seeks to purchase a burial cave for her east of Mamre near Hebron. Abraham engages with the native "Hittites" in Canaan in a Near Eastern bargaining session that involves a show of what seems on the surface to be extreme generosity by the "Hittites" who offer Abraham the field with the "cave of Machpelah" as a free gift. Under the rules and custom of Near Eastern bargaining, Abraham must match their extravagant generosity by insisting that he will pay the very high price of 400 shekels for the land that the Hittites mention as the value of their "gift" of the field. Although an expensive purchase in the end, Abraham thereby obtains a small piece of Canaan to call his own in which to bury his wife Sarah. It is a small down payment on God's future gift of the land to his descendants. The cave of Machpelah will also become the burial place for Abraham (25:8–10), Isaac (35:27–29), Rebekah, Jacob, and Leah (49:29–31).

24:1–67. Isaac Obtains a Wife, Rebekah, from Family in Mesopotamia. A very elderly Abraham instructs his chief servant not to get a wife for his son Isaac from among the Canaanites but rather to go "to my country and to my kindred" in Mesopotamia and obtain a wife for Isaac there. Abraham still feels himself to be an alien in Canaan, and "home" remains in some sense still in Mesopotamia (24:4). At the same time, Abraham knows that God will one day give the land of Canaan to his descendants, so he does not want his son Isaac to migrate out of Canaan back to Mesopotamia (24:5–8). The servant travels to Mesopotamia and finds, by divine providence, a wife for Isaac named Rebekah. The servant also meets Rebekah's brother, Laban (24:29–32). It will be this same Laban, uncle to Jacob, who will prove to be equal to Jacob as a con artist and swindler (29:15–30; 31:1–9; see 25:29–34; 27:1–45). Rebekah's father and brother acknowledge that God has brought Abraham's servant to them and that Rebekah should become Isaac's wife (24:50–51). The marriage of the Mesopotamian Rebekah and Isaac back in Canaan (24:59–67) is a sign of a hybrid identity, with one foot still in Mesopotamia and the other in Canaan but not fully at home in either place.

25:1–18. Abraham's Death and the Descendants He Leaves Behind. After the death of Sarah (23:1–2), Abraham marries a second wife or "concubine" (25:1, 6) named Keturah and together they have several children, including Midian who is the ancestor of nomadic tribes called the Midianites who dwell east of Canaan (25:4, 6). It will be Midianite traders who rescue Joseph from a pit but then sell him as a slave to Ishmaelites who take him to Egypt (37:28). Later, Midianites will also welcome Moses into their family, and Moses will marry a Midianite wife (Exod 2:15–22). The Ishmaelites comprise twelve tribes, similar to the twelve tribes of Israel; they dwell in the deserts of Arabia (25:16–18).

Abraham dies at the age of 175. Ishmael joins his brother Isaac one last time to bury their father, Abraham, at the same cave of Machpelah where Isaac's mother, Sarah, was buried (25:9–10; 23:19). Isaac then settles at Beer-lahai-roi, the same place where the Lord had comforted and rescued Ishmael's mother Hagar when she was pregnant (25:11; 16:14). The genealogies in Gen 25 list the descendants of Abraham from his two concubines, Keturah and Hagar. These descendants are all portrayed as the ancestors of nations and peoples that surrounded ancient Israel, thereby fulfilling God's earlier promise that Abraham would become the father of "a multitude of nations" (17:5).

B. The Family Stories of Isaac's Son, Jacob (25:19–36:43)

The Abraham cycle of stories (Gen 12–25) focused on God's faithfulness in keeping alive the promises of God to Abraham and Sarah in the face of difficult obstacles and near death (such as the barrenness of Sarah in 11:30 and God's command to Abraham to sacrifice his son Isaac in Gen 22, respectively). The stories about Jacob in Gen 25–36 will also focus on God's blessing of Jacob in spite of conflict, suffering, and the threat of death. The intersections between Jacob and other nations will also remain as a theme as it was throughout the Abraham cycle (Laban in Mesopotamia, ch. 29–31; Esau as ancestor of Edom, 25:30; 36:1; and the people of Shechem, Gen 34).

25:19–34. The Twins Jacob and Esau: Birth and Rivalry. Isaac's wife, Rebekah, was barren as her mother-in-law, Sarah, had been (11:30), but Isaac prays for her and she becomes pregnant with twins. The two boys are already wrestling fiercely in Rebekah's womb when the Lord reveals to her that these two sons are "two nations" who "shall be divided," the one stronger than the other and "the elder shall serve the younger." Once again, the reader encounters the common Genesis theme of the selection and favoring of the younger sibling over the elder (see the commentary on 17:21). When the twins are born (25:24–26), the first son came out "red" (*'admoni*), which is a word play on "Edom" (*'edom*), the nation for which Esau is the ancestor (36:1). The elder Esau's body is "hairy" (*se'ar*), another word play; it identifies the region of "Seir" (*se'ir*), which is where Esau eventually will settle (36:8, 20). The younger twin brother came out, "gripping Esau's heel," in effect, hitching a free ride through the birth canal. The younger twin is thus called "Jacob," meaning in Hebrew "he grabs by the heel" or "he supplants." Jacob will gain a reputation for swindling and conning whatever he is able from his older brother Esau and supplanting Esau's privileged status as the eldest son, when Jacob steals his blessing and birthright.

Esau grows up to become a skillful hunter and outdoorsman whereas Jacob is a more "quiet" or domestic man, living in tents rather in the outdoors. The father, Isaac, loves Esau, while the mother, Rebekah, loves Jacob. The division in parental devotion has dysfunction written all over it. The conflict between Jacob and Esau begins early with Jacob at home cooking a red-colored stew. A hungry and weary Esau comes in from the field and demands from Jacob "some of that red stuff" (*'adhom*), another pun on "Edom" (*'edhom*), the other name for Esau and the nation he represents (36:1, 8). Sensing desperation in Esau's voice, Jacob strikes a deal and offers a bowl of the red stew in exchange for Esau's birthright as the eldest son. Esau agrees (25:29–34). Jacob is on his way to ensuring that "the elder shall serve the younger" (25:23).

26:1–33. Isaac and the Philistine King Abimelech: Echoes of Abraham. Several episodes involving father Isaac in Gen 26 echo and parallel events in the life of Isaac's father, Abraham. A famine forces Isaac and Rebekah to migrate to another area (26:1), just as a famine forced Abraham and Sarah to migrate to Egypt (12:10). God promises Isaac land and innumerable descendants (26:1–5, 24) as God had done to Abraham (12:1–3, 7; 15:5). Isaac builds an altar for worship (26:25) as Abraham had done (12:7–8; 13:18). Isaac passes his wife Rebekah off as his sister and comes into conflict with the local King Abimelech (26:6–11) as Abraham had done with Sarah with the same king Abimelech (20:1–18). The story puns on the name "Isaac" (*yitskhaq*–"he laughs") and the Hebrew verb used for Isaac "fondling" (*metsakheq*) his wife Rebekah (26:8), echoing numerous such word plays on the name "Isaac" and "laughter" in the Abraham cycle of stories (17:17; 18:12–15; 21:6, 9). Isaac digs wells and has disputes over the ownership of the wells (26:17–25) as Abraham also did (21:25–34). Isaac negotiates a covenant of reconciliation with Abimelech (26:26–31) in parallel with Abraham's covenant with the same Abimelech (21:22–24).

This long list of echoes and parallels across the two generations of Abraham and Isaac achieves the rhetorical effect of presenting a number of divinely guided patterns and recurring deep harmonies that are footprints of the same God who works from generation to generation in consistent but also surprising ways. The contemporary reader is thereby encouraged to discern and explore deeper patterns, analogies, and harmonies that may emerge as the Genesis ancestral stories are placed side by side with the rest of Scripture and the stories, events, and concerns of contemporary life, faith, and world.

26:34–28:9. Jacob Steals the Blessing of the Elder Esau and Flees. The story of Jacob and Rebekah's scheme to deceive the elderly, blind father Isaac and steal the blessing that rightfully belonged to the firstborn Esau is a well crafted tale of suspense. Rebekah disguises Jacob by putting on him the rustic-smelling garments of Esau and goat skins to simulate Esau's "hairy mantle" (27:15–16, 27; see 25:25, 27). While Esau had been sent out to hunt game for his father Isaac, Jacob brings Rebekah's specially prepared meat dish to Isaac instead, posing as his older brother Esau. After some close calls of being found out, Isaac in the end blesses Jacob, thinking that he is Esau. Part of the blessing is that "nations will bow down to you" and you will "be lord over your brothers" (27:29). The blessing fulfills the Lord's prediction to Rebekah while the twin boys were still in her womb: "the elder would serve the younger" (25:23). There is a synergy between God's predestined plans for Jacob, on one hand, and the human striving by Rebekah and Jacob to ensure Jacob's wellbeing, on the other. God's predestination does not exclude but works through human decisions and bold actions.

Esau returns and discovers that Jacob has stolen his blessing as the eldest son. An angry Esau resolves that "I will kill my brother Jacob" (27:41). The Jacob-Esau relationship is a replay in many ways of the Cain-Abel story–two brothers, different vocations, an experience of perceived injustice by the elder brother, envy and anger, and a plan to kill the younger brother (Gen 4:1–16). Rebekah intervenes and convinces Jacob that he must flee to Mesopotamia to avoid Esau's murderous plot under the guise of seeking a wife from kindred in Mesopotamia rather than from the native Canaanite women (27:41–28:5; see 26:34–35). One of the overarching questions of the Jacob cycle is whether or not God will be able to work with this family of Abrahamic descendants to bring a new ending to this brother-against-brother hatred that ended with murder in Gen 4. Will God achieve a new way of reconciliation within the family of Abraham?

28:10–22. God's Blessing of Jacob at Bethel.
Two dramatic encounters with God bracket Jacob's leaving the land of Canaan on the way to Mesopotamia (28:10–22) and Jacob's return to the land of Canaan twenty years later (Gen 32:22–32). Jacob's first encounter with God involves God's generous blessing of Jacob, all promise and pure gift. The second encounter will involve wrestling and conflict with God and will end with a haggard Jacob defeated, limping, but also finally blessed.

On his way out of Canaan, Jacob stops to sleep at a certain spot and then begins to dream that there was "a ladder" or ramp set up between earth and heaven at that spot with "angels of God" moving up and down the ladder (28:10–13). Jacob has unknowingly stumbled on a portal between heaven and earth, a holy place not built by humans but revealed by God. Although the tower builders of Babel (Gen 11) had been unsuccessful in their human attempt to build a tower with "its top in the heavens" that would link earth and heaven (11:1–9), God here provides such a stairway in Jacob's dream. Dreams in the ancient world were important ways by which the divine communicated with human beings (20:3; 31:24; 37:6–9). As part of the dream, the Lord stands before Jacob and affirms that all the promises of the land of Canaan and of innumerable descendants that God gave to Abraham are now given to Jacob as the chosen carrier of the promised line. God promises Jacob that "I am with you" and "will bring you back to this land." God will not leave Jacob until God has done what God has promised (28:13–15). Jacob awakens and designates the spot as a holy place and names it "Bethel," meaning "house of God" (28:17, 19).

29:1–31:55. Jacob and Laban: Jacob Prospers in Mesopotamia.
Jacob sets out on a journey to "the land of the people of the east," or Mesopotamia, both to escape his brother Esau (27:41) and to find a wife from among his kindred in Haran in Mesopotamia (27:46–28:5). Jacob comes to a well and "by coincidence" (or divine predestination) meets Rachel, the daughter of Laban who is Jacob's uncle and brother to Jacob's mother Rebekah. The scene at the well replays the finding of Isaac's wife at the well near Haran in the previous generation (24:1–67). The same theme of God's hidden providence and guidance of events animates the scene.

Laban has two daughters, the elder Leah and the younger Rachel. When Laban asks Jacob what his wages should be, Jacob offers to work seven years for the hand of Rachel in marriage (29:15–20). Jacob's favoring of Rachel over Leah (29:16–18) is yet another instance of the recurring Genesis motif of the younger being favored over the elder (Cain and Abel in 4:1–16, Ishmael and Isaac in 17:20–21, Esau and Jacob in 25:23–26, and Joseph and his brothers in 37:2–8). Rachel is described as "graceful and beautiful" (29:17). Leah is described as having eyes that were "lovely" in the NRSV translation. However the same Hebrew word may also be translated as "weak," so Leah's eyes may not necessarily have been "lovely" but weak and unattractive. Laban tricks Jacob into marrying Leah first after working seven years for Rachel. Jacob is then forced to work another seven years so he can also marry Rachel, the wife he wanted all along (29:21–29).

Jacob's love for Rachel, and not Leah, sets up the potential for another dysfunctional set of family relationships and conflicts, similar to the Sarah-Hagar rivalry (16:3–6; 21:9–11) and the competition between Jacob and Esau (25:27–28; 27:41; 28:6–9). Rachel and Leah and their respective slave girls engage in anguished competition over who will produce the most children for Jacob. Eventually eleven sons will be born with a twelfth son born later to Rachel in Gen 35. These twelve sons will become the ancestors of the twelve tribes of the people of Israel (Gen 46:8–27). The relative status of the mother of each son (Rachel favored over Leah, Rachel's maids favored over Leah's maids), likely reflects the relative status of the corresponding tribe at some point in Israel's history. Thus, the Joseph tribe was likely one of the more powerful tribes at some point since Joseph's mother, Rachel, was the favored primary wife of Jacob. Leah's sons and her maid's sons reflect tribes that were likely of lower status at another time. The name of each son carries with it some significance, typically expressing thanksgiving or delight at the birth.

The Lord compensates Leah as the "unloved" wife by giving her four sons: Reuben, Simeon, Levi and Judah. By doing so, Leah hopes that now "my husband will be joined to me" (29:31–35).

Rachel, on the other hand, is barren, and, like the earlier Sarah, Rachel is envious of Leah and her children. In desperation and anger, she gives Jacob her slave-girl Bilhah, just as Sarah had given Hagar to Abraham in order to have a son and heir (16:1–6). After Bilhah gives her two sons, Rachel boasts that she has wrestled with her sister Leah and "prevailed"; God will later describe Jacob also as one who has wrestled with God and humans and "prevailed" (32:28).

Leah's maid Zilpah has two more children with Jacob, Then Leah barters away some mandrakes to Rachel for an opportunity for Leah to spend the night with Jacob. As the primary wife, Rachel has the first rights of sleeping with Jacob, so she trades that right to Leah for the mandrakes. Mandrakes were herbs that were thought to enhance fertility in women. Leah has two more sons with Jacob along with a daughter, Dinah (30:21), who will be featured in a later narrative in Gen 34. The mandrakes apparently work, because Rachel conceives and has her one son, Joseph. Rachel also attributes her release from barrenness to divine help (30:22–24). Rachel will eventually die in childbirth as she gives birth to her second son, Benjamin (35:16–21). Rachel's two sons, Joseph and Benjamin, will be Jacob's two youngest sons and also his most favored sons (37:3; 42:35–38).

Laban had earlier outsmarted Jacob in order to have Jacob work for him fourteen years in order to marry Rachel (29:15–30). Jacob returns the favor and outsmarts the deceptive Laban in an elaborate scheme of genetic engineering and selective breeding involving spotted and black sheep and goats (based in part on recessive genes for hair color being repressed in one generation and reappearing in another generation). Jacob builds up a large herd of strong sheep and goats and becomes "exceedingly rich" (30:25–33). Jacob's human actions and schemes to gain blessing and wealth join implicitly with the hidden working out of God's blessing activity, which God had promised to Jacob (28:13–15). Likewise, the strategies used by Leah and Rachel to have children through their maids or through bartering mandrakes were also ways by which human activity cooperated with God's guidance and work to achieve the blessing and fertility that God had promised. Trusting in God's promises and blessing does not entail passivity but requires persistent human activity and

ingenuity alongside the divine guidance of events (see 31:10–12).

Jacob had first fled from Canaan to Haran in Mesopotamia to avoid the jealousy and conflict with his brother Esau (27:41–45). In Gen 31, Jacob flees from Mesopotamia back to Canaan to avoid the jealousy and conflict with Laban and his sons (31:1–2). Laban chases after Jacob, but they eventually work out a covenant of reconciliation (31:43–55). Their reconciliation mirrors the covenants of peace that Abraham (21:22–34) and Isaac (26:26–33) negotiated with the Canaanite Abimelech. The theme of conflict and reconciliation with foreigners as well as within the family of Abraham runs throughout Genesis

32:1–33:17. Jacob Wrestles with God and Reconciles with Esau. Jacob prepares to encounter his brother Esau as he returns from Mesopotamia to Canaan after being away for twenty years (31:38, 41). The last words that the reader has heard from Esau is that he planned to "kill my brother Jacob" (27:41). When Jacob left Canaan twenty years earlier, Jacob had negotiated a contract with God that God would ensure that Jacob could "come again to my father's house in peace" (28:21). That agreement is about to be put to the test. Jacob begins by sending messengers with extravagant gifts of livestock herds and servants ahead of him to give to Esau in order to find favor in Esau's eyes (32:5). The messengers return to Jacob, reporting that Esau is coming with an army of four hundred men to meet Jacob and his family. Jacob assumes Esau's intentions are hostile and so decides to divide his family and herds into two groups so that if Esau destroys one group, the other group may be able to escape (32:3–8). Jacob pleads for God's protection in fulfillment of the promises God had made earlier when Jacob had first left Canaan (28:13–15). Jacob combines his trust in God's protection with his own actions of sending herds upon herds of livestock designed to bribe Esau and soften his anticipated hostility (32:13–21). Again, trust in God's promises is combined with active human intervention on Jacob's part.

God had encountered Jacob in a dramatic way at Bethel twenty years earlier when Jacob was leaving Canaan (28:10–22). God had then been gracious and generous in offering promise and protection to Jacob. Now, as Jacob returns to Canaan, God encounters Jacob again in a dramatic encounter. However, this time God attacks Jacob in a wrestling match that leaves him wounded, limping, but blessed in the end. A mysterious "man" suddenly attacks Jacob at the crossing or "ford of the Jabbok" in an all-night wrestling match after Jacob has sent the rest of his entourage across the river (32:22–24). "The man" sees that he cannot "prevail" against Jacob, and so he touches Jacob's thigh and dislocates his hip, rendering him helpless. Although now defeated, Jacob will not let go his grip on the "man." Jacob demands a blessing from this "man," whom Jacob eventually realizes is actually "God" (32:26, 30).

Changes in names in Genesis signal major transitions and new blessings as in the change from Abram to Abraham (17:5) and Sarai to Sarah (17:15). The "man-God" who wrestles Jacob also blesses Jacob, giving him a new name, "Israel" (meaning in Hebrew, "the one who strives with God") because Jacob has "striven with God and humans" and has "prevailed" (32:28). Jacob's many conflicts and struggles with Esau, Laban, and Laban's sons are intertwined with Jacob's struggles with God. The change in name from Jacob to Israel is a sign that Jacob's life as an individual is also a metaphor for the whole people of Israel and their relationships to other peoples and nations.

The morning after the wrestling with God, Jacob looks up and sees Esau coming with his army of four hundred men. Jacob meets Esau, bowing down to the ground seven times in a sign of humility as he approaches Esau in an effort to save himself and his family from being killed by Esau and his men (33:1–3; see 27:41; 32:7–8, 11). Unexpectedly, Esau's reaction to seeing Jacob is to run and embrace him, kiss him, and then weep together with him (33:4). Jacob introduces his large family to Esau as a gift that "God has graciously given" to him (33:6). Esau asks the purpose of all the herds upon herds of livestock that Jacob had earlier sent ahead with messengers and tells Jacob that these gifts are not necessary, suggesting that Jacob ought to take the gifts back (33:8–9; see 32:3–5, 13–21).

Jacob insists that Esau accept this present or gift with these words to Esau, "Truly to see your face is like seeing the face of God." The encounter with Esau echoes in some way the prior encounter with God ("Peniel" in 32:30 means "Face of

God"). Esau had been gracious in embracing and not killing Jacob and his family (33:10). God the wrestler had been gracious in blessing and not killing the weak and defeated Jacob. Now Jacob returns the favor by giving a gift without ulterior motive back to his brother Esau in gratitude for the graciousness that God and Esau have both shown him. The Hebrew word used to describe the "gift/blessing" (*berakhah*) that Jacob give to Esau (33:11) is the same Hebrew word for the "blessing" (*berakhah*) of the eldest son that Jacob had originally stolen from Esau twenty years before (Gen 27:35–36, 41).

On the one hand, the reconciliation of Jacob and Esau in Gen 33:4 is a glimpse of another way that enemy-brothers may resolve their mutual hatreds and jealousies, a hopeful alternative to the story of Cain and Abel. On the other hand, Genesis is also realistic. After the reconciliation, Esau suggests that their two family groups should journey together to his homeland of Seir or Edom and live together as one people. Jacob agrees but then promptly heads away from Edom and heads to Canaan, where he settles at Succoth (33:14–17). The welcome reconciliation of Jacob and Esau is tempered by Jacob's continued fear and felt need for some separation between him and his brother Esau.

33:18–34:31. Rape and Revenge: Jacob's Daughter Dinah. Jacob moves his family to the Canaanite city of Shechem and buys there a "plot of land" from "the sons of Hamor" on which to pitch his tent. One of the sons is named Shechem (33:18–20). Abraham had been the first of the ancestors to buy a plot of land in which to bury his wife Sarah (23:1–20). Jacob's purchase of the small plot means that he is the second ancestor who secures a small down payment on God's promise that one day the whole land would belong to his descendants. Jacob erects an altar to God as a theological claim on the land. In the meantime, however, Jacob remains an alien in the land of Canaan and without the protections of native citizenship.

The story of the rape of Jacob and Leah's daughter, Dinah, in Gen 34 wrestles with this alien status of Jacob and his family and how to respond to a violent attack against a member of the family when in a position of vulnerability as aliens in the land. Dinah is raped by Shechem, the son of Hamor and "prince of the region"

(34:1–2). This act of violence against Dinah by Shechem incites the sons of Jacob to retaliate violently. Jacob's sons devise a scheme of weakening the males of Shechem and then killing all of them. The relationships between the ancestors of Israel and the Canaanites have been peaceful and positive up to this point in Genesis. Genesis 34 is the first example of violence between the two groups. The narrative is designed to raise a number of moral dilemmas that draw the reader into the story and the moral quandries it presents. Shechem rapes Dinah and then "loved the girl and spoke tenderly to her," seeking to marry her as his wife (34:3–4). Although he is prince of the region and could take Dinah as a wife without consulting them, Shechem generously and honorably offers to pay as high a marriage present to Jacob's family as they demand (34:11–12). Dinah's reactions or feelings are not presented, and thus the reader must consider the possibilities of what is best for Dinah in this case. As a victim of sexual assault by a foreigner, she will bear much shame within her own community and may have difficulty finding a husband. Thus, it is possible that her interests may best be served in this tragic situation by marrying Shechem. And yet Shechem raped her. Could Dinah feel anything but revulsion toward him?

The sons of Jacob deceptively agree to allow Shechem to marry their sister Dinah, but only on condition that every male in the city of Shechem be circumcised. (Circumcision, cutting off the foreskin of the penis, was a sign of belonging to God's covenant people [17:9–14].) Jacob's sons, however, use this religious ritual cynically as a ploy to weaken the males of the city so that they can go in and kill all the males in revenge for the rape of their sister (34:13–24). Two of Jacob's sons, Simeon and Levi, are full brothers of Dinah, with Leah as their mother (29:31–34; 30:21). They are the first to enter the city and kill all the males. Their motivation is focused on maintaining family honor (34:30–31).

The other sons of Jacob "plunder" the city, stealing all their wealth and capturing all their wives and children and making them "their prey" (34:27–29). Did this include raping the women of Shechem in revenge? The phrase made them "their prey" is ambiguous but troubling. These other brothers of Dinah seem more focused on their own self-interests rather than the interests of

Dinah and her wellbeing. In 34:26, the reader is informed that Dinah has been staying in Shechem's house all along. Is she there because she wanted to be? Or was she being held by Shechem against her will? This is another of the unresolved issues in the narrative that preserve the complexity and moral ambiguity concerning the use of violence by the weak Israelites against the more powerful Canaanites.

In the end, Jacob focuses on the pragmatic and long-term effects of his son's violent actions. Jacob fears that their violence will endanger his family's welfare in future interactions with the Canaanites because Jacob's family is "few" in number and thus vulnerable (34:30). Simeon and Levi appeal to moral principle and the attack on the family's honor as justification for their act of violence without regard for the consequences. The story rightly ends with a question for the reader to ponder (34:31). Later, in his deathbed blessing of his twelve sons, Jacob will condemn Simeon and Levi for their violence by condemning them to being "scattered" within Israel. The scattering of Levi is an allusion to the Levites' lack of any tribal land of their own in Canaan and their presence in cities scattered among the other tribes (Num 18:23; Deut 10:9; Josh 14:3; 18:7). Simeon's "scattering" included its absorption into the tribe of Judah (Josh 19:9). God had earlier imposed the same punishment of being "scattered" upon the arrogant tower builders of Babel as a limit to the potential violence they might inflict if all the nations continued to join together as one imperial community (see commentary on 11:9).

35:1–29. Jacob's Return to Bethel: Birth and Death. Jacob engages in religious house cleaning and collects all the foreign gods and idols that his wives had taken from their father Laban (31:19, 30–35) and buries them under a tree near Shechem. Jacob and his family then travel to Bethel where he builds an altar and receives again God's promises of land and offspring (35:1–15). The episode seems to be an alternate and briefer version of a story set in Bethel (28:10–22).

Jacob's favored wife, Rachel, suffers through a difficult birth with her second son and then dies in childbirth. She names her son "Ben-oni," meaning "Son of My Sorrow" as she dies, but Jacob renames the son "Benjamin," meaning "Son of the Right Hand" (35:18). Sitting at the right hand of a patriarch or other authority indicates a favored position. Benjamin is one of two favored sons of Jacob, the other being Joseph. Both sons were born to Rachel, Jacob's favored wife (37:3; 42:35–38). Benjamin is favored, although he is the youngest of Jacob's twelve sons. This is another example of the favoring of the younger sibling over the eldest, a recurring theme in Genesis (4:1–16; 17:20–21; 25:23–26; 29:16–18; 37:2–8). Just as Sarah's death accompanied the purchase of a small part of the promised land of Canaan (23:1–20), so Rachel's death accompanies the addition of one more offspring in fulfillment of God's promise to Jacob of many offspring. Throughout Genesis, the partial fulfillment of the promises of God often happens in the context of struggle, conflict, difficulty, and even death.

After Rachel's death, the eldest of Jacob's twelve sons, Reuben, has illicit sexual relations with one of Jacob's concubines or secondary wives, Bilhah, who was also the maid of Rachel. "Israel [Jacob] heard of it" (35:22). In his deathbed blessing, Jacob will proclaim the demotion of his firstborn son, Reuben, because of this incident, yet another example of the Genesis motif of the demotion of the elder in favor of the younger (49:3–4). The recurring theme in Genesis affirms God's favor and election of the smaller and "younger" nation of Israel in relation to the greater and "older" civilizations of empires who rose and fell during the course of ancient Israel's history (Assyria, Babylon, Persia).

Jacob visits his elderly father, Isaac, in his last days. The last recorded encounter between Jacob and Isaac had occurred decades earlier when Jacob deceived his father in regard to Esau's blessing (27:35). Jacob and Esau come together as brothers to bury their father, Isaac (35:29), just as the brothers Isaac and Ishmael had come together to bury their father, Abraham (25:9).

36:1–43. The Family Line of Esau. The momentary reappearance of Esau in 35:29 becomes the occasion for the listing of Esau's extensive genealogy in Gen 36. Esau is the ancestor of the nation of Edom, a country that lies just to the east and south of Canaan (36:1). The land of Canaan will later become the nation of Israel, whose ancestor is Jacob (25:23, 30; 28:13). The long listing of Esau's descendants affirms both the partial fulfillment of divine promises to Abraham that he would be the

father of "a multitude of nations" (17:4) and the inclusion of other nations like Edom in the broad horizon of God's concern to bless "all the families of the earth" (12:3). Ancient Israel's interactions with the nation of Edom during its history varied between positive relations at times (Deut 23:7; 2 Kgs 3:1–12) and hostile relations at others (Num 20:20; 2 Sam 8:13–14; 1 Kgs 11:14; Ps 137:7; Jer 49:7–22; Ezek 25:12–14).

C. The Family Stories of Jacob's Sons: Joseph and Judah (37:1–50:26)

The last cycle of stories in Genesis features Jacob's son, Joseph, who is one of two younger sons born to Jacob's favored wife, Rachel (30:22–24). Benjamin, the other son of Jacob and Rachel, is the youngest of Jacob's twelve sons and will also play a role in the story (35:16–20). Joseph as the favored son participates in the repeated theme in Genesis of the younger being favored over the elder (4:1–16; 17:20–21; 25:23–26; 29:16–18; 37:2–8; 48:1–22). Jacob's son, Judah, also plays a prominent role at certain points in chapters 37–50, reflecting the favored status of the tribe of Judah and the southern kingdom of Judah in much of ancient Israel's history. The overall theme of the Joseph story is God's faithful protection and guidance through experiences of great suffering as God works to preserve life and make good come out of evil (45:7; 50:29).

37:1–36. Joseph and His Brothers: Dreams and Schemes. The chapter opens with a superscription or title, "this is the story of the family of Jacob" (literally in Heb., "these are the generations of Jacob"). This is a formula that occurs six times throughout Genesis and marks the beginning of each major new section (2:4; 6:9; 10:1; 11:27; 25:19).

Jacob favors the younger Joseph and provides him alone with a special "long robe with sleeves," a public sign to the other brothers that Joseph was their father's favorite. As a result, the brothers "hated" Joseph (37:4). Sibling conflict and jealousy and the violence that threatens to erupt as a result is a key theme that weaves its way in and out of the chapters of Genesis (4:4–8, 23–24; 16:3–6; 19:4–9; 27:41; 31:1–2; 32:11; 34:25–31; 37:4, 18–20). Joseph adds to the brothers' jealousy and hatred by reporting to them two dreams that imply that all of Joseph's brothers and even his parents will one day bow down before him (37:5–11). Joseph's dreams are literally fulfilled later in the story (42:6; 43:26, 28). Three dream sequences are central to the Joseph story, each sequence containing two paired dreams that reinforce their authenticity as divinely inspired and reliable predictions of the future (37:5–11; 40:5–23; 41:1–36; see 41:32).

Joseph's brothers initially conspire to kill Joseph (37:18–20) but throw him into a pit instead. In the process, the brothers strip Joseph of his special robe with long sleeves (37:23–24). Clothing will mark major transitions throughout Joseph's life (39:12, 15–18; 41:14, 42); here it marks the transition from favored son to a slave (37:23–24). The brothers decide to sell Joseph as a slave to a passing caravan that takes him to Egypt. There he becomes a slave to an Egyptian captain of the guard named Potiphar (37:36). The brothers dip Joseph's robe in the blood of a goat and bring it to their father, Jacob, who is devastated by grief and assumes a wild animal has killed Joseph (37:31–35).

38:1–30. Judah and Tamar: Deception, Death, and New Life. The story of Judah and Tamar in Gen 38 interrupts the Joseph narrative of Gen 37–50. Joseph plays no role as a character; Gen 38 may thus represent a secondary addition to the larger Joseph story. However, a number of motifs and images do intersect with the surrounding chapters of the Joseph story: a goat (37:31 and 38:17, 20), the use of clothing as a source of deception and recognition (37:31–33 and 38:13–17, 26), and a woman luring a man into a sexual relationship (38:14–18 and 39:7–18). On a deeper thematic level, both the Judah-Tamar and the Joseph stories affirm God's guidance and providence through often unusual, irregular, or unexpected means.

The Judah-Tamar story begins with Judah having three sons—Er, Onan, and Shelah. Tamar is married to Er, and Er dies childless. Under such circumstances in ancient Israel, the next oldest brother-in-law (Onan) has an obligation to have sexual relations with the wife of the deceased brother in order to produce a child heir for the deceased brother (see Deut 25:5–10). Onan fails to live up to his obligation, and he also dies. Judah is afraid to allow Shelah to lie with Tamar, fearing the loss of a third son. Tamar takes matters into

her own hand, dressing up as a prostitute, having sexual relations with Judah, and becoming pregnant. In the end, Judah must acknowledge his own guilt and negligence and Tamar's righteousness in doing what she did (38:24–26). Tamar gives birth to twins; the younger of the two boys becomes the ancestor of King David and his divinely chosen royal line (38:27–30; see Ruth 4:18–22; 2 Sam 7). Once again, contrary to expectations, the younger is favored over the elder.

39:1–23. Joseph and Potiphar's Wife. Potiphar's wife seeks to lie with the "handsome" Joseph, but Joseph refuses because to do so would betray both his master Potiphar and God (39:8–9). During one attempt at seduction, Potiphar's wife grabs Joseph's "garment" and uses it against Joseph as evidence to her husband that Joseph had tried to sexually molest her (39:10–18). Potiphar is enraged and has Joseph thrown into prison where Joseph rises again as second in command next to the chief jailer, by God's guidance (39:19–23).

40:1–23. Joseph and the Two Dreams of the Prisoners. This scene involves the second of the Joseph story's three dream sequences (37:5–11; 40:5–23; 41:1–36). Joseph interprets a pair of dreams, one for the cupbearer of Pharaoh and the other for Pharaoh's baker. Joseph has shifted his role from being the dreamer (37:5–11) to being the interpreter of someone else's dreams. (40:5–23). The two interpretations that Joseph offers concerning the dreams of the cupbearer and the baker begin with an identical phrase: "Pharaoh will lift up your head" (40:12–13; 40:18–19). However, the implication of the phrase for the two individuals is totally different. For the cupbearer, the phrase means that Pharaoh will exalt the cupbearer and restore him to his former position. For the baker, the phrase means that Pharaoh will lift up his head in a public execution by hanging. The cupbearer will be the one who will eventually tell Pharaoh about Joseph's abilities as a dream interpreter.

41:1–57. Joseph and the Two Dreams of Pharaoh. Two years pass, and Pharaoh has a set of two dreams (the third of three dream sequences in the Joseph narrative). Pharaoh dreams of seven "sleek and fat cows" that come out of the Nile River who are then eaten up by seven "ugly and thin cows" (41:1–4). In a second dream, Pharaoh sees seven plump ears of grain swallowed up by seven thin and blighted ears of grain (41:5–7). None of Pharaoh's magicians or wise men could interpret the dreams, but the cupbearer recalls Joseph as an able dream interpreter from his time in prison. Joseph is called out of prison, and his clothes are changed. As before, clothing signals a change of fortune for Joseph (37:23; 39:12; 41:42).

According to Joseph, the dreams predict seven years of plentiful harvests followed by seven years of severe drought and famine. The dreams are doubled, indicating that "the thing is fixed by God" and will shortly occur (41:28–32). Pharaoh chooses Joseph to oversee a national food storage and distribution program and exalts him as second-in-command to Pharaoh himself. Again, a change of clothing marks the transition to Joseph's new status (41:37–44). Pharaoh gives Joseph an Egyptian wife, Asenath, and Joseph has two sons, the firstborn Manasseh and second born Ephraim. Their names signify that God has made Joseph forget his misfortunes and that God has made Joseph "fruitful in the land of my misfortunes" (41:50–52). A worldwide famine sets in for seven years, just as Joseph had predicted and "all the world came to Joseph in Egypt to buy grain" (41:57). Joseph's distribution of food to starving nations becomes a concrete way in which God's promise that Abraham's descendants would be "a blessing to all the families of the earth" comes to fulfillment (12:3).

42:1–43:34. Joseph and His Brothers: Two Encounters in Egypt. The father Jacob sends ten of his remaining sons down to Egypt to buy food because of the famine. Jacob keeps only his youngest and favored son, Benjamin, home in Canaan. Joseph recognizes his brothers when they arrive in Egypt, but they do not recognize Joseph. The brothers bow before Joseph, unwittingly fulfilling the predictive dream that Joseph shared with them as a seventeen-year-old (37:5–11). Joseph accuses his brothers of being spies as a pretext to demand that they bring their youngest brother, Benjamin (Joseph's only other full brother born to Joseph's mother Rachel–30:22–24; 35:16–20), to Egypt. Joseph keeps one of his brothers, Simeon, in Egypt as a guarantee that the other brothers will return with young Benjamin.

The brothers return to Canaan and report to their father, Jacob, that they must bring Benjamin back with them to Egypt in order to retrieve Simeon, who remains there, and in order to buy more grain. Jacob initially refuses but then relents and allows his favored son Benjamin to go with his brothers to Egypt. When the brothers arrive in Egypt, Joseph sees his beloved brother Benjamin and is overcome with emotion (43:29–31) as he sets out a feast for his brothers. Although the oldest and firstborn of the brothers would be most honored, Joseph ensures that Benjamin, the youngest of the brothers, receives preferential treatment—five times the food and drink of the other brothers (43:33–34). Once again, the younger is favored over the elder, a prevalent theme throughout Genesis (4:1–16; 17:20–21; 25:23–26; 29:16–18; 37:2–8). Joseph also restores Simeon to his brothers (43:23).

44:1–34. The Test: Judah Offers Himself as a Substitute for Benjamin. Joseph sends the brothers on their way back to Canaan, but he has his steward secretly plant Joseph's special silver cup in Benjamin's grain sack. When the brothers have gone some distance, the steward catches up with them and declares that the brother with whom the cup is found shall become a slave and the rest of the brothers may go free. The search reveals that the silver cup is hidden in Benjamin's sack (44:1–13). The brothers return to Joseph. Judah then steps forward, explains how dear Benjamin is to his father, and offers himself as a substitute to remain in Egypt as a slave instead of Benjamin. Judah offers up his own life to preserve Benjamin's freedom and to save the life of his father ("when [my father] sees that the boy is not with us, he will die," 44:31).

Judah's offer to substitute himself as a slave instead of Benjamin redeems his earlier role in selling Joseph as a slave to the Ishmaelites (37:26–28). Judah's willingness to make the ultimate sacrifice and offer his life for Benjamin's freedom in obedience to the agreement he made with his father, Jacob (43:8–10), recalls another episode when Abraham was tested and offered up his life and future in the form of his son Isaac in obedience to God (22:1–19).

45:1–28. Joseph Reveals Himself to His Brothers. When Joseph hears Judah's offer of himself to save Benjamin, Joseph reveals his true identity to his brothers for the first time and weeps uncontrollably as his pent-up emotion is released. The brothers are dismayed, afraid of what the powerful

Joseph will do to them. But Joseph reassures them that it was not they who sent him to Egypt, but it was God who "sent me before you to preserve for you a remnant on earth" (45:7). As God had chosen Noah and his family to preserve a remnant on earth in the great worldwide flood (Gen 6–9), so God chose Joseph to preserve life and a remnant in the great worldwide famine (45:4–8).

Joseph invites his brothers to go back to Canaan and retrieve their father, Jacob, so that they can all return to Egypt and live in the land of Goshen: "the best of all the land of Egypt is yours" (45:20). Goshen provided lush grassland in the delta region of the Nile River in northeast Egypt, ideal for grazing livestock (47:1–6).

46:1–47:31. Jacob and His Sons Join Joseph in Egypt. As Jacob sets out with his sons to leave Canaan behind and to journey to Egypt, God speaks to Jacob in a vision or dream at night and assures Jacob that God "will go down with you to Egypt" and God "will also bring you up again" (46:1–4). God had made those same assurances earlier in Jacob's life in another nighttime vision or dream at Bethel when Jacob was on his way out of Canaan to live with his uncle Laban in Mesopotamia (28:15). Jacob will go to Egypt and live there for some time, but Jacob will be brought back to Canaan only after he dies in Egypt. Joseph and his brothers will return their father's body and bury him in the cave of Machpelah, the burial site that Abraham purchased for his wife Sarah (47:29–31; 50:12–14; see 23:1–20).

A census list of all of Jacob's family lists a total of seventy members, a modest but important step toward God's earlier promises of innumerable descendants (46:8–27; see 13:16; 15:5). Jacob sends Judah to confer with Joseph about preparations for his family's settlement in the land of Goshen in Egypt (46:28). The younger Judah has displaced Reuben, the firstborn, as the representative of Jacob's sons and emerges as a favored son alongside Joseph, yet another example of the Genesis motif of the younger being favored over the elder.

After a long separation, Joseph is finally able to see and embrace his father "Israel" (the other name for Jacob, 32:28; 35:10) as Joseph falls on his neck and weeps. The scene recalls a similar emotional reunion of Jacob and his brother Esau after

many years of separation (33:4). The poignancy of the moment is captured in father Jacob's words, "I can die now, having seen for myself that you are still alive" (46:30).

Joseph advises his brothers to tell the Egyptians that their vocation is shepherding so that they will be settled in Goshen, somewhat separate from the rest of Egypt. Joseph explains that shepherds "are abhorrent to the Egyptians" so that it would be good for Jacob's family of shepherds to live apart from the other Egyptians (46:31–34). Agriculture in ancient Egypt, with the seasonal rise and fall of the Nile River, primarily involved field-based crops. Egyptian crop farmers were wary of shepherds with grazing animals wandering about their land. The Egyptians' warm embrace of Joseph's family tempered with Joseph's advice that his family remain separate from the Egyptians recalls the similar balance or tension between embrace and separation expressed between Esau/Edom and Jacob/Israel in Gen 33. Moreover, the implied enmity between shepherds and farmers is a distant echo of the rivalry between the two brothers, Cain the farmer and Abel the shepherd. The echo sounds an ominous note for the future in the otherwise upbeat narrative. The shepherds of Israel will eventually experience the wrath of Cain; the Egyptians will become resentful of the favored Israelites and murder their young male babies (Exod 1:8–22). As the reader moves from Genesis to Exodus, the violence of a family will become the violence of an empire against its citizens.

Joseph's brothers and father have an audience with the Egyptian Pharaoh who grants them land in Goshen (47:1–6). The patriarch Jacob blesses Pharaoh when they first meet (47:7) and again when they depart (47:10). By his blessing of Pharaoh, Jacob provides another modest fulfillment of the promise that Abraham's descendants would be a blessing to "all the families of the earth" (12:3).

The increasingly severe famine forces Egyptian families to give up all their money, their livestock, their land, and, finally, their freedom in exchange for the food that Joseph and Pharaoh provide to them (47:13–26). As Abraham and Sarah had enslaved the Egyptian Hagar, so Joseph participates in enslaving the whole Egyptian population. The tables will be turned on Joseph and his family years later when a new Pharaoh who "did not know Joseph" will turn the tables and make Joseph's family of Israelites into slaves (Exod 1:8–14).

48:1–22. Jacob Blesses Ephraim and Manasseh, Sons of Joseph. The patriarch Jacob is ill and near death. Joseph brings his two sons, the elder brother Manasseh and the younger brother Ephraim, to Jacob for a blessing. Just as Jacob himself experienced the preferred blessing from God as the younger brother of Esau at the hands of his blind father Isaac (27:1–40), so Jacob insists on laying the right-handed and preferred blessing on the younger Ephraim and only the left-handed blessing on the older Manasseh (48:10–20). Once again, the younger is favored over the elder, a consistent theme that runs throughout Genesis (4:1–16; 17:20–21; 25:23–26; 29:16–18; 37:2–8; 43:33–34). The recurring theme affirms God's favor and election of the smaller and "younger" nation of Israel in comparison to the greater and "older" civilizations or empires that rose and fell during the course of ancient Israel's history (Assyria, Babylon, Persia).

49:1–33. Jacob's Deathbed Blessing of His Twelve Sons. After blessing Joseph's two sons, Jacob gathers his twelve sons together for a final blessing and description of their future destinies (49:1). The blessing of Jacob's sons is poetry rich in imagery, metaphor, and word play. The blessing of each son reflects narrative events in Genesis or elsewhere in Scripture as well as the histories of the tribes and kingdoms (northern Ephraim and southern Judah) of ancient Israel (49:28).

The demotion of Reuben as the exalted firstborn son stems from the story about Reuben "defiling his father's bed" by sleeping with his concubine (35:22). Jacob's "blessing" of Reuben echoes the recurring theme in Genesis of the demotion of the eldest and firstborn and the raising up of the younger and the unlikely ones (here Joseph and Judah). The condemnation of Levi and Simeon and their "scattering" among the tribes of Israel (Levi–Num 18:23; Deut 10:9; Josh 14:3; 18:7; Simeon–Josh 19:9) results from the excessive and vengeful violence of the two brothers against the people of Shechem when their sister Dinah was raped (34:25–26, 30).

The narrative of Gen 37–50 raises up Joseph (37:5–11; 48:21–22) as well as Judah (44:18–34;

46:28) as favored, virtuous, and exalted tribes. Jacob's blessing provides five verses for Joseph and Judah, and only one to three verses for each of the other sons of Jacob. This highlighting of Joseph and Judah reflects not only narrative dynamics but also political realities in ancient Israel's history. The northern kingdom of Israel came to be identified with Ephraim, the favored son of Joseph (Isa 11:13; Ezek 37:19; Hos 5:9–14; 11:8–9). The southern kingdom came to be identified with the tribe of Judah from which the royal Davidic line traces its roots (Gen 38:27–30; Ruth 4:13–21; 1 Sam 17:12; 2 Sam 7:8–17). Thus, Jacob's blessing prophesies that "the [royal] scepter shall not depart from Judah" (49:10).

Jacob concludes his blessing, charging his sons to bring his body to Canaan when he dies so that he may be buried "in the cave in the field at Machpelah." Abraham bought the field as a burial place for his wife Sarah (23:1–20). Abraham, Isaac, Rebekah, and Leah are all buried there as well (49:29–33). Jacob had earlier given Joseph the same instructions to bury him in the land of Canaan, not Egypt (47:29–31). The burial plot owned by Abraham represents a small piece of the promised land, a down payment of sorts on God's assurance that one day the whole land would belong to Abraham's descendants (12:7; 13:14–17; 15:7–19; 17:8; 26:2–3; 28:13; 35:12). After delivering the blessings upon his twelve sons, Jacob breathes his last and dies.

50:1–26. Jacob's Death and Joseph's Forgiveness of His Brothers. As their father requested, Joseph and his brothers travel back to the promised land of Canaan and bury their father Jacob in the cave at Machpelah. When they return to Egypt, the brothers of Joseph are afraid that with their father, Jacob, gone, Joseph may decide at last to take his revenge upon them for their treachery in selling him as a slave many years earlier (37:25–28). The brothers tell Joseph that their father, Jacob, had instructed them to urge Joseph to "forgive the crime of your brothers" (50:17). Joseph weeps when he hears their words (50:17). Joseph weeps at several points in the story (42:24; 43:30; 45:2; 45:14–15; 46:29; 50:1). On all of these occasions, only Benjamin among the brothers of Joseph had ever wept alongside Joseph (45:14). However, now all the other brothers join Joseph in their weeping and thereby demonstrate deep remorse for their earlier actions (50:18). They fall before Joseph and offer to become Joseph's slaves, again fulfilling the prophecy of Joseph's first two dreams regarding his brothers bowing down to him (37:5–11; see 42:6; 43:26, 28).

Joseph responds magnanimously, urging his brothers not to be afraid. Joseph asks, "Am I in the place of God?" Joseph's question is rhetorical and implies that he is not in the place of God nor does he wish to be. Joseph's resistance to take on the role of God and judge his brothers in revenge for what they did to him offers a counter-voice to Adam and Eve's succumbing to the serpent's tempting offer to eat the fruit and become "like God" (3:5). The first human couple's desire to be "like God" led to the violence of the next generation in which Cain killed his brother Abel (4:1–16). Joseph's response stops the potential cycle of vengeance and violence and offers another way forward. Joseph looks back over his long life of struggle with the threat of violence, slavery, and prison and sees the hand of God at work: "Even though you intended to do harm to me, God intended it for good" (50:20). Such a response is not appropriate in every experience of suffering. However, Joseph has been richly blessed by God after enduring a life of much adversity. From that vantage point, Joseph has the benefit of hindsight. He sees that God has made good come out of his suffering, preserving the life of his family and many other "families of the earth" (12:3; see 45:5–7). Thus, his brothers need not fear; Joseph will care for them and the "little ones" (50:21). Joseph affirms the theme of the Joseph story that God can be trusted to guide events toward the fulfillment of God's promises, often working in hidden and unexpected ways, even at times turning evil into good. The theme is a fitting commentary on Genesis as a whole. The stories of Genesis affirm God's surprising faithfulness in working toward the preservation and blessing of Abraham and his family as well as "all the families of the earth," even in the face of continuing human evil, violence, and hatred. Throughout Genesis, God has made good come out of evil.

Joseph lives long enough to see his grandchildren and great-grandchildren (50:22–23), but he eventually dies in the land of Egypt. As Jacob had asked to have his body returned to the land of Canaan, Joseph on his deathbed asks his brothers to do the same so that his body would be buried in the land of Canaan. Joseph left Canaan as a young man by being taken out of a pit (37:28), and Joseph desires to return to Canaan in his death by being placed in a cave at Machpelah (50:24–25). The Joseph story concludes without resolution or closure. Joseph's body is embalmed in a coffin, waiting expectantly to be carried back some day to Canaan at a time "when God comes to you" (50:24–26). Joseph's coffin will have to wait for many years before reaching its place of final rest in Canaan (Exod 13:19; Josh 24:32). Similarly, God's promises in Genesis to Abraham, to his descendants and to all humanity continue to await their full completion.

BIBLIOGRAPHY

R. Alter. *Genesis, Translation and Commentary* (New York: W. W. Norton, 1996); W. Brueggemann. *Genesis*. IBC (Atlanta: John Knox, 1982); E. Fox. "Can Genesis Be Read As a Book?" *Semeia* 46 (1989) 31-40; _____. "Stalking the Younger Brother: Some Models for Understanding a Biblical Motif." *JSOT* 60 (1993) 45-68; T. Fretheim. "Genesis." NIB (Nashville: Abingdon, 1994) 1:317-674; D. Olson. "Untying the Knot? Masculinity, Violence, and the Creation-Fall Story of Genesis 2–4." *Engaging the Bible in a Gendered World: Essays in Honor of Katharine Doob Sakenfeld*. C. Pressler and L. Day, eds. (Louisville: Westminster John Knox, 2006); P. Trible. *God and the Rhetoric of Sexuality*. OBT (Philadelphia: Fortress, 1978); C. Westermann. *Genesis 1–11, A Commentary*. John Scullion, trans. (Minneapolis: Augsburg, 1984); _____. *Genesis 12–36, A Commentary*. John Scullion, trans. (Minneapolis: Augsburg, 1985); _____. *Genesis 37–50, A Commentary*. John Scullion, trans. (Minneapolis: Augsburg, 1986).

EXODUS

BRENT A. STRAWN

OVERVIEW

Titles. The English title comes via Latin from Greek *exodos*, literally, "the way out," which is shortened from the longer *exodus Aigyptou*, "the departure from Egypt." This title nicely captures the central event that transpires in the first half of the book. The Hebrew name of the book, *shemot*, "names," is abbreviated from *we'eleh shemot*, "and these are the names ..." in the opening verse. "Names" too captures something important about the book, given personal names in the book:

- *Israel*, which becomes a people, not just an extended family, in Exodus. The transition from an extended family of individuals to a large group, a nation, ultimately the people of God, is facilitated precisely by the exodus and within the book that recounts it;

- *Moses*, who is born in Exod 2, and dominates the rest of the Pentateuch and Israel's legal imagination;

- and, finally and especially, the divine name *Yahweh*.

The personal name of Israel's God is said to be revealed for the first time in 6:3 (see also 3:14–15; cf. Gen 4:26). The meaning of this name (and how it is given) is enigmatic so that, in one sense, one discovers what Yahweh means and who Yahweh is by reading the book of Exodus itself. God's name is defined by what God does in Exodus and in the exodus. Certain key texts throughout Exodus are central in the definition of the divine name (Exod 3:14–15; 6:2–8; 15:3, 26; 20:2, 5–6; 29:45–46; 31:13; 33:19; 34:6–7).

Significance. Exodus is arguably the most important book of the OT. The exodus itself dominates the narrative history of Israel—again, it represents the starting point of Israel as a people (cf. 1:9; 15:13)—and recurs frequently in poetic articulations of that event. The latter include the Psalms (see Pss 78, 105, 114, 135) and also Second Isaiah (Isaiah is thought to be two books in one with the second book beginning at ch 40), which portrays the return from exile as a new and improved exodus from Babylon (see Isa 43:14–21;

48:20–21; 51:9–11; 52:11–12). These examples, along with references to the exodus elsewhere in the OT (e.g., Lev 19:36; Num 24:8; Deut 5:6; Josh 24:17; Judg 2:1; 1 Sam 8:8) and beyond (e.g., 1 Macc 4:9; Bar 1:19–20; 2 Esdras [5 Ezra] 1:7; [4 Ezra] 3:17) indicate that Exodus and the events it recounts lie very close indeed to the heart of the OT and its faith.

The same holds true for the NT. It is no accident that the passion takes place during Passover. There are deep structural connections between Exodus and the Christ event. While the chronology of the Gospels differs somewhat, the last supper may have been a Passover meal (see Matt 26:17–19; Mark 14:14–16; Luke 22:8–15; cf. John 18:28; Exod 24:8). According to John's chronology, Jesus dies on Passover, the very day when the lambs were slaughtered in the Temple prior to the paschal meal (cf. John 19:14, 29); this connection eventuated in specific Christological titles ("Lamb, Lamb of God"; see John 1:29, 36; Rev 5:6, 8–9, 12–13; 7:10; 21:9, 14, 22; cf. Acts 8:32–35; 1 Peter 1:19) as well as particular creedal affirmations (1 Cor 5:7; cf. Rev 5:6; 12:11; 13:8), and, perhaps, certain details in the passion accounts (cf. Exod 12:46 with John 19:33, 36; cf. also Num 9:12; Ps 34:20).

The NT has thus constructed the Christ event on the foundation laid in Exodus. Three important ramifications follow: first, the exodus is *the* redemptive activity of God in all of Scripture— even what happens later in the NT cannot be discussed apart from resonances with it. Many subsequent movements for liberation have been similarly inspired by Exodus. Second, the interrelationships between the exodus and Christ events demonstrate that it is the same God who acts in both—the same God, moreover, who acts in similar and recognizable ways in both. Third, the connection between Christ-event and exodus appears to reflect various analogues:

Exodus-event:

    Slavery > Exodus > Covenant (Sinai)

Christ-event:

    Crucifixion > Resurrection > Pentecost

Such analogues are instructive for both "versions." They suggest, for example, that the deliverance from Egypt is no less about *sin* than is Christ's death. The exodus is salvation from the sins of Egypt and its oppressive pharaoh. The analogues also suggest that the salvation that comes through the crucifixion is no less *real* or *political* than is the exodus from Egypt's tyrannical king.

Such connections and analogues indicate that Exodus is arguably the most important book, not only of the OT, but of the entire Christian Bible. The exodus is the foundational salvific act of God in all of Scripture, providing the root metaphor not only for Israel's subsequent life with God, but also for the NT authors and their attempts to understand God at work in Christ.

Structure and Theology. Exodus can be outlined several different ways, each highlighting something distinctive about the book. That granted, the book divides nicely into two roughly coequal parts, the first detailing the departure from Egypt (Exod 1–18) and the second with the covenant at Sinai (Exod 19–40). These movements of *rescue*, followed by covenantal *relationship*, can be correlated with familiar and formal theological categories: *grace* (or *gospel*) followed by *law* or *justification* followed by *sanctification*. What is most important about the book's two halves, however, is their *theological order*. Exodus narrates in large scale the precise movement evident in the prologue to the Decalogue (20:2): namely, from the revelation of who God is and what God has done for Israel (and these two are inextricable) to the giving of the commandments in the Decalogue proper (20:3–17). In a Christian context, it was not Paul who saw this, nor Luther or Calvin or some other; it is built, rather, into the very structure of Exodus itself, in the ordering of the exodus followed by Sinai. Simple observation of this fact might prevent many Christians from egregious misunderstandings of the religion of ancient Israel, let alone contemporary Judaism. No one knows better than enslaved Israel that God's gracious deliverance preceded God's covenant. Prior to both still was God's election of the ancestors (cf. 2:24; 3:6, 15–16; 4:5; 6:3, 8; 32:13; 33:1; cf. Deut 4:37; 7:8; 8:18; 9:5; 29:13). There is no "earning salvation" here. It is *given* in the ancestors and in the exodus. The covenant with God,

which is marked by the gift of torah, follows those prior gifts.

As crucial as this ordering is, there is also some overlap. Instructions concerning Passover, Unleavened Bread, and the Firstborn occur already in the first half of the book (Exod 12:1–28; 12:43–13:16); in the second half one finds the narrative of the golden calf and the renewal of the covenant (Exod 32–34). Such overlap does not contradict the dominant order; it merely underscores the interrelationship and unity of God's work in Israel and Israel's work in God. The work of creating, redeeming, and sustaining are profoundly connected.

Overlap between the two halves of Exodus is also evident in the mixing of genres: *narrative* dominates Exod 1–14, 16–19, and 32–34; whereas *law* is the primary genre in 12:1–28; 12:43–13:16; 20:1–31:18. Exodus 35–40 is itself mixed, a narrative execution of the legal instructions in 25–30. Finally, Exod 15 captures the power of the exodus in *poetry*.

Exodus also appears to be a complex combination of preexisting sources—preeminently Priestly (P) texts and non-Priestly sources. At four key junctures (Exod 3–4, 14–15, 19, 32–34), it appears that the major sources have come together in especially complicated ways. Each juncture concerns a crisis: God's calling of Moses (3–4), God's deliverance of Israel (14–15), God's covenant at Sinai (19), and God's restoration of Israel after a violation of the covenant (32–34).

OUTLINE

I. The Exodus from Egypt (1:1–18:27)

    A. Background to Deliverance (1:1–2:25)
        1:1–7. The Flourishing of Israel in Egypt
        1:8–22. The Oppression of
           Israel in Egypt
        2:1–10. The Birth of the Deliverer
           and His Deliverance
        2:11–15*a*. Early Failure:
           Moses the Murderer
        2:15*b*–22. Early Promise: Midianite
           Deliverer and Shepherd

DETAILED ANALYSIS

I. The Exodus from Egypt (1:1–18:27)

A. Background to Deliverance (1:1–2:25)

1:1–7. The Flourishing of Israel in Egypt. The opening chapters provide background, especially of the problem of Egyptian servitude. At the beginning, however, Israel is flourishing. The opening unit (1:1–7) serves as a bridge to the end of Genesis. All twelve sons of Israel (Jacob) came to Egypt, joining Joseph there. The seventy persons of 1:5 probably counts only Jacob's sons and grandsons; though not an insignificant number, especially when wives, daughters, and granddaughters are considered, this figure is still within the realm of the extended family. But 1:7 makes clear that this large group outgrows the notion of family very quickly. The "sons of Israel" (NRSV, "Israelites")

of 1:7a are no longer only the immediate sons (or grandsons) of Jacob (cf. 1:1). Instead they are "the Israelites"—capable of filling the land (1:7b) and able to be called the "people (of the sons of Israel" (1:9; NRSV, "the Israelite people"). This is no accident: the verbs used in 1:7 (being fruitful and prolific, multiplying and growing strong) hearken back to Genesis, either to the Priestly account of creation there (see, e.g., Gen 1:20–22, 28–29) or to the promises to the ancestors, especially Abraham (see, e.g., Gen 16:10; 17:2, 6, 20; 22:17; cf. 26:4, 24; 28:3; 35:11; 41:52; 47:27; 48:4). These links demonstrate that God's purposes in creation and promises in the election of the ancestors are coming to pass. The only problem is that they are coming to pass in Egypt.

1:8–22. The Oppression of Israel in Egypt. Israel's fortunes change when a new king "who did not know Joseph" arises (1:8). Joseph's deeds that put Pharaoh and Egypt in his debt (see Gen 41, 47) are a thing of the past. Worse still, Pharaoh sees Israel's growth with different eyes. Israel's blessing is Pharaoh's bane; Pharaoh lives in a non-Yahwistic world (cf. Exod 5:2). Fearing that Israel might aid his enemies in war, he enslaves them in a preemptive strike, returning them to Joseph's prior state (1:10–11; see Gen 37:25–38; 41:37–45). The tactics of the dictator do not work, however: "the more they were oppressed, the more they multiplied and spread" (Exod 1:12a). The recurrence of the important verbs from 1:7 and Genesis (see 28:14; 30:43) can only mean that God lies behind Israel's resilience. But, again, Israel's blessing is misinterpreted: all the Egyptians now share Pharaoh's sentiment. It is already clear that Israel and Egypt cannot coexist and that Israel's blessings will not be tolerated on foreign soil.

Egypt escalates its oppression. Israel's forced labor is constantly described as ruthless oppression (1:11–14). But Pharaoh is still not satisfied. He attempts full genocide. First, he asks the Hebrew midwives to kill all the male children as they are birthed, sparing the daughters. This would effectively eliminate Israel, which depended on patrilineal descent, as a distinct nation within a generation. Ironically, it is the midwives who begin Pharaoh's downfall. When they disobey because they "fear God" (1:17) and lie to cover it up (1:19), Pharaoh extends the directive to all of

Egypt. Daughters may live, but the Nile will run red with the blood of baby boys (1:22; cf. 7:14–25).

This unit raises historical questions, which recur throughout the book. First is the matter of Israel's size. Exodus 12:37 indicates that Israel departs as a group of 600,000 men in addition to children. How could such a large group be served by only two midwives? One must posit that the exchange with the midwives is simply illustrative, or that the figure in 12:37 is exaggerated, or both. While there is debate over the precise meaning of the Hebrew term 'elef "thousand," it is easiest to find in 12:37 another instance of the widespread ancient Near Eastern literary convention of inflating numerical figures.

Second is the placement of the exodus in history, time, and space. None of these matters is uncontroversial in biblical studies with some scholars preferring to see the stories in Exodus as largely late in origin, fictional in genre, or a historicization of a cult legend. The questions are many and are complicated by the fact that both of the pharaohs mentioned in Exodus go unnamed (contrast 1 Kgs 14:25; 2 Kgs 19:9; 23:29; Jer 44:30; cf. also 2 Kgs 17:4). In the absence of a specific name, one must consider other data to identify the "exodus era" and the specific kings involved (if one assumes some measure of historical veracity). While the internal biblical chronology (see Exod 12:40–41; cf. Gen 15:13; 1 Kgs 6:1) would locate the exodus in the 15th century, most scholars agree on a later date in the 13th century. This corresponds with the rise of highland villages in the central hill country of ancient Palestine that are associated with early Israel. It also fits with the only secure reference to Israel in Egyptian records: the stela of pharaoh Merenptah (1213–1203 BCE), which refers to that king's clash with a people called "Israel" (ca. 1209 BCE, see COS 2:2.6:40–41; ANET 376–78). The 13th-century horizon would probably make the pharaoh of the oppression Seti I (1294–1279 BCE) and the pharaoh of the exodus, his successor Ramesses (II) the Great (1279–1213 BCE). At this point, the name of one of the supply cities said to have been built by the Israelites, Rameses (Exod 1:11; 12:37), becomes quite important. It may be the same site known as Pi-Ramesse in Egypt (probably Qantir; the other city, Pithom, may be Tell el-Retabeh).

That the pharaoh goes unnamed remains a significant problem for historical reconstruction, though various reasons have been offered for it. One such reason could be theological: in Exodus the pharaoh has become a larger-than-life figure, transcending the *individual* who wears the crown. "Pharaoh" is instead an *entity* that includes the office and those who inhabit it. Exodus' use of the generic term "Pharaoh" may thus indicate that the problem is largely with the royal office—considered divine in ancient Egypt—with the specific person being immaterial (see below on 7:8–13:16). This non-descript ("Pharaoh" can then become a *symbol*: "the Enemy" par excellence.

2:1–10. The Birth of the Deliverer and His Deliverance.
This unit serves as a bridge from Pharaoh's genocidal edict to the event that prompts Moses to kill and flee Egypt. We hear about Moses' parents (named in 6:20) and his Levite lineage (2:1–2). As the previous unit showcased women who thwarted Pharaoh, so also does this one: Moses' mother successfully hides her "fine baby" (2:2); Pharaoh's daughter rescues Moses from the Nile and raises him as her own (2:5–6, 10; cf. Acts 7:22); and Moses' sister (named in 15:20; Num 26:59) successfully reconnects Moses with his true mother, even arranging for her to be paid for nursing her own baby (2:7–9)!

Moses' birth account has been widely compared to the birth legend of Sargon of Akkad (COS 1:1.133:461; ANET 119). Such a comparison highlights Moses' humble origins as well as his "royal" destiny. How these intersect must be worked out in the rest of the narrative. Other scholars have compared 2:1–10 to Egyptian stories about the birth of the god Horus. This comparison underscores the Egyptian origin (or coloring) of the account as well as the high status of Moses, which puts him on par with Pharaoh (see 4:16; 7:1; 34:29–35; cf. also 33:11, 17; 34:5; Num 12:3; Deut 34:10–12). Equally crucial are the links between Exod 2:1–10 and the story of Noah. The term used for basket in 2:3, 5 occurs elsewhere only for Noah's ark (Gen 6–8). This inner-biblical connection is of greater significance than the comparisons with the births of Sargon and Horus insofar as it figures Moses as a new Noah, who will prove instrumental in God's plans of restoration, salvation, and, also, judgment.

2:11–15a. Early Failure: Moses the Murderer

2:15b–22. Early Promise: Midianite Deliverer and Shepherd

These two vignettes demonstrate that Moses has the blood of a deliverer coursing through his veins. In the first unit Moses acts prematurely and too violently (Exod 2:11–15a). Though motivated by compassion for a fellow Hebrew, his act is too much, too soon. The murder cannot be covered up, and Moses is now a wanted man (2:15a). Though Moses' act estranges him from his fellow Hebrews and from Pharaoh, it is clear that he is one to watch: he has an eye for injustice, and he is willing to do something about it. Pharaoh wants someone like that put down; God wants someone like that called up (see 3:1–12).

After fleeing from Pharaoh, Moses finds himself in Midian (2:15b–22). Here too he proves an able deliverer, this time without going too far. In this case Moses' eye for injustice concerns the mistreatment of foreign women. Not only does he come to their defense, he also waters their flock (2:17).

Moses is in between: estranged from Israel in Egypt and from his adoptive family there, he is nevertheless identified as an Egyptian by Reuel's daughters (2:19). He settles in Midian and marries Zipporah (2:21). They have a son, Gershom, which sounds like the Hebrew for "a sojourner there" (2:22). In a word, Moses experiences the same alienation and loss as his fellow Hebrews back in Egypt.

2:23–25. The Turning Point: Israel in Pain, the God Who Knows.

Back in Egypt, things are getting worse. The pharaoh who instigated the terrible policies of ch. 1 has now died (2:23a). While his death will facilitate Moses' return (4:19), it also suggests a possible change of fortune for Israel because regime changes were often marked by beneficent acts from the new king. But no. All we hear of is Israel *in pain*. Four different verbs for groaning or crying out are packed into two verses (2:23–24); these cries emerge from Israel's bondage (2:23). Their cry for help rises up to God (2:23b). And this inarticulate lament is enough to rouse God. Now, four different verbs describing God's attention to Israel are packed into two verses: God heard, remembered, looked, and "knew" (NRSV, "took notice of them"). All of God's perceptions are open to Israel in their pain. This is the turning point and the beginning of the end of Pharaoh and the end of the oppressive politics of Egypt. It all begins with Israel's agony.

B. The Calling of the Deliverer (3:1–4:26)

3:1–12. Encounter at the Mountain of God, Part I.

This unit contains the first instance of an important pattern found elsewhere in the OT: the prophetic call narrative (see Isa 6:1–13; Jer 1:4–10; Ezek 1:1–3:15; Judg 6:11–17; Luke 1:26–38). The form comprises six elements: the divine confrontation (Exod 3:1–4a), the introductory word (3:4b–9), the commission (3:10), the objection (3:11), the reassurance (3:12a), and the sign (3:12b). Several aspects of Moses' call are significant. First, God calls Moses in the midst of his regular activities (3:1a) and in continuity with his past history of deliverance (2:5–6, 12, 17). Second, there is much repetition between 3:7, 9 and 2:23–25. What is new in Exod 3 is that God has now decided to do something about Israel's pain; this involves deliverance *from* Egypt *to* a good land (3:8; cf. 3:17). It also involves a human agent, creating for Moses a specific and dangerous human responsibility. Third, given this danger, it is not surprising that Moses objects to this call. Objection to God's calling is a standard and expected element in the form. True prophets do not seek their callings and do not want them when they come. And yet, fourth, with the call form the objection is heard and answered in the reassurance and sign. Although Moses ("I" in 3:11a) appears puny when compared to Pharaoh, the Israelites, and Egypt (3:11b), the point is not who he is but, instead, Who is with him (3:12a).

3:13–4:17. Further Discussion: More Objections and More Answers.

Despite God's presence, Moses is not satisfied. His call narrative is thus expanded by four more objections (3:13; 4:1, 10, 13). These become increasingly less compelling but nevertheless introduce information about God, Moses, and Aaron that is crucial for the plot. (The expansion is also due to the confluence of several different traditions in 3:1–4:17; this feature marks the unit as one of four especially important loci in the book [see the Overview].) The significant issues in Exod 3–4 include the role of human vocation in God's delivering acts along with God's revelation of the divine identity.

The most important of the additional objections is the first one, in which Moses asks for God's name (3:13). Given the importance of names in antiquity, it may be that Moses is asking not only for insight into the divine nature but even for a measure of control (deities were invoked in prayers, oaths, blessings, and curses by name). If control is what Moses seeks, it is flatly denied. God's "name" is enigmatic at best. The Hebrew *'ehyeh 'asher 'ehy* "I AM WHO I AM" (3:14; NRSV) is perhaps better translated "I WILL BE WHO I WILL BE." This latter translation better reflects the verbal aspect employed and ties 3:14 to 3:12. Part of what God "will be" is "with you" (3:12: *'ehyeh 'immak*). Juxtaposed, then, are (1) God's unwillingness to be mastered in a way that would make God an object rather than the Subject who calls and delivers; and (2) God's willingness to be known in what transpires in the future (3:14 could even be translated "I will be *what* I will be"). If there is mystery and hiding in the first point, there is promise of more revelation in the future in the second. In effect: "I am who I will be in the exodus. Wait and see." Further insight into the meaning of the name will be revealed at key junctures throughout Exodus (see 6:2–8; 15:3, 26; 20:2, 5–6; 29:45–46; 31:13; 33:19; 34:6–7).

The divine name is immediately rephrased as "the Lord." This appears to be the third-person articulation of the first-person version in 3:14, both related to the verb *hyh* "to be". While God can say "I am," humans must say "he is" (cf. the LXX at 3:14, which translates "I am the one who is"), probably a causative form: the one who causes to be—that is, who creates, the creator (note "the Lord of Hosts," i.e., "he who creates the heavenly hosts"). At an early point, out of reverence, the divine name was not spoken; its original vocalization, however, was probably something like "Yahweh" ("Jehovah" is a, secondary combination of those consonants with the vowels from the Hebrew word for Lord).

Not unlike the objection in 3:11, Moses' second objection is also met with reassurance (3:18–22; cf. 12:36). In the course of further objections (4:1, 10, 13), God provides Moses with the miraculous signs of his staff (4:2–5), his leprous hand (4:6–9a), water from the Nile that becomes blood (4:9b; cf. 7:14–25), further assurance of divine presence (4:12; cf. 3:12), and, finally, the assistance of Aaron (4:14–16). There is nothing left for Moses to do but take his staff and go (4:17).

4:18–20. Permission from Jethro. First, Moses seeks permission from his father-in-law, now called Jethro (cf. Reuel in 2:18; Hobab in Num 10:29; cf. Judg 4:11). Moses receives Jethro's blessing and returns to Egypt with his wife and sons (note the plural; see 4:20; 18:3–4).

4:21–23. Anticipation of Events to Come. These verses anticipate what will transpire with Pharaoh (cf. also 3:18–22; 6:28–7:7). Here is the first mention of the hardening of Pharaoh's heart (see 7:8–13:16 below) and a foreshadowing of the tenth plague (12:29–32). As horrific as the latter is, its first reference in Exodus is set within a parent-child metaphor; God figures as a parent who will go to any lengths to rescue his or her child from an abusive, murderous situation (cf. Isa 43:1–7). That metaphor does not make the tenth plague less horrific, but it may make it more understandable—at least at the emotional level.

4:24–26. A Frightening (and Confusing) Episode. The Lord does not pose a threat solely to Egypt, however. In one of the most disturbing episodes in the entire OT, the Lord tries to kill Moses. This passage is difficult in Hebrew as the pronouns are often unspecific (e.g., who is the antecedent of "his feet": Moses, Gershom, God?). Zipporah's quick-thinking action clearly bears some relationship to circumcision but also, apparently, to marriage practices. She now joins the list of key female figures who act in salvific ways in the opening chapters of Exodus. The oddity of Yahweh's assault remains, however. It appears to be connected to Yahweh's claim on the firstborn (see Exod 13:1–2, 11–16; 22:29a–30; 34:19–20), the tenth plague (cf. 4:21–23), and the destructive power of God that can even strike Israel if not for the averting power of blood (12:7, 13, 22–23; cf. 29:19–21). The Lord is not to be trifled with—neither by Pharaoh and Egypt (5:2) nor by Moses or Israel.

C. Moses, Israel, Pharaoh: Prelude to a Conflict (4:27–7:7)

4:27–31. Reunion with Aaron, First Overture to Israel. Moses is reunited with Aaron, who is informed of the plan (4:28) and accepts his intermediary role (4:30; cf. 4:14–16). The brothers meet with success: "the people believed" (4:31).

Moreover, once the people learn that God has visited them ("given heed") and seen their misery (cf. 2:25; 3:7, 9), they are moved to worship (cf. 12:27). Israel has a united front with empowered leaders. They are ready to face Pharaoh.

5:1–6:1. The First Unsuccessful Parley with Pharaoh.
The first meeting with Pharaoh is unsuccessful, however. The initial request to let Israel go is couched in liturgical language (or disguise?): so that they might worship Yahweh (5:1, 3; cf. 3:12b, 18; 4:23; cf. on 12:43–13:16 below). But if the earlier pharaoh did not know Joseph, the new one does not know the Lord (5:2). He has little respect for what is a minor deity—*of slaves* no less—compared to the gods and goddesses of ancient Egypt, guarantors of the status quo that kept Egypt on top and Israel on bottom. But here is a great irony because Pharaoh will come to know the Lord in excruciatingly intimate ways (see 7:5, 17; 8:22; 9:16; 14:4, 18; cf. 10:2).

The new pharaoh is as despotic as his predecessor. He does not care if his slave force is diminished by their lack of worship (5:3b). He interprets their desire to worship as laziness (5:8, 17) and requires them to work harder: the same daily quota of bricks but without provision of straw (5:7–8, 10–11, 13, 18). "Thus says the LORD" (5:1) has led to "Thus says Pharaoh" (5:10). Pharaoh's dictum means the people must scour the land looking for straw (5:12) while their supervisors are beaten for reduced productivity (5:14). They "cry out" (*tsaʿaq*) to Pharaoh (5:15)—a term rich with meaning, often used of social injustice (cf. 2:23; 22:22, 26)—but he will not listen, not even when the supervisors state that he is unjust to his "own people" (5:16). Pharaoh does not see Israel as his own people but simply as lazy slaves.

Israel's problems with Pharaoh lead to problems with their leaders (5:20–21). Israel's united front is threatened. But, when Israel's cry to Pharaoh (5:15) proves ineffectual and is turned in anger against Moses and Aaron (5:21), Moses intercedes with Yahweh on Israel's behalf (5:22–23). The cry to Yahweh leads to divine (re)assurance that deliverance will take place. Moses is an effective intercessor (cf. 32:11–14, 31–32; 33:12–17; 34:9), in part because he is a skilled orator. In his prayer he shifts from speaking of Israel as "this people" (5:22) to "your people" (5:23). God responds

when it is God's people who are involved (6:1; cf. 6:2–13; 32:11–14; 33:13b, 15–16).

6:2–13. Further Reassurance.
The exchange in 5:22–6:1 is subsequently expanded by a lengthy assurance where the divine name Yahweh is said to be revealed for the first time (cf. 3:14–16; Gen 4:26b [both J]; Exod 6:3 is P). Yahweh reiterates knowledge of Israel's plight and memory of the oath to the ancestors, before promising deliverance, relationship, and delivery to the promised land (6:4–8). The entire speech is framed by "I am the LORD" (6:2, 8), indicating that these acts shed insight into the definition of "I AM/WILL BE" and the One whose name that is (cf. 3:14 above). But the Israelites cannot hear this reassurance; they are too broken (6:9).

6:14–27. The Pedigree of Moses and Aaron.
The plot is interrupted by a digression concerning the genealogy of Moses and Aaron. It functions to clarify their relationship (6:20; cf. 4:14; 7:1–2; 28:1–2, 4, 41), provides the names of their parents (6:18, 20; cf. 2:1), and establishes their Levitical heritage (cf. 2:1). We also learn that Jochebed was Amram's aunt (6:20; cf. Num 26:59), making Moses and Aaron "illegitimate" according to later legislation (Lev 18:12; 20:19). The birth of many important biblical figures is marked by sexual controversy (e.g., Isaac, Jephthah, Solomon, Jesus). Here the emphasis is probably on the pure pedigree of Moses and Aaron; the marriage legislation in Leviticus, at any rate, had not yet been given.

6:28–7:7. Another Reassurance and Another Anticipation.
The narrative resumes with a repetition of 6:10–13 in 6:28–30. The Lord responds to Moses' objection that he is a poor speaker (6:12, 30; cf. 4:10) in a passage (7:1–2) that is very similar to 4:10–12, 14b–16. The two passages are typically ascribed to different sources, but the continuation of the call-objection-reassurance schema in two different places indicates that the called need continual reassurance just as divine revelation is continually ongoing.

This section contains another anticipation of what will take place in the narrative (cf. 4:21–23). This one also refers to God hardening Pharaoh's heart (7:3; cf. 4:21), a particularly complicated topic. While three different verbs are used (all translated by NRSV with "harden" or "hardened") to describe this situation, the total number of instances of the motif is divided precisely in two: in half of the instances the Lord hardens Pharaoh's heart (4:21; 7:3; 9:12; 10:1, 20, 27; 11:10; 14:4, 8); in the other, Pharaoh hardens his own heart (7:13, 14, 22; 8:15, 19; 32; 9:7, 34, 35; some of these latter are somewhat ambiguous, however). The distribution is also important: the Lord does not harden Pharaoh's heart directly until 9:12, in the sixth plague. Prior to that, all hardness is due to Pharaoh's own obduracy. Pharaoh's last self-hardening is in the seventh plague (9:35), after which all hardness is the Lord's work. Both the Lord and Pharaoh are involved in this scenario, even *concurrently* (plagues 6–7). One must not, therefore, ascribe the hardening entirely to Pharaoh, in some sort of psychological interpretation, or to the Lord, in some sort of theological determinism.

The hardening motif is closely connected to the plague narratives, which follow immediately (see 7:8–13:16 below; cf. 11:9). The plagues make the Lord known—not only to Pharaoh, but also to Israel, Egypt, and the whole earth (9:16; cf. 9:29). This larger function indicates that more is occurring in the plagues and the hardening of the heart than simply setting Israel free. Indeed, especially since Pharaoh no longer hardens his heart after the seventh plague, Yahweh's work is in no small measure a means to "get glory over Pharaoh" (14:4, 17–18), thereby exalting Yahweh and severely undercutting Pharaoh (9:16–17), Egypt (10:2), and the entire religious apparatus of Egypt (see below).

D. War of the Gods: Yahweh vs. Pharaoh (7:8–13:16)

In Hebrew the ten acts against Egypt are regularly called "signs" or "wonders," not "plagues" (see, e.g., 7:3; 10:1–2; 11:9–10). This terminology indicates that the acts are symbolic, reflecting something beyond their immediate content. This includes pointing backward to Pharaoh's genocidal acts (especially plagues one and ten) and forward to what takes place at the Reed Sea (Exod 14–15).

The plagues also symbolize a contest between the Lord and Egypt, especially its religion that guarantees Egypt's oppression of Israel. Some scholars have attempted to tie the plagues to specific gods—e.g., the first plague and gods associated with the Nile (Hapi, perhaps, or Sobek), the fifth plague and the goddess Hathor, often depicted as a cow, or the ninth plague and the sun-god Ra. In 12:12 Yahweh states "on all the gods of Egypt I will execute judgments" (cf. Num 33:4). However, apart from 12:12, the gods are not mentioned by name, perhaps because the Lord will not share the stage with any other deities.

There is, however, another supernal entity that is mentioned throughout the plagues: the god-king Pharaoh. While debate continues as to whether the pharaoh was always considered divine, it seems safe to say that the king was at least semi-divine as the offspring of Ra and the incarnation of Horus; the office itself was fully divine. The plague narrative, then, is a cosmic battle of the gods: Yahweh, the God of Israel, vs. Pharaoh the archenemy of Israel, who represents Egypt and its massive religio-economic apparatus. In these chapters, the Lord toys with Egypt, making the Egyptians and their king look like fools (10:2). Pharaoh now knows who Yahweh is (cf. 5:2). In the process, Yahweh demonstrates control over all of Egypt—including not only natural objects that were typically the purview of the Egyptian gods but also over Pharaoh himself. This should not be interpreted "egotistically," so much as revelationally: Yahweh is establishing who he is and who he will be (cf. 3:14) to all concerned—Pharaoh, Egypt, Egypt's gods (12:12), Israel, the whole earth (9:16).

The cosmic nature of the battle between the Lord and Pharaoh sheds light on other matters. First, some scholars have attempted to explain the signs and their sequence as naturally occurring phenomenon, such an interpretation surely misses the point. Ultimately, there is nothing natural about the plagues. Second, the plagues can be understood as signs of ecological disaster. Creation is being unmade, returning to a pre-creational chaotic state of darkness. This means Israel will be re-created in the exodus, especially in the crossing of the sea. Third, the sins of Pharaoh (cf. 9:27, 34; 10:16–17) are shown to be opposed to God's creational purposes in Israel and, through Israel, in the whole world (9:16, 29; cf. Gen 12:1–3; Exod 19:3–6). Since they are cosmic, anti-life, anti-creational sins, they must be met with signs that are equally cosmic and deadly. Finally, what transpires in the signs is God's action (see 8:19; cf. 9:20). Moses and Aaron play distinctive roles, but divine power and action are prominent, especially in the most violent strike. This means that, despite the violence of the plagues, they can actually be understood pacifistically: Israel does not fight for itself, does not take up arms, does not kill Egyptian children or damage Egyptian property. Instead all it needs do is sit back, keep still, watch, and learn who the Lord is and see the lengths to which the Lord will go to save them.

7:8–13. Aaron's Rod: Prelude to Battle. The war begins with a vignette about Aaron's staff. Differences from 4:2–5 reflect different source materials (E vs. P, respectively; for an explanation of the documentary hypothesis, see the commentary on creation stories in Gen 1–2), but they may also reflect plot development (the increased role of Aaron) and Egyptian allusions. The term for "snake" in 7:9 (different from 4:3) could also be translated "crocodile"—both animals were important in Egyptian and Pharaonic symbolism (cf. Ezek 29:3; 32:2). Swallowing was a metaphor for control in ancient Egypt, so Aaron's "snake" demonstrates control over Egypt (see also Exod 15:12).

7:14–25. The First Plague: Blood. The first sign is an ominous "flashback" to 1:22. It is as if the Lord is announcing his knowledge of Egypt's past genocidal acts. It also trumps Pharaoh because the king's plan was thwarted; the Lord will succeed.

8:1–15. The Second Plague: Frogs. As with Aaron's rod and the water-into-blood, the Egyptian magicians are able to replicate the sign of the frogs (8:7; cf. 7:11, 22). Hereafter, however, they will be unable to match the power of God. This sign is the first to elicit Pharaoh's request for prayer (8:8). Moses intercedes and the Lord listens—a characteristic aspect of their relationship throughout Exodus (3:1–4:17; 5:22–6:8; 32:11–14; 32:31–33:3; 33:12–34:28).

8:16–19. The Third Plague: Gnats. The "secret arts" of the Egyptian magicians have now failed (8:18). They declare to Pharaoh that this is "the finger of God!" (8:19). The magicians are not the last in Pharaoh's circle to understand exactly with whom they are dealing (cf. 9:20).

8:20–32. The Fourth Plague: Flies. The fourth sign is the first in which the Israelites are not affected, miraculously, by the plagues. This motif will recur as Israel and the land of Goshen, where it resides, are protected from negative effects. Exodus 8:23 says this is "a distinction" (NRSV)

that the Lord sets between Israel and Egypt. The Hebrew (MT 8:19) is more accurately translated "a redemption/liberation." While the text here is somewhat difficult, and the LXX, Vulgate, and Syriac's reading "distinction" more understandable (so NRSV), the notion of the Lord's setting "redemption" between Israel and Egypt is evocative, foreshadowing what will take place in the next few chapters and what is already taking place now.

9:1–7. The Fifth Plague: Diseased Livestock. The fifth sign maintains the distinction between Israel and Egypt (9:4), this time concerning livestock. Exodus 9:6 is overstated in light of 9:19. Such hyperbole is part of the totalizing language that pervades the plague narrative (e.g., 7:19–20; 8:4, 17, 24; 9:6, 9, 11, 22, 24–25; 10:6, 12–15, 19, 22; 11:5). The *entirety* of the land—*all* of Egypt—experiences the Lord's signs. One expects no less in a battle of cosmic proportions.

9:8–12. The Sixth Plague: Boils. Notable here is that the Egyptian magicians are not only ineffective, they must flee from Moses because the boils affect them (9:11). They are now completely removed from the battle, unable even to attempt replication via their secret arts. Moreover, once Pharaoh's coterie is directly afflicted by the signs, it is just a matter of time before the king himself feels them (note 9:14). Perhaps for this reason the sixth sign is the first to state that the Lord hardens Pharaoh's heart (9:12).

9:13–35. The Seventh Plague: Thunder and Hail. Although thunder and hail may not seem as exotic as the previous signs, they occur in the normally arid climate of Egypt. It rarely rains in Egypt; these climatological phenomena are, in that geographical context, as awesome and unnatural as what has come before.

The Lord threatens that the seventh sign will come upon Pharaoh himself and claims to have preserved Pharaoh's life up to this point. The reason for this appears in 9:16, a key verse in the plague unit: "to show you my power, and to make my name resound through all the earth." The acts of God have creation-wide ramifications and purposes. The acts are working too. Some of Pharaoh's officials are said to "fear the word of the LORD" (9:20; cf. 9:30) and to respond to God's instructions. This language is fraught with theological significance. "To fear" is associated with reverence and worship. The Lord and the Lord's word is becoming known in Egypt, even respected, even in Pharaoh's closest circles.

The severity of the seventh sign elicits Pharaoh's first confession of sin (9:27). His repentance, however, is short-lived: After agreeing to let Israel go (9:28), he hardens his heart one last time (9:34–35).

10:1–20. The Eighth Plague: Locusts.
In 10:1, the Lord takes credit for what was Pharaoh's self-hardening in 9:34–35. Again we see that the subject and causes of hardening are intermixed. The eighth sign indicates that God has transgenerational purposes in mind (see also 12:26–27; 13:8–9). The Lord has "made fools" of the Egyptians so that children and grandchildren "may know that I am the LORD" (10:2). The (re)formation of Israel that is prominent in Exod 15–24 is at work here as well.

Pharaoh's officials now openly encourage him to let Israel go, stating flatly that "Egypt is ruined" (10:7). But Pharaoh insists on conditions for an exodus (10:8; cf. 8:25; 10:24). His monstrosity—in line with his predecessor (1:16, 22)—is revealed when he swears (by Yahweh, no less!) that Israel's "little ones" will not depart (10:10a). The term used here typically refers to toddlers. The only mind with an "evil purpose" (cf. 10:10b) is thus Pharaoh's. But, after Pharaoh admits his sin and requests forgiveness (10:16–17), Yahweh relents regarding the locusts (10:19). But not regarding Pharaoh's heart (10:20).

10:21–29. The Ninth Plague: Darkness.
With the ninth sign, the impact of the plague on the created order is complete: the land returns to pre-creational darkness, one "that can be felt" (10:21). Miraculously, "all the Israelites had light where they lived" (10:23b). Israel experiences the first day of creation: God spoke light and it was (Gen 1:3). This situation prefigures the re-creational activity that transpires in chapters to come (esp. Exod 14–18).

Pharaoh attempts one final compromise, wishing to keep at least some economic advantage for himself. When this is denied, he threatens Moses with death. Here again this Pharaoh emulates his predecessor (2:15), but his threat is empty: he will summon Moses and Aaron again

(12:31). The threat is also ironic, leading directly into the tenth and final sign.

11:1–10. The Tenth Plague Announced.
The Lord announces one last plague to Moses, who relays the details to Pharaoh in hot anger (11:4–8). The final strike has been is announced, but its enactment is delayed until 12:29–32. This builds tension, with the intervening material functioning as the quiet before the storm.

The Lord will again make a distinction between Egypt and Israel (11:7): while Egypt is wailing (*tsa'aq*, see under 5:1–6:1), not so much as a dog will bark to disturb the Israelites (11:6–7). Moreover, Pharaoh's officials will come and bow down to Moses, not Pharaoh, and beg the people to leave (11:8; cf. 10:7; also 8:19; 9:20). But again—and not for the last time (cf. 14:4, 8; cf. 14:17)—Yahweh hardens Pharaoh's heart "in order that my wonders may be multiplied in the land of Egypt" (11:9).

12:1–28. Instructions for the Passover.
The interlude before the tenth plague is filled with instructions for Passover. In the immediate context, Passover provides protection from the plague (12:23), but the instructions envision that Passover is equally about the future. It will function as a ritual reenactment and remembrance of the tenth plague and, thus, the exodus from Egypt. In this way, the exodus is memorialized forever—it will not be forgotten, but taught to future generations in different circumstances (12:24–27a; cf. 12:17). It is even impressed upon the calendar: the exodus marks the first month of the New Year (12:2).

The Feast of Unleavened Bread also commemorates the exodus (12:14–20; cf. 23:15; 34:18). As with the hurried consumption of the Passover lamb (12:11), the lack of leaven is due to the hastiness of Israel's departure. There simply was not time enough to let the dough rise (12:34, 39).

Many scholars believe that both of these celebrations, along with the consecration of the firstborn, may well have had distinct and disparate origins—in agricultural rites of various sorts, for example (cf. 23:14–19a). Regardless, they are now drawn to the foundational salvific act in all of Scripture, the exodus, and made to serve as handmaidens of it.

These verses end on two important notes: first, the people bow down and worship (cf. 4:31). This represents a return to the united front established in the first overture to Israel (4:27–31). Gone is the strife caused by Pharaoh (5:19–21). Nine signs and divine protection have restored leaders and people, people and God. Second, so restored, the people are said to be perfectly obedient (12:28). This unity and obedience will also mark Israel at the end of Exodus (Exod 35–40).

12:29–32. The Tenth Plague: Death of the First-born. After the tension-filled exchange regarding the tenth plague (10:27–11:8) and then the interlude in 12:1–28, the tenth plague is narrated tersely. It happens just as Moses spoke (12:29; cf. 11:5); the "loud cry" that results is identical (12:30; cf. 11:6). It is hardly an accident—and more like poetic (better: prophetic) justice—that this cry is the same word as used earlier for Israel's suffering (*tsa'aq*, see 2:23). The correspondence between sin and judgment is also present in the strike itself. Echoes with 1:16 and 1:22 have long been recognized. Exodus 4:22–23 is also important, but so is the first sign (7:14–25). The current pharaoh reaps what a previous pharaoh sowed. What's more, Pharaoh learns that what his despotic predecessor attempted to do over a period of time—without success—Yahweh accomplishes, with ease, in a single night: "There was not a house without someone dead" (12:30*b*; cf. 12:33), except, of course, in Israelite houses, protected, as they were, by the blood of the lambs (12:6–7, 13, 23, 27; cf. 4:24–26; also 1 Peter 1:18–19; Rev 7:14; 12:11; Matt 27:25).

The hardening of Pharaoh's heart is over; judgment has been served and all concerned now know the Lord and the power of his might. Pharaoh no longer refuses, no longer attempts compromises. Now there are only a string of commands for Israel to depart immediately (12:31–32*a*). Pharaoh even realizes that the Israelites' exodus will mean a blessing on him as well (12:32*b*). This blessing could simply be the cessation of plagues, but the word used and the syntactical construction evoke the call of Abraham (Gen 12:2) as well as the blessings Jacob pronounced on a Pharaoh long past (Gen 47:7, 10). This shows the exodus to be part of God's mission to bless all the families of the earth. It puts that mission back on track (cf. 1:1–7, complicated by 1:8–22); it also represents

something of a return to non-hostile relationships between Israel and Egypt—a point continued in the next unit but unfortunately short-lived.

12:33–36. Plundering Egypt. True to prior statements (3:22; 11:2; Gen 15:14), the Egyptians now urge the people to leave and give them jewelry and clothing: "And so they plundered the Egyptians" (Exod 12:36*b*). In the context of the cosmic battle between the Lord and Pharaoh, this plundering is a sign that the war is over. The Lord has won and his people take the spoils. These spoils will prove both useful (cf. 25:3–7; 35:22–29; 38:24–25) and detrimental (cf. 32:2–4; 33:5–6) in the narratives to come.

12:37–42. The Journey from Rameses to Succoth. For Rameses (Qantir), see under 1:8–22 above; Succoth is often identified with Tell el-Maskhuta in the Wadi Tumilat. Exodus 12:38 suggests that non-Israelites also went up with Israel out of Egypt (see also Lev 24:10; Num 11:4; Deut 29:11; Josh 8:35; Neh 13:3). Perhaps the knowledge of the Lord learned in the signs has proven transformative for some Egyptians (cf. Philo, *Mos.*, 1.147; *Exod. Rab.* 18.10; Josephus, *Ag. Ap.*, 1.233–235).

12:43–51. Further Instructions for the Passover

13:1–2. Instructions Regarding the Firstborn

13:3–10. Instructions for the Festival of Unleavened Bread

13:11–16. Consecration of the Firstborn

Four sections containing instructions for the feasts of Passover, Unleavened Bread, and the consecration of the firstborn follow. The first two are already familiar from 12:1–28. Indeed, the discussion of Passover/Unleavened Bread brackets the tenth plague and its aftermath:

12:1–28 Instructions for the Passover and Unleavened Bread
    12:29–32: The Tenth Plague
    12:33–42: Aftermath: Plundering Egypt and the Journey to Succoth
12:43–51 + 13:3–10 Instructions for the Passover and Unleavened Bread

The violence of the tenth plague is now contained by the ritual celebration of the event. It is no longer enacted, only *re*enacted in liturgical and ritual mode.

Similarly, though the consecration of the first-born is new, it is split into two sections (13:1–2, 11–16), interleaved between the Passover/Unleavened Bread instructions even as it bears obvious connection to the tenth plague as those instructions do (cf. also 4:22–23, 24–26). Note:

> 12:1–28 Instructions for the Passover
> and Unleavened Bread
>> 12:29–32: The Tenth Plague
>> 12:33–42: Aftermath
> 12:43–51 Instructions for the Passover
>> 13:1–2: Instructions Regard-
>> ing the Firstborn
> 13:3–10 Instructions for Unleavened Bread
>> 13:11–16: Consecration of the Firstborn

Such interleaving signifies that the Lord's claim on the firstborn is related to God's awesome power, manifested in the tenth plague, on the one hand, and to God's profound parental passion mobilized on the part of weak children, on the other hand (cf. 4:21–23).

Consecration of the firstborn is discussed elsewhere (22:29b–30; 34:18–20; Num 3:11–13, 41, 45; 8:17; 18:15–18; Deut 15:19–16:8) where it is clear that, in the case of animals, the statute is closely connected to sacrifice. Animals not suited for sacrifice, like the donkey (Exod 13:13a), are thus "redeemable" (an important notion, used here for the first time with reference to economic substitution) for ones that are. Human children are redeemable as a matter of course (13:13b).

Rituals are a way the exodus is reenacted and made visible, even on the body (13:9). These "incarnated" traces of the exodus serve as reminders (13:9, 16) of what the Lord "did for me when I came out of Egypt" (13:8)—that is, they make the exodus a personal, existential reality. They are also an ideal mechanism by which children are instructed in the faith (13:8, 14–15; cf. Deut 6:20–25). It is as if Exodus knows that its events are singular and unrepeatable. They will only be available, hereafter, in ritual remembrance (or metaphorical reuse; see the Overview). Such remembrance is crucial so that even those who were not present and did not see can nevertheless avow: "the LORD brought *us* out of Egypt" (13:16b, emphasis added; cf. 13:8).

E. Fire and Flight (13:17–15:21)

13:17–22. The Pillars of Cloud and Fire. Although the Israelites were prepared for battle (13:18b; cf. 12:39), God is apparently concerned that they will lose heart and turn back (13:17). This is evidently what leads to God's accompanying presence in "a pillar of cloud by day … and in a pillar of fire by night" (13:21; cf. 14:19; 23:20–23; 32:34; 33:2 on angelic accompaniment). This enables round-the-clock travel not to mention travel on the best, though "roundabout," route (13:18a). The early departure from Egypt is thus marked by the miraculous power of the Lord, as were the plague narratives. This trend will continue because the route God has selected leads straight toward the Reed Sea.

14:1–31. The Crossing of the Re[e]d Sea

15:1–21. The Song of Moses

In chs. 14–15, one finds another place in which multiple sources are present. There are at least three versions of the crossing at the sea—two prose versions in Exod 14 and a poetic version in Exod 15.

The Priestly version is marked by the splitting of the sea when Moses reaches his hand out over it (14:21a, c, 27a); this is in response to the cry of the people (14:10b). The people must go forward (14:15b), walking through two walls of water on dry ground (14:16, 22, 29). The non-Priestly version recounts the Lord fighting for the people; all they must do is "stand firm," "keep still," and observe the Lord's deliverance (14:13–14). In this account, the Lord drives the sea back with a strong east wind all night (14:21b), then throws the Egyptians into a panic, clogging the wheels of their chariots, before ultimately tossing them into the sea (14:24–25, 27b; cf. 15:1, 4). The poetic version in Exod 15, while after the fact (see 14:30–31), nevertheless contains additional details that are at times akin and at times opposed to the prose accounts. In context, this poem, the "Song of Moses," is Israel's doxological response to their deliverance. It is often thought to be among the earliest compositions in the OT, with some scholars believing that the song was originally attributed to Miriam (cf. 15:21 with 15:1; in antiquity compositions were often cited by first lines only)—who is notably called a prophet (15:20)—and only later ascribed to Moses. While it may be early, the poem is not a contemporaneous account, since it appears to know of later realities: God's abode, Philistia, the taking of the land, and, perhaps, even Mt. Zion and the Temple—or, at least, Mt. Sinai and the tabernacle (see 15:13–17).

While it may be impossible to extricate these versions, let alone harmonize them, it is important to note the recurrence of: (1) the hardening motif (14:4*a*, 8, 17*a*), correlate with God's "gaining glory" over Pharaoh (14:4*b*, 17*b*, 18) so that all Egypt will know "that I am the LORD" (14:4*c*, 18). This ties the crossing of the sea to the plague narratives, making it God's final sign. (2) The notion that it is the Lord who acts decisively in the exodus such that Israel is largely a passive, observant beneficiary. Any and all violence remains the sole prerogative of the Deity. (3) The re-creation motif. It is hardly unimportant that the people are said to cross the sea "on dry ground" (*yabashah*), which outside of Exodus occurs in the Pentateuch only in Gen 1:9–10 (note also Exod 14:16, 22, 29; cf. 4:9 ; 15:19). One hears, then, a strong echo of the Priestly creation story: after the destruction of the plagues, Israel is now being re-created. The crossing of the sea is, in a sense, the third day of creation all over again.

But what sea is being discussed? NRSV translates "Red Sea," on the basis of the LXX, though often with a footnote offering an alternative: "Or *Sea of Reeds*." The latter option is due to the Hebrew (*yam suf*), and its probable relation with the Egyptian word for "reed." "Red Sea" evokes the formidable body of water by the same name, or, perhaps its western branch, the Gulf of Suez. Given its size, some scholars have argued that "Red Sea" is a later (mis)interpretation of the Hebrew phrase, an attempt, perhaps, to historicize or localize the event from a later period. "Reed Sea," on the other hand, is rather non-descript. On the basis of the term "reed" as well as geographical hints (e.g., 14:2, 9; 15:22), some scholars argue that the sea in question was one of the lakes in the Isthmus of Suez: the Ballah lakes, Lake Timsah, or the Bitter Lakes region (cf. 15:23 on the latter). Yet another proposal should be mentioned: a few scholars have taken *suf* to be related to *sof*; this turns the "Reed Sea" into "Sea of the End." Such an eschatological connection, if it is that and if it is valid, may well be secondary—a later pun. But it does pick up on

several mythological elements that are evident in the story, especially in the poetic version.

The event at the sea is an ending: the end of Israelite slavery, perhaps even the end of the world in a proleptic or eschatological way (cf. the Passover Haggadah). If so, then "Reed Sea" is analogous to "Pharaoh": in the description and use of these terms, one sees a mixing of historical and mythological elements. There is a king, but his significance goes far beyond a specific name (which in this case is notably absent) or personage. Similarly, there is a sea, but its importance lies far beyond its precise location (cf. Pss 74:12–15; 77:16–20; 114:1–8). What matters for Exodus, ultimately, is that the Lord saved Israel "that day," that Israel witnessed this awesome deed, and that Israel feared and believed in the Lord and "in his servant Moses"(14:30–31). At the sea, Israel learns something crucial about who "I AM/WILL BE" is (3:14): Yahweh is a warrior, Yahweh is his name (15:3).

F. In the Wilderness (15:22–18:27)

Though Israel is liberated, the people do not arrive at Sinai for three months (see 19:1; but cf. 18:5). Moreover, while Israel's *liberation* is complete, their *formation*—or perhaps better: *re-formation* or *re-creation* from slaves of Pharaoh to slaves of Yahweh—is only begun. The material between the crossing of the sea and the arrival at Sinai is especially important with regard to this re-formation/creation.

15:22–27. The Bitter Water of Marah

16:1–36. Manna from Heaven

17:1–7. Water from the Rock at Massah and Meribah

In these three accounts, Israel learns that their God can and will provide for them. The first needed commodity is water (15:22–27). As earlier in the book (see Exod 2–3, 5–6, 14), crying out (*tsa'aq*) to the Lord leads to God's deliverance (15:25*a*; similarly 16:2–3, 7–9, 12). Israel also learns more about who Yahweh is and will be (cf. 3:14): Yahweh is Israel's healer (15:26*b*), but Yahweh is also the Lord who instructs; gives statues, ordinances, and commandments (15:25*b*–26); and offers the conditional "if" of obedience and covenantal responsibility (15:26*a*; cf. 19:5–6).

Next, God provides quail for meat and the manna from heaven (16:1–36). This provision is brought on by a more strident complaint (16:2–3; cf. 15:23; 14:11–12); hence, the gift is more extensive. Like the water at Marah, the manna is connected to Israel's ethics (16:4; cf. 15:25*b*). It is a trial run in covenantal obedience, especially the observance of the Sabbath (see 16:28; cf. Deut 8:2). The gathering of manna evokes the gathering of straw in Exod 5; the only difference is the master Israel now serves. The current one is trustworthy to provide enough for each day, double for the Sabbath (16:22–26), from this point forward until they reach Canaan (16:35; cf. Josh 5:12). So, a jar of manna is to be kept as a perpetual memorial. It reminds Israel Who it is that provides food, as well as that hoarding is not a way of life endorsed by Yahweh (Exod 16:18; cf. 2 Cor 8:1–15).

17:1–7 contains a third provision—another one having to do with water. In this instance, the people "quarrel" with Moses (17:2). Moses interprets this as testing the Lord (cf. 16:7–8); indeed, the Israelites' question seems to forget who brought them out of Egypt in the first place (17:3). Moses cries out (*tsa'aq* again) and this again leads to God's action (17:4–5). Seeing water gush from the rock gives Israel an answer to their question: "Is the LORD among us or not?" (17:7).

In addition to providing insight into the divine nature, these three units attest to re-creational themes. In the plagues, nature was out of control, as it moved to "uncreation" and the nadir in the ninth and tenth plagues. Now, Israel experiences the re-creation of nature: bitter waters are made sweet, meat and bread rain down in the wilderness, and water bursts forth from a rock.

Israel again complains about food and drink, later, after they depart from Sinai (Num 11; cf. 20:1–13). In Numbers, their complaint is met with provision but also with the Lord's anger, fire, and plague (Num 11:1–3, 10, 20, 33–34). What might explain the difference in divine response there versus in Exodus? One insightful possibility is that Yahweh acts with great patience in Exod 15–17 because Israel is still being formed or reformed—learning to see themselves (and their God) as a loved and cared-for child (with nurturing parent) rather than as an abused slave. But Num 11 follows Sinai. In a real sense, Sinai is Israel's bar mitzvah. At Sinai, Israel grows up, becoming not only Yahweh's firstborn (Exod 4:22) but a "son of the commandment." After Sinai, then, complaints are not tolerated as they are prior to Sinai—no doubt in part because they reflect a much more profound lack of trust in the God who not only delivered, but who has come near in covenant (cf. Deut 4:7–8).

17:8–16. The Attack of Amalek

18:1–27. Interlude: Jethro and Jurisprudence

These two narratives concern two paradigmatic but contrary non-Israelite responses to Israel and its deliverance. First, negatively, comes Amalek, an Edomite tribe (Gen 36:12), that dwelled in the Negev (Num 13:29). Without provocation or explanation, Amalek attacks Israel. Joshua and others fight back, triumphing as long as Moses' hands are upheld. Joshua is victorious, and Israel again learns more about "I AM/WILL BE" (cf. 3:14): "The LORD is my banner" (17:15): both that the Lord's might is efficacious outside of Egypt and Joshua's efficacy as war-general prefigure things to come. The paradigmatic nature of Amalek's response to Israel is signified by 17:16 (cf. Deut 25:17–19).

But non-Israelites can also respond paradigmatically to Israel in positive ways. Jethro reappears in Exod 18:1–27 (cf. 2:18; 4:18). His is a non-Israelite response that hears of God's deliverance (18:1, 8) and rejoices over it (18:9). Indeed, Jethro's subsequent doxology (18:10–11) is nothing short of an affirmation of faith (cf. 18:11 with 15:11) accompanied by requisite sacrifices (18:12). It is not surprising that he was often treated as a convert in later interpretation. What *is* surprising is that Jethro is the impetus behind a major change in Israelite jurisprudence (18:13–26). Jethro advises Moses to delegate judicial matters and tells him how to pick suitable judges. Jethro even speaks of and for God (18:19, 21, 23). Moses listens and obeys (18:24). Jethro, then, offers a second, more positive option for how the non-Israelite world can receive, interact, even join in with God's people.

II. The Covenant at Sinai (19:1–40:38)

A. The Theophany and the Commandments at Sinai (19:1–24:18)

19:1–25. Encounter at the Mountain of God, Part II. With ch. 19 Israel arrives at Sinai. Here,

the second half of the book of Exodus commences. Israel will be at Sinai for the rest of the book—indeed, until Num 10:11. The first chapter of the Sinai pericope, Exod 19, is another place where multiple traditions have come together (cf. Exod 3–4, 14–15, 32–34). Priestly and non-Priestly traditions are here, as, perhaps are two distinct versions (J and E) of the latter and even a few touches from a final redactor (R). The confluence of at least two if not four different sources attests that the contents of Exod 19 are of great importance. The issue that attracted such attention is the (re)formation of Israel. This (re)formation has already been initiated in Exod 15–17, but it is especially pronounced beginning with Exod 19 and running through Exod 24, at least, but really all the way through Num 10:10. Israel will forever remember that what took place at Sinai was foundational and unrepeatable (cf. Deut 4:9–20, 32–40).

The covenant that is enacted in Exod 19–24 is nicely encapsulated in 19:3b–6. God's gracious acts are followed by a conditional "if": *if* Israel obeys, *then* Israel will be God's treasured possession, a priestly kingdom, and a holy nation. While this is a unique relationship, Israel is reminded that the Lord claims ownership of everything (19:5b). This claim chastens Israel's election; more importantly, it highlights the intercessory, even missiological, role that Israel serves in the divine economy vis-à-vis "the whole earth." Israel answers the "if" with a resounding "yes" (19:8), and the people made ready "to meet God" (19:17) and receive the Lord's commands. The encounter is nothing short of volcanic (19:16–19).

The introductory matters in Exod 19 are concluded by the ceremony in Exod 24:1–18. In between comes Israel's most important and most ancient law.

20:1–17. The Decalogue

20:18–21. The People's Response

Israel hears the Ten Commandments—or "ten words" (see Exod 34:28; Deut 4:13; 10:4)—directly from God. After that, they are afraid and ask Moses to intercede for all that follows (Exod 20:18–21). This underscores Moses' import but also sets the Decalogue apart as the most important piece of OT law. Its primary position, its place in the ark, and its repetition in other parts of the OT (e.g., Exod 34:11–26; Lev 19; Deut 5:6–21;

further Deut 6–11; 12–26) all make the same point. In one sense, all of the law that follows can be seen as dependent on, related to, and/or an explication of the Ten Commandments.

One cannot do justice to the Decalogue in a short space. Only a few comments can be offered. First, the Decalogue includes a condensation of the entire narrative of liberation that has transpired in Exod 3–15. The so-called prologue to the Decalogue reminds Israel about who "I AM/WILL BE" is (cf. 3:14)—namely, the God who delivered—and thus about what God has done for Israel (20:2). The law-giving and the law-keeping that follow are predicated on the prior grace of the Lord. The Jewish tradition counts this "prologue" as the first commandment. Thus, before all else, one must remember what God has done for us.

The first commandment (in Christian enumeration) forbids other gods priority before Yahweh (20:3). This is not a monotheistic statement so much as a monolatrous one. There may be other gods—indeed there are other gods (cf. 12:12)!—but Israel is not to traffic with them. The only monotheism that matters, ultimately, is an *ethical* one. The second commandment (in Reformed enumeration) concerns the prohibition of images (20:4–6). In Hebrew, this commandment is closely tied to the first (the "them" in 20:5 refers back to "other gods" in 20:3), hence their combination in Jewish, Lutheran, and Catholic numerations. At one point, this commandment may have prohibited images of Yahweh. Now it refers to created things, which are not to be worshipped as the Creator.

The third commandment prohibits wrongful or trivial use of God's holy name. The verb used here (literally, "take up") may specify wrongful use in public contexts. That could relate to court scenarios (cf. 20:16), use in oath formulae, or even—more broadly—in any way that brings the name into ill repute. At issue, then, is hypocrisy.

The Sabbath commandment was given and narrated in the story of the manna (Exod 16). Here it is tied to the Lord's rest in creation (cf. Deut 5:15, where it is tied to Egyptian servitude). The fifth commandment regarding parents may relate to the fourth insofar as it probably concerns aged parents. As the Sabbath commandment demonstrates, there is more to life than work, so the parent commandment dictates proper treatment for elders who are no longer viable economic producers.

The remaining commandments are especially terse and concern treatment of other people (so also the fifth commandment). The terseness of these directives—and, indeed, of the whole Decalogue—means that much of Israel's legal corpus will contain case law explicating the "constitutional law" of the Decalogue. "You shall not kill" (Exod 20:13, author's translation). But what does this mean? Does it apply to war? Unintentional homicides (see 21:12–14)? These questions are taken up in subsequent laws.

Finally, the tenth commandment includes interior states as well as outward action—perhaps interior affects that lead to external action (cf. Micah 2:2). This prompts one to reread the entire Decalogue and consider how it might apply to the internal world as well as the external one. This too is apparently how Jesus understood matters (see Matt 5:22, 28)

20:22–23:33. The Book of the Covenant. The "Book of the Covenant" (see 24:7a) is widely thought to be among the oldest parts of OT law. It is introduced in 20:22–21:1, a passage detailing laws about worship and specifying that what follows are "ordinances" (21:1)—a term used extensively for law based on but distinct from the Decalogue (cf. Deut 12:1). It concludes in Exod 23:20–33, a passage describing what God will do for Israel if the people obey (23:22). By framing the central laws of the Book of the Covenant, this introduction and conclusion indicate that Israel's observance of these laws is both an act of worship and a measure of their covenant fidelity upon which their future success in Canaan and subsequent relationship with God will depend.

As a collection, the Book of the Covenant is disparate, containing laws that run the gamut from religious to civil matters. In addition to the introductory laws on worship (20:22–26), one finds laws pertaining to personal injury (21:12–27), property (21:28–36), compensation for wrongdoing (22:1–15), and so on. This is not a "collection" marked by obvious coherence or unity. "Collection" also signals that this unit may not have functioned as a law code proper. Many legal issues are not discussed in the Book of the Covenant;

even punishment for violation is often left unmentioned. The Book of the Covenant may have been a compilation of legal wisdom or a compendium of principles for judges as they made decisions about related matters.

A few points about the Book of the Covenant should be underscored.

1. Although it may be an early collection, it contains pieces that obviously stem from later periods.

2. Laws concerning slavery (21:2–11, 20–21, 26–27, 32; 23:12; already in 20:10, 17) are a case in point. They are also odd considering the dominant liberative thrust of Exodus. How could Israel enslave others, playing the part of Pharaoh to another, especially given the Sabbath command (20:17; cf. 5:6–9; Deut 5:15)? Do these slave laws indicate that Israel failed to live up to a life marked by exodus? One might first reply that these laws surely come from a later point in Israel's history. Second, in most cases, the kind of slavery discussed in these laws is intra-Israelite and is of a different kind than Egyptian slavery. Most laws about slavery in the OT concern persons who work to pay off economic debts; the laws typically insure a limited period of service (Exod 21:2; cf. Deut 15:12–18), except in very rare circumstances (Exod 21:5–6). This is quite different from Egyptian slavery, which was ethnically demarcated and indefinite in duration. Most, but not all (see, e.g., Lev 25:44–46), Israelite slave practices thus do not undercut the primary liberative thrust of the exodus. Indeed, some have argued that even the slave laws are marked by humanitarian concerns (e.g., limiting the length of servitude, circumscribing the power of the slaveowner).

3. If so, and certainly in others places in the Book of the Covenant, Israel begins to model within its community something of God's redemption of the people (see esp. 22:21–27; 23:6, 8–9, 11–12). This is clearly a process, though, and not yet complete. Israel is still very much in the process of (re)formation. It is left to a later law collection to abolish Israelite slavery (Lev 25) and a still later writer to come close to abolishing slavery altogether (Gal 3:28; Philemon).

4. Insofar as the ordinances concern the good of the community and its life, they become part of God's (re)creative work in the world. Law in the

OT thus becomes a picture of the way in which the community should live.

5. The *lex talionis*, the so-called "eye for an eye" law (21:23–25), deserves brief comment. In its ancient context, this law is *not* a vindictive prescription. To the contrary, the talion law is a measure of proper justice, making sure that punishment matches the crime.

24:1–18. Sealing the Covenant. The people respond to the ordinances (24:3; cf. 21:1) as they did at the very start: with full agreement (24:3; cf. 19:8). The covenant is marked by a written document (24:7a), the building of an altar, and sacrifices (24:4–6). After hearing the Book of the Covenant, the people again reiterate their commitment (cf. 19:8; 24:3), adding "and we will be obedient" (24:7b). Moses then sprinkles them with "the blood of the covenant" (24:8).

As a final act of covenantal agreement, Moses, Aaron, Nadab, Abihu, and seventy elders ascend the mountain, see God, and share a meal (24:1–2, 9–11). Despite some confusion about who is present (cf. 24:1–2 with 9–11, 12–13, 15), perhaps due to the blending of different sources, the statement that these individuals saw God (twice, with two different verbs) is remarkable. Despite the fear that is often associated with seeing God (see, e.g., 33:20; Deut 18:16; Judg 6:22), people do frequently encounter God in the OT and survive

(see, e.g., Gen 16:13; 32:30; Judg 13:22). In Exod 24, seeing God signals the proximity of the Deity and the people in the unique bond of covenant (cf. 25:8; 29:45–46).

Exodus 24:12–18 provides a transition to what follows. It mentions the tablets of stone that Moses will receive from God and states that Moses remained on the mountain for forty days and forty nights—a generic number that designates a lengthy and full period. Much will happen during this time.

B. Instructions for the Lord's Tabernacle (25:1–31:18)

Moses receives extensive instructions for the tabernacle (for a reconstruction see fig. 1). The tabernacle is critical because it serves as the physical sign of God's presence and movable center for worshiping the Lord in the wilderness (cf. 2 Sam 7:6). (The ark of the covenant plays similar functions, functioning as the mobile throne by which God goes into battle [cf. Num 10:35; 1 Sam 4:3–5] and from which the Lord delivers additional commandments [Exod 25:22].) The tabernacle also provides a model for the Temple (1 Kgs 5–7). The importance of the tabernacle as the physical habitation of the Deity explains the detail that marks Exod 25–31. Little is left unspecified; the style of the chapters is fulsome. Care for God's

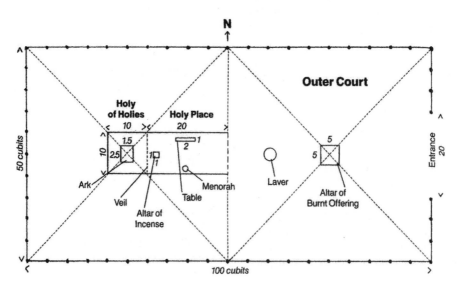

Fig. 1. Plan of the Tabernacle (from N. M. Sarna, *Exploring Exodus: The Heritage of Biblical Israel* [New York: Schocken, 1996], 192).

tabernacle includes special attention to those who serve therein (Exod 28–29; 30:17–30). Also of great import are the specific practices that take place in the tabernacle (29:38–46) and provisions for its ongoing maintenance (30:11–16). These details concerning the tabernacle, along with its personnel and rituals, are all repeated, in virtually identical form, in Exod 35–40. This repetition is of crucial theological importance, since it follows the report of Israel's violation of the covenant and God's renewal of the covenant (Exod 32–34, on which see below).

This repetition also signals something about the larger structure and meaning of Exodus. Exodus 25–31 and 35–40 may be seen as parallel panels, the first planning a place for God's presence, the second preparing that place. Exodus 1–24 and 32–34 may also then be construed as parallel panels, each having to do with God's acts to facilitate the people's arrival at this place of presence as well as to deal with the problems that complicate the achievement of that goal. A two-act outline of Exodus results (Janzen):

Act 1

A   1–24: Oppression, Redemption, Covenant

B   25–31: Planning a Place for Presence

Act 2

A'   32–34: Sin, Redemption, Covenant

B'   35–40: Preparing a Place for Presence

In each act, God delivers Israel from evil to enable the move to B/B'. In the first act, the evil is Egyptian oppression. In the second, it is the evil of Israel's own sin in the golden calf episode. This structure suggests that Exodus focuses on God's redemption—the salvation (or justification) of the people—so as to bring them into intimate relationship (6:7; 19:5–6; Lev 11:45; 22:33; 25:38; 26:12; Num 15:41; Deut 26:17; 29:13)—the covenant with God (or sanctification of the people). The latter is the special emphasis of Exod 25–31. Here Israel receives two additional insights into the nature of "I AM/WILL BE" (3:14), first, in 29:45–46: "I will dwell among the Israelites .... I am the Lord their God, who brought them out of the land of Egypt that I might dwell among them"; then in 31:13: "that you might know that I am the Lord, who sanctifies you" (author's translation).

C. The Covenant Violated and Renewed (32:1–34:35).

Exodus 32–34 is the fourth place at which various sources that make up the Pentateuch have come together in particularly complicated ways (cf. Exod 3–4, 14–15, 19). The crucial issue in this case is restoration: can Israel be restored after violating the covenant in such a devastating way and at the worst of times—immediately after the covenant has been made? Given the seriousness of this question, it is not surprising that several traditions offered responses to it.

32:1–35. The Golden Calf Debacle. Chapter 32 returns to the foot of the mountain, where Israel has been waiting for Moses since he disappeared into the cloud (24:18). While "forty days and forty nights" is a generic term, it is nevertheless a considerable time for Israel to be without its leader. The people's request that Aaron make them "gods for us, who shall go before us" is directly related to Moses' delay (32:1).

The narrative that follows is not without some ambiguity. Is Aaron's declaration of a festival to the Lord (32:5) an attempt to set things right after the people's idolatrous definition of the calf (32:4*b*)? Or is his declaration the worst kind of syncretism? On balance, Exod 32 as a whole presents Aaron in a distinctly unfavorable light (32:21–24, 35*b*).

Several issues seem to lie just beneath the present form of the chapter. One of these concerns the calf itself. Only one calf is made, but the Israelites designate it with a plural: "your gods" (contrast Neh 9:18). Is the calf envisioned as an animal mount—perhaps a divine one—with a god riding upon it? Such iconography is common in the ancient Near East. Or is the plural form of Exod 32:4 a not-so-subtle polemic against Jeroboam, who speaks virtually identical words (1 Kgs 12:28*b*) after making two calves of gold, one for Dan and one for Bethel (1 Kgs 12:29)? And why a calf or young bull? Bull imagery is largely eschewed for the Lord in the OT, probably because it was frequently associated with both El and Baal—gods of the Canaanite pantheon. Is the calf a Canaanite motif? Alternatively, bovine imagery is used extensively in Egypt, especially of the cow-goddess Hathor (note also Apis and Mnevis, who have been proffered as possible referents). In this reading, does the calf evoke a desire for things

Egyptian, perhaps even an attempt to "marry" the goddess Hathor to the god Yahweh?

These questions permit no firm answers. What is certain, however, is that the calf violates the first and second commandments (20:3–6). This serious violation happens at the very moment place of covenant-making. Adding further to this irony is that the people apparently want proof of divine accompaniment (32:1). At the very moment of their apostasy, Moses is receiving instructions for how God's presence will accompany Israel in the tabernacle (recall 20:18–19; cf. 28:35)! Perhaps worst of all, Israel takes a key aspect of the divine name—"I am the LORD who brought you out of the land of Egypt" (20:2)—and applies it to the calf. This, too, violates the Decalogue (20:2, 7), but is equally at profound odds with the entire revelation of Yahweh throughout Exodus.

It is no wonder that God immediately disowns the people (32:7) and plans to start again, with Moses as Abraham *redivivus* (32:10; cf. Gen 12:2). Destruction is only narrowly averted by Moses' intercession (32:11–14; cf. 33:12–23). He reminds Yahweh that Israel belongs to him, no one else (32:11*a*; cf. 32:7), and he restores the epithet "bringer out of Egypt" to Yahweh, to whom it belongs (32:11*b*). Moses suggests that Yahweh consider the divine reputation in Egyptian eyes (32:12), and, failing all else, remember the ancestors (32:13; cf. 2:24). Remarkably, God does exactly what Moses asks and foregoes the planned destruction (32:14; cf. 32:12*b*; Jonah 3:10).

Though the people are spared, the covenant is declared null and void by the breaking of the tablets (32:19; cf. 32:15; 31:18; 24:12). Moses destroys the calf thoroughly (32:20), reprimands Aaron (32:21), and calls those still faithful to Yahweh—the Levites—to fight the apostate, whomever they may be (32:25–29).

The "great sin" (32:21, 31) of the golden calf, therefore, threatens to undo all that has come before. The parallel structure of Exod 1–24//32–34 shows that evil and sin can be theological (32) as much as socio-political (2–5). Evil and sin can be individualized (cf. 32:26) and systemic (a la Pharaoh's sin). Both types must be redeemed; both require atonement and forgiveness (6:6; 10:17; 32:30; 34:9).

Following the re-creation of Israel in Exod 15ff., Exod 32 can be seen as "the Fall"—Israel's primal sin. The remainder of Exodus considers if and in what way that Fall can be countered in (new) re-creation. Already in Exod 32, it is clear that not all of Israel will survive the process (32:28, 33, 34*b*–35).

33:1–6. The Command to Leave Sinai Without God's Presence

33:7–11. The Tent of Meeting Outside the Camp

33:12–23. Moses' Intercession

In 32:4 Yahweh commanded Moses to lead the people on, saying that the angel would accompany them. No mention is made, however, of the Lord's own presence (contrast 13:21; 29:45–46). What was just a hint in 32:4 becomes explicit in 33:1–6. Yahweh returns to distanced speech about Israel, attributing them to Moses (33:1*a*; cf. 32:7, 11). Although Yahweh does mention the ancestors (33:1*b*; cf. 32:13), the first element in Moses' intercession has apparently failed. Instead, the Lord declares that he will not go up in Israel's midst (33:3*a*); their rebellion would lead God to consume them (33:3*b*).

After the people react appropriately to "these harsh words" (33:4–6) and an aside about Moses' tent of meeting, a kind of precursor to the tabernacle (33:7–11; cf. 27:21), the narrative resumes with Moses interceding yet again (33:12–25; cf. 32:11–13). Here too he proves a skillful orator by first discussing himself and his role (33:12–13*a*)—which is not under negotiation—and only then, quickly and briefly, reminding Yahweh that Israel is "your people" (33:13*b*). Again, Yahweh listens to Moses (cf. 32:14), promising his presence—at least with Moses ("you" in 33:14 is singular). But Moses presses for Israel, speaking of "us" and stating that only God's presence will make him favored and Israel (again described as "your people") "distinct" (33:16)—an important aspect in the plagues (see 8:22; 9:4, 26; 10:23; 11:7; 12:23). Yahweh accedes, apparently solely because of Moses (33:17): Moses has again proved instrumental in redeeming the people, now from their own sin. But still Moses presses for more: not satisfied with seeing God's ways (33:13), he now asks to see the Lord's "glory" (33:18). Exodus 33:11 already stated that Yahweh and Moses spoke "face to face, as one speaks to a friend," but Moses seeks more: insight into the divine nature. Like his earlier attempt to know God's name (3:13), Moses' current request will be partially granted and partially denied. Moses will not see God's glory but only God's "goodness" (33:19) and "back" (33:23) "for no one can see me and live" (33:20, author's translation, cf. 24:10). And Moses receives further insight into the meaning of the divine name: "I will be gracious to whom I will be gracious, and will show mercy on whom I will show mercy" (33:19). This is quickly revised in 34:6–7.

34:1–9. The Revelation of Yahweh

34:10–28. The Covenant Renewed

As a sign that the covenant is renewed, Moses again ascends the mountain, bringing new tablets to be reinscribed (34:1–4). Yahweh then passes before Moses and proclaims the name "The LORD" (34:5). But what seemed to be capricious in 33:19—giving grace and mercy however God saw fit—is now clarified and extended into a creedal statement that is repeated in various parts of the OT (34:6b–7; see Num 14:18; Jer 32:18; Joel 2:13; Jonah 4:2; Nah 1:3; Pss 86:15; 103:8; 145:8; Neh 9:17). This is the final and fullest clarification of "I AM/WILL BE" (3:14). At crucial points, the book of Exodus has offered insight about the nature of the Lord. Here, at the most crucial point of covenant renewal, we hear of the Lord's mercy, grace, patience, steadfast love, and forgiveness (contrast 20:5–6). To be sure, there is also punishment and requiting, but the divine scales are decisively tilted toward grace and mercy: thousandth generation to fourth. Moses bows in worship (34:8). But ever the model leader, he also capitalizes on God's mercy and grace to intercede again for Israel. For the first time, Moses himself admits that Israel is stiff-necked, but he knows that the Lord will pardon (34:9; cf. 34:7a).

The Lord agrees by reinstating a covenant (34:10, 27), which includes a reiteration of several of the covenantal laws that have come before (cf., e.g., 34:17 with 20:4, 23; 34:21 with 23:12; etc.). Contrary to 34:1 and 28, however, 34:11–26 are not identical with the Ten Commandments. Scholars often call 34:11–26 the "ritual Decalogue" since it focuses primarily on worship. While this ritual Decalogue has a distinct origin from the "ethical" one, in the literary context, its emphasis

on worship makes sense because the threat to the covenant has been posed precisely by and within a liturgical context (the calf). Moreover, the fact that the ritual Decalogue begins with the prohibition of worship of other gods like 20:3–4, and ends with a law that parallels the last one in the Book of the Covenant (34:26b//23:19b), suggests that this unit is meant to stand in as a summary of in continuity with 20:1–23:19.

34:29–35. Moses' Visage. At the conclusion of his second stay on the mountain (34:27), Moses returns and his face "shone" (34:29). The verb used here (*qaran*) is a denominative from the noun "horn" (*qeren*). While most ancient versions translated the verb with words meaning "shine" (so also NRSV), the Vulgate understood that Moses' face was horned. Such an interpretation was memorialized in art by Michelangelo's famous statue. Other perspectives are possible, but the horned one is intriguing given the long-standing practice in ancient Near Eastern iconography to depict divinities with horns (the motif is neither restricted to bovine deities nor to just one type of god). Moses' being horned, in this light, would be a sign that he has been exposed to divinity, even taking on some of those characteristics himself. Alternatively, it might be noted that pharaohs in Dynasties 18–19 frequently wore a ram's horn on their face representing, apparently, their deification. Whether this depiction derived from general ancient Near Eastern or Egyptian iconography or simply designating an unusual radiance, Moses' close encounter with God is now physically manifest, visible to all. He has become, more than ever before, God's stand-in. Not surprisingly, the people are afraid (34:30; cf. 20:18–19). But Moses, like Yahweh, calls to them nevertheless and tells them everything (34:31–32). Subsequently, when Moses speaks with Yahweh and delivers Yahweh's words, his face is seen shining (or horned); otherwise, he veils his face, not unlike Yahweh himself (34:33–35; cf. 33:20).

D. Israel at Full Stretch (35:1–40:38)

The final six chapters of the book of Exodus are often undervalued. This is undoubtedly due to the repetitive nature of these materials: the instructions laid out in chs. 25–31 are enacted in chs. 35–40 in close detail. On the face of it, there is little new here, and so scholars often give the final unit short shrift. This practical result is that many treatments end with an exposition of chs. 32–34, which are then touted as the theological climax of Exodus. In point of fact, chs. 35–40 are of equal or greater theological significance.

The Sabbath regulations in 35:1–3 pick up where 31:12–17 left off, almost as if ch 32 never happened. In light of the extensive work to follow, the Sabbath command reminds Israel of the importance of rest. After this comes preparation for the construction, including offerings for the tabernacle's materials (cf. 35:4–9 with 25:1–7), an overview of what will be constructed (35:10–19), response to the instructed offering (35:20–29), and mention of Bezalel and Oholiab (35:30–36:2; cf. 31:1–11). The request for offering is open-ended (35:5: "whoever is of a generous heart"), but the response is overwhelming, moving quickly from all whose heart was stirred and whose spirit was willing (35:21) to "both men and women; all who were of a willing heart" (35:22a) until finally it is simply "everyone" (35:22b, 23, 24 [twice]) or "all" (35:25, 26, 29). The offerings brought exceed the need (36:3–7). These Israelites have been reformed: from Egypt, through the wilderness, into the covenant and out of it through the calf debacle, only to be brought near again in chs. 33–34. They no longer have stiff necks (32:9; 33:3, 5; 34:9) but willing hearts and spirits (35:21–22, 26, 29; cf. 25:2).

In contrast to the order in chs. 25–31, the tabernacle is constructed before the ark (36:8–38; cf. 26:1–37), probably because the structure that houses the ark should be built before the ark itself. The construction of the ark follows immediately (37:1–9; cf. 25:10–22), then the table for the bread of the presence (37:10–16; cf. 25:23–30), and the lampstand (37:17–24; cf. 25:31–40). For some unexplained reason, 37:25–28 then moves to the altar of incense—a major dislocation vis-à-vis chs. 25–31, which doesn't discuss the incense altar until 30:1–10. As part of this dislocation is another: 37:29 briefly recounts the making of the anointing oil and incense (cf. 30:22–37). It may have simply made sense to associate the incense with the incense altar so that chs. 35–40 present a streamlined version of chs. 25–31. With Exod 38 we return to the order of chs. 25–31, discussing the altar of burnt offering (38:1–8; cf. 27:1–8) and the courtyard and its hangings (38:9–20; cf. 27:9–

19). Exodus 38:21–31 is a brief digression, "the records of the tabernacle" (38:21), after which 39:1–31 parallels 28:1–43 regarding the priestly vestments. The ordination of the priests (29:1–37) is delayed until Lev 8 and the sacrifices of Exod 29:38–46 are discussed extensively in Lev 1–7 and inaugurated in Lev 9. The half-shekel offering (30:11–16) is taken up in 38:25–28, where it directly contributes to the decoration of the tabernacle. The completion of work is recounted in 39:32–43 with the erection and consecration of the tabernacle coming in 40:1–33. Yahweh then fills the tabernacle (40:34–38), one year after the Israelites departed Egypt (see 12:2). Yahweh now dwells with the people (cf. 29:45–46), and the tabernacle assumes the role formerly played by the pillar of cloud and fire (13:17–22).

The strong similarities between chs. 25–31 and chs. 35–40 are significant. Both sections derive from the Priestly source; detailed and precise instructions for ritual practice are important. Although the dating of "P" is debated, there can be no doubt that P was important in exile and beyond—during times when the proper tools or locus of priestly worship were inaccessible. At such times, the repetition of chs. 25–31 and chs. 35–40 could function as a kind of visionary experience, even something on which to meditate; one could compare mystical developments known later in Judaism which focused on the Temple (Hekhalot mysticism; cf. Ezek 40–43; Pss 48, 122), heavenly worship (the *Songs of the Sabbath Sacrifice* from Qumran), or God's throne (Merkabah mysticism; cf. Ezek 1). Perhaps Exod 25–31 + 35–40 stands as a precursor of such mysticism.

If chs. 32–34 represent Israel's fundamental sin, then the repetition of chs. 25–31 in chs. 35–40 plays another important theological function. The "creation" that began in chs. 25–31 and threatened by the "fall" in chs. 32–34 is set back on the right course (re-creation) in chs. 35–40. The way this repetition is presented is crucial. Everywhere the repetition underscores *exact obedience* in a precise command-execution format. This obedience marks *all involved in the work* and *all that the* Lord *commanded* (39:42–43). "As the Lord had commanded Moses" occurs eighteen times in two chapters (39:1, 5, 7, 21, 26, 29, 31, 32, 42, 43; 40:16, 19, 21, 23, 25, 27, 29, 32). Some of this obedience is Bezalel's and Moses', but the work culminates in a three-fold citation of the people's obedience (39:32, 42, 43a), which leads directly to Mosaic blessing (39:43b). The repetition at work in chs. 35–40, then, is far from redundant, but literary proof of complete obedience, which is in turn proof that God's second act of redemption worked and that the second attempt at covenant "took." Israel's vows in 19:6; 24:3, 7 are proven, in the end, not to be delusional but true—thanks to the forgiveness of God. That forgiveness-empowered-obedience leads directly, even inevitably, to the indwelling of the tabernacle and God's presence—in many ways the goal of the book of Exodus—now fully realized (40:34).

This is how Exodus ends, then, in *human obedience* and in *divine presence*—indwelling—with Israel. So, much later, when John 1:14 describes God's word becoming flesh and living (literally, "tabernacle-ing," *eskēnōsen*) among us, it is not simply the vocabulary but the very thought itself that is rooted in Exodus. The tabernacle-ing of God in Exodus is facilitated, if not actually caused, by human obedience. Humans can and do disobey—in the worst of ways and at the worst of times (Exod 32)—but they can be restored. That restoration can in turn become manifest in precise obedience to the Lord's commands. To use later theological vocabulary, such a movement is one of sanctification. That is how Exodus ends.

There is another sense, however, in which the book of Exodus refuses to end. Disobedience remains a lively issue, as is clear in Lev 1–7 (also Lev 16), which contains extensive instructions regarding sin and impurity. And there are numerous texts narrating further disobedience (e.g., Lev 10; Num 11, 13–14, 16, 20, 21, 25). The issues raised in Exod 32–34 are thus not yet definitively settled; Israel's sanctification is ongoing.

Additionally, the Sinai pericope runs through Num 10:10. Only then do the Israelites finally depart from God's mountain (see Num 10:11–13). It is within this large block that Israel placed her most important law, even if much of that is now obviously anachronistic in such a context. By means of this extension of the Sinai pericope into Leviticus and Numbers, Exodus has a hard time ending in ch 40.

Even after Numbers comes Deuteronomy, which does not advance the movement from Egypt into Canaan but instead circles back, reiterating much of the story and much of the law—in revised fashion—for a new generation camped in the plains of Moab opposite Jericho. In its distinctive way, Deuteronomy situates that second generation (or any subsequent reader) over and over again at the seminal moments: as beneficiaries of the Lord's deliverance (e.g., Deut 6:21–22) and recipients of the Lord's commandments (e.g., Deut 4:10–20; 5:2–4), but also as worshipers of the golden calf (Deut 9:8–21) and rebels in the spy disaster at Kadesh (Deut 1:19–45; see Num 13–14). This strategy constantly presses the question of covenantal obedience upon the reader. Even (maybe especially) here, then, Exodus has not ended but is repeated, re-appropriated, and reapplied for a new generation facing new circumstances in a new land. Deuteronomy's "upgrade" becomes foundational for much of the rest of the OT, especially the Deuteronomistic History of Joshua–Kings, all of which, in this light, traces itself back to Exodus. But this should come as no surprise. Exodus is, after all, arguably the most important book in the Bible, recounting the foundational salvific act of God in all of Scripture. One never finishes with or "ends" something that important.

BIBLIOGRAPHY

W. Brueggemann. "The Book of Exodus: Introduction, Commentary, and Reflections." *NIB* (Nashville: Abingdon, 1994) 1:675–981; B. S. Childs. *The Book of Exodus: A Critical, Theological Commentary.* OTL (Louisville: Westminster, 1974); T. E. Fretheim. *Exodus.* Interpretation (Louisville: John Knox, 1991); _____. "Creation in Exodus." *God and World in the Old Testament: A Relational Theology of Creation* (Nashville: Abingdon, 2005) 109–31; J. K. Hoffmeier. *Israel in Egypt: The Evidence for the Authenticity of the Exodus Tradition* (New York: Oxford University Press, 1997); C. Houtman. *Exodus.* 4 vols. HCOT (Leuven: Peeters, 1993–2002); J. G. Janzen. *Exodus.* WestBibComp (Louisville: Westminster John Knox, 1997); D. T. Olson. "The Book of Exodus." *A Theological Bible Commentary.* G. O'Day and D. L. Petersen, eds. (Louisville: Westminster John Knox, 2009); G. V. Pixley. *On Exodus: A Liberation Perspective.* R. R. Barr, trans. (Maryknoll: Orbis, 1987 [Spanish orig., 1983]); W. H. C. Propp. *Exodus 1–18.* AB 2

(New York: Doubleday, 1999); _____. *Exodus 19–40*. AB 2A (New York: Doubleday, 2006); G. A. Rendsburg. "Moses as Equal to Pharaoh." *Text, Artifact, and Image: Revealing Ancient Israelite Religion*. BJS 346. G. Beckman and T. J. Lewis, eds. (Providence: Brown Judaic Studies, 2006), 201–19; N. M. Sarna. *Exploring Exodus: The Heritage of Biblical Israel* (New York: Schocken, 1996); J. A. Wilcoxen. "Some Anthropocentric Aspects of Israel's Sacred History." *JR* 48 (1968) 333–50.

LEVITICUS

BARUCH J. SCHWARTZ

OVERVIEW

The name Leviticus derives from the Greek *Levitikon*, "things pertaining to the Levites," expressing the fact that much of this book has to do with the laws of worship and purification, for which the priests in ancient Israel, who were of the tribe of Levi, were primarily responsible. The Hebrew equivalent, *torat kohanim* "instruction of (or 'for') priests," is the standard name for Leviticus in Talmudic literature. The book is also called *wayyiqra'* ("and [the LORD] called"), the Hebrew word with which the book opens.

Leviticus must be read as part of the larger literary complex extending from Exod 25 to Num 10. According to that literature, when the Israelites' arrived at Mount Sinai, God instructed Moses to supervise the manufacture of a tabernacle, a portable abode for the divine Presence (or Glory), and to consecrate his brother Aaron and the latter's sons to serve there as priests. The tabernacle was also to be the place of lawgiving, where God would meet with Moses and convey all of God's commands (Exod 25:22); thus it is also called "tent of meeting." After the tabernacle and all its appurtenances were completed, the Glory of the Lord took up residence, the priests were consecrated, worship commenced, the laws were conveyed, the tribes were mustered and arranged, and instructions for the journey to Canaan were given. Then the Israelites finally departed from Sinai and began their journey to Canaan.

All of these events are said to have taken place in just under a single year. The portion of the narrative that constitutes the book of Leviticus covers precisely one month of that period: the first month of the second year after the exodus. It comprises (Lev 1–7; 11–23; 24:10–27:35) a detailed report concerning the commandments conveyed to Moses in a series of meetings with the Lord in the tabernacle. Only two passages refer to events other than the lawgiving itself (Lev 8–10 and 24:1–9), and they are intimately connected with it.

The first laws given are those pertaining to sacrifice (chs. 1–7). These are followed by the account of the consecration of the priesthood and the inauguration of the tabernacle service, culminating in the crime of Aaron's sons and the consequences thereof (chs. 8–10). The law-giving then continues with the commandments concerning permitted and forbidden foods (ch. 11), the purification and atonement following physical defilement (chs. 12–15), the annual Day of Atonement (ch. 16), the prohibitions of profane slaughter and blood (ch. 17), sexual crimes (chs. 18 and 20), miscellaneous regulations assuring Israel's holiness (ch. 19), the sanctity of the priests (ch. 21) and the qualifications for sacrificial animals (ch. 22), the annual holy days (ch. 23), the oil for the tabernacle lamp (24:1–4) and the bread of presence (24:5–9). The account of the crime of the blasphemer follows (24:10–16, 23), after which the concluding laws are given, pertaining to the sabbatical and jubilee years and to slavery and property rights (25:1–26:2). These are followed directly by God's promises of reward for compliance and his threat of dire measures if compliance is not forthcoming (26:3–45). The laws about vows and tithes (ch. 27) are then appended.

The tabernacle narrative, including the entire book of Leviticus with all of the laws it contains, belongs to the Priestly document, or P, the largest of the four narrative strands that were woven together to create the Pentateuch. This portion of the Priestly document narrative is an independent and autonomous account of the Sinai events and cannot be harmonized or reconciled with the three other accounts of how Israelites received their laws. (For a brief explanation of the other traditions in the Pentateuch, see the commentary about the creation stories in Gen 1–2.) Similarly P's version of the laws themselves constitutes a complete and independent law code that neither complements nor supplements the laws contained in the other sources. In P's view, only the events recounted in its own narrative took place, and only the laws contained in its legal passages—a large portion of which are in Leviticus—were commanded. For this reason, no attempt will be made here to explain P's laws in conjunction with the laws in J (the Yahwist document), E (the Elohist document), or D (the Deuteronomist document); rather they will be considered on their own terms, with the legal traditions reflected in the non-Priestly sources serving for the purposes of contrast. The aim of the interpretation is thus to demonstrate the uniqueness of the Priestly legal tradition.

The Priestly document (P) achieved its final form after the Holiness Legislation (H, see the introduction to ch. 17) was added to it. Biblical scholars once unanimously embraced the idea that P is the latest of the sources and assigned it to the exilic or post-exilic period, and many critics still adhere to this view. However, a significant number of scholars now assign the Priestly literature to the pre-exilic period, adducing weighty literary, historical, and linguistic arguments in favor of this. According to this view, which seems preferable, the Priestly source was the product of learned scribes of the Jerusalemite priesthood during the last centuries of the Judean kingdom, and it took shape in two phases, the Holiness Legislation being added to the earlier Priestly work in the final years before the exile. However, the dissemination of P took place only much later, when P was combined with the other sources to create the Pentateuch, in the post-exilic period. For this reason, the widespread influence of Priestly law on Israelite religion did not begin in earnest until a relatively late date. The division of the Pentateuch into five scrolls, or "books," became necessary when the sources were combined, since the resulting text, the Pentateuch, was so lengthy that it could not be written on a single scroll; that is how the *book* of Leviticus, like the other four books of the Pentateuch, came into existence.

OUTLINE

I. The Laws of Sacrifice (1–7)

    A. The Five Types of Lord Offering (1:1–6:7)
        1–3. Gift Offerings
        4:1–6:7. Expiatory Offerings

    B. Additional Instructions Pertaining to Each Type of Offering (6:8–7:38)

II. The Inauguration of Worship (8–10)

    A. Consecration of the Priests (8)

    B. The Initial Worship and God's Appearance;

the Calamity and Its Ramifications (9–10)

III. The Laws of Purity and Purification (11–16)

    A. Forbidden Foods from the Animal Kingdom (11)

    B. Bodily (and Related) Impurities and Their Disposal (12–15)
        12. Women after Childbirth
        13–14. Scale Disease and
            Related Conditions
        15. Genital Impurities

    C. The Annual Purification of the Tabernacle and the People (16)

IV. The Holiness Legislation (17–27)

    A. The Sanctity of Slaughter and Prohibition of Blood (17)

    B. Avoiding the Abominations of Canaan and Their Consequences (18)

    C. "You Shall Be Holy" (19)

    D. Penalties for Offering to Molech, Consulting Spirits, and Sexual Crimes (20)

    E. Requirements and Disqualifications for Holy Persons and Sacrificial Animals (21–22)

    F. Sacred Times (Sabbaths and Festivals) (23)

    G. Oil for the Lamp and the Bread of Presence (24:1–9)

    H. The Crime of the Blasphemer and Laws Conveyed in Its Wake (24:10–23)

    I. Concluding Commands and Exhortation (25–26)
        25:1–26:2. God's Lordship over
            the Land of Canaan
        26:3–46. Reward and Threat, and
            Conclusion of the Lawgiving

    J. Appendix: Pledges and Their Valuation, and Repeated Conclusion (27)

DETAILED ANALYSIS

I. The Laws of Sacrifice (1–7)

The Book of Exodus concluded with the Lord's Glory, i.e., the fiery cloud encasing his manifest

Presence, taking up residence in the Tabernacle (Exod 40:34–35). Immediately thereafter God begins to issue his commands—just as had been announced in advance (Exod 25:22). In the speeches that comprise the first seven chapters of Leviticus, he commands how to perform each of the five types of sacrificial offering, detailing the materials required, outlining the procedure to be followed, prescribing the manner in which the portions are to be consumed or disposed of and, where appropriate, indicating the result thereby accomplished. Two sets of commands are given (1:1–6:7 and 6:8–7:38); each set relating to all five types of offering. In the first set, the main focus is on the altar ritual and what precedes it; in the second, further instructions are given, pertaining primarily to how the offering is to be apportioned and handled thereafter.

The offerings are prescribed here as occasional offerings made by individuals. However, they are mandated frequently in other texts as well, either as individual offerings to be made in certain circumstances (e.g., 12:6–8; 15:9–20; Num 6:10–17; 8:8) or, in the case of the first four of the five, as sacrifices to be made on behalf of the Israelite people, either in connection with the dedication of the tabernacle and the inauguration of the priesthood, in which context they have actually been mentioned earlier, in anticipation of this passage (e.g. Exod 29:14, 18, 28), and will also be mentioned again (see 8:2, 14, 18; 9:2–4 etc.) or as part of the statutory regimen of worship to be carried out on regularly occurring, prescribed occasions (see Exod 29:38–42 and Num 28:1–30:1).

A. The Five Types of Offering (1:1–6:7)

The five types of sacrifice divide into two distinct groups. In the first group (chs. 1–3) are gift offerings, of which there are three types: burnt offerings, grain offerings and sacrifices of well-being. When offered by individuals, these are expressions of the worshiper's spontaneous desire to present something to the Lord and are thus essentially voluntary. In the second group (4:1–6:7) are expiatory (or "atoning") sacrifices, of which there are two types: the "sin" or purification offering and the "guilt" or reparation offering. These are required in consequence of specific circumstances and are thus obligatory.

1–3. Gift Offerings. An "offering" in Hebrew is literally "that which is brought near," i.e., presented to God. Any Israelite, male or female, may make a gift offering at any time. Typical occasions might be the fulfillment of vows, moments of distress, gratitude for recovery from illness or deliverance from danger. Beyond this, any time a person is simply moved to pay homage to God, the private visit to the sanctuary and the sacrifice of a gift offering is the accepted expression of piety.

The section outlining the three types of gift offering begins with the stipulation that animal sacrifices are to be made "from the herd or from the flock"; i.e., of domesticated livestock: cattle, sheep or goats (1:2). It then goes on to delineate how this is to be carried out, if the worshiper has decided to make a burnt offering (1:3–13), and how it is to be performed, if the worshiper has decided to make a well-being sacrifice (3:1–16). Sandwiched in between these two sections, which actually form a continuous text, are two additional laws: the provision for a burnt offering from fowl (1:14–17) and the law of grain offerings (2:1–16). These have presumably been inserted in order to enable those without access to herd and flock animals to perform acceptable acts of devotion.

The burnt offering (1:1–17) is the gift offering par excellence; the Hebrew term means "that which goes up [in smoke]." The flesh of the animal is consumed on the altar in its entirety; all of it, so to speak, becomes God's food, and the person who makes the offering derives no personal benefit from it. Leviticus does not explain what might move a person to make a burnt offering; it is simply taken for granted that a wholly consumed animal sacrifice is the most elementary form of devotion. For this reason, the burnt offering was also the central, indispensable component of public worship: two sheep were offered daily as a perpetual burnt offering (Exod 29:38–42; Num 28:1–8) and this number was duly augmented on Sabbaths, New Moons, and festivals (Num 28:9–30:1).

The person making the offering places his hand upon the animal's head as an act of presentation. The Hebrew indicates that the worshiper also performs the slaughter, which was done by slitting the throat, and the flaying of the animal. As for the priest, his task is to receive and present the blood, dashing some of it round about the altar, and to place the flesh on the altar fire—which the priests were to stoke and keep burning constantly—so that it is consumed completely, entrails and legs included. Thus the worshiper is responsible for transferring ownership of the animal to God and for transforming it from a living animal into food fit for divine consumption; the priests, as God's palace servants, are responsible for the sacred tasks of dashing the blood and offering the flesh as a gift to the Lord.

The references to "acceptance" in vv. 3 and 4 express concern about the worshiper's need to know that his offering has been accepted. According to 22:17–20, if the worshiper sees to it that the animal is without any disqualifying blemish, acceptance is assured. The significance of the statement that the burnt offering secures "atonement" (v. 4) is uncertain; the sense may be that it is accepted as a sort of payment, which some have taken to mean as a substitute for the worshiper himself. However, it is neither the death of the animal nor the dashing of the blood that results in "atonement"; rather, in this case, the presentation of the animal as an offering to God provides for "atonement."

The expression "an offering by fire" (vv. 9 et al.) is now known to be a mistranslation; the Hebrew word actually means "gift." Only burnt offerings, grain offerings, and sacrifices of well-being are thus in view; the expiatory sacrifices are not gifts but rituals of purification. As for the oft-recurring statement that the smoke rising from the altar is a "pleasing odor to the LORD," the Priestly legislation is perfectly comfortable with depicting God as inhaling the fragrant odor of roasting flesh and deriving pleasure from it.

Just as the quadrupeds acceptable for sacrifice are the domesticated livestock, so too the birds that may be offered as burnt offerings, turtle doves and pigeons, are the two types of domesticated fowl used for human consumption.

The second type of gift offering is the grain offering (2:1–16). The Hebrew term for this offering means "tribute," expressing the basic idea that God is Israel's suzerain and that the Israelites are expected to pay him that which is his due. In the Priestly sacrificial texts, this general term has received its specialized sense of "offering made of

grain." The two ingredients needed to make such an offering, "choice flour," i.e. semolina, and olive oil, would be available even to the poorest Israelite, suggesting that the law was introduced so that even persons of humble rank might visit the sanctuary and pay "tribute," i.e. perform a respectable act of devotion. The grain offering also plays an important role in the regimen of statutory public offerings, accompanying the burnt offerings made each morning and evening (see Exod 29:40; Num 28–29).

The individual who has decided to present a grain offering has several options regarding its preparation. He may present the mixture of flour and oil uncooked (v. 1); this is the simplest to prepare, but, because it requires the addition of frankincense, it is quite costly. The remaining types, which require no frankincense, compensate for the smaller financial investment by involving some exertion in preparation of unleavened cakes: oven-baked (as loaves or wafers, v. 4), griddle-toasted (and crumbled, vv. 5–6), and pan-fried (v. 7). Only a representative, or "token," portion of the grain offering is consumed on the altar (if the offering is offered in its uncooked form, this includes all of the frankincense, since this is God's alone); the remainder is eaten by the priest (see 6.18; 7.9). For the rationale behind this, see 6:17. Before the priest places the token portion upon the altar, the entire offering is presented by the worshiper. Analogous to the placement of the hand on the animal (see 1:4), this serves as an indication that the cakes, loaves, or wafers are not from the worshiper's everyday pantry but have been prepared specifically for use as an offering to God.

The grain offering too is called a "gift" and is said to be "of pleasing odor to the LORD." Outside of the Priestly laws, it is assumed that the addition of fragrant spice is what renders the offering pleasing (see Isa 1:13; 43:23; Jer 6:20; 17:26; 41:5; Ps 141:2), but in Leviticus this is not stipulated; here the Lord's food gifts are intrinsically pleasing. The grain offering is also referred to as "most holy" (vv. 3, 10); for the significance see 6:24–29. In the Priestly system for worship, offerings are classified according to precisely defined ascending grades of sanctity, as are the sections of the tabernacle and all its appurtenances.

Neither leaven (sourdough) nor honey (the nectar of dates and figs) may be used in any grain offerings (vv. 11–12). To be precise, these may be offered but not placed on the altar, suggesting that it is specifically the fermentation of the grain offering, but not these substances per se, that is to be avoided—probably in order to ensure that the preparation, offering, and eating all take place within a brief time period and in proximity to the altar. The requirement to salt the grain offering (v. 13) is a corollary of this condition, since salt was thought to be an anti-fermentation agent. The expression "the salt of the covenant with your God" should not be over-interpreted; it simply means that the salting of grain offerings is a solemn obligation to be observed for all time.

In what reads like something of an afterthought, the possibility that one might bring a grain offering "of first fruits" is mentioned (vv. 14–16). The English word "fruits" is used here in its general sense of "produce of the soil"; the text actually refers here too to grain, grain that has not fully matured so that flour cannot be made from it. It is prepared and offered in the same way as the uncooked grain offering mentioned above. Thus the law provides a means for an Israelite to visit the sanctuary and present tribute to God from the very first moment his grain begins to ripen.

The third and final form of gift offering (ch. 3) is the sacrifice of well-being (an approximate translation): the sacrifice of an animal from the herd or flock of which the worshiper partakes in the form of a festive meal; this is performed as an expression of joy, gladness, gratitude, or relief. According to Priestly law, this is the only way domestic livestock are permitted to be eaten (see 17:3–8).

Ownership of the entire animal is transferred to God, but only the blood and "fat," i.e., the suet, which is the hard, subcutaneous fatty tissue surrounding the internal organs, is actually consumed on the altar; the remainder of the animal is eaten by the priests and the worshipers. This constitutes a sacrificial meal because the celebrants eat it in the Lord's presence, i.e., as subjects privileged to be hosted in the palace of a ruler, and because the portions eaten by the priest and the worshiper are understood to have been given to them by God.

The command follows the form of the burnt offering law (1:2–13), first stating the procedure for an animal from the herd (vv. 1–5) and then for an animal from the flock (vv. 6–15)—this time

keeping sheep and goats separate, since the heavy broad-tail characteristic of the former is included among the portions placed upon the altar (v. 12). The worshiper's role is similar to that for a burnt offering; the altar ritual, in which the blood is dashed against the sides of the altar as a libation and the fatty portions and suet are turned into smoke as a "pleasing odor to the LORD," is then performed by the priest.

Burning suet provides a dense smoke of rich and meaty fragrance, suggesting that the deity to whom it is offered derives pleasure from it. In biblical ritual, therefore, the suet of sacrificial flesh is offered to God, along with the kidneys and the "appendage of the liver" or caudate lobe (and, in the case of sheep, the broad-tail; see above). The blood of gift offerings is also thought of as reserved for God so that "suet and blood" make up the divine repast (see Ezek 44:7, 15). The Priestly legislation prescribes further that these substances, since they belong to the Lord alone, are not to be eaten by humans; all blood and suet are therefore prohibited (v. 17); see 7:22–27 and 17:10–16. The words "all fat" (correctly: "all suet") in v. 16 are a scribal error; the verse should conclude "a food-gift of pleasing odor to the LORD," cf. vv. 5 and 11.

4:1–6:7. Expiatory Offerings.

There are two types of expiatory sacrifice. The first, treated in 4:1–5:13, is traditionally referred to as a "sin offering," but the Hebrew term should properly be translated as "purification offering." The second, detailed in 5:14–6:7, has usually been called a "guilt offering"; this too is a misnomer and should be replaced by "offering of reparation." Offerings of expiation are not voluntary, spontaneous acts of adoration; rather, they are required rituals, occasioned by specific circumstances. Unlike the laws pertaining to gift offerings, therefore, the rituals are prescribed along with the circumstances that give rise to them. The focus is on expiation necessitated by cases of a person's wrongdoing; other situations in which similar expiation rituals are required, for individuals as well as in the public cult, are described elsewhere.

Expiation, or "atonement," in the Priestly legislation is not a means for making amends, either by appeasing God—such as by paying him a sort of fine—or by inflicting some deprivation upon oneself as a form of penalty. Nor is the sacrifice of the animal a substitute for one's own death. The

Hebrew word translated by "expiate" or "atone" conveys none of these post-biblical ideas; rather it means "wipe clean." The purifying act consists of the application of the blood of the slaughtered animal to the tabernacle and objects within its confines. As in Mesopotamian ritual texts, where the same verb is used to refer to the ritual cleansing of temples, "atonement" in P is thus a ritual by which the divine abode is purged of unwanted substances said to have accumulated there. These consist of the Israelites' bodily impurities, as explained in chs. 12–15, and certain acts of wrongdoing that they commit—as described in this section. If this contamination is allowed to accumulate, it threatens the community's survival. Thus its removal, or "atonement," is of critical importance (see 15:31).

The commands concerning the purification offering are given first (4:1–5:13). This offering is required when an Israelite becomes aware of having unwittingly transgressed a prohibition. Inadvertent acts are not ignored in Priestly law, and, when errors are made, atonement is necessary. In order for this to occur, the offending parties must come to realize their wrongdoing; it must either be brought to their attention by another person or dawn on them somehow.

The details differ according to the identity of the person, the main distinctions pertaining to the animal required (the higher the rank, the larger the animal), and the precise location within the tabernacle at which the blood is to be applied. The first two sections speak of offenses committed by the "anointed priest," i.e., the high priest (vv. 3–12), or by "the whole congregation of Israel" (vv. 13–21), thereby bringing guilt upon the community. The contamination having entered the tabernacle, purgation of the outer sanctum is required; this is done by sprinkling blood towards the curtain (see Exod 27:31–24) and daubing blood on the horns of the incense altar (see Exod 30:1–10). The next three sections pertain to offenses committed by a "ruler," i.e., a person of exalted status within his tribe (vv. 22–26), or an ordinary Israelite (vv. 27–31 and 32–35). These generate a less powerful contamination, and therefore require only the purgation of the tabernacle's exterior. The blood of the animal is thus applied to the horns of the sacrificial altar that stood in the courtyard. In all cases, the assigned portions of the sacrificial animal are consumed on the altar; on the disposal of the remaining flesh see 6:24–30 and 10:16–20.

The sixth section (5:1–10) adds four very specific cases of wrongdoing by an individual. These are all acts of omission rather than violations of prohibitions. The offender, though initially aware of his neglectfulness, has subsequently put it out of mind. When realization and remorse finally occur, the purification is to be performed in the tabernacle court as prescribed above. Unique here is the requirement that the guilty party supplement his remorse and sacrificial expiation with verbal confession. These four cases refute the idea that obligations evaporate with time, asserting instead that one's culpability for negligence intensifies the longer it lasts. The references to being "guilty" in vv. 2–4 are inaccurate translations; the Hebrew conveys the sense of *realizing* one's guilt, as in the opening phrase of v. 5.

The laws of the purification offering (5:7–13) conclude by prescribing how persons of limited means are to comply with the obligation to make expiation when required. The sacred precincts must be decontaminated—remarkably, even by means of a grain offering, if that is all the person can afford. There are no exemptions.

The second expiatory sacrifice is quite similar in its ritual to the purification offering. Its name comes from a word meaning "to incur liability," and as a noun it denotes the payment of damages. It is mandated in cases of trespass against sacred objects and the sacred domain (5:14–16), in cases of undiscovered violations, presumably involving trespass as well (5:17–19), and in cases of fraud accompanied by false oath, i.e., trespass against the sacred name of the Lord (6:1–7). The term "reparation offering" is thus preferable to "guilt offering." This sacrifice embodies the crucial importance that Priestly laws attach (as do Mesopotamian ritual texts) to the need to guard the sacred sphere from unauthorized access and to prevent the misuse of items believed to be sacrosanct—the tabernacle and its furnishings, offerings and gifts that have been brought to it, and the name Yahweh—the most widely accessible sacred "object," and the most susceptible to misuse. When these are mistreated, the ritual purgation is not sufficient; some form of restitution is needed. The value of the ram that is offered, to which one-fifth is to be added as a payment of damages beyond the restitution itself, is viewed as symbolic compensation for that of sacred property. In the final section, the case of fraud accompanied by false oath, the restitution and fine are paid to the injured party; see also Num 5:5–8.

The recurring refrain throughout 4:1–6:7 states that the parties "shall be forgiven." Forgiveness in the Priestly sacrificial system is not an act of grace for which one can only hope and pray; it is the stated outcome of the prescribed expiation rituals.

B: Additional Instructions Pertaining to Each Type of Offering (6:8–7:38)

In this section, further regulations are provided regarding each of the five types of sacrifice prescribed in chs. 1:1–6:7. Each new topic is introduced by the phrase "this is the ritual of ...", or better: these are *the instructions* regarding etc. (6:2, 7, 18; 7:1, 11). With a few exceptions, these instructions relate primarily to how each sacrifice is to be apportioned and disposed of following the altar ritual.

First (6:8–13) are the instructions for the burnt offering. Complementing 1:3–13, this paragraph adds the requirement that the flesh may burn on the altar throughout the night, but by morning the ash must be removed. Linen vestments are required of the priests in close proximity to the altar, but upon exiting the holy area, non-sacred clothing is donned. As for the altar fire itself, once ignited (see 9:24) it must be kept burning at all times, a perpetual sign that God's worship continues without interruption. These regulations are the counterpart of the corresponding instructions for distribution and consumption given below for the remaining types of sacrifice, parts of which are eaten.

These are followed by the instructions for the grain offering (6:14–18). Pursuant to 2:1–13, they add what comes next: how the priests are to prepare and consume their portion of the grain offering, as well as a warning that the offering may not leave the sacred precincts and may not come into contact with the laity. Direct contact communicates dangerous, contagious holiness (see v. 20; Exod 29:37; 30:29; Num 17:1–4). Most significant is the statement that priests do not receive their share of the sacrifice from the person who presents the offering. Rather, the worshiper gives the entire sacrifice to the Lord; he then "shares" it with the priests in recognition of their service (see 2:1–8; cf. 7:34).

The text goes on (6:19–23) to describe the personal grain offering required of "Aaron and his sons," i.e., the high priests: Aaron and all of his successors. This offering is consumed in its entirety on the altar so that the priest does not receive a share of a gift that he himself offers. The words "on the day when he is anointed" (v. 20) mean "from the time of his anointment [onward]," i.e., in perpetuity. Lesser priests, too, receive no share of any grain offering they make on their own behalf.

The next instructions (6:24–30) pertain to the purification offering; see 4:1–5:13. The paragraph stipulates where it is to be slaughtered, defines its degree of sanctity as "most holy," prescribes who may eat of its flesh and where (offerings so defined are to be eaten only by priests within the tabernacle confines), and sets forth the ramifications of lay contact with the flesh (7: 20–21). It concludes by spelling out a crucial distinction between purification offerings whose blood has been used to decontaminate the interior of the tabernacle (4:2–21) and those whose blood has been applied to the outer altar (4:22–5:10). The flesh of the former may not be eaten and must be burned; the flesh of the latter *must* be eaten—by the officiating priest, who may share it with other priests (7:26 and 29). Thus are severe and minor impurities, respectively, disposed of and the purification process made complete (see on 10:16–20). Flesh and blood that have not been disposed of communicate impurity to objects with which they come in contact, requiring the latter to be cleansed.

Next (7:1–7) come the instructions concerning the reparation offering; these are predicated on 5:14–6:7. Most of the details correspond with those given in the laws pertaining to the other sacrifices. As with the purification offering (6:29), only priests are eligible to eat the flesh; here too the officiating priest receives the flesh and is given the option of sharing it with other priests.

A short conclusion (7:8–10) follows the instructions pertaining to the four "most holy" sacrifices, filling in the remaining details regarding the distribution of the priestly portions of each one.

The instructions for the well-being offering (7:11–34) are to be read in conjunction with the ritual described in ch. 3. There are three types of well-being offerings (see 19:5–8 and 22:29–30): the sacrifice of thanksgiving, designed to demonstrate to all present the beneficence of God enjoyed by the worshiper, and consumed, along with "cakes," i.e., baked loaves, within a single day (vv. 12–15); the votive offering, made in fulfillment of a vow; and the freewill offering, a spontaneous feast of joy (vv. 16–18). In the latter two cases, no loaves are offered and two days are allowed for the consumption of the flesh. Violating the time restriction (presumably in both cases, although this is made explicit only with regard to the second) invalidates the sacrifice retroactively and brings severe guilt upon the offender. Sacrificial flesh may not be eaten once it has come into contact with a source of physical impurity; an impure individual who actually eats sacrificial flesh is "cut off from his kin" (vv. 19–21). This threat recurs numerous times in Priestly law; it is not excommunication but rather extirpation, i.e., the eventual total extinction of one's line, by whatever means God sees fit to cause this to happen (see 20:2–9).

Verses 22–27 elaborate on 3:17. The "fat"— i.e., the suet—and blood of permitted animals, whether sacrificed or not, may not be eaten (see 17:10–16). An exception is domestic animals that have been killed by beasts or died of themselves. Their flesh may be eaten (see on 11:40, 17:15–16 and 22:8) and household use (but not consumption) of the suet is permissible.

The section concludes with the instructions for distribution of the well-being sacrifice. The altar portions are presented by the worshiper to be turned by the priest into smoke on the altar. The priests' portion is given to them by God, not by the worshiper, as remuneration for their service (see also Num 18:8–24). In Priestly legislation, this portion consists of "the breast of the elevation-offering," referring to the custom of elevating the offering in order to present it, and "the thigh that is offered"; according to Deuteronomic law they are to receive "the shoulder, cheeks and the stomach" (Deut 18:3). At the temple in Shiloh, they received "all that the fork brought up" from the cauldron of boiling flesh (1 Sam 2:14)—yet

another way of indicating that the priest's portion is allotted to him by God alone.

Verses 37–38 summarize the whole of chs. 1–7 and close the account of what was communicated to Moses on the day that the divine Glory entered the tabernacle (see 1:1). Mention of the "the offering of ordination" (see 8:22–29) is something of a discrepancy, since this offering was not referred to in these chapters. The words "on Mount Sinai" (7:38) should be translated "*at* Mount Sinai"; i.e., "[in the tabernacle that stood] at [the foot of] Mount Sinai" (similarly 25:1; 26:46; 27:34).

II. The Inauguration of Worship (8–10)

Having imparted to Moses the instructions needed to perform all of the types of sacrifice to be offered henceforth, God now commands that the inaugural rituals commence. First comes the "ordination," or consecration, of the priests, without whom the regimen of worship cannot begin (ch. 8); this is followed by the first sacrificial service and dedication of the tabernacle, climaxing in the public appearance of God's Glory.

A. Consecration of the Priests (8)

Several months earlier, when God announced to Moses that his brother Aaron and his sons were to become his priests (Exod 28:1), he outlined the details of this ceremony (Exod 29). Now he informs Moses that it is to be carried out, in the presence of the whole people, and Moses complies. Most of ch. 8 thus consists of a repetition, with minor differences, of Exod 29, with the actions related in the past tense and the recurring refrain "as the LORD had commanded Moses."

The ceremony consists of five elements: 1. Investiture: the priests are clothed for the first time in the garments required to perform their service (vv. 7–9 and 13). 2. Invocation: the priests present a burnt offering (vv. 18–21). 3. Consecration: the blood of a ram of offering is smeared on the priests' bodies (vv. 22–24*a*). 4. Ordination, literally, "filling the hands," so called because the priests receive for the first time their assigned share of the sacrifices; they offer a portion to the Lord (vv. 26–29) and eat what remains (v. 31). This ordination offering resembles a well-being offering (3:1–16, 7:29–34) of the thanksgiving type (7:12–15). 5. Anointment: the priests are anointed (the extremities of the body representing the whole) with the sacred oil, later mixed with blood from the offering, infusing them with holiness (vv. 12, 30). Until such time as the induction is complete, Aaron is in the role of the worshiper while Moses assumes the role of priest, receiving on this occasion the "priest's share" of the sacrificial flesh.

Before their investiture, the priests must be bathed (v. 6); before the first sacrifices are made, the tabernacle and its furnishings must be anointed (vv. 10–11); in order for the altar to be used, it must be purified (vv. 15–17) from the impurities that have collected there. Thus, the consecration of the tabernacle itself takes place while the priests are being purified. Following these ceremonies, the priests remain within the tabernacle's confines for seven full days, strictly avoiding all contact with the non-sacred. With this their consecration is completed (vv. 31–36). According to Exod 29:35–37, on each of the seven days another purification offering is to be made, the altar is to be cleansed and anointed, and the ordination ceremony is to be repeated (cf. Ezek 43:25–26). Exodus 29:30 also mandates that the same ritual is to be repeated whenever a new high priest is installed.

B. The Initial Worship and God's Appearance; the Calamity and Its Ramifications (9–10)

The narrative continues with the events of the eighth day (9:1–10:19 is a single unit in the Hebrew text). Moses orders the priests to emerge from their seclusion and to perform their first sacrificial service (9:1–6). This consists of a purification offering (to decontaminate the tabernacle once again) and each of the three types of gift offering: a burnt offering (to invoke the presence of God), a grain offering, and a well-being offering in celebration of the great event—a rare well-being offering made on behalf of the public in Israelite ritual (see also 23:19). Moses has Aaron instruct the people to prepare the communal sacrifices; thus the high priest performs, for the first time, his task of informing the Israelite people of their cultic duties. The stated purpose of these rituals is "for today the LORD will appear to you" (9:4; see 9:6), i.e., they are carried out in order to prepare for a theophany. The instructions are carried out in logical sequence, and Aaron blesses the people. He and Moses then enter the tabernacle and invite the Lord to emerge, after which they bless the people again, this time apparently

praying that God favor them with his manifest presence. Finally the glory of the Lord shines forth from the inner sanctum. Flames emerge, igniting the altar fire and consuming the sacrificial portions. Thus the Lord signals that he is pleased with his people's homage and will indeed reside in the abode they have built for him.

At this, the people burst into rejoicing (9:23b–24), but the celebration and sacred meal that were naturally to follow are sadly aborted. Suddenly, two of Aaron's sons, Nadab and Abihu, take up censers—metal utensils with handles used for offering smoking incense—place unlit coals in them, and sprinkle incense upon them, intending to attract the divine fire. The term "fire" (10:1) refers to the kindling material, and the word rendered "unholy" actually means "alien" or "unauthorized" (10:1). In the public institutions of worship, ritual crimes are dire. Only what is prescribed is legitimate, and what is not commanded is sacrilege (for the acceptable uses of incense see Exod 30:7–8 and Lev 16:12). The Lord thus sanctifies his name by striking them down on the spot (10:2–3): fire emerges again from the Holy of Holies and incinerates them.

The surviving members of the priestly family are forbidden to engage in any of the mourning rituals (10:4–7); feelings aside, their task as priests is to carry on with the day's ceremonies (10:12–15). Moses becomes agitated upon learning that they have deviated from the normal manner of disposing of the sacrificial flesh (10:16–18), but when Aaron assures him that what has occurred is not a reform but a one-time exception to the rule in light of the tragic circumstances, his fears are allayed (10:19–20).

A parenthetical section (10:8–10), which would serve well as the introduction to the next passage, cautions the priests to refrain from alcohol when engaged in their ritual duties or in giving instruction, since drinking alcohol might diminish their ability to make precise distinctions "between the holy and the common, and between the unclean and the clean."

III. The Laws of Purity and Purification (11–16)

God continues to communicate his laws to Moses. In Priestly thought, the distinction between prohibited and permitted is not identical to the distinction between "clean and unclean," but the two are not entirely unrelated. Thus, before proceeding to the laws of purity and purification (chs. 12–16), God issues commands regulating prohibited and permitted food.

A. Forbidden Foods from the Animal Kingdom (11)

According to Gen 9:1–4, humans may eat all vegetation and the flesh of all living beings, but they must abstain from eating blood. The Israelites, however, are under additional restrictions. These pertain to each category of the animal kingdom. a) In addition to domestic livestock, which are fit for the altar and therefore obviously permitted, Israelites may eat the flesh of large non-domestic land animals (vv. 2–8) only if they have true (NRSV, "divided") hoofs and cloven feet and chew their cud, i.e., only if they possess the features most characteristic of cattle, sheep, and goats; see Deut 14:5. b) They may eat the flesh of beings that populate the waters (vv. 9–12) only if these have the markings peculiar to fish, i.e. fins and scales. c) They may not eat the flesh of the birds listed (some of the translations are uncertain); the list enumerates all known fowl that are dissimilar in their appearance and habits to the fowl used in sacrifice, i.e., the turtle dove and the pigeon (vv. 13–19). d) Among the "winged insects" (vv. 20–23), they may eat only those that have "jointed legs above their feet, with which to leap on the ground" (v. 21), i.e., that diverge from their class, resembling birds more than insects. e) Last, all "creatures that swarm upon the earth" (vv. 41–42, the direct continuation of v. 23), i.e. small land animals, are prohibited. Thus, Israelites may only eat domestic livestock and fowl, wild animals that resemble them, and a few species of flying insects.

While impurity is properly the subject of the next portion of Leviticus (chs. 12–16), its implications for the law in this chapter are given here in a parenthetical section (vv. 24–40). Prohibited land animals are not only forbidden as food; their carcasses also communicate impurity when humans touch them. The impurity is minor, only a brief time, until sunset, followed by laundering (and, presumably, bathing). Since the carcasses of small land animals may occasionally come into contact with foodstuffs, vessels, utensils, seeds, and the water supply, the text describes how each of these is affected and how the impurity is to be dealt with. The translation of v. 34 is misleading; water does not make food unclean! Rather, like seeds and grain (v. 38), food becomes *susceptible to* impurity only if, prior to coming in contact with the unclean object, it has been moistened at any time.

In Priestly law, Israelite lay persons may eat the flesh of an animal that has died by itself rather than being slaughtered, as long as the animal is one of a permitted species. Impurity results and must be remedied, but no sin has been committed. Leviticus 17:15–16 and 22:8 provide further details about this issue. Verse 39 probably means that the carcass of a permitted animal communicates impurity *only* if the animal has died on its own or been killed by a beast, whereas if it has been slaughtered, no impurity results.

The Israelites are commanded to regard as "detestable" the animals that they are forbidden to eat. This may imply that while these animals are not intrinsically loathsome, the Israelite is to cultivate an attitude of abhorrence toward them simply because they are prohibited. By maintaining a set of dietary restrictions corresponding to distinctions present in the natural world, the Israelites, in Priestly thought, are kept holy, that is, separate from the remainder of humanity (vv. 44–45; see also 20:25–26) and closer to the divine.

B. Bodily (and Related) Impurities and Their Disposal (12–15)

In these chapters God commands how to dispose of the several types of impurity (NRSV, "uncleanness"), an approximation of a Hebrew term meaning contamination or defilement. In the Priestly law, this is something like an atmospheric layer, enveloping and coating persons or objects. It is believed to emanate from human corpses, carcasses of animals, genital fluids, and a specific skin condition treated in chs. 13–14, all of which involve the escape of a person's life force. Defilement, once produced, behaves like a vapor, expanding to fill available space and contaminating persons and objects with which it comes into contact, communicating to them various degrees of impurity, which in turn need to be eradicated.

This impurity is a simple fact of life. The phenomena that produce it are neither evil nor sinful; people and objects routinely and unavoidably contract it at all times. The only sin involved is that of allowing impurity to come into contact with sacred objects and sacred space, and these are considered especially vulnerable to its effect. In Priestly thought, if impurity is allowed to penetrate the divine abode and to accumulate there, the Lord's presence will depart and Israel will not survive (15:31). For this reason, priests, who are in constant contact with the sacred sphere, are explicitly cautioned to shun all but the most unavoidable impurity. Moreover, since all unchecked impurity, no matter where it may be, is believed to contaminate the sanctuary, even from afar, the lay Israelite, while he is under no obligation to avoid impurity, is warned not to remain unclean, i.e., not to neglect his solemn responsibility of doing away with impurity once he has contracted it, for this would inevitably allow it to contaminate the divine abode, posing a threat to everyone.

Three elements participate in the disposal of impurity: the elapse of time, cleansing (usually in water), and the purification offering (see 4:1–5:13). The first two purify the individual; the third, required only in cases of major impurities, purges the sanctuary of the impurity that the affected individual has inevitably caused to accumulate there.

12. Women after Childbirth. The woman who has given birth needs to be cleansed "from her flow of blood" (v. 7), i.e., the discharge of dark fluid that typically lasts for a few days and is followed by a lighter flow that may last for a number of weeks. These two phases correspond to the two stages of the mother's purification. Two uniform periods, defined by the stereotype numbers seven and forty (33 + 7) used throughout the Bible, are prescribed. No reason is given for doubling the length of each phase when a female child is born. The ancients may have supposed that the post-partum genital flow was of longer duration after the birth of a girl, or they may have noted that there is occasionally vaginal flow from the infant girl herself and seen this as conferring an additional measure of impurity.

During the first phase, the mother is severely unclean: she communicates minor impurity by contact ("as at the time of her menstruation"; see 15:19–24), and her impurity affects the sanctuary from afar. During the second phase, the impurity is less intense. It no longer contaminates persons or mundane objects, nor does it spread aerially to the sanctuary, but direct contact with the sacred must still be avoided. Only at the end of the second phase can the woman attend to the purification of the sanctuary; this she must do whether she is a person of means (vv. 6–7) or not (v. 8). The expiation is carried out by means of the purification offering (see Lev 4). A burnt offering too is required (see ch. 1); the reason for this is not stated. Circumcision (v. 4) is not a stage in the purification process; it is mentioned here by association (cf. Gen 17:9–14).

13–14. Scale Disease and Related Conditions. The next set of commands prescribe how to dispose of the impurity caused by the condition known as tsara'at. The translation "leprosy" (or "leprous disease") is misleading, since the disease currently called by this name was not known in biblical times and the description given in the Bible is not consistent with it. Biblical *tsara'at* is said to afflict not only humans but also fabrics (13:47–59) and building materials (14:33–47), so it cannot be identified with any single known medical condition.

With regard to humans, the word *tsara'at* refers to certain scale-like eruptions of the skin stemming from a number distinct causes, while *tsara'at* in fabrics and building materials may be identified as certain types of mildew. Before microbiology, conditions sharing similar outward manifestations were referred to by a single name.

Disease per se does not produce impurity; those suffering from ailments other than *tsara'at* (and abnormal genital fluxes; see 15:1–15, 25–30) are not considered to be impure. Only *tsara'at*, because the person afflicted with it is looked upon as potentially dead (see Num 12:12; Job 18:13), is viewed as a manifestation of the gradual escape of the life-force, which is the definition of impurity in the Priestly legislation.

The priest has no role in the healing process; throughout biblical tradition, the onset, progress, and cure of disease are believed to be outside of human control. The priest's only task is to determine if the lesions that appear are indeed *tsara'at*, and this is the sole reason for the lengthy, detailed instructions given in this passage. If *tsara'at* is not present, the priest's task is over: the person is evidently suffering from some other ailment, and the priest declares him pure. If it is found, the patient is declared impure and placed in quarantine until his disease is healed. This is not in order to arrest the spread of the disease but rather to check the spread of the potent impurity that it is believed to produce, lest this have an irreversible effect on the sanctuary. If a conclusive diagnosis cannot be made, a seven-day waiting period ensues (involving isolation, to be on the safe side), after which the condition is examined again. After the person's healing is complete, the priest is to supervise the person's purification and, because the potent impurity of *tsara'at* has inevitably affected the sanctuary, expiation as well (see 14:19).

Indicative of the unique severity of the impurity associated with *tsara'at* is the fact that no other impure individuals are instructed to remain "outside the camp" (13:46), or in later periods, outside the city (2 Kgs 7:3). During his quarantine, the afflicted individual is to "wear torn clothes and let the hair of his head be disheveled" and to "cover his upper lip"; these are the outward signs of distress. He is also required to cry out, "Unclean, unclean" as a warning to others that his impurity is contagious. The Priestly legislation passes no moral or religious judgment on the afflicted individual; he is accountable only if he fails to attend to the prompt eradication of his impurity as soon as his disease has disappeared.

Mildew that causes the erosion and eventual disintegration of fabrics (vv. 48–58) is deemed a manifestation of the very same leakage of life-force as *tsara'at* in humans. The fabric suspected of having *tsara'at* is subjected to a diagnostic procedure similar to that used with human patients, but confirmed cases of *tsara'at* in fabrics cannot be "cured," and no purification rituals are prescribed. Only the prompt disposal of the impurity, accomplished through the destruction of the affected fabric, is required.

The next section, resuming 13:47, prescribes how the person cured of *tsara'at* must rid his person and his environment of the impurity generated by his disease. This indispensable safeguard against the threat posed to the community by the accumulation of impurity is the responsibility of the person who has suffered the affliction; the

priests' role is to see that it is carried out and to perform the necessary rituals. The purification and expiation take place in three stages. The first, occurring as soon the priest pronounces the afflicted person cured and while he is still outside the camp, drives off the impurity that envelops his physical person. The purging agent is the blood of the first of two birds. This is the only instance in the Priestly legislation in which purifying blood is actually applied to a human. The second bird is set free to carry off the impurity; this is similar in some ways to the scapegoat ritual described in ch. 16. Cedar wood, crimson yarn, and hyssop are agents of purification throughout biblical and ancient Near Eastern traditions (see, e.g., Ps 51:9).

Stage two, on the seventh day, consists of the final cleansing of the individual. In stage three, on the eighth day, he makes his offerings. The need for a purification offering (v. 19) is perfectly obvious; this rids the sacred sphere of the impurity that has accumulated there. But the reparation offering (v. 12) is incongruous since no evident trespass against the sacred has taken place. No satisfactory explanation for this requirement has been given. The application of consecrated oil (vv. 14–18) apparently adds a measure of sanctification to the purification process, while the burnt offering and grain offering are acts of homage. The section concludes with the provisions for the person of modest means (vv. 21–32; cf. 4:7–13;12:8).

The final section of the law confirms that certain types of mildew or rot in the walls of a house were sufficiently evocative of *tsara'at* in humans to be equated with it and were taken as manifestations of the very same deadly leakage of life. The measures taken depend on the reexamination of the house after a seven-day quarantine; if the condition has spread the affected stones and plaster are removed and replaced. Thereafter, if it returns, it is considered incurable and the house must be demolished. If it does not, the condition is said to have run its course and the priest pronounces the house clean. Clearing the house of foods and other objects in advance of the priest's visit so that they are not pronounced impure is a legal fiction designed to prevent undue economic hardship. To eradicate the impurity that has accumulated, a ritual similar to the first stage in the purification of the affected human (vv. 3–7) is performed (vv. 49–53). No purification of the sanctuary is prescribed; the phrase "make atonement" in v. 53 is used anomalously, to refer to the decontamination of the house.

3. Genital Impurities (15). This chapter deals with defilement caused by the flow of life fluids from the genital organs: semen, menstrual fluid, and the discharge accompanying gonorrhea or other genital or urethral infection. None of these is considered sinful, nor are they thought of as punishments; they are simply facts of nature: some normal, some pathological. It is taken for granted that impurity and contact with impure persons will occur in the normal course of everyday life. The only sin connected with them is failure to purify oneself from them.

The first section (vv. 2*b*–15) deals with abnormal discharge from a male. The symptoms are indicative of various urethral infections. In ancient times, these were not known to be sexually transmitted. This is paralleled by the fifth section (vv. 25–30), which speaks of abnormal discharge from a female, also taking into account menstrual flow of abnormal duration. These are severe impurities, lasting for seven days after the condition has passed, after which the final cleansing of the person takes place and purification offerings are made to decontaminate the sanctuary. Inexpensive animals are prescribed—by analogy, for males as well as for females—since prolonged menstrual flow or irregular discharges in women are relatively frequent.

The second section (vv. 16–17) speaks of normal discharge from a male, i.e., the emission of semen; this parallels the fourth section (vv. 19–24), which deals with normal discharge from a female, i.e., menstruation. These are lesser impurities; they require only the cleansing of the individual, which, if performed promptly, arrests any possible contamination of the sanctuary. They differ in that the impurity resulting from the emission of semen, which is momentary, lasts only until nightfall, while that resulting from menstruation, which continues several days, lasts a week. The third section, at the center of the chapter (v. 18), deals with the impurity contracted during sexual intercourse by both males and females. This minor impurity, after cleansing, lasts until nightfall.

Unclean individuals are not "off limits," but since direct or indirect contact with them communicates minor impurity, appropriate measures must be taken to rid oneself of it. This chapter provides the details relating to this communication of impurity to persons and to objects. These regulations apply, by appropriate analogy, in other cases of bodily impurity of similar degree (see, e.g., 12:2; 13:46). Such secondary impurity is less severe than that borne by the affected person himself; after washing and laundering it dissipates by nightfall and does not spread to the sacred sphere. One exception is sexual intercourse with the menstruant: it communicates a more severe impurity lasting seven days (v. 24). Nevertheless it is not prohibited here; if the necessary purification takes place no sin has been committed. The law in 18:19 thus directly contradicts ch. 15 on this issue.

The laws of purity and purification in Leviticus conclude with a warning that includes a clear statement of their rationale (v. 31). Failure to adhere to the laws of purification brings about death, i.e., the collective destruction of the Israelite people, since when impurity accumulates unchecked in the Lord's abode, he will leave and Israel will not survive (cf. 16:16; Num 5:3; 19:13, 20).

C. The Annual Purification of the Tabernacle and the People (16)

Verse 1 indicates that in the narrator's reconstruction of events, this law was communicated to Moses immediately after the events described in vv. 9–10. The laws in vv. 11–15, he thus informs us, were actually given somewhat later and have been placed here in order to delineate the types of impurity and to explain the crucial importance of sanctuary purification, before proceeding to the command that serves as the culmination of the purity laws.

A certain amount of tabernacle defilement inevitably remains despite all of the purification rituals prescribed thus far. Regular, public rituals of purification are therefore required; these are calendrical and are prescribed in Num 28–29. In addition, and especially because deliberate crimes, which contaminate the inner sanctum, are not expurgated by these rituals, once a year it is necessary to decontaminate the inner sanctum along with the rest of the tabernacle and to see to the final removal of all sins and impurities from Israel's midst. This annual ritual is the subject of ch. 16. It is to be performed on the tenth day of the seventh month (v. 29). Elsewhere (23:27,28; 25:9) this date is referred to as the "Day of Atonement," with "atone" once again meaning "cleanse [the sacred precincts] of sin and defilement" (cf. Lev 23:26–32; Num 29:7–11).

The chapter begins by prescribing the thorough purification of the tabernacle, focusing on the inner sanctum (vv. 3–22). Since this is the spot where God's Glory resides, egress is fatal and must be avoided. The need to cleanse the entire sanctuary once a year is the one exception (v. 2). To avoid death, the priest creates a cloud of incense as he enters, preventing himself from viewing the Glory (v. 13). Since these rituals essentially amount to a large-scale clean-up operation, the priest wears simple linen garments, which are easily laundered (v. 4).

The ritual includes two purification offerings: a bull on behalf of the high priest and his household (cf. 4:3–12) and a goat on behalf of the Israelite people. Aaron thus enters the inner sanctum twice, sprinkling the blood of these offerings in order to decontaminate the sacred space; this is followed by the cleansing of the outer sanctum (v. 16b) and then by the purging of the courtyard altar (vv. 18–19), first with the blood of the bull and then with that of the goat.

The procedure also requires a live goat; a lottery (vv. 8–10) determines at random which goat is to be used for which purpose. The live goat is needed to carry away the deliberate transgressions of the Israelites; v. 21 makes it clear that unlike the impurities, which have been destroyed by the purification ritual, these have been removed from the tabernacle but still need to be disposed of. This is accomplished by transferring them—manually and verbally—onto the goat's head and then driving the goat into the wilderness (vv. 20–22). There it will be received as an offering by Azazel (literally: "fierce god"), a demon or deity believed to inhabit the wilderness, and thereby eradicated once and for all. Remarkably, this is not seen as the worship of another god but rather as an act of obedience to Yahweh.

Two burnt offerings are also prescribed, one on Aaron's own behalf and the other on behalf of the people.

In addition to decontaminating the sanctuary, the annual Day of Atonement also brings about a sort of purification of the Israelite people, since the removal of their sins and impurities serves as a catharsis; thus the text says "you shall be clean" (v. 30). The people play a role in this process: vv. 29–34a prescribe that they must observe a fast (the phrase "deny yourselves" in v. 29 literally means "deprive your throats," i.e., fast) and a cessation of labor. Without the active participation of those whose impurities and offenses are being purged, the ritual would be ineffective.

IV. The Holiness Legislation (17–27)

Up until this point, the Priestly work has conveyed the sense that the commandments given at Sinai had to do only with the worship of God and the purity of his earthly abode. By inference, at least, P seems to be saying that proper conduct in other spheres is a matter of common sense and universal morality, not of command. Chapters 17–26 correct this impression by supplying civil and criminal legislation pertaining to social behavior as well as ritual activity. These chapters report that at Sinai God's will in these areas also became explicit in the form of commands and prohibitions, and, moreover, that failure to adhere to them also has a negative effect on the sacred. Most scholars see this as a progression, even a transformation, in Priestly thought, and as an indication that these chapters were composed by Priestly authors later than those responsible for the bulk of P. This conclusion seems to be confirmed on stylistic grounds as well. By inserting their legislation here (and at a few other points in P), these authors thus expanded the pre-existing Priestly account of lawgiving in the tabernacle.

The most characteristic feature of the laws in these chapters is their concern for holiness. Here alone it is maintained that holiness of persons is not restricted to the realm of the tabernacle and the priesthood but is rather attainable, in some measure at least, by the Israelite people as a whole (chs. 19–20). As well, one hears explicitly about the holiness inherent in the slaughter of certain animals for food (ch. 17), the holiness of the priests and of sacred offerings (chs. 21–22), the annual "holy times" (ch. 23), the holiness of the name of Yahweh (ch. 24) and the holiness of the fiftieth year (ch. 25). Implied also is the holiness of the land of Canaan (chs 18; 26). For this reason, scholars refer to this portion of Leviticus as the Holiness Legislation (or Holiness Code) or H.

A. The Sanctity of Slaughter and Prohibition of Blood (17)

The next three laws communicated to Moses are concerned with the proper disposal of the blood of slain animals. Formally these laws are not expressed as prohibitions ("you shall not...") but as threats, pronouncing that those who commit certain acts are condemned to be "cut off" (see 7:19–21).

The first law (vv. 3–8) prescribes that Israelites may not simply slaughter animals from the herd and flock for food. They must be offered as sacrifices of well-being (see 3:1–17 and 7:11–34), after which the worshipers may partake of their share of the flesh. Failing to comply is tantamount to having slain the animal in the antediluvian period when such an act was considered murder (see Gen 1:29–30), i.e., it is a capital crime. This law rests on the postulate that whereas, prior to the establishment of the Israelite cult at Sinai, slaughter of domestic livestock was devoid of sanctity, from that time forth it became a sacrificial act. Once the tabernacle is in operation, however, the slaughter of domestic livestock at any other location is a sacrifice to the "goat-demons" believed to inhabit the wilderness and is strictly prohibited.

The unambiguous statement that this is "a statute forever to them throughout their generations" (v. 7b) cannot be reconciled with the more practical law in Deut 12:15, 20–27, according to which non-sacrificial slaughter of livestock would eventually become permissible. In the Priestly view, no such relaxation of the law was ever given.

The second law (vv. 8–9) outlaws all sacrifice that is not offered at "the entrance of the tent of meeting," i.e. the tabernacle. The clear implication for the future is that Israelites are to worship the Lord only where he resides: at the one legitimate sanctuary. The Priestly legislator thus agrees with Deut 12 in its demand that all sacrificial worship be centralized in one location, but disagrees on whether non-sacrificial slaughter may be practiced after the centralization has been accomplished.

The third law forbids the "eating" of blood, i.e., the eating of flesh without first draining the blood. The Priestly writer has already recounted that after the flood all humans were commanded to refrain from blood (Gen 9:4) and that the same command was later given to the Israelites (3:17; 7:26–27). By recounting here that this law was now repeated, H is able to supply it with a unique and highly complex rationale. It may be paraphrased thus (v. 11): the life-force of every living being is contained in the blood (observable from the fact that loss of blood brings about death), and it is this that God has assigned to the altar (in expiatory sacrifices; see 4:1–6:7), there to serve as *ransom* (NRSV, "atonement"), i.e., as a symbolic, "blood-for-blood" (or life-for-life) exchange for one's own life; therefore the blood of all flesh is strictly forbidden. Deuteronomy also records this prohibition, explaining it somewhat differently (Deut 12:16, 23–24; 15:3).

This law draws in its wake two corollaries: the requirement to drain the blood of wild animals hunted and killed for food (vv. 13–14; see 11:1–19) so that it becomes mixed with earth and therefore inedible, and the need to dispose of the impurity contracted by eating carrion (vv. 15–16). The latter point too was mentioned earlier (see 11:40); it is repeated here because it constitutes an exception to the blood prohibition: blood that has coagulated is no longer thought to contain the animal's life-force, so the flesh may be eaten. The non-Priestly law codes, in contrast to this, expressly forbid eating such flesh (i.e., Exod 22:30; Deut 14:21). In P, only those belonging to the innermost sphere of sanctity, namely the priests, must observe this restriction (22:8) while lay Israelites are not so obligated; this is Ezekiel's view as well (Ezek 44:31).

B. Avoiding the Abominations of Canaan and Their Consequences (18)

In ch. 18, the Israelites are warned not to practice the "abominations" of the Egyptians and Canaanites (vv. 2–5 and 24–30) so as to avoid suffering their fate. Incorporated in this address is a list of prohibited sexual unions (vv. 6–23), including incestuous relationships (vv. 6–18), to which the prohibition of sacrificing children to Molech (v. 21) is also added. Refraining from these, no less than the scrupulous maintenance of the divine abode as emphasized earlier in Leviticus, is the key to Israel's national survival. In addition, the individual perpetrator is punished by being "cut off" (see 7:20–21).

Biblical tradition assigns to the Egyptians and Canaanites a reputation for sexual licentiousness and perversion. It is unlikely, however, that this reflects reality; the biblical writers, who had little or no first-hand knowledge of Egypt and Canaan, seem to have attributed these abominations to Israel's long-extinct enemies as a means of stigmatizing the cultural "other" and as a means of condemning the behavior itself—since the fate supposedly suffered by these nations served as an obvious cautionary lesson. This tradition also provided a morally plausible explanation for the apparent disappearance of the "Canaanites," the peoples who, the biblical authors assumed, must have occupied Israel's land before they did.

The phrase "uncover nakedness," which means "uncover the sexual organ," is used throughout vv. 6–19 (see also 20:11) to expresses the ignominy of engaging in sexual relations with a family member despite the revulsion that viewing the genitals of a close relative was supposed to arouse. The statement that the nakedness of one's mother is the nakedness of one's father (v. 7), like similar statements that follow, conveys the idea that a woman's sexual organs should be accessible only to her husband.

The list of prohibited sexual unions with "anyone near of kin" (an expression for the extended family; see 25:49 and compare 21:2) covers four generations, with the male addressed in the text placed in the second generation. In this way, all female relations who might be the object of his sexual desire at some point during his adulthood are named. Directly related women: in the generation preceding him, his mother (v. 7) and stepmother (v. 8); in his own generation, his sister (v. 9); in the vertical line, his granddaughter (v. 10). (The daughter should have been included between vv. 9 and 10; she has accidentally been omitted.) The step-sister too is considered of the same degree as a true sister (v. 11). Indirectly related women: in the generation preceding him, his true aunt (vv. 12–13) and his aunt by marriage, said here to be of the same degree (v. 14); in the next generation, his daughter-in-law (v. 15); in his own generation, his brother's wife (v. 16; this in direct opposition to Deut 25:5–9). Women related to each other—mother and daughter, grandmoth-

er and granddaughter (v. 17) sisters (v. 18)—are all forbidden. This is a stringent view; the non-Priestly sources relate that Abraham was married to his half-sister (Gen 20:12) and that Jacob was married to two sisters (Gen 29:16–28). Even P reports that Amram was married to his aunt (Exod 6:20)—presumably an act of the sort that these laws sought to remedy.

Additional sexual prohibitions are intercourse with one's own wife when menstruating (v. 19; cf. 15:19–24—this is one of H's most significant divergences from P); intercourse with another's wife, i.e., adultery (v. 20); non-procreative intercourse, i.e., with a male (v. 22), an animal (v. 23a), and between a woman and an animal (v. 23b). The mention of sacrificing children to Molech (see on 20:2–5) indicates that H, like D (see Deut 12:31 and 18:9–12), sees child sacrifice as one of the abominable practices for which the Canaanites were expelled from their land. He therefore adds it to the list of sexual offenses, which he believes are comparably heinous.

Biblical and ancient Near Eastern cultures were not familiar with homosexuality as a sexual orientation or lifestyle; it took notice only of the occasional act of male anal intercourse (see Gen 19:4–5 and Judg 19:22). Among the law codes, only H mentions it (see also 20:13), apparently viewing as aberrations all sexual acts that are not potentially procreative.

The imagery in the concluding section (vv. 24–30) depicts the land of Canaan as so sensitive to the behavior of its inhabitants that when abominable acts are performed, "defiling" the land, it ceases to yield its bounty and its population is forced to emigrate. This idea is unique; elsewhere it is presumed that the pre-Israelite inhabitants of Canaan were either destroyed or expelled by the conquering Israelites.

C. "You Shall Be Holy" (19)

This collection of commands teaches that there is no such thing as a divine law that pertains only to ethics; every commanded or prohibited action affects the realm of the sacred and is thus in the category of ritual law as well. The text expresses this idea by mixing together laws touching upon various areas of life—sacrifice, commerce, legal institutions, the Temple, idolatry, family relations, oaths, alms, first fruits, theft, fraud and more—

thus placing all of them on a single plane. For example, the legislation in the chapter (vv. 3–36) begins by juxtaposing reverence for parents with observance of the Sabbath in order to convey the idea that all laws are in a single category: obedience to the divine command. Almost every paragraph concludes with the same refrain "I am the LORD" (or "I am the LORD your God"), essentially a way of saying "Do this/refrain from doing that because I, Yahweh, say so." Taken together, the opening and closing verses (vv. 2, 37; 20:7–8) of this miscellany imply that only through the faithful observance of God's commands can the Israelite fulfill his sacred charge of being holy. The opening words "You shall be holy, for I the LORD your God am holy" (v. 2) are thus a caption and not a separate command. God's holiness is his quality of "otherness," of being separate from all that is not him, whereas holiness in humans is a matter of *belonging to* God and being designated his "personal" property. While outside of P, Israel is holy simply by virtue of having been chosen (see Exod 19:5–6; Deut 7:6, 14:2, 21), here Israel's holiness is a goal to be accomplished through obedience to the laws and statutes of God.

Some of the topics of the legislation in the chapter are mentioned elsewhere in the Priestly account of the lawgiving, while others are mentioned only here. After citing parents, Sabbath-observance (see Exod 31:12–17; 35:2–3; Lev 23:3; 26:2 and v. 30 below) and idolatry (vv. 2–3; see 26:1), the text returns to the well-being offerings of the votive and freewill types discussed in 7:16–18 and 22:21–23 (for the third type of well-being offering, that of thanksgiving discussed in 7:12–15, see 22:29–30). The added statement that the offender has "profaned what is holy to the LORD" (v. 8) provides the connection to the theme of holiness. This is followed by two pairs of prohibitions to be observed in the field and vineyard respectively (vv. 9–10). The first in each pair is observed while reaping, the second in each pair during ingathering. The concluding command "you shall leave them for the poor and the alien" is thus fulfilled by inaction, cf. Deut 24:19–21.

The next four sets of laws (vv. 11–12, 13–14, 15–16 and 17–18) share a common theme: decency and honesty in what appear to be interpersonal affairs are concerns of the deity. All four paragraphs deal with matters of conscience: since all of the crimes mentioned are in some measure committed in secret, the offenders think they are undetected. The progression is from the crimes most difficult to conceal to those that can never be proven and whose victims have no remedy, leaving punishment in the hands of God alone. When false oath follows theft and cover-up (vv. 11–12; 6:1–7), God becomes a party to what began as a civil matter. Unknowing victims of exploitation (vv. 13–14) may never find out that they have been mistreated, so fear of God is the only real sanction (see also v. 32; 25:17, 36, 43). The perversion of judicial proceedings follows (vv. 15–16—the second verse refers to making unjust charges against one's fellow), and the final set (vv. 17–18) also forms a unit, relating to pent-up hatred and its consequences. As v. 18 explains, bearing of grudges results ultimately in vengeance; but by refraining from such behavior one treats his fellow with the same "love," i.e., understanding and forgiveness, one normally extends toward one's own shortcomings. In later Jewish and Christian interpretation, of course, the words "love your neighbour as yourself" were generalized to serve as a blanket command covering all ethical duties.

Next comes the injunction to uphold the boundaries fixed by God in the natural world (v. 19; Deut 22:9). Wool and linen are, however, woven together in the priestly vestments (Exod 28:6, 39:29) and in the fringes (Num 15:37–40). What is used in sacred garments is taboo for mundane use. This is followed by a case law relating to sexual relations with a female slave who is "designated" for marriage to another man (vv. 20–22). Since the woman is technically not yet free, she is not strictly "betrothed," but the offense against God needs to be expiated. The translation "an inquiry shall be held" is not certain.

The fruit of a tree is off limits for the first three years and is offered to the Lord in the fourth; only then may it be eaten (vv. 23–25). The expression "set apart" is actually a translation of "sacred"; thus this law too is connected with the theme of holiness (see also Judg 9:27).

The prohibition of eating "anything with its blood" (v. 26a; see 17:10–14 and 1 Sam 14:32–35) refers to an act probably associated with augury and witchcraft (v. 26b). The next two verses forbid extreme expressions of grief and mourning (see Deut 14:1–2, 1 Kgs 18:28), as they are associated with conjuring up the dead and communicating with gods of the nether world (see on 21:5). This section closes with the command not to "profane" one's daughter (v. 29) by consigning her to harlotry; the term "profane" indicates that this is the opposite of holiness.

The main body of the chapter (vv. 3–32) closes with three verses that develop themes with which the chapter opened. Conjuring up mediums and wizards (v. 31, NRSV; others "ghosts" and "familiar spirits"), while it is admitted to be an effective method of gaining hidden knowledge (see 1 Sam 28:3–25), is strictly off limits for Israelites; see 20:6, 27 and compare Deut 18:9–14.

The concluding section (vv. 33–36) makes up an appendix, extending to the resident alien two of the laws mentioned in the main body of the chapter: love of neighbor (v. 18) and fairness in "judgment" (v. 15), here reinterpreted to mean "correct measure." The law in vv. 35–36 probably refers to the fact that the non-native is unlikely to be familiar with local weights and measures, cf. Deut 25:13–16. Thus the Israelite is expected to treat the alien with the same decency he is required to show his countryman. The prohibition of exploiting the non-Israelite is grounded in Israel's own experience, cf. Exod 22:20, 23:9; Deut 10:19.

D. Penalties for Offering to Molech, Consulting Spirits, and Sexual Crimes (20)

Sacrifice to Molech and sexual crimes were treated in ch. 18. There, however, the laws are direct prohibitions, whereas those appearing here are phrased conditionally and prescribe specific penalties. The lack of correspondence between the two chapters with regard to the specific crimes enumerated, along with the fact that ch. 18 actually does include a penalty clause (v. 29), shows that this chapter should not be read as providing the punishments for the crimes enumerated in ch. 18. The existence of two separate chapters devoted to one theme, with an entire chapter standing between them, indicates that ancient compilers had enormous reverence for the texts that they inherited from earlier bearers of tradition.

Sacrificing to Molech is a capital offense (vv. 2–5; see 18:21). Molech is the name of a deity associated with the world of the dead. The worship of Molech consisted of the sacrifice of

children; there is evidence that this was occasionally practiced in Israel, sometimes in the false belief that this was Yahweh's will. In addition to requiring death by stoning, the law states that God will attend to the eventual extinction of the perpetrator's line (see 7:20–21). This is extended to the criminal's family if those charged with prosecuting the crime neglect their duty. The contamination of God's sanctuary results from this crime wherever it is committed.

Verse 6 deals with those who consult "mediums and wizards" (see 19:31), and v. 27 below prescribes the penalty for the practitioners themselves (on vv. 7–8, see the discussion at the beginning of ch. 19).

Now follows a series of prescribed penalties for sexual and other crimes (vv. 9–21). For those in vv. 9–16, the death penalty is prescribed, with burning mentioned as the method in one case (v. 14). The remainder are under the threat of being "cut off" (see 7:20, 21), either explicitly or by implication. No reason for this distinction is given, nor is there any clear indication of why only some verses contain characterizations of the crime (such as "they have committed perversion" in v. 12 and "it is a disgrace" in v. 17) and others do not. The expression "their blood is upon them" (e.g., v. 9) means that the guilty parties have justly incurred the death penalty and the executioners are not accountable.

Adultery (v. 10) is defined as sexual relations between any man, married or single, and a woman betrothed or married to someone else. Both parties to the crime are guilty, cf. Deut 22:22. Being cut off "in the sight of their people" (v. 17) occurs only here; it is probable that the penalty is carried out by God, cf. 7:20, 21. On relations with the menstruating woman (v. 18), see 15:19–24 and 18:19. The style of v. 19 is inconsistent with the conditional formulation in the rest of the chapter; no explanation for this is apparent. Dying childless (vv. 20, 21) is a specific form of being "cut off" since the person's line is thereby made extinct.

The concluding exhortation (vv. 22–26) returns briefly to the themes of 18:24–30, and introduces the motif of distinction: as God has distinguished Israel from the other nations, so the Israelites must distinguish clean from unclean foods, and thus be holy—since "holy" means designated or set apart. The final two verses appear to be loosely connected to this chapter, cf. 11:43–45.

E. Requirements and Disqualifications for Holy Persons and Sacrificial Animals (21–22)

God now addresses the issue of holiness in the tabernacle cult (chs. 21–22). All persons and objects that have become "holy," that is, have the status of belonging to the Lord, are subject to desecration, either through contact with impurity, by disqualifying blemish, or by unauthorized use; these must therefore be avoided so that Yahweh's earthly abode and holy name are not desecrated in turn.

The first topic is the holiness of the priesthood (21:1–15); priests are charged with preserving the boundaries between holy and profane (see 10:10). Since they enter the sacred precincts and must handle and eat sacrificial flesh, they must avoid impurity and refrain from approaching the sacred when they do become impure. Lay Israelites are not subject to the former prohibition, but they too must observe the latter. The priests must also abstain from observing the rituals of mourning detailed here (see 10:6–7), as they too are considered to desecrate their bodies (in 19:27–28, similar acts are also forbidden to lay Israelites). Further, since the holiness of the priests is genetically transmitted, they may marry only women about whom there is no suspicion of the presence of another man's seed. And while lay Israelites too are forbidden to allow their daughters to engage in harlotry (19:29), the priest's daughter's prostitution is a capital case, since her father's sanctity—and through it, God's—would thereby be desecrated.

The high priest is subject to even greater restrictions: he must refrain even from benign expressions of grief, must avoid contact with the corpse of even his closest relations, and must marry a virgin: even a widow is off-limits.

The next topic is the prevention of desecration resulting from priests (21:16–24) who have disqualifying physical defects. The priest, as God's palace servant, profanes the abode of the deity if he cannot adequately embody the divine form in whose image humans are made (Gen 1:26–27; 5:1). The absence, or permanent malformation, of external characteristics distinctive of the human species thus disqualifies a person born into the priesthood from officiating. He, of course, remains a priest and is, therefore, entitled to eat the priestly portions of the sacrificial flesh.

Another measure to be taken in order to avoid desecrating the sanctuary and the sacred offerings is to prevent their coming into contact with impure priests and, in the case of the offerings, their consumption by ineligible persons (22:1–16). Allowing impurities, even minor ones, to come into contact with the sacred profanes the divine name, since Yahweh's abode and the gifts presented to him are thereby treated as though they were common. The specifics, including the procedures required for cleansing and disposal of each type of impurity, are treated in chs. 11–15. Sacrificial portions that may only be consumed by priests are "most sacred" (see 6:24–29); contact between them and a lay person leads to their desecration. Non-priests who are formally a part of the priest's household may however share in them. On unwitting desecration of the sacred (v. 14) see also 5:14–16.

The physical defects that render animals unfit for the altar (vv. 17–25) are analogous to those that disqualify priests from officiating, but deformed animals do not cause desecration; they are simply not accepted (see 1:3–4; 7:18; 19:5–8) and the person's sacrifice is deemed not to have been offered. What is placed on God's table must be without defect (cf. Mal 1:6–14). From vv. 21–23 it may be deduced that the offering made in fulfillment of a vow is of a greater sanctity than the freewill offering, since the deformities mentioned in v. 23 are acceptable in the latter case. Together with 7:12–18, whence it is learned that the thanksgiving offering is the most sacred of the three, these verses thus confirm the hierarchy of the three classes of well-being offering.

The final section (vv. 26–30) deals with offerings that are not accepted due to time factors. The law in vv. 26–27 is based on the idea that an animal is not considered fit for the divine table until it is viable, i.e., has safely gotten beyond the stage of a newborn and is a creature in its own right. The law in v. 28, in contrast, seems to be motivated by humane concerns (see Exod 23:19; 34:26; Deut 14:21; 22:6–7). The law in vv. 29–30 must be read along with that in 19:5–8; together they restate the law in 7:12–15.

This passage concludes with a general exhortation (22:31–33). Just as compliance with the commandments enables the Israelites to absorb the holiness of God (19:3, 37; 20:7–8), failure to obey the commandments desecrates the name of God. In Priestly thought, Israel exists in order to sanctify God's name, and their failure to do so has the opposite effect: God's name is profaned, that is, God's fame is diminished and his reputation tarnished.

F. Sacred Times (Sabbaths and Festivals) (23)

The laws in this chapter provide a glimpse into the unique Priestly vision of the annually occurring special occasions. The word translated as "festivals" means, in fact, "times" or "dates," and the term translated "holy convocations" means simply that these dates are to be proclaimed as holy; no convocation or gathering is implied. Thus in P these annual dates are conceived of not as celebrations but as "sacred times." Like sacred objects, persons, areas and utterances, they may not be treated as common, and this is accomplished by observing them, like the Sabbath, as days of cessation from daily activity. This is unique to P. As the Lord's dates, they are envisaged in P primarily as days on which the Lord is worshiped in a manner exceeding the daily routine. The focus of the chapter is almost entirely on rituals on those days performed by the priests in the Temple, while the participation of the lay population is incidental. Only two of the sacred times, the unleavened bread observance (v. 6) and the days of dwelling in booths (v. 34 and vv. 41–42) are also days on which the laity is expected to make a pilgrimage to the Temple; this too is obscured by the translation where the word for "pilgrimage" is rendered as though it too meant "festival." An important distinction between this and the non-Priestly law is that in the latter there are three pilgrimages, and they are incumbent upon all males (Exod 23:14, 17; 34:23–24; Deut 16:16), whereas here no such obligation is stated.

Another Priestly calendar of sacred dates appears in Num 28–29. The main difference between the two passages is that Lev 23 elaborates on the distinctive observances connected with each occasion whereas the passage in Numbers provides a full listing of the required offerings for each day. The full impact of the unique Priestly view of Israel's so-called festivals can only be appreciated if this chapter is contrasted with the non-Priestly calendars in Exod 23:14–19; 34:17–26 and Deut 16:1–17.

Following the caption (v. 2), the chapter opens with mention of the weekly Sabbath (v. 3), consecrated according to P at Creation (Gen 2:1–3) but instituted only when the tabernacle was built (Exod 31:12–17; 35:1–3; see also Lev 19:3, 30; 26:2; Num 15:32–36). Only Priestly law mentions it alongside the festivals, and in Lev 23 it may be secondary; note the repeated caption (v. 4).

The sacred times per se (vv. 5–43) begin with the annual passover sacrifice (v. 5), which is not a sacred occasion but which immediately precedes the first of these, the Pilgrimage of Unleavened Bread (vv. 6–8). P provides details concerning these in Exod 12; here only what pertains to the calendar of sacred occasions is mentioned. P nowhere provides the rationale for the Unleavened Bread; it thus preserves a more natural, agricultural origin of the practice as associated with the beginning of the barley harvest in early spring. The observance of the first and last days of the two long pilgrimages as full holy days is also peculiar to the Priestly tradition (see vv. 36 and 39; Exod 12:16; Num 28:25; 29:35).

Next come the elaborate instructions for the Temple rituals performed by the priests, commencing on the first day of the week after the Unleavened Bread pilgrimage and culminating seven weeks later. A first sheaf of the new barley harvest (NRSV, "first fruits" is misleading), with its accompanying offerings, is presented each year in order to secure divine blessing for the new crops. The new grain may not be partaken of until the ceremony has taken place. Seven weeks are then counted so that the sacred occasion observed at their conclusion, elsewhere called the Day of the First Fruits and Weeks (Num 28:26), will coincide with the Temple rituals to be observed thereon— since in P this date is not marked by a pilgrimage. On this date, the priests are to present two leavened loaves called the "bread of first fruits" (see v. 20), offered in thanks for the new grain harvest and accompanied by appropriate additional offerings. The partial quotation from 19:9–10 appearing in v. 22 is added here because of its association with harvest time.

On the first day of the seventh month, i.e., at the approach of the fall equinox, when the agricultural year closes and recommences, P ordains a sacred date for "remembrance by shouting" (NRSV, "commemorated with trumpet blasts") (vv. 23–25). This is only one of several observances in P designed to call God's attention to the Israelite people and their needs (Exod 28:12, 29; 30:16; Num 31:54). The day seems to be envisaged as a day of crying out to God—presumably by the priests in the Temple—so as to beseech his aid in the new agricultural year.

In later tradition the "shouting" ordained here was deemed to be the sounding of the ram's horn, and with the eventual adoption of the autumnal New Year, the first day of the seventh month in the vernal calendar became New Year's Day.

The Day of Atonement (vv. 26–32), also unknown outside of P, is explained in ch. 16. The cessation of labor, which serves (along with the fast) to effectuate the purification and atonement rituals performed, marks this day too as a sacred occasion; Lev 23 thus incorporates it into the annual cycle of such dates.

Last are the laws for the Pilgrimage of Booths (vv. 33–43). The name of the annual fall pilgrimage refers to the huts that serve as temporary shelters from the elements, because the duration of the pilgrimage necessitates the erection of such shelters for the many pilgrims staying in the Temple city for seven days. In vv. 39 and 42, as well as Num 29:12, this is referred to as "the pilgrimage of the LORD"—*the* pilgrimage par excellence. The eighth day, known only to the Priestly tradition, is observed as day of abstaining from labor (NRSV, "a holy convocation" interprets otherwise, v. 36) but not as a "pilgrimage." Still it is a "sacred occasion," and a cessation from labor is to be observed by all, those who make the pilgrimage, those who do not, and those who do so but return home for the eighth day.

Since the additional observances of the Pilgrimage of Booths are not sacrificial rites performed by the priests but are rather observed by the public at large in the course of their week-long visit to the Temple-city, they are not included in what comes before the caption in vv. 37–38.

Taking branches and boughs (v. 40) is evidently a ritual of joyous acknowledgment of the current year's agricultural abundance. The rationale suggested here for the obligation to dwell in booths (vv. 42–43) seems to be a retrojection: just as Israelites gather to live in makeshift huts on their annual visit to the Temple, the text seems to be saying, their ancestors dwelled in proximity to the Lord's portable abode, the wilderness tabernacle, living in temporary dwellings until they reached the promised land.

G. Oil for the Lamp and the Bread of Presence (24:1–9)

This section contains two brief laws. The first (vv. 2–4), providing the instructions for the oil to be used for the tabernacle lampstand, is an almost exact repetition of Exod 27:20–21 and provides the explicit connection between it and Exod 25:31–40. The second (vv. 5–9), detailing the procedure for the loaves to be displayed (thus: "showbread" or "Bread of Presence") on the table in the tabernacle without ever being sacrificed on an altar, completes the legislation of Exod 25:23–30 by elaborating on its last verse. The twelve loaves represent the tribes of Israel and suggest their constant devotion. Conceptually, the loaves are a gift made by the Israelite people to the Lord, who in turn bestows it upon the priests in recognition of their service (see 6:10–11). Both of the rituals mentioned here pertain to the complex of acts performed by the high priest inside the tabernacle. These constitute a perpetual, symbolic pageant of worship. The daily lighting and tending of the lampstand is also mentioned in Exod 30:7–8, in the context of the high priest's incense offering, which is the other component of this complex of rituals. In the Priestly tabernacle, Yahweh is enshrined in the inner sanctum, but all acts of devotion are performed in the outer sanctum, and the partition dividing the two is never breached. The mention here of laws relating to the perpetual tabernacle routine may serve as a supplement to the preceding chapter, which details the calendar of regularly recurring special occasions.

H. The Crime of the Blasphemer and Laws Conveyed in Its Wake (24:10–23)

The incident recounted here appears unrelated to the laws that precede and follow it. It is, however, connected intimately with the theme of holiness that pervades these chapters, since the divine name is the one sacred "object" that can be used by anyone at any time (see on 6:1–7); it is only logical that *mis*using it is *the* sacrilege par excellence. The crime of blasphemy described here consists of cursing God (see Exod 22:28; 1 Kgs 21:10–13), that is, maligning God or uttering an imprecation against God in which his name is included.

Thrice more in the Priestly literature (Num 9:1–14; 15:32–36 and 26:1–11), one reads about Moses' inability to render a decision before consulting God (probably by means of the *urim* on Aaron's breastplate; see Exod 28:15, 30). Each time, the remedy pronounced becomes a permanent law applicable for future generations as well.

As the author imagines it, the only non-Israelites present in the wilderness period would have been the offspring of Israelite women and Egyptian men, conceived and born while still in Egypt. Since he wishes to extend his legislation to "aliens as well as citizens" (vv. 16 and 22) and thus to stress that the desecration of Yahweh's name is a capital offense by definition, whether performed by an Israelite or not, he casts such a person in the central role of the narrative.

The short collection of additional laws (vv. 17–22) is parenthetical. It has a simple theme: as opposed to the obligation to worship Yahweh, which rests upon Israel alone, the measure-for-measure ("eye for eye") rule in crimes and damages is incumbent upon the resident alien precisely as it is also required of the citizen (v. 22). The similar statement in the law of the blasphemer (v. 16) accounts for this section being added here. The narrative flow of vv. 10–16 continues, and concludes, in v. 23.

I. Concluding Commands and Exhortation (25–26)

Leviticus 25–26 is a single divine speech, indicating that the author intended for them to be viewed as a single rhetorical unit. It is communicated to Moses at Mount Sinai (25:1; 26:46; see also 7:38; 27:34), that is, in the tabernacle, which stood at [the foot of] Mount Sinai—precisely as were the rest of the laws in Leviticus (NRSV, "on" Mount Sinai is misleading). The first section, the laws of the sabbatical and jubilee (25:1–26:2), leads uninterruptedly into the second, the speech of promise and threat (26:3–45). The connection between the two sections is in the theme of the

Yahweh's ownership of the land of Canaan. The first explores the legal ramifications of the Israelites' status as indentured servants on Yahweh's estate, and the second details the wages promised to the tenants if they comply with his demands and the measures he will take in order to compel them to do so if they are unwilling. The legal section thus flows directly into the concluding exhortation, and the division into two chapters during the medieval period is not warranted.

25:1–26:2. God's Lordship over the Land of Canaan. Only in Priestly legislation is the seventh year (25:2–7) referred to by the name "Sabbath." Further, only here is it forbidden to work the land in the seventh year, even though its produce may be gathered and eaten. Whereas non-Priestly law commands the Israelite to "release and abandon" the produce of the seventh year (Exod 23:11) so that the poor may gather it, Priestly law provides for the poor in other ways (19:9–10; 23:22). The seventh-year "release" in Deuteronomy pertains only to the annulment of debts (Deut 15:1–6). The law as envisaged here is wholly sacral in character: since the land of Canaan is Yahweh's estate, it is, in a sense, sacred. The Israelites are thus required to enable it to observe a "weekly" (in terms of agricultural years) cessation from productive activity, just as they themselves are obligated to do in their own lives. The prohibition pertains to normal, wholesale sowing, reaping, and harvesting only. As much food as needed may be gathered from what grows on its own, and livestock may graze.

The law of the jubilee (25:8–55) concentrates on its two central features: the land release and the release of indentured persons. The fiftieth year, which, unlike the seventh, is referred to as holy (25:10, 12), follows the seventh sabbatical, entailing a two-year cessation of agricultural activity. It commences in the seventh month which is the beginning of the annual agricultural cycle. The name "jubilee" has no connection to Latin *jubilare* "shout for joy" (cf. English "jubilation"); rather, it seems to be derived from a root meaning "bring" and to mean "homebringing," i.e., liberation (see 25:10).

The underlying idea of the jubilee is that the division of the land of Canaan among the Israelite tribes, clans, and families (see Num 33:54) is to be permanent. The land of Canaan is not the Israelites' property, it is rather a "holding" (see

25:24)—not theirs to buy, sell, and reapportion. "Buying" and "selling" of land in Canaan is actually a matter of leasing it until the jubilee. The jubilee is thus primarily an affirmation of God's exclusive dominion, designed to demonstrate that the Israelites are God's indentured servants (25:42, 55). Once again, the lawgiver expresses the idea that social legislation is included among God's commands only insofar as it impinges on the sacred.

The text responds to the anxiety the jubilee law arouses (25:20–22) by ordering the Israelite to do as commanded and trust in God, promising that the produce of crops sown in the fall of the sixth year will suffice as long as necessary.

"Redemption" in the Bible refers to the obligation to enable one who has lost his property or liberty to regain it. This obligation rests both upon the buyer, who must allow the person in question to repurchase his property or liberty as soon as his means suffice, and upon the kinsmen of the person in question, who must assist him if his means do not suffice. The laws of redemption in 25:23–55 demonstrate that the jubilee is actually the remedy of last resort, and that, prior to its advent, society must provide for the restoration of property and liberty whenever possible; otherwise the jubilee, when it arrives, affects the redemption by default.

An exception is the "sale" of urban property (25:29–34). The seller and his kinsmen have only a year to pay the redemption fee; if they cannot, the sale is final. If the property is in an unwalled town, or is in one of the Levites' designated cities that include the surrounding fields (Num 35:1–8), the jubilee is in force.

The prohibition of interest (25:37), which outside of the Priestly law applies in all circumstances (Exod 22:24; Deut 23:20–21), is restricted here to the specific case of the live-in relative attempting to redeem his property or liberty.

In contrast to the picture emerging from the non-Priestly law codes (see Exod 21:2–11; Deut 15:12–18), where Israelite slavery is recognized, in the Priestly legal tradition an Israelite forced to "sell" himself to another Israelite has the status of a hired laborer and must be treated as such. His servitude is temporary, and the option of electing to remain in perpetual servitude does not

exist (25:39–43). Israelites, like land holdings in Canaan, are Yahweh's property. He took them out of Egypt not in order to make them free but to make them slaves: *his* slaves. Only non-Israelites may be enslaved, and they and their progeny become the permanent property of their master (25:44–46). As with land holdings, the redemption price for indentured persons is a function of the number of years remaining until the jubilee (25:47–54), since at that time any Israelite will be released.

Although the chapter division views 26:1–2 as the introduction to what follows, it is preferable to take these verses as a caption to the preceding material. By expressing three of the basic concerns of the Holiness Legislation (see 19:4, 30), the text thus signals the end of the Priestly body of laws, after which it precedes to the concluding oration (26:3–45).

26:3–46. Reward and Threat, and Conclusion of the Lawgiving. This oration describes the rewards for compliance (26:3–13) and the divine response to failure to comply. If the Israelites agree to adhere to the commands as given in all of the chapters preceding, God will provide peace, prosperity, safety, population increase and swift and decisive victory over all enemies. The aim of the exodus will be accomplished: Israel will become God's people, and God will take up residence in their midst and reign over them. Thus God will maintain the covenant (16:9)—which in Priestly tradition means that God will uphold the commitment made to Abraham (Gen 17:4–8) and repeated to Moses (Exod 6:2–8)—to make Israel numerous and to give them the right to use the land of Canaan as a "holding" (see above).

Much more space is given to the threats than the promises (26:14–45). In contrast to the Deuteronomic tradition (Deut 11:13–17; 28:15–68), the disasters threatened here are not punishments but warnings. They appear as a series of successive attempts to "chastise" (NRSV, "punish" [e.g., 26:18], which does not convey this) the Israelites, i.e., to coerce them into submission if they refuse to accept his yoke. Even the final stage, expelling the Israelites from Canaan (26:27–39), is not aimed at bringing Israel's national existence to an end (as in Deuteronomy); rather it is the ultimate means to force Israel into line. The misery of exile will lead to remorse, following which

Yahweh will remember his covenant and implement his original plan once and for all. Yahweh thus appears here not in the role of the offended tyrant getting even for each infringement but rather as a determined ruler who realizes that severe measures may be necessary in order to achieve his end—and who will not shirk from using them. God is pictured here not so much as *willing* to give repeated second chances as *compelled* to do so, since, in Priestly thought, the covenant cannot ever become null and void.

If the Israelites refuse to accept God's terms, his first attempt to coerce them will consist of diseases and enemy incursions (26:16–17). If this fails, it will be followed by the withholding of rain and the resultant crop failure (vv. 18–20); the expression "sevenfold for your sins" signifies that the coercion imposed will be unimaginably greater than the offense they commit by spurning God. If this too is unsuccessful, the third attempt (vv. 21–22) will follow: an onslaught of wild beasts, the precise reverse of v. 6. The word translated "hostile" here and below is of uncertain meaning; it may mean "uncaring, indifferent." The fourth attempt (vv. 23–26) will consist of sword, pestilence, and famine. These, along with wild beasts, are God's four weapons of destruction in Ezek 14:12–23. This makes the total number of measures employed by God to pressure God's people into compliance add up to seven, the typical way of expressing completeness in the Bible.

If all of these prove ineffective, the final stage will ensue (vv. 27–38). Israel's land will be overrun by an invading enemy; all the local shrines and cultic objects (whose very existence is an anathema) will be destroyed, the land will become a ruin, and the population will flee fearfully into exile where they will all but cease to exist. In an ironic aside (vv. 34–35), God points out that although, during Israel's long refusal to obey God's commands, many cycles of seven years will have gone by and the land will not have observed its Sabbaths, when Israel goes into exile and its land is deserted, it will be repaid the rest it was denied.

Those who go into exile will become fewer and fewer with the passage of time. At last, the remaining survivors, moved by their misery to consider its cause, will realize it was their own (and their ancestors' own) fault and will acknowledge their guilt and that of their ancestors. When they finally commit themselves to comply fully with God's demands, the slate will be wiped clean of the accumulated guilt. The expression "uncircumcised heart" (v. 41) refers to their obduracy. The phrase, along with the entire process predicted here, expresses the notion that the refusal to accept the yoke of God's commands was immediate and unrelieved. Thus it is incorrect to speak of the final stage as repentance, since repentance consists of the return to former righteousness.

The Priestly history of Yahweh's active relationship with the people of Israel began when he heard their cry in bondage and was moved to remember his covenant with the patriarchs (Exod 6:5; see Gen 17:4–8; 28:1–4; 35:11–12). Thus its ending, as envisaged here (26:42–45), is an appropriate one: in the predicted future, Yahweh will hear their confession of guilt, will recall again his promise to the patriarchs, and will finally succeed in implementing his plan. The expression "the covenant with their ancestors whom I brought out of the land of Egypt" (v. 45) indicates that the promise made to Abraham, Isaac, and Jacob was indeed communicated in P to the generation of the exodus as well, and this is confirmed by Exod 6:6–9.

The text does not tell us what is expected to happen if the predicted remorse and confession fail to materialize; the prophecies of Ezekiel address this issue when it arises.

The caption in v. 46 indicates that this is the end of the Priestly account of the lawgiving in the tabernacle and that the laws in the next chapter are an added appendix.

J. Appendix: Pledges and Their Valuation, and Repeated Conclusion (27)

A person may make a monetary donation to the sanctuary by a procedure called consecration. In the first type (vv. 1–8), the Priestly legislator preserves the notion of self-consecration without requiring a person actually to sacrifice himself; rather one may contribute the monetary value of oneself or a member of one's household. What is otherwise a purely fiscal matter thus becomes a sublime act of devotion. The values are fixed; but if a poor person wishes to consecrate himself or a member of his family the scale is flexible (v. 8).

The second type of consecration (vv. 9–13) pertains to animals. Those fit for the altar (vv. 9–10), once consecrated, must be offered and no substitutions are to be made. Those that may not be sacrificed (vv. 11–13) may be consecrated only in order to be sold by the sanctuary for their monetary value. Unlike persons, animals have their values determined on the spot by the priest. One who opts to make his contribution and also keep his animal may redeem it for silver, but must add a 20% surcharge.

The third type of consecration is that of houses (vv. 14–15). One may actually donate one's house to the sanctuary for sale, or one may consecrate the house and then redeem it for silver, again adding 20% to the value. The redemption fee goes to the sanctuary, and the house returns to its owner.

The final type of consecration is that of real estate (vv. 16–25). Fields and ancestral lands may be donated for sale, the proceeds going to the sanctuary treasury; or the donor may redeem them, again at a 20% surcharge. Here, however, proper adjustment must be made for the number of years remaining until the jubilee. The sum of fifty shekels mentioned in v. 16 probably means one shekel per year, maximally fifty, if the jubilee is 50 years away. A homer of barley seed is an amount equal to the normal load carried by an ass.

Such voluntary contributions are an important source of revenue for the Temple, and they are also the only way that individual Israelites can participate in the regimen of public worship performed by the priests on their behalf. The complicated procedure by which one must consecrate and then redeem the object, instead of simply donating the monetary value up front, is something of a legal fiction, designed to impart the sense that one has given to God a portion of one's tangible wealth.

The remainder of the chapter (vv. 26–33) deals with objects that cannot be consecrated to the Lord since they belong to him already. Firstlings of the flock and herd (vv. 26–27; see Exod 13:2; Num 3:40–51) must be sacrificed and cannot be redeemed; firstlings of non-sacrificial animals may be redeemed or sold. The term translated "ransomed" in vv. 27, 29 is used to express the fact that the item in question is the property of God to begin with, so the person is not actually regaining ownership.

Next are objects that have been "devoted to destruction" (vv. 28–29). This seems to mean objects that have been proscribed, i.e., become taboo, as the result of a pledge that no use would ever be made of them and that they would become the permanent property of the Lord, never to be sold, redeemed, or exchanged. These are to be destroyed, and if they are humans, this means that they are destined for death. It is difficult to imagine that one may sentence oneself, one's slave, or a household member under one's authority to death as a consecration to the Lord, and that once this is done, there is no reprieve; but there may have been times when such a law was implemented.

Finally, tithes, which belong to God already, cannot be consecrated (vv. 30–33). The crop tithe mentioned here may be in addition to the one in Num 18.21–32. As for the tithe of herds and flocks, it is unique, not mentioned elsewhere in the Torah; from Samuel's words in 1 Sam 8:15–17, however, one may deduce that kings were in the practice of imposing such tithes as a form of taxation.

Since a section of this chapter (vv. 16–24) depends upon the laws of land tenure, it would have been unclear if the chapter had been placed before ch. 25, while placing this chapter between chs. 25 and 26 would have interrupted their thematic continuity. This explains why this chapter appears after the conclusion of the Priestly lawgiving, after which the caption of 26:46 is repeated in abbreviated form (v. 34).

BIBLIOGRAPHY

G. A. Anderson. "Sacrifices and Offerings in Ancient Israel. Studies in their Social and Political Importance." HSM 41 (Atlanta: Scholars Press, 1987); R. E. Gane. *Cult and Character: Purification Offerings, Day of Atonement, and Theodicy* (Winona Lake, Ind.: Eisenbrauns, 2005); M. Haran. *Temples and Temple-Service in Ancient Israel* (Oxford: Clarendon Press, 1978); J. Klawans. *Purity, Sacrifice, and the Temple: Symbolism and Supersessionism in the Study of Ancient Judaism* (Oxford: Oxford University Press, 2006); I. Knohl. *The Sanctuary of Silence: The Priestly Torah and the Holiness School* (Minneapolis: Fortress, 1995); B. A. Levine. *Leviticus: The Traditional*

Hebrew Text with the new JPS Translation. JPS Torah Commentary (Philadelphia: Jewish Publication Society, 1989); J. E. Hartley. *Leviticus.* WBC 4 (Waco: Word, 1992); J. Milgrom. *Leviticus 1–16.* AB 3; *Leviticus 17–22.* AB 3A; *Leviticus 23–27.* AB 3B (New York: Doubleday, 1991, 2000, 2001); B. J. Schwartz. *The Holiness Legislation: Studies in the Priestly Code* (Jerusalem: Magnes, 1999 [Hebrew]).

NUMBERS

Thomas B. Dozeman

OVERVIEW

Title. Two titles are associated with the fourth book in the Pentateuch. The title, "Numbers," derives from the Vulgate (Vg, *Numeri*) and the Septuagint (LXX, *Arithmoi*). A second title, "In the Wilderness," comes from the Masoretic Text (MT, *bemidbar*), in which pentateuchal books are named either by their opening word or by a significant word in the first sentence. These two names imply separate themes and divergent literary structures. "Numbers" accentuates the two accounts of the census taken of the Israelite people, which divides the book between the first (Num 1–25) and second (Num 26–36) generation of Israelites to leave Egypt. "In the wilderness" focuses instead on the theme of journey with God, which yields a three-part structure to the book: Num 1:1 10:10 contains revelations in the wilderness camp; 10:11–21:35 narrates the tragic wilderness journey of the first generation; and 22:1–36:13 describes the second generation of Israelites on the plains of Moab as they prepare to enter the promised land.

Composition. Statements reporting divine revelation frame the book of Numbers. Numbers 1:1 introduces the book with the statement: "The LORD spoke to Moses in the wilderness of Sinai, in the tent of meeting." The closing verse of 36:13 states: "These are the commandments and the ordinances that the LORD commanded through Moses to the Israelites…." The opening and closing verses emphasize the authoritative nature of the literature as law, which is composed by Moses. A careful reading of the book, however, reveals a wide variety of literary genres and a number of distinct authors. The book of Numbers includes poetry (e.g., the song of the ark, 10:35–36; an excerpt from the Book of the Wars of Yahweh, 21:14–15; the song of the well, 21:17–18; the ballad over Heshbon, 21:27–30; and the oracles of Balaam, 23:7–10, 18–24; 24:3–9, 15–24); liturgy (e.g., the Priestly blessing, 6:24–26); travel and inheritance records (e.g., the itinerary list, 21:10–20; 33; the inheritance of the land, 32); Priestly law (e.g., the law of restitution, 5:5–10; the law of sacrifice, 15:1–31; the law of the red heifer, 19;

the law of homicide, 35:9–15); and prose tales about the wilderness journey (e.g., the selection of the seventy elders, 11–12; the story of the failed conquest, 13–14; the battle against Sihon and Og, 21:21–35).

This diverse literature has been fashioned into a larger narrative of the wilderness journey from Egypt to the promise land, of which there are at least two versions, the non-Priestly (NP) and the Priestly (P) histories. The P history is the most prominent in the book of Numbers, including the camp legislation in Num 1–10 and nearly all of the literature on the inheritance and cultic laws in Num 26–36, as well as conflict stories of the wilderness journey in Num 11–25 (e.g., the departure from Sinai, 10:11–28; a version of the loss of the land, 13–15; conflict over the priesthood, 16–19; the sin of Moses and Aaron, 20:1–13; the death of Aaron, 20:22–29; and the sin at Baal Peor, 25:6–18). The NP history is concentrated in the story of the wilderness journey in Num 11–25, including an account of the departure from Mount Yahweh (10:29–36), conflict over the leadership of Moses and the selection of the seventy elders (11–12), a version of the loss of the land (13–14), further conflict over the leadership of Moses by Dathan and Abiram (16), the wars of conquest east of Jordan (20:14–21; 21:1–20; 21:21–35), the story of Balaam (22–24), the sin at Baal Peor (25:1–5); and the summary accounts of the wilderness journey and the inheritance of the Transjordanian land (32–33).

Central Themes. The central themes of the book of Numbers include the purity of God and its influence in cultic practice, the formation of community and ethical behavior (1–10, 15, 19), the wilderness journey as a place of testing and a model story of how the people of God live out their faith in this world (11–21), and the promised land as the goal of the religious pilgrimage (22–36).

OUTLINE

I. The Tabernacle Camp (1:1–10:10)

    A. The Camp and Community (1:1–6:27)

DETAILED ANALYSIS

I. The Tabernacle Camp (1:1–10:10)

The central theme in the description of the Israelite camp and the divine sanctuary is the holiness of God and how it transforms human society. The layout of the camp (1:1–6:27) in relation to the tabernacle (7:1–10:10) introduces degrees of holiness, depending on how close a person or place is in relation to the tabernacle. There are degrees of holiness among priests, Levites, and people as well as among the tabernacle, the camp, and the wilderness area outside of the camp. The closer to God, the holier. The authors describe how holiness emanating from the tabernacle creates a new social, political, and environmental order for Israel. The arrangement of the camp, the order for marching, and the role of the priests and the Levites outline the ethics of holiness.

A. The Camp and Community (1:1–6:27)

These chapters represent divine instruction to Moses within the tent of meeting, which outline the effects of divine holiness on Israel's social organization in the camp of the tabernacle. The holiness of God creates separation between the sacred and the profane worlds. God is holy; humans are not. Thus care must be taken in bringing the two together. Humans must conform to divine holiness. The concern for order in the Israelite camp represents the desire to conform to holiness.

1:1–47. Census of the First Generation. The deity demands a census of all Israelite males, twenty years of age and older, by tribe. The description of the census in v. 3 as "enrolling" (Heb.: *paqad*) the males means it is a census for military purposes. Verses 4–16 indicate that leaders are chosen from each tribe. The tribes are listed with Reuben as the first. The tribes are listed in a stereotypic manner, beginning with the name of the tribe, the chosen leader, and his father's name. Verses 17–47 provide the summary of the census by tribe, excluding the Levites. The total number of males over twenty years of age is 603,550, which repeats the number from Exod 38:26. The number most likely has symbolic value for the ancient authors, but that meaning eludes modern interpreters.

1:48–54. Separation of the Levites. The Levites are not included in the census. Verses 48–50a provide the reason. The Levites are not to be numbered because they are assigned special duties in caring for the tabernacle. Verses 50b–54 state three duties of the Levites: they perform service for the tabernacle, they carry the tabernacle and its vessels, and they provide a protective buffer around the tabernacle by pitching their texts between the sanctuary and the Israelite camp. Verse 54 concludes the account of the census by stating that all of the divine commands were completed. The Levites will also be separated out from the tribes in the promise land, where they will dwell in cities rather than receive an inheritance of land (Num 35).

2:1–34. Arrangement of the Camp. Once the Israelites are numbered, the divine instructions shift to the arrangement of the campsite. The tabernacle is situated at the center of the Israelite camp with the tribes distributed evenly on its four sides in the following manner. The tribes camping on the east side of the tent of meeting are Judah, Isaachar, and Zebulun (vv. 3–9); on the south of the tent of meeting, Reuben, Simeon, and Gad (vv. 10–16); at the center closest to the tent of meeting, the Levites (v. 17); on the west side of the tent of meeting, Ephraim, Manasseh, and Benjamin (vv. 18–24); and on the north side of the tent of meeting, Dan, Asher, and Naphtali (vv. 25–31).

This geographical distribution of the tribes highlights the status of certain tribes, with those on the east side of the camp receiving the highest honor. The first tribe listed in each group is assigned a leadership role over the "regimental encampment," which has its own insignia or banner. The arrangement of the camp indicates the primary position of Judah, with the tribe of Reuben as leader of the second regimental encampment. The arrangement of the campsite also provides the order for marching. Verse 17 reports that the tabernacle is at the center of camp and that it is surrounded by the Levites. According to Num 2 the sanctuary is located at the holiest place on earth. It becomes the center of all life for the Israelite tribes, which are organized around the tabernacle. The role of the Levites to safeguard the sanctuary reflects both the power and the danger of holiness in the midst of the people of God. Thus the Levites both serve the sacred for the Israelite people and also protect the holiness of God from the danger of the people's impurity.

3:1–10. Genealogy of the Levites. The section begins with the genealogical phrase, "This is the lineage of Aaron and Moses," known as the Toledot formula. Most instances of the Toledot occur in Genesis, where the story of creation and the ancestors is read as an evolving genealogy, first of the world (Gen 1–10) and then of the Israelite nation (Gen 11–50). The reference to the Toledot in 3:1 narrows the focus of the biblical narrative even further from the nation of Israel to the priestly family of Aaron. Verses 5–10 return to the topic of the relationship of the Levites to the Aaronide priesthood and to Israelites in general. The Levites are positioned between the priesthood and the congregation for the purpose of serving both groups in front of the tabernacle (vv. 6–7). The description of the Levite's work as "to perform duties," likely indicates guard duty, in which the Levites protect the sacred space of the tabernacle from encroachment. The Levites also transport the tabernacle, when the Israelites journey through the wilderness.

3:11–13. Levites as Substitutes for Firstborn.
God states that the Levites are substitutes for all Israelite firstborn. The command indicates the divine claim on firstborn males. Exodus 22:29 provides the rationale, when God states: "The firstborn of your sons you shall give to me." The few passages that mention the divine claim on the firstborn do not explain the reason for the holy status of the firstborn or the cultic implications of the law. The divine claim on the firstborn may have been associated with first fruits (Exod 23:14–17) or the role of the firstborn in ancestral worship (Deut 26:1–14). Whether there was a special ritual, redemption, or even sacrifice of the firstborn is difficult to determine. (The story of the sacrifice of Isaac in Gen 22 is a polemic against child sacrifice, suggesting some form of child sacrifice may at one time have taken place.) Verse 13 roots the holy status of the Israelite firstborn in the exodus, when the Israelite firstborn were spared death on the night of Passover.

3:14–51. Census of the Levites.
The role of the Levites as substitutes for the Israelite firstborn requires that they be counted. All Levitical males from one month of age and older are to be numbered according to their three ancestral houses, the house of Gershon numbers 7,500 males (vv. 21–26), Kohath has 8,600 males (vv. 27–32), and Merari 6,200 males (vv. 33–37). Verses 38–39 locate the Aaronide priests in the camp as dwelling on the east side of the tabernacle, while also contrasting their labor within the sanctuary from the Levites who work outside it, before noting that the total number of Levitical priests is 22,000. Verses 40–51 return to the topic of Levitical substitution for the Israelite firstborn. In cases where there are more firstborn than Levites, the redemption of the firstborn is achieved through a Temple tax.

4:1–49. Tasks of the Levites.
The chapter begins with a second census of the Levites, who are between the ages of thirty and fifty years. All the Levites are placed under the direction of the Aaronide priests. Eleazar supervises the Kohathite Levites (v. 16), while the Gershonites and the Merarites are under the oversight of Ithamar (vv. 28, 33). The Kohathites carry the most holy objects of the tabernacle on the wilderness march, including the ark, the table of showbread, the lamp stand, the golden altar, and all the utensils (vv. 5–15). The Gershonite Levites carry the curtains of the tabernacle (vv. 21–28), and the Merarites carry the frames, bars, and pillars of the tabernacle with its court (vv. 29–33).

5:1–4. Purity Laws for the Camp.
The holiness of God requires not only the separation of the sacred and the profane but also involves the distinction between health and disease. Holiness is the source of human health and purity. It must be protected from human infection, contamination, pollution, and impurity. Verses 1–4 state three forms of impurity that threaten the camp: (1) a skin disease described as *sara'at*, sometimes translated as leprosy; (2) abnormal bodily discharges from the genitals; and (3) contact with a corpse. Each of these conditions represents a form of death, which stands in conflict with the life-giving power of holiness centered in the tabernacle. These laws are designed to protect holiness from defilement and thus safeguard the presence of God in the camp; they are not to protect humans. Any male or female with these conditions threatens the purity of the camp and must be expelled.

5:5–10. Law Regulating Community Relationships.
These verses deal with the breakdown of communal relationships that create impurity and threaten holiness. The focus of the law is not secular crime, but the violation of the sacred. Verse 6 states that cheating and stealing "break faith with the LORD." The Hebrew verb, "to break faith" (*ma'al*) when used with the prepositions *with/against* (*be*) indicates some form of sacrilege. The sacred character of the law is further reinforced when the offender is described as "incurring guilt." Guilt in this instance describes a state or condition incompatible with holiness. The imagery is medical. Such a person infects the camp with pollution and thus must be cured through confession and repayment of the offense.

5:11–31. Law Regulating a Woman Accused of Adultery. The concern for social relationships (vv. 5–10), which may defile the camp, focuses here on marriage. The law is aimed at a wife who is suspected of "going astray" (*sata*), meaning to commit adultery. Verses 15–31 outline a judicial procedure for determining the guilt or innocence of a suspected adulteress. The rationale for the ritual is that adultery is sacrilege. A woman guilty of such an action threatens the camp with contamination, not because she is ritually unclean from sexual intercourse, but because she is ethically unclean from violating her marital relationship. The aim of the ritual is not to assuage the husband's jealousy but to avoid defilement of the camp.

The magical character of the ordeal described in vv. 15–28 for determining the guilt or innocence of the woman underscores the sacred dimension in which the law is meant to function. The priest is instructed to take the accused woman before God (v. 16), mix holy water with dust from the floor of the tabernacle (v. 17), loosen the woman's hair, and place an offering of jealousy and remembrance in her hands (v. 18). Verses 19–26 stipulate an oath, which functions as a self-curse upon the woman, should she be found guilty. The priest writes the oath on parchment in the mixture of water and dust as a potion named "the water of bitterness," which the woman must drink. Verses 27–28 indicate that the woman's reaction to the potion will determine her guilt or innocence, suggesting a trial by ordeal. The closest parallel in the Hebrew Bible is Exod 32:20 where Moses makes the Israelites drink water mixed with powder from the destroyed golden calf. If guilty, the curse will take effect causing the woman's uterus to drop, most likely indicating the aborting of a fetus; if innocent she will conceive the child.

Interpreters have struggled with the technical language of the ritual and its larger meaning. The various descriptions of the offering such as "offering of jealousy," "offering of remembrance," "bringing iniquity to remembrance," and "holy water" lack precise parallels in the Hebrew. The setting of the sanctuary for the ordeal places the law of adultery within the realm of sacred law as compared to civil law, perhaps protecting the wife from the rage of her husband. The law is intended to protect the holiness of the camp from the impurity of sexual defilement.

6:1–21. Law of the Nazirite. The name *Nazirite* comes from the Hebrew verb *nazar*, meaning "to separate." A Nazirite is potentially any woman or man from the congregation who makes a vow to be separate or dedicated to God for a period of time, resulting in the holy status of the person for a set period of time. The law of the Nazirite appears in three parts: vv. 1–8 describe the restrictions that apply to the Nazirite; vv. 9–12 focus on cleansing from accidental defilement; and vv. 13–20 outline proper procedures for ending the vow. Verses 1–8 describe three restrictions on Nazirites, while they are in their holy state: Nazirites cannot drink wine (vv. 3–4); cut their hair during the period of the vow (v. 5); nor touch a corpse, since holiness and death are incompatible (v. 6). Should a Nazirite accidentally break his or her vow, vv. 9–12 outline the procedures for decontamination so that the person can begin the vow anew. A contaminated Nazirite must undergo a seven-day period of purification, at the end of which his or her hair must be shaved. On the eighth day, two turtle doves or pigeons are presented to the priest for sacrifice, followed by a guilt offering of a one-year-old male lamb, which expiates the person, allowing that person to begin the Nazirite vow anew. Verses 13–20 outline the proper ritual for leaving the holy state of the Nazirite. Self-removal from the sacred is a dangerous procedure, requiring a complex series of sacrifices, including a burnt offering, a sin offering, an offering of well-being, and grain and drink offerings.

6:22–27. Priestly Blessing. A Priestly blessing on the congregation concludes the section of laws concerning camp defilement, which began in Num 5. The act of blessing is deeply rooted in Israelite culture, perhaps even protecting humans from the contamination of the dead. The Priestly blessing consists of three poetic lines (vv. 24–26), each of which contains two verbs: *bless-keep*; *shine-grace*; and *lift-peace*. The name *Yahweh* appears once in each line, as the subject of the first of the paired verbs. The first verb in each line summarizes an activity of God upon the worshiper (*bless, shine, lift*), and the second describes the results of God's actions (keep, grace, peace).

Verses 22–23, 27 provide the literary context for the poem. Verses 22–23 indicate that the blessing functions as a concluding benediction to the instructions about purity in the camp. Verse 27 clarifies that it is God, rather than the priest, who blesses. The blessing provides a safeguard against defilement by infusing the camp with the power of divine blessing. It also provides a portrait of the ideal camp, where God pays attention to persons, where blessing and security drive out the power of death, and where the achievement of wholeness and peace is possible.

B. The Tabernacle (7:1–10:10)

The scope of the laws narrows in this section from the effects of holiness on the camp to the tabernacle at its center. The subject matter also changes from the social organization of Israel and their ethical relationships to the cultic rituals associated with the care and dedication of the sanctuary.

7:1–88. Offerings of Dedication. Verse 1 refers to Moses' dedication of the tabernacle (cf Exod 40:1, 16, where Moses also dedicates the sanctuary). The repetition suggests a suspension of time from Exod 40 to Num 7, before the twelve days of dedicatory offerings in 7:2–88. The central theme in the chapter is sacrifice, which in the present context constitute dedicatory gifts to God. Verses 2–9 describe the dedicatory offerings as spontaneous gifts from the laity. The initial gifts include six wagons and twelve oxen for the transportation of the tabernacle. Verses 10–88 offer an extensive account of gifts presented by each tribal leader over a twelve-day period. The order of the gift-giving follows the sequence of tribes, in which Judah rather than Reuben is first. Each tribe brings identical gifts including grain offering on 1 silver plate and 1 silver basin; incense offering in 1 gold dish; burnt offering of 1 bull, 1 ram, and 1 male lamb; sin offering of 1 male goat; and well-being offering of 2 oxen, 5 rams, 5 male goats; and 5 male lambs. The sacrifices are presented to the priesthood as resources for the cult.

7:89. Moses in the Tabernacle. God speaks to Moses in the most holy place of the tabernacle. The iconography within the tabernacle and the actions of Moses reflect the Priestly theology of divine presence. The voice of God is heard from between the two cherubim that frame the mercy seat and form the top of the ark of the congregation. The word *cover* is a more accurate translation of the Hebrew word (*kapporet*) than "mercy seat."

The translation *mercy seat* may derive from the rite of atonement that takes place at the ark in Lev 16. The iconography of the tabernacle represents the cherubim and ark from the Jerusalem Temple of the monarchical period now used to describe the ways in which God was present with Israel even during the exile. In the Jerusalem Temple, God was described as being enthroned upon two cherubim (Ps 99:1–5), massive winged statues ten cubits in height (1 cubit = 18–22 inches), each with a single wingspan of five cubits (1 Kgs 6:23–28; 8:7). Their wings stretched the width of the inner chamber of the Temple, providing a throne for God, with the ark in front of the wings of the cherubim as a footstool for the enthroned deity (Ps 99:1–5). The tabernacle retains the cherubim, but they are smaller and function as guardian angels of divine law within the ark. No mention is made of the royal imagery of divine enthronement.

8:1–4. Menorah. The lamp stand or menorah is described in Exod 25:31–40. Its shaft is called a stem, and its receptacles for the lamps are branches. The imagery may represent a stylized tree of life, which symbolizes both fertility in nature and the life-giving power of God. Verses 1–4 focus on the location of the menorah within the tabernacle. The lights on the menorah must burn toward the altar, accentuating the presence of God in the tabernacle.

8:5–26. Dedication of the Levites. The Levites were distinguished from rest of the Israelites in 1:48–53. Numbers 3–4 recounted their separate census, service to the tabernacle, and role as substitutes for the Israelite firstborn. The present section focuses on the purification and dedication of the Levites. In contrast to the consecration of the Aaronide priests, the Levites undergo a process of purification. The process includes sprinkling with water, shaving their entire bodies, and washing their clothes (vv. 5–8). Rites of sacrifice follow the rituals of purification (vv. 9–13). The Levites lay their hands on two bulls, who are then sacrificed as a means of atonement for the Levites, one as a sin offering and the other as a burnt offering. Verses 14–18 make clear that the ritual process of purification and sacrifice results in the Levites becoming a divine possession, thus fulfilling their role as substitutes for the Israelite firstborn. Verse 19 notes that the Levites also atone for the Israelites through their position in the camp, where they protect the people from the danger of holiness by creating a buffer between the sanctuary and the tribes.

9:1–14. Passover. The law of Passover frames the story of the exodus, appearing first during the exodus when Israel is in the land of Egypt (Exod 12) and again at the conclusion of the revelation at Mount Sinai (Num 9). Passover functions as the Israelite's constitutional festival: it saves the firstborn from death in Egypt, and it defines Israel as a nation. Participation in Passover creates the congregation as the people of God, whether native Israelite or resident alien. Verses 1–14 presuppose the earlier instruction on Passover from Exod 12. This passage addresses problems that might arise with observing the Passover on the fourteenth day of the first month. Israelites who are not able to observe Passover on its designated day because of issues of impurity are allowed to observe the festival one month later. All Israelites must observe Passover.

9:15–23. Cloud and Wilderness March. The section describes the cloud that is associated with the tabernacle and that symbolizes the presence of God. The cloud is a common symbol throughout the ancient Near East to indicate the presence of the divine. It often appears as a halo or bright disk, most likely symbolizing the sun, which would surround a god or person with divine power. Verses 15–16 state that when Moses set up the tabernacle, a cloud covered it continually, day and night. During the night the cloud appeared as fire. The cloud first appears on the day that Moses sets up the tabernacle (Exod 40:1, 16). Verses 17–22 provide a detailed summary of the way in which the cloud guides Israel in the wilderness march. The cloud signals when Israel must march and when they must camp. The periods of marching and camping vary, according to vv. 19–22. Rest periods may include one night (v. 21), days, a month, and even longer periods of time (v. 22). The periods of rest may reflect the Priestly ritual calendar (Num 28–29), according to which feasts require diverse periods of rest.

10:1–10. Trumpets. God commands Moses to make two silver trumpets, which were likely narrow tubes, roughly eighteen inches in length with a bell-shaped end. The trumpets, blown by the Aaronide priests, were used to summon the congregation and to prepare the camp for travel in the wilderness. Once the people reach the promise land, the trumpets would summon the people to war and to observe feast days. Verse 10 concludes with the divine promise that God will remember the Israelites upon hearing the trumpet blasts. The instruction concludes with the phrase, "I am Yahweh, your God," which reveals the divine name. This phrase, known as the self-introduction, appears throughout the important events of the exodus (Exod 6:2, 7; 7:17; 10:2; 14:4, 18) and the wilderness journey (Exod 29:46; Lev 19:11, 13, 16; 18:2, 5; 25:17–38).

II. The Wilderness Journey (10:11–21:35)

Israel departs from Mount Sinai. This section depicts the journey of the first generation of Israelites as a tragic story leading to death. The section is dominated by conflict between God, Israel, and Moses in the wilderness. Conflicts over leadership focus on Moses, whose authority is challenged twice. The prophetic leadership of Moses is central to Num 11–12 whereas chs. 16–17 address his priestly leadership. Resolution of the conflicts through divine judgment defines more clearly these distinct leadership roles. Chapters 13–14 describe the failure of the first generation of Israelites to secure the promise land. Their failure provides guidelines for success by a future generation (15, 18–19). Chapters 20–21 provide transition from the failed journey of the first generation of Israelites to the second generation.

A. Leaving Sinai (10:11–36)

There are two accounts of Israel's departure from Mount Sinai. Numbers 10:11–28 is the Priestly version of the departure, which incorporates the language, characters, and tribal organization from 1:1–10:10. This account highlights the Israelite nation as a whole. Numbers 10:29–36 is the first portion of the NP history. It describes Israel's departure from Mount Yahweh, with the ark of the covenant leading the people three days in advance. Here the focus is on God leading the people rather than on the journeying of the people.

10:11–28. Organization of the Wilderness March. The date for the departure from Mount Sinai is month 2, day 20 of the second year after the exodus, allowing for the completion of the second Passover prescribed in 9:1–14. The cloud guides Israel as was described in 9:15–23. Verse

12 describes the travel route of the Israelites as a journey "by stages" from Sinai to Paran. The P history repeats this information in Num 12:16. The location of Paran is unknown. It is described as a desert site between Midian and Egypt in 1 Kgs 11:18. The location bears theological significance in ancient poetry as the desert home of Yahweh, who is described as "the Holy One from Mount Paran" (Hab 3:3). Verses 13–28 depict the organization of the wilderness march with military imagery, which consists of four standards. The first standard includes Judah, Issachar, Zebulun, and the tabernacle transported by the Gershonites and Merarites. The second standard includes Reuben, Simeon, Gad, and the Holy Objects carried by the Kohathites. The third standard consists of Ephraim, Manasseh, and Benjamin. And the fourth standard, forming the rear guard, includes Dan, Asher, and Naphtali.

10:29–36. Leading of the Ark. These verses constitute a second account of the departure, this time from Mount Yahweh rather than from Mount Sinai. Verses 29–32 report an exchange between Moses and his father-in-law, Hobab the son of Reuel (also named Jethro in Exod 3:1; 4:18; and 18:1). Moses requests his guidance and promises him a share in the goodness that Yahweh promises Israel. Hobab refuses, prompting Moses to repeat the request for leadership. Moses receives no response from Hobab, but the ark immediately begins to guide Israel following this exchange (vv. 33–36), suggesting that God replaces Hobab as a leader of Israel on their wilderness journey. Verses 33–34 describe the departure of Israel from Mount Yahweh, with the cloud of God traveling in front for the three days journey in search of a resting place. In a short poem, vv. 35–36 characterize the ark as a guide in the wilderness. In contrast to the Priestly account of travel in Num 10:11–28, where the ark traveled in the midst of Israel, the poem places the ark ahead of the people in their journey, while also emphasizing the role of the ark in holy war. The first line of the poem describes Yahweh's ability to attack the enemy, while the second line envisions the successful return of Yahweh from battle. The ark is one of the most significant cult objects in Israel's history, appearing in a number of different roles throughout the Old Testament. 1 Samuel 4–7 follows the imagery of this poem, narrating the role of the ark in war. Psalm 99:1–5 reinterprets the ark as the footstool of the enthroned

God in the Jerusalem Temple. Deuteronomy 10:8 reinterprets the ark once again as the container for the Ten Commandments, which form the basis of covenant between God and Israel.

B. The Prophetic Spirit of Moses (11:1–12:15)

Numbers 11–12 explores the leadership of Moses through a series of complaints. The stories of complaint (also described as murmuring stories) organize the wilderness journey of the first generation of Israelites. The complaint stories begin immediately when the Israelites leave Egypt and continue through the entire wilderness journey (Exod 14:11–12; 15:22–26; 16; 17:1–7; Num 11:1–3, 4–35; 14; 16–17; 20:2–13; 21:4–9). The murmuring of the Israelites arises during threatening situations in the wilderness: the lack of food and water, disease, or the fear of the inhabitants of Canaan, all of which cause Israel to protest their present condition. Their complaint is accompanied by a longing to return to slavery in Egypt, which represents a lack of faith in the leadership of Yahweh and Moses and eventually leads to the death of the first generation. The murmuring stories intensify from episodes of testing (Exod 14–18) before the Israelites receive the law at Mount Sinai (Exod 19–Num 10) to instances of disobedience after the revelation of law (Num 11–21).

Numbers 11–12 consists of three stories of conflict. Numbers 11:1–3 introduces the section with a general story of complaint by the rabble in the camp, who are destroyed by fire. A second story of complaint in 11:4–35 focuses on the lack of food, prompting Moses to complain to God. Numbers 12 recounts the challenge of Aaron and Miriam's challenge to Moses as a unique prophetic leader. The stories describe the nature of Moses' charismatic leadership. The word *charisma* means "gift" in Greek. Moses is presented as a gifted leader, someone filled with the divine spirit, who speaks with God face to face, conveys the divine word to the people, and intercedes on behalf of the people. The section explores the nature of Moses' charismatic leadership from different perspectives. Numbers 11:4–35 explores the way in which Moses' charismatic spirit can be transferred to other leaders, while Num 12 emphasizes the unique quality of Moses' prophetic spirit.

11:1–3. Complaint at Taberah. The first incident after the departure from the divine mountain is reported in a story of complaint, for which the reader is unprepared. The story signals a change of mood in the book of Numbers—from the formation of the community at Sinai (Num 1–10) to conflict in the wilderness journey (Num 11–21). The complaint in 11:1–3 lacks specific details, stating simply that people rebel and God responds by sending down fire to destroy the rebels. The location of the story, *Taberah*, meaning "burning," identifies the story as an etiology, since the geographic setting is meant to provide commentary on the event. The sequence of events provides the pattern for many of the murmuring stories in Numbers: (1) complaint by the people; (2) divine punishment; (3) the cry of the people; (4) the intercession of Moses; (5) and the end of the divine judgment.

11:4–35. Moses and the Seventy Elders. Two themes are interwoven in the second murmuring story, the complaint of the people about the lack of meat in the wilderness (vv. 4–9, 13, 18–23, 31–34) and Moses' protest about the burden of leadership (vv. 10–12, 14–17, 24–30). The distribution of Moses' charismatic spirit to others, first to the seventy elders and then to Eldad and Medad, involves both themes. The story is made up of three scenes: the murmuring of the people and the protest of Moses over leadership (vv. 4–15), the divine response to Moses (vv. 16–23), and the selection of the seventy elders to assist in the leadership of the people (vv. 24–35).

11:4–15 provides the setting and circumstances of the story. Verse 4 states that certain members of the camp, described as "rabble," have a strong "craving" (*ta'awa*) for meat. The description of this group as craving meat provides the location of the story, Kibroth-hattaavah ("graves of craving"). The craving for meat is a rejection of manna, the wilderness food given to Israel in Exod 16. The literary relationship between the stories is underscored when manna is described in Num 11:7–9. What begins as a murmuring story, takes an unexpected turn when Moses complains about the burden of leadership (vv. 11–15). The burden of Moses' leadership was first introduced in Exod 18, when Jethro, the father-in-law of Moses, advised him to select more leaders to govern the people. The divine promise to Moses (Exod 33) of guidance in the wilderness journey provides further background for the complaint of Moses. Moses' complaint, "Why have I not found favor in your sight?" repeats the divine promise to him found in Exod 33:12–23. In this way, Moses accuses God of abandoning him in the wilderness, which prompts his request for death (v. 15).

11:16–23 contains the divine response to the Israelite's craving for meat and to Moses' complaint about the burden of leadership. God instructs Moses to select seventy elders who will share his spirit and thus aid him in leadership (vv. 16–17). The transfer of Moses' spirit will take place at the tent of meeting, a sacred tent pitched outside of the Israelite camp, as compared to the Priestly tabernacle, which is placed at the center of the camp. God responds to the request for meat (vv. 18–20), repeating the complaint of the people by quoting their earlier words as an indictment: "You have wailed in the hearing of the Lord, saying 'If only we had meat to eat. Surely it was better for us in Egypt.'" Yahweh states that the people will eat meat for one month until it becomes repulsive to them. Moses responds to the divine prediction by reminding God that there are not less than 600,000 Israelites (see Exod 12:37) who will need meat. The deity responds with the rhetorical question: "Is the Lord's power limited?"

11:24–35 narrates the resolution. Verses 24–30 recount the selection of seventy elders at the tent of meeting outside of the camp, where God takes a portion of Moses' spirit and places it in them, prompting the leaders to prophesy. Verse 25 reports that the seventy elders become ecstatic prophets upon receiving the spirit of Moses, but only momentarily as they take on the role of scribes. The episode involving Eldad and Medad, who unexpectedly received a portion of Moses' spirit even though they were not part of the seventy elders, underscores the uncontrollable character of charismatic power. The spirit blows where it will, and it is not always possible for the community of faith to control it. The complaint of Joshua, that Eldad and Medad should not be allowed to prophesy, represents the community's attempt to control the charismatic power of the spirit (v. 28). Moses' response affirms the unpredictable nature of the spirit throughout the community: "Are you jealous for my sake? Would that all the Lord's people were prophets, and that the LORD would put his spirit on them?" (v. 29). Verses 31–35 describe the feeding of meat to the people as an act of divine judgment. Quails drop from heaven all around the camp, but not in it, until they are piled up over three feet deep. The people who leave the Camp to eat the meat collect not less than eighty-nine bushels of quail per person. But they die, eating the feast at the "Graves of Craving." Those who remained in the camp live and are able to journey on with God in the wilderness.

12:1–16. Conflict Between Moses, Miriam, and Aaron. The charismatic leadership of Moses remains the central issue in the controversy between Miriam, Aaron, and Moses. But the story moves in the opposite direction of ch. 11, where the central problem was how the spirit of Moses could be passed on to the seventy elders and even influence all the members of the camp (11:29). The central message in Num 12 qualifies the previous story. Miriam and Aaron claim the same prophetic authority as Moses, which sets in motion a story about the unique character and status of Moses.

12:1–3 isolates the three leaders of the exodus—Moses, Miriam, and Aaron—in a controversy over prophetic authority. This controversy is underscored by the fact that Aaron (Exod 7:1) and Miriam (Exod 15:20) are designated as prophets during the events of the exodus. Aaron and Miriam challenge Moses' prophetic authority with two arguments: (1) he is married to a Cushite woman and (2) they doubt that God only speaks through him. The marriage of Moses to a Cushite woman stands in uneasy tension with the tradition of Moses' marriage to Zipporah, the Midianite, suggesting a range of folklore about Moses. The combination of intermarriage and prophetic authority likely reflect debates in the Second Temple period surrounding intermarriage (see Ezra–Nehemiah). The marriage of Moses to a Cushite woman, the biblical reference to Ethiopia, stands in tension with the authoritative teaching on intermarriage that emerges in the post-exilic period. It challenges the prescribed boundaries of the community. Their challenge concerning the special status of Moses as the authoritative voice for God (v. 2) cannot be separated from their complaint concerning his marriage to the Cushite (v. 1). The two reinforce each other. By arguing that God also speaks through them, Miriam and Aaron are adding authority to their criticism of Moses' intermarriage. Verse 3 sets the stage for refuting the challenge to Moses' authority, stressing his special quality as a devout person.

12:4–10 describes God's response to the challenge, summoning the three characters to the tent of meeting outside of the camp. God responds in an oracle (vv. 6–8), defending the incomparable nature of Moses and stating that prophets receive messages in dreams and riddles (v. 6). But to Moses, God speaks "mouth to mouth" (v. 8). The phrase is unique to this story. Yet similar language is used to describe Moses in Exod 33:11, where God speaks to Moses face to face as a friend, and in Exod 34:29–35, where the divine light invades the face of Moses. Moses' direct communication with God is different from the way that God interacts with prophets, thereby placing Moses in a special category. Consequently, prophets like Miriam and Aaron should fear Moses and not challenge his charismatic authority or his actions, including his intermarriage with the Cushite woman. God strikes Miriam with leprosy as a result of the challenge to Moses' prophetic authority

12:11–15 illustrates the special status of Moses as a charismatic leader. Aaron requests special intercession for Miriam, whose leprosy threatens to make her like that of a stillborn baby (v. 2). Moses responds, interceding for Miriam, and prompting divine healing, which illustrates his special relationship with God.

C. The Story of the Spies and the Loss of the Promised Land (13:1–15:41)

Chapters 13–15 are pivotal in the book of Numbers. They tell the story of why the first generation of Israelites to leave Egypt lost the gift of the promise land (chs. 13–14). The story concludes with legislation concerning the sacrifices that Israel must offer when the next generation eventually enters the land (ch. 15).

13:1–20. Selection of the Spies. The section begins with the divine instruction to Moses that he send out men into the land of Canaan. The NRSV translates the activity of the men as "spying out the land." The NIV translation, "to explore," is closer to the meaning of the Hebrew word. Verses 4–16 provide a list of the leaders from each tribe who are sent into the land. Most names on the list are unique to this passage. Noteworthy is the listing of Caleb and Hoshea (= Joshua), who emerge as heroes in the story.

13:21–33. Mission and Report of the Spies. Verses 21–24 describe the mission of those sent into the land. Verse 21 states that the men must explore Canaan and provide an evaluation of the land, which requires the group to travel to the northern most boundary of Lebo-hamath. Verses 22–24 limit the travel of the group to the southern border of the land for the purpose of reconnaissance in preparation for conquest. Two points are emphasized in the latter version. First, the land is rich, producing lush grapes. The region is even named as the Wadi Eschol, meaning "grape-cluster" (v. 24). Second, the land is populated by a race of fearful giants descended from Anak (see also Deut 1:19–46; Josh 14:12, 15; 15:13–19). Goliath, the giant slain by David, is a descendent of this race (1 Sam 17).

13:25–33 contains two versions of the spies' negative report. In the first version (vv. 27–31), the spies declare the land rich in resources. It even "flows with milk and honey." But they also note the fearful character of the giants, as well as other indigenous nations, who will prevent the Israelites from conquering the land. Verses 32–33 provide a second report in which the land, itself, is declared so bad that it eats its inhabitants. Taken together the two reports reflect a rejection of the goodness of the promise land and a fear to follow God by engaging in holy war against the inhabitants.

14:1–45. Response to the Report of the Spies. This section recounts various responses to the report of the spies. The people react by murmuring (vv. 1–4). They complain about divine leadership in the wilderness, fear for their children's lives, and wish that they had remained in Egypt. Moses and Aaron fall on their faces (v. 5), which in this context signifies anger against the Israelites (cf. the similar action in Num 16:4). Joshua and Caleb counter the complaint of the people by reaffirming the goodness of the land (v. 7), the power of God to fulfill the promise of land (v. 8), and the need for people to engage in holy war (v. 9).

God provides two responses to the murmuring of the people in vv. 11–38, which are signaled by the repetition of the statement of disgust to Moses: "How long ..." (vv. 11 and 27). In the first response (vv. 11–25), God complains that the people have rejected divine leadership and do not believe in divine power, even though they have seen signs of it in Egypt and in the wilderness. As a result, God decides to destroy all the adult Israelites except for Caleb and to make a new nation from Moses. Moses intercedes for the people (vv. 13–19), repeating many of the same arguments that he used to rescue the people from divine destruction after the sin of the golden calf (Exod 32). First, he cautions God that killing the Israelites would lead the nations to conclude that Yahweh is unreliable and unable to fulfill God's promise of land. Second, Moses calls upon the merciful character of Yahweh to forgive sin, which was revealed to him on Mount Sinai (Exod 34:6–7). God agrees to forgive, as Moses requested (vv. 20–24). The entire nation is not destroyed instantly, although they are denied the gift of the promise land. The divine gift of the land is transferred to their children, while the first generation of Israelites is commanded to travel back into the wilderness on the Red Sea road (v. 25). In the second response (vv. 26–38), God provides greater detail about how divine punishment will be enacted, stating that persons will be punished according to what they actually said (v. 28). The divine speech accentuates individual responsibility for sin instead of the collective guilt of the people. Those who murmured and were over the age of twenty will die in the wilderness (v. 29). Joshua and Caleb are the only exceptions. The children will inherit the land instead of their parents (v. 31). And the length of the punishment is determined by the offense. Thus, the forty days in which the land was explored is translated into forty years of wilderness wandering (vv. 34–35). Finally, the leaders who provided a bad report of the land will die instantly (vv. 36–37).

14:39–45 concludes the story of the loss of the promise land with a failed account of holy war. When Moses tells the people of the divine decision to defer the gift of the land, the people panic, confess their sin, and decide to invade (v. 40). Moses condemns this decision as yet another transgression against God, which can only lead to the slaughter of the people, since God will not fight for them (vv. 41–43). The closing scene of the story pictures the people entering the hills for battle, while the ark of Yahweh remains in the camp (v. 44). The inevitable consequence is recounted in v. 45: the people are destroyed all the way to the city of Hormah, a location south of Hebron.

15:1–41. Legislation for Israel's Future Life in the Land. The loss of the land is followed by a series of laws that point ahead to the Israelite's future life in the promise land. The chapter offers two sets of laws concerning the future life in the land, vv. 1–16 and 17–31. Each one is introduced by the phrase, "the LORD spoke to Moses, saying: Speak to the Israelites and say to them" (vv. 1–2a, 17–18a). The chapter closes with additional laws (vv. 32–41) that pertain to the wilderness march.

Verses 1–16 provide instruction on the ingredients for sacrifices. Similar laws occur in Lev 2 and Ezek 46:5–14. The law in Num 15:1–16 differs from the other law codes in that it extends the law of sacrifice to the non-Israelite, resident alien, should such an individual choose to participate in the sacrifice cult.

Verses 17–31 include two types of laws. Verses 17–21 state the requirement for a donation from the first batch of dough whenever anyone eats "bread in the land." Verses 22–31 shift the topic to forgiveness according to three distinct types of transgression. First, if an act of transgression is committed without the people's knowing it, corporate forgiveness of both native Israelites and resident aliens is possible, requiring the sacrifice of a bull for a burn offering and a male goat for a sin offering (vv. 22–26). Second, the sacrifice of a female goat is able to atone for unintentional individual sin (vv. 27–29). Third, there is no forgiveness for intentional sin (vv. 30–31). Such a person must be "cut off" from the people, meaning excommunication or execution.

15:32–41 turns to a case set in the wilderness: a law concerning a person who collects sticks on the Sabbath. The law is presented as a narrative, in which a person from the wilderness camp is caught in the infraction and taken to Moses, who lacks legal precedent. There is Sabbath law in the Decalogue (Exod 20:10–11) and in the revelation of the tabernacle (Exod 31;12–17; 35:1–3). But these laws do not address the setting of the wilderness. Thus, the story requires a special revelation, in which God states that Sabbath law applies both to the Israelites' future life in the land and during their wilderness journey. The Sabbath law is universal in scope regardless of the setting.

Violation of the Sabbath law requires the death penalty. Verses 37–41 contain the divine instruction that the people sew blue tassels to the corners of their garments as a reminder of the law that all Israelites must remember and obey (see the same law in Deut 22:12).

D. The Conflict over Priestly Leadership (16:1–19:22)

The section explores priestly leadership in the wilderness community through a series of challenges to the authority of Moses and Aaron. The theme of priestly leadership provides a counterpart to Num 11–12, where charismatic, prophetic leadership was at stake.

16:1–40. Conflict with Korah, Dathan, and Abiram. The central conflict in the story is between the Levite, Korah, and Moses and Aaron over priestly leadership, specifically over the nature of holiness and who has the power to approach God in the sanctuary. Korah and 250 followers state that the entire congregation is holy, because God dwells in its midst, and therefore all the people should be allowed to approach God in the same manner as the Aaronide priests (v. 3). A second conflict between Dathan, Abiram, and On over the leadership of Moses in the wilderness is also woven into the story, although it assumes a subordinate role to the dispute involving Korah (vv. 1–2).

16:1–17 establishes the setting of the conflict over priestly leadership. A group charges Moses and Aaron that "they have gone too far" in "exalting themselves above the assembly of the LORD" (v. 3). The expression signifies oppression when it is exercised for self-gain (Ezek 29:15). The response of Moses (vv. 4–17) is separated into two parts. First, vv. 4–11 are directed toward Dathan and Abiram, where the charge of the abuse of power concerns civil authority. They accuse Moses of abusing his role of leadership by proclaiming himself leader and, in the process, "lording it over" (*sarar*, v. 13). Rather than executing judgment on his own, Moses turns the matter over to God and provides evidence that he has not abused his leadership office (v. 15). He has not taken a single donkey from any of his accusers, nor has he harmed them in any way. Second, the challenge of Korah dominates the present form of the text (vv. 4–11, 16–17), shifting the theme from civil to religious leadership. Although the theme changes, Moses responds as he did to Dathan and Abiram. Moses does not adjudicate the conflict, but turns the matter over to God. A ritual with cultic censers and incense is devised to determine who will achieve holy status and thus be able to draw near to God.

16:18–35 describes the divine execution of Dathan, Abiram, and Korah. The confrontation between Moses and Dathan and Abiram takes place at their tents, rather than at the sanctuary (vv. 24–34). Moses states that if Dathan and Abiram have made a just complaint, they will die of natural causes; but if their complaint is unjust, the ground will swallow them up. The divine execution follows immediately with the ground consuming the households of Dathan and Abiram. The confrontation between Moses and Korah occurs at the sanctuary (vv. 18–23, 35). The performance of the ritual act with censers (v. 18) prompts a theophany of Yahweh's glory before the entire congregation (v. 19). The deity commands Moses and Aaron to separate from the people so that all Israel can be destroyed. Moses and Aaron intercede for the people so that God only destroys the guilty, thus emphasizing the theme of individual responsibility. Moses is successful in this intercession, leading to the death of only the guilty parties.

16:36–40 concludes the episode with a cultic etiology concerning the origin of hammered plates on the altar. These plates are made from the censers of the 250 participants in Korah's company who challenged the special status of the Aaronide priesthood. The censers are a warning about non-authorized persons encroaching upon the holiness of God.

16:41–17:13. The Authority of Aaron.

Two stories underscore the special status of Aaron as priest, his ability to atone for the people (16:41–50), and his magical staff (17:1–13). The story of priestly atonement (16:41–50) begins when the conflict over priestly leadership from 16:1–40 spills over into the following day, with the congregation murmuring against Moses and Aaron at the sanctuary, accusing them of murdering the "people of Yahweh." Yahweh appears in response to the complaint and advises Moses and Aaron to separate from the people so that their opponents can be consumed instantly with fire. As in the pre-

ceding story, Moses and Aaron intercede for the people, but not before God launches a plague in the camp. Moses directs Aaron to perform a ritual of atonement for the people against the divine plague. Aaron takes his censer, puts fire on it from the altar with incense, and appeases the avenging wrath, which reinforces his special role as priestly mediator, but not before 14,700 Israelites are killed. The authority of Aaron is underscored in 17:1–13, through a ritual concerning the staff of each of the tribal leaders. God commands Moses to collect the staff from each leader and to place them in the sanctuary. The next day only Aaron's staff has budded with ripe almonds, signifying his special status as priest, which warns the Israelites about the danger of encroaching on the sacred and the need for priestly representation.

18:1–19:32. Guidelines for Approaching God.

The stories of conflict over priestly leadership are followed by detailed guidelines of how God is to be approached in the sanctuary. The guidelines provide a response to the statement of the Israelite people at the conclusion of the conflict stories in Num 16–17, when they express their fear to approach God with the words, "We are perishing" (Num 17:12).

Verses 1–7 are a divine speech to Aaron, rather than Moses. The speech outlines the safeguards that will protect the Israelite people from perishing in the presence of God. The deity states that priests protect the Israelites from divine holiness. By performing their duties at the sanctuary and at the altar, divine wrath will not strike the Israelite people. Verses 8–20 outline the compensation that Aaronide priests will receive for performing their sacred duties. Priests receive compensation from the most holy offerings (vv. 8–10), holy offerings (vv. 11–14), and from a Temple tax on the redemption of first born humans and animals (vv. 15–18). Priests are not allowed to own land (v. 20). Levites receive a tithe for their service of maintaining the sanctuary and performing guard duty (vv. 21–24), but they are also required to pay a separate tithe to the Temple (vv. 25–32).

19:1–22. Corpse Contamination.

Death represents the most potent form of impurity and thus must be kept separate from the holiness of God within the sanctuary. Those contaminated by death through the handling of the corpse of a family member are banished from the camp. The background for this teaching may be the rejection of ancestral worship, known as the "cult of the dead." Thus, rather than worshiping the dead, Num 19 declares the dead to be a danger to divine holiness. The chapter outlines procedures to purify Israelites from corpse contamination in the ritual of the "water of cleansing" and thus to reenter the camp and the worship life of the community of faith.

19:1–13 describes the ritual that decontaminates persons from defilement through contact with the dead. The ritual requires a red cow without blemish, which has never been yoked—used for profane labor. The high priest must slaughter the cow and burn it in fire outside of the camp. The blood of the cow must be sprinkled seven times in the direction of the sanctuary. This is an unusual ritual for several reasons. It suggests a sacrifice, even though the actions do not take place at the altar. The blood of the cow is burned in the fire along with the skin, flesh, and dung, none of which is permitted at the altar. The presence of blood in the ashes of the cow is a ritual detergent, along with cedar wood, hyssop, and crimson, aimed at purifying those contaminated by death. The ingredients create the "water of cleansing," which allows the contaminated Israelite to reenter the camp, even while it contaminates those who perform the ritual. Verses 10–13 state that the ritual requires seven days of purification and that both Israelites and resident aliens must undergo purification from corpse contamination.

19:14–22 clarifies the circumstances under which someone becomes defiled from contact with the dead (vv. 14–16), and it provides more detailed instructions for using the water of cleansing (vv. 17–22). When a person dies within a tent, all persons and objects in the tent become contaminated for seven days. Contamination in the open field results from direct contact with the corpse. Purification requires that ashes from the red cow be mixed with running water, meaning water that is spring fed and not stagnant. A ritually clean person is required to apply the ingredient to the contaminated person, making the ritual celebrant unclean until evening. Failure to follow proper procedures leads to an individual being cut off from the assembly.

E. Leaving the Wilderness (20:1–21:35)

Numbers 20–21 contain a loose collection of stories that provide a transition from the wandering and death in the wilderness to holy war in the Transjordan. The stories trace of the death of the first generation and the emerging leadership of the second generation.

20:1–13. The Sin of Moses and Aaron. The section begins with a report about Miriam's death in the first month (v. 1). Reference to the same event in Num 33:38–39 indicates that it is the fortieth year of wilderness wandering. Verses 2–13 recount a story of disobedience by Moses and Aaron, which results in their not being able to enter the promised land. The story opens with a report about drought, prompting the people to murmur (vv. 2–5). God responds to the complaint by instructing Moses to (1) take the staff that is in the sanctuary, which is likely the budding staff of Aaron (see Num 17); (2) assemble the people; and (3) speak to the rock in order to bring forth water for the Israelites and their cattle. The story is set at Meribah, a name meaning a legal dispute. The absence of divine punishment against the people suggests that their complaint is not an instance of disobedience, but a legitimate dispute with the deity. Moses sins in that he judges the complaint of the people to be an instance of disobedience, accusing the people as being "rebels," and, as a consequence, he does not follow the divine instructions. He strikes the rock rather than speaking to it, and thus fails as a leader. God describes the disobedience of Moses as a lack of trust in the deity, which prevents the holiness of God from being displayed for the entire people. Moses and Aaron are thus excluded from entry into the promise land.

20:14–21. Conflict with Edom. The story recounts diplomatic correspondence between Israel and Edom, in which the Israelites request passage through Edomite land. The request for passage is couched in the language of brotherhood (v. 14), recalling that the eponymous ancestor of the Edom is Esau, the older brother of Jacob (Gen 25:19–33:20). The Israelites describe their salvation from Egypt, before requesting passage on the King's Highway (v. 17). Edom refuses the request and even threatens war (v. 18). Israel responds by offering to pay for water (v. 19), an offer also refused by Edom. The story concludes with the

Israelites forced to travel around the land of Edom, which stands in conflict with another version of this same story (Deut 2:3–13), according to which the Israelites travel through the territory of the Edomites.

20:22–29. Death of Aaron. Aaron dies when the Israelites arrive at Mount Hor, which prompts significant rites of mourning. Like Moses (Deut 34:1–8), Aaron dies on a mountaintop, which is followed by thirty days of mourning, as compared to the normal seven-day period of mourning the dead (Job 2:13). The death of Aaron provides the occasion for the Priestly author to model the transition of leadership in the high priestly office. There is not transfer of a prophetic spirit or even the laying on of hands. Instead, Eleazar, the son of Aaron, becomes high priest by taking the vestments of Aaron and putting them on. The full ritual of investiture is described in Exod 29:29–30.

21:1–3. War Against the King of Arad. This story narrates divine deliverance and a successful holy war against the Canaanite king of Arad in the Negeb at Horman. The king of Arad is described as having successfully attacked the Israelites and taken captives. Israel asks God for help, vowing to place all the cities of Arad under the ban (*herem*), which means that all property would be given over to God through destruction, rather than becoming booty for the warriors. God hears the request and aids the Israelites in the defeat of the king of Arad. The story reverses the negative account of war at Horman in Num 14:39–45, when the first generation of Israelites disobeyed the deity and waged an unsuccessful war. The story of the successful holy war marks a transition from the wilderness wandering to the conquest of the promise land.

21:4–9. The Serpent of Bronze. The final murmuring story occurs when the Israelites leave Mount Hor and journey south around Edom on the Red Sea road (v. 4). The story recounts a general and incoherent complaint by the Israelites against Moses and God, about both the absence of bread and water and the miserable quality of the food in their possession (vv. 4–5). God responds (v. 6) by sending poisonous serpents to bite and kill many of the people. The serpents are described as "seraphs," suggesting supernatural agents of divine punishment. The same creatures are described as protecting God in the call of the prophet Isaiah (Isa 6). The point of the story is not

so much the deadly bite of the seraph snakes, but their healing property. Once the people confess their sin, God instructs Moses to make a seraph and to place it on a pole or banner as an antidote to the snakebites (v. 8). Moses makes a bonze replica of the seraph, called *Nahash Nehoshet*, "the serpent of bronze," which has the power to heal anyone who looks at it. The story is related to the cultic icon of Nehustan in the Jerusalem Temple, which was destroyed by King Hezekiah (2 Kgs 18:4). The theme of divine healing in the final murmuring story is important, because it fulfills the promise of God in the first wilderness story (Exod 15:22–26), when Yahweh promised to be a God of healing for the Israelites.

21:10–35. War Against the Amorite Kings, Sihon and Og. Verses 10–20 recount the final stages of Israel's wilderness march to Mount Pisgah, a location in the fields of Moab (see also Num 33 and Deut 2). Two songs are embedded in the travel notices. The first song (vv. 14–15) is a fragment of poetry from an anthology of war poems, entitled The Book of the Wars of Yahweh. The meaning of the poetic fragment is obscure. The title suggests a war poem, but the text highlights place names, without a clear reference to holy war. The second song (vv. 17–18a) is about water. The location of the song is Beer ("well"), shown as a divine gift.

21:21–35 narrates the defeat of the Amorite kings Sihon and Og. The story also appears in Deut 2:26–3:7 and Judg 11:19–26. The story begins with the Israelite people requesting to pass through the kingdom of Sihon (vv. 21–22), pledging to stay on the King's Highway and to eat no food, drink no water, nor trespass in the fields. Sihon attacks the Israelites in the wilderness Jahaz (v. 23). Verses 24–25 and 31–32 describe the Israelite conquest of Sihon. The central location is Heshbon, the city of King Sihon. The Israelites also conquer the northern kingdom of Sihon to the city of Jazer, which leads to the defeat of Og of Bashan (vv. 33–35). Og is mythologized in Deut 3:11 as one of the last of the Rephaim giants. The author of Deuteronomy informs the reader that his bed was sixteen feet long and on display at the Ammmonite city Rabbah. The accounts of conquest frame a poem about Heshbon (vv. 26–30). The song may be an Amorite poem, celebrating Sihon's defeat of the Moabites, now taken over by the Israelites as a taunt against the king of Heshbon. Verses 27–29 recount the defeat of the Moabites, identifying Heshbon as the city of King Sihon.

III. Preparing for Canaan on the Plains of Moab (22:1–36:13)

This section is the third and final portion of the book of Numbers. The central theme of preparation for entry into Canaan builds upon the two previous sections and involves a change of setting—from the wilderness to the plains of Moab. In this new section external threats to the community from other nations replace the problems of internal conflicts within the wilderness camp over leadership and the challenge of following God on the journey. The first threat is the danger of being cursed by another nation (chs 22–24). The second external threat is the danger of worshiping the gods of another nation (25:1–18). Chapters 26–36 conclude the book by looking ahead to Israel's future life in the land. It includes a new census of the second generation (ch. 26), followed by a series of inheritance laws (chs. 27, 32, 36), guidelines for worship (chs. 28–30), and instructions for holy way (chs 31).

A. Balaam and Baal Peor (22:1–25:18)

The focus of tension in Num 1–21 has been on the internal life of the Israelite people. Numbers 1–10 probed the life of Israel within the camp. The danger of holiness within the tabernacle gave rise to the lay of the camp as a means to protect the Israelites as they lived in proximity to God. The journey of the Israelites in the wilderness (Num 11–21) continued to focus on the Israelites' relationship with God, highlighting internal conflicts over leadership, faith, and the promise of land. The internal threats in Num 1–21 give way to external challenges to the community in 22:1–25:19. These chapters explore two external threats to the religious life of the Israelite community. The first is the danger of being cursed by another nation (Num 22–24). The story of Balak and Balaam probes the protective role of God outside of the boundaries of the Israelite community. Israel plays no active role in this story. The second external threat is the danger of worshiping the gods of another nation (Num 25). In contrast to the threat from Balak and Balaam, Israel plays a central role; their sin at Baal Peor illustrates how other nations might defile the community through intermarriage and syncretistic worship.

Balaam is an ambiguous character in the Hebrew Bible and in the New Testament. The commentary will illustrate that the story of Balaam in Num 22–24 portrays a non-Israelite seer positively. He knows Yahweh independently of Israel's history of salvation and rescues the nation from the threat of Balak, the Moabite king. The story of Balaam demonstrates that the power and revelation of God cannot be limited to one people or one religious tradition. This insight rests uneasily in the Bible as is evident in the tendency to reinterpret Balaam negatively as a threat to the worship of Yahweh (Deut 23:1–6) and as a human who is greedy for divine power (Rev 2:14; Jude 11; and 2 Pet 2:15).

22:1–14. First Mission of Balaam. The story opens by describing the nature of the Israelite threat to Balak and the Moabite nation. The Moabites "dread" and the Israelites and are "overcome with fear." Both words describe the fear that overcomes people at the threat of holy war. The king of Egypt is described with the same reaction to the Israelites in Exod 1:12 as a result of their rapid population growth. The same reason for fear also influences Balak. He too fears the size of Israel and the impact that they will have on his country.

22:5–7 introduces the character of Balaam, who is presented as a well-known diviner whom Balak wishes to hire in order to curse the Israelites. Balaam is identified as the son of Beor, whose home is Pethor located on the Euphrates River. Pethor may be Pitru a city in Syria, south of Carchemish. The location is unclear and may be intended for literary purposes now lost to the reader. The discovery in 1967 at Tell Deir 'Alla of a text about a diviner name Balaam son of Beor has provided unexpected information concerning the significance of Balaam. The text recounts Balaam's vision of a natural disaster brought on by Shagar, a fertility goddess, and the Shaddai-gods.

In Num 22:1–7, Balak sends messengers to Balaam stating his fear of the Israelite nation, which has come out of Egypt and whose population growth threatens the surrounding nations. The reader is told that Balaam possesses the power to curse and to bless, and Balak hopes that the diviner will curse the Israelites (v. 6). Balaam's power to bless and to curse is described in v. 7 as "divination" (*qesem*), a practice condemned in the Hebrew Bible (Deut 18:9–14), making Balaam an ambiguous character, since "diviner" is not a title that Balaam claims for himself.

Balaam's intercession with God (vv. 8–14) to discern whether or not to curse Israel further complicates his character. Balaam states to Balak's messengers that he is unable to make a decision without instruction from his God, Yahweh, whose direction he seeks during the night (vv. 8–11). Balaam's reference to Yahweh is surprising, since his nighttime exchange with God makes it clear that he has no knowledge of the Israelites. Thus he knows Yahweh and has a relationship with the deity independent of the salvation history of Israel. In fact, Balak has no knowledge of the Israelite people; he simply refers to "a people" that has come out of Egypt. The divine response to Balaam reinforces Balaam's special and independent relationship with Yahweh. Yahweh never refers to the Israelites by name, but simply instructs Balaam not to curse "the people," because they are blessed (v. 12). The episode concludes with Balaam denying the request of the messengers of Balak. Throughout these events, the Israelites remain unaware of the external threat posed by Balak and the role of Yahweh in their protection.

22:15–35. Second Mission of Balaam. The second mission of Balaam includes two stories. Verses 15–21 recount the second request of Balak for the assistance of Balaam. Verses 22–35 comprise a separate folktale about the confrontation of Balaam and the messenger of Yahweh and the clairvoyance of Balaam's donkey.

The language intensifies in the second mission of Balak to request the aid of Balaam in vv. 15–21. The messengers plead and even demand the assistance of Balaam, assuring him that no price is too high (vv. 16–17). Balaam's response is equally emphatic, stating that no amount of money could make him act contrary to the command of Yahweh, his God (v. 18). Thus, the portrayal of Balaam remains positive in the second request by Balak. As in the first story, Balaam leaves the messengers to consult God during the night for an answer to Balak's request (vv. 19–20). This time God instructs Balaam to return with the messengers of Balak, but to speak only the words

that God commands him. The narrative concludes with Balaam saddling his donkey and accompanying the messengers to meet Balak (v. 21). At an earlier stage of composition, the narrative likely progressed immediately to 22:36–38, where the arrival of Balaam is noted and the seer repeats his message to Balak that he can only speak what God puts in his mouth.

22:22–35 is a separate story in which Balaam journeys with his servants to Moab, but not with the messengers of Balak. The separate character of the narrative is evident in the anger of Yahweh (v. 22) at Balaam's decision to travel to Moab, which contradicts the divine instruction in v. 20. The unexpected response of God is accompanied by a new divine figure, the messenger of Yahweh. The portrayal of Balaam also changes significantly in this tale—from a diviner who carefully discerns the will of Yahweh to a blind and impatient seer, whose donkey is more clairvoyant than he. The story that is critical of Balaam is part of the larger negative reinterpretation of Balaam throughout the biblical literature noted above. The tale narrates a confrontation with the messenger of Yahweh (vv. 22–27) and the interpretation of the message (vv. 28–35).

22:22–27 describes the messenger of Yahweh blocking the road and functioning as Balaam's adversary (*satan*), an opponent who is seeking to kill him. The messenger of Yahweh often functions in stories of holy war (Exod 23:20–33). The messenger of Yahweh confronts Balaam three times, all seen by the donkey (vv. 23, 25, 27), but not by Balaam. The encounters are increasingly intense. First, the messenger of Yahweh forces the donkey from the road (v. 23). Then he forces the donkey against the wall (vv. 24–25). Third, he blocks the donkey's path causing the animal to lie down (vv. 26–27). In each case, the donkey saves Balaam's life, while the seer is blind to the rescue and responds with increasing violence toward the donkey.

22:28–35 provide an interpretation of the event to Balaam. First, the donkey addresses the seer, asking why Balaam has beaten it three times (vv. 28–30). Balaam misinterprets the actions of the donkey as ruthless, stating that if he had a sword, he would kill the animal. The donkey replies with common sense, asking if he has ever acted ruthlessly in the past toward the seer. The implication of the question is that Balaam should trust the animal based on past experience, even if he is unclear about the present circumstances. Then, the messenger of Yahweh addresses the seer (vv. 31–35), explaining the nature of the threat to Balaam. The messenger of Yahweh reinforces the statements of the donkey, noting that if the animal had followed Balaam's direction, the seer would now be dead. The story concludes with Balaam confessing his sin, claiming ignorance, and offering to return to his home.

22:36–23:12. First Oracle of Balaam. Verses 36–40 narrate the meeting of Balaam and Balak at Ir-Moab. Balak asks why Balaam has been delayed and whether the seer understands his power to honor him. Balaam dismisses the comments of Balak and repeats that he can only speak the words that God puts in his mouth.

The first oracle of Balaam in 22:41–23:12 is made up of three parts, the location of the seer at Bamoth-baal (vv. 22:41–23:6), the oracle (23:7–10), and the concluding dialogue between Balaam and Balak (23:11–12). The ability of Baal to see the Israelites is important for effective divination. 24:41–23:6 locates Balaam at Bamoth-baal, where he is able to see only a fraction of the Israelite nation. The process of divination requires the sacrifice of a bull and a ram on seven altars, after which Balaam departs to a barren height to meet Yahweh (23:3–5). 23:7–10 contains the oracle of Yahweh to Balaam as a poem. The poem occurs in three parts. Verses 7–8 state that Balaam is unable to curse if it is not God's will. Verse 9 describes the distinctive character of the Israelites, while v. 10 makes reference to the fertility of the Israelites instead of cursing them. 23:11–12 concludes the first oracle with Balak complaining that instead of cursing Israel, Balaam has blessed them.

23:13–26. Second Oracle of Balaam. Verses 13–17 introduce a new location for the next oracle of Balaam—the top of Mount Pisgah in the field of Zophim. Once again a bull and a ram are sacrificed on seven altars before Balaam departs from Balak to receive a divinatory word from God. Upon his return Balak asks, "What has Yahweh said?" Verses 18–24 contain the oracle, which Balaam delivers as a response to Balak's inquiry. The oracle comprises three stanzas. First, vv. 18–19 emphasize that human attempts to manipulate the future as Balak desires are useless, because God fulfills

all divine promises. Second, vv. 20–22 recount Israel's history of salvation as an outgrowth of divine blessings. Third, vv. 23–24 move from the past events of salvation history to the present by comparing Israel to a lion that eats it prey. Balak is angry and prefers that Balaam say nothing at all, to which Balaam responds that he can only say what God tells him (vv. 25–26).

23:27–24:14. Third Oracle of Balaam. Balak takes Balaam to a new location, Peor, where seven more altars are constructed with the appropriate sacrifices of a bull and a ram. It is not clear that Balaam is initially able to see the Israelites from the new location of Peor, which overlooks the wasteland. The introduction of the "spirit of God" (24:2) suggests that Balaam achieves a new level of clairvoyance in the third oracle (vv. 3–9). The content of the oracle supports this interpretation, with its repetition of the technical word for "oracle" (ne'um), which often accompanies prophetic discourse in the Hebrew Bible. Balaam identifies himself as clairvoyant, whose eyes are opened, who has a vision of the Almighty, and who hears the words of God (vv. 3–4), before describing the Israelite nation with fertility imagery of palm trees, gardens, the aloe tree, and cedars. He concludes ominously that those who curse Israel will be cursed and those who bless Israel will be blessed. Verses 10–13 conclude the unit with an angry exchange between Balak and Balaam. Balak repeats his demand for a curse against Israel, while Balaam repeats his constraint that he can only speak what God tells him.

24:15–25. Fourth Oracle of Balaam. The final scene contains an oracle against Moab (vv. 15–17) and Edom (vv. 18–19), as well as an additional series of oracles against the nations that will surround Israel (vv. 20–24). The vision of Moab is eschatological in nature, including Messianic motifs. The destruction is "not now," nor is it "near." The vision contains royal imagery of a star coming from Jacob with a scepter. This figure will destroy Moab along with the Sethites, perhaps a reference to all humanity, since Seth is the third son of Adam and Eve (Gen 4:26; 5:1–8). Verses 18–19 predict the future destruction of Edom. Verses 20–24 are not related to the poetry in vv. 15–19. The section begins with a new introduction, which broadens the scope of Balaam's final oracle to include judgment on Amalek (v. 20), the Kenites (vv. 21–22), and an unnamed nation (vv. 23–24). The Amalekites are remembered for attacking the Israelites on their wilderness journey (Exod 17:8–16). The reason for the judgment on the Kenites is unclear, since they are remembered for showing kindness toward the Israelites as they came out of Egypt (1 Sam 15:4–9). The story of Balaam ends in v. 25 with the seer returning to his home.

25:1–18. Sin of Israel at Baal Peor. There are two versions of Israel's sin at Baal Peor. Verses 1–5 are a story of idolatry involving the Moabites, and vv. 6–19 are an account of intermarriage with the Midianites.

25:1–5 comprise an account of Israelite idolatry with Moabites at Shittim. The idolatry is anchored in sexual imagery: "The people began to have sexual relationship with the women of Moab" (v. 1). The Hebrew is less explicit about the role of sex in the story, since the verb, *halal*, means, "to pollute." Biblical writers often use the imagery of sexuality as a metaphor to describe false worship, which may be the case in this story. Verse 2 introduces the theme of false worship, which results in the Israelites becoming "yoked" to the Baal of Peor (v. 3). The deity responds angrily. All of the chiefs of the people are singled out for judgment by the God (v. 4). Their punishment is to be hanged in the sun, suggesting a pubic execution. Such execution without burial indicates divine curse (Deut 21:22–23). Moses executes the divine command, but limits the punishment to the guilty, rather than all of the chiefs. Moses' departure from the divine command has caught the eye of interpreters. It suggests that Moses is following legal precedent from God's earlier instruction in Num 14:11–25, where punishment was reserved for the guilty.

25:6–18 describes a second incident at Baal Peor, which threatens the purity of the Israelite camp. An Israelite man, Zimri son of Salu from the tribe of Simeon (v. 14), marries a Midianite woman, Cozbi the daughter of Zur (v. 15). The couple enters the camp in the sight of the entire congregation, while the people are still in mourning before their tents. Phinehas, the son of Eleazar and the grandson of Aaron, kills the couple in the tent by stabbing the woman through her belly while also piecing the man. The Hebrew word translated tent (qubba) may specify a mar-

riage tent, since the description of the execution of the couple suggests the act of intercourse. The execution of the couple halts a plague, which has already killed 24,000 Israelites. The divine speech in vv. 10–13 commends the action of Phinehas by giving him a "covenant of peace." The covenant of peace may indicate either health in general or the protection of Phinehas from bloodguilt and revenge by Zimri's clan. God also establishes a second covenant with Phinehas, in which the deity promises that his family will be priests forever. The story concludes (vv. 16–18) with the divine command to Moses that he show hostility toward Midian, because of the deceit of the Midianites in the intermarriage with Israel. The command is paradoxical, since Moses is also married to the Midianite, Zipporah, the daughter of the priest Jethro (Exod 2:15–22), who functioned as Moses' advisor in Exod 18 and in Num 10:29–35. The divine command points the reader ahead to the war against Midian in Num 31.

B. Instructions for Inheritance (26:1–36:13)

Chapters 26–36 signal a change in the book of Numbers from the wilderness wandering of the first generation to the preparation for conquest by the second generation of Israelites. The central theme, inheritance, provides a new beginning to the Israelites' quest for the promise land, an issue repeated throughout the book. The census of the second generation (Num 26) repeats the first (Num 1). There is also a change of leadership. Eleazar replaces Aaron as high priest (Num 26:1) and Joshua succeeds Moses to lead Israel into the promise land (Num 27:12–13).

26:1–65. Census of the Second Generation. The reference to the plague in 25:19 ties the introduction of the census to the story of the sin at Baal Peor, where God unleashed a plague on the Israelites, killing 24,000. The story of second census occurs in three sections: the divine command and setting (24:1–4), the record of the census (24:5–56), and the conclusion (24:57–65).

26:1–4 loosely parallels the divine command for a census in 1:1–4. In each case, the census is presented as a divine command; the command focuses on males, twenty years of age and older, who are able to go to war. The divine command in 26:1–4, however, is directed to Moses and

Eleazar, signaling progression in the story from the first to the second generation.

26:5–56 records the census. A literary relationship exists between the list of tribes in Num 26 and Gen 46. However, the list in Gen 46 is about individuals, while Num 26 is about clans. The census in Num 26 follows a two-part pattern in which each tribe is identified by clan, followed by the total number of able-bodied fighting men over the age of twenty years. Commentary concerning the tribes of Reuben, Judah, Manasseh, and Asher is interspersed throughout this pattern. The order and number of male warriors in each clan is as follows: Reuben, 43,730; Simeon, 22,200; Gad, 40,500; Judah, 76,500; Issacher, 64,300; Zebulum, 60,500; Joseph, including Manasseh, 52,700 and Ephraim, 32,500; Benjamin, 45,600; Dan, 64,400; Asher, 53,400; Naphtali, 45,400, Levi, 23,000. The total number of the census is 601,730 (26:51). The census is intended to determine the proportion of inheritance for each tribe, of which two methods are presented: land will be determined by the size of the tribe (26:52–54) and by the casting of lots (26:55).

The genealogy of Reuben (vv. 4–7) departs from the structure by extending the genealogy down three generations to include Dathan and Abiram, the central characters from the episode concerning conflict with Moses over leadership (Num 16).

The numbering of Judah (vv. 19–22) departs from the expected format in two ways. First, the death of Er and Onan in the land of Canaan is noted. Second, the genealogy extends through the line of Perez. Both additions tie the census of Judah to the story of Judah and Tamar in Gen 38, which explores the significance of the levirate law for inheritance rights. The levirate law requires that when a husband dies without leaving offspring, the dead man's brother must produce children with his sister-in-law in order to carry on the clan of the lost brother. The literary relationship between the census of Judah and Gen 38 suggests that the author of Num 26 affirms the continuing practice of the levirate law for purposes of inheritance.

The splitting of Manasseh (vv. 29–34) and Ephraim (vv. 35–37) with reference to Joseph is unique among the census of the tribes. It relates the census to Gen 48, where Manasseh and Ephraim are introduced as sons of Joseph. Noteworthy is the reversal of order between Manasseh and Ephraim, which places Manasseh in the special seventh position within the census. The number seven tends to mark moments of transition in the Priestly history including the completion of creation (Gen 2:1–3), the construction of the tabernacle (Exod 24:15–18), and the law of Jubilee (Lev 25). The transitional role of Manasseh as representing something new in tradition is reaffirmed by the linear depth of the genealogy, which also extends to seven generations: Joseph, Manasseh, Machir, Gilead, the six offspring of Gilead, Zelophehad, and the daughters of Zelophehad. Manasseh is the seventh tribe, and the daughters of Zelophehad are the seventh generation of Manasseh. They are the ones who represent something new in Israelite tradition, the right of daughters to inherit apart from levirate law.

The genealogy of Asher (vv. 44–50) is the last to depart from the standard format of the census. The new feature in his genealogy is the listing of Serah as the daughter of Asher. She is the only recorded daughter of an eponymous ancestor; her place in the genealogy of Asher is also noted in Gen 46:17 and 1 Chr 7:30. The purpose of her status in the genealogy is not immediately clear. But it likely also relates to inheritance law, perhaps illustrating the rights of daughters to inherit independent of the levirate law.

26:57–62 reports the separation of the Levites from the other tribes as was also the case in the first census.

26:63–65 states that, with the exception of Caleb, the entire first generation of Israelites, who rebelled against God in the wilderness, are now dead,

27:1–11. Daughters of Zelophehad. This section recounts a legal claim by the daughters of Zelophehad from the tribe of Manasseh (see 26:28–35) for the right to inherit. They present their legal case at the door of the tent of meeting before Moses, Eleazar the priest, the leaders, and the entire congregation (vv. 1–2). The daughters describe their problem in vv. 3–4. Their father died in the wilderness leaving no sons to inherit. The daughters explain that he "died for his own sins," suggesting the principle of individual responsibility—neither entire families, nor successive generations should be punished for the sins of a single member of the family. Thus, in order to perpetuate the family name, they request the right of inheritance. There is no legal precedent for adjudicating the claim of the daughters of Zelophehad, which forces Moses to seek a ruling from God (vv. 5–11). First, God concurs with the legal claim of the daughters and instructs Moses to transfer the inheritance of Zelophehad to his daughters. Verses 8–11 extend the claim of the daughter in four general case laws. The first codifies the present situation: If a man dies without sons, then the inheritance is passed on to his daughters (v. 8). The next three laws underscore the right of male inheritance in a patrilineal society: (1) if a man dies without sons or daughters, then his inheritance would pass on to his brother (v. 9); (2) if there are no brothers, then the father's brothers would inherit (v. 10); and (3) if there are no uncles, then the nearest kinsmen of his clan would inherit (v. 11).

27:12–23. Leadership of Joshua. Verses 12–14 contain the divine announcement to Moses of his impending death. God commands Moses to ascend the Abarim mountain range, located on the northern end of the Dean Sea. From there he will be able to see the promise land before he dies. The inability of Moses to enter the promise land is a result of his sin (20:1–13). No specific dates are given for the divine announcement to Moses. The announcement of the death of Moses is repeated in Deut 32:48–52 before it is fulfilled in Deut 34:1–8. This structure of divine announcement and fulfillment demonstrates that the book of Numbers is meant to be read within the larger context of the Pentateuch. The present literary structure suggests that Num 27–Deut 34 contain the final address of Moses to the Israelites before his death on Mount Nebo. The remainder of Numbers focuses on inheritance law, while in Deuteronomy, Moses recounts the exodus and wilderness journey (Deut 1–11) to the second generation, as well as the content of the private revelation that he received from God (Deut 12–26).

27:15–23 describes the transfer of Moses' spirit to Joshua. Moses addresses Yahweh as the "God of the spirits of all flesh," in requesting a new civil leader for the Israelites (vv. 15–17), who can lead the people in war and fulfill the role of a shepherd. The divine response appears in the selection of Joshua (vv. 18–21). The reference to the spirit of Joshua and the notice that only a portion of Moses' spirit is transferred to him recalls the selection of the seventy elders in Num 11. The transfer of Moses' spirit to Joshua is accomplished through the laying on of hands under the supervision of the high priest Eleazar, who must discern the character of Joshua by consulting the Urim. The Urim and Thummin are divining stones used by the priest to inquire judgment from God (Exod 28:30).

28:1–29:40. Priestly Sacrifices and the Cultic Calendar. The priestly duties for public sacrifices during "appointed times" are outlined in Num 28–29. The "appointed times" refer to sacred moments in the day, week, or month, as well as seasons of the year. A similar cultic calendar with a focus on the role of lay Israelites occurs in Lev 23. The cultic calendar is arranged by the frequency of sacrifices, beginning with daily sacrifice (28:2–8), progressing through Sabbath or weekly sacrifice (28:9–10), and continuing with monthly sacrifice (28:11–21), before concluding with the list of yearly festivals (28:16–29:38). The section concludes by noting that private sacrifices must be performed separately from the public sequence of sacrifices (29:39–40).

28:3–8 describes the daily sacrifice or "the regular burnt offering." The daily offering of the priests was also known as the *tamid*, from the Hebrew word meaning "regular." The daily offering was performed twice each day, once in the morning and again at twilight. The sacrificial victim was a one-year-old lamb without blemish, which was offered with a grain and drink offering.

28:9–10 outlines the special requirements for the sacrifice on the Sabbath. The amount of offering on the Sabbath was equal to the daily offering, which meant that the Sabbath sacrifice consisted of a double portion of two lambs.

28:11–15 describes the monthly offering of the priests. The sacrifice was to take place on the first day of the month or new moon. The offering included two bulls, one ram, and seven lambs, as well as grain and drink offerings.

28:16–29:38 outlines the yearly sacrificial festivals. The festivals are concentrated in the first and seventh months, with the only exception being the Festival of Weeks or Fruits Fruits, which occurs between the these months.

28:16–25 describes the festivals in month one, which includes the Festival of Passover and the Feast of Unleavened Bread. The Passover offering is observed on month 1, day 14 (28:16). The details of Passover are absent because there are no separate offerings by priests during this festival, which is the focus of the text. The Passover is described in detail in Exod 12 and Num 9:1–14. The Feast of Unleavened Bread was observed on month 1, days 15–21 (28:17–25). A convocation of all Israelites was required on the first and last days of the feast. In addition, priestly sacrifice was required on all seven days. The sacrifices are the same for new moon, although no drink offering is mentioned. They include two bulls, one ram, and seven lambs.

28:26–31 describes the Feast of Weeks, an agricultural festival that is not fixed in the calendar. Calculations for determining its date are not provided. Lev 23:9–22 states, however, that the feast was determined by counting fifty days, seven Sabbaths from the day on which the sheaf of the first fruits was presented to the priests. The Feast of Weeks required a convocation of all Israelites and the cessation of work. The amount of the burnt offering required by priests includes two bulls, one ram, and seven lambs.

29:1–21 lists the festivals in month seven, which includes the Blowing of the Horn, the Day of Atonement, and the Feast of Booths. The Blowing of the Horn was on month 7, day 1 to separate the new moon of the seventh month from the other months of the year (29:1–6). The priests were required to sacrifice one bull, one ram, and seven lambs on this day. The Day of Atonement was observed on month 7, day 10 (29:7–11). The name of the festival does not appear in these verses, but is derived from Lev 23:27. The ritual is outlined in Leviticus 16. The purpose of the Day of Atonement is to purge the sanctuary of the defilement accumulated through human use. The contamination from human sin is transferred to a goat, which is then sent out into the wilderness (Lev 16:20–22). 29:7–11 stipulates the day to be one of rest and fasting. The priests are required to sacrifice one bull, one ram, and seven lambs. The Feast of Booths was celebrated on month 7, days 15–21, with an extra day of sacrifice on day

22 (29:12–38). Once again the name of the festival is absent in these verses, but is derived from Lev 23:34. The reference to "booths" (*sukkot*) is meant to recall Israel's wilderness travels (Lev 23:43). The priestly sacrifices were extensive, which occur in a descending number of bull sacrifices—from thirteen on day 15 to seven on Day 21, while on each day there are also sacrifices of two rams and seven lambs. On day 22 the priestly sacrifice includes one bull, one ram, and seven lambs.

29:39–40 underscores that the list of sacrifices are meant to be public. The section closes by indicating that Moses fulfilled the divine instruction by relaying the information concerning public offerings.

30:1–16. Vows by Women. The chapter contains instruction by Moses concerning vowing. Vows are promises in which a person invokes God's name, making a binding covenant with God. Vows were most likely accompanied by private offerings, since they included dedication to God at the sanctuary. Two words are used to describe the ritual process. The first word is *neder* which is translated as "vow" and the second is *issar*, "pledge." The word *vow* indicates a situation in which a person promised to do something for God in exchange for divine help, while a *pledge* involves an action of self-denial. Nazirites make a pledge to enter their special state of service. Jacob makes a vow, when he promises to construct a sanctuary for God at Bethel in exchange for divine protection (Gen 28:20–22).

The central topic in the chapter is vows by women. The legislation describes situations in which women are able to make and to fulfill vows. The primary concern is the financial obligations that accompany vows and the conditions under which either fathers or husbands are able to annul them. The legislation is made up of two parts, vv. 2–8 and vv. 9–15, with each section divided into three parts. Verses 2 and 9 describe binding oaths by men (v. 2) and by widows and divorced women (v. 9). Verses 3–5 and 10–12 describe vows by women that can be annulled either by a father (vv. 3–5) or by a husband (vv. 10–12). Verses 6–8 and 13–15 address specific situations in which a husband might desire to annul a vow of his wife after a period of time. Verses 6–8 address a situation in which a husband might wish to annul a vow that was made by his wife and approved by her father prior to their marriage. In this case the husband may annul the vow without penalty. Verses 13–15 states that if a husband does not act immediately to nullify a vow of his wife, he must bear the guilt for any future action on his part to annul the vow.

31:1–54. War Against Midian. The chapter is a fictional account of the destruction of the entire Midianite nation by the Israelites, without their losing a single casualty. The story provides the Priestly writer's version of holy war. Joshua is not the leader. Instead Moses and the priests oversee the event, Eleazar the high priest determines acceptable booty from holy war, and Phinehas the son of Eleazar actually leads the troops.

31:1–18 focuses on the actual holy war. God instructs Moses to take vengeance on the Midianites as a response to intermarriage at Baal Peor (Num 25:6–18). One thousand soldiers are chosen from each tribe. Verses 5–12 describe the battle, anchoring the institution of holy war in the cult, under the leadership of the priest Phinehas, who takes the vessels of the sanctuary into battle. The battle results in the death of all the Midianite males (v. 7); the five kings of Midian, Evi, Rekem, Zur, Hur, and Reba (v. 8); and Balaam son of Beor (v. 8). The booty includes all Midianite women and children, all cattle and flocks, and all goods (v. 9). Moses responds angrily in vv. 13–18.

He commands that all male children and non-virgin women must be killed, but that virgins are acceptable booty, meaning that the male warriors may marry them. The focus on intermarriage reinforces the close tie between this story and the account of Israel's sin at Baal Poer (Num 25:6–19).

31:19–24 describes the procedures for purifying humans and objects from the pollution of war. War pollutes according to the Priestly writer. (It does not sanctify its participants as is the case in Deut 20–21.) Purification is necessary because death defiles all participants and threatens the purity of the camp. Soldiers must undergo a seven-day ritual of purification outside of the camp, with cleansing taking place on the third and seventh days. Objects must also undergo purification with fire and water, while all clothing must be washed. The purification process is similar to the instruction concerning corpse contamination in Num 19.

31:25–47 reports the inventory and distribution of the booty. The booty is divided equally among warriors and all other Israelites. The booty from the war with Midian is exceptionally large: 675,000 sheep, 72,000 oxen, 61,000 donkeys, and 32,000 virgins.

31:48–54 closes the account of the war against Midian with a census of the warriors. Not a single soldier is killed in the battle with Midian. The warriors bring a gift of gold and jewelry to Moses, weighing 16,750 shekels, that is intended to make atonement for themselves to God. The gift is a ransom to God in order to avoid divine wrath, perhaps associated with the census, or from their participation in war, in which case there is no such thing as "holy war" according the Priestly author.

32:1–42. Inheritance East of the Jordan. The story opens with the tribes of Gad and Reuben requesting land east of the Jordan, because it is rich for grazing and they own a great number of cattle. The tribes petition Moses, Eleazar, and the entire congregation for the land of Jazer and Gilead (vv. 3–5). Moses interprets the request as a desire for the two tribes to inherit land without participating in holy war (vv. 6–15). He angrily recalls the story of the spies and accuses the two tribes of discouraging the entire nation from waging holy war (v. 7) and of instigating disunity (v. 6). Reuben and Gad forge a solution (vv. 16–19). They will first fortify cities in the Transjordan region in order to provide for the security of their families and livestock. Then they will join the other tribes in waging holy war west of the Jordan River. Moses accepts the solution and restates it as law (vv. 20–24). If Reuben and Gad fulfill their obligations, they will be free to live in the Transjordan. If they do not fulfill the agreement, they will incur guilt, but no punishment is stated. The agreement is ratified in vv. 28–32 before Eleazar the priest, Joshua son of Nun, and the heads of the tribes.

33:1–56. Wilderness Journey. This chapter creates a transition in the book. It looks back to Yahweh's leading Israel in the wilderness by listing stopping points on the march (vv. 1–49), and it looks ahead to the conquest of the promised land, with an admonition that Israel continue to engage in holy war after crossing the Jordan (vv. 50–56). The reason for identifying stopping points in the wilderness locations is unclear. A comparison of Num 33 with other ancient Near Eastern texts suggests that the list may be a record of military campaigns, or, perhaps, of pilgrimage sites. The toponyms differ significantly from the travel account of Exodus-Numbers, which creates further questions about the role and meaning of the text.

33:1–11 emphasizes the military nature of the chapter. Israel is envisioned as an army under the command of Moses and Aaron. The exodus is described in vv. 3–8 and Israel's wilderness journey in vv. 9–11. The description of the exodus distinguishes the death of the Egyptian firstborn (vv .3–4) from the confrontation at the sea (vv. 5–8). The accounts tend to follow the story of the exodus in the book of Exodus, with the exception of v. 4, which states that the exodus took place in full sight of all the Egyptians, who are still burying their firstborn dead. The account of Israel's entry into the wilderness (vv. 9–11) diverges from that in the book of Exodus, since the Red Sea is not associated with the crossing of water. It is rather a campsite that Israel reaches only after several days of travel from Elim.

33:12–37 describes twenty-four stopping places on the march of Israel from the Wilderness Sin (v. 12) to the Wilderness of Zin (v. 37). Only five of the locations occur in Exodus-Numbers (the Wilderness of Sin, Rephidim, the Wilderness of Sinai, Kibroth-hattaavah, and Hazeroth).

33:38–56 narrate Israel's travels from Kadesh to the Plains of Moab. These verses accentuate the theme of holy war. The death of Aaron at Mount Hor begins the section. His death notice (vv. 38–39) includes information that is lacking in Num 20:22–29 concerning the date, Year 40, month 5, day 1 from the exodus, and he is 123 years old. Verse 40 provides commentary on the Canaanite king of Arad, against whom the Israelites wage a successful holy war (Num 21:1–3). The story is followed by instruction (vv. 50–56) about Israel's need to wage holy war in Canaan. The theme of holy war continues in vv. 50–56 with commands that Israel exterminate the indigenous population.

34:1–29. Boundaries to the promised land. Verses 1–12 contain the description of the promised land, which does not correspond to the boundaries of the land of Israel at any time in its history.

It is an idealized vision of the land as a divine gift. The description of its borders progresses in a circle that moves in a clockwise direction from south (vv. 1–15, wilderness of Zin along Edom, Dead Sea, Akrabbim, Zin, Kadesh-barnea, Hazar-addar, Azmon, and the Great Sea)) to west (v. 6, the Great Sea), to north (vv. 7–9, the Great Sea, Mount Hor, Lebo-hamath, Zedad, Ziphron, and Hazar-enan) and to east (vv. 10–12, Hazar-enan, Shepham, Riblah, Sea of Chinnereth, Jordan, and Dead Sea). The circle begins and ends with the Dead Sea. The boundaries of the promised land exclude the Transjordan. The eastern boundary indicates as much, since it runs along the Jordan River.

34:16–29 names ten tribal leaders who are to assist Eleazar and Joshua in distributing the land. The order of the tribes follows the direction of the boundaries from vv. 1–15, moving from south to north. The tribes who will settle in the south include Judah, Simeon, Benjamin, and Dan. The Joseph tribes, Manasseh and Ephraim, will settle in the central portion of Canaan. The northern tribes include Zebulun, Issachar, Asher, and Naphtali. Similar descriptions of Canaan's boundaries occur in Josh 15:1–12 and Ezek 47:15–20.

35:1–15. Levitical Cities of Refuge. The Levites are separated from the other tribes in the promised land, just as they were in the wilderness camp. The Levites were counted separately in 1:48–53, they camped in a separate section (2:17), they were given special tasks in caring for the tabernacle (Num 3–4), and they atoned for the Israelite firstborn by acting as substitutes for the divine claim on the firstborn (Num 8). In vv. 1–8, God states that the Levites will receive no land, because they are a divine possession. Instead, they receive specific cities located throughout the land. Verses 2–8 describe the boundaries of each city, the size of its pastureland, the numbers of cities, and the process by which they will be selected from each tribe's territory. The relation of Levites to specific cities stands in conflict with the account in Deut 18:6, which suggests that Levites are scattered throughout all of the cities of the promised land and Ezek 48:3–22, which states that the Levites do in fact inherit land. Num 35:6–8 states that there are forty-eight Levitical cities, with six of the cities having the status of a "city of refuge."

35:9–15 focuses on the Levitical cities of refuge, stating that they will be places of asylum or refuge. The six cities of refuge are not named in this chapter, but they are listed in Deut 4:41–43 and Josh 21:21. The crime for which the cities of refuge are intended to provide asylum is homicide. Verse 12 reports that asylum is granted to protect someone from the avenger, or next of kin, who is responsible for redeeming the debt of blood that is created by a homicide. The law of asylum does not eliminate the role of the avenger, but it does transfer the execution of justice surrounding homicide from the family to the state.

35:16–34. Laws of Homicide. This section explores the distinction between intentional and unintentional homicide. Verses 16–21 provide criteria for determining intention and the procedure to be followed in executing punishment. Guilt can be determined in two ways. First, the object used to kill indicates motive. The use of an iron object, a stone, or piece of wood indicates motive since these objects are considered to be weapons. Second, motive can also be discerned by the emotions. If someone kills another out of hatred, then that person is guilty of murder. Verses 22–28 describe instances of unintentional homicide. Accidental death through pushing or while working with stone requires a trial. Absence of motive still leaves the problem of bloodguilt, which requires the one at fault to seek out a city of refuge. Only the high priest can atone for the guilt of shedding blood unintentionally. Upon his death, all persons guilty of unintentional homicide are atoned and allowed to leave the city. The section concludes by articulating the rules surrounding homicide. Verse 30 states that no person can be convicted of murder on the basis of only one witness. Verse 31 reports that no ransom is possible for convicted murderers under any circumstance; they must be executed. Verse 32 mandates that no person guilty of manslaughter is able to ransom an early release from a city of refuge. Verses 33–34 offer the rationale for the laws regarding homicide: the shed blood pollutes the land, which is able to drive the deity away.

36:1–13. Daughters of Zelophehad. The original claim of the daughters of Zelophehad from the tribe of Manasseh was that they be able to inherit land, because their father died without leaving any sons (Num 27:1–11). The claim is supported by God and codified into case law by Moses. The elders of the tribe of Manasseh present Moses with a new problem embedded in the earlier ruling—intertribal marriage. Under the present law, the possession of land by the daughters of Zelophehad would be transferred to their husband upon marriage, which would diminish Manasseh's territory. The elders state that according to the law of Jubilee (Leviticus 25), the land will permanently transfer to the husband's tribe.

36:5–12 presents the response of Moses. He agrees with the elders and writes an addendum to the previous ruling (see 27:8–11), maintaining the inalienable right to possession of land by the tribes. The section concludes by naming again the daughters of Zelophehad and by stating that they have fulfilled the new law, since each married within the clan of Manasseh.

36:13 concludes the book by stating that the commandments within it are of divine origin and were delivered to Moses on the plains of Moab.

BIBLIOGRAPHY

T. R. Ashley. *Numbers.* NICOT (Grand Rapids: Eerdmans, 1993); P. J. Budd. *Numbers.* WBC 5 (Waco, Tex.: Word, 1984); E. W. Davies. *Numbers.* NCB (Grand Rapids: Eerdmans, 1995); T. B. Dozeman. "Numbers." *NIB* (Nashville: Abingdon, 1998) 2:3–267; B. A. Levine. *Numbers 1–20.* AB 4A (New York: Doubleday, 1993); _____. *Numbers 21–36.* AB 4B (New York: Doubleday, 2004); J. Milgrom. *Numbers.* JPS Torah Commentary (Philadelphia: JPS, 1990); M. Noth. *Numbers.* OTL (Philadelphia: Westminster, 1968); D. T. Olson. *Numbers.* Interpretation (Louisville: Westminster John Knox, 1996); K. D. Sakenfeld. *Journeying with God: A Commentary on the Book of Numbers.* ITC (Grand Rapids: Eerdmans, 1995); G. J. Wenham. *Numbers: An Introduction and Commentary.* Tyndale Old Testament Commentaries (Leicester: Inter-Varsity, 1981).

DEUTERONOMY

Mark Biddle

OVERVIEW

Deuteronomy or "second law" takes its name from the title provided in the Septuagint. The title does not suggest that Deuteronomy contains a different law from that given at Mt. Sinai. Instead, the title recognizes its central nature as a restatement and reapplication of the one law formulated for a new generation facing new circumstances.

Deuteronomy insists that there is but one covenant and that each generation, like the second generation since Mount Sinai, which is addressed in this book, must apply the requirements of that covenant to concrete circumstances of its life. In so doing, Deuteronomy offers a warrant and a model for interpreting scriptural tradition. Only a fixed covenant with unchanging principles can provide continuity and identity for God's people. At the same time, no statement of particulars can anticipate all the challenges that may arise over time. How could Moses have anticipated the need to apply the central principles of God's covenant to the demands and challenges facing modern medical practice, for example? Each generation must faithfully interpret the principles of the covenantal relationship with God in new settings.

This insight about the ongoing need to interpret covenantal principles may account for the seminal influence that the book exerted on the development of the Bible itself and on the traditions that view Deuteronomy as Holy Scripture. Second Kings 23–23 report the discovery of a "scroll of the law" (Torah) during the renovation of the Temple under King Josiah (623/622 BCE). In response, Josiah undertook an extensive reform that reflects Deuteronomy's focus on cultic centralization, in particular. The description even involves language characteristic of Deuteronomy. Together, the nature of the reform and evidence of Deuteronomy's style and vocabulary have prompted scholars to refer to Josiah's Reform alternatively as the Deuteronomic Reform. Deuteronomy's influence seems to have extended to the major historical narrative in the Bible, the former prophets, or as modern scholarship terms them, the Deuteronomistic History (Joshua, Judges, 1 and 2 Samuel, 1 and 2 Kings). The language and central thesis of

this account of Israel's history clearly derives from Deuteronomy's understanding of God's relationship with Israel. Beyond the Old Testament, Jesus debated the Pharisees, not over the validity of the Law, but over the principles of its interpretation, demonstrating his own preference for a Deuteronomy-like extension and radicalized notion of the principles of covenant fidelity.

Given all this, the churches' neglect of Deuteronomy is difficult to understand. It offers a nuanced theology of grace and obedience, calling for the people of God to live out their identity and modeling ways to move from principle to practice.

OUTLINE

I. Moses' Introductory Speech: On the Journey (1:1–4:49)

    A. Introduction (1:1–5)

    B. Events on the Journey (1:6–3:22)
        1:6–18. Moses Appoints Assistants
        1:19–46. Rebellion at Kadesh-barnea
        2:1–23. Passage Through
            the Transjordan

    C. Conquest of Israel's Transjordanian Territories (2:24–3:22)
        2:24–37. Heshbon
        3:1–11. Bashan
        3:12–22. Allocation of Territory

    D. Moses' Death Presaged (3:23–29)

    E. A Sermon Interpreting the Sinai/Horeb Experience (4:1–40)

    F. Cities of Refuge (4:41–43)

II. Moses' Second Address: Covenant (4:44–28:68)

    A. Introduction (4:44–49)

    B. Sermons on Key Covenant Themes (5:1–11:32)
        5:1–33. The Sinai/Horeb Covenant
        6:1–25. "No Other Gods"

DETAILED ANALYSIS

I. Moses' Introductory Speech: On the Journey (1:1–4:49)

A. Introduction (1:1–5)

Deuteronomy begins with a geographical puzzle. Apparently, the place names represent the itinerary for the last leg of Israel's journey in the wilderness and provide the immediate background to the exposition of the Torah that begins in 1:6; i.e. Moses began to expound the law "after smiting Sihon, etc."[1] Moses appears here as the unique divine spokesman, the first, and perhaps most authoritative, interpreter of the Torah. The pregnant verb translated "to explain" (v. 5) anticipates Moses' fundamental concerns in the series of addresses in Deuteronomy, namely, not merely to restate the covenant but to explicate it for a new generation—to offer its members the opportunity to "sign on" to the ancestral covenant—and to launch and define a tradition of faithful but adaptive interpretation.

B. Events on the Journey (1:6–3:22)

1:6–18. Moses Appoints Assistants. The first unit in the historical preamble, marked by the parenthetical phrase "at that time" (vv. 9, 16, 18), begins with Israel's departure from Mt. Horeb (Sinai). Immediately, Moses recognizes the scope of the task he faces leading a people so numerous (v. 10, cf. Gen 15:5; 26:4), blessed (v. 11, an allusion to the ancestral promise), and destined to occupy such a vast territory (v. 7). As in related passages in Exodus (18:13–26) and Numbers (11:10–25), although with significant differences (i.e., whether Moses appointed judicial aids *before* or *after* departing from Horeb, whether Jethro was involved, who selected them), Deuteronomy records the measures Moses took to alleviate the burden of leadership. Even Moses was subject to fatigue, ill-temper, and disappointment. In comparison to the versions in Exodus and Numbers, Deuteronomy reveals a special focus on the qualifications (v. 13) and responsibilities (vv. 16–17) of Moses' assistants. Moses instructed Israel to choose competent ("wise"), perceptive ("understanding"), and experienced men. Such judges and arbiters will bring insight, wisdom, and life experience to resolving disputes. Moses defines the tasks of these judicial assistants in terms of four principles: their jurisdiction extends even to the resident alien; their jurisprudence must be impartial (v. 17); their authority derives from God; and, their task requires humility in the face of challenges beyond their competence.

---

1 Unless otherwise indicated by NRSV or RSV, the quotations are direct translations by the author.

Deuteronomy discusses this incident because it signals two features central to its message that Israel's covenant relationship with God will continue in ever new circumstances. First, soon after God made a covenant with the people at Horeb, Moses required skilled and wise assistance. In its earliest days, Israel established a tradition of leadership that would survive Moses' death. Second, Deuteronomy argues that the implementation of the covenant will require skilled and wise interpretation, especially as generations pass and circumstances change.

1:19-46. Rebellion at Kadesh-barnea. Deuteronomy 1:19-46 recounts the events that brought Israel to Moab, poised to enter the promise land. The passage is notable particularly for its puzzling relationship to Num 13-14, a relationship characterized both by differences of emphasis and Deuteronomy's brevity. The two accounts differ about who first suggested the reconnaissance (Deuteronomy—the people; Numbers—Yahweh), its extent (Eshcol; all the way to Syria), whether the people's rebellion motivated Yahweh to prohibit Moses' entry into the land (yes; no, cf. Num 20:12), the hero (Joshua; Caleb), the potential enemy (Amorites; Canaanites and Amalekites). Deuteronomy abbreviates significantly (it offers no list of the spy party, no reference to the grapes of Eshcol [Eshcol means "(grape) cluster" in Hebrew]), even omitting details necessary to follow the storyline (a summary of the spies' report, reference to Caleb's speech, the people's consideration of a return to Egypt, their threat to execute Joshua and Caleb). These features suggest that Deuteronomy assumes its readers' knowledge of Numbers. Deuteronomy's synopsis results in a version with distinct emphases—not etiology as in Numbers, but Israel's remarkable mistrust, its disingenuous repentance, and the close identity of leader and people.

Deuteronomy's account divides neatly into six sub-sections: 1:19-21 (Horeb to Kadesh-barnea), 1:22-25 (espionage), 1:26-28 (Israel Refuses entry), 1:29-33 (Moses' exhortation), 1:34-40 (Yahweh's anger), and 1:41-46 (Israel's untimely repentance and obedience). The first sub-section begins with a travel notice (cf. 1:6*b*, 19; 2:1, 3, 8, 13, 24, 34; 3:1, 4, 29; 31:1; 32:44; 34:1), which constitutes the narrative structure for the "outer framework" of Deuteronomy. Israel moves from

one stop to the next, Kadesh-barnea (possibly modern Tel el-Qudeirat) along the King's Highway from Syria to the Arabah. Here, on the southern border of the promised land, Moses encourages the people to take possession of Yahweh's gift, the objective of their journey and the consummation of Yahweh's deliverance from bondage. Moses' encouragement (v. 21), however, hints at a problem: the inhabitants of the land are powerful; Israel, on the other hand, is a band of wandering refugee slaves. The people propose a reconnaissance mission; Moses agrees and appoints a representative from each tribe. The spies return from the Valley of Eshcol with ample evidence of the bounty awaiting them (vv. 22-25), but, unlike the account in Numbers, do not mention the might of the current inhabitants. Deuteronomy's omission highlights the shocking character of Israel's response to the spies' report (vv. 26-28). Their fear quickly becomes outright disobedience and rebellion. The people "murmur" that Yahweh has tricked them, promising deliverance while, all along, intending to abandon them to destruction (v. 27). Moses quickly points out that their mistrust is all the more astonishing based on what Yahweh has just accomplished on their behalf (vv. 29-33). Surely the God who delivered Israel from Pharaoh's hosts can bring them into possession of his promise (v. 30). Surely the God who has carried them in the wilderness "as a man carries his son" will not forsake them in the land (v. 31). Surely the God who guided them from camp to camp will guide them as they take possession of his promise (v. 33). Yet, Israel does not believe (v. 32) and, in response, Yahweh angrily metes out three limited penalties (vv. 34-40): first, none of the rebellious generation, excepting the faithful spy Caleb, will be permitted to enter the promise land(vv. 35-36); second, Moses' must share the fate of his people—Joshua will lead the people into Canaan (vv. 37-38); third, the current generation will wander until its extinction, but their children will receive the benefits of Yahweh's promise in full (vv. 39-40). To modern sensibilities, Moses' fate seems wholly unfair. One can speculate that Moses' agreement to the spy mission opened the door for or even encouraged the people's disobedience. In response to God's harsh sentence, the people facilely reverse their course (vv. 41-46). In typically belated, human semi-honesty, they express regret, not apparently over their disobedience, but over its consequences. Despite God's warning that the opportunity has passed, that he will not accompany them in battle (v. 42), they persist in charting their own course, only to face an enemy comparable to a hive of angry bees. Defeated, they return the Kadesh-barnea sorrowful. In the ultimate judgment against their inconstancy, Yahweh ignores their weeping (45).

2:1–23. Passage Through the Transjordan.
Deuteronomy's historical retrospective shifts between succinct statements such as the remark that Israel wandered near Mt. Seir for "many days" (2:1; cf. 1:46) and longer descriptions of events it considered particularly important. Deut 2:1–23, for example, provides an expansive treatment of Israel's migration through and conquest of areas east of the Jordan river (Israel's passage through Edom, vv. 1–8; Moab, vv. 9, 13; and Ammon, vv. 17–23; and the "passing" of the rebellious generation, vv. 14–16), apparently in order to develop the theme of Yahweh's involvement in human affairs beyond his covenant relationship with Israel.

Two puzzling phenomena in this section merit mention. First, an extended section (vv. 1–8a) parallels materials found in Numbers (20:14–21; 21:4) and raises the question of literary relationship and dependence. Deuteronomy portrays Israel's uneventful passage through Edom whereas Numbers depicts a hostile confrontation in which the king of Edom succeeded in repelling Israel's incursion, compelling Israel to circumnavigate southward (Num 21:4) and eastward (Num 21:10–12). The argument that Deuteronomy and Numbers relate independent traditions here fails to account for the clear commonalities. Instead, it is likely that Numbers was the source for Deuteronomy since Deuteronomy's silence on Israelite-Edomite hostilities conforms with its favorable stance regarding Edom (see 23:7).

Second, and related to Deuteronomy's sympathies with Edom, Deuteronomy narrates encounters with Moab and Ammon not recorded elsewhere. Just as Yahweh had instructed Israel simply to pass through Edomite territory without designs on conquest (2:5), he commands them not to "harass Moab/Ammon, etc." because their lands are their inheritances from Yahweh through Lot. Evidence suggests that the Edomite passage served as the model for these Deuteronomic expansions (2:5 employs second person plural forms while 2:9, 19 employ singular forms [this singular/plural shift occurs throughout Deuteronomy]; vv. 9, 19 add the reference to harassment; vv. 9, 19 omit certain key phrases found in 2:5; vv. 18–23 interrupt the sequence).

These two features point to an important theme in this passage, namely, that Israel's God is also God of all humanity. Just as Yahweh gives Canaan to Israel in fulfillment of a promise and recognition of a relationship, Yahweh has given possessions to Israel's "relatives"— Edom, Moab, Ammon—and even to the entirely unrelated Philistines (= "Caphtorim"). Yahweh's removal of the original inhabitants of the territories of Moab and Edom (vv. 10–12) and of Ammon and Philistia (vv. 20–23) provides an important additional clue. By dispossessing one people in favor of another, Israel's God manages the course of human history with an efficiency of agency. In one act, God punishes the guilty nation and meets the obligation of his promise. While Israel inevitably views God's relationship to human affairs through the single lens of the covenant, Deuteronomy 2:1–23 reminds Israel and the reader that the special character of Israel's relationship with God neither limits God's capacity to nor *relieves God from* managing the whole economy of human affairs.

C. Conquest of Israel's Transjordanian Territories (2:24–3:22)

In contrast to Israel's passage through the territory of its kindred Edomites, Moabites, and Ammonites, its encounters with the Amorite kingdoms of Heshbon (2:24–27) and Bashan (3:1–11) and their kings Sihon and Og, respectively, were openly hostile. These accounts exhibit Deuteronomy's characteristic perplexing shift in person and number (cf. v. 24), manifest the problem of Deuteronomy's relationship to Numbers (vv. 26–33 parallel Num 21:21–25 and Judg 11:19–26, the simpler and therefore probably earliest version), and continue Deuteronomy's emphasis on international relations as a mechanism for administering justice. Theologically, this section raises two new issues for readers: the fundamental question of human free will in the face of statements that God "hardened" Sihon's heart and the Israelite institution of "holy war" with its apparent insistence on the total eradication of Israel's enemies.

The passage grounds Israel's claims to the upper Transjordan in its earliest days in the land.

2:24–37. Heshbon. The relative length of this section suggests that the author has used the opportunity to expand the brief tradition concerning victory over Heshbon by attention to two issues: God's engagement with Sihon (vv. 28–29) and holy war (vv. 34–37). The account describes God's instruction to challenge Sihon (vv. 24–25) after first offering peace (vv. 26–29) and then the defeat of Heshbon (vv. 33–37) after Sihon refuses the offer (vv. 30–32). In contrast to the instructions concerning the Edomites, Moabites, and Ammonites, Yahweh delivers Sihon, the Amorite conqueror (Num 21:26; Josh 12:2) of the region, into Moses' hands, charging Moses to treat Sihon according to the provisions of holy war (vv. 24–25; cf. v. 25 and Exod 15:14, 16). Nonetheless, Moses' overture to Sihon offers essentially the same terms made to Edom and Ammon (cf. 2:6 and 2:28), promising that Israel would not stray from the roadway (apparently the north-south "King's Highway"; cf. Num 21:22) and citing Israel's peaceful encounters with Edom and Moab as evidence of their irenic intentions. Sihon's reaction, then, was entirely unprovoked and unfounded, but, from Yahweh's perspective at least, not unexpected. The Amorites' guilt has reached critical mass and Sihon's reaction only gives an opportunity for Yahweh's judgment administered by Moses and Israel.

Sihon's stubborness parallels Pharaoh's. Sihon is "not willing" to accede to Moses' request (cf. Exod 8:15, 32; 9:34; 10:27) "because" or "so that"—both translations are plausible—"Yahweh hardened his spirit and made his heart obstinate" (cf. Exod 7:3; 9:12; 10:1, 20, 27; 11:10; 14:4, 8, 17). Do such texts mean to suggest that Sihon exercised no volition or that, when Sihon chose to resist, Yahweh "cooperated," as it were, in Sihon's self-condemnation? At any rate, Yahweh has long since anticipated the outcome of Sihon's interaction with Moses, namely, Israel's victory at Jahaz (Deut 2:32).

Indeed, Israel's victory was, more precisely, Yahweh's victory (vv. 34–35). Holy war regulations require that enemy women and children be spared (20:13–14), yet the text apparently reports that Israel annihilated the entire population of Sihon's major cities. Verses 34–35 (and 3:6–7), may be translated, alternatively, "we … utterly destroyed the male population of every city; we allowed none of the women and children to flee; only the cattle we took as spoil," thereby aligning Israel's actions with the requirements for holy war.

The section concludes with a description of the conquered territory (v. 26) and Israel's caution not to involve the Ammonites (v. 37). The people's boastful claim that there was no city "too high" for them stands in tension with their timidity at Kadesh-barnea (cf. 1:28).

3:1–11. Bashan. Deuteronomy abridges the tale of Israel's encounter with Og, the king of Bashan, (cf. Num 21:33) since it closely paralleled the encounter with Sihon. It offers, instead, a detailed list of the conquered towns and villages and reports that Og was a giant, a descendent of the legendary Rephaim.

3:12–22. Allocation of Territory. Having led Israel to conquer these territories in the Transjordan and having brought the people to the threshold of the promise land, Moses takes the opportunity to apportion this territory to the tribes of Reuben and Gad (half of Gilead) and the half-tribe of Manasseh (the other half of Gilead and all of Bashan), at their request. Since these tribes now have a possession acquired before Israel's entry into the promised land, Moses also stresses the notion that Israel is one people (cf. Num 32, which reports that the now-settled tribes request exemption from further military duties, and Deut 3:19). Just as their brothers assisted them in the conquest of Gilead and Bashan, Reuben and Gad must assist their brother-tribes in the conquest of Canaan until God gives all Israel rest from its enemies in the land (cf. Deut 12:10; 25:19; Josh 1:13, 15; 22:4; 23:1; 2 Sam 7:1, 11; Neh 9:28; Esth 9:16–22).

The conquest of Canaan has been anticipated, indeed, even performed as a prelude, with the conquest of Gilead and Bashan. Now, Moses turns to Joshua, who will lead Israel in the actual conquest, to encourage Joshua in that task. Since Joshua has witnessed God's intervention on behalf of Israel in the conquest of its Transjordanian territory (v. 21a), Joshua can expect God to continue to fight with and for Israel (v. 21b). Joshua must not fear (v. 22a) because Yahweh "himself fights for you" (v. 22b).

D. Moses' Death Presaged (3:23–29)

Hearing that he will not enter Canaan (cf. 1:37–38), Moses responds with an exemplary and moving prayer begging God to reconsider. Moses' strategy hinges, not on his own faithfulness, but on Yahweh's greatness. Word play propels the unit. Moses asks only to "cross over" and "see" the land "over" the Jordan. Yahweh becomes "cross" (v. 26). Joshua will lead the people as they "cross over" (v. 28). God will allow him to "see" the land, but only from a distance. Joshua will lead the people into the land that Moses had only "seen." What was the source of God's displeasure with Moses? Numbers points to a specific sin Moses committed in a moment of pique (Num 20:10–13; 27:12–23). Deuteronomy offers only the ambiguous phrase "on [Israel's] account." Israel's sin is, in some sense, his responsibility.

The final travel notice reports Israel's stop in Moab. The narrative suspends accounts of Joshua's commissioning, anticipated in 3:21, and Moses death, anticipated in 3:23–28, to resume them later (vv. 31–34). First, Moses will discuss the nature of Israel's covenant responsibilities (vv. 4–11) and specify examples of its application (vv. 12–26).

E. A Sermon Interpreting the Sinai/Horeb Experience (4:1–40)

Deuteronomy 4 opens with an extended instruction (vv. 1–40) reflecting on Israel's obligation to the Horeb covenant. Two concluding sections (vv. 41–43, cities of refuge, and 44–49, which offer a transition to Deut 5) function as largely unrelated appendices. In turn, Deut 4:1–40 is loosely related to Deut 1–3. The former is historical narrative, the latter a rather loosely structured and a far-reaching, covenantal exposition. In character, Deut 4 resembles theological reflection more closely than prophetic preaching, drawing implications from experiential data garnered at Mt. Horeb/Sinai. For the first time, the otherwise confusing interchange between plural and singular forms of the pronoun "you" seems to reflect a rhetorical strategy. The reader must distinguish between the plural "you" addressed to Moses' presumptive original audience, the plural "you" addressed to the ancestral generation actually present at Horeb (vv. 9–24, 34–36), and the plural "you" of the generation that will later face a profound national crisis and even exile (vv. 25–31), and, finally, the "you" of the readership, itself. This subtlety conflates the generations into a single trans-historical Israel, which stands before God.

Moses' opening admonition to Israel differentiates between "statutes" and "ordinances" that Moses will "teach," presumably in contrast to the "law" that God "commands" Israel to obey. The Hebrew term translated "statutes" describes the collected wisdom of "rulings" issued by authorities in interpreting the "law" (cf. Num 35:12; 2 Kgs 25:6; Jer 1:16; Prov 16:10)—analogous to modern "case law." Similarly, the etymology of the word translated "ordinances," which refers in its most simple use to "boundaries" (cf. Jer 5:22; Job 38:10), can describe the "principles" applicable in a system (i.e., the created order [Jer 31:35–36]). Although the Decalogue articulates the "law," Moses' recognizes that, as a statement of fundamentals, it requires interpretation and application. With Israel facing the promised land and Moses facing his impending death, Moses thought it wise to instruct Israel in the "case law" and "principles of application" necessary for bringing fundamental norms to bear on real-life circumstances. As the so-called "canonical formula" (v. 2) makes clear, however, this need to interpret the Decalogue does not involve changing the fundamental principles.

At Mt. Horeb, God had commanded Moses to instruct Israel about the principles for interpreting the law. Among the purposes, according to vv. 6–8, was that Israel's neighbors might be impressed with the superiority of Israel's covenant, its unparalleled access to its God (v. 7). and its unsurpassed laws (v. 8).

What, precisely, are the fundaments Moses teaches Israel to interpret? How will Israel have access to them? First, Israel must remember its experience, actively preserve that memory, and propagate it in subsequent generations (v. 9). Israel's God reveals himself to Israel experientially. Even though the generation Moses addresses was not present at the foundational moment, through memory and tradition it too can stand at the shore of the Reed Sea and at the foot of Mt. Horeb! It too can hear Yahweh's very voice (4:11–12, 33, 36; cf. Exod 19) and view the tablets (4:13).

Deuteronomy 4:15–20 develops a syllogistic deduction about God derived from their foundational experience at Horeb. (1) Israel witnessed no perceptible figure at Mt. Horeb (v. 15); instead, Yahweh spoke "from the midst of the fire." (2) Therefore, Israel should not depict its God visually (v. 16–19). (3) Israel should remember that the creator God—acting majestically but unseen, and not a component of creation—delivered Israel from Egypt (v. 20).

Unlike their literary context, vv. 21–24 state the principle that obedience is necessary (v. 23) after the case in evidence (vv. 21–22), which does not allude to what happened at Mt. Horeb, but to some unspecified instance involving idolatry (perhaps Beth-Peor, v. 3) and somehow implicating Moses. Verses 25–28 return to the themes of memory and theophany, warning that the collective memory of Horeb may wane and the people may turn to idolatry, thereby "provoking" (Jer 7:18, 19; 8:19) God's wrath. This term, together with the abrupt transition between vv. 24 and 25, suggest that this unit may be a Deuteronomistic addition. If so, it recalls the central theme of the Deuteronomistic History: Israel's history was a long series of "provocations" that ultimately bankrupted even God's patience. Indeed, vv. 24–28 sound like a historical retrospective on the Babylonian crisis.

The reference to exile elicits a promise of restoration, if these exiles "seek" Yahweh (note the very close parallel with Jer 29:13), if they "return" to him and "heed his voice" (again, with close parallels in Jeremiah), then God, who is merciful (v. 31), will bring them home again.

Deuteronomy 4:32 returns suddenly to Horeb (probably further evidence that vv. 25–31 are a later insertion) and God's voice to draw yet another theological conclusion, namely, that Yahweh is the sole God. Yahweh's voice (v. 32), the people's survival after the encounter (v. 33) and Yahweh's act to deliver Israel from Egypt are all without rival or parallel. The God who authored these unique events is also unique, the *only* God (v. 35). Yahweh's act of deliverance implies Yahweh's dominion over human history. Pharaoh's gods proved to be no gods at all. Yahweh's ability to dispel the Amorites and bestow Canaan upon Israel also implies that Yahweh is no mere national deity. Yet, lest God's revelation in the theophany at Horeb be confused with evidence for a local deity, v. 36 in particular makes it clear the Yahweh was not *located* at Horeb, nor *present* in the fire. Instead, from heaven, he spoke *through* the fire. Finally, the text extrapolates a familiar conclusion from this inference of Yahweh's uniqueness: Israel must obey the terms of its covenant with its God; after all, Yahweh is the *only* God.

F. Cities of Refuge (4:41–43)

This transition from historical retrospective (1:1–4:40) to the preamble (5–11) of the Deuteronomic Code (12–26) includes Moses' designation of three Transjordanian "cities of refuge" (vv. 41–43, anticipating 19:1–13) and offers a final introduction to the upcoming treatment of hermeneutical principles. Four passages deal with the cities of refuge (Num 35:9–15; Deut 4:41–43; 19:1–13; Josh 20:1–9). They disagree somewhat as to who founded the Transjordanian cities (Moses or, as Josh 20 maintains, probably Joshua). Scholars differ concerning the interrelationship. Deuteronomy 4:41–43, in contrast to the other three texts, pays little attention to procedures regarding refuge, presumably because it can rely on one or more of the other texts to supply that information.

II. Moses' Second Address: Covenant (4:44–28:68)

A. Introduction (4:44–49)

Finally, Moses' exposition of the law (1:5) can begin. A double introduction (vv. 44 ‖ 45) identifies what follows, alternatively, as the "Torah" or as "testimonies, statutes, and ordinances." *Testimonies*, a technical term for the memorial to the covenant, occurs only here and in 6:17 and 20. The compound phrase may point forward to the Decalogue (Deut 5) as this "testimony" and to the "commandments, statutes, and ordinances" that begin in Deut 6:1–2. Verses 45–46 give the impression that Moses taught the content of Deuteronomy immediately upon Israel's departure from Egypt. They may be evidence of an early form of Deuteronomy minus the historical preamble.

B. Sermons on Key Covenant Themes (5:1–11:32)

5:1–33. The Sinai/Horeb Covenant. A hermeneutical preamble (chs. 5–11) to the law code (chs. 12–26) follows the historical preamble (chs. 1–3[4]). This hermeneutical preamble begins with the Decalogue, before discussing the methods and motivations for interpreting it.

Moses emphasizes three essential issues: his role as mediator (vv. 4–5; cf. vv. 25–31), the transgenerational nature of this covenant (v. 3), and the distinction between the Decalogue and its explication in the Deuteronomic Code. Several general observations concerning the Decalogue set the boundaries for its interpretation. First, although it states the fundamental principles of Yahweh's covenant with Israel, it does not constitute the basis for that relationship. Yahweh delivered Israel from Egypt before establishing this covenant because Yahweh meant to be faithful to his promise to the ancestors. Canonically and theologically, then, "grace" precedes "law." Second, the Decalogue does not consist of "laws." Just as the Hebrew term *torah* derives from a verb "to point out, to indicate" and therefore refers to "instruction, guidance," the "laws" in the Decalogue lack the formal elements of genuine laws—they include no clear definitions, no statement of penalties, no assignment of enforcement authority. Instead, these "laws" constitute the fundamental principles of the covenant relationship (e.g., "apodictic" law). Third, a few cases include so-called "motivational clauses"—rationales for observance of a particular commandment. Fourth, as long noted, the Ten Commandments constitute two groupings: four commandments deal with the people's relationship to its God and six deal with relationships between persons. Biblical faith knows no distinction between religion and ethics.

The Decalogue begins (v. 6) with a reminder of the essential foundation for the covenant relationship: Yahweh delivered. The principles given in the Decalogue do not *constitute* the relationship, they *configure* it. The configuration on two tablets suggests the proper relationship between worship and ethics: both are grounded in the community's relationship to God.

The *first commandment* (5:7) describes the nature of relationship to God in terms of *exclusivity*. Yahweh delivered Israel from Egypt. In return, Israel owes Yahweh exclusive allegiance. Similarly, because God is jealous, the *second commandment* (in the Jewish enumeration; 5:8–10) warns Israel against the manufacture and worship of any representation of God. Although no Scripture passage provides a concise rationale for this prohibition, it probably reflects a concern for maintaining God's priority in the relationship. Idols can be localized and controlled, but God will not be manipulated. God's prerogatives continue as the theme of the *third commandment* (5:11). Yahweh insists that his proper name be used properly, not "emptily," "vainly," or "lightly." The commandment implies a proper use of the divine name in oath-taking (see Jer 4:2; 5:1; 13:25–27). The converse, then, would be to invoke God as witness to an oath made rashly or deceptively, thereby involving God's name and reputation in a sham or deception. The *fourth commandment* (Sabbath), in three sections (the commandment proper, 5:12; an expanded "motivational clause"; and a definition of the precise intention of "keeping" the Sabbath, i.e., the total cessation of work), emphasizes, once again, that God delivered Israel from Egyptian bondage. Deuteronomy understands (cf. Exod 20), the Sabbath as a weekly commemoration and celebration of God's gift of freedom. Israel must celebrate the gift of rest and further emulate its God by granting rest, in turn, to its servants and resident aliens of both genders.

The *fifth commandment* (v. 16) states a subtle rationale for trans-generational loyalty. If adult children care properly for their parents, the example they set will ensure that they too can expect to be honored in their advanced age. The commandment does not state what "respecting" one's parents involves.

Subsequent tradition will have to elaborate the application of the *sixth commandment*. This apparently categorical prohibition against killing cannot be easily harmonized with other biblical attitudes toward capital punishment and war. The simplest suggestion that "kill" means "murder" conflicts with evidence concerning the most ancient biblical usage of the verb to denote killing that requires tribal or family revenge (cf. Num 35:27, 30). Interpreters wrestle with whether to understand the commandment as a prohibition against feuds and vigilante justice or to expand it as a principled statement about the supreme value of human life.

A hermeneutical challenge also arises with respect to the *seventh commandment* prohibiting adultery since the modern conventional definition of marriage as involving "one man and one woman" did not pertain in ancient Israel. In effect, only sexual relations between a married woman and someone other than her husband were defined as adultery. The Deuteronomic Code recognizes the need for refinement and deals with a number of related cases in the effort to broaden the application of the principle of sexual purity.

Not surprisingly, perhaps, a similar dynamic manifests itself in relation to the *eighth commandment* (v. 19). Based on the use of the verb, translated here "to steal," in Exod 21:16, where it means "to kidnap" (i.e. "to steal" a person), many scholars hypothesize that the commandment must have also originally referred to kidnapping. In this interpretation, the eighth commandment involves crimes against the worth of persons. The Decalogue regularly focuses on relationships, not ownership. Thus, the *ninth commandment* (v. 20) deals with the serious damage that can result from dishonesty in the law court. Only the *tenth commandment* (v. 21) addresses an attitude instead of an overt action and focuses on property instead of persons. To deprive a person of property, especially of livestock in an agrarian society, is to mount an attack on the person's very livelihood. The warning against improper desire, however, stands in the Decalogue as a unique recognition that volition and action are intimately intertwined.

A report of the people's reaction to events at the foot of Mt. Horeb/Sinai follows the Decalogue proper. First, Yahweh spoke audibly to Israel, appeared to them in fiery darkness, and with his own fingers wrote the Decalogue for all of those gathered (5:22–23). They were witnesses. Second, this encounter with Yahweh was so terrifying that the people immediately sought to place distance between themselves and God, filling the gap with Moses' mediation (vv. 24–28). Third, their eyewitness experience of the revelation of God's will and their dependence on Moses' as mediator of the covenant highlights the central theme of Deuteronomy, obedience to the covenant.

6:1–25. "No Other Gods." Situated between the Decalogue (5) and its explication (12–26), Deut 6–11 concentrates on the first commandment as the statement of the essence of Israel's relationship with its God. This theological reflection on Yahweh's claim to exclusive relationship occurs in four sections: vv. 1–3 introduce Moses' teaching, vv. 4–9 formulate the "Shema," vv. 10–19 catalogue the blessings of fidelity to Yahweh and the curses of infidelity, and vv. 20–25 explain the extreme importance of transmitting the covenant tradition to the next generation.

Obedience to the covenant brings benefits (vv. 1–3): reverence for Yahweh, long life, individual blessings, and Israel's numeric growth. Key Deuteronomic themes echo in the statements concerning Moses' "teaching" the covenant tradition and in the encouragement to "teach" subsequent generations.

Named for its incipit, the "Shema" (vv. 4–9) paraphrases the first commandment and extends it to radical limits. The Shema calls for radical, total, whole-hearted, full-bodied devotion. This radicality finds expression in the Shema's insistence on Yahweh as Israel's *only*, not merely *first* God. Israel's devotion, therefore, must be *total*, involving the whole heart (the seat, not of emotion, but of volition and decision making in the Hebrew understanding; cf. Prov 27:19), the whole self, and the whole of one's strength. Yahweh demands a radical decision ("heart") affecting all of life ("all one's soul") without restriction ("all one's might").

The Shema constitutes such a quintessential statement of the covenant that steps must be taken to locate it at the center of the individual Israelite's life. Its words are to be recited to begin and end the day, at home and abroad; they are to be worn on one's hands and forehead; they are to be inscribed on the doors of homes and the gateposts of cities; they are to be taught each new generation.

The covenant principle embodied in the Shema comprises the chief criterion for gauging the health of Israel's covenant relationship with its God. Radical devotion to Yahweh brings blessing; violation brings curse. In vv. 10–19, the statement about God's plan to fulfill his promise to Israel's ancestors by displacing the Canaanites (vv. 10–11, 18–19) surrounds the focal injunction to obey the covenant (vv. 12–18*a*), which focuses, now, on the ironic danger that Israel's initial blessing may seduce it to forget that these blessing were the unmerited gift of God's grace (6:15). This recognition will motivate Israel to serve Yahweh only, swearing oaths (authentically) in Yahweh's name (v. 13). Put negatively, Israel should not serve other gods (v. 16) lest Yahweh, who is "a jealous God" (cf. 5:9), replace blessing with curse.

Incidentally, Moses' admonition in v. 18 employs, not the technical language of covenant, but the everyday language of "right" and "good." Deuteronomy may acknowledge here that the standards of decency, which are the common heritage of all humankind, form a foundation for the specific requirements of Torah/covenant. In other words, even when the Torah fails to address a particular life situation, Israel knows right and wrong and is without excuse.

This sermon concludes with a so-called "didactic question" (v. 20) found throughout Deuteronomic/Deuteronomistic literature (see Exod 12:26–27; Deut 29:24–28; Josh 4:6–7; 1 Kgs 9:8–9; Jer 5:19; 16:10–13). In response to a child's inevitable question concerning the importance of the covenant, parents should recall Yahweh's act of deliverance from Egyptian bondage as the foundation for the covenant relationship (vv. 21–23) and describe its redemptive and salutary purpose (vv. 24–25). Characteristically, the parent employs first-person plural forms: "By redeeming our ancestors, Yahweh redeemed *us*."

7:1–26. The Threat of Syncretism. Good leaders not only admonish their followers to pursue their core principles but to anticipate possible threats. In Moses' view, the chief danger awaiting Israel consisted of the temptations presented by the Canaanites. The biblical witness attests that, throughout its history in the land, Israel often failed the test of maintaining cultural and religious integrity, regularly turning aside, instead, to "follow after other gods." Moses offers three specific suggestions: avoid assimilation, avoid arrogance, and avoid anxiety.

Deuteronomy 7:1 lists seven Canaanite tribes awaiting Israel. They were more numerous with a highly developed society and fortified city-states. Now that the Canaanites' sin had reached maturity, however, Yahweh would deliver them into Israel's hands in "holy war" (cf. 3:1–7 and, especially,

20:1–18). Israel was to annihilate the Canaanite population, to eschew treaties and intermarriage with them (a provision suggesting that the injunction to annihilate them was either hyperbole or later proved impracticable), and to eradicate all Canaanite culture and religion.

Does the call to remain separate, distinct, "holy" somehow imply Israelite superiority? No, Israel's holiness derives entirely from Yahweh's free choice. Israel did not earn its status. The danger, of course, is that Israel could come to regard itself as *inherently* superior. Neither Israel's size nor strength motivated Yahweh's decision to choose Abraham and his descendants (v. 7). Yahweh's choice was entirely unmotivated. Israel's success in the land will depend on Yahweh to keep his promises (vv. 8–9, 12). While Israel's election had no basis in Israel's merit, the biblical witness clearly indicates that it had a purpose: Israel's calling to be God's holy, covenant people (vv. 9–12). Again, vv. 12–16a stress that fidelity to the covenant will bring fertility, both human and agricultural. Grown strong and numerous, Israel will be able to expunge the Canaanites, removing the threat to Israel's holiness.

Interpreters must place this passage in the context of the biblical witness to Israel's role as the mediator of blessing to the nations. The specific challenge of resisting Canaanite religious and cultural influence called for extreme measures, apparently. This text's call for holiness expresses God's universal will; the call to eradicate strangers does not.

The reminder that Israel did not earn God's attention was meant primarily as a warning against self-importance. It could have almost the opposite effect, however. If Israel is so insignificant, then it has good reason to fear its more powerful enemies (cf. 1:19–33). Just as Israel becomes holy before God (v. 6), so also its strength is solely the product of its relationship with God. This encouragement to trust in Yahweh's protection is more than deductive logic. Israel's brief history as the covenant people was already replete with examples of God's intervention in Egypt (v. 18) and during the exodus (v. 19ab). Yahweh will continue so to act when Israel confronts the Canaanites (v. 19c–20). Fear, then, would be entirely unfounded (vv. 21–25), so long as Israel remembers not to take possession of any of the "abominations" they may find in the land, being careful to destroy "the idol images of their gods," in particular, and refraining from illicit plunder (v. 25).

Verse 22 presents a special problem—or opportunity—for interpreters. Although Deut 7 calls for the eradication of the Canaanites, v. 22 describes a process that will be phased. The text offers an inventive rationale: should the eradication be immediate and instantaneous, given Israel's insignificant population, the countryside would soon be overrun with wildlife. This tension between the radical program and its phased implementation suggests that Deut 7 may best be understood as a hyperbolic statement of the urgent priority of maintaining distinction from corrupting cultural influences and not as an endorsement of genocide.

8:1–20. Poverty and Prosperity. Deuteronomy 8, a warning against apostasy in conditions of extreme lack (vv. 1–10) and rich abundance (vv. 11–20), is the third sermon expounding the first commandment. Its two sections, indicated by the new beginning in v. 11, the transition from past to future, the reflection of the first half in the second, and the focal significance of a hymn in each section (vv. 7–10 and vv. 14–16), highlight the balanced construction of the sermon.

After a standard summons to obey the commandments supported by the promise that obedience brings blessing (v. 1), the summons to recall the wilderness experience (v. 2) announces the topic of the sermon. Normally understood from the perspective of punishment for Israel's rebellion at Kadesh-barnea (cf. 1:19–46), this sermon regards the wilderness experience as a period of education when Yahweh "humbled" and "tested" Israel to determine its willingness to obey. Yahweh sought to teach Israel a fundamental lesson, namely, that in a situation of extreme want, when mere survival demands one's total attentions and energies, Yahweh provides. In the wilderness, Israel did not enjoy fine cuisine in abundance. Yahweh met its fundamental needs, sufficiently (and no more) and daily (but only so). Their clothing lasted for the entire journey. God preserved them alive and healthy; God did not, however, lavish upon them extravagance and luxury.

It is important always to remember that even the basics of life are God's provision (v. 3). *In*

extremis, even an everyday loaf of bread signifies God's sustaining provision. How much more so, then, will the abundance and plenty of the promised land signify God's abundant provision? Having learned the lesson of desert dependence on Yahweh, Israel should now be eager "to obey his commandments, to walk in his ways, and to fear him" (v. 6). In the land, Israel will know no lack, it will "eat and be satisfied."

This very abundance presents a new danger. "Watch yourself" (v. 11) the sermon warns. Complacency can quickly develop when one forgets the desert, when one comes to presume that one's wealth is the product of one's own hands, when one neglects to express gratitude in obedience. The hymn-like section in vv. 14–18 celebrates the history of Yahweh's provision. Prosperity cannot be allowed to obscure Israel's memory of the God "who brought out" from Egyptian bondage (v. 14), "who led in the wilderness" (v. 15). In the desert, water and bread are clearly God's gifts. In the rich promised land, it becomes easy to deceive oneself: "My strength and the might of my hand have gotten me this wealth" (v. 17). Such a claim is tantamount to rejecting God's essential role in bestowing the land upon Israel and in sustaining its plenty; it is tantamount to idolatry; it brings the loss of blessing, the painful reminder that, in fact, Israel is not the source of its own prosperity.

9:1–10:11. Election and Presumption. Deuteronomy 9 supplements the treatment of the election theme in Deut 7:6–11 (Yahweh's unmerited choice) and, in a way, in Deut 8:11–20 (Israel's unearned prosperity). Just as Israel had not attracted God's attention because of its strength or skill, Moses explains in Deut 9, it did not distinguish itself for its exemplary righteousness either. In fact, Israel demonstrated a contrary trait from its earliest days. Before Moses could return with the tablets of the Law, Israel had committed one of the most egregious acts of idolatry and rebellion in its entire history. Indeed, similar acts of infidelity would come to characterize Israel's history.

This discussion of Israel's rebellion with the golden calf (Exod 32) does not, as one might expect, issue in a call to covenant obedience (but see 10:12–11:32). Deuteronomy 9:1–10:11 focuses, instead, on the danger of self-delusion concerning Israel's propensity to wander. Israel is God's chosen people only by virtue of God's free choice, not because of Israel's merit. Indeed, God continues in relationship with Israel *despite* its behavior, not because of it.

After the familiar summons to hear, the issue of Canaanite opposition facing Israel across the Jordan raises once again the specter of weak Israel falling victim to Anakim, a fear immediately dismissed by the promise that Yahweh will be "a consuming fire" annihilating Israel's enemies (v. 3). Why, however, the text asks, should Yahweh act on Israel's behalf? The Canaanites have earned the punishment coming to them (v. 4); Yahweh's intervention on Israel's behalf reflects faithfulness to the promise made to Abraham, Isaac and Jacob (v. 5). Israel should remember its history of rebelliousness whenever it is tempted to vaunt its own character.

The evidence of Israel's *unrighteousness* is so strong that Deuteronomy elaborates the warning. Israel must always "remember" (v. 7) its historical propensity to rebel against its God. In a confused retelling of the golden calf incident (cf. Exod 32), Deuteronomy 9 narrates how Yahweh gave the tablets of the law to Moses (vv. 8–11), told Moses to descend the mountain to see the people's rebellion (v. 12) and announced his decision to annihilate Israel and substitute Moses' descendants (vv. 13–14). At the foot of the mountain, Moses shattered the tablets and interceded for Israel, and for Aaron, over a period of forty days and nights *before* destroying the golden calf (vv. 18–21). Deuteronomy omits reference to the violent aftermath. Clearly, Deuteronomy has little interest in the details. Instead, for Deuteronomy, the raw fact of Israel's idolatry *at the foot of Mt. Horeb while Moses is receiving the tablets of the Law* once and for all refutes any claim to inherent righteousness Israel may ever make.

The theological import of this event in Israel's history should not be overlooked. Within days of Yahweh's theophany and Israel's acceptance of God's covenant offer, they violate the quintessential principle of that relationship. Moses broke the tablets of the law just as Israel had broken the covenant, violating its exclusive devotion to the God who delivered from Egyptian bondage. Yahweh's anger was justified, as was Yahweh's readiness to accept the people's de facto decision to end the relationship. Similarly, the theological import of Moses' intercession should not be overlooked.

Without it, Israel (and Aaron) would have been lost (v. 20). The high stakes involved account for the extremity of Moses' intercession: fasting for forty days and nights "prostrate before Yahweh." Understandably, Deuteronomy sets aside the content of Moses' prayer for special attention (9:25–29).

Between the narrative (vv. 7–25) and the content (vv. 25–29) of Moses' intercession, this comment listing other incidents of rebellion in Israel's history underscores the gravity of the warning against pretentious claims of righteousness. At Kadesh-barnea, Israel refused God's charge to take possession of the promise land; at Taberah ("Fire," cf. Num 11:1–13), Israel murmured; earlier, at Massah ("Proof") and Meribah ("Contention"), Israel faulted Moses' leadership; at Hibroth-hataavah ("Graves of craving," cf. 11:4–32), the Israelites complained about their diet of manna. These incidents illustrate not only Israel's propensity for disobedience but also Israel's petty habit of complaining. Like spoiled children, rather than express gratitude that God had liberated them and met their basic needs, they whined for more exotic foods!

Since Israel has broken the covenant even before it could be documented, a question may now arise: why, then, did God not discontinue the relationship. Moses' intercessory prayer (vv. 25–29) answers this question in a theologically profound appeal, not to Israel's character, but to God's. In four phases, Moses develops an argument that Yahweh must spare Israel: (1) Israel is the elect because God made the choice freely, without regard to Israel's merits (v. 26). (2) In order to be true to God's nature, God must honor God's promise (v. 27). (3) Otherwise, God risks God's reputation (v. 28). (4) Ultimately, the relationship between Yahweh and Israel depends, historically and existentially, not on Israel's obedience, but God's promise (v. 29). Israel's status as the elect, covenant people has nothing to do with Israel's righteousness and everything to do with God's grace!

Moses' appeal to God's very nature succeeds. God reconsiders, replacing the broken tablets of the covenant and resuming the relationship. Israel continues on its journey, now provided with the Ark of the Covenant as the symbol of God's continued presence and a forgiven priest (10:6–9) as the founder of a priestly line of intercessors.

10:12–11:32. Covenant Obedience. The paraenetic introduction to the Deuteronomic Code (12–26) concludes with a series of brief exhortations and admonitions. Thought by some to reflect the outline of an ancient Near Eastern treaty (declaration of principles, 10:12–11:1; historical summary, 11:2–7; blessings and curses, 11:16–17, 22–31), it summarizes the major points already annunciated in the preceding chapters, especially in the Shema. The two chapters provide a catch-all repository of Deuteronomic preaching.

The first "unit" consists of a sequence of exhortations and statements linked in a chain of clauses introduced by the Hebrew conjunction *and*. The Shema serves almost as the text for this "sermon," which reiterates the notion that Yahweh chose weak Israel as an act of grace and extrapolates the requirement that Israel imitate its God by "loving" (v. 19) the weakest and most vulnerable persons: widows, orphans and resident aliens (v. 18). The opening rhetorical question (v. 12) expects that the hearers/readers can easily and quickly respond. God expects neither mysteries nor particular difficulties. God simply anticipates that Israel will live out its covenant relationship, wholeheartedly and vigorously respecting ("fear") God, "walking" in God's ways, "loving" and "serving" God (see on 6:4–5). Israel's God can claim this level of devotion because, as the Creator and Lord of all, God chose Israel. Therefore, Israel must "circumcise the foreskins of their hearts" (v. 16; cf. Jer 31:31–34; Ezek 11:19; 36:26), and prepare the seat of the will, the heart, to obey. Israel, that is, must end its rebellion against God's will. Typical for Deuteronomy, the implications of Yahweh's claim to exclusive and wholehearted devotion culminate in an ethical obligation. Since Israel's God intervenes on behalf of the downtrodden, Israel's devotion to its God will take the form of intervention on behalf of those who need protection. God watches over them and so should God's people.

This "unit" reprises the Shema's focus on Yahweh's uniqueness and exclusivity. Yahweh is to be the focus of Israel's service, devotion, ethics and worship (vv. 20–21) because, simply put, "He is [Israel's] God" (v. 21). Evidence that God has and will fulfill God's obligation in the relationship includes the wonders and horrors God performed on Israel's behalf (v. 21), and Israel's prosperity and fertility even in Egyptian bondage (v. 22). The unit ends with the refrain charging Israel to love Yahweh and obey his commandments (11:1).

Normally, Deuteronomy stresses that, even though later generations of Israel may not have actually been present in Egypt, God's grace persists across generations. Effectively, all generations of Israel were present in that one generation (see commentary on Deut 4). Deuteronomy 11:2–7, consisting of a single, complicated sentence, departs from this normal pattern. It insists that Moses' hearers "know" that their sons "did not see" (v. 2); they did (v. 7). Their "vision" includes a standard series of phenomena, "Yahweh's discipline, greatness, mighty hand, outstretched arm, and signs and wonders," which reflect different places and persons, e.g., "in Egypt, to the Egyptian army, in the wilderness, to Dothan and Abiram." In the context of Deuteronomy's otherwise consistent contention concerning the generational solidarity of Israel, this assertion defies explanation.

The land represents perhaps the most tangible fruit of Israel's relationship with Yahweh. As God's gift (vv. 9, 17, 21), it is the means of God's blessing (vv. 9–12, 14–15, 17, 21), but also the medium of God's punishment for Israel's disobedience (v. 17). This unit (11:8–31) deals with a number of circumstances involving the land: (a) vv. 8–15 describe the advantages the land affords, contrasting the labor intensive irrigation of Egyptian crops with the rain-watered produce of Israel; (b) vv. 16–17 warn against apostasy and describe the effects on life in the land brought about by disobedience, namely, severe drought; (c) vv. 18–21 reiterate parts of the Shema, encouraging Israel to focus on the centrality of the covenant in order to prosper in the land and confronting Israel with a clear and obvious choice; (d) vv. 22–25 promise Yahweh's assistance in taking possession of the land, driving out the inhabitants in fear before Israel—if Israel keeps the covenant; (e) vv. 26–30 summarize, employing key Deuteronomic concepts of blessing and curse, reinforcing the notion that Israel has a clear choice to make (see 27:1–14); (f) vv. 31–32 offer a concluding exhortation for Israel to "keep" and "do" the commandments of the covenant.

C. The Covenant Elaborated: The Deuteronomic Code (12:1–26:19)

Scholars have identified Deut 12–26, termed the "Deuteronomic Code" in contrast to the "Covenant" (Exod 20–23) and "Holiness" (Lev 17–26) Codes, as a more-or-less self-contained collection of case law ("statutes and ordinances") meant to illustrate the principles of interpreting and applying the fundamental ideals of the Decalogue. Deuteronomy, the more comprehensive of the three, shares with the Covenant Code an interest in civil and criminal issues and with the Holiness Code an interest in cultic matters. Such similarities and differences between these codes call attention to the development of Israelite case law and to their respective theological perspectives. For Deuteronomy, the hermeneutical principles exemplified in the Code are more important than the specific laws. Given the primacy of the injunction to "love" Yahweh wholeheartedly, in view of the urgency actively to transmit the covenant tradition to successive generations, and with an awareness that, although the principles of covenant relationship may be enduring, conditions of life change, the Code should be understood as offering early documentation for Israel's interpretation of the covenant. It establishes precedent much in the same way modern American jurisprudence involves case law in determining the application of constitutional and statutory law to specific cases.

This observation also accounts for the outline of the collection. The first century CE Jewish interpreter Philo of Alexandria argued that Deut 12–26 arranges its material according to the structure of the Decalogue. Calvin and Luther argued similarly. Recent scholarship has identified structural and verbal features that call attention to the parallels. The commentary that follows will treat this arrangement as of central importance to the interpretation of the Deuteronomic Code.

12:1–13:18. "No Other Gods." The first section of the Deuteronomic Code explicates the first commandment. The principle operative throughout this material, based on the centrality and priority of Yahweh's claim to Israel's exclusive devotion, concentrates on two measures designed to protect Israel from any possible contamination by foreign religion. Cultic activity is restricted to a central supervised location (12:2–28); and Israel is charged to eradicate, without mercy, all idolatrous influence (12:29–13:18). Orthodox worship is so vital that Deut 12 offers three forms of a law requiring its centralization (vv. 2–7, 8–12, and 13–28]). They agree that the sacrificial cult may only be practiced at the central sanctuary; they differ only about the rationale for this requirement. The first version (vv. 2–7) contrasts centralization with the practices of Israel's neighbors, the second (vv. 8–12) concerns Israel's practice during the wilderness wandering, and the third (vv. 13–27) deals with a potential unintended consequence.

Israel must maintain its distinctiveness over against the Canaanites (vv. 2–7). The danger of assimilation is so great that Israel must wholly eradicate Canaanite religious sites and objects (vv. 2–34). Specifically, Israel must destroy the "high places" associated with the fertility cult ("every green tree") and the "pillars" and "asherim" (= "sacred trees"?) sacred to it. Absolutely no room can be left for confusing or identifying Yahweh with Baal (cf. Hos 1–2). Positively, Yahweh will choose a place for Israel to establish its own cult.

Centralization of the sacrificial cult is an innovation (vv. 8–12). During the wilderness period, the Israelite sanctuary was mobile; and during the judges period, Israelites sacrificed at a number of local sanctuaries. Indeed, the mobile sanctuary embodied a key element of Israel's theological witness, namely, that Yahweh cannot be bound to a place. Centralization therefore requires a rationale (cf. 1 Sam 4–6; 1 Kgs 8:27). Deuteronomy emphasizes, first, that Yahweh is not, in fact, tied to the sanctuary in any way. Rather, Yahweh allows his "name" to dwell there; the central sanctuary symbolizes God's presence amid Israel, it does not constitute it. Second, because *Yahweh chooses* the site of the central sanctuary, the people have no control in the matter. Ultimately, the centralization of Israelite worship manifests a tension present throughout biblical theology: Israel's God is both *immanent* and *transcendent*.

The innovation of centralized worship also raised an unintended practical difficulty (vv. 13–28). Owing to Israel's understanding of the sacredness of blood (see Gen 6:11; 9:2–6), it did not distinguish between profane slaughter and sacred sacrifice. Any act of taking an animal's life was a sacred act. Centralization of sacrifice would mean, however, that a person could not consume meat unless an animal had been slaughtered sacrificially, that is, by a priest at the central sanctuary. Obviously, this would be impractical for Israelites living significant distances from the central sanctuary. The provision occurs in a negative (vv. 13–14) and two parallel positive forms (vv. 15–19 and vv. 20–27). Deuteronomy permits the consumption of meat slaughtered away from the central sanctuary so long as the sacred blood is treated with the proper respect (vv. 16, 23–24). In addition, vv. 18–19 admonish Israel to treat the Levites properly. Obedience to these stipulations in these verses will create trans-generational benefits (v. 25).

Although the destruction of Canaanite cultic objects and the centralization of Israelite worship should greatly diminish the threat of apostasy, Deuteronomy (12:29–13:18) recognizes that people may still be tempted. A second category of four provisions supplements the explication of the first commandment by addressing the threat posed, not by material objects but by human choices. These provisions envision someone contemplating or advocating the worship of other gods: an individual (12:29–31), a false prophet (12:32–13:5), a family member or confidant (13:6–12), or a whole city or community (13:13–18).

An individual may become curious about the religious practices of those who preceded Israel in the land (v. 30). Although the Bible rarely identifies the features of Canaanite religion that make it so abominable, it refers occasionally to an obscure ritual involving "passing [one's children] through fire." This has been understood as a reference to child sacrifice, although some scholars have recently proposed that it may refer to a ritual of dedication or purification. In either case, it clearly violated the requirement to worship Yahweh only and, as biblical history attests (2 Kgs 3:27; 16:3; 17:17), continued to represent a temptation for Israel centuries after Moses. Individual Israelites must, therefore, at all costs, distance themselves from it.

Deuteronomy encourages Israel to keep its covenantal tradition alive, ever interpreting it and adapting it to meet new demands. Moses stands as the model interpreter; further, Deuteronomy embodies one stage of this interpretation. The fact that the fixed statement of the covenant requires interpretation raises a danger, however. How, in the future, will it be possible to discern the authenticity of diverse voices claiming to offer valid interpretations of the tradition? Later, Deuteronomy (18:22) and the prophets (Jer 23:18, 22; 28:8–9;

Amos 3:7; cf. Ezek 13:9) will develop a series of criteria for this problem. Deuteronomy 13:1–3 offers the first, very practical and applicable, test: If a prophet contradicts the basic principles of the covenant, he is manifestly a false prophet. No true prophet of God will advocate violation of the first and central commandment of the covenant, "teaching rebellion against Yahweh" (v. 5)!

If the false prophet hails from a distant village or city, it may be easy to recognize his apostasy; if a close family member or intimate friend should advocate apostasy, however, emotions may cloud judgment and weaken resolve (13:7–12). Nonetheless, violation of the first commandment represents such a threat that even these intimates, who may have spoken in confidence (v. 6), must be treated with the same severity as the stranger. Obedience to the first commandment may even require that one ruthlessly take the lead in executing an apostate so that news of such horror may deter others (v. 11).

The progression from an individual's curiosity to private discussion among intimates culminates in the public act of an entire community (vv. 13–19). Should "certain base fellows" (RSV; Heb.: "sons of Belial") convince the population of a city to engage in idolatry, Israel must treat that city as though it were no longer in Israel, waging "holy war" against it as against a Canaanite city, but not before a careful consideration of circumstances. Apparently imagining a situation in which rumor and innuendo could result in catastrophic injustice, Deut 13 requires that any such case be carefully investigated. The punishment prescribed is of such severity and irreversibility that it can only be executed should the charges be proven.

14:1–21. Misuse of God's Name. First impressions of Deut 14:1–21 seem to challenge the assumption that the Deuteronomic Code explicates the Decalogue. How do habits of personal grooming and diet relate to the commandment against employing the divine name "lightly" or "falsely" (cf. 5:11)? In Deuteronomy's view, one "takes the name of Yahweh," not just when pronouncing it, but also by the physical identity of God's people (cf. vv. 1–2, 21). To be set apart as "a people holy to Yahweh" involves the testimony of lives lived in accordance with the will of God. As God's children (v. 1) who bear the family name, all of life, including dress and diet, becomes a (true or false) statement in God's name.

In contrast to Deut 12–13, this passage closely parallels texts in Leviticus (14:2*a* ‖ Lev 21:5; 14:3–21*a* ‖ Lev 11:2–45; 14:21*a* ‖ Lev 17:15, compare Exod 23:19; 34:26). Deuteronomy 14:1–21 explicates the commandment concerning God's name by categorizing existing traditions and, in so doing, offering creative theological interpretation. Deuteronomy shares with Leviticus a respect for life and the divine order reflected in classes of animals. Genesis 9:3 suggests that God originally intended that human beings, and probably animals too, be herbivores. As a result, the killing of animals for food creates tension. Despite generations of efforts to find some hygienic rationale (e.g., pork is the source of trichinosis) or religious polemic (e.g., prohibited animals were holy to pagan deities), careful analysis of these dietary regulations reveals that the animals classified as improper for consumption fall into two broad categories, reflecting concerns for the holiness of life and of the created order. First, all the animals permitted for food are herbivores, while many prohibited are either raptors who take life (cf. 11–18), scavengers who benefit from death, or carrion (v. 21*a*). In all these cases, proper respect for the lifeblood of the (original) victim demands abstention. The otherwise enigmatic regulation against boiling a kid in its mother's milk (v. 21*b*) extends this respect for life by prohibiting a culinary practice that must be viewed as perverse from the Priestly perspective: cooking an animal in the substance that once sustained its life. Second, all other animals unsuitable for consumption betray characteristics suggesting mixture of species. Animals that chew the cud normally have cleft hooves; any animal exhibiting only one of these characteristics occupies a marginal place in God's created order and must not be eaten (vv. 7–8). Fish have fins and scales; animals that live in water but have none or only one of these characteristics exists as an anomaly in God's order and are therefore off-limits for human consumption (vv. 9–10).

If Israel is to bear God's name authentically, it must respect the sanctity of life and the boundaries established between life and death. Israel reflects its own status as a people "set apart" to God by honoring the boundaries and categories, as understood by a pre-scientific culture, that God established in the created order.

14:22–16:17. The Sabbath. Both versions of the Decalogue (Exod 20; Deut 5) relate the Sabbath to a positive theological principle: either God's hallowing of the day of rest in creation (Exod) or God's liberation of Israel from slavery (Deut). Both emphasize the blessing of liberation and rest. Indeed, Deuteronomy's interpretation exhorts Israel to engage in a wide variety of restful, liberating, and celebratory behaviors. Deuteronomy achieves this interpretation by classifying disparate materials under the Sabbath heading, thereby expanding and deepening the principle of Sabbath rest and celebration.

The editors clearly indicate that this material relates to the Sabbath. Units of seven (15:1, 9, 12, 18; 16:3–4, 8, 9, 13, 15) and three (14:28–29; 16:16–17) dominate; worship is a central focus (14:22–27); the so-called "motive clause" from Deuteronomy's version of the Sabbath commandment, "Remember that you were a slave," recurs (15:15; 16:12) and echoes in regulations concerning the Passover (16:1–8). The Sabbath commandment's requirement that it apply to all (Ex 20:10; Deut 5:14) surfaces in the determination that even, or especially, those on the fringes of society should enjoy Sabbath rest and freedom (cf. "sojourners" in 14:22–27, 28–29; 15:1–6, 7–11; "slaves" in 15:12–18; and even "livestock" in 15:19–23). Finally, all celebrations of God's provision of bounty and freedom involve a Sabbath element (15:19; 16:8). Rest is possible only because of God's blessing on Israel's work during the week (14:29; 15:6, 10; 16:15). Good, honest work, God's blessing, and Sabbath freedom and rest constitute a grand harmony.

It is difficult to construct a coherent model of the Old Testament system of tithes and offerings (compare, e.g. 14:22–29 and Num 18:8–32). Difficulties arise in part because Deuteronomy does not understand itself to be a procedural handbook but a hermeneutical guide. Deuteronomy focuses on the central requirement that the tither share with the disenfranchised that portion of the tithe not burnt in sacrifice or reserved for the priests. A key feature is the joy the tither expresses in worship. The worshiper, his household, and his guests are to celebrate extravagantly ("whatever your soul desires"). Furthermore, Deuteronomy insists that, since Israel's God is a liberator, Israel must also liberate. Sabbath, a weekly commemoration of freedom, must be an opportunity for extending freedom to others. The most horrible perversion imaginable of God's intervention on Israel's behalf would be for Israel, itself, to become an oppressor.

Every third year the distance from the central sanctuary is to be transformed into an opportunity for extending Sabbath liberty (vv. 28–29). Rather than traveling to the central sanctuary, Israelites should share their tithes with the underprivileged, the landless Levite, the disenfranchised immigrant, and widows and orphans without means of support. By extending Sabbath liberation, Israel ensures God's continued blessing (14:29).

Deuteronomy's treatment of the Sabbath establishes connections between the celebration of Israel's God, who frees slaves, and a wide range of apparently unrelated circumstances. Economic debt, which could drive one into slavery, appears prominently (Deut 15). Every seventh year is to be a year of Sabbath "release (from debt)." Exodus prescribes a fallow year for crops so that poor people may glean freely (23:10–11); Deuteronomy goes much farther, prescribing the forgiveness of all debts. Apart from the somewhat illiberal and inconsistent attitude toward foreign debt (vv. 3, 6) and a contradictory effort to mitigate the image of Israel implicit in a need to forgive debts, Deuteronomy's version of the Sabbath is a radical economic implementation of fundamental theological insights.

Although Sabbath forgiveness offers hope to debtors, creditors have reason to fear it. Crafty lenders may refuse to make a loan immediately prior to a Sabbath year since they may not recover their investments. In contrast to Lev 25, Deuteronomy focuses on the lender's attitude. Cold calculation and hard-hearted stinginess are the polar opposites of the joy and freedom celebrated in the Sabbath. The proper Israelite response to need emulates God's response. To behave otherwise is to risk becoming an oppressor, one against whom the oppressed may "cry out" as the Israelites cried out against the Egyptians (15:9).

Ancient Israel practiced "debt slavery," repayment by indentured servitude for a period limited by the Covenant (Ex 21:1–11) and Deuteronomic Codes to six years (15:12–18). Four features highlight Deuteronomy's concept of Sabbath freedom in relation to debt slavery. First, female slaves must be treated equally. Second, whereas the Covenant Code specifies that wives given to men during their servitude and any children born of these unions remain the property of the master, Deuteronomy's silence suggests that wives and children are subject to the rules that apply to their husbands and fathers. Who would choose to go free if to do so meant to abandon a beloved wife and children? Third, Deuteronomy omits any reference to a sacral setting for the ceremony that establishes permanent servitude. Fourth, only Deuteronomy requires that a slave be freed with ample provisions for starting a new life (vv. 14), reminding the erstwhile master that he too was once a slave.

The regulations concerning the sacrifice of firstborn males of herd and flock (15:19–23) do not appear to recall the Sabbath commandment. However, key phraseology (cf. v. 19 and Exod 20:8 ∥ Deut 5:12) employs the language of the Sabbath commandment; and Deuteronomy's familiar emphases confirm the relationship between Sabbath and sacrifice: celebration, centralization, profane slaughter, and respect for the life-blood.

Israel's earliest ritual calendar included three annual festivals: Passover-Unleavened Bread, Harvest-Pentecost, and Booths-Ingathering. By discussing them here (Deut 16), including language that recalls the Sabbath commandment ("to keep," v. 1; the number *seven*, vv. 3, 4, 8, 9, 13; the prohibition of work), and linking these inherently agricultural festivals to the exodus event (16:3, 12), the Deuteronomic Code maintains that they too embody the Sabbath principles of rest, joy and liberation.

Deuteronomy's provisions for Passover (vv. 1–8) differ significantly from those in Exodus. Exodus (12:5) specifies a lamb or a kid for Passover; Deuteronomy also allows for larger cattle (16:2). Exodus views Passover as a family holiday observed at home (12:3–4, 7, 21–24); Deuteronomy prescribes the observance of Passover at the central sanctuary (16:2, 5–6). Exodus (12:9) specifies that the meat for the Passover meal be roasted, *not* boiled; Deuteronomy (16:7) explicitly requires the opposite (perhaps to allow the preparation of larger animals). These details have little significance, however, in light of Deuteronomy's association of Passover with the Sabbath. Just as Passover is the annual commemoration of God's deliverance from Egyptian bondage, the Sabbath is the weekly commemoration of Israel's freedom.

Deuteronomy's unique treatment of the Feast of Weeks (16:9–12; cf. Exod 23:16; 34:22; Lev 23:15–16; Num 28:26) expresses Deuteronomy's program: the relationship between blessing, bounty, and commemoration (v. 10), joyous celebration (v. 11), extension of Sabbath rest, liberty, and joy to dispossessed and disadvantaged Levites, aliens, orphans, and widows (v. 11), centralization, and, above all, the fundamental link between the Feast of Weeks and the exodus.

Although Deuteronomy does not specifically relate the Feast of Booths (16:13–15) to the exodus, the periscope includes three of the book's central emphases: rejoicing (vv. 14, 15), sharing, and centralization. In Post-biblical Judaism, the Feast of Booths celebrated the reception of the Torah.

Deuteronomy concludes its discussion of the major festivals with a summary of the essentials (16:16–17). These three festivals are obligatory for Israelite males; further, the rites are restricted to the central sanctuary; above all, they celebrate God's freedom and bounty.

16:18–18:22. "Honor Your Parents." What is involved in honoring parents? Deuteronomy answers by gathering probably once-independent material under the rubric of authority and its exercise. Deuteronomy both supplies the notion of "honoring parents" with content and extends the principle stated in the commandment to apply to other figures in society who exercise authority worthily and within proper limits.

Deuteronomy 16:18–17:13 combines several distinct sub-units into an extended treatment of the limits and duties of judicial authority. Deuteronomy does not focus on judicial structures (e.g., qualifications, appointment, and terms of office) but rather on the dangers of the misuse of authority. The first such danger, corruption, invalidates the authority of the judge because it influences judges to render false judgments. Judges must not "pervert" justice by taking into account the status and social class of parties or by taking a bribe. Israel's present and future prosperity depends, in part, on its judicial integrity (16:18–20). Deuteronomy 16:21–17:1, which reiterate prohibitions

against idolatrous practices, may allude to the first commandment, reminding readers of the relationship between legitimate human authority and its ultimate origin. Alternatively, this subsection may serve as the preamble to the following unit, citing the statute before outlining the suitable judicial treatment (17:2–7). In either case, 17:4–7 bring the issue of judicial authority to its apex. Given the gravity of the punishment for idolatry, the valid exercise of authority demands the highest standard of circumspection on the part of the judge(s). They must disregard hearsay, investigate diligently, require multiple witnesses, and, finally, require the entire community, starting with the star witness, to perform the execution (forcing everyone involved to face the awesome finality of the outcome). Finally, vv. 8–13 explicitly state the notion that underlies the preceding material, namely, that all human authority confronts limits. A local judge may occasionally hear a case that exceeds his expertise (v. 8). He must admit his limits and turn to "the Levitical priests and the judge" for assistance. Their ruling must be honored without exception or omission. Verse 12 reminds readers not to take the concern with the abuse and limits of authority as license to denigrate or disregard properly exercised judicial authority; any who legitimately exercise authority in the service of Yahweh, the supreme authority, deserve honor and respect.

Deuteronomy turns now to the monarchy; one of only three texts in the Old Testament to describe that institution (Deut 17:14–20; 1 Sam 8:11–22; 10:25). The book stresses the limits of royal authority in four sections (qualifications for selection as king, vv. 14–15; prohibited actions, vv. 16–17; the king's subjection to the Torah, vv. 18–19, and a concluding admonition, v. 20). Acknowledging that sometime in the future the people may wish to establish a kingdom, Deuteronomy establishes guidelines for any future monarchy. Israel's king must not be an absolute despot: Yahweh will choose for the people from among the people (v. 15). Further, this fellow Israelite should exercise only limited power (vv. 16–17): he must not succumb to the temptations of military might (horses) acquired with the fruits of forced labor (apparently "Egypt" as a symbol of servitude), of diplomatic entanglements (perhaps many wives as a tool of statecraft), or of wealth (v. 17b)—all measures designed to demonstrate Israel's reliance, not upon worldly power but divine guidance and protection. These three temptations parallel precisely Solomon's errors (cf. 1 Kgs 5:13; 9:15–22; 12:18; Exod 1:11; and 1 Kgs 11:1–13). Finally, to ensure that the king remember that his authority derives from and is subject to the superior authority of Israel's true king, Deuteronomy requires that a personal copy of the Torah be prepared for the king upon his assumption of the throne and that he study it daily and thus "learn to fear Yahweh" (v. 19). In short, the king must guard against arrogance in relation to his brother and sister Israelites *and* in relation to God and the requirements of God's covenant.

It is unclear whether 18:1–8 means to comment on the relative authority of kings and priests, especially since it does not address expressly the limits of priestly authority, but concentrates on providing food for the landless Levites. It may be, of course, that the landlessness of the Levites itself constituted a limit to Levitical authority. In any case, owing to their special status among the tribes of Israel, the Levites deserve the same respect owed one's parents. At a minimum, the Levites merit provision for their basic needs (vv. 3–8; cf. Lev 7:28–36; Num 18:18). Perhaps as a concession to the impact cultic centralization may have on Levites serving in regional sanctuaries (now deprived of their means of livelihood), Deuteronomy stipulates that these priests be admitted to the priesthood at the central sanctuary with equal rights and responsibilities and an equal share in the priest's portion (vv. 6–8).

Among those who exercise authority in the context of Israel's relationship with its God, Deuteronomy reserves pride of place for prophets (Deut 18:9–22). Prophets may exercise authority abusively or without authenticity. Deuteronomy prohibits various forms of magic ("divining," "soothsaying," "hydromancy," "sorcery, astrology," "spellcasting," "necromancy") because magic perverts the proper relationship toward the Lord of all creation. Prophets serve God; God cannot be coerced by technical mechanisms. True prophets speak on God's behalf only when God commissions them. God's people need prophets since the fixed/canonical tradition cannot anticipate all the circumstances in which they may need God's guidance (vv. 16–17). When the need arises, God will commission a prophet like Moses who must

be respected because of his God-given authority (vv. 18–29). Thus, the community will encounter two categories of persons claiming prophetic authority: those speaking for themselves (whether in Yahweh's name or in the names of other gods) and those speaking based on their divine commission. The community may safely dismiss any prophet who speaks in the name of a god other than Yahweh. Such a prophet has transgressed the foundation of the covenant, devotion to Yahweh only (v. 20). Prophets who speak a false message but do so in the name of Yahweh are more difficult to identify. If a prophet speaks in Yahweh's name but his prophecy does not come to pass, he is a false prophet (v. 22). As later biblical tradition will demonstrate, this criterion offers little help in certain circumstances when, by the time the prophecy has come true, it may be too late to respond (see Jer 18:26–29).

19:1–22:8. No Killing. Deuteronomy interprets the prohibition against killing through a wide variety of case studies. Three "transitional" sections (21:10–14, 15–17; 22:5) divide the macro-unit into four sub-units: the protection of innocent life (19:1–21), limitations on taking life in war (20:1–20), situations that obscure the boundaries between life and death (21:1–23), and the demand, inherent in the commandment against killing, to enrich life (22:1–8). Thus, Deuteronomy defines the prohibition against killing quite broadly to include prophylactic measures, limits on revenge and retribution, protections for non-human life, and, finally, destructive measures short of actual killing.

Three categories of persons deserve protection. Cities of refuge provide sanctuary for those who have accidentally caused another's death (19:1–13). Fraudulent real estate dealings can deprive small farmers of their sole livelihood (v. 14). Lying witnesses can use the system as a weapon (vv. 15–21).

Deuteronomy 19:1–13 requires that cities of refuge be dispersed equitably throughout Israel (vv. 1–3), defines accidental manslaughter (vv. 4–7), provides for the addition of cities should Israel acquire new territory (vv. 8–10), and defines murder (vv. 1–13). Manslaughter and murder must be distinguished so that people involved in accidents can be protected from clan vengeance. Clan law obligated one's nearest kinsman, or the "kinsman-redeemer-avenger," to protect clan honor and property (cf. Lev 25:25, 39–55). Chief among his obligations was revenge. The system of cities of refuge, based on the distinction between accident and intention, were designed to restrain the inevitable feuds, or cycles of blood vengeance. The central problem involves the subjective nature of intent. Two tests of the killer's actions can suggest his intentions. *Motive*, indicated by previous animosity between the parties (vv. 4–7), suggests intention. Absent motive, one can assume accident. *Premeditation*, suggested by preparations ("lying in wait," v. 11), clearly indicates intention. Verse 13 should be seen as a restriction on clan vengeance. Any retribution must be equitable and must be exacted only of the actual offender.

Deuteronomy 19:14 ingeniously applies the commandment against killing to property theft. Since, according to Mosaic law, land—God's perpetual trust—could not be transferred; no legitimate reason could account for moving boundary markers (cf. Prov 22:28; 23:10). Any such movement could only be interpreted as theft (cf. Amos 2:6–8; 4:1–3; 5:10–13; Mic 2:1–3). Since, in an agrarian culture, land is the principle source of livelihood, property theft was tantamount to robbing a subsistence farmer of the very source of life. Any offense against the essentials for living or even, as Jesus argued (Matt 5:21–26), against a person's character, differs from murder only in degree.

Similarly, Deuteronomy regards error or deceit in the judicial system as a threat to the life of an accused innocent and enumerates several steps to protect against wrongful conviction (19:15–21): (1) The testimony of a single eyewitness—who could make an honest error or intentionally deceive—is insufficient (v. 15). (2) Judges must beware of "violent" (i.e., intending to do harm, the motive, v. 16) and "lying" (i.e., with intent, not in honest error, the means, v. 19) witnesses who may seek to usurp the court as a weapon. (3) Israelite authorities must be diligent, assuming nothing, examining all witnesses carefully (vv. 17–18). (4) As a deterrent, the penalty for perjury is the same assigned to the charge brought against the accused (vv. 18–21). The presumption of innocence must be protected. The second cluster of cases (20:1–20) deals with conflict between competing demands. Nothing in the

Bible seems to contradict the bias toward preserving life as fundamentally as does the concept of "holy war" discussed here. Ancient Israel's perceptions of the will of God were necessarily context-bound. Since Deuteronomy treats holy war in the context of the interpretation of the commandment against killing, the editors must, themselves, have recognized the conflict between war and respect for (all) life. The rules propounded here limit life-taking in martial contexts in four sub-sections: the theological basis for holy war (vv. 1–4), deferments from service (vv. 5–9), and rules of engagement (vv. 10–18), including regulations against slash and burn techniques (vv. 19–20).

Holy war presents a special case. Yahweh wages war against *his* enemies; the battle, the victory, and the spoils are Yahweh's (cf. Josh 7:1, 23–24; 9:1–3; Judg 7:1–23; 1 Sam 7:10; etc.). Theologically, then, holy war is one of Yahweh's tools for executing justice on the international scale. Holy war is not an act of Israelite aggression but of divine judgment.

The initial restriction on warfare (5–9) dismisses from military service new homeowners, owners of newly planted vineyards, those engaged to be married, and those who are simply afraid. Deuteronomy supplies a clear rationale only for the final exemption (v. 8). The explanation given for the first three categories emphasizes the folly of risking one's life instead of enjoying its benefits and pleasures.

Two interpretations of vv. 10–18 are possible. One views vv. 10–15 as rules governing holy war with distant cities and vv. 16–18 as those governing neighboring cities. Israel could sue for peace with remote enemies, but not neighbors. In war, Israel could kill only males among distant enemies, but must exterminate neighboring populations. It could plunder distant enemies, while nearby cities must be totally destroyed. Another interpretation, found in the Talmud (*y. Shevi'it* 6:1), understands vv. 10–11 to refer to all enemies whereas vv. 12–15 and vv. 16–18 apply to distant cities and nearby cities, respectively, who reject the peace offer. The second interpretation not only represents a less bloodthirsty approach, it also reflects Israelite practice recorded elsewhere (Deut 2:26–30; Josh 11:19–20; 1 Kgs 9:20–21). Still, the requirement to eradicate total populations under certain circumstances seems harsh.

In the context of surrounding cultures, however, Deuteronomy's effort to limit war reflects its view of the sanctity of life. Ancient Near Eastern invaders commonly demolished their enemy's resources, destroying crops and cisterns (cf. 2 Kgs 24). Deuteronomy prohibits such tactics (vv. 19–20). Israel must spare trees, especially fruit trees, in war. Israel may eradicate human populations, but must spare apple trees. Deuteronomy understands that the prohibition against killing extends to the protection of the ecology that sustains human life. Sometimes, the sanctity of life and the reality of death clash, making it difficult to act appropriately (21:1–23). Five specific situations model such dilemmas: unsolved homicides (vv. 1–9), captive wives (vv. 10–14), paternal favoritism (vv. 15–17), an incorrigible son (vv. 18–21), and the treatment of the corpse of an executed criminal (vv. 22–23).

The blood of an innocent victim pollutes the land (Num 35:33; cf. Deut 19:10) and cries out for justice (Gen 4:10). Only the guilty party can expiate for the crime. What can the community do? First, since the corpse was found in the countryside (v. 1), the leaders of the two nearest towns determine which is nearer (v. 2). That community then sacrifices an unworked heifer near a running wet-weather stream by breaking its neck (shedding no further innocent blood). Before priests, the leaders then wash their hands over the heifer with water from the running stream, pronouncing themselves innocent of bloodshed and seeking Yahweh's absolution. The priests then grant absolution because the leaders have done "the best they could" (v. 9). The procedure recognizes the mysterious organic connection between human ethical behavior and the health of the ecosystem.

The text regulating marriage to women captured in warfare (21:10–14) begins by reporting details of the situation (vv. 10–11). It then calls for the woman to engage in ritual mourning for her parents for one month (vv. 12–13) before the marriage. The regulation culminates in the prohibition, should the man later divorce her, against returning her to slave status. She must be released as a freedwoman. In a dual sense, this man has *forced* this woman *against her will* into the borderland between death and new life. The regulation, apparently more suited to the treatment of slaves or the conduct of holy war, explicates the commandment against killing by insisting that the husband respect both the captive woman's need to mourn her loss and her new status. He may not further diminish her.

In ancient Israel, the first-born son inherited an additional share and assumed the responsibilities of patriarch. The regulation propounded in 21:15–17 prohibits the violation of this practice in favor of a younger son. The text is not concerned with fairness but with the father's attitude toward the first born as the assurance of the family line. At the extreme end of the spectrum from the negative "do not kill" to the positive "promote life," this celebration of the first born represents an affirmation of life.

Deuteronomy 21:18–21 deals with the incorrigible son, not in relation to the commandment to honor parents, but here because both the son's actions and the prescribed penalty involve life and death. The circumstance envisioned involves an adult son, a rebellious, incorrigible, drunkard, whose profligacy threatens the estate and the welfare of his aging parents. His behavior endangers them all. In antiquity, the public display of corpses of executed criminals and prisoners of war was considered a deterrent against crime and a means of humiliating enemies (see 1 Sam 31:8–13; 2 Sam 2:4–7). Deuteronomy 21:22–23 acknowledges the practice, but severely limits it, requiring that the corpse be taken down and buried by the end of the first day. Deuteronomy frowns upon depriving even a criminal of a proper burial, without which, in the ancient view, the deceased could find no rest. The Talmud (*Sanh.* 46*b*) warns against an "affront to God" because such disdain for a human being created in God's image implies disdain also for God.

The explication of the commandment against killing culminates in a series of cases that convert the negative into a positive requirement to promote and protect all life (22:1–8). Life is so precious that one must nurture it however and whenever possible.

Ancient Israel's "Good Samaritan Law" (22:1–4) requires one to take positive steps to aid another in distress. One may not stand by while another suffers injury or loss (v. 1). Rather, one must assist (v. 3) whenever needed (v. 4). Oxen were the tractors of the ancient world. Sheep were the sources of milk and wool. Loss of or injury to these animals brought hardship, threatening the owner's ability to provide for himself and his family. One must not kill by disregarding the interconnection between life and the conditions necessary for sustaining it.

Deuteronomy 22:5 is virtually impossible to translate, much less interpret. The key term describing something prohibited to women can best be translated "thing." Men, in turn, may not wear a woman's "wrapper." Parallelism suggests that the prohibited "thing" is some article of men's clothing. The term translated "man" here is not the generic noun, but a term for "warrior, champion," prompting the suggestion that the "thing" is some instrument of warfare. Neither of these translations is assured (in the ancient world, both genders wore robes), nor is a conceivable relationship to the commandment against taking life readily apparent. It is better to acknowledge the limits of knowledge than to press speculative interpretations.

The biblical concern for life extends beyond humans. Deuteronomy 22:6–7 prohibits taking a mother bird *and* her young. Mother birds can lay more eggs. One may take the young and the species can survive. While animal life is not of equal value with human life, animals are living beings, created by God, deemed good, and commissioned to multiply and fill the earth (Gen 1:22, 28). Biblical reverence for the sanctity of life includes respect for God's creation.

Finally, just as the principle underlying the cities of refuge depends on intention, the macro-unit on killing ends with an admonition dealing with recklessness (22:8). In fact, the two circumstances may constitute an inclusio, bracketing this unit. Lest a reader conclude that lack of intent to kill completely exonerates one from responsibility in the accidental death of another, Deut 22:8 holds that recklessness, the failure to take reasonable precautions, violates the regard for life inherent in the prohibition against killing.

22:9–23:18. No Adultery. Marriage fixes boundaries of relationships. Adultery represents disregard for these boundaries. In keeping with Deuteronomy's propensity to explicate a commandment by extrapolating applications inherent, but not expressed, in the commandment, the Deuteronomic Code extends adultery to include a wide range of boundary transgressions or inter-mixtures. It deals with sexuality and gender and, more broadly, with an overarching respect for order in nature (22:9–12), in human sexual relationships (22:13–30), and within the community (23:1–18).

The English word *adulterate* aptly describes the issue concerning mixtures in nature (22:9–12): mixed crops, a mixed brace of draft animals, clothing made of a mixture of fabrics (cf. also Lev 19:19). Judging by a similar text (Num 15:37–41), tassels on the fringes of one's garment (absent in Lev 19:19) aided memory, reminding the Israelites of their holy status, i.e. of the boundary between them and other nations. The tassels symbolically warn against cultural "adulteration."

Patriarchal Israel defined adultery proper in terms of the (future or actual) husband's confidence that his wife's children are his offspring. The double standard offends moderns. Yet, Deuteronomy also represents an advance in its broader cultural environment. Deut 22:13–30 seeks to protect women against predatory or manipulative men. Still, male sexuality was relatively unrestricted.

Seven cases illustrate the spectrum of rules concerning female sexuality: (1) the slandered bride (13–19) ; (2) the guilty bride (20–21); (3) adultery with a married woman (22); (4) adultery with an engaged woman (23–24); (5) the rape of an engaged woman (25–27); (6) the rape of a single woman (28–29); and (7) the prohibition against marrying one's (widowed?) step-mother (30 [Hebr. 23:1]). The order generally reflects descending magnitude both regarding the woman's status (wife, fiancée, single woman, widow) and the pertinent penalty (death, fine).

(1) To retain her dowry, a disgruntled husband may falsely accuse his new wife of adultery rather than simply divorce her. If her parents, with both reputation and estate at risk, can produce "evidence" of her virginity "in the gate" (v. 15), they can expose the groom's lie. Community elders "correct" him (by flogging?, cf Deut 25:2–3), he must pay his father-in-law, who "controls" his daughter's virginity, 100 shekels of silver or twice the normal bride-price (see v. 29), and he may never divorce the slandered bride. Notably, the

woman finds little solace; the crux is the value of her virginity.

(2) Should, however, a groom's charges prove true, the bride is to be stoned at her father's door. The dowry and the father's reputation are forfeit. The bride pays with her life. Her husband's sexual history is not an issue. Her lover goes free.

(3) Clear cases of adultery present no difficulty for Deuteronomy. If a man and another man's wife have consensual sex, both are guilty of a crime punishable by stoning.

(4) An engaged woman who has consensual sex with a man other than her fiancé in a populated area, on the other hand, raises two legal questions. First, is she married? She is considered married since her fiancé has paid the dowry. Second, what is the criterion for determining consent (cf. v. 22)? The regulation relies on the "cry for assistance." In a populated area, the woman could have cried out if she were non-consenting and, presumably, someone would have come to her aid. The attacker would have been guilty of rape. The woman's silence signifies consent. She is an adulteress and both are guilty. The interpretive tradition recognizes that a rapist may coerce silence and adds additional tests of consent.

(5) A similar incident in a rural setting does not allow for the silence test. The man is assumed to be a rapist. This situation involves a unique case of the double standard working to the disadvantage of the male involved.

(6) The first case involving a single woman concerns rape (v. 28). The rapist must pay the bride-price and marry his victim. Apparently, a man may either "buy" the woman's virginity either before or after taking it. Even more troubling is the lack of provision for cases in which the attacker escapes discovery (cf. v. 28).

(7) The final regulation prohibits one category of "post-marital" adultery in which the injured party is not the potential, but the deceased husband. Treated elsewhere in the context of incest (Lev 18:6–30), marriage between a man and his step-mother ("his father's wife") is forbidden. Although she is not directly related to the man in question, his relationship to his father accounts for the impropriety.

"Adultery," i.e., the violation of boundaries, surfaces in yet another class of circumstances: the purity of God's people. The cases gathered in Deut 23:1–18 examine (1) the identity of the cultic community (vv. 1–8 and vv. 15–16), (2) the purity of the camp (vv. 10–14), and (3) the exclusion of prostitution and its wages from the community and its sanctuary (vv. 17–18).

(1) Six categories of people may not become members of the community: mutilated or emasculated men (vv. 1–8; either because mutilation is associated with pagan cults, because it blurs gender boundaries, or because it renders one unable to fulfill the injunction to procreate); those of mixed ancestry for ten generations; Ammonites and Moabites, also for ten generations, because they did not show Israel hospitality en route to Canaan (cf. 2:8–30); and, for three generations, Edomites and Egyptians (vv. 7–8). This interpretation of adultery contradicts passages such as Isa 56:3–8 and, thus, represents another example of the context-bound nature of sections of the Bible. Surely the people of God must maintain its purity, but surely too the loving God welcomes all who would worship him. The interpreter is challenged to balance two principles: purity and inclusivity.

(2) The camp is holy (v. 14) and must be kept pure. Nocturnal emissions and open latrines are, therefore, problems. Since, in Israel's view, all aspects of reproduction involve holiness, an individual who has experienced "a chance occurrence in the night (v. 10; cf. Lev 15:16–18) must be "set apart" for a period. After washing, he may return to the camp. A latrine outside the camp and a spade for each warrior not only provides for hygiene, but respect God's presence in the camp. Israel ought not to expose Yahweh to such indecency (Heb. lit. "nakedness of a thing," v. 14). The prescription concerning the universal offer of asylum for escaped slaves sounds a noble tone. Or, perhaps better, it echoes a note of thanksgiving for God's gift of freedom. Notably, the placement of this regulation underscores the notion that the acceptance of such escapees does not threaten the purity of the cultic community, rules concerning Edomites and Ammonites notwithstanding. (3) Finally, God's holy people must not include prostitutes (compare Lev 19:29) nor should their earnings be accepted in the Temple treasury. The connotation of the phrase "wages of

a dog" is unclear. Literally, dogs were carnivores and scavengers and therefore unclean. Dogs were associated the certain pagan gods among Israel's neighbors. The phrase, probably an idiom, most likely refers to prostitution.

23:19–24:7. No Stealing. Two pairs of cases dealing with theft form a parenthesis around this section; three laws at the core expand the application of the commandment against stealing. Without the framework, the relationship of these cases to theft might go unnoted. They apply the commandment to abstractions, identify God as a potential victim, focus on the harm to victims generally, and exemplify the close interrelationship between the several commandments.

In contrast to its parallels (Exod 22:25; Lev 25:35–38), Deut 23:19–20 widens the restriction against charging interest to exclude all Israelites and, specifically, interest on necessities, illustrating the close relationship between stealing and killing. In Deuteronomy's view interest is theft.

Vows are promises to do something in the future, usually contingent upon the deity's fulfillment of a request. In contrast, oaths are affirmations with the deity as security. Unfulfilled vows are tantamount to stealing *from God*.

The situation described in 23:25–26 was common in ancient agrarian cultures. Roads were few and a direct route is always preferable. To refuse bypassers hospitality is theft. Instead of protecting the farmer from loss, Deuteronomy requires him to share his bounty. The conversion of the negative into a positive typifies the Deuteronomic Code. Not giving is stealing!

Deuteronomy 24:1–4 contains the most comprehensive information available concerning ancient Israelite divorce law. While the prohibition is straightforward, the rationale is entirely unclear, as is its placement. A man may not remarry a former wife who has since remarried. Apparently, fearing that the couple may have continued to have feelings for one another, the law intends to guard the second marriage against the influence of the first husband. If he were to sabotage the second marriage in order to remarry his wife, he would, in effect, be stealing.

The bridegroom must not risk his life in military service, stealing from himself the blessing of marriage and family (24:5–7). One must not steal from oneself God's gift. Israelite creditors may not claim as collateral (cf. Exod 22:25–27; Lev 25:35–38) any of life's necessities or the means for procuring them. Finally, kidnapping and enslaving a fellow Israelite is a capital offense. It is "stealing a life."

24:8–25:4. No False Witness. Lying, either through speech or action, can damage another, impugning the fundamental honor due one who bears the image of God. The eight brief cases examined here (cf. Lev 13–14; Exod 22:26; Lev 19:9, 13; 23:10, 22) involve, in descending order of status, virtually every social class known in ancient Israel—including even foreigners, criminals, and oxen. No one is so lowly as to deserve dishonest treatment.

(1) Against the background of Miriam's leprosy resulting from her slanderous accusations against Moses (v. 9; cf. Num 12), this admonition to respect priestly teaching warns against slandering—speaking falsely of—priests. As Moses' successors, they hold positions of particular responsibility and authority.

(2) Collateral for loans (cf. Exod 22:25–27) may not be seized lest the debtor be publicly dishonored. Rather, the creditor must wait until the debtor produces the collateral. Poor persons' only valuable possessions may be articles of clothing. The text mentions an outer garment used as bedding by night. The creditor must return it each day before sunset so that the poor person may sleep in warmth. Clearly, Deuteronomy has shifted the focus along a continuum—false witness to slander and now to humiliation. The dignity, even of the poorest, must be preserved. To denigrate the poor is to lie.

(3) Day laborers fall just below poor homeowners in Israel's social hierarchy. Only those with no patrimony or trade would resort to hiring themselves out. Employers sometimes capriciously withheld wages. Deuteronomy (24:14–15; cf. Lev 19:13; Mal 3:5) demands that workers, regardless of nationality, be paid at the conclusion of each day's labor—otherwise, they go to their families empty-handed. If employers fail to meet this simple requirement, their laborers may cry out to God as Israel did in Egyptian bondage. Promising without paying is bearing false witness.

(4) Deut 24:16 explicitly forbids executing one generation for the crimes of another. The argument hinges on the notion that it is dishonest to judge one generation by the behavior of another.

(5) At the bottom of the Israelite class structure one finds foreigners, orphans, and widows. Deuteronomy 24:17–22 prohibits maltreatment of these persons (vv. 17–18); it enjoins providing for their basic needs (vv. 19–22). The rationale for respecting the lowliest is the reminder that Israel once sojourned as foreigners in a foreign land, so it owes foreigners fundamentally just treatment. (6) Similarly, it is impermissible to take advantage of widows. To treat individuals as though they did not deserve fundamental respect is to bear false witness concerning a child of God. Indeed, more prosperous Israelites must make efforts to meet the basic needs of these needy persons—without unnecessarily humiliating them. Deuteronomy calls upon Israelite farmers not to harvest thoroughly so that underprivileged classes of people can support themselves with the fruits of their own labor. Deuteronomy converts the requirement that no harm be done into a requirement to do good.

(7) Deuteronomy 25:1–3 further radicalizes the principle that bearing false witness is a form of attack. Even criminals must receive appropriate and proportionate penalties (not to exceed 40 lashes), and the judge responsible for the sentence should be present for its execution. These measures not only spare the criminal undue humiliation, but protect the community from coming to despise a fellow human being.

(8) To be as clear as possible concerning the extent to which the prohibition against bearing false witness applies equally to everyone, Deut 24:4 concludes with the case of a laboring animal that must be permitted to graze as it works. Even members of the animal kingdom deserve fundamental respect.

25:5–12. No Coveting Another's Wife. Toward the end of the Deuteronomic Code, treatments of individual commandments become shorter and interpretations become more innovative. Deuteronomy regards the commandments against coveting the neighbor's wife and coveting the neighbor's property as distinct commandments (nine and ten). The two cases examined here constitute an exemption (25:5–10) and a limitation on that exemption (25:11–12).

In "levirate marriage" (Lat.: *levir*, "brother"), the oldest surviving brother of a man who died childless marries the widow and fathers a child in the name of the deceased, preserving his memory and heritage. The practice borders dangerously, however, on incest and, in terms of the Decalogue, "coveting" another's wife. The extreme importance of family lineage and the preservation of estates outweigh these dangers. Death without an heir was so horrendous that it simply must be avoided. With no heir, rights to the deceased's estate would become legally unclear. The text is silent on an equally important benefit of levirate marriage, namely, the widow's status. Technically she would continue as a member of her husband's family, but with no male responsible for caring for her. Deuteronomy understandably disdains a brother who refuses the levirate. His squeamishness or selfishness endangers his brother's memory, estate, and widow. The ritual involving a sandal described here has parallels in nomadic divorce rites.

It is difficult to imagine a woman becoming involved in a fight between her husband and another by grasping the opponent's genitals. The punishment is equally absurd and any possible connection with coveting is puzzling. The solution may involve the phrase "a man and his brother." Literally, this text may warn against understanding the power to defend a deceased husband's memory to extend to such overt aggression. While symbolic attacks may be suitable in some cases, such physical threats to an offender's ability to procreate go beyond the pale. Ironically, her actions could render her brother-in-law unfit to act as a *levir*.

25:13–26:15. No Coveting Another's Property. The final two commandments deal not with objective acts but subjective intentions. Since intentions can only be discerned through the actions they motivate, the explication of the final commandment focuses on acts that arise from "covetousness." It involves cases, first, in which covetousness can motivate one to deceive others (25:13–16) or take advantage of their weakness (25:17–19) and, second, in which the negative prohibition against coveting is converted into positive injunctions of gratitude (26:1–11) and generosity (26:12–15).

The reasoning for the first regulation (vv. 15b–16) follows the statement of the situation (vv. 13–15a). Each of these sections occurs in two sub-units arranged in an ABB'A' structure. A prohibition (negative) against false measures is restated as an injunction (positive) to keep only true measures. The promise that observance of the law will bring long life (positive) precedes a statement of its opposite (negative). Notably, the regulation does not deal with *using* two sets of measures but with *possessing* them. Possession of false measures suggests an intention to use them.

The Bible reports the genesis of Israel's historical animosity toward the Amalekites (Gen 14:7) in the period before Israel came to Mt. Horeb (Exod 17:8–15) when the Amalekites attacked Israel at Rephidim in an opportunistic attempt to gain advantage over a weaker opponent (25:18). Covetousness can motivate aggression.

Deuteronomy 26:1–15 deals with the offerings of first fruits and tithes and focuses not on the procedures for the ritual, but on the confessions of faith to be offered on these occasions. The thrust of the passage, together with the unit that follows, concerns Israel's reaction to God's generosity and recalls the emphases found in Deuteronomy's exposition of the Sabbath law. Israel is to celebrate God's gifts in God's presence (vv. 5, 13). The so-called "historical confession" ("A wandering Aramean was my father...") links salvation history with the agricultural cycle, recalling the fact that the redeemer of the exodus is the Lord of creation. It identifies the Israelite farmer with his patriarchal ancestor, Abraham. Verses 5–10 unfold the history of Yahweh with Israel in simplest terms, recounting Israel's slavery in Egypt (v. 6) and celebrating God's deliverance and guidance on the journey to Canaan (vv. 7–9). The summary consistently refers to its speakers in the first person plural "we" or "us" in another example of Deuteronomy's insistence that the one covenant made with Yahweh applies to Israel in all its generations (cf. vv. 6, 7–8, 15), an insistence underscored by the shift to the individual speaker in the moment of offering the first fruits. In the third declaration accompanying the "poor tithe" (see 14:22–29), the worshiper stresses another aspect of solidarity—not across time with ancestral generations, but across Israelite society with less fortunate Israelites. The worshiper affirms that he has shared God's bounteous gifts with Israel's disenfranchised (v. 13; cf. the commentary on Deut 10:12–19; 14:28–29) and denies that he has been involved in the cult of the dead. The banquet associated with the "poor tithe" may have externally resembled the banquets held annually in honor of the dead (cf. 1 Sam 28:3–25; 2 Sam 18:18; 2 Kgs 21:6; Isa 8:19–20; 28:15, 18; Jer 16:5–8; Amos 6:7; Ps 106:28) forbidden by the Torah (Lev 19:31; Deut 14:1; 18:9–11) have been confused with them. Deuteronomy's transgenerational emphasis must not be mistaken for such idolatry. A petition to Yahweh (v. 15), which includes a request for God's blessing, concludes this section.

A brief, but pregnant, conclusion (vv. 16–19) alludes to the Shema (v. 16; cf. 6:5) and to Moses' instructions dealing with Mt. Ebal (cf. 11:29–30). This text exemplifies the importance of understanding the Deuteronomic Code within the context of the book's overall focus on loyalty to Israel's one God. Further, Deuteronomy continues to insist that there is only one Torah by clearly alluding to the original establishment of Yahweh's covenant with his people (Exod 19–20). The phrases "treasured people" (Exod 19:5; Deut 26:19) and "holy people" (Exod 19:6; Deut 26:19) establish this connection beyond question. The same God who offered a covenant relationship to the ancestors gathered at the foot of Mt. Horeb now offers the same covenant in the same key language to a later generation. As the phrases "this very day" (v. 16) and "today" (vv. 17, 18) intimate, the vitality of this covenant relationship depends, not on the historic relationship, but on present realities. The current generation, and every subsequent one, must maintain the tradition, keeping it fresh and realizing it in the community.

D. Covenant Curses and Blessings (27:1–28:68)

Deuteronomy concludes with a series of units that witness to the covenant: instructions regarding a rite of witness (Deut 27) involving the recitation of covenant blessings and curses (Deut 28), a renewal of the covenant by the second generation (Deut 29–30), Moses' farewell (Deut 31–32), his final blessing (Deut 33), and the account of his death (Deut 34).

These materials focus on the historic transition faced by Israel at the shift from the wilderness to settlement in the land, from Moses' leadership to

Joshua's. The second-generation will confront situations unimagined by its ancestors. Deuteronomy, addressed as a book to even later generations of *readers*, concentrates on the notion that such transitions, which each subsequent generation will face, are times of crisis fraught with danger and ripe with opportunity at the same time. Deuteronomy encourages generations of readers to maintain covenant traditions while adapting and extending them in the face of new challenges.

Moses' third major address deals with rooting Israel's new life in the land by adherence to Torah. Three disproportionate sections, each indicated by an introduction (vv. 1, 9 and 11), constitute a framework (vv. 1–8 and 11–26) of ceremonial instructions surrounding a restatement of the Shema (vv. 9–10). Deuteronomy 27 describes four rituals in a loosely structured composition (reflecting a complicated tradition history?) that emphasizes the importance of ceremonial (re-)affirmation of the covenant at such times of transition.

27:1–10. Stone Memorial and Altar. For the first time in the book, Moses is no longer the sole speaker; now he speaks as one of "Israel's elders" (v. 1) or of the "levitical priests" (v. 9). Moses prepares to transfer authority. The theme of transition is central to the conclusion of the book. Following reminders to "keep all the commandments" (v. 1), Moses and the elders restate (see 11:19–23) instructions to erect monumental stones immediately upon entry into the land (vv. 2, 4) inscribed with "all the words of this Torah" (vv. 3, 8) on Mt. Ebal (v. 4). These stones stand as permanent reminders of the centrality of the Torah to Israel's public life. Covenant is a public matter. A somewhat redundant (cf. vv. 2 and 4 and vv. 3 and 8) addition deals with the parallel erection of an altar of unhewn stones where Israel is to sacrifice in thanksgiving (cf. Deut 14). Stele and altar remind Israel of the public nature of Torah as a gift from God. Finally (vv. 9–10), Moses and the levitical priests, who will assume responsibility after him for interpreting the Torah, call on Israel to hear and obey commandments and the statues explicating them. These statements are directly related to the Shema.

27:11–26. Covenant-Making Rituals. Editors combined elements from instructions concerning two rituals. According to one ancient tradition (vv. 12–13), after Israel has crossed the Jordan,

six tribes each will take positions on Mt. Gerizim and Mt. Ebal to declare the covenant blessings and curses, respectively. According to the other (vv. 14–26), Levi—now not merely one of the twelve tribes, but priests for the entire people—is to lead them in a litany of curses. How can Levi be two places fulfilling two roles simultaneously? Mt. Ebal, the location of the covenant stele and altar, is not suitable as the site for the annunciation of covenant curses. The tension probably arose as the result combining originally independent sources.

The litany of curses is complex. First, it does not, in fact, contain formal curses but instead oaths. They do not so much invoke disaster as elicit the people's assent. God will both ascertain the appropriate consequence and enforce it. The people agree that the offenses listed merit such an outcome and submit themselves to the regime. Second, the list of offenses corresponds largely to the Decalogue so that scholars sometimes refer to it as the "Shechemite Dodecalogue." Third, the structure of the list highlights the first and tenth items—actions done "in secret," although, in fact, virtually none of the actions described in the litany would likely be committed in public. In other words, these oaths assign to Yahweh's direct oversight those crimes that might go unnoticed by the community.

The contents deal with five categories of offense: idolatry (v. 15), four instances of the abuse of power (regarding v. 16, see the commentary on Deut 5; regarding the neighbor's landmark, see the commentary on Deut 19:14), four instances of sexual misconduct (bestiality, v. 21; three varieties of incest, vv. 20—with one's father's wife, 22—with one's sister, either whole or half, and 23—with one's mother-in-law; cf. Lev 18:6–23 and the commentary on Deut 5:18 and 22:13–30), two cases of secret aggression against a fellow Israelite (physical violence, v. 24; conspiracy to commit such violence, v. 25), and a final general curse (v. 26) designed to cover any accidental omission.

The language of the eleventh item deserves comment. It employs a term sometimes erroneously translated "soul" (cf. NRSV, "person"). Clearly, Deut 27:25 cannot refer to an instance in which someone accepts money to smite another Israelite's eternal soul. Instead, in the Hebrew conception, a human being is a psychosomatic whole, a person.

28:1–68. Covenant Blessings and Curses. To underscore the covenantal character of Yahweh's relationship with Israel and particularly the role of Deuteronomy as an adumbration of the covenant's terms, the editors of the book add to the Deuteronomic Code a collection of blessings and curses similar to those found at the end of ancient Near Eastern vassal treaties—similar, but not identical, since, strictly speaking, only vv. 28–33 and 38–42 are true "curses" and only vv. 3–6 and 16–19 true "blessings." With curse and related materials outnumbering blessing and related materials three to one, this section—dealing with virtually every area of life from nature to international relations, and calling for the most horrendous outcomes—clearly emphasizes the costs to Israel should it forsake its covenant. The composition possesses an intricate, almost baroque, structure. It is divided between blessings (vv. 1–14) and curses (vv. 15–68), with frameworks delineating the two major sections (cf. vv. 1–12 and v. 13 and vv. 4 and 11 surrounding the blessings), although these designations do not include vv. 47–68 of the curses (cf. vv. 15 and 45–46 framing the curses) suggesting that they may be later insertions in the composition. A series of sometimes parallel, sometimes chiastic citations and allusions across the two major sections up to v. 46 (cf. vv. 1–2 with 15, 3–6 with 16–19, 7 with 25, 8 with 20–21, 9–11 with 36–37, and 12–13 with 43–46) complements the framework, sets the curses and blessings in an inverse relationship and confirms suspicions regarding the secondary character of vv. 47–68. Three sections within vv. 15–46 have no parallels to the blessings and, consequently, may also be secondary.

The blessings (28:1–14) contain four familiar themes: (1) the charge to heed Yahweh and do his commandments, (2) the promise that, in view of such obedience, Yahweh will elevate Israel on the world stage (cf. vv. 9–13*a*), (3) the admonition against straying either "to the right or to the left," and (4) the excoriation of idolatry. The blessings offer something new, however, Yahweh's offer of *bounty* and *security.* Verses 3–6 seem to be a coherent, probably liturgical, collection of blessings that probably predated the larger composition; it may have been the seed that gave rise to the larger unit. Their offer of bounty in every aspect of agrarian life resurfaces in the more general promise of v. 8. Yahweh also promises Israel *secu-rity* against attack. The promise of international prominence differs in perspective. This Israel does not reside at home, secure from attack, but steps onto the international stage as the aggressor. Its enemies will fear. Israel's bounty will be the envy of the world and the source of the capital that will permit it to lend without borrowing (v. 12).

The covenant curses (28:15–46) appear as inversions of the blessing (cf., e.g., vv. 3–6 and 16–19). The themes of bounty, security, and prominence are both inverted and reordered. The "Yahweh will smite" sayings and the futility curses interrupt this structure and take up novel themes, "madness" and "pestilence," suggesting that they represent editorial insertions in their current context.

Whereas the blessings promise bounty, the curses threaten that infidelity will bring natural disasters that will turn bounty into deprivation, ultimately resulting in Israel's demise (vv. 20, 21, 22, 24). Illnesses, weather disasters, and plant diseases (v. 22) will ensue. While obedience motivates Yahweh to open his "storehouse" (v. 12), infidelity moves him to withhold the rains. In a striking metaphor, he will turn the heavens to bronze so that the earth below will become iron (v. 23). Obedience brings Israel security; infidelity subjects Israel to the fate that should pertain to its enemies. Israel will flee in chaos; Israelites will die in battle to be left unburied on the battlefield (cf. 21:22–23).

Verse 27 begins a series of interruptions and displacements. First, it introduces material that does not mirror, as expected, the "prominence" theme, but deals instead with "pestilence," specifically various skin ailments and lesions that will befall disobedient Israel. Second, it stands apart from vv. 28–34, which deal, instead, with "madness." The motif of "pestilence" reappears only in vv. 35–42, which may have been the original context for v. 27. Disregarding v. 27, vv. 28–34 represent a coherent and cohesive exposition of the madness that will come upon unfaithful Israel. Blind and bewildered, confused and disoriented, Israel will become easy prey for its enemies (v. 29). A sequence of futility curses depicts circumstances certain to bring madness (v. 34). A range of apparent blessings become void before Israel's eyes—brides will be raped; houses and vineyards abandoned.

Verse 27 departs from the "madness" theme, but fits well in the discussion of physical destruction and deterioration in vv. 35–42. In contrast, vv. 36–37 seem to belong better with vv. 43–44. The verses depicting "madness" reflect situations involving human agents that cause Israel's suffering, those recounting "pestilence" materials deal with natural pests and decay. "Yahweh will smite" sayings are coupled with futility curses describing hope disappointed by decay and destruction.

The counterpart to vv. 12*b*–13*a* also views Israel's fate in local terms whereas the interpolation in vv. 36–37 takes a much grander view. Israel becomes the victim of an aggressively expansionistic world empire. This interpolation succinctly anticipates the Babylonian crisis, employing key features of the dominant theology of the Babylonian period (sixth-century BCE): Israel's kings will have misled their people; Israel's infidelity will result in exile where Israel will be compelled to worship strange gods; Israel will be scattered among the nations. Disobedience will threaten Israel's national survival.

A reprise of v. 15 in v. 45 is coupled with the statement that the covenant curses will function forever as a "sign" for Israel. This statement participates in the overall structural scheme for Deut 27–34. Deuteronomy describes each of the institutions and offices discussed in this section in turn as "signs," "testimonies," or "witnesses" to the nature and purpose of God's covenant. Moses will cease to lead God's people, but they will not be left without guides: Joshua and his successors, the Song of Moses, the memorial stones on Gerizim and Ebal, the tablets of the covenant. The people cannot plead ignorance of the covenant.

Nothing of the intricate structure that shapes vv. 1–46 continues into vv. 47–68. Whereas the topics of vv. 1–46 are natural phenomena and Israel's fate among its neighbors, vv. 27–68 describe very specifically the fates of a nation besieged and exiled (cf. the allusions to bondage in vv. 60, 68) The tone becomes much more acrid, threatening not correction but annihilation. Notably, the mood shifts from the conditionals of curses and blessings to a narrative unmistakably mirroring the crises when the Assyrian and Babylonian armies attacked Israel in the eighth and sixth centuries, respectively. Finally, vv. 47–68 seem to be aware of Deuteronomy as a book (vv. 58, 61), suggesting

that an earlier form of the book already existed when this interpolation was added. These observations strongly suggest that vv. 47–68 constitute an expansion to the curses material intended to draw the connection between the warnings voiced in vv. 16–46 and the horrors Israel/Judah actually experienced at, especially, the hands of Babylon.

While vv. 1–46 follow a thematic arrangement, vv. 47–57 narrate, in great and graphic detail, a linear plot: (1) Ungrateful (instead of the expected disobedient) Israel fails to serve Yahweh wholeheartedly so that God hands them over to an enemy (vv. 47–48). (2) This enemy (described much as sixth-century authors described Babylon; cf. Jer 4:13; 5:15) comes from far away, swooping like an eagle, speaking a foreign language, and showing no compassion (vv. 49–50). (3) The enemy will burn, pillage, and destroy without restraint (vv. 51–52). (d) Israel's reaction will be even more horrendous than the invader's tactics. Under siege, the nobility will be reduced to cannibalism, eating their own children and refusing to share the flesh (vv. 53–57; cf. 2 Kgs 6:24–32 and Lam 2:20; 4:10).

The final section (vv. 58–68) offers theological commentary on the preceding materials and introduces the topic of exile (vv. 64–68). A number of features suggest that it represents the final stage in the literary growth of Deut 28: (a) The commentary seems to have in view the *book* of Deuteronomy, which it describes as "this book of the Torah" (v. 61). (b) Similarly, the reference to the patriarchs seems to reflect knowledge of the written patriarchal tradition. (c) It seems to assume that its readers are already in the land (v. 63).

The memory of Egyptian bondage hovers over both of the two sub-sections of the unit (vv. 58–62, the contents of the book of the Torah; vv. 58–63, exile). The first subsection admonishes Israel to observe the provisions *in the book* lest God bring upon them every calamity described, and even some "not recorded in this book" (v. 61), resulting in total destruction. The book is the key to Israel's survival. The text then turns to a renewed description of exile. Methodically, it describes the experience of banishment from the land, of dispersal among the nations, of coerced idolatry, and, ultimately, of despair. Disobedience will, in essence, result in a return to slavery from which there will be no redemption, because Israel will have chosen this course.

III. Moses' Third Speech: Succession and Farewell (29:1–34:12)

Deuteronomy 29:1 may introduce Moses' third major speech or conclude Deut 4:1–28:68. Regardless of one's judgment about this issue, the material in this section depicts a Moab covenant, distinct from the Horeb covenant. The notion of a covenant made in Moab is complicated for two reasons: first, Deuteronomy has consistently maintained the exclusivity of the Horeb covenant (see 4:10–14), and second, Deut 29–32 contains a collection focused around the theme of decision in transition, not a covenant. Its three subsections (Deut 29–30, a covenant sermon; Deut 31, Moses' parting address and the transfer of leadership; and Deut 32, the "Song of Moses") summarize and reprise the great Deuteronomic ideas.

A. Covenant Renewal in Moab (29:1–30:20)

The reference to a covenant ceremony stands alone, serving a solely homiletical purpose, calling upon Israel to choose life! Even its structure points to its homiletical nature: It discusses the covenant *past* (29:2–8), *present* (29:9–15), and *future* (29:16–29; 30:1–10) as the motivation for a *call to decision* (30:11–20).

The retrospective (*past*) briefly recalls events discussed earlier (to v. 2 cf. 4:34; 7:19–20; 10:21–22; etc.; to v. 3 cf. 4:34; 7:19; etc.). Such retrospectives, which characterize Deuteronomistic literature (e.g., Josh 24:1–13), rehearse the basis for Israel's confidence in Yahweh's gracious favor. The long history of Yahweh's benevolence contrasts with Israel's historical failure to understand (v. 3 [4]).

The text shifts to the narrative *present* (cf. v. 8 [9]), reprising a number of themes: obedience and prosperity (v. 9), the all-Israel character of the covenant (vv. 10–11, 14–15), and the "voluntary" nature of Israel's participation in the covenant relationship (v. 12). The dialectic implicit in vv. 12–13 expresses a key biblical polarity: the legal, contractual nature of covenant and the free, unmerited nature of promise (see above on 7:6–16).

The discussion turns from present to *future*, promise to pessimism. It assumes that Israel will inevitably stray from the covenant. Alternatively, this section may constitute an editorial on Israel's actual history of unfaithfulness. Regardless, two cases of disloyalty form the focus: secret individual or group disloyalty (vv. 16–21) and national apostasy (vv. 22–29). As early as the wilderness, Israel became familiar with "detestable things," idols of wood and stone, gold and silver (vv. 16–17). Even an individual or a small group attracted to worship these idols can poison the entire nation (v. 18). Should such apostasy occur, the text warns, Yahweh will take severe action. It violates the very foundation of Israel's relationship with Yahweh—Yahweh's absolute claim to Israel's devotion. Infidelity will invoke "every curse recorded in this book" (v. 20).

The second subsection contemplates the reaction of post-catastrophe generations (and foreigners) to the total destruction of the land as the result of such apostasy. The tone reflects either an assumption that Israel will inevitably fail or historical knowledge that Israel has, in fact, failed. The result will be or has been a desolate land and an exiled people. In the future (from Moses' perspective), Israel will lie smitten, unproductive, like Sodom and Gomorrah, devastated. In response to the question, "Why?" passers-by will formulate Deuteronomic/Deuteronomstic theology: This desolation occurred "because they abandoned the covenant of Yahweh, ... they followed after and served other gods ... and Yahweh's anger burned against this land.... Yahweh sent them away from their land" (vv. 25–27). The proverbial conclusion unites the sub-sections: private apostasy cannot be hidden from Yahweh; it will eventually have public ramifications.

Deuteronomy does not grant finality to the assumption that Israel will inevitably stray and suffer Yahweh's displeasure. Even beyond that future horror, it argues, will lie a future restoration. One day, exiled Israel will "return to [its] heart" (v. 1), initiating a process of return and restoration. Links to earlier sections demonstrate such events will constitute Israel's return to life in covenant with Yahweh (e.g., citations of the Shema in vv. 2, 6, 10) including return from exile (v. 5). The word-play manifest in vv. 1–10 on the Hebrew word that can be translated "to repent," "to return" or "to restore" is theologically significant. When Israel *repents*, Israel can *return* because Yahweh will *restore*. At the core of the term is the image of turning around. In the Hebrew Bible/Old Testament, repentance is not an emotion or a feeling (i.e., "regret") but an action, a change of direction: Israel will one day "return to its senses" (v. 1), choosing to direct its step solely toward Yahweh and according to his will (vv. 2, 8, 20); in response, Yahweh will reassert his intention to bless Israel (vv. 3, 9). At the very center of this discussion of repentance (v. 6), one finds a fundamental question. Why must Israel repent? Why has Israel so long been stiff-necked and rebellious? Deuteronomy asserts that something has been amiss with Israel's "heart," its organ of decision and volition. The problem has not been ignorance; Israel knows the Decalogue, the revealed will of God. The problem has not been capability; Yahweh's principles for living are not beyond humanity's abilities. No, the problem seems to have been intention, desire, volition. Israel knew what was right; Israel could easily have done what was right; Israel did not *want* to do right, however. The solution? Yahweh will "circumcise" Israel's heart, enabling repentance and return.

Like all good sermons, this unit concludes with a *call to decision*. The options have been laid before the reader. In a final effort to anticipate possible objections, vv. 11–14 make two significant claims: first, the covenant does not make impossible demands and, second, God's expectations are not mysterious. Christian theology, emphasizing the universality of human sin, is sometimes uncomfortable with Deuteronomy's claim that keeping the covenant is not that difficult. One stream of Christian theology has even suggested that human beings, after the Fall, are so depraved that doing right is impossible. Deuteronomy argues, rather, that human beings are *capable*, but *unwilling* to do right. Further, the basic principles of life in relationship with Yahweh have been clearly announced and carefully explained. God, in God's grandeur, may be mysterious, but God's will for humankind is, or should be, "on your lips and in your heart" (v. 14).

Deuteronomy has presented ancient Israel and all subsequent readers with a choice. They can choose faithful relationship and life or infidelity and, cut off from the source of life, death. The most profound matters are often that simple.

B. Moses' Successors (31:1–32:47)

Deuteronomy turns attention to pragmatic concerns at this moment of transition, in particular, to questions surrounding Moses' departure. Stylistic features (e.g., first person divine speech) of this section reveal its complex compositional history (repetitions such as vv. 6–7 and 23 and discontinuities such as those between vv. 15–16 and 22–23; etc.). The narrative recounts and interprets events from Israel's distant past, continuing the account broken off in 3:23–29. Together with Deut 1–3, this material forms the framework to the book, probably representing the last stage in its growth and integrating Deuteronomy into the "Deuteronomistic History."

The structure of the narrative highlights the ways in which Israel can think about a time after the death of Moses: Joshua will succeed Moses (vv. 1–8, 14–15 and 23), the Torah scroll will bear witness to the covenant with Yahweh (vv. 9–13, 24–29), and the Song of Moses will bear witness to Moses' wisdom long after his parting (vv. 16–22). The resulting structure (ABACAB) calls attention to the interrelationship of these three "successors" to Moses.

31:1–8. Joshua. Ancient manuscripts offer conflicting testimony about whether this unit continues the speech recorded in Deut 29–30 or marks the beginning of a new one. In either case, its substance revolves around Moses' health (v. 2) and the fact that he will not enter the promised land. How can they go on without Moses, their only leader, the covenant-bringer, an intimate companion of God? First, even during Moses' lifetime, Israel's true guide was Yahweh. This relationship will neither end nor alter. Second, in principle, Moses has been Yahweh's spokesman. Joshua and others after him will now fill that role.

31:9–13. The Torah Scroll. The biblical texts that discuss Joshua's commission imply one difference between Moses and Joshua, however. None mention that Joshua will succeed Moses as the chief interpreter of the covenant. Instead, he is to be Israel's military leader. After Moses, it seems, "this Torah," Deuteronomy, the record of Moses' principles of Torah interpretation, will be the foundation for Israel's tradition of Torah interpretation. While priests will bear particular responsibility for studying and applying the principles in "this Torah," it will, nonetheless, be the heritage of all

Israel, to whom it will be publicly read on a seven-year cycle. Moses insists that the study of the Torah results in obedience. All future generations of Israel must take great care that knowledge of the Torah be perpetuated.

31:14–22. Moses' Song. In this second sequence, Yahweh addresses Moses directly concerning the urgency of this transition (v. 14). The mood is unprecedented in Deuteronomy. This is the only reference to the tent of meeting in the book. Here only does God appear in the book. Moses' death is near; God is present; leader and successor stand in the divine presence. The stage is set.

Yahweh interrupts the commissioning of Moses to compose a song (vv. 16–18). Every indicator marks vv. 16–21 as an insertion. It interrupts; it describes the Song in terms usually reserved for the Torah (to vv. 19, 21–22; cf., e.g., 4:1, 5, 10, 14; 5:31; 27:3, 8; 30:14); the sequence of events remains unclear; the Song, itself, will appear only later. Nonetheless, the rhetorical purpose of the Song is clear (vv. 19–22). It calls attention to the fact that, like Joshua, Moses' personal successor, and the Torah scroll, Moses' authoritative principles of interpretation, the Song will bear witness to the covenant's central claim: Israel's fidelity is to Yahweh alone.

31:23. Joshua. Verse 23 offers the content of Yahweh's commission stated in vv. 14–15. Yahweh's statement repeats vv. 7–8. Now, however, Yahweh does not speak through Moses, but directly to Moses' successor.

31:24–29. The Torah Scroll. The sequence of events has become wholly confused. Has Moses already written the Torah (v. 9) or does he do so now (v. 24)? Because Moses expects Israel to rebel soon and severely, he accentuates the roles of the Ark of the Covenant, the Torah, and the Song as "witnesses" against them in that rebellious future. The Torah scroll, bearing the commandments and Moses' model for interpreting them, will leave them without excuse. Invoking even heaven and earth to witness his admonitions, Moses offers the Torah as the instrument for interpreting not only God's will but Israel's history.

31:30–32:47. Moses' Song. One of the most intriguing passages in the Bible, it is redundant (vv. 48–52; 44–47) in its context. It exhibits affinities with non-Deuteronomic material (cf.

Num 20:1–13 and 27:12–14); ancient manuscripts offer significantly different readings; its language intermixes archaic and late biblical Hebrew, first and third person speech, and an array of theological stances—all with parallels in several similar didactic Psalms (esp. 78 and 82); references to Israel's history entice historians, but are vague enough ultimately to frustrate attempts to clearly identify places and times (e.g., the unnamed enemy). Nevertheless, this Song transforms the book of Deuteronomy into a key for understanding Israel's history.

The Song functions on many levels: as Moses' address to the people (31:30), as a witness to the covenant (32:1), as Moses' teaching (32:2), and as a summons to praise (32:3). This interplay of law, instruction, and praise is pregnant theologically. It reminds readers of the instructional purpose of the law and of the ultimate objective of both law and instruction, namely, life lived in worship of God.

The Song's basic thesis is that, despite Yahweh's fidelity, Yahweh's people repeatedly and ineluctably break faith. It begins as a hymn in praise of "the Rock," a relatively common epithet (1 Sam 2:2; Isa 17:10; Hab 1:12; Ps 19:15[14 Eng]) accentuating God's constancy and reliability. "The Rock" always acts with integrity, justly, and without caprice. These statements focus on observable behaviors. Yahweh has been and ever will be faithful in relationship to his people. Israel, on the other hand, behaves corruptly; with twisted, blemished motives, it is altogether unreliable (v. 5). Israel breaks faith with a parent (v. 6) whose love and loyalty are rock firm.

Rather than merely assert Yahweh's loyalty, the Song documents it: in Israel's election (vv. 8–9), during the wilderness period (vv. 10–12) and in the upcoming fulfillment of the promise of the land (vv. 13–14). Indeed, God's fidelity has roots before history when "God Most High" chose not to assign Israel to any of his assistants (v. 8–9). God's fidelity reaches back to the beginning of their national existence when Yahweh discovered them in the harsh desert (cf. Hos 2:16–17 [14–15 Eng]; Jer 2:2–3; Ezek 16) and guarded them as a most cherished possession. God taught fledgling Israel to fly, always vigilant to guide and protect (v. 11). Finally, Yahweh's provision and protection manifest themselves in the rich abundance of the promised land. Yahweh's steadfastness is sure.

Israel did not respond to Yahweh's provision with gratitude and obedience, but with arrogance and a sense of entitlement. Israel should remember Yahweh's deliverance from Egyptian bondage, Yahweh's guidance and provision in the wilderness, Yahweh's gracious gift of the land. Yet, prosperity will obscure their memory. The Song compares this unfathomable behavior to that of a wild animal (v. 15). "Jeshurun" is an infrequent term for Israel with obscure roots (v. 15; see also Isa 1:3). The final form of the Song represents the awareness that the book actually addresses generations of readers. An aside abandons narrative to confront directly these readers who "grew fat" and rebelled. Of course, Israel's ingratitude expressed itself as idolatry. Israel turned to novelties, turning its back on Yahweh. To emphasize adequately the horror of Israel's behavior, the Song likens it to that of an ungrateful child who neglects his or her parent. "The Rock" (Yahweh) has been steadfast, Israel has wavered like a spoiled child. The final verse comes very close to applying maternal imagery to Yahweh. Significantly, "father" is a theological metaphor; this text, at least, suggests that God also behaves toward his children as does a "mother."

"Yahweh saw" all this apostasy and was moved to turn away, hiding his face, allowing Israel to experience what it seems to want—life apart from Yahweh's provision and protection. Exposed, Israel will experience the full force of Yahweh's absence: no rain, famine, illness, infestation of vermin. The whole cosmos will suffer (v. 22) and Israelite society will collapse (v. 25).

Yahweh's deliberations take a new turn (v. 26). Thinking beyond just what Israel deserves, Yahweh anticipates that Israel's enemy will likely have no greater understanding (v. 28) than does Israel, and may misinterpret events as evidence that Yahweh was impotent to provide for his people. The enemy's arrogance, moreover, suggests a comparison with Sodom and Gomorrah!

How can Yahweh's profound love for Israel, Israel's ingratitude, and the arrogance of Israel's enemies be reconciled in the course of human history? Yahweh announces in vv. 34–35 that he will mete out "vengeance" and "repayment"

when the time is right. But upon whom? Israel or its equally deserving enemy? One might expect Israel to be the target, but situated immediately following vv. 26–33, which turn attention to Israel's enemy, the likeliest interpretation is that Yahweh will not allow the enemy's arrogant assumption that Yahweh is powerless to go unchecked. Indeed, the opposite is true; the enemy was only able to prevail over Israel because Yahweh allowed it! Yahweh will indeed "vindicate" Israel—but not before visiting upon it the consequences of its apostasy.

The ambiguity that continues to surface (vv. 37–38, 41–42) concerning the identity of Yahweh's "adversaries" (v. 41) accentuates the overall theme of Yahweh's lordship over human history. Yahweh holds both Israel and the foreign nations accountable. Any nation can become Yahweh's enemy by failing or refusing to recognize his exclusive sovereignty over human history (vv. 39b–42). Yahweh "will repay those who hate [him]," whether the haters be Israel or Babylon! The ambiguity concerning the targets of Yahweh's anger that runs throughout the second half of the Song is integral to the message of the Song. Who are these enemies of Yahweh? Everyone is a candidate.

The manuscript evidence for the text of v. 43 suggests a complicated historical problem. The likely earliest reading found in a Qumran manuscript and supported by the Septuagint, depicts Yahweh at the head of the heavenly council whose members bear responsibility for guiding the affairs of the nations. Again, the underlying theological assumption is that Yahweh cannot rule the world as though Israel, his chosen, alone can claim Yahweh's justice. Yahweh cannot favor Israel *to the disadvantage* of the other nations of the world. Indeed, Israel's role in human history is that of mediator (cf. Gen 12:1–3).

At last, the Song, and with it the Torah, come to an end (32:44–47). The conclusion returns to narrative. Moses and Joshua conclude the public reading of the Song and admonish the audience to consider it and to obey the Torah, therein lay life and prosperity (v. 47). Joshua appears as "Hoshea" here (cf. Num 13:8, 16; 32:44).

C. Moses' Death (32:48–34:12).

32:48–52. Predicted. Yahweh informs Moses of certain details concerning his impending death. Moses is to ascend Mt. Nebo where he will die, just as Aaron had died atop Mt. Hor (Num 33:38–39) and for the same reason (cf. Num 20:1–13). From the vantage point of Mt. Nebo, Moses will be permitted to survey the promised land, but not to enter it. The material is repetitive, but significant because of its affinities with Priestly perspectives on Moses death (cf. Num 27:12–14).

33:1–29. Moses' Farewell Blessing. Moses' final address contains his blessings for the individual tribes (cf. Gen 27:27–29, 39–40; 49:1–28); in effect, the whole book represents Moses' parting words to Israel. Together with Moses' Song, these blessings replicate Deuteronomy's blessing and curse pattern. The framework surrounding the Deuteronomic Code subsumes the law code into a larger context of teaching, admonition, promise, and warning.

Much suggests that Moses' blessings derive from a period late in the book's growth: historical references reflect the monarchial period; it has a psalmic framework (vv. 2–5, 26–29); Moses is spoken of in the third person; and the theology and diction are uncharacteristic of Deuteronomy ("man of God," v. 1; Sinai, v. 2; Jeshurun, v. 5; etc.). The blessings mirror particular moments in Israel's history. Further, many of the tribes addressed had already virtually ceased to exist well before the exile. The psalmic framework, finally, recontextualizes these blessings, and the whole composition has been further recontextualized: the law code concludes with a psalm of praise!

Deuteronomy 33:1 offers no narrative setting. Yahweh "shines forth" from Mount Paran "with myriads of holy ones at his right hand." The Hebrew is replete with obscurities, translation difficulties, and interpretive challenges. The unexpected, but not unique reference to Sinai, Seir, and Paran (see Exod 15:15; Judg 5:4–5; Hab 3:3; Ps 68:8) reflects ancient traditions. Who are the "holy ones"? Israel as in v. 3 or the heavenly hosts as in Num 10:36; Ps 3:6; Dan 11:12? Who are "the peoples" whom Yahweh loves? Israel's tribes (vv. 2, 3; cf. v. 5) or the nations of the world? The psalm concludes with a clause that celebrates Yahweh's rule over his people (cf. v. 26).

In contrast with Jacob's blessings (Gen 49), Moses' blessings generally focus on some undertaking of the tribe instead of a salient characteristic. Hence, they sometimes provide tantalizing data for the task of historical reconstruction.

Moses' blessing for *Reuben* exemplifies the contrast between Deut 32 and Gen 49. Jacob condemned his first born for the Bilhah incident (Gen 35:22). Moses offers a limited pardon. Reuben will survive, at least. Similarly, whereas Jacob emphasized *Judah*'s role as leader, Moses prays for Yahweh's assistance against Judah's enemies, which may reflect hopes for the restoration of the united monarchy ("one people," v. 5). The contrast between Jacob's and Moses' blessings for *Levi* could hardly be sharper. Jacob refers to the dangerous revenge taken against Shechem (Gen 34) when he foretells the dispersal of Levi (and *Simeon*—Moses' blessing omits Simeon altogether). Moses views this scattering as a function of Levi's priestly role and relates Levi's reputation for revenge to the annihilation of idolaters after the golden calf affair (Exod 32:26–29). Again, Moses' blessing for *Benjamin* contrasts sharply with Jacob's focus on his son's "ravenous" appetite. Moses echoes the status of Benjamin's eponymous ancestor as his father's favorite, depicting the tribe as dwelling "between his hills/shoulders." The most direct blessing goes to *Joseph* who will know agricultural bounty, military success, and political supremacy (v. 16, the northern kingdom, also known as Ephraim). *Zebulon* and *Issachar* commonly appear together. In the far northwest, they faced significant challenges. Zebulunites, neighbors of the Phoenicians, alone among Israel's tribes, went to sea while Issacharites (note the etymology of the name, Gen 30:14–18) were hired laborers. The thrust of Moses' blessing, however, deals with the sanctuary the two tribes shared in the north (v. 19; perhaps Mt. Tabor, see Hos 5:1). Given Deuteronomy's insistence on cultic centralization, this affirmation ("right sacrifices") surprises, as does the statement that this sanctuary will attract worshipers from the nations. *Gad*'s territory in the Transjordan was the object of territorial wars throughout Israel's national existence. Syria, Ammon, Israel, and, sometimes, Judah all claimed the territory (see Judg 3:12–14; 1 Sam 11:1–11; Amos 1:3). *Dan* set out from its original home between Judah and Ephraim for more space, capturing Laish near Mt. Hermon (Josh 19:40–48;

Judg 18:1–31). Moses' blessing involves a play on words with the meaning of *Laish*, "lion." Dan is a lion's whelp. Moses affirms *Naphtali's* expansion from south of Hermon toward the Sea of Galilee as Yahweh's blessing. Although *Asher* held prime agricultural land, it was also situated along a path often traveled by campaigning armies. Its name may be etymologically related to words for "blessed/fortunate" or for "foot." Moses' blessing plays on all these circumstances: blessed, foot, (olive) oil, with bars of iron as protection against invading armies.

A psalm (33:26–29) completes the poetic frame. Israel's God is incomparable. Israel is incomparably blessed (*asher*) with protection and bounty.

34:1–12. Moses' Death. Deuteronomy ends enigmatically, combining Deuteronomic tradition (cf. 34:1b–6 and 31:23–29) with material (vv. 7–9) akin to the "Priestly" tradition (cf. Num 27:18), juxtaposing the two major traditions concerning Moses prohibition from entering the promised land with a unique tradition defending Moses' reputation (vv. 10–11).

Atop Mt. Nebo, Moses commanded a view of the promised land, according to the text, thereby at least symbolically taking possession of the land. Still, he was not permitted to enter. As important as Moses may have been, not even he, accompanied Israel to its final destination. Moses' life is complete, but the story of Yahweh's relationship with Israel is not. When Moses had earlier ascended a mountain and did not return quickly, the insecure people resorted to idolatry. What will they do now that Moses will never return?

Deuteronomy first reports Moses' death (120 years old, still strong and healthy, v. 7; but contrast 31:1–8). He was not sick and had not been injured. He had simply completed his task. Israel mourned his passing for the extraordinary period of a month (v. 8) before Joshua took the reins of leadership (v. 9). The foundation for Israel's future had been firmly established. Now, a new generation with a new leader would face new challenges of life in the promised land.

Always, however, Deuteronomy bears witness to the covenant, to a tradition of covenantal interpretation, to covenant blessings and curses, and to the call to choose life over death. An editor concluded Deuteronomy with an evaluation of Moses' unique stature. As prophet, friend of God, and mediator of Yahweh's power, Moses was absolutely unparalleled (vv. 10–12).

BIBLIOGRAPHY

M. Biddle. *Deuteronomy.* Smyth & Helwys Bible Commentary 4 (Macon: Smyth & Helwys, 2003); W. Brueggemann. *Deuteronomy.* AOTC (Nashville: Abingdon, 2001); I. Cairns. *Word and Presence: A Commentary on the Book of Deuteronomy.* ITC (Grand Rapids: Eerdmans, 1992); D. Christensen. *Deuteronomy 1–11.* WBC 6A (Dallas: Word, 1991); S. Kaufman. "The Structure of the Deuteronomic Law." *Maarav* 1/2 (1979) 105–58; A. D. H. Mayes. *Deuteronomy.* NCBC (Grand Rapids: Eerdmans, 1979); J. G. McConville. *Law and Theology in Deuteronomy.* JSOTSup 33 (Sheffield: JSOT Press, 1984); R. D. Nelson. *Deuteronomy: A Commentary.* OTL (Louisville: Westminster John Knox, 2002); D. Olson. *Deuteronomy and the Death of Moses: A Theological Reading.* OBT (Minneapolis: Fortress, 1994); J. Tigay. *Deuteronomy.* JPS Torah Commentary 5 (Philadelphia: Jewish Publication Society, 1996); G. von Rad. *Deuteronomy: A Commentary.* OTL (Philadelphia: Westminster, 1966); M. Weinfeld. *Deuteronomy and the Deuteronomic School* (Oxford: Clarendon, 1972).

JOSHUA

Richard Hess

OVERVIEW

The book of Joshua is named for its dominant human character. The name Joshua derives from the Hebrew root "to save" (Heb.: *yasha'*). The figure of Joshua first appears in Exod 17, where he leads the Israelites in their battle against the Amalekites. Joshua is Moses' assistant and qualified to assume the role of his successor. From the perspective of plot, the book moves Israel from its wilderness wanderings to its victories in Canaan and its allotment of that land.

From the perspective of textual criticism, the Masoretic Text and the Septuagint texts of these books have several important differences. Chief among these are the different positions of the Mount Ebal altar account. In the MT it appears in Josh 8:30–35, while in the LXX it occurs at the beginning of ch. 5. The Qumran evidence, chiefly 4QJos[a] and 4QJos[b], share the position of the altar story with the LXX. 4QJos[a] adds an additional and otherwise unattested paragraph after the altar account and before Josh 5:2. The MT and LXX also differ in many details of the place names in chs. 13–21. For example, after Josh 15:59, there is an additional district (that includes Bethlehem) in the LXX not present in the Judean districts of the MT. The LXX has a note after Josh 21:42 that does not appear in the MT. In Josh 24:29-31, the sequence of the leader's death and the note concerning Israel's faithfulness appear in different order in the two versions, with the LXX following the order of Judg 2:6-9. While recognizing the importance of the LXX, the MT text will be used throughout this commentary.

Given the close similarity in language and theology with Deuteronomy, this book has sometimes been understood as a seventh-century BCE composition that Josiah created in order to justify his plans for the expansion of the Judean kingdom. Some scholars have spoken of the first six books of the Hebrew Bible as a Hexateuch that existed as a single unit until the danger of such a propagandistic book as Joshua in the period of the Persian Empire (with its emphasis on the divine gift of land on both sides of the Jordan River that included much more territory than the small province of Yehud) caused it to be separated from the Pentateuch and hidden or at least de-emphasized. The book forms a part of what has been termed the Deuteronomistic History; i.e., the narrative sections of Deuteronomy followed by Joshua, Judges, 1 and 2 Samuel, and 1 and 2 Kings.

Despite clear linguistic indications that the final edition of Joshua dates to the late Monarchy, there are hints in the text of greater antiquity than the seventh century BCE. Among these, the following may be noted. The descriptions of the borders of Canaan match those of Egypt's New Kingdom Empire in the second millennium BCE, but do not occur later. The Hivites, the Perizzites, and the Girgashites of Josh 3:10 have all been identified with proper names or elements of such names found in second millennium BCE extrabiblical texts, but which do not appear in later periods. Specifics surrounding the stories of Rahab (a woman managing an inn on the city wall), Jericho (the divinely caused collapse of the walls), and Achan (the wedge [literally "tongue"] of gold) all have parallels found in Hittite and Babylonian texts of the second millennium BCE, but not later. The names of the Canaanite and Amorite kings in Josh 10 and 11 (as well as the name Rahab), and of the sons of the Anakim (Josh 15:14) all have their closest parallels with personal names of the second millennium BCE but not later. Some of these, such as Piram, Sheshai, and Talmai, seem to be Hurrian; a language and culture for which there is no evidence after the tenth century BCE.

Modern literary methods have appreciated the tensions within the text at numerous places, e.g., the apparently repeated crossings of the Jordan River in Josh 3–4 and the observations that all the land was subdued versus the lists of unconquered territories and cities in Josh 13–21. Comparative approaches have noted the similarity between the book as a whole and early West Semitic land grants. Indeed, one grant of the city of Alalakh is particularly important. This city is located north of ancient Israel, near to the New Testament site of Antioch. It shared Israel's West Semitic language background and culture. The cuneiform tablet discovered there dates from the early second millennium BCE. It parallels the book of Joshua with a history of a war necessary to acquire the territory, a list of towns so obtained, and a covenant-making ceremony that formally ratifies the gift from the greater king to his vassal in exchange for the exclusive loyalty of the vassal. This same pattern occurs in the book of Joshua. Chapters 1–12 describe the war that resulted in the acquisition of the land. It constituted a battle led by "the greater king," in this case the God of Israel. There follow town lists and boundary descriptions that define the gift of the land and the places in it. This material appears in chs. 13–21 of Joshua. Finally, there is the covenant renewal in which the people pledge their exclusive loyalty to God and, in return, they receive the land as a gift for that loyalty. This occurs clearly in Josh 24, but is anticipated in Josh 8:30–35 and in chs. 22 and 23.

Theological emphases in the book include the importance of obedience to God's instructions, the danger of division and loss of unity, the gift of the land as God's covenant blessing to the people of Israel, and God's holiness that will allow for no compromise. Probably the chief theological issue in the text of Joshua is the question as to how a loving God could command Israel to commit genocide against the people of Canaan. While part of this problem concerns texts outside of Joshua, such as Deut 20, a few observations should be made here regarding what the text actually says as opposed to what is often assumed. Israel does indeed attack Jericho and Ai. The absence of archaeological evidence for Canaanite occupation of these sites is well known. However, this absence may also suggest that these sites were not civilian population centers but rather military forts, perhaps constructed in part from pre-existing walls. This may explain why nowhere in the text are specific noncombatants mentioned aside from Rahab and her family. Indeed, the lists of slain in Josh 6:21 and 8:25 may be stereotypic rather than intended to specify particular groups such as non-combatants. Beyond this, the remaining wars of Israel in Josh 9 and 10 are defensive. In both cases, either Israel or its ally is attacked and Israel must defend itself to survive. Even in the sequence of attacks on the various Canaanite cities in these chapters, it is important to keep in mind that they took place after the major battles. The civilians, with their armies decimated, would not have been likely to seek shelter in the fortress cities. Instead, they would have fled into the rural

hills and have hidden. This view is supported in its context by the subsequent generation where plenty of Canaanites appear for intermarriage and contacts (Judg 2:10–12). That is not to say that no civilians were killed. However, the narrative of Joshua can be read without explicit evidence of widespread genocide.

OUTLINE

I. Israel's Victories Against the Canaanites (1–12)

    A. Joshua Establishes His Leadership (1:1–18)
        1:1–9. God's Appointment of Joshua
        1:10–18. Joshua Recognized
           as Leader by Israel

    B. Rahab's Faith (2:1–24)
        2:1–8a. Rahab Hides the Spies
        2:8b–13. Rahab's Confession
        2:14–21. The Negotiations
        2:22–24. The Spies Return to Joshua

    C. Israel Crosses the Jordan (3:1–4:24)

    D. Israel Celebrates Passover (5:1–12)

    E. The Victory at Jericho and the Salvation of Rahab (5:13–6:27)

    F. The Sin of Achan (7:1–26)
        7:1–5. Defeat at Ai
        7:6–21. Identification of Achan
        7:22–26. Achan's Punishment

    G. The Second Assault on Ai (8:1–29)

    H. The Altar at Mount Ebal (8:30–35)

    I. The Gibeonite Alliance (9:1–27)

    J. Victory Against the Southern Coalition (10:1–43)
        10:1–5. Formation of the
           Southern Coalition
        10:6–15. Response of Israel and God
        10:16–27. The Five Kings
        10:28–39. Defeat of the Southern
           Fortified Centers
        10:40–43. Summary of the
           Southern Campaign

    K. Victory Against the Northern Coalition (11:1–11)

DETAILED ANALYSIS

I. Israel's Victories Against the Canaanites (1–12)

A. Joshua Establishes His Leadership (1:1–18)

The first chapter of Joshua is sometimes ignored as a mere collection of phrases gathered from Deuteronomy. However, it provides the crucial story of the transition from the death of Moses to the establishment of a new leader for the nation of Israel. As such, it is unique in biblical literature. The text represents one of the finest collections of exhortations on leadership found in the OT and one of the most important sources for a study of the subject. Within a narrative describing the transition of leadership, these eighteen verses depict the key features of leadership as understood by the OT in terms of God's sovereign choice, the privileges and responsibilities that accompany that call, and the manner in which Joshua establishes the recognition of such leadership at a crucial moment in Israel's history.

The first five verses of the chapter also form a Table of Contents for the whole book of Joshua. The divine speech lays out the manner in which God will work for the people of Israel to bring them into the land and to give it to them. The remainder of the chapter places its emphases on the call for faithfulness to God's Word and on the enlistment of all the tribes of Israel, even those who already possess their inheritance. This section foreshadows the unity of Israel and its faithfulness before God throughout its battles, its allotments of land, and its covenant renewal.

1:1–9. God's Appointment of Joshua. Verse 1 establishes the death of Moses as a given fact, which emphasizes the need for a new leader to fill the power vacuum left by the death of the former one. The "servant of the LORD" describes Moses for the first time in Deut 34:5, at the death of the leader. In the same manner, Joshua will receive this accolade only at his death (Josh 24:29). The epithet measures the life of service of a person who receives it only after the life has been lived. Later OT literature uses it more generally. Jesus raises the relationship of his disciples from servants to friends (John 15:15), but apostles such as Paul continue to apply it in a spirit of joyful service (Rom 1:1).

Verse 2 outlines chs. 1–5 as it describes the crossing of the Jordan. The verb, "to cross" (Heb.: 'avar) refers to crossing the Jordan River and is a keyword repeated several times in the first five chapters (Josh 1:11; 2:10, 23; 3:1, 2, 4, 6, 11, 14, 16, 17; 4:1, 3, 5, 7, 8, 10, 11, 12, 13, 22, 23; 5:1), tying together all the movement into this one great event. Likewise, the emphasis on "all this people" establishes the theological importance of the unity and totality of the nation in their loyalty to God and Joshua. When they are united, they know only victory. When they are divided, they experience only defeat.

Verse 3 promises victory "every place" that Israel goes. It anticipates the victorious battles of chs. 6–12. The "every," like the "all" of v. 2, translates the same Hebrew word, *kol*, and correlates the unity of the people with the complete fulfillment of the promise of the land. Although the promise was originally given to Abram (Gen 12:1–3 et passim), it is here ascribed to Moses, which recalls Deut 34:4. God gives all that was promised to Moses to his successor, Joshua.

Verse 4 describes southern Canaan (the wilderness), northern Canaan (the Lebanon), the north-eastern border of the Euphrates River, the Egyptian (and later Mesopotamian) term for northern Canaan (Hatti or Hittite land), and the western boundary of the Great Sea or Mediterranean. This forms the outline of Canaan as known to Egypt in the second millennium BCE and to Israel (Gen 10:19; Num13:17, 21–22; 34:3–12). It summarizes the boundary descriptions of Josh 13–21.

Verse 5 emphasizes "all the days of your life." It looks forward to the final years of Joshua as outlined in chs. 22–24. This verse forms a hinge between the promises of vv. 1–5 and the responsibilities of vv. 5–9. The promise of God's presence here and in v. 9 enable the mission that Joshua and all Israel have received. If they are to enter and acquire the land, it will occur only because God is present with them to lead them to this goal. In fact, this phrase frames a chiastic literary construction in vv. 5–9. Within this envelope lies the twofold command, "Be strong and courageous." This exhortation appears before a great task, whether the pursuit and defeat of the southern coalition (Josh 10:25), the construction of the Temple (1 Chr 28:20), or the defense of Jerusalem against Assyria (2 Chr 32:7). Between the second and third of these charges lay the threefold reference to the torah or instruction of Moses in vv. 7 and 8. Meditation and obedience lead to success. But within this chiastic context, Joshua will not succeed because he obeys God's Word. Joshua will succeed because God is present with him to enable him to obey God's Word. Thus the mission and its success depend on God's presence in the same manner as the Great Commission of the New Testament that Jesus gives to his disciples depends on Jesus' presence with his disciples (Matt 28:18–20).

1:10–18. Joshua Recognized as Leader by Israel. Verses 10–11 describe Joshua's response to all Israel. The "officers of the people" are the civil counterparts to the priests, charged with administrative responsibilities (Exod 5:6–19; Deut 20:5–

9). Joshua's practical implementation concludes with a recollection of God's promise in v. 2.

The unusual focus on the two and a half tribes in vv. 12–18 provides an example of Joshua's assumption of leadership at a point when he was most vulnerable. Moses had given these tribes their land and so they could expect no personal gain in following Joshua across the Jordan River and in risking their lives. Yet if Joshua could not command their allegiance in this matter, the unity of the tribes would fracture. This would politically compromise Joshua's leadership and theologically end the unity of Israel emphasized in v. 2. Joshua plays his "trump card" by calling upon Moses' own words from Deut 3:18–20. Moses placed a condition on the gift of the land to these tribes; they promised to follow Israel and fight with it west of the Jordan River. The tribes affirm their loyalty in an elaborate oath (vv. 16–18), an oath probably taken by the other tribes just as the Canaanite princes took an oath to each new pharaoh who gained power during the New Kingdom Empire. The Hebrew root for "rebels," *mrd*, occurs in Deuteronomy for crimes that carry the death penalty (Deut 1:26; 9:7, 23, 24; 21:18–21; 31:27). Thus the oath includes a curse so that the enemies of Joshua become the enemies of these tribes. The final phrase, "be strong and courageous," ties this incident with the earlier charge by God to Moses and confirms its place in the establishment of Joshua's leadership over Israel. Thus, God's leader is appointed by God and also recognized by all the people. The leader obeys God, and also identifies key areas of potential problems where proactive confrontation diffuses potential rebellion.

B. Rahab's Faith (2:1–24)

Rahab forms the Canaanite counterpart to Joshua, as the representative of her people who responds in faith to the divine message, and leads her people to salvation. The juxtaposition of this chapter immediately after ch. 1 demonstrates the grace of God made available to those of Canaan as well as Israel. The story begins with an assignment to spy out the land and ends with a tale of redemption for the spies as well as Rahab and her family.

2:1–8a. Rahab Hides the Spies. Joshua initiates this action just as he exercised leadership in 1:10–18. The word translated spies (Heb. *meraggelim*) appears in 2 Sam 15:10 to describe agents of Absalom who spread information, rather than those who gather it. The spies of Josh 2 do both, examining the land around Jericho and seeking supporters. Thus, they come to the house of Rahab the prostitute, most likely a hostel or inn for travelers. Here they might make contact with any who would ally with Israel. Obviously, they made their purpose known, for the king receives a report and searches for them. Rahab, however, has hidden them. Repetitions in the story emphasize the great risk that she takes: "search out the land," which describes the known purpose of the spies and clarifies that any aid would constitute aid to the enemy (vv. 2 and 3); "I did/do not know" demonstrates Rahab's willingness to lie to protect the spies and thus to risk her life if discovered (vv. 4 and 5); "the gate" closed or shut identifies how the only means of escape for the spies has been cut off, requiring the spies to rely completely on Rahab (vv. 5 and 7); and "on the roof" describes how thoroughly Rahab opened up her house to hide the spies (vv. 6 and 8).

2:8b–13. Rahab's Confession. Rahab begins what may be the longest prose speech by a woman in a biblical text. She asserts the positive statement beginning with "I know." This contrasts with what she did "not know" in conversation with the agents of the king. Her confession of faith in vv. 8–11 forms a chiasm framed by God's gift of the land and God's sovereignty in heaven and on earth. Within this envelope, the fear of the Canaanites appears in vv. 9b and 11a. In particular, the phrases "dread of you has fallen" and "melt in fear" recall the Song of the Sea's prophecy that this would happen to the Canaanites when they learned of Israel's defeat of Egypt (Exod 15:15b, 16a). Rahab's confession of this fulfillment introduces the heart of the chiasm, v. 10 and God's historic acts of redemption toward Israel at the Red Sea and with Sihon and Og, east of the Jordan River. Thus at the heart of Rahab's faith lies God's historic acts of redemption, just as in the New Testament Jesus' death and resurrection are the historic acts of redemption that form the basis for believers' faith (Rom 10:9).

In the second half of her monologue (vv. 12–13), Rahab turns to her request for aid from the spies. Her observation that she has "dealt kindly" with the spies uses a phrase consisting of the common verb, "to do, make" (Heb. *'asah*) followed by the important noun for "love, covenantal loyalty" (Heb. *khesed*). This phrase appears in Gen 24:12 when the servant of Abraham searches for a wife for Isaac and prays that God may show her to him. It occurs in Exod 20:6 and Deut 5:10 where God "shows kindness" to thousands of generations of those who are obedient and loving. Thus, the phrase implies that "dealing kindly" points to the preservation of the family for future generations. This occurs with Rahab. She seeks a "sign of good faith" that the spies will preserve her family from death when Israel attacks Jericho. She explicitly mentions the members of her immediate family but not herself in the list of those to be saved. Her concern for her family outweighs matters of self-preservation.

2:14–21. The Negotiations. The spies' speech is recorded here for the first time. They seek from Rahab the guarantee that she will not tell Jericho's officials of their presence in the city or the region. They also indicate that Rahab's family must be in her house at the time of Israel's attack. Anyone outside will lose his or her life. Finally, they require a red cord to be tied to her window to identify her house. The presence of the family together in the house and something red at the door or (here) the window recalls the Passover that Israel will celebrate before it attacks Jericho. The original celebration of this festival required that all the family be together in their home and that they place the blood of the lamb on the doorposts of the house (Exod 12:1–14). Verse 15 describes how Rahab let the spies down from her window on the wall. However, to avoid the odd appearance of the spies negotiating (in vv. 16–20) while dangling on the wall or shouting from the ground below, it seems best to understand v. 15 as a summary statement that is followed by the details of the negotiations. Verse 21 concludes with the actual act of the spies' departure from Rahab's house.

2:22–24. The Spies Return to Joshua. Following the advice of Rahab, the spies remain hidden in the steep ascents to the west of Jericho, a source of innumerable hiding places. The "three days" of their remaining hidden may be a general length of time, or it may correspond to the three days of Josh 3:2. During this time, the camp of Israel prepares to cross the Jordan River. The spies cross the Jordan River (see comment on 1:2 for this verb) and return to Joshua. Their report does not consist of details concerning geography or of the defenses of Jericho. Instead, they quote the first part of Rahab's confession (Josh 2:9). One may compare the majority report of the ten spies at Kadesh Barnea who felt the land could not be taken due to the strength of the enemy (Num 13:28–33). The victory at Jericho will not be one of military strategy but rather one of faith in divine leadership.

C. Israel Crosses the Jordan (3:1–4:24)

For Israel to occupy the land, the nation needed to enter it. This required them to journey westward from Abel Shittim, where they had been camped since Num 25:1 (33:49), across the Jordan River and onto the plains of Jericho. God chose to mark this first passage of the nation into the promised land by a miracle corresponding to the crossing of the Red Sea (Exod 14—15). As there, the waters would "stand aside" and allow God's people to pass through on dry ground. This would happen in springtime when the Jordan River was at its widest and deepest, wider than its average of ninety to one hundred feet and deeper than the average three to ten feet. The current would then be at its strongest. However, unlike the previous generation, this one was not running from an enemy. Instead, they organized and proceeded in a careful, ceremonial order. For this reason, the priests who carry the ark of the covenant took the place of priority in the crossing. Literarily, this account occupies a series of "panels," each of which focuses on a different group, that goes through two cycles: Josh 3:1–6, the tribes of Israel; Josh 3:7–13, Joshua; Josh 3:14–17, the priests; Josh 4:1–9, the stone bearers; Josh 4:10–13, the tribes of Israel; Josh 4:14, Joshua; Josh 4:15–18, the priests; Josh 4:19–24 the meaning of the stones. As in Exod 26–40 and the construction of the tabernacle, so here in this holy ceremony, divine instructions are given and there follows a word-for-word narrative that describes how these instructions were obeyed.

The "three days" of preparation (Josh 3:2) correspond to the three days that the spies remained in the region of Jericho (Josh 2:22). This anticipates careful coordination of time, festivals, and miracles that will continue into chs. 5 and 6. The distance of "two thousand cubits" that the people kept between the ark and themselves would equal three thousand feet or more than half a mile. This emphasized the holiness of the ark as the symbol of God's unique presence among the Israelites. The command for the people to "sanctify yourselves" recalls similar words at Mt. Sinai in Exod 19:10–15, where washing one's clothes and abstaining from sexual intercourse formed physical signs of the obedience. Consecration and preparation are key aspects of all ministry on behalf of God (Eph 6:10–18).

The miracle of the crossing serves to "begin to exalt" Joshua (Josh 3:7), so as to further confirm his position as successor to Moses, already discussed in ch. 1. Here Joshua will instruct the priests through whom the miracle will take place. The priests who bear the ark of the covenant of the Lord must march directly into the Jordan River. When they touch the water, they shall stand in it and the waters will cease to flow. This miracle will also assure the people that God will drive out the inhabitants of the land (Josh 3:9). Theologically, it demonstrates that God, symbolized by the ark, will not be thwarted in the divine plan by powerful forces of nature, such as the Jordan River in full flow. Thus, Israel will understand that, as it follows the presence of God, no barrier, natural or human, can stand in its way. Rivers dry up and walls collapse before the ongoing movement of the ark, of God, and of God's people. The priests regularly represent the people before God in presenting sacrifices (Lev 1–7, 16) and they represent God to the people in teaching about the divine will (Lev 10:10–11). Thus, the people see their ministers going before them in leadership and risking their lives as they plunge into the rushing current of the Jordan River. The people follow at a distance and, through the obedience and courageous leadership of their ministers, they come safely to the other shore.

The Adam of Josh 3:16 lies almost seventeen miles north of Jericho. Zarethan lies farther north. This miracle affected nearly thirty per cent of the Jordan Valley, a dramatic example of the "wonders" that God promised to do for Israel. Twelve stones symbolized the twelve tribes of Israel (Josh 4:2–3) and became a marker at Gilgal (the name means "circle," perhaps describing the circle of stones) where Israel first entered the promise land. They serve as a pedagogical tool to explain to each new generation the significance of the miracle at the Jordan River. In a similar fashion Christians undergo baptism and receive the bread and wine of communion to remember and to teach the meaning of their salvation to each generation of believers (Luke 22:19–20; 1 Cor 11:24–26; Rom 6:4; Col 2:12; 1 Pet 3:21). Israel will celebrate Passover at Gilgal in the next chapter. The Passover will take on new meaning, enhanced by the miraculous crossing of the Jordan River by this new generation.

D. Israel Celebrates Passover (5:1–12)

As the first Passover in Egypt, Israel celebrated deliverance from its enemy, the Egyptian king and his army. The Passover for this new generation anticipates the victory over the enemies who will gather against the new nation. The fear that these enemies experience is described with the same language as that used by Rahab in Josh 2:9. Joshua prepares knives, made of obsidian and potentially sharper than the metal blades of that time, to circumcise Israel. Just as the crossing of the Jordan imitates Israel's previous generation who crossed the Red Sea, so this generation needs to be circumcised as the previous generation was. The previous generation "perished," literally "completed" (Hebrew root *tmm*) in the wilderness just as this generation remained where they were until the circumcising "was done," literally "completed" (Hebrew root tmm). God instituted circumcision in Gen 17:8–14 along with the promise of the land that Israel had now entered. Circumcision brought upon this generation all the responsibilities of the covenant, as seen in the Passover they were about to celebrate. It also brought upon the people all the promises and blessings of the covenant; chief among these was the inheritance of the land. The "disgrace of Egypt" (Josh 5:9) describes the rebellion of the generation of the exodus and their subsequent loss of access to the promise land. The circumcision of the new generation replaced rebellion with obedience at Gilgal; the root of whose name, "circle," can carry the sense, "to roll (away)."

The Passover forms the key celebration. In Exod 12:1–13:16 Israel celebrated the Passover when they began their journey into the wilderness. Here the nation concludes that journey by keeping the festival. Early in the wilderness journey, God provided manna for the people to eat (Exod 16:1–36). With the end of this journey, the manna ceases and the people eat from the firstfruits of the land. The "parched grain" or roasted grain consisted of the barley that Israel found growing near Gilgal and whose harvest time coincided with the Passover and Days of Unleavened Bread (Lev 23:10–14). These firstfruits constituted the "down payment" that God gave to Israel at this point, a literal foretaste of the blessings of the fullness of the land. In a similar manner, the resurrection of Jesus Christ becomes the firstfruits of the resurrection of all Christians who have died (1 Cor 15:20–23), and the gift of the Holy Spirit forms the firstfruits of the fullness of Christian redemption (Rom 8:23).

E. The Victory at Jericho and the Salvation of Rahab (5:13–6:27)

The scene of Josh 5:13–15 introduces the assault on Jericho as Joshua meets his heavenly counterpart, the leader of the heavenly army. A heavenly messenger with a drawn sword commands serious attention because it indicates that God has come to bring judgment (Num 22:23; 1 Chr 21:16). The "commander of the army of the LORD" receives Joshua's worship. As in Gen 18 and 22, the distinction between an angel and God fades. It is truly God whom Joshua addresses. The reference to "holy ground" recalls God's command to Moses that inaugurates his mission to lead Israel out of Egypt (Exod 3:2–5). Joshua stands at the beginning of his mission to lead Israel into the promised land. Such demonstrations of divine holiness regularly precede the bestowal of a mission (Isa 6; Ezek 1; Luke 1:26–3:8; Matt 17:1–13), as the saving presence of Christ comes before the call to Christian discipleship (Rom 5–6; Eph 2:8–10; 4:1–16).

Joshua 6:1 reaffirms the important imagery of the gate and of access to the fortress of Jericho (see Josh 2:5, 7). The "shut up" posture positions Jericho as an obstacle in the ongoing advance of God and the mission of Israel, just as the literary position of this verse "obstructs" the call of Joshua and the following success over Jericho. The daily march around the site for seven days corresponds to the seven days of Unleavened Bread following Passover. As in the first Passover, Israel will see the defeat of its enemies. This is a holy time when the presence of God in the form of the ark accompanies the warriors to "march around the city." This verb (Hebrew root, *nqp*) occurs in Ps 48:12, when the pilgrim walks around Jerusalem to admire its defenses; and in 2 Kgs 6:14, when a king surrounds a city with his army in order to capture its occupants. Thus, the march constitutes a ceremonial inspection of the defenses to see if there is any opening or willingness to negotiate entrance. It also suggests a martial intent toward Jericho. The procession of the ark of the covenant began at Mount Sinai. The story of Jericho forms part of the ongoing movement of the ark until it reaches its resting place in Jerusalem (2 Sam 6). The people of God are led by faith in their Lord into the promised rest (Heb 13:7–16). The details of the march, the commanded silence on the seventh day, and the times of shouting and horn blowing all attest to a disciplined force following the divine commands through Joshua.

On the seventh day, Joshua promises the people that, after circumnavigating Jericho seven times and shouting as the trumpets blow, the Lord will give Jericho to them. However, they are warned not to take any booty for themselves. Everything is "devoted to destruction" (Heb. *kherem*; Josh 6:18–21). All living things are to be destroyed and all property belongs to the treasury of the Lord. This edict anticipates the disobedience of Achan and the story of Josh 7. It also fulfills the command of Deut 20:16–18 in which those who have resisted the Lord, in this case Jericho, are forcibly repossessed. Nothing remains to tempt Israel to follow the gods and ways of the Canaanites. From this perspective, the seven days of marching become one final and direct opportunity for Jericho, its king, and its soldiers to turn to God as Rahab had done.

Joshua 6:16–25 describes the fall of Jericho just as Joshua had promised. It also details the salvation of Rahab and her family. By one count of the Masoretic text, eighty-six Hebrew words recount the story of Rahab's salvation whereas one hundred two words tell of the destruction. For the writer of this chapter the story of God's mercy toward Rahab was virtually as important as the account of God's judgment on the fortress. Rahab and her family live among the Israelites and eventually become part of Israel and part of the promised line that leads to Jesus (Matt 1:5). In the midst of divine judgment, Rahab corre-

sponds to the Good Shepherd's search for the one lost sheep (Matt 8:12–14; Luke 15:4–7). Joshua curses Jericho and his words are fulfilled when it is rebuilt (1 Kgs 16:34). Joshua's "fame was in all the land" because "the LORD was with Joshua" and he was successful in his first military conflict.

F. The Sin of Achan (7:1–26)

If Rahab corresponds to Joshua as a leader of her people who acted in faith, Rahab contrasts with Achan. She represents a Canaanite coming to faith in Israel's God and acting to assist that nation, whereas Achan depicts an Israelite acting contrary to that faith and putting the community in jeopardy. In the end, Rahab and her family join God's people while Achan and his family are excluded from the covenant community. Having Abraham for one's father does not guarantee divine favor (Luke 3:8).

7:1–5. Defeat at Ai. Israel "broke faith" (Heb. *m'l*), a verb always used to describe faithlessness toward God. The unique genealogy of Achan in v. 1 (only here in the book of Joshua are four generations described) connects his transgression with his family, clan, tribe, and ultimately with the whole nation of Israel. Ai guarded the central one of three Iron Age roads from Jericho into the hill country. The planned movement into the central area of Cisjordan could occur only if Israel gained access to the plateau region of Benjamin. Ai, like Jericho, may well have served primarily as a fortress guarding these routes of access. The focus in both is on the soldiers and on the king, a term whose Semitic root (*mlk*) can designate civil or military officials in fourteenth century BCE Amarna letters from Palestine. Unlike the spies' report of ch. 2, where faith in God's work was key, these spies describe the strength of the military force and recommend a small contingent of Israelite warriors. The decision to send part of the army may have seemed to be a good strategy. However, it divided the whole people and thus compromised the important theological consideration that the nation as a whole would take possession (Josh 1:2). The loss of life and humiliating rout of this force led to a reversal of fortunes. In ch. 5 the Canaanites feared Israel; now Israel becomes afraid of Canaan (Josh 7:5).

7:6–21. Identification of Achan. The acts of tearing clothes, falling on one's face, and putting dust on the head describe mourning (1 Sam 4:12; Job 2:12). The refocusing on God, with the extended question of why God would do this, brings Israel back into the proper attitude of consulting God for every concern. The concern that this would encourage the Canaanites was a real one (Josh 7:9). Until this defeat, Israel had not lost a battle since they attempted to invade Canaan a generation earlier (Num 14:45). Now the nations of Canaan would know that this generation of Israelites could be defeated. They would no longer fear as they had.

God communicates to Joshua that some of the *kherem* (see Josh 6:18–24) has been stolen by one of the Israelites. Joshua's identification of the perpetrator begins with the sanctification of the people, something that took place before the Israelites crossed the Jordan River (Josh 3:5). This becomes the first step in the process of reversing the manner in which Israel has become *kherem* in the eyes of God (Josh 7:12–13).

The identification will take place according to tribe, clan, and household. This reverses the order of the genealogy at the beginning of the chapter. These groups form the major social divisions of ancient Israel. Joshua's verdict concerning the perpetrator and all related property consists of consigning everyone and everything to destruction by fire (Josh 7:15). This penalty corresponds to the original command to burn all Jericho by fire (Josh 6:18–24). The identification of Achan, probably by means of the high priest casting lots (especially the Urim [and Thummim]; Num 27:21), leads to his admission of guilt. It begins with a general confession of sin and moves to the specific action. Achan "saw" something "beautiful" (Josh 7:21). Using the same Hebrew verb and adjective, Eve also "saw" something "beautiful" (NRSV has "good"; Heb. *tov*) in Gen 3:6. Both Eve and Achan coveted and this led to the additional sin of taking what God had forbidden.

7:22–26. Achan's Punishment. They brought Achan, his family, and all his property to a valley, perhaps the Buqeiah, about eight miles south of Jericho, i.e., in the opposite direction from where Israel was headed. Capital punishment was required. Stoning may have provided a more merciful death than burning alive. It may also have involved all of Israel in the execution. Israel burned the bodies with fire, an application of the

kherem (see Josh 6:18–24), and covered them with a pile of stones (Josh 7:26). This memorial reminds Israel of the need to eradicate sin in its midst, just as the stones at Gilgal commemorate God's salvation of the people. God's "burning anger" threatened to destroy Israel when it worshiped the golden calf (Exod 32:12), when it engaged in immorality at Baal-Peor (Num 25:4), if the Transjordanian tribes refused to assist Israel west of the Jordan River (Num 32:1), and—especially in this case—if Israel did not do away with all the things devoted to destruction (Deut 13:17). The name, Achor (Heb. root '*kr*), derives from a term meaning to bring trouble. It forms the basis for Joshua's question in Josh 7:25. Christians learn from this example concerning the terrible effect of sin, which elicits a particularly strong judgment from God here and in the early church's story of Ananias and Sapphira (Acts 5:1–11).

G. The Second Assault on Ai (8:1–29)

The second attack on Ai differs from the first. It begins with God's word and promise of success, rather than someone else's speech. It emphasizes the whole army acting together (and thus all Israel; Josh 1:2) rather than one faction of a divided force. It also involves a ruse rather than a direct attack. This last point prevents additional loss of lives among the Israelites. The Israelites position their main force in a ravine north of Ai. They place a smaller ambush to the west of the fortress, at a hiding place between Ai to the east and Bethel to the west. The traditional site of Ai, Et Tell, fulfills these topographical requirements. The problem of the absence of evidence of occupation at the traditional time when these events would have taken place may argue for their legendary nature, or it may suggest that Ai was a makeshift fortress used to defend one of the main roads from Jericho to Bethel and the highlands of Palestine. Such a fort would leave little evidence of occupation based on the finer (and datable) pottery that occurs in domestic sites. The defenders could have made use of the older walls at the site. The figures of "thirty thousand warriors" and "five thousand men" (Josh 8:3, 12) could actually represent smaller numbers. The Hebrew word for "thousand" (*'elef*) can mean a squad or unit, especially in military contexts. Thus, here and elsewhere in Joshua, the thousands could refer to squads each containing far fewer numbers than one thousand.

At daybreak, the king of Ai and his forces leave Ai to confront Joshua and his army. They appear to give way before Ai's army and flee eastward just as in the first assault (Josh 7:4–5). This action draws out all the forces of Ai and leaves it open to the Israelite ambush hiding to the west. At the proper moment, Joshua responds to God's command and holds up his sword (Josh 8:18). Perhaps the gleam of the sword in the morning sun provided an adequate signal for the ambush to recognize that the time had come to enter the fortress and set on fire whatever would burn. The ambush now comes behind the army of Ai and thus catches them in a pincer movement as Joshua turns his soldiers to face their enemy. With the ambush to the west and the main Israelite force to their east, the army of Ai loses all will to fight and Israel easily puts them to the sword. Only the king is left alive. Joshua brings him to Ai's gate and hangs him in front of the burning mound. As with Achan (Josh 7:26), they raise a pile of stones over the king's body. Ai means "ruin" and this describes what remains after the victory. The smoothness of the operation and the total defeat of the enemy contrasts with the events of ch. 7 and demonstrates for the people of God the importance of removing sin from among the people and of following the will and the word of God.

H. The Altar at Mount Ebal (8:30–35)

The Septuagint and the fragments from the Dead Sea Scrolls place this section in ch. 5 where it fits better as part of the ceremonies completed at the time of the entrance into the promised land. However, the geographical understanding of the events would suggest that Israel could not celebrate at Mt. Ebal until it reached the hill country. This did not happen before the victory over Ai and Bethel (Josh 8:17). On Mt. Ebal they constructed an altar of field stones (Exod 20:25) and "offered on it burnt offerings to the LORD, and sacrificed offerings of well-being." According to Lev 1:3–17, burnt offerings provided for atonement. By virtue of the fire consuming everything, the burnt offerings become an illustration of total dedication of the offerers to God. The offerings of well-being were the only sacrifices in which some of the meat could be eaten by the offerers (Lev 7:11–34), symbolizing their fellowship with God. The altar and Joshua's writing of the law of Moses on (plastered) stones is understood to fulfill the divine command

of Deut 27:1–10. The blessings and especially the curses that are pronounced recall the remainder of Deut 27. The unique stone structure on Mt. Ebal, dating to c. 1200 BCE, remains an enigma that some have related to the altar described here. However, that claim remains unproven. These verses emphasize the obedience of Israel to God's word and their desire to hear that word and to renew their covenant with God.

I. The Gibeonite Alliance (9:1–27)

Has the sin of Achan and the resultant defeat at the first assault on Ai changed the attitude of fear in Canaan (Josh 2:10; 5:1) to one of courage to attack Israel? The text does not say, but the first two verses do demonstrate a change of attitude to one of aggression. The results of sin may have far-ranging effects, whether with the first human couple (Gen 3) or with Israel under Joshua. Like the kings "beyond the Jordan," "the inhabitants of Gibeon" also "heard" of God's work in Israel. However, their response differed. Gibeon (el-Jib) lay north of Jerusalem and southwest of Bethel. Like all the other Cisjordan events in the first nine chapters of Joshua (except Josh 8:30–35), this site lay in the later tribal territory of Benjamin.

The action of a people offering themselves as slaves in exchange for their lives forms a common theme in ancient Near Eastern accounts of victorious kings. However, in the story of Joshua, Israel had nothing about which to boast. Gibeon's ambassadors disguised themselves so as to appear to have come from a long distance. According to Deut 20:10–18, God commanded Israel to treat their enemies differently, depending on whether they came from outside the promised land or from within it. The former were subject to labor and servitude whereas the latter were doomed to extermination. The Gibeonites knew of this. They disguised themselves so as to make it appear that they did not come from Canaan. As with Rahab, the heart of their confession of faith has to do with God's historic acts of redemption for Israel against Egypt, Sihon, and Og (Josh 2:10; 8:10). Apparently the Gibeonites were ruled by elders (Josh 8:11) since no king is mentioned. Their Hivite origins (Josh 8:7) may suggest a background within the Hittite sphere of culture, where a council of elders handled local affairs. Without any mention of consulting God, Joshua and the Israelite elders make a treaty, so they are all held responsible for this transaction (Josh 8:15). When the Israelites learned that their treaty partners were Gibeonites, they obeyed the commands regarding the responsibilities of aliens living in the land, forcing them to become "hewers of wood and drawers of water" (Deut 29:11). This responsibility would connect Gibeon with the tabernacle and later the Temple, and the sacrifices that required wood and water. Israel "murmured" against their leadership when they learned how they had made a treaty contrary to God's will. This verb, "to murmur" (Heb. root *lwn*), appears in Exodus and Numbers to describe the murmuring of Israel against God and Moses in the wilderness. However, here the Israelites would not violate the treaty they had made, although the lesson not to swear hastily needed to be learned (cf. Matt 5:33–37; Jas 4:13–17). Joshua's question and the Gibeonites' response (Josh 9:22–25) exonerated Israel from knowingly allowing Canaanites to live. Ironically, the only people whom the Bible records that Joshua "saved" were the Gibeonites (Josh 9:26), despite the fact that the name Joshua derives from the same Hebrew root for "to save; salvation" (Heb. *yasha'*).

J. Victory Against the Southern Coalition (10:1–43)

As in the crossing of the Jordan River (chs. 3–4) and in the story of Ai's capture (ch. 8), here as well the author writes with a series of literary panels that enable descriptions of both the work of God and of Israel simultaneously taking place. Unlike the previous victories, this one considers an entire region with only a few verses devoted to each of the places mentioned. Thus, the speed of the action increases. More than any other chapter in Joshua, this one parallels Egyptian, Hittite, Babylonian, and Assyrian annalistic conquest narratives. Especially in vv. 28–42, the text presents a repetitive description of a king moving his army from one city to another in conquest. Similar verbs and phrases occur with reference to each city, despite minor variations. Even the formation of the rebellion (vv. 1–5), the nighttime march and the divine miracles (vv. 6–15), and the fate of the kings (vv. 16–27) have direct parallels in comparative ancient battle narratives. This is not the genre of an account that would have been developed by pacifistic, egalitarian villages in the highlands of early Israel. Instead, it derives from a context of warfare, common to other ancient nations. Theologically, the Christian is reminded of Eph 6 and the description of the disciple's life as one of spiritual warfare. Success requires divine assistance, and a knowledge of and obedience to God's word.

10:1–5. Formation of the Southern Coalition. An alliance with Gibeon gave Israel control of the Benjaminite plateau of the central highlands. This also included the Beth Horon pass westward to the coastal plain. This pass formed the most important route to the hill country and to cities such as Jerusalem. Thus the king of Jerusalem, the first city to the south of Gibeon, was threatened with the loss of his ally to the north, "a large city." The leader, Adoni-Zedek, turned to his remaining friends to the south and west. He contacted four major city-state forts. The names of the leaders and of their cities represent the strength of the region that will unite to fight the perceived Israelite threat. By making this first move, the Canaanites threaten Gibeon and its ally, Israel. Thus, Israel's response in what follows is a defensive one.

10:6–15. Response of Israel and God. The Gibeonite request for Israel's aid based on the aforementioned treaty and their response recalls the corresponding dependency of God's people upon their (treaty) covenant relationship, whether Old Testament or New, and the need to claim that relationship by means of prayer (e.g., Matt 6:9; 26:41; 2 Cor 13:7). Like Joshua's ambush at Ai (Josh 8), this all-night march created another ruse that surprised the enemy and enabled Israel to drive them westward into the Shephelah (low hill country) to Azekah, and then to Makkedah (Khirbet el-Qom). Azekah is close to Jarmuth whereas Makkedah would be nearby the remaining three cities of the coalition. The names of these two sites summarize the battle. They also indicate places from which the coalition survivors might seek refuge in their hometowns (an option that v. 19 seeks to close). While vv. 6–10 summarize the human part of the battle, vv. 11–15 outline the divine role. God fights for Israel with "huge stones" from heaven and by stopping the sun at Joshua's command. The former anticipates the "large stones" (the same expression in Hebrew) that seal the five kings in the cave (vv. 18, 27). The "standing" of the sun has evoked much controversy. It has been variously identified as a miracle where the sun did not move, a solar eclipse, and an omen. Whatever took place, the text emphasizes the divine decision to grant Joshua some control over the heavenly bodies. God's participation in the battle, with (hail?) stones and the standing of the sun, results in victory. As at Jericho, Israel seems to follow behind and to have little to do to complete the work (cf. v. 11).

10:16–27. The Five Kings. The capture of the five kings of the coalition took place in the cave in which they were hiding at Makkedah. This itself was a humiliation, as was the loss of their army. The coalition's army perished on that day, except for a few survivors who escaped to their towns and would be exterminated in the remainder of ch. 10. The kings of southern Canaan faced further humiliation as "the chiefs of the warriors" in Israel put their feet on the necks of these leaders. This display, like the hanging of the kings after their execution, was intended to proclaim publicly their defeat and to encourage Israel's army for future battles. As noted above, the same expression identifying the hail stones that God sent from heaven also identifies the "large stones" used to seal the tomb and to provide yet another memorial for Israel to remember these important events in the creation of the nation in Cisjordan (Josh 4:8–9, 19–24; 7:25–26; 8:29).

10:28–39. Defeat of the Southern Fortified Centers. Those who survived the first day's conflicts and escaped to the fortified cities in the area now become objects of a hunt through virtually seven major city fortresses in the south. Indeed, this seems to comprise largely a sweep from the northwest southward and eastward and then to the northeast of the southern areas (Hebron) before returning westward. Using a variety of repeated phrases—took, fought against, the Lord gave it, its king, he struck it with the edge of the sword, he utterly destroyed every person in it, he left no one remaining, he did to its king as he had done—the text describes the destruction (but not burning; cf. Josh 11:13) of each fortified center. The manner in which no two cities are described with an identical set of phrases suggests variation in tactics. At the center of the city list lies Gezer, which was not attacked. Its king and his army were defeated. Yet its central position suggests that this was a key victory. Gezer was one of the three major Canaanite cities defeated by pharaoh Merneptah according to his 1209 BCE account; and

it was remembered as an important city controlled by Egypt during the time of Solomon (1 Kgs 9:16). This repetitive style for the seven cities resembles the annals of ancient Near Eastern kings throughout the second and first millennia BCE.

10:40–43. Summary of the Southern Campaign. Verse 40 summarizes the victories in the south by region and v. 41 by boundaries. Phrases such as "he left no one remaining, but utterly destroyed all that breathed," may reflect hyperbole characteristic of the annalistic genre. Here it emphasizes the complete obedience of Joshua. Verse 42 gives the credit to God who "fought for Israel." Verse 43 marks the end of this episode with the return to the Israelite camp at Gilgal. Neither here nor elsewhere in the first twelve chapters does Israel occupy the defeated cities and regions. They fought a defensive battle for their survival, and then returned to their home.

K. Victory Against the Northern Coalition (11:1–11)

Unlike the southern coalition, the northern one appears to have a clear leader, the king of Hazor (Tel el-Qedah). This site expanded to cover an area of more than 170 acres, the largest Old Testament site in Palestine. As in ch. 10, the basic themes of a coalition that initiates the attack, Israel's successful response, and the destruction of the cities and regions involved in the attack all appear. The narrative is shorter, however. There are no lengthy chases, details of miracles, or gory descriptions of the execution of the leadership. Instead, one has the sense of a speedy completion to these events. The region stretches from the Sea of Galilee and the Huleh basin westward to the Mediterranean Sea. Although the focus of the towns lies around the Galilee, it is not clear how far north Mizpeh may reach, perhaps into the Beqa Valley of Lebanon. The "very many horses and chariots" (Josh 11:4) describes the most advanced military technology available. These armies were beyond the strength of the smaller and poorer southern coalition. The battle takes place at the "waters of Merom," identified either as Tel Qarnei Hattin west of the Sea of Galilee or as Tel Merom in the upper highlands of the eastern Galilee. The Israelite chase proceeds in a counter-clockwise fashion. From the battle site they moved westward in the Jezreel Valley and then north across the Plain of Acco and past

Tyre to Sidon. From here the army turned southeast and passed along the Marj 'Ayyun Valley and along the Litani River. From there it entered the Huleh Valley and continued south to Hazor. In this manner, all the rebels and their fortified sites would have been attacked. Only the destruction of Hazor is described, however. Using the same expressions as found in Josh 10:28–39, this town experienced the same assault by Israel, as had those in the southern coalition. The additional description of Hazor as at "the head of all those kingdoms" is an accurate description of the (extrabiblical) textual and archaeological record of the site before its destruction in the thirteenth century BCE. It may also explain why Joshua "burned Hazor with fire" (Josh 11:11). It forms an inclusio or envelope with Jericho and Ai, as places devoted to God at which nothing was allowed to remain. As Israel defended itself from these forces who attacked it, so the narrative emphasizes the terrible consequences of resisting God's will; something that can appear in the forms of war and other types of oppressive conduct (Rom 1–5).

L. Summary of the Battles (11:12–23)

The passage begins with a statement that summarizes all the towns and their leaders that Israel defeated. The text emphasizes the obedience of Joshua to Moses. As God recognized Joshua as Moses' successor, so they have now acknowledged Moses' will. Joshua's obedience occupies v. 15 as well. In between, Hazor's distinctive treatment forms the conclusion to the battles. Elsewhere Israel killed the people and took the property as their booty, but they did not burn the towns. Only Hazor was burnt. Verse 15 emphasizes Joshua's obedience with a chiasm:

A   As the LORD had commanded his servant Moses, so Moses commanded Joshua,

B   and so Joshua did;

B'   he left nothing undone

A'   of all that the LORD had commanded Moses.

The second part of the section (vv. 16–20) begins with another summary of the battles, describing the land taken by noting the extremities from the Negeb in the south to the Lebanon valley (the Beqa) in the north. Verse 18 mentions that the war lasted a long time. This may include

some of those conquered entities mentioned in ch. 12 that do not appear elsewhere in the first eleven chapters of the book. The report highlights the kings. It was the elite that opposed Joshua and the Israelites; repeatedly little or nothing is said of the citizenry who seem not to have participated in the battles. If Hazor was the central concern of the first part of the summary, the peace treaty with the Gibeonites seems to be the concern of this second part. As opposed to the kings who fought Israel (v. 18), the citizens of Gibeon (who did not appear to have a king; cf. Josh 9:11) made peace with God's people (v. 19). The towns of these other kings were destroyed according to God's will.

Verses 21–23 describe the defeat of the Anakim. The Anakim were a social group, elsewhere called by the name of the Nephilim (Num 13:33) and the Rephaim (Deut 2:11). These were legendary warriors slain early in Israel's history. Mention of Hebron and Debir anticipates the remaining two battle narratives, those of Caleb (Josh 14:6–15) and of Othniel (Josh 15:13–19). Verse 23 explicitly looks forward to those allotments in chs. 13–21. While "Joshua took the whole land" (v. 23), some of the Anakim "remained in Gaza, in Gath, and in Ashdod" (v. 22). This suggests that not all the land was captured and anticipates the descriptions of unconquered areas elsewhere in Joshua and in Judg 1. The "rest from war" indicates that the battles have now ended, if only for a while. The writer of Hebrews contrasts this temporary rest (Heb 4:8) with the eternal rest promised in Christ (Heb 4:9–10; cf. 1 Pet 1:4–5).

M. Summary of Lands and Cities Defeated by Moses and Joshua (12:1–24)

Verses 1–6 provide an overview of the lands and cities acquired by Israel's victories over Sihon and Og, while vv. 7–24 do the same for the victories over the kings west of the Jordan River. Joshua's work as recorded in the first eleven chapters thus becomes part of the larger purpose of God's plan in giving the land east as well as west of the Jordan. The regions described by vv. 1b–5 include the region east of the Jordan River from the Wadi Arnon that empties into the Dead Sea in the south to Mount Hermon in the north. Sihon ruled the southern half of this and Og the northern half. Generally speaking, the Jabbok Valley formed their common border. For Og's connection with the Rephaim (v. 4), compare Josh 11:21 and the associated Anakim, all of whom were legendary heroes. The towns of the Ashtaroth and Edrei are mentioned in the Ugaritic myths of the thirteenth century BCE and associated with a deity Rapiu (cf. Rephaim). Moses received the credit for the acquisition of these lands and for the allotments to the two and a half tribes (Num 21:21–30; Deut 1:4; 2:24–37; 29:6–7; Josh 1:12–18), in a verse that appears again in Josh 13:8 and 32.

Verses 7–8 repeat the listing of regions where victories occurred, beginning in the north in the Lebanon and moving south as far as the Negeb. Verses 9–24 list thirty-one kings, as noted in the summary. This literature recalls the itineraries of Egyptian pharaohs who recorded campaigns into Canaan from the sixteenth to the tenth centuries BCE. These itineraries do not necessarily assume that every city was destroyed; only that the armies were defeated. The sequence initially follows the first ten chapters of Joshua. However, from v. 13 onward additional towns appear that had not been mentioned previously. Only Bethel has no king listed. Perhaps the king of Ai governed both places. The text demonstrates God's faithfulness and presence with Israel to give them "every place that the sole of your foot will tread upon" (Josh 1:3).

II. The Allotments (13–21)

A. Allotments East of the Jordan River (13:1–33)

Verses 1–7 form an introduction. Joshua's advanced age appears again after the end of this major section (Josh 23:1). As elsewhere (Gen 18:1; 24:1; 1 Kgs 1:1), this description anticipates a major responsibility that the aged person(s) will still need to accomplish. In this case, it is no longer the acquisition of the land. Rather, it is to allot the land. The division begins with what has already taken place; the land not yet conquered and the areas already allotted. Those areas not yet conquered create a tension with the remainder of these chapters that describe the land as a whole that is allotted. This culminates in the expression of complete fulfillment in Josh 21:43–45, a passage that seems to allow no alternatives. The text appears to develop God's promise that "I will myself drive them out from before the Israelites"

(v. 6) and thus act as though the land is fully conquered even though these verses record that such is not the case at this point.

Verses 8–33 begin with a definition of Israel's territory east of the Jordan. It resembles the lands of Sihon and Og from Josh 12:1–6. From south to north, the town lists identify the tribes of Reuben (vv. 15–23), Gad (vv. 24–28), and half of the tribe of Manasseh (vv. 29–31). At the beginning and end of this description, in vv. 14 and 33, as well as in Josh 14:4, readers learn that the Levites had no inheritance in the allotted land. Like the land given to the tribes east of the Jordan, the lack of a physical inheritance for the Levites goes back to Moses (Exod 32:25–29; Num 18:20–24; 26:62; Deut 10:9; 14:27; 18:1–2). The Levites represent all Israel, on both sides of the Jordan, before God. They will receive towns in which to live (Josh 21) but they will not possess the lands on either side of the Jordan River. Here at the beginning of this most materialistic of sections, the distribution, the constant reminder of the status of the tribe of Levi emphasizes the point that the most important values lie beyond the success of this world.

B. Allotment of Judah (14:1–15:63)

Verses 1–5 introduce the allotments that Joshua and Eleazar, the high priest of Joshua's generation, would distribute. They had seen this land defeated and now they would distribute it by lot, according to divine command (Num 26:5, 56; 33:54; 36:2). Although consideration was given to the size of the tribe (Num 33:54), the casting of lots was the key. By expressing God's will, this act determined the allotment for each tribe (Prov 16:33). In place of an inheritance for the Levites (see comment on Josh 13:14, 33), the tribe of Joseph would receive two portions, one for Manasseh and one for Ephraim. Verse 5 caps the introduction with a statement observing the obedience of God's people in this matter.

In Num 13–14 Caleb, along with Joshua, had delivered a favorable report. He believed that God would give Israel the land. Israel did not follow him and lost forty years in the wilderness. Caleb had faithfully waited all that time for his inheritance. Now at 85 he was given his inheritance at Hebron in southern Judah. He is a model of patience and faithfulness. As a Kenizzite, perhaps related to the Kenites, he was not originally an

Israelite. The Kenizzites were apparently incorporated into the tribe of Judah (Num 13:6). As in the case of Rahab, so Caleb formed a model of another non-Israelite who received the promises of God. Thus, Caleb models the acquisition of one's inheritance for the rest of Judah and for all Israel, just as his patience, faithfulness, and courage remain virtues for Christians today.

Joshua 15:1–12 provides a summary of the boundary description and vv. 20–63 set forth twelve districts of Judah with their town lists. This is the largest and the most complete boundary description and town list of any tribe. It would appear to indicate the greater importance of the tribe of Judah as well as its conformity to divine order and organization. The text portrays Judah as the most blessed of the tribes in its allotted lands.

Verses 13–19 form an interlude that returns to consider the story of Caleb. Despite Caleb's age, the account describes how God gave the fearful Anakim (Josh 11:21–22; 15: 13–14) into Caleb's hand and how he received his inheritance. He also promised his daughter in marriage to the one who would conquer Debir. Othniel captured the town and received Achsah as wife. She then negotiated from her father additional springs, an invaluable resource in a desert. This story, repeated in Judg 1:13–14, anticipates the era of the judges, for Othniel becomes the first judge and a model one (Judg 3:9–11).

C. Allotments of Ephraim and Manasseh (16:1–17:18)

Ephraim and Manasseh are the two sons of Joseph. Their tribal territory will form the center of the northern kingdom. They are bounded on the south by the tribes of Dan and Benjamin, and on the north by the Jezreel Valley. The Archites and Japhletites, inhabitants of this region, are otherwise unknown, except for the observation that Hushai, David's diplomat, was an Archite (Josh 16:2–3; 2 Sam 15:32; 1 Chr 27:33). Ephraim was the southernmost of the two tribes. Its boundary list appears first (there is no town list), followed by the unconquered towns (Josh 16:5–10), as occurred in the Judean allotment.

Chapter 17 records the allotments of Manasseh, west of the Jordan River. Unlike other tribes whose territories are defined by towns and districts, this distribution is based on the sons of Manasseh.

The firstborn, Machir, received two regions to the east of the Jordan River (see Josh 13), Gilead and Bashan. The remaining six brothers received allotments that are preserved as places named in the eighth century BCE Samaria ostraca. The one exception among these was Hepher, whose son Zelophehad had no sons. Instead, he had five daughters. They received a special dispensation from Moses to preserve their father's inheritance (Num 27:1–11). The five sons inherited districts in the southern and western regions of Manasseh's territory; while the five daughters of Zelophehad received areas in the northern and eastern parts of the tribal lands. As with Ephraim, Manasseh has a boundary description. However, in light of the evidence from the Samaria ostraca and elsewhere, the sons and daughters already mentioned function as town lists. The same is true of the list of Manasseh towns within the territories of Issacher and Asher.

Joshua 17:14–18 provides a note on the development of the upper forest region of the hill country for the excess population of Manasseh. They could not settle in the neighboring Jezreel Valley or the valley of Beth-shean due to the iron chariots of the Canaanites. These would apparently describe chariots that had some sort of simple iron plating attached; but they would provide a significant military threat for any people not possessing these expensive and advanced weapons. Although the day would come when Israel had superiority over the Canaanites, for the present they are to clear the thick undergrowth and other obstacles in the highlands, and to settle there. The necessary terraces that would allow for farming in these ecosystems are scattered throughout the region. Some from sites such as Ai and Raddana have been dated to c. 1200 BCE and the time of the explosion of a village culture throughout the region. These more than three hundred villages, not present in the previous centuries, may be identified with the settlement of earliest Israel.

D. Allotment of Benjamin (18:1–28)

The remaining allotments are mapped from Israel's new center at Shiloh, which will remain the religious center for Israel until the time of Eli (1 Sam 1–4). The land is a gift of God's blessing. Mapping it corresponds to the writing and observance of the law of Moses. Both form essential books of the covenant. One contained the promises and the other provided details of the fulfillment of the promises. Joshua will cast lots for the distribution of the seven remaining territories. Israel continued to seek God's direction through the casting of lots. The centrality of the sanctuary at Shiloh reflects the central location of Josh 18:1–10 in chs. 13–21 of the book. Central in the lives of the people of God is the regular practice of meeting for worship and instruction (cf. Heb 10:25).

The territory of Benjamin is described first. Benjamin was Joseph's full brother in the stories of Genesis. Here they remain tied together by receiving adjacent territories and by their allotment descriptions following one after the other. Although some of the boundary information was given earlier (e.g., the southern boundary of Benjamin coincides with the northern boundary of Judah in ch. 15), the full boundary description is provided along with lists of towns in the eastern (Josh 18:21–24) and in the western parts of the territory (Josh 18:25–28). Again, this comprehensive and orderly account suggests a tribe organized according to God's will.

E. Remaining Allotments of the Land (19:1–51)

These remaining allotments include the town list of Simeon (vv. 1–9), the boundary description and partial town list of Zebulun (vv. 10–16), the town list of Issachar (vv. 17–23), the (partial?) boundary and town list of Asher (vv. 24–31), a boundary description and partial town list for Naphtali (vv. 32–39), and a town list for Dan (vv. 40–48). The report about this last tribe includes a note about the migration of the tribe away from their divinely allotted territory northward to the city of Dan. All these texts preserve incomplete descriptions and ones that are much smaller than Judah and Benjamin. The text depicts a lack of orderliness and completeness; something that does not correspond to God's will.

The tribal allotments west of the Jordan River began with the example of Caleb for Judah in Josh 14:6–15. The other hero of faith from the wilderness generation, Joshua, concludes the allotments with his inheritance in his tribal territory of Ephraim. Not only do the stories about Joshua and Caleb form an envelope for the whole allotment of the land, the story of Joshua also demonstrates the virtues of true kindness, sacrifice, and humility in leadership (cf. Gal 5:22–26). Joshua waits until all the others have received their allotments and then he receives his own share. He does not seek to claim the best or the most choice of these lands for himself. Nevertheless, this minister of God's people does receive a fair share for his own family (cf. 1 Tim 5:17–18).

F. The Towns of Refuge (20:1–9)

The principle of sacrifice and of the Sabbath teaches that while God has given Israel bountiful harvests and all the days of their lives, they recognize this by returning to God the firstfruits and one day in seven as a token of what Israel has received. This applies to the promise land as well. As God had given Israel its land in fulfillment of the divine responsibilities of the covenant, so Israel would now return back to God certain towns for divinely mandated purposes. Towns of refuge for the inadvertent killer of another person had been described earlier (Exod 21:12–14; Num 35:9–15, 22–28; Deut 4:41–43; 19:1–10); three were designated west of the Jordan River and three to the east. Deuteronomy 19 affirms an additional three towns on the west side. Their absence here may reflect the lack of a complete conquest. The killer stands at the city gate and sets forth his/her case. That person remains in the town of refuge until a trial where the incident occurred (Num 35:22–28). Even if the killer is acquitted of premeditation at this point, the blood avenger, a family relation of the victim, is obligated to seek redress. So the killer lives in a town of refuge where protection is guaranteed "until the death of the one who is high priest" (Josh 20:6). The high priest symbolizes all Israel in its sin before God (Lev 16). The death of the priest is accepted in place of the killer and blood vengeance is satisfied.

G. The Levitical Towns (21:1–42)

The second manner in which Israel returns to God a portion of its inheritance takes place with the setting aside of towns as a gift to the Levites, who otherwise have no land (Num 35:1–8). This principle of God's people returning to God a portion of their material blessings remains active in the New Testament (Acts 2:44–47; Rom 15:26–27; Phil 4:10–18). The Kohathites who were descendants of Aaron's line would function in a priestly capacity. Their location in the south, near to the tabernacle and the later Jerusalem Temple, seems reasonable (Josh 21:4). The remaining Kohathites, the Gershonites, and the Merarites each had different functions related to the care of the things of God (Num 1:47–53; 3:1, 25–26, 33–37; 4:15–33; 7:9), and each received inheritance from different tribes. The forty-eight towns that the Levites would occupy were spread throughout Israel and formed the foci for Levitical and priestly duties of teaching their fellow Israelites the instructions of God (Lev 10:11). The towns included former Canaanite strongholds and those near the frontiers of Canaanite lands so that all the inhabitants of the land might have the opportunity to learn of God.

H. Conclusion to the Allotments (21:43–45)

These verses emphasize the fulfillment of God's promises. Three times this realization is repeated. The Hebrew for "all, every," *kol*, appears six times in this passage, highlighting the completion of God's blessings to Israel. Is this not a contradiction of Josh 13:1–7, where the lands remaining to be captured were listed? Israel had realized victory over the nations round about them as a group; however, there remained the need to deal with specific towns and areas among the allotments. God's power has accomplished redemption for the land, just as it will ultimately bring full redemption to Christians. However, towns and regions remain unconquered just as sin and suffering remain in the lives of Christians.

III. Proper Worship of God (22–24)

A. An Altar East of the Jordan River (22:1–34)

Joshua discharges the Transjordanian tribes to their inheritances, with commendation as to how they fulfilled their agreement to fight for Israel (Josh 1:13–18; 22:1–4). He recognizes that these tribes are fully part of the covenant community. The tribal identity now becomes the pressing issue of this chapter. The Transjordanian tribes built an altar in Canaan but one that was apparently visible across the Jordan River in their homeland (Josh 22:10). The remaining tribes saw this as an affront and gathered for war. They sent the new generation's priest, Phinehas son of Eleasar, accompanied by ten representatives from each of the tribes west of the Jordan River, to negotiate with the Trans-

jordanian tribes. They accused the Transjordanian tribes of turning away from God by building this altar and they feared that God's wrath would fall on all Israel, as had happened at Peor (Num 23) and with Achan (Josh 7). The tribes east of the Jordan began their response with a repeated confession of the Lord as the "God of gods!" They thus recognized no other deity nor did they wish to compromise their faith in any way. They wanted the altar to function as a memorial, rather than as a place of (false) worship. Future generations would remember that the tribes east of the Jordan built it to express their unity and identity in religious as well as political matters with the other tribes of Israel. The explanation satisfied Phinehas and the tribal representatives, and then all Israel. The name of the altar, "Witness," signified its role as "a witness between us that the LORD is God" (Josh 22:34). Just as with this story of early Israel, so in the life of the church the maintenance of unity (John 17) and holiness (2 Cor 6:14–18) before God become essential elements of the church's mission on earth (2 John 7–11).

B. Joshua's Farewell Address (23:1–16)

As with Moses in the book of Deuteronomy, so here Joshua presents a farewell address in which his focus concerns Israel's future and the choices it has. Little occurs here that has not already appeared in Deuteronomy or elsewhere in the Pentateuch. Joshua thus does not announce new ideas but rather repeats time-honored truths. The note that "Joshua was old and well advanced in years" recurs here, as it first appeared in Josh 13:1. There it preceded the allotments; here it precedes the people's agreement to follow God and the actual habitation of the land. As in Josh 13, so here there is a recollection of what remains to be done and a promise that "God will push them back before you" (v. 5). Repeated items in the address of this chapter emphasize aspects of concern to Joshua: "it is the LORD your God who has fought/fights for you" (vv. 3, 10); "those nations that remain / these nations left here among you" (vv. 4, 7, 12); and "be very steadfast/careful" (vv. 6, 11). God will fight for Israel, but the nation has a responsibility to participate as well (v. 5). As in Josh 1:7 so in Josh 23:6, "the book of the law of Moses" plays a key role in guiding Israel to live faithfully. Verses 9–10 connect God's faithfulness in fighting for Israel with the ability of Israel to defeat superior forces. The theme of wholehearted commitment and devotion to God remains a key one for Christians as well (Rom 12:1–2).

The blessings of victory come with faithfulness. As in the covenant of Deuteronomy (ch. 28) there follow the curses for disobedience. Specifically, Joshua envisions three aspects of covenant violations: alliance and intermarriage with Canaanite survivors who will then destroy the Israelites (vv. 12–13); just as God has been faithful in blessings so God will be faithful in bringing judgment upon the nation for its sins, and this will continue even after Joshua's death (vv. 14–15); and idolatry leads to God's anger and Israel's destruction (v. 16). As with the covenant of Moses and Joshua, so also for the Christian there are judgments associated with departing from faithfulness (Heb 6).

C. Joshua's Covenant Renewal with Israel (24:1–28)

This last formal gathering under the leadership of Joshua recounts a covenant renewal ceremony. The covenant bore a resemblance to the political treaty, especially the Hittite suzerain-vassal treaty discovered among the Hittites and found as late as the early twelfth century BCE. As a narrative report of the event, this chapter does not explicitly contain all the elements of this structure but some do appear. The titulary identifies the suzerain to the vassal. In this case, Joshua begins, "Thus says the LORD, the God of Israel" (Josh 24:2). This historical prologue follows and serves to motivate the vassal to continued loyalty and obedience by pointing out how much such obedience benefits the vassal. In Josh 24:2–13, the historical review begins with Israel's ancestors who worshiped other gods east of the Euphrates River. God's deliverance of Abraham from this and the lives of his successors in Canaan develop the theme of divine providence. The sojourn in Egypt ended with the divine choice of Moses and Aaron. There followed the deliverance from Egypt and its destruction in the sea, the wilderness wanderings, the failure of Balaam who tried to curse Israel but could only bless the nation (Num 22–24), and the victories over Jericho and all the peoples of Canaan. Throughout this description, emphasis remains with God's deliverance of Israel from its enemies. Thus the drying up of the Red Sea mentioned by Rahab (Josh 1:10) and the manna in the wilder-

ness do not receive mention; nor, of course, do the events at Mt. Sinai. Israel defeated Amorites east and west of the Jordan River. God's sending of "the hornet" symbolizes the terror that has manifested itself in fear throughout the book of Joshua (Josh 2:9, 24; 5:1; 9:24; 10:2; 14:8). This hornet fulfills the promise made in Exod 23:27–28. In a similar manner Josh 24:13 fulfill the promise of Deut 6:10–11. It emphasizes God gracious gift for Israel, just as Eph 2:8–10 does for Christianity.

Joshua 24:14–24 corresponds to the legal stipulations of the covenant and treaty documents. As in ancient treaties and in biblical covenants such as Deuteronomy, the basic legal element is grounded in exclusive loyalty to the suzerain, in this case loyalty toward God. The dramatic challenge that Joshua gives to Israel to put away the gods of Israel's ancestors across the Euphrates and the deities of the nations surrounding them concludes with Joshua's own example of serving only the Lord. The people of Israel respond with a similar reflection of their God's deliverance from Egypt, guidance in the wilderness, and victory over the Amorites. They conclude with a similar affirmation of loyalty to God. Not content with giving Israel a choice, perhaps because he knows their hearts so well, Joshua challenges them directly, "You cannot serve the LORD, for he is a holy God" (v. 19). He wants them to count the cost, to realize how dangerous it is for them to make this commitment and then turn their backs on it. Implied in v. 20 are the covenantal blessings and especially cursings. If they do not obey, then Israel will lose their lives and their identity. Israel's response and insistence that they will follow God leads to Joshua's reference to the one remaining element that regularly occurred in Hittite suzerain-vassal treaties; the witnesses. Usually the witnesses were the deities of both nations. Here, however, the invocation of other gods would violate the basic command of loyalty to God alone. Therefore, Joshua identified two witnesses: the people themselves and a large stone that he set up at Shechem (vv. 22 and 27). At this point, Joshua wrote the words of the covenant requirements in the book of God's law. Like the stone and their own words, it would remind them of what they had promised.

All may seem well as Joshua sends Israel to their homes. However, two ominous elements remain. First, when Joshua charged the people specifically to "put away the foreign gods that are among you" (v. 23), the people's general response to obey God alone omits any mention of agreement with this specific element. Second, the text does not record that the people of Israel made any effort to put away their gods. Unlike their ancestor Jacob and his family, who buried their images at Shechem (Gen 35:2–4), these people do nothing. James' assertion that actions must accompany faith (Jam 2:14–16) comes to mind. Judges 2:11–13 suggests that it did not take long for Israel to fall into the sin of idolatry after the death of Joshua and his generation.

D. The Deaths of Joshua and Eleazar (24:29–33)

As with Moses (Deut 34:5), so Joshua at the end of his life received the accolade, "the servant of the LORD." Joshua and Joseph both died at the age of 110 (Gen 50:26). Since Joshua's inheritance was the last one (Josh 19:50), his death and burial closed the era of the allotments. Verse 31 reflects how the generation of Joshua and the elders was one of faithfulness to God just as it was one that had witnessed God's miracles. The reports about their final resting place match and enhance the connection between Joseph and Joshua in terms of age (Josh 24:32). Joseph's burial recalls his death (Gen 50:24–26) and Jacob's purchase of the burial ground (Gen 33:18–20). Thus, the deaths of Joshua and Joseph connect the beginning of Israel's history with its final settlement in the land. The death of Eleazar brings to an end the priestly generation of Joshua and anticipates the next generation with reference to his priestly son, Phinehas. The importance of the death of the high priest has already been noted (Josh 22:14). The conclusion of the book reflects on faithfulness in leadership and ministry, not unlike the apostolic testimony found in 2 Tim 3:7–8.

The concluding verses of Josh 24:29–33 are virtually repeated in Judg 2:6–9. They not only summarize the great story of Israel in the Pentateuch; these words also prepare for the next generation by anticipating the death of the generation of Joshua and dramatic apostasy that arises (already noted in Judg 2:10–13) after the passing of this godly leadership. The theological message forms a bridge with the beginning of the book of Joshua as well. There the focus was on God's will for the leadership of the people of God as represented in the figure of Joshua. Here, the importance of that leadership is remembered for its positive influence. The book of Joshua in many ways reflects the ideals of this godly leadership and the faithful obedience of the people. This is true despite the clear imperfections of that people, as for example in the account of the Gibeonites in Josh 9. The book of Judges will contrast this ideal with the reality of a settled people struggling with the daily temptations of seeking after other gods and becoming like the surrounding peoples. God's plans for leadership will adjust to meet these new challenges.

BIBLIOGRAPHY

A. G. Auld. *Joshua: Jesus Son of Naue in Codex Vaticanus.* Septuagint Commentary Series. (Leiden: Brill, 2005); T. Butler. *Joshua.* WBC 7 (Waco: Word, 1983); R. S. Hess. "A Typology of West Semitic Place Name Lists with Special Reference to Joshua 13–21." *BA* 59/3 (September 1996) 160–70; "The Book of Joshua as a Land Grant." *Bib* 83 (2002) 493–506;_____. "Early Israel in Canaan: A Survey of Recent Evidence and Interpretations." *PEQ* 125 (1993) 125–42; *Joshua. An Introduction and Commentary.* TOTC. (Leicester: IVP, 1996); "Non-Israelite Personal Names in the Book of Joshua." *CBQ* 58 (1996) 205–14; "War in the Bible: An Overview." *War in the Bible and Terrorism in the Twenty-First Century.* R. S. Hess and E. Martens, eds. Bulletin for Biblical Research Supplement (Winona Lake, Ind.: Eisenbrauns, forthcoming); "West Semitic Texts and the Book of Joshua." *BBR* 7 (1997) 63–76; D. M. Howard, Jr. *Joshua.* NAC (Nashville: Broadman, 1998); R. D. Nelson. *Joshua: A Commentary.* OTL (Louisville: Westminster John Knox, 1997); K. L. Younger, Jr. *Ancient Conquest Accounts: A Study in Ancient Near Eastern and Biblical History Writing.* JSOTSup 98 (Sheffield: Sheffield Academic Press, 1990).

JUDGES

JEROME F. D. CREACH

OVERVIEW

The book of Judges receives its name from the statement in Judg 2:16 that, when Israel suffered at the hands of enemies, "the LORD raised up judges, who delivered them out of the power of those who plundered them." As this verse indicates, the judges are primarily military leaders. Nevertheless, those individuals said to have "judged" Israel (2:7; 15:20; 16:31) do lead Israel in other ways as well. For example, Deborah acts as a judge in the traditional sense of the term (4:5, "the Israelites came up to her for judgment") and as a prophet (4:4).

Judges is set in the time between Israel's exodus and wilderness wandering (led by Moses and Joshua) and the establishment of the monarchy. Many historians once thought Judges provided significant information about a definite historical era, 1200 to 1020 BCE. As the theory goes, the Israelites during this time organized as a league of tribes with the judges leading them in war. This portrait of early Israel now seems difficult to maintain. Most of the stories in Judges involve local heroes and a small number of Israelite tribes. Such a portrait of "all Israel" appears to be a creation of writers and editors from a later time. Nevertheless, the period of the judges remains very important theologically in the biblical narrative. It represents a time in which the Israelites struggled to live into the promises of the land Joshua had conquered. Whereas the time of Joshua is remembered as a period of obedience and the realization of divine promises (2:7), the time of the judges is marked largely by disobedience and decline. The main sign of Israel's failure is its inability to secure the land God gave (2:20–21).

Some scholars propose that Judges portrays Israel's disobedience in order to prepare the reader for the Davidic monarchy, introduced in 1 and 2 Samuel. This idea is thought to be supported by the recurring refrain, "In those days there was no king in Israel; all the people did what was right in their own eyes" (17:6; 18:6; 19:1; 21:25). But Judges' understanding of Israel's sinfulness and the leadership of the judges is more complex than this argument allows. Some of the judges are por-

trayed as heroic and honorable, but they do not take up the mantle of kingship. The one figure who declares himself king (Abimelech in Judg 9) is sharply criticized for the ruthless means by which he gains power. The note that Israel had no king seems to have a more subtle meaning that is related to God's role as sovereign. That is, Judges contains narratives about an Israel that does not recognize the king it does have, namely the God who has given Israel the land (see 8:3).

The book of Judges is closely related to Deuteronomy in its theological interests. In fact, Judges seems to be part of a literary complex (excluding Ruth) that runs from Deuteronomy through 2 Kings (called the Deuteronomistic History). One of the major Deuteronomistic interests in Judges is the concern for Israel to separate itself from those living in the land and to avoid worshiping their gods. Judges presents Israel's experience in terms of a recurring pattern of apostasy, defeat, and deliverance (2:11–19). As the book unfolds, however, it becomes apparent that the cycle of rebellion, oppression, and salvation reveals the larger picture of Israel caught up in a world of lawlessness and violence.

Many modern interpreters have been concerned about the portrayal of violence in Judges. Portions of the book seem to glorify the violent acts of Israel's judges. The exploits of Ehud (3:12–30), Deborah (4–5; cf. the act of Jael [4:17–22; 5:24–27]), and Samson (16:28–30) are prime examples. When the book gives tacit approval of such violence, however, it seems to recognize Israel as a victim in the grips of an oppressive and powerful enemy. In other situations, however, violence is a primary sign of Israel's deterioration. Indeed, Judges depicts Israel in a downward spiral in which violence is a sign of Israel's disorder. The final section of the book (chs. 17–21) shows the outbreak of violence and warfare as evidence that Israel failed to acknowledge properly God's sovereignty (see 17:6; 18:6; 19:1; 21:25).

The declining status of and violence done to women signifies Israel's deterioration as narrated in the book. Near the beginning, Caleb's daughter Achsah seeks a blessing from her father and he grants it (1:14–15). Deborah appears early in the cycle of judges as one of the most influential leaders in Israel (4–5). As the book progresses, however, women suffer more and more. Jephthah sacrifices his daughter (11:34–40). The men of Gibeah rape and murder a Levite's concubine (19:22–30). At the end of the book Israel traffics in women in an effort to restore the tribe of Benjamin (21). In other words, the violent treatment of women symbolizes the way in which Israel has lost its way during a time when "there was no king in Israel."

OUTLINE

I. After Joshua, the Canaanites Remain (1:1–3:6)

   A. Israel Fails to Secure the Land (1:1–2:5)

   B. Apostasy, Defeat, Deliverance (2:6–3:6)

II. The Judges (3:7–16:31)

   A. Othniel (3:7–11)

   B. Ehud (3:12–30)

   C. Shamgar (3:31)

   D. Deborah (4:1–5:31)
      4:1–24. Narrative Account
      5:1–31. Song of Deborah and Barak

   E. Gideon (6:1–8:35)
      6:1–32. Call of Gideon
      6:33–8:3. Defeat of Midian and Amalek
      8:4–35. Gideon's Fall

   F. Abimelech (9:1–57)

   G. Tola and Jair (10:1–5)

   H. Jephthah (10:6–12:7)
      10:6–16. Rebellion, Oppression, and Divine Sorrow
      10:17–11:28. Rise of Jephthah
      11:29–40. Jephthah's Vow and the Death of His Daughter
      12:1–7. Jephthah's Violent Legacy

   I. Ibzan, Elon, Addon (12:8–15)

   J. Samson (13:1–16:31)
      13:1–25. Samson's Birth
      14:1–15:20. Marriage at Timnah

      16:1–3. The Prostitute at Gaza
      16:4–31. Delilah and the Death of Samson

III. Downward Spiral of Violence (17:1–21:25)

   A. Micah, the Levite, and the Danites (17:1–18:31)

   B. The Violent End (19:1–21:25)
      19:1–30. The Levite's Concubine
      20:1–48. Civil War
      21:1–25. Reconciliation Through Violence

DETAILED ANALYSIS

I. After Joshua, the Canaanites Remain (1:1–3:6)

Judges begins with a two-part introduction (1:1–2:5; 2:6–3:6) that draws attention to the failure of the Israelites in the period following Joshua's death. The first part focuses on military failure: Israel cannot drive out the Canaanites. This section ends with Israel weeping over its inability to secure the land (2:4–5). The second part deals with religious or covenantal failure. It introduces a pattern of apostasy, judgment, and divine deliverance that structures much of the rest of the book (2:11–19). The two panels cannot be sharply separated theologically. Israel's efforts to secure the land symbolize its obedience to the covenant; the land represents God's blessings on an obedient people (2:20–21).

A. Israel Fails to Secure the Land (1:1–2:5)

Judges 1:1–2:5 begins with the death of Joshua (1:1) and picks up where the book of Joshua left off, with the Israelite tribes going out to secure the territories assigned to them by casting lots (see especially Josh 15:1; 16:1; 17:1, 14, 17). Whereas Josh 1–12 suggests God's people acquired the land easily and quickly, Judg 1:1–2:5 presents a more complex picture. For this reason some scholars have characterized Judg 1:1–2:5 as more historically accurate than Josh 1–12 (and more in line with Josh 13–19, which differs from the prior chapters).

Judges 1:1–2:5 highlights the importance of Judah above the other tribes, which suggests this first section was written at a time when Judah was the dominant tribe and Jerusalem (1:8) was centrally important (perhaps after 722 BCE when the northern tribes were in exile). When the Israelites inquire as to which tribe should go up to take the allotted territory, God appoints Judah. He is initially successful (1:1–10), but the section as a whole portrays the progressive failure of the Israelites. Although Simeon is presented positively, he succeeds only under the auspices of Judah ("Judah said to his brother Simeon, 'Come up with me;' " 1:3). The rest of the tribes falter: the tribe of Benjamin, though represented well by Caleb (1:20), is not able to drive out the Jebusites (1:21); Joseph's tribes (Ephraim and Manasseh) are endowed with divine presence just as Judah ("the LORD was with them"; 1:22; cf. 1:19), and experience some success (1:22–26), but their achievements are qualified by the assessment that they "did not drive out" the residents of their territories (1:27, 29); the same is said of Zebulun (1:30), Asher (1:31–32), and Naphtali (1:33). The summary of the tribes' accomplishments and failures ends with the wholly negative portrait of Dan: "The Amorites pressed the Danites back into the hill country" (1:34).

Judah and Simeon defeat and capture Adoni-bezek (1:5–7), known in Josh 10:1–5 as leader of a royal coalition against the Israelites. Verses 6–7 depict the king as sub-human (like a dog beneath the table), typical treatment of a conquered enemy. Adoni-bezek's confession in v. 7 ("as I have done, so God has paid me back") is a warning about the ultimate punishment of one who uses power to practice cruelty (it is God who pays him back).

Judges 2:1–5 is linked to 1:1–36 by the theme of driving out the residents of the land (2:3). This section begins with "the angel of the LORD" going from Gilgal to Bochim. Gilgal was the place Joshua's army camped upon crossing the Jordan (4:19–24), the place Joshua circumcised those who were born in the wilderness (Josh 5:2–9), and the place the Israelites first celebrated Passover in Canaan (Josh 5:10–12). The identity of Bochim is uncertain, but it may well be another name for Bethel (see 21:2). The move from Gilgal to Bochim represents failure and disobedience. The angel declares that God will not abandon his covenant (2:1), but the Israelites have been unfaithful by making covenants with the people of the land (2:2). With

such an indictment, the people weep (2:4) and the place is called Bochim, meaning "weeping" or "weepers."

B. Apostasy, Defeat, Deliverance (2:6–3:6)

This second introductory panel seems out of place. It begins with the final acts of Joshua, though 1:1 already reported what happened after his death. This may mean that 2:6–3:6 was the original beginning to the book of Judges. In any case, Judg 2:6–3:6 begins much like the book of Joshua ends, but with important differences that reflect the context of Judges. Like Josh 24, this section of Judges includes references to Joshua sending the people away to their inheritance (2:6; Josh 24:28), to Joshua's generation being obedient (2:7; Josh 24:31), and to Joshua's death and burial (2:8–9; Josh 24:29–30). Judges 2:6–10, however, focuses on the rise of the disobedient generation after Joshua. Judges 2:10b notes that the new generation "did not know the LORD," a line reminiscent of Exod 1:8 ("a new king arose over Egypt, who did not know Joseph").

Judges 2:11–23 then presents a pattern that highlights Israel's sinfulness on the one hand and God's graciousness on the other hand. The Israelites "did what was evil in the sight of the LORD" by worshiping other gods (2:11). Specifically, they followed after the Baals, local expressions of the Canaanite storm god, and the Astartes, representatives of a fertility goddess, the consort of Baal (2:13). As a result of this unfaithfulness, the Lord gave the Israelites over to their enemies (2:14–15). But God raised up judges to deliver them (2:16–17) because God was "moved to pity" by their suffering (2:18). Despite God's graciousness, however, the Israelites reverted to their unfaithful ways whenever a judge died (2:19).

The introduction to the book ends with a theological explanation for why the nations remained in Israel's midst; namely, God refused to drive out the nations because of Israel's disobedience to the covenant (2:20–21). Hence, God left the nations to test Israel's faith (2:22–23; 3:1–2). Israel would live among the nations (listed in other texts such as Deut 7:1). The final word of the introduction concerns Israel's failure to abide by the covenant in this context, as signaled by intermarriage with the people of the land and the worship of their gods (3:6; see Deut 7:3–4).

II. The Judges (3:7–16:31)

A. Othniel (3:7–11)

The report of the work of the first judge (known already from 1:13), though brief, includes the entire pattern introduced in Judg 2:11–19: the people did "what was evil in the sight of the LORD" (3:7); the "anger of the LORD was kindled" against them and the Lord gave them over to enemies (3:8); the Israelites cry to the Lord and he raises up Othniel as a deliverer (3:9); the spirit of the Lord is upon Othniel and he is successful (3:10); as a result, the land "had rest forty years" (3:11). The judges who follow may be evaluated by how their work follows or departs from this sequence.

B. Ehud (3:12–30)

The account of Ehud in Judg 3:12–30 makes for a great story: an intriguing hero, a suspenseful plot, and a mysterious murder. The story is set when the Moabites, led by King Eglon, oppress the Israelites and demand tribute from them. Ehud is chosen to deliver the yearly offering as a sign of Israel's loyalty. The intrigue begins with Ehud's tribal identity and his mode of operation as a soldier. As a Benjaminite he is literally a "son of the right hand." Judges 3:15 notes, however, that Ehud is "a left-handed man." The reference to his use of the left hand bears practical military importance. Literally v. 15 reports Ehud was "bound concerning his right hand." Judges 20:16 uses the same language to report that the Benjaminites had 700 soldiers specially trained as left-handed slingers. This perhaps means the Benjaminites restricted their soldiers' right arms in order to produce left-handed (or ambidextrous) fighters. This ability gave them a distinct advantage against other soldiers who assumed and were equipped for right-handed opponents. In the case of Ehud, use of the dagger with his left hand (which meant he placed it upon his right thigh; 3:16) allowed him to pass through King Eglon's security with the weapon undetected and to attack King Eglon without him suspecting foul play.

Judges 3:17 depicts Eglon as "a very fat man." Fat here is both a description of Eglon's physical appearance and a statement about his opulent lifestyle. The story is about the disadvantaged underdog, Israel, who defends itself against one of the biggest "fat cats" of the day.

Another key element of the story is the place King Eglon receives state visitors. The account seems to imply Ehud meets Eglon in a two-storied palace with a portico and public reception hall on the first floor and private chambers for the king on the second floor. The king's chamber includes a bathroom with a toilet (the "cool roof chamber" in 3:20). Such buildings have been discovered in northern Syria.

When Ehud returns (3:19) to seek a private audience with Eglon, he apparently meets the king on the second floor. The "secret" Ehud has for Eglon is perhaps news of another vassal's unfaithfulness, sensitive enough that it required a private conversation. Ehud reaches for his dagger with his left hand and drives it into Eglon, whereupon "the fat closed over the blade" (3:22). Then v. 23 reports that Ehud went out, closed the doors, and locked them, presumably from the outside. But at least two questions remain concerning the murder. One question is how Ehud escaped unnoticed. The sequence of events in v. 23 may indicate that the doors featured a tumbler lock accessible from the outside through a fist-sized hole (as described in Song 5:4–6). The door would have been secured by means of a bolt that was released by raising the pins that held the bolt in place with a key that fit over the ends of the pins. Or Ehud may have exited through the toilet by lowering himself to the floor below, and then gone out through an access door used by royal janitors. However, this interpretation fails to take seriously the order of events in v. 23 and it ignores the lock system just described, which allows an easier explanation.

Another question is the meaning of the word rendered "dirt." This translation follows the Aramaic and Latin versions, which attempt to interpret a Hebrew word that they did not fully understand. There is a similar word in Akkadian that means "excrement" and the first three letters of the word form a Hebrew noun that does clearly mean "the contents of the intestines" (Lev 4:11). So apparently when Ehud's weapon goes into the belly of Eglon it ruptures his intestines, thus causing feces to emerge from the wound.

The story of Ehud concludes with him rallying the Israelites against Moab, thus giving the land "rest" for eighty years (vv. 26–30). The reference in 3:29 to the 10,000 Moabite soldiers all being "strong" could also mean "fat" (see the use of this word in v. 22 ["fat closed around the blade"] and see Hab 1:16 where this word is paired with the term used to describe Eglon in v. 17). Hence, the entire Moabite army is like King Eglon. This portrait enhances the idea that underdog Israel triumphs over a more wealthy and powerful enemy.

C. Shamgar (3:31)

Based on Shamgar's name (which is non-semitic) and his identification as "son of Anat," some scholars have proposed he was a Canaanite warrior devoted to the goddess Anat (Baal's sister) and who may have served the Israelites as a mercenary. Such a claim is also strengthened by the pairing of his name with Jael (5:6); Jael was also a non-Israelite. All that can be said with certainty, however, is that Shamgar is presented as a mighty warrior who, like Samson, kills a multitude of Philistines with an unconventional weapon. Perhaps that similarity to Samson caused the report about Shamgar to appear at the end of ch 16 in some Greek manuscripts.

D. Deborah (4:1–5:31)

Judges 4–5 describe Deborah and her general Barak defeating Canaanite forces at Mount Tabor and then celebrating with a victorious hymn. The hymn in Judg 5 is one of the oldest passages in the OT, likely dating to the twelfth century, close to the events it recounts. Judges 4 is a later narrative account that appears to use the poetic version as its main source. However, the hymn now appears at the end of the narrative as a celebrative song performed by Deborah and Barak (note the way in which the two sections are linked by the comment in 5:1, "Then Deborah and Barak son of Abinoam sang on that day, saying").

It is important to assess the differences between Judg 4 and 5. The differences can be explained largely by considering how the writer of ch. 4 interprets and sometimes expands ch. 5. One may identify two primary tendencies: (1) the author of Judg 4 sometimes reads the poetic parallels in Judg 5 as though they are narrative and not poetry (hence, the writer treats them literally); (2) the writer of the narrative fills in the gaps of the poetic version by drawing upon other traditions that seem relevant (see below). As a result, it is appropriate to read ch. 4 both as a derivative

account that has used ch. 5 as a source (noting how the author interpreted and supplemented the existing account) and as a coherent narrative.

4:1–24. Narrative Account. Verses 1–3 provide an introduction to the work of Deborah like that given for Othniel (3:7–9) and Ehud (3:12–14): Israel "did what was evil in the sight of the LORD" (4:1); the Lord "sold them" to their enemies (4:2); then the Israelites "cried out to the LORD for help" (4:3).

Judges 4:2 presents two figures who oppose the Israelites—Jabin and Sisera—though Judg 5 mentions only Sisera (5:20, 26; cf. 5:28–30 in which Sisera's mother awaits his return with the spoil). The addition of Jabin is likely influenced by the note in Judg 5:19 that Sisera led the forces of the "kings of Canaan." Joshua 11:1 identifies Jabin as king of Hazor, whereas Judg 4:2 knows him as the king "of Canaan."

Judges 4:3 reports Jabin's forces were formidable because they had "chariots of iron" (v. 3); the actual places iron was used on such vehicles is uncertain; perhaps the wheels were iron-covered or the poles at the front were made of iron. Chariots were important since they allowed infantry to move swiftly into position against an enemy. There is no record of the Israelites having chariot forces before the time of David (2 Sam 8:4).

Verse 4 introduces the unlikely hero Deborah. Translations of v. 4, however, may actually conceal some of the radical nature of Deborah's leadership. The label, "wife of Lappidoth," identifies her in a domestic role. The expression, however, could also be translated, "woman of Lappidoth" (thus identifying her with a place rather than with a husband) or perhaps "woman of fire." If understood this way, the focus is on Deborah's charisma. She is a fiery figure, one chosen by God and endowed with extraordinary gifts. As such, she is far different than the domestic figure one might expect.

Deborah's roles of prophetess and judge are a remarkable sign of God's favor. As with Greek oracles, Deborah is identified with a tree where the Israelites seek her for "judgment." They come for "decisions" (as JPS renders), that is, for divine judgment that she gives by virtue of her role as mediator between God and humans (the basic role of prophet).

Barak acknowledges Deborah's special status when he responds to her request that he lead in battle, "If you will not go with me, I will not go" (4:8b). Deborah affirms her prophetic gifts when she declares that Barak will not win glory for himself; instead, Sisera will fall to the hand of a woman (4:9). Ironically, however, the woman to whom he will fall is not Deborah the warrior but Jael, the tent-dwelling wife of Heber (4:17).

Although Deborah is identified as a judge for "Israel," the story of her battle with Sisera includes only two northern tribes, Zebulun and Naphtali (4:6, 10). Judges 5:14–18 hints at the involvement of other tribes, but their role is not clear. Hence, Judg 4's listing of only two tribes likely reflects the author's conservative approach to the original source.

Mount Tabor, where the battle takes place, is in the Lower Galilee, just to the south of the territory occupied by Zebulum and Naphtali. The Israelite troops are presented as militia fighters, summoned when needed, pitted against Sisera's standing army. The battle itself is described much like the defeat of Pharaoh at the Red Sea. Just as God did to the Egyptian troops, the Lord "threw Sisera and all his chariots and all his army into a panic" (4:15a; Exod 14:24). Indeed, the victory is attributed to divine action: "the Lord will sell Sisera into the hand of a woman" (4:9a); "the LORD has given Sisera into your hand. The LORD is indeed going out before you" (4:14); "So on that day God subdued King Jabin of Canaan before the Israelites" (4:23).

The account of Sisera's death and the defeat of his army begins with a brief explanation of why the tent of Heber the Kenite might seem to Sisera a hospitable place to escape from Barak (4:11). The Kenites were descendants of Moses' father-in-law and thus might be friendly to the Israelites. Heber, however, had separated from the other Kenites and migrated far to the north near Kadesh. This focus on Heber also paints Jael as a domestic figure (the wife of Heber), just as many translations of 4:4 present Deborah (as "wife of Lappidoth"). It is worth noting, however, that the tent in 4:17 is identified with Jael, not her husband.

Verses 12–16 portray Barak routing the forces of Sisera. Sisera escapes on foot while Barak pursues Sisera's chariots in another direction.

Sisera's retreat to the "tent of Jael, wife of Heber the Kenite" assumes a world dominated by tribal chieftains (v. 17). Sisera believes Heber is sympathetic to him and Jael confirms that impression by welcoming Sisera into the tent (v. 18). Jael here is portrayed either as Sisera's mother who dotes over him or as his lover, or perhaps as an ambiguous mixture of the two. She feigns affection for Sisera by giving him milk to drink when he asked only for water (v. 19). When he falls asleep beneath the cover Jael places over him she approaches him "softly" (v. 21), a statement that has sexual overtones (see Ruth 3:7 in which Ruth comes "softly" to Boaz at the threshing floor). She then takes in her hands a tent stake and mallet and drives the stake through Sisera's temple. The language here too has sexual overtones, but it reverses the typical aggressor (male) and victim (female) roles. The woman, who is often vulnerable to sexual assault by the soldier, becomes the aggressor and pierces the soldier.

5:1–31. Song of Deborah and Barak. Chapter 5 is a song that recalls the victory of ch. 4 and attributes the victory to God (see the same pattern of victory hymn following narrative in Exod 15). The song is addressed to God ("to the LORD I will sing," v. 3); twice the singer calls for participants to "bless the LORD" (vv. 2, 9); and the victory is cast as the outcome of God's mighty rule over cosmic forces (vv. 4–5). Even when human agents such as Deborah, Barak, and Jael appear, the hymn recognizes that heavenly forces assured the victory ("The stars fought from heaven, from their courses they fought against Sisera," v. 20). The hymn, which celebrates God's justice and judgment over oppressive forces, presents the deity as a divine warrior.

The song is attributed to Deborah and Barak (v. 1), but the verb "sing" is feminine singular, which implies that Deborah voices the hymn. Deborah's leadership of the celebration is understandable in light of women's roles in such rituals (see Exod 15:21; 1 Sam 18:6–7). Verse 7 also seems to identify Deborah as the speaker. Although NRSV renders "you arose" the verb is actually first-person singular, "I arose."

"When locks are long" (v. 2a) may refer to willing service in warfare (see v. 2b), though the exact inference here is debated. Free-flowing hair can be a metaphorical expression of the warrior's lack of restraint. Indeed, ancient Near Eastern iconography often depicts warriors with long and sometimes disheveled hair. But the long locks could also refer more specifically to Israel bursting free of oppression. This language (and the expression, "offer themselves willingly" in 2b) may be related to the nazirite vow not to cut the hair (see 13:5, cf. the free-flowing locks in Num 6:5).

Verses 4–5 describe a theophany (God's appearance in natural phenomena) typical of other victory hymns (Ps 68:7–10). The Lord's appearance from Seir/Edom in the Transjordan is present elsewhere (cf. God's appearance from Sinai in Ps 68:17 and the association of God with Sinai here).

Verses 6–9 set the battle in a time of social upheaval and relate the event to specific human characters (Shamgar; see 3:31; and Jael; see 4:17–22). Concerning the former, the time of the fight is marked by the prosperity of the "peasantry" under the leadership of Deborah. The label "mother" for Deborah refers to her authority and may apply to her prophetic role, just as Elijah and Elisha were called "father" (2 Kgs 2:1–2; 13:14). The plundering activity may reflect Robin Hood-like action against rich traders. Choosing "new gods" may refer to the rise of the Israelites under Deborah. Treaties were typically sealed by recognizing the deities as witnesses. Verse 8b indicates the miraculous rise of the Israelites who operated without the conventional military weapons (see 4:13).

Throughout vv. 10–13 there are hints that Israelites exist outside the typical power structures. They dwell in rural areas beyond the power of cities; hence, they march "down to the gates" (that is, to walled settlements), not from them (v. 11b; see also v. 13b, "they marched down for him against the mighty").

Verses 14–18 are often thought to distinguish those who answered the call to battle from those who did not, i.e., Ephraim, Benjamin, Machir (western part of Manasseh), Zebulun, and Issachar fought with Barak (vv. 14–15a), while Reuben, Gilead (not one of the tribes, but listed here), Dan, and Asher did not. Though vv. 15b–17 are often interpreted as statements of non-participation, however, the verbs translated "tarry" and "sat still" (vv. 16a, 17b) and "stayed" (v. 17a) typically mean "sit" or "dwell," but not "stay behind." Furthermore, the question about Dan (which is iden-

tical in form to that about Reuben) includes a verb that simply means "sojourn" or "live temporarily." The only clear statement about non-participation concerns Meroz (v. 23), an otherwise unknown group. Therefore, it cannot be determined with certainty what vv. 14–17 (and especially vv. 15b–17) say about these tribes. Perhaps for this reason the author of ch. 4 only named Zebulun and Naphtali as those who fought with Barak. Verse 18 praises them as those who "scorned death."

Verses 24–27 recount how Jael killed Sisera, albeit with strikingly different details than in 4:17–24. Verse 24 pronounces blessing on Jael in a poetic line that begins and ends with the expression, "May you be blessed" (NRSV, "Most blessed"). The expression "wife of Heber the Kenite" could also be translated "woman of the company of the Kenites" (see comment on 4:17 above). The poetry of vv. 25–27 suggests a very different sequence of events than those in the narrative in 4:19–21. The parallel expressions in v. 25, "he asked water"/"she gave milk"/"curds in a lordly bowl" do not suggest she provided something more than requested. Rather, this is a poetic device used to heighten and intensify the statement of what she provided (the substance provided becomes richer and more calorie-laden as the poetic line moves from start to finish, a common technique in Hebrew poetry; see Ps 51:5). Similarly, v. 26 suggests Jael hit Sisera with a blunt object, probably while he consumed what she had given him. Tent pegs could be substantial (Isa 33:20) and might well have been an object tent-dwellers would have grabbed in an act of self-defense (as some have proposed, Jael might have been fending off a rape). At any rate, the parallel expressions, "her hand to the tent peg"/"her right hand to the workmen's mallet" do not suggest that Jael used two objects to kill Sisera. Rather, this is a poetic way of saying Jael used something available in the tent. This picture of the event is confirmed by v. 27, which reports Sisera fell at Jael's feet after she hit him. Verse 27 uses another technique common in Hebrew poetry to describe Sisera's end; it presents a miniature narrative in short parallel units: "he sank/ he fell/ he lay still at her feet/ at her feet he sank/ he fell/ where he sank, there he fell dead."

The song's penultimate section (vv. 28–30) portrays Sisera's mother waiting for her son to return from battle with the spoil. She is presented as the mirror opposite of Deborah. Both are "mothers" (v. 7), but Deborah represents the weak and oppressed Israelites (as prophet and warrior) while Sisera's mother is the picture of aristocracy (pampered and at leisure).

E. Gideon (6:1–8:35)

The name Gideon means "hacker." The title indicates his role as religious reformer, one who hacks down the idols of foreign deities (6:28–32). Despite his zeal for the purity of worship, however, his last act is the making of a cult object, an ephod, that leads Israel into idolatry (8:22–27). Hence, he is an ambiguous leader.

6:1–32. Call of Gideon. Judges 6:1–10 is an extended prelude to the call of Gideon. This section expands the pattern of activity in 2:11–23: Israel sinned against the Lord; the Lord gave them over to enemies; Israel cried to the Lord; the Lord sent a judge to deliver them. This lengthy prelude develops the basic pattern in three ways. First, the nature of the enemy's oppression is described in greater detail: The Midianites and the Amalekites decimated Israel's crops and impoverished them (6:3–6). Second, Israel's rebellion against God is characterized specifically as idolatry (6:10); Israel is tempted to pay heed to the deities of the peoples who oppress them. Finally, these verses describe an elaborate provision of a deliverer. God first sends a prophet who reminds Israel of how God delivered them in the exodus. Then the prophet indicts them for their disobedience (6:7–10). Only later does the narrator identify Gideon as the deliverer. This prophetic word hints at one of Gideon's main tasks, namely to rid Israel of its idol worship. The lengthy call of Gideon (6:11–32) implies that he bears great responsibility.

The commissioning of Gideon takes the form of other such stories in OT and is especially similar to the story of the call of Moses (Exod 3:1–4:17). Such accounts typically include the appearance of God or an angel. In this case "the angel of the LORD" appears to Gideon when he is threshing grain (6:11). As the story proceeds, however, the one speaking to Gideon is alternatively identified simply as "the LORD" (6:14, 16). The uncertain identity of the visitor is reminiscent of Jacob's nocturnal encounter with "a man" (Gen 32:22–32). The angel's visit also includes fire as a sign of his presence (6:21); hence the scene echoes that of Moses at the burning bush (Exod 3:1–6).

Such stories also include a divine address to the one being called and a specific task to be performed (Exod 3:7–10). In Judg 6:14 the angel says, "Go in this might of yours and deliver Israel from the hand of Midian; I hereby commission you."

Judges 6:11–32 is also like other commissioning stories in that the one being called expresses doubts about the mission, whereupon the divine visitor provides a sign of assurance that the mission will be successful. Gideon expresses repeated doubts, asking for multiple signs. In this way, Gideon is just like Moses who continued to object to the mission until God became angry with him (Exod 4:14). Gideon first questions the angel's address to him, "The LORD is with you, you mighty warrior" (v. 12). Although Gideon does not mention it directly, he might have questioned the label "mighty warrior." At the time of the angel's appearance, Gideon is doing the unassuming work of a farmer and hiding the produce from the enemy. What Gideon questions, however, is the notion that God is present. Gideon complains that God has "cast us off," language common in the Psalter (Pss 74:1; 88:14). Typical of such exchanges, the Lord then commissions Gideon to deliver the people (6:14). To this, Gideon objects that he is from a clan with no power or influence (v. 15; see the similar objection of Moses in Exod 3:11). But Gideon's unassuming family and his own low status as youngest child put him in the company of others like Jacob and David. The truth communicated here seems to be what Paul would later say to the Corinthian church, "God chose what is low and despised in the world, things that are not, to reduce to nothing things that are" (1 Cor 1:28). Indeed, the point is not that Gideon is strong, but that God is with him (v. 16; see 1 Cor 1:29).

After the Lord commissions Gideon, Gideon then asks for a sign, another typical feature of commissioning stories. The sign that follows, which involves Gideon setting up an altar at the place of the Lord's appearance, associates Gideon with Israel's patriarchs (Gen 12:7, 8; 13:18; 26:23–25). The sign of God's presence is a fire that springs from the rock of the altar when Gideon places his sacrifice there.

After the scene of commissioning, God instructs Gideon to tear down his father's altar to Baal. His father, Joash, is a member of Canaanite society and thus adheres to the idea that Baal brings fertility to the earth and economic prosperity to the people. Baal's altar is flanked by a "sacred pole" or Asherah. The sacred pole may represent a goddess associated with Baal. Gideon's action is a sign that his altar to the Lord has replaced the altar to Baal and that the Lord is in fact superior to the Canaanite deity. The ultimate sign of this transfer of allegiance is that the wood from the sacred pole by the altar to Baal is to be used as wood for the fire on the Lord's altar (6:25).

Gideon's destruction of his father's altar amounts to a complete rejection of the Canaanite worldview. It challenges strongly held ideas about the forces that control the world and what allegiance to such forces means. It is not surprising, therefore, that Gideon performs his act at night and in secret. After Gideon is determined to be guilty of the iconoclastic act (perhaps by the people inquiring through a prophet; see v. 29), the people of the town call on his father to bring him out to be killed. Joash recognizes, however, that power rests with Gideon's God. He therefore responds with legal language, let Baal "contend for himself" (v. 31). This expression thus explains the origin of Gideon's other name. He is called Jerubbaal which means, "let Baal contend" (v. 32). Although the story presents Jerubbaal as a name given when Gideon contended with Baal, it may have been his original name since the rest of the story refers to him primarily by this title (see 7:1).

6:33–8:3. Defeat of Midian and Amalek. After Gideon's initial success in destroying the altar of Baal, the enemies mentioned in 6:3 appear again (6:33). As before, the foe is portrayed as a group of allies consisting of the Midianites, Amalekites, and the "people of the east." Gideon seems prepared to lead the Israelites against the enemy since "the spirit of the LORD took possession of Gideon" (6:34). When the spirit came earlier upon Othniel (3:10) he delivered Israel from its enemies. Now, however, the divine spirit seems to have little effect upon Gideon, even though the tribes respond to Gideon's call to battle (6:34–35). Instead of leading the troops with confidence he instead asks for another sign of assurance.

Gideon's second request for a sign (6:36–40) suggests a lack of faith that might engender God's anger (6:39). Gideon asks two times for God to give a sign. The first request involves Gideon placing a fleece of wool on the threshing floor and asking God to fill the material with water from the dew, while the ground around remains dry (6:36–38). This sign may not have been that difficult to accomplish. It is a common practice to acquire fresh water in places without fresh-water streams. But then Gideon asked for the sign to be reversed, with the ground being wet with dew but the fleece remaining dry (6:39–40). God provides the miraculous signs that Gideon requested.

The subsequent account of Gideon's battle with the Midianites (7:1–8:3) reinforces God's support of and presence with Gideon, but it also subtly portrays Gideon's misplaced trust. The story begins with God ordering Gideon to reduce the number of troops going to battle in order to make clear that God alone would deliver Israel from its enemy. The warriors are not to say, "My own hand has delivered me" (7:2). Two tests reduce the number of troops. The first test reflects Moses' instructions to allow any warrior who was fearful to return home (Deut 20:8). This reduces the force from 32,000 to 10,000. The second test involves Gideon watching the troops as they drink from the stream. Only those who lap water like a dog are kept for the battle. So, with only 300 soldiers Gideon goes out to face the multitude of Midianites, Amalekites, and people of the east who "lay along the valley as thick as locusts" (7:12).

The account of the battle resembles the story of Joshua's battle at Jericho (Josh 6). Gideon's men blow trumpets to signal the fight (7:18, 19, 22), and the battle is won because God gives it into their hands (7:9, 14). The main difference is that Gideon also claims part of the credit for the victory. He instructs his troops to shout, "For the LORD and for Gideon" (7:18; cf. 7:20). Gideon claims for himself something that should be reserved only for God.

8:4–35. Gideon's Fall. The conclusion to the story of Gideon shows him to be an ambiguous figure. As 8:4–21 indicates, Gideon is successful as a commander in battle. The timid thresher of grain has indeed become a "mighty warrior" (6:11–12). It is possible to interpret these verses as an account of brutality that God does not mandate. Gideon treats his enemies cruelly, cutting off the hands of

Zebah and Zalmunna (8:7) and killing the people of Succoth and Penuel (8:16–17). Nevertheless, Gideon's leadership in battle leads the Israelites to ask him to be their king (8:22). To his credit, Gideon responds by saying that only the Lord can rule over Israel (8:23).

What comes next, however, is a puzzling turn in the Gideon story. He asks the people to give him golden earrings they acquired as booty and with them he makes an ephod, an object associated with divination (8:27). The reason for making this object is not clear. It is possible that Gideon's fashioning of the ephod indicates that he abdicates his own responsibility as leader. Instead of "ruling" Israel, he provides an object meant to help them seek God's guidance. Regardless of the rationale for the ephod, it leads Israel astray. As 8:27 says, "all Israel prostituted themselves to it." At the end of his life Gideon is given a hero's burial (8:32), but his legacy is ambiguous. As soon as Gideon dies, the Israelites returned to worshiping the Baals and practicing idolatry (8:33–35).

F. Abimelech (9:1–57)

Gideon's son Abimelech is the first Israelite in the Bible to take the title "king." The fact that his story portrays his rule so negatively is evidence that Judges is not simply intended to prepare readers for the monarchy. Instead, the account shows how unjust monarchy can be.

Since ch. 9 never says that Abimelech "judges" Israel, his story should in fact be read as a continuation of the story of Gideon. His name ironically means "my father is king." Titles like this typically indicate that the person descended from a king or that his own kingship has been approved by the deity, the divine monarch. The first possibility does not apply since Gideon declared that neither he nor his son would rule over Israel. Indeed, he said only God could be Israel's king (8:23). The second scenario also does not apply. God does not give Abimelech his authority; he takes it by force.

Though Abimelech seeks to be king, his rule is not an attempt to create a national political entity. Rather, his authority is limited to a territory associated with his own kinship group. He convinces the "lords of Shechem" to anoint him alone as their ruler rather than have Gideon's seventy sons as authorities over them. They agree and provide him with money to form an army (9:4). Soldiers in such an army were typically at the bottom of the social order, without inheritance or standing (see 11:3; 1 Sam 22:2), but their identity here as "worthless and reckless fellows" also paints them with disdain (2 Sam 6:20). This characterization of Abimelech's troops is consistent with the description of Abimelech and his actions to secure his rule. After receiving the support of the people of Shechem, Abimelech murders his brothers in order to ensure his place as king. He was born to Gideon's concubine and thus had less status than the sons of Gideon's wives (on the significance of the concubine see the discussion of 19:1). Hence, Abimelech attempts to gain power and influence through means other than an inheritance. The people of Shechem then make Abimelech king at a sacred location, marked by a tree (see the reference to the palm of Deborah in 4:5).

Jotham, Gideon's youngest son, is the sole survivor of Abimelech's murderous plot. He denounces Abimelech's actions with a parable delivered from Mount Gerizim, a place outside Shechem closely associated with covenant-making (Josh 8:30–35). Jotham recounts that the trees looked among themselves for a king (9:8). But neither the olive tree (9:9), nor the fig tree (9:10–11), nor the vine (9:12–13) would accept the position. Each had its own important work to do, producing fruit that sustains and enriches life. Only the worthless bramble agrees to be king (9:14–15). The poem ends with the bramble's ironic declaration of its desire to provide "shade" or "refuge" for the other trees. As a mere scrub bush it cannot provide shade. The fable may not be intended as a critique of monarchy in general, but of the type Abimelech established, namely, rule founded on murder and deceit.

The remainder of the story of Abimelech narrates his downfall (9:22–57). God sends "an evil spirit" that creates dissention between Abimelech and the lords of Shechem. God's disapproval comes specifically because of Abimelech's violent killing of his seventy brothers (9:24). Thus, Abimelech must fight for control of his kingdom. At this point, two new characters enter the story—Gaal, who opposes Abimelech and wins the support of the lords of Shechem (9:26–29), and Zebul, the "ruler of the city" who continues to support Abimelech (9:30–33). With the help of Zebul, Abimelech fights Gaal for control of Shechem.

Abimelech wins the battle, razes the city, and kills all who are within its fortifications (9:45). This act shows how violent Abimelech really is. His dispute was with the lords of Shechem, not the commoners in the city, but he kills all of them. Moreover, after destroying Shechem he "sowed it with salt," which may mean he poisoned the ground so crops could not be grown in the territory again. Then Abimelech turns to the lords of Shechem who retreat to the Tower of Shechem, a fortified portion of a temple (9:46). Abimelech burns the tower and kills all those inside.

The victory of Abimelech at Shechem, however, comes back upon him when he continues to pursue his enemies at the city of Thebez (9:50–57). The people of Thebez retreat into a tower fortress just as the people of Shechem had done and Abimelech proceeds to burn the tower as he had burned the tower of Shechem. But Abimelech approaches the wall too closely and a woman drops a millstone on him. The millstone was an object a woman could hold in her hand, not what one imagines as a lethal weapon. That fact, and the fact that a woman dropped it on Abimelech is the ultimate sign of shame. Although Abimelech's armor bearer actually kills him with his sword to avoid it being said that "A woman killed him" (9:54), the manner of Abimelech's death was remembered for generations (2 Sam 11:21). To the extent that he is killed by a woman, Abimelech is like Sisera who is killed by Jael (4:9).

The story of Abimelech concludes with the statement that "God repaid Abimelech" for his violent acts (9:56) and God brought on Shechem the curse of Jotham. It is significant that in a book that seems to favor the Israelites over the Canaanites and supports the Israelite "conquest" of Canaan, God punishes Israelites when they behave inappropriately.

G. Tola and Jair (10:1–5)

These two judges provide a respite from the tumultuous times associated with Abimelech. They are often called "minor" judges because no narratives have survived about their activities. Both are said to have "judged" Israel (10:2, 3) and both are said to have ruled for an extended period (Tola, twenty-three years, 10:2; Jair, twenty-two years, 10:3).

H. Jephthah (10:6–12:7)

10:6–16. Rebellion, Oppression, and Divine Sorrow. This section describes the Israelites' rebellion against God according to the pattern introduced in 2:11–23: Israel worshiped the Baals and Astartes; the Lord was angry and allowed their enemies to defeat them. However, here the rebellion and subsequent punishment is intensified by the additional note that the Israelites serve the gods of Sidon, Moab, the Ammonites, and the Philistines. In other words, they worship the deities of all their enemies identified to this point (plus Sidon, which has not appeared until now). In turn, the Israelites are "sold" by God to two enemies—the Philistines and the Ammonites—not just one as before.

To their credit, the Israelites confess their unfaithfulness (v. 10). God responds, however, by reminding Israel of this recurring pattern; from the time of their oppression in Egypt (see the reference to the Egyptians in v. 11) the people have cried to God when their enemies oppressed them. Each time God delivered them from bondage, but each time Israel turned to other gods. Hence, God's declaration in v. 13a, "You have abandoned me" seems like a summary concerning Israel's disobedience rather than simply a declaration of one more instance of unfaithfulness. The pronouncement in v. 13b, "I will deliver you no more" is likewise a final statement. The character of vv. 10–15, however, provides the context for a radically different conclusion in v. 16. Verse 16a reports that Israel "put away the foreign gods" and "worshiped the LORD" (even without a promise of deliverance). Verse 16b then records one of the greatest expressions of divine pathos in OT. NRSV renders, "he could no longer bear to see Israel suffer," but this is a circuitous translation that does not adequately reflect the deep emotion the Hebrew communicates. The subject is actually "his soul" or "his life" (NRSV, "he"). The verb means "to be cut short." Although the meaning of this expression is uncertain (cf. RSV, "became indignant"), it probably means that God experienced sorrow, hence, God's life was diminished. Next comes an expression that explains the cause of God's disquietude, cf. Num 23:21; Isa 53:11. God was saddened (perhaps "cut to the quick") by Israel's suffering. This portrait of God provides an important balance to the frequent statement that God's anger "was kindled" against Israel (2:14, 20; 3:8; 10:7). The notion that God suffered because of Israel's suffering is consistent with the summary statement in 2:18, that God "would be moved to pity by their groaning."

10:17–11:28. Rise of Jephthah. Jephthah is introduced as an unlikely hero, the son of a prostitute who is rejected by his half brothers (11:1–3). His identity as the son of a prostitute has more to do with his place (or lack of a place) in the father's lineage than with any stigma attached to such disreputable birth. Being born to a woman other than his father's wife allows the sons of the legitimate wife to exclude him from the inheritance (v. 2). The omniscient narrator identifies Jephathah's father as Gilead.

The story of Jephthah is similar to those of Abimelech (Judg 9) and David (1 Sam 16:1–13), men forced to find wealth and position apart from the resources of the household of the father (David being the youngest of seven sons, thus virtually assured of inheriting nothing). Jephthah gathers around him others who were economically disadvantaged. They "went raiding," that is, they became mercenaries or guerrilla fighters (again, like David [1 Sam 22:2], as well as Jeroboam [2 Chron 13:6–7] and Abimelech [Judg 9:4]).

Jephthah wins the support of the elders of Gilead and then leads them successfully against the Ammonites. He shows himself particular adept at negotiation by arguing on the basis of Israel's history for the territory they possess (11:12–28). When the Ammonites fail to solve territorial issues through negotiation, Jephthah then leads the people of Gilead militarily.

11:29–40. Jephthah's Vow and the Death of His Daughter. Despite Jephthah's successful beginning, his story turns tragic when he makes a vow to enlist God's help in his battle with the Ammonites. The vow is a pledge that implies a self-curse if not upheld. In this case, the vow is part of Jephthah's preparation for battle, a practice attested elsewhere (Judg 21:1–3). The content of the vow, however, eerily anticipates the tragic end of the story. Jephthah's promise is ambiguous and open-ended; according to NRSV, he pledges to sacrifice "whoever comes out of the doors of my house" (11:31). But the expression, "whoever comes out" translates a participle that is masculine singular and could be translated "whatever comes out." It is possible to speculate that Jephthah assumed a domestic animal would emerge first when he arrived home. The first floor of houses in this period typically had a central courtyard where domestic animals were kept. But the courtyard was also used for cooking and other domestic chores and would have been a typical work place for women. Therefore, it should also not be a surprise that Jephthah's daughter, his only child, was the first to come out of the house.

The daughter in fact came out specifically to meet her father "with timbrels and with dancing" (11:34a), which would also not be unexpected. Women had a particular role as leaders in victory celebrations (see the same expression, "with timbrels and dancing" in Exod 15:20). When Saul's army returned victorious the women of the villages met them with celebrative songs (1 Sam 18:6–7).

It is possible to read into the story divine neglect of Jephthah's daugther. The story has parallels to Gen 22:1–19. Jephthah's daughter is called the "only" child (v. 34), as Isaac is also identified (Gen 22:2, 12, 16). But while a voice from heaven directs Abraham not to sacrifice Isaac, in Judg 11:34–40 God is silent here. The story itself, however, provides no information about either divine approval or disapproval.

The ambiguity of Jephthah's vow is probably best left unexplained and the story is probably best read as a tragedy, similar to Greek tragedies. Jephthah has a fatal flaw that finally undoes him and his daughter. One main issue that plays out is Jephthah's lack of inheritance. Being excluded by his half brothers from a share in the father's property, Jephthah works his way into power and wealth by means of military and negotiating skills. When he oversteps his bounds ("negotiating" with God) by making his vow, however, he ensures that his own property, and his name, will not be passed on. The emphasis on his daughter being his "only" child suggests this point is primary. Further, Jephthah's comment to his daughter when he sees her coming out of his house should be understood in this light ("Alas, my daughter! You have brought me very low; you have become the cause of great trouble to me;" 11:35ab). His "great trouble" refers to his loss of his progeny.

The story ends with the daughter taking initiative: she responds to her father with a request to go for two months with her friends to "bewail" her "virginity" (11:37). After Jephthah grants her request (11:38a), she departs (11:38b). When the daughter returns, she gives herself over to the vow (11:39a). A final note then links the lament over her virginity to a custom among daughters in Israel of lamenting Jephthah's daughter for four days each year (11:39b–40).

The main question regards the meaning of the daughter lamenting her virginity. The word for virginity refers to the state of a woman who has not had sexual relations (Deut 22:14–15, 19ab; cf. "young woman" in Deut 22:19a). The emphasis in this case, however, may be more the young woman's marriageable age than her lack of sexual experience. The daughter perhaps "bewails" (literally, "weeps over") something related to this state, the major time of transition for a young woman in ancient Israel. But why did she weep over "her virginity" and why would this one woman's tragic experience produce a ritual for all daughters in Israel, as 11:40 indicates? One key may be in the broad similarities between this story of Jephthah's daughter and European folk tales about young women held captive in towers (Rapunzel) or otherwise captured (as in "Beauty and the Beast") or put to sleep ("Sleeping Beauty" and "Snow White"). In each case, the resolution of the story—release from the tower, from a beast, or from a death-like sleep—leads to the young woman becoming a wife. Hence, the stories both recognize the anxiety-producing nature of the time between childhood and womanhood, and reinforce the role of women in patriarchal society, namely as daughter and as wife/mother. The story of Jephthah's daughter particularly emphasizes the relationship between father and daughter.

The relationship between the two primary characters here is not a caricature of father/daughter relations in patriarchal social structures. First, it should be noted that the daughter's centrality to inheritance implies a higher status for her than one might expect. Only sons were to inherit property (Deut 21:17) unless the inheritance could only be passed on to daughters (Josh 17:3–8; see also the special case of Job 42:15). Here her role as heir to Jephthah's property provides the crux for the story. Second, the daughter appears as an actor in the story, not just as a victim of her father's vow. Although she acquiesces to her father's vow, nevertheless she expresses her opinion, makes a request of her father, and creates the ritual that is passed on to the daughters in Israel. In the end the story remains androcentric, but the daughter is not simply a silent pawn in its plot.

12:1–7. Jephthah's Violent Legacy. Jephthah's story ends sadly, with this once successful negotiator unable to maintain peace between the Israelite tribes. Conflict arises when the tribe of Ephraim complains that Jephthah did not include them in battle against the Ammonites (12:1). The complaint probably stems from the Ephraimites' desire to share the spoils. Jephthah says he called the Ephraimites to aid him, but they did not respond (12:2b–3). The story in Judg 11 does not report this. Hence, it is not clear whether the account implies that Jephthah is lying, or perhaps that such a call to arms was implied when tribes in coalition were engaged in conflict with outside forces. What is clear is that Jephthah could not avert violence between Ephraim and Gilead, as Gideon has earlier had done (the Ephraimites made the same complaint to Gideon; see 8:1). Instead, "Jephthah gathered all the men of Gilead and fought with Ephraim" (12:4).

I. Ibzan, Elon, Abdon (12:8–15)

The brief accounts about Ibzan, Elon, and Abdon provide little information except that Ibzan and Abdon had numerous sons, a sign of their influence as tribal chiefs. Brief accounts like these perhaps helped establish the paradigmatic number twelve as the number of judges who ruled Israel (the text never says Abimelech "judged" Israel; thus he stands outside this number).

J. Samson (13:1–16:31)

Samson is a famously flawed hero, known best for his incredible strength. The most positive aspect of Samson's story perhaps lies in the battles with the Philistines that shape Samson's "public" life. Samson represents Israel in its marginal state as victim of an oppressive power. Indeed, Samson's life is framed by the Philistine conflict (13:1; 16:23–30) and his role as deliverer.

Despite the potentially positive value of the Samson story, he also embodies much of what is wrong with Israel in the book of Judges. Samson sleeps with a prostitute (16:1–3) just as Israel "prostituted" itself with foreign gods (the same root is used in 2:17 and 8:33). Although the story begins with the lofty portrayal of Samson as a nazirite, he eventually breaks every vow. As the last judge, Samson stands in contrast with Othniel, the first and model judge, in two important ways: (1) unlike Othniel, who married an Israelite woman from a devout family (1:11–15), Samson has a string of bad relationships with foreign women who lead him astray; (2) Othniel delivered Israel from its enemies and gave them "rest" for forty years (3:9, 11), but Samson could only "begin to deliver Israel" (13:5). The end of his life marks no period of relief from Israel's enemies (16:35).

Samson's career as Israel's deliverer also marks the culmination of the worst impulses of previous judges. Gideon and Jephthah at times were given over to revenge and settling personal vendettas (8:4–9, 13–17; 12:1–6), but now Samson is consumed with such acts (14:19; 15:7, 14–17; 16:28–30). Hence, Samson's career punctuates the period of decline that is the period of the judges; it anticipates the complete lawlessness with which the book ends.

13:1–25. Samson's Birth. The opening verse of the Samson story (13:1) repeats part of the established pattern for the work of the judges: the Israelites "did what was evil" and the Lord handed them over to the Philistines for forty years. But what typically comes next—the Israelites cry to the Lord for deliverance—is missing (2:11, 14; 3:7–8, 12; 4:1–2; 6:1; 10:7–8). This missing element is a subtle sign that God's use of judges to rescue the Israelites has become ineffective. The failure of Israel to cry out to God implies that they do not even know how to call for help. This implication of the missing element is evident in 15:11 where the Israelites protest Samson's challenge to the Philistines by saying, "the Philistines are rulers over us." At the end of the Samson story, the relief from Philistine rule is only partial, with no summary statement concerning the number of years the Israelites had peace after Samson's time as judge.

The birth of Samson is foretold by the angel of the Lord to Samson's mother, the wife of Manoah. She is identified as barren (v. 2), which, along with the angelic visit, signals the extraordinary nature of the birth and the importance of the child (see

similar stories of Isaac in Gen 11:30; 21:1–7; and Samuel in 1 Sam 1:1–28).

The angel instructs the woman not to drink wine or to touch anything unclean (v. 4) because the child will be a nazirite. The word nazirite means "separated one" or "consecrated one" and normally refers to an adult who takes a vow for a limited period of time (see Num 6:1–21). Samson, however, is to be a nazirite from birth and, apparently, for life. Numbers 6:1–21 stipulates three requirements for the nazirite: to abstain from wine, not to cut their hair, and to avoid touching a corpse. Samson's mother in essence begins to fulfill two aspects of the vow for him in-utero. All three of these requirements eventually play an important role in revealing Samson's weaknesses and failure to remain true to his nazirite identity.

After the angel appears to the woman, she reports the experience to her husband Manoah who, in turn, asks God to repeat the experience for him. The appearance of the angel of the Lord to Manoah seems to be written with knowledge of two stories in Genesis. Manoah's hospitality (v. 15) is like that Abraham extended to the three visitors who came to him (Gen 18:1–15). The attempt to learn the angel's name (v. 17) is similar to Jacob's effort to learn the name of the visitor with whom he wrestled (Gen 32:29). These allusions to the stories of the patriarchs, plus the motif of angelic visitation to a barren woman, suggest God is expending all possible effort in the birth of Samson. The previous judge's work (Jephthah) ended in failure, marked by intertribal conflict. Hope now rests on Samson.

14:1–15:20. Marriage at Timnah. The account of Samson's birth in ch. 13 raises great expectations for him to deliver Israel. The first story of Samson as an adult, however, immediately shatters those expectations. Samson marries a Philistine woman in violation of covenant regulations (Deut 7:3–4). In route to and during his wedding he breaks one, and possibly two of his nazirite vows. Throughout chs. 14 and 15, Samson seeks vindication on the Philistines who have wronged him, thus misusing his physical strength. Despite the selfish motivation of these acts, however, the story claims that God uses them to bring about Israel's deliverance (14:4).

Samson is born in Zorah, a town on the border between Israelite and Philistine territory. The account in chs. 14–15 turns on issues especially pertinent to residents of such an area. The covenant God established with Israel demanded separation from the people of the land, with particular emphasis on avoidance of marriage contracts with them (2:2; Deut 7:3–4). Samson's first act is to request his father and mother to arrange a marriage with a Philistine woman at Timnah, another town on the border between Philistine and Judahite territory. Recognizing the covenantal implications, his parents suggest marriage to an Israelite woman. But Samson insists, "Get her for me, because she pleases me" (v. 3; see v. 2). His words, "she pleases me" is, literally, "she is pleasing in my eyes." This statement anticipates the refrain that will appear later in the book, "all the people did what was right in their own eyes" (17:6; 21:25). Samson's disregard for the covenant seems to symbolize Israel's turn away from God's expectations.

Judges 14:5–9 is the first account of Samson breaking his nazirite vows even as he displays his legendary strength. Reference to the "vineyards of Timnah" (v. 5) is a subtle indication that Samson disregards his vow since he is to refrain from any product (food or drink) from the vine (13:14; Num 6:3–4). The portion of the vow he actually breaks in ch. 14, however, is the prohibition against touching a corpse (Num 6:6). On the way to Timnah, Samson kills a lion barehanded because the "spirit of the Lord rushed on him" (v. 6). According to Lev 11:27, the lion itself is ritually impure, thus rendering Samson unclean. But when he returns from meeting the woman at Timnah he takes honey from the beehive in the lion's carcass, a breach of nazirite regulations.

The next portion of the story (vv. 10–20) turns on the difficult union of rival groups—Philistines and Israelites—through marriage. The feast (v. 10) indicates the groom's contribution to the proceedings were meant to bring the two groups together. This event also seems to be the occasion for Samson to break the restriction against partaking of strong drink (Num 6:3–4; 13:4). The wedding feast is identified by a Hebrew word that implies drinking. So, although the story does not report it directly, Samson appears to violate his nazirite status. A significant feature of the feast

is the assignment of thirty Philistine companions for the Israelite groom. The attempt to bring the two groups together, however, ultimately fails. Samson proposes a riddle, based on his discovery of the honey in the lion's carcass: "Out of the eater came something to eat. Out of the strong came something sweet" (v. 14). The riddle in turn is the center of a wager of sixty garments. When the Philistines cannot solve the riddle, they threaten Samson's wife and her family. She then nags him for the length of the festival until he reveals the solution to the riddle. When she discovers the answer to the riddle and provides it to the thirty Philistines, they give Samson the answer just before their time is up ("before the sun went down," v. 18). Their response, however, is not straightforward. Rather, it is formed as a question, "What is sweeter than honey? What is stronger than a lion?" (v. 18). Hence, their answer both solves the riddle (they identify lion and honey and eater/strong and sweet) and poses another one. The answer to their counter-riddle seems to be love or human passion (Song 8:6, "love is strong as death").

Samson's offers a poetic response to his companions that is also filled with sexual (and chauvinistic) overtones: "If you had not plowed with my heifer, you would not have found out my riddle" (v. 18). Throughout the Samson story (and throughout much of Judges) women are treated as commodities, as those owned or controlled by men. So here Samson refers to his wife as "my heifer," and his charge that the companions have "plowed" with her may imply that they have used her sexually. Whoever is in control of the woman sexually has advantage in the narrative. But ironically, the women Samson tries to control end up controlling him (the wife at Timnah in 14:17 handles Samson like Delilah does in 16:16). After being bested by the Philistines at Timnah, Samson goes into a rage, attributed again to the spirit of the Lord (v. 19), and kills thirty men at Ashkelon, an important Philistine city (see Josh 13:3). Then Samson abandons his wife, an act tantamount to divorce. Hence, her father gives her to Samson's best man.

Chapter 15 continues the story of Samson's wedding at Timnah with Samson returning to reclaim his wife whom he left earlier. Themes from the previous chapter continue, particularly the picture of women as desirable property used by husbands and fathers (v. 3) and of Samson's hot-headed action. Verses 4–8 narrate the first story of Samson's Herculean strength and v. 6 confirms that he uses it to settle a personal vendetta against the Philistines. When the men of Judah bind him and hand him over to the Philistines and he breaks the ropes, the scene anticipates the Delilah story in which he will twice be bound and break free (16:7–12).

In a more positive way, however, Samson fulfills a role in this story best characterized by the label "wild man." Every culture seems to know such characters, from the Gilgamesh epic (the character Enkidu) to Medieval stories of wild men raised by animals. Wild men are closer to the untamed wilderness than to urban culture; they live alone in desolate places; they have power over wild animals; they use crude or unconventional implements (usually from the natural world) to conquer foes; and they are hairy! Samson has already been characterized as a person with long hair (as part of his nazirite identity). In 14:6 he kills a lion with his bare hands. Now in 15:4–5 Samson uses an army of foxes with fiery tales to get back at the Philistines. Later (15:15) he uses the jawbone of a donkey to kill 1, 000 Philistines. In 15:8 Samson hid "in the cleft of the rock of Etam," thus confirming his loner status.

Nonetheless, Samson's wildness is a mark of God's favor (for example, Samson's long hair ensures his strength and God's favor), whereas typically such characters become acceptable to God only when they are tamed. This view of Samson's wildness probably reflects the way in which Samson represents Israel in these stories. In terms of culture and military sophistication, Israel is inferior to the Philistines. But as outsiders and underdogs, Israel is favored by God (cf. Deut 32:10–13 which depicts Israel as a wilderness creature adopted by God and nursed with wild honey). Perhaps for that reason, God's spirit is with Samson, the wild man. His wildness represents the opposite of the sophistication and oppressiveness of the Philistines. Hence, Samson, with all his rash reactions and seemingly selfish acts of revenge, at some level represents liberation from oppression for Israel.

16:1–3. The Prostitute at Gaza. Samson's second sexual encounter is with a prostitute at Gaza, one of the five major Philistine cities. This brief story alludes to much of what has already been revealed about Samson in chs. 14–15: he lusts after foreign women; these women lead him into encounters with Philistine adversaries; the trysts do not lead to permanent relationships; Samson maintains his status as a loner. Samson's visit with the prostitute of 16:1–3 gives the men of Gaza opportunity to kill him. They lay a trap, waiting for his appearance at morning. But Samson tricks the Philistines by leaving the prostitute at midnight. Not only does he escape their trap, he also takes the city gate with him. The scene is Paul Bunyan-like. Genesis 22:17 refers to Israel's dominance over its enemy as "possessing their gate," and here Samson takes the gate, literally. He moves it from Gaza to the Israelite city of Hebron, some forty miles away.

16:4–31. Delilah and the Death of Samson. The final story of Samson's love life is much like the one in ch. 14. Samson is attracted to a woman who lures him into a trap for the Philistines. The name Delilah in Hebrew means "flirtatious," which fits her role in the story. Unlike Samson's first two lovers, however, her ethnic identity is uncertain. She lives in the valley of Sorek, an area within Israelite territory, some thirteen miles southwest of Jerusalem. Perhaps this means Samson finally listened to his parents and sought after an Israelite woman. Still, the area in which she lives is border territory and the Philistines use her to capture Samson. Whatever Delilah's ethnic identity, she differs from the first two women since she gets information from Samson for money.

Verses 4–22 narrate the way in which Delilah coaxes from Samson the secret to his strength. Two themes dominate the story. First, Delilah deceives Samson, just as the wife at Timnah had done, through constant nagging (14:17; 16:16). Second, Samson is overconfident, apparently believing he is the author of his own strength when in reality it comes from God. He knows, of course, that his strength derives from his nazirite vow to God (16:17), but his willingness to play with Delilah and the Philistines concerning the source of his strength exemplifies an overconfidence in his control of it (see especially 16:20).

The story has four movements. Each movement includes Delilah asking Samson to reveal the source of his strength (vv. 6, 10, 13, 15); Samson revealing, or supposedly revealing it (vv. 7, 11, 13,

17); Delilah acting on Samson's information (vv. 8, 12, 14, 19); and Delilah calling the Philistines to take Samson (vv. 9, 12, 14, 20). It may be tempting to think Samson a dolt since he revealed the source of his strength after Delilah called the Philistines on him three times before. The sequence of four episodes, however, is a typical storytelling technique that builds suspense (cf. Matt 13:1–9) and, if anything, it underscores Samson's arrogance, not his stupidity.

The final movement ends with the Philistines seizing Samson, gouging out his eyes, and making him grind at the prison mill. Since grinding grain was the work of women in the ancient Near East, this may be an attempt to feminize Samson, a common treatment of enemy soldiers (2 Sam 10:4). The movement ends, however, with a hint of what is to come: Samson's hair begins to grow back and, with it, his strength.

Verses 23–31 present a later scene as the Philistines gather to sacrifice to Dagon, their chief god of fertility. Samson's final act is a repudiation of the Philistines and their deity. His prayer is followed by the return of his strength. The conclusion to his story (v. 31) presents an honorable burial in his family tomb and a positive note that "he had judged Israel twenty years."

III. Downward Spiral of Violence (17:1–21:25)

The final major section of the book of Judges provides testimony concerning the failure of the era of the judges and of their leadership. This portion of the book is punctuated by the repeated refrain, "In those days there was no king in Israel; all the people did what was right in their own eyes" (17:6; 18:6; 19:1; 21:25). These final chapters show the Israelites at the end of a downward spiral that is narrated throughout the book, but especially since the judge Jephthah (see 12:1–7).

A. Micah, the Levite, and the Danites (17:1–18:31)

Judges 17:1–18:31 reports the first scene in the decline of the Israelites in a story about an idolmaker and an opportunistic Levite who hires himself out as a priest. The account is set in northern territory. The story centers on a certain Micah and his mother. The name Micah (v. 1) is ironic in that it means "Who is like the Lord?" and yet the bearer of the name, and the other characters in the story seem to act in opposition to God. Micah initially embezzles money from his mother (17:2, "I took it"). When he returns it, his mother dedicates the money to the construction of an idol (17:3). The refrain in 17:6 offers indirect disapproval of this behavior. It is the act of an individual who creates a shrine without approval from a centralized authority. Although the story portrays a time when such images may have been accepted at local shrines, the reference to the house of God at Shiloh (18:31) hints at what would become official policy later: only one sanctuary is designated as the place of God's presence, first Shiloh and later Jerusalem (Jer 26:6).

Micah steals a sum of eleven hundred pieces of silver. The amount draws the reader back to the story of Samson, for this is the same amount each Philistine gave Delilah to betray the Israelite strong man (16:5). Although the story does not explicitly refer to the Samson account, the amount of money suggests that no good will come in the following events.

The description of the idol in 17:3 uses two words, one indicating something hewn (perhaps from wood) and the other an object cast with metal. This figure was probably an image carved out of wood and then overlaid with precious metal (a silver-plated calf similar to the one described here has been discovered at Ashkelon). In addition to this object, Micah also constructs an ephod and a teraphim, objects used for divination, and sets them up in his personal shrine. He then installs his son as priest.

Judges 17:7–13 introduces a Levite from Bethlehem who goes out looking for employment and a place to live. As one who did not inherit property, the Levite was to be supported by the community through its offerings at the sanctuary (Deut 18:1–8). This story may come from a time before such institutional support, or after the exile when support was difficult to find. In this narrative, the Levite hires himself out to Micah and becomes his private priest. Micah provides wages and essential goods. Micah believes that hiring the holy man brings God's favor on him, that he has, in effect, hired God (17:13).

The story of Micah and the Levite illustrates well the situation when "there was no king in

Israel," that is, when the Israelites did not properly recognize God's authority over them (17:6). The subsequent story also begins with the same reference to there being "no king in Israel" and it too demonstrates the lawless character of Israelite behavior. Judges 18 recounts how the tribe of Dan searched for a territory to occupy and acquired one by attacking the innocent and defenseless people of Laish.

Judges 18:1 explains that the tribe of Dan had no allotted territory and therefore needed a place to live. This report directly contradicts Josh 19:41–46, which says Dan was given territory just to the north of Judah and extending west into traditional Philistine areas. Joshua 19:47 notes, however, that Dan lost its southern territory and moved north to the area at the center of the account in Judg 18.

The Danites begin their quest for a homeland by sending out spies. Given the negative assessment of spy missions in Num 13 and Josh 2, this does not speak well for them. The spies come to the home of Micah and encounter the Levite through whom they inquire about the success of their mission (18:5). Their target is the city of Laish (18:7). The people of the town are described as remarkably peaceful ("quiet and unsuspecting"; v. 7), simply minding their own business. Moreover, their distance from any of Israel's enemies indicates they are completely without malice and pose no threat to the Danites. This situation stands in contrast to other stories that depict Israel's "legitimate" conquest and holy war. Numbers 13:27–33; Josh 6; 10:1–11; and 11:1–5 describe powerful and aggressive enemies who oppose Israel. In Judg 18 the Danites are powerful and aggressive and take land from the weak and unsuspecting.

The Danites ironically carry out their mission with the tacit approval of God. The Levite indicates that God had given them the land (18:6), a claim one of the spies later states as well (18:10). But given the Levite's character, his declaration should not be taken at face value. He has simply sold out and now gives words in the name of God for pay. In the end, the Danites take the Levite and the elements of Micah's shrine and make both part of their own system of worship (18:27–31). The story ends with the subtle note that the Danites kept Micah's idol "as long as the house of God was

at Shiloh" (18:31). Their sanctuary had no more divine approval than did their land-grabbing.

B. The Violent End (19:1–21:25)

19:1–30. The Levite's Concubine. The story in Judg 19 is one of the most horrifying accounts in the Bible. It recounts a Levite's concubine who was wantonly raped and killed during an attack on her family and the family that gives them refuge in the city of Gibeah. While the men of Gibeah are portrayed in the darkest way possible, the most sinister character in the story may be the Levite. After apparently abusing his concubine and thus causing her to leave him, he woos her back only to give her over to the ravenous crowd. Later he lies about what happened and incites an inter-tribal war. The picture of the Levite is subtly drawn. It is consistent in style, however, with the rest of Judges, which uses subtlety and irony to portray the condition of Israel when it does not follow its God.

The story begins appropriately with the note that "In those days, there was no king in Israel" (19:1). Although the full summary formula is not present, it is clear that the Levite in the story "did what was right in his own eyes" (see 17:6; 18:1; 21:25). He did not act as though God was king and as though justice and righteousness prevailed.

The story centers on the Levite's concubine and the fact that she has left him and returned to her father's house. A concubine is a wife of secondary status, sometimes obtained from an impoverished family as a slave and then designated by the master as his wife (Exod 21:7–11). The translation of v. 2, "his concubine became angry with him (the Levite)" follows two ancient manuscripts, one Latin and one Greek, that suggest the concubine has cause to leave her husband. The Hebrew of the verse, however, uses a verb that is usually translated "to commit adultery" (as NIV translates; see the same verb in Deut 22:21; Hos 1:2). This is probably due to the fact that Israelite law had no provisions for a woman to divorce her husband and, thus, the concubine's leaving could only be characterized as unfaithfulness. Marriage contracts were male-centered. The fact that the Levite sought to bring the concubine back and that he "spoke tenderly to her," however, probably indicates he had abused or mistreated her (see the same language in Gen 34:3; Shechem tried to get Dinah to marry him after he had raped her).

Verses 4–9 present an exaggerated display of hospitality as the concubine's father bids the Levite stay as his guest for five days. Hospitality was an important institution that offered protection for sojourners (Exod 22:21; Lev 19:33–34; Deut 16:14). It also served as a primary illustration of God's love for Israel who had been a "stranger" in the land of Egypt (Deut 10:18–19). The portrait of hospitality here also reveals the male-centered world in which the main benefits of hospitality are shared between men. The concubine who had been wronged is not even part of the conversation.

Verses 10–21 continue the story's focus on hospitality, but now the account turns to the problem of hospitality denied to the Levite and his concubine. The Levite departs his father-in-law's house in Bethlehem at a late hour, so it is necessary to find shelter for the night. He does not want to stop in Jerusalem because it is populated with Jebusites (thus the name Jebus for the city), and so he continues on to Gibeah, a city that should welcome the travelers as fellow Israelites. The Levite and his company, however, wait in vain for someone to offer them shelter. Only a resident alien from the hill country of Ephraim (the area to which the Levite is traveling) takes them in.

The next scene (vv. 22–26) echoes the account of Sodom and Gomorrah in Gen 19. As in the Genesis account the men of Gibeah surround the house, pound on the door, and demand that the traveler (the Levite) be sent out "that we may have intercourse with him" (v. 22; see Gen 19:5). "Have intercourse" translates a verb that literally means "to know." The old man responds to the crowd by saying, "Since this man is my guest, do not do this vile thing" (v. 23). The characterization of their intent to have sex with the Levite as "a vile thing" is probably not a statement about same sex relations in general (though see Lev 18:22). Rather, for the men of the city to have intercourse with him would be to treat him as an enemy. By this act, they would "feminize" him just as victorious armies often treated those they defeated as women.

Perhaps the greatest horror in the story, however, regards the action of the Levite who is under attack. As in the Sodom and Gomorrah

story (Gen 19:8), the owner of the house offers his daughters to the crowd, along with the Levite's concubine (19:24). This in itself is unthinkable. But the Levite goes further by putting his concubine out to the ravenous crowd. Verse 25 says the Levite "seized" his concubine and put her out. The term translated "seize" is sometimes used to denote the force a man exerts over a woman when raping her (2 Sam 13:14). Therefore, the text suggests that the Levite is guilty not just of cowardice and lack of compassion, but of the rape also. His crime is emphasized further by the twofold notice that he stayed in the house until it was light (vv. 26, 27). Then, when he leaves the house and finds his concubine lying with her hands on the threshold he shows no emotion or remorse. When asked how the crime occurred, the Levite is disingenuous. He speaks as though he and his concubine were together through the ordeal and as though his life was threatened as well (20:5).

The scene in vv. 27–28 is remarkable in that it does not say whether the woman is dead or alive; the Levite does not express any concern over the matter. His silence is far removed from his "speaking tenderly" to the concubine when he sought to bring her back from her father's house.

20:1–48. Civil War. As the book of Judges nears its end, it is clear that the Israelites have moved far from the ideals of life in the land with which the book began. Judges started with an account of the Israelite tribes attempting to secure the territory God had given them, but it ends with the Israelites fighting each other. The Israelite tribes begin a civil war over the death of the Levite's concubine. Judges 20:1–2 emphasize that "all" Israel came together to inquire about the Levite's concubine. The irony, of course, is that not all the tribes are present and the ones who gather at Mizpah will attempt to annihilate the one tribe that is absent.

The Levite's testimony (20:4–7) is correct in labeling the rape of the concubine as a "vile outrage," but several features of his testimony are less than honest. He reports that the "lords of Gibeah" rose against him (20:5), but the account indicates the perpetrators were a perverse group in the city (19:22), not necessarily the city's leaders. The Levite also says the men of the city intended to kill him (20:5). Judges 19:22, however, only says they wanted to have intercourse with him. He also does not report that he "seized" his concubine and put her out to the crowd (19:25), which, as already noted, implicates the Levite in the rape as well as the men of Gibeah. By distorting the story in these ways, the Levite creates a conflict between the tribe of Benjamin and the other Israelite tribes that diverts attention from his own guilt.

Those who hear the Levite's carefully edited story respond with what is perhaps an unknowing distortion of justice. The law of Moses stipulates that punishment of a crime should be proportional, "an eye for an eye" (Exod 21:24). This means that more than "an eye for an eye, a tooth for a tooth" is a miscarriage of justice. The Israelite tribes, however, respond to the rape and death of the Levite's concubine by destroying the entire city of Gibeah (20:37).

The sequence of battles in Judg 20:18–48 shows the results of a civil war in which no one really wins, but all parties experience God's judgment. Before each battle, the Israelites ask the Lord whether they should go out to battle or not. Each time the Lord tells them to go, but initially God does not promise victory and the Israelites suffer defeat (20:18, 21). Finally, in Judg 20:28 God tells the Israelites they will be victorious. The text makes clear, however, that "the LORD defeated Benjamin before Israel" (20:35).

21:1–25. Reconciliation Through Violence. The book of Judges ends with the Israelite tribes attempting to reconcile with the tribe of Benjamin, but the effort at peace is fraught with difficulty. The tribe of Benjamin is cut off from the other tribes and threatened with extinction since no one will give their daughters to the Benjaminites as wives (21:7). The people weep over Benjamin's fate (21:2). In a society based on kinship, which assumes stable families and male heirs are necessary for survival, the absence of potential wives is indeed lamentable. But the solutions the other tribes propose lead to more violence against women like the violence done to Jephthah's daughter and the Levite's concubine. The final chapter portrays Israel trafficking in women to benefit Benjamin (vv. 12, 14) and Benjamin's stealing of women to ensure a future for itself (vv. 20–23).

Although the text does not outwardly condemn these practices, the treatment of women in this chapter and in the final section of Judges (chs.

19–21) is a clear sign of Israel's deterioration. At the beginning of the book, women like Achsah are held in high honor, they take initiative, and they effect positive change (1:13–15). Deborah successfully liberates Israel from its foes (chs. 4–5). But by the end of the book women are reduced to chattel, commodities traded, stolen, and abused. The final verse of the book ("there was no king in Israel"; v. 25) might be read rightly as an ironic statement about Israel's failure to recognize God's rule over God's people.

BIBLIOGRAPHY

R. Boling. *Judges.* AB 6A (Garden City, N.Y.: Doubleday, 1975); B. Halpern. "The Assassination of Eglon: The First Locked-Room Murder Mystery." *BR* (December 1988) 33–44; _____. "The Resourceful Israelite Historian: The Song of Deborah and Israelite Historiography." *HTR* 76 (1983) 379–401; P. J. King and L. E. Stager. *Life in Biblical Israel* (Louisville: Westminster John Knox Press, 2001); L. R. Klein. *The Triumph of Irony in the Book of Judges.* BLS 14 (Sheffield: Sheffield Academic Press, 1988); J. C. McCann. *Judges.* Interpretation (Louisville: Westminster John Knox, 2002); G. Mobley. "The Wild Man in the Bible and the Ancient Near East." *JBL* 116 (1997) 217–233; S. Niditch. *Judges: A Commentary.* OTL (Louisville: Westminster John Knox, 2008); D. T. Olson. "The Book of Judges: Introduction, Commentary, and Reflections." NIB (Nashville: Abingdon Press, 1998) 2:721–888; J. L. Thompson. *Writing the Wrongs: Women of the Old Testament among Biblical Commentators from Philo through the Reformation* (Oxford: Oxford University, 2001); P. Trible. *Texts of Terror: Literary-Feminist Readings of Biblical Narratives.* OBT (Philadelphia: Fortress, 1984).

RUTH

Katharine D. Sakenfeld

OVERVIEW

A longtime favorite among Christians and Jews, the story of Ruth's commitment to Naomi is upheld as a model for the deep and active caring of one human being for another. The story moves from brokenness to wholeness, from death to life, from hunger to food in abundance, from anxiety to security, from exclusion to inclusion, from barrenness to birthing, from bitterness to rejoicing. The various characters constantly invoke God's blessing upon one another, and the story develops toward its positive ending because those same characters undertake actions that enable the fulfillment of their prayers. The town of Bethlehem at the end of the story can be viewed as a "peaceable village," a microcosm of the peaceable kingdom anticipated in Isa 9.

More recent reflection on the narrative has raised questions, however, about this idyllic perspective. Ruth has been portrayed as seeking her own self-interest, determined to escape from an undesirable life in Moab; Naomi has been portrayed as disliking Ruth but taking advantage of her. Boaz also has been portrayed as focused on self-interest (romantic and economic) rather than genuinely concerned with Ruth's welfare. These "against the grain" interpretations arise, and indeed are viable, because the narrator does not attribute motivations to the characters, and because it is possible to assume hidden motives underlying the characters' own words. This commentary works primarily with the traditional, more idyllic or positive perspective, while recognizing that biblical characters may have mixed motives for much of what they do.

The idyllic character of the story should not, however, blind readers to hidden dangers in applying its themes to contemporary life. Among these dangers are several implicit assumptions: that marriage and children are the only or even best or most desirable way to provide economic security for women; that outsiders should be fully included in a community only to the extent that they abandon their own cultural identity; and that Ruth provides the one proper model for a woman's relationship to her mother or to her mother-in-law.

Scholars disagree about the date of composition of the story, with options ranging from the era of King David ca. 1000 BCE (the earliest possible date, since the story is designed to establish his ancestry) to the Persian era ca. 450 BCE, when Ezra's insistence that foreign wives and children be sent away (Ezra 9–10) might have led an opposition group to highlight a tradition that even King David himself had a Moabite great-grandmother. Whenever the story emerged, it would have stood as a challenge to Israel's stereotyping of all foreign women as likely to lead Israelites away from the worship of God alone (e.g., Num 25; Deut 7:3–4; 1 Kgs 11:3–5; 16:31–32).

Set in the era of the Judges, the upright living characteristic of Ruth stands in sharp contrast to the violence and mayhem of that period. In the Christian canon, Ruth is placed chronologically, between the book of Judges and the story of David in 1 Samuel. Jewish tradition associates Ruth with the Feast of Weeks, and thus in the Hebrew Scriptures Ruth is placed with other short books read on festivals in the Jewish liturgical year.

OUTLINE

I. Setting the Stage (1:1–22)

    1:1–5. Arrival in Moab; Marriages and Deaths

    1:6–9. Naomi Sets Out for Bethlehem and Bids Her Daughters-in-law Farewell

    1:10–18. Orpah Returns Home; Ruth Insists on Accompanying Naomi

    1:19–22. Naomi and Ruth Arrive in Bethlehem

II. Ruth Spends a Day Gleaning in the Field of Boaz (2:1–23)

    2:1–7. Ruth Arrives in Boaz's Field and Boaz Finds Out Her Identity

    2:8–16. Conversation Between Boaz and Ruth

2:17–23. Ruth Returns to Naomi and Reports on Her Day

III. Ruth Spends a Night with Boaz at His Threshing Floor (3:1–18)

3:1–5. Naomi Gives Instruction to Ruth

3:6–13. Conversation Between Boaz and Ruth

3:14–18. Ruth Returns to Naomi and Reports on Her Night

IV. A Happy Ending? (4:1–22)

4:1–12. Legal Proceedings Before the Village Elders

4:13–17. Marriage, a Baby Boy, and a Blessing

4:18–22. The Ancestral Genealogy of King David

DETAILED ANALYSIS

I. Setting the Stage (1:1–22)

1:1–5. Arrival in Moab; Marriages and Deaths. The opening verses introduce two of the three main characters (Naomi and Ruth) and provide the geographic, cultural, and theological context for what is to follow. Hunger is a classic reason for migration both in the biblical tradition (e.g. Gen 12; 42) and in the modern world. The move from Bethlehem ("House of Bread") to Moab places the family squarely in the territory of one of Israel's traditional and most hated enemies. Moabites were remembered as descendants of the incestuous union between Lot's elder daughter and her father (Gen 19:37), and they were singled out as a people forbidden to enter Israel's house of worship (Deut 23:3). King Balak of Moab opposed the Israelites on their journey from Egypt to Canaan (Num 21–23), and King Eglon oppressed them in the era of the Judges (Judg 3). Tensions and battles continued throughout the monarchy, and prophets announced dire judgments upon Moab (e.g., Isa 15–16; Jer 48).

Awareness of this long history of animosity sharpens the impact of the narrative from beginning to end. According to one Jewish tradition, Naomi's husband Elimelech dies because he led

his family to Moab, and her two sons die because of their foreign marriages. Yet by the end of the book, Ruth "the Moabite" will not only be married to a Bethlehemite but will also be remembered as the great-grandmother of King David.

As this section ends, Naomi's status is measured explicitly in terms of the absence of husband and sons. It seems that the two daughters-in-law do not count, and indeed vv. 11–13 will explain why this is true from Naomi's point of view.

1:6–9. Naomi Sets Out for Bethlehem and Bids Her Daughters-in-law Farewell. The ending of the famine in Naomi's homeland (1:6) is the first of only two events in the story attributed directly to God; the other is Ruth's conceiving of a child (see 4:13). Of all that transpires, these moments would be understood by the ancient hearers as the events least subject to human control.

Naomi soon dismisses her daughters-in-law. Yet she recognizes their goodness to her and prays that God will treat each of them as "kindly" (v. 8) as they have treated her family, and indeed that they will be able to marry again among their own people. Underlying the word "kindly" is the Hebrew term *khesed*, a key thematic concept in the story. *Khesed*, variously translated as "kindness," "lovingkindness," "loyalty," or (of God) "steadfast love," represents both attitude and action. It describes commitment in a relationship that takes shape in actions that go beyond what would normally be required or expected, actions that support and even rescue the other in times of deep crisis or distress. Here Naomi remarkably calls upon God to measure up to the standard of such human loyal love that her daughters-in-law have shown to her and to their Israelite husbands.

1:10–18. Orpah Returns Home; Ruth Insists on Accompanying Naomi. The younger women's unwillingness to return home evokes a long and despairing response from Naomi (vv. 11–13). The initial reasoning of her response turns to a wail of anguish in her assertion that God has turned from her.

The Israelite practice of levirate marriage may help to explain Naomi's reference to other sons, although the parallel is not exact. According to this custom, when a man died before his wife bore a son, one of his surviving brothers was expected to marry the widow for the purpose of producing an heir for the man who had died (see Deut 25:5–10; Gen 38; and the possible reprise of this theme in Ruth 4:5–8). The theme of marriage between a widow and a deceased husband's brother is present here, but Naomi's stated goal is security for her daughters-in-law rather than descendants for her dead sons.

Orpah goes "back to her people and her gods" (v.15), following her mother-in-law's advice and urging. The narrator makes no criticism of Orpah's decision; she simply disappears from the story. Yet Ruth will not follow Orpah's example. Ruth's statement of determined and unwavering lifelong commitment to Naomi (vv. 16–17) echoes Naomi's references to Orpah's people and gods, as Ruth declares her allegiance to Naomi's people and Naomi's God.

These words of commitment of a daughter-in-law to her mother-in-law resonate differently in different contexts. In Judaism, Ruth is remembered as the model convert, and the various phrases of her extended statement to Naomi are sometimes given symbolic associations with various aspects of the conversion process. Many Christian readers are surprised that the words were not originally related to a wedding context. Ruth's declaration stands in dramatic contrast to a steady stream of mother-in-law jokes and stereotypes that reflect the tensions frequently experienced in such relationships. Yet one should be wary of viewing Ruth's commitment as a norm. Her commitment represents precisely what was *not* culturally expected, as it manifests her continuing *khesed* toward Naomi.

1:19–22. Naomi and Ruth Arrive in Bethlehem.
In response to the women of the town, Naomi asks to be called "Mara," meaning "bitter" (v. 20). Her lament made first to Ruth and Orpah reaches a second crescendo in a four-fold report about God's terrible dealings with her. Ruth receives no mention by Naomi or by the women; it is as if Ruth and her *khesed* count for nothing, as if she is not even present. Naomi's grief is center stage.

II. Ruth Spends a Day Gleaning in the Field of Boaz (2:1–23)

2:1–7. Ruth Arrives in Boaz's Field and Boaz Finds Out Her Identity.
The action of ch. 2 covers a single day and is introduced by an aside from the narrator explaining the identity of Boaz, whom Ruth will soon meet. The description of Boaz as *ish gibbor khayil*, "a prominent rich man" (2:1), anticipates Boaz's subsequent description of Ruth as a *esheth khayil*, "worthy woman" (3:11). The phrases, translated according to context, indicate one who is well respected in the community.

Gleaning was the principal economic "safety net" for the destitute in ancient Israelite society, specifically for widows and resident aliens like Ruth (Deut 24:19–22 and Lev 19:9–10; 23:22). Although the narrator's "as it happened" (v. 3) might suggest coincidence, the reader is invited to imagine God at work behind the scene in bringing Ruth to the very field of Naomi's kinsman, whose family connection is reiterated here. Equally providential is Boaz's arrival ("just then"), whereupon he notices and inquires about the unknown person in his field. The explanation of the head reaper (vv. 6–7) mentions Ruth's Moabite ancestry two times, highlighting a theme that will persist throughout the story.

2:8–16. Conversation Between Boaz and Ruth.
Boaz's opening words to Ruth indicate the potential danger associated with gleaning, particularly for an unattached foreign woman, as the phrase translated "not to bother you" (2:9) has overtones of sexual molestation. Boaz's advice and his offer of precious drinking water are quite extraordinary responses to a foreigner. Boaz attributes his good will solely to what he has been told of Ruth's character and behavior; conspicuously absent from his response is any reference to his kinship to Elimelech. His references to an unknown people and to "the LORD, the God of Israel" (vv. 11–12) harken back to Ruth's commitments to Naomi's people and God (1:16–17). The theme of God's wings of refuge (compare Ps. 91:4) will reappear in 3:9 within the context of a human relationship.

As he had made the unusual offer of water, so Boaz also offers food in abundance, and then grain in abundance as sheaves are actually to be placed in Ruth's path. The theme of Ruth's overflowing care and commitment to Naomi is mirrored by Boaz's generosity to Ruth.

2:17–23. Ruth Returns to Naomi and Reports on Her Day.
Naomi's amazement at the large quantity of grain and leftovers from the midday meal

reaches a climax when Ruth speaks the name "Boaz," whom Naomi now reports to be among near kinsmen of the family. Naomi's words in v. 20 mark the beginning of Naomi's turn from despair and provide a key theological clue for interpreting the story. The Hebrew construction is richly ambiguous because the relative pronoun "whose" may refer either to the Lord or to Boaz; theologically it surely refers to both. In Ruth's "chance" encounter with Boaz and Boaz's generosity, God's "kindness" (*khesed*; see above 1:6–9) has not forsaken Naomi, Ruth, or Elimelech and his sons. God's *khesed* is not an abstraction, but has taken concrete form precisely in Boaz's *khesed*, which extends beyond Ruth to Naomi and her family. For his part, Boaz's *khesed* has been inspired by Ruth's own *khesed* to Naomi. A web of human kindness reflects, refracts, and embodies God's kindness.

III. Ruth Spends a Night with Boaz at his Threshing Floor (3:1–18)

3:1–5. Naomi Gives Instruction to Ruth. As Naomi had earlier urged the "security" of Moabite marriages for her daughters-in-law (1:9), so now again she plans "security" for Ruth (3:1) through a man. She gives Ruth highly detailed instructions about bodily and clothing preparations, and is even more specific about the timing, location, and actions Ruth is to undertake at the threshing floor (vv. 3–4).

3:6–13. Conversation Between Boaz and Ruth. The Hebrew of this scene is filled with words that may have either ordinary meanings or sexual overtones, especially the words "feet" (used euphemistically for genitals) and "lie down" (for sleeping or sexual relations). Both in content and in choice of vocabulary, the storyteller establishes the possibility for a sexual tryst outside of marriage, yet draws back from saying exactly what took place.

When Boaz awakes in surprise, even shock, to discover a young woman next to him, Ruth diverges from Naomi's plan by announcing what Boaz should do. Her phrase "spread your cloak over your servant" (3:9) is in effect elevated language for a marriage proposal (compare Ezek 16:8). Furthermore, the Hebrew word for "cloak" is the same word that Boaz used for God's "wings" (2:12), suggesting a connection between divine refuge and human protection. Ruth is challenging Boaz

to bring to fruition by marriage the "full reward" that he himself had earlier wished God to bring to Ruth. Boaz's response in praise of Ruth is even more fulsome than his initial words in 2:11. Again he refers to her *khesed* (here translated "loyalty"); "this last instance" points to her suggestion of marriage. Boaz's assumption that she might have gone after younger men suggests that he is considerably older than she is; more than that, it brings to mind the wilderness era story (Num 25) of Moabite women who enticed Israelite men into sexual relations and thereby into idolatrous practices. By contrast, Ruth the Moabite is here portrayed as behaving uprightly, even in her lying beside Boaz in the dark of night.

Boaz also speaks of Ruth as *esheth khayil* ("worthy woman"; see comment at 2:1). This expression appears elsewhere in the OT only in reference to a "capable wife" (Prov 31:10). Many of the characteristics of the wife described in Prov 31 are exemplified in Ruth's caring for Naomi. Unlike the woman in Proverbs, Ruth is poor and a foreigner, but her personal qualities (cf. Prov 31:11, 12, 13, 20) commend her to Boaz and to the larger Bethlehem community as one worthy of praise.

Having affirmed Ruth's intent, Boaz introduces an unexpected twist to the plot as he refers to a nearer kinsman who has first refusal rights for marriage to Ruth. Boaz's instruction to Ruth to "lie down until the morning" (v. 13) may be intended to protect Ruth from the danger of travel by night or from the suspicion that might come upon her if she were observed away from home at night. Nonetheless, her "[lying] at his feet" (v. 14) develops the ambiguous sexual overtones of the scene.

3:14–18. Ruth Returns to Naomi and Reports on Her Night. Ruth departs in the earliest predawn, in those moments when vague shapes may be seen but individuals not identified. As he had done before, Boaz again provides abundant grain for Naomi.

In selecting details of the conversation between the two women upon Ruth's return, the storyteller focuses not on the expected theme of Ruth's security, but rather upon Boaz's gift of grain, a symbol of his concern for Naomi's security. This focus reinforces the theme of Naomi's movement out of despair and emphasizes that the lives of all the major characters are intertwined.

IV. A Happy Ending? (4:1–22)

4:1–12. Legal Proceedings Before the Village Elders. Ruth now disappears as a speaking character for the remainder of the story. She is talked about, and indeed she conceives and gives birth, but she is no longer a principal actor on stage.

As Naomi had predicted, Boaz wastes no time in resolving the matter of who will marry Ruth. The gate of a town or city was the usual place for conducting legal proceedings in Israelite society. The immediate arrival of the unnamed nearer kinsman is reminiscent of the providential moments in 2:3, 4.

Many details of the proceedings described here remain obscure. What is the status of the plot of land belonging to Naomi, and why have we not heard of it earlier? If she owns land, why is she destitute? Why must the nearer kinsman marry Ruth if he takes control of Naomi's land? How exactly would marriage to Ruth damage his inheritance? While scholars are not sure of the answers to such questions, inheritance rights were certainly carefully regulated (e.g., Num 26; 27; 36). Whatever the system of inheritance at work in this scene (presumably clear to ancient hearers of the story), the underlying problem is the death of Naomi's husband and sons. Boaz's approach to the case heightens the drama. He first offers the nearer kinsman the opportunity to redeem Naomi's land, i.e., to make a financial arrangement to keep it within the extended family holdings. Only after receiving an affirmative reply does Boaz note that "Ruth, the Moabite, the widow of the dead man" comes with the deal—"to maintain the dead man's name on his inheritance" (v. 5). This explicit naming of Ruth's undesirable ethnic and marital status stands in tension with inheritance custom. It is reasonable to suppose that the redemption of Naomi's land represented a legal obligation with a sequence of rights of refusal, while the marriage to Ruth was understood as a concomitant moral obligation that could somehow have an economic impact on the value of the real estate transaction. Thus the nearer kinsman does not violate any customary law by his refusal, while Boaz is able to take the moral high ground regarding the opportunity to marry Ruth. The custom of sandal

removal to seal a decision appears elsewhere only in Deut 25:9, which concerns levirate marriage. Although the two texts also share the motif of the name of a dead husband, the circumstances differ significantly in other respects; thus it seems that Ruth's case is at best tangentially related to levirate marriage.

The two-fold use of the verb *acquire* for both land and wife (vv. 9, 10) focuses on the legal transaction; the verb does not connote that Ruth is merely chattel or property. The witnesses to the transaction include not just the elders, but "all the people" (vv. 9, 11). The whole town, apparently including the women, joins in praying a blessing on Ruth. Remarkably, they invoke a favorable comparison to the great matriarchs Rachel and Leah, progenitors of the Israelite tribes. Ephrathah (compare 1:2) is the home region of the family of King David. The story of Judah and Tamar, Perez's parents (Gen 38) has many resonances with the story of Ruth, but also many differences in detail. One common thread is the birth of an important child to a woman who has challenged many societal norms. In Christian tradition Ruth and Tamar are connected as two of the four women mentioned in the genealogy of Jesus in Matt 1.

4:13–17. Marriage, a Baby Boy, and a Blessing. The marriage is consummated, and immediately Ruth conceives (see comment on 1:6). The women who greeted Naomi upon her return to Bethlehem (1:19–21) and heard her cry of bitterness now reappear to bless God for the goodness showered upon her. Ruth's son will become "restorer" and "nourisher" (4:15) for Naomi, terms that connote not only physical sustenance but comfort, encouragement, and support. Now the women also acknowledge Ruth, who had been totally ignored in the arrival scene, praising Ruth's love for Naomi. The comparison they offer, "more to you than seven sons" (v. 15), places Ruth on the highest possible pedestal according to the norms of Israelite culture.

The women then name the baby. In the OT, naming is done more frequently by mothers than by fathers, without any obvious pattern of circumstances, but only here are neighborhood women rather than either of the parents involved in the naming. The story also differs from other naming scenes because scholars can discern no apparent wordplay or other substantive connection between the name Obed and the women's explanatory statement that "a son is born to Naomi." Rather, the women's statement ties the entire story together by looking back to Naomi's lament in 1:11. Naomi is finally made whole. From this perspective, the book is Naomi's story even more than it is Ruth's.

The story ends well, in that food is in good supply; the outsider, Ruth, has been included not just by Boaz but by all the people; a child is born and celebrated; and Naomi's sadness is reversed. Yet, as indicated in the introduction to this commentary, this ending carries hidden dangers if it is viewed as a narrow prescription for happy endings in contemporary societies. Each community needs to examine afresh God's vision for its own wholeness, with care not to adopt uncritically the sociological patterns of previous societies, whether those of ancient Israel or of more recent history.

4:18–22. The Ancestral Genealogy of King David. The book concludes with an expansion of the three-generation genealogy that introduced David in v. 17. In this male-descent, linear genealogical form, familiar from Genesis and 1 Chronicles, there is no place for Ruth or Naomi. Despite all the language earlier in the narrative about the importance of maintaining the name of the dead, the genealogical line runs through Boaz, with no mention of Elimelech or his sons. The genealogy focuses the reader's attention squarely on David (the last word of the book) and provides in the Protestant canonical order a link to the story of David's rise to leadership that follows in 1 Samuel.

BIBLIOGRAPHY

A. Brenner, ed. *A Feminist Companion to Ruth* (Sheffield: Sheffield Academic Press, 1993); F. W. Bush. *Ruth, Esther.* WBC 9 (Waco, Tex.: Word Books, 1996); D. N. Fewell and D. M. Gunn. *Compromising Redemption: Relating Characters in the Book of Ruth.* Literary Currents in Biblical Interpretation (Louisville: Westminster/John Knox Press, 1990); E. F. Campbell Jr. *Ruth: A New Translation with Introduction, Notes, and Commentary.* AB 7 (Garden City, N.Y.: Doubleday, 1975); J. Lapsley. "Seeing the Older Woman: Naomi in High Definition." *Engaging the Bible in a Gendered World: An Introduction to Feminist Biblical Interpretation in Honor of Katharine Doob Sakenfeld.* L. Day and C. Pressler, eds. (Louisville: Westminster John Knox, 2006) 102–113; E. P. Lee. "Ruth the Moabite: Identity, Kinship, and Otherness." *Engaging the Bible in a Gendered World: An Introduction to Feminist Biblical Interpretation in Honor of Katharine Doob Sakenfeld.* L. Day and C. Pressler, eds. (Louisville: Westminster John Knox, 2006) 89–101; K. Nielsen. *Ruth: A Commentary.* OTL (Louisville: Westminster John Knox Press, 1997); K. D. Sakenfeld. "Naomi's Cry: Reflections on Ruth 1:20–21." *A God so Near: Essays on Old Testament Theology in Honor of Patrick D. Miller.* B. A. Strawn and N. R. Bowen, eds. (Winona Lake, Ind.: Eisenbrauns, 2003) 129–43; _____. "Ruth 4: An Image of Eschatological Hope." *Liberating Eschatology: Essays in Honor of Letty Russell.* M. A. Farley and S. Jones, eds. (Louisville: Westminster John Knox Press, 1999) 55–67; _____. *Ruth.* IBC (Louisville: Westminster John Knox Press, 1999); P. Trible. *God and the Rhetoric of Sexuality.* OBT (Philadelphia: Fortress Press, 1978).

1 SAMUEL

STEVE MCKENZIE

OVERVIEW

Originally one work, 1 and 2 Samuel were first distinguished in the LXX. Though they bear the name of Samuel, he is the focal character only in the first eight chapters of 1 Samuel, dies before 1 Samuel ends (25:1), and is not mentioned in 2 Samuel. Most scholars view Samuel as part of a larger work encompassing Deuteronomy plus the Former Prophets in the Hebrew Bible (Joshua, Judges, 1 and 2 Samuel, 1 and 2 Kings) and known as the Deuteronomistic History (DtrH).

The author(s) of the DtrH is/are unknown. It was apparently completed shortly after 562 BCE, the date of the last event it records (2 Kgs 25:27–30). Some scholars think that there were earlier editions of the DtrH, especially one from the time of King Josiah of Judah (640–609 BCE). The DtrH authors composed their work by making use of older sources, integrating them, and supplementing them with speeches and narratives in their own "Deuteronomistic" (Dtr) style.

Debate over the date and identification of those sources is part of a larger debate over the character of history of 1 and 2 Samuel. The fact that no reference to the person of David outside of the Bible had been found suggested to some scholars that he did not exist. The discovery of a ninth-century Aramaic stele referring to Judah as the "house of David" (Judah) has assuaged these doubts, but this does not mean that all of 1 and 2 Samuel functions as a neutral account of past events.

Further reason for caution regarding the work's historicity is its high literary quality. However Samuel was written and whatever its character as history writing, it is a literary masterpiece. Many of its passages are filled with puns and word plays; its characters are complex, its plots intricate. The author(s) who produced this work was/were very creative.

The main interest of 1 and 2 Samuel is David, who is also, in many ways, the central character of the DtrH. First Samuel tells of his rise and 2 Samuel of his kingship. The prophet Samuel introduces monarchy into Israel, and Saul is a foil to David. As is widely recognized, 1 Samuel is pro-Davidic. Saul can do nothing right and David nothing wrong. Many scholars regard 1 Samuel, if not 2 Samuel too, as an apology for David. That is, the work was written as a literary defense especially against the charge that David was a usurper who seized the crown from his predecessor. This charge is met, above all, by the claim that David was divinely chosen and guided to the throne.

OUTLINE

I. Samuel the Prophet (1–7)

    A. Samuel's Birth and Dedication to Yahweh's Service (1:1–2:11)
        1:1–28. Hannah's Request for a Son Is Answered
        2:1–11. The Song of Hannah

    B. The Rejection of Eli's Priestly House (2:12–3:21)
        2:12–17. The Sin of Eli's Sons
        2:18–21. The Visitation of Hannah
        2:22–26. Eli's Parental Failing
        2:27–36. Oracle Against Eli's House
        3:1–21. Samuel's Call to Prophesy

    C. The Ark Narrative (4:1–7:1)
        4:1–22. The Philistines Capture the Ark
        5:1–12. The Ark as a Scourge to the Philistines
        6:1–7:1. The Return of the Ark

    D. Samuel Judges Israel (7:2–17)

II. The Rise and Fall of Saul (8–15)

    A. Saul Becomes Israel's First King (8–12)
        8:1–22. Samuel Reacts to Israel's Cry for a King
        9:1–10:16. Saul Is Anointed Privately
        10:17–27a. Saul Is Chosen Publicly
        10:27b–11:15. Saul Proves Himself
        12:1–25. Samuel's Farewell

    B. Saul's Failings (13–15)
        13:1–22. Saul Is Rejected for Failing to Wait
        13:23–14:52. Saul's Foolish Oath
        15:1–35. Saul's Disobedience.

III. David's Ascent (16–31)

A. David Comes to Saul's Attention (16–17)
16:1–13. Anointing of the Shepherd David
16:14–23. David Becomes Saul's Armor-bearer
17:1–58. David and Goliath

B. David in Saul's Court (18–20)
18:1–16. David's Military Success
18:17–30. David Marries Michal
19:1–24. Saul's Moves Against David Become Overt
20:1–42. Jonathan's Failed Reconciliation

C. David the Fugitive (21–31)
21:1–9. David Seeks Help from the Priests of Nob
21:10–15. David Feigns Madness Before the Philistines
22:1–5. David Gathers an Army and Provides for His Parents
22:6–23. Saul Annihilates the Priests of Nob
23:1–29. Providential Escapes in the Wilderness
24:1–22. An Opportunity to Kill Saul in a Cave in En-gedi
25:1–44. David, Nabal, and Abigail
26:1–25. Another Opportunity to Kill Saul in the Wilderness of Ziph
27:1–28:2. David Becomes a Philistine Mercenary
28:3–25. Saul Consults a Medium at Endor
29:1–11. David Is Sent Away by the Philistine Commanders
30:1–31. David Avenges the Sack of Ziklag
31:1–13. Saul Dies on Mt. Gilboa

DETAILED ANALYSIS

I. Samuel the Prophet (1–7)

A. Samuel's Birth and Dedication to Yahweh's Service (1:1–2:11)

1:1–28. Hannah's Request for a Son Is Answered. The barren wife who has a son due to divine intervention is a common motif in the Bible. This story also puns repeatedly on Saul's name with the Hebrew root *sh'al*, "to request" (vv. 17, 20, 27–28, variously rendered). Hanna was the first wife and Peninnah the "second" (v. 2; NRSV, "other"). Elkanah apparently married Peninnah because Hannah could not bear children. While her husband was on his annual journey to the temple (v. 7; "house"), Hannah prayed outside of the temple where Eli, seated at the doorway (v. 9), could see her. She promised to make her son a "nazirite" or "devoted one" (v. 11). Samuel was to be a nazirite for life (cf. Num 6:1–21). Hannah fulfilled her vow when Samuel was weaned (v. 24). In Hannah's statement that her son is "given" to Yahweh (v. 28), the word "given" in Hebrew is identical to the name Saul, leading some scholars to believe that this story originally narrated the birth of Saul rather than Samuel.

2:1–11. The Song of Hannah. Originally a hymn of national thanksgiving, this poem was adopted for the story of Hannah because of its reference to God reversing the fate of the disadvantaged (esp. vv. 4–8). The line in v. 5 about the barren woman who bears children seems particularly appropriate for Hannah. The references to Yahweh's "king" and "anointed" (v. 10) indicate that the poem was written during the period of the monarchy and thus significantly later than the time of Hannah. The poem features in Mary's Magnificat (Luke 1:46–55).

B. The Rejection of Eli's Priestly House (2:12–3:21)

2:12–17. The Sin of Eli's Sons. Priests were given a portion of sacrifices as their livelihood (Lev 7:28–36; Deut 18:3). At Shiloh, they apparently received whatever meat a fork dredged up from a boiling pot. Eli's sons demanded the fat portion, which properly belonged to the deity, and thus they showed no respect for God.

2:18–21. The Visitation of Hannah. Samuel's ephod was a simple loincloth that signaled his status as a priest. Eli's reference to "the gift that she made" is another pun on Saul's name in Hebrew.

2:22–26. Eli's Parental Failing. The further sin of Eli's sons—lying with the women at the entrance to the tent of meeting (v. 22)—is not present in some of the best textual witnesses to

Samuel and was probably borrowed from Exod 38:8. It disagrees with previous descriptions of the shrine at Shiloh as a building (temple) rather than a tent. The behavior of the sons contrasts with that of Samuel (v. 26), whose description here may have served as a pattern for Luke's portrait of Jesus (Luke 2:52).

2:27–36. Oracle Against Eli's House. This oracle was inserted by the Deuteronomistic author probably in anticipation of Saul's slaughter of the priests of Nob (1 Sam 22) and the later replacement of Abiathar's priestly line by the Zadokites (1 Kgs 2:27, 35). "Your ancestor" (v. 27) may be Moses, from whom many scholars think Eli traced descent, or Levi, because of the reference to choosing him from "all the tribes of Israel" (v. 28). To "go up to my altar" is to offer sacrifices, one of the duties of a priest, along with offering incense and wearing the ephod. This ephod may refer to an instrument used to divine Yahweh's will and mentioned later (1 Sam 23:9) rather than to Samuel's loincloth (2:18). The one who will survive (v. 33) is probably Abiathar, and the "faithful priest" (v. 35) Zadok.

3:1–21. Samuel's Call to Prophesy. Since prophetic revelation was rare (v. 1) and it was Samuel's first prophetic experience (v. 7), he did not immediately recognize God's call (vv. 2–9). Samuel slept in or near the "holy of holies" where the ark resided. Since the ark symbolized Yahweh's presence, this was an appropriate place for a revelation. The fact that Yahweh appeared to Samuel, not Eli, and that it took Eli three times to realize that Samuel was receiving a divine call were further indications of the growing separation between God and Eli. The divine message to Samuel (vv. 10–14) reiterated and confirmed that of the man of God in ch. 2. Eli's sons had so profaned the sacrifices that might be used to atone for sin that now no sacrificial atonement would be accepted (vv. 13–14).

C. The Ark Narrative (4:1–7:1)

4:1–22. The Philistines Capture the Ark. Some scholars consider 4:1–7:1 an independent source reporting the capture and return of the ark, since Samuel is not mentioned in these chapters. The story begins with a battle between Israel and the Philistines. They had entered Canaan from the western Mediterranean at the same time that Israel was emerging as a nation in the central highlands, so that clash between them was inevitable. After losing the first battle (v. 2), the Israelites bring the ark to the front in order to secure divine aid (v. 3). But the ark is captured and Israel soundly defeated (v. 11). The narrative makes clear that Yahweh is punishing Eli and his sons by removing the ark from Shiloh. Eli's own death is occasioned by shock at the news of the ark's capture rather than that of his sons' deaths (v. 18). He is placed in the line of the judges, who ruled Israel before the monarchy. However, the "forty years" ascribed to his rule is probably a round number for a generation.

5:1–12. The Ark as a Scourge to the Philistines. The Philistines take the ark to Ashdod, one of their main cities, and place it in the temple ("house") of their god, Dagon, beside Dagon's statue or idol (vv. 1–2). This act symbolizes Dagon's defeat of Yahweh, since wars between peoples in the ancient Near East were often conceived as contests between their deities. Dagon was a Canaanite god of grain who is portrayed in these stories as the Philistines' principal god. The Philistines find Dagon's statue lying prostrate before the ark with its head and hands cut off, as was often done with enemy soldiers captured or killed in battle (vv. 3–4), thus showing that Yahweh is superior to Dagon. Yahweh's demonstration of power continues in the form of a pestilence that some identify as bubonic plague because of the symptomatic tumors, its spread by mice, and its beginning in the coastal city of Ashdod (vv. 6–12). Following Ashdod, Gath and Ekron each experience plague. These were three of the five prominent Philistine cities (plus Ashkelon, Gaza) whose rulers made up the "lords" of the Philistines.

6:1–7:1. The Return of the Ark. The Philistines have learned that the ark is a sacred object. They return it with a "guilt offering" to atone for handling it and to stem the plague (vv. 1–5). The offering that is sent back is also a kind of test. One would expect two "milch cows" that have never been yoked to wander aimlessly in search of their calves. That they head straight for Israelite territory indicates that the plague was Yahweh's doing and not happenstance (vv. 7–12). The new cart and previously unyoked cows are appropriate for sacrifice, and the people of Beth-shemesh use them as such (v. 14). Kiriath-jearim, where the ark was sent (7:1) was on the border between Benjamin and Judah.

D. Samuel Judges Israel (7:2–17)

Samuel, who has served as priest and prophet, now is presented as Israel's national leader, the last of the judges and a transitional figure between the judges and the monarchy. The "twenty years" (v. 2) fits into the Dtr. chronology established in the book of Judges. It represents half a generation and the period of foreign oppression prior to deliverance brought by a judge. Before God will deliver them, the people must repent of worshiping other gods and turn to Yahweh (vv. 3–4). Baal and Astarte were the principal male and female Canaanite deities. Samuel then gathers all Israel to Mizpah for a rededication ceremony (vv. 5–6). The four ritual activities mentioned here—libation, fasting, confession, and prayer—do not occur together elsewhere in the Bible and seem to represent a combination of functions—repentance, purification, rededication, and, perhaps, preparation for war. Samuel's leadership is not as a warrior but as an intercessor; it is God's "mighty voice," i.e., thunder, that routs the Philistines (v. 10). The other adversary here, the "Amorites" (v. 14), is a Deuteronomistic term for the pre-Israelite inhabitants of Canaan. As the book of Judges depicts two types of leaders—military deliverers and legal functionaries—so Samuel embodies both roles. Having effected victory over the Philistines, he rides an annual circuit (v. 16) administering justice in towns, all within the tribal territory of Benjamin.

II. The Rise and Fall of Saul (8–15)

A. Saul Becomes Israel's First King (8–12)

8:1–22. Samuel Reacts to Israel's Cry for a King. Having presented Samuel as the last judge, the book describes the beginning of kingship in Israel. Samuel's sons, like Eli's before him, are unfit to succeed him (vv. 1–2). The leadership vacuum occasions the elders' call for a king, but it is also motivated by their desire to be "like the nations" (vv. 4–5). The request for a king is interpreted as a rejection of Yahweh's sovereignty (v. 7) in line with a long history of disobedience (v. 8). Yahweh's granting the request for a king (v. 9) may indicate that the evil lies not in the institution of kingship but in the people's lack of faith. The

"ways of the king" about which Samuel warns the people are the customary trappings of ancient Near Eastern kingship, such as conscription and taxation (vv. 11–18). This list may draw from an older document detailing a king's rights and privileges. They also resemble practices enacted by Solomon (1 Kgs 4:7; 5:13). The people "refused to listen" to Samuel's warning and insist on having a king (vv. 19–20). Here and elsewhere in this chapter, the verb "listen" or "hear" puns on Samuel's name. The verb "govern" here means "judge." Despite God's repeated prior deliverance of Israel through the judges, they now demand a king for military protection and rule.

9:1–10:16. Saul Is Anointed Privately. Chapters 9–11 contain three stories about Saul's election as king. The first of these was a folktale about Saul's recovery of lost donkeys that has been revised to report his private anointing as king. Saul's father, Kish, is a man of "prominence" or "wealth" (v.1; NRSV). Saul himself is tall and "handsome" (v. 2; NRSV, lit., "good"), and thus is an ideal candidate to be king, since leaders are often described in the Bible as handsome (Gen 39:6; Exod 2:2; 1 Sam 16:12). Saul and a servant search throughout the tribal areas of Benjamin and Ephraim (vv. 3–4), finally arriving at Zuph, the home of Samuel's father (1:1). The locations of Shalishah and Shaalim are uncertain, but both pun on Saul's name. It was customary to pay a man of God for the service of divine inquiry (vv. 7–8), and the servant proposes a quarter shekel (about 1/8 ounce) of silver for the purpose. The "shrine" or "high place" where sacrificial worship was carried out was outside of the city gate (vv. 11–14). Sacrifices marked occasions when people ate meat, i.e., the portions not offered to the deity (entrails and fatty portions). At the sacrificial meal (vv. 22–24), Saul is given the seat and portion (the thigh) of honor. At least a portion of these verses, that which concerns Samuel's foreknowledge of Saul's arrival, is also editorial. The editor makes clear that Samuel's anointing of Saul the next morning was an absolutely private affair between just the two of them (9:27–10:1); this permits the editorial inclusion of another story about Saul's designation in public (10:17–27a). Saul is anointed over Yahweh's "heritage," i.e., Israel; other nations are conceived as the heritage of their respective national gods. In the original folktale, it was apparently only at Saul's encounter with the men at Rachel's tomb that he learned the fate of the donkeys (10:2). The two loaves of bread are actually two offerings of bread according to the reading of the LXX and a Dead Sea Scroll fragment, indicating that Saul again receives a portion of honor (10:3–4). Saul's encounter with the prophets (10:5–6, 10–13) endows him with Yahweh's spirit as was the case with the judges. Music could be used to induce an ecstatic trance in which prophets delivered their oracles (v. 5). The story seems to be interrupted by vv. 7–8, which commission Saul to military action ("Do whatever you see fit to do"), and are part of the story of his failure (13:7b–15). The story ends with Saul's interview upon his return home (vv. 14–16). The interview with Saul's uncle rather than his father is unexpected since the uncle plays no role in the story. That interview emphasizes the private nature of Saul's first anointing, thus preparing the way for his public designation in the next episode.

10:17–27a. Saul Is Chosen Publicly. The process described in vv. 20–21 illustrates the social structure of Israel, consisting, in ascending order, of the individual, extended family, clan, and tribe. Designating by lot was a means of choosing akin to modern techniques like drawing straws. However, in the OT, God is typically understood to make the choice. Elsewhere, lots are used to designate offenders (Josh 7:14; 1 Sam 14:41), suggesting that the choice of Saul here may not be viewed positively. The verb "inquired" here puns on Saul's name. His height is a sign of his suitability to be king and perhaps another reason why he is chosen (vv. 23–24). The "rights and duties of the kingship" may allude to the "ways of the king" in 8:9, 11. Those who refuse to bring Saul a present (v. 27) in effect reject him as their king.

10:27b–11:15. Saul Proves Himself. This paragraph (10:27b), present in the NRSV and based on a Dead Sea Scroll reading, provided the information necessary for understanding the following story. The Gadites and Reubenites lived east of the Jordan in territory claimed by Nahash. Jabesh-Gilead lay outside of this territory, but when Nahash attacked, the Gadites and Reubenites fled there. Nahash pursued them and threatened Jabesh with the same treatment feared by the fugitives, namely, the loss of the right eye as punishment for their encroachment and a sign of submission (11:1–2). The city elders negotiate the opportunity

to seek aid in Israel (11:2). The fact that they send "through all the territory of Israel" (11:3) rather than directly to Saul shows that this story did not originally assume Saul's kingship and was therefore independent of the previous two stories. In fact, Saul finds out about the plight of Jabesh only when he providentially hears the people weeping as he is returning from working in the field (v. 5). The spirit of God comes upon him as it had upon the judges (v. 6). Dismemberment was a punishment for treaty violation, so Saul's dismembering of his oxen and distribution of the pieces may have been a way of summoning the tribes to fulfill their treaty obligation (v. 7). Having received the news that Saul is coming to save them, the people of Jabesh tell Nahash, "Tomorrow we will give ourselves up to you" (v. 10). Literally, "we will come out to you," is ambiguous, since it could refer either to surrender or to do battle. The "next day" is that same night, since the day was measured from sunset to sunset (v. 11). Thus, Saul's army marches all night to reach Jabesh "at the morning watch." The reference to those who rejected Saul's kingship (vv. 12–13) links this story to the previous one (10:27a). The link was necessary because the story behind 10:27b–11:15 was originally independent, reporting how Saul was anointed king following a military victory (v. 15). The editor has added the reference to *renewing* the kingship (v. 14), so that Saul's victory now answers those who doubt his martial prowess.

12:1–25. Samuel's Farewell. This farewell speech of Samuel's is a composition of the Deuteronomistic Historian, who, like other ancient historians, often created speeches for major characters. Samuel begins by pointing out his age and his integrity in leading the people (vv. 1–5). His deeds contrast with the "ways of the king" (8:11–18). He reviews Israel's historical traditions, culminating in the recent request for a king (vv. 6–12). The name Bedan (v. 11, Heb.) either preserves a tradition not found in Judges or another name for Jephthah. The Greek reading, Barak, represents a different sequence of judges from the book of Judges. (Deborah, rather than Barak, is the real judge according to Judg 4–5.) The Hebrew text also has Samuel instead of Samson in this verse, and the former is likely a scribal error. Samuel indicates that it was the threat of Nahash, not the Philistines as in 1 Sam 8, that impelled the Israelites to request a king (v. 12). Samuel places the burden for the choice of Saul as king upon the people and puns on Saul's name ("asked," v. 13). He concedes that God will not reject Israel for requesting a king, so long as they remain obedient (vv. 14–15, also 19–25). He then offers a sign of Yahweh's power and presence with Samuel that hints at his displeasure with their request for a king (vv. 16–18).

B. Saul's Failings (13–15)

13:1–22. Saul Is Rejected for Failing to Wait. The next three chapters contain episodes from Saul's reign and battles, showing his disobedience and ineptness. Not much is known of Saul's reign, including its length or his age at accession. The appearance of Jonathan, Saul's son, for the first time here as a grown man (v. 2) implies a considerable lapse in time since the young man Saul became king. Jonathan wins a victory over the Philistines while Saul, following Samuel's order (10:8), waits in Gilgal (vv. 3–7). As directed by Samuel, Saul waits seven days before offering the sacrifices himself (vv. 8–9), though the stories narrated since 10:8 imply the passage of a much longer period of time. Samuel condemns Saul (vv. 13–14), but the nature of Saul's offense is unclear, especially since he later builds an altar (and offers sacrifices?) without condemnation (14:31–35). Saul's punishment is the rejection of the continuation of his dynasty, clearing the way for David, the "man after God's own heart" (v. 14). This expression does not imply any special quality on David's part but merely states that Yahweh favors him as Israel's "ruler," i.e., king designate, instead of one of Saul's sons. The Philistines have been making raids against Israelites (v. 17–18), who have no iron weapons because that metallurgic technology is controlled by the Philistines (vv. 19–22).

13:23–14:52. Saul's Foolish Oath. The battle in this chapter reflects poorly on Saul since it is Jonathan who takes the initiative. "Gibeah" (14:2) should probably be read as "Geba"; the two names are very similar in Hebrew and appear to be confused in this chapter. Saul's priest, Eli's grandson (v. 3), carries the divinatory ephod. It is striking, particularly in contrast to David's use of the ephod later, that Saul has not consulted Yahweh yet. Again, this reflects badly on Saul. In contrast to his father, Jonathan shows himself to be a man of great courage and faith, as he trusts in Yahweh to

give him victory (vv. 4–10). Yahweh aids Jonathan and Israel by sending "a very great panic" (lit. "a panic of God") and an earthquake upon the Philistines (v. 15). Saul first tries to determine who has left the camp and is engaging the Philistines (v. 17), and then he calls for the ephod, presumably to determine what move to make (v. 18, where the Greek reading "ephod" is preferable to the Hebrew "ark"). However, the increasing tumult among the Philistines induces him to halt the consultation of Yahweh before the priest is finished (v. 19). The identity of the "Hebrews" in v. 20 is uncertain. They are evidently not identical with the Israelites and may be mercenaries who first sided with the Philistines and then rallied against them.

Saul's foolish oath in the remainder of the chapter spoils the victory. The oath imposing a fast on the army is intended as an act of piety (v. 24). But it has disastrous consequences, first because the soldiers would have fought better if they had not suffered weakness from hunger (vv. 30–31). Their hunger then leads to a ritual offense as they eat meat "with the blood" (v. 32), contrary to law (cf. Lev 19:26; Deut 12:16). Saul corrects this problem by ordering the troops to slaughter the animals on a large rock so that the carcasses could be leaned against the rock and the blood drained (v. 34). He also builds an altar to sacrifice those parts of the animals designated for God and perhaps to atone for the ritual violations.

In addition, Jonathan unwittingly breaks Saul's oath by eating honey (vv. 27–29). The statement that Jonathan's "eyes were brightened" means that the honey's nourishment energized him for battle. Later, however, when Saul tries to inquire of Yahweh about his next step, he receives no answer because someone has violated his oath (vv. 36–37). The verb "inquire" here puns on Saul's name. Ironically, though, it is the priest, rather than Saul, who proposes consulting God. The lack of an answer may suggest divine disfavor with Saul as well as displeasure at the violation of the oath. The Urim and Thummim were a form of "lot" used to divine the will of God by answering yes-or-no questions and choosing between alternatives (cf. Exod 28:6–30). They were also capable of yielding no response as suggested in this story. Saul's readiness to have Jonathan executed is another indication of his rash foolishness (vv. 43–46).

The final segment of this chapter summarizes Saul's reign (vv. 47–52), especially since his war with the Amalekites is related in the next chapter. Saul's victories and his valiant rescue of Israel (v. 48) hint that his reign may have been more successful than indicated in 1 Sam.

15:1–35. Saul's Disobedience. This story of Saul's disobedience may duplicate 13:8–15a. since both explain God's rejection of Saul as king. However, the focus in the earlier episode was on Saul's line, which would not continue, while the present episode is more a rejection of Saul's own kingship. Saul is ordered to avenge the Amalekites' opposition of Israel after the exodus (Exod 17:8–15; Deut 25:17–19) by annihilating them completely, a technique of "holy war" as attested in other ancient Near Eastern documents.

Saul warns the Kenites before his attack (v. 6). These were another clan in southern Judah known as metalworkers. Saul's preservation of King Agag and the best of the animals is viewed as disobedience by God and Samuel (vv. 9–14). Saul, though, intends to sacrifice the animals to Yahweh (v. 15), and he may be saving Agag for ritual execution (see below). Samuel's response (vv. 22–23) resembles the oracles of the eighth century prophets that denounce hollow ritual (Hos 6:6; Am 5:21–24; Mic 6:6–8).

Saul grasps the hem of Samuel's robe and unintentionally tears it (v. 27). Samuel likens the robe to the kingdom, which Yahweh will tear from Saul and award to his "neighbor," i.e., David. The statement that Yahweh ("the Glory of Israel") will not change his mind (v. 29) is in tension with the fact that he had changed his mind about Saul being king. It may be a later addition, as signaled also by its introduction with the particle *wegam* ("moreover," lit., "and also"). Samuel also curiously changes his mind about returning with Saul (vv. 30–31, cf. v. 26). Samuel then dismembers Agag "before Yahweh" in a ritual execution typically employed for treaty breakers (vv. 32–33). This may have been the fate Saul had in mind for Agag all along, as suggested by his dread (so NRSV following the Greek). The statement that "Samuel did not see Saul again" (v. 35) is contradicted by 19:18–24 but well anticipates the story in ch. 28.

III. David's Ascent (16–31)

A. David Comes to Saul's Attention (16–17)

16:1–13. Anointing of the Shepherd David. This chapter begins the story of David. God tells Samuel to prepare a horn of oil for the purpose of anointing a new king (v. 1). The title "Messiah," meaning "anointed," was used for kings and derives from this practice.

Jesse presents his sons to Samuel in birth order. Eliab, the oldest, is like Saul in appearance—tall and handsome (v. 6). But also like Saul he is rejected from kingship because he lacks the inner qualities that God seeks (v. 7). David appears as the youngest of Jesse's sons (v. 11), and God's favoring of the youngest is a theme found elsewhere in the Bible (e.g., Jacob, Rachel, Joseph). The word "youngest" also means "smallest," further highlighting the contrast with Saul.

The portrait of David as a shepherd foreshadows David's kingship, since kings in the ancient Near East were often described and depicted as shepherds (cf. 2 Sam 5:2). While "handsome" is a typical descriptor for the king, the further details about David's physical appearance—beautiful eyes and ruddy, i.e., of reddish complexion—are unusual (v. 12). The contrast with Saul is highlighted above all by the notice that Yahweh's spirit "came mightily upon David from that day forward" (v. 13). From this point on in the narrative God is with David and against Saul.

16:14–23. David Becomes Saul's Armor-bearer. The introduction of David in this episode was originally independent from 16:1–13. There David was a youth tending sheep. Here, he comes to Saul's court as an experienced warrior (v. 18). In the present sequence, the spirit of Yahweh leaves Saul (v. 14) only after it has already come upon David (v. 13). Together, the two stories drive home the point that God is with David and against Saul. The "evil spirit from Yahweh" reflects ancient theology in which Yahweh is the author of both good and ill. Evil spirits were conceived of as being all around, and music was understood as a way of keeping them at bay. Hence, it was common for a king to employ a musician as a regular figure in his court. The basic tradition behind this narrative, then, may have been simply that David came into Saul's service as a court musician. David's instrument was the lyre, a portable stringed instrument resembling a small harp.

The description of David is unusual for its detail (v. 18). "Man of valor" probably refers to social prominence or wealth, since the next item in the list is "warrior." "Prudent in speech" implies astuteness as well as eloquence. Yahweh's presence with David is a central theme in 1 Samuel, especially in contrast with Saul. The author depicts the relationship between David and Saul as a very close one at the beginning (v. 21). Saul is a sort of father figure to David and effectively "adopts" him as his son, thus hinting at David's succession as king.

17:1–58. David and Goliath.

This famous story is actually a composite of two versions, which can be easily distinguished from one another because the Greek text (LXX) contains only the initial version (vv. 1–11, 32–49, 51–54), which has been supplemented in the Hebrew text with the remaining verses in this chapter and 18:1–5. The composite nature of the present story accounts for certain inconsistencies. Both versions were evidently drawn from a legendary story about David's defeat of a Philistine champion.

The familiar name of the Philistine champion, Goliath, occurs only twice in the story (vv. 4, 23), which generally refers to "the Philistine." While the name is genuinely Philistine, it was probably not original to this story and came in under the influence of 2 Sam 21:19, which says that a Bethlehemite named Elhanan killed Goliath. The champion's height in the Hebrew text, nine and one-half feet, is also likely an unintended exaggeration. The Greek reading, "four cubits and a span"—some six and one-half feet—is more realistic.

The Philistine's armor (v. 5) does not match depictions of Philistine soldiers in Egyptian reliefs and is probably borrowed from that of different cultures and different periods with an interest in presenting him as invincible. The bronze coat of mail, for instance, at five thousand shekels would weigh about 126 pounds! However, the "helmet of bronze," if modeled after Assyrian styles, which did not possess nose guards, would permit David's sling stone to strike the Philistine in the forehead. The "javelin" slung over his shoulder was probably more like a "scimitar." The weight of the spear-

head at 600 iron shekels was more than fifteen pounds, suggesting that it was designed for hand-to-hand combat rather than hurling. The Philistine's proposal of combat between representatives of the two armies (vv. 8–10) has been likened by some scholars to examples of individual battles in Greek literature (esp., the *Iliad*).

The second version of the story begins with v. 12, where David is introduced as though for the first time. This version identifies the same three sons of Jesse named in 16:1–13. Here, David is a shepherd and errand boy rather than a warrior (v. 15, cf. 16:18). Here also the Philistine has been reproaching Israel for forty days, while the other version has him face David the same day he issues his challenge. Saul's promised reward to the successful Israelite champion includes making his family "free" (v. 25), which refers to exemption not only from slavery but also from conscription and taxation.

The initial version of the story resumes in v. 32 where David accepts the Philistine's challenge. Saul's reluctance to send David because of his youth (v. 33) contrasts David's trust in God with Saul's lack thereof. The contrast is further drawn in the comic scene of Saul's effort to equip David with protective armor and David's inability to maneuver in it (vv. 38–39). The sling that David produces (v. 40) was not a toy but an effective weapon commonly used in ancient Near Eastern warfare. It had the advantages of being easily portable, easily hidden, and deadly accurate from a distance.

The effort to demoralize one's enemy through taunting and threat (vv. 41–47) was a tactic in ancient Near Eastern warfare comparable to "trash talking" in modern sporting events. The Philistine's disdainful perception of David as a boy with sticks (vv. 42–43) hints that he may not have seen the sling. David invokes God as the true source of his victory, of which he is certain because of the Philistine's defiance of Yahweh and his people. Verse 50 is an insertion from the secondary version, which has the sling stone killing the Philistine. In the initial version, the stone merely felled him, and David finished him off by beheading him (v. 51). In the present compilation, the Philistine actually appears to be killed twice, though v. 50 could be read as an out-of-place summary of the story.

Following David's victory, the Israelites chase the Philistines deep into their own territory (v. 52). The current ending of the story (vv. 55–58) stems from the second version and stands in tension with the story at the end of chapter 16. There, Saul was said to love David, while here he does not know him.

B. David in Saul's Court (18–20)

18:1–16. David's Military Success. The first five verses of this chapter are lacking in the LXX and thus continue the supplemental version of the Goliath story. Nevertheless, this passage introduces the theme of the close relationship between David and Jonathan. While Jonathan's love is that of a close personal relationship (v. 1), "love" in the ancient Near East is also a way of conveying political loyalty. Thus, Jonathan, heir to Saul's throne, is loyal to David! His bestowal of his robes upon David (v. 4) is tantamount to an abdication in favor of David as Saul's successor. David's success as a military commander (v. 5) also wins him the loyalty of the army. As the writer presents it, everyone in Saul's kingdom favors David—except Saul himself.

Saul's jealousy of David is sparked by the victory celebration that allots David a status equal and even superior to Saul's (v. 7). This episode marks the turning point in the relationship between Saul and David. The remainder of this chapter and the next two recount subtle attempts Saul makes to rid himself of David. The schemes grow more and more overt until Saul begins openly to seek David's life. Saul's attempt to spear David (19:8–10) originally marked the climax of this series of subtle plots and the first overt attempt to kill David in the initial narrative. The gradual increase in the overtness of Saul's actions in the initial narrative has been broken by the insertion of an earlier attempt by Saul to spear David (18:10–11), which is again supplemental as shown by its absence from the LXX. Thus, in the initial story, Saul first removed David from his presence and gave him a military command, apparently in the hope that David would be killed in action (18:12–13). The plan backfired when David's constant success won him the loyalty of all Israel and Judah (vv. 14–15).

18:17–30. David Marries Michal. Saul's next subtle move was the offer of his daughter, Michal, in exchange for 100 Philistine foreskins, again hoping that David would fall to the Philistines in the attempt (v 20–30). "Foreskins" likely refers, perhaps euphemistically, to uncircumcised penises collected as war trophies, a practice attested on Egyptian reliefs. The terminology exemplifies "dark humor" on the author's part as a classic case of "adding insult to injury"; David "converts" the Philistines into Israelites by "circumcising" them. The stakes are high in this episode. Saul risks bringing David into his family and thus giving him a claim, albeit an indirect one, on the throne. Thus, the narrative speaks of becoming "the king's son-in-law," which is precisely the incentive behind David's risking his life. David's ambition is thinly masked here. The text states that Michal loved David but never that David loved Michal. Her love for David is yet another example of David's universal appeal and support in the story. Later texts report that he took her from her husband (2 Sam 3:14–16) and that she bore him no children, who would have been heirs to Saul (2 Sam 6:23). He seems to have been interested in her purely to legitimate his claim to Saul's throne.

19:1–24. Saul's Moves Against David Become Overt. Saul next tries to talk his servants and Jonathan into killing David, but Jonathan thwarts his father by warning David and then by convincing Saul that David is innocent (vv. 1–5). He secures an oath from Saul that David will not be killed (v. 6) and thus reconciles the two of them (v. 7). The reconciliation is temporary, though, as Saul is roused to jealousy by the evil spirit after David's next successful encounter against the Philistines and tries to kill David with his spear (vv. 8–10). This narrow escape initiates David's flight; from now until Saul's death David will be on the run. The episode in vv. 11–17, therefore, is probably out of place. It appears to reflect David and Michal's wedding night and thus probably originally came directly after the story of their marriage. It shows Michal helping David to escape and thus choosing him over her father. The household idols used by Michal to fool Saul's messengers are referred to elsewhere in the Bible, where they seem to have been used for divining and may have represented property rights (Gen 31:33–35; Judg 17:5).

David's first stop upon leaving Saul, Ramah (vv. 18–24), appears to make little sense historically or geographically, since it was north of Gibeah. This episode is included here for ideological reasons, because Ramah was Samuel's home:

Samuel and the prophets add their support to David. Even more important, Yahweh uses prophecy as a tool to protect David from Saul's envoys and then to disable Saul himself.

20:1–42. Jonathan's Failed Reconciliation. David again seeks help from Jonathan, who does not believe that his father would act against David without consulting him. The two of them concoct a plan to test Saul's true sentiments toward David. The new moon was celebrated with sacrifice and feasting (v. 5). David's absence would be noted, and Saul's reaction to it would reveal his attitude toward David. The covenant in this chapter is about more than friendship; it involves political loyalty, implied by the term "love" (v. 17). Hence, Jonathan's wish that Yahweh will be with David as he has been with Saul (v. 13) portends David's kingship. Jonathan's concern for David's treatment of his posterity ("my house," vv. 14–15) also assumes David's future reign and is the basis for his treatment of Jonathan's son Mephibosheth (2 Sam 9). Jonathan's oath (v. 16) was probably originally an imprecation against David himself as an assurance against future violation of the treaty. A scribe probably altered the language out of reverence for David. Ironically, "the enemies of David" would include Saul.

Saul does not initially remark on David's absence from the sacrificial meal, assuming that it is because of ritual uncleanness, which might have a variety of causes (v. 26; cf. Lev 11–15). But when Jonathan informs him that he has excused David from the sacrifice, Saul becomes angry, insulting and even attacking Jonathan (vv. 26–34). Saul refuses to call David by name, disparaging him as "the son of Jesse" (v. 27). Saul, in effect, accuses Jonathan of treason by saying that he has chosen David over himself (v. 30). Making such a choice shames his mother's "nakedness," a euphemism for the genitals and thus for Jonathan's own origins. Saul recognizes that if David lives he will be the next king in Jonathan's place (v. 31). The theme of David and Jonathan as rivals or alter-egos is further apparent when Saul tries to kill Jonathan with his spear just as he had tried to kill David (v. 33). Jonathan faithfully signals David as promised (vv. 35–40).

C. David the Fugitive (21–31)

21:1–9. David Seeks Help from the Priests of Nob. Lying between Gibeah and Jerusalem, Nob was evidently the home of Eli's line after the fall of Shiloh (Ahimelech was Eli's great grandson). Ahimelech greets David uneasily (v. 1), perhaps suspecting that he is on the run from Saul. But David convinces him that he is on a secret mission and about to rendezvous with his men (v. 2). The only food Ahimelech has is holy bread, which he offers to David if he and his men are ritually pure. (In the NT, Jesus cites this story to illustrate human need transcending ritual law [Matt 12:3–4; Mk 2:25–26; Lk 6:3–4].) The transaction is ominously witnessed by Doeg, an Edomite and a leading official in Saul's administration (v. 7). David also requests a weapon and receives Goliath's sword (vv. 8–9).

21:10–15. David Feigns Madness Before the Philistines. The story of David's flight to the Philistine king Achish of Gath (vv. 11–15) seems out of place, especially in view of chs. 27–29, where David serves him as a mercenary. David's feigning of madness in order to escape danger indicates that the mentally ill were considered divinely "touched" on the order of prophets and were therefore protected from harm. It is unlikely that the Philistines would have been familiar with the victory song of the Israelite women (v. 11). It is also peculiar that they refer to David as the "king of the land." Is it possible that David was already the effective ruler of the Negeb long before Saul's death?

22:1–5. David Gathers an Army and Provides for His Parents. Adullam, the site of a small fortress about 17 miles southwest of Jerusalem, becomes David's headquarters. "Cave" (v. 1) should probably be emended to "stronghold" (v. 4), the two words being very similar in Hebrew. Apparently fearing for the safety of his parents in Bethlehem, David sends them to Moab (vv. 3–4), perhaps because he was partly of Moabite ancestry through Ruth (cf. Ruth 4:17–22).

22:6–23. Saul Annihilates the Priests of Nob. Saul is cast in the typical, royal posture of a king seated under a sacred tree (the "tamarisk") judging the people (v. 6). Saul tells his fellow Benjaminites that they cannot expect rewards for supporting the Judahite, David. Ahimelech's inquiring of Yahweh on David's behalf (v. 10) is not reported in chapter 21, but it proves important when Saul confronts the priest. Ahimelech does not deny that he helped David. His defense, rather, is that he has often inquired of God for David, who is among Saul's most loyal servants (vv. 14–15). Both statements only fanned Saul's rage. Ahimelech also pleads ignorance, but Saul does not listen and orders the execution of the priests (v. 17). Doeg alone carries out the order, presumably because as an Edomite he does not have scruples against attacking Yahweh's priests (v. 18). Ironically, Saul devotes the city of Nob to destruction, thus committing an act of war against Yahweh himself. Abiathar's lone escape (vv. 20–23) fulfills the oracle in 2:27–36. He will prove an invaluable ally to David in avoiding capture by Saul and will eventually become one of David's high priests.

23:1–29. Providential Escapes in the Wilderness.
This chapter recounts a series of narrow escapes from Saul in the wilderness, illustrating the benefit to David of having Abiathar and the ephod (v. 6). Following the directives of Yahweh, David rescues Keilah (vv. 1–5) and then escapes when he learns of Saul's approach (vv. 6–14). These incidents exhibit not only God's protection of David but also David's trust in and regular consultation of Yahweh. Jonathan's support of David (vv. 16–18) is both moral and tangible ("strengthened his hand"). Jonathan's willingness to yield his place as king to David and to agree to serve as his second in command (v. 17) illustrates the writer's apologetic contention that everyone—even the crown prince—recognized David's kingship. The final episode (vv. 19–29) is perhaps the best example of divine protection of David. Saul has David trapped but is forced to withdraw at the last moment by news of a Philistine incursion (v. 27).

24:1–22. An Opportunity to Kill Saul in a Cave in En-gedi.
The remainder of 1 Samuel seems focused on demonstrating that David had nothing to do with Saul's death. This is the first of two stories (ch. 26) that show David having opportunities to kill Saul and refusing to do so. The point seems to be that if David did not kill when he had the chance, he certainly would not have been involved in Saul's final demise.

In a denigrating portrait, especially for a king, Saul enters a cave in the vicinity of En-Gedi, in order to "cover his feet," an idiom for defecation. David and his men are hiding in that cave, and the men see this as an opportunity. Refusing to kill Saul, David cuts off a portion of his garment, which might be viewed as symbolic emasculation

or usurpation (v. 4b). David refuses to harm Saul because as Yahweh's "anointed" he is sacrosanct (v. 6). For the same reason, when David speaks to Saul outside of the cave, he is very respectful and self-deprecating. He denies that he intends any harm against Saul and displays the piece of Saul's garment as proof that he could have harmed Saul (vv. 8–11). Still, there is an edge, or double entendre to David's words. His designation of Saul as "my father" is respectful but also implies his right to succeed (v. 11). He also expresses confidence that Yahweh will vindicate him against Saul (v. 15). Saul's weeping confession is another sign of his instability, but it shows that, when rational, even he recognizes that David is in the right (vv. 16–25). He acknowledges that David will succeed him (v. 20) and begs him not to annihilate his line, as was common practice for usurpers (v. 21). David's oath (v. 22) anticipates his treatment of Saul's grandson, Mephibosheth (2 Sam 9).

25:1–44. David, Nabal, and Abigail.
This story is placed between two stories of opportunities that David has to kill Saul and refuses (ch. 24; 26). Here, David vows to kill a wealthy, Saul-like figure out of personal revenge, but is prevented from doing so by the man's wife. Meaning "fool," Nabal seems an unlikely personal name. Its original meaning might have been different or the man's real name may have been different and "Nabal" adopted as fitting the character in this story. It is also similar to Hebrew words for "wine bottle" and "corpse," both of which appropriately characterize Nabal at different points in the story. Nabal's wife, Abigail, was his exact opposite.

Sheep shearing was a time of celebration, so David is hoping to catch Nabal in a generous mood (v. 4). The ten men he sends are intended both to intimidate Nabal and to indicate what size gift David has in mind (v. 5). As David presents it (vv. 6–8), he and his men have protected Nabal's flocks in the wilderness, so that Nabal is indebted to him. David's request is answered with insults by Nabal (vv. 10–11). David is furious and orders his men to arm themselves (v. 13). Nabal's servants immediately recognize the danger they are in and appeal to Abigail, acknowledging that Nabal cannot be reasoned with (vv. 14–17). Abigail wisely gathers provisions and sets out to intercept David (vv. 18–20). At this point, the narrator reveals David's true intention: to kill all of the males (lit. "everyone who urinates on the wall") in Nabal's household (v. 22), leaving Abigail, a woman, as the only one who could avert the crisis.

Abigail does obeisance to David as to a king (v. 23). Her speech is a model of eloquence and diplomacy, both soothing his bruised ego and gingerly reasoning with him. She dismisses Nabal and his actions as insignificant (v. 25) and offers him a "present" for his men (v. 27). She argues that it is in David's own self-interest not to attack Nabal's household, because the shedding of innocent blood would be a blot on David's kingship (vv. 30–31). Rather, he should trust Yahweh to avenge him. She concludes with a marriage proposal ("remember your servant"). "When the LORD has dealt well with my lord" is ambiguous and may refer either to Nabal's death or to David becoming king.

The chapter ends with the names of three of David's wives. All three marriages likely reflect political maneuvering. The only other Ahinoam in the Bible was Saul's wife (14:50). The only other Abigail was David's sister (1 Chr 2:16). It is uncertain whether these are the same women. In any case, Ahinoam's Jezreel was also in Judah near Carmel, so that she and Abigail represent David's hegemony over the Calebites. The reference to Michal prepares for 2 Sam 3:13–16, where David demands her return because through her he has a claim to Saul's kingdom. The fact that she was married to another man raises the possibility that she was not really previously married to David.

26:1–25. Another Opportunity to Kill Saul in the Wilderness of Ziph. This story is similar to the one in chapter 24. This time, Saul is sleeping with his army around him (v. 5). David sneaks down with Abishai, the brother of Joab, two of the rough and ready "sons of Zeruiah" (v. 7). Abishai encourages David to have Saul killed with, ironically, the same spear he had thrown at David (v. 8). As in chapter 24, though, David piously refuses to harm Yahweh's anointed (vv. 9–11). Going to "the other side," where he can lead Saul's men away from his own camp should Saul pursue him, David addresses Saul as in chapter 24, though here he speaks directly to Abner, Saul's commander. David curses anyone who may have accused him (falsely) to Saul because they have forced him to leave Yahweh's "heritage," i.e., Israel. The idea here is that

each country had its own god, and each god its own country or "heritage." In other countries, therefore, one would "serve other gods" (v. 19). As in ch. 24, Saul admits that he is in the wrong and promises not to harm David, and he alludes to David's future kingship (v. 25).

27:1–28:2. David Becomes a Philistine Mercenary. David seeks refuge with the Philistine king, Achish, in the city of Gath. It seems unlikely that Achish would have accepted David if David had previously feigned madness to escape (21:10–15), so these two anecdotes stand in tension. The city of Ziklag, granted to David by Achish, lay on the southern Philistine frontier (v. 6), so that David and his men served as mercenaries guarding that frontier. From Ziklag, David conducted raids against settlements of people hostile to Judah (v. 8). He brought the spoils to Achish, claiming to have attacked Judah and its constituents (v. 10), and since he killed all the inhabitants of the places he attacked, no one could tell Achish the truth (vv. 9, 11). Thus, Achish became convinced that he had David's loyalty (v. 12), so much so that he takes David and his men with him to war against Israel (28:1). The statement, "Then you shall know what your servant can do" (28:2), is a double entendre; what Achish hears as a pledge of loyalty and promise of potential is a veiled warning about David's duplicity.

28:3–25. Saul Consults a Medium at Endor. Saul is anxious about the impending battle with the Philistines (v. 5). But having alienated himself from Yahweh, he receives no response using the customary means of divination (v. 6). He violates his own order and Israelite law banning those who consult the dead (v. 3; Lev 19:31; 20:6, 27; Deut 18:10–11) by going in disguise to consult a medium. Verses 11–12a anticipate the identification of the ghost or "divine being" (lit., "god") as Samuel. The ghost comes up from the underworld (v. 13), where the dead are understood to reside. Saul recognizes Samuel from his robe (v. 14), the same one that Saul tore and Samuel used as symbol that God would tear the kingdom from him (v. 17; cf. 1 Sam 15). Saul is told that he and his sons will be with Samuel the next day, meaning that they will be dead (v. 19). Saul's terror at this news (vv. 20–21) ill befits a king and suggests that he is unqualified to continue as such. He is hungry probably because he fasted in anticipation of consulting the medium.

29:1–11. David Is Sent Away by the Philistine Commanders.

In reviewing their troops for war, the Philistine commanders notice David and his men. Since it is they rather than the "lords of the Philistines," the rulers of the Philistine city-states, like Achish, who will actually fight the battle, they demand that the "Hebrews" be dismissed, fearing that David will revert to Israel (v. 4). Achish remains convinced of David's loyalty to him, but goes along with his fellow Philistine lords and dismisses David, sending him back to Ziklag, "the place that I appointed for you" (v. 10). David's reference to "the enemies of my lord the king" (v. 8) is again duplicitous. David's "lord" and "king" is Saul, making Achish and the Philistines the enemies against whom David desires to fight. This story makes clear that David did not participate in the battle in which Saul lost his life. Not only had the Philistines dismissed him, but he was on his way to Ziklag, far away from the northern town and valley of Jezreel, where the battle is joined (v. 11).

30:1–31. David Avenges the Sack of Ziklag.

This episode both continues the defense of David in the face of Saul's death and presents him as a royal figure. The fact that it took three days for David to reach Ziklag (v. 1) emphasizes David's distance from the dying Saul. David faced a mutiny as a result of the raid and the loss of his men's families (vv. 2–6). But his reaction was exemplary as he "strengthened himself in Yahweh" (v. 6) and then called for Abiathar to consult God about his next move (vv. 7–10). In contrast to God's "silent treatment" of Saul (28:6), he answers David, telling him to pursue the raiders and attack them. The Egyptian servant found on the way (vv. 11–15), having been providentially abandoned to die by his master, has no qualms about leading David to the Amalekite camp. The defeat of the raiders garners David great booty (vv. 16–20), which he distributes among the elders of cities in southern Judah (vv. 26–31) as a way of securing their support for his kingship. The decree that David issues concerning the men who guarded the equipment (vv. 21–25) both shows him to be a decisive and effective leader and provides an etiology for the practice of equally distributing spoil.

31:1–13. Saul Dies on Mt. Gilboa.

The scene switches back to Saul in battle on Mt. Gilboa. His sons have been killed, and he is seriously wounded (vv. 1–3). Wishing to avoid torture ("sport"), he asks his armor-bearer to finish him off. But the man refuses, presumably out of reverence for Saul's status as Yahweh's anointed. So Saul commits suicide (v. 4). (Suicide is not prohibited in the Hebrew Bible; it occurs elsewhere in desperate circumstances [2 Sam 17:23; 1 Kgs 16:18; cf. Matt 27:5].)

Those "on the other side of the valley" apparently refers to the Israelites who lived north of the Jezreel, where the battle occurred, and "those beyond the Jordan" to those whose homes are east of the Jordan. As a result of their flight, the central section of Israel falls to Philistine domination. This would have included the Jezreel and meant that the Philistines controlled access to the roads and thus trade through Israel, both east-west along the Jezreel Valley and north-south along the coast and through the Jordan Valley. Beth-shan guarded the eastern end of the Jezreel.

Just as David cut off Goliath's head and took his armor (17:51, 54), so the Philistines dismember Saul's corpse and seize his armor as war trophies (vv. 9–10). They credit their gods with the victory. The people from Jabesh-Gilead were indebted to Saul for rescuing them from Nahash (10:27b–11:15), which was probably why they undertook the mission of retrieving the corpses of Saul and his sons (vv. 11–13).

BIBLIOGRAPHY

R. Alter. *The David Story* (New York: Norton, 1999); D. M. Gunn. *The Story of King David: Genre and Interpretation.* JSOTSup 6 (Sheffield: JSOT, 1978); B. Halpern. *David's Secret Demons: Messiah, Murderer, Traitor, King* (Grand Rapids: Eerdmans, 2001); S. Isser. *The Sword of Goliath: David in Heroic Literature.* Studies in Biblical Literature (Atlanta: SBL, 2003); R. W. Klein. *1 Samuel.* WBC (Waco, Tex.: Word, 1981); N. P. Lemche. "David's Rise." *JSOT* 10 (1978) 2–25; P. K. McCarter Jr. *I Samuel.* AB 8 (Garden City, N.Y.: Doubleday, 1980); S. L. McKenzie. *King David: A Biography* (New York: Oxford, 2000); L. E. Stager. "The Archaeology of the Family in Ancient Israel." *BASOR* 260 (1985) 1–29.

2 SAMUEL

STEVE McKENZIE

OVERVIEW

The book of 2 Samuel is the continuation of 1 Samuel. Since 2 Sam 1 provides another report of Saul's death (1 Sam 31), it literally takes up where 1 Samuel leaves off.

The prophet Samuel, after whom the book is named, is long dead when 2 Samuel begins and is never mentioned in the book. At the same time, the story narrated in 2 Samuel extends beyond that book, continuing in 1 and 2 Kings. Thus, 1 and 2 Samuel are part of the much larger Deuteronomistic History (= Deuteronomy, Joshua, Judges 1 and 2 Samuel, 1 and 2 Kings).

With Saul gone, David immediately becomes king of Judah. A protracted civil war with Saul's heir, Ish-baal (-bosheth) ensues. The assassinations of Abner and then Ish-baal open the way for David to unite Israel with Judah under his rule. This he does, conquering Jerusalem and designating it as his capital, installing the ark there as well. All this takes place in the first six chapters. The book tells how God responds to David's suggestion about building a temple by promising him a dynasty. It reports his military successes, and in the midst of one of these, his adultery with Bathsheba, murder of her husband, and Nathan's denunciation of the affair. Further trouble plagues David's reign in the rape of his daughter, Tamar, by her half-brother and crown prince, Amnon, and then the murder of the latter by Absalom, her full brother, who subsequently leads a successful, albeit short-lived, revolt against his father. After the report of another, less successful revolt, the book ends rather abruptly with a collection of texts (narratives, military anecdotes, and poems) that are out of chronological order but reflect careful arrangement. David's death is left to be recounted in 1 Kings.

The main feature in the literary-critical landscape of 2 Samuel is the so-called "Succession Narrative," otherwise known as the "Court History" of David. This hypothetical document was initially posited as an early work of historiography—essentially contemporaneous with the events it reports—underlying much of 2 Samuel, including David's dealings with Mephiboshet (2 Sam 9), the Ammonite campaign (2 Sam 10), the Bathsheba affair (2 Sam 11–12), the revolts of Absalom and Sheba (2 Sam 13–20), and Solomon's accession (1 Kgs 1–2), that sought to explain how Solomon came to succeed David. In recent decades, the date, purpose, characteristic—even the bare existence—of this document have been questioned by scholars. The designation "Court History" for what amounts to the bulk of 2 Samuel places in relief just how little of David's reign is actually reported in 2 Samuel—a handful of events over what is supposed to have been a forty-year reign.

There is much less unanimity among scholars about the overall interpretation of 2 Samuel than there is for 1 Samuel. Some, including the present author, find a continuation of the apologetic tendency of 1 Samuel; the author defending David in the face of allegations that he was responsible for the assassinations of the Saulides—Abner, Ish-baal, and most of Saul's other sons and grandsons—as well as his own sons, Amnon and Absalom. Others see the Court History as a scathing condemnation of the Davidic line and even of monarchy in general. The majority view probably lies between these two positions. The author of 2 Samuel is sympathetic toward David but faults him for personal and familial failings and traces the troubles during his reign to these failings.

OUTLINE

Detailed Analysis

I. David's Accession to Kingship (1:1–5:5)

A. David Learns of Saul's Death (1:1–27)

1:1–16. Interrogation of the Amalekite. The book of 2 Samuel begins with a second account of Saul's death in battle, parallel to 1 Sam 31. The two versions need not be taken as variants from different sources. Rather, it seems likely that the Amalekite in the present account should be understood as lying. Hence, his claim to have been on Mt. Gilboa while the battle was raging (v. 6) is unbelievable. Moreover, Amalekites are depicted elsewhere as untrustworthy scavengers and enemies of Israel (1 Sam 15; 30). The reader is to surmise that he pilfered the royal effects from Saul's corpse (v. 10) and then, aware of the rivalry between Saul and David, brought them to David, along with his contrived story about finishing Saul off, in anticipation of a reward. The man's status as a "resident alien" (*ger*) makes him subject to Israel's laws and therefore liable for having killed Yahweh's anointed (1:13–14). This episode also shows David's respect for Saul and the position of Yahweh's anointed. "Anointed" is a royal title; it could be transliterated into English as "messiah."

1:17–27. Lamentation over Saul and Jonathan. The "lamentation" or "dirge" (Heb: *qinah*, v. 17) was a particular kind of poem marked by a distinctive meter. For "The Song of the Bow" (v. 18), the Hebrew text reads only "bow." This may be a copyist's error or perhaps a musical notation. The "Book of Jashar" was apparently a collection of poems; it is cited elsewhere (Josh 10:13). David orders that the poem be taught in Judah, i.e., among his fellow tribesmen, who rivaled the house of Saul and the tribe of Benjamin for leadership over Israel, in order to show David's high regard for Saul. "Glory" and "mighty" (or "warriors") allude to Saul and Jonathan (v. 19). The poem commands that the news of their deaths not be proclaimed among the Philistines, who would celebrate it (v. 20). The rejoicing of the Philistine "daughters," i.e., women, may be contrasted to the victory songs of the Israelite women in 1 Sam 18:6–7 and to their weeping in v. 24. Next, the poem curses the "mountains of Gilboa" where Saul died (v. 21). Leather shields were "anointed with oil" to keep them from becoming brittle and ineffective. The Israelite women lament Saul's death because his military conquests brought them items from the spoils of battle (v. 24). The reference to Jonathan's love "passing the love of women" (v. 26) is hyperbole; scholars disagree about whether it implies a sexual relationship between David and Jonathan.

B. Civil War (2:1–5:5)

2:1–4a. David Made King of Judah. The writer depicts David as still looking to Yahweh for direction. The verb "inquired" or "asked" (*ša'al*, v. 1) is a pun on Saul's name. Formal inquiry probably involved use of the ephod, Urim and Thummim, or some other divinatory device. Hebron was the principal city of the Calebites, the leading clan in Judah. Ahinoam and Abigail (v. 2) were both from this region (1 Sam 25:43), and their presence lent support to David's bid to be king of Judah. David's previous gifts to the elders of Judah from his despoiling of the Amalekites might also have won him supporters.

2:4b–7. David's Overture to Jabesh-Gilead. Not content to be king of Judah, David immediately begins moving toward the Israelite throne. Jabesh-Gilead was an enclave of loyal Saul supporters because he had rescued them from the Ammonites

(1 Sam 11). Those from Jabesh retrieved Saul's corpse for burial (1 Sam 31:11–13). David's letter suggests that he, rather than one of Saul's sons, is Saul's successor and that the Jabesh-Gileadites should support him.

2:8–11. Ishbaal Succeeds Saul. Ishbaal is presented as something of a figurehead, with Abner, the commander of the army, holding the real power. The Hebrew actually reads "Ishbosheth," the word *bosheth* ("abomination") having been substituted for –*baal* by a pious scribe because the latter is the name of a Canaanite god. However, *baal* means "master, lord" and may have once been an epithet for Yahweh. The location of Mahanaim east of the Jordan indicates that following Saul's death and Israel's defeat, the Philistines controlled most of the territory west of the Jordan, despite Ishbaal's claim to be king "over all Israel" (v. 9). "Geshurites" should probably be read instead of "Ashurites"; Geshur was a territory and sometimes independent kingdom directly east of the Sea of Galilee (2 Sam 3:3; 15:8). Ishbaal's reign overlaps with only two of the seven and one-half years that David reigned over Judah (vv. 10–11). It is unclear whether the remaining five and one-half years occurred after Ishbaal's death or before his reign, while Saul was still king of Israel.

2:12–32. The Battle at Gibeon and the Death of Asahel. The exact nature of the contest in vv. 12–17 is unclear. The episode provides an etiological explanation for the place name Helkath-hazzurim, meaning "field of the flint blades." It also initiates the battle and subsequent war that follow. David's forces win the day and eventually the war. Of crucial importance in this narrative of the first battle is the death of Asahel in vv. 18–23. Asahel was the brother of Joab and Abishai, two of David's leading commanders (v. 18). He is depicted here as a young man, fleet of foot and trying to build his reputation as a warrior—a depiction that stands in tension with his inclusion as a leading figure in the list of David's military heroes (23:24). His death at Abner's hand furnishes a motive for Joab's assassination of Abner in the next chapter.

3:1–5. David's Sons Born in Hebron. Of the sons listed here, Amnon, Absalom, and Adonijah will play roles in futures stories. However, nothing more is known of Chileab (v. 3), Shephatiah (v. 4), or Ithream (v. 5). It is often supposed that Chileab died young, since he was David's second son, yet he does not appear again. David's marriage to Absalom's mother, Maacah, likely sealed a treaty with her father, Talmai, who was the king of Geshur (see on 2:9).

3:6–39. Abner's Defection and Assassination.
Ishbaal's questioning of Abner in the matter of Saul's concubine, Rizpah (v. 7), led Abner to defect to David. A "concubine" was a slave-wife used for sexual purposes, whose children were not considered heirs. Sleeping with one of the king's harem would amount to a claim to the throne, so that Ishbaal's question is effectively an accusation of treason. Abner does not deny his relationship with Rizpah but is offended by the disrespect and implication of disloyalty from Ishbaal, whom he placed on the throne (2:8–9). "Dog's head" is an expression unattested elsewhere in the Bible; the context as well as comparable references to dogs indicate that it is an expression of reproach (cf. 1 Sam 17:43; 24:14; 2 Sam 9:8; 16:9; 2 Kgs 8:13). Abner may have been seeking a pretext to defect to David's side, which was winning the civil war. "Dan to Beersheba" represented the traditional north-south extent of Israel (v. 10).

David's demand that Abner bring Michal (v. 13) is politically motivated; as Saul's daughter, she symbolizes his claim to Saul's kingdom. It is not clear why Ishbaal complies with David's demand (vv. 14–16), though some scholars have suggested that he was legally compelled to do so. It is possible that Paltiel (or Palti, cf. 1 Sam 25:44) was Michal's real and only husband and that the stories about her marriage to David are to legitimate his claim to be Saul's successor as his son-in-law.

Abner first lobbies the Israelites and Benjaminites on David's behalf (vv. 17–19). The promise from Yahweh that he cites in v. 18 is not attested in exactly this form elsewhere and is probably the author's synthesis, presented as a rhetorical device by which Abner seeks to convince the Israelite leaders. The author makes a point of claiming that David treated Abner hospitably (v. 20) and then dismissed him peaceably, indicating that he had nothing to do with Abner's death. Thus, the text repeatedly states that Abner left in peace (vv. 21, 22, 23). Joab is upset that David released Abner, whom he accuses of spying (vv. 24–25). The text also makes clear that David was ignorant of Joab's actions (v. 26) and that Joab acted out of revenge

for Asahel (v. 27, 30). David affirms his innocence in the matter, denouncing and cursing Joab (vv. 28, 29), but does not punish him until many years later, in what is patently an act of retribution for Joab's having supported Adonijah instead of Solomon (1 Kgs 2:5–6). The harshness of the "sons of Zeruiah" becomes a theme in 2 Samuel, as they shoulder the blame for the violent deaths of leading individuals whose removal benefited David. David also laments Abner's death and orders the people to do the same (vv. 31–34). He fasts as a sign of mourning (v. 35), and praises Abner as a great man (v. 38). The author reports that David's actions convinced the Israelites that he was not responsible for Abner's death (vv. 36–37).

4:1–12. Ishbaal's Assassination.
Since Abner was the commander of the army and the real power behind the throne, his death effectively meant the end of the civil war and of Ishbaal's kingdom. The original form of the name Mephibosheth was probably Meribbaal (1 Chr 8:34; 9:40). His disability, described here, made him unsuitable to be king, and, as a result, he was later kept alive instead of being executed along with Saul's other sons (see on ch. 9). As in the case of the Amalekite who claimed to have killed Saul (2 Sam 1) and which David cites here (v. 10), the two captains who assassinated Ishbaal brought his head to David anticipating a reward. David does not call Ishbaal Yahweh's anointed as he did Saul (1:14), but refers to him as a "righteous man" (v. 11), and he has the two assassins executed and dismembered in ritual fashion (v. 12), perhaps because he considered them traitors.

5:1–5. David Made King of Israel.
With Saul, Jonathan, Abner, and Ishbaal all dead, "all the tribes of Israel" (i.e., the northern tribes, excluding Judah), turn to David for leadership. They claim kinship with David ("your bone and flesh") and say that it was he who brought them military success ("led out Israel and brought it in") even while Saul was reigning. The quotation attributed to Yahweh (v. 2) is not attested elsewhere; it expresses the author's view and perhaps that of the Israelites that David is divinely chosen to be king, and it is a device by which the Israelites seek to ingratiate themselves to David. "Shepherd" was a common metaphor in the ancient Near East for the king. The term "ruler" (naghidh) means "king designate." The figure of "forty years" for the total

length of David's reign may be a round number for a generation, as it is elsewhere in the Bible.

II. David Builds an Empire (5:6–12:31)

A. Consolidating the Kingdom (5:6–25)

5:6–16. Establishing Jerusalem as the Capital. One of David's priorities upon becoming king was the establishment of a capital. Scholars have long observed that Jerusalem was a perfect choice because of its geographical and political neutrality. As a Jebusite city, it did not belong to either Israel or Judah and was roughly between them geographically. The choice of Jerusalem thus helped to unite Israel and Judah under David's rule.

Exactly how David conquered Jerusalem is unclear. The interpretation reflected in the NRSV that his army entered through a water shaft may be correct. But it lacks definite archaeological confirmation and does not explain the references to the blind and lame. Another proposal translates the phrase "get up the water shaft" as "strike at the wind pipe" and takes it to mean that David orders his men to kill the enemy rather than maiming them (cf. Lev 21:18). "Millo" (v. 9) means "fill" and may refer to an artificial landfill between different hills on which Jerusalem was built. Yahweh's presence with David (v. 10) was a major motif in 1 Samuel and continues in 2 Samuel as well. David's house in Jerusalem is built with Phoenician materials and expertise (v. 11), illustrating his regional dominance. A further symbol of regnal power in the ancient Near East was a large harem; hence, David's addition of more wives and concubines (v. 13). Solomon's birth is recounted later, so that his mention in v. 14 is anticipatory.

5:17–25. Defeating the Philistines. David's battles with the Philistines likely preceded his conquest of Jerusalem, since they opposed his efforts to unite Israel and Judah. Thus the "stronghold" in v. 17 refers not to Jerusalem but probably to Adullam. Both accounts depict David inquiring of Yahweh (see on 2:1) about military strategy. In both battle accounts, it is Yahweh who fights for Israel and gives victory. The first (vv. 17–21) is based on an etiology for the name Baal-perazim. It is noteworthy that the etiology identifies Yahweh as the "lord" or Baal in the name. In line with ancient Near Eastern practice and in reversal of the Philistines' capture of the ark (1 Sam 4:5–11),

David takes the Philistine idols as trophies of Yahweh's superiority and victory (v. 21). As a result, David drives the Philistines back to their own territory on the coastland west of Gezer (v. 25).

B. David Brings the Ark to Jerusalem (6:1–23)

6:1–19. Transfer of the Ark. The transfer of the ark takes place in two stages, separated by a three-month hiatus when the ark resides at Obed-Edom's house after Uzzah's death. The episode begins as a celebration (vv. 1–5). Viewed as Yahweh's throne, the ark was an important religious symbol, so that moving it into Jerusalem would make the city a religious as well as political capital. "Cherubim" were not the winged infants of Renaissance art but mythical, griffin-like creatures that guarded palaces and temples. The story of Uzzah's death is an etiology for the name Perez-Uzzah (vv. 6–11) as well as an illustration of the ark's holiness. As a sacred object, it is not to be touched; Uzzah's offense (or "breach") in this regard may have occurred because the ark was not being transported correctly. Wary of the ark's potential danger, David leaves it in Obed-Edom's house until the blessings it brings to that household show that it bears no inherent danger. Then David has it carried to Jerusalem—this time by humans and with frequent sacrifices to appease Yahweh (vv. 12–19). David himself officiates as a priest, wearing an ephod (v. 14) and sacrificing (vv. 17–18). This ephod was apparently a scant apron, and judging from Michal's reaction (v. 16), David wore little else.

6:20–23. David's Encounter with Michal. Michal accuses David of demeaning the office of king by uncovering himself in front of the lowest element of society. David responds that he is honored by Yahweh, who chose him to replace her father, and by his people. Although v. 23 implies that Michal's childlessness was the result of David's or Yahweh's displeasure with her because of this incident, it may actually have been a political strategy on David's part to prevent Michal from bearing a son who would have been Saul's heir and hence a potential rival to David.

C. Yahweh's Promise to David (7:1–29)

Yahweh's promise of an enduring or eternal dynasty is a key passage in the DtrH since it explains why Judah was ruled by a single dynasty and why it outlasted Israel. There is general agreement that the chapter is a Deuteronomistic composition. The point of the passage is presented as a kind of word play: David expresses interest in building Yahweh a house (= temple), and Yahweh says that instead he will build David a house (= dynasty).

The statement that David had rest from his enemies (v. 1) may be textually corrupt. It stands in tension with the accounts of his wars in the following chapters and with 1 Kgs 5:3–4. David makes no explicit proposal, but it seems clear that he has in mind building a temple for Yahweh, and Nathan initially approves of the idea (vv. 2–3). Similarly, Yahweh does not categorically refuse a temple, but suggests that he does not need a temple yet and that David's son rather than David himself is the one to build it (vv. 4, 12–13). The statement that Yahweh has not had a "house" (v. 5) overlooks the temple in Shiloh (1 Sam 1–3). Yahweh then says that just as he chose David to be king, he will choose the "place" for the temple to be built by David's son after God has given Israel peace (vv. 8–17). David's son, therefore, connects the two meanings of "house," since he will both establish and continue David's dynasty and build the temple. The word "forever" (vv. 13, 16) does not mean endless time but simply a long time. Another key word here is "steadfast love" (*khesed*), which refers to Yahweh's loyalty or commitment to David. The chapter ends with David's lengthy prayer, again in Deuteronomistic style, thanking Yahweh for his promise.

D. David Defeats Neighboring Countries (8:1–18)

8:1–14. David's Victories. These verses recount victories of David over the peoples surrounding Israel: Philistines (v. 1), Moabites (v. 2), Aram-Zobah (vv. 3–12), and Edom (vv. 13–14). In contrast to the two stories in ch. 5, David is here the aggressor against the Philistines, and v. 1 reports his decisive defeat of them. The identity of "Metheg-ammah" is unknown; NRSV renders it as a place name. David's treatment of the Moabites is somewhat surprising if, as the book of Ruth suggests, he was of partial Moabite descent (cf. 1 Sam 22:3–4). The "monument" in v. 3 must have belonged to David, since Hadadezer could have traveled from Aram (Syria) to the Euphrates

without encountering David. David's crippling of the rear legs of the chariot horses (v. 4) has been taken as an indication that Israel did not yet have an extensive chariot force in its army. Hamath (v. 9) was another Aramean city-state, and a rival of Zobah. "Joram" is a Yahwistic name and unexpected for an Aramean. The Chronicles parallel (1 Chr 18:10) has "Hadoram," a more fitting Aramean name. In addition to the countries in these anecdotes, v. 12 mentions David's defeat of Ammonites and Amalekites. Verse 14 offers a theological synthesis: David's victories were the gift of Yahweh.

8:15–18. David's Cabinet. It was the king's responsibility to administer justice and equity for all of his people, especially the poor and disadvantaged (v. 15). A similar cabinet list occurs in 20:23–26. The precise functions of the different cabinet posts are uncertain, for instance, the difference between the "recorder" (v. 16) and the "secretary" or "scribe" (v. 17). The exact identity of the "Cherethites and Pelethites" is also uncertain, though scholars have typically identified them as "Cretans" (i.e., from Crete) and "Philistines." They apparently comprised a kind of elite bodyguard for David. The mention of David's sons as priests (v. 18) suggests that an exclusively Levitical priesthood was not yet in place.

E. David's Treatment of Mephibosheth (9:1–13)

David's question, "Is there still anyone left of the house of Saul?" presupposes the execution of Saul's heirs and indicates that 21:1–14, which recounts that execution, originally preceded ch. 9. "Kindness" (*khesed*) involves covenant fealty and recalls David's promise to Jonathan (1 Sam 20:15). However, David's motive in caring for Mephibosheth likely had more to do with his being "crippled in his feet" (v. 3). Since this disability made Mephibosheth less of a threat to rival David, he was not executed as were Saul's other heirs but was moved to David's residence where he could be watched (v. 13). At the same time, David allowed Mephibosheth to retain the income from Saul's estates (vv. 9–12).

F. War with the Ammonite-Aramean Coalition (10–12)

10:1–19. Defeat of the Arameans. War with the Ammonites is sparked after the death of Nahash, their king. This is presumably the same Nahash against whom Saul fought (ch. 11), yet David's words in v. 2 indicate that he had a treaty with Nahash. Hanun's actions suggest that Ammon was the inferior partner in the treaty and that he was trying to extricate himself. Shaving half of the beards of David's men and cutting off their garments below the waist (v. 4) were symbols of emasculation and were therefore insulting and humiliating both to the men and, by extension, to David.

Recognizing David's superior military might, the Ammonites seek reinforcement from several Aramean city-states—Zobah, Rehob, Maacah, and Tob. The "gate" (v. 8) is the city gate of Rabbah or Rabbat-Ammon, the Ammonite capital. The Israelites besiege Rabbah but are attacked from behind by the Arameans, so that Joab is forced to fight on two fronts (vv. 9–10). The "cities of our God" (v. 12) are Israelite cities east of the Jordan; Joab is rousing the troops by giving them a righteous cause to fight. After an initial defeat by the part of the Israelite army commanded by Abishai, the Arameans under Hadadezer rally other Arameans to their side but are defeated by David and the full Israelite army (vv. 14–19). This war with the Arameans may be the same one described in other terms in 8:3–8.

11:1–27. David's Adultery with Bathsheba and Uriah's Death.

Verse 1 is not a general statement that kings went or should have gone to war in the spring as it is translated in the NRSV. Rather, the verse dates the events in ch. 11 one year after the kings in ch. 10 had come out to battle. There is, therefore, no implication that David should have gone to war rather than staying in Jerusalem. No reason is given for David staying behind. It is worth noting that he did not initially accompany Joab in the siege of Rabbah in the previous chapter and only came out secondarily to face the Arameans. What is clear is that his remaining behind in this instance has a literary function since it introduces the story of his adultery with Bathsheba. This story may be a later addition to Samuel; it differs from the surrounding material in that it is not apologetic but baldly admits David's crimes without attempting to deflect them.

Though the text does not say that David's couch was on the roof, he may have gone there in the heat of the afternoon to nap where he could catch the cool breeze. When he awakens he strolls on the roof and sees a woman bathing (v. 2). Her location is not given; she may have been inside a walled courtyard. Some have speculated that Bathsheba seduced David by bathing where she knew he would see her. The present narrative, however, focuses on David's responsibility and blames him entirely for the liaison. "Uriah" is a Yahwistic name, even though he is identified as a "Hittite," a term used in the Bible for one of the indigenous peoples of Canaan. Bathsheba's bath was part of her ritual purification following her menstrual period (Lev 15:19–28), meaning that she was at peak fertility when David slept with her. There is, therefore, no doubt that David is the father of the child she conceived.

It was unusual for Uriah to be summoned for a personal audience with the king—all the more so since he was one of the best soldiers in the army according to 23:39. His summons is made even more unusual by the fact that David asks him only general questions about the welfare of the army and the progress of the siege—questions that would have been answered by regular communiqués between Joab and David. Uriah, therefore, would have been suspicious that the king had some other reason for summoning him. He may have thought his loyalty was being tested and determined to be on his best behavior. Thus, the more David tried to get him to go home, the more Uriah resisted in order to prove his devotion to duty and his consecration for war (cf. 1 Sam 21:5). "Feet" is a common euphemism for the genitals, so that "wash your feet" is likely a euphemism for having sexual relations (11:8). David wanted Uriah to have sex with his wife, so that the child she had conceived would appear to be his (Uriah's). Ironically, David was confident enough in Uriah's loyalty to send him back to Joab carrying his own death warrant (11:14–15).

Following David's order, Joab placed Uriah opposite the enemy's best warriors (11:16). Uriah's death, however, resulted from a tactical error on Joab's part; he allowed his men to get too close to the city wall, and several of them in addition to Uriah were killed (11:17). Joab used Uriah's death to cover up his mistake just as David was covering up his (11:18–21). The well-known story of Abimelech's death (Judg 9:50–57) suggests that David's cover-up will be as successful as Abimelech's attempt to mask the fact that he was killed by a woman. The story ends with an expression of Yahweh's displeasure at David's deed that links it with the account of Nathan's oracle of condemnation in the next chapter.

12:1–25. Nathan's Denunciation and the Death of David's Son. Nathan comes to David with what is ostensibly a legal case, though the lack of specifics hints otherwise. It is actually a parable of sorts designed to get David to pronounce judgment on himself. David's anger (12:5) is reminiscent of his response to Joab's news (11:20). In each case, an embarrassing revelation follows. Here, it is that David himself is the rich man who has stolen from his neighbor. The Hebrew words for "house" and "daughter" are similar and may have been confused in 12:8, so that the verse originally reported that God gave David Saul's daughter (Michal) and all the daughters of Israel and Judah. The point is that David had many women yet stole his neighbor's wife. The references to the sword (= violence) and trouble within David's own house (12:10–12) allude to the events in chs. 13–20, especially Absalom's revolt. The taking of David's wives really threatens his kingdom as represented by the harem. One of Absalom's first acts after driving his father from Jerusalem was to sleep publicly with concubines David had left behind (16:21–22).

David himself does not die for his crime, but his guilt is transferred to the son conceived in the adultery. David's responses at the baby's illness and death are unconventional (12:15–23). He mourns and fasts while the baby is alive, trying to convince Yahweh to let it live. But after the baby has died, he stops mourning and eats. "House of Yahweh" (12:20) is the Temple. Its use here is anachronistic, since the Temple was not yet built. Solomon's birth is reported as the next son of David and Bathsheba (12:24–25). The name Solomon means "his replacement," alluding most likely to the dead baby. Curiously, the name Jedidiah ("Yahweh's beloved") is never again used for Solomon.

12:26–31. The Fall of Rabbat-Ammon. The chapter ends by returning to the siege of Rabbah (12:26–31). Joab conquered the royal citadel and took the water supply and then notified David to join him for the final fall of the city. "People" in vv. 28–29 transparently means "army." Milcom

was the Ammonite god. This explains why his crown (v. 30) was so heavy (a talent of gold weighs about 75 pounds).

III. Absalom's Revolt (13–20)

A. The Rape of Tamar and Murder of Amnon (13:1–39)

13:1–22. Amnon Rapes Tamar. In the present narrative, David's troubles in this and the following chapters are the punishment for his sin with Bathsheba. However, the Bathsheba episode may be a later insertion, as chs. 13–20 can be read independently, Absalom's revolt having its own causes, apart from David's sin, in Amnon's rape of Tamar and in Absalom's ambition. Amnon was the half brother of Absalom and Tamar, all three being children of David with different mothers. Amnon was the oldest son and crown prince. Assuming that Chileab died young (see on 3:3), Absalom would have been the next in line for the throne. As a virgin daughter of the king, Tamar may have been guarded, making it difficult for Amnon to be alone with her; hence Jonadab and Amnon had to concoct a plan (13:2–5). The word for "cakes" in Amnon's request (13:6) resembles the Hebrew word for "heart" and thus alludes to Amnon's intentions and the sexual overtones of the story. The words "brother" and "sister" (13:11–12) are also used in erotic literature (e.g., Song of Solomon) as terms of desire and endearment and further hint at the sexual nature of this story. It is unclear whether "such a thing" (13:12) refers to rape or incest. Tamar's suggestion that David would allow an incestuous marriage (13:13) may reflect contemporary practice or her effort to buy time.

Amnon's despicable treatment of Tamar is epitomized by his contemptuous reference to her in 13:17, where the word "woman" does not occur, so that it might be rendered, "Put this *thing* out of my presence." The type of garment worn by Tamar, "a long robe with sleeves" (13:18), is mentioned elsewhere in the OT only for Joseph (Gen 37:3). Tamar tears the garment (13:19) in lamentation for what has happened to her and perhaps because she is no longer a virgin. The consequences of Amnon's deed are devastating to her, as she remains unmarried and childless, living with Absalom (13:20). The narrator does not explain what happened to her subsequently. The narrator's report of David's response (13:21) suggests his apologetic stance: David was very angry but would not punish Amnon out of love for him; he would not, therefore, have been complicit in Amnon's later murder. Absalom, on the other hand, hides his hatred for Amnon by not speaking to him, all the while plotting his murder.

13:23–39. Absalom Kills Amnon. After two years of harboring his rage, Absalom chooses his moment to strike. His invitation of David (13:24–25) raises the question whether he was already planning full-scale revolt. Sheepshearing was a time of celebration; in fact the word "feast" actually refers to a drinking bout. Absalom waits to kill Amnon until he is drunk and vulnerable. David at first suspects a revolt but then is assured that Absalom murdered only Amnon for revenge (13:30–35). David's profuse weeping (13:36) is another technique of the writer's to assert David's innocence. Absalom fled to his maternal grandfather, with whom David had a treaty (see on 3:3), so it would have been odd for David not to suspect where he had gone. Verse 39 is best understood as reporting that after three years David was consoled about Amnon's death and his desire ("spirit") for going out in search of Absalom was exhausted; hence, his willingness in the next chapter to allow Absalom back into Jerusalem.

B. Absalom's Return from Exile (14:1–33)

14:1–20. The Wise Woman of Tekoa. Again, David is presented with a legal case that is designed to provoke him to pronounce judgment on himself. This time it is Joab who initiates the matter by hiring a wise or skilled woman to petition David. The woman's fictional case is similar to David's in that one of her sons killed the other, and the offender's life is now sought. The fact that the woman has only two sons while David has many more—a crucial difference—is ignored by both the woman and David in applying his decision and oath to her case. Verses 15–17, where the woman continues to plead her case after David has rendered his decision, may be out of place and fit better after v. 7. David perceives Joab's hand in the matter (14:18–20), presumably in part because the woman, a stranger, would have no particular stake or interest in David's treatment of Absalom.

14:21–33. Absalom Returns. Initially, David allows Absalom to return home but refuses to see him (14:21–24). The description of Absalom's hair foreshadows the way in which he will die (18:9–15). Two hundred shekels would be about five pounds, an enormous amount of hair. The mention of Absalom's daughter is a poignant reminder of her namesake and hints at Absalom's abiding animosity toward David.

After two years, Absalom determines to enhance his status and appeals to Joab. But this time Joab refuses, perhaps because he does not perceive it to be in David's best interests. Absalom then adopts more extreme measures, setting Joab's fields on fire. The stratagem, illustrative of Absalom's rash nature, works but gives Joab cause for revenge.

C. Absalom Seizes the Throne (15:1–16:23)

15:1–12. Absalom Launches the Revolt. Absalom pretends to the throne by adopting a king's entourage (15:1) and by claiming himself as a better judge—one of the roles of kings in the ancient Near East—than his father (15:2–4). He also casts himself as one of the common people (15:5). By these various means Absalom "stole the hearts" (an idiom for deception, so also Gen 31:20) of the "people of Israel." This likely refers to the entire nation, not just to the northern tribes, since the scene takes place in Hebron, which is in Judah. Absalom's choice of Hebron as a launching place for his revolt harks back to David's having been crowned king of both Judah and Israel in Hebron (5:1–7). Ahithophel was a famous advisor of David's (16:15–23).

15:13–16:14. David Flees Jerusalem. This section reports a series of encounters between David and various groups and individuals as he flees Jerusalem, crossing the Kidron Valley and the Mount of Olives. (1) The first encounter is with the Cherethites and Pelethites (see on 8:18) and Gittites, i.e., people from the Philistine city of Gath, who, David notes, display greater loyalty to him by their presence than do his own people of Judah (15:20–21). (2) Next come the priests, Abiathar and Zadok, along with the Levites bearing the ark. David sends them back to Jerusalem, perhaps because properly caring for a sacred object like the ark would slow David's retreat. The sons of the two priests will serve as covert informants to David of events in Jerusalem (15:28). (3) The appearance of Hushai answers David's prayer that God thwart the advice of Ahithophel (16:23). Hushai also completes David's spy network (15:32–37). The words David gives to Hushai (15:34) are duplicitous; he will serve David by pretending to serve Absalom. Hushai's epithet, "David's friend" (15:37) seems to be a title, but its exact sense is uncertain. (4) Ziba, the servant of Mephibosheth, comes with provisions but without his master, who, he claims has stayed behind in Jerusalem hoping to receive the throne by virtue of being Saul's grandson and Jonathan's son (16:1–4). David responds by awarding Saul's lands and property to Ziba, who may, in fact, be lying in the hope of receiving such a reward (19:24–30). (5) Another relative of Saul's named Shimei is less sympathetic, cursing David and pelting his entourage with stones as they flee (16:5–8). Shimei's accusation that David is a murderer with the "blood of the house of Saul" on his hands indicates an awareness of the executions of Saul's sons recounted in ch. 21 and may suggest that the accusation of David's complicity in Saul's own death was commonplace. Like his brother Joab, Abishai is portrayed as rash, violent, and fiercely loyal to David, here volunteering to kill Shimei (16:9–14).

16:15–23. Absalom Enters Jerusalem. The narrative scene now switches back to Absalom's entry into Jerusalem. Hushai is appropriately duplicitous: in referring to the one whom God and Israel have chosen, he means David, not Absalom. He also says, in effect, that by acting in Absalom's service, he is in fact serving David. Absalom is blinded by the flattery, a hint of his conceit. His first act as king, following Ahithophel's advice, is to cuckold his father publicly in a defiant claim of power (16:20–23). Exactly why Ahithophel joined Absalom's revolt is never explained, though it has been postulated that he was Bathsheba's grandfather, based on the name of Eliam as her father and his son (11:3; 23:34).

D. Hushai Buys Time for David (17:1–29)

While Ahithophel advises Absalom to pursue David immediately with the singular purpose of killing him, Hushai counsels waiting (17:1–14). Ahithophel's advice is sounder but suggests that people will turn to Absalom only because David is dead. Hushai plays on Absalom's ego, suggesting

that loyalty for Absalom will only grow with time. Hushai also gives a vivid description of the great victory that Absalom will personally have as commander. Ahithophel's better advice is defeated by Yahweh (v 14), leading him, either in shame or with foresight about Absalom's inevitable defeat, to commit suicide (v 23).

As prearranged, Hushai sends word to David through the sons of Zadok and Abiathar. Thanks to Hushai, David has time to recoup his forces rather than having to worry about immediate pursuit. The priests' sons survive by hiding in a well whose simple opening—a hole in the ground—is camouflaged (17:15–22). This is the final reference to Hushai, leaving one to speculate whether his duplicity was uncovered by Absalom and he was executed.

Mahanaim, where David flees (17:24), was the site east of the Jordan where Ishbaal and Abner fled after the Philistine defeat (2:8). It will be strategically important in David's defeat of Absalom. He is provided for in Mahanaim by Barzillai, who is apparently wealthy (17:27–29). Meanwhile, Absalom has placed his cousin Amasa over his army (17:25). The curious reference to Abigail as the "daughter of Nahash" rather than of Jesse is probably a simple scribal error occasioned by the occurrence of "Nahash" in v 27.

E. Absalom's Defeat and Death (18:1–18)

David used the time won for him by Hushai to prepare for Absalom's attack. Perhaps aware of his focus on killing David, his men insist that he not go into battle with them (18:3–4). The narrative thus distances David from Absalom's death. David's order to deal gently with Absalom (v 6) further absolves him of responsibility. David's military expertise is suggested by his choice of the battleground—the forest of Ephraim—where Absalom's superior numbers are neutralized by the terrain (18:6–8).

Mules were the mounts of royalty (13:29; 1 Kgs 1:38), so that Absalom's unseating from his mule signals his loss of the throne. His hair may also be a symbol of his pride (14:26), which occasioned his downfall. It is not clear exactly how Absalom died; it may be that Joab uses three spears or sticks to beat on Absalom's chest and knock him from the tree (v 14) before he is surrounded and killed by the ten young men (v 15).

Piles of stones are used elsewhere to bury cursed persons (Josh 7:26), as may be the case here too. However, the monument to Absalom mentioned here is not to be confused with the Hellenistic or Roman tomb, belatedly dubbed "Absalom's tomb," that stands in the Kidron Valley outside of modern-day Jerusalem.

F. David Mourns for His Son (18:19–19:8)

The remainder of this chapter and the first part of the next one contrast David's reaction at the news of Absalom's death with the expected and typical response at an enemy's defeat. Ahimaaz wishes to carry the news to David because he thinks the king will be pleased about the victory. But David is fixated on his son, and Ahimaaz may not know Absalom's fate (18:29). The notice of Absalom's death is conveyed by the Cushite, a designation for a Nubian or Ethiopian. David's debilitating sorrow at the news can be compared to his profuse lamentation over Saul and Jonathan (1:11–27) and Abner (3:31–39). All three were political rivals whose deaths benefited him. David's mourning on this occasion is depicted as excessive to the point that it causes his army to be ashamed of their victory rather than celebrating it. Hence, Joab intervenes to persuade David of the necessity of welcoming and congratulating the army, lest he lose their loyalty (19:5–7). "Love" and "hate" in Joab's speech carry political overtones for loyalty and rebellion. Joab scolds David for mourning over the rebel, Absalom, as though he were a loyal servant and for shaming his loyal soldiers as though they were the ones who revolted.

G. David Returns to Jerusalem (19:9–43)

The narrative of David's return consists of two passages concerning the rivalry of the northern tribes and army with those of Judah over who would welcome David back first (19:9–15, 41–43). The two passages enclose repeat encounters with Shimei, Mephibaal, and Barzillai. The issue of who would welcome David first is not a hollow one; both Israel and Judah seek to curry David's favor now that he is back in power militarily and fiscally. David naturally favors Judah because it is his home tribe (vv. 11–12), although the army of Judah denies that it has received any special rewards or bribes from David (v. 42). His appointment of Amasa, his nephew (17:25), in place of Joab may have been intended to appease the army

of Judah, which Amasa had commanded under Absalom. It also gave Joab a motive to do away with Amasa.

David's first encounter is with Shimei, who cursed and mocked David when he fled Jerusalem (16:5–13). The presence of 1,000 fellow Benjaminites (19:17) with Shimei likely influenced David to grant his plea for forgiveness in avoidance of another civil war. David's mercy is also part of the writer's contrast between him and the brutal "sons of Zeruiah," represented here by Abishai, who still wishes to kill Shimei (16:9–10).

Ziba may have been among the 1,000 Benjaminites with Shimei. Having received from David the holdings of Saul's house (16:1–14), he is pleased to welcome David back. However, Mephibosheth also appears this time and denies Ziba's accusations (19:24–30). He defends himself with the claim that his disability kept him from joining David in his flight from Jerusalem, and Mephibosheth supports this defense by his appearance, which suggests that he has been in mourning since the king's departure. Caring for his feet here probably means cutting his toenails, and his "beard" is more properly his moustache (v. 24). Mephibosheth's reference to his family being "doomed to death" (v. 28) reflects the typical practice by a usurper of executing all the males in the line of his predecessor. David's decision to divide the property (v. 30) suggests that he is unsure whom to believe.

H. Sheba's Revolt (20:1–26)

20:1–13. Amasa's Assassination. The statement that Sheba was present at the argument with Judah (19:41–43) indicates that his revolt was occasioned by David's favoritism toward Judah. His rallying cry calls for the Israelite army to withdraw from David's service to its "tents" (v. 1). Despite the claim that all Israel joined Sheba (v. 2), the rest of the chapter indicates that not all Israel was involved. It may have been much smaller than Absalom's revolt. Joab assassinates Amasa in much the same way that he killed Abner (3:26–39). His ostensible motive was Amasa's replacement of him as army commander and Amasa's ineffectiveness (vv. 4–6). The real motive may have been political—to rid David of a former enemy and potential future rival.

20:14–22. Sheba's Demise. Abel Beth-Maacah was a large, fortified city on Israel's northern frontier. It is described here as one of Israel's "mothers" or largest, founding cities (v. 19). While feminine imagery is typical for cities, it is especially intriguing here, since Abel's leader is a nameless "wise woman" (v. 16). While she seems to know who Joab is, she seems entirely unaware of the reason for the siege or of Sheba and his revolt. Joab's identification of Sheba (v. 21) suggests that his revolt was limited to Benjamin and the hill country of Ephraim rather than involving all Israel. The woman's wisdom and negotiating skill are apparent in the story, where she saves her city from destruction by delivering up Sheba.

20:23–26. David's Cabinet. While some scholars think that this list represents a historical change in the make-up of David's cabinet as depicted in 8:16–18, they may have originated as two versions of the same list that came about with the displacement of 21:1–14 from before 9:1. One interesting difference between them is the presence here of an overseer of the "forced labor," indicating that it was David who began the practice of conscription of the northern tribes, which eventually led to the split between Israel and Judah (1 Kgs 12:18).

IV. The Appendix (21–24)

A. Narrative: The Execution of Saul's Heirs (21:1–14)

The last four chapters of 2 Samuel reflect a clear symmetrical (chiastic) structure: narrative, military anecdotes, poem, poem, military anecdotes, narrative. It has long been surmised that the narratives once stood together and were separated editorially by the insertion first of the anecdotes and then of the poems. The narratives themselves may have been placed at the end of the book because they reflect negatively on David. The first one, which tells of the execution of Saul's heirs, seems presupposed by David's question in 9:1 as to whether any heir remains to Saul's house and thus must once have preceded this verse. The story, furthermore, seems patently apologetic in nature as it explains David's execution of Saul's heirs as something he was forced to do in order to save Israel from a famine that itself resulted from an offense by Saul. Joshua 9 recounts the treaty between Israel and the Gibeonites that Saul is evi-

dently accused of breaching. But there is no story elsewhere that details Saul's assault. Additionally, 1 and 2 Kings make clear that usurpers in Israel commonly executed the male members of the previous royal house as a way of securing power. David was likely doing the same thing, and his motive was strictly political. Hence, David's execution of Saul's heirs probably occurred early in his reign. The sparing of Jonathan's son, "Mephibosheth" (originally named Meribbaal, see on 4:4) may have led to the theme of David's special affection for Jonathan. The real reason that he was spared probably had to do with his disabled status. The "sons" of Saul includes grandsons, and Jonathan's son Meribbaal is to be distinguished from Saul's son Mephibosheth (v. 8). The courageous vigil of Rizpah, Saul's concubine, compelled David to honor Saul's and Jonathan's remains.

B. Military Anecdotes: Heroes of the Philistine Wars (21:15–22)

The anecdotes in these verses also probably originated early in David's reign during his battles against the Philistines. Some have suggested that David's near escape lies behind his not going into battle in 11:1 and 18:3. The reference to Goliath (v. 19) is a tradition that has influenced the story in 1 Sam 17 in the name of the Philistine hero and in the description of his spear. The confusion was early, as indicated by the Chronicler's attempt at correction (1 Chr 20:5). The name of Elhanan's father also reflects textual corruption; *'oreghim* is the Hebrew word for "weavers" that occurs later in the verse. The Chronicles version of the name, Jair, is probably an attempt at correction. If so, this may be the same Elhanan son of Dodo mentioned in 23:24.

C. Poem: David's Song of Deliverance (22:1–51)

This psalm is essentially the same as Psalm 18. Its references to the Temple (v. 7), built after David's death, and to his descendents (v. 51), indicate that he did not write it. In this context it appropriately expresses the sentiments attributed to David for God's protection. The psalmist called upon Yahweh when his life was threatened (vv. 4–7). Yahweh's rescue of the psalmist is depicted as a cosmic theophany of the storm god as a warrior (vv. 8–20). The psalmist then praises Yahweh for his faithfulness and his help against enemies. "Anointed" (= messiah) was a royal title;

this verse suggests that the psalm may have been composed in the royal court of Judah.

D. Poem: David's Last Words (23:1–7)

Like Jacob (Gen 49) and Moses (Deut 32–33), David's "last words" are conveyed in a psalm. Scholars debate the date of this poem, with some attributing it to David himself based on its epithets for God, and others arguing that its references to David as a prophet (v. 1) and to his dynasty ("house," v. 5) and the covenant with him indicate a much later date. The function of the poem in this context seems to be to praise David as the model of a righteous king (vv. 3–4) and to stress the divine promise to him of a dynasty.

E. Military Anecdotes: David's Military Honor Roll (23:8–39)

The first section of this "honor roll" (vv. 8–12) concentrates on exploits of the "three," whose heritage and deeds are otherwise unknown. The episode in vv. 13–17 is apparently to be understood as the deed of the "three" mentioned earlier (v. 17). However, the introduction in v. 13 suggests that it was originally an anecdote about three anonymous captains. The meaning of David's reaction to their exploit (vv. 16–17) is also unclear. Some think that he is upset that they risked their lives for such a frivolous purpose; others suggest that pouring out the water was a libation and a great honor to the men.

Abishai and Benaiah (vv. 18–23) are both known from other texts. Abishai was Joab's brother. Benaiah commanded David's bodyguard (20:23) and was Solomon's army commander who killed Joab (1 Kgs 2:28–35). Asahel, Joab's other brother, heads the list of the "thirty" (v. 24). His presence here among David's best warriors stands in tension with the description of his death as a youth (2:18–23), which may have been composed for the apologetic purpose of providing Joab a motive for the murder of Abner. Also notable among the thirty are Eliam (v. 34), the son of the famous counselor, Ahithophel, and possibly the father of Bathsheba (11:3), and Uriah the Hittite, Bathsheba's husband (v. 39). The total of "thirty-seven" apparently includes the "three" as well as Abishai and Benaiah. There are also textual variations in the present list of thirty where additional names may have been present. If so, the designation of the honor roll as the "thirty" may have been a round number or a constant number of living soldiers who were replaced as they died but whose names remained on the list as a memorial.

F. Narrative: David's Census (24:1–25)

The final narrative of Samuel looks forward to the building of the Temple in 1 Kings, the books originally being parts of a united work. "Again" alludes to an earlier story of punishment from Yahweh—probably the one in 21:1–14, which likely immediately preceded the present narrative. The parallel to this narrative in 1 Chr 21 states that it was Satan (or "an adversary") who incited David to take a census, the Chronicler evidently being troubled by the idea that God could incite someone to sin. At the time Samuel was written, the idea of Satan as a representative of evil had not yet developed. Rather, Yahweh, as the only God, was understood as the source of both calamity and prosperity, and disaster was typically seen as a response to human wrongdoing.

Different explanations have been offered as to why taking a census was sinful. Was it because of David's pride and his trying to take credit for what God had done in making Israel grow? Was it because a census was usually taken in preparation for conscription or taxation, measures that the author wished to denounce? Or was it that the Israelites were not all ritually pure as a census required? The narrative is more interested in the result of the sin than in its cause.

The census begins east of the Jordan at Aroer, proceeds north to Dan, and then goes south on the west side of the Jordan to Beer-sheba. The figures reported, 800,000 for Israel and 500,000 for Judah (v. 9), are of men of military age. They may be exaggerated, or the word "thousand" may refer to a military unit (e.g., "platoon") of an undetermined number. Israel and Judah may be distinguished because Judah, as David's home tribe, was to be exempted from taxation and conscription, as was implemented under Solomon.

David's choice of plague as punishment proves effective because Yahweh halts the plague after less than a day—from morning until the "appointed time," perhaps the evening meal. Still, there are 70,000 casualties, though again this figure may be exaggerated or a way of referring to seventy military units (v. 15). But Jerusalem is also spared.

The angel of death is stayed at the threshing floor of Araunah the Jebusite, that is, one of the pre-Israelite inhabitants of Jerusalem, as David pleads for mercy for his subjects ("these sheep," v. 17). This may mark the end of the original story, since, in the verses that follow, the plague is stopped not because of David's pleas and Yahweh's mercy but because of the burnt offering. The story is thus transformed into what appears to be an etiology or ordination of sorts for the site of Solomon's Temple, and this is made explicit in Chronicles.

BIBLIOGRAPHY

R. Alter. *The David Story* (New York: Norton, 1999); A. A. Anderson. *2 Samuel.* WBC 11 (Waco, Tex.: Word, 1989); I. Finkelstein and N. A. Silberman. *David and Solomon: In Search of the Bible's Sacred Kings and the Roots of the Western Tradition* (New York: Free Press, 2006); B. Halpern. *David's Secret Demons: Messiah, Murderer, Traitor, King* (Grand Rapids: Eerdmans, 2001); P. K. McCarter Jr. *II Samuel.* AB 8 (Garden City, N.Y.: Doubleday, 1984); S. L. McKenzie. *King David: A Biography* (New York: Oxford, 2000); M. J. Steussy. *David: Biblical Portraits of Power.* Studies on Personalities of the Old Testament (Columbia: University of South Carolina Press, 1999).

1 KINGS

IAIN W. PROVAN

OVERVIEW

As the name of this book indicates, 1 Kings describes part of the period of the monarchy in ancient Israel—from the end of the reign of David over all Israel down to the reigns of Jehoshaphat king of Judah and Ahaziah king of Israel. It was evidently written along with 2 Kings at some point after the middle of the sixth century BCE, since 2 Kgs 25:27–30 looks back upon the release of King Jehoiachin from prison in Babylon in 561 BCE. Its authors are unknown, but are often referred to as "Deuteronomists" because of the marked influence of the book of Deuteronomy on 1 and 2 Kings, in terms of language, literary style, and theology. For example, it is to Deuteronomy that the language of David's parting speech to Solomon points in 1 Kgs 2:1–4 (note "observe what the LORD your God requires," Deut 11:1; "walk in his ways," Deut 8:6; "keep his decrees and commands," Deut 6:2; "that you may prosper in all you do," Deut 29:9; "that the LORD may keep his promise," Deut 9:5; "with all their heart and soul," Deut 4:29).[1] "Deuteronomic" language of this kind recurs throughout 1 and 2 Kings, as first Solomon (1 Kgs 11), then almost all the succeeding kings of Israel and Judah, are weighed according to the Mosaic law code and found wanting (e.g., Jeroboam, 1 Kgs 12:25–33; 14:1–16). The era during which the book was written helps us to explain this phenomenon. The northern kingdom had fallen to the Assyrians around 722 BCE; Judah had fallen to the Babylonians in 587 or 586 BCE after a two-year siege of Jerusalem. First and Second Kings were composed when the city still stood in ruins, as was its Temple—one of the great symbols of the Lord's presence with Israel. The surviving descendant of King David, Jehoiachin, had only just been set free from prison. Questions abounded about the meaning of these events. Was Israel's God not in fact in control of nature and history, as Mosaic religion claimed? Were there other, more powerful gods in Babylon who had engineered the Babylonian victory over Israel? If the God of Moses really *did* exist, and really

was good and all-powerful, how was it that God's chosen city and Temple had been destroyed, and how was it that God's chosen royal line (the line of David) had all but come to an end? First and Second Kings represent a sustained response to these questions, in the light especially of Deuteronomy's teaching. Israel's God is indeed in control of nature and history, the authors maintain; there are no other, more powerful gods anywhere. This good and all-powerful God has overseen the destruction of God's chosen city and Temple, and the exile of Israel to Assyria and Judah to Babylon respectively. The reason for these actions lies in Israel's great sinfulness. Israel has not obeyed God, nor heeded God's word through the prophets, from the reign of Solomon onwards (a king who turned away from the true God to worship other gods, 1 Kgs 2:12–11:43). In 1 Kings this truth is illustrated most importantly by Jeroboam, son of Nebat, who leads northern Israel into independence from Rehoboam and Judah (12:1–24) and into institutionalized idolatry (12:25–33); by Rehoboam himself, along with his successor Abijam (14:22–24; 15:3–5); and by Ahab, who compounds Jeroboam's sins with others of his own (16:29–22:40). It is such unfaithfulness to the Lord that has ultimately led to the demise of both Israel and Judah, as 2 Kgs 17 makes especially clear.

OUTLINE

I. The Reign of King Solomon (1–11)

    A. Solomon Becomes King (1:1–2:46)

    B. More on Solomon and Wisdom (3:1–28)

    C. Solomon's Rule over Israel (4:1–20)

    D. Solomon and the Nations (4:21–34)

    E. Preparations for Building the Temple (5:1–18)

    F. Solomon Builds the Temple and His Palace (6:1–7:51)

    G. The Ark Brought to the Temple (8:21)

    H. Solomon's Prayer (8:22–53)

---

1   Unless otherwise indicated by NRSV, the quotations from 1 Kings are direct translations by the author.

DETAILED ANALYSIS

I. The Reign of King Solomon (1–11)

A. Solomon Becomes King (1:1–2:46)

The opening narrative of 1 Kings constitutes the last chapter of the story about David as well as the first chapter of the story concerning Solomon. The prophet Nathan had promised David that his dynasty would last forever; God would raise up one of his sons and establish his kingdom forever (2 Sam 7:12–13). First Kings 1 recounts the ways in which Solomon, and not someone else, succeeded David, whereas ch. 2 reports David's final instructions to Solomon and reports what Solomon did immediately after his father's death to consolidate his power.

The "someone else" who *might* succeed David is Adonijah, the fourth of David's sons born in Hebron (2 Sam 3:2–5). He takes the risk of trying to seize the kingship because the king appears impotent, both generally and in the very precise sense that he is unable to "know" Abishag sexually (1 Kings 1:1–4). Gathering the symbols of kingship around him ("chariots ... horsemen" and a regiment of soldiers, cf. 1 Sam 8:11), Adonijah organizes a coup with the help of the military commander Joab and the priest Abiathar (cf. 1 Sam 22:20–23; 2 Sam 2–3). He is opposed by people like Nathan the prophet and Bathsheba, Solomon's mother, whose strategy is to remind David of an oath (intriguingly not mentioned in 2 Samuel) that he swore to Bathsheba about Solomon's succession (1 Kgs 1:11–27). This strategy turns out to be successful (vv. 28–40). Adonijah's dinner guests disperse, and he himself seeks refuge in the Tabernacle (vv. 41–51) until he receives clemency from King Solomon in return for an (implied) promise of good behavior. He apparently believes that the altar in the Tabernacle, as a holy place, provides him with some protection from Solomon's vengeance (cf. Exod 21:12–14). Chapter 2 opens with some important words directed by David to Solomon. First he talks to him about his conduct as king (2:1–4), enjoining him to rule within the framework of obedience to God. The exercise of royal power is not to be arbitrary; it is to be in accordance with the law of Moses—in particular, with the law code of Deuteronomy, whose language is clearly evoked here. If Solomon should fail in this obedience, his dynasty will be in jeopardy.

David addresses Solomon, secondly, about certain "loose ends" from his long reign, which must be tied up if Solomon is to reign in peace (1 Kgs 2:5–9). Barzillai is to be recognized for his kindness (2 Sam 17:27–29); this inhabitant of Transjordan represents the ideal citizen of Solomon's kingdom, his dutiful service to his king rewarded with peaceful fellowship around the king's table. The northern Israelite Shimei and the Judean Joab, by contrast, are to be punished for their crimes—albeit that Shimei has already repented of his wrongdoing and been guaranteed safety by David (cf. 2 Sam 16:5–14; 19:16–23), while Joab's behavior has not concerned David sufficiently before this point in the story to make him take his own action against his close ally (cf. 2 Sam 3:22–30; 20:4–10). This suggests that it is not the need to deal with blood-guilt that drives David in 1 Kgs 2, so much as the need to remove people from David's past who are likely (as partisans of north or south) to disrupt Solomon's rule. The pragmatism at the heart of this course of action that is designed to bring each one's "gray head down with blood to Sheol" (i.e., to prevent these men from entering the underworld via a peaceful and natural death in old age) is significantly described in terms of "wisdom." Solomon must not act rashly, suggests David, but should use his brain and find some clever justification for removing Joab and Shimei from the scene (2:6, 9). There will be a great stress on Solomon's wisdom in the following chapters also (1 Kgs 3; 4:29–34; 10:1–13), but it will never again be used to such ruthless effect as it is in ch. 2.

First Kings 2 closes with a description of how this "wisdom" was enacted (2:13–46). Adonijah's request for David's concubine Abishag is apparently interpreted by Solomon as an attempt to revive his claim to the throne (cf. 2 Sam 16:20–22, which suggests that sexual liaison with the king's concubines amounted to such a claim). He is killed; and Abiathar and Joab are found guilty by association. The former is banished to his family estate; the latter grasps the horns of the altar in the Tabernacle (1 Kgs 2:28), apparently believing (like Adonijah earlier) that this offers him safety—but he also is killed. The occasion for the execution of Shimei (2:36–46) is his apparent infringement of a ban on traveling outside Jerusalem (despite that Solomon's generalized description of this ban in v. 42, indicated in NRSV's "any place whatever," does not in fact correspond to the much more specific wording in v. 37 about crossing the Wadi Kidron). By one means or another, Solomon has made sure that his control of the kingdom is secure.

B. More on Solomon and Wisdom (3:1–28)

The first thing that the new king does, after the ruthless acts of 2:13–46, is to make a marriage alliance with the pharaoh of Egypt—contrary to the teaching of Deuteronomy that warns against "a return to Egypt" (Deut 17:16) in terms of too-close relations with that nation and explicitly forbids intermarriage with foreigners, lest the Israelites should be led into apostasy (Deut 7:3). Solomon is not keeping the law of Moses, in spite of David's words in 1 Kgs 2:1–4, although he *has* paid attention to David's advice in the same chapter about using "wisdom" to rid himself of

his enemies. His inattention to important religious matters is also suggested by his failure quickly to build the Temple and thereby deal with the problem of people worshiping at local cultic sites (NRSV, "high places"). He "loved the LORD" (v. 3), but there are question marks over the depth of this love. Hitherto in the story, Solomon has been ruling based on his own "wisdom" (1 Kgs 2:6, 9). In 1 Kgs 3:4–15, however, the deficiency of this wisdom is acknowledged. Solomon confesses ignorance (3:7) in the face of a task that is too great for him (3:8) and asks for "an understanding mind to govern your people, able to discern between good and evil" (3:9). It is essentially a confession that Solomon has not ruled well up until now, and wishes to make a fresh start. God is "pleased" with Solomon's prayer precisely because he has not sought to confirm his own position in life (3:10–11). He has not asked for "long life or riches," nor has he sought (as in ch. 2) the life of his enemies. Moreover, when God promises to give Solomon the things for which he had *not* asked (3:13–14), the death of enemies is not mentioned (although long life and riches are). The implication is that Solomon has recognized and God is confirming that the "wisdom" of ch. 2 was of an unenlightened, self-serving kind and must now be replaced with a higher kind, so that the king may rule justly and well over his subjects (3:9, 11). This event evokes an important theme of the OT: that it is the fear of the Lord that is truly the beginning of wisdom (Job 28:28; Ps 111:10; Prov 15:33).

First Kings 3:16–28 illustrates how this *new* wisdom makes all the difference to Solomon's ability to administer justice to his subjects (cf. 3:11). The king in ancient Israel was the highest court of appeal and the foundation of justice. That is why he hears the difficult case of the two prostitutes, each of whom claims a newborn child as their own. His success in judging claim and counter-claim reveals him to be one who has "the wisdom of God . . . in him, to execute justice" (v. 28).

C. Solomon's Rule over Israel (4:1–20)

The kingdom that results from the gift of wisdom in ch. 3 is well-ordered (4:1–19), happy and prosperous (4:20)—the kind of kingdom one would expect to find if its king has been gifted by God to rule (cf. Ps 72, "Of Solomon"). Its order is facilitated first by Solomon's "high officials" (vv. 1–6), including "the (high) priest," the "recorder" (perhaps the state prosecutor), and the "king's friend" (his personal advisor). Next come the "twelve officials over all Israel" who were to provide food for the royal household month by month. The regions over which they governed almost certainly included Judah, since "all Israel" in 1 Kgs 1–11 typically refers to the whole kingdom of Israel, north *and* south (3:28; 8:62, 65; 11:42), and Solomon's "all Israel" in 4:1 clearly correlates with "the people of Judah and Israel" in v. 20. NRSV is surely incorrect, therefore, in adding a thirteenth official in v. 19 who was allegedly "in the land of Judah." The Hebrew text itself only says that there was "one governor who was over the land"—using a Hebrew word that is different from the word used elsewhere in the passage for the district "officials." The reference is most likely to Azariah (v. 5), the person to whom the twelve district officers were responsible. The consequence of Solomon's wise administrative arrangements was that, even though his subjects were "as numerous as the sand by the sea" (a fulfilment of the Abrahamic promise in Gen 22:17), they were happy (v. 20).

D. Solomon and the Nations (4:21–34)

The Hebrew text understands what appears in the NRSV as 4:21–34 to be part of a single unit, beginning in 4:21 and extending through 5:18. This unit is distinct from what precedes it, moving on from Solomon's rule over Israel to his dominion over "all the kingdoms from the Euphrates to the land of the Philistines, even to the border of Egypt." Israel's peace and prosperity are related to this wider Solomonic dominion. The surrounding kingdoms contribute to the prosperity and present no military threat (vv. 21–28), so that all the Israelites live "under their vines and fig trees" (i.e., under God's blessing, each one having a degree of economic independence; cf. Joel 2:22; Mic. 4:4; contrast Ps 105:33; Jer. 5:17). This is also the context in which the district "officials" do their job of supplying "provisions for King Solomon and for all who came to King Solomon's table, each one in his month." We further discover just how great Solomon's wisdom is: it is unsurpassed throughout the world (vv. 29–34), exceeding even the wisdom of nations like Egypt.

E. Preparations for Building the Temple (5:1–18)

The Hebrew text treats NRSV's 5:1–18 as part of the same unit that began 4:21. As a result, the preparations made for the building of the Temple take place in the context of Solomon's sovereignty over the surrounding nations. The story about the gathering of building materials for the Temple project illustrates this reality. Solomon suggests to Hiram, king of Tyre, a co-operative venture ("my servants will join your servants," v. 6) in which Hiram should set the level of wages to be paid to his men. Hiram responds with proposals of his own: first, that his own men alone should cut and transport the wood down the coast to Israel, and that Solomon's men should only be involved after this has been done; and secondly that the wages are not to be paid to his laborers, but in the form of supplies of food for *his* royal household (v. 9). Solomon complies with the second proposal (v. 11), but ignores the first (vv. 13–18). There is cooperation; but it is cooperation between a vassal (Hiram) and a suzerain (Solomon). Such a high view of Solomon will become even more apparent in 1 Kgs 9:10–10:29.

F. Solomon Builds the Temple and His Palace (6:1–7:51)

The historian moves on to a detailed description of the building itself, beginning with the external structure: its overall proportions (v. 2) and its basic form (a tripartite arrangement, comprising the vestibule or entrance hall, the nave or main hall, and the inner sanctuary, vv. 3–5). One hears about its windows (v. 4); and of the strange structure around it with its side rooms (vv. 5–6, 8, 10). The work was carried out with reverence, avoiding the use of iron tools at the Temple site (v. 7; cf. Exod 20:25; Deut 27:5–6). Solomon receives an oracle concerning the entire project (vv. 11–13), which places the Temple in its proper theological context: God will "dwell among" his people once it is built, but God still requires obedience to the law (cf. Lev 26:11–12). The building of the Temple does not change anything about the nature of the divine-human relationship (or, indeed, about the nature of God, as 1 Kgs 8:27–30 later make clear). This was something that the Israelites were apt to forget in later times (e.g. Jer 7:1–34).

The author then proceeds to a description of the *interior* of the Temple, paying primary attention to the inner sanctuary (vv. 16, 19–32), because this was the very dwelling place of God (cf. 1 Kgs 8:1–13; 1 Sam 4:4; Ps 80:1; 99:1). One reads about its separation from the larger nave (v. 16); its measurements (v. 20); its decor (vv. 20, 29–30); its doors (vv. 31–32); its altar (vv. 20, 22); and its cherubim (vv. 23–28)—large, winged creatures which dominated the sanctuary, reaching half-way up to its ceiling and all the way across the walls. The other parts of the Temple were less significant. They receive little attention, although there is much interest in the splendor of the decoration. The predominant word in this respect is "gold" (vv. 20–22, 28, 30, 32, 35).

One might naturally expect to hear next about the way in which the whole Temple project was finished through completion of the interior furnishings; but this issue is not addressed until 7:13–51. Instead the historian narrates the construction of the royal palace complex. Significant here is the wording of 6:38–7:2. NRSV translates: "the house was finished in all its parts, and according to all its specifications. He was seven years in building it. Solomon was building his own house thirteen years, and he finished his entire house." A slightly different translation of 7:1 brings out better the contrast that is intended here: "But his *own* house Solomon spent thirteen years building; and he completed the *whole* of *his* house." Solomon spent much more time on the palace complex than on the Temple; and pushed it through to completion before fully completing his work on the Temple. This explains why the account of the building of the palace has been inserted between 6:38 and 7:13. The positioning is itself intended to indicate the way in which Solomon's energies were diverted from Temple-building to palace-building, to the detriment of the Temple project. He may be "wise," but this does not mean that he always makes good decisions.

First Kings 7:13–51 then picks up the Temple-building account. A second Hiram of Tyre (not the king) is employed to complete the Temple furnishings made of bronze, while Solomon is responsible for the furnishings of gold. Notable in this account is the "molten sea" (a large, metal basin designed to hold water, possibly symbolizing the forces of chaos subdued and brought to order by the Lord

who is creator of the world; cf. Gen 1:1–23; Ps 74:12–17; 89:5–11; 93).

G. The Ark Brought to the Temple (8:1–21)

The ark of God—the great symbol of the Lord's presence and the place where the tablets of the law were kept (Exod 25:10–22; Deut 10:1–5; Jos 3–6)—had hitherto remained in a tent-sanctuary somewhere in the old city of David (2 Sam 6:16–17; 7:2; 1 Kgs 3:15). Now it is carried to the Temple, during the festival of Tabernacles in "the seventh month" (cf. 1 Kgs 8:65–66; Lev 23:33–43). No sooner have the priests withdrawn from the inner sanctuary than another well-known symbol of God's presence—the cloud—appears (v. 10; cf. Exod 13:21–22; 16:10; 19:9; 40:34–38). Like Moses, the priests could not do their job because of this cloud that symbolized "the glory of the LORD" (1 Kgs 8:11; cf. Exod 40:35 and Rev 15:8). The presence of the cloud is a sure sign that the new arrangements for worship have received the divine blessing, as Solomon himself perceives (vv. 12–13) when he turns to address the people about God's promise to his father David (vv. 14–21; cf. 2 Sam 7:1–17).

H. Solomon's Prayer (8:22–53)

The speech is followed by a prayer. The main concern of its first part (vv. 22–26) is again the promise to David: Solomon asks God to fulfill the promise of an eternal dynasty. He quickly moves on, however, to the significance of the Temple as a place for prayer, uttering seven petitions, each of which contains a plea that God should "hear in heaven" (vv. 32, 34, 36, 39, 43, 45, 49)—for that is where God really is (8:27–30). The first petition (vv. 31–32) involves a difficult legal case in which a person must make an oath (cf. Num 4:11–31). The second, third, and fourth petitions concern various disasters that might befall the people of Israel: defeat in battle and subsequent exile (vv. 33–34); drought (vv. 35–36); and dangers such as famine, plague, and siege (vv. 37–40). In each instance, the cause of the problem is sin, and the main requirement of the situation is forgiveness. The fifth petition (vv. 41–43) addresses a foreigner who prays towards the Temple. Solomon desires that this person, too, would know that God answers prayers and that "all the peoples of the earth" would know God's name and fear him (cf. Isa 2:1–4; 56:6–8). The sixth petition

(vv. 44–45) is, like the second, concerned with war. This time the focus is not on defeat as a result of sin, but on victory in God's cause ("by whatever way *you* shall send them," v. 44). The seventh petition (vv. 46–51) returns to the question of defeat and exile. If exile should take place, and if the people should repent and pray towards land, city, and temple (v. 48; cf. Dan. 6:10 for the practice), then God is asked to regard them once more as his people and "maintain their cause" (v. 49, cf. v. 45).

Solomon's prayer is of the utmost importance, for it places both the Temple and the law in a wider perspective. The Temple is an important building, but God is not confined by a building, and certainly does not depend upon it. He will survive even its destruction, to hear his people's prayers in exile. Likewise, obedience to the law is very important, yet Solomon holds out hope, beyond failure, for restoration.

I. The End of the Temple Narrative (8:54–9:9)

Solomon addresses the people for a second time (8:54–61) and the festivities come to a conclusion (8:62–66). God then appears to Solomon a second time, responding to Solomon's prayer with solemn words about dynasty and temple, people and land (9:1–9). God's first appearance to Solomon (1 Kgs 3:4–15) marked the beginning of his rise to greatness; he was endowed with heavenly wisdom. The second marks the end-point of his upward mobility, and points ahead to disaster. Israel will be cut off from the land, transformed from a nation renowned for its wisdom (1 Kgs 4:21–34) into a nation that is a "proverb and a taunt" (9:7; cf. Deut 28:37).

J. Glory Under a Cloud (9:10–10:29)

Solomon's rule over the surrounding kingdoms, combined with his status in the world in general (4:21–34), put him in a position first to prepare for the building of the Temple (5:1–18) and then to build and dedicate it (6:1–8:66). First Kings 9:10–10:29 now reconsider the glory of this Solomonic empire in the context of 8:22–53 and 9:1–9 and their warnings of exile, which suggest an ominous future. Themes from chs. 4–5 are picked up again (Solomon's dealings with Hiram, 9:10–14; his use of forced labor, 9:15–23; foreigners coming to listen to his great wisdom, 10:1–13),

but they are repeated in ways that hint, not of wisdom, but of foolishness (9:24; 10:26).

There was initially no reference to gold in the agreement struck between Solomon and Hiram (5:1–18), but the author now reports that Hiram supplied Solomon with as much gold as he desired (9:11). This is the first mention of gold in a section of Kings littered with such references (9:28; 10:2, 10–11, 14, 16–18, 21–22, 25)—a stark contrast to chs. 4 and 5, in which prosperity is described in terms of food, not gold. This is significant, since Deut 17:17 warns the king that excessive wealth brings with it the danger of apostasy (cf. Prov 30:8).

First Kings 9:15–23 alludes to 5:1–18, which reports that Solomon used conscripted labor to build the Temple. Solomon did not use this task-force only for the Temple, but also for his other building projects (vv. 15–19). Those forced to work did not include his Israelite subjects, but only the descendants of those Canaanite peoples "whom the Israelites were unable to destroy completely" (v. 21). The point of this new information becomes clear when one remembers that the book of Deuteronomy identifies intermarriage with foreigners as apostasy (Deut 7:1–6). The foreigners mentioned there include precisely those Amorites, Hittites, Perizzites, Hivites, and Jebusites mentioned in 1 Kgs 9:20. First Kings 9:24 underlines this concern about foreigners by referring to Solomon's marriage to Pharaoh's daughter.

Another foreigner in the story is the queen from Sheba (cf. Gen 10:28), who visits Solomon "to test him with hard questions" (1 Kgs 10:1). The ease with which he deals with these questions, combined with her own observation of his wealth, leaves the queen breathless (10:5; NRSV, "there was no more spirit in her"). It is interesting, however, that whereas the authors of Kings in ch. 4 stress the benefit of Solomon's wisdom to all his subjects (4:20, 25), focusing on its practical effects for the life of the nation, she refers in the first instance much more narrowly to the blessing Solomon must be to his men (NRSV, "wives," v. 8) and his "servants." This comment is consistent with the theme of ch. 10, where the focus is upon the benefit of wisdom to the royal court, and particularly to Solomon himself, rather than to the people. The influx of food described in chs. 4–5 has been replaced by an influx of luxury goods

(vv. 2, 10–12, 22, 25); and Solomon's use of all this wealth is entirely self-indulgent (vv. 14–29). Gold is mentioned no fewer than eleven times in these verses. Solomon uses it to decorate his palace (v. 16); to overlay the finest throne ever seen (vv. 18–20); and to make household items with it (v. 21). If he does not bother much with silver in his royal court (cf. Deut 17:17), it is only because it was of little value in Solomon's day (1 Kgs 10:21). This does not prevent him from accumulating it anyway (vv. 22, 27), along with chariots and horses from Egypt (vv. 26 and 28, recalling 4:26). All but one of the instructions about kingship in Deut 17:16–17 have now been abrogated by Solomon. First Kings 11 will address the remaining one, "he must not take many wives."

K. Solomon's Apostasy, Opponents, and Death (11:1–43)

First Kings 1–10 has hinted that all is not well with Solomon's heart. First Kings 3:1–3 juxtaposed affirmation of his love for God with suggestions of divided loyalties, revealed in his choice of marriage-partner and his priorities in building projects (linked with his attitudes to worship). First Kings 4:26 and 4:28 report that he accumulated many horses. First Kings 6:38–7:1 then pursued the question of building priorities; and 10:26–29 did the same with regard to horses, a context in which the topic of Solomon's great wealth was introduced, and the marriage/worship question again briefly addressed (9:10–10:29). Chapter 11 now voices open criticism of Solomon and tells of the inevitable consequences of all that has gone before. His sins have found him out; and they have led him to apostasy. Although he loved the Lord (3:3), he also "loved ... the daughter of Pharaoh" and many other women besides (11:1–2); and these women "turned away his heart" from God (11:3–4). He worshiped their gods and built sanctuaries for them on the Mount of Olives (the "mountain east of Jerusalem," v. 7) and elsewhere. As 1 Kgs 2:4, 8:25, and 9:4–5 have led readers to expect, God's judgment follows. The kingdom is to be torn away from David's family, albeit not in Solomon's lifetime and not quite all of it. "One tribe" remains for the sake of David and Jerusalem (11:9–13). First Kgs 11:14–40 narrates the difficulties that Solomon now confronts. Whereas in the midst of God's blessing Solomon had peace on every side (1 Kgs 5:4), now the blessing has departed and the peace is fractured. Two adversaries from the south and from the north oppose the apostate king in his old age: Hadad (cf. 2 Sam 8:13–14), and Rezon son of Eliada (cf. 2 Sam 8:3–4). Solomon's most important enemy, however, is to be found closer at hand: Jeroboam son of Nebat, to whom Ahijah offers a forecast about his future kingship (v. 29). A cloak is torn and divided into twelve pieces, of which ten, symbolizing ten tribes, are given to Jeroboam (vv. 30–31). One tribe is to remain for the sake of David and Jerusalem (although actually this "one" includes "two"—Judah and Benjamin, 12:21). This concession marks out the narrative that follows, all the way through to near the end of 2 Kings; for the house of David is never judged as severely as are the royal houses of the northern kingdom, and it outlasts them all.

II. The Kingdom Is Divided (12–14)

A. The Kingdom Is Torn Away (12:1–33)

The narrator now describes the tearing away of the kingdom from David's family, which was threatened in ch. 11. Solomon's son Rehoboam goes to Shechem to be crowned king—a town with a long history in Israel (the place of covenant renewal in Josh 24:1–27; and the place where kingship first intruded itself into the tribal life of Israel in Judg 8:22–23; 9). The people complain that they are no longer a people living in freedom in the promised land; they have become once more a people under "hard service," as they were in Egypt (1 Kgs 12:4; cf. Exod 1:14; 2:23). Jeroboam appears in this story as a kind of second Moses, leading Israel out of bondage, even as Rehoboam plays Pharaoh, increasing the oppression by replacing mere whips with "scorpions" (perhaps a particularly vicious form of whip, 1 Kgs 12:14; cf. Exod 5:1–21) and thus fulfilling God's will even as Pharaoh did in the hardening of his heart (1 Kgs 12:15; cf. Exod 7:13). However, Jeroboam quickly becomes "Aaron" instead of "Moses" (1 Kgs 12:25–30). Fearing that the presence of the "house of the LORD at Jerusalem" (12:27) will undermine his rule of the northern tribes, he builds his own centers of worship in the far north of his territory (Dan) and in the far south (Bethel). Two "calves of gold" are created to act as focal points of worship there, introduced to the people by the very words used by Aaron in Exod 32:4 of his own golden calf (cf. 1 Kgs

12:28). Bethel is of primary interest to the biblical author, because that is where the story of ch. 13 will take place. The historian refers specifically to the temple at Bethel (a house on high places, v. 31; NRSV, "houses"), to the priests appointed to serve there, and to the new "festival on the fifteenth day of the eighth month" designed to replace the Feast of Tabernacles celebrated in Jerusalem in the *seventh* month (cf. 1 Kgs 8:2; cf. Lev 23:33–43).

B. The Man of God from Judah (13:1–34)

Jeroboam stands at the altar of his new temple as Solomon had stood at his (1 Kgs 8:22), ready to dedicate it; but he does not have the opportunity to speak, since this temple is illegitimate in the eyes of the deuteronomist. Jeroboam had been promised a dynasty as enduring as David's, if only he would obey God (1 Kgs 11:38); his various acts of disobedience now elicit prophetic opposition in the shape of a man of God from Judah, whose prophecy points forward to a time when all northern dynasties will have come to an end, and only the house of David remains to take action against Bethel (2 Kgs 22:1–23:30). In the meantime, the prophet provides a sign, indicating that the prophecy is true (vv. 3, 5): the altar is then torn down, and "the ashes poured out from the altar." The God who can ensure that prophecy comes to pass in the short term can surely also do so over the longer term. There can be no escape for disobedient kings. The strange sequel to this story (13:7–32) emphasizes that disobedient prophets will also not escape God's punishment.

God's law stands over everyone—even those who deliver it. Despite the strictest of divine commands, that he must "not eat food, or drink water, or return by the way" that he came, the man of God from Judah is persuaded by another prophet to accept hospitality in his house by the (false) claim that he too has had a prophecy from God (vv. 11–19). As a result, the man of God "disobeyed the word of the LORD" (v. 21) and he died. He ought to have heeded the word of the Lord that *he* had received rather than being led off his path by another's claim that God has spoken to *him*.

C. The End of Jeroboam (14:1–20)

These verses describe what happened as a result of Jeroboam's desire to have the two houses he wanted (dynasty and temple) instead of the one he was promised (dynasty); and they do so in a way which makes clear the essential differences between David's house, which endures, and Jeroboam's, which does not (see the comments on 11:1–43). Jeroboam's wife thinks that *she* has been sent to *Ahijah* to find out about her sick child; but she discovers when she arrives at his house that in fact *he* has been sent to *her* with a message about the kingship (v. 6). Jeroboam has failed to be like David (14:8; cf. 11:38), and has worshiped other gods as Solomon had done before him (v. 9). Therefore, God will "bring evil upon the house of Jeroboam," forcing the dynasty to an end for want of male descendants. It will be a dishonorable end, since human bodies will not be buried, but eaten by dogs and birds (vv. 10–11; cf. 1 Sam 31:8–13 for evidence of the importance of proper burial). This further horizon of prophecy is once again accompanied by a more immediate sign, as in 1 Kgs 13: "the child shall die" (14:12). A still further horizon relates to the distant future (vv. 14–16). In the absence of a strong dynasty to rule them, the northern Israelites are destined to know only the instability of "a reed … shaken (i.e. swaying) in the water," and eventually exile to a land beyond the river Euphrates. That is where persistence in the sins of Jeroboam will lead them (cf. 2 Kgs 17:1–6, 21–23).

D. The End of Rehoboam (14:21–31)

The story of Rehoboam's reign, begun in ch. 12, has been delayed, since the historian has followed Jeroboam through rebellion to idolatry and judgment and on to death. Meanwhile, in Judah, people have been doing "evil in the sight of the LORD" (14:21): setting up high places at which idolatrous worship could take place, and installing there "pillars" (cf. Deut 12:3 for reference to these Canaanite cult objects that the people must destroy upon entry to the land) and Asherim (NRSV, "sacred poles"—wooden objects used in the worship of the goddess Asherah, who was the consort of Baal, the Canaanite god of fertility; cf. 1 Kgs 16:32–33). They have embraced local fertility religion, indicated further in the existence of "male temple prostitutes in the land" (cf. Hos 4:14; Deut 23:17–18). No prophetic oracle about the end of David's house ensues, however, because Judah is not to be torn away from David as Israel was torn away from Jeroboam. Instead the historian reports a lesser reversal suffered by Rehoboam at the hands of Shishak of Egypt, representing the fatherly discipline of God described in 2 Sam 7:14.

III. Abijam and Asa (15:1–24)

The deuteronomist continues with Rehoboam's immediate successors, Abijam and Asa—the latter of whom will reign throughout a period in which the northern kingdom will see five kings come and go (15:25–16:28) before Ahab comes to the throne in Asa's thirty-eighth year (16:29–30). Abijam is the characteristically bad Judean king, indulging in the idolatry of the later Solomon and of Rehoboam, yet surviving to produce an heir because "for David's sake the LORD his God gave him a lamp in Jerusalem, setting up his son after him, and establishing Jerusalem" (15:4). Asa, in contrast, is the characteristically good Judean king, behaving relatively faithfully like David and the earlier Solomon. Thus he took action against the "male temple prostitutes" mentioned in 14:24 (v. 12) and removed both the idols made in previous reigns and his own idolatrous mother who had made an "abominable image for Asherah" (v. 13). Although he did not likewise remove the high places and focus his reformed worship only on the Temple in Jerusalem, he was generally exemplary in his religious policy. These two kings between them—Abijam and Asa—set the pattern for all the Judean kings who follow; they are measured on the basis of whether they have been "like David" or not.

IV. From Nadab to Ahab (15:25–16:34)

The fulfillment of the prophecy against the house of Jeroboam (ch. 14) was delayed until it became clear how different it will be from God's treatment of David's house. Now readers discover what Ahijah meant by describing Israel as a reed swaying in water (14:15), as one northern dynasty follows another in quick succession. Nadab son of Jeroboam is murdered by Baasha, who in turn kills all the other members of Jeroboam's family (15:25–32; cf. 14:10–11). Baasha himself then walks "in the way of Jeroboam and in the sin that he caused Israel to commit," with predictable consequences (15:33–16:7). A prophet appears to announce that the fate of Baasha's house will be the same as Jeroboam's (16:3–4). His son Elah lasts no longer than Nadab (two years, 16:8–14). Elah is murdered at home in Tirzah by Zimri, who

kills not only the family of Baasha, but also family friends (v. 11). Zimri only reigns for a week; and after fighting off the challenge of Tibni, Omri assumes the kingship (16:15–22). The only event of his reign that is recorded is his purchase of the hill of Samaria and his building of the new northern capital there (16:23–28). The last Israelite king to gain the throne in this period is the most famous one: Ahab son of Omri (16:29–34). He is also the worst, walking in the sins of Jeroboam but also marrying a foreign woman, Jezebel, who inevitably leads him into the worship of foreign gods. To the temple and altar for the calf at Bethel is added now an altar for Baal in a temple of Baal in Samaria.

V. Elijah and Ahab (17:1–22:40)

A. Elijah and the Drought (17:1–24)

Prophets had addressed the preceding northern royal houses, proclaiming that idolatry would lead to their demise. Elijah now appears to challenge the house of Omri. The doom that he announces will, however, not occur until 1 Kgs 21:21–24. His first task is to inveigh against the Baal-worship that Ahab has introduced into Israel—to demonstrate that Baal is no more a god in any real sense than Jeroboam's calves are. Chapter 17 provides the context—the divinely-ordained drought of 17:1—and demonstrates that it is the Lord, and not Baal (nor any other "god"), who controls both life and death, both fertility and infertility. In Canaanite religion, it was Baal who had authority over the rain and brought fertility to the land. Its absence meant the absence of Baal, who must periodically submit to the god Mot (death), only to be revived at a later date and once again water the earth.

Elijah begins to challenge this cyclical and polytheistic view of reality in 17:1–7. The Lord, and not Baal, brings rain, being sovereign over creation. This sovereignty extends to the Lord's ability to look after Elijah in an inhospitable area east of the Jordan River where there is no normal food supply. Elijah is miraculously fed there, just as the Israelites had once been the beneficiaries of Gods provision of "bread and meat" in the wilderness (cf. Exod 16, esp. vv. 8, 12–13). The theme of miraculous provision continues in 17:7–16; the Lord is able to bring drought even in what is (1 Kgs 16:31 implies) the very heartland of Baal-worship, the region of Sidon. Yahweh is God of all, and not just a local Israelite god. The *threat* of death having twice been overcome, 17:17–24 tells about the overcoming of death itself. A child dies, and the question that arises is: when faced by "Mot" (death), must the Lord, like Baal, submit? Even the underworld is not a place from which the Lord can be barred, however (Ps 139:1–12); and the child is brought back to life.

B. Elijah and the Prophets of Baal (18:1–46)

The day for the Lord once again to "send rain on the earth" arrives; but prior to this there must be a public demonstration of what has been established in private in ch. 17—that the Lord truly is God. The deuteronomist addresses the question as to who is the real "troubler of Israel," Elijah or Ahab (v. 17; cf. Josh 6–7, esp. 6:18 and 7:25). Elijah's view is that the trouble has religious roots, namely the forsaking of the commandments of the Lord and the worship of the Baals (the various local manifestations of the god Baal, 1 Kgs 18:18; cf. 2 Kgs 1). The contest on Mount Carmel is designed to settle the question of who is really God, the Lord or Baal (v. 21). It is a contest that involves "fire" (v. 24), perhaps because both Baal (the Baal myth) and the Lord (cf. Lev 9:24; 10:2; Num 16:35) were associated with fire and lightning. Baal fails to deliver such fire, even though his followers engage in extravagant actions apparently designed to elicit his support. Elijah saturates the whole area around the altar with water, precisely to make clear that there is no natural connection between what the human participants are doing and what God will do; and the "fire of the LORD" falls, consuming not only the burnt offering but everything else associated with it. The rain falls; and Ahab and Elijah run for Jezreel, where Jezebel awaits.

C. Elijah and the Lord (19:1–21)

Elijah appears to believe that he has won a decisive battle; yet a still more formidable opponent than Ahab awaits him: Queen Jezebel. Her ongoing resistance, apparently unexpected, sends Elijah into retreat, both physically and mentally. Even though no word of the Lord instructs him (cf. 17:2, 8; 18:1), he flees to the very south of the promised land, as far away from Jezebel as possible. He looks for a lonely place in which to die. He has had "enough" (v. 4). Here God gently inter-

venes to lead him back onto the right path, first with food and then with instruction. At "Horeb the mount of God" he is asked what he is doing there (v.8); and his answer is strangely selective; he does not speak of previous successes but only of Israelite apostasy and prophetic casualties. He needs to be reminded more fully of the past—to remember who God is and what God has done. This may well be one of the intentions behind the "wind … earthquake … fire" of vv. 11–12; they are a reminder of Mount Carmel. Yet there is also an apparent intention to teach Elijah something beyond what he has learned already; for while the emphasis at Carmel was on God's spectacular ways, the emphasis in 19:11–12 is on God's quiet ways. God is not to be found in the spectacular elements of the storm outside the cave; he reveals himself on this occasion in "a sound of sheer silence" (NRSV) or, better, in "a barely audible whisper." There is no evidence that Elijah understands the significance of this (notice that his answer to the second asking of God's question in v. 13 is exactly the same as before, vv. 10, 14). Most likely it is connected to the instructions he receives next: to "anoint Hazael … Jehu … Elisha" (vv. 15–16). A new order will bring about the final victory over Baal worship; it will come as a result of political process (God's "quiet ways"), not as a result of obviously spectacular demonstrations of divine power. It will arrive, not as a result of Elijah's efforts, but as a result of the efforts of others. Elisha, who is recruited by Elijah as the chapter closes, will play an important role in that political process.

D. Ahab's War Against Aram (20:1–43)

Since Elijah has recruited Elisha one expects the deuteronomist to report that Elijah now anoints Hazael as king over Aram and of Jehu as king over Israel (19:15–18). Instead, one finds a story involving "a certain prophet" (v. 13, Elijah does not appear at all), and in which a different king of Aram (Ben-Hadad) loses a war with Ahab. These events underscore the purport of ch. 19. Elijah is not the only servant of God left, in spite of what he has claimed (19:10, 14). Moreover, the quiet ways of God must take their course before the events spoken of in 19:17 will occur. As ch. 20 opens, the king of Aram is trying to reduce Israel to vassal status. His terms are at first accepted by Ahab (v. 4), only later to be rejected after a revision which apparently makes them more oppressive (vv. 5–9). This leads to a battle, which a prophet correctly predicts will have a successful outcome (v. 13–15), if Israel fights according to an implausible divine battle plan in which untrained servants (NRSV, "young men") strike the first blow. The plan benefits from the fact that Ben-Hadad is the worse for drink (vv. 12, 16), and seemingly incapable of uttering coherent or sensible instructions (v. 18), and victory is won. Further warfare the following spring (v. 22; cf. 2 Sam 11:1) leads to the same outcome, for the Aramean plan to fight the Israelites in the plain (v. 23)—although it is sound military strategy if one possesses superior cavalry and chariotry—is based on faulty theological reasoning ("their gods are gods of the hills"). Ahab is found disobeying a divine commandment in pursuit of financial gain, however, and is confronted by a member of a prophetic group (20:35–43; cf. 2 Kgs 4:1; 6:1) who tricks the king into pronouncing judgment upon himself. Like Saul, Ahab has released an enemy king whom God had "devoted to destruction." His life is therefore forfeit.

E. Naboth's Vineyard (21:1–29)

Having already given notice of Ahab's death (20:41–42), the author now announces judgment on his house, which has been delayed since ch. 16, as an apparently reinvigorated Elijah appears again in Jezreel to denounce a new and heinous crime. The crime arises out of a dispute about a vineyard in that city, which Ahab wants (21:2) but Naboth (the owner) refuses to give up, because it is his "ancestral inheritance" (v. 3). Land in Israel belonged, not to the families who technically owned it, but to God (Lev 25:23) who had driven out the previous inhabitants and allocated its various parts to the tribes as their inheritance (see especially Josh 13:7). An Israelite was not supposed to sell land in perpetuity; and a complicated set of laws existed that were designed to keep land in the family and to prevent its accumulation in the hands of a few (e.g. Lev 25:8–24; Deut 25:5–10). Naboth is bound to refuse Ahab's offer; and in making it, Ahab disregards Israelite law. His own initiative frustrated, Jezebel steps in with a different plan (21:4–14), which is to have Naboth executed on false charges. The two witnesses required by OT law are paid off (v. 10; cf. Deut 19:15–21), and Naboth is duly stoned to

death (v. 13; cf. Exod 22:28; Lev 24:14–16). This clears the way for Ahab to take possession of the vineyard (21:15–24), where he is confronted by Elijah. Ahab's house, the prophet announces, is to suffer the same fate as the houses of Jeroboam and Baasha (v. 22; cf. 1 Kgs 14:10–11; 16:3–4), because Ahab has (like them) provoked the Lord to anger and caused Israel to sin (cf. 14:9, 15–16; 16:2). The chapter nevertheless closes in a surprising way (21:25–28). Ahab repents; and God delays the disaster that Elijah has foretold (v. 28). God is gracious to even the most wicked of people.

F. The Death of Ahab (22:1–40)

Ahab's own death, foretold by two different prophets (20:41–42; 21:19), is now described in the context of a story about a third prophet. Its occasion is a campaign that Ahab launches to win back from the Arameans the strategically important city of Ramoth-gilead in Transjordan (v. 2) with the help of Jehoshaphat king of Judah (about whom the author will soon offer more information, 22:41–50). Jehoshaphat is prepared to accompany Ahab, but first he wants to "inquire ... for the word of the LORD" (vv. 4–5). The prophets are gathered (22:6–8), with the exception of the allegedly difficult Micaiah, at the threshing-floor of the city (an open space at which people could assemble). They speak and act in ways that imply the military campaign will be successful. Micaiah, at first, apparently agrees (cf. vv. 12 and 15), but under questioning pronounces a negative oracle (vv. 17, 19–23). In fact, he provocatively claims, God's plan to lure the king to his death at Ramoth-gilead (v. 20) involves precisely those prophets whom Ahab first summoned into his presence (cf. Ezek. 14:1–11). They are being influenced by "a lying spirit" (vv. 21–23; cf. 1 Sam 16:14–15, a story in which Saul is afflicted by "an evil spirit). Ahab chooses to go with the overwhelming prophetic majority in favor of military action, but evidently not with great conviction, for he disguises himself before going into battle (vv. 29–30). Such a disguise is an evident harbinger of disaster, for it recalls the action of Jeroboam (1 Kgs 14:1–18), and before him Saul (1 Sam 28) just before their own deaths. So it proves, as Jehoshaphat (though alone wearing royal robes, v. 30) is saved from death because of his Judean shout and Ahab (playing the ordinary soldier) is struck down by an arrow shot at random yet piercing his armor at a weak point.

Like Solomon, Ahab had married unwisely. He was led even further astray than Jeroboam. But like Jeroboam, he was not of David's house, and he was not therefore exempt from being treated like Saul (2 Sam 7:14–16), whose story echoes at various points. He, too, loses his kingdom.

VI. Jehoshaphat and Ahaziah (22:41–53)

Both Jehoshaphat and Ahaziah have already entered the narrative as characters in Ahab's story—comrade in arms and successor, respectively (1 Kgs 22:2, 40). Now they find their own place in the story as 1 Kings comes to an end. Stability has been the norm within the southern kingdom as chaos has afflicted the north, as the good Asa has been succeeded by the equally good Jehoshaphat, who "walked in all the way of his father" and reigned for a substantial length of years. The length of Ahaziah's reign, on the other hand, is exactly what we expect of the son of an Israelite king who receives an oracle of judgment: two years (v. 51; cf. 15:25; 16:8). His religious commitments are also entirely predictable. Like his father, he walked "in the way of Jeroboam son of Nebat" (cf. 16:31), and "served Baal and worshiped him" (cf. 16:31–32).

BIBLIOGRAPHY

J. S. Ackerman. "Knowing Good and Evil: A Literary Analysis of the Court History in 2 Samuel 9–20 and 1 Kings 1–2." *JBL* 109 (1990) 41–60; W. Brueggemann. *1 & 2 Kings* (Macon, Ga.: Smyth & Helwys, 2000); T. E. Fretheim. *First and Second Kings.* Westminster Bible Companion (Louisville: Westminster John Knox, 1999); P. R. House. *1, 2 Kings.* NAC (Nashville: Broadman & Holman, 1995); B. O. Long. *1 Kings, with an Introduction to Historical Literature.* FOTL (Grand Rapids: Eerdmans, 1984); J. G. McConville. *Grace in the End: A Study in Deuteronomic Theology* (Grand Rapids: Zondervan, 1993); R. D. Nelson. *First and Second Kings.* IBC (Louisville: John Knox, 1987); I. W. Provan. *1 and 2 Kings.* NIBC (Peabody: Hendrickson, 1995); I. W. Provan. *1 & 2 Kings.* OT Guides (Sheffield: Sheffield Academic, 1997); _____. "Why Barzillai of Gilead (1 Kings 2:7)? Narrative Art and the Hermeneutics of Suspicion in 1 Kings 1–2." *TynBul* 46 (1995) 103–116; R. S. Wallace. *Readings in 1 Kings* (Grand Rapids: Eerdmans, 1996); J. T. Walsh. *1 Kings.* Berit Olam (Collegeville, Minn.: Liturgical Press, 1996).

2 KINGS

Iain W. Provan

Overview

Second Kings describes part of the period of the monarchy in ancient Israel—from the reign of Ahaziah as king of Israel to the reign of Judah's last king, Zedekiah. It was written along with 1 Kings at some point after the middle of the sixth century BCE, since 2 Kgs 25:27–30 looks back upon the release of an earlier Judean king, Jehoiachin, from prison in Babylon in 561 BCE. Its authors are unknown, but are often referred to as "Deuteronomists" because of the marked influence of the book of Deuteronomy on 1 and 2 Kings (see the introduction to 1 Kings for details). In particular, almost all the kings of Israel and Judah are assessed in relation to the laws in Deuteronomy and are found wanting (e.g., Jehoram, 2 Kgs 3:1–3). It is this corporate failure to obey God that the authors of 2 Kings identify as the fundamental reason for the fall of the northern kingdom to the Assyrians around 722 BCE and the fall of Judah to the Babylonians around 587 BCE.

These events did not signify (as many might have thought) that Israel's God was not in fact in control of nature and history; nor that there existed other, more powerful gods than he. Second Kings is adamant that there is only one God in the world (5:15); Yahweh is not to be confused with the other gods worshiped within Israel and outside. These are simply human creations (17:16; 19:14–19), and as such powerless, futile entities (17:15; 2 Kgs 18:33–35). It is the Lord, and no one else, who controls both nature and history (1:2–17; 4:8–37; 5:1–18; 6:1–7, 27; 10:32–33; 18:17–19:37)—something that is perhaps illustrated most clearly in the way prophets function within 2 Kings, describing the future before God brings it about (19:6–7, 20–34). The events of 722 and 587 BCE signified that Israel's good and all-powerful God had been angry with his people and because of this anger had overseen the destruction of Jerusalem and its Temple, and the exile of Israel to Assyria and Judah to Babylon respectively. Israel had not obeyed God, nor heeded God's word through the prophets, from the reign of Solomon onwards—that is why disaster fell (2 Kgs 17:7–23; 23:26–27; 24:1–4).

Two exceptions to this rule are, however, included in 2 Kings. The first is Hezekiah (2 Kgs 18:1–20:21), who trusts God like no one before him; and the second is Josiah (22:1–23:30), who reforms worship like no one before him, in line with Deuteronomy's religious vision (note the many references in 22:1–23:30 to "the book of the law" that guides Josiah's reform—a phrase used in the Pentateuch only of Deuteronomy, e.g. Deut 28:61; 29:21). These kings stand as righteous models for a future Davidic king, as the Israelites return from exile and rebuild their community in Palestine—a hope that still exists by the end of the book, albeit in fragile form, associated with Jehoiachin (2 Kgs 25:27–30). His continuing existence hints that the promise of God to David of an everlasting dynasty may still remain in force, even after judgment has fallen on Israel and Judah.

Outline

I. The Death of Ahaziah (1:1–18)

II. Elisha and Israel (2–10)

    A. Elijah Gives Way to Elisha (2:1–25)

    B. Elisha and the Conquest of Moab (3:1–27)

    C. Elisha's Miracles (4:1–44)

    D. An Aramean Is Healed (5:1–27)

    E. Elisha and Aram (6:1–23)

    F. The Siege of Samaria (6:24–7:20)

    G. The Shunammite's Land Restored (8:1–6)

    H. Hazael Murders Ben-hadad (8:7–15)

    I. Jehoram and Ahaziah (8:16–29)

    J. The End of Ahab's House (9:1–10:17)

    K. Jehu Destroys Baal Worship (10:18–36)

III. Joash (11–12)

IV. Jehoahaz and Jehoash (13:1–25)

V. Amaziah, Jeroboam, and Azariah (14:1–15:7)

DETAILED ANALYSIS

I. The Death of Ahaziah (1:1–18)

Ahaziah's reign is introduced in 1 Kgs 22:51–53. The occasion for the confrontation with the prophet Elijah in ch. 1 is an injury sustained when the king falls out of the window (NRSV, "lattice") of his upper chamber in Samaria (1:2). He sends messengers to consult one of the many local manifestations of the god Baal about his fate—Baal-zebub, the god of Ekron (a Philistine city about 25 miles west of Jerusalem). The name Baal-zebub (lit. "lord of the flies") is probably a deliberate corruption of "Baal-zebul" ("Baal the exalted"), intended to express the authors' scorn of or hostility towards this so-called "deity." Elijah intercepts the messengers on the road with a prophecy about Ahaziah's death; and not for the first time in Kings an attempt is made to capture the deliverer of such a negative word from God (cf. 1 Kgs 13:1–7; 18:9–10). The attempt fails and the oracle stands. The manner of Ahaziah's death is however unexpected—there is no revolution, and Ahab's royal house is not destroyed in line with Elijah's prophecy (1 Kgs 21:21–24). Has the prophecy partly failed? It seems so at first sight; but it will later turn out (2 Kgs 3:1) that there is another son of Ahab, Ahaziah's brother Jehoram. It is this son whose reign shall see the true fulfillment of Elijah's prophecy.

II. Elisha and Israel (2–10)

A. Elijah Gives Way to Elisha (2:1–25)

First Kings 19:15–18 makes clear that the end of the war with Baal-worship will not occur until Elisha has succeeded his mentor Elijah, and Hazael and Jehu have appeared on the scene. The first of these events is described here in 2 Kgs 2. In the course of a journey among different prophetic communities in Israel, Elijah, despite the fact that he has been told by the Lord to make Elisha his successor, keeps trying to leave him behind (2:1–6). He appears to want to deny Elisha the inheritance of the prophetic spirit that should be his (cf. vv. 9–12)—an indication, perhaps, that he is reluctant to endorse God's plans for the future. A "double portion" of land (v. 9) is what an eldest son would expect of a father as his inheritance (Deut 21:15–17; cf. 1 Kgs 2:12 for the "father-son" relationship between the two prophets). Elisha persists, however; and in a scene reminiscent of Moses at the Sea of Reeds, both men cross the Jordan on dry land (vv. 7–8; cf. Exod 14:15–31, esp. vv. 21–22) and Elisha does receive this gift of the spirit after all (2 Kgs 2:11–12), as chariots (NRSV, "chariot") and horsemen of fire take Elijah up into heaven. He is consequently able to repeat Elijah's action in parting the waters (vv. 13–14), proving himself to be Joshua to Elijah's Moses. His tearing of his clothes (v. 12) signifies both mourning for Elijah and the final transition from his old to his new life. The "company of prophets" in Jericho, not privy to what has happened in the storm's midst, assume that perhaps Elijah has simply been picked up and deposited in a different place, and go looking for him, perhaps at least to bury him; but to no avail (vv. 15–18).

The chapter closes with two stories that further authenticate Elisha as Elijah's prophetic successor—a man able both to bless and to curse in the Lord's name (vv. 19–25; cf. Moses in Deut 28). He purifies the water of Jericho; and he curses some boys from Bethel who adopt a disrespectful attitude towards a prophet of the Lord. This narrative of prophetic succession ends with Elisha's trip to Mount Carmel (v. 25)—the scene of Elijah's great victory over the priests of Baal. Elisha is ready to pick up where Elijah left off in the war against Baal.

B. Elisha and the Conquest of Moab (3:1–27)

Ahab's son Jehoram is a wicked king but "not like his father and mother" (2 Kgs 3:1–3). He does not worship Baal, although he tolerates the cult (cf. 3:13; 9:22; 10:18–28) and continues in Jeroboam's sins. His response to the rebellion of Moab (already mentioned in 2 Kgs 1:1) is to seek help, like his father before him, from Jehoshaphat—readers are in fact explicitly reminded of that earlier chapter by Jehoshaphat's response to this request in 3:7 (cf. 1 Kgs 22:4). Jehoshaphat is not concerned on this occasion to discover the counsel of the Lord before going off to war (cf. 22:5). Disaster follows, in the context of which Jehoshaphat recovers his memory: "Is there no prophet of the LORD here, through whom we may inquire of the LORD?" (2 Kgs 3:9–12; cf. 1 Kgs 22:7). Elisha's name is mentioned as one who used to "pour water on the hands of Elijah" (i.e., serve him), whereupon the kings agree to consult him. His two-part prophecy in 2 Kgs 3:13–19 foresees that the immediate crisis will be dealt with by a miracle (water deriving from "neither wind nor rain") and that, thereafter, God will grant the alliance a comprehensive victory over Moab. Events quickly begin to unfold in line with the prophecy (vv. 20–27). Water mysteriously appears, providing the troops and their supply animals with what they need but also fooling the Moabites into thinking that the allies have slaughtered one other. Their reckless advance on the Israelite camp is met with force, as their opponents drive them back and point by point act out Elisha's words (v. 25, cf. v. 19). However, on the verge of the total victory that Elisha had apparently prophesied, the Israelites encounter unexpected difficulty. "Great wrath" comes upon Israel from an unspecified quarter (v. 27). The reference is probably to the superhuman fury of Mesha's troops upon seeing the sacrifice, as they counter-attack with renewed strength. The Lord does hand Moab over to the alliance (v. 18)—but not completely. It is probable that this was God's intention from the start. Once again a wicked Israelite king has been lured to disaster, not this time by a lying spirit speaking through false prophets (1 Kgs 22), but by the Spirit of God revealing partial truths through a true prophet—for Elisha did not in fact say that the kings would *conquer* every fortified city in Moab (as per NRSV, v. 19), but only that they would *attack* them.

C. Elisha's Miracles (4:1–44)

The Moabite affair has further established Elisha's credentials as a prophet in the line of Elijah; for both are now associated with the God who provides water at will (cf. 1 Kgs 18). Chapter 4 includes more miracles that are reminiscent of Elijah. The first is occasioned by a crisis that faces the widow of a man from one of the prophetic groups over which Elisha exercises leadership (2 Kgs 4:1–7; cf. 1 Kgs 17:7–16). Her sons are to be taken as slaves in payment of debt (cf. Isa 50:1; Neh 5:4–5), but Elisha solves the problem. The major part of the chapter is then taken up with a sequel to the "widow narrative" of 1 Kgs 17:7–16 (2 Kgs 4:8–37; cf. 1 Kgs 17:17–24). Unexpected life (a son is conceived when the husband of Elisha's Shunammite hostess is too old to father a child, 2 Kgs 4:8–17) gives way to unforeseen death (vv. 18–21). The mother goes to see Elisha, even though it is not one of the days on which it is customary to consult prophets (4:23; cf. Amos 8:5). She is not willing to accept his plan to resurrect the boy from a distance by means of his staff (2 Kgs 4:29–30)—she wants his personal attention, which does in fact prove crucial, as Gehazi fails to evoke any response from the corpse (v. 31). It is only Elisha's own prayer and mysterious actions that succeed in bringing the boy back to life (cf. 1 Kgs 17:19–23). The third miracle of the chapter is reminiscent of the healing of the water of Jericho (2 Kgs 4:38–41; cf. 2:1–22), but this time it is food rather than water that is in an unsatisfactory state. Elisha knows what to add to the pot to make it safe to eat. Fourthly and finally, food is once again multiplied (4:42–44; cf. 4:1-7), so that it not only provides people with their immediate needs, but also produces a surplus.

D. An Aramean Is Healed (5:1–27)

The account of Elisha's miracles continues with the story of Naaman the Aramean, during which the Lord is recognized as God, not only of Israelites, but also of foreigners (cf. 1 Kgs 17:17–24), and is acknowledged as the only real God there is (cf. 1 Kgs 18:20–40). The sovereignty of Israel's God over the whole world is clear at the beginning of the story; the author reports that Naaman's success in life was a gift from the Lord (2 Kgs 5:1). Yet he has a skin disease (not necessarily "leprosy," NRSV), and this is what brings him to Elisha (vv. 9–12). The meeting does not go well. Naaman apparently expects personal attention from Elisha and a healing on the spot; what he receives is a messenger (v. 10) who *apparently* addresses him, not about healing, but about ritual cleansing. He would have been able "to wash …

and be clean" in that sense using the rivers in his homeland (v. 12; this language echoes that of the cleansing ritual in Lev 13–14). He has failed to listen carefully; Elisha's words in fact include the promise that "your flesh shall be restored" (2 Kgs 5:10). His more attentive servants are able to persuade him to reconsider his hasty interpretation of Elisha's words (v. 13), with the result that Naaman is healed and comes to believe that the Lord is God (v. 15). Elisha did not, in fact, heal Naaman. Keen to drive home this lesson, he refuses to accept any payment from the Aramean (v. 16). However, his servant Gehazi has no such scruples about benefiting from God's work (vv. 20–27), and he suffers serious consequences as a result. Naaman's disease becomes Gehazi's own.

E. Elisha and Aram (6:1–23)

Elisha's activity as a prophet has thus far had a relatively private character (2 Kgs 2:19–25; 4:1–44), and this is briefly continued in ch. 6 with the short story about the ax head that floats so that it can be retrieved (6:1–7). However, it is Elisha's destiny also to be involved in important upcoming national and international events, presaged in his dealings with Naaman in ch. 5, where Elisha involves himself with Aram for the first time. That involvement with Aram occupies much of the next two chapters, which prepare the way for the bloody events of still later ones. Second Kings 6:8–23 contribute to this preparation by showing Elisha now fully drawn into the politics of the region. The uneasy peace of 2 Kgs 5 has given way to sporadic fighting involving Aramean raids into Israelite territory. The king of Aram is infuriated that Elisha is alerting Jehoram on a regular basis to Aramean troop movements. He tries to capture him at Dothan, about 11 miles north of Samaria. Elisha is unconcerned, because he knows that he is surrounded by the army of the Lord and that the Arameans are outnumbered (6:16–17). Their blindness to the odds is quickly compounded by a blindness to their surroundings, which puts them entirely at the mercy of the seer they had come to capture. Dependent upon him for guidance, they are led to the Israelite capital where, after a great feast, they are sent home.

F. The Siege of Samaria (6:24–7:20)

The historian now describes a full-blown invasion of Israel by the king of Aram, who besieges Samaria (2 Kgs 6:24–33). There is a famine so severe that one woman is driven to cannibalism. King Jehoram is powerless to help, lacking supplies. Only the Lord who provides such things can deliver, as Jehoram himself affirms (v. 27); and this is what happens, in line with another prophecy from Elisha (7:1–2). Normal business "at the gate of Samaria" (the marketplace) will be resumed on the following day. Produce worth eating will change hands once again at much lower prices than are presently the case (7:1; cf. the prices in 6:25). The king's skeptical right-hand man will see this miracle happen; but he himself will not eat—since to mock the prophetic word is to mock the Lord. The prophecy is fulfilled through the agency of four men with skin diseases (7:3–11). Faced with certain death if they go into the city or stay where they are (v. 4), these men instead choose *possible* death in the Aramean camp. Seen in the half-light of the late evening, with "the sound of chariots, and of horses, the sound of a great army" in the background (v. 6), they are perceived by the Arameans to be mercenaries. The Arameans flee from the field, abandoning their possessions where they lie (v. 7). General plunder of the Aramean camp follows (v. 16), with the consequence that economic conditions in Samaria immediately become better. The skeptical officer of 7:2 is trampled in the scramble to acquire goods (vv. 17–20). He stood in the way of God's salvation, as kings and their officials often do in these stories about Elisha; and he has died in a rush of judgment. It is the humble—in this case the "lepers"—who are the channels through which God's blessing comes to Israel.

G. The Shunammite's Land Restored (8:1–6)

There has been a concern throughout the Elisha story to portray the prophet as a channel for God's salvation, not simply to Israel as a whole, but also to individuals—Israelites and non-Israelites. Now, after the long narrative about the siege of Samaria, but before the report about Hazael, the historian writes again about the Shunammite woman of 2 Kgs 4:8–37. Whereas in 4:13 she had a home among her own people and did not need Elisha's patronage, now in 8:1–6 she does. While she has been avoiding the famine by sojourning in Philistia, someone has taken her land. Providentially, however, just at the moment she arrives at the royal court after seven long years to beg for her house and land, Gehazi is telling the king all about her. The king takes steps to ensure the return of everything that belonged to her, as well as all the income from her land that she would have received had she stayed in the country.

H. Hazael Murders Ben-hadad (8:7–15)

Ben-hadad becomes ill and consults the Lord about his illness (v. 8). Hazael is the man sent to find the answer from Elisha, the general thrust of which is that Ben-hadad is going to die (v. 10). Elisha encourages some deception on this point, however, so as to lull Ben-hadad into a false sense of security. Elisha also looks beyond the king's death into Aram's future—a future in which Hazael will be king, and will inflict great suffering on Israel (vv. 12–13), as he ravages the land and brutalizes the people (cf. Amos 1:13; Hos. 13:16; 2 Kgs 15:16). Hazael duly smothers his master with a wet bed-cover (if that is what the unusual Hebrew word in v. 15 means) and takes power. He has come from nowhere to the throne. He is a "mere dog" as he puts it—the "son of nobody" according to an Assyrian source.

I. Jehoram and Ahaziah (8:16–29)

The historian last referred to Judah in 2 Kgs 3, when King Jehoshaphat was involved in the ill-fated campaign against Moab. Another Judean king has come and gone in the meantime; the reader must be told about him and introduced to his successor in order to understand the story that follows (2 Kgs 9–10). That king is Jehoram (1 Kgs 22:50; 2 Kgs 1:17), a wicked ruler who is apparently a Baal-worshiper (8:18). The Davidic dynasty survives in these circumstances only because God has promised David a "lamp" that keeps on burning (cf. 1 Kgs 11:36; 15:4). Jehoram's successor Ahaziah also possesses habits of religion to match those of the family to whom he is related by marriage ("he was son-in-law to the house of Ahab") and with whom he has close contact. It is in fact as he is visiting the wounded King Jehoram in Jezreel in the aftermath of another joint campaign against Ramoth-gilead (2 Kgs 8:28–29) that he is caught up in Jehoram's troubles and killed.

J. The End of Ahab's House (9:1–10:17)

Of the players in the last act of Ahab's drama who were mentioned in 1 Kgs 19:15–18 only Jehu remains. Elisha sends a servant to find him among the army still encamped at Ramoth-gilead (2 Kgs 9:1–13). A secret anointing takes place (vv. 2, 6), and although Jehu is reluctant to respond to questions about this act (v. 11) his reticence is overcome by the persistence of his companions, who immediately proclaim him king (v. 13). The terms of the prophecy received by Jehu are broadly in line with those of Elijah's in 1 Kgs 21:21–24 (cf. also 1 Kgs 14:6–11; 16:1–4): Ahab's house is to be destroyed, with special attention to Jezebel. Jehu now sets about his task, traveling to Jezreel with an army (2 Kgs 9:14–16). Jehoram, accompanied by Ahaziah, goes out to meet him "at the property of Naboth the Jezreelite" (v. 21)—a name with fateful connotations (cf. 1 Kgs 21, esp. vv. 1–2; 16–24). Jehoram is killed, and Ahaziah shares in his fate.

Jehu now approaches the city itself, in pursuit of Jezebel (2 Kgs 9:30–37). He discovers her sitting at a window, adorned as a prostitute (v. 30; cf. Ezek 23:36–49). She taunts Jehu as one unlikely to survive his own revolution (his reign will be a "seven-day wonder," like Zimri's in 1 Kgs 16:8–20) and is thrown down to the ground beneath by a number of eunuchs (royal officials). Some time later Jehu orders her burial; but while he has been eating and drinking the dogs have also been consuming Jezebel—just as Elijah had predicted (1 Kgs 21:23; cf. 2 Kgs 9:10).

Elijah had also prophesied that the Lord would consume Ahab's descendants and cut off from him every last male in Israel (1 Kgs 21:21); the story goes on to recount in 2 Kgs 10:1–17 Jehu's crusade against Ahab's family that accomplishes this end. The first to be dealt with are the seventy sons of the house of Ahab who are living in the capital Samaria under the tutelage and care of the leading men of the city (v. 6). These are the people from among whom a successor to Jehoram would normally be chosen. By writing letters to the leading citizens challenging them to place one of these "sons" on the throne and fight for their master's house, Jehu makes them choose sides. Jehu himself then goes on to kill the remaining members of the house of Ahab in Jezreel, as well as those closely associated with Ahab there (v. 11). His work in Jezreel complete, he leaves for Samaria; and on the way, he meets some relatives of Ahaziah (v. 13), who are duly murdered as well.

K. Jehu Destroys Baal Worship (10:18–36)

Samaria had been the focal point for the Baal cult (cf. 1 Kgs 16:32–33); and it is that cult to which Jehu now gives his attention, although his approach is a subtle one. The dynasty may have changed, he tells the people of Samaria, but the religious policy will remain the same (2 Kgs 10:18). A religious festival is organized and all the servants of Baal are gathered together, unsuspecting, under one roof (vv. 19–21), where they are massacred. The "pillar … in the temple of Baal" is destroyed and the temple of Baal demolished (vv. 26–27; cf. 1 Kgs 16:32–33; 2 Kgs 3:2). Baal-worship in Israel is officially at an end. Jehu does nothing about the worship of "the golden calves that were in Bethel and in Dan," however (10:29). It is therefore surprising to find him addressed by God in v. 30 as one who has "done well in carrying out what I consider right." Apart from 2 Kgs 10:30 the authors of Kings only use such language of David (1 Kgs 15:5) and of the relatively good (i.e., non-idolatrous) kings of Judah (e.g., 1 Kgs 15:11; 22:43). It is even more surprising to find Jehu receiving a David-like dynastic promise (2 Kgs 10:30). Evidently the eradication of Baal-worship is so significant that, for the moment, participation in the sins of Jeroboam pales into insignificance. What Jehu has done that is right outweighs what he continues to do that is wrong (vv. 29, 31). The chapter ends by returning to Hazael king of Aram, who now begins a period of sustained aggression against Israel (10:32–36), conquering Transjordan as far south as the Arnon Gorge, the southern limit of Israelite territory there (Josh 12:2).

III. Joash (11–12)

The destruction of the house of Ahab has impinged to an unsettling extent upon the house of David. Ahaziah has been killed, just like Jehoram; and a number of his relatives have suffered the same fate as Ahab's relatives (2 Kgs 10:12–14). Have the two royal houses become so identified in intermarriage (8:18, 27) that a distinction is no longer to be found between them? Second Kings 11 intensifies this question by reporting the attempt of Athaliah (possibly a daughter of Jezebel) to wipe out the entire royal family, thus bringing the line of David to an end (just as Ahab's line has come to an end). Happily one royal prince survives. Joash is smuggled to safety and hidden with his nurse in the Temple, where he remains unrecognized for the six years of Athaliah's rule. Eventually a coup is organized by the chief priest Jehoiada (vv. 4–16), who conspires with the commanders of the various military units in Jerusalem and manages to ensure sufficient security for a coronation to take place within the Temple precincts. Part of the ceremony involves the presentation of a list of divinely-ordained laws (v. 12; NRSV, "covenant") by which the king shall govern (cf. Deut 17:18–20). Athaliah, rushing to the Temple precincts to find out what is happening, discovers the conspiracy much too late, and is executed (2 Kgs 11:15–16). There follows a covenant-renewal ceremony (vv. 17–21), in which the king and the people once more identify themselves (in the aftermath of the idolatrous interlude represented by the reigns of Jehoram and Ahaziah), as "the LORD's people" (cf. Josh 24:1–27; 2 Kgs 23:1–3). At the same time, a covenant is made "between the king and the people" (2 Kgs 11:17; cf. 2 Sam 5:1–3). It is important to re-define kingship in distinctively Israelite terms after a period in which thinking about such matters has no doubt been influenced by foreign ideas (cf. the kingship described in 1 Sam 8:11–18). The identity of Judah having thus been re-established, steps are taken to remove the worship of Baal from the city (v. 18).

Joash turns out to be a king who fundamentally "did what was right in the sight of the LORD" (2 Kgs 12:2; cf. the verdict on the idolaters Jehoram and Ahaziah, 2 Kgs 8:18, 27). He gave attention to the Temple of the Lord (12:4–16), which had suffered from neglect during the years in which the worship of Baal was encouraged. His initial plan is to leave the repairs to the priests themselves (vv. 4–5); but this plan fails because (it is implied) the priests are not anxious to spend money on mere buildings (vv. 6–8)—they care more for their own well-being than for the Temple, and divert funds to their own benefit even though they are well provided for under the normal laws of sacrifice (v. 16; cf. 1 Sam 2:12–17, 27–29, for a similar situation). Joash himself therefore takes control of the project, ensuring that money is truly set aside for it and is used properly (2 Kgs 12:9–12). The repairs are duly carried out, although it is a humble restoration that results. There are "no basins of silver, snuffers, bowls, trumpets, or any vessels of gold, or of silver" in this Temple (v. 13). Joash, like Solomon, reigns for forty years (cf. 1

Kgs 11:42); but the Temple is a poor reflection of its former glory (contrast 2 Kgs 12:13 with 1 Kgs 7:50). The house of David is still being "humbled" in the aftermath of Solomon's sins, as 1 Kgs 11:39 predicted. This theme is also visible in the closing verses of 2 Kgs 12. It is not just Israel (2 Kgs 10:32–33) but also Judah that is oppressed by Hazael king of Aram (12:17–18). The nation is far from the days when the king of Israel had peace on every side (1 Kgs 5:4).

IV. Jehoahaz and Jehoash (13:1–25)

Having just been told about events in Judah during the reign of Joash, the reader is now updated on what has been happening in Israel during the reigns of those two kings who acceded to the throne within Joash's lifetime. Both kings survive (if only just) the Aramean onslaught initiated by Hazael in 2 Kgs 10. The first is Jehoahaz (13:1–9)—a wicked king, indulging as his predecessors had done in the sins of Jeroboam. Under normal circumstances one might expect the appearance of a prophet to announce the end of Jehu's house (cf. 1 Kgs 14:6–14; 16:1–4; 21:21–24); but the divine promise to Jehu has created a new situation (2 Kgs 10:30). His house survives, although there *is* divine punishment in the form of an Aramean oppression so severe that it reduces the army of Jehoahaz to little more than a remnant (13:3) as insubstantial as "the dust at threshing" time that is caught by the wind and blown away (v. 7). There is also "a savior," however—perhaps a foreign king, distracting Aram from its war with Israel (v. 5). The second Israelite king in this period is named Joash/Jehoash (13:10–25). His reign provides the context for the death of Elisha. The prophet falls ill in a period when the "chariots of Israel and its horsemen" have been decimated by the Arameans (v. 14; cf. v. 7) and the king arrives to consult him. Elisha is able to offer Jehoash words of some comfort (vv. 15–19). They are not unqualified, however, apparently because the king's response to prophetic commands is not unreserved. The destruction of the Arameans will not be complete, because the king did not obey the prophetic word sufficiently enthusiastically. These are Elisha's last words; but his powers live on in the grave (13:20–21). The historian no doubt reported this because of the connection between this story and the verses that follow (13:22–24), which indicate that even in the living death of

exile God has not banished the Israelites from his presence. If contact with the great prophets of the past is maintained through obedience to their teachings, it is implied, death may yet be followed by an unexpected resurrection (cf. Ezek. 37:1–14; for God has made a "covenant with Abraham, Isaac, and Jacob" (v. 23), committing himself to Israel as a people and promising her a land.

V. Amaziah, Jeroboam, and Azariah (14:1–15:7)

Second Kings 13 ended with the description of a modest upturn in Israel's fortunes (v. 25). The impetus of that recovery continues in ch. 14. Amaziah of Judah is a relatively good king who keeps the law of Moses in dealing with the families of those who had murdered his father (cf. Deut 24:16). Yet he foolishly challenges Jehoash of Israel to a fight, and ignores his warning (2 Kgs 14:9) that Amaziah is only a puny thornbush, easily trampled upon by any wild animal, in comparison to Jehoash's mighty and immovable cedar of Lebanon. Amaziah is duly defeated at Beth Shemesh, a city 20 miles west of Jerusalem (2 Kgs 14:11–12). This leads on to an Israelite assault on the capital of Judah itself (vv. 13–14), in which a section of the wall of Jerusalem is destroyed (cf. Jer 31:38; Neh 8:16 for the gates mentioned here). The humbling of the house of David thus continues (cf. 1 Kgs 11:39; 15:16–22; 22:48–49; 2 Kgs 11–12), and is not materially affected by the succession to the throne of Azariah (15:1–7; he is also called Uzziah in 15:13, 30, 32, 34). Israel, on the other hand, is resurgent—not just in the reign of Jehoash, but also in the reign of his son Jeroboam (14:23–29), who restores the border of Israel from Lebo-hamath (an unknown city located somewhere to the north-east of Hamath) to the Sea of Arabah (i.e., the Dead Sea; cf. Josh 3:16; 12:3). In so doing, Jeroboam recovers all the territory in Transjordan captured by Hazael in 2 Kgs 10:32–33 and reestablishes the ideal borders of northern Israel as they had existed under Solomon (cf. 1 Kgs 8:65). This happens not because Jeroboam is a good king (2 Kgs 14:24) but because the promise to Jehu stands (10:30) and God remains compassionate (13:23). Specifically, "the LORD had not said that he would blot out the name of Israel from under heaven" (14:27), so that when there was a danger of this happening, during the time of Jehu's dynasty, he took steps to deliver Israel from her enemies.

VI. Israel's Last Days (15:8–31)

The death of Jeroboam II marks the fourth generation of the divine promise to Jehu (2 Kgs 10:30). One, therefore, expects a return to the unstable government of the northern kingdom implied by 1 Kgs 14:15, before the houses of Omri and Jehu were established. Reign now follows reign in quick succession, as the nation plunges speedily towards defeat and exile at the hands of the Assyrians. Scarcely has Jeroboam's son Zechariah begun to rule (15:8–12) when he is assassinated by Shallum, who holds on to power for a mere month before losing both crown and life to Menahem (15:13–16). Menahem reigns for ten years (15:17-22), in which time Pul, king of Assyria, (also known as Tiglath-Pileser) invades his land and forced him to pay him tribute (v. 19). Menahem's son Pekahiah (15:23–26) lasts just two years. He, too, is the victim of conspiracy, as one of his chief officers, Pekah, launches an attack on the royal palace and Pekahiah is assassinated. Pekah then reigns for twenty years (15:27–31)—enough time to see Tiglath-Pileser demonstrate that he has replaced the Aramean king as Israel's greatest enemy by annexing much of Israel's northern and eastern territory and deporting to Assyria a significant percentage of her population. Pekah is in turn assassinated by Hoshea son of Elah—the king during whose reign Samaria and the northern kingdom will fall. Before narrating the demise of Israel, however, the historian describes events in Judah under Jotham and Ahaz.

VII. Jotham and Ahaz (15:32–16:20)

Jotham has already been exercising power in Judah because of his father Azariah's illness (15:5); but now he becomes king in his own right (15:32–38). He rebuilds the upper gate of the house of the Lord (presumably damaged in the course of Jehoash's incursion into Jerusalem in 14:13–14). He himself also suffers an assault from the north led by Rezin king of Aram and Pekah. This is the beginning of the Syro-Ephraimite war that features so prominently in the early chapters of Isaiah (Isa 7–9).

Jotham's son Ahaz permits the return to a period of officially sanctioned idolatry in Judah (16:1–20). The language in which his religious policy is described is in fact largely that of 1 Kgs 14:23–24, where Judah's adherence to idolatrous worship was first described (compare 2 Kgs 16:3*b* with 1 Kgs 14:24*b*; and 2 Kgs 16:4*b* with 1 Kgs 14:23*b*). The new element is the sacrifice of his son in the fire (v. 3*a*), which is an allusion to participation in the cult of Molech mentioned in 1 Kgs 11:7 (cf. Ezek 16:20–21; 20:26–31; Lev 18:21; Jer 32:35). The Syro-Ephraimitic alliance besieges Ahaz in Jerusalem; and he responds by sending messengers to the king of Assyria, accepting vassal status and requesting his help (2 Kgs 16:5–9). This intervention by Assyria into Judean affairs is fateful in its consequences, not simply in terms of politics but also in terms of religion (vv. 10–20). A new altar for the Temple of the Lord displaces the old one (cf. 1 Kgs 8:64), which is now to be used only for Ahaz "to inquire by" (2 Kgs 16:15)—perhaps for sacrifice in relation to divination. There are also various other innovations at the Temple (vv. 17–18). Ahaz has been influenced by what he saw in Damascus (v. 12), and wishes to imitate it, possibly in part to please the king of Assyria (v. 18).

VIII. The End of Israel (17:1–41)

The exile of Israel has been foretold (1 Kgs 14:15), although it has long been delayed because of God's promises and God's character (2 Kgs 10:30; 13; 14:23–29). The third siege of Samaria that is now described will, however, be the last (cf. 1 Kgs 20:1 ff.; 2 Kgs 6:24 ff.). It occurs during the reign of Hoshea (17:1–6), whose political manoeuvering between Assyria and Egypt leads to his imprisonment and the capture of his capital city by the new Assyrian emperor Shalmaneser. The Israelites are carried off to Assyria and dispersed in various places throughout the empire. A number of different explanations might be given for these events, but the authors of Kings are interested only in one (17:7–17): "the people of Israel had sinned against the LORD their God" (v. 7). As the Lord once drove other peoples out of the land because of their sins (v. 8), so Israel now meets the same fate—as will Judah eventually, it is hinted (vv. 13, 19). Into the land of Israel, conversely, are now imported various other peoples (17:24–41) from places both close at hand (e.g., Hamath) and further away (e.g., Babylon). It is their religion that is the subject of interest in the last section of the chapter. From their own point of view, "they worshiped the LORD but also served their own gods" (v. 33). From the point of view of the authors of Kings, however, they neither worshiped the Lord nor adhered to his laws (v. 34); for the Lord is not simply a local god who can be worshiped alongside others, but the Lord of all peoples and all history.

IX. Hezekiah (18:1–20:21)

The account of Israel's exile in 2 Kgs 17 has introduced the possibility that Judah, like Israel, may be heading for exile, unless she heeds the prophetic warnings she has received and turns away from her sins. It is at this point in the narrative that a king appears who resembles David more closely than any Davidic king so far and leads Judah in a very different direction from his father Ahaz. He is, first, a king who reforms Judean worship. Even the most righteous of Judean kings thus far has failed to remove the high places—but Hezekiah does this (18:4). He also takes action against "the bronze serpent that Moses had made" in the wilderness (Num 21:4–9), which has evidently become an object of worship. He is, secondly, a king who displays unparalleled trust in the Lord (2 Kgs 18:5). The consequence of Hezekiah's faithfulness is that his military exploits parallel David's in a way that is not true of any of the rest of David's descendants. Only of David and Hezekiah among the Davidic kings is it said that "the LORD was with him" (v. 7; cf. 1 Sam 16:18; 18:12, 14; 2 Sam 5:10) and that the king "prospered" in war (2 Kgs 18:7; cf. 1 Sam 18:5, 14, 15). Only David and Hezekiah, furthermore, are said to have defeated the Philistines (2 Kgs 18:8; cf. 1 Sam 18:27; 19:8). Hezekiah was like David; he was at the same time unlike Ahaz, for he rebelled against the king of Assyria. To remind readers of the kind of environment in which Hezekiah pursued this bold policy, the historian reiterates the fate of the northern kingdom at the hands Shalmaneser (18:9–12; cf. 17:1–6). This reminder creates a transition into an account of what happened when the new king of Assyria, Sennacherib, attacked Judah (18:13–19:37). The beginning of the attack is reported in vv. 13–16, and does not augur well for Judah as "all the fortified cities" fall. Hezekiah attempts to buy off Sennacherib with an apology as well as gold and silver. Sennacherib does not accept this apology and tribute, but sends an army from

Lachish (southwest of Jerusalem) to the capital to persuade Hezekiah to surrender (18:17–25). The persuasion focuses on the issue of "trust" that has been introduced in v. 5. Hezekiah should neither trust in Egypt nor in the Lord, who is unlikely to help since Hezekiah has just removed his "high places and altars." The people should make peace with the king of Assyria and surrender the city, going into exile only to find a new "promised land" like their own (v. 32; cf. Deut 8:7–9); for no god has ever been able to deliver its land out of the hand of the king of Assyria (2 Kgs 18:33–35), and it will be no different with the Lord. These disparaging remarks about the power of God are followed up with further remarks in 19:10–13 about his integrity: Hezekiah has been deceived by the God in whom he trusts.

The reality is of course very different and is outlined in Isaiah's prophecy in 19:1–7 (God is certainly powerful enough to assure Jerusalem's deliverance); in Hezekiah's prayer in 19:14–19 (He is God alone, creator of heaven and earth, "God … of all the kingdoms of the earth," whereas the other "gods" are only "wood and stone," cf. Deut 4:28); and in Isaiah's further prophecy in 19:20–34. In the last passage, it is clear that Sennacherib's blasphemy and pride will bring about his downfall (vv. 21–22). His great mistake has been to imagine that what he has accomplished in his military campaigns has been achieved in his own strength (vv. 23–26). This is not so; and he will be forced by the Lord to return to Assyria (vv. 28, 32–34). Recovery in Judah afterwards will be slow but sure (vv. 30–31)—initially the people will be able to survive only because of the crops that spring up from what is already in the ground, but in the third year normal agricultural practice will resume (v. 29). Chapter 19 concludes with the fulfillment of the first part of the prophecy, as the "great army" outside Jerusalem's gates (18:37) suffers enormous casualties and Sennacherib returns with all his forces to his capital Nineveh (vv. 35–36), where he is killed.

Jerusalem has survived and Hezekiah's trust in God has been vindicated. It seems that the veiled threats in 2 Kgs 17 about Judah suffering the same fate as Israel have come to nothing. Second Kings 20, however, persists in the idea that ultimately Judah will fall. The chapter opens with a "flashback" to the period around 713/712 BCE, fifteen years before Hezekiah's death, when Hezekiah contracts a life-threatening illness (20:1–7). He receives a promise that he will live for another fifteen years (v. 6). Throughout this period (it is implied) God will deliver the king and the city out of the hand of the king of Assyria. The immediate sign that the prophecy is true involves the movement of a shadow on some steps (NRSV, "dial" v. 11) associated with the name of his father Ahaz. The shadow miraculously recovers ground just as Hezekiah is (metaphorically) destined to do. What of the period after the fifteen years are complete, however? The story in 20:12–21 alludes to this. What Hezekiah's Babylonian visitors *see*, Isaiah tells the king, they will one day *take away* to Babylon, along with some of the king's descendants (v. 18). Hezekiah is surprisingly unmoved by this news. A man recently rescued from death, he is content simply to have "peace and security" in his lifetime (v. 19).

X. Manasseh and Amon (21:1–26)

Second Kings 17 and 20 had hinted that Judah will ultimately share Israel's fate, the deliverance of Jerusalem under Hezekiah notwithstanding. With Manasseh, God's patience breaks; and hints of disaster give way to explicit prophetic announcements of it. Manasseh is the worst of the Judean kings, indulging in all that has been most reprehensible in the religion of Israel in the preceding chapters of Kings and adding to it. His father's reforms are reversed, as the high places are rebuilt so that idolatry can resume there, and a new sacred pole for Asherah replaces the one Hezekiah removed (21:3; cf. 18:4). Like Ahaz, he sacrifices his own son in the fire and practices divination (21:6; cf. 16:3, and possibly 16:15). Like Ahab, he builds altars to Baal (21:3; cf. also the Asherah pole in 1 Kgs 16:33) and worships idols (2 Kgs 21:11; cf. 1 Kgs 21:26). Behind Ahab stand Jeroboam and the other Israelite kings who caused Israel to commit sin (2 Kgs 21:16; cf. 1 Kgs 14:16; 15:26, 30, 34; 16:2, 13). Manasseh also consults mediums and wizards (2 Kgs 21:6; cf. Deut 18:9–13) and takes it upon himself to install "the host of heaven" (sun, moon, and stars) as fit objects for worship alongside the Lord in the Temple (2 Kgs 21:5, 7).

Other nations had been driven out of the land for such crimes (vv. 2, 9); this is how it will be also

with Judah (vv. 10–18). Jerusalem will be assessed by the divine architect (v. 13; note the use of the measuring line in Isa 34:11 and Lam 2:8) and, like a dangerous building, condemned. It will be emptied of all that is in it, wiped clean like a dish after a meal is finished (2 Kgs 21:13). Judah, the remnant of the Lord's inheritance left in the land, will be handed over to her enemies just as Israel was (v. 14; cf. 17:18; 19:4, 31). In the shadow of such momentous events, the reign of Manasseh's son Amon has the appearance of a relatively unimportant footnote (21:19–26).

XI. Josiah (22:1–23:30)

It is at this juncture in Judean history that Judah ironically finds herself with yet another righteous king—a second Moses to match her second David in 2 Kgs 18–20. This is Josiah, a king long-awaited (cf. 1 Kgs 13:2) and the best of all. The verses that introduce him (2 Kgs 22:1–2) already alert the readers to the kind of person he is going to be with their allusion to Deut 17:20, where the ideal king is said to be one who does not "turn" from the law of Moses "to the right or to the left." This is only the first of many references in 2 Kgs 22–23 that link Josiah with the figure of Moses in particular and "the book of the law" (22:8) in general—that is, with Deuteronomy (cf. Deut 28:61; 29:21; 30:10 for the phrase). As ch. 22 opens, however, this book has been lost (22:3–13). It has been generally available to the kings of Israel and Judah in previous times (1 Kgs 2:3; 2 Kgs 10:31; 14:6; 18:6); but it has disappeared from public view during the long reign of the apostate Manasseh. It is, however, found during Josiah's eighteenth year while the Temple is being repaired. Its contents lead to the king tearing his robes in grief and despair and sending various officials to "inquire of the LORD" about it (vv. 11–13). The prophet chosen by Josiah's officials for consultation is (perhaps surprisingly) not Jeremiah or Zephaniah, but Huldah, the wife of the "keeper of the wardrobe" (v. 14—perhaps a Temple official, cf. 2 Kgs 10:22). Her words confirm what the historian had already reported from the unnamed prophets of 2 Kgs 21. However, because Josiah has humbled himself before the Lord he will not personally see the disaster that is to fall on Jerusalem (v. 20). He will instead be "gathered to [his] grave in peace," that is, while Judah and Jerusalem still know peace, rather than the sword.

Since Josiah is a pious king, Huldah's oracle about the future does not deflect him from the path of religious reform despite its foretelling of doom (23:1–3). He gathers all the people together to hear "all the words of the book of the covenant" (v. 2; cf. Deut 31:9–13); and a covenant-renewal ceremony follows (cf. 2 Kgs 11:12–14), during which all concerned promise to follow the Lord and wholeheartedly to keep "his commandments, his decrees, and his statutes" (v.3; cf. Deut 6:17; 1 Kgs 2:3). The destruction of Baal-worship in Jerusalem and Judah immediately follows (2 Kgs 23:4–14), during which (and among other things) the apartments of the male temple prostitutes are broken down (where ritual garments were manufactured for use in the worship of Asherah, v. 8) and horses and chariots associated with the worship of the sun are destroyed (v. 11). The Josianic reform also embraces the northern cultic site of Bethel (23:15–20), to which Josiah takes the ashes of the idolatrous vessels brought out from the Temple (v. 4). He defiles Bethel's altar with bones taken from the surrounding tombs, in accordance with the prophecy of the man of God in 1 Kgs 13:2 (cf. also 13:11–32 for the background to vv. 17–18). For the first time since Solomon, a king has been able to treat the northern area of Israel as if it were part of the same kingdom as the south. A Passover follows (2 Kgs 23:21–25) in accordance with the stipulations of Deuteronomy (Deut 16:1–8, noting esp. v. 6; and see Josh 5:10–12 for the last mention of Passover in the narrative). There was simply no king like Josiah when it came to turning to the Lord (2 Kgs 23:24–25; cf. Deut 6:5). Yet Judah's fate was already settled and even Josiah himself did not come to a happy end (2 Kgs 23:26–30).

XII. The End of Judah (23:31–25:30)

The story of 1 and 2 Kings now comes to its end. The first of Josiah's successors is Jehoahaz, but he reigns for only three months (23:31–32). He is not a ruler acceptable to the Pharaoh of Egypt, who is temporarily Judah's new overlord in the aftermath of Josiah's death at Megiddo. Jehoahaz is therefore replaced with his brother (v. 34). It is during Jehoiakim's reign that readers hear for the first time about the armies of Babylon, the ultimate agent of divine judgment upon Judah (cf. 2 Kgs 20:12 ff.). It is Babylon that has been gradually replacing Assyria as the region's dominant imperial power in the preceding period; and

it is the king of Babylon who now appears at the head of the army sent by the Lord to destroy Judah because of the sins of Manasseh (24:2–4). He subdues Egypt, and comes into possession of the whole Solomonic empire, "from the Wadi of Egypt to the River Euphrates" (v.7; cf. 1 Kgs 4:21, 24; 8:65). Jehoiakim's son Jehoiachin succeeds him and has to pay the price for his rebellion against Babylon, as Jerusalem is besieged (24:8–17). Jehoiachin surrenders (v. 12) and is carried off into exile (v. 13). A remnant of sorts still remains—but only the poorest people of the land (v. 14). Jehoiachin is replaced by his uncle Mattaniah (v. 17); but Mattaniah, under his new name of Zedekiah, also rebels against the king of Babylon (v. 20). The result is a new siege of Jerusalem. The city falls; "every great house" in Jerusalem is burned down, including Solomon's Temple and palace (25:9); and the walls around Jerusalem are broken down as well (v. 10). More of the population is exiled (vv. 11–12), and some are executed (vv. 18–21). The threats of 1 Kgs 9:6–9 have become a reality. Judah, like Israel, has gone "into exile out of its land" (2 Kgs 25:21; cf. 2 Kgs 17:23). Gedaliah, the grandson of Josiah's secretary Shaphan (23:12) is appointed to govern what is left, but he does not survive long. Ishmael son of Nethaniah, who apparently has ambitions to be the next king (he is a member of the royal family, 25:25), slaughters everyone at Mizpah. The final exile of the book of Kings is a voluntary one, as the remaining people flee to Egypt (v. 26; cf. Jer 40:7–43:7). The epic saga that began with Exodus from that land has ended with the remnants of Israel returning whence they came. The only hope that remains lies with Jehoiachin (2 Kgs 25:27–30), released from prison and given a seat of honor at the king of Babylon's table. He is the only son of David left; and his survival hints that the promise to David of an everlasting dynasty may not yet have failed—that somehow the words of 2 Sam 7:15–16 remain true, that "my love will never be taken away from him ... your throne shall be established forever."

BIBLIOGRAPHY

W. Brueggemann. *1 & 2 Kings*. Smyth and Helwys Bible Commentary (Macon, Ga.: Smyth & Helwys, 2000); M. Cogan and H. H. Tadmor. *2 Kings*. AB 11 (Garden City: Doubleday, 1988); R. Cohn. *2 Kings*. Berit Olam (Collegeville,

Minn.: Liturgical Press, 2000); T. E. Fretheim. *First and Second Kings.* Westminster Bible Companion (Louisville: Westminster John Knox, 1999); V. Fritz. *1 & 2 Kings.* CC. A. Hagedorn, trans. (Minneapolis: Fortress, 2003); T. R. Hobbs. *2 Kings.* WBC 13 (Waco: Word, 1985); P. R. House *1, 2 Kings.* NAC (Nashville: Broadman & Holman, 1995); B. O. Long. *2 Kings.* FOTL (Grand Rapids: Eerdmans, 1991); J. G. McConville. *Grace in the End: A Study in Deuteronomic Theology* (Grand Rapids: Zondervan, 1993); R. D. Nelson. *First and Second Kings.* IBC (Louisville: John Knox, 1987); I. W. Provan. *1 and 2 Kings.* NIBC (Peabody: Hendrickson, 1995); _____. *1 & 2 Kings.* OT Guides (Sheffield: Sheffield Academic, 1997).

1 CHRONICLES

Alejandro Botta

OVERVIEW

The book of Chronicles (called *sefer divre hayamim* in the Babylonian Talmud, which is best translated "Annals") is the last book of the "Writings" (*ketubim*), the third section of the Hebrew Bible. The Babylonian Talmud refers also to a *sefer yochatzin*, "the book of the genealogies" (Talmud *b. Pesah. 62*) that Rashi associated with Chronicles. In the Hebrew Bible and in Jewish tradition both books of Chronicles comprise a unity (the Masoretic scribes consider 1 Chron 27:25 as the middle verse of the whole book).

Christian Bibles include 1 and 2 Chronicles among the so-called "Historical Books" after 1 and 2 Kings. The book itself, like most of the literary works composed before the Hellenistic period, doesn't include a title or the name of its author. The name given to it by the sages and church fathers reflects their intention to describe or qualify its content. The LXX calls Chronicles *ta paraleipomena* ("the things omitted or left out")—i.e. from the books of Samuel and Kings—and the LXX Codex Alexandrinus adds *Basileon Iouda*, "regarding the Kings of Judah." The Vulgate followed the LXX and called 1 and 2 Chronicles *Liber (Primus* and *Secundus) Paralipomenon*. The modern title *Chronicles* goes back to Martin Luther's German translation *Das Erste* and *Das Zweite Buch Der Chronik* (following St. Jerome, who referred to Chronicles as *Chronicon Totius Divinae Historiae,* or "Chronicle of the Entire Divine History.")

The Wisdom of ben Sirach's picture of David seems to reflect Chronicles' depiction of David as founder of the cult (Sir 47:9–10), indicating that Chronicles had already achieved authoritative status by the second century BCE. Mathew's reference to the death of "Zechariah son of Barachiah" is also evidence of the acceptance of Chronicles as part of the authoritative corpus (Matt 23:35 ref. to 2 Chr 24:20–22).

Authorship and Relationship with Ezra and Nehemiah

The Talmud ascribed part of the authorship of Chronicles and Ezra-Nehemiah to Ezra, and part of it to Nehemiah. "Ezra wrote the book that bears his name and the genealogies of the Book of Chronicles up to his own time. This confirms the opinion of Rab, since Rab Judah has said in the name of Rab: Ezra did not leave Babylon to go up to Eretz Yisrael until he had written his own genealogy. Who then finished it [the Book of Chronicles]?—Nehemiah the son of Hachaliah" (Talmud *b. Bat. 15a*). Medieval Christian scholars were not so certain. Hugh of Saint Cher (ca. 1200–1263 CE), a French Dominican, affirmed that the author was unknown, although he trusted the veracity of its content. That was also the opinion of Stephen Langton (ca. 1150–1228 CE), Archbishop of Canterbury, and the Franciscan scholar Nicolaus Lyranus (ca. 1270–1349 CE).

Until recently, the great majority of biblical scholars had considered the book of Chronicles to form a unity with Ezra and Nehemiah. This position was supported by the overlap between 2 Chr 36:22–23 and Ezra 1:13a; a supposed linguistic identity between them, the use by 1 Esd of 2 Chr 35–36, Ezra 1–10, and Neh 8:1–13a; and similarities in their theology and purpose. Nowadays, pioneered by the work of Sarah Japhet and Hugh G. M. Williamson, the consensus has moved into considering the book of Chronicles and Ezra–Nehemiah as two different and independent works.

Date

There is a certain agreement among scholars that Chronicles is a post-exilic composition. The suggested dates by scholars range from 520 BCE to 160 BCE, although there is some consensus to date the book during the fourth century BCE.

Chronicles as Legitimate Historiography

The positive valorization of Chronicles by the church fathers and medieval scholars suffered a strong blow at the hands of nineteenth century and early twentieth century Protestant scholarship. For Julius Wellhausen (1844–1918), and Charles. C. Torrey (1863–1956), the work was historically unreliable and an extreme distortion of the history of ancient Israel. A more positive attitude toward the Chronicler was developed during the second half of the twentieth century under the influence of scholars like Gerhard von Rad (1901–71) and Martin Noth (1902–68). Contemporary scholarship seems to be more willing to accept Chronicles as a valid historiographical work. The Chronicler acts as a historian when he gathers material and sources about the past of his community, decides what is significant for his time, and connects diverse events from his sources to produce a coherent narrative about the past. The difference between a past event and a historical event is, after all, how significant that event is for the present community.

Sources

Chronicles abounds in citations of works used by the author to compose his narrative. The book of the kings of Israel and Judah is cited several times, although sometimes with a slightly different name (2 Chr 16:11; cf. 20:34; 25:26; 27:7; 28:26; 32:32; 33:18; 35:26; 36:8); there is also a mention of the midrash of the books of Kings (2 Chr 3:22 and 24:27). The Chronicler also refers to prophets or prophetic records like the acts of Samuel the seer, the acts of Nathan the prophet, the acts of Gad (1 Chr 29:29), the prophecy of Ahijah, and the visions of Iddo (2 Chr 9:29). The Chronicler is also familiar with the genealogical information provided by the books of Genesis, Exodus, Numbers, Joshua, Samuel, and Ruth. There is a citation of what is written "in the law of the LORD" (1 Chr 16:40) which possibly refers to the Pentateuch; and a reference to a book of laments, unknown to us, that included a "lament of Josiah" (2 Chr 35:25). The author seems to know the books of Isaiah (2 Chr 28:16–21), Jeremiah (2 Chr 36:21), and Zechariah (2 Chr 36:9). The Chronicler also used information from lists (1 Chr 6:1–15), and three canonical psalms (Pss 96; 105; 106) are cited in 1 Chr 16. Without being exhaustive, this list of sources shows evidence of a dedicated historian at work.

OUTLINE

I. Genealogical Lists (1:1–9:44)

A. Israel's Ancestors (1:1–2:2)

B. Judah's Lineage (2:3–4:23)

2:3–9. Judah to Hezron

2:9–17. Descendants of Ram

2:18–24. Descendants of Caleb

2:25–41. Descendants of Jerahmeel

2:42–55. An Additional List of Descendants of Caleb

3:1–24. Descendants of David

4:1–23. Other Descendants of Judah

C. Descendants of Simeon (4:24–43)

D. The Tribes of Transjordan: Reuben, Gad, and Manasseh (5:1–26)

E. Descendants of Levi (6:1–81)

F. Tribes of the Central Mountainous Region (7:1–40)

G. Additional Descendants of Benjamin (8:1–40; 9:1 *a*)

H. The Post-Exilic Community (9:1 *b*–44)

II. The Reign of David (10:1–29:30)

A. Death of Saul (10:1–14)

B. David's Coronation (11:1–12:40)

C. Transferring the Ark to Jerusalem (13:1–16:43)

13:1–14. Failed Attempt to Bring the Ark to Jerusalem

14:1–17. Three success stories

15:1–16:3. Transporting the Ark to Jerusalem

15:1–3. Preparations for the Transportation

15:4–10. List of Levites Who Participate in Transporting the Ark

15:11–15. Summons and Purification of the Levites

15:16–24. Appointment of Singers and Others at the Service of the Ark

15:25–16:3. Transporting the Ark

16:4–42. Worship Organization Concerning the Ark

16:4–6. Personal Service

16:7–38. Psalm of Thanksgiving

DETAILED ANALYSIS

I. Genealogical Lists (1:1–9:44)

A. Israel's Ancestors (1:1–2:2)

The first chapter of Chronicles is based on a list of genealogies from the book of Genesis and serves as an introduction to the book. The chapter is divided in three parts: (a) 1–23, the descendants of Adam; (b) 24–54, the descendants of Abraham, (c) 2:1–2, the descendants of Israel. In the same way as in the Assyrian and Babylonian cosmogonic genealogies, the author distinguishes an antediluvian generation (1:1–23) and a postdiluvian generation (1:24–2:2). The mention of Peleg (1 Chr 1:19) serves as a pivot for the Chronicler to highlight the original unity of humanity, as the author mentions that it was in times of Peleg (Heb.: "division") "the earth was divided." The Chronicler begins the genealogy with Adam in order to emphatically place the people of Israel in the context of universal history.

B. Judah's Lineage (2:3–4:23)

This section consists of three parts: (a) 2:3–55, the genealogies of the tribe of Judah; (b) 3:1–24, the house of David; and (c) 4:1–23, additional genealogies of the house of Judah. Here begins the section which will cover the longest part of the genealogical material of Chronicles.

2:3–9. Judah to Hezron. This section is based on Gen 46:12 and Num 26:19–22. The Chronicler stresses both the divine election of Judah and his intolerance with unfaithfulness in the cases of Er, who "was wicked in the sight of the Lord and he put him to death," and of Achar, "the troubler of Israel who transgressed in the matter of the devoted thing."

2:9–17. Descendants of Ram. The importance of Ram, who is not the firstborn but occupies the first place on the list, is due to his being one of David's ancestors. Verses 10–12 are based on Ruth 4:19–22. David's sisters are only mentioned here.

2:18–24. Descendants of Caleb. This is not the only place where the name Caleb is mentioned (cf. 2:42–55; 4:1–8) and could refer to two different people. The first part of the genealogy (18–20) deals with Bezalel, a silversmith (cf. Ex 31:2; 35:30), who although belonging to a period prior to David, is associated with David and the tabernacle in view of the future construction of the Temple by Solomon. The second part (21–24) establishes a connection between Judah and a group of descendants of Gilead.

2:25–41. Descendants of Jerahmeel. This section includes two lists of names (25–33 and 34–41) which appear only here in the Hebrew Bible.

2:42–55. An Additional List of Descendants of Caleb. Continuing the section 2:18–24, it includes two lists (42–50*a* and 50*b*–55). The first one enumerates the sons of Caleb from a wife whose name is omitted (42–45); the descendants of Caleb through his concubine, Ephah (46–47); and the sons of Caleb with his second concubine, Maacah (48).

3:1–24. Descendants of David. The line of David's descendants is the centered of Judah's genealogy and continues the section of vv. 2:1–17. David's nineteen sons are enumerated (1–9); the kings of Israel (10–16); and the post-exilic generation (17–24). The extension of David's genealogy to such a late period reflects the importance of David's descendants even during the restoration period (cf. Hag 2).

4:1–23. Other Descendants of Judah. This section contains various genealogies with no parallel in the Hebrew Bible. The best known of these is the one dedicated to Jabez (9–10) and his prayer granted by God. The Hebrew version of this prayer presents some difficulties and would be best translated "if you blessed me and enlarged my borders, and if your hand might be with me, and that you would extend lands of pasture." This way, the greatest honor Jabez deserves could be attributed to the extension of his territory due to prayer and not to military force.

C. Descendants of Simeon (4:24–43)

The tribe of Simeon comes after that of Judah due to proximity. The cities that are listed in vv. 28–33 (cf. Josh 19:2–8) were considered part of Judah from ancient times.

D. The Tribes of Transjordan: Reuben, Gad, and Manasseh (5:1–26)

This section enumerates the descendants of Reuben (1–10), Gad (11–22), and the half-tribe of Manasseh (23–26). At the beginning of this section the Chronicler clarifies the reason by which Reuben, Jacob's firstborn (cf. Gen 29:31–32), does not come first in his genealogy. The interest of the author to demonstrate that God often discards the firstborn (cf. 1 Chr 2:3 and 26:10) seems to emphasize the fact that before God there are no natural rights, only the benefit of divine election. The section dedicated to Gad points to the theology of the Chronicler when explaining the reason for military success: they cried to God in the battle (cf. 2 Chr 14:11–15; 20:5–30; 32:20–21) and God granted their wish (cf. 1 Chr 12:19; 15:26; 2 Chr 25:8; 32:8) because they trusted in him (cf. 2 Chr 32:10); therefore, the Hagrites and all those who were with them "were given into their hands" (vs. 20). The section dedicated to Manasseh explains the reason for the exile of the northern tribes (cf. 2 Kgs 17:7–23). Israel had transgressed against God (cf. 2 Chr 36:14), idolatry being one of the main issues; God sends a foreign army to punish his people (cf. 2 Chr 36:17), and the consequence is the exile (cf. 2 Chr 36:18–20).

E. Descendants of Levi (6:1–81)

The importance that the Chronicler attributes to the Levites is evident in the amount of verses dedicated to the tribe of Levi. Together with Judah and Benjamin, they capture the attention of the Chronicler in the genealogy section. The section is divided into two parts: the genealogy of the Aaronite priests and other Levites (1–53), and the settlements of the Levites (54–81). The lineages of David and Aaron (cf. 1 Chr 2:10–17; 3:1–16) are the only cases in which the generations are enumerated from the patriarchal era until the exile.

F. Tribes of the Central Mountainous Region (7:1–40)

Issachar (7:1–5)

Benjamin (7:6–12)

Naphtali (7:13)

Manasseh (7:14–19)

Ephraim (7:20–29)

Asher (7:34–40)

The Chronicler has ordered the genealogies of Issachar, Benjamin, and Asher in a similar fashion: using the formula "son of…" followed by the list of leaders of the family clans, using military terminology (7:6; 7:11; 7:40); the use of exaggerated quantities to describe the men apt for war in each tribe (cf. 5:11 and 40); and finally the lack of narrative material as can be found in the genealogies of Manasseh and Ephraim.

Concerning the genealogy of Ephraim, it is noteworthy that in this brief text three literary genres can be found: a genealogy (vv. 20–21a), in which Ephraim's sons are mentioned; a brief narrative section (vv. 21b–24), which tells about the death of Ephraim's children by Gath, Ephraim's mourning, and the births of Beriah and Seerah; and Joshua's pedigree (vv. 25–27). The difference between a "genealogy" and a "pedigree" is that the first emphasizes the principal ancestor (in this case Ephraim) and later relates the descendants, while the second is centered on the final descendant (Joshua in this case).

Surprisingly, in the genealogies of both Manasseh and Ephraim there is no mention of any stay in Egypt. Manasseh appears to be associated with Aramaic elements in Palestine, from where he takes his wife (1 Chr 7:14ff), leaving aside the tradition of the stay in Egypt and emphasizing the continuity of the occupation of his territory (the northern part of the territory east of river Jordan). Something similar happens with the genealogy of Ephraim (1 Chr 7:20ff), who according to the Genesis narrative is born and dies in Egypt (Gen 41:50–52; Exod 16). However, in Chronicles Ephraim is in no way associated with Egypt. Rather, Ephraim is presented as originally from and settled in Palestine. The narrative of the murder of his sons as a result of a conflict with Gath's men and the foundation of three cities by his daughter Seerah "who built both Lower and Upper Beth-horon, and Uzzen-sheerah" located in Palestine, does nothing but reinforce the local Pal-

estinian emphasis which the author of Chronicles places on Ephraim's sons.

Verses 25–27 include a list of ancestors, or pedigree, of Joshua, son of Nun. Due to the narratives about Joshua included in the book of Exodus, we know that Joshua was born in Egypt and was the leader who conducted the people across the Jordan and in the later conquest of the land. None of this is important to the author of Chronicles. In 1 Chr 7:25–27, Joshua is presented as already established on the land, in contrast with the conqueror role with which he is presented in the book that bears his name. His leadership in the conquest is omitted in Chronicles.

G. Additional Descendants of Benjamin (8:1–40; 9:1a)

This new chapter concerning the tribe of Benjamin is structured in two sections, a list of Benjaminite ancestral houses (vs. 3–32) and a genealogy of the family of Saul. While the previous section dedicated to Benjamin (7:6–12) was centered on the military census, the current chapter is centered on the geographical distribution.

H. The Post-Exilic Community (9:1b–44)

On concluding the descendants of Jacob (1 Chr 1–8), the Chronicler adds a final section listing the inhabitants of Jerusalem, paying special attention to the priestly families (10–13), the Levitical families (14–16), and the gatekeepers (17–33).

II. The Reign of David (10:1–29:30)

After the genealogies, a narrative section begins which follows the structure of 1 Sam 31–2 Kgs 25. The Chronicler presents us with the particularities of his theological perspective through additions, alterations, and omissions of the text used as a base.

A. Death of Saul (10:1–14 // 1 Sam 31:1–13)

The Chronicler begins this section with the death of Saul forming an *inclusio* with 2 Chr 36. The death of Saul and the dispersion of his people is a foreshadowing of the end of the Judaean dynasty and the subsequent exile of the southern kingdom. The section is structured in three parts:1–7, the narrative of the war with the Philistines and its consequences; 8–12, the destiny of Saul and his sons; 13–14, summary and final thoughts. The Chronicler is not really interested in the reign of Saul more than as a prologue to the story of David. Saul's disobedience contrasts with David's faithfulness, while at the same time serving as a prototype for subsequent evil kings. Saul's unfaithfulness will be remembered throughout the Chronicler's work (2 Chr 26:16, 18; 28:19, 22; 29:5–6, 19; 30:7; 33:19; 36:14). It is summarized in 10:13, where Saul dies for his unfaithfulness to the Lord because he did not keep his commands and had consulted a medium seeking guidance instead of seeking the Lord's guidance. This chapter, nevertheless, serves as a paradigmatic anticipation of the exile, at the same time that David's serves as paradigm of the postexilic restoration.

10:1–4. A repetition of 1 Chr 8:29–38, acting as a transition between the genealogy section and the narrative section which begins at this point. The battle takes place on Mount Gilboa. The results are disastrous. The use of archers was a common tactic in the ancient Near East; the wounds of other kings due to enemy arrows are described in similar manner in other Scripture passages (1 Kgs 22:34; 2 Kgs 9:24; 2 Chr 35:23). Saul's suicide on the battlefield is, on the other hand, the only case of suicide in the OT.

10:5–6. Chronicler replaces "his armor-bearer and all his men" of 1 Sam 31:6 for "all his house died together," highlighting the end of the dynasty.

10:7–10. The narrative of this episode in 1 Sam 31 concentrates on the fate of Saul's body. Although the Chronicler does omit the fact that Saul is decapitated, he does pay attention to the fate of the head. The cutting of the head and disposing of the armor is a literary motif that also appears in the story of David and Goliath (1 Sam 17:54). It is possible that many stories on the death of Saul circulated in Israel.

10:13–14. These verses have no equivalent in 1 Samuel. This is the only place in Chronicles in which Yahweh directly intervenes in a dynastic change. Saul's dynasty could have endured if he had remained faithful to the Lord. It is clearly pointed out that the death of Saul is a punishment for his sins, "therefore the LORD put him to death," and with his death the Lord turns the kingdom over to David.

B. David's coronation (11:1–12:40)

Even though basically the material for this section comes from 2 Sam 5, the Chronicler presents his material with the intention to highlight the divine intervention in favor of David. Verses 11:1–3, 10–40 and 12:1–41 form a chiastic structure aimed at emphasizing Hebron as the place in which the troops from different parts of the country concentrate to march towards the conquest of Jerusalem. The structure, as is common with the Chronicler, follows a thematic order rather than a chronological one:

a.	Hebron		11:1
b.	Ziklag		12:1
c.		stronghold	12:8
c'.		stronghold	12:16
b'.	Ziklag		12:20
a'.	Hebron		12:21

11:1–3. During Saul's reign, David had established his power's center in Hebron (1 Sam 30:31) and according to 2 Sam 2:4 it is exactly there where he is anointed king over the house of Judah. Nevertheless, this is not mentioned by the Chronicler, nor is the confrontation with Ishbaal. In this way the absolutist character of the Davidic dynasty is emphasized. In Chronicles, all Israel is "together with" David, while in Samuel the tribes only "came" to David. In this way the common destiny of all Israel and the Davidic dynasty is demonstrated.

Then David made a covenant with all the elders who had declared their union with the house of David: "we are your bone and flesh." According to the Chronicler's theological perspective, all this happened in accordance with what God had already announced through Samuel (1 Sam 15:28; 16:1–3).

11:4–9. The new dynasty needs a capital in neutral territory and Jerusalem is the chosen place. Once again it is "all Israel" who marches instead of "the king and his men" (2 Sam 5:6). All this serves the Chronicler to mark a break with the city's past and proclaim a new beginning. From this moment, and till present times, Jerusalem will be the city of David *par excellence.* The verse summarizes the essential elements of David's ascent to the throne, taken from 2 Sam

5:10. David's power will increase under the protection of the Lord of Hosts.

11:10–47. David's heroes. This section is taken from 2 Sam 23:8–39. In 2 Samuel the last name is that of Uriah the Hittite (Bathsheba's husband), whom David sent to die in battle.

C. Transferring the Ark to Jerusalem (13:1–16:43)

13:1–14. Failed Attempt to Bring the Ark to Jerusalem. 13:1–4. Chapter 13 begins with a prologue which is original to the Chronicler and is not found in the book of Samuel (13:1–4). It describes the first failed attempt to transfer the ark to Jerusalem. The Chronicler's intention to highlight David as being superior to Saul is set out, "for we did not turn to it in the days of Saul" (v. 3), and it is David who initiates the sequence of events which will finally bring the ark to Jerusalem. Jerusalem could in no way be the religious center of Israel if the ark was not there. David's procedure indicates his role as popular leader of the people. It is not by royal decree that the decision is made but rather after consulting with the commanders and leaders (v. 1). The decision to transfer the ark could not be made lightly; such a move needed to have the support of all Israelites, and their priests and Levites (v. 2). On other occasions the Chronicler points out the consultation carried out with the leaders of the people when important decisions have to be made for the cultic life of the people. In 2 Chr 30 it will be Hezekiah who consults with the leaders and "all the assembly in Jerusalem" to celebrate Passover.

13:5. David then assembled all Israel "from Shihor of Egypt" to "Lebo-hamath." Shihor is the literal Hebrew transliteration of the Egyptian expression "channel of Horus" and indicated the southern limit of Israel (= *Sihor Mizrayim* "channel of Egypt," cf. 1 Kgs 8:65; 2 Kgs 24:7) set by one of the eastern branches of the Nile (Pelusium) which no longer exists.

13:6. The Chronicler omits "Lord of Hosts" (2 Sam 16:2), a title for God only used in connection with David (and which refers only to the fact that "God's name is invoked").

13:8. A narrative climax prepares for the tragedy which follows—from general rejoicing to experiencing the fear of divine mystery.

13:9–14. Uzzah's death, who with all good intentions tries to stop the ark from falling, causes quite a stir. Verses 10–13 describe a sequence of events which begins with the "anger of God" (v. 10) and continue with the "anger" and "fear" of David (vv. 11–12), concluding in v. 13, in which David repents of his original idea as a response to the uncontrollable divine action and decides not to take the ark "into his care into the city of David." Rather he takes it to the house of Obed-edom the Gittite. Paradoxically the ark ends up in the house of a Philistine at the service of the royal household (cf. 2 Sam 5:18). Contrary to David's fears, "the Lord blessed the household of Obed-edom and all that he had" (v. 14).

14:1–17. Three Success Stories. In 2 Samuel the first intent of taking the ark to Jerusalem is a failed one and is followed by a second try, this time successful (2 Sam 6:12–19). In Chronicles the narrative is interrupted to include between these two attempts, three success stories: King Hiram of Tyre's messengers (vv. 14:1–2); the increase of David's harem and family (3–7); and the story of the victory over the Philistines (8–12 and 13–17), basically following the narrative of 2 Sam 5:11–25.

15:1–16:3. Transporting the Ark to Jerusalem. In his description of the now successful move of the ark to Jerusalem, the Chronicler follows the model of 2 Sam 6:13–23.

15:1–3. Preparations for the Transportation. In 2 Sam 6:12 the beginning of the movement in the narrative is triggered by the news that David receives of the Lord's blessing of the house of Obed-edom. In Chronicles it is David's religious zeal which is presented as the initial cause of this new intent. David prepares a place for the ark, anticipating its arrival. On this occasion it will not be the lay people who will bring in the ark, but it will be carried by the Levites, as David declares in v. 2 (cf. Deut 10:8). The popular character of this enterprise is maintained in the narrative when it mentions that David assembled "all Israel" (v. 3).

15:4–10. List of Levites Who Participate in Transporting the Ark. The Chronicler, as he usually does, points out the distinction between the Levites and the "descendants of Aaron," i.e. the Aaronite priests (v. 4), and then sets out the list of Levites according to their families (Kothar, Merari, Gershom, etc).

15:11–15. Summons and Purification of the Levites. In accordance to David's original summons that "no one but the Levites were to carry the ark of God" (15:2), the Chronicler relates the sanctification of the Levites. This sanctification was necessary to bear the ark on their shoulders (cf. Exod 19:10, 15; Deut 23:10; 1 Sam 21:5), and explains the reasons for the original failure (cf. 1 Chr 13:1–14) when the ark had not been transported according to God's orders.

15:16–24. Appointment of Singers and Others at the Service of the Ark. After the Levites have been sanctified, the Chronicler narrates the selection of singers with musical abilities. First three singers of the same order are appointed and then fourteen of the second order, who at the end of v. 18 are called "gatekeepers".

15:25–16:3. Transporting the Ark. Here the Chronicler goes back to the narrative of Samuel. In Samuel the ark is transferred by David, while in Chronicles this is a collective endeavor in which the elders of Israel and the military leaders also take part. In Chronicles it is emphasized that the Levites (helped by God) are the ones who carry the ark; followed by the main strata of the Israelite society, the military, civilian, and religious groups. All Israel is behind this endeavor (v. 28). At the end of the story the Chronicler leaves aside the criticism of Michal, Saul's daughter—the Chronicler had mentioned the disdaining attitude when seeing David dance in 15:29.

16:4–42. Worship Organization Concerning the Ark. This long section has no parallel in the Deuteronomistic history and can be attributed to the Chronicler's composition, with certain ulterior editing and additions.

16:4–6. Personal Service. Once again David is the one to name ministers, to invoke—lit. "remember"—to praise, and to thank the Lord.

16:7–38. Psalm of Thanksgiving. As a corollary to the above description, the Chronicler includes a song of thanksgiving and praise ordered by David, "by Asaph and his kindred." The reference to Asaph is important, as the texts that mention him in place of Heman or Ethan are considered very ancient. The psalm of the Chronicler includes parts of Ps 105 (vv. 1–5); 96 (vv. 1–3); and 106 (vv. 47–48).

16:39–42. Worship at the Gibeon Sanctuary. Gibeon is located five miles northeast of Jerusalem. The last reliable historical mention of the tabernacle is that of Num 25:6. Here the Chronicler possibly follows an oral tradition which finally places it close to Jerusalem. The "high place," basically a place of worship often associated with different constructions (2 Kgs 17:29; 23:19), in Scripture usually represents the presence of syncretistic worship harshly criticized by prophets. Until Josiah closed down all places of worship to concentrate worship in Jerusalem, these were tolerated on the condition that Yahweh was the worshiped god (1 Sam 9:16–24; 1 Kgs 3:4–5; 2 Chr 1:3–7).

D. David's Kingdom Is Consolidated (17:1–21:30)

17:1–27. Nathan's Prediction. Nathan's prediction is of fundamental importance for the development of the theology of the covenant between God and Israel. From here onward, the covenant will not only be with the people but also with the Davidic dynasty. Through the covenant with David, God renews the covenant with all the people (2 Sam 23:1–7). Nathan's prophecy legitimizes the institution of the monarchy in the name of God, and can be taken as a starting point for the messianic dynasty that characterizes the theology of the house of David.

17:1–6. Oracle on the Temple (2 Sam 7:1–7). Both in Samuel and Chronicles, the prediction is preceded by an introduction (1 Chr 17:1–2; 2 Sam 7:1–3). Though here the Chronicler faithfully follows the text of Samuel, he omits the second part of 2 Sam 7:1: "the LORD had given him rest from all his enemies around him." In addition, the Chronicler substitutes the rhetorical question in Samuel "Are you the one to build me a house to live in?" (2 Sam 7:5) for a negation "You shall not build me a house to live in." This clarifies that God is not against the construction of the Temple, but rather against the man who was ready to begin the construction. The reasons offered by God by means of the prophet are that since leaving Egypt God has previously lived in a tent and tabernacle, both of these are synonymous and contrast with "house," which indicates a construction with walls. The second reason is that even during the following period, after leaving Egypt (the time of judges) and while the ark lodged in Shiloh, God did not ask for a temple.

17:7–15. Oracle on the Davidic Descendants (2 Sam 7:8–16). In this passage the oracle turns from the negative form (it won't be David who builds the Temple) to the positive form: it will be God who builds the house of David to assure his descendants, and it will be from these descendants that the person who will build the Temple will come. As in other texts of renewal or establishment of a covenant, the narrative begins with a historical prologue in which the benefits that God has bestowed on David (7–8a) are pointed out. God has taken David from the pastureland to make him king over Israel, protecting him from his enemies. Now, then, is the time to formulate the promises of the covenant which include the greater glory of the name of David, a secure place for the people of Israel, and the assurance of the dynastic continuity. It will be a son of David who will build the Temple, and God's covenant with David will be perpetuated in Solomon, from whom God will never withdraw his love, that is, the election (the opposite from what happened with Saul, David's predecessor).

17:16–27. David's Prayer (2 Sam 7:18–29). David responds to Nathan's oracle with a prayer taken from 2 Samuel with no significant alterations aside from the substitution of Yahweh for Elohim (17:2, 3) or "the ark of God" for "the ark of the covenant of God" (17:23).

17:16. David "sat before the LORD" in prayerful attitude. The supplicant could stand (Gen 18:22; 1 Sam 1:26), kneel (1 Kgs 8:54; Ps 95:6; Dan 6:10), or fall on his face (Deut 9:15; Josh 7:10). The verb used to describe David's posture (lit. "sitting") is quite surprising.

David's prayer consists of two parts: 16–22 and 23–27. The first responds to the content of the first part of Nathan's prophecy: God's benevolence towards David (7–8). David responds, praising God for his promise to establish David's house; to the enumeration of God's promise to Israel (9–10a), David refers to the exodus and conquest and the covenantal relationship between God and Israel (20–22). The second part of the prayer (23–27) claims from God the fulfilling of God's promise on the establishment and continuity of the Davidic dynasty.

18–20. The Battles of David and the Establishment of His Kingdom. These chapters represent a summary of 2 Sam 8–21, with no significant additions by the Chronicler:

1 Chronicles	2 Samuel
1 Chr 18	2 Sam 8
——	2 Sam 9
1 Chr 19	2 Sam 10
1 Chr 20:1a	2 Sam 11:1
——	2 Sam 11:2–27
——	2 Sam 12:1–25
1 Chr 20:1b	cf. 2 Sam 12:26
——	cf. 2 Sam 12:27–29
1 Chr 20:2–3	cf. 2 Sam 12:30–31
——	2 Sam 12:1–21:14
——	2 Sam 21:15–17
1 Chr 20:4–8	2 Sam 21:18–22

In this summary, the Chronicler tries to present David's military success against the Philistines, Moabites, Ammonites, and Arameans.

21:1–22:1. David Orders a Census and Acquires the Land to Build the Temple (2 Sam 24:1–4, 8–25)

The Chronicler follows the narrative of 2 Samuel in this case as well. The variations we find between the texts are attributed not so much to the particular perspective of the Chronicler, but to a slightly different version of the text of Samuel used by the Chronicler.

E. Preparation for Building the Temple (22:2–27:34)

This section is structured around the decisions made by David before his death regarding the building the Temple. This is the most extensive contribution of the Chronicler with no parallel in the Deuteronomistic history. After the promise to David that it would be his son who was going to build the Temple (ch. 7), the Chronicler presents the way David left everything ready for what Solomon was to carry out.

22:2–19. David Gives Instructions for Building the Temple. Chapter 22 consists of three sections:

vv. 2–5 describe David's initial preparations; vv. 6–16, the charge to Solomon; vv. 17–19, his command to the leaders of Israel. Each of these sections is centered around a rhetorical nucleus—David's thoughts (v. 5); David's words to Solomon (vv. 7b–16); words to the leaders (vv. 18–19). Each of the following sub-sections begins with "David said" or "David commanded," emphasizing David's leadership in the whole project. This way, Nathan's omen in 1 Chr 17:11–14 begins to happen: "I will raise up your offspring after you, one of your own sons, and I will establish his kingdom. He will build a house for me and I will establish his throne forever," referred to by Solomon in 1 Kgs 5:5.

22:2–5. David Recruits Workers and Gathers Materials for the Temple.

In this project, it will not be the Israelites who will be submitted to forced labor (as Solomon would do in 1 Kgs 5:27), but rather "aliens residing in the land." The term *gerim* is used in Chronicles when referring to the Canaanites who had remained in Israel (2 Chr 2:16ff; 8:7–10), free men but with no legal rights. The basic task these workers have to face is to cut the stone for the Temple. It does not say from where David imports iron and bronze. Usually iron was imported from Anatolia. In the times of Samuel, the Philistines exercised a form of monopoly (1 Sam 13:19–22). Tyre and Sidon, Phoenician cities which usually appear together (1 Kgs 5:15, 20; Ezra 3:7), are the places from which cedar wood came. The description of Solomon as "young and inexperienced" is in harmony with the description of himself in 1 Kgs 3:7, a young child "who does not know how to go out or come in," and with the introduction by David of him in 1 Chr 29:1 as "young and inexperienced." It is interesting that Rehoboam is the other king to whom a similar description applies ("young and irresolute" 2 Chr 13:7), which suggests that these are not mere descriptive terms but rather something pejorative which reflects the immaturity that characterizes both kings.

The greatness of the building task contrasts with the youth of Solomon. The building will be "famous and glorified throughout all lands" and reminds us of the failed intention of Gen 11:4 "let us make a name for ourselves; otherwise we shall be scattered abroad upon the face of the whole earth."

22:6–16. David Charges Solomon with Building the Temple.

David's discourse consists of two parts, a historical prologue (v. 7–10) and an exhortation to Solomon (11–16). In the prologue David recalls his intentions to build the temple "to the name of the LORD my God" (v 7), bringing to mind the Deuteronomistic theology (cf. Deut 12:11) and the Deuteronomistic history (1 Kgs 8:16, 19, 20, 29). These verses are a programmatic discourse (cf. 2 Sam 7 // 1 Chr 17; Josh 1:1–9; 1 Kgs 2:1ff.) which will be repeated in 1 Chr 28:1–10. All ideas anticipated in verses 9–10, quietness, the "house"—both as a dynasty and as a temple—the adoption as son of God, and the everlasting kingdom are the components of the ideal paradigmatic king. "Peace" is a characteristic of this king, which contrasts with the violent times of David. Though in 1 Chr 17 we are not told the reason why it is David who will not build the Temple, here it is clearly stated that David has "shed much blood and [has] waged great wars" (already in 1 Kgs 5:3 it had been pointed out that David "could not build a house for the name of the LORD, because of the warfare"). "Peace and quiet to Israel" (v. 9), then, becomes an indispensable requirement for the construction of the Temple. At the base of this idea is Deut 12, which establishes that God will give you "rest from your enemies all around" (Deut 12:10).

David exhorts Solomon, who "will prosper if you are careful to observe the statutes and the ordinances that the LORD commanded Moses for Israel," making clear the conditional characteristics of the divine promises. Only obedience to the law of the Lord guarantees the promised prosperity.

22:17–19. David's First Discourse to the Leaders.

This short pericope is addressed only to the leaders of Israel, whom he exhorts to seek guidance of the Lord with mind and heart, to concentrate all efforts on building the Temple, and, in so doing, support (cf. 1 Chr 5:20) Solomon in this project. This discourse is also divided in two parts. Verse 18 is a historical prologue for the exhortation of v. 19 which demands seeking God with "mind and heart" (cf 1 Chr 28:9; 2 Chr 15:12; 34:31) and building the Temple.

23:1–24:31. Organization of Levites and Temple Priests.

Chapters 23–27 are generally considered a later addition to the Chronicler's work. Even if different stages can be identified in the composition, they should be considered as a unit on their own. The information presented here belongs to an ulterior period to Chronicles and cuts the preceding narrative. "Levite" is here used in a general manner, referring to all those who serve in the Temple as priests (ch. 24), musicians (ch. 25), gatekeepers and treasurers (ch. 26).

Preparation for the building of the Temple is not reduced to gathering materials and designing plans for the building. A precise definition of who will be serving in the sanctuary is an essential aspect of the project for the Chronicler.

23:1–32. List of Levites. Chapter 23 consists of three sections. Verses 2b–6a describe the obligations of the Levites; 6b–24 presents three lists of the three family leaders; and 25–32 returns to the duties of the Levites.

23:2b–6a. Enumeration and Division of the Levites. These verses calculate the total number of Levites over 30 years of age as is specified in Num 4:3; 23:30 (though in Num 8:24 age is established at 25) as 38,000. David assigns the division of tasks that they are to carry out: 24,000 supervisors, a quantity which largely exceeds the 8,580 Levites of Num 4:48.

23:6b–24. Levites to Service of the Temple. The Chronicler has previously introduced some of these names in relation to the role assigned to Levites by David in 1 Chr 6. Some narrative verses interrupt the lists. Verse 13 anticipates the privileged status of Aaron and his descendants. Verse 24 reduces the necessary age to be accepted among the Levites from 30 to 20 years old (23:3).

23:25–32. Description of the Tasks of the Levites. The changes in the obligations of the Levites, after the construction of the Temple, are explained in vv. 26–28. Due to the fact that they will no longer need to transport the tabernacle, they are assigned with additional tasks established in the Pentateuch (vv. 25–26) as assistants to the Aaronite priests, emphasizing the subordination of the Levites to the priests (vv. 28–32). While v. 24 is based on Num 1, vv. 25–26 follow the outline of Num 3–4.

24:1–19. The Sons of Aaron. This directly follows the previous chapter. In 23:23 the sons of Moses are mentioned, and now the sons of Aaron are mentioned. The genealogy of Aaron follows Num 3:2–4, though details about the deaths of Nadab and Abihu are omitted (cf. Lev 10:1–2). Most of the chapter is dedicated to describing the way the priests are organized and distributing their responsibilities.

24:20–31. Expansion of the List of Levites. The additional list of Levites of these verses is a complement to 23:6–24.

25:1–31. List of Musicians and Singers. This passage is directly linked to 1 Chr 23:6b–24a, repeating parts of those verses in the same order. Special emphasis is put on the musical ministry of Asaph, Heman, and Jeduthum, and that their appointments came directly from David. The chapter is divided into two sections. The first (1–7) is an introduction to the musicians, their respective family ancestors, a brief description of their obligations, and their numbers. The second section (8–31) introduces casting lots for their duties and a subdivision in 24 classes similar to the priests (1 Chr 24). Tradition which affirms David's relation with music is well documented in biblical texts (cf. 1 Sam 16:23; 18:10; 19:9; 2 Sam 1:17ff; 6:5, 14). Music is central to the worship service and here related to the task of worship prophets. It seems evident that Levites also played this role (cf. 2 Kgs 23:2 // 2 Chr 34:30). In 2 Chr 20 the Levite prophesies in response to the prayer of Jehoshaphat. Asaph and Jeduthum are mentioned with the Levites in Neh 11:17ff. Two titles of the psalms include Jeduthum's name, (Ps 39, 62); twelve include Asaph's name (Ps 58, 73–83); and one includes Heman's (88).

26:1–32. A List of Gatekeepers and Officers. In its current form, chapter 26 can be divided into three sections. The first (vv. 1–19) is a genealogy of gatekeepers (vv. 1–11) and their tasks (12–19); the second section (20–28) is an additional list of Levites in charge of the treasury and their tasks; and the third (29–32) is a list of supervisors.

26:1–19. Gatekeepers. Besides this, Chronicles includes two other lists of gatekeepers (1 Chr 9:17ff; 16:37ff). Gatekeepers did not belong to the Levites in Ezra 2:42, 70; 7:24; 10:24; Neh 10:28; 11:19. Here the Temple gatekeepers descend from the two Levitical families of Kore (vv. 1–3, 9) and Merari (vv. 4–8, 10–11). Kore is identified in 1 Chr 6:37–38 as one of the sons of Izhar. The most prominent figure of the group is Meshelemiah (mentioned in 1 Chr 9:21). Merari's family is divided in two groups, Obed-edom (vv. 4–8) and Hosah (vv. 10–11).

26:20–28. Treasurers. This group of Levites is responsible for the administration and care of two types of "treasures": the "treasures of the house of God" (v. 20)—this includes "offerings" (cf. 9:28–29; 23:28–29)—and the "dedicated gifts."

26:29–32. Outside Duties. After the administrators of the Temple, the Chronicler includes a list of people whose duties are carried outside of the Temple. Chenaniah and his sons are "officers and judges" (v. 29), while Hashabiah is responsible for "oversight of Israel west of Jordan" (vv. 30, 32), because of the pedigree of Izhar and Hebron (see 1 Chr 6:2, 18; 23:12, 18–19). Even in the Priestly tradition (P), Levites do not carry out priestly duties, although this role does appear in Deuteronomy (Deut 17:8–13; 21:5) and in Ezek (44:24).

27:1–34. List of Civic Officials. Concluding the list of duties assigned to the Levites, ch. 27 describes the civil organization of David's kingdom. The list of officers is preceded by a summary in v. 1 which specifies it "is the list of the people of Israel," that is to say, no longer the tribe of Levi but rather the whole people.

27:2–15. The Army. These verses present the organization of the army in twelve divisions, each of them of 24,000. All the chiefs are part of the list of the heroes of David (2 Sam 23:8 ff; 1 Chr 11:10–30). Jashobeam of the tribe of Judah (Perez his father in v. 3) is one of the sons of Judah, and is assigned to lead the first division during the first month (Nisan = March–April). He is also named commander-in-chief of all the army during that period. In a similar fashion all commanders for the rest of the other months are listed.

27:16–24. Leaders of the Tribes. The second group of officials corresponds to the tribal leaders. Following the criteria to distinguish between priests and Levites, chiefs are introduced for Aaron and Levi (v. 17). The tribe of Manasseh is also divided in two (v. 20b–21a), a division based on what could be geographical reasons. Gad and Asher are not listed. The passage contains a critical note on the census of the population ordered by David (cf. 1 Chr 21 / 2 Sam 24). The condemnation is not against the census as such, rather

against counting those under twenty. Taking into account that the census is used to estimate the payment of taxes and the number of men in case of war and for the need of public labor, counting those under twenty means increasing the burden that communities must suffer, and as such is condemned.

27:25–31. David's Stewards. The following list enumerates those in charge of administrating David's private property (cf 1 Chr 28:1). Twelve officers are also assigned in charge of three areas. The first two of these officers are in charge of the king's property in Jerusalem and the fields, five stewards in charge of crops, and five in charge of cattle.

27:32–34. David's Personal Assistants. That there are seven counselors named in this list is probably due to Persian influence, where the emperor had seven counselors. It is not clear whether Jonathan should be identified with the son of Shimea (1 Chr 20:7 // 2 Sam 21:21). The title "king's friend" applied to Hushai is an administrative title (the same as in Egypt).

F. Solomon's Investiture (28:1–29:25)

These chapters relate Solomon's enthronement, barely referring to the Deuteronomistic's sources (cf 1 Kgs 1–2). The central figure is David: David gathers all Israel's officers (28:1); David says (28:2); David provides (29:1); David says (29:10, 20); David calls to bless the Lord (29:20).

Different from the story in 1 Kgs 1–2, where the people play a mere anecdotic role (cf. 1 Kgs 1:39b–40), in these two chapters they play a fundamental role: Solomon's investiture takes place before all the people; most of David's speech is addressed to the people (28:2ff; 29:1ff; 29:20ff); the people play an important role providing the necessary elements for building the Temple (28:1; 29:1); the people also participate in the blessing of God (29:20) and in worship and celebration of religious festivities (29:21–22).

28:1. Assembly in Jerusalem. This is the most complete listing of the Israelite officers in Chronicles. This verse is an appropriate summary of the list of officers presented in the previous chapter, to which three groups are added: eunuchs ("palace officials," NRSV), mighty warriors, and all warriors.

28:2–10. David's Second Speech. David's speech is introduced by a typical expression in Chronicles, "Hear me" (cf. 2 Chr 13:4; 15:2; 20:20; 28:11; 29:5) and centers round three topics: construction of the Temple, Solomon's divine election, and an exhortation to keep the commandments of God. David begins by reminding the people of his wish to build the Temple, denied by God because he was a man of war and he shed much blood. It is Solomon, chosen by God among David's sons to take his place on the throne, who will build the Temple. The same way as Moses could not enter the promised land (Deut 4:21–22) and it fell to Joshua to lead in the final possession of this promised land, so it will be Solomon and not David who will embark on the enterprise of concluding the Temple. The promise of a lasting kingdom for Solomon, which in 1 Chr 17:4 is unconditional, here appears conditioned to his efforts in keeping God's commandments and ordinances, which is reinforced in 28:9b: "if you seek him, he will be found by you; but if you forsake him, he will abandon you forever." The conditional character of the divine promise extends to the leaders of all Israel (28:8). They too must observe and search out "all commandments of the LORD your God" so as to possess the land and leave it as an inheritance forever to their children. From the perspective of the post-exilic community it is clear that the motive by which the Davidic dynasty has been displaced and the people were taken into exile has been the lack of observance of the divine commandments by the king and his leaders.

28:11–22. Plans of the Temple. The same way the plans of the tabernacle were revealed to Moses and then drawn (Exod 25:9, 40), so the plans of the Temple are revealed to David and then drawn up (28:2, 12, 18, 19). The difference between the times of Moses and the Chronicler is that Moses receives the revelation orally, while the revelation to David is in writing (28:19). For the post-exilic community the inspired word has become the inspired text.

David is not only the architect of the Temple but also the one who dictates the order of service and establishes the hierarchical order of the staff who serve the Temple. Even if Solomon is the builder, it is David who is the intellectual author of the whole project.

29:1–9. David's Third Speech. These verses follow a concentric structure centered on David's exhortation, "Who then will offer willingly, consecrating themselves today to the LORD?" (29:5). At the extremes David provides for the construction of the Temple (gold, silver, bronze, iron, wood, precious stones) (29:2–3) and the people provide for the construction of the Temple (gold, silver, bronze, iron, wood, precious stones) (29:7–8). The people "offer willingly" as in the building of the tabernacle (Exod 25:1ff.), an issue which dominates the entire section (29:5, 6, 9).

29:10–19. David's Prayer. These verses begin with a blessing: "Blessed are you, O LORD, the God of our ancestor Israel" which is a recurrent expression in the book of Psalms (Ps 41:13; 72:18; 89:52; 106:48), and constitutes David's prayer, which although similar to the psalms of thanksgiving, is written in prose. It is possible that the Chronicler decided to present it in such a way due to the fact that at the time the singing of psalms was related mostly to the adoration in the Temple and basically the responsibility of the Levites. The prayer is composed of three parts: the doxology (v. 10b–13), the presentation and dedication to God of the voluntary offering (vv. 14–17), and the supplication (18–19). David asks God that Solomon may faithfully uphold "your commandments, and your decrees, and your statutes," a clear reference to the Torah, so the Temple may be built.

29:20–25. Solomon's Anointment and the Beginning of His Reign. If it were not for the narrative in 1 Kgs 1–2 about the way Solomon reaches the throne, it would be impossible to perceive in the narration of the Chronicler the bloody family conflicts and palace intrigues which facilitated his ascent to the throne. The Chronicler adds to the narrative of 1 Kings the offering of sacrifices by "all the assembly" (v. 21), pointing to the unity of the people in support of the new king ("and all Israel obeyed him," v. 23).

G. Summary of David's Reign (29:26–30)

In the same way he will do with the other kings, the Chronicler here presents a summary of David's reign, highlighting that David reigned over "all Israel" (v. 26) without mentioning that while he reigned in Hebron the territory under his command covered only the tribe of Judah (cf. 1 Kgs 2:11). In v. 28 he points out that David achieved everything that a king could wish and died "in a good old age, full of days, riches, and honor."

BIBLIOGRAPHY

P. C. Beentjes. *Tradition and Transformation in the Book of Chronicles* (Leiden: Brill, 2008); E. Ben Zvi. *History, Literature and Theology in the Book of Chronicles* (London; Oakville, Conn.: Equinox, 2006); P. B. Dirksen. *1 Chronicles* (Leuven: Peeters, 2005); M. Eisemann. *Divrei Hayamim / Chronicles: A New Translation With a Commentary Anthologized From Talmudic, Midrashic and Rabbinic Sources* (New York: Mesora Publications, 1987–1992); S. Japhet. *The Ideology of the Book of Chronicles and its Place in Biblical Thought.* 2nd rev. ed. (Frankfurt am Main; New York: P. Lang, 1997); _____. *I & II Chronicles: A Commentary* (Louisville: Westminster John Knox Press, 1993); I. Kalimi. *An Ancient Israelite Historian: Studies in the Chronicler, His Time, Place and Writing* (Assen: Van Gorcum, 2005); _____. *The Reshaping of Ancient Israelite History in Chronicles* (Winona Lake: Eisenbrauns, 2005); R. W. Klein. *1 Chronicles: A Commentary* (Minneapolis: Fortress Press, 2006); G. N. Knoppers. *I Chronicles 1–9: A New Translation with Introduction and Commentary* (New York: Doubleday, 2003); _____. *I Chronicles 10–29: A New Translation with Introduction and Commentary* (New York: Doubleday, 2004).

2 CHRONICLES

Alejandro Botta

See 1 Chronicles for Overview.

Outline

DETAILED ANALYSIS

I. The Reign of Solomon, Son of David (1:1–9:31)

Although the recounting of the reign of Solomon occupies nine chapters in 2 Chronicles, most of the narrative focuses on the construction and dedication of the Temple as it brings David's preparations to fruition.

A. Wisdom and Wealth of Solomon (1:1–17 // 1 Kgs 3:1–15 & 1 Kgs 10:26–29)[1]

1:1. Solomon's Kingdom Established. The last verses of 1 Chronicles showed Solomon already sitting on David's throne; this first section of 2 Chronicles documents his prosperity. The opening verse states that he "established himself in his kingdom" (cf. 1 Kgs 2:12 and 2:46b), an expression that denotes the overcoming of certain obstacles or conflicts by the king (cf. 1 Chr 11:10; 2 Chr 12:13; 13:21; 17:1; 21:4).

1:2–6. Solomon Offers Burnt Offerings in Gibeon. Solomon's convocation resembles the one made by David (1 Chr 28:1). The purpose is to demonstrate that "all Israel" was present in this act of worship. The central verb in v. 5 is *darash*, which the NRSV translates as "to inquire." It is used in Chronicles in the sense of "to worship." The Chronicler feels the need to justify Solomon's worship at one of the high places (1 Kgs 3:4 "for that was the great high place") by adding that "God's tent of meeting ... was there" (1:3) and by mentioning the altar built by Bezalel.

1:7–13. Solomon Asks for Wisdom. The Chronicler omits God's appearance to Solomon in a dream and moves directly to God's speech. The passage

follows its parallel in 1 Kgs 3:5–14. God's question (1 Kgs 3:5b = 2 Chr 7b); Solomon's response (1 Kgs 3:6–9 = 2 Chr 1:8–10); and God's reaction (1 Kgs 3:10–14 = 2 Chr 1:11–12). Solomon, previously described as "young and inexperienced" (1 Chr 29:1), will demonstrate maturity and humility when he asks for wisdom to lead his people. Because of this request, God provides him with "riches, possessions and honor" (v. 12).

1:14–17. Wealth of Solomon. God's promise is fulfilled. During Solomon's reign, chariots began to be used in Israel. First Kings 9:19 says that Solomon built "the cities for his chariots, the cities for his cavalry."

B. Construction of the Temple (2:1–5:1)

2:1–18. Procuring the Material and the Craftsmen. David had already charged Solomon with completing the preparations for the building of the Temple (1 Chr 22:14). Solomon will force seventy thousand men "to bear the burdens" and "eighty thousand to quarry in the hill country" (v. 2). He will also request the help of Hurram ("Hiram" in Kings), king of Tyre, who provided skilled craftsmen, cedar, cypress, and algum timber for the project. The Chronicler emphasizes that the laborers forced to work on the Temple were not native Israelites but foreigners (2 Chr 2:17–18; cf. 1 Chr 20:3; 22:2 and 1 Kgs 5:13–18).

3:1–17. The Building. Solomon builds the Temple on the site that God has shown to David (1 Chr 21:28–22:1); the site is also identified as Mt. Moriah, where Abraham was ordered to sacrifice Isaac (Gen 22:2) and which is described as God's mountain (Gen 22:14). The date for the beginning of the construction coincides with the date provided in 1 Kings (2 Chr 3:1–5:1a // 1 Kgs 6:1–30; 7:15–51), but the reference to the exodus from Egypt is omitted, as is usual in Chronicles.

4:1–5:1. The Furniture. The making of the bronze altar (v. 4:1) is not mentioned in 1 Kings, but its existence is assumed in 1 Kgs 8:64; 9:65; 2 Kgs 16:14. The description of the rest of the bronze objects manufactured for the Temple closely follows 1 Kgs 7:40b–47, and the description of the gold objects follows 1 Kgs 7:48–50. The Chronicler clarifies the use of the "ten lavers" (v. 6). Ten tables are listed (v. 8) instead of only one in Kings (1 Kgs 7:48).

---

1   The symbol // means parallel, or that the material in Kings is very similar to the material in Chronicles.

C. Dedication of the Temple (5:2–7:22 // 1 Kgs 8:1–9:8)

5:2–6:2. Bringing the Ark of the Covenant // 1 Kgs 8:1–13. The assembly gathers in Jerusalem on the seventh month (named Tishri after the exile but Ethanim in the pre-exilic period, cf. 1 Kgs 8:2) to bring the ark to the Temple. The assembly includes the leaders and "all the Israelites" (v.3). The seventh month is the month of the feast of the Tabernacles (Sukkot, Lev 23:34; Deut 16:13–16; 31:10). In 1 Kings the priests are in charge of moving the ark, but here the task falls to the Levites, according to what David had prescribed (1 Chr 15:2; cf. Deut 10:8; 31:25; Num 3:31). The sacrifices offered by Solomon and "all the congregation of Israel" resemble the sacrifices offered by David and the people when the ark was moved from Kiriat-jearim to Jerusalem (1 Chr 13:5). The climax of this section is achieved when a cloud fills the house of the Lord (v. 13b–14 // 1 Kgs 8:10b). God has previously inhabited a dark cloud (this is the meaning of 'arafel, translated sometimes "thick darkness," NRSV, or "thick cloud," JPS) which carries the sense of a provisional habitat. From now on, God will dwell permanently in the Temple.

6:3–42. Speech and Prayer of Solomon. Solomon's speech follows the pattern of David's speech in 1 Chr 28:2–10. After his speech, Solomon turns to the bronze altar, extending his hands in prayer (cf. Exod 9:29). The Chronicler is careful to put some distance between the altar, reserved for the priests, and the king, adding v. 13 to the narrative in 1 Kings. Solomon praises God for fulfilling his promise to David and asks that God keeps his promise that the Davidic dynasty be perennial, as long as "your children keep to their way, to walk in my law as you have walked before me" (v. 16). The general statement of 1 Kings "to walk before me as you have walked before me" becomes in Chronicles more specific: "to walk in my law as you have walked before me." After the exile, to walk before God has become to walk in God's law (torah). Verses 18–21 reflect tension between a belief in God's transcendence (cf. 2 Chr 2:4–5; Isa 56:7) and his presence in the Temple. Solomon's prayer (vv. 22–23) suggests that oaths previously made in the tent of meeting or other sacred place (cf. Lev 6:3–6; Num 5:13; Judg 11:11; Amos 8:14) are now made in the Temple. The Chronicler also

thinks it possible for foreigners to pray to God (v. 33b).

7:1–10. Sacrifice and Theophany // 1 Kgs 8:54–66. The final act of the Temple's dedication is the offering of sacrifices. The Chronicler adds two miracles to the story narrated in 1 Kings. First, fire descends from heaven, consuming the burnt offering (v. 1), in the same way that fire from heaven had consumed David's offering (1 Chr 21:26). Second, God's glory fills the Temple, preventing the priests from entering the precinct.

7:11–22. God Answers Solomon's Prayer // 1 Kgs 9:1–9. Verses 13–15 offer a good example of the Chronicler's theology of retribution. Four actions by the people lead to God's forgiveness: "if my people who are called by my name humble themselves, pray, seek my face, and turn from their wicked ways, then I will hear from heaven, and will forgive their sin and heal their land" (v. 14). The notion of humbling oneself appears previously in 1 Chr 17:10; 18:1; 20:4, and becomes a key element in the Chronicler's theology from this point forward (cf. 2 Chr 16:6–7; 30:11; 32:26; 33:12, 19, 23; 34:7; and 36:12). Praying has been connected to the rebuilding of the Temple (cf. 1 Chr 17:25 and 2 Chr 7:1) and to petitions for rescue (2 Chr 32:20–24 and 33:13). To seek God's face (2 Chr 11:16; 15:4, 15 and 20:4) and "to turn from their wicked ways" as theological concepts also appear in 2 Chr 15:4; 30:6, 9; and 36:13).

D. Solomon's Achievements (8:1–9:28)

8:1–18. Building and Settlement // 1 Kgs 9:10–28. Here the Chronicler contradicts the story in 1 Kgs 9:11–14. In 1 Kings, it is Solomon who gives away the cities to Hiram of Tyre for one hundred twenty talents of gold. The Chronicler considers the promised land sacred and giving it away is not a proper act for a king like Solomon.

9:1–28. The Queen of Sheba // 1 Kgs 10:1–28. The visit of the Queen of Sheba follows, with little variation, the parallel story in Kings. Solomon's wisdom has transcended the limits of his kingdom. As no other king before or after, he is a source of wisdom beyond the borders of Israel. Verses 13–28 highlight again the wealth of Solomon and his passion for luxury items: he orders "two hundred large shields of beaten gold" (v. 15) and three hundred smaller shields also of beaten gold (v. 16).

9:29–31. Death of Solomon // 1 Kgs 11:41–43. The Chronicler adds a few interesting details to the story in 1 Kings, such as the mention of additional sources about the life of Solomon: "the history of the prophet Nathan," "the prophecy of Ahijah the Shilonite," and "the visions of the seer Iddo concerning Jeroboam son of Nebat" (v. 29), Solomon's years on the throne (forty), and his burial (v. 30–31).

II. Kings of Judah (10:1–36:23)

A. The Schism of the Kingdom (10:1–11:4)

The assembly of northern tribes challenge the oppressive taxes that enabled Solomon to pursue his building projects. Instead of following the advice of Solomon's advisers, Rehoboam chose to heed the advice of his young friends and to punish the people's disrespect with additional oppressive measures. As a result, the northern tribes reject Rehoboam as their king and secede. The intervention of the prophet Shemaiah prevents Rehoboam from engaging in a fratricidal war (11:2–4). The Chronicler thinks that Judah is still part of his ideal "all Israel" by replacing "all the house of Judah and Benjamin" (1 Kgs 12:23) with "all Israel in Judah and Benjamin" (v. 3).

B. Rehoboam, Son of Solomon (11:5–12:16)

11:5–12. Rehoboam's Fortifications. The list of cities fortified by Rehoboam does not have a parallel story in Kings, but there is no reason to doubt its authenticity.

11:13–17. Migration of the Levites // 1 Kgs 12:31–32; 13:33. Jeroboam undertakes religious reforms in the northern kingdom that revoked the Levites' ability to function as priests. As a result, they migrated to the southern kingdom. For the Chronicler, everything that Jeroboam does in matters of religion is reprehensible.

11:18–23. Wives and Children of Rehoboam. In addition to the reference to David's wives and concubines, this is the only place in Chronicles where the author mentions the names of wives, concubines, and children of a king. Comment on the fortified cities connects the passage with vv. 5–12. Following Solomon's example, Rehoboam appoints his sons in strategic positions to assure his control of the country.

12:1–12. Pharaoh Shishak Attacks Judah // 1 Kgs 14:25–28. Chronicles adds parenthetical comments to the parallel story in Kings. The first refers to the consolidation of Rehoboam's dominion and his unfaithfulness to God's law (v. 1). The narrative sequence makes clear that Shishak's attack results from Rehoboam's and the people's infidelity. Shishak lists one hundred and fifty cities captured during his campaign in his inscription at Karnak, most of them situated in northern Israel. This passage is composed with Sennacherib's campaign in mind (2 Kgs 18–19). In the case of both kings, Rehoboam vs. Shishak and Hezekiah vs. Sennacherib, the story highlights their consolidation of power and the subsequent arrogance that brings divine punishment. Also in both cases, the humbling of the leaders and the king prevents the destruction of Jerusalem.

12:13–16. Conclusion of Rehoboam's Reign. The Chronicler adds two sources not mentioned in Kings: "the records of the prophet Shemaiah and of the seer Iddo, recorded by genealogy" (v. 15). Rehoboam does not receive a favorable judgment: "He did evil, for he did not set his heart to seek the LORD" (v. 14). "To set one's heart to seek the LORD" will become an essential component of the Chronicler's definition of faithfulness. Not to do so leads one to sin.

C. Abijah, Son of Rehoboam (13:1–14:1 // 1 Kgs 15:1–2; 6–8)

The sermon of Abijah in vv. 4–12 is a literary form (sometimes called "levitical sermons") important in Chronicles. The theological message is clear: the northern kingdom has not only rebelled against the Davidic dynasty but against God himself. In vv. 13–21, Chronicles departs from the narrative in Kings to tell the story of the victory of Judah against Israel. Israel has a larger army, but regardless of their numbers or Jeroboam's military strategy, they are no match for God's chosen dynasty. Judah triumphs "because they relied on the LORD, the God of their ancestors" (v.18). Further on, the Chronicles makes clear that it is God himself who strikes Jeroboam, causing his death. Verse 22 cites another extra-biblical document, "the story of the prophet Iddo," as a source of his narrative.

D. Asa, Son of Abijah (14:2–16:14 // 1 Kgs 15:1–24)

14:2–15. Shalom and Foreign Intervention. Asa enjoyed ten years of peace. He acted as Davidic kings should (v. 2). Asa "took away the foreign altars and the high places, broke down the pillars, hewed down the sacred poles"(v. 3) and also kept the laws and commandments. The blessings are manifested in a period of peace and in the success of his building program. According to the Chronicler, prosperity is a direct consequence of being faithful. God's peace is challenged by a foreign invasion (vv. 9–15). An Egyptian army attacks Judah and Asa brings his troops to face an enemy much more numerous and powerful. But Judah is not alone. Asa cries to the Lord and the Lord acts, defeating the Ethiopians (who originated like Egyptians in North Africa and are known as Cushites).

15:1–7. Oracle of Azariah, Son of Oded. The spirit of God commands his prophet to address the king. The speech is another example of the theology of the Chronicler and has also been characterized as a Levitical sermon. In it, the Chronicler promises peace, prosperity, and blessings to those who seek the Lord (vv 3–6, cf. Hos 3:4).

15:8–19. Reforms and Covenant. Asa reacts immediately to the prophet's demands. He receives the support of all the people of Judah, Benjamin, and the refugees that fled the northern kingdom of Israel and who remained faithful to God. The reforms conclude with a covenant renewal, where the people "with all their heart and with all their soul" commit to the Lord. As a consequence, God gives them rest and peace. King Asa even decides to remove his mother, Maacah, as the queen mother because of her devotion of Asherah, although she is not put to death, as the oath of the people in 15:13 would have implied. The Chronicler states that Asa was not completely effective in removing all the high places of worship (in clear contradiction with 14:3), but he is described by the Chronicler as a king with a true heart.

16:1–14. War and Prophetic Reprehension. Asa cannot counteract Israel's strategic fortification of Ramah, a city in the territory of Benjamin (4.3 miles N. of Jerusalem), and has to resort to an alliance with the King of Aram, Ben-hadad, who resided in Damascus, to prevent its completion. Hence, he took "silver and gold from the treasures of the house of the LORD and the king's house" (v. 2) and sent them to Ben-hadad. The alliance produced the expected results. After Ben-hadad attacked the northern kingdom, Asa was able to take the fortification materials from Ramah to fortify Geba and Mizpah, two other cities in the territory of Benjamin. The story in Kings does not pass judgement on Asa's actions, but the Chronicler was very critical of this foreign alliance. The prophet Hanani came to Asa (vv. 7–10) and expressed God's condemnation of Asa's lack of trust in the God of Israel. The theology of the Chronicler demands that kings should put their trust only in God. Asa's reaction was very different from his reaction to the oracle of the prophet Azariah (15:1–7); instead of obeying, he became angry. Instead of returning to God, Asa throws Hanani in jail (v. 10). In the following verse the Chronicler comments that, at the same time, Asa oppressed some of the people of Judah. A king that leaves God cannot act justly with the people or his prophets. When Asa became sick, he failed again to look for God's assistance (cf. Exod 15:26). Of course, nothing good can come from this act of disloyalty to the Lord. Asa did not recover and died.

E. Jehoshaphat, Son of Asa (17:1–21:1 // 1 Kgs 15:24*b*; 22:1–36, 41–50*a*)

17:1–19. A Faithful King. Jehoshaphat is one the favorite kings of the Chronicler (along with Josiah and Hezekiah). The ongoing hostilities between the northern and southern kingdoms led Jehoshaphat to fortify cities and to establish garrisons and outposts to prevent Israel from invading Judah. In this unstable situation, he showed his faithfulness to God by rejecting Baal (v. 3) and trusting God. The Chronicler will make clear that the earlier ways of Asa were right and the final one wrong (v. 3). Jehoshaphat's loyalty to God will bring him prosperity and security. The mention of "great riches and honor" is similar to the Chronicler's rendering of the reigns of David and Solomon (cf. 1 Chr 29:28; 2 Chr 1:12). His educational efforts offer a concrete example of Jehoshaphat's faithfulness. He sends officials, Levites, and priests to teach God's law in the cities of Judah. This "mission" is, however, peculiar since teaching God's law was a prerogative of the priests (Jer 18:18; Ezek 7:26; Lev 10:11). The exact nature of the "book of the law" that the group carries with them is uncertain. The existence of such a book is assumed in Deuteronomistic texts (Deut 28:61; Josh 1:8; 2 Kgs 14:5). As a result of Jehoshaphat's faithfulness, God imposes fear on the surrounding countries, which not only will refrain from attacking Judah, but will bring Jehoshaphat tribute, increasing his wealth.

18:1–19:3. Impious Alliance. This section describes an alliance between Judah and the northern kingdom, designed to attack the Aramaean enclave of Ramoth-gilead. "Jehoshaphat had great riches and honor" (v.1) and did not need to enter into an alliance with Ahab, king of the unfaithful northern kingdom. He is, however, "incited" to do it (NRSV, "induced"), which in the Bible always has a negative connotation and outcome, by Ahab. In the midst of optimistic oracles of victory and triumph, Jehoshaphat wants to hear what Micaiah son of Imlah has to say, a prophet whom Ahab dislikes because he always prophesies disasters. Micaiah reluctantly declares the word of God: disaster will indeed be the outcome of the battle (v. 16). The parallel text in Kings reports that during the battle, Jehoshaphat, surrounded by the enemy, cried to his soldiers for help (1 Kgs 22:32); in Chronicles, he asks God for help and is rescued (v. 31). Ahab is wounded and does not outlive the day. He dies at sunset (v. 34). Jehoshaphat returns to Jerusalem only to be reprehended by the seer Jehu, son of Hanani (19:2).

19:4–11. Judicial Reform. Jehoshaphat continues his reforms by traveling around the country to bring the people back to the Lord and by appointing judges that would "judge not on behalf of human beings but on the LORD's behalf" (v. 6). A final appeals court is set up in Jerusalem, presided over by Amariah, the chief priest for religious matters, and by Zebadiah, son of Ishmael, for civil matters (v. 11).

20:1–21:1. War and Final Disappointment. The Chronicler reformulates the story in Kings to focus on God's reward for Jehoshaphat's piety. The description of the invasion by Moabites, Ammonites, and Meunites (cf. 2 Chr 26:7) fits well with the narrative of 2 Kgs 1:1; 3:5 and the Mesha inscription. As is usual in Chronicles, the author highlights the religious elements, leaving aside the political or economic aspects of the conflict. The Chronicler reports that Jehoshaphat's reaction to the invasion was religious: "he set himself to

seek the LORD, and proclaimed a fast throughout all Judah" (v. 3). The Levite Jahaziel, son of Zechariah, proclaims an oracle of salvation: "Do not fear or be dismayed; tomorrow go out against them, and the Lord will be with you" (v. 17; cf. Exod 14:13–14; 1 Sam 17:47). In the final section the Chronicler reports again about the destiny of any alliance with the unfaithful: Jehoshaphat of Judah accepts a partnership with Ahaziah of Israel to build a fleet. As expected, the ships were wrecked and were not able to reach their destination.

F. Jehoram, Son of Jehoshaphat (21:2–22:1 // 1 Kgs 22:50b; 2 Kgs 8:17–24)

Jehoram marries a daughter of Ahab and falls to her idolatrous practices. He systematically kills every other possible candidate to the throne. The bad behavior of the king naturally brings political calamities and Jehoram is unable to maintain control over his dominion: the Edomites achieve liberation from the Judahite yoke (vv. 8–11). The Chronicler includes in this section a letter from the prophet Elijah (vv.12–15), which is absent in the parallel story in Kings. The letter reflects very clearly the Chroniclers's theology of immediate retribution. In vv. 12b–13, Jehoram's sins are enumerated, and in vv. 13–15 the prophet foretells the consequence of his behavior. Verses 16–20 fulfill the prophecy: Jehoram dies a painful death.

G. Ahaziah, Son of Jehoram (22:2–9 // 2 Kgs 8:25–10:14)

The youngest son of Jehoram is made king by the people. All of his older brothers had perished. Several kings appear in the Bible as being put in office by the people (Joash, Uzziah, Josiah, and Jehoahaz, 2 Kgs 11:12–20; 14:21; 21:24; 23:30 // 2 Chr 23:1ff; 26:1; 33:24; 36:1). The Chronicler adds to the story in 2 Kings that it was his mother and bad counselors who led him astray (vv. 3–4). Ahaziah's death story is altered by the Chronicler to reflect his pernicious alliance with the northern kingdom. His father's piety, however, prevents him from the ultimate dishonor and his body is properly buried.

H. Athaliah, Mother of Ahaziah (22:10–23:21 // 2 Kgs 11:1–20)

In this section, the Chronicler follows with only minimal variations the parallel story in

Kings. Details surrounding the foreign character of the troops brought to the house of the Lord (2 Kgs 11:4) are omitted because they do not suit the theology of the Chronicler. Joash is made king and Athaliah is sentenced to death by the priest Jehoiada, who led a religious reform to return to traditional Yahwism.

I. Joash, Son of Ahaziah (24:1–27 // 2 Kgs 11:21–12:21)

Joash's reign is clearly demarcated by the life and death of Jehoiada the priest. While Jehoiada was alive, Joash acted faithfully (v. 2). After Jehoiada dies, the king abandons the beliefs of his advisor and faces the disastrous consequences of such defiance. During his faithful period, the king restores the Temple (the Chronicler highlights the role of the Levites in this task), but after the death of Jehoiada, the king and the nobles reject the faithful priest's reforms and even kill Jehoiada's son, the prophet Zechariah. His last wish "May the LORD see and avenge!" (v. 22) will be fulfilled. Verses 23–27 provide additional information to the story about Joash in Kings: the army of Aram attacks Judah and Jerusalem "with few men" (v. 24), but they achieve a decisive victory because God had abandoned Joash. He is wounded in battle and killed in his bed by his own servants.

J. Amaziah, Son of Joash (25:1–26:2 // 2 Kgs 14:1–17)

25:1–16. First Years and the Campaign Against Edom. The reign of Amaziah follows a similar pattern to the reign of Joash. There is a period of faithfulness and prosperity when the king listens to God's prophet and follows his advice (vv. 1–13), followed by unfaithfulness and disaster when the king disregards the message of the prophet (vv. 14–24). His first action is to take revenge for his father's death, killing those responsible but not their children (cf. Deut 24:16; Jer 31:29–30; Ezek 18:20). The Chronicler expands the only verse in Kings about the campaign against Edom. There is a census before the campaign (cf. 1 Chr 21; 2 Chr 14:8; 2 Chr 17:14–19), and the king also hires mercenaries from the northern kingdom, but a prophet prevents them from participating in the battle. God was not with Israel. Still, if the people of the northern kingdom return to God with all their hearts, God will return to them (cf. 2 Chr 15:2). The victory is not the result of human

efforts but the direct consequence of relying on God. God fights for his people. Paradoxically it is the booty that Amaziah brings with him that causes his future downfall. He takes the Edomite gods and, as might be expected, worships them. A prophet rebukes the king but is threatened. Amaziah's destiny is sealed.

25:17–28. War Against Joash, King of Israel. The theology of the Chronicler is evident here again in the differences from the story in Kings. The announcement of the prophet of God to Amaziah will be fulfilled (v. 20) and the king will face a terrible defeat, followed by the plundering of the royal residence and the Temple.

K. Uzziah, Son of Amaziah (26:3–23 // 2 Kgs 14:21–15:4)

Two different periods marked again by the king's faithfulness (vv. 3–15) and unfaithfulness to God (vv. 16–23) also characterize the reign of Uzziah. In his youth, the king follows the good counsel of Zechariah, "who instructed him in the fear of God" (v. 5) and "as long as he sought the Lord, God made him prosper." But arrogance leads again to transgression and the king encroaches upon the privileges of the priests to make the offerings (v. 18). The story in Kings does not explain why Uzziah became leprous. For the Chronicler it is clear; God struck him (v. 20). Before falling in disgrace Uzziah had led successful military campaigns against the Philistines, Arabs, and Meunites and took tribute from the Ammonites. His building projects helped improve the defense system of the city of Jerusalem and supported agriculture "for he loved the soil" (v. 10). His last days were spent in isolation due to his illness; his son Jotham exercised authority until Uzziah died. The sequence of faithfulness, prosperity, arrogance, and disgrace is apparent here once more.

L. Jotham, Son of Uzziah (27:1–9 // 2 Kgs 15:33–38)

His father's leprosy was a living example for Jotham of the consequences of violating the sanctuary's holiness. He continued to reinforce the defensive fortifications in Judah. Verses 3b–6 are additions of the Chronicler to his canonical source; his triumphs in battle and the tribute he received were the result of his faithfulness because "he ordered his ways before the LORD" (v. 6).

M. Ahaz, Son of Jotham. (28:1–27 // 2 Kgs 16:1–12)

Chronicles' portrays Ahaz quite negatively. While in Kings one finds the expression "the LORD his God" (2 Kgs 16:2), the Chronicler omits "his God," emphasizing the distance between this king and God.

The most important event during his life was the Syro-Ephraimite war (cf. 2 Kgs 15:27; 16:5; Isa 7:1–17; Hos 5:8–15). The result of this war that exemplifies Ahaz's unfaithfulness differs considerably in Chronicles from the text in Kings. Jerusalem does not fall in Kings; it does in Chronicles, and booty and captives are taken away from the sacred city. The captives taken by the northern kingdom will return, however, due to the intervention of the prophet Oded. The prophet points out that despite the constant strife between the northern and southern kingdoms, they are still one people. God shows his displeasure with both Judah and Israel, but denounces the northern kingdom as having been repeatedly guilty of unfaithfulness (28:13b).

The war leaves Judah vulnerable, whereupon the Edomites and the Philistines take advantage of the situation. Ahaz should have asked the Lord for help, but against Isaiah's advice (Isa 7), he asks the king of Assyria for help (v. 16). Help comes but at a heavy price. Ahaz is forced to accept Assyrian hegemony. The Temple of God is shut down and the Baals are worshiped. It is possible that Ahaz even used the Temple to worship pagan deities (cf. 2 Kgs 16), but the Chronicler omits that possibility in order to preserve the sanctity of the Temple. According to the Chronicler, Ahaz's burial outside of the royal burial ground, separated from his ancestors, will be his punishment (cf. 2 Kgs 16:20).

N. Hezekiah, Son of Ahaz (29:1–32:33 // 2 Kgs 18:1–6; 13–17; 19:14–19, 35–37; 20:1–3, 12–21 // Isa 36:1–22; 37:14–20, 36–38; 38:1–3; 39:1–8)

29:1–36. Purification of the Temple. The restoration of the Temple and the renovation of the covenant (v. 10) are the first steps in a religious reform. Hezekiah's speech offers another good example of the Chronicler's theology. The sin of the ancestors has brought God's ire upon the people, but reconciliation is possible and Hezekiah will become

an agent of divine reconciliation. The sacrifices for the re-dedication of the Temple follow the instructions of Lev 17:6 and Num 18:17; offerings and burnt offerings (cf. Lev 1) and sacrifices of peace (cf. Lev 7:11) follow.

30:1–27. Passover Celebration. From a private family celebration (Exod 12:1–2), the now Passover becomes a public festival. It also offers the occasion to call the northern kingdom to return to God (v. 6). The Passover will be celebrated by all the people at the Temple. Letters are sent to all Israel emphasizing the religious unity of the people. The invitation, however, is not to celebrate the Passover meal, but to return to the Lord (vv. 6, 9). The holy city is cleansed from shrines for Baal and the Levites offer sacrifices for the people. The arrival of ritually impure refugees from the northern kingdom presents a theological challenge that the Chronicler resolves by inserting Hezekiah's prayer, asking God to pardon those people. This prayer contains an important theological innovation, placing internal intent ahead of external purity.

31:1–21. Religious Reforms. After the purification of the Temple and the celebration of the Passover, Hezekiah reorganizes the Levites and priests to serve in the Temple and provides the logistical support for the regular Temple sacrifices and worship activities. The just king is able to achieve all of this because he sought God with all his heart (v. 21).

32:1–33. Assyrian Invasion and Death of Hezekiah. Sennacherib reigned in Assyria from 721–681 BCE. His Palestinian campaign aims, among other things, at punishing disloyal vassals. The story in Chronicles presents differences from the story in Kings: it adds a description of the defense system prepared by Hezekiah; omits the alliance with Egypt (an act for which previous kings have been punished); and omits the pay of tribute to Assyria. These omissions are meant to uphold the image of Hezekiah as a just king. Hezekiah dies full of honor and respected by all the people (v. 33).

O. Manasseh, Son of Hezekiah (33:1–20) and Amon, Son of Manasseh (33:21–25)

Manasseh becomes king when he is only twelve years old, and the first part of his long reign of fifty-five years is portrayed by the Chronicler as a systematic program to overturn the religious reforms of his father Hezekiah. God speaks to Manasseh and his people, but they reject the word of God. Immediate retribution follows and Manasseh is taken captive by the Assyrians. When he prays to God (v. 12), God hears his prayer and restores him (something not mentioned in Kings). The Chronicler demonstrates that God hears the prayers of the humble (cf 2 Chr 6). After Manasseh turns back to God, he begins a building program to repair the walls of Jerusalem (v. 14; cf. 1 Chr 11:8; 2 Chr 26:9; 27:3–4), reorganizes the army in Judaean cities (cf 2 Chr 11:5–12; 14:6; 17:12–19), and restores the Yahwistic faith. All of these actions are those appropriate for a just king. The summary of Manasseh's reign reflects the two aspects of his behavior: his apostasy and his repentance. The brief reign of Amnon (vv. 21–25) follows closely the description of Kings (2 Kgs 21:21–22), adding that Amnon never repented (v. 23). He is portrayed as an evil king whose death at the hands of his servants seems just the natural consequence of his impiety.

P. Josiah (34:1–36:1 // 2 Kgs 22:1–23:30 // 1 Esd 1:1–33)

Josiah (together with David, Solomon, Asa, Jehoshaphat, and Hezekiah) belongs to a select group of kings favored by the Chronicler. He becomes king at a very young age, which suggests that most of his policies were dictated by the group who brought him to power, the "people of the land."

34:1–7. Introduction. The Chronicler reinforces the positive evaluation of Josiah found in Kings (2 Kgs 22:1–2) by adding information about his early piety. Josiah sought God since he was sixteen years old, and at twenty he led the persecution and execution of priests of Baal (v. 5).

34:8–33. The Book of the Law. In Chronicles, the discovery of the book of the law is the consequence of a program of religious reform already in place, whereas in Kings the book of the law triggers Josiah's reform. In this way, the Chronicler does not base Josiah's reform on a fortuitous finding, but as the consequence of the king's fidelity to God. The precise content and extension of the book found by the priest Hilkiah (v. 14) is a matter of debate, but it almost certainly contained material found in Deuteronomy. Josiah's reform

seems to have been patterned according to the regulations of Deut 12 (cf. 2 Chr 34:24; Deut 27:9–26; 28:15–68); the celebration of the Passover follows the regulations of Deut 16 (cf. 2 Chr 34:22–28; Deut 18:9–22). The book makes Josiah aware of how unfaithful his father has been. His sense that God's punishment is on the horizon is confirmed by the prophet Hulda (v. 24). The imminence of the punishment does not prevent the renewal of the covenant. The book of the law then becomes the book of the covenant (v. 30). The narrative closely follows the story in Kings, but prophets become Levites in Chronicles (v. 30, cf. 2 Kgs 23:2) in harmony with the Chronicler's attribution of prophetic ministry to the Levites (cf. 1 Chr 25:1; 2 Chr 20:14; 29:30).

35:1–19. Passover Celebration. The text presents a more elaborate version than the brief narrative in Kings (2 Kgs 21:21–23), emphasizing liturgic details and the participation of the Levites. The Passover celebration is the climax of Josiah's reign. It takes place in Jerusalem, following the precedent established by Hezekiah. The Chronicler considers this celebration a return to the faithful days of Samuel.

35:20–27. Last Days of Josiah. Paradoxically, the faithful king (2 Chr 34:27; 35:6, 12) finds a tragic death for not heeding the word of God conveyed to him by Pharaoh. Instead of retreating from battle, Josiah rides to his death. The Chronicler follows a pattern similar to the one used to describe the death of Ahaz: both kings try to disguise themselves (v. 22; cf. 2 Kgs 18:19), both die as consequence of an arrow wound (v 23; cf. 2 Kgs 18:33); both are taken away in a chariot (v. 24; cf 2 Kgs 18:34).

Q. Final Kings of Judah: Jehoahaz (36:2–4); Eliakim–Jehoiakim, Brother of Jehoahaz (36:5–8); Jechoiachin, Son of Eliakim–Jehoiakin (36:9–10); Zedekiah brother of Jehoiachin (36:11–13 // 2 Kgs 23:30–35 // 1 Esd 1:34–38; 2 Kgs 23:36–24:7 // 1 Esd 1:39–42; 2 Kgs 24:8–17 // 1 Esd 1:43–46; 2 Kgs 24:18–25:21 // 1 Esd 1:46b–58)

Babylon assumed control of the Middle East after the fall of the Assyrian Empire in 610 BCE. After they defeat the Egyptian army in 605 BCE, there was no one who could oppose their might. The city of Jerusalem was captured on March of

597 BCE and the elite deported to Babylon. In July 587, after a short-lived rebellion, the Babylonians destroyed the city and the Temple and took thousands as exiles to Babylon.

36:1–4. Jehoahaz. The death of Josiah leaves the "people of the land" in power again. They skip the firstborn Eliakim and set Jehoahaz on the throne. Pharaoh Neco intervenes, deposing and deporting him to Egypt. Neco declares Eliakim the new king, changing his name to Jehoiakim.

36:5–8. Eliakim–Jehoiakim. Jehoiakim will reign eleven years, but the destiny of Judah has already been decided. Their alliance with Egypt makes them an enemy of Babylon, and Egypt is no match for the powerful Babylonians. According to Kings, Jehoiakim dies in Jerusalem, but in Chronicles he is taken captive to Babylon.

36:9–10. Jechoiachin, Son of Eliakim–Jehoiakin. Jehoiachin seemed to have been a precocious rebel, as the Chronicler reports that already at the age of eight he began to do what was bad in the eyes of the Lord. Immediate retribution followed, and within a year he was taken captive to Babylon together with the rest of the vessels of the Temple.

36:11–13. Zedekiah, Brother of Jehoiachin. Zedekiah was supposed to rule under Babylonian supervision, but the urge to rebel was growing among the elite and the people. After eleven years, Zedekiah rejected Jeremiah's message and rebelled against Nebuchadnezzar. The consequences were tragic; in July 587, Jerusalem and the Temple were destroyed.

R. Deportation and Cyrus' Edict (36:14–23 // Ezra 1:1–3)

The last verses in Chronicles fulfill Jeremiah's words of hope (Jer 25:11–12; 29:10). The exile comes to an end and the people return to the land. God has kept his promise.

BIBLIOGRAPHY

P. C. Beentjes. *Tradition and Transformation in the Book of Chronicles* (Leiden: Brill, 2008); E. Ben Zvi. *History, Literature and Theology in the Book of Chronicles* (London; Oakville, Conn.: Equinox, 2006); M. Eisemann. *Divrei Hayamim / Chronicles: A New Translation with a Commentary Anthologized From Talmudic, Midrashic and Rabbinic Sources* (New York: Mesora Publications, 1987–1992); S. Japhet. *The Ideology of the Book of Chronicles and Its Place in Biblical Thought.* 2nd rev. ed. (Frankfurt am Main; New York: P. Lang, 1997); _____. *I & II Chronicles: A Commentary* (Louisville: Westminster John Knox Press, 1993); I. Kalimi. *An Ancient Israelite Historian: Studies in the Chronicler, His Time, Place and Writing* (Assen: Van Gorcum, 2005); _____. *The Reshaping of Ancient Israelite History in Chronicles* (Winona Lake, Ind.: Eisenbrauns, 2005).

EZRA

Jacob Wright

OVERVIEW

In many manuscripts of the LXX and in the Masoretic tradition, the books of Ezra and Nehemiah comprise a single book. Although the Vulgate and some of the early church fathers separate it into two distinct works, this book was likely composed as a unity and should be appreciated as such.

The book of Ezra–Nehemiah recounts the Judean reconstruction during Persian rule (539–430 BCE), after the devastation wrought by the Babylonians (586 BCE). It may be divided into three general sections: Whereas the first one (Ezra 1–6) relates primarily to a construction project (the Temple) and the second one (Ezra 7–10) to reforms for the community, the third (Neh 1–13) integrates the two themes by addressing a construction project and internal reforms.

Within these sections, there is room for a wide range of subjects. Yet they all relate to the fundamental question of Judah's identity—which institutions stand at its center and which practices demarcate its boundaries. It is the question, not the answers to it, that unifies the work. Yet the authors have also created a sophisticated narrative that aligns the physical with the spiritual: The building of Jerusalem's Temple and the municipal Wall runs hand-in-hand with the construction of the Judean community as whole. ("Wall" is capitalized since it represents in Ezra–Nehemiah the pendant to Temple and includes much more than Jerusalem's physical ramparts.)

Within the corpus of biblical literature, Ezra–Nehemiah is distinctive in its citation of many sources. The genre of these sources include lists (Ezra 2; Neh 3; 7; 11–12), official correspondence and edicts written in Aramaic (Ezra 4–6, 7), and first-person memoirs (Ezra 7–9; Neh 1–7, 13). The sources have been subjected to heavy criticism with respect to their authenticity, and this criticism has provoked interest in the book as a work of literature. Ezra–Nehemiah reflects a new form of historiography, which may be influenced by Greek forms of history-writing. It also testifies to the growing importance of texts as sources of author-ity in a new post-monarchic age. Even the Persian kings first consult their records before making an imperial decision. They then supplement earlier decrees with new edicts (=commentaries). In this way, they model a *hermeneutical* method of survival for the Judeans themselves, who find their way by searching in their own texts.

As for the problems the sources pose for historians, one should not confuse authenticity with historical worth. That the Persian letters and decrees in Ezra 1–7 may stem in large part from Judean hands should neither dismay the biblical reader nor lead to a wholesale dismissal of the book. Rather, it should foster a greater appreciation for the ideals of the book expressed through the writings of foreign kings and Judean heroes.

The completion of Ezra–Nehemiah is usually dated to the late Persian period (end of the fourth century BCE). The Artaxerxes mentioned in Ezra 7–8 and Neh 2 is most likely Arxtaxerxes (d. 424 BCE). The identity of the Darius in Neh 12:22 is difficult to determine, but he may be Darius III (336–330 BCE). Aside from these datable rulers, a handful of evidence suggests that the composition of the book (esp. the final chs. in Neh 8–12) continued in the early Hellenistic period, if not even in the times of the Maccabees. If so, the combination of Torah piety and a well-fortified Jerusalem in Neh 1–13 would have provided an important model for polities at this time. Furthermore, the book depicts an ideal history of relations between Judah and a foreign empire, from its inception (Ezra 1:1) until its end (Neh 12:22). This scope likely presupposes the fall of that empire and the need to reflect on past history in the face of succeeding empires.

The title of the book commemorates two figures who differ starkly from each other in their (portrayed) personality and approach to problems. Much contemporary homiletic literature devotes a great deal of attention to this contrast, using Ezra and Nehemiah as leadership case studies. Such use of these figures is by no means unprecedented; it can be traced throughout the book's long reception history and probably informed the composition of the book itself.

OUTLINE

DETAILED ANALYSIS

I. First Movement: Rebuilding Altar and Temple (1:1–6:22)

The first six chapters of Ezra treat the construction of the altar and Temple, and the problems encountered during the course of the project. In explaining the delay of the construction (from the reign of Cyrus to Darius), this section also serves as a kind of historical reflection on prophets, especially Haggai and Second Isaiah (see especially 5:1–2).

The section has its own distinctive character and themes. Especially prominent is the motif of seeking-and-finding in texts. Indeed, the narrative is governed by the fate of Cyrus's decree: Readers are introduced to it at the outset (ch. 1). Yet in the course of time, this document gets lost in the imperial bureaucracy and archives, which results in a lengthy delay of the project (chs. 4–5). When the decree is finally found again (6:1–2), the Judeans can finally complete the project. Rather than mere narrative conceit, this motif of seeking-and-finding expresses a fundamental message of the book: the potential as well as the perils inherent in textual authority.

A. The Cyrus Edict (1:1–4)

Because EN seems to represent one book, some commentators read this paragraph as an introduction to the entire work. The "house of the LORD" represents accordingly the city or community rather than just the Temple. However, the book lacks a grand conclusion and thus perhaps one should not expect an introduction to the whole.

The deity is said to "stir up the spirit" of Cyrus. In Hag 1:14 the same expression refers solely to local Judeans who build in the time of Darius. The author of our passage seems to have transferred the inspirational moment to an earlier point and to a foreign king (see, however, v. 5), constructing thereby a much different historical account from that in Haggai (and Zechariah). The notice that the decree was "also in writing" is important for the subsequent narrative (see esp. 6:1–2).

The decree responds to any doubt as to where this House should be built. The likely reason for the stress on location is the existence of communities who considered themselves equally to be "the people of Yahweh" (v. 3) yet built temples in other locations (e.g., Samaria). Cyrus's words implicitly proscribe these competing temples. If a group really belonged to Yahweh's people and heeded imperial (as well as divine) orders, it would contribute solely to the building project in Jerusalem.

The decree may be based in some way on a historical edict. The Persian rulers followed a long-established tradition of reversing earlier policies in order to gain the loyalty of their subject peoples. However, the formulation of these verses betrays a Judean theological perspective that the historical Cyrus would have considered heretical, and it differs from the quotation of the decree in 6:3–5 (see also 5:13–15). By allowing Cyrus to proclaim that Yahweh granted him all the kingdoms of the earth (v. 2) and charged him to build his house in Jerusalem (temple construction often followed conquest in ancient Near Eastern royal ideology), the author introduces a central message of the book: The role of native Judean kings has been assumed by *foreign* imperial rulers. The continuity between native and foreign kingship is underscored by the use of vv. 1–3*a* in 2 Chr 36:22–23.

B. Return of Yahweh's People and Vessels (1:5–11)

The people of Yahweh (v. 3) who heeded the response are solely the former inhabitants of Judah and Benjamin (v. 5). The remaining verses present the return of this people in a direct relationship to the return of the vessels (see esp. v. 11*b*), which are mentioned throughout the book (5:14–15; 6:5; 7:19; 8:25–33; Neh 10:39[40];13:5, 9). The cultic vessels represent the essential continuity between the First and Second Temples inasmuch as they are the same items that Nebuchadnezzar had despoiled from the First Temple (v. 7). (Despoliation of cultic inventory was widely practiced in the ancient world; cf. especially 1 Sam 4–7; 2 Sam 5:21; and—with respect specifically to the vessels/people—Jer 27–28.) The identity of Sheshbazzar (Zerubbabel?) is a mystery. Here he is called the prince of Judah, while according to 5:14–16 he was appointed governor by Cyrus and later laid the Temple foundation (cf. however 3:8–10).

C. The Plurality and Boundaries of the Community (2:1–70)

This chapter consists primarily of a list of names and numbers of Judeans who could trace their roots back to exilic origins. The list is interrupted by a reference to groups who could not prove their genealogies (2:59–62). This attention to ethnic continuity echoes the emphasis on cultic continuity in 1:7–11 (compare Nebuchadnezzar's actions in 2:1 with 1:7). For a community in the midst of upheaval and struggling to negotiate its

survival in a new imperial, multicultural environment, such concern with identity and tradition is to be expected. In the absence of clearly demarcated political borders and a native Judean army to defend those borders, the community notably turns to texts (=written tradition), such as genealogies and registers, imperial edicts, and the Torah—the text par excellence (see, e.g., 3:2, 4). By means of these texts and sophisticated methods of interpretation, the community not only demarcates their social, ethnic, and religious boundaries but also determines how they should proceed into an unprecedented future.

The list probably represents an ideal vision of Judah. For the narrative, it serves various purposes: It fills the gap between chs. 1 and 3, and may be compared to the voyage accounts in the subsequent two movements (from Mesopotamia to Judah: Ezra 8 and Neh 2). By the end of the chapter, the author can report that the Judeans (identified with "all Israel"!) were now residing in their cities (v. 70). As a hybrid between clan and territorial register, it also functions as a map of Judah in compendium form. Finally, the list serves, as in Neh 7, to express the plurality of the community and to replace the otherwise anonymous, general designations (such as "people of Judah") with actual names.

The central role played by the kings of Judah and Israel at an earlier time is now filled by numerous names of clans and families, who are guided by a lay leader (Zerubbabel) and a priest (Jeshua). In this respect, the community's leadership may be compared to that of pre-monarchic Israel as depicted in Exodus–Joshua. Moreover, whereas earlier only the king contributed to the building of the Temple (1 Kgs 5–7; 1 Chr 22; 2 Chr 2–4), now the people themselves assume this responsibility (vv. 68–69), as the exodus generation did with respect to the tabernacle (Exod 35–36).

D. Building the Altar (3:1–7)

This passage, which seems to have been created as a preface to 3:8–13, tells of the construction of the altar. By virtue of this passage, the book presents concentric spheres of sacrality, each marked by the verb "to build": altar, the House of God, and the Wall of Jerusalem. The narrative will progressively refocus attention from the center (altar and priesthood) to the periphery (the Wall and entire community).

If the altar was built already in the seventh month, the community had little time to make the voyage back and settle in their new homes. Yet it is important to re-inaugurate the festival calendar on the first day of the year (3:6). The community also works quickly because of "the terror of the peoples of the lands"[1] (3:3), who later attempt to disrupt their progress (4:1–5:5). It then takes measures to prepare for the second phase of construction (3:6b–7, compare 1 Chr 22:2, 4, 15; 2 Chr 2:15–16 as well as the prophecy in Isa 60:13). These measures once again involve private donations "in keeping with authorization from Cyrus" (3:7). The latter point is noticeably absent in 1:1–4 (but cf. 6:4). Its inclusion here further illustrates not only the imperial support for the project but also the community's strict adherence to imperial orders. It may be compared to the emphasis on adherence to the Torah (3:2, 4, 5). The community is ultimately governed by two texts: the Torah and the Cyrus edict.

E. Construction of the Temple (3:8–6:22)

Up until this point the narrative has treated important preliminary matters relating to preparations for the building of the Temple, which are dated to the first year of Cyrus. Beginning in 3:8, which is dated to the second year, the account will now focus on the construction of the Temple and reasons why its completion was delayed until the reign of Darius.

3:8–13. Laying a Foundation. The second phase of building involves the appointment of Levites to oversee the rest of the construction of "the House of Yahweh," the laying of the foundation of the sanctuary proper (hekhal), and a festive "groundbreaking" ceremony. That this event is dated to the second month (of the second year) should be read in connection with 2 Chr 3:2 relating to the work on the First Temple. Here again the text stresses historical continuity in this fledgling community (see also the reference to David in v. 10).

The antiphonal musical celebration is led by the priests and Levites (v. 10) and consists of two types of song: praise (hallel) and thanksgiving (hodot). The quoted psalm (v. 11) appears often in the book of Chronicles in relation to the First Temple (1 Chr 16:3; 2 Chr 5:13; 7:3). Its popularity in the post-exilic period is likely related to its affirmation of Yahweh as the source of the community's connection to a prior glorious period of Israel's history. The narrator notes that the community was moved to praise, while some of the elderly wept at the sight. The notice may be responding to the same reaction that the prophet Haggai addresses (Hag 2:3). If so, it declares that the disappointment Haggai observed was counterbalanced by joy.

4:1–5. Interruptions to the Building Project. The concluding statement in ch. 3—that the sound of the celebration was *heard far away* (3:13)—leads directly to ch. 4, which begins with the enemies of Judah and Benjamin *hearing* about the construction project. These enemies identify themselves as non-natives who began sacrificing to "your God" after they had been settled in their land by the Assyrians (4:2). Their petition to join the project is briskly rebuffed by the leaders of the community. The reason offered is strikingly similar to that of Nehemiah in Neh 2:20. Yet in contrast to Nehemiah's response, Zerubbabel et al. can refer to a decree from Cyrus, which is addressed solely to the people of Yahweh (1:3). Although these "enemies" seek Yahweh and sacrifice to Yahweh, the authors do not consider them to be the people of Yahweh (see however 6:21). Spurned, the enemies adopt various machinations to disrupt the project, which include both scare tactics and bribing officials in the imperial bureaucracy. That this harassment continues from the reign of Cyrus to the reign of Darius (4:5) reflects the historical likelihood that the construction of the Temple *commenced* in the reign of Darius rather than the reign of Cyrus (see Hag 1).

4:6–24. Seeking-and-Finding in the Imperial Archives, Part I. After referring to two letters (4:6–7), the narrator cites the correspondence between Artaxerxes and two of his officials in the West, Rehum and Shimshai (4:8–23; the language switches here to Aramaic). They write to the imperial court with accusations against the Judeans. Artaxerxes responds and commands the work be brought to a halt. The narrator then reports that the construction ceased until the second year of

---

1   Unless otherwise indicated by NRSV, the quotations from Ezra are direct translations by the author.

Darius (cf. 4:5). Thus, the narrative jumps ahead to the reign of Artaxerxes (d. 424 BCE) and then back to Darius (d. 486 BCE). These letters also refer to the work on the city walls rather than the Temple.

How can one explain these incongruities? First, the letters illustrate and provide concrete evidence for the claims made in 4:5–7. Second, the possibility that the decree could be reversed (4:21*b*) anticipates the permission this same king later grants Nehemiah. But before this happens, the narrator reports the completion (chs. 5–6) and beautification (chs. 7–8) of the Temple. In this way, the book illustrates how the imperial court favors the Temple, whereas the Wall project (initially) jeopardizes the success of the Restoration. Third, Artaxerxes *seeks* and *finds* in his records before making a decision (4:15, 19). His behavior provides a model for the Judeans, who can seek and find matters in their records (cf. 2:62; 7:10; Neh 7:5, 64; 8:14; 13:1) at a time when they no longer have a king of their own.

5:1–2. The Role of the Prophets. A new era begins with the prophets, Haggai and Zechariah, encouraging Zerubbabel and Jeshua to "rise and build" (5:1–2). Although the community thereby implicitly disobeys the orders of Artaxerxes (4:21), the authors can, in this way, harmonize the books of Haggai and Zechariah with the prophecy of Second Isaiah. The reader now knows that Haggai and Zechariah did indeed play an essential role in initiating the construction of the Temple. But the preface to this history provided in Ezra 1–4 shows how the prophecy in Second Isaiah pertaining to Cyrus and his declaration (e.g. Isa 44:28) was also fulfilled. This sophisticated exegesis resolves the tension between these books. However, in contrast to Hag 1, the authors of Ezra 1–6 present the work as merely *resuming* in the second year of Darius (instead of commencing) and the community being concerned with this project since the first year of Cyrus.

5:3–6:12. Seeking-and-Finding in the Imperial Archives, Part II. Like ch. 4, this section pivots on the king's activity of seeking-and-finding. This time, however, the king does not search in a book but rather in the imperial archives for a particular document: the Cyrus edict. Because it had been lost, enemies could interrupt the building project.

The plot of Ezra 1–6 is thus propelled by the Cyrus edict—both its fate and its interpretation.

A brief narrative (5:3–5), consisting mainly of an excerpt from 5:8–10, prefaces the letters themselves (5:6–6:12). (For "the eye of their God," see Ps 33:18 and Job 36:7.) The letters closely resemble those in ch. 4 in both form and content, yet they present a scenario that is more historically tenable. Tattenai and Shetharbozenai do not accuse the Judeans (in contrast to Rehum and Shimshai; 4:11–16) but merely report about their inquiry. When asking the king to undertake a search, they also employ more polite language (cf. 5:17 with 4:15). Like Neh 1:1–4, the history recounted by the Judean elders (5:11–13) notably lacks any reference to a collective return, as told in Ezra 1–2. Sheshbazzar is the governor of the community (in contrast to 3:1–5:2, but see 1:7–11). Moreover, one hears nothing about opposition as in 3:1–5:5.

The sense of identity and history mirrored in the elders' response is noteworthy. They are the servants of the sovereign God ("the God of heaven and earth"). Surprisingly, they do not say anything about being Darius's servants. Yet they claim authorization from Cyrus, whose edict they link historically to the work of a great king of Israel (Solomon). What separates the two sides of history is destruction and exile—attributed emphatically to the *Babylonian–Chaldean* king—in direct response to their ancestors' act of *angering* the deity.

Darius's role as interpreter figures prominently in this passage. The Persian king presents a new reading of the Cyrus decree that focuses on the dimensions/location of the Temple as well as the return of the vessels. He also discovers that, according to Cyrus, the royal treasury should bear the costs of the building project (6:1–5; for kings sponsoring the Temple construction, see comments on 2:1–70). On the basis of what he finds in the text, he then acts, issuing a new decree that confirms and supplements what he found.

6:13–22. The Completion of First Phase of the Building Project. Once the new decree is issued by Darius, the House of God is finally completed after more than two decades. The agreement between the divine command and the imperial decrees is noteworthy (6:14). Moreover, this passage emphasizes, in contrast to the letters, the exilic origins of the community; they represent the twelve tribes of Israel (6:17). After describing the dedication, the narrator notes the celebration of Passover (and Mazzoth) a month later (6:19–22; now reverting to Hebrew). The returning exiles are joined in the festivities by those "who had separated themselves from the nations of the land to seek Yahweh …" (i.e., the non-exiled population or, as Rashi claims, proselytes). Reference to the Assyrian king (6:22) is anachronistic, but it agrees with the emphasis on all Israel (the Assyrians exiled the ten northern tribes/Israel).

II. Second Movement: Ezra, the Temple, and Community (Ezra 7:1–10:44)

Ezra 7 marks the beginning of the second movement. It is once again (cf. ch. 4) set within the reign of Artaxerxes. Yet it revolves around the person of Ezra, who represents an ideal figure of the new post-monarchic age. Chapters 7–8 recount his commission and voyage to Jerusalem; its focus is primarily the Temple. In contrast, chs. 9–10 shift abruptly to recount his approach to a communal crisis.

A. Ezra Is Sent to Jerusalem (7:1–8:36)

The preceding movement (chs. 1–6) presents the community building the Temple with the help of texts, in which they together with the Persian kings *seek-and-find*. This section now focuses attention on the activity itself of seeking-and-finding by portraying an individual who "had set his heart to *seek* the Torah of the LORD, and practice and teach Israel laws and commandments" (7:6, 10).

7:1–10. Introducing Ezra. The account begins with Ezra's priestly genealogy (7:1–5). The genealogy, however, is not complete; rather, it highlights the most prominent names connecting him to *Aaron*, "the first/chief priest." Ezra's later partner, Nehemiah, identifies himself in his introductory prayer as a servant of Yahweh like *Moses* (Neh 1:5–11).

Second, the narrator, like the king (7:12), identifies Ezra as a proficient scribe of Torah (7:6, 10–11). Ezra's dual identity (priest-scribe) mirrors the book's ideals: birth supplemented by action/merit. His genealogy establishes his personal con-

tinuity to earlier generations that inhabited the land and, more specifically, his connection to the first priest in Israel's history. Yet the narrator also shows how Ezra complemented his inheritance by birth with meritorious performance in studying the Torah.

Third, in 7:9 the narrator expresses the beginning of the return in architectural terms (*yesud hama'alah*), which are employed elsewhere in the books for, respectively, the *foundation* and *ascents/elevations* in Jerusalem. Accordingly, Ezra's mission is presented as continuing the project of building the House of God.

7:11–26. The Artaxerxes Decree. Whether Artaxerxes' decree (in Aramaic) corresponds to an authentic imperial document is a matter of debate among scholars. Whatever the case may be, its presence in the book reiterates one of its primary emphases, viz., that the Persian court looked favorably upon the Temple, which served as the conduit of imperial benefaction to Judah. The heart of the decree (vv. 15–24) parallels the decrees in ch. 6 inasmuch as it prescribes donations for the Temple from the royal treasuries. Here, however, the king (and his court) also make "freewill offerings" (7:16; cf. 1:4; 2:68; 3:5); and he also exempts Temple officials from taxes (7:24). Artaxerxes' words leave no doubt that the king acts out of fear and respect for Ezra's God (see esp. 7:23). The framework of the decree grants Ezra permission to go up to Jerusalem with anyone who wishes to accompany him (7:13), to inquire (lit. "seek") in Judah according to the law/wisdom of God (7:14, 25), and to appoint a government to administer these laws, executing corporal punishment if necessary (7:25–26). It should be noted that chs. 9–10 do not depict Ezra either appointing judges or threatening corporal punishment.

7:27–8:36. Transporting the Vessels. After the decree is cited, the narrative moves seamlessly into a first-person account, which begins with Ezra's blessing (7:27–28a). The attention devoted to the Temple in the preceding decree underscores the continuity between Ezra's commission and the larger building project. The same is reaffirmed in Ezra's blessing: God is praised as the one who guides the heart of the foreign king to "glorify" the Temple.

The actual narrative begins in 7:28*b*, where Ezra tells his readers how he took immediate action to fulfill his commission. His first move is to assemble representative leaders. The account here continues in 8:15 after being interrupted by a list of clans that accompanied him from Babylon. This list consists of three individuals followed by twelve larger groups. (One may compare this constellation to the three patriarchs and twelve tribes, or three major and twelve minor prophets.) Based on the number of males (1,513), the whole congregation would have exceeded 5,000. Nevertheless, Ezra notices that the entire community was not represented: The Levites were absent, and hence he takes measures to remedy the situation (8:15–20). The passage resembles others in the book that highlight the importance of the Levites (see esp. Neh 13:10–14, 22).

Second, Ezra proclaims a fast during which the people petition their God for a safe journey (lit. "straight path"—cf. Isa 40:3) for themselves, their children, and their possessions (8:21–23). The fast replaces the imperial soldiers. After they had just expressed their unequivocal trust in God's providential care for those who seek him, Ezra says that he was ashamed to ask the king for a military escort "to aid" them (*azar*, a play on the name Ezra, lit. "[God is] aide"). This verse (8:22) accentuates the already implicit contrasts between Ezra and Nehemiah. Nehemiah's trip is much more about himself: He travels alone and is accompanied only by an entourage of imperial soldiers (Neh 2:9). In contrast, Ezra makes a concerted effort to bring a large and representative group.

Third, Ezra identifies twelve priests to carry the cultic vessels and offerings; both objects and their bearers are declared holy. Ezra's act and instructions to the group (8:24–30) have ritual, symbolic qualities communicating the significance of the move from Babylon to Jerusalem.

The rest of the chapter (8:31–36) recounts the voyage and arrival. The description of the journey is reported in very few words, emphasizing the deposition of the vessels in the Temple as well as the concluding sacrifices and the delivery of the king's edicts. The closing line expresses the happy ending and overriding theme of this first episode of the Ezra account: The Persian governors "supported (lit. "lifted up") the people and the House of God."

B. Ezra's Approach to a Communal Problem (9:1–10:44)

After the happy ending in 8:36, the narrative takes a sharp turn. Persian patronage for the Temple now becomes the backdrop (9:9) against which a communal crisis and Ezra's response are portrayed. These chapters have Nehemiah's memoir in view: What is only one of several abuses that Nehemiah confronts (Neh 13:23–30) is here presented as *the* fundamental problem facing the community—one of existential proportions (9:14). In this way, the authors of the book provide a preface to Nehemiah's work, whose Wall and reforms can now be read as a response to the problem Ezra faced. The book also invites its readers to compare and contrast Ezra's and Nehemiah's approaches.

9:1–15. Ezra's Own Account. The account is extremely precise in both the narrative order and word-choice. First, Ezra is confronted with a problem; he does not notice it himself (cf. Neh 13:23). Second, the problem itself is presented in historical terms: The Judeans (Israelites, priests, and Levites) have failed to separate themselves from the peoples of the lands, whose abominations resemble the land's prior inhabitants and neighbors (9:1). Third, the problem of non-separation expresses itself in the activity of intermarriage. The "holy race" (lit. "seed"; see Isa 6:13) becomes in this way "mixed up." The statement may be compared to Exod 19:6, in which the holiness that defines priests is applied to the whole nation; yet here the stress is not on the closeness of priests to the deity but rather the distance that holy priests must maintain from the profane. Fourth, the leaders are identified as especially culpable.

In his mourning behavior, Ezra manifests in his own body what is happening to the communal body. By rending his clothes and pulling out his hair, he performs his message. In the end, however, his dismay is beyond words and actions, and thus he sits the entire day in silence (cf. Job 2:12–13). The silence adds gravity to the moment he speaks, so that his words provoke collective action. But he does not address the community directly; rather he turns to his God in prayer. The contrast to Nehemiah's approach is pronounced (Neh 13:25–27).

Ezra's prayer is not concerned with purity of race but rather with issues that govern the book's account of post-exilic history: separation, solidarity, and survival. Without ethnic, social, and religious boundaries, the community by definition does not exist. But making a bold reductionist move, Ezra's prayer reveals the deeper theological principle underlying this sociological truism: The community is on the brink of destruction because it has failed to appreciate the divine favor (9:7–9) and mercy (9:13) manifested in recent history in that it has disregarded the commandments communicated through the prophets (9:10–12). The potential result is that they would be punished to the point that now not even a remnant would escape (9:14–15). Intermarriage does not threaten Judean cultural-ethnic superiority but rather its very attempt to survive in a situation of foreign "bondage" (9:8–9). In the words of the poet Rainer Maria Rilke, "Who is talking about great triumph? It is all about simply survival!"

10:1–44. A Report about Ezra's Actions. After his prayer, Ezra's first-person account stops and a third-person narrative begins. This switch reflects how Ezra simply catalyzes a movement that is really propelled by others: The shift from first- to third-person account corresponds to the shift from Ezra to community.

Chapter 10, like the preceding accounts, focuses on the *approach* to the problem. Ezra's prayer elicits a collective response (10:1). One leader, Shecaniah ben Jehiel, proposes to make a communal pact to "put away" all the wives and their children. This proposal, which is disturbing for modern readers and was probably for many ancient ones as well, is then adopted by Ezra (10:2–4).

Significantly, the narrative never reports the execution of the proposal. Instead one reads at length about an assembly in Jerusalem (10:6–16). Everyone (man) who did not appear is subject to loss of property and membership in the "exilic congregation" (10:8). Here one encounters a sectarian or communal polity that differs starkly from the authority over territory and body granted by Artaxerxes in ch. 7. Accordingly, Ezra does not call for the expulsion of women and children from Judah in 10:11 but rather a "separation" from the congregation (cf. 10:8). Elsewhere the word for "separation" bears predominantly a ritual association or refers to formal status (see esp. 8:24–29). The particulars of this legal ritual are not spelled

out (10:14). Yet it is unlikely, contrary to the insistence of many commentators, that 10:6–44 (in contrast to 10:2–5) refers to a mass divorce and banishment of women and children. Only the priests, in keeping with ancient law, are said to have pledged to divorce their wives (10:18–19).

The interpretation adopted here explains why the account seems to taper off without a conclusion (KJV/JPS 10:44; the RSV/NRSV translates a later Greek version). It concludes in this manner because it does not have the actual expulsion of women and children in view. Rather the author points the finger at the numerous *men* (10:20–43) who were culpable yet had been faithful to appear before the council in order to undergo the "separation," whatever it entailed.

Although the immediate narrative concludes here, the story of rebuilding identity told by this book continues in Neh 1.

BIBLIOGRAPHY

J. Blenkinsopp. *Ezra–Nehemiah: A Commentary.* OTL (Philadelphia: Westminster John Knox, 1988); M. J. Boda and P. L. Redditt, eds. *Unity and Disunity in Ezra–Nehemiah: Redaction, Rhetoric and Reader.* Hebrew Bible Monographs 17 (Sheffield: Sheffield Phoenix, 2008); D. J. A. Clines. *Ezra, Nehemiah, Esther.* NCB (Grand Rapids: Eerdmans, 1984); T. C. Eskenazi. *In an Age of Prose: A Literary Approach to Ezra–Nehemiah.* SBLMS 36 (Atlanta: Scholars Press, 1988); R. W. Klein. "Ezra, Nehemiah." *NIB* (Nashville: Abingdon, 1999) 3:661–851; Y. Rabinowitz. *The Book of Ezra: A New Translation with a Commentary Anthologized from Talmudic, Midrashic and Rabbinic Sources.* ArtScroll Tanach Series (Brooklyn: Mesorah, 1984); H. G. M. Williamson. *Ezra, Nehemiah.* WBC 14 (Waco: Word, 1985); J. L. Wright. *Rebuilding Identity: The Nehemiah-Memoir and Its Earliest Readers.* BZAW 348 (Berlin: De Gruyter, 2004).

NEHEMIAH

JACOB WRIGHT

OVERVIEW

Nehemiah comprises together with Ezra one book, and an overview of this work is provided in the preceding chapter. The problems posed specifically by Neh 1–13 will be treated in the course of the commentary. One issue, however, must be addressed at the outset: the relationship between the narrative in Neh 8–10 and the rest of the book.

Nehemiah 8–10 stand out within Neh 1–13 for a number of reasons. Rather than being narrated by Nehemiah, these chapters are formulated about him. Moreover, not only does Neh 8 focus on the figure of Ezra, but also much of the narrative in this chapter represents the continuation of Ezra 10 in the Greek version of 1 Esdras. These and other observations have led many scholars to conclude that Neh 8 was originally formulated as part of the Ezra account. According to this position, the chapter was formerly positioned, along with portions of Neh 9, either between Ezra 8 and 9 or after Ezra 10. The communal pact in ch. 10 is said to represent an independent document found in the Temple archives and included by the editor of the book.

While this position deserves consideration, it creates more problems than it solves. The mention of Nehemiah in 8:9 would have to be attributed to a gloss in order to attribute the narrative to the Ezra account. Furthermore, the mention of Ezra at key points elsewhere in Neh 1–13 suggests that the original formulation of Neh 8 could have also presented these two figures cooperating. That 1 Esdras removes the reference to Nehemiah from Neh 8 is not surprising: This late book is characterized by an almost complete erasure of Nehemiah's memory from this history (presumably because his account criticizes the high-priestly line). Based on undeniable lexical and stylistic parallels between Neh 7–8 and Ezra 2–3, it is much more likely that Neh 8–10 was composed from the beginning for its present literary setting.

OUTLINE

I. First Movement: Rebuilding Altar and Temple (Ezra 1–6)

II. Second Movement: Ezra, the Temple, and Community (Ezra 7–10)

III. Third Movement: Nehemiah, the Wall, and Community (Neh 1:1–13:31)

A. Rebuilding the Wall (1:1–6:19)
1:1–11a. First Pivotal Conversation
1:11b–2:9. Second Pivotal Conversation
2:10–20. Initiation of the Project
3:1–32. An Account of Building the Wall
4:1–23 (Heb 3:33–4:17).
  Animosity Intensifies
5:1–13. The Fraternity of the Judeans
  and Socio-Economic Reforms
5:14–19. Nehemiah's Munificence
6:1–14. Attempts to Assassinate
  Nehemiah or His Character
6:15–19. The Climactic Statement
  of Completion

B. Repopulation and Dedication of Jerusalem (7:1–13:3)
7:1–73 (Heb 72). Fortifying and
  Repopulating Jerusalem
8:1–12. Reading Torah
8:13–18. Celebrating
9:1–37 (Heb 38). Confessing
  and Petitioning
9:38–10:39 (Heb 10:1–40).
  Covenanting Together
11:1–12:26. The Commemoration
  of Leaders
12:27–13:3. The Day of Dedication

C. Enforcing the Communal Pledge (13:4–31)

DETAILED ANALYSIS

III. Third Movement: Nehemiah, the Wall, and Community (Neh 1:1–13:31)

Within the third movement of the book, one can likewise distinguish three sections: The first allows Nehemiah to recount the building of the Wall (1:1–6:19), the second section is told—with few exceptions—in the third-person and involves

---

271

important events leading up to the dedication of the Wall (7:1–13:3), and in the third small section Nehemiah resumes the narration to complete the book (13:4–31).

A. Rebuilding the Wall (1:1–6:19)

These first six chapters consist almost exclusively of first-person passages ascribed to the Nehemiah Memoir (see however 3:1–32). As such, the section has its own distinctive character: it depicts the construction of the Wall in various building stages, beginning with the prehistory of the project (chs. 1–2). Each stage is demarcated by a response from Judah's enemies when they "hear" of the progress: 1:1–2:10; 2:11–20; 3:1–4:5; 4:6–15; 4:16–23; 6:1–19 (the account of the reforms in ch. 5 interrupts this schema). Moreover, each stage corresponds to a specific problem facing the community and progress in the project of rebuilding identity.

1:1–11a. First Pivotal Conversation. The narrative begins with a conversation through which Nehemiah learns about the problem he will later address. The condition of Jerusalem's wall and gates, although representing the focus of Nehemiah's project, is identified by Hanani and the Judeans as a part of a larger *social* problem facing the entire province of Judah: great trouble and shame. Throughout Nehemiah's memoir, these terms bridge the building report (e.g. 3:33–35/4:1–3) and the accounts of social reforms (e.g. 5:9; 6:13; 13:7, 17, 27).

The passage refers to the Judeans who escaped the deportations and *remained* in Judah, but surprisingly ignores the numbers of those who, according to Ezra 1–10, had recently *returned* from exile. Only a late addition to the first-person Nehemiah account (7:4–73) is cognizant of the Babylonian/exilic origins of the Judeans. This reveals the historical problems posed by the references to massive returns.

Nehemiah's reaction to the news—mourning, fasting, and praying (1:4)—may be understood as "performed theology." It affirms that the solution to Judah's distress ultimately lies with divine hands rather than in Nehemiah's clever tactics and leadership, which are depicted throughout the memoir. The prayer itself (1:5–11a) pauses narrative time and allows the protagonist to reveal his theological motivations. It is framed by petitions that past prayers be heard (1:6, 11). Situated between these petitions are (1) an affirmation that sin had caused the present calamities, (2) a reference to a divine promise, and (3) a reminder of the community's special identity.

Most of this passage (1:1b–11a) is not presupposed in the following scene. The expansion of Nehemiah's building report with accounts of reforms (esp. chs. 5 and 13) would have necessitated a new introduction, which 1:2–4 provides. Likewise, the insertion of the narratives in chs. 8–10, which emphasize Torah-piety, seems to correspond to the insertion of the prayer in 1:5–11a (see esp. 1:7).

1:11b–2:9. Second Pivotal Conversation. This paragraph describes a (second) pivotal conversation, now between Nehemiah and Artaxerxes. It takes place in the first month, perhaps during a New Year's celebration. As the royal cupbearer, Nehemiah is serving wine to the king. Because Nehemiah enjoyed the king's favor, he is granted a request. Yet by telling his readers that he prayed right before responding (2:4), Nehemiah ascribes ultimate responsibility for the positive outcome to divine providence (see 1:4–11).

Nehemiah is granted only a leave of absence; he is not appointed governor, which seems to contradict 5:14. He must also ask for letters granting him safe passage and providing him lumber for the project. In contrast, Artaxerxes grants Ezra generous gifts and makes the royal treasuries available to him. Still, Artaxerxes provides Nehemiah with a retinue of soldiers and cavalry, which Ezra does not receive (see Ezra 8:22 and comments there). The disparities between Ezra's and Nehemiah's account may be related to tensions between Nehemiah and the Temple circles, which seem to have had a hand in the composition of Ezra 7–8.

2:10–20. Initiation of the Project. Opposition to Nehemiah is presented already in 2:10. Similar notices, which begin with "as _____ heard," punctuate the building narrative and create discrete building phases (2:19–20; 4:1–5; 4:7–9; 6:1–14); they conclude in 6:16 after the statement of completion. The three figures that are the subject of these notices are Sanballat, Tobiah, and Geshem/Gashmu. Sanballat was probably the governor in Samaria; he is attested in extra-biblical sources. Tobiah likely oversaw the administration in the

Transjordanian/Ammonite region. There is also independent evidence for Geshem as a sheikh in the southern Arabian/Edomite region.

The first notice (2:10) presents Nehemiah's agenda in broad terms, i.e., to seek the welfare of the people. It is also more radical than the subsequent notices inasmuch as it identifies Sanballat and Tobiah as opposed to "the people of Israel." Both figures would have most probably worshiped Yahweh and have identified themselves as belonging to "the people of Israel." In comparison, the second notice (2:19–20) is much tamer: All three now accuse the Judeans of rebuilding the Wall in order to rebel against the empire.

In between these two notices is an account of Nehemiah's arrival in Jerusalem, his night ride during which he inspects the ruins, and his address to the community leaders that convinces them to embrace his building program (2:11–18). As elsewhere, the narrative attributes success at critical junctures to Nehemiah's savvy approach. Here the account emphasizes his decision to wait to reveal his plan (2:12, 16) and the way he goes about presenting it (2:17–18).

3:1–32. An Account of Building the Wall. This passage poses a problem: It not only recounts the completion of the work but it also lacks references to interruptions or opposition that characterize Nehemiah's account elsewhere. Due to similarities in expression between 3:1 and 2:18 (and 2:20), the passage was likely created for its present context rather than originating as an independent archival document. It was probably inserted at a relatively early point in the composition of the memoir and, if so, testifies to the originally brief and un-polemical nature of the building report.

The passage both describes the topography of the Wall and memorializes the donors—all the guilds, groups, and regions that contributed to the project. They are "the servants of the God of heaven" who "have share, claim and right in Jerusalem" (2:20). The Wall is formed literally by the names of the builders, who work collectively and in collaboration.

The passage mentions no fewer than 10 gates. This unusually large number, rendering it vulnerable to penetration, corresponds to the way the construction of the Wall symbolizes the demarcation of Judahite identity: Although a barrier to the outside, the Wall does not hermetically seal off Jerusalem but rather offers many points of access.

4:1–23 (Heb 3:33–4:17). Animosity Intensifies. The present arrangement of the building account alternates between passages reporting progress on the Wall and passages reporting attempts to thwart this progress. This back-and-forth is especially apparent in the present section. In the first paragraph (3:33–37/4:1–5), Sanballat and Tobiah taunt the Judeans, and Nehemiah responds with an imprecation.

Sanballat's insult expresses one of the main messages of the account itself: the correspondence between the restoration of the ruins and the revivification of the community. Similarly the joining of the Wall (3:38/4:6) corresponds to the enemies joining together in a military coalition (4:2/4: 8).

The account highlights, and depicts at length, the leadership skills Nehemiah displays during this crisis. He mobilizes the builders in preparation for the impending attack by arranging them into armed militia companies and rallying them with stirring speeches (4:8, 13–14/4:14, 19–20). These speeches resemble the great addresses delivered at the time of the first Conquest (e.g., Josh 10:25).

The present section contains the image that is most widely associated with Nehemiah: working with one hand and wielding a weapon with the other. Building becomes a means of fighting. This image also marks the great conceptual disparity with the preceding narrative in Ezra 1–10: The Judeans do not wait patiently for the empire to protect their interests, nor are they focused on the Temple as the conduit of imperial benefaction. Rather, they create a larger space (symbolized by the Wall) in which they can flourish; and they are prepared to fight their neighbors who attempt violently to disrupt this project.

5:1–13. The Fraternity of the Judeans and Socio-Economic Reforms. This passage evinces many parallels with the three reform accounts in ch. 13: Nehemiah witnesses an abuse, indicts the offenders, takes various corrective measures, and then utters a concluding prayer of remembrance (see 5:19).

The first paragraph (5:1–5) delineates the formal complaints of "the people and their wives against their Judean kin" (5:1). At issue is a situation of increasing economic disparities: some families are becoming wealthier at the expense of others, who are losing possession of both property and children. The female children in particular are being abused. Due to these financial injustices and loss of familial property rights, the fabric of the Judean community is being torn apart. If the problem is not addressed, the Wall—both in the physical and larger social sense—would not be built. The solution is a complete restoration of all property and interest (5:11–12), a major imposition on any economy.

As an ideal leader, Nehemiah hears this complaint and responds effectively (5:6–13). He calls for the wealthy to "walk in the fear of God" (=ethically) in order to prevent the "reproach" of the surrounding nations. Earlier, he refers to this "reproach" in order to convince the Judeans to rebuild the Wall (2:17); hence the reform and the building project address a common problem.

Yet Nehemiah is not satisfied with mere preaching and promises. Rather he institutionalizes the change through legal actions, which include a formal oath and a curse; readers are told that such measures proved to be effective (5:13b).

5:14–19. Nehemiah's Munificence.
This paragraph, which continues the theme of 5:1–13, describes Nehemiah fiscal policies as governor. This is the first time he is described this way. It is quite possible that later authors identified him as a governor in order to present a model of behavior for—or polemics against—later governors.

Nehemiah claims that, because of his fear of God (5:15), he did not place any extra burdens on the people in order to pay his own salary. In addition he displays generosity by hosting many guests each day at his table. Such commensality would have helped consolidate political and social bonds.

Uniting this paragraph with the preceding one is a petition that his God not "forget" (or "erase," 13:14) everything he had done for "this people" (5:19). This prayer presumes that the deity keeps a written record of human deeds. Because the prayer is addressed directly to God (as in 3:36–37/4:4–5; 6:14; 13:14, 22, 29, 31 and in contrast to 1:5–11 and 2:4), the memoir (or a version of it) may be meant primarily for a divine readership and only secondarily for a human audience.

6:1–14. Attempts to Assassinate Nehemiah or His Character.
After the interlude in ch. 5, the theme of building and opposition from chs. 2–4 resumes. The first three episodes (6:2–4, 5–9, 10–14) of this section are dated to the final phase of the project (6:1). They all concern the person and work of Nehemiah, mirroring an emphasis of 5:14–19. The texts allow one of Judah's "founding fathers" to address important questions facing later generations of readers. Thus, the first paragraph (6:2–4) presents Nehemiah focusing on the "great work" and refusing to be distracted (see 5:16). The second paragraph (6:5–9) allows Nehemiah to affirm that his intention in building was not to establish a monarchy or rebel against the empire. The author alludes here to the corruptibility of prophets—and the danger it poses for Judean rulers (6:7); this point becomes central to the message of the following paragraph (6:10–14).

6:15–19. The Climactic Statement of Completion.
Now, finally, the Wall was finished—in just 52 days (6:15). Responsibility for such quick work is attributed to divine assistance (6:16; see Ps 118:23). Here also one reads for the last time that the enemies "heard" the news, yet now they must admit their defeat (6:16). What necessitated the project ("disgrace and reproach," see 1:3 and 2:17) has now finally been alleviated.

The twenty-fifth of Elul marks a great reversal of fortune, for not only had the ramparts been restored but the community had also undergone a major social and spiritual transformation. To underscore this point, all the reforms are dated to the period of construction. This is not only the case for ch. 5 but also for the reforms reported in ch. 13. Nehemiah 13:15–22 and 13:23–30 begin with expression "in those days," which also introduces 6:17–19, and the "days" in 6:17 clearly refers to the 52 days in 6:15. Moreover, 6:17–19 most likely originally continued, before the insertion of the largely third-person narrative material in 7:1–13:3, in the account of 13:4–9(10–14). Tobiah had to send letters to his Judean alliance partners (6:17–19) because when Nehemiah came to town, he removed Tobiah from his apartment in Jerusalem (13:4–9; on the date in 13:6, see ad loc.). Accordingly, the reforms recounted in ch. 13 are presented as taking place during the construction, so that the twenty-fifth of Elul becomes truly climactic. Support for this reading is provided by structural observations: Five consecutive accounts beginning in ch. 5 conclude with prayers for remembrance (5:1–19; 6:1–14; 6:17–19 + 13:4–14; 13:15–22; 13:23–31), and the final three of these accounts begin with the phrase "in those days," referring to the 52 days in 6:15–16.

B. Repopulation and Dedication of Jerusalem (7:1–13:3)

Whereas 13:4–31 seems to have been originally connected to 6:17–19, a large block of material in 7:1–13:4 now severs the earlier narrative. This block appears to have gradually grown to its present proportions. The first insertions are probably the texts relating to the fortification and repopulation of Jerusalem in chs. 7 and 11 as well as the account of the dedication ceremonies in 12:27–43. By citing the list of Ezra 2, the author of Neh 7 provoked the composition of Neh 8–10 (cf. Ezra 2–3); these important chapters expand on the theme of the internal reforms in Neh 5 and 13. Nehemiah 8–10 were composed with the climatic celebration at the dedication of the Wall in view. The reader should understand that the people studied Torah, confessed their sins, and made a pact before celebrating that momentous day.

7:1–73 (Heb 72). Fortifying and Repopulating Jerusalem. After finishing the building project, the people appoint gatekeepers, a commander of the city, as well as a militia to protect the city and their homes. Jerusalem is now fortified and rests fully within Judean hands. The martial elements of the account, which are introduced in ch. 4, continue in ch. 11. That singers and Levites also are appointed (7:1) has to do with the fact that the gates, as thresholds, are also religiously precarious places (see 3:1 and 12:27–43).

In the process of fortifying Jerusalem, Nehemiah repopulates the city (7:5–72/73). This theme too continues in ch. 11. God is said to "place this idea in [his] heart" (7:5). This expression, which is used first in 2:12 with reference to the building project, appears here to introduce a new project, one that relates specifically to the people.

Significantly the method Nehemiah employs for repopulating the city is "seeking-and-finding" (see commentary on Ezra 4–7). The text he "finds" is "the book of the genealogy of those who were the first to come back" (7:5). This may be the author's description of Ezra 1–6, since the passage he "finds" in it, and then quotes at length (7:6–72(73)), parallels closely Ezra 2. This discovery results in a new understanding of the Judeans' identity, since up until now Nehemiah had never acknowledged any collective return from Babylon (see esp. 1:2–3).

This harmonization of Nehemiah's account with the historical conceptions in Ezra 1–10 has likely been provoked by the mention of mixed marriages and alliances in 6:17–19. The need for internal social-religious reforms is answered with the composition of Neh 8–10.

As to why the author listed all the names again (after Ezra 2), one should note that the numbers in ch. 11 are precisely 10 percent of those in ch. 7, corresponding to the "tithe" in 11:1. From the perspective of ch. 8, the repetition of Ezra 2 also grants names and identity to the otherwise anonymous mass of people in ch. 8.

Finally we may appreciate an element of "realized eschatology" here: Only those whose names were "found written" in this book are permitted to inhabit the new(ly built) Jerusalem.

8:1–12. Reading Torah. This passage takes its point of departure from the repetition of Ezra 2 in Neh 7. In contrast to the account of the rebuilding of the altar and the numerous sacrifices in Ezra 3, this description of the seventh month (the central month in the cultic calendar) noticeably lacks any reference to the Temple or the High Priest Eliashib.

Herewith the narrative shifts the perspective from the center (priests sacrificing on the altar) to the periphery (the people beckoning Ezra to read the Torah to them). In the course of the month, the leaders (8:13) and then people (9:1) learn to read for themselves. In keeping with his portrayal in Ezra 9–10, Ezra responds to communal petition and only then becomes a catalyst for collective action. When he ascends the platform to read, he takes with him a group of leaders, symbolically demonstrating that he cannot lead alone. Later the Levites are involved in interpreting the text to the congregation (8:8).

The activities are performed ceremoniously in keeping with the reverence for the Torah; many of these features anticipate later rituals of reading in the synagogue. Yet the account also underscores general comprehension (8:8–12). Earlier we are told that not only men but also women and "all who could understand" were present. After the loss of territorial statehood and living in the context of imperial rule, broad participation and education have become critical to the formation and survival of the community. In keeping with the festive nature of the day (later known as Rosh Hashanah), the people celebrate with feasting, drinking and merrymaking—"because they had understood the words that words that were declared to them" (8:12).

8:13–18. Celebrating.

The second part of ch. 8 is about not just the celebration of the Feast of Booths (Sukkoth) but also an ideal form of communal action. The lay leaders, priests, and Levites gather around "the scribe Ezra in order to study the words of the Torah." Through their seeking in the scriptures, they "find" (see on "seeking-and-finding" in Ezra 4–7 and Neh 7) a particular commandment. However, what is said to be written is not found word-for-word in the Pentateuch. Rather it represents a product of constructive exegesis called "midrash" (derived from the word "to seek"). By means of this sophisticated technique of interpretation, ancient law and the sacred writings as a whole are applied to new circumstances.

The innovative way the festival is celebrated—by making booths throughout Jerusalem and dwelling in them—corresponds to the building theme in the surrounding narrative, but it also expresses a theological message: the festival celebrates divine providence and commemorates a time when Israel did not yet possess its land (see Lev 23:42–43). The reference to "the days of Jeshua son of Nun" is probably to be explained by the fact that this epoch marks the zenith in the biblical memory—when Israel successfully occupied the land and followed their leader Joshua in observing Torah. Not surprisingly the narrator notes that "he" or "they" read Torah each day of the weeklong festival.

9:1–37 (Heb 38). Confessing and Petitioning.

After celebrating throughout the month, the people reassemble in Jerusalem, now in a much more somber mood: fasting and wearing sackcloth with dust on their heads. They first ritually separate themselves from foreigners (see comments on Ezra 10), and thereafter engage in confession and Torah reading—now significantly on their own and without the help of Ezra.

The brief narrative is followed by a lengthy prayer uttered by a group of Levites. The complex text deserves attention not least because of its distinctive reading of biblical history. The paramount concern of the prayer is the land. After praising the deity's creative and sustaining acts, it begins with the election of Abraham and the fulfilled promise to give his descendants a land possessed by other peoples (9:8). The prayer alternates between enumerations of divine benevolent acts (9:9–15 and 19–25) and descriptions of Israel's stubbornness and disobedience (9:16–18 and 26–31) that result in the loss of sovereignty. The cyclical judgment-restoration schema that characterizes "the period of Judges" has been applied to all of Israel's subsequent history, so that the catastrophe of 586 BCE is no longer central (9:26–31). In fact, the construction and destruction of the Temple are passed over in silence, in keeping with distinctive emphases of the preceding chapter and of Nehemiah's account.

The final section (9:32–37/38) consists of a petition that the deity once again regard the people's plight. In what way God should respond is not spelled out. Nevertheless, the problem is clearly stated: "We are slaves in our own land." As recompense for past sins, foreign kings possess "power over our bodies and livestock." This note of protest stands out in the context of the book, which presents foreign rule otherwise in ultimately favorable terms. While the yearning for Judean territorial sovereignty also deviates from many passages in the book, it dovetails with the emphases in Nehemiah's account.

9:38–10:39 (Heb 10:1–40). Covenanting Together.

Proceeding from the close interdependence between Torah-obedience and land-tenure affirmed by the prayer, the community responds to "all this" (the "great distress" in 9:37) with a communal pact. The word here for "pact" is constructed from the same root as that for Abraham's "faithful" heart. God rewarded it with a covenant that was likewise upheld (9:8). Mirroring the importance assigned to texts in the book, the pact is explicitly said to have been put in writing and sealed with names of communal leaders (Nehemiah sets the example; 10:1/2). The list of names is followed by a general declaration of intent: "to walk in the Torah of God" (10:28–29/29–30). What such obedience entails is spelled out in the subsequent stipulations.

Most of these stipulations relate specifically to contributions for the Temple and cultic officers (10:32–39/33–40). Yet the wording of the final line as well as the first two stipulations (10:30–31/32–33) are drawn from Nehemiah's indictments in ch.13. This citation necessarily affects the reading of the final chapter of Nehemiah's account: Instead of introducing new reforms, Nehemiah must now be understood to be enforcing prior communal resolutions. Yet the authors' aim was likely not to diminish the importance of Nehemiah's actions. The intention is probably rather to demonstrate the importance of a strong leader: The community ultimately fails in its commitment to uphold the pact. Hence they require someone like Nehemiah who, through his preaching, identifies abuses, reaffirms the community's earlier pledge, and institutes proactive measures that ensure its fulfillment. A similar compositional history and reading strategy inform the relationship of pentateuchal law to the preaching of the prophets.

11:1–12:26. The Commemoration of Leaders.

The narrative continues here with a brief note regarding the repopulation of Jerusalem, followed by several lists. Thematically the account resumes the thread in ch. 7 regarding both Jerusalem's repopulation and fortification (see the references to warriors in 11:6, 14). The difference is that in ch. 7 Nehemiah is the subject of the action; here the people act on their own, in keeping with the transition depicted in chs. 8–10.

One may wonder why the closely related chs. 7 and 11 are so widely separated. In addition to the initial compositional move to create a parallel to Ezra 2–3, the larger motivation was likely to show that the community first undergoes a deep spiritual transformation (recounted in chs. 8–10) before it finally inhabits Jerusalem, "the holy city" (11:1).

The method employed to select the city's new residents is casting lots. One tenth of Judah's population must relocate to Jerusalem. But they are said to "volunteer" for this move and thus receive a blessing from their neighbors.

The following list shares much with 1 Chr 9 and may be based on an independent source. The whole chapter, and especially 11:25–36, constructs an ideal map of greater Judah (and Benjamin). It draws on conceptions and antiquated names from the book of Joshua, and it includes places that were not integrated into Judah until the Maccabees (who may have viewed Nehemiah as a great hero). At the center of the province is Jerusalem (containing 1/10 of the population), and this center is circumscribed by towns with their dependent villages.

These lists of cultic officers who resided in Jerusalem provoked the addition of other registers of cultic officials. One can still detect some of the ancient priestly disputes under the surface of this material.

12:27–13:3. The Day of Dedication.

Now finally we are told about "the dedication of the wall of Jerusalem" (12:27). This account is predominantly a third-person report, but in 12:31–43 Nehemiah's voice makes itself heard again after a long pause. Originally a brief account of how he organized celebrations must have stood close to the notice of completion in 6:15–16. This account is still preserved in our text. In it Nehemiah tells how he choreographs two large thanksgiving companies from among the princes of Judah. Separately they circumambulate the Wall, singing in stereo, and in the end they come together for sacrifices and celebrations at the Temple. The depiction of a closing circle or two halves joining together, which can be found elsewhere (see esp. chs. 3–4), expresses symbolically one of the central messages of the Nehemiah Memoir: the social and spiritual unification of Judah through the Wall-building project. The text deserves to be appreciated for its deliberate liturgical or performed theology.

As the book developed, the account was both amplified internally and successively distanced from 6:15–16. Now the Judean princes are joined by Ezra the scribe, priests, Levites, and cultic musicians (12:27–30, 33–36, 41–42). The celebration is also called a "dedication," and the people, gates, and Wall are purified (see already 3:1). In addition to these cultic officials, others are appointed (12:44–47). The expression "on that day" (12:43, 44, 47, and 13:1) has eschatological significance in prophetic books and refers to a coming age. Here, however, it refers to a historical moment as a kind of "realized eschatology." Jerusalem has been rebuilt and the people dwell in peace. The messianic hope associated with David is fulfilled here above all in the Temple and cult (12:46).

That these dedication ceremonies are so far removed from their original proximity to 6:15–16 has to do with same redactional dynamic informing the separation of chs. 7 and 11. Before the people can celebrate and properly dedicate the Wall, they must first experience the events recorded in 6:17–12:26. What they then celebrate is not just the building of the Wall but other major achievements (e.g., social reforms, a communal pact).

13:1–3 reports further that "on that day" the people engaged in scriptural seeking-and-finding, and what they "found" relates to the expulsion of Ammonites and Moabites. The paragraph bridges the narrative to the following section, which relates to various measures to demarcate boundaries to non-Judeans (13:4–9, 16, 20–21, 23–30). This preface identifies Nehemiah's practical-political measures as in keeping with a prior communal resolution and as based on scriptural precedent.

C. Enforcing the Communal Pledge (13:4–31)

The book concludes in this last section by giving Nehemiah the final word. This section includes three discrete paragraphs, each of which resembles ch. 5 both in structure and in style: first he observes a problem, then he indicts the offenders and takes various corrective measures, and finally utters a prayer that his God will remember his good deeds.

Originally these accounts told what Nehemiah undertook soon after arriving for the first time in Jerusalem (13:6a–7); they were formerly linked directly to 6:17–19: Because Nehemiah had "before this" (13:4) removed Tobiah from Jerusalem, Tobiah's alliance partners in Judah were forced to write letters in order to maintain relations with him (6:17–19). As seen in the commentary on 7:1–13:3, these passages have gradually grown apart due to the insertion of new material.

Nehemiah 13:6b dates the events to a time twelve years after the twentieth year of Artaxerxes (the year to which everything narrated in ch. 1:1–13:3 is dated). The date in this half-verse however was most likely secondarily interpolated and drawn from 5:14. Such editorial activity would have been elicited by the composition of the communal pact in ch. 10. The inserted date in 13:6b allows Nehemiah to leave the province and then return a long time thereafter, only to witness that the community had failed to follow through with

its pledge (ch. 10). The addition of 13:6b thus adds a new dimension to these texts: What were originally descriptions of how Nehemiah introduced new reforms become now accounts of how he reminds the community of the pact and enforces it.

All three units in ch. 13 include secondary yet thematically related material. Thus 13:10–14 treats the larger theme of the Temple as in 13:4–9. Here Levites had not received their "portions" (i.e., livelihood) and therefore had "fled" to their properties elsewhere (13:10). Nehemiah gathers them back to Jerusalem and institutes measures to correct the problem. The second account relates primarily to native Judeans engaging work on the Sabbath (13:15–22). But it also includes a superimposed layer that treats the problem posed by foreign traders (13:16, 20–21).

The problem posed by "others" in Judah is presented also in 13:4–9 and especially in 13:23–31. There readers are told about Nehemiah's response to intermarriages in Judah. With respect to a culpable son of the high priest, Nehemiah "made him flee" (13:28; note the contrast to the Levites who "fled" in 13:10). As for non-priestly Judeans, however, he does not expel them nor does he manifest his anger against their foreign wives.

Undeniably, his direct approach to the mixed-marriage problem contrasts starkly with that of Ezra. Moreover, he is also disturbed by a different aspect of the issue: The children could not speak "Judean"—that is, the intermarriages posed a serious threat to the survival of Judean language, culture, and traditions. Yet despite the differences from the Ezra account, one must appreciate the editors' choice to allow this passage to serve as the book's conclusion. The problem that Ezra witnesses and introduces to the narrative of the book (i.e., mixed marriages and the paradigmatic issue they pose for the project of rebuilding identity) is answered in Neh 1–13 with its complex depiction of the community constructing for themselves a physical and spiritual Wall. This Wall both unites the people in an unbroken circle (see esp. Neh 3) and serves as a barrier to deleterious practices and influences.

BIBLIOGRAPHY

J. Blenkinsopp. *Ezra–Nehemiah: A Commentary.* OTL (Philadelphia: Westminster John Knox, 1988); M. J. Boda and P. L. Redditt, eds. *Unity and Disunity in Ezra–Nehemiah: Redaction, Rhetoric and Reader.* Hebrew Bible Monographs 17 (Sheffield: Sheffield Phoenix, 2008); D. J. A. Clines. *Ezra, Nehemiah, Esther.* NCB (Grand Rapids: Eerdmans, 1984); T. C. Eskenazi. *In an Age of Prose: A Literary Approach to Ezra–Nehemiah.* SBLMS 36 (Atlanta: Scholars Press, 1988); R. W. Klein. "Ezra, Nehemiah." *NIB* (Nashville: Abingdon, 1999) 3:661–851; Y. Rabinowitz. *The Book of Ezra: A New Translation with a Commentary Anthologized from Talmudic, Midrashic and Rabbinic Sources.* ArtScroll Tanach Series (Brooklyn: Mesorah, 1984); H. G. M. Williamson. *Ezra, Nehemiah.* WBC 16 (Waco: Word, 1985); J. L. Wright. *Rebuilding Identity: The Nehemiah-Memoir and Its Earliest Readers.* BZAW 348 (Berlin: De Gruyter, 2004).

ESTHER
Nancy Bowen

OVERVIEW

Esther is one of the five festival scrolls in the Writings of the Jewish Bible. The story is an etiology of the Purim Festival, which is not legislated in the Torah. Its location in Christian Bibles, after Ezra and Nehemiah, reflects its historical setting of the Diaspora. Thus, this story addresses issues related to Israel's life in exile as a minority among a potentially hostile majority. Since some of the story's features correspond to what is known from Persian sources, it may have been composed in Persia. However, discrepancies suggest Persia was a convenient background for raising issues involving life in the Diaspora.

Esther presents a two-fold threat of annihilation: destruction of Jewish identity by assimilation to Persian culture and complete elimination of the Jews by Haman's genocidal plot. The plot revolves around these threats and suggests how Jews might respond whenever they arise. The story illustrates that salvation from these threats requires solidarity, courage, cleverness, and chance. Combining these elements yields surprising reversals—the powerful lose their power and the powerless gain it. The book's genre is that of a novella or short story. The use of literary (narrative) exegetical methodologies dominates contemporary Esther studies. These show that exaggeration plays a major role throughout the story. Descriptions of lavish banquets, extensive beauty treatments, and a gallows' height, as well as how individuals overreact to relatively unimportant slights, are examples of how exaggeration leads to irony.

Esther is similar to the stories of Joseph (Gen 37, 39–50) and Daniel (Dan 1–6), as all three recount how a follower of Yahweh achieves great status within a foreign court despite great danger. Esther is also similar to the stories Judith and Ruth, stories where the main characters are women whose actions save others. Esther differs from all of these stories in that there is no explicit mention of God or God's role. In the other stories, deliverance results from God's intervention in the situation. As this is a story of planned genocide, God's absence is noteworthy. In this story, the people are forced to rely on one another, rather than on God. Throughout Esther, hiding and revealing are important actions. Disclosure or non-disclosure of identity motives, piety, and ideology will decide events and their eventual outcome.

OUTLINE

I. Introductions (1:1–3:6)

    A. Introducing Ahasuerus (1:1–22)

    B. Introducing Mordecai and Esther (2:1–23)

    C. Introducing Haman (3:1–6)

II. The Plot Thickens (3:7–6:13)

    A. Haman's First Plot (3:7–19)

    B. Mordecai's and Esther's Counter Plot (4:1–17)

    C. Esther Acts: First Banquet (5:1–8)

    D. Haman's Second Plot (5:9–14)

    E. Haman Mortified (6:1–13)

III. Resolution (6:14–10:3)

    A. Esther Acts: Second Banquet (6:14–8:2)

    B. Undoing Haman's Plot (8:3–17)
        8: 3–8. Esther's Petition
        8:9–17. Mordecai's Decree

    C. Enemies Destroyed (9:1–19)

    D. Purim Established (9:20–10:3)

DETAILED ANALYSIS

I. Introductions (1:1–3:6)

A. Introducing Ahasuerus (1:1–22)

The name "Ahasuerus" may be a Hebrew rendering of the Persian word for "mighty man," a common epithet for Persian rulers. Ahasuerus was a generic ruler, like the unnamed Pharaoh in Exodus. Thus, the issues presented in Esther are not a matter of a particular king's policies, but arise whenever Jews are subject to foreign rule.

The word "banquet" (*mishteh*) is derived from the Hebrew verb "to drink," making them wine-drinking events, not eating events. These occur frequently throughout the story (1:3–9; 2:18; 5:4–8, 12, 14; 6:14; 7:2, 7–8; 8:17; 9:17–22). The opening scene alone consists of three banquets: the 180-day banquet for the officials (1:3–4), the subsequent 7-day banquet for all the people (1:5), and a concurrent women's banquet given by Queen Vashti (1:9).

Ahasuerus summons Vashti to his banquet, and she refuses him (1:11–12). Why she refused is a matter of speculation. Perhaps she did not wish to be displayed like a trophy before a room of drunken men. Some speculate she was to come naked, "wearing the royal crown," and nothing else. Whatever her reason, she is a subordinate resisting authority—one of the major themes of this story. Ahasuerus is "enraged" by this, but, unsure how to respond, he willingly accepts Memucan's advice (1:13, 21). Patriarchal and political control are reestablished by decree: all wives must obey their husbands and Vashti is banished (1:19–20). Vashti's downfall makes possible Esther's eventual elevation, but it also warns possible successors they will be expected to obey all the king's commands.

B. Introducing Mordecai and Esther (2:1–23)

This chapter establishes Ahasuerus' character. The lavish banquets indicate he is generous and benevolent. But benevolence hides a petty tyrant who drinks too much, is short tempered, and is easily influenced by others. Once Ahasuerus' anger abates, he realizes he has no queen (2:1). Again uncertain what do, his servants propose a solution he happily accepts—to hold a Miss Persia contest where the winner becomes queen (2:2–4).

Readers are now introduced to Mordecai, a "Jew" (2:5; 3:4; 5:13; 6:10; 8:7; 9:29, 31; 10:3). His lineage obliquely connects him to Saul (1 Sam 9:1, 21; 10:21 14:51; 2 Sam 16:5–14). The Hebrew text implies that Mordecai was among the first group of Jerusalemites deported by Nebuchadnezzar in 597 BCE (2:6; cf. 2 Kgs 24:10–12), making him more than 100 years old! Whether this is an editorial error or an instance of exaggeration, the narrative clearly identifies Mordecai as a foreigner in Persia.

Esther, who lives with and is cared for by Mordecai, is introduced with Hebrew (*Hadassah* means "myrtle," hinting at her sweetness) and Persian names (cf. Dan 1:6–7). Esther (*'ester*) can be considered a word play on the Hebrew verb "to hide" (*satar*), which would refer to Esther hiding her Jewish identity (2:10) and/or to God's hiddenness in the story.

Since Esther is "fair and beautiful," she is one of those selected to participate in the contest to become Ahasuerus' queen (2:7–8). Within the citadel she wins the "favor" of Hegai, the chief eunuch (2:9). "Favor" (*khesed*) might also be translated "loyalty" or "devotion" (e.g., Josh 2:12, 14; 1 Sam 2:5–6; Prov 19:22; Ruth 3:10). Hegai's loyalty to Esther translates into giving her special treatment, perhaps providing her an edge in the competition.

The twelve-month beauty treatment that follows is another example of exaggeration and Ahasuerus' generosity—no expense is spared (2:12–14). It also illustrates Esther's compliance with her indoctrination into the role of royal concubine. To the extent that assimilation poses a threat to Jewish existence, the community is in danger; Esther has succumbed. She neither engages in distinctive Jewish practices nor has physical characteristics that set her apart. Only self-disclosure would reveal her kindred (2:10). Unlike Daniel's resistance to the Babylonian assimilation (Dan 1:3–5, 8), Esther does not resist Persian assimilation. In the end, Esther wins Ahasuerus' "favor" (or "loyalty"; cf. 2:9). Furthermore, Ahasuerus "loved" Esther, a word elsewhere associated with covenantal loyalty (cf. Deut 6:5).

As Esther gains the king's loyalty, so does Mordecai. He sits "at the king's gate" where he overhears two royal eunuchs plotting against the king (2:21). Mordecai demonstrates his loyalty to the king by telling Esther the plot. She reports it to Ahasuerus, and he orders the eunuchs hanged. The event, and Mordecai's role in it, is recorded in the king's annals, which later becomes significant (6:1–11).

C. Introducing Haman (3:1–6)

Like Esther and Mordecai, Haman is a foreigner. He is a descendant of King Agag, whose destruction God commanded of Saul (1 Sam 15). Hence, before Mordecai and Haman even meet, one can anticipate their hostilities. Haman also achieves a rapid rise in the Persian court, and Ahasuerus issues a command that all his servants should "bow down and do obeisance" before Haman, which Mordecai refuses to do (3:1–2). Infuriated by Mordecai's noncompliance, Haman overreacts (3:5–6). Considering it "beneath him" to retaliate against Mordecai only, he plans to destroy all the Jews, which ironically mirrors God's plan for the total destruction of the Amalekites as a form of punishment (1 Sam 15:2-3; cf. Exod 17:8). Haman's character is thoroughly despicable—proud, self-centered, greedy, and vindictive.

II. The Plot Thickens (3:7–6:13)

A. Haman's First Plot (3:7–19)

Haman's threat to destroy the Jews creates the story's key conflict and drives the plot for the remainder of the story. To ensure success, Haman casts a lot to determine an auspicious day for battle (2:7; cf. Judg 20:28; 1 Sam 14:37; 23:4; 2 Sam 5:19; 1 Kgs 22:6). "Lot" (*pur*) is a Persian loan word associated with the festival's name, Purim (9:26). Haman's inquiry takes place "in the first month," when Passover is celebrated (Exod 12:1–2; Lev 23:5; Deut 16:1–8). Ironically, the month celebrating deliverance now foreshadows destruction. The lot selects the thirteenth day in the twelfth month, which gives everyone almost a year to plot further.

Haman needs Ahasuerus' consent to carry out his "final solution." Playing to Ahasuerus' fear of disobedience as a destabilizing force, Haman argues that the Jews are insubordinate, following their own laws and not the king's (3:8). Like most racist propaganda, there is no evidence to verify his claim. Haman also employs financial persuasion, depositing an excessive amount of money in the king's treasuries. Ahasuerus' reply, "The money is given to you" (3:11), might imply he refused the bribe. Mordecai's report to Esther of the sum (4:7) and Esther's claim that the Jews were "sold" (7:4) suggest the king accepted the money. Perhaps Ahasuerus permits Haman use of the money for implementing his plan.

A decree ordering wholesale annihilation of the Jews is sent to "every province in its own script and every people in its own language"

(3:12). Clearly, this was a multiethnic empire, suggesting that the existence of the Jews was not an inherent problem. The decree commands all "to destroy, to kill, to annihilate" the Jews (3:13; cf. 8:11). The language reveals Haman's excessive anger; it takes three verbs to eradicate the Jews. The Hebrew text does not provide a rationale for attacking the entire Jewish population, including women and children. Would other ethnic groups obey lest they are labeled insubordinate, or would they resist this unethical decree? As if anticipating resistance, the decree includes financial incentive—citizens will be allowed to plunder the goods of those they kill. Inside the citadel, Haman and Ahasuerus drink to their agreement. But outside the citadel, things are far from settled; there is chaos (3:15).

This episode reveals the dangers of vengeance, hate-filled speech, racial profiling, prejudice, and stereotyping. It serves as a warning of what happens when one group demonizes another. The episode ironically mirrors Israel's treatment of "others" among them (Deut 7:1–6, 22–26; 9:1–5; Josh 6:21; 11:16–20). Israel's history witnesses to their own acts of annihilating those who were different. If "genocide" is to disappear from contemporary vocabulary, the story encourages readers to challenge any similar act.

B. Mordecai's and Esther's Counter Plot (4:1–17)

When Mordecai hears of the decree, he performs actions of mourning seen elsewhere in the Bible (4:1; cf. 2 Sam 3:31; 1 Kgs 21:7; 2 Kgs 19:1; Isa 37:1; Jer 6:26; Dan 9:3; Jon 3:6). Although "loud and bitter" cries appear in psalms petitioning divine help (Pss 22:5 [6]; 107:13, 19; 142:1 [2], 5 [6]), the text does not clearly state that Mordecai is appealing to God. There is solidarity among the Jews who join Mordecai in mourning their anticipated death. Since Esther demonstrates that identity can be hidden by non-disclosure, these public actions would reveal identity. Threatened with annihilation, instead of choosing to conceal their identity, the Jews reveal it. Esther's servants bring news of the decree and Mordecai's actions to her attention (4:1). Since she does not join in mourning, Esther continues to hide her identity. Perhaps sending clothes to Mordecai (4:4) expresses her wish that he similarly conceal his identity.

What ensues is a series of messages relayed by the eunuchs, who are important characters throughout Esther. As castrated men, they exist at the boundary of gender—male, yet not male. They are thus able to cross other boundaries, conveying information between separated spaces—between men and women (1:10–11; 3:3–4) and citadel and city (2:21; 3:4–15; 6:14; 7:9). In the first exchange (4:5–8), Mordecai tells Esther of the situation and sends a copy of the decree. He charges Esther to intercede with the king on the Jews' behalf, but offers no specific strategy for countering the decree.

Esther replies that intercession is impossible (4:9–11). The law states that an individual can see Ahasuerus only if that individual is summoned, and he has not called for her in thirty days. His disinterest hints at limits to her influence. The penalty for violating this law is death. Although it is possible that Ahasuerus might spare her life, his previous over-reactions to disobedience suggest otherwise. Besides, disobedience goes against everything Esther has been trained and told to do all her life. Her obedience is why she is where she is. She is now faced with competing demands—does she violate Mordecai's request or the king's law?

Mordecai's reply (4:13–14) is the most often cited and preached upon statement in the book, even though the interpretation of key phrases remains contested. Mordecai points out that Esther can die going before Ahasuerus or she can die when the decree is executed—her position and rank will not save her. If she does act, that "relief and deliverance will rise for the Jews from another quarter" is traditionally interpreted as referring to divine deliverance. But it could refer to another human willing to help, unlike Esther. Whether Esther has "come to royal dignity for just such a time as this," may be interpreted as a reference to God's guiding hand working behind the scenes for the benefit of God's people—or as a moment of chance. Either way, Mordecai challenges Esther to take advantage of the situation, now.

Esther responds with a command for the Jews to fast. Since she will also fast, this act moves her to solidarity with the Jews and begins to reveal her identity. A public fast means others (though not the king?) will notice her association with the Jews (4:15–16). The fast is not necessarily a religious act. It may be interpreted as a means of preparation for her audience with Ahasuerus, including coming to terms with revealing her Jewish identity. Esther's statement, "if I perish I perish," acknowledges that she acts with no assurance of what the outcome will be. There is no certainty there will be deliverance (Dan 3:17–18); however, regardless of consequences, she is determined to take a particular course of action.

C. Esther Acts: First Banquet (5:1–8)

Dressed in royal robes, Esther approaches Ahasuerus (5:1). Although her clothing continues to hide her Jewish identity from the king, it emphasizes her power and authority as queen. Esther again wins the king's favor (5:2; cf. 2:17). Ahasuerus' character has changed; he does not fly into a rage. By holding out the scepter and letting Esther live, Ahasuerus holds out hope of deliverance to the Jews.

Continuing to display benevolence, Ahasuerus asks Esther what her request is, offering to give her whatever she wants, even to half of his kingdom. (5:3). She requests a banquet (*mishteh*), with him and Haman (5:4). Knowing that Ahasuerus never refuses a banquet and that he is easily influenced when drunk, Esther's request displays crafty planning. Mordecai asked her to approach the king, but how she does so is her own plan.

As they are drinking, Ahasuerus asks Esther again for her request (5:6, cf. 5:3). The repetition suggests he did not interpret the invitation to the banquet as her request. He would view her failure to make a request as insubordination. Since he is drinking, one might imagine an edge to his voice. "What do you really want Esther." In reply, Esther piles on the flattery (5:7–8). She repeats Ahasuerus' words, "petition" and "request," stating what he wants to hear. She thrice addresses him as "king," emphasizing his superior position. Besides asking, "if it please the king" (cf. 5:4), she emphasizes winning his "favor" (cf. 2:17; 5:2), to remind him of their bond. Esther asks that Ahasuerus and Haman attend a second banquet on the next day, promising to reveal her real request then, assuring Ahasuerus of her obedience. Why she does not "entreat him for her people" at this banquet is an open question. One possibility is that another banquet builds suspense. Esther has not yet revealed her identity to Ahasuerus. Will she have the courage to do so? How will he respond? Will she save her people?

D. Haman's Second Plot (5:9–14)

Haman leaves the party "happy," evidently believing that he is continuing to rise in the king's inner circle. He is also drunk. "Good spirits" is identical in Hebrew to Ahasuerus being "merry with wine" (1:10). Haman's contentment soon dissipates to be replaced by fury (2:9). As he leaves, Haman passes by Mordecai, who again shows disrespect, this time by refusing to stand instead of refusing to bow. Nor does Mordecai "tremble," a word that can indicate fear (Dan 5:19; Hab 2:7).

Why Haman "restrained himself" is unstated (5:10). He may be waiting to seek advice before acting on his rage, a pattern for both him and Ahasuerus (1:13; 3:6; 7:8–9), or may be afraid to act without the king's permission. Returning home he calls his friends and his wife, Zeresh, and recounts his woeful condition (5:11–13). In advising her husband, Zeresh stands in the biblical tradition of women who advise men, for good or ill (e. g., Gen 27:5–10; 1 Sam 25:26–31; 2 Sam 13:12–13; 14:4–17; 20:16–19; Job 2:9). On the advice of those assembled, Haman builds a gallows fifty cubits high, planning to tell the king in the morning to hang Mordecai on it. He will then go to the banquet in the evening happy (5:14). The gallows' height of seventy-two feet (twenty-two meters) is another exaggeration. The word for "gallows" is literally "tree" (*'ets*). So the wording, "hang on a tree," reminds readers of God's curse in Deut 21:22–23.

E. Haman Mortified (6:1–13)

The next episode relies on fate and leads to one of the story's many ironic reversals. On the night before the banquet, by chance, Ahasuerus has insomnia and cures it by having someone read to him from his annals (6:1). By chance, the episode recounting Mordecai's thwarting of the eunuch's assassination plot is read (6:2). Haman arrives just as Ahasuerus is inquiring whether anything had been done to honor Mordecai (6:3–5). Ahasuerus seeks Haman's advice on what to do "for the man whom the king wishes to honor" (6:6), and Haman thinks that Ahasuerus wishes to honor him. Knowing that Ahasuerus always does what others advise, Haman suggests an outrageous list

of things that he considers honorable (6:7–9). The tables are turned on Haman as Ahasuerus tells him to do exactly those things to his enemy, Mordecai. But Haman obediently complies (6:10–11).

Here, the text focuses on Haman's reaction (6:12*b*) to this humiliating turn of events. He rushes home. Instead of revealing himself so all could bow to him, he hides his identity by covering his head, a gesture of shame (2 Sam 15:30; Jer 14:3–4). He also mourns, but for what? The death of his prestige? His loss of honor? A bruised ego? Does Haman foresee his impending death? The response of his wife and friends to his predicament is unsympathetic. They are certain that Haman cannot defeat his enemy. There are many possibilities for the basis of their certainty. It may be a hidden reference to Yahweh who is with the Jews and fights for them, an overt reference to previous biblical claims to destroy Haman's people (Exod 17:14–16; Num 24:20; Deut 25:17–19), an acknowledgement that Mordecai's star is on the rise, or due to some inherent quality in the "Jewish people." Haman's decline is emphasized by the three-fold repetition of the verb "to fall" (*nafal*) (evident only twice in translation)—"downfall ... will surely fall."

III. Resolution (6:14–10:3)

A. Esther Acts: Second Banquet (6:14–8:2)

This is the turning point in the story. From now on the plot works to eliminate the threat of Jewish annihilation. Haman hurried home the night before; now he is "hurried" off to Esther's second banquet by royal eunuchs (6:14). The Hebrew states that Ahasuerus and Haman went in "to drink" with Esther, not NRSV's "feast" (7:1). In Hebrew, the same phrase, "wine banquet" (*mishteh hayyayin*), is repeated three times (7:2, 7, 8), though translated differently in NRSV. Ahasuerus' language is identical to his previous queries to Esther (7:2; cf. 5:3, 6), as is her answer (7:3; cf. 5:8). She again uses flattery and court language to smooth the way with the king. She finally reveals her real "petition"—let my life be given me—and "request"—and the lives of my people. The equation of "my life" and "my people," demonstrates that Esther has become fully Jewish.

Esther uses the exact phrasing of the decree's language (3:13) to explain to Ahasuerus the need for clemency. Her claim that if they "had been sold merely as slaves," she would have held her peace is probably exaggeration (7:4). The remainder of her speech is difficult to translate and interpret, but the general idea is that acting on her request will be to Ahasuerus' advantage.

The realization that his queen's life is threatened seems to sober Ahasuerus, and he demands to know the evildoer (7:5). Haman is revealed as the perpetrator of this racist crime (7:6). The story reminds readers that the way to deal with such evils is to expose them. As long as they remain hidden, they cannot be changed. Ahasuerus is enraged and storms off to the garden.

Haman seizes the king's absence to beg for his life. Again fate intervenes. As Haman is appealing to Esther, Ahasuerus reenters the room and believes Haman is assaulting his wife. If the stakes were not so high, the scene would be a comedy of errors. This gives the king a good explanation for why he is punishing Haman, someone he had promoted, given permission to write the decree, and from whom he had taken a sizable bribe. An anonymous "they" (the eunuchs?) cover his face, signifying shame (e.g., Pss 44:15 [16]; 69:7 [8]; Jer 51:51). The eunuchs point out Haman's gallows and remind Ahasuerus that Mordecai had saved his life. Ahasuerus' command to hang Haman on the gallows he intended for Mordecai is the story's central reversal and an "eye-for-an eye" variety of justice. Such an approach began this catastrophe. Hanging Haman assuages Ahasuerus' anger and brings many benefits to Esther and Mordecai. Esther inherits Haman's house, she is able to reveal Mordecai's relationship to her, the king gives Mordecai the ring he had previously given to Haman (3:10), and Esther sets Mordecai over the house (8:1–2). This brief interlude is reminiscent of the stories of Joseph and Daniel who, even in the midst of calamity, find themselves promoted. It also builds further suspense since Haman's death does not overturn the looming edict.

B. Undoing Haman's Plot (8:3–17)

8:3–8. Esther's Petition. Instead of rational appeal, Esther employs dramatic emotion (8:3). She employs even more flattery than in 7:3. The expressions, "if the thing seems right" and "I have his approval (lit. I am good in his eyes)," occur only here (8:5). Since Ahasuerus throughout is

incapable of or unwilling to come up with his own solutions to crises, Esther now tells Ahasuerus what to do. Esther suggests that the previous order be revoked, making it as if the letters stating Haman's decree had never been sent. For Esther, this will prevent the calamity coming to "my people" and "my kindred" (8:6). Now Esther is fully identified as a Jew. Her people and kindred were exactly what she had concealed (2:10).

Ahasuerus statement to Esther and Mordecai is fraught with ambiguity (8:7). Is he suggesting he has already done enough for them? Or is this a veiled threat? If one moment Haman is writing decrees in the king's name and the next he is hanged, then Esther and Mordecai could also be subjected to Ahasuerus' fickleness. Ahasuerus does not directly accede to Esther's request. He gives them permission to "write as it please you (pl.)."

One of the vexing plot devices is that a written law cannot be revoked. Not even Ahasuerus can change it. A law's morality cannot be challenged, only obeyed. Letters once sent cannot be returned. As a consequence, writing functions throughout the story both to reveal and reinforce existing realities. The first decree reveals and reinforces patriarchal fears and ideology. Haman's decree reveals and reinforces ideologies of racism and violence. Such ideologies are not easily reversed. Outlawing slavery did not end racism, and enfranchising women did not end sexism. In Esther, writing also seeks to create an alternative reality—where women are obedient and Jews no longer exist. What ideologies will Esther and Mordecai's writing reveal and reinforce? What new reality will they seek to create?

8:9–17. Mordecai's Decree. Mordecai alone dictates the decree. Except for brief appearances (9:12–13, 29–32) Esther disappears; as if having served her "moment such as this," she becomes dispensable and can be set aside. One wonders whether Esther's decree would have differed. On one level, the counterdecree changes everything. Instead of sackcloth and ashes, Mordecai parades through the city in royal garb (4:1; 8:15). Instead of weeping and lamenting (4:3), the people celebrate with gladness and joy (8:16–17; cf. 9:22). On another level, nothing changes. The language of decree (3:12–15) and counterdecree (8:8–14) is nearly identical. Drinking continues (8:17; "festival," *mishteh*). There is nothing to prevent the story from repeating.

C. Enemies Destroyed (9:1–19)

Esther 9:1–10:3 consists of several episodes that were added later to the story, which successfully concludes at 8:17. The first episode relates the events of the day chosen by lot, when power reverses in favor of the Jews (9:1–19). Shifting power is evident in the Jews' actions, which sound more offensive than defensive (9:2). That "the fear of them" had fallen on everyone (9:2) indicates reaction to rising Jewish power rather than divine miracle (9:3–4). The day's mayhem is reported incrementally, moving from the citadel outward to the city and to the provinces.

Five hundred Gentiles are killed in the citadel, including Haman's ten sons (9:6–10). When this is reported to Ahasuerus, he seeks out Esther to find out what is happening in the provinces. He asks if she has a request and asks that the Susans be allowed another day of defending their lives (9:11–13). This explains the different customs regarding which day to celebrate Purim (9:17–18, 21). She further requests to hang Haman's sons (who are already dead). What she requests is as an act of proof, shaming, and warning, analogous to the public display of photographs of the dead bodies of Saddam Hussein and his sons during the Iraq War. The photos offered proof they were dead, shamed the Hussein family and Baathist party, and warned others who might behave similarly that the same could happen to them. Ahasuerus, of course, grants Esther's request (9:14–15). The death count in city and provinces combined is 75,800 over two days. The enormous number symbolizes how widespread and pervasive the anti-Semitic sentiment was.

D. Purim Established (9:20–10:3)

Deliverance from annihilation is officially ritualized through the yearly commemoration of Purim (9:20–32). Since it is not legislated in Torah, letters from Mordecai and Esther sent to all the Jews authorize Purim. Mordecai's writing, though not officially a "law," functions similarly. His record of the events reveals interethnic conflict as the key issue and emphasizes the importance of human actions (9:25). The holiday's repetition reinforces the ethic necessary for confronting the ongoing conflict: whether or not relief is gained from enemies this year, destruction is certain if humans do not act. A ritual aspect of Purim is to send "gifts of food," the same word for the "portion of food" that Hegai gives to Esther when she wins his favor (2:9). Hegai's favoring Esther is arguably what puts Esther in the right place at the right time. Reenacting Hegai's kindness will hopefully spur similar coincidences resulting in deliverance. Mordecai's writing does not envision the elimination of interethnic conflict, but occasional reversals, where there is joy instead of sorrow (4:1–3), "feasting" (*mishteh*), instead of fasting (4:16–17). This future will happen only if all Jews, everywhere, through all time commemorate Purim (9:27–28).

Esther writes the final letter in the book (9:29–32). Esther is described by both her Persian ("Queen") and Jewish ("daughter of Abihail") identities. Unlike Mordecai, she is never only "the Jew." As a result, Esther bears multiple identities, one is characteristic of Jewish existence in the Diaspora. The only detail recorded is the inclusion of "fasts" and "lamentation (lit. outcry)" in Purim regulations. This is the language describing the responses to Haman's decree (4:1, 3, 16). Although the wish is for "peace (*shalom*) and security," Esther's writing acknowledges that as long as the ideology of racism and the violence that attends it remain inscribed, so will sorrow and sadness.

On the surface, the final verses celebrate the theme of reversal by describing how Mordecai advanced in the kingdom (cf. Gen 40:40–45; Dan 5:29). A series of parallel statements suggest how he uses his privilege. He uses his "power" for "the good" of "the Jews/his people," suggesting he continues to thwart any would-be Hamans. Mordecai is "popular" with "his many kindred" because he seeks their "welfare (*shalom*)." What he had done only for Esther (2:10), he extends to all "his descendants." This positive outlook, however, hides something more sinister, namely, that Ahasuerus "laid tribute" on the entire empire. The word for tribute (*mas*) describes coerced labor (Exod 1:11; Josh 17:13; 1 Kgs 5:13). Now everyone, not just one ethnic group, have been "sold into slavery." Is Mordecai involved in any way? Does this hint at the oppressed becoming the oppressor? If so, from where will relief and deliverance come?

BIBLIOGRAPHY

T. K. Beal. *Esther. Ruth and Esther.* D. W. Colter, ed. Berit Olam (Collegeville: Liturgical Press, 1999); J. A. Berman. "*Hadassah Bat Abihail*: The Evolution from Object to Subject in the Character of Esther." *JBL* 120 (2001) 647–69; S. Crawford. "Esther." NIB (Nashville: Abingdon, 1999) 3:855–941; L. Day. *Esther.* AOTC (Nashville: Abingdon, 2005).

JOB

Adele Berlin

OVERVIEW

What is the book of Job about?

The meaning of the book of Job is not easily captured in a single phrase, for it touches on a number of the most important issues in religious thought, including the reason for suffering, divine justice, human intellectual integrity, and the motivation for piety. More broadly, it is a quest for knowledge about the nature of God and the universe, and the place of humans in it. It is essentially an inquiry into human and divine wisdom, about the possibility of arguing against accepted truths, and about exploring in the most abstract way the human condition and the morality of the universe.

Literary character, structure, and language

Job is usually placed under the rubric of wisdom literature, a modern scholarly category that includes biblical and ancient Near Eastern works that address questions of how to live one's life, the meaning and purpose of life, human and divine justice, and other perennial inquiries into the nature of the world and the place of humans in it that range from the practical to the theoretical or philosophical. Biblical wisdom literature— Proverbs, Ecclesiastes, and Job——is written in poetry, as are the psalms and other poems found throughout the Hebrew Bible. But nothing in wisdom literature, or in all of biblical poetry, approaches the sustained intensity or the linguistic virtuosity of the poetry of Job. The vocabulary is extensive and, at times, esoteric, with a number of terms that are found nowhere else in the Bible. The numerous Aramaisms add to the foreignness and the learnedness of the discourses. Parallelisms often extend beyond the requisite two lines into multiple-line parallelisms; and metaphors, often one-liners in other books (like Proverbs) are stretched into long conceits (elaborate comparisons). Rhetorical questions abound, drawing the reader, as well as the participants in the dialogues, into pondering the issues raised. Rational thought is wedded to aesthetically beautiful expression in a way that may seem unexpected to a modern reader, for whom the rational stands in opposition to the emotional, with poetry a form generally reserved for the emotional. The book of Job combines high verbal art and sophisticated inquiry— an intellectual and aesthetic treat.

The book is formally structured, again showing its artifice, although parts of the structure are incomplete. A prose frame, chs. 1–2 and 42:7–17, surrounds the poetic dialogues. The first two prose chapters are further structured as scenes that alternate between earth and heaven. The poetic speeches in 3:1–42:6 alternate between Job and each of his three friends, Eliphaz, Bildad, and Zophar, for almost three rounds (Bildad's third speech is short and Zophar lacks a third speech). A fourth speaker, Elihu, is introduced in chs. 32–37. God too speaks, in chs.38–41, with Job responding. Standing outside of the dialogic structure is ch. 28, a poem about wisdom.

The dialogue, or disputation, is a familiar form in ancient Near Eastern wisdom literature, both in Egypt ("A Dispute Between a Man and His Ba [Soul]") and in Mesopotamia ("A Dialogue Between a Master and His Slave"). Mesopotamia had earlier disputation literature both in Sumer and in Babylonia, in which two parties, usually natural phenomena, argue about which is superior (e.g., the dispute between summer and winter or the tamarisk and the palm). Literature structured on dialogue is perhaps best known from the symposia of ancient Greece.

Most of the Mesopotamian dialogue literature is lighthearted in tone; more serious and closer to Job in contents is "The Babylonian Theodicy," a dialogue between a sufferer and his friend in which the sufferer bemoans the injustices of society while the friend attempts to reconcile these injustices with the accepted views on the divine ordering of the universe. Another Babylonian composition often compared to Job is a monologue called "I Will Praise the Lord of Wisdom" (sometimes called "The Poem of the Righteous Sufferer" or "The Babylonian Job") describing various calamities that a certain noble experienced and his restoration to health and prosperity by Marduk (the Lord of Wisdom) to whom he offers praise.

Date and Composition

Despite some archaizing vocabulary, the book is generally dated to the Persian period, probably during the fifth to fourth century BCE. The role of the "Satan" resembles that in Zech 3:1 and 1 Chr 21:1, and allusions to Isa 40–66 (postexilic prophetic literature) also support this late dating. Considerable discussion has been devoted to the source-critical question of whether the book was written as one piece or evolved in several stages. Some scholars think that the Elihu speeches are a later addition. Most agree that there existed a folktale about a righteous man named Job (cf. Ezek 14:14, 20) that the author called upon for his main character, although the form in which this tale is recounted in our book seems to have been the product of a sophisticated writer, most likely the author of the poetic sections.

OUTLINE

I. The Prologue: Job's piety (1:1–2:13)

    A. Introducing Job (1:1–5)

    B. The Scene in Heaven: The Test Proposed (1:6–12)

    C. The Scene on Earth: The Test Enacted (1:13–22)

    D. The Scene in Heaven and on Earth: The Second Test (2:1–10)

    E. Job's Friends (2:11–13)

II. Job Curses His Existence (3:1–26)

III. The Dialogues Between the Three Friends and Job (4:1–27:23)

    A. The First Cycle (4:1–14:22)
        4:1–5:27. Eliphaz's First Speech
        6:1–7:21. Job's Response to Eliphaz
        8:1–22. Bildad's First Speech
        9:1–10:22. Job's Response to Bildad
        11:1–20. Zophar's First Speech
        12:1–14:22. Job's Response

    B. The Second Cycle (15:1–21:34)
        15:1–35. Eliphaz Speaks Again
        16:1–17:16. Job Responds to Eliphaz
        18:1–21. Bildad Speaks Again.
        19:1–29. Job Responds to Bildad
        20:1–29. Zophar Speaks Again
        21:1–34. Job Responds to Zophar

    C. The Third Cycle (22:1–27:33)
        22:1–30. Eliphaz Speaks for
          the Third Time
        23:1–24:25. Job Responds
        25:1–6. Bildad Speaks Briefly
        26:1–27:23. Job Responds

IV. A Poem about Wisdom (28:1–28)

V. Job's Concluding Speech (29:1–31:40)

VI. The Elihu Speeches (32:1–37:24)

VII. God Speaks from the Whirlwind (38:1–42:6)

VIII. Epilogue: Job Is Vindicated and Restored (42:7–17)

DETAILED ANALYSIS

I. The Prologue: Job's Piety (1:1–2:13)

The scenes of the prose prologue alternate between heaven and earth. They are preceded by the narrator's introduction of Job and his family, providing the setting and characterization of Job; and they are followed by the arrival of his three friends to comfort him. The prose frame reappears as an epilogue at the conclusion of the book (42:7–17). Written in an apparently simple style, like other postexilic books such as Jonah and Ruth, the prologue is actually carefully contrived and tightly structured——not at all the way folktales are typically told. It may draw on an ancient folktale, but its present form bears the marks of the Persian period (the character of the Satan and the word q-b-l, "to receive" [2:10], which occurs almost exclusively in late books). It is likely from the same hand responsible for the rest of the book. The author, like the author of Jonah, chose as a main character a figure mentioned in the biblical tradition (2 Kings 14:25 for Jonah and Ezek 14:14 for Job) but about whom little or nothing was said.

A. Introducing Job (1:1–5)

The story opens with a "once upon a time" construction, suggesting to even the ancient reader that the story of Job is not intended as a historical account. Indeed, the set-up is entirely theoretical, for it focuses on a sinless man (patently impossible) and the absurd situation in which God is forced to test a person he knows to be perfect. But such a setting is necessary in order to press in its most extreme and abstract form the questions of the book—God's justice vs. the suffering of the righteous, the accessibility of wisdom, etc. Job is presented as a prosperous aristocrat from Uz, an area equated with or south of Edom (or perhaps associated with Aram, northeast of Israel). Though not an Israelite, he is nevertheless God-fearing and blesses Yahweh, the God of Israel (1:21). The adjectives that describe him, "blameless and upright, one who feared God and turned away from evil" (v. 1) mean that he is morally perfect. The same adjectives will be used by God (1:8; 2:3), confirming the narrator's description and adding that there is no one else on earth like Job. "Greatest of all the people of the east" (v. 3) may refer to Job's wealth or to his wisdom; the men of the east were known for their wisdom, as was Job. The point of making Job a non-Israelite is to add to the theoretical nature of his character, and the point of making him a man of the East is to epitomize his wisdom.

The perfect Job has a family perfect in size (seven and three are favorite biblical numbers for perfection) and gender distribution (more sons than daughters), and a full complement of wealth, a sign of his success and his blessing. He will lose his wealth and children in the reverse order of their mention. Job's exaggerated piety is exemplified by his "preventative" offerings for his adult children (who should be responsible for their own sin-offerings), just in case they may have thought, not uttered, blasphemy while they were feasting. The idea of cursing God, the antithesis of fearing God, is central to the test (1:11, 22; 2:5, 9).

B. The Scene in Heaven: The Test Proposed (1:6–12)

Each scene opens with "one day" (1:6; 1:13; 2:1), focusing attention on a particular moment. God is in the company of a council of heavenly beings, among them the Satan, that is, the Adversary or the Accuser or the Prosecutor (the definite article in the Hebrew indicates that this is not a personal name). Only centuries later does Satan become God's rival, an autonomous power opposed to God (cf. Mark 3:22–30; Luke 22:31; John 13:27; Rev 20:1–10). To test whether Job's piety is motivated by a reward, the Satan proposes to deprive Job of all that signals a reward for piety: wealth and family in the first test and physical health in the second. God has no choice but to accept the Satan's challenge and agree to the test, which places the ultimate blame for Job's loss and suffering on God. The question of why a person should fear God is never fully answered in the book. It is perceived as an absolute value.

C. The Scene on Earth: The Test Enacted (1:13–22)

The test is carried out in a most unrealistic and highly structured manner, whereby Job is informed, in rapid succession, by a sole surviving messenger in each of four instances, that his wealth and children have been destroyed by human attacks (marauding tribes, the Sabeans and the Chaldeans) alternating with natural disasters (lightening and a wind-storm). Job's reaction is to bless God, not to curse him. In the prologue, Job seems passive and accepting of the terrible tragedies that befall him.

D. The Scene in Heaven and on Earth: The Second Test (2:1–10)

The first test having failed to make Job curse God, Satan ups the ante, now requesting that Job suffer physically in his own body in the form of a loathsome skin disease. Yet he still refuses to curse God. He maintains his integrity, another theme-word (from the same Hebrew root as *blameless* in 1:1) that occurs in God's speech (2:3) and in Job's wife's speech (2:9). Job's wife appears in v. 9, urging him to curse God and die. Cursing God was a capital offense (Exod 22:27; Lev 24:10–16; 1 Kings 21:10) and would result in Job's death, presumably here by the hand of God. But Job rejects her advice, insisting that people must accept both the good and the bad from God. If written during the Persian period, this may be a subtle polemic against the dualism of Zoroastrianism, which posits that good and evil originate from separate sources. Interpreters differ on their assessment of Job's wife: was she an agent of the Satan or a loving wife who could not bear to see her husband suffer? "Foolish woman" (v. 10) is a woman who rejects wisdom teaching and speaks disgraceful words (cf. "fool" in Ps 14:1; Deut 32:6).

E. Job's Friends (2:11-13)

Three friends from three unidentifiable places in the vicinity of Uz come to comfort Job, as friends are formally required to do for a mourner. Silent at first, out of respect for Job's suffering, they adopt the signs of mourning along with Job. When they do speak, in the poetic sections, they draw on wisdom ideas that they think will lead Job to an acceptance of his condition; but Job will refuse to be comforted by arguments he cannot accept.

II. Job Curses His Existence (3:1–26)

The poetic section of the book opens with an angry lament by Job, despairing that he had been born. He does not curse God, but curses the day of his birth, wishing it had been erased from the calendar. Words for darkness and gloom predominate in vv. 1–10, as Job attempts to undo the creation of light and revert to the darkness before the creation of the world. *Leviathan* (v. 8), the primordial sea monster, signals a return to chaos (cf. Ps 74:14; Isa 27:1).

If he had to be conceived, he then wishes that he had perished in the womb or in the birth process or at his first suckling at the breast. His view of death is positive, a relief from suffering. The realm of death is not a place of reward and punishment (that idea comes later), but of a peaceful shadowy existence. Most important, although not explicit here, in the realm of death one is cut off from God (cf. Ps 6:6); and Job would like nothing more than that God would leave him alone. "Fenced in" (v. 23), used here in a negative sense, is, ironically, the same word that the Satan used in a positive sense for God's protection of Job (1:10). The end of the chapter (vv. 20–26) raises the question of why people in despair continue to live when they would prefer to die. However much Job would welcome death, he never contemplates suicide or euthanasia.

III. The Dialogues Between the Three Friends and Job (4:1–27:23)

The dialogues begin at this point, with cycles of speeches alternating between each of the three friends—Eliphaz, Bildad, and Zophar—and Job, who responds to each friend in turn, refuting the argument just offered at greater length than it was stated. Consistent with the Bible's narrative convention, no more than two parties can participate in a conversation, so it is literally a dialogue, a two-way conversation; there is never a three- or four-way debate among the speakers. There are three rounds of speeches, although Bildad's third speech is short and Zophar lacks a third speech altogether. Perhaps these missing speeches were lost, or, alternatively, this structure signals an intentional petering-out of the debate with no side declared the winner. The argument is not linear, but traverses the same topics, escalating at different points. The friends try various arguments to rationalize and justify the condition in which Job finds himself, while Job vehemently rejects their assumptions and their reasoning, insisting that there is no valid reason for his suffering. Both sides employ emotional language loaded with metaphors as well as logic.

A. The First Cycle (4:1–14:22)

4:1–5:27. Eliphaz's First Speech. Eliphaz, the first to break the silence of 2:13, begins softly and solicitously, reminding Job of his (Job's) wisdom and how he had helped others in the past. But, he adds, when Job himself is afflicted, he seems unable to offer himself the same wise and comforting advice he had offered to others. This is a subtle rebuke to Job that he should rely on the traditional answers to the problem of suffering, summed up by "See, we have searched this out; it is true" (5:27). Indeed, Eliphaz offers the conventional wisdom—that the innocent are not destroyed; only those who do evil are punished (4:7–11). "Fear of God and integrity" (4:6) are both attributes of Job (1:1, 8; 2:3) and are so recognized by Eliphaz, who suggests that they should provide the explanation Job seeks. While the terms are near synonyms, the modern reader may think of integrity as maintaining what one thinks is right, which in Job's case is his innocence. This type of integrity risks undermining Job's fear of God.

Eliphaz then (4:12–21) describes a revelatory vision he had, an eerie dream-like experience of communication with the divine (dreams were thought to be a way in which the deity communicated with humans), in which he was told that no human can be more righteous than God. This passage is difficult; some scholars think it is misplaced and should be assigned to Job, following his lament in ch. 3, rather than to Eliphaz. Most important is the rhetorical question, implying a negative answer, "Can mortals be righteous before God" (4:17), that is, can humans prove they are righteous if God has condemned them (suffering being a sign of God's judgment of one's guilt). To be righteous before God is precisely what Job seeks to accomplish, but the friends declare that it is impossible, that God's standard of justice, as they understand it, cannot be overridden. Cf. 9:2; 15:14–16; 25:4–5. Humans are frail and transient, and they fall short of God's standard. Humans lack the ultimate wisdom that is God's. This lack of parity between God and humans will continue to play out in the book, especially in God's speeches in chs. 38–39. "Even in his servants he puts no trust, and his angels he charges with error" (4:18) shows that even the divine beings in the heavenly court fall short of perfection; an ironic statement hinting that the Satan was wrong, although, of course, Eliphaz knows nothing of Satan's actions in ch. 1.

Implying that Job has become a fool (5:2), one who rejects the teachings of the wise, Eliphaz urges Job to seek God, to acknowledge that God does great and mysterious things, that he frustrates the wise but ultimately saves the needy. In other words, trust in God takes precedence over rational understanding of the situation. "How happy is the one whom God reproves" (5:17) suggests that Job should welcome his suffering as divine correction, a way of improving Job. At the same time, says Eliphaz, trying to have it both ways, suffering is temporary, and God will ultimately heal Job, end his suffering, and grant him the ideal life with many children and death at a ripe old age with undiminished strength (5:24–27).

6:1–7:21. Job's Response to Eliphaz.

Job's words echo Eliphaz's, but with a different twist. He opens with a description of his suffering, as if to intimate that that is the reason he spoke so rashly, seeming to agree with Eliphaz's judgment about Job's earlier speech. But Job is not about to apologize for what he said, nor to retract his words. Here and throughout, Job maintains that he is correct. And in the last part of his speech, in ch. 7, he reiterates even more strongly his thoughts about the misery of life and the injustice he feels.

Eliphaz counseled Job to seek God; Job says that he wishes that God would grant his request, which is that God should let him die (6:8–10). Job questions his ability to remain patient much longer, and insists that he has not "denied the words of the Holy One" (6:10), as Eliphaz implied. This phrase may mean that Job has not cursed God, even under duress; or it may mean, rather, that Job has not hidden the suffering that God has caused him.

In 6:14–27, Job lashes out in a biting critique of his friends, whom he compares to the treacherous and undependable waters of the desert wadis that flood in the winter and dry up in the summer, leading rich caravans from distant places to get lost in the desert wasteland. The friends have, likewise, let Job down. He never asked them for money, only comfort and wisdom; but they have offered nothing to comfort Job or to instruct him. Eliphaz accused Job of wrongful speech, but Job finds nothing in Eliphaz's speech that is right.

Chapter 7 begins with a description of Job's condition, similar to some of the psalms of lament. But unlike the psalms of lament, this is not a prayer to God but rather an angry outpouring, parodying the psalms, about the frailty and transience of human life, so incommensurate with the blow dealt by God against Job. "Am I the Sea, or the Dragon, that you set a guard over me" (7:12), asks Job, meaning that he is not a powerful cosmic force like the primeval waters that God subdued at the time of creation. He is insignificant vis-à-vis God and wants only to be left alone, away from God's scrutiny. "What are human beings, that you make so much of them" (7:17) is a parody of Ps 8, and vv. 19–21 echo Ps 39 with a twist. What sin could Job have committed that would harm God? Why does not God just wipe it away and be done with it (7:20). Job is not admitting here that he sinned, only that for whatever reason (which he cannot fathom) God has made him a target; God's reaction is all out of proportion. The only way Job can avoid God's scrutiny is by dying, for then God cannot find him any longer (7:21). This speech, like ch 3, views life as burdensome, akin to the hard service of a laborer (7:1; similar to parts of Ecclesiastes), and it views death as a release (7:15–16; cf. 3:18–20). Job has ostensibly been addressing Eliphaz, but his words are really aimed at God.

8:1–22. Bildad's First Speech. As is common in disputation literature, where the debaters must refute the words of their opponents, Bildad reacts to the last speaker's (Job's) words, characterizing them as a lot of hot air. Bildad asks a leading question: "Does God pervert justice?" (8:3). Of course, Bildad does not think so, but this is precisely what Job accuses God of doing, and it is the crux of the dialogues. Bildad makes the extremely uncomforting observation that if Job's children were destroyed, they must have done something to deserve it. (Job's earlier critique about the lack of support he got from his friends is amply justified here.) As for Job, if he will supplicate God and if he is pure and upright (readers know that Job is and Job knows it, but Bildad seems uncertain), then God will restore him. Bildad paints a lovely picture of the future while omitting the darkness of Job's present suffering. Like Eliphaz, he urges Job to accept the wisdom of previous generations. The end of the chapter contains a plant metaphor equating a plant without water to a person without God, a common image found also in Ps 1 and Jer 17:5–8. Both the plant and the person who ignores God will perish. (The text is difficult in vv. 16–19).

9:1–10:22. Job's Response to Bildad. Ostensibly agreeing with Bildad that God does not pervert justice, Job asks if, theoretically, a human could win a legal case against God. God is so great, says Job, describing him in the cosmic terms of creation and control over the forces of nature, that who could stand up to him? Even a righteous person would have no chance against such power. In some ways, this section anticipates God's speeches in chs. 38–39, but in their present context the words express Job's hopeless inadequacy and frustration; God is too large for a human to deal with, too preoccupied with big things to even notice the trouble of one insignificant human.

9:25–10:22. Job then contemplates his own life, transient and miserable, wondering yet again what he could possibly do to prove his innocence. Job calls for an arbiter to settle the case between himself and God; for as it stands now, God is both the judge and a party to the dispute. Job requests to know what error he has committed. Is God sadistic, Job asks; and if not, why does he pick on

Job so much, discovering faults that do not exist? Job accuses God of having created him with the intent to find sin in him. (Cf. Ps 139 for a more positive view of God's formation of the individual.) Better, then, that Job had never been born or that he be permitted to die, for only in Sheol, the realm of the dead, can he escape God's scrutiny and condemnation. Verses 18–22 echo ch. 3. The speech as a whole inverts tropes that are usually invoked to praise God—God's mastery over the cosmos and his intimate knowledge of the humans he has created—using them to criticize God.

11:1–20. Zophar's First Speech. Like Bildad but in even stronger language, Zophar criticizes Job's speech concerning both its quantity and quality, pointing out that a lot of babble does not make the speaker correct. "My conduct is pure" (v. 4) is better rendered "my teaching is pure." Zophar is paraphrasing and criticizing Job's earlier words. "But O that God would speak" (11:5), wishes Zophar, thinking that God would contradict Job's claim of innocence. Of course, in line with so many ironies in the book, Job has been hoping all along for God to speak, but for the opposite reason. God does finally speak beginning in ch. 38. In vv. 7–10 Zophar describes the impossibility of understanding God's ways, specifically God's limits, which extend beyond the cosmos. In one sense, this is an answer that the book provides to the problem of the righteous sufferer. But Zophar offers this advice in a belittling manner, not taking Job's words seriously and in essence calling him as stupid as an ass (the apparent meaning of the unclear Hebrew phrase in v. 12). Here, as at several other points in the book, a solution to Job's inquiry is glimpsed, but the context makes it unacceptable. Zophar concludes by advising Job to act with proper contrition (since Zophar is certain Job has sinned), and then his condition will improve.

The friends have offered the conventional answers: only sinful people suffer, God forgives sin if the sinner repents, suffering is good discipline for a person, and one cannot understand God's ways. These points may seem contradictory, but each has merit on its own and some or all of them are still offered today when one is confronted with tragedy. Yet Job will not settle for easy answers; answers that are dissonant with his experience bring him no comfort.

12:1–14:22. Job's Response. This long speech evinces several moods. Job opens with a response to his friends, especially Zophar, that is angrily sarcastic (12:1–13:19), but then addresses God (13:20–14:22), first using a legal metaphor followed by contemplative remarks on the transience of human life.

In 12:1–13:19 Job reacts angrily to Zophar's insult about his lack of wisdom, arguing that he is no less wise than the friends, who present themselves as the epitome of wise men. Yet Job has become a laughingstock to them—another injustice that he suffers. 12:6, somewhat obscure, seems to point out the unfairness of the world in which those who provoke God are not punished, contrary to what the friends preach. That God is responsible for this state of affairs is readily apparent, even to dumb animals. This is a rebuttal, in the form of a parody of a wisdom discourse, to Zophar's calling Job a stupid ass and to the notion that wisdom is difficult to obtain but can be achieved if one tries hard enough.

In 12:13–13:2, on the other hand, wisdom and strength are the properties of God, who uses them to control the world. No one can undo what he does. Most of what God does, according to this passage, is destructive and negative; this is a satirical reversal of a hymn of praise for God. Job concludes that what he knows he has learned from his own experience, unlike the friends who rely on conventional assumptions. He insists that he is not inferior to his friends.

Still addressing the friends, in 13:3–19, Job insists that he wants to argue his case directly with God. The friends, he says, have spoken falsely about God (God will agree in 42:7), and they are taking God's side unfairly. In fact, if Job can indeed come before God, that will vindicate him, for "the godless shall not come before him" (13:16). The legal metaphor is prominent in this passage. Verse 15 is a famously difficult passage, sometimes translated "Though he kill me, yet I will hope in him."

In 13:20–14:22 Job pleads with God to desist from troubling him, or at least, as if in a legal scenario, to reveal to him what sin he may have committed. In despair he notes that human life is fleeting and is determined by God. If so, why does God not turn away and let humans enjoy whatever short life he has allotted them? For when humans die, they are dead forever. Job then imagines a temporary death (14:12–17), hiding in Sheol until God's anger passes; afterwards he would live again, this time as a person whose sin is out of God's sight. It is doubtful that the idea of resurrection or a belief in the next world had developed by the time the book was written, although perhaps the idea was beginning to be formulated. More likely, this is a poetic metaphor for an unrealistic situation, a wish on Job's part for a temporary reprieve. 14:1, "a mortal, born of woman," has the nuance of human frailty (see 15:14). 14:2, the imagery of grass and flowers signifies transience, whereas a tree (see 14:7–9) can regenerate.

B. The Second Cycle (15:1–21:34)

With some of the same ideas they used earlier, the friends and Job engage in a second round of dialogues. Here the tone is less sympathetic and more abstract. The focus is on the defense of accepted religious ideology, particularly on the punishment of sinners.

15:1–35. Eliphaz Speaks Again. Eliphaz, using rhetorical questions typical of wisdom dialogue, again criticizes Job's speeches but attributes them to Job's sinfulness, not to his anguish, as he did earlier. Does Job possess some secret wisdom that no one else has, asks Eliphaz with sarcasm. Wisdom that goes back to the time of creation and is therefore like God's wisdom? The implied answer is "no," that Job's wisdom is of recent vintage whereas the friends have the weight of generations of wisdom on their side. Moreover, no human is perfect; even the divine beings are less than perfect (15:15–16; cf. 4:18). But those who are indeed wicked will meet a bad end, described by Eliphaz in lavish detail and with great assurance. The portrait of the sinner includes pain, despair, and destitution; and the absence of the ideal life, for he will die before his time (not in a ripe old age) without progeny to survive him (15:32–33). The emphasis is on retribution, which will come in this life, although the description sounds in part like later images of hell. This chapter is the counterpart of Eliphaz's speech in ch. 5, where he describes the reward of the righteous.

16:1–17:16. Job Responds to Eliphaz. The verbal insults continue as Job dismisses the words of his friends. But the greater criticism is leveled against

God for his savage violence against Job, described in the most physical terms, with a military metaphor added (16:12–15). God has handed Job over to the wicked (16:11) who jeer at him (16:10). But the real enemy is God, who has decimated Job. This discourse is similar to psalmic laments (see also Lam 3:21) but unlike typical laments, it never resolves itself in the sufferer's plea for God to save him and the assurance that God will do so. Legal discourse then takes over, with Job calling upon witnesses to testify on his behalf. "O earth, do not cover my blood" (16:18) is a plea, in legal terms, that the crimes against him be avenged (see Gen 4:10). Parallel to the earth's crying out for him, Job also seeks a heavenly witness ("my witness is in heaven," 16:19), an angel-like figure who can serve as witness and judge in the law suit between Job and God. Chapter 17 expresses Job's despair at his situation—mocking and social ostracism are common motifs in laments—and his sense that the solution to his predicament is death, a thought that he earlier welcomed as an escape from God but here mentions sardonically as the only place he can find a secure home, given the social rejection he finds in life.

18:1–21. Bildad Speaks Again. Less patient than before, Bildad chastises Job, warning him that the natural order of the world will not make an exception in his case, and that the wicked person will receive the harsh punishment he deserves. That punishment is described in graphic detail, including the failure of his schemes, the ensnarement of the wicked, an assault by terror, and the destruction of his home and family, until in the end he is entirely cut off from society; there is no continuity of his family line and no memory of him, except for horror at his fate. The metaphors are largely military and/or hunting images, followed by loss of security and family. The loss of progeny and the family line is especially devastating in the ancient context. The wicked is defined (17:21) as one who does not know God. While Bildad does not say that Job is wicked, and that therefore his situation was deserved, some interpretations infer it. Alternatively, Bildad may be speaking more theoretically, reinforcing the certainty of the traditional claim that sees the moral order reflected in the just awarding of reward and punishment.

19:1–29. Job Responds to Bildad. The war of words continues. Job accuses Bildad of verbal abuse, insisting that God has wronged him (Job) and that he has not sinned. Job's reply calls on military imagery that is reminiscent of Bildad's imagery for the wicked, including darkness, tearing him down, troops advancing against him and encircling him (in a siege). Job has been alienated from his family, friends, and servants. Job is, then, suffering in some ways as Bildad described for the wicked, but Job's description is aimed at evoking sympathy, not condemnation. In fact, he calls for pity from his friends instead of their constant accusations against him. They persecute him as God does rather than offering him support. "O that my words were written down" (19:23): Job wishes to preserve his words, either written in a book or engraved on a rock or monument, presumably so that in some future time he will be proved right. "For I know that my Redeemer lives" (19:25): this famous verse and the following ones are often interpreted Christologically (hence NRSV's capitalization of "Redeemer") to refer to the distant future when Job will be vindicated. It is also used to support the notion of bodily resurrection. However, in the context of the book, it makes more sense to understand this phrase as referring to a time near the present, while Job is still alive, not after his death. The Hebrew term for "redeemer" is *go'el*, meaning a kinsman who is responsible for protecting the interests of the family when the normal avenues of protecting were not present (Lev 25:25, 28; Deut 19:6–12; Ruth 4:4–6; Jer 32:6–7), be it the buying back of inherited land, the ransoming of someone from slavery, or the avenging of a murder. Although Job may wish to have his words preserved, he really wants his vindication now, while still in his flesh (19:26), and here he is expressing the hope that, although there is no one in his immediate family to defend him (since he has been alienated from them), there may yet arise a kinsman to take his side and defend his interests. Better, then, to translate the Hebrew copula *waw* that precedes the word "redeemer" as "but" rather than "for." It is open to interpretation whether Job has an actual person in mind or is using the term metaphorically for a heavenly intercessor like the one in 16:19. Verses 25–29 present a number of textual difficulties but one can discern a hopeful note here, that Job still believes in himself and in the rightness of his cause, which he expects will be demonstrated, and that ultimately the friends will be judged to have been wrong.

20:1–29. Zophar Speaks Again. Zophar is agitated by Job's words, which threaten to undermine the friends' basic principle of reward and punishment. He insists that since the beginning of time, the wicked thrive only briefly and are then sure to be punished. The chapter is devoted to the punishment of the wicked, portrayed in mounting intensity. Verses 4–11 elaborate on the ephemeral nature of the wicked, who "fly away like a dream" (v. 8) and will no longer be remembered. Any happiness that the wicked enjoy will be fleeting, and any wealth they acquire will quickly disappear so that their children "will seek the favor of the poor" (v. 10). Wealth was thought to be a sign of God's blessing, as in the description of Job in 1:2–3, so the wealth of the wicked could not be lasting. The wicked may seem to prosper for a while, but ultimately they will get what they deserve. Verses 12–23 use metaphors related to eating. The wicked person savors evil, holding it in his mouth and enjoying its taste. But this delicious food soon turns into venomous poison in his body, making him sick and ultimately killing him. The wicked is unable to ingest the truly good food, "honey and curds" (v. 17), a symbol of plenty, as in Isa 7:15 (see also the related phrase describing the promised land as a land flowing with milk and honey [Exod 3:8, 17]). Although the wicked person "eats," he cannot "digest" that which he has taken unlawfully; he cannot benefit from his ill-gotten gain, obtained by oppressing the poor. Verse 23 forms a transition between the imagery of the wicked person's eating and God's punishment; God will rain down punishment upon the wicked like food (the Hebrew is obscure). The following verses describe the punishment in terms of metal weapons that attack the wicked and destroy his body. The image begins as a description of a human battle and then turns into a cosmic destruction of the wicked by darkness, fire, and flood. ("The possessions of their house will be carried away" in v. 28 is better rendered "A flood will carry away his house.") Heaven and earth reveal his iniquity and rise up against him. Ending as he began, Zophar declares that this dreadful punishment was ordained by God.

21:1–34. Job Responds to Zophar. Job refutes Zophar's picture of the punishment of the wicked, and by so doing he overturns the foundation of the moral order of the world, as perceived by the friends and the tradition they represent. The principle that the righteous are rewarded and the wicked punished is the foundation of traditional wisdom, as taught in Proverbs and by Job's friends. But Job's personal experience contradicts this principle; and Job's wisdom comes from experience (and later from the revelation of God), not from the traditional wisdom teachings of the ages. We can sympathize with Job, for how often in our own lives do we see the wicked prosper, yet we try to maintain our faith in a moral order. Sometimes, we do so by projecting the time of reward and punishment into the future, after death. But this option was not available to Job; for him and the people of his time, reward and punishment must occur in this life. For Job, then, his own experience stands in direct contradiction with traditional teaching, and that contradiction cannot be harmonized.

The wicked live on, says Job (vv. 7–8), living to a ripe old age, gaining power, and having many children. Old age and much progeny are the blessings of the pious, here portrayed as the fortune of the wicked. The picture of a secure and happy life is further developed: secure homes, successful animal husbandry, an expanding family that brings delight. Furthermore, their wickedness is manifest in their rejection of God (vv. 14–15). And, lest one say that the punishment comes in the time of the children (5:4; 18:19; 20:10), Job replies that the wicked cannot know or care what happens after they are dead, hence it is no punishment at all. Job concludes that reward and punishment are random, without reason (vv. 23–26). Those who think that ultimately the house and the memory of the wicked will perish should consult world-travelers who have seen more than most people. They will report that even after death the wicked are honored (vv. 28–33). In describing the fate of the wicked, Job's friends have brought him not consolation but rather nonsense (*hevel*, the theme-word of Ecclesiastes) that is sacrilege (*ma'al*; NRSV, "falsehood").

C. The Third Cycle (22:1–27:33)

This last round of dialogues among the three friends is shorter than the first two. Bildad's speech is unusually short and under-developed as it stands in ch. 25, although it seems to continue in 26:5–14 under what is labeled as Job's speech. Zophar does not speak at all in this cycle (although some scholars ascribe 27:13–23 to him). Many scholars suspect that part of what was once a more complete cycle, modeled on the first two cycles, had been lost in antiquity and some of the remaining parts have been dis-arranged (before the time of the Septuagint and the Targum of Job at Qumran, which contain the same speeches as the MT). An alternative explanation is that the dialogue intentionally breaks down at this point, the two sides (Job vs. his friends) having made their arguments many times over but being unable to resolve their differing views. To the extent that there is a satisfying solution in the book, it will come later and not from the three friends.

22:1–30. Eliphaz Speaks for the Third Time. Human piety can neither harm nor benefit God, says, Eliphaz, so therefore God is an objective judge of human behavior. Reiterating the accepted principle of reward and punishment, Eliphaz here declares in no uncertain terms that Job has acted wickedly, a point that had been suggested before but only tentatively. Job's wickedness is exemplified by moral and social wrongdoings: economic oppression of family and of the underprivileged in society (the poor who are hungry, widows, and orphans). Similar tropes are used by the prophets in their criticisms of Israelite society. Verse 6 speaks of pledges for loans, here seized "for no reason"—apparently suggesting that the borrower was not given the chance to repay the loan. A person who had nothing of value would give his clothing as a pledge for a loan (Exod 22:25–26; Deut 24:17). NRSV's "from your family" is actually "from your brothers/ fellows" in Hebrew and refers to Israelites in general. The portrait is of a greedy and uncaring person.

In vv. 12–14 the normally positive description of God's position in the heavens is twisted into a negative one. Echoing Job's statement in 21:22b, Eliphaz ascribes to Job the idea that God is so high up in the heavens that he cannot see what is happening on earth. The clouds that envelop God (typical of theophany language; the clouds shield humans from direct contact with the divine) block out his vision (compare Lam 3:44 where the clouds block out prayer). The notion that God does not know what people do is typical of the wicked (e.g., Pss 10:11; 73:11). Eliphaz warns Job not to side with the wicked but to learn from the punishment that they have suffered in the past. The wicked will always be cut off, much to the satisfaction of the righteous. Eliphaz ends by entreating Job to agree with God rather than opposing him, to repent and to pray. Then will God favor him and grant him success.

23:1–24:25. Job Responds. Job seeks God but not the way Eliphaz intended. Using some of the same images for quite different effect, Job insists that he is pious and that if he could find God, he would present his case to him and be acquitted of guilt. Far from suggesting that God cannot see what happens on earth, Job insists that God knows that Job is innocent (23:10). Yet God acts in his own way, doing as he likes, which is what terrifies Job. Indeed, as Eliphaz intimated, there are moral and social injustices in the world, but they are not of Job's doing. Why does God allow them to continue? If he is a just God, why does justice come so slowly?

Job's list of wrongs in the world (24:2–17) is longer and more rhetorically developed than Eliphaz's. It begins with items that one finds in legal collections and prophetic chastisements, like moving boundary markers, oppressing the poor, seizing pledges, and even committing murder, theft, and adultery. But the picture of misery that these wrongs generate is stronger than any condemnation of the evildoers. The poor are completely impoverished, forced off their land, hungry and without shelter against the weather, serving as day laborers who cannot benefit from the food they gather and process for the wealthy. In their weakened and unprotected state, they fall victim at night to murderers, thieves, and adulterers. But it is not so much the criminals who are condemned; rather it is God, who permits his world to deteriorate into lawlessness and social breakdown. God, who knows the time of justice (24:1), does not bring it about in a timely manner.

These chapters are linguistically difficult, and not all passages (especially 24:18–24) altogether comport with their contexts.

25:1–6. Bildad Speaks Briefly. This snippet of a speech may continue in 26:5–14, in what is now included in Job's speech. In terms that echo ancient myths of creation, Bildad declares the superiority of God over everything. "He makes peace" (v. 2) among the rebellious members of the heavenly court (perhaps an ironic nod to the Satan in ch. 1). "How then can a mortal be righteous before God … one born of woman" (v. 4); see 4:17–19 and 15:14–16. Verses 5–6 remind us of Ps. 8, which, for a different purpose, puts humans low on the divine hierarchy; cf. also Job 4:18.

26:1–27:23. Job Responds. Job's first words are sarcastic questions, asking how Bildad has helped him. The attribution of the passage from 26:5–14, describing God's power in creation, is uncertain. Perhaps it is the continuation of Bildad's speech in ch. 25; or perhaps these are Job's words, seemingly agreeing with Bildad's description of God but actually opposing him by describing a God who is cruelly powerful. There are strong echoes of the combat myth of creation. In 26:5–6 the emphasis is on the reaction to God in the netherworld, the place of the dead, especially the "shades," the spirits of dead kings and heroes. The formation of Zaphon, God's cosmic mountain, is mentioned next, followed by the creation of the celestial domain. Verse 10 describes the horizon set upon the waters (cf. Prov 8:27), the place where light and darkness meet. God's defeat of the primordial waters or water-monsters (Sea, Rahab, serpent) form the climax of God's awesome power that none can withstand.

27:1–23. Swearing by God's name (a serious act in the ancient world that makes God a party to the oath), the very God who deprived him of justice, Job insists that he will maintain his integrity (cf. 2:3, 9), meaning that he will not speak falsely nor admit any wrongdoing. In vv. 7–10 Job curses his enemy, whose fate, Job hopes, will be like that of the wicked, described graphically by Zophar in ch. 20 and echoed here. But who is the "enemy"? If it is God, as some suggest, the curse that God will not hear his cry makes little sense. If it is the friends, this is indeed far stronger language against them than has occurred before. Or it may be a rhetorical mode of expression in which Job is actually describing himself, who is being treated by God as if he were wicked. In fact, the resemblance to Zophar's earlier speech in ch. 20 makes Job's speech here look like a parody of it whereby Job is implying his rejection of Zophar's traditional pre-packaged ideas. Job may appear to others to be wicked, to judge by his abject condi-tion, but it is his "enemy" or opponent who is the wicked one, not himself.

IV. A Poem about Wisdom (28:1–28)

This gem of a poem is justly famous, but its place in the structure of the book is uncertain. Since it has no introductory heading to identify the speaker, most scholars think it stands outside the dialogues, either as a later addition or as an original interlude. Others take it as part of Job's preceding speech or even as part of Elihu's speeches that follow in chs. 32–37 (ch. 28 having been misplaced). It seems best to understand the chapter as an interlude that is integral to the book—the linguistic style is similar to the book's other poetry—but not part of any character's speech. The poem focuses on the question of the accessibility of wisdom that has been an underlying subject of the dialogues and that will be further developed when God speaks from the whirlwind (chs. 38–41). The poem falls into three sections: vv. 1–11, 12–19, 20–28, marked by "But where shall wisdom be found?" (v. 12) and "Where then does wisdom come from?" (v. 20).

28:1–11. While most commentators understand this section as a description of mining, some think that it is really about creation, or perhaps a combination of the two in which human mining is analogous to God's creating the world. In any case, this section portrays the world underneath the ground, a world very different from that above the ground (see v. 5). The underneath world is the source for precious metals and stones, to whose value wisdom may be compared (see Prov 3:13–15); in ancient Near Eastern thought, the underneath world is also a potential place where wisdom may be located. Wisdom, like these precious materials, is hard to find and requires great effort to extract. "A mine for silver" (v. 1) in Hebrew is "a source for silver." NRSV chooses the "mining" interpretation. "Miners" (v. 3) is in Hebrew "he." Some commentators think the reference is God rather than a human miner. Verses 7–11 say that humans can seek out places and extract treasures where no other creature can, even birds of prey, which have extraordinarily fine eyesight, and wild animals who roam far to find their prey.

28:12–19. Wisdom is even more difficult to find than precious materials. Humans do not know how to find it. It is not in the land of the living, nor is it in the deep primordial waters, the deep (sweet waters) or the sea (salt waters)—the waters which lie beneath the earth and are even deeper than the mines of the previous section. Wisdom's value is far above the most expensive commodities and the most exotic gems.

28:20–28. No living creature knows where to find wisdom, not even the far-seeing birds. It is neither in the land of the living (v. 13) nor in the realm of death (v. 22). Only God, all-seeing and all-knowing, knows where wisdom is, for he used it to create the world. (On the idea that wisdom was used in creation see Prov 8:22–30 and Ps 104:24.) Wisdom, then, belongs to God, and humans can acquire it only through fearing God. The culmination of this chapter agrees with Prov 1:7 and Eccl 12:13—that the prerequisite for wisdom is the fear of the Lord. "Fear of the Lord ... depart from evil" (v. 28) echoes the description of Job in 1:1. One may conclude, then, that Job is indeed wise. In that light, readers can appreciate Job's final speeches.

V. Job's Concluding Speech (29:1–31:40)

Coming after the interlude of ch. 28, these speeches of Job are not to be taken as concluding his argument to his friends, but as a self-standing speech, different in tone from the dialogues, in which Job presents himself and his situation to anyone who will listen (the implied audience is unclear). Job has actually not had the opportunity to do this earlier: in the prologue he is presented by the narrator; and in the dialogues by the friends, with Job providing "corrections" to their estimate of him; but here he speaks for himself, telling his story in his own words. He begins (ch. 29) by wishing for the good old days when God was beneficent to him and he was successful in life, enjoying high status and the respect of his community, where his every word was valued (unlike the reception his friends gave his words now). He then laments (ch. 30) that now younger men deride him and God does not heed his cry. He reiterates his innocence (ch. 31) using the language of oath-taking—if he did X, may Y happen to him—whereby a person legally proclaims his innocence. This section has often been compared with the Egyptian Book of the Dead, wherein the deceased declares to Osiris, the divine ruler of the realm of the dead, and to forty-two judges that he is innocent of a specific list of offenses. It also bears some resemblance to Samuel's farewell address (1 Sam 12:1–5) in which he rhetorically asks the community if he has defrauded anyone and the Israelites answer formulaically that he has not.

29:1–25. Job wishes for life as it was before his suffering, when he felt cared for by God, as evident by the fact that he led a successful life, surrounded by his immediate family (vv. 4–6), respected by his peers at the upper echelons of society (vv. 7–11), and a benefactor to those at lower socio-economic levels (vv. 12–17). No one spoke when Job spoke (vv. 9–11; speech is important at the end of the chapter as well, and at the beginning of ch. 30). He aided the unfortunate and saw to it that the wrong-doer did not oppress them. In a nutshell, the social values of society—honor and social justice—were embodied in Job. This section provides a complement, with different emphasis, to the narrator's description of Job in 1:1–3, a God-fearing person of substance and social standing. Job expected to live this way forever (there was no reason he should not), enjoying a long and vigorous life with his family and the continued respect of the community who looked to him for counsel and approval.

30:1–19. Now, in the language that combines lament and anger, Job describes his fallen social state, when even younger men with no status mock him. Job describes these people as outcasts and scavengers who shame and abuse Job. Job has lost his honor and his place in society. He suffers mentally and physically; physical pain and disease is often the way mental anguish is described, here and in the psalms.

30:20–31. Addressing God (as he might have been doing all along), Job complains that God has not heard his cries and has not helped him. In fact, God is cruel to Job, harassing him and bringing him close to death (which earlier Job wished for but here uses as a sign of extreme suffering). Despite his care for the needy, which should have brought him God's blessing, Job is beset with misery, socially isolated in the mirror image of his former state. The description echoes Lamentations: the ostrich and the jackal were thought to be nasty animals who frequented ruins or lived in the wasteland (cf. Lam 4:3, where they are considered bad parents); blackened skin and bones dried out from the heat render the person unrecognizable (cf. Lam 4:8, where they are the result of starvation in the siege). Job's former public persona has been erased; hence, he ceased to exist. In a society where one's identity was a function of one's belonging to and hierarchy in a group, and where the individual was of little import, this is the equivalent of identity-theft.

31:1–40. Believing in both himself and in God, Job seeks a way out of the conundrum in which he finds himself. He declares God's omniscience, which must include the knowledge of Job's righteousness. Job insists, indeed, formally declares in an oath-like formula ("If I have done X, let Y happen to me"), that he has conducted himself properly in a long list of situations.

31:1–12. The first theme is sexual propriety. Job has not lusted after women nor committed adultery (a capital offense). Warnings against such behavior are directed at young men in Proverbs; here, then, Job portrays himself as the "wise" person that Proverbs seeks to produce. Had he engaged in inappropriate sexual behavior, Job would deserve severe punishment, which he states not in terms of legal penalties but in terms of measure for measure retribution. In v. 8, sowing and reaping may be taken literally or may be metaphors for having sex. A clearer case is in v. 10, where "grind" and "kneel" have sexual connotations. If, says Job, I have violated another man's wife, let my own wife be violated.

31:13–23. The second theme is care for those who are lower on the socio-economic scale: servants and the poor. Job has not ignored or rejected the grievances of his servants, for they, like he, are God's creations (v. 15). Job speaks here not as a powerful owner of slaves or as a judge, but as one who can empathize with his fellow human beings. An extension of that sentiment is his generosity to the poor, including the orphan and the widow (who often exemplify disadvantaged members of society). Charity to the poor is a common biblical trope. The punishment suggested by Job if he had not been charitable is that his shoulder and arm, symbols of his strength and control, be broken. He would then be subject to superior power, as the poor were to his own power.

31:24–28. The third theme is loyalty to the important values, mainly to the fear of God. Job has not been seduced by money, nor has he been enticed by false worship of the celestial bodies. Rather, he remained loyal to God.

31:29–34. This section deals with proper behavior to outsiders: enemies and sojourners. Job did not rejoice at the downfall of his enemies, and he specifically did not curse them. And he provided hospitality for wayfarers. The last phrase in v. 33 may be rendered as "like Adam" instead of "as others do." The allusion is to Adam's hiding his disobedience from God (Gen 3:8). The effect is to make any failure of Job's social conduct equivalent to disobeying God; and, more to the point, it also makes any attempt to hide a sin from God impossible. Just as Adam could not hide his sin, so Job could not hide any sin from God. Therefore, Job must be sinless. Why, then, must he fear everyone and remain isolated?

31:35–37. Job pleads for God to hear his case, to provide a response to his declaration of innocence, or to draw up an accusation against him that Job would proudly display. This would give Job an even better chance to prove his innocence.

31:38–40. These verses return to the formula "If I have done X, may Y happen to me." They concern proper disposition of the land and its produce. On one level, Job is saying that if he has taken from the land anything that does not belong to him, may the land never produce food for him again. On a second and more serious level, Job alludes to the idea that the land of Israel rids itself of anyone who has polluted it by immoral offenses (Deut 24:3). This is an allusion to national exile, which seems to be applied here to Job's sense of personal exile from God and from his society.

The words of Job are ended (31:40). The narrator or editor signals the end of the dialogues. (Cf. Ps 72:20; Jer 51:64, which mark the end of a major section or subcollection.)

VI. The Elihu Speeches (32:1–37:24)

Most scholars think the Elihu speeches are a later addition to the book. The end of Job's speeches, and the friends' speeches as well, is formally noted in 31:40 and 32:1, so the introduction of Elihu is certainly a new move in the book. That this character is not mentioned among the friends in the prologue (chs. 1–2) or the epilogue (42:7–17) suggests that he was not originally present. He seems to know the earlier speeches since he quotes from them more frequently than the earlier speakers do. The style of his discourse is different from the earlier dialogues, with more Aramaisms and a preference for the divine name "El." Elihu presents himself as something of an upstart, a younger man who thinks he can accomplish what the three friends failed to do. Modern readers often find him to be a windbag, a portrait with which Elihu might agree (see 32:18–20). He speaks at length; there are four speeches, as marked by editorial phrases like "Then Elihu continued," but they follow one another with no interruption or response from Job or anyone else. While he does not actually add a new line of thought to the previous arguments, he emphasizes the idea of speaking even more than the others and also the idea of "knowledge." His main line of argument is that God is just. He agrees with the three friends that Job must have sinned, but he focuses less on Job's sin and more on the greatness of God, arguing that Job cannot put himself on the same level as the deity. His description of God's power, especially in ch. 37, prepare the way for God's speeches that follow immediately in ch. 38.

32:1–5. The narrator introduces Elihu in a few prose lines telling us four times that he was angry, at Job because Job thought himself more righteous than God and at the friends because they could not convince Job otherwise.

32:6–22. Elihu's first speech. Elihu begins his poetic discourse by addressing all present. In 33:1 he directs his words to Job, and in 34:1 he speaks to the "wise men." Job is the addressee in 35:1. Elihu opens by challenging the accepted notion that to be older is to be wiser. Wisdom, he opines, is not a factor of age but of the knowledge given by God. He waited patiently for his elders to speak, he explains in a quasi-humble manner, but he found their words unenlightening. Now, bursting with eagerness to voice his own views, he can hold himself back no longer.

33:1–31. Elihu takes God's side against Job. In order to persuade Job, to soften him up, as it were, Elihu points out that both he and Job are equal in that both are creatures of God (33:6–7), so Elihu is not trying to overwhelm Job with superior power, but to convince him as an equal. Job was wrong, says Elihu, to think that he was innocent and was being persecuted by God. Elihu argues that God is greater than humans, and that he does, indeed, reply to humans but in indirect ways, through dreams and night visions (both were accepted modes of divine revelation), which Job earlier found terrifying (7:4). The main point is that pain and suffering are God's means to discipline people, to turn them away from wrong actions. The description of illness in 33:19–22 is quite vivid. The sufferer is rescued by a mediator (the Hebrew term is *melitz*, "an angel, a mediator" in NRSV; others take it as a human intercessor), who declares the innocence of the sufferer before God. Then God returns him to health. This is a later take on the psalmic laments in which the sufferer appeals to God directly and is saved. The idea of an angelic intermediary reflects later Judaism, as does the emphasis on prayer and repentance (33:26–27; the growth of penitential prayer is a phenomenon of the Second Temple period). While Eliphaz contended (5:17) that Job's suffering could be seen as divine correction, Elihu has a much more developed system whereby God regularly brings a person to the brink of death as a way to shape him morally, with repentance being the key ingredient to deliverance. Thus, by insisting on his innocence, Job defeats Elihu's system for he has no reason to repent. That is why Elihu was angry at Job.

34:1–37. Elihu's second speech. Elihu addresses the wise men, presumably not Job's friends whom he castigated in ch. 32 for their ineffective arguments, but a wider implied audience of wise men, the community's bearers of wisdom. Elihu aligns them with himself as opposing Job, and he proposes that they can assay Job's arguments with their own minds, that is, through reason. He quotes Job's earlier words in a belittling manner, implying that these words make no sense and are contrary to what is known of the world. He deems Job, who insists that God has been unjust to him, to be among the wicked, for Job denies the basic principle that God rewards or punishes people for just cause. Most of the chapter, its central section from vv. 10–33, is a description of God's nature and his governance of the world, which is intended to refute Job's argument. In the concluding verses (34–37) Elihu again addresses the wise men, requesting that they verify Elihu's estimation of Job's wickedness.

34:1. Then Elihu continued. The Hebrew uses the same expression, literally "then Elihu said and replied," that was employed in the dialogues when the speaker changed, but here Elihu is the only speaker. The phrase marks a new section or speech and is thus well-rendered in NRSV.

34:7. "Who is there like Job" is somewhat ironic to the reader who knows there is no one on earth as perfect as Job (1:8), but Elihu means it in a derogatory sense: there is no person who mocks God as Job does.

34:10–37. Arguing against Job, Elihu notes that a main attribute of God is that God does not act wickedly, for he repays people for their deeds as they deserve. God is, then, a just God. The "proof" is that God created the world and continues to maintain it; if God were to disappear, so would the world. God as creator is a common trope, most often used to demonstrate God's power over enemies and his care for the righteous, but here it supports the assertion that God is just. The "logic" with which Elihu backs up this statement is "Shall one who hates justice govern?" (34:17). It is inconceivable to Elihu that the ruler of the world, who chose to create and govern the world, would be unjust; and he illustrates this point by showing how God addresses injustice in the world, even when it comes from kings. God shows no partiality to the rich and powerful. Moreover, he sees every human action and there is no place to hide from him, even in the darkest shadows. This statement refutes Job's in 24:13–17 that criminals operate in darkness unbeknownst to God. It may also be a subtle reproof of Job's wish to escape from God's sight and a warning to Job that he cannot get away with his "lies." Verse 23 is difficult; it seems to mean that there are no set times to come before God for justice; rather, God carries out justice in his own good time and it is not for humans to compel him to do so. Nevertheless, God is sure to carry out justice, sometimes suddenly and without warning (34:20, 24–27). Even if God apparently remains silent and hides his face, he will eventually render justice (v. 29 is difficult) for in that way does God prevent the wicked from triumphing.

Verses 31–37 are difficult and have been variously interpreted as Elihu's advice to Job, or Elihu's construction of what Job expects God to say, or, perhaps best, a concluding address to the wise men, condemning once again Job's lack of understanding of God's justice.

35:1–16. Elihu's third speech. Directing his remarks to Job, Elihu continues his argument along the same lines as before but with a slightly different focus. He does not argue that Job was inaccurate to say that he had not sinned, but rather that saying so showed a lack of justness (*mishpat*, a term that occurs several times in Elihu's speeches). The point Elihu makes is that whether a person sins or not does not affect God in the least, and similarly, being righteous offers no benefit to God. It is human beings who are affected by righteousness or wickedness. God remains true to his nature whatever people do. That does not mean, however, that God pays no heed to human behavior. On the contrary, God is ever vigilant.

35:9–16. If the oppressed cry out but are not answered, it is because "no one says, 'Where is God my Maker' " (35:10), that is, they do not call upon God in the manner proper to prayer (or, alternatively, those seeing oppression in the world complain about it but do not seek God's help). They do not recognize that God gave them more knowledge than he gave the animals (or, alternatively, that humans learn from the animals about God's nature; compare Job's words in 12:7). If God fails to respond immediately, it is because of "the pride of evildoers" (35:12), that is, the oppressed are evildoers in that they did not say "Where is God my Maker." Their cry is, then, "an empty cry" (v. 13) which goes unheeded: "Surely God does not hear an empty cry." An alternative interpretation is that this phrase means "Surely it is false that God does not listen" (NJPS). Whatever the precise meaning of this difficult passage may be, Elihu is insinuating that Job, who is a prideful evildoer (because he has accused God of injustice), has by his own words prevented or delayed God's proper response. Elihu moves from generalities to Job's particular case in v. 14, which, according to NRSV, means that Job's cry to God is even less valid than that described in the previous verses. The chapter concludes by summing up Job's words as *hevel*, worthless, empty words, since they are uninformed by true knowledge.

36:1–37:24. Elihu's fourth speech. In contrast to Job's worthless words (35:16), Elihu characterizes his own speech as "not false" because he is "perfect in knowledge" (36:4), that is, his knowledge is complete whereas Job's falls short. He then reiterates at greater length and intensity his previous point that God is just, that he punishes the wicked and rewards the righteous.

36:5–15. If God's justice appears delayed, it is because the righteous are arrogant and need to be shown the error of their ways (cf. 35:12). Suffering is a wake-up call to obey God: "He delivers the afflicted by their affliction" (36:15). If the sufferers listen and serve God, they will be granted prosperity, but if not, they will perish, "without knowledge."

Knowledge or its absence is a repeated theme in this chapter. Worse than righteous sufferers who calls upon God (even imperfectly) are the "godless in heart" who do not cry out (to God) when they suffer (36:13). This is a more pointed critique of Job, who never asks God to save him but only rants and rages against what God has done to him. The idea that the godless meet an early death (36:14) is a rhetorical exaggeration, suggesting that they have no chance to change their ways and be delivered; it obviously cannot apply to Job, who is no longer young.

36:16–21. Elihu now switches from making general statements in the third person to addressing Job in the second person. This section is difficult to understand (especially v. 19) and has provoked different renderings. The gist is that God has granted beneficence to Job (presumably in the past) but Job is concerned only with the question of God's justness. Job should beware that his anger at God should not lead him to mock God or accuse him falsely of being unjust. Verse 21, as rendered by NRSV, seems to explain Job's current situation by the earlier point that affliction is a warning to avoid iniquity.

36:22–37:24. Elihu concludes his discourse with praise of God's power. He employs many rhetorical questions, as God will do in chs. 38–39. These rhetorical questions draw in the listener (Job), who can easily supply the answers, thereby supporting Elihu's argument. The tone of the discourse gradually changes from annoyed impatience at the lack of knowledge of God displayed by Job to a calmer, hymn-like expression of awe and appreciation for God's immense power and presence in the world. The main point is that God is in no way comparable with humans.

36:22–33. This section may be subdivided into three parts, each beginning with Hebrew *hen*, "indeed" (rendered in vv. 22 and 30 in NRSV by "see," and in v. 26 by "surely.") God's power, says Elihu, is far above everyone and everything; no one teaches him what to do and no one can accuse him of error. Rather, Job should extol God in songs of praise, as others do. Humans observe God's greatness from a distance, a thought that leads to the point that God is ultimately unknowable (36:26a), that God and humans are not comparable. "The number of his years is unsearchable" (36:26b), or, "the number of his years is infinite." The crucial distinction between God and humans is that God lives forever while humans are mortal (cf. Gen 3:22).

Evidence for God's superiority to humans is the divine creation and control of the cosmos (a common biblical trope). The primary example is the cycle of rain, which is both beneficent, bringing the water necessary to grow food, and also frightening and dangerous, with its storms and lightning (cf. 37:13). The imagery in vv. 29–33 is reminiscent of Ps 29 and elsewhere where God is depicted as a storm-god. Verse 33, as rendered by NRSV, interprets lightning and thunder as God's anger at iniquity (the verse is difficult).

37:1–13. The theme of God's power manifested through thunder and lightning is developed further, along with related meteorological phenomena. This is a wonder that humans are unable to fathom (37:5).

The less common phenomena of snow and ice, infrequent but not unknown in Israel, are even more wondrous. Ice comes from the breath of God and the expanse of water is frozen (37:10). When a snow storm or rain storm occurs, this is a sign of God's power. Even animals must take shelter. Again, Elihu does not stop at the mention of these marvelous divine acts, but explains them as being either for correction or for love (37:13).

37:14–24. Addressing Job by name, Elihu urges Job to consider God's wondrous works, posing rhetorical questions (much as God will do in ch. 38) calculated to emphasize Job's ignorance and powerlessness versus God's cosmic power. God's "knowledge is perfect" (37:16) recalls Elihu's claim that his own knowledge is perfect (36:4). This is not to suggest that Elihu's knowledge equals God's, but to focus on Job's imperfect, incomplete knowledge and to intimate that Elihu is correct about God's nature while Job is mistaken. The theme of "knowing" is emphasized in these verses when Elihu asks Job "Do you know" (37:15, 16) and "Teach us" (37:19; literally, "cause us to know"). "Whose garments are hot" (37:17) is a way of saying that Job is at the mercy of the weather and cannot control its effect. "Spread out the skies, hard as a molten mirror" (37:18). The verb "spread out" is from the same root as "firmament" or "dome" (NRSV) in Gen 1:6–7, and it means something hammered out like metal. (Compare the different and softer image in Isa 40:22: "stretches out the heavens like a curtain.") Verses 21–22 describe a theophany; God appears as brightness, as golden splendor (compare the similar and more elaborate description in Ezek 1). This is a foreshadowing of the theophany that follows in the next chapter and suggests that even if the Elihu speeches were a later addition, they have been neatly stitched into their present context. The speech culminates with Elihu's main point: that God is inscrutable and awesome in power and in justice. A play on the similar-sounding Hebrew words "to see" and "to fear" informs the last verse and introduces the common wisdom trope of fearing the Lord.

VII. God Speaks from the Whirlwind (38:1–42:6)

Rightfully considered the climax of the book, God at last appears to Job in a theophany (theophanies are often accompanied by thunder and lightning, as at Mt. Sinai). God does not answer Job's questions, but instead he reveals to him something of divine wisdom, the wisdom whereby the cosmos was created. Several scholars have described these Godspeeches in terms of the sublime—the description of something that is indescribable, that exceeds the imagination, that evokes the feeling of being overwhelmed by something too vast or too powerful to be fully grasped. The divine speeches present verbal pictures of the edge of the cosmos where chaos and creation meet—the mysterious place far from human habitation where darkness turns to dawn, where snow and hail are stored, where wild and exotic animals go about their lives. The purpose of these speeches was not to frighten Job into submission, but rather to lift Job to a new level of reality, a

God's-eye view of the universe, where all things, even suffering and death, have their place and need no justification. From a human perspective this is not a perfect place, for it includes elements of chaos, which, though under God's control, continue to be present in the universe; moreover, even these elements of chaos are cared for by God. For all that, God's speeches may appear terrifying, but they are also comforting, for they reassure readers and Job that the world was indeed created through divine wisdom and that it continues to operate that way.

There are two speeches, 38:1–39:30 and 40:1–41:34 (MT: 26), with short responses by Job at 40:3–5 and 42:1–6. As in the speeches of the human characters, there are many rhetorical questions. In these chapters they highlight the contrast between God's power and knowledge and Job's lack of these attributes. The description of creation moves in general from the founding of the universe to celestial and meteorological phenomena, and then to wild and exotic fauna, including the war-horse, the Behemoth, and the Leviathan. The descriptions are highly poetic and highlight God's understanding and care of his creations vis-à-vis Job's inability to do so.

38:1–39:30. God's first speech. God's first speech sets Job's lack of knowledge against God's perfect knowledge, as shown by his creation of the world and his ongoing care of it. It begins with the creation of the universe, the control over the sea, and the creation of light. It then moves to meteorological phenomena, the constellations, and again to the rain. Finally, it speaks of wild animals—mountain goats, wild asses and oxen, birds of prey— whose ways only God understands and whom God provides for. These animals are not under the sway of humans. Somewhat anomalously, from the modern perspective, the ostrich and the war horse are included in this picture, perhaps because of their energy and their nonconventional behavior that puts them at odds with human tastes and values, as the other animals in this speech are.

38:1–3. God responds to Job's challenge with a challenge of his own. Echoing Elihu, God declares that Job lacks knowledge, as the "examination" that follows will prove.

38:4–7. Where was Job when God created the universe? In a society that prized antiquity, the first question shows that Job is a recent newcomer to the world. In any case, he would not have been able to construct it as God did. The imagery is architectural—laying a foundation and a cornerstone, taking measurements. Verse 7 introduces the idea of the cosmos as God's temple, in which the heavenly beings sing his praise.

38:8–11. The restraining of the sea, the primordial waters of chaos, is a major feature in creation imagery (see Gen 1:6–10). Normally, the sea is depicted as a powerful force of evil that needs to be prevented from overrunning the created world and returning it to chaos, but here that image is softened. The sea is likened to a newborn whom God swaddled in the clouds.

38:12–15. Interpretive problems abound, but the sense is that Job cannot control the cycle of day and night.

38:16–21. Job has never been to the far reaches of the cosmos; he has never traversed the cosmos and therefore has no direct experience of it. Verses 16–17 refer to the vertical axis, the deepest places of the universe, the realm of darkness and death below the earth. Verses 18–19 refer to the horizontal axis, the places from which light and darkness, day and night, originate. Verse 21 is obviously ironic.

38:22–30. Meteorological phenomena, located far from human habitation: snow, hail, east wind (also the source of the light), rain, dew, and ice. Job knows neither the origin of these phenomena nor how to direct them. These "exotic" meteorological events are distant from humans; even the rain is in the desert where no one lives. In v. 28–29 God is imagined as both father and mother to the various forms of water, much as he parented the sea (38:8–9).

38:31–33. The constellations, which rise and set and change their positions in the sky throughout the year. The identity of *Mazzaroth* is unknown. For the other names see 9:9. *The Pleiades* is in Hebrew "the herd," *Orion* is "fool," and *the Bear* may be "lioness."

38:34–38. Job lacks the wisdom to know when and how to send the rain to water the earth; that is, he is unable to provide sustenance for the universe as God does (also 38:39–41). The imagery in vv. 37–38 is evocative—the clouds as rain-jars and the rain pouring down onto the earth, forming mud. In v. 36 the terms "inward parts" and "the mind" are obscure in Hebrew and may refer either to proper names (perhaps of Egyptian deities) or to birds who could tell when rain would fall.

38:39–41. God provides for the wild animals and birds, far from human habitation, while Job cannot. The lion, a predator, and the raven, a scavenger, seem most able to provide for themselves, yet is it really God who provides their food.

39:1–4. Job does not know the gestation cycle of the wild mountain goats. Unlike domestic animals, these animals are not bred by humans.

39:5–12. The wild ass and the wild ox run free in uninhabited areas. Like the wild goats, they are the antithesis of domesticated asses and oxen. These animals resist human domination over them. This is a part of nature that humans cannot control.

39:13–18. The ostrich, an ungainly and flightless bird that can run very fast (v. 13), was widely considered throughout the ancient Near East to be a negligent parent (cf. Lam 4:3) because it deposits its egg in a hole in the sand rather than in a conventional nest (although it is not accurate that it abandons its egg or its young). Its poor parenting is explained here by God's depriving it of wisdom. The ostrich is also a loner or outcast (30:29). The stereotypical hiding of its head in the sand (or in a bush) is not biblical but is mentioned by the Roman writer Pliny the Elder.

39:19–25. The final phrase of the ostrich passage, "the horse and its rider" (v. 18), forms a transition to the war horse, also fast running. The horse pulled the chariot and the rider rode in the chariot, not on the horse. This horse is eager for battle, undaunted by the sight and sound of weapons.

39:26–30. The hawk and the eagle are birds of prey that soar high above the earth. Job is no more responsible for their instinctive behavior than he is for the behavior of the other creatures. This is the natural world that God has made, with its own rules that humans cannot understand or regulate. If Job cannot understand the natural world, how can he understand God's actions vis-à-vis humans?

40:1–5. Job's response. Job now understands that he is unworthy in comparison to God and says that having spoken before when he had no right to, he will now keep silent. Notwithstanding Job's admission of unworthiness, God continues to speak. Job's more contrite response will come at 42:1–6.

40:6–14. God's second speech. God's second speech begins with words similar to his first (38:1–3), but then raises the stakes by daring Job to make himself as powerful and majestic as God is, so that he is able to bring low the proud. Verse 8 articulates the way Job has set up the contest between himself and God into a zero-sum game: will Job condemn God so that he (Job) may be justified?

40:15–41:34. The Behemoth and the Leviathan. Having dared Job to vanquish the proud and powerful, God describes the archetypes of powerful creatures, the Behemoth and the Leviathan (cf. 41:34). It is not clear whether these are mythical beasts or actual animals. Many identify the Behemoth as the hippopotamus, since he lives in the marsh, or perhaps as a bovine creature, since he eats grass like cattle and his description implies the virility often associated with bulls. The word "Behemoth" is a plural form of "cattle" or "beast," a land animal in contrast to the Leviathan, a sea monster. The Leviathan has been identified as the crocodile although elsewhere in the Bible it is a mythical sea serpent or sea dragon associated with the forces of chaos. Its description here is as much mythical as real. Both the hippopotamus and the crocodile are known in Egypt, in real life and as mythological creatures whom the god Horus slays, although it is not clear why Egyptian cultural symbols would be used here. My own preference is to think of the Behemoth and the Leviathan as mythical animals that are modeled on exaggerated descriptions of real creatures. I would liken the Behemoth to a dinosaur, a real animal that has taken on mythic dimensions. The counterpart for the Leviathan is the Loch Ness monster, a creature that occupies the space between real and mythic.

40:15–24. The Behemoth is the first of the great acts of God (v. 19; cf. v. 15) meaning that this beast is venerable compared to the newcomer, Job. His body is compared to the tallest of trees and the hardest of metals. The stiff tail in v. 17 may be a euphemism for an erect penis.

41:1–34 (40:25–41:26 in Hebrew). The Leviathan, like the Behemoth, cannot be hunted, nor can it be tamed. The Leviathan is even more frightening than the Behemoth, with impenetrable armor-like skin, spewing fire from its mouth and nostrils. This sea dragon is undaunted by any weapon. It thrashes about in the water and frightens even the gods (divine beings, 41:25).

42:1–6. Job's second response. Job now recognizes that God is beyond human comprehension, and that the world is not run by human rules of order or moral justice. Quoting God (42:3–4; cf. 38:2–3), he admits that he spoke before from a lack of knowledge. Now, after the theophany, Job has a deeper, more direct understanding of God, not just through hearing about him from traditional teaching but through "seeing," that is, experiencing God firsthand (Job did not literally see God). Before, Job's experience was incongruent with traditional teaching about God. Now, though, from his position of greater understanding, that tension is gone, for Job sees the world differently. The world that he sees is not neatly divided into good and evil, righteousness and sin; rather, it is a world in which elements of chaos—and that includes suffering—remain, under God's watchful eye. Job suffers not because he sinned, but because he is human.

42:6 is enigmatic. Whatever its exact meaning, Job does not repent of sin (of which he was free) but of his accusations against God. In the end, as at the beginning, Job is God-fearing.

VIII. Epilogue: Job is Vindicated and Restored (42:7–17)

The prose narrative that opened the book concludes here, forming a frame around the poetic speeches and providing closure. God deems Job correct and his friends wrong in the way they spoke about God (42:7–8). Many interpreters find this statement inconsistent with the dialogues, but it may mean that Job was more honest than his friends in trying to understand God's ways, and in the end more successful, whereas the friends maintained a more simplistic view of God.

Job is restored twofold, including a new set of children (which seems not to have raised ancient eyebrows). Special attention is granted the daughters, who are named, declared most beautiful (a favorite biblical attribute for women), and receive an inheritance along with their brothers (this is highly unusual). Job lived for 140 years, twice the natural lifetime of 70 years (Ps 90:10) and had four generations of descendents. Long life and great progeny is the traditional reward for piety and wisdom. And so Job "lives happily ever after," having successfully undergone a quest for wisdom like no other man.

BIBLIOGRAPHY

S. Balentine. *Job* (Macon, Ga.: Smyth and Helwys, 2006); D. Clines. *Job 1–20.* WBC 17 (Dallas: Word Books, 1989); _____. *Job 21–37.* WBC 18A (Nashville: Thomas Nelson, 2006); K. Dell. *The book of Job as skeptical literature.* BZAW 197 (Berlin; New York; De Gruyter, 1991); E. Good. *In Turns of Tempest: A Reading of Job, with a Translation* (Palo Alto: Stanford University Press, 1990); N. Habel. *The Book of Job. A Commentary.* OTL (Philadelphia: Westminster, 1985); Y. Hoffman. *A Blemished Perfection. The Book of Job in Context.* JSOTSup 213 (Sheffield: Sheffield Academic Press, 1996); C. Newsom. "The Book of Job." NIB (Nashville: Abingdon, 1996) 4:317–637; _____. *The Book of Job: A Contest of Moral Imaginations* (New York: Oxford, 2003); M. Pope. *Job.* AB 15 (Garden City: Doubleday, 1973); R. Scheindlin. *The Book of Job. Translation, Introduction, and Notes* (New York and London: Norton, 1998); R. Whybray. *Job.* Readings (Sheffield: Sheffield Academic Press, 1998); G. H. Wilson. *Job.* NIBCOT 10 (Peabody, Mass.: Hendrickson Publishers; Bletchley, Milton Keynes, UK: Paternoster, 2007).

PSALMS

Rolf A. Jacobson

OVERVIEW

The Psalter is a collection of 150 prayers, songs, liturgies, and poems. The various psalms were composed by a variety of authors, all of whom are anonymous.

Many psalms are introduced with superscriptions such as "of David" or "of Asaph." Such superscriptions do not identify the author of these compositions, but rather indicate that the psalm is to be associated with these figures in some fashion. Most scholars believe that these superscriptions were not originally a part of the psalms that they introduce. They were most likely added at a later date, sometime during the process through which the individual psalms were collected together. These superscriptions often include terms and phrases that interpreters believe are musical notations referring to how the psalms were performed. These include "for the flutes" (Ps 5), "with stringed instruments" (Ps 4), and the like. The meaning of other terms in the superscriptions is simply unknown, such as "according to the Sheminith" (Ps 6), "according to the Gittith" (Ps 7), and so on. The meaning of *Selah*, which occurs 71 times in the middle of various psalms as well as 3 times in Habakkuk 3, is also unknown; most believe that it was a liturgical direction, perhaps calling for a pause or a musical interlude.

The interpretation of the psalms has been dominated by a method called Form Criticism. This approach categorizes the psalms into various genres, or forms, and interprets the psalms in light of these categories. The most significant forms are:

Prayers for Help—Also called "laments," these are prayers that request divine rescue from various crises. Most of the time, little specific information about the situation that gave rise to these prayers is discernible. Perhaps specific information was deliberately obscured in the editing process so as to make the prayers available to future generations to be prayed in many circumstances. Prayers for help come in both individual and communal forms. For a representative prayer for help, see the commentary on Ps 13. There are more prayers for help than any other type of psalm.

Hymns of Praise—Also called psalms of "descriptive praise," these songs were composed for the community to sing in worship. The purpose of praise is not to flatter God but to bear witness to God's character, actions, and blessings. There are subgroupings of hymns, such as the "songs of Zion" (see Ps 46) and "enthronement psalms" (see Ps 47). For a representative hymn, see Ps 117.

Songs of Thanksgiving—Also called psalms of "declarative praise," these songs were composed to praise God following an experience of having been rescued by God from some crisis. Songs of thanksgiving come in both individual and communal forms. In the Psalter, the appropriate way for one to offer thanks to God is to publicly praise God so that others may hear about and learn from what God has done. For a representative song of thanksgiving, see Ps 30.

Instructional Psalms—Also called "wisdom psalms," many of the poems in the Psalter show the influence of Israel's wisdom tradition and seem to have been written in order to offer instruction. For a representative instructional psalm, see Ps 41.

Royal Psalms—Many of the prayers, hymns, and poems of the Psalter were written either about Israel's kings or composed for them to perform. Royal psalms are not properly a "form," since there are royal hymns, royal liturgies, and royal prayers for help. Yet there are enough psalms that clearly relate in some way to the king that scholars have assigned them the category of "royal psalm." For a representative royal psalm, see Ps 2.

Liturgies—Many of the psalms seem to have been liturgical compositions, in which various sections may have been spoken or sung by different parties. These psalms both offer clues as to how Israel worshiped and also may hint at how all of the psalms were performed in the Temple. For a representative liturgy, see Ps 15.

Other Psalm Forms—In addition to these major types of psalms, there are also acrostic poems (see Pss 9/10), historical psalms (see Pss 103 and 104), festival psalms (see Pss 50, 81, 95), and other genres that have been proposed by various scholars.

The upside of form criticism is that it helps interpreters to see recurring patterns in the psalms and to remember that these are the real prayers and songs of ancient people. The downside of form criticism is that it sometimes causes interpreters to flatten individual psalms. This can result in a tendency to fail to appreciate the unique aspects of various psalms and to reduce all prayers for help (for example) into a single, aggregate prayer.

Perhaps the most salient feature of the psalms is that they are Hebrew poetry. Hebrew poetry is both like and unlike English poetry. Like English language poetry, Hebrew poetry tends to be richly symbolic, metaphorical, and imaginative. It often makes non-linear leaps (for example, expressing deeply anguished pain in one verse and expressing stolid trust in the very next) or indulges in counterfactual imagery (e.g., describing a river in the midst of the city of Jerusalem, in which there is no actual river; cf. Ps 46:4). The imaginative and often playful nature of this poetry contributes both to the joy and difficulty of reading the psalms.

Unlike English poetry, end rhyme is not an important feature in Hebrew poetry. But in the same way that end rhyme lends structure and a sense of completion to English poetry, a feature called "parallelism" serves a similar purpose in Hebrew poetry. Parallelism can be described as the balancing of two or more sections of grammar by placing one after the other. For example:

> Have mercy on me, O God, according to your steadfast love;
>
> > According to your mercy, blot out my transgressions. (Ps 51:1)[1]

Or

> My heart is steadfast, O God, my heart is steadfast;
>
> > I will sing and make melody. Awake, my soul!
>
> Awake, O harp and lyre!
>
> I will awake the dawn. (Ps 108:1–2)

Although some scholars have tried to capture the different ways in which Hebrew parallelism functions by assigning categories and labels to it, it is most helpful simply to be aware that parallelism exists. It works by taking a word or phrase and then building on it by attaching another word or phrase.

The 150 psalms of the Psalter are divided into five books, each of which closes with a verse or more of doxological praise. The most likely reason for this five-book division was to put the Psalter on even footing with the Pentateuch, which also has five books. In recent years, some scholars have argued that there is a discernible progression and argument in the arrangement of these psalms. It is apparent that the psalms move generally from individual psalms to communal psalms, from prayers for help to songs of praise, and from psalms of David to psalms associated with other figures. According to one major interpretation, the Psalter tells the story of the rejection of the Davidic covenant—which had accented the eternal nature of the Davidic monarchy—and the embrace of the Mosaic covenant, which had emphasized the responsibility for all Israelites to keep the law. An alternative viewpoint notes that both royal and instructional psalms were placed at key seams between various of the Psalter's five books. According to this view, the placement of these psalms serve to teach that the Psalter is both a book of instruction (for all Israelites) and a book of promise (that God would send the Davidic messiah sometime in the future).

OUTLINE

I. Book I (1–41)

    41:13. Closing Doxology

II. Book II (Pss 42–72)

    72:20. Closing Doxology

III. Book III (73–89)

    89:52. Closing Doxology

IV. Book IV (90–106)

    106:48. Closing Doxology

V. Book V (107–150)

    150. Closing Doxology

---

1 Unless otherwise indicated by NRSV, the quotations from Psalms are direct translations by the author.

Detailed Analysis

I. Book I (1–41)

Psalm 1

Psalm 1 contrasts the "way of the righteous" (v. 6) and the "way of sinners/the wicked" (vv. 1, 6). The first stanza (vv. 1–3) portrays the way of the righteous; the second stanza (vv. 4–6) portrays the way of the wicked.

In the first stanza, the one who is "happy" is described first negatively and then positively. Negatively, this one does *not* follow the advice of the wicked, take the "way" of sinners, or sit in the seat of scoffers. Positively, this one delights in God's *instruction*, which is a better translation of *torah* than *law*—the term here could almost be translated *scripture*. The happy one will flourish, like a tree that bears fruit even in a brutal environment. The connection between the tree that drinks of the water and the happy one who drinks of the Lord's instruction/scripture is obvious.

The second stanza also begins negatively, by describing the "way of the wicked." They do not bear fruit and flourish. Quite the opposite from one who is deeply rooted in God's instruction, the wicked lacks roots and thus is like dried up leaves in autumn, lacking substance and subject to the wind. The poem ends with the promise that God watches over the chosen people. The wicked choose their own way and thus lead themselves to destruction. The righteous surrender self-mastery and give themselves to the Lord's way, becoming objects of the Lord's care.

Psalm 2

Psalm 2 is a royal psalm, perhaps originally used at the coronation of a new king in Jerusalem. The psalm consists of four stanzas (vv. 1–3, 4–6, 7–9, 10–12), which play out a drama; each stanza changes the scene of the drama and the first three stanzas close with a different voice being quoted. The entire action of the psalm occurs via *speech*.

The first stanza begins with a rhetorical question—Why do the nations rage against God? To conspire against heaven is futile, and the rest of the psalm describes the reason for such futility. The stanza describes the nations' rebellion against God's reign and the authority of God's "anointed"

(*mashiakh*) as rebellious speech: They "conspire" and "plot," and the stanza closes by quoting the speech of the rebellious rulers.

In stanza 2, the action shifts to heaven, where the Lord laughs—a form of speech—at human rebellion. This laughter is not mean-spirited, but underscores the futility of human rebellion. The stanza closes with the Lord's speech, which gives God's answer to the rebelling human speech of stanza 1.

The third stanza moves the drama to Jerusalem's Mt. Zion, where the king reports God's promise—one characteristic way in which God responds throughout Scripture to human rebellion.

In the closing stanza, the psalmist enjoins the "kings" and "rulers" to serve God and use their mouths to kiss the king, rather than speak rebellious words. When interpreting this psalm, it is important to include ourselves among those rebelling against God, otherwise the psalm might be employed triumphalistically.

Psalm 3

Psalm 3 is a prayer for help from foes who oppress. The superscription identifying the poem with David's escape from Absalom's treachery (see 2 Sam 15–18) is not original to the psalm, but indicates the earliest interpretation of the psalm. It underscores the Lord's sustaining love for those who suffer, even those who suffer familial betrayals. The poem has four stanzas plus a closing declaration.

The psalmist begins by repeating three times how "many" foes oppress. The enemies' malice toward the psalmist is exacerbated by their impious belief that God lacks the power to deliver the psalmist. The psalmist, by contrast, trusts exclusively in the Lord's faithfulness and delivering power. The words *help* (v. 2), *deliver* (v. 7) and *deliverance* (v. 8) all derive from one Hebrew root. The psalm paints a vivid scene of chaos and security: many foes encircle the psalmist all around, but because the Lord is the psalmist's shield, the poet can sleep in security and awake sustained.

Psalm 4

Psalm 4 is a prayer for help, perhaps from one who has been falsely accused (v. 2) or from one who is beset by worshipers of false gods (vv. 3, 7). The poem is paired with Ps 3; both use the phrase "many are saying" (3:2; 4:6), both speak of sleeping securely (3:5; 4:8), and both are prayed with the assurance that the Lord responds to the cries of the faithful (3:5; 4:3).

The situation that originally generated this cry for deliverance cannot be determined, but that is appropriate, since the psalm is meant to be prayed in any situation in which a sufferer desires God's righteousness and graciousness (v. 1). The psalm contrasts proper trust and joy with improper trust and joy. The psalmist trusts in and finds true joy in the Lord and the light of the Lord's face, which is a metaphor for God's favor and deliverance (v. 6). The wicked seek after lies (which may mean either that they lie or that they worship gods who cannot keep promises, v. 2) and they rejoice in material prosperity (v. 7).

The psalm draws an inseparable connection between right worship and right living: "Do not sin ... put your trust in the LORD" (vv. 4–5).

Psalm 5

Psalm 5 is a cry for help from one who prays "in the morning" (twice, v. 3). Break of day was both a time for offerings (Amos 4:4; 2 Kgs 3:20;), for prayer (Pss 55:17; 88:13; Mark 1:35), and for the manifestation of God's deliverance (Ps 46:5; Isa 33:2). It is impossible to pinpoint the situation that gave rise to this prayer in any particular morning ritual or sacrifice. Rather, the psalm should be interpreted in light of the hope that God's deliverance would arise like the sun, driving darkness and threat away.

The psalm's five-stanza structure is informative. Stanzas 1 and 5 (vv. 1–3, 11–12) are about God—who hears the prayers of those who cry out and receives the praise of those who have been delivered. Stanzas 2 and 4 (vv. 4–6, 9–10) are about the wicked—those who boast, lie, breathe threats, and rebel against the Lord. The middle stanza is about the faithful supplicant—the one in need of God's steadfast love, God's presence, God's guidance; the one who worships the Lord. This structure sets off the sufferer from the wicked, whose violence threatens God's people. It also emphasizes God as the only agent capable of offering deliverance.

Psalm 6

Psalm 6 is the first of seven poems the Western Church later classified as "penitential psalms" (Pss 32; 38; 51; 102; 130; 143). This classification would not have been recognizable to the ancient psalmists, but reflects a particular understanding in the Pauline-Augustinian tradition concerning the role of confession and forgiveness in the life of faith. The category is part of the history of the interpretation of the psalms rather than part of composition of the psalms. The psalm does not formally ask for forgiveness, though the references to God's "anger," "wrath," and "discipline" may indicate a sense of guilt due to sin. Whether or not the psalm originated from some instance of guilt, it is nevertheless a passionate prayer for deliverance from a near-death experience. The poem may be prayed by or on behalf of anyone undergoing intense suffering.

The psalm is at its most poignant in its desperate cries for help ("do not rebuke," "be gracious," "heal," "save," etc.) and in the eloquent portraits of pain ("I am languishing," "my bones are shaking with terror," and the entirety of vv. 5–7). The painful metaphors and images haunt the reader and point to a God so near as to care deeply when any suffer.

In some prayers for help, the psalmist closes by praising and trusting God (cf. Ps 13:5–6). Here, such trust/praise takes the form of a scathing rebuke of those who wish the psalmist ill (vv. 8–10). This address to the enemies highlights the social aspects of trusting and praising the Lord.

Psalm 7

Psalm 7 is an intense plea for God to deliver the psalmist from enemies. While some interpreters see the poem as the words of one falsely accused, such precision is impossible. The declaration of innocence in v. 3 may not relate to a specific event or accusation, but may indicate the psalmist's claim to a more general innocence in comparison with persecuters (cf. vv. 4, 8, 14–16). It is unclear whether vv. 12–13 refer to God or the enemy.

The dominant metaphor for God in Ps 7 is the common OT metaphor of God as judge (vv. 6–11). The judgment in question here is not the final judgment at the end of life or time, but an immediate judgment of a violent clash between the supplicant and those who threaten violence. The attribute of God that goes along with the judge metaphor is righteousness (vv. 8–11, 17). The image of God as an angry (v. 6) and righteous judge offends many today. But the anger and judgment of God are the flip side of the love and forgiveness of God. Because God loves all creation, God is angry with any who cause suffering.

Psalm 8

The first hymn of praise in the Psalter begins and ends with praise of God "in all the earth" (vv. 1a, 9). The middle of the psalm continues this theme, touching on God's glory in the heavens (vv. 1b–3) and the vocation of responsibility for creation that God has entrusted to humanity (vv. 5–8). Set in the middle of the psalm is a question (v. 4).

The first section of the poem ruminates on the glory of God in the heavens. The meaning of v. 2 is unclear, but the sense of vv. 1b–4 is clear. The psalmist considers the magnitude of the Creator's work—the heavens, the moon, the stars—and is led to a question: why, in light of a vast creation, should the powerful Creator be mindful of one human being, or even all human beings?

Other parts of Scripture answer this question differently, but Ps 8 responds: because God has a vocation for humanity. In vv. 5–8, the poem magnificently portrays humans as the royalty (v. 5) to whom God has given the responsibility for caring for creation (vv. 6–8). This responsibility extends over domesticated animals, wild animals, birds, and even sea creatures.

Psalm 9/10

For many reasons, Pss 9 and 10 are considered one unified psalm. The chief reasons are that together they form an extended alphabetic acrostic poem, and multiple ancient manuscripts and translations considered them one psalm.

An alphabetic acrostic is a poem in which each section begins with a successive letter of the Hebrew alphabet. The acrostic structure may simply have been a device to help people memorize poems, although the length of certain acrostics casts doubt on this as a universal conclusion about all acrostics. To the extent that the conclu-

sion is valid, however, it indicates that the psalm was composed in part to instruct people in prayer and praise. The structure may also be a clue to an early theology of the word in Israelite religion, in which the written word itself was understood as sacred because the development of the alphabet allowed writing to preserve theological testimony.

The general themes of this unified psalm are trust and praise in the Lord's just judgment and longing for God's intervention on behalf of the oppressed. Among the notable poetic devices in Pss 9/10 is the quotation of the words of the enemies (10:4, 11, 13). In these verses, the enemies are quoted saying that God does not "see" or "seek out" the wicked for judgment. The psalmist, living a countercultural faith, avers that "you do see!" (10:14) and begs God to "seek out their wickedness." The enemies are also quoted as saying that God has "forgotten." But the psalmist avers that the nations have "forgotten" God, and God will not forget the poor and needy (9:17–18).

The chief characteristics of the wicked are arrogance and persecution of the poor. The arrogant mindset of those who imagine themselves as completely autonomous and independent leads them to oppress the poor (10:2). Those who "fear" God understand their dependence, and thus trust in and pray for God's just intervention.

Psalm 11

The poem of trust embodies the difference between alarm and trust. There are four players in this poetic drama: the psalmist, some wicked people who pose a threat to the psalmist and his/her community, a group of righteous who advise the psalmist to flee, and the Lord.

The psalmist begins with a here-I-stand declaration, "In the LORD I take refuge." Then the psalmist poses a rhetorical question, asking the panicking righteous why they advise flight. The speech of these advisors extends from v. 1b through v. 3; the final verse sums up their terror: What can the powerless righteous do?

The psalmist's answer comprises vv. 4–7. The psalmist asserts a confidence that is not based on anything that is visible, but on God, who cannot be seen and whom only faith can apprehend. The psalm plays poetically with the metaphor of vision. The Lord is in the heavenly temple, where no human can see, but from which God's eyes can see and test all (v. 4). The righteous live now by faith and will one day see God's face (v. 7).

Psalm 12

Psalm 12 is a prayer for help. The poem displays signs of liturgical use, but it is impossible to reconstruct an original liturgical setting or sequence with any certainty. It may have been the prayer of an individual (v. 1), or of the community (v. 8), and may have featured a priest speaking a promise on behalf of God (v. 5). That promise, spoken in v. 5 and elaborated upon in v. 6, is the heart of the psalm.

The psalm begins and ends with assertions that the psalmist and the community are isolated, surrounded by wickedness and those whose tongues breed malice (vv. 1, 8). Speaking is a major metaphor in the psalm—the wicked lie, speak with false hearts, have flattering lips, and boasting tongues. In response to this speech, the psalm quotes the promise of the Lord. The Lord says, "I will now rise up." In many psalms, the supplicant begs God to arise. The promise here indicates that deliverance will come soon. A second promise should be translated, "I will place in safety ...." The psalm then reinforces the word of promise with a poetic reflection upon the surety of God's promises (v. 6)

Psalm 13

This short poem is often considered the model prayer for help. The basic elements of this psalm genre occur once each, in a neat order: a threefold complaint ("I," "You," and "They" complaints; vv. 1–2); a petition (v. 3); a motivating clause (v. 4); an expression of trust (v. 5); a promise to praise (v. 6).

The psalm begins intensely and then intensifies further. The sufferer's fourfold "how long" complaint is quite literal (vv. 1–2)—suffering is intensified when one does not know how long it will last (cf. Ps 74:9). The psalmist's accusation that God has "hidden your face" is matched by the psalmist's plea that God "look!" (v. 1; NRSV, *consider*) and "give light to my eyes." The prayer elegantly matches the threefold complaint about *self*, *God*, and *"my enemy"* in vv. 1–2, with what one might call a threefold request in vv. 3–4. The

petition asks *God* to deliver *me* lest *"my enemy" rejoice*. Continuing the play on words, the psalm closes by expressing trust in God's deliverance and a promise to *rejoice* in divine deliverance. The psalmist's community-building attitude of rejoicing over God's salvation is implicitly compared with the enemies, who rejoice over the pain and defeat of others.

Psalm 14

Psalms 14 and 53 are nearly identical poems (see commentary on Ps 53). The best rubric under which to understand the literary nature of this psalm is "wisdom" or "instruction," because the poem contrasts the "fool" and the "wise" (vv. 1–2), which is typical of wisdom literature (see Prov 30:21–28). Although v. 7 grants the end of the psalm a prayer-like quality, this verse was probably added later by editors.

The best rubric under which to understand the theological nature is "the unity of thought and action." In respect to both the fool and the wise, the poem underscores the basic unity between thought and action. The fool says "there is no God" and does "abominable deeds" (v. 1); has "no knowledge" and thus does evil (v. 4). The wise, by contrast, "seek after God" (v. 2) and make God "their refuge." To make God one's refuge (cf. Pss 7:1; 11:1) is actively to seek God's help in times of danger. The danger that threatens the psalmist's community is described in absolute terms: "There is no one who does good, there is no one, not even one" (v 3; NRSV, *no, not one*). The comfort and refuge that God provides is likewise stated absolutely (v. 5).

Psalm 15

Psalm 15—similar to Pss 2, 24, 118:19–21, and 121—shows signs of probable liturgical use. Each poem takes a question/answer shape. Psalms 15, 24, 118:19–21 and Isa 33:13–16, furthermore, share the common theme of entrance into God's presence, indicating they may have functioned as entrance liturgies. When one compares these with similar liturgies from Israel's neighbors, it is striking that these liturgies do not include commands pertaining to ritual or physical purity (see Num 19:10*a*–22; Lev 21:10–24). Rather, the concerns are ethical. Similar to Jesus' teaching that one should make peace with one's neighbor before approaching God's altar (Matt 5:23–24), the concern here is on the impact one's actions have on the community.

Who "sojourns" (v. 1; NRSV, *abide*) in God's presence? The answer is given both positively and negatively. Positively, the one who is blameless and is a doer of right sojourns with God. Negatively (the Hebrew word for *not* occurs six times in vv. 2–5), the one who does not harm a neighbor by means of speech (v. 3), attitude (v. 4), or wealth (v. 5) sojourns with God. The psalm closes with the promise that matches these criteria: Those people "will not be moved."

Psalm 16

The psalm begins with one brief word of petition (vv. 1–2) and then shifts to an extended expression of trust (vv. 3–11). The psalmist first confesses to worship and seek good from God alone and later rejoices in manifold blessings received.

The meaning of vv. 3–4 is disputed, so it is better not to center any interpretation of the psalm on these verses. It does seem clear, however, that the psalmist is rejecting a false way of worshiping false gods (v. 4b–c). Verses 5–8 form the center of the psalm both literarily and theologically. Based on the psalm's vocabulary, the psalmist was probably a priest. The terms *portion, lot, boundary lines*, and *heritage* describe the distribution of the land among God's people. The Levites, notably, were given no land; the offerings of the land (Lev 6:9–10) and the Lord (Num 18:20) are described as their portion. The term *cup* symbolizes both the abundance of God's gifts (cf. Ps 23:5) and also a ritual celebration of thanksgiving (cf. Ps 116:13).

The message of these verses suits a materialistic time when money is worshiped rather than God. The supplicant celebrates the spiritual, intangible blessings of God as if they were tangible property.

Psalm 17

Psalm 17, a prayer for deliverance from danger, builds on Pss 15 and 16. Psalm 15 declared that those who "speak the truth" and "do not slander" (vv. 2–3) may sojourn with God; here the psalmist asserts "my mouth does not transgress" (v. 3). Psalm 16 rejoiced in the "portion" God has granted (vv. 5–6) and confessed "I shall

not be moved" (v. 8); here the psalmist prays for protection from those "whose portion in life is in this world" (v. 14) and asserts "my feet have not slipped" (v. 5).

The supplicant asserts innocence and demands to be heard on that basis (vv. 1–5). This assertion is not an abstract claim of absolute moral perfection, but a provisional appeal for help based on the rightfulness of the psalmist's situation vis-à-vis those who attack. The psalmist is beset by those whose hearts are closed to pity (v. 10); the issue is the fairness of the psalmist's cry for deliverance.

The psalm vividly contrasts the enemies' violence ("They track me down … like a young lion lurking in ambush," vv. 11–12) and the protection of the Lord ("Guard me as the apple of the eye … in the shadow of your wings," v. 8).

Psalm 18

Psalm 18 is a hymn of thanksgiving sung by one who had experienced divine deliverance (v. 6). Both the superscription, which situates the poem in David's life, and a very near parallel of this psalm in 2 Samuel 22, near the end of the narrative of David's life, indicate the types of situations in which such psalms were appropriate. They indicate that praise of God is not reserved for public worship occasions, but is to be spoken in the midst of daily life when God's deliverance and blessing are experienced. The psalm's structure is:

Introduction (vv. 1–3)

Praise of God's appearance and deliverance (vv. 4–29)

Center confession (vv. 30–31)

Praise of God's blessings for the king (vv. 32–45)

Conclusion (vv. 46–50).

God as rock is prominent at both the beginning and end of the psalm (vv. 2, 46) and in the theological and literary center of the psalm (vv. 30–31). This central section confesses that the Lord alone is God because God's way is perfect, God keeps promises, and God is the rock who provides refuge.

Psalm 19

This praise poem is a composite poem formed in two or three phases. The psalm is unified by the twin motifs of "word(s)" and "creation."

The first section (vv. 1–6) refers to God (*'el*) and explores the paradox of creation's inaudible praise of the Creator. The paradox is that nature has no discernible language ("There is no speech, nor are there *words*; their *voice* is not heard," v. 3) and yet those who worship Creator can nevertheless hear nature's praise ("their *voice* goes out ... their words to the end of the world," v. 4). Among Israel's neighbors, the sun was the god of law and justice, so the image of the sun in vv. 4b–6 can be interpreted as praising God's endowment of natural law in creation.

The second section (vv. 7–10) refers to the Lord (*yhwh*) and praises the "torah" (v. 7; NRSV, *law*); vv. 7–9 contain six parallel lines, which together describe what the Lord's word is (perfect, "pure, etc.) and what it does (revive the self, make wise the simple, etc.). The creation theme is continued by natural metaphors (gold, honey) in v. 10.

The last section is a recognition that while God's word is perfect and following it is rewarding, those who keep it are not, so forgiveness is a necessary part of the life of faith (v. 12). The psalm ends with a closing prayer for protection from violence (v. 13) and the request that this prayer might be accepted by God.

Psalm 20

This elegant composition was originally a liturgy intended for use by the king (vv. 6, 9). The military (vv. 5–7) and cultic (vv. 2–3) terminology indicate either a time of war or some other occasion in which the king's military leadership would have been important symbolically. The poem has two stanzas (vv. 1–5, 6–9), with vv. 1 and 9 forming an inclusio—both verses include the words LORD, *answer*, and *day of* (v. 9; NRSV, *when*, is literally *day of*). The message of the psalm can be asked rhetorically: where should we look for answers in times of trouble—to ourselves and our military strength or to God?

The first stanza consists of a series of benedictory prayers offered on behalf of the king. The petitions intensify as the stanza progresses, culmi-

nating in the overarching prayer: "May the LORD fulfill all your petitions" (v. 5). The second stanza is a response to these prayers, bearing witness to the confidence that the king and community have in God's deliverance. Although the prayer was originally composed for an ancient king, it is appropriate now for anyone struggling with difficulties that seem beyond his or her abilities and powers.

Psalm 21

Similar to Ps 20 in many ways, this royal psalm first gives thanks for the Lord's faithfulness to the king (vv. 1–7) and then speaks words of either promise or trust, depending on one's interpretation (vv. 8–12). The psalm ends with a verse of praise.

The poem's first movement praises and thanks God for the fidelity that God has shown to the king. This section offers a litany of gracious deeds that the Lord has done on behalf of the king. The theological center of the entire psalm in v. 7b summarizes this litany of gracious deeds by ascribing them to the fidelity or "steadfast love" of God.

The second section of the psalm may be interpreted either as speech to God (and thus an expression of trust) or words spoken by a priest or prophet to the king (and thus as a set of promises). These two interpretive options are not as different as one might suspect. Is not trust based on faith in what is promised? Are not promises spoken to engender trust? The language of the closing paean of praise (v. 13) echoes the vocabulary of v. 1, bringing the poem to a fitting end.

Psalm 22

Psalm 22 may be the most poignant and famous cry for help in the Psalter. Perhaps because of its raw power and pain, Jesus later echoed its opening cry while on the cross. Although the early church interpreted the psalm as messianic prophecy, the psalm remains an actual prayer available for any sufferer to take up, a reminder that faith in God includes room for doubt and even despair.

The first section of the psalm (vv. 1–21a) is comprised of alternating sections of lament (vv. 1–2, 6–8, 12–18), trust (vv. 3–5, 9–10), and requests for deliverance (vv. 11, 19–21b). The poem alternates between metaphors that are viscerally excruciating (vv. 2, 6–7, 12–18, 20–21a) and touchingly hopeful (v. 3, 9–10). This part of the psalm roars to its crescendo with the petition of vv. 19–21a.

Many have puzzled over the sudden change of mood and circumstance that governs the second half of the psalm (vv. 21b–31). Has the psalmist received a promise of help, or the actual help, or even just had a psychological shift in perception? All that may be said with certainty is that in some way the deliverance of the Lord has become real to the psalmist. Therefore, the psalmist's song changes into a soaring song of praise. The images of vv. 21b–31 portray an entire gallery of metaphors of God's faithfulness on behalf of Israel.

Psalm 23

One of the most loved passages in all of Scripture, this poem draws on the metaphors of shepherd and table host to express trust and confidence in the Lord. The psalm combines two movements—one movement from the metaphor of shepherd to that of host, and a second from third-person creedal language spoken about God to second-person prayer language spoken to God.

In the ancient world, the shepherd metaphor always carried royal connotations (see 1 Kgs 22:17–18; Jer 23:1–4). Thus, far from being a bucolic image, the shepherd of Ps 23 is a royal figure. The metaphor confesses the faithfulness with which God provides food, safety, and guidance. In v. 4, when the psalmist is "in the darkest valley," the divine pronouns shift from third-person to first-person. This reflects the reality that creedal information one memorizes about God quickens into a second-person relationship when one experiences the paradox that God's care becomes known in suffering.

The image of God setting a table in the midst of violent pursuers draws on the social values of honor and shame. Although the enemies desire the psalmist's shame, God provides a place of honor. God's faithfulness is not merely passive acceptance of the psalmist, but active pursuit. Normally, in the psalms the enemies "pursue" the psalmist to do violence, but here, God's "goodness and mercy" pursue (v. 6; NRSV, *follow*) the psalmist. The original meaning of v. 6b was that the psalmist was promising to return to God's

Temple throughout life. The later Christian interpretation of this verse as confidence of eternal life in God's heavenly house is a faithful expansion of this image.

Psalm 24

Similar to Pss 15, 118:19–21, and Isa 33:13–16, this poem seems to have been used liturgically accompanying entry into the Temple compound. The psalm begins with a confessional statement (vv. 1–2), continues with a question and answer regarding who may enter the Temple (vv. 3–6), and closes with a praise of the Lord's entrance into the Temple (vv. 7–10). The psalm envisions the mutual movement in which the Lord's people (vv. 3–5) and the Lord (vv. 7–10) enter into each other's presence in the Temple.

The psalm concentrates theologically on the identity of these two parties who move to meet each other. There are two complementary questions in the psalm: "Who is the King of glory?" and "who shall stand in his holy place?" In answer to the first question, the Lord is the God who has created all (vv. 1–2) and who remains active in its history (vv. 8–9). The opening verses retain vestiges of the ancient mythological conception that creation was a battle in which God defeated the forces of chaos (*sea* and *rivers*). Similarly, God's activities in history are portrayed via a military metaphor (v. 8). In answer to the second question, those whose intimate relationship with the Lord leads them to live ethically exemplary lives may enter into God's presence.

Psalm 25

Psalm 25 is an acrostic psalm (see commentary on Ps 9/10), although two letters are repeated and two omitted. Similar to other acrostic psalms, the argument of the psalm does not proceed smoothly, but is repetitive and irregular, most likely because of the need to start each verse with a successive letter. Nevertheless, three main motifs are noteworthy: the "way" of the Lord (vv. 4–5, 8–10, 12), the appeal not to be put to "shame" (vv. 1–3, 19–21), and the appeal for forgiveness, which is rare in the psalms (vv. 11, 17–18).

God's "way" or "path" (see Pss 1; 23) is a common metaphor in the psalms. The metaphor implies the promise that those who follow God's way in life will travel life's road more safely and will arrive at a better destination. This psalm particularly connects the metaphor with instruction regarding sin. God's way is for sinners (v. 8), meaning both that God forgives sin and that God shows an alternative way of life. Finally, the way of God leads to the place of honor, where those who seek violence will be put to shame and those who "fear the LORD" (v. 12) will not be put to shame.

Psalm 26

This prayer for deliverance echoes both the concerns of Ps 1—with its emphasis on avoiding the company of evildoers (cf. Pss 1:1; 26:4–5)—and Pss 15 and 24—with their emphases on the moral requirements of those who will enter God's presence (cf. Pss 15:2–4; 24:4–5; 26:1, 6). The psalm may have originated as a prayer of someone facing formal indictment, but is now appropriate for anyone who feels judged or rejected by the community.

Two main motifs dominate the poem. The first motif is the assertion of innocence. The psalmist asks God to "judge me" (v. 1; NRSV, *vindicate*); and through many metaphors such as walking in integrity, not wavering, walking faithfully, having a pure heart, not sitting with evildoers, and the like, the psalmist asserts innocence. The psalmist is not claiming to be sinless in the absolute sense, but in regards to specific charges. The second motif has to do with the body and bodily postures. The psalmist walks in integrity and faithfulness, asks God to test the heart, does not sit with the wicked, washes hands in innocence, moves around God's altar, is not like those whose hands are full of evil, and has feet planted on upright ground. The point is that God's righteous way is one that people are to follow.

Psalm 27

The unity of Ps 27 has often been questioned, because the first half of the poem (vv. 1–6) appears to be a song of trust in the midst of a military threat (v. 3), whereas the second half (vv. 7–14) appears to be a prayer for help of one suffering false accusations and familial betrayal (vv. 10–12). It is possible that these two segments originally arose independently, but are trust and petition really that different? Every psalm of trust assumes real and immediate threats, such as "the

darkest valley" of Ps 23:4 or the foaming seas and roaring nations of Ps 46:3, 6. And every prayer for help except one (Ps 88), includes explicit affirmations of trust (cf. Pss 13:5; 22:3–5). Moreover, the psalms slip so fluidly in and out of various metaphors that the interpreter cannot safely conclude that the image of the threatening host (v. 3) or false witnesses refers to literal life situations.

The opening metaphor of God as "my light" occurs only here in the Old Testament. Another key motif is "seeking" or "inquiring" of (vv. 4, 8) God's face. Literally, the metaphor refers to an intentional journey to a sanctuary to request a word from the deity. Symbolically, it expresses both the psalmist's trust in and longing for God.

Psalm 28

As with many prayers for help, this petition is spoken out of a complex, three-way relational web. The supplicant is caught between God and a hostile community. The psalm at once adjures God to end the divine silence by simultaneously rescuing the psalmist from a desperate situation and also imposing judgment on those who persecute the psalmist. This so-called dual wish—to be rescued and to have the enemies judged—troubles many modern readers, but the psalmist suffers a reality in which there is no other deliverance than the destruction and removal of the threat.

The poem employs two plays on words. First, as the psalm begins, the petitioner "lifts" (v. 2; *nasa'*) hands to God's sanctuary in petition and praise. The psalm correspondingly ends with the request that God would be Israel's shepherd and "lift" (v. 9; NRSV, *carry*) them out of danger. The closing request that God "shepherd" (*ra'a*) the people also is part of the poem's linguistic play, the petitioner having earlier complained about enemies working evil (*ra'a*) even as they speak peace with their "neighbor"(*rea'*).

Psalm 29

This hymn of praise is replete with the ancient mythological symbolism with which modern readers struggle to identify. Without ears to hear this symbolism, the poem falls on deaf ears. In ancient Israel's imagination, the one God was surrounded by lesser "heavenly beings" (v. 1), the council of God (cf. Isa 6:1–5), some of whom may be hostile to God's rule (cf. Ps 82). The Lord earns lordship by defeating the powers of chaos—here portrayed as "the waters" (v. 3) and "the flood" (v. 10; cf. Gen 1:1).

Psalm 29 is a hymn that celebrates the Lord's triumph over these powers of chaos. The psalm begins by calling on the beings in God's heavenly house to acknowledge the Lord's kingship by acknowledging God's "glory" (v. 1); the psalm ends in a similar fashion as those in God's earthly house (the Temple) also speak God's "glory" (v. 9). The middle section speaks seven times of the "voice of the LORD"—the cacophony of a thunderstorm—triumphing over waters, mighty waters, cedars, and so on. The psalm ends by celebrating the Lord as enthroned over the forces of chaos, and thus as the only power worthy of glory and able to grant true blessing and peace (v. 11).

Psalm 30

Psalm 30 is a song of thanksgiving celebrating God's faithfulness as experienced in the psalmist's delivery from a near-death crisis. The structure of the psalm is clear: thanksgiving for deliverance (vv. 1–3); call for others to join in thanks (vv. 4–5); recollection of the crisis (vv. 6–7); repetition of the petition (vv. 8–10); closing word of praise (vv. 11–12).

A key motif is the image of the psalmist having nearly "gone down to the Pit" (v. 3; the pit could be a well or cistern, and thus is a metaphor for death), but of God having "drawn me up" (v. 1) and "brought up my soul" (v. 3). In v. 9, the psalmist recalls an earlier prayer for deliverance: What profit is there if I "go down to the Pit?" (v. 9).

The psalm also employs pairs of words and images that contrast the despair of the crisis with the wonder of God's deliverance: God's anger/God's favor; for a moment/for a lifetime; weeping/joy; night/morning; mourning/dancing; sackcloth/clothed with joy; silence/praise. The creedal confession in v. 5 and the prayer confession in v. 11 together summarize the message of the psalm.

Psalm 31

This poem alternates between poignant pleas for help (vv. 1–2, 9, 16–18), a profound expression of pain (vv. 10–13), and expressions of trust and praise (vv. 3–8, 14–15, 19–24). As a whole, the psalm moves from petition to praise to instruction (vv. 23–24). The psalm is replete with formulaic language. The text borrows from other texts and is in turn borrowed from—compare vv. 1–3a with Ps 71:1–3; v. 5a with Luke 23:46; v. 9a with Ps 6:3; v. 12 with Jer 22:28; v. 13 with Jer 22:10; v. 17 with Jer 17:18; v. 24 with Josh 1:6, 7, 9.

The dominant theological note of the psalm is sounded in vv. 5 and 14. The psalm as a whole explores what it means to entrust and commit one's life to God. Such a life will be dually marked: on the one hand, by the opposition and scorn of those who reject the way of God (vv. 6, 11), and on the other hand, by a steadfast "hope" (v. 24; NRSV, *wait*) that is able to take a long view of life and rely on God in the face of persecutions and suffering.

Psalm 32

This psalm of thanksgiving after deliverance from a crisis was later counted as one of the penitential psalms (see commentary on Ps 6). In place of a call to praise (cf. Ps 30:1–3) the psalm starts with a wisdom-like beatitude celebrating the joys of forgiveness. The psalm recalls the crisis as a bodily illness (vv. 3–4) and recounts how a confession of sin led to forgiveness (v. 5) and restoration. Three different terms for sin are used in vv. 1–2 and again in v. 5, emphasizing via both repetition and variety the necessity for the sinner to seek forgiveness from God. At the close, the sufferer transforms into preacher. The psalmist offers instruction about the benefits of "the way" (v. 8) of the Lord, and, with wonderful imagery, warns against mulish stubbornness (most likely the psalmist is recalling his or her own earlier silent reluctance to confess sin).

One interpretive issue that the psalm raises is the connection between sin/guilt and suffering/disease. As Job's misguided counselors illustrate, one cannot automatically conclude that those who suffer illness have violated some law. The fact that the psalmist interprets the past health crisis as God's judgment does not mean that all such crises are the results of sin.

Psalm 33

This moving hymn of praise bears witness to several cardinal elements of Old Testament theology: worship, (vv. 1–3), creation (vv. 4–9), the word of God (vv. 4, 6, 9, 11), providence (vv. 10–18), and hope (vv. 20–22).

The psalm teaches that worship is both a human response that is fitting, but also that it is the way in which the "word of the LORD" (v. 4) shapes and renews (this is the force of "new" in v. 3) the people. Worship is not merely a human activity; the primary actor in worship is God. The psalm also connects the Lord's word with both God's creating and sustaining works. Similar to Genesis 1, this poem portrays creation as an act of God's word by which God *ordered* a chaotic environment into a hospitable one (vv. 6–7). The existence of life depends on the ongoing creative activity of God. Moreover, God remains an active subject within creation, frustrating the chaotic wishes of those who oppose God's reign (vv. 10–11) and ordering human society into hospitable community (vv. 11–15).

The psalm ends on a high note concerning trust and hope. Hope and trust are not merely beneficial attitudes, they are attributes of the life of faith. To belong to God is to wait on and trust in God.

Psalm 34

This acrostic psalm (see commentary on Ps 9/10) is similar to Ps 25; both omit the letter *waw* and both add an extra *pe* verse at the end. Unlike many acrostic poems, Ps 34 has a clear structure and form. It is a psalm of thanksgiving that, like Ps 32, moves from a call to praise (vv. 1–3), to thanksgiving (vv. 4–10), to instruction (vv. 11–22). The Davidic superscription is not original to the psalm; it suggests that one read the psalm against the background of 1 Sam 21:10–15 (assuming that the superscription's *Abimelech* is a mistake for *Achish*). The psalm is heavily influenced by Israel's wisdom tradition.

A notable element of the call to praise is the call for the community to join the psalmist's thanksgiving for an act of divine deliverance. For the congregation to be God's community, it must join in the praise of those whom God has redeemed. As other psalms show, inability or unwillingness to join thusly ruptures the community. The thanksgiving section emphasizes the fear of the Lord (vv. 4, 7, 9). To fear God is to acknowledge one's

dependence on God and to reject the false lure of self-sufficiency. The last section of the psalm emphasizes God's agency as the one who hears, sees, rescues, saves, and redeems the righteous.

Psalm 35

This cry for help can be understood as an unpacking of the petition, "Deliver us from evil"—this is a prayer meditation of one caught in the nets of evildoers. A sufferer marshals military (vv. 1–3), natural (vv. 5–8, 17), legal (vv. 11–12), and grieving (vv. 13–14) imagery to portray a crisis fraught with threat and pregnant with deliverance.

An interesting element in the psalm is the various voices that the psalmist quotes: God's voice (v. 3), "my bones" (v. 10), the enemies (vv. 21, 25), and the community who desires "my vindication" (v. 27). As one traces the progression of these attributed words, one can map the psalmist's desired movement from crisis to rescue to rehabilitation. Of special note is the psalmist's plea for God to declare, "I am your salvation" (v. 3). Many interpret this as a message of salvation announced by a priest in a temple (similar to Eli in 1 Sam 1:17), but it may simply express the psalmist's desire for rescue. Of equal interest is the closing request in v. 27 for the congregation to praise the Lord. This indicates that divine deliverance must be matched by communal rehabilitation; God's saving act is not complete until God's people join in welcoming the sufferer.

Psalm 36

The psalm seems like a prayer for help, but its vocabulary betrays wisdom tradition influence. Prayers for help often include complaint about foes, trust in God, and cries for help. Here, complaint is replaced by description of "the wicked" (vv. 1–4); trust is replaced by praise of God (vv. 5–9). The petition occurs in vv. 10–12.

The psalm's first two sections contrast a description of the "wicked," whose flaw is that they are self-governed (vv. 1–4), with praise of "the LORD" (vv. 5–9). Given the occurrence of wisdom terminology, this is surprising; in wisdom literature one expects "the wicked" to be contrasted with "the righteous" (cf. Pss 1; 37). Instead, Ps 36 contrasts the wicked with the Lord! The praise lauds God's *character*, which is described by pairing key theological words about God's character—*steadfast love* (*hesed*), *faithfulness*, *righteousness*, and *judgments*—with poetic metaphors drawn from the domain of creation—*heavens*, *clouds*, *mighty mountains*, and *great deep*. This poetic strategy of pairing culminates with the confession "in your light we see light," where the natural and theological metaphors become one.

The psalm closes with the petition that God would stay true to the divine character by continuing to act faithfully on behalf of the people.

Psalm 37

Like most acrostic poems (see commentary on Ps 9/10), this psalm lacks a discernible progression. The influence of the wisdom tradition is evident both in the contrast between "wicked" and "righteous" and in the self-consciously instructional nature of the psalm. If the reference in v. 25 to being old is taken literally, this poem is the sage advice of an elder. Taken canonically, the poem comes to new generations as the advice of spiritual ancestors.

Two repeated motifs in the psalm can serve as foci for interpretation. First, the psalm warns do not "be obsessed" (vv. 1, 7, 8; NRSV, *fret*) with the success of the wicked. Similar to Ps 73:2–20, the psalm warns that if one focuses either on the seeming reward of the wicked or on their unrighteous behavior, one might be tempted to follow their path. Second, the psalm promises that the righteous shall "inherit the land" (vv. 3, 9, 11, 22, 34; cf. vv. 18, 27). This allusion to God's promise to Abraham (Gen 12:1–3) invites the reader to imagine living life for the long haul, trusting that in the end God keeps promises—as God did for Abraham and Sarah. The rhetoric about age in v. 25 underscores this point.

Psalm 38

This prayer for forgiveness, healing, and rehabilitation is one of the seven penitential psalms (see note on Ps 6). The psalm is almost certainly the prayer of one suffering from a grave illness (vv. 5–10). This suffering is increased by the fact that in addition to the physical suffering, the illness has isolated the psalmist from the community. It may be that members of the community,

similar to Job's friends, interpreted the psalmist's illness as evidence of sin (v. 19). Or, it may be that the community simply remained aloof to the psalmist's pain and offered neither support nor comfort (v. 12)—either because they were afraid of contagion or because, as often happens, they did not know how to bring comfort.

For the psalmist, the answer to the crisis is found first in the decision to "declare" his or her sins (v. 18; NRSV, *confess*), and second, in the hoped-for forgiveness of God. With humans, forgiveness does not automatically mean reconciliation; but with God, it does.

Psalm 39

This psalm can be understood through the lens of paradox. The psalmist claims more than once to be silent (vv. 2, 9), yet speaks this prayer and begs, "Give ear to my cry" (v. 12). The sufferer desires both more and less of God's attention—asking God both to "turn away" (v. 13) and to "hear my prayer" (v. 12). The singer desires to "know my end" (v. 4), even while acknowledging that attempts at knowledge are fruitless (v. 6). The psalmist experiences life as toil and trouble (v. 6), yet begs for more (v. 13). The keystone that holds together the paradoxical arch under which the psalmist lives is God, whose faithfulness is experienced both in punishment for sin (v. 10) and in forgiveness (v. 8).

The metaphor of the psalmist as a "sojourner" (v. 12; NRSV, *passing guest*) "like all my forebears" has captured the imagination of many interpreters. The metaphor, which conjures echoes of the ancestral narratives in Genesis, proclaims both law (that humans are mortal) and promise (that eternal God watches over and values human life).

Psalm 40

As in other psalms of thanksgiving, the psalmist recalls the past crisis (vv. 1–3), then offers renewed praise of God (vv. 4–7). Verse 7 should likely be translated, "I have come, in this scroll is written what happened to me"—the psalmist came to the sanctuary and presented a written testimony of God's act of deliverance.

Such testimony is a necessary part of the life of faith. To refrain from such testimony is to hide God's saving help selfishly in one's own heart

(v. 9)! Whereas our culture privatizes faith, this psalm teaches that faithfulness to God requires public testimony, lest one conceal God's grace (v. 10). The psalm closes with a renewed prayer for help (vv. 11–15) and the wish that God would manifest deliverance so powerfully that all might join the psalmist in a new song (vv. 16–17). Verses 13–17 also appear as Ps 70 (see commentary there).

Psalm 41

Book I of the Psalter closes as it began, with an instructional psalm that begins with the term *happy*. Similar to Ps 1, this poem promises that God sustains the righteous through troubles and tribulations (vv. 1–3). This opening stanza is a thumbnail sketch of the psalmist's theology. The remainder of the psalm (vv. 4–12) functions as a case study of this theology. Both the psalmist and the community interpret the psalmist's illness as evidence that the psalmist has sinned. The community includes both ill-wishers who delight at the prospect of the psalmist's demise (vv. 5–7) and well-wishers who have given up hope in the psalmist's recovery (vv. 8–9). Rejection by the community both multiplies the psalmist's suffering and paradoxically drives him or her to rely even more deeply on God (vv. 10–12). Verses 11–12 may indicate that the psalmist has already experienced healing or completely trusts in God's faithful promise of healing. Either way, the personal case study in the psalmist's theology climaxes with the psalmist's solid expression of trust and hope.

The doxology in v. 13 is not properly a part of Ps 41, but is the editorial closure of Book I of the Psalter.

II. Book II (42–72)

Psalm 42/43

For several reasons, Pss 42 and 43 are judged to comprise one poem: a refrain occurs three times across the two psalms (42:5–6a; 42:11; 43:5), Ps 43 lacks a superscription, and the theme of the Temple unifies the entire poem. The superscription assigns this to "the Korahites," probably a group of Levitical musicians in the Second Temple (cf. 1 Chr 9:19; 2 Chr 20:19) who are identified with a group of psalms (see introduc-tion). The psalmist's memories of leading the musical temple procession for the festival (42:4) suggest that the singer should be understood as one of the Korahites. But the references to enemies who taunt "where is your God?" (42:3, 10) and to physical separation from the Temple (42:6; 43:3) suggest that the Levite is in exile. Who are these enemies? Certainty eludes the interpreter. All that can be said is that they are those who separate the singer from God.

The governing theological motif of this psalm is separation from God's presence. The governing poetic motif is water—the psalmist thirsts for God as a deer longs for streams, the psalmist weeps, pours out his soul, and feels like the thundering deeps and waves are drowning him. Like one dying of thirst who is tortured by memories of water, the psalmist's very memories of joyful singing in God's presence torture him in exile from the Temple. Yet, paradoxically, these memories also promise the psalmist hope. Three times in the chorus, the psalmist addresses himself, adjuring himself to hope and singing the promise, "I shall again praise him, my help and my God."

Psalm 44

The community prayer for help may have been composed for use either after a particular national defeat or for annual temple use as part of a liturgy enacting a drama of defeat and rescue. In either case, the theological challenge to God's faithfulness and plea for deliverance resonates in any age. The fact that the speaking voice alternates between an individual (vv. 4, 6, 15–16) and community probably indicates that the king or some other leader spoke the prayer on behalf of the people.

The poem has three movements. In the first (vv. 1–8), the language is creedal. The psalm recites God's mighty deeds on behalf of the nation, emphasizing that Israel's fortunes were not their own doing but the gracious action of God. This sets up the second movement, in which the singer accuses and questions God, transforming the language of confession into accusation (cf. vv. 7, 10). In the third movement, the psalmist questions God: Since "we have not forgotten you" (v. 17), "why do you forget our affliction and oppression?" (v. 24). Then the poem calls for God to reverse the nation's fortunes. The closing verses (23–26) resound with bold pleas for God to remain faithful to the promises of the covenant "for the sake of your steadfast love" (cf. Exod 34:6–7).

Psalm 45

This psalm is unique in the Psalter, a song of praise addressed to the ancient king and his bride, most likely on the occasion of their wedding. A psalm of the Korahites (see commentary on Ps 43/44), the singer likely was a temple musician. In the ancient world there was no concept of separation of "church and state," and thus the state and its head were directly associated with the nation's faith. Although Israel's prophets, laws, and scriptures often criticized the king (cf. Deut 17:14–20; 1 Sam 8:4–22; Jer 23:1–4), the king was nevertheless understood as akin to a means of grace, one of the ways in which the Lord acted to bless the people (cf. Ps 72). Thus, the king was a means by which God protected the people militarily (v. 3), provided justice and equity (v. 4), established righteousness (v. 7), and kept faith with the ancestral promises to give the people land, a name, and descendants (vv. 16–17).

Israel's kings universally failed to live up to the divine standards, for kingship and the monarchy failed. In both Rabbinic Judaism and Christianity, this psalm became reinterpreted as a promise of the coming messianic king.

Psalm 46

This communal song of trust is composed of three stanzas (vv. 1–3, 4–6, 8–10). The refrain that follows the second and third stanzas (vv. 7, 11) can be seen as the central confession of trust in the psalm (see also vv. 1, 5). Like other psalms of trust such as 23 and 27, the poem names forces that pose mortal dangers. The poetic imagery of the psalm describes both the threatening powers and God's protecting presence in ways that merge mythological features with historical and natural features.

In the first stanza, the focus is on the earth— the raging seas and roiling earth encompass both the natural threats of earthquakes and storms as well as the mythological hazard of cosmic chaos. In the second, the focus is the nations (cf. Ps 2:1). God's presence in Jerusalem and gracious protection are portrayed mythologically as a river (v. 4).

There is no river in Jerusalem (the Gihon spring does not qualify); but the image is a frequent mythological symbol of blessing, protection, and new life (cf. Ezek 47). The last stanza portrays God paradoxically as a warrior who brings peace. The voice of God crowns the psalm (v. 10) with the promise that God is exalted in both the nations (stanza 2) and the earth (stanza 1).

Psalm 47

This psalm is one of a group of psalms that have been labeled "enthronement psalms," because they celebrate the Lord as king (v. 7). It has been proposed that each year—possibly during the Festival of Tabernacles at the time of the fall harvest or during the celebration of the new year—Israel liturgically enacted the enthronement of the Lord. Some believe that at this worship service the Israelites proclaimed, "The LORD has become king!" (Ps 93:1; NRSV, *the LORD is king)*—in much the same way that Christians annually enact Jesus' resurrection at Easter with the words, "Christ is risen!" According to this view, the liturgical cry "The LORD has become king!" renews—reenacts—the reality of God's kingship, which God had established in the past.

This hymn of praise has two stanzas, each of which follows the normal pattern for such poems—a call to praise (vv. 1, 6) followed by testimonies or reasons for praise (vv. 2–5, 7–9). Whether such an annual celebration of the Lord's kingship ever happened is unknown, but the message of Ps 47 is indeed that the Lord reigns over both Israel and all the earth, which is reason for praise. Human praise is the subversive announcement that the powers that claim dominion over the earth are fraudulent. Praise announces a different Lord, and thus undermines the claims of all others who would rule over us.

Psalm 48

This psalm, with 76, 84, 87, and 122 (46 and 132 are related), is a "song of Zion" (cf. 137:3). Zion refers both to Jerusalem as a whole and to God's Temple specifically. The songs of Zion share some unique features: the psalms personify Zion, often addressing it directly; they praise Zion's beauty and glory; they emphasize that God has chosen to dwell or cause God's "name" to dwell in Zion; they emphasize that God protects the city.

The literary device of praising the city may seem odd to modern readers, but the city functioned in Judean theology in ways similar to the concept of "means of grace" in Christian theology. God was understood as present on behalf of the people "in, with, and under" the city (48:3, 8–10)—so much so that the psalm can even say of the city, "This is God" (v. 13!). As such, this motif picks up God's promise of "a land" to Abraham (Gen 12:1–3). "In the far north" (v. 1) is not literal (Jerusalem is in Israel's south), but refers to the mythological Canaanite Mount *Zaphon* (which in Hebrew means "north") that was the imagined residence of the gods. Likewise, vv. 4–8 probably do not refer to any historical attack on Jerusalem, but are a mythological depiction of the nations' rebellion against God.

Psalm 49

This song of instruction levels the unlevel earthly playing field by asserting that all humanity, "low and high, rich and poor together" are mortal and thus are alike in God's sight. The message of the psalm is that the righteous should not be afraid when others, especially the wicked, achieve earthly success, for all such victories are temporary. Rather, trust in God who alone has eternal power.

The structure of the psalm is straightforward. A four-verse introduction calls on the audience to listen to "wisdom" (vv. 1–4). Two eight-verse stanzas follow, each of which culminates with a refrain that announces that all flesh is mortal (vv. 12, 20). A key concept in the poem is that of "ransom" (vv. 7–8, 15), which plays on the theme of wealth that dominates the psalm. The term means to "rescue" a person or animal from an obligation by paying a price either in money or in kind (Exod 34:20; Num 18:17). The point here is that no amount of earthly wealth can ransom human life from the obligation flesh owes to death. Only God can "ransom ... from the power of Sheol" (v. 15). While some doubt that this verse promises life after death, it seems likely that in this late psalm, the promise of eternal life is implied.

Psalm 50

Psalms 50, 81, and 95 have been labeled as "festival psalms" because they probably were used liturgically at one of Israel's three major annual festivals (Passover, Weeks/Pentecost, or Booths/Succoth)—major elements of which included animal sacrifice (Lev 23:33–36). These psalms share an admonishing tone, the call to "obey" (v. 7; NRSV, *hear*) as God testifies against the people, the quotation of God's voice as the culmination of the psalm (vv. 5–23), and the reference within these quotations to the Decalogue (vv. 18–20). The presence of the voice of God in these psalms underscores that worship is not primarily a human activity, but a sacred time when God encounters humanity. The admonishing tone of God's voice underscores that discipline and even reproach are important parts of a healthy relationship with God.

God's speech to the people in Ps 50 is underscored by the motif of "silence." God says that while the people transgressed the commandments against theft, adultery, and false witness (vv. 18–20), "I have been silent" (v. 21). But now God is breaking this silence (v. 3) and testifying "against" the people (v. 7). God denounces the sacrifices of the festival as penultimate (vv. 8–14). Instead, God desires covenant obedience and a sacrifice of "thanksgiving" (vv. 14–15, 23).

Psalm 51

One of the seven penitential prayers (see commentary on Ps 6), this prayer for help is a passionate plea for forgiveness. The superscription that connects this prayer with the affair between David and Bathsheba (see 2 Samuel 11–12) is not original to the psalm, but reflects the earliest layer of interpretation of the psalm. It offers one example of an instance in which this prayer for forgiveness would be appropriate.

The opening two verses of the psalm use three different Hebrew words for sin, emphasizing by repetition and variation the psalmist's complete sense of sin. The psalmist matches this with three different words for forgiveness, accentuating the desperate need for forgiveness. The phrase "against you, you alone, have I sinned" (v. 4) does not deny that sin has human victims, rather it emphasizes that God cannot and will not be separated from the equation. The basis of the psalmist's plea for forgiveness is God's character ("steadfast love" and "abundant mercy," v. 1), rather than any action or quality of the sinner.

The central section of the psalm includes two passages that are well known because they have been adopted widely in worship. In the first, "create in me ..." (vv. 10–12), the psalm employs the metaphor of *re-creation* to ask for forgiveness. In the second, "O LORD, open my lips ..." (vv. 15–17), the psalmist promises that forgiveness will be met with a response of praise.

The last two verses are a later Priestly addition to the psalm, probably added to balance the criticism of sacrifice in vv. 16–17.

Psalm 52

This poem moves from the announcement of judgment upon one of the wicked (vv. 1–7), to a song of trust and praise in God's steadfast love (vv. 8–9). Because the psalm addresses the wicked directly (vv. 1–5; cf. 2:1–22; 4:2–5; 6:8–10), some have compared this psalm to prophetic texts, in which judgment is often proclaimed directly to the wicked.

The wicked are marked by two complementary characteristics. First, they do evil to their neighbors primarily with their words (vv. 1–4). Second, the wicked do not trust in God, but instead trust in "abundant riches" (v. 7) and, by extension, in earthly understandings of power and success. God's anger here is related to God's love. Because God loves the oppressed, God's judgment is announced. The psalmist is loyal to both God and God's "faithful," presumably the powerless who are oppressed by the wicked (vv. 8–9).

Psalm 53

This psalm is identical to Ps 14 in all but a few minor details, primarily that whereas Ps 14 uses the Hebrew proper name for God *yhwh* (*The LORD*), Ps 53 uses the more generic *'elohim* (*God*). This is generally the case in Pss 42–83, which are therefore labeled the Elohistic Psalter. For commentary, see Ps 14. Note the resonance between Ps 52, which emphasizes that the wicked do evil because they have chosen to trust in wealth rather than God, and Ps 53, in which the "fool" rejects both God and doing good (v. 1).

Psalm 54

The brevity of this prayer for help serves to magnify the intensity of the psalmist's crisis.

Words are not wasted. The psalm opens with a fourfold cry for deliverance; the first two phrases beg for salvation, the second two ask to be heard (vv. 1–2). The description of the enemies is typically opaque. No one situation can be discerned behind the clouded glass of the text; rather, the words are sufficiently ambiguous to allow sufferers in many different crises to make this prayer their own. In that light, the superscription that connects the prayer with a time in David's life (cf. 1 Sam 23:19) offers one situation appropriate for this psalm, but does not reflect the setting in which it was authored.

The center of the prayer, both textually and theologically, is v. 4, which expresses the psalmist's trust in God. God is confessed as "helper," the same word used in Gen 2:18 to describe the partner that the man needs. The word does not imply a diminutive or inferior person, but one with the necessary power and fidelity to help. The "freewill offering" (v. 6) that the psalmist promises is a type of offering that is not required by cultic legislation, but a gift offered solely in grateful response for deliverance.

Psalm 55

This prayer for help may have been first uttered by a Temple priest, as indicated by the reference in v. 14 to processing in the Temple with "the fellowship" (NRSV, *throng*). The psalmist is in desperate straits, but that is not unusual in the psalms. What marks this psalm as singular is that the betrayal has not come from "enemies ... I could bear that" but from "my equal, my companion, my familiar friend" (vv. 12–13). The force of this threefold, emphatic utterance in Hebrew can scarcely be overstated. The pain that gave rise to this prayer makes it appropriate for anyone who has experienced a similar betrayal by a friend, neighbor, or family member. This personal treachery is exacerbated by the psalmist's sense that similar brokenness stalks the walls and markets of the city (vv. 10–11). The reference to crying out evening, morning, and noon (v. 17) may echo daily ritual activities in the Temple.

A surprising and unexpected confidence in the Lord arises out of the midst of this anguish. The psalmist is confident in the face of daunting earthly odds, because of the character of God, "who is enthroned from old" (vv. 18–19). Verse

22 is a promise that undergirds the prayer; it is a reminder that prayer is a relational activity based on trust in God's character.

Psalm 56

This poem opens with a cry for help, but is dominated by powerful expressions of trust, which begin in v. 3. Something akin to a refrain occurs in vv. 4 and 10–11, sounding the psalm's leitmotif of trust: why fear human beings when one can trust in God?

The psalmist's trust is built upon the twin foundations of God's word (v. 4, 11) and God's providence (v. 8). The two go together. The psalmist trusts in the promise that God keeps watch over the faithful and, in fact, that God has written the psalmist's name in a book—signifying the surety and steadfastness of the divine-human relationship. It is not clear how the psalmist knows God's word. Does this refer to a promise received from a priest or prophet? Does this refer to a promise made in the distant past or one recently received? Does the "word" refer to Scripture (assuming this is a late psalm)? As the reference to God collecting the psalmist's tears indicates, trust in the promise of providence is not a naïve assumption that God's people are immune to suffering, but a more nuanced trust that God transforms suffering and gives life meaning.

Psalm 57

Similar to Ps 56, this psalm begins with an appeal for help (vv. 1–4), but the second half of the psalm is dominated by praise (vv. 5, 7–11). The psalm has two halves, as the praise refrain in vv. 5 and 11 indicates. The turning point of the psalm comes in v. 6, as the psalmist confidently announces, in traditional wisdom vocabulary, that the enemies have fallen into the very trap that they had set.

This poem features powerful metaphors that communicate both the psalmist's desperation (the enemies are greedily devouring lions, the psalmist takes refuge under God's wings) and also the psalmist's praise (the psalmist calls for "my heart," "lyre and harp" to awake). In the psalms, sufferers often call on God to awake as part of the cry for help. Here, the language is reversed. In light of trust in God's "unfailing love," the cry to awake

is an expression of spontaneous, joyful praise. The psalm closes with images of creation (heavens, clouds, heavens, earth). These metaphors communicate both the vast reach of God's hand and the sudden "shine" of God's deliverance.

Psalm 58

This poem begins with a textual problem and ends with a theological problem. The textual problem regards how to unravel v. 1. The Hebrew word for *silence*, *'elem*, makes little sense here, so most translations emend the word to *'elohim*, meaning either *gods* (NRSV) or *mighty ones* (NIV). The first option assumes the psalm is directed at the false gods of the nations, similar to Ps 82. The second view interprets the psalm as aimed at corrupt judges and leaders within the community, as v. 3 suggests. Either way, this prayer is rare in that it opens by being directed not at God but at someone other than God.

The harsh wishes of the destruction of the enemies in vv. 6–10 raise a theological problem for many readers. While it is tempting to try to diminish the raw impact of these curses, it may be more honest to admit that such rage can be a part of the life of faith—especially when one has been deeply hurt. The psalmist, as far as we know, does not take vengeance into his or her own hands, but takes it to the Lord in prayer and, one can hope, leaves it there. The psalmist also trusts that God will have the last word, in spite of the harsh reality of evil.

Psalm 59

Psalm 59 is a prayer for help that is woven artfully around the root metaphor of speech. The psalm has three stanzas (vv. 1–5, 7–13, 15–17) and a refrain that separates the stanzas (vv. 6, 14). The first stanza employs formulaic language. It begins and ends with appeals for deliverance; in the middle the enemies are described and the psalmist asserts innocence. The refrain portrays the enemies as predatory dogs (cf. Ps 22:16), who growl threateningly—in Ps 46:3, 6, the word translated here as "growl" describes the threatening roar of the sea and the nations. Here, the word denotes both the violence that the wicked achieve with their speech (vv. 3, 7a) and the fact that they do not believe God has the power to intervene and judge them (v. 7b).

The second stanza describes God's reaction to their "words," "cursing," and "lies" (vv. 12–13); God "laughs" (v. 8). God's laughter here portrays the rebellious threat of the enemies as insignificant in the grand scheme. The last stanza describes the psalmist's reaction to the enemies' speech. The psalmist sings praise of God. Praise may seem an insignificant response to the violent speech of the enemies, but it names God as an active agent in the world, thus it is a form of speech that sustains the psalmist in a faithful relationship with God.

Psalm 60

Psalm 60 is a corporate prayer for help that may cause modern readers difficulty, both because of its many geographical references and because of its theology. The poem may have been composed in light of a particular military crisis, or it may have been used liturgically on an annual basis.

The geographical references (vv. 6–9) remind the reader that God's ancient promise of the land (cf. Gen 12:1–2) was a vital part of ancient Israel's faith. The land was seen in ancient Israel as akin to a "means of grace" in Christian theology. The land was God's paramount gift. It simultaneously provided *identity*, *sustenance*, and *protection* for the people. For modern readers who may take for granted citizenship in a peaceful country, the poem is a reminder of the crisis that *the loss of place* can lead to. The ancient promise that is quoted in vv. 6–8 fuels the request that God restore the land.

The theology in this psalm does not support a nationalistic triumphalism or a view that a military victory is automatically a sign of God's favor. Ps 60 is the prayer of an oppressed people; it underscores God's presence among the defeated and reminds that "human help [Heb.: *salvation*] is worthless" (v. 11).

Psalm 61

Similar to many other prayers for help, the circumstances that gave rise to this prayer are lost. The opening appeal indicates that the psalmist desires rescue, but other than the obscure reference to a faint heart (v. 2), there are no clues to the psalmist's situation.

The psalm draws on spatial metaphors to make its appeal. The psalmist calls "from the end of the earth" (v. 2). This is most likely not a literal reference to exile from the Temple, but a theological reference to a situation of crisis—the psalmist is distant from God in a spiritual sense. Balancing this lament, the psalmist seeks refuge and sanctuary in the Temple (v. 4). Again, this is most likely not a literal request for sanctuary, but a spiritual request for protection and deliverance.

The petition on behalf of the king (vv. 6–7) recognizes that a prosperous government benefits society at large. The psalm personifies God as "steadfast love and faithfulness" (v. 7), indicating that God's character and person are inseparable.

Psalm 62

This instructional poem moves from personal trust to public instruction. Building on the foundation of a refrain, which expresses a trusting faith that waits only for God (vv. 1–2, 5–6), the psalmist first admonishes the wicked about the violence of their ways (vv. 3–4) and then exhorts the faithful to trust in God (vv. 8–11).

The poem is shaped by a staccato, pedagogical rhythm. The refrain gives voice to the theological center of the psalm, emphasizing the faithful posture of trusting and waiting in God. To wait "in silence" does not literally mean to refrain from all speech; after all, the psalmist *speaks* in this poem. Rather, it emphasizes a dimension of faith that trusts steadfastly in God *alone*. Verse 8 begins, "Trust in [God] at all times," whereas v. 10 starts, "Do not trust in oppression" (NRSV, *put no confidence in extortion*). This complementary structure can be seen as a commentary on the first commandment. To trust in God is to denounce faith in other powers and protections. Here, the tempting gods of oppression and riches are specifically named. God's trustworthiness is imagined metaphorically as a fortress or refuge—one of the most common metaphors in the Psalter.

Psalm 63

Drawing upon the metaphor of nutrients that sustain life, Ps 63 confesses that God true life depends on a relationship with God. The psalm is launched by the powerful metaphor of thirsting for God "as in a dry and dreary land" (v. 1). Even for readers who do not live in an arid climate, the metaphor translates powerfully, since thirst—and even extreme thirst—is a basic human experience. The psalm builds on this metaphor in v. 5, "my soul is satisfied as with a rich feast." Again, because hunger and satiation are basic human experiences, the metaphoric force is powerful. "Soul" does not refer to a spiritual counterpart of the body, but to the psalmist's "inmost being," or "vital center." The point is that God is the necessary and only central sustaining force of life.

The psalmist further declares that God's "steadfast love is better than life" (v. 3). Although this verse may hint at life beyond the grave, the real sense is that God's steadfast love is the one thing needful for life. Because of this, the psalmist promises to "praise you with my life" (NRSV, *bless you as long as I live*). The sense here is that having found the one thing necessary to sustain true life, one's life becomes completely caught up in bearing witness to God's sustaining love.

Psalm 64

As with so many prayers for help, this prayer begins with an appeal for help (vv. 1–2) and ends with confident trust and the call for praise (vv. 7–10). Because the tense of the verbs in vv. 7–9 is uncertain, it is unclear whether this poem is best understood as a prayer for help in the midst of crisis or a psalm of thanks after deliverance from crisis.

The psalm is composed of the twin elements of "speech" and "ambush." The enemies are portrayed as doing violence with the speech, by shooting verbal arrows at the blameless from ambush (v. 4). How the enemies' speech does violence is not spelled out. They may make false accusations (v. 4) or perhaps they merely plot evil (vv. 2, 5). As in many psalms, the wicked feel free to make mischief because they believe God lacks adequate power to "see" or to hold evildoers accountable (v. 5). But the psalmist confesses faith that God will in turn "shoot his arrow at them" (v. 7), because God does see and will hold the wicked accountable for the crimes of "their tongue" (v. 8). The psalmist further promises that there will be a time when people will "tell" what God has done (v. 9).

Psalm 65

This hymn praises God for answering prayer and forgiving (vv. 2–3), for electing Israel and

being present in the Temple (v. 4), for achieving victory over the cosmic forces of chaos through the act of creation (vv. 5–7), for providing deliverance from the nations (v. 7*b*), and for providing a bountiful harvest (vv. 9–13). The hymn refuses to draw neat lines between God's various gracious activities on behalf of creation. Theologians often prefer to compartmentalize God's various deeds and deal with them cleanly, but this psalm serves up a messy plate. The attempt to link the various activities of God in this psalm in a clear, causal sequence is ill advised. The poem is an effusive pouring forth of praise that transgresses the boundaries of such categories and causal links.

At its heart, the psalm praises God for the ongoing sustenance and bounty of harvest (vv. 9–13). Although some interpreters have tried to locate the psalm at the time of the end of a drought, such a setting is unlikely. The psalm is a more general praise for the blessings of harvest. These blessings are not seen as distinct from or available apart from God's other actions, such as forgiveness, creation, and the like, but as one aspect of God's multifaceted grace.

Psalm 66

Psalm 66 is a poem that morphs through three types of praise—a hymn of praise (vv. 1–7), a communal song of thanksgiving (vv. 8–12), and an individual song of thanksgiving (vv. 13–20)—introducing the history of God's actions on behalf of Israel and inviting all to join themselves to this story. One can understand the movement of the psalm by tracing the words *come* and *bless*. The psalmist bids the peoples to "come and see what God has done" (v. 5). The language of coming (cf. Ps 95:1) means to enter into a relational space with God. Here, the purpose is to hear of what God has done for Israel in the exodus and the entry into the land (v. 6). The psalm then invites the peoples to "bless" (which means praise) God, who has sustained the people through many hardships. Verses 10–12 present God's sustaining help by means of vivid imagery.

The psalmist presents himself or herself as a personal example, doing personally what the nations were exhorted to do: "I have come ... " (NRSV, *I will come*). The psalmist describes the gift of exorbitant offerings (v. 15), a ritual means of joining oneself to God. On this basis, the psalmist renews the call for the peoples to "come" (v. 16). The poem closes with the psalmist again fulfilling his or her own imperative: "Blessed be God" (v. 20).

Psalm 67

Psalm 67 is part priestly prayer for blessing and part hymn of praise. The psalm has three stanzas (vv. 1–2, 4, 6–7), separated by a refrain (vv. 3, 5). Both the refrain and the central stanzas are calls for the nations to join in praise of the Lord. The call to praise is substantiated by two reasons: God's saving deeds (v. 2) and God's justice (v. 4). As the phrases "among all nations" (v. 2) and "the peoples/the nations" (v. 4) indicate, the *universal* frame of God's actions are emphasized. Thus, the psalm's exhortation to praise transcends national and ethnic boundaries—praise is the activity that breaks down the walls that divide.

The opening and closing stanzas of the psalm are prayers for blessing. Verse 6b should be translated, "may God, our God, bless us" (NRSV, *has blessed us*). The connection of this prayer for blessing with "all the ends of the earth" recalls the ancestral promise of Gen 12:1–3 that God's blessing of Israel is for the purpose of blessing all the nations of the earth. As part of the divine mission to bless all the families of the earth, God uses the priestly nation Israel as a means of blessing.

Psalm 68

This lengthy poem is most likely the oldest psalm in the Psalter and is certainly the most difficult to interpret. It is so filled with unclear terms (15 Hebrew words occur only here in the Old Testament) and obscure phrases that some scholars have concluded that the poem is comprised of the fragments of other psalms. Given the psalm's length and obscurities, commentary here will focus on one major theme of the psalm.

One major theme of the psalm is the revelation of God's presence (vv. 5–10, 15–18, 29, 35). The psalm recalls God's presence as made known at Mt. Sinai, during the march through the wilderness, in the blessings of harvest, in the establishment of the Temple in Jerusalem, and above all in the history and fortunes of the nation Israel. Of interest here is the *particularity* of God's revelation. Like the Christian witness to God's incarna-

tion in the person and flesh of a crucified messiah, Israel's witness to God's presence in her history is a scandalous claim that the eternal has become available in one particular people and place. The ways and wisdom of God's reign break into the world through this ancient people and its story.

Psalm 69

Similar in many ways to Ps 22, this individual prayer for help is often cited in the New Testament, especially in the passion narratives. The imagery and emotions of this lyric are volatile, particularly in the opening description of crisis (vv. 1–5) and in a long section that curses the psalmist's oppressors (vv. 22–28). As with Ps 22, the turn to confident praise at the end of the psalm has caused confusion. Although some explain this change as the result of a divine promise delivered by a priest, it is more likely that lament and confidence are psychologically enmeshed emotions.

It is impossible to translate for the modern mind the intensity and force of the metaphor of drowning in water (vv. 1–3, 14–15). Among ancient Israel's neighbors, the river was both god and judge. Within Israel, water and sea symbolized the anti-creation forces of chaos. It is striking, then, that in the trusting conclusion of the psalm the sufferer confesses, "Let... the sea and everything" in them praise the Lord. The only ground for such a breathtaking reversal is the rescue of the Lord. The psalmist is a figure typifying God's action. The pray-er is oppressed and lowly, admits to sin (v. 5), and yet is faithful and trusts in the Lord's deliverance.

Psalm 70

These verses are repeated, with very minor differences, in Ps 40 as part of a song of thanksgiving (vv. 13–17). Here, they comprise an independent prayer for rescue from personal oppressors. One salient feature of the psalm is the contrast between the quoted speech of the enemies in v. 3, and the called-for speech of the community in v. 4. The enemies' speech has no denotative content; it consists solely of a destructive mood that rejoices in the downfall of the psalmist. The community, in contrast, is enjoined to "love" God's salvation and thus to sing, "God is great!" This points to a foundational quality of the community that God calls forth to share in God's mission: the community rejoices in the deliverance of others and resists rejoicing in the suffering or downfall of others.

Psalm 71

Rhetorically, this poem is the anguished prayer of an elderly member of the community (vv. 5–6, 9, 17–18). Literally, it is a composite prayer for help assembled in part from elements of other psalms (vv. 1–3//31:2–4; v. 6//22:9; v. 12//22:11, 38:22; v. 13//35:4; v. 18//22:30; v. 22//33:2, 98:5; and so on). Combining the rhetorical and literary, one gets the impression that a person who has drunk deeply from the Psalter's tradition of prayer and praise now draws near to the end of life.

Theologically, the psalmist's trust bears comparison with the concept of faith in Hab 2:1–5. Having been afforded a broader perspective by a life long in days and deep in experiences of both joy and sorrow, the psalmist trusts in God's deliverance and providence even in the midst of calamity. Thus, the psalm swings back and forth between praise and petition, complaint and confidence, honor and shame. The present moment of suffering is the time in which the psalmist experiences all of those emotions and prayer postures. Furthermore, the psalm is a teaching testimony (v. 18), a witness of one wise with age, who has recorded this instruction for a future generation. It is included in the Psalter for the edification of those who have ears to hear.

Psalm 72

It is no accident that Ps 72, a royal psalm, closes Book II of the Psalter. In the editorial shaping of the Psalter, royal psalms were placed at key junctures between books (see Pss 2, 72, 89) as part of the reinterpretation of these psalms in the tradition (more on this below). The superscription identifies this psalm as written for Solomon, probably because of the theme of the king judging the people in righteousness.

As noted in the commentary on Ps 45, in ancient Israel the monarchy was understood as something akin to a means of grace in Christian theology. One sees that connection clearly in Ps 72 in the way that the poem can move seamlessly from petitions asking that the king judge righteously and defend the poor, to petitions asking that mountains and hills provide prosperity

(vv. 2–4). Both king and land were seen as gifts from God through which God blesses and provides. The special emphasis on the government's responsibility to the needy and poor (vv. 12–14) is noteworthy.

The fact that Israel's human kings did not live up to their divine calling was interpreted by Israel as one of the reasons that the monarchy failed. Precisely after the monarchy failed, the royal psalms were retained in the Psalter and reinterpreted. Both Christianity and Judaism interpreted the inclusion of Ps 72 in the Psalter as a messianic promise of a perfect Davidic king to come. Some scholars have detected signs of that reinterpretation present already in v. 17.

Verses 18–20 are not part of the psalm. Each of the five books of the Psalter concludes with a doxology; vv. 18–19 are the doxological conclusion of Book II. Verse 20 is an editorial insertion signaling the close of the major collection of Davidic psalms.

III. Book III (73–89)

Psalm 73

Book III of the Psalter begins with an instructional psalm; such psalms have been placed editorially at key seams in the Psalter (see Pss 1, 41, 73, 90)—a clue to read the psalms not just as ancient prayers, but as instruction in the way of faith. This poem is a confession of God's faithfulness. Similar to a song of thanksgiving, the psalmist recounts a time of crisis; after this narration, rather than turning to praise as is typical in a song of thanksgiving, the psalm turns to instruction.

The confession of faith is summed up in the opening phrase: "Truly God is good to Israel" (NRSV, *to the upright*). This opening declaration provides the context within which the psalmist narrates a past crisis in which the temptation to give up on God and God's ways was so strong, that the psalmist almost joined the wicked. This temptation arose from the apparent prosperity of the wicked (vv. 3–14).

What helped the psalmist avert this temptation was an experience of God's presence (vv. 17, 23–24, 28). The experience occurred in worship and afforded the psalmist a wider perspective on life, the perception that the apparent prosperity of the wicked is a phantom prosperity (v. 20) in comparison with the richer gifts that God grants.

Psalm 74

Psalm 74 is a communal prayer for help. Although the poem may have been composed for annual liturgical use in some Temple commemoration, the descriptions of the Temple destruction and certain vocabulary in vv. 3–8 suggest that the psalm was written (similar to the Book of Lamentations) soon after the Babylonians destroyed Jerusalem and the Temple c. 587 BCE.

A key word in the psalm is the imperatival petition, "Remember!" While the term is not uncommon in prayers for help, its threefold occurrence here (vv. 2, 18, 22) is telling. The fact that this imperative also occurs twice in Ps 89:47, 51, another lament likely written after Jerusalem was destroyed, signals the important theological conviction that new life for the people could only be generated by the agency of God. The call was for God to remember the covenantal promises (v. 20) and thus restore the nation.

Two other theological motifs are employed to move God. First, the scoffing of the enemies who destroyed is quoted, and God is urged to remember those taunts (vv. 8, 18, 22). Second, the psalmist recalls God's primeval creative activity—understood mythologically as the defeat of the anti-creation forces of chaos (vv. 12–17). The poem intimates that as God once fashioned life and order where there had been no life and chaos, God can again create new life for the people.

Psalm 75

This communal song of thanksgiving may have been placed after Ps 74, a communal prayer for help, both to balance its despair and to illustrate the full cycle one finds in Israel's prayer of the movement from crisis to petition to deliverance to thankful praise. Similar to the three great festival psalms (50, 81, 95), this liturgical poem features the voice of God speaking words of admonition to the worshiping congregation.

After opening sentences of thanksgiving (v. 1), the Lord speaks—most likely through a prophetic or priestly figure. God assures that justice will be established "at the set time"—meaning when God decides the time is ripe, perhaps to be understood

as an answer to the cry "how long" in 74:9. God also admonishes the wicked against their pride (vv. 4–5). The psalm continues with an affirmation that judgment comes only from God. The cup of wine is a metaphor for God's judgment (cf. Isa 51:17; Rev 14:10). The psalm ends with a second speech from God. The psalm paints an especially vivid portrait of the wicked as those who live under a false sense of autonomy, whereas the righteous are those who depend on God.

Psalm 76

This hymn of praise is similar to other "songs of Zion" that praise God's election of Jerusalem as the divine dwelling place and God's protection of the city against cosmic and human threats (cf. Pss 46; 48; 84; 114). Although some scholars have tried to identify the psalm with a specific military victory in Israel's history—such as the exodus, one of David's triumphs, or the defeat of Sennacherib in 701 BCE—it is more likely that the psalm was composed for annual, liturgical use in the Temple.

Verse 1 of the psalm indicates that God's choice of Zion is a means of revelation, a channel through which God has revealed the divine character. The remainder of the psalm unpacks two expressions of God's character—God's activities of stopping war (vv. 3, 5–6; cf. Ps 46:9) and God's righteous judgment of oppressors (vv. 7–12). To some modern minds, these two activities seem contradictory. But in the ancient view they were seen as complementary. God's desire to end war is based in God's love for all creation and the divine desire that society be ordered in such ways that all can thrive. When the wicked do evil, God's love for the oppressed is expressed in judgment of the oppressors.

Psalm 77

Memory often plays a significant role when people of faith endure times of crisis. This prayer for help is testimony to the power of memory both to torment sufferers and also to help them come to grips with questions of faith in the midst of suffering. The psalmist is in the midst of a personal crisis that keeps sleep from coming (vv. 1–3). In the middle of the sleepless night, the sufferer's racing mind returns again and again to God and the history of God's saving deeds (v. 5). At first, this knowledge causes despair, as the psalmist wonders if God has forsaken love and recanted the divine promises (vv. 7–10). The complaint section of the prayer climaxes in v. 10 as the psalmist quotes his or her own conclusion that God has repented of love.

But then the psalmist's rumination on God's history takes on a new role. The psalmist narrates the deeds of God in such a way that the psalmist's understanding of God's presence in suffering is reframed. God's way is "holy" and "your footprints were unseen" (vv. 13, 19), meaning that God's presence is often mysterious and beyond the capacity of human comprehension. Nevertheless God is present and active. God's way is "through the sea," meaning God does not promise the absence of suffering, but God leads in the midst of and through chaos.

Psalm 78

When the Old Testament narrates history, it is never simply for the purpose of recounting what happened. Rather, history is recited for the purpose of theological witness. That is the case with Ps 78, in which Israel's history is told in order to teach "the next generation" (v. 6) to know God, by knowing what God has done in the past. Following an introduction (vv. 1–8), the psalm narrates Israel's dealings with God during the wilderness wanderings (vv. 9–41), the exodus (vv. 42–51), and from the time of the settlement of the land down through King David (vv. 52–72). Similar to 2 Kings 17, a major concern of Ps 78 involves God's rejection of the northern kingdom and election of both David and Jerusalem (v. 67–70).

Similar to the Deuteronomic History (Judges through 2 Kings, except for Ruth), the poem relates a long story of the people's unfaithfulness. They tested (vv. 18, 41, 56), forgot (v. 11), lacked faith in (vv. 22, 32, 37), and did not obey God (vv. 10, 56). God met this constant infidelity with compassion and forgiveness (v. 38), although at times God exercised anger in order to bring about repentance (vv. 34–35). This story serves as both a warning not to repeat the sins of the northern kingdom and a promise that God remains faithful in spite of human infidelity. Even in the rejection of the northern kingdom God remains faithful, since the southern people are still present as God's inheritance (vv. 71–72).

Psalm 79

This psalm follows Ps 78, which details the rejection of Israel and the destruction of the sanctuary at Shiloh, and precedes Ps 80, which pleads for communal restoration. This location suggests that the poem be understood in light of Jerusalem's destruction c. 587 BCE at the hands of Babylon. The violence of that destruction challenged Judah's faith, which was in part built on the promises that God would protect Jerusalem and the Davidic line.

At the heart of Ps 79's faith struggle is the question quoted in v. 10: "Where is their God?" This typical "taunt" (vv. 4, 12; cf. Pss 42:3, 10; 115:2) reflects the ancient belief that the destruction of a nation was equivalent to the defeat of that nation's god—that the destruction of a god's temple (v. 1) in effect made that god homeless. The words quoted in v. 10 are placed on the lips of the enemies, but they also reflect Israel's own doubts and pain. By quoting the enemies, Israel could both voice its own struggles but also distance themselves from responsibility for the words. By quoting the enemy's taunt—like Hezekiah, who "spread" a taunting Assyrian letter before the Lord (Isa 37:14–17)—the psalm presents God with the enemies' challenge to the Lord's strength and fidelity. By asking God to hear the "groans of the prisoner" (v. 11), the psalmist asks God for a new exodus deliverance (cf. Exod 2:23–25).

Psalm 80

The threefold refrain (vv. 3, 14, 19) summarizes the driving concern of this prayer: restore the people! The request for God's face to shine is simultaneously a prayer for blessing (Num 6:25) and a plea for a new revelation of divine power (Ps 67:1–2). Many elements tie Pss 78–80 together, including the motif of shepherd. Ps 78 describes the Davidic kings as the shepherds of God's sheep (v. 71). Psalm 79 prays for God to tend "your people, the sheep of your pasture" (v. 13). Psalm 80 begins by addressing God as "shepherd of Israel," a title that occurs only here. Some scholars have interpreted this sequence to the rejection of the Davidic monarchy; at the least, God's lordship is here elevated to a degree that relativizes all human claims to rule God's people, even the claims of God's earthly servants.

Similar to the parable in Isa 5, vv. 8–13 recall God's history of gracious deeds by drawing on the metaphor of the people as God's vineyard. But whereas the prophet sought to move the people to repentance, the psalmist seeks to move God to repentance (*turn again* in v. 14 renders *shuv*, which is normally translated *repent*). As "give us life" in v. 18 indicates, the prayer is literally a prayer for new life and existence for people.

Psalm 81

As with the two other great festival psalms (50, 95), this hymn of praise features a call to praise (vv. 1–5) and the words of God, which were probably spoken by a priest or Temple leader (vv. 6–16). Verses 3–5 identify the psalm with the Festival of Tabernacles, Israel's fall harvest feast. During the Old Testament period, this was the major festival of the liturgical year.

The most striking aspect of this liturgy is the admonishing tone. Modern worshipers expect festival days to be joyous celebrations, but the words of admonition and moral exhortation here call this assumption into question. As with the divine speeches in the other festival psalms, there is a direct connection with a part of the Decalogue. Here, the first two commandments are reinforced (vv. 9–10; cf. Exod 20:1–6). The call to obey the Lord (vv. 11–13) is driven by the reminder of God's loving actions for the people (vv. 6–7) and God's promise to care for the people, especially the continuing providential gifts of the fruits of the harvest (vv. 10*b*, 16).

Psalm 82

Psalm 82 is the most explicitly mythological poem in the Psalter. Its background—the concept of the "divine council" (v. 1)—represents an ancient worldview that is foreign to modern readers. The divine council consists of the Lord as the chief God presiding over other subservient beings (see Isa 6:1–6; 1 Kgs 22:19–22; Job 1:6–12; Jer 23:18). The psalm takes the form of a drama. The Lord plays the role of the universal judge who assembles the divine council for trial. The Lord charges the gods of other nations with failing in the fundamental obligation to establish justice, especially for the unprotected classes— the orphan, the "poor" (v. 3; NRSV, "lowly"), and the needy. Justice, a fundamental biblical concept,

refers to the *external social order in which all life can prosper*. Verse 5 is a description of the gods who are blind and ignorant. In v. 7, the Lord sentences the gods to mortal death because they have failed to provide justice.

As the dramatic sentence in v. 6 indicates, the psalm is a transitional poem on the way from a polytheistic worldview—which many in Israel held—to a monotheistic view, which is the end product of the OT canon (cf. Ps 115:3–8). The closing appeal for God to rise up and judge the earth may be an exclamation of praise, but it may also be an appeal for the Lord to perform justice— as the Lord had expected the gods of the nations to do.

Psalm 83

Various dates have been proposed for this communal prayer for help, based on the names of the ten threatening nations mentioned in vv. 6–8. A precise date cannot be determined; in fact, it is likely that the psalm represents a liturgical poem composed for regular liturgical use in the Temple, rather than for any one crisis. The mention of the nations reflects the perpetual threats that Israel experienced from many nations. The accusation that "they conspire with one accord" (v. 5) does not mean that there was a literal league among these nations, but rather that Israel interpreted the history of hostility as an overall opposition of other nations to God's mission to bless the nations of the earth through Israel (cf. Gen 12:1–3).

After an opening appeal (v. 1), vv. 2–7 consist of complaint about the nations, while vv. 8–18 are a mirroring section of petition. At the center of each of these sections is a verse in which the words of the enemies are quoted. In v. 4, the nations say, "let the *name* of Israel be remembered no more." Such boasting taunts were typical in the ancient world, as is attested in Pharaoh Merneptah's famous boast on a victory monument: "Israel lies in waste, its seed is no more." The poem closes by turning the vocabulary of the nations on its head: "Let them know that you alone, whose *name* is the LORD, are the Most High" (v. 18).

Psalm 84

This bright lyric is part pilgrimage psalm, part song of Zion, and all hymn of praise. That is to say, this is a song that praises God for the wonders of divine grace that God showers (literally, v. 6) on Israel by virtue of the Temple. It is also a poem with significant pilgrimage themes (vv. 5–7); it may have been sung by worshipers who were on their way to Jerusalem to observe one of the three annual pilgrimage festivals, most likely the fall harvest Festival of Tabernacles (cf. Exod 23:16–16). The psalm praises God by lauding the Temple—God's holy dwelling place (v. 1), the nexus point between heaven and earth—and by lauding the worshipers—God's holy people. The Temple is conceived of as an incarnational space where the divine and human realms intersect. Thus, it is the space where human beings become God's people—the channel through which God's blessings, such as harvest/fertility (v. 6), protection (v. 9), and "favor and honor" (v. 11), are made available. God's hospitality is portrayed via the image of the lowly sparrow finding a home in the Temple (v. 3). The surpassing joy and grace that are manifest in the Temple are pictured through the contrasting images (one day versus a thousand; better a doorkeeper than a dweller) of v. 10. The "doorkeeper" is not a priestly office, but should be understood as one who sleeps outside awaiting entrance into the Temple.

Psalm 85

Psalm 85 consists of four stanzas: a communal thanksgiving for past deliverance (vv. 1–3), a communal petition for national restoration (vv. 4–7), a prayer for God's word to be revealed (vv. 8–9), and a promise of deliverance (vv. 10–13). Interpretations of the psalm as a whole differ. The view taken here is that the psalm is a liturgy in which the community requests divine restoration and then receives that promise from God. Exactly what "restoration" entails is unclear: perhaps return from exile (vv. 1b, 4–6), perhaps forgiveness for some national sin (v. 2), perhaps deliverance from a national threat (vv. 7, 9), perhaps a bountiful harvest (v. 12).

Seen from a bird's-eye view, the psalm bears witness to God's past acts of deliverance (vv. 1–3), to the ongoing human need for divine intervention (vv. 4–8), and to the promise that the one who established a covenant with Israel will remain faithful and continue to deliver Israel (vv. 10–13). In the last stanza, the divine attributes of stead-

fast love, faithfulness, righteousness, and peace are personified as tangible forces that act at God's behest and on the people's behalf. The text of v. 8c is difficult and thus not too much weight should be placed on any interpretation of it.

Psalm 86

This is the touching, three-stanza prayer of a sufferer who has nowhere to turn "in the day of trouble" but to God (v. 7). The first stanza (vv. 1–7) consists of confident yet vulnerable petitions for God to rescue the sufferer. Taken together, these verses offer rich insight into the reasons supplicants can have confidence that their petitions are heard. Every verse, with the exception of v. 6, includes a clause that contributes something to the understanding of why the psalmist hopes for the prayer to be answered. These reasons include God's character, the nature of the relationship between God and the psalmist, and the psalmist's desperate situation.

The second stanza picks up the theme of God's character and magnifies it. None is like the Lord, because none has the power to accomplish what God has and will accomplish, and because none has God's faithful and steadfast character. Even though a major theme of the first stanza is the strong relationship between God and psalmist, the psalmist knows that God always has more to teach about the divine way (v. 11).

The last stanza consists of renewed appeals, this time focusing on the threat of the enemies (v. 14) and again on God's character (v. 15). The closing request for a sign—some hint of deliverance—is a prayer to which anyone who has suffered can relate.

Psalm 87

This "song of Zion" is perhaps the most obscure and difficult psalm in the Psalter. How to translate much of the psalm is unclear. Those parts that can be translated with confidence still often remain obscure. Those difficulties granted, the psalm praises the city Jerusalem directly as a stand-in for God (v. 3). It praises Zion as the favored point of contact between the heavenly and earthly spheres (v. 5). In particular, Jerusalem is praised above Jacob (the northern kingdom), while the residents of various foreign counties—Rahab (a mythical beast that here symbolizes Egypt), Babylon, Philistia, Tyre (a city of the Phoenicians), and Ethiopia—are portrayed as honoring those born in Jerusalem. The Lord singles out those born in Jerusalem (v. 6). The meaning of the last verse is not clear, although if one takes "singers and dancers" as a reference to worshipers, then the verse has those worshipers recognizing in some way the singular blessings that God pours out in and through Zion. The psalm's emphasis on Zion's blessings should be balanced by a reminder that in the OT, God's blessing of the chosen people was for the purpose of blessings all the nations of the earth (Gen 12:1–3).

Psalm 88

This psalm is widely regarded as the darkest of all the prayers for help. Of all the laments, Ps 88 alone lacks any sign of confidence in rescue or hope in the future. The psalm's desperate gloom is magnified by its artistic construction. The psalm has a three-stanza structure (vv. 1–9a, 9b–12, 13–18). Each section is structured similarly, containing an appeal to the "LORD," a reference to a different part of the day—"at night" (v. 1), "every day" (v. 9b), "in the morning" (v. 13)—and a reference to a different body part—"incline your ear" (v. 2), "I spread out my hands" (v. 9b), "you hide your face" (v. 14). In those laments that move toward hope, a reference to the morning would signal hope (cf. Pss 5:3; 30:5; 143:8). The morning of Ps 88 dawns upon only more pain and despair. The sufferer is ill onto death (vv. 3–9) and expects no new life after death (vv. 10–12). The illness is caused by God (vv. 14–17). The psalms usually portray God as defeating the forces of chaos that are metaphorically pictured as the "flood" (v. 17). But here, *God's activity is portrayed as the flood*. The psalm's climactic verse (v. 18) repeats the complaint of v. 8a and punctuates it with a dark exclamation: "my companion is darkness" (the translation of this last phrase is disputed; NRSV, "my companions are in darkness" is unlikely).

As noted already, the artistry of this poem only serves to makes its painful cry more poignant. The only glimmers of hope are the three mentions of the Lord, signaling that even in complete suffering, a relationship still exists between the sufferer and the "God of my salvation" (v. 1). Perhaps the best that can be said is that even cries of pain this stark are part of a life of faith.

Psalm 89

This lengthy royal psalm brings Book III of the Psalter to a close. The psalm is comprised of an introduction (vv. 1–4) followed by three distinct sections (vv. 5–18, 19–37, 38–51). It begins in praise but closes in pain. The introduction sounds both the psalm's praise keynote—God's covenant with David (vv. 3–4; cf. 2 Sam 7:1–17)—and also introduces the theological grounds for the closing lament, God's "steadfast love" and "faithfulness" (vv. 1–2). The first section of praise emphasizes the Lord's universal kingship, which the Lord earned through the complementary actions of creation and of defeating the powers of chaos (vv. 9–14).

Section two transitions from God's kingship to God's election of the Davidic monarchy. This section emphasizes God's promises to David, specifically God's assurance that although wayward Davidic kings would be disciplined, "I will not remove him from my steadfast love, or be false to my faithfulness" (v. 33). Section three turns to lament, accusing God of having "renounced the covenant" (v. 39). It asks, "where is your steadfast love … your faithfulness you swore to David?" (v. 49). The psalm seems to reflect the fall of Jerusalem c. 587 BCE. As mentioned, the theological issue is God's faithfulness to the Davidic covenant. Having accused God of renouncing the covenant, the psalm's only petition is "Remember" (vv. 47, 50; see also the commentary on Ps 74).

Verse 52 is not properly a part of Ps 89, but a doxology that closes Book III.

IV. Book IV (90–106)

Psalm 90

Book IV begins with a wisdom psalm. Some interpreters have argued that the arrangement of Ps 89 (which laments the destruction of the Davidic monarchy) at the end of Book III and of Ps 90 (the only "song of Moses") at the start of Book IV is a major clue to the theology of the Psalter. According to this view, the Psalter tells the story of the failure of the Davidic covenant and a corresponding move to embrace the Sinai covenant (cf. Exod 19–20). But wisdom psalms are placed at the junctures of several of the books of the Psalter (cf. Pss 1; 41; 73). It is more likely that this arrangement signals that the Psalter is a book of instruction.

Psalm 90 begins with the image of God as the people's eternal "dwelling place." This establishes the psalm's poetic contrast between God's eternal nature and the mortal existence to which humans are consigned. The psalm expresses the notion of human mortality through the metaphors of fleeting dreams, withering grass, evening and morning, sin, and flight (vv. 5–10). The span of life is seventy or eighty years (v. 10). The psalm applies this wisdom in three requests. It asks God to grant a wise perspective (so that life may be well lived; v. 12), to "turn back" God's wrath (grant longer life; v. 13), and to "prosper the work of our hands" (to bless the work of one's life; v. 17).

Psalm 91

One of the key theological images of the Psalter is God as "refuge"—the protecting place and person to which a sufferer can flee from enemies, illness, threats from nature, and even from personal sin. Psalm 91 can be understood as an extended meditation on that metaphor.

The poem begins by pairing the image of God's protective refuge with the act of the follower confessing faith—divine refuge is available for anyone who confesses the Lord as refuge and places trust in that refuge (v. 2). The images of "shelter," "shadow," and "wings" may have been associated with the Temple as a place of sanctuary and the image of the cherubim's wings (cf. 1 Kgs 6:22–28), which may be a clue that the psalm was a liturgy for individuals who came to the Temple seeking assurance of God's protection. Alternatively, the metaphor may stem simply from the tradition elsewhere in the Bible that depicts God's guidance using the metaphor of the eagle (Deut 32:10–11; Exod 19:4). The body of the psalm consists of a sequence of divine promises, which are summed up "no evil shall befall you" (v. 10). In Luke 4:10–11, Satan quotes the promise of vv. 1–12—a possible warning to those who might take the promises of Ps 91 out of context.

Psalm 92

The superscription that identifies this as "a song of the Sabbath Day" reflects the later application of this song of thanksgiving. This emphasis on joyful music and singing in the call to praise (vv. 1–4) and the praise of the congregation gathered in the Temple (vv. 12–13) fit well with this Sabbath application. Categorized according to form, the psalm is a song of thanksgiving, expressing the praise of one whom God has sustained through a personal crisis. Categorized according to content, the psalm is an instructional psalm, because of its wisdom-like contrast of the "wicked" (also *dullard* and *stupid*) with the "righteous." Similar to many other instructional psalms, this poem emphasizes the limited perspective of the wicked, whose short-timeline worldview leads them to eschew the narrow path of God's way in favor of the quick fix and fast payoff. The righteous, on the other hand, take a broader view of life. They have learned to trust God through times of crisis. This longer view affords them the strength to flourish even into old age.

Psalm 93

This hymn of praise is one of a group of psalms that have been labeled "enthronement psalms" (see commentary on Ps 47), because the argument has been made that they were part of a liturgical celebration that announced, "The Lord has become king" (v. 1a). The argument has also been made that the Lord's kingship is the central theological affirmation of the Psalter. Such a broad conclusion may not be merited, but Ps 93 does bear witness that the Lord's kingship was established through the act of creation. Even the "floods" (v. 3, NRSV; a literal translation would be "rivers," cf. Ps 46:4)—a mythological symbol of the anti-creation forces of chaos—praise the Lord's majesty. The Lord's dominion, based in creation, is eternal and the Lord's "decrees" are sure (v. 5). The psalm thus makes the connection between God's nature and God's instruction.

Psalm 94

This intense prayer for rescue is one part petition for divine vengeance and one part meditation on divine providence. As a prayer for vengeance, the poem numbers among the so-called imprecatory psalms that actively call evil down upon the enemy (cf. Pss 69:22–26; 137:7–9; 139:19–22). As a meditation, the psalm poetically addresses those who deny God's providence and asserts that God is both aware of human rebellion (vv. 8–11) and has the capacity to discipline and judge (vv. 12–23). The enemies are characterized by their rebellion against God and God's ways, which leads them to commit deliberate acts of evil, including the murder of society's most vulnerable members (vv. 5–6). The wicked feel licensed to engage in such immorality because they do not believe that the Lord is aware of human evil or has the power to hold evildoers accountable (v. 7). The prayer's plea for judgment against the wicked offends some modern readers. It should be noted both that genuine evil is a part of fallen human existence and that outraged emotions are part of a life committed to God's just ways. The community asks for God's judgment but does not take vengeance into its own hands.

Psalm 95

Similar to Pss 50 and 81, this hymn of praise betrays signs of having been composed for one of the three major festivals of the Israelite year (probably Tabernacles, the fall festival) and includes a section in which the divine voice admonishes the congregation (vv. 8–11). It may be that the psalm enacts a liturgical procession in which the fellowship first enters the sanctuary (v. 2) and then bows down before God (v. 6). Whether this is true or not, the theological pairing of *praise* and *entering in God's presence* is instructive. Praise is speech that names God as the indispensable actor in the world's drama. Praise is not song and speech designed to flatter God; rather, by naming God as lord, it creates the theological space in which the worshiping community enters anew into relationship with God.

The hymn is one of the enthronement psalms (see commentary on Ps 47). God's kingship is based on the acts of creation (v. 5) and of electing Israel (v. 7). The divine admonition reminds the people of the history of testing and rebelling against God during the wilderness years (cf. Exod 17:1–7; Num 20:1–13).

Psalm 96

This hymn of praise accentuates the universal kingship and judgment of God. One of the so-called enthronement psalms (see commentary on Ps 47), it praises the Lord as king (v. 10). The psalm has two stanzas (vv. 1–6, 7–13). Each stanza starts off with three verses (six clauses) of imperative exhortations to praise. The first stanza calls for "a new song." This phrase may have been a technical term for a song of thanksgiving sung after experiencing divine rescue, as the clause "tell of his salvation" in v. 2 may indicate (cf. Ps 40:3). This stanza also praises God as unequaled by other powers. Israel worships the creator; other peoples worship humanly fashioned idols (vv. 4–5).

The second stanza calls on all the nations and families of earth (vv. 7, 10) to worship the Lord by bringing offerings and praise to Jerusalem ("his courts," v. 8). The song calls on the nations to sing Israel's song (v. 10), and poetically depicts creation as already praising the true creator (vv. 11–12). The reference in v. 12 to God's coming in judgment does not refer to the New Testament concept of the end of time, but to God's rescuing actions within history.

Psalm 97

This hymn of praise is one of the enthronement psalms (see commentary on Ps 47). The dramatic focus of this song is on the revelation of God by means of a thunderous theophany (vv. 2–9). The point of the metaphor is not that God is literally in the thunderstorm, but that the Lord's presence is like the storm—an immanent presence that overshadows and destabilizes earthly powers, yet a transcendent mystery surrounded in "clouds and thick darkness" (v. 2). The "heavens proclaim his righteousness" is a double entendre that continues the metaphor. The heavens are both the thundering skies, but also the heavenly realms in which the righteous God dwells. "Zion hears and is glad" continues the double meaning; Zion hears both the storm and the spiritual realm's testimony to the true God, who surpasses any human idols or images.

The psalm makes a characteristic Israelite connection between God's revelation and God's ongoing providence and guidance. The God revealed in Zion loves those who hate evil. In v. 11, the abstract concepts of light and joy portray God's presence.

Psalm 98

A communal "new song" (see commentary on Ps 96) that celebrates an experience of God's deliverance of the people, this hymn calls for exuberant praise. The hymn occurs in three stanzas. The first calls for praise because God has delivered Israel. The song may have been composed after a specific experience of rescue, such as deliverance from military threat, but is general enough to be applied to many circumstances. The point is that in the experience of deliverance, God has revealed the divine character: steadfast love and faithfulness.

The second stanza calls on "all the earth" to praise God, but focuses on human praise—that of song, lyre, trumpet, horn, and voice. The praise names God as king (this is an enthronement psalm; see commentary on Ps 47). The final stanza picks up the call for "all the earth" to praise and enjoins the sea, world, floods, and hills to praise. This poetic flourish is more than a mere anthropomorphism. It is a metaphoric description of the universal rule of the faithful Lord, whose reign bears not just on people, but also on plants, animals, earth, and even the anti-creation forces of the chaotic flood.

Psalm 99

The first three verses of this enthronement hymn (see commentary on Ps 47) poetically pair the particular and universal aspects of Israel's theological witness. The first phrase of each verse names the particular: "The LORD" is the proper name of God revealed to Israel, the cherubim are the winged lions represented in Jerusalem's Temple (cf. 1 Kgs 6:22–28), "Zion" is a name for Jerusalem. The second phrase of each verse names the universal: God's lordship extends over the peoples, the earth, and all the peoples. Together, these verses capture the particular and universal scandal of Israel's good news: The Lord revealed particularly to Israel is king (v. 1) of all creation.

The Lord's kingship is not merely objective, however. God is committed to justice and righteousness both within Israel and throughout the nations. This characteristic commitment to justice is as much the basis for the Lord's reign as any objective qualities of God. The psalm bears further witness to the Lord's faithfulness by narrating God's fidelity in *answering* Moses, Aaron, Samuel, in giving the *law*, and in *forgiving* sin.

Psalm 100

Perhaps the best known of all psalm paraphrases in hymns, "All People That on Earth Do Dwell," captures both the universal scope of this song's witness and its joyful mood. The psalm has two stanzas (vv. 1–3, 4–5), each of which includes both imperative calls for praise and a reason to praise. There are seven imperatives—make a joyful noise, worship, come, know, enter, give thanks, and bless—a number symbolic of perfection. The center imperative sums up the psalm's theology: "Know that the LORD is God" (v. 3a). To "know" God however is never simply a matter of intellectual assent. The Hebrew term does not distinguish between intellectual knowledge and moral obedience, but includes both. To know God is also to obey God (cf. Hos 4:1–4).

The first of the two reasons for praise names God's act of creating the nation (v. 3). The phrase "it is he who made us" refers to the act of electing the people, not the more universal act of creation. The second reason for praise (v. 5) lauds God's goodness, steadfast love, and faithfulness—terms that bear witness to God's faithful character, which is the heart of the theology of the Psalter.

Psalm 101

The singer of this song is not named explicitly anywhere in the text, but most interpreters identify the singer as the king, because the statements "I will destroy" the wicked (vv. 5, 8) fit best with the monarch's role in ancient Israel. That interpretation makes this a royal psalm, expressing the king's role as one of the means through which the Lord's reign is realized. The poem may have been composed for a king's coronation, or more likely, for the king to speak during an annual Temple ritual. It fits within Israel's conception of the ideal Davidic monarch, whose reign the prophets anticipated (cf. Isa 9:1–7; 11:1–9).

As an expression of God's action in the world, the poem affirms that God's commitment to a just order requires judgment of those who oppress the neighbor (v. 5). As an expression of what God requires of human beings, the psalm affirms that the call to leadership within God's people is also a call to follow God's "way that is blameless" (vv. 2, 6). More to the point, the call to join oneself to God's house (vv. 2, 7) is a call to be accountable to and for other members of the community. The psalm makes this point poetically when the speaker pledges to "study the way that is blameless" but also trusts that "whoever walks in the way that is blameless shall minister to me" (v. 6).

Psalm 102

The superscription labels this "a prayer of one afflicted, when faint and pleading before the LORD." The superscription is not original to the psalm, but a clue to the earliest interpretation. This description also indicates that the poems and prayers of the Psalter were collected in part so that other men and women could pray them. This prayer is for one who seeks divine intervention due to illness or a similar crisis. The psalm was also identified by the Western Church as one of the penitential psalms (see commentary on Ps 6), although confession and forgiveness are not explicit themes in the prayer.

One dominant motif is the sufferer's contrast between human mortality and divine immortality. For instance, the poem contrasts "my days" (vv. 3, 11, 23, 24; NRSV, "my life" = "my days" in Hebrew) and "your years" (vv. 24, 27). This stark contrast is accentuated by the apposition of a description of the psalmist's suffering (vv. 3–11) with a description of God's glory (vv. 12–22). Particularly poignant is the simile of the psalmist lying awake through the night, groaning like a lonely owl (vv. 5–7). Prayed from this depth of pathos, the psalm expresses confidence that God can offer healing, because God hears the groans and prayers of the lowly (vv. 17, 20).

Psalm 103

Psalm 103 combines praise, thanksgiving, and instruction. An artistic masterpiece, the song opens with imperative calls to "bless" (that is, to praise) the Lord. In vv. 1–5, the psalmist poetically exhorts "my soul" to praise God. By *soul* is meant the psalmist's most essential self, not some eternal, spiritual counterpart to the body—the Israelites knew no such concept. The reasons to praise God are summed up in v. 2*b*: because of "all his benefits." The reformer Philip Melanchthon famously taught that to know Christ is to know his benefits. Similarly, when the psalm recounts the Lord's benefits in vv. 3–19, it seeks to make God known others. In vv. 3–5 the psalmist testi-

fies to the benefits that God has shown the psalmist. The *your* and *you* in vv. 3–5 refer to *my soul*, thus the psalmist testifies that God has forgiven, healed, redeemed from near death, given long life, and renewed.

In vv. 6–19 the psalmist broadens the description of God's benefits "for all who are oppressed." These benefits include the gift of the law (v. 7), acts of compassion (v. 13), and especially God's gracious forgiveness (vv. 8–12). The closing crescendo of four imperative calls to "bless the LORD" offers a bookend to the psalm, in which all the hosts of heaven join the psalmist's "soul" in praising God for his benefits.

Psalm 104

This hymn is a twin to Ps 103. Both begin and end with the self-exhortation, "Bless the LORD, O my soul." But whereas Ps 103 praises the wondrous *acts of salvation* of God for both the psalmist and the people, Ps 104 praises God's magnificent *acts of creation.*

The order in which creation unfolds is similar to the liturgical description of creation in Gen 1—first the heavens are created (vv. 2–4), followed by earth and sea (vv. 5–9), animals, plants, and people (vv. 10–26)—but the order is not exactly the same and the Gen 1 emphases on Sabbath and creation in the image of God are lacking in Ps 104. As lyric poetry, Ps 104 is both more metaphorical (see the anthropomorphic descriptions of God stretching out, riding, setting, building, rebuking, etc.) and more mythological (see the references to the fight against chaos and the reference to the mythological Leviathan, vv. 2–4, 26) than Gen 1.

Creation is both a one-time and an ongoing divine event. God's creations in turn "bring forth" (v. 14) other creations. The psalm emphasizes both that creation function orderly according to laws and rhythms (vv. 19–25) and that God's ongoing presence and guidance within creation is reason to praise (vv. 27–30).

Psalm 105

The second of three lengthy historical psalms (see 78 and 106). The center of this hymn's proclamation is that throughout the people's history God has kept the promises that were made in the ancestral covenants with Abraham, Isaac, and Jacob. To put this a different way, the psalm describes the history of Israel as the history of God's faithfulness to the promises God made to Abraham. The psalm narrates this history, with its "wonderful works," "miracles," and "judgments" (v. 5), as the story of God remembering the covenant. *Promise* is the key term in the psalm; it is translated variously as *word*, *promise*, and *what he had said* in vv. 8, 19, 27, 28, and 42.

The psalm spends the bulk of its historical narration on the story of Israel's early period, from Joseph's slavery in Egypt (vv. 16–23), through the exodus events (vv. 26–39), God's guidance and provision in the wilderness (vv. 40–41), and the gift of the promised land (v. 44). This history is sung both so that new people will come to know God through the psalm's praise (v. 1) and also so that people might participate in the covenant and obey God's laws (v. 45).

Psalm 106

This historical psalm plays off its twin, Ps 105 (cf. also Ps 78). Whereas Ps 105 focuses on the story of Israel's sojourn in and exodus from Egypt, Ps 106 briefly relates the story of the exodus (vv. 7–12), but goes into far greater depth about the events of Sinai (vv. 19–23), the wilderness years (vv. 24–33), and the first generations in the land (vv. 34–43). Whereas Ps 105 emphasized the people's history as the story of God's faithfulness, Ps 106 narrates the history of a people who repetitively sin against God. Whereas Ps 105 is a hymn of praise, Ps 106 begins and ends with praise, but the body of the psalm is as much a prayer for forgiveness and rescue as it is a hymn.

As a prayer for forgiveness, the psalm multiplies various expressions for sin: sinned, committed iniquity, did not remember, rebelled, forgot, put God to the test, had no faith, did not obey, and so on (vv. 6–7, 13–14, 24–25). As the psalm progresses through the story of Israel's history, the perversity of the people's sins increase. For example, early on the people merely "did not remember the abundance of your steadfast love" (v. 7). Later they "provoked God to anger with their deeds" (v. 29). Finally, they "sacrificed their sons and daughters" and "poured out innocent blood" (vv. 37–38). The poem brings this dramatically building intensity to a climax with the announcement of a gracious surprise: God "remembered his covenant and

showed compassion according to the abundance of his steadfast love" (v. 45).

Verse 48 is not properly a part of the psalm, but the closing doxology of Book IV of the Psalter.

V. Book V (107–150)

Psalm 107

An artfully balanced liturgy of thanksgiving, Ps 107 calls for praise in response to the Lord's acts of steadfast love on behalf of many people. After an opening call to praise (vv. 1–3), the psalm includes four tightly composed, parallel stanzas (vv. 4–9, 10–16, 17–22, 23–32) and ends with a more freely composed stanza of praise (vv. 33–43).

The introductory call to praise exhorts those whom the Lord has redeemed from the east, west, north, and south to thank God. Each stanza begins with a description of "some" who suffered some peril or crisis (vv. 4, 10, 17, 23), then continues that "they cried to the LORD in their trouble, and he delivered/saved them from their distress" (vv. 6, 13, 19, 28). Finally, each stanza enjoins, "Let them thank the Lord for his steadfast love" (vv. 8, 15, 21, 31). This fourfold pattern is presented as a model for the life of faith. The Lord intervenes to move people from lamentation in the midst of crisis to praise after experiencing deliverance. To praise, therefore, is to place one's own life within the overarching narrative of God's deliverance. It is to sing oneself into God's story.

The final stanza praises God's characteristic actions of providing for the hungry and thirsty (vv. 33–38) and of overturning the oppressive orders of society on behalf of the lowly oppressed (vv. 39–43).

Psalm 108

A composite poem made up of Pss 57:7–11 and 60:5–12, this psalm may be a clue that some psalms were created by borrowing sections from various earlier compositions. See commentary on Pss 57 and 60, but also consider this psalm in its own integrity. The persona of this psalm seems to be speaking on behalf of the people as a whole, and a key theme is Israel's role and fate "among the nations" (v. 3). Appeal is made to God on the basis of the steadfastness of the singer's heart, on the singer's witness among the peoples, on

God's strength, and most importantly, on the basis of God's character (v. 4). The psalm quotes a past promise (vv. 7–9) in which God pledged to establish Israel in the land and give them victory over threatening powers. On the basis of this past promise, the singer closes the psalm in complaint over Israel's situation (vv. 10–11) with a renewed request for help (v. 12) and confidence in God's intervention. This confidence is based both on God's character and on God's power.

Psalm 109

This prayer for help is all about speech, as the manifold references in vv. 1–5 indicate: *do not be silent, praise, deceitful mouths, speaking, lying tongues, words of hate, accuse,* and *prayer.* The psalmist has been accused and asks God to pronounce innocence. Following the opening verses, there is a long section in which the enemies' false speech is quoted (vv. 6–19). The introductory words *They say* (v. 6) are not present in the Hebrew, but for a variety of reasons the passage is best understood as the psalmist's quotation of the enemies' words. The enemies desire the psalmist to be tried and punished. The references to *children* and *posterity* (vv. 10–13) may indicate that a guilty verdict would result in the sale of the psalmist's children as slaves to pay off a debt (cf. Lev 25:39). The reference to the sins of the parents (vv. 14–15) reflects the ancient belief that personal misfortune stemmed either from personal sin or the sins of one's parents.

After quoting the violent speech of the enemies, the psalmist appeals to God for deliverance (vv. 20–31). The entire psalm can be understood as a commentary on the false-witness commandment. The psalmist's request may be summed up: "Let them curse, but you will bless" (v. 28*a*). Both cursing (accusing) and blessing are speech acts—actions one does with words (like making a bet). The psalmist requests an irrevocable divine blessing in the form of a declaration of innocence.

Psalm 110

Psalm 110 contains some of the most obscure lyrics in the Psalter. In spite of many scholarly attempts, textual corruptions and confusion about how to understand certain terms and sentences have prevented a clear interpretation of the text, so readers must proceed with caution. What is clear

is that this is a royal psalm dealing with God's gracious activities through the person of the human king. The psalm seems to quote various promises of the divine king to the human king, consisting of assurances of God's presence and blessing, particularly in battle. The reference to being a priest "according to the order of Melchizedek" (v. 4) is a reminder that the monarch also served priestly functions on behalf of the people. The title refers to a pre-Israelite king of Jerusalem who was called a "priest of God Most High" (cf. Gen 14:17–20). Early Christians interpreted the psalm as a messianic promise; it is frequently cited in the New Testament (cf. Mark 12:36; Acts 2:34–35; Heb 5:6; etc.).

Psalm 111

Psalms 111 and 112 are alphabetic acrostics (see commentary on Ps 9/10), with each half verse beginning with a successive letter of the Hebrew alphabet. Both are concerned with the divine-human relationship; but whereas Ps 112 majors in the human side of that relationship, Ps 111 concentrates on the divine side.

The psalm focuses on God's agency within the human-divine relationship. It names many "works of the LORD" (v. 2), such as provision of food, remembering the covenant, giving the land, issuing the law, and rescuing the people from foreign tyranny (vv. 5–7, 9). The closing wisdom-like instruction that the "fear of the LORD is the beginning of wisdom" (v. 10) further reinforces the conclusion that the psalm was intended as instruction in the godly way.

Psalm 112

Like its twin Ps 111, this poem is an alphabetic acrostic (see commentary on Ps 9/10). Psalm 112 picks up the concluding admonition of Ps 11 to "fear the LORD" and restates it in v. 1. Continuing along this line, the poem focuses on the human side of the divine-human relationship. Although the psalm does laud the blessings and benefits of those who fear God and follow the commandments (v. 1), the emphasis is actually on the blessing that God's followers are to their neighbors. To put this another way, this psalm is a commentary on following God's way as the means to love the neighbor. Those who follow God's laws become a beacon for those in darkness, are generous in lending, conduct their affairs with justice, and give freely to the poor (vv. 4–5, 9). They even begin to take on some of God's qualities: righteousness, graciousness, and mercy. This is so because in loving the neighbor (by following the law), the believer exhibits these divine characteristics.

Psalm 113

In Jewish liturgical usage, Pss 113–118 form the Egyptian Hallel (*praise*). The first two psalms are sung before the Passover meal and the last four after.

This masterful lyric is also a classic hymn of praise, consisting of both an artful call to praise (vv. 1–3) and poetically crafted reasons for praise (vv. 4–9). The call to praise begins with a thrice-repeated imperative call to praise (v. 1) followed by a shift to the synonym *bless*. After asserting that the name of God be praised "from this time on and forevermore," the psalmist engages in some poetic play. "From the rising of the sun to its setting" means both *all day* (from dawn to dusk) and *everywhere* (from the east to the west).

The psalm also explores the gracious activity of God by means of a poetic progression that descends along an imagined vertical axis: "high above all nations" > "above the heavens" > "seated on high" > "looks far down" (vv. 4–6). Who does God find at the bottom? God finds the lowliest of humans: the poor man and the barren woman. What does God do? God "raises" them up. The NRSV phrases *seated* (v. 5), *make them sit* (v. 8) and *gives a home* (v. 9) all reflected the same Hebrew verb (*yashav*), suggesting that when God condescends from on high to raise up the lowly, God is exchanging some part of God's nature and character with the humans that God is saving.

Psalm 114

Psalm 114 is a tightly composed four-stanza hymn, with an A–B–B'–A' chiastic pattern. The first stanza dramatizes the exodus from Egypt and the division of the land. The "house of Jacob" refers to the Israelite people as whole, whose twelve tribes are described as descending from the ancestor Jacob. In v. 2, *Judah* refers to the southern kingdom, in which the Lord's Temple ("sanctuary") was located; *Israel* is the northern

kingdom, God's "dominion" (where God reigns rather than dwells).

The second stanza describes the entry into the land, while the third stanza transforms the assertions of the second stanza into rhetorical questions, which are a familiar motif (cf. Ps 113:5–6). The answer to the rhetorical questions occurs in v. 7. Why flee and turn back? Because of the "presence of the God of Jacob." To worship *is* to enter God's presence. Although the psalm never directly calls on the people to praise, it does address the terrain of the land: "Tremble, O earth." In v. 2, the terms *Judah* and *Israel* equated people with land and land with people. Thus, to call for the land to praise both calls for the people to praise and underscores their connection with the land.

Psalm 115

Similar to Pss 2, 15, and 121, this hymn is structured around an opening question (vv. 1–2) followed by a longer answer. The opening question, "Where is their God?" was a taunt in the ancient world (cf. Pss 42:3, 10; 79:10; Joel 2:17; Mic 7:10). The taunt reflects the ancient belief that a national defeat meant that the victorious nation's god had triumphed over the defeated nation's god. The psalm rejects that belief. In a daring poetic move, the psalmist interprets the enemies' rhetorical taunt literally and gives a literal answer: "Our God is in the heavens" (v. 3*a*). There follows a substantial ridicule of human-made idols "and all who *trust* in them" (vv. 4–8; cf. Isa 44:9–20).

The word *trust* becomes the hinge of the poem, as the psalmist turns and exhorts Israel to "*trust* in the LORD." *Israel* (vv. 9, 12) refers to the laity gathered for worship, *house of Aaron* (vv. 10, 12) refers to a priestly group, descended from Aaron. Those *who fear the LORD* may refer to uncircumcised proselytes, who have not fully joined the people (vv. 11, 13).

The psalm's conclusion plays on two different meanings of the Hebrew term translated as *bless*. Worship is the sacred space where humans "bless the LORD" (meaning *praise*) and where the Lord "will bless" humans (meaning *bestow blessings*; vv. 13–15). Idols, it is implied, are not worthy of praise because they cannot bless.

Psalm 116

This is a song of thankful praise sung following divine deliverance from a personal crisis. A normal part of a prayer for help is the vow to praise God once the crisis has passed (cf. Ps 13:6). Corresponding elements of a song of thanksgiving are descriptions of the crisis (v. 3), of the cry for help (v. 4), of the divine deliverance (vv. 5–11), and the announcement that the vow to praise is being kept in the form of renewed praise of God (vv. 12–19). The crisis from which the psalmist was rescued may have been a grave illness, but the psalm is general enough that anyone who has received God's help and passed through a crisis may sing its words.

The reference to the "cup of salvation" most likely reflects a ritual meal celebrating the deliverance (cf. Lev 7:11–18). Verse 15 should be translated "Grievous in the sight . . ." (NRSV, *precious*). The Temple is the sacred space where the psalmist returns to offer thankful praise, but it is also the place where the community is restored, as the congregation hears the testimony of the one who was delivered and receives that one again as a healthy and full member of the body (vv. 14, 18). As is indicated by the deep anguish and complaints over the enemies that one finds in the prayers for help, the loss and restoration of this community is no small matter.

Psalm 117

The shortest of all psalms also provides a clear model for a hymn of praise and a thumbnail sketch of the theology of the Psalter. A hymn includes two elements: a call to praise (v. 1) and reasons for praise (v. 2). Hymns also often include a closing renewal of the call to praise (v. 2c). The call to praise has a universal flair, enjoining all the nations to praise Israel's God. The reasons for praise given in this psalm are the Lord's steadfast love and faithfulness. These two finite terms succinctly bear witness to the character of the infinite Lord. The central affirmation of the Psalter, and this psalm, is that God is faithful.

Psalm 118

Similar to Ps 116, this is a song of thanksgiving of one who has experienced divine deliverance and has passed through a crisis, such as a severe illness. Many have speculated that the psalm reflects a Temple liturgy for those who come to the Temple to fulfill vows of thanksgiving that were uttered during times of crisis. Reasons for this conclusion include apparent references to various groups in the Temple (Israel, house of Aaron, fearers of the Lord; vv. 2–4, see commentary on Ps 115), liturgical directions (v. 15), an entrance liturgy (vv. 19–20), and a description of a worship procession (vv. 26–27). It is impossible, however, to reconstruct such a Temple liturgy on the basis of the text of this psalm.

Many affirmations of the psalm are characteristic of the Psalter: God's characteristic steadfast love (vv. 1–4), God's faithful commitment to hear the cries of the lowly (v. 5), the wisdom of trusting in God rather than earthly forms of refuge (vv. 8–9), and the restoration of the one who was rescued with the larger community (vv. 15–16, 22–23). Verse 24 should be translated, "This is the day that the Lord has acted [to rescue], let us rejoice and be glad in him." Verses 1 and 29 form an inclusion around the psalm, affirming the central confession of the Psalter's theology.

Psalm 119

The blue-ribbon winner of acrostic poems (see commentary on Ps 9/10), Ps 119 is comprised of 22 stanzas, each one having eight lines and each line beginning with a successive letter of the Hebrew alphabet. The acrostic pattern provides the only discernible structure. There is no other development in the poem.

Along with Pss 1 and 19, the central motif of this psalm is God's *torah* (translated in NRSV as *law*, but properly rendered as *instruction*). This theme is developed by the nearly constant repetition of nine synonyms for divine instruction: *law, decrees, ways, precepts, statutes, commandments, ordinances, word, promise*. The poem is part meditation on, part love song about, part prayer for God's instruction. Its message can be summed up by v. 97: "Oh, how I love your law! It is my meditation all day long."

As its length, plodding style, and theme indicate, this poem is neither for life's high or low moments, but for the long and steady walk of faith. The psalm commends God's guiding word as the light for the lifetime journey of faith.

Psalm 120

"A Song of Ascents"—Pss 120–134 bear this superscription. The meaning of the title is unclear, but many scholars believe it refers to those on pilgrimage ascending the mountain to Jerusalem's Temple. Perhaps these psalms were collected for those making pilgrimage and were sung at various points along the journey. Supporting that conclusion, Ps 120 speaks of being an "alien," distant from the Temple, and Ps 121 would be fitting for one departing on a journey, whereas Pss 133 and 134 fit the arrival at the Temple.

Psalm 120, the first psalm of ascent, is a prayer for help that expresses the distress of one forced to live far from home. The psalmist complains of living in the midst of warring hearts "who hate peace" (v. 6). The psalmist refers to the enemies as "lying lips," "deceitful tongue" (twice), and "sharp arrows." This objectification of the enemies has the effect of magnifying their violent actions. The psalmist, on the other hand, is exiled—Meshech refers to an area near the Black Sea, while Kedar to a part of the Arabian peninsula. The point is not that the psalmist is literally in one of these places, but separated (spiritually or physically) from home, people, and God.

Psalm 121

"A Song of Ascents" (see commentary on Ps 120). One of the most well-loved lyrics in Scripture, this poem may have originated as a liturgy for those leaving on a journey, possibly a pilgrimage. The psalm is replete with promises of protection and is thus also suitable for those going through the pilgrimage of life.

Although the syntax is unclear, NRSV is probably correct in translating v. 1 as a question. The *hills* may refer to the mountains around Jerusalem (cf. Ps 125:2) and thus to the psalmist's destination. Or the hills may signify a source of threat, behind which dangers lie hidden. Either way, the psalmist confesses that the one who created those hills, the maker of "heaven and earth," is the psalmist's helper.

The remainder of the psalm is a series of promises, perhaps delivered by a priest. These promises feature the sixfold repetition of the word *keep/ keeper* (*shamar*). The word means to guard or watch over, as the use of the term in Pss 127:2

and 130:6 indicates. The balanced images of God keeping watch through day and night, no matter where one places foot and right hand, symbolize that God's care is constant and all-encompassing.

Psalm 122

"A Song of Ascents" (see commentary on Ps 120). This "song of Zion" (see commentary on Ps 46) was probably part of a pilgrimage observance, as the references to going to the "house of the LORD" "as was decreed for Israel" indicate. The decree in question was most likely the law requiring all males to journey to Jerusalem for the three pilgrimage festivals (cf. Exod 23:14–19). Employing a poetic device common in the songs of Zion (see commentary on Ps 46), the song speaks directly to Jerusalem as a cipher for God. This song praises Jerusalem (vv. 3–4) as the place where God's just judgment occurs. It also prays for Jerusalem (vv. 6–9) as a source of the blessing of peace—the name *Jerusalem* and the Hebrew word for peace (*shalom*), which each occur three times in the short poem, are etymologically related. Jerusalem is celebrated because it is the place where God's blessings of justice, prosperity, and peace converge; and from Jerusalem they emanate outward for the world (cf. Isa 2:1–4).

Psalm 123

"A Song of Ascents" (see commentary on Ps 120). This brief communal prayer for help is uttered from a profound posture of humility. The psalm has two stanzas, each with two verses. The first stanza draws on the poetic motif of the eye to emphasize the community's humility. It has an A-B-B-A chiastic structure. In the first and last phrases, the eyes of the community look to God in prayer "until he has mercy on us" (v. 2). The two middle phrases are similes that support the petition for mercy. The psalmist compares the humility of the community before God to that of slaves before the hand of their master, or a servant maid before the hand of her mistress.

The plea for mercy at the end of v. 2 is immediately repeated twice more in v. 3, making it the hinge and center of the psalm. The poem's conclusion continues the theme of humility by describing the humiliation Israel has received at the hands of arrogant, proud powers. The ancient cultural values of honor and shame lie behind the psalm's posture of humility. The psalm pleads with God to reverse the unjust conditions of the world and to act on behalf of the lowly.

Psalm 124

"A Song of Ascents" (see commentary on Ps 120). Psalm 124 is a communal song of thanksgiving, most likely prayed after deliverance from a crisis, such as a military threat (v. 2). The phrase "let Israel now say" in v. 1*b*, followed as it is by a repetition of v. 1*a*, may indicate that the entire psalm was sung responsively by half-verse. It may even give a clue that many psalms were chanted in this manner, although such a conclusion cannot be drawn with confidence. As it is, the text only repeats the phrase one time (v. 2*a*). This repetition emphasizes the basic tenet of Israel's witness to its history: if the Lord had not been there—in the flood, in droughts, in Egypt, in the wilderness, in the exile—Israel would have been swallowed up. As with so many psalms, this poem conflates the threats of human enemies (who are in this poem portrayed as devouring predators; vv. 3, 6) and of cosmic enemies (the anti-creation powers of chaos; vv. 4–5).

The psalm closes with praise of God, whose merciful intrusion not only sprung Israel from the snare but broke the snare for good (v. 7). The closing confession of God as "our help" is an echo of the promises of Ps 121.

Psalm 125

"A Song of Ascents" (see commentary on Ps 120). This is a communal song of trust, which expresses confidence that the Lord will faithfully provide for and protect Israel. The psalm also is meant as instruction for the people of God concerning the value of properly trusting God. Those who trust in the Lord's provision are compared to the holy city Jerusalem. The city was understood both as an instrument through which God blessed the people (cf. Ps 122:3–5) and as part of God's covenantal promise to protect (cf. Ps 46:5). By identifying the people with the city, the psalm underscores the people's participation in God's blessings and God's promises. The enemies are pictured metaphorically as a scepter, a symbol of human lordship (v. 3). The subtle imbalance between the contrasting images of the righteous like mountains and the wicked like a scepter is

meaningful. To human perception, the oppressing foreign powers may have seemed an imposing, even dominating, threat. But consistent with so many psalms, this poem bears witness that it is better to trust in God than in mortals.

Psalm 126

"A Song of Ascents" (see commentary on Ps 120). This communal prayer for help pairs the complementary notions of restoration and rejoicing. The psalm consists of two stanzas (vv. 1–3, 4–6). The first stanza recalls God's past act of restoration (v. 1) and the memories of rejoicing and laughter that accompanied God's rescue. The psalm probably has in mind the return of the people following the Babylonian exile. The stanza also contains the surprising affirmation that when God delivered Israel, *the nations*—that is, the people who worship other gods and often threaten Israel (cf. Ps 124:2)—*praised God*. Even more surprising, the nations' praise of God inspires Israel to echo that praise, which they do verbatim in v. 3. Often in the Psalter the enemies' words are quoted as reason for God to punish them, but here, the righteous echo the words of the nations.

The second stanza picks up the themes developed in the first stanza and rephrases them in the form of petitions. God is asked to restore the people again that they may rejoice again. The images of dry riverbeds teeming with water and harvesters singing joyfully may reflect a prayer for rescue from drought. The recollection of past deliverance and renewed call for restoration are reminders that divine help is a constant need.

Psalm 127

"A Song of Ascents" (see commentary on Ps 120). Similar to God's covenantal promise to David in 2 Sam 7:1–17, this brief instructional poem is crafted around the multiple meanings of the Hebrew term translated *house* (v. 1; *bayit*). The term can refer to the Temple (God's house), to a human home or dwelling, and to human offspring. In 2 Samuel 7, after settling into his newly constructed palace, David thinks to build God a house. But God refuses and in turn promises David a house (dynastic lineage). Psalm 127 affirms that all human work, including the construction of houses and cities, is vain without God's blessings. It goes on to affirm that children are one of

God's ultimate blessings. The psalm may reflect traditions about Solomon, who was the builder of the First Temple, a fortifier of cities (1 Kings 8; 9:15). The psalm bears witness to the penultimate frustration that human efforts are tenuous and the ultimate promise that with God's blessings almost anything is possible.

Psalm 128

"A Song of Ascents" (see commentary on Ps 120). Psalm 128 continues several themes of the preceding psalm: children as a blessed heritage (127:3–4; 128:3, 6), the concept of *house* (127:1; 128:3), concern for *labor* (127:1; 128:2; although the two psalms use different Hebrew words for *labor*), the presence of *Happy is ...* statements (127:5; 128:1). Also present in the psalm are two characteristic themes of the songs of ascent: the Lord's blessing (v. 5; cf. Pss 133:3; 134:3) and a concern for the welfare of Israel (v. 6; cf. Pss 130:7; 131:3). The twice-repeated theme of the "fear of the LORD" also lends the psalm a wisdom hue. The ancient worshipers did not make pilgrimage merely out of obedience, but also because they experienced God's blessings in the Temple. The psalm is a reminder that in spite of the appearance that worship is a human act, the true actor in worship is God.

Psalm 129

"A Song of Ascents" (see commentary on Ps 120). Psalm 129 is a communal song of trust. This classification depends on translating the verbs in vv. 5–6 as declarations rather than wishes: "All who hate Zion will be put to shame and turned back. They will be like ...." The psalm begins with a liturgical call for Israel to recall the constant stress under which it endured as a community and thus the constant deliverance experienced at the hand of the Lord. The first-person reference refers to the community as a whole, as the liturgical call "let Israel now say" indicates (on this phrase, see commentary on Ps 124). The psalm teems with agricultural metaphors—the wicked "plowed my back" (v. 3), they will be like grass that withers so that reapers may not harvest it. According to Ruth 2:4, harvesters would call out blessings on one another: "The LORD bless you!" The last verse of the psalm says that because the wicked will be like grass that does not grow and thus is never harvested, they will never hear the blessing of the Lord called upon them.

If the conclusion is correct that the psalms of ascent were connected with a harvest pilgrimage, then the agricultural image fits well. But the imagery is employed here to confess confidence in God's ongoing providence and protection.

Psalm 130

"A Song of Ascents" (see commentary on Ps 120); one of the penitential psalms (see commentary on Ps 6). A prayer for help from a crisis that the psalmist believes was brought on by some unnamed sin (vv. 3–4). The psalmist calls out from the watery "depths," a metaphoric description of the crisis that draws on the mythological concept of the floods as the embodiment of chaos (cf. Ps 69:1–3). The psalmist does not explicitly confess sins, but such a confession is implied in vv. 3–4. God's grace, rather than God's wrath, is given as the reason God is to be revered. Because the one thing that the psalmist needs, the word of forgiveness and restoration, can come only from God, the psalmist does the only thing possible: wait. The twice-repeated metaphor of the watchers was interpreted in later Judaism as priests who wait for the dawn in order to offer sacrifice, but more likely it refers to guards (cf. Ps 127:1) who keep watch. The morning is often the time when God's help is revealed (see commentary on Ps 5). The psalm ends with an appeal for the entire community to hope in the Lord with the same steadfast resolution as the psalmist.

Psalm 131

"A Song of Ascents" (see commentary on Ps 120). Regarded by some as the prayer of a woman, the psalm expresses the humble confidence of one who has given up the illusory quest for self-determination and has found peace in God's lordship. The dominant note of v. 1 is humility. In the psalms, arrogance and pride are characteristics of the wicked, who do not submit themselves to God's ways. The psalmist rejects the folly of prideful self-mastery and submits humbly to God. The translation of the last phrase of v. 2 is disputed. The psalmist may be comparing "my soul" to a "weaned child that is with me," implying that the psalmist is a woman. Or, "like the weaned child within me," the psalmist may be claiming to have a quiet, childlike faith. How to interpret the metaphor of the weaned child is also unclear, since nursing children are usually those who are quiet. Perhaps the point is that weaned children have reached a stage of semi-autonomy in which they are no longer totally dependent but still recognize their dependence. The closing exhortation calls upon all of Israel to hope in the Lord with this sort of humble dependence.

Psalm 132

"A Song of Ascents" (see commentary on Ps 120). A royal liturgy that celebrates David's recovery of the ark of the covenant and transportation of the ark to Jerusalem (1 Sam 7:1–2; 2 Sam 6). The psalm also celebrates God's twin election of David and his line to be God's king—"son"—forever (vv. 11–12) and of Jerusalem as God's "resting place forever" (vv. 13–14). These two tenets were foundational expressions of the theology of Zion. Accompanying these promises, God also promises that blessing will emanate from Zion for the sake of David and the covenant (v. 15).

It is probably the motifs of blessing, of David's first "pilgrimage" to Jerusalem, and of God's past actions for Israel that resulted in the inclusion of this royal psalm in the songs of ascents. The psalm differs from the other songs of ascents in its length and the fact that it seems to be an older psalm than the others. But its emphases on blessing and Jerusalem made it appropriate for the collection.

Psalm 133

"A Song of Ascents" (see commentary on Ps 120). This brief poem focuses on the unity of God's people. Many modern readers understand v. 1 as relating to the contemporary, nuclear family; the psalm has in mind the larger family, the people of God. Following Solomon's reign, the people split into two countries. The psalm is a prayer for unity for the people, a unity centered in God's blessing. The poem employs a radical strategy to make its case for unity: it poetically describes an abundant act of hospitality and then an impossible scene of unity. The abundant act is the anointing of the head with oil. This act symbolized hospitality and welcome (cf. Pss 23:5; 92:10; 141:5; Mark 14:3–9). It also was an act of consecration for priests (cf. Exod 29:7). Both acts are in mind here, the former to signify the call for unity, the latter to signify the Temple and its priests as a mediating source

of blessing for the entire people. The Hebrew word *descend* (a nice counterpoint in the songs of ascents) is translated twice as *running down* (v. 2) and once as *falls* in the impossible metaphorical scene of the dew of the northern Mount Hermon falling on the southern Mount Zion. The metaphor describes the gathering of the two people around God's blessings, as they emanate from Zion.

Psalm 134

"A Song of Ascents" (see commentary on Ps 120). The last of the songs of ascents takes place in the Temple at night. The poem plays on two meanings of a Hebrew verb that can mean both *bless* and *praise* (vv. 1, 2, 3; *barakh*). The adherents arrive to "praise" God and find that God blesses them. The theme of blessing is a red thread running through the entire songs of ascents collection. That theme reaches its climactic moment in Ps 134, which declares the blessing of the Lord "maker of heaven and earth" (an echo of Ps 121:1) upon all those who gather. There may also be a subtle poetic play in the poem on body parts. Those who *stand* in the Temple raise their *hands* to bless God (or perhaps to *kneel down*). The previously mentioned verb *bless* is derived from the Hebrew root that means *knee* and thus can mean to *kneel down*. The meanings *bless* and *praise* may have developed from the posture one took to receive a blessing or to praise.

Psalm 135

This hymn of praise begins and ends with calls for praise (vv. 1–3, 19–21). The opening call to praise features a fourfold repetition of the imperative call "praise!" while the closing section has a corresponding fourfold repetition of "bless!" In between, the psalm recounts various reasons for praising the Lord, all of which are summed up in the introductory reasons of vv. 3–4: the Lord is good and has chosen Israel. In vv. 5–6, the setting is the heavenly realm and God's action of creation is stressed, especially God's ongoing actions of making creation fertile (v. 7). "Above all gods" refers to the ancient conception of God ruling as the king of the divine council (cf. Isa 6:1–6). In vv. 8–12, the setting shifts to the earth and the focus is on God's interventions in history on behalf of Israel, culminating in the gift of the land. The psalm's ridicule of human-made idols and those who worship them is typical of post-exilic literature (cf. Ps 115:4–8; Isa 44:9–20). To praise God is to confess the person in whom one places trust (v. 18). To praise the Lord of Israel is to align one's voice and life with the one who delivered Israel from Egypt and is known in the ongoing history of that people.

Psalm 136

Like Ps 117, this hymn of praise bears witness to the central confession of the Psalter's theology: the Lord is a God of steadfast love. Whereas Ps 117 succinctly confesses that witness in two verses, Ps 136 sounds that note with every breath, making the confession an antiphon that occurs in every verse. Similar to the structure of other hymns, such as Ps 135, the song opens and closes with calls for praise, and in between recounts first God's gracious action of creation (vv. 4–9) and then God's gracious acts of deliverance in history (vv. 10–25). Those two complementary tenets form the poles around which Israel's praise resounds. The historical actions of God cited are those that formed the core of Israel's identity: the deliverance from Egypt (vv. 10–16), the guidance through the wilderness and into the land (vv. 17–22), and God's ongoing protection from foes and gift of sustenance (vv. 23–25).

Psalm 137

The composer of this song was a Temple musician who had been hauled into exile when the Temple was destroyed. In Babylon, he was tormented by requests for a "song of Zion." Songs of Zion, such as Pss 46, 48, 76, and 84, often praise Zion directly (cf. 76:4) as a stand-in for God. They celebrate God's protection of the city and the Temple as God's abode. The request for such a song was a painful barb at both the psalmist's vocation and his faith.

The psalmist confesses being caught up in a painful paradox. Ironically addressing a question to Zion, he asks, "How could we sing?" As such, this is a song of Zion sung in a new key, place, and theme. If he does forget the city, he invokes curses on his "right hand" that plucks the harp and "tongue" that sings. In spite of the pain, the psalm is nevertheless a song.

The closing prayer for the destruction of the enemies (vv. 7–9) is perhaps the most vitriolic curse

in the Psalter. There is no softening its venom or explaining away its violent wish. Considered in a canonical scope, the psalm does remind that vengeance belongs to God and human beings are not to act out on wishes to see the enemy punished (cf. Rom 12:17–21).

Psalm 138

Psalm 138 is a song of thanksgiving sung in response to deliverance. The opening expression of praise (vv. 1–2) celebrates God's characteristic steadfast love and faithfulness. The phrase *before the gods* reflects the ancient view of God presiding over the heavenly council (cf. Isa 6:1–6). The last phrase of v. 2 is unclear, but it may reflect the psalmist's experience of God proving faithful to a divine promise. The psalm lacks a description of the past crisis and only mentions that the psalmist called out in the day of trouble and God answered (v. 3).

Because vv. 4–5 call on the kings of the earth to praise the Lord, some have identified the speaker as the king. This conclusion is unwarranted, however, since the confession that the nations shall bear witness to God is also characteristic of post-exilic theology. Verse 6 describes the countercultural nature of God's actions, honoring the lowly and humbling the arrogant (cf. Ps 113:5–8; Luke 1:51–53). The psalmist's experience of deliverance leads the psalmist to a new understanding of God's guidance, so the psalm ends with a renewed confession of trust (vv. 7–8; cf. Ps 23:4).

Psalm 139

One of the most-loved psalms, this well-balanced, four-stanza poem moves from an intense meditation to passionate petition. The first stanza meditates on God's supreme knowledge of the psalmist. Employing key words that will return later—*search, know, thoughts, way* (vv. 1–3)—the psalmist confesses that there is nothing about the psalmist that God does not know. The second stanza modulates to the theme of God's presence and confesses that there is no place where God would not be with the psalmist, including the realm of the dead (Sheol), the watery deeps where chaos was thought to reign, and the place of utter darkness. The third stanza meditates on the relationship between the psalmist and the creator. Earlier, the psalmist confessed that "you discern my thoughts from far away" (v. 2). Here, the psalmist confesses that God's thoughts are as far beyond human comprehension as the grains of sand are beyond mathematics.

The closing stanza picks up the vocabulary of the opening verses—*search, know, thoughts, way* (vv. 23–24)—in a plea for deliverance from the wicked. The psalmist tenders the self to God's searching in a plea of innocence. Perhaps the psalmist had been falsely accused by enemies. The psalmist's claim to "perfect hatred" troubles many; the psalmist is rejecting the ways of evil and oppression that characterize the wicked. But the ancients knew no distinction between a person's deeds and the person. To hate their evil deeds is to hate them, according to the ancient grammar.

Psalm 140

Many scholars consider this psalm the prayer of one who has been falsely accused, because of the references to the violence that the enemies do with their tongues (vv. 2–3, 11). Such a conclusion is not warranted, however. The term translated *slanderer* in v. 11 literally means "a man of the tongue," which does not necessarily imply false accusation. As in many other prayers in which the sufferer complains about the speech of the wicked, it is most likely that the enemies use their tongues to plot evil against the psalmist: "The arrogant have hidden a trap for me" (v. 5*a*). As is also typical of many psalms (and as influenced by Israel's wisdom tradition), the sufferer prays that the wicked will be caught in their own traps: "Let the mischief of their lips overwhelm them!" (v. 9). The language of God covering the psalmist's "head in the day of battle" (v. 7) should also be understood as metaphorical, rather than taken as a literal clue to the psalmist's situation.

The psalmist is besieged by those who use speech to plot evil. For this reason, the psalmist stresses that his or her own speech is a confession of faith: "I say to the LORD, 'You are my God.'" Speech may be used for evil or for good. The psalmist employs the tongue to confess faith in God and on that awaits vindication from God.

Psalm 141

In both Second Temple Judaism and in Christianity, this psalm was assigned for use during evening prayer services, because of v. 2. The refer- ence to prayer rising "as an evening sacrifice" may not mean that this prayer originally accompanied the offering (cf. Num 28:1–8), but that the prayer was offered in substitute of the offering (because the supplicant was not present in the Temple). Psalm 40:6 recounts how God did not require sacrifice from that psalmist, but praise (cf. Pss 50:8–23; 51:16–17). A similar understanding may be reflected in Ps 141.

This prayer accentuates the psalmist's humble *vertical* orientation ("my eyes are turned toward you, O God," v. 8*a*) and guarded speech (vv. 3, 6). The motif of guarded speech reflects the psalmist's prayer to be protected from temptation. Speech reflects internal attitudes and internal attitudes lead to action. Verses 5–7 are corrupt and impos- sible to translate with certainty. Typical of many psalms and of Israel's wisdom tradition, the psalm- ist prays that the wicked will be caught in the very traps that they lay for others (v. 10).

Psalm 142

This prayer for help has two stanzas (vv. 1–4, 5–7), with the argument of the prayer turning at the end of v. 4. In the first stanza, the psalm- ist complains bitterly to God, employing intense first-person language throughout. Only once, in the very center of this stanza, does the psalmist use second-person language: "you know my *way*" (v. 3*a*). The psalmist immediately contrasts this confession of faith with the dangerous reality: "In the *path* where I walk they have hidden a trap for me" (v. 3*b*). The psalmist sums up the crisis: "no refuge remains for me" (v. 4).

Refuge becomes the hinge on which the psalm swings, as the psalmist immediately confesses, "I say, 'You are my refuge ...'" (v. 5). Although two different Hebrew words for *refuge* are used in vv. 4 and 5, the concept provides the turning point of the psalm. The psalmist even emphasizes the confession of trust with the emphatic introduc- tion, "I say ...." The psalmist then offers petitions for rescue (vv. 6–7*a*), followed by a vow to praise and an expression of trust (v. 7*b*). The contradic- tory references to being pursued and in prison are best understood metaphorically, rather than literal clues to the psalmist's situation.

Psalm 143

A prayer for help, one of the penitential psalms (see commentary on Ps 6). This intense plea for rescue is one of the places in the Bible where the connection is made between God's actions on behalf of the people and God's actions on behalf of the individual. The psalmist cries out for personal intervention (vv. 1–4, 6–12). As part of the prayer, the sufferer recalls God's wondrous deeds for the people as a whole (v. 5; cf. Ps 22:3–5). The theological basis for this connection is the character of God. As the Lord has proven to be a God of "faithfulness," "righteousness," and "steadfast love" (vv. 1, 8, 11–12) through God's wondrous deeds for Israel, so God is enjoined to demonstrate God's character by delivering the psalmist from a personal crisis.

The psalm is replete with potent imagery and concepts: no one is righteous before God (v. 2; cf. Rom 3:10); a soul thirsting for God (v. 6); God's steadfast love in the morning (v. 8; cf. Ps 30:5); a request for instruction in God's ways (v. 8; cf. Ps 1). Perhaps because of v. 8, the Greek church assigned this psalm for morning prayer.

Psalm 144

A royal prayer for help, the king probably prayed this prayer before battle, although it is possible that the poem was a liturgical composition intended for use in an annual Temple festival. The king's prayer is not primarily for himself, but for himself as the leader of the national community (vv. 1–2, 9–11). The psalm begins with a praise confession of faith, reminiscent of Ps 18, another royal psalm. The meditation on human mortality in v. 3 is similar to Ps 8:4, but in this context it serves rhetorically to fuel a plea for help, rather than praise (as in Ps 8). Verses 5–8 comprise an imaginative request for a theophany, in this case meaning a display of God's power in victory. Verses 9–11 are the vow to praise following the crisis; "new song" is a technical phrase referring to a song of thanksgiving after deliverance (cf. Ps 40:3). The enemies are twice referred to as those "whose mouths speak lies" (vv. 8, 11). Perhaps the lies that the enemies speak are that God lacks the power and fidelity to save Israel (cf. Isa 37:17–20; Ps 10:4, 11; etc.). Although vv. 12–14 may have been prayed by a priest, they nevertheless reflect a proper royal concern for the nation.

Psalm 145

As much as any other hymn, this song indicates that a primary purpose of praise is to confess one's faith. Praise is not intended to please or flatter the deity. Praise is sung as a means of bearing witness and confessing faith. The psalm makes this transparent in the description of how the psalmist's praise (vv. 1–3) is part of a domino-like progression in which the praise of one generation is passed to another (v. 4), so that *they* (v. 7; meaning future generations) will continue to praise and laud God's wondrous deeds. This is also the force of the last verse of the psalm. The song scores this point again through its creed-like testimony to God's character (8–9, 13*b*–20). Even the alphabetic acrostic structure of the poem may subtly underscore that language exists for the purpose of praising God.

The witness underscores God's faithfulness, especially in keeping faith with divine promises (v. 13*b*, the phrase *The Lord ... his deeds*, is not found in the Masoretic Text, but was restored from other Hebrew and ancient texts). Verses 15–16 testify to God's gracious action of continuing to provide sustenance through creation; they serve in some traditions as a table prayer.

Psalm 146

Psalm 146 is the first of five hymns of praise that close the Psalter. Each of these psalms begins and ends with the call, "Praise the Lord!" Similar to Ps 8, this hymn may be the praise performance of an individual, because it lacks the typical call for praise. If so, this psalm bridges the categories of the hymn of praise and the song of thanksgiving. The song alternates poetically back and forth between heaven and earth. The psalmist starts by praising God "as long as I live" (v. 2) to admonishing the congregation not to trust "in mortals in whom there is not help" (v. 3) and who "return to the earth" (v. 4). The psalm then transitions back to a heavenly focus with the testimony that the Lord "made heaven and earth" (v. 6). It then returns to the earth, with a description of the Lord's gracious deeds for the lowly (vv. 7–9). The emphasis here is on God's counter-worldly preference for the oppressed, the hungry, prisoners, the blind, the bowed down, the righteous, the stranger, and the orphan and widow. Standing against all of these are the wicked (v. 9), whose ways God derails.

Psalm 147

Psalm 147 is a tripartite hymn of praise, in which each of the three stanzas (vv. 1–6, 7–11, 12–20) could just as well have stood separately as an independent hymn. Each stanza calls for praise (vv. 1, 7, 12) and offers as reason for praise Israel's characteristic dual testimony for God's transcendent heavenly activities (vv. 4, 8, 15–18) as well as for God's immanent earthly actions (vv. 2–3, 6, 9–11, 13–14, 19–20). The hymn places special emphasis on God's election of Israel. The emphasis spells out both the particular benefits to Israel, such as security, peace, and prosperity (vv. 2, 13–14) and also the special revelation that Israel received in the form of the law (vv. 19–20). It is worth stressing that the psalm, while distinguishing between the dual heavenly and earthly actions of the Lord, holds them together as a consistent unity. The *command* (v. 15) and *word* (v. 18) that God sends out effect God's will in the natural sphere; this same *word* (v. 19) is revealed only to Israel in God's *statutes and ordinances*. The connection between God's creative word and revelatory word seen here is found also in Genesis 1.

Psalm 148

A hymn of praise in which the call for praise element (vv. 1–5a, 7–13a) begins to dominate over the reasons for praise element (vv. 5b–6, 13b–14). This shift anticipates the climax of the Psalter in Ps 150. The two stanzas (vv. 1–6, 7–14) each display a parallel structure. In the first stanza, the extended call for praise exhorts the heavens and all their residents to praise the Lord (cf. Ps 96:11). The reason for praise, fittingly, is God's action of creation. In the second stanza, various earthly characters are called to praise God, including the mythological forces of the storms and the earthly terrain (v. 9; cf. Pss 97:1 114:5–8), wild animals, and the kings of the nations (v. 11; cf. Ps 96:7). Both the call for the heavens and the various earthly subjects to praise the Lord may represent a polemical edge in Israel's praise, since Israel's neighbors deified the heavenly bodies, certain forces of nature, and human royalty.

The fictive audiences that the psalm addresses (heavens, sea monsters, kings, etc.) are a cipher for the actual Israelite congregation worshiping in the Temple. That audience would have understood the call for them to praise.

Psalm 149

This psalm most likely was composed and performed during a liturgical Temple celebration, such as the fall harvest Festival of Tabernacles. The references to song, musical accompaniment, and Zion mark the song as a Temple composition (vv. 1–3). The references to military victory, weapons, and the subjugation of enemies suggest the mythological conception that the harvest was a celebration of the Lord's defeat of the anti-creation powers of chaos (vv. 4–8). The psalm's placement as the next-to-last psalm in the final form of the Psalter suggests that the original liturgical testimony to the Lord's victory was later interpreted eschatologically, with an eye on the future deliverance of both Israel and the world from the powers of evil.

Psalm 150

This hymn places a final exclamation mark of praise on the theological witness of the Psalter. In general, the Psalter moves from lament to praise and from individual to communal songs. This hymn is the appropriate conclusion to that general progression, because it takes one element of the hymn—the call for praise—and develops that call into an independent and complete poem. The psalm offers little along the line of reasons for praise (cf. v. 2b), but the rest of the instructional witness of the Psalter can be taken as the summative reasons for praise. The song calls for praise of the Lord to be sounded everywhere (v. 1), upon every musical instrument (vv. 3–5), and by every living thing (v. 6).

BIBLIOGRAPHY

W. Brueggemann. *The Psalms and the Life of Faith* (Minneapolis: Fortress, 1995); T. Craven. *The Book of Psalms* (Collegeville, Minn.: Liturgical Press, 1992); J. Limburg. *Psalms*. Wesminster Bible Companion (Louisville: Westminster John Knox, 2000); J. L. Mays. *Psalms*. Interpretation (Louisville: John Knox, 1994); J. C. McCann. *A Theological Introduction to the Book of Psalms: The Psalms as Torah* (Nashville: Abingdon, 1993); P. D. Miller. *Interpreting the Psalms* (Philadelphia: Fortress, 1986); C. Westermann. *The Psalms: Structure, Content & Message* (Minneapolis: Augsburg, 1980).

PROVERBS

Glenn D. Pemberton

OVERVIEW

Proverbs is one of three canonical books (Job, Ecclesiastes) associated with Israel's wisdom tradition. In its broadest sense, wisdom (*khokhmah*) denotes any expertise or skill (e.g., a professional sailor [Ezek 27:8] or mourner [Jer 9:17]). Among the sages, however, wisdom came to denote expertise in life based on careful observation of God's created and moral order. Thus, wisdom had primary concern for practical success in everyday life, a goal at the heart of Proverbs (1:2–4).

Proverbs and Israelite wisdom developed over a long period of time within the broader international wisdom traditions from Mesopotamia and Egypt. Despite formal attribution to Solomon (1:1), Proverbs explicitly identifies several other individuals or groups responsible for large portions of the book: anonymous sages (22:17; 24:23), Agur (30:1), Lemuel (31:1), and the scribes of Hezekiah (25:1). Implicitly, the materials of Proverbs also denote diverse origins such as the family farm (10:4–5; 14:4), home (13:24), city (11:10), and the royal court (25:2–7). Thus, while the book of Proverbs comes from an urban setting in the postexilic period, much of the book's contents originate from other places many years prior.

A brief prologue (1:1–7) provides the title (v. 1), objectives (vv. 2–4, 6), audience (vv. 4–5), and primary theme of the book: the key to genuine wisdom is one's relationship to the Lord ("fear of the Lord," v. 7). Form and content then coincide to divide the book into two halves. The first half of the book (1:8–9:18) consists of ten speeches from a parent to a child (literally, a father to a son, e.g., 1:8–19; 2:1–22) and four interludes that feature wisdom personified as a woman (e.g., 1:20–33; 8:1–36). The cumulative aim of these materials is to convince the reader of the importance of choosing wisdom as a way of life, a choice nothing less than a decision between life and death (4:13, 22; 5:7–14, 23).

The second half of the book (10:1–31:9) presents the content of wisdom through individual sayings that describe wise and foolish behavior. Six sections or collections provide minimal structure to these diverse proverbs. The first and longest is a collection of "the proverbs of Solomon" (10:1–22:16) that has little discernable internal order other than beginning with a large group of antithetical proverbs (10:1–15:33). The second and third collections derive from anonymous sages (22:17–24:22, 23–34), the second is related to the Egyptian wisdom text of *Amenemope*. The fourth section is again attributed to Solomon through the hands of Hezekiah's scribes (25:1–29:27) who either inherited or arranged some of their materials according to theme. Finally, the book credits the fifth (30:1–33) and sixth sections (31:1–9) to non-Israelites: Agur and King Lemuel.

An acrostic poem regarding the woman of noble character comprises the epilogue to the book (31:10–31). Although this poem may describe an ideal wife, it is more likely that the woman is personified Wisdom from chs. 1–9. Earlier the sages had urged the son to pursue and marry Woman Wisdom (4:5–9); now the sages present the benefits of having chosen Wisdom as one's life partner. The one who responds to the book's invitation to decide for wisdom (1:8–9:18) and adopts a life-style of wisdom (10:1–31:9) will receive great blessings.

OUTLINE

I. Prologue (1:1–7)

II. An Invitation to Choose Wisdom (1:8–9:18)

III. The Content of Wisdom (10:1–31:9)

    10:1–22:16. The Proverbs of Solomon (i)

    22:17–24:22. The Sayings of the Sages (i)

    24:23–34. The Sayings of the Sages (ii)

    25:1–29:27. The Proverbs of Solomon (ii)

    30:1–33. The Sayings of Agur

    31:1–9. The Sayings of Lemuel

IV. Epilogue: Woman Wisdom as Wife (31:10–31)

DETAILED ANALYSIS

I. Prologue (1:1–7)

The prologue identifies youths with little life experience as the primary audience for the book (v. 4, see 14:15), with secondary concern for the continued learning of sages (v. 5). A series of infinitives (*for, to*) identify two goals for that audience: (1) an intellectual grasp of wisdom (vv. 2, 6), and (2) an ethical response of "righteousness, justice, and equity" (v. 3). Both depend on a theological conviction ("the fear of the LORD," v. 7), a reverence of God that leads to life (Prov 15:33; Job 28:28).

II. An Invitation to Choose Wisdom (1:8–9:18)

Chapters 1–9 interweave three themes within a collection of ten lectures from a parent to a "child" (literally, a father to his "son" who is coming of age) and four interludes: (1) the importance of wisdom for a successful life (e.g., 3:13–18), (2) wisdom as a way of life or a path upon which one walks, not a one-time decision (e.g., 6:20–23), (3) the necessity of making a proactive choice for wisdom (e.g., 2:24–25; 7:1–5; 9:3–6), and (4) not to choose it is to accept a foolish life-style.

In the first lecture (1:8–19) the parents urge the child to accept rather than reject their teaching (vv. 8–9) and then caution against the seductive allure of sinners and their greed. The sinners' speech attempts to circumvent the parents' appeal for a disciplined life and invites the child to participate in an exciting illicit adventure (vv. 11–12) that leads to fast wealth (v. 13) and membership in a one-for-all community (v. 14). The parents implore the child to see through the rhetoric (vv. 15–19) and warn that these people are rushing toward violence that will ultimately take their lives. Even a bird avoids an obvious trap, but not these people. Greed will destroy them (v. 19).

Wisdom, personified as a woman, makes her first appearance in 1:20–33 (Interlude 1) with tones reminiscent of a prophet ("how long?") or a woman scorned. Wisdom is not elusive but shouts at every public location (vv. 20–21); the child has no excuse for missing her call. Tragedy awaits those who ignore her counsel (vv. 24–26). Such people will turn to her only when calamity

strikes (and it will), but then it will be too late (vv. 26–28). Wisdom explains that their fate rests on their prior decisions. Since they did not choose a relationship with God (v. 29) and would not accept Wisdom's counsel or correction (v. 30), they will reap the consequences of their behavior (v. 31). The time to accept wisdom is now; those who do will live securely (v. 33).

The acquisition of wisdom is no easy matter. In the second lecture the parent asserts that intense effort is necessary to gain wisdom (2:1–22). The child must not only accept the parent's words but pay close attention, cry out for insight, and seek wisdom like a buried treasure (vv. 1–4). Only if a person fully invests herself in the pursuit of wisdom will she come to have a genuine relationship with God (v. 5) and be able to enact ethical behavior ("righteousness and justice and equity," v. 9). Indeed, the Lord stores up and gives away wisdom (vv. 6–7), but the gift must be sought through diligence with an integrity of character appropriate to wisdom's aims (v. 7). The result of acquired wisdom is a relationship with God that is not only pleasant (v. 10) but provides protection or rescue from two dangers: (1) the alluring speech of evil men who abandon ethical behavior for the so-called joy of devious schemes (vv. 12–15), and (2) the smooth words of the adulteress who abandons her marriage vows and leads her male victims to death (likely metaphorical, living death, vv. 16–19). In both instances, the parent's primary concern is for the words these people speak to lure and then entangle the child in deadly conduct. Wisdom, however, will enable the child to see reality through the deceptive rhetoric and escape the danger of both evil men and women. Therefore, the parent concludes, the child must stay on the path of just behavior. To do so means security and stability (v. 21); to fail will result in loss of home and livelihood (v. 22).

The third lecture reminds the child of parental instruction regarding fundamental character qualities and their value (3:1–12). The reminders alternate between warnings ("do not"—vv. 3–4, 7–8, 11–12) and admonitions ("do"—vv. 5–6, 9–10). A good reputation depends on an unflinching commitment to be loyal or reliable (vv. 3–4). Rather than relying on oneself due to an inflated sense of one's own abilities (v. 5) or arrogance ("wise in your own eyes," v. 7), a person should "fear" or fully trust in the Lord (vv. 5–8). Such reliance on God may be demonstrated by giving the first or best of one's profits and trusting God to provide an abundance in return (vv. 9–10). The parent urges the child, however, also to regard hardship or a lack of blessing as a sign of the Lord's favor, the discipline of a much-loved child (vv. 11–12).

The second interlude in chs. 1–9 consists of an ode to wisdom (3:13–18): it was by wisdom that the Lord created the heavens and the earth (vv. 19–20). The ode again personifies Wisdom as a woman (cf. 1:20–33) who offers benefits to those who grasp and hold onto her. She offers riches (v. 16) and an income better than money (v. 14). She provides quality of life ("long life"): honor (v. 16), peace, and pleasantness (v. 17). She is more precious than anything else (v. 15). Woman Wisdom is nothing less than a tree of life restored and within the grasp of all people (cf. Gen 2:9; 3:22).

The fourth lecture again implores the child not to lose sight of wisdom, but to practice a prudent life-style, upheld here as the key to a secure life (3:21–35). One who maintains wisdom will walk without stumbling, sit without fear, and lie down to sleep soundly (vv. 23–24). He will not fear disaster (reading with the NJPS "you will not fear" rather than the NRSV "do not be afraid") because the Lord will be his security (vv. 25–26). The remainder of the lecture defines a prudent life-style in attitudes and actions toward others: prompt repayment of loans or other "good" due to another (vv. 27–28), not taking advantage of a person's trust or good will (vv. 29–30), and not being enamored with the apparent success of the violent (vv. 31–32). In fact, the Lord's curse is on the wicked, while the righteous, humble, and wise receive God's blessing (vv. 33–35).

In the fifth lecture the father recounts his training from his own father (the child's grandfather) in order to persuade his children to accept wisdom (4:1–9). When the father was young, the grandfather spoke to him to convince him (the father) to hear, remember, and obey his appeal to acquire wisdom (vv. 4–5). In order to accomplish this rhetorical goal, the grandfather personified wisdom as a woman, either as an influential patron or spouse, who protects, honors, and rewards the child who loves and embraces her (vv. 6–9).

Lecture six urges the child to accept parental guidance by contrasting the path (life-style) of wisdom and the path of the wicked (4:10–19). Though it may not seem so dire to the child, he or she must realize that the decision between wisdom and folly is a life-or-death decision. On the one hand, Wisdom provides a smooth and well-lit path on which the child may walk or even run without stumbling (vv. 11–12, 18). On the other hand, those walking on the path of the wicked cannot rest until they cause someone to stumble. They thrive ("eat" and "drink") on violence and stumble about in darkness (vv. 16–17, 19). The child must not step foot on their path (v. 14) but accept the parent's way of wisdom (v. 10).

Once again, in the seventh lecture the parent urges the child to remember his teaching because it alone offers genuine life (4:20–27). The speech unpacks the anatomy of wisdom: heart (v. 23), lips (v. 24), eyes (v. 25), and feet (vv. 26–27). The heart denotes a person's innermost being, the source of the will (3:1) emotions (12:25; 13:12), desire (6:25; 23:17), and trust (3:5; 31:11). Consequently, the heart determines the course of a person's life (21:1).

A contrast between the danger of the "other" woman and the benefits of fidelity to one's spouse governs the eighth lecture (5:1–23). After a brief appeal for the son's attention (vv. 1–2), the parent warns against any association with a "loose" woman, any woman other than the son's wife. Her speech allures (v. 3; cf. 2:6; 7:5, 21) but the consequence of swallowing her words is nothing less than a living death. This woman leads young men straight to the grave ("Sheol") although she is so deluded that even she is unaware of her true course (vv. 5–6). A man who does not stay away from her gives away his life to the "alien" (vv. 8–10). *Alien* may denote a non-Israelite or more likely is metaphorical for the "otherness" of any woman who is not the son's spouse. Only at the end, when all is lost, will the son realize and confess his foolishness: the folly of not listening to correction or accepting instruction (vv. 11–14).

The parent advises the son to find sexual fulfillment with his wife (vv. 15–19). "Water," "springs," and "fountain" are erotic imagery (Song 4:12, 15). To drink from "your own cistern" denotes sexual intercourse with one's own wife (Prov 5:15), a pleasure that should be reserved for the son and his spouse (vv. 16–17). The parent further pronounces a blessing on the son's sexual relationship with his wife, that it be fully satisfying and even intoxicating in its passion (vv. 18–19). If so, the parent cannot imagine any reason why the son would seek sexual fulfillment in another woman (v. 20).

Two final arguments clinch the parent's appeal. The first is theological; the Lord sees everything; there are no secret affairs (v. 21). The second is practical; every sinful activity produces results that destroy the sinner (vv. 22–23). The lecture is obviously androcentric; it is to a young man about the sexual dangers of the "other" woman. Nonetheless, the same message to women would vary only in detail. The danger of "other" men is just as real for young women.

A third interlude from the lectures brings together sayings that warn against practices that may seem innocent or inconsequential but are in fact dangerous (6:1–19). First, vv. 1–5 warn against the risks of pledging financial security for a loan (e.g., collateral or co-signing). Such a reckless action puts a person entirely at the mercy of the lender ("your neighbor's power") and the only escape is an immediate release from the obligation (see also 11:15). A second reckless practice that may seem harmless is "just a little" laziness. In reality, just "a little slumber" or "folding of the hands to rest" will cause poverty to attack like a thief or warrior (vv. 10–11; cf. 24:33–34); it is better to observe and follow the example of an industrious ant (vv. 6–8). Third, those who devise deceptive schemes against others through their misleading speech, winks, and other gestures are in imminent danger of calamity (vv. 12–15). Finally, a graded numerical saying concludes the interlude. In the pattern of x/x+1, the emphasis sometimes falls on the final item, here the Lord's feeling ("hate") regarding those who disrupt family relationships (cf. ch. 30).

The opening appeal of the ninth lecture (6:20–35) again introduces concern for the son's interaction with the "wife of another" ('esheth r'a, lit., "evil woman," v. 24a) or "adulteress" (nokhriyah, lit., "foreign woman," v. 24b). This woman may attract the son with her beauty (v. 25), but her most potent weapon is her seductive speech ("smooth tongue," v. 24). Only acceptance of

parental wisdom will provide an effective defense to her persuasive words (vv. 23–24).

The remainder of the lecture advances two arguments against sexual liaisons with a married woman. First, adultery comes at a high cost. Verse 26 compares the cost for a prostitute ("a loaf of bread") with the price of adultery ("a man's very life"), not to condone prostitution but to assert the much higher cost of adultery (see also vv. 32–33). Second, no one can avoid paying the price for an adulterous affair. No one can play with fire and not be burned (vv. 27–28). A community might understand ("not despise") a thief who steals only to eat, even though the thief will still pay in full (vv. 30–31). But no one will have compassion for an adulterer (vv. 32–33), especially not the woman's husband (vv. 34–35). The son (and daughter) must realize that illicit affairs come only at a high cost that is certain to be paid; only a fool thinks he or she can "get away with it."

The tenth lecture (7:1–23) continues the theme of the danger of illicit sexual liaisons. Here, the remedy for keeping the son away from the other woman is not only for the son to remember parental instruction, but to develop an intimate, even marital relationship with Woman Wisdom. "You are my sister" (v. 4) is an expression of endearment between a husband and wife (Song 4:9).

From his window, the father (or mother) claims to have witnessed just how an adulteress seduces young men. She dresses like a prostitute (v. 10; although married, v. 19) and looks everywhere for her next victim when she sees and approaches a young man (vv. 11–12). She seizes, kisses, and then brazenly speaks to him (v. 13). In fact, her speech is the power of her seduction (vv. 5, 21). She claims the recent fulfillment of a vow and peace offerings (shelamim), which featured the return of meat to the worshiper to eat (Lev 7:11–18). In other words, she claims to have fresh meat for dinner at home. She also claims that she has been looking just for this particular young man (v. 15), a rhetorical ploy to flatter him. The woman goes on to describe the erotic preparations she has made (vv. 16–17) before finally making a direct proposal for sex (v. 18). With her intentions now explicit, the woman anticipates possible objections: where is your husband? (not home, v. 19a), how long will he be gone? (a long time, v. 19b), how do you know? (he took a bag of money, v. 20). Her speech is smooth and seductive, and the young man believes it like a dumb animal senselessly walking to his own death. He fails to see through the rhetoric and realize that his life is on the line (vv. 21–23). The parent has seen this episode happen so many times that it seems like the house of the adulteress (or adulterer) is the gateway to living death (vv. 26–27).

Personified Wisdom makes her third appearance in chs. 1–9 (interlude 3), again to implore the child to accept her instruction (cf. 1:20–33; 3:13–20). As before, she appears in every public space inviting all to listen (8:1–5). Wisdom gives several reasons why people should respond to her teaching. First, the quality of her speech is noble; Wisdom speaks only what is right, true, and straight—and nothing that is twisted or deceptive (vv. 5–9). Second, her instruction is better than the acquisition of any other aspiration or desire, especially wealth ("jewels," vv. 10–11). Third, Wisdom's character is impeccable. She lives with "knowledge and discretion" and hates pride and corrupt speech (vv. 12–13). Fourth, she supplies the insight and strength for those who govern justly (vv. 14–16). Fifth, while Wisdom is better than riches (cf. vv. 10–11), she does reward those who diligently seek her with "enduring wealth and prosperity" that is better than gold or silver (vv. 17–21).

The sixth argument for accepting Wisdom vividly expands her personification to include direct descent from God. Wisdom was "created" (qanani, v. 22) or "brought forth" (kholalti, vv. 24–25) by the Lord before the creation of the earth or heavens (vv. 22–25). Both verbs suggest the process of birth; God gave birth to a daughter—Woman Wisdom. As a result, Daughter Wisdom was present when God created the land, the sky, and restrained the waters (vv. 26–29). At that time she was beside the Lord as a "master worker" ('amon, v. 30). As translated by the NRSV (drawing from the LXX), Woman Wisdom worked beside God in creation as a master artisan. The context, however, better supports the translation "little child" (NRSV footnote) or "infant" (KJV, REB). Wisdom was born prior to creation (vv. 22–25) and at creation "dances about" (sha'shu'im, NRSV, "his delight," v. 30), rejoicing and delighting in creation, especially humanity (vv. 30–31). Because of Wisdom's presence at cre-

ation, she knows how the world works, including what is best for humans. Therefore, people should listen to her to gain life (vv. 32–36).

Chapters 1–9 conclude with a final appeal from Woman Wisdom (9:1–6), instruction to teachers of wisdom (9:7–12), and a warning about Woman Folly (9:13–18). Woman Wisdom has made every arrangement for a splendid banquet: built a large house, prepared meat and wine, set the table, and sent out invitations to all the simple or naïve (vv. 1–8). Her food and drink denote laying aside immature behavior in order to act with insight or understanding, in other words, to truly live (vv. 5–6). Personified Folly appears in stark contrast to Wisdom. Folly is loud and ignorant (v. 13). And yet she extends the exact same invitation as Woman Wisdom: "You who are simple, turn in here!" (v. 16, cf. v. 4a). Woman Folly also offers food and drink, including the exciting allure of danger and secrecy. "Stolen water" and secret bread most likely denote illicit sex (cf. 5:15–17). Although initially similar to Wisdom's call and perhaps even more appealing, the child (son) must employ wisdom to see through the guise. Those who follow Woman Folly walk to their own death (v. 18).

Instruction to teachers of wisdom lies between the two contrasting invitations (vv. 7–12). In Proverbs the terms describing foolish or wicked behavior exist on a graduated scale of character deformation with "simple" (pethi) as the least severe and most correctable and a "scoffer" (lets) or "fool" ('ewil) as the most extreme and least correctable. The text warns against attempting to correct a scoffer; the wise will only be hurt by the attempt because a scoffer is beyond correction. However, rebuking and teaching the wise will lead to their further character development (vv. 8b–9). Wisdom is ultimately rooted in a proper relationship of respect to God (v. 10, cf. 1:7, 15:33) that alone promises genuine life (v. 11).

III. The Content of Wisdom (10:1–31:9)

10:1–22:16. The Proverbs of Solomon (i)

The first and longest collection of sayings in Proverbs begins with five chapters of primarily antithetical proverbs, the first line asserting a truth or observation which is then contrasted by a second line (e.g., "A wise child ... but a foolish child" [10:1] or "the wise of heart ... but a babbling fool" [10:8]). Despite many recent efforts to identify purposeful arrangement of these proverbs, close literary connections do not appear to extend beyond small clusters of two or three proverbs (e.g., 10:1–2, 3–4, 6–7). Recurring topics in chs. 10–15, however, are clear. Most proverbs in these chapters regard one or more of four thematic contrasts: (1) righteous/wicked, (2) appropriate/inappropriate speech, (3) prosperity/poverty, and (4) wisdom/folly. The density of these themes in chs. 10–15 is far greater than their appearance in other chapters, suggesting a deliberate emphasis on these contrasts. As a result, the commentary will review each of these themes with special attention to select verses.

The first and most prominent theme in chs. 11–15 is the contrast between the righteous and the wicked. Apparently, a key concern of the editors was to address misperceptions regarding the life and fortunes of the wicked. Despite appearances, the sages claim that the wicked do not possess any true or lasting prosperity, e.g., "Treasures gained by wickedness do not profit" (10:2*a*), "The wicked earn no real gain" (11:18*a*), and "No one finds security by wickedness" (12:3, see also 10:3, 6, 16, 24, 28; 11:23; 13:25; 14:19). Instead, the lives of the wicked "are filled with trouble" (12:21*b*) and "trouble befalls their income" (15:6*b*, see also 11:8, 21). The wicked will collapse under the weight of their wrongdoing (10:25; 14:32). They will not remain in the land (10:30), their years will be short (10:27; 12:7; 13:9; 14:11), and their expectations and hopes will come to nothing (10:3, 28; 11:23). In contrast, it is the righteous who achieve or who are blessed with real and enduring prosperity (10:2, 6; 11:18; 14:11; 15:6), enjoy stability in times of crisis (10:25, 30; 11:8; 12:3), and find their dreams and hopes fulfilled (10:24, 28; 11:23). The emphatic rhetoric suggests that then, as now, the presence of wicked people who appear to flourish posed a special problem for sages who wanted to encourage righteous behavior.

These proverbs, as others, should not be read as a guarantee that the righteous will always prosper and the wicked always suffer. Neither ancient nor modern proverbs function in such absolute ways. Rather, these proverbs assert in general terms that the way to genuine prosperity and security is by means of integrity, fairness, and just business practices—not shortcuts, dishonesty, or oppression. Despite appearances, the sages warn, people do not really admire the wicked. The community will rejoice when the wicked perish (11:10*b*; 10:7). Further, the religious practices and the life-style of the wicked are an abomination to the Lord (15:8–9), and the "Lord is far from the wicked" (15:29*a*).

A second thematic contrast involves speech. Lack of restraint characterizes foolish speech. A fool babbles on and on without self-control (10:8, 14; 13:3; 15:2, 28). Wise speech, however, is restrained (10:19), appropriate (10:32; 15:23), guarded (13:3), thoughtful (15:28), and sometimes even silent (11:12; 12:23). Disciplined speech both enables and results from listening—to instruction (15:31–32; 10:8, 17; 15:5), advice (12:15; 13:10), and rebuke (13:1, 18). To listen and learn, however, would require a fool to stop talking, which is an impossible task for him (10:8, 14). The collection also emphasizes the power of the tongue for good and ill. Foolish or wicked speech may bring ruin (10:8, 14; 13:3), ensnare the speaker (12:13), ambush the listener (12:6), thrust like a sword (12:18), destroy friends (11:9), stir up anger (15:1), and even overthrow communities (11:11). But wise or righteous speech is like valuable silver (10:20); it brings healing (12:18), encouragement (12:25), and nourishment to the listener and speaker (10:21; 12:14; 13:2). Such talk preserves and fosters life (13:3; 14:3, 25) primarily because of its honesty (12:17, 22; 14:5, 25). Godly speech is a fountain of life (10:11) and a tree of life (15:4).

Third, many proverbs in chs. 10–15 contrast the ideas of wealth and poverty. Although addressed to the wealthy rather than the poor, the sages are realists. The poor have a hard life (10:15; 14:20; 15:15) while wealth provides security to the rich (10:15; 13:8). Further, while the proverbs draw extensive attention to self-induced causes of poverty (e.g., laziness [10:4, 5; 12:24; 13:4; 15:19], wickedness [10:3; 11:18; 13:21, 22, 25; 15:6], stinginess [11:24–26], greed [11:26; 15:27], chasing worthless pursuits [12:11], and all talk with no work [14:23]) so that the reader will avoid these behaviors, the sages also acknowledge that poverty may come due to injustice (13:23). Over against causes of poverty, the sages identify appropriate means to long-lasting prosperity (e.g., righteousness [10:3, 6, 16, 24; 11:18, 28; 12:12; 13:21–22, 25, 15:6], diligent work [10:4; 12:11, 14*b*, 24, 27; 13:4; 14:23], and generosity [11:24–25]) as well as the proper use of wealth (e.g., kindness to the poor [14:21, 31]). And yet, despite their positive attitude toward wealth (it is the Lord's blessing [12:2]), the sages emphasize that some things are far more important (e.g., righteousness [11:4], fear of the Lord [15:16], and love or harmony [15:17]) and mock those who pretend to be rich in order to impress others (12:9; 13:7).

The final thematic contrast in these chapters consists broadly of the ideas of wisdom/folly, good sense/lack of understanding, and other similar terms. A fundamental precondition for wisdom is humility (11:2) with an openness to learn (12:15; 13:10). Wise behavior is especially exhibited in self-control (14:16), mentioned here in regard to various contexts (e.g., temper [12:16; 14:17, 29], speech [10:14, 19], and wealth [12:11]). The sages show their disapproval of an out-of-control life by scorning those who act without sense (11:22; 14:1) and emphasizing the public support for those with good sense (12:8; 14:35). Because of their careful, disciplined actions, the wise have direction in life (14:15; 15:21, 24) that brings joy to their parents (10:1; 15:20), benefits to those around them (13:14, 20; 14:7), and pleasure to themselves (10:23). While folly is the reward of fools (14:18), wisdom crowns the life of the wise (14:24).

Although not a contrasting theme or more prevalent than elsewhere in the book, these chapters also have much to say about the Lord's active presence in human affairs (15:3, 11). Unfortunately, much of what the Lord sees is an insult (oppression of the poor, 14:31; cf. 17:5) or an "abomination (*to'evah*) to the Lord," i.e., things that are offensive, repulsive, or repugnant (e.g., false balances [11:1], lying lips [12:22], the sacrifice of the wicked [15:8], the ways of the wicked [15:9], and evil plans [15:26]; cf. 6:16–19). While the Lord works against the proud (15:25), security and well-being come to those who follow the way of the Lord (10:3, 29; 12:2; 14:9; 15:29) and have a proper relationship with God ("fear of the Lord," 10:27; 14:26–27; 15:33).

The following comments address problems in the following proverbs:

10:2, "delivers from death"—In Proverbs the terms *life* and *death* are often symbolize a person's quality of life, a full and vibrant life or the lack joyful living (e.g., 10:16, 17, 21, 27).

10:10, "winks the eye"—a gesture to plan or coordinate deceptive or harmful actions (6:12–14; 16:30; Ps 35:19).

10:12, "love covers all offenses"—to forgive or pardon, not improperly cover-up or condone sin (cf. 1 Pet 4:8).

10:15, "the wealth of the rich"—a realistic observation about the benefits of wealth. Wealth provides security unavailable to the poor. Elsewhere the sages warn against overestimating the security wealth provides (see 18:10–11; cf. 13:8; 14:20–21; 19:4).

10:22, "and he adds no sorrow with it" or "and toil adds nothing to it"—reading *'etsev* (*toil* or *sorrow*) as the subject of the sentence. While other proverbs affirm the importance of human effort (10:4; 14:23), with exaggeration characteristic of many proverbs, this text emphasizes that the Lord is the ultimate source of blessing.

11:1, "false balance" and "an accurate weight"—balances with weights were a basic form of measurement for trade or commerce. True balances and weights denote honest business practices (see 16:11; 20:10, 23).

11:15, "guarantee loans"—to be held responsible for repayment should the debtor default, a practice similar to co-signing for a loan. Several proverbs caution against this risky practice, especially on behalf of a stranger (see 6:1–5; 17:18; 20:16; 22:26–27; 27:13). While Proverbs upholds generosity (e.g., 11:24–25), the danger of financial ruin is to be avoided.

11:16, "A gracious woman ... aggressive gain riches"—The NRSV adopts the Greek text, which adds lines b and c to this verse (alone, lines *a* and *d* reflect the Hebrew). The primary antithesis in the proverb is ambiguous. The contrast may be between honor (long lasting) and riches (temporary), female behavior (*gracious*) and male behavior (*aggressive*), or gentleness (*gracious*) and violence (*aggressive*).

12:4, "she who brings shame"—like most proverbs this saying and those regarding the "contentious wife" come from a male's perspective.

With imagination and humor, the sages bemoan the plight of a man married to a quarrelsome and argumentative wife; better to suffer the discomforts of the desert (21:19) or the corner of a housetop (21:9; 25:24)—to live anywhere but endure the torture of her arguing, an unstoppable dripping of rain (19:13; 27:15–16). The principle is just as valid for hypercritical, domineering, and verbally abusive husbands—better to live anywhere but with them.

12:27, "The lazy do not roast their game"—because they do not hunt or capture game to roast (cf. NAB, NJB, RSV). The Hebrew is difficult but the main idea is clear; the lazy have nothing, but the diligent obtain wealth.

13:8, "but the poor get no threats (*ge'arah*)"—or "does not listen to rebuke" (cf. NJB, NAB). The contrast with *ransom* in 8*a* supports understanding *ge'arah* as *threat*. Wealth is a relative good. It may provide ransom or relief from kidnapping or other danger, but wealth also raises a higher possibility for some dangers.

13:9, "lamp of the wicked goes out"—metaphorical. A lamp or light that goes out is a sign of death (Job 18:5, 6; 2 Sam 21:17) or disaster (Job 21:17; see also Prov 20:20; 24:20).

13:24, "spare the rod"—a commonly held principle in Israel and the ancient Near East, namely, that corporal punishment improves character. Paradoxically, the motivation for physical punishment was to come out of love for the child, not hate or anger. Other proverbs urge parents to discipline children in order to drive out folly (22:15), instill wisdom (29:15), and save their lives (23:13–14; 29:17). The concept of the rod or corporal punishment does not advocate child abuse or mistreatment of prisoners but wisely measured discipline within the context of love.

14:9, "Fools mock at the guilt-offering (*'asham*)"—ambiguity in the Hebrew has spawned several emendations (e.g., RSV, NAB, NJPS). Fools have so little concern for their sin that they act with contempt toward a guilt offering that would atone for their sin, a rare reference to sacrificial atonement in wisdom literature (cf. Lev 5:14–6:7; 7:1–6).

14:13, "Even in laughter the heart is sad"—human emotions are complex. A happy appearance may mask inner turmoil, and our greatest joys hold the potential of our greatest sorrows, even at the same moment. As with other proverbs, the text does not assert an absolute truth but makes a general observation.

14:15, "the simple (*pethi*)"—a young person who stands at a crossroads in his or her character development (1:4; 7:7). In contrast to the clever (*'arum*), the simple lack training and knowledge and so tend to believe everything (14:15, 18); they also fail to recognize danger and suffer for it (22:3). Though ignorant, the simple are open to learning (19:25; 21:11), but because of their inexperience they are also prone to wander into the wrong path (1:32). As a result, the book of Proverbs records something of a battle between wisdom (1:22; 8:5; 9:4) and folly (9:16) for the life and character of the simple. The book itself enters the fray by identifying the simple as the book's primary audience (1:4).

14:20–21, "the poor ... the rich"—see 19:4.

15:11, "Sheol" (synonym "Abaddon")—the underworld or realm of the dead (see also 1:12; 5:5; 27:20; Job 26:6; Ps 139:8).

15:13, "glad heart ... sorrow of heart"—*heart* (*lev*) denotes a person's all-important inner being or psyche (4:23) made visible in one's facial appearance ("countenance") and powerful enough to crush hope or strength ("the spirit"; cf. 4:23; 17:22; 18:14).

15:24, "Sheol"—see 15:11.

15:30, "The light of the eyes"—may denote the joy of good news reflected in the face of a messenger (NIV; cf. 16:15) or the inner courage and strength given by God (Ezra 9:8; Ps 13:3). Chapter 16 begins with two short thematic collections. The first stresses the presence and activity of the Lord in human affairs (vv. 1–11). Over and above human efforts, the Lord determines plans (v. 1), steps (v. 9), and outcomes (v. 3). The Lord exercises insight into a person's inner disposition (v. 2) and may respond with favor (v. 7) or disgust and punishment (v. 5). The Lord is sovereign, even over those who reject his rule (v. 4). But those who commit their plans to the Lord succeed (v. 3) and those who live in reverence and respect of the Lord ("fear the Lord") are able to avoid evil (*ra'*) or trouble (v. 6).

The second collection regards the king (vv. 10–15) and is closely related to vv. 1–10. In ancient Israelite thought the king was God's representative and the mediator between God and the people (e.g., Ps 2:6–9). So here the ideal king, like the Lord, is a wise judge (v. 10; cf. 16:2), views evil as abomination (v. 12; cf. 16:5), and delights in honest and righteous behavior (v. 13; cf. 16:11). His favor brings blessing (v. 15; cf. 16:3, 7), and his anger is deadly (v. 14; cf. 16:5).

The following comments address problems in the following proverbs.

16:4, "even the wicked for the day of trouble"—not that the Lord forces some people to be wicked. Rather, the Lord's dominion is absolute, including punishment ("day of trouble") of the wicked.

16:6, "By loyalty and faithfulness iniquity is atoned for"—genuine devotion erases or cancels the effects of sin with God (and others; cf. 10:12) while a proper relationship of reverence ("fear of the LORD") prevents sin. The proverb does not reject sacrificial atonement (Lev 1–7), but emphasizes vital attitudes necessary for atonement (cf. Hos 6:6; 1 Sam 15:22).

16:10, "Inspired decisions (qesem)"—elsewhere this term denotes divination, forbidden to Israel (e.g., Deut 18:10; 1 Sam 15:23). Here, used in a positive sense, the term metaphorically refers to God enabling the king to make wise judgments as if the Lord himself had spoken.

16:11, "Honest balances and scales"—see 11:1.

16:15, "In the light of a king's face"—see 15:30.

16:30, "winks the eyes"—see 10:10.

16:33, "the lot is cast into the lap"—a way of reaching a decision, especially that of divine will (e.g., 18:18; see also Jonah 1:7; Acts 1:26). While the precise procedure for casting lots is uncertain, ancient Israel regarded the Lord's control of the outcome as certain. Chapter 17 has no obvious literary structure although three themes reverberate in the text: the fool, friendship, and family. A fool is nothing but trouble for his or her parents (vv. 21, 25) or those who encounter him (v. 12); fools refuse to learn (vv. 16, 24) or accept correction (v. 10), and the only hope for their speech is not to speak (vv. 7, 27–28). Friendship relies on forgiveness (v. 9), not returning evil for good (vv. 13–14),

and faithful love (v. 17; cf. 18:24). And healthy families choose peace over abundance (v. 1), wisdom over shameful behavior (v. 2), and justice over unfairness (v. 13). Naturally, grandchildren are the pride of their grandparents (v. 6).

17:8, "A bribe is like a magic stone"—a realistic observation about the power of a bribe. Bribery or gift-giving often achieves its goals, at least in the eyes of the person offering the gift (18:16; 21:14; cf. 6:35). Proverbs condemns bribery for illegitimate purposes (17:23; 15:27; see Exod 23:8; Deut 16:19).

17:18, "pledge" and "surety"—see 11:15.

17:19, "one who builds a high threshold"—either elaborate architecture of the door or the whole house (synecdoche) expressive of pride, or "his opening" (pithkho; NRSV, "threshold") denotes the mouth, thus haughty or proud speech. In either case, pride leads to destruction ("broken bones," see also 16:18).

17:24, "the eyes of a fool to the ends of the earth"—fools are incapable of concentrating on their true needs. Instead, they are continually distracted and their attention wanders from one thing to another. The topic of speech dominates ch. 18. Words possess tremendous power, even the power of life and death (v. 21); a fool's talk is his or her undoing (vv. 6–7) while good lips produce fruit that sustain life or bring satisfaction (vv. 20, 4). A wise person listens before speaking (v. 13; cf. 2, 15, 17) and will avoid the tasty words of a gossip (v. 8). On the topic of the court and justice see verses 5, 17–18, and 23.

18:1, "The one who lives alone is self-indulgent"—a person who isolates himself from the community and pursues selfish desires. Such anti-social behavior is contrary to the collective identity and values of the Old Testament. Self-centered commitments lead a person to reject wisdom from the community ("sound judgment," 1b) and value only his own personal opinion.

18:4, "The words of the mouth are deep waters"—either (1) a contrast between words that derive from deep within a person and are thus ultimately incomprehensible (v. 4a; cf. 20:5) and wisdom that is readily available (v. 4b; so NRSV, NIV), or (2) the three images of water in lines a and b describe ideal speech as "deep waters" (inexhaustible), a "fountain of wisdom" (wise), and a "gushing stream" (refreshing; so NAB, NJB, NJPS).

18:16, "A gift opens doors"—see 17:8.

18:18, "Casting the lot"—see 16:33.

18:19, "An ally offended is stronger than a city"—the meaning of the Hebrew is uncertain (see the diversity of translations: NIV, NAB, RSV [following the LXX], NJB). Reading 19a with the NRSV, a close relationship (friend or family) damaged by a dispute or offense is more difficult to reconcile than capturing a fortified city. Line b is more obscure; it likely emphasizes the difficulty of resolving a broken friendship.

18:23, "The poor use entreaties"—because of their marginal social location, the poor must present requests with care and deference to superiors (cf. 19:4, 7). Because of the security of their resources and position (cf. 10:15; 14:20; 22:7) the wealthy may respond ("answer") rudely, without concern for the feelings or reactions of the poor. The proverb is an implicit rebuke of such common social conditions and behavior (see also 13:23; 22:16).

Wealth and poverty are the most prominent theme in ch. 19. The proverbs identify regrettable social realities: people flock to those with money to spend (vv. 4a, 6), but avoid those who lack resources (v. 4b, 7). Only one specific cause for poverty is recognized: laziness (v. 15, comically portrayed in verse 24). Genuine prosperity comes as a result of wisdom (v. 8), obedience (v. 16), kindness to the poor (v. 17), and, above all, a proper relationship to the Lord (v. 23). However, integrity not wealth should be a person's upmost aspiration. Even if the result is poverty, it is better not to become perverse (v. 1) or a liar (v. 22). Other themes prominent in the chapter include family life (vv. 13, 14, 18, 26), the court (vv. 5, 9, 28, 29), and anger (vv. 11, 12, 19).

19:4, "poor are left friendless"—a troubling but common feature of human society; people befriend those who advantage them (the rich) and avoid social entanglement with those who drain them (the poor). A similar proverb pair in 14:20–21 condemns such behavior, not only as shallow but sinful (cf. 10:15; 18:23; 19:7).

19:7, "are hated"—the term *sane'*, encompasses a broad spectrum of feelings: intense hatred (1 Kgs 22:8), aggravation (25:17), avoidance (11:15, translated as "refusing"), or preference for one person over another (Gen 29:31, 33).

19:7, "when they call ..."—an ambiguous third line (literally, "one pursuing words, they are not [or 'they are']"). Some devise a translation that relates the line to the previous couplet (e.g., NRSV, NIV). Others regard it as a remnant of an unrelated lost proverb (e.g., NJB).

19:13, "a wife's quarreling"—see 12:4.

19:19, "if you effect a rescue ..."—the Hebrew is ambiguous. Either: (1) "you will have to do it again" (NRSV, NAB), or (2) you will only make matters worse (NJPS, NJB). In either case the counsel is the same; the only hope for a hot-tempered people is for them to endure the consequences of their behavior. Attempts to help by extricating them from their punishment are ineffective or even harmful.

19:25, "Strike a scoffer (*lets*)"—a scoffer is one of the final stages in the character deformation of a fool. A scoffer not only acts foolishly but refuses to listen to rebuke (13:1; 15:12) and turns on those who try to help (9:7–8). Above all, a scoffer "acts with arrogant pride" (21:24) and so is an abomination to all (24:9).

19:25, "the simple"—see 14:15.

Chapter 20 features a number of proverbs that describe or comment on the human condition. The human heart (or mind) is complex (v. 5). The Lord searches out and weighs the heart (v. 27; 21:2), but the intelligent also can discern a person's intentions (v. 5). Although a person's actions reveal his or her inner character (v. 11), it remains impossible for a person to understand fully his or her own way (v. 24), just as it is impossible to make oneself pure from sin (v. 9) or find a trustworthy person (v. 6).

With three exceptions (vv. 25, 29–30), all the proverbs from 20:22 to 21:3 regard either the Lord, the king, or both. The Lord is the creator (v. 12) and not only understands humans (vv. 27; 21:2) but can order a person's steps (v. 24), turn a king's heart (21:1), and help the wronged repay evil (v. 22). Deceptive trade is an abomination to the Lord (vv. 10, 23), but righteousness and justice "is more acceptable than sacrifice" (21:3; cf. Hos 6:6; Mic 6:6–8). Like the Lord, the ideal king has dangerous power (20:2), sifts out the wicked (vv. 8, 26), and his reign is characterized by righteousness (v. 28).

Several other verses in ch. 20 concern business and finance (vv. 4, 10, 13, 16–17, 21, 23, 25).

20:5, "like deep water"—symbolizes the intentions and plans concealed deep within a person, accessible only to a wise person who knows how to fish the water (see 18:4).

20:10, "Diverse weights and measures"—see 11:1.

20:14, "'Bad, bad,' says the buyer ..."—a humorous glance at the marketplace. During the bargaining process a prospective buyer will question or deny the value of a product in order to drive down the price ("Bad, bad"). Then, once purchased, the buyer will boast to others about the product and his or her great bargain.

20:16, "pledge given as surety"—see 11:15.

20:20, "your lamp"—see 13:9.

20:23, "weights" and "false scales"—see 11:1.

20:25, "to say rashly, 'It is holy' "—to make a vow dedicating something to the Lord (e.g., a sacrifice [Lev 7:16; 22:18], person, animal, house, or land [Lev 27:1–27]). Once made, a vow could not be revoked (Num 30:2; Eccl 5:4; cf. Judg 11:29–40). A rash vow might derive from a dangerous situation (asking God to save) or out of great joy for God's intervention.

20:27, "The human spirit is the lamp of the Lord"—the "human spirit" (*nishmath 'adam*) is the life-breath by which God animates flesh (Gen 2:7, "the breath of life" [*nishmath khayyim*]). Since this life-breath enters deep within a person, it is a fitting figure for God's lamp that searches a person's inner motives and thoughts (see also 15:11; 16:2; 21:2).

Like ch. 20, ch. 21 highlights personal business or finances, especially misguided efforts to obtain wealth (hastiness [v. 5], deception [v. 6]) or character traits opposed to gaining and keeping wealth (laziness [v. 25], miserliness [v. 13], loving luxury [v. 17], quickly spending resources [v. 20]). This chapter also features the character and destiny of the wicked (*rasha'*). The wicked are utterly corrupt: their desires are evil (v. 10), they are brazen (v. 29), they covet all day long (v. 26), and their sacrifices are an abomination (v. 27; cf. vv. 8, 15, 24). Just retribution will come on the wicked (vv. 7, 12, 18, 28; cf. v. 16); they cannot prevail against the Lord (v. 30). But those who pursue righteousness will be rewarded (vv. 21, 23).

21:4, "the lamp of the wicked—are sin"— the meaning of this phrase in relation to 4*a* is uncertain. Elsewhere extinguishing the "lamp of the wicked" means death or a difficult life (13:9; 24:20; 20:20). Perhaps because of their arrogance (4*a*), even what should give light and direction to their lives is sin—corrupt and darkened (e.g., Matt 6:22–23). Or "lamp" may be a symbol for any endeavor (so in the NIV, NAB, NJPS). Because of their pride, anything the wicked undertake will be sinful.

21:9, 19, "a contentious wife"—see 12:4.

21:14, "a gift in secret" and a "concealed bribe"—see 17:8.

21:18, "The wicked is a ransom for the righteous"—enigmatic, perhaps best understood as a metaphor for the concept of just rewards: the wicked suffer, not the righteous. The righteous and upright are not perfect (Mark 10:18), but they do not walk on the path of the wicked (Prov 11:5; 15:9). In some sense (collectively?), the wicked and faithless are the ransom or payment (*kofer*, see 6:35; 13:8; Exod 21:29–32) that allow the righteous to go free (cf. Isa 43:3). Or in a broader view, justice is established by a reversal of positions—the righteous away from a place of suffering and the wicked toward punishment (see 10:2, 28; 11:8, 21; 12:21).

21:22, "one wise person"—one might question the wisdom of a lone sage attacking a fortified city (cf. Eccl 9:14–16), but the hyperbole establishes the key idea: wisdom is more powerful than brute strength (cf. 20:18; 24:5; Eccl 7:19).

Proverbs 22:1–6 concludes the collection that began in 10:1. These verses, like preceding chapters lack any evident structure. They do, however, continue the emphasis on wealth and business from chapters 20–21 with an unusual density of the terms *'osher* ("riches," vv. 1, 4) and *'ashir* ("rich," vv. 2, 7, 16; see similar ideas in vv. 9, 13).

22:6, "Train children in the right way"—like other proverbs, a statement of general truth, not an absolute guarantee or sweeping judgment of parents. Early and consistent training has lasting effects upon a child, for which parents (especially) are responsible (cf. 19:18; 23:13; 29:15; see also on 20:30). Children, however, are ultimately responsible for their own decisions and life (13:1; 15:5).

22:8, "rod of anger"—the Hebrew in line *b* is difficult and has led to various translations (e.g., NJPS, NAB). *Rod* (*shevet*) symbolizes rule or power (as in Isa 14:5–6); taken with line *a* the image is that of a cruel tyrant who rules unjustly and in anger.

22:17–24:22. The Sayings of the Sages (i)

After initial debate following its discovery in 1923, most scholars now recognize a close relationship between the Egyptian text of *Amenemope* and Proverbs 22:17–24:12. Israelite sages were likely familiar with, influenced by, and perhaps even made direct use of *Amenemope*. This section of Proverbs especially addresses young men from the upper class who are near the beginning of their careers on how to succeed or advance in their professions. The opening verses define such success as a pleasant life (22:18), living out trust in the Lord (22:19), and reliability and competence in one's work (22:21). To these ends, the sages offer cautions regarding common missteps taken to advance one's career (e.g., taking advantage of the powerless [22:22–23], risky financial practices [22:26–27], an unhealthy ambition for wealth [23:4–5], and losing self-control [23:19–21, 26–28]) and admonitions toward best practices for achievement (e.g., skill in one's work [22:29], listening to wise counsel [24:3–6], and faithful service to the Lord and king [24:21–22]).

22:20, "thirty sayings (*shalishiwm*)"—the Hebrew text is uncertain. Most translations and commentators adopt the emendation "thirty" (*sheloshim*) based on a similar statement in *Amenemope*, "Look to these thirty chapters. They inform, they educate." On this basis the NIV, GNB (TEV), and CEV not only adopt this emendation but also identify the thirty sayings by inserting headings into their translations, although each differs. Most interpreters identify only 24–28 sayings in the collection.

22:21, "to those who sent you?"—common language for a messenger who must convey his master's message, bring back an accurate reply, and perhaps even represent his master in any negotiations (see 10:26; 13:17; 25:13; 26:6).

22:22, "at the gate"—the place for public business and legal trials (see Deut 21:18–21; Ruth 4:1–12; cf. Prov 8:1–3, 24:7).

22:26, "pledges ... surety"—see 11:15.

22:28, "Do not remove the ancient landmark"—ancient landmarks consisted of pillars or stones set out to mark property lines. To remove or move such a stone would be to encroach on and claim someone else's property, most likely individuals who are poor or cannot defend their rights (e.g., 1 Kgs 21:1–16; Isa 5:8). Chapter 23:10–11 repeats verse 28*a* and adds that God is the protector of those who are vulnerable (cf. 15:25). See also Deut 19:14; 27:17; Job 24:2.

23:7, "like a hair in the throat"—the meaning of the Hebrew is uncertain. Most translations read the rare word (*sha'ar*) as a verb for "calculate, reckon" (e.g., NIV, NJPS, RSV). The NRSV follows the Greek and a similar passage from *Amenemope* (regarding a person who confiscates the property of a poor man, "it [is] a blocking to the throat; It makes a vomiting to the gullet") and renders (*sha'ar*) as a noun: a "hair" in the throat that causes a person to vomit (v. 8). As a whole, verses 6–8 warn against accepting an invitation from a begrudging or two-faced host.

23:10, "ancient landmark"—see 22:28.

23:13, "Do not withhold discipline"—see 13:24.

23:20, "winebibbers (*sob'e-yayin*)"—those who drink to excess. With the "gluttonous eaters of meat," these two groups symbolize extravagant and self-centered life-styles (see Deut 21:20 and Prov 21:17; on alcohol in Proverbs see 20:1; 23:29–35; 31:4–5).

23:29–35, "Who has woe?"—an extended lampoon of excessive drinking. An initial riddle of six questions (v. 29), leads to an answer (v. 30), a warning (v. 31), and then a vivid description of the "bite" of drunkenness (vv. 32–35). The text includes a full range of consequences for drunkenness: emotional ("sorrow," v. 29), relational ("strife," and "complaining," v. 29), mental (hallucinations, v. 33), and physical (red eyes, v. 29; the sensation of seasickness, v. 34; injuries without awareness or memory, v. 35a; and addiction, v. 35b).

24:7, "the gate"—see 22:22.

24:16, "fall seven times"—a symbolic number of completeness (6:31; 26:16, 25; Job 5:19). No matter how many times the righteous may fall, they will recover. The wicked, however, will not recover from even one calamity (v. 16).

24:17, "do not rejoice"—the sages advance a challenging ethic regarding a person's enemy. Instead of taking revenge (20:22; 24:29) a person is to help an enemy (25:21–22), and when misfortune befalls, one should not rejoice or gloat (Job 31:29; cf. Ps 35:13–15). Verse 18 is more difficult and may be read in at least three different ways: (1) God will stop punishing the enemy because of your reaction, (2) public celebration preempts the divine process of justice, or (3) the Lord is so repulsed by self-righteous gloating that he will turn away from the enemy to punish you.

24:20, "lamp of the wicked"—see 13:9.

24:21, "do not disobey either of them"—the text is uncertain. The NRSV reads with the Greek while most English translations follow the Hebrew ("and do not join with rebellious officials," NIV; cf. NAB, NJPS, NJB, NRSV margin). The underlying idea, however, is much the same for both translations: faithfulness to God and the king, God's earthly representative. The warning presupposes an ideal king who exercises justice and righteousness (see 27:23–27; 28:2–3, 15–16; 29:4, 14).

24:23–34. The Sayings of the Sages (ii)

The editorial heading, "These also are sayings of the wise," sets these verses apart as an appendix to the previous section (22:17–24:22, "The Words of the Wise"). The contents of this section fall into two parallel parts of three sections each: Part I—(a) the law court—admonition to judges for impartiality (24:23b–25), (b) a related proverb on honesty (24:26), (c) an admonition regarding diligent and timely work (24:27), and Part II—a) the law court—admonition to witnesses for honesty (24:28), b) a related proverb on vengeance (24:29), c) a tale and admonition regarding diligent and timely work (24:30–34).

24:27, "after that build your house"—literally, prepare your fields before building a house; figuratively, acquire a means of support first and then build a family.

24:33–34, "A little sleep, a little slumber"—perhaps the lazy person's excuse: just a little more rest will not hurt anyone. Verse 34 responds: a little more sleep and poverty will attack you (cf. 6:10–11).

25:1–29:27. The Proverbs of Solomon (ii)

The superscription attributes the compilation of Prov 25–29 to scribes during the reign of King Hezekiah of Judah (ca. 715–687 BCE). The first half of the collection contains a number of thematically related verses (25:1–27:27) while the second half contrasts the righteous and the wicked (28:1–29:27).

The opening verse (25:2) establishes the first topic (the royal court) while vv. 3–15 address courtiers with advice for success. First, court ministers should be wary of overconfidence regarding their insight into the king's mind, just as a king should respect God's unsearchable wisdom (vv. 2–3). Second, wicked officials pollute the kingdom and must be removed to provide the purity of righteousness that establishes a king's reign (vv. 4–5). Third, self-advancing courtiers are put on notice; it is best to act humbly rather than claim a place of prestige only to be humiliated (vv. 6–7; Luke 14:7–11). Fourth, one should not be hasty to bring a matter to court (royal or civil, vv. 7c–8) or betray a confidence in order to win a case (vv. 9–10). Like claiming a place of prestige, such unethical actions lead to shame, not advancement. Fifth, a good decision or rebuke ("a word fitly spoken") and a receptive attitude ("a listening ear") are both highly valued (vv. 11–12). Sixth, a faithful servant is refreshing and life-giving (v. 13), but an unreliable person who makes empty promises only disappoints (v. 14). Finally, words are powerful, especially patient and gentle speech that may change a superior's mind (v. 15).

The rest of the chapter is loosely based on the ideas of friendship (vv. 16–22) and appropriateness or self-control (vv. 16–17, 20, 27–28).

25:20, "one who sings songs"—the NRSV reconstructs the Hebrew from the Greek. A person who sings cheerful songs, as opposed to laments, to someone overwhelmed by grief inappropriately disregards the impact of sorrow on the human heart.

25:21–22, "heap coals of fire"—a person should provide for the needs of an enemy in order to bring about the enemy's contrition or perhaps add to their punishment (vv. 21–22). The phrase "heap burning coals on their heads" is obscure. Many interpreters follow Augustine and Jerome who claim the action helps the enemy by softening his heart or pricking his conscience. More recent work has suggested an Egyptian ritual of placing coals in a bowl on one's head in order to represent burning shame and penitence. On the other hand, in the Old Testament fire upon the head typically denotes punishment (Pss 18:12; 120:4; 140:10; Ezek 10:2; 2 Sam 22:13).

25:27, "to seek honor on top of honor"—the Hebrew of v. 27b is unintelligible and requires emendation. In the NRSV, line a describes moderation in one's appetite for a good thing (honey). Assuming synonymous parallelism, line b identifies another good ("honor") that should also be pursued in moderation, if at all (cf. 27:2).

Three themes about fools are interwoven throughout 26:1–12. First, the true character of a fool is like a reluctant horse or stubborn donkey (v. 3), unreliable in the completion of any assignment (vv. 6, 10). Fools proudly think that they know everything ("wise in their own eyes," vv. 5, 12), although they do not learn from their mistakes (v. 11), are unable to deploy a proverb properly (vv. 7, 9), and speak ineffective curses (because the curses are undeserved, v. 2). Second, because of their character, fools are a danger to the community. Their unreliability will hurt the one who hires them (v. 6), and the employed fool will endanger the public (v. 10). A fool is not only inept with proverbial wisdom (v. 7) but apt to hurt others by his or her use of proverbs (v. 9). Third, the collection offers guidelines for how a community should deal with fools. Honor for a fool is out of place (v. 1); it will only expose the community to further harm (v. 8). A person should not employ a fool (v. 6, 10) and should be careful when and how he or she interacts with fools. Sometimes it is best not to answer a fool, lest one be drawn into acting like a fool (v. 4). But other circumstances require a response that will deflate a fool's pride (v. 5).

Verses 13–16 use hyperbole to ridicule the lazy person or "sluggard" (KJV). Such a person makes ridiculous excuses to avoid activity (v. 13), stays in bed so long that he or she is like a hinged door turning back and forth (v. 14), and lacks even the energy to put food into his or her mouth (v. 15). And while the lazy person thinks that he or she is wiser than anyone else (v. 16), in truth one who is so wise "in self-esteem" (literally, "wise in his own eyes") is really a fool (cf. 25:6, 12).

The remainder of ch. 26 consists of two interlocking themes: quarrelsomeness and speech. Persons who meddle in other's quarrels (v. 17) or who mislead a neighbor (and claim innocent intentions, vv. 18–19) are both acting like lunatics. Quarrels would die out if only people would stop "whispering" about matters that are none of their business (v. 20). A quarrelsome person, however, keeps trouble stirred up (v. 21). One particular challenge is that a whisperer's words taste good (v. 22). A listener would be wise to remember, however, that such smooth speech covers an evil heart (v. 23) and disguises deceitful intentions (v. 24). So, one should exercise care when an enemy has kind things to say; most likely, he or she is hiding perfect ("seven") hatred (v. 25). Such duplicity will eventually come to light. Those who lay a trap (e.g., deceive) or start a stone rolling (e.g., a rumor) will be caught by what they started (v. 27). Lies and flattery are not innocent or harmless but destroy both the victim and the oppressor (v. 28).

Chapter 27:1–10 consists of proverbs, often in pairs, without any clear overarching theme.

27:10, "do not go to the house of your kindred"—the proverb assumes that one's family ("kindred") is far away. In such a case it is vital not to forsake personal or family friends who are nearby (v. 10a). Then when calamity comes one can seek support from these friends who are nearby (v. 10c) and not a relative who is far away (v. 10b). See also 17:17; 18:24.

Reminiscent of chs. 1–9, in 27:11–22 the parent urges the child to accept wisdom (v. 11) so that the child may see the danger in what might otherwise appear to be harmless practices (v. 12). For example, persons who secure a loan for a stranger do not see the jeopardy in which they have placed themselves (v. 13). Nor does a person who rises early and speaks loud greetings ("blesses") realize that his or her action will not be appreciated (v. 14). Verses 15–16 warn the child against the danger of marrying a contentious spouse (see 12:4). On a more positive note, the parent reminds the child of the value of friendships that make a person better (v. 17) and the honor of reliable service to a superior (v. 18). The parent also provides insight into human nature. The expression on someone's face reflects the inner person ("one human heart reflects another," v. 19), and the human desire to see or experience is never satisfied (v. 20). Finally, a most telling test of character is how a person responds to praise (v. 21). However, no test or manner of correction will drive folly out of a fool (v. 22).

At first glance, 27:23–27 appears to address shepherds. Inclusion of v. 24, however, and its reference to "a crown" that does not last forever indicates that the agricultural language is being used of a king or courtier. Thus, these verses remind leaders to be attentive to the needs and condition of their people (v. 23) and the profit that comes from a well-tended populace (vv. 25–27).

Chapters 28 and 29 are given shape by several proverbs that contrast the righteous and the wicked (28:1, 12, 28; 29:2, 16, 27). The first of these proverbs compares the insecurity of the wicked with the confidence of the righteous (28:1). Recurrence of key ideas in vv. 2–11 may explain how the righteous come to have such confidence. They listen (v. 9), obey (v. 7), and do not forsake instruction (v. 4). They recognize the greater value of being blameless rather than being wealthy (vv. 6, 11). Unlike evildoers, they are discerning or understanding (vv. 2, 7, 11) and knowledgeable (v. 2). And their treatment of the poor provides evidence of their attention to instruction. They do not oppress the poor to enrich themselves (vv. 3, 8).

The next unit (28:12–28) continues to contrast the righteous and wicked (vv. 12, 28) and develops the theme of wealth and poverty. Those who truly prosper are those who confess rather than conceal their sin (vv. 13–14), hate illegitimate profit rather than charging ruthlessly over the helpless (vv. 15–16), are blameless (v. 18), trust in the Lord rather than self (vv. 25–26), and give to the poor rather than neglecting their needs (v. 27). Several verses further contrast appropriate

and effective means of acquiring wealth against ineffectual and unethical methods. On the one hand, a person who works hard (v. 19), is reliable (v. 20), has the courage to speak an honest rebuke (v. 23), trusts the Lord (25), and is generous to the poor (v. 27) will gain an abundance of food, blessing, and favor. On the other hand, those who are eager to get rich (vv. 20, 22), chase pipe dreams (v. 19), show favoritism (v. 21), are stingy (vv. 22, 27), speak only what others want to hear (v. 23), take advantage of parents for monetary gain (v. 24), and are greedy (v. 25) should expect nothing but poverty (vv. 19, 22), punishment (v. 20), and disfavor or curses (v. 27). Ultimately, it is those who trust the Lord and walk in wisdom who truly prosper (vv. 25–26).

Chapter 29:1–14 draws special attention to the contrast between what happens when the wicked are in power and when the righteous thrive (vv. 2, 16). When the wicked rule, people suffer (v. 2) because wealth is squandered (v. 3), extortion or bribery tears down the country (v. 4, NIV), concern for the poor is lacking (v. 7), mockers keep cites in an uproar (v. 8), the bloodthirsty seek to kill the upright (v. 10), and lies corrupt the government (v. 12). But when the righteous thrive, people rejoice because justice gives a country stability (v. 4), evildoers are caught by their own actions (v. 6), wisdom calms cities (v. 8) and settles the rage of fools (v. 11), and justice for the poor becomes a priority that secures the kingdom (vv. 7, 14).

The last unit of ch. 29 distinguishes between the discipline associated with righteous behavior and the consequences of the failure to administer or respond to correction (29:15–27). Accepted with humility, discipline imparts wisdom (v. 15), peace (v. 17), blessing (v. 18), and honor (v. 23). But failure to correct or a refusal to listen to instruction leads to disgrace for parents (v. 15), a lack of restraint (v. 18), insolence or disrespect (v. 21), and disgrace (v. 23).

30:1–33. The Sayings of Agur

This chapter consists of an introduction (vv. 1b–6) and conclusion (vv. 32–33), three short sayings or proverbs (vv. 10, 17, 20), three numerical sayings (vv. 7–9, 15a, 24–28), a list without numbering (vv. 11–14), and four graduated numerical sayings (x/x+1; vv. 15b–16, 18–19, 21–23, 29–31).

At times, the final item of a numerical list is the climax or key point of the saying (e.g., vv. 18–19, vv. 29–31); at other times the enumeration is for rhetorical effect—to build tension or attention (cf., 6:16–19; Amos 1:3–2:4).

30:1, "Agur son of Jakeh. An oracle."—The term *hammassa'* ("An oracle," NRSV) better designates Agur as a non-Israelite from "Massa" (RSV, NJPS, NJB, NAB), a people of North Arabia (cf. Gen 25:13–14; 1 Chr 1:29–30). Nothing else is known about this sage.

30:1–6, "The words of Agur, son of Jakeh"—with the exception of this phrase, the Hebrew of v. 1 is so difficult that commentators question the text and/or meaning of almost every word. As a result, major English translations differ significantly (cf. NRSV, NIV, NJPS, NAB, NJB, RSV). The best solution is to read v. 1 in light of the context of vv. 2–6. Agur confesses his inability to acquire genuine wisdom (vv. 2–3). He then turns to a series of rhetorical questions (cf. Job 38–39) with the only possible answer: God. God alone is the all-powerful creator (v. 4). Finally, Agur directly asserts the reliability of God's word (vv. 5–6). In view of this context, it seems best to read 1*bc* with the NRSV ("I am weary, O God") or NAB ("I am not God"). As a human, Agur's efforts to gain perfect wisdom only weary him.

30:23, "an unloved woman"—literally "a hated woman" (*shenu'ah*). The term may denote an older unmarried woman who unexpectedly marries (NRSV), or perhaps a second, unfavored wife of a polygamous home who suddenly comes to rule the house (cf. Deut 21:15–17; 1 Sam 1:1–2:10).

30:23, "a maid when she succeeds (*tirash*) her mistress"—the verb has two possible meanings: (1) to inherit (NJB) or succeed (NRSV) after the death of the mistress, or (2) to displace (NIV, NAB) or supplant (NJPS) her position in the house (e.g., Hagar and Sarah, Gen 16; 21). While either scenario is an unexpected social reversal, the second is more shocking, and thus, may be preferred here.

30:31, "the strutting rooster ... and a king striding"—the Hebrew of v. 31 is unintelligible. In line *a* most translations adopt "strutting rooster" from ancient translations and for line *b* rely on the Greek ("he harangues his people," cf. NJB) or work from the context ("a mighty lion," 31*a*)

and emend the text to read: "striding before his people" (NRSV, cf. NAB).

31:1–9. The Sayings of Lemuel

This short instruction not only comes from a non-Israelite (on "oracle" or "Massa" see 30:1), but from a woman, King Lemuel's mother, the only instruction from a woman—extant in the ancient Near East. The text consists of two warnings and two commands; it begins with warnings about sex (vv. 2–3) and alcohol (vv. 4–5). Lemuel's mother is not clear how women might destroy the king's reign (v. 3), perhaps by his own obsession with sex or manipulation by his harem. She is clear, however, about the detrimental effects of alcohol on the king's exercise of justice (vv. 4–5).

The commands correspond to the warning about alcohol. While the king should not drink to excess, he should give alcohol to those in bitter distress so that they might have relief, albeit temporary (vv. 6–7). Such advice would be cynical if not for the second command with its proactive stance on behalf of the destitute (vv. 8–9). Together these commands administer both a short-term immediate relief and a long-term solution that gets to the root of the problem—injustice. The king's power should not be for the unrestrained pursuit of luxury but for action on behalf of the unfortunate (cf. 31:20; 28:3, 15; 29:7, 14).

IV. Epilogue: Woman Wisdom as Wife (31:10–31)

An acrostic in Hebrew, starting with *'aleph* each verse begins with the next consonant of the alphabet (with *sin* and *shin* taken as one letter; the poem describes either an ideal woman or wife (so the NRSV heading "Ode to the Capable Wife") or returns the reader to the concept of Woman Wisdom from chs. 1–9 (or perhaps has both meanings in mind).

As an ideal wife, this woman is a hard worker (vv. 15, 18, 19, 27), an expert in domestic management (vv. 13–15, 21–22, 27) and commercial enterprise (vv. 16, 24), of great monetary and social benefit to her husband (vv. 11, 23), and is a wise woman who has a proper relationship to the Lord (vv. 26, 30). Her husband should acknowledge her value and is ordered to give her a share of her own profits (vv. 10, 31).

The lack of advice to women in chs. 10–31 and the rather unrealistic portrait of this woman (e.g., when does she sleep?) has led a number of commentators to identify this figure as Woman Wisdom. Many similarities exist: both Woman Wisdom and the woman of Prov 31 are more precious than jewels (3:14–15; 8:11, 19: cf. 31:10*b*); both provide security (1:33; cf. 31:21, 25), riches, and honor (3:16; 8:18, 21; cf. 31:11*b*, 13–14, 16, 23–24); and both open their mouths with wisdom (1:20; 8:1; cf. 31:26). Woman Wisdom promises that those who keep her ways will be happy (8:32) and in Prov 31 the sons of the woman call her happy (v. 28). Finally, wisdom is the fear of the Lord (1:7; 9:10) and the woman of Proverbs 31 fears the Lord (v. 10). In Prov 1–9, Wisdom appeared as a young woman seeking relationship with young men, even marriage (4:5–6). In Prov 10–31, the sages explored what life with wisdom would look like. Now, Proverbs concludes with a description of the immense benefits that derive from having an intimate marital relationship with Woman Wisdom. Such a person "will have no lack of gain" (31:11*b*).

BIBLIOGRAPHY

W. P. Brown. *Character in Crisis: A Fresh Approach to the Wisdom Literature of the Old Testament* (Eerdmans: Grand Rapids, 1996); R. J. Clifford. *Proverbs.* OTL (Louisville: Westminster John Knox, 1999); M. V. Fox. *Proverbs 1–9.* AB 18A (New York: Doubleday, 2000); L. G. Perdue. *Wisdom & Creation: The Theology of Wisdom Literature* (Nashville: Abingdon, 1994); _____. *Wisdom Literature: A Theological History.* (Louisville: Westminster John Knox, 2007); G. Von Rad. *Wisdom on Israel* (Nashville: Abingdon, 1972); R. C. Van Leeuwen. "Proverbs." NIB (Nashville: Abingdon, 1997) 5:17–264; R. N. Whybray. *Proverbs.* NCB (Grand Rapids: Eerdmans, 1994).

ECCLESIASTES

Katherine J. Dell

OVERVIEW

The book of Ecclesiastes takes its name from the Greek (LXX) translation of the Hebrew *Qoheleth* ("one who assembles"). The designation of Qoheleth in English is traditionally *Preacher*, but in the NRSV (1:1) we find *Teacher*. The book is, along with the other wisdom books (Proverbs, Job) a part of the Writings. Like Proverbs, it is attributed to Solomon. However, its language and style suggest a post-exilic origin (third century BCE is most likely, although some scholars date it to the fifth century). Like other wisdom literature, it has a timeless quality and is concerned with human experience rather than containing any reference to Israelite history. However, the persona of Solomon is an inspiration for the book, as indicated by the royal testament in 1:12–2:26. The book is basically the work of one author, although the epilogue in 12:9–14 may be added or even be a later reflection by the same author. Although Ecclesiastes' roots lie in the wisdom literature of the Old Testament, it offers a distinctive message and represents a significant development away from the optimism of Proverbs. It breaks away from belief in life's certainties and in the principle of just reward and punishment to express profound doubt and to question any principle of fairness in life. The frequent catchword *hebel, vanity* (e.g., 1:14) gives the book a pessimistic air. However there are moments of optimism—or at least realism—that create a positive/negative tension in the book. Like other wisdom books, God is portrayed as the creator and orderer of human life, and yet the author doubts whether human beings can truly apprehend that order. He sees wisdom's limitations; he notes the fleetingness and yet the value of enjoyment, the reality of hard work, and the repetitiveness of experience; he is preoccupied with the transience of life and of death as the final leveller of rich and poor, righteous and wicked alike; and he is well aware of life's ambiguities.

OUTLINE

I. The Introduction (1:1–11)

II. The Solomonic Experiment (1:12–2:6)

    A. The Quest for Wisdom (1:12–18)

    B. Solomon's Test of Pleasure (2:1–11)

    C. The Vanity of It All (2:12–26)

III. The Poem on Time (3:1–8)

IV. Musings on God (3:9–22)

V. Musings on Human Activity (4:1–6:12)

    A. Society, Toil, and Friendship (4:1–16)

    B. Proper Reverence, Money Matters, and Ultimate Contentment (5:1–20)

    C. The Futility of Life Without Enjoyment (6:1–12)

VI. Observation and Advice (7:1–9:18)

    A. Facing Human Limitations (7:1–14)

    B. Testing by Wisdom (7:15–29)

    C. King and God (8:1–17)

    D. Life and Death (9:1–18)

VII. Miscellaneous Sayings (10:1–20)

VIII. The Mystery of Life (11:1–10)

IX. The Poem on Old Age (12:1–8)

X. The Epilogue (12:9–13)

DETAILED ANALYSIS

I. The Introduction (1:1–11)

"The Teacher" (Eccl 1:1), thought to be the proper name of the author, is described as the son of David and king in Jerusalem, by inference Solomon, who succeeded to the throne of the united kingdom (1 Kgs 2:12). He was also famed for his wisdom (1 Kgs 3; 4:29–34). It seems here that the author is deliberately taking on the persona of Solomon—as becomes apparent in 1:12–2:8—

perhaps to show that he, Qoheleth, stood within the venerated tradition of wisdom. The pessimistic tone of the book is set in v. 2 with the opening phrase, "Vanity of vanities." This phrase and its variant, "All is vanity," are repeated approximately 50 times throughout the book. The Hebrew *hebel* is usually translated *vanity* (as NRSV), although *futility* and *worthlessness* are possible. The word signifies something insubstantial that is fleeting or fruitless. Qoheleth's first question (v. 3) is about human toil and what people gain from it. He infers that human toil is fruitless. The author then (vv. 4–7) comments on cycles of natural phenomena. This may mean, from the perspective of v. 3, that toilers come and go while the earth remains forever. These verses are not necessarily negative; they are simply a comment on known observations of the time. On a flat earth the sun appears to rise and disappear with nowhere to go until rising again; winds blow around on known circuits, and there is a similar cycle of rain causing streams to flow into the sea; and, since the sea is not full, the cycle must somehow go around. The cycle of human life with each generation succeeding another is a similar cycle, but changing generations contrast with the seeming permanence of the earth. In v. 8 Qoheleth seems to explore a new line of thought—that everything is wearisome. The human eye and ear are never satisfied—human beings want to see and hear new things and may think they are doing so—and yet in fact the human race has seen everything before. One has the sense here of an aged man who sees patterns being repeated. This is a variation on the idea of cycles—everything comes around again. According to v. 9 the past repeats itself in the future, and what appears new is not so in reality. In v. 10 he explores the irony of people thinking something is new and not remembering that it has gone before. The people of long ago (v. 11) are not remembered and their deeds with them, and this pattern will repeat itself in the future. People make the same mistakes over and over again and do not learn from history or their predecessors.

II. The Solomonic Experiment (1:12–2:6)

A. The Quest for Wisdom (1:12–18)

The function of a Solomonic persona is made clear. Verse 12 restates v. 1; this Qoheleth was king over Israel in Jerusalem. Qoheleth is putting himself into the role of the wise king Solomon in order to provide an experiment concerning the quest for wisdom. Wisdom is meant to be the key to understanding all that is done under heaven, but Qoheleth relativizes this statement when he describes it as an unhappy business designed by God to keep humans busy (v. 13). Qoheleth has observed others and has claimed to have seen all the deeds that are done under the sun and declared them vanity. In v. 15, Qoheleth apparently quotes a proverb, which he then relativizes. Straightening out what is crooked and numbering nothing are both impossible and, in like manner, so is his task here. The autobiographical tone resumes (v. 16)—this author, as did Solomon, acquired great wisdom and knowledge, and yet that led him to know its opposites, madness and folly. Verse 18 also looks like a quotation from the tradition, or one made up by Qoheleth to express his sentiments about the futility of seeking wisdom.

B. Solomon's Test of Pleasure (2:1–11)

The Solomonic guise continues with "a test of pleasure." He tries enjoying himself, but laughter is deemed mad and pleasure useless (v. 2). He drinks wine—for his body not his mind—trying to lay hold on folly, to see if there is any pleasure in it (v. 3). He constructs "great works" (vv. 4–6). He builds houses, vineyards, gardens, and parks full of trees. The text gives the impression of great riches, not just his property, but in his descriptions of fruit trees and his possession of slaves and herds (the markers of wealth in those days) as well as silver and gold (v. 8*a*). Singers and concubines (cf. Solomon's concubines in 1 Kgs 11:3) are also part of the attempt to gain satisfaction (v. 8*b*)—he tries entertainment, both spiritual and physical. The king's greatness was unsurpassed, his wisdom was intact, and every desire was fulfilled (vv. 9–10). He even found pleasure in all his toil. This passage is mainly positive until v. 11, which provides the relativizing statement that the toil was indeed vanity and led to no real gain under the sun.

C. The Vanity of It All (2:12–26)

The Solomonic persona continues his reflection about wisdom, madness, and folly. This is an unusual juxtaposition; normally wisdom and folly stand in opposition to one another. He resumes the theme of nothing being new—the king's successor will only do what has already been done (v. 12). He cites what appears to be a traditional proverb (v. 14) on wisdom being as preferable to folly as light to darkness. However, death relativizes everything, so what is the point of having been so very wise (v. 15)? For this author, since death is the ultimate fate, everything in human life, including all striving and toil, is rendered ultimately pointless. What distinguishes a wise man from a fool when both are dead? Neither is remembered after death (v. 16). With the inevitability of death in mind, Qoheleth says that he hated life (v. 17). There is not even a legacy of wisdom from one generation to another, for the one who follows the wise person may be a fool (vv. 18–20). He thinks specifically in terms of inheritance, the result of all his toil, which may well go to a fool who did not toil for it (v. 21). All the pain, vexation, and sleeplessness are for nothing (v. 23). There is a slight mood change (v. 24) when the author has one of his moments of optimism, celebrating eating and drinking and finding enjoyment in one's toil. This is God-given. This is the first reference to God, perhaps suggesting that God gives a person a reason to live after all—for apart from him who can eat or who can have enjoyment (v. 25)? Verse 26, another quotation from the wisdom tradition that is relativized in v. 26a, states the traditional doctrine of retribution, that to one who pleases him God will give wisdom and all good things, while, ironically, the one who displeases him will serve the very one who pleases him.

III. The Poem on Time (3:1–8)

This poem, with an almost liturgical use of repetition, illustrates Qoheleth's views on the cyclical nature of time. Human beings live out their lives according to fixed times. This poem celebrates the diversity of human life and activity. However, humans are not in control of their own destiny. These expressions of time occur mainly as opposites, such as a time for breaking down and a time for building up (v. 3). The formulations are general, as is usual in poetry—the poem does not report what is being broken down or built up. Some of the references are obscure, e.g., a time to throw away stones, and a time to gather stones together. Does this refer to demolition and rebuilding, or is it a metaphor for keeping and throwing away as in v. 6? The pair may derive from an agricultural context, i.e., clearing out stones from a

field. Verse 7b, a time to keep silence and a time to speak recalls the emphasis on communication found in Proverbs (e.g., Prov 10:14, 19).

IV. Musings on God (3:9–22)

Verse 9 echoes an earlier refrain (1:3) about the point of toil. In v. 10 the "business" described echoes 1:13, typical of repetition in this short book. Qoheleth seems to provide commentary on the poem about time—God has made everything suitable for its time (v. 11) Still, though human beings have a sense of past and future, their knowledge of God's actions from the beginning to the end of time is beyond human grasp. Qoheleth returns to the thought of enjoyment being God's gift (vv. 12–13, cf. 2:24–5) and wonders at God's works (v. 14). The permanence of God's actions stands in contrast with human transience. Qoheleth then returns (v. 15) to a cyclical view of human life, and yet here with the idea that God seeks out what has gone by, i.e., what has been forgotten. The final section of ch. 3 concerns justice. Even in a pure place—that of justice—wickedness exists (v. 16). He is probably thinking of the corruption of courts. Qoheleth knows the traditional formulation that God rewards the righteous and punishes the wicked in their due time (v. 17). He then makes a comparison between human beings and animals—their fate is the same—as one dies, so dies the other (v. 19). There appears to be no difference. Does one even know if the human spirit will rise and that of the animal descend(v. 21)? One wonders whether Qoheleth's purpose here is to downgrade human beings or whether he has a particularly high view of animals. Qoheleth concludes with the idea that all should enjoy their work—a positive note rather than the previous negative idea that toil is meaningless (cf. 2:22–3).

V. Musings on Human Activity (4:1–6:12)

A. Society, Toil, and Friendship (4:1–16)

The author airs his ideas on all kinds of human activity. He sees oppression of the weak by the powerful and concludes that those already dead are more fortunate than the living (v. 2). It is even better not to have been born at all so as never to have seen all the evil deeds that are done under the sun (v. 3). This is a moment of particular despair—this author's moods swing from one extreme to another, and in the context of oppression here he commends non-existence (cf. Job 3). This chapter contains a number of separate proverbs, probably quotations of traditional wisdom sayings. He notes that envy of another person is often a strong motivation for working (v. 4)—an apt comment on human nature but regarded by him as vanity (v. 4). Verse 5 is a proverb about the dangers of laziness (cf. Prov 19:15, 24)—fools are so lazy they metaphorically eat their own flesh rather than going out to gather food. Verse 6 is a proverb that recommends peace and quiet over toil. These two proverbs contradict one another and create a tension, in this case the truth that work is a necessity but moderation is best and doing no work leads ultimately to ruin. Qoheleth enjoys reflecting about particular cases, e.g., persons with no siblings or descendants (vv. 7–8). Their motivation for toil is personal riches, but they deprive themselves of pleasure in their life and will have no one to whom to pass on this gain. Qoheleth understands this as vanity and an unhappy business (v. 8). This comment contradicts Qoheleth's view that there is no point in toiling since a person will not enjoy the fruits of labor after death (2:21). Verses 9–12 contain a final musing on toil in the context of friendship. Qoheleth decides that two is better than one (this follows on from consideration of the loner in verses 7–8). With two, one can lift up and help the other (v. 10); two can keep each other warm (v. 11); and two are stronger against an enemy (v. 12). The image of a threefold cord in verse 12b reinforces the point—the thicker the cord, the stronger it is. Verses 13–16 contain another test case; this time a poor but wise youth is compared with an old but foolish king. Qoheleth infers that in time the wise youth becomes the foolish king despite the initial hope in the youth—everything comes around.

B. Proper Reverence, Money Matters, and Ultimate Contentment (5:1–20)

Qoheleth turns his attention to Temple life and warns that a cautious listening is better than rushing in with a sacrifice as fools do (v. 1), for they do not know how to keep from doing evil. As in the prophets (e.g., Amos 4:4–5) right living is more important than the offering of sacrifice. Qoheleth gives a different reason for speaking carefully chosen works than does traditional wisdom (cf. Prov 10:19). He draws a sharp contrast between God in his heaven and humans upon earth, expressing his sense of the otherness of God before whom few words should be spoken. The importance of actually fulfilling vows to God is pursued in vv. 4–6. Words and dreams seem to be associated in vv. 3 and 7—he is clearly against too much daydreaming. Dreams probably come from people's own imaginations—better to fear God (v. 7). Verse 8 provides another test case—the author describes injustice and is not surprised to see corruption at the highest level. Verse 9 quotes a proverb that seems to advocate the presence of a king, the highest power in the land. His theme then changes to money, appearing again to cite proverbial wisdom. Money does not ultimately satisfy; it is vanity (v. 10). Verse 11 states the point that increased wealth never goes as far as expected—the cost of acquiring it has to be offset against the gain from it. Increased wealth brings anxiety (v. 12). An ordinary laborer does not have such worries—he sleeps peaceably while the surfeit of the rich will not let them sleep. Another test case appears in vv. 13–17—that of parents who lose all their money and have nothing to pass on—as they came from their mother's womb, so they shall go again (v. 15). Qoheleth disapproves since it makes a mockery of all the work they have done and causes them much vexation (v. 17). In the final verses of ch. 5, Qoheleth summarizes his view that eating, drinking, and enjoying one's work are keys to contentment in human life (v. 18). Money is a gift of God (v. 19), if one is able to enjoy it and not look to it for ultimate satisfaction.

C. The Futility of Life Without Enjoyment (6:1–12)

Qoheleth is concerned about evil in the world, again using test cases to make his points. He starts (v. 2) with the wealthy person who has everything, but is unable to enjoy it all. He is concerned that a stranger enjoys them, perhaps after the person's death. His next thought is of someone who has had many descendants and a long life—again if it has not been an enjoyable life, it was not worth living. The absence of a burial (v. 3) may indicate a convicted criminal or simply that at death some people are not honored. Better is a stillborn child who has not seen the sun or known anything (vv. 3–4). Life is about enjoyment, and death is the fate of all (v. 6). In v. 7–9 he airs a few of life's ironies; e.g., in v. 7, humans toil for food but the appetite is never satisfied. This could be a metaphor for never being satisfied with enough money. Qoheleth's cyclical view of life seems to reappear in v. 10; whatever has come to be has already been named. Presumably this means named by God. In v. 11 he seems to tire of words and wonders how anyone knows what is good for mortals in their short lives (v. 12). The inference is perhaps that God does know, but humans do not. The phrase "like a shadow" (v. 12) indicates that human beings are dim figures to be likened to shadows that are fleeting and impermanent.

VI. Observation and Advice (7:1–9:18)

A. Facing Human Limitations (7:1–14)

This chapter opens with a string of proverbs. Qoheleth nevertheless puts them in a new framework and relativizes traditional wisdom ideas. His choice of proverbs is a pessimistic one, favouring reputation over precious items, death over birth (v. 1), and mourning over feasting, all in the light of death (v. 2). Awareness of death colors his approach to life so that he commends sorrow and sadness rather than excessive laughter—the heart of the wise is in the house of mourning, but the heart of fools is in the house of mirth (v. 4). A number of proverbs warn against fools and their song (v. 5) and laughter (v. 6). Traditional wisdom themes continue: human beings are easily corrupted (v. 7); patience is better than pride (v. 8); beware of anger (v. 9); don't spend your time looking back (v. 10). In a moment of optimism, he moves on to praise wisdom over all things (vv. 11–12)—it protects and ultimately gives life. All things are the work of God, both good and bad; and human beings cannot change anything (vv. 13–14).

B. Testing by Wisdom (7:15–29)

Qoheleth continues his commentary on different types of people, following the traditional wisdom distinction between the righteous and the wicked (v. 15). However, he advises not being over-righteous or its opposite. Humans live in a tension between opposites, and the fear of God is at the heart of it all (v. 18). Wisdom gives strength (v. 19), but no one is so righteous as to have never sinned (v. 20). Furthermore one should make allowances to people who may talk about you behind your back—your heart knows that many times you have yourself cursed others (v. 22). Wisdom is not easily attainable (vv. 23–25, 27). In v. 26 he echoes Proverbs 6:20–7:27 in his description of a woman who ensnares men. Qoheleth claims that he has found one man among a thousand, but not a woman. It is not clear whether he means a righteous man or woman or something else. Could this be an echo of Solomon and his thousand women as mentioned in 1 Kgs 11:3? If so, it is more of a warning to men about their attitude to women.

C. King and God (8:1–17)

Qoheleth begins by extolling wisdom (v. 1). He then moves (vv. 2–5) to consider the king (cf. Prov 15). He is aware of the immense and unchallengeable power that the king wields. The wise person will need to steer a careful path with the king as in all life. Verse 6 echoes the poem on time. Human lack of power in general receives comment—humans cannot tell the future (unlike God is the inference) (v. 7), nor can they control elements, the timing of events, or indeed effect deliverance (v. 8). Qoheleth muses on the enigma that, almost inevitably, one person's authority leads to another's hurt (v. 9). He goes on to talk about the wicked and their dissembling (v. 10) and regrets that the human heart is fully set to do evil (v. 11). His view of human nature is pessimistic. Yet, unlike the wicked, those who fear God will have nothing to fear (v. 13). Another irony is that righteousness is sometimes mistaken for wickedness and vice versa. He repeats his injunction to enjoy life in (v. 15). Verses 16–17 express the thought that only God knows his work, and humans will continue to seek but never find it (cf. Job 28).

D. Life and Death (9:1–18)

Qoheleth sees the usual categories of righteous and wise people, and he notes that only God knows what is truly in their hearts. Human beings, whether righteous or wicked, suffer the same fate. This irony of life makes one question the worth of good behavior. However, Qoheleth ultimately decides that life is better than death. The living know that they will die, unlike the dead who know nothing, have no reward, and of whom no memory lasts (vv. 5–6). Qoheleth is more positive concerning joy in life (v. 7). He elaborates on the wearing of white garments, a sign of joy since white was reserved for special festive occasions, and on enjoying one's wife (v. 9). He mentions Sheol (v. 10), the place of the dead; there will be no work to do there. He airs the thought (v. 11) that while human beings would like there to be certainties (e.g., the fastest person wins the race), it is not always so. Time and chance happen to all. Disaster can strike quickly, like a net for a fish or like birds caught in a snare (v. 12). The final part of ch. 9 contains a story of a poor wise man who saved the city by his wisdom, and yet he was not remembered. So, though wisdom is better than might, since this man was not heeded it puts a different gloss on wisdom's value. The chapter ends with several traditional proverbs on the importance of quiet words by the wise rather than shouting from a ruler and on wisdom's worth over weapons of war (v. 18).

VII. Miscellaneous Sayings (10:1–20)

This collection of maxims is akin to that found in Proverbs. The author may have borrowed some and created others. Much of it reads like traditional wisdom, but Qoheleth juxtaposes proverbs in order to highlight contradictions, unafraid to add his own comment. There is much preoccupation with wisdom and folly (vv. 1–3). Verse 4 highlights the anger of rulers—power is dangerous and it is better to sit tight and let the anger pass. In v. 5 Qoheleth bewails the apparent disorder of society's hierarchy—folly sits in many high places, and the rich sit in a low place. Living life is a dangerous exercise (vv. 8–9); even physical exercise has its risks. Blunt tools need more strength (v. 10). Such sayings are truisms about life. Concern about communication returns (vv. 12–14) with a depiction of fools who talk on and on. Qoheleth enjoys painting a picture of the unwitting fool (v. 15). Verses 16–17 concern the relationship of king to land—the proper hierarchy is the right order of things. Verse 18 condemns sloth, a common proverbial theme (e.g., Prov 10:26). Verse 19 speaks of the need for gladness and makes a positive statement about money as necessary. The danger of speaking out against people—especially the king—is aired in v. 20. It is surprising how words carry!

VIII. The Mystery of Life (11:1–10)

The chapter opens with a short series of proverbs. The first two (vv. 1–2) concern keeping options open—send out your bread upon the waters is probably a metaphor for spreading the risk, as in dividing one's means. The second two (vv. 3–4) are about the ways of nature, including tips about farming—clouds spilling their rain, trees falling, not sowing on a windy day, and not reaping when rain is due. Qoheleth wonders (v. 5) at the mystery of life given to an unborn child—a mystery at that time and likened to the mysterious purposes of God. Spreading risk comes back as a theme in an agricultural context (v. 6). In v. 7, Qoheleth observes that it is pleasant for the eyes to see the sun, which stands in contrast with the long years of darkness when dead. The commendation of enjoyment is reiterated. A note of judgment is also sounded—youth should not be irresponsibile. He decides (v. 10) that youth is a vanity after all—he also advises not worrying and ignoring pain.

IX. The Poem on Old Age (12:1–8)

In contrast to youth, the author now turns to figurative descriptions of old age. Human life is on an inevitable cycle from youth to old age to death. The trembling guards of the house (v. 3) symbolize shaking limbs; the strong men bent reflect the stooped posture of some aged people. The women who grind may refer to teeth that fall out. Seeing dimly may well be a reference to the eyes dimming with age. Verse 4 probably alludes to the dead of night when elderly people are often awake, their need for sleep diminished. The daughters of song (v. 4) may refer to what one can no longer hear. Verse 5 concerns being more fearful when older. The almond tree blossoming may refer to the hair going white, as the almond tree does when it flowers. The image of a grasshopper dragging itself along indicates weak legs, perhaps painful movement or a broken limb, or it may indicate overeating (which is the only time a grasshopper appears to drag itself along). Sexual desire fades too; ultimately death is in store. Images of brokenness (v. 6) describe the descent to death (cords, bowls, pitchers, and wheels, which can all be broken). The silver cord and golden bowl (possibly an oil lamp suspended by a cord) may indicate former glory and riches, its recipient brought low by sickness and finally death. In v. 7 a distinction is made between the dust and the breath, an interesting dualism, atypical of the Hebrew Bible. The dust represents the body and the breath returns to God. Qoheleth concludes the chapter with his usual refrain about life as vanity.

X. The Epilogue (12:9–13)

Beginning in v. 9 Qoheleth is no longer speaking, but is spoken of in the third person. Qoheleth is described as not only wise but as having taught many things. He took care over the words he used and wrote words of truth plainly. He may have taught in a school; he was an educator and steeped in the wisdom tradition. However, he was not afraid to question the essential elements in that tradition. In v. 11 wise sayings are praised as fixed points and derive from "one shepherd," a phrase that may refer to God. The work ends on a note of there being too many books written and study itself being a weariness of the flesh (v. 12). There is also a pious note—fear God and keep his commandments, cf. 3:14. The author sees God as holding the key to all understanding and being in a position to judge every deed (v. 14). Trusting in God is thus good, pragmatic advice, as has been the character of this short, yet profound book.

BIBLIOGRAPHY

E. S. Christianson. *A Time to Tell: Narrative Strategies in Ecclesiastes.* JSOTS 280 (Sheffield: Sheffield Academic Press, 1998); J. L. Crenshaw. *Ecclesiastes.* OTL (Philadelphia: Westminster, 1988); K. J. Dell. "Ecclesiastes as Wisdom: Consulting Early Interpreters." *VT* 44 (1994) 301–29; M. V. Fox. "Frame Narrative and Composition in the Book of Qoheleth." *HUCA* 48 (1977) 83–106; _____. *A Time to Tear Down and A Time to Build Up: A Rereading of Ecclesiastes* (Grand Rapids: Eerdmans, 1999); T. Krüger. *Qoheleth.* Hermeneia (Minneapolis: Augsburg Fortress, 2004); E. P. Lee. *The Vitality of Enjoyment in Qoheleth's Theological Rhetoric.* BZAW 353 (Berlin: Walter de Gruyter, 2005); N. Lohfink. *Qoheleth. A Continental Commentary* (Minneapolis: Augsburg Fortress, 2003); C. Seow. *Ecclesiastes.* AB 18C (New York: Doubleday, 1997); R. N. Whybray. *Ecclesiastes.* NCB (London: Marshall, Morgan and Scott, 1989).

SONG OF SONGS

FRED W. DOBBS-ALLSOPP

OVERVIEW

The Song of Songs is a collection of lyric poems that celebrates human love. It features the voices of two lovers, a girl and boy, and their professions of love for one another (the description "girl" and "boy" convey the youth and inexperience of the lovers). At times the two voices join in dialogue (e.g., 1:9–17; 2:1–7), while at others they speak separately, addressing each other or the girl's companions, the "daughters of Jerusalem." The title, "Song of Songs" (*shir hashshirim*) is a superlative construction in Hebrew, i.e., "the most sublime of songs," like "king of kings" (Dan 2:37). However, the phrase may be taken more literally still as "a song of (many) songs," suggesting a collection or anthology of songs. The sequence as a whole exhibits cohesiveness, and yet the multiple poems or fragments of poems require the reader to negotiate the junctures and disjunctions between the poems.

Structurally, the Song remains stubbornly open and idiosyncratic. There is some intentional shaping of the sequence's beginning and end. It starts with the voice of the girl yearning for her lover, followed by fragments of poems. Only in ch. 2, especially with the ode-like celebration of springtime (2:8–17), does one begin to encounter the articulated poems that comprise the main body of the collection (e.g., 3:1–5; 4:1–7; 5:2–6:3; 6:4–10). The sequence then seems to unravel, much as it started, among fragments and bits of poems (esp. 8:5–14). In its last lines, readers once again hear the girl's voice, and thus the collection ends very much as it began. Aside from this overarching movement, the Song resists all attempts to map, paraphrase, or otherwise reduce to logical or thematic content. What stands out most conspicuously, then, are the individual poems and peak moments whose effects are mostly ephemeral. Whatever underlying structure there is reveals itself organically as the poems wind their way from one peak moment to the next. In the end, this kind of lyrical structure invites and even necessitates readerly focus on single fragments and individual poems.

This love poetry has ancient parallels in the Mesopotamian sacred marriage texts and in Egyptian love poetry. Moreover, Isaiah of Jerusalem uses a love poem in his "Song of the Vineyard" (Isa 5:1–7). And the editor(s) of the Psalter, who created the various psalmic superscriptions, know about love songs (Ps 45:1; cf. Ezek 33:32).

The date of the Song is debated. There is nothing in the poems that ties them to a specific historical setting. The language, including Aramaisms and Persian loanwords, strongly suggests a relatively late date, sometime between the fourth and second century BCE. The Song, either in whole or in its several component poems, may have had some prehistory (oral or written). Later Jewish and Christian interpreters eventually appropriated the Song for explicitly religious purposes by way of allegory, explaining the relationship between the two lovers as if it referred to the relationship between God and Israel or Christ and the church (or the individual believer). Ironically, such claims bring the Song closer to the ways in which the poetry of love in Mesopotamia was most commonly staged, through the voices of gods and goddesses or the king and divine consort.

The allegorical tradition of reading the Song is a strategy imposed on the text. That is, there is nothing within the Song itself or within the tradition of love poetry from the ancient Mediterranean world that requires (or authorizes) such a strategy of reading. Allegories tend to prescribe a particular interpretation and are normally not very subtle (e.g., 2 Sam 12:1–7; Isa 5:1–7). Yet there is nothing allegorical about the Song and no textual, historical, or cultural warrant for reading it allegorically. The Song, like much ancient Egyptian love poetry, is what it appears to be, a celebration of the love of two flesh-and-blood people.

OUTLINE

I. Superscription (1:1)

II. First Poem (1:2–4)

Detailed Analysis

I. Superscription (1:1)

The initial line of the Song is often construed as assigning authorship to Solomon—"the Song of Songs, by Solomon" (NJV). However, it was common practice in antiquity to attribute authorship to a well-known figure (e.g., David [Pss 3:1; 4:1], Solomon [Prov 1:1]). The line is most likely an editorial superscription. The ascription to Solomon is not totally unmotivated since he is mentioned (possibly) a half-dozen other times in the Song (1:5; 3:7, 9, 11; 8:11, 12).

II. First Poem (1:2–4)

The Song opens with the love affair in full bloom. The first poem is voiced by the girl and consists of two brief stanzas (vv. 2–3 and 4), each beginning and ending with like sounds or the same words. The whole is shaped through repetitions (e.g., the eightfold occurrence of the second person pronominal suffix), wordplays and puns, and an intermingling of pronominal references that all but defies logical ordering. These combine to express the girl's desire and the topsy-turvy world of young love.

1:2. In the phrase "let him kiss me with kisses" (*yishaqeni minneshiqoth*) verb and object share the same Hebrew root, which allows for some pleasant alliterating and redoubles the depth of the desire named. The addition of the last word in the line, "his mouth," signals hyperbole; first love and young love by its nature must be over the top, the very definition of hyperbole. It also elicits a play in the Hebrew between the verbs for kissing (*nshq*) and drinking (*shqh*; cf. 8:1–2). The longing here is for the deep-throated kiss of lovers that can only be gulped greedily for fear that the thirst (for love) will be too quickly quenched. The second line of the couplet cinches the play as the best wine is used as the standard of comparison. This "love" is to be tasted, smelled, felt, and ultimately praised and reveled in (v. 4). "Wine" is the drink most emphatically associated with lovemaking in the Song (1:2, 4; 2:4; 4:10; 5:1; 7:9; 8:2).

1:3. The extolling of the fine "fragrance" of the boy's "anointing oils" plays on the designation for the finest virgin olive oil (esp. 2 Kgs 20:13=Isa 39:2) Olive oil was a chief staple of the ancient Levant and was used for many purposes, including to oil skin and hair. "Poured out" (NRSV) measures the depth of the girl's longing for her lover by the image of expensive oil being poured out. The "maidens" (NRSV) are either the girl's companions, who are more commonly referred to as a the "daughters of Jerusalem" (e.g., 1:5), or some non-specified other young women who potentially pose a threat to the lovers.

1:4. The string of first common plural verb forms ("let us ... we will ... we will") gives some cohesion to the stanza. The "king," i.e., the boy (also in 1:12 and 7:6)—is, perhaps, a pet name or an erotic fantasy, though the royal motif is significant throughout the sequence of poems. *Extol* (NRSV), or more technically, *savor* (as in the breathing in of burnt offerings, cf. Lev 24:7; Isa 66:3; Ps 20:4), evokes the senses.

III. Second Poem (1:5–8)

In moving to the second poem, the reader notices that nothing joins the two poems, except voice, which in 1:5–6 is finally identified clearly as female, and the tone, which is self-assertive and exuberant, but also light and playful. Reference to Solomon (v. 5) continues the royal motif. The poem breaks into two main sections, vv. 5–6 and vv. 7–8. The first section features the voice of the girl addressing her girlfriends and extolling the beauty of her sun-darkened skin. The second section of the poem highlights the banter of the two lovers. That the lovers are in conversation is significant, because Egyptian love poetry, by contrast, is almost all monologic. In the Song, readers are treated to (at least) two different views about love.

1:5. The phrase "I am black and beautiful," is affirmative, not apologetic. The girl extols the beauty of her own sun-darkened skin. The girl's blackness is clearly identified within the poem as resulting from exposure to the sun as she tended the vineyards. She is emboldened by the reassuring knowledge that she and her blackness are loved by the boy (who addresses her as "most beautiful of women," v. 8). The boast, then, is the healthy braggadocio of one newly in love and eager to share her happiness.

The first person pronoun is used only by the girl in the Song (1:5, 6: 2:1, 5,16; 5:2, 5, 6, 8; 6:3; 7:11; 8:10) and effectively centers the Song's discourse on her.

The reference to "the tents of Kedar" is wonderfully multivalent. *Tents* could refer literally to the tents themselves (if they are made in Bedouin fashion, from the wool of black goats), or intended as a metonym for the Kedarites, a North Arabian nomadic tribe. The Hebrew root (*qdr*) itself implies "darkness" (esp. Sir 25:17).

1:6. The language throughout these lines is layered with plays, puns, and double entendre. One example is "they were angry with me" (from *kharah*), which may also be read as "they burned against me" (from *kharakh*), playing on the scorching sun that burns the skin.

"Mother's sons" is a synonym for "brother" (Gen 27:29; Deut 13:7; Ps 50:20) and serves as a counterpoint to the earlier "daughters of Jerusa-

lem." The girl says, "They made me keeper," a task typical for older children in a family. The term *vineyard* is used here (as elsewhere) both literally (cf. 7:12)—vineyards were conventional settings for love in ancient love poetry—and figuratively as an image for the girl herself (esp. 4:12–5:1; 6:2), and as a symbol of female sexuality (cf. 8:12).

1:7. The imagery shifts from vineyards to shepherding. The girl speaks first in a mock pout, wondering where her lover grazes his flocks that she may join him during the afternoon siesta—"noon" in warm climates is a time for rest and repose, and thus convenient for an amorous tryst.

1:8. The boy stands his ground, replying that if she truly does not know—and of course he implies that she *does* know—then she should go right ahead and "pasture" her "kids" among his companions' flocks. She is here imagined as a shepherdess, but *kids* may signify figuratively the girl's breasts, as with the *gazelles* and *fawns* in 4:5 and 7:3.

IV. Third Poem (1:9–17)

Dialogue dominates the next several poems. This poem has three stanzas of six lines apiece. In the first stanza (vv. 9–11), the boy's voice carries over from the end of the last poem. He uses the image of a fine mare fitted out with decorative bridle and halter to express the girl's beauty (cf. 1:5). By way of response (vv. 12–14), the girl imagines wearing her kingly lover as a "bag of myrrh." The whole stanza is shot through with references to the pleasing and alluring scents of exotic spices and flowers. The final stanza (vv. 15–17) features the couple's mirrored exclamations of admiration and ends with reference to their union—"our couch ... our house ... our rafters."

1:9. The point of comparing the girl to a "mare among Pharaoh's chariots" affords an image of fierce beauty (a literary commonplace) and also her sexual allure. The chariotry is made up of only stallions, and a mare in their midst would cause a stir. The simile takes its point of departure in the harness and other fineries with which the finest royal horses were commonly fitted out, and thus suggests the girl's bejewled head and neck. "My love" is the boy's preferred term of endearment for the girl (1:9, 15; 2:2, 10, 13; 4:1, 7; 5:2; 6:4).

1:10–11. The imagery of ornaments and jewels may well have both mare and girl in mind.

1:12–14. Nard and myrrh are fragrant spices; henna is the aromatic flower of the cypress. The spices complement the gold and silver, just as imaging the boy as king echoes the identification of the chariotry as belonging to Pharaoh. *My beloved*, which plays on the term for lovemaking (see esp. 7:8–14), is the girl's pet name for the boy, occurring more than two dozen times in the Song.

"En-gedi," an oasis on the western shore of the Dead Sea, literally means, *kid-fountain*, a pun that confirms the earlier erotic metaphor of *kids* (1:5).

1:15–17. The boy's and the girl's professions of admiration mirror each other. One of the lovers plays on the phrasing or imagery used by the other.

The rock dove's dark upper torso and characteristic head-bobbing symbolize the sparkle and aliveness of the girl's dark irises set against the white of the eye (cf. 5:12).

V. Fourth Poem (2:1–7)

This poem continues the dialogic form of the last several poems. The first section (vv. 1–3) is comprised of flattering compliments in which each lover builds on the language of the other and suffuses it with images of fragrant flowers and fruit trees. The second section (vv. 4–6) shifts scenes. Now the girl finds herself in a "house of wine" and sick "with love." The poem closes (v. 7) with an adjuration addressed to the girl's companions (cf, Song 3:1–5; 8:1–4). The poem is highly fragmented, with only a few words (*apple tree/ apples, love/love/love*) and phrases (*I am/I am, so is among/so is among*) providing a sense of a larger whole.

2:1. The nature of the girl's self-appraisal here— whether boastful or self-deprecating—is unclear. *The Sharon* probably refers specifically to the fertile coastal plain of Israel.

2:2–3. The alternating compliments intentionally mirror one another. There is no ambiguity about the boy's intentions. He takes up the image of the lily, and by contrasting it to the noxious *bramble*, he makes clear his own sense of his beloved's singular brilliance. *Maidens* likely means *young women* (of marriageable age).

2:3. It is the girl's turn to speak again. This time she fashions her own eroticized comparison. The Hebrew term routinely translated *apple* (*thapuakh*) likely refers to the apricot or possibly even the quince, as both are indigenous to the greater Levant. But whether apple, apricot, or quince, the erotic symbolism of the fruit is not in doubt (2:5; 7:9), nor are the girl's ambitions. In Mesopotamia, the male lover is frequently symbolized and imagined (most phallically) as what is conventionally glossed as an *apple tree*.

2:4. "Banqueting house" (lit. *house of wine*) is a unique term in the Bible. Given the erotic associations of wine in the Song, it surely means to allude to another of the couple's trysting places (as in 1:17).

2:5. Raisins and apples were thought to have aphrodisiac qualities; hence the rich fruit is symbolic of lovemaking. Beyond an expression of affection or tender feeling, the term *love* refers as well more specifically to the act of lovemaking (so also in 2:7; cf. Jer 2:33; Prov 5:19).

2:6. The girl's wish, "O, that his left hand were under my head and his right hand embraced me!" is similar to an Old Assyrian love spell in which the girl is rendered "lovesick" and unable to "rest" until her neck is "entwined" with her lover's. Love is the cause of the girl's malady, and more love is its only cure.

2:7. "By the gazelles or the wild does" stands here in place of an oath sworn in the name of the deity. In the naturalistic vernacular of the poetry, the *gazelles* and *wild does* are emblems of love (this is especially clear for the gazelle, which appears in 2:9, 17 and 8:14 with reference to the boy and in 4:5 with reference to the girl's breasts). Thus, the girl swears by her love instead of her god. The final couplet (repeated in 3:5 and 8:4) may be taken as a warning about arousing *love* prematurely or unmindfully.

VI. Fifth Poem (2:8–17)

Up to this point in the Song, the poems have a pronounced sense of fragmentation about them. Only with this ode-like celebration of springtime love does the reader begin to encounter more perceptibly articulated poems. The beloved's coming and going as a gazelle, at beginning and end, effectively frames the poem, and the fivefold repetition of "my beloved" (vv. 8, 9, 10, 16, 17) and the interlacing of animal imagery (gazelle, dove, jackal) help join the stanzas (vv. 8–9, 10–13, 14, 15, 16–17) into a whole.

2:8–9. The first stanza invokes the experience of sighting a shy and skittery gazelle, almost as if it has been conjured by the oath at the end of the previous poem. The abbreviated lines and choice of active verbs convey the characteristic speed and agility of the gazelle.

2:8. The gazelle is the male lover. The girl first hears his approach— as "the voice of my beloved." She catches sight of him ("look, he comes!") leaping and bounding playfully in the distance. A palpable sense of excitement and expectation courses through these opening lines.

2:9. And then just as suddenly ("look, there he stands!"), the gazelle/lover appears at the wall of the family compound, peering in at the girl as she is peering out at him. The woman-in-the-window is a common motif in ANE art. The poet transforms this motif (cf. Judg 5:28; 2 Kgs 9:30), allowing readers to see both the girl and the boy as they are framed for each other by the window.

2:10–13. The second stanza is framed by the words "Arise, my darling, my fair one, and come away" (vv. 10, 13). This is the only time in the Song where any direct discourse is introduced formally (v. 10), perhaps because it is unequivocally the girl's telling of what the boy said to her. The entire poem, after all, is written from the perspective of the girl. He beckons her to join him, enticing her through a beautifully evocative depiction of the awakening of spring, a perennial time of love.

2:11–13. Winter is the rainy season in Palestine, usually ending in mid-April. Spring, the time described in these verses, arrives with flowers blossoming, figs and vines blooming, and migrant birds reappearing.

2:14–15. The next two stanzas (vv. 14 and 15) feature animal figures. In the first (v. 14), the girl is imagined as a "dove," literalizing the boy's term of endearment for her (*my dove*, cf 5:2; 6:9), and thereby figuring her inaccessibility (cf. 7:8). The wild rock dove, common to the region, nests in rocky crags, in part, to stay out of reach of predators, such as a fox or jackal. But in this case, the

metaphorical cliffs also stand in for the wall and house that keep the boy out of reach of his beloved.

There follows in v. 15 an apostrophe imploring the capture of the scavenging foxes or, as likely, jackals, before they *ruin* the vineyards. The vineyards of ancient Palestine were walled and guarded for just this reason. Possibly the dove and gazelle are in danger too as prey. The *blossoming vineyards* recall the girl's earlier reference to her budding sexuality (1:6) and more immediately to the blossoming vines of spring (v. 13). There is something of a tease, then, in these lines, especially if heard as voiced by the girl—far from being inaccessible, her sexuality (*our vineyards*) is in full bloom and in danger of being raided by others (i.e., jackals).

2:14. The girl's next lines may be heard as a response to the "voice" (v. 8) and then "sound" (vv. 10–13) of her lover and as the "voice" that the boy so desires to hear (v. 14). These "voicings," then, join in with the other "voices"/"sounds" of spring (v. 12) to form a virtual chorus.

2:16–17. The final section of the poem begins again with reference to the girl's lover and reprises the gazelle and stag imagery from vv. 8–9, though this time as a plea for the boy to leave at the coming of dawn.

2:16. The mutual pledge of love echoes ANE marriage and adoption formulas. *His flock* of the NRSV is an overly literal translation that stresses only one of the senses of this line: the image of the boy as shepherd. The Hebrew is more nuanced. "He pastures among the lilies" intimates the erotic and provocative image of the lover himself, grazing among the lilies, the choicest and most delicate portion of the pasturage, i.e., the girl herself.

2:17. As the shadows of night recede, the beloved, imagined (again) as a "gazelle," is warned to flee. The NRSV's *turn* is overliteral; the Hebrew imperative focuses on the lover's "becoming like a gazelle." The bounding and skipping *gazelle/ young stag* which came up to the window at the poem's beginning, must go back from where he came.

VII. Sixth Poem (3:1–5)

This poem features a nighttime search for the beloved. The opening line (lit. "on my bed in the nights") cues readers to think of their meeting as occurring nightly. Indeed, in coming to the poem from what precedes it, a narrative-minded reader might well imagine the girl by her window waiting night after night for another sighting of her gazelle-like lover. This impulse toward story is aided by an obvious narrativity that infuses these verses. Its base story-line may be simply stated: the girl, desiring her absent lover, searches the city for him and eventually finds him, though not before she herself is found by the nightwatch. She seizes him and brings him to her mother's house. At this point the story breaks off, and the poem ends with the girl adjuring her girlfirends (as in 2:7 and 8:4).

3:1. The transition from the first ("upon my bed nightly") to the second line ("I seek him whom my soul loves") is all important, as it disturbs from the outset any straightforward narrative construal. Is the girl dreaming or thinking to herself, longing for her lover? Does she actually leave her bed to search for her lover? Or is it all imagined? None of these questions can be answered definitively and thus should serve as the reader's initial cue that something more than a charming story is afoot.

3:2–4. The heart of the story (such as it is) unfolds through iteration. Almost all of the language (e.g., "him whom my soul loves") is repeated, as many as four times over. There are even some phrases repeated from 2:8–17 (*to arise, to go around*). Two times the girl seeks her lover but cannot find him. The third time (typical of stories) also fails, as the girl is herself "found" by the nightwatch, who, like her, go "about in the city." They offer no reply to her query about her lover's whereabouts, and it is only after this last encounter that she finally finds "him whom her soul loves." She seizes him and "does not let him go." The phrasing "my mother's house" (cf. 8:2) is striking. Its rarity (occurring elsewhere only in Gen 24:28 and Ruth 1:8) deviates from the otherwise ubiquitous designation "house of the father." When set alongside the Song's other furtive mentions of the girl's mother (1:6; 6:9; 8:1, 2, 5), the poet's references to motherhood begin to seem less accidental, perhaps flavoring the Song with an awareness of a social reality in which women had an important role in family life and household decisions, a notion that comports with the important role of the female voice throughout the Song.

3:5. But whatever more happens is left to the reader's imagination, with only a bit of prompting from the closing address to her girlfriends—not to arouse or disturb love (v. 5). The constant repetition of seeking and finding (or not finding) articulates well the basic nature of human love and desire.

VIII. Seventh Poem: Solomon's Wedding Procession (3:6–11)

Solomon's wedding procession. Elsewhere in the Song, the boy is imagined as a royal figure (1:4, 12; cf. 7:6), even as Solomon (1:5; 8:11, 12). So there is no reason not to think that in this passage too the reference is to the boy—the king, after all, is one of the major personas in Mesopotamian love poetry. In this instance, the royal motif may have been chosen for its "sexual allure." Royal rhetoric in the Bible, as in Mesopotamia, occasionally presents the body of the king as alluring, desirable, beautiful (e.g., 1 Sam 16:12; Ps 45:3). Indeed, Solomon is heralded as a paradigmatic lover (e.g., 1 Kgs 11:3). The poem itself falls into three uneven parts. The first stanza (v. 6) is comprised of a rhetorical question, "who is this?" which the long middle stanza (vv. 7–10) answers (rhetorically, if not otherwise). The poem concludes in v. 11 with an apostrophe (this one addressed to the "daughters of Zion"), a favored closing gesture (cf. 2:7; 3:5; 8:4).

3:6. The Hebrew term rendered here as *coming up* is commonly used to designate travel to Jerusalem. It is a homonym of the Hebrew noun for "whole burnt offering." Thus, the image of the procession, viewed from afar, appears as a column of smoke—like one would associate with sacrifice and the burning of incense—winding its way up the mountainous approach to Jerusalem. The allusions to sacrifice lend the scene an otherworldly and spiritual appearance as well. The aromas, *myrrh* and *frankincense*, have associations with the cult and trade, and also with love (cf. 4:6; 5:13).

3:7–8. At one level, the image of the royal retinue is realistic and projects onto the boy a strong sense of masculine desirability. The bed, if a *litter* (so NRSV) by the logic of v. 6, is also just an ordinary *bed* (2 Kgs 4:10)—a place for sleeping or love. Whatever more may be intended by the mention of the "alarms in the night," it injects a sense of unease or foreboding, which often accompanies the Song's darker tonalities (e.g., 5:7; 8:5–7).

3:9–10. The fineness of Solomon's wedding bed is invoked (Amos 6:4; Esth 1:6). Indeed, it is not uncommon for the aesthetic appeal of the love bed to be stressed (e.g., 1:16–17; Prov 7:16–17).

3:11. The mention of the "wedding day" here (and the allusion in 8:8) recalls that bridal songs were a popular genre of love poetry in Mesopotamia. Although the Song's celebration of love is not staged with marriage narrowly in view, marriage, children, and a continuing life lived among family and kin would have been the normal horizon of expectation for young lovers.

IX. Eighth Poem (4:1–7)

This poem (see also 5:10–16; 6:4–10; 7:1–7) prefigures the later Arabic *wasf,* a poem or a section of a poem that elaborates an extended description of a person or other object. Sung in the voice of the male lover, it proclaims the beauty of the girl he loves. The opening and closing couplets (vv, 1*a*, 7), which form an inclusio, plainly express the poem's sole preoccupation: "Wow! You are so beautiful, my love/ Wow! You are so beautiful!" (v. 1*a*).

The structure of the poem is very intentional. Its main body is divided into two symmetrical halves (vv. 1*b*–2, 3–4). In the first section, an aspect of the woman's beauty —"your eyes," "your hair," "your teeth"— is fronted and compared to a domestic animal—"doves," "goats," and "sheep." In the second section, the similes—"like a scarlet thread," "like a slit of pomegranate," and "like the tower of David"— are now fronted and feature products of human culture—textiles, fruits, architecture. The descriptive aspect of this *wasf*-like poem is brought to a close in v. 5 with the boy's appreciation of his lover's breasts. He then resolves to join his lover (v. 6), and the poem concludes with a reprise of the opening exclamation.

4:1. Much of this poem's charm lies in the play of metaphor at the heart of its several similes. "Your eyes are doves" features the image of the rock dove (see comment on 1:15). Visually, the image is that of the girl's dark eyes, perhaps hiding bashfully behind the veil, but very much alive, darting like the dark, bobbing head of the dove. The image projected in the comparison of the girl's hair to a flock of goats meandering down a mountainside is of her dark hair cascading down her back.

4:2. The girl's teeth are white, like the prevailing color of the fleece of sheep (especially after shearing and washing).

4:3. The Hebrew word translated *mouth* only occurs here. It designates both the mouth and speech. The comparison of the girl's *cheeks* (cf. Judg 4:21; 5:26; lit. *temple, forehead*?) with the half of a pomegranate is perhaps intended to convey the image of rosy cheeks. The metaphor of "scarlet thread" and a "half of pomegranate" provide provocative color against the black and white palette of the earlier lines.

4:4. The mention of David's name might be intended to lend the girl a bit of the warrior-king's regality and ability to intimidate. Alternatively, the name "David," Hebrew *dwyd* (*dawidh*) puns the girl's favorite pet name for the boy, *dwdy,* "my lover" (*dodhy*). The architectural imagery used here of the girl (cf. also 6:4; 7:4, 5) may draw on the biblical tradition of personifying cities as women (e.g., Isa 47:1–15; 52:1–2; 54:1–17; Lam 1:2).

4:5. The "gazelle" embodies grace and beauty (see at 1:8). The erotic connotations of "feed among the lilies" recalls 1:8 and 2:16.

4:6. Here the boy mirrors the words uttered earlier by the girl in 2:17. Inspired by the vision of his lover's beauty, he insists that, instead of retreating into the hills at the coming of dawn, he will go at sunset to the "mountain of myrrh" and "hill of frankincense," that is, to the girl's breasts, for she is "perfumed with myrrh and frankincense" (3:6). His ambition to rest among these hills of spices echoes the girl's earlier exclamation (1:13).

4:7. The attributes inscribed here praise the beauty of the girl's entire self—body, mind, and soul—which has "no flaw."

X. Ninth Poem (4:8–5:1)

These verses offer another dialogic poem. The boy's voice is dominant (4:8–15, 5:1). The poem is filled with puns, wordplays, and repetitions that help structure and bind the whole together.

4:8–15. The first section features the voice of the boy, who again (cf. 2:8–17) aims to entice his beloved to come away with him. This time she is portrayed as being sequestered in the Lebanon mountains (cf. v. 15).

4:8. The references to the "Lebanon" and the Anti-Lebanon mountain ranges, which are located north of Israel in modern day Lebanon and Syria, symbolize danger (backed up by the menacing mention of "lions" and "leopards") and the girl's inaccessibility (cf. 2:14). The poem moves geographically from the inaccessible mountains to the (ultimately accessible) garden.

4:9. A paradigm example of staircase parallelism—each successive line elides an element from the previous line while adding a new element. *Ravish* can be considered either in a privative sense (i.e., "you take my heart away") or with more specific connotations of sexual arousal.

4:10. Here the boy echoes the girl's language from 1:2–3. The boy's repetition of the woman's words is a gesture of the mutuality and parity that characterizes these lovers' relationship. The variation in the boy's words inscribes, just as importantly, an awareness of their individuality.

4:11. The metaphors of nectar, honey, and milk focus on the sweet taste and allure of the girl's lips and tongue, as well as the honeyed nature of her words (cf. Prov 16:24).

4:12. "A garden locked" means she is unavailable to other men.

4:14. The profusion of exotic spices and fruits is deliberate and exaggerated to suggest the intensity of feeling and also to continue layering the whole with erotic overtones (Prov 7:17; Ps 45: 9). Many of these products were not indigenous to Palestine (e.g., nard, myrrh, frankincense) and would have been imported, a detail that suggests they are expensive. *Chief spices* is better translated *best spices*.

4:15. The water imagery alludes to v. 12 and helps to bind vv. 12–15 to this section. The girl is the figurative source of life for the boy.

4:16. The boy summons the winds of love using the same word (*awake*) that the girl used earlier to warn about not summoning love prematurely (3:5; cf. 2:7; 8:4). Lest the reader miss the sexual overtones, *come* is used elsewhere for

sexual intercourse in the Hebrew Bible (esp. Gen 16:2; 38:16). The second couplet is spoken by the girl. Both agree that the "garden"—the girl!—is the boy's.

5:1. The boy accepts the girl's invitation (4:16) and enters the garden of his delight. Eating and drinking as elsewhere in the Song have palpable erotic overtones.

XI. Tenth Poem (5:2–6:3)

The longest poem in the collection. The absent lover and the "sickness" induced (5:2–8) provoke the girl's description of him (5:10–16), which in turn eventually conjures him (6:2–3). The boy ends up in "his garden" (6:2) where he was at the end of the previous poem (esp. 4:16–5:1), gathering and sampling its various delights.

5:2–9. A companion piece of sorts to 3:1–5.

5:2–6. Contrary to 3:1–5, the focus here is on the action that happens prior to the search itself. Separation, not absence, is the poem's initial preoccupation. The boy comes to the door, knocks, and begs to be let in out of the heavy nighttime dew (v. 2). The girl, who has already gone to bed, is somewhere (in the sleeping room) on the other side of the door. She dithers. By the time she opens the door, her lover has fled (v. 6). Readers are allowed to sense how very close to a union the lovers come—the boy even managing to reach through the lock, the very lock the girl eventually manipulates to open the door (vv. 4–5)—whatever allusions to sexual intercourse that this sequence of events may conjure are left, quite wonderfully, to the readerly imagination. Readers, like the girl herself (v. 4), feel in their own stomachs the tumble of excitement at these prospects and just as surely register the ache of her disappointment.

5:7–9. The pace picks up and vocabulary familiar from 3:1–5 begins to recur. She seeks but does not find, and, again as in 3:3, the nightwatch find her instead. The reader takes all in stride, having quite literally been down this road before. And then comes the hammer. The guards beat, batter, and (literally) disrobe the girl. End of story, but the poem continues. The reader, reeling from the girl's brutal violation, hardly is able to take in the closing adjuration, which either asks rhetorically about what the girl's friends will tell her lover—namely, that she is lovesick—or makes them swear not to tell him what has happened.

5:10–16. The girl's response comes in the form of her only *wasf*. The section as a whole is framed by two general statements of admiration: "my lover is radiant and ruddy" (v. 10) and "this is my lover" (v. 16). In contradistinction to the other three *wasf*s, the girl's admiration is frequently relayed in terms derived from sculpture. To what end is this inflection of sculpture in the round put? Literally, it is offered as an answer to her girlfriends' question in v. 9: what distinguishes your beloved from other men? The *wasf*, then, is intended to say that he is beautiful, vital, and sexually alluring (esp. v. 16: "and all of him is desirable"). She is evidently successful since as her girlfriends agree to help in the search (6:1).

5:12. The image is wonderfully complex, suggesting both the whiteness of the dove and the image of the dark pupil set within the white iris, and lush. *Milk*, in particular, is associated elsewhere with the idyllic, human flourishing and prosperity (Exod 3:8, 17; 13:5; 33:3; Num 13:27; Deut 6:3; Isa 55:1; 60:16; Joel 3:18; Job 29:6; Song 4:11; 5:1; Lam 4:7). The *whiteness* of the *milk* also contrasts with the *blackness* of the *raven*.

5:14–15. The imagery in these verses suggests a statue, the great value and surpassing beauty of which is uppermost in mind.

XII. Eleventh Poem (6:4–10)

Another *wasf* (cf. 4:1–7; 5:10–16; 7:1–7), staged almost as if in answer to the girl's immediately preceding *wasf*-like admiration of the boy. The four *wasf*s of the Song clump together here in the middle of the sequence, anchoring the whole in the singularity of genre. The body of the poem is framed with an inclusio (v. 4, 10), featuring repeated vocabulary and multiple similes with the same concluding line, "terrible as an army with banners." The body is composed of the *wasf* proper, which is the most limited *wasf* in the Song, focusing only on the beloved's face.

6:4. Tirzah was the capital of the northern kingdom in the late tenth and early ninth centuries. Comparisons to the beauty of capital cities likely draws intentionally on the biblical tradition of personified cities (cf. 4:4), e.g., Jerusalem was "perfect in beauty" (Lam 2:15).

6:8–10. The singularity of the girl is stressed in these lines, a point underscored in the Hebrew by the juxtaposition of the numbers *sixty* and *eighty* in v. 8 with *one* repeated twice in v. 9, and then elaborated for good mearsure in v. 10 (cf. 3:7).

6:10. *Moon/sun* are not the common terms for these heavenly bodies, but are highly elliptical poetic metonyms, *whiteness* and *heat* (cf. Isa 24:23; 30:26), which more eloquently evoke dawn imagery, the point at which the moon is still visible but the heat of the sun can already be felt. The image conveys a sense and feeling of freshness, newness.

XIII. Fragments (6:11–12)

The exact connection of these fragments to the immediately surrounding material is not obvious. The garden imagery and the royal theme are obviously common to the larger sequence.

6:11. The identity of the speaker is ambiguous. The garden imagery, usually associated with the girl (e.g., 4:12), may suggest that the boy is speaking. If not, the girl at last responds positively to the boy's invitation in 2:10 to accompany him.

XIV. Twelfth Poem (7:1–7)

This final *wasf* is framed by an inclusio, consisting of couplets that laud the girl's beauty. The boy's admiring gaze travels in trepidation from sandaled-foot to the regal braids that hold him captive. With only one exception ("your feet" displaced by the opening exclamation of beauty), each of the ten body parts admired head their lines. The framing inclusio makes evident the loving and admiring nature of the boy's gaze.

7:1. The identity of the voice(s) heard in the opening couplets is unclear, and while a curiosity, knowing who is speaking is not crucial to the experience of the poem. The voice implores four times over for the girl to "(re)turn" that she may be looked upon. Only here in the Song is the girl provided with a designation, the "Shulammite." The second couplet ("why do you look …"), whether or not it is uttered by a different voice (e.g., the boy's), may be heard as a response to the opening request for the Shulammite to "(re)turn" (cf. 5:8–9).

7:2. "How graceful are your feet in sandals"—adornment (here the sandals) is important in this culture's ideal of beauty. *Your rounded thighs*, better, t*he curves of your thighs.* Here too the adorned nature of beauty's conceptualization is patent, as the curve of the girl's thigh is likened to jewelry (Hos 2:15; Prov 25:12) made by a master artisan.

7:3. *Navel* (cf. Ezek 16:4; Prov 3:8) is commonly thought of as a euphemism or double entendre for *vulva*, but this may be doubted. When taken straightforwardly, the simile would appear to suggest that "the navel was considered pretty." If reference is made at all to the girl's vulva, it is made allusively, triggered by the mention of a bowl never lacking mixed wine. In Sumerian love poetry the goddess's vaginal juices are imagined as a "sweet drink" for her lover. Here, as elsewhere in the Song, the phrasing is far more delicate and discrete than what is often found in the Mesopotamian love poetry. The following simile, "your belly is a heap of wheat," works on a variety of levels. The term for *belly* frequently designates more specifically a woman's *womb* (e.g., Gen 30:2; Judg 16:17; Isa 13:18). When combined with the image of "a heap of wheat," the associations with fertility and nourishment are palpable, and thus eroticism and fertility imagery are closely linked. At another level, the image of heaped wheat suggests the softness and gentle curve of the woman's stomach, as well, perhaps, as its golden and tawny hue.

7:5. Each of the images in this verse has the personified city in their background. For the image of the girl's neck as an "ivory tower," compare 4:4. *Ivory* is likely meant to convey a notion of splendor and opulence (cf. 1 Kgs 10:18; 22:39; Amos 3:15; 6:4; Ps 45:8).

7:6. Carmel is the mountain range that runs southeast of modern Haifa. Though not incredibly tall (552 m at its highest), its headland juts out prominently into the Mediterranean Sea. The western slopes catch the breezes off the Mediterranean, and thus are lush and fertile and beautiful.

XV. Thirteenth Poem (7:8–14)

The next poem, shaped as an asymmetrical dialogue (vv. 8–10*a*, 10*b*–13), is distinct from the *wasf* that precedes it. The boy speaks first; his part turns out to be the shorter of the two sections. The second and longer half of the poem (vv. 10*b*–13) is rendered in the girl's voice.

7:8–10*a*. The girl's intimidating inaccessibility is once again depicted (cf. 2:14). She is imagined as a beautiful, stately palm, one of the oldest cultivated fruit trees in the ancient world and rich in cultural symbolism. The girl's breasts are high and out of reach. And though the boy repeats his determination to scale the scary height (the date palm grows to be between eighty and a hundred feet tall) and to lay hold of the desired fruit, the poetry reflects—laments!—his doubts about accomplishing such a feat. And thus readers are not surprised to find the boy's closing lines pitched more as a wish ("Oh, may your breasts ...") and the image shifted ever so slightly but crucially. Would that the girl's breasts were more like clusters of grapes on the vine, down low and quite reachable, than the date clusters of the tall palm.

7:9. As if energized by the accessibility implied by the vine imagery, the boy can now even taste the girl's kisses—the imagery echoing the girl's opening ejaculation (1:2–3), and thus symbolizing (yet again) the lovers' harmonious commensurability. The next line enacts another of the Song's high moments. The image of wine continues, literally "going down ... smoothly." But the movement is directed specifically "to my lover," the girl's pet name for the boy. Apparently, she now is the speaker, interrupting and completing the boy's speech. And what is so very delectable is just how the poet musters language to depict a kiss (even *the* kiss the girl has longed for from the beginning of the sequence), linguistic intercourse both literal and figural. Here is as close as the Song comes to actually showing the lovers joining together, each satisfying their own and the other's want. And yet, of course, the joining is not itself represented or narrated. All that is said is that the fine wine to which the girl's mouth is likened goes down smoothly.

7:12–13. This section is given over to the girl's invitation to her lover to join her in the garden. The desire for the garden is shared by two: "let *us* go forth ... let *us* ... see" The lusciousness of the garden imagery here matches in tone and tenor the fruit-full imagery in the first part of the poem, binding the poem together as a whole.

7:12. The girl is in the midst of urging her lover to rise early in the morning and accompany her to the garden, which is both a favorite place for the couple's tryst and an emblem of the girl herself and her budding sexuality (esp. 4:12–15). The final line breaks off the invitation and description of the garden to announce, with some emphasis: "There I will give my love to you!"—the Hebrew of "my love(making)" playing on the fourfold repetition of the girl's favorite designation for the boy, "my love(er)."

7:13. The closing lines echo and play off language used elsewhere in the poem and the poem itself ends with the girl's comment that she has stored up the choicest fruits "for you, my lover" (NIV).

XVI. Fourteenth Poem (8:1–4)

A poem of yearning. The girl speaks throughout, continuing from the previous poem. The clustering of second person masculine suffixes (7:12, 13; 8:1) helps connect the two poems to one another and emphasizes the girl's agency, effectively complementing her willed passivity. The language and imagery throughout draw most explicitly on language and imagery already encountered in the Song.

8:1. The girl wishes her lover was "like a brother" so that they could express their love freely and publicly without rebuke.

XVII. Conclusion (8:5–14)

The sequence unravels to a close, much as it started, among poetic fragments.

8:5a. The first part of this verse appears to be one of the several floating fragments that surface here and there in the Song (e.g., 5:1; 6:11–12; 7:1). It is a reprise of 3:6, only now the girl is in focus, not the boy imagined as Solomon.

8:5b–7. The consistency of voice—the girl speaks throughout—gives this fragment its greatest sense of cohesion.

8:5b. For the eroticism inherent in the girl's imaging the boy as an "apple tree," see the comment on 2:3. To "rouse" a boy so, by means of his lover and under such a symbol laden tree, hardly requires Freud to appreciate the implication of the boy's "arousal." The eroticization of

the boy's mother is explicit—earlier (3:4; 6:9; 8:2) the girl's mother was similarly eroticized. Such transgressive imaginings—here the mother viewed as sexually alluring, the idea of making love on the very spot where the girl's beloved was conceived, where, once upon a time, another pair of young lovers made love—provide the electric charge required to ignite the erotic. By figuring the mother's lovemaking in terms of conception and childbirth, the poet fixes on the outcome of the event, the birth of the girl's lover, while lending a darker hue to the image—childbirth was a common literary trope for extreme pain.

8:6. Seals were made of precious and semi-precious metals and stones and were used to seal documents and to indicate ownership. They were worn on a cord around the neck (Gen 38:18) or as a ring (Gen 41:42; Jer 22:24; Sir 49:11) and were considered a valuable possession. The image, not uncommon, signifies belonging and special intimacy. The girl desires to be bound closely and always to her lover. "Love is as strong as death" (*maweth*) is usually (and not inaccurately) glossed as denoting love's ultimate ineluctability. But it is doubtful whether the simile can finally be reduced to any one paraphrasable gloss. For instance, not to be missed is the allusion to the mythic image of "strong Mot," the Ugaritic god of death, who battles and defeats equally strong Baal. Thus, one might infer that love, or at least this particular love, is to be imagined as locked in mortal combat with Death—all love inevitably comes to an end, even if only through the actual death of (one of) the lovers. And, in fact, the Song is aware of the dark side of love that is always at risk of being unleashed—the girl is beaten by the night guard for love (5:7), becomes sick (2:5; 5:8), and warns her girlfriends three times over not to arouse love prematurely (2:7; 3:5; 8:4); her lover is assaulted by her very glances (4:9; 6:5) and not infrequently imagines her through a militaristic lens.

8:7. "Many waters" in the Ugaritic myths are associated with the god Yam (*Sea*) whom Baal conquers. This mythological overlay lingers in biblical tradition as well, where the "many waters" are similarly associated with the powers of chaos which Yahweh dominates (Gen 1; Isa 51:9–10; Ps 74:12–14). Here then "love" successfully resists that which only Yahweh is able to withstand.

8:8–10. Another fragment. Perhaps the playful banter between the girl (8:10) and her brothers (cf. 1:6). The "little sister" in question is surely fictive, but there is no reason not to think that as with the boy's periodic inflection as Solomon the one elsewhere called "sister" (4:9, 10, 12; 5:1, 2) is not also here in view, especially since she appears to speak in the final couplet. *Little* and *she has no breasts* stress the girl's sexual immaturity. The girl counters (8:10) that her maturity is beyond doubt. The language foregrounds city imagery throughout (*wall, battlement, door, towers*). In the eyes of her lover she finds peace and well-being; she is, that is, like that ancient Mediterranean paradigm of safety, a walled and fortified town.

8:11–12. Solomon is addressed. The speaker is likely the boy, who extols the unparalleled value of his own vineyard, the girl.

8:13–14. The concluding poetic fragment ends on a note of anticipation. The boy asks to hear the girl's voice (v. 13), echoing his own earlier plea (2:14) and answering in kind the girl's initial request for a kiss (1:2). She complies and beckons him, as in 2:17, to flee to the mountains (v. 14).

8:14. The closing lines of the Song, like the opening lines, are the girl's, and thus they form an inclusio, featuring her voice and effecting one last rendition of desire, the ebbing and flowing that is love. By figuring the mountains as "the mountains of spices," the girl's closing command is made enigmatic. These spice-filled mountains are surely a figurative reference to the girl herself, and thus the ultimate instability of love—to want it and at the same time to not want it—is wonderfully figured (i.e., flee ... to me). And with the addition of the final word (*spices*) and its transformative self-reflexivity, readers are sent back to the beginning of the Song. A fitting, albeit relentlessly circular, close to the Song.

BIBLIOGRAPHY

F. W. Dobbs-Allsopp. "Late Linguistic Features in the Song of Songs." *Perspectives on the Song of Songs—Perspektiven der Hoheliedauslegung* (2005) 27–77; J. C. Exum. *Song of Songs.* OTL (Louisville: Westminster John Knox, 2005); M. Fox. *The Song of Songs and the Ancient Egyptian Love Songs* (Madison: University of Wisconsin Press, 1985); O. Keel. *Song of Songs: A Continental Commentary* (Minneapolis: Fortress, 1994); C. Meyers. "Gender Imagery in the Song of Songs" *HAR* 10 (1986) 209–23; R. Murphy. *Song of Songs.* Hermeneia (Minneapolis: Fortress, 1990); M. Pope. *Song of Songs.* AB 7C (Garden City, N.Y.: Doubleday, 1977); J. Westenholz. "Love Lyrics from the Ancient Near East." *Civilizations of the Ancient Near East.* Vol. 2 (New York: Scribners, 1995) 2471–84 .

ISAIAH

John Goldingay

Overview

The book of Isaiah is the first of the three "major prophets," that is, the three longest prophetic books. Its position as the first reflects the fact that Isaiah himself lived in the eighth century, whereas Jeremiah and Ezekiel lived 150 years later. It thus has its scale in common with those two books, but it also deserves setting alongside Hosea, Amos, and Micah, who were contemporaries of Isaiah ben Amoz (especially alongside Micah, who like Isaiah prophesied in Judah).

The book's opening reports that Isaiah ben Amoz was active during the reigns of Uzziah, Jotham, Ahaz, and Hezekiah over Judah. Chapters 1–39 indicate that this was a time when Judah came under considerable political pressure through the expansionist policies of the first great Middle Eastern empire, that of the Assyrians; the question was, how is the people of God to cope with that kind of situation? These chapters also reflect the social changes that had come upon Judah over two centuries and more, a time of increasing urbanization and a divide between people who were quite comfortably off and people who had a hard time making ends meet. Finally, the chapters attest to the temptation to look to religious resources other than Yahweh in order to cope with such political and economic pressures. They urge people to turn back to Yahweh, but they also promise that even if Yahweh brings calamity upon the people, there will be restoration.

The second half of the book begins with a different tone as it reports Yahweh's proclamation, "Comfort, O comfort my people" (40:1). It presupposes that Yahweh has indeed brought calamity on the people but has now said "Enough is enough"; the time for restoration has arrived. It is coming about through the Medo-Persian king Cyrus (44:28), who led the Persians in conquering the Babylonian Empire, taking Babylon in 539 BCE. This part of Isaiah thus presupposes a setting and an audience living two centuries after Isaiah ben Amoz. So, this prophet is someone different from Isaiah ben Amoz, and this part of the book deserves setting alongside Jeremiah and Ezekiel, who preceded it by a short period and also looked forward to Yahweh's restoration of Judah. Lamentations provides further background to some of the conditions presupposed by chapters 40–55.

Chapters 56–66 in turn combine a confrontational tone like that of chs. 1–39 with promises that elaborate on ones in chs. 40–55. Chapters 56–66 make best sense if one reckons that they come from a time soon after chs. 40–55, when something of the restoration that those chapters promise has come about, but things are not nearly as glorious as they would have made one expect. This part of the book thus deserves setting alongside Haggai and Zechariah.

The book as a whole reflects several different periods, but it is not merely an anthology of unrelated prophecies. Chapters 40–66 continue on from chs. 1–39. In all three parts of the book, Yahweh is "the Holy One of Israel." This title appears 25 times throughout the book and only five times in the rest of the Old Testament. The entire book is a message from the Holy One. Other motifs in one part of the book are taken up in another, such as the people's blindness and deafness, the image of Yahweh as the potter, and the notion of the nations being drawn to Jerusalem. Yahweh used the messages in chs. 1–39 to inspire the anonymous prophet or prophets whose words come in chs. 40–55, and later used the words of that "Second Isaiah" to inspire a "Third Isaiah" whose words come in chs. 56–66. (It may be that within chs. 1–39, too, there is material that was inspired by Isaiah ben Amoz rather than that came directly from him, particularly in chs. 24–27; but there are fewer explicit markers of this.)

Outline

(Repeated headings indicated by (i), (ii), or (iii) denote similar sets of oracles.)

I. Judah in the Time of Ahaz (1:1–12:6)

DETAILED ANALYSIS

I. Judah in the Time of Ahaz (1:1–12:6)

Chapters 1–5 alternate two kinds of message. There are accounts of why and how things have gone wrong for Judah and how things will get worse; interwoven with these are promises of how Yahweh will transform Jerusalem on the other side of these calamities. Isaiah 6:1–9:7 then focuses more on narrative accounts of Isaiah's ministry, but with the same threefold implications. Isaiah 9:8–12:6 returns to direct warnings and promises, but now with the emphasis more on the latter.

A. Confrontations and Promises (i) (1:1–5:30)

1:1–2:1. Judah's devastation (i)

1:1. What we are to read is a "vision." These prophecies are not mere human insight or opinion but a divine revelation; readers need to be open to them as that. Yet they are a vision of "Isaiah ben Amoz." They came via this particular human person. Isaiah's angle of vision is different from that of other prophets, and his person is part of his ministry. His very name, which means "Yahweh is deliverance," expresses a central theme of his message. His vision concerns "Judah and Jerusalem." Judah, a tiny people in the southern part of Syria-Palestine, is the entire book's consistent focus; and even when it talks about other nations, it does so because of their significance for Judah, whether as threats or as allies. The problems, danger, and destiny of Jerusalem, Judah's capital, are also the whole book's consistent focus. Then the names of the kings remind readers that the chapters need to be understood against the background of this particular period. What Yahweh has to say to Judah and Jerusalem is different in other times.

1:2–4. Judah is actually called "Israel"; it is a partial embodiment of "my people." They are Yahweh's "children." But they do not behave like it. They no longer accept the authority of the head of the family. They do not "know" their father; in the OT *know* often implies "acknowledge," recognize the authority of, obey.

1:5–9. Their rebellion against Yahweh eventually issued in invasion by the Assyrians, rendering Jerusalem like a man who has been mugged or like a bivouac in the middle of a field, almost as devastated as Sodom and Gomorrah. The implication is that although this chapter comes at the beginning of the book, its message relates to events quite late in Isaiah's own ministry, i.e., during the time of King Hezekiah (the back story comes in chs. 36–37). These verses indicate where Judah's story is going; succeeding sections and chapters will indicate how it got there.

1:10–20. Jerusalem has ended up like Sodom and Gomorrah because it has behaved like Sodom and Gomorrah. There is a mismatch between its worship and its life outside worship. People made costly offerings, celebrated great festivals, and prayed fervently, and as far as one can tell, meant every word. But their lives did not match the nature and concerns of the God they worshiped. Their hands were full of blood: the community includes powerful people who can swindle the vulnerable out of their rights, their land, their livelihood, and thus ultimately of their lives (1 Kgs 21 describes an extreme example). The rest of this community tolerates that and fails to protect such people. They need to remove the blood from their hands if Yahweh is to be able to tolerate looking at these hands raised in worship and prayer. Verse 18 describes the change Yahweh demands, and vv. 19–20 lay alternative destinies before the community.

1:21–31. The prophet again speaks of oppression, of the neglect of the vulnerable, and of the people's worship, though here not orthodox worship of Yahweh whose problem is that it is not matched by a life worthy of Yahweh, but an inclination

to traditional, Canaanite-style forms of worship (vv. 29–30). People may have seen this as worship of Yahweh, not worship of other gods, but it was far away from the worship Yahweh could accept, because it again did not match who Yahweh really was. The tragedy of the situation in the city is that it has fallen so short of its destiny and of how things used to be (vv. 21–22). The threat against the people (v. 20) is now expressed more chillingly. But Yahweh's action is designed to purify and restore as well as punish (vv. 25–27). Even shame at those spiritual practices (v. 29) is a positive thing if it turns people back to Yahweh.

2:1. A conclusion closes off this opening summary of Isaiah's ministry.

2:2–5. Jerusalem's Transformation (i)

2:2–4. The vision of Jerusalem's transformation had spoken of justice and judges (1:21, 26, 27), which are related words in Hebrew and reflect people with authority exercising their authority in the right way. This more far-reaching vision speaks of Yahweh "judging" between the nations. The implementing of proper authority will not characterize Jerusalem alone. Jerusalem will be the base from which Yahweh effects that in the world, stopping the nations fighting one another by deciding who is in the right, in the manner of the judges (the body of elders) at the village gate resolving community conflicts. The geophysical transformation (v. 2) is presumably a metaphor; the promise does not indicate how Yahweh will accomplish this goal. But Yahweh will not merely make decisions for the nations in an authoritarian way. The nations will come to be "taught" and receive "instruction." These two words are also related. "Instruction" is *torah*, often translated "law"—but "instruction" or "teaching" gives a better idea. Yahweh will teach them so that they walk in Yahweh's ways, behavior that might even reduce their conflicts.

2:5. This verse both concludes vv. 2–4 and introduces what follows. "Come, let us walk" takes up the nations' words in v. 3. It is not Jerusalem's job to transform itself in the spectacular fashion of v. 2 so that it may draw the nations, but the people of God are supposed to embody God's vision for the whole world. Perhaps God will use that to draw the world to Zion.

Verses 2–5 appear in a slightly different form in Micah 4:1–5. It is impossible to know which prophet actually uttered them or whether they come from yet another prophet. One need not assume that all the material in a prophetic book came from the prophet whose name stands at the top.

2:6–4:1. Judah's Devastation (ii)

2:6–9. These verses, like 1:1–2:1, indict Judah for its waywardness. The section again begins from the disaster that has already overcome the community. The judgment has issued from the people's inclination to trust in resources other than Yahweh—political, religious, financial, and military. This motif will recur in the book. A prophet's job includes praying *for* the people, so the frightening prayer in v. 9c likely presupposes that the people do not repent, and also that it is designed to frighten them into doing so. Prophets' words were often designed to avoid being fulfilled.

2:10–22. Such humbling and false trust relate to questions the community needs to take seriously; otherwise it is in danger of calamity. The main focus is on "pride" or "haughtiness," though those English words give only a narrow impression of what the prophet refers to. Verses 12–13 help to make the point clear as they refer to what is "lofty," "lifted up," and "high," and in the subsequent illustration—such as Lebanese cedars and Bashan oaks—the emphasis lies on their impressiveness, not on the attitude they take. So the problem lies in Judah's ability to stand so tall. It is impressive, and it knows it. That means it compromises Yahweh's majesty rather than testifying to it; the word describing Yahweh's majesty (*ga'on*) is closely related to the word describing the people as proud (*ge'eh*). So describing the people as of haughty eyes need only imply that they stand tall and look tall and are entitled to do so. The passage doubtless presupposes that the people have become overattached to their impressiveness, but part of its significance is that people find it hard not to do that. Powerful and impressive people start thinking of themselves that way. They are then are on the way to disaster.

The day when human impressiveness will be put down is "the day of Yahweh" (v. 12). "Yahweh's day" was a day people anticipated as a time of great blessing, but prophets warned that they could make it the opposite (cf. Amos 5:18). Sometimes "Yahweh's day" appears to be far off, but here it is a day that will come in people's experience. Yahweh's purpose will be implemented in spectacular fashion in their lives, and this will not be pleasant (if they carry on as they are). That day will also expose some of the inappropriate resources in which the people now trust (vv. 20, 22).

3:1–8. Issues concerning Judah's leadership come into focus. First, an aspect of the trouble that will come upon the community is that all its leadership will be gone. "Support and staff" is a metaphor for leadership, while v. 1b describes the results of chaos in the land, and vv. 2–8 itemize the literal reality of the loss of leadership. The community will be driven to recognizing and following the leadership of people who are unqualified and inadequate for the task (some of whom will be wise enough to recognize their inadequacy and resist being drafted), resulting in further social breakdown.

3:9–12. Since vv. 1–7 presuppose that calamity has not yet taken place, v. 8 presumably reflects the situation after Jerusalem and Judah will have fallen. Verses 9–12 fit with that. The people have brought this trouble on themselves; it has not yet happened, but it is inevitable, unless the community does something about it. They attack and defy Yahweh (v. 9a—they will not see themselves as doing that, but it is the implication of their stance). And one reason calamity will take the form of removing their leadership is that the leadership is already a disaster (v. 12). Verses 10–11 make an aspect of Isaiah's challenge more explicit. If the community as a whole has brought this trouble on itself, this action does not rule out the possibility of dissociating oneself from its causes and thus from its effects.

3:13–15. The three little messages about leadership close by explicitly confronting the elders and princes (that is, the government). In the OT, government's central task is to care for ordinary people's needs and rights. But government regularly uses its power to look after itself. It is "my people" you are thus abusing, says Yahweh. The solemnity of that charge is increased when the passage closes with the description of Yahweh as "the Lord GOD of hosts," as it began with the description of Yahweh as "the Sovereign, the LORD of hosts." The expressions are virtually identical in Hebrew; more literally, they mean "the Lord Yahweh of Armies." The expression is difficult to translate, but it clearly means that this sovereign God controls mighty power.

3:16–4:1. In a patriarchal society, the men's job is to exercise the leadership, while their women's job is to exemplify beauty. Presupposing that arrangement, Isaiah complements the indictment of the men regarding their role with a shorter confrontation of these women regarding theirs. Their being able to strut their stuff in their finery depends on their men being involved in the abuse that 3:14–15 described. And the decimating of the men in war that will be their punishment will have its implications for their women (4:1).

4:2–6. Jerusalem's Transformation (ii)

As was the case in 2:2–5, the declaration that trouble is coming is balanced by a promise that this will not be the end of the story. The city's population will be decimated, but there will be "survivors," people who "remain"; the verb links with the word "remnant," which will be important in Isaiah. And these "remains" will see the city and the land beautified and fruitful once again. As 1:25–27 promised, the calamity will be designed not merely to destroy but to purge and cleanse. People do not survive because they are holy (disaster is not selective); they are made holy because they survive. They are not the remnant because they are faithful; because they are a remnant, they are to be faithful. Yahweh will then establish a wall of protection around the city.

5:1–30. Jerusalem's Devastation (iii)

At this point in the book, however, devastation not transformation has the last word. Prophets have to balance the way they talk about these two realities, giving people enough encouragement to motivate them but not so much that they avoid the issues they need to face.

5:1–7. A love song would continue the positive tone of 4:2–6, and vv. 1–2a would give that impression. But the love song changes, and then things get worse and worse. A song about a vineyard would puzzle people less than it puzzles readers today; Israel was often pictured as a vine or an olive tree. But in case people had not gotten the point, v. 7 makes it explicit. The scandalous

difference between what Yahweh looked for and what happened is underscored by the words Isaiah uses, whose similarity underscores that contrast. "Justice" is *mishpat*; "bloodshed" is one letter different, *mispakh* (literally, "flowing"; it comes only here, and maybe Isaiah invented it to make the point). "Righteousness" is *tsedaqa*; "a cry" is again one letter different *tse'aqa*. The word for Israel's own cry under oppression in Egypt now comes from the lips of people oppressed by fellow-Israelites.

5:8–24. A series of "Ah"s ("Hey" would give more the impression) protests more concretely the wrongdoing that earns Yahweh's punitive action. The land-grabbing that prevents families from farming their own land will result in the devastation of the houses and land that people have accumulated (vv. 8–10). The self-indulgent party-people will die of hunger and thirst (vv. 11–17). The people who pervert the legal system to their own ends, and do not believe Yahweh will act, will find that Yahweh does (vv. 18–24), because they have rejected Yahweh's instruction, despised Yahweh's word. "Instruction" (*torah*) may refer to the teaching in *the* Torah, in Genesis–Deuteronomy, but the parallelism with Yahweh's "word" suggests it refers to Isaiah's own message.

That is all the more solemn against the background of a particularly significant definition of who Yahweh is (v. 16). This first brings together in parallelism the expressions "Yahweh [of?] Armies" (see comment on 3:13–15) and "Holy God," the short version of Isaiah's distinctive "Holy One of Israel." Yahweh is the frighteningly awesome, overwhelmingly transcendent God. It is unwise to violate Yahweh's Torah; Isaiah 6 will spell out the implications.

Here, the verse itself spells out how Yahweh's awesomeness expresses itself. The verb that speaks of Yahweh being exalted is related to the word for "haughty" in the previous verse. Human majesty is put down as Yahweh's majesty asserts itself. But Yahweh is not just concerned to safeguard divine majesty for its own sake, nor is Yahweh irrationally and unpredictably intense and fierce. Yahweh asserts this majesty and demonstrates holiness by "justice" and "righteousness." These two words attempt to express in English the meaning of Hebrew words that do not have English equivalents. "Justice" is *mishpat*, the exercise of leadership or authority, which can apply to the implementation of legal justice by judges but has much wider implications. "Righteousness" is *tsedaqa*, which denotes doing the right thing by people in your community, a righteousness embodied in the way one protects and serves other people. Yahweh, then, expresses divine power and holiness by exercising authority in such a way as to do the right thing by "my people" in Israel (3:15). This is a frightening prospect for the powerful, wealthy people in the nation who hear Isaiah's words.

5:25–30. The move between past tense verbs and future tense verbs again suggests that Judah is challenged to respond to the calamity that has come, lest a worse one follow with the arrival of the terrifying Assyrian army. The Assyrians will come because they want to enlarge their empire, but they will come because (unbeknown to them) Yahweh is whistling for them.

B. An Account of Isaiah's Ministry (6:1–9:7)

The book makes a transition to talking primarily about Isaiah's ministry rather than only relating messages from Yahweh, and from mostly poetry to mostly prose.

6:1–13 Isaiah's Vision of the Holy One, and the Message Isaiah Is to Give

6:1–8. This account of Isaiah's ministry starts by describing how he came to be a prophet. Initially it describes a vision of Yahweh, specifically of Yahweh as the great king (in the context of the earthly king's death) and as the holy one: not just holy but utterly holy. This vision explains why Yahweh's being "the Holy One" is so important in Isaiah. The seraphs come only here in the OT; because *saraf* means "burn," and on the basis of OT references to fiery serpents, they are usually reckoned to be serpent-like.

6:9–13. This is not really a story about Isaiah's call, because actually Isaiah volunteers, and he is then commissioned to declare a frightening message. Understandably, then, readings in church commonly stop at v. 8, but vv. 1–8 lead inexorably into vv. 9–13. Isaiah's ministry is to stop people from understanding anything, so that terrible punishment falls on them; Jesus says the same applies to his ministry (Mark 4:11–12). The people are already willfully resistant to Yahweh's

message; this persistent lack of understanding is one form that punishment will take. At the same time, the point of telling people that this is Isaiah's commission (as with other prophetic declarations of judgment) is presumably in part to shake them into a response that will mean the declaration does not need to be implemented.

7:1–25. Isaiah's Fulfillment of His Commission (i)

7:1–9. An opening summary of the story, like a newspaper headline, is followed by the details. The kings of Judah's northern and eastern neighbors want Judah to join in rebelling against their Assyrian overlords, and if Ahaz is unwilling to do so, they are prepared to depose him. Isaiah wants Ahaz to trust Yahweh such that he need not worry about these two kingdoms. Aram and Ephraim (the northern kingdom, also referred to as "Israel") are not more impressive than their capital cities, and these cities are not more impressive than those two kings. Isaiah's son's name is nicely ambiguous: only remnants of Ephraim and Syria will survive, or only remnants of Assyria will survive, or only remnants of Judah will survive if it does not trust in Yahweh, or at least remnants will survive, or the remnants must return to Yahweh. Isaiah's subsequent words suggest that the first meaning is the primary one in this context.

7:10–17. Isaiah offers Ahaz a sign to bolster his faith; he cannily declines (he would then have no option but to trust Yahweh). Isaiah says he will receive one anyway. A young woman who is present, perhaps Isaiah's wife (as their other children are also given significant names), will have a baby and call it "God-is-with-us." The implication is not that the baby *is* "God-with-us," any more than that the son in v. 3 *is* the remnant. Rather the baby's birth will follow the moment when Judah experiences a deliverance that indicates Yahweh has indeed acted, that "God is with us." NRSV assumes that the word for a young woman does not mean virgin; if it does (and the woman is therefore not Isaiah's wife), Isaiah likely means that by the time a woman who is at the moment a virgin but is about to marry conceives and has her first child, the crisis will be over and she will be able to give her baby that name. The further description of the child then elaborates the point. But the sign will do Ahaz no good (v. 17). As is often the case, the New Testament gives the passage new significance in using it to illumine Jesus' story.

7:18–25. Four further declarations elaborate not only on the way Yahweh will bring the Egyptians and Assyrians, but also on the way life will be able to continue after the devastation.

8:1–15. Isaiah's Fulfillment of His Commission (ii)

8:1–4. Names and the birth of a baby are once again means of Isaiah's fulfilling his prophetic commission. This baby is called "Pillage speeds, loot hastens." It is thus again cryptic, like "Remnants will turn," and like Jesus' parables. It draws people's attention and makes them think. The closing words again clarify the meaning in the immediate context. The message is parallel to that of the baby's birth (7:10–17). Getting people to witness the inscription on the tablet will provide evidence in the future that Yahweh really had said this through Isaiah and thus that people should take it seriously then even if they do not now.

8:5–15. Isaiah declares the consequences of ignoring his message about the need to trust Yahweh. "Shiloah" refers to the Siloam stream, Jerusalem's water supply, which is a metaphor for Yahweh's supplying Jerusalem's needs. Alternative waters will all but drown Judah, but not quite do so. Verses 9–10 explain how. "God is with us" recurs at the end of vv. 8 and 10. Countries can plot against Judah, as Ephraim and Aram have done, but they will not succeed. Yet people are inclined to be more awed by Ephraim and Aram than they are by God (vv. 11–15). "Sanctuary" is literally "holy place," so v. 14 picks up the warning in v. 13. Being like a holy place or a rock, Yahweh should provide safety for the people, but they are making Yahweh a threat to themselves.

8:16–22. Isaiah's Gloomy Conclusion

Once again, v. 16 presupposes that people are ignoring Isaiah's warnings. They are more inclined to resort to traditional means of receiving divine guidance such as consulting dead people, who might be expected to know more than the living. So Isaiah puts this message into writing and again has it sealed against the day when his warnings have been fulfilled and the day of darkness has fallen.

9:1–7. The Promising Coda

As usual, Isaiah does not let calamity have the last word; darkness, gloom, and anguish are succeeded by glory, light, and joy. Strikingly, v. 1 begins with a promise for Ephraim, the sibling nation with whom Judah is in conflict and whose devastation Isaiah has promised. For what happened before Ephraim's final fall and is presupposed by v. 1, see 2 Kgs 15:29. But presumably vv. 2–7 apply to Isaiah's actual audience in Judah as well as to Ephraim. The promise is expressed in the past tense, a vivid way of describing something that is certain and guaranteed by God and is therefore in effect on the way, though the very last line ("the zeal of the LORD of hosts will do this") speaks more literally. This is something that Yahweh will definitely make happen.

Christians have used some aspects of the passage to help them understand the significance of Christ, but the passage as a whole does not directly apply to Christ and the NT does not so apply it. Verse 7 does express what Christ will yet do. So far, most if not all the significant children have been Isaiah's; but this is a royal child, perhaps one already born but not yet on the throne (Hezekiah?), or perhaps a Messiah-like figure not yet born. Like the names of those other children, the name in v. 6 does not describe him but describes the reality he points to. Like Immanuel, the name is a description of God, the God who guarantees the ultimate destiny of the people. The day of Midian's defeat (see Judg 6–8) provides an image for Judah's deliverance by Yahweh from Assyria.

C. Confrontations and Promises (ii) (9:8–12:6)

Isaiah returns to words of prophecy directly confronting Judah, though they again look beyond disaster to deliverance and renewal.

9:8–10:4. His Anger Has Still Not Turned Away

The link with 1:1–5:30 is explicit in the refrain (9:12b, 17b, 21b; 10:4b), which takes up that in 5:25b. But 9:8 also follows neatly on 9:7b in describing the power and effectiveness of Yahweh's word. The sequence again speaks of troubles that have already come and of people's unwillingness to learn the lesson from them.

9:8–21. Why does Isaiah focus on calamities that have come to Ephraim, and specifically on its capital city, Samaria (the kind presupposed by 9:1)? Isaiah lived in Jerusalem; as far as one can know, he never went to Samaria, in a foreign country with which Judah had an uneasy relationship. The people who heard these messages would be the Judeans themselves. This message might make them feel comfortable; bad news about another country can do that. But they could undergird Isaiah's emphasis on not being afraid of its big and apparently impressive neighbor. The calamities that had come on Ephraim provide evidence of the truth of Isaiah's message in 7:1–17.

10:1–4. There is something else. In 9:8–21, it is all about "them." But much of the description of Ephraim repeats features of Isaiah's critique of Judah, which ought to make Judah feel uncomfortable as it listens; Ephraim is only the same as Judah. This final part of the sequence (ending with the final occurrence of the refrain, in v. 4b) makes that explicit: it addresses "you." One function of 9:8–21 is to set up the people in Judah who are Isaiah's actual audience. If they have said "Yes" to 9:8–21, these verses make them see they have been challenging themselves. They, too, are people who think they can solve their own problems and turn a crisis into a challenge (9:8–12). They, too, are people who will not let trouble make them turn back to Yahweh (9:13–17). They, too, risk being torn apart by their own greed (9:18–21; Ephraim and Manasseh are the two big clans within Ephraim—the northern kingdom—as a whole). They, too, make the legal system work against the interests of the needy (10:1–2). So they, too, stand in peril of Yahweh's anger.

10:5–23. The Downfall of Assyria and the Restoring of Israel (i)

10:5–19. The means for expressing Yahweh's anger and raising Yahweh's hand (v. 4) is Assyria and Assyria's hand (v. 5). Yet Assyria does not act like a law court judge, who is there simply to serve the people, but does what it does for its own reasons, pursuing its own expansionist policies. It treats Yahweh as just the same as any other "idol," and it is naturally but unwisely rather proud of its achievements. So Judah is not only just the same as Ephraim; in its natural pride in itself it is just the same as Assyria. But Assyria, too, must be put in its place. The Holy One is a threat to Assyria, just as the Holy One is to Judah. Remains of Assyria

will be left, but only enough to witness to the fact that it once existed.

10:20–23. For Israel, the survival of some remains bears a more positive significance. Admittedly, 10:20–23 holds in sharp tension the fearsomely bad news and the gleam of good news. Catastrophic destruction is decreed in the land (so the note to v. 23 in NRSV). But something will be left. Isaiah does not imply that this remnant deserves to survive; they are simply people who are fortunate enough to escape. But they can then be the nucleus of a new Israel, if they choose to be. The question is whether the surviving remnant makes a commitment now to become the faithful remnant. The marker of that will be a commitment to leaning on Yahweh instead of leaning on Assyria, which turned into the one that struck them (v. 20). That is what the Judah of Isaiah's day has refused to do.

10:24–11:16. The Downfall of Assyria and the Restoring of Israel (ii)

Once again the sequences of prophecies come in pairs; this pair parallels 10:5–23.

10:24–34. Yahweh promises that Assyria's attacks and domination will not go on forever; in fact they will soon cease (10:24–27a). The model for the act of deliverance is again what Yahweh did at the exodus and in Gideon's day (Judg 6–8). The promise of speedy action makes this a good example of the possibility that later disciples of Isaiah were inspired to update his prophecies during the time when Assyria actually was about to fall, a century after Isaiah's own time. The imaginary account of the Assyrians advancing on Jerusalem from the north through the area now dominated by Ramallah (10:27b–32) does not correspond to any known attack, but it gives a vivid picture of what an advance might be like, to feed people's imagination. It culminates in the army's arrival at a point where they can see the city and plan to attack it next day. But Yahweh then intervenes. Once again, the Assyrian forces are pictured as a mighty forest (cf. 10:16–19), which Yahweh intends to cut down (vv. 33–34).

11:1–10. Related to that victory is the promise of Israel's restoration, initially focusing on the restoration of the Davidic monarchy. David's line, which goes back to David's father Jesse, has also become like a tree that Yahweh has cut down, as subsequently happened with the fall of Jerusalem in 587. But sometimes a felled tree can grow again, and Yahweh declares that this will indeed happen. This "shoot" or "branch" becomes an image for what was later called the Messiah. He will be all that a king is supposed to be, and more. He will have the insight to lead Israel, being the sort of person who acknowledges and reveres Yahweh. That will mean he governs the land with the right combination of concern for the needy, intolerance about the way they can be abused by the legal system, and ruthlessness with the people who do abuse them (vv. 3b–5: in the context, the "earth" likely refers to the "land" of Israel in particular, as in 10:23). Whereas his actual growth might be seen as a natural process (felled trees sometimes do produce new shoots), what he will do cannot be understood in that way. He will achieve what he achieves not because of his innate insight or spirituality but because Yahweh's spirit will rest on him. In this context, the vision in vv. 6–9 is likely then another image for the peace that the new David will achieve. The weak will be safe. Indeed, by implication there is here a positive message even for the people in power, the abusers. They can decide to live in peace with the weak rather than behaving with the ruthlessness that characterizes Judah's authorities.

11:11–16. What the "shoot" will achieve will draw the nations to him and to the place where he lives (v. 10; compare 2:2–4). That last note forms a segue to a vision of Yahweh not only drawing the nations themselves but commissioning them to bring back the peoples of both Judah and Ephraim from their dispersion around the Middle East and the Mediterranean (vv. 10–16). The mutual hostility of Ephraim and Judah will dissolve, they will be able to repossess the whole of the land, and the obstacles to their return will disappear.

As is commonly the case with prophecies, these promises in 10:24–11:16 saw some fulfillment in Isaiah's day and over succeeding centuries. Isaiah 36–37 relates some cutting down of Assyria to size, and Assyria fell to Babylon in the next century. When Babylon fell to the Persians, they freed Judean exiles and refugees to return to Judah. Such partial fulfillments are part of what encourages Israel to continue to look for more complete fulfillment. Similarly, the extent to which Christ fulfills something of these prophecies (see Rom 15:12) encourages us to look for his

complete fulfillment of the promise expressed in (for instance) 11:1–10.

12:1–6. A Song to Sing in that Day

Giving Judah a song of praise to sing when those promises have been fulfilled is another way of underlining the certainty that fulfillment will come. Divine anger and thus chastisement will then have given way to comfort (see 40:1) and deliverance from Assyrian (and Babylonian) control (49:8). Withering will give way to wells for drawing from (41:17–18—"fountains" there is the same word as "wells" here). Whereas Isaiah has been unable to persuade people to trust, now they will do so, and they need not be afraid (cf. 44:8). It will be an experience like the Red Sea deliverance, and the song will be able to pick up the themes of Israel's song then (Exod 15:1–18). Like the thanksgivings in the Psalms, it will deserve to be sung so that the whole world can hear, because what Yahweh does for Israel is also good news for the whole world. Chapters 1–12 close with an acknowledgment of Yahweh as "the Holy One of Israel," Isaiah's signature way of proclaiming God.

II. The Nations (13:1–23:18)

Isaiah has already referred to nations other than Judah such as Aram and Assyria, but now these other nations come into focus. Sometimes the prophecies are addressed to these other nations, but even when that is so, they are directly intended for Judah's hearing. It is doubtful whether the other nations ever heard them, or were intended to do so. They are designed to help Judah to understand the nations of its day in the right way. Chapters 1–12 attest that Judah was naturally inclined either to fear them or to establish alliances with them. Isaiah 13–23 seeks to wean them from either attitude.

A. The Northern Powers (13:1–14:27)

The chapters begin with the two great empires that impinged on or controlled Judah from the late eighth century till 539.

13:1–14:23. Babylon

In Isaiah's day, Babylon was a medium-sized power south of Assyria, under Assyrian domination. It was interested in making common cause with Ephraim and Judah, which also had an ambivalent relationship with Assyria (cf. Isa 39). Yet this interest offers no explanation for its occupying nearly a quarter of the chapters concerning the nations. But it would make entire sense in the sixth century, when Babylon had taken Assyria's place as the imperial power, destroyed Jerusalem, and taken many Judeans to Babylon. Perhaps these prophecies come from Isaiah, but they have been arranged and/or expanded in that later context.

13:1–16. Here, with the exception of the heading, there is no overt reference to Babylon. Yahweh summons unnamed warriors to come and make a desolation of the earth. This could easily describe Yahweh's summoning Babylon itself to bring desolation to Assyria. But the lack of specificity makes it open to being applied to Babylon's own fall. By implication, Assyria's fall to Babylon and Babylon's fall to Persia are instances of a recurrent pattern in Yahweh's activity. Empires think the sun will never set on them, but Yahweh brings them down by using another empire that does not realize it is Yahweh's servant, an army made holy (v. 3) through being drafted by Yahweh. The sequence of superpowers is not meaningless chance but something in which Yahweh is involved, in their rise and their demise.

The superpower's fall occurs on "the day of the LORD" (vv. 6, 9). This is not a far-off day or a final one but one that happens in the experience of the hearers of this prophecy. Yet the fact that the protagonists are unnamed and Isaiah speaks about "the world" and "the whole earth" also implies that this particular day is one embodiment of Yahweh's ultimate purpose.

13:17–22. Only now does it become clear that it is the Medes whom Yahweh is stirring to put the Babylonians down. The Medes controlled an empire east of Babylonia (in roughly contemporary terms, Media was equivalent to Iran, Babylonia to Iraq). Yahweh is happy to use the Medes with their violent instincts as a means of bringing about Babylon's downfall. Like the imaginary picture of the Assyrians approaching Jerusalem (11:27b–32), the picture of the Medes conquering Babylon is not a literal prediction of what would happen. The people of Babylon wisely surrendered to the Medo-Persian army and the city was not destroyed. Scriptural thinking does not assume that prophecies need to be literally fulfilled; they

are works of a divinely inspired imagination. The total collapse of the Babylonian Empire to the Persians was enough to count as fulfillment of this prophecy.

14:1–2. For Israel, the significance of Babylon's fall is that their oppression by Babylon will not be the final chapter. The ruled will become the rulers, the served will become the servants (TNIV; "slaves" is likely misleading).

14:3–23. Two related pictures portray the death of the Babylonian king. Verses 3–11 imagine a funeral dirge to lament this death, portraying the king's arrival in the abode of the dead. His victims rejoice at the security this brings; other world leaders comment on his ending up just like them. Verses 12–21 then take up an ancient Near Eastern myth to portray his fall. Each morning the Venus star (the "day star") rises just before the sun but is then eclipsed by the sun itself. In the myth, that suggested a subordinate god trying to become the chief god but failing. The prophecy turns this plot into an allegory of the Babylonian king who had wanted to be the king of the world, in effect to be God, but one who would be put down. The reason for this is the king's abuse of his own people (v. 20). For "Day Star," the KJV has "Lucifer," which presupposed and encouraged the assumption that vv. 3–11 refer to the fall of Satan. This interpretation corresponds to the meaning of the ancient Near Eastern myth but not to the meaning of this passage in Isaiah, where the myth has become a parable, a way of picturing the historical event of the king's pretensions and his fall.

14:24–27. Assyria

In Isaiah's own day, Assyria is the empire that matters. The prophecy again speaks in terms of "the whole earth" and "all the nations," showing how Yahweh's dealings with one empire express Yahweh's intentions for the entire world. This declaration concerning Assyria indeed came true; so Yahweh could also bring to fulfillment the declaration concerning Babylon.

B. Judah's Neighbors (14:28–17:11)

After paying attention to the imperial setting of Judah's situation, the book focuses on the people's immediate context. It moves through Judah's neighbors in a circle from Philistia in the west and southwest via Moab in the southeast to Aram and Ephraim in the northeast and north.

14:28–32. Philistia

The Philistines occupied an area on the Mediterranean including Gaza. The link with Ahaz's death (about 715 BCE) may mark this time as one of anxiety and uncertainty about what policy changes a new king will bring. Perhaps it is in this connection that Philistia is sending envoys to Jerusalem. But the reference to a broken rod indicates that the context also includes the recent death of an Assyrian emperor who had invaded the area. Philistia was more vulnerable to such attacks, sitting on the main route between Assyria and Egypt. It may hope to get Judah to ally with it against the imperial power. Isaiah resolutely opposes Judah's substituting political maneuvers for trust in Yahweh's commitment to Zion (v. 32b). Perhaps giving Philistia this message even invites them to put their trust in Zion.

15:1–16:14. Moab

The Moabites, Judah's neighbor to the southeast, occupied the territory across the Dead Sea. They, too, were inclined to try to get Judah to join them in rebelling against Assyria. For them, too, Isaiah warns of disaster; but the message is designed for the Judeans to hear, again to bolster their resistance to talk of alliance and rebellion. The passage brings together a sequence of originally separate poems about Moab, arranged so that portrayals of disaster (15:1–9; 16:6–14) stand on either side of a more promising vision (16:1–5).

15:1–9. Once more, the portrayal of disaster hitting Moab does not describe something that has already happened in the way that it happened, nor something that is to happen in the way it is to happen. It is an imaginary scenario, a picture of what another invasion could be like for Moab and what its implications could be for the people. In the aftermath of such devastation throughout the different Moabite cities and regions, people make pilgrimage to the land's sanctuaries to mourn and lament there. Paradoxically, Isaiah or Yahweh cries out for the Moabites in their suffering and declares that there will be even more.

16:1–5. This invitation makes more explicit than 14:32 that Judah's neighbors are invited to have recourse to Yahweh when they suffer disaster. They can bring gifts to the Davidic king and the God of Zion and seek their wisdom and refuge, fulfilling the vision of 2:2–4.

16:6–14. This picture of tough love or loving toughness adds a note of rationale for the disaster, which lies in Moab's majesty and self-assurance that need to be exposed. At the same time, the passage again grieves over the people's suffering, declares that even this will not be the end of disaster, and adds that having recourse to their sanctuaries (to have their gods to protect them) will not help them.

17:1–11. Aram and Ephraim

17:1–9. Completing the circle around Judah, Isaiah comes to Aram and Ephraim (cf. 7:1–9; 8:1–4). There is something shocking about the inclusion of Ephraim, which includes most of the clans that were supposed to comprise Israel (they are called Jacob in v. 4); they are thus bracketed with a foreign people. They stand together with them in their politics and they will be together with them in their fate. As with Moab, one of the disaster's consequences will be to convince Aram that its humanly devised religion is useless (vv. 7–8).

17:10–11. "You" is feminine singular, suggesting it addresses a city; the indictment implies an Israelite city that has turned away from Yahweh to use the methods of traditional religion to seek to ensure a harvest. Is this Samaria, Ephraim's capital? Or has Isaiah turned round to address Jerusalem itself? Or does either city have to ask, "Is it I?"

C. The Empire (17:12–14)

At the center of this sequence of declarations about individual nations is one about "the nations," which in the prophets is often a term for the imperial power of the day that comprises and controls many individual peoples. This multinational entity is pictured as thundering and roaring as it asserts itself and seeks to extend its tentacles over a little people such as Judah. Nonetheless, they will vanish with the dawn.

D. The Southern Powers (18:1–20:6)

Judah and its neighbors sat between the great powers to the north and east and the great powers to the south. In Isaiah's day an Ethiopian dynasty ruled in Egypt, so "Ethiopia" or "Egypt" refers to the same power. Egypt was sometimes a threat to Judah, sometimes a resource it relied on as it played one great power off against another, sometimes a temptation as it could itself seek to get Judah to collaborate in resisting Assyrian power and domination. Like the prophecies regarding Moab, 18:1–20:6 sit at the center of promises of a positive future for Egypt, but frame them with warnings of disaster.

18:1–7. Ethiopia

Isaiah himself was in no position to dismiss Ethiopian envoys seeking Judean cooperation to conduct their foreign policy. His message is for Judean politicians who would actually decide how to respond to these diplomatic approaches. Once again the political oracle closes by noting how these foreign peoples will come to recognize Yahweh.

19:1–25. Egypt

19:1–15. Initially everything is negative; Judah must not take Egypt too seriously as a potential ally. Egypt was famed for its intellectual resources, and intellectual resources are also a political resource; Egypt has plans for its role in the Middle East and Judah is inclined to go along with them in formulating its own plans. It is not surprising that Egypt ignores the fact that Yahweh also has plans. It is sadder that Judah does so: see vv. 3, 11 ("counsel" is the same word), 12, and 17 (also 5:19; 8:10; 14:24–27; 30:1). A major aim here is to get Judah to see that its own plans are based on false premises and that Egypt's policy-making will let it down. Egypt is destined to experience being under a "hard master" (maybe Assyria) just as it had long ago been a hard master over Israel. The Nile's affliction also recalls the exodus story. But the Nile was Egypt's great pride. Egypt never had to worry about drought as Judah did. But the resource Egypt thought it could always rely on will let it down.

19:16–25. These verses provide a transition to looking at Egypt quite differently. A bridge passage (vv. 16–17) continues the warning tone of vv. 1–15 and the theme of planning, but it is the first of five prose prophecies about features of "that day," a day that lies beyond current circumstances, a time when Yahweh's purpose will be fulfilled. That need not make it a far-off day, but it is marked off from the present, as the message

in vv. 1–15 is not. On that day, confidence will be turned into fear, an appropriate stance to Yahweh (the words for "tremble," "fear," and "terror" can all have a positive meaning in connection with awe). Egyptians will speak Hebrew and swear allegiance to Yahweh. Yahweh will relate to Egypt in the same way as to Israel (vv. 19–22). Egypt and Assyria will worship together; they will be "my people" and "the work of my hands," like and with Israel. Thus Israel will fulfill its Abrahamic vocation to be a blessing in the midst of the earth as it stands between them geographically and mediates between them.

After the exile, Egypt became a major center of Jewish life and thus a place where Yahweh was worshiped. It was eventually the place at which the Scriptures were translated into Greek so that Greek-speaking Jews and Gentiles could read them. Nothing like vv. 24–25 came true, yet Israel held onto these promises and incorporated them in their Scriptures, apparently in the conviction that they were still true prophecies, expressions of Yahweh's purpose that would still be fulfilled one way or another.

20:1–6. Egypt and Ethiopia

In the context of events taking place in 711 BCE (also reported in Sargon's own records), Isaiah makes more concrete his declaration concerning Assyria's defeat of Egypt and Ethiopia, and dramatizes it. Since Isaiah's speaking of Yahweh's words is Yahweh's means of implementing them (cf. 9:8), so is acting out what Yahweh intends. Isaiah need not have spent three whole years going about virtually naked (in the freezing cold of a Jerusalem winter); perhaps he appeared from time to time like that. But perhaps that is to try to rationalize what he did and reduce it to something we can more easily envisage.

E. The Northern Powers, and Jerusalem Itself (21:1–23:17)

21:1–17. Babylon

21:1–10. In returning to the northern powers, only with v. 9 does one discover that the first message concerns Babylon; "wilderness of the sea" presumably meant something to Isaiah's hearers but it remains a mystery to us. Verse 1*b* describes the coming of an unidentified army, also conveying a tone of mystery and terror (cf. vv. 3–4). Once again Yahweh is commissioning conquerors to put Babylon down (cf. 13:1–22). This will apparently involve deceit; allies will turn into attackers (vv. 2, 5). Elam and Media are beyond Babylon to the east. Verses 6–9 describe the commissioning of a lookout on the walls of the city that sent off the attacking army, waiting for news to come of whether they have been successful; in v. 9*b* he declares that they have been. Babylon's fall in 539 would be a fulfillment of the vision, and v. 10 might reflect the way this is good news for Judah.

21:11–12. Dumah is an oasis near Babylon, perhaps inevitably sucked into the kind of conflict vv. 1–10 describe. Here, people who fear a surprise night attack wait anxiously for the morning; the lookout reminds them that surviving one night only means facing another.

21:13–17. Dedan and Tema in turn are oases near Dumah, and Kedar is a people (rather than a place) in that area. "Desert plain" is *'arav*; these people live in northwest Arabia. They too are apparently affected by these events. Verse 14 attests to a need for people to have compassion on fugitives. Verses 16–17 recognize that these events in far-off lands take place within Yahweh's sovereignty.

22:1–25. Jerusalem

22:1–14. The audience might again be unsure what city the enigmatic heading refers to, but might assume it was another obscure foreign city, which apparently had a narrow but rather ignominious escape from destruction (vv. 1–3). Then they discover that the prophecy is talking about—themselves (vv. 4–14); see further chs. 36–37. This section also presupposes that the great escape is not the end. People have failed to learn the lesson from what happened. As usual, Isaiah berates them for thinking they were responsible for their own destiny and not letting a crisis make them turn to Yahweh. As usual, he puts the implications of their words into their mouths (they did not actually utter the words in v. 13*b*). By simply rejoicing in Yahweh's deliverance and not turning to Yahweh, they were signing the death warrant that would be delivered when Jerusalem fell in 587 BCE.

Ironically, Jerusalem's eventual captors are to be the same sort of people that in the previous chapter destroyed Babylon. They will not actually be the identical people, but referring to these people helps to underline a point. In one sense, and theologically, Jerusalem is a city with a very different status and significance from all the other places in chs. 13–23. But the unexpected incorporation of Jerusalem here suggests to its people that in a sense it is just another city. It behaves that way, and it will be treated in such a way.

22:15–25. Isaiah turns to Shebna, a senior politician of the day, who is building an impressive tomb for himself in the city. Because of his commitment to this memorial, he will be ignominiously cast out and replaced by Eliakim, who will exercise his important role.

23:1–18. Tyre

23:1–14. The declarations concerning the nations close with Tyre, south of modern Beirut. Tyre, the great trading and maritime power to the northwest of Jerusalem, and Babylon, the great political and military power to the northeast, thus form a bracket around these declarations. The prophecy works by imagining peoples' horror and astonishment when its trading and maritime power collapses. Sidon, its neighbor, is naturally associated with Tyre's fate. Like other powers, it is put down precisely because of its greatness, which causes it to be rather impressed with itself (vv. 9–12). And like other powers, it is thus the victim of Yahweh's capacity to make a plan and implement it (v. 9).

The old city of Tyre is a small island half a mile off the coast, located in a very strong defensive position. It is "the fortress of the sea" (v. 4), always hard to conquer. It was better placed than most Levantine cities to resist incorporation into one of the great empires or engage in successful rebellion against a superpower. Even Nebuchadnezzar failed to capture it (Ezek 29:17–18), and Alexander the Great did so only by building a causeway to the city.

23:15–18. Again paralleling other declarations, these final verses indicate that destruction is not the end of the story. Tyre can turn to Yahweh. After the regular "seventy years," it will eventually return to trading, but now dedicating its profits to Yahweh, supporting the worship of

Yahweh. The declaration presupposes that trading is like prostitution (it turns relationships into a means of making money?). (Prophets can use bold imagery.)

III. The World (24:1–27:13)

Through chs. 1–23, the geographical and temporal horizon keeps broadening. Chapters 24–27 have a yet wider horizon. They make little reference to concrete peoples or events and talk rather about the wasting of the whole earth, about the swallowing up of death, and about Yahweh's dealing with cosmic forces of resistance. They do refer to Judah and Jerusalem (e.g., 24:23; 26:1). Those whom Isaiah addresses are still the people living there, confronted by a world that ignores Yahweh's expectations and purposes and by an empire with its great capital that abuses a little people such as Judah.

A. The Earth Laid Waste (24:1–16)

24:1–13. A Horrifying Vision (i)

The imagery is dominated by a wasting of the world, from which no one is protected by their status or resources (the "now" in v. 1 is a logical "now," not a temporal one). The author (vv. 5–6) assumes that Yahweh has made known basic expectations to the whole world, and in fact made an everlasting covenant with the earth. The passage refers to the Noachian covenant or something like it. Humanity's failure to live up to those basic expectations leads to a curse that devours the world. The language of curse also recalls Gen 3–4, though the word for curse here is different (strictly, it denotes an oath).

24:14–16. A Response of Praise and Dismay

The prophet hears voices praising Yahweh (vv. 14–16a). The passage does not indicate whose voices these are. Nonetheless, the prophet is unable to join with them, because of a sense of horror at the current state of affairs (v. 16b).

B. Earth and Heaven in Tumult (24:17–25:5)

24:17–23. A Horrifying Vision (ii)

The second vision of total devastation briefly recapitulates the first one (vv. 17–20), then adds another dimension (vv. 21–23). Whereas the first confined itself to this world and emphasized how the calamity affected all sorts of people, the second adds reference to "the host of heaven" and "the kings of earth." The former stand over against "the LORD of hosts" and the latter stand over against the idea of Yahweh "reigning" (v. 23; in Hebrew "king" is *melekh*, "reign" is *malakh*). This perspective offers a different way of describing the world's sin. "Transgression" is here *pesha'*, which denotes rebelling against authority. The prophet sees the world's sin as lying in the way entities that were supposed to accept Yahweh's authority rebelled against it. There are such entities on earth; the passage assumes that there are similar heavenly powers. The reference to the sun and the moon perhaps reflects astrological religions' belief in the authority of heavenly powers, exercised via the stars and planets. There seems to be something demonic (we might say) about the way human authorities behave. Wittingly or unwittingly, they seem to be related to something bigger than themselves. But Yahweh will punish them as well. And thus Jerusalem will become the place from which Yahweh reigns (cf. 2:2–4).

25:1–5. A Willing Response

There is no equivocation about the response to the second vision (contrast 24:14–16). The putting down of the heavenly and earthly powers proved Yahweh to be the refuge of the needy, amongst whom Judah could see itself. Perhaps the implication is that the heavenly and earthly authorities are their oppressors. Or perhaps Yahweh has proved to be the refuge of the needy by protecting them in the midst of the calamity that overwhelmed the earth. Either way, even the strong and ruthless now acknowledge Yahweh. The parallelism with "glorify" suggests that "fear" has the common connotation of "revere/acknowledge/worship." Once again there is good news as well as bad news for the victims of Yahweh's judgment. They come to see the truth and acknowledge it.

C. The World Rejoicing, Moab Humiliated (25:6–26:19)

25:6–12. An Encouraging Vision (i)

All peoples will come to Mount Zion, as Yahweh brings war to an end. The ensuing celebration eliminates the experience of death, grief, and mourning associated with war. There will be a feast resembling a great festival such as Passover or Tabernacles or such as the Israelite elders feasting with Yahweh at Sinai (Exod 24). These occasions were not confined to people who were born Israelites; foreigners in Israel who chose to become full members of the community could participate. This celebration is more deliberately an occasion for all peoples (cf. 2:2–4), other victims of the power that is being destroyed. At the same time, it is still good news for Israel, because God removes the disgrace that has come upon Israel through its many military defeats. Yahweh's bringing peace to the world also means that he is delivering Israel.

God's decisive action does not remove from people the necessity to make their response to Yahweh. While the banquet is for all peoples and Moab has already been singled out and implicitly invited (16:1–5), if it prefers to hang onto its pride and its own strength, it will pay the price (vv. 10b–12).

26:1–19. A Response of Praise and Yearning

Whereas the responses in 24:14–16 and 25:1–5 come in the present, as reactions to what God intends to do, this response initially takes the form of a song that will be sung at the time when Yahweh does what the visions declare; cf. 12:1–6. But the response of praise (vv. 1–6) gives way to a response of yearning for God to act in accordance with the vision (vv. 7–19), cf. 24:14–16, which contained two comparable elements. When the people of God stand between God's making promises and God's fulfilling them, then both praise and prayer are appropriate.

26:1–6. Judah will be in a position to give praise for the strength of its city. It looks so much less impressive than a city such as Babylon, but is much stronger because Yahweh protects it (the word translated "victory" is *yeshu'a*, usually translated by words such as "deliverance"). Once again the prophecy pictures Jerusalem open to other peoples. The people who live there are to open its gates so that any nation that keeps faith can enter.

26:7–19. But all this lies in the future. In the manner of a psalm, vv. 7–8 go on to declare that the people believe those declarations, but do not experience them at the present time. Yahweh is the God of mercy and grace (the word translated "favor" also means "grace") and is therefore

inclined to postpone the moment of putting down the oppressor, but if Yahweh does so forever, he would encourage people to think they can get away with anything (vv. 9–11). Verses 12–19 then mix future tense and past tense verbs, but vv. 14–15 denote what will be true when Yahweh has acted (as was the case in 9:2–4). Yahweh will have put down the nation's foreign overlords in such a way that they will never come back to life and power, and, as a result, Yahweh's own people, which seemed dead, will be brought back to life. The imagery of death and resurrection thus involves the entire people of God, as is the case with Ezekiel's vision of the dry bones (Ezek 37:1–14), not those of a single person.

D. Israel Protected and Restored: An Encouraging Vision (ii) (26:20–27:13)

26:20–21. These verses, too, are similar to the discourse of psalms. When people pray, Yahweh responds; psalms sometimes include this response (notably, Ps 12). Here Yahweh responds to the reflections and yearning expressed in 26:7–19. People cannot see any sign that deliverance is coming or that the moribund nation is going to be revived as the "lofty city" is brought down. The prophecy declares that this is such a real and certain event that Yahweh's people need to prepare for that dire time.

Chapter 27 adds four more promises about how things will be "on that day" or "in days to come." Admittedly such expressions imply a disjunction between the present and the future. Things that will take place "on that day" may be certain, but there is no sign of them arriving. The people of God have to live by faith that Yahweh's word will indeed be fulfilled.

27:1. First, Yahweh will complete the task of subduing the powers of disorder and resistance that was begun at creation, the powers embodied in the "lofty city." When the OT refers to "Satan," it does not imply a figure with the profile of Satan in the NT, but when it speaks of Leviathan, the serpent, or the dragon, it can imply a figure rather like that (cf. Rev 12:9).

27:2–5. Second, the relationship between the vinedresser and the vine will be restored to one of protection rather than attack (contrast 5:1–7). As NRSV understands v. 4, the vine itself will still need to make sure it generates no thorns and briers; but other translations take these thorns and briers to be attackers of the vine, with whom Yahweh relishes the idea of fighting.

27:6–11. Third, the vine will thus flourish and so the fortunes of the people will be reversed. Israel has paid the price for its guilt, but that means it can now be restored; the destruction it has experienced means the forms of worship that offended Yahweh have been destroyed. The fortified city (vv. 10–11) is presumably again the lofty city that symbolizes the oppressive superpower, as in 25:2; it has proved unwilling to face the facts about its position and about God's expectations of it, and it pays the price, so that its oppression comes to an end.

27:12–13. Fourth, Yahweh will bring the scattered people home from both ends of the world to which they have been scattered so that they can join in worship again.

IV. Judah in the Time of Hezekiah (28:1–33:24)

Chapters 28–33 comprise five sections, all beginning *hoy*. The exclamation resembles the English "Hey" in drawing people's attention to what follows, but it can have various nuances (NRSV translates "Ah," "Oh," and "Alas"). Whereas earlier chapters have referred to King Ahaz, chs. 28–33 is the time of King Hezekiah, who will himself eventually appear in chs. 36–39. Isaiah's critique of the people in the context of Ahaz's reign in chs. 1–12 emphasized the way the haves were abusing the have-nots, though it also referred to the nation's need to trust in Yahweh rather than in political alliances. In this new context, the minor theme has become the major theme. Ephraim has fallen to the Assyrians, who are now threatening Judah. Judah is therefore inclined to look in the opposite direction for support, to Egypt (see 30:1–7; 31:1–3).

A. A Covenant with Death (28:1–29)

28:1–6. This chapter takes its time about revealing the real agenda, the theme of trust that will run through the chapters (see vv. 11–12, 15–16). First (vv. 1–4) it again expresses judgment on Ephraim, in a way that might be calculated to make the people of Judah cheer, though it also speaks about the way this act will not be Yahweh's last word (vv. 5–6). It is odd that by this time Ephraim has already fallen to the Assyrians. Perhaps Isaiah is referring to people living in the capital, Samaria, who escaped deportation, or perhaps he is recalling a message he delivered in those earlier decades.

28:7–13. Either way, the point lies in the way he turns to his own people to say "You are just as bad." His particular focus is the self-indulgence of the people who were supposed to guide people in the right way (vv. 7–8) and their related scorn for Isaiah's message (vv. 9–13). They think that message is too juvenile to take seriously. It means declining to take adult responsibility. But ignoring it will be their downfall.

28:14–22. In making treaties or covenants with a nation such as Egypt, they think they are safeguarding their lives but actually they are committing suicide. Of course they do not see themselves as having made an alliance with Sheol, the abode of the dead, but that is the implication of their having made a treaty with Egypt. They are bringing disaster on themselves; Sheol is where they will end up. Trust in Yahweh is the key to security, whereas trusting in something else will destroy the people. Yahweh in person will bring that about. It will be a great act such as the one described in 2 Sam 5:17–25 and 1 Chr 14:8–16; except that this time Yahweh will be acting against Israel, not for Israel. Isaiah notes that it seems strange that Yahweh would bring such a calamity on Israel. The natural thing for Yahweh to do is be faithful and merciful. But people need to be aware that Yahweh will enact punishment when it is appropriate.

28:23–29. Isaiah then speaks in the manner of a teacher whose insight appears in Proverbs. This is paradoxical because Isaiah has been challenging people not to rely too much on human wisdom. But he points out that the wisdom of a farmer, who knows how and when to plow as well as how and when to sow, illustrates the wisdom with which Yahweh operates in Israel's life (not surprisingly, because the farmer's wisdom comes from Yahweh). Yahweh plows, which is an unpleasant experience for the ground, but Yahweh also sows, and knows how to do both. The close of the chapter thus offers allusive encouragement after Isaiah has once again warned of disaster to come.

B. Disaster Threatened and Averted (i) (29:1–24)

29:1-8. This chapter unfolds dramatically. First it speaks of Jerusalem as the city David camped against and captured, so that it became the city where Israel worshiped. Now it seems as if David is again besieging Jerusalem, except that Israel is David's victim, and Yahweh's victim. Only here is Jerusalem called "Ariel"; the name sounds like the term for the hearth round the altar where animals were burned as a sacrifice. The whole city is going to be consumed by fire; except that, at the last minute, Yahweh reprieves it, changes sides, and defeats its attackers. The warning and promise correspond to two sides of Yahweh's relationship with Israel. The people's faithlessness means Yahweh has to take action against it, but Yahweh's faithfulness means Yahweh will finally be merciful.

29:9-16. The faithlessness and the imperative of chastisement are developed, with further paradox and an awareness of the mystery of human willfulness. The people are blind and deaf to what Yahweh is doing. They will not see the truth; indeed they seem unable to do so. What stops them? It is their own unwillingness to see and hear. Yet a person cannot help being blind and deaf. Yahweh has already told Isaiah that he is to be the means for making them deaf and blind; it is part of the punishment for their turning away from Yahweh (6:9–10). The people are engaged in joyful worship, they know all the words to sing, but their true attitude as expressed in their life does not correspond to what the words say. In the OT, the heart usually refers not to the emotions but to what one may call the mind, the inward person forming attitudes and making decisions about how to live. The people's hearts being far from Yahweh when they worship means there is a mismatch between their worship, which might be full of enthusiasm, and the way they live. In worship they acknowledge Yahweh's wisdom, but they live on the basis of their own wisdom. As in 28:15, they may not literally say that Yahweh has no understanding, but that is implied by the way they decide to run their political affairs.

29:17-24. In turn, the divine faithfulness and mercy reappear. The movement of forest becoming farmland and farmland becoming forest is another image for the way Yahweh's wisdom works (cf. 28:23–29). The time will come when the deaf and blind will see, the needy will have reason to rejoice, their abusers will be put down, the shamed will be honored, and the faithless will acknowledge Yahweh as the holy one.

C. The Wisdom of Relying on Yahweh (i) (30:1–33)

30:1–7. The context continues to be the Assyrian threat to Judah, but the focus moves to political policy in Jerusalem, seeking alliance with and support from Egypt. Isaiah presses the scandalous nature of this action in two ways. First, Judah is contravening the alliance it has already made with Yahweh. The words tell the story, especially the word *plan*: Yahweh is supposed to be the one who makes plans for Judah. Second, Yahweh is supposed to be the people's refuge, protection, shelter, shadow, help (cf. Ps 91). Once more, the words tell the story. It is blasphemous to treat Egypt as if it could have that significance (again, no doubt Isaiah is interpreting the politicians' actual words), and this will not only fail but have the opposite effect. *Rahab* (the name is differently spelled in Hebrew from the Rahab in Joshua) is another term for an embodiment of dynamic power asserted against God; it is associated with the battle at the Red Sea (cf. Isa 51:9). If Egypt could only live up to its reputation, it might be of some use to Judah, but it will turn out to be too weak to do so.

30:8–14. In further expounding the nature of Judah's rebellion and seeking to bring Judah to its senses, the prophecy invites them to see how their reputation for rebellion will haunt them forever. The words attributed to them reflect their behavior rather than constitute their actual words, but v. 11*b* is especially chilling. Isaiah indicts them for blasphemy, "trusting in" and "relying on" something other than Yahweh: indeed, in oppression and deceit. So disaster will follow. This process as described does not require the direct action of Yahweh but is the natural outworking and inevitable result of their own action.

30:15–17. Deliverance and strength lie in Judah's doing nothing on its own. It is very hard to make politicians live on the basis of that principle. They normally seek to take what they see as responsible action, but events will turn their aims upside down.

30:18. NRSV's layout of the chapter reflects the critically important role of v. 18; the verse reflects a paradox prominent in the book. The people's policies require that Yahweh is held back from showing grace. Yet there is another logic afoot: Yahweh will indeed show them compassion, one way or another. Yahweh is a God of justice—that is, one who takes the right kind of decisive action. So the negative waiting on Yahweh's part is paired with an encouragement to a positive waiting on the people's part.

30:19–22. The content or basis for hope is expressed in three ways. First, the people's relationship with Yahweh will be put back on its proper footing. At the moment they do not turn to Yahweh when they are under pressure, so Yahweh may not answer. However, when the people cry out and when they abandon their idols, Yahweh will respond graciously to them.

30:23–26. Second, the practicalities of their life will work out. Though this idyllic picture is interrupted by the reference to slaughter and towers falling, the people's restoration requires these events.

30:27–33. The time of well-being is developed, thirdly, in the promise of Assyria's downfall. Only then will Judah be able to enjoy full life. A people oppressed or controlled by an imperial power knows that putting down that imperial power is vital to its future.

D. The Wisdom of Relying on Yahweh (ii); Disaster Threatened and Averted (ii) (31:1–32:20)

These two chapters are about the same length as chapters 28, 29, 30, and 33, and they have one *hoy* in 31:1 to introduce them; that suggests chs. 31 and 32 belong together.

31:1–9. They begin by re-expressing the challenges in 29:1–8 and 30:1–7. Similar to 30:1–7, they again make the point by talk of trust, reliance, wisdom, and help; Judah associates these with its Egyptian policy rather than with Yahweh. Verse 3 reformulates the point by an instructive contrast of "human-God" and "flesh-spirit." In Paul, the latter would imply the sinfulness of the flesh, but in the OT, "flesh" simply suggests weakness over against the dynamic power of the spirit of God. Refusal to recognize this reality will mean Yahweh

swooping down on Jerusalem like a lion or vulture (vv. 4–5). But then, as in 29:1–8, the attacker suddenly becomes the protector. Once again, Isaiah is addressing both the necessity for Yahweh to act against Jerusalem and the necessity for Yahweh to deliver it. Related to this is the necessity for Judah to turn to Yahweh (vv. 6–7). This action of the people may have to be a response to Yahweh's act of deliverance, not a reason for it; the deliverance issues simply from Yahweh's mercy (vv. 8–9).

32:1–8. Judah needs decent leadership to pull it away from the life-style that makes Yahweh take it to the brink of destruction. Yahweh promises to provide such individuals. Good leaders will protect the weak, make discerning decisions (that is, decisions that take God into account), and encourage the community to recognize villainy as villainy and goodness as goodness. Such actions will transform the society.

32:9–14. Whereas the willfulness that 31:1–32:8 presupposes may be traced to the male leaders in the society, vv. 9–14 turn to their wives, who have little opportunity to do anything but enjoy the fruits of their husbands' folly. "Complacent" comes from the verb "trust" and thus takes up Isaiah's recurrent critique of Judah; the women share the attitude of their husbands who reckon it is safe to trust themselves, their policies, or their allies. Everything in which they trust will collapse. In light of the catastrophe Yahweh is bringing, which will mean the end of their pleasant life-style, Isaiah bids the wives to prepare to behave like mourners. An invading army will destroy the fields as well as the cities and turn the cities themselves into wilderness.

32:15–20. Once more Isaiah turns things round. Verse 15 marks the transition by means of another reference to the power of God's dynamic spirit, which can transform the devastated landscape. Crops will flourish again, and so will proper relationships in the society. The nation will know the peace and security that the politicians seek by the wrong means, and proper trust will be possible. The last two verses presuppose the notion that urban life is really unnatural and that people will return to something more like the Garden of Eden.

E. Yahweh Exalted in Majesty (33:1–24)

Throughout chs. 28–33, the ratio of threat to promise keeps changing, with the stress on threat in chs. 28–29 and more of a balance in chs. 30–32, until in ch. 33 all the stress lies on promise. But the chapter does not develop in a logical way like chs. 28–32 because it takes up themes and expressions from throughout chs. 1–32 and turns them into a kaleidoscope of promise. There is no pattern to the arrangement of the pieces of glass or paper in a kaleidoscope (except the one produced by its mirrors). Verse 2, for instance, takes up 30:18–19; v. 8 compares with 24:5; 28:15, 18; v. 9 repeats 24:4 and summarizes 32:9–14; v. 11 takes up 26:17–18; and so on. These are only examples of the ways specific words and phrases from chs. 1–32 recur throughout the chapter.

Chapter 33 thus rounds off chs. 1–33, taking us halfway through the book. And whereas chs. 28–32, like the earlier part of the book, refer to specific times, people, and places, here there is little of that. The chapter is more broadly applicable. The opening words about the destroyer who has not been destroyed, for instance, can apply to any instance of such a superpower. Within OT times, that phrase might have been understood to refer to Assyria, Babylon, Persia, and Greece, but it has been applied to superpowers after OT times as well.

The chapter promises that the superpower will not stand (v. 1). It provides Yahweh the response and the testimony that Yahweh looks for but has usually not received (vv. 2–6). It laments the experience of hardship that the people bring on themselves but then declares that Yahweh will act decisively (vv. 7–12). It challenges Judahites to acknowledge Yahweh's deeds (vv. 13–16). Finally, it promises good leaders and a restored city (vv. 17–24).

V. Ultimate Redress and Transformation (34:1–35:10)

These two chapters continue the promise in ch. 33, which concluded the first half of the book: Yahweh's ultimate purpose will be fulfilled. Chapters 34–35 provide a double introduction to the book's second half. Whereas the first half reports considerable indictment of Israel for its waywardness, there is much less in the second half. And whereas there was less encouragement of Israel in the first half, there is more in the second. These changes presuppose a situation in historical context. In the early sixth century BCE, Yahweh brought on Jerusalem the kind of catastrophe that chs. 1–33 had threatened; many people from Judah were taken into exile. Now, after that catastrophe, the time has come to put down Judah's attackers and to restore Judah. These two chapters introduce those themes.

A. Redress (34:1–17)

34:1–4. The chapter begins by summoning the nations to hear of the doom that is to come on them and on their deities (cf. 24:21–23).

34:5–7. It then focuses on Edom. Edom is thus in the position occupied earlier in the book by the Assyrian and Babylonian superpowers. All are national embodiments of power and aggressiveness. They are unwitting servants of Yahweh in bringing calamity on Judah, but they act for their own reasons and they are subject to Yahweh's judgment. Edom was never a superpower but a power of similar status to Judah itself, with its heartland to the southeast of Judah and southeast of the Dead Sea. But it gradually took over vast areas of Judean land over a period beginning in the seventh century and extending through the Second Temple period.

34:8–17. Any restoration of Judahite land would require the removal of Edom (see the parallelism in 35:4); this is action undertaken "by Zion's cause." The action will give Judah its land back. The chapter gives no reason for Yahweh's anger, beyond the need to restore Zion to its land. It simply declares that Edom will become a kind of sacrifice. "Doom" translates the verb *kharam*, which refers to the total destruction that Israel reports took place when it conquered Canaan (see Josh 11:20). "Lilith" is a Mesopotamian demon or spirit or goddess; vv. 8–17 indicate that the land will be devastated in the manner of Sodom and Gomorrah and thus left for the wildest of animals and demons to inhabit.

"Vengeance" (*naqam*) does not suggest revenge but proper redress for wrongdoing (see the parallelism in 35:4). The destruction of Edom itself is not actually required to put right its occupation of Judean land; this action has melded into an act of final judgment on a serious evildoer. In Roman times "Edom" became a code word for the Roman

Empire itself, and the focus on Edom here, standing for the nations as a whole, perhaps already suggests it has become a kind of cipher for an evil empire. Edom is mentioned only in vv. 5–7; no doubt it is assumed in vv. 8–17 (see NRSV in v. 9) but since it is not named explicitly readers should not focus exclusively on this particular embodiment of aggressiveness but understand that it symbolizes national aggression against God's will and people.

B. Transformation (35:1–11)

Edom's streams will be turned into pitch and habited land will be given over to wild animals, whereas Judah's streams will flow in the desert and the territory of wild animals will become habitable by human beings. These two chapters thus mirror each other. The deposition of Edom makes possible the restoration of Judah. The chapter brings together four separate pictures.

35:1–2. First, wilderness that grows only enough grass to support a few sheep will be transformed so that it resembles forested Lebanon or wooded and flowered Carmel; its splendor will thus proclaim Yahweh's splendor.

35:3–4. Second, Yahweh's coming with recompense will mean deliverance from Babylon or Edom or whomever, and mean that people who are discouraged by being in exile in Babylon, by living under Persian imperial control, or by having lost their land to Edom can have hope.

35:5–7. Third, these great acts of God will break through the people's blindness and deafness in relation to Yahweh, which Isaiah had lamented, and will cause people to jump and shout in praise.

35:8–10. And the people who have been cut off from Jerusalem by exile or flight will be able to return safely, grief at their fate being replaced by joy.

VI. Judah in the Time of Hezekiah (36:1–39:8)

Despite the presence of stories about Isaiah in chs 6–7 and 20, these chapters are the most sustained narratives in the book. They are actually variants of 2 Kgs 18:13–20:19, but they include more of Isaiah's prophecies (2 Chr 32 offers another, shorter version of the story). In each book the narratives have a logical place as part of the whole. In Isaiah they link both backwards to what has preceded and forwards to what will follow (and in that respect they parallel chs. 34–35). Insofar as they are about events in Hezekiah's reign, particularly the political and religious crisis of Assyrian invasion, they are related to chs. 28–32, which derive from Isaiah's activity in that period. But insofar as they close with the prospect of exile in Babylon, they belong with chs. 40–55, which presuppose the fulfillment of Isaiah's prophecy about that exile.

A. Sennacherib's Challenge to Hezekiah, and Isaiah's Response (i) (36:1–37:7)

36:1. The Assyrians' desire to extend their empire to include Judah, which occupies a strategic position at the tipping point between the area of Assyrian control and the area of Egyptian dominance, provides the background for these narratives. As chs. 28–32 indicate, Hezekiah saw alliance with Egypt as the lesser of these two evils, but he perhaps miscalculated the Assyrians' determination. Verse 1 summarizes their devastating achievement. Only Jerusalem remains for Sennacherib to conquer. Located on the top of the mountain ridge that runs north-south between the Mediterranean and the Jordan valley, it is less accessible than other cities such as Lachish, near the coastal plain. And it is in a strong position on a spur of that mountain ridge, so that when an army arrives there, it will have a hard time capturing the city; its best bet is to starve the residents into surrender.

36:2–10. From Lachish, then, the king sends his commanding officer and his army up to Jerusalem and he attempts negotiations for the city's surrender, shouting across one of the ravines that protect the city. He points out the fallacy (as he sees it) in relying on any of the resources on which the king might rely.

36:11–20. The king's staff amusingly ask him to speak in the international language, which they understand but ordinary people do not. That only prompts him to restate his case for the sake of the ordinary people who are going to be devastatingly affected by what happens.

36:21–37:7. His staff report to Hezekiah, who knows the two things he must do; he is the model king in this story. King and staff know that belittling Egypt is all very well, but the commander has made a fatal mistake in belittling Yahweh. In a situation of peril such as the city is in, a prophet's job is to mediate between the people and Yahweh by bringing their needs to Yahweh and bringing Yahweh's word to them.

B. Sennacherib's Challenge to Hezekiah, and Isaiah's Response (ii) (37:8–38)

The dynamics of this episode parallel those of the first (some interpreters think it is an alternative version of the first episode (vv. 37–38 report Sennacherib's return to his own land and his death, in fulfillment of v. 7). But the text presents this episode as following on the first.

37:8–20. The king indeed hears a rumor (v. 7) and goes off to pay attention to trouble elsewhere (the word for "rumor," *shemu'a,* usually means "report" and need not mean the news is untrue). Meanwhile Sennacherib sends Hezekiah a message implying "I'll be back." But his mistake is to speak even more disparagingly of Yahweh's capacity to protect Jerusalem (vv. 8–13). Hezekiah again knows what to do and how to press Yahweh to take action (vv. 14–20).

37:21–29. Isaiah brings a reply, which expands significantly on vv. 6–7, thus becoming the dominant feature of this second episode. The poetic message is formally addressed to Sennacherib, but it is a message to Hezekiah, encouraging him with the promise that Jerusalem is destined to see Sennacherib depart (v. 22) because of the mistake he has made in the way he thinks and speaks of Yahweh and of his own achievements (vv. 23–29). Isaiah thus takes up characteristic emphases of chs. 1–12, including the declaration that the key factor in these events is not the plans of the great Assyrian king but the plans of Yahweh, of which Sennacherib is the unwitting executor.

37:30–35. The prose supplement to the poetic message then addresses Hezekiah directly. Its opening presupposes the devastating effect that military invasion brings. The army both eats everything that grows and makes it impossible to plant and grow for the next year; still normal life is destined to resume. This might seem an unspectacular promise, but is actually a remarkable one, as is suggested by the declaration that the zeal or passion of Yahweh will accomplish it. It means that a "remnant" of the Judean people who

have had to take refuge in Jerusalem will be free to take possession of the land again. Verses 33–35 re-express Yahweh's intention about Sennacherib, with the significant double theological rationale present in v. 35*b*.

37:36–37. There follows a devastating disaster, followed by events that fulfill Yahweh's words.

C. Hezekiah's Illness, and Isaiah's Response (38:1–22)

38:1–8. As is often the case, Isaiah mediates between the king and the heavenly cabinet, though (as in the psalms) the passage also assumes that the king himself can approach Yahweh with his pleas, and assumes that the object of that is not to conform his will to God's but to change God's mind; and he succeeds in doing that. Hezekiah's plea changes the divine decision announced in v. 1. As the NRSV margin notes, the meaning of vv. 7–8 is not clear, though evidently Hezekiah was given an extraordinary sign that Yahweh had heard his prayer.

38:9–20. The prayer of thanksgiving parallels such thanksgivings in the Psalter. Indeed, there is nothing that refers concretely to Hezekiah's own experience, which suggests that Hezekiah is using a "standard" psalm. Verse 9 could be translated "a writing for Hezekiah" and there is no need to think that he personally wrote it; it might be more natural to assume that it was written for him. Thanksgiving psalms are commonly dominated by a recollection of the straits from which God rescued a person, a feature that dominates this thanksgiving. Thus whereas it often looks as if the psalm is describing Hezekiah's current suffering, it is actually describing how things were when he was sick and how he prayed then. The poem also speaks of Sheol in the manner of a psalm, though in the book of Isaiah this motif recalls previous texts that mentioned Sheol (5:14, this is where the nation is bound; 14:9–20, this is where the Babylonian king is bound; 28:14–19, this is the fate the nation thinks it can avoid, in Hezekiah's time). Hezekiah knew he was bound for Sheol and that there he would not be able to praise Yahweh for showing faithfulness in delivering him; but actually Yahweh *has* delivered him from arriving in Sheol before his time, and he can therefore praise Yahweh.

As a prayer of thanksgiving, it sometimes addresses God (v. 17–19), but like other such psalms, it more often speaks of God in the third person because it is giving testimony to other people; this is how it opens and closes (vv. 10–11, 20). Such prayers encourage other people to acknowledge and trust Yahweh for themselves. That practice is reflected in the combination of "me" and "we" in v. 20, and in the comment about a father (the word is actually singular) and his children in v. 19.

38:21–22. The closing verses provide further background to vv. 9–20 and 1–8.

D. Envoys from Babylon to Hezekiah, and Isaiah's Response (39:1–8)

Babylon's dual roles emerge in this final scene about Isaiah ben Amoz. Babylon is both an up-and-coming power in Isaiah's own day and one destined to be the superpower one century later. Merodach-baladan's envoys reflect that earlier time and attest to Babylon's desire to encourage the various nations within the Assyrian Empire to assert their independence. (Chronologically, the invasion to which chs. 36–37 refers thus actually followed on the events in chs. 38–39, but the absence of a chronological order makes for a good link between chs. 39 and 40.) Isaiah is unhappy that Hezekiah reveals the character of his resources to Merodach-baladan; perhaps such action illustrates the kind of false trust that chs. 30–31 attack. Isaiah 39 thus contributes to an ambiguous portrait of Hezekiah. In chs. 36–37, he shows just the right attitude of commitment to Yahweh; here and by implication in chs. 30–31 his stance is different. And there is a further ambiguity in his response to Isaiah (v. 8): is it appropriately trustful or cynical? In the context of the entire book, 39:6–8 prepares the way for chapter 40.

VII. Israel in the Time of Cyrus (40:1–48:22)

The historical background of chs. 40–48 is very different from that of preceding chapters. After Hezekiah's day, the seventh century was dominated by the religiously bleak reign of Manasseh, who encouraged adherence to deities other than Yahweh and forms of worship very different from the ones the OT approves. Toward the end of that century, Josiah attempted to return

the community back to the kind of stance taken by Hezekiah, but in the long term he failed. His own death came about as part of the process that led to Assyria's replacement by Babylon as superpower. Judean rebellion against Babylon led to a series of reprisals against Jerusalem, culminating in the city's catastrophic fall and destruction in 587 and the exile of much of its population. Around 540 BCE, however, Babylon was in turn about to be replaced by Persia as superpower. This is the historical context addressed by chs. 40–55. These chapters speak to the situation of Judeans in Babylon and those left behind in Jerusalem.

The prophet responsible for these chapters is not Isaiah ben Amoz, promising what Yahweh will do two centuries after his day, but someone actually living in the 540s when the moment for comfort has arrived. The author of these verses is not Isaiah ben Amoz himself but someone who takes up his prophetic work at a later time. This prophet might be with the exiles in Babylon or might be with the people who had stayed behind in Judah; the message would be relevant to both. This prophet—or perhaps prophets—remains anonymous. Likewise, the person's gender remains unknown (though a female perspective is more prominent in these chapters than anywhere else in the Prophets).

A. Introducing a Message of Comfort (40:1–31)

40:1–11. In chs. 1–39 Isaiah has confronted the people and warned them about punishment to come from Yahweh. All was not bleak; the people might avoid trouble if they changed their ways. Even if they did not do so and Yahweh did punish them, there could be comfort the other side of calamity. Isaiah 12 thus spoke about comfort as something belonging to "that day," the future day of restoration. In the meantime, after the fall of Jerusalem in 587 BCE (see 2 Kgs 25), people lamented that the city has no one to comfort it (Lam 1:2, 9, 16, 17, 21).

Isaiah 40:1–11 brings a quite different message from chs. 1–39 as it declares that the time for comfort has arrived and the time of punishment is now past. Whereas Yahweh had said, "You are not my people and I am not your God" (Hos 1:9), now Yahweh says "my people ... your God" again (vv. 1–2). The prophet overhears an unidentified voice (probably one of Yahweh's heavenly aides) commissioning a great highway for Yahweh (vv. 3–5). Another voice commissions a proclamation to Jerusalem that Yahweh is coming back on this highway, along with the people (vv. 9–11). The poem presupposes that Yahweh had abandoned Jerusalem (cf. 49:14), but is now returning. The prophet is commissioned to proclaim this good news. But the people are too withered by the hot breath of Yahweh's wrath to be able to hear what is being said (vv. 6–7). Yahweh responds by pointing out that there is nothing wrong with the prophet's assessment of the people's state, but there is something else that needs to be taken into account (v. 8).

40:12–31. The opening to the chapters presupposes that the people will have a hard time accepting this message, and much of these chapters is a battle to help them to do so. This process starts in vv. 12–31. The prophet knows that people are naturally overwhelmed by an imperial power (vv. 12–17), of the images of peoples' gods (vv. 18–20), of the rulers of the nations (vv. 21–24), and of the planets and stars that these nations reckoned determined what happens on earth (vv. 25–26). In connection with each, the prophet declares, "Don't you realize Yahweh is greater than that?" All this provides anticipatory warrant for the exhortation in vv. 27–31. It begins by reformulating the idea of being like withered grass, and then summarizes the purport of vv. 12–26: Yahweh is capable of acting along the lines the prophet will promise; hence, the people who wait expectantly for Yahweh to act will find strength to walk on that highway.

B. Yahweh's Commitment to Israel as Servant (41:1–20)

41:1–7. Whereas 40:12–31 directly addresses Judeans during the exile, 41:1–7 addresses the surrounding nations and asks what they make of a victor from the east. In some ways the figure recalls Abraham (see Gen 14), in some ways Cyrus the Persian who is rampaging through the Middle East turning the Babylonian Empire into a Persian empire. The connotations of both individuals, both chosen by God, help the people understand that Yahweh's purpose is being achieved. The word "victory" is *tsedeq*, which more literally suggests what is faithful and right (cf. 45:19; 64:5), so that it issues in deliverance (cf. 51:5); NRSV regularly translates "righteousness." Abraham and now

Cyrus are the means through which Yahweh executes a faithful, right, or righteous purpose in delivering Israel, one that will indirectly be an act of deliverance for the world as a whole.

41:8–13. Indirectly, of course, Yahweh was addressing the Judeans, and Yahweh now does that directly. Whereas the arrival of Cyrus seems like a threat to other peoples, the fact that Yahweh is behind him means it is not a threat to Israel, because as a people they are Yahweh's servant. Being someone's servant means being protected and supported. The head of another household will be punished for mistreating the servant. So Israel has no reason to fear anyone who oppresses it. The exile might have seemed to signify that Yahweh had thrown out this servant (who, after all, had not been very committed to his master), but the passage reassures Israel that this is not so. The assurance and security still hold.

41:14–16. Indeed, the prophet makes that point in a novel way. Isaiah ben Amoz wanted people, symbolized by an insect, to take seriously the fact that Yahweh is the Holy One of Israel. Verse 14 also wants people to take seriously this particular character of God. Yahweh is the Holy One *of Israel*. Yahweh is committed to this people as the Holy One. The claim that Yahweh is the Holy One of Israel appears throughout the book of Isaiah.

This Holy One is "your Redeemer." A redeemer (*go'el*) is the member of an extended family who has the resources to come to the assistance of someone in the family when they have difficulties and might (for instance) lose their land and their independence, or when they have been wronged. This person is under moral obligation to use these resources to help vulnerable persons to keep or gain their freedom and independence. Calling Yahweh Israel's Redeemer ("restorer" might be a better word) means viewing Israel as members of Yahweh's family to whom Yahweh has made a commitment that Yahweh intends to show by delivering them from their overlords. Verses 15–16 probably speak of the same mountains and hills mentioned in 40:3–4: the exiles will be able to overcome all obstacles in order to make the journey home.

41:17–20. Israelites are like people parched with thirst in the desert. Verses 17–20, particularly the notion of God answering the people, are similar to the discourse of psalms, in which Israel prays to God when they are in a crisis. Whereas Cyrus's coming arouses panic in other peoples (vv. 5–7), Yahweh's support means Israel's rejoicing in Yahweh (v. 16b), and the result of Yahweh's gift of abundant water will be the whole world's recognition of Yahweh (v. 20).

C. The Servant Commitment Yahweh Looks for (41:21–42:17)

This section repeats and then develops the argument of 41:1–20.

41:21–29. First, Yahweh asks another question about this victor, who can also be described as from the east (the literal direction across the desert). Yahweh now poses a question to the gods of the other nations rather than to the nations themselves. It is now a question concerning the identity of the one who said that this conqueror was going to come rather than about who made him come. Since Israel's God had proclaimed what would happen, Yahweh is truly God. "Do good, or do harm": do anything! Yahweh had declared the intention to put Babylon down by means of the Medes (Isa 13) and is now doing so. The other peoples' gods had not declared that intention. Further, since Yahweh through Isaiah ben Amoz had demonstrated being in control of such events, there is good reason to take seriously what Yahweh now says through this new prophet.

42:1–9. Second, the prophet returns to the image of Yahweh's servant, again taking the argument further. During much of the twentieth century, it was customary to link vv. 1–4 with some later passages that refer to Yahweh's servant and call these "servant songs." However, these passages make more sense when read in their individual literary contexts. In 41:8–16 the master-servant relationship was intended to encourage Israel; here it is a challenge. A servant is supposed to be committed to his master as the master is committed to the servant. The verses outline the nature of this commitment—the role Yahweh's servant is supposed to fulfill. He is to be the means by which Yahweh's "justice" is proclaimed in the world. Concerning this word, see the comment on 5:16. Proclaiming Yahweh's justice means making known in the world the way Yahweh is making decisions and implementing them in order to take the world to its proper destiny. Israel is to be a covenant to the

people (vv. 5–9): that is, an embodiment of what being in covenant with Yahweh looks like. It is thus to be a light to the nations.

However, Israel is in no state to fulfill this vocation. Yahweh's servant will not cry out or grow faint (vv. 2–4), but Israel in exile is doing exactly those things. Thus the movement between 41:8–16 and 42:1–9 is significant. Here Israel is not actually named as Yahweh's servant. It is supposed to fulfill that role, but it cannot. So the servant vocation requires fulfillment; the Gospel of Matthew claims that Jesus is someone who fulfills the role of servant (Matt 12:15–21).

42:10–17. Third, vv. 10–17 take up the image of the transformation of nature from 41:17–20, and makes this a topic for praise. The verses resemble a psalm of praise, with vv. 10–12 exhorting praise and vv. 13–17 giving the basis for it. Yahweh has been silent and holding back from action but is now bringing about the tumultuous events that will make Judah's restoration possible.

D. The Blind Servant Whom Yahweh Still Intends to Use (42:18–43:21)

42:18–25. The tension between calling Israel Yahweh's servant (41:8) and describing the role of Yahweh's servant in terms that Israel can hardly fulfill (42:1–4) now becomes explicit. Yahweh's servant is deaf and blind (in fulfillment of Yahweh's intention in 6:9–10). The plan was to commend Yahweh's teaching to the world through this servant (v. 21), but a people living in exile in Babylon or in the midst of devastation in Judah cannot do that (v. 22), especially when they do not comprehend what has been going on (vv. 23–25). "Why have you treated us thus?" they ask. "There is a perfectly coherent answer," Yahweh replies.

43:1–7. That confrontational response might have been expected to lead Yahweh to discharge this servant and find another. But Yahweh does not follow with logic. In Genesis, Yahweh bade people such as Abraham, Hagar, Isaac, and Jacob not to be afraid when they were faced with a difficult future; here Yahweh gives the same bidding to Jacob-Israel. The present Jacob-Israel is in the same frightening position as the Jacob-Israel Yahweh originally brought into being. Yahweh has not given up on the project initiated then and will not do so now. At the exodus Yahweh gave up claims on Egypt and its associates in order to have

Israel (but see 45:14). Yahweh intends to bring the scattered people back to their land.

43:8–13. The prophet develops this point by repeating the challenge to the nations and their gods, cf. ch. 41. These gods had no one to testify to their having spoken and then acted. Israel's role as Yahweh's servant is to testify as Yahweh's witnesses. The blind and deaf witnesses will testify to what they have seen and heard.

43:14–21. The background to these chapters is the situation of Judah under Babylonian domination, with many of its people exiled to Babylon. Only now is Babylon actually mentioned for the first time. In stating that Yahweh intends to destroy Babylon, the prophet in effect promises an act that will be like the exodus, but then tells people to forget about those former events because what Yahweh intends to do now will eclipse Yahweh's previous deeds.

E. The Servant Who Made Yahweh Serve (43:22–44:23)

43:22–28. The argument of 42:18–43:21 is repeated but developed further, just as 41:21–42:17 moved beyond 41:1–20. So this accusation, or rather self-defense, corresponds to the one in 42:18–25. The language of 43:26 implies that Israel is trying to take Yahweh to court, and 43:28 contains the charge Israel is bringing (the "princes of the sanctuary" could be any sacred leaders in Jerusalem). "Yes, I did do that," says Yahweh, "and I had every reason." Further, since the fall of Jerusalem the people have not been calling on Yahweh to restore them, even though they did not have to offer sacrifices, because the Temple has been destroyed (vv. 22–23). Literally, they have not had to "serve" Yahweh in this way, though they have made Yahweh serve them—it is their sins that they have presented to Yahweh. Talking thus of "serving" appropriates ironically the "servant" language of, e.g., 42:1; 43:10. Against this background, v. 25 offers an extraordinary statement of grace.

44:1–5. That note continues in the passage corresponding to 43:1–7. The new promise it adds is the confession of Yahweh described in v. 5. The language might imply Israelites owing their allegiance to Yahweh or other peoples coming to acknowledge Yahweh. The latter will be more explicit in, e.g., 45:14–17, but the former would

be significant in itself given the implication that many people had lost faith in Yahweh while they were in exile.

44:6–23. Verses 6–8 expand on the claims and argument of 43:8–13, with an unequivocal declaration that Yahweh is the only God. It is not merely a statement about monotheism. It does not merely say that there is only one God, but rather that Yahweh is the only God. The gods of Babylon with whom the Judeans were sometimes impressed are not worthy of such behavior. Yahweh alone has demonstrated the capacity to declare what will happen, so that Yahweh's witnesses can then say, "You see: Yahweh said this would happen, and it has." Talk in terms of mere "prediction" misses the point, which is that Yahweh can declare what will happen because Yahweh is the one who makes it happen.

The main body of this section (vv. 9–20) forms much the most extensive polemic against making images that appears in Isa 40–55. Through the centuries before the exile, Israel was tempted to make images of Yahweh in the way that other peoples made images of their gods and also to make images of those other gods. In Mesopotamia that temptation would take new form as people were impressed by the magnificent images of the Babylonian gods. In theory no one would ever think that the image *was* the deity; they knew that El or Marduk (or Yahweh) was much bigger than that. But in practice, that distinction could doubtless be hard to maintain. Here the prophet largely ignores it and satirizes the nonsensical implications of image-making. In closing this section (vv. 21–23), the prophet brings Israel back to thinking about its status in relation to Yahweh and the grace of Yahweh affirmed in 43:25. "Return" (*shuv*) is a verb commonly translated "repent"; it implies that people have indeed turned away from Yahweh to other deities and need to turn back. But the order of events is significant. It is not "return to me and I will forgive you and redeem you" but "return to me because I have forgiven and redeemed you." The renewal of the people and their relationship with Yahweh will not be complete until they return to Yahweh. But Yahweh's forgiving and redeeming is not contingent upon that return. Yahweh's relationship with Israel is not contractual. Yahweh's forgiving and redeeming provides the inspiration for their returning. The section concludes with an admonition for the cosmos to praise Yahweh for having redeemed Israel.

F. The Anointed Through Whom Yahweh Intends to Restore Jerusalem (44:24–45:25)

44:24-28. The initial verses depict Yahweh as Israel's creator, the world's creator, the one who is sovereign in political events and who thus fulfills the words of prophets such as Isaiah and frustrates the predictions of other supposed prognosticators (vv. 24–26a). These prophetic words are germane to the present situation and promise a new version of the deliverance at the Red Sea (vv. 26b–27). These claims are then followed by a quite new statement (v. 28). Though Cyrus's work has been presupposed, only now is he named. "Shepherd" is a standard ancient Near Eastern description of a ruler, so "my shepherd" would not be a very revolutionary way of describing Cyrus as Yahweh's agent. Yet prophets usually refer to foreign rulers as agents of punishment (e.g., 10:5–6). A foreign ruler commissioning the rebuilding of Jerusalem and its Temple bears a different significance.

45:1-8. The prophet now describes Cyrus in more revolutionary fashion as Yahweh's "anointed," the word that is Anglicized as "messiah." In the OT, this word does not refer to a future redeemer (the OT uses other words for that) but to an Israelite king such as David (or to an Israelite priest), who by his anointing is designated and authorized by Yahweh to fulfill that role. Using the word to refer to a pagan king, as if the pagan king takes the Davidic king's place, is extraordinary and unprecedented. But the prophet declares that Yahweh will indeed give this king the kind of victories David had, even though Cyrus does not acknowledge Yahweh. Yahweh's aim is that Cyrus and the world as a whole will come to recognize Yahweh as the one who brings about weal (*shalom*) for people who are being delivered, such as the victims of the Babylonians, and woe (calamity) for the people Yahweh is putting down, which in this context means Babylon. (KJV has God creating "evil," but this gives a misleading impression.) In part, though only in part, all this does come true; Cyrus did in a formal sense recognize Yahweh (see Ezra 1:1–4), though not to the exclusion of other gods. The heavens and the earth are personified and summoned to enact this purpose of Yahweh (v. 8).

45:9-13. The Judeans will be scandalized at the idea that Yahweh can use a pagan king in such a fashion. The prophet thus acknowledges the people's challenge and reasserts its truth. Who are they to decide how Yahweh's purpose should be fulfilled?

45:14-17. An oracle offers a new perspective on the Egyptians and their neighbors. The peoples who held Israel in servitude and whom God gave up temporarily in order to deliver Israel at the beginning of its story (43:3) will now come to recognize Israel and Israel's God. Yahweh had been hiding from Israel by letting the people be ravaged, but now Yahweh is reversing course and delivering Israel. NRSV treats the confession in vv. 15–17 as the prophet's words, but there is no indication that the other peoples' words concluded at the end of v. 14; it makes better sense to construe vv. 15–17 as a continuation of the peoples' confession.

45:18-25. That spectacular series of declarations closes with another. Yahweh denies having truly hidden from Israel ("in secret," *beseter*, is related to the verb "hide," *satar*). Yahweh had always been speaking to the people; the problem was their inabililty to listen. Once more, the nations are commanded to assemble, to admit that their trust in their gods with their images was foolish, but in doing so they are also challenged and invited to find deliverance with Yahweh, the true God.

G. A Vision of Babylon's Gods Falling (46:1–13)

46:1-7. This chapter imagines what the fall of Babylon will be like: in a panic, the Babylonian priests move the precious divine images away from the city to prevent their being destroyed or desecrated. It did not happen that way. When the Persians came up against Babylon the priests changed sides and welcomed Cyrus, at least according to Cyrus's account on the "Cyrus Cylinder." But that version makes the prophet's point about the helplessness of the images and thus of their gods. Gods are supposed to support the people. What is the value of gods people must carry? The prophet once again underlines the difference between these so-called gods and Yahweh, the only real God.

46:8-13. The prophecies in chs. 40–45 have been implicitly critical of the Judean community during the exile and have grown increasingly so (see 45:9–13). They now confront it quite directly and with a growing sense of urgency and frustration. Yahweh's act of deliverance is near; the closer Cyrus comes, the nearer it becomes. The fact that he is a bird of prey is good news for the Judeans, since their overlords are his target. But they are "far from deliverance," in danger of missing out on it because of their unwillingness to recognize the way in which Yahweh is bringing it about. "Deliverance" is *tsedaqa*, virtually a synonym for *tsedeq* (see on 41:1–7). Thus one could say they are "far from righteousness," as other translations have it; they are far from recognizing that Yahweh is doing right by them.

H. A Vision of Babylon Falling (47:1-15)

47:1–4. The prophet depicts Babylon as a woman, the mistress of an impressive household or a queen, who is losing her position and being turned into an ordinary housewife. There is no inherent suffering or humiliation in the role she will have to perform. Her nakedness results from the removal of her ladylike apparel so that she can do her work; her shame lies in the contrast with the position she formerly held, and "vengeance" suggests redress for her oppressive rule.

47:5–7. Her demotion results from the lack of mercy she showed for Israel. She was Yahweh's agent in bringing punishment, but she behaved like a woman who did not care at all for an elderly person whom she ought to respect. It is an indictment of her womanhood, because "mercy" or compassion (*rakhamim*, the plural of the word for a womb), is a distinctive womanly virtue.

47:8–11. Like anyone in a position of power, she assumed she would be there forever, but she was wrong. "Lover of pleasures" could give a misleading impression; she is simply someone who is naturally used to the good life of a wealthy person. A more serious indictment is the way in which she understands herself: "I am, and there is no one besides me." Only God can say that (cf. 43:10, 13; John 18:6), and a human being or a human power that thinks in those terms takes a terrible risk.

47:12–15. Her conviction that she is unassailable stems in part from her vast resources that enable her to discern future events and the ways to cope with them before they happen. Babylon indeed possessed vast information that enabled it to project the future on the basis of the movements of the planets and other forms of divination. The prophet declares all this will be exposed as futile.

I. A Final Challenge to the Rebels (48:1–22)

48:1–11. The prophet's confrontational stance becomes most aggressive here. This section begins by addressing the community in the terms that should apply to it and that it no doubt claimed, but then questioning whether it has a right to them (vv. 1–2). The prophet recalls the way Yahweh has spoken to the people in the past but now says Yahweh spoke in this way only because they would otherwise attribute events to their images (vv. 3–5). Yahweh is saying new things now; if Yahweh had said them in the past, the community would have taken no notice (vv. 6–8). Yahweh has been merciful in the past, but only to avoid looking stupid by destroying Yahweh's own people (vv. 9–11). The passage vividly illustrates the desperate way the prophet is trying to knock some sense into the community, sometimes by speaking encouragingly, sometimes by depicting the downfall of its enemies, but here by trying to shake it to its senses.

48:12–19. The confrontation now takes gentler form. Familiar themes recur (vv. 12–16*a*): Yahweh as first and last, Yahweh as creator, Yahweh as the only one who had spoken of current events before they happened. Here these themes reaffirm Yahweh's intention to make Cyrus the means of overthrowing Babylon. This is re-expressed in another scandalous form as "the LORD loves him." That verb is the one that underlies the earlier description of Abraham as Yahweh's "friend" (41:8) and it thus again closely aligns the pagan conqueror and the great ancestor. Both of them have a vital place within Yahweh's purpose. Verse 16*b* then provides a special introduction to the solemn and striking words that follow in vv. 17–19. Here alone in the OT does Yahweh say "if only" about something that has happened (Yahweh does say "if only" in Ps 81:13, but there about something that could still happen). Alongside the aggressiveness of vv. 1–11 is a poignant divine sadness over Israel's condition. Yahweh is all-powerful, but does not treat people like puppets or children and thus cannot stop them from making stupid decisions.

48:20–22. There is a third challenge. Babylon is about to fall, and the Judeans there need to pack their bags, mentally and emotionally, convinced that they will soon be able to make the declaration in v. 20*b* and encouraged by the way Yahweh looked after Israel on their journey from Egypt to Canaan; Yahweh will surely do that again. But the chapter ends on a final confrontational note (v. 22). Unless they turn from their rebelliousness and their resistance to Yahweh's plans, they will not enjoy any of the fruit of these promises, any *shalom*, any flourishing and well-being. This solemn note brings the first half of Isa 40–55 to a close.

VIII. Jerusalem in the Time of Cyrus (49:1–55:13)

There is both continuity and discontinuity between chs. 40–48 and chs. 49–55. The context is the same. The Babylonian Empire is still about to fall to Cyrus. The prophet is still concerned to help the Judean community in Babylon or Jerusalem or both to wake up to the fact that these events are destined to bring about the freeing of the exiles and the restoration of the city. But the focus moves from the former to the latter, to the restoration of Jerusalem. Further, chs. 40–48 have made much of the place and calling of Israel as Yahweh's servant, but they have exposed a problem about that which they have not solved. The latter chapters alternate between a focus on one or the other of those two issues; there are passages in which Yahweh's servant speaks or is described and passages that bring encouragement to Zion.

A. A Servant to the Servant (i) (49:1–13)

49:1–6. The prophet once again gives testimony, but at greater length than in 40:6 and 48:16b, and thus more like Isaiah giving his testimony (6:1–13). It resembles Jeremiah's account of his call (Jer 1:4–10); Paul will take up the same way of speaking to describe his own call (Gal 1:15). The unfolding of this prophetic testimony further parallels the call of Jeremiah (and that of Moses) in relating how the prophet objected to the call, and how Yahweh overruled the objections; but here the objection is not "I won't be able to do it" but "I have tried to do it and failed (though I still trust Yahweh)." The testimony also parallels the description of Isaiah as Yahweh's servant in 20:3

(indeed, 44:26 assumes that every prophet is Yahweh's servant); this prophet, too, has that servant calling. The prophet is called to be a servant to the servant.

What is novel here is that Yahweh also declares, "you are … Israel, in whom I will be glorified." What could that mean? Verses 5–6 make explicit that Yahweh is still concerned for the people Israel itself. So there is a sense in which the prophet is Israel and a sense in which Israel itself is Israel. We have seen that Israel is in no condition to fulfill its vocation as Yahweh's servant and Yahweh's witnesses, yet Yahweh is still committed to its doing so. But it has a long way to travel before it can fulfill this vocation. In the meantime, the prophet is called to fulfill it, to embody what it means to be Israel and what it means to be Yahweh's servant, and to do that for Israel's sake so as to bring Israel back to Yahweh and bring about its restoration as a people (vv. 5*a*, 6*a*). That is not all. By doing that, this prophet-servant will also be a means of bringing light to the world. Perhaps that implies people such as the Babylonians hearing the prophet's message; perhaps it refers to people seeing what Yahweh does in restoring Israel through the prophet's ministry. Paul sees this promise fulfilled in his and Barnabas's ministry (Acts 13:47).

49:7–12. We could see these subsequent promises to Israel as the prophet fulfilling this ministry. The Judeans are people despised by their overlords (v. 7*a*), they resemble people in dark imprisonment (v. 9*a*), they are scattered in exile (v. 12), they are suffering (v. 13). But Yahweh intends to restore them to honor (v. 7), the honor of being chosen, chosen to serve Yahweh. "Slave" is the word elsewhere translated "servant" (*'ebed*); the people will be taken out of this inappropriate service and restored to their proper position of servanthood. Reestablishing their land and nationhood will be a means of making them "a covenant to the people," the people in the world in general, the intention announced in 42:6–7. It will make them an embodiment of what it means to be in a covenant with Yahweh.

49:13. All that will be reason for celebration.

B. Encouragement for Zion (i) (49:14–50:3)

49:14. Jerusalem-Zion had a prominent place in 40:1–11 but has since been largely in the shadows. The prophet has focused on the events that will bring Babylon's downfall and immediately affect the Judeans living there. But these are also the events that will make possible Jerusalem's restoration. That claim is no more believable in Jerusalem than it is in Babylon.

49:15–50:3. Yahweh has four responses to the charge in v. 14. Necessarily, perhaps, they amount simply to further promises of what Yahweh intends now to do. There is no evidence that can be given except the evidence of who Yahweh is. First (49:15–21), it really is the case that people are coming back, so that instead of being devastated and bereft the people multiply. The prophet thus challenges people to look at Yahweh in a different way. Yahweh is like a mother who cannot avoid motherly feelings for her child even if it behaves inappropriately. And what Yahweh does will raise questions to which Zion will have no answer except that Yahweh has done it. Second (49:22–23), imperial powers that are Zion's oppressors will be turned into its servants, and that will convince Zion that Yahweh is Lord. Third (49:24–26), the victims of these imperial powers will be freed as the powers themselves turn to fighting each other; that will convince the world about who Yahweh is. Fourth (50:1–3), Yahweh does have the power to bring all this about. This final response also relates to that opening charge of having abandoned Zion. Yes, I divorced her, says Yahweh. You can look at her divorce certificate and see the basis for that act. But even divorce does not mean Yahweh is finished.

C. A Servant to the Servant (ii) (50:4–11)

50:4–9. One could say the prophet has been seeking to sustain the weary with an appropriate word in 49:14–50:3 and throughout 40:1–50:3. The weary are the Judeans in Babylon and/or in Jerusalem, and the word is the message that has run through these chapters. The prophet tried to keep them going in light of what Yahweh is doing and is about to do; it would be tragic if they are not ready to enjoy the fruits of it. To this end, the prophet has needed to have the tongue of people who are taught (see NRSV margin at v. 4), a disciple's tongue. "Disciples" (*limmudim*) is the same word that appeared in 8:16; the prophet is a disciple of Isaiah ben Amoz as well as a disciple of Yahweh. It is only because of being a disciple and a listener that it is possible to be a speaker. The trouble is that delivering this message has been

very costly, not merely unsuccessful. The attackers of vv. 5–6 might be members of the Judean community who opposed the prophet; perhaps they were people who had come to live successful lives in Babylon and did not want trouble to be caused by someone taking the side of its attackers. Or perhaps they were Babylonians who could not tolerate that. Nonetheless, the prophet is sure of vindication (vv. 7–9).

50:10–11. The point of that testimony lies in vv. 10–11. It places a choice before the audience. People must either identify with the prophet or with the attackers. (It is usual to assume that the one who speaks in vv. 4–9 is the same "servant of Yahweh" as in 49:1–6, though only in v. 10 does the word *servant* come and thus confirm this.) There is no promise attached to identifying with the servant; in the short term, at least, it will mean darkness not light. There is a threat attached to identifying with the attackers. They will find that their actions work against them.

D. Encouragement for Zion (ii) (51:1–52:12)

51:1–8. This opening exhortation addresses people who "pursue righteousness" and "know righteousness." In what sense do they do that? "Righteousness" is *tsedeq*, the word also translated "deliverance" in v. 5. As usual in these chapters, this "righteousness" is not a human characteristic but a principle of divine action. It is Yahweh doing the right thing by Israel in delivering them from their overlords (see on 41:1–7). The verses address people who are pursuing righteousness in the sense that they are longing for Yahweh to bring about that deliverance. That is also the sense in which they are seeking Yahweh, seeking for Yahweh to act, and the sense in which they know righteousness and have Yahweh's teaching in their hearts. They know Yahweh is the only one who can deliver, and they know that Yahweh intends to be revealed to the world. They are seeking this, but they have a hard time believing in it. So vv. 1*b*–2 reminds them of a reason for doing so.

The rest of vv. 1–8 reaffirms Yahweh's promises. Yahweh *will* comfort Zion (v. 3). The parallelism in this verse makes clear that while "comfort" sometimes denotes offering words of encouragement, as in English, sometimes it denotes taking action to relieve people's sadness. Yahweh's teaching *will* go out to bring light to the peoples as they see Yahweh's "justice" at work. On "justice," see the comment on 42:1–4; vv. 4–5 as a whole reaffirm 42:1–9. The cosmos could dissolve, but Yahweh's deliverance will stand forever. The people who revile Israel and who look so threatening and impressive will turn out not to be so.

51:9–11. The words recall exhortations that come in prayers within psalms; they would then be the prophet's exhortation to Yahweh. But since Yahweh is the speaker in the preceding and following lines, the words are best understood as a self-exhortation on Yahweh's part. They add a further basis for people to believe that Yahweh will act: Yahweh brought them out from Egypt and through the Red Sea, defeating hostile forces there (on Rahab, see 30:1–7). Verse 11 repeats the promise in 35:10.

51:12–16. Israel therefore can stop fearing its current overlords. Yahweh can again exercise lordship over the sea, which symbolizes devastating forces that are actually under Yahweh's control.

51:17–23. Encouragement to Zion now becomes exhortation as the exhortation addressed to Yahweh's arm (51:9) becomes one addressed to Zion; the verb in v. 17 is a form of the same verb as 51:9. "Awake," says v. 9; "you need to rouse yourself, too," says v. 17. Zion is like a woman who has been knocked to the floor by disaster, a disaster brought about by Yahweh. But Yahweh does not remain in a disaster-bringing mode, and that stage in Zion's life is now over. Yahweh is now going to turn on the people who assaulted her. Externally nothing has changed yet, but everything is about to change. Zion has to adopt a new stance, ready for a new life to begin.

52:1–6. The verb *awake* appears in v. 1 in exactly the same form as 51:9. Zion is urged to see herself as not merely able to get up again after being assaulted but as able to make herself look lovely again. Her act of re-clothing is the converse of the fate envisaged for Babylon in Isaiah 47. And Zion will no longer be defiled. The uncircumcised and defiling people might be Israelites who are uncircumcised in heart or might be foreigners who treat her the way depicted in vv. 3–6. (Other nations that want to come to worship Yahweh will be able to come to the city, even though they are foreigners; uncircumcised and unclean foreigners will be the people who just want to destroy and defile it.)

52:7–10. The prophet imagines that the process whereby the city is to be liberated is imminent, rather in the way Isa 46–47 imagines the process of Babylon's fall is taking place. Isaiah 40:9–11 commissioned an announcement that Yahweh was coming back to Jerusalem, and here a messenger gives the announcement: Yahweh reigns (one could translate the verb "has begun to reign").

52:11–12. The same imperative verb, *depart*, introduces this section. The Judeans in Babylon are to be ready to leave there when the city falls, dissociating themselves from the impurity of the worship of other gods and bringing back to Jerusalem the vessels that had been taken from the Temple when the city fell, long ago. It will be a new exodus, even better than the first exodus (v. 12).

E. A Servant to the Servant (iii) (52:13–53:12)

Yahweh reverts to the way of speaking about a servant that appeared in 42:1–4; that is, the passage does not identify Israel as the servant (like, e.g., 41:8–9), nor does the servant speak as "I" and thus give us the impression it is the prophet (as in Isa 49:1–6 and 50:4–9). So 52:13–53:12 is more a vision of a role to be fulfilled than a description of a person. The fact that Israel has been described as Yahweh's servant suggests that Israel might be being invited to see itself here. But in 42:1–4, the description made it look like a role that Israel needed to have fulfilled for its own sake before it could fulfill it for someone else, and the same is true here; if Israel appears in the passage, it is as the "we" who have to come to a new view of the servant. Yet the fact that Yahweh has kept affirming that Israel is still destined to be Yahweh's servant means that it is indeed entitled or invited to see itself here. The literary context also invites readers to see the vision as a description of the prophet, or at least as based in part on the prophet's experience as described in 49:1–6 and 50:4–11. Perhaps it is the prophet's self-description in the third person, as when Jesus refers to himself as "the Son of Man." Although the passage sees him as giving up his life and having been in a tomb, it need not imply that he is actually dead.

The poem focuses on the role rather than on the identity of the person. Whoever is Yahweh's servant, this is the role and the promise. One can see why Jesus found this passage playing a crucial role in enabling him to understand the nature of his ministry. The NT also understands it as offering the church a way of seeing itself and helping it to cope with its affliction.

52:13–15. Yahweh declares that like both Israel and the prophet, this servant is someone who has been humiliated but is to be taken to a place of great honor and to be recognized by the nations.

53:1–11a. The bulk of the description takes the form of testimony by people who understood this servant in a new way. He was someone totally unimpressive and dishonored, and people therefore thought he was under Yahweh's punishment, as his friends thought about Job. That he took his affliction so silently made them realize they must be wrong. He shared their affliction when he did not need to; for instance, they were transgressors or rebels against Yahweh; he was faithful to Yahweh. Indeed, he was experiencing affliction that they did not experience (cf. 50:4–9). But the fact that he experienced suffering that he did not deserve but that came from his faithfulness to Yahweh opened up a new possibility for the people. He lived as "an offering for sin" like the offerings in the Temple (the term *'asham* usually refers to an offering that makes compensation for wrongdoing.)

53:11b–12. The vision closes with Yahweh speaking and affirming that this will be so.

F. Encouragement for Zion (iii) (54:1–17a)

54:1–3. The prophet goes back to addressing Zion with imperative verbs. Once again the basis for the imperatives is something Yahweh is going to do rather than something that has already happened. The imperatives invite the prophet's hearers in Babylon or Jerusalem to imagine Zion rejoicing now because she knows she is going to be surrounded by all these children—for instance, by the Judeans in Babylon who will have returned to Jerusalem.

54:4–8. Moreover, her husband has returned to her. Yahweh admits to having abandoned her and does not offer any defense for that here (50:1–3 has already provided the kind of defense Yahweh would offer) but offsets this by declaring that this abandonment is only temporary and that Zion's current suffering will be eclipsed by the compassion and love Yahweh will now show.

54:9–10. "Love" is khesed, suggesting "commitment," and that promise is then undergirded by one of the very few references to Noah outside Genesis. Yahweh's commitment to Noah had a similar background; people had proved incorrigibly willful and Yahweh had acted in devastating wrath, but had then sworn unconditionally never to do that again.

54:11–17a. Yahweh spells out the implications of Zion's restoration. It will be as if Zion is not merely rebuilt with stone but with precious stone. The problem that led to Yahweh's abandonment will not recur because her children will be turned into Yahweh's disciples (v. 13; the same word as in 50:4). NRSV assumes that *shalom* (v. 13) refers broadly to "prosperity" or well-being, but it also provides a segue to the promise of peace (vv. 14b–17a). In the past Yahweh has been the one who stirred up trouble for Zion, but that will not happen again; therefore any threats that come will not emanate from Yahweh and will, therefore, not succeed.

G. The Heritage of the Servants (54:17b–55:13)

54:17b. Zion's children, "Yahweh's disciples" (54:13), are now also "Yahweh's servants"; the expression appears in the plural form for the first time in Isaiah. Whereas 54:1–17a addressed Zion, 54:17b now addresses these people themselves, in the plural, which suggests it is the introduction to ch. 55 at least as much as the conclusion to ch. 54.

55:1–5. People are seeking to take responsibility for their own future. They need instead to look to Yahweh for that which truly satisfies. The prophet restates declarations about covenant and *khesed*, now given another new twist. Yahweh had made a covenant with David, but now there is no Davidic king. So where is the *khesed* Yahweh showed to David (Ps 89:49)? The answer is that Yahweh now intends to relate to and work with the whole community in the fashion Yahweh once worked with David. It will now be the whole community that witnesses to the nations through what Yahweh does with it, and draws them to Yahweh.

55:10–13. The people are to "seek Yahweh" in the sense of looking to Yahweh for their future, and to give up their sinful way of resisting Yahweh's thinking about how to take them to their destiny (vv. 6–9). Yahweh's plans are certain to find fulfillment (vv. 10–13).

IX. Judah After the Exile (56:1–66:24)

The last eleven chapters contain no references to Cyrus or Babylon. They focus on Jerusalem and provide even more glorious promises about the city's transformation. They also critique aspects of Judean worship and life. It makes sense to assume that the book is arranged in roughly chronological order and that these last chapters speak to Judah's life after the exile, the same context addressed by Haggai, Zechariah, and Malachi. Some passages imply the time before the Temple has been rebuilt (see 64:11; 66:1), which would suggest the beginning of that period; others suggest a later stage. The prophecies are arranged in pairs, in ABCDEEDCBA order rather than in linear, chronological order. Reading them is like climbing stairs then coming down the other side.

A. An Open Community and Its Responsibility (i) (56:1–8)

56:1. "What is right" and "deliverance" are both used to translate the word *tsedaqa*, which in chs. 1–39 tended to refer to Israelites doing the right thing in light of relationships with one another (see commentary on 5:16), but in chs. 40–55 tended to refer to Yahweh doing the right thing in light of a relationship with Israel (see on 46:8–13). The beginning of these final chapters sets the two in vital relationship with one another, a motif that underlies the chapters. The community is to do what is right because Yahweh does what is right. As usual, it is not quite the case that their deliverance is conditional on their right behavior; rather, since Yahweh is committed to doing right by them, they must do what is right by one another. But if they fail in their obligation, they cannot complain if Yahweh's promise does not come true.

56:2–8. Observing the Sabbath is a practice unique to Israel. It is thus capable of being *the* marker of commitment to Yahweh, and if foreigners keep the Sabbath, they deserve to be regarded as true members of the covenant people. The same applies to eunuchs, who can make no biological contribution to the future survival and flourishing of Israel. The passage makes enthusiastic promises to foreigners and eunuchs whom some people in Judah might have excluded from membership in the community. In light of 58:13–14, these verses likely challenge Judeans about their own Sabbath practices.

B. Warnings and Challenges (i) (56:9–59:8)

56:9–57:2. Confrontation (i): The Leadership

This ironic invitation shows that in the Judean community nothing has changed. Unprincipled people can again take advantage of the weak because the people who should protect the "sheep" are stupid, asleep, and preoccupied by self-indulgence. With further irony, the fact that this malfeasance must issue in calamity means that people who are its victims are fortunate because they escape the calamity that must follow on this wrongdoing in the community.

57:3–13. Confrontation (ii): Dissolute Religion

57:3–4. There is another respect in which nothing has changed; people are still disposed to follow their traditional religious practices. Sorcery involves rituals of divination that are designed to discover what is going to happen, and then rituals to forestall any negative events that the divination reveals. Adultery and whoring suggest unfaithfulness to Yahweh and/or religious rites involving sexual activity designed to encourage fertility. People are inclined to scorn the narrow-minded faith that says one should simply rely on Yahweh in connection with such needs. That makes them rebels against Yahweh and deceivers who pretend to be committed to Yahweh but secretly practice heterodox rites.

57:5–9. The prophet is also scandalized by people's willingness to sacrifice a child to try to avert some disaster. Leviticus 18:21 bans such sacrifices to the god Molech, and here the parallelism in v. 9 suggests that Molech was a god in charge of the realm of the dead.

57:10–13. People have not recognized that their costly efforts to bring life into being or to ward off death have been in vain (v. 10). Yahweh's turning away from them in the exile has not driven them to return to Yahweh; in fact, just the opposite has occurred (v. 11). Their religious commitment is not something that impresses Yahweh when it is so misguided (vv. 12–13).

57:14–21. The Alternative that Stands Before People (i)

57:14–19. Yahweh again speaks of preparing a highway, as in 40:3–5, but this time it is "my people's way," cf. 35:8–10. By no means have the people arrived where they need to be in order to reach their destiny. But Yahweh is committed to getting them there. Being majestic and holy does not mean being unwilling to associate with ordinary mortals. Words such as "contrite" suggest a challenge to the hearers, though the word *dakka'* simply means "crushed," which suggests that this is another promise that Yahweh will be present with people who have been afflicted and broken by Yahweh's wrath in order now to revive them. So the people can look forward to real shalom.

57:20–21. But if v. 15 does not impose upon them the requirement of contrition, this does not mean nothing is expected of them. The prophet repeats 48:22. They cannot continue to behave as is described in 57:3–13.

58:1–14. Confrontation (iii): Fasting, Fraud, and Sabbath

58:1–9a. The prophet addresses people who indeed worship Yahweh. This does not preclude their also being involved in the kind of practices critiqued in ch. 57. The denunciation reflects their life in society rather than their religious life. They are, indeed, religiously observant. They seek blessing from Yahweh and celebrate what Yahweh has done for Israel, but there is a mismatch between their religious life and their life in society. The prophet castigates the same attitudes as prevailed before the exile; for biblical comments about this period after the exile, see Neh 5. Instead of caring for people who have become the victims of circumstances such as poor harvests, by making sure they have enough to eat and somewhere to live, they take advantage of them as employees who have no way of negotiating a living wage. Yahweh does not respond to the oppressors when they come to pray for Yahweh to restore their situation because they have ignored the cause of the poor. Only when they become more generous will Yahweh respond to them.

58:9b–12. There is another classic way whereby people who are doing well ensure they do better, by inappropriate legal activity, "pointing of the finger" (v. 9b, cf. Prov 6:13). In contrast, v. 10a describes the behavior that Yahweh expects, whereas vv. 10b–12 elaborate on the promises of restoration.

58:13–14. A further "if—then" challenge and promise follow, stressing the Sabbath (cf. 56:2–8). While letting people have a Sabbath rest is another way of treating them properly, the prophet emphasizes the significance of the Sabbath as a sign of revering Yahweh. This day belongs to Yahweh; it was not created for business or comparable pursuits.

59:1–8. The Alternative that Stands Before People (ii)

Verse 1 suggests that the people were asking in their prayers, "Is your hand too short to save, is your ear too dull to hear?" The prophet responds that Yahweh *could* raise a hand or lift an ear, but *will not* do so. The people cannot come into Yahweh's presence to pray. This is not because there are temporary ritual barriers between them and God such as are caused by contact with a corpse. These can be removed by time and/or by a cleansing ritual. The nature of their contact with death has generated barriers of the kind that rituals do not address. They do not behave with *shalom*; so they will experience no *shalom* (v. 8).

C. The Prayer that Needs to Be Prayed (i) (59:9–15a)

Nevertheless, a prayer follows. As a result of being admitted into Yahweh's council (see commentary on 38:1–8), a prophet is in a position to mediate in both directions, bringing Yahweh's word to people and people's needs to Yahweh. At the same time, putting this prayer here suggests that the prophet wants people to see the prayer as part of this message. This fits with the prayer's content. People pray as if they practice righteousness, but there is actually no justice in their paths (58:2; 59:8). That is why justice and righteousness are far from them (vv. 9a, 14a)—that is, Yahweh is not acting in relation to them with *tsedaqa* and *mishpat*. Verses 12–13 and 14b–15a thus offer contrition appropriate to the people's condition.

Yet it seems that the prophet is making it on the people's behalf.

D. The Answer to Prayer (i) (59:15b–20)

When prophets such as Hosea and Jeremiah pray on behalf of the people, Yahweh is inclined to refuse to listen because the people themselves are not committed to acknowledging their wrongdoing before God in the way that the prophet does on their behalf (Jer 14:1–15:4; Hos 6:1–6). One would then expect that Yahweh would take the same stance in relation to the prayer in vv. 9–15a. However, instead of pointing out that there is every reason for Yahweh to ignore their prayer (cf. 1–8), the prophet declares that Yahweh is concerned for them and is dismayed that there is no justice, i.e., that no one is acting on their behalf. The prophet thus takes the same stance that appears in chs. 40–45: it is no good for Yahweh simply to wait until the people themselves change; that could mean waiting forever. Yahweh has to act on their behalf; then they will "fear the name of the Lord." The passage combines past-tense verbs (which declare that Yahweh has made a decision and that the act is as good as done) and future-tense verbs (which recognize that it has not actually happened).

Who did Yahweh think should act to restore Israel (v. 16a)? Perhaps it is a Cyrus-like figure. But in the absence of any such person, human or heavenly, taking action, Yahweh has determined to take action personally (cf. 42:13–17). It is not so much a matter of attacking Israel's enemies but of putting down Yahweh's own enemies, people who oppose Yahweh's purpose, with the aim that the rest of the world should come to acknowledge Yahweh. Yahweh will then act as Zion's redeemer or restorer (see 41:14–16). But this will be effective only for people who turn from their rebellion against Yahweh (v. 20). Yahweh takes the initiative, but the people must respond.

E. Zion's Transformation (i) (59:21–60:22)

The center of chs. 56–66 is a series of promises that Yahweh will gloriously restore Jerusalem. The events that followed the fall of Babylon had freed Judeans to return and had led to the rebuilding of the Temple, but sources such as Nehemiah indicate that this restoration fell far short of the promises in Isaiah 49–54. These chapters reaffirm those promises in even grander fashion. In these first promises about a gathering of the nations and of the city's children, the opening and closing sections (60:1–3 and 17b–22a) form a pair, as do the two central sections (60:4–8 and 9–17a). The entire chapter portrays a great reversal for the city, especially in its relationship with the nations.

59:21. The promises begin with a divine commitment. Yahweh makes a covenant with the *people* to keep speaking through the *prophet* and through the prophet's successors. Thus Yahweh promises to keep speaking to them.

60:1–3. This opening commission to "shine" is a figure of speech. The city cannot decide to shine, but it will do so involuntarily because Yahweh will shine on it and it will reflect Yahweh's brightness, as Moses once did. Such brightness will not scare the nations but attract them from their darkness.

60:4–8. The implications are spelled out primarily in three overlapping ways. The nations will bring the city's children (back). They will also bring fabulous wealth to the city. Not only will the city enjoy this wealth, but it will also take the form of flocks and other gifts to enhance the worship of Yahweh.

60:9–17a. The three themes are elaborated. The returning offspring will be so numerous they will fill scores of ships. The nations that shamed, destroyed, and domineered the city will rebuild, beautify, and serve it. Their resources will beautify Yahweh's house.

60:17b–22a. The last section in turn elaborates on the first. Devastation will be replaced by *shalom* (well-being) and *tsedaqa* (Yahweh doing right by the city). The brightness of the light that comes from Yahweh's presence will eclipse the light of sun and moon.

60:22b. Yahweh's own person stands behind these promises. And Yahweh will bring their fulfillment with speed. Yet that fulfillment will come "in its time." When Yahweh decides this time has come, the fulfillment will happen in an instant. But this does not mean the instant starts now. Evidently the people who received this prophecy had enough experience of something they could call a degree of fulfillment of it (e.g., in Nehemiah's building of the city's walls) to believe that it was a word from Yahweh and not mere fantasy. They then held onto it as a promise of something ultimate to which Yahweh was committed.

F. Zion's Transformation (ii) (61:1–62:12)

61:1–4. A distinctive feature of this parallel account of Yahweh's promises is the way the prophet speaks as a person, as in 49:1–6; 50:4–9. First comes testimony of the one commissioned to proclaim the promises. "The spirit of the Lord Yahweh is upon me" is an initial fulfillment of Yahweh's earlier promise (59:21); "Yahweh has anointed me" is a more surprising description, because anointing usually applies to priests or kings (cf. 45:1) not prophets. It is thus a distinctive way of claiming a divine commission. It undergirds the message that follows. The good news is that Yahweh is bringing redress to the city's overlords and thus liberation to its oppressed people.

61:5–11. Thus whereas other peoples have prevented Israel from offering proper worship of Yahweh, or have sought to do so (see Ezra 1–6 as well as the earlier story of the Temple's destruction), now they will make it possible for Israel to do so. Shame gives way to great honor, blessing, and joy. Yahweh will stop oppression by other peoples and implement the covenant relationship (v. 8). And for the prophet, proclamation to the people is accompanied by joy in Yahweh (vv. 10–11). In praising Yahweh with such enthusiasm, the prophet is doing what Israel is destined to do, behaving even now as if Yahweh's promises have been fulfilled. The verses recall psalms of thanksgiving, which also give anticipatory praise even before the event has actually happened (v. 11b).

62:1–5. The prophet next declares a commitment to pray that Yahweh will indeed fulfill these promises and to maintain that active prayer until it happens. The verses pick up and elaborate the promises in ch. 54, using similar words such as "sons" (banim) and "builders" (bonim).

62:6–9. As well as making a personal commitment to prayer, the prophet commissions other people to keep making a nuisance of themselves to Yahweh until the time of fulfillment comes, like the woman who keeps knocking on the judge's door (Luke 18:1–8). They are like lookouts since they are committed to the city's welfare and since they are committed to staying alert at all times to fulfill their task.

62:10–12. Finally the prophet commissions some people to leave the city and construct a road. The imagery is familiar (e.g., 35:8–10; 40:3–5; 48:20), but it is reworked in a new direction (cf. 57:14–19). The roadmakers are once more unnamed, but their road is for the people to come back to Jerusalem. Moreover, other peoples are accompanying them and presumably (to judge from other declarations in chs. 60–62) making that journey possible. As was also the case in passages such as 48:20, the declaration is designed to help the people of Jerusalem understand that Yahweh is committed to bringing its people back.

G. The Answer to Prayer (ii) (63:1–6)

These verses correspond to 59:15b–20, though they also follow on 59:21–62:12. The prophet imagines an anonymous questioner (perhaps a lookout) asking about an impressive warrior who arrives covered in red, which suggests blood, though it is literally grape juice. Although he comes from the direction of Edom, this need not mean he has been fighting Edom; indeed, the last verse indicates that this is not so, unless Edom stands for nations in general (as in ch. 34). The figure turns out to be Yahweh, who has acted to do right by Israel (tsedaqa, v. 1b) to put down these nations and thus redeem and restore Israel (see commentary on 41:14–16) because no one else was doing so (cf. 59:15b–20).

H. The Prayer that Needs to be Prayed (ii) (63:7–64:12)

The second prayer follows; it is parallel to 59:9–15a but much longer. Indeed, some time elapses before its character as a prayer becomes clear. Further, the passage implies that the Temple is still in ruins, which may suggest the prayer originally belonged in the exilic period, before the time during which Isa 40–55 was composed. Its presence here reflects the sense runnning through chs. 56–66 that the exile continues into what is often called the post-exilic period.

63:7–14. The prayer begins as a twofold review of Israel's story. First, it recalls Yahweh's deeds at the exodus, though Yahweh's hope that they would respond to such an expression of love was disappointed. But Yahweh's chastisement won their return and Yahweh delivered them again at the Red Sea. Yet that raises the question why Yahweh is not relating to them in this way now. Their experience in the exile and after the exile is very different from the experience of their ancestors. The references to Yahweh's "holy spirit" and "the spirit of Yahweh" are noteworthy. The phrase "holy spirit" comes in the OT only here and in Ps 51:11. It makes clear that "his holy spirit" was active in Israel, though the phrase is not a technical term in the OT as it became in Christian doctrine.

63:15–19. At this point the passage becomes overtly a prayer, addressing Yahweh in light of that difference between Yahweh's activity in Israel's life at the beginning and Yahweh's behavior now. As in vv. 7–14, the prophet moves between speaking as "I" and as "we"; once again, this is a prayer the prophet articulates on behalf of the people. As happens in the psalms, the first thing the prayer seeks is Yahweh's attention; in a way this is all it needs, because if the people gain Yahweh's attention, surely God will respond. So the prayer looks up to Yahweh's heavenly dwelling and urges Yahweh to look down on what is happening—or not happening—to Israel. Their unrestored state means that their great father-figures would not recognize them. If Yahweh is their father and redeemer, then certain actions should follow. In the typically bold nature of Israelite prayer, the people accuse Yahweh of making them stray from Yahweh's ways and hardening their hearts, as if they were Egyptians not Israelites. Accusing Yahweh in this way risks the danger of excusing ourselves, but it does take seriously the fact that Yahweh is Lord, i.e., a ruler responsible for Yahweh's people.

64:1–14. The second thing the prayer asks is for Yahweh to act. It is again typical of OT prayer that it is does not request something in concrete terms. Although the prayer is bold in the way it confronts Yahweh, it is reticent in telling Yahweh what to do, perhaps in the conviction that if it can gain Yahweh's attention, then Yahweh will decide what course of action is needed. So it asks for Yahweh to come in spectacular fashion and take action against the nations—Israel's overlords—who oppose Yahweh in the world.

64:5–7. The prayer once more makes Yahweh responsible for the people's failure. It was after Yahweh got angry and chastised Israel that Israel sinned (the prayer ignores the causes of Yahweh's anger), so that the right deeds Israel might have accomplished it no longer does, and it risks paying the ultimate price for that. Yahweh has hidden and abandoned the people to their sins, so it is understandable if people have given up praying.

64:8–12. The prayer finally appeals once more to the fatherhood of Yahweh. Surely a father will care about his children. But the subsequent appeal to Yahweh as potter suggests that the prayer takes up Yahweh's own words—as expressed in 45:9–11—and turns them into a challenge for Yahweh. Yahweh allegedly has the wisdom to know when enough is enough (cf. 28:23–29), but is Yahweh displaying that wisdom? Yahweh has spoken of abandoning coolness, silence, and self-restraint (42:14–15), but when will this happen?

I. Warnings and Challenges (ii) (65:1–66:17)

This further set of warnings and challenges balances 56:9–59:8.

65:1–7. Confrontation (i)

Israel assumes that it can say anything to Yahweh in prayer, but also that Yahweh has the same freedom in replying. Thus this second set of warnings and challenges responds with a vigor and straightness that matches those of Israel's prayer. Yahweh indicts vigorously their inappropriate religious practices and promises that judgment will be the consequence.

65:8–16. The Alternative that Stands Before People (i)

The promised judgment (vv. 6–7a) will not mean indiscriminately destroying the people. Yahweh affirms the intention to restore the people and the land, but for the first time (with the book almost over) speaks overtly about distinguishing between the faithful and the faithless within Israel. Isaiah 54:17b, for the first time in the book, referred to Yahweh's servants (plural); moreover, the prayer in 63:17 appealed to the people's status as servants (cf. also 56:6). This chapter takes up the servant's talk but suddenly applies the terms to a group within Israel, set over against those who forsake Yahweh (vv. 8, 9, 13, 14, 15). It is the former who will enjoy Yahweh's blessing in the land. Being servants means responding when

Yahweh summons; the others fail to respond and make up their own minds about what to do, how to worship, and how to find guidance (v. 12). That group will "be put to shame."

65:17–25. The Associated Promise

Yahweh now speaks to the people as a whole. Talk of a new heavens and a new earth (v. 17) in later apocalyptic literature came to suggest the creation of a new cosmos, but the present context makes clear that the prophet refers to a new Jerusalem (v. 18). Indeed, paradoxically, the distinguishing feature of the new Jerusalem will be that it realizes the intention of Yahweh's original creation—for humanity (vv. 20–23) and the rest of nature (v. 25).

66:1–6. The Alternative that Stands Before People (ii)

Whereas the people have attempted to use the devastated state of the Temple as a basis for encouraging Yahweh to take action (64:11–12), Yahweh again undercuts their argument. The verses thus take a very different attitude to the Temple from the one present in Haggai and Zechariah. Thus between them these prophets testify to the way having a temple both does and does not make theological sense. Indeed, one might have thought that vv. 1–2a would exclude any divine dwelling among humanity, but vv. 2b–4 rework the basis on which Yahweh chooses to live somewhere. People who offer the right sacrifices (the first alternative in each line in v. 3a) can be no more acceptable than people who offer abominations (the second half of each line). Verses 5–6 develop the motif of division within the community that appeared in 65:8–16 and make explicit that this is not a division between people who worship Yahweh and people who do not but a schism between two groups who worship Yahweh.

66:7–17. The Alternative that Stands Before People (iii)

The book almost closes with a series of further promises of Jerusalem's transformation, but these are now set in the context of the division within the community. These verses nuance what was said earlier about the transformation that the chapters have been describing by declaring that it

will benefit only "his servants," only people who are properly committed to Yahweh.

J. An Open Community and Its Responsibility (ii) (66:18–24)

The book closes with the worldwide vision with which chs. 56–66 began. Once again Yahweh declares that the nations will bring the scattered Judean community back to Jerusalem, but here the emphasis is on the gathering of the nations to "see my glory." To that end Yahweh will commission some of the surviving Judeans to proclaim this glory and draw the nations into worship of Yahweh. The notion of being witnesses (e.g., 43:9–12; 55:4–5) thus receives sharper profile. Further, the role of priests and Levites will no longer be confined to Israelites; some of these Gentiles will be able to share in teaching and leading the worship in the new Jerusalem.

Such an inclusive verse would make for a fine ending to the book, but to the very end it refuses to stop surprising readers, ending with a warning that challenges them (v. 24).

BIBLIOGRAPHY

W. Brueggemann. *Isaiah*. 2 vols., Westminster Bible Companion (Louisville: Westminster John Knox, 1998); B. S. Childs. *Isaiah*. OTL (Louisville: Westminster John Knox, 2001); J. Goldingay. *Isaiah*. NIBCOT 13 (Peabody, Mass.: Hendrickson, 2001); W. Holladay. *Unbounded by Time: Isaiah Still Speaks* (Cambridge, Mass.: Cowley, 2002); P. D. Miscall. *Isaiah*. Readings (Sheffield: JSOT, 1993); J. A. Motyer. *The Prophecy of Isaiah* (Downers Grove, Ill.: InterVarsity, 1999); C. R. Seitz, ed. *Reading and Preaching the Book of Isaiah* (Philadelphia: Fortress, 1988); C. Westermann. *Isaiah 40–66*. OTL (Philadelphia: Westminster, 1969).

JEREMIAH

James M. Kennedy

OVERVIEW

The book of Jeremiah takes its name from the prophet whose words it contains and whose actions it describes. No other prophetic book in the Old Testament gives as much biographical information about its namesake as the book of Jeremiah. Yet Jeremiah's biography is not the point. What one learns about his life in the book is related to the book's message. Interestingly, readers know nothing of how and when he died. Instead the book attests that he spoke God's word and performed God's directions, and for the compilers of the book that was enough.

The book began to take form in the exilic era, which commenced with the first deportation of Judahites to Babylon in 597 BCE. The Greek version, the Septuagint (LXX), exhibits a different order from the Masoretic Text (MT) in significant ways, most substantially in the sequence of the oracles against Israel's national neighbors. The discovery of the Dead Sea Scrolls revealed the existence of Hebrew manuscripts of the book of Jeremiah that closely relate to LXX. Many scholars have concluded that the differences between MT and LXX are not from textual dislocation but involve two different Hebrew versions of the book. The New Revised Standard Version (NRSV) is a translation of MT and provides the basis of the following commentary.

Perhaps more so than the other two lengthy prophetic books—Isaiah and Ezekiel—Jeremiah displays sequences that seem unrelated. The implications of this are multiple, but of paramount importance is the necessity for patience on the part of readers. The commentary that follows views the difficult sequences as planned. The book of Jeremiah asks its readers to enter a world marked by confusion, fear, hope, despair, joy—a world of seriously ambivalent and conflicting emotions. It is the world of Judah's catastrophic fall to the Babylonian Empire and the events that led to it. Perhaps the book's complicated literary structure invites its readers to experience a mental simulacrum of the conditions that appeared to whirl out of control around its central human figure, a human being whom the God of history called on to do an impossible task.

OUTLINE

I. Prologue (1:1–19)

    A. Superscription (1:1–5)

    B. The Call of Jeremiah (1:6–10)

    C. Divine Promise and Warning (1:11–19)

II. Destruction (2:1–25:28)

    A. Oracles of Judgment (2:1–10:25)
        2:1–4:31. Appeals for Repentance
        5:1–6:30. Indictment and Sentence
        7:1–10:18. Corruption of the Temple

    B. Jeremiah's Response (10:19–22:30)
        10:19–11:17. Covenant and Apostasy
        11:18–22:30. Jeremiah's
            Debate with God

    C. Prophetic Conflict (23:1–28:17)
        23:1–7. A Glimpse of Hope
        23:9–28:17. Jeremiah and Hananiah

III. Promise of Restoration (30:1–33:26)

    A. The New David (30:1–34)

    B. Return of the Exiles (31:1–30)

    C. The New Covenant (31:31–40)

    D. Signs of Assurance (32:1–33:26)

IV. Judah's Last Days (34:1–45:5)

    A. Collapse of Trust (34:1–22)

    B. Sign of the Rechabites (35:1–19)

    C. Jehoiakim and the Scroll (36:1–32)

    D. Jeremiah's Imprisonment (37:1–38:29)

    E. The Fall of Jerusalem and Aftermath (39:1–45:5)

V. The Nations (46:1–51:64)

DETAILED ANALYSIS

I. Prologue (1:1–19)

A. Superscription (1:1–5)

The first two words in the book bear more significance than the simple translation "the words of Jeremiah" allows. The Hebrew word *davar*, "word," may mean "chronicle" or "event." As readers proceed through the book, it becomes clear that the superscription means more than "words," but something like "the events" or "deeds" of Jeremiah. The autobiographical and biographical elements are definitive components of the book.

The text dates the coming of the Lord's word to Jeremiah beginning in 628/7 BCE and lasting until the fifth month of 587 BCE. Jeremiah's hometown of Anathoth relates him to the ancestor, Abiathar, whom Solomon exiled there generations earlier (2 Kgs 2:26). Jeremiah's heritage of exile may have played a role in his enemies' reactions to what the Lord tells him to announce (Jer 29:27). Nevertheless, the book reminds its readers that Anathoth itself harbored many of the prophet's foes (Jer 11:21–23).

B. The Call of Jeremiah (1:6–10)

From before Jeremiah's birth, the Lord intended him to be "a prophet to the nations" but Jeremiah protests that his youth disqualifies him from such service. His demurral evokes an image of Moses' insistent argument with God at the burning bush in Exodus 3. Jeremiah's exact age does not figure, only that he asserts he is a *na'ar*, that is, a youth (Jer 1:6; NRSV, "boy"). God is unimpressed with his lack of credentials and insists that Jeremiah speak as commanded. The prophet has no choice. Readers learn of Jeremiah's underlying concern in the Lord's command "do not be afraid of them." To whom "them" refers is ambiguous. Such an ambiguity may be by design and so leave Jeremiah in a state of anxiety as well as communicate a similar mood to the book's readers. God has looked into Jeremiah's heart, seen his fear, and speaks to it; it is a lesson that will figure later in the book (Jer 17:9, 10; 20:12). Jeremiah informs his readers that God instilled the divine message by touching his mouth. Jeremiah's task as prophet will be both destructive and constructive. His words not only will participate in the dismantling of Judah but will exert their inexorable power over other nations and kingdoms as well (Jer 46:1–51:64).

C. Divine Promise and Warning (1:11–19)

With the vision of the "branch of an almond tree," the Lord secures Jeremiah's attention to the inevitability of the divine word's success. In Hebrew, the word for "almond" (*shaqed*) is phonemically similar to the word for "watching" (*shaqod*). Jeremiah understands what the almond branch means and instantly transfers the literal content of the vision into comprehending it as expressing the Lord's assurance of fulfillment.

The vision of "a boiling pot, tilted away from the north" unfolds the general message, namely, that the Lord is going to send a scalding destruction over the land from out of the north. Indeed, the Babylonian advance on Judah will be from the north because of the desert that lies to the east of Judah and west of Babylon. Tellingly, the Lord does not identify the attackers from the north but depicts them as "all the tribes of the kingdoms of the north." The reference to the multiplicity of kingdoms suggests that the Babylonians will use the empire's vast resources of conquered peoples to descend on Judah, like the varied contents of the pot set to boil.

With the threatening promise "I will utter my judgments against them" (v. 16), the Lord acts as both prosecutor and judge. This declaration exhibits the actions of a prosecutor making a case against a defendant as well as the judge pronouncing sentence. Here is the basic crime that Jerusalem and the cities of Judah have committed: by way of "offerings to other gods," they have offered sustenance to the other gods and have rendered adoration to their own creations instead of to the Creator. "Gird up your loins" is a figurative expression deriving from the need to secure the bottom part of one's garments to engage in toil or to do something quickly. What Jeremiah is about to do, that is, "tell them everything that" the Lord commands, will be toilsome and laborious. The labor finds expression in the Lord comparing Jeremiah to a city under siege that must make preparations to hold back a besieging army (here Jeremiah's own compatriots). As toilsome and troublesome as his situation may be, Jeremiah can only accept the Lord's promise of his eventual security. With the divine promise in v. 19, "for I am with you," the text alludes to the Lord's promise to Moses (Exod 3:12).

II. Destruction (2:1–25:28)

A. Oracles of Judgment (2:1–10:25)

Jeremiah 2–38 contains disparate materials that seem at times not to follow any logical sequence. Some scholars attribute the difficult order of the text to a complex textual history of copying and editing. As plausible as this is, the text's organization could also be by design. The text that seems to be disordered might reflect the disordered character of the situation to which Jeremiah must speak. Text and reality merge in the apparent jumble. Furthermore, the text's seemingly disordered nature provides readers with an experience that will compel them into imaginatively identifying with the kind of inner struggle Jeremiah will endure. Just as the prophet must deal with what may seem like a world out of control, the book's readers must work in unusual ways to make sense of what seems like a text out of control. There are a few clues along the way that provide useful guidance. Indeed, by the time one has read the entire book and viewed chs. 2–38 in their literary context, the end to which the text's editors arranged the material sheds light on its beginning. In part, the book of Jeremiah works on the assumption that a comprehensive understanding of what is happening can come only from the perspective of looking back, as an anonymous prophetic voice announces in Jer 23:20 and 30:24, "In

the latter days you will understand this." Charles Tindley's hymn truly captures the essence of this interpretive maneuver with the famous line, "We will understand it better by and by."

2:1–4:31. Appeals for Repentance. In this section, the book of Jeremiah configures the Lord's accusations against Israel as a way to convince Israel of the need to turn back to God. Rhetorically, the accusations imply God's appeal for Israel to stop such behavior and to return. Verse 5 expresses the Lord's amazement that, instead of clinging closely to the divine guide through the desert, "they went far from me." Why would a migrating people simply abandon the knowing guide in such dangerous territory to follow "after worthless things"? If the ancestors had found wrong in the Lord, then there would be no question. "Wrong" (*'awel*) refers to mistreatment, malice, or crookedness. Although Israel cannot point to any maltreatment from God, they followed "worthless things." The term for "worthless things" is *hebel*, elsewhere translated as "vanity" (Eccl 1:2), and allows for the connotations of "breeze" or "wind." The accusation constructs a picture of people leaving off from following a guide to chase after dust devils and becoming just as confused in their whirling about as is the whirling wind. That the Israelites' ancestors followed wrong (*hevel*) alludes to the issue of the "wrong" (*'awel*) about which the Lord asks.

The description of the alien terrain in v. 6 only adds to the wonderment of Israel's leaving off from following the Lord. Navigating through such dangers, they never asked, "Where is the LORD?" That God brought them into the garden that was Canaan in v. 7 implies the character of God as gracious. Yet, once in Canaan, Israel's lack of concern for the Lord continues. Verse 8 reframes the question concerning the presence of the Lord in a liturgical context and as absent from the mouths of the priests. Furthermore, interpreters of the law did not know or recognize the Lord, Israel's rulers transgressed, and the prophets prophesied by Baal, the Canaanite god of fertility. In the desert, the ancestors scrambled after "worthless things"; in the land they "went after things that do not profit" (v. 8), most likely a reference to idols.

A brief excursus on idols in the Old Testament will clarify the book of Jeremiah's polemic against them. Readers of the Old Testament will know that it records God's denunciation of idolatry, as for example in Exod 20:4–6, 23 and Lev 26:1. Not just any statue could be an idol. An idol was a representation of a deity in animal or human form that served a focusing function in liturgy. Idols were cult statues. Throughout the ancient Near East, the statue destined to become a cult statue underwent a ceremony known by various names. In Egypt, it was called The Ceremony of the Opening of the Mouth. In Mesopotamia, it was The Ceremony of the Washing of the Mouth. Both were variations of the same basic concept, namely, that after the ceremony was complete, the spirit of the god the statue represented took up residence in it. Because the ancients thought of the spirit as giving life, the cult statue required care. This care amounted to a place to live, namely, a shrine in a temple and something to eat, namely, sacrifice. A key component of the use of the cult statue was divination. The ancients believed that the god could communicate with the appropriate cultic official through the statue. The prophets of the Old Testament protested the use of cult statues with vigor. Habakkuk 2:18–20 offers evidence that the Israelites had their own variation of the ceremony by which the statue could be summoned to divine life and offer instruction. In contrast, Habakkuk proclaimed, "But the LORD is in his holy temple" (Hab 2:20).

In Jer 2:9–11, God challenges the accused to look about them and to find a nation that has changed its gods. Framed as a rhetorical question, the Lord's challenge demands a negative answer. Yet, Israel has changed its supreme devotion—their glory—into "something that does not profit" (Jer 2:11). Here is a reference to cultic statues that denies them any ability to act. They are not capable of transmitting a divine oracle. In vv. 12–13, the Lord addresses the divine council (see Jer 23:18, 22). The vocative, "O heavens," exhibits the figure of metonymy, whereby a word represents a given entity or entities by association. The Lord uses strong verbs that depict deep horror at Israel's misdeeds. Jeremiah's readers learn that much more is at stake than one people. Jeremiah will express this later in ch. 4.

The Lord compares Israel's change of worship to their having dug out "cracked cisterns that can hold no water" when all along they have had available "the fountain of living water," an arte-

sian well that forces its water to the surface and requires no descent into dark holes. The book may be foreshadowing one of Jeremiah's darkest moments—being abandoned to die in a muddy cistern (Jer 38).

Against the background of Josiah's death and Neco's triumph, the prophet examines Israel's condition. Second Kings 23:29–35 provides the background for the despoiling that vv. 14–19 describe. Jeremiah's pondering takes the literary form of describing the Lord continuing to speak to the divine council (see Jer 2:11). Like a master taking away the belonging of a slave, Neco has plundered Jerusalem and its surroundings, so Jeremiah fitfully muses on the question, "Is Israel a slave? Is he a homeborn servant?" These questions refuse an affirmative answer and so the Lord asks, "Why then has he become plunder?" Verse 17 expresses the tragic answer. Israel invited the disaster by abandoning the Lord. The phrase "while he led you in the way" reprises the accusation from 2:6–8.

Presumably, v. 19 represents a component of the Lord's address that Jeremiah will convey to the people. The word "apostasies" translates the Hebrew word *meshuvah*, a noun that derives from the verb *shuv*, "to turn." It designates wandering or rambling around. It is the same root the prophet will employ (3:14, 22; 4:1) when he urges his people to turn to God, which, in effect would mean to stop wandering and to follow God. The phrase "evil and bitter" is the kind of condition that compels the Lord to summon the heavens to be shocked and horrified (v. 12). The Hebrew word for "evil" bears the sense of calamitous or catastrophic as well as evil. "Bitter" carries forward the conditions that prevail from having dug out useless cisterns that can yield only puddles of bitter water. Along with the word "forsake," "bitter" ties the thought more securely to 2:13.

That the Lord can assert "the fear of me is not in you" presupposes that Israel does not see itself as having abandoned the Lord. Verses 20–22 describe Israel's transference of loyalty from the Lord to the Canaanite fertility cults. Having planted a choice vine, the Lord expresses deep dismay at the results, namely, the choice vine becomes a wild vine, a quickly propagating, useless weed. The evidence of Israel's guilt is ineradicable (2:22) and prompts the Lord's troubled bemusement in

v. 23, "How can you say, 'I am not defiled, I have not gone after the Baals'?"

Israel cannot deny its guilt. The nation's leaders, who call on the cult statues, will find them powerless (2:26–28). Verses 26–27 explain the nature of the shame the officials will suffer. The impotence of the idols will come to light and. thereby, the leadership's dereliction of duty will be obvious to all. Verse 29 implies that the Lord is having a conversation; someone has been complaining. The Hebrew word for "complain" (*riv*) suggests a legal argument. Presumably, the nation has lamented the disaster of Neco's victory and now, in vv. 30–32 the Lord corrects the record by reminding Israel that its rebellion against God is the cause of its military failure against Egypt. In v. 30, the Lord recalls unnamed moments in Israel's history in which punitive guidance has failed. The prophets who spoke God's word loyally met with violent death at the hands of their own people. Verse 31 recalls the imagery of the land as a garden (2:7) as God rhetorically asks if the care the land requires has not been given. Indeed, the question may assume the declarative form, "I have been neither a desert nor a land of darkness to Israel."

Behind the argument of v. 31 lies the sad truth that Israel has sought what it needs from Baal, as if the Lord were of no value. Completely unaware of their culpability in the national disaster, the people throw up their hands not in worship but in exasperation as they assume that God has failed them. They take the privilege of rejecting the Lord because they interpret the present crisis as a failure of the suzerain of Mount Sinai. Verse 32 expresses yet again God's bewilderment. How can a girl forget her jewelry or a bride her attire on the wedding day? Yet, Israel has neglected God "days without number."

Israel's wandering after Baal is so skillful that it can serve as an example to "wicked women," presumably, prostitutes (2:33). Yet, such skill cannot conceal the evidence of Israel's crime as "on your skirts is found the lifeblood of the innocent poor." The use of the adjective "innocent" to describe the poor suggests that persons without recourse to adequate defense have been falsely charged with crimes the punishment for which is death. Jeremiah sees a close connection between Israel abandoning God and the social elite's perversion

of power to suit their own schemes. In spite of this evidence, Israel insists "I am innocent" and "I have not sinned" (2:35). Verse 36 describes Israel's turning from God as frivolous and carefree, with no forethought of consequences. Therefore, the Lord will nullify any help that may come from Egypt or Assyria. Israelite emissaries will return with their hands on their heads, a sign of shame and failure (cf. 2 Sam 13:19).

Jeremiah 3:1 alludes to a law about marriage in Deut 24:1–4. If a man divorces his wife, she may marry another man. If the second husband divorces her, the first husband may not take her back. The answer to the question of v. 1 is therefore "no," the land would be defiled. The Lord applies the conditions to Israel. Having "played the whore with many lovers," would the nation dare think of returning to the first husband, the Lord? In v. 2, the evidence for Israel's adultery from the Lord mounts. No place is clean from Israel's adultery. The term, "bare heights," renders a Hebrew word that can refer to caravan trails. The sense appears to be that Israel has lain in wait like a roadside prostitute to take advantage of the goods and services available along the trade routes. The second half of v. 2 carries this image forward by comparing Israel to just such characters. For this reason, the Lord has held back the rains (v. 3). God's explanation of drought conditions relates to 2:29, where the divine Lord reminds Israel of the real identity of the guilty party. God's acknowledgment of having heard Israel's call in vv. 4–5 continues a string of occurrences wherein the Lord quotes something Israel has said (2:20, 23, 25, 31). Regardless of the words God hears, v. 5 confirms that Israel's conduct has not shifted to exhibit sincere returning.

In 3:6–14, Jeremiah conveys what the Lord said to him in the days of King Josiah. The basic message is that, given the northern kingdom of Israel's apostasies (vv. 6–10), Judah has surpassed them. The fate of the northern kingdom should have been Judah's object lesson, but Judah's confession of loyalty to the Lord was "only in pretense." In the light of 3:4–5, Jeremiah's readers will see that Judah has habitually wandered away from the Lord. The implication of the Lord's command to Jeremiah to proclaim a divine plea to Israel in the north to return (3:11–14) seems to be that perhaps Judah will outdo her northern sister in sincere repentance. Unlike Judah, who will not acknowledge guilt, perhaps Israel will acknowledge its own (3:13) with the result of reunification with Zion.

In vv. 15–18, Jeremiah depicts the momentous character of what God ultimately promises to do. Instead of corrupt rulers, the Lord will install "shepherds after my own heart." These leaders will nourish the new kingdom with "knowledge and understanding." Verse 16 conveys a component of the message that may have shocked the priestly hierarchy in Jerusalem, namely, the absence of the ark of the covenant of the Lord in the future scenario. The ark functioned as the throne of the invisible Deity who dwelled over the cherubim (cf. 1 Sam 4:4). Instead of the ark as God's throne, Jerusalem itself will serve that role. The Lord's presence will be unmediated and obvious to all the nations who will assemble before God.

Verses 19–20 exhibit the theme of the divine pathos. With the imagery of a wife who abandons her husband, the text conveys the sense of bitter disappointment that God endures as Israel wanders away. Having given Israel a beautiful and productive land in which to live, the Lord muses, "I thought you would call me, My Father." In Jeremiah, the word *father* first occurs in 2:27 where Israel's leaders "say to a tree, 'You are my father.'" Reference to God as father in the Old Testament is not frequent, yet frequent enough to know that it functioned in a meaningful way to express the implications of God's covenant relationship with Israel (Deut 32:6, 19; Isa 64:8; Hos 11:1). In v. 20, the Lord accuses Israel of having "been faithless" (NRSV).

Verse 21 presents an anonymous voice in the divine council; perhaps it is Jeremiah, opining "A voice on the bare heights is heard." "Bare heights" may refer to the high ridges on which caravans made their way along trading routes. The imagery portrays Israel as orphaned children crying out for any sustenance they can find along the routes that wayfarers and caravans take. It is a heart-rending image. At v. 22, the Lord speaks up with the plea, "Return, O faithless children, I will heal your faithlessness." "Faithlessness" describes the act of wandering or meandering, turning this way and that (Jer 2:19, NRSV, "apostasies"). To return to the Lord is to reverse and to straighten the meandering course that led Israel into dire conditions.

The promise "I will heal your faithlessness" parallels the divine promise that Hos 14:4 quotes.

Verses 22b–25 display the ideal response for which God hopes, but that will turn out to be unrealistic. As if responding to the divine appeal for repentance in v. 22a, the penitent nation alerts God to its intent to come to God. The Hebrew is emphatic (NRSV, "Here we come").

In v. 24, "the shameful thing" may refer to the cult statue in a way that underscores its complete failure to respond to Israel's needs. That it "has devoured all for which our ancestors had labored" alludes to the material sacrifices that were believed to maintain the presence of a deity's spirit in the statue. "Shame" in v. 25 is the same word that depicts the cult statue in the previous verse. It refers to Israel's failure to have heeded God's plea. To cover with "dishonor" (NRSV) conveys the awareness of anyone who sees an exhibition of shame. The ideal confession of sin admits that Israel's entire history has been one of rebellion against the divine sovereign. The admission, "We have not obeyed the voice of the LORD our God," is characteristically Deuteronomic and takes its substance from alluding to texts such as Deut 8:20; 13:4, 18; 15:5.

Israel, having correctly admitted its crimes against God and having accepted its shame and dishonor, must do more. Jeremiah 4:1–4 expresses God's instructions concerning what it means to return to obedience and how to regain honor among the nations of the world. The word "abominations" (4:1; NRSV) also bears the sense of "detestable thing" or "filth." Ostensibly, it refers to the cult statue. That Israel is to remove such things "from my presence" could mean that Israel must remove them from the Temple in Jerusalem as well as from the land itself. The further condition, "and do not waver" (NRSV), may also mean "wander" or "roam." Israel's devotion to repentance not only involves turning back to follow the Lord, but refusing to allow its resolve to weaken, which could then lead to wandering away from the Lord again.

The oath, "as the LORD lives," commits the one making the oath to live up to a prior agreement. To swear it "in truth, in justice, and in uprightness" is to do so with integrity and commitment. In Jer 38:16, King Zedekiah will swear this oath as his guarantee that he will not allow harm to come to Jeremiah if Jeremiah will tell him the truth from God. Jeremiah is completely honest, but Zedekiah finally sets a condition of safety on his prior oath. Regardless of having sworn, "as the LORD lives," he warns Jeremiah to keep their meeting a secret, or Jeremiah will die. Verse 2b relates the consequences of Israel's sincere turning to God; the nation will regain its honor as the Lord's people among the nations of the earth. "Then nations shall be blessed by him" evokes the ancestral promise of blessing to all humankind in Gen 12:1–3; 26:1–5; 28:13–15.

The word "for" with which v. 3 begins relates vv. 3–4 to what has come before. The actions that the Lord urges in vv. 3–4 reinforce the appeal to repent in vv. 1–2. The appeal from God employs agricultural metaphors that describe actions taken to prepare land for sowing seed. "Fallow ground" (NRSV) describes land that once had been plowed and seeded but then allowed to go unattended for a time. Breaking up the fallow ground removes from it the thorns that would have inevitably grown in the meantime. Ostensibly, the command in v. 3, with its agricultural metaphors of breaking up the fallow ground and removing its thorns, carries forward and reinforces the description of true repentance that vv. 1–2 express.

Verse 4 conveys the command "Circumcise yourselves to the LORD" (NRSV) but could just as well be rendered "Be circumcised by the LORD." To the ancient Israelites, this command would not make sense insofar as Israelite boys were circumcised on the eighth day after their birth. The parallel text, "remove the foreskin of your hearts" (NRSV) reveals the symbolic nature of the previous command. The origins of circumcision are lost in the distant reaches of human history. The Hebrews were not the only ancient people to practice circumcision. It was common among other Semitic cultures of Syria and Palestine. The Israelites traced its origin to the divine command to Abraham in Gen 17. Exodus 12:48 reasserts the rite in the context of Israel's exodus from Egypt. Theories concerning the meaning of circumcision abound; this commentary works on the hypothesis that circumcision was a rite related to what the ancient Semitic peoples believed about human reproduction. The removal of the foreskin was the removal of a possible obstacle to the transfer of seed from the man to the woman. Circumcision essentially prepared the male human to father children. Because mystery and anxiety veiled the process of reproduction, anything related to it became a matter of ritual concern and control. In Jer 4:3–4, the agricultural imagery of preparing the ground for productivity and the removal of the foreskin of the heart therefore complement each other. To remove the foreskin of the heart is therefore a symbol of preparing the heart to receive the productive power of God's blessing. Verse 4b sets out the alternative. God's rage will erupt like an unquenchable fire and, to carry forward the agricultural metaphor, burn the thorns into ashes.

In vv. 4–8, the Lord's command to Jeremiah casts him as an informant, ostensibly from the divine council, who is to alert the appropriate authorities to sound an alert from Jerusalem regarding an advancing invading army. A warning is to go out to the settlements around Jerusalem for the inhabitants to flee into the city for refuge. Verse 6 recalls Jer 1:14–15, where the Lord informs Jeremiah that devastation will come to Judah from the north.

In v. 7, the metaphor of a lion depicts the disaster approaching from the north. A lion emerging from its cover to hunt for prey might seem a small matter to contemporary city dwellers, but in the ancient Near East, a marauding lion could strike terror in the hearts of the inhabitants of villages and settlements without walls. Proverbs 30:30 describes the lion as the mightiest of beasts, never backing down from pursuing what it wants. Second Kings 17:25 preserves the memory of a pride of lions attacking a settlement and killing many people. Jeremiah's ancient audience would have fearfully appreciated the metaphor.

Immediately the metaphor of a lion shifts to something much more ominous, "a destroyer of nations." The ambiguity of the actual agent of disaster (Jer 4:6; NRSV, "the evil") provokes anxious reflection. It will "make your land a waste" and depopulate the cities. Verse 8 calls for a response from the people. Wearing sackcloth suggests repentance, but mourning is also an occasion for wearing it (Gen 37:34). Here the emphasis falls on mourning. Verse 8 continues the oracle that God tells Jeremiah to "declare in Judah, and proclaim in Jerusalem" (v. 5). It is not an oracle calling for repentance but announces the imminent disaster to descend from the north. The only thing for the land's inhabitants to say involves the recognition that the Lord's burning rage (4:8; NRSV, "fierce anger") has not turned back.

Verse 9 offers a fuller description of "that day" of disaster; the social system disintegrates. Courage will fail the king and his cronies. As Jer 39:4 reports, when the Babylonians breach Jerusalem's defenses, Zedekiah and his guard flee in terror from the city under cover of night, hoping to find refuge in the desert to the south. They will not succeed.

Presumably standing in the divine council (Jer 23:18, 22), Jeremiah objects in v. 10. He accuses the Lord of having deceived the people with protestations of their security, knowing full well that "the sword is at the throat." To what promise of protection Jeremiah refers is a puzzle. To this point in the book, God has not assured Judah or Jerusalem of divine protection in any terms that do not presuppose the nation's repentance. The prophet's response may exhibit his own lack of perception of God's command. Jeremiah will become aware of his own need for instruction (Jer 10:23, 24).

Verse 11 portrays the Lord re-engaging the people in debate. A message will arrive from the advancing front with the dreadful announcement of a desiccating, destructive storm close behind. In v. 13, the Hebrew word translated "Look!" (hinneh) conveys both the suddenness and nearness of the invading force. The depiction of the enemies' chariots as "like the whirlwind" carries forward the metaphor of the desiccating, destructive wind from v. 11. As the Lord and Jeremiah confront each other, it is still not too late. Jerusalem may yet turn and "be saved" (v. 14). Verses 15–17 suggest, however, that the time of decision is short. The enemy may not yet be at the gates, but their advance is relentless. As if responding to Jeremiah's accusation of deceit from v. 10, the Lord lays the blame at the feet of the disloyal people. Verse 18 concludes with an assertion that Jerusalem's inhabitants finally comprehend the true nature of their dire predicament.

Verses 19–21 record Jeremiah's pained response and suggest that the prophet has himself learned something about the true nature of the situation. The painful, visceral reaction Jeremiah experiences compels him to speak out. The speech is not to the people, however, but is an exclamation of distress in the context of the divine assembly's deliberations. Jeremiah's distress is strong enough to induce physical pain. As if recognizing that etiquette in the council requires him to remain quiet, he cries aloud, "I will not be silent" (v 19; NRSV, "I cannot keep silent")! The verbs in v. 21 are difficult to translate. Jeremiah's question may express his dread of experiencing a prolonged time of suffering. Conceivably, he opines, "How long shall I have to see the standard and hear the sound of the trumpet?"

The Lord speaks in v. 22 and tells the troubled prophet that the people are vacuous, void of any awareness of God, prone to folly and without capacity for understanding. Nevertheless, they possess the wisdom (NRSV, "they are skilled) for doing evil. Their wisdom does not extend to doing what is good, i.e., to perform in such a way as to live in obedience to God's instruction. Against this background, readers may justifiably think that Israel's protestations of innocence (Jer 2:23) are sincere. Thus, Jeremiah faces a situation in which the Lord compels him to proclaim the divine word of judgment but to an audience that cannot respond obediently.

Jeremiah 4:23–26 conveys a vision of cosmic horror. Creation crumbles into the same state of chaos out of which Gen 1 portrays God as calling it. In the divine assembly, the Lord allows Jeremiah to witness the consequences of Israel's ignorance of the divine teaching and reveals to the horrified prophet that the consequences reach far beyond Israel's dissolution and exile. The vision expresses total destruction in several scenarios. The earth essentially liquefies and the luminaries of the heavens go dark (v. 23). The mountains quiver and collapse (v. 24). All life vanishes from the surface of the earth and the birds of the air flee (v. 25). Areas that once produced abundant agriculture become sterile, with the result that civilization collapses (v. 26). Other prophetic books in the Old Testament employ similar imagery to depict the juggernaut blast of the Lord's rage (Isa 24:1–8; Joel 2:1–11; Hab 3:2–16; Zeph 1:2–3).

In v. 27, the Lord brings the horrific vision to a close and then reveals that the vision was of something that could be, but that, mercifully, will not transpire. "I will not make a full end," the Lord states. Whether this is an editorial expansion by a late hand is possible, but it now functions to mitigate the scene of cosmic destruction. Indeed, God has proclaimed that the heavens will grow dark, but this is not of the same devastating quality that v. 23 describes; and indeed the earth shall mourn. From this the divine judge will not relent (v. 28).

Jeremiah 4:29 evokes the image of a panicked urban population fleeing into wooded areas and looking for refuge among rocky crags at the sound of an approaching cavalry with its steeds and archers, leaving towns depopulated. In a similar but lengthier text, Isa 2:10–21 describes the inhabitants of Judah's cities fleeing into desolate places to escape the terror of the Lord. Judges 6:2 refers to the oppressed Israelites as hiding from the Midianites in wild areas where there is cover in mountain caves.

In 4:30, the prophet poses a question that expresses amazement or surprise. Given the desolate conditions of having to flee the towns, the prophet is surprised to see women still concerned with their finery. In the final analysis, it will be in vain. The enemy has no romantic interests, but only in killing (vv. 30–31).

5:1–6:30. Indictment and Sentence. In Jer 5:1–2, the Lord challenges Jeremiah to canvass the streets of Jerusalem to see if he can find anyone "who acts justly and seeks truth." The presence of one such person will mean pardon for Jerusalem. The Lord warns Jeremiah not to take at face value hearing people say, "As the Lord lives" because it is a false oath. Imagining how Jeremiah's words to God in v. 3 relate to v. 2 allows any number of scenarios. This commentary envisions Jeremiah as returning to the divine assembly with a negative report. The streets are busy with people who have taken no heed to God's disciplinary acts in past times. Indeed, Jeremiah reports that they have only grown more stubborn (v. 3).

In v. 4, Jeremiah observes that the people he questioned "are only the poor" who "have no sense." The literacy rate in Jeremiah's time would not be high; most people had to spend almost every waking hour in making ends meet. Jeremiah decides to confront the rich, that is, the class of people who would be in a social situation more conducive to education. Verse 5a portrays the prophet as confident that the social elite will "know the way of the Lord, the law of their God."

Yet even among the privileged that had access to the necessary documents and traditions, he finds transgression. With the image of yoke and bonds, the prophet implies the simile that the social elite are like a domesticated animal that has escaped its confines and run wild (v. 5b). Verse 6 carries this simile forward by reference to the kinds of dangers a recalcitrant domesticated animal will face in the wild.

Jeremiah 5:7 draws the readers' attentions once again to the divine assembly. The Lord's question, "how can I pardon you?" is related to Jeremiah's failure to find one righteous person in Jerusalem. As v. 1 indicated, if Jeremiah found a good person, God would pardon the city. That is now not an option. Verses 7–8 summarize God's indictment. In v. 9, the Lord asks two rhetorical questions that if answered negatively would mean that God would deny the validity of the divine commandment for Israel to be loyal.

In vv. 10–11, the Lord commands the divine assembly to disperse into Judah and cause havoc. The verses employ the metaphor of a marauding army despoiling its prey's agriculture. The Lord's instructions include a caveat in v. 10a; the havoc is to be limited. Verses 12–13 configure the Lord's command as a response to the people's confidence that God will not, in fact, do anything. Indeed, the prophets have promised national security, but God will reveal their promises as mere wind.

Verse 14b characterizes the divine word that Jeremiah must speak as a fire that will consume dead wood, a metaphor for the people. In vv. 15–17, the Lord promises to bring on the house of Israel an invading army that will consume both human and natural resources. However, God's purposes do not include total destruction (v. 18). Enough of the population will remain to ask the question "Why has the Lord our God done all these things to us?" Jeremiah will remind the people that they abandoned the Lord to worship foreign gods. Verse 19 concludes with a foreshadowing of the deportations that will begin in 597 BCE.

Verse 20 indicates that the Lord continues to instruct Jeremiah on what he shall say to the people. Following the summons to hear, Jeremiah is to address the people as "mindless" or "lacking a mind" (v. 21; NRSV, "senseless"). Having the ability to see and hear, they yet do not reverence the Lord. Just to the west, the Mediterranean Sea constantly pounds the sands of the coast, and yet it gains no foothold. "The waves toss," the Lord says, "they cannot prevail" (v. 22). This is the doing of the Lord and Israel lacks the intelligence to extrapolate from this phenomenon a sense of God's power. The Lord set a boundary the sea cannot cross and gives the rain in its appropriate season, but senseless Israel refuses to fear God (vv. 23–24). Israel fails to recognize that its sin has become as fast a barrier to the coming of rain as is the land to the rolling waves of the sea (v. 25).

Verses 26–28 portray Israel's social elite as scoundrels who have grown wealthy by treachery and deceit. The basic metaphor is that of a fowler who catches birds, creatures that find themselves unwarily trapped in snares. In v. 28, the phrase "fat and sleek" implies a nearly carefree life-style but it is one derived from depriving the most vulnerable in the land of justice. Ostensibly addressing the divine council, the Lord sets out a declaration clothed as a rhetorical question, "Shall I not punish them for these things?" The misdeeds of both prophets and priests have produced an "appalling and horrible thing," a phrase that describes one's hair bristling with horror. Incredibly, the people are content with the situation but they have not faced the question of its consequences (v. 31b).

If one thinks of its setting as the divine assembly, Jeremiah 6 presents a dramatic and emotional interchange between the angry Lord and a prophet who desperately wants to serve both. As vv. 27–30 will reveal, part of the Lord's agenda is to educate Jeremiah concerning the wayward paths of the people. In v. 1 the Lord bids trumpets to blare in Tekoa and directional signs on Beth-haccherem. Tekoa was approximately 10 miles south of Jerusalem. The exact location of Beth-haccherem is not known, but best estimates put it just under 5 miles south of Jerusalem. The flight takes place toward the opposite direction from which the disaster will break, namely, the north.

In vv. 2–3, the Lord compares "daughter Zion" to the best of pastures. Such lush abundance will attract aggressive shepherds who will bring their sheep. The implication is that the sheep will devour the resources of the land. Although the poetic image is of the shepherd's temporary tents, it evokes mental pictures of the tents the

Babylonian army will pitch during the siege to come. Verse 4 turns to describing that specific context. This verse gives voice to an army eager to attack before the night falls. Verse 6 begins with the prophetic messenger formula and alerts readers that what follows is God's decree. Like a military field commander, God commands the setting up of the siege ramp against Jerusalem and, as if providing strategic intelligence to the enemy, points to Jerusalem's location. The Babylonians will be seeking plunder, but God's reasons for giving them the city are different. As the arbiter of true justice, he demands that "this city must bear the consequences" (Jer 6:6; NRSV, "this city must be punished"). Like a well that keeps its water fresh and cool (v. 7), Jerusalem contains oppression within her. The simile of a well implies that Jerusalem's corruption is deep and deliberate; wells are the work of human engineering. Verse 8 yields a hint that disaster can yet be averted. The Lord pleads with Jerusalem "to be disciplined" (NRSV, "take warning"). The Hebrew follows this plea with the word *pen*, literally, "lest I shall turn from you" (NRSV, "or I shall turn from you"), thus allowing for a different conclusion to the matter.

Verses 10–11 convey the prophet's sense of frustration as he complains before the Lord that Israel holds the divine word in contempt as the people refuse to listen and obey. Jeremiah, in contrast, is filled with the anger of God and has grown weary with not expressing it. God directs Jeremiah to pour it out into the streets on both young and old. Verses 13–15 describe greed as permeating every level of society, including priest and prophet. Nevertheless, the social elite insist that all is well (v. 14) by asserting "peace, peace." That the people do not blush indicates that they do not see their condition as embarrassing but their behavior dishonors the reputation of God.

Verses 16–17 portray God as having provided guidance and warning, but Israel has repeatedly refused. In vv. 18–19, all nations are addressed. The poetic figure of apostrophe allows God to address Israel obliquely as the Lord promises to bring disaster on the people. The refusal of Israel to follow the Lord's teaching invalidates the nation's public worship (v. 20). Insofar as the nation chose the wrong way (v. 16), they must follow a path studded with causes for stumbling. Verses 22–23 reprise the theme of the enemy from the north

(1:13–15; 4:6; 6:1). Verses 24–25 portray an imaginary crowd of worriers whose fear of the foe from the north will impede the normal processes of society.

Ostensibly standing in the divine assembly (v. 6), Jeremiah verbally expresses his desire for the people to recognize the seriousness of their plight by engaging in the customary rituals of mourning and grief. The divine judge replies in vv. 27–30 that Jeremiah's role as assayer of the population is to educate him, implying that his task is not to side with the people. Verse 29 depicts a foundry worker ceaselessly bellowing the blaze of refinement but to no avail. There is nothing to gain from the refining process. Jeremiah must learn that there is nothing of value that remains among his people.

7:1–10:18. Corruption of the Temple.

Knowing something about the symbolism of temples in the ancient Near East contributes significantly to one's understanding of these chapters. Ancient Near Eastern cultures generally thought of temples as models of the cosmos. They were microcosms of the greater cosmos that stretched out around them. The *hierodules*—persons in charge of a temple's various operations—saw in their temple an earthly manifestation of cosmic order. To desecrate a temple was to attack the very foundations of cosmic order as the hierodules of any particular temple would think of it. Thus, the destruction of a temple would have frightened its caretakers and the community of faith that revolved around it to a degree similar to how the threat of nuclear terrorism would evoke dread in contemporary times.

The ritual slaughter of appropriate animals was a central component of temple activity. According to the Priestly worldview in the Old Testament, a relationship existed between the appropriate disposing of the blood of a sacrificed animal and the maintaining of the cosmic order the temple symbolized. The Priestly documents give no theoretical explanation as to why the two are related except to imply that as long as Israel obeys the Lord and offers the divinely sanctioned sacrifices, the forces of impurity would remain powerless. Thus, Israel was to offer sacrifices because the Lord commanded it. The book of Jeremiah reflects the belief that sacrifices at the Temple were necessary. For Jeremiah verbally to assault the Temple of Jerusalem, and to do so claiming to be speak-

ing on behalf of God, would have outraged the royal and priestly bureaucracies. As Jer 7 begins, the Lord tells Jeremiah "to stand in the gate of the Lord's house, and proclaim" a message of subversion related to the people's naïve assumption that the presence of the Lord's house guarantees the nation's continued survival.

God and people will dwell together in this place contingent only on Israel's making good (7:3; NRSV, "Amend") its ways. The prophet urges his hearers not to rely on what he calls "these deceptive words." The threefold exclamation of "the temple of the Lord" may have been meant to mock the repetitious nature of the liturgical words spoken there. Most likely, in a mimicking way, it echoes the claims of the priests, who in defense of the Temple, only feel the need to assert that it belongs to God.

Verses 5–6 amplify what it means to "truly amend your ways and doings." Here the prophet calls his hearers to cease their exploitation of the most vulnerable in Judahite society, namely, "the alien, the orphan, and the widow." "Innocent blood" suggests the execution of people for crimes they did not commit. Furthermore, recalling Jer 4:1, Jeremiah presses the people not to follow other gods, which can only lead to disaster (v. 6; NRSV, "your own hurt").

In vv. 8–12 the prophetic word confronts the people with the inconsistency between how they live (v. 9) and how they worship (v. 10). The prophet warns them (vv. 13–15) to consider the fate of Shiloh, where a temple of the Lord once stood. The Bible is not explicit about what befell Shiloh, but it is possible that the Philistine war that 1 Sam 4 describes may have resulted in the temple's destruction. Perceiving Jeremiah's sense of solidarity with Israel, the Lord commands the prophet not to speak on the nation's behalf (7:16). Jeremiah may not protest either Israel's innocence or ignorance as God points out that adoration of the "queen of heaven" is rampant (v. 18). The reference here is possibly to Asherah, whose likeness possibly appears on a potsherd from the ninth century BCE on which is etched the blessing, "May you be blessed by Yhwh and his Asherah." Verses 21–26 deliberate on the theme of obedience from the perspective of the Deuteronomic traditions. The book of Deuteronomy repeatedly underscores the necessity for Israel to obey the Lord's teachings (Deut 6:1–3, 17, 18; 8:1–3; 12:1), to remain in the land, and to receive the Lord's blessings. In Jer 7:21, the Lord mockingly encourages the Israelites to slaughter more and more animals in sacrifice; it will avail them nothing. Instead, it is the sacrifice of Israel's stubborn will that can fulfill the requirements God has set before the nation.

Jeremiah 7:27–8:3 continue the Lord's accusations of disobedience and refer to the horrific practice of human sacrifice (vv. 30–32). The destruction that will befall Israel will be so extensive that there will be no one to bury the dead (v. 33), the creation of new families will vanish (v. 34), and the bones of the social elite will be disinterred and scattered before the celestial objects that the Israelites venerated (8:1–2). Who remains will prefer to die than to live (8:3).

Jeremiah 8:4–10:25 seem to be a loosely stitched series of oracles on different topics. They address conditions that derive from the perversion of animal sacrifice from a means to an end as well as the use of the cult statue. Verses 4–7 set out God's argument against the people on the basis of the nation's stupidity. Normally, when someone falls down, he or she gets up again, but Israel falls and decides to keep falling (vv. 4–6)! As if in response to pleas from Jeremiah, the Lord informs the prophet (v. 6) that, having given heed and listened, God can find no honest intent in what the Israelites say. God tells the prophet that even birds know when to migrate and to return (v. 7) but "my people do not know the ordinance of the LORD." Here the Lord presses the central issue: Israel's ignorance. Thus, Jer 8:7 is related to Jer 4:22 and 5:4–5; together they create a picture of Israel as unable to turn back to God because the nation cannot comprehend itself as needing to return.

Verses 8–12 repudiate any claim the Israelites might make to support their having knowledge. The fact that scribes have purposely miscopied God's teachings (v. 8) leads logically to the nation's state of ignorance. Verse 9 promises that the mischief of the scribes and the wise will not remain hidden. Their perversion of the written record will rise up to shame them. Verses 10–12 delineate how the Lord will reveal their fraud. The well-being they promise (v. 11) will not occur; indeed, they themselves will be among the dead on the day of disaster (v. 12). In v. 13, the Lord uses the metaphor of a fruitless garden to describe Israel.

Verses 14–17 offer an imaginative scene depicting the response of people who live in outlying areas to the imminence of the arrival of the destruction from the north. In the face of invasion, such populations flood into cities to find protection behind the walls. "Poisoned water" (v. 14) renders a Hebrew phrase that also occurs in Jer 9:14 and 23:15. Its precise meaning is not known but it may refer to water that has come to have the taste of bile. Some older English translations render it as "water of gall." Such water would be impossible to stomach. It is a fitting metaphor to depict the bitterness of the situation of people having to abandon homes and farms for safety elsewhere. Verse 15 is related to the false proclamation of security in v. 11. Instead of peace, terror comes. Verse 17 uses a metaphor that evokes Num 21:6, where the Lord sends venomous snakes into the Israelite camp. The Lord releases snakes that "cannot be charmed" (NRSV), that is, no amulet can serve as a charm to ward off the snakes' infestation. In the ancient Near East, wearing charms inscribed with spells to ward off snakes was a widespread practice.

In these chapters, speakers change suddenly. Jeremiah 8:18–19a suggests that the prophet speaks, lamenting his loss of joy and describing the poor of the land reassuring themselves that they will find safety in Jerusalem; after all, they reason, "Is the LORD not in Zion? Is her King not in her?" Verse 19b conveys the Lord's exclamation of dismay concerning the peoples' use of the cultic statue. Then Jeremiah speaks out again in 8:21–9:2. Almost as if there had been no interruption, he continues in v. 20 with what he hears the refugees saying as they make their way to the city and its presumed safety. Even after the harvest, there is not enough to sustain. He expresses profound grief for his people and rhetorically inquires about the failure of the "balm in Gilead" (v. 22), by which he possibly refers to the mastic resin of the *Pistacia mutica*. Physicians applied the resin to seal wounds and it did so as it hardened. Essentially, v. 22 asserts that no medicine can answer the desperate need of restoring the nation's relationship to God.

Jeremiah's reputation as a weeping prophet probably stems from 9:1–2. He bewails having run dry of tears, he has wept so much; he wishes he had a desert retreat to which he might flee to get away from traitorous adulterers who are his people. In v. 3, the Lord accuses the people of speaking crookedly, hence the simile of the bent bow. Truth is a casualty in Israel's social structure, a condition deriving from Israel's failure to acknowledge God. In vv. 4–9, the Lord offers an extensive warning to Jeremiah not to trust his neighbors. Fraud is rampant and lying is a skill the Lord accuses the people of cultivating (v. 5). "Friendly words" mask deceitful intent (v. 8). As if alluding to Jeremiah's expression of grief in 8:21–9:2, the Lord tells the prophet to lament that even the dwelling place of wild animals has become devoid of life (v. 10). With a sterile countryside surrounding it, Jerusalem will become a pile of rubble fit only for jackals (v. 11).

Jeremiah speaks in v. 12 and bemoans in rhetorical questions the condition of his people. In v. 14, the plural "the Baals" designates the various cult statues of Baal found at his numerous shrines. The bitter wormwood (*Artemisia absinthium*) and poisoned water (8:14) will be Israel's only food, a metaphor for the bitterness of their situation.

Verses 17–22 urge what amounts to planning a funeral. Professional mourning women will have much to wail about as death has invaded the homes and streets of Jerusalem (v. 21). Not only will death prevail in the city but in the countryside as well (v. 22).

In vv. 23–36, the Lord subverts the standard signs of status and replaces them with knowledge of who God is (v. 23). To know the Lord implies an active concern for the things that concern God, namely, "steadfast love, justice, and righteousness in the earth, for in these things I base my policy" (v 24; NRSV, "for in these things I delight"). Verses 25–26 promise destruction to "all those who are circumcised only in the foreskin" and not in the heart. To be circumcised in the heart is to be receptive to God's word.

Jeremiah 10:1–18 develops the theme of Israel's lack of knowledge. In vv. 2–5, the Lord encourages the people not to fear the divinatory practices of the nations; whereas in vv. 6–10, a member of the divine assembly speaks up to praise the Lord's incomparable wisdom and power and to denounce the cult statues. Verse 8 indicates that divination

was indeed an important component of the cult statue's use.

B. Jeremiah's Response (10:19–22:30)

Jeremiah's response to the situation he faces is that of a finite human being struggling heroically to comprehend. Compelled to obey the Lord and deeply empathetic with his people, Jeremiah experiences emotions that to describe as ambivalent would be an anemic understatement. He is psychologically wounded from both his loyalty to God and his passionate feelings for Israel.

10:19–11:17. Covenant and Apostasy. Some scholars read Jer 10:19–22 as an expression of personified Jerusalem; this is plausible. Yet, just as plausible is to read it as displaying the prophet's empathy. He characterizes what will happen to his people as if it were happening to him. Unlike the shepherds who led Israel astray and did not inquire of the Lord (v. 21), Jeremiah is one with his people.

Jeremiah, ostensibly standing in the divine assembly and speaking in solidarity with his people, refers to his personal pain and its justice. He concedes, "I must bear it." The image of the tent and lost children derives historically from Israel's nomadic heritage and does not suggest that Jeremiah is actually living in tents. Using the metaphor of tent and lost children, Jeremiah establishes a sense of solidarity with this peoples' history. Their story is his story.

As noted earlier, "shepherds" alludes to kings, who typically portrayed themselves as their peoples' shepherd. In v. 21, the prophet muses on the shepherds' incompetence (NRSV, "are stupid"). Their ignorance is so profound that they do not know where to go for guidance; Jeremiah opines, they "do not inquire of the LORD."

Verse 22 continues to convey Jeremiah's voice as he pauses to note aloud the sound of a thundering rumble. It is the disaster from the north (Jer 1:14–16; 4:6; 6:1, 22). With the terms "desolation" and "jackals," the verse evokes the Lord's declaration of intent from Jer 9:11.

Verse 23 expresses a sentiment that seems to deny the authenticity of the prophet's appeals for Israel to turn back to the Lord. What seems to be a denial of human freedom is, in fact, an expression of the prophet's keen awareness that as an individual member of the nation, he cannot control or determine what will happen to him in the heart-wrenching days to come. He did not choose to be a prophet; he did not choose to be born; he did not choose to be in the situation where he finds himself. The acknowledgment of his finitude precedes a request that his chastisement be just (v. 24). He cannot escape the disaster that will come to the nation. He is in solidarity with his people in their sin and in their punishment (vv. 19, 20). As a result, he appeals to God's justice.

Verse 25 anticipates the oracles against the nations that are penultimate to the book's last chapter. It is also related to the first words that God directed to Israel in Jer 2:2, 3. Verse 25 portrays the prophet, perhaps tentatively, alluding to the Lord's memories and daring to introduce a nuance of hope into the situation. After all, why should he ask the Lord to punish the nations specifically for devouring Israel if Israel remains forever outside God's covenant loyalty?

Perhaps this is why the editorial plan of the book immediately takes its readers into a text, namely Jeremiah 11, in which God directs Jeremiah to address the inhabitants of Jerusalem about the responsibilities of the covenant relationship. Verses 1–8 sustain a strong Deuteronomic ambience as it closely associates God's blessings and curses with Israel's obedience or disobedience. The Lord commands Jeremiah to remind the people of Judah and Jerusalem of the exodus from Egypt (vv. 1–5), of solemn warnings against disobedience (vv. 6–7), and of Israel's history of disobedience (v 8). Verses 9–13 bring the brief Deuteronomic recital of history to Jeremiah's contemporary situation. The basic disobedient act is the worship of foreign gods (v. 12–13). Verse 9 has configured this multiplication of deities as a deliberate act, that is, a conspiracy. As noted in the excursus on cult statues, one of the basic functions of the statue was to serve as a vehicle for divination. Essentially, the biblical prophetic literature accuses ancient Israel of taking its cues for social and religious order from a multiplicity of authorities, authorities that the prophets insist do not exist (Jer 2:11).

The Lord commands Jeremiah (v. 14) not to take the people's part in his role as prophet. As Gen 20:7 indicates, prophets were to intercede for other humans, but here God demands that Jeremiah not do so for Judah and Jerusalem. Possibly alluding to the covenant implications of Jeremiah's request regarding the nations in 10:25, the Lord counters with the question, "What right has my beloved in my house, when she has done vile deeds?" (11:15). The destruction of the olive tree—a metaphor of Israel—in vv. 16–17 evokes the practice of a besieging army setting fire to the agricultural areas that surround cities. Thus, when the army leaves, the devastation will inhibit the growth of resistance. After all, a hungry people may rebel, but unless they find a way regularly to satisfy their need for food, they cannot succeed.

11:18–22:30. Jeremiah's Debate with God. Jeremiah 11:18–12:4 presents what scholars often refer to as Jeremiah's first lament. The others occur in 15:10–21; 17:14–18; 18:18–23; and 20:7–18. This commentary depicts them as a part of a debate between God and Jeremiah in the divine assembly. In its current literary context, v. 18 refers to what the Lord says in v. 9 about a conspiracy, but it also fits well with earlier accusations that the Lord has made against Israel. Verse 19 conveys Jeremiah's awareness of a conspiracy against himself, describing himself as an innocent lamb about to be sacrificed. One cannot help but recall Jeremiah's first protest, "I am only a boy" (Jer 1:7) and read v. 20 as the prophet reminding the Lord of the divine promise of protection (Jer 1:18–19). Verse 21 surprises the reader with the Lord referring to Anathoth, Jeremiah's own hometown, as a site of conspiracy against Jeremiah's life. Why residents of Anathoth might want to silence Jeremiah could stem from their having suffered acts of retribution from Jerusalem because of the words of one of the town's sons. In any case, not even the prophet's hometown is safe for him, as the Lord concedes in vv. 5–6.

The forensic terminology of Jeremiah's statement in 12:1a—"lay charges ... put my case"— again suggests the context of the divine assembly. In 12:1b–4, the prophet seeks to understand his situation. In v. 3, given that the Lord knows of Jeremiah's loyalty, the prophet ponders the apparent contradiction between the material realities that confront him and the Lord's commitment to his well-being. The Lord replies in vv. 5–6 in a way that does not appear to answer Jeremiah's questions. The basic gist of these two verses only confirms Jeremiah's sense of danger. If he is not safe in Anathoth, there is no place he can go to find refuge. God warns Jeremiah against trusting even his relatives. Who then can the prophet trust? The question attracts a more developed answer as the book unfolds (Jer 17:5–7).

Verses 7–17 convey the Lord's sentence of judgment on the wayward people. That the Lord asserts in v. 8 "therefore I hate her" (NRSV), namely Judah and Jerusalem—indeed greater Israel—is to assert that the people are no longer God's covenant people. The Hebrew imperatives that conclude v. 9 are plural. Verse 9 thus portrays the Lord commanding members of the divine assembly to disperse into the world to gather scavenging animals for a feast. Readers might initially think of "many shepherds" (v. 10), referring to past foreign kings who have beset Israel (Jer 6:3), but Jeremiah has elsewhere portrayed Israel's own shepherd-kings as exploiting the nation for their own gain (10:21). Ironically, there is ultimately no difference between how Israel's own kings have treated their people and how the foreign kings have at times ravaged them.

The symbolic act of burying a loincloth (13:1–11) works on the basis of its condition when Jeremiah digs it up again. It is ruined and so represents Israel's condition. Where Jeremiah buried the loincloth is not clear; the Hebrew word *perath* (vv. 6–7) may refer to a town near Anathoth. Nevertheless, the point seems clear: Israel is unfit to cling to the Lord. In vv. 12–14, Jeremiah's full wine jars lend themselves to the divine message that God will fill Jerusalem's leaders with wine, a metaphor that implies that they are incompetent. The decisions such leaders make will mean the death of many people (v. 14).

Verses 15–19 urge the social elite to humble themselves before the darkness of the times catches them, engulfing them in a darkness that will compel them into ruin. If they ignore Jeremiah, the prophet will weep bitterly in secret because of Jerusalem's pride. The essence of v. 18 is an appeal to the king and the queen mother to abdicate their positions; after all, soon there will be no kingdom to rule (v. 19).

Verses 20–21 urge the royal figures to look northward over a depopulated realm and ask about the whereabouts of their flock. They are to contemplate being under the rule of former allies who have turned to treachery (v. 21). The social upheaval will be like the pains of childbirth. Verses 22–27 portray Jerusalem with the image of a raped woman. Having abandoned the Lord's protection, Jerusalem is vulnerable to being violated.

A serious drought (Jer 14:1–6) compels Jeremiah to speak in the divine council on behalf of his people. Verses 7–9 appeal to the reputation of the Lord's name. The prophet asks why the Lord would act as if there were no history between God and the nation (v. 8) when, in fact, the prophet states, "we are called by your name." Verse 10 conveys God's response: the nation has grown fond of wandering. In v. 11 the Lord commands Jeremiah a third time not to intercede on Israel's behalf (Jer 7:16; 11:14); the divine judge will not change the decree. Jeremiah persists and blames the people's condition on lying prophets (v. 13). The Lord replies that the lying prophets will meet their end with the ones who took them as valid messengers from the Lord (vv. 14–16).

In vv. 17–18, the Lord instructs Jeremiah to make his expressions of grief public. Everywhere he goes there is death in the wake of the deceitful priests and prophets who, having no knowledge, convincingly pose as knowledge-mongers. Still Jeremiah persists in interceding for the people (vv. 19–22), but the Lord declares that not even Moses and Samuel could change the divine sentence of judgment (15:1). Warfare and scavenging animals are God's weapons (vv. 2–3). Verse 4, like 2 Kgs 21:10–15 and 23:26–27, traces the disaster back to the policies of Manasseh.

The Lord ignores Jeremiah's expressions of pity with the rhetorical question asserting the absence of pity for Jerusalem (v. 5) and with the comment that widowhood will permeate the nation. Jeremiah's expression of woe focuses on his status as a troublemaker among the Israelites (vv. 10–12). In vv. 11–14, the Lord assures Jeremiah that he will be safe and describes the plundered city (vv. 13–14).

Jeremiah 15:15–21 conveys Jeremiah's second lament. He expresses joy at finding the words of the Lord (v. 16) and testifies that he did not participate in the frivolous merriment of his fellow Israelites. Nevertheless, he feels that God has betrayed him (v. 18). In vv. 19–21, the Lord tells

Jeremiah to reorient his concerns so that he may remain in the divine assembly. God reassures the prophet of his security (vv. 20–21). The Lord then (16:1–18) commands Jeremiah to set aside his pathos for his people and to convey God's word with greater determination than before. Indeed, Jeremiah is to remain a bachelor to dramatize the nearness of conditions that will make starting a family a foolish endeavor (vv. 1–4). Jeremiah must not mourn regardless of the carnage around him (vv. 5–9). When asked why such a disaster has fallen, the prophet must confront the people with their history of rebellion, which included polluting the land with the cult statues (vv 10–18). Jeremiah then denys that humans can make gods (vv. 19–20).

In Jer 17:1–4, the Lord characterizes Judah's apostasy as indelibly recorded in the celestial records of the divine assembly and follows with a description of that apostasy.

Verses 5–8 convey the Lord's curse on those whose hearts turn away and a blessing on those who are obedient. Because the people are deceitful, the Lord warns them that no one can fool God with false claims of repentance (vv. 9–10). Jeremiah then prays for restoration (vv. 12–18).

In vv. 19–27, the Lord instructs Jeremiah to give instructions to Judah regarding Sabbath observance. Refraining from carrying a burden on the Sabbath and honoring the Sabbath as holy will yield great prosperity (vv. 24–26), but failure in this regard will make Jerusalem into God's kindling (v. 27).

Jeremiah 18:1–11 presents the lesson of the potter. Just as a potter reworks a vessel to produce a useful one, so God will rework Israel to make the nation fit for its divine destiny. Verse 12 communicates the response, essentially declaring to God their independence. The cold streams from Lebanon's peaks do not run dry, but Israel has cut itself off from the source of life (vv. 13–17). A desiccating wind from the east will easily disperse the nation.

Verse 18 informs readers of plots to silence Jeremiah; plots to which he reacts by appealing to God for justice (vv. 19–23). In Jeremiah 19, God dramatically demonstrates the divine power to annul any plots. He commands Jeremiah to shatter an earthen pot in the presence of the people, drawing attention to the act as a symbol of the nation's immediate future. Part of that future means that so many people will die that disposal of the bodies will become a matter of simply dumping them at the Baal shrine in Jerusalem to be scavenged (vv. 7–8). Famine due to the siege will force Jerusalem's inhabitants to resort to cannibalism for survival. The image evokes the horrors that Deut 28:53–57 forecasts.

For such frightening words, Pashhur, a priest and the chief of the Temple's security forces, arrests Jeremiah and has him beaten and put in the stocks (20:1–6). Jeremiah unleashes a curse from the Lord on Pashhur to the effect that Pashhur and his family will die in Babylon. The Lord seals the curse by changing Pashhur's name to the similar-sounding "the encompassing terror."

Jeremiah 20:7–18 contains two laments from Jeremiah that express his inner conflicts while simultaneously displaying hope. He regrets that his message offers nothing but doom (v. 8), but when he tries not to speak the Lord's word, it bursts out like fire (v. 9). Although he complains of his enemies' treatment of him, he clings to God's promise of protection (vv. 11–13). Nevertheless, his burden is nearly unbearable, leading him to wish he had never been born (vv. 14–18).

Jeremiah 21–22 contains a series of oracles against Judah's royal family. The word "Chaldeans" occurs for the first time in the book in 21:4. Originally it referred to the ethnic or tribal background of the dynasty of Nebuchadnezzar, but over time it came to refer to the Babylonians as a whole. In ch. 21, Zedekiah asks Jeremiah to intercede with God to turn Nebuchadrezzar back (vv. 1–2); but Jeremiah announces the Babylonian king's victory (vv. 3–10). Jeremiah (ch. 22) urges the Judahite king to live up to the highest standards of royal justice to avert disaster; otherwise the Lord will send destroyers like loggers in Lebanon cutting down cedars and burning them (v. 7). The woe saying of vv. 13–17 implicates the king in the exploitation of labor to build large houses and in the denial of justice to the poor and needy. The details of Jehoiakim's death are not known, but the prophet promises an ignominious disposal of his body (vv. 18–19). Jehoiakim's successor, Coniah (Jehoiachin) will go into exile, never to return to Judah (22:24–30).

C. Prophetic Conflict (23:1–28:17)

23:1–7. A Glimpse of Hope. Jeremiah 23–28 does not consistently develop any one specific theme, but it comes close as it unfolds the drama of prophetic conflict that took place between 597 and 587 BCE. After the first deportation in 597, the understandable hope that God would reverse the Babylonian victory and return the deported Judahites and the royal family to Jerusalem found itself fueled by what appears to have been a sizable portion of the Judahite prophetic voices of the time. Along with a few companions, Jeremiah stood against this hopeful outlook with a message that the social elite easily cast as treasonous.

Jeremiah 23:1–8 offers a word of hope. The word of hope, however, says that Judah's plotting powerbrokers will endure a crushing defeat of their plans. The prophet utters an oracle of woe against the shepherds who destroy and scatter the sheep of God's pasture. Ostensibly addressing a situation of assigning blame for the Babylonian imposition of control, the oracle (v. 2) sets responsibility firmly at the feet of the highest levels of bureaucratic control, the kings. *Shepherd* was a term that ancient Near Eastern monarchs often used to present themselves as the beneficent protectors of the nation. Instead of guiding the nation to safety under divine guardianship, the shepherds have "driven them away" and not attended to their needs. For a shepherd to disperse the flock into a chaotic charge is an image that any culture would find ridiculous. Yet Judah's kings have done just that. God promises (v. 3) to gather the dispersed flock and set over them shepherds who will establish the kind of social conditions necessary for security and fruitful living.

Verse 5 conveys the Lord's declaration of the inevitable rise of a "righteous Branch" who will belong to the Davidic dynasty. Unlike the kings of whom Zedekiah will be the last (Jer 52:1–11), the new king will fulfill the job description the word *shepherd* implies. The designation *Branch* plausibly alludes to Isa 11:1 and is part of the tradition that eventually finds expression in Zech 3:8 and 6:12 as well. It builds on the image of a felled tree's stump growing a new shoot. The Branch will be "righteous," meaning that the shepherd will act in a trustworthy way and thereby evoke the confidence of the nation. Verse 4 sustains this description with the Lord's promise that the people "shall

not fear any longer, or be dismayed, nor shall of any be missing." Verses 7–8 promise renewal comparable to the Lord's actions in the past. In the days to come, Israel's confession of faith will no longer commemorate the exodus from Egypt, but a new exodus involving the return of the "house of Israel out of the land of the north and out of all the lands" where the Lord had driven them. This new confession is related to Jer 3:15–18, which declares that the ark of the covenant will find no place in the future worship of God.

23:9–28:17. Jeremiah and Hananiah. A brief superscription, "concerning the prophets," opens the series of oracles and narratives that comprise 23:9–28:17. The word *prophet* (*navi'*) does not involve the truth or falsehood of the one who speaks a message, but the claim of a divine origin for the message. In this instance, Jeremiah insists that the prophets are lying or deluded. The text reflects Deuteronomy's norms about prophetic behavior. Deuteronomy 18:15–22 contains Moses' instructions to Israel concerning prophetic leadership. If a prophet's word fails to come to pass, then the Israelites can know that the prophet has spoken a word the Lord did not send. Jeremiah 23:9–28:17 raises the question of whom the Lord has truly sent and concludes with a narrative that answers the question.

Jeremiah 23:9 introduces a compilation of texts that depict prophetic opposition to Jeremiah's message. As is the case in other parts of the book, these texts do not make clear where the prophet leaves off speaking and the Lord begins.

Judah's condition is lamentable in the deepest sense of the term. Jeremiah is nearly a broken man as he confesses that his "heart is crushed within me" (v. 9). The word *crushed* translates the same word as the Lord employs in 2:13 to describe Judah's cisterns as cracked. Conceivably, Jeremiah believes himself near death as not only is his heart failing, but his bones quiver. Like a drunken person, he experiences the world around him as whirling out of control. The reason is that "the land is full of adulterers" (v. 10). First occurring in Jeremiah at 9:2, the word *adulterers* summarizes the nature of what it means to abandon the Lord to worship foreign gods. The word for "curse" reflects the discourse of Deuteronomy. The Hebrew word *'alah* may mean "oath" as well as "curse," as in Deut 29:12, 14, 19. The book of

Deuteronomy consistently warns Israel that to worship foreign gods will mean, among other disasters, that the land will become unproductive.

In v. 10, "course" renders a Hebrew word that refers to the way someone or something runs. The word for "evil" not only designates moral evil but can involve the disastrous consequences that result. "Their might is not right" speaks to the issue of how the prophets acquired their influence and power. They have stolen the people's trust and misplaced it with a "course" that will lead to disaster. With the phrase "in my house I have found their wickedness," v. 11 informs the reader that somewhere in the text the Lord has begun to speak. Conceivably, vv. 9–10 convey Jeremiah's lament, with the Lord speaking up in v. 11 to declare that both "prophet and priest are ungodly." Jeremiah and the Lord appear to be speaking to each other in the divine council.

Verse 12 unfolds in more extensive terms the ruinous consequences of the course that brings v. 10 to a conclusion. Paths and trails in the Judahite hill country are treacherous under good conditions. One wrong footfall and a traveler can plunge into a ravine and experience a shattering death. At night, with only a torch to light the way, the trails are particularly dangerous. In a downpour, they may become slippery or "smooth" and not allow a traveler to make a secure foothold. Verse 12 indicates that it will be along such ways the Lord will drive the prophets so that they will slip and plunge into the ravines and canyons below. The course they ran while in power led to disaster, and the way they will someday be compelled to run—"in the year of their punishment"—will lead to shattering.

What the Lord saw in Samaria's prophets was revolting. Samaria was the capital of the northern kingdom. There, the Lord declares (v. 13), the prophets "prophesied by Baal and led my people Israel astray." As if that was not bad enough, the Lord reports (v. 14) having seen "in the prophets of Jerusalem ... a more shocking thing." From the Deuteronomic perspective, Jerusalem was the place where the Lord had put the divine name to dwell (Deut 12:5). The presence of the divine name in the Temple in Jerusalem made what the prophets did there even more appalling than what the prophets of Samaria had done. Verse 14 suggests that the prophets of Jerusalem have assisted in the consolidation of power in "the hands of evildoers." Instead of serving the needs of God's people, they have worked to enhance their own social and political positions by pandering to the unconscionable ways of Judah's social elite.

That the social elite and the prophets have become like Sodom and Gomorrah (Gen 19) bears ominous implications. Wormwood (*Artemesia absinthia*) is a noxious herb that can discourage other plants from growing near it and can repel some insects. For "poisoned water," see comment on Jer 8:14.

In vv. 16–17, Jeremiah conveys God's appeal to whoever will listen—that they not act on the basis of "the prophets who prophesy to you; they are deluding you." These prophets are declaring a message of well-being, asserting that "No calamity shall come upon you." The source of their message is their own imagination; it does not derive "from the mouth of the LORD." Interestingly, the Lord does not at this point accuse the prophets of deliberately lying.

Verse 18 explicitly mentions "the council of the LORD." Any prophet who, like Jeremiah, had stood there and listened, would know that a hopeful message about Jerusalem would not be forthcoming. More generally, v. 18 poses two questions. The answers are clear. No one but Jeremiah has stood in the divine council. His words are trustworthy, even if they are not being obeyed.

Verse 19 challenges readers to imagine the kind of scene the prophet points to when he cries out, "Look, the storm of the LORD! Wrath has gone forth, a whirling tempest; it will burst upon the head of the wicked." Texts such as Isa 30:30; Pss 50:3; 83:15 describe the Lord as surrounded by whirling winds, lightning, and dense clouds when the divine sovereign descends to earth. Elsewhere in the Old Testament, destructive weather occurs as a symbol of being under siege by an enemy army (Amos 1:14; Nah 1:3). The prophet may be pointing to an impending thunderstorm as an advance signal of the disaster the Lord is about to bring on Judah. Verse 20 promises that the rage of the Lord's anger will not dissipate—like a strong approaching storm—until "he has executed and accomplished the intents of his mind." Since humans cannot understand the "intents" of the deity, the prophet adds, "In the latter days [literally, after the days] you will understand it clearly." The book of Jeremiah hints that careful consideration of its contents will help people understand the disaster that befell Judah.

The description of the storm (vv. 19–20) seems to interrupt the divine council passage which, after v. 18, resumes in v. 21. Because the storm passage ends with a promise of eventual understanding, it underscores the significance of the divine assembly. The Lord, as the divine judge over the council, has decreed destruction for them. As herald of the divine council, Jeremiah announces that disaster is coming. Moreover, in the years that will follow, people will come to understand such celestial jurisprudence.

In vv. 21 and 22, as if pounding the arm of the divine throne, God describes the prophets as eagerly setting about the prophetic task; although they do so without having received a divine commission. That divine commission would have derived from their presence in the Lord's council, where they would have heard the Lord's words, would have told the people, and would have diverted them from the catastrophic path they chose. The book of Jeremiah unveils something of the divine pathos; the Lord sadly and angrily muses on what could have been.

Verses 23–40 underscore the serious harm that the lying prophets do. They are announcing an imminent end of the first deportation and the return of the exiles. Jeremiah 24 answers with the vision of the good and bad figs. The former represents Jehoiachin and the first of the deported Judahites, concerning whom the Lord says, "I will set my eyes upon them for good" (v. 6). The latter represent the partisans of Zedekiah and his handlers of whom the Lord says, "I will make them a horror" (v. 9).

Jeremiah 25 rehearses the Lord's many attempts to convince the people of Judah to turn back to God (vv. 1–7). No such turning having occurred, the Lord declares that "King Nebuchadrezzar ... my servant" (v. 9) will bring disaster to the nation. In a visionary trance, the prophet receives a cup from the Lord's hand and gives it to the nations to whom the Lord sends the prophet (vv. 17–26). The nations will fall like drunken revelers. The Israelites must also drink of God's wrath (vv. 27–29). What follows (vv. 30–38) is an international drunken orgy of violence and destruction.

Jeremiah 26–27 set out a narrative revolving around the Temple sermon (Jer 7). The social elite among the people demand the death penalty for Jeremiah because of what he has said against the Temple (26:7–11). Some of the officials present, however, are sympathetic and remind the crowd about Micah of Moresheth and about the effective nature of his word, quoting Mic 3:12. This appeal to an earlier prophet saves Jeremiah's life. Jeremiah was remanded to Ahikam son of Shaphan who apparently was his friend. The reference to the death of an earlier prophet, Uriah son of Shemaiah, suggests just how close Jeremiah came to meeting a similar fate (vv. 20–23).

In Jer 27:1, the Hebrew manuscripts do not uniformly present Zedekiah as king. The Masoretic Text is the basis for most contemporary translations and reads *Jehoiakim*. The more likely reading is *Zedekiah*. The rest of the narrative names him as king. Envoys from the kings of Edom, Moab, Ammon, Tyre, and Sidon have arrived in Jerusalem ostensibly to plot a strategy against Babylon. Jeremiah is to wear a yoke of straps and bars as a symbol of the Lord's command for the nations to yield to Babylon and submit to Nebuchadrezzar. Jeremiah assures the envoys that their prophets are misleading them (v. 9). Verses 12–22 portray Jeremiah as turning the same word to the people of Jerusalem and Judah. He urges them not to heed the words of the prophets who speak in the Lord's name that the exiles of the first deportation and the vessels of the Lord's house will soon be returned. They are deceiving the people and themselves.

Jeremiah 28 narrates a showdown between Jeremiah and the prophet Hananiah. Hananiah breaks Jeremiah's yoke to demonstrate that God will break the power of Babylon. Jeremiah simply replaces them with a nearly unbearable yoke of iron. He confronts Hananiah about his false claims and announces that Hananiah will be removed from the earth within a year (v. 16). In what is possibly a deliberate understatement, the narrator tells readers that in the same year Hananiah died. The lack of details as to the cause of his death and any lack of reference to its effects testifies to the final vacuity of his words.

III. Promise of Restoration (30:1–33:26)

Jeremiah 30–36 comprise a collection of oracles and narratives that focus on Israel's destiny of redemption beyond the disaster of the nation's destruction. Readers at the beginning of the twenty-first century might consider it strange that such a text occurs where it does and not at the end of the book. Yet the book of Jeremiah's sequential arrangement is theologically significant. In part, the book is designed to involve readers' imaginations. The book of Jeremiah remains a sealed text to the impatient and incurious. For those who take the time and effort to plumb it, it can lead not only to a greater comprehension of the book's message to the ancient exiled Judahites, but also to a deepening awareness of how it speaks to the contemporary situation.

A. The New David (30:1-24)

The Lord commands Jeremiah to write in a scroll (30:2; NRSV, "in a book") all the words that the Lord has spoken. Presumably, these words comprise the Lord's accusations against Israel as well as the dreadful divine sentence of destruction. The word *for* at the beginning of v. 3 signifies that the Lord is about to give the reason for having Jeremiah write this text. If ancient or contemporary readers expected a continuation of indictment and judgment, there is a surprise waiting. Verse 3 portrays God as promising to reverse the deportation and bring both Israel and Judah back to the land sworn to the ancestors. In generations to come, therefore, there will be a written testimony of disobedience and destruction, but the future generations will also possess a written testimony of divine mercy.

In poetic form, vv. 4-7 encapsulate Israel's experience of destruction. Men are doubling over in pain like women about to give birth (v. 6). Verse 7 reinforces the incomparable nature of the horrors of "that day." Indeed "there is none like it." Verses 8-9 express the promise that the Lord will break the powers of oppression, that the people will serve God, and that God will raise a new David. Against the background of the incomparable nature of the disaster of "that day," this is all the more striking. Not even the oppression of Israel in Egypt is an appropriate analogue. There can be no hope for Israel to extricate itself from the suffering; yet what is not possible for Israel to achieve is possible for God.

Jeremiah 30:10-31:22 contains a series of poetic oracles that proclaim and reinforce the message of the good that God has planned for Israel's destiny beyond destruction. The admonition not to be afraid and God's reference to Jacob as "my servant" (Jer 30:10) may bring to many readers' minds texts such as Isa 41:8-10 and Isa 44:1-2. Jeremiah 30:11 makes clear that the grace v. 10 displays is not cheap. The Lord promises to chastise Israel "in just measure," that is, the divine punishment will not exceed what God intends to accomplish.

Verses 12-15 describe a shattering (Jer 30:12; NRSV, "hurt") that is beyond repair. From the human point of view, there is absolutely no hope. The words "enemy" and "merciless foe" underscore the implacable hatred and a corresponding level of violence that aims not simply to kill, but to render the victim into tangled flesh and pulverized bones. The depth and magnitude of Israel's rebellion against the Lord call for the divine chastisement to be profound.

A surprising shift occurs with v. 16. The Hebrew word that begins v. 16, *lakhen* (NRSV, "therefore"), may at times mean "in such manner" or "in similar manner." The Lord thus asserts that Israel's enemies will receive punishment that corresponds to the disaster they brought on Israel. Whereas vv. 12-15 underscore Israel's condition as beyond all hope, the case is not hopeless for God. Verse 17 addresses the issue of God's power to restore by evoking an image of divine jealousy on behalf of Israel. Israel's enemies devastated the nation on the assumption that none of the national powers would care: "It is Zion; no one cares for her!" God shows they are seriously mistaken.

The general image of Israel's destiny that vv. 18-22 conveys is one of joyful and productive autonomy from foreign power. "Their prince shall be one of their own" (v. 21). The divine assurance (v. 22) that Israel will be God's people and that the Lord will be Israel's God implies the establishment of a new covenant by which to consolidate and define the relationship. In the circumstances of the moment, the surviving Israelites might wonder how the imperial powers can possibly fall. The promise of divine restoration seems an unrealistic dream. Verses 23-24 speak to this issue. A prophetic voice declares that God's storm, fueled by the Lord's fierce rage, will accomplish God's purpose. The oracle concludes with the assurance of understanding in the days to come. Indeed, a key component of the canonical prophetic witness is that it is only from the perspective of the end, or the goal, that full comprehension of the mysteries of the apparent chaos of history can emerge.

B. Return of the Exiles (31:1–30)

Jeremiah 31 begins to lead the book's readers from a hint about a new covenant (Jer 30:22) to an explicit reference about such a covenant (31:31–34). Verse 1 reprises 30:22. Following this affirmation, the Lord explains why the redemption of the nation is not only possible but inevitable. Verses 2–3 remind readers of God's commitment to the ancestors and configure God's commitment as "an everlasting love." The Hebrew for "everlasting," *'olam*, is significant. It not only refers to something as everlasting, but as of great antiquity. Jeremiah 31 moves beyond Israel having been destroyed and into a depiction of Israel "re-storied," as it were.

As Jer 3:1 indicates, a man who has divorced a wife may not take her back if she has married another man. Accusations of adultery abounded earlier in the book of Jeremiah (3:9; 5:7; 7:9; 23:14; 29:23). In v. 4, the Lord addresses the new nation as "virgin Israel!" Israel's virginity is a clear sign of a new reality, not merely a restored relationship. That the land of Israel will yield luxuriant productivity implies that God's love for Israel is not unrequited. Verse 6 makes this point explicit with the description of the people gathering to "go up to Zion, to the LORD our God." That this summons relates to the hill country of Ephraim speaks of the new unity between Israel and Judah.

Jeremiah 31:7–14 portrays a future of relentless joy. God promises to lead the remnant of Israel back to their ancestral home. The language evokes the exodus from Egypt, but the gathering of the people will encompass not simply one geographical area but the widest expanses of the earth (v. 8). Jeremiah 3:9 portrays God as bitterly disappointed that Israel did not cry out, "my father;" but 31:9 speaks of a day to come when God will say, "I have become a father to Israel, and Ephraim is my firstborn." Verses 10–14 focus on the blessing of agricultural bounty and suggest a sharp contrast between what shall be and the devastation that once was (Jer 5:15–17).

Jeremiah 31:15 seems out of place, but the juxtaposition of this brief note of grief is brilliantly executed. Rachel, whose story unfolds in Genesis 29, here personifies the voice of sorrow. The reference to such profound grief jars readers back to the tragedy of the moment. Jeremiah's editors will not permit the divine promise of restoration to reside in an idealistic framework, unrelated to tragic historical realities. Furthermore, the one who hears the voice is God. The prophetic messenger formula, "thus says the LORD," introduces the quotation. The book of Jeremiah thus conveys God's pathos for the suffering people.

In v. 18 God acknowledges having heard Ephraim's confession of gamboling off "like a calf untrained." The phrase "I struck my thigh" (v. 19) signifies an outward sign of the distress that leads to repentance. Presumably speaking to the divine council, God reveals deep emotion when saying, "I groan inwardly for him," (31:20; NRSV, "I am deeply moved for him"). In vv. 21–22, the metaphor for Israel shifts to the language of betrothal. God is not commanding here, but pleading with a relentless pathos that will not rest. The Lord directs Israel to consider the paths that led it astray and to retrace its steps. Israel wavers, unsure, frightened, and bewildered. Verse 22b conveys God's encouragement to virgin Israel's hesitation in terms that render void the standard patriarchal expectations of gender relations. The word *created* recalls Gen 1:1, thus reminding readers that the creator has the power and right to do something unheard of. The new thing that God has created is a situation in which "a female encircles a hero" (NRSV, "a woman encompasses a man"). This phrase bears multiple meanings. It can describe a woman making her way through dangerous territory without needing a male companion to ward off attackers. And it can just as well work on the metaphorical level: God as groom and Israel as the bride. In such a case, it describes the groom as a hero who stands before the woman's deciding gaze. God's deepest yearning for Israel to return will compel the Lord to act in surprising, creative new ways.

C. The New Covenant (31:31–40)

The prophetic literature in the Old Testament never allows Israel's rebellion against God and the nation's destruction at the hands of the Babylonians to be the final word. Uniformly, the prophetic books convey a portrait of God acting to redeem. The concept of covenant is often a component of such portraits. Isaiah 54:10; Ezek 34:25; and Hos 2:18 describe the Lord establishing a covenant of peace between all living things. Isaiah 55:3 promises that the Lord will make an everlasting covenant with Israel that will take the model of the Davidic covenant. In Isa 61:8, God promises to make an everlasting covenant that will lead to the blessing of the nations. In Jer 31:31–34, the prophet uses a distinctive phrase—a new covenant. The phrase "new covenant" occurs in the Old Testament only here. The prophet describes it as a thorough replacement of the covenant that God made with Israel when God "took them by the hand to bring them out of the land of Egypt" (v 32).

The Lord reminds Israel of its having broken that earlier covenant. The Deuteronomic writers described that covenant as documented in writing and as requiring reading, study, meditation, and teaching (Deut 5:1; 17:19; 31:10–13). Under the stipulations of the new covenant, God will make all Israelites "know" the teaching (v 33; NRSV, "law"). The problem of ignorance about which Jeremiah complained (Jer 5:4) will cease to exist.

D. Signs of Assurance (32:1–33:26)

An exilic reader could have responded to Jer 30–31 with derisive laughter or, perhaps, with a cautious, fragile sense of hope.

These two chapters exhibit a future that is exceedingly difficult to imagine. The autobiographical narrative of Jer 32 speaks, in part, to the issue. God gives a sign to Jeremiah that confirms future restoration. Verse 1 sets the events Jeremiah is about to describe in Jerusalem's darkest days. In the tenth year of Zedekiah, the end is imminent. Engaging in business as usual seems a completely irrational act. The Babylonian army has besieged Jerusalem; Zedekiah has confined Jeremiah in "the court of the guard" (v. 2). Furthermore, Zedekiah had asked Jeremiah why the prophet claims that God gave him a message of disaster. The king even repeats the grim details about his own capture and deportation to Babylon (vv. 3–5).

Perhaps intentionally, Jeremiah's answer is cryptic and seems to avoid Zedekiah's concerns. Instead of preaching the same message that the earlier parts of the book contain, Jeremiah tells the doomed king about a real estate transaction.

The Lord instructs Jeremiah to purchase the field of his cousin, Hanamel. Hanamel agrees and the appropriate papers are drawn up, signed, and witnessed. The Lord tells Jeremiah to store the documents of the transaction in an earthen jar, to preserve them for an extended amount of time. In v. 15, Jeremiah tells the king the point of the story. The land will someday be cultivated and normal real estate transactions will once again take place.

Presumably still in the presence of the king, Jeremiah then prayed "to the LORD" (v. 16). His petition began with praise, acknowledging the limitless capacity of God's power as creator. Zedekiah might not have understood what Jeremiah was doing, but the prophet is actually answering the question the king had posed in vv. 3–5. After testifying to Israel's deliverance from Egypt, Jeremiah praises the Lord for bringing Israel into a fertile land. At v. 23, the prophet more sharply focuses on Zedekiah's question. Israel disobeyed the teachings of the Lord and made no effort to do what God directed. Then the prophet describes the siege machines battering the walls and says to God, "What you spoke has happened." But to whom does the prophet address the words, "as you yourself can see" (v. 24)? One is tempted to imagine Jeremiah looking into the king's eyes and obliquely speaking to him. Jeremiah concludes his request for understanding by summarizing to God what God had told him to do.

At v. 26, the interview between Zedekiah and Jeremiah has presumably concluded. In Jer 32:17 Jeremiah admitted to God, "Nothing is too hard for you." Verse 27 recalls that confession with God asserting, "I am Yahweh" (NRSV, "the LORD"). Biblical scholars generally agree that the divine name signifies God's role as creator. Thus, it is as the creator that the Lord asks Jeremiah "is anything too hard for me?" Verses 28–35 offer the reason for Jerusalem's disaster.

IV. Judah's Last Days (34:1–45:5)

Following oracles that convey a message of consolation, Jeremiah 34–45 comprise a narrative of unrelenting tragedy. Perhaps the point is the contrast between an undeserved act of divine grace and the relentless march of Judah toward the consequences of its rebellion. Jeremiah's God simply will not give up, even though Judah refuses to turn from its course. As Jeremiah's readers move through 34:1–45:5, the light that is the grace of God shines brighter than it would had the texts of consolation appeared at the end of the book.

A. Collapse of Trust (34:1–22)

Mere weeks before the Babylonian siege of Jerusalem begins, the Lord commissions Jeremiah to tell Zedekiah of the king's fate. Zedekiah will not escape from Nebuchadrezzar (vv. 3–6). The Babylonian king will confront Zedekiah personally. Jeremiah is to let Zedekiah know that he will not die violently but "in peace" (v. 5). Furthermore, mourners will perform rituals of burning incense and lamentation. Verses 6–7 indicate that it was not until the actual siege of the city had begun that Jeremiah so informed the king.

Verses 8–22 convey a story of treachery that reveals Jerusalem's government as unworthy of trust and hopelessly riddled with the self-interests of the social elite. Zedekiah had issued a covenant of manumission concerning all Hebrew slaves. According to v. 9, the basic reason was "so that no one should hold another Judean in slavery." The manumission may have been intended to provide more human resources to resist the Babylonian siege. Approximately one and a half years after the siege began, word apparently came to Jerusalem that Pharaoh Hophra was on the way with forces to relieve the city. Conceivably, in the hope of such deliverance, the social elite broke the covenant of manumission and reclaimed the slaves. Hophra's advance forces a Babylonian retrenchment and the siege lifts but only for a brief time (v. 21). Hophra falls back and the Babylonian siege continues. The breaking of the covenant is the cause for a divine word of destruction in which the Lord promises that the covenant breakers will be split like sacrificial calves (v. 18). This punishment corresponds to the ceremony of the making of the covenant that involved the killing of a calf and cutting it into two pieces. The calves represented the fate of anyone who broke the covenant (cf. Gen 15). Zedekiah will fall into the hand of enemies and the Babylonians will decimate Judah and its towns (vv. 21–22).

B. Sign of the Rechabites (35:1–19)

Jeremiah 35 presents a narrative that describes the Lord instructing the prophet to gather the Rechabites in a room located in the Temple. One of the Rechabites' practices involved abstaining from wine, a regulation that the group's founder, Jonadab ben Rechab, had issued generations earlier. In the presence of selected leaders of the social elite, Jeremiah tells them to drink wine. They refuse and, in so doing, stand as an example of loyalty to an ancestral decree. In vv. 12–17, the Lord reiterates the sad story of Israel's failure to obey the divine sovereign as a stark contrast to the Rechabites' stubborn loyalty to their founder's directions. For their loyalty, the Lord rewards the Rechabites with a promise of generational continuity (vv. 18–19).

C. Jehoiakim and the Scroll (36:1–32)

Jeremiah 36 presents an intricate narrative about a prophetic text and a wicked king. In Jehoiakim's fourth year (605 BCE), Jeremiah dictated the Lord's words to the scribe Baruch son of Neriah. Barred from entering the house of the Lord, Jeremiah tells Baruch to read the scroll aloud there. Word eventually reaches the king, who calls for a personal audience. As Baruch reads, the king takes the section Baruch read and burns it until the scroll is gone. Why Jehoiakim burned the scroll is not revealed, but it may have been a demonstration of his disdain for the prophet. Perhaps he hoped that by burning the scroll its words would not come to pass; but Jeremiah simply dictated another and added more words to it. The new scroll included a description of Jehoiakim's death and something worse, namely, that his body would remain unburied and exposed (vv 30–31).

D. Jeremiah's Imprisonment (37:1–38:29)

In 588 BCE, Egyptian forces were able to force a brief halt to the Babylonian siege. Nine years earlier, Nebuchadrezzar had installed Zedekiah on the throne of Judah and deported Coniah (Jehoiachin) to Babylon. Zedekiah did not remain a loyal vassal, an act of treachery that brought Babylon back to Judah to besiege Jerusalem. Zedekiah sends messengers to Jeremiah to request the prophet's intercession. When the Egyptian forces then set out to rout the Babylonians, it appeared the Lord had answered the prophet's prayer.

According to Jer 37:6–8, the Lord instructs Jeremiah to inform Zedekiah that the Babylonian retreat is temporary. During the lull, Jeremiah attempts to go to Anathoth to claim the field he had purchased from his relative, Hanamel (Jer 32). A sentinel named Irijah arrests the prophet and accuses him of deserting to the Babylonians. Jeremiah is beaten and imprisoned. The "cistern house" (v. 16) would have been a small structure built over a cistern to protect it from the elements. Thus begins the ordeal that will mean the end of Jeremiah's freedom until the fall of the city.

Verses 17–21 report that Zedekiah secretly visits the prophet and consults with him. Jeremiah informs the king that Zedekiah will fall into the hands of the king of Babylon. Jeremiah successfully requests that the king move Jeremiah into "the court of the guard" (v. 21). The prophet is allowed a ration of bread until it finally runs out during the siege the Babylonians are soon to renew.

Jeremiah's enemies are powerful and are aware of the demoralizing effect the prophet's words might have on the city's defenders. Having spun Jeremiah's words into a cloak of treason, they force Zedekiah's hand to have the prophet left to die in an abandoned cistern (38:5–6). The cistern was a bottle-shaped chamber and was empty. It was damp enough, though; Jeremiah sank into the mud. The stench and vermin aside, the prophet was left in total darkness to die.

If not for the intercession of an Ethiopian named Ebed-Melech, a servant in Zedekiah's house, Jeremiah would never have been seen again. Ebed-Melech may have placed himself in serious jeopardy. The men to whom he refers as acting wickedly are powerful and privileged; as Zedekiah realizes, they wield greater influence than does the king himself (38:5). Nevertheless, Jeremiah is hauled out of the cistern and returned to the guard house.

Although Zedekiah promises Jeremiah's safety in return for his services as a prophet, the king nevertheless refuses to act on the oracular charges the prophet delivers. Surrendering to the Babylonians, the king would save Jerusalem from an inevitable conflagration (v. 17). The king threatens Jeremiah with death if the prophet reveals their secret meetings (vv. 24–28).

E. The Fall of Jerusalem and Aftermath (39:1–45:5)

Jeremiah 39 describes the fall of Jerusalem to the Babylonians in 587 BCE. The Babylonians capture Zedekiah trying to escape the city (vv. 4–6). Nebuchadrezzar decimates Zedekiah's family, blinds the fallen king, and orders his deportation to Babylon (v. 7). The king's palace and the Temple are dismantled along with the city's walls. There follows a redistribution of land among the poor who previously had owned nothing (v. 10). Nebuchadrezzar provides a security detail for Jeremiah, who conveys to Ebed-Melech a divine promise of safety (vv. 11–14).

The narrative in Jeremiah 40–45 carries forward an important theme of the book, namely, Israel's inability to obey the Lord's word. The death of Hananiah (Jer 28) and the fall of the city demonstrate Jeremiah's trustworthiness as a prophet of the Lord according to the standards provided in Deuteronomy 18.

The Babylonians appoint Gedaliah son of Ahikam governor of Judah and allow Jeremiah to choose to remain in the land (40:1–6). Ishmael son of Nethaniah was a member of the royal family and undertook a conspiracy to assassinate Gedaliah. Ostensibly, he hoped to rise to a position of power. Gedaliah ignores warnings of the plot (40:13–16) and unwittingly makes himself vulnerable to Ishmael as they ate together; Ishmael kills Gedaliah. Ishmael resorts to robbery and murder, essentially becoming an outlaw (41:4–8). Although Gedaliah's friends try to capture Ishmael, Ishmael escapes across the Jordan into Ammonite territory (41:11–17).

The remaining Judahites are terrified that Nebuchadrezzar will retaliate for Gedaliah's assassination; they ask Jeremiah for guidance from the Lord concerning whether they should flee to Egypt. They promise to do whatever the Lord says (42:1–6). When Jeremiah returns to them after ten days to tell them to remain in the land, they refuse to believe him. Jeremiah warns the refugees that the Lord will punish them in Egypt, but they resist the message, abduct Jeremiah, and flee (43:1–7). In spite of all they have witnessed, they take their rebellion against the Lord to Egypt where they continue to make offerings to the queen of heaven (Jer 7:18; 44:17–19, 25). As a consequence of their actions God denies them the privilege of calling on the divine name (vv. 26–27). Jeremiah 45 depicts a divine promise of safety to Baruch who had himself expressed lamentations to God

(vv. 2–3). For his loyalty, his life shall be "a prize of war" wherever he goes.

V. The Nations (46:1–51:64)

This section bears a superscription, "The word of the Lord that came to the prophet Jeremiah concerning the nations." To some scholars, the superscription suggests that the oracles preserved here originally comprised a separate collection of sayings. Whatever the origins of these oracles, they bring the words of Jeremiah to an end. Jeremiah 51:64 concludes this section with the phrase, "Thus far are the words of Jeremiah." This notation complements the first verse in the book, and, consequently, could be translated "thus far the chronicles of Jeremiah" (see commentary on Jer 1:1). The prophet's name will not occur in Jeremiah 52. (The name "Jeremiah of Libnah" [52:1] does not designate the prophet from Anathoth.)

This section begins and ends with oracles concerning the competing empires of Jeremiah's time, Egypt and Babylon. The oracles are an elaborate figure of speech known as an apostrophe. The literary figure of apostrophe implies that the real audience for these oracles is the one to whom the book of Jeremiah originally spoke, that is, the exilic community in Babylon. Nevertheless, these oracles also demonstrate that the standards of human life that God demands are not peculiar to the Israelites and that all nations share in the responsibility of demonstrating righteousness and justice. Of the nations singled out, the Lord promises future restoration for Egypt (46:26), Moab (48:47), the Ammonites (49:6), and Elam (49:39). The other nations, Philistia (47:1–7), Edom (49:7–22), Damascus (49:23–27); Kedar and Hazor (49:28–33), and Babylon (50:1–51:64) do not receive words of consolation.

Readers must linger over these oracles to discern their significance. One important issue is the status of the Babylonian Empire. It had destroyed not only Israel but neighboring nations as well. From a human point of view, it brooks no rival and seemingly may last forever. As a result, it is no accident that the last oracle, which addresses Babylon, is the longest and most complicated. Its length and rich texture underscore for the exilic audience the Lord's superior power to determine Babylon's ultimate fate. Jeremiah 50:1–3 begins the oracle against Babylon with an ironic gesture.

The prophet describes the destruction that will befall Babylon as something falling on the city from the north, thus recalling that Babylon was the foe from the north that decimated Judah (Jer 1:13–15; 4:6; 6:1, 22; 10:22; 25:9, 26). The northern origin of Babylon's destruction also finds expression in 50:9, 41, and 51:42.

When Babylon falls, Judahite exiles will be liberated and return to Zion, weeping as they seek God (vv. 4–5). Portions of this oracle describe the inevitability of Israel's restoration (50:4, 5, 17–20, 33–34; 51:5–10). These promises reinforce the literary and theological significance of the consoling texts in Jeremiah 30:1–33:26. Redemption lies at the literal and theological heart of the book of Jeremiah.

This section concerning Babylon includes an exclamation by an anonymous voice, possibly from a member of the divine assembly, acclaiming the Lord's incomparable majesty and power (51:5–19). The one who created the cosmos (v. 5) and sustains it (v. 6) will demonstrate the vacuity of the cult statues of Babylon. As a result, God has the power to bring about the Babylonian Empire's dissolution.

VI. Epilogue (52:1–34)

With minor variations, the epilogue of Jeremiah 52 duplicates the narrative of the destruction of Jerusalem and the disposal of the sacred vessels of the Lord's house found in 2 Kgs 24:18–25:30. Elsewhere, Deuteronomic language permeates the book of Jeremiah, thus suggesting that the editors were themselves proponents of Deuteronomic theology. Readers can surmise that those who edited the book of Jeremiah deemed Jeremiah to exemplify Deuteronomic thought. The Deuteronomic History portrays figures such as Joshua, Samuel, Elijah, and Elisha as prophets like Moses (see Deut 18:15–22). By concluding the book of Jeremiah with a variation of the conclusion of 2 Kings, the book's editors have set Jeremiah into that prophetic line.

BIBLIOGRAPHY

R. P. Carroll. *Jeremiah: A Commentary.* OTL (Philadelphia: Westminster, 1986); M. B. Dick, ed. *Born in Heaven Made on Earth: the*

Making of the Cult Statue in the Ancient Near East (Winona Lake, Ind.: Eisenbrauns, 1999); W. L. Holladay. *Jeremiah 1: A Commentary on the Book of the Prophet Jeremiah, Chapters 1–25.* Hermeneia (Philadelphia: Fortress, 1986); _____. *Jeremiah 2: A Commentary on the Book of Jeremiah, Chapters 26–52.* Hermeneia (Philadelphia: Fortress, 1986); P. J. King. *Jeremiah: An Archaeological Companion* (Louisville: Westminster John Knox, 1993); J. R. Lundbom. *Jeremiah 1–20.* AB 21A (New York: Doubleday, 1999); _____. *Jeremiah 37–52.* AB 21C (New York: Doubleday, 2004); W. McKane. *A Critical and Exegetical Commentary on Jeremiah.* Vol 1. ICC (Edinburgh: T&T Clark, 1986); _____. *A Critical and Exegetical Commentary on Jeremiah.* Vol 2. ICC (Edinburgh: T&T Clark, 1996); P. D. Miller. "Jeremiah." NIB (Nashville: Abingdon, 1994–2004) 6:553–926; J. Rosenberg. "Jeremiah and Ezekiel." *Literary Guide to the Bible.* R. Alter and F. Kermode, eds. (Cambridge, Mass.: Harvard University Press, 1987) 184–233; L. Stulman. *Jeremiah.* ABOTC (Nashville: Abingdon Press, 2005).

LAMENTATIONS

CARLEEN R. MANDOLFO

OVERVIEW

The book of Lamentations consists of five distinct poems (the first four are alphabetic acrostics), commemorating the annihilation of Jerusalem in 587/6 BCE at the hands of the Babylonians, who are understood—both in this book and in much of the prophetic tradition—as doing Yahweh's bidding. The English title is a translation of the Latin (*threni*) and Greek (*threnoi*) meaning "laments." In Hebrew, *quinot* (also meaning "lamentations") is a title for the book attested in the Babylonian Talmud. Otherwise in Jewish tradition, as well as in the Hebrew Bible itself, the title is *'eykah*, after the first word of the book, "How!" The alphabetic acrostic functions to give form and structure to otherwise unmanageable grief.

Unlike biblical prose texts devoted to recounting the events of the invasion (2 Kgs 24–25; Jer. 25), the poet (or poets) of Lamentations was far more interested in providing a series of visceral tableaux on the experience of devastation. Generically, it is simplest and most useful to categorize these poems as psalms of lament, i.e., they share formal and conceptual elements with laments in the biblical Psalter. It is also clear that they rely on other forms of ancient Near Eastern literature, such as the dirge and city lament—the latter of which was a common form of lamentation used by Israel's Mesopotamian neighbors in which the wounded party (i.e., the city itself) was frequently figured as a woman—often the consort of the city's deity. Nonetheless, biblical laments diverge from their Mesopotamian counterparts. The city laments of Sumer, for example, offer praise in response to the eventual restoration of the city by the gods. In contrast, the biblical book of Lamentations is devoid of any suggestion of rehabilitation. God is utterly silent throughout the book.

In the Jewish tradition, the book is placed in the latter third of the canon among the "Writings" and is recited in the Jewish liturgical calendar on the "Ninth of Av," which commemorates the destructions of the First and Second Temples in 586 BCE and 70 CE, respectively, as well as more recent catastrophes suffered by the Jewish people.

The first two poems were composed in a dialogic fashion, with the voice of Jerusalem appearing as a bereaved woman antiphonally responding to a second voice, sympathizing with and yet once removed from the woman's experience of anguish. The third poem most closely resembles a typical lament psalm, with a supplicant alternately lamenting, appealing to, and praising God. Chapter four reads like a cross between a lament psalm and a prophetic dirge in which the suffering of the people is recounted and blamed on the unjust and ritually impure actions of the city's leaders. The final poem paints a picture of complete political, economic, and personal upheaval. The poem (and book) ends on a note of near hopelessness. Still, the determined reader can find hope in a relationship between humans and the divine that persists against all odds.

While the book does not shy away from placing blame at the feet of the people, on the whole the tone is not so much penitential as overwhelmed with pathos.

OUTLINE

I. Poem One (1)

    A. Daughter Zion as Widow (1:1–11*b*)

    B. Daughter Zion Describes Her Anguish at the Hands of Yahweh (1:11*c*–16)

    C. Daughter Zion Has No Comforter (1:17)

    D. Daughter Zion Admits Fault, but Demands Retribution Against Her Enemies (1:18–22)

II. Poem Two (2)

    A. Visceral Recounting of God's Vengeance Against Zion (2:1–10)

    B. Zion or a Prophetic Voice Mourns the Fate of the Children (2:11–12)

    C. Impossibility of a Comforter (2:13–17)

    D. Zion Implored to Cry Out to God (2:18–19)

E. Zion Cries Out to God in Anger and Betrayal (2:20–22)

III. Poem Three (3)

A. Grievance Against God (3:1–18)

B. Supplicant's Confidence in the Covenant (3:19–24)

C. God Is Just and Trustworthy (3:25–41)

D. Reprise of Grievance (3:42–54)

E. Qualified Thanksgiving (3:55–58)

F. Plea for Retribution Against Enemies (3:59–66)

IV. Poem Four (4)

A. The Abandonment of Zion's Children (4:1–5)

B. God's Treatment of Zion Compared to Sodom (4:6–10)

C. The Culpability of the Priests and Elders (4:11–16)

D. No One to Protect Zion from Her Enemies (4:17–20)

E. Oracle Against Edom (4:21–22)

V. Poem Five (5)

A. Plea that God Remember the People (5:1)

B. Breakdown of All Social Structures (5:2–18)

C. A Final Plea for Mercy (5:19–22)

DETAILED ANALYSIS

I. Poem One (1)

The chapter begins with a cry, "How!" ('eykah), which sets the tone for the entire book. Expressions of despair, anguish, and betrayal dominate the emotional terrain of these poems. Chapter one focuses on Jerusalem, personified as a princess who has been reduced to widowhood by her former lovers and friends (1:1–2), probably an allusion to former political and military allies. The female representation of the city recalls the prevalent use of the marriage metaphor in several

of the prophetic books (e.g., Hos 1–3; Jer 2–3; Ezek 16:23). In those texts, Israel/Jerusalem is understood to be the adulterous wife of Yahweh, who, because of her betrayal and ingratitude, is punished by her "husband," who sends the nations against her and her children. It is impossible to know whether the poet(s) of Lam 1–2 was explicitly making reference to this tradition. However, the theological implications of such references are profound. Reading Lam 1–2 in relation to these prophetic texts sets up a dialogic encounter between voices—God's and Israel's. Whereas the voice of the people, now spoken by a woman, is nearly absent from the prophetic texts, the first two chapters of Lamentations permit the people to speak back to the deity, offering their point of view on the situation described earlier by the aforementioned prophets. Despite the extremity of Jerusalem's suffering, this human perspective does not deny the claims made against Jerusalem in the prophets, but rather offers a new perspective.

Although both the narrator's voice and Daughter Zion make reference to Zion's sins (vv. 5 and 14), the primary purpose of this lament is not to have Jerusalem appear as penitent, but rather to enable her to give voice to the extreme suffering she and others endured during the siege and destruction wrought by King Nebuchadnezzar's forces. Jerusalem's voice serves as a counterpoint to the main thrust of much of prophetic rhetoric, which is primarily concerned with establishing the culpability of the people, that justifies the destruction of the city. The poet(s) of Lamentations (with the possible exception of ch. 3) makes clear that the people are suffering more than they deserve to suffer.

Conspicuous throughout ch. 1 is repeated reference to the absence of a comforter for Zion (vv. 2, 9, 16, 17, 21). There has been much speculation about the identity of the comforter, but it is clear from the level of despair and hopelessness conveyed by the poet that only God could provide true comfort for Daughter Zion. Thus, that God seems utterly deaf to Zion's cries is the real tragedy of the book. Second Isaiah will try to rectify this sense of abandonment by proclaiming "comfort" to the people and insisting that their period of punishment is over (Isa 40:1).

The choice of gendered imagery in chs. 1–2 is theologically significant. In the book of Lamentations, women's suffering is closely related to their familial status—the loss of a husband meant the loss of prestige and security in ancient Israel. The heartbreak involved in the loss of a child meant then what it means now, perhaps the ultimate hardship a woman can endure, and thus a particularly effective way for the poet to express the magnitude of suffering experienced by the people, personified as Daughter Zion.

II. Poem Two (2)

The emphasis on suffering over culpability is even more pronounced in ch. 2 than it was in ch. 1. The vitriol unleashed at God is unparalleled in biblical literature (with the possible exception of sections of Jeremiah and Job). The verbs used in the first nine verses to portray the actions of the deity against Daughter Zion are relentlessly harsh: God "casts down," "lays waste," ravages," "slays," "rejects" to name just a few. In v. 4, God is described "like an enemy," a conflation of God with the Babylonians that reflects prophetic texts, which were wont to portray God as the source of Babylon's military successes. Prophetic rhetoric emphasizes divine power over mercy, a theological perspective that can be troubling for contemporary readers. This focus on God's might derives from the realities of ancient Near Eastern politics and religious rhetoric. Still, Lamentations should be seen as a text that reminds the deity of the human toll when power supersedes mercy. The Hebrew Bible is rife with examples of humans confronting God in order to remind him that covenantal values require a careful balance between divine justice and mercy to ensure that humans not be mortally overwhelmed (e.g., Gen 18 in which Abraham bargains with God to spare Sodom).

In v. 11, third-person speech switches to first-person (a stylistic feature common to other biblical poetic texts, such as Psalms and the Prophets); readers may now be hearing the voice of Daughter Zion herself. The shift in voice lends a dynamic quality to the poetry that enhances the poignancy of the content. The poem provides different points of view from which to witness Jerusalem's wreckage. The more intimate tone of vv. 11–12 reflects the content of the passage—the focus is once again on the misery of the children. Babies perish in the arms of their mothers who are help-

less to feed them. Echoing ch. 1, v. 13 reprises the impossibility of comfort. Instead, Daughter Zion is entreated to lift her hands in supplication to the only possible source of comfort, God (v. 18), which highlights both the dilemma and possibilities of monotheistic faith. That Israel does not have the option of turning to other deities for relief might be a terrifying reality, but such a situation provides the occasion for intense intimacy between God and the people. They are compelled to find a way to reestablish their bond or both will suffer the consequences of a failed relationship.

Daughter Zion responds with a series of passionate rebukes of the deity: "Look, O LORD, and consider!" (v. 20). Both the chapter and Daughter Zion's speech ends with a reprimand that refutes one of the main accusations brought against her in the prophetic texts—infanticide (Ezek. 16:20)— and turns it back on the deity, whom she accuses of being the actual murderer of her children.

III. Poem Three (3)

In ch. 3, the emphasis shifts away from women and children, and a male voice comes to the fore. The descriptions of extreme hardship continue, but this chapter takes the edge off some of the harsh rhetoric of the first two chapters. One of the ways in which this is apparent has to do with the formal characteristics of the poetry. Chapter 3, more than the other four poems in the book, is a typical lament psalm, albeit somewhat stylized. Lament psalms typically oscillate between grievance and praise, and Lam 3 shares this aspect with them. The beginning of the poem strikes a tone that is nearly indistinguishable from that in chs. 1–2, but in vv. 19–41 the tone softens to a degree that finds no parallel in chs. 1–2: "the steadfast love of the LORD never ceases, his mercies never come to an end" (v. 22).

The positioning of the praise portions at the center of the poem as well as the poem's centrality in the book suggests a deliberate attempt to concentrate attention on the positive qualities of God that are called into doubt in the remainder of the book. At the same time, the inclusion of praise gives the grievances formal legitimacy and ensures that protest not be equated with blasphemy. The poem never loses sight, however, of the overall theme of the book, which is the people's torment bordering on despair. Verse 42 renews the grievance, after which the poem expresses the hope that God will look and see the pain of his people (v. 50).

The poem ends with an expression of confidence that God will do precisely that (vv. 55–58), followed by a final request that God bring retribution on those who have mistreated God's people (vv. 59–66). The request for revenge is reminiscent of the oracles against the nations, a prominent part of prophetic literature (e.g., Isa 13–23; Jer 46–51; Ezek 25–32; Amos 1–2). Both Lamentations and the oracles against the nations reflect Israel's covenantal theology, which understands God to be a protector of his people.

IV. Poem Four (4)

On the continuum between the unmitigated bleakness of ch. 2 and the more formally typical and theologically palatable complaint of ch. 3, the fourth poem edges closer to the former, but has faint echoes of the hope present in ch. 3.

The first five verses rehearse the poignant theme of starving children, but with a twist. The poet ascribes the suffering of the children to the "cruelty" of the people, whose maternal instincts are not as well developed as those of animals (v. 3). This claim is not meant to be an indictment of the people, but rather an attempt to demonstrate the degree to which the severity of Yahweh's wrath has diminished Israel's basic human instincts. The issue of class also emerges in this poem. Reference to gold, purple, and feasting on delicacies emphasizes the devastation experienced by the elite.

The comparison of Israel to Sodom (v. 6) not only emphasizes the totality of destruction but also implies a degree of arrogance on the part of the Israelites. This motif may be connected to the spotlight trained on the elite. This emphasis on the powerful citizens in Jerusalem continues with reference to the former physical prowess of the princes of the city, who have now become "blacker than soot" and "shriveled" (v. 8). The "cruelty" to the children is further defined in v. 10; women are described as feeding on the flesh of their own children.

The apparent compassion offered the rich and powerful who have fallen so far is nuanced and tempered in vv. 11–16. The priests and prophets, the religious and moral leaders of the people, are accused of shedding innocent blood in the midst of the city (v. 13). This indictment probably alludes to the sins of social injustice, so often inveighed against in the prophets (Isa 1:27; Amos 5:10–13). Whatever the details of the crimes, the priests and prophets are described as social outcasts, so impure that the people banish them from their midst.

The poem concludes with an oracle against Edom, which sets up a contrast with Israel that works to the latter's benefit. While Edom will continue to suffer God's wrath for their treatment of Israel, Daughter Zion's punishment will come to an end (v. 22).

V. Poem Five (5)

The fifth and final poem assumes the formal features of a fairly typical communal lament. It is the only poem of the five that is not composed in acrostic form, though it is made up of twenty-two verses, as are the first, second, and fourth poems (the Hebrew alphabet contains twenty-two letters). The absence of an alphabetic acrostic may signal a descent into chaos and serves as a fitting counterpart to the unresolved conclusion of this poem (and hence the book).

The poem opens with a plea reminiscent of many lament Psalms, "Remember, O Lord" (cf. Ps 74, which shares similar imagery and themes and probably reflects the exilic experience as well). This chapter is the only poem in the book that begins with a plea; the others all forcefully commence with images of affliction, though absent an explicit appeal. As a result, this poem exhibits a less rebellious tenor than the other poems (except arguably Lam 3).

The body of the poem rehearses many of the same themes as the rest of the book—the utter dissolution of social order and the unspeakable suffering of Jerusalem's people. More prominent, however, is the idea of communal culpability (vv. 7, 16). Taking some of the onus off the deity gives this poem a family resemblance to the penitential poems in the Psalter (e.g., Ps 130). This reference to the community's sins is another element that sets it off from the rest of the collection in this book. Nonetheless, unlike a typical penitential psalm, this poem ends on a note of despair, rather than praise or expression of hope common to laments in the Psalter (penitential or otherwise). The penultimate note struck, however, is faintly hopeful. God's power is highlighted, suggesting that if he should choose, he could alleviate the suffering of his people (v. 19). However, this glimmer of hope does little to mitigate what has come before and, especially, the tone on which the poem ends—the acknowledgment that perhaps Yahweh has "utterly rejected" his people (vv. 20–22).

In part due to its ending, Lamentations is Scripture particularly apt for the post-Holocaust world, in which it is no longer appropriate to attach meaning or salvation to radical suffering, such as that attested in this poetry.

BIBLIOGRAPHY

A. Berlin. *Lamentations: A Commentary* (Louisville: Westminster John Knox Press, 2002); F. W. Dobbs-Allsopp. *Lamentations.* IBC (Louisville: Westminster John Knox Press, 2002); E. Gerstenberger. *Psalms, Part 2, and Lamentations.* FOTL 15 (Grand Rapids: Eerdmans, 2001); N. Gottwald. "Lamentations." *HBC* (San Francisco: Harper & Row, 1988) 646–51; D. Hillers. *Lamentations.* AB 7A (New York: Doubleday, 1972; rev. ed., 1992); T. Linafelt. *Surviving Lamentations: Catastrophe, Lament, and Protest in the Afterlife of a Biblical Book* (Chicago: University of Chicago, 2000); N. Lee. *The Singers of Lamentations: Cities Under Siege, from Ur to Jerusalem to Sarajevo.* BI (Brill Academic Publishers, 2002); C. Mandolfo. *Daughter Zion Talks Back to the Prophets: A Dialogic Theology of the Book of Lamentations.* Semeia Studies (Society of Biblical Literature/Brill, 2007); K. O'Connor. *Lamentations and the Tears of the World* (Maryknoll, N.Y.: Orbis Books, 2002).

EZEKIEL

JACQUELINE E. LAPSLEY

OVERVIEW

Ezekiel is one of the strangest books of the Bible. Bursting with bizarre symbolism and sexually explicit language, the book seethes with divine fury even while simultaneously offering some of the most powerful expressions within the OT of God's desire to restore humanity and creation to wholeness. Both Jewish and Christian traditions have long puzzled over what to do with this book, which fascinates even as it repels. Many have intuited that Ezekiel has something of considerable significance and power to say about God and about Israel's relationship to God, but have been frustrated by the book's seemingly deliberate obfuscations, by its raw anger, and by its apparent resistance to conventional modes of biblical interpretation.

Despite its length and canonical status as one of the major prophets, Ezekiel is not widely cited in the NT (apart from its significance in the book of Revelation, and perhaps an allusion in 2 Cor 6:16), nor are its texts favored by preachers, with the exception of Ezek 37 (the dry bones). It offers little by way of messianic hope or pithy, comforting, quotable thoughts about God's love and promises of redemption. It resists being used for the interpretive purposes of others; rather, it demands to be read as a whole, for the integrity of its profound claim that though humanity's relationship with God is broken, and indeed, that human moral agency itself is broken beyond repair, God nevertheless reaches into that seemingly irreparable brokenness and makes humanity whole again. Israel's long history has shown how human effort to maintain covenant relationship with God has failed, and indeed, it has shown how the endless human striving to contain and control God has failed. The book reveals Yahweh as one who cannot and will not be contained or domesticated. In its understanding of the human condition and of the divine-human relationship as being irremediably broken unless healed by divine unilateral action, the book of Ezekiel bears some resemblance to the writings of Paul in the NT.

Ezekiel was a priest and a prophet in the years leading up to and following the Babylonian inva-

sion of Judah in the early sixth century BCE. The prophecies in the book are generally dated to the period 593–571 (though they do not follow a clear chronological pattern within the book). Having been deported from Jerusalem with the first wave of exiles in 597 (mainly composed of the leadership class), Ezekiel has been in Babylon for several years by 593. The end of Judah as a quasi-autonomous political entity occurs in 587 with the destruction of Jerusalem and the Temple, along with further deportations, at the hands of the Babylonians.

These events provoked an unparalleled theological crisis in Israel's life, the depth of which is everywhere evident in Ezekiel. The Temple was widely understood in several of Israel's dominant religious traditions (Zion theology, Priestly theology) to be the unique locus of God's presence in and with and for Israel. The destruction of the Temple that looms on the horizon throughout much of Ezekiel's prophecies is thus tantamount to God's total abandonment of Israel—Israel whom God had chosen to be a "treasured possession" (Exod 19:5), with whom God was understood to be in a covenantal relationship of loving and enduring loyalty. For Ezekiel as a priest, the destruction of the Temple seems to signify both the end of his own identity (what does it mean to be a priest without the Temple in which to serve?) and, more importantly, the end of Israel as God's covenantal people.

The severity of this theological crisis requires language, imagery, and ideas that are out of the ordinary. (This theological crisis also involves political, social, and economic factors—these modern categories ill fit their indissolubility in the ancient context; basically, the crisis is theological, with political, social, and economic consequences.) So the bizarre and offensive features of the book should not surprise, for they are part of the attempt to articulate the depth of the crisis at hand—a crisis both bizarre and offensive. Ezekiel's language moves at the boundaries of meaning, because the situation he describes moves at the boundaries of what is expressible, even thinkable. Indeed, the book makes claims that, on the surface, seem to be inconsistent: that

Israel must take responsibility for its failures, and that due to the irreparably damaged human condition, Israel is incapable of changing its behavior. Another paradox lies at the heart of the book as well: that where God seems most present, God is absent, and where God appears to be absent, God is present. Thus all human efforts to domesticate God will fail. These paradoxes lie at the heart of the book's theological power, for they are finally not contradictions, but productive tensions that lead to new insights about God and about human beings.

The book appears on the surface to fall neatly into three parts (God's judgment of Israel, God's judgment of the nations, God's restoration of Israel), but within that threefold structure it resists easy organization. Perhaps this is deliberate: one of Ezekiel's themes is to reject the way humanity attempts to tame and domesticate God. Frustrating our desire to divide the book into nice, digestible chunks emphasizes that God will not be controlled by human will.

OUTLINE

I. God's Judgment of the Covenant People and Departure of the Divine Presence (1:1–24:27)

    A. Divine Presence and Absence (1:1–11:25)
        1:1–3:27. Divine Presence and
            the Prophet's Call
        4:1–7:27. Signs of Impending Judgment
        8:1–11:25. Judgment and
            Divine Absence

    B. Signs of the Judgment (12:1–24:27)
        12:1–23:49. Signs and
            Announcements of Judgment
        24:1–27. Two Signs Summarizing
            Israel's Predicament

II. God's Judgment of the Nations (25:1–32:32)

    A. Ammon, Moab, Edom, Philistia, Tyre, Sidon (25:1–28:23)

    B. An Explicit Word of Hope for Israel (28:24–26)

    C. The Special Case of Egypt: Israel's Double (29:1–32:32)

III. God's Transformation of the Covenant People and Return of the Divine Presence (33:1–48:39)

    A. After Disaster, Signs of Hope (33:1–35:15)
        33:1–33. The Fall of Jerusalem
        34:1–31. False Shepherds and
            the True Shepherd
        35:1–15. Judgment on Mount
            Seir (Edom)

    B. Transformation of Land and People (36:1–37:28)
        36:1–38. The Re-Creation of Land
        37:1–28. The Re-Creation of
            People and Nation

    C. God's Final Triumph over All External Threats (38:1–39:29)

    D. The Final Temple Vision—Divine Presence Restored (40:1–48:35)
        40:1–43:11. Tour of the New Temple
            and Return of the Divine Glory
        43:12–46:24. The *Torah* of the Temple
        47:1–48:35. The Effect of the
            Divine Presence on the Land

DETAILED ANALYSIS

I. God's Judgment of the Covenant People and Departure of the Divine Presence (1:1–24:27)

A. Divine Presence and Absence (1:1–11:25)

1:1–3:27. Divine Presence and the Prophet's Call

1:1–28. **Visions of God at Chebar Canal.** Ezekiel's inaugural vision is vital for understanding the theology of the book as a whole. The vision itself is stunning—there is nothing like it elsewhere in the Old Testament. It overpowers the prophet at the moment of the vision, and the description has continued to overwhelm believers who have received it over millennia. The elements of the vision tumble off the page, with the prophet consistently resorting to analogical language ("something like . . .") to convey what he sees: cloud, fire, amber, living creatures, wings, legs, bronze, hands, faces, lion, ox, eagle, burning coals, torches, lightning, wheels, rims, eyes, spirit, dome, deafening sound, throne, sapphire, human form, amber, fire, splendor. He can only give an *approximate* description of God's glory; the vision is both orderly and chaotic—it does not cohere in one clear depiction of what is seen. Ezekiel experiences the *mysterium tremendum* of God's presence in what he sees and hears, yet God is also not fully present in the vision. In this massive sensory overload, the prophet glimpses God, and yet that glimpse also points away from God; it simultaneously reveals and obscures. Ezekiel 1:28 sums up the vision: "This was the appearance of the likeness of the glory [*kabod*] of the LORD." The paradox at the heart of the vision—the simultaneous presence and absence of God—is also one of the central paradoxes and main theological claims of the book itself.

It is 593 (five years after the first wave of deportations in 597), and Ezekiel and the other exiles have been in Babylon about five years. The prophet is by an irrigation canal in Babylon when the heavens are opened and he has a vision of the divine realm that exists above the earthly realm. Many modern readers now assume God can be present anywhere, but for Ezekiel and his audience the presence of God is closely tied to a particular place: the Temple in Jerusalem. For them, the possibility of a destroyed Jerusalem Temple and their exile to Babylon seemed to signal the unthinkable—namely, the defeat of their God, Yahweh, and the triumph of the Babylonian gods. To encounter Yahweh anywhere outside of the Jerusalem Temple would be not only unprecedented but difficult even to imagine. Thus Ezekiel's vision makes a powerful and astounding theological claim: Yahweh has not abandoned the exiles to foreign gods and is not bound by spatial limitations, as appearances suggest. On the contrary, extraordinarily, Israel's God is present with the exiles in the backwaters of Babylon itself! The vision itself thus serves as comfort to the exiles that they have not been abandoned, but God's continuing presence also bears ominous overtones: it means that God will not allow the people to forgo an accounting of their failures that have brought them to this point.

The vision has both troubled and fascinated believers for millennia. The early rabbis were concerned that the vision might lead the faithful into unsound mystical speculation, and those under thirty were forbidden, at least by some, to read the book, especially the beginning and the end (chs. 40–48 propose rules that seem to contradict the *torah*, or law/instruction, of Moses). And indeed, the vision was a catalyst for *merkavah* mysticism (*merkavah* refers to the throne-chariot of God), a rich and dynamic Jewish interpretive tradition. Christian traditions found the vision to be an important source of iconography; for example, the lion, ox, eagle, and human faces are understood to represent the four gospels in visual representations, and the wheels appear in everything from paintings to African-American spirituals.

2:1–3:27. The Prophet's Call. As in other prophetic books, Ezekiel offers a narrative of his call by God to the prophetic task. Ezekiel's response to the vision described in ch. 1 had been to fall down and worship, and it is from that posture that he is lifted by the spirit of God and set upon his feet to hear the divine commission. A new theme is introduced here: the sinfulness of Israel as the primary problem that God seeks to address through the work of this exiled prophet (2:3–4). Significantly, whether the Israelites will be responsive to the prophet's words and actions is irrelevant; Ezekiel's activity will let the people know that a prophet has been among them, not so they will change their behavior (2:5–7; 3:7–11). This signals another important theme: knowledge. The people have no genuine knowledge of who they are or of who God is—and the prophetic task is to fill these two voids in the people's understanding. Whether they are willing, or even able, to change their ways is a secondary matter, for behavioral change can only be achieved after the people understand the identity of God, and their own identity in relation to God.

Ezekiel literally eats the grim prophetic words he is to proclaim (3:1–3), an entirely fitting beginning to his prophetic activity since much of what he will convey to the Israelites throughout the book is symbolically enacted on his own body. He will literally embody God's word to Israel. In some ways, he points toward the beginnings of an incarnational theology—the word of God in human form.

Given the reservations expressed in these chapters about whether Israel will change their behavior, it seems odd to hear the emphasis on individual responsibility that characterizes 3:16–21. Yet Ezekiel consistently claims that both are true: people cannot change their behavior, yet they are responsible for their actions. But the issue in this particular section is not the people's response, per se; rather it concerns the prophet's responsibility to fulfill the divine commission. The image of Ezekiel as a sentinel—as one who proclaims the danger on the horizon—will appear again in 33:1–9.

Finally, God commands Ezekiel to engage in three sign-actions (the first three of many): to withdraw to his house, be bound with cords there, and to remain speechless except to deliver the word that God chooses (3:22–27). Ezekiel's dumbness has long puzzled commentators (since so much of the book is his speech!), but the point here is that Ezekiel is not to fulfill the traditional prophetic role of trying to bring the people to repentance for their sins. True, the people are accountable for the piteous state to which Israel has descended; but paradoxically, the prophet's task is not to make them shape up, for they are incapable of taking responsible action on their own. The prophet is only to offer to the people an account of the gravity of their situation and of how God will act to deliver them from it.

4:1–7:27. Signs of Impending Judgment

4:1–5:17. The Prophet's Sign-actions. Ezekiel continues to bear the word of God on his body in a series of sign-actions in chs. 4 and 5. A shift is noticeable from the sign-acts commanded in 3:22–27, however: there the acts pertained to the nature of the prophetic task itself, whereas beginning in 4:1 the prophet's sign-acts convey God's judgment of Israel, beginning with Jerusalem in particular, for its failure to live in covenantal relationship with God.

The brick diorama (4:1–3), the prophet's lying on his side for 430 days (4:4–8), and the shaving of his hair (5:1–4) all symbolically enact the siege and final fall of Jerusalem, which will take place between 589 and 587. The mixed-grain bread cooked over dung and eaten with a small ration of water symbolizes the deprivations of life under siege (4:9–17). Israel has broken its covenant with God (mainly by idolatrous worship, but also by breaking other commandments), and they will

live out the consequences of that brokenness. The fear and wasting (4:16–17) that characterizes life under siege closely mirrors the curses imposed for breaking covenant (see Lev 26:26, 39).

Because the sign-acts encode the word of God on the prophet's body, they are rhetorically more effective than plain prophetic speech. The difference is a bit like that between hearing a script read and seeing the play performed on stage—the power is in the performance. That Ezekiel engages in so many sign-actions, that his body becomes the divine word because words alone are not effective, points toward one of the underlying issues in the book: the people have difficulty hearing what God is trying to get across to them, and this problem in communication cripples the divine-human relationship. They are presently either unwilling or incapable, or both, of understanding the word of God. The problem is not that Jerusalem, in its total disregard of the requirements of God's covenant, has become like the nations around it; rather Jerusalem is *more wicked* than other nations (5:5–7)—an astonishing claim for an Israelite prophet to make about Israel! And one that forcefully articulates the depth of Israel's unfaithfulness.

While the main point of these sign-actions is to convey God's judgment on the people, a minor but significant feature of these sign-acts is the way in which they threaten the Priestly understanding of purity. At first, Ezekiel is to eat the bread cooked over human dung, which repels, of course, but also profoundly contaminates. The requirement is softened to cow dung, a common fuel; God's reduction of the command recalls the pattern of divine amelioration in Gen 1–11 (God sews clothes for the exiled couple, the mark on Cain, etc.). In the same way, the people will be defiled as they are carried off to live in a foreign land, and yet God promises to be present with them while they are exiled, not fully perhaps, but partially (11:16). Ezekiel himself, whose priestly identity is so central to him, is defiled along with the other deportees by the experience of exile.

6:1–7:27. Judgment on the Land. The next two chapters continue the theme of God's judgment of Israel, no longer by means of sign-actions, but by addressing the mountains of Israel (6:2). The choice of Israel's mountains as the object of judgment has puzzled modern readers (some scholars

even accuse Ezekiel of contributing to environmental degradation). It is, of course, the people whom God judges for their failures, not literal mountains; thus here the mountains symbolize the people as a whole. Yet the prevalence of indictment language about the land itself reveals something significant about the way Ezekiel thinks: land and people are inextricably bound together. Ezekiel's view of land and people as an integrated part of creation is, in some ways, more in keeping with the views of modern environmentalists who argue for the interdependence of humanity and the environment. For Ezekiel it is precisely because they are bound together that the land may be appropriately personified and also suffer destruction along with the people.

This is no ordinary punishment, however. The land, along with the people, must suffer a totalizing destruction, a form of *erasure*, of death itself. Consider the verbs in 6:6: "In all your settlements the towns will be decimated [*khrb*], and the high places laid waste [*yshm*], so that your altars may be decimated [*khrb*] and may bear their guilt, your idols shattered [*shbr*] and destroyed [*shbt*], your incense altars hacked up [*gd'*], and your deeds wiped out [*mkhh*]" (author's translation). Ezekiel strains here to find more synonyms for *destroy* despite a relative wealth of options in the biblical Hebrew thesaurus. As the last verb makes clear, those deeds, and the land they were done on, must be completely annihilated. The land suffers for the sins of humanity. The same verb appears in Gen 6:7, 7:4 and twice in 7:23 to describe what God does by means of the flood: "He wiped out [*mkhh*] every living thing that was on the face of the ground, human beings and animals and creeping things and birds of the air; they were wiped out [*mkhh*] from the earth" (7:23, author's translation). Ezekiel's use of this verb in Ezek 6:6, as the final in a relentless series of synonymous verbs, contributes to the audience's sense of the inalterable force of the divine will to eradicate completely both the people responsible for polluting the land and the land itself. They are of a piece and cannot be extricated from each other.

This erasure of people and land seems, on the surface, theologically indefensible to modern readers, yet it is necessary within Ezekiel's theological framework: Israel has reached a point where remediation is not possible, only divine re-

creation can restore Israel as God's people. That will be the subject of the last part of the book, with the re-creation of land and mountains in ch. 36 playing a crucial role in "answering" the devastation announced in ch. 6.

The refrain, "they/you shall know that I am the LORD"—often called the "recognition formula"—appears for the first time (of over 70 occurrences in the book) in this section (6:7, 10, 14). The central theme of the knowledge of God is underscored with every repetition. In what does such knowledge consist? To begin with the negative: it does not involve intellectual knowledge of Yahweh's transcendent being. Rather, it is the people's acknowledgment of the sovereignty of God following a divine action; it is the people's recognition that God is creator and redeemer of the world, and, crucially, that *they* are not. Knowledge of God for Israel means that they internalize completely the proper relationship between themselves and this God who made them, brought them out of Egypt, entered into covenantal relationship with them, and who still longs to be in that relationship despite Israel's sins (6:9: "you ... shall remember me ... how I was crushed by their wanton heart").

As John Calvin famously recognized, the necessary flip side to knowledge of God is knowledge of self, a concern that also appears in this section. Once the people remember clearly the truth of their history—how they abandoned the Lord—they will loathe themselves (6:9). Distressing as the language of self-loathing is to modern ears, this is Ezekiel's way of speaking about self-knowledge. The language of loathing (and later in the book, of shame) does not connote a psychologically damaging self-examination for Ezekiel. Rather, it involves the people's internalizing a truthful account of their history that leads them to see themselves as God sees them, and to experience an appropriate and healthy sense of humility and shame in light of that truth (more on shame in the discussion of ch. 16).

Chapter 7 introduces a new and important concern of Ezekiel's: the prevalence of violence in Israel and its connection to economic status. The first part of the poem refers to the disasters and destruction that will befall Israel as a result of the impending Babylonian invasion and makes clear that these events function as divine punishment for Israel's sins (7:1–9). The second half of the poem speaks specifically of the violence perpetrated by the wealthy and of the divine punishments that result. Here, as elsewhere in prophetic texts, Ezekiel makes a connection between wealth, pride, and violence. This toxic mixture leads to idolatry (7:19–20) and blood: "For the land is full of bloody crimes; the city is full of violence" (7:23). A lack of self-knowledge leads to an over-reliance on wealth, and the desire to increase that wealth leads to violence.

8:1–11:25. Judgment and Divine Absence

8:1–9:11. Temple Abominations and Judgment.
Chapter 8 begins the description of the second of the three structuring visions of the book (ch. 1; ch. 8; ch. 40). It is apparently the same figure described in the inaugural vision (1:26–27) who brings Ezekiel from Babylon to Jerusalem "in visions of God" (8:3). There he witnesses the abominations in the Temple that will ultimately drive the Lord out of it. It is difficult for contemporary readers, so far removed from the biblical worldview, to understand the gravity of the crisis at hand. God's presence among the people, dwelling first in the tabernacle, and then in the Temple once the people are settled in the land, has been a given in Israelite thought since the wilderness period (Exod 29:45; 1 Kgs 6:13). The people will thrive and flourish as long as God chooses the Temple as an earthly dwelling place. The idea that God might remove the divine presence from their midst was close to unthinkable for Israel. Yet Ezekiel's tour of the Temple, where he witnesses the unspeakably offensive idolatrous worship practices taking place there, provides the justification for God's abandonment of the Temple in ch. 10.

Ezekiel describes four scenes in the Temple (8:5–18), each one moving closer and closer to the holiest part of the sanctuary ("the holy of holies"), and each one describing an act more offensive and defiling than the last. The final scene depicts men, their backs to the altar, worshiping the sun, a total rejection of Yahweh at the very locus of the divine presence. Everything that Ezekiel sees in the Temple to this point has been a gross violation of the first and second commandments against worshiping other gods and against the making of images (see Exod 20:3–6; Deut 4:1–20; 5:7–12). Furthermore, all of these acts defile the holiness of the Temple. In the Priestly worldview that Ezekiel shared, the distinction between that which is holy (God, but also sacred space and that which is in it) and that which defiles holiness (human sinfulness among other things) is crucial. If the Temple becomes "polluted," even the sacrifices designed to cleanse the Temple would not be adequate and God would leave the Temple. The holiness of God cannot abide in a contaminated place.

Significantly, Yahweh names a further transgression after all these abominations have been described: the people fill the land with violence. Violence—crimes committed against other people—are considered on a par with the idolatry going on in the Temple (8:17). The Hebrew in 8:17*c* actually reads "See, they are putting the branch to my nose!" which seems to be a euphemistic way of saying—and this would have shocked Ezekiel's audience even more than it does modern readers—that they are sticking their penis in God's face! With their idolatrous worship and their violence, the people are making an unimaginably vulgar gesture in the Lord's face.

It is worth asking what the people involved in these rituals hope to accomplish by them. What has driven them to these acts that so flagrantly violate the covenant with God? The answer would seem to be desperation. As their world crumbles around them (the Babylonian invasion, the seeming absence of Yahweh), they cast about wildly for some means of controlling what is happening to them. Yet this urge to control is deeply misguided; the human desire to control the divine—to make the deity/ies "fix" things— must be decried and repudiated as nothing but the chaff of false hope.

In an extremely disturbing scene that recalls the devastating slaughter in Exod 32:26–28, the Lord calls for the slaughter of the old and the young in the city as punishment for the abominations in the Temple. As in the case of the golden calf, the slaughter reveals the depth of the crisis generated by the people's sin. The people say that God has abandoned the land and does not see, but the situation is precisely the opposite: God will hold them accountable for their idolatry and their violence (9:9-10). Here again is the paradoxical claim: God is in fact present when the people believe God to be most absent.

10:1–11:25. Departure of the Divine Glory. At the end of this first major section of the book, the event that was at once so menacingly certain and yet so impossible to conjure in the imagination, finally occurs: the divine "glory"—the very presence of God—departs from the Temple. While this is a previously unthinkable event, it is also a logically inevitable one given the situation in Jerusalem and in the Temple that Ezekiel has been describing to this point. The people's flagrant sinfulness, their violence and their idolatrous worship, has led the Lord to abandon the divine dwelling on earth. Whereas the first chapter of the book offered an overpowering image of the divine presence (in Babylonia no less!), this first section ends with an overpowering image of the divine absence (from the Temple, from Jerusalem!). Ezekiel is at pains to show that the divine glory he saw in Babylon is the very same that he now watches leave the Temple (10:15). The people sin through their idolatry, the misrepresentation of God's presence, and the result will be the removal of God's presence. Yet, by emphasizing the *absence* of God, both the absence of physical representations of God and the actual absence of God from the Temple, Ezekiel makes it possible for his audience to perceive God's *presence* in exile.

Prior to the final departure of the divine glory from the city itself (11:22–23), Ezekiel is privy to God's scathing indictment of Jerusalem's leaders, as well as a divine promise to the exiles of eventual return and restoration. The judgment against the leaders is in keeping with attention to the failures of leaders elsewhere in the book (chs. 12; 21; 34). They are indicted for gloating over the departure of those exiled in the first deportation and for taking over their homes (11:2–3), and again, for their violence ("You have killed many in this city," 11:6). These malignant rulers invoke the image of the city as a pot and themselves as the good meat in the pot, but the Lord refutes their claim (11:7–11), announcing judgment on them for their covenantal failures. The pot imagery will be completely reworked in 24:2–14 as Ezekiel struggles with the notion that the city, that is the people of the city, are inherently sinful and cannot be restored except by God's unilateral saving action. Thus the promise of God in 11:19–20 ("I will give them one heart, and put a new spirit within them; I will remove the heart of stone from their flesh and give them a heart of flesh, *so that* they may

follow my statutes and keep my ordinances and obey them" [emphasis added]) stands in considerable tension with Ezekiel's repeated claim that the people are responsible for the disaster that is befalling them. The tension between these two claims, that the people are responsible and that they are incapable of changing their behavior, is ultimately a productive one theologically. Ezekiel's most profound claims about the human condition emerge from this paradox.

B. Signs of the Judgment (12:1–24:27)

12:1–23:49. Signs and Announcements of Judgment

12:1–17:24. Signs, Oracles, and Metaphors About the Nature of Israel's Failure and Obligations to God. The material in chs. 12–23 is an uneven mixture of poetry and prose. Dense allegories and sign actions intersperse with prose accounts of Israel's history. This analysis will be able to highlight only some of these chapters.

After a prophetic sign-action designed to emphasize that the events of the exile are at the instigation and under the control of God (12:15–16), attention once again focuses on the leaders of Israel: they are the primary target of the Lord's withering judgments in Ezekiel. God will punish those prophets who have misled the people into believing that all would be well, "who ... saw visions of peace for [Jerusalem], when there was no peace" (13:16; cf. 13:10). Other prophets, this time specifically women, are also indicted for victimizing the people for their own economic gain (13:17–23).

In ch. 14 it is the elders' turn to hear a word of judgment. This theme of responsibility runs like a melody through Ezekiel (it appears in chs. 3; 14; especially in 18; and 33). In ch. 14 the prophet receives a divine word about the nature of Israel's accountability: in stark contrast to the situation in Gen 18:23–33 where Abraham argues with God about the number of righteous persons needed to save Sodom (the golden number is ten), in Ezekiel there is no golden number. The presence of even the most legendary righteous persons (Noah, Daniel, Job) will not save the people; righteous individuals (what few there are) will save only their own lives. The drumbeat of Israel's accountability for its sins beats steadily throughout the book, of which ch. 14 is but one example, yet another drumbeat, in apparent countertempo, also beats throughout the book: although the people are entirely accountable, they also are incapable of improving their situation on their own.

Even though ch. 23 appears in the next section, it is best addressed in conjunction with ch. 16 because they both portray Israel's history of sin in an extended allegory that is highly sexualized, even pornographic. There are two trajectories in recent interpretation of these chapters. First, ancient and modern readers alike have been offended by these chapters, and recently women scholars have drawn attention to the dangers of these difficult passages: the sexualized violence perpetrated against these metaphorical women seems to authorize male violence against real women, which is a serious, widespread, and ongoing global tragedy. Second, some scholars have suggested that the feminization of Israel depicted in these chapters is related to real experiences of victimization at the hands of imperial powers: being overrun by a massive army *is* emasculating, figuratively, and perhaps also literally as well.

It is entirely appropriate to be concerned about the effects of these texts on real women and yet still to ask how this appalling imagery functions in Ezekiel as a whole. These images are *designed* to shock those hearing or reading them. Ezekiel believes his audience to be suffering from a spiritual complacency and listlessness that can only be blasted away by rhetorical strategies that turn their theological assumptions upside down. In chs. 16 and 23, Ezekiel simultaneously depicts God as faithful and Israel as rapaciously and inherently unfaithful, worse even than the nations around her (see Ezek 5:7). Through these offensive images, Ezekiel helps his reader pay attention to the depth of the problem facing the people, who will not be able to save themselves.

The idea of self-loathing as a form of self-knowledge was introduced above regarding ch. 6, and the language of shame functions similarly here when, at the end of ch. 16, God promises a future deliverance (16:53–54, 60–63). Although it may be perplexing for modern readers, for Ezekiel feeling ashamed is part of the divine restoration and mercy; and the people will only begin to experience their shame once they are made

new and are back in the land. For Ezekiel this kind of shame is not toxic, but restorative; it is a form of self-knowledge. To experience this kind of shame is to penetrate all the self-deception in which human beings tend to wrap themselves, to see themselves as God sees them. Thus, one of the hallmarks of the new identity of the restored people will be the self-knowledge resulting from the shame they experience.

18:1–23:49. More on the Nature of Israel's Failure and Obligations to God. Many scholars have been interested in ch. 18 because it seems to move from an understanding of corporate responsibility, that is Israel's dominant way of thinking about accountability, to an understanding of responsibility as accruing to an individual, which is a more modern way of thinking. Thus, for a time in scholarship, Ezekiel was thought to have initiated a fundamental shift toward individualism. But this reading has not stood up to scrutiny.

Ezekiel is instead disputing a view apparently widely held by his audience: that their own generation, the one currently suffering the disastrous punishment of exile, is not responsible for what is happening to them. Their view is that their ancestors sinned, and now they are suffering the consequences (18:2). The idea that the consequences of sin are transmitted generationally is not unbiblical—indeed it is prominently expressed in the Pentateuch (Exod 34:7; Lev 26:39–40; Deut 5:9). Ezekiel's position in ch. 18, which stands in some tension with these pentateuchal texts, is that each generation is responsible for its own sins—the exilic generation cannot get off the hook by blaming their parents and grandparents for their current predicament (18:4).

This text also affirms the possibility that at least some Israelites are capable of repentance (18:27–28). Indeed God exhorts the people: "Get yourselves a new heart and a new spirit!" (v. 31). The implicit theological anthropology assumes that people are capable of changing their behavior, their orientation to God, themselves, and the world around them. Yet, in other places in the book (e.g., chs. 16; 20; 23; 36; 37), it is precisely the people's *incapacity* to change themselves that is affirmed. So, twice God promises to *give* the people a new heart and a new spirit, a gift that will enable them to obey the *torah* (36:26–27; cf. 11:19) and, in ch. 37, the details of this promise are literally enfleshed. The book wrestles with the tension between these views, but ultimately Ezekiel leans toward the idea that fundamental change in human moral agency must be a unilateral saving action on God's part. Yet even so, the paradox remains: human beings are entirely responsible for their sins even as they are incapable, without divine help, of fundamentally changing their situation.

In keeping with the more deterministic half of this paradox, ch. 20 offers a strikingly revisionist account of Israel's history with God (which is also in keeping with the grim allegorical readings of Israel's history in chs. 16 and 23). Many of Israel's prophets recall Israel's beginnings, its time in Egypt and the wilderness, as the golden "honeymoon" period when God and the people were in right relationship with each other, before the people fell into unfaithfulness (Hos 9:10; Isa 1:21, 26; Jer 2:2). Ezekiel's early history of Israel is at odds with the corporate memory of these other prophets: the version Ezekiel offers is one of Israel's unremitting failure from its very beginnings in Egypt (20:8). There was no honeymoon period; the people—every single one of them (v. 8)—have been incapable of faithfulness from the very outset. Forged in the fires of the exile, Ezekiel's reading of Israel's history is unlike that of any other biblical writer: it is a tale of unfaithfulness because the human condition is such that people can strive for obedience but they can never attain it.

As enigmatic and disturbing as it is, the divine pronouncement that God "gave them statutes that were not good and ordinances by which they could not live" (v. 25) underscores the total corruption of the human condition. Earlier in the passage God's gift of life-giving laws is affirmed three times (vv. 11, 13, 21), and Israel's incapacity to obey those life-giving laws is repeatedly decried. The "not good" laws they obey, however—in fact, perversely, the only laws the people obey are the ones that do not give life! The mystery of this verse (why would God give laws that were "not good"?) cannot be fully resolved, but the verse serves Ezekiel's purposes in that it emphasizes the hopelessness of the human condition under the present circumstances.

Ezekiel is not usually known for his emphasis on social justice, but his indictment of the way vio-lence and oppression are wielded against the powerless is actually quite pronounced, as is evident in other chapters. In ch. 22, Ezekiel makes it especially explicit that violence (22:3, 6, 9, 12, 25, 27), the abuse and oppression of the weak (22:7, 10, 11, 29), and unjust economic practices that exploit the poor (22:7, 12, 13, 25, 27, 29), are all violations of what lies at the heart of covenant faithfulness and will not be tolerated—they are as serious as the idolatry and cultic violations with which Ezekiel is customarily more closely associated.

24:1–27. Two Signs Summarizing Israel's Predicament

24:1–14. The Filthy Pot and the Intractability of Sin. It is appropriate to highlight the two halves of ch. 24 because together they cogently summarize Israel's predicament and the divine judgment that has been proclaimed in the book up to this point. Once again, Ezekiel uses two highly symbolic, enigmatic images to communicate God's judgment: a filthy pot that cannot be cleaned (24:1–14) and sign-actions following the death of the prophet's wife (24:15–27).

On the day that the siege of Jerusalem is announced (24:2), Ezekiel is commanded to share an image with Israel ("the rebellious house" [24:3]) in words that echo a variety of phrases from the first half of the book, thus encapsulating in one metaphor many imagistic features of Ezekiel's judgments. The judgment apparently begins benignly, with a kind of cooking song (vv. 3b–5) that seems to confirm in the minds of its hearers the privileged relationship between Israel and the Lord. The Jerusalemites, and particularly those left in the city after 597, are the "good pieces" in the cooking pot (v. 4).

But this "happy cooking song" version of reality is vigorously disputed in the first rejoinder that follows (vv. 6–8). The messenger formula introduces a scathing indictment of the perspective espoused in the song: "Woe to the bloody city, the pot whose rust is in it, whose rust has not gone out of it!" (v. 6). *Rust* might be better translated as "corruption," and the question arises: what is corroded, the pot itself or the meat in it? Putrid meat is easily dumped out; a diseased pot poses a more serious problem. As the rest of the passage bears out, the corruption appears to be internal: the metal itself is corroded, rendering the pot useless for any purpose; the corrosion is *intractable*.

On the face of it, v. 7 poses a logical problem by simultaneously making two apparently contrary assertions: that "the blood she [the city] shed is inside it" and that "she placed it [the blood] on a bare rock." How is the blood both within the pot *and* placed on the rock? Just as in the vocative "Woe to the bloody city" (v. 6), the meaning of blood in this passage is multivalent: it refers both to the blood that Jerusalemites have shed, that is, violence, but also to the blood that contaminates and defiles according to the Priestly worldview. Once the blood (of the meat) has been poured out on the rock, the blood (violence) is still embedded in the pot as part of its corrosion. The blood here recalls the blood of the infant (actually the mother's blood) in ch. 16, and the blood of the menstruating woman (22:10), both of which are defiling. Blood, with its connotations of both faithless violence and impurity, functions a peculiarly appropriate image for the type of corruption that Ezekiel ascribes to the inhabitants of Jerusalem.

Instead of pouring out her blood on the ground and covering it, the pot/city has poured it out on the bare rock. This surely refers to the levitical law requiring the blood of an animal to be poured out and covered with earth (Lev 17:13). Israel's failure to comply with this basic law symbolizes the totality of its covenantal failures. In a literarily fitting retaliation for this sacrilege, Yahweh will spill *their* blood upon a bare rock (v. 8).

A second rejoinder (vv. 9–13) to the cooking song of vv. 3*b*–5 follows the first rejoinder of vv. 6–8. The second rejoinder is not a continuation of the first; rather each one offers a distinctive view of the pot, changing the angle of the lens in order to emphasize different aspects of the image. In the first rejoinder, the blood that is in the pot—seemingly permanently—is highlighted (vv. 7–8), whereas in the second it is the corrosion of the pot itself that takes over and dominates the rest of the rejoinder (vv. 11–13). Indeed, the first words of this second rebuttal announce that the disease of the pot is still within it. Thus what connects the two rejoinders is not so much the image of the pot, but the repeated emphasis on the *intractable disease* of the pot. Ezekiel picks up on the image of the pot's inherent corrosion in his refutation, and, by the end of v. 13, obsesses about its recalcitrant filth in the manner of Lady MacBeth.

When the contents of the pot have burned away, the pot is left on the fire empty, in a vain hope that its corruption will finally burn off (v. 11). But the disease inherent in the pot will not dissipate, becoming a source of deep frustration and weariness to God. "In vain I have wearied myself; its thick rust does not depart" (v. 12). By this time a slippage has occurred in the way the original metaphor of the pot and meat has evolved. In ch. 11, the people saw themselves as the meat and Jerusalem as the pot (11:3), and this division seems to have held true in the first rejoinder (the people, like the meat, were being emptied out by deportation, but the city itself remained). Although it is the pot that is addressed in v. 13, and therefore ostensibly the city and the people are conflated here. Thus the apparent distinction between the people and the city (cited in ch. 11), in the end, collapses. And if this distinction collapses, then the traditional belief in the inviolability of Jerusalem must also collapse, for the second rejoinder heralds the destruction of the city itself, since both the meat and the pot are to be destroyed.

With this image of the people's *inherent* and *permanent* wickedness that not even God seems able to correct, the passage forcefully yet poignantly summarizes the first twenty-four chapters of the book. The location of the disease *within* the substance of the pot itself (and not something that is stuck to the pot) suggests that to Ezekiel's mind the people's wickedness, the disease of their being, is inherent in them. And this disease within the nature of the people is permanent in that not even *divine* cleansing can remove the corrosion. Something more radical is called for, which is here envisaged as a complete expression of the divine fury (v. 13*b*), resulting in the destruction of Jerusalem. Yet in the same breath, Ezekiel hints that a different future lies ahead, in which the city will be cleansed of its disease ("you shall not again be cleansed until ..."). But, as is frequently the case with Ezekiel, it is not clear how the movement from a disease to health will actually occur. Ezekiel is seeking to convince his hearers of the ineradicable truth that Jerusalem will be destroyed. The naive hope of the exiles that they might return to the city, and the even more naive hope of the present inhabitants of Jerusalem that they might escape punishment, must be exposed as false. Underlying this rhetorical strategy is an implicit belief that the people are indelibly wicked, diseased, like the pot.

24:15–27. Prohibition on Mourning and the Human Condition. The sign-act in 24:15–27, involving the death of Ezekiel's wife, and its interpretation are in some ways the last word of judgment against Israel before the oracles against the nations and the words of hope that mark the second half of the book. The power of the divine word here relies on an analogy between the death of the prophet's wife and the death/destruction of the city of Jerusalem. Most commentators on this passage understand Ezekiel to be prohibited from engaging in the customary mourning rituals following the sudden death of his wife (vv. 16–17), an act of suppression that serves as a sign in the second half of the passage (vv. 21–27)—that the Israelites too will be prohibited from ritually expressing their grief over the loss of the Temple, as well as the loss of their children. But why prohibit mourning a loss so deep? The answer is intimately connected to Ezekiel's struggle to articulate the problem of human nature and what he views as its inherent defectiveness. Ezekiel understands the people's love and desire to be once again misdirected (within the book, Ezekiel never depicts the people's desire as appropriate)—but here he leaves open the possibility that their love might one day find its true object, i.e., God.

A classic critique of the pervasive Temple theology is evident here. The people idolatrously placed their confidence in this "stronghold," and now Yahweh will be the one to destroy that confidence along with the Temple. While the passage relies on the wife/Temple analogy for its power, the language describing the people's feelings for the Temple suggests an intensity of feeling that is not present in the description of Ezekiel's feelings for his wife. The people's passion for the Temple is extreme, as the piling on of appositional phrases suggests ("the pride of your power, the delight of your eyes, and your heart's desire" [v. 21]). If these are indeed the passionate feelings of Ezekiel for his wife and even more so of the people for the Temple, then their anguish at the loss of wife and Temple respectively must be equally intense. Yet Yahweh wills that such intensity of feeling not be permitted traditional expression. Neither the prophet nor the people are allowed to perform the customary rituals mourning the dead, nor are they even allowed to weep. Every customary human action expressing loss, and especially the conventional rituals of structured mourning, are actions denied both prophet and people.

Understanding mourning and weeping as distinctively human behaviors is important for seeing the contrast to what follows. In v. 17, the prophet is commanded to "Groan softly [NRSV: Sigh, but not aloud]; make no mourning for the dead." The type of groaning this verb envisions is the primal, inarticulate groaning of the wounded (Jer 51:52; Ezek 26:15) or the equally primal groaning of those who react viscerally to the abominations in the Temple (Ezek 9:4). The primal nature of this type of noise contrasts with the now prohibited, but structured, "mourning" (*sapad*) from the previous verse. This is made quite explicit in the subsequent clause: "make no mourning for the dead." "Mourning" (*'ebel*) here includes all of the conventional mourning customs from the beginning to the end of the mourning period. Inarticulate "groaning" is permissible, then, but formal mourning is not. A quiet primal moan is allowed, but nothing that might provide a structure within which the prophet and people might make sense of their overwhelming experience of loss.

Those actions that might provide a framework within which the prophet could assign meaning to his wife's death are prohibited (v. 17). Human beings are meaning-makers, but it is specifically this human desire for meaning that is excluded here. The accrual of prohibitions against specifically human activities, however, suggests something beyond the simple withdrawal of human structures for interpreting experience. It goes further to evoke a process by which the prophet is *dehumanized*; he is stripped of those features that make him human. The prophet must confront loss without those structures of meaning that human beings need in order to interpret their complex experience. Instead, the Lord requires him to have the complex experience, but withdraws the means of interpreting it: he feels the loss of what he loved, but is incapable of anything but inarticulate groaning.

And so it will be for the people when Yahweh pollutes the object of their desire, the Temple. The language becomes even more vivid. Like the prophet confronting the death of his wife, the people, faced with the loss of their beloved Temple, will "not mourn or weep" (v. 23). But new elements appear here that were absent earlier. Not only will there be no customary mourning ritual, but the people shall "rot" (nemaqqotem; NRSV softens to "pine away") in their iniquities. This verb is elsewhere used to describe the decaying and festering of organic substances (Ps 38:6; Isa 34:4; cf. Lev 26:39; Ezek 4:17; 33:10). The image of organic decay evoked by this verb in 24:23 contributes to the sense that the people are undergoing a process of dehumanization—they are literally decaying. The very last phrase of v. 23 intensifies this effect. As they decay, the people will "groan (nehamtem) to one another." The English translation disguises a significant difference between this type of groaning and the groaning in v. 17. With the earlier verb (he'aneq), the sound was animal-like in its inarticulacy, but the attested subjects of the verb were human. By contrast, the verb in v. 23 almost always occurs with non-human subjects (e.g., animals, the sea). This choice of verbs is thus crucial: now the people will be rotting away and groaning explicitly as animals groan. The progressive dehumanization of the people, and of the prophet as a sign to the people, has now reached its completion.

What is the point of prohibiting mourning rituals? Why this diminishment of the human to what is less than human? For punishment alone, or for some larger purpose? Ezekiel continually reiterates that all of God's actions have one goal: so that the people may know God. But how does the stripping away of human categories of meaning here serve this end? How does the resulting emotional chaos help the people gain knowledge of God? For Ezekiel, the people's love/desire for the Temple, intense as it is, is misdirected. They loved the Temple, but they failed to love the One whom the Temple represents. The only cure for this, in Ezekiel's view, is radical indeed: it is a process by which the people are stripped of what makes them human, reduced to an animal-like state.

Strong emotions related to the death of a loved one require ritual acts of mourning in order to rein in the potential chaos of uncontrolled emotions. Yet Ezekiel skewers the Israelites' tendency to make order out of chaos for its naive self-sufficiency; it leaves no room for the activity of God. This critique of the human propensity for order is reminiscent of the divine speech in Job, in which Job's desire for structures of value and meaning is contrasted with the chaos represented by Leviathan. In Ezekiel the stripping away of

orders of value and meaning to the point where people resemble animals embodies the unstructurable, unorderable elements of the cosmos. For Ezekiel, human-generated categories are closing the people off, shielding them from knowing the presence and activity of God. Eliminating these meaning-making forms leaves the people with the chaos of their raw emotion, and so prepares them to receive the activity and knowledge of God. The Israelites' tendency is to resolve their grief over the Temple too easily and only by means of their own ritualized mourning, a mourning in which God is not an active player. Their reduction to an animalistic state allows them to feel their loss with all its attendant pain. The irresolvability of their grief leaves open a space for the radical action of God, space that was previously closed off in the well-ordered culture of ritualized mourning.

This is a very hard ethic. The necessity of being denuded of precisely that which makes us human cannot, should not, be integral to anyone's theology. Having examined this austere logic, should one not reject its claims? Possibly, but not without first considering what insights it might reveal. Ezekiel relativizes all human categories of meaning—they are inadequate and insufficient to deal with reality, and they deny the radical action of God. For Ezekiel, only through a progressive dehumanization can the people be prepared for new life. Nothing of the old nature can be retained. Later in the book (ch. 37), the re-creation of humanity can only be initiated after the people are declared dead—they are brought to new life with nothing of the old life remaining except their bones. The people must be crushed so low that they no longer seek piecemeal solutions for their desperate situation, such as setting their hearts on the Temple, or mourning its loss in the usual, customary ways. The symbolic ordering of experience (religion, culture) must be violently disturbed before the people can perceive the divine action that ultimately seeks to restore them to their full humanity.

II. God's Judgment of the Nations (25:1–32:32)

A. Ammon, Moab, Edom, Philistia, Tyre, Sidon (25:1–28:23)

As in many other prophetic books (Isaiah, Jeremiah, Amos), Ezekiel includes a set of chapters in which judgments are directed at nations other than Israel. These chapters appear to be directed at seven different nations, yet it is clear that the nations themselves are not the real intended audience at all (nor was Ezekiel in a position to present these oracles to them!): it is Israel in exile who is to "overhear" these judgments and to be comforted by the knowledge that God, despite the harsh judgments in the first half of the book, has not abandoned Israel to its enemies, but rather is holding these nations responsible for their actions just as Israel is held accountable for its failures.

What word of hope is this that consists of bad news for a neighboring country, albeit a historic enemy? Yet this is not an opportunity for smugness on Israel's part. Rather, God's judgment of the surrounding nations demonstrates that the Lord is sovereign over all lands, that God is in control of historical events that, to Israel's eyes, seem to be spinning out of control. The oracles against these nations signal that God's will is unfolding, and Israel's fate is therefore not subject to the whims of any nation. For the exiles, this is a word of hope. But the hope is mixed with warning. The foreign nations are judged for their economic and military ambitions, for their overweening pride, and for the idolatry that undergirds it all (this is particularly true for Tyre, Sidon, and Egypt). Israel cannot but observe that divine judgment for these failings is both swift and complete.

Israel's immediate neighbors (Ammon, Moab, Edom, and Philistia, 25:1–17) appear first among the seven nations. They are smaller than the nations further along on the list, and neither their presence on the international scene nor their transgressions are as prominent as those of Tyre, Sidon, and especially Egypt, which is the subject of the fiercest expressions of divine wrath. Significantly, Babylon nowhere is judged, though it is the dominant imperial power of the moment, has deported the exiles—Ezekiel's audience!—to its own lands, and is about to destroy the Temple along with Jerusalem. Ezekiel understands Babylon to be operating at the Lord's behest; that empire does not act independently but only as the means by which God punishes Israel (in much the same way as Isaiah understood Assyria to be an agent of the divine will in the eighth century BCE).

The small but economically prosperous island city-state of Tyre, situated off the cost of Lebanon,

is the subject of a lengthy judgment, followed by an ironic, mocking lamentation over its fall (26:1–21; 27:1–36). These are immediately followed by a lengthy proclamation against, and subsequent mocking lament over not the city, but the *king* of Tyre (28:1–10, 11–19). Why does the small kingdom of Tyre get such lengthy treatment? Tyre had become very prosperous from its seafaring merchant economy and, according to the prophetic accusation, therefore set itself above other nations, subtly claiming to be a seat of the gods. The prophetic judgment skewers this claim, and with a high degree of literary artistry employs a metaphor that Tyre might use to understand itself (as a great ship carrying a grand cargo) in order to reveal the city's true fate—to be crushed and destroyed as even the finest ship will be by a powerful storm.

Sidon, a city on the Phoenician coast just north of Tyre, is often paired with the great island city-state, which perhaps explains its role here as recipient of a very brief and generic accusation and proclamation of judgment (28:20–24). Worth lifting from this short oracle is the divine motivation: God acts so that all people will perceive rightly the holiness of God. For Ezekiel, divine action, whether of judgment or deliverance, always occurs in order to reveal the holiness and the glory of God. Part of the problem with the nations, as with Israel, is their failure to perceive and respect the chasm that differentiates the unholy human realm of ambitious self-interested politics and avaricious economic scrambling from the unfathomable holiness of God.

B. An Explicit Word of Hope for Israel (28:24–26)

The oracles against foreign nations, so characteristic of the prophetic material, have long been understood as implicit words of comfort to Israel. But here, when the first six of the seven nations subject to judgment have been identified and accusations against them enumerated and decisions rendered, Ezekiel inserts an explicit word of hope: "The house of Israel shall no longer find a pricking brier or a piercing thorn among all their neighbors who have treated them with contempt" (v. 24). Thus the previous chapters, laying out the charges that God holds against Israel's enemies, are explicitly understood as signs of hope for Israel: God is sovereign over these foreign nations, and God is still, in spite of everything, *for* Israel.

This brief, but important, message of comfort concludes with a promise that in the future Israel will dwell securely in their land (repeated twice in v. 26), the same land from which they have been forcibly removed and which is currently under foreign occupation. The idea of living securely, in safety, is one Ezekiel repeats eight more times in chs. 34–39 to describe Israel's future. They will once again build houses, plant vineyards, and enjoy the life of *shalom* that comes from being in right relationship with God and with one another. Their neighbors will no longer threaten them. Ezekiel discloses a glimpse of this future of safety without spelling out the details of how such a future will be realized. The details of how to get from the despair of exile to this vision of new life in the land remain murky.

The placement of this expression of comfort is odd. It occurs, as a kind of summary of the meaning of the oracles for Israel, after the judgments against six of the seven nations. Why doesn't it come after the final nation, Egypt, has been targeted for divine accusation and punishment (chs. 29–32)? Of the seven nations, Egypt receives far and away the most attention (half of the total number of chapters), yet the summary statement of the meaning of the oracles comes in the *middle* of the set, not at the end. I suspect that the function of the oracles against the first six nations is precisely to comfort Israel—its enemies will be punished; God acts on Israel's behalf still. But the oracles against Egypt do not serve this purpose and thus the summarizing message of 28:24–26 would be ill-placed at the end of ch. 32, despite appearances to the contrary. In Ezekiel's mind, Egypt serves a much more complicated, tortured, and unique relationship to Israel than any of the other nations.

C. The Special Case of Egypt: Israel's Double (29:1–32:32)

While Egypt—the nation out of which Israel first emerged as a people via the exodus—is the focus of the second half of the oracles against nations, the nation has appeared before in the book. Indeed, the revisionist history of ch. 20 focuses obsessively on Israel's time in Egypt as the crucible in which Israel's (mal)formation as a

people took place. Chapter 23 likewise reveals an unusual fixation with Egypt and its decisive, torturous effect on Israel's corporate identity. Ezekiel zeroes in on Egypt and its Pharaoh with four chapters of relentless, scathing judgment oracles. Why such an intense negative spotlight on Egypt?

The most obvious answer is that during the period Ezekiel is writing, Israel turned to Egypt repeatedly as a political ally in the ultimately futile hope of avoiding Babylonian hegemony. But something deeper is going on than the customary prophetic repudiation of political alliances that demonstrate a lack of trust in the Lord. Ezekiel returns repeatedly to Egypt, in chs. 17, 20, 23, and then relentlessly in chs. 29–32. As he describes Egypt's failings, and Israel's failings in connection with Egypt's failings, the line between Israel and Egypt grows fuzzier. Israel begins to look much like Egypt, which for Ezekiel is symbolized by the primordial chaos monster (29:3–7). Egypt's idols become Israel's idols, Egypt's corrupt ways, Israel's corrupt ways (20:7, 8, 16, 18, 24, 31, 39; "So I will put an end to your lewdness and your whoring brought from the land of Egypt; you shall not long for them, or remember Egypt any more," 23:27). Furthermore, the announcement that God will "scatter" Israel among the nations (11:16; 12:15; 20:23; 22:15; 36:19; cf. the sheep in ch. 34) is echoed by a promise to "scatter" Egypt (29:12; 30:23, 26). And where God will "gather" Israel back together after such scattering (11:17; 20:34, 41; 28:25), so Egypt too will be gathered (29:13–14) after having been scattered (albeit as the lowliest of nations).

Ezekiel seems to understand Egypt as a kind of double for Israel, a dark "other self" through which Ezekiel explores the underside of Israel's identity—the part of Israel that troubles Ezekiel's God so: the proud, faithless idolaters with rapacious appetites (esp. ch. 23). By subtly identifying Israel with Egypt in this way, Ezekiel works through what he perceives as Israel's deepest flaws, and then by casting Egypt down into the pit of Sheol (32:17–32), Ezekiel symbolically binds and controls the part of Israel's character that too closely resembled Egypt. Egypt, the chaos monster who unleashed chaos within Israel's very identity and who has haunted Israel since the exodus, is finally brought under the sovereign control of the Lord.

III. God's Transformation of the Covenant People and Return of the Divine Presence (33:1–48:39)

A. After Disaster, Signs of Hope (33:1–35:15)

33:1–33. The Fall of Jerusalem

As the first half of the book prepared for the destruction of Jerusalem (through ch. 24) and struggled to express the reality and meaning of divine absence in Jerusalem, so now the second half of the book, beginning in ch. 25 with the first oracle against a foreign nation, but gaining more focus in ch. 33 and following, looks toward the restoration of Jerusalem, the Temple, and the return of the divine presence into the heart of Israel's life. More specifically, ch. 33 is a hinge chapter between the two halves of the book. Chapters 34–37 announce the transformation of Israel, both land and people; chs. 38–39 develop the claims of chs. 25–32 by announcing God's victory over all other powers, even cosmic ones. All of this is by way of preparation for the return of God's glorious presence to Jerusalem and for a new Temple (chs. 40–48).

As a hinge chapter, ch. 33 points back to the first half of the book with its unrelenting judgment and also toward the future, since the tragedy of Jerusalem's fall no longer looms as it did in the first half of the book, but is now announced as something already accomplished. Chapter 33 is related directly to ch. 3. First, Ezekiel's responsibility to be a sentinel for the people, warning them of the impending divine judgment, is reiterated (see 3:17–21). As in ch. 3, the emphasis on the prophet's responsibility to warn the people that God does see and judge is part of the drumbeat of human responsibility running throughout the book. The prophet's responsibility is a model for the people's responsibility explicitly articulated in vv. 10–20: as the prophet is responsible to God for his actions, so the people are responsible to God for their actions.

A second connection to ch. 3 concerns the prophet's ability to speak: where Ezekiel's mouth had been shut in 3:26, God now opens it, thus inaugurating a new phase in his ministry. This startling reversal occurs at the precise moment when the news of the fall of Jerusalem reaches Ezekiel and the exiles in Babylon (33:21–22). The date in the text suggests that the news of Jerusalem's fall in July 587 reaches Ezekiel in January of 586, so in the twelfth year of the exile of the first round of deportees. The meaning of the prophet's temporary muteness from ch. 3 until ch. 33 has been much debated. After all, Ezekiel has been quite vocal during the intervening chapters! It seems that while Jerusalem and the Temple still stood, the prophet was authorized to speak the deity's words announcing the coming judgment and the reasons for it, but was prohibited from speaking any words of hope because the Temple had become a false symbol of divine presence. Now, with the Temple fallen and any misconceived notion of having captured God's presence in Jerusalem fallen with it, Ezekiel may now speak genuine words of hope for the future to his fellow exiles, based not on false claims to control God's presence and action in the world, but on God's will to transform the people (chs. 34–37) and to return in glory to Jerusalem (chs. 40–48).

But first, any notion the remaining survivors in Judah may harbor that they are somehow *entitled* to restoration (relying on cheap grace, v. 24) is here disabused, as Ezekiel affirms that all of Judah and Jerusalem will be decimated and laid waste (vv. 27–29). Why such harsh judgment at this particular moment, on the cusp of a new era of hope? While it seems excessive at first glance, to scathe Israel without remainder at this moment serves an important function: it eliminates any lingering, vestigial thought that some remnant of the old Israel will continue into the new era. On the contrary, nothing is left of the old people or land (even the mountains will be desolate, v. 28), and thus God will have to start anew, re-creating both land and people from scratch. This final announcement of the irrevocability and totality of the judgment bears theological implications: the people and even the land are too corrupt, too damaged (see the pot in ch. 24) to be repaired; what is required is re-creation *de novo*, a completely new beginning, a divine transformation of the human condition, creating the possibility for a new relationship between God and humanity.

The chapter ends with a revealing vignette of life in exile, of the challenges facing Ezekiel as he seeks to convey the divine word to a people finally unable to hear it. They *seem* willing to attend to what the Lord might be saying through the prophet ("Come and hear what the word is that comes from the LORD," v. 30), but the words do not sink in ("they hear your words, but they will not do them [NRSV, obey them] v. 31). The people do not act upon the prophetic words because "lust is in their mouths and their heart goes after unjust gain" (v. 31b, a more literal translation than NRSV, "for flattery is on their lips, but their heart is set on their gain"). The *lust* and the *unjust gain* both denote conditions where something normal has been carried to an abnormal excess (uncontrolled desire; profit gained by violence). While the following verse suggests that the word *'agabim* is something lovely and pleasant, in this verse it denotes something lovely and pleasant that has been carried to such an extreme that it is worthy of condemnation (lust). Both the people's speech (external behavior) and their heart (internal disposition) are distorted by excess desire.

Because inordinate desire is in the people's own mouths ("lust," v. 31) their hearing is impaired and they consequently hear only what they want to hear, which, not surprisingly, is the same thing which is on their own lips ("lust," v. 32). They hear a song of sensuous lust because that is what they hear coming from their own mouths; it sounds very beautiful to them (v. 32). In v. 32 they listen to the prophet's words, which are harsh words of judgment, but they do not, cannot, accurately perceive the negative as negative. The distortions of normal human behavior (profit and desire become greed and lust, respectively) have in turn distorted the people's capacity to understand correctly what they hear and see.

This is another occasion where Ezekiel's implicit view of human motivation is apparent. This text, along with others, notably chs. 16 and 23, suggest that the people seek primarily the fulfillment of their own desires. For Ezekiel, however, human desire is never depicted as normal; on the contrary, it is always excessive and monstrously out of control. This is unusual in Israelite traditions. In Deuteronomy, just to take one example, desire has a proper role when it is directed toward God ("You shall love the LORD your God with all your heart, and with all your soul, and with all your might," Deut 6:5). But Ezekiel does not speak in these terms; the language of love, whether divine or human, is missing from the book—it is

an appropriate motivating force for neither God nor human beings.

As in the earlier passages dealing with the prophetic vocation (2:5, 7; 3:11, 27), whether the people are capable of hearing the prophet's words or not is irrelevant to the prophetic call in ch. 33. The judgment, that is, the events the prophet proclaims in his words, will take place irrespective of the people's response ("When this comes—and come it will!" v. 33). It is at this moment, "when it comes," that the people "shall know that a prophet has been among them." This sequence of events bears a curious consequence for thinking about time in Ezekiel. The whole point of the prophetic mission cannot be understood from the point in time of the prophet's speaking; it can only be understood from a vantage point in the future, once the events to which the prophet refers have taken place. At that time, the people will be able to look back on the past and understand that the prophet had been sent by the Lord and had been speaking the Lord's words. This is why Ellen Davis views Ezekiel's writing as marking a shift away from the oral and toward the textual, toward an archival function. The word of God can no longer be frustrated by one generation's inability to hear it; the text will wait until a generation comes who can hear its word(s). Thus the purpose of the prophet's activity is not to bring about a change in the people's behavior in the present, but to instill a particular kind of knowledge in them in the future.

34:1–31. False Shepherds and the True Shepherd

While ch. 33 marks the shift from judgment toward hope, that hope is not unalloyed. Rather it is mixed with judgment in chs. 34 and 35. Or, to be more precise, hope for the people as a whole is inherently connected to judgment of particular groups who have wielded power abusively and stand under God's judgment. Such is the case for Israel's leaders in ch. 34 and their neighbors to the southeast, the Edomites, in ch. 35.

Ezekiel takes up the classic Israelite metaphor of the people of Israel as sheep, with shepherds representing Israelite kings (e.g., 2 Sam 5:2; Jer 3:15; 10:21; 12:10), as well as other leaders (e.g., 2 Sam 7:7; Isa 44:28; Jer 17:16). In Ezekiel, it seems that the shepherds refer to Israelite kings, but also more broadly to other members of the ruling elite (those who wield political, religious, and economic power). The indictment, laid out in 34:1–8, is not simply that the powerful have been tending to their own needs instead of the needs of the people, but that they have been using the sheep for their own unjust gain—the failure is not one of neglect, but of abuse: "You eat the fat, you clothe yourselves with the wool, you slaughter the fatlings; but you do not feed the sheep" (34:3). This particular accusation has appeared repeatedly in the book, that the political, economic, and religious establishment use their power for their own gain, at the expense of those whose interests these elites are supposed to serve (22:12, 13, 27; 33:31).

The accusation acquires even more specificity: Israelite leaders have not healed the sick, bound up the injured, or gone in search of the lost sheep (34:4). The metaphor of the shepherd is powerful because of the range of duties of an effective shepherd: not simply to herd and feed the sheep, but to tend them all, the vulnerable and lost as well as the strong, with care and compassion. Instead of tenderness, those in power in Israel have ruled with "force and harshness."

The result is that the sheep, God's people, have become prey to wild animals (34:5) and are scattered over all the earth without the protection they should expect from a shepherd (34:6). This indictment suggests that due to not only incompetent but also malign leadership, the people have been subject to economic and political injustice and violence, as well as the incursions of foreign powers. The responsibility for the "scattering" of the people over the earth, that is, the exile, is also here clearly laid at the feet of Israel's leadership (as opposed to the widespread belief among Ezekiel's audience that Yahweh's defeat at the hands of foreign gods explains the exile).

The judgment on these actions begins in v. 10 and is shocking in its imagery: "I will rescue my sheep from their mouths, so that they may not be food for them." Again, the reader is startled to imagine these shepherds as guilty not of neglect, but of the outright villainy of exploiting their power and authority for their own pleasure. They do not feed the sheep, *they eat the sheep*. This situation is even more dire than the one depicted in Matt 9:36, where the sheep suffer with no shepherd at all; there they are "harassed and helpless."

Better to have no shepherd than the ones Ezekiel describes!

More startling still is what comes next: "I myself will search for my sheep, and will seek them out" (34:11). Through the shepherd metaphor, God is revealed as one who searches for a people who are scattered and lost (v. 12), brings them home again (v. 13), nourishes them with good food and a healthy environment (vv. 13–14), and heals them by binding up their wounds and strengthening the weak and vulnerable (v. 16). In v. 16 the metaphor shifts: where the elite had been cast as the malevolent shepherds, now with God as the shepherd the powerful become the strong, fat sheep who will not escape punishment because they made life miserable for the leaner, weaker sheep (vv. 17–22). The governance of this divine shepherd, who is both compassionate to the vulnerable and committed to justice for the oppressors, provides a stark contrast to life under Israel's leaders.

The image of God as the one to shepherd God's people with compassion and love is, of course, present elsewhere in Scripture, most famously in Ps 23 and in John 10, where Jesus is depicted as the good shepherd. The relationship of the various OT texts to each other is uncertain, but the imagery in Ezek 34 was very likely a resource for the writer of John 10. Not only do a number of parallels appear (the bad shepherd/hired hand, the vulnerability of the sheep to predation, etc.), but in both texts the role of shepherd passes from God to a trustworthy vice-regent, one who can care for the people as God would care for them. In John this is Jesus, of course, whereas in Ezekiel this is "my servant David" (vv. 23–24)—a more muted messianic hope than those expressed elsewhere in the prophets, especially in Isaiah, where the messianic figure is a king of the Davidic line. Ezekiel does not understand this shepherd as a king, but as a prince (*nagid*). Not only is Ezekiel's terminology less politically fraught, but it expresses the need to imagine a shepherd/leader to care for the sheep/people who is *not* a king (since the disastrous leaders included Israel's kings), but who still represents God's commitment to the house of David.

35:1–15. Judgment on Mount Seir (Edom)

The transition from the promises to Israel of a compassionate shepherd, with its renewal of covenant relationship with God, to the judgment on Mount Seir, in Edom, seems abrupt. What does one have to do with the other? The judgment against Edom is especially puzzling since an oracle against Edom already appears in 25:12–14 with all the other oracles against foreign nations. The oracle in ch. 35 is sandwiched between the promises to Israel in ch. 34 and the promises to Israel in ch. 36, a strange arrangement. Of course, the oracles against nations also serve as implicit promises to Israel, but still, why Edom, and why here?

First, Edom is one of Israel's neighbors who apparently took most advantage of Israel's dire situation at the time of the first Babylonian incursions by actively participating in their destruction (vv. 5, 10). They are accused of nurturing an ancient grudge, verbal abuse (v. 12), and acting from hatred and envy (v. 11), all of which evokes the brotherly rift between Jacob and Esau (Gen 25:22–23; 27:41–45; 32:4–22; 33:1–16; Amos 1:11–12), the eponymous founders of Israel and Edom, respectively. Edom's actions toward Israel (saying, e.g., "They are laid desolate, they are given us to devour," v. 12), and toward God ("you magnified yourselves against me with your mouth," v. 13) are all the more egregious for being, in a sense, within the family.

So Edom's attitude and behavior toward Israel are particularly heinous, but still one may wonder why this oracle against Edom appears here. The key lies in the connections between this oracle, against Mount Seir in Edom, and the promises to the mountains of Israel in ch. 36. Judgment against Edom's mountains and promises to Israel's mountains are an implicit connection, but that connection becomes explicit in 36:5: "I am speaking in my hot jealousy against the rest of the nations and against all Edom, who, with wholehearted joy and utter contempt, took my land as their possession, because of its pasture, to plunder it." The language of punishment against Edom ("I will make you a perpetual desolation, and your cities shall never be inhabited," 35:9; repeated in vv. 3, 4, 7, 14, 15!) is repeated as a promise to Israel: it is precisely Israel's "desolate wastes and ... deserted towns, which have become a source of plunder and an object of derision to the rest of the nations all around" (36:4) that will once again become lush and populated (36:34, 35, 36). Edom will suffer the same fate that they inflicted on Israel, even as Israel's land will become abundant once again.

One final detail is worth noting: Edom is accused of claiming Judah and Israel for itself, even though the Lord was there (35:10). Three words ("Yahweh was there") appear almost as an afterthought here, yet they subtly express one of Ezekiel's main claims: that though the Lord is not constrained by Israel to "be" in the Temple in Jerusalem, neither is God absent from Israel even at its most desperate moment. God can be in Babylon with the exiles (ch. 1) as well as in Israel when all appears to be death and destruction. And the claim that God was present at one of Israel's darkest moments anticipates the claim of eternal divine presence with which the book concludes (48:35).

B. Transformation of Land and People (36:1–37:28)

36:1–38. The Re-Creation of Land

To understand the promises to the mountains of Israel, one must return to the judgment against the mountains in ch. 6. There the Lord announced that the mountains would be stripped bare and laid waste, that they would undergo a kind of erasure, becoming a *tabula rasa*. The totality of that destruction recalled that of the primeval flood—nothing was left. Now the promise is to renew the land, in fact, to re-create it all over again. The language of creation that saturates chs. 36 and 37 only makes sense when one recognizes that for Ezekiel human identity (as it was previously conceived), along with the land itself, have been wiped away. The intensity and extent of the eradication—its totality—is not simply a function of the intensity of the divine wrath. Rather, from Ezekiel's point of view, nothing of the old is usable; God *must* start from scratch. A new earth and a new humanity are possible, but only by the unilateral action of God that begins the work of creation all over again. In chs. 36 and 37, God acts not simply to *renew* Israel and the land, but to *re-create* them entirely. Chapter 36 has the re-creation of both people and land in view, whereas 37:1–14 famously focuses on the rebirth of the people alone. Both are deeply connected.

Of particular interest is the creation imagery present, especially in 36:8–11. Although the vocabulary is not identical, the imagery is very similar to that found in the creation accounts of Gen 1–3:

> But you, O mountains of Israel, *shall shoot out your branches, and yield your fruit* [cf. Gen 1:11, 12, 29] to my people Israel when they draw near to enter. See now, I am for you; I will turn to you, and *you shall be tilled* [cf. Gen 2:5, 15; 3:23] and *sown* [cf. Gen 1:11, 12, 29]; and *I will multiply human beings* [cf. Gen 1:22, 26, 27, 28] upon you, the whole house of Israel, all of it; the towns shall be inhabited and the waste places rebuilt; and *I will multiply human beings and animals upon you* [cf. Gen 1:24–26; 2:20]. *They shall increase and be fruitful* [cf. Gen 1:22, 28; 9:1, 7] and I will cause you to be inhabited as in your former times, and will do more *good* [cf. Gen 1:4, 10, 12, 14, 18, 25, 31] to you than ever before. Then you shall know that I am the Lord. (author's translation and emphasis)

The italicized words reflect vocabulary and images found in the Genesis accounts of creation. The promise in v. 11 is particularly striking: "I will cause you [i.e., the mountains] to be inhabited as in your former times and will do more good to you than ever before." The language of the goodness of creation is echoed here, but with the twist that this *new creation will be better than the first one*, which, as Genesis 1 was at pains to claim, was not only good, but *very good* (Gen 1:31; emphasis added). For Ezekiel, the new creation really must be better than the first one if all the dismal history of failure, idolatry and *torah* violation are not to be repeated. This new creation has to be better than "very good."

With the mountains restored, the second part of ch. 36 turns to God's creation of a new humanity. Not surprisingly, the Priestly language of purification is important (v. 25), but the metaphor shifts in the next, oft-quoted verse: "A new heart I will give you, and a new spirit I will put within you; and I will remove from your body the heart of stone and give you a heart of flesh" (v. 26). The result of this divine surgery is that the people will be able to obey the *torah*: "my spirit I will set within you, and *I will make it so that* in my statutes you walk and my ordinances you keep and do" (v. 27, author's translation). Although

the original creation was *good*, it was not *good enough*, in Ezekiel's view. Now the unilateral action of God to re-create human beings results in their new capacity to live as God's people (v. 28); it was precisely that capacity that was lacking in the original human nature.

The rest of the chapter returns to the image of the land as newly fruitful: an abundance of grain, fruit, and other produce removes the threat of famine (vv. 29–30), and the land will once again be tilled as it was in the original garden of Eden: "This land that was desolate has become like the garden of Eden; and the waste and desolate and ruined towns are now inhabited and fortified" (v. 35). This new land is an Eden for this new people.

37:1–28. The Re-Creation of People and Nation

Much has been said about the dry bones in 37:1–14, probably the most famous passage in Ezekiel, and certainly one that has nourished Jewish and Christian faith communities for millennia. Immediately one realizes that this passage expands in great detail the concise promise of 36:26–27 (and 11:19–20) that the people will be made new by the gift of a new heart and a new spirit, indeed the very spirit of God. In much the same way that the imagery in ch. 36 recalled other Israelite creation traditions, so 37:1–14 also evokes God's first creation of humankind: the spirit/breath/wind of Yahweh animates this people, created from the dust of their bones instead of the dust of the earth.

The passage depicts the corporate re-creation of Israel. As God's people, Israel has died, which explains the totality of the destruction language elsewhere in the book, and the presence of the birth imagery in the re-animation of the bones here. John Kutsko, in claiming that the process of revivification in Ezek 37 uses imagery of human creation, cites its similarities to Job 10, where Job accuses the deity of destroying what God had made:

> "Your hands fashioned and made me;
>   and now you turn and destroy me.
> Remember that you fashioned me like clay;
>   and will you turn me to dust again? . . .
> You clothed me with skin and flesh,
>   and knit me together with bones and
>   sinews." (Job 10: 8–9, 11)

Kutsko cites this text, with its birth imagery, to argue that what Ezek 37 describes is in fact a new birth. God redeems Israel from death by birthing a new Israel. This act of re-creation, not quite *ex nihilo*, but certainly from bones alone, transforms a people who were previously incapable of obedience into a people—now for the first time!—capable of obeying the *torah*, of living in covenantal relationship with God. No simple resuscitation, this rebirth morally and spiritually transforms the people into something new.

The form of the vision mirrors its content. This is no static image; rather, it leaps across the imagination of the hearer in a dynamic movement. Four elements of this movement are worth noting. First, the inadequacy of the old self has led to its death. The description of the bones as "very dry" (v. 2), the people as "slain" (v. 9), and the Lord as bringing the people up from their graves (v. 12, 13) all make clear that the old self is quite literally dead. Second, the importance of knowledge is reiterated when Ezekiel announces that God possesses knowledge that he, Ezekiel, does not have (v. 3). This helps to align Ezekiel with his audience, which both lacks knowledge and is surely incredulous at the possibility of life for these bones. Yet, when the people are made new, they will have the crucial knowledge of God's identity (vv. 6, 13–14) and power. The rhetorical goal of this whole vision, as in so many other places in Ezekiel, is to instill this knowledge in the people.

Third, the new human creation is incomplete with only the sinews, flesh, and skin; it requires a new spirit to give it life (vv. 8–10). And finally, as in 36:27, the spirit that gives life must come from God (v. 14), in keeping with the idea, negatively articulated in the first half of the book, that human beings do not have it within themselves to regenerate; new life must come unilaterally from God. The inpouring of the divine spirit is not a mere restoration of a previous existence, but a transformation of the very character of the people. The mistakes of the past will not be repeated because the old self will be replaced by a new and improved self, filled with the knowledge of God.

At the moment when the bones come together, there is a tremendous shaking (*ra'ash*, the NRSV's "rattling"; cf. Ezek 3:12; 38:19). The Septuagint calls it a *seismos*, an earthquake, recalling the thunderous *seismos* that shakes the foundations of the earth when Jesus breathes his last (Matt 27:51; cf. 28:2). It is the sound of life coming out of death. Of course, the people initially find the notion of new life from death ridiculous. "Our bones are dried up, and our hope is lost; we are cut off completely," they say (v. 11). Their imaginations are crippled in that they think death is always an end, not a beginning. Certainly the god they have tried to control (through their Temple rituals, their belief that God would always be in the Jerusalem Temple) would not be able to do much about their dry bones. But Ezekiel holds up for them the vision where death becomes the occasion for new life. They rise as a vast multitude, transformed and animated by the very breath/wind/spirit—*ruach*—of God, to become the people of God, now ready to embody God's covenantal justice for the sake of the world.

This is an absurd vision—it defies all logic. How can Ezekiel make such a vision compelling to the withered imaginations of his audience? Walter Brueggemann speaks of the prophetic task as precisely one of re-imagining, of slicing through the layers of numbness that encase us, to pierce our self-deception, "so that the God of endings is confessed as LORD." How does Ezekiel do this?

He does not do it by rational argumentation, by appealing to the people's reason. Instead, Ezekiel affirms the absurd by offering them an image that re-organizes their view of reality. While he has an important role in the vision itself, speaking the words that bring the bones to life, it is a curiously passive role, one devoid of ego. Ezekiel does not function here as the quintessential prophetic messenger, as one who bears God's words aimed at a particular audience: "Thus says the Lord GOD." Rather Ezekiel stands with his audience, aligned with them, and points to the image without advocating for its truth value. He simply shares with them the vision that he saw of what God is doing, making a new creation, forming a new people for God's mission in the world.

As one can see in so many passages in the book, the old Israel—people and land—have been destroyed because they were not capable of being God's covenant people—that is Ezekiel's ghastly message. Yet that corporate death makes it possible for God to intervene decisively in their catastrophic freefall and to make a way for them to once again be the covenant people. Understanding

Ezekiel's claim in this way helps to make sense of what otherwise seems to be needlessly horrific and unrelenting judgment language in the book.

The second half of chapter 37 (vv. 15–28) seems anti-climactic. Indeed, of the myriad interpretations of the dry bones passage, very few continue into the second half of the chapter. Yet the two halves are connected, for where the people are created anew as God's people in the first half, in the second half that people, historically divided into two separate nations, are permanently reunited and gathered back into the land.

Two features of the passage are especially important. First, unlike his previous circumspection in speaking of a future Davidic leader (in 34:24 David is the promised "prince"), Ezekiel here emphatically promises reunited Israel a king (37:22) who will be in the Davidic line (37:24, though he is again dubbed "prince" in the following verse). So although heavily muted in Ezekiel, the messianic promise of an endless reign of just kings who will also be shepherds does make its quiet appearance in Ezekiel ("they and their children and their children's children shall live there forever; and my servant David shall be their prince forever" (v. 25).

Having been newly transformed by the spirit of God, this people will now be able to "follow my ordinances and be careful to observe my statutes" (v. 24). What had been Israel's struggle and its failure, keeping the *torah*, is now firmly asserted. Infused with the spirit of God, a new people is equipped for a new life.

As in 34:25, when God promised a covenant of peace (*berit shalom*) to the "sheep," here the Lord renews the promise to make with this new people an everlasting covenant of peace (v. 26). The relationship between God and God's people will be devoid of strife when God acts to bless and multiply the people, and promises to be present in the sanctuary forevermore (v. 26). It is possible to envision such a covenant of peace only when it is God who makes it, not the people. It is a glorious vision of the divine-human relationship, but it is one in which human beings are strangely passive. It is characteristic of Ezekiel in the latter part of the book to conjure a vision of the future that is gloriously re-created and made new, complete with a newly transformed people of God, but it is almost always one in which human beings have

almost no active part. Ezekiel cannot imagine a "covenant of peace" in conjunction with an active human will; bitter experience constrains his imagination on this point.

C. God's Final Triumph over All External Threats (38:1–39:29)

These chapters read quite differently from all that has preceded, or indeed, that follows them. They are widely considered to be proto-apocalyptic because in their description of the Lord's defeat of a distant, symbolic figure (Gog of Magog) and his massive army of allies, there is no effort to establish these events within history, and Israel's role is to remain patient and trust in the sovereignty of God over all forces. It is Yahweh who summons Gog to battle, ironically with the goal of inflicting a massive defeat on this epitomic, fierce enemy bent on Israel's destruction. While markedly different in style and tone from the other material in the second half of the book, Yahweh's defeat of Gog and defense of Israel vividly underscore God's commitment to Israel's protection, and God's power to make good on that commitment. The ultimate goal, from the divine perspective, is for all nations to perceive the sovereignty and holiness of Yahweh. In this sense, although the Gog pericope can be sharply distinguished from the rest of Ezekiel in terms of its literary features, it stands in thematic continuity with what precedes and follows it.

In the depiction of Gog of Magog and his devastation of Israel and subsequent defeat by Yahweh, three elements are of particular interest. First, the Israelites are depicted as living a very subdued and peaceful existence in the land. Indeed they are described as the "quiet ones, living in safety, all of them" (38:11, author's translation). The Israelites are essentially bystanders in what is depicted as a massive military spectacle. This depiction of the people as placidly watching events unravel by the hand of Yahweh may be contrasted to Ezekiel's portrayals of the people's previous history, when they themselves raucously and dangerously *made* history (e.g., chs. 16; 20; 23). The people's new disposition to trust God in quiet tranquility thus distinguishes them from their old selves. On this day the people live quietly and safely, acting only when the word of Yahweh compels them to do so, not on their own initiative (such as burning weapons and burying enemies, 39:9, 12).

The second element of note in these chapters is the recurrence of shame language at the end, which leads to self-knowledge. In the final section (39:21–29), a truncated summation of exile and return, the first several verses (vv. 21–24) give the reasons for exile, followed by, beginning in v. 25, a description of the quality of life in the restoration. It is a time of reconciliation: Yahweh will show mercy to the whole house of Jacob, bringing it out of captivity (v. 25). This mercy paradoxically means that the people will experience shame: "They shall bear [NRSV wrongly says "forget"] their shame, and all the treachery they have practiced against me, when they live securely in their land with no one to make them afraid" (v. 26). As noted before in the discussion of chs. 6 and 16, the knowledge of self afforded by a searing experience of shame is prerequisite to a renewed life with God.

The third element of note is related to self-knowledge: it is the knowledge of God. Using proto-apocalyptic elements, these chapters reflect a concern for Israel's restoration in so far as they highlight the vital importance of both Israel's and the nations' knowledge of Yahweh (38:23; 39:6, 7, 13, 21, 22, 27, 28). In this respect, the Gog episode is in keeping with chs. 33–37 and 40–48, where the knowledge of God as a goal of divine action is reiterated. The recognition formula appears seven times in these two chapters—more densely than anywhere else—thereby linking these chapters closely to the rest of the book. As elsewhere, the recognition formula reveals a concern for a moral, spiritual, and thus holistic knowledge of God (as opposed to merely cognitive knowledge). With the defeat of Gog, who represents any and all enemies Israel might ever have, both the nations and Israel will come to a knowledge of Yahweh that will transform the way they understand themselves in relation to the deity and to one another—it will be life-changing knowledge.

D. The Final Temple Vision—Divine Presence Restored (40:1–48:35)

40:1–43:11. Tour of the New Temple and Return of the Divine Glory

Ezekiel's book began with a vision of the presence of the Lord (chs. 1–3), continued with a vision of the departure of that presence (chs. 8–11), and now ends with a vision of God's return to a transformed Temple and a transformed people (chs. 40–48). Another way of putting it: At the beginning of the book one learns that God is not in the Temple but on the move (ch. 1), then Ezekiel is taken on a tour of the Temple to find out the reasons for God's absence (chs. 8–11), and now the prophet is taken on another Temple tour, this time one which reveals the Lord's return. Thus the promises of divine return and restoration, offered throughout the book (e.g., 20:40–44; 37:23–28), are now realized. With this vision, the drama of presence and absence is complete. The vision forms a fitting conclusion to the "story" that began in the first chapter with Ezekiel's overwhelming encounter with God by the Chebar canal.

Many interpreters understand the legislation in these final chapters to be casting itself as a second giving of the divine law, with Ezekiel in the role of Moses. Thus the vision forms a fitting sequel to the new creation of people and land promised in chs. 36–37. This pattern of new creation followed by new law further supports the idea that Ezekiel believes the life of Israel must begin all over again, with a new human identity capable of fulfilling the new laws. Only with a new humanity on a regenerated land is God's continuing presence both possible and assured.

The vision is dated to 573, about fourteen years after the fall of Judah and about two years before the end of Ezekiel's prophetic career. The nature of the material in chs. 40–48 has been the subject of much discussion, without winning anything approaching unanimous support. The attention to detail is certainly in keeping with Ezekiel's Priestly background (and vividly recalls the construction of two other divine places of indwelling—the tabernacle in Exod 25–31; 35–40 and Solomon's Temple in 1 Kgs 6–7). Most interpreters concur that the temple described in the vision is not meant to be a blueprint for the actual Temple that was rebuilt in Israel around 520. Rather, as Susan Niditch argues, the vision functions more as a verbal icon—it symbolically orders and categorizes the world, much in the way that Gen 1–11 symbolically orders the world and allows the viewer to see the transcendent. Like that earlier creation account, Ezekiel's vision conjures a new world ordered by hierarchy and work roles, geographic boundaries, and the divisions between peoples and places, which make for a coherent map of reality. This world is marked by harmony between God and humanity (so like the Priestly Gen 1, but unlike the non-Priestly Gen 2–11), a harmony established by the reordering of sacred time and space and sustained by meticulous attention to the new laws of the Temple.

The vision offers Ezekiel's audience a symbolic picture of the future that is hopeful because it is centered on God's life-giving presence. As throughout the book, God's presence or "glory" (Heb: *kabod*) is not construed as passive or static; rather the presence of God is always active, demonstrating God's desire to be in relationship to God's people, whether expressed in acts of judgment or of deliverance. In the final vision, the Temple is first restored (40:1–42:20), making possible the return of God's *kabod* to the new sanctuary (43:1–11). In the next section, Ezekiel receives the instructions (the *torah* of the Temple, 43:12) for how people will live in such a way that their sin does not once again drive God from the sanctuary (43:12–46:24). The return of God's life-giving presence described in 43:1–4 literally gives life to the land (see 47:1–12) and restores the relationship between people and land to a healthy interdependence, undergirded by their mutual dependence on God's presence. The final part of the vision describes, with the Priestly concern for detail characteristic of the whole vision, the boundaries of this newly fertile land (47:13–48:35). The last line encapsulates one of the book's major themes, the presence of God, by concluding with a new name for the city: "The Lord is There" (48:35).

This first section (40:1–43:11) recounts the prophet's tour of this new Temple, as he is guided by an ethereal man equipped with a linen cord and a measuring reed, the presence of which testifies to the significance of order and precision in the new creation. The details of the arrangement of space in the new Temple, seemingly arcane to most readers, are designed to create a buffer between the sacred and the profane: a core goal of this new space is to protect the holiness of God from the contaminating potential any human activity may bring. God departed the Temple in ch. 10 because it had become too defiled to host the presence of a holy God any longer. Ezekiel 43:8 explains that part of the problem was the architecture itself of the first Temple: "In their

setting of their threshold by my thresholds, and their post by my posts, and the wall between me and them, they have even defiled my holy name" (author translation). The walls were just too thin to maintain the appropriate boundaries between holy and that which defiles. The new Temple architecture addresses that danger: it has multiple layers that protect the holiest inner sanctum like layers of an onion, beginning with an outer wall that is about ten feet high and amazingly, equally as wide.

Ezekiel witnesses the divine return to the Temple in 43:1–11, and he is careful to connect it to his two other encounters with the divine *kabod* recounted in chs. 1–3 and 8–11 (43:3). While several promises of God's *future* presence appear in the book, here that promise is at last realized: "I will reside among the people of Israel forever" (43:7, 9). Yet, one may well wonder how Ezekiel imagines this harmonious relationship between God and the people to be sustained, given the unmitigated disaster of Israel's history. However, God created the people anew, gave them a "new heart" and a "new spirit," and infused them with God's own spirit (37:14)—this will make it possible for the people of God to obey the *torah* and live in covenantal faithfulness with the Lord.

There are not a lot of people in this last vision, which suggests that Ezekiel is not too sure how it will all work out "on the ground." It seems that Ezekiel is very concerned about the capacity of human beings to destroy the paradise envisioned, and steps must be taken to avoid this eventuality. Throughout the final vision, for example, the behavior and even the movement of human beings are severely restricted (e.g., ch. 46 prescribes precisely how the people are to enter and exit the Temple, never exiting whence they entered [46:9–10]). Those groups chosen to lead the restored Israel are those who were among the least guilty in the past (the Zadokites), while those deemed especially at fault are demoted (the Levites; 44:10–16). The people themselves play no significant role in the new Temple because their sins were so egregious in the past. The dearth of people is thus meaningful in and of itself: Ezekiel is deeply concerned not to let human actions result in a repeat of Israel's disastrous history.

One way to prevent problems is to hit the theme Ezekiel has drummed many times: knowledge, both of God and of self. For Ezekiel, knowledge of God and self is the necessary prerequisite to any right action. In the final vision as elsewhere in the book, the people cannot faithfully be the people of God until they know themselves and know their God. The task of both priest (44:23) and prophet (40:4; 43:10–11) is to convey knowledge to the people because it is knowledge that will shape their moral understanding of the new reality and their place in it. The new humanity does not obviate the need for a sacrificial system—Ezekiel retains the cultic system, much as the priests had conceived it, which is in some tension with his claims elsewhere that the new heart and new spirit infused by God will make the people obey divine commands (36:27).

As elsewhere (chs. 6; 16; 38–39), shame plays a vital and positive role in forming the new moral identity of the people of God; it is a means of liberating self-knowledge. The order of events is important: "When they are ashamed of all that they have done, make known to them the plan of the temple" (43:11). For Ezekiel, the self-knowledge facilitated by an experience of shame—the internal realization and acceptance of the people's responsibility for the past—is a prerequisite for receiving the knowledge of the divine plan for a harmonious future relationship with God. Without true understanding of the past, a different future is not possible.

43:12–46:24. The *Torah* of the Temple

The tour of the Temple has been moving progressively inward, peeling the "onion" of the Temple layers, each layer growing in holiness. In this middle section of the vision, Ezekiel and his guide arrive at the altar, which is described with meticulous attention to detail and is followed by directions for its consecration and purification (43:13–26). At the end of seven days, the altar is ready, and divine favor is bestowed (43:27). The gate by which the Lord enters the Temple is shut (44:2–3), so that no one else may enter by that same way, again preserving the necessary space between holy and profane. Yet for Ezekiel the closing of this door also symbolizes the fulfillment of God's promise to reside amongst the people forever; its sealing means that God will never again depart from the Temple—the closed door is a potent architectural sign of the hope at the core

of Ezekiel's Temple vision. Ezekiel also devotes considerable attention to the Temple personnel, with the stock of the Levites falling and that of the Zadokite line of priests rising (44:4–31). Unifying the various directions concerning the holy district, weights and measures, offerings, festivals, and assorted other commandments (45:1–46:24) is the Priestly focus on holiness and appropriate boundaries, but also a pronounced concern for economic justice (45:8–9, 10–12; 46:18). The future will not be marked by the voracious, uncontrolled appetites and resulting oppression that characterized the past.

All this detail and precision is entirely in keeping with the Priestly framework in which Ezekiel operates. But it also testifies to a strained desire for the control that meticulous order confers, a desire to address the threat posed by any potential chaos (and Israel's history suggests to Ezekiel that there is enormous reason to be concerned!) with a maximum of control and regulation. The detail and precision in Ezekiel's vision bespeaks a regulated architecture of hope, that is, the orderliness and structure of the Temple vision work to guarantee that what happened before—human sin contaminating the holiness of the Temple—will not happen again. For Ezekiel hope lies in sound architectural plans, good construction, precise directions for building use, and crucially, really thick walls. For him, God's power and promise are reflected in the closed door, in the thick walls that allow God to be present amidst the people.

There is an irony here. One of Ezekiel's indictments of Israel was its attempt to control God by Temple rituals, by its misplaced trust that God would not desert the Temple (see discussion for chs. 8; 12). The Israelites' rage for order in a chaotic world had become an impediment in their relationship to God, yet is Ezekiel not trying the same gambit here? The Temple vision projects a world in which order and structure are the keys to salvation—they will reconcile God with God's people.

Nonetheless, for Ezekiel a key difference separates the Israelites' efforts to control the Lord, and the "regulated architecture of hope" in the last vision: the problem with the false hope that the people clung to through order and structure was that that order and structure was of their own making. In the Temple vision, Ezekiel transfers the order and structure to the architecture of the Temple itself—for Ezekiel this is a source of genuine hope. Moreover, the similarity between the people's sin in trying to control God and Ezekiel's effort to regulate the future through precise architecture, reveals unresolved issues in the book. The strained precision of Ezekiel's ending discloses his continuing ambivalence over human identity, his doubt that even God's action can re-create people in such a way that the threat to the holiness of God, and thus to the continuation of the divine-human relationship, can be adequately defused. The tidiness of Ezekiel's ending belies the unresolved conflicts that characterize the rest of the book. He wants everything to be wrapped up neatly in a "happy marriage" between people and deity.

The ending of Ezekiel is not only about order and containment, however. In the midst of so much measured, static imagery, one immeasurable, extremely dynamic, image bursts forth: the water that flows from the sanctuary itself, bringing life to everything around it (47:1–12).

47:1–48:35. The Effect of the Divine Presence on the Land

Water gushes out of the Temple (47:1). This crucial aperture in the Temple contrasts sharply with the otherwise restricted space and movement in this exact and exacting structure. Not surprisingly, given the role of measurements in the rest of the vision, the first half of the passage (47:1–6) describes the mysterious guide's efforts to measure the water, with prophet in tow. The measurements suggest that the water begins gently— the disruption of the closed sanctuary surface is only a small one—but it gathers tremendous force once outside of the sanctuary. At first, the water is only ankle deep, then knee deep, then up to the waist, and finally too deep to cross. The impassibility is repeated twice in one verse: "it was a river that I could not cross, for the water had risen; it was deep enough to swim in, a river that could not be crossed" (47:5). This gushing water—a potent symbol of God's saving power—is the only immeasurable thing associated with the Temple. Initially just a trickle, these waters gushing forth from the Temple to revive the land are simply too powerful to be appraised by a yardstick (so

to speak). "Do you see, mortal?" the guide asks (47:6, author translation)—do you see that what God is doing now can neither be contained nor measured by instruments or calculations? This is God's healing power on the loose, unleashed from the Temple, now on the same side of the Temple wall as the people.

The second half of the passage conveys the way the river revivifies both land and sea—"everything will live where the river goes" (47:9). The creation vocabulary of Genesis is prominent here—a withered world is re-created by the life-giving water, in much the same way the withered bones were re-created by the life-giving breath/wind/spirit of God in ch. 37. The growth that the water initiates is also immeasurable: "a great abundance" of trees and fish, in "many" kinds (47:7, 9, 10; cf. the dry bones in ch. 37). Here precise measurements cannot express the immense hope unleashed by the torrent of the life-giving river.

The salvific action of divine water (ch. 47) and breath (ch. 37) cannot be quantified; the imprecision of their description indexes the power of God, in much the same way that the imprecise language of Ezekiel's vision of God in ch. 1 discloses the divine power and transcendence. Ezekiel's ending thus contains and reveals some of the same tensions stirring under the surface of the rest of the book: hope for the future is manifest in the controlled environment of the Temple, but also in the dynamic power of God to burst through the Temple walls and heal both land and people with an incalculable flow. The hope embodied in the quantifiability of the Temple measurements thus stands in some tension with the unquantifiable power and reach of both the healing water (ch. 47) and the life-giving breath (ch. 37).

After the land has been made fertile in this way, Ezekiel ends the book by describing its equitable distribution (47:13–23; 48:1–29). The land is apportioned without regard for geography, topography or hierarchy (other than the necessity of appropriate boundaries to keep the Temple holy); the principle of distribution is equality. Thus the end of the book recalls the Jubilee year, with its ample provision for all (Lev 25). In the very last verse, the city, peopled by God's newly formed people on God's newly formed land, is renamed: "The Lord is There" (v. 35). So Ezekiel's last words proclaim that the Lord dwells in this place, banishing all the sins that have plagued the people and that Ezekiel has so forcefully catalogued in earlier chapters. Gone forever are the violence, oppression, and idolatry; in their place God and God's people are bound together in a covenantal life of justice, equity, and peace.

BIBLIOGRAPHY

D. Block. *The Book of Ezekiel.* 2 vols. NICOT (Grand Rapids: Eerdmans, 1997); W. Brueggemann. *The Prophetic Imagination* (Philadelphia: Fortress, 1978); E. Davis. *Swallowing the Scroll: Textuality and the Dynamics of Discourse in Ezekiel's Prophecy.* JSOTSup 78 (Sheffield: Almond, 1989); M. Fox. "The Rhetoric of Ezekiel's Vision of the Valley of the Bones." *Hebrew Union College Annual* 51 (1980) 1–15; R. W. Jenson. *Ezekiel.* Brazos' Theological Commentary on the Bible (Grand Rapids: Brazos, 2009); P. Joyce. *Ezekiel: A Commentary.* Library of HB/OT Studies 482 (London; New York: T&T Clark, 2007); J. Kutsko. *Between Heaven and Earth: Divine Presence and Absence in the Book of Ezekiel* (Winona Lake, Ind.: Eisenbrauns, 2000); J. Lapsley. *Can These Bones Live? The Problem of the Moral Self in the Book of Ezekiel.* BZAW 301 (New York: W. de Gruyter, 2000); _____. "Doors Thrown Open and Waters Gushing Forth: Mark, Ezekiel, and the Architecture of Hope." *The Ending of Mark and the Ends of God: Essays in Honor of Donald Harrisville Juel.* B. R. Gaventa and P. D. Miller, eds. (Louisville: Westminster John Knox, 2005); A. Mein. *Ezekiel and the Ethics of Exile* (Oxford: Oxford University Press, 2001); S. Niditch. "Ezekiel 40–48 in a Visionary Context." *CBQ* 48 (1986) 208–224; M. Odell. *Ezekiel.* Smith & Helwys Bible Commentary (Macon, Ga.: Smith & Helwys, 2005).

DANIEL
Matthias Henze

Overview

The apocalypse is a form of revelatory literature. It is governed by the view that salvation from this alien and threatening world is possible only through the revelation of divine secrets. These secrets include information about the end of time, which is thought to be imminent, and about a new eon, a perfect reality that awaits the faithful and that will replace this imperfect and broken world. These divine secrets are typically transmitted by an angel to an individual chosen by God to receive and to record for future generations what he has learned.

The book of Daniel is such an apocalypse. In it, Daniel is told "what is inscribed in the book of truth" (Dan 10:21). An interpreting angel appears to Daniel and explains that he has come to help Daniel understand what will happen to all of Israel "at the end of days" (Dan 10:14). And even though the angel strengthens Daniel physically and interprets for him his apocalyptic visions, in the end even Daniel has to concede, "I heard but could not understand" (Dan 12:8). The words and their ultimate meaning remain a secret until "the time of the end" (Dan 12:4).

Not all modern readers will be comfortable reading an apocalypse, a text which, according to its self-understanding, is esoteric rather than exoteric. The fact that in the modern world apocalypses have become the domain of extremist millennial movements does not make apocalyptic literature any more endearing. But a book like Daniel should be read on its own terms. Then the reader will discover that Daniel is not so difficult to understand after all, that this is not a violent text of fire and brimstone but a book deeply rooted in the prophetic tradition of ancient Israel that gives encouragement and hope to its readers. The attentive reader will immediately notice that the book of Daniel readily falls into two halves, the cycle of court legends about Daniel and his three companions in chs. 1–6, and Daniel's apocalyptic visions in chs. 7–12. The two parts are connected in several ways. Dreams are an important vehicle for divine revelation, for King Nebuchadnezzar in chs. 2 and 4 and for Daniel in chs. 7, 8, and 10–12;

and the division of the last installment of history into four kingdoms is introduced in ch. 2 and then repeated in ch. 7. But there are also important differences between the two parts. The predominant theme of the cycles is the life of the Jews in the Diaspora and the question of how they can preserve their Jewish identity and still make a career at the foreign court. The encounter of the Jewish and the non-Jewish world is amicable. Also, there is nothing apocalyptic in chs. 1–6. All this changes dramatically in the second half of the book. Daniel begins to have visions in which Gentile empires turn into apocalyptic beasts (ch. 7), and the main topic now is the *eschaton*, that is, the fate of Israel in the end time.

The biblical narrator is explicit about when chs. 7–12 were composed. At the center of his attention one finds Antiochus IV Epiphanes (175–164 BCE), the Seleucid king who appears in Daniel either as "the little horn" (7:8, 11; 8:9–12, 22–25) or simply as "a contemptible person" (11:21). In 167–164 BCE, Antiochus persecuted the Jews and profaned the Jerusalem Temple. The persecutions led to the Maccabean revolt, and scholars agree widely that Dan 7–12 was composed, and the book of Daniel reached its present form, toward the end of the revolt, possibly in the year 164 BCE. This makes Daniel the youngest book in the Hebrew Bible. The legends in chs. 1–6 are older and most likely circulated independently, possibly in smaller collections first, before they were added to the visions, possibly by the same circles who composed the visions. The tales now introduce Daniel and explain why God chose this wise and righteous man (cf. Ezek 14:14; 28:3) to be the recipient of the apocalyptic lore.

The book of Daniel has been popular and influential in early Judaism and early Christianity, in spite of—or, perhaps, precisely because of—its esoteric nature. In the library of Qumran, home of the Dead Sea Scrolls, eight fragments of the book were discovered. The worldview and language of Daniel had been a major influence on the Qumran group and on its own thinking. Early Christians found in the son of man figure in Dan 7 a prophecy about Jesus, and so "Son of Man" has become a messianic title in the New Testament Gospels (Mark 2:27; Matt 8:20; 18:11).

OUTLINE

I. The Court Tales (1:1–6:28)

A. The Four Youth at the Babylonian Court (1:1–21)

B. Nebuchadnezzar's Dream: The Composite Statue (2:1–49)

C. The Fiery Furnace (3:1–30)

D. Nebuchadnezzar's Dream: Nebuchadnezzar's Madness (4:1–37)

E. Belshazzar's Feast (5:1–31)

F. Daniel in the Lions' Den (6:1–28)

II. The Apocalyptic Visions (7:1–12:13)

A. The Vision of the Four Beasts and the Son of Man (7:1–28)

B. The Vision of the Ram and the He–Goat (8:1–27)

C. Daniel's Prayer (9:1–27)

D. The Final Revelation (10:1–12:13)

DETAILED ANALYSIS

I. The Court Tales (1:1–6:28)

The story of Daniel and his three companions stands at the beginning of the book and introduces not only the cycle of court legends in Dan 1–6 but the book as a whole. It may well have been composed specifically for that purpose. Chapter 1 introduces the book's fictitious setting, its main characters, and the central theme of the court tales: the youth have to negotiate how to preserve their Jewish identity while cooperating closely with, and indeed working for, the foreign monarchs at whose courts they serve.

A. The Four Youth at the Babylonian Court (1:1–21)

1:1–2. The first verses of the book connect the narrative of Daniel with the description of King Nebuchadnezzar's destruction of Jerusalem in 587 BCE as found in the other books of the Bible (2 Kgs 23–25; Jer 39–45; 52). By telling the story of Daniel and his three friends, the biblical narrator gives the exiles a face and picks up the story where the historian in 2 Kgs 25 left off. In a sense, the transition from 2 Kgs to Daniel is emblematic of the history of Judaism in general: for Daniel and his three companions, the temporary exile imposed by the Babylonian king has turned into a permanent Jewish Diaspora.

The date in v. 1 has long puzzled interpreters. The "third year of ... Jehoiakim" is the year 606 BCE (2 Kgs 23:36–37), whereas Nebuchadnezzar captured Jerusalem only in 597 BCE. Such historical inaccuracies are not uncommon in post-exilic Jewish legends (2:1; Jdt 1:1–6) and underscore the fictional character of the literature. *Shinar* is a traditional name for Babylon (Gen 10:10; 11:2; Zech 5:11).

1:3–7. The four youth receive a three–year training in the "literature and language of the Chaldeans" (v. 4), which is Akkadian. The term "Chaldean" either refers to the Babylonian courtiers as a professional group (2:4–10; 3:8–12; 4:7), or it is used as an ethnic designation for the Babylonians (5:30; 9:1; 2 Kgs 25:4; Jer 24:5; Ezek 1:3). As is customary in such situations, the youth receive new names (Gen 41:45; Esth 2:7), which, unlike the royal food rations they are given, they receive without any objections, presumably because they are able to keep their Hebrew names (2:17; the *Prayer of Azariah*).

1:8–17. Life in the Diaspora meant that dietary restrictions played an especially important role (Tob 1:10–11; Jdt 10:5; 1 Macc 1:62–63; 2 Macc 5:27; cf. Lev 11 and Deut 14). Daniel refuses to "defile himself" (v. 8). The concern for proper food clearly overrides any concern Daniel has about the Babylonian education and his Gentile name. The narrator emphasizes that the youth's health is God's doing and not the result of their diet.

1:18–21. The story ends as it began, with a chronological notice. The "first year of King Cyrus" (v. 21) is 538 BCE. Daniel 10:1 dates Daniel's final apocalyptic vision recorded in chs. 10–12 to "the third year of King Cyrus of Persia." The note in 1:21 anticipates that Daniel will outlast

Nebuchadnezzar and serve monarchs from subsequent empires.

B. Nebuchadnezzar's Dream: The Composite Statue (2:1–49)

The story of Nebuchadnezzar's first dream (cf. ch. 4) introduces a recurring motif in the court tales, the contest between the Babylonian courtiers and Daniel. In this case, however, the Babylonian sages never threaten Daniel but, instead, benefit from him. It is only because of Daniel's unique ability *both* to tell the content of Nebuchadnezzar's dream and to interpret it that they are pardoned and are given their lives.

2:1–12. Since Daniel was trained for three years at Nebuchadnezzar's court before he was brought before the king (1:5, 18), he can hardly have interpreted the dream "in the second year of Nebuchadnezzar's reign" (2:1). It could be that Daniel is interpreting the dream while still in training, though it is more likely that the author of our story did not know ch. 1, which was added later as an introduction to the collection of court tales as a whole.

There are numerous reports in the ancient Near East about the interpretation of royal dreams (Gen 40–41), though no courtier is ever asked to recount the dream itself first. The impossibility of the task sets the stage for Daniel to shine and, more importantly, for the biblical narrator to make the point that the situation is resolved because of the God of Israel, not because of Daniel's gifts.

The chapter begins in Hebrew and switches abruptly to Aramaic in the middle of v. 4 (Aramaic in 2:4*b*–7:28; Hebrew in 11–2:4*a* and 8:1–12:13).

2:17–23. Nebuchadnezzar's dream is a "mystery" (2:19, 27–30, 47; 4:9), which only becomes intelligible when Daniel receives "a vision of the night" (2:19; 4:5; 7:1). The Aramaic word for the dream's interpretation, *peshar* (in 2:4–7; 4:18–19; 5:12; 7:16), in the library from Qumran is used for a special kind of biblical interpretation known as *pesher*.

Daniel responds with a prayer (vv. 20–23), a hymn in praise of the God of Israel, who possesses the qualities Nebuchadnezzar was initially seeking in his courtiers: he "reveals ... hidden things" and "knows what is in the darkness."

2:24–45. Brought before the king, Daniel agrees with the courtiers that Nebuchadnezzar's demands are unreasonable (v. 27) but then adds that it is his God alone "who reveals mysteries" (v. 28; similarly Gen 41:16). The enormous statue is made of different metals of declining value, which represent four kingdoms: Babylonia, Media, Persia, and Greece (the "prince of Greece" in 10:20 brings the four-kingdom schema to its conclusion). The feet of iron and clay represent the Greek empire divided into Ptolemaic and the Seleucid kingdoms. The four kingdoms recur in ch. 7, though there the emphasis is on the succession of the kingdoms; they also increase in their use of violence rather than decrease in value.

The stone "cut out, not by human hands" (v. 34; see the similar phrase in 8:25) signifies the divine intention to destroy the kingdoms. Early Jewish and Christian interpreters have found in the stone a symbol of the messiah (Matt 21:42–44; Luke 20:17–19).

2:46–49. Nebuchadnezzar's euphoric response seems awkward, not least because Daniel has just predicted the demise of the Babylonian kingdom. Also, the Gentile monarch and tyrant now worships Daniel and even brings him offerings (v. 46). Jewish and Christian interpreters were at pains to explain Daniel's rather friendly and close rapport with Israel's archenemy. The episode demonstrates Nebuchadnezzar's acceptance of, and implied conversion to, the God of Daniel, who is the "God of gods" (v. 47).

C. The Fiery Furnace (3:1–30)

The motif of the conflict between the courtiers and Daniel's companions, introduced in the previous chapter, is here propelled to its extreme. The story is filled with gross exaggerations, used primarily for their satirical effect: the statue's proportions are gigantic (v. 1), the list of court officials is unnecessarily repeated verbatim (vv. 2, 3), the list of instruments appears multiple times (vv. 5, 7, 10, 15), the furnace is heated up seven times (v. 19), so that the executioners themselves die in its flames (v. 22). The tale is both hilarious and deeply revealing. It sharply contrasts Jewish monotheism with Babylonian idol worship, a popular theme in post-exilic literature—with deep roots in Isa 40–55—and ridicules the king's idolatry with much irony.

Daniel is conspicuous for his absence from the tale. Some scholars therefore hold that originally the story circulated independently and was only later incorporated into the cycle of stories about Daniel because of its thematic resemblance.

3:1–18. King Nebuchadnezzar erects a golden statue (Isa 40:19–20; Jer 10:2–4; Bel). The Greek historian Herodotus reported a massive statue of solid gold in a temple in the center of Babylon (*History* 1.183). Dedication ceremonies are well attested in the ancient world (1 Kgs 8:63; Neh 12:27), but the religious intolerance at the center of our tale is not. The accusation and interrogation of the three youth by the Gentile tyrant seems fabricated and provides the narrator with a formidable opportunity to have the three men bear witness to their God. Nebuchadnezzar's exclamation, "Who is the god ...?" (v. 15), nicely captures his own presumptuousness.

The response of the youth (vv. 16–18) has long puzzled interpreters. Their reply, "If our God ... is able to deliver us" (v. 17), implies that they harbor some doubt whether their God is willing, or even able, to save them. By contrast, "the wise" in Dan 11–12 chose death, confident that they will be rewarded in the resurrection of the dead (see 11:33 and 12:3; also 1 Macc 1:62–63; 2:19–22; 2 Macc 6:27–28; 7:1–2).

3:19–30. Nebuchadnezzar comes across as a dullard, whose extreme emotional responses quickly shift from total rage to profound devotion in just a few verses. The religious intolerance toward the youth is simply replaced by another form of religious intolerance in the final decree (v. 29). Similarly, the transition from the king's fury in v. 19 to his astonishment in v. 24 to see four men walking in the fire seems rather abrupt, and so the Greek and Latin versions insert at this point the *Prayer of Azariah*, one of three Additions to Daniel. As in 2:49, the youth are promoted again in 3:30.

D. Nebuchadnezzar's Dream: Nebuchadnezzar's Madness (4:1–37)

Scholars have long assumed that the king of the story's original version was not Nebuchadnezzar but Nabonidus (556–539 BCE), the last Neo–Babylonian king and father of Belshazzar (the author of Daniel erroneously claims that Belshazzar is the son of Nebuchadnezzar; see chapter 5).

Nabonidus spent ten years in Teima, an oasis in the Arabian peninsula, while his son Belshazzar served as regent. This assumption was then corroborated with the discovery of the "Prayer of Nabonidus" (4Q242), a fragmentary text from Qumran, in which Nabonidus relates how he was afflicted for seven years while praying to his gods of silver and gold (cf. 5:23), until an anonymous Jew cured him and told him of the God of Israel.

4:1–3. The story about Nebuchadnezzar's second dream is framed in vv. 1–3 and 34–37 by two doxologies (a doxology is a "praise of God"; cf. 6:26–27). The doxologies are expressions of Nebuchadnezzar's newly found faith and, at the same time, capture the main message of the stories: they demonstrate the absolute sovereignty of the God of Israel. Nebuchadnezzar, architect of the Babylonian exile, looms large in the collective memory of ancient Israel. By putting two doxologies in honor of the God of Israel into the mouth of Israel's archenemy, the biblical author strips the Babylonian villain of his gruesome qualities. Instead, the king becomes rather benign, even comical, and in the end turns into a faithful proselyte.

The chapter begins and ends as a first-person account of Nebuchadnezzar, a literary style known elsewhere from Neo-Babylonian inscriptions and letters, which here lends the story the character of a confession of faith. The story takes the form of a royal edict, sent "to all peoples" (v. 1; cf. 6:26), in which the king relates the story that provoked the two doxologies.

4:4–18. Whereas Nebuchadnezzar never told the diviners his first dream (2:5), he willingly gives Daniel a detailed description of his second dream. The "tree at the center of the earth" (v. 10) is a common motif in the ancient Near East, representing great emperors (Ezek 17:1–24; 31:1–14; see also Herodotus 1.108 about Cambyses' vision; and 7.19 about King Xerxes). The "holy watcher" (vv. 13, 17, and 23) is an angelic figure not attested elsewhere in the Hebrew Bible. Watchers appear in several Jewish texts of the late Second Temple period and at Qumran (*Jub* 4:22; 7:21; 10:5), though they are perhaps best known from the *Book of the Watchers* (*1 En* 1–36).

4:19–33. Daniel again articulates the main lesson to be learned, that God is sovereign and gives dominion "to whom he will" (v. 25). When

Nebuchadnezzar is stripped of his royal power, transformed into an animal and forced to roam the steppe, he remembers Daniel's words (vv. 33-36) and is promptly reinstalled on his throne.

Daniel is visibly troubled by the dream and the interpretation he has to give. Not only is he reluctant to speak (v. 19), he readily offer his advice on what the Babylonian king can do to postpone the divine sentence. Early interpreters were divided over their reading of the story. The rabbis saw in Nebuchadnezzar's transformation into an animal a just and well-deserved punishment for Israel's worst enemy, whereas Christians noted that the king is reinstalled in the end and hence saw in him a model penitent.

E. Belshazzar's Feast (5:1–31)

The tale of Belshazzar's feast picks up and develops further stylistic elements and motifs from the preceding stories: as in ch. 3, there are several exaggerations, most of all the description of the royal banquet (cf. Esth 1), which is blasphemous, idolatrous, and excessive; Belshazzar's profanation of the Temple implements, which will cost him his life (v. 23), harks back to Nebuchadnezzar's original sacrilege (1:2; Isa 52:11; Ezra 1:7–11); the queen (probably the queen mother, wife of Nebuchadnezzar) alone remembers Daniel and his God-given endowment (v. 11), which in turn leads to a brief recollection of Daniel's promotion under Nebuchadnezzar; and the first part of Daniel's oration recalls in detail the events of the previous chapter (vv. 18–21).

5:1–12. Belshazzar was the son of Nabonidus, the last Neo-Babylonian king, and viceroy during his father's absence in Teima (cf. ch. 4), not the son of Nebuchadnezzar. Readers are not told why the banquet is celebrated, though the reference to "the gods of gold and silver" (v. 4) brings up the familiar topic of idol parody (Isa 44:9–20; Wis 13–15; Bel).

5:13–31. Only Daniel is able to read the writing on the wall. The three words—MENE (erroneously repeated by a scribe?), *TEKEL*, and *PARSIN*—can be read as nouns or as verbs. As nouns, they refer to three weights. *MENE* in Aramaic is a mina or about 600 grams, a *TEKEL* is a shekel or 10 grams, i.e., less than half an ounce, and *PARSIN* is a half (some interpreters read the ending –*IN* as a dual,

hence two halves, which seems unlikely), though the text does not make clear whether this means a half-mina or a half-shekel. By themselves, the measurements make little sense. In his interpretation, Daniel takes the three terms to be verbal forms, in which case *MENE* means "numbered," *TEKEL* "weighed," and *PARSIN* "divided." Together, they predict the fate of the Babylonian empire. Some scholars have proposed that each is associated with the fate of an individual monarch (e.g., Nebuchadnezzar, Nabonidus, and his viceroy Belshazzar), but this is unwarranted. The point of the omen is to predict the imminent end of the Babylonian kingdom.

As in 2:46, the king responds favorably and rewards Daniel, as he had promised. Unlike the previous tales, however, this one does not conclude with the king's doxology and conversion but with his death. The God who "desposes kings" (2:21) put an end to Belshazzar's life and kingdom. His successor is "Darius the Mede" (v. 31), the protagonist of the next tale. No such figure is known to have existed. The Persian king who defeated Nabonidus, Belshazzar's father, was Cyrus the Great (560–530 BCE), who was followed by his son Cambyses II (530–522 BCE). Darius then succeeded Cambyses and was king of Persia from 522 to 486 BCE. The Greek historian Herodotus reports that Darius divided the Persian Empire into twenty provinces and determined their tributes (Herodotus, 3.89–90; Dan 6:1; Est 1:1; 8:9).

F. Daniel in the Lions' Den (6:1–28)

The conflict between the courtiers and Daniel escalates in the tale of Daniel in the lions' den. The initial equilibrium among the three presidents (compare the seven counselors in Est 1:14 and Ezra 7:14) is disturbed when the king plans to appoint Daniel "over the whole kingdom" (v. 3; 2:49; cf. Gen 41:45; Est 3:1).

The story of Daniel in the lions' den has some close parallels with the apocryphal story of Bel and the Dragon, one of the three Additions to Daniel: both legends revolve around a conflict at a foreign court, both have as their central motif the lions' den, and in both tales the accusers are thrown into the den in Daniel's stead. Daniel 6 and Bel have therefore been called "variations" or "duplicate narratives" of the same original story. Some scholars think that Bel and the Dragon is the more developed of the two narratives. But one should be careful not to exaggerate the similarities, nor do the parallels imply that one version developed out of the other. Neither story shows clear signs of depending on the other.

6:1–9. On Darius and his efforts to divide the kingdom into twenty provinces, see the comment on 5:31. The numbers here are gravely overdrawn (Est 1:1; 8:9). The Persians, who brought an end to the Babylonian exile and, upon defeating the Neo-Babylonians, allowed the Jews to return home, are well known for their religious tolerance. The edict calling for the deification of the king and the prohibition to pray to other gods is historically implausible and serves the dramatic purpose of setting the stage for the legend. The presence of a lions' den, a pit to be closed with a stone (vv. 17, 23–24), may have been inspired by Ezek 19:4, 8–9; Ps 57:6–7.

6:10–18. Daniel retreats to the "upper room" (Judg 3:20; 1 Kgs 17:19), a quiet place for his prayers (Jdt 8:5; Matt 6:6; Acts 1:13; 9:37). Daniel prays three times a day (Ps 55:17; Jdt 9:1) "toward Jerusalem" (*m. Ber.* 4.5).

Like Nebuchadnezzar before him, Darius shows sincere concern for Daniel's wellbeing. Still, like Cyrus in Bel, Darius comes across as a weakling, who lacks the capacity to resist his own advisors and is easily manipulated.

6:19–28. In the end, it is not Darius but the God of Israel who rescues Daniel. The legend ends, like the one in chapter 4, with a doxology (6:26–27), which again takes the form of an edict sent "to all peoples" (v. 25; cf. 4:1), in which the king confesses the supremacy of the God of Daniel.

The quasi-martyrdom of Daniel enjoyed great popularity with later interpreters (1 Macc 2:60; Heb 11:33–34).

II. The Apocalyptic Visions (7:1–12:13)

A. The Vision of the Four Beasts and the Son of Man (7:1–28)

Placed at the center of the book of Daniel, ch. 7 serves as the transition from chs. 1–6, the first part, to chs. 7–12, the second part of the book (see Introduction). Speaking in the first person, Daniel relates the first of his three end-time visions (the first vision is in ch. 7, the second in ch. 8, and the third in chs. 10–12). From now on, the book's main topic is no longer the life of Daniel and his companions in the Diaspora but God's eschatological plan for Israel. According to its literary genre, narrative voice, and content, ch. 7 marks a clear shift from the didactic court tales in the first to the apocalyptic visions in the latter half of the book.

All the while, Dan 7 has several close links with the six preceding chapters. Indeed, the parallels are so obvious that they must be considered intentional. Like chs. 2–6, for example, ch. 7 is written in Aramaic, and the shift back to Hebrew only occurs with ch. 8. The affinities are especially close between Dan 2 and 7. Both stories include a dream interpretation that revolves around the division of history into four kingdoms: in Dan 7, the *lion* represents the Neo-Babylonian, the *bear* the Median, the *leopard* the Persian, and the *beast* the Greek empire. The fourth kingdom is the fiercest and most destructive. The eleventh horn in 7:8 and 7:11–12 (see also 8:9) clearly refers to Antiochus IV Epiphanes (175–164 BCE; see the account about him in 1 Macc 1:16–28), the focal point of the vision. Daniel 7 is also linked to ch. 4 (the description of the first beast in 7:4 refers back to Nebuchadnezzar's madness in 4:33), as well as to ch. 5 (through Belshazzar, who is mentioned in 5:1 and 7:1). Since the first half of the book predates the visions, Daniel's initial vision is an appropriation of the four kingdom schema already introduced in Dan 2 in light of the persecutions under Antiochus.

7:1–8. Daniel's nocturnal Vision of the Four Beasts is dated to "the first year of King Belshazzar" (7:1). However, Belshazzar already died at the end of chapter 5 (5:30). Chapter 7 thus begins a new chronological sequence: 8:1, the third year of Belshazzar; 9:1, the first year of Darius; 10:1, the third year of Cyrus; and 11:1, the first year of Darius.

As is characteristic of all early Jewish apocalyptic visions, the Vision of the Four Beasts blends imagery from the Hebrew Bible with images from ancient Near Eastern myths. The scriptural basis for the historical scheme, including the Medes, is Isa 13:17; 21:2; Jer 51:11, 28; the motif of the four winds representing the four points of the compass (in a vision about four kingdoms!) are also found in Jer 49:36; Ezek 37:9; Zech 2:6 and 6:5; the great sea refers to the primordial ocean mentioned in Gen 7:11; Isa 51:10; and Amos 7:4 (also *4 Ezra* [2 Esd] 13:2); and references to sea monsters are found in Isa 27:1; 51:9; Ps 74:13–14; and Job 41:1 (for composite creatures in general see also Ezek 1). As for the ancient Near Eastern background of Dan 7, some have found allusions to the Babylonian creation epic *Enuma Elish*, in which Marduk defeats the sea monster Tiamat, while others point to Canaanite mythological imagery, and specifically to the myths from Ugarit, in which Baal, the storm god, overpowers Yam, the sea god. Most significantly, ancient mythology here supplies the imagery for the final sequence of world history. The current persecutions under Antiochus, which mark the beginning of history's final installment, conjure up images of the primordial conflict.

7:9–14. The blend of biblical and ancient Near Eastern images continues into the next section, Daniel's Vision of the Heavenly Throne Room, in which Antiochus, the blasphemous little horn, is put to death and eternal governance is given to the "one like a human being." The scene as a whole is reminiscent of the heavenly assembly of gods in ancient Near Eastern texts (see also Ps 82; Job 1), though the parallels are particularly striking with the Ugaritic texts, in which El, the supreme god, also known as the "the eternal" and "father of years," sits on the throne to preside over the divine council.

Daniel sees God sitting on his throne, with wheels of burning fire. Once again, the scene combines diverse motifs from Isa 6; Ezek 1; 10; and *1 En* 14 (for fire in association with a theophany, the "appearance of God," see also Exod 24:17; Deut 4:24). God is surrounded by the ministering angels (Dan 10:20–21; Deut 33:2; 1 Kgs 22:19; *1 En* 1:9; 71:8, 13). The extreme arrogance of the *little horn* (similarly 5:2–3, 30) is here contrasted with the righteousness of the "one like a human being," lit. the "son of man." The identity of the son of man is never disclosed. Within the narrative logic of the book, the son of man is most likely a heavenly agent, possibly the archangel Michael (10:13, 21; 12:1). Early Jewish interpreters understood "son of man" to be a messianic title (*4 Ezra* [2 Esd] 13:3; *1 En* 46:1; 62:14). Similarly, in the Gospels, "Son of Man" is a Christological title of Jesus (Mark 2:27; Matt 8:20; 18:11; et al.).

7:15–28. Greatly disturbed by what he saw in his dream (2:1; 4:5), Daniel, whose ability to interpret the dreams of others set him apart in chs. 1–6, is now in need of an interpreter himself (note the visions in Zech 1–6). The anonymous interpreting angel (perhaps Gabriel, see Dan 8:16) explains that dominion will be given to "the holy ones of the Most High" (7:18, 27). This could be a reference to the angelic host (*1 En* 14:22–23). Alternatively, it could designate the persecuted Jews (the list of Antiochus' offenses in vv. 19–27 supports this reading), or, more narrowly interpreted, "the holy ones" could be the circle of Jews that produced the book. In any case, Daniel is terrified by the angelic announcement, but keeps the matter in his mind (cf. 8:27; 12:4; Gen 37:11; Luke 2:19).

B. The Vision of the Ram and the He-Goat (8:1–27)

8:1–2. In ch. 8, the book reverts to Hebrew. Daniel's Vision of the Ram and the Goat follows directly on the heels of the Vision of the Four Beasts in ch. 7, and the two visions are closely connected. Indeed, the latter is set only two years after the former (see dates in 7:1 and 8:1), and in its opening verse Daniel, who is still speaking in the first person, explicitly refers back to the vision "that had appeared to me at first." Both chapters have a similar literary structure (date formula, vision report, interpretation by the angel, and Daniel's bewilderment) and largely overlap, as both predict the downfall of Antiochus IV Epiphanes, the "little horn" (7:8, 11; 8:9–12, 22–25). And yet, ch. 8 is considerably more specific in its reference to Antiochus' tyrannical behavior.

8:3–14. The apocalyptic beasts of ch. 7 have been replaced by two domestic animals. The two horns of the ram represent the empire of the Medes and of the Persians, the great horn of the goat represents Alexander the Great, who in 323 BCE suddenly died, "at the height of its power" (8:7), and the "four prominent horns" represent the Diadochi, i.e., the four generals who succeeded Alexander. All of this culminates in the description of Antiochus' defilement of the Jerusalem Temple (8:9–12; the same events are told in greater detail in 1 Macc 1:54–61). In his arrogance,

Antiochus "grew as high as the host of heaven," an allusion to Isaiah's song (Isa 14:12–15), in which the prophet taunts a Babylonian king (2 Macc 9:9–10). According to 7:14, the desolation of the Temple will last 1,150 days, roughly the length of the three-and-a-half years in 7:25; 9:27; and 12:7 (1 Macc 4:52–54).

8:15–27. Whereas the heavenly interpreter in 7:16 remained anonymous, Daniel now learns that the name of the interpreting angel, is "Gabriel," meaning "man of God" (or, possibly, "God is my warrior"). The name is a play on his description in 8:15 as having "the appearance of a man" (v. 15; repeated in 9:21 in the phrase "the man Gabriel"). Gabriel (8:16; 9:21; also Luke 1:11, 19, 26; 2:9) and Michael (10:13, 21; 12:1) are the only two angels in the Hebrew Bible with proper names (*1 En* 9:1; 20:5, 7).

Gabriel explains that "the vision is for the time of the end" (8:17, repeated in 8:19, likely modeled after Hab 2:3; see also 9:26; 11:27, 35, 40; 12:4, 9, 13). This could mean that the defeat of Antiochus will usher in the end of history in general, but it is more likely that "the time of the end" here refers specifically to the end of Antiochus' oppressive reign. The point of the vision, then, would be to provide the persecuted community with the assurance that Antiochus' fate has already been sealed in heaven.

Gabriel's interpretation of Antiochus' reign in 8:23–25 is a good example of an *ex eventu* prophecy, that is, an after-the-fact "prophecy": the biblical author "predicts" events that have already happened in the past or are currently unfolding. This includes Antiochus' surprise attack on Jerusalem (8:25, "without warning he shall destroy many"; cf. 1 Macc 1:29–30) and Antiocus' blasphemous behavior (8:25, "he shall even rise up against the Prince of princes," a reference to God). But the author errs in his prediction of the tyrant's death in 164 BCE (see also 11:45), when he claims that Antiochus died "not by human hands" (8:25; an allusion to Zech 4:6). Such an error on the part of the author is helpful for the modern interpreter, since it shows that the vision was written while Antiochus was still alive.

The announcement of Antiochus' imminent death provides little relief for Daniel, who falls sick (8:26) and, even after his recovery, remains dismayed and bewildered (8:27; cf. 7:28). Daniel's strong, even physical, reaction and his lack of understanding, made explicit again in 12:8, have important implications for an understanding of the apocalypse. It shrouds the book in a veil of mystery and preserves the sense of secrecy characteristic of this literature (see Overview).

C. Daniel's Prayer (9:1–27)

Daniel's prayer in ch. 9 interrupts the sequence of visions in the second, apocalyptic part of the book of Daniel and clearly stands out in several ways. What distresses Daniel now is not a vision but what he "perceived in the books" (9:2), namely Jeremiah's prophecy that the devastation of Jerusalem would last seventy years. Also, Gabriel does not assist Daniel with an angelic interpretation of a symbolic dream vision but instead talks about the events of the end time. Jeremiah's prophecy serves as his point of departure, though it is hardly interpreted in detail like the dreams in the previous chapters. Most strikingly, Daniel's lengthy prayer is a penitential prayer whose Deuteronomic language is strangely at odds with its apocalyptic context.

9:1–3. The chapter begins with a date formula (1:1; 2:1; 7:1; 8:1; 10:1). On Darius the Mede, see the commentary on 5:31 (he is mentioned again in 11:1). Ahasuerus is Xerxes, King of Persia (485–465 BCE), son and successor of Darius I, also not a Mede (cf. Ezra 4:5–6).

The scene begins when Daniel reads Jeremiah's seventy-year prophecy (Jer 25:11–12; 29:10; see also Zech 1:12; like Daniel, 2 Chr 36:20–22 also explicitly refers to Jeremiah); that is, Daniel "perceived" (9:2, NRSV) the number of years. The Hebrew, *binoti*, literally means "understood" (cf. 10:1). For Daniel, there is nothing unclear about Jeremiah's prophecy, he therefore does not ask for an interpretation. In a sense, it is precisely because he understands Jeremiah's promise of restoration (Jer 29:10–14) that he responds in prayer.

9:4–19. Daniel's penitential prayer, a communal confession of Israel's sin, consists of the initial confession (vv. 4–10), followed by an acknowledgment of divine justice (vv. 11–14, Daniel confesses that Israel has suffered what Moses had already predicted), and a plea for mercy (vv. 15–19). The theology of Daniel's prayer is Deuteronomic: it is predicated on the notion that the desolation of the Temple is the result of Israel's sin, and that, if Israel repents, God will forgive. Such penitential prayers are common in post-exilic literature (Ezra 9:6–15; Neh 1:5–11; 9:5–37; Bar 1:15–2:19; and the Prayer of Azariah), but Daniel's prayer seems strangely out of context here.

Interpreters who have questioned the authenticity of Daniel's prayer point out that its deterministic, apocalyptic understanding of history stands in conflict with the Deuteronomic notion that penitence can alter the course of historical events. They also observe that the Hebrew of the prayer is smooth and Deuteronomic and lacks the Aramaisms we find in the rest of Dan 8–12. Those who argue in favor of the text's unity observe that the prayer is linked to its context by several key words (e.g., *desolation* in vv. 17 and 27) and that Daniel's penitence is a direct response to his reading of Jeremiah. It is likely that the author of Daniel adopted a traditional prayer and integrated it into his book.

9:20–27. Gabriel (see 8:16) arrives and, rather than interpreting Jeremiah's prophecy, asks Daniel to consider the following "vision" (9:23) about future events. Gabriel's historical scheme is based on the revocalization of the Hebrew text. Jeremiah's number of "seventy" (Heb.: *shiv'im*) years, Gabriel explains, really means seventy "weeks" (Heb.: *shavu'im)* of years, i.e., 490 years, a periodization of time based on the jubilee year (Lev 25). The time of Jerusalem's destruction has been predetermined by God.

During this time, an "anointed prince" (v. 25; Heb.: *mashiah)* will come, a reference either to the governor Zerubbabel or to Joshua the high priest (Zech 3–4; Ezra 3:2). The "anointed" (Heb.: *mashiah*) in v. 26 who will be assassinated is most likely the high priest Onias, who was murdered in 171 BCE (also 11:22; 2 Macc 4:30–34). The violent prince in v. 26, finally, is Antiochus. He is responsible for "an abomination that desolates" (v. 27; 11:31; 12:11; also 1 Macc 1:54–58; 2 Macc 6:1–5), the incident during which Antiochus put pagan altar stones on the altar in the Temple.

D. The Final Revelation (10:1–12:13)

Daniel's final revelation in chs. 10–12 regarding the last days, the longest unit in the book, recounts in considerable detail the course of Hellenistic history as inscribed in "the book of truth"

(10:21). The vision takes the form of a prophetic commissioning, which is to be recorded in a book but has to remain secret and sealed "until the time of the end" (12:9; *1 En* 14–15). The vision is clearly structured: an anonymous angel appears (10:1–9) and speaks of a celestial battle between Michael and the princes of Persia and Greece (10:10–11:1). He then gives a historical "preview" from the Persian and Hellenistic rulers down to Antiochus IV Epiphanes (11:2–45). The vision ends with a prediction of the resurrection of the dead (12:1–3) and the book's epilogue (12:5–12), which is framed by the final address to Daniel (12:4, 13).

10:1–9. The unit begins with a date formula (the "third year of King Cyrus of Persia," 536 BCE) and the note that the vision concerns "a great conflict"; the celestial (10:10–11:1) and terrestrial (11:2–45) warfare are two sides of the same conflict. 10:2–4 describe the setting of the vision. Daniel prepares himself through mourning and fasting (*4 Ezra* [2 Esd] 5:13, 20; 6:35; *2 Bar* 9:1; 12:5; et al.). While standing along a river (already in 8:2; also Ezek 1:1–3), Daniel sees a man—possibly Gabriel—whose appearance is like that of an angel (Ezek 1:4–14; 9:2–3; Rev 1:13–16; see also the birth of Noah in the *Genesis Apocryphon* from Qumran), though only Daniel can see him (10:7; Acts 9:7).

10:10–11:1. The angel explains that he has come to Daniel to help him understand what will befall Israel "at the end of days" (10:14; however, see 12:8). He speaks of a celestial conflict between the angelic princes that is currently raging, in which each prince represents a nation: the "prince of Persia" and the "prince of Greece" are fighting against Michael, the warrior and defender of Israel (12:1; *1 En* 9:1; Rev 12:7; see also the *War Scroll* from Qumran).

11:2–45. Whereas the angelic description of the war in heaven remains somewhat sketchy, his after-the-fact "prophecy" about the current earthly conflict is much more detailed and increasingly so as we approach the time of the actual author of the vision. The divine interpreter divides his account into two parts; he begins with the war between the Seleucid empire of Syria, the "king of the north," and the Ptolemaic empire of Egypt, the "king of the south" (11:2–20), and then in the second part follows the career of Antiochus IV

Epiphanes, "a contemptible person," to his death (11:21–45).

The angel begins in 11:2 with a terse reference to four kings of Persia; the fourth could be Artaxerxes I (465–424 BCE; also mentioned in Neh 2:1), or, more likely, Darius III (336–331 BCE; he is not mentioned elsewhere in the Hebrew Bible). 11:3–4 summarize the reign of Alexander the Great, the "warrior king," whose kingdom was divided after his death.

In 11:5–20 the interpreter turns to the period in between the death of Alexander (323 BCE) and the reign of Antiochus IV (175–164 BCE). The "king of the south" (11:5) is Ptolemy I Soter (323–285 BCE), founder of the Ptolemaic Kingdom in Egypt. Another of Alexander's officers, Seleucus I Nicator (358–281 BCE), founded the Seleucid Kingdom. The "alliance" in v. 6 refers to Ptolemy II Philadelphus, who married his daughter Berenice to Antiochus II; however, Berenice and her son were later murdered. 11:7–9 tells the story of Berenice's brother, Ptolemy III Euergetes (246–221 BCE), king of Egypt, who launched several campaigns against Seleucia. Then, in 11:10–13, the author refers to the sons of Seleucus II, the "king of the north" (v. 7): Seleucus III (227–223 BCE) and Antiochus III the Great (223–187 BCE). Ptolemy IV Philopator (221–203 BCE) recaptured Seleucia in 219 BCE. 11:15–19 relate how in 200 BCE Antiochus III initially launched a campaign against Egypt and was able to capture "the beautiful land," i.e., Judea, and then went on to take control of territories in Asia Minor. He died in 187 BCE.

11:20 relates the story of Seleucus IV Philopator (187–175 BCE), successor of Antiochus III, who, according to 2 Macc 3, sent one of his officers, a certain Heliodorus, to Jerusalem to rob the Temple, where Heliodorus is repelled because of a divine intervention and converts to the God of Israel.

11:21–45. The account turns to Antiochus IV Epiphanes (175–164 BCE), successor of Seleucus IV, a "contemptible man" (11:21; cf. 1 Macc 1:10), and the "little horn" of 7:8 and 8:9. Verses 22–28 provide a quick summary of his reign. Antiochus rose to power by eliminating those who were in his way, including "the prince of the covenant" (v. 22), probably a reference to the murder of the high priest Onias III (9:26; 2 Macc 4:34–35).

11:25–28 relate how, in 170 BCE, Antiochus invaded Egypt and, on his way home, plundered the Temple in Jerusalem (1 Macc 1:20; 2 Macc 5:11–21). In 168 BCE, 11:29–30 reports, Antiochus moved again against Egypt, but this time was repelled by the *ships of Kittim* (v. 30; the term is derived from Citium, a city on Cyprus, and used here and in the scrolls from Qumran as a designation for Rome). In frustration, he turns against the Jerusalem Temple.

In 11:31–39 Antiochus desecrated the Temple (2 Macc 5:23–27), abolished the daily offerings (9:27; 1 Macc 1:54), and "set up the abomination that makes desolate" (see comment on 9:27). He tried to "seduce" (v. 32; 1 Macc 2:17–22) some Hellenizing Jews but was opposed by the faithful. One of the resisting groups is referred to as "the wise" (11:33–35; 12:3). Their task is to instruct others, presumably in their resistance, and among them will be found the first martyrs in Jewish history (v. 35; 1 Macc 1:31–38, 54–64; 2 Macc 6:11; 7:1–41). Unlike the Maccabees, however, "the wise" do not appear to have propagated the use of violence. Some modern interpreters argue that the book of Daniel stems from the circle of "the wise."

Antiochus grew exceedingly arrogant, rejecting "the gods of his ancestors" (v. 37), imposing the worship of Zeus Olympios instead (2 Macc 6:2), and paying no respect to the god "beloved by women" (v. 37), the Mesopotamian god Tammuz (Ezek 8:14). In 11:40–45, the after-the-fact "prophecy" switches to become genuine, albeit erroneous, prophecy. The biblical author predicts that Antiochus will die in a cataclysmic battle "at the time of the end" (v. 40; Ezek 38–39; see also the *War Scroll* from Qumran). The inaccuracy of the predictions implies that the author was composing his account while Antiochus was still alive, i.e., between 167 and 164 BCE (other legendary accounts of Antiochus' end are found in 1 Macc 6:1–17; 2 Macc 1:14–16; and 2 Macc 9:1–29).

12:1–4. The last chapter opens with a judgment scene, not unlike 7:10. Michael, the protector of Israel (8:15–16; 10:13), "shall arise" (v. 1), presumably in the divine assembly, to advocate for those "found written in the book" (v. 1). The book (10:21) keeps a record of those destined for life (Exod 32:32–33; Isa 4:3; Rev 20:12, 15), though it may not include everybody but "many of those who sleep in the dust" (v. 2). Earlier prophets have used resurrection language metaphorically for the rebirth of Israel (Isa 26:19; Ezek 37). In Dan 12:1–3, however, one finds the first unambiguous expression of the belief in the physical resurrection of the individual, a belief that became central in both Judaism and Christianity. "The wise" (see 11:33–35) are singled out; they will "shine ... like the stars," that is, assume a quasi-angelic status (8:10; Mark 12:25; *1 En* 104). Daniel is advised, once again (8:26), to keep the revelation a secret.

12:5–13. The book's epilogue includes a final vision, though it is not formally introduced as a new unit. Daniel sees two individuals, presumably angels, standing by a river, their hands raised in a gesture of swearing (Deut 32:40; Rev 10:5–6). The angels offer several schedules for the advent of the end, which is imminent: three and a half years (7:25; 9:27; and 12:7; compare the 1,150 days in 8:14), 1,290 days (12:11), and 1,335 days (12:12). The exact meaning of the dates remains obscure, and, understandably, Daniel remains confused (12:8). Since the number of days increases, it may be that, once the previous prediction had proven to be wrong, a higher number was added. The book ends with the promise to Daniel that he will be included in the resurrection.

BIBLIOGRAPHY

J. J. Collins. *Daniel, With an Introduction to Apocalyptic Literature.* FOTL 20 (Grand Rapids: Eerdmans, 1984); _____. *Daniel.* Hermeneia (Minneapolis: Fortress, 1993); J. E. Goldingay. *Daniel.* WBC 30 (Dallas: Word Books, 1989); M. Henze. *The Madness of King Nebuchadnezzar* (Leiden: Brill, 1999); G. W. E. Nickelsburg. "Apocalyptic Texts." *Encyclopedia of the Dead Sea Scrolls.* L. H. Schiffman and J. C. VanderKam, eds. (New York: Oxford University Press, 2000) 29–35; _____. *Jewish Literature between the Bible and the Mishnah.* 2nd ed. (Minneapolis: Fortress Press, 2005); C. Rowland. *The Open Heaven: A Study of Apocalyptic in Judaism and Early Christianity* (New York: Crossroad, 1982); C. L. Seow. *Daniel.* Westminster Bible Companion (Louisville: Westminster John Knox, 2003); E. Ulrich. *The Dead Sea Scrolls and the Origins of the Bible* (Grand Rapids: Eerdmans, 1999); L. M. Wills. *The Jewish Novel in the Ancient World* (Ithaca and London: Cornell University Press, 1995).

HOSEA

BETH L. TANNER

OVERVIEW

The book of Hosea is the first of the twelve minor prophets. The title of "minor" is not a measure of significance but of length. Like many of the Minor Prophets, the message of the book of Hosea is powerful and moving. Among all the prophetic books, Hosea is predated only by the book of Amos. Its origin lies in the northern kingdom, Israel, before its destruction in 722 BCE, so it stands as a reflection on a great loss that changed the fortunes of both Israel and Judah forever.

The Hebrew text of the book is difficult with multiple differences between Hebrew and early Greek manuscripts. This situation accounts for the significant differences among contemporary English translations; but, although the translation of individual lines varies, the overall message of the book remains clear.

The text was edited early in its history, possibly in Judah after the destruction of Israel and again after the exile in 586 BCE. The process by which the book grew testifies to the fact that these words spoke to communities of the faithful long after Hosea's prophetic mission to Israel ended.

Everything known about Hosea is contained in verse 1:1, which reports his father's name as "Beeri" and the kings who reigned when he was active as a prophet. It is curious his work is identified with only one northern king, Jeroboam II (786–746), but four Judean kings (approximately 750 until 698). These southern kings could have been added when the book was brought to Jerusalem after 722 to make the point that all Hosea said came to pass, but this suggestion is far from certain. Because of the unusual way Hosea's activity is reported, an exact date of his prophetic activity is impossible to pinpoint, but it was probably near the end of Jeroboam II's reign until sometime before the Assyrian invasion in 722. This period reflects great changes in Israel's history; from a time of independence and peace, through the rise of the powerful Assyrians when Israel becomes a vassal state, and finally up until the destruction of the northern cites and scattering of the people (2 Kgs 15:1–17:41).

Hosea's prophecies are directed at Israel and Ephraim. Ephraim is often a synonym for Israel, but it also is a specific region that consists of the heart or center of Israel, including its major cities and worship centers. Indeed, if the cities mentioned in Hosea are plotted on a map, they run in a line almost up the middle of the country, which means he is prophesying to the geographic, economic, and religious heart of Israel.

One of the greatest controversies concerning the book is Hosea's marriage (chs. 1–3). Hosea 1:2 reports that God told Hosea to "go, take for yourself a wife of whoredom." Scholars and the faithful alike have struggled to decide if this command is an actual command from God or if its language is symbolic. While the debate still continues, a reading of the full verse is enlightening, "go, take for yourself a wife of whoredom and have children of whoredom, for the land commits great whoredom by forsaking the LORD." It seems anyone who lives in God's promised land is involved in the same "great whoredom" against the Lord. In other words, the unfaithfulness includes all of the people, not just one particular woman. No matter whom Hosea marries, the woman would be part of this broken system. Indeed, Israel's unfaithfulness to God is the primary theological theme of the entire book. The book of Hosea describes the people's forsaking of the Lord in terms that are designed to demonstrate the pain in the heart of God, even as the judgment falls.

OUTLINE

I. Superscription (1:1)

II. Israel Goes After Other Gods (1:2–5:7)

    A. Report of Hosea's Prophetic Acts (1:2–11)

    B. Second Prophetic Act (2:1–13)

    C. Restored Relationship (2:14–23)

    D. A Future for Unfaithful Israel (3:1–5)

    E. God's Indictment (4:1–19)

    F. God's Coming Judgment (5:1–7)

493

III. Israel Has Turned from God and Places Trust in Other Nations (5:8–7:16)

    A. Announcement of Exile (5:8–15)

    B. Call for Repentance (6:1–3)

    C. God's Agony (6:4–7:10)

    D. Lament over Israel (7:11–16)

IV. Israel Has Broken the Covenant (8:1–13:16)

    A. Broken Covenant (8:1–14)

    B. The Coming Exile (9:1–17)

    C. Israel Depends Only on Israel (10:1–15)

    D. God's Broken Heart (11:1–11)

    E. Sin that Stretches Back to the Ancestors (12:1–13:16)

V. A Final Plea to Return (14:1–8)

VI. Later Wisdom Addition (14:9)

DETAILED ANALYSIS

I. Superscription (1:1)

Verse 1 provides the only information given about Hosea. It orients the reader to the historical period during which Hosea prophesied but offers no information on Hosea the person. The absence of such information reminds readers that the point of the book is not to present information about Hosea, but to convey the words of the Lord contained in this book.

II. Israel Goes After Other Gods (1:2–5:7)

The first major section is set against a background of Canaanite religion generally and the fertility cult specifically. This religion was the greatest rival to the worship of Yahweh in preexilic times (see 1 and 2 Kings). Baal was the storm and fertility god, and most myths and rituals associated with him centered on fertility. Fertility of the land was of central importance to people who scratched out a living in arid lands. Canaanite religion included the practice of cultic imitation where human sexual acts were part of the ritual believed to cause Baal to mate with his consort bringing the rains necessary for the crops to grow. The references to prostitution or whoredom in Hosea are in response to these Baal rituals. The metaphor operates on two levels. The first condemns the ritual act of sexual encounter (Hos 4:11–19), and the second symbolizes the central metaphor of broken relationship experienced by God as the people turn to Baal, other gods, and other nations. The people have broken their covenant promises to God by turning to the fertility cults. This prophetic word is vivid and shocking and meant to get the attention of the people in the strongest way possible.

A. Report of Hosea's Prophetic Acts (1:2–11)

This opening section is not an oracle, but a report of God's instructions to Hosea concerning his wife and children. As noted in the Overview, Hosea does not necessarily marry a prostitute. All of the people of Israel are unfaithful (v. 1:2). Verses 3–9 narrate the birth of Hosea and Gomer's three children; each is given a name that reflects God's anger at the people: *Jezreel* signifying the place where Jehu slaughtered two other kings in a coup (2 Kgs 9:14–29); *Lo-ruhamah* meaning "not pitied"; and *Lo-ammi* meaning "not my people." Symbolic names are common during this period; these reflect God's message to the people. The chosen people of God are reminded that because of their unfaithfulness they are no longer God's children.

Without any transition, vv. 10 and 11 report the eventual restoration of the people using imagery similar to promises made to Abraham (Gen 22:17). In addition, v. 11 tells of a time when the north and the south will be reunited under one king (1 Kgs 4:20). It is the hope of a future restoration as "You are not my people" become "children of the living God" (v. 10). Just as Hosea's children will pass from memory so will the time of Israel's exile from God.

B. Second Prophetic Act (2:1–13)

There may be no more shocking words in the entire Bible than here. If read literally, its language is violent. It treats women as property that can be abused and imprisoned, and children as something that can be discarded (vv. 2–7). However, what is clear by vv. 8–11 is that the mother and wife here is not Gomer, but Israel. The oracle begins with sympathy for the betrayed spouse and anger toward the wayward Gomer; but, beginning at v. 8, Hosea's audience is the unfaithful spouse and God is the one crying out in sorrow and anger. The poetry evokes the intense feelings and then turns those feelings into a powerful lesson about God's love. The image works as well today as it did in ancient days, for most people know the deep pain of being betrayed by those with whom we share the most intimate of relationships. Hosea's words illumine the sort of feeling that God must have had when dealing with a disobedient Israel. God does not automatically punish all who stray, but exists in a loving and committed relationship that is often very painful to both parties.

C. Restored Relationship (2:14–23)

Just as ch. 1 transposed judgment and hope, vv. 14–23 depict a God who will indeed have a change of heart toward wayward Israel, and the loving relationship will be restored with a new covenant (v. 18). Today it is hard to imagine that a betrayed spouse would choose to enter into a new covenant of love, but in ancient times this act would have been unbelievable. The price for adultery was death (Lev 20:10–11). This shocking chapter also attests to God's great capacity for love and grace toward the people who have transgressed to the point of receiving a sentence of death. The chapter takes a reader from sympathy and judgment to a conviction of his or her own sin and a hope of restoration—all in twenty-three verses.

D. A Future for Unfaithful Israel (3:1–5)

God again speaks to Hosea telling him to marry an unfaithful woman because "the LORD loves the people of Israel" even though they follow other gods. The message here is the same as ch. 2. Israelites will lose their independence because of their unfaithfulness (vv. 1–4) but will be restored by God in the future (v. 5). The point is not to speculate on the identity of the woman but to realize this is a metaphor for God's own hurt when God's people break the covenant relationship.

E. God's Indictment (4:1–19)

This oracle was created in the form of a lawsuit that God brings against the people (v. 1). Hosea contends that the elders have no loyalty to God

and are not teaching the next generation; as a result, there is no knowledge of God among the young (vv. 6, 13, 14). The priest and the prophets have failed in their responsibilities to teach the people to remain faithful to God (vv. 4–10). As a result, all of creation suffers (v. 3).

Verses 11–19 should be understood as a response to Canaanite fertility rituals. They took place at sacred places on mountains (v. 13), were marked with wooden idols (v. 12), and sexual intercourse was part of the ritual (vv. 13–14, 17–18). These acts were an abomination to God, not only because they involved sexual behavior but because they were a complete abandonment of the covenant and a violation of the commandment to "love the LORD your God with all your heart, and with all your soul, and with all your might" (Deut 6:5). The people have shown they do not trust God to bring the rains that allow life to continue. They would rather consult "a piece of wood" (v. 12). Others may worship multiple gods, but Israel was to venerate only Yahweh.

F. God's Coming Judgment (5:1–7)

This pronouncement is chilling. It opens by calling on the priests, kings, and others to hear the proclamation (v. 1). Hope is lost as Hosea declares God's message that "their deeds do not permit them to return to their God" (v. 4). When Israel turns and seeks the Lord, the Lord will not be found (v. 6). The betrayal is too great, and God has finally left the people to their own devices. Verse 7 matches ch. 1, since Israel, just like Hosea, has birthed a generation of illegitimate children, illegitimate because they do not even know enough to realize their actions are wrong. This first section ends with the verdict delivered. God has finally turned away.

III. Israel Has Turned from God and Places Trust in Other Nations (5:8–7:16)

The next major section has a specific historical referent. As the Assyrians became more and more of a threat, Israel was forced to pay heavy tribute (2 Kgs 15:19) and became a vassal state to them. Seeing the Assyrian threat grow stronger, Pekah, Israel's king, joined with Remaliah of Syria to form a coalition to remove the threat. Judah wanted no part in this coalition. In 735 BCE, Pekah and Remaliah sent an army to attack Jerusalem to remove the king and force Judah to join the coalition (2 Kgs 16:1–5). This is known as the Syro-Ephraimite war. Judah turned to Assyria for help against this coalition, and the result was that both Syria and Israel were destroyed by 722 and Judah became a vassal state of Assyria, paying heavy tribute as had the Israelites (2 Kgs 15:7–17:41). In these chapters, the focus is not on going after other gods but after other nations.

A. Announcement of Exile (5:8–15)

This oracle opens with a cry of alarm moving through the heart of Israel from the far south to the north (vv. 1–2). The blowing of the *shofar* signals either a festival or an alarm, and in this case it is the announcement of the Lord's judgment on the people. Verses 8–9 deal with Israel, and in v. 10 Judah is also condemned. Reference to a "landmark" (v. 10) may reflect God's two countries—Israel and Judah—fighting each other. God is not sending punishment for the sake of punishment but so the relationship can be restored (v. 15). The horn blast is not a call to arms and war, but a call to return to God.

B. Call for Repentance (6:1–3)

The speaker changes from God to one of God's people, probably the prophet who calls on "us" to return to God. The plea offers one last opportunity to prevent the coming armies by making an about-face to the Lord. Verse 2 refers back to the fertility cults attested in ch. 3. In Canaanite mythology, the god Baal rises up from the world of the dead to bring the needed rain. The prophet is warning that there will be a time of alienation from God because of the people's actions, but God will not abandon them forever and will soon come with the needed rains that will revive the lives of the people.

C. God's Agony (6:4–7:10)

God's voice returns with questions of bewilderment in v. 4, "what shall I do with you?" Verse 6 echoes other passages in which God explains that what God desires from the people is not ritual and sacrifice, but love and faithfulness (Isa 1:10–17; Ps 51:17; Mic 6:6–8). God does not have a problem with ritual itself, but with ritual that is done only for the sake of ritual. Verses 7–11 tell the tale of how the people have responded

to God's love, and the focus again is on a broken covenant. The multiple geographic references, as in previous texts, demonstrate that all of the land of promise is under indictment and, also, that the problem is ongoing, since Adam is the site where Israel first crossed into the promised land (Josh 3:16). The people are compared to a burning fire, a fire that destroys all the rulers (7:7), which is probably a reference to the succession of kings who were murdered by military officers as the country fell into a state of anarchy at the end of Israel's existence (2 Kgs 15–16). Hosea 7:10 summarizes Israel's behavior in this period of history. In contrast to God's questions at the beginning of the section, the speaker is probably now a narrator or the prophet. As God wonders what to do, Israelites keep right on doing the very same things they had always done, oblivious to the searching questions posed by God about their future.

D. Lament Over Israel (7:11–16)

Description of Israel's behavior turns into lament when God sees that, instead of returning to the Lord, the people turn to Egypt and Assyria to seek aid (v. 11). Verses 12–13 describe God's dilemma: the wayward people will be punished, but God's desire is to "redeem them" (v. 13). The people are in despair and cry out, but not to God even though it is God that trained them and gave them strength (vv. 14–16). Instead, they plot and turn to Egypt, and so their fate is sealed by their own acts. They turned to other gods and now to other nations, and all the while God is standing by waiting for them.

IV. Israel Has Broken the Covenant (8:1–13:16)

The final large section turns from the Syro-Ephraimite crisis to the time immediately before Israel's destruction and scattering. All of the previous themes reappear: Israel's infidelity, Israel's transgression of the covenant, Israel's turning to other nations, Israel's dependence on themselves and their institutions instead of God, and a history lesson on Israel's long pattern of disloyalty. These chapters present vivid imagery about Israel's sin and punishment. The voices alternate between description of Israel's acts and words of the heartbroken God. Even as the Assyrians approach, God is still calling the people to return.

A. Broken Covenant (8:1–14)

This chapter begins with another trumpet call (cf. 5:8). Israel has broken the covenant and ignored God's laws. They have done this by setting up rulers without consulting God (vv. 1–6). "The kings" (vv. 4, 10) are those who ruled in quick succession during the final years of the northern kingdom. The instability in government was clear. The leaders were busy grabbing power by assassination, relying on their swords instead of on God (2 Kgs 15–16). Hosea also refers to idols or calves in Samaria (vv. 5–6). Reference to a calf may imply that this generation is like the generation in the wilderness, which worshiped a calf that Aaron had made (Exod 32). Or it may allude to the calf idols that Jeroboam set up in Dan and Bethel (1 Kgs 19:16). In either case, Hosea indicts breaches of the covenant and also attests that God has continued to be loyal to the covenant even while the people continued to sin.

Verses 7–10 focus on Israel's turning to other nations. Israelites may think they are powerful, but their prosperity is like stalks of straw with no heads of grain (v. 7). Even if there was something to harvest, other nations will take it for their own (v. 7). Israel may not know it yet, but they are already under the control of other kings (v. 10).

The prophet tells the people the more altars they build, the more sin there is in the land (vv. 11–14). This does not necessarily mean that they are worshiping other gods, but that the Lord does not accept their sacrifices because sacrifice without fidelity to God and justice to neighbor is meaningless. The reference to Egypt (v. 13) is a look backward to a time when they were slaves and foreshadows what is coming. Verse 14 makes clear that Israel and Judah will suffer the same fate. They have built up their own human-made cities and fortifications instead of building up their relationship with God.

B. The Coming Exile (9:1–17)

The prophet's words continue in vv. 1–9 and return to the topic of Israel's worship. The background here is one of a festival (vv. 1, 5), probably the harvest festival of *Sukkoth* (v. 2). This is a seven-day festival, celebrating the harvest and all of its bounty, an ancient type of Thanksgiving. The sermon begins with a start (vv. 5:8, 8:1) and calls on those present to stop rejoicing (v. 1). The message—Israel's infidelity to God (v. 1)—has been prominent through the book. They will go into exile, whether to Egypt or Assyria (v. 3). Verses 4–9 interpret their celebrations as useless and their sacrifices as more like the elements at a funeral. God is coming not in a great festival but in judgment (v. 7).

God speaks in vv. 10–17; the words are even harsher than those of the prophet. Verse 10 moves from tender beginnings to Israel's first encounter with Baal while still in the wilderness (Num 25). The rest of the oracle is as harsh as any words in the Bible, declaring barrenness and death for Israel's children. As in ch. 4, this oracle needs to be understood in terms of fertility religion and the veneration of Baal. The people are going to Baal to secure the fertility of the land and their future children, but it is the Lord who is the Creator (v. 10). Their acts with Baal will yield "no birth, no pregnancy, no conception" (v. 11). Even if the children live, they will die in the coming destruction and exile (v. 13). These words are as surprising as the ones in ch. 2 and are designed to shock the hard hearts of the people into changing their course.

C. Israel Depends Only on Israel (10:1–15)

Verse 1–8 are spoken by the prophet and begin positively with the image of Israel as a luxuriant vine. Verse 2 attests that, as Israelites prospered, so did their building of worship centers. What could be better? But vv. 3–4 make clear, that with the growth of the country, the people begin to depend on themselves instead of the Lord. They spend their time speaking with empty words and clogging the courts with nonsense. The signs of their prosperity will be destroyed, including the big and ornate places of worship for they have put their trust in ornate shrines instead of in God.

God's speech begins at v. 9; it offers another history lesson. The days of Gibeah refer to either the tribal war in Judg 19–21 or to its function as an important city during the time of Saul. Either way, God declares that since the very beginning Israel has violated its covenant. Verses 10–11 interpret this long history as a time when God often "spared her fair neck": now it is time for the people to work at breaking up the hard-packed soil of their hearts. Verse 12 offers an invitation for the people to sow righteousness in that hard soil. Despite their long history, God is still calling them back. Verses 13–15 depict Israel's response to God's calling. They will continue in their ways and trust not in God but in themselves, and for this they will be destroyed.

D. God's Broken Heart (11:1–11)

This chapter may be the most deeply emotional poetry in all of the prophetic literature. It presents familial imagery, this time with God as the long-suffering parent to the rebellious child Israel. As was the case with the familial imagery in the first three chapters, this poetry is also meant to create strong feelings and to show the pain of God as Israel continues to sin and turn away from the deity.

Verses 1–3 offer a reprise of God's long history with Israel, this time with the metaphor of a parent helping a young child, a metaphor that represents Israel in Egyptian slavery and in the wilderness. The prophet characterizes God as calling, teaching, leading, and feeding Israel, diction consistent with God's interactions with the people during the exodus period as God called them out of Egypt, guided them with the pillar and cloud, and fed them with manna. But even despite all of these gifts, Israel still venerated other gods.

Verses 5–7 are not unexpected since Hosea has consistently affirmed that Israel will be exiled and scattered. The reference to both Egypt and Assyria (cf. 7:11) may either signal Israel's earliest (slavery in Egypt) and final (exile to Assyria) moments or allude to the exile to Assyria and the later presence of Judahites in Egypt (Jer 43). In either case, the people will be taken by force from the promised land.

The next four verses (vv. 8–11) offer vivid insight into the very heart of God. God is in agony over the coming exile of the people. As in 6:4–10, God is having a conversation with God's self, wondering how it might be possible to punish Israel and let it become like "Admah" and "Zeboim," two cities destroyed with Sodom and Gomorrah (Deut 29:22–23). At the thought of destruction, God's heart churns as compassion and love grow within the divine breast. The image painted with words is one known to most people who have been hurt by a child. It is that sinking, hollow feeling as anger and love crash against each other in the soul of the suffering parent. This is not a God who simply punishes without remorse; leaving the people to

what they have long deserved is agonizing for God. Verse 9 summarizes the very heart of God. The great Creator king who could destroy everything with a word, uses the restraint that humans do not possess. God's power is manifest in grace and love, not in the ability to destroy. There will be a time of exile, of punishment, but this God is not a god of retribution but restoration; those sent away will come trembling back home.

E. Sin that Stretches Back to the Ancestors (12:1–13:16)

These oracles return to the theme of Israel's long history of turning away from God. Verses 1–6 open by declaring that Israel is faithless while Judah remains steadfast in its fidelity to the Lord. The prophet recounts moments in the life of their ancestor Jacob, which serve as a plea for the people to return to God and what is right (v. 6). Without missing a beat, the oracle switches to Israel's dependence on its own resources (vv. 7–8) and God's pronouncement that they will return again to living in tents (v. 9), not as a show of God's favor as in the wilderness but as a punishment for their infidelity.

Chapter 13 once again tells of God's long-suffering love for the sinful people. It begins with the people going after Baal (vv. 1–3), followed by God telling them exactly how God has cared for them, but they turn away (vv. 4–6). Consistent with the wilderness theme, God will become a wild animal and pounce on the defiant Israel with no one to come to their aid (vv. 8–13). Verse 14 presents the third instance in which God questions that which is about to happen (cf. 6:4, 11:8). Even at this late hour, God agonizes over the coming judgment. The meaning of the second half of v. 14 is ambiguous: does it mean that God has given up and summoned death and "Sheol" to swallow the people, or should it be read as God wondering when these things will come to pass? In either case, God is still struggling with the decision. Verses 15–16 offer a gruesome and realistic picture of war. Like the images of the unfaithful spouse, these images are shocking and meant to shake Israel out of its confidence in everything other than God.

V. A Final Plea to Return (14:1–8)

The prophet begins his final plea of the book with the imperative cry, "Return, O Israel!" Hosea's shocking images of betrayal and war are meant to stop Israel from what they have been doing, and lead them to ask forgiveness from the Lord (v. 2) and to renounce dependence on other nations (v. 3). It is not too late. As confirmation of the prophet's plea, God's final words offer forgiveness (vv. 4–8). God wants to heal and love Israel "freely" (v. 4). God wants to restore Israel and their land. God's final word in the moments before the destruction offer mercy. God cannot turn away, for, as the deity states, "I am God and no mortal" (11:9).

VI. Later Wisdom Addition (14:9)

This final verse is an addition from a later time. Hosea's words were delivered to a country on the brink of destruction, and in a few short years all that Hosea anticipated came to pass. When the book was brought to Judah after the destruction of Israel by the Assyrians, it ceased to be prophecy and became a lesson on what happened when the people turned away from God. This final verse encourages later generations to learn their lesson from Israel's past behavior and fate and to see the grace that God continued to offer even as the Assyrians marched into Israel.

Hosea's words are indeed shocking with images that are dangerous and powerful. Yet as shocking as they are, the images are meant to show just how radical God's love and grace really are. Hosea's words can speak today just as they did in ancient times as a call to return to the God who loves humanity instead of choosing other things that pave the way to death and destruction.

BIBLIOGRAPHY

E. Ben Zvi. *Hosea.* FOTL (Grand Rapids: Eerdmans, 2005); B. Birch. *Hosea, Joel, and Amos.* Westminster Bible Companion (Louisville: Westminster John Knox, 1997); J. Limburg. *Hosea–Micah.* Interpretation (Atlanta: John Knox, 1988); R. Patterson. "Parental love as metaphor for divine-human love." *Journal of the Evangelical Theological Society* 46.2 (June 2003) 205–216; D. Stuart. *Hosea–Jonah.* WBC 31 (Waco, Tex.: Word, 1987).

JOEL

PABLO ANDIÑACH

OVERVIEW

The name Joel ("Yahweh is God") is present in many OT texts (1 Sam 8:2; 1 Chr 5:4, 8, 12; 7:3; 27:20; also in the post-exilic community: Ezra 10:43; Neh 11:9), but none of them refers to the prophet of this book. Though the book presents minimal information about this prophet, it provides clues to the time the book was composed. The book attests to the important role that the elders and priests played in that society (1:2, 13–14; 2:16–17). They function as role models and are authoritative for the population of the city. When the prophet summons the people, the absence of any reference to a king points to a period when the monarchy no longer existed. As a result, the most probable date for the final redaction of the book is during the Persian period (539–333 BCE).

As part of the Book of the Twelve, Joel sits between Hosea and Amos, probably because of the continuity of expressions (4:16 with Amos 1:2). The NT includes many quotations from Joel, especially in apocalyptic texts. Matthew 24:29 quotes 2:10 and alludes to 2:31 (also Mark 13:24–25; Luke 21:25). Paul quotes 2:32 in Rom 10:13 as proof that salvation is given to all who invoke the name of God. There is a long list of citations in Revelation (6:12–13, 17; 8:7, 12; 9:7–9; 14:5, 8; 19:15; 22:1). The most important quotation is Joel 2:28–32, which is found in the words of Peter during the feast of Pentecost in Jerusalem (Acts 2:14–36); he interprets the text as a prophecy fulfilled in that moment. These references show that Jews in the first century were awaiting a realization of the promises in the book. The book's structure orients readers to its message. The prologue (1:2–4) announces a tragedy of such magnitude that it will be remembered for many generations. The next section describes a locust plague, but there are some hints that lead the reader to think of an army invasion (v. 6). Reference to the Day of the Lord, a theme that will grow in importance as the book develops, first appears (v. 15). The devastation of nature follows the pattern of a military invasion, as it is built on the description of hungry locusts (2:1–11), which attack Jerusalem in a way that resembles a professional and well-trained army. The first major section of the book ends when the people are summoned to call upon God and ask for compassion, and where they are called to return with sincerity to the Lord (2:12–17).

The call of the people presented in the first part receives a response in the following section (2:18–3:17). Joel 2:18–27 declares the promise of God to restore everything that was destroyed by the army/locust invasion: food, peace, and cult (v. 27). The desolation will be transformed into fertility and prosperity. The next unit (2:28–32) describes the blessings promised by God to the whole people, especially those who are marginalized and poor, and concludes with the promise of liberation forever from foreign domination (3:17). The end of 2:18–3:17 provides the answer to the call in the book's first section. However, the scope of the text has broadened—from an initial reference to a locust plague to the judgment of the oppressed nations (3:19). The epilogue that closes the book describes a new situation created by the intervention of God.

OUTLINE

I. Prologue: The Tragedy (1:1–4)

II. The People Call to God (1:5–2:17)

    A. Summoning the People (1:5–14)

    B. Devastation of the Land (1:15–20)

    C. Military Invasion (2:1–11)

    D. Asking for Mercy (2:12–17)

III. God's Answer (2:18–3:17)

    A. Restoration of Life (2:18–27)

    B. Promise of the Spirit (2:28–32)

    C. God's Judgment (3:1–17)

IV. Epilogue: God's Justice (3:18–21)

DETAILED ANALYSIS

I. Prologue: The Tragedy (1:1–4)

The prologue announces an extraordinary event that grabs readers' attention. Many imperative verbs appear together in vv. 2–3: "hear," "give ear," "tell." They create a dramatic expectation for something that has not yet been revealed. The reader has to reach v. 4 to understand that there has been a powerful invasion of locusts. It is described using a formula that is repeated: what one left, another has eaten. The poetry presents a nightmarish scenario.

The locusts are mentioned with four different names, probably referring to the insect's life cycle. But the contemporary reader senses that the ancient audience does not encounter an ecological and short-lived disaster—one which occurs periodically and is followed by renewal—but instead confronts a great tragedy that needs to be remembered and recorded because nothing like it has ever happened. The prophet is certain that, even in the future, nothing comparable will take place.

II. The People Call to God (1:5–2:17)

A. Summoning the People (1:5–14)

This unit is made up of four stanzas headed by imperative verbs and addressed to different sectors of the population. The first (vv. 5–7) begins with "wake up" and is addressed to the drunkards. These are the drinkers who will wake up to discover that there is no more wine for them. This theme permits the reader to see—even if it is not explicit—that the absence of wine will affect ritual activities in the Temple. The second stanza (vv. 8–10) begins with "lament" and is addressed to the wife who cries for the lost husband of her youth. This widow, who symbolizes those who have survivied the disaster, will no longer receive the love that she deserves. In the next stanza (vv. 11–12), the farmers and vinedressers are called to lament and wail for the tragedy. Four verbs in v. 12 derive from the same Hebrew root with the meaning "to be dry." This diction reveals that the experience reflected in this text is a drought in which the temperature and the lack of moisture have killed not only crops but all plants. The final stanza addresses the priests with many imperative verbs: "put on sackcloth," "lament," "wail," "sanctify," "call," "gather." The text emphasizes that the priests are responsible for the destiny of the people.

B. Devastation of the Land (1:15–20)

The text opens with the announcement that the Day of the Lord is imminent. Next come five stanzas in which the victims of this tragedy are listed. In the first place are the people and the Temple (v. 16). Then come crops and plants (v. 17), and after these the cattle (v. 18). Verses 19–20 mention pastures, trees, wild animals, and streams. This gradual buildup in the description of all that is being destroyed demonstrates that the disaster affects all known reality. It is important to note that there is no reference to locusts in this unit.

C. Military Invasion (2:1–11)

The description of the army—using imagery inspired by a plague of locusts and by the consequences of a long drought—provides the literary context for developing the theme of judgment on the oppressor nations in the next part of the book (2:18–3:17). It is well known that ancient Near Eastern authors often made the comparison between armies and locusts. The Ugaritic legend of King Keret reports that his army was "like locusts that dwell in the land." Sumerian and Assyrian texts also used this image: "In huge numbers, like locusts, they covered the land," is said of the Gutean soldiers in a text from the third millennium. In the Bible one finds similar statements. Judges 6:3–5 speaks of the Midianite people as "thick as locusts," and Jer 46:23 describes the army of the Assyrian king as "more numerous than locusts."

D. Asking for Mercy (2:12–17)

This first part of the book closes with a summons to ask God for mercy. These verses present a call to every group and generation of the people; it is astonishing that even children and babies are mentioned. This inclusive call affirms that no one lies beyond the judgment of God or beyond God's blessing. At the end of this unit, the question, "Where is their God?" exemplifies Israel's status in the eyes of foreign nations. They mock Israel, challenging the power of Israel's God.

III. God's Answer (2:18–3:17)

The second part of the book clarifies the characters at work in the first part. Specific nations are now named. Specific acts of violence against Israel—e.g., the sale of its citizens into slavery—allow the reader to understand the actual dimensions of the tragedy described earlier in more general terms. This second part must be understood as an outgrowth of the book's first part.

A. The Restoration of Life (2:18–27)

This unit is built on a parallel structure:

18	Introduction	A	The Prophet Speaks
19–20	1st stanza	B	God Answers
21–24	2nd stanza	A'	The Prophet Speaks
25–27	3rd stanza	B'	God Answers

Following a brief introduction announcing that God will now speak are three stanzas in which the voice of God alternates with that of the prophet. God acts by restoring the natural environment that had been destroyed by the enemy. In v. 25, the voice of God refers to the prologue (1:4), saying that the people will be repaid for the years of destruction created by the locusts, "my great army, which I sent against you." This reference is part of the continual semantic play in Joel where the text continually moves between the historic and the eschatological realms.

B. The Promise of the Spirit (2:28–32)

The irruption of God in the middle of the community will transform it. The spirit will be poured over all people, even over those whose life is normally excluded from the divine blessing. To give the spirit to "sons and daughters … old people … youths … male and female slaves" stands in tension with some of Israel's religious traditions, especially since the priests are not included in this list. The primitive Christian community read this text as prophecy fulfilled before their eyes in the events of Pentecost (Acts 2:17–21).

C. God's Judgment (3:1–17)

From a literary point of view, this unit may be divided into two subunits: an announcement (vv. 1–8) and a call (vv. 9–17) to judgment. The first part proclaims that God will judge the nations in the valley of Jehoshaphat. The location of this valley is unknown (the naming of the modern Jehoshaphat Valley occurred at a much later time). The nations will be judged because they destroyed the land, sold Israelite children as prostitutes, and sent youths to the Greeks as slaves. They have taken the treasure of the Jerusalem Temple to use as ornamentation for their own temples. The subsequent call to war stands in direct contrast to the famous texts of Isa 2:4 and Mic 4:3, as it here urges the people to "beat your plowshares into swords."

IV. Epilogue: God's Justice (3:18–21)

There are many points of contact between the prologue and epilogue. For example, the tragedy (1:2b) corresponds with the blessing (3:20); the devastation of the land (1:4) corresponds with the promise of fertility (3:18). In the prologue, there is a reference to the origin of the disaster (1:3) whereas now a better future is envisioned (3:18a; 21b). At the beginning of the book, the locusts/army brings destruction and death, while now God is the giver of restoration and salvation. The text moves from a time of catastrophe to a time of well-being, making clear the basic message of the book: There will be justice for those who have suffered oppression, and that day will be one of abundance and blessing for them.

BIBLIOGRAPHY

P. Andiñach. "Joel." *Global Bible Commentary.* Daniel Patte, ed. (Nashville: Abingdon, 2004) 272–76; J. Barton. *Joel and Obadiah* (Louisville: Westminster John Knox, 2001); J. Crenshaw *Joel.* AB 24C (New York: Doubleday, 1995); G. Ogden and R. Deutsch. *A Promise of Hope: A Call to Obedience: A Commentary on the Books of Joel and Malachi.* ITC 10 (Grand Rapids: Eerdmans, 1987); M. Sweeney. *The Twelve Prophets.* Berit Olam. 2 vols. (Collegeville: Liturgical Press, 2000) 147–87; H. W. Wolff. *Joel and Amos: A Commentary on the Books of the Prophets Joel and Amos* (Philadelphia: Fortress, 1977).

AMOS

M. Daniel Carroll R.

OVERVIEW

The book of Amos is renowned for championing social justice. Its best-known verse perhaps is 5:24—"Let justice roll down like waters, and righteousness like an everflowing stream." Dr. Martin Luther King Jr. appealed to these powerful words as part of his "I Have a Dream" speech at the Lincoln Memorial in August, 1963.

Amos often is considered to have been the first writing prophet, and not a few commentators defend the authenticity of much of the book. Critical scholars have suggested successive stages of editorial expansion of the original prophet's words. A recent trend is to attribute the production of Amos, along with much of the Old Testament, to a circle of scribes in Jerusalem during the post-exilic, or Persian, period. There also is a growing appreciation for the literary artistry of the book. Several verses connect Amos to surrounding Minor Prophets (1:2, Joel 3:16 [Heb 4:16]; 9:12, Obadiah).

The heading (1:1) and other historical allusions place the prophet in the long reign of Jeroboam II, who ruled Israel during the first half of the eighth century BCE. For a portion of that time the nation was prosperous and strong. As the years progressed, the country began to suffer military setbacks. The internal situation also was precarious. The luxurious lifestyles enjoyed by those in power came at the expense of the poor, and the court system was corrupt.

Scholars have tried to identify specific features of Israel's socioeconomic system that resulted in the exploitation of certain segments of the population, e.g., rent capitalism, a tributary mode of production. Such suggestions may help readers understand particular passages, but there is not enough archaeological or textual data to identify with certainty the realities of eighth-century Israel. The book provides moral commentary, not sociological analysis. Nonetheless, the external pressures on and the domestic problems within Israel took their toll. After the death of Jeroboam the political situation quickly unraveled. In 722 BCE, the Assyrian armies conquered Samaria, the capital of Israel, after a lengthy siege, and the region became a province of the Assyrian empire.

The central focus of the book is the person of God. Amos' favorite name for God is "the LORD [God] of hosts" (Heb.: *yhwh ['elohe] tseba'oth*; 3:13; 4:13; 5:14–15, 27; 6:8; 9:5). In climactic declarations, three hymn-like passages assert that God is powerful (4:13; 5:8–9; 9:5–6). The fundamental message is that the all-powerful God will judge Israel because of its social injustice and military pride. The national religion propounded a view of the Lord that sanctioned a distorted view of reality (7:10–13). Confident in God's sure provision and protection, the people crowded the sanctuaries for celebrations (4:4–5; 5:4–6). But the god of their rituals and temples was a very different deity, not the God of the exodus (2:9–10; 3:1–2). Israel's political, economic, and religious system stood condemned: the military pretense would be exposed as groundless, the powerful punished for their oppression of the poor, and the sanctuaries destroyed. Beyond the judgment lay the hope of a restored land and a proper relationship with God (9:11–15).

OUTLINE

I. The Preface (1:1–2)

II. The Oracles Against the Nations (1:3–2:16)

    A. The Oracle Against Surrounding Nations (1:3–2:3)

    B. The Oracle Against Judah (2:4–5)

    C. The Oracle Against Israel (2:6–16)

III. The Words of God and the Prophet (3:1–6:14)

    A. Divine Exposure of Israel's Guilt (3:1–4:13)
        3:1–4:3. The End of Samaria and Bethel
        4:4–13. Religion Can Be Blind

    B. Lament for the Death of Israel (5:1–6:14)

DETAILED ANALYSIS

I. The Preface (1:1–2)

This is one of the most complete superscriptions among the prophetic books. Tekoa is a town in Judah, about ten miles south of Jerusalem. Amos was a southerner commissioned to prophesy against the northern kingdom of Israel. The term translated "shepherd" (*noqed*) is not the usual word for shepherd (*ro'eh*) and appears in only one other passage (2 Kgs 3:4). The significance of the term is debated, but at the very least it suggests that Amos was not a poor sheepherder (cf. 7:14–15).

Verse 1:2 introduces the entire book. In so doing, it includes words and motifs that appear throughout the book: the roar of the Lord (3:4, 8; cf. 3:12); the hymnic tone (4:13; 5:8–9; 9:5–6); the mourning; and Carmel (9:3). God is the Divine Warrior, who comes in might to judge (cf. Judg 5:4–5; Mic 1:3). The roar portends disaster, which will be manifest in an earthquake (cf. Zech 14:5) and war. There is death in the offing. A better translation of "wither" is "mourn" ('*abal*; cf. NASB, ESV). This verb reoccurs in 8:8, 10; 9:5 (cf. 5:16–17).

The Lord speaks from Jerusalem, the capital of Judah, implying that the government and religion of Israel are illegitimate. In addition, 9:11–15 announces that hope lies with a Davidic kingdom,

not with Israel's present regime. This Judean perspective can explain the accusation of conspiracy leveled against Amos by Amaziah (7:10).

II. The Oracles Against the Nations (1:3–2:16)

This section contains oracles against eight nations, including Judah and Israel. Many scholars consider the oracles against Tyre (1:9–10), Edom (1:11–12), and Judah (2:4–5) to be secondary. There is historical evidence, however, to connect them to the period during which Amos was active. Moreover, catch-words link these three oracles to others, creating a coherent literary pattern.

The opening formula uses an $x/x+1$ pattern, with three as "x" (cf. Prov 30:18–19, 21–23, 29–31), and the phrase "I will not revoke the punishment." "Punishment" is an interpretive translation of the Hebrew, which actually reads, "I will not cause it to return" (NRSV note). The oracles are inconsistent in the number of transgressions listed, perhaps citing those considered the most heinous.

A. The Oracles Against Surrounding Nations (1:3–2:3)

There are several possible reasons for these judgments. It may be that God is responding to actions taken against his people (1:3, 13). Yet, not all these barbarities were directed at Israel. For example, the tomb of the king of Edom had been violated (2:1). In several oracles the victims are not identified (although they could be Israelites, e.g., 1:6, 9). The moral vision of the book reflects a concern for all peoples.

Cruelty in warfare is condemned throughout these oracles. The threshing of Gilead in Transjordan (1:3) could refer to physical torture or could be a figurative expression for brutality (cf. Isa 41:15). The buying and selling of slaves (1:6, 9) also correspond to that context. While in the ancient world some fell into slavery because of debts (2:6; 8:6), many slaves were the victims of armed conflicts. The similarity of vocabulary in the oracles concerning Philistia (1:6–8) and Tyre (1:9–10) and the similar fate of Edom suggest that these nations will be punished in a coordinated way.

The punishment in every case involves defeat. These nations' important cities would be razed

(1:7, 10, 12, 14; 2:2) and their own people and leadership punished and sent away (1:8, 15; 2:3). Cruelty would beget cruelty, a judgment in kind. The instrument of divine chastisement is not specified. These words found fulfillment when the Assyrian Empire conquered the nations of this region.

B. The Oracle Against Judah (2:4–5)

The fact that the oracles against Judah and Israel begin with the same formula indicates that at one level these two nations were no different than those who did not claim the Lord as their god. In addition, although Amos was from Judah, he was not reluctant to rebuke that nation as well. The prophet is not a narrow-minded nationalist.

Many readers assume that religious defection—following after other gods—is indicted in v. 4, but another interpretation is possible. Judah had rejected the law (*torah*) of the Lord, and that law covered every sphere of life. Parallels in Isaiah about rejection of divine instruction confirm that such sin is not limited to cultic matters (Isa 5:24; 30:9). "Lies" could refer to words of false prophets (Mic 2:11) or to wrong-headed decisions of national leaders (Hos 7:13; Isa 28:15, 17), which would result in destruction (Mic 3:5; Isa 3:12).

C. The Oracle Against Israel (2:6–16)

This indictment is the longest and most detailed. The transgressions of Israel do not include military violence, however. Seven abuses are enumerated in 2:6–8. Commentators differ on the meaning of each, but there is no doubting that they all constitute some sort of injustice against the vulnerable.

The nation had forgotten the Lord's gracious acts in its past (2:9–10; cf. 3:1–2) and now tried to compromise his representatives (2:11–12). Consequently, Israel's army would be routed (2:14–16). Seven kinds of soldiers are listed: perfect sin (2:6–8) yields perfect defeat. Israel's "day," like that of the other nations (1:15), will be a time of military disaster (cf. 5:18–20).

III. The Words of God and the Prophet (3:1–6:14)

This major section is usually associated with the "words of Amos" (1:1). It can be subdivided into two parts, 3:1–4:13 and 5:1–6:14. Chapters 3–5 begin in similar fashion: "Hear this word."

A. Divine Exposure of Israel's Guilt (3:1–4:13)

3:1–4:3. The End of Samaria and Bethel. This subsection can be divided into various segments. The first two verses emphasize that Israel has violated its unique relationship with the Lord, which had been certified at the exodus (cf. 2:9–10). The seven questions in 3:3–6 describe a series of encounters. They move from a vague question to an encounter with God, and all but the first involve death. An *inclusio* connects 3:1–2 with 3:3–8 ("the Lord [God] has spoken"), while the "roars" of 3:4, 8 remind the reader of 1:2.

This ominous tone continues in 3:9–4:3. There is a call for other nations to witness the sin in Samaria, the capital, where abuses abound (3:9–10). An invasion has been decreed as Israel's punishment. The enemy will destroy the strongholds, the sanctuary at Bethel, and the fine homes of the royal family (3:11–15). The powerful, who coldly take advantage of the poor, will lead the way into exile (4:1–3). This is the doing of the roaring divine lion, who has caught his prey and left but scraps (3:12).

4:4–13. Religion Can Be Blind. These verses censure religious practices. The Lord evaluates the rituals at the sanctuaries as sin. They were designed to fulfill the religious desires of the people. There was no sacrifice for sin, just thanksgiving for the goodness of God (4:4–5). This religion was totally disconnected from the realities of hunger, drought, agricultural failure, and defeat (4:6–11).

These five disasters are accompanied by the fivefold refrain, "yet you did not return to me." The afflictions had been designed to force the people to seek the true Lord, but they preferred the religion of national blessing. Israel must prepare for an encounter with God, who is described with five participles that emphasize his incomparable might (4:12–13).

B. Lament for the Death of Israel (5:1–6:14)

This section is made up of three parts, each of which includes a chiasm—that is, a concentric ring structure whose climax is at its center.

5:1–17. What Is in a Name? The announcement of an encounter with the Lord in 4:13 is followed by a lament (5:1–3). This woe concerning a terrible defeat in battle is matched with mourning in city and countryside alike (5:16–17). The charge to seek God instead of the historic sanctuaries (5:4–6) is echoed in 5:14–15, a charge that makes clear that genuine faith requires establishing justice. The metaphor of twisting God's demands in poisonous ways (5:7) is made concrete by the accusations in 5:10–13.

The first hymnlike passage appears in 5:8–9. This powerful God will destroy the defenses of Israel. At the center of these lines, and of the entire passage, is the statement "The LORD is his name." He is the main point of the prophetic message. The misrepresentation of God has yielded—and authorized—an oppressive society.

5:18–27. The Delusion of Religion. A second woe hits at the conviction that the day of the Lord would be the occasion of victory. It would be nothing of the sort! Instead, it will be utter darkness and inescapable ruin (5:18–20). These verses are matched with 5:26–27, which reiterate that military defeat would result in exile (cf. 4:1–3). Verse 26 is difficult to translate but probably refers to Mesopotamian astral deities that would accompany the people into exile.

5:21–23, 25 condemn the religious practices of Israel. 4:4–6 had urged the people not to look for God at the holy places; these verses denounce every kind of ritual (seven are listed in 5:21–23). The visceral response of God to this unacceptable worship is manifest in the verbs. True worship had not been like this in the past; it cannot be that way now (5:25). The center of this passage is v. 24. It underscores the inseparable connection between ethics and worship.

6:1–14. The Delusion of Power. The last segment of this section also begins with an expression of woe. The opening verses that decry the complacency of the leaders find their parallel in the false confidence in military might in 6:13–14. They had conquered Lo-Debar, literally "no-thing"!.

6:4–7 describe a *marzeach* feast. These were gatherings of the well-to-do, perhaps to honor the dead. They were renowned for excessive drinking and consumption. The corresponding verse (6:12) questions the nonsensical nature of this lasciviousness (cf. 5:7). God rejects this state of affairs and will tear down their cities (6:8, 11). The center of this chiasm is 6:9–10. Although the details are hard to reconstruct, the scene seems to portray a kinsman who must burn the corpses of those who have died (in the war or an earthquake).

IV. Visions of Israel's Future (7:1–9:15)

The final three chapters contain five visions (continuing the penchant for series of five). Visions three through five are followed by explanatory expansions.

A. Two Visions of Natural Disaster (7:1–6)

In the first two visions the prophet pleads with the Lord, asking him to "forgive" and "cease" (7:2, 4). Amos intercedes when he sees the agricultural devastation to be wrought by locusts (cf. Deut 28:42; Joel 1) and a fire strong enough to dry up the cosmic deep (cf. Gen 7:11). Some scholars suggest that these visions come from early in Amos' career, when there was still the possibility that God might not punish Israel. Such reconstructions are hypothetical. The literary mood is one of impending doom that is withheld only momentarily. In stark contrast to the proud self-assurance of the nation, Amos understands that Israel is "small," incapable of defending itself against the coming enemy invasion and helpless before these natural disasters.

B. A Vision of Military Defeat (7:7–9)

Although the traditional translation for the term *'anak* is "plumb line," this Akkadian loan word actually means "tin." The image again is of self-delusion. The walls of the strong fortresses are like walls of tin. The Lord has torn off a piece and thrown it in scorn amongst the people.

C. Expansion: The Confrontation at Bethel (7:10–17)

This passage illustrates how compromised the religion of Israel had become. Amaziah accuses Amos of conspiracy and makes clear the bond between the national ideology and the worship of God (7:10–13). The high priest and his family will personify Israel's judgment of death and exile (7:16–17).

There is further information concerning the prophet. He was not from a prophetic guild before his calling by God. He had been a "herdsman" (*boqer*, a term that implies he owned sheep and cattle). In addition, he worked with sycamore trees (there is little agreement as to what this entailed). These do not grow in the area of Tekoa, so it is possible that the prophet owned multiple properties. This reinforces the impression of 1:1 that Amos was a man of means.

D. A Vision of Religious Failure (8:1–3)

The fourth vision is a basket of summer fruit (*qayits*). This term offers a word play with "end" (*qets*). Israel's hour had come; the joyous celebrations in the temple decried earlier will be replaced by wailing for the dead.

E. Expansion: The Cost of Religious Perversion (8:4–14)

Amos 8:4–6 recalls the avarice and the exploitation of the poor in 2:6. The Lord's response is swift. Prior vocabulary and themes reappear in 8:7–13, such as the descriptions of God in 5:8, the mourning of 5:16–17, the "day" of 5:18–20. Ironically, those who silenced the prophets (2:11–12) will not find a word; the "pride of Jacob" does not refer here to the arrogance of Israel (6:8) but to the glory of God.

Scholars disagree about whether 8:14 refers to other deities or whether these were various names for the Lord in different sanctuaries. This decision depends in part on the translation of *'asmat semeron*, whether as the goddess "Ashimah" (NRSV) or as the "guilt of Samaria" (NASB, NIV, NKJV). The former would point to syncretism, the latter to a heterodox Yahwism.

F. A Vision of Divine Sovereignty in Judgment (9:1–6)

The fifth vision shows the Lord beginning to punish Israel at a temple, most likely the sanctuary at Bethel (cf. 3:15; 5:5; 7:10). He strikes at the center of the religious system, which consecrated the social world of Israel in God's name. Although such destruction could stem from an earthquake, reference to "the sword" suggests a war (9:1). Again, there is no escaping (9:2–4; cf. 2:14–16; 5:19). Like the other hymnic passages, 9:5–6 emphasizes the power of the Lord of hosts, who commands the earth and the heavens.

G. Expansion: The Hope Beyond the Ruins (9:7–15)

God disabuses Israel of any misplaced confidence in its election (9:7–10). That special relationship left the nation without excuse (2:9–10; 3:1–2), and it did not mean that the Lord was not involved with other peoples. All nations must respond to the demands of God. Israel would suffer at his hand, but some from Israel would survive. This motif had been hinted at earlier (3:12; 5:14–15; 6:9–10).

Amos 9:11–15 declare that a future lay beyond the catastrophe. Many scholars attribute these verses to an author other than Amos. Still, one must recognize that the oracle reverses the conditions wrought by earlier disasters. There will be food and drink, not hunger and thirst; the towns will be rebuilt, and the land tilled and harvested in contrast to the dismantling of the fortresses and homes in the invasion. This is a picture of plenty and of a people at peace. This will occur under the rule of a Davidic monarch, and those nations with whom Israel had been at war (chs. 1–2) will become members of that kingdom. "On that day," the Lord of hosts will become "the LORD your God." The relationship with his people will be fully restored.

BIBLIOGRAPHY

F. I. Andersen and D. N. Freedman. *Amos: A New Translation with Introduction and Commentary.* AB 24A (Garden City: Doubleday, 1989); M. D. Carroll R. *Amos—The Prophet and His Oracles: Research on the Book of Amos* (Louisville: Westminster John Knox, 2003); J. H. Hayes. *Amos the Eighth-Century Prophet: His Times & His Preaching* (Nashville: Abingdon, 1988); J. Jeremias. *The Book of Amos: A Commentary.* OTL (Louisville: Westminster John Knox, 1998); P. J. King. *Amos, Hosea, Micah: An Archaeological Commentary* (Philadelphia: Westminster, 1988); S. M. Paul. *Amos: A Commentary on the Book of Amos.* Hermeneia (Minneapolis: Augsburg Fortress, 1991); G. V. Smith. *Amos: A Commentary* (Grand Rapids: Zondervan, 1989); H. W. Wolff. *Joel and Amos.* Hermeneia (Philadelphia: Fortress, 1977).

OBADIAH

Carol J. Dempsey

OVERVIEW

The shortest of all the Old Testament books, Obadiah consists of twenty-one verses. Nothing is known about the prophet. His name, which means "worshiper of Yahweh," was common in Israel. The book of Obadiah was written sometime between the late sixth century and the early fifth century BCE. The prophet's message, which is directed primarily against Edom, focuses on the "day of the Lord." For Edom, this day will be dreadful; for Israel, it will be hopeful and promising.

Obadiah's prophecy against Edom is part of a series of prophecies against foreign countries. An invective against Edom appears in several prophetic texts, including Isa 34:5–17; 63:1–6; Jer 49:7; Ezek 25:12–14; Amos 1:11–12; and Mal 1:2–4. In Obadiah, the Edomites are guilty of deeds that exploit Judah in its time of weakness. Edom reaps God's righteous anger on account of its deeds.

The book focuses on justice, power, and divine sovereignty. God will exercise divine justice on Israel's behalf. Together with the other nations, Edom will be made to suffer when the day of the Lord dawns. Embedded in the text is the ancient belief in *lex talionis*—eye for an eye, tooth for a tooth, fracture for a fracture, life for a life (see Obad 1:15; cf Lev 24:18–21). What Edom has sown, Edom will reap: the strong and powerful become the powerless, while the one restrained from exercising power, namely Judah, becomes powerful (v. 18). God will vindicate Israel through a display of power that brings liberation for one group of people at the cost of another. The text betrays the violent climate of the day, and shows how violence can be used to color religious imagination. Finally, not only will the exiles be restored to their land but also, and perhaps more importantly, the kingdom will be restored to God (v. 21). Obadiah's vision celebrates a new world order, with God reigning over all people and nations.

OUTLINE

I. Introductory Statement (1a)

II. Prophecy Against Edom (1b–14)

    A. Divine Indictment Against Edom (1b–4)

    B. Proclamation Outlining Edom's Demise (5–9)

    C. Description of Edom's Transgressions (10–14)

III. Prophecy Concerning the Day of the Lord (15–21)

    A. Word of Judgment Against Edom (15–16)

    B. Word of Hope and Promise to Israel (17–21)

DETAILED ANALYSIS

Verse 1a indicates that Obadiah's prophecy originated in a vision, most likely an intuitive experience that engaged the prophet's entire being. Verses 1b–14, a divine indictment against Edom, features the prophet delivering God's message in poetry. Multiple voices can be heard throughout the text. The poet begins with God quoting the Edomites (v. 1c), a technique that provides the poet's audience with the necessary material to set the stage for subsequent proclamations. The Edomites have heard a "report from the Lord"—presumably a bad one (v. 1c)—and responded in a hostile manner (v. 1d). Here the poet depicts God quoting the Edomites directly. Verses 2–4 describe God's response: God will make Edom "least" among the nations; Edom will be despised (v. 2). Edom is then shown to be proud and self-exalted, two characteristics captured metaphorically through the image of a soaring and high-roosting eagle. This people, however, will suffer humiliation (v. 4). Central to Edom's downfall is the people's haughty "heart," the seat of intelligence and central place for all relational activity in ancient Israel (see, e.g., Deut 6:4–6; 7:7; 10:16).

Verses 5–9 outline Edom's demise. Edom will be plundered (v. 5), pillaged (v. 6), deceived by trusted allies (v. 7), stripped of wisdom and understanding (v. 8), and defeated militarily (v. 9). Edom will become weak and vulnerable.

Verses 10–14 expose Edom's transgressions, which include brutality against the Israelites, symbolized by the reference to Jacob (v. 10), participation with other nations in treachery against Jerusalem and Judah (v. 11), and most detestably, the gloating over and boasting about Judah's misfortune (vv. 12–13*b*), not to mention Edom's looting of Judah, along with handing over Judah's survivors during its time of distress and misfortune (vv. 13*c*–14). Edom is guilty of abusing "Jacob" in countless ways, all of which incites divine fury that comes to a climax in vv. 15–16.

Verses 15–16 focus on the day of the Lord and begin the second part of the book (vv. 15-21). God warns Edom and the nations that "the day of the LORD" is imminent and that those found guilty of injustice and oppression will reap what they have sown. Implied in the imagery of drinking is the metaphor of God's cup of wrath from which Edom and all the nations will have to drink on the day of the Lord. The cup's contents will cause suffering, pain, helplessness, and disgrace (cf. Isa 51:17, 22; Jer 25:15–29).

Images shift in vv. 17–21. The poet proclaims God's message of hope and promise to a community scorched by military invasions, deportations, the loss of land and Temple, and exile. These verses outline the various territories that Judah will acquire, and foreshadow a day of celebration and jubilation when Judah is liberated from exile and restored to the land. The graphic metaphor in v. 18 depicts Jacob and Judah as representative of the Northern and southern kingdoms, respectively. With this metaphor, the poet points to a time when Judah will overtake Esau (Edom) and all the other countries that Esau represents. The "fire" and "stubble" symbolize divine judgment on Edom. Judah's resurgence as a country is linked to its restoration to the land which, in turn, is related to covenant renewal with God. A people once oppressed by an enemy will now govern that enemy. Although hopeful, the text reflects the imperialistic attitudes embedded in an ancient world and culture, many of which remain present in today's world and which require transformation.

BIBLIOGRAPHY

E. Ben Zvi. *A Historical-Critical Study of the Book of Obadiah.* BZAW 242 (New York: Walter de Gruyter, 1996); W. P. Brown. "Obadiah." *Obadiah through Malachi.* Westminster Bible Companion (Louisville: Westminster John Knox Press, 1996) 7–14; C. J. Dempsey. *The Prophets: A Liberation Critical Reading* (Minneapolis: Fortress, 2000); P. R. Raabe. *Obadiah.* AB 24D (New York: Doubleday, 1996); M. A. Sweeney. "Obadiah." *The Twelve Prophets. Volume One.* Berit Olam (Collegeville, Minn. The Liturgical Press, 2000) 279–98; H. W. Wolff. *Obadiah and Jonah.* CC. Margaret Kohl, trans. (Minneapolis: Augsburg, 1986).

JONAH

BARBARA GREEN

OVERVIEW

It is difficult to know when the book of Jonah was written. A Jonah ben Amittai appears in 2 Kgs 14:23–27, but, given the Bible's propensity to assign fresh adventures to its heroes, it is possible, though not necessary, to hypothesize an eighth-century backdrop for the book. Assyrian Nineveh was a bitter enemy of Israel from the ninth to seventh centuries, possibly before and not afterward. Those favoring a post-exilic date for the writing of most biblical material will be persuaded that the anxiety of post-exilic Jerusalem, threatened, spared, but existing under further threat, may find in the city of Nineveh—also condemned, reprieved, but destroyed—a provocative analogue. Some scholars have claimed that a theme of universalism in the book helps to date it as exilic, in opposition to the more restrictive viewpoints of Ezra and Nehemiah. However, such a view represents a primarily Christian assessment of the book, with centuries of Jewish commentators reading the story quite differently. The book of Jonah is wonderful literature. The literary structure of the book is symmetrical and balanced. Its two halves are closely related at both the macro- and micro-levels. The genre of the book has been variously understood—as a parable, a riddle, a satire. The plot of the story has been scrutinized and anomalies uncovered. If earlier commentators tended to rearrange the story where logic seems deficient, now scholars highlight these moments: That Jonah does not leave the environs of Nineveh after many think he should (4:5) and that he provides information about his motives tardily (4:1–3) afford space for the interpretation of the character and meaning of the book. Scholars draw attention to use of words that tie sections together (*great, appoint, wicked, hurl*), the book's tendency to use unusual vocabulary (*show concern* in 4:10–11), and the ambiguity of the central word, *overthrow*, with which Jonah addresses the city at 3:4. Such literary analysis has displaced some of the attention once paid to historical questions.

Scholars offering diverse opinions about the meanings of the book have pointed out the vast network of choices any interpreter must face and have shown that reading is more a matter of the stance of the interpreter than had once seemed the case. The characterization of the prophet as churlish or fearful, the importance accorded to the Gentile sailors and Ninevites, and the nature of the relationship between deity and prophet can be and have been read in ways that seem contradictory.

OUTLINE

I. In Flight (1:1–17)

    A. Superscription (1:1)

    B. Call and Flight (1:2–5)

    C. On Board the Ship (1:6–14)

    D. Overboard (1:15–17)

II. In the Fish (2:1–10)

    A. Swallowed (2:1)

    B. At Prayer (2:2–9)

    C. Landed (2:10)

III. In Nineveh (3:1–10)

    A. Preaching (3:1–4)

    B. Response of Nineveh (3:5–9)

    C. Response of God (3:10)

IV. Outside Nineveh (4:1–11)

    A. Response of Jonah (4:1–4)

    B. Awaiting Results (4:5–8)

    C. Final Questions (4:9–11)

DETAILED ANALYSIS

I. In Flight (1:1–17)

1:1. The superscription identifies the object of the address as Jonah son of Amittai.

1:2–5. Jonah is commanded to cry out against the city Nineveh, whose wickedness was evident to God. Neither the content of the cry nor the nature of the evil is specified. Jonah's response is acted rather than spoken: he flees to Jaffa, finds a ship, pays the fare and boards, heading away from Nineveh to escape God's commission. God hurls such a storm that the sailors begin to jettison the cargo to lighten the ship and keep it from sinking. Jonah sleeps, the word conveying a condition beyond natural slumber (1 Kgs 19:5) or, alternatively, irresponsible laziness (Prov 19:15).

1:6–14. The captain rouses Jonah and asks him to pray to his deity in the hopes that God might respond. Throughout the book, the deity is variously named: as God/Elohim, as Yahweh, or with both names, allowing—in a book involving both Jews and Gentiles—appropriate ambiguity. The word *Elohim* does double duty as distinctive designation for the one God and as a common plural for others. The sailors cast lots, assuming correctly that the guilty party will be selected. Jonah is identified and questioned urgently about his mission, origin, homeland, and ethnic identity. The interrogation generates not name and mission but Jonah's ethnic and religious commitment: a Hebrew with allegiance to the God who made heaven and earth. Commentators point out the irony in Jonah's readiness to identify the God from whom he has sought to escape overland and by sea as master of just those realms. Also provocative is Jonah's admission of responsibility for the storm, which the narrator summarizes rather than letting us hear just how Jonah would describe his behavior for his fellow-travelers. Such reticence is one of the ways the narrator manages to keep complex and uncertain the character of the hero. The sailors evidently recognize the deity in question, for their fear and their outrage increase. They ask Jonah what they might do. He offers one option: that the sailors throw him overboard—whether as appeasement to the deity or removal of a sinner is not clear. He does not volunteer to jump but hints that he would not resist their action. They seem loath to do it and attempt to return to shore, but to no avail. Finally, with conditions worsening, they pray to not be held guilty of shedding innocent blood, acknowledge God's sovereignty, and hoist their troublesome passenger overboard.

1:15–17. The sea calms at once, and the sailors are last seen revering God, offering sacrifices, and making promises to Jonah's deity who has assisted them. The deity who hurled the storm accepted the jettisoning of Jonah and appointed a large fish to swallow him. For three days and three nights the prophet remains within the fish and prays to his deity from there. The identity of the fish has been a question for centuries; translations starting with the Septuagint specify it as a whale. The ancients—Jewish and Christian—understood it allegorically as the underworld, death, a synagogue, or the like.

II. In the Fish (2:1–10)

2:1–9. Some commentators have thought that the prayer was extraneous, different in tone from the tale in which it was embedded. It recalls in form and phrasing various laments and thanksgivings (e.g., Pss 31:22; 69:1–2; 88:7–8). The language suits sojourn in the sea better than within a fish. Others note that Jonah never specifically asks for rescue. The fish tends, on the whole, to be viewed negatively by commentators, though nothing in the story demands such a view; the fish saves Jonah.

2:10. At God's prompt, the fish disgorges its passenger onto dry land.

III. In Nineveh (3:1–10)

3:1–4. The narrative resumes without reference to Jonah's previous effort to evade the commission. Nor is the content of Jonah's preaching specified. A string of verbs characterizes Jonah's obedience: He proceeds to the large city and begins his preaching at once; its effect is immediate. Jonah's pronouncement is most terse: "Forty days more and Nineveh shall overturn" (3:4, author's translation; NRSV, "shall be overthrown"). The utterance is a mere five words in Hebrew, making Jonah the Bible's most laconic prophet, and possibly the most direct! What remains unspecified is the significance of the word *overturn*. The Hebrew word was used to depict the violent fate of Sodom and Gomorrah (Gen 18). But the verbal form in question here occurs in the reflexive or passive aspect of the verb, allowing for the possibility that the overturning can be the city turning itself around.

3:5–9. The words have a phenomenal impact on the citizens of the city. The people believe God. And then first the citizenry and then the king fast and don sackcloth. Though people and animals have already done so, the king and nobles issue a decree commanding the fast and the turning from violence contemplated against others. The king concludes, like the captain of the ship, that God may repent and turn away from anger so that the city will not perish.

3:10. Readers learn from the narrator that God observed the Ninevites' deeds, changed his mind, and did not carry out the threatened destruction.

IV. Outside Nineveh (4:1–11)

4:1–4. Jonah is upset at something not precisely specified in the Hebrew, though clarified in translation: *it was very displeasing* (4:1) should refer to something Jonah witnessed, plausibly the Ninevite behavior (alternatively, though popularly in commentary, God's change of mind that Jonah learns outside the narrative). Jonah, ruminating on his experience in prayer, offers a flashback from his moment of flight, revealing that he fled toward Tarshish because of God's propensity toward mercy and habit of relenting from disaster. The encomium describing God's ways in 4:2 occurs numerous times in the Bible, with similar wording (e.g., Exod 34:6–7; Deut 4:31; Ps 145:8). Jonah ends this prayer with no request but that his life be taken. Readers may choose to infer negativity about the Ninevites, but it is explicit in neither discourse nor narrative. God responds, querying the appropriateness of the prophet's anger. Jonah maintains the justification of his feelings.

4:5–8. The narrator provides fresh information about Jonah's actions: he leaves the city going east (rather than homewards), builds a shelter, and waits to see what will happen next. God appoints a plant (of disputed type) to shelter him. Jonah rejoices. But God next appoints another animal (worm rather than fish) to attack the plant, which is vulnerable under the hot sun and fierce east wind, also appointed by God. Jonah opines that death is better than life.

4:9–11. The book's final section features a final intervention from God, in the form of an analogy. God remarks that the prophet's distress over the plant resulted from neither labor nor long acquaintance. It emerged quickly and disappeared as rapidly. Yet Jonah evinced concern for it. God now asks Jonah: Should not I show concern for a whole city of creatures, unable to distinguish right hand from left? Jonah remains silent. Scholars have for millennia speculated about the meaning of the analogy. It seems a matter of relationship: Jonah's experience with the plant was brief; yet he felt concern for it. God has, arguably, been in a relationship with a city of people for a longer time, has expended labor on its behalf, thus justifying God's concern for the city. Readers may also find here evidence of God's care for Jonah, given the time and energy expended on him!

Jonah's non-response to God's question (v. 11) provides readers with another conundrum. Can one imagine what Jonah would have said? That Jonah is deeply upset is clear. That he has reproached God about mercy is also clear, though he stopped short of wishing God had not spared the city. That Jonah has not left the environs is apparent, though what he expects to see is not stated. The book ends somewhat in the manner of a NT parable, which prompts response from those who heard it. If Jonah's silence is to be broken, interpreters must do it. Readers can think about the book in various ways: To struggle to understand God's ways with large cities that do evil but turn from it as well; to contemplate the nature of prophecy itself. A Hebrew and Gentiles (mariners and Ninevites) exist in the book. How do they interact? What possibilities of change of heart are manifest here, and what may one learn from such behavior? There are many ways to interpret this short narrative, though it may be better to ask the kind of probing questions that conclude the book rather than to assert firm conclusions.

BIBLIOGRAPHY

A. K. M. Adam. "The Sign of Jonah: A Fish-Eye View." *Semeia* 51 (1990) 177–91; E. Ben Zvi. *Signs of Jonah: Reading and Rereading in Ancient Yehud* (Sheffield: Sheffield Academic Press, 2005); B. Green. *Jonah's Journeys* (Collegeville, Minn.: Liturgical Press, 2005); J. M. Sasson. *Jonah.* AB 24B (New York: Doubleday, 1990); P. M. Trible. *Rhetorical Criticism: Context, Method, and the Book of Jonah* (Minneapolis: Fortress, 1994).

MICAH

Carol J. Dempsey

OVERVIEW

Rich in imagery, metaphors, and intricate wordplays, the book of Micah presents itself as a word addressed to the people of Israel and Judah in the latter half of the eighth century BCE during the reigns of Jotham (742–735 BCE), Ahaz (735–715 BCE), and Hezekiah (715–685 BCE). Though Micah's career as a prophet appears expansive, most likely it spanned only the last quarter of the century when Hezekiah reigned. Together with Amos, Isaiah, and Hosea, Micah was one of the four great prophets of the eighth century BCE. Little is known about his person. His name means "Who is like the Lord," and although the name is common in ancient Israel, he is distinguished from others by being identified with Moresheth—otherwise known as Moresheth-gath (1:14)—located twenty-one miles southwest of Jerusalem.

The book reflects a period in Israel and Judah's history that was plagued by Assyrian military invasion, beginning with the Syro-Ephraimitic War (734–732 BCE) down through Sennacherib's invasion of Judah in 701 BCE. In the midst of these turbulent years, however, Judah experienced religious reforms and an economic revolution that left the wealthy landowners growing in prosperity at the expense of small peasant farmers. Religious and political leaders began to view their vocations and positions as business careers with opportunities to assert their power for purposes of self-interest instead of for the common good. The times, then, became fraught with injustice, oppression, and corruption. The prophet Micah addresses the political, social, and religious climate of his day as he rails against the perpetrators of graft (see, e.g., Micah 1–3) while offering not only a vision of a new world order (see 4:1–5) but also a message of hope (e.g., 2:12–13; 4:6–8).

Micah makes clear that Israel's God will not tolerate injustice rooted in and flowing from apostasy, idolatry, hypocrisy, the disregard for the Torah, and a break in the covenant relationship. Divine justice will be meted out, and yet, the final word of the book as a whole offers a word of universal compassion (7:18–20), but not before the prophet intercedes on behalf of the people (6:6–8) and, in so doing, creates one of the most-often-quoted passages of the entire Bible (see 6:8).

The book of Micah grew over time. Micah 1–3 is generally accepted as authentic to Micah; Mic 2:12–13 could be a later addition, but evidence remains inconclusive. Micah 6:1–7:6 may also be attributed to Micah with the remainder of the book consisting of a compilation of later additions. The book includes a wide array of literary forms and techniques, i.e., judgment speeches (1:2–7; 3:1–2), laments (1:8–16; 7:1–7), a lawsuit (6:1–5), prayers (7:14–17, 18–20), reflections (6:6–8), and metaphors (e.g., 1:2–4; 2:12–13; 3:1–3; 4:1–5, 8–13; 7:1).

OUTLINE

I. Superscription (1:1)

II. Proclamation of Judgment; Word of Hope (1:2–3:12)

    A. Judgment Speech (1:2–7)

    B. Dirge-Lament (1:8–16)

    C. Woe Proclamation (2:1–5)

    D. Disputation Prophecy (2:6–11)

    E. Salvation Proclamation (2:12–13)

    F. Address to Israel's Political Leadership (3:1–4)

    G. Proclamation concerning the Prophets (3:5–7)

    H. Interlude: Statement of Confidence (3:8)

    I. Address to Israel's Leadership (3:9–12)

III. Proclamation of Future Restoration (4:1–5:15)

    A. Prophetic Vision (4:1–5)

    B. Divine Promise (4:6–5:15)

IV. Words of Judgment, Lament, Trust, Promise, Petition, and Compassion (6:1–7:20)

DETAILED ANALYSIS

I. Superscription (1:1)

The book of Micah opens with a superscription (1:1) typical of many prophetic books (see, e.g., Isa 1:1; Jer 1:1–3; Hos 1:1; Amos 1:1; Zeph 1:1) that situates both prophet and proclamation in a particular time period, and here specifically in the latter part of the eighth century BCE. All three kings mentioned ruled over Judah. The prophet's proclamation is the result of something that "came" to him, which he "saw" concerning Samaria and Jerusalem, the capital cities of the northern and southern kingdoms, respectively. The prophet seems to have had an intuitive experience that involved a vision.

II. Proclamation of Judgment; Word of Hope (1:2–3:12)

A. Judgment Speech (1:2–7)

The first major section of the book (1:2–3:12) includes a proclamation of judgment (1:2–2:11; 3:1–12) and a word of hope (2:12–13). Micah 1:2–7 is a judgment speech. The poet calls his listeners and the whole earth to attention, and also calls upon God to be a witness among the inhabitants of the land (v. 2). With metaphorical language he next describes an impending theophany (vv. 3–4). God's coming is imminent and will have devastating effects. The poet uses imagery from the natural world as metaphors for Israel and Judah, which will eventually be destroyed through military invasions. Together, vv. 3–4 disclose the power of God and the powerlessness of creation before God.

With two rhetorical questions (v. 5), the poet next indicts Israel and Judah, and specifically their capital cities Samaria and Jerusalem, the seat of leadership. Both cities were associated with idolatry in the latter part of the eighth century BCE (cf. Mic 1:6–7). In Mic 1:6–7, God, speaking through the prophet, announces a plan to destroy Samaria because of its transgressions (v. 5b) and idolatry. Samaria represents Jacob/Israel, the northern kingdom. Samaria's fate symbolizes the fate of the entire kingdom.

Micah 1:2–7 presents a hierarchical and patriarchal picture of God and God's power. This God dwells in "his holy temple" (v. 2), enthroned in the heavenly court, who will "come down" (v. 3), creating quite a different picture from the God who walked in the garden in the cool of the evening (Gen 3:8) and who spoke with Moses as a friend (Exod 33:11).

B. Dirge-Lament (1:8–16)

Micah 1:8–16 is a dirge-lament. Verse 8 is a pivotal verse that looks backwards to vv. 5–7 and forward to v. 9. God will lament, wail, go barefoot and naked, make lamentation like the jackals and mourning like the ostriches because of the peoples' transgressions, the impending loss of the kingdoms, and the sad state of Jerusalem. Here nakedness is associated with sin (see Gen 3:10). God will perform all of these actions and sounds of lamentation through the prophet who will be a sign to the community of its sinfulness, while also being a sign of God's presence and an expression of God's righteous anger yet steadfast love. The "incurable wound" is the blow dealt by God (see Jer 15:18; 30:12–15; and Jer 1:14) that Judah and Jerusalem will soon endure, specifically, devastation at the hands of the Babylonians.

Verses 10–15 resemble a funeral song. All of the cities mentioned are located in the Shephelah—the lowlands of the region. When God comes down and treads upon the high places of the earth (1:3), not only will the mountains and the hilltops of Samaria and Jerusalem be destroyed but also the lowlands. The historical setting for this dirge-lament is most likely the Assyrian invasion by Sennacherib in 701 BCE (see v. 15b).

Verse 16 closes the dirge-lament. The poet exhorts his listeners to lament. The verse foreshadows the exile after the fall of Jerusalem in 587 BCE.

The use of the present perfect tense, otherwise known as the prophetic perfect tense of vision, for an event that has not yet happened, signifies that what is predicted will, in fact, happen.

C. Woe Proclamation (2:1–5)

Micah 2:1–5 is a woe proclamation. Together with Mic 2:6–11, these verses convey a stinging message of judgment. In v. 1, the poet proclaims a warning to those guilty of premeditated injustices, which he enumerates in v. 2. Verses 3–5 are an announcement of judgment composed of a proclamation of intended chastisement (v. 3), a prediction of disaster (v. 4), and a threat (v. 5). Here the poet depicts God as a schemer of actions that will take place to "get even" with those who have transgressed others. Those who have taken land will lose their fields (v. 4) and be banned from further acquisition of property. The text makes the point that God asserts divine power on behalf of those victimized by the abuse of power of others. Lastly, vv. 1 and 3 exemplify the principle of *lex talionis* (see Lev 24:18–21), which was part of Israel's social culture and which became part of its religious culture and Torah. Those who used power oppressively will experience the punitive power of God.

D. Disputation Prophecy (2:6–11)

Micah 2:6–11 is a disputation prophecy. God, speaking through the prophet, quotes the prophet's adversaries, a comment that reveals a strained relationship between God and some of the Israelites due to the Israelites' smug attitude (v. 6) and their deeds of injustice (vv. 8–9). The rhetorical question in v. 7 highlights the distance that exists between the people and their God. Verses 8–9 add new transgressions to the list already begun in Mic 2:1–2. The punishment for wickedness is expulsion from the land (v. 10). Hence, the people's ill-gotten land will provide no place for the guilty to rest, especially because it has become "unclean" because of the people's sinfulness (see Lev 18:24–25). The poet ends the prophecy on a note of sarcasm (v. 11), which is God's final response to the objection raised by the opponents in v. 6 who do not want to hear an honest prophetic word proclaimed.

The tone of the poet's message changes in Mic 2:12–13, a salvation proclamation that promises divine care to those exiled, the remnant of

"Jacob." Here "Jacob" does not refer to the northern kingdom; instead, "Jacob" refers to Judah as the remnant of Israel which, in turn, sets the stage for restoration promised in Mic 4–5. Verses 12–13 will serve as a consolation for the people when they are exiles, if only they remember them.

E. Salvation Proclamation (2:12–13)

Micah 2:1–13 makes several theological points. First, the community addressed is struggling and living under a divine threat (vv. 1–11) and divine promise (vv. 12–13). Second, even those people closest to God are liable to sin and must accept the consequences of their actions. Third, since land is a divine gift, others' property rights and boundaries must be respected (see Exod 20:15, 17; Deut 15:4–5). Fourth, power, wealth, and status are not to be used to exploit others. Last, Israel's God is a God of justice who will not tolerate injustice.

F. Address to Israel's Political Leadership (3:1–4)

G. Proclamation concerning the Prophets (3:5–7)

The poet now returns to his proclamation of judgment (3:1–12). This new unit consists of an address to Israel's political leaders (vv. 1–4), a proclamation concerning the prophets (vv. 5–7), an interlude (v. 8), and another address to Israel's leadership (vv. 9–12). The poet exposes the overt and subtle abuse of power. In vv. 1–4, 5–7, and 9–12, the poet outlines the injustices and sins of Israel's political and religious leadership. The rhetorical question in v. 1 indicts Israel's leadership who do not act justly and who are the "haters of good and the lovers of evil" (v. 2*a*; author's translation). The poet continues his invective with a brutal metaphor in vv. 2*b*–3 that compares Israel's leaders to savage butchers and voracious cannibals who treat people like animals ready to be consumed. The poet next assaults verbally Israel's prophets (vv. 5–7), who are guilty of leading the people astray, who have corrupted their prophetic office for personal satisfaction and gain, and who will lose their prophetic gifts on account of their corruption.

H. Interlude: Statement of Confidence (3:8)

In v. 8, the poet sets himself apart from those whom he has been attacking and, in so doing, he becomes a refreshing contrast to the corrupted leaders of his day. To be filled "with power" is to be filled with God's Spirit and, consequently, with justice and might; such a person is responsible for exposing injustice. Thus, the prophet performs his tasks, proclaims God's word, and lives his life in the power and Spirit of God.

I. Address to Israel's Leadership (3:9–12)

In Mic 3:9–12, the poet again rails against the political and religious leaders of his day, inclusive of the community's priests (v. 11). He lists the wrongs of which his addressees are guilty and then mocks them by quoting their own words. He proceeds to inform his audience that because of the leaders' injustices, and all the other social injustices (see Mic 2), Jerusalem and the Temple—symbols of God's presence—will be destroyed. And yet, the presence of the Spirit-filled prophet remains among the people as a sign of God's enduring love for the people.

III. Proclamation of Future Restoration (4:1–5:15)

A. Prophetic Vision (4:1–5)

B. Divine Promise (4:6–5:15)

The second major section of the book (4:1–5:15), a proclamation of future restoration, consists of a prophetic vision (4:1–5) and a divine promise (4:6–5:15). Verses 1–5 offer a vision in which weapons are destroyed and transformed into tools of production at the peoples' initiative. The prophecy promises (v. 1) the reestablishment of Mount Zion—the Lord's mountain—which was considered a sacred mountain that had great importance for the whole world. The image of all the countries streaming to Zion to learn God's ways suggests a sense of unity as well as a certain religious solidarity that the countries will have with Judah (v. 2). Verse 3 depicts God as a judge who arbitrates in an effort to establish universal peace and security among all peoples of the earth (v. 4). Verse 5 suggests and celebrates a common vision of faith shared among world religions. In this poem, the poet offers a prophetic message: the peace that can exist among all countries and the unity with the Divine can be a goal and can become a reality for world politics and world religions.

Micah 4:6–5:15 is a divine promise of restoration after exile. God will heal and transform the weak and afflicted into a strong nation, and will establish divine reign over them on Mount Zion (4:6–8). The mention of God having caused the affliction of the people harks back to Mic 1:9. Images of childbirth in 4:9–10 hint at the new life soon to be experienced. The language of harvesting in 4:11–13 symbolizes Israel's victory over hostile nations.

The language of Mic 5:1 is curious. Here the poet points to the time when Jerusalem will be invaded and its present ruler will be insulted by a slap on the face. The image shifts quickly in vv. 2–5, where the poet describes a new messianic ruler soon to be born in Bethlehem, who will be "the one of peace" (v. 5a). Verses 5b–6 offer another reference to peace, this time when Assyria is conquered. Verses 7–9 continue the theme of Israel's transformation heard earlier in Mic 4:6–8. The remnant of Jacob, once weak, will now be made strong like a lion, capable of defeating all its enemies. The poet closes this section of the book with a description of what God intends to do to Israel in the "new day." God will cleanse Israel of all its idols (vv. 10–14) and, in anger and wrath, will execute vengeance on the nations that did not obey (v. 15). This last verse is harsh. The poet is proclaiming that Israel's God—the sovereign one—is not only Lord of creation but also Lord of history. Again, language about God reflects the historical background and backdrop of life lived in the latter part of the eighth century BCE.

IV. Words of Judgment, Lament, Trust, Promise, Petition, and Compassion (6:1–7:20)

A. Covenant Lawsuit (6:1–5)

B. Torah Lawsuit (6:6–8)

The third major section of the book (6:1–7:20) includes words of judgment, lament, trust, promise, petition, and compassion. Micah 6:1–5 is a covenant lawsuit. In vv. 1–2, the poet prepares the audience to hear God's case against Israel, which a bewildered God lays out in vv. 3–5 in conciliatory fashion while recounting past events (see Exod 1–15; Num 22–24). The people have forgotten their story and, in the process, have forgotten the graciousness of their God. Verses 6–8, a torah liturgy, are a response to God's questions, plea, and demand for an answer. Here the prophet stands in a humbled, self-reflective, penitential state, representing his people who have yet to come before the Lord. Micah raises three soul-searching questions aimed at atonement. Each question reflects a willingness to offer some sort of sacrifice, culminating in the offer to sacrifice one's firstborn for the sake of one's sin. What God requires, however, is justice, lovingkindness, and a humble walk together (v. 8). The humble walk with God will reveal what needs to be done by way of justice and lovingkindness.

C. Judgment Speech (6:9–16)

A raging voice from God, angered over the people's transgressions, is heard once again in vv. 9–16, a judgment speech. Following an initial statement that calls his listeners to attention (v. 9), the poet depicts God enumerating a list of the Israelites' unjust behaviors, and the divine plans to be executed upon the guilty parties (vv. 10–16). The poet describes a punitive God who uses the natural world to chastise a wayward people. This situation triggers a lament from the poet (7:1–7).

D. Lament (7:1–7)

E. Statement of Trust (7:8–10)

F. Divine Promise (7:11–13)

G. Petition (7:14–17)

In Mic 7:1–7, the poet uses similes and metaphors created from the natural world to describe the condition of his society; it is a wasteland, totally corrupt. The prophet, however, does not lose heart: he places his confidence in his God (v. 7) and utters a profound statement of trust (vv. 8–10). Another divine promise of restoration follows next (vv. 11–13; cf 4:6–5:15), accompanied by the prophet's petition that God care for the people as in the days of old (vv. 14–17), which in turn would serve as an instruction to all the nations.

H. Statement of Divine Love (7:18–20)

The book of Micah closes with what is, perhaps, the most poignant of all words within the prophetic corpus. In Mic 7:18–20, the prophet asks a simple rhetorical question (v. 18a) that leads into a heartfelt statement that describes God's compassionate and faithful love for all time (vv. 18b–20). Although the text as a whole is filled with biting words of judgment, with some sections sprinkled with promises of restoration, the final word of the prophet and the text is a word of hope, a word of love, and herein is revealed the true God of Israel.

BIBLIOGRAPHY

E. Ben Zvi. *Micah*. FOTL 21B (Grand Rapids: Eerdmans, 2000); C. J. Dempsey. "Micah." *The Prophets: A Liberation Critical Reading* (Minneapolis: Fortress, 2000) 23–33; W. McKane. *The Book of Micah* (Edinburgh: T&T Clark, 1998); M. A. Sweeney. "Micah." *The Twelve Prophets. Volume 2.* Berit Olam (Collegeville: The Liturgical Press, 2000) 339–416; B. K. Waltke. *A Commentary on Micah* (Grand Rapids: Eerdmans, 2007).

NAHUM

James D. Nogalski

OVERVIEW

The prophet Nahum comes from Elkosh (1:1), a town whose location is not known. The prophet's name, ironically, means "comfort," yet the bulk of Nahum presents a message of devastation. Nineveh/Assyria is the primary object of God's wrath in Nahum (though it is explicitly mentioned only in 1:1; 2:8; 3:7, 18). This concentration on Assyria, and its capital Nineveh, is explained by historical circumstances of the seventh century BCE. The book appropriately comes after Micah (the last eighth-century prophet) and before Habakkuk (a book that anticipates the rise of Babylon). Nahum represents Judah's seventh-century concern about Assyria before Nineveh passes from the political scene in 612 BCE.

Judah became a de facto vassal of Assyria in the last third of the eighth century and remained so for the better part of a century until Assyrian hegemony weakened to the point at which Josiah was briefly able to assert some level of political independence at the beginning of his adult reign (622), well before his death at the hands of the Egyptian Pharaoh Necho II (609).

The book of Nahum consists of three independent poetic pieces joined together by editorial transitions. The structure of Nahum probably represents a post-exilic expansion of an earlier collection of poetic pronouncements celebrating Assyria's downfall. The expansion incorporated the theophany (1:2–8) as a theological reflection upon divine punishment of the wicked, thus interpreting the judgment that follows as part of God's cosmic justice—overthrowing even powerful nations who dare to act against the God of creation.

OUTLINE

I. Superscription (1:1)

II. Semi-acrostic Theophany Anticipating God's Wrath and an Editorial Transition (1:2–8, 9–15)

III. First Song of Destruction and Transition (2:1–12, 13)

IV. Second Song of Destruction and Conclusion (3:1–17, 18–19)

DETAILED ANALYSIS

I. Superscription (1:1)

The superscription of Nahum actually contains two titles, a clue that it may result from more than one level of editorial activity. The first part of the superscription focuses on the object of the following judgment ("an oracle concerning Nineveh"). Nineveh was the capital city of Assyria for much of the period of Assyrian domination, from the end of the eighth century to Nineveh's destruction at the hands of the Babylonians and Medes in 612 BCE. The second part introduces the prophetic figure to whom the message is attributed (the book of the vision of Nahum the Elkoshite). Neither this prophet nor his hometown is mentioned elsewhere in the Old Testament.

II. Semi-acrostic Theophany Anticipating God's Wrath and an Editorial Transition (1:2–8, 9–15)

1:2–8. Semi-acrostic Theophany. Nahum 1:2–8 has been placed at the beginning of the book by editors for literary, historical, and theological purposes. Nahum 1:2–8 was originally an independent poem that used an acrostic style to describe the awesome power of Yahweh's appearance as a threat to Yahweh's enemies. Unlike other acrostic poems in the OT (see Lam 1–4; Pss 9–10; 119), however, Nah 1:2–8 appears to have been designed to proceed only halfway through the alphabet with each subsequent line beginning with the next letter of the alphabet (though this pattern is disturbed in four lines (vv. 2b, 2c, 4b, 6a). These disruptions to the acrostic pattern echo ideas from Mic 7 and other texts in the Book of the Twelve. The theophanic orientation likely prompted the poem's incorporation into the Book of the Twelve. A similar theophanic poem, probably added at the same time, concludes the book of Habakkuk (3:1–19).

In addition to the acrostic pattern, Nah 1:2–8 exhibits a clear rhetorical logic. Yahweh's character (jealous and avenging) provides the rationale for a description of Yahweh's appearance in a storm that also draws upon traditional creation images of the Divine Warrior battling the forces of chaos to reestablish order in the world (1:2a, 3b–4). This action causes all creation (the mountains, hills, land, and world, 1:5). to tremble. Nahum then calls for a response with a rhetorical question (who can endure Yahweh's wrath?) while 1:7–8 respond to this question from two directions. Those who take refuge in Yahweh will find protection (1:7) while Yahweh's enemies will be utterly destroyed (1:8).

Editorial Transition (1:9–15). Nahum 1:9–15 functions as an editorial transition between the theophany proclaiming Yahweh's vengeance on his enemies and the introduction to the earlier collection celebrating the demise of Nineveh. Parts of 1:9–15 presuppose the theophany of 1:2–8 by addressing those plotting against Yahweh. For example, Nah 1:9–10 uses plural verbs. In contrast, other portions of the passage address three different characters using singular pronouns: (1) the personified Lady Nineveh (indicated by second-person, feminine singular "from you") address in 1:11, 12a; (2) her king ("one has gone out who plots evil against the LORD" in 1:11)[1] who will soon be destroyed for his (third-person, masculine singular in 1:13) hostility toward Yahweh; and (3) Lady Zion (1:12b, see also 1:15 about the removal of her oppression). The presence of these separate characters makes the passage difficult to follow in English translation. The address to Lady Nineveh and her king probably constitute an earlier introduction to the corpus before the addition of the theophany. However, the combination of the theophany with this expanded introduction equates the enemies of Yahweh in 1:2–8 with Assyria, its king, and its capital city as it announces reprieve for Jerusalem. Nahum 1:9–15 thus provides a theological framework from which to understand Assyria's destruction so powerfully depicted in the two poems that comprise the bulk of Nah 2–3. Two motifs in the editorial transition

reappear at the end of the book (thereby creating an inclusio): the futility of Assyrian might (1:12; 3:15b–17) and the direct address of the Assyrian king regarding his imminent death (1:14; 3:18–19).

III. First Song of Destruction and Transition (2:1–12, 13)

2:1–13. First Song of Destruction. Chapter 2 forms the first of two composite units setting forth graphic descriptions of the downfall of Nineveh. The extent to which this chapter represents a single composition is debated, but there is little doubt that both chs. 2 and 3 are compiled in such a way as to portray two parallel descriptions of Nineveh's destruction. The subunits in ch. 2 include an address to Lady Nineveh announcing the impending attack as the work of Yahweh to relieve Jacob/Israel (2:1–2); a description of the warriors (2:3); the initial onslaught of chariots and the hapless Assyrian nobles (2:4–5); a poetic depiction of the city destroyed (2:6–8); a description of the aftermath of the city's destruction (2:9–10); and a satirical reflection on the illusion of Assyrian power using the metaphor of Assyria as a lion whose strength is no match for Yahweh (2:11–12). This poetry functions more like an impressionist painting than a narrative account. Image is piled upon image to create the sense of Nineveh's inevitable destruction, the futility of its defenses, and the totality of its defeat. The descriptive language is framed by claims that the destruction is the work of Yahweh, against whom earthly power is no match (2:1–2, 13). The concluding verse, placed in the mouth of Yahweh, summarizes the message using the images of chariots, lions, prey, and messengers from the preceding text, while at the same time anticipating the image of the sword in 3:3.

IV. Second Song of Destruction and Conclusion (3:1–17, 18–19)

3:1–19. Second Song of Destruction. Nahum 3 functions similarly to Nah 2. Its three subunits (3:1–7, 8–17, 18–19) each have their own internal logic, but function together within this context by depicting Nineveh's destruction, before returning to the motifs of the inadequacy of Assyria's strength (3:15–17) and the death of its king (3:18–19) with which the early corpus began (1:12, 14).

---

1   Unless otherwise indicated by NRSV, the quotations from Nahum are direct translations by the author.

Nahum 3:1–7 conforms to typical patterns for a woe oracle: the initial accusation beginning with "alas" (3:1); a description of the disaster (3:2–3); a rationale for the punishment (3:4); and a divine response (3:5–7). Like 2:3–8, Nah 3:2–3 produces a series of images that convey a battle scene of deadly proportion. The rationale in 3:4 personifies Nineveh as a prostitute whose seduction of other nations leads them into slavery and debauchery. The divine response (3:5–7) depicts Yahweh abusing and humiliating this prostitute. Rhetorically, the shocking images of sexuality and violence underscore the severity of Assyria's punishment for the ancient reader even while they will likely offend the sensitivity of modern readers more accustomed to speaking of God's judgment in less explicit terms.

Nahum 3:8–17 is a composite taunt song made up of two main sections. It begins in 3:8–11 by drawing an analogy between the destruction of the mighty city of Thebes, the capital of the Egyptian empire (destroyed in 663 BCE) and the impending destruction of Nineveh in 612 BCE. Both cities were capitals of these powerful empires. Both cities were strategically situated on rivers that were used for defensive purposes. And both cities were thought to be impenetrable. Yet, both cities succumbed to the onslaught of superior power. The satire of this unit should not be lost. It was Assyria who destroyed Thebes in 663, but now the tables will be turned according to 3:8–11, with Assyria now destroyed. Nahum 3:12–17 begins and ends with botanical metaphors depicting Nineveh as a ripe fig tree whose fruit is ready for the taking (3:12), but it will be devoured by locusts (3:15–17). In between, Nineveh's troops (3:13) and its defenses (3:14) are mocked as ineffectual. The locust imagery in 3:15–17 functions in two ways: (1) locusts are used to convey Assyria's power through numerical superiority; (2) Assyria's locusts will be overrun by more powerful locusts.

Nahum 3:18–19, like 1:14, addresses the king of Assyria directly, using second masculine singular forms of address to speak of his imminent demise. Whereas Yahweh prepares the grave of the king in 1:14, Nah 3:19 speaks of the king's mortal wound, thus bringing death closer.

The book of Nahum, read in isolation, has sometimes been interpreted as a xenophobic rant, its message reduced to a celebration of the downfall of a hated enemy. Undoubtedly, the almost gleeful presentation of a nation's destruction should be assessed critically. However, recent work concerning the editorial shaping and placement of Nahum for the Book of the Twelve suggests that a broader purpose was at work in the incorporation of Nahum into its current canonical setting. The editorial hands that compiled the vivid depictions of Nineveh's destruction emphasized two theological claims, which need to be heard when one interprets Nahum. First, Assyria was not an innocent bystander on the political stage. For more than a century, Assyria's expansionistic and militaristic tendencies had terrorized the region and impoverished smaller nations from whom it exacted exorbitant taxes. Judah was no exception to this oppression. The editorial shaping of Nahum interprets Assyria's destruction as a potential end to Judah's oppression (1:12b, 15; 2:2). Second, the downfall of Assyria is portrayed as the work of Yahweh. Theologically, the power of God used to thwart the brutality and oppression of so powerful a force as the Assyrians is presented as a source of hope and justice. The book assumes that if God is a just God, then at some point God must intervene against a country that so blatantly flaunts its own power to do as it chooses. In the logic of the theophany at the beginning of the book, God appears in order to bring judgment against the guilty (1:3), while offering refuge to those who seek God (1:7). In this sense, Nahum makes a theological affirmation that Yahweh ultimately controls the powers of this world.

BIBLIOGRAPHY

R. Coggins and S. P. Re'emi. *Israel Among the Nations: A Commentary on the Books of Nahum, Obadiah, Esther.* ITC (Grand Rapids: Eerdmans, 1985); J. O'Brien. *Nahum, Habakkuk, Zephaniah, Haggai, Zechariah, Malachi.* AOTC (Nashville: Abingdon, 2004); J. J. M. Roberts. *Nahum, Habakkuk, and Zephaniah.* OTL (Louisville: Westminster John Knox, 1991); M. Sweeney. "Nahum." *The Twelve Prophets. Vol. 2.* Berit Olam (Collegeville, Minn.: Liturgical Press, 2000).

HABAKKUK

James D. Nogalski

OVERVIEW

The name Habakkuk is unusual; it derives from an Akkadian word for a garden plant. Thus, unlike many prophetic names (e.g., Isaiah), it has no theophoric element. The plant name attests to the way in which Mesopotamian culture influenced Judah in the seventh and sixth centuries BCE.

Nothing is known about the individual named Habakkuk, although he is mentioned in Bel and the Dragon (1:33–39), a Greek Addition to the book of Daniel. There, Habakkuk is the prophet miraculously transported by the messenger of God to deliver food from Palestine to Daniel who is in the lions' den in Babylon.

At its canonical place in the Book of the Twelve, the book named for Habakkuk is presumed to have a seventh-century setting, though the final form of the book may date to the exilic or post-exilic period. The internal literary flow of the book and its position in the Twelve should be taken into account when interpreting Habakkuk. The bulk of the first two chapters functions as a prophetic complaint against the prosperity of the wicked and Yahweh's subsequent promise to send the Babylonians to punish them. Habakkuk 3 consists of a theophanic description of the Divine Warrior battling the elements of chaos (3:3–15) followed by the prophet's affirmation of confidence in Yahweh's decision (3:16–19).

Habakkuk is closely related to themes prominent in surrounding books, particularly the literature that extends from Micah to Zephaniah. Habakkuk follows Nahum's pronouncement of the end of Assyrian hegemony, but portrays the situation in Judah in terms similar to Mic 6:1–7:7 (note especially the similarity of Mic 7:7 and Hab 3:16). In the chronology and logic of the canonical order, a reader of the Book of the Twelve finds that the behavior confronted by the prophet remains virtually unchanged from the accusations that occur in Mic 6:1–7:7, even though the reader must assume that nearly a century has passed. Hence, the severity of Yahweh's response to the prophet's complaint (Hab 1:2–4), namely, that Yahweh will send the Babylonians (Hab 1:5–11), can be interpreted as part of Yahweh's ongoing frustration with people who continue to turn their back on Yahweh and on their covenantal obligations.

The book reflects multiple historical contexts. It presumes traditions regarding Babylon's rise to prominence in the seventh century BCE, but the theodicy comprising the foundational core of the book has parallels in exilic/post-exilic literature, the time when it reached its final form. However, the core of the third chapter (3:3–15) is a theophanic poem that exhibits archaic linguistic characteristics, though the frame around it may be attributed to a later setting.

OUTLINE

I. Superscription (1:1)

II. Complaint About the Wicked (1:2–4)

III. Divine Response (1:5–11)

IV. Renewed Complaint (1:12–17)

V. Vision Recounted (2:1–5)

VI. Five Woe Oracles (2:6–20)

VII. The Prayer of Habakkuk (3:1–19)

    A. Theophanic Petition and Vision (3:1–15)

    B. A Prophetic Response (3:16–19)

DETAILED ANALYSIS

I. Superscription (1:1)

The first superscription (1:1; see also 3:1) functions as a title attributing chs. 1–2 to a prophet named Habakkuk. No other biographical information is provided.

II. Complaint About the Wicked (1:2–4)

In its current form, 1:2–4 begins with a prophetic complaint regarding the prosperity of the wicked and Yahweh's failure to act against them. The prophet articulates accusations of violence and wrongdoing as a perversion of the orderly world expected by God. Similar ideas are taken up again in 1:12–17 in what may have been the original continuation of this complaint.

III. Divine Response (1:5–11)

A divine speech comprises 1:5–11 by announcing impending punishment (1:5–6a) and describing the perpetrators of that punishment (1:6b–11). Even though addressed to a group, this unit responds to the prophetic complaint of 1:2–4. The unit begins with an admonition to read the signs of Yahweh's activity in the world, then identifies the Chaldeans (Babylonians) as the instrument Yahweh will use to punish the wicked in Judah (1:5–6a). The remainder of this response focuses its attention upon the fierceness of the Babylonians. The description of the Babylonians in 1:6b–11 appears designed to trump the description of Nineveh in Nah 3 with an even more imposing portrayal of Babylon as a ruthless, brutal enemy whom no one can stop. Its army marches through other lands as if they were not there (1:6–7), it relies on its own massive military power (1:7–8, 11), and it mocks those who stand in its way (1:10).

IV. Renewed Complaint (1:12–17)

Habakkuk 1:12–17 returns to the prophet confronting God regarding the prosperity of the wicked as in 1:2–4. However, in places, 1:12–17 expands this message to include the Babylonians among the wicked. Thus, while the prophet pleads that Yahweh rid the world of the wicked (1:12–13), the enemy is also described in corporate terms as one who conquers nations (1:17). This artful blending of wisdom motifs with prophetic judgment creates a theological paradox dealing with the question of God's role in history: Why would Yahweh allow the wicked in Judah to prosper and then punish them by sending the Babylonians?

V. Vision Recounted (2:1–5)

In Hab 2:1–5, the prophet continues to speak, announcing his decision to await a response from Yahweh (2:1), which the prophet announces (2:2a), then recounts (2:2b–5) as a message to resolve the theodicy question. This "vision" admonishes patience to the righteous, because a time of judgment will come even though it may seem to be delayed. The vision pronounces judgment upon the proud and arrogant whose greed leads them to Sheol and death. The righteous, by contrast, are those who live by faith (2:4). Embedded in this description of the fate awaiting the wicked, one hears an implied response to the initial complaint of 1:2–4: God will punish the wicked, but in God's own time. The final line of 2:5, however, appears to have in mind the punishment of the wicked nation sent by God who will "gather all nations to [himself]/and collect all peoples for [himself]." Thus, Hab 2:1–5 anticipates not one but two judgments in its final form: one for the wicked against whom the prophet railed at the beginning of the book, and one for the Chaldeans who will invade Judah. This same image of two stages of judgment comes back into play at the end of Hab 3. This image derives from theological reflection upon the events that transpired in the sixth century. Jerusalem's destruction in 587 was interpreted as punishment from God, as was Babylon's implosion as a regional superpower replaced by the Persians in 539 BCE.

VI. Five Woe Oracles (2:6–20)

Habakkuk 2:6–20 contains a collection of five small units organized around the formulaic presence of "woe" or "alas" (NRSV; Heb.: *hoy*) as an introductory marker (2:6, 9, 12, 15, 19). These oracles begin with an introduction (2:6a) to orient the reader to the collection's role. The content demonstrates the same dual focus on wisdom and political elements that appeared in Hab 1. A foundational composition warns readers to avoid certain destructive behaviors (greed, lust, violence, and idolatry). An application of this admonition to a corporate entity follows, which in the context of Habakkuk can only be interpreted as Babylon. The first thematic focus has as much in common with the wisdom tradition as with the prophetic tradition, whereas the second likely serves as the reason for incorporating Habakkuk into the Book of the Twelve. Habakkuk 2:6–8 begins with an introductory statement (2:6*a*) orienting the reader to the collection that follows as "mocking riddles." Habakkuk 2:6–7 admonishes against greed. Greed leads to overextending credit in the perpetual desire to increase one's tangible assets, only to find that one's own creditors suddenly appear to collect their due. Habakkuk 2:8 expands this admonition onto the political level by condemning the greedy as one who has "plundered many nations" and has caused bloodshed and violence to the earth. This application refers back to the violence about which the prophet complained in 1:2–3 as well as the description of the Chaldeans who mercilessly attack other countries (see 1:6–10).

The second woe (2:9–11) initially warns against powerful persons who oppress others to build their own houses, only to find that these actions will bring shame upon their own house. The house they build will itself become a testament to their greed, as noted in the language of personification: the stones and plaster crying out. The rationale expressed in the last half of 2:10*b*, however, once again expands the horizon of the wicked to one who has "[cut] off many peoples" as a means of applying this admonition, not to a wealthy individual, but as a warning to Babylon.

The third woe (2:12–14) differs from the first two in two ways. First, it focuses attention on acts of a powerful oppressor (one who builds a city with bloodshed and iniquity) and needs no reformulation to evoke the image of Babylon's impending attack. Second, it does not offer an explicit word of judgment. Rather, the result of the woe is a statement of confidence that the earth will recognize Yahweh's glory.

The fourth woe (2:15–17) returns to the pattern of condemning ethical misdeeds, in this case condemning the prurient behavior of getting one's neighbors drunk with the purpose of seeing them naked (2:15). The act will bring punishment from Yahweh by bringing shame upon those who perpetrate it (2:16). This fourth woe is also reinterpreted to apply to Babylon in 2:17, whose actions have devastated humanity and the animal kingdom.

The final woe (2:18–20) deviates from the stylistic and thematic pattern of the previous four. It is the only one of the five that does not begin with "alas" as the first word of the unit. Instead, it first introduces a new topic, idolatry, a religious rather than an ethical violation. Then, 2:19 condemns those who worship idols. The unit concludes (2:20) with a theological affirmation functioning as an implicit warning. In this sense, it has a universal theological point to make, like the end of the third woe: Yahweh is in his holy temple, and all the earth should keep silent before him.

These woe oracles, like Hab 1:5–2:5, show evidence that ethical and religious admonitions have been reinterpreted as judgments against Babylon. In their final form, they accuse a nation (Babylon) of behavior (greed, lust, and idolatry) worthy of judgment in the eyes of God. A foreign nation stands accountable to Yahweh's ethical pronouncements.

VII. The Prayer of Habakkuk (3:1–19)

Habakkuk 3 offers numerous interpretive challenges due to its linguistic difficulties, tradition history, and transmission. Portions of Habakkuk 3 are often cited as some of the oldest Hebrew poetry in the OT, though some argue this linguistic style imitates ancient patterns rather than presenting an authentic archaic form. This archaic poetic style is made more complicated due to the presence of ancient mythical traditions, which have been used to describe Yahweh. Finally, the transmission of this chapter is unusual on two fronts. First, this chapter bears the hallmarks of cultic transmission, which make it resemble a psalm more than a prophetic pronouncement. The chapter has a psalm-like superscription (3:1), a subscription (3:19*b*), and a triple use of *selah* (3:3, 9, 13)—an enigmatic musical notation that elsewhere appears only in the Psalter. The ritual character of the chapter makes it unusual for prophetic literature in general, not just the book of Habakkuk. Second, Hab 3 is nowhere attested in the Qumran scrolls. The *Habakkuk Pesher* (an ancient biblical commentary found at Qumran) stops at 2:20, despite having more room on the scroll, and no other fragment contains verses from Hab 3. Despite the absence of Hab 3 from the Qumran scrolls, most scholars think the chapter was an integral part of the book long before the time of the Qumran community.

A. Theophanic Petition and Vision (3:1–15)

Habakkuk 3:1–2 contains the second superscription of the book (see 1:1) and introduces the following verses as a prayer, a designation that reflects the function of the language of the chapter's framing elements (3:2, 16–19). The frame contains a petition to Yahweh (3:2) and an affirmation of confidence in Yahweh's strength and power to deliver (3:16–19). The first-person speaker petitions Yahweh for mercy even while anticipating judgment "in the midst of years" (not "in our own time" as NRSV in 3:2).

Habakkuk 3:3–15 conveys a complex theophanic portrait in two parts. The first part (3:3–7) functions as a theophany report proper in which God's appearance from Teman/Paran is announced (3:3), followed by a description of God's appearance (3:4–5) and a recounting of its effect on the created order (3:6) and the regions of Cushan and Midian (3:7). These place names are associated with the mountainous Sinai region, a place frequently present in theophanic portrayals. The responses of creation and the nomads of Cushan/Midian convey the fear that Yahweh's presence elicits. Nonetheless, these areas are not the target of the Warrior. This language of fear and the mountain regions are quite at home in Divine Warrior texts in which Yahweh goes to battle against an enemy (Judg 5:4–5; Deut 33:2; Pss 18:7–15; 114:3–8; Isa 30:27–28; Jer 25:30–31).

The second portion of the theophanic portrait, 3:8–15, provides a hymnic description of Yahweh's battle against the enemy, a description that draws upon Divine Warrior traditions to depict Yahweh's defeat of chaos. These ancient images have roots in Canaanite and Mesopotamian mythology where the respective deities battle the Sea and the River in narratives recounting creation. However, the Canaanite and Mesopotamian traditions in Habakkuk have been transformed into a story of *Yahweh* defeating the enemy. In the context of Habakkuk, the unnamed "enemy" is appropriately interpreted as Babylon—even if it was not originally the opponent (see reference to the nations [plural] in 3:12 and "the people [singular] to attack us" in 3:16*b*).

The second theophanic element begins with a rhetorical question (3:8). It presumes a negative response, turning the imagery of chaos on its head (since in the non-Israelite versions, a deity did battle Sea and River).

In Hab 3:9–11, the Divine Warrior attacks (3:9) and cosmic imagery attests to the fear of those who stand in Yahweh's way. The cosmic elements in 3:8–11 (river, sea, earth, mountains, the waters, great deep, sun, moon) evoke the ancient story of the deity taming the elements of creation.

The response implied by the rhetorical question of 3:8 is finally answered explicitly in 3:12–13. The target of Yahweh's appearance is "the nations" and the purpose of the battle is "to save your people" and "your anointed." How the reference to the nations is interpreted depends largely upon the context one identifies. Those paying attention to the entire canonical context of Habakkuk or its position in the Book of the Twelve tend to interpret the nations as those nations involved in the destruction of Jerusalem and its aftermath. Those who interpret Hab 3 as a separate poem tend to interpret the nations' relation to Yahweh as primarily a theological issue.

Habakkuk 3:13–14 make clear that the people and king are the ones for whom Yahweh does battle. Nevertheless, tension remains with the larger context of Habakkuk, which anticipates that this deliverance will happen only after the Babylonians punish Judah. Thus, the book assumes a twofold judgment, one from Babylon roused by Yahweh to attack Judah (1:5–11) and the second against Babylon by Yahweh (3:14, 16).

Habakkuk 3:15 reflects tension concerning the question with which the second part of the hymn opened (3:8). Verse 15 highlights the reinterpretation of the chaos battle hymn in 3:8–14. While 3:8 implied that Yahweh came against his enemies, not against the Sea, the allusions to the chaos battle reinterpret the enemy as the nations (3:12), meaning the statement that Yahweh did trample the Sea becomes a statement about the ultimate destruction of the enemy (Babylon).

B. A Prophetic Response (3:16–19)

Habakkuk 3:16–19 constitutes the remaining portion of the editorial frame that surrounds the theophany. Like 3:2, Hab 3:16–19 anticipates a time of inevitable judgment, which causes great consternation and trepidation. Nevertheless, this speaker also affirms trust in Yahweh (3:18–19) even while acknowledging difficult days ahead (3:17). These verses appear designed to comment on the theophanic vision of 3:3–15. The prophet recognizes Yahweh will ultimately prevail against the enemy (assumed to be Babylon when read with Hab 1–2), but the enemy will still attack the prophet's people.

The response to the vision (3:16–19) framing the theophany appears to have been expanded in two ways in 3:16b–17. First, 3:16b shows awareness that the independent hymn (3:2–15, 16a, 18–19) has interpreted the enemy as Babylon as in Hab 1–2 (note the enemy is "the nations" in 3:12, but one people in 3:16b). Second, this additional material demonstrates awareness of other writings in the Book of the Twelve in two specific ways. First, the reference to God's appearance as a "day of calamity" recurs in three successive prophetic books (Nah 1:7; Hab 3:16; and Zeph 1:15; see also Obad 12) referring to the downfall of Assyria, Babylon, and Jerusalem respectively. Second, the (for Habakkuk) unusual motif of the land's fertility draws on imagery from Joel 1–2, as do other texts in the Book of the Twelve. In such editorial expansions, editors invite readers to contemplate the ways in which various texts in the Book of the Twelve reinforce each other. This literature perceives the continuity of God's message to the prophets, proclaiming that God is at work in and through history.

BIBLIOGRAPHY

F. I. Andersen. *Habakkuk*. AB 25 (New York: Doubleday, 2001); J. M. O'Brien. *Nahum, Habakkuk, Zephaniah, Haggai, Zechariah, Malachi*. AOTC (Nashville: Abingdon, 2004); J. J. M. Roberts. *Nahum, Habakkuk, and Zephaniah*. OTL (Louisville: Westminster John Knox, 1991); M. A. Sweeney. "Habakkuk." *The Twelve Prophets*. Vol. 2. Berit Olam (Collegeville, Minn.: Liturgical Press, 2000).

ZEPHANIAH

James D. Nogalski

OVERVIEW

The name Zephaniah means "the LORD hid" (i.e., "hid from danger"). Following the superscription, the book may be divided into three thematic groupings of short sayings and speeches (see outline). In many respects, Zephaniah functions as the southern counterpart to Amos in the Book of the Twelve, with the bulk of the message pronouncing judgment against Judah (instead of Israel) and the nations. From the beginning, judgment is inevitable, unavoidable, and imminent. Judgment against Judah (1:4–6, 9–13) intertwines with words of universal judgment (1:2–3) and pronouncements concerning the day of the Lord (1:7, 8, 14–18; 2:1–3). Like Amos, Zephaniah's oracles against the nations (2:4–15; 3:8) essentially end with judgment against God's own people (3:1–7). Zephaniah concludes with a series of promises, both for the world at large (3:9–10) and for Zion (3:11–20). Unlike Amos, however, Zephaniah depicts the Lord, not a Davidic monarch, as king of the restored Zion.

OUTLINE

I. Superscription (1:1)

II. Judgment Against Creation and God's People (1:2–2:3)

III. Oracles Against the Nations and Judgment Against God's People (2:4–3:8)

IV. Promises of Deliverance for the Nations and for Zion (3:9–20)

DETAILED ANALYSIS

I. Superscription (1:1)

The superscription of Zeph 1:1 contains three elements: a word-event formula, a regnal formula, and an extended genealogy. Mention of the word of the Lord is a recurring element at the beginning of prophetic books (see Hos 1:1; Joel 1:1; Mic 1:1); it emphasizes the source of the prophet's authority.

The presence of Zephaniah during Josiah's reign is significant on two fronts. First, it sets the historical context for reading Zephaniah (even though the final form reflects a later period). Second, reference to Josiah and Hezekiah accounts for Zephaniah's placement as the final prophetic writing in the Book of the Twelve that presumes a pre-exilic literary setting.

Other prophetic superscriptions cite a prophet's ancestry (Hos 1:1; Joel 1:1; Jonah 1:1; Isa 1:1; Jer 1:1; and Zech 1:1 [two generations]), but only Zeph 1:1 traces a prophet's heritage back four generations, presumably to demonstrate his royal lineage by portraying Zephaniah as a descendant of Hezekiah (the last Judean king mentioned in the Book of the Twelve [Mic 1:1]).

II. Judgment Against Creation and God's People (1:2–2:3)

A series of sayings pronounces judgment on creation (1:2–3) and Judah (1:4–6), then explores various features of the day of Lord (1:7–17) before calling Judah to seek the Lord (2:1–3).

Zephaniah 1:2–3 draw upon language from the Priestly story of creation (Gen 1) and the flood story (Gen 6–9) to introduce the book's message. In so doing, 1:2–3 pronounce judgment upon the created elements in reverse order to their appearance in Gen 1. By itself, 1:2–3 suggest universal judgment, but, given its position at the outset of the book, this cosmic language interprets the significance of the judgment to follow as something akin to the undoing of creation. Zephaniah 1:2–3 does not speak of a universal judgment followed by a second stage of judgment on Judah and Jerusalem (1:4–13). The integration of allusions to the Priestly account suggests a post-exilic provenance for the composition and placement of these verses.

The next subunit, 1:4–6, pronounces judgment upon Judah and Jerusalem because a number of groups have broken faith with the Lord (the remnant of Baal, the idolatrous priests, those worshiping astral deities, and those blending the worship of the Lord and other deities). The actions condemned fit relatively well in a late seventh-century setting, at least as described by the biblical accounts of Josiah's reforms. Given the previous reference to Josiah (1:1), 1:4–6 give the impression of judgment pronounced for many of the same behaviors that motivate Josiah's reforms in 2 Kgs 23.

The next thematic group, 1:7–18, revolves around the impending day of the Lord and its implications. Many short sayings (1:7, 8, 9, 10–11, 12–13, 14–18) are loosely connected by "on that day/time" formulas, but together they paint a portrait of impending disaster sent by the Lord. Zephaniah 1:7 introduces the theme to follow by calling for silence in anticipation of the day of Lord as a cultic sacrifice. In 1:8, the day of sacrifice will result in punishment of the political leaders for their tendency to ingratiate themselves to foreign overlords (the officials, the sons of the king, and all those wearing foreign garments). Zephaniah 1:9 announces punishment "on that day" for the superstitious (or syncretistic) practice of jumping over thresholds out of fear of evil spirits who might reside there (see 1 Sam 5:5). Zephaniah 1:10–11 changes the focus of judgment to the broader community of Jerusalem's inhabitants, an emphasis that continues into 1:12–13. Given the specific judgments against particular groups in the preceding "day of the LORD" statements, the inclusion of various districts in Jerusalem as the object of destruction eliminates any suggestion that the impending day of Lord will only affect a select few.

In Zeph 1:14–18, a series of short statements reflects upon the nature of the impending day of the Lord. Several phrases associated with the day of the Lord have parallel expressions elsewhere in the Book of the Twelve. The end of this unit (1:18) exhibits the same universal perspective concerning the day of the Lord as that in 1:2–3, but most of 1:14–18 coincides with the previous pronouncements against Jerusalem and Judah, again suggesting the judgment's scale and significance.

Zephaniah 2:1–3 calls on the pious in Judah to seek the Lord in the hope that the Lord will allow them to survive the coming destruction on "the day of the LORD's wrath." This oracle presumes the possibility of a remnant that will survive, surviving because they seek the Lord, righteousness, humility, and justice (*mishpat*). Since the idea of judgment on all the earth (1:18) serves as an introduction to the oracles against the nations (2:4–3:8), 2:1–3 seem out of place.

III. Oracles Against the Nations and Judgment Against God's People (2:4–3:8)

The oracles against the nations (OAN) in Zephaniah cover four regions: two smaller kingdoms to the west (Philistia) and east (Ammon/Moab) followed by two major powers of the seventh century (Egypt and Assyria) with whom Judah had to contend prior to the rise of Babylon. Inclusion of the larger powers distinguishes Zephaniah's oracles from those of Amos (Amos 1:3–2:16), but the surprise ending of the OAN switches to judgment against Jerusalem, much like Amos' OAN conclude with judgment against Judah (2:4–5) and Israel (2:6–16). Despite reference to Zephaniah as a prophet from the time of Josiah (Zeph 1:1), several allusions to Judah as a remnant suggest these oracles have been edited for an exilic/postexilic community.

The oracle against the Philistines (2:4–7) uses eight names to identify the region: the same four Philistine cities mentioned in Amos 1:6–8 (Gaza, Ashkelon, Ashdod, Ekron); two ethnic terms (Philistines and Cherethites); and two geographic terms (Canaan and the seacoast). In its current form, 2:4 and 2:5 are oddly positioned since the opening of 2:4 ("for …") does not make sense as the cause for seeking the Lord in 2:3, and the first word of 2:5 (*hoy*) usually signals a new unit. Zephaniah 2:4–7 provides no reason why the Philistines are singled out for judgment. This oracle promises that the "remnant of the house of Judah" will take over the land and houses of Philistia (2:7). As such, this oracle probably presumes the destruction of Jerusalem, though this has been debated.

The next oracle (2:8–11) pronounces judgment against the Moabites and Ammonites for taunting the people of the Lord (2:8) who are again called a "remnant" (2:9), suggesting an exilic or early post-exilic date. Ammon and Moab will suffer the fate of Sodom and Gomorrah, an allusion to the destruction recounted in Gen 19:24–29.

The oracle against the Ethiopians (2:12) is generally interpreted to mean Egypt. The reasons for referring to Egypt as Cush (Ethiopia) are not entirely clear since Ethiopia was not a major power in Josiah's time. At any rate, the brief, vague, ungrounded judgment against Ethiopia (meaning Egypt) suggests a symbolic function, since Assyria is the next nation mentioned. The Assyria/Egypt polarity is common in many prophetic texts, especially Isaiah and the Twelve (see 2 Kgs 17:4; 23:29; Isa 7:18; 11:11, 16; 19:23–25; 20:4; 27:13; Jer 2:18, 36; Lam 5:6; Hos 7:11; 9:3; 11:5, 11; 12:1; Mic 7:12; Zech 10:10–11), and Cush appears elsewhere in Zephaniah (1:1; 3:1).

The oracle against the Assyrians (2:13–15) comments on the fall of Assyria. The latter half of the seventh century saw a gradual decline in the power of Assyria, until its final demise in 612 when Nineveh was destroyed. During its latter years, Assyria allowed Egypt to control parts of the trade routes. Only 2:15 implies a reason for judgment: Assyria's pride in its own strength. This charge appears elsewhere in prophetic literature (see Isa 10:12–15; Nah 3:8–13), but it is leveled against other countries as well, including Edom (Obad 3) and Babylon (Hab 1:15–17). The motif of nations mocking Assyria concludes Nahum (3:19). This oracle portrays Nineveh's destruction as a past event, which means it would have been written sometime after 612.

The oracle against Jerusalem appears unexpectedly in 3:1–7. When a woe oracle against the "soiled, defiled, oppressing" city begins in 3:1, nothing prepares the reader for the realization that the nation being condemned has changed. At first the reader assumes Nineveh continues to be addressed, but the accusations that it has not trusted in the Lord (3:2) and that its prophets and priests have broken faith with *torah* make clear that 3:1–7 concerns Jerusalem. This oracle against Jerusalem thus evokes a reminder of the main focus of 1:2–2:3, that Jerusalem will be punished.

Zephaniah 3:8 concludes the OAN with a statement characterizing judgment against the nations as a result of the Lord's indignation toward their behavior. The effect of the oracle against Jerusalem (3:1–7) followed by the conclusion to the OAN (3:8) implies the same dialectic with which Zephaniah began—pronouncements of broader judgment—and thus frames the specific pronouncements against Jerusalem. This judgment also anticipates motifs similar to those in the first vision of Zechariah, combining punishment of the nations after Jerusalem's judgment with the Lord's zeal (see Zech 1:14–15).

IV. Promises of Deliverance for the Nations and for Zion (3:9–20)

The last major section of Zephaniah (3:9–20) focuses upon Yahweh's salvific acts, both for the nations and Jerusalem, rather than on judgment. These promises have long been treated as post-exilic additions to the book. The first unit (3:9–10) reverses the message of the OAN by pronouncing a blessing upon the nations (even using an artful allusion to reverse the situation of the tower of Babel story; cf. purified speech [*brr* + *sph*] in Zeph 3:9 and confused speech [*bll* + *sph*] in Gen 11:7).

The next unit, 3:11–13, addresses the personified Lady Zion directly (using second-person, feminine singular speech) announcing an end to the punishment in the distant future ("on that day") when Zion will be filled with a humble remnant that seeks Yahweh (3:12).

The address to Lady Zion continues throughout most of 3:14–20 (only 3:20 changes to a plural addressee). Zephaniah 3:14–17 announces the return of the victorious Warrior, calling Jerusalem to rejoice over the removal of the enemies (3:15) and twice reiterating the Lord's presence in the city (3:15, 17). The final promise (3:18–20) has likely been created for this particular place in the Book of the Twelve, since it draws upon Mic 4:6–7 and Joel 3, books that precede Zephaniah, while anticipating a return of the exiles, which reflects the situation in Haggai, a book that follows Zephaniah. The final verses of Zephaniah expect an eschatological renewal of the Lord's kingdom with Jerusalem as its center.

BIBLIOGRAPHY

A. Berlin. *Zephaniah*. AB 25A (New York: Doubleday, 1994); J. O'Brien. *Nahum, Habakkuk, Zephaniah, Haggai, Zechariah, Malachi*. AOTC (Nashville: Abingdon, 2004); J. J. M. Roberts. *Nahum, Habakkuk, and Zephaniah*. OTL (Louisville: Westminster John Knox, 1991); M. Sweeney. "Zephaniah." *The Twelve Prophets*. Vol. 2. Berit Olam (Collegeville, Minn.: Liturgical Press, 2000).

HAGGAI

Stephen L. Cook

OVERVIEW

The prophet for whom the book of Haggai is named was an important Persian-era figure, principally responsible, along with Zechariah, for the rebuilding of the ruined Temple of Jerusalem (cf. Ezra 5:1; 6:14). In 520 BCE, near the start of the reign of King Darius I of Persia, he insisted that work on the Temple resume after two decades of stalled progress. The Persian ruler Cyrus the Great had conquered Babylon and allowed a return of Judean exiles in 539–538 BCE, but their efforts to raise a new Temple had faltered after the erection of an altar and a repair of the shrine's foundations (Ezra 3; 5:16). The exhortations of Haggai and Zechariah resulted in a new Temple's dedication in the spring of 515 BCE.

Although the Scriptures reveal little biographical information about Haggai, his perspective coheres closely with the Priestly theology behind Ezekiel and portions of the Pentateuch known as the Holiness School. Thus, he may have been among Ezekiel's followers in Babylonian exile. Neither clericalism nor ceremonialism drives his temple-centeredness, but a cogent insistence that buildings and rituals really do matter in cementing a transformative relationship with God. For Haggai, nothing is more crucial than the Temple, because it represents God's indwelling presence.

OUTLINE

I. A Call to Rebuild the Ruined Temple (1:1–11)

II. The People Begin Work (1:12–15a)

III. Encouraging the Workers Through Apocalyptic Imagination (1:15b–2:9)

IV. Preparing for Ceremonial and Ethical Wholeness (2:10–19)

V. Expecting the Messiah (2:20–23)

DETAILED ANALYSIS

I. A Call to Rebuild the Ruined Temple (1:1–11)

On August 29, 520 BCE, Haggai launched a prophetic dispute with the governor and high priest of the Persian province of Yehud, once called Judah, over the dismal state of the Temple, destroyed by the Babylonians in 586 BCE. The people enjoyed sturdy, "finished houses" (v. 4; NRSV, "paneled houses"), he noted, but God's house lay desolate. They experienced futility at agriculture, a direct result of their misplaced priorities. No automatic linkage of sin with natural calamity was causing their frustrations but their neglect of the divine covenant of the Holiness School, which included specific "futility curses" for unfaithfulness (see Lev 26:20, 26). Haggai uses a Hebrew pun to stress God's application of covenantal sanctions: since the Temple is in "ruins" (v. 9), he says, God has sent a "drought" (v. 11).

A particular point of dispute was over timing. The Hebrew of v. 2 emphasizes the problem of relating any rebuilding effort with God's consummation of history. A new Temple that did not cement God's permanent presence would do more harm than good (see Ezek 43:7). Learned study of Jer 25:11–12 and 29:10, however, left Haggai with no doubts that God's prescribed seventy-years of exile were concluding, that God was now coming to Jerusalem (cf. Hag 2:4–7; Zech 8:3). A new global stability under King Darius, which allowed for Temple construction, was the first stage of God's advent.

II. The People Begin Work (1:12–15a)

On September 21, 520 BCE (v. 15a), within one month after Haggai's initial exhortation, the people began to work. The Lord's stirring (v. 14) aroused a people reluctant to arouse themselves to grasp hold of God (see Isa 64:7, 11). Both here (v. 13) and in 2:4–5, God spurs the people on with a promise that God will dwell with them (viz. Exod 29:46): God is present, guiding their steps, determined to dwell openly among them in

529

a Temple. This is the theological heart of Haggai: God among us, sanctifying us (cf. Ezek 37:28).

III. Encouraging the Workers Through Apocalyptic Imagination (1:15b–2:9)

On October 17, 520 BCE, during the Festival of Booths, Haggai fielded concerns the new Temple would not measure up (v. 3; cf. Ezra 3:12). In response to grave doubts, he upheld God's transcendent perspective (v. 4 repeats "says the LORD" three times). He offered an apocalyptic imagination to the people (cf. Zech 4:10), invigorating their resolve (cf. Zech 8:9, 13).

Just "one moment yet" and the construction effort will issue in unimagined "splendor" (vv. 7–9). The tribute of the nations will adorn Jerusalem, and God's presence will perfect the Temple. The Hebrew of v. 7 echoes the ideal of God's glory filling God's house (Exod 40:34–35; cf. Ezek 43:5; 44:4; Zech 2:5). In v. 9b, an idiom of the Holiness School points ahead to an ideal messianic harmony between God, people, and environment (see Lev 26:6; cf. Ezek 34:25–28).

IV. Preparing for Ceremonial and Ethical Wholeness (2:10–19)

On December 18, 520 BCE, Haggai argued that ongoing Temple construction should become a spiritual discipline preparing for holiness (see Lev 19:2). Priestly rulings were his pedagogical device. Defilement germinated at present like corpse contagion (vv. 13–14; cf. Zech 3:3; Lam 4:14–15; Isa 64:6), necessitating God's planned indwelling and cleansing of the land (cf. Zech 3:9; 13:1). Religious discipline would be needed as groundwork, however. The workings of ritual show that sanctity is not haphazard (v. 12).

Verses 15–19 reveal that Haggai is speaking at a re-foundation ceremony for the new Temple (cf. Zech 4:9). Echoing points made in 1:1–11, Haggai describes the day as a turning point from covenantal curse to covenantal blessing.

V. Expecting the Messiah (2:20–23)

The same day, December 18, Haggai asked governor Zerubbabel to consider himself God's Messiah (cf. Zech 4:10). His allusive language explicitly reversed Jer 22:24–30, where messianic

hopes were put on hold. An apocalyptic breakpoint was imminent, he said; the time for rekindling hope had come (see Jer 23:5).

Haggai's word was not false prophecy. Zerubbabel remained a mere governor, but he earned a place in Scripture as a *micro-christus*, a figure presaging God's Messiah. A son of David in both blood and spirit, his work at Temple building brought to focus an earthly Zion indwelt by God's glory, radiating wholeness. In his labors, messianic reality received a preview (cf. Mark 9:1–4).

BIBLIOGRAPHY

J. G. Baldwin. *Haggai, Zechariah, Malachi: An Introduction and Commentary.* TOTC (Leicester, England: InterVarsity, 1972); C. L. Meyers and E. M. Meyers. *Haggai, Zechariah 1–8.* AB 25B (New York: Doubleday, 1987); J. A. Motyer. "Haggai." *The Minor Prophets. Volume 3: Zephaniah, Haggai, Zechariah, and Malachi.* T. E. McComiskey, ed. (Grand Rapids: Baker, 1998); D. L. Petersen. *Haggai and Zechariah 1–8: A Commentary.* OTL (Philadelphia: Westminster, 1984); J. E. Tollington. *Tradition and Innovation in Haggai and Zechariah 1–8.* JSOTSup 150 (Sheffield: JSOT Press, 1993).

ZECHARIAH

Stephen L. Cook

OVERVIEW

In the early restoration era (520–518 BCE), the prophet Zechariah urged returning exiles and those who had never left to rebuild God's house, purify their community, and await the dawning of God's reign. He shared the zeal of Haggai for getting the Temple ready for God's tangible presence (1:16; 4:9–10; cf. Hag 2:7, 9). Although sharing a common goal with Haggai (see 8:9), Zechariah never mentions him by name. Embracing his position as a Temple official (see 7:2–4), Zechariah may have felt some distance from prophets outside God's sacral establishment.

Zechariah was likely a Zadokite priest, aligned with portions of the Pentateuch known as the Holiness School (see Lev 17–26). This corpus prioritizes an ideal sacral wholeness of people and land centered on God's indwelling presence. Zechariah echoes Ezekiel, a Zadokite (see Ezek 44:15–16), who treasured the Holiness School Scriptures. He was eventually priest-in-charge of an entire priestly household, the clan of his grandfather Iddo (Neh 12:16; cf. Zech 1:1, 7; Ezra 5:1; 6:14; 1 Esdr 6:1), which he probably accompanied in its return from exile (cf. Neh 12:4).

Seventy years or so after Zechariah's time, his disciples added the apocalyptic prophecies of chs. 9–14. His protégés advanced his Priestly theology, so 11:4–17. True to their founder, they remained Temple officers, wedded to the Holiness School. Times had changed, however. The Greco-Persian wars were upturning the world. Persia's defeats at Marathon in 490 BCE and at Salamis in 480 BCE were shaking the empire, throwing everything off balance. Egypt revolted in the 450s. What is more, Yehud's civil leaders, now unconnected to David's royal line, were failing their people (10:2–3). To those who knew the Scriptures, it felt as if God's new world was kicking in the womb.

OUTLINE

DETAILED ANALYSIS

I. First Zechariah (1–8)

A. A Call to Repentence (1:1–6)

In October/November 520 BCE, around the time of Hag 1:15*b*–2:9, Zechariah called on the people of Yehud to turn to God and abandon their ancestors' entrenched disobedience. "Did the prophets talk idly to them?" Zechariah asked (v. 5[1]; NRSV, "do they live forever?"). Clearly not! They marched into exile for not listening (v. 5; cf. 7:14), finally admitting their thoroughgoing culpability (v. 6*b*; cf. Lam 2:17).

As in Hag 2:17, Zechariah's call to return is a summons to renew the covenant relationship of the Holiness School and to rebuild Jerusalem's Temple. Such tokens of repentance would invite God's radical presence, God's "return" (v. 3) to "dwell in the midst of Jerusalem" (8:3; cf. the Holiness School in Exod 25:8; 29:45; Num 35:34).

B. The Eight Visions of Zechariah (1:7–6:15)

1:7–17. First Vision: Horses and Riders. On February 15, 519 BCE, apocalyptic revelation illumined the "night" (v. 8), probing God's hidden mystery. Zechariah received a series of eight apocalyptic visions, each with a touchstone in the structures, symbols, and rites of the Temple. Empowered through revelation, Zechariah even saw colors in the dark! An interpreting angel (here, a horseman) assists him (v. 9; cf. Dan 8:16; 9:22; Rev 1:1; 22:6), revealing heaven's keen awareness of how much work remains preparing for God's new world (vv. 11, 15–16).

Before the prophet's eyes, the Temple's floral décor (cf. 1 Kgs 6:18, 29) and molten sea (cf. 1 Kgs 7:23) transfigure, unveiling their deeper significance. Zechariah finds himself in God's garden, decked with "myrtle trees" (cf. Isa 55:13), irrigated by "the cosmic deep" (v. 8; NRSV, "the glen"; cf. Ezek 28:2). The grounds quarter God's steeds, which have been out on patrol (v. 11). Their riders have returned with disappointing news. The anticipated cosmic shakeup of Hag 2:6–9 is nowhere in sight. Heaven must get to work.

---

1 Unless otherwise indicated by NRSV, the quotations from Zechariah are direct translations by the author.

1:18–21. Second Vision: Four Horns and Four Workers. Heaven's work is unveiled to Zechariah in a transfiguration of the altar's "horns," projections extending in the cardinal directions and signifying God's cosmic might. God's enemies arrogate this might to themselves (cf. Dan 7:7–8, 20–21), sealing their doom on judgment day (cf. 1:15; 2:9; 6:8; 8:2).

The "horns that scattered Judah" are obliterated, the wicked are cut off (cf. Ps 75:10); this is hope with teeth! Significantly, "construction workers" (v. 20, cf. Ezra 3:7; NRSV, "blacksmiths") initiate the apocalypse. Temple construction is no sideshow in earth's widescreen drama, but a sacrament of kingdom come (cf. 1:16).

2:1–5. Third Vision: A Surveyor's Work Aborted. Ezekiel had envisioned an angel surveying Jerusalem for walls and gates (Ezek 40:3; 47:3; cf. Zech 1:16), and Zechariah is shown this very angel. Ezekiel also envisioned Jerusalem electrified by holiness, bustling and ballooning (Ezek 36:37–38). As Zechariah looks on, ballooning holiness trumps wall building. A glowing, bustling city "without walls" will host God's glory, fulfilling expectations of the Holiness School for divine glory to dwell amid the people (v. 5; cf. Exod 29:45; 40:34–35). This future will break with the present; Jerusalem's current population was under five hundred.

2:6–13. A Summons to the Exiles. All remaining exiles must hurry home from Babylonia, the "land of the north" (cf. Jer 3:18; 31:8). The divine glory that commissioned Zechariah (v. 8; cf. Ezek 1:28) will soon overthrow Zion's plunderers (vv. 8–9) and come home to dwell (*shakhan*, vv. 10, 11; language of the Holiness School). God's concrete, tangible indwelling will create a "holy land" arrayed about a holy center, the supreme hope of the Holiness School (Ezek 37:28; Lev 22:32; Num 5:3; 35:34). This shining land (cf. Zech 9:16) will attract the nations to become God's people (v. 11; cf. 8:20–23).

3:1–10. Fourth Vision: The Cleansing of High Priest Joshua. Having been exiled outside the Temple's umbrella of holiness, the priesthood was now "filthy" (v. 3; see Ezek 4:12–13; Amos 7:17). God's planned land of holiness must have pure priests (cf. Num 18:7), so heaven plucks their representative Joshua from oblivion (v. 2; cf. Amos 4:11) and purifies him (vv. 4–5).

To ward off clericalism and complacency, the Temple's inner cabinet must concentrate on being "stewards of key symbols" (v. 8; NRSV, "omen of things to come"). They must hold vigil for King Messiah, the "Branch" (v. 8; 6:12; cf. Jer 23:5; 33:15; Ezek 29:21), ever mindful of such symbols as the Branch's unclaimed crown (6:14) and God's messianic inscription on the Temple's foundation stone (v. 9; cf. 4:7). Unlike Hag 2:23, this text neither mentions Governor Zerubbabel nor reifies the messianic ideal in any way.

4:1–14. Fifth Vision: A Lampstand and Two Olive Trees. The Temple's tree-shaped lampstand (the menorah, cf. Exod 25:31–40) now unveils itself as an archetypal cosmic tree (cf. Dan 4:10–12). Its "seven lamps" (v. 2) transmute into God's all-seeing eyes (v. 10b; cf. 3:9; Ezek 1:18; 10:12). The archetype marks the Temple as an axis of earth and a conduit of God's presence. Just as a cosmic tree fructifies everything within reach (see Dan 4:12), this menorah blesses God's dyarchy, both high priest and son of David (the "two olive trees," vv. 3, 11–14). They become "children of bounty/fresh oil" (v. 14; NRSV, "anointed ones"), witnessing to God's power, assisting in God's outreach.

An oracle inserted in vv. 6–10a interrupts the vision with words of hope and messianic imagination. Temple construction is but a prelude, a "day of small things" (v. 10; cf. Hag 2:3). God's open reign is coming, and the community's overtures toward it brim with grace and favor. Shouts of "Grace, grace" rightly accompany Zerubbabel's presentation of the Temple's "foundation stone" (v. 7; NRSV, "top stone"; cf. 3:9). Still, until the vision is fulfilled, vigilance (cf. 3:8–10) and humble reliance on God's spirit (v. 6; cf. 9:9) are required.

5:1–4. Sixth Vision: A Flying Scroll. The Temple vestibule (cf. 1 Kgs 6:3), used for reciting the covenant, transfigures into a flying embodiment of the Holiness School's theology and covenantal sanctions. The sanctions root out all stubborn immorality (e.g., stealing) and all sacrilege (e.g., swearing falsely), creating a "whole land" fit for God's indwelling (cf. 2:12; 9:16).

5:5–11. Seventh Vision: A Woman in a Ephah. God's holy land is rid of demonic, counterfeit worship in a vision with its touchstone in a typical jar-housed figurine, of the sort used in ancient Near Eastern shrines as deposits and offerings. Desecrating its symbolic homeland, "Wickedness" returns to roost in idolatrous Babylon. Occupying its own anti-temple, its jar serves as its ark and weird storks serve as its cherubim.

6:1–8. Eighth Vision: Four Chariots. Sun chariots of the Temple (see 2 Kgs 23:11) transfigure and are hitched to God's horses (cf. 1:7–17). Twin peaks on earth's horizon, freshly morphed from Temple pillars (see 1 Kgs 7:15–16), grant them entrance into space-time. Particularly in the north, the fabled terrain of evil (cf. 2:6; Ezek 39:2; Joel 2:20), they "vent the anger of [God's] spirit" (v. 8; NRSV, "set my spirit at rest"). They win apocalyptic victory.

6:9–15. The Two Crowns. Zechariah fashions two symbolic "crowns" (v. 11; see NRSV note), since a dyarchy of king and priest will preside in God's coming new era (see 4:11–14). At that time, harmony will reign between "the two" leaders (v. 13). For now, to keep Persia appeased, Governor Zerubbabel takes no crown. Joshua is crowned as high priest, but is cautioned to hold vigil for God's royal "Branch" (v. 12; see 3:8) and to sit as "a priest by his throne" (v. 13) when he is revealed.

C. An Inquiry About Fasting and Prophetic Responses (7:1–8:23)

7:1–6. An Inquiry About Fasting. On December 7, 518 BCE, Zechariah responds to an inquiry from longtime inhabitants about whether their mourning rites over the Babylonian destruction of Judah should continue. He raises the question of motives (cf. Isa 58:3): Was their fasting merely self-pity? Was it jockeying for favor? He postpones specific counsel until 8:18–19.

7:7–14. The Causes of the Exile. The people's fasting should (but did not) reflect the lessons of exile and aim to undo the type of "adamant" heart that caused the disaster (v. 12; cf. Ezek 3:7–9). A truly penitent spirituality would rend the heart, opening it to "love truth and peace," "compassion and supplication" (see 8:19; 12:10).

8:1–17. Envisioning Jerusalem's Future. God's presence will come "dwell in the midst of Jerusalem" (v. 3; cf. 2:10–11), fulfilling the deepest hopes of the Holiness School (see Exod 25:8; 29:45; Num 35:34). The promised indwelling should occasion the sort of moral reformation that the people's fasting had not begun to achieve (vv. 16–17).

8:18–23. Fasts Will Give Way to Feasts. Inquiries about fasting (viz. 7:3) will soon be obsolete. "Impossible" joy is in the wings (see 8:6), the joy of harvest feasting (8:12; 14:16). The prospects for joy should spawn shalom, the very shalom to which a genuine penitence would have aspired (see Isa 58:4).

Verses 20–23 depict a contagious excitement about joining God's worshiping community spreading among the nations (cf. the similar universalism of 2:11; 14:16).

II. Second Zechariah (9–14)

A. The First Burden (9:1–11:17)

9:1–8. The Lord Takes Control from North to South. God's word first "focuses in" on Syria/Aram (vv. 1–2a; NRSV, "is against"), which willingly joins forces with "all the tribes of Israel." Further south, an obstinate Phoenicia digs in and is overthrown (vv. 2b–4). Then Philistia's pride is broken and a purified Philistine remnant integrates with Israel (vv. 5–7). Thus, God establishes security for an ideal Israel in the end times.

9:9–10. A Humble Messiah. Enacting Gen 49:10–12, fulfilling archetypal hopes for Judah's royal dynasty, the Messiah enters fair Zion on the sacred donkey of lore. He inherits a peaceable world, for God declares, "I will cut off the chariot" (v. 10; NRSV, "He will …"). Beyond peaceable, his nature is "humble" (v. 9; a biblical ideal: Num 12:3; Prov 3:34; 16:19). He embodies the same reliance on God's spirit advocated in 4:6 and 7:12. In accordance with Ps 33:16–17, his mount is no warhorse. He knows that salvation comes to earth only through deflating the self, not through horse power (cf. v. 10; 10:5; 1 Kgs 1:5). His commitment to withdraw the ego climaxes later in the book, in 12:10 and 13:7.

9:11–17. God's Victory of Abundant Life. Plundering Sheol, God restores dispersed Israel (v. 11). Incarnating the Divine Warrior of lore (cf. Ps 68;

Hab 3), God defeats all powers holding back the new age.

The Divine Warrior's victory brings bounty, banqueting, and brilliant new life (vv. 15–17; cf. Ps 68:7–10; Deut 33:26–29). Having conquered "like slingstones" (v. 15a, cf. Josh 10:11; NRSV, "the slingers"), God's people now shine like crown jewels (v. 16). Emulating a brimming Temple basin, they now "drink and get boisterous" (v. 15b; NRSV, "drink their blood").

10:1–12. Reviving Lost Israel. As Ezekiel observed, Israel suffers like scattered sheep. Two main ingredients formed a recipe for chaos: failure to seek God directly (vv. 1–2a; cf. Ezek 13) and a failure of leadership (vv. 2b–3; cf. Ezek 34:2–4). God intervenes, raising up messianic commanders out of Judah (v. 4; cf. Ezek 34:23–24). Under new command, a victimless victory is won. What is conquered is the chaotic sea of dispersion and oblivion (v. 11).

11:1–3. Toppling All Proud "Trees." The thought of Lebanon deforested at an inrush of returnees (10:10b) conjures a vista of human pride toppling like timber at God's apocalyptic appearance. The haughty cedars of Lebanon and the lofty oaks of Bashan are paradigmatic of the hubris and tyranny to be felled by God (see Ezek 27:6; 31; Isa 2:12–13). The Hebrew translated as "thickets … destroyed" (v. 3) also means "pride brought to ruin" (as in Ezek 32:12).

11:4–17. Playing the Part of Israel's Shepherds. Zechariah, given new life as a literary construct, plays two separate shepherds in a symbolic drama about failed leadership (see 10:2b–3). Verses 4–6 recount the self-centered rule that brought on the exile (cf. Ezek 34:1–10). Verses 7–14 have Zechariah enact the part of God, the ultimate shepherd (Ezek 34:15), who corrected Israel in pre-exilic times by destroying "three shepherds" (i.e., the totality of failed rule) in "one month" (i.e., decisively). The staff "Favor" represents the broken covenant (v. 10; cf. Ezek 16:59); "Unity" symbolizes the "family ties" of Judah and Israel (v. 14; Ezek 37:15–23). The symbolic actions of vv. 12–13 convey what minimal value everyone seemed to place on God's interventions. Truly, this flock was doomed to exile.

In vv. 15–17, the action shifts to the future, when a "worthless shepherd" will arise as an anti-messiah. The mounting messianic fervor of Zechariah has brought an archetypal shadow of the Messiah to consciousness. Now activated, this shadow will reappear later as the boastful horn of Dan 7 (second century BCE) and as the "wicked Branch" of the "Vision of Gabriel" (first century BCE).

B. The Second Burden (12:1–14:21)

12:1–9. The End-Time Assault on Jerusalem. The book's final section (Zech 12–14) is chiastic in structure, with paired passages arrayed symmetrically. Paired with Zech 14, this passage portrays the overthrow of an end-time horde swarming against Zion (see Ezek 38:9, 16; Joel 3:11–13). The Holiness School guards the dignity of the rural populace (see Lev 25:10, 23–24; Ezek 45:8–9; 46:18), so the clans of the countryside, besieged along with Jerusalem, are first in victory.

12:10–13:1. The Sacrifice of the Pierced One. A future godly ruler of Israel dies sacrificially according to both this passage and 13:7–9, its twin within the book's chiastic structure. He is representative of an ideal Israel and is mourned in a manner befitting the fall of God's entire elect (see Amos 8:10; Jer 6:26). As God mercifully pours out the spirit on the perpetrators (12:10), the death of the messianic "shepherd" (see 13:7) brings on a massive mourning that is both cathartic (13:1) and restorative. Restoring the fundamental connectedness of community was the aim of all traditional mourning in tribal Israel. Mourning was an act of re-membering, in which all community members, both living and dead, were united, healed, and redeemed.

13:2–6. Holiness Spreads Through the Land. Idolatry, false prophecy, and the "unclean spirit" are all banished here at the heart of the chiasm of Zech 12–14 (cf. 14:20–21), fulfilling the dreams of the Holiness School for a pure land (Num 5:3; 35:34). In a wondrous age when all people are visionaries (cf. 12:10; Joel 2:28–29), claimants to privileged revelation are God's clear enemies. To fail to "pierce" them is effectively to "pierce" God (12:10 and 13:3 use the identical verb, *daqar*).

13:7–9. The Good Shepherd Stricken. God invites the tragedy that emerged in the matching passage, 12:10–13:1. God's royal vicar (see Ezek 34:23), God's interlocked companion (Ezek 34:24), dies as a means to catalyze the rebirth of the covenant people (v. 9c; Ezek 34:25). Such catalysis is archetypal: to create afresh, one grapples with chaos; to birth new life, one suffers through labor; to make space for new being, one deflates the ego, rending the self.

14:1–21. The Divine Warrior's Triumph at Jerusalem. The tribulation is more painful and the vision of rebirth more cosmic in this radical reprise of 12:1–9. God wins apocalyptic victory and "living waters" restore paradise to earth (v. 8; cf. 13:1; Gen 2:10; Ezek 47:1–12; Joel 3:18). A universalistic worshiping community (cf. 2:11; 8:20–23) now joins in celebrating Judah's new preternatural fertility (cf. 4:12–14; 8:12; 9:15) at the Festival of Booths.

BIBLIOGRAPHY

J. G. Baldwin. *Haggai, Zechariah, Malachi: An Introduction and Commentary.* TOTC (Leicester, England: InterVarsity, 1972); M. J. Boda and M. H. Floyd, eds. *Bringing Out the Treasure: Inner Biblical Allusion in Zechariah 9–14.* JSOTSup 370 (London: Sheffield Academic Press, 2003); S. L. Cook. *Prophecy and Apocalypticism: The Postexilic Social Setting.* (Minneapolis: Fortress, 1995); C. L. Meyers and E. M. Meyers. *Haggai, Zechariah 1–8.* AB 25B (New York: Doubleday, 1987); _____. *Zechariah 9–14.* AB 25C (New York: Doubleday, 1993); D. L. Petersen. *Haggai and Zechariah 1–8: A Commentary.* OTL (Philadelphia: Westminster, 1984); _____. *Zechariah 9–14 and Malachi: A Commentary.* OTL (Philadelphia: Westminster, 1995); E. J. C. Tigchelaar. *Prophets of Old and the Day of the End: Zechariah, the Book of Watchers and Apocalyptic.* OtSt 35 (Leiden: Brill, 1996); J. E. Tollington. *Tradition and Innovation in Haggai and Zechariah 1–8.* JSOTSup 150 (Sheffield: JSOT Press, 1993).

MALACHI

Stephen L. Cook

Overview

A repeating superscription—"An Oracle" (Mal 1:1)—links Malachi with the sections of Zechariah immediately before it (see Zech 9:1 and 12:1). Like the preceding oracles, Malachi presents rich, Persian-era apocalyptic prophecy. "The great and terrible day of the LORD comes," he announces (Mal 4:5).

At the same time, Malachi's "oracle" has its own integrity. His personal life is obscure, since his book volunteers no biography; his name may be only a title ("my messenger"). Malachi's message, however, has unique contours that reveal how differently from Zechariah he thinks about the endtimes. His stance is that of a Levite.

In contrast to Zechariah, Malachi orients himself on the Sinai covenant and functions as its mediator in the tradition of Moses and other Levites of renown (see Deut 18:15–19). He links his title, "my messenger," with the Levitical duty to teach the covenant (Mal 2:7). He holds all priests to the standard of the "covenant with Levi" (Mal 2:4–6).

Repeatedly, Malachi's words align with Deuteronomy, Jeremiah, Hosea, and the Elohistic source (E hereafter), which derive from like-minded Levites. The Levites are the heroes of E, as texts such as Exod 32:26–29 (E) show; Deuteronomy robustly advocates for the Levites (e.g., Deut 12:12, 19; 14:27; 17:18; 18:6–8; 26:12); and Jeremiah and Hosea, whose books resonate with Deuteronomy, seem to have been Levitical priests.

Like Zech 9–11 and 12–14, the book of Malachi likely stems from the difficult period leading up to the mid-fifth century BCE. Perhaps it was written during the reign of the Persian king Artaxerxes I (465–424 BCE). Many experienced this era before Ezra and Nehemiah as a time of "great trouble and shame" (Neh 1:3). Religious apathy had set in as a result of Persian pluralism, faded dreams, loss of messianic and eschatological vision, and a revival of pre-exilic syncretistic and occult practices. Malachi's chief concern was the unfaithfulness of worshipers and priests at the Temple, rededicated in 515 BCE. From within Temple circles, Malachi

countered the current malaise with a Levitical and apocalyptic ideal of worship and covenantal community, which, he proclaimed, would triumph suddenly despite all current skepticism (Mal 2:17).

Outline

I. The Lord's Covenant Love for Israel (1:1–5)

II. Rebuking Faithless Temple Priests (1:6–2:9)

III. Three Examples of Judah's Covenantal Infidelity (2:10–16)

IV. God's Coming Day: Countering Disillusionment and Cynicism (2:17–3:5)

V. A Call to Repentance (3:6–12)

VI. Judgment and Vindication (3:13–4:3)

VII. Moses and Elijah, the Famed Covenant Mediators (4:4–6)

Detailed Analysis

I. The Lord's Covenant Love for Israel (1:1–5)

Following a superscription in v. 1, the book launches the first of a series of six back-and-forth disputes. These interchanges, which counter the people's lapsed faithfulness, typically begin with a statement of God's perspective (here, v. 2a), turn to quote the audience's objections (here, v. 2b), and then lay out a prophetic response (here, vv. 2c–5). Renewing the covenantal relationship with God is central to each dispute.

Malachi's first dispute insists that covenantal election (God's "love"; cf. Hos 11:1; Deut 10:15) and privation (God's "hate"; cf. Hos 9:15) make a real difference in history. In particular, no one can ignore that the land of Jacob's twin Esau now lies in ruins. The Babylonian emperor Nabonidus campaigned against Edom in 553 BCE (cf. Obad 7), and the Nabateans were now overrunning it. The "Esaus" of the world—profane and without covenantal tutelage—have no future. The "Jacobs," in contrast, will benefit from the reign of God, not via worth or merit (see Deut 7:7–8), but due to God's summons. With the advent of God's reign, people far and wide will worship God (see Mal 1:5, 11, 14). The covenant's expansive goal will burst "beyond the borders of Israel!" (v. 5).

II. Rebuking Faithless Temple Priests (1:6–2:9)

At the beginning of the second dispute (1:6–11), Malachi rebukes his fellow priests for despising God's "name" (1:6). Their shoddy, defiling worship (1:7) is degrading God's uniquely chosen shrine, where God's "name" dwells (see Deut 12:11; 16:2, 6). They plead ignorance, but God's standards for sacrifice leave them without excuse (1:8; cf. Deut 15:21). In fact, a closed Temple would be preferable to their lax, grudging service (1:10)! As in 1:5 (and cf. 1:14), God's imminent reign proves to be the ultimate reference point (1:11). Though contested at present (see 1:4; 2:17), God's reign offers a doxological and eschatological truth, unmasking the audacity of lackadaisical worship. God is lord from east to west (cf. Ps 50:1). All around the world, sacrifice and pure oblation are "about to be offered" God (1:11 author's direct translation; NRSV, "is offered").

The Temple is now corrupt, vv. 12–14 reiterate. The priests practically stick up their noses at God (1:13). The cheap worship they conduct is a nuisance to them and an open invitation for fraudulence among the populace (1:14a). How can this be happening, given the doxological truth that God inspires universal reverence (1:14b; cf. Ps 76:12)?

In 2:1–9, Malachi reminds the priests of their special clerical covenant, which includes sanctions for unfaithfulness (2:2; cf. 3:9; Deut 28:15–68). Shocking language about "dung" (2:3) personalizes the looming threat. Malachi argues that all priestly subgroups (the Zadokite and Aaronide lineages included) are bound by the overarching "covenant of Levi" (see Deut 18:5; 33:8–11; Jer 33:20–22; Ps 16:4–6). All are responsible for teaching God's covenantal ways (2:6–7; see Deut 17:8–11; 31:9; 33:10; Jer 2:8). The grim current reality (2:8–9) could not contrast more sharply with Malachi's covenantal ideal.

III. Three Examples of Judah's Covenantal Infidelity (2:10–16)

Malachi's third dispute confronts his audience with three specific examples of covenantal betrayal. First (v. 10), he cites the betrayal of the covenant of Levi (cf. 2:4, 8). How can the current vitriol between priests (cf. 2:3) be acceptable, given their "one father"? *Father* points to several figures: Levi (cf. Exod 3:6; 1 Sam 2:27–28), Abraham (cf. Josh 24:3), and God, Israel's true parent (1:6; cf. Deut 32:6) and creator (Deut 32:6).

Second (vv. 11–12), Malachi cites spiritually mixed marriages. Neither parochial thinking nor ethnic bias propels his concern (see 1:5, 11, 14). Marrying foreigners was fine (see Num 12:1), just not devotees of a "foreign god" (v. 11; cf. Deut 31:16; 32:12; Ps 81:9). Israel's binding, exclusive relationship with the "one God" (v. 10; cf. Deut 6:4) was easily undermined by marrying outside the covenant (see 1 Kgs 11:2).

Third (vv. 13–16), Malachi cites the affront of letting enmity break up a legitimate marriage, considered a covenant in the Scriptures (Prov 2:17; Jer 31:32; Ezek 16:8). The text is uncertain at places. The "one" in v. 15 is likely father Abraham (see the comments on v. 10; cf. the NET and the NIV's alternate reading), not "one God" (NRSV). As long as "flesh and spirit" (v. 15) were his, Abraham maintained covenant loyalty with Sarah, "the wife of his youth." He swallowed his anger at her and dismissed Hagar (Gen 21:11–12 [E], even though Hagar had met his "desire" for "offspring." Verse 16 likely reads: "If one hates one's wife and divorces her … then one covers one's garment with violence" (cf. ESV, LXX, Vulg.; vs. NRSV, "For I hate divorce …"). The language of hating and divorcing has Deut 24:3 in mind. "Covering one's garment with violence" means "wearing" a crime openly, like a scarlet letter.

IV. God's Coming Day: Countering Disillusionment and Cynicism (2:17–3:5)

Malachi's fourth dispute confronts disillusionment at the delay of God's justice. Observing an apparent triumph of evil, people felt defeated. Judgment felt so unreal, some virtually dared God to punish their sin (3:15; cf. Zeph 1:12). The prophet fires back with an apocalyptic vision forged on the basis of Deuteronomy and E.

Even now, God's messenger waits in the wings, ready to clear the way for God. The E strand describes this same messenger blazing the hoary exodus trail (Exod 14:19; 23:23; 32:34; Num 20:16; cf. Josh 5:14). Marked verbal parallels between this disputation and Exod 23:20 and 33:2 betray Malachi's reliance on E in describing the figure. The loaded language assures readers that God's apocalyptic advent will result in a new exodus, renewing the people as God's "special possession" (Mal 3:17; cf. Exod 19:5 [E]; Deut 7:6).

The mission of the messenger is merely preparatory. There follows a momentous arrival of the Lord, God's self, in an epiphany (3:2–5). Present despair of judgment ever arriving will vanish "suddenly" (3:1), as a reverent "fear" of God washes over the land (3:5; cf. Gen 20:11 [E]; 22:12 [E]; 28:17 [E]; Deut 4:10; 5:29; 8:6). At God's chosen shrine, all priests, no matter their lineage, will become ideal Levites, their previous grudging manner a casualty of lye soap and smelting heat (3:3).

The passage also announces the arrival of a third eschatological figure, "the messenger of the covenant" (3:1; cf. 2:7; 4:5). He plays the mediatory role of Moses (see Deut 18:15–19 and Num 12:6–8 [E]), standing in for a people who must hide from God's numinous, awe-inspiring epiphany (see Exod 19:16 [E]; 20:19 [E]; Deut 5:26; 18:16). He trains the people in the covenant's structures for right living.

V. A Call to Repentance (3:6–12)

Malachi's fifth dispute urges a return to God. What other response makes sense, given the coming apocalypse he has described? The divine arms are open to receive the people back, he stresses, because the God of the covenant does not "change" (v. 6; cf. Num 23:19 [E]). Because of God's unswerving commitment to the Sinai covenant, it is open to renewal by those who return heart and soul (see Deut 30:2). (An alternative translation of v. 6, "I, the LORD, have not hated [you]," equally stresses the Lord's covenantal commitment [see above on Mal 1:3; cf. Deut 1:26–

27].) God's constancy is downright eerie (cf. Hos 11:9), given how often the people have "turned aside" and "have not kept" the covenant (v. 7; cf. Deut 5:32; Josh 1:7; 23:6; 2 Kgs 18:6).

The people ask what they are supposed to do, and Malachi confronts them with their betrayal of Temple worship. In Deuteronomy's spirituality, the people's tithes and offerings in support of God's one sanctuary honored God's singular claim on their lives and the integrity of their communal life under the covenant (v. 8; see Deut 12:5–7). If they would only start embracing God's claim in a wholehearted and materially tangible way, Malachi argues, they could resurrect the covenant both economically and spiritually.

In calling for a "test" of God's will to bless (v. 10; cf. Ps 34:8), Malachi is far from encouraging a selfish spirit ("What do we profit?" 3:14). Rather, he doggedly maintains that the covenantal relationship makes a positive difference in the real world (see the first dispute). His emphasis on successful agriculture (vv. 10–12) is no "prosperity gospel," but a stress on the relationship between human faithfulness and flourishing soil. Human reverence and mutuality set the stage for the good earth's recovery.

VI. Judgment and Vindication (3:13–4:3)

Malachi's sixth (concluding) dispute counters a knee-jerk impatience with his theology. People wanted the Sinai covenant to be a "prosperity gospel," guaranteeing that each person would inevitably get ahead. They wanted a "test" that would box God in, forcing God to meet their terms and their timetable (vv. 13–15; cf. 1:2; 2:17).

Happily, not everyone misheard Malachi. Some of his contemporaries knew a reverent "fear" of God (v. 16; 4:2; cf. 1:14; 2:5; 3:5). Awe of God evokes the kind of right living that brings spacious, fulfilling life.

As in E, God's day of discrimination holds no threat for the God-fearing remnant, whose names are in God's book of life (v. 16; Exod 32:33–34 [E]). Until that day, when righteousness dawns upon them, they will embody God's covenantal purposes as God's "special possession" (v. 17; cf. Exod 19:5 [E]; Deut 7:6; 14:2; 26:18).

VII. Moses and Elijah, the Famed Covenant Mediators (4:4–6)

Verses 4–6 draw Malachi, and the Bible's entire collection of prophecy, to a close. They remind readers to attend to both past and future. Deuteronomy 34:10–12 concludes the Torah on a similar note: The Sinai experience will remain foundational, but the covenant has a prophetic future. The revelation to Moses was definitive, but Moses was himself a prophet, and he had prophets as successors (cf. the comments on Mal 3:1).

BIBLIOGRAPHY

J. G. Baldwin. *Haggai, Zechariah, Malachi: An Introduction and Commentary.* TOTC (Leicester, England: InterVarsity, 1972); S. L. Cook. *The Apocalyptic Literature.* IBT (Nashville: Abingdon, 2003); A. E. Hill. *Malachi.* AB 25D (New York: Doubleday, 1998); J. M. O'Brien. *Nahum, Habakkuk, Zephaniah, Haggai, Zechariah, Malachi.* AOTC (Nashville: Abingdon, 2004); D. L. Petersen. *Zechariah 9–14 and Malachi: A Commentary.* OTL (Philadelphia: Westminster, 1995); D. Stuart. "Malachi." *The Minor Prophets. Volume 3: Zephaniah, Haggai, Zechariah, and Malachi.* T. E. McComiskey, ed. (Grand Rapids: Baker, 1998).

TOBIT

LOREN STUCKENBRUCK

OVERVIEW

The book of Tobit is a fictional story of pious and faithful Jews exiled in Assyria. Tobit, the alleged author, is the subject of the first part of the book. He suffered blindness and financial ruin because of his exemplary piety. The story then moves to Sarah, a blameless young woman who was unable to marry because a demon was killing her fiancés on their appointed wedding days. These two stories are linked when Tobit's and Sarah's prayers are answered at the same time by the sending of the angel Raphael, who helps Tobit's son Tobiah marry Sarah, heal Tobit, join the families, and bring about financial security. It is an entertaining tale that emphasizes the importance of piety and familial loyalty, making the point that ultimately God protects and rewards the righteous.

OUTLINE

DETAILED ANALYSIS

I. Tobit's Exemplary Piety in Israel and in Exile (1:1–2:1)

The book opens in the third person (1:1–2), claiming to be the words of Tobit, the main character who is later told to record all the events which happened to him in the story (12:20). Tobit is presented as a Jew who belongs to the tribe of Naphtal (in the northern kingdom of Israel). Though his capture during the reign of the Assyrian king Shalmanesser (726–722 BCE, but see 2 Kgs 15:29) locates most of the story's events in the Eastern Diaspora, the first part of Tobit's life is lived out in the land of Israel. The chronology is confused: Tobit was young when his tribe, along with Israel, revolted against the Jerusalem Temple (late 10th cent. BCE, after Solomon's death), while his capture to Nineveh corresponds to events two centuries later. Tobit's wide-ranging chronological and geographical profile is constructed to emphasize his impeccable religiosity. This lends a certain timelessness and consistency to his piety, the expression of which does not depend on location or an ability to make pilgrimages to Jerusalem.

What aspects of Tobit's piety does the story consider so exemplary? For one thing, he worshipped at the Temple as long as that was possible (1:4). His trips to Jerusalem would involve him in the bringing of tithes and offerings to the Temple, as well as his giving to the poor while there (1:6–8). Though worship in Jerusalem is not emphasized in the main part of the book, the theme is picked up again at the end (chs. 13–14) when Tobit sings in praise of the heavenly Jerusalem and anticipates its future glory. Further activities, directed at other Israelites, play a more prominent role in the following narrative: almsgiving, familial loyalty, and burying the dead. As a giver of alms, Tobit would feed the hungry and give clothing to the naked. Loyalty to family, developed later in the book, is already implied as he follows his grandmother's instructions (1:8), marries Hannah who is from his tribe (1:9), and gives alms to his kinsmen (1:16–17). Tobit's burying the dead is specifically linked to his exilic setting, when the corpses of murdered Jews were left exposed and unburied by Gentile persecutors (1:17–19). It is thus because of burying the dead that Tobit finds himself persecuted and loses the prominence and possessions he had acquired under Shalmaneser.

By the end of this section, Tobit has been presented as a pious Jew who is acquainted with suffering. His good deeds are rewarded after a frightening period of persecution. Tobit is also presented as a savvy caretaker of his wealth, some of which he entrusts to Gabael as an investment during his business trips to Media (1:14). It is on the basis of Tobit's established character as a righteous sufferer who has already experienced vindication that the book begins to explore the problem of suffering and piety in more depth.

A. Tobit's Blindness and the Problem of Piety (2:2–3:1)

In ch. 1 Tobit seems to have overcome problems that resulted from his burial of the dead. Chapter 2 takes a different turn: Tobit's burial of the dead leads to further troubles, this time to blindness, ridicule from other Jews, and a sharp rebuke from his own wife! The story, then, is not simply about someone who suffers for being obviously righteous; Tobit even finds his own character being questioned and thus reaches the point of despair. Instead of being rewarded for his fidelity to Jewish tradition, he is blinded.

The occasion that inaugurates the episode is the Feast of Weeks (Gk.: "Pentecost," meaning "fiftieth"), which celebrates the presentation of the first sheaf of wheat seven weeks after the initial planting. The sumptuousness of the festal meal (2:1–2) serves to highlight Tobit's ardent piety; his search for someone poor to share the meal with leads to a report about the corpse of a Jew lying in the street. Tobit is not only prepared to leave the feast to organize the burial (2:4,7), but also demonstrates his piety by scrupulously observing purity regulations (2:5,7,9)—through washing, delaying the burial itself until sundown, and not re-entering his home that night.

The immediate cause of Tobit's blindness, the droppings of sparrows, is at once humorous and problematic. The randomness of his condition makes the question of theodicy (i.e. how could God allow something like this happen to a pious person?) all the more acute. The force of Tobit's physical impairment is compounded as the efforts of doctors to heal him with their "medicines" only worsen the condition (2:10; cf. Mk. 5:26), and his wife questions the value of his piety (2:14).

B. Tobit's Prayer (3:1–6)

In his despair, Tobit utters a prayer, the first of six formal prayers in the book. Tobit has a two-fold petition: (1) he asks God, in his justice, to forgive and hold him responsible for his wrongdoings, including unintentional sins (3:3–5); and (2) he begs God to let him die so he will be liberated from his physical distress and social ridicule (3:6). Tobit's plea for forgiveness also acknowledges Israel's disobedience to God and need for pardon. In this way, the text presents Tobit as a figure with whose ups and downs Jewish readers were meant to identify.

C. Sarah's Plight and Prayer (3:7–15)

The scene shifts from Tobit's predicament in Nineveh to that of another pious Jew, a young woman named Sarah who lives in Ecbatana of Media. The story is no longer from Tobit's point of view. Sarah's troubles, on the surface, seem of a very different kind from Tobit's. An only child, she has been unable to marry, since seven men engaged to her died on their wedding nights before they were able to consummate the marriage. For this Sarah is accused by one of her father's maidservants of killing (the Old Latin says "suffocating") each of her husbands. Like Tobit, she begs God to let her die (3:13), she is the target of reproach (3:7, 15), and she petitions that she not have to suffer reproach (3:15). However, unlike Tobit, her prayer suggests a more straightforward character: the direction of her "face" and "eyes" toward God (3:12) implies a Temple piety; she protests her innocence and does not ask for forgiveness (3:13–14; see the elaboration in the Vulgate), and she reasons that it would ultimately be best not to die since she would then dishonor her father by leaving him without an heir (3:15). Readers are not yet informed that the cause of the men's deaths is demonic (cf. 3:17).

II. The Angel Raphael is Enlisted to Help Tobit and Sarah (3:16–17)

A temporal literary device (3:16, "at that very moment"; cf. 3:17) links the stories of Tobit and Sarah, whose prayers are finished, heard and answered at the same time by the same means: the sending of Raphael "to heal them both." The description of Raphael's activity would almost have been superfluous for a Hebrew speaking audience, since the angel's name itself means "El has healed."

In this section the narrator's voice provides readers with a bird's eye view of most of the storyline. Readers are told in advance that the demon Asmodeus lies behind the deaths of Sarah's husbands, and they now know for the first time that Tobit's son Tobiah will play a vital role in the story and become Sarah's husband.

A. Tobit Instructs Tobiah and Tells Him about the Invested Money (4:1–21)

Chapter 4 is framed by Tobit's decision to send Tobiah away to collect the invested monies from Gabael in Rages of Media (4:1–2, 20–21). The collected investment will serve as Tobiah's inheritance, as Tobit thinks the death he prayed for is imminent. Tobit's instructions suggest a concern with the handling of money, whether through the enjoinder to give to the needy (4:6–11, 16), the payment of employees' wages (4:14) or, implicitly, through the directive that Tobiah bury him and, after his death, not to neglect his mother (4:3–

4). The advice, however, ranges more widely: a caution against having illicit sex, which is interpreted as marrying outside one's own tribe and related to arrogance and time-wasting (4:12–13); a command to avoid drunkenness, which is combined with a saying that sounds like the Golden Rule, "Don't do to anyone what you don't like to be done to you!" (4:15); and general exhortations to seek advice from sensible people and to praise God and seek his counsel (4:18–19). The latter advice to praise God is a salient feature of each of the six main prayers recorded in the book (cf. 3:2, 11; 8:5,15; 11:14; 13:1).

B. Azariah Hired to Accompany Tobiah to Media (5:1–6:1)

From here until the end of the book, Tobit's son Tobiah takes over as its main character. As Tobiah does not know the way to Rages, Tobit sends him out to hire a guide. Tobiah finds a man who identifies himself first as an Israelite relative (5:5) and then with the name "Azariah" (5:13, meaning "Yahweh has helped"), though readers are informed from the start that he is the angel Raphael (5:4). Again, as in 3:16–17, readers are openly given a perspective on the story that its characters do not share. Tobiah's travelling companion is approved by Tobit, especially when Tobit learns that he is a relative (5:13–14). The "recognition" of Azariah as a relative reinforces the emphasis of the book on the advantages of family loyalty.

As the parents send Tobiah and his companion on their way, the impression is left that Tobit's wife Hannah approves of the journey (5:17). Again, however, she argues with Tobit, stating her fear that the journey is too much of a risk to take simply for the sake of money. She contrasts her view that one ought to be content with what one has (5:18, 20) with the claim that Tobit is overly interested in money. Tobit's reassurance that all will be well with their son is uttered ironically: "a good angel will go with him" (5:22).

C. Tobiah and Raphael at the Tigris River (6:2–9)

As the two travellers, joined by a dog (6:2; cf. 11:4), approach Ecbatana (east of Nineveh), they come to the Tigris River (which in fact was west of Nineveh). This reinventing of geographical details serves the storyline, as it is at the river where the solution to Tobit's and Sarah's problems becomes apparent: parts of a fish. The angel's role is primarily to give Tobiah instructions about what to do. Thus when the fish attacks Tobiah as he nears the river to wash, Raphael does not subdue the fish himself but rather tells Tobiah to overpower it. The angel's instructions about what to do with the fish's heart and liver in 6:5 are taken from a widely circulating recipe: when heated to smoke, they liberate "*a man or woman* under attack by a demon or an evil spirit" (6:8). Similarly, it is possible that using gall on the eyes was a common remedy (6:9). Readers, however, will already be aware from 3:17 that these fish parts will be used as "medicine" to cure Tobit's blindness (11:11–13) and to help Sarah become a wife (8:2–3).

D. Raphael's Instructions to Tobiah near Media (6:10–18)

Again, Raphael's special knowledge comes into play: he tells Tobiah about Sarah, who lives with her father and mother in Ecbatana, and announces that it has been predetermined that she should become his wife. The case for Tobiah to marry Sarah, however, is also a legal one that the angel explains (6:11–13). Tobias has the legal right to marry her as her closest remaining male relative and to become her father's heir. The legal reasoning described here (6:12; cf. 6:13 and 7:10–12, where the practice is expressly derived from "the book of Moses") finds a more tightly defined counterpart in the law for levirate marriage in Deut. 25:5–10, according to which the closest single brother is required to marry his widowed sister-in-law (cf. Gen. 38:6–26). Tobiah, however, is not a brother, nor have any of the seven dead men consummated their marriage to Sarah. A tradition that better approximates the practice adopted in this book may be found in Ruth 3:9–13, according to which the nearest kin after the parents can marry the widow.

Great care is taken, both in 6:12 and 8:7, to emphasize that marriage is not based on lust after beauty, but on character. Though Sarah is initially described as "beautiful" in 6:11 (Gk. omits "beautiful"), the following verse mentions her beauty only after she is portrayed as "sensible and courageous."

E. Tobiah and Raphael's Arrival at the House of Raguel (7:1–17)

When Tobiah and Raphael enter the house of Sarah's father, the first thing they establish is that they are relatives (7:2–8) close enough to have recognizably similar appearances. This lays the basis for the negotiations of terms for marriage to Sarah that follow between Raguel and Tobiah. Raguel, having acknowledged his legal responsibility to give Sarah to Tobiah (7:10), goes on, as did Raphael in the previous chapter (6:14–15), to rehearse Sarah's troubled history.

Until now, Tobiah has essentially been following the instructions of his father and the angel in the story. A point of transition in his character occurs in 7:9–10. Despite Raguel's bad news about Sarah's past, Tobiah proceeds confidently, much in contrast to the worries he expressed to Raphael in 6:14–15. Thus by the time he marries Sarah and consummates his marriage to her, Tobiah is a pious and responsible adult.

The story is sensitive to the feelings of the women. Having prepared the bedroom, Edna shares in her daughter's tears as she seeks to encourage her. Her words, "May the Lord of Heaven give you joy in place of your pain" (7:17), signal a reversal of the quotation from Amos 8:10 in 2:6. Edna's words thus occur at the cusp of the U-turn about to unfold on behalf of the righteous.

F. Deliverance from the Demon on the Wedding Night (8:1–21)

As Tobiah enters the bridal chamber, he follows Raphael's instructions on what to do with the fish's heart and liver: he smokes them over the incense coals to produce a pungent odor that drives Asmodeus away to distant "parts of Egypt," where the angel binds him with chains. The demon now gone, consummation of the marriage happens only after both Tobiah and Sarah utter a prayer of praise (which in 8:6 alludes to the institution of marriage in Gen. 2) and petition for deliverance. The oddity of a deliverance prayer after the demon is gone is explained by the petition for continued protection so that as a couple they might "grow old together" (8:6). Marriage is not simply for having children; significantly, the text celebrates the value of the husband-wife relationship within marriage.

Irony, even humor, comes through in the activities of Raguel during the wedding night. Raguel, thoroughly expecting Tobiah to meet the same fate as his predecessors, has a grave dug to receive and bury husband number eight during the night (8:9–11). Readers, of course, know these efforts are going to be unnecessary! Upon learning that Tobiah and Sarah are soundly asleep together, Raguel has the grave filled before dawn (presumably to keep up appearances), though not before he and Edna have uttered a threefold praise to God and have begged that mercy and deliverance ("to bring both their lives to completion", 8:16) be shown the couple.

The chapter closes with Raguel requesting that Tobiah stay an additional fourteen days to celebrate the marriage. He promises, in addition, that Tobiah will inherit his possessions, half now and the other half after he and Edna have died.

G. Raphael Collects the Money from Gabael in Rages (9:1–6)

The marriage, the wedding feast, and the events leading up to the occasion have distracted the story from the original purpose of Tobiah's journey. The collection of Tobit's deposit of money from Gabael comes as something of an anticlimax. Tobiah finds himself unable to leave the wedding feast, and so asks Azariah to complete the task for him.

III. Tobiah and Sarah's Departure for Nineveh (10:1–13)

The first scene (10:1–7a) constitutes the last of three arguments between Tobit and Hannah (cf. 2:11–14; 5:18–6:1). Readers would not have missed the husband and wife telling each other, "Be quiet!" Since Tobiah has not yet returned him, Hannah's old worries return as she expresses regret that she let her son go (10:6, an allusion to 5:18) and thinks her son must have died (10:6). Though Tobit, as before (5:19–22), reassures his wife that Tobiah will return safely, the text makes clear that he too is worried (10:1–3). The couple's tension, then, is the result of their shared concern.

The second scene (10:7b–13) continues to reflect Tobiah's character as one who is now acting with initiative and responsibility (cf. 7:9–10). Whereas Raguel attempts to persuade Tobiah

to stay a little longer while sending news to his parents through messengers that all is well (10:8), Tobiah, knowing his parents (10:7b), insists that he himself must go (10:9). Coming through with his promise, Raguel gives Tobiah half his possessions. In presenting the farewell, the storyteller does not miss the opportunity to include admonitions, first by Raguel to Tobiah and Sarah in turn (10:11,12a) and then by Edna to them both together (10:12b). Raguel instructs Sarah to honor her parents-in-law, while Edna directs Tobiah not to be a source of grief to Sarah.

The chapter concludes with Tobiah praising God and calling upon God to honor his parents-in-law (10:13). This is the first time in the book that Tobiah calls for a blessing upon others.

A. Tobiah's Return to Nineveh (11:1–9)

As Tobiah and Sarah draw near to Nineveh, Raphael once again seizes the initiative. Since Tobiah's parents do not yet know about his wife, the angel suggests that he and Tobiah, with the fish's gall in his hand, go ahead of the group (11:2–4). In addition, Raphael instructs Tobiah more precisely than before (cf. 6:9) in how to apply the medicinal gall when he sees his father (11:8). In the meantime, Hannah has spotted them coming from a distance (11:5), and announces their arrival to her husband; she then receives her son, declaring her readiness now to die (11:9).

B. Tobit's Blindness is Healed (11:10–19)

When the sightless Tobit stumbles out to greet his son, Tobiah applies the medicine to his father's eyes, following Raphael's instruction. The burning effect of the gall makes it possible for Tobiah to peel off the white film so that Tobit can see. As Hannah has done before (cf. 10:5), Tobit calls Tobiah "light of my eyes" (11:14). In the story, then, both the smoked liver and heart and the gall are regarded and treated as "medicine" (11:11; cf. 6:5, 8); procedures used to drive away a demon and to peel off film causing blindness in the eyes are not distinguished in kind.

Tobit then utters praise, not only to God but also to God's "holy angels" (twice in Codex Sinaiticus). Sarah, who has arrived a little later, is welcomed into the household by Tobit, who blesses her and praises God (11:16–17). Celebrations "among all the Jews of Nineveh" ensue, attended by Ahiqar and Nadin, thus making the joy a matter for the extended family. The mention of "Jews" (i.e. "Judaeans") is anachronistic, as at this time (late 8th cent. BCE) no Judaeans had been exiled. The designation betrays the period of the storyteller who expects his readers to resonate with the activity of this group.

C. Raphael Reveals His Identity (12:1–22)

The chapter begins with Tobit wishing to settle accounts with Azariah by paying him the promised wages (12:1–5). From v. 6 until the end of the chapter, the meeting between Azariah, Tobit and Tobiah is presented as private, signalling that information (much of which is already known to the reader) will be divulged. However, before Azariah discloses his true identity to the characters, the text has him give out a few more ethical instructions (12:6–10), which include the importance of praising God, keeping a king's secret, praying while fasting, doing good, and giving alms. This last mention in the book of almsgiving underscores its significance as a marker of piety: in addition to saving "from death" (an echo of Tobit's earlier instruction to Tobiah; cf. 4:10), it also "purifies (from) sin."

In 12:11–15 Raphael finally reveals his identity to Tobit and Tobias. He is the one who brought to God the requests of Tobit and Sarah (ch. 3) and the report about Tobit's burying the dead (ch. 2). Raphael was then sent "to test" Tobit and to heal him and Sarah (12:13). At this Tobit and Tobiah's response is a combination fear and reverence. To readers this response may have seemed appropriate, not only given Raphael's determinative role in the storyline but also because of the inclusion of angels in Tobit's prayer of praise in 11:14. Raphael, however, clarifies to both the characters (and the readers) that they should praise God. Though Raphael was with them, it was the will of God which made all of this possible (12:17–18). As an aside, the angel also explains what readers do not know: he did not actually eat anything, but only appeared to do so (6:6, only "he" i.e. Tobiah eats, a detail changed in the shorter Greek version to "they").

IV. Tobit's Song of Thanksgiving (13:1–18)

Chapter 13 follows on from the angel's instruction to praise God in 12:20 and provides formal expression to the statement in 12:22 that Tobit, together with Tobiah, continued to praise God. Its text is easily divided into two parts. The first is a hymn of praise to God (13:1–8) for his discipline and mercy, which essentially weaves together the story of Tobit with that of Israel (who are scattered now on account of sin, but will be the object of divine mercy when they turn to God). The theology of the song is not entirely consistent with the angel's description of what happened to Tobit as a "test" (cf. 12:13), though in 3:1–6 Tobit confesses his own wrongdoing (alongside that of Israel). The second part, in the wake of the theme of God's mercy on Israel, focuses on Jerusalem, which will be restored in all her glory as the eternal dwelling place for God (13:9–17).

A. Tobit's Final Instructions and Death (14:1–11)

What transpires here is what Tobit originally thought he was doing in ch. 4: giving last instructions to Tobiah before his death. In the ancient world, this kind of written instruction was called a "testament," an influential and widespread literary genre. The patriarch or venerable figure's words of advice were disseminated to his offspring at the moment before death, that is, when he had gained maximum wisdom.

Oddly, Tobit's death (14:1, at 112 years) is narrated before the presentation of his final instructions to both Tobiah and his grandsons (cf. 1 En. 91:1–2). Initially, Tobit's words are primarily concerned with the immediate and longer term future. He advises Tobiah, after his parents' deaths, to leave Nineveh with his family for Media, appealing to Nahum's prediction of Nineveh's destruction (Nah. 1:1; 2:8–10, 13; 3:18–19). Tobit insists that the prophets' predictions will not go unfulfilled (14:4). And so, beyond this, Tobit is made to predict that after a period of exile, the returnees will rebuild the Temple in Jerusalem, but not to the same standard as the first one (14:5), bringing Tobit's words to bear on the time of the narrator and his contemporary readers. The storyteller is clearly unimpressed by the Jerusalem Temple of his day, and goes on to have Tobit predict an event that lies in the future to both narrator and readers: the rebuilding of Jerusalem and Temple to a grandeur that outclasses anything that has come before (cf. 13:16–17). This unprecedented event will lead to a turning of "every nation of the whole earth" to worship (literally, "fear") God, leaving behind the idols that have deceived them.

B. Hannah's Death, Tobiah's Return to Ecbatana and His Death (14:12–15)

After Hannah's death, Tobiah buries her next to his father and, heeding Tobit's instructions, leaves for Media where he takes care of Sarah's parents and buries them honorably. The story rounds out the loyalty and responsibility shown towards the parents of both the husband and wife. Tobiah's age at death is given at 117 years. The advanced ages of Tobit and Tobiah at their deaths, as well as their privilege of seeing grandchildren—in Tobiah's case, children to the fifth generation—signals a happy outcome and reward for the piety and values commended in the book.

BIBLIOGRAPHY

M. Bredin, ed. *Studies in the Book of Tobit: A Multidisciplinary Approach.* Library of Second Temple Studies 55 (London: T&T Clark, 2006); J. A. Fitzmyer. *Tobit.* Commentaries in Early Jewish Literature (Berlin/New York: Walter de Gruyter, 2003); L. L. Grabbe. "Tobit." *Eerdmans Commentary on the Bible.* J. Rogerson and J. D. G. Dunn, eds. (Grand Rapids: Eerdmans, 2003) 736–47; M. Hallermayer. *Text und Überlieferung des Buches Tobit.* Deuterocanonical and Cognate Literature Studies 3 (Berlin/New York: Walter de Gruyter, 2007); C. Moore. *Tobit.* AB 40A (Garden City: Doubleday, 1996); L. T. Stuckenbruck. *Angel Veneration and Christology.* WUNT 2/70 (Tübingen: Mohr Siebeck, 1995); _____. "'Angels' and 'God': Exploring the Limits of Early Jewish Monotheism." *Early Jewish and Christian Monotheism.* L. T. Stuckenbruck and W. North, eds. JSNTSup 263 (London: T&T Clark International, 2004) 45–70; S. Weeks, S. Gathercole, and L. T. Stuckenbruck. *The Book of Tobit. Texts from the Principal Ancient and Medieval Traditions.* Fontes et Subsidia 3 (Berlin/New York: Walter de Gruyter, 2004); G. G. Xeravits and J. Zsengellér, eds. *The Book of Tobit. Text, Tradition, Theology.* JSJ Supplements 98 (Leiden/Boston: Brill, 2005).

JUDITH

SIDNIE WHITE CRAWFORD

OVERVIEW

Judith is a Jewish novel, a work written by one author and meant to be read. Although the book survived in only Greek and Latin, its original language was Hebrew, and it was written in Palestine between 135 and 100 BCE. While it did not become part of the Jewish canon of Scripture, as part of the LXX it was part of the Christian Bible and is found in the Apocrypha; it is considered deuterocanonical by the Roman Catholic and Eastern Orthodox churches.

The literary artistry of the anonymous author of Judith is evident. The book falls neatly into two parts, each with its own "envelope" construction (see Outline). Nebuchadnezzar, the powerful pagan king, dominates the first half; Judith, the pious Jewish widow, the second. The author uses humor, irony, and double entendre to make his theological points.

Judith is a work of historical fiction; the historical "mistakes" that introduce the book (1:1) would have been obvious to its original audience, and one can imagine the author "winking" at them, inviting them to share the joke (see Detailed Analysis). Judith is fiction and meant to be enjoyed as such, but it is fiction with a serious purpose.

The theological message of Judith is disarmingly simple: God will protect his people provided that they remain loyal to the covenant. The importance of observing Jewish law is a frequent motif, and the centrality of the Temple and the Jews as a worshiping community are emphasized.

To accomplish the divine purpose, God can and does use the apparently weakest instruments. Judith, the heroine, is a Jew, a woman, and a widow. In a reversal of gender roles, she defeats Holofernes and thus Nebuchadnezzar, ruling Gentiles and powerful men. Further, she does this by her own action; no miracle is required. The message is clear: God acts through human initiative, and a person of faith, no matter how lowly, can perform the seemingly impossible. To drive his point home, the author draws on the stories of earlier biblical heroines who saved their people: the judge Deborah and Jael, who slew the general

Sisera by driving a tent peg through his skull (Judg 4–5), and Esther, who saved the Jews of Persia from annihilation. In later Christian tradition Judith becomes a model of fortitude, chastity, and humility, often compared with the Virgin Mary and St. Joan of Arc.

OUTLINE

I. First Half (1:1–7:32)

    A. Campaign Against Disobedient Nations (1:1–3:10)
        1:1–16. Campaign Against Arphaxad
        2:1–13. Plan to Punish Disobedient Nations
        2:14–3:10. Holofernes' Campaign

    B. Israel Prepares for War (4:1–15)

    C. Holofernes Expels Achior (5:1–6:13)
        5:1–21. Achior's Speech
        5:22–6:13. Holofernes' Response

    C'. Achior Is Taken into Bethulia (6:14–21)

    B'. Holofernes Prepares for War (7:1–5)

    A'. Campaign Against Bethulia (7:6–32)

II. Second Half (8:1–16:25)

    A. Introduction of Judith (8:1–8)

    B. Judith Plans to Save Israel (8:9–10:9a)
        8:9–36. Judith Speaks to the Elders
        9:1–10:9a. Judith's Prayer and Preparations

    C. Judith and Her Maid Leave Bethulia (10:9b–10)

    D. Judith Overcomes Holofernes (10:11–13:10a)
        10:11–12:9. Judith in Holofernes' Camp
        12:10–13:10a. Judith Kills Holofernes

    C'. Judith and Her Maid Return to Bethulia (13:10b–13:11)

    B'. Judith's and Israel's Victory (13:12–16:20)

DETAILED ANALYSIS

I. First Half (1:1–7:32)

A. Campaign Against Disobedient Nations (1:1–3:10)

1:1–16. Campaign Against Arphaxad. The story begins with an obvious historical error, signaling to its audience that it is fiction, not fact. Nebuchadnezzar was the king of the Neo-Babylonian Empire, not the Assyrian Empire, and his capital was Babylon, not Nineveh. Nineveh was the capital of the Assyrian Empire, but it had been destroyed in 612 BCE. The combination of the two "evil empires" of Assyria and Babylon into one overwhelmingly evil symbol makes its eventual defeat an even greater illustration of God's power. Arphaxad is also a fictitious character. The measurements given for Ecbatana's walls are immense, and meant to emphasize King Arphaxad's glory and Nebuchadnezzar's overwhelming power. Nebuchadnezzar's war involves the entire known world; Samaria and Jerusalem, the ancient capitals of Israel and Judah (v. 9), are only a tiny piece of it.

2:1–13. Plan to Punish Disobedient Nations. Nebuchadnezzar instructs his general Holofernes to destroy those nations that refused to act as his allies in his war with Arphaxad. The rhetoric of these verses is inflated, meant to convey the power and threat of Nebuchadnezzar. His revenge is purely political; it has no religious overtones. However, the author's use of irony is visible in his use of the title "the Great King, the lord of all the earth" in v. 5; he will use the word *lord*, Gk. *kyrios*, with double intention throughout the story, as a title for the earthly rulers Nebuchadnezzar and Holofernes, and more importantly for Israel's God.

Several references in these verses had negative implications for the readers, setting them up for the crisis to come. The eighteenth year of Nebuchadnezzar (v. 1) was 587 BCE, the year in which he destroyed the kingdom of Judah, exiled its inhabitants, and razed Jerusalem and its Temple to the ground. The name Holofernes also had negative associations for the Jews. Artaxerxes III Ochus, a Persian king who campaigned against Judea in 350 and 343 BCE, had a general named Holofernes, who in turn had a servant named Bagoas (see 12:11). And vv. 8–9 would remind the reader of the historical Nebuchadnezzar's destruction of Judah and the exile of its inhabitants in 587 BCE, as well as the Assyrian exile in 722 BCE (2 Kgs 17:5–6) and the first Babylonian exile in 597 BCE (2 Kgs 24:10–16).

In verse 12, Nebuchadnezzar's boast that he will accomplish his plan "by my own hand" stands in ironic contrast to Judith's statement in 8:33 that "the Lord will deliver Israel by my hand." God's *hand* is used throughout the OT as a symbol of God's power (e.g., Exod 15:6; Deut 6:21). Judith's hand literally becomes God's instrument. The question is raised: Who is more powerful, Israel's God or Nebuchadnezzar?

2:14–3:10. Holofernes' Campaign. The focus of these chapters gradually narrows from the entire earth to the western region of the empire to the small seacoast towns that are Israel's neighbors. The size of Holofernes' army is emphasized by the author's use of biblical metaphors. A "mixed crowd" accompanies the Israelites in their flight from Egypt during the exodus (Exod 12:38). The metaphor comparing an army to a "swarm of locusts" occurs in Joel 1:4. The phrase "dust of the earth" is actually "sand of the earth" in Greek, thus mixing the two metaphors "dust of the earth" and "sand of the sea," common biblical phrases for an innumerable multitude (e.g., Gen 13:16; 32:12). These metaphors are used ironically; Holofernes is not coming to save, like the God of Israel, but to destroy. Holofernes' initial campaign is striking in its rapidity, violence, and success. The author piles up synonyms of destruction, creating the impression that Holofernes is conducting a "scorched earth" campaign.

The geography of these verses is confused. Some of the locations are known (e.g., Put and Lud), while others are unidentified (e.g., Bectileth). If these geographic locations are taken literally, Holofernes and his army accomplished a three-hundred-mile march in only three days; they then began marching back and forth across northern Mesopotamia and Syria in a zigzag fashion, destroying nations as they went. These details should not be taken seriously, but as artistic license to illustrate the fearsomeness of the Assyrian attack. In v. 28, Holofernes reaches the Mediterranean coast, thus drawing closer to Israel, which lies just inland of these cities. When these cities surrender, Israel is left unprotected to the north and west.

In v. 8, religion enters the narrative and with it a threat to Israel's single-minded loyalty to its God. Nebuchadnezzar had not ordered Holofernes to destroy cultic establishments, and he certainly had not demanded to be worshiped as a god. The demand, however, intensifies the threat to the Jews.

Holofernes reaches the borders of Israel in v. 9. Esdraelon (Jezreel) is a great valley that separates the hills of Galilee from those of Samaria. Dothan lies to the south of Esdraelon; Geba lies at the western end of the valley, while Scythopolis (modern Beth Shean) lies at the eastern entrance. Holofernes is thus approximately forty miles north of Jerusalem.

B. Israel Prepares for War (4:1–15)

The Israelites react to the news of Holofernes' victories by praying, performing acts of ritual penitence, and preparing for war. The emphasis shifts from the political to the religious implications of Holofernes' threat; the Israelites have heard that Holofernes had destroyed the temples of the coastal cities, and they fear for their own Temple in Jerusalem. Thus the author of Judith identifies the Jews as a worshiping community centered on the Temple.

The identification of the inhabitants of Judea as "Israelites" rather than "Jews" in v. 1 is an anachronism, indicating a hope for a return of the united kingdom of David and Solomon, and perhaps a gesture toward the Samaritan community, who actually inhabited the central hill country north of Judea; the district of Samaria is mentioned by name in v. 4. The office of high priest was an important one all throughout the post-exilic period, but only the Hasmonean high priests Jonathan, Simon, and John Hyrcanus I exercised the broad civil and military powers demonstrated by the high priest in vv. 6–8. Both Bethulia and Betomesthaim are unknown and probably fictional. Their importance lies in their

location, guarding the mountain passes that were the only access route to Jerusalem.

The Jews' first line of defense is God, to whom they turn in prayer and penitence. Fasting is an act of humility, while the wearing of sackcloth is a mourning gesture (see Esth 4:1–3). In this emergency, the Israelites take this gesture to extremes, even putting sackcloth on their cattle and the altar (cf. Jon 3:8)! The prayers have their desired effect; God "hears" and "has regard for" the Jews. At this early stage of the book, the outcome is no longer in doubt; God will rescue the Jews. The remaining question is "How?" The performance of all the required ritual activities indicates that this generation of Jews, unlike previous ones, do cleave to the Law and therefore deserve God's protection and care (Deut 28:1, 7).

C. Holofernes Expels Achior (5:1–6:13)

5:1–21. Achior's Speech. Achior, an Ammonite general, recites Israel's history to Holofernes and explains that God defends them. The Moabites, Ammonites, and Canaanites, all mentioned in vv. 2–3, were historical enemies of Israel, so it is ironic that Israel's sacred history is articulated so well by an Ammonite. Achior is an example of a wise, righteous Gentile such as the prophet Balaam (Num 22–24), who speaks the truth about Israel regardless of its political expediency.

Holofernes unknowingly articulates, through his questions in vv. 3–4, the book's central message: Israel's power and strength reside in God, who is their king and rules over them. Therefore, they will not submit to any earthly ruler. Achior gives a brief synopsis of Israel's history, extending from Abraham through Joshua. The mention of the Shechemites in v. 16 ties his statement to Judith's in 9:2, where she recounts the vengeance of Simeon and Levi upon the Shechemites. In his recital, Achior embraces the Deuteronomic theology, which argues that obedience to the Law will bring prosperity for the Israelites, while disobedience will bring punishment (Deut 28–32). Achior's final statement in v. 21 is prophetic; Holofernes and his army will become a laughingstock.

5:22–6:13. Holofernes' Response. Holofernes recognizes Achior's words as prophetic, but he rejects them in favor of a prophecy of his own. Holofernes' speech is unintentionally ironic; many of his questions and statements carry double meanings recognized by the reader. He speaks in the name of a false god, but makes true statements about the actual God. In v. 2, Holofernes asks the question that underlies the whole book; the answer, of course, is the God of Israel. The language that Holofernes uses to describe Israel's anticipated destruction is reminiscent of the language of holy war used to describe Israel's destruction of its enemies (e.g., Josh 8:24–29; Isa 34:2–7).

Holofernes' speech in vv. 5–9 is ironic in the extreme; his words will come true, but not in the way that he anticipates. The next time Achior sees his face, Holofernes' head will be severed from his body!

C'. Achior Is Taken into Bethulia (6:14–21)

Holofernes has shown no mercy to Achior; but the Israelites, although they are in a dangerous situation, are merciful toward him. The story's focus narrows to the small town of Bethulia.

In 6:14–15, the leaders of Bethulia are introduced. The author again employs irony by naming the chief magistrate Uzziah, which means "my strength is the LORD." Uzziah's strength will prove no match for Judith's. The tribe of Simeon is obscure; although it is one of the twelve tribes, it disappears early from the tribal lists (e.g., Judg 5; Deut 32), and its territory shifts around. The Israelites' reaction to Achior's tale is humble and pious, in sharp contrast to the arrogance and braggadocio of Holofernes and his men.

B'. Holofernes Prepares for War (7:1–5)

Holofernes now prepares for the siege of Bethulia. The mention of the spring is ominous, since towns in the ancient world were built next to natural water sources on which they were absolutely dependent. Although the Israelites are terrified, they are still braver than the peoples of the seacoast, since they prepare to defend themselves instead of surrendering.

A'. Campaign Against Bethulia (7:6–32)

Holofernes' seizure of the springs dooms the Bethulians to slow torture by thirst. The list of Holofernes' allies now includes the Edomites, another ancient enemy of Israel (Jer 49:7–22). Once again Israel's adversaries are unintention-

ally ironic; the Israelites don't rely on their spears (v. 10), but on God. The advice to Holofernes to seize the springs is a little strange, since he has already done so in v. 7, but the intention is the same: to force the Israelites to surrender because of lack of water.

The plan of Holofernes and his advisors begins to work; the Israelites are perishing from thirst (vv. 20–22). They have held out for more than a month, but their courage has finally deserted them, and they wish to surrender. Their complaint to Uzziah that slavery is preferable to death by thirst is similar to that of the Israelites in the wilderness to Moses (Exod 17:1–7). Uzziah is hoping for a miracle (as at Meribah), so he strikes a compromise with the Bethulians. When the miracle comes, it will take an unexpected form.

II. Second Half (8:1–16:25)

The events of the second half of the book focus on the heroine Judith and the destruction of Holofernes. An important theme in this half of the story is the reversal of gender roles, culminating in the beheading of the mighty man by the supposedly weak widow.

A. Introduction of Judith (8:1–8)

The heroine Judith is finally introduced. Like Deborah (Judg 4–5), Judith arises in a scene with erotic overtones. And like Esther, she uses her beauty and wits to achieve her goal. The name *Judith* means "Jewess" and identifies her as the ideal type of the Jewish heroine. Judith is given the longest genealogy of any female character in the Bible; it is significant that the last ancestor mentioned is Israel, the eponymous ancestor of all Israelites. Her genealogy also connects Judith to the tribe of Simeon (Num 1:6).

Judith's husband, Manasseh, is a shadowy character, only important for giving Judith her status as a wealthy widow. Judith's status as a widow is important to the story, since only a widow would have the freedom of action to carry out her plan. An unmarried girl was controlled by her father, a wife by her husband, but a widow was under her own control. Judith also appears to be childless. Thus Judith's situation as a Jewish woman is anomalous in several ways. As a pious widow, Judith practices a rigorous asceticism. She only breaks her fast on festival days when fasting was forbidden. Her rooftop tent may be a reminder of the booths used in the Festival of Sukkot (Lev 23:42) and of the tabernacle in the wilderness (Exod 26). However rigorous her asceticism, Judith is still beautiful, as befits a heroine in the ancient world. Judith's reputation for piety and devotion allow her to flout the conventions of women's behavior in that time period without negative ramifications.

B. Judith Plans to Save Israel (8:9–10:9a)

8:9–36. Judith Speaks to the Elders. Judith's speech to the elders comprises one of the major theological statements in the book. Judith upbraids Bethulia's leaders for their lack of faith and cajoles them into permitting her to carry out her plan. Her high standing in the community is demonstrated by the fact that the leaders drop everything and go to her tent. When they arrive, Judith rebukes them for acquiescing to the people's demand in 7:23–31. While the people understood the situation through the lens of the Deuteronomic theology, according to which God was punishing them for sins, Judith understands the situation differently. According to Judith, Uzziah's five-day deadline puts God to the test. This is wrong, because God is beyond human comprehension; God may have some purpose behind the siege that the Bethulians do not understand. God has the choice of saving the Bethulians or destroying them, but it is according to God's own timetable. While prayer is efficacious because it pleases God, bargaining is not, and the Bethulians risk God's wrath by resorting to it.

Judith goes even further in vv. 18–23 by declaring that the people's interpretation of the situation must be wrong, since they have renounced idol worship. It was idol worship that led to both the Assyrian and the Babylonian destructions (2 Kgs 17:7–18; 21:5–10), but since now the people are innocent, they have no reason to suppose God wishes to destroy them. Using the language of honor and shame, Judith states that Israel's defeat in this situation would shame God in the eyes of other nations. The implication is that God will not allow this to happen. In v. 24, Judith reminds her listeners that Bethulia is the only obstacle between Holofernes and Jerusalem, so their actions affect not only themselves but also the Temple.

Judith understands the present situation as a test of faith, much as God tested Abraham and Isaac in the sacrifice of Isaac (Gen 22:1–14). According to this theology, faith is refined through hardship. Uzziah's response (vv. 28–31) reveals only partial understanding. He realizes that Judith is wise, in the tradition of Joseph, Solomon, and Lady Wisdom from the book of Proverbs. However, he only asks her to pray for rain, at best a temporary reprieve. Although Uzziah's oath was wrong, since he swore it to God he cannot break it. Judith once more attempts to make them understand that the situation calls for much more drastic action than a mere prayer for rain. She makes an astonishing statement: if they allow her to leave the besieged town (making her an easy target for the enemy forces), she will deliver them within the allotted five days. Further, they must trust her enough not to question her intentions. Judith, like Esther, intends at this time of crisis to take matters into her own hands. Even more astonishingly, Uzziah and the others agree. Although their faith in God is weak, they are willing to put their faith in Judith.

9:1–10:9a. Judith's Prayer and Preparations. Before undertaking her mission, Judith naturally turns to God. Her prayer is humble, but no mention is made of sin or repentance; according to Judith the Jews are innocent victims. The prayer's theology is typical of Second Temple Judaism: God is omniscient and omnipotent, a defender of the downtrodden. The prayer embraces the doctrine of retributive justice, in which even a weak woman could prevail.

The time of Judith's prayer aligns her with the Temple ritual, thus continuing the Temple focus. She begins by recalling with approval the episode of the revenge of Simeon and Levi on Shechem for the rape of Dinah (Gen 34). She is identifying herself not with Dinah, but with her ancestor Simeon; she too will be an avenger. The reminder that she is a helpless widow is a superb touch.

Verses 5–6 emphasize that God is the omnipotent Creator, and thus the outcome of this struggle is already decided. To emphasize this message, v. 7 contains a quotation of Exod 15:3, the Song of the Sea, which celebrates God's victory over the Egyptians in the exodus. The Temple focus returns in v. 8.

In vv. 9–14, Judith emphasizes her feminine frailty; for a man to be defeated by "the hand of a woman" would be an unbearable shame, but God is the god of the weak and powerless, and Judith the Jewess here stands for the weakness of all the Jews against the might of Holofernes. Judith asks for the ability to deceive with words, which may seem an ethical lapse, but is consistent with the doctrine of retributive justice.

Following her prayer, Judith leaves the safety of both her old self and Bethulia by changing her persona from pious widow to beautiful seductress and by stepping through the gates of Bethulia into enemy territory. Judith's toilette is voyeuristic; bathing scenes became popular in Second Temple literature, e.g., the Additions to Esther and Susanna. The lack of water in Bethulia does not deter the author. Judith's beautification ritual is elaborate, emphasizing the great transformation taking place. She can be compared to a warrior putting on his armor for battle. Judith also prepares ritually pure food to take with her to the enemy camp. The town elders are astonished at Judith's now-revealed beauty, as are all who encounter her from now on.

C. Judith and Her Maid Leave Bethulia (10:9b–10)

The gate is opened, and Judith and her maid make their symbolic way through the gate, down the mountain, and through the valley. They will retrace their steps exactly when they return (13:10b).

D. Judith Overcomes Holofernes (10:11–13:10a)

We have now reached the denouement of the central conflict in the book: the struggle between Judith and Holofernes, the proxies for the God of Israel and Nebuchadnezzar.

10:11–12:9. Judith in Holofernes' Camp. Judith is promptly captured by the enemy and taken to Holofernes. From now on Judith will employ "deceptive speech"; all of her dialogue will be ironic, full of double meanings and outright lies. Her beauty works to lull the Assyrians' suspicions, enabling her to carry out her plan without hindrance. Judith's promise to the guards to give a "true report" of the situation in Bethulia is only truthful from the point of view of an Israelite. The use of the word *lord* in verse 15 and in the ensuing

scenes will always have a double meaning: the literal one of the human potentate, Nebuchadnezzar or Holofernes, and the hidden one of Israel's God. In Judith's initial dialogue with Holofernes she continues to speak deceptively, successfully employing irony and humor to disarm him. Holofernes on the other hand unwittingly speaks the truth, although the truth is apparent only to the reader. He also reveals himself as vain, obtuse, and a braggart. His twofold admonishment to Judith to "take courage" is humorous; Judith is in no need of courage. For her part, Judith employs gross flattery. 11:6 is particularly ironic; God will accomplish his purposes through Holofernes, but not in the way Holofernes imagines!

Judith's tale includes references to Jewish law that Holofernes cannot have understood. It was forbidden to eat meat that was improperly slaughtered (Lev 17:10–16). The tithes of the first fruits were considered sacred to the priest and the Levites (Num 18:8–32). However, at least one strand of Jewish interpretation then, and the prevailing one today, declared that any violation of the Law was acceptable to preserve human life (1 Macc 2:29–41).

In vv. 16–19, Judith speaks as a prophet, making several references to OT texts (Ps 89:4; Ezek 34:1–10; Isa 56:10–11). However, her prophecy is a false one. Holofernes also speaks prophetically; Judith is indeed "renowned throughout the whole world." What he means by "your God shall be my God" is unclear; does he intend to worship Judith's God as pagan kings did in the book of Daniel? Or does he anticipate Judith's worshiping Nebuchadnezzar?

In 12:1–9, Judith establishes a routine in the enemy camp that will eventually allow her to escape without hindrance. Judith continues to evince concern for the proper observance of ritual purity.

12:10–13:10a. Judith Kills Holofernes. Judith has only five days in which to accomplish her mission. On day four Holofernes decides to seduce her, thus unwittingly setting in motion the final events of the plot. Holofernes uses the language of honor and shame in v. 12; although he means to shame Judith, she is about to shame him. Bagoas' invitation actually invites Judith to become Holofernes' mistress; Judith's response is as usual laced with ironic double entendres. The author must intend for his readers to laugh at v. 18; we know what Judith means, although Holofernes does not. Holofernes, although he appears to be controlling the situation, is rapidly losing control, as evidenced by v. 20. Judith, while seeming to relinquish control, actually continues to control both herself and Holofernes.

In 13:1–10a the long-anticipated climax to the story occurs. Judith cuts off Holofernes' head and escapes back to Bethulia.

The translation "dead drunk" in 13:2 captures the Greek well and delivers a good pun, for Holofernes will soon be dead period! At the climactic moment, Judith pauses for prayer, reminding us that her action is not motivated by personal vengeance but by the safety of the Israelites and the Temple. Judith's action is loaded with sexual innuendo; the line between sex and death was very close in pre-modern times. Holofernes' decapitation is a symbolic castration; he loses his potency and his power to harm the Israelites.

C'. Judith and Her Maid Return to Bethulia (13:10b–13:11)

Judith and her maid, retracing the same path they took in 10:10, reenter the symbolic safety of Bethulia's gates. Judith displays her trophy and, together with the Bethulians, blesses God, who is the true victor. Judith's victory cry is reminiscent of Ps 24, which also calls for gates to be opened in triumph.

B'. Judith's and Israel's Victory (13:12–16:20)

13:12–14:10. Judith's Plan and Achior's Conversion. In 9:2, Judith had prayed for this result; now she praises God for bringing it about. Holofernes' defeat is made more shameful because Judith is a woman. Uzziah's blessing recalls other OT blessings: Jael (Judges 5), Ruth (Ruth 3:10), and Melchizedek's blessing of Abram (Gen 14:19–20).

The danger is not completely gone, however. Now the Bethulians must defeat the Assyrian army. In 14:1–10, Judith reveals herself as not only a cunning assassin but also a military strategist. Judith's strategy includes a ruse that will lead to the discovery of Holofernes' headless body, thus sending the Assyrians into a panic (cf. 2 Kgs 19:35; 2 Chr 32:21).

Achior reappears to bear witness to the fulfillment of the prophecy he gave in 5:20–21. His faint, in contrast to Judith's fortitude, once again illustrates the reversal of gender roles in the book. Achior's conversion, symbolized by the physical act of circumcision, is an example of a strand in Judaism that welcomed conversion, illustrated by the books of Ruth and Jonah. Deut 23:3, in contrast, forbids the conversion of Ammonites.

14:11–16:20. Israel's Victory and Celebration. The Assyrians discover Holofernes' headless body and are routed by the Israelites. The Israelites win a military victory against the seemingly invincible Assyrian army, and Judith leads them in celebrations at the Temple.

Bagoas' final statement in 14:18 summarizes the reversal of honor and shame that has taken place: the least powerful member of a powerless group has defeated the representative of the most powerful force on earth. The oppositions of female/male, Hebrew/Assyrian, and one/many are all present. Now that the Assyrians are "headless," they flee in panic, and the Israelites are able to defeat them easily. The slaughter and plunder are typical of warfare in the ancient Near East.

Beginning in 15:8, Judith, the Bethulians, and all Israel rejoice and praise God for Judith's victory. The reader is constantly reminded that God is the real victor, the power behind Judith. The centrality of Jerusalem is emphasized. It was unusual for the high priest and his entourage to leave Jerusalem for any reason; thus the extraordinary nature of this victory is emphasized. However, Judith is given full credit for her deed; it was not divine intervention but human initiative that saved the day, and God fully approves.

In 15:12–16:17, Judith leads the women of Israel in celebration. There is a strong tradition in Israel of women leading celebratory processions (see Exod 15:21; Judg 11:34; 1 Sam 18:7; and, in the NT, Mary's hymn in Luke 1). Judith's hymn of victory is modeled on other victory hymns such as Exod 15 (Miriam) and Judg 5 (Deborah). The song falls into three parts: Introduction (vv. 1–2), narration of the event (vv. 3–12), and response of praise (vv. 13–17). Verse 2 contains a quotation of Exod 15:3; see also 9:7.

Judith, the childless widow, speaks in maternal terms about her people. In 16:5, the phrase "hand of a woman" appears for the third time, again with connotations of shame for the defeated (9:10; 13:15). The dichotomy of the downtrodden and the powerful is reiterated in vv. 11–12. Although the reference to "sons of slave-girls" is not literally true, it emphasizes the shame of the Assyrian defeat.

Verses 13–17 are replete with biblical allusions: God as creator (Gen 1:2; Ps 33:6), the upheaval of nature in the face of the Divine Warrior (Exod 15:18; Ps 18:7–15; Isa 64:1), and God as avenger (Isa 66:24).

The worship of God, including sacrifice, which takes place in 16:18–20, is centralized in Jerusalem, as mandated by the book of Deuteronomy. Holofernes' canopy falls under the ban (Heb.: *kherem*), according to which the spoils of war belong to the true victor, God (Josh 6:19).

A'. Epilogue Concerning Judith (16:21–25)

The epilogue describes the remainder of Judith's life. She retires to Bethulia, although not specifically to her rooftop tent. She refuses to remarry; in Christian tradition Judith is upheld as a model of chastity, although in Jewish tradition her unmarried state is anomalous. Judith reaches a very old age and is exemplary to the end; she frees her maid and gives generous bequests. Finally, like the judge Deborah (Judg 5:31), her legacy to Israel is a long period of peace.

BIBLIOGRAPHY

T. Craven. *Artistry and Faith in the Book of Judith.* SBLDS 70 (Chico, Calif.: Scholars, 1983); A. LaCocque. *The Feminine Unconventional: Four Subversive Figures in Israel's Tradition* (Minneapolis: Fortress, 1990); C. A. Moore. *Judith: A New Translation with Introduction and Commentary.* AB 40 (Garden City, N.Y.: Doubleday, 1985); L. M. Wills. "The Book of Judith." NIB (Nashville: Abingdon, 1999) 3: 1073–1183.

THE ADDITIONS TO ESTHER

NANCY BOWEN

OVERVIEW

The story of Esther exists in both a Hebrew (MT) and Greek version. The NRSV translates the text of the major Septuagint (LXX) manuscripts, which are fairly faithful renderings of MT's Esther plus six extended Additions. The Additions derive from different contexts and languages, and were probably added at different times. They add religious elements lacking in the Hebrew, most notably references to God and elements of Jewish piety, and enhance the theme of conflict between Jews and non-Jews.

OUTLINE

I. Addition A (11:2–12:6)

    A. Mordecai's Dream (11:2–12)

    B. The Eunuchs' Plot (12:1–6)

II. Addition B, Haman's Decree (13:1–7)

III. Addition C (13:8–14:19)

    A. Mordecai's Prayer (13:8–18)

    B. Esther's Prayer (14:1–19)

IV. Addition D, Esther Approaches the King (15:1–16)

V. Addition E, Mordecai's Decree (16:1–24)

VI. Addition F (10:4–11:1)

    A. Mordecai's Dream Interpreted (10:4–13)

    B. Greek Esther Authorized (11:1)

DETAILED ANALYSIS

I. Addition A (11:2–12:6)

A. Mordecai's Dream (11:2–12)

Addition A consists of two sections. The first reports a dream that Mordecai had (11:2–12).

There will be a "fight" between two "dragons," a creature symbolizing danger and chaos (Isa 27:1; Dan 7:23–27; Rev 12:3–4). The encounter is "a day of darkness and gloom" (11:8) like the "day of Yahweh" (Joel 2:1–2; Zeph 1:15). God responds to the righteous nation's cry (11:10) as God did in Egypt (Exod 2:23–24; 3:7–9). The dream's language establishes a theme of conflict between righteousness and evil, where, with God's help, righteousness prevails. The dream reveals "what God had determined to do." In the MT humans control the outcome; here God controls the future.

B. The Eunuchs' Plot (12:1–6)

Addition A also recounts a plot by two eunuchs to kill the king (12:1–6). Mordecai successfully thwarts the plot, and the king rewards him. A similar story occurs in 2:19–23. The suggestion that Haman is behind the plot and seeks revenge against Mordecai for his interference (12:6) differs from his motivation 3:1–6. The MT identifies Haman as an Agagite, a historic enemy of the Jews (1 Sam 15:8–33). Here he is identified as "a Bougean," an uncertain identification. He will later be identified as a Macedonian, a historic enemy of the Persians (16:10).

II. Addition B, Haman's Decree (13:1–7)

Additions B (13:1–7) and E (16:1–24) fill gaps in the MT by providing copies of the royal decrees dictated by Haman and Mordecai respectively (3:12–13; 8:9–10). Addition B records Haman's proposal to destroy the Jews with harsher language than in 3:8. It is cunning propaganda, demonizing the Jews as Other (cf. 3 Macc 3:12–29). They are depicted as different, and therefore dangerous. Homeland security motivates taking action—difference threatens the empire's stability (13:4–5). Typical of racist propaganda, the accusations are false. There is no evidence that the Jews threatened the Persian Empire. Accusation alone becomes sufficient cause for annihilation "without pity or restraint," language that ironically echoes what Israel is commanded to do to the Canaanites (Deut 7:16) and contradicts Artaxerxes assertion of "kindness" (13:2).

III. Addition C (13:8–14:19)

Addition C records prayers by Mordecai (13:8–18) and Esther (14:1–19), portraying them as devout Jews. The prayers are similar to individual complaint psalms, which petition God to save from the "enemy" (e.g., Pss 3; 6; 22). They differ on why God should act. Mordecai appeals to covenant; God's special "inheritance," or "portion," is in danger (13:15, 16–17), terms characterizing Israel's special relationship to God (e.g., Deut 32:9; Zech 2:12; 2 Macc 1:26; 3 Macc 6:3). Esther appeals to the people's needs; they are in trouble and have no escape (14:5, 9, 19). God is omniscient and omnipotent in the prayers, knowing the situation and having the power to change it (13:9, 11–12; 14:12, 15–16, 19). Indeed, these prayers are answered, establishing a theology of prayer's efficacy in dire circumstances and removing MT's ambiguity as to God's knowledge or power.

The prayers provide motivations and feelings absent in the MT. Mordecai refuses to bow to Haman because, though willing to debase himself to save Israel (13:13), he will bow only to Yahweh (13:14). This is still ambiguous since no law prohibits honoring foreign rulers. The desire not to elevate human glory hints that Haman may have claimed divine status, rendering bowing a form of idolatry (Exod 20:3–5; Dan 3:1–18). Esther hates her royal life. Her attitude toward Gentiles in general, and Persians in particular, is one of overt hostility. She strongly identifies with the Jewish people (14:5) and seems obsessed with separating herself whenever possible from court life, including regarding her crown as unclean as a menstrual rag (14:16; "filthy rag"; cf. Lev 15:19–24). She abhors having sex with the king (14:15), perhaps reflecting post-exilic anxiety about intermarriage. Sadly, this shows the same demonization of the Other as does Addition B.

IV. Addition D, Esther Approaches the King (15:1–16)

Addition D elaborates MT's much briefer account of Esther's approach to the King (MT 5:1–2). Additions C and D emphasize Esther's fear. It drives her to prayer, overwhelms her before the king, and heightens the sense of danger she, and her people, face. This emotion presents several possibilities for describing her character: she is an accomplished actress, pretending to be something she is not, "happy"; she is stereotypically female, physically and emotionally weak; or she is a courageous hero, carrying on with her mission though afraid. Esther's initial approach to the king is successful because God actively intervenes to change his spirit from anger to gentleness (15:7–8), an answer to her prayer (14:13).

V. Addition E, Mordecai's Decree (16:1–24)

Addition E details Mordecai's decree countermanding Haman's previous decree (Addition B). The empire changes its view of the Jews by judging them "with more equitable consideration" (16:9). A minority group is seen as contributing to the empire's peace and stability; difference becomes an asset. Jews are permitted to live under their own laws, removing the threat of annihilation through cultural assimilation (16:19). There is solidarity as Persians defend Jews and celebrate victory with them (16:20, 22–23). Addition E offers a peaceful model of tolerance and cooperation between groups, except that it proceeds to vilify the Macedonians who replace the Jews as Other (16:10–14). Repeating the dynamic that started the conflict suggests violence will continue as long as there are those who scheme and rulers who can be persuaded.

VI. Addition F (10:4–11:1)

A. Mordecai's Dream Interpreted (10:4–13)

B. Greek Esther Authorized (11:1)

Mordecai's dream is interpreted in Addition F. Mordecai credits God for everything that has happened, affirming the theology that God saves the righteous when they cry out in distress. Purim celebrates God's victory instead of human victory. The interpretation of Esther as the river that grew from a tiny spring perhaps references her growing maturity and authority in the story. Addition F closes with a note intended to authenticate the Greek version of Esther, or maybe just the Purim festival (11:1). The existence of multiple authoritative versions and the freedom to change and add to the story reveals the dynamic process of canonization. Because of the story's importance, new generations adapted the text to offer new interpretations in new contexts. Contemporary communities should consider whether new interpretations might be needed to reflect contemporary issues and experiences of God.

BIBLIOGRAPHY

S. W. Crawford. "The Additions to Esther." NIB (Nashville: Abingdon, 1999) 3:945–72; L. Day. *Three Faces of a Queen: Characterization in the Books of Esther.* JSOTSup 186 (Sheffield: Sheffield Academic Press, 1995).

THE WISDOM OF SOLOMON

Walter T. Wilson

OVERVIEW

Neither part of the title of this work should be taken at face value. To begin with, scholars agree that the author is not in fact the Israelite king and renowned patron of wisdom, but an anonymous Jew writing in the late first century BCE or early first century CE. Composed in an eloquent, sometimes lyrical, Greek, this book is among the most Hellenized works of the Apocrypha. As such it evidences numerous interactions with Greek culture, especially Greek philosophy (e.g., 7:22b–8:1). The vehement attack on Egyptian animal-worship in 15:14–19 suggests that the author is writing in Alexandria, where conflicts between Jews and non-Jews were common. The language of 6:3 indicates a date of composition sometime after the Roman occupation of Egypt in 30 BCE, but precision beyond this is difficult to achieve.

Questions have also been raised as to what type of "wisdom" this work represents. To be sure, the author draws freely on classic wisdom texts like Proverbs and Sirach, and the figure of divine wisdom plays a prominent role in his reflections (e.g., 6:12–20). At the same time, Wisdom also incorporates ideas and imagery familiar from Jewish apocalyptic literature (e.g., 3:7–9), and in this the book resembles certain wisdom writings found among the Dead Sea Scrolls. As with these writings, Wisdom represents an effort to transform earlier genres and traditions into a vehicle for conveying a more complex worldview, one that integrates sapiential and apocalyptic perspectives.

In the hands of our author, such integration is pressed into the service of his overarching theme: the deliverance of the righteous, specifically, those who obey "the law" (see on 6:4), and the punishment of their ungodly oppressors. In an environment where Jews were often viewed with suspicion and often faced with inducements to abandon their distinctive way of life, the pertinence of such a theme would have been obvious. The book encourages the readers' adherence to their faith traditions in difficult circumstances by dramatizing how divine judgment is manifested in human existence. The wicked experience divine retribution, while those who remain faithful will be vindicated and exalted, enjoying immortality (see on 3:4).

Like Sirach, Wisdom enjoys canonical status in the Roman Catholic Church, while in Protestant denominations it is relegated to the Apocrypha. A number of ancient Christians, including Clement of Alexandria (ca. 150–211/215 CE), regarded the book as Scripture.

OUTLINE

I. The Righteous and the Wicked Contrasted (1:1–6:25)

    A. Appeal to Seek Wisdom and Righteousness (1:1–15)

    B. The Deluded Reasoning of the Unrighteous (1:16–2:24)

    C. Reward and Retribution After Death (3:1–4:19)

    D. The Final Judgment (4:20–5:23)

    E. Appeal to Seek Wisdom and Righteousness (6:1–25)

II. Solomon's Quest for Wisdom (7:1–10:21)

    A. The King's Need for Wisdom (7:1–14)

    B. Wisdom's All-Embracing Excellence (7:15–8:1)

    C. Solomon's Love Affair with Wisdom (8:2–20)

    D. Solomon's Prayer for Wisdom (8:21–9:18)

    E. Wisdom's Agency in Salvation History (10:1–21)

III. Divine Justice in the Exodus Story (11:1–19:22)

    A. First Comparison: The Plague of the Nile and Water from the Rock (11:1–14)

B. Second Comparison Begun: The Plague of Small Animals and the Sending of the Quail (11:15–20)

Digressions on the Nature of Divine Justice (11:21–15:19)

B'. Second Comparison Concluded: The Plague of Small Animals and the Sending of the Quail (16:1–4)

C. Third Comparison: The Plague of Insects and the Bronze Serpent (16:5–14)

D. Fourth Comparison: The Plague of Storms and the Rain of Manna (16:15–29)

E. Fifth Comparison: The Plague of Darkness and the Pillar of Fire (17:1–18:4)

F. Sixth Comparison: The Destruction of the Egyptians and the Deliverance of the Israelites (18:5–25)

G. Seventh Comparison: Death and Salvation at the Red Sea (19:1–21)

H. Concluding Doxology (19:22)

DETAILED ANALYSIS

I. The Righteous And The Wicked Contrasted (1:1–6:25)

A. Appeal to Seek Wisdom and Righteousness (1:1–15)

The address of "King Solomon" to his Gentile peers ("you rulers of the earth," 1:1; cf. 6:1–2) belongs to the book's fictional setting; the actual readers are Jews governed by such rulers. Advice on kingship is a prominent feature of another book attributed to Solomon, Proverbs (e.g., 16:10–15; 20:26–28; 25:1–7; 29:4, 12–14). The author begins by identifying the basis of right rule: wisdom (cf. Prov 8:15–16).

1:6–11. The description of wisdom as a "kindly spirit" that "has filled the world" and "holds all things together" (1:6–7) and that can "dwell" in the righteous (1:4) reflects Stoic teachings on the world soul, the rational principle that pervades and sustains the universe (cf. 7:22b–8:1). Here the author emphasizes wisdom's role as an instrument of divine justice that holds people accountable for

their words and deeds (cf. 4:20; 11:20; 12:25–26; 14:31).

1:12–15. In contrast to certain biblical traditions according to which death is an aspect of human existence decreed by God (e.g., Deut 32:39; 1 Sam 2:6), our author asserts that God created humanity "for incorruption" (2:23) and is not the direct source of death (cf. 1:16; 2:24; Jas 1:13–15).

B. The Deluded Reasoning of the Unrighteous (1:16–2:24)

In a manner familiar from the Hellenistic diatribe, the author ascribes to his opponents an imaginary speech that expresses their views about life in an exaggerated form (2:1–20). The comments in 2:12 may suggest that the opponents are apostate Jews, though it is more likely that they include "the ungodly" in general (1:16). It is their "covenant" with death (1:16; cf. Isa 28:15) and not any direct action on God's part that accounts for how death corrupted the world (2:24).

2:1–5. Similar laments about the finality of death can be found especially in the book of Ecclesiastes, e.g., 2:16; 3:19–22; 4:2–3; 6:12; 9:5–6.

2:6–20. The failure of the ungodly to recognize the true nature and purpose of life leads them into three forms of unrighteousness, each more deplorable than the last: they revel in sensual pleasures (2:6–9), they exploit the weak (2:10–11), and they persecute the righteous unto death (2:12–20).

2:21–24. The author now gives his assessment of the speech that he has just put into the mouths of the ungodly. Blinded by their unrighteousness, it is impossible for them to comprehend God's "secret purposes" (2:22; cf. 13:1; 14:22; 16:16). Instead they have been corrupted by the "devil's envy" (2:24, a reference to the temptation story of Gen 3:1–24). The righteous, by contrast, are by definition those who possess such knowledge (2:13; cf. 6:22; 10:10). They are destined for "incorruption," i.e. immortality (2:23; cf. 1:15; 3:4), which represents the true purpose of human life (cf. 2 Esd 7:113; 1 Cor 15:42–54; 1 Pet 1:3–6, 23).

C. Reward and Retribution After Death (3:1–4:19)

The views expressed in 2:1–20 are now refuted by alternating descriptions that contrast the rewards conferred on the righteous (3:1–9; 3:13b–15; 4:1–2; 4:7–15) with the punishments meted out to the unrighteous (3:10–13a; 3:16–19; 4:3–6; 4:16–19). Even if the righteous lack the blessings customarily associated with success (a long life, a life free from suffering, many children), they will be more than compensated for this at the final judgment. The unrighteous, meanwhile, are miserable in both this life and the next.

3:1–9. Lacking knowledge of God's ultimate purpose for humankind (2:22), to the ungodly the righteous people that they condemned to death "seemed to have died" (3:2), but in fact their souls were in God's care all along (3:1). Their suffering is not punishment, but a brief moment of divine testing and discipline (3:5–6; cf. 11:9–10; 16:6, 11; 18:20; Deut 8:5; Prov 3:11–12; 17:3; Sir 2:1–5; 18:13–14; 32:14; 2 Macc 6:12–16), while their death is the inauguration of a higher form of existence: they will "shine forth" (3:7; cf. Dan 12:3; Zech 9:16; 2 Esd 7:97; Matt 13:43) and "govern nations" (3:8; cf. Dan 7:22; Rev 20:4). No indication is given as to the condition of the righteous between the moment of death and the time of their "visitation" (3:7), indicating that the author is not operating with a fully developed eschatology.

3:10–13a. The unrighteous acts of the ungodly listed in 2:6–20 are now depicted as rebellion against God.

3:13b–4:6. In the ancient world, children were considered a blessing (e.g., Ps 127:3–5), while barrenness could be interpreted as a sign of divine displeasure (e.g., Gen 30:23). The author counters this by arguing that true blessedness and renown do not derive from physical progeny but from the fruit of virtue (3:15; 4:1). Similarly, in response to the biblical injunction barring eunuchs from the cultic assembly (Deut 23:1), he draws on Isa 56:4–5 to promise them a place in God's heavenly temple (3:14). The quest of the righteous for virtue is represented figuratively as an athletic "contest," immortality being one of its "prizes" (4:2; cf. 4 Macc 17:11–16; 1 Cor 9:24–27). For the condemnation of parents who bear illegitimate children (3:16–17; 4:3–6), cf. Sir 16:1–4; 23:22–26;

such people will have no hope on "the day of judgment" (3:18; cf. 2 Esd 7:38; 2 Pet 2:9).

4:7–19. It was customary to associate old age with wisdom (e.g., Job 15:7–10; Prov 3:16). The author counters this by alluding to the story of Enoch (Gen 5:24), who is identified as a paradigm of righteous individuals "taken up" (4:10) by God in order to preserve their souls from "the fascination of wickedness" (4:12). From this perspective, premature death is not a curse but an act of divine mercy (4:15). It is also interpreted as an act of retribution: in the afterlife, the righteous will condemn the ungodly (4:16), just as the ungodly had condemned them to death (2:20).

D. The Final Judgment (4:20–5:23)

Many elements of this depiction derive from the book of Isaiah. When the unrighteous witness the deliverance of the righteous, they are filled with fear and amazement (for the eschatological scenario, cf. 2 Esd 7:36–38; Luke 16:22–25). The author juxtaposes their remorseful speech of self-condemnation in 5:4–13 with the arrogant speech that they had delivered earlier in 2:1–20. The assertion made there that "our allotted time is the passing of a shadow" (2:5) is now ironically fulfilled (5:9).

4:20–5:8. The astonished reaction of the unrighteous to the righteous is modeled after the fourth Servant Song (Isa 52:13–53:12), which portrays the vindication of "the righteous one" after enduring affliction and death at the hand of his oppressors. The confession of guilt uttered by the unrighteous in 5:6–8 is paralleled also by Isa 59:2–3, 7–10, and for the idea in 4:20 of being convicted by one's sins, see Isa 59:12.

5:9–14. The ephemeral nature of human life is a recurring theme of biblical literature, e.g., Isa 40:6–8; Hos 13:3; 2 Esd 7:61; Jas 4:14. The comparisons in 5:10–11 may be adapted from the riddle in Prov 30:18–19.

5:15–23. We now learn that divine judgment will occur on a cosmic scale, when God "will arm all creation" (5:17) in order to crush the forces of unrighteousness (cf. 19:6; Sir 39:28–31). The righteous, meanwhile, will be numbered among the heavenly hosts (5:5; cf. Dan 12:2–3) and receive a divine crown and diadem (5:16; cf.

Isa 62:3). The imagery in 5:17–20 of the Divine Warrior donning various attributes as armor is based on Isa 59:17–18; cf. Ps 7:12–13; Eph 6:13–17. The author will use this imagery again in 18:14–16. The descriptions in 5:21–23 recount some of the standard trappings of divine judgment; cf. Isa 28:2; 29:5–6; 41:15–16; Ezek 13:11; 38:22; 2 Esd 15:40–44; Rev 16:18.

E. Appeal to Seek Wisdom and Righteousness (6:1–25)

The previous section had concluded by raising the prospect of God overturning the thrones of unrighteous rulers (5:23). This provides an occasion for Solomon to renew the appeal for his fellow kings to pursue wisdom (cf. 1:1–15).

6:1–11. Since their sovereignty is granted them by God (cf. Prov 8:15–16; Sir 10:4–5; Rom 13:1), the actions of kings are subject to divine scrutiny. Indeed, "the mighty will be mightily tested" (6:6; cf. Jer 25:15–29; Ezek 21:25–27; Sir 10:8–18). The reference in 6:4 to their failure to observe "the law" is ambiguous. Since he expects even pagan rulers to follow it, the author is probably referring to the law of nature, i.e., universal principles of justice, though, like other philosophically inclined Jews of the era, he probably believed that this law comes to expression most perfectly in the law of Moses (cf. 6:18; 16:6; 18:4, 9). The Greek term for "dominion" in 6:3 is used elsewhere in ancient sources for the Roman conquest of Egypt.

6:12–20. The personification of wisdom as a desirable woman is based on Prov 8:1–21. The sentence in 6:17–20 is a good example of a chain argument, or "sorites" (cf. Rom 5:3–4; 2 Pet 1:5–7). In this case it connects the acquisition of rule and immortality with the observance of wisdom's laws.

6:21–25. The switch to the first-person singular signals a transition to the second major part of the book. For the idea that wisdom played a role in "the beginning of creation" (6:22), see on 8:2–8.

II. Solomon's Quest for Wisdom (7:1–10:21)

A. The King's Need for Wisdom (7:1–14)

Even though Solomon is a king, he is still a mortal, a "child of earth" (7:1; cf. Gen 2:7; Sir 17:1; 1 Cor 15:47), and so must pray to God for wisdom like anyone else. His story thus serves as a model for all those who desire wisdom.

7:1–6. The description of the king's birth in 7:1–2 reflects ancient assumptions about human pregnancy; cf. Job 10:9–11; Ps 139:13–16. For the idea in 7:6 that everyone enters and exits life the same way, cf. Sir 40:1.

7:7–14. The section's opening reference is to the prayer of Solomon in 1 Kgs 3:6–9, which our author paraphrases in 8:21–9:18. Not only is wisdom greater than power, wealth, health, or beauty, Solomon learns that she is the source of these and of "all good things" (7:11; cf. Job 28:15–19; Prov 2:4; 3:13–16). She can even be referred to as the "mother" of all blessings (7:12), an image that extends the personification of wisdom as a female figure in 6:12–20.

B. Wisdom's All-Embracing Excellence (7:15–8:1)

This encomium of divine wisdom combines earlier biblical descriptions with concepts derived from Greek philosophy.

7:15–22a. Since wisdom is "the fashioner of all things" (7:22a; cf. 8:4–6), those who possess her understand all forms of human knowledge, including everything from cosmology to botany (7:17–20; cf. 1 Kgs 4:29–34).

7:22b–8:1. In antiquity divine beings were believed to have many names and appellations. Most of the twenty-one (the product of three and seven, numbers signifying perfection) attributes listed in 7:22b–23 are familiar from Greek philosophical writings, e.g., Pseudo-Aristotle, *On the Cosmos* 400B–401B. The depiction of wisdom as "a pure emanation" pervading all things (7:24–25) reflects the influence of Stoic philosophy in particular; see on 1:6–11; cf. Sir 1:9–10. For wisdom's function as a "reflection" of the divine (7:26), cf. Heb 1:3.

7:27. Abraham was known both as a friend of God (2 Chr 20:7; Isa 41:8; Jas 2:23) and as a prophet (Gen 20:7; Ps 105:15); that status is now available to anyone who possesses wisdom; cf. 7:14.

C. Solomon's Love Affair with Wisdom (8:2–20)

Having described wisdom in general terms, the king now recounts the many benefits that he has personally obtained from his relationship with wisdom, whom he loved like a bride (cf. Prov 7:4; Sir 15:2; 51:15, 21).

8:2–8. That wisdom was God's agent in the creation of the world (8:4–6; cf. 6:22; 9:1–2, 9) is a fundamental tenet in the Jewish tradition, e.g., Prov 3:19; 8:5, 7, 22–31; Sir 24:4–6, 9. As such she bequeaths everything that is necessary for "life," including the four forms of moral excellence mentioned in 8:7, which constitute the standard "canon" of virtues in Greek philosophy.

8:9–18. On account of his superior wisdom, Solomon earned both the admiration of his people and the respect of his fellow rulers (cf. Job 29:7–11, 21–23; Sir 15:4–6). Achieving personal "rest" (8:16), or tranquility, is an important goal of the sage, as in Sir 6:28; 28:16. Greek philosophers held that human beings have a "kinship" with the gods by virtue of their common possession of reason; in 8:17 this extends to the sage's possession of immortality (cf. 6:18–19; 15:3).

8:19–20. Solomon's description of his birth may be influenced by Platonic doctrines concerning the pre-existence of the soul; cf. 4 Macc 18:23.

D. Solomon's Prayer for Wisdom (8:21–9:18)

This section, notable for its lyrical expression, is an expanded version of the prayer in 1 Kgs 3:6–9; cf. 2 Chr 1:8–10.

8:21–9:3. After an introduction (8:21; cf. Sir 1:10), the prayer opens with an address to God (9:1–3) that recounts how humankind was created through God's wisdom to "rule the world" (9:3; cf. Gen 1:26, 28; Ps 8:6; Sir 17:2–4). In order to do so rightly, they need wisdom.

9:4–12. The body of the prayer consists of two parallel petitions, 9:4–9 and 9:10–12. Each begins with a request that God send Solomon the wisdom that resides beside the divine throne (9:4, 10), further personifying wisdom as God's female consort (cf. 6:12–20; 18:15; Prov 8:30; Sir 24:4).

9:8. That Solomon's Temple (see 1 Kgs 6:1–38) was only a copy of a heavenly archetype may be inferred from Exod 25:9, 40; 26:30 (cf. Heb 8:5; Rev 11:19).

9:13–18. The prayer concludes with a meditation on the futility of human efforts and humankind's dependence on God; cf. Job 38:31–38; Isa 40:12–14; Jdt 8:14; Sir 1:2–6; Bar 3:29–31. That the human body "weighs down the soul" (9:15) is an observation borrowed from Platonic philosophy.

E. Wisdom's Agency in Salvation History (10:1–21)

The preceding section concluded with the claim that people are "saved by wisdom" (9:18). This gives the theme of the current section, which offers seven illustrations of wisdom's providential ordering of history. In each case a righteous hero is contrasted with one or more unrighteous adversaries. Personal names are eschewed throughout, indicating that they all are to be understood as generic types. For a similar catalog of biblical figures, see Sir 44:17–45:26 (cf. Heb 11:4–31).

10:1–3. Adam and Cain (Gen 1:26–5:5).

10:4. Noah (Gen 5:28–9:29). The author interprets Cain's sin as the cause of the flood (cf. 14:6).

10:5. Abraham (Gen 11:26–25:10) contrasts with "the nations" of the Tower of Babel story (Gen 11:1–9).

10:6–8. Lot (Gen 19:1–29) escaped the destruction of Sodom and Gomorrah.

10:9–12. Jacob and Esau (Gen 27–33). The "arduous contest" is a reference to Gen 32:22–32 (cf. Hos 12:3–4).

10:13–14. Joseph (Gen 37–50) contrasts with those who falsely accused him (Gen 39:6a–23).

10:15–21. Moses (Exod 1–17) prevailed over Pharaoh and his armies.

III. Divine Justice in the Exodus Story (11:1–19:22)

11:1–20; 15:20–19:22. The discussion of Moses in 10:15–21 leads seamlessly into an elaborate comparison (or "synkrisis") of God's dealings with the Egyptians and the Israelites during the exodus. Although it is much longer, this section follows the same principle as that of 10:1–21: the respective fates of the righteous and the unrighteous are contrasted through a series of seven historical illustrations (supplemented by a series of digressions in 11:21–15:19), with no personal names being used. The author's apologetic interests are evident in the manner in which he consistently magnifies the Egyptians' culpability while never mentioning any of the Israelites' failures.

A. First Comparison: The Plague of the Nile and Water from the Rock (11:1–14)

The logic informing all of the comparisons is announced in 11:5: God employs the same means for saving the righteous and punishing their adversaries (cf. 11:13; 16:24; 18:8). In this case the former drink while the latter thirst. The idealized portrait of the Israelites in 11:4 may be inspired by Ps 107:6; cf. Exod 7:14–24; 17:1–7; Num 20:2–13.

11:9–14. On the surface, the suffering of the righteous and the unrighteous might appear to be the same. The former, however, experience suffering as an expression of divine discipline and testing (11:9–10; cf. 3:5), while the latter experience it "in a different way" (11:14) because they recognize that their suffering benefits the righteous (11:13).

B. Second Comparison Begun: The Plague of Small Animals and the Sending of the Quail (11:15–20)

The comparison will not be concluded until 16:1–4. The author's interpretation of the exodus story (cf. 12:23) assumes the biblical principle of retribution in kind, for which see Exod 21:23–25; Lev 24:18–20; Deut 19:18b–21. For the "unknown beasts" of 11:18, see Job 40:15–41:34.

Digressions on the Nature of Divine Justice (11:21–15:19)

The second comparison is interrupted by a string of loosely connected arguments meant to demonstrate that the unrighteous deserve the punishment that they receive.

11:21–12:2. Since they are part of God's creation, God shows love and mercy to all people, especially by granting them the opportunity to repent when they sin (cf. 12:10, 13, 16, 19; 15:1; Sir 17:24; 18:11–14; Pr Man 1:7; 2 Esd 7:132–33; 8:45).

12:3–11. God showed mercy even to the "accursed race" of the Canaanites (12:11; cf. Gen 9:25–27) and demonstrated forbearance by sending wasps against them in advance of human armies (cf. Exod 23:28). Their failure to recognize God's displeasure with them and repent (12:10) is seen as justification for the Israelites' "colonization" of the holy land (12:7). Among the Canaanites' most heinous practices was child sacrifice (12:5–6), in observation of the Molech cult (Lev 20:2–5).

12:12–18. Legal terminology is employed to depict God as a righteous and merciful judge (cf. Job 9:12, 19; Ps 76:7–9; Isa 40:13–14; Rom 9:14–21). In this capacity God will "rebuke any insolence" among those who doubt the reality of divine justice (12:17; cf. Ps 119:21; Isa 13:11; Jer 48:30; Sir 35:22b–24; Bar 4:34).

12:19–22. God's forbearance toward the wicked serves as a model for the righteous, who should be merciful in their dealings with them as well (12:19). If God makes repentance available to the unrighteous, it is all the more available to God's children (12:20–22).

12:23–27. Animal worshipers receive "mild rebukes" from God at first (12:26) when they are punished by the very creatures they think to be gods (cf. 11:15–16). But when they continue in this abomination, they receive "the utmost condemnation" (12:27).

13:1–15:19. The author reproves, with increasing severity, the worship of nature (13:1–9), of idols (13:10–15:13), and of animals (15:14–19).

13:1–9. The worship of the heavenly bodies was common in antiquity (cf. Deut 4:19; 2 Kgs 21:3–5; 23:4–5; Gal 4:3, 8–9). While the effort to find God in the created world is understandable (13:6), it is misguided, because it puts too much confidence in what can be seen (13:7), and therefore fails to discern the world's Creator (13:5) and Lord (13:9).

13:10–19. In constructing this section the author would have had a long tradition of Jewish polemic against idolatry upon which to draw, e.g., Ps 115:3–8; Isa 40:18–20; 44:9–20; Jer 10:1–16. He begins with a sarcastic description of how idol "gods" are crafted from discarded wood (13:10–16;

cf. 15:7–19). To pray to such worthless and help-less objects is preposterous (13:17–19).

14:1–11. Safety in a voyage is assured not by a flimsy piece of wood, but by divine providence (14:1–5; cf. 17:2; 4 Macc 9:24), just as Noah and his family were saved from the waters that destroyed the "arrogant giants" (14:6–7; cf. Gen 6:1–9:29; 3 Macc 2:4). The idolater is just as hateful to God as what he worships, upon which there will be a divine "visitation," i.e., judgment (14:8–11; cf. 3:7; Sir 16:18; Luke 19:44).

14:12–21. In contrast to divine wisdom (see on 8:2–8), idols have not existed since the beginning of creation (14:13). They are, instead, the product of human vanity. The arguments of 14:17–21 resemble those of the Greek writer Euhemerus (ca. 300 BCE), who suggested that the "gods" were in fact human kings who after their deaths had been deified by their subjects.

14:22–31. Idolatry is seen to lead its followers into other sins, especially murder, adultery, and perjury, a fact that only increases their culpability; cf. Jer 7:9; Rom 1:28–31.

15:1–6. Idolaters are briefly contrasted with those who are God's own, i.e., those who know God's power and righteousness (15:3). The allusion to Exod 34:6–9 in 15:1–2 indicates that the latter are the Israelites.

15:7–13. A second attack on those who manu-facture idols (cf. 13:10–19). Here the emphasis is on the cynicism and greed of those who sell what they know to be "counterfeit gods" (15:9). To them life is nothing more than "a festival held for profit" (15:12; cf. Isa 22:12–13). That human souls are only borrowed and must someday be returned (15:8) was a popular concept of Platonic origin (cf. 15:16).

15:14–19. The series of digressions culminates with an attack on the Egyptians, who are casti-gated as the "most foolish" (15:14) both because they oppressed God's people and because they worship animals, indeed the most vile and sense-less of animals (15:18).

B'. Second Comparison Concluded: The Plague of Small Animals and the Sending of the Quail (16:1–4)

The series of comparisons that had begun in 11:1–20 resumes here. The Egyptians are torment-ed by the very creatures they worship (16:1; cf. Exod 8:1–15), while the Israelites enjoy delicacies (16:2–3; cf. Exod 16:9–13; Num 11:16–23, 31–34). The author assumes that both the Israelites and the Egyptians are aware of what the other side is experiencing (16:4; cf. 11:13–14; 16:8, 22; 18:1).

C. Third Comparison: The Plague of Insects and the Bronze Serpent (16:5–14)

The bites are a warning to the Israelites, who quickly find healing (16:5–6, 10–11; cf. Num 21:4–9), but to the Egyptians they are death (16:9, 13–14; cf. Exod 8:20–32; 10:1–20). The author is careful to point out that the bronze serpent was only "a symbol of deliverance" (16:6): the real Savior was God (16:7).

D. Fourth Comparison: The Plague of Storms and the Rain of Manna (16:15–29)

The Egyptians endure "unusual rains" that destroy their crops (16:16, 19; cf. Exod 9:13–35), while heavenly food descends on the Israelites like snow (16:20, 22; cf. Exod 16:1–8, 14–36; Num 11:4–9). The author apparently believed that the plague of thunder and hail occurred simultaneous-ly with the plagues of frogs, gnats, and flies (16:18; cf. Ps 105:30–32). The idea that the manna was "suited to every taste" (16:20) is found also in later rabbinic sources. At this point an explanation for how the miracles were accomplished is also pro-vided: the very elements of creation itself undergo internal transformations (16:23–25) so that the fire sent upon the Egyptians was not extinguished by the relentless rains (16:16), while the snow-like manna "withstood fire without melting" (16:22; 19:18–21).

E. Fifth Comparison: The Plague of Darkness and the Pillar of Fire (17:1–18:4)

The longest of the comparisons, this section is noteworthy for its unusual, poetic language and its attention to the psychological dimensions of terror. Features of the narration in 17:2–21 are familiar from the "descent into Hades" genre, of which Book 6 of Virgil's *Aeneid* was a well-known example. Thinking that their sins were hidden, the Egyptians themselves are enveloped in darkness (17:3; cf. Exod 10:21–29), afflicted by their guilty consciences (17:11; cf. 1 Tim 4:2; Titus 1:15), and forced to endure nightmares (17:14–16; cf. 18:17–19; Job 7:14; Dan 4:5; Sir 40:5–7). Those who had imprisoned God's holy ones (18:4) are now bound by a "chain of darkness" (17:17). The righteous, meanwhile, are led through the wilderness by a pillar of fire (18:3; cf. Exod 13:21–22; 14:24) so that they might become instruments through which "the imperishable light of the law" might shine on the world (18:4; cf. Isa 49:6; Bar 4:1–2; 2 Esd 14:20–22).

F. Sixth Comparison: The Destruction of the Egyptians and the Deliverance of the Israelites (18:5–25)

Both groups experience death, though the reasons and ends are different. In retribution for killing the Israelites' male children (18:5; cf. Exod 1:22), the Egyptians' firstborn are killed on the night of the first Passover (18:6–19; cf. Exod 11:1–12:32) so that they finally "acknowledged your people to be God's child" (18:13; cf. 5:5; 12:27; Exod 4:22–23; Hos 11:1). The enigmatic "destroyer" of Exod 12:23 is personified in 18:15–16 as the word of God, which earlier had been identified with divine wisdom (9:1–2). The Israelites experience a plague of death as well (18:20–25; cf. Num 16:41–50) though, unlike the Egyptians, they have a savior to intervene on their behalf, i.e., Aaron. No mention is made of what caused the plague, i.e., the Israelites' rebellion against Moses and Aaron (Num 16:41).

G. Seventh Comparison: Death and Salvation at the Red Sea (19:1–21)

The water of the Sea drowns the Egyptians' armies, filling up their punishment (19:1–5; cf. Dan 8:23; 2 Macc 6:14), while it parts for the Israelites, allowing them to pass through on dry land (19:6–9; cf. Exod 14:1–31). The author explains that this and the other miracles were accomplished when the material elements "changed places with one another" (19:18–21), i.e., they were transformed so as to accomplish divine providence; cf. 16:23–25.

H. Concluding Doxology (19:22)

The main point of the section and the book is summarized: God's people will always receive "help."

BIBLIOGRAPHY

S. Burkes "Wisdom and Apocalypticism in the Wisdom of Solomon." *HTR* 95 (2002) 21–44; S. Cheon. *The Exodus Story in the Wisdom of Solomon: A Study in Biblical Interpretation.* JSPSup 23 (Sheffield: Sheffield Academic Press, 1997); J. J. Collins. *Jewish Wisdom in the Hellenistic Age.* OTL. (Louisville: Westminster John Knox Press, 1997) 178–221; P. Enns. *Exodus Retold: Ancient Exegesis of the Departure from Egypt in Wisdom 10:15–21 and 19:1–9.* HSM 57 (Atlanta: Scholars Press, 1997); L. L. Grabber. *Wisdom of Solomon.* Guides to Apocrypha and Pseudepigrapha (Sheffield: Sheffield Academic Press, 1997); M. Kolarcik. *The Ambiguity of Death in the Book of Wisdom 1–6: A Study of Literary Structure and Interpretation.* AnBib 127 (Rome: Biblical Institute Press, 1991); M. McGlynn. *Divine Judgement and Divine Benevolence in the Book of Wisdom.* WUNT 2.139 (Tübingen: Mohr Siebeck, 2001); A. Passaro and B. Giuseppe, eds. *The Book of Wisdom in Modern Research: Studies on Tradition, Redaction, and Theology.* Deuterocanonical and Cognate Literature: Yearbook 2005 (Berlin: Walter de Gruyter, 2005); J. M. Reese. *Hellenistic Influence on the Book of Wisdom and Its Consequences.* AnBib 41 (Rome: Biblical Institute Press, 1970); S. Schroer. "The Book of Sophia." *Searching the Scriptures, Volume Two: A Feminist Commentary.* E. Schüssler Fiorenza, ed. (New York: Crossroad, 1994) 17–38; D. Winston. *The Wisdom of Solomon.* AB 43 (New York: Doubleday, 1979).

SIRACH

Benjamin G. Wright III

OVERVIEW

The Wisdom of Jesus son of Sirach, also known as Ecclesiasticus (often Sirach for short). This Jewish wisdom book goes by three different names depending on the language tradition. The title above derives from superscriptions to Greek manuscripts. The Hebrew title was evidently "The Wisdom of Joshua son of Eleazar son of Sira," hence the short title the "Wisdom of Ben ('son of') Sira." The name *Ecclesiasticus* derives from the Vulgate (Latin) version and means "belonging to the church."

Sirach was written by a sage who identifies himself as Jesus son of Eleazar son of Sirach of Jerusalem (50:27). He wrote at the beginning of the second century BCE, probably between 200 and 180, and he likely witnessed the turbulent changeover of control of Judea from the Ptolemies in Egypt to the Seleucids in Syria.

The original language was Hebrew, but the primary form of transmission was the Greek translation made by the author's grandson around 117 BCE. The book was not accepted into the Jewish biblical canon, and although the rabbis knew proverbs connected with Ben Sira, the Hebrew fell into obscurity and disuse. The Greek translation, included in the Septuagint, became part of the scriptures of the Christian church. Sirach survives in important Latin and Syriac translations. In the late nineteenth century, a discovery of Hebrew manuscripts in a *genizah* (storeroom) of a Cairo synagogue brought to light six fragmentary medieval manuscripts. Excavations at Masada revealed a first-century BCE manuscript containing portions of 39:27–44:17. At Qumran, 2Q18 preserves only a few words of 6:20–31 and some letters at the ends of lines that could be 6:14–15 or perhaps 1:19–20. 11QPs^a preserves parts of 51:13–20, 30b. In all, the Hebrew manuscripts preserve approximately two-thirds of the book.

The foundation for Ben Sira's literary efforts is the proverb (*mashal*), expressed mostly in two-line couplets called *bicola*. He often combines these bicola into larger units of poetry on thematic topics typical of ancient Near Eastern wisdom, like speech, friends, women, and business. In addition to practical advice, Ben Sira instructs his students about more speculative topics, such as the wonders of creation. Besides the proverb, he employs other literary forms, including prayers, autobiographical poems, and woes (often found in prophetic books).

As a wisdom teacher, Ben Sira draws on diverse sources for his teaching. Traditions of wisdom transcended ancient Israel and were common to most of the ancient Near East, and Ben Sira knows wisdom material from other contexts, particularly from Egypt. He also seems to be acquainted with some Greek traditions. Another major source of Ben Sira's wisdom is observation of the natural world. In a long poem on the wonders of nature, he begins, "I will now call to mind the works of the Lord and will declare what I have seen" (42:15). Most important, Ben Sira has command of the literary heritage of ancient Israel, many works of which were later included in the Jewish and Christian biblical canons. While scholars do not know exactly what would have constituted scripture in Ben Sira's time, he certainly valued the Pentateuch highly. He undoubtedly had access to other literary works and traditions, but at times it is difficult to determine their exact form, partly because Ben Sira does not explicitly quote other literature. He uses his source texts to suit his agenda, shaping them in ways that often obscure the precise form in which they came to him.

OUTLINE

The Wisdom of Ben Sira has no discernible structure on which scholars agree. The praise of Wisdom (ch. 24) occupies a pivotal position in the center of the book, dividing it roughly in half. Scholars recognize larger sections with sub-units on specific topics. I have followed that practice below.

The Prologue (to the Greek translation)

I. Sirach 1:1–4:10

Detailed Analysis

The Prologue (to the Greek translation)

Ben Sira's grandson introduces his translation with three Greek sentences. In the first he speaks of his grandfather's reasons for writing. When Ben Sira had become proficient in the "Law, the Prophets, and the other books of our ancestors," he wrote in order to assist others who wanted to live "according to the law." Some have identified these three categories with the three divisions of the Hebrew canon, although this is unlikely. While "Law" probably intends the Pentateuch or Torah, we do not know what constituted the prophets for Ben Sira, and certainly there was no identifiable third group in his time. In the second sentence the grandson reflects on the problems of translation. Here he offers an apologia for his translation should anyone think it lacking, noting that the translations of the Scriptures have the same character. The third sentence gives the circumstances of the translation. The grandson attributes to his own work the same motivation as his grandfather.

I. Sirach 1:1–4:10

A. Praise of Wisdom (1:1–10)

Ben Sira sets the stage with a poem emphasizing Wisdom's cosmic nature, in which he personifies her, the first of God's creations (cf. Prov. 8:22–30), as a woman. The rhetorical questions focus on her hiddenness from human ken (cf. Job 28), since God alone knows the answers to these questions. Yet, she is at the same time "poured out" on all creation and "lavished" on "those who love him" (v. 10).

B. Fear of the Lord Is Wisdom (1:11–30)

Already in 1:8, Ben Sira notes that God is to be feared, that is, to be regarded with awe. In this poem, he links wisdom to "fear of the Lord," another central theme. In an identical construction in vv. 14, 16, 18, and 20, he says that fear of the Lord is the "beginning," "fullness," "crown," and "root" of wisdom. The one who fears God finds wisdom and reaps benefits such as long life. Several important topics of wisdom teaching that occur frequently in Sirach reinforce the importance of fearing the Lord, especially control of anger, speech, and the importance of honor. In contrast to earlier Israelite wisdom literature, Ben Sira also enjoins "keeping the commandments," and in the programmatic vv. 26–27 he creates a central nexus of ideas that undergird all of his teaching: wisdom, fear of the Lord, and keeping commandments (Mosaic Law).

C. Trusting in God (2:1–18)

Verse 1 begins in the usual manner of a wisdom teacher addressing a student—"my son." In this three-stanza poem, Ben Sira observes that even the one who fears God will experience trials.

The remedy is to "cling to him" (v. 3), since God will show mercy to such a person. In claiming that faithfulness will bring prosperity, Ben Sira accepts the deuteronomistic view that God blesses the faithful. As he does elsewhere, here Ben Sira appeals to the past—"consider the generations of old" (v. 10)—to illustrate the truth of what he says. Verses 12–14 employ the prophetic form of the "Woe."

D. Duty to Parents (3:1–16)

Ben Sira comments on the commandment to honor parents unconditionally (Exod 20:12; Deut 5:16). His appeal to his students as their father effectively establishes his parental authority over them (v. 1). As in the pentateuchal commandments, honoring parents brings reward, including "long life" (cf. Deut. 5:16). Ben Sira accepts that God keeps an account of one's sins and good deeds, and thus, honoring parents "atones for" (v. 3) and counts against one's sins, melting them away (v. 14–15). The last stanza (vv. 12–16) discusses care for elderly parents, and in the comparison to blasphemy (v. 16), Ben Sira reinforces the religious duty of honoring them.

E. Humility and Almsgiving (3:17–4:10)

This passage concludes a three-section discussion of obligations to God, parents, and society. Humility is an important virtue in wisdom instruction (cf. Prov 15:33). Ben Sira warns against speculation into the secrets of the universe and the future (vv. 22–24), a likely target being Jewish apocalyptic speculation like that in 1 Enoch. Yet knowledge is necessary for wisdom, and the knowledge revealed to his students is the Torah. As with honoring parents, almsgiving, a central ethical/social act, "atones" (cf. Tob 4:10–11). As in the Torah and earlier wisdom teaching, care for the marginalized—the poor, hungry, orphans—is obligatory. On God hearing their cries, see Exod 22:22–23; Deut 15:7–11.

II. Sirach 4:11–6:17

A. Submission to Wisdom (4:11–19)

In Hebrew this section is a first-person speech of Wisdom resembling passages from Prov 1–9. Although she is pictured as a teacher, remarkably v. 14 uses the Hebrew verb *sharath*, a cultic

term (cf. Deut 10:8), to equate service to Wisdom with service to God. The claim that those who obey Wisdom "will judge the nations" indicates that Ben Sira was training a professional class of scribes, a class to which he belonged. Wisdom is a stern taskmistress, who, like human teachers, severely tries her pupils before revealing her secrets (v. 17–19).

B. Shame and Speech (4:20–31)

Sayings beginning with "do not" are typical of wisdom instruction. The section's overarching topic is shame oriented mostly around proper and improper speech. Accruing honor and avoiding shame determined one's social status in ancient Mediterranean society. Ben Sira counsels that some types of shame are appropriate—so, for example, confession of sin—which ironically bring honor (Heb.: *kavodh*; Gk.: *doxa*). Negative kinds, such a displaying ignorance, must be avoided. Verse 24 points to the primarily oral context of ancient wisdom instruction.

C. Practical Wisdom—Presumption, Speech, Passion (5:1–6:4)

Ancient wisdom teachers spoke about wealth frequently (cf. Prov 13:11, 22). In ancient Israel it was sometimes thought to indicate God's favor. Here Ben Sira warns against the presumption of relying on wealth. Yet, his is not a blanket criticism, as the qualifier "dishonest" suggests (v. 8). The adjective "double-tongued" (v. 14) likely refers to slander, which brings not only shame but destruction. Finally, sexual relations comprised another popular wisdom topic, and Ben Sira warns against unbridled or uncontrolled passion. Throughout the book he uses a variety of euphemisms for human sexuality; here the language is agricultural (6:3). Note the relationship between shame and a "bad name" or reputation. Ben Sira highly values cultivating a good reputation, which equals accruing honor.

D. Friendship (6:5–17)

The mention of friendship in 6:1 might have precipitated the placement of this longer poem. Ben Sira holds faithful friends in high regard (vv. 14–16), comparing them to "treasure." He also understands that one must test potential confidants before trusting them with secrets, since many will be fair-weather friends. Verse 17 provides one example of how interpersonal relationships can influence others, so a literal translation of 17*b* (Hebrew): "for like himself, so is his neighbor."

III. Sirach 6:18–14:19

A. Submission to Wisdom (6:18–37)

This poem has three parts: (1) the discipline of wisdom (vv. 18–22), (2) the benefits of wisdom (vv. 23–31), (3) the student-teacher relationship (vv. 32–27). Wisdom is acquired through discipline and life experience (note the reference to "gray hairs" in v. 18). Verse 22 contains a play on words. The Hebrew word *musar*, discipline/instruction (Gk.: *sophia* [wisdom]), can also be construed as coming from the verb meaning "withdrawn"—thus, "she is not readily perceived." The references to a "glorious robe" and "splendid crown" symbolize both royalty and priesthood (cf. 50:11). For "purple cord," see Num 15:38–39. The last section shows that education in antiquity was fundamentally a disciple-teacher relationship.

B. Miscellaneous Advice (7:1–17)

The material in 7:1–9:16 is characterized by the negative injunction, translated "do not." Ben Sira personifies evil in vv. 1–2, but not in the form of the strange woman of Proverbs, as might be expected. Verses 4–7 emphasize the difficult position of the scribe/sage, since holding public office brings with it attendant dangers. Ben Sira understands the value of hard work (cf. 38:24–34). Verse 17 does not point to post-mortem punishment, which is not in Ben Sira's worldview. The Hebrew reads "the expectation of humans is worms," that is, decay.

C. Household, Priests, the Poor (7:18–36)

Administering one's household is an important wisdom topic. The list of cattle, sons, daughters, and wives constitutes a man's "possessions" (also including slaves). Wives and daughters are especially noteworthy, because they have tremendous influence on a man's honor and social status. Ben Sira was a strong supporter of the priests in Jerusalem. Here he connects proper worship of God with proper respect for his priests. "All your heart"

and "all your strength" allude to Deut 6:5. Caring for the socially marginalized forms an important aspect of God's covenant with Israel (see Exod 22:21–23; Deut 15:7–11).

D. Circumstances to Avoid (8:1–19)

Ben Sira counsels caution, a frequent topic for him, when dealing with a range of different people and situations. The section points to Ben Sira's social context. He has to deal with the wealthy and powerful (v. 1–2), but he also serves those same people. As such he is part of a retainer class—he works for the upper elites, but is not one of them. At the same time he is not counted among the poor.

E. Women and Friends (9:1–16)

Ben Sira warns his male charges about the dangers of relationships with women. For an example of the image of the "loose woman," see Prov 7:4–27. The reference to "destruction" in v. 9 might be to the penalty for adultery—death (see Lev 20:10; Deut 22:22). Perhaps the proverbs about drinking with another's wife forged the connection to choosing friends, since new friends are like "new wine." The exhortation to avoid sinners and be intimate with the righteous reinforces the influence that associates can have.

G. Rulers (9:17–10:5)

Ben Sira expresses confidence in God's control over human government. Most of the "offices" enumerated here are likely to be local Temple-state officials—magistrate, judge, ruler—with whom Ben Sira would have been familiar. A good ruler is known through wise words and education. The idea of the "right time" occurs frequently in Sirach (cf. 1:23, 24).

H. Pride (10:6–18)

Pride and sin go together and begin when one forsakes God. Ben Sira's warnings treat primarily those in power, following up on the previous section. He might be commenting on contemporary politics, but this is not certain. He argues that no one should be proud, not even kings, since everyone suffers the same fate—"maggots," "vermin," and "worms." In vv. 14–17, Ben Sira establishes that God can reverse human circumstance by replacing the powerful with the humble.

I. Honor and Humility (10:19–11:6)

The use of rhetorical question and answer is a popular wisdom device. Ben Sira reorients true honor to mean fear of the Lord. Even though the rich and the powerful receive human honor, the one truly worthy of honor fears the Lord—and that could be a poor person just as readily as a rich person. Later, in his meditation on the sage, Ben Sira will argue that the person in the best position to accrue such honor is the wise scribe (38:34b–39:11). The following sayings extend the idea by linking true honor to humility.

J. Deliberation (11:7–28)

Ben Sira holds that piety brings prosperity and God's blessing. In fact, every human condition is God's responsibility (v. 14). Verses 26–28 contain Ben Sira's thoughts on individual theodicy. Even if the pious do not appear to prosper, God will reward them at death. Since he does not believe in post-mortem rewards and punishments, "reward" likely refers to the persistence of one's good reputation and pious children, which elsewhere constitute immortality (see 30:4–5; 40:19; 41:12–13). Verse 28 suggests that a good death signals a pious person.

K. Friends and Associates (11:29–13:24)

Ben Sira's ethic of caution characterizes this section. One needs to be careful when trusting others. The image in 12:11 is of a copper mirror—keeping it polished enables one to see better. The value of caution extends especially to sinners. In order not to be harmed by them, one should not help them in any way—an idea that extends Ben Sira's conviction that God repays both the pious and the evil. Ben Sira also warns about the troubles that attend attempts to bridge social gaps, particularly between rich and poor. Even though 13:24 leaves room for righteous wealth, this passage intimates that riches "free from sin" are very rare.

L. Happiness (13:25–14:2)

The word *heart* (13:25, 14:2) forms an inclusio for this short section. The heart is the seat of emotion and thought, hence its effect on one's countenance. Notice the continued importance of speech.

M. Wealth (14:3–19)

For Ben Sira, greed makes no sense in the face of the finality of death. Therefore, one should make responsible use of wealth—particularly by being generous with others. *Hades* is the Greek term for *she'ol*, the place of the dead in Hebrew thought. Ben Sira encourages his students to enjoy what they have, since, proverbially, they cannot take it with them. For the phrase "old like a garment" (v. 17), see Isa 50:9. The decree, "You must die," alludes to the story of Adam and Eve in Gen 2 and 3.

IV. Sirach 14:20–23:27

A. Seeking Wisdom Brings Happiness (14:20–15:10)

Sirach 14:20–27 forms a complex beatitude, beginning with "Happy is the person." The following verbs metaphorically emphasize the importance of single-mindedly seeking wisdom. Ben Sira returns, in 15:1, to the connections between fear of the Lord, obeying commandments, and acquiring wisdom, which forms the transition from seeking to the results of finding wisdom. The portrayal of Wisdom as a young bride evokes sexual imagery that occurs often in Sirach. Verse 7 introduces the fool, who in traditional wisdom literature serves as a foil/anti-type to the wise.

B. Free Will and God's Justice (15:11–16:23)

Even though Ben Sira attributes all of human fortune to God (11:14), he holds human beings responsible for their sin. People have always had "free choice," the translation of the Hebrew *yetser*. In later rabbinic literature, the word means "inclination," and humans are thought to have two competing ones, the inclination for good and the inclination for evil. That humans choose between "two ways," such as life and death, is a common feature of Jewish and early Christian ethical instruction. Ben Sira dismisses the idea that many children signify God's favor. Dying childless would significantly compromise one's chances at an eternal memory, so important to Ben Sira. In 16:5–9, Ben Sira appeals to "historical" examples to show that God does not overlook sin.

C. Wisdom and God's Creation of Human Beings (16:24–18:14)

Ben Sira's meditation emphasizes the orderliness of the created order, which reinforces God's control. In 17:1–8, he relies on the two Genesis creation stories, freely intermixing them. He also departs from Genesis in one important respect. Whereas Genesis understands death as an aberration, 17:2 suggests that a limited lifespan was always God's intention. A hierarchy of God, humans, and animals is built into the structure of the passage. Verse 17:11 collapses the time between creation and the Sinai event, thus moving from universal humanity to the particularity of Israel's relationship to God. In calling people to repentance, Ben Sira notes the insignificance of a human life span and human inability to fathom God's ways. For this reason, God "pours out his mercy upon them" (18:11).

D. Self-Control and Speech (18:15–19:17)

This section contains practical proverbs on almsgiving, self-control, and holding one's tongue. Verse 18:27 encapsulates Ben Sira's view: "One who is wise is cautious in everything." The repeated use of the verb *question* in 19:13–17 makes for a memorable refrain, which could represent Ben Sira's reflections on Lev 19:17. Note the contrast of the fool and the intelligent/wise so common in wisdom literature.

E. Wisdom Contrasted with Cleverness (19:20–30)

This section is characterized by the Greek word *panourgia*, translated "cleverness," a morally neutral or even positive term elsewhere in Sirach (cf. 1:6; 6:32). Here it is associated with people who use their cleverness for morally suspect ends. Moreover, Ben Sira claims that appearances really do provide insight into someone's character.

F. Topics Related to Speech (20:1–31)

Speech dominates this section. For the most part, line one of a proverb states the opposite of line two, employing the contrast of the wise and the fool. Silence generally is virtuous, but sometimes one should speak. The wise know the appropriate time (kairos) for both (v. 7). The appearance of words such as *hated, ridicule, shame,* and *dis-*

grace testifies to how central the system of honor and shame is to Ben Sira's instruction.

G. Sin (21:1–10)

In several places Ben Sira claims that God hears the prayer of the poor (e.g., 4:5–6), but he does not argue that God prefers the poor due to their poverty. The theme of vv. 8–10 restates the idea that the death of sinners will not be a good one, even if they appear to have prospered in this life.

H. Wisdom and Folly (21:11–22:18)

The overall topic of this passage is education and the inability of fools to learn. "Fulfillment of the fear of the Lord" reprises the connection between fear of God, wisdom, and obedience to the law. Water as a metaphor for wisdom (v. 13) returns in 24:25–33. Note the contrast with the broken-jar mind of the fool. Since Ben Sira's students were to enter public service as scribes, good manners were vital (vv. 18–24). Sirach 22:3–5 highlights Ben Sira's notorious misogynism. A daughter's behavior can bring shame to father or husband—therein lies the "loss." Ancient parents and teachers apparently did not hesitate to use corporal punishment (v. 6).

I. Preservation of Friendship (22:19–26)

Ben Sira comments on the bonds of friendship, which can survive many difficulties. He does note, however, that some actions, like revealing secrets or treachery, will destroy a friendship. The switch from third person to first person reinforces the importance of being true to a friend, since, even if one suffers for it, the one inflicting the harm will be revealed publicly as untrustworthy.

J. Prayer for Protection from Sin (22:27–23:6)

The first person continues in this short prayer for God's protection from sins of the tongue, sinful thoughts, and wrong desire. The theme of not falling before adversaries is common in the Psalms (cf. Ps 39). The prayer contains three separate invocations: "Lord" (likely the four-letter name), "Father," used in Jewish literature as both a corporate and personal invocation, and "God/ Master of my life."

K. Speech and Sex (23:7–27)

The verses on oaths concern proper use of God's name and making false oaths. Ben Sira thinks that habitually swearing oaths inevitably leads to breaking them and misusing the name of God. On such abuse, see Exod 20:7; Lev 19:12; Deut 5:11. Foul language brings shame, and it reflects on one's parents (v. 14). The specific note that one cannot hide sexual sins from God follows on passages like 15:18–19 and 17:19–29. Note how the woman's sin is said to be against her husband, but not vice versa. That punishment extends to children (vv. 24–26) could mean that they will die prematurely or suffer shame throughout their lives (cf. Wis 3:16–19; 4:3–6).

V. Sirach 24:1–33:18

A. The Praise of Wisdom (24:1–34)

Verses 1–22 form a praise of personified Wisdom in the tradition of Prov 8:22–31 and Job 28. Wisdom is the first of God's creations (see ch. 1) and spreads across the earth—that is, she has a universal aspect. She also has a particular aspect in that God chooses her dwelling place among the Israelites where she serves in the holy tent, i.e., the Temple in Jerusalem. The comparisons to plants and spices in vv. 13–17 symbolize beauty, fragrance, and usefulness. The substances in v. 15 also connect to the Temple, since they were used in cultic ritual there. Some of these images reemerge in ch. 50 in the description of Simon II. In vv. 19–22, Wisdom issues an invitation to a feast where she is the food. Ben Sira then makes the remarkable claim that not only is Wisdom found in the Temple, the provenance of priests, but she is embodied in the "book of the covenant of the Most High God," which is accessible to the entire people but especially to the scribe. The rivers call to mind paradise and fecundity, since the Gihon, Pishon, Tigris, and Euphrates surround Eden in Gen 2:10–14. In a continuation of the fluvial metaphor, Ben Sira derives his own teaching from that same wisdom, and he likens it to prophecy. In this way, he forges a relationship between cult, Torah, and the sage, whose wisdom constitutes a type of revealed knowledge, largely derived from study of the Law and traditional wisdom.

B. Praiseworthy Things (25:1–11)

Ben Sira employs numerical proverbs and beatitudes. Usually a numerical proverb has the form a and a+1 (see 23:16–17, 25:7), although vv. 1 and 2 do not have the a+1. On plowing with an ox and ass together, see Deut 22:10. Most significantly, at the end of the list of beatitudes, Ben Sira claims that nothing surpasses fear of the Lord, not even social status, which ideally levels the social playing field. Thus a scribe like himself might actually be higher on the ideal social ladder than the rich and powerful whom he serves.

C. Evil and Good Women (25:13–26:18 [verses 19–27 are a later addition])

A discourse on wives that alternates evil wife–good wife–evil wife–good wife, with much more attention paid to the evil wife. Ben Sira adopts what became the standard interpretation of Gen 3:1–24, that the woman's disobedience caused human death. This view differs from ch. 17 where limited days were God's intention from the start. The subject of 26:10 is likely a wife as in the Syriac version, not a daughter. The images in v. 12 are transparently sexual. Most significantly, all the actions described here are either good or bad depending on how they affect the husband, a reflection of an honor/shame culture that revolved around men.

D. Integrity (26:28–27:15)

Honesty and integrity are important wisdom topics. 26:29–27:3 contains a harsh criticism of business. Usually honesty in business, such as using accurate scales, is a central wisdom idea (see 42:4; Prov 11:1; 20:10), but Ben Sira seems convinced that sin is potentially inherent in any transaction. Ben Sira often takes his examples from the life of artisans and farmers (27:4–6; see 38:24–34a). A person's speech reveals one's interior condition, both good and bad.

E. Relationships with Companions (27:16–28:26)

Ben Sira observes that betraying a secret will certainly destroy a friendship (cf. 22:19–26). Winking is a sign of duplicity (Prov. 6:13; 10:10). Since Ben Sira does not recognize post-mortem reward and punishment, his notion of theodicy requires that God knows people's sins so that God can repay them before or at death. The idea that God's forgiveness depends on forgiveness of neighbor is widespread in early Judaism and Christianity (cf. Mark 11:25). Verse 28:5 makes effective sacrifice dependent on righteous behavior (see ch. 35).

F. Lending and Surety (29:1–20)

The Torah forbids taking interest on loans (Exod 22:25; Lev 25:35–37). Ben Sira encourages lending to a neighbor in need as an act of mercy, even though it is fraught with danger. The Torah also enjoins almsgiving (cf. Deut 15:7–11), which Ben Sira values highly. On v. 12, see 3:30. Surety, providing collateral, could be doubly dangerous, since the one guaranteeing the loan was dependent on both lender and borrower to regain his property. Ben Sira expresses his ethic of caution in v. 20.

G. Home and Children (29:21–30:13)

Ben Sira warns against being dependent on others; thus, one must be content with life's necessities. He recognizes that the poor have some means, which separate them from destitution and begging (cf. 40:28). His advice about children is harsh, but consistent with ancient attitudes towards childrearing (cf. Prov 13:24). A disciplined son will carry on the father's name and uphold the family. The comparison of an unbroken horse to a son reveals Ben Sira's attitude to discipline, which insures against shame for both parent and child.

H. Food and Health (30:14–25)

The thought continues the previous idea of contentment with one's circumstances. Throughout his book Ben Sira advises his students to enjoy what they have (cf. 14:11–16). The images in vv. 18–20 illustrate those who cannot enjoy "good things": for the dead and idols—food, for the eunuch—sex. Ridicule of idols is common in biblical and early Jewish texts; see Isa 44:9–20; Bel and the Dragon; the Letter of Jeremiah. The point of the passage is to assure long life, since after death there is only Sheol.

I. Wealth (31:1–11)

Inability to sleep signals anxiety (see also 42:9). Ben Sira does not condemn wealth, but the series of rhetorical questions in vv. 9 and 10 indicate that he thought the combination of righteousness and wealth highly unlikely at best. After all, what rich person does not "go after gold" (v. 8)? The Hebrew word translated "gold" is the earliest example of the term mammeon, which appears as a loan word in the New Testament (Matt 6:24; Luke 16:9, 11, 13).

J. Table Manners (31:12–32:13)

These three discreet sections on food, wine, and banquet behavior emphasize moderation and modesty. Ben Sira trained his students for public careers, and banquets could be filled with social land mines that could affect them. Thus, proper social etiquette was essential. He also includes the value of generosity with one's resources. His advice concerning food and wine is eminently practical. Banquets, however, had formal rules of etiquette, which Ben Sira reinforces, such as when one can/should speak.

K. Divine Providence (32:14–33:18)

Verse 32:23 forges an odd connection between caution and fulfilling the law. Perhaps Ben Sira has something like Deut 4:9 in mind. The idea that no evil comes upon the one who fears the Lord ignores reality, but it appears often in wisdom literature and in Sirach. In 33:7–15 Ben Sira illustrates how God's works come in pairs: festival versus ordinary days, blessed (Abraham) and holy (priests) versus cursed (Canaanites) people, good versus evil, and life versus death (see 42:24–25). The first person conclusion links Ben Sira to earlier prophets and sages.

VI. Sirach 33:19–39:11

A. Independence (33:19–24)

Ben Sira observes that independence depends on control of property, and doing so brings honor. Distributing property "in the hour of death" enables one to enjoy it throughout life, but also to determine how it will pass to the next generation.

B. Slaves (33:25–33)

Slave systems were normative throughout antiquity. Israelite law recognized slavery, even if Israelite slaves were thought to be different from Gentile slaves (see Exod 21:2–11, 20–21, 26–27;

Lev 25:44–46; Deut 15:12–18). Ben Sira's advice is thoroughly practical, since idle slaves will try to get away. For the person who has only one slave, Ben Sira recognizes his/her importance. The phrase "bought him with blood" equates life with resources. (For this idea see also 4QInstruction from the Dead Sea Scrolls.)

C. Dreams (34:1–8)

Ben Sira rejects the idea that knowledge comes through dreams and visions. He may be reacting against apocalyptic dream visions like those reported in 1 Enoch. He also rejects divination and omens (see Deut 18:10–11). In arguing that dreams are a projection of the dreamer, his attitude sounds modern. He does make room for dreams sent by God (e.g., Joseph), although he does not say how one can differentiate legitimate from illegitimate dreams. In his view, God has shown everything necessary in the Torah (v. 8).

D. Education, Experience, Fear of the Lord (34:9–20)

By affirming that education comes from wide experience and then claiming such experience for himself, Ben Sira establishes his own credentials. Verses 14–20 further explicate his idea of fear of the Lord. God will protect the one who fears God and will make him or her prosper (vv. 19–20).

E. Sacrifices and True Worship of God (34:21–35:26)

This section weaves together ethical/moral and Temple piety. Although God desires sacrifices, only the righteous offer acceptable ones. To offer sacrifices from property taken from the poor is the moral equivalent of murder, as is depriving the poor of a living generally (34:24–27). Offering kindness is the same as offering a cereal sacrifice (35:3). The remark that God does not accept bribes segues to remarks about God's justice, similar to those in other places in the book. Ben Sira's claim that God will do justice (35:22) transitions to God's protection of Israel and the prayer in 36:1–22.

F. Prayer for the Deliverance of Israel (36:1–22)

Ben Sira's prayer is in the style of a number of Psalms. In the context of a wisdom book, this prayer surprises with its emotional tine. It has an eschatological orientation that is national— Ben Sira implores God to "gather all the tribes of Israel"—but not messianic. Verses 6–7 allude to the story of Israel's deliverance in the exodus. Verse 20 reflects a developing idea, also found in other early Jewish literature (especially some of the Dead Sea scrolls) and early Christianity, that the prophets were predicting future events.

G. Wives, Friends, Counselors (36:23–37:15)

Ben Sira returns to practicality in this section. Verse 29b recalls the description of Eve in Gen 2:18 and further reinforces that a woman's importance revolved around her husband. The phrase "a fugitive and a wanderer" describes Cain in Gen 4:12. Finding and keeping true friends is an important topic in Sirach; see, for example, 6:5–17. Ben Sira warns against trusting counselors, since they will act out of self-interest. As proof, he offers a list of nine examples of people to avoid. In the end, God and one's own heart prove most trustworthy.

H. Deliberative Speech and Moderation (37:16–31)

Ben Sira moves from choosing counselors to effective public speech. Wisdom characterizes the difference between an effective teacher or public speaker and an ineffective one. Verse 26 invokes the idea that honor brings reputation ("his name"), which constitutes a kind of immortality. The short unit on moderation in eating leads to the next section on physicians and illness.

I. Sickness, the Physician, Mourning (38:1–23)

Ben Sira combines a traditional notion that sin causes illness, which then requires God's forgiveness, with consultation with a physician, whom God "created" (Heb.: "allotted"). In vv. 9–12, he recommends prayer and sacrifice to atone for sin before seeking a doctor. Verse 5 alludes to the story in Exod 15:23–25 as proof of the inherent healing properties of natural substances used by both physician and pharmacist. Ben Sira next enjoins the traditional religious duties of mourning and burial. Verse 17 is unusual in that the normal period of mourning was seven days not one or two (cf. 22:12). He gives the practical advice that overwrought mourning does neither the mourner nor the departed any good.

J. The Superiority of the Scribe (38:24–39:11)

Ben Sira praises the scribe in two poems (38:24–34b; 38:34c–39:11). The first has been compared to the Egyptian *Satire of the Trades*, but Ben Sira does not engage in satire. In fact, he shows high regard for farmers, artisans, smiths, and potters. They cannot be scribes, however, because the required attention to their tasks does not provide the necessary leisure time. They enable society to survive, but they do not serve as rulers or in courts and assemblies. The scribe differs in this respect. He plumbs the depths of the tradition, and in v. 6, Ben Sira employs the language of prophecy, as he has elsewhere, to characterize the scribe's words. The result for the wise scribe is eternal renown and a lasting memory—immortality in the community.

VII. Sirach 39:12–43:33

A. Praise of the Creator (39:12–35)

Following the description of the ideal scribe, Ben Sira reverts to the first person as if to emphasize his own scribal achievement. The images of vv. 13–14 recall the flourishing of Wisdom in ch. 24. He calls his students to recite this hymn praising God. All of creation is "very good" (cf. Gen 1), obeys its creator, and has a purpose. The righteous receive good things from God and the wicked, bad things. Even life's necessities turn out evil for the wicked—how Ben Sira does not say. Verse 17 could refer to the crossing of the sea (Exod 15:8) or to creation (Gen 1:9–10). Verse 23 alludes to the destruction of Sodom and Gomorrah (Gen 19:24–28).

B. Life's Joys and Miseries (40:1–41:13)

Ben Sira notes that people of all social strata share the same exigencies of life, particularly the certainty of death. Yet, given his concept of theodicy, he insists that sinners suffer seven times worse. Several biblical allusions inhabit the initial section: Gen 3:17–19 ("hard work"); Gen 3:20 ("mother of all the living," but here the *earth* not *Eve*); Gen 6–8 ("the flood"); Gen 3:19 ("returns to earth"). Sirach 40:18–26 consists of a series of "better than" proverbs, where two initial elements (here good things) are compared to a third, which is superior. These proverbs culminate in the highest value, fear of the Lord. For Ben Sira,

begging constitutes a form of social death, and he prefers real death to it. He contrasts the attitudes toward death of the rich and healthy with those of the poor and frail, but since death is inevitable, one should not fear it. Finally, in 41:11-14 Ben Sira reemphasizes the importance of a lasting name and reputation as a way of transcending the end that comes to all.

C. Shame (41:14–42:8)

Shame can be both proper and improper. The section highlights the centrality of the honor/shame system to Ben Sira's understanding of social status and relations, and it follows, probably intentionally, right after mention of the importance of a virtuous name and reputation. The topics treated vary widely, from table manners to business to lechery. Most remarkable is the injunction not to be ashamed of the law of the Most High and the covenant. Some scholars think that not sinning to save face reflects competing Jewish and Hellenistic values, although it might just as readily refer to any social situation in which one compromises one's values in order to gain approval or acceptance.

D. Daughters (42:9–14)

A section that might offend modern sensibilities, the main point is that a father needs to do everything he can to avoid shame that comes via a daughter's possible misbehavior. The key is v. 11 where the daughter puts her father to public shame. Even though the general sentiment is consistent with ancient codes of honor and shame, v. 14 is an unusually harsh assessment and reveals something of Ben Sira's personal attitude toward women.

E. The Works of God in Nature (42:15–43:33)

A three-part hymn of praise that leads to the Praise of the Ancestors (chs. 44–50)—first, marveling at God's omniscience (42:15–25), second, describing the wonders of nature (43:1–26; showing the influence of texts like Job 38 and Pss 104; 105), and third, calling others to praise God (43:27–33). By referring to creation by God's word, Ben Sira alludes to Gen 1:1–31. God knows all of creation, including past and future as well as the human heart. Thus, Ben Sira's theodicy makes sense, since by knowing everything, God can mete out reward and punishment justly. On the idea of opposites in creation, see 33:15. Among the natural wonders, the moon stands out for its role in determining the calendar, but see Gen 1:14 where sun and moon together set the signs, seasons, days, and years—perhaps Ben Sira's response to Jews who advocated a solar calendar. His claim that God's word holds the cosmos together and that God is "the All" may reflect knowledge of Stoic notions of the *logos* (cf. the Gospel of John and Philo of Alexandria) that brings order and stability to the world. At the same time, Ben Sira takes pains to note that God and creation are different—God is "greater than all his works."

VIII. Sirach 44:1–50:24

A. Introductory Praise of the Ancestors (44:1–15)

Ben Sira introduces his Praise of Famous Ancestors (author translation) by mentioning a series of types of people who have gained renown, among them kings, prophets, and scribes/sages. He also notes that some have died and left behind no memory; they thus have truly perished. The text does not make clear whether these are pious people, as some scholars think, or wicked people who deserve such a fate. Given Ben Sira's theology elsewhere, it seems likely that they are wicked or impious people and that the pronoun "these" in v. 10 refers not to the people of v. 9, but to those already singled out in vv. 1–8. The main point of the poem comes in vv. 14–15—their names and memory still live on, and they exemplify the immortality that the pious earn through their faithfulness.

B. The Early Covenantal Figures: Enoch, Noah, Abraham, Isaac, Jacob (44:16–44:23e)

Enoch's status in the list is debated. While many scholars think it original, others consider it a later addition, in part because Enoch does not have a covenant made with him, as do the seven figures after him. In light of Enoch's widespread presence in Second Temple literature, the notice itself is rather unremarkable. He is the only person in the Praise to be called an example—of "repentance" (Greek) or "knowledge" (Hebrew). The short section on Noah focuses on his continuation of the human race. For Abraham, the covenant in the flesh is circumcision and the test was the offering of Isaac. Ben Sira claims that Abraham kept God's commandments, even before they had been given to Moses. Jacob's inheritance is the land, which gets divided among the twelve tribes.

C. The Later Covenantal Figures: Moses, Aaron, Phinehas (44:23f–45:26)

Ben Sira concentrates on Moses' role as the one to whom God gave the law. Although he notes Moses' great glory and respect, his brother Aaron, who receives a perpetual priesthood, garners more attention. The focus on Aaron is primarily two-fold: his cultic and teaching roles. The reference to Korah's rebellion might be addressed to contemporary conflicts within the priesthood. Ben Sira notes specifically that Aaron and his sons can wear the high priestly vestments. The verses on Phinehas parallel the biblical information, but Ben Sira contrasts David's and Phinehas's covenants. David's only extends to one son at a time, whereas Phinehas's covers all of his descendants. This observation probably reflects Ben Sira's historical situation in which there was no king, but a high priest who also served as the leader of the people. The second-person address of v. 26 is probably directed at contemporary priests.

D. Joshua, Caleb, the Judges, Samuel (46:1–20)

In the Praise Ben Sira emphasizes faithfulness. Joshua and Caleb were the two who "opposed the congregation," that is, believed that God would give the land to the Israelites (see Num 14:6–10). Ben Sira praises judges who "did not fall into idolatry." The hope that the judges' bones bring forth new life could be an allusion to a story like 2 Kgs 13:20–21 in which Elisha's bones revivify a corpse. Because he was faithful, Samuel was proved to be a prophet, whose prophecies came true. He anointed two kings, Saul and David, although Ben Sira does not mention Saul.

E. Nathan, David, Solomon (47:1–22)

The appearance of Nathan leads directly to David, whom God "set apart" to be king, as vv. 2–11 demonstrate. Even as a youth, David displayed kingly characteristics, especially in his defeat of Goliath. Ben Sira also mentions David's installation of Temple singers, a tradition known from Chronicles. The reference to God removing his sins alludes to the incident with Bathsheba.

Solomon, however, faces more explicit criticism. Although he built the Temple and was wise, Ben Sira highlights his failings. Yet, despite Solomon's problems, Ben Sira claims that God will not destroy David's line—perhaps a reference to the promise in 2 Sam 7.

F. The Establishment of the Northern Kingdom, Elijah, Elisha (47:23–48:16)

Ben Sira turns to the division of Solomon's kingdom. Jeroboam sins because he set up cult shrines at Dan and Bethel (1 Kgs 12:25-33). Elijah operated in the northern kingdom (see 1 Kgs 17–19; 2 Kgs 1–2). The intent of v. 11 is unclear due to textual problems. For Elisha's career, see 2 Kgs 2–13. Verse 15 refers to the destruction of Samaria, the capital of the North. A Davidic ruler remained in Judah (the southern kingdom), even if most of them sinned; and in fact, Ben Sira singles out only two, Hezekiah and Josiah, for praise.

G. Hezekiah and Isaiah (48:17–25)

Hezekiah famously constructed a water tunnel to supply Jerusalem with water throughout an Assyrian siege. On the manner of rescue, see 2 Kgs 19:15–35//Isa 37:21–38. The prophet Isaiah counseled Hezekiah, so they are praised together. In the verses on Isaiah, Ben Sira reveals his understanding of prophecy as prediction of future events and the end of time (v. 25).

H. Josiah and Succeeding Ancestors (49:1–13)

Ben Sira remembers Josiah for eliminating idol worship and removing the "high places" in favor of the Temple in Jerusalem. Somewhat surprisingly, he does not mention the discovery in the Temple of a book of the law that prompted the reforms (see 2 Kgs 22–23). Ben Sira attributes the destruction of Judah and Jerusalem to abandonment of the law. He singles out Jeremiah as one who predicted these events, and in v. 7 he alludes to Jer 1:5 and 10. Ben Sira's remark that Ezekiel saw God's chariot is the first mention in Jewish literature of the *merkevah*, God's chariot-throne, which in later Judaism became an object of mystical speculation. He also mentions "the Twelve," indicating that in this period the Minor Prophets already existed together in a single corpus. Finally, Ben Sira offers brief notes on post-exilic reestablishment of the Temple under Zerubbabal and the

rebuilding of Jerusalem's walls under Nehemiah. Curiously, he does not mention Ezra, a priest and scribe and a central figure in the narratives of post-exilic Jerusalem.

I. Miscellaneous Ancestors (49:14–16)

This unit sits uncomfortably in its present place. Four of the six figures are predeluvian. Adam ends the unit, making the transition to Simon II in ch. 50 difficult, even though Simon probably concludes the Praise.

J. Simon II (50:1–24)

Ben Sira portrays his contemporary as the ideal royal high priest. His eulogy of Simon is reminiscent of Wisdom's self-praise and of his praises of Aaron and Hezekiah. Like a beneficent king, he repaired Jerusalem (probably after the Seleucid–Ptolemaic conflicts over Judea)—fortifying city and Temple and bringing in water. The ritual described in vv. 14–21 has been variously identified as being for the daily offering, for Yom Kippur (the Day of Atonement), or Rosh Hashanah (the New Year). The "blessing of the LORD" could refer to the priestly blessing given in Num 6:24–27 (cf. Lev 9:22–23). The benediction in vv. 22–24 differs between Greek and Hebrew—the NRSV translates the Greek. The Hebrew reads: "May his kindness to Simon be enduring; may he fulfill for him the covenant of Phinehas that it not be cut off for him or for his seed, for the days of heaven."

IX. Sirach 50:25–51:30

A. Epilogue (50:25–29)

Ben Sira takes a short opportunity to excoriate the Edomites, the Philistines, and the Samaritans. The epilogue provides us with the author's name and ends with the characteristic idea of the fear of the Lord.

B. Ben Sira's Hymn of Thanksgiving (51:1–12)

Ben Sira offers a prayer of thanksgiving for deliverance from enemies that employs the language of psalms. Some have questioned its authenticity, but nothing suggests decisively that Ben Sira did not compose it. The long litany that appears in Hebrew MS B between v. 12 and v. 13 is not original.

C. Ben Sira's Search for Wisdom (51:13–30)

The book's final poem describes the sages's search for Wisdom with a decidedly erotic tinge— although scholars disagree about the extent of the eroticism. The language is similar to other places where Ben Sira encourages his students to pursue Wisdom. Fragments of the poem in 11QPsa demonstrate that it was originally an acrostic. Verse 23 mentions Ben Sira's house of instruction (beth midhrash). What such an institution would have looked like is debated, but it certainly indicates some context for educational purposes.

BIBLIOGRAPHY

R. A. Argall. *1 Enoch and Sirach: A Comparative Literary and Conceptual Analysis of the Themes of Revelation, Creation and Judgment* (Atlanta: SBL, 1995); P. C. Beentjes. *The Book of Ben Sira in Modern Research* (Berlin: Walter de Gruyter, 1997); C. V. Camp. "Understanding a Patriarchy: Women in Second Century Jerusalem through the Eyes of Ben Sira." *"Women Like This": New Perspectives on Jewish Women in the Greco-Roman World.* A. Levine, ed. (Atlanta: Scholars Press, 1991) 1–39; J. J. Collins. *Jewish Wisdom in the Hellenistic Age* (Louisville: Westminster John Knox, 1997); J. L. Crenshaw. "The Book of Sirach." NIB (Nashville: Abingdon, 1997) 5:603–867; R. A. Horsley. *Scribes, Visionaries, and the Politics of Second Temple Judea* (Louisville: Westminster John Knox, 1997); B. L. Mack. *Wisdom and the Hebrew Epic: Ben Sira's Hymn in Praise of the Fathers* (Chicago: University of Chicago Press, 1985); B. L. Mack. Introduction and Notes to "Ecclesiasticus, or the Wisdom of Jesus Son of Sirach." B. G. Wright III. *Harper Collins Study Bible.* H. W. Attridge, ed. (San Francisco: HarperSanFrancisco, 2006); L. G. Perdue. *Wisdom Literature: A Theological History* (Louisville: Westminster John Knox, 2007); J. T. Sanders, *Ben Sira and Demotic Wisdom* (Chico, Calif.: Scholars Press, 1983); P. W. Skehan and A. A. Di Lella. *The Wisdom of Ben Sira* (New York: Doubleday, 1987); G. G. Xeravits and J. Zsengfellér, eds. *Studies in the Book of Ben Sira* (Leiden: Brill, 2008).

BARUCH

Patricia K. Tull

Overview

The deuterocanonical book of Baruch, written most likely in Jerusalem in the second century BCE, is associated with the book of Jeremiah in the Septuagint and Latin Vulgate. It is considered canonical by Roman Catholic and Eastern Orthodox churches, but not by Jews or Protestants. The final chapter appears during advent in Catholic and Anglican lectionaries.

Like many works written during and after the Second Temple period, the book introduces an authorial fiction: that it was composed by Jeremiah's friend and scribe Baruch, son of Neriah (see Jer 32:12–16; 36:4–32; 43:3–6; 45:1–5). According to Jer 43:6, Baruch and Jeremiah were taken to Egypt after Nebuchadnezzar destroyed Jerusalem. But according to this book's opening, Baruch lived and wrote among Babylonian exiles. Several other historical inaccuracies reflected in the introduction suggest that Baruch's biographical and historical features are fictional.

Baruch is deeply scriptural and theological, however, freely partaking of themes and language from Deuteronomy, which is echoed throughout the book, as well as from several other major sections of the Hebrew Bible. The book sets side by side five genres well known from Scripture: (1) prose narrative (1:1–9), which introduces (2) a letter (1:10–14), modeled on Jer 29:1–23, which contains (3) a prayer of repentance (1:15–3:8), modeled on Dan 9; (4) a poetic hymn to divine Wisdom, who is the Torah of God (3:9–4:4), modeled on Job 28; and finally (5) poetic words of consolation addressed from and to Mother Jerusalem, modeled on Isa 40–66 (4:5–5:9).

Because obvious transitions at 3:9 and 4:5 are lacking, and because of the genre shifts, many readers view Baruch as a composite document comprised of pieces written by at least three authors. But citing especially the echoes of Deuteronomy and Deuteronomic theology throughout the book, some recent commentators have seen continuity among the book's parts. Even though the medium of communication changes over the course of the book, as do the names by which God

is remembered, all sections share common characteristics: concern for Jerusalem and traditional understandings of the human relationship to God, responsiveness to Torah, exegetical reutilization of Scripture, and a chastened quest for God's will and for Israel's restoration. Unlike some other roughly contemporary works, Baruch exhibits no interest in messianic or apocalyptic discourse. Rather, its author offers the community models for learning from their ancestors' mistakes and living in humble piety in the here and now.

Outline

I. Introduction (1:1–14)

II. Baruch's Prayer (1:15–3:8)

III. Wisdom's Call (3:9–4:4)

IV. Jerusalem's Consolation (4:5–5:9)

Detailed Analysis

I. Introduction (1:1–14)

The book is presented as the words of Baruch, writing in Babylon "in the fifth year," probably, that is, five years after the destruction of the Temple in 587 BCE. After Baruch reads the book that follows to the exiled King Jeconiah (Jehoiachin) and all the Judeans in Babylon, they weep, pray, fast, and take up an offering to be sent to Jerusalem, along with the Temple vessels that had been carried to Babylon. Ezra 1:7–11 presents Cyrus of Persia restoring these implements much later, but the story here requires this action, since the funds being sent to Jerusalem are intended to buy sacrifices for offering on the altar.

Beginning in v. 10, a letter from the exiled community addresses Jerusalem's high priest Jehoiakim, who is otherwise unknown, and the people with him. This letter asks them to offer incense, burnt, grain, and sin offerings on the altar, praying for the exiled community as well as for King Nebuchadnezzar of Babylon and for his "son" Belshazzar—whom Dan 5:2 likewise erroneously identified as Nebuchadnezzar's son, though he was actually the son of Nabonidus, Nebuchadnezzar's son-in-law's son's successor. The introduction evokes Jeremiah's letter exhorting the exiled community in Babylon to reconcile themselves to their new life (Jer 29), as well as Ezra's public reading of Torah, inspiring repentance (Neh 8). The Jerusalemites are asked to read the contents of this scroll aloud as a confession of sin on behalf of both the exiles and themselves.

II. Baruch's Prayer (1:15–3:8)

The fifty-one verse prayer of confession that follows is similar to Daniel's much briefer prayer in Dan 9:4–19. The prayer's opening in Bar 1:15–18 echoes Dan 9:7–10 rather precisely, and the supplication at the prayer's turning point in Bar 2:11–18 echoes the conclusion at Dan 9:15–19. Interwoven with this prayer, a retrospective of Deuteronomistic theology, are a variety of phrases from the books of Deuteronomy and Jeremiah. Prominent especially in Bar 2:21–26 are echoes of Jeremiah's exhortation in Jer 27 to serve the king of Babylon.

The prayer is general rather than specific, and all-encompassing in its scope. Israel's sin began with the ancestors who were brought out of Egypt, and includes all the people of Judah and inhabitants of Jerusalem along with all their public leaders. Sins include disobedience (1:18, see Dan 9:10), serving other gods and doing evil in the Lord's eyes (1:22; see Deut 4:25; 11:16), and failing to heed God's command to submit to Babylon (2:24; see Jer 27:13). As a result of this sin, Israel has incurred the curses Moses warned of in Deut 28: cannibalism (Bar 2:3, see Deut 28:53), being scattered among the nations (Bar 2:4; see Deut 28:64), and being left few in number (Bar 2:29, see Deut 28:58, 62). Now, recognizing divine justice in the calamities they have endured, they quote a pastiche of passages from Exodus, Deuteronomy, 2 Kings, and Jeremiah, as divine promises that in exile they will come to recognize, obey, praise, and remember God, and will return to their ancestral land forever (Bar 2:29–35). The prayer concludes with a plea for mercy and a reassurance that the people have repented.

Remarkable in both its humility and its exegetical study of Scripture, the prayer recalls the entire story of Israel's birth, prosperity, destruction, and struggling rebirth as a nation that was, by the author's time, "exiled" within its own borders.

III. Wisdom's Call (3:9–4:4)

Baruch 3:8 concludes with a reminder to God that "we" are in exile. After a call that repeats precisely the Deuteronomic phrase "Hear, O Israel" (Deut 5:1, 6:4, obscured in the NRSV translation, which reverses the word order), Israel is asked rhetorically *why* the people are in enemy land. The answer is supplied immediately: "you have forsaken the fountain (see Jer 2:13, 17:13) of wisdom." Indeed, in Deut 4:5–6 Moses had drawn a close link between obedience to the law and wisdom, and this link is exploited in a poem that draws upon the personification of wisdom in Job 28, with assistance from Deut 30, Job 38, and Prov 3:13–18.

The poem progresses through a series of questions and answers concerning the quest for wisdom, based on Job 28's poem concerning where wisdom is to be found, with generous contributions from the poem about finding God's commandments in Deut 30:11–14. It was not found by rulers who schemed to gain wealth (Bar 3:16–19, see Ezek 28:2–10 on the wise ruler of Tyre), nor by those in Teman, who were likewise renowned for wisdom (Bar 3:22–23, see Jer 49:7 and Obad 8–9), nor by the giants of old (Bar 3:26-27, see Gen 6:4). God alone has found the way to wisdom (Bar 3:32, 36, see Job 28:23). But whereas in Job, wisdom was simply the fear of the Lord, Baruch agrees with the understanding found in Sirach 24, in which Wisdom searches for a dwelling place and is told by God to make her dwelling with Israel (Sir 24:8): God has found the way to Wisdom and has given her to Israel. Baruch also agrees with Sirach that wisdom is "the book of the commandments of God" (Bar 4:1, see Sir 24:23). Although Deut 30:11–14 does not spell out why Israel need not go to heaven or beyond the sea to find God's decree, Baruch draws the exegetical connection: "the word is very near to you" (Deut 30:14) because God has already sought it out and given it to Israel, who must now hold it fast and live (Bar 4:1, see Prov 3:18).

In this section God is no longer called *kyrios*, "Lord," but "the one who knows all things" and "the one who prepared the earth for all time," "the one who sends forth the light," and "our God" (Bar 3:32–33, 35). Wisdom is known by other names as well. She is not only *sophia* (wisdom, 3:12, 23; see Prov 1:20), but also *phronēsis* ("understanding" or "prudence," 3:9, 14, 28; see Prov 3:13), *synesis* ("intelligence," 3:14, 23, 32; see Prov 9:6), *ischys* ("strength," 3:14; see Prov 8:14), and *epistēmē* ("knowledge," 3:20, 27, 37; Job 28:12)—all feminine nouns. In Baruch she is not presented, as in Proverbs, as a quasi-sexual partner for a male audience, but is commended to "you, Israel" (second person common plural). If her appearing on earth to live with humankind sounds familiar to Christians, it is because the idea of Wisdom as the divine Torah dwelling with Israel is echoed in John's formulation "the Word became flesh and lived among us" (John 1:14). Indeed, many patristic writers, including Irenaeus, Clement, Origen, Tertullian, Ambrose, and Hilary, used this poem, especially "she appeared on earth and lived with humankind" (3:37; see John 1:14) to support their understanding of the preexistent Christ.

The nature of life-giving wisdom is important to this writer. It is not information, nor is it cleverness. Wealth and power cannot buy it. It does not even consist of aphorisms based, like much of the wisdom of Proverbs, on observations concerning the created world or human behavior. Here, not only is reverence for God the beginning of wisdom, but wisdom entirely consists in adherence to God's commandments revealed in the Torah. Following the law is posed not simply as a means to avoid divine punishment, but as the only way to gain a coherent grasp of life itself.

IV. Jerusalem's Consolation (4:5–5:9)

Wisdom is only one of the two major personified female figures in the Hebrew Scriptures. The other is the city of Jerusalem, or Zion, who appears in Psalms, 2 Kings, and several biblical prophets, but is best known from Lamentations and Isaiah 40–66. Nowhere else in Scripture do the two figures, Wisdom and Zion, appear side by side as they do in Baruch.

As in the previous two sections, the topic announced from the beginning is exile, still understood in Deuteronomic terms. An anonymous speaker (presumably Baruch) addresses "my people," reminding them that they were handed over to their enemies because they angered God

(Bar 4:5–6). Combining the claims of Deut 32:18 ("you forgot the God who gave you birth"), Isa 1:2 in which God says, "I reared children and brought them up,/but they have rebelled against me," and Lam 2:22 where Zion says, "those whom I bore and reared my enemy has destroyed," the speaker poses God and Zion side by side as grieving co-parents: "You forgot the everlasting God, who brought you up,/and you grieved Jerusalem, who reared you" (Bar 4:8). The verb used of God, *tropheuō*, is otherwise attested in the LXX only to describe Moses' mother, the "nursing woman" (Exod 2:7). The verb used of Zion, *ektrephō*, describes God in Ps 23:2 (see also Isa 49:21; Prov 23:24). A subtle wisdom theme emerges in the reminders of the hopes and expectations of both father and mother (see Prov 1:8, etc.).

The next verse introduces Zion's own speech, which continues through Bar 4:29. Following her speech the anonymous observer resumes, this time speaking to Zion herself. This structure of interaction between Zion and a sympathetic observer who speaks both about and to her resembles that found in Lam 1 and 2. Unlike Lamentations, however, Baruch presents both Zion and the other speaker as articulating hope and comfort. The refrain "take courage" structures this poem, appearing first in the mouth of "Baruch" (4:5), speaking to the people, and subsequently twice more in Zion's words, also addressed to her children (4:21, 27), and finally directed back to Zion herself (4:30).

The theology is the same as in previous sections of Baruch. Only the perspective from which it is viewed differs. Zion's sorrow is caused by the sins of her children (Bar 4:12; see Isa 50:1). Here Zion endures none of the sexually abusive imprecations of Hosea, Jeremiah, and especially Ezekiel, in which gender is integral to sin and God is the jealous husband. Instead, Baruch holds the mother city to be the innocent victim of her children's disregard for God's commandments. Daughters are specifically mentioned along with sons (4:10, 14, 16), and "children" appears seven times as the neuter term *tekna* rather than *huioi*, "sons." Confession of sin and the hope for restoration have already been articulated in the initial letter and prayer; the alternative path of wise obedience has already been traced. Here the pathos of a mother longing for her children's return creates a relationship within which wayward Israelites can envision themselves assuming responsibility for the welfare of their society as a whole.

Baruch 4:5–20 presents the sin and exile of Zion's children as a situation over which Zion mourns, though she considers herself helpless to assist them except by her prayers. "I have taken off the robe of peace/and put on sackcloth for my supplication;/I will cry to the Everlasting all my days" (4:20), she says. However, she does more than simply pray. She expresses confidence in God's deliverance and recommends patient endurance with prayer. A turning point is reached midway through her speech when Zion finds joy in God's mercy and articulates hope for the future in tones similar to those of Second Isaiah: "I sent you out with sorrow and weeping, but God will give you back to me with joy and gladness forever" (4:23, see Isa 49:22; 51:11).

In Baruch Zion offers her most fully reasoned understanding of herself, her children, and her God, who in this section is also called "Holy One" (Bar 4:22, 37; 5:5) and "Everlasting" (Bar 4:8, 10, 14, 20, 22, 24, 35; 5:2). She advises her children to "endure with patience the wrath that has come upon you" (4:25) until they are remembered by God and brought to everlasting joy. Though weeping and sorrowful (4:11), widowed, bereaved, and desolate (4:12), Zion neither accuses nor excuses her children, but urges acceptance, repentance, and expectancy. Though the book echoes the suffering of Zion that was articulated so brutally in Lamentations when the Babylonian exile was still fresh and shocking, time and distance have conferred on Zion more dignity, control, and motherly counsel.

In Baruch's first section the people are forced to articulate their own sorrow, and in the middle section a more dispassionate speaker touches only briefly on present sufferings. In the final section, however, Zion as mother represents transcendent compassion, moved by human suffering, grieving both over and with her children. She mediates the tension between respect for divine order, which moves her to plead with her children, and compassion for human failure, which moves her to plead with God.

As Zion has comforted, so she too is comforted. The sympathetic voice that introduced her speech returns in the conclusion of this section and of the book of Baruch, reassuring her of God's comfort (4:30, see Isa 51:12 and Lam 1:2, etc). As in Isa 47, a wretched fate is predicted for Jerusalem's unnamed enemies who "rejoiced at your fall" (Bar 4:31) and especially for the city that "received your offspring" (Bar 4:32) and will be "grieved at her own desolation" (v. 33). In expressions echoing Isa 43:5, 49:18, and 60:4, Jerusalem is told to "look toward the east" to see her children returning to her from east and west (4:36–37). They are carried in glory (5:6; Isa 49:22; 60:4) and led joyfully by God (5:9; Isa 52:12; 55:12). Zion herself is invited to don new clothing (5:1–3; Isa 52:1–2) and receive her new name (5:4; Isa 62:2, 12). The poem concludes with creation's response: helped by hills that become low and valleys that fill up to make level ground (5:7; 40:4), and shaded by woods and fragrant trees (5:8; Isa 55:12–13), Zion's children are led back by God in "the mercy and righteousness that come from him."

Unlike Isa 40–66, in which Zion is told to sing aloud (Isa 54:1) but never actually speaks, Baruch represents Zion as a theologically articulate figure whose conversation partner complements her speech and transforms her hope into immanent reality. By the conclusion of the book, hearers in a century quite distant from the Babylonian exile, who are nevertheless still suffering foreign domination, have been beckoned by Torah, prophets, and wisdom, all three speaking in concert, to reclaim their scriptural and religious heritage, to repent of sin, to seek wisdom through obedience, and to be rejoined with their consoling Mother Jerusalem.

BIBLIOGRAPHY

D. Burke. *The Poetry of Baruch: A Reconstruction and Analysis of the Original Hebrew Text of Baruch 3:9–5:9.* SBL Septuagint and Cognate Studies 10 (Chico, Calif.: Scholars Press, 1982); W. Harrelson. "Wisdom Hidden and Revealed according to Baruch (Baruch 3:9–4:4)." *Priests, Prophets and Scribes.* E. Ulrich et al., eds. JSOTSup 149 (Sheffield: Sheffield Academic Press, 1992); C. A. Moore. *Daniel, Esther, and Jeremiah: The Additions.* AB 44 (Garden City, NY: Doubleday, 1977); A. Saldarini. "The Book of Baruch." NIB (Nashville: Abingdon, 2001); E. Tov. *The Book of Baruch* (Missoula, Mont,: Scholars Press, 1975).

THE LETTER OF JEREMIAH

PATRICIA K. TULL

OVERVIEW

The Letter of Jeremiah, a treatise on the absurdity of idol worship, was originally written in Hebrew, but was passed down from ancient times in Greek translation. In some LXX manuscripts it was placed after Lamentations, but in others it appeared as the final chapter of the book of Baruch.

Modeled on Jer 29:1–23, it purports to be a letter of instruction from Jeremiah to Judahites soon to be exiled to Babylon. As many commentators note, however, it is neither a letter nor is it Jeremiah's. Its date is uncertain, but most scholars place it in the Hellenistic period, no later than 2 Macc 2:1–3, which refers to it. The book expands upon criticisms of idolatry found not only in Jer 10:1–16, but in several chapters of the exilic portion of Isaiah (40:18–20; 42:17; 44:9–20; 45:16–20; 46:1–7) as well as some late Psalms (115:3–8; 135:15–18).

OUTLINE

I. Introduction (6:1–7)

II. The Gods Are Made, Dressed, and Treated Like Human Beings (6:8–16)

III. The Gods Are Powerless to Offer Protection, Even for Themselves (6:17–23)

IV. Humans Have to Care for Them and Carry Them Around (6:24–29)

V. The Gods Can Do Nothing for Their Worshipers (6:30–40a)

VI. Even Their Own Worshipers Dishonor Them and Show Them No Real Reverence (6:40b–44)

VII. Human Hands Made the Gods, and Humans Are Mortal (6:45–52)

VIII. The Gods Do Not Control Nature and Cannot Protect Even Themselves (6:53–56)

IX. Thieves Can Steal or Disfigure the Gods (6:57–65)

X. All Created Things, Even Wild Animals, Have a Purpose, While the Gods Have None (6:66–73)

DETAILED ANALYSIS

In the introduction, Jeremiah explains that the exiles will remain in Babylon up to seven generations (revising the "seventy years" in Jer 29:10), and warns them against fearing the Babylonian gods, which are made of silver, gold, and wood, and are carried about on human shoulders. The rest of the book debunks these gods, using a variety of arguments for their lifelessness and uselessness, as well as for the dishonesty of their priests and the ritually objectionable practices that surround their worship.

The arguments are punctuated by a summarizing refrain that appears at irregular intervals. The first three and final two instances of the refrain exhort: "From this it is evident (or from this you will know, etc.) that they are not gods, so do not fear them." The middle several refrains are formulated as rhetorical questions, such as "Why then must anyone think that they are gods, or call them gods?" Along with implicit negative comparisons with the God portrayed in the OT, the "do not fear" refrains keep the contrast alive between the gods who are too powerless to inspire fear and the invisible God whom they must worship (v. 6). The rhetorical questions invite readers to ponder the evident ignorance of those who fear these gods.

Although the letter calls them "gods" (*theoi*) throughout, and "idols" (*eidola*) only in the final verse (NRSV's wording in vv. 44 and 63 notwithstanding), it is clear that the author follows biblical polemics in equating Babylonian gods with the human-made icons that represent them. Several arguments are mounted against fearing these objects. First, they are made by mortals out of earthly materials, and as such they are perishable: their gold tarnishes, their clothing rots, their hearts are eaten by crawling creatures from the earth. Second, and most prevalently, these gods are powerless. They cannot speak, much less make or depose kings, give wealth, save anyone from death, rescue the weak, restore sight to the blind, answer prayers, provide rain, judge, or deliver. They cannot even take care of themselves: others must keep the dust and tarnish off of them, protect them from thieves, light lamps for them, carry them about, pick them up if they fall, and protect them from harm. Even the weapons in their hands are useless, and they are unaware of the smoke that blackens them and the bats, swallows, birds, and cats that sit upon them. Common household objects such as columns and doors are more useful than these gods. The sun, moon, and elements of nature, though they are not gods themselves, through their obedience to God serve greater purposes than these gods. Even wild animals are better, since they can protect and care for themselves.

As if these arguments are not enough, the writer also impugns the integrity of those who serve them. Priests steal from worshipers by appropriating the gold and silver, sacrificial meat, and clothing offered to the gods, and they do not share with those in need. They also "sit with their clothes torn, their heads and beards shaved, and their heads uncovered," howling and shouting before the gods (vv. 31-32)—several practices foreign and even forbidden (Lev 10:6; 21:5; Ezek 24:17). Ritually unclean women touch the sacrificial meat. Prostitutes compete with one another to solicit sexual partners. From a Judahite perspective, practices surrounding the worship of these gods are ethically and ritually abhorrent.

Although some of the satirical images it conjures up can be amusing, the book has been roundly criticized for its repetitive, sarcastic, and even imperious style. The writer's aim is to render the worship of other gods thoroughly unpalatable and implausible to readers. No attempt is made to understand the foreign practices on their own terms.

While such arguments must have served the social and theological purpose for which they were intended, their intolerant tone would be met with objections today. Though demonstrating detailed knowledge of the mundane aspects of the gods' creation and maintenance, the writing exhibits no interest in worshipers' own understanding of the cult objects' meaning.

Fortunately, contemporary archaeologists are well informed about the initiation rituals of Babylonian idols. According to texts from the library of Ashurbanipal, each image was initiated in an elaborate symbolic ritual in which the craftsmen denied having manufactured it, and it was taken back to its origin as a tree in the forest, so that the god could be created not by human hands but by the deities in heaven, and descend to earth to "participate" in the image, transubstantiating it. While aspects of the care of these cult objects did verge on fetishism, analogies to later Jewish and especially Christian attachments to objects such as Torah scrolls, the eucharistic host, and icons— even the Bible itself—help modern readers understand the extent to which humans rely on inert objects that we can see and touch to bring us into communion with the invisible God.

BIBLIOGRAPHY

T. Jacobsen "The Graven Image." *Ancient Israelite Religion: Essays in Honor of Frank Moore Cross.* P. D. Miller et al, eds. (Philadelphia: Fortress Press, 1987); C. Moore. *Daniel, Esther and Jeremiah: The Additions.* AB 44 (Garden City, NY: Doubleday & Co., 1977); A. J. Saldarini. "The Letter of Jeremiah." *NIB* (Nashville: Abingdon, 2001); P. K. Tull. "The Letter of Jeremiah." *Women's Bible Commentary.* C. A. Newsom and S. H. Ringe, eds. Expanded ed. (Louisville: Westminster John Knox Press, 1998).

THE PRAYER OF AZARIAH

Matthias Henze

OVERVIEW

The apocryphal Prayer of Azariah and the Song of the Three Jews is the first of three extended Additions to the book of Daniel in the Greek and Latin versions of the Bible (the other two are the story of Susanna and the story of Bel and the Dragon). Composed originally in Hebrew, no Semitic source text survives, and, like the other two Additions, the Prayer is now preserved in two Greek versions, the Old Greek (LXX) and the younger Theodotion, which has since replaced the Old Greek in the Bibles of the Roman Catholic and Orthodox Churches. The two Greek versions diverge only slightly from one another, which suggests that they both go back to the same Semitic original.

The Prayer of Azariah and the Song of the Three Jews is inserted into the Aramaic narrative between Dan 3:23 and 3:24 (Dan 3:24–90 in the Greek and Latin Bibles). Daniel 3 tells the story of Daniel's three companions, who refuse to worship a golden statue set up by Nebuchadnezzar in the province of Babylon. In Dan 3:23 the three young men are tied up and thrown into the fiery furnace, and in 3:24–25 the Babylonian king is astounded to see four men, the three companions and an angel, walking freely and unharmed in the flames. The insert in the Greek text bridges the somewhat abrupt transition from Nebuchadnezzar's fury to his astonishment and tells the reader what happened in the furnace. It also shifts the emphasis in Dan 3 from prose narrative to liturgical poetry, and underscores the miraculous nature of the episode.

The Prayer of Azariah and the Song of the Three Jews consists of three parts, the Prayer of Azariah, one of Daniel's three friends (vv. 1–22); a short prose insert, describing the extreme heat of the furnace and explaining the mysterious appearance of the angel (vv. 23–27); and the Song of the Three Jews (vv. 28–68).

OUTLINE

I. The Prayer of Azariah (1–22 [24–45 in the Greek])

II. Prose Interlude (23–27 [46–50 in the Greek])

III. The Song of the Three Jews (28–68 [51–90 in the Greek])

DETAILED ANALYSIS

I. The Prayer of Azariah (1–22 [24–45 in the Greek])

The Prayer begins with a brief narrative introduction (vv. 1–2). As the three young men walk around unharmed in the midst of the flames, Azariah begins to pray and blesses God. The names of Daniel and the three youth, Hananiah, Mishael, and Azariah, were changed to Belteshazzar, Shadrach, Meshach, and Abednego in Dan 1:7, but the Prayer only uses their Hebrew names (vv. 2 and 66). Daniel is conspicuous for his absence from both Dan 3 and the Prayer of Azariah and the Song of the Three Jews.

In form, the Prayer of Azariah is a communal confession of sin, with the community (not Azariah, as the narrative introduction would suggest) as its subject. Such prayers are common in post-exilic literature, and parallels are found in Dan 9:4–19; Ezra 9:6–15; Neh 1:5–11; 9:5–37; and Bar 1:15–3:8. The Prayer closely adopts the covenant theology that was characteristic of its period. It follows deuteronomic theology (see especially Deut 28–32), according to which obedience brings the blessings of the covenant and disobedience its curses. The psalm begins in vv. 3–10 with an affirmation of God's justice. God is just, and his judgment is true. Israel is currently delivered to their enemies and lives under an unjust king. Israel deserves her present plight, however, because the people have broken the law and have not kept the commandments.

586

The prayer proceeds in vv. 11–13 with a plea to God not to abandon Israel or to annul the covenant, for the sake of God's name, and for the sake of God's covenantal promise to Abraham to make him a great nation (v. 13; Gen 15:5). In vv. 14–17, the psalmist continues his plea for mercy. Israel has become the smallest of all nations, without a leader, a prophet, or even the possibility of bringing offerings. In language borrowed from David, the finest biblical poet and model penitent (Pss 51:16–17; 141:2), the psalmist asks that "a contrite heart and a humble spirit" be acceptable to God in place of the sacrifices of lambs and bulls (vv. 14–17). Some modern interpreters assert that the three men not only offer their contrite hearts but their lives to God, as they are ready to die in the fiery furnace so that sacrifice in the Prayer is replaced with martyrdom (Dan 11:33–35), but this ignores the fact that the Prayer was not composed for its present context.

The Prayer of Azariah ends in vv. 18–22 with a prayer of deliverance. The congregation is now ready to seek God's presence and appeals to God to be merciful. Instead of putting them to shame, it is Israel's enemies who deserve to be shamed (Pss 25:3; 40:15). The call in vv. 21–22 for their enemies to be overthrown so that all nations come to realize that the God of Israel alone is God fits well with the present literary context of the Prayer, since the stories in Dan 1–6 frequently end with a doxology from the foreign monarch in praise of the universal sovereignty of the God of Daniel (Dan 2:47; 3:28–29; 4:35–37; 6:26–27; Bel 41).

There are several reasons why the Prayer was most likely not composed for its present context but at some point existed independently and only later was interpolated here. One is its deuteronomic theology with its belief that the people's current affliction is the result of Israel's sin, a theology nowhere to be found in Dan 1–6 (it has a striking parallel in Dan 9:4–19, however). Another reason is that the situation presumed in the Prayer is at odds with the present plight of Azariah. According to the Prayer of Azariah, Israel is currently living among her enemies under a wicked king. The king in question could of course be Nebuchadnezzar, the king in Dan 3, but in Dan 1–4 Nebuchadnezzar's encounter with Daniel in general is rather amicable. The Prayer's implied context fits better the general conditions of the Jews during post-exilic times, particularly during the time of Antiochus Epiphanes in the second century BCE, when the Prayer may have been composed, though this has to remain conjectural. Yet another reason why the Prayer is most likely a secondary insertion is its very form, a communal confession of sin and a petition for mercy, not exactly the kind of prayer one would expect from a youth in the fiery furnace.

II. Prose Interlude (23–27 [46–50 in the Greek])

The Prayer of Azariah and the Song of the Three Jews are bridged by a short prose narrative. The prose section links not only the two psalms but also the Addition as a whole to its narrative context in Dan 3.

Verses 23–25 exaggerate the gigantic proportions of the blaze and relate how the king's servants keep adding more fuel to the fire, including napthta (possibly petroleum, 2 Macc 1:36), pitch, tow, and brushwood. As a result, the flames reach a height of close to 80 feet, or 49 cubits, so that even some of the royal workers are consumed by the fire (Dan 3:22). Verses 26–27 speak of the surprising appearance of the angel, also noticed by Nebuchadnezzar in Dan 3:24–25 (see also Sus 44–45 in the Old Greek). The angel appears in order "to be with Azariah and his companions" and to drive the flames out of the furnace so that the men can survive. His intervention makes the three sing hymns and glorify God.

III. The Song of the Three Jews (28–68 [51–90 in the Greek])

The Song of the Three Jews is a hymn of praise that calls on the entire creation to join in the praise of God, much like Ps 148, which may have inspired its composition. Unlike the Prayer of Azariah, the Song does not presuppose a situation in which the community is persecuted and lives under a wicked king. Apart from an editorial gloss at the end (vv. 66–68), it has nothing in common with Dan 3. The Song of the Three Jews therefore is most likely an independent composition that may well have originated in a context different from the Prayer of Azariah, though given its timeless motifs and the lack of any historical references it is difficult to determine when it was written.

The Song of the Three Jews begins in v. 28 with a brief introduction. Verses 29–34 open the hymn with a sequence of blessings that amount to a majestic doxology in praise of God who is enthroned in the heavenly temple and who is praised by the universe (Pss 96 and 97).

Verses 35–65 are distinct in form, in that each line ends with an identical antiphonal refrain, "sing praise to him and highly exalt him forever," a liturgical form known from Ps 136 in the biblical psalter. This part of the Song can further be subdivided into three roughly parallel sections. Verses 35–51 call on the heavens and all that is in them—angels, waters above the heavens, powers, sun, moon and stars, rain and wind, etc.—to join in the hymn of praising God. Verses 52–60 then turn to the earth and all that is in it—mountains, all that grows on the ground, seas and rivers, whales and all that swim in the waters, etc. The last to be called on to praise God are "all people on earth" (v. 60). The order in which the constituents of creation are listed roughly follows the order of the same groups in the creation account in Gen 1 (also Ps 104). Verses 61–65, finally, presents an appeal to Israel to join in the hymn—Israel, the priests of the Lord, the servants of the Lord, the spirits and souls of the righteous, and those who are holy and humble in heart.

The conclusion of the Song of the Three Jews in vv. 66–68 brings the reader back to the situation that provoked the Song in the first place. The three men call on themselves to exalt God and to thank him for delivering them from the fiery furnace. Verses 67–68 recall Ps 136:1–3. This last section feels somewhat strained. It interrupts the cadence created by the recurring refrain and may well have been added by a redactor who adopted a previously existing hymn and tried to tie it to its new literary context.

The liturgical character of the Prayer of Azariah and the Song of the Three Jews is evident, though we do not know of any employment of either text in the Jewish liturgy. However, the Song of the Three Jews is attested in some Christian hymnals and liturgies, where it is known as the *Benedicite opera omnia.*

BIBLIOGRAPHY

D. Harrington. *Invitation to the Apocrypha* (Grand Rapids: Eerdmans, 1999) 185–206.

SUSANNA

Matthias Henze

OVERVIEW

The apocryphal and popular story of Susanna and the Elders is one of three extended Additions to the book of Daniel in the Greek and Latin versions of the Bible (the other two are the Prayer of Azariah and Bel and the Dragon). The tale is about a devout Jewess in Babylon, who is wrongfully accused of adultery, condemned to death, but vindicated due to Daniel's last-minute intervention. Modern interpreters have found in Susanna the Jewish reworking of a pagan folklore about the wise and righteous protagonist, who is accused and condemned to death but rescued by God and ultimately vindicated (Gen 37–50; *Ahiqar*; Wis 2–5).

Not much is known about the origin of the story. Composed originally in Hebrew, or perhaps in Aramaic, no Semitic source text survives, and, like the other two Additions, the story is now preserved in two Greek versions, the Old Greek/the Septuagint and the younger Theodotion, which has since replaced the Old Greek in the Bibles of the Roman Catholic and Orthodox Churches. In genre and setting, the story of Susanna resembles the legends about Daniel in Dan 1–6 as well as other Jewish novels of the period, such as Esther (including the Greek Additions) and the apocryphal books of Judith and Tobit. The fact that a woman plays a leading role links this book to the books of Esther, Ruth, and Judith, though by comparison Susanna remains surprisingly passive. She is set apart not by her deeds (it is Daniel, after all, who rescues her) but by her piety.

Susanna's date of composition is not known, though the third or second century BCE is likely. The two Greek versions diverge significantly from one another. In the Old Greek, Susanna follows the book of Daniel as the thirteenth chapter together with Bel and the Dragon, whereas Theodotion places Susanna before ch. 1, presumably because Daniel is here called "a young lad" (v. 45). Theodotion is significantly longer than the Old Greek and adds numerous details.

OUTLINE

I. Introduction (1–4)

II. Introduction of the Elders (5–14)

III. The Attempted Seduction of Susanna (15–27)

IV. The Trial (28–43)

V. Divine Intervention (44–64)

DETAILED ANALYSIS

I. Introduction (1–4)

These verses, which are only attested in Theodotion (the Old Greek lacks an introduction), set the scene for the book. Susanna, the daughter of righteous parents, is the wife of Joakim, an eminent Jew living in Babylon. Three of Susanna's attributes are emphasized from the outset, all typical of the Jewish novel and with parallels in related literature, and all essential for the plot of the story: Susanna is "a very beautiful woman" (repeated in v. 31; see Esth 2:7; Tob 6:12; Jdt 8:7–8); she was trained by her parents "according to the law of Moses," which means that she is very pious, even in the face of persecution (Jdt 8:6–8; Dan 3:17); and she is married to a husband of great wealth and social standing, in whose house the Jews gather frequently (Esth 2:15–18; Jdt 8:7).

Unlike the other Jewish novels to which Susanna can be compared—Esther, Dan 1–6, Tobit, Judith—the story of Susanna and the Elders unravels entirely in the Jewish world of the Diaspora community. There is no Gentile king here, no threat to Jewish existence, and no rivalry between the Jewish protagonists and the Gentile court officials. Such a portrayal of a fully autonomous, self-governing, and highly affluent Jewish Diaspora community at the time of the Babylonian exile was probably not intended to be historically accurate. Rather, the story of Susanna wants to delight and entertain the reader. More importantly, by focusing exclusively on the Jewish community, the story teller exposes some of its most precarious shortcomings: in spite of their social standing, the two elderly judges are corrupt; the community's judicial system is defunct; and the same assembly that is quick to condemn Susanna only a few verses later has the elders executed and praises God "who saves those who hope in him" (v. 60).

II. Introduction of the Elders (5–14)

Two of the appointed judges that year, who gather daily in Joakim's house to administer justice, fall in love with Susanna and, without telling anyone, lust after her (Exod 20:17). One day, when they discover their unchecked passion, they conspire how they can find Susanna alone.

The storyteller prefaces his account of the two elders with a derogatory saying, so the reader already anticipates their wicked intentions. The origin of the saying is unknown, though the portrayal of the two scoundrels is remarkably reminiscent of the two false prophets mentioned in Jer 29, which contains a letter sent by Jeremiah to the exiles in Babylon. In it the prophet accuses the two prophets of telling lies and committing adultery with their neighbors' wives (Jer 29:20–23). Earlier in the same chapter of Jeremiah, the prophet encourages the exiles to build houses and plant gardens (Jer 29:4–7), which reinforces the impression that the setting of the story of Susanna presupposes a world similar to that of Jeremiah's letter and may even have been modeled after it.

III. The Attempted Seduction of Susanna (15–27)

The scene is rather terse in the Old Greek. There the elders simply approach Susanna and try to force her into having intercourse with them, with no further description of the circumstances. Only Theodotion has the famous episode of Susanna's bath in the orchard (vv. 15–18), which is well known from artistic and musical depictions of the story.

On a hot day, Susanna takes a bath in the garden. As soon as she sends her two maids away, the two elders, who had been spying on her, seize the opportunity and force her to make a decision: either to have intercourse with them or be accused by them of adultery with a young man. Susanna refuses them, as this would entail "sin[ning] before the Lord" (v. 23), and so she cries out for help.

The erotic element of the bath scene has been compared to the Greek romance. But the first crucial moment in the story is not a scene of sexual pleasure or violence but of theological decision (Gen 39:9). Being raised according to the Law of Moses (v. 3), Susanna knows that the punishment for adultery is death (Lev 20:10; Deut 22:22)—though her wording suggests that it is not death she fears but sin against God, another indication of her piety. Susanna cries out "with a loud voice" (v. 24), which in and of itself is an affirmation of her innocence (Deut 22:24); and at once the elders too begin to shout, though not out of innocence, but, as the text puts it, "against her." When help rushes in, it is only the elders who tell their fabricated version of the story.

IV. The Trial (28–43)

The next day during the gathering of the community, the elders bring their case against Susanna and again tell their story. The narrator leaves no doubt about their true intentions and again introduces the scene with a derogatory remark, the elders came to Joakim's house "to have Susanna put to death" (v. 28). The scoundrels claim that, when they perchance witnessed Susanna's sexual encounter with an unidentified young man in the garden, they rushed to the scene, yet found themselves unable to restrain the young man because he was stronger than they. However, they were able to seize "this woman" (v. 40), who refused to tell them who the young man was. Since they are elders of the people and judges, their testimony is well received by the assembly, and Susanna is promptly condemned to death. Once again Susanna cries out "with a loud voice" (v. 42), though this time in prayer (vv. 42–43). The prayer is not a prayer for intercession, as is sometimes asserted (Susanna does not ask God to intercede), but another affirmation of Susanna's innocence. Susanna chooses to defend herself against the twisted accusations of the elders, not by addressing the elders directly or, for that matter, by bringing her plea before the assembly that just condemned her. Instead, she says a prayer before God, the supreme Judge (Jdt 9:2–14; Add Esth 14:3–19). Since God knows all secret things, she prays, God surely knows that Susanna is innocent. Before she prays, Susanna "looked up toward Heaven" (v. 35), which recalls the earlier description of the two lecherous elders, who, overcome by their lust, "turned away their eyes from looking to Heaven" (v. 9). The contrast between them could not be starker.

The scene of the trial differs in the two Greek versions. The Old Greek specifies, for example, that Susanna came to her trial together with her parents, four children, and five hundred maids. In the Old Greek, the elders demand that Susanna be stripped naked in front of the assembly, "in order that they could be sated with lust for her beauty" (v. 32 author's trans.; see Ezek 16:37–39; Hos 2:3; m. Sotah 1:5–6), while Theodotion inserts the phrase, "for she was veiled" (v. 32), implying that Susanna merely had to take off her veil to expose her face. In the Old Greek, Susanna prays before the elders testify against her, whereas in Theodotion her prayer comes after the accusations.

As the elders get ready to deliver their arraignment, they lay their hands on Susanna's head. The gesture carries a wide range of meanings in the Jewish Bible, and its meaning here is not clear. This is the only explicit bodily contact between the seducers and Susanna, though it is also possible that the gesture follows an ancient rite, according to which witnesses lay their hands on the victim's head in a capital case before the punishment is carried out (Lev 24:14); two witnesses are required for a capital punishment (Deut 17:6; 19:15).

V. Divine Intervention (44–64)

Susanna is vindicated. Just as Susanna is being led to her execution, God stirs up the holy spirit in Daniel (in the Old Greek an angel gives Daniel a spirit of understanding), and so it is now Daniel who shouts "with a loud voice" (v. 46), rebuking the assembly for not having cross-examined the elders properly on their false testimony. The community leaders quickly realize that "God has given [Daniel] the right of an elder" (v. 50 author trans.). Daniel separates the two judges and interrogates them independently (Deut 19:15–21). Each questioning consists of two parts: Daniel first denounces each of the elders for his lifelong perversion of justice and effectively convicts him prior to the interrogation, but then proceeds to ask him under

which tree the purported sexual encounter took place. Each gives a different location, and so their perjury is quickly exposed. Each interrogation has a certain comic effect and revolves around a pun: the name of each tree anticipates the elder's punishment. It has been suggested that the Greek wordplay proves that the story of Susanna was originally composed in Greek, but this ignores the possibility that the Greek translator introduced the pun into the story. The punishment of the elders corresponds to the punishment they had intended for Susanna, they are executed in her stead (Dan 6:24; Bel 22, 42; Esth 7:10). Modern interpreters often point to Deut 19:16–21, which stipulates that one shall do to the false witness as he intended to do to the wrongly accused. By the time of the Mishnah, i.e. about four or five centuries after Susanna was written, the ways of dealing with false witnesses had been much mitigated, and the witnesses would hardly have been executed (m. Mak 1:1; m. Sanh 5:1–2).

The two Greek versions end on different notes. The Old Greek ends in praise of the youth and with the admonition, "let us watch out for young able sons" (v. 62), whereas Theodotion concludes with a praise of Daniel, who became great from that day onward.

BIBLIOGRAPHY

J. J. Collins. *Daniel*. Hermeneia (Minneapolis: Fortress, 1993); E. S. Gruen. *Heritage and Hellenism* (Berkeley: University of California Press, 1998); C. A. Moore. *Daniel, Esther and Jeremiah: The Additions* (New York: Doubleday, 1977).

BEL AND THE DRAGON

MATTHIAS HENZE

OVERVIEW

The apocryphal story Bel and the Dragon is the last of three extended Additions to the book of Daniel in the Greek and Latin versions of the Bible (the other two are the Prayer of Azariah and the story of Susanna). Bel and the Dragon consists of two, roughly parallel tales. In the first (vv. 1–22), Daniel uncovers the fraud of the Babylonian priests of Bel, who secretly consume the daily food rations prepared for their idol while claiming that it was Bel who ate them. In the second tale (vv. 23–42), Daniel kills a large serpent that is worshiped by the Babylonians. Daniel is then thrown into the lions' den but survives miraculously, while the prophet Habakkuk provides him with food.

The two tales may well have originated independently (in the Old Greek the king remains anonymous; in Theodotion the king of the first tale is Cyrus the Persian, whereas in the second episode he remains nameless), yet in their present form they are woven into a single story by a number of elements: the central topic of both tales is the satirical polemic against idols and idolatry, a prominent theme in exilic and post-exilic literature (Isa 40:18–41:7; 44:9–20; 46:1; Wis 13:1–15:17; Ep Jer; *Apoc. Ab.* 1–8; *Jub.* 12:2–5; 20:8–9); both tales draw a sharp contrast between the worship of idols and Jewish monotheism, insisting that only Daniel worships "the living God" (v. 25) besides whom there is no other God (v. 41; Isa 45:5–6); and the tales are linked by the motif of food, which Bel cannot consume, which promptly destroys the giant serpent, and which Daniel receives from Habakkuk.

The original language of Bel and the Dragon is unknown, though Hebrew, or perhaps Aramaic, seem most likely. No Semitic original survives, however, and, like the Prayer of Azariah and the story of Susanna, Bel and the Dragon is preserved in two Greek versions, where it is placed at the end of the book of Daniel. The Greek versions are the Old Greek (the Septuagint) and Theodotion, which has replaced the Old Greek in the Bibles of the Roman Catholic and Orthodox Churches. The date of composition is likewise unknown,

with most scholars proposing the third or second century BCE.

OUTLINE

I. Introduction (1–2)

II. Daniel Exposes the Fraud of the Babylonian Priests (3–22)

III. Daniel Kills the Serpent (23–27)

IV. Daniel in the Lions' Den (28–32)

V. The Prophet Habakkuk feeds Daniel (33–42)

DETAILED ANALYSIS

I. Introduction (1–2)

Both versions introduce the story rather differently. The Old Greek begins in v. 1, "From a prophecy of Habakkuk,"[1] thereby attributing Bel and the Dragon to the corpus of texts associated with the prophet Habakkuk; even though the two tales were originally independent, the superscription treats them as a unit. Verse 2 introduces Daniel as if he was unknown to the reader, "There was a certain person, a priest, whose name was Daniel." The verse then continues to speak of Daniel as "a companion of the king of Babylon," suggesting that the king in Bel and the Dragon is a Babylonian king. Theodotion, by contrast, begins in v. 1 with a superscription that is modeled after the prophetic books of the Bible, "And King Astyages was added to his ancestors, and Cyrus the Persian received his kingdom." According to Theodotion, then, the king of Bel and the Dragon is the Persian King Cyrus. In 550 BCE, Cyrus dethroned Astyages (585–550 BCE), the last king of Media. Here Bel and the Dragon differs form the book of Daniel,

---

[1] Unless otherwise indicated by NRSV, the quotations from Bel and the Dragon are direct translations by the author.

where Cyrus replaced an otherwise unknown "Darius the Mede" (Dan 5:31; 6:28).

II. Daniel Exposes the Fraud of the Babylonian Priests (3–22)

The Babylonians worship the god Bel, whom they serve daily with lavish portions of flour, sheep, and wine. Confronted by King Cyrus about why he does not join in the worship, Daniel replies that he only reveres his God, the creator of heaven and earth, not "idols made with hands" (v. 5; Jdt 8:18). Thereupon the king confronts the priests with an intimidating proposition: unless they tell him who eats the provisions they will die, but if Bel is eating them, Daniel shall die (vv. 8–9). One evening, when Bel is again brought his food rations, Daniel has ashes scattered secretly on the floor of the whole shrine. When the king returns early the next morning, the food is gone and the king rejoices. But Daniel points to the traces on the floor, whereupon the king has to concede that he has been tricked, and the seventy priests of Bel reveal the hidden door through which they used to enter at night to consume the food. In the Old Greek version, their fate remains unclear, and the king destroys Bel, whereas in Theodotion the king puts the priests to death together with their families, as he had previously ordained (vv. 8–9), and delivers Bel into the hand of Daniel, who destroys both the idol and his temple.

This brief episode is a fine example of an idol parody. The idol in question is Bel (meaning "lord"), the Akkadian pendant to the Canaanite god Baal. In Babylon, the same deity is known as Marduk, or Merodach (Isa 46:1; Jer 50:2; 51:44). Herodotus (*History* 1.183) describes a massive statue of solid gold, sitting at a golden table on a golden chair in a temple in the center of Babylon, which still received offerings in the days of Cyrus and was later destroyed by Xerxes. Daniel shows no sympathy for Bel and ridicules the idol, which, in his words, merely has "clay inside and bronze outside" (v. 7; Dan 2:33), a phrase reminiscent of the idol polemic in Isa 40:18–20. The God of Daniel, who alone is the living God, emerges the clear winner. But Bel is not the only looser in this story; the Gentile king is likewise portrayed in a less than favorable light. Cyrus comes across as gullible and easily manipulated. In fact, Daniel outright laughs at him twice in this short episode,

first after the king claimed that Bel is truly a living god, since he consumes the food he is served (v. 7), and then again when the king sees the food gone and hastily proclaims that "there is no deceit" in Bel (v. 17–19)—only to discover, of course, that he had been deceived all along by the priests. Thus, both Bel *and* the Gentile monarch become the target of our author's penetrating ridicule (1 Esd 3–4).

III. Daniel Kills the Serpent (23–27)

The second tale begins somewhat abruptly, without any transition. It can be further subdivided into three scenes: Daniel blows up the serpent (vv. 23–27); Daniel survives in the lions' den (vv. 28–32); and Daniel receives food from the prophet Habakkuk and is vindicated (vv. 33–42).

The key phrase in the first of the three scenes, like in the previous one, is "living god" (in Theodotion). The king (he remains anonymous from now on, though interpreters generally assume that he is still Cyrus) points to a giant snake revered by the Babylonians as a god and challenges Daniel. Since this one plainly does consume food, Daniel won't be able to claim that "this is not a living god" (v. 24). Daniel, once again unimpressed, counters that only his God is a "living God" (v. 25) and asks for permission to kill the dragon without the aid of a weapon. As soon as the king agrees, Daniel boils together pitch, fat and hair into a cake and feeds it to the serpent, which promptly bursts open. The episode ends when Daniel exclaims, not without a little *Schadenfreude*, "See your objects of reverence!" (v. 27).

The serpent as a deity has deep roots in the ancient Near East. In the Babylonian creation myth *Enuma Elish*, Bel/Marduk, the chief deity of Babylon, is said to have vanquished Tiamat, the embodiment of primordial chaos. Remnants of the motif of the serpent as a mythological monster are found in the Hebrew Bible (Job 7:12; Pss 74:13–14; 104:26; Isa 27:1).

Some interpreters have suggested that Bel and the Dragon is drawn in part from Isaiah 45–46: there the God of Israel speaks to Cyrus too (45:1–3); there is not other god besides the God of Israel (45:5–6), who is the creator (45:18); and Isaiah 46:1 opens with the words, "Bel has fallen!" (LXX)—all *theologumena* with close parallels in Bel and the Dragon. Other interpreters have pointed to Jer 51:34–35, where the inhabitants of Zion mourn their own defeat by King Nebuchadnezzar by comparing the Babylonian tyrant to a monster, who "has filled his belly with my delicacies" (Jer 51:34). There is, of course, no reason why Bel and the Dragon can't have been inspired by more than one motif or text. The reader is struck, above all, by the lightheartedness and humor of Bel and the Dragon, which is completely absent from any of the alleged biblical base texts such as Job, Isaiah, and Jeremiah.

IV. Daniel in the Lions' Den (28–32)

Greatly outraged by what Daniel has done to their god, the Babylonians conspire and now turn against the monarch. The destruction of their god is for them a clear sign that the Gentile king has become a Jew. Threatening to kill the king, they demand that Daniel be delivered into their hands. The monarch is compelled to comply, and they throw Daniel into the lions' den. The Old Greek adds, not without irony, that the pit was intended for the king's conspirators, and that Daniel was thrown to the lions in order to deprive him of "the good fortune of a burial" (v. 32).

The accusation that the Gentile king has become a Jew is reminiscent of the story in 2 Macc 9:17, in which Antiochus Epiphanes promises to convert to Judaism, if the God of Israel cured him of his affliction (Jdt 14:10; Dan 4).

Bel and the Dragon has some obvious affinities with Daniel 6: both have as their central motif the lions' den; both are legends set at the court of a foreign monarch; in both stories the king's signet ring is instrumental (vv. 14 and 17); and both stories end with the death of the accusers and their families. Bel and the Dragon and Dan 6 have therefore been called 'variations' or 'duplicate narratives' of the same story, with Bel and the Dragon the more developed of the two narratives. But we should be careful not to exaggerate the similarities, nor do the parallels imply that one version developed out of the other. Neither story shows clear signs that it depends on the other.

V. The Prophet Habakkuk Feeds Daniel (33–42)

An angel appears to Habakkuk in Judea and tells him to take the food he has just prepared to Daniel in Babylon. When the prophet responds that he doesn't know the place, the angel transports him "by the hair of his head" (v. 36) straight to the lions' den (Ezek 8:3). The king arrives at the den on the seventh day, rejoices to find Daniel unharmed, pulls him out, and has the villains thrown into the den instead, who are devoured at once.

The Habakkuk scene begins abruptly and may well be an interpolation. Its main connection with Bel and the Dragon is the subject of food. There are more affinities with Daniel 6 here: Daniel's confession in v. 38, for example, that God has not forgotten him (Dan 6:22), and the reversal of fortunes in vv. 40–42 (Dan 6:24).

Bel and the Dragon concludes with the king's solemn acclamation of the uniqueness of Daniel's God, "You are great, O Lord, the God of Daniel, and there is no other beside you" (v. 41; Isa 45:3–5). Similar doxologies are found in the book of Daniel (Dan 2:47; 3:28–29; 4:34–37; 6:26–27). The story as a whole thus has the ending of a conversion story.

BIBLIOGRAPHY

J. J. Collins. *Daniel.* Hermeneia (Minneapolis: Fortress, 1993); E. S. Gruen. *Heritage and Hellenism* (Berkeley: University of California Press, 1998); C. A. Moore. *Daniel, Esther and Jeremiah: The Additions* (New York: Doubleday, 1977); G. W. E. Nickelsburg. *Jewish Literature between the Bible and the Mishnah.* 2nd ed. (Minneapolis: Fortress Press, 2005).

1 MACCABEES

JOHN B. F. MILLER

OVERVIEW

First Maccabees is one of the most important primary sources for a fascinating period in Jewish history. It describes the Maccabean revolt and the initial stage of its aftermath: a brief period of Judean independence in an epoch otherwise marked by foreign rule under the Babylonians, Persians, Macedonians, and finally the Romans. This is a text that helps one understand what Jews in the time of Jesus may have been hoping for in their expectations of the long-awaited Messiah. The freedom and autonomy enjoyed during this brief period of independence (142–63 BCE) loomed large in the historical memory of some Jews suffering under the yoke of Roman rule in the first century CE (see, for example, Josephus, *J.W.* 7.253–55).

The text receives its title from the nickname of one of its principal figures, Judas Maccabeus; similarly, Hasmoneus is mentioned by Josephus as an ancestor of Judas's father, Mattathias (*Ant.* 12.265). Thus, Maccabean and Hasmonean have come to be used as terms describing the family and political dynasty that lie at the center of 1 Maccabees even though neither adjective appears in the text itself. The precise meaning of "Maccabeus" remains a matter of debate; some have suggested that one possible meaning, "Hammer," is a descriptive reference to Judas's physical appearance or personality

Focusing on the period from 169 BCE to 134 BCE, 1 Maccabees describes the following: a persecution of observant Jews during the reign of the Seleucid ruler Antiochus IV Epiphanes; the response to that persecution, now known as the Maccabean revolt, under the leadership of a priest named Mattathias; the exploits of Mattathias's sons (especially Judas, Jonathan, and Simon) in an ongoing struggle with Seleucid rulers; the initial stages of a period of Judean independence under Mattathias's last surviving son, Simon; and the beginning of the reign of Simon's son, John Hyrcanus. There is general agreement among scholars that 1 Maccabees functions propagandistically as a pro-Hasmonean version of the period of history it describes.

First Maccabees was probably written shortly before or after the death of John Hyrcanus (104 BCE). Although scholars agree that the text was composed originally in Hebrew, the earliest extant version is in Greek. There are also texts bearing the titles 2, 3, and 4 Maccabees, but they do not share the same author. First Maccabees offers significant details concerning the early stages of the Maccabean revolt—events that figure prominently in Dan 7–12. The style of presentation bears strong similarities to biblical "histories" (e.g., 1–2 Samuel). Indeed, the author of 1 Maccabees frequently connects events described in the text with God's saving acts at earlier points in Israel's history. The absence of divine intervention and miracles in the text is, therefore, striking. Scholars have commented frequently on the writer's familiarity with the geography of the region; reading this text with a map at hand will illuminate the experience considerably.

OUTLINE

I. Persecution of Israel under Antiochus IV Epiphanes (1:1–64)

    A. Alexander the Great and the Diadochi (1:1–9)

    B. The Rise and Corruption of Antiochus IV Epiphanes (1:10–64)

II. Rebellion of Mattathias (2:1–70)

    A. Mattathias Laments and Refuses to Acquiesce (2:1–27)

    B. The Uprising (2:28–70)

III. Leadership of Judas Maccabeus (3:1–9:22)

    A. Judas Defends Judea Against Retaliatory Attacks and Cleanses the Temple (3:1–4:61)

    B. Judas Attacks Territories Outside of Judea and Brings Jews to Safety (5:1–68)

    C. Death of Antiochus IV Epiphanes and Succession of Antiochus V Eupator (6:1–17)

DETAILED ANALYSIS

I. Persecution of Israel under Antiochus IV Epiphanes (1:1–64)

A. Alexander the Great and the Diadochi (1:1–9)

1:1–4. Alexander Establishes His Kingdom. Alexander ascended to the Macedonian throne in 336 BCE. In just over twelve years, he amassed one of the largest empires the world had ever known; it extended from Macedonia and Greece to the western regions of India. Compared to other Jewish writers (e.g., Dan 7:7, 23), the author of 1 Maccabees describes Alexander in somewhat neutral terms. More severe judgment is reserved for Alexander's successors, who "caused many evils on the earth" (1:9).

1:5–9. Alexander Establishes Generals as His Successors and Dies. Alexander died young, lacking a legitimate heir. In this power vacuum, Alexander's generals (often referred to as the Diadochi, "successors") carved up his empire; he did not divide the empire among his generals, as 1:6 suggests. The two who took the most territory, and who were of greatest concern for the history of Judea, were Ptolemy and Seleucus. Ptolemy took Egypt; Seleucus took the eastern portion of Alexander's empire. Both Ptolemy and Seleucus had designs on the other's territory. Because it lay between these two kingdoms, Judea and the surrounding region was regarded by both as an important buffer zone and staging area from which to launch attacks on the other. During one such campaign, dating roughly from 200–198 BCE, Antiochus III (the Great) wrested control of Judea from the Ptolemaic kingdom. Judea then remained under Seleucid control until the events described in 1 Macc 13.

B. The Rise and Corruption of Antiochus IV Epiphanes (1:10–64)

1:10–15. Antiochus's Rise to Power and Collusion of "Renegades" in Israel. Time was designated in antiquity according to the reign of a particular ruler, or the number of years since a particular kingdom had been established. The "kingdom of the Greeks" (1:10) is a reference to the establishment of the Seleucid kingdom. Converting the dates given in 1 Maccabees into our own chronological standard is complicated by two factors. First, there are disagreements in the source material as to when precisely the "kingdom of the Greeks" began. Some suggest the equivalent of 312 BCE, others the equivalent of 311 BCE. Second, people in the eastern portion of the Seleucid kingdom observed the new year in spring, while those in the western portion observed it in autumn. The dates provided in the present discussion, therefore, should be read as commonly accepted approximations.

Antiochus IV usurped the Seleucid throne in 175 BCE, and had grand designs for expanding his kingdom. Helpful for this endeavor were pro-Hellenistic Judeans (i.e., Jews who were more concerned with assimilating into Hellenistic culture, and less concerned with observing Torah, which required a degree of separation from certain aspects of Hellenistic culture). 1 Maccabees 1:11 refers to such Jews as "renegades" (*paranomoi* literally means "one who acts contrary to the law"). The author does not dwell on the political machinations of these "renegades," whose exploits are described in 2 Macc 4–5.

1:16–19. Antiochus's Successful Military Incursion into Egypt. With Judea more securely allied to his cause, Antiochus launched a successful campaign into Egypt in 170 BCE. Antiochus's forces took much of lower Egypt, with the exception of Alexandria, and Antiochus briefly controlled this territory using his nephew, Ptolemy VI Philometor, as a puppet ruler.

1:20–40. Antiochus Robs the Temple of Jerusalem and Establishes the Citadel. Temple-robbing was a tempting endeavor for the successors of Alexander. It was a relatively quick, albeit dangerous, way to acquire funds. Antiochus's own father, Antiochus III, died attempting to rob a temple in 187 BCE.

Antiochus's forces fortified an area near the Temple and garrisoned "renegade" Jews there in 167 BCE (1:33–34). Referred to more than two dozen times in 1 Maccabees, this "citadel" became a lasting point of contention. Despite the many victories of Judas Maccabeus and his brothers, the citadel was held by Seleucid forces until 141 BCE (see 1 Macc 13:49–51). The exact location of the citadel continues to be a matter of debate.

1:41–64. Antiochus Attempts to Compel Jews to Forsake Their Religious Customs. According to 1 Maccabees, the final straw leading to the Maccabean revolt is an ever-intensifying environment of religious persecution. Although religious persecution is mentioned from time to time in Jewish Scripture (e.g., Esth 3–9), it was rare in the Hellenistic period. Tolerant polytheism was the general rule for the Macedonians. Josephus, for example, describes an edict from Antiochus III that granted Jews the freedom to observe their ancestral religion (*Ant.* 12.142). Oddly, 1 Maccabees ascribes no particular motivation for Antiochus IV to overturn such a decree, nor does it ascribe a significant motive for the persecution that ensues. Indeed, despite the straightforward manner in which 1 Maccabees presents a causal relationship between Antiochus's persecution and the Jewish revolt against that persecution, there are reasons to suspect a different sequence of events. Many scholars are more convinced that Antiochus's persecution was an attempt to restore order during a period of infighting between differing Jewish factions (see earlier comment on "renegades" in 1:10–15).

II. Rebellion of Mattathias (2:1–70)

A. Mattathias Laments and Refuses to Acquiesce (2:1–27)

2:1–14. Mattathias's Lament. The general tone of Mattathias's lament is similar to that found in a number of biblical passages. See, for example, the reference to the "destruction of my people" in Lam 2:11.

2:15–27. Mattathias's Initial Clash with the Officers of Antiochus. The explicit comparison drawn between Mattathias's and Phinehas's respective acts of zeal (see Num 25) invites a comparison of the more implicit similarities between the two. Both are of priestly lineage (Num 25:7; 1 Macc 2:1), and both kill an Israelite/Jew who is in collusion with worshipers of false gods (Num 25:8; 1 Macc 2:24–25). The implied connection pertains to the results of their zeal. Phinehas's act pleased the Lord so much that the Lord granted Phinehas a covenant of peace and perpetual priesthood (Num 25:11–13). Thus, the author of 1 Maccabees creates a sense of legitimacy for the way in which Mattathias's sons will ultimately be granted the position of high priest later in this narrative (see 1 Macc 10:20). Although 1 Maccabees is silent on the subject, there was significant Jewish opposition to the Maccabean high priesthood. Scholars have argued convincingly, for example, that it was a reaction against the high priesthood of Jonathan or Simon that led some Jews to establish a religious community at Qumran—a community that would be responsible ultimately for the Dead Sea Scrolls.

B. The Uprising (2:28–70)

2:28–41. Flight into the Wilderness and the Question of Fighting on the Sabbath. Even defending oneself was regarded by some Jews as profaning the Sabbath (cf. 2 Macc 6:11). The decision of Mattathias and his followers to defend themselves against attack even on the Sabbath is vindicated later in the narrative (see 1 Macc 9:43–49).

2:42–48. Mattathias and Hasideans Form an Army and Begin a Rebellion. The "Hasideans" are a group of pious Jews who initially join Mattathias's revolt. Some scholars have argued that this was a sect within Judaism that would eventually become known as the Pharisees.

2:49–70. Testament of Mattathias. The testament of a patriarchal figure on the verge of death is common (see, for example, Gen 49). The individuals selected in Mattathias's final exhortation are remarkable primarily for their willingness to keep the commandments of the Lord even in the face of death.

III. Leadership of Judas Maccabeus (3:1–9:22)

A. Judas Defends Judea Against Retaliatory Attacks and Cleanses the Temple (3:1–4:61)

3:1–9. Heroic Depiction of Judas. In these verses Judas takes on an almost mythical dimension. Note, for example, the term *giant*, which is used of

the Nephilim in LXX Gen 6:4, and of the Anakim (i.e., the "giants" in the promised land) in LXX Num 13:33. This poem also contains other biblical allusions, including the turning away of God's "anger from Israel" in v. 8. The same language is used in Num 25:4, introducing the story of Phinehas's zeal (see comment above on 2:15–27).

3:10-4:35. Judas Secures Judea. The author of 1 Maccabees never uses the words "God" or "Lord" to refer to the God of Israel, but instead prefers the more reverent circumlocution "Heaven" (see 1 Macc 3:18, 19, 50, 60,; 4:10, 24, :40, 55; 5:31; 9:46; 12:15; 16:3). This is very similar to the language found in the Gospel of Matthew (e.g., "kingdom of heaven," Matt 5:3 and *passim*).

One finds the author's first extended depiction of a cultic ritual sandwiched between accounts of Judas battling Apollonius, Seron, Gorgias, and Lysias (1 Macc 3:42–53). Since the Temple has been profaned, Judas and his followers go to Mizpah to entreat the help of "Heaven." This passage is an unmistakable allusion to 1 Sam 7, which describes the Israelites at Mizpah before they engaged the Philistines in battle. Language of the "sanctuary" being "trampled" is allusive as well: Isa 63:18 makes a similar reference to the Temple in an entreaty for the Lord to avenge Israel against its enemies. It is important to notice both that Judas and his followers are invoking God's assistance, and that the depiction of this invocation draws heavily on earlier accounts of God's saving acts in the history of Israel.

4:36–61. Judas Cleanses the Temple and Dedicates the New Altar. The peculiar reference to a "prophet" who might come "to tell what to do with" the profaned altar stones alludes to references in Deut 18:15, 18 of God raising up a prophet like Moses. A similar reference is made in 1 Macc 14:41 as part of the author's attempt to legitimize the Maccabean high priesthood (see also the comment above on 2:15–27).

The narrative presents the celebration of dedication taking place three years to the day (25 Chislev 167–25 Chislev 164) after the Gentiles profaned the altar by offering sacrifice on it (1 Macc 1:54–59; 4:52–54). The dedication of this new altar in the Temple is to be celebrated for eight days each year. This marks the inception of the Jewish festival of Hanukkah.

B. Judas Attacks Territories Outside of Judea and Brings Jews to Safety (5:1–68)

This portion of the narrative makes explicit what has been a pervasive implication in 1 Macc 2–4: Mattathias and his sons are specially designated to bring deliverance to Israel (see comment above on 2:15–27 and compare 5:61–62). It is because they do not share this familial distinction that Joseph and Azariah are said to be defeated in battle (5:60–61). Furthermore, the narrative clearly indicates that Judas is not merely fighting for the sake of territory, but to cleanse the land of pagan worship (see, for example, 5:44, 68; cf. the similar actions of Mattathias in 2:45, and see Exod 34:13 and Deut 7:5).

C. Death of Antiochus IV Epiphanes and Succession of Antiochus V Eupator (6:1–17)

The claim that Antiochus's death was a direct result of his disappointment and worry over the wrongs he did to the Jews (6:8–13) is a tendentious fabrication. The historian Polybius states that Antiochus IV was repelled in his attempt to rob the temple of Artemis in Elymais. Antiochus retreated and died at Tabae in Persia. Interestingly, people of that region also claimed that Antiochus was struck down by a divinity, only they claimed it was Artemis (*Histories* 31.9).

Antiochus V Eupator was still a young boy at the time of succession. Real power lay in the hands of his guardian, Lysias.

D. Encounters at Beth-zur and Beth-zechariah (6:18–63)

6:18–27. Judas Assails the Citadel, and the Besieged Appeal to Antiochus V Eupator. As one reads about Mattathias's and Judas's military feats within Judea in the early chapters of 1 Maccabees, it can be easy to forget about the citadel near the Temple in Jerusalem and the Seleucid forces and renegade Jews who continue to occupy it. Brief references in the text, however, indicate it was a perpetual source of danger (1 Macc 1:33, 36; 3:45; 4:2, 41; 6:18, 20, 24, 26, 32; 9:52–53; 10:6–7, 9, 32; 11:20–21, 41; 12:36; 13:21).

6:28–46. Battles at Beth-zur and Beth-zechariah, and the Death of Eleazar. Aside from being noted as sons of Mattathias in 2:2–5, Eleazar and John are mentioned only in their respective deaths

(6:45–46 and 9:36). Despite the fact that his sacrifice did not bear the fruit he had hoped, Eleazar is depicted as one who gave his life "to save his people" (6:44); similar language of "saving Israel" is used to describe Judas after his death in 9:21.

6:47–63. Lysias Routs the Forces of Judas, but then Persuades Antiochus V Eupator to Return to Antioch. The rescue of fellow Jews described in 1 Macc 5 now threatens the safety of Judas and his followers in Judea. Lysias's siege being executed during a sabbatical year for the Judean farmlands, combined with the significant influx of refugees, creates a food shortage. For a brief moment, the Maccabean revolt seems to be in grave jeopardy. The circumstances described in 6:47–61, however, presage events that will lead ultimately to Judean independence. Despite the advantage of superior numbers and the very real potential to crush Judas and his followers, Lysias must counsel Eupator to make terms quickly so that they can turn their attention to internal political threats within the Seleucid government at Antioch. Through various savvy political alliances with competitors for the Seleucid throne, Jonathan and Simon will win eventual autonomy for Judea (see 11:30–37 and 13:31–53).

E. Coup of Demetrius and New Internal Struggles Within Judea (7:1–50)

7:1–20. Demetrius Usurps Seleucid Throne and Appoints Alcimus as High Priest. This passage marks the first time the author of 1 Maccabees addresses the significance of Seleucid appointments to the high priesthood. The position of high priest was paramount from the time of the Persian empire to the Seleucid reign: during this period of occupation and foreign rule, the high priest in Jerusalem was both the highest religious authority and highest civic authority in the area (see, for example, 1 Macc 7:20).

The author of 1 Maccabees, who only rarely offers direct quotations or paraphrases of Jewish Scripture, suggests in vv. 16–17 that the actions of Alcimus were "in accordance with" the words of Ps 79:2–3. Not surprisingly, this psalm invokes God's wrath on those who have harmed Israel.

7:21–50. Judas Exacts Vengeance on Alcimus and Defeats Nicanor. When Demetrius sends Nicanor to exact retribution for the expulsion of Alcimus, both the Temple priests (7:36–37; cf.

1 Kgs 8:20 and Isa 56:7) and Judas (7:41–42; cf. 2 Kgs 19:35) offer invective prayers reminiscent of those in earlier Jewish Scripture entreating God's help in battle.

F. Fame of Rome and Judas's Alliance with the Romans (8:1–32)

The narrative space devoted to an overwhelmingly positive depiction of Rome (8:1–16), and Judas's subsequent success creating an alliance with this western power (8:17–32), strikes a note of tragic irony; in 63 BCE, it will be the Romans who bring an end to the Judean independence that 1 Maccabees celebrates.

G. Judas Dies in Battle Against Demetrius's Commander, Bacchides (9:1–22)

First Maccabees 9:22 offers a striking play on statements found in 2 Kings and 2 Chronicles. In those texts, it is customary to conclude the description of a figure with a statement about where the rest of the individual's deeds are recorded (see, for example, 2 Kgs 14:18; 15:11, 15, 21, 26; 20:20; 24:5; and 2 Chr 13:22; 25:26; 32:32). Instead, the author of 1 Maccabees states that other deeds of Judas "were not recorded because they were so numerous" (author's trans.).

IV. Leadership of Jonathan (9:23–12:48)

A. Distress in Judea and the Selection of Jonathan (9:23–31)

As problems of famine continue (see comment above on 6:47–63), the situation in Judea turns from bad to worse in the absence of Judas's leadership. "Renegades" (see comment on 1:10–15 above) are once again powerful and "the country went over to their side" (9:24), a shift the author attributes to the famine rather than to a lack of faith. "Since the time that prophets ceased to appear among them" (9:27) refers to the belief that Haggai, Zechariah, and Malachi were the last of the prophets.

B. Jonathan's Battle Against, and Eventual Treaty with, Bacchides (9:32–73)

In 159 BCE, Alcimus attempts to remove the wall separating the inner court of the sanctuary. Precisely what this means is unclear and remains a subject of debate. In any case, he is prevented from completing this outrage by a paralyzing illness. The narrative does not state that God struck Alcimus down, but such is implied.

Following the failed plot of the "renegades," described in 1 Macc 9:58–69, Jonathan is able to create a treaty with the retreating Bacchides—a treaty that leads to five years of peace for Jonathan and his forces in Judea. This marks the first of several treaties or alliances that Jonathan will create during his period of leadership.

C. Jonathan Exploits the Rivalry Between Demetrius and Alexander Epiphanes (10:1–66)

10:1–47. Respective Offers of Alexander Epiphanes and Demetrius. In 152 BCE, another claimant to the Seleucid throne, Alexander Epiphanes (referred to in other sources as Alexander I Balas), son of Antiochus IV Epiphanes, challenged the rule of Demetrius. In return for Jonathan's loyalty, Alexander offers Jonathan the office of high priest, which Jonathan accepts. (On the significance of this position in terms of both religious and civic authority, see earlier comment on 7:1–20.) Wanting the help of Judea, Demetrius makes an even more elaborate offer. Jonathan does not trust Demetrius (10:46), but the terms of his offered alliance (10:27–45) illuminate the Judeans' situation under Seleucid rule. Very high taxes on produce (10:30), other taxes and tributes (10:29–33), and confiscation of personal property (10:43) were regular burdens on the Judeans.

10:48–66. Jonathan Honored by Alexander Epiphanes. Although the benefits bestowed on Jonathan by Alexander will be challenged soon enough, this event marks a significant step in the road to Judean independence: Jonathan is made a "Friend" of the king and a legitimate "governor" of his province (10:65).

D. Demetrius II, Ptolemy's Shifting Alliance, and Jonathan's Alliance with Demetrius II (10:67–11:53)

The same nephew, Ptolemy VI Philometor, through whom Antiochus IV Epiphanes briefly ruled parts of Egypt (see comment above on 1:16–19) now attempts to gain control over Seleucid territory by repudiating his alliance with Alexander Epiphanes in favor of one with Demetrius II (11:8–18).

Jonathan's tenuous alliance with Demetrius II is tested quickly, when Demetrius requests Judean troops. Although the numbers in 11:47 are surely hyperbolic, the loyalty, valor, and military might of these troops in 11:47–51 is juxtaposed with Demetrius's refusal to honor his agreement with Jonathan.

E. Jonathan's Alliance with Antiochus VI Epiphanes and Battle Against the Forces of Demetrius II (11:54–74)

The alliance offered by Trypho through Antiochus VI (11:57–59) around 145 BCE expands the territory under Maccabean control significantly. The outlying areas of this territory must be taken with force, however, as indicated by Jonathan's battles in Gaza and the plain of Hazor. Although the description of Jonathan's prayer (11:71) is more perfunctory than that found in earlier passages like 3:50–53, it nevertheless includes God in the focus of this military success.

F. Jonathan Renews Earlier Alliances with Rome and Sparta (12:1–23)

Although the narrative describes alliances with both Rome (cf. 1 Macc 8) and Sparta, the latter is far more intriguing. Scholars disagree on the veracity of this material. Some argue that the letter from Arius (12:7) is a complete fabrication, while others attempt to demonstrate the plausibility of some communication between King Areus I of Sparta (309–265 BCE) and either Onias I or Onias II.

G. The Ongoing Struggle with Demetrius II and Trypho's Deception (12:24–48)

As Jonathan and Simon continue the struggle to maintain their territory, Jonathan succumbs to the treachery of Trypho in approximately 143 BCE.

V. Leadership of Simon (12:49–16:3)

A. Distress in Judea and Simon's Successful Bid for Power (12:49–13:9)

The transition of leadership from Jonathan to Simon parallels that from Judas to Jonathan (cf. 1 Macc 9:23–27). As the people mourn the loss of a great leader, enemies inside and outside of Judea seek to take advantage of their dire circumstances. The people's reply, "all that you say to us we will do" (13:9), echoes the people's response to Moses in the recounting of the Sinai theophany in Deut 5:27. The connection between Simon and Moses will become even more explicit later in the narrative, when it is determined that Simon should hold both civic and religious authority over the independent state of Judea, "until a trustworthy prophet should arise" (14:41; cf. Deut 18:15, "The LORD your God will raise up for you a prophet like me from among your own people").

B. Simon Faces Off Against Trypho (13:10–24)

Simon is portrayed as a very shrewd political figure, navigating a delicate situation with an enemy he cannot trust (13:17) and with his own people, who may turn on him (13:17–18).

C. Simon Establishes a Memorial to Honor His Family (13:25–30)

Simon's lavish memorial honoring his family presages the independence to be described shortly in the narrative. Such memorials were common in antiquity, both as a means to honor individuals and as a means to commemorate military victories.

D. Simon Renews Alliance with Demetrius II and Achieves Judean Independence (13:31–42)

In 142 BCE, Simon was able to obtain freedom from taxation and tribute to the Seleucids. For the first time since the Babylonian exile, Judea experiences true independence: "the yoke of the Gentiles was removed from Israel" (13:41).

E. Peace and Prosperity in the Reign of Simon (13:43–14:49)

13:43–53. Simon Takes Gazara and the Citadel. Gazara is mentioned less frequently than the citadel in the narrative of 1 Maccabees, and the problems surrounding it are described less clearly. A careful look at passages like 4:15–16 and 9:52, however, reveals the city's importance. It is described as the point at which Judas's pursuit of his enemies must cease, and as one of the cities fortified by Bacchides to "harass" Israel.

The citadel had been a threat in Jerusalem from the days of Antiochus IV Epiphanes. Its final capture and cleansing are celebrated, understandably, with great joy.

14:1–49. Repeated Descriptions of Simon's Accomplishments. From the perspective of the author, Simon's reign marks the golden years of this new period of independence. The effect of repeating Simon's accomplishments and hard-won popularity in the statements of alliance renewal from Sparta and Rome is to emphasize Simon's significance dramatically.

The depiction of life in Judea during Simon's reign is filled with possible scriptural allusions. Some scholars argue that the author of 1 Maccabees is describing something akin to a messianic age. In the mention of the land giving forth its produce in 14:8, for example, one may find an allusion to the eschatological language of Zech 8:12. On the other hand, one could suggest that it is an allusion to Lev 26:4, a passage portraying the benefits that will come to Israel when it keeps God's statutes and commandments (Lev 26:3; cf. 1 Macc 2:27, 64). Other verses in 1 Macc 14 allude more clearly to biblical passages describing times of peace and prosperity (cf., for example, 1 Macc 14:12 and 1 Kgs 4:25).

F. Simon Encounters the Treachery of Antiochus VII Sidetes and Passes Leadership to His Son John (15:1–16:3)

In a way that closely parallels the tenuous alliance between Demetrius II and Jonathan (11:24–53), Antiochus VII initially confirms his alliance with Simon, only to become "estranged" from him (15:27).

VI. Leadership of John (Hyrcanus) (16:4–24)

A. John Repels the Advance of Antiochus's Commander, Cendebeus (16:4–10)

John's pursuit of Cendebeus to Kedron, approximately twenty miles southwest of Modein, again suggests the difficulty of controlling the territory surrounding Judea.

B. Murder of Simon (16:11–22)

Ptolemy is Simon's son-in-law. The author of 1 Maccabees glosses over the aftermath of the assassination, a grizzly affair in which John was prevented from exacting revenge on Ptolemy because the latter held John's mother hostage.

According to Josephus, Ptolemy eventually escaped after killing John's mother; John was too busy dealing with another siege being executed by Antiochus VII to pursue him (*Ant.* 13.230–237).

C. Summary Conclusion (16:23–24)

As noted by many scholars, the summary statement contained in the last two verses suggests that the narrative of 1 Maccabees was written near the end of John's life, or shortly after his death.

BIBLIOGRAPHY

H. Attridge. "Historiography." *Jewish Writings of the Second Temple Period: Apocrypha, Pseudepigrapha, Qumran Sectarian Writings, Philo, Josephus.* M. Stone, ed. CRINT 2 (Philadelphia: Fortress, 1984). B. Bar-Kochva. *Judas Maccabaeus: The Jewish Struggle Against the Seleucids* (Cambridge: Cambridge University Press, 1989); J. Bartlett. *1 Maccabees.* Guides to Apocrypha and Pseudepigrapha (Sheffield: Sheffield Academic Press, 1998); E. Bickerman. *The God of the Maccabees: Studies on the Meaning and Origin of the Maccabean Revolt.* Translated by H. Moehring. SJLA 32 (Leiden: Brill, 1979); J. Goldstein. *1 Maccabees.* AB 41 (Garden City: Doubleday, 1976); L. Grabbe. *Judaism from Cyrus to Hadrian. Volume One: The Persian and Greek Periods* (Minneapolis: Fortress, 1992); D. Harrington. *The Maccabean Revolt: Anatomy of a Biblical Revolution.* OTS 1 (Wilmington, Del.: Michael Glazier, 1988); M. Hengel. *Judaism and Hellenism: Studies in Their Encounter in Palestine During the Early Hellenistic Period.* J. Bowden, trans. (London: SCM, 1974); D. Mendels *The Land of Israel as a Political Concept in Hasmonean Literature: Recourse to History in Second Century B.C. Claims to the Holy Land.* TSAJ 15 (Tübingen: J. C. B. Mohr (Paul Siebeck), 1987); P. Schäfer. "The Hellenistic and Maccabaean Periods." *Israelite and Judaean History.* J. H. Hayes and J. M. Miller, eds. (Philadelphia: Trinity Press International, 1977); V. Tcherikover. *Hellenistic Civilization and the Jews.* S. Applebaum, trans. (Philadelphia: Jewish Publication Society of America, 1959. Repr., Peabody, Mass.:Hendrickson, 1999); S. Tedesche and S. Zeitlin. *The First Book of Maccabees.* JAL (New York: Harper & Brothers, 1950).

2 MACCABEES

SHANE BERG

OVERVIEW

Second Maccabees provides an account of the military successes of Judas Maccabeus in the mid-second century BCE against the forces of the Seleucid kingdom, to whom Judea was subject. It also relates some of the events that led up to the outbreak of the fighting. The book is characterized by a strong theological outlook, especially in comparison with 1 Maccabees. The God of Israel is portrayed as actively working in and through the events and people described to reward faithful obedience to the covenant and punish those who act wickedly. On occasion God even sends angelic beings who mete out punishment to evildoers or bring timely aid to the faithful.

God's defense of the integrity of the Temple is a prominent theme in 2 Maccabees. Attacks on the Temple are featured in three key episodes in the book, and in each case God intervenes to ward off the threat or, in the case of the sacrileges of Antiochus IV Epiphanes, to bring about restoration after defilement. The purification of the Temple by Judas Maccabeus in 164 BCE gives rise to the annual eight-day Hanukkah commemoration. One of the primary rhetorical goals of the author of 2 Maccabees is to legitimate the festival of Hanukkah and recommend its observance by Jews in the Diaspora.

The author explains at the outset that his book represents an abridgement of a five-volume history by a certain Jason of Cyrene (a city in North Africa). Second Maccabees was written in Greek, and most likely the history of Jason of Cyrene was also a Greek work. This longer historical work is not extant, so it is difficult to assess its nature and purpose, especially since the author of 2 Maccabees acknowledges that he has added his own literary and rhetorical embellishment to the details he culls from Jason's history (2:29).

It is not possible to fix the date of 2 Maccabees precisely. Jason of Cyrene must have composed his historical work after 161 BCE, the year of the latest events described in 2 Maccabees. The book opens with two letters addressed to Jews living in Egypt; it is not clear whether these letters were included by the author or added by a later hand to the completed work. The first of the letters prefixed to Second Maccabees is dated 124 BCE (1:9), and it is likely, though not certain, that the entire work was completed at that point. 2 Maccabees was thus most likely written between 161–124 BCE.

First and Second Maccabees recount many of the same events, though it does not appear that either one was a source for the other. Despite their overlapping content (2 Maccabees covers roughly the same time period as 1 Macc 1–7), 1 and 2 Maccabees differ in key ways. First Maccabees covers a longer span of time and covers events related to several members of the Maccabeus family, while 2 Maccabees is focused on a relatively short stretch of time and is concerned with the deeds of Judas Maccabeus alone. Another important difference is the view of history in the two books. First Maccabees conforms in many ways to the principles of causality typical of Hellenistic historiography, while 2 Maccabees exhibits a more explicitly religious view of causality in which history is regarded as the working out of divine punishment and reward.

OUTLINE

I. Preliminary Material (1:1–2:32)

    A. A Letter to the Jews of Egypt (1:1–9)

    B. A Letter to Aristobulus and the Jews of Egypt (1:10–2:18)

    C. The Author's Prologue (2:19–32)

II. Events Leading up to the Maccabean Revolt (3:1–7:42)

    A. A Thwarted Attempt to Rob the Temple (3:1–4:6)

    B. The Hellenistic Program of Jason (4:7–22)

    C. The Crimes of Menelaus (4:23–50)

    D. The Desecration and Pillage of the Temple by Antiochus IV (5:1–27)

Detailed Analysis

I. Preliminary Material (1:1–2:32)

A. A Letter to the Jews of Egypt (1:1–9)

This first prefixed letter is brief and conforms to typical epistolary conventions. It is dated 124 BCE, and refers to a previous letter sent in 143 BCE in the tumultuous period that followed on Jason's usurpation of the office of high priest (1:7–8; see 4:7–29, 5:1–14). In the letter the "Jews in Jerusalem" exhort "their Jewish kindred in Egypt" (1:1) to observe the festival of Hanukkah (1:9).

B. A Letter to Aristobulus and the Jews of Egypt (1:10–2:18)

This second prefixed letter is much longer than the first and purports to be written by the "people of Jerusalem and Judea and the senate and Judas" just prior to the first celebration of Hanukkah in 164 BCE (1:10, 18). This claim in uncorroborated by any other independent evidence, however, and the letter is more likely to be dated to the decades following the purification of the Temple in 164 BCE. In addition to the "Jews of Egypt," the letter is addressed to Aristobulus, who is described as a teacher of King Ptolemy (1:10). Aristobulus is a Jewish philosopher of the second century BCE from Alexandria known from several ancient sources, but the claim that was a teacher of Ptolemy is not attested outside 2 Maccabees.

The author of the letter seeks to highlight historical precedents for the festival of Hanukkah, which would seem to indicate that there was some dispute at this time concerning its inclusion in the Jewish festal calendar. The somewhat long and meandering series of episodes from Israel's past recounted in 1:19–2:15 are intended to legitimate two central aspects of the Hanukkah celebration—its eight-day length and the lighting of the menorah. In order to demonstrate that the fire of the Hanukkah lamps is an appropriate symbol for the purification of the Temple, the author recounts several stories—most of them not attested anywhere else—associated with what he calls the "festival of the Fire" (1:18). This otherwise unknown festival commemorates Nehemiah's purification of the slabs that would become the altar in the Second Temple. This task was accomplished by means of a fire fueled by a thick liquid that was the residue of the fire from the altar of the First Temple, which had been hidden by the priests in advance of the Babylonian invasion (1:19–36). The examples of sacrifices being consumed on the altar by heavenly fire in the times of Moses, Solomon, and Nehemiah are offered as further justification for the propriety of the symbolic purifying light of the Hanukkah festival (2:9–13).

The author also attempts to legitimate the length of Hanukkah—eight days—by suggesting that Moses, Solomon, and Nehemiah observed eight days of purification and sacrifices after erecting their respective temples (2:11–13). The point of all these vignettes is that the Jews of Egypt should observe Hanukkah (2:16–17) because its symbolism is grounded in the precedents of Moses, Solomon, and Nehemiah, who each purified the sacred altar with fire for eight days.

C. The Author's Prologue (2:19–32)

The author claims that the five-volume history of Jason of Cyrene that he has condensed treated the wars of Judas Maccabeus against Antiochus IV and V and Judas' purification of the Temple (2:19–23). This statement would seem to suggest that Jason's historical account was limited to the same time period and range of topics presented in 2 Maccabees. The alternative is that Jason's historical account was a broader work, an excerpt of which was epitomized by the author of 2 Maccabees. If indeed Jason's history was limited to the time and events covered by 2 Maccabees, then his five-volume work must have been characterized by staggering detail.

The author states that his purpose in condensing Jason's history is to make for a more enjoyable experience for the reader, to facilitate the memorization of the text, and to reach a broader readership (2:24–25). In an artful characterization of his abridgement of Jason's history, he compares Jason to the builder of a house while he likens himself to one who merely paints and adorns it (2:29). A similarly self-deprecating rhetorical flourish is found at the very end of the work (15:38–39).

II. Events Leading up to the Maccabean Revolt (3:1–7:42)

A. A Thwarted Attempt to Rob the Temple (3:1–4:6)

This account of a successfully defended assault on the Temple sets the stage for the rest of the narrative by emphasizing God's willingness to intervene in human affairs to protect the holy site. During the high priesthood of Onias III, whom the author presents as exemplary in every way, a disgruntled Temple official named Simon falsely reports to the provincial governor, Apollonius, that incredible sums of money had been deposited in the Temple that could easily be confiscated (3:4–6). Simon appears to have wished to cause trouble for Onias III, who had denied him an appointment to a desired post.

Apollonius takes the bait and informs the king, Seleucus IV, who dispatches a high-ranking aide, Heliodorus, to make his way to Jerusalem and procure the Temple deposits (3:7–8). Though upon his arrival in Jerusalem Heliodorus discovers that the amount of money held in the Temple fell far short of what Simon had claimed, Heliodorus decides that he must take it nonetheless to satisfy the king (3:9–14). Despite the fevered prayers of the residents of Jerusalem (3:14–22), Heliodorus makes his way to the Temple treasury. In what is probably a conflation of two stories, Heliodorus is run down by a divinely sent war horse ridden by an angelic armor-clad warrior who is seen by all present (3:25), and then he is beaten by two young angels who seem to be visible only to him (3:26). Heliodorus is rendered paralyzed and mute by his encounter, and he and his retinue recognize the

"sovereign power of God" (3:28; cf. 3:24, "Sovereign of spirits"). Onias III prays for Heliodorus, who recovers and makes vows and sacrifices to the God of Israel and bears witness to all concerning what happened to him (3:31–36). This episode foreshadows one of the central themes of 2 Maccabees—that those who attack God's Temple will suffer divine retribution.

B. The Hellenistic Program of Jason (4:7–22)

Jason, the brother of Onias III, took advantage of the accession of a new king, Antiochus IV, to secure the high priestly office that belonged to his brother by offering a considerable sum of money to Antiochus (4:7–9). Though commentators often refer to this payment as a bribe, bidding for important offices was in fact a fairly standard practice in Hellenistic kingdoms.

Jason secured the right to establish a *gymnasion* and an *ephebeion*, key social institutions in Greek cities that provide a public place for exercise and socializing (the *gymnasion*) and a formal course of training in Greek culture for adolescents (the *ephebeion*). He also requested that the residents of Jerusalem be enrolled as citizens of the city of Antioch (4:9–10; cf. 1 Macc 1:11–15).

The author of 2 Maccabees presents Jason's actions as an assault on the Jewish way of life under God's Torah for which he will be divinely punished (4:11–17). But Jason's actions are quite comprehensible in light of the general tendency in the Hellenistic age for citizens of small or remote cities to attempt to elevate their status by formally adopting the institutions and customs of more cosmopolitan Greek cities. Scholars tend to take as historically accurate the state of affairs in Judea presented by the author of 2 Maccabees—namely, that a Torah-observant populace was forced to adopt a foreign culture by a few radical advocates of "Hellenism." This simplistic historical portrait, however, can and should be subjected to critical scrutiny. It is more judicious to assert that in this era there was a "culture war" raging between those who wanted to advance Judea's standing in the Seleucid kingdom by adopting cosmopolitan institutions and customs and those who wanted to reject such cultural changes and instead adopt Torah as the governing charter for Judea. The populace of Judea was caught in between these zealous parties with robust agendas.

C. The Crimes of Menelaus (4:23–50)

In 172 BCE Menelaus, the brother of Simon (see 3:4–12, 4:1–6), outbid Jason for the high priesthood and drove his supplanted rival into exile in Ammon (4:23–29). Menelaus and his brother Lysimachus turn out to be cruel and greedy. Menelaus, for example, sells off precious Temple objects in order to pay off the tribute he owes to the king and then arranges for Onias to be murdered when he exposes this vile act (4:30–38). Menelaus and Lysimachus, according to our author, gained a notorious and widespread reputation for theft, murder, and all sorts of other evil deeds.

It is important to note that unlike the description of Jason's tenure as high priest, no mention is made of "Hellenizing" on the part of Menelaus, a distinction that scholars sometimes fail to make. Menelaus and Lysimachus are presented as simply resorting to violence and deceit to satisfy their greed, not as implementing some Hellenistic cultural agenda.

D. The Desecration and Pillage of the Temple by Antiochus IV (5:1–27)

When Antiochus IV is away preparing for a second invasion of Egypt (presumably in 169 BCE; according to 1 Macc 1:16–28, this second invasion took place in 168 BCE), Jason gathers some forces and attempts to drive Menelaus from Jerusalem (5:1–5). Menelaus retreats to the citadel, however, and Jason engages in reckless slaughter of the residents of Jerusalem (5:6). Jason eventually flees into exile and dies unmourned and unburied abroad, which the author considers a fitting punishment for his crimes (5:10).

This fighting in Jerusalem leads Antiochus to fear that Judea is in revolt, so he breaks from his preparations for invading Egypt and leads his troops into Jerusalem, where they engage in the indiscriminate slaughter of thousands of inhabitants (5:11–14; the author's figure of 80,000 slain or enslaved is certainly grossly exaggerated). Despite the magnitude of the carnage, the author counts Antiochus' entry into the forbidden areas of the Temple and his plundering of the holy vessels and Temple deposits as even greater crimes (5:15–16; cf. 1 Macc 1:21–24). In the wake of this desecration and plundering, Antiochus leaves deputies in charge at Jerusalem and Samaria who continue to persecute and murder the inhabitants (5:21–26; cf. 1 Macc 1:29–40).

The author's theology of divine retribution is prominent in the description of Antiochus' crime against the Jewish people and the Temple. Antiochus, overwhelmed by glee, fails to perceive that his success was not of his own doing but rather brought about by God in order to punish the sins of the Jerusalemites (5:17–18). This state of punishment is not permanent, however, and the Temple will be restored when God again exercises mercy toward the people (5:19–20). The Temple's restoration, and Antiochus' well-deserved downfall, are foreshadowed by the brief mention that Judas Maccabeus and a few compatriots escaped the onslaught and made their way up into the remote parts of the hill country (5:27).

E. Persecution of the Jews Under Antiochus IV (6:1–7:42)

Not long after his brutal siege of Jerusalem, Antiochus IV takes steps to alter the Temple worship of both the Samaritans at Gerizim and the Jews at Jerusalem (167 BCE). Both were renamed in honor of Zeus, and new ritual activities like sacred prostitution were introduced and existing customs such as Sabbath observance and the celebration of traditional festivals were forbidden (6:1–11; cf. 1 Macc 1:41–64; Dan 11:31). While conflation of Greek and indigenous religious practices was common in Hellenistic kingdoms, Antiochus IV seems to have been particularly aggressive and confrontational in these policies, and the author of 2 Maccabees regards them as almost unspeakably evil.

The suffering of the Jews that resulted from the compulsion to participate in pagan rituals and the prohibition of their traditional practices is explained by the author in terms of the logic of divine retribution. That the Jews are suffering, according to the author, is in fact a sign of God's favor; that God punishes the Jews immediately for their transgressions curbs further sinfulness and thus prevents a catastrophic future punishment such as the Gentiles will receive for the accumulated mass of their evil deeds (6:12–17).

This rationalization of the suffering of the Jews is necessary to mitigate the impact of the two gruesome scenes of martyrdom that immediately follow it. Both accounts seem to be independent tales that have been incorporated into the present work. The first is the story of Eleazar, an elderly and venerable scribe who refused the order to eat a piece of pork (6:18–21), for which he was tortured and killed on the rack (6:29–30) He steadfastly refused an offer, made in light of his stature and dignity, to substitute a piece of *kosher* meat and so only feign to eat pork (6:21–22). He refuses this accommodation, expressing his concern that the young Jews who see it will be disheartened by seeing an old man adopt a foreign religion, and so he chooses a noble death in order to remain faithful to God's laws to the very end (6:23–28; Eleazar's martyrdom is related in greater length in 4 Macc 5–7).

The second martyrdom tale relates the torture and execution of seven brothers and their mother, a longer account of which is found in 4 Maccabees 8–18). This story, which has been famous in both the Jewish and Christian traditions since antiquity, unfolds in a most grizzly fashion. Like Eleazar, this entire family is compelled by Antiochus to eat pork (7:1). The brothers refuse, professing loyalty to the laws of their ancestors, and each in turn is cruelly dismembered and roasted alive on a pan over an open fire (7:3–39). The mother encourages each boy to face death courageously, and finally is killed herself (7:41). One of the distinctive features of this tale is the prominence of the hope in bodily resurrection as a reward for faithful to God's laws (7:9, 11, 14, 23, 29). There are also several references to God's retribution for evildoers (7:14, 17, 19, 31–36), a theme that grows ever more prominent as the narrative of 2 Maccabees proceeds.

III. The Wars of Judas Maccabeus Against the Seleucids (8:1–15:36)

A. The Campaigns of Judas Against the Forces of Antiochus IV (8:1–9:29)

Having established the dire situation for Jews under Antiochus IV, the stage is set for the military actions of Judas Maccabeus, whose exploits are the focal point for the rest of 2 Maccabees. The rise of Judas is associated by the author as a major turning point in the narrative in which God's wrath gives way to mercy in the form of divine aid to Judas' cause. Judas is portrayed as God's chosen deliverer who is faithful to God in

every way (8:16–24, 36), and 6,000 loyal soldiers are represented as the models of courage, piety, and compassion (8:1–4, 12–14, 24–29).

One of the difficulties of interpreting 2 Maccabees is assessing the historical accuracy of the stark contrast set up by the author between the noble and courageous Judas and the depraved Seleucid officials and their lackeys. It makes little sense for a ruling overlord like Antiochus IV to harass a subject people with such cruelty and wanton abandon, and it seems hard to believe that Judas' motives were as disinterested as they are represented here. The Maccabees won this contest, and the histories that we have in 1 and 2 Maccabees are written from the victor's perspective. It is probably much more plausible to imagine that Judas and his followers were a theocratic faction whose rhetoric about absolute fidelity to "ancestral traditions" was an agenda they were pursuing rather than a description of "facts on the ground" in Judea at the time. This theocratic party opposed the cosmopolitan agenda of individuals like Jason, and they were willing to fight for their vision of Judea under no law but God's.

Judas and his small fighting band of 6,000 square off against the Seleucid general Nicanor and his 20,000 troops and rout them in short order (8:24–29; cf. 1 Macc 4:13–25), and soon thereafter win surprising victories over other forces (killing 20,000 in the process) under the control of Timothy and Bacchides, both Seleucid commanders (8:30–34; cf. 1 Macc 5:6–7 and 7:8–25).

Turning from these various conquests, the narrative shifts to Antiochus IV, who, while carrying out a humiliating retreat from an unsuccessful campaign in Persia, decides to find a vent for his rage by turning Jerusalem into a "cemetery for the Jews" (9:1–4, author's trans.). On his way to Jerusalem, however, he is stricken with a series of gruesome maladies and injuries that bring him to his deathbed, all of which the author attributes to God's righteous punishment of Antiochus for his arrogance and wickedness (9:5–10). Being at death's door humbles Antiochus, who even attempts to forestall God's wrath by promising to lavish the Jews with privileges, honors, and gifts, and even to become a Jew himself (9:11–17).

When this attempt to win God's favor fails, Antiochus resigns himself to death and writes a letter to the Jews (9:18), the text of which is given by our author (9:19–27). The content of the letter, however, does not seem to match the narrative description that leads up to it. Antiochus refers to his illness as "annoying," and states that recovery is likely (9:21–22). He announces that he has decreed that his son, Antiochus (V), will be king his place, and he asks the Jews to maintain good relations with him. The likely explanation for the lack of fit between the letter and the narrative is that the letter is in fact authentic, and our author has take the liberty of constructing a dramatic and exaggerated literary context for it that emphasizes the theme of divine retribution. For other versions of the death of Antiochus IV, see 1:13–17, 1 Macc 6:1–17, and Dan 11:40–45.

B. The Purification of the Temple (10:1–9)

This section of 2 Maccabees appears to have been displaced from its original sequence in Jason of Cyrene's history, evidence for which can be seen in the awkward notice in 10:9, "Such then was the end of Antiochus, who was called Epiphanes." This concluding statement should follow directly on 9:28, where Antiochus' death is narrated. It would appear that the brief account of the purification of the Temple (10:1–8) should come immediately after 8:36 and be followed by the chapter on the death of Antiochus (9:1–28). This arrangement of the sections would also bring the chronology of events into line with 1 Maccabees.

The victories of Judas and his forces results in the liberation of Jerusalem and the purification of the Temple in 164 BCE. They construct a new altar and resume the suspended sacrifices, light the lamps, and celebrate for eight days (10:6). The whole of 2 Maccabees has been building to this climax, and indeed one of the central rhetorical purposes of the book seems to be to elevate the festival of Hanukkah to the same status as other major Jewish holidays.

C. The Campaigns of Judas Against the Forces of Antiochus V (10:10–13:26)

The narrative now begins to relate a series of military victories by the increasingly powerful Judas Maccabeus and this army. After the death of Antiochus IV, his nine-year-old son Antiochus V

Eupator took the Seleucid throne, and Lysias became the regent for the child king after forcing out Philip from the role, who had been chosen by Antiochus IV (see 1 Macc 6:55–56).

Shortly after the accession of Antiochus V, Judas engages in a successful campaign in Idumea (10:14–23; cf. 1 Macc 5:1–54) and crushes an army of mercenaries commanded by Timothy, whom he had defeated before (see 8:30–33), not far outside Jerusalem (10:24–31); Timothy himself is eventually cornered and killed (10:32–38). During this battle against Timothy, five riders on horses appear from heaven and give aid to the forces of Judas (10:29–30).

The episode found in 11:1–15 is out of place in the narrative and belongs to the time before the purification of the Temple (cf. 1 Macc 4:26–35). In it Lysias, who is nursing a desire to turn Jerusalem into a respectable Hellenistic city (11:2–3), invades Jerusalem and besieges Beth-zur, a Judean fortress. A heavenly horseman appears and sends Lysias and his men into panicked retreat in response to the prayers of Judas and his men for God to intervene in the siege (11:6–12).

A collection of four brief letters is found in 11:16–38. Though the author associates them with the peace agreement forged by Lysias with the Jews, the scholarly consensus is that these letters are out of chronological order; they should most likely be arranged in order as follows: 16–21, 34–38, 27–33, 22–26. Furthermore, the first three of these letters belong to the reign of Antiochus IV, but here they are placed in the reign of Antiochus V. All four letters deal with some aspect of peace negotiations between the Seleucids and the residents of Judea.

A number of Judas' military victories are described in rapid-fire fashion in 12:1–45. He avenges the persecution of the Jewish populace in Jamnia and Joppa (12:2–9), wins several battles in Gilead (12:10–16; cf. 1 Macc 5:9–36), and then decisively defeats the army of Timothy (12:17–25; cf. 1 Macc 5:37–43), who presumably is a different Timothy than the one defeated twice and then killed by Judas earlier in the narrative (8:30–33, 10:24–37). Other military successes are described in 12:26–37 (cf. 1 Macc 5:46–54). Judas pauses after these campaigns to gather up his dead and to make a sin offering (12:43), an act that in Scripture is intended to be effective for the living (see Lev. 4:13–21) but that is interpreted by the author as made on behalf of the dead and thus gives evidence of Judas' belief in the resurrection of the dead (12:43–45).

Another instance of the author's emphasis on fitting retribution for evildoers is found in the account of the death of Menelaus, who inadvertently angers Antiochus V and Lysias while trying to promote his self-interest with them and is scapegoated and executed for the unrest in Judea (13:1–8). As Antiochus V prepares for a vicious attack on the Jews, Judas calls for three days of fervent prayer, after which his forces rout the king's troops in a series of skirmishes (13:9–21). In light of these defeats, as well as news of a potential revolt in Antioch, Antiochus V negotiates a hasty treaty with the Jews and withdraws (13:22–26).

D. Nicanor's Treachery and the Campaign of Judas Against Nicanor (14:1–15:36)

After Demetrius I usurps the throne from Antiochus V in 161 CE, he installs a man named Alcimus as high priest and sends Nicanor to lend military support to the installation of Alcimus in Jerusalem and to put an end to Judas once and for all (14:1–14; the events in 14:1–15:36 are paralleled in 1 Macc 7). Alcimus refers to Judas as leader of the "Hasideans" (10:6; they are regarded as distinct from Judas' band in 1 Macc 2:42, 7:13), whom he characterizes as a guerilla force that destabilizes and harasses the Seleucid-appointed government in Judea (10:6–10).

Nicanor decides to strike up a friendship with Judas rather than risk facing him in open battle (14:15–25), a narrative element that is not mentioned in 1 Maccabees. This stratagem seems to have been designed to keep close tabs on Judas, whom Nicanor convinces to settle down and start a family (14:23–25), thereby ensuring that he is not in the field carrying out attacks on Seleucid forces.

The goodwill between Nicanor and Judas does not last because Alcimus reports to Demetrius that Nicanor has not followed through on the order to kill Judas (14:26–27). Nicanor is reluctant to heed Demetrius' reiterated order, but knows that he must do so or face dire consequences (14:28–29). Judas perceives Nicanor's change in attitude and withdraws into hiding (14:30; 1 Macc 7:29–30

blames Nicanor rather than Alcimus for this development). Nicanor tersely demands that the priests in the Temple disclose Judas' location, and in response to their refusal he stretches forth his arm and threatens to destroy the Temple and set up a cult of Dionysus (14:31–33), a threat for which he later receives what the author considers an apt punishment (see 15:28–35, where the tongue and arm of Nicanor's corpse are mutilated because of his arrogant words and gestures).

After a description of the martyrdom of a certain Razis (14:37–46; it does not fit well into the narrative and seems primarily aimed at making yet another defense of the notion of bodily resurrection), Nicanor's inglorious defeat and death at the hands of Judas and his men is related (15:1–35; cf. 1 Macc 7:40–50). God's favor and aid for Judas is again a prominent narrative motif; Judas sees a vision of Onias III praying for the Jews, who is then joined by the prophet Jeremiah who gives Judas a golden sword with which to slay his enemies (15:12–16).

The author chooses to bring the narrative to a close on a high note with Judas and his compatriots celebrating their victory in Jerusalem rather than moving on to Judas' death at the hands of Bacchides nor his brothers' difficult and lengthy struggle to win full independence for Judea (for which see 1 Macc 9–13).

IV. The Author's Epilogue (15:37–39)

The author closes with a brief and playful epilogue that compares his literary achievement to a strong wine (=Jason's history) that is mixed with water (=his editing and abridging of Jason's history) in order to create a sweet and pleasing drink.

BIBLIOGRAPHY

E. Bickerman. *The God of the Maccabees.* Trans. H. Moehring. (Leiden: Brill, 1979); J. J. Collins and G. Sterling, eds. *Hellenism in the Land of Israel* (Notre Dame, Ind.: University of Notre Dame Press, 2001); J. Goldstein. *II Maccabees.* AB 41A (New York: Doubleday, 1983); M. Hengel. *Judaism and Hellenism.* 2 vols. John Bowden, trans. (Philadelphia: Fortress, 1974); E. Schürer. *The History of the Jewish People in the Age of*

Jesus Christ. Vol. 1. G. Vermes, F. Millar, P. Vermes, and M. Black, eds. (Edinburgh: T&T Clark, 1973); M. Smith. "Hellenization." *Palestinian Parties and Politics That Shaped the Old Testament* (New York and London: Columbia University Press, 1971); V. Tcherikover. *Hellenistic Civilization and the Jews.* S. Applebaum, trans. (Philadelphia: Jewish Publication Society, 1973).

1 ESDRAS

CAMERON HOWARD

OVERVIEW

The LXX contains two texts bearing the name "Esdras," the Greek form of "Ezra." First Esdras, known as "Esdras a" in the LXX, precedes "Esdras b," the canonical text of the biblical books of Ezra and Nehemiah. First Esdras is a book of the Apocrypha, and the Eastern Orthodox traditions consider it deuterocanonical, part of the "second canon." Although 1 Esdras is not considered authoritative by the Roman Catholic Church, the book, labeled as Third Esdras in the Vulgate, is appended after the New Testament in Bibles that are based on the Vulgate.

Much of 1 Esdras aligns closely with the material in canonical Ezra, as well as with small portions of Chronicles and Nehemiah. The book begins with an account of the last kings of Judah, largely identical to 2 Chr 35–36. It then includes the entire text of Ezra, with some minor variants and one major addition: the "Story of the Three Youths" (1 Esd 3–4), which has no canonical parallel. The book ends with the account of Ezra's reading of the law paralleled in Neh 8, but that account breaks off in mid-sentence, indicating that the original conclusion to 1 Esdras has been lost.

Most scholars date 1 Esdras to the mid- to late-second century BCE It appears that its "author" was more like an editor, choosing the relevant Chronicles, Ezra, and Nehemiah passages from Hebrew and Aramaic, translating them into Greek, making small alterations to the narrative, and adding the Story of the Three Youths. First Esdras adds little historical clarity to the reports of the return to Jerusalem in Ezra and Nehemiah; in fact, the chronology of Persian kings and Jewish leaders in 1 Esdras is even murkier than in the canonical accounts. Instead, the book subtly recasts the details of Chronicles–Ezra–Nehemiah to offer a differently nuanced perspective on Judah's path from righteousness into exile and ultimately to its reconstitution as a faithful community.

OUTLINE

I. The Last Days of Judah (1:1–58)

A. Josiah's Kingship (1:1–33)

B. Apostate Kings (1:34–58)

II. The Return Begins (2:1–30)

A. Cyrus' Authorization of the Return and Rebuilding Projects (2:1–15)

B. Correspondence with Artaxerxes Regarding the Return (2:16–30)

III. The Story of the Three Youths (3:1–4:63)

A. The Contest (3:1–4:41)

B. The Aftermath of the Contest (4:42–63)

IV. The Return Continues (5:1–7:15)

A. The Returnees (5:1–46)

B. Progress in Rebuilding (5:47–65)

C. Opposition (5:66–34)

D. Completion of the Temple (7:1–15)

V. Ezra's Return (8:1–9:55)

A. The Details of Ezra's Mission (8:1–90)

B. The Renouncement and Expulsion of Foreign Wives and Children (8:91–9:36)

C. Ezra Reads the Law (9:37–55)

DETAILED ANALYSIS

Because 1 Esdras is dominated by the text of Ezra, it echoes many of that book's themes: the persistence and success of the returnees in the face of repeated opposition, the difficulties of defining the "insiders" and "outsiders" of the new community, the reinstitution of right religious practices, and the sovereignty of God—the God who "stirred up the spirit of King Cyrus" (2:2)—over Judah and Persia alike. Nevertheless, 1 Esdras is not simply a duplication of the book of Ezra; instead, it reworks the Ezra materials, reordering them and adding to them, in order to make a distinct narrative.

First Esdras distinguishes itself from its canonical parallels by juxtaposing Judah's rapid fall from glory in 2 Chr 35–36 with the book of Ezra's painful ascent back into a reconstituted community, omitting the extended historical background the rest of Chronicles provides. By beginning with Josiah's observance of the Passover, 1 Esdras showcases Judah at its best: a pious king follows the Law, the vessels and officials of the Temple are in place and in order, and animals for sacrifice abound. The account of Judah's decline in 1 Esd 1 is rapid and terse. Judah quickly falls from the apex of Josiah's celebration through a line of apostate kings and into exile. Yet 1 Esdras does not dwell on the exile itself. Instead, the book immediately recounts the decree of Cyrus and the beginning of the exiles' return to Judah. Unlike the road to exile, the path to rebuilt community is slow and winding, with multiple starts and stops along the way. The structure of 1 Esdras poignantly contrasts a quick, easy slip into sinfulness with a slow, difficult recovery from the disaster that sin has bred.

Although it contains a structure unique from its canonical counterparts, the heart of 1 Esdras' distinctiveness lies in the Story of the Three Youths (1 Esd 3–4). The story is a "court legend," a genre well-attested in the ancient Near Eastern and Hellenistic worlds. In these types of stories a courtier, usually a member of a subject people, rises to prominence in the foreign king's court because of the courtier's wisdom and righteousness. Analogous stories in the Old Testament include Gen 37–40, Dan 1–6, and Esther. The Story of the Three Youths was most likely a popular folktale that circulated independently of the Ezra–Nehemiah account, either in Greek or Aramaic. The Jewish editor of 1 Esdras then inserted the story into the Ezra materials, altering the details of both to fit the needs of the new narrative.

The Story of the Three Youths bolsters Zerubbabel's role in the rebuilding of the Temple and the city walls. As the courtier whose answer to the riddle proves wisest, he not only showcases his own sagacity but also becomes responsible for procuring deeper support and additional resources from King Darius, who encourages him to ask for rewards "beyond what is written" (4:42). References to Zerubbabel not attested in Ezra–Nehemiah are present elsewhere in 1 Esdras (6:17, 26, 28). At the same time, except for one brief mention at 1 Esd 5:40, the figure of Nehemiah remains conspicuously absent from 1 Esdras, even as it preserves textual parallels from the book of Nehemiah. First Esdras credits Zerubbabel, rather than Nehemiah, as a leading figure of the restoration.

The reason the author of 1 Esdras drew attention to Zerubbabel over Nehemiah remains unclear. The author may have wished to use Zerubbabel's Davidic ancestry to draw attention to the Davidic line, which otherwise is largely ignored in Ezra–Nehemiah, but 1 Esdras does not otherwise expound upon that theme. Yet the Story of the Three Youths develops the meaning of the return accounts beyond emphasizing one figure. The story underscores the agency of the Jewish people and their God—"the God of truth" (1 Esd 4:40)– in the restoration process. In Ezra the fate of Judah's building projects rests largely on the reliability of the Persian archives. Artaxerxes' search of the archives shows that Jerusalem was a rebellious city, and he orders its rebuilding to cease (Ezra 4:17–24). Darius' search of the archives shows that Cyrus decreed that the Temple in Jerusalem be rebuilt, and so the work of building begins again (Ezra 6:1–15). First Esdras preserves these "paper-shuffling" exchanges but adds a story of court wisdom that personalizes an otherwise impersonal, almost arbitrary process. In the Story of the Three Youths, it is Zerubbabel's testimony to truth that restarts the building process, and Zerubbabel attributes both that truth and his victory to God. The Story of the Three Youths indeed moves the 1 Esdras narrative "beyond what is written," supplementing the Ezra account to take the returnees' success out of the machinations of a foreign government and to put it more explicitly into the hands of their God.

BIBLIOGRAPHY

R. J. Coggins and M. A. Knibb. *The First and Second Books of Esdras* (Cambridge: Cambridge University Press, 1979); J. M. Myers. *I and II Esdras.* AB 42 (Garden City: Doubleday, 1974); Z. Talshir. *I Esdras: From Origin to Translation.* SCS 47 (Atlanta: Society of Biblical Literature, 1999); _____. *I Esdras: A Text Critical Commentary.* SCS 50 (Atlanta: Society of Biblical Literature, 2001). L. M. Wills. *The Jew in the Court of the Foreign King: Ancient Jewish Court Legends.* HDR 26 (Minneapolis: Fortress, 1990).

THE PRAYER OF MANASSEH

CASEY D. ELLEDGE

OVERVIEW

This apocryphal prayer attributed to the infamous Judahite king Manasseh explores a range of traditional themes in Jewish penitential prayer.

The Prayer of Manasseh builds upon the same traditions found in 2 Chr 33:11–19, where the reign of the wicked king concludes with his capture by the Assyrians, public repentance, and restored rule. Unlike the traditions found in 2 Chronicles, however, the Prayer gives a living voice to Manasseh's actual plea for divine mercy. Using autobiographical features, the Prayer employs the phraseology of the Chronicler's version of Manasseh's reign (cf. 2 Chr 33:6–7, Pr Man 10; 2 Chr 33:11–12, Pr Man 10–11). Such literary dependence demonstrates that the Prayer, like other apocryphal prayers, represents an expansion of earlier scriptural tradition. The Prayer of Azariah and Song of the Three Young Men, provide comparative examples.

The Prayer's dependence upon 2 Chronicles would date its composition to the eras subsequent to Chronicles (fourth century BCE), yet prior to its quotation in the third century CE *Didascalia Apostolorum*. Within this range, an absence of Christian references suggests a date of composition within the last two centuries before the Common Era. The original language of the Greek prayer remains uncertain. A different Hebrew prayer of Manasseh found at Qumran may increase the likelihood that the Greek version could be the translation of an originally Semitic prayer. In the opinion of some scholars, such earlier Hebrew prayers of Manasseh may even have antedated the composition of 2 Chr 33:11–19 itself, thus providing a source for the Chronicler's own distinctive account of Manasseh's repentance.

OUTLINE

I. Manasseh Praises God's Power, Wrath, and Mercy (1–7)

  A. The Creator's Majesty (1–4)

  B. God's Wrath upon Sinners (5)

  C. "Unsearchable is your promised mercy" (6–7)

II. Manasseh Pleads for Mercy (8–15)

  A. God invites repentance (8)

  B. Confession of sins (9–10)

  C. Plea for redemption (11–14)

  D. Concluding promise to praise the deity (15)

DETAILED ANALYSIS

With economy and beauty, the prayer dramatically develops its wide-ranging themes, beginning with God's power in creation and ending with the penitent speaker's vow to praise the deity for the mercy bestowed upon him. The prayer opens by directly addressing God's creative power, wrath, and mercy (1–7). The God of the Jewish ancestors is the creator of all things (1), whose might made heaven and earth and the sea, "who confined the deep/and sealed it with your terrible and glorious name" (3). The penitent is certain that the creator's wrath and mercy are equally encompassing: "the wrath of your threat to sinners is unendurable;/yet immeasurable and unsearchable/is your promised mercy,/for you are the Lord Most High,/of great compassion, long-suffering, and very merciful,/and you relent at human suffering" (5b–7c). Through the skillful use of poetic parallelism, the prayer achieves a striking balance of divine justice and mercy.

As the prayer develops beyond this cosmic tableau, the penitent begins to plead his own case (8–15). The "God of the righteous" need not grant repentance for those who are already innocent—but rather "for me ... a sinner" (8). A series of stylistic repetitions intensifies the speaker's desperation, as he confesses his own sins: "My transgressions are multiplied, O Lord, they are multiplied" (9b); "I have sinned, O Lord, I have sinned" (12a); "Forgive me, O Lord, forgive me" (13b). The autobiographical content of the prayer

613

alludes specifically to Manasseh's religious crimes: "I have provoked your wrath ... setting up abominations [i.e., idols]" (10*d*, *f*). Conflicted and on the verge of despair, he declares himself unworthy to lift up his eyes to the heavens (9*c*); he is convinced, "I am rejected because of my sins" (10*c*).

Yet even so, "now" he bows "the knee of [his] heart," beseeching the divine graciousness (11), hopeful that the "God of the righteous" ancestors is also "the God of those who repent" (13*f*). Rather than judging the sinner, God will do a greater work by revealing the divine glory even in the person of the wicked king himself: "in me you will manifest your goodness;/for, unworthy as I am, you will save me according to your great mercy" (14*a–c*). The prayer concludes as the speaker, graciously redeemed, makes good on this promise, joining "all the host of heaven" in singing hymns of praise to God (15).

This intensely personal, as opposed to national, psalm of repentance embodies in its own distinctive way a number of themes to be found in other biblical and early Jewish literature. It employs traditional features of penitential psalmody found in other writings, including reflections upon God's mercy and grace (Pr Man 1–7; cf. Pss 32:10; 51:1; 130:3–4, 7–8), a confession that often acknowledges the deity's wrath upon the speaker is just (Pr Man 8–10; cf. Pss 32:5; 38:1–4, 18; 51:3–5; 130; 3, 8; 143:2; Syr. Ps 155:8), the speaker's petition for divine mercy and cleansing from evil (Pr Man 11–13; cf. Pss 6:1–4; 38:1, 15–22; 51:1–2, 7–12; 130:1–2, 5–6; 143:1–2, 7–12; Syr. Ps 155:1–15), and the promise that the speaker will offer continual praise for the deity's compassion (Pr Man 14–15; cf. Pss 6:5, 51:14–15; Syr. Ps 155:19). Further comparisons may be made to contemporary psalms discovered within the *Great Psalms Scroll* from Qumran. Manasseh's prayer also displays the well-known motif of the wicked ruler who comes to acknowledge the might of Israel's God (cf. Dan 2:46, 3:28, 4:34–37; 6:25–27; 2 Macc 9:1–18), thus affirming the deity's moral governance of history. The autobiographical features of the prayer further advance the theme that if the notorious Manasseh can receive pardon for his transgressions, then no human wickedness can outreach the grace of God.

BIBLIOGRAPHY

J. H. Charlesworth."Prayer of Manasseh." In *The Old Testament Pseudepigrapha*, ed. J. H. Charlesworth. 2 vols. (New York: Doubleday, 1985) 2:625–37; W. Schniedewind. "A Qumran Fragment of the Ancient 'Prayer of Manasseh.'" *ZAW* 108 (1996) 105–107.

PSALM 151

MATTHEW GOFF

OVERVIEW

Psalm 151 is a brief hymn, seven verses in length, in which David recounts in the first person his selection by God to be king and his defeat of Goliath. The poem stresses that God exalted David, a lowly shepherd, rather than his brothers. Psalm 151 draws extensively from 1 Sam 16–17. The hymn appears at the end of Psalter not in the Hebrew Bible but rather in the Septuagint (LXX), or Greek Old Testament. The psalm is not in the Jewish, Protestant, or Catholic canons but is revered as scripture in the Eastern Orthodox tradition.

Because of the Dead Sea Scrolls, we now have an ancient version of Ps 151 in Hebrew. A large work, known as the Psalms Scroll (11QPsa), was found in Cave 11 of the Qumran site. This document contains thirty-nine hymns that correspond to biblical psalms and several others that do not. Column 28 of this scroll contains a version of Ps 151. It has significant differences from the form of the poem in the Septuagint. This Qumran composition indicates that the hymn was composed originally in Hebrew and then translated into Greek. In the Hebrew text there is a clear break in the manuscript between a poem that deals with David becoming king (Ps 151:1–5) and another that involves his battle with Goliath (Ps 151:6–7). Scholars classify the first Qumran hymn as Ps 151A and the second as Ps 151B. The Psalms Scroll suggests that LXX Ps 151 is a combination of two originally distinct compositions.

OUTLINE

I. Superscription

    A. Attribution to David

    B. Development of the Psalter into Its Final Form

II. God's Selection of David as King (vv. 1–5)

    A. God Chooses David, Rather than His Brothers

    B. David as a Musician

III. David's Defeat of Goliath (vv. 6–7)

DETAILED ANALYSIS

The superscription stresses that the poem is "outside the number," referring to the 150 poems of the psalter. The hymn is thus presented as a kind of appendix to the Book of Psalms. Concern that the poem is "outside the number" may explain the superscription's assertion that the psalm was written by David himself. The attribution to David functions as a justification for the hymn's inclusion in the psalter. The superscription of the Qumran version of Ps 151 is much briefer than that of LXX Ps 151. It reads: "A Hallelujah of David the Son of Jesse." The claims that the psalm was written by David himself or that the hymn is "outside the number" were added later. The Qumran version of the hymn reflects an earlier stage of the biblical psalter in which its canonical form with 150 psalms had not fully taken shape.

Psalm 151 contains two sections. The first (vv. 1–5) recounts God's selection of David as king. It relies on 1 Sam 16. In v. 1 David declares: "I was small among my brothers,/and the youngest in my father's house;/I tended my father's sheep." Verse 5 similarly stresses that David's brothers were "handsome and tall," but that God did not choose any of them to be king (v. 5; cf. 1 Sam 16:7–11). Theologically, a key message of this hymn is that God's blessings do not always work in ways that make sense in human terms. Psalm 151 enumerates several factors, such as David's youth and small stature, that would suggest he would be the least likely child of Jesse to become king. David ascended to the throne not because of his own charisma or talents but because God appointed him for the royal office.

God's selection of David is also stressed in Ps 151:4, which asserts that God "sent his messenger" to anoint David. This "messenger" (Gk.: *angelon*) can be understood as an angel, but in the Bible it is Samuel who anoints David as king (1 Sam 16:13). The Qumran version of Ps 151, in contrast to the Septuagint version of the poem, explicitly states that the prophet Samuel anoints David.

Another important trope of Ps 151 is that David is a musician. This motif is drawn from 1 Sam 16 (vv. 16–18). In Ps 151:2 David claims that he has fashioned a harp and a lyre. The next verse reads: "And who will tell my Lord?/The Lord himself; it is he who hears" (v. 3). This somewhat obscure statement can be reasonably understood as a reference to God hearing David's musical praise of God. The Qumran Psalms Scroll indicates that Ps 151:3 is a truncation of an originally longer text. In the Hebrew version of the poem David makes musical instruments, as in LXX Ps 151, but then goes on to assert: "And [so] have I rendered glory to the Lord, thought I, within my soul. The mountains do not witness to him, nor do the hills proclaim; the trees have cherished my words and the flock my works." Nothing whatsoever in these lines corresponds to LXX Ps 151. The next line in the Qumran poem is similar to, but longer than, Ps 151:3 in the Septuagint: "For who can proclaim and who can bespeak and who can recount the deeds of the Lord? Everything has God seen, everything has he heard and he has heeded." The Qumran poem stresses the difficulty of praising God because his accomplishments are innumerable and he has, literally, heard it all. This motif fell out of the psalm in the course of its scribal transmission and is not present in its Greek translation. It is easier to draw the conclusion that God hears David praise him from the Septuagint version of the hymn than the Qumran form of the composition.

The second section of Ps 151 (vv. 6–7) concerns David's defeat of Goliath. This story is recounted in 1 Sam 17, and the hymn draws on this biblical narrative. Goliath is never referred to by name in the psalm but is rather called "the foreigner" (the Philistine). Psalm 151:6 states that he cursed David (cf. Sam 17:43). David also asserts that he beheads Goliath with his own sword (Ps 151:7), an act described in 1 Sam 17:51.

Theologically, the overall message of Ps 151 is that God has the power to exalt the lowly (David) and bring down the mighty (Goliath). The hymn, by stressing that God selected the most unlikely son of Jesse to be king of Israel, teaches that the deity works in unexpected ways. The psalm, with its singular focus on David, concludes the biblical psalter as a whole in the Septuagint. In this arrangement the psalter ends on a strongly Davidic note, which is not the case in conventional translations of the OT. Psalm 151 asserts not only God's selection of David as king of Israel but also the traditional attribution of the psalms to this venerable figure of ancient Israel.

BIBLIOGRAPHY

P. W. Flint. *The Dead Sea Psalms Scrolls and the Book of Psalms* (Leiden: Brill, 1997); D. J. Harrington, S.J. *Invitation to the Apocrypha* (Grand Rapids: Eerdmans, 1999); N. F. Marcos. "David the Adolescent: On Psalm 151." *The Old Greek Psalter.* Ed. P.J. Gentry et al. (Sheffield: Sheffield Academic Press, 2001) 205–17; J. A. Sanders. *The Psalms Scroll of Qumran Cave 11* (Oxford: Clarendon, 1964).

3 MACCABEES

JEREMY F. HULTIN

OVERVIEW

The title 3 Maccabees is misleading, for the events in this book take place half a century before the Maccabean revolt. The title likely arose when this text was placed after 1 and 2 Maccabees in Greek manuscripts. The book describes how God delivered the Jews from two major crises under Ptolemy IV Philopator, king of Egypt from 221–204 BCE. In the first, the king threatened to enter their Temple (3 Macc 1–2); in the second, he subjected the Jews to slavery and, ultimately, to systematic destruction (3 Macc 2:28–6:29).

The work may well have been composed in Alexandria, the site of most of the story's action and home to a sizeable Jewish community. Because the book exhibits familiarity with the Greek translations of Esther and Daniel, it must have been composed after the mid-second century BCE. It is possible that the "registration" or "census" described in 2:28 was modeled on the registration for a poll tax introduced by Augustus in 24/23 BCE. Some scholars also detect echoes of the crises of Caligula's reign (37–41 CE). Thus the book could date from the Roman period. Ultimately, any date between 150 BCE to 50 CE is possible.

Although the historical value of 3 Maccabees has had its scholarly defenders, it seems best to consider it a work of historical fiction, a Jewish "novel" that includes real historical figures (e.g., Philopator) and perhaps memories of one or more historical incidents. Josephus gives a brief account of a similar crisis in Egypt, but he sets events in the 140s BCE (*Against Apion* 2.53–55). Thus there were apparently diverse legends explaining the origin of a contemporary celebration for divine deliverance.

Given the king's terrible persecution of the Jews, it would be tempting to infer that the author viewed the Gentile government with suspicion or hostility. But in fact, the author insists that true, law-abiding Jews were a bulwark for the king. Jews "continued to maintain goodwill and unswerving loyalty toward the dynasty" (3:3) even when the king began to mistreat them. At the end of the book, the king recognizes that the Jews are "those who faithfully kept our country's fortresses" (6:25) and that they were distinguished "in their goodwill towards us" (6:26 author's trans.; cf. 7:7 and 5:31). Such statements could hardly be made by an author who considered support of the government inherently incompatible with Judaism. In fact, it is the apostates, who violated divine commandments "for the belly's sake," who would never be favorably disposed toward the king's authority (7:11). In other words, faithfulness to the Jewish religion is the marker not of a traitor but of a good royalist.

Nor are the Gentiles in the book unremittingly hostile to the Jews. There are a few Gentiles who help (cf. 3 Macc 1:27; 3 Macc 3:8–10, where they are called the Jews' "neighbors ... and business associates"). But these passages remain exceptions to the overall tenor of the book. On the whole, the outlook of 3 Maccabees is strikingly different from that of the Letter of Aristeas, which envisions Greeks and Jews enjoying pleasant, respectful conversations about God and wisdom.

The author may exhibit ambivalence and inconsistencies in his attitudes toward Gentiles or the king, but the book's central theme is unequivocal and frequently reiterated: God is mighty and will come to the aid of his people when they call upon him. Even Philopator realizes in the end that anyone who would cause the Jews harm has "the Ruler over every power, the Most High God, in everything and inescapably as an antagonist to avenge such acts" (7:9). This emphasis on God's surpassing greatness is echoed throughout the book: God is king, lord, all-powerful, most great. Hence prayer is more effective than any human resistance, and lengthy prayers bring about resolution to the book's two major crises.

To judge from the paucity of ancient references to 3 Maccabees, the book was not widely read either by Jews (there are in fact no Jewish references to the book) or by Christians. Theodoret summarizes the book in his commentary on Daniel. It is not rendered in the Vulgate, but there were Syriac translations.

OUTLINE

I. The Battle of Raphia (1:1–7)

II. Threat to Temple in Jerusalem (1:8–2:24)

A. Philopator Denied Entrance to the Sanctuary (1:8–15)

B. Jewish Uproar in Response to the King's Intention (1:16–29)

C. Prayer of the High Priest Simon (2:1–20)

D. God Heeds Prayer, Shakes Philopator (2:21–24)

III. Crisis in Egypt (2:25–6:21)

A. Philopator's Retaliatory Decrees Against Jews (2:25–33)
  2:25–28. Jews Forced to Sacrifice and to Be Registered for Poll-tax
  2:29. Jews to Be Branded with Ivy Leaf as Symbol of Dionysus
  2:30–33. Some Jews Apostatize; Majority Remains Steadfast

B. Philopator Orders Egyptian Jews Gathered for Execution (3:1–30)
  3:1–10. Variety of Views About the Jews
  3:11–30. Philopator's Letter

C. Jews Gathered for Execution (4:1–21)
  4:1–15. Jews Arrested and Imprisoned
  4:16–21. Impossibility of Enrolling All the Jews

D. God Prevents Philopator's Plans to Execute the Jews (5:1–51)
  5:1–9. Hermon Prepares the Elephants to Trample the Jews
  5:10–17. God Causes Philopator to Oversleep
  5:18–35. Renewed Preparation of Elephants; Divinely Induced Amnesia
  5:36–51. Philopator Renews His Threats, and Promises Destruction of Jerusalem

E. Prayer of Eleazar (6:1–15)

F. Angelic Deliverance and Reversal of Fortune (6:16–29)

IV. Celebrations for God's Deliverance (6:30–7:23)

A. Jews Celebrate for Seven Days (6:30–35)

B. A festival of Commemoration Is Instituted (6:36–41)

C. Royal Decree on Behalf of the Jews (7:1–9)

D. Revenge Against Apostates (7:10–16)

E. Peaceful Return Home (7:16–23)

DETAILED ANALYSIS

1:1–5. The book opens with Ptolemy IV Philopator (221–204 BCE) preparing to battle Antiochus III (223–187 BCE), king of Syria, at Raphia, a city near Gaza (217 BCE). One Dositheus, son of Drimylus, who is said to be an apostate Jew (1:3), saves Philopator from a plot on his life. The detail about Dositheus's having apostatized is odd given the animus directed against apostates elsewhere in this book (2:33; 7:10–16), and the claim that they were less committed to the wellbeing of the kingdom (7:11). A lengthier account of these events, with some variation in the details, is contained in Polybius, *The Histories* 5.79–86.

1:6–15. Following his victory, Philopator made offerings to the sanctuaries of various local cities, including the Temple of Jerusalem. But although he was allowed, even as a Gentile, to make a sacrifice and to offer gifts (1:10), he was forbidden by biblical law from entering the sanctuary itself (Exod 30:10; Lev 16:2, 11–12, 15; Heb 9:7). Angered by this distinctive Temple law, the king decides to enter despite all Jewish remonstrance. (Pompey the Great actually entered the Temple in 63 BCE; it was widely believed that God punished him for this impiety; and in 40 CE, Caligula planned to have his statue set up in the Temple.)

1:16–29. The author vividly depicts the distress Philopator's plan causes the Jews of Jerusalem. Some Jews called for armed resistance (1:23), but the elders—no doubt representing the author's own sympathies—persuade them to join in supplication to God rather than taking up arms. Indeed, heartfelt entreaty to God characterizes this entire scene (1:16, 21, 24), and even some of the Gentiles around the king join in urging God to intervene (1:27)!

2:1–20. Simon II was high priest from 219 to 196 BCE. He was renowned for fortifying and beautifying the Temple (Sir 50:1–21), making him an especially appropriate person here to pray for the Temple's protection. Simon's prayer resembles the prayers of Ezra 9, Neh 9, and Dan 9.

Simon begins by listing God's attributes. As is often the case in 3 Maccabees, the emphasis falls upon God's power. This implicitly contrasts God with Philopator: God is *truly* "Lord," "king," "sovereign of all creation," "*only* ruler," and "almighty"; and whereas the Jews suffer at the hands of an "*impious* and *profane* man," God is "*holy* among the *holy* ones" (2:2).

Having listed several attributes of God, Simon recounts God's past punishment of the insolent and arrogant. First he says that God destroyed the "giants" with the flood. In Gen 6:1–4, when the "sons of God" took women as wives, their offspring were called "Nephilim," which the LXX rendered "giants." Ancient Jewish texts such as *1 Enoch* say a good deal more about these fallen angels and their giant offspring than does Genesis, and make explicit that the flood was meant to obliterate the giants (e.g. Wis 14:6). Simon also states that God overthrew Sodom and Gomorrah (2:5) and destroyed Pharaoh (2:6–7). In the NT, Jude also mentions the punishment of "the angels who did not keep their own position" (Jude 6) and the punishment of Sodom and Gomorrah (Jude 7).

Simon next appeals to God's choice of Jerusalem as the place for his "name" (cf. Deut 12:11) and his "magnificent manifestation" (2:9). The latter could refer to visions of God's glory (e.g. Isa 6), but even more appropriate for the present prayer would be a reference to the fiery manifestation of God's presence in Solomon's Temple (2 Chr 7:1; cf. 2 Macc 1:19–23).

Indeed, the fact that God had chosen Jerusalem forms a central motif of Simon's prayer (2:10, 14–18). God has promised to hear petition "when we come to *this place* and pray" (2:10, emphasis added). Such a focus on Jerusalem is all the more noteworthy in a book that was most likely composed in the Diaspora, and reminds us that Jews throughout the ancient world viewed Jerusalem as *the* holy city and its Temple as the only true dwelling of Israel's God. Simon acknowledges that God's true dwelling is in heaven (2 Macc 2:10; cf. 1 Kgs 8:27), but this observation was rarely felt to be incompatible with God's sanctifying and even inhabiting the Temple in Jerusalem. Christian readers often forget that Jesus also affirmed that God "dwelt" in the Temple (Matt 23:21).

Although Simon mentions of the sins of Israel (2:13, 19), he does not dwell on national culpability for the present distress. Ultimately, Simon prays like the Psalmist (Ps 79:9–10) and reminds God of the honor God would lose if he let the Temple be destroyed. The horrifying thought of Gentiles speaking arrogantly (2:17; cf. 4:16; 6:4–5) is invoked to prompt God to action. It is almost as though Simon reminds God of two possible linguistic outcomes: either the Gentiles will boast that they have "trampled down the house of the sanctuary" (2:18), or there will be "praises in the mouth of those who are downcast and broken in spirit" (2:20).

2:21–24. God heeds the "lawful supplication" of Simon and scourges Philopator, shaking him "as a reed is shaken by the wind" (cf. Matt 11:7). In an ironic scene, the king's "bodyguards" can do nothing to protect their master other than to drag him away from the Temple, paralyzed and speechless. Whereas Heliodorus (2 Macc 3:26–40) and Antiochus IV Epiphanes (2 Macc 9:5–29) both repented after being punished by God for their insolence, Philopator uses his recovered speech to utter "bitter threats" against the Jews.

2:25–33. Philopator returned from Jerusalem to Egypt with a vendetta against the Jews, at whose hands he had just been humiliated. The king now acts in tandem with his "previously mentioned drinking companions and comrades." (These men have in fact *not* been previously mentioned in 3 Maccabees, an indication that the book may be missing an earlier reference to them, perhaps because the author was using a source that had previously mentioned them.) To punish the Jews, the king composes a decree stating that: (1) all peoples must sacrifice as a prerequisite for entering their sanctuaries, (2) the Jews are to be "subjected to a registration involving poll tax" and reduced to the "status of slaves." Furthermore, those who were registered were to be branded with the ivy leaf, the symbol of Dionysus (2:29). The only way to avoid such registration and reduction of status was to join the initiates of Dionysus and thus to enjoy equal citizenship with the Alexandrians (2:30; this offer of Alexandrian citizenship is mentioned again at 3:21 but, strangely, is not mentioned at the end of the book when the Jews' fortunes are restored).

The precise details of this decree and any possible relationship it might have to an historical registration have been much debated. The reference to a registration for the poll tax may reflect historical circumstances of the Roman period. In 24/23 BCE Augustus introduced a census to determine how many would be liable to pay the poll tax. Jews, unlike Greek citizens of Alexandria, were deemed liable to the tax. Although there is little evidence that Ptolemaic leaders ever tried to compel the Jews to abandon their religion in the way depicted here, there is ample evidence from the Roman period that Alexandrian citizens objected to Jews enjoying citizenship when they would not worship the same gods as the Alexandrians did. Thus it is possible that the author has projected back into the reign of Philopator not only the census for taxation, but also the connection between worship of Greek gods and the privilege of citizenship.

"Being reduced to their former limited status" (2:29) refers to the fact that in the early third century BCE, Jews had been deported to Egypt by Ptolemy I Soter and held as slaves until they were manumitted by his successor, Ptolemy II Philadelphus (285–47 BCE) (*Letter of Aristeas* 22).

2:31–33. Jewish response to the king's decree is divided: some capitulated (cf. 7:15), but "the majority" maintained their religion by paying money, that is, apparently, by paying bribes to avoid the registration. These latter Jews considered the former as "enemies" of the Jewish nation, a sentiment that will reach its strongest expression at the close of the book (7:10–16).

3:1–30. Because of the failure of his plan, Philopator is now enraged not only against those in Alexandria but also those in the countryside. Why the Alexandrian Jews are still free in 4:12 is not clear.

Fictive letters and decrees were a regular component of ancient literature, especially Greek novels. For instance, in the Greek version of the Book of Esther, a fictive letter (and one quite similar in content to Philopator's here) was included after 3:13 (*Additions to Esther* 13:1–7). Philopator views the Jewish refusal to let him worship in their Temple as stemming from their "traditional arrogance" (3:17–18). From the king's perspective, a generous offer had been made to the Jews, namely, Alexandrian citizenship and participation in religious rites (3:21). Hence he describes those Jews who cooperated not as "apostates" but rather as the "few among them who are sincerely disposed toward us" (3:23). The king invokes several of the more widespread elements of ancient Alexandrian anti-Jewish sentiment, such as the charge of impiety and a wariness about Jewish separateness (3:24).

4:1–21. The author paints a lachrymose portrait of the imprisonment of Jews (note the reversals of 4:6–8). While the pathos of the scene is unmistakable, the details of the narrative are not entirely coherent. For instance, it is not clear why the king is so insistent that the Jews be "enrolled individually" when he is planning to execute all of them in a single day (4:14). Be that as it may, this element of the plot lets God's "providence" shine forth, as the Jews turn out to be too numerous to be counted.

The king's idols cannot "come to one's help" (4:16)—that is, they are precisely the opposite of God, who "was *aiding* the Jews from heaven" (4:21). The reference to the king's "profane mouth" and "improper words" against God are reminiscent of Dan 7:8, 20.

5:11–31. God puts the king into a deep sleep, which gives the Jews a reprieve and issues in further praise and supplication (5:13). Furthermore, this particular intervention by God also occasions an unexpectedly lovely comment about the divine gift of sleep (5:11), a sentiment with many more parallels in Greek and Latin literature than in the Bible (though cf. Ps 127:2). Having first put the king to sleep, God then causes him to forget why he has assembled the elephants in the first place; the king declares that he has no complaint against the Jews (5:31)!

Ultimately, the king renews his oath to massacre the Jews held captive in Alexandria, and adds to this that he would level Judea and burn the Temple in Jerusalem (5:42–43). Not only is the drama heightened by the repetition of threat and rescue, but the scale of the crisis has now grown beyond the boundary of Egypt and affects all who worship the God of Israel.

5:50–6:15. Facing certain death, the Jews "considered the help that they had received before from heaven," and prayed all the more fervently for God's help (5:50–51). These two verses nicely encapsulate one of the central hortatory purposes of the entire book: because God has so dramatically saved Israel in the past, earnest prayer is the appropriate response to any present crisis.

Just as Simon's prayer in 3 Macc 2 prevented the destruction of the Temple, so the prayer of "a certain Eleazar" (6:1–15) leads to the ultimate deliverance of the Jews. The appearance of an aged, distinguished figure named "Eleazar" recalls the like-named martyr of 2 Macc 6:18–31 and 4 Macc 5–7, as well as the high priest in the *Letter of Aristeas* 1, 41.

Eleazar's prayer is similar to Simon's. He invokes God's might (6:2) and recalls God's former deliverance from threatening rulers such as Pharaoh (6:4) and Sennacherib (6:5; cf. 2 Kgs 18–19). Also like Simon, Eleazar urges God not to let the Gentiles boast (6:11), and even suggests that if punishment is truly necessary, God should first rescue the Jews and then destroy them himself.

But unlike Simon, who prayed from the chosen city Jerusalem, Eleazar states that he and his fellow Jews are "perishing as foreigners in a foreign land" (6:3, emphasis added). Hence it is appropriate that he invokes instances in which God rescued individuals who were far from the promised land, such as the "three companions" of Daniel, whom he notes were in Babylon (6:6). And by stating that Daniel was thrown to the lions because of "envious slander" (6:7), Eleazar helps to liken Daniel's situation to that facing the Jews (3 Macc 2:26; 3:7; 7:3–4). Finally, Jonah (6:8) is the classic example of a prophet rescued while far from home. Eleazar concludes his prayer with a reference to Lev 26:44 (emphasis added), reminding God that he had never neglected his people even "when they were in the land of their enemies."

6:16–29. God finally and conclusively delivers the Jews. When the Ptolemaic troops are thrown into confusion by two terrifying angels,

the elephants begin to trample the soldiers. Now, finally, Philopator repents. Much as in 5:28–34, Philopator blames his advisors for having initiated the foolish and cruel plan to destroy the Jews. He insists that the Jews have served his country well (6:25–26) and that their God has sustained his government (6:28).

6:30–41. In a scene of reversals, the very place meant for the Jews' destruction becomes one of joy. Dirges are replaced by songs of praise. Instead of being branded with the ivy leaf of Dionysus, the Jews are now supplied *wine* for a festival of seven days (6:30). Even the king thanks God for his own rescue (6:33). The festival is instituted for future observance in much the way Esth 9 recounts the establishment of Purim. Josephus in fact mentions a festival celebrated in Alexandria commemorating the deliverance from the elephants (*Against Apion* 2.25).

7:1–16. Philopator reiterates in writing his newfound appreciation for the Jews and their God, summarizing a central theme of the entire book, namely, that the "God of heaven" defends the Jews as his own children (7:6), and hence that anyone who opposes them opposes the "Ruler over every power" (7:9). In Esth 8–9 the Jews are permitted to avenge themselves against their *Gentile* antagonists; in 3 Macc 7:10–16, they are granted permission to execute renegade *Jews*. Finally (7:17–23), in a storybook dénouement, the Jews are returned to their homes and recover any lost property; their neighbors now fear them (cf. Esth 8:17).

BIBILIOGRAPHY

J. J. Collins. *Between Athens and Jerusalem.* 2nd ed. (Grand Rapids: Eerdmans, 2000); N. C. Croy. *3 Maccabees.* Septuagint Commentary Series (Leiden: Brill, 2006); C. W. Emmet. "The Third Book of Maccabees." *The Apocrypha and Pseudepigrapha of the Old Testament.* R. H. Charles, ed. 2 vols. (Oxford: Clarendon, 1913); M. Hadas. *The Third and Fourth Books of Maccabees* (New York: Harper, 1953); V. A. Tcherikover. "The Third Book of Maccabees as a Historical Source of Augustus' Time." *Scripta Hierosolymitana* 7 (1961) 1–26.

4 MACCABEES

JEREMY F. HULTIN

OVERVIEW

The present work was included in some early Christian codices of the Bible (Alexandrinus, Sinaiticus, and Venetus) with the simple title "Fourth Maccabees." Eusebius and Jerome referred to the work more descriptively as "On the Supremacy of Reason," and attributed it to the first-century Jewish historian Flavius Josephus. The text does occur in some editions of Josephus's works under the related title, "On Temperate Reason," but both the details of the account and its language confirm that the attribution to Josephus was erroneous.

As the author himself notes (3:19), the work is divided into two main parts. In the first section (1:1–3:18), the author uses a variety of arguments and biblical illustrations to demonstrate that "devout reason is sovereign over the emotions" (1:1). In the second portion of the book, the author recounts the fates of nine Maccabean martyrs: the aged priest Eleazar (5–7), the seven brothers (8–14), and their widowed mother (14–17). The noble conduct of these martyrs is presented as further evidence that "devout reason" can triumph over any emotion or agony. But the accounts of the martyrs are certainly more than just further illustrations of the book's thesis. In an age when the temptation to abandon a distinctively Jewish way of life could be powerful, these heroes' steadfast adherence to the Mosaic law is put forward as a moving example worthy of imitation (18:1–2).

Little can be said with certainty about the author or when and where he wrote. He was clearly a devout Jew who had the benefit of an education in Greek rhetoric (cf. 1:12) and had some acquaintance with Stoic philosophy. But such an education could have been obtained in any major city of the Hellenistic Diaspora, or even in Palestine. Although the events he describes transpire in Jerusalem (4:22; 18:5), the early Church commemorated the martyrs in Antioch, making that one attractive possibility (but only a possibility) for the book's provenance. Regarding the date of composition, the references to the Temple (4:9; 4:20) cannot count as evidence that the cult in Jerusalem was still operational, for other Jewish

texts written after the destruction of the Temple in 70 CE also describe cultic activities in the present tense. One possible clue about the date can be found in the fact that Apollonius is called governor of Syria, Phoenicia, and Cilicia (4 Macc 4:2; cf. 2 Macc 3:5). Elias Bickerman observed that Cilicia was only governed along with Syria between 20 and 54 CE; if the author wrote during this period, he could have projected the administrative circumstances of his own day into the past. As attractive as Bickerman's proposal is, subsequent scholarship has complicated the question. Ultimately, a date between the middle of the first century and the early second century CE is reasonable; recent scholarship has tended to favor the later end of this spectrum.

The division of the work into two parts creates a challenge for defining its genre. The opening portion (1:1–3:18) is well described as a literary diatribe, in which the author addresses imagined objections to his thesis (1:5; 2:24). The latter portion of the book is a form of epideictic rhetoric, the rhetoric of praise and blame. In particular, it resembles Greek funeral orations, which praised the piety and bravery of the dead so as to encourage the imitation of their virtues. Although there is a clearly marked division between the two halves of the work (3:19), there is no reason to doubt its overall unity. The first part of the book also makes use of historical examples (such as Joseph, Moses, and David) to demonstrate the supremacy of reason over the passions; and the praise of the Maccabean martyrs in the second part of the book is punctuated with reflections on their evidentiary value for the same thesis (6:31–35; 13:1–5). It has been argued that this speech was originally presented orally, perhaps at Antioch, the traditional burial site of the martyrs (17:8–10 refers to their tomb). The references at 1:10 and 3:19 to "this anniversary" and "the present occasion" could indicate that we have a commemorative funeral oration. But an author trained in rhetoric would have been able to simulate the language used in funeral orations, so there is little to say whether it was actually delivered or was composed simply to be read.

Significance and Influence. 4 Maccabees was translated into Syriac, but no Latin translations survive and it was not made part of the Vulgate. Without question, the literary influence of 4 Maccabees on Christian authors can be seen in second-century literature about martyrdom, especially in the letters of Ignatius of Antioch and in the *Martyrdom of Polycarp*. It was also an important book for major patristic authors such as John Chrysostom, Augustine, and Jerome. The story of the mother and her seven sons is preserved in rabbinic sources (discussed by Hadas); but the rabbinic accounts seem not to be literarily dependent on 4 Maccabees, for they place these events in the reign of the Roman Emperor Hadrian rather than the Seleucid king Antiochus IV Epiphanes.

Among the most striking teachings of 4 Maccabees is its claim that the deaths of the martyrs functioned as a "ransom" and an "atoning sacrifice" for Israel (see the comments on 6:29; 17:20–22). Because similar language is used of Jesus' death in the NT, some have proposed 4 Maccabees as an inspiration for this idea. Students of the apostle Paul may be particularly interested in the way 4 Maccabees portrays the role of the Mosaic law in the pursuit of self-control. Throughout 4 Maccabees it is taken for granted that it is possible to adhere to the law and that the law helps individuals to triumph over passions. For instance, 4 Macc 2:5–6 cites the commandment not to "covet" (Exod 20:17; Deut 5:21) as *evidence* that reason can control desires (i.e., God would not command what was impossible); Paul, on the other hand, claims that through this very commandment the power of sin "produced in me all kinds of covetousness" (Rom 7:7–8).

OUTLINE

DETAILED ANALYSIS

I. The Supremacy of Devout Reason over the Emotions Proven Philosophically (1:1–3:18)

1:1–12. The author presents the thesis to be defended and explains (1:7–12) that he will do so both by argument (1:1–3:18) and by considering the conduct of the Maccabean martyrs (3:19–18:24). The thesis is that "devout reason" is overeign over the emotions. With the adjective "devout" or "pious," the author sounds at once his distinctively Jewish approach to the broader philosophical question of the relation of reason to the passions. For him, true reason is "devout" because it is directed toward God and nurtured by the God-given law of Moses.

The Greek word *pathos*, commonly rendered "emotion," could also be translated by "passion" or "affection." All schools of Greek philosophy were in agreement that reason should be superior to the passions or emotions, but they disagreed about the degree of mastery possible and the means of achieving such mastery. The earliest Stoics had argued that the emotions must be extirpated entirely, resulting in a state of *apatheia*, passionless perfection. Thus the author's claim that reason does not *destroy* the emotions but only resists yielding to them has been cited as evidence that he diverges (intentionally or otherwise) from pure Stoic dogma. But Stoics such as Posidonius (ca. 135–51 BCE) had modified the older Stoic teaching about the passions, arguing that they were in fact innate to a person (cf. 2:21–22), and hence that they were to be controlled rather than eradicated. Thus it is possible that the author may be entirely consistent with a later Stoic position. On his claims about the passions, see also 1:28–29; 3:2–5.

The author also explains (1:10–12) how the praise of the martyrs is related to his principal theme: the martyrs' ability to despise suffering illustrates his claim that "reason controls the emotions." To be sure, the martyrs are more than simply evidence of a thesis: they are also national heroes, for their virtue and steadfastness resulted in the downfall of the "tyrant," the Seleucid king Antiochus IV Epiphanes.

2:7–23. The author was clearly aware of the charge that the Mosaic law seemed too arbitrary and particular for it to count as philosophical. Before illustrating the way that Eleazar was a "true philosopher" (5–7), he first notes that the legislation itself has the power to improve people morally. For instance, if one follows the law, one is forced to lend without interest (2:8; cf. Exod 22:25; Lev 25:35–37; Deut 23:19–20) and to cancel debts in the seventh year (Deut 15:1–11), and hence, even a "lover of money" is forced to overcome his or her base inclination. A host of related examples are adduced. Importantly, the author notes that the law is superior to the power of familial and friendly attachments (2:10–13) in that it enjoins rebuke. This prepares the way for the author's reflections on the family affections of the brothers and their mother (4 Macc 13–14). With the examples of Moses and Jacob, the author argues that the law and reason can master even anger: Moses did nothing rash to Dathan and Abiram when they grumbled against him (Num 16:12–15, 23–25, although the biblical account does claim that Moses was "very angry"!); and Jacob censured Simeon and Levi for their savage treatment of the Shechemites (Gen 34). In a fascinating theological reflection on the source of the emotions, the author affirms that God "planted" the emotions and inclinations in humans, but that God also set the mind as governor over them (2:21–22). To this enthroned mind God gave the law. The claim that those obedient to the law have a "kingdom" echoes the famous claim of the Stoics that only the wise man was truly a king (cf. 14:2).

2:24–3:5. The author concedes that reason cannot deal with "its own emotions," such as forgetfulness and ignorance; rather, its proper control is over the emotions of the body. Nevertheless, even passions of the mind, such as anger or malice, can be resisted by reason so that they do not gain the upper hand.

3:6–18. The example of King David's ability to resist his irrational thirst is perhaps not best suited for the problem of reason's ability to rule over its own passions (e.g. forgetfulness and ignorance). The illustration is, however, a fascinating interpretation and expansion of the incident recorded in 2 Sam 23:13–17 and 1 Chr 11:15–19. Several details are added to the biblical account to accentuate the irrationality of David's thirst and the challenge of resisting it: David was *extremely* thirsty; there were springs where he was; the two young soldiers who fetched the water did so at tremendous risk (in the books of Samuel and Chronicles it is *three* warriors, and the dangers of their mission are not so great).

II. Reason's Supremacy Demonstrated from Maccabean Martyrs (3:19–17:6)

3:19–4:26. An abridged version of the events of 2 Macc 3–6 sets the scene for the martyrdoms, which will occupy the remainder of the book (4 Macc 5–18). In condensing 2 Maccabees the author has changed and garbled a few details. The attempted seizure of the Temple funds (3:20) took place not under Seleucus Nicanor (311–281 BCE) but Seleucus IV Philopator (187–175 BCE); furthermore, Seleucus was not the *father* of Antiochus IV Epiphanes (4:15) but his brother. Finally, in 2 Macc 3 it is Heliodorus, not Apollonius, who is prevented from stealing funds from the Temple treasury. None of these details is as important for the author as giving an explanation for why God allowed such terrible persecution. So long as there was a righteous high priest and good conduct in Jerusalem, God came to the Temple's defense (3:19–4:14); it was the *unlawful* reforms of the high priest Jason (175–72 BCE) that angered "divine justice" and brought Antiochus's persecution as punishment (4:15–26). Because it was unlawful behavior that brought about the dire persecution, it is fitting that the deaths of the martyrs "for the sake of the law" (6:27) reverse Israel's fortunes (cf. 17:22).

5:1–7:23. Whereas the events leading up to the persecution under Antiochus have been condensed, the relatively brief account of Eleazar's martyrdom (2 Macc 6:18–31) is here greatly expanded so that the philosophical validity of Eleazar's actions—and indeed the philosophical nature of the law itself—can be defended. At stake is nothing less than whether the practice of Judaism is consistent with the highest principles of philosophy. Most schools of ancient philosophy were in agreement that life should be lived "according to nature." Antiochus thus questions whether Eleazar can really be a "philosopher" when he "senselessly" refuses something nature has given, such as pork (5:5–12). Furthermore, Antiochus adds, God would surely forgive a *minor*

transgression committed under such duress (5:13; cf. 8:22).

5:14–38. Eleazar replies to both arguments. To eat defiling food would *not* be a minor transgression, for it would be tantamount to despising the whole law, since all transgressions are of equal value (5:19–21). Furthermore, the Jews' reputation for piety was at stake (5:17–18; cf. 6:18), and, as Eleazar will note later, he should not set a bad example for others (6:19). As for the weightier charge that the particular food laws were irrational and unnatural, Eleazar responds along two lines. First, he claims that the law engenders such universally recognized virtues as "self-control," "courage," "justice," and "piety" (the first three of these belong to the four "cardinal" virtues), and therefore the law is philosophically worthy. Second, he notes that God the lawgiver is also God the Creator of all things; hence God's particular stipulations in the law must reflect what is best for his creatures (5:25–26).

6:1–35. The gruesome details of Eleazar's torture and death demonstrate the extent of his self-mastery and introduce the athletic motif (6:10) that will recur in the other martyrdoms (9:8; 11:20–21; 14:5; 15:29; 16:16; 17:11–16). Eleazar's concern for setting a good example means that he cannot even *pretend* to eat pork (6:15–23). Eleazar prays that his voluntary ("I might have saved myself") suffering and death could count vicariously for the Jewish people (6:27–29). His blood is to purify them and his life is given as ransom for theirs, an idea that is later echoed by the first brother (9:24) and developed by the author (17:20–22).

From this lurid account of torture the author draws a conclusion relevant to his initial thesis: Eleazar's conduct illustrates that "devout reason is sovereign over the emotions" (6:31) for it "has mastered agonies" (6:35).

7:1–23. Eleazar is praised in terms reminiscent of a Stoic sage: by his deeds he has proven that his "divine philosophy" is true (7:9). Because Eleazar's death constituted an "atoning sacrifice" that saved Israel (17:22; 6:27–29), he is compared to Aaron, who "made atonement for the people" to stop the plague (Num 16:46–50). Like Isaac (Gen 22:1–19), Eleazar was willing to be slain.

As earlier (1:5; 2:24), the author now addresses imagined objections (7:17–23). In this case the question does not go to the heart of his claim that reason can control the emotions; rather, the counter argument simply notes that not all people have "prudent reason." The author is actually in agreement with this "objection," for he claims that only those who "attend to religion with a whole heart" (7:18), only the "wise and courageous" (7:23), master their emotions. Once again, philosophy and "faith" in God are combined (7:21) in a uniquely Jewish synthesis.

8:1–9:9. In order to show just how great a temptation the brothers overcame, the author first imagines how they might have spoken had they been "cowardly and unmanly" (8:16–26) before he reports what they actually said (9:1–9). Likewise the mother's hypothetical speech (16:6–11) is presented before her actual response (16:16–23). In both cases, the hypothetical discourse proposes various plausible reasons to submit to the king's order. One suspects that some such arguments in favor of assimilation were current in the author's day and that he sought to counter their seductive logic. The brothers are introduced as "handsome," and their beauty makes an impression on the king (8:4, 5, 10), suggesting that it is he, rather than these young men, who is the victim of his passions.

9:10–12:19. In an almost formulaic fashion, each of the seven brothers endures brutal torture and speaks defiantly to the king before dying. Their bold responses to the tyrant cast them as true philosophers who take no notice of human status. The fact that the brothers appear from oldest to youngest heightens the pathos of the account and illustrates that reason can overcome the innate weakness of youth. In fact, the seventh brother (12:1–19) is so young that even the king feels compassion and allows him to speak with his mother. She, however, advises him in the "Hebrew language" (12:7), a detail that not only invokes the unique heritage of the Israelites but also heightens the suspense, as it leaves both Antiochus and the readers unsure what she has advised him to do. The king and his friends believe that the boy has come to his senses, and they set him free (12:9), but, just as his brothers had done, he audaciously informs Antiochus that eternal "tortures" await him (12:12, 18; cf. 9:32; 10:11, 21; 11:3, 23) and

chastises him for ignoring the fact that his victims "are made of the same elements" as he is (12:13). As will his mother (17:1), the last brother takes his own life (12:19). Stoics and some Jews believed that suicide was permissible—and even noble—in certain dire circumstances (cf. 2 Macc 14:37–46).

13:1–14:10. After noting that the brothers' triumph over their passions demonstrates the initial thesis (13:1–7), the author then (13:8–14:10) reflects on the power of their brotherly affection. Although the author praises such familial affection as a gift of "all-wise Providence" (13:19), he also recognizes that brotherly love was an emotion to be "overcome" (14:1; cf. 2:9–12).

14:11–20. He makes a similar argument about the mother's overcoming her love for her children. Even in "unreasoning animals" the parental instinct to protect progeny is strong. Hence the mother's dramatic choice of religion over her own children is all the more remarkable, and she can be likened to Abraham (14:20), who was willing to sacrifice Isaac in obedience to God. When faced with a choice between "religion" and her children, the mother rightly chose religion; but it is a religion "that preserves them for eternal life" (15:3), so that in a sense, she, like Abraham, will get her children back. That the mother belongs to the "weaker sex" (15:5) represents a widespread prejudice (cf. 1 Pet 3:7). The ability of a woman—and a *mother*—to control her passions is the greatest proof of the author's central thesis. It is obvious just how gendered a virtue self-control was in the ancient world, for the author claims that the mother showed "a *man's* courage" (15:23) and indeed acted more courageously than "males" (15:30; cf. 16:14).

16:15–23. Whereas 5:4 and 8:3 suggest that the mother and her sons were brought into Antiochus after Eleazar had been killed, here the author reports how the mother exhorted her children to martyrdom as though they had witnessed his death. Her argument emphasizes shame and honor: if an elderly man can endure such torments, it would be shameful for these young men to cower.

17:1–18:5. After the gory and detailed treatment of the demise of Eleazar and the brothers, the mother's death is announced with striking brevity (17:1–6): she commits herself to the flames lest the guards touch her body, thus highlighting her modesty. (On voluntary death, cf. 12:19.) This final praise of the mother likens her and her sons to the stars, perhaps indicating a sort of astral mode of immortality (cf. Dan 12:3). The author believes in the immortality of the soul (9:22; 14:5; 15:3; 16:13; 17:12; 18:23) rather than in the resurrection of the body (cf. Philo and the Wisdom of Solomon).

III. Concluding Encomium (17:7–18:24)

In a concluding reflection on the accomplishment of the martyrs (17:7–18:5), they are presented as victorious *athletes* who triumphed over the tyrant before the entire world (17:11–16; cf. 6:10; 9:22). Such metaphors were common in philosophical language as well as in early Christian discourse (cf. Heb 12:1).

17:20–22. The martyrs' deaths are said to have caused the overthrow of Antiochus and the purification of the homeland (cf. 6:27–29; 9:22). The language used for the martyrs' deaths bears striking resemblance to that used by Christians for the death of Jesus, as their deaths are called a "ransom" (cf. Mark 10:45) and an "atoning sacrifice" (cf. Rom 3:24; cf. also 1 Tim 2:6; Titus 2:14; 1 Pet 1:19). The idea of one person's death applying vicariously to others is uncommon in the OT and in other ancient Jewish writings, but was well known from Greek literature.

18:10–19. The mother recounts that her deceased husband had faithfully taught their sons "the law and the prophets." Jews in the ancient world took great pride in their ancestral scriptures and in the fact that they saw to the education of their young.

18:20–24. The entire work concludes with a recapitulation of the torture the martyrs underwent. The author understands that it would be natural to lament such suffering. But because the martyrs will receive "immortal souls from God" (18:23), any lament must be paradoxical: their trial was "bitter ... and yet not bitter" (18:20), for through their steadfast piety, they saved their country, brought down the tyrant, and won themselves a place in the heavenly chorus.

BIBLIOGRAPHY

E. J. Bickerman. "The Date of Fourth Maccabees." *Studies in Jewish and Christian History.* 3 vols. (Leiden: Brill, 1976) 1:275–81; J. J. Collins. *Between Athens and Jerusalem.* 2nd ed. (Grand Rapids: Eerdmans, 2000); D. A. deSilva. *4 Maccabees: Introduction and Commentary on the Grek Text in Codex Sinaiticus.* Septuagint Commentary Series (Leiden: Brill, 2006); M. Hadas. *The Third and Fourth Books of Maccabees* (New York: Harper, 1953); S. K. Stowers. "4 Maccabees." *The HarperCollins Bible Commentary.* J. L. Mays, ed. (San Francisco: HarperSanFrancisco, 2000); R. B. Townshend. "The Fourth Book of Maccabees." *The Apocrypha and Pseudepigrapha of the Old Testament.* R. H. Charles, ed. (Oxford: Clarendon, 1913) 2:653–85).

2 ESDRAS

Bruce W. Longenecker

OVERVIEW

Is God really just? Are God's ways knowable? If they are, are they understandable, and are they fair? Might God say one thing and do another? And what happens when the experiences of life don't seem to match up to traditionally-established doctrines? How reliable are scriptural accounts of God's ways and character? Might the Scriptures even be misleading in what they depict as fundamental realities of life?

In the course of their lives, many people in the Judaeo-Christian tradition have undergone crises of faith, in which questions of this sort are probed with existential urgency. This is no less the case for the author of 4 Ezra (i.e., the main text in a collection of three that were written separately by different authors, but which are now assembled together to form a document called 2 Esdras). In fact, the unnamed (and presumably male) author of 4 Ezra strides into the deepest and most troubling theological waters without hesitation. The main character of 4 Ezra holds his fists up high in defiance as he relentlessly pursues both a truthful and a theologically acceptable answer to his probing questions, with a deep aversion to trite theological reasoning. In the process, he tackles some of the toughest issues regarding God's own character and justice, and does so in a manner that is virtually uncontested in the ancient world in its indefatigable wrestling with the perceived contradictions between the mainstays of mainstream theology on the one hand and, on the other, key experiences and observations on life.

People of faith are often forced to probe pressing issues of theodicy, such as: If God is all-powerful, merciful, and loving, why is there evil in the world, to the extent that the innocent suffer tragically at the hands of perpetrators of horror? If the author of 4 Ezra probes these issues obstinately, he does so not in relation to his own individual experiences of life *per se*. Instead, he asks them on behalf of the suffering people of Israel, to whom he belonged. The event that triggered his reflections was the humiliating destruction of the Jerusalem Temple in 70 CE by Rome (although he writes as if he were the prophet Ezra of old).

When the forces of Rome took on the all-sovereign power of the almighty creator God in the Jewish war of 66–70 CE, the vile evils that prop up the rule of Rome should have been overthrown in an almighty victory that established the people of Israel as the apple of God's eye at the expense of the Gentile nations. Instead, the people of Israel have been humiliated and the name of Israel's God has been shamed and disgraced, with the gods of pagan Rome having triumphed. How can this be?

OUTLINE

I. A Christian Prophecy and Apocalypse 1:1–2:48

    A. The Rejection of Israel as God's People (1:1–2:9)

    B. The Election of the Church as God's People (2:10–48)

II. A Jewish Apocalypse 3:1–14:48

    A. The First Dialogue (3:1–5:20)

    B. The Second Dialogue (5:21–6:34)

    C. The Third Dialogue (6:35–9:25)

    D. The Vision of the Woman in Mourning (9:26–10:59)

    E. The Vision of the Eagle and the Lion (11:1–12:51)

    F. The Vision of the Man from the Sea (13:1–58)

    G. Ezra the Scribe (14:1–48)

III. A Christian Prophecy and Apocalypse 15:1–16:78

    A. Oracles of Doom Against the Nations (15:1–16:34)

    B. Exhortations to God's Suffering People (16:35–78)

DETAILED ANALYSIS

The theological project of 4 Ezra is contained within seven distinct sections within chs. 3–14 of 2 Esdras (with the later texts 5 Ezra comprising 2 Esd 1–2 and 6 Ezra comprising Esd 15–16; these texts are discussed below). The first three sections of 4 Ezra are lengthy dialogues between Ezra, who probes into the ways of God, and the angel Uriel, who responds (often in frustratingly curt and lackadaisical ways), giving Ezra what appears to be the divine perspective on things. Throughout these dialogues (2 Esd 3:1–5:20; 5:21–6:34; and 6:35–9:15), Ezra insists that God must be a merciful God, for his people and the whole of humanity have no hope unless God's grace meets their failings (see esp. his three appeals to God in 7:132–8:62). On the other hand, Uriel leaves little room for mercy in the character of God; only those who are completely without failings in this age will enjoy God's gracious salvation in the age to come (see esp. 7:45–61). Ezra intimates that Uriel's understanding falls short of the depiction of God known in Israel's Scriptures, for without the mercy of God, no one can enjoy God's salvation. Uriel responds that a few will benefit from God's salvation, but only a few, a tiny handful. Moreover, their salvation will be attributed not to God's grace but to the perfection that they have exhibited throughout the whole of their life. Ezra is baffled and dissatisfied.

Although the fourth section (2 Esd 9:26–10:60) begins as if it were yet another dialogue, it quickly changes its format, as Ezra is overcome by a vision of a woman weeping over her lost son, much like Ezra was in despair over the loss of almost all of the people of Israel, who will no doubt fail to experience God's salvation. The experience allows Ezra to externalize his despair, allowing him to move on to a new phase of his quest, as in the final three episodes of 4 Ezra. In the fifth and sixth episodes (2 Esd 11:1–12:51 and 13:1–58 respectively), Ezra is shown further visions of the overwhelming power of God, who demolishes the all-encompassing control of evil within this world (including Rome itself) and who saves Israel—a twelve-tribe Israel comprised of (1) a few from the two tribes of Israel who have remained in Judea and (2) a ten-tribe conglomerate who have been living perfectly in a land far away (see esp. 13:21–52). In the final seventh episode (2 Esd 14:1–48), Ezra is instructed to restore the Scriptures to the people of Israel, and to write a further seventy books wherein real knowledge and understanding of God's ways reside. Meanwhile, the people of Israel are kept in the dark about their desperate situation, but are to continue to praise God in the expectation that he will be merciful to them.

We cannot tell whether the author was ultimately satisfied with his own theological probings. But later authors were, it seems, as Christian authors elaborated the text of 4 Ezra with their own textual additions. The other two texts in 2 Esdras include 5 Ezra (= 2 Esd 1–2) and 6 Ezra (2 Esd 15–16). Both were written by Christian authors. Fifth Ezra was probably written in the middle of the second century CE, with the author seeking to demonstrate that God's favor had been transferred from Israel to the Gentiles. Sixth Ezra, written in the second half of the third century, piggy-backs onto the end of 4 Ezra, drawing out themes of the solemn judgment of God against sinners and the consequent requirement for God's people to live a godly life. But it is 4 Ezra that is the theological giant of the three texts of 2 Esdras, standing high above much of the theological literature of the ancient world in terms of its theological acumen and profundity.

BIBLIOGRAPHY

R. J. Coggins. *The First and Second Books of Esdras.* CBC (Cambridge: Cambridge University Press, 1979); D. Harrington. *Invitation to the Apocrypha* (Grand Rapids: Eerdmans, 1999) 185–206.

MATTHEW

STEPHEN WESTERHOLM

OVERVIEW

The Gospel of Matthew stands appropriately at the beginning of the NT, in closest proximity to the Old. Like all the writers of the NT, Matthew believes that the God who spoke to Israel in the past through prophets has now spoken—"in these last days," the days of fulfillment—through the Son of God himself (so Heb 1:1–2; cf. Matt 17:5). But more than any other evangelist, Matthew is concerned to link the old revelation with the new, to show the latter as the culmination rather than the abrogation of what went before.

Early church tradition explained this emphasis by saying that Matthew, a disciple of Jesus, wrote the Gospel for the Jewish people, and in Hebrew, though the work was later translated into Greek. That the original audience of the Gospel was primarily Jewish seems likely enough; but in the view of most scholars today, the Gospel was composed not in Hebrew, but in Greek, and in fact takes over the basic structure and often the very wording of another Greek composition, the Gospel of Mark. Some scholars allow some truth to the church tradition by suggesting that the Apostle Matthew may have put together a collection of sayings of Jesus that was then drawn upon by the writer of our (Greek) Gospel. But the Gospel writer himself is unknown, though it is customary and convenient to refer to him as "Matthew."

If Matthew used the Gospel of Mark as a source, then he must have been writing after 70 CE, the approximate date of Mark's composition. (We may note as well that Matt 22:7 appears to reflect an awareness of the fall of Jerusalem to Roman forces in 70 CE.) Since the Gospel was familiar to Ignatius of Antioch, writing in the early second century, its own date of composition was presumably in the decade of the 80s or early 90s. Antioch is perhaps the city most often suggested as the place of origin for the Gospel; but other areas where Jewish believers in Christ rubbed shoulders, and disputed questions of faith, with non-Christ-believing Jews are also possibilities.

Matthew's evident concern is to tell the story of Jesus, who is center stage in nearly every episode in the Gospel. Jesus is important for Matthew, not as a gifted human being whose religious intuitions, insights, and experiences can inspire others, but as the focus and instrument of God's activity on earth. That activity is seen as the continuation and climax of the OT drama of God's dealings with the covenant people of Israel. Matthew's main theme is an OT theme, the "kingdom of God" or "of heaven," where "heaven" serves as a circumlocution for "God." In one sense, God's kingdom (or rule) is a universal and eternal reality, whether or not humans choose to submit to it (cf. Ps 103:19; 145:13; Dan 4:3). But in the face of human hostility to that rule, God established a covenant with Israel in order that, among the covenant people, and as a model for all the peoples of the earth, God's rule might be realized (note the reference to the "throne of the LORD" in Israel in 1 Chr 29:23).

Yet even in Israel the rule of God remained an ideal, or a future hope, far removed from the everyday reality of human frailty and faithlessness, and from the brutal reality of suffering and oppression to which the people of God were subjected. The good news of the Gospel is that, in the person of God's Son, God has intervened to reassert the rightful rule of "the kingdom of heaven" and to impart its blessings to the covenant people of Israel and, ultimately, to all nations. In Jesus, the power of God's rule is at work, freeing the sick and oppressed from their afflictions, anticipating the day when all evil will be banished. Through Jesus, God's forgiveness and a place in the kingdom is offered to all, even to those whose lives of open sin have hitherto cut them off from the company of the devout (cf. Matt 9:9–13; 11:19). Indeed, not only does Jesus offer to all God's forgiveness; in the end, he offers his own life to make such forgiveness possible (26:28). But participation in the blessings of God's kingdom presupposes submission to its rule, and in much of Matthew's Gospel Jesus spells out the demands of that rule: those who would obey God are to listen to the voice of God's Son (17:5; cf. 10:40) and become his disciples (28:19–20). Such discipleship is costly, for a world in rebellion against God's rule will prove hostile to its subjects (10:16–39). But they may rest assured of God their Father's provision and care (6:8, 25–33; 10:29–31), and of the reward that awaits them when Jesus returns in power and glory and the kingdom of God is consummated (16:27; cf. 25:14–30).

One way of summarizing the *content* of Matthew's Gospel, then, is to say that the God who spoke to Israel of old through the prophets has now spoken decisively in the person of God's Son. But the conviction underlying the *writing* of Matthew's Gospel is that the God who *has spoken* through the Son still *speaks* to the hearts of those who listen attentively to the stories and words of Jesus. In the words of the Gospel, Matthew intends his readers to hear for themselves the invitation to God's kingdom, the summons to discipleship. Not that Matthew addresses his readers directly with these challenges; in this respect he is like the authors and editors of the prophetic books of the OT who collected, shaped, and transmitted the words God spoke through the prophets in the belief that, though originally directed to a particular context in the past, they remain vehicles through which God addresses later generations. In the truth of that conviction lies the justification for the never-ending process of interpreting and proclaiming the ancient texts of Holy Scripture.

OUTLINE

I. The Coming of Messiah (1:1–4:11)

A. Jesus' Genealogy and Birth (1:1–25)

B. Worship from Afar, Hostility at Home (2:1–23)

C. Messiah's Forerunner (3:1–12)

D. The Baptism and Temptation of Jesus (3:13–4:11)

II. The Mission of Messiah (4:12–28:20)

A. The Launch of Messiah's Ministry (4:12–25)

B. Messiah, Mighty in Word (5:1–7:29)
 5:1–16. The People of God in the Midst of the World
 5:17–48. The Greater Righteousness of God's Rule
 6:1–34. Children of the Heavenly Father

 7:1–29. Accountability and the Judgment

C. Messiah, Mighty in Deed (8:1–9:38)
 8:1–17. Initial Healings
 8:18–27. The Cost of Discipleship
 8:28–9:38. Deeds that Offend

D. The Disciples' Mission (10:1–42)
 10:1–4. Empowerment for the Mission
 10:5–15. The Disciples' Task
 10:16–42. The Response to the Disciples

E. Responses to Jesus (11:1–12:50)
 11:1–19. Jesus and John
 11:20–30. Woes for the Unrepentant, Rest for the Weary
 12:1–21. Sabbath Controversies
 12:22–37. Blasphemy Against the Spirit
 12:38–50. Unbelief and Its Consequences, Obedience and Its Rewards

F. The Mysteries of the Kingdom in Parables (13:1–52)
 13:1–9, 18–33, 36–50. The Parables
 13:10–17, 34–35, 51–52. Why Parables?

G. The Mysteries of God's Son (13:53–17:27)
 13:53–58. Offense in Nazareth
 14:1–12. The Death of John the Baptist
 14:13–36. Bread for the Hungry, Peace in the Storm
 15:1–20. Religion of the Lips
 15:21–39. The Cry of a Heart and the Feeding of a Crowd
 16:1–12. Blind Foes and Dense Disciples
 16:13–17:8. The Revelation of Jesus Christ
 17:9–27. Earthly Realities

H. Church Matters (18:1–35)
 18:1–14. The Community of Little Ones
 18:15–35. Dealing with Offenders

I. On the Way to the Cross (19:1–23:39)
 19:1–15. Family Matters
 19:16–30. The Lure of Wealth
 20:1–34. Serving Self or Others?
 21:1–22:14. The Kingdom Offered— and Rejected—in Jerusalem
 22:15–46. Putting Jesus to the Test
 23:1–39. Woes and Warnings

J. The Last Days (24:1–25:46)
 24:3–31. The Troubles of the Last Days
 24:32–25:46. The Call to Readiness

K. Death and Resurrection (26:1–28:20)
    26:1–27:66. The Passion of the Savior
    28:1–20. The Risen Lord

Detailed Analysis

I. The Coming of Messiah (1:1–4:11)

A. Jesus' Genealogy and Birth (1:1–25)

Matthew links the old revelation with the new by tracing the genealogy of Jesus back to Abraham, forefather of God's covenant people Israel. The genealogy is carefully structured around pivotal points in Israel's history, reaching its climax in the coming of Messiah.

The opening words ("account of the genealogy") are ambiguous ("genealogy" [Greek *genesis*] may also mean "birth" [as in 1:18], or even "history") but suggestive: borrowing words that appear in the Greek translation of Gen 2:4 and 5:1, Matthew implies that the story he tells represents both a new beginning ("genesis") and the culmination of the sacred history begun in (the old book of) Genesis. The juxtaposition (in 1:1) of "Jesus" with "the Messiah" (or "Christ") indicates that the significance of neither name is properly understood apart from the other. Though Matthew will insist that Jesus is more than (merely) the "son of David" (22:41–46), the latter title is nonetheless important as a designation of the Messiah (cf. 2 Sam 7:12; Jer 23:5). In addition to showing Jesus' Jewish ancestry, "son of Abraham" suggests that he represents the fulfillment of promises given to the patriarch.

Following the custom of Jewish genealogies, Jesus' fore*fathers* are listed (1:2–16), even though this entails giving the ancestry of Joseph, his adopted father, rather than that of Mary, his real mother (note the careful wording of 1:16). The artificial division of Jesus' ancestors into three groups of fourteen generations (note, e.g., the omission—necessary if the number fourteen is to be achieved—of three generations in 1:8–9 from the list found in 1 Chr 3:11–12) marks the genealogy as a vehicle designed to convey a gospel truth rather than merely inform curiosity: the appearance of Jesus (Matthew wants readers to know) represents the next great event—after the call of Abraham, the reign of David, and the

Babylonian exile—in God's dealings with Israel. Equally telling is the inclusion of selected women in the genealogy. These are not, as one might at least have expected, the matriarchs of Israel, but women whose foreign roots (Tamar, Rahab, Ruth) or immoral past (that "David was the father of Solomon *by the wife of another man*" [1:6] highlights the adultery involved) might be thought to exclude them from a place in God's program for Israel. Mention of precisely *these* women serves to highlight the universal embrace of the gospel.

The birth of any human being is a miracle (cf. Ps 139:13–16); that of the Son of God was, appropriately, more miraculous still, though unfolding according to divine plan (Matt 1:22–23; cf. Isa 7:14). Between the betrothal and the wedding of Mary to Joseph (1:18), and apart from any sexual relations between them (1:25), Mary conceived a child by the power of the Holy Spirit (1:18). (Chrysostom notes that, since neither the angel nor Matthew could say more than that the conception was the work of God's Spirit, human inquisitiveness should proceed no further.) The event (like others in the story that follows) carried with it its own possibility of misunderstanding and offence (1:19; cf. 11:6); but Joseph, believing the divine word he received, took Mary as his wife. That word (1:21) indicated that the child to be born would "save his people [in the first place, Israel, but ultimately, all who believe in him; cf. 26:27–28] from their sins." Salvation from sins begins with their forgiveness, but includes as well the enablement of those forgiven to live as God's children (cf. 5:13–48), and the hope, one day, of deliverance from the very effects of sin, including disease and death (cf. 8:1–17, 28–9:8, etc.).

The significance of Jesus' appearance is further indicated by the name Emmanuel, "God is with us" (1:23). At the least, the name indicates that the birth of the Messiah is a fresh token of God's favor toward Israel. But the term also suggests that Jesus' appearance brings the presence of God into the midst of the covenant people, a suggestion confirmed by later echoes of the promise in which Jesus substitutes his own presence for that of his heavenly Father (18:20; 28:20).

B. Worship from Afar, Hostility at Home (2:1–23)

In writing of "wise men from the East" who worship Christ, Matthew wants to move his readers to do the same. At the same time he shows how the coming of Christ encounters hostility from the start. The story also provides further opportunity to show how all Scripture points to Christ.

The OT scriptures had spoken of a day when, drawn by the appearance of God's glory, the kings and peoples of the earth would bring treasures ("gold and frankincense") to Jerusalem (Isa 60:1–7); Israel's king would receive the tribute of rulers and nations (Ps 72:10–11, 15). In a story that recalls these expectations, Matthew tells how mysterious "wise men from the East," bearing precious gifts ("gold, frankincense, and myrrh") for Israel's new-born king, are guided by a miraculous star (cf. Num 24:17) to the infant Jesus. The Greek verb rendered "pay homage" (2:2, 8, 11) is elsewhere translated "worship" (e.g., 4:10; 28:17). Jesus is repeatedly the object of such "homage" or "worship" in Matthew's Gospel; it is never suggested to be inappropriate (contrast Acts 10:25–26; Rev 19:10; 22:8–9) in spite of the reminder that worship belongs to God alone (Matt 4:9–10).

Foreign "wise men" gladly submit to the revelation they receive; not so, Herod and "all Jerusalem" (2:3). King Herod (2:1, 3) finds the reference to a new king's birth (2:2) threatening. Jerusalem, whose religious leadership is able to cite Scripture to identify Messiah's birthplace (2:6, which combines Mic 5:2 and 2 Sam 5:2), is equally troubled. Its inhabitants find disruptive and disturbing the notion that the God whom they worship might be about to act in their midst. The opposition of "chief priests" and "scribes" is a motif that runs throughout the Gospel; that of Herod comes to an immediate head as he seeks, first surreptitiously, then with open savagery, to kill the Christ-child (2:7–8, 16). His actions recall those of the Pharaoh who oppressed the Israelites in Egypt (Exod 1:15–22). In both stories, innocent children die, but the designs of the tyrant are foiled by the preservation of one destined to be the instrument of his people's redemption (Exod 2:1–10; Matt 2:12–18). That Matthew wants readers to see Israel's story recapitulated in Jesus is evident when he tells of the infant's forced sojourn in Egypt (2:13–15; cf.

Ps 105:16–23), when he applies to Christ the prophetic text "Out of Egypt I have called my son" (2:15; cf. Hos 11:1), and when he draws upon a prophetic lament over past devastations in Israel to characterize the grief that followed Herod's massacre of Bethlehem's children (2:17–18; cf. Jer 31:15).

In response to an angelic message (2:19–20, echoing Exod 4:19), Joseph returns with Mary and her child to the land of Israel, settling in the Galilean town of Nazareth. Again, Matthew sees a fulfillment of divine purposes set forth in Scripture, though 2:23 recalls the purport of several passages rather than any one particular text (note that Matthew refers in the plural to "prophets"): Isa 4:3; 11:1; 49:6; and even Judg 13:5 are among those that have been proposed. By a play on words, "Nazorean" suggests both the city of Jesus' upbringing and the holiness associated with Nazirite vows (Num 6:1–21; cf. Judg 13:3–7).

C. Messiah's Forerunner (3:1–12)

The work of Jesus is not to be understood apart from that of John the Baptist. Scripture itself—foreseeing, in advance of the appearance of the Lord, a "voice" preparing his way (Matt 3:3, where the "Lord" of Isa 40:3 is understood as Christ)—requires the linkage. Moreover, by its very nature, the rule of God that Jesus inaugurates *requires* the judgment of which John speaks: given that participation in God's kingdom is only possible for those prepared to submit to its rule, exclusion is inevitable for those who do not.

"In those days" (3:1; i.e., while Jesus was still in Nazareth, before beginning his messianic activity), John announced the imminent coming of God's kingdom and called for a repentance that signaled both penitence for the past and a determination to make oneself ready for the advent of God's rule (3:2). John's austere lifestyle (recalling that of Elijah; cf. 2 Kgs 1:8) comported well with the seriousness of his message, prioritizing obedience to God over earthly comfort (3:4). Religious leaders—including both Pharisees, known for their exacting interpretation and scrupulous observance of the ancestral law, and Sadducees, from whose ranks were drawn the upper levels of the priestly hierarchy—were warned that the impending judgment respects no persons, that leaders of others cannot afford not to examine themselves. The criterion of judgment for all is that of appropriate conduct; such externalities as physical descent from Abraham are irrelevant (3:7–9). John's announcement of impending doom was itself an indirect summons to produce "fruit" that would prove to be "good" on the day of judgment (3:10).

The repentance that John urged was outwardly expressed by baptism, accompanied by the confession of sins (3:5–6). Unlike the repeated washings prescribed for ritual uncleanness in Mosaic law, John's baptism represented a once-for-all commitment to a lifestyle befitting one who welcomes the arrival of God's kingdom. John distinguished this preparatory baptism "with water" from the baptism "with the Holy Spirit and fire" to be brought by the Messiah (3:11). "Holy Spirit and fire" may refer separately to the grace of the Holy Spirit granted to the repentant and the ("fiery") judgment that awaits the impenitent. Alternatively, the words may together refer to the divine holiness that must consume, whenever it comes in contact with, all wickedness.

D. The Baptism and Temptation of Jesus (3:13–4:11)

Honoring John's divine mission (cf. 11:7–11; 21:23–27), modeling the humility he will require of his followers (cf. 20:20–28), and identifying himself with those whose sins he will bear (cf. 3:5–6; 8:17; 20:28), Jesus begins the work he has been given to do (cf. John 17:4) by coming to John to be baptized. John humbly protests his unworthiness, then shows the true humility of obedience. As soon as Jesus is baptized, "the heavens ... opened" to signal a divine communication. God's Spirit "like a dove" descends on Jesus (thus fulfilling Isa 42:1; cf. Matt 12:18), a sign that his mission, empowered by God's Spirit (cf. 12:28), is about to begin. And God the Father himself speaks the Word that must be inwardly heard by all who follow Jesus (cf. 16:16–17): "This is my Son, the Beloved, with whom I am well pleased" (3:17; cf. Ps 2:7; Isa 42:1). Luther's paraphrase captures Matthew's message: "If you desire that I be a gracious Father, you may rest assured. Only hold fast to my Son, with whom I cannot be at enmity, and you will be beloved of me also because of him. So hear him and do what he says to you." Following his identification as God's Son, Jesus proves

himself a *loyal* son before beginning his public activities. Like Israel (also called God's "son"; cf. Exod 4:22–23) in the wilderness, Jesus is tempted by hunger (cf. Exod 16:3), by the impulse to put God to the test (Exod 17:1–7; Ps 95:7–11), and by the worship of false gods (Exod 32:1–8). Unlike Israel of old, he withstands each temptation.

Even temptations find a place in God's purpose, though they are neither to be sought (Matt 6:13; 26:41) nor entered with any presumption of strength (contrast 26:31–35): Jesus is led "by the Spirit" to be tempted (4:1). His forty-day fast recalls those of Moses (Deut 9:9, 18), as well as Israel's forty years in the wilderness (Deut 8:2). In the first temptation, Jesus is urged to use his power as God's Son to satisfy his hunger, and thus to fend for himself apart from the Father's will. He responds to Satan, here and in the temptations that follow, not by invoking his unique prerogatives as God's Son, but with the tools available to any tempted human being, and with the spirit of all who are faithful: Scripture is cited, the will of God obeyed. More essential to life than bread itself is the spiritual nourishment provided by the Word of God (4:4, citing Deut 8:3).

Satan then seeks to exploit Jesus' very trust in his Father to tempt him to depart from his Father's will: should he not demonstrate his great faith by exposing himself to a danger from which only the miraculous intervention of God could deliver him? But those who truly trust God allow God to determine their steps; to attempt to dictate what God must do is an expression of human presumption, though disguised as extraordinary faith.

Satan then abandons all deception, blatantly offering power and glory in return for misdirected worship. Jesus repulses the temptation, reserving for his Father the worship and service that are due God alone. Only by taking the path of obedience will he come to possess "all authority in heaven and on earth" (28:18).

II. The Mission of Messiah (4:12–28:20)

A. The Launch of Messiah's Ministry (4:12–25)

The public work of Jesus' forerunner ends when John is "arrested" (literally, "handed over," a verb used of Jesus in 17:22; 20:18, etc.; in the service of God's kingdom, John and Jesus share the same fate), a signal that the time of preparation is over. Matthew speaks of Jesus' move to Capernaum (4:13) in terms that echo a text from Isaiah that he then quotes (4:15–16; cf. Isa 9:1–2): as Isaiah foresaw, Jesus brings light to those in darkness. The reference to "Galilee of the Gentiles" hints at the day when Gentiles will be numbered among Jesus' followers (28:19–20).

Jesus' message is summed up (4:17) as an announcement (also made by John; cf. 3:2) that "the kingdom of heaven has come near"; i.e., God, the rightful ruler of all, is about to reassert that rule and put things right that have gone terribly wrong where people have refused to acknowledge God's sovereignty. The news demands immediate action: those who hear it must either welcome it with a demonstration of their allegiance to God's rule or face exclusion from its blessings.

From the very beginning Jesus is accompanied by disciples who will later be responsible for the extension of his mission (10:1–42; 28:18–20; cf. Acts 10:36–42). Matthew's account of the calling of four disciples (4:18–22; cf. 9:9) is sparse in details, focusing on exemplary aspects. The mere words "Follow me" would never have elicited the response they received had the hearers not sensed in them a divine summons; the same is true of the proclamation of the Christian gospel (cf. 1 Thess 2:13). Believers in the gospel, like the first disciples of Jesus, are thus "called of God" (cf. 1 Thess 2:12). Accepting the call means, negatively, abandoning other pursuits. Positively, it means embarking on a life of following Christ.

The chapter concludes (4:23–25) with a summary of Jesus' activities: announcing the good news about the kingdom of God and demonstrating its power, not gratuitously or ostentatiously, but in healing the sick and bringing deliverance to the oppressed. As a result, crowds—though not disciples—multiply.

B. Messiah, Mighty in Word (5:1–7:29)

In the first of five discourses of Jesus in the Gospel (the "Sermon on the Mount," 5:1–7:27), Matthew shows him to be "mighty in … word" (Luke 24:19; cf. Matt 7:28–29). The focus of the sermon is on the character and behavior of those who participate in God's rule. Spoken originally on a mountain (5:1, recalling the mountain from which Israel received God's law [Exod 19:16–

20:21]) by Jesus to his disciples, Jesus' words come to later disciples from their risen Lord, in possession of "all authority in heaven and on earth": it is at the behest of the risen Lord that they are taught to obey his commands (28:18–20). The identity of the speaker is crucial: the (counterintuitive) declaration that "the meek … will inherit the earth" (5:5), the command (counter to human instinct) not to "resist an evildoer" (5:39), the assurance (counter, at times, to all appearances) that the heavenly Father will provide for the needs of those who seek God's kingdom (6:33); these are not the quixotic ideals of a deluded prophet, but reality as disclosed by the Lord of all, a reality now hidden within the kingdoms of this world, but destined one day to supplant them.

5:1–16. The People of God in the Midst of the World. The sermon begins (5:3–12) with a series of beatitudes, a familiar form (cf. Ps 1:1–3; 128:1–4) that identifies first who it is who enjoys God's favor ("the poor in spirit," "those who mourn," etc.), then the manner in which that favor is revealed ("theirs is the kingdom of heaven," "they will be comforted," etc.). The pronouncements, which overturn worldly values and expectations, remain hopeless ideals at odds with reality *unless* they come from One whose word creates and shapes reality.

The "poor in spirit" are those who, in their desperate need, cry to God for help (cf. Ps 34:18). "Those who mourn" are those grieved by all that is evil in the world and by their own part in its waywardness. The "meek" are those who want no part in the world's pursuit of power, but become like children and serve others. "Those who hunger and thirst for righteousness" are those who long to see all that is good and right prevail in the world—and in their own lives. The "merciful" are those eager to aid all in need, ready to forgive all who wrong them, and charitable in assessing the deeds and motives of others. The "pure in heart" are those who singlemindedly pursue the will of God. The "peacemakers" are those who subordinate their own rights and interests to maintain peace, overcoming evil with good (cf. Rom 12:21). Misfits and persecuted on earth, the poor in spirit, mourners, and meek who follow Jesus will be rewarded with a part in the kingdom of heaven.

Yet followers of Jesus must be faithful to their calling, to the way of life prescribed for them by Jesus, if they are to be a good, not useless, presence in the world (v. 13). The good they do can no more be hidden than can a city built on a hill; but it elicits praise for the divine Source of all good rather than for the conduits of God's goodness (vv. 14–16).

5:17–48. The Greater Righteousness of God's Rule.

The grace of the gospel and Jesus' compassion for sinners have at times been mistaken for an acceptance of all kinds of human behavior, erasing distinctions between good and evil (in effect, abolishing God's law [5:17]). In this section of the Sermon on the Mount, the same Jesus who befriends tax collectors and prostitutes declares insults and lustful looks to be sins that deserve damnation. In both cases, God's incarnate goodness is at work: a love that reaches out to the wounded and broken while inexorably opposing every trace of the evil responsible for their brokenness.

Jesus does away with none of God's demands—indeed, as guides to a life in harmony with the wisdom of God's creation, they *cannot* be done away as long as creation lasts (5:18); rather, he brings them to their intended "fulfillment" (v. 17). While extending forgiveness to every repentant sinner who falls short, he makes no compromise in spelling out the righteousness of God's kingdom, a righteousness far surpassing mere compliance with any legal code, including that comprised by the legal enactments of "scribes and Pharisees" (5:20). He "fulfills" the law, then, not by simply restating its provisions, but rather by vividly portraying the righteousness of God's rule that underlies the Mosaic code, but which that code, as the law of an earthly society of imperfect human beings, can only approximate.

Thus a legal code can prohibit murder and adultery but not outbursts of anger, expressions of contempt, or lustful looks. Jesus does (5:21–30), since these too express human willfulness, not God's rule. Regulated divorce, oaths that guarantee truth-telling when invoked (but presuppose more laxity on other occasions), and retributive justice may be necessary evils in a society of sinners (cf. 19:8), but they can have no place in lives governed by God's goodness (5:31–42). And inasmuch as God's goodness and compassion extend to "all

that he has made" (Ps 145:9; cf. Matt 5:45), the love and benevolence of God's children cannot be exclusive, but must be shown even toward those who mistreat them (vv. 43–47). In short, the moral vision of Jesus' followers finds its inspiration, its goal, and its delight in the perfection of divine goodness (5:48).

The language Jesus uses is typically dramatic, even hyperbolic, rather than legal, conveying a vision without attempting to spell out how God's children are to behave in every situation. Reflecting on the pictures Jesus uses, they must understand that they cannot serve God acceptably when they are at odds with other human beings; every attempt must be made to be reconciled at once with any whom they have wronged (vv. 23–26). They must be vigilant in shunning all avoidable temptations to sin and rigorous in resisting the unavoidable (vv. 29–30). When ill-treated, they are to respond with a love that seeks the wrongdoer's good, "overcom[ing] evil with good" (v. 39; Rom 12:21). As children of the Lord of heaven and earth, they need hardly fend for themselves and their rights; they can afford to be magnanimous toward all as God their Father is magnanimous (vv. 40–42, 44–48).

The intensification of punishments listed in v. 22 appears rhetorical; the wrongs condemned are equally sinful. The point of v. 32 is that the God who ordained marriage does not recognize divorce (cf. 19:4–6); hence second marriages, in the eyes of One for whom the first marriage is still in force, entail an adulterous relationship. The husband who (in Jewish practice of Jesus' day) initiates the divorce bears responsibility for his (remarried) wife's adultery unless it was her unfaithfulness that precipitated the divorce ("except on the ground of unchastity"). The logic of vv. 34–36 is that true reverence for God means avoiding all oaths, not simply those that explicitly mention the divine name; after all, any circumlocution inevitably remains within the sphere of God's domain.

6:1–34. Children of the Heavenly Father.

When children of God do good, they shun rather than seek a human audience (6:1, illustrated in vv. 2–6, 16–18). They serve God single-mindedly (vv. 19–24), assured that their heavenly Father knows, and will provide for, all their needs (vv. 25–34).

In doing good for God's eyes alone, followers of Jesus are unlike hypocrites whose ostentatious deeds of charity, prayer, and fasting Jesus memorably caricatures (vv. 2, 5, 16). The reward that follows good deeds, whether human applause or divine favor, is determined by the intended audience.

In the confidence with which Jesus' followers approach God in prayer, they are unlike Gentiles who vainly attempt to secure divine attention with drawn-out invocations (v. 7). Knowing that God already knows what they need, they nonetheless show to what source they look for all good by bringing their requests to God (v. 8). As children to a caring parent, so followers of Jesus speak to God their Father trustingly and simply (vv. 9–13).

The first concern of their hearts is that God's name will be acknowledged and revered by all, that all will submit to God's rule, and that all, on earth as now in heaven, will do God's will (vv. 9–10). In effect, each of these initial petitions expresses a yearning for the day when God's kingdom comes and all is put right on earth; at the same time each implies the desire of petitioners to realize God's rule in their own lives. Intent only on serving God, they ask no more for themselves than provision of their daily necessities, forgiveness for their every failing, and deliverance from temptations to which they know themselves prone to fall (vv. 11–13). Grateful for God's forgiveness, they spontaneously meet its condition that they in turn grant forgiveness to others (vv. 14–15).

No one enters God's service on a part-time basis (v. 24): God is truly *God* only of those whose devotion to God encompasses all they do. Such single-minded service is spoken of as the "healthy" eye that signals a body "full of light"; its absence betokens a life "full of darkness" (vv. 22–23). Its reward—unlike the pursuit of earthly goods—lasts eternally (vv. 19–21).

The trust of God's children in the goodness of their Father relieves them of the anxieties that plague those who, not knowing God, are left to fend for themselves (vv. 31–32). Such worry is unnecessary because God, who bestows the greater gifts of life and body, will surely grant the lesser gifts of food and clothing as well (v. 25b); because the heavenly Father who feeds the birds and "clothes" the flowers will surely provide for the needs of his children (vv. 26, 28–30); because worry achieves nothing—the lives of God's children are in God's hands in any case (v. 27); and because worry about the future is a pointless luxury when there are concerns in the present that demand attention (v. 34). In short, those who live to promote God's kingdom and to practice its righteousness may confidently leave their needs in the hands of an all-knowing, benevolent God (v. 33).

7:1–29. Accountability and the Judgment. No single theme unites all that Jesus says in 7:1–27, but human accountability before God is repeatedly emphasized.

The root of human sinfulness lies in humanity's unwillingness to acknowledge God and give God due worship and obedience (cf. Rom 1:21); conversely, human sinfulness finds constant expression in an eagerness to assume the prerogatives of God (cf. Gen 3:5). Thus the reality that human beings are moral creatures accountable to God their Judge finds perverted expression in a proclivity to judge the actions and character of one's fellow-creatures. Jesus' injunction not to judge (Matt 7:1; cf. 1 Cor 4:5; Jas 4:11–12) does not eliminate the need for moral discernment (cf. 7:6, 15–20), nor does it mean that sin should not be recognized as sin. It does mean that human beings should look for sin first in themselves (vv. 3–5) and interpret the actions of others in the most charitable way possible—as they themselves would be charitably judged by God (v. 2; cf. 1 Cor 13:4–7; 1 Pet 4:8).

God's love and forgiveness are freely offered, in the gospel, to all. But what God offers, and the message that conveys the offer, are both sacred, to be joyfully and reverently received. What is sacred must not be heedlessly exposed to the ridicule of those who despise it or to the practical contempt of those who claim to enjoy God's grace while exhibiting no concern to pursue God's righteousness (7:6).

God, the Father in heaven, is good and more willing than any loving parent on earth to give what is good to his children. As Father, he invites his children to trust him and come to him with their needs: "Ask!" "Search!" "Knock!" (vv. 7–11).

What God wants of human beings is spelled out in "the law and the prophets," but in its essence it is known in human hearts: the goodness that people want others to show to them is what they ought to show to others (v. 12).

The kingdom of God is only gained by those (the "few") who refuse to be guided by the spirit, values, and ambitions of this age, and who live disciplined lives devoted to God's service: the "gate" to the kingdom is "narrow," the road that leads to it "hard" (vv. 13–14).

As the path to life is easily missed, so there are many who, though innocent in appearance, would lead others astray (v. 15). In the end, however, their actions reveal the orientation of their hearts: "you will know them by their fruits" (vv. 16–20). Those who would be guides to God's kingdom must themselves have submitted to its rule.

Such submission requires more than *calling* Christ "Lord"; nor are mighty deeds done in Jesus' name themselves evidence of compliance with God's will. Apart from a serious striving for the righteousness that Jesus has elucidated in the Sermon on the Mount, pious words and eye-catching deeds lead only to judgment (vv. 21–23). Only as Jesus' words are heeded as well as heard do they lead, not to judgment, but to life (vv. 24–27).

The forthrightness and authority with which Jesus proclaimed the requirements of God's rule amazed his hearers: they had not heard the like before (vv. 28–29). Amazement, to be sure, is not discipleship.

C. Messiah, Mighty in Deed (8:1–9:38)

8:1–17. Initial Healings. The Messiah who is mighty in word (Matt 5–7) now proves mighty in deed as well: Matthew highlights first his healing of a leper (8:1–4), a foreigner's servant (vv. 5–13), and a woman (vv. 14–15). The healings serve to announce the program and to demonstrate the power of God's kingdom to do away with all the effects of sin. At the same time, each act of healing represents the response of Jesus' compassion to the need of a particular person.

Matthew's healing stories frequently highlight the importance of faith. A leper, approaching Jesus with reverence (the verb translated "knelt before" here is rendered "paid homage" in 2:11, "worshiped" in 28:17) and complete confidence in his ability to heal, appeals to Jesus' compassion: "If you choose [literally, "If you will"—a condi-

tion appropriately attached to all prayer; cf. Rom 1:10; 1 John 5:14], you can make me clean." Jesus responds with a touch and word that bring instant healing. Avoiding ostentation ("say nothing to anyone"), Jesus instructs the man to comply with the requirements of Mosaic law (cf. Lev 14:1–32) as a "testimony" to the officiating priest and his fellows of Jesus' power to heal and of his conformity to God's law. Carrying out the required procedure would also pave the way for the former leper's acceptance back into the community.

A centurion, recognizing that, just as his own commands are backed by the authority of Rome, so Jesus speaks with divine authority, is confident that Jesus' mere word will heal his paralyzed servant. Jesus commends the extraordinary faith of this Gentile "outsider," and indicates that many such "outsiders" will join the patriarchs at the festivities of the kingdom of heaven, while unbelieving "insiders" will be excluded from the company. Jesus heals the servant with words that formulate an important principle: God helps those who in faith look to God (here in the person of Jesus) for help (8:13; cf. 9:29).

Matthew proceeds to tell of the healing of Peter's mother-in-law, then of all the sick who were brought to Jesus. He concludes the section by quoting Isa 53:4.

8:18–27. The Cost of Discipleship. The episodes that follow reveal something of the rigors and perils of discipleship. Matthew does not say what happened to the would-be followers of 8:18–22, nor is the hindrance alluded to in v. 21 clarified. The evangelist recounts the episodes merely to make the point that followers of Jesus must be prepared to share his deprivations and suffering (cf. 10:24–25) and to recognize his claims on their obedience as overriding all other demands (burial of the [physically] dead can be left to those not in the service of the kingdom of God [the spiritually "dead"]). Here, as elsewhere in the Gospel (see on 10:37–39), the absolute devotion and obedience humans owe God is formulated as duty to Jesus. Yet it is in this context that Jesus first uses the self-designation "Son of Man" (8:20). The phrase recalls Daniel's reference to "one like a human being" (literally, "one like a son of man") who comes "with the clouds of heaven" and receives "dominion and glory and kingship" (Dan 7:13–14; cf. Matt 24:30; 26:64); but its use in Matthew (cf.

17:22–23; 20:18–19) indicates that Jesus' path to glory is one of suffering and the cross.

Turning from Jesus' would-be followers, Matthew tells of what happened (and illustrates what happens) to actual disciples (who "*followed* him"). They are overtaken by a great storm to which their master seems oblivious. Jesus, awakened, makes the most of the teaching moment (he is with them; they should trust him and not be afraid) before calming the sea. The episode recalls Ps 107:23–30, with Jesus playing the role of "the LORD" in the psalm. The astonished reaction of the disciples (8:27) is appropriate, but their question is left (for the moment) unanswered (cf. 16:15–17).

8:28–9:38. Deeds that Offend. Even Jesus' healings provoke offense. He frees from their oppression two demoniacs who had terrorized all who came near them. But because he does so by allowing the exorcised demons to spend their destructiveness on a herd of pigs, the local townspeople are only too anxious to have him leave their neighborhood (8:28–34). Jesus then heals a paralytic, but first pronounces the forgiveness of the man's sins—to the consternation of scribes who inwardly protest that forgiveness is God's prerogative. The healing then becomes not simply an act of compassion, but a demonstration of Jesus' authority: though it is easy enough to *say* that another's sins are forgiven, Jesus' performance of the more difficult feat of healing shows that he acts, when healing *and* forgiving, with the authority of God (9:2–8).

Jesus' call of a tax collector (see on 4:18–22) and willingness to fraternize with the latter's cohorts proves a further occasion for offense (cf. 11:19; Luke 15:1–32): is he not condoning the behavior of "sinners" (Matt 9:9–11)? No, replies Jesus; as sick need the physician, so "sinners" need to hear the summons to God's kingdom that it is his mission ("I have come to call ...") to proclaim. The point of v. 13*b* is not to distinguish between those who do and those who do not need to repent (in fact, the call to repentance is general [3:2; 4:17]), but to highlight why "sinners," of all people, are not to be excluded from Jesus' mission.

In a further complaint, the question is raised why Jesus' disciples, unlike others, do not fast. Jesus replies, in effect, that "to everything there is a season"; but in the presence of the bridegroom, the wedding party cannot fast. Similarly, those who fast now fail to recognize the appearance in their midst of the herald of God's kingdom (cf. 12:6, 28, 41–42; 13:16–17). To insist on the traditional practice of fasting when a new and joyous stage in salvation history has come is like trying to patch an old cloak with a new (still unshrunk) piece of cloth or to keep new wine contained in old wineskins.

Matthew (9:18–26) drastically reduces Mark's account (Mark 5:21–43) of the raising of Jairus' daughter and the healing of a woman with a hemorrhage, but preserves enough to stress: (1) the power of Jesus, who heals in a moment an affliction of twelve-years standing, and even raises the dead; (2) Jesus' willingness to aid all who look, for God's help, to him; and (3) the ridicule he attracts from those without faith.

The next episode (vv. 27–31) focuses again on Jesus' willingness to help in response to faith. Two blind men, addressing him as the Messiah ("Son of David"; cf. 1:1), appeal to his compassion and affirm their confidence in his ability to heal. The gift of sight they receive is explicitly linked to their faith (9:29; cf. 8:13). As in 12:15–21, Jesus commands those he has healed not to spread the news, choosing to advance God's kingdom with deeds of mercy but no display.

The final story in this narrative section of the Gospel (9:32–34) sums up the divided response with which Jesus meets, even when healing. Crowds, lacking the insight of faith, at least acknowledge with amazement the unprecedented nature of Jesus' miracles. Pharisees, vexed by the popular response, sinisterly suggest that Jesus is in league with the devil. Matthew introduces this ominous charge here, though reserving its discussion for 12:22–37.

Undeterred by criticism, Jesus continues his mission in both word and deed (9:35; cf. 4:23). Recognizing, however, the dearth of spiritual leadership in Israel, the need of the people—like scattered sheep—to be brought back to their divine Shepherd (9:36; cf. Ezek 34:1–31), and perhaps the reality that, physically, he himself can only reach so many, Jesus tells his disciples to pray that God would send new "laborers" out into the "harvest." In ch. 10, the disciples find themselves the answer to this prayer.

D. The Disciples' Mission (10:1–42)

Matthew 10 contains the second of Jesus' extended discourses in the Gospel: himself sent on a mission by God his Father (10:40), Jesus now expands his outreach by sending (10:5) his disciples on a mission focused on the same people (10:5–6; cf. 15:24), communicating the same message (10:7; cf. 4:17), demonstrating the same power (10:1, 8; cf. 4:23–24; 11:4–5), and anticipating the same hostility (10:24–25, 38). In responding to Jesus' disciples, people are responding to Jesus (10:40).

As elsewhere, Matthew here collects and passes on material that is both precious and pertinent to his readers because it comes from their Lord. Some of what Jesus says is not to be forgotten because it reminds us of the scope and purpose of his own salvific activities, even though the latter were subject to limitations transcended long before the Gospel was written (compare 10:5–6 with 28:18–20). Some of Jesus' directives, though permitting literal compliance only in the context in which they were originally given, outline areas of concern and a manner of living that must characterize all his adherents (compare 10:9–10 with 6:19–34). Some, indeed, of what Jesus says in this chapter would find fulfillment first in the period between Easter and the Parousia (e.g., 10:17–23). Matthew shows no concern to define (and thus restrict) the relevance of the material he preserves. Confident that the words of the Lord will bear fruit in the lives of his followers, the evangelist confines his task to that of collecting, shaping, and transmitting the material.

10:1–4. Empowerment for the Mission.

Matthew assumes his readership's familiarity with the (hitherto unmentioned) circle of twelve disciples. Sent to do the work of Jesus, they receive the necessary empowerment from him (v. 1). Their names are given inasmuch as their part in the church's story—as those who attended and were commissioned by Jesus—is both foundational and unrepeatable. As "apostles" they are invested with the authority of the one who commissioned them. Still, the Gospel is not *their* story: few details accompany their names. "Cananaean" (of the second Simon), from an Aramaic term, speaks of this disciple's "zeal" (cf. Luke 6:15), though probably not here a technical term for a member of a Jewish revolutionary group. "Iscariot" is uncertain, though commonly taken to identify Judas's place of origin (Kerioth).

10:5–15. The Disciples' Task.

The choosing of *twelve* disciples is likely itself intended to reflect a mission to (the "*twelve* tribes" of) Israel; and during Jesus' life on earth (contrast 28:19), their mission, like his, is confined to Israel (10:5–6). That priority, clear in other NT texts as well (e.g., Acts 3:26; Rom 1:16), serves to demonstrate God's faithfulness to promises to Israel without, ultimately, excluding Gentiles from participation in their blessings (Rom 15:8–12). The message of the disciples is that of Jesus (cf. Matt 3:2; 4:17). Their words are to be accompanied (as they are with Jesus) by deeds demonstrating the power of the kingdom in beneficial, not gratuitous, ways. In doing good, the disciples are mere instruments of divine benevolence; they are not to bring disrepute on their mission by exploiting it for personal gain (v. 8). The extreme restrictions on the provisions they take (vv. 9–10) compel them to trust their heavenly Father to care for their needs: the importance of such dependency pertains to all followers of Jesus even where the explicit demands do not. Having found accommodation in a receptive ("worthy") home, they are to be content, not seeking better conditions elsewhere (v. 11). Their initial greeting on entering the house is no mere formality, but a prayer that God will grant peace to its inhabitants; its efficacy depends on the response of the household to the disciples' mission (vv. 12–13). Where that mission is rejected, the disciples are to enact symbolically their own fulfilled responsibility, and the liability to judgment of those who oppose them (v. 14). Since forgiveness and salvation are available to all who do not reject the message of forgiveness and salvation, such rejection proves unpardonable; indeed, it incurs even greater judgment than that of cities proverbial for their wickedness (v. 15).

10:16–42. The Response to the Disciples.

The inbreaking of God's kingdom inevitably disrupts life on an earth where God's sovereignty is not acknowledged. Beginning at 10:16, Jesus prepares his disciples for the (largely negative) response they will receive.

They are not to invite persecution by their behavior, but to exercise prudence in avoiding it, wherever possible ("wise as serpents"; cf. Rom 12:18). Still, such prudence must be combined with an "innocence" that hides no agendas and harbors no ill will ("innocent as doves"). While those who oppose them are, in their hostility, like wolves bent on devouring sheep, from another perspective they are themselves "lost sheep" (cf. 10:6); the mission to rescue them must not be curtailed because of opposition (v. 16).

Disciples of an ill-used master, Jesus' followers can expect no better treatment (vv. 17–25). Like Jesus, they will be "handed over" to trial, flogged, tried by governors, even put to death. They will be betrayed by their closest kin, hated by all, driven from one city to another. No assurance of protection or deliverance is given: they are to be content to share the same slander and abuse to which their Lord was subjected (vv. 24–25; cf. Acts 5:41; Phil 1:29). They do know that they venture into danger at Jesus' command (v. 16); that even in these situations they serve a divine purpose ("as a testimony," v. 18); that the Spirit of their heavenly Father will enable them to bear effective testimony before those who try them (v. 20); that they will "be saved" (i.e., will participate in the glories of God's kingdom) if they remain faithful to the end (v. 22); and that as they proclaim the kingdom in Israel (a mission that is to continue until the end), they will not have exhausted their places of refuge before the coming of Jesus as "the Son of Man" (v. 23, alluding to Dan 7:13–14).

Persecution will test the genuineness of the disciples' loyalty and faith. Like Jeremiah, they will find themselves fearless only as they actively fulfill their commission, the charge to proclaim openly what Jesus has disclosed to them in private (vv. 26–27; cf. Jer 1:17–19). Like Isaiah, they must live so conscious of the presence of God that they fear, not humans, who can only kill the physical body, but God alone, by whose judgment all live or die eternally (v. 28; cf. Isa 8:11–13). Moreover, the God they fear is also their heavenly Father, whose providential care extends to the least significant of his creatures (the sparrows) and the least significant aspect of his children's lives (the hairs on their head). Confident of their Father's watchful care and loving design, they need not fear their persecutors (vv. 29–31).

Verses 32–33 envisage situations when disciples are put on trial for their faith, though the terms permit wider application: before God his Father, Christ will acknowledge as his own—

implicitly, at the Last Judgment—those who are willing to confess before others their allegiance to him. Conversely, those who deny him before humans, he will deny before his Father. That Peter, who three times denied his Master, was a leader in the early church shows that even for this sin the contrite can find forgiveness.

Jesus' proclamation of the kingdom of God offers peace and salvation to all—even the most notorious of sinners—who submit to the proclamation of the kingdom; of its very nature, it cannot bring peace to those who oppose God's reign. Hence the division, even within families and households, between those who welcome and those who resist the offer (vv. 34–36). As Jesus' followers find themselves betrayed by their own kin (v. 21), so they must not allow loyalty to kin to deflect them from their life of discipleship (v. 37); rather they must embrace the life of self-denial and suffering ("take up [their] cross"; cf. 16:24) entailed in following Jesus, prepared to sacrifice everything—even life itself—for his sake. What they offer up ("lose") for him they will "find" eternally; what they cling to ("find") rather than sacrifice, they will eternally "lose" (vv. 38–39). Here the absolute duty of human beings, as creatures, to God—to love God above all else and with all their being (Deut 6:4–5); to follow God and none other (cf. 1 Kgs 18:21); to offer everything they have, even life itself, in God's service—is stated as an absolute duty to Jesus (see on 8:18–22).

Indeed, one's response to Jesus is, in effect, one's response to the God who sent him, and it is reflected in one's response to Jesus' messengers. Many oppose them, but not all; and what is decisive is not the apparent impact of one's activities, but whose side one is on (cf. 12:30). Jesus promises that those who receive his messengers will share in the messenger's reward; nor will the slightest gestures of kindness done for disciples of Jesus *because they are his disciples* go unrewarded (vv. 40–42).

E. Responses to Jesus (11:1–12:50)

With a transitional, summary statement (11:1) Matthew launches into a new section of narrative material (11:1–12:50). No single heading captures the essence of all its pericopes, but the emphasis shifts from Jesus' mission itself to the response it provokes. God's claim on people's lives permits no shrugging off; in the ongoing struggle between good and evil, the kingdom of God versus that of Satan, neutrality is not an option. In this section, what is at stake in people's response to Jesus' mission is clarified and—one way or another—people declare their allegiances.

11:1–19. Jesus and John. Nothing in this world is more precious, and nothing more vulnerable, than faith. Imprisoned, perhaps troubled by the evident discrepancy between the deeds of the Messiah (related in 4:12–11:1) and his own anticipation of imminent judgment (3:7–12), John wonders whether Jesus is, after all, the One he expected. Jesus summarizes his own activities in a way that echoes prophetic promises (11:5; cf. Isa 26:19; 29:18; 35:5–6; 61:1), indicating that, with those activities, the day of fulfillment has indeed come. To its appearance all must, and will, respond: with faith that, however weak, is blessed; or with offense that *this* man—the friend of sinners (11:19), son of a carpenter (13:55), who chooses, and proclaims the necessity of choosing, the path of the cross (16:21–26)—could be the instrument of God's salvation.

John's messengers gone, Jesus publicly honors his forerunner, underlining in the process the link between their respective missions (vv. 7–15). The crowds attending John were drawn neither by ordinary desert sights nor by paraded human opulence, but by the presence of a prophet (vv. 7–9). Yet John was more: as the herald of the Messiah (v. 10), the Elijah who precedes and marks Messiah's coming (v. 14; cf. Mal 4:5; Luke 1:17), John stood on the threshold of the new age (v. 13), honored above all who belong to the old order, though not as blessed as the least who participates in the new (v. 11).

But from its first announcement by John, the kingdom of heaven has met with the violent assaults of opponents (v. 12) and the petulance of the "generation" as a whole (vv. 16–19). The latter, like children who pout when others will not play *their* game, have found reason to object to the divine message both in the asceticism of John and in the conviviality of Jesus. But activities—such as those of John and Jesus—planned by divine wisdom will inevitably prove to be right (v. 19).

11:20–30. Woes for the Unrepentant, Rest for the Weary. The kingdom is offered to all, but open only to the repentant. Jesus' summons to repentance was accompanied by mighty works that themselves called for a response to the manifest presence of God. Such moments, when God's claims on people's lives are specially, even tangibly, real must not go unheeded. The liability to judgment of those too complacent or proud to respond will match the magnitude of their spurned opportunity (11:20–24; cf. 10:15; Luke 12:48).

In the words and deeds of Jesus, his Father—the "Lord of heaven and earth"—is addressing human beings. Jesus gratefully acknowledges that the openness to his mission shown by the lowly ("infants"; cf. Matt 18:1–5; 19:14) corresponds to his Father's will; so too its rejection by those too knowing to listen, too confident in their own wisdom to heed God's call (vv. 25–26; cf. 1 Cor 1:18–31). Those who refuse to recognize Jesus, the Son, withhold honor from the One to whom the Father has entrusted all things (v. 27; cf. 28:18). Thus knowing God the Father and acknowledging God's Son go together: the Son is known only by the Father and those whose eyes the Father has opened (vv. 25, 27; cf. 16:17); the Father is known only by the Son and those to whom the Son reveals him (cf. John 1:18).

Jesus invites all who live in quiet desperation, wearied with the troubles of a sin-marred existence, burdened by religious obligations that bring them no nearer God (cf. 23:4), to become his disciples. His are not the demands of one bent on asserting his authority, but of one meek, who promises "rest": a life of discipleship, learned at Jesus' feet ("learn from me" [v. 29]), reflecting undivided devotion to God, with childlike trust in, and obedience to, the Father's will (vv. 28–30).

12:1–21. Sabbath Controversies. The Sabbath activities of Jesus and his disciples provide the occasion for two controversies recounted at the beginning of ch. 12. In the first (vv. 1–8), hungry disciples pluck heads of grain as they pass through a grainfield, an activity permitted on other days of the week (cf. Deut 23:25), but construed by Pharisees as reaping, a category of work forbidden on the Sabbath (cf. Exod 34:21). Jesus counters the charge with a series of arguments and claims. First, God's will is not promoted by casuistically interpreting and rigidly applying legal texts while ignoring human need: after all, Scripture itself countenances David's violation of the law when he satisfied his and his companions' hunger with consecrated bread reserved for the priests (1 Sam 21:1–6; cf. Lev 24:9). Second, since the demands of the Temple take priority over Sabbath laws, so must the service of "something greater than the temple" (vv.5–6): the implicit claim is that the presence of God is more immediate in the person and work of Jesus than in the Temple itself. Third, those who condemn the hungry for plucking grain on the Sabbath are out of step with a God who prioritizes compassion above fulfillment of ritual laws (v. 7, citing Hos 6:6; cf. 9:13). Fourth, since the God who instituted the Sabbath is free to define its true observance, so the One through whom God's reign is realized is "*lord*" of the Sabbath (12:8).

In the second incident (vv. 9–14), Jesus defends a Sabbath healing by demonstrating that, even when less is at stake, common sense dictates that help be given on the Sabbath. In general, Sabbath laws must not be used to prevent doing what is good. Those vexed that Jesus would heal on the Sabbath then devote the hallowed day to plotting his destruction.

Rather than aggravate the situation ("his hour had not yet come" [cf. John 7:30]), Jesus withdraws. He continues to heal all comers and to forbid them to publicize what he has done. In the unobtrusive, compassionate way in which he heals the effects of sin, advancing the cause of God's just rule (vv. 18–20), Matthew sees a fulfillment of Isa 42:1–4; appropriately too the Isaiah text refers to *Gentile* faith in God's humble servant.

12:22–37. Blasphemy Against the Spirit.

When, as the result of an exorcism performed by Jesus, a blind and dumb man was able to speak and see, the awestruck crowd wonders whether Jesus might be the Messiah ("son of David"). Provoked by the suggestion, Pharisees contemptuously dismiss it, attributing Jesus' powers to Beelzebul (i.e., Satan; compare vv. 26 and 27, and note already 9:34). Jesus shows first the *folly* of this claim (it entails Satan fighting against himself [vv. 25–26]; it is inconsistently directed against Jesus, not against other exorcists [v. 27]); then its *seriousness*: if (as is indeed the case) Jesus casts out demons by the power of God's Spirit, then the kingdom of God is already making its presence felt in their midst, overpowering Satan and setting Satan's captives free (vv. 28–29). To oppose this work of Jesus—indeed, even to fail to align oneself with it—is to side with the powers of evil at a time when lines are being drawn, and those who will enter God's kingdom are being "gathered" (v. 30). God is ready to forgive all other sins, including blasphemy and opposition to Jesus rooted in a failure to discern the nature of his mission; but there can be no forgiveness for the determined opposition to God's rule that perversely, and blasphemously, labels evil the manifest good that it brings (vv. 31–32).

In attributing Jesus' powers to Satan, his opponents have revealed the malice of their hearts (vv. 33–34). Since "no one can tame the tongue" (Jas 3:8), the good or evil stored up in people's hearts is bound to find expression in their words; hence people's own words provide an adequate and irrefutable basis for their approval or condemnation on the day of judgment. Those who heedlessly disparage the work of Jesus are reminded that, on judgment day, people are accountable for even the careless words they have spoken (vv. 35–37).

12:38–50. Unbelief and Its Consequences, Obedience and Its Rewards.

The appearance of God's kingdom in the words and work of Jesus demands a response of faith: to begrudge God one's faith, spelling out terms that God must meet before one will yield it (12:38; cf. 1 Cor 1:22), betrays a heart unwilling to submit to God's rule. Such resistance is typical of the "evil and adulterous [i.e., faithless] generation" Jesus encountered. The only "sign" it would be given would be one of God's own choosing, the resurrection of Jesus (to which veiled reference is made in v. 40). The indifference and hostility shown by Jesus' contemporaries in the presence of God's kingdom appears all the more inexcusable when compared with the positive response of the Ninevites to a prophet's word and that of the queen of Sheba to Solomon's wisdom (vv. 41–42; cf. Jonah 3:4–9; 1 Kgs 10:1–10). In a graphic picture, Jesus warns of the sorry end that awaits those who fail to follow up an initial interest in God's kingdom (cf. 3:5–6; 4:25) with true repentance and faith (vv. 43–45).

Jesus uses the appearance of his mother and brothers to highlight the very different state of those who follow him: they do the will of God his Father and are thus the true (or spiritual) kin of God's Son (vv. 46–50).

F. The Mysteries of the Kingdom in Parables (13:1–52)

The limited headway made by Jesus' mission and the opposition it provoked are among the "mysteries" (NRSV footnote in 13:11; cf. "what has been hidden" in v. 35) treated in his third discourse in Matthew's Gospel. The chapter includes both parables of Jesus and reasons for the adoption of this method of teaching.

13:1–9, 18–33, 36–50. The Parables. These verses contain a series of seven parables, together with the explanations given to the disciples for the first two parables. The opening parable of the sower (vv. 3–9, 18–23) stands on its own. The other six parables are made up of three groups of two parables each: that of the weeds among the wheat (vv. 24–30, 36–43) finds a parallel in the parable of the net that catches good fish and bad (vv. 47–50). The parable of the mustard seed (vv. 31–32) goes with that of the yeast (v. 33). The parable of the treasure hidden in the field (v. 44) goes with that of the pearl of great value (vv. 45–46).

The parable of the sower, spoken to "great crowds," clarifies—for those with "ears" to hear and understand (v. 9)—why the message of the kingdom meets with varying responses; at the same time it challenges listeners to respond appropriately. The message is like seed that is sown: depending on the type of soil on which it falls, it may or may not bring a harvest of grain. Those with no understanding of the message are like a beaten path that seed cannot penetrate: the "evil one" has no problem keeping those "tone deaf" to the summons to God's kingdom from responding when they hear it. Rocky ground has enough soil to allow seed to spring up, not enough to let it grow; similarly, some people are glad enough when invited to God's kingdom, but put off when they encounter the hostility it provokes among others. As seed sown among thorns yields no grain, so those unwilling to put aside the cares of the present age and the allurement of wealth are thus prevented from seeking God's kingdom and righteousness (cf. 6:19–33). Only those who "bear fruit" so grasp (and are grasped by) the call of God that they single-mindedly pursue it, regardless of the troubles it brings, and disregarding all other calls for their devotion. "Let anyone with ears listen!"

The parables of the weeds among the wheat (spoken to the crowd, explained to the disciples) and that of the net that catches good fish and bad (spoken to the disciples) explain that evil will co-exist with the good—the "children of the evil one" with "the children of the kingdom"—until the end of the age. Judgment is to be reserved for that day, when the good and the evil will be assigned their separate destinies.

The parables of the mustard seed and yeast (both spoken to the crowd) give assurance that God will bring to its glorious consummation the kingdom of God, even though its dawn, in the ministry of Jesus, commands little attention.

The parables of the treasure hidden in the field and the pearl of great value are spoken to the disciples: however unaccountable their way of life may appear to outsiders, those who have glimpsed the glories of God's kingdom will gladly seek it to the exclusion of all other pursuits.

13:10–17, 34–35, 51–52. Why Parables? In fulfillment of scripture (13:34–35, citing Ps 78:2), Jesus uses parables to communicate the mysteries of the kingdom. The stories challenge listeners to reflect on how the everyday events they relate have points of similarity with truths about God's kingdom. Teaching in parables itself reinforces a fundamental principle of the kingdom: as one act of obedience, or one sin, leads to another, so openness to the message of the kingdom leads to greater and greater insight (v. 12a), while resistance to its invitation renders one increasingly impervious to its message (vv. 12b, 13–15).

Specially blessed are Jesus' disciples: favored beyond "prophets and righteous people" of old who yearned for, but did not see, the dawn of God's kingdom; and favored beyond their contemporaries, who see but fail to grasp what is happening in their midst (vv. 16–17). Granted insight by God (v. 11a) and explanations by Jesus of what they do not understand (vv. 18–23, 36–43), they are equipped to convey to others both Jesus' ("new") message of the kingdom and how it was anticipated in God's ("old") dealings with the covenant people of Israel (vv. 51–52).

G. The Mysteries of God's Son (13:53–17:27)

Again, no single theme unites all the narrative material between Jesus' third and fourth discourses in Matthew's Gospel, but the mysteries surrounding Jesus' own person are the focus of a number of episodes. Outsiders express their bewilderment (13:54–56; 14:2; 16:13–14). The disciples are granted treasured but fleeting moments of luminosity in which they recognize the Son of God (14:33; 16:16–17; 17:1–8).

13:53–58. Offense in Nazareth. Like the Galilean cities denounced in 11:20–24 for their failure to repent, the people of Nazareth are put off rather than drawn to faith by the presence of Jesus. The contrast between his humble roots, which they know all too well, and the power of his words and deeds leaves them astonished; but astonishment here induces only offense. Where eyes are shut to the glory of God (cf. 13:15), familiarity breeds contempt (13:57). Nor does Jesus challenge their dismissive response with further miracles; "according to" their *un*belief, they experience little of God's power (v. 58; cf. 8:13).

14:1–12. The Death of John the Baptist. For Herod Antipas (son of the Herod of 2:1) too Jesus' mighty works demand explanation but prompt no repentance. Prodded by conscience, he suspects that John the Baptist, whom he executed, has returned to life with supernatural power. Herod had arrested John to silence the latter's fearless rebukes of his immorality (14:3–4; cf. Lev 18:16; 20:21), then executed him rather than publicly renege on a fatuous commitment. The episode is one of the few in the Gospel in which Jesus is not the center of attention; nonetheless, the parallels between John the Baptist's death and that of Jesus are clear (see 17:11–13).

14:13–36. Bread for the Hungry, Peace in the Storm. Jesus withdraws, but the pursuit of the crowds and his own compassion make respite impossible. Practicality suggests that, after a day of meeting their needs, Jesus dismiss the crowd to find food; but Jesus insists that those who have come to him need go nowhere else for nourishment. As Jesus feeds the crowd, the God who "gives food to the hungry" is at work (Ps 146:7; cf. Matt 6:25–26, 33); at the same time, the story anticipates both Jesus' last supper, where the bread and wine he provides represent the gift of his own body and blood (26:26–28), and the feast of the kingdom of heaven, likewise furnished by Jesus the Messiah (cf. 8:11; 26:29).

In the verses that follow, Matthew invites his readers to join the disciples in seeing and worshiping God's Son (14:33). After communing alone with his Father (v. 23), Jesus comes to his disciples in a way that recalls divine appearances and activities in the OT: walking on water (cf. Job 9:8; Hab 3:15); speaking the divine "I am" (NRSV, "It is I," v. 27; cf. Exod 3:14); bidding his people not to fear (v. 27; cf. Isa 41:13, 14; 43:1, 5); calming the sea (v. 32; cf. Job 26:12; Ps 107:29). Matthew's desire, however, is not to drive readers to consult a concordance, but to encourage them to identify themselves and their troubles with the beleaguered disciples in the boat; to sense in the approaching presence of Jesus the goodness and greatness of God; to focus, not (as Peter did) on the hardships that surround them, but on the One who summons them to trust and come to him; and to acknowledge and worship Jesus as God's Son.

Coming to Gennesaret on the northwest shore of the Sea of Galilee, Jesus heals all who seek his aid (vv. 34–35).

15:1–20. Religion of the Lips. Religious observances can be a means of serving God; but they can also be a means of concealing, from oneself as well as from others, a heart that is not submissive to God's will. A dispute over handwashing gives Jesus the opportunity to distinguish between true service of God and false.

Religious Jews of Jesus' day were united in believing that faithfulness to God required observance of the laws of God's covenant with Israel; they differed in their interpretation of particular laws and in whom they recognized as Torah's legitimate interpreters. Pharisees distinguished themselves by their recognition of non-priestly experts in the law ("scribes") as authorities, by their broad application of the laws governing ritual purity (e.g., Lev 11–15; Num 19), and by their adherence to, and advocacy of, a body of traditions that supplemented biblical law: the "tradition of the elders" of Matt 15:2, the forerunner of the "oral law" of rabbinic Judaism. Handwashing (to remove certain ritual impurities) before eating belonged to these extrabiblical traditions (though presumably an extension of such laws as Exod 30:19–21; 40:30–31; Lev 15:11); according to Matt 15:1–2, Pharisaic authorities who came from Jerusalem (perhaps to investigate the activities of

Jesus) object to the failure of Jesus' disciples to observe this tradition.

Jesus responds by attacking the tradition itself as a substitute for, and even circumvention of, the radical demands of God. He cites an example whereby *God's* command to honor one's parents is effectively set aside by *human* tradition: by pronouncing one's property to be dedicated to God (whether or not it was actually given to the Temple), one was able to prevent its use by others, in this case for parental support (vv. 3–6). The words of Isaiah (Jesus says) apply to these "hypocrites" whose service of God is a human construction, a lip service that is not matched with the devotion of the heart (vv. 7–9, citing Isa 29:13).

To the crowd as a whole, Jesus enunciates a fundamental principle (v. 11, explained in vv. 17–20; cf. Rom 14:14): the "defilement" that matters is that conveyed, not when something external enters the mouth (i.e., by the food one eats or the way in which one eats it), but by that which emerges from the mouth (i.e., coming from the heart). No show of religiosity that leaves untouched the malicious, or lustful, or slanderous thoughts of the heart can claim God as its source; nor will it survive divine judgment (vv. 10–13, 18–19).

15:21–39. The Cry of a Heart and the Feeding of a Crowd.
In dramatic contrast with the contrived and superficial religiosity of complacent insiders is the extraordinary faith of a desperate outsider: a Canaanite woman begs Jesus to heal her demon-possessed daughter. Jesus never actually denies her request; his initial responses seem designed to discourage all but the most persevering of petitioners. First, he is silent, suggesting even to the disciples that he does not want to be bothered (v. 23). Then he remarks that her request exceeds his commission (v. 24; see on 10:5–6). When she persists with her pleas, he offers the common sense (and perhaps proverbial) observation that one does not give bread meant to nourish one's children to pet dogs—implying, again, that his mission is limited to Jews. Undaunted, she turns the latter observation to her advantage: pets *are* allowed a place beneath their masters' tables, where crumbs that fall become their food. As in 8:10–13, Jesus commends the faith of an outsider and grants her request.

The narrative continues with yet another summary of Jesus' healing of all who come to him with their needs; unlike the carping of religious leaders, the crowds are prepared to acknowledge in Jesus' miracles the goodness of God to the covenant people (vv. 29–31). The chapter concludes with a second story in which Jesus meets the physical needs of a crowd by multiplying the provisions that are put at his disposal (vv. 32–39; cf. 14:13–21).

16:1–12. Blind Foes and Dense Disciples.
In the religious leadership of Israel, Jesus encounters willful blindness. Here Pharisees and Sadducees, united (for once) in their desire to embarrass Jesus before a crowd, demand that he "show them a sign from heaven"—a falling star would do, or perhaps a darkened sun at midday—to legitimate his claims. But Jesus, who performs many miracles in Matthew's Gospel for the good of others and *in response to* faith, here as elsewhere (see 4:5–7; 12:38–40; 13:58; 27:42) refuses to work gratuitous wonders in the absence of faith: not thus are true disciples gained (cf. Luke 16:31; John 2:23–25; 6:26–27). Instead he laments the lack of spiritual discernment among people capable of advanced scientific observations (Matt 16:2–3) and dismisses their imperious demand in the same terms as in 12:39 (16:4).

Jesus' disciples are more compliant but (apart from divine enlightenment) scarcely more perceptive. Not only do they misconstrue Jesus' warning for the teaching (in this case, God-talk that substitutes for faith and obedience) of the Pharisees and Sadducees, but they do so in a way that reveals their continuing anxiety for "what [they would] eat" (cf. 6:25) even after Jesus has proven himself able to meet all such needs (16:7–11). Again, Jesus rebukes their "little faith" (cf. 8:26; 14:31) and corrects their misunderstandings.

16:13–17:8. The Revelation of Jesus Christ.
This section speaks of the revelation of Jesus' identity (16:13–20), of the nature of his mission (vv. 21–28), and of his glory as God's Son (17:1–8). In each case, the confusion of human perceptions apart from divine enlightenment is apparent.

Having journeyed northward into Gentile territory and arrived at Caesarea Philippi, at the foot of Mount Hermon, Jesus asks his disciples what *people* make of his identity (16:13). The disciples confine their response to a series of well-intentioned (contrast 9:34) but nonetheless confused perceptions, all of which grant that Jesus is some sort of prophet (16:14). Only through God the Father is God the Son known, even by Jesus' disciples (vv. 16–17; cf. 3:17; 11:27).

Jesus is "the Messiah, the Son of the living God" (v. 16). "Messiah" (or "Christ," the Greek equivalent) here refers to the expected descendant of David who would establish God's righteous rule over Israel, to the benefit of all nations: through the Messiah, God would put things right on earth (cf. Isa 9:6–7; 11:1–10; Jer 23:5–6). Since the Messiah was a "son of David" (cf. Matt 1:1), and since the sons of David who sat on "the throne of the LORD" over Israel (1 Chr 29:23) were spoken of metaphorically as God's "sons" (2 Sam 7:14; Ps 2:7; 89:26–27), "Son of God" is at times a mere equivalent of the title "Messiah" (cf. Matt 26:63). But when affirmed of Jesus in Matthew's Gospel, it means much more: the relationship between the divine Father and Jesus, the Son, is unique (11:27); indeed, the Son is himself "God with us" (1:23), and to him divine prerogatives are ascribed throughout the Gospel (see, e.g., on 2:2, 8, 11; 9:2–3; 10:37–39; and below, on 16:24–27).

According to 2 Sam 7:12–14, David's son, called God's son, will build a house for God. In Matt 16:18, Jesus speaks of a fulfillment of that promise surpassing anything done by Solomon: Jesus himself will build his "church," the Christ-confessing people who form God's spiritual temple (cf. Eph 2:19–22). Of that temple Christ himself is the irreplaceable foundation (1 Cor 3:11). Yet since Christ is known through the testimony of his apostles, they may be spoken of in similar terms (Eph 2:20; Rev 21:14). In Matt 16:18, the "rock" (Gk.: *petra*) on which the church is built is identified specifically as Peter, first of the apostles (10:2) and leader of the church in its earliest days: the very name "Peter" (Gk.: *Petros*; cf. *Cephas*, the Aramaic equivalent, in Gal 2:9, 11) was given by Jesus to mark him for this role. The gospel entrusted to Peter (and to the other apostles) is the "key" that opens the door to God's kingdom, the message that brings salvation or condemnation to its hearers, depending on their response (cf. Matt 10:7, 14–15, 40). And to Peter (and the other apostles; cf. 18:18) is assigned the task of adjudicating issues within the community as they

arise. That the forces of evil (the "gates of Hades") will oppose Christ's church is taken for granted; but they cannot overcome it.

Yet any proclamation of Jesus as Christ that does not speak of Christ *crucified* invites misunderstanding; not yet, then, are the disciples to tell of his Messiahship (Matt 16:20). Indeed, the disciples themselves are ill-prepared to accept God's agenda for the Messiah—rejection, suffering, death, and resurrection—when Jesus reveals it. Peter attempts to dissuade him and is sharply rebuked by Jesus (vv. 21–23). Jesus goes further: the path of self-denial and self-sacrifice that he takes is the path prescribed for all who would be his followers (v. 24; see on 10:37–39). Through the centuries Christians have been no less creative than the Pharisees of 15:1–9 in contriving pious substitutes for obedience to Jesus' radical demands. Yet only when life centered on the self—its ambitions and gratification—is renounced for Jesus' sake is eternal life gained; and Jesus pointedly notes that gaining possessions at the cost of one's life—one's *true* life—is no way to do business (vv. 25–26).

The absolute devotion humans owe God—because God is *God* and because humans owe God everything—finds expression here in the call to follow Jesus, to sacrifice all for his sake (16:24–25; cf. on 8:18–22; 10:37–39); at the same time, the divine prerogative of judging humankind is here assumed by Jesus (16:27). But he comes again "in the glory of the Father" to repay all for the good or evil they have done (v. 27). Jesus encourages his disciples with the assurance that some of them will live to see him come in his kingdom (v. 28). Matthew proceeds immediately to tell how three disciples were granted an anticipation of that vision (17:1–8), and concludes his Gospel with the post-resurrection inauguration of Christ's reign (28:18)—though its consummation is reserved for an unknown hour (24:36).

What follows (17:1–5) is a narrative expression of the truth of 2 Cor 4:6 (cf. also Matt 11:27): the God who created light "in the beginning" must illumine the hearts of believers—here represented by Peter, James, and John—to enable them to see God's glory in the person of Jesus Christ. A glimpse of that glory makes the sacrifices of 16:24–25 worthwhile (cf. 13:44–46) and strengthens faith in the coming glory of God's kingdom (16:27; cf. 13:43). Moses and Elijah are seen with Jesus, stressing the continuity between old revelations ("the law and the prophets") and the new. But old revelations find their fulfillment in the new (5:17), and it is to Jesus, the divine Son, that God the Father directs attention and obedience (17:5, first repeating 3:17, then echoing Deut 18:15).

The transfiguration of Jesus represents a momentary glimpse in time of eternal reality. But not yet can Jesus and his disciples rest in heavenly glories (cf. 17:4). Much remains to be accomplished in time.

17:9–27. Earthly Realities. Jesus and his disciples (not unlike the Moses of Exod 32!) descend from the mountain to face earthly realities: a question from skeptics (17:9–13), a demon-possessed boy and a faithless generation (vv. 14–20), imminent suffering (vv. 22–23), and the demand that taxes be paid (vv. 24–27).

That the dawn of God's kingdom could be seen in the work of Jesus was dismissed by some on the grounds that Elijah, who must come first (cf. Mal 4:5–6), had not yet appeared. When Jesus' disciples voice this objection, Jesus confirms the timetable it implies but affirms that "Elijah" has already come and has gone unrecognized; he encountered the same fate as that which awaits Jesus. John the Baptist is meant, and the parallels between his life and that of Jesus are again underlined (see on 14:1–12).

In retelling (in a sharply abbreviated form; compare vv. 14–20 with Mark 9:14–29) the healing of a demon-possessed boy, Matthew focuses on the need for faith. Jesus' rebuke of the "faithless and perverse generation" among which he lives (v. 17; cf. 12:39; 16:4) here includes the disciples, whose faith was too "little"—even after all the time they had spent with Jesus—to enable them to perform an exorcism that they had been empowered to do (10:1). With a graphic picture (v. 20, echoed in 1 Cor 13:2), Jesus declares that the power of the God for whom nothing is impossible is accessible to those with faith.

The imminence of Jesus' suffering, death, and resurrection is the subject of another reminder in Matt 17:22–23 (cf. 16:21; 17:12). Nothing Jesus says or does in Matthew's Gospel is rightly understood if detached from the climax of the Gospel here anticipated (Matt 26–28).

Matthew 17 closes with the issue of paying taxes, here that which provided for the daily Temple sacrifices. If taxes paid to the Temple are taxes paid to God, then God's own Son and his followers should be exempt from paying them: no king demands taxes from his offspring. But Jesus is not inclined to disclose the secret of his divine sonship (cf. 16:15–20) merely to avoid paying taxes. Matthew tells how Jesus arranges—as only Jesus can!—for the tax to be paid (v. 27).

H. Church Matters (18:1–35)

In the fourth discourse of Jesus in the Gospel, Matthew turns to matters within the community of Jesus' followers. Jesus requires that his disciples practice self-effacement, acknowledge the seriousness of sin, show concern for the erring, and be willing to forgive.

18:1–14. The Community of Little Ones. The discourse is prompted by an inquiry from the disciples (v. 1), itself prompted by their (all too human) desire for a prominent place in God's kingdom. Jesus addresses not so much their question as the mindset that underlays it: any who would enter God's kingdom must abandon thoughts of self-promotion and embrace the lowliness of a child. Embraced lowliness is demonstrated in part by embracing the lowly (cf. 19:13–15; Rom 12:16): to welcome a child is to welcome Christ (Matt 18:5).

In the verses that follow (6–14), "little ones" appears to refer to all who, by believing in Christ, have become "little" (i.e., have embraced lowliness; see v. 6). Their faith is precious in God's sight but vulnerable in a hostile world (see on 11:1–6): woe betide any who cause "little ones" to lose their faith or to wander into sin (vv. 6–7). That sin—unrepented and unforgiven—excludes from God's kingdom is presupposed throughout the discourse. As limbs are amputated to preserve physical life, so Jesus' followers must ruthlessly remove from their lives whatever entices them to sin (vv. 8–9; cf. 5:29–30).

God has charged angels with the care of these "little ones" (v. 10; cf. Ps 34:7; 91:11–12; Heb 1:14). If all are precious to God, none is to be disdained. Should any wander from the path of faith and obedience, every effort must be made to restore them, for God their Father wants none of them to perish (vv. 12–14).

18:15–35. Dealing with Offenders. The discourse continues with instructions given to Jesus' disciples on how they are to treat a brother or sister who sins against them. Love does not permit them to turn a blind eye to such sin, thus abandoning the wrongdoer to the consequences of their misdeed (note the connection between Lev 19:17 and 18; also Prov 3:12; 27:5–6), but nor will it want to embarrass them before others: only if a private word is disregarded are others to be brought in to add their voices. If the counsel of two or three is also rejected, then the whole church is to be enlisted in the effort to restore the offender. From any who nonetheless persist in sin the church is to disassociate itself—in the hope that this action of last resort will prompt repentance (vv. 15–17; cf. 2 Cor 2:5–11; 2 Thess 3:14–15). God in heaven, by forgiving or not forgiving the sin of the offender, will ratify the decision of a church that acts thus in love (v. 18).

Indeed, God will always hear and answer the united prayers of Christ's followers, however few they be, for God is bound to honor the presence of Christ who is with them when they meet in his name (vv. 19–20). The promise of Christ's presence (cf. 28:20) is reminiscent of Jewish texts that speak of the presence of God in the midst of those who meet to study Torah.

Human willingness to forgive has its natural limits (18:21); but God's does not, and those who would live in God's kingdom must choose God as their model. Jesus illustrates the point with a parable of a king who mercifully cancels an astronomical debt, but who reimposes it when he learns that the forgiven servant would not overlook the trifling sum he was owed by another. Followers of Jesus are to give as they have received (10:8), love as they have been loved (John 13:34), and forgive as they have been forgiven (Matt 18:35; Eph 4:32) if they would have a part in God's kingdom.

I. On the Way to the Cross (19:1–23:39)

In this section, Jesus and his disciples leave Galilee for Judea and Jerusalem, where he encounters the hostility that will lead to his crucifixion.

19:1–15. Family Matters. Having journeyed to Judea, Jesus is met with a trap-question ("Is it lawful for a man to divorce his wife for any cause?") designed to draw attention to the discrepancy between his (presumably well-known) opposition to divorce and certain provisions of the law of Moses (cf. 19:7, citing Deut 24:1). For Jesus no less than the Pharisees, Scripture defines right behavior ("Have you not read … ?" [v. 4]), but the provisions cited by the Pharisees represent a concession to, and regulation of, human sinfulness rather than what God intends for marriage (Matt 19:8). God created human beings "male and female" so that the two might unite in one indissoluble family unit (vv.4–6, citing Gen 1:27; 2:24). God instituted marriage for the good of humans, providing a lasting framework to encourage and support mutual love (cf. Gen 2:18). It is wrong, then, for humans to opt out in pursuit of their own agendas. Indeed, God does not recognize the dissolution of a marriage, but sees sexual union—even after a divorce—with anyone other than one's original spouse as an act of adultery (19:9, which excuses, however, a husband who divorces—as Jewish law appears to have required him to divorce—an unfaithful wife).

Jesus' disciples suggest that, if marriage is a school of love with demands so rigorous, one is perhaps well advised not to apply for admission (v. 10). Jesus grants that marriage is not for everyone: not for those rendered unfit—by birth or the violence of others—for the procreative act, nor for those divinely enabled to overcome sexual temptation while living a single life in the service of God's kingdom (19:12; cf. 1 Cor 7:7, 32–35).

The narrative moves from a discussion of marriage to a story about children. Jesus' disciples think children too insignificant to warrant their master's attention. Jesus rebukes them, repeating the lessons of 18:3 (it is those who embrace the lowliness of a child who find a place in God's kingdom) and 18:10 (none of God's "little ones" is to be despised), and blesses the children (19:13–15).

19:16–30. The Lure of Wealth. To a young man who inquires what "good" he must do to gain eternal life, Jesus replies that the good that God—the source of all goodness—requires is apparent already in the commandments of the Decalogue and that of neighbor-love; it need hardly be the subject of further inquiry (19:16–19, citing Exod 20:12–16; Lev 19:18). The young man claims to have observed these commandments, but Jesus reveals the divided loyalties of his heart when he invites him to make up what still lacks in his obedience by selling his possessions, giving the proceeds to the poor, and becoming Jesus' disciple. As elsewhere in the Gospel, the absolute duty humans owe God finds expression in the requirement to become a follower of Jesus. Unwilling to decisively choose God over wealth (cf. 6:24), the young man regretfully quits the scene.

Jesus seizes the occasion for a teaching moment with his disciples. Only of those whose lives are governed by devotion to God can it truly be said that God is their *God*; and only for such does God's kingdom have a place. Love of wealth makes this impossible. A love for God that reduces all other loves to their proper place is itself a gift of God (vv. 23–26); and in the day when God puts all things right, God will reward those who have demonstrated a love for Jesus greater than their attachment to possessions or kin. His immediate disciples will rule a restored Israel. Others, too, will be rewarded "a hundredfold" for sacrifices they have made (vv. 27–29). But the promise is meant to encourage Jesus' followers, not to invite their self-congratulation: on the day when all secrets are revealed, many who expect to be first will find themselves last, and *vice versa* (v. 30).

20:1–34. Serving Self or Others? The promise that sacrifices for Jesus' sake will be rewarded (19:29) might suggest that God's kingdom is a meritocracy, or invite a preoccupation with one's perceived entitlements. Jesus counters such notions with a parable (20:1–16) in which the number of hours people work makes no difference in their pay. A generous landowner gives a full day's wage not only to those who agreed to that sum at dawn, but also to those hired at intervals throughout the day. Given the tendency of human beings to focus on how any eventuality affects themselves, those who worked longest immediately take offense, construing the landowner's munificence as a depreciation of their labors. The landlord reminds them that they had not been wronged, and that he had the "right" to be generous! Jesus may well be using the parable (like that of the prodigal son, Luke 15:11–32) to defend his outreach to the disreputable: "respectable" people are outraged by the grace shown to "sinners" (Matt 9:11; Luke 15:2; this outrage is depicted in Matt 20:11–12; Luke 15:25–30), whereas Jesus wonders how they can begrudge God his generosity. Though this age is peopled by those absorbed in their own feel-

ings and agendas, children of the heavenly Father find immunity from self-absorption in being "lost in wonder, love, and grace" (to quote the Wesley hymn).

An act of self-promotion sparks the exchange in Matt 20:20–28 as well; and it follows, most inopportunely, yet another announcement of Jesus' pending condemnation, suffering, death, and resurrection (vv. 17–19; cf. 16:21; 17:22–23). Demonstrating the insensitivity of the self-preoccupied, James and John (the "sons of Zebedee") choose this time to seek—through the appeal of a devoted mother—positions of honor and power in Christ's kingdom (vv. 20–21). Jesus reminds them that those who participate in his kingdom must first share his suffering (the "cup" prepared by God for him to drink), then declares that the mission he has come to fulfill is not that of assigning positions within the hierarchy of God's kingdom (vv. 22–23). Since James and John differed from the other disciples only in the brazenness of their request, Jesus explains to them all that though greatness in this age is measured by one's domination of others, the greatness that counts among his followers is that of mutual service (vv. 25–27). Indeed, his own mission is devoted to serving others, not to finding ways of being served, and it culminates in the sacrifice of his very life to procure their deliverance from the bane of sin (v. 28; cf. 1:21).

The chapter concludes with a miracle story distinguished from other such stories by the actions of the crowd: attributing their own sense of self-importance to Jesus, they attempt to silence two blind men whose cries for help they regard as a nuisance. Jesus, whose mindset is totally different, pauses to hear the blind men's request and compassionately grants them sight (20:29–34).

21:1–22:14. The Kingdom Offered—and Rejected—in Jerusalem. As prophets at times conveyed their message through symbolic acts (e.g., Ezek 12:1–16; 24:15–24), so Jesus now makes, of his entrance into Jerusalem, a symbolic offer of the kingdom that (since 4:17) has been the subject of all his teaching and activity: he deliberately enters the city as Zech 9:9 said Israel's king would do in the day of God's salvation. His entry on a donkey's back reflects the meekness of the king and the peaceable nature of the kingdom. As throughout the Gospel, the (now acted out) message of the kingdom meets both with popular, but little comprehending, enthusiasm (21:8–9, where "Hosanna" [lit. "Save now!" cf. Ps 118:25] has become an acclamation of the Messiah ["Son of David"]) and with the dismay (v. 10; cf. 2:3) of those whose way of life brooks no interference—even from God.

Nonetheless, with the authority of a king, Jesus does interfere with the trafficking (i.e., the selling of animals for sacrifice and the changing of currency into that approved for payment of Temple dues) that had turned the Temple courtyard from a "house of prayer" into a "den of robbers" (21:12–13, echoing Isa 56:7 and Jer 7:11). Again, deliberate fulfillment of prophecy may be, in part, the point (cf. Zech 14:21 and, perhaps, Mal 3:1–4). The religious authorities who had tolerated the abuses in the Temple that Jesus attacked were far less tolerant of the healing of the blind and lame and the praise of children that, in Jesus' presence, replaced them. In reply, Jesus underlines that God's purposes are embraced and fulfilled by those little esteemed in society (vv. 14–16, citing Ps 8:2; cf. Matt 11:25–26).

In yet another symbolic act, Jesus curses a fig tree that had none of the fruit for which he was looking (21:18–19). The immediate withering of the tree provides an opportunity to underline the importance of trusting God when one prays (vv. 21–22; cf. 17:20). At the same time, the curse represents a warning to those who claim to be God's people that (the "fruit" of) their lives must match their pretensions (cf. 3:8–10; 7:21–23, and the parables that follow in ch. 21).

A pivotal exchange follows (21:23–27) in which those angered by Jesus' activities challenge him to declare by what authority he does them. Jesus counters by asking whether John the Baptist was divinely sent or acted of his own (human) initiative. His opponents' refusal to acknowledge the prophetic character of John's activities, and their apparent concern, not with the truth of this crucial issue, but only with avoiding personal embarrassment, reveal the insincerity of their question and the pointlessness of answering it. Jesus refuses to articulate the claims of God for those who lack ears to hear them (cf. 7:6).

Still, the message of the three parables that follow is unmistakable. In the first (vv. 28–32), the disreputable people who responded positively to John's message are compared to a son who initially refused but later obeyed his father's instructions. They (Jesus indicates) will enter God's kingdom long before religious leaders whose evident religiosity is like the spoken assent which the second son in the parable gives to his father's command, but whose rejection of John's message of the kingdom shows their unwillingness to act on their promise of obedience.

In the second parable (vv. 33–44), Jesus echoes a famous lament of Isaiah. The prophet had compared God's people to a vineyard whose owner did everything possible to ensure its fruitfulness, but which yielded only wild grapes (Isa 5:1–7). In Jesus' reshaped parable, the tenants placed in charge of the vineyard both refuse to turn over its produce to the owner and maltreat the messengers sent by the owner to collect it. Their mismanagement and malice reach their climax when they murder the owner's son, but they receive just retribution when the owner himself appears. The point of the parable—that Israel's leaders, in opposing Jesus, are acting like their forebears who mistreated the prophets; that God will vindicate Jesus, punish the corrupt leadership of Israel, and reconstruct as the people of God those who would bear appropriate "fruit" (see on vv. 18–22 above)—is not lost on "the chief priests and the Pharisees"; but their desire to arrest Jesus is hindered by their fear of the crowds (vv. 45–46; cf. v. 26).

The third parable (22:1–14) highlights both the insolence and the judgment of those who reject the offer of God's kingdom. The joys of the kingdom are pictured as a wedding banquet prepared by a king. The ostensible people of God are represented by those invited to the feast who, incredibly, respond (to their king, no less) with contempt and hostility (vv. 5–6). Their punishment (Matthew no doubt sees v. 7 as speaking of Jerusalem's destruction in 70 CE) is followed by the extension of the invitation to the banquet to anybody who would come. (We may think here both of the disreputable people whom Jesus "called" to the kingdom [cf. 9:10–13] and of the apostolic proclamation of the gospel to Gentiles [28:19].) The appearance at the banquet of a man improperly attired (representing those who see themselves, but do not live, as followers of Jesus [cf. 7:21–27]) leads to his banishment from the feast (vv. 11–14). The parable thus warns both those who reject and those who appear to accept Jesus' message of the perils that accompany their unprecedented opportunity.

22:15–46. Putting Jesus to the Test. In the verses that follow (15–46), three questions are put to Jesus with hostile intent before Jesus in turn poses a question of his interlocutors. In each case Jesus confronts his insincere questioners with the demands of life lived before God; in each case he leaves them speechless, but with their hostility intact.

A number of Jews felt religious qualms about supporting with their taxes a Roman regime that worshiped gods other than the Lord. The question whether it was lawful (i.e., in keeping with the law of God) to pay such taxes was thus a real one, but posed here not by religious seekers but by those intent on exposing Jesus to the charge of insurrection. Jesus responds that the emperor and God should both be given their due: those who use Roman coinage are bound to pay Roman taxes; those whose lives are a gift from God are bound to give God their wholehearted devotion (vv. 15–22).

Saducean opponents posed a question (based on the law of Deut 25:5–6; cf. Gen 38:8) intended to mock Jesus' evident belief in the resurrection (vv. 23–33). Jesus corrects their misunderstanding of what belief in the resurrection entails (it does *not* mean a mere continuation of earthly life and relationships), then confronts their unbelief with a reminder of the power of God and the implications of Scripture: if God, in the time of Moses, was still the God of the patriarchs, then those patriarchs must be living in God's presence long after their death on earth.

The lawyer who asks Jesus to identify the greatest commandment in the law perhaps hopes he will speak dismissively of parts of the law. Jesus responds by identifying the fundamental duty of human beings, apart from which *any* fulfillment of the law is meaningless: the duty to love God with all one's being and to show the same devotion to one's neighbor's well-being as one naturally devotes to one's own (vv. 34–40; cf. Deut 6:5; Lev 19:18).

To those eager to discuss religion but not to yield God obedience, Jesus asks whose son the Messiah is (vv. 41–46). The obvious answer—"the son of David"—is correct (cf. 1:1), but insufficiently indicative of the authority with which the Messiah speaks. The Messiah whom David speaks of (in Psalm 110) as "Lord" must be more than his son. Readers of the Gospel know that Jesus, the Messiah, is the Son of God (3:17; 16:16; 17:5). To the words of David's Lord, the Son of God, it is crucial that all give heed (17:5).

23:1–39. Woes and Warnings. Human religiosity is by no means always opposed to human self-assertion. On the contrary, apparent devotion to God easily masks—even from the religious themselves—a pursuit of prestige and power that is antithetical to true devotion. In Jesus' denunciation of the vices that marred much religiosity in his day, Matthew highlights once again the opposition between Jesus and Jerusalem's religious leadership at the same time as he warns the pious of all ages of the perils that attend religiosity.

The objects of Jesus' denunciations are the scribes (the experts in the law) and the Pharisees (reputed to be its strictest observers). Jesus' endorsement of their teaching (23:2–3a) is, as later charges show (see vv. 16–22; also 15:1–20), merely rhetorical, intended to heighten the contrast between what they demand of others and what they do themselves (vv. 3b–4). Failure to practice what one "preaches" is a perennial danger for teachers (cf. Jas 3:1). Where religion requires visible tokens of obedience, those for whom it serves as a path to prestige show exaggerated conformity (v. 5; phylacteries were small leather boxes containing texts of Scripture worn on the left arm and forehead [cf. Exod 13:9, 16; Deut 6:8; 11:18]; for fringes, see Num 15:37–40; Deut 22:12]. The same people relish occasions in which they encounter respect and the honorific titles with which they are addressed (vv. 6–7). Jesus' disciples are to eschew such titles, reserving all honor for God their Father and Jesus, God's Messiah, and seeking greatness only in service (vv. 8–12; cf. 20:25–28).

Seven "woes" follow, each directed against the "hypocrisy" (i.e., the discrepancy between appearance and reality) of "scribes and Pharisees," each—like prophetic pronouncements of judgment (cf. Jer 18:1–11)—indirectly inviting repentance from all in whom the fingered vice is found. The false teaching and priorities of the "scribes and Pharisees" prevent both teachers and their converts from entering God's kingdom (vv. 13–15). The attempt to distinguish between binding and non-binding oath formulas leads to conclusions both absurd (vv. 16–19; the basis on which the distinctions mentioned in these verses was drawn remains unclear) and—like many attempts to define casuistically the divine will in "gray" areas—incommensurate with the radical obedience and honor which are God's due (vv. 20–22): regardless of the formula, every oath is, effectively, an oath "by God" (cf. 5:33–37).

Punctilious observance (even to the point of seeing that every herb is tithed, in exaggerated obedience to Num 18:21–24; Deut 14:22–29) of commandments requiring visible and tangible compliance easily becomes a preoccupation substituting for, rather than accompanying, the justice, compassion, and faith that are at the heart of God's demands (vv. 23–24). Indeed, just as humans are typically more concerned to avoid being *seen* to do what they ought not than they are to avoid doing it, so the appearance of righteousness may be anxiously pursued as a cover for evil activities (vv. 25–28).

Finally, expressions of devotion to God's messengers who were mistreated in a bygone era are exposed as mere hypocrisy when those who express them oppose God's messengers among their contemporaries (vv. 29–33; the command of v. 32 is of course ironic). The "prophets, sages, and scribes" who, according to v. 34, will be sent by Jesus are messengers of the Christian gospel; the reception they encounter will match that of the prophets of old (cf. 5:11–12), thus provoking at last an outpouring of long accumulated divine wrath (vv. 35–36; on Zechariah, see, apparently, 2 Chr 24:20–22).

Jerusalem's destruction in 70 CE is in view both in vv. 35–36 and in v. 38 ("left desolate" means "abandoned by God"). Divine judgment only follows Jerusalem's persistent rejection of God's messengers and of the shelter from judgment that would have followed acceptance of Jesus' passionate appeals for repentance (v. 37). The judgment is not, however, final: like Paul (Rom 11:25–27), Matt 23:39 appears to envisage a day when Israel will welcome, in faith, its returning Messiah.

J. The Last Days (24:1–25:46)

Christian faith, inevitably and from its very beginnings, includes an eschatological hope: if God, Creator of all, is both good and all-powerful, then evil, though tolerated for a time, will not be allowed to spoil God's creation forever. God will see that goodness, righteousness, and peace prevail in the end.

The fifth and final discourse of Jesus (24:1–25:46) picks up where chap 23 ended, with the "desolation" of Israel's "house" and the return of Christ (23:38–39). Jesus' disciples, pointing out the splendors of the Temple as rebuilt by Herod, are told of its pending destruction (24:1–2). Their question (or *questions*; but the destruction of the Temple, the return of Christ, and the end of the age all appear to be linked in the disciples' minds [v. 3]) prompts Jesus to characterize the troubles of the period leading up to his return and to summon his followers to faithfulness.

24:3–31. The Troubles of the Last Days. Jesus begins with a general characterization of the days to come (vv. 3–8): they will be marked by the claims of false messiahs, by warfare, and by "natural" disasters. Jesus' followers are to be neither deceived nor dismayed. They will find themselves the objects of persecution and hatred, which in turn will lead to apostasy, betrayal, and diminished fervor within their own communities (vv. 9–12). Before the end comes, however, the gospel proclaimed by Christ himself must be brought to all the world (v. 14; cf. 28:19–20). Those who remain faithful to the end will be saved (v. 13).

The verses that follow (15–28) speak of troubling times ahead in Judea. Though referring in the first place to events leading up to the fall of Jerusalem in 70 CE, the account is taken by many interpreters to have an eschatological referent as well. The desecration of the Temple site (v. 15; cf. Dan 9:27; 11:31) should be taken by Jesus' followers in Judea as a signal to flee without delay, for unprecedented suffering will follow (vv. 15–21, reminiscent of Gen 19:12–26). They are to pray that their flight may not be impeded by weather or by the difficulties of Sabbath travel (though Jewish law would not have forbidden such travel where life was endangered) (v. 20). Claims of false messiahs and prophets may be rejected outright, for Christ's return, when it happens, will require no investigation: it will be as evident to all as lightning, as certain as the gathering of vultures around a corpse (vv. 23–28).

Using the time-hallowed language of apocalyptic accounts, Jesus speaks of cosmic catastrophes preceding his return "on the clouds of heaven" (vv. 29–30; cf. Isa 13:10; Dan 7:13–14). That return will mean judgment for "all the tribes of the earth," deliverance for the faithful (vv. 30–31).

24:32–25:46. The Call to Readiness. Christ's followers, seeing these signs, should be prepared for Christ's return (vv. 32–33): the generation that sees the signs will also experience his coming (v. 34). Verse 34 is understood most naturally to refer to the generation of Jesus' own contemporaries (cf. 16:28), though the early Christians, recalling the contingent nature of prophecy (cf. 1 Sam 2:30; Jer 18:1–11), interpreted the delay of Christ's return as a God-given opportunity for people to repent and be saved (cf. Luke 13:6–9; Acts 3:19–21; 2 Pet 3:9).

The timing of Christ's return remains a mystery, however, to all but God the Father: even the Son in his humanity is ignorant here (v. 36). Its uncertainty is both a temptation to indifference and moral laxity and a call for readiness. Those prepared will be "taken" and delivered from the judgment that comes to all who are "left" (vv. 40–41; cf. v. 31). The chapter concludes with a parable illustrating the readiness to which Christ's followers are called: they keep faithfully at the tasks they have been given (vv. 45–47) rather than becoming lax in their duties and indulgent in their lifestyles (vv. 48–51).

The call to readiness remains central in the two parables that begin ch. 25. In the first (vv. 1–13), ten bridesmaids await the appearance of the bridegroom, whom they are to accompany to the wedding festivities. Five bridesmaids show themselves wise by equipping their lamps with sufficient oil to last even if the bridegroom's appearance should be delayed. Conversely, five foolish bridesmaids are compelled to go and procure more oil just as the bridegroom approaches; they then arrive after the festivities have begun and find themselves excluded. The point of the parable is summed up in v. 13: given the certainty of Jesus' return but the uncertainty of its timing, one should maintain a constant state of readiness, living at all

times with the same moral earnestness, the same fervor and focus in one's service, as one would show if one knew Christ's return was imminent.

In the second parable (vv. 14–30), enormous sums of money (an ordinary laborer would need to work fifteen to twenty years to earn the equivalent of a single "talent") are entrusted, in differing amounts, to servants with the intention that they would use them to increase their master's property. The talents represent the different responsibilities entrusted to Christ's followers: the resources, gifts and aptitudes, relationships, and circumstances that are a part of everyone's life and that are to be put to good use in the service of God's kingdom. Those who do so faithfully will, like the first two servants in the parable, be commended and rewarded abundantly at Christ's return. Those who fail to live for God's kingdom, whatever their declared allegiance ("Master" in v. 24 is the same word as "Lord" in 7:21–22, though in neither case is profession matched with obedience) or excuse (the misplaced fear expressed in vv. 24–25—that any venture might result in losses rather than gains—does not absolve the servant of his indolence) will share the fate of the kingdom's opponents.

The chapter closes with a dramatic portrayal of the final judgment (vv. 31–46). As elsewhere in the Gospel, Jesus' disciples are warned that professions of allegiance to the "Lord" (vv. 37, 44) must be matched by appropriate deeds (e.g., 5:20; 7:21–27): here deeds of charity are cited (cf. 5:7; also Jas 2:14–17; 1 John 3:16–18). Many interpreters understand the "brothers" (NRSV, "members of my family," v. 40) with whom Jesus identifies (cf. Prov 14:31; 17:5; 19:17), and who ought to have been the beneficiaries of such charitable acts, as impoverished members in the Christian community (cf. 18:5), or those who propagate the Christian gospel (cf. 10:40–42). But the Jesus of Matthew's Gospel demands that his followers show love to all they encounter (5:43–45; cf. Luke 10:25–37).

K. Death and Resurrection (26:1–28:20)

26:1–27:66. The Passion of the Savior. For Matthew, the crucifixion of Jesus represents the intended climax, not the tragic curtailment, of Jesus' mission. It has been anticipated (cf. 10:38; 12:14; 16:21–23; 17:12, 22–23; 20:17–19, 22, 28;

21:37–39) and foreshadowed (2:13–18; 14:1–12) throughout the Gospel. Now, when Jesus has finished "all" that he has to say (26:1; cf. John 17:4), the time has come (Matt 26:18, 45) for him to fulfill his Father's will (26:39, 42; cf. 6:10) and the divine plan announced in Scripture (26:54, 56) by giving his life to "save his people from their sins" (1:21; cf. 26:28).

As in John's Gospel (cf. John 10:17–18), so in Matthew, Jesus is shown to give up his own life freely. Repeatedly, Jesus announces what is about to happen (26:2, 21–25, 31 [citing Zech 13:7], 34). Knowing he is about to be betrayed and arrested, Jesus prepares himself, in prayer, for the event (vv. 36–44) rather than taking measures to evade it; nor does he call on his Father's resources to deliver him (vv. 53–54). Indeed, when the case against him disintegrates for lack of credible testimony (vv. 59–61; for v. 61, cf. John 2:18–22), Jesus provokes the charge of blasphemy that leads to a guilty verdict (vv. 65–66) by boldly announcing that he, as the Son of Man, will be exalted to God's right hand and will return to earth in judgment (v. 64, echoing Dan 7:13–14). At all times Jesus, not his foes, is in control of events—though this does not prevent them from mocking him when they appear to gain their purpose (vv. 67–68).

The significance of the events is summed up in Jesus' words at the Passover meal he shares with his disciples (vv. 26–28). When, in the course of the meal, Jesus gives his disciples bread to eat and wine to drink, he illustrates the giving of his body and blood for their benefit: as the Passover celebrated Israel's deliverance from slavery and entry into a covenant with God, so the shedding of Jesus' blood secures for his followers a covenantal relationship with God, one in which his self-sacrifice procures their sins' forgiveness (cf. Exod 24:8; Jer 31:31–34). They, the beneficiaries, are invited to "take," "eat," and "drink" of what he offers them.

Readers find it natural to identify with Jesus' disciples who, notwithstanding good intentions (vv. 41, 51) and self-assurance (v. 35), fail Jesus at each turn of the narrative. Their "righteous indignation" at the perceived wastefulness of a woman's act of devotion is singularly insensitive to the feelings of both the woman (note v. 10) and of Jesus, as he anticipates his death and burial (vv. 6–13). Judas, "one of the twelve" (v. 47) who ate at the same table with Jesus (v. 23), betrays

him (as David was betrayed by his trusted counselor Ahithophel; cf. Ps 41:9, and note the parallels between the fate of Ahithophel and that of Judas, 2 Sam 17:23 and Matt 27:5). The disciples closest to Jesus, whose companionship he seeks as he approaches with dread his suffering and death, fall asleep rather than pray at the crucial hour (vv. 36–45). Nor are any of the disciples able to live up to their promise to be true to Jesus (v. 35): when trouble comes—and after an initial resort to violence, checked by Jesus, that completely misrepresents his mission (vv. 51–54; cf. 5:38–39)—their resolve vanishes, the instinct for self-preservation takes over, Peter denies Christ, all forsake him, and Jesus is left alone.

The story that portrays the failed intentions of the disciples also features the relentless hostility to God's Son of the leadership of God's covenant people; the judicial irresponsibility of the governor and the thuggery of soldiers of the greatest empire the world had known; the mob mentality that turned common people into a throng crying for Jesus' execution. Matthew 27 shows that the humanity for which the Son of God died was also the humanity that crucified God's Son.

The religious and political leadership of Israel ("the chief priests and the elders of the people") initiate the action against Jesus (26:3–5, 14–16, 47; 27:1), and it is their relentless hostility that drives the process to its predicted conclusion (cf. 16:21; 20:18). It is not to be thwarted by the lack of credible evidence (26:59–60), nor moved by the anguished repentance of the traitor they had suborned (27:3–4), nor shamed by the governor's ploy to force them to choose between a notorious criminal and "Jesus who is called the Messiah" (27:15–23). Nor are they content with gaining Jesus' crucifixion. They join the passersby (27:39–40; cf. the language of 4:3, 6) in mocking the crucified "King of Israel," even using his healing of the sick as the basis for taunting him with his apparent inability to save himself (vv. 41–43, echoing Ps 22:8). Indeed, their hostility extends beyond death to attempts to prevent belief in Jesus' resurrection (27:62–66; 28:11–15): so deeply ingrained, even in the leadership of God's covenant people, is the universal human tendency to protect pride, position, and prerogative from any infringement. Yet their murderous hostility toward God's Son is combined with—and its evil perhaps concealed even from themselves by—punctilious attention to details of religious law (27:5–7; cf. John 18:28).

For his part, Pilate attempts to conceal his irresponsibility (highlighted by the story of his wife's dream [27:19]) by washing his hands of the whole affair (27:24). His attempt to shift responsibility ("See to it yourselves") is as futile as that of the "chief priests and the elders" who spoke the same words to Judas (v. 4). Roman soldiers show the depravity of the human heart by mocking—with imitation robe, crown, and scepter—and brutalizing the "King of the Jews" (vv. 27–31).

The crowd of common people allows itself to be swayed by the suggestions of its leaders in crying, without cause, for Jesus' death (vv. 20–23). The words with which they accept responsibility for Jesus' execution (27:25) are certainly linked by Matthew to the destruction of Jerusalem in 70 CE, interpreted as divine judgment (cf. 23:34–36). Readers of every race and generation—and in particular those who acknowledge that "Christ died for [their] sins" (1 Cor 15:3)—should acknowledge their solidarity with the crowd whose sinful cries resulted in Christ's death.

In the face of the charges brought against him, and even when taunted, abused, and crucified, Jesus remains silent (27:12–14), thus both fulfilling Scripture (cf. Isa 53:7) and illustrating the meekness and non-resistance to evil that he enjoined on his disciples (5:5, 38–42; cf. 1 Pet 2:19–25). After responding to Pilate's "Are you the King of the Jews?" with an ambiguous "You say so" (perhaps "Well, yes, but not as you understand the phrase" [27:11]), Jesus does not speak again until he cries from the cross the opening words of Psalm 22, "My God, my God, why have you forsaken me?" (v. 46): like righteous sufferers in the psalms and throughout all ages, though to a degree known by no other, he experienced what it means to suffer in faithfulness to God while the face of God remains hidden, and divine deliverance is not forthcoming (cf. Ps 10:1; 13:1; 44:17–26). The apparent remoteness of God is yet another consequence of human sin, and must be borne by the Savior.

The universal significance of what is happening is underlined by the "darkness" that "came over the whole land" during the hours of Jesus' agony, and, at his death, by the tearing of the Temple curtain (cf. Heb 9:3, 8; 10:19–22), an earthquake, the resurrection of "many . . . saints" (cf. 1 Cor 15:20, 22), and the acknowledgement, by Gentiles, of Jesus as God's Son (vv. 45, 50–54).

Jesus is buried by a rich follower, Joseph from Arimathea, in Joseph's own new family tomb. Two of the women who accompanied Jesus from Galilee observe Joseph as he does so (vv. 55–60).

28:1–20. The Risen Lord. Undeniably, evil has found a place in God's world: its presence was never more in evidence than when God's Son was crucified. Yet evil cannot have the *last* word in God's world: its defeat was sealed by the resurrection of the crucified Son.

Matthew 27 closes with Jesus' opponents seemingly in control, their maneuvers successful in securing both his execution and a guard for his tomb, their taunts unanswered, that God had no interest in rescuing his self-proclaimed Son (27:43). Yet throughout the Gospel readers have been made aware that God's plan (announced in Scripture) *includes* Messiah's rejection and crucifixion. That claim, together with all of Jesus' words and activities, is vindicated by the resurrection. Indeed, the resurrection marks the inauguration of Christ's reign (cf. 28:18), the "kingdom of heaven" whose coming has been the focus of Jesus' message throughout the Gospel (e.g., 4:17; 12:28; 13:1–52; 26:64). Without the resurrection, Jesus' claims are the product of delusion or deceit; the resurrection proves them true.

Matthew's account is typically concise. At dawn on "the first day of the week" (hereafter "the Lord's day" celebrated by his followers [Rev 1:10; cf. Acts 20:7; 1 Cor 16:2]), two women express their undying devotion to what appears a lost cause by going "to see the tomb" (Matt 28:1). As, in Matt 1, an angel of the Lord announced Christ's birth, so, in ch. 28, an angel announces his resurrection and gives the women instructions to convey to Jesus' disciples: they will see him in Galilee. The women, moved to both "fear and great joy" by this sign of God's presence and activity, meet Jesus himself on their way to fulfill their commission. He speaks lovingly of the disciples who failed him as his "brothers" whom he intends to see. The women worship him.

Sandwiched between this encounter with the risen Jesus (vv. 8–10) and that of the disciples (vv. 16–20) is a reminder that the world that rejected Jesus remains unmoved: as, in 21:23–27, Jesus' opponents were more interested in saving face than in discovering the truth of Jesus' claims, so here the extraordinary turn of events moves them, not to faith, nor even to wonder that seeks an explanation, but rather to use the tools at their disposal (i.e., bribery) to undermine a message that implies their part in opposing God's purposes. The rule of Christ has been inaugurated, but until "the end of the age" it will encounter denial and opposition.

As Jesus appeared in glory to three disciples on the mountain of transfiguration (17:1–8), so now, on a mountain, the risen Lord appears to all his disciples. As, on a mountain, Jesus rejected the tempter's shortcut to the rule of this world (4:8–10), so now, having fulfilled the Father's will, he declares on a mountain, "All authority in heaven and on earth has been given to me" (28:18). It was on a mountain that Jesus first instructed his followers on the ethics of the kingdom (5:1–7:27); so now, on a mountain, he commands them to "go" and "make disciples of all nations." They do this in the first place by baptizing people of all nations in the name of the one God who is at the same time a Father in whose providential care they may trust (6:7–13, 25–34; 7:11; 10:29–31), a Son who reveals the Father (11:27) and who accomplishes the divine plan for the salvation of lost humanity (1:21), and a Spirit through whom God's presence and power are made real in the world (3:16; 10:20; 12:18, 28); and they make disciples in the second place by passing on the teaching of Jesus (28:19–20). The disciples charged with this mission, like followers of Jesus in every age, are the same disciples who have shown their "little faith" throughout the Gospel and who harbor uncertainty even as they worship their resurrected Lord (6:30; 8:26; 14:31; 28:17). Yet they are assured of the accompanying presence of the one born Emmanuel ("God is with us" [1:23]) even "to the end of the age" (28:20).

BIBLIOGRAPHY

D. C. Allison. *The Sermon on the Mount: Inspiring the Moral Imagination* (New York: Crossroad, 1999); F. D. Bruner. *Matthew: A Commentary. Volume 1: The Christbook, Matthew 1–12* (Grand Rapids: Eerdmans, 2007); _____. *Matthew: A Commentary. Volume 2: The Churchbook, Matthew 13–28* (Grand Rapids: Eerdmans, 2007); W. D. Davies and D. C. Allison, Jr. *A Critical and Exegetical Commentary on the Gospel According to Saint Matthew.* Vols. 1–3. ICC (Edinburgh: T&T Clark, 1988–97); R. T. France. *The Gospel of Matthew.* NICNT (Grand Rapids: Eerdmans, 2007); D. A. Hagner. *Matthew 1–13.* WBC 33A (Dallas: Word, 1993); _____. *Matthew 14–28.* WBC 33B (Dallas: Word, 1995); C. Keener. *A Commentary on the Gospel of Matthew* (Grand Rapids: Eerdmans, 1999); U. Luz. *Matthew 1–7: A Commentary.* Hermeneia (Minneapolis: Fortress, 2007); _____. *Matthew 8–20: A Commentary.* Hermeneia (Minneapolis: Fortress, 2001); _____. *Matthew 21–28: A Commentary.* Hermeneia (Minneapolis: Fortress, 2005); S. Westerholm. *Understanding Matthew: The Early Christian Worldview of the First Gospel* (Grand Rapids: Baker Academic, 2006).

MARK

C. Clifton Black

OVERVIEW

Origin and Sources. Mark's Gospel may have been the first sustained, literary interpretation of the traditions about Jesus in primitive Christianity. Although traditions from as early as the second century CE ascribe the Second Gospel to "Mark," Peter's companion in Rome (1 Pet 5:13), nowhere in the Gospel is its author identified or correlated with other NT figures. Mark's presumption that its readers are unfamiliar with Jewish customs, Aramaic terms, and Palestinian geography (7:2–4, 31, 34) suggests an origin beyond Palestine. The pervasiveness of Latin customs and vocabulary (5:9; 10:12; 12:42) points to a provenance in Syria, Italy, or elsewhere in the Roman Empire. If the tumult forecast in 13:5–23 mirrors that of Mark's readers, then the Gospel may have arisen during the era of Nero's persecution of Christians (64 CE) and the Jewish revolt against imperial Rome (66–73 CE). Such a setting is consistent with Mark's emphasis on the tribulations of Jesus and his followers (4:17; 10:30, 33–34). Such dating squares with the judgment, accepted by most scholars, that Mark was a source for Matthew and Luke, both of which may have been written toward the end of the first century CE. Mark's own sources appear to have included miracle stories (4:35–5:43), sayings (9:42–50), and an account of Jesus' final days in Jerusalem (14:1–15:47).

Genre and Style. Mark bears the stamp of many genres: OT prophetic and apocalyptic narratives (1 Kgs 17–2 Kgs 9; Dan 1–6), legends of the rabbis, and lives of Hellenistic philosophers. Like the other Gospels, Mark is essentially a religious proclamation based on historical event. Though vivid, its Greek is cruder than that of Matthew or Luke. Closely examined, however, Mark exhibits care in composition, creatively juxtaposing disparate traditions.

Preeminent among Mark's *emphases* is an interpretation of Jesus that recognizes his authority (1:21–27; 2:1–3:6) yet stresses his suffering and death (8:31; 9:31; 10:33–34, 45). Authentic discipleship is depicted as self-sacrificial service to God for the sake of the gospel (8:34–9:1; 9:33–50; 10:35–45). Ironically, Jesus' disciples (10:35–41; 14:66–72) display such discipleship less often than do a cast of minor characters (5:21–43; 12:41–44) and Jesus himself (14:32–42). Jesus' followers are summoned to faithful vigilance during an arduous, ambiguous time between the inauguration and consummation of God's kingdom (1:14–15; 4:1–34; 10:1–31; 13:28–37).

Mark's relation to other Gospels. Compared with Matthew and Luke, Mark contains much less of Jesus' teaching (cf. Matt 5:1–7:27) and none of the infancy narratives (Luke 1:1–2:52). Only later endings to Mark describe appearances of the risen Christ. Unlike John, whose Jesus unveils himself at length (6:35–51; 10:1–18), Jesus in Mark is a cryptic figure who conceals as much as he reveals (4:1–34; 9:2–13). Despite its mysterious character, Mark's place in the NT has been secure, perhaps because no Gospel probes more intensely the implications of "proclaim[ing] Christ crucified" (1 Cor 1:23).

OUTLINE

I. Prologue: Introducing Jesus (1:1–15)

II. The Early Days (1:16–10:52)

    A. Jesus' Galilean Ministry and Its Opposition (1:16–3:12)

    B. "Who Then Is This?" (3:13–6:6a)

    C. Revelation over Bread (6:6b–8:21)

    D. Christology and Discipleship (8:22–10:52)

III. The Final Days (11:1–15:47)

    A. Jerusalem and the Temple (11:1–13:37)

    B. The Passion Narrative (14:1–15:47)

IV. Epilogue: The Empty Tomb (16:1–8) [The Shorter Ending of Mark]

[The Longer Ending of Mark (16:9–20)]

DETAILED ANALYSIS

I. Prologue: Introducing Jesus (1:1–15)

Mark's prologue consists of five seamless segments: the title and epigram (1:1–3), a description of John the Baptist (1:4–8), the stories of Jesus' baptism (1:9–11) and temptation (1:12–13), and a transitional passage that opens Jesus' Galilean ministry (1:14–15). This introduction orients the reader to several interrelated themes.

A christological concentration: Jesus Christ ("messiah" or "anointed one": 8:29; 9:41; 12:35; 13:21; 14:61; 15:32) stands at the beginning of this Evangelist's "good news" or "glad tidings of salvation" (vv. 1, 14; cf. Isa 52:7; 61:1; Matt 11:5; Rom 1:1; 1 Cor 15:1; 1 Thess 2:2, 8–9). Although missing from some ancient witnesses, "Son of God" is another significant title for Jesus in Mark (1:11; 3:11; 9:7; 15:39); in the OT it connotes an obedient servant within God's salvation history (2 Sam 7:13–14; Hos 11:1; Wis 2:18).

An Old Testament backdrop: The epigram in vv. 2–3 conflates material from Isa 40:3 with Exod 23:20 and Mal 3:1, suggesting that John's ministry fulfills Scripture and prepares the way of one mightier than he (v. 4). In the wilderness (vv. 3, 12, 13) Israel rebelled against God (Pss 78:17–18; 106:13–33) yet was delivered (Exod 19–24). The Baptizer shares the prophets' concern for repentance and forgiveness (Isa 1:10–20; Jer 31:34; Joel 2:12–13; Zech 1:4) in association with baptism (v. 4; Ezek 36:25–28); his attire recalls that of Elijah (v. 6; 2 Kgs 1:8). The heavenly acclamation of Jesus at his baptism (v. 11) combines elements of Ps 2:7 and Isa 42:1, with possible allusions to Gen 22:2–16 and Exod 4:22–23. A sojourn of forty days is reminiscent of Exod 34:28 and 1 Kgs 19:8. Though the significance of Jesus' being with the wild beasts (v. 13) is unclear, it may suggest the restoration of a paradise-like condition before the fall (see Gen 2:19–20; Isa 11:6–9; 65:25) or, in conjunction with angels, providential protection (Ps 91:11–13).

An apocalyptic aura: Elijah's return was sometimes regarded as a sign of the age's end (Mal 4:5). In John he has indeed returned (Mark 9:13); the whole countryside around Judea's capital, Jerusalem, is responding to his message (v. 5). Israel's reinfusion with the Holy Spirit was expected in the last days (vv. 8, 10; Isa 11:1–2; Joel 2:28–32; Acts 2:17–22); the Spirit hovers over Jesus at his baptism (vv. 9–10; Gen 1:2) before driving him into the desert (v. 12). The rending of the heavens is an apocalyptic image of divine disclosure (v. 10; 15:38; Isa 64:1 Ezek 1:1; John 1:51; Acts 7:56; Rev 4:1; 11:19; 19:11). By the NT era Satan, Jesus' tempter (v. 13), is considered God's eschatological adversary (Mark 4:15; John 13:27; Acts 5:3; 26:18; 2 Cor 11:14; 1 Tim 5:15; Rev 20:1–10). The pith of Jesus' proclamation, repentance and trust on the threshold of God's sovereign reign (v. 15b; 4:11; 9:1; 15:43), is apocalyptically tinged: "The time"—God's appointed moment—"is fulfilled" (v. 15a; 11:13; 12:2; Ezek 7:12; Dan 7:22; Gal 4:4). Such a time is painful (13:1–23): Jesus' own ministry in Galilee, a region of northern Palestine, begins only after John's arrest (v. 14), which presages Jesus' own (14:16).

II. The Early Days (1:16–10:52)

A. Jesus' Galilean Ministry and Its Opposition (1:16–3:12)

Mark's first major section comprises a series of five anecdotes that characterize Jesus' earliest ministry (1:16–45) and its stimulation of five controversies (2:1–3:6).

At the beginning of each of Mark's major sections (3:12–19a; 6:6b–13; 8:27–9:1; 11:1–11; 14:1–11) Jesus' disciples are prominent. In 1:16–20 the first disciples are summoned along the Sea of Galilee, an inland fresh-water lake. Fishermen enjoyed a lucrative business, as suggested by Zebedee's hired men (1:20). Brief though it is, this passage highlights features that will recur: the extraordinary authority of Jesus' actions (1:27; 4:41), his initiative in making disciples (2:14; 3:13–19a), and the rupture such discipleship creates within families (3:19b–21; 10:28–30).

Jesus' casting out of an unclean spirit in Capernaum (1:21–28), on the northwestern shore of the Sea of Galilee, is the first of four such stories in Mark's four major sections (see 5:1–20; 7:24–30; 9:14–29). Jesus triumphs over the demon's attempt to wrest power through assertion of his antagonist's identity (v. 24b; cf. Gen 32:27–29). Subtle details cast long narrative shadows: Jesus wields authority over Satan's dominion (vv. 24a, 27c; 1:32; 3:11–12), which astounds (vv. 22a, 27a;

2:12; 5:20, 42*b*; 7:37; 11:18) and causes his fame to spread (v. 28; 3:7–10; 5:20; 6:14, 53–56). Jesus' teaching is fresh (v. 27*b*; 2:21–22), unlike that of the scribes (v. 22), the professional interpreters of the law who will return as Jesus' nemeses (2:6, 16; 3:22; 11:27). This healing takes place on the Sabbath in a synagogue (v. 21; also 3:1–2), a place of teaching and prayer, even as Jesus will resist later attacks in Jerusalem's Temple (11:27–12:27).

Describing Jesus' cure of all of Capernaum's sick, including Peter's mother-in-law (1:29–34), Mark generalizes the exorcism's effect. Three other nuances are introduced: the ministry of women to Jesus (v. 31*b*; 14:3–9; 16:1); his silencing of demons, who know his true identity (v. 34*b*; 3:11–12); the impossibility of keeping Jesus' power a secret (vv. 32–33; 1:43–45; 7:36).

Jesus' ministry begins with preaching (1:14–15); Mark broadens that aspect by narrating the build-up to a preaching tour throughout Galilee (1:35–39). More details are introduced for later development: Jesus as a person of prayer (v. 35*b*; 6:46; 14:32–42); his distance from the multitudes and their incursions upon him (vv. 35, 37; 1:45; 2:1–2; 3:7, 19*b*–20; 6:31–34; 9:2–15); and those searching for Jesus, often with hostile intent (vv. 36–37; 3:32; 11:18; 12:12; 14:1*b*).

Jesus' healing of a leper (1:40–45) declares many of Mark's remaining preoccupations. This tale demonstrates Jesus' compassion for those in distress (v. 41; 5:21–24*a*; 6:34–36, 48*a*; 8:2–3) and his divine power for its alleviation (v. 42; 4:39; 6:41–44, 48*b*–51*b*; 8:7–9; cf. 2 Kgs 5:7). Because leprosy (Hansen's disease) was regarded as contagious impurity (Lev 13:1–14:47), its sufferers were subject to banishment (2 Kgs 7:3–10; 2 Chr 26:19–21). Accordingly, Jesus insists that this leper's cleansing be ratified by a priest and honored with an offering (v. 44; cf. Lev 14:48–57). Social reintegration of outcasts and appreciation of genuine piety recur throughout Mark (3:4; 5:19, 23–34; 7:18*b*–23; 12:29–31).

Mark 1:16–45 highlights Jesus' power while resistance stirs in the shadows. In 2:1–3:6 opposition to Jesus moves onto center stage. Controversy stitches together five anecdotes arranged as a chiasm, or inverted ladder:

A   Dispute over blasphemy: a paralytic (2:1–5, 10*b*–12) and some scribes (2:6–10*a*)

B   The scribes' challenge to the disciples about Jesus' eating (2:13–17)

C   The disciples' feasting and the bridegroom's removal (2:18–22)

B'   The Pharisees' challenge to Jesus about his disciples' eating on the Sabbath (2:23–28)

A'   Dispute over Sabbath: Pharisees (3:1–2, 6) and a man with a withered hand (3:3–5)

Two healings (2:1–12; 3:1–6) encompass three debates, all of which involve eating (2:13–17, 18–22, 23–28). The two bookends, tainted by spiritual heart disease (2:6, 8; 3:5), conflate common elements in a mirror image: the first healing (2:1–4, 10*b*–12) frames an accusation (2:5–10*a*); murderous suspicion (3:1–2, 6) frames the second healing (3:3–5).

The scribes' repudiation of Jesus' healing of a paralytic (2:1–12) is the first instance of Mark's characteristic technique of "sandwiching" two traditional pieces in such a way that each provides commentary on the other (see also 3:1–6; 3:19–35; 5:21–43; 6:6*b*–30; 11:12–25; 14:1-11; 14:53–72). The primary concern of 2:1–12 is Jesus' authority, manifested in his extraordinary ability to heal (vv. 10–11); the passage's theological springboard is the OT's correlation of healing with forgiveness (2 Chr 7:14; Pss 41:4; 103:3; Isa 57:17–19). Other issues rise to the fore. The scribes' rejection of Jesus' pronouncement of forgiveness is framed as blasphemy (v. 7*a*), a capital offense (Lev 24:15–16) with which Jesus will ultimately be charged by Jerusalem's high priest (14:64). Its relevance here presumes that forgiveness was God's exclusive prerogative (v. 7*b*; Exod 34:6–7; Isa 43:25). As elsewhere (3:4; 11:30) Jesus counters with an ambiguous question that puts his accusers on the spot (v. 9); the paralytic's healing suggests Jesus' authority to forgive sins without proving it. By contrast, faith (v. 5) manifests itself as aggressive confidence in Jesus' healing power (see also 5:34, 36; 10:52). Though he exhibits unusual discernment (v. 8), the only authority Jesus claims for himself is that of "the Son of Man" (v. 10), his customary yet obscure expression of self-reference throughout Mark (2:28; 8:31, 38; 9:9, 12, 31; 10:33, 45; 13:26; 14:21, 41, 62).

The summoning of Levi from a roadside toll-house (2:13–14) dissolves into a larger tableau: disgruntlement among Pharisaic scribes over Jesus' eating with social outcasts (2:15–17). Jewish tax collectors were despised for their presumed dishonesty, interaction with Gentiles, and collaboration with Roman authorities. "Sinners" were the notoriously wicked who flouted Jewish law. In Mark, the Pharisees are ranged among Jesus' typical adversaries (v. 18; 2:24; 3:6; 7:1, 5; 8:11; 10:2; 12:13), even though they were a popular reform movement within Judaism that piously applied the law to all aspects of life (Josephus, *B. J.* 2.162–66). Here the dispute turns on the proper expression of righteousness: distancing one's self from sinners or fraternizing with them, as a physician consorts with the infirm (vv. 16–17).

A criticism of eating shifts into one of *fasting* (2:18–11), a Jewish rite observed annually (Lev 16:29; Zech 7:5) and occasionally (Ezra 8:21–23; Jonah 3:7–9) as a sign of contrition. Early Christians eventually adopted the practice (Acts 13:2–3; 14:23), as Mark 2:20*b* suggests. Jesus' rejoinder challenges not the act but its timing: The time to mourn is not at a wedding (cf. Isa 54:5–6; 62:4–5; Ezek 16:1–63; Hos 2:19; Eph 5:32; Rev 19:7) but rather when the bridegroom is taken away (vv. 19–20*a*; 14:21). Jesus' ministry represents something new (cf. 1:27) that the old cannot contain (vv. 21–22).

Another dispute erupts over plucking grain on the Sabbath (2:23–28). During and after the biblical era Jews debated the legality of particular activities on the Sabbath, the day set apart from all work (Exod 20:8–11; Deut 5:12–15; *m. Sabb.* 1.1–24.5). Plucking heads of grain (v. 23) may have been considered a violation of the proscription of reaping on the Sabbath (Exod 34:21). In rabbinic style Jesus defends his disciples' actions by countering with scriptural precedent (Lev 24:5–9; 1 Sam 21:1–6) whose effect is more liberal (Mark 7:1–23). The underlying question—Who decides?—is resolved in favor of Jesus, "the Son of Man [who] is lord even of the sabbath" (v. 28; cf. 2:10).

The healing of the man with a withered hand (3:1–6) is the last in this series of initial disputes. The narrative pattern inverts that of 2:1–12: a mighty work (vv. 3–5) is sandwiched inside a controversy (vv. 1–2, 6). The issue is the same as in 2:23–28: Jesus' contemporaries would have accepted a violation of the Sabbath to save life but would have questioned that exception's relevance in this case. Jesus attributes pitiless legality to "hardness of heart," stubborn obtuseness (see also 6:52; 8:17; 10:5; Exod 9:34–35; 1 Sam 6:6; 2 Chr 36:13; Ps 95:8). The climax of this passage, indeed of 2:1–3:6, lies in 3:6. The Herodians may have been partisans of the Herodian dynasty or officials appointed by Herod Antipas, tetrarch of Galilee and Perea (4 BCE–39 CE). Either way Mark foreshadows a conspiracy of Jewish and Roman authorities to destroy Jesus (see also 6:14–29; 12:13; 15:1).

Mark 3:7–12 is a transitional summary that underscores Jesus' growing popularity (1:28, 35–37, 45) while foreshadowing his ministry beyond Palestine (7:24–31). Judea and Jerusalem (v. 8) lay south of Galilee; Idumea ("Edom," Gen 32:3) was a region southeast of Judea. Beyond the Jordan was Perea, northeast of Judea and southeast of Galilee; Tyre and Sidon were cities northwest of Galilee. Mark gathers several threads in this digest: the enormous, life-threatening crowds (vv. 8–10; 3:20; 6:31) that want to touch Jesus (1:41; 5:27–28; 6:56); the unclean spirits' submission to him (v. 11; 1:23–26; 5:1–13; 9:25–26); their recognition of Jesus as the Son of God (see also 1:24; 5:7) and his silencing of that acclamation (v. 12; 1:34).

B. "Who Then Is This?" (3:13–6:6*a*)

Mark's previous section crystallized Jesus' ministry and its ensuing controversy; this one focuses on Jesus' mysterious identity and its challenge to faith. Opening and closing with disputes in which Jesus' family is implicated (3:21, 31–35; 6:1–6*a*), two episodes highlight Jesus' contest with unclean spirits (3:22–30; 5:1–20) and a trio explores the dynamics of faith amid hopeless circumstances (4:35–41; 5:21–43). At this section's heart is Jesus' teaching in parables (4:1–34), addressing God's kingdom while characterizing its principal herald.

Mark's first major section opened with Jesus' calling of his first disciples (1:16–20); this section begins with the filling out of the Twelve (3:13–19a). The setting is a mountain or "the hill country" (v. 13), a typical place for special disclosures in the OT (e.g., Exod 19:3–25) and elsewhere in Mark (9:2–13; 13:3–37). Jesus "makes" (3:14, 16) twelve whom he wants: a number that may symbolize Israel's twelve tribes (Num 1:4–16; 13:1–16; cf. Matt 19:28; Luke 22:30). The term "apostles" is rare in Mark (elsewhere only at 6:30). Its basic meaning, emissaries who discharge a specific commission, is its likely connotation (see 6:7–13). Besides affording him company, the Twelve are authorized to do precisely what Jesus has done in 1:21–3:12: to preach and wield authority over demons (3:14–15; 6:12–13). The names and ordering of the Twelve (3:16–19a) vary across the NT (see Matt 10:2–4; Luke 6:14–16; John 1:40–49; 21:2; Acts 1:13). Jesus gives Simon the name *Petros* (Greek for "stone" or "rock"; 1:16; cf. Matt 16:18–19 and its Aramaic equivalent "Cephas" in John 1:42; 1 Cor 1:12; Gal 1:18). Despite Mark's translation (3:17), the derivation and meaning of "Boanerges," nicknames for James and John (1:19), remain obscure. The "Cananaean," applied to another Simon (v. 18), may derive from an Aramaic term denoting religious zeal (*qananan*; see Luke 6:15; Acts 1:13). The meaning of "Iscariot" (3:19a) is cloudy; it could be rooted in different Semitic terms for "one from Kerioth" (see Josh 15:25; Jer 48:24) or "a fraud" (*sakar*), perhaps even in a Latin word for an "assassin" (*sicarius*). Mark immediately identifies Judas as the one who will hand Jesus over: the same verb used to describe John the Baptist's arrest (1:14).

The embedding of a harsh controversy over Jesus' authority (3:22–30) inside a framing narrative that redefines his family (3:19b–21, 31–35) exemplifies a classic Markan technique first witnessed in 2:1–12. Indeed, that traditional sandwich and this one evince interesting parallels. In both cases the setting is "at home" (2:1; 3.19b), where an overflow crowd has gathered, impeding access (2:2; 3:20). Accusatory scribes are present in both cases (2:6; 3:22); here they have come "from Jerusalem," where Jesus' death awaits (10:32–34). Coloring both scenes are spirits, whether discerning (2:8) or unclean (3:30), and a charge of blasphemy (2:7; 3:28–29) associated with Jesus' healing power (2:9; 3:22) and his forgiveness of sins (2:7; 3:28–29). Both tableaux turn on the scope or source of Jesus' authority: either to forgive sins (2:7) or to cast out demons (3:22). The cords braiding 3:22–30 with its surrounding material in 3:19b–21 and 3:31–35 are (1) a serious misapprehension of Jesus as "out of his mind" (v. 21) or demon-possessed (v. 22; cf. John 8:48–52; 10:20) and (2) the division of households revealed by that charge. While Jesus counters his attackers with the claim that a house internally divided cannot stand (3:25–27), his own family show themselves as divided against Jesus (3:21, 31–32). Jesus suggests that his ministry spells the toppling of Satan (vv. 26–27) or "Beelzebul" ("lord of the flies" [2 Kgs 1:2] or "lord of the dwelling" [Matt 10:25]); strangely, the lord of an ancient household—the father—is absent from among Jesus' mother and brothers (Mark 3:31–32). Both components of this Markan sandwich of traditions end on a jarring note. In 3:28–30 Jesus solemnly affirms that confusing the Holy Spirit (see 1:8, 10, 12) or the Spirit's agent (3:30) with unclean spirits is tantamount to commission of an unforgiveable sin—perhaps because a patient so gravely ill will never solicit the physician's healing (2:17). In 3:33–35 Jesus radically redefines members of the family, antiquity's most basic social organization. No longer are they his relatives by blood; now they are all who do God's will. The broadening of that family to include "sister[s]" (v. 35) probably bespeaks female disciples in the earliest churches.

Mark characterizes Jesus' speech "in parables" (3:23), which in the OT are riddles or enigmatic stories that provoke without necessarily illuminating (Ps 78:2; Prov 1:6; Ezek 17:2; Hab 2:6). The stage is set for 4:1–34, Mark's largest cluster of parables, which, like 2:1–3:6, is chiastically arranged:

A Introduction (vv. 1–2)

  B The sower (vv. 3–9)

    C The parables' purpose: Mystery given or withheld (vv. 10–12)

      D The sower explained (vv. 13–20)

    C' The parables' purpose: Disclosure and secrecy (vv. 21–25)

  B' The growing seed (vv. 26–29) and the mustard seed (vv. 30–32)

A' Conclusion (vv. 33–34)

The setting (vv. 1–2, 10, 33–34) swings between poles of publicity and privacy, between distance and proximity, between parables and explanation. Three parabolic stories (vv. 3–9, 26–29, 30–32) liken God's kingdom (v. 11) to seeds whose inauspicious origins—random or inattentive sowing, minute size—eventuate in astonishing outcomes: a hundredfold yield (v. 8), automatic growth (v. 28), "the greatest of all shrubs" (v. 32). Fertility and fruitlessness are common metaphors in Jewish and early Christian apocalypticism (2 Esd 4:26–32; 1 Cor 3:6–8), even as sickle and harvest (v. 29) refer to final judgment (Joel 3:13a; Rev 14:14–20) and nesting in large branches (v. 32) suggests protection of God's elect (Ezek 17:23; 31:6; Dan 4:12, 21).

Punctuated by prophetic exhortations to listen and to look (vv. 3, 9, 23–24a; cf. Isa 28:23; Rev 2:7, 11), apocalypticism is even more pronounced in Jesus' baffling reasons for the parables (vv. 10–12, 21–25). In Daniel (2:18–19, 27–30), intertestamental Judaism (1 En. 63:3), the Pauline tradition (Rom 11:25; 1 Cor 4:1; Eph 3:3–9), and Revelation (10:7), the "secret" or "mystery" (Mark 4:11) refers to God's cosmic purposes, graciously disclosed to a select few. Things temporarily hidden are intended for disclosure (vv. 21–22). Attending that revelation, however, is a paradoxical concealment, a deafening and blinding, which the parables themselves are meant to inflict (v. 12). Like other NT authors (John 12:40; Acts 28:26–27), Mark adapts Isa 6:9–10 to interpret rejection of the gospel: preaching the word both gives to and deprives those mysteriously disposed to receive or to refuse (vv. 24–25; cf. 2 Esd 7:25). Even more puzzling is the reality that "those outside" (v. 11) can be those seemingly closest to Jesus (3:31–32). Mark sustains this enigma. Parables told as his listeners "were able to hear it" (v. 33) is highly ambiguous; disciples to whom everything is explained (v. 34) persistently do not understand (v. 13; 6:52; 7:18a; 8:17, 21; 14:68).

The heart of this section (vv. 13–20) is an allegorical interpretation of the sower (vv. 3–9), which may have originated among early Christians in reflection on their missionary hardships and the difficulty of discipleship (cf. 2 Cor 4:7–12; 2 Thess 1:4). The seed of Jesus' original parable is inconsistently interpreted as "the word" (i.e., the gospel: vv. 14, 15b) and various responses to it (vv. 15a, 16–20; cf. 2 Esd 8:41–44; 9:31). Mark 4:13–20 is a précis of his entire narrative, which recounts the vicissitudes of Jesus' ministry in the face of satanic temptation (v. 15; 1:13; 8:33), his disciples' temporary acceptance but apostasy under fire (vv. 16–17; 9:42–47; 14:27), and this world's lures of wealth and prestige (vv. 18–19; cf. 9:33–37; 10:17–27). At the end, in spite of everything, good soil bears astonishing fruit (v. 20)—perhaps an allusion to Jesus' own vindication by resurrection (14:28; 16:6–7; cf. John 12:23–24).

If Mark 3:19b–4:34 bespeaks tacit christology, then 4:35–6:6a pointedly raises the question "Who is Jesus?" This segment exhibits balanced architecture:

A "Who then is this?" Jesus stills a storm (4:35–41)

B Three healings: The Gerasene demoniac (5:1–20), Jairus' daughter (5:21–24, 35–43), the woman suffering from hemorrhages (5:25–34)

A' "Where did this man get all this?" Jesus provokes controversy (6:1–6a)

Mark's christological question generates human reactions of faith, fear, or disbelief: the other thread tying these passages together (4:40; 5:15, 33, 34, 36; 6:3, 6a).

Jesus' stilling of a storm (4:35–41) is a mighty work that reverberates with both the OT and Mark's exorcism narratives. The windstorm, waves, and boat's being swamped (v. 37) recall Ps 107:23–25 and Jonah 1:4. Jesus' sleep in the stern (v. 48) suggests the repose of trust in God (Job 11:18–19; Pss 3:5; 4:8). In its desperation (Pss 44:23–24; 59:4b) the disciples' plea for deliverance (v. 38) recalls the Psalms (69:1–2, 14–15; 107:26–28a). Like unclean spirits in Mark 1:25 and 9:25, the wind is "rebuked" and the roiling seas are "muzzled" (v. 39a; cf. Ps 104:6–7). The quelling of chaotic waters (vv. 39a, 41b) implies divine power (Gen 1:2, 6–9; Pss 65:5–8; 74:12–14; 93:3–4; Isa 51:10); great awe (v. 41a) characterizes human response to divine manifestations (Isa 6:1–5; Jonah 1:10, 16). The most obviously Markan stamp on this tale is the sharp contrast between Jesus' serenity and his disciples' terror: "Why are you afraid? Have you still no faith?" (v. 40).

After the storm's stilling, likened to an exorcism, Mark recounts an actual *exorcism* on Galilee's east bank, in Gerasa (modern Jerash: 5:1–20; cf. 1:21–28; 7:24–30; 9:14–29). The story comprises Jesus' contest with a demon (vv. 1–13) and its social consequences (vv. 14–20). As before (3:11), the unclean spirit bows before a superior force (v. 6) even while attempting to repel the exorcist with divine adjuration (v. 7b). The battle ensues with retaliatory commands (vv. 8, 12–13) and incantation of names (vv. 7a, 9; cf. 1:24). Defilement pervades the scene. The victim, possessed by an unclean spirit (v. 2), lives among tombs, the abode of the dead and of social outcasts (v. 3; cf. Isa 65:1–7). Gentiles applied the title "The Most High God" (v. 7a) to Israel's God (Gen 14:18-20; Num 24:16; Dan 3:26). A Roman "Legion" (v. 9), a regiment of about six thousand soldiers, is a massive Gentile occupation; equally defiling is a herd of two thousand swine (vv. 11–13; cf. Lev 11:7–8; Isa 65:4). The duel's outcome is simultaneously satisfying and terrifying: thousands of demons take possession of thousands of swine; all are drowned in chaotic waters (v. 13; cf. 4:41). The aftermath (5:14–20) abounds with conflicting emotions—fear (v. 15), gratitude (v. 18), amazement (v. 20b)—and social tensions. After the swineherds publicize the occurrence in city and countryside, the populace comes out, broadcasts its own witness, and entreats Jesus to depart (vv. 14, 16–17). Now clothed and calm, the erstwhile demoniac begs for Jesus' fellowship (vv. 15, 18). Jesus refuses his request (v. 19), instead commissioning him to tell his friends of the Lord's mercy: presumably that of God (see 12:11, 29–30, 36; 13:20), though this new missionary proclaims Jesus (v. 20; cf. 2:28; 11:3; 12:37). The news spreads throughout the Decapolis (v. 20a), ten cities lying within a predominantly Gentile region west and east of the Jordan River (see also 7:31).

While the raising of Jairus' daughter (Mark 5:21–24a, 35–43) is reminiscent of healings by Elijah (1 Kgs 17:17–24) and Elisha (2 Kgs 4:18–37), the deepest reverberations are those with the interrupting story of the healing of a woman with hemorrhages (Mark 5:24b–34). Each tale mirrors the other, down to the smallest details. Both center on women—"daughters" (vv. 23, 34)—whose lives are running out after twelve years (vv. 25, 42). The sufferers' medical conditions—chronic menstruation (v. 25) or death (v. 35)—restrict or exclude them from normal social relations (see Lev. 12:1–8; 15:19–30). Circumstances are hopeless and growing worse (vv. 23a, 26b, 35). In both tales someone pitifully falls at Jesus' feet (vv. 22, 33); in both he displays uncommon insight that appears laughably absurd (vv. 30–33, 39–40). Jesus' power trumps that of professionals: physicians (v. 26) and mourners (v. 38). By touch (vv. 23b, 27–28, 41a) both women are healed (*sozo*: vv. 23b, 28, 34a) and restored to wholeness (vv. 34b, 43b). Most important, both stories pivot on faith that penetrates fear (vv. 33–34, 36; cf. 4:40; 9:23–24). Mark stipulates that the little girl is "at the point of death" (v. 23b; cf. Matt 9:18) before recounting at excruciating length the tale of the older woman, capped by a false ending (v. 35). This is performative theology: the narration itself raises the stakes for *the reader's* trust in God.

With Jesus' return home (6:1–6a) Mark's second major segment ends as it began: With the disciples in tow (cf. 3:13–19a) Jesus is repudiated by association with his family (3:31–32). This passage recalls much that has occurred to this point: Jesus' teaching in the synagogue (1:21, 39; 3:1–4), astonishment over his powerful deeds (1:22, 27; 2:12), and rejection by those nearest him (3:19b–21). Here they "stumble" (v. 3b; the same Greek verb translated as "fall away" in 4:17) because they think they know him, his everyday occupation (carpentry, or any material craftsmanship), and his kinfolk (v. 3a; as in 3:19b–35 Jesus' father remains curiously missing). Insiders again stand on the outside (4:11–13); honorable prophets divide their households (v. 4; 3:25). The conclusion is sadly predictable and doubly ironic: Hometown folk receive from their native son the very nothing they expect (v. 5a; 4:24–25)—though he *does* cure a few (v. 5b). Now it is *Jesus* who is amazed (v. 6a; cf. 1:27; 2:12; 5:42)—by their lack of faith (cf. 4:40).

C. Revelation over Bread (6:6b–8:21)

Pulsing throughout Mark's third major section is the capacity of Jesus' ministry to reveal the kingdom's "insiders" and "outsiders" in surprising ways. Curiously, most of these episodes have something to do with food: a royal banquet (6:14–29), two wilderness feedings (6:30–44; 8:1–10), and a debate over kosher practice (7:1–23). A woman pleads for crumbs from Israel's loaf (7:24–30); the disciples bumble over bread (8:14–21).

Food is conspicuous by its absence in the commissioning of the Twelve (6:6b–13). In 3:13–15 Jesus assembles the Twelve to extend his ministry; after a transitional summary of his work (6:6b), that is precisely what happens. Their assignment consists of exorcism, healing, and preaching repentance (vv. 7, 12), all of which they accomplish (v. 13). Sending in pairs (v. 7) reflects biblical custom, in the interest of safety and corroboration (Deut 17:6; 19:15; 1 Tim 5:19). For room and board they are utterly dependent on others' hospitality (v. 10). Their traveling gear—a mere staff and sandals (vv. 8–9)—is extraordinarily sparse; other itinerant preachers in antiquity carried with them bread in a beggar's bag.

The tale of John the Baptist's death (6:14–29) is Mark's only anecdote in which, not Jesus, but a contemporaneous political figure predominates. True, Jesus' fame occasions its placement here (v. 14); debate over his true identity (vv. 14b–16) recalls earlier encounters (3:22; 4:41; 6:2–3) and anticipates later ones (8:28–30; 9:11–13; 12:35–38; 14:61; 15:2). The protagonist is Herod Antipas, son of Herod the Great and tetrarch of Galilee and Perea (4 BCE–39 CE), popularly acknowledged as "king." His conclusion that Jesus is John raised from the dead (vv. 14b, 16) is the first intimation of the latter's death (cf. 1:14). As retold by Mark, the miserable tale in 6:14–29 recalls personages and events in Israel's history. John is a righteous man like Eleazar (2 Macc 6:18–31; 4 Macc 5:1–7:23), martyred for his fidelity to the law (vv. 18, 20, 27–28; cf. Lev 18:16; 20:21). Herodias is a schemer like Jezebel (1 Kings 19:1–3; 21:5–15), bent on destroying a prophet who challenges her (vv. 19, 24). Like Ahab (1 Kings 21:1–4, 27), Herod is a weak ruler, manipulated by his shrewd wife (vv. 16–17, 20, 26–27a). Herod presages Pilate: both seemingly in control, both easily outmaneuvered (vv. 21–25; 15:1–15). John's disciples give their teacher's body a decent burial (v. 29). How will Jesus' disciples dispose of his remains?

The apostles' (or emissaries') report of all they have done and taught (v. 30) harks back to vv. 13–14, suggesting that 6:14–29 has been another Markan intercalation, casting a shadow on the Twelve's success-stories. The feeding of five thousand (6:31–44) offers sharp contrast between two very different meals: a private state banquet, twisted into an innocent man's execution (6:21–28), and a public feast in the wilderness, refreshing the lives of all. This tale also chimes with remembrance of things past and hope for things to come: Israel's miraculous sustenance by God in the wilderness (Exod 16:13–35; Num 11:1–35) and Jewish expectations of an end-time feast for God's elect (Isa 25:6–8). Although retreat to the desert is intended for restful solitude (vv. 31–32; 1:35), Jesus' compassion for the multitude, "like sheep without a shepherd" (vv. 33–34), is a poignant reminder of a faithful king's proper response to needy Israel (Num 27:15–17; Ezek 34:1–31). The disciples' suggestion that the throng be disbanded elicits Jesus' command that they be fed (vv. 35–37a): a manifestly impossible assignment, whose cost would require two-thirds of a day-laborer's annual income (v. 37b). Equally ridiculous are Jesus' query of how much food is available and the puny reckoning (v. 38). No matter: The crowd is divided into "groups" (literally, *symposia*, suggesting a banquet's conviviality, v. 39), companies "of hundreds and of fifties" (v. 40) like Israel's jurisdictions in the wilderness (Exod 18:21, 25). Jesus' look to heaven (v. 41a) indicates the source of his power (also 7:34; Ps 121:1); his taking, blessing, breaking, and giving (v. 41b) are a host's customary actions at a Jewish meal, prefiguring Jesus' last supper (14:22). The symbolic significance, if any, of twelve baskets and five thousand men (*sic*) is obscure (v. 44; so also 8:8–9). Clearer is the miracle's confirmation by the multitude's satisfaction and the plentiful leftovers (vv. 42–43; cf. 2 Kings 4:42–44).

Reminiscent of appearances of the risen Christ in Luke (24:36–37) and John (21:1–14), Mark 6:45–52 presents this Gospel's second epiphany of Jesus on the sea (see 4:35–41). Again Jesus removes himself for prayer (v. 46; 1:35; 3:13) as evening falls (vv. 35, 47). Events unfold "early in the morning" (v. 48b: "around the fourth watch of the night," between three and six a.m.). The imagery reaches deep into the OT: Jesus' bestriding the waves (v. 48b) recalls the Lord God's own power (Ps 93:3–4); "It is I" (*egō eimi*: v. 50), a classic expression of divine self-identification (Exod 3:13–15; Isa 43:10–11); the numinous evokes human terror (Exod 3:6b; Jonah 1:9–10). Jesus' intent to bypass them (v. 48c) may allude to God's veiled self-disclosure to Moses (Exod 33:18–23) and Elijah (1 Kgs 19:11–12), though Jesus in Mark is typically ahead of his disciples (10:32; 16:7). The climax in 6:51 is much like 4:39*b*–41, but here Mark emphasizes the Twelve's incomprehension (cf. 4:13), attributed to their hardness of heart (v. 52; 3:5; Ps 95:8) and focused on "the loaves," a veiled reference to their earlier incredulity (v. 37).

Their misperception of Jesus (vv. 49–52) is immediately juxtaposed with another throng's recognition of him as one with power to heal (6:53–56). This transitional summary (see 3:7–12) is located at Gennesaret (v. 53), on the lake's northwest shore, instead of Bethsaida on the northeast, where the boat was headed (v. 45). Mark emphasizes Jesus' openness to Galilee's widespread need of healing (1:28–45), communicated through a simple touch of his tassel (v. 56; 5:27–28; Num 15:37–41).

From destruction (6:14–29) to nourishment (6:30–44), from obtuseness (6:45–52) to recognition (6:53–54): Between such poles Mark's narrative swings. From beseeching (6:55–56) to criticism—Jesus and the Pharisees' mutual rejection (7:1–23)—the pendulum swings again, with a discernible arc.

1. The Pharisee's critique of eating with unwashed hands (vv. 1–2, 5) seems decades ahead of its time: The earliest mishnaic prescription for scrupulous washing among priests is about 100 CE (cf. *m. Ber.* 8.2–4). By Mark's day some laity may have adopted this pious practice. The parenthetical explanation (vv. 3–4) assumes Gentile readers unfamiliar with Jewish customs. Some Pharisees (2:16) from Jerusalem (the place of danger: 3:22; 10:32) challenge the disciples' ritually unclean "eating [of] the loaves" (7:2): a Semitic expression that recalls 6:38*b*, 41, 44, 52.

2. Disregarding the point at issue, Jesus sets the written Law—"the word of God"—over "the [oral] tradition of the elders" (vv. 6–8, 14). Quoting Isa 29:13, he likens eating with unwashed hands to vacuous worship, castigated by Israel's prophets (Isa 1:10–20; 58:1–14; Amos 5:21–24). Jesus extends his critique (vv. 9–13) to Corban, a ritual offering (Lev 1:2) withdrawn from secular uses like parental support, as violating the Fifth Commandment (Exod 20:12; Deut 5:16).

3. Jesus' answers the Pharisaic critique with a blatant repudiation of laws for keeping a kosher table (vv. 15, 18–19; cf. Lev 11:1–47). All hear this "parable"; privately the disciples, who "still fail to understand" (v. 18; 6:52), receive extended interpretation (vv. 14, 17; 4:34). Adopting a list of vices common in ancient exhortations (vv. 21–22; see Rom 1:29–31; Gal 5:19–21; 2 Tim 3.2-5), Jesus reasons that the organ in need of purification is not the stomach but rather the heart, the seat of moral sensibility and religious conduct (Ps 24:4; Jer 32:39–40). Defilement comes not from without but from within (vv. 18–20, 23). Mark draws the obvious if scandalous conclusion: "Thus he declared all foods clean" (v. 19*b*).

Immediately following this controversy are two healings in disreputable Gentile territory (Tyre, Sidon, the Decapolis: vv. 24, 31; cf. 3:8; Ezek 26:1–28:19). The healings themselves—the daughter of a Syro-Phoenician woman (7:24–30) and a deaf-mute (7:31–37)—do not receive as much attention as the tensions attending them. There is the pull between seclusion and disclosure (vv. 24*b*, 33*a*; cf. 1:44–45; 6:31–33). The infirmities (possession by an unclean spirit, v. 25; deafness and speech impediment, v. 32) place the sufferers at odds with their own bodies. Suspense is further created by Jesus' responses—at first, refusal (v. 27); later, a "gag-order" (v. 36*a*)—which others immediately overturn (vv. 28–29, 36*b*). The focus of 7:31–37 is on the healer's technique (vv. 33–35) and the astonishment his work evokes (v. 37; cf. Isa 35:5). In 7:24–30 the dynamics are reversed: the healing occurs at long distance (vv. 29*b*–30), while the foreign woman's acceptance of Jesus' harsh rebuff ("dog"; cf. 1 Sam 17:43), her insistence on receiving even the crumbs of Israel's "bread" (vv. 26–28), stand at the center.

The feeding of four thousand (8:1–10) parallels the tale in 6:30–44, reprising the same narrative components: desert ambience (6:31; 8:4), a famished horde (6:34–36; 8:2), Jesus' compassion (6:34; 8:2), the disciples' hesitation (6:37; 8:4), meager provisions of bread and fish (6:38; 8:5, 7), their offering to God (6:41; 8:6*b*–7) and orderly distribution (6:39–40; 8:6*a*), satisfaction of everyone's hunger (6:42; 8:8*a*) with abundant leftovers (6:43; 8:8*b*). Although Dalmanutha's location is unknown (8:10), the overarching setting is Gentile (7:31).

The earlier feeding miracle triggered misunderstanding (6:51b–52); so it is here, twofold. First, certain Pharisees return (8:11–13; cf. 7:1), demanding that Jesus verify his divine authority (as though heavenly feedings of thousands were an inadequate "sign"; cf. Num 14:11). Jesus refuses to comply with this generation's faithlessness (v. 12; 8:38; 9:19; cf. Deut 32:5, 20; Ps 95:10). Second, Jesus' own disciples have forgotten the bread (8:14–21). Their hardened hearts (v. 17; see 4:13) align them with the Pharisees (3:5) and Herod (6:14–29) when by now they should beware their antagonists' insidious corruption (the "yeast" that ferments within bread: 8:15; cf. 1 Cor 5:6) and recognize in Jesus the power of God (8:19–20). This section of Mark, which opened with the Twelve's ability to follow Jesus (6:7–13, 30), ends with an off-key demonstration of their resistance and incomprehension (8:17–18, 21; cf. Jer 5:21; Ezek 12:2), pointing the way into Mark's fourth major section.

D. Christology and Discipleship (8:22–10:52)

This section is the pivot around which this Gospel turns. To this point Jesus' identity and activity have been correlated with that of his disciples (1:9–20; 3:7–19a; 6:1–13). In this section, lying near the Gospel's center, the character of Jesus' messiahship and the responsibilities of his disciples forcefully converge in the dawning light of Mark's passion narrative, which immediately follows (11:1–15:47). This section adopts a tripartite structure that is framed by the Gospel's only two stories about the healing of blind men.

A Two-Stage Healing: Mark 8:22–26.

Prediction of the Son of Man's Destiny	The Disciples' Misunderstanding	Teaching about Discipleship
8:31	8:32–33	8:34–9:1
9:31	9:32–34, 38	9:35–37, 39–50
10:33–34	10:35–41	10:42–4

The Calling of Bartimaeus: Mark 10:46–52. The intercalated correspondences between blindness and incomprehension (4:12; 8:18), between healing and teaching (1:27), are unmistakable.

The first healing-story (8:22–26) returns the reader to Bethsaida (6:45), as well as to the motifs healing by touch (5:23), with saliva (7:33), in seclusion (5:37, 43; 7:24, 36). This story's anomalous feature is its sufferer's progressive relief, requiring more than one touch by the healer (vv. 23–25). Likewise, the Twelve's perception of Jesus is fuzzy, requiring of their teacher multiple corrections.

The first of Jesus' pointed exchanges with his disciples (8:27–9:1) occurs at Caesarea Philippi (v. 27). As in 6:14–15, those with whom Jesus is identified (v. 28) were popularly regarded as harbingers of "the Day of the Lord." While correct (1:1), Peter's identification of Jesus as "the Messiah" (v. 29) is susceptible of misunderstanding and, therefore, is sternly silenced (literally, "rebuked": v. 30; see 3:12).

Cryptically referring to himself as "the Son of Man" (2:10, 28), Jesus foretells his suffering, death, and vindication in twenty-five words (v. 31) that synopsize Mark's last seventy-five verses. The elders were senior Jewish lay leaders (Luke 7:3) who with the chief priests and the scribes constitute the Sanhedrin, or supreme Jewish council, in Mark (14:43, 53–55). That the Son of Man "must undergo" all these things is a way of expressing its conformity to God's will. This is no parable; it is said as plainly as Peter rebukes it (v. 32). Regarding all his disciples (vv. 33, 34), Jesus rebukes his rebuker as offering a satanic deviation from God's intentions (v. 33; cf. 1:13). Jesus then draws Mark's clearest connection between his own destiny (the cross) and his followers' responsibility to deny themselves, even to the point of death, for the sake of the good news (vv. 34–37; 1:1, 14). Honor and shame preoccupied ancient society (Xenophon, *Hiero* 7.3); here Jesus associates shame with alignment to the values of "this adulterous and sinful generation," honor with fidelity to God (v. 38). Jesus' first reference in Mark to an apocalyptic Son of Man (8:38; also 13:26–27; 14:62; cf. Dan 7:13–14) is ambiguous. In this figure is he pointing to another or to himself? Perhaps the latter (v. 31), as early Christians deduced (Matt 19:28; Acts 7:55–56). Equally mysterious is Jesus' promise in 9:1, so easily disconfirmed in Mark's own day— unless the kingdom's coming with power points to the very next episode.

Jesus' transfiguration (9:2–8) and its ensuing deliberation (9:9–13) are saturated with apocalyptic imagery. A high mountain (v. 2) is a place of divine disclosure in the OT (Exod 19:3–25; 1 Kgs 19:8). Here the revelation is privately witnessed by an inner circle (cf. 5:37; 13:3), ordered to withhold report of their experience until after the resurrection (v. 9). Transfiguration is rooted in Jewish apocalypticism (Rom 12:2; 2 Cor 3:18; Phil 3:21); dazzling whiteness often connotes glorification (Dan 12:3; 2 Esd 7:97; Rev 4:4). In Mal 4:4–5 Moses and Elijah (v. 4) are linked as heralds of the Lord's day. A cloud (v. 7) often accompanies OT theophanies (Exod 24:12–18; Isa 4:5; Ezek 1:4), which characteristically evoke terror (v. 6; Exod 3:1–6; Isa 6:1–5). What sets this theophany apart is the heavenly voice's identification of Jesus as God's beloved or unique Son, comporting with Jesus' singular transfiguration. This divine announcement recalls that of Jesus' baptism (1:9–11); this time, however, an audience beyond Jesus is addressed and instructed to pay attention to him (v. 7). Rather than housing God's self-revelation on a mountain-top (v. 5; cf. Exod 25:1–9), the disciples are redirected to the world below (v. 9). Their questioning (vv. 10–11) elicits from Jesus another pronouncement of the divine necessity of his many sufferings (v. 12) with the assurance that his precursory Elijah, John the Baptist, has come and was similarly received (v. 13; see 1:6; 6:15).

The last of four exorcisms in Mark (1:21–28; 5:1–20; 7:24–30), the healing of an epileptic child (9:14–29) counterpoises desperate anguish (vv. 18, 20–22, 26) against the requisite of faith (vv. 19, 23). Whereas the scribes, like the disciples, are divided (vv. 10, 14) and the boy's father sways from trust to unbelief (v. 24), Jesus exerts mastery over the demonic (v. 25) so that its victim may arise (v. 27; cf. 5:41–42). Nothing is possible apart from faith and prayer (vv, 19, 23, 29), a lesson reiterated in Mark 11:22–26.

With another change of scene (Galilee, v. 30), Mark unfolds the second of Jesus' predictions and corrections of his disciples (9:31–50). The major differences between the wording of 9:31 and 8:31 are the former's simplicity and emphasis on the Son of Man's betrayal (cf. 1:14; 3:19). The disciples are typically uncomprehending and fearful (4:13, 40), evidenced by their private argument in Capernaum over who among them is greatest (vv. 33–34), a common point of debate within antiquity's social groups (Luke 22:24–25). Jesus upends the conventional premise by demanding of his disciples servanthood (v. 35), exemplified by accepting a little child—an exemplar of powerlessness—as one would accept Jesus himself (vv. 36–37). Nor are there rigid boundaries between disciples and other sympathizers, like the exorcist casting out demons in Jesus' name (vv. 38–39). If the bar for those receiving Jesus' disciples is low and easily reached (vv. 40–41), that for faithful discipleship is high indeed. On that note this segment concludes, with a chain of what may originally have been detached sayings about radical self-sacrifice, now linked by catchwords ("causes to stumble," vv. 42, 43, 45, 47; "fire," vv. 48, 49; "salted," vv. 49, 50a, 50b). The primary exhortations are for protection of Jesus' "little ones" (disciples: v. 42), elimination of any impediment that might prevent entry into eternal life, or God's kingdom (vv. 43–48), and the importance of vital peace among disciples (vv. 49–50).

Focused on life within the family, Mark 10:1–31 explores the ethics of discipleship. Appropriately, the subject opens with marriage (vv. 2–12). Proper grounds for divorce were debated among later rabbis (m. Git. 9.10); their Pharisaic antecedents raise the question here (vv. 2–4). Jesus argues (vv. 5–12) that their cited precedent (Deut 24:1) arose from human stubbornness (cf. 3:5) and is trumped by Genesis (1:27; 2:24; 5:2). God wills union, not division (see 9:50b). As elsewhere in the NT (Matt 5:32; 19:9; 1 Cor 7:10–16), Mark 10:11–12 seems to relax absolute prohibition of divorce. By OT definition (see Exod 20:14; Deut 5:18; 22:22) adultery violates only the husband's prerogative. By contrast, Jesus asserts also the wife's protection against adultery (v. 11) and assumes her right to initiate divorce (without remarriage, v. 12). Effectively placed on a level plane, wives and husbands owe each other mutual rights and responsibilities.

The subject turns to children brought to Jesus for blessing but rebuked by his disciples (vv. 13, 16). Jesus defends these little ones as candidates for God's kingdom (v. 14) and urges upon his disciples a child's vulnerable receptivity (v. 15; 9:36–37). Before the kingdom's demands Jesus himself renounces any claim of goodness (v. 18; cf. 2 Cor 5:21). Such a disposition differs sharply from the man wanting to do something to inherit eternal life (v. 17), God's new creation in the age to come (9:43–47; Dan 12:2; 2 Macc 7:9). Though religiously observant (vv. 19–20; Exod 20:12–17; Deut 5:16–20; 24:14), he cannot satisfy the outstanding requirement: to relinquish his riches for heavenly treasure—to receive God's kingdom like a child (v. 15)—and to follow Jesus (vv. 21–22). Read in context, the problem with wealth (vv. 23–25) lies in its inhibition of self-denial (8:35–37) and unreserved dependence on God, for whom nothing is impossible (vv. 26–27). Jesus accepts Peter's affirmation that he and others have indeed abandoned all for the gospel (v. 28), promising them that they shall inherit a new family in this life and eternal life in the coming age (vv. 29–30). That promise is, however, laced with surprises: no *paterfamilias* (the supreme head of antiquity's households) replaces an earthly father (v. 29); the rewards to come are comparatively modest (cf. 1 Esd 7:88–89); persecutions remain on the horizon (v. 30); God retains sovereignty for reversing expectations (v. 31).

Mark 10:32–45 presents this section's third contrast between suffering christology and recalcitrant discipleship, set amidst the disciples' fearful amazement as they approach the Judean capital from which hostility to Jesus has radiated (v. 32; 3:22). Verses 33–34 offer the most detailed forecast of the Son of Man's destiny; verses 35–41, the most blatant display of his followers' failure to get the point. The wording of James and John's request (vv. 35–37) echoes Herod's impetuous offer to Herodias' daughter (6:22); moreover, they mistake the cup they must drink as that of bliss (Pss 23:5; 116:13) not woe (Isa 51:17, 22). The rest of the Twelve are predictably indignant (v. 41); Jesus implies that all of them still construe authority in the Gentiles' self-aggrandizing terms (v. 42), not as the radical inversion of social norms that obtains in God's kingdom (vv. 43–44; 9:35). Discipleship derives from christology: the Son of Man who gives life as ransom or compensatory redemption for many (v. 45; 14:24; cf. Isa 43:1–7; 1 Tim 2:5–6).

The healing of blind Bartimaeus (10:46–52) in Jericho (v. 46) bookends the healing of Bethsaida's blind man (8:22–26). Many themes are reprised in this brief encounter: partial apprehension of Jesus ("Son of David," vv. 47–48; cf. 12:35–37);

refusal to be diverted (v. 48a, 51b; 8:33; 9:43–47); faith that heals (v. 52a; 9:23; 10:27). Timaeus' son not only receives his sight; he acts toward Jesus, who calls him (v. 49: 1:17, 20), as a disciple should (vv. 50, 52b; 9:23b; 10:14).

III. The Final Days (11:1–15:47)

A. Jerusalem and the Temple (11:1–13:37)

Mark's fifth major section narrates Jesus' last days, spent in Jerusalem. The focal point is the Herodian Temple, Israel's religious and political center. There Jesus performs and interprets a prophetic act (11:12–26). Later, facing the Temple, he speaks of its annihilation within the context of God's final judgment (13:1–37). The heart of this section (11:27–12:44) is a series of controversies arising from Jesus' teaching in the Temple court about God's will.

In Jerusalem Mark slows down the narrative by clocking days (11:11, 12; 14:1, 12) then hours (14:17, 72; 15:1, 25, 33, 34, 42; 16:1–2). The first day is marked by Jesus' arrival (11:1–11), whose description in Mark is less lofty (cf. Matt 21:1–11; Luke 19:28–40; John 12:12–19). Bethpage's location is uncertain; Bethany was about two miles southeast of the Judean capital (John 11:18). The Mount of Olives, a high hill east of Jerusalem (Ezek 11:23), was associated with both the city's defeat (2 Sam 15:15–30) and hope for God's end-time triumph (Zech 14:4). Speculation about pre-arrangements for the colt (vv. 2–4) is pointless; the point is acknowledgment of Jesus' authority (vv. 5–6; cf. 1 Sam 10:1–8). Apart from the textually suspect 16:19, "the Lord" appears only in v. 3 with clear reference to Jesus. The animal (v. 7) may allude to a humble king's conveyance (Zech 9:9); its having never been ridden (v. 2) is reminiscent of unyoked, consecrated animals (Num 19:2; Deut 21:3; 1 Sam 6:7). Spreading of cloaks and branches on the road (v. 8) is a motif in Israel's royal and festal processions (2 Kgs 9:13; 1 Macc 13:51; 2 Macc 10:7), accented here (vv. 9–10) by acclamations approximating Ps 118:25–26 (a thanksgiving for military deliverance). "Hosanna" (literally, "Save now!") was a liturgical formula for God's praise. "The kingdom of our ancestor David" recalls Bartimaeus' recognition in 10:47–48, which Jesus himself will challenge in 12:35–37. Jesus' visit to the Temple, refurbished by Herod the Great (37–4 BCE), is anticlimactic and suspenseful (v. 11). Jesus' arrival does not neatly match customary expectations of Israel's king.

Mark 11:12–25 comprises one of the evangelist's characteristic narrative insertions (see 2:1–12). In the center is the cleansing of the Temple (vv. 15–19): a debatable characterization, as its defilement is not evident. Purchasing cultic paraphernalia in the Court of the Gentiles, the outermost plaza of the Temple complex, was legitimate, even necessary. Jesus' bewildering conduct—affronting both buyers and sellers (vv. 15–16)—suggests the Temple's destruction (see also 13:1–2). Those seeking refuge there, as bandits regard a secure lair (Jer 7:1–11), must look elsewhere for "a house of prayer for all the nations" (v. 17; Isa 56:7). The understandable animosity of chief priests and scribes (v. 18) harks back to 3:22 and 8:31, and will be amplified in 11:27–33.

Surrounding Jesus' prophetic action is the withering of a fig tree and its interpretation (vv. 12–14, 20–25). OT prophets likened Israel to a fruitless fig tree (Jer 8:13; Joel 1:7; Mic 7:1; cf. Luke 13:6–9). That it was not the season for figs (v. 13) holds an important clue: a season—*kairos*, climactic time appointed by God (see 1:15)—of fruitlessness (on a tree, in the Temple) invites judgment, which Jesus twice invokes (vv. 14–17; also 13:28–29). From a chain of exhortations with catchwords ("faith," "believe," vv. 22, 23, 24; "prayer," "praying," vv. 24, 25; cf. 9:42–50) Mark constructs Jesus' consolatory instruction about prayer, emphasizing forgiveness among disciples (vv. 14*b*, 20–21, 25). Because the Temple was situated on a rise, faith's moving of a mountain is apropos (v. 23). Trusting in God is itself promised to rescue from calamity (v. 24; see also 2:6; 5:34, 36; 9:23–29; 10:26–27).

Recalling the controversies of 2:1–3:6, Mark 11:27–12:44 comprises another five controversies in Jerusalem (11:27–12:34), to which are appended three provocative barbs about christology (12:35–37), destructive piety (vv. 38–40), and authentic discipleship (vv. 41–44).

The controversy is a frontal assault on Jesus' authority to challenge the Temple's cultic practice (11:15–19) by those most heavily invested in it: chief priests, scribes, and elders (vv. 27–28). From Mark's beginning, Jesus' authority has occasioned

amazement (1:22, 27) and contention (2:7–8). As elsewhere (2:25–26; 10:3), in rabbinic fashion Jesus counters one question with another: the origin of John the Baptist's authority (vv. 29–30). This was a delicate matter. Ancient Jews (Josephus, *A. J.* 18.117–18) and Christians (Matt 21:32; Luke 7:28–30; Acts 19:1–7) esteemed John and his baptism of repentance for their alignment with God's righteousness. Verses 31–32 capture the Hobson's choice Jesus offers his antagonists. As earlier (2:6; 3:4; 9:10), his interlocutors are divided (v. 31), finally copping a plea of ignorance (v. 33*a*) that justifies Jesus' reply: If his accusers are in no position to adjudicate John's credibility, then neither can they judge Jesus' (v. 33*b*).

Jesus elaborates his parabolic answer with a controversial parable (12:1–12), Mark's longest and most allegorical (cf. 3:23–27; 4:1–34). The planter's procedure (vv. 1–2), customary for its era, recalls Isaiah's identification of God's vineyard with wayward Israel (5:1–7; cf. Jer 2:21; Ezek 19:10–14). The coming of the season (v. 2, *kairos*) strikes an eschatological note (see 1:15; 11:13). OT prophets, styled as God's slaves (Jer 7:25; 25:4; Amos 3:7; Zech 1:6), suffered comparable brutality at the hands of their countrymen (vv. 2–5; 1 Kgs 18:12–13; 2 Chr 24:20–22; Neh 9:26). "A beloved son" (v. 6), murdered for being the true heir (vv. 7–8), is a veiled yet direct pointer to Jesus (1:11; 9:7); likewise, the religious leadership (11:27) recognize themselves as the parable's killers (v. 12; 3:6). Psalm 118:22–23 is cited to interpret Jesus' rejection by his coreligionists and to assert the church's vindication (cf. Acts 4:11; Eph 2:20; 1 Pet 2:7).

The third controversy (vv. 13–17) features Pharisees (first appearing in 2:16) and Herodians (3:6), whose identification is pertinent to the trap they lay (vv. 13–15*a*): Poll (per capita) taxes were a detested aspect of subjugation to imperial Rome. If Jesus can be maneuvered into sanctioning their payment, his piety is compromised; if he advocates nonpayment, sedition is whispered. Jesus recognizes their hypocrisy (v. 15*b*); Mark's reader perceives the truth in their obsequiousness (v. 14). The head (literally, "image") on the requested denarius (a laborer's daily wage; v. 15) is the emperor's (v. 16); its title (literally, "inscription"), "Tiberius, Emperor, Son of the Divine Augustus." Jesus evades the trap with a neat double entendre: Caesar is entitled to his own (see also Matt 17:24–27; Rom 13:1–7; 1 Pet 2:13–17), as is God (to whom belongs everything).

Next come the Sadducees (vv. 18–27), the priestly aristocracy (Acts 23:6–8), whose denial of resurrection was likely based on its absence from the Pentateuch (cf. Isa 26:19; Dan 12:2–3; 2 Macc 7:14, 23; Josephus, *A. J.* 13.197; 18.17). Presupposing the law of levirate marriage (Deut. 25:5–6), their question issues from an absurd exaggeration: Whose wife will a seven-time widow be after she herself dies (vv. 19–23)? Jesus' initial answer rejects the question's premise: In post-mortem life there is no marriage (v. 25). More to the point (vv. 26–27a), the wording of God's self-identification to Moses (Exod 3:6, 15–16) implies that Abraham, Isaac, and Jacob still live under divine dominion. Formally, Jesus' argument resembles rabbinic exegesis and reasoning. Its point is emphatic: His social superiors are altogether wrong about "the scriptures [and] the power of God" (vv. 24, 27b). The end of Mark's Gospel will verify that soon enough.

The final controversy in the Temple proves unexpectedly noncontroversial (vv. 28–34). Since scribes have opposed Jesus since Mark's beginning (1:22), the reader anticipates the same here (v. 28), yet this scribe simply inquires about first principles, a question of scriptural precedent debated among the rabbis (*m. Ber.* 2.2, 5; *b. Mak.* 23b–24a; *Sifra* Lev 19:18). Jesus' reply to a sincere question is an impeccably orthodox answer (vv. 29–31): love of God and neighbor, the *Shema* (Deut 6:4–5) wedded to the Holiness Code (Lev 19:18). Jesus' questioner not only commends but amplifies his assessment (vv. 32–33: Deut 4:35; 1 Sam 15:22; Isa 45:5, 21; Hos 6:6). Jesus has the last, enigmatic word (v. 34a): If the scribe were any closer to God's kingdom than this, would he then be Jesus' disciple?

Having silenced all further debate (v. 34b), Jesus takes the initiative with three brief rejoinders, linked by catchwords ("scribes," vv. 28, 32, 38; "widow[s]," vv. 40, 42; cf. 9:42–50; 11:22–25). His first challenge (vv. 35–37a) mysteriously questions the Messiah's Davidic sonship (2 Sam 7:4–17; Ps 89:3–4; cf. Matt 1:1; Rom 1:3; 2 Tim 2:8) by assuming the traditional attribution of Psalm 110 to "David himself." Since his audience hears this with delight (v. 37b), the force of Jesus'

remark is worth teasing out. First, the utterance "by the Holy Spirit" is with presumed prophetic authority (Acts 1:16; 28:25; Heb 3:7; 10:15). Second, Mark may concur with other NT authors in regarding Ps 110:1 as descriptive of Jesus' ultimate exaltation (Acts 2:34–35; 1 Cor 15:25; Heb 1:13). Most important, David's concession of a Lord greater than himself (v. 37a) may be Mark's way of qualifying the suffering Son of Man's superior messiahship (8:29–31).

Denunciation of pretentious scribes follows in vv. 38–40. The OT castigates oppression of economically vulnerable widows (Ps 94:1–7; Isa 10:1–2; Zech 7:10; Mal 3:5). Speaking of widows, Jesus concludes his teaching in the Temple with a surprising comment made opposite the treasury (v. 41), a Temple chamber that abutted the Women's Court as well as a receptacle for offerings (John 8:20). By contrast with the wealthy, making large donations, a poor widow offers two small copper coins (the smallest in circulation at that time), equal in value to a penny (a Roman *quadrans*, about one-sixty-fourth of a laborer's daily wage; v. 42). The surpassing value of her gift is a lesson for disciples, underlined by Jesus' solemn assurance (v. 43; see 3:28; 9:1, 41). Like another nameless woman memorable for her extravagance (14:3–9), this widow gives "all she had to live on": literally, "her whole life" (v.44), as Jesus himself will do (10:45). The irony that she gives everything for a seemingly lost cause (13:1–2) is no greater than Jesus' own sacrifice soon to come.

Mark 13:1–37 is Jesus' last extended discourse to members of the Twelve, some of whom comment on the Temple's massive stones and wondrous structures (v. 1). The Jewish historian Josephus corroborates just how magnificent the Temple was: Soaring fifty meters into heaven and covered on all sides with massive golden plates, "The outside of the building lacked nothing to astonish the mind or eye" (*J.W.* 5.222). Examining the Temple's remains, today's visitors to Jerusalem observe building blocks whose weight ranges from two to nearly four hundred tons. Whether or not Mark knew of the Romans' destruction of the Temple in 70 CE, as Luke seems to (19:41–44), Jesus' forecast of its future is prescient (v. 2), much as OT prophets accurately predicted devastation of its predecessor, Solomon's Temple (Jer 26:18; Mic 3:12).

More than an architectural marvel, the Temple represented Israel's sacrifice of itself to the God who had called it into covenant existence. Its decorative tapestry "typified the universe" (Josephus, *J.W.* 5.212–14), suggesting to worshipers that the world itself was held together by the divine-human interaction occurring within these sacred precincts. No little anxiety percolates in the questions of the disciples (v. 3).

The discourse that follows (vv. 5–37) is a familiar genre in antiquity: a farewell address of leaders to their followers (see Gen 49:1–33; Deut 33:1–29; Josh 23:1–24:30; Tob 14:3–11; John 14:1–17:26; Acts 20:18–35). Jesus' address at Olivet is braided with common forms of expression: exhortations to vigilance, predictions of things to come, commissions or prohibitions, and authoritative pronouncements. Moreover, Jesus' address is clearly structured. About three-quarters is devoted to the *second* of his disciples' queries, "the sign when these things will be accomplished." Jesus' offers not one sign but many, each more obvious than the last.

1. *Earthly calamities that will befall everyone* (vv. 6–8): While images of socio-political turbulence are common in prophetic portents (Isa 19:2; Jer 22:23; Rev 6:8; 11:13), first-century Jews and Christians were aware of specific tumults (Acts 5:36–37). Jesus warns that such lie within divine providence and are not in themselves proof of the end (cf. 2 Thess 2:1–12).

2. *Particular forms of stress that believers will undergo* (vv. 9–13): As Jesus himself must suffer (14:17–21), his disciples will be targeted for arrest before sanhedrins (local Jewish courts) and suffer abuse. All is for the sake of the good news (Mark 1:1, 14) proclaimed to all nations (11:17): an OT theme (Isa 49:6; 52:10) adapted in the NT (Mark 16:20; Rom 11:11–32; Eph 3:1–10). Anxiety is answered by reassurance that in the hour of trial God's Holy Spirit will support those suffering for the gospel (also Matt 10:19–20; Luke 12:11–12; John 14:26). Interfamilial betrayal is a stock apocalyptic motif (Mic 7:6), yet such divisions occurred among first-century Christians (John 9:18–23; 16:2), even as the Roman historian Tacitus attests to widespread hatred of early Christians (*Annals* 15.44).

3. *Particular human reactions to the great tribulation* (vv. 14–23)—especially flight—are triggered by "the desolating sacrilege," pagan desecration of the Temple (see Dan 9:27; 11:31; 12:11). This is an era of unparalleled tribulation, sometimes expected to precede the end (Dan 12:1; Rev 7:14. 13:20); if occurring in winter, heavy rains would impede travel. Again believers are assured of their election by God (cf. Ps 105:6; Rom 8:33; Eph 1:4–5) and are warned against losing their heads over signs performed by false prophets (v. 6; Matt 7:15–23; 2 Thess 2:9–10).

4. *Particular supernatural responses* (vv. 24–27): Celestial convulsions are commonplace in OT prophecy (Isa 13:10; 34:4; Ezek 32:7–8; Joel 2:10, 31). Expecting the advent of an end-time Son of Man may have its origins in Daniel (7:13–14); Christian apocalypticism associates that figure with Jesus (Rev 1:7, 13). The ingathering of God's dispersed elect is a pervasive biblical hope (Isa 11:11; Ezek 39:25–29; Bar 5:5–9; 1 Thess 4:15–17).

The disciples *began* by asking when these things will happen. Jesus defers this until last, reworking the question into a matter of discipleship.

5. *Predictable imminence and assurance of the time* (vv. 28–31) are parabolically represented by a maturing fig tree (cf. 11:12–14, 20–21). The language here is vague yet urgent: exactly who "is near, at the very gates" is unclear; "this generation" is regarded pejoratively in Mark (8:11). Still, all these things are soon to happen (see 9:1); all else may fade, but Jesus' promise is dependable.

6. There remains, nevertheless, *unpredictable suddenness and ignorance of the precise time* (vv. 32–37). "That day" likely refers to "the day of the Lord" (Isa 2:12; Jer 46:10; Ezek 30:2–3; Amos 5:18–20; Zeph 1:14–18); "that hour," God's appointed time for the consummation of the age (cf. 1:15; 14:35; Dan 8:17–19). Instead of futile attempts to clock that hour, faithful disciples remain vigilant and accountable (see also Matt 25:1–30; Luke 12:35–40; Rom 13:11–14). The stages of night on v. 35—evening, midnight, cockcrow, and dawn—may refer to the Romans' four nocturnal watches (6:48).

In presentation and substance the Olivet discourse is apocalyptic pastoral care: dialing down anxiety, reminding disciples that God remains mysteriously and faithfully in control.

B. The Passion Narrative (14:1–15:47)

Mark's last major section recounts events culminating in Jesus' betrayal and arrest (14:1–52), his arraignment (14:52–15:15), his execution (15:16–41), and burial (15:42–47). Appreciation of Mark's irony-saturated treatment is critical.

The anointing of Jesus (14:3–9) is illuminated against a conspiracy for his arrest (14:1–2, 10–11). Entwining two sharply contrasting anecdotes that complement each other, Mark frames a theologically significant gift for Jesus from an unnamed woman (vv. 3–9) with the consummation of long-standing machinations against him by religious authorities (3:6; 8:31; 11:18; 12:12) assisted by a named member of the Twelve (vv. 1–2, 10–11; 3:19a). The effect is one of ironic simultaneity: The woman is publicly, albeit unwittingly, preparing Jesus' body for burial (v. 8) while others aggressively seek (vv. 1, 11; 1:37) his secret betrayal (9:31). Her gift is incredibly lavish: fragrant perfume (Song 1:12; 4:13, 14), worth over three hundred denarii (almost a full year's wages for a day-laborer; cf. 6:37), seems wasted from the viewpoint of conventional religiosity (v. 5; see also 12:38–44; Deut 15:11). Colluding with the religious establishment, Judas is promised an unspecified reward (vv. 10–11). Pouring the ointment on his head (v. 3) suggests Jesus' royal anointment (1 Sam 10:1; 2 Kgs 9:6); this is a messianic coronation (1:1). Later Jesus will be crucified as "King of the Jews" (15:26). Here (14:9) as elsewhere in Mark (1:14; 8:35; 13:9–10), "gospel" is embedded in suffering that God's will be done. Mark's timing for these events (v. 1) is apparently Wednesday, 13 Nisan (March–April), two days before Passover: the annual celebration of God's liberation of Israel from captivity (Exod 12:1–13:16), later conjoined with the seven-day harvest festival of Unleavened Bread (2 Chr 35:17; Ezek 45:21–24). In spite of concern that it not happen during the festival (v. 2), Jesus' arrest occurs on Passover evening (14:12–50).

Jesus' last observance of Passover (14:12–31) comprises four vignettes: preparation for the feast (vv. 12–16), his betrayal's prediction at table (vv. 17–21), the institution of the Lord's Supper (vv. 22–26), and a foretelling of all the Twelve's desertion (vv. 27–31).

The preparation (vv. 12–16) is introduced by one of Mark's anomalies regarding the calendar: The first day of Unleavened Bread (v. 12; usually 15 Nisan) seems inconsistent with 14 Nisan, when the Passover lamb is sacrificed (Exod 12:1–20; cf. John 18:28; 19:14, 31, which locates Jesus' last day twenty-four hours later than in the Synoptics).

The prediction of betrayal (vv. 17–21) occurs after all have taken their places ("were reclining," the customary posture at banquets: Luke 5:29). Jesus' poignant language (v. 18) echoes earlier phrases in Mark: "Truly I tell you" (also vv. 25, 30; 3:28), "will betray" (9:31). The betrayer at table—the last place a friend should knife his host in the back—chimes with Ps 41:9. Elsewhere in Mark (2:10; 10:33) "the Son of Man" speaks of himself with authority about the suffering he must endure. He goes "as it is written," meaning in accordance with the divine purpose (also 8:31; 1 Cor 15:3–4).

Passover slides into institution of the Lord's Supper (vv. 22–26), variously expressed elsewhere in the NT (cf. Luke 22:14–23; John 6:48–58; 1 Cor 11:24–25). At previous banquets in Mark (6:41; 8:6) Jesus "took, bless[ed], broke, and gave" (v. 22); likewise he earlier spoke of his sacrifice for many (v. 24; 10:45). In Greek as in English, one's "body" is a flexible metaphor: "My selfhood" or "personality" may capture some nuances here (cf. 1 Cor 10:16–17). "Blood of the covenant" (v. 23) is a classic OT image for ratification (Exod 24:6–8; Jer 31:31; Zech 9:11), christologically developed in Hebrews (9:11–10:18). "That day … in the kingdom of God" suggests the new eschatological age, sometimes envisioned as a magnificent banquet (1 Chr 12:38–40; Isa 25:6–8; Matt 22:1–4).

Jesus' prediction of the Twelve's desertion (vv. 27–31) occurs en route to the Mount of Olives (see 11:1; 13:3). The sheep's scattering after their shepherd's smiting accords with Scripture (Zech 13:7; cf. Mark 6:34; 14:21). To "become deserters" (vv. 27, 29) is tantamount to "falling away," much as rocky, rootless hearers of the word fold under pressure (4:16–17). One such "rock"—Peter (petros, 3:16)—twice repudiates his threefold defection (vv. 29–31a); his peers join in for a third denial (v. 31b). Jesus promises his own post-mortem fidelity in Galilee (v. 28; 16:7). The mind reels at ironies past and to come: Jesus' injunction that his followers must deny themselves (8:34), their precipitate denial of their denials, Jesus' denial of himself out of loyalty to the traitorous.

At Gethsemane (14:32–52) Jesus is arrested as all of the Twelve forsake him. Verses 32–42 present Jesus' most extended crisis of faith in Mark. In many ways it is a flashback to Jairus, his daughter, and the woman with chronic bleeding in 5:21–43. All these stories are drenched in apocalyptic imagery: Jesus' declaration that the woman depart in peace (5:34), his raising of the little girl (5:41–42), his references to "the cup" (14:36; see also 10:38–39; Isa 51:17, 22) and "the time of trial" (14:38; cf. Jas 1:2; 1 Pet 1:6; Rev 2:10), and his repeated rousings (14:34, 37–38, 41ab) of disciples who cannot stay awake (vv. 37, 40, 41; cf. 13:34–37). All culminates in his announcement that "the hour" has come (vv. 35, 37, 41c; cf. 13:11, 32). Present in all three stories are Peter, James, and John (5:37; 14:32–33), who characteristically flout their teacher (5:31; 14:34, 37–38, 40). Suffusing these tableaux is utter hopelessness: Jairus's little girl is at death's door (5:23a); the woman's bleeding has only worsened (5:25–26); here Jesus is tormented, even to death (14:34a). All the protagonists' initial responses to crisis is fear (5:33, 36; 14:33): distress that throws its victims to the ground (5:22, 33; 14:35), a grief whose source is human frailty, "weakness of the flesh" (14:38; cf. Isa 31:3; 40:6; Rom 8:1–17). "Daughters" (5:23a, 34) and a "beloved son" (1:11; 9:7) addressing "Abba" (Rom 8:15; Gal 4:6) beg for relief (5:23b, 27–28; 14:36, 39, 41). Like the woman (5:28), Jesus temporarily resists discovery yet ultimately steps forward to face the truth (5:32–33; 14:36): the Son of Man's ordained betrayal into sinful hands (14:41–42, 49b).

Immediately Jesus' arrest (14:43–52) compounds the irony. The betrayer is Judas (v. 43; 3:19; 14:10), using as his signal the kiss to which a rabbi was entitled from his disciples (Prov. 27:6; Luke 7:38). Just as he predicted (Mark 8:31), those to whom Jesus is delivered are the religious elite who first challenged him in the Temple (11:27): chief priests, scribes, and elders, whose associates Jesus implicated for the very banditry for which

he is now apprehended (11:17–18; 14:48–49a). Various interpretations have been proposed for the mysterious incident in 14:51–52. Is it an anticipation of the linen shroud in 15:46, soon to be discarded? Is this the same young man in 16:5? Should we recall naked flight in Gen 39:12 or Amos 2:16? None is compelling. Perhaps Mark intends a contrast between Jesus' calm courage and his followers' panicked flight (14:50).

"On the night he was betrayed" (1 Cor 11:22) not one but two interrogations took place at the high priest's house. Mark heightens the irony by folding one (that of Jesus: 14:55–65) inside the other (that of Peter: 14:53–54, 66–72). Inside Mark portrays a kangaroo court, with Jesus the silent center (v. 61; cf. Ps 38:12–14) amidst a rash of judicial irregularities. A formal trial by the entire council, or Sanhedrin (v. 55; cf. 13:9), should not be convened at night, especially on a festal evening; nor should a verdict to convict be reached in a single day (m. Sanh. 4.1). The charge that Jesus threatened to destroy the Temple is bogus (vv. 57–58) and contradicted (vv. 56, 59; cf. Deut 19:15; Ps 109:2–3). The Temple's replacement with one not made with hands braids a strand of the OT (2 Sam 7:4–17) with later Christian reflection (Acts 7:48; 1 Cor 3:16; 1 Pet 2:4–6). Finally (v. 61b) the high priest, presumably Caiaphas (18–37 CE; Matt 26:3; John 18:13, 24), oddly charges Jesus as the Messiah, the Son of the Blessed One: all terms central to Christian preaching (Mark 1:1; John 20:31), none culpable of capital punishment. Jesus accepts that claim (v. 62), again predicting the advent of an apocalyptic Son of Man (8:38; 12:36; 13:26) along the lines of Ps 110:1 and Dan 7:13–14. Rending his garment (v. 63; Gen 37:29), the high priest charges blasphemy (v. 64), which here seems unfounded (see Lev 24:16; cf. Mark 2:7). The court's conduct in v. 65 is reminiscent of Isa 50:6; 53:3–5; at the precise moment they taunt him to "prophesy," Jesus' prophecies are fulfilled in the courtyard outside (vv. 66–72). There a motley group, chiefly the high priest's maid, accurately spots Peter as having been "with Jesus" (v. 67; 3:14). Not only does Peter lie about his discipleship (v. 71); he does so in a manner revealing unintended truth about all of the Twelve: "I do not know or understand" (v. 68; see 4:13; 6:52; 8:17, 21; 9:32). The cock crows (whether a bird or a Roman signal: 13:35), Peter remembers (14:30–31) and collapses (v. 72):

one who lost himself by trying to save himself (8:35).

Jesus' arraignment continues by his transfer to Roman jurisdiction (15:1–15). Mark's specification of morning (15:1) is the first of five carefully measured, temporal indicators in this chapter (vv. 25, 33*a*, 33*b*, 42). The Pharisees, Jesus' antagonists earlier in Mark, have faded from the picture; henceforth the chief priests, representing the entire Sanhedrin, are his principal accusers (vv. 3, 10, 11, 31). Recalling the second passion prediction in 9:31, Mark emphasizes Jesus' being handed over (15:1, 10, 15) to Pontius Pilate, fifth Roman prefect of Judea (26–36 CE). Philo (*Legat.* 301–2) and Josephus (*Ant.* 18.55–57; *B. J.* 2.169–77) characterize Pilate as stubbornly vicious; the Evangelists, as a reluctant pawn (Matt 27:18–25; Luke 23:1–24; John 18:28–19:16). Appearing for the first time in Mark 15:2, the title "the King of the Jews" is the first of five ironic acclamations of Jesus by Roman agents (vv. 9, 12, 18, 26; cf. v. 32). Their unbelieving affirmation chimes with the high priest's in 14:61, as does Jesus' silence in 15:5. The trial before Pilate concludes with the so-called Passover amnesty (vv. 6, 8), evidence for which is uncorroborated outside the Gospels. Benefiting from this custom is one Barabbas (literally, "Son of the Father"). In which insurrection he may have committed murder (v. 7) is uncertain; Luke (13:1; Acts 5:36–37) and Josephus (*Ant.* 18.55–62, 65–87; *J.W.* 2.167–77) report numerous Jewish revolts against their Roman overlords. Pilate's offer to release Jesus and the crowd's decision for Barabbas underscore two further ironies: yet another authority in Mark proves feckless (see 6:14–29); a known malefactor goes free while a righteous innocent (cf. 6:20; 15:15) pays the ultimate penalty.

The execution of Pilate's sentence (15:16–47) begins with Jesus' humiliation by the Roman guard (15:16–20). A whole cohort numbered between 200 to 600 soldiers; if this be exaggeration, its effect is to dramatize the enormous odds against Jesus. Like the crown, purple suggests royal raiment (15:17; see 1 Macc 10:20). Bowing in worship (v. 19) while uttering, "Hail, King of the Jews!" (v. 18) is altogether ironic, possibly a cruel parody of the legionary salute, "Hail, Caesar, conqueror, emperor" (Suetonius, *Claudius* 21.6). Mockery by physical abuse (vv. 19–20) recalls Jesus' prediction in 10:34, which in turn recalls Isa 50:6 and Mic 5:1.

A condemned prisoner like Jesus carried only the crossbar (v. 21); the gibbet awaited at the place of execution. By reporting that a passerby named Simon (cf. 14:37) was pressed to carry his cross (cf. 8:34), Mark may cut the irony deeply indeed. Evidently Mark's audience would have recognized Rufus and Alexander; identification of the former with Paul's associate (Rom 16:13) is impossible to confirm. Though it can no longer be certainly located, Golgotha (v. 22) was apparently outside Jerusalem's city walls (John 19:20; Heb 13:12). Myrrh–spiked wine (v. 23) was likely offered as an analgesic (cf. Prov 31:6); because he has chosen to drink from another cup (10:38; 14:36), Jesus refuses this one.

Cicero describes crucifixion—impaling a victim onto a stake and crossbar—as the supreme penalty (*In Verrem* 2.5). It was commonly used in cases of imperial sedition, which matches several of Mark's details: the placard of the charge, "the King of the Jews" (v. 26); the identification of fellow victims as revolutionary bandits (v. 27; cf. 14:48). The intent of crucifixion was sadistic: cruel, shameful, protracted torture of society's most heinous offenders of lower class. In that context Mark's portrait of Jesus' crucifixion is in four respects noteworthy. First, the evangelist does not milk the event for pity: he simply states the matter (v. 24). Second, the details of Jesus' final hours, effectively tolled (vv. 25, 33), remind a biblically knowledgeable reader of Pss 22 and 109, two classic laments: casting lots for a victim's clothes (v. 24/Ps 22:18), taunting by head-shaking (v. 29/Ps 22:7; 109:25), the cry of dereliction (v. 34/Ps 22:1). For those able to perceive, "the scriptures [are being] fulfilled" (14:49*b*; made explicit in 15:28, which is absent from the oldest manuscripts). Third, reminiscent of Jesus' prediction at Olivet (13:24), midday darkness over the whole land (v. 33) is an apocalyptic portrayal of divine judgment (Amos 8:9).

The fourth characteristic of Mark's narration is by now predictable: its hellish irony. Malefactors are crucified on Jesus' right and left (v. 27): the places of honor that James and John had requested (10:37). Even Jesus' fellow victims join with bystanders in ridiculing him (v. 32*b*; cf. Luke 23:39–43). The mockery, rendered in the

NRSV as "derision" (v. 29), is described in Greek as "blaspheming" (see 14:64); singled out among the blasphemers are the chief priests and scribes (v. 31). The substance of their jeer in v. 29, like the testimony of impeached witnesses in 14:58, demonstrates that to the very end most of Jesus' auditors have misunderstood him altogether. The taunt that he save himself (v. 30) directly contradicts the Son of Man's mission in 8:35; that he is the Messiah, Israel's king (v. 32a) who cannot save himself as he saved others (v. 31), is exactly right (1:1; 10:45; 14:24; 15:2). In effect Golgotha's audience is enacting the attitude of the unrighteous in the Wisdom of Solomon (2:12–24); their insistence on signs as a basis of faith (v. 32a) Jesus has already repudiated (8:11–12). In Mark the relationship between faith and mighty works is precisely opposite: nothing can happen unless first one trusts God (2:5; 5:34; 9:23; 11:22–24).

Irony persists in Mark's depiction of Jesus' death and its immediate aftermath. His lament in Aramaic (v. 34; see also 5:41; 7:34) occasions still more misunderstanding by his audience (see also 4:12; 8:14–21): they mistake "Eloi" (God) as a cry to Elijah (v. 35). Perhaps evolving from 2 Kgs 2:9–12, later Jewish tradition envisioned Elijah as protector of the righteous in distress. In John the Baptist, however, Elijah has already returned and been disposed of (1:6; 6:27–28; 9:11–13). While an allusion to Ps 69:21 may be intended, sour wine, a common drink of the time, is offered in a final, unavailing attempt to pump a miracle from heaven (v. 36). After a final shriek lacking either confidence (Luke 23:46) or triumph (John 19:30), Jesus dies (v. 37). Immediately (v. 38) Mark redirects the reader's attention to the curtain of the Temple, perhaps that which veiled the Holy of Holies (Exod 26:31–37), ripped from top to bottom. As a bookend to the heavens' rending at Jesus' baptism (1:10), this is surely a revelatory sign. Just what it reveals is debatable. It may symbolize the Temple's eventual eradication (see also 11:15–19; 13:1–2); another possibility, effectively developed in Hebrews (9:1–28; 10:19–20) is unmediated access to God created by Jesus' death. Equally ironic and no less ambiguous is the centurion's reaction (v. 39). For the first and only time in Mark, a human being besides Jesus identifies him as God's Son (cf. 1:1; 3:11; 9:7; 13:32). This person is a Gentile, and Gentiles have been receptive to Jesus (3:8; 5:20; 7:24–31; 11:17; 13:10).

Ironically this Gentile is one of Jesus' executioners, facing Jesus who has thus expired (cf. Matt 27:54). Whether his assertion betokens sincerity or sarcasm (15:9, 32) is impossible to determine. Only the reader who faithfully accepts the Son of Man's self-assessment (8:31; 10:45) is in position to judge the accuracy of the centurion's verdict and the basis on which it is reached (cf. 1 Cor 1:18–2:5).

Women observing from a distance (v. 40; cf. Ps 38:11) perform three important functions. First, they remind the reader of those *absent* from the scene: the Twelve, who have long since abandoned Jesus (14:50). Second, their presence clarifies that Jesus' ministering entourage has included from the beginning many women, disciples beyond the Twelve (v. 41; see also 1:31; 14:6). Third, Mary Magdalene, Mary the mother of Joses, and Salome know where Jesus was buried (v. 47), anticipating any objection that they later visited the wrong tomb (16:1). Whether Mary the mother of James and of Joses is the same woman as Jesus' mother (6:3) is impossible to determine. The negotiations for disposition (vv. 42–45) of Jesus' body ring true, and archaeological remains confirm the burial customs implied (v. 46; see also Deut 21:22–23; Isa 22:16). It is unclear on which council Joseph of Arimathea (in northwest Judea) served, but respected membership could have allowed him access to Pilate as Mark describes (v. 43, 45). If not a disciple as such, Joseph was "himself awaiting expectantly" the kingdom that Jesus preached (1:15); with courage Joseph performs for the body those services John's disciples rendered for their dead teacher (6:29). Since death after crucifixion often occurred after "long drawn-out agony" (Seneca, *Dialogue* 3), Pilate's surprise that Jesus was gone after only six hours is as understandable as his determination to verify it (vv. 44–45)—confirmation that may have served as additional defense against later charges of Christian fraud (cf. Matt 27:62–66). Evening on the Day of Preparation (v. 42) suggests the three hours before sundown on Friday; even a hurried burial before the Sabbath suggests Jewish piety and provides reason for the women's return to anoint the body after the Sabbath was past (16:1).

IV. Epilogue: The Empty Tomb (16:1–8) [The Shorter Ending of Mark]

[The Longer Ending of Mark (16:9–20)]

The earliest and finest manuscripts of Mark end at 16:8. This Gospel's textual tradition includes three other endings, two of which the NRSV places in brackets. The latter two are obvious attempts by scribes to close this Gospel in conformity with the other Gospels' conclusions. (The fourth ending, an expansion of "the Longer Ending," is not rendered in the NRSV and will not be discussed further.)

The Shorter Ending of Mark, thirty-four Greek words in length, was added not earlier than the fourth century CE This conclusion offers the women's report to the eleven and others (see Matt 28:8; Luke 24:9) and a variant of Matthew's "Great Commission" (28:19–20). Through "Peter and those with him," the risen Jesus disseminates "the sacred and imperishable proclamation of eternal salvation" (cf. 1 Tim 1:11; 2 Tim 1:10; 1 Pet 1:23–25). This announcement's sweep "from east to west" presumes, or at least aspires for, subsequent expansion of the Christian proclamation (cf. Mark 13:10; Acts 1:8; Rom 15:22–29).

Dating to the late second century and present in a majority of witnesses is the Longer Ending of Mark (16:9–20), well known to readers of the KJV. Mixing a variety of NT motifs, many foreign to Mark, this ending reads as a pastiche of the other Gospels. The risen Jesus' first appearance to Mary Magdalene (v. 9) recalls different traditions in Matt 28:9–10 and John 20:11–18. From Luke 8:2 is probably derived the detail that he had cast out seven demons from Magdalene. The disbelief confronting Mary's testimony (vv. 10–11) is reminiscent of Luke 24:9–11. Mark 16:12–13 seems an abbreviated version of the Emmaus Road episode in Luke 24:13–35. The clearest intersection of this ending's theology with that expressed elsewhere in Mark lies at 16:14: Jesus appears and upbraids the eleven for their "lack of faith" (see 4:40*b*; 6:6*a*; 9:24) and their "stubbornness" (literally, "hardness of heart": see 3:5; 6:52; 8:17; 10:5). Recalling Mark's opening reference to the good news (1:1), 16:15 and 20 paraphrase Matt 28:19, with additional cautions and encouragements. "The one who does not believe will be condemned" (16:16*b*) is without precedent in Mark

but akin to John (3:18; 16:17). "The one who believes and is baptized will be saved" (16:16*a*) approximates assertions made elsewhere in the NT (Matt 28:19; Acts 2:38; Titus 3:5; 1 Pet 3:21). Though Mark is suspicious of signs as warrants for belief (8:11; 13:22; 14:32), the Longer Ending accords credibility to many signs done in Jesus' name (vv. 17, 20; cf. 9:39; John 2:23; 4:48; 6:30). Casting out demons is not beyond the purview of Jesus' disciples in Mark (3:15; 6:7; cf. 9:38). Other convincing signs (16:17–18) are characteristically Lukan: speaking in tongues (Acts 2:4–11; 10:46; 19:6), safely picking up snakes (Luke 10:19; Acts 28:3–6), healing the sick by the laying of hands (Acts 3:1–10; 5:12–16; 9:12, 17–18; also Jas 5:14–15). Divine cooperation with and confirmation of Christian believers (Mark 16:20) is assured throughout the NT (Matt 28:20; Acts 4:30; 6:8; 14:3; 15:12; Rom 15:19; Heb 2:3–4). Even more prevalent is the image, developed from Ps 110:1, of the Lord Jesus as gloriously seated at God's right hand (Acts 2:33–34; 5:31; 7:55–56; Rom 8:34; Eph 1:20; Col 3:1; Heb 1:3; 8:1; 10:12; 12:2; 1 Pet 3:22). His being "taken up into heaven" (Mark 16:19) recalls Jesus' ascension in Luke (24:51; see also Acts 1:2, 11; 1 Tim 3:16) as well as Elijah's departure in a chariot of fire (2 Kgs 2:11).

What, then, of Mark's original epilogue (16:1–8), on which all other endings are based? As elsewhere in the passion narrative (14:1, 12, 17; 15:1, 25, 33, 42), Mark sets the stage with temporal precision: "when the Sabbath was over [after six o'clock on Saturday evening] ... very early on the first day of the week [Sunday]" (vv. 1, 2). Those visiting the tomb are the same women named as witnesses of Jesus' death (15:40). They have come to anoint the hastily buried body (15:42, 46). Their mission is doubly futile: Another woman has already performed that task (14:8); repeatedly Jesus has promised that his body would be raised three days after his death (8:31; 9:31; 10:34). While superficially an expression of poor planning, their concern for moving from the tomb's mouth a stone so large (vv. 3–4) tacitly rebuts any accusation that the body was stolen (thus, Matt 28:11–15). Again their concern proves needless: The stone has already been rolled back (v. 4). Entering the tomb they are astonished to see a young man dressed in white (v. 5), suggesting apocalyptic glorification (9:3; Dan 7:9; 12:3; Matt 13:43; Rev 7:9, 13). In v. 6 he assures them

(a) there's no reason for alarm: (b) Jesus, the crucified Nazarene they are seeking, (c) is not there because (d) he has been raised from death (implicitly, by God). This is one of the NT's fundamental claims (John 5:21; Acts 4:10; 13:30; Rom 4:24; 1 Cor 15:3–4; 2 Tim 2:8). Verse 7 is an assignment: (a) Go and tell his disciples, especially Peter (see 14:30–31, 66–72), (b) that Jesus is going ahead of them back to Galilee (the starting point: 1:9, 14), (c) where they will see him (cf. Acts 2:32; 3:15; 10:40–41; 1 Cor 9:1; 15:5–8), (d) just as he said (Mark 14:28). Verse 8 describes the women's response: (a) they flee the tomb, (b) tremulous and bewildered, (c) and say nothing to anyone (d) because they were afraid. The final irony: Even these women, who followed Jesus longer than anyone else, fall short from fear—as his disciples have done as far back as Mark 4:40–41. When all else and all others fail, God remains faithful to the promise relayed by Jesus himself (8:31; 9:31; 10:33–34). Mark's Gospel is but the beginning of the good news (1:1), now sandwiched into its readers' lives, where it may continue to unfold as a parable most surprising (4:1–34).

BIBLIOGRAPHY

C. C. Black. *Mark: Images of an Apostolic Interpreter.* SPNT (Minneapolis: Fortress, 2001); M. E. Boring. *Mark: A Commentary.* NTL (Louisville: Westminster John Knox, 2006); A. Y. Collins. *Mark.* Hermeneia (Minneapolis: Fortress, 2007); R. A. Culpepper. *Mark.* SHBC (Macon, Ga.: Smyth & Helwys, 2007); M. D. Hooker. *The Gospel according to Saint Mark.* BNTC (Peabody, Mass.: Hendrickson, 1991); D. H. Juel. *A Master of Surprise: Mark Interpreted* (Minneapolis: Fortress, 1994); J. Marcus. *Mark 1–8: A New Translation with Introduction and Commentary.* AB 27 (Garden City: Doubleday. 2000); _____. *Mark 9–16: A New Translation with Introduction and Commentary.* AB 27A (New Haven: Yale University Press, 2009); F. J. Moloney. *The Gospel of Mark: A Commentary* (Peabody, Mass.: Hendrickson, 2002); P. Perkins. "The Gospel of Mark: Introduction, Commentary, and Reflections." *NIB* (Nashville: Abingdon, 1995) 8:503–733; H. N. Roskam, ed. *The Purpose of the Gospel of Mark in Its Historical and Social Context.* NovTSup 114 (Leiden: Brill, 2004).

LUKE

John T. Carroll

Overview

Genre and character of the work. The Gospel of Luke, with its sequel, the Acts of the Apostles, is a narrative of Christian origins; it grounds the spread of the gospel ("good news") to all nations in the public career of Jesus, the prophet-Messiah commissioned by God and empowered by God's Spirit for a ministry of word and deed in Galilee and Judea. Luke embeds the story of Jesus in the history of Israel, whose hopes and scriptural promises find fulfillment in the story Luke tells.

A central concern of Luke's two-volume narrative is legitimation. How can Israel's hopes for salvation be realized in a community composed increasingly of Gentiles, with Jews dividing in response to its message? How can Israel's Messiah face the scandalous death of crucifixion? Luke shows how these surprising developments represent the working out of the divine purpose for Israel and the nations.

Luke gives distinctive shape to a story others told before him, reworking Mark's narrative of Jesus' ministry and weaving it with other sources (written and oral): birth stories, teachings of Jesus (many shared with Matthew, others found only in Luke), and resurrection appearances.

Author and audience. Tradition assigns the Gospel of Luke (and Acts) to a physician, occasional companion of Paul (see Col 4:14). While authorship by Luke is *possible*, no positive indicators point to Luke or to a physician as author, and interpretation is not aided by such an identification. As with the other Gospels, anything that is to be learned about author, audience, and circumstances of composition must be inferred from the story Luke tells.

Themes. Luke highlights God's work of salvation in Israel, fulfilling scriptural promise, through the agency of Jesus, the Spirit-empowered Messiah and prophet. In Acts salvation extends to the whole world, a move anticipated in the Gospel, even if Jesus mostly confines his activity to Jewish circles. He launches his ministry in his hometown, an episode that prefigures both the character and the outcome of his career: Jesus brings hope and liberation to the poor, sick, and lost; salvation thus effects radical role reversals, both vertical (rich and poor, powerful and powerless exchanging positions) and horizontal (sinners displacing the righteous in God's realm).

While Jesus is the chief actor, the purpose that drives the story is God's. Divine empowerment ("Holy Spirit") authorizes Jesus and his apostles; their message, acts of healing, and inclusive hospitality embody God's rule. Restoration comes to God's people but in the process subverts prevailing cultural scripts. People lacking status and power model the life of God's realm. This countercultural vision provokes opposition, eventually leading to Jesus' execution—prelude to divine vindication in resurrection and mission to the whole world as the story continues in Acts.

Outline

Preface (1:1–4)

I. Beginnings (1:5–4:13)

    A. Narrative of the Birth and Childhood of John and Jesus (1:5–2:52)

    B. Preparation for the Ministry of the Messiah (3:1–4:13)

II. Ministry (4:14–19:27)

    A. Galilean Ministry (4:14–9:50)
    B. Journey to Jerusalem (9:51-19:27)

III. The Final Days (19:28–25:53)

    A. Climactic Teaching Ministry in Jerusalem (19:28–21:38)

    B. Ministry During the Passion (22:1–23:56)

    C. Easter: Ministry of the Risen Jesus (24:1–53)

DETAILED ANALYSIS

Preface (1:1–4)

Luke begins the Gospel with a formal preface, signaling that the work, addressed to "most excellent Theophilus," seeks a hearing from cultured audiences in the Greco-Roman world. Luke sketches the scope and aims of his literary project, presents his credentials to deliver a trustworthy narrative, and characterizes the story as one about fulfillment. Having conducted careful research, and building on the narrative tradition crafted by predecessors, Luke, a second-or third-generation Christian teacher, retells the story in a way that accents narrative design ("an orderly account") in which events are not random but fulfill divine promise. The goal is a reliable account, so that Theophilus—whose name means "lover of God," probably a person of status—and others who hear the story "may know the truth concerning the things about which you have been instructed." Luke opens his second book with a briefer preface (Acts 1:1–2) that links the two writings, recalling the content of the Gospel.

I. Beginnings (1:5–4:13)

A. Narrative of the Birth and Childhood of John and Jesus (1:5–2:52)

Like Matthew, Luke begins the story by relating Jesus' birth. However, Luke develops the significance of Jesus' arrival by setting it in three distinct contexts. (1) Luke first narrates the birth of the precursor prophet John. (2) Luke's account of the births of John and Jesus evokes scriptural promises to Israel, celebrating hopes fulfilled. (3) At the same time, John and Jesus step into human history at a particular geopolitical moment, when Rome and its emperor hold sway. It remains to be seen how Israel's hope and Rome's power will collide.

1:5–38. Twin Announcements: the Coming of Prophet and Son of God. Having garnered the attention of a cultured, Greek-speaking audience, Luke begins the story with a move of cultural reorientation, borrowing language, character types, and plot twists from Jewish Scripture. In a narrative that will close in the Jerusalem Temple (24:52–53), where better to begin than in this same sacred space, observing rituals faithfully performed by an aging priest? Heaven claims his attention with surprising news, soon to be followed by an even more stunning revelation to a young peasant girl—the first of many accounts pairing male and female characters (e.g., 2:25–38; 10:25–42; 13:10–17 with 14:1–6; 15:3–10).

1:5–25. Pious, yet childless, the first characters in Luke's story reprise a role played by many in Israel's history, notably Abraham and Sarah (Gen 16–18) and Hannah (1 Sam 1–2). A heavenly messenger (Gabriel) interrupts the priest Zechariah in the course of his Temple service and announces that his wife Elizabeth will give birth to a son, whom they are to name John. As with their biblical predecessors, the promise of a child is not a private matter; God's promise concerns the formation and now restoration of a people. John will play a special role; in the mold of Elijah, he will call the people back to their God, readying them for their "Lord" (cf. Mal 4:5–6).

This is extraordinary news, warranting suspension of the sacred routine, but Zechariah is slow to believe because he and his wife are so old. The priest is unable to speak until the promise he could not trust has been realized. Events will have to speak for themselves—until, that is, Elizabeth becomes pregnant and, in a voice reminiscent of Rachel's (Gen 30:22–23), celebrates God's gracious reversal of her position as a childless woman in a society that privileges households with children. So Luke narrates the first of many inversions of status in his story.

1:26–38. The young woman Mary also receives an unexpected heavenly visitor, though in her home far from the Temple. She too receives the promise of a son, whose stature will surpass even John's. With the name Jesus (its significance ["God saves"] is not developed as in Matt 1:21), he will be known as holy, Son of God, and he will reign over Israel forever (Luke 1:32–33), fulfilling Nathan's promise to David (2 Sam 7:12–14). Like the priest Zechariah, the socially marginal young woman answers Gabriel with a question: "How can this be, since I am a virgin?" (Luke 1:34). Unlike Zechariah, however, she accepts God's promise, after the angel offers news of the pregnancy of Mary's relative Elizabeth as proof that "nothing will be impossible with God" (vv. 36–38). If Mary's trust in divine promise is not misplaced, this will be an occasion for joyful celebration.

1:39–56. Elizabeth and Mary Meet, Celebrate Their Pregnancy. Praise for a God who delivers on promises to the people finds voice as Mary visits Elizabeth and bursts into Spirit-inspired song. Prophetic speech articulates the meaning of the events now set into motion.

1:39–45. Mary visits her relative Elizabeth, staying for three months (until Elizabeth is ready to deliver). Only Luke forges kinship ties between Jesus and John, who are also yoked as agents of God's work of salvation. Especially remarkable is the part played by two women and their conversation at the start of the narrative. Anticipating the end of the story, when women will be the first to proclaim Jesus' resurrection (24:1–11), Luke highlights the words of two women, who interpret what God is doing in Israel. On Easter, the apostles (men) will receive the message of women disciples with skepticism; in a story that aims at reliable narration (1:4), how will Luke's readers respond to women's prophetic witness as the story begins?

Elizabeth finds voice first. The son she carries in her womb, Gabriel had prophesied, would be "filled with the Holy Spirit" even before birth (1:15). When Elizabeth hears the greeting of Mary, "the child leap[s] in her womb," yet *Elizabeth* is the one who is "filled with the Holy Spirit" and speaks (v. 41): the mother of a future prophet invests his leap with meaning: "the child in my womb leaped for joy" (v. 44). Elizabeth discerns Mary's trusting reception of God's word; she also knows who is Lord—the unborn child Mary now carries, whom John will acknowledge as greater than himself (3:15–17). Elizabeth's greeting discloses that while God is sovereign, the "Lord" to whom all people owe loyalty and service, God's Son (Jesus) will also bear that authority. Elizabeth's "blessing" of Mary prompts the younger woman to pick up this theme. She will not focus her prophetic speech on her own good fortune, however, but on the character of God's activity in the world.

1:46–56. Mary's song (the "Magnificat": the passage's first word in Latin translation) praises a God who has launched a social revolution. These are neither gentle nor tame words; the coming of John and Jesus enacts a divine reign that effects wholesale reversal of status and power in the world. Elevation of the one low in status (like Mary herself), unending mercy tempering the exercise of might: God exerts power by deposing the powerful and lifting up the powerless, nourishes the poor and turns away the wealthy. So, in a socially and politically subversive way, the God of Israel fulfills ancient promises to Abraham and his descendants.

Echoing Hannah's prayer in 1 Sam 2:1–10, Mary's song characterizes the divinely initiated events that now unfold as the fulfillment of God's promise to Abraham *and* as the expression of God's commitment to power and status inversion. The social order that will mark the realm of God, in Luke's narrative description, will disenfranchise those with power and resources, and honor the powerless and impoverished. How will the agents of salvation whose births Luke chronicles enact such a bold social program? Will Roman power stand aside without a fight?

1:57–80. John's Birth and Prophetic Interpretation by His Father. The next scene, chronicling John's birth, pictures his parents' fidelity to divine purpose and presents the father's Spirit-impelled declaration of praise to God, reinforcing Mary's celebration of divine activity.

1:57–66. Luke briefly mentions John's birth, which the village marks as an expression of divine mercy to Elizabeth. When the community gathers eight days later for the child's circumcision and naming, attention focuses on his name; defying expectation, Elizabeth and then Zechariah (with the aid of a tablet) insist that the infant receive the name "John." Zechariah moves from his initial skepticism to fidelity, and at once "his mouth was opened and his tongue freed" (v. 64). Behind these passive-voice verbs lies the activity of God, yet God does not restore capacity for speech as a reward for obedience, or to cancel punishment for earlier lack of trust. Instead, John's father regains his voice so as to speak, "filled with the Holy Spirit," the prophetic declaration that follows— another in a series of inspired speeches that articulate the meaning of what is happening.

1:67–80. Like Mary, Zechariah praises God and in so doing interprets God's activity. Verse 67 describes the source of his words—the Spirit—

and characterizes them as prophetic speech (Mary's song is prophetic in function but not in label). "Blessed be the Lord God of Israel," he begins (v. 68)—deserving of blessing, of praise (*benedictus* in Latin), because God has decisively intervened in Israel's history to fulfill ancient promise, keep covenant relation with the people, effect their salvation, and conduct them in the ways of peace. As in Mary's song, the prayer of Zechariah highlights the fulfillment of scriptural promise, mentioning Abraham, David, and more generally ancestors and prophets. The images multiply: mercy, salvation, divine visitation to liberate the people, and peace. From beginning to end, chapter one kindles hopes for Israel's future, raising expectation of imminent liberation. By the end of the story, many of these images will have been turned on their head: divine visitation will be neither recognized nor welcomed (19:41–44); redemption will fail to materialize, at least as expected (24:21); "things that make for peace" will be hidden from a recalcitrant people (19:42). What manner of salvation is this?

Zechariah's hymn-prayer hints that the salvation God effects in Israel will not meet expectation; there will be surprises, even provocations, on the road to liberation. Though not as radical as Mary's song, Zechariah's, too, rewrites conventional scripts. Salvation, pictured as a mighty "horn," as rescue from enemies, has as its aim righteous service of God and assumes the form of forgiveness of sins, the outcome of divine mercy. Luke does not "spiritualize" salvation, however, for Jesus, the embodiment of salvation for both Israel and the nations, will engage in a mission that not only delivers forgiveness but also challenges the structures of economic and political power and social privilege.

For now, reinforcing Mary's song, and picking up threads from Gabriel's earlier announcement to him, Zechariah illuminates the future roles of John and Jesus as agents of divine liberation. John will prepare the people for Jesus' ministry of liberation, pointing them toward the one who will enact salvation and mediate God's forgiveness.

2:1–20. Jesus' Birth and Prophetic Interpretation by an Angelic Choir.

The Roman emperor's directive ushers Mary and her future husband to Bethlehem, where Jesus is born. Yet as the occupying power counts heads in a census, God delivers more than Caesar had counted on. The story of Jesus' birth points beyond Rome to the sovereignty of God, and to the significance of this newborn through whom divine rule comes to be exercised in the world. A third message from heaven confirms and extends the good news about Jesus earlier proclaimed by Gabriel and seconded by Mary and Zechariah.

2:1–7. The narrator supplies a dose of geopolitical reality: the emperor Augustus issues decrees that affect the whole world (exaggeration, to be sure, but not by far, at least from the vantage of occupied Palestine). No historical records confirm that an empire-wide census, or even a regional one during the governorship of Quirinius, occurred, though a limited census, inciting vigorous protest (cf. Acts 5:37), did follow the deposing of Herod Archelaus in Judea in 6 CE. Whatever the historical details, the census aligns the tradition of Jesus' birth in Bethlehem with the fact of his family's residence in Nazareth and introduces into the narrative a tension between two world rulers, Caesar and God's Messiah. Power appears to belong to Rome, yet fidelity to God on the part of law-abiding people generates outcomes the emperor could scarcely have imagined.

So Jesus is born at Bethlehem, David's city, an apt birthplace for a descendant—through Joseph, introduced here for the first time—of David. The last line of the passage, "there was no place for them in the inn" (2:7), highlights the deep irony. A child born in conditions of marginality and poverty (a feeding trough for animals) will challenge Caesar's claim to universal dominion, but only by way of radical reversal of conventional notions of power and status. The stage is set for acclamation of an infant born to be king, not by wealthy and powerful magi (Matt 2) but by shepherds.

2:8–20. Heaven again disrupts routine human activity, as socially marginal shepherds in the countryside near Bethlehem encounter divine glory in the form of angels who announce the birth of a Savior. Disclosure of Jesus' identity and vocation—"a Savior, who is the Messiah [i.e., Christ], the Lord" (v. 11)—and affirmation of God's gift of peace prompt the shepherds to investigate and, ultimately, to praise God. When the shepherds report their experience, it astonishes everyone who hears. News about Jesus' words and actions will repeatedly amaze people (e.g., 2:47; 4:32; 5:26; 8:25, 56; 9:43). Astonishment at God's powerful work is not yet faith, but Mary has stepped onto the path toward authentic faith: while she has already heard firsthand something resembling the shepherd's report (1:32–35), she must mull over (2:19) the extraordinary meaning of the birth of a child who begins life away from home, outside any home. (He will later describe his life as one well acquainted with homelessness, 9:58.)

So arrives the one who will enact God's salvation, as Israel's anointed ruler (Messiah), and exercise sovereignty in the world on behalf of God as "Lord." The era of fulfilled promises has begun, yet will Caesar willingly relinquish his own claims to universal sovereignty, as the source of peace on earth? What manner of Messiah, Savior, and Lord will the manger-boy wrapped in cloths grow to be? *Will* peace find a home on earth (cf. 19:38, 42)?

2:21–40. Preview of Jesus' Destiny: The Child and Israel's Salvation. The outer frame of this passage displays the fidelity of Jesus' family, but the accent falls on the fulfillment of divine promise, articulated by a pious old man in the Temple in a way that foreshadows the conflict that will accompany God's offer of salvation to Israel. Like John, Jesus is nurtured in a pious Jewish family. At his circumcision, Mary and Joseph honor the angel's directive to name the boy Jesus and observe the purification rituals prescribed by Mosaic law (cf. Lev 12:6–8) when they present their firstborn son at the Temple—an occasion for another prophetic oracle about Jesus' vocation and destiny, one that will that add chords of conflict to the symphony of promise and fulfillment.

Luke introduces an aging prophetic duo (2:25–38, again pairing male and female). Though not labeled a prophet, the devout Simeon, directed by the Spirit, encounters Jesus and his parents in the Temple and delivers an oracle that celebrates the presence of salvation in this child but also prophesies the conflict that will greet him. Israel will receive honor ("glory") through him, to be sure, but divine revelation will extend to the nations (or "Gentiles") as well—the first of many anticipations of the inclusion of Gentiles in the people of God (e.g., 3:6, 38; 4:25–27; 7:1–10), a story Luke will tell in Acts. Moreover, the Messiah

will not only restore God's people but also divide them. Some will rise, while others will oppose him and fall, a division-through-conflict that will touch even Mary.

The extraordinarily devout widow Anna adds her prophetic testimony. The narrator labels her a prophet but does not report any oracles spoken by her, instead providing a general summary. (Acts 21:9 presents similar treatment of Philip's four prophetic daughters.) Following the oracle of Simeon, the subtle phrasing of the narrator's profile of Anna raises questions. She praises God and talks about "the child" to all who were "looking for the redemption of Jerusalem" (Luke 2:38), but what form will that redemption take? Who will recognize and accept it, and who will resist it?

Luke's selective account of the infancy of Jesus closes by repeating the theme of his parents' fidelity to "the law of the Lord" (v. 39), and a narrative summary takes notice of the child's growth as one marked by the grace, or favor, of God.

2:41–52. Jesus, Son of God, Among the Teachers in the Temple (Part One). The narrative jumps ahead to Jesus' twelfth year. Continuing an annual custom of traveling to Jerusalem for the Passover, the family does so again, but when Jesus fails to appear among the company returning to Nazareth, Mary and Joseph finally locate him in the Temple, listening to the teachers and impressing them with his understanding. The point of the story becomes clear in the spirited exchange that ensues between Jesus and his mother. Already at age 12, Jesus knows who he is, and whose son he is. In response to the distress Mary voices for "your father and [me]," the son responds that his place is "in my Father's house" (lit., "among the things of my Father," vv. 48–49). Mary's incomprehension may seem puzzling; after all, Gabriel had told her that her son would be the Son of God and sit on David's throne (1:32–33, 35). Perhaps that message was more for Luke's audience than for the young girl Mary. In a real way, though, Mary models for readers a genuine faith that does not arrive fully formed but, taking note of the complexity of life in this world and grappling with the sometimes inscrutable, expectation-shattering activity of God, relentlessly seeks until it finds. In any case, the son begins to surpass his parents, yet returns home and remains an obedient son. Verse 52 repeats the refrain of 2:40, marking Jesus' growth in wisdom (already on display among the teachers in the Temple), and in favor both divine and human. When Luke's audience next observes him, he will be on the verge of assuming his vocation as Messiah, Son of God.

This is the first of two teaching sessions in the Jerusalem Temple. Luke will not narrate another visit by Jesus to Jerusalem and the Temple until the last week of his life. Then he will take possession of the Temple, making it the setting for his final teaching before his arrest (19:47–21:38). The teachers who greet him then will not judge his answers so kindly.

B. Preparation for the Ministry of the Messiah (3:1–4:13)

Fast-forward nearly two decades: John the baptizing prophet steps back into the story to begin his ministry. So the narrative preparation for Jesus' own career gains momentum.

3:1–20. John's Prophetic Ministry. The passage begins with a list of political leaders, notably the emperor Tiberius; the tetrarch of Galilee, Herod Antipas; the Roman governor of Judea, Pontius Pilate; and the high priestly duo of Annas and (his son-in-law) Caiaphas. By linking the prophet's call to the reign of particular rulers, and by employing the phrasing "the word of God came to John" (3:2), Luke recalls the prophetic books of the OT (e.g., Jer 1:2–3; Hos 1:1; Mic 1:1). The question again arises: How and with what outcome will political power and prophetic message authorized by God collide?

John receives his prophetic call while in the wilderness near the Jordan (where Jesus' messianic call will soon be validated) and conducts his ministry there. Through a purifying ritual bath in the river, John baptizes all who are willing to reorder their lives ("repent"), orienting commitments and actions toward the coming reign of God—a "baptism of repentance for the forgiveness of sins" (3:3), thus fulfilling his father Zechariah's prophecy (1:77). John's message, drawing from Isa 40:3–5, pictures him as the wilderness herald who prepares the way of the Lord (cf. Luke 1:76), a way that extends salvation to all people. John joins Simeon as a prophetic witness to the universal scope of salvation.

Verses 7–14 expand John's proclamation, first with an urgent summons to repentance in view of imminent judgment, then through moral instruction that accents generous, just, and honest handling of material goods, anticipating a theme Jesus will develop in radical terms in his teaching (e.g., 12:13–21; 14:33; 16:13, 19–31; 18:18–30). Finally, John distinguishes his role from that of Messiah, the more powerful one still to come. Despite the austerity and urgent tenor of John's message, the narrator characterizes it as "good news" (or "gospel," v. 18). For John, and later for Jesus in Luke's Gospel, good news of salvation and moral seriousness are two sides of one coin.

Luke brings John's ministry to a sudden end, reporting his arrest by Herod Antipas. Such is the destiny of a prophet who not only admonishes soldiers but also dares to rebuke a powerful ruler (for Herod's decision to marry his brother's wife). This is the outcome of the first direct collision between prophet and "king" in Luke's story. Opposition to the agents of God's deliverance is real—and potent. Luke keeps the stage uncluttered; one character (John) exits the story before another (Jesus) takes his place (cf. 1:56 for a similar departure by Mary before Elizabeth gives birth to John). This narrative sequence reinforces the image of John as the precursor who goes before the Lord (Jesus) to prepare his way; their ministries do not overlap. Nevertheless, in a temporal flashback, one significant baptism remains to be narrated.

3:21–4:13. Jesus' Identity and Vocation: Baptism, Genealogy, and Testing. This section of the Gospel brings into focus the identity and vocation of Jesus as Messiah, Son of God. At his baptism he receives direct divine confirmation of his status as Son of God, and the Spirit anoints him for the work that lies ahead. Then a genealogy ascribes honor to Jesus as "son of Adam, son of God." Finally, Jesus demonstrates, against demonic opposition, his resolve to accept his vocation as Messiah, Son of God.

3:21–22. In the course of John's baptizing ministry, Jesus, too, received baptism—presumably by John, though this is only implicit. What matters is not John's role in the event (after all, Jesus is the "greater one" of the two) but heaven's. The Spirit of God (Holy Spirit) descends upon Jesus (tangibly, as a dove). Luke will not often mention the Spirit during the ministry of Jesus; however, a cluster of references at the outset (also 4:1, 14, 18) supplies the divine signature on Jesus' activity. He speaks and acts under the direction and empowerment of God's Spirit (cf. Acts 10:38). The Spirit is not alone in bearing witness to Jesus; a voice from heaven addresses Jesus: "You are my beloved Son; I take delight in you" (Luke 3:22; author's trans.). In God's authoritative voice, the baptism seals Jesus' identity as Son of God.

3:23–38. Genealogies serve various interests, including ascription of honor through recall of one's ancestors. Luke does this and more, as he presents a genealogy (substantially different from the one in Matt 1:1–17) that locates Jesus on a family tree that, proceeding backward in time, includes King David; patriarchs Judah, Jacob, and Abraham; and Adam, "son of God." By tracing Jesus' roots to Adam, Luke again affirms that Jesus brings God's salvation not only to Israel but also to all people (cf. 2:32; 3:6). Mention of Adam as "son of God" (3:38) prepares for resumption of the theme of Jesus' divine sonship, the implications of which will be probed in the next scene.

4:1–13. At Jesus' baptism, the divine voice marked Jesus as beloved Son of God, confirming Jesus' self-understanding and the Lukan audience's previous information, and God's Spirit came to rest upon Jesus. Yet neither knowledge of divine sonship nor anointing by the Holy Spirit sets Jesus on an easy path. In fact, the devil—chief enemy of God's purpose and architect of evil opposition to its accomplishment—seizes the opportunity to challenge Jesus' fidelity to his vocation as God's Son. (To dramatic effect, the narrative presents as a dialogue with an external entity what one might today describe as an internal struggle to discern and embrace God's will.)

Like Matt 4:1–11, Luke narrates a threefold test in which both the devil and Jesus appeal to Scripture (OT). The devil, with support from Ps 91:11–12, prods Jesus to tap divine power to make a splash in the world: (1) breaking his 40-day fast in the wilderness—replication in miniature of Israel's 40-year wilderness ordeal?—by turning stone into bread (Jesus will later speak of stones acclaiming God's royal Messiah, Luke 19:40); (2) seizing power over the nations (though at the cost of abandoning loyalty to God); and (3) claiming angelic protection from destruction at the Temple mount. Jesus counters this "scriptural paradigm"

for his messianic vocation by appealing to texts from Deuteronomy (8:3; 6:13 and 10:20; 6:16): (1) not bread but God's word sustains (though Jesus will interpret reliance upon divine nourishment as a practice that calls for robust response to human hunger, Luke 9:10–17); (2) worship and loyalty are due God alone (from whom the Son of God does receive "the ends of the earth [as] your possession," according to Ps 2:8); and (3) not even God's Son should presume to place a demand upon God, inverting the testing scenario by putting God to the test. Jesus' ensuing ministry will reject the flashy, power-centered ministry urged by the devil, but neither he nor his followers will neglect the physical needs of people. Indeed, he will feed a large crowd and restore health to the sick. The focus is instead on the temptation to use power to serve self-interest. By the story's conclusion, Jesus' radical rejection of that approach will be evident. The one who saves others will not save himself from the cross, even if he does ask to be spared the ordeal (see 22:42; 23:35, 37, 39).

The unit closes on a foreboding note; the devil, though bested by Jesus, will at "an opportune time" again challenge Jesus' fidelity to his messianic vocation (4:13; cf. 22:3). For the time being, however, Jesus—Spirit-empowered, his mission in sharp focus—is ready to launch his ministry. Where better to begin than at home?

II. Ministry (4:14–19:27)

A. Galilean Ministry (4:14–9:50)

Luke blends the roles of prophet and Messiah as Jesus begins his ministry in Galilee. He makes a formal beginning in his hometown synagogue, an inaugural scene that defines the program of his ministry and previews its outcome. Jesus then moves from town to town, teaching, proclaiming the good news of God's reign, and embodying it in grace-filled acts of healing, forgiveness, and hospitality.

4:14–44. Jesus' Spirited-empowered Ministry Begins at Home, with Mixed Results. The same Spirit that came to Jesus at his baptism and sustained him through his wilderness ordeal now energizes an itinerant ministry in Galilee, and those who hear Jesus' teaching respond with praise. But he also provokes a hostile response in Nazareth, his childhood home. In a dramatic scene in the synagogue, Jesus reads from Scripture, selecting a passage from Isaiah (61:1–2*a*, but adding a line from Isa 58:6), and then claims that the Scripture "has been fulfilled in your hearing" (Luke 4:21).

With help from Isaiah, Jesus interprets the Spirit's (i.e., God's) action in his life (itself the result of the Spirit's work [1:35]). Jesus believes himself to be commissioned—indeed, anointed (*echrisen*, word-relative of "Christ") by the Spirit—to engage in a ministry that brings good news to the poor, liberates those who are bound, and restores sight to the blind, enacting the scriptural paradigm for the Spirit-anointed, God-commissioned Messiah. So the Spirit of God places its signature on Jesus' activity. The larger context of the verse Jesus draws from Isaiah 58 suggests the future directions of Jesus' ministry, including a bold critique of inauthentic Temple worship near the end of his life (Luke 19:45–46): No worship of God is genuine if it coincides with unjust actions, with neglect of the needs of the poor. Jesus will make their plight a central concern of his ministry.

The synagogue audience, though puzzled because they know Jesus to be only "Joseph's son" (partial truth, as readers recognize; cf. 2:48–49; 3:23), nevertheless receive gladly such hope-inspiring words. Surely this is good news for them, Jesus' own people (doctors take care of their own, right?). However, Jesus immediately challenges any such presumption; the good news he brings is for outsiders, not for his own people. After all, no prophet is accepted at home. Jesus illustrates the point by recalling episodes from the careers of Elijah and Elisha when they brought help not to people in need within Israel but to outsiders. The implication is twofold: Jesus, too, has a prophet's task, and it will shatter traditional barriers and transgress conventional boundaries, benefiting outsiders. Luke shows the direction the narrative will eventually take, including Gentiles in God's people (culminating in Acts 28:28). The scene previews the story's plot in another sense. Enraged by Jesus' words, the Nazareth audience seeks to put him to death, but without success, as his appointment with a prophet's destiny lies ahead at Jerusalem (cf. Luke 13:33–34). For the present, Jesus has more work to do among his people. How will nearby Capernaum respond to him?

As Jesus begins his career, his way of enacting Israel's salvation—hopes such as were celebrated in the speeches of Luke 1–2—indicates that the "smooth" way of salvation proceeds through conflict, role reversals (both vertical and horizontal), and radical revision of expectations. Mary's song and Simeon's oracle had it right. Status inversion (1:51–53) and the division of the people in response to the work of the Messiah (2:34–35) have begun.

Superficially, Capernaum (on the north shore of the Sea of Galilee), the next stop on Jesus' tour of Galilee, forms a stark contrast to Nazareth. Where Nazareth rejects, Capernaum enthusiastically accepts Jesus' ministry. After Jesus has taught with impressive authority, freed a man from debilitating demonic control and a woman (the mother-in-law of Simon, to be more fully introduced in ch. 5) from a high fever, and healed others of illness or demonic possession, the people of Capernaum attempt to keep him from leaving. Yet this response, too, is misguided. By claiming for itself the healing power of the Messiah, Capernaum would set itself against the purposes of God. Jesus answers with a mission statement: "I must proclaim the good news of the kingdom of God to the other cities also" (v. 43). So Jesus departs, to continue his teaching mission elsewhere. Jesus actually returns to Capernaum in the very next chapter, but the last word on the town is one of judgment (10:15).

This passage highlights the activity of demons, especially their knowledge of Jesus' identity as "Holy One of God" (4:34) or "Son of God" (v. 41). Jesus silences their witness which, though accurate, is not helpful advocacy; 11:14–26 shows the potential for misinterpretation of his exorcisms. Nor is this the way in which Jesus seeks to invite authentic faith, which joins attentive listening and faithful obedience (e.g., 6:46–49; 8:19–21). Faith is more about how one lives, in grateful response to God's gracious work, than having the right label for Jesus. Clinical diagnosis today may employ categories other than demons and unclean spirits for the conditions from which Jesus restores such people, but the distortions of human well-being he attacks are familiar enough.

After the success of his activity in Capernaum, Jesus withdraws to pray and gains clarity about his mission, just as he had sought clarity of vocation in the desert following his baptism. This is the second time readers have observed Jesus at prayer (the first notice immediately preceded the divine voice at his baptism, 3:21). Jesus finds guidance for his work through prayer (6:12; 9:18, 28–29; 10:21–22; 11:1; 22:41–42; 23:34, 46), a distinctive feature of Luke's portrayal of Jesus, and a model for readers to emulate (11:1–4).

5:1–11. Jesus Begins to Gather Disciples. The focus of Jesus' ministry is clear: teaching; announcing the good news of God's saving reign, especially for the poor and marginalized; and restoring health. Now he begins to recruit followers to aid him. He will ask them to leave everything behind—home, family, occupation—to accompany him, forming a community of "disciples" (learners) to convey the same good news and receive empowerment to bring the same healing, first alongside him and then (in Acts) after him.

He begins with a fisherman, Simon (Peter), whose mother-in-law he has just healed, and who will emerge as chief among the apostles ("ones sent") in Acts. Simon does not strike an impressive pose at the moment of his call; aware of his failings, he responds to Jesus' teaching and an extraordinary catch of fish engineered by Jesus: "Go away from me, Lord, for I am a sinful man!" (5:8). Undeterred, Jesus summons Simon and his fishing partners, the brothers James and John, to a new fishing vocation, "catching people" (v. 10; i.e., for God's realm). Jesus will later define his mission as seeking and saving "sinners" like Simon (5:32; 19:10), so this first call to discipleship scripts an apt headline for the ministry to come. Leaving everything behind, as disciples in Luke are expected to do (5:28; 14:26, 33; 18:28), these recruits join Jesus' band.

5:12–6:11. Healing and Feasting—and Escalating Conflict. A series of episodes probes the connections between Jesus' religious practice (fasting, Sabbath observance, hospitality) and social conventions, as well as Mosaic law. Healing events frame the section, each developing the implications of Jesus' activity for religious practice and conviction. Throughout the narrative, Luke weaves together mutually interpreting words and actions of Jesus. The result is escalating conflict between Jesus and other teachers over both his authority and the interpretation of Scripture.

In the first episode (5:12–16), Jesus encounters a man afflicted with leprosy, a skin ailment (not identical to the disease called by that name today) that rendered him ritually unclean and gave him a socially marginal existence (see Lev 13–14). Jesus "touched" the man, and at his word "the leprosy left him" (Luke 5:13). Jesus sends the man to the priest to make an offering "as Moses commanded"; his ministry of healing does not conflict with the Torah (v. 14).

A second healing disrupts Jesus' teaching in the company of "Pharisees and teachers of the law" from every part of Palestine (5:17–26). When a paralyzed man is lowered into the room, Jesus, struck by this display of faith, says to him, "Friend, your sins are forgiven you" (v. 20)—an assertion that strikes observers as blasphemous, for only God can forgive sins. Jesus, discerning prophet that he is, reads their minds and responds by adding to the (weightier) declaration of forgiveness the (easier) command to walk, thus showcasing his authority as Son of Man to forgive. The man gives proof of his healing by carrying his bed home, filling the village streets with praise of God.

The passage links physical restoration and forgiveness but does not *explain* the man's physical condition as the result of sin. Nor does Jesus offer healing as a *reward* for faith, even if it is the bold faith of the man and his friends that opens up access to the gift of restored movement. On the theological point at issue: Jesus' declaration "your sins are forgiven you" employs a "divine passive"; God is the source of forgiveness, even if Jesus is its mediator. So the charge of blasphemy is wide of the mark. Jesus' authority to forgive derives from God. As Son of Man, a self-identifying image Jesus likely has drawn from Dan 7:13–14 (where "one like a human being" [lit., like a son of man] receives from God eternal dominion; cf. Luke 22:69), Jesus rightly exercises judgment—and mercy—on behalf of God.

Luke 5:27–39 develops the theme of forgiveness of sins as a central concern of Jesus' ministry. The call of the tax collector Levi—like other disciples in Luke, he abandons "everything," including his occupation, to follow Jesus—culminates in a festive banquet at Levi's home (he obviously did not relinquish all his possessions!). Pharisees and experts in Torah interpretation criticize the disciples' meal fellowship with "tax collectors and sinners." (Tax agents were widely regarded as dishonest and as disloyal collaborators with Rome; cf. 18:13; 19:7.) Jesus defends his social intimacy with religious outsiders, employing a medical metaphor: doctors treat sick people; Jesus calls sinners—to repentance (a reordered life, 5:32). This will be the focus of Jesus' mission, over the objections of the "righteous."With the image of repentance, the passage moves seamlessly into a discussion of fasting (often associated with repentance; note the fasting imagery in Isa 58:1–9, a passage echoed in Luke 4:18). Followers of both the Pharisees and John the Baptizer regularly engage in fasting and prayer, while Jesus' followers "eat and drink" (5:33). To a query prompted by these contrasting expressions of piety, Jesus replies with two parabolic images (fabric and wineskins) that picture the incompatibility of old and new, even if people still typically prefer the old. Jesus' teaching and embodiment of God's reign, while faithful to Scripture and to authentic Jewish religious practice, proves to be innovative, radical, and controversial (as previewed in 4:16–30). The present, in Jesus' view, is a time not for fasting and mourning but for festive joy that expresses communally an inclusive vision of God's realm. Fasting will be apt later, when the bridegroom is forcibly taken from the disciples—first foreshadowing by Jesus of his destiny (cf. 9:22, 44; 13:31–35; 18:31–33). Luke 7:31–35 will return to this contrast between John's austere discipline and the celebration that marks Jesus' practice of hospitality.

The religious practice of Sabbath keeping and the related matter of Torah interpretation come into view in the next two vignettes (6:1–11). Pharisees chastise Jesus' disciples for failing to keep the Sabbath when they pluck grain and eat (Exod 34:21 prohibits harvesting on the Sabbath). Although Jesus might have defended his disciples' behavior by appealing to Deut 23:25 (which distinguishes plucking from harvesting), he finds warrant instead in King David's emergency appropriation of sacred bread (1 Sam 21:1–6), thus setting up Jesus' own claim to sovereignty: "The Son of Man is lord of the Sabbath" (Luke 6:5). The next scene shows how Jesus chooses to exercise that sovereignty; not only hunger but also the need for healing justifies action on the Sabbath.

Luke 6:1–5 pictures Jesus' sovereign authority (as "lord") over the Sabbath, and he claims, with scriptural warrant, that genuine human need (such as hunger) should guide conduct on the Sabbath. In vv. 6–11, encountering a man with a physical disability (a "withered" hand), Jesus presses further. In such a case, fidelity to Torah *requires* one to act: "I ask you, is it lawful to do good or to do harm on the sabbath, to save life or to destroy it?" (v. 9). By refraining from action, one actually harms and therefore fails to keep the law. Not convinced by Jesus' interpretation, enraged observers debate what to do. Conflict intensifies, yet despite vigorous criticisms of Jesus' religious practice, his ministry is pictured as shaped by faithful interpretation of Scripture.

6:12–49. Jesus Names Twelve Apostles and Reveals the Character of Life in God's Realm. After an all-night prayer session on a mountain, Jesus commissions twelve disciples to be "apostles" ("ones sent"). The number twelve expresses symbolically that Jesus' ministry aims at Israel's restoration—all twelve tribes (cf. 22:30; Acts 1:15–26). Simon, to whom Jesus gives the name Peter, heads the list, and Judas Iscariot, "who became a traitor," comes last, both names prefiguring momentous events to come. The mountain setting is a prime location for reception of divine revelation, from Moses on Mount Sinai onward (see Exod 19–24, echoed in the Sermon on the Mount in Matt 5–7, a passage that parallels Luke's "Sermon on the Plain," 6:20–49). Having chosen twelve authorized agents to expand the scope of his ministry (9:1–6; cf. 10:1–12), Jesus shows a vast crowd what it means to be his disciple, and so reveals the content and character of the reign of God the apostles will represent in their mission on his behalf.

6:17–49. When a crowd assembles, Jesus gives his longest discourse so far, profiling the commitment to which he summons disciples (vv. 20–49). Beginning with *grace* notes, he pronounces the disciples "blessed" (implicitly, by God). What is the nature of their happy fortune? With four beatitudes (a more elaborate set of nine appears in Matt 5), Jesus pictures the radical role reversals in God's domain. The recipients of God's favor are those who are poor, hungry, weeping, and hated now, not those who enjoy good fortune—the wealthy, sated, laughing, and honored. With these contrasting beatitudes and woes, Jesus begins to enact in word the status inversion for which Mary's song praised God (Luke 1:51–53).

If God's salvation effects reversal of circumstance, what are the implications for human relationships? Jesus provides a concise sketch: (1) when met with hatred and harm, one should respond with love and compassionate mercy, modeled after God's own merciful character (6:27–36); (2) when facing another's failings, one should refrain from judging and instead forgive, aware of one's own failings (vv. 37–42). The discourse concludes with imagery that appeals for action embodying the message one has heard. As fruit indicates the quality of a tree, one's way of life indicates the character of the heart (vv. 43–45); hearing Jesus' word without performing it will only bring ruin (vv. 46–49). Having impeccable christology ("Lord, Lord") is no cover for disobedience—including disobedience expressed in a refusal to extend grace and mercy to others.

7:1–35. Jesus Restores Health and Life, Thereby Revealing His Identity.

Another round of healing elicits a query from John the Baptizer regarding Jesus' identity and vocation, and both the narrator and Jesus then draw contrasting profiles of these two figures, and of the people's response to them.

7:1–10. For the first time, Jesus extends his ministry of healing to a Gentile household. Inside-out reversal, already evident in Jesus' acceptance of "sinners," over the objection of Pharisees and specialists in Torah interpretation (5:27–32; cf. 5:8, 20), reaches a new level. After the pattern of Elisha (as previewed in 4:27), Jesus restores health in response to the request of a Gentile military officer, aided by others' mediation (cf. 2 Kgs 5:1–19). The Roman soldier, a centurion (head of a company of 100), is a curious blend of deferential humility and bold assertiveness. A person with authority himself, he acknowledges Jesus' power to heal, even at a distance; yet, realizing that he is not worthy to host Jesus under his roof, he sends two delegations to present his request to the "Lord." Like another centurion in Acts 10 (Cornelius), this soldier has close ties to the Jewish community (he even built the Capernaum synagogue). The point of the story is not the healing of the centurion's slave, though the narrator does report it; rather, Luke emphasizes the extraordinary faith of this Gentile: "[N]ot even in Israel," Jesus exclaims, "have I found such faith"

(Luke 7:9). God's gracious favor comes to outsiders, even Gentiles, just as Jesus had said it would (4:25–27)—the first enactment of the prophecies voiced by Simeon (2:32) and John the Baptizer (3:6). Although Jesus will direct his ensuing ministry to Jewish communities (with the exception of 8:26–39), the encounter with this remarkable Gentile soldier gives a preview of the direction the story will take in Acts.

7:11–17. After the pattern of Elijah (as previewed in Luke 4:25–26), Jesus restores life to a widow's son (cf. 1 Kgs 17:17–24; also Elisha in 2 Kgs 4:32–37). The narrator reports Jesus' motive: compassion, a notice heightened by the mother's vulnerable position after losing both her husband and her only son. His method? A simple command to "rise." Impressed by the Messiah's prophetic ministry of teaching and healing, reminiscent of Elijah and Elisha, the people recognize God's gracious visitation (cf. 1:68) and acknowledge Jesus as the "prophet" through whom that grace has come to them. Word continues to spread, reaching even that other prophet, John, who languishes in Herod Antipas's prison.

7:18–23. John, the imprisoned prophet who was to "prepare the way" for Jesus, sends his own disciples with a question for the acclaimed prophet-healer: "Are you the one who is to come?" (7:20). Do Jesus' activities follow the script for the mighty one who would bring the decisive judgment John had announced as imminent (3:9, 17)? For confirmation of his identity and calling, Jesus points to his acts of healing, echoing Isa 35:4–6 with its images of the future restoration of the land ("when God comes to save you," Isa 35:4). A whirlwind tour with Jesus, the mighty healer, shows the arrival of the era of salvation—an indirect answer to John's query. But will John and other observers discern the moment as one of fulfillment, the year of God's favor? Jesus is indeed the Spirit-empowered herald of good news as he aids people in desperate need: "[B]lessed is anyone who takes no offense at me" (Luke 7:23).

7:24–35. After the departure of John's messengers, Jesus evaluates the people's response to John and himself. They were right to esteem the Baptizer as a prophet, yet he was even more—indeed, the end-time prophet who prepared for the Lord's coming (citing Mal 3:1 and recalling Luke 1:76). Still, John belongs to the time of preparation; the era of fulfillment in God's realm surpasses even his greatness (cf. 16:16–17). A narrator's aside interrupts Jesus' address to the crowd, observing the wedge John's ministry has driven between receptive crowds (including tax collectors) and resistant Pharisees and Torah experts. Jesus' ministry likewise divides the people between responsive sinners and righteous critics, as exemplified in the next episode (7:36–50). First, though, Jesus borrows an image from village life to clinch his point about a people dividing in response to God's emissaries, John the austere ascetic and Jesus the "friend of tax collectors and sinners" who enjoys a good feast. Like children who refuse to play a street game because they cannot agree on the rules (is it about dancing or mourning?), the people have no excuse for remaining uncommitted because John and Jesus are a study in contrasts; after all, God's wisdom merits acceptance when it appears in any of "her children," no matter how diverse.

7:36–8:3. Grateful Response of Several Women to Jesus' Benefaction: Role Reversal at a Pharisee's Home and Funding Jesus' Itinerant Ministry.

Two prominent themes—divergent responses to Jesus' ministry and the inside-out status inversion it provokes—are spliced together in this scene, a dinner set at a Pharisee's home. This is the first of three such occasions, each surfacing conflict between host and guest (cf. 11:37–54; 14:1–24). A woman enters the house uninvited and in a gesture of shocking intimacy bathes, kisses, and anoints Jesus' feet. The impropriety of the woman's behavior prompts the Pharisee (Simon) to doubt Jesus' status as prophet: everyone knows she is a sinner, yet he lets her touch him. Jesus reads Simon's mind and answers with a parable and a rebuke, defending the woman and honoring her at the host's expense. Just as a person forgiven a larger debt shows greater love (i.e., gratitude) than one forgiven a smaller debt, so this woman's extravagant affection expresses the grace she has received (presumably in an earlier, untold encounter). The Pharisee host, by contrast, withholds even basic tokens of hospitality. Host and guest, righteous man and sinful woman, exchange places. Other dinner guests are left with the question, "Who is this who even forgives sins?" (v. 49). Who, indeed! The woman—a model of faith that receives the gift of mercy and responds with gratitude and love—enters the inside-out domain of God's grace, of salvation and peace, mediated by Jesus.

8:1–3. Jesus resumes his travels as herald of God's reign, the twelve apostles accompanying him, along with several women Jesus has restored to health. These women, including Mary Magdalene (liberated from seven demons), Joanna (married to Herod's property manager), and Susanna, cover the expenses of Jesus' itinerant band, thus exemplifying the hospitality and generous sharing of possessions to which Jesus summons all disciples (12:13–21, 33; 16:19–31; 18:18–25). Divine grace again elicits the human response of gratitude and generous service (cf. 4:39).

8:4–25. With Parable, Provocation, and Power, Jesus Forms a New Family Defined by Faith.

Jesus has already employed the teaching device of the parable, a brief fictional narrative that illuminates some aspect of life or God's realm (5:36–38; 7:41–42; cf. 6:39, 48–49). Beginning with 8:4–15, which presents and then interprets a parable commenting on Jesus' ministry of proclamation, parables become increasingly prominent, including several unique to Luke: a compassionate Samaritan (10:30–35), a rich fool (12:16–20), a widow's lost coin (15:8–10), a father and his two sons (15:11–32), a dishonest but savvy manager (16:1–8), a rich man and Lazarus (16:19–31), a widow and a judge (18:2–5), and a Pharisee and a tax collector (18:10–13).

An opening parable pictures a sower planting seeds in various soil conditions. Even if many seeds do not produce, a bountiful harvest is sure. Jesus appends an explanation of the purpose of parabolic teaching; presenting indirectly revelation ("mysteries") the disciples receive more directly, parables frustrate listeners' ability to perceive. Jesus then explains the parable of the sower as a symbolic narrative about diverse responses to the proclamation of God's word. Not hearing the word but enduring fidelity is the goal of Jesus' teaching (and later the disciples'), a point Jesus reinforces when he redefines his family as "those who hear the word of God and do it" (8:21). (Jesus' mother and brothers later appear in the company of the faithful, Acts 1:14.) Attentive listening to the word matters; Jesus does not intend to keep people from perceiving the word and work of God, despite the explanation of parables in vv. 9–10. Shifting to visual imagery, he affirms that what is temporarily hidden will eventually come to light. God's work of salvation seeks attentive listening and enduring commitment of life in response.

8:22–25. Life presents challenges to faith, as exemplified in a scene set on the lake. The disciples struggle to survive a menacing storm in their wave-tossed boat, while Jesus sleeps. Awakened by their cries of distress, he calms wind and wave and then asks, "Where is your faith?" (8:25). The amazed disciples wonder who can command even the forces of nature. The disciples are growing toward more perceptive faith—and understanding of Jesus' identity—but have a long way to go, much of that ground to be covered in the next chapter. This passage invites deep trust in God's care, even though endangered boats often do capsize (metaphor for all manner of perils) and people perish.

8:26–39. Life for a Tormented Tomb-dweller in Gentile Territory. A mood of awe and fear continues as Jesus' band is greeted across the lake by a demon-tormented man whose appearance (naked) and residence (among the tombs) show that he no longer lives within human community. Like others before him who were afflicted by malevolent spiritual beings, this man knows who Jesus is ("Son of the Most High God," 8:28; cf. 4:34, 41). Jesus has already commanded the spirit to depart, though further dialogue reveals that the man ("Legion") is actually in the grip of a demon army. The demons beg to be dispatched into a herd of pigs (this is Gentile territory), resulting in the animals' self-destruction; ironically, while seeking to avoid "the abyss," the demons drive the pigs off a cliff into the lake.

Contact with this kind of spiritual power is frightening. Loss of an entire herd is even more distressing, and the herders spread the news. Yet when all gather to see the spectacle, what terrifies is not the awesome power unleashed in the event but the sight of the man sitting—clothed, sanity restored—with Jesus. Among Gentiles, too, Jesus' ministry provokes divided response. The Gerasenes ask Jesus to depart, but the healed man desires to stay with him; Jesus asks him instead to tell in his own region what "God has done for you" (i.e., what God's agent of salvation, Jesus, "had done for him," v. 39)—another preview of the Gentile mission to be narrated in Acts.

8:40–56. Jesus Restores Health and Life to Two Women. Jesus returns to Galilee and enthusiastic crowds, only to be met by desperate pleas for the healing of two women, in a hybrid narrative Luke has adapted from Mark 5:21–43. First, a synagogue leader named Jairus requests the healer's intervention to save his dying daughter. Suspense builds when Jesus stops to deal with a woman in the crowd who has stealthily touched his clothing and found healing of her chronic bleeding condition; the disorder placed her in the socially marginal position of continual ritual impurity. The two women are twins of a sort, having in common their gender, need of healing, and the number 12 (the young woman is 12; the bleeding woman has suffered from her disorder for 12 years and spent all her resources seeking a remedy). Jesus commends the woman's faith and dismisses her in peace, but at that very moment word comes from Jairus's house that his daughter has died. Undeterred, Jesus urges stubborn, against-the-evidence trust, enters the girl's room, restores her to life, and instructs her parents to give her food and keep the event private. Jesus' ministry brings help to both a woman on the social margins and the child of a prominent leader—an inclusive, status-transcending community shaped by divine grace. The surprising appeal for silence at the story's end (reversing Jesus' command to "Legion" to tell his story, 8:39) is no blanket appeal for secrecy in mission, for in the next passage Jesus dispatches his twelve apostles to broadcast the ministry of healing and word far and wide.

9:1–9. The Twelve Extend Jesus' Ministry, and Herod Antipas Is Perplexed. The twelve disciples selected by Jesus as apostles (6:13) now receive their first missionary assignment. Jesus dispatches them to expand the sphere of his ministry, proclaiming God's reign and healing just as they have seen him do. He charges them to "[t]ake nothing for your journey," relying on the hospitality of a household within each village, and taking nothing with them (not even the dust of the street!) when they leave a place that does not welcome them (9:3–5).

When the Twelve take their good news in word and healing deed "everywhere" (v. 6), news reaches the tetrarch of Galilee, Herod (Antipas, a son of Herod the Great). Herod dismisses the speculation that this is the work of the baptizer

John, raised from death (Luke's first notice of the previously imprisoned John's execution): "John I beheaded" (v. 9). While others maintain it is Elijah, whose return was anticipated before the last days (see 1:17; Mal 4:5), Herod muses: "Who is this?" (a query the disciples, too, posed in Luke 8:25). Given John's demise, the desire of Herod to see Jesus creates suspense, which will be sustained as the narrative unfolds (13:31; 23:6–12).

9:10–17. Jesus and the Twelve Feed a Large Crowd.

The apostles report their activities to Jesus, and he attempts unsuccessfully to retreat with them. When large crowds follow, Jesus resumes speaking about God's realm and healing. At day's end, the Twelve are eager to dismiss the crowd to seek food and shelter, but Jesus directs them to provide nourishment instead, their meager resources notwithstanding. Jesus then "blessed and broke" the loaves and fish, acts that will gain ritual significance later in the story (22:19; 24:30; cf. Acts 27:35). Twelve baskets of left-over food, one for each apostle, show that by God's gracious provision, the generous sharing of resources is more than ample to meet the need of all God's people (whether five thousand or, with appreciation of the symbolic cast of the narrative, all twelve tribes).

9:18–27. Jesus Teaches Disciples About His Identity and Vocation of Suffering.

Finally alone with the disciples, Jesus is praying again and seizes the opportunity to probe the disciples' grasp of the events they have been experiencing, and their developing interpretation of his identity and role. Pressing beyond the crowd's (partially correct) perception of him as a prophet (though he is not, as some think, John the Baptizer or Elijah; cf. 9:8), Peter brands Jesus "the Messiah of God" (v. 20). Despite the truth of the label, Jesus commands silence. Why? The next line supplies a hint, in a first unambiguous prediction of his coming suffering and death at the hands of the religious leaders—and subsequent resurrection vindication—as Son of Man. Jesus' messianic vocation embraces shame, suffering, and death. All who follow Jesus, moreover, should expect to share in his vocation, taking up their own cross each day; the temporal qualifier ("daily") indicates that the cross image works metaphorically. Seeking honor from God may mean accepting dishonor, even if not actual crucifixion, in one's social world.

Nevertheless, the reality of death, whether real or metaphorical, cannot prevent the imminent appearance, even in a world hostile to God's purposes and messengers, of God's reign, at least for those with eyes to see it (cf. 17:20–21).

9:28–36. Heaven Confirms Jesus' Identity and Provides a Glimpse of His Future Exaltation.

Confirmation of Jesus' teaching about his identity and vocation now comes from the most reliable source—God—in a setting that primes readers to expect divine revelation: Jesus at prayer on a mountain, with Peter, John, and James. Jesus' transformed appearance ("transfigured," revealing his heavenly glory), illustrious company (Moses and Elijah), and the topic of conversation (Jesus' coming departure—exodus—at Jerusalem) give the three disciples a behind-the-curtain glimpse of Jesus' glory in the realm of God, anticipatory fulfillment of Jesus' prophecy in 9:26–27. What the disciples cannot yet comprehend, Luke's audience is primed to discern. A voice from a cloud, traditional choreography of divine revelation, provides public endorsement of the private disclosure Jesus heard at his baptism: "This is my Son, my Chosen" (v. 35; cf. 3:22). The appended command, "[L]isten to him," echoing Deut 18:15–20, implies that Jesus is the "prophet like Moses" whom God promised to send (cf. Acts 3:22–23; 7:37). Jesus takes up in his own figure, for the decisive era of Israel's salvation, the roles of both Elijah and Moses, a point scored symbolically when the cloud's lifting reveals only Jesus. The "exodus" image suggests that Jesus' journey to Jerusalem—the focus of a long section in the center of Luke's Gospel (9:51–19:27)—is both an exit from life and a journey from wilderness testing to liberation.

9:37–50. Greatness Divine and Human: Vanquishing Demons and Rewriting the Scripts for the Messiah and His Loyal Followers.

A mountain-top glimpse of glory gives only temporary reprieve from insistent crowds, including desperate pleas for help from the father of an only child tormented by a malevolent spirit, which even the disciples were unable to banish. Impatient with the faithlessness of his contemporaries, Jesus nevertheless frees the boy from the spirit—an outcome the narrator labels healing, signaling that for Luke diseases and demons are related expressions of disordered human life. Divine grace restores well-being: the enacted good news of God's reign in a world marked by evil. Such is the "greatness of God" (v. 43).

In 9:43*b*–50, Jesus again pictures his vocation as one of suffering, yet the disciples do not understand, a point the narrator makes emphatically, in three waves. (1) God is implicated, as Jesus' meaning is "concealed" from the disciples (the passive voice implies divine agency) and they are afraid to ask. Not until the disciples have experienced the shattering of their hopes in Jesus' crucifixion will their eyes be opened (24:13–35). (2) Disciples then debate among themselves: Which of them is the greatest? Such status-seeking is discordant with Jesus' vision of God's realm, which brings radical status inversion for both Messiah and people. So Jesus embraces a young child as a paradigm of greatness in God's realm, turning social convention upside down (cf. 18:15–17; 22:26). (3) The disciples win Jesus' rebuke for opposing competitors who are exorcising demons in Jesus' name but do not belong to his disciple team: "[W]hoever is not against you is for you" (9:50). What matters is not one's position inside or outside, but doing the work of God (cf. 6:46; 8:21).

B. Journey to Jerusalem (9:51–19:27)

Jesus begins a circuitous journey to Jerusalem, where his destiny lies. In alternating scenes, he nurtures the disciples' formation in faith, teaches crowds, and spars with other teachers who oppose his religious vision and its embodiment in practice.

9:51–62. Resistance to Jesus' Summons into God's Realm. Jesus makes a decisive turn, "set[ting] his face to go to Jerusalem" (v. 51). Jesus has been engaged in an itinerant ministry all along, but now the journey (however vague its markers of place and chronology) is defined by its destination. Like all other prophets, Jesus must face rejection in the holy city (13:33–35)—an exaggerated, yet symbolically and theologically profound affirmation. The disciples again show the dissonance between Jesus' vision and theirs. When advance messengers are rebuffed in a Samaritan village, James and John propose prayer for the town's destruction, and win Jesus' rebuke. The advocate of love of enemies (6:27–28) has no interest in violent reprisal, though he will return to the theme of divine judgment upon towns

within Israel that have turned away from God's reign (10:13–15).

9:57–62. What does it mean to follow a Messiah who is determined (pun intended) to go to Jerusalem? Will Simeon's oracle ("a sign that will be opposed," 2:34) dominate the headlines? Repudiation by a Samaritan village supplied the first hint. The second follows swiftly, as Jesus encounters three potential followers. Discipleship en route to Jerusalem means (1) homelessness, (2) willingness to abandon sacred familial duties (burying a parent) to proclaim God's reign, and (3) uncompromising commitment to the hard work of God's realm, at the cost of loyalty to family. The response of these characters to Jesus' radical, countercultural demand goes unreported; it is up to Luke's audience to answer.

10:1–24. Mission in Expanding Circles, and Divided Response. To judge from Jesus' exchanges with three potential disciples at the end of ch. 9, the turn toward Jerusalem has heightened the mission's urgency. Jesus again enlarges the scope of his mission, increasing its stakes by terming it a "harvest" (stock image of end-time judgment, as John also knew, 3:17). Jesus sends out seventy-two disciples, in pairs—two witnesses are needed to offer credible testimony—to supplement the work of the apostles (in some manuscripts this team numbers 70). As in the earlier mission of the Twelve (9:1–6), the seventy-two are to announce the approach of God's reign and heal the sick. They are also to rely upon the hospitality of the villages they visit, eating whatever food is offered (laying aside kosher purity concerns). Yet they will also meet rejection (God's offer of salvation divides God's people, as Simeon prophesied), and that amounts to rejection of Jesus, God's agent of deliverance, and therefore of God—a recipe for judgment, even for Capernaum, so enthusiastic in its initial response to Jesus' activity.

When the seventy-two return celebrating their success in freeing people from demons (a far cry from the failure in 9:40), Jesus graphically depicts that success as the result—or indicator—of Satan's fall from heaven (cf. 11:14–26). No less important is the divine approval that embraces disciples ("names written in heaven," 10:20). That divine grace is to be found, and celebrated, in the most unexpected of places: not among the wise and powerful, but among babies; not among kings and prophets, but among disciples and those whose eyes they open. This is the mysterious working of God, who (not the devil, 4:6) has given Jesus authority.

10:25–42. Parable and Hospitality: Doing and Hearing the Word. Jesus' message has emphasized the dual necessity of attentive hearing and faithful doing of the word (e.g., 6:46–49; 8:21). The next two scenes reinforce this theme, highlighting first doing (10:25–37), then hearing (vv. 38–42).

10:25–37. A "lawyer" (specialist in interpretation of Torah) puts Jesus' practical wisdom to the test: "[W]hat must I do to inherit eternal life?" (v. 25). Jesus counters with a question of his own: What does the expert in the law find there? As Jesus does elsewhere in the Gospels (e.g., Mark 12:28–31), the man responds with a hybrid commandment. One who seeks enduring life must love God with one's whole being (citing Deut 6:5, a primary identity-shaping command for Jews) and also "love your neighbor as yourself" (citing Lev 19:18). Jesus commends the answer, which points to the source of real life—provided that people actually "do this" loving of God and neighbor.

Since the lawyer's motive was to test Jesus, he persists in interrogating, to "justify himself": Who is the neighbor one is directed to love? Self-justification is *not* a practice Jesus commends (Luke 16:15), but he responds as if his conversation partner is earnest. The answer takes the form of a provocative parable featuring a man severely beaten while on the road that descended sharply from Jerusalem to Jericho, together with a trio of potential rescuers. For undisclosed reasons, two men whom readers would expect to offer aid—a priest and another with a priestly role in the Temple (a Levite)—continue on their way without stopping. Jesus springs a surprise when he introduces as the story's hero a Samaritan, whom Jewish listeners would be inclined to despise (cf. 9:52–54). The narrator details the compassion-prompted aid the Samaritan renders. Then Jesus subverts the lawyer's previous question, which had probed the limits in the obligation to love neighbors, with a counter-question: "Which of these three ... was a neighbor to the man who fell into the hands of the robbers?" (v. 36). In Jesus' reframing of the matter under debate, "neighbor" is no longer the recipient of love but the *way* in which one lovingly

engages others. Since a detested Samaritan is the one whose compassionate action must be emulated (even the lawyer admits as much), love not only of enemies (6:27) but *from* enemies expresses God's gracious will for human life. So the parable challenges conventional social maps and boundaries.

10:38–42. If the preceding passage accented compassionate action that embodied the divine purpose, Luke now balances the mandate to "do" with a summons to attentive listening. The model to be emulated is a woman, Mary, whose desire to attend to Jesus' teaching contrasts with her sister Martha's preoccupation with the tasks of hospitality for their guest. This vignette scores two points simultaneously: women are equal partners with men in the company of disciples (cf. 8:1–3), and to be a disciple means to hear Jesus' word, a necessary step on the way to performing it. Hospitality is important, too (e.g., 14:10–24), but attending to "the word" is crucial.

11:1–13. Jesus Models and Commends Persistent Prayer. The disciples, who have observed Jesus' practice of prayer and know that John taught his disciples to pray, ask Jesus to give them similar instruction. He provides a model prayer, which has formed faith and voiced the heart's deep need for two millennia. Luke presents the prayer in a more compact form than Matt 6:9–13. The prayer's first line accents the honor of God, the "Father" whose gracious provision calls for answering love and allegiance and forms the basis for the ensuing petitions for (1) realization of God's reign; (2) provision of needed nourishment; (3) forgiveness, as petitioners themselves forgive all debts owed them; and (4) protection from overwhelming testing. Though not a comprehensive enumeration of human need, this is a suggestive template for prayer that voices need, relying in trust on God's gracious care.

11:5–13. With multiple images, Jesus develops the basis for sustained practice of prayer: trust in a gracious God. In a culture that placed great stock in the values of hospitality, friendship, and public reputation (honor), even a reluctant neighbor, despite personal inconvenience, will get up at midnight and share bread at a friend's over-the-top, shameless request (not *persistent*, as rendered in the NRSV). God may be trusted much more to provide for the needs of God's people. Jesus reinforces the point with a series of sayings that commend active, persistent prayer. Good results from continual asking, seeking, and knocking (the nuance of the present-tense imperatives in vv. 9–10). What is the ground for such seeking? The grace of a loving God whose gifts to human beings transcend the good gifts even fallible human parents offer their children—above all, the Holy Spirit. This last line guards against the potentially damaging interpretation that God is a cosmic goods-dispenser at one's beck and call and that faith means expecting God to meet one's every request. Whatever the request, God provides the empowering divine presence that humans *need*. While Jesus assumes, in support of his appeal for trusting prayer in God, that even "evil" fathers routinely give their children good gifts, the reality is often harshly and harmfully different. The lesser-to-greater argument Jesus is making is that God's gracious kindness toward people surpasses human parents' care for their children.

11:14–36. Jesus Answers Critics of His Ministry of Liberation. Conflict with Jesus' critics had faded to the background but now resumes, with a new focus of debate: the source and meaning of Jesus' exorcisms. Observers accuse Jesus of casting out demons "by Beelzebul, the ruler of the demons" (v. 15), while others "test" him by pressing for a "sign from heaven" (v. 16; cf. 4:3, 9). Jesus answers his critics with a series of counter-assertions. (1) The charge that Jesus' exorcisms betray alliance with the prince of evil is absurd, for Satan would be undermining his own regime. (2) None level similar charges at other Jewish exorcists. (3) In decisive, positive terms, Jesus' exorcisms point to the presence of God's powerful reign (the "finger of God," 11:20 echoes Exod 8:19). Jesus adds interpretive commentary: he is overpowering Satan and releasing people bound by evil forces. Reversing an earlier generous statement (9:50), he then declares, in the context of heated debate about his ministry's character and source, that anyone who is not allied with him (hence with God's reign) is "against me" (11:23). So Jesus turns his opponents' criticisms on their head. The activity they ascribe to evil Jesus reframes as the operation of God's realm, defeating evil powers and bringing "release to the captives" (cf. 4:18).

Jesus concludes his defense of his ministry with an arresting image: removal of an oppres-sive, distorting reality needs to be accompanied by positive construction of a new reality. Otherwise, a banished demon will bring back to an empty home seven spirits "more evil than itself" (11:26). Attentive listeners who hear Jesus' words and do them (a theme repeated in the next paragraph), who participate with him in acts of compassion and hospitality, will have houses filled to overflowing with good.

11:27–36. Swelling crowds are not necessarily a positive sign. For a second time, Jesus castigates his contemporaries (cf. 9:41), this time for seeking signs (cf. 11:15) while refusing to embrace the reordered life ("repentance") to which prophetic signs point. Unlike the queen of Sheba (1 Kgs 10:1–13), they fail to discern the moment (cf. Luke 12:54–56), and unlike the people of ancient Nineveh (Jonah 3), they fail to repent at the word of God's prophet. Even a woman who pronounces Jesus' mother blessed (cf. Luke 1:42, 48) receives correction: "Blessed rather are those who hear the word of God and obey it" (11:28). Verses 33–36 add sight to sound, stressing the importance of clear vision. Luke 11:27–36 thus emphasizes the integrity of self that results from sound perception—hearing God's word and seeing clearly—and faithful action. Jesus, perceiving with prophetic clarity, realizes that the fidelity of enthusiastic crowds has yet to be tested.

11:37–54. Conflict at Table (Again): Jesus Turns Up the Heat on His Critics. For a second time, Jesus accepts a Pharisee's dinner invitation (cf. 7:36–50), and the meal again becomes the occasion for conflict. The host's astonishment that Jesus neglects to wash his hands—where is his concern with ritual purity?—elicits from Jesus a sharp critique of Pharisees' practice. Preoccupation with outer purity cannot cover over interior "greed and wickedness" (cf. 16:14). The external practice that *does* align with interior purity is generous giving to the poor ("almsgiving," 11:41). Jesus intensifies his critique of Pharisees' practice: they are careful to tithe when it comes to spices, yet "neglect justice and the love of God" (v. 42). Without cancelling the obligation to tithe, Jesus makes clear which claim on human obedience is primary. He also faults Pharisees for concern with public affirmation, and closes with a stinging, ironic rebuke for a group that prizes ritual purity: "[Y]ou are like unmarked graves, and people walk over them [becoming ritually impure] without realizing it" (v. 44).

Another meal guest, a teacher of the law, objects to Jesus' rebuke of Pharisees, feeling himself implicated, too, and Jesus turns up the heat. Teachers of the Torah weigh others down with burdensome obligations and withhold the beneficial knowledge they possess, even aligning themselves with ancestors who murdered the prophets. The long-standing clash attested in Israel's Scripture between divine servants and a resistant people will culminate in the response of "this generation" to "prophets and apostles" whom God sends. Eventually, violent repudiation of God's messengers will bring judgment.

The meal's aftermath is unsurprising; teachers whom Jesus has criticized reciprocate the hostility and seek opportunities to spring a verbal trap on him. In an era when polarizing conflict immobilizes church and political system alike and when it is easy to lob verbal missiles at others with whom one disagrees, it is imperative to temper the harsh polemic of this passage with Jesus' call elsewhere in Luke to "love enemies" and emulate God's mercy (e.g., 6:27–36). Nevertheless, people who hold power but "neglect justice" and mercy do deserve to be "called out."

12:1–12. Directions for Witness in the Face of Conflict. Despite enormous crowds, the road to Jerusalem will bring intensifying conflict, as Simeon predicted (2:34–35), and the apostles' later mission will immerse them in conflict as well (e.g., Acts 5, 7, 22). Jesus therefore begins the disciples' formation for witness in the face of conflict. First, he warns against hypocrisy—maintaining appearances, but allowing action to be out of sync with heart. What is hidden will come to light, and what is whispered in secret will become public.

Jesus urges courageous witness before hostile rulers, trusting in God's care ("even the hairs of your head are all counted," v. 7) and relying upon the empowerment of the Holy Spirit. Loyal witness will receive divine affirmation, even if that witness results in suffering and death (cf. 21:12–19), while those who deny the Son of Man "will be denied before the angels of God" (12:9). Yet forgiveness extends even to those who speak against the Son of Man—a good thing for Peter, for whom denial of his Lord will not be the last word (22:54–62).

If one slanders (NRSV, "blasphemes") the Holy Spirit, however, one is beyond hope, for one can no longer perceive the holy, powerful working of God as good. The cutting edge of these words is sharpened by the earlier repudiation of Jesus' acts of healing as demonic (11:14–23).

12:13–34. Teaching on Wealth and Well-being. Jesus often addresses the subject of wealth and poverty in Luke's Gospel, and does so in radical ways (already anticipated by Mary's song, 1:46–55). How will one whose mission delivers good news to the poor (4:18; cf. 6:20) and bad news to the rich (6:24) respond when asked to divide a family inheritance (a household scenario to which Jesus will return in 15:11–32)? In an ironic reversal of Moses' spurned mediation attempt in Exodus ("Who made you a ruler and judge over us?" Exod 2:14), Jesus refuses to mediate: "Who set me to be a judge or arbitrator over you?" (Luke 12:14). He warns against the greed he discerns in the request, which misses the truth that "life does not consist in the abundance of possessions" (v. 15). To illustrate, Jesus tells a parable about a rich man whose abundant harvest outpaced his storage capacity. Rather than share his good fortune—his food—with others, he tears down his barns and builds larger ones to "store all *my* grain and *my* goods" (v. 18) and ensure a life of comfort and security. All an illusion! What happens to his abundance if he dies that night? Jesus clinches the point: preoccupation with treasure for self and wealth that honors God (and thus is shared with others; cf. vv. 33–34) are mutually exclusive.

12:22–34. Jesus now reinforces the lesson for his disciples. They should take their cue not from the anxiety-driven acquisitiveness people exhibit but from nature. One may trust in the gracious provision of God, who clothes flowers and nourishes birds and will certainly care for human children. Strive not for goods but for God's reign, Jesus urges, and God will provide what is needed; indeed, the loving "Father" to whom one prays (11:2, 13) will even make a *gift* of God's realm. This life freed from oppressive concern with possessions and security will grasp less and release more (for the benefit of the poor) and open up access to enduring treasure. In an age dominated by concerns with economic systems, financial security, and the quest to acquire goods or to maintain what one already possesses, Jesus' teaching in 12:22–34 is countercultural. He employs exaggeration, for one still needs to work to obtain food and clothing (birds work for food, too). Yet these words have a strange appeal, as they invite—while also challenging—readers to make God's concerns their primary commitment. Thus they may live by trust in God's generosity, and emulate it in their dealings with others, rather than by acquisitiveness that seeks to maintain self-advantage.

12:35–13:9. Instruction on Discerning the Moment. Jesus continues his project of (trans) forming disciples for God's realm, addressing first disciples (12:35–53) and then crowds (12:54–13:9) on the topic of discernment. How should one order life in the present moment, when God's reign is at hand?

12:35–53. Still speaking to disciples, Jesus shifts to a new topic: knowing what time it is and ordering life accordingly. Contrasting images picture the importance of vigilant preparation: (1) slaves are rewarded for remaining alert to open the door for their master at his late-night return from a wedding banquet; and (2) knowledge of the timing of a potential burglar's intrusion enables a homeowner to take preventive action. Just so, disciples must remain vigilant as they await the Son of Man's unpredictable arrival, first appearance of a motif that will become increasingly prominent: Jesus' future (post-Easter) return, or parousia (see 17:22–37; 21:27; cf. 19:11–27).

Peter presses for clarification: does Jesus intend this message for disciples or for a wider audience? Jesus explains the parable with another, this time featuring a household manager (steward) who supervises other slaves. A faithful manager stays on the job and treats his supervisees fairly, even if the master delays in returning. Those entrusted with greater responsibility are expected to produce accordingly. While everyone is called to be faithful in the time before the Lord's return, leaders of the community of disciples (e.g., apostles) bear special responsibility. Throughout the remainder of his ministry, Jesus will equip them to perform wisely their particular leadership role (carried out in Acts).

The apostles' leadership role involves more than relationships within the household (community of disciples), for the arrival of God's reign provokes intense opposition in the world.

Elsewhere, Jesus speaks of his mission in terms of seeking and saving the lost (19:10; cf. 5:32; 15:1–32). In 12:49–53, he inscribes the other side of the coin: in a world that repudiates concern with people located on the social margins, Jesus came to kindle a blazing fire, to undergo a baptism (of death), and to bring division—even disrupting intimate household relationships, and so rewriting the script for the mission of John, the latter-day Elijah (cf. 1:7; Mal 4:6). From beginning to end, he restores God's people but also is a "sign that [is] opposed" (Luke 2:34). God's reign is countercultural, not least in its demand for commitment that transcends allegiance to family (cf. 9:59–62).

12:54–13:9. Jesus shifts attention to the crowds, summoning them, too, to wise discernment of the historical moment, and what it asks of them. They may be able to read the weather but they fail to read the times—the appearance of God's reign among them, liberating the oppressed, saving the lost, deposing evil powers, and fashioning a community marked by God's expansive grace (the "year of the Lord's favor," 4:19). What does such an extraordinary moment ask of God's people? They must recognize the present as the time for decisive action, whether setting things right with a legal adversary or reordering life to align with God's purposes ("repenting"). The misfortunes of others (e.g., worshipers killed by order of the brutal Roman governor Pontius Pilate and victims of a tower's collapse) do not result from their wickedness. But such disasters should prompt honest self-examination and reordering of one's commitments and actions; it would be foolish to presume that life will go on forever and that one can delay getting it right.

Jesus reinforces this appeal with another brief parable (unique to Luke) about a fig tree that fails to bear fruit. The owner is ready to chop it down, but when the farmer who tends the tree pleads to give it another year, he agrees. God, too, is patient and merciful, but now is the time to reorient life toward God's purposes. Next year the ax may be called into action. Jesus' message here recalls that of his predecessor John (3:9). There is no time like the present to discern well, and to act courageously, allowing one's life to be shaped by, and for, God's transformation of the world.

13:10–21. Sabbath Liberation for a Woman. For the second time, Jesus interrupts a synagogue teaching session on the Sabbath to heal a person (cf. 6:6–11), again inciting hostile response; the synagogue leader urges him to heal on the other six days (14:1–6 narrates a third healing controversy on the Sabbath). In his messianic ministry, though, Jesus liberates the oppressed—this woman's physical ailment is depicted as an eighteen-year binding by Satan—in a Jubilee year of release (4:18–19, 21) that knows no "sacred" day interruptions. Even farm animals are released from their stalls to get water on the Sabbath, so why not set this woman free? The contrasting reactions to the event speak volumes: the healed woman praises God and the crowd rejoices, while Jesus' critics are "put to shame" (v. 17). God's people are being restored, and at the same time divided, by Jesus' ministry.

With two compact parables (actually, similes), Jesus interprets the healing that has just occurred. It is God's reign in action, transforming human life. Often this happens in improbable ways, where the outcome belies insignificant or obscure beginnings. Imagine a tiny mustard seed growing into a tree that offers birds a home, or a woman adding a small amount of yeast to flour and so producing fully leavened bread. So it is with God's realm; the world is undergoing transformation, but only faith discerns it and praises God.

13:22–35. More Images of God's Reign: Reversal—and a Prophet's Destiny.
Luke reminds readers of the goal of Jesus' journeying; mention of Jerusalem frames the unit, which highlights the inside-out reversal effected in God's realm and graphically pictures the destiny awaiting Jesus. Perhaps reacting to the growing hostility to Jesus' activity, someone from the crowd queries whether only a few would "be saved" (v. 23). With the image of difficult entrance through a "narrow door," Jesus confirms that many will fail to enter (i.e., the domain of God, or life), though he does not say that only a few will experience salvation. Undermining presumption of inclusion in God's realm, Jesus offers no guarantee for those who have known the Lord's presence or heard his teaching or even enjoyed meal fellowship with him, nor for those who belong to God's chosen people. God's realm belongs instead to outsiders, people from every corner of the earth, and those who are at the bottom ("last," v. 30). So the dramatic inside-out, upside-down reversal that marks

God's realm is a matter of divine grace. Yet, as the warning to "all you evildoers" shows (v. 27), those who answer God's gracious welcome respond by both hearing and doing God's will. Intimate association with Jesus and affirmation of his status as Lord cannot replace living by the vision for human life that he advocates (cf. 6:46–49; 8:19–21).

Prophets whose words point to God's ways typically meet rejection, and Jesus entertains no illusion that he will fare differently. When Pharisees warn him of Herod's designs on his life, Jesus dismisses the notion, confident that his mission of healing has not run its course and that his prophet's date with death will come later, at Jerusalem. The holy city's penchant for violent rejection of God's messengers elicits from Jesus a lament for "your house" (i.e., Temple), left empty until he will be greeted with acclamations—but even then only as prelude to his crucifixion (see 19:38). The sword prophesied to pierce Mary's soul (2:35) now takes direct aim at her son's.

14:1–24. Table Talk Once More: Redrawing Social Maps in the Light of God's Reign.
A third meal in a Pharisee's home provides the occasion for another Sabbath healing, this time of a man with dropsy (a condition marked by fluid retention and swelling, interpreted in that social world as evidence of greed). Posing questions before and after the healing, Jesus implies that healing on the Sabbath does not conflict with the Torah; this merciful rescue is no more problematic than the accepted action of lifting an ox or a child from a pit. His critics fall silent.

The behavior of status-conscious meal guests prompts Jesus to offer advice on meal practices, and then a parable, challenging conventional notions of honor. At a wedding banquet, one should "take the lowest place"; honor (public reputation)—a prized value in Jesus' culture—will be enhanced when the host invites one to take a position conveying greater honor. Indeed, in God's topsy-turvy world, the humble will receive greatest honor (a line repeated in 18:14; cf. 1:48, 51–53). Jesus then addresses the host. While it was customary to invite to a meal persons capable of reciprocating and thus enhancing one's honor, Jesus gives countercultural counsel: "[I]nvite the poor, the crippled, the lame, and the blind" (14:13). God, source of the only honor that matters, will be the one to reciprocate, granting a share in the "resurrection of the righteous" (v. 14). There is hope for persons with wealth, it seems, if they share generously with those in need, joining Jesus in "bring[ing] good news to the poor" (4:18; cf. 6:20; 7:22).

At mention of the "resurrection of the righteous," a dinner guest toasts the good fortune of those who "will eat bread in the kingdom of God" (14:15). Jesus responds with a parable challenging complacent assurance that one will have a place at that table. What happens when everyone who had accepted a dinner invitation requests, at the last minute, to be excused? The host fills the hall, drawing guests from the "poor, the crippled, the blind, and the lame" and even outsiders to the village, effectively excluding those originally invited. One would only miss the greatest party in town, opting instead to tend to routine business, because one has failed to discern the moment (cf. 12:54–59). This parable depicts God's realm as a domain of grace, where all sorts of people find welcome and nourishment. But one does need to accept the invitation.

14:25–35. The Cost of Following Jesus. All is not festive banquets in Jesus' company. With the crowds swelling, Jesus issues a sharp warning; one must become a disciple with eyes wide open, counting the cost. As a wise builder does not start a major project without sufficient funds and a king does not start a war if he lacks the forces needed to win, potential disciples should consider the demands of that vocation: placing commitment to God's realm above all else, even allegiance to family (the practical meaning of the insistence that one "hate" family [v. 26]); bearing a cross (cf. 9:23); and surrendering possessions (generously sharing with those in need). God's realm is marked by radical grace, but no less by radical, costly discipleship.

Luke appends obscure sayings about salt. Disciples are worth their salt only when they actually perform the job to which they have been recruited—announcing and embodying in actions and relationships the good news of God's reign.

15:1–32. Invitation to Party: Three Parables Interpreting Jesus' Ministry to the Lost. Jesus' ministry, including the intimacy of shared meals, again provokes criticism. Defending his embrace of sinners, Jesus offers three parables that picture God's gracious acceptance of those who are "lost." First, heaven's delight at the restoration of a sinner is like that of a shepherd who (improbably) abandons ninety-nine sheep to locate one that is lost and throws a party to celebrate its rescue. The implication is that Jesus risks alienating the righteous in order to restore hope to those who have lost their way. Pairing the shepherd with a woman who has lost one of her ten coins, Jesus repeats his affirmation of God's gracious care for the lost. The third parable, the longest extant parable of Jesus, initially follows the structure of the first two. A lost son is welcomed (though not sought) by his father, who invites the whole village to celebrate his return. The parable of the prodigal (extravagantly forgiving) father departs from the preceding pattern—and gives voice to the complaint of the righteous against Jesus' acceptance of sinners even before they have tangibly demonstrated their repentance, in the role played by the dutiful older son. The last part of the story narrates his understandable protest against his father's excessive mercy toward "this son of yours" (v. 30) and the father's plea to him to join the party to welcome "this brother of yours" (v. 32). Jesus' audience is left wondering what the older son will do, and Luke's audience ponders the response of Pharisees to Jesus' invitation. He welcomes sinners, yet has no desire to exclude the righteous. However, they have a decision to make.

16:1–31. Wisdom and Integrity in Use of Wealth. Jesus shifts attention from Pharisees back to disciples, though Pharisees remain interested, if skeptical, listeners. Chapter 16 probes wise use of material resources, expressing fidelity to God's ways as revealed in Scripture.

16:1–13. An enigmatic parable features a manager who engages in questionable business practices, and Luke appends brief sayings on faithful use of wealth that tame the difficult parable. Fired for "squandering [a rich man's] property" (v. 1), his business manager concocts a shrewd survival plan. By reducing the amounts owed by the rich man's debtors, the manager ("steward") ensures that he will receive a friendly welcome, if not employment, in their homes. The rich man, his hands tied by the manager's generosity, on his behalf, toward the debtors—he would not dare to reinstate the forgiven debts, thus forfeiting honor in the community—can only commend his cunning former manager. Ironically, the manager wins his master's praise by doing what got him fired, squandering the rich man's property.

The parable plays with a prominent Lukan concern, responsible use of material resources, but its message is elusive. Evidently Luke found the parable difficult; the following sayings counter the notion that Jesus is commending dishonesty as a business practice. Far from it, to judge from vv. 8b–13. Only persons who handle money honestly will have anything of value entrusted to them. Indeed, allegiance to money and allegiance to God are fundamentally conflicting values (v. 13). Verses 8b–9 spin the parable's plot in a more positive direction: God's people ("children of light") must be wise just like the manager, making "friends" by using "unrighteous wealth" (author's trans.)—sharing generously with the poor.

16:14–31. Pharisees who overhear the assertion that service to God is incompatible with service to wealth mock Jesus, prompting him to affirm the law's enduring validity, then tell a parable that connects the claim of the law to wise use of possessions. First, Jesus redirects the quest for honor from a human public to God and declares that the claim of God's law remains even in the new reality of God's realm inaugurated by John the Baptizer, illustrating that claim with a difficult saying about divorce and remarriage (v. 18; though the statement goes beyond what Mosaic law says about divorce; see Deut 24:1–4).

Then, countering the Pharisees' dismissal of his teaching about wealth, Jesus tells a parable that enacts the role reversal announced by Mary's song (Luke 1:53) and his earlier pronouncement of blessing for the poor and woe for the rich (6:20, 24). A destitute man named Lazarus unsuccessfully begs for food, day after day, at a rich man's gate, but when they die, their roles are reversed. Lazarus enjoys the company of the patriarch Abraham (cf. 13:28–30), while the rich man suffers torment. The last movement of the parable returns to the theme of the law's enduring validity. If the rich man's brothers do not practice what both law and prophets teach about right use of wealth, even the message of one raised from death will have no impact. The realm of God, including resurrection, does not nullify God's claim on human obedience, as expressed in law and prophets alike. Jesus did not invent the call to generous

sharing of resources with the poor; it is a profound biblical theme. He does, however, give the theme radical expression as he embodies God's upside-down realm: "Blessed are you who are poor . . . . But woe to you who are rich, for you have received your consolation" (6:20, 24).

17:1–19. Images of Grace, Faithful Service, and Boundary-transgressing Gratitude. Jesus turns his attention to the disciples, accenting forgiveness, faith, and service. First, a dose of realism: mistakes that cause others difficulty are inevitable, but that does not lessen accountability, especially when it is "one of these little ones" (presumably a child) who is affected (vv. 1–2; cf. 9:47–48; 18:15–17). Those who do wrong are accountable and must reorder life, but disciples are also to forgive, and forgive again. Forgiveness is difficult, however, so the disciples ask to have their capacity for faith expanded. With hyperbole—the image of mustard-seed faith planting a tree in the sea— Jesus replies that the disciples have enough faith but need to exercise it. And faith and service go hand in hand; disciples may rely, but not presume, on divine grace. Jesus later reverses the image, picturing himself serving the disciples at table—but to inspire, not cancel, their own humble service toward others (22:27).

17:11–19. Life-transforming faith is not the disciples' exclusive property. On the route to Jerusalem (aptly in a liminal space "between Samaria and Galilee," v. 11), Jesus encounters ten lepers who seek healing. When he sends them to the priests (to attest their restoration to purity) and they find themselves made clean, only one—a Samaritan—returns, praising God, to thank Jesus. Astonished that "this foreigner" alone modeled grateful praise of God, Jesus comments that his "faith has made [him] well," v. 19). God's saving work continues to turn the social world—and the domain of faith—inside out. Outsiders receive welcome into God's realm.

17:20–18:8. Authentic Faith(fulness) When God's Reign Delays. God's reign is already evident in Jesus' ministry, which proclaims good news and embodies salvation for all who are open, in faith, to receiving it. Nevertheless, full realization of God's purposes for the world remains a matter of hope. This section of the Gospel highlights the tension between present and future expressions of God's realm, and its implications for human faith.

17:20–37. Pharisees, who share with Jesus an expectation of God's coming rule (including resurrection; see 20:27–40; Acts 23:6–9), query him about its timing. In reply, Jesus affirms God's reign as present, though unrecognized. Those who cannot discern God at work now will not be helped by the enumeration of signs for which to watch. However, Jesus provides disciples a more specific scenario for the coming of the Son of Man, an event associated with the future expression of God's reign. Life and history will test faith, for the completion of God's purposes, symbolized by the glorious arrival of the Son of Man, will not occur promptly and will be preceded by his suffering and death. During a time of waiting, routine activities of life will take over, so that on "the day that the Son of Man is revealed" (v. 30), vigilance will be a challenge, as it was for the contemporaries of Noah and Lot. The ensuing images continue a tone of urgency and crisis for both life and faith. When "the day" comes, one should not retrieve possessions, return home, or hold securely onto life. The unstated positive appeal is to entrust one's future entirely to God. So humanity will be divided, with one of a pair taken and the other left, and those left behind will inhabit a world marked by the reality of death (v. 37). The path to divine glory passes through suffering and death (cf. 24:26). In a world, and a future, such as this, will faith persist?

18:1–8. Jesus adds a parable that affirms the importance—and challenge—of trusting faith in a world where realization of God's rule delays. A widow's quest for justice must overcome not only her legal adversary but also the inaction of a contemptuous judge who should have respected her vulnerable situation. Her persistent demands for justice wear down the judge, and out of his own self-interest he finally vindicates her. If such a judge will deliver justice, how much more may people of faith trust in God for vindication! Nevertheless, lived experience and ongoing historical struggles will test faith and lead to discouragement, so that one must persist in trusting prayer. Only so will faith endure until the coming of the Son of Man.

18:9–30. Status Inversion in God's Realm. A parable, an object lesson on the character of God's realm, and a dialogue with a man on a religious

quest highlight the reversals of role and status in Jesus' ministry.

18:9–14. Despite heated debates between Jesus and Pharisees (5:17–6:11; 7:36–50; 11:37–54; 14:1–24; 15:1–2; 16:14–15), his audience would perceive Pharisees as models of piety, religiously and morally serious people who seek to be faithful to God's will as revealed in Torah. Tax collectors, by contrast, would be viewed as models of sinfulness, disloyal and dishonest. Yet Jesus tells a parable in which a tax collector's humble plea for mercy, not a Pharisee's confident prayer of gratitude for his impeccable faithfulness, is heard; it is the sinner who leaves Temple worship "justified" (vindicated by God). The narrator's description of the parable's audience and Jesus' clinching statement of its point leave little to speculation. Role reversal in God's dominion is both horizontal and vertical. (1) Only God's assessment of righteousness (or sinfulness) matters, and sinners who accept God's gracious forgiveness, not righteous Pharisees who protest, have inside position. So with this parable, Jesus again explains and defends his embrace of sinners. (2) God's realm honors the lowly and humble, and demotes the self-important. The next two vignettes further develop this latter, upside-down reversal.

18:15–30. For a second time, Jesus presents children as exemplars of God's work in the world (cf. 9:46–48). Disciples obstruct babies' access to Jesus (evidently having forgotten Jesus' warning in 17:2!), but he welcomes the children and affirms them, low in status, as model participants in God's realm.

A wealthy "ruler," who enjoys status children lack, brings his quest for "eternal life" to Jesus. If children are paradigm-setters for God's reign, what place will a member of the social elite have? Jesus points him to a sampling of the Ten Commandments, which the man has faithfully kept. The enduring life of God's realm is defined by grace, to be sure, but it also means doing God's will (cf. 8:21; 10:25–28; 16:16–17). However, an obstacle still blocks the man's quest. Jesus challenges him to divest himself of wealth to benefit the poor, and to become a disciple. Unable to abandon his wealth, he departs with resigned sorrow, prompting Jesus to comment on the impossible possibility of wealthy people entering God's realm. What human beings cannot accomplish, however (camels navigating needles?), God is able to do, as readers soon discover (19:1–10). Unlike the rich ruler, Peter remarks, disciples have left everything, including home and family, to follow Jesus; indeed, they will have their reward both now and in the life that is still to come.

18:31–19:27. Images and Acts of Salvation near Jerusalem: Divergent Responses to God's Realm. As Jesus approaches Jerusalem, a preview of coming danger collides with images of salvation. With a last parable before entering the holy city, Jesus interprets the divergent responses attending his ministry as bearer of God's rule.

18:31–34. Disciples are not the only ones called to sacrifice for God's realm. For a fourth time, and in vivid detail (including mention of Gentile participants), Jesus explicitly announces his coming suffering and death—fulfilling prophetic Scriptures (cf. 9:22, 44; 17:25). Still, the disciples fail to understand (cf. 9:45). Such a horrific outcome to the Messiah's career defies comprehension.

18:35–43. Ironically, a blind beggar perceives more clearly. Despite the crowd's efforts to silence him, he petitions the "Son of David" for mercy, and Jesus delivers: "Receive your sight; your faith has saved you" (v. 42; or "made you well," as in 7:50; 17:19). Salvation is evident in the gift of sight, but even more in the man's response. He "sees" what God's grace has provided and follows Jesus, his praise of God inspiring praise from "all the people." Sight and salvation, discipleship and praise: positive images of God's reign accumulate on the eve of Jesus' arrival in Jerusalem.

19:1–10. Inside-out reversal that typifies salvation recurs when Jesus encounters a wealthy "chief tax collector," Zacchaeus, in Jericho. The diminutive tax collector finds himself up a tree attempting to see Jesus, who calls him down and insists on staying with him. The crowd, picking up the Pharisees' refrain, grumbles at Jesus' intimacy with a notorious sinner. Yet the social transaction at Zacchaeus's home reveals that "[t]oday salvation has come to this house" (19:9), to a child of Abraham whose membership in God's people is not forfeited by conspicuous wealth (contrast the misfortune of another child of Abraham in 16:24–30), social marginality, or dishonest business practices. Disqualifying wealth is no hindrance for Zacchaeus's entry into life, as the head of local

taxation pledges to compensate people he has cheated and to give half his wealth to the poor—another image of salvation, a life transformed in response to Jesus' acceptance.

19:11–27. Arrival at Jerusalem, just after mention of the presence of salvation "today" at Zacchaeus's home, triggers hope that God's realm is imminent. Jesus counters this expectation with a parable explaining that the Messiah, Israel's rightful ruler, will receive royal honors only after his people have rejected him. In Jerusalem, not the realm of God but crucifixion awaits.

Luke stitches this royal claimant sub-plot to a parable that describes the varying success of investments made by the ruler-in-waiting's slaves during his absence. Only those who risk letting the money go (as they do business) prove obedient to their master and win his praise—and a share in his political power (authority over cities). The slave who banked on security, keeping the money safe and returning it without profit, loses everything. Discipleship, like Messiahship, exposes one to risk; those who play it safe will find themselves left out of the Messiah's grace-filled, power-sharing dominion. This parable advocates courageous, faithful service; the followers Jesus leaves behind to continue his mission are accountable for what they do with what he has entrusted to them.

III. The Final Days (19:28–25:53)

A. Climactic Teaching Ministry in Jerusalem (19:28–21:38)

Jesus finally reaches the holy city, goal of his journeys since 9:51, and teaches in the Temple. As before, his activity evokes sharply divergent responses, but now the stakes are higher; the power-wielding elite in Jerusalem look for a way to eliminate him.

19:28–44. Divine Visitation Welcomed and Resisted. Jesus prepares to enter Jerusalem, descending from the Mount of Olives. He sees to the choreography himself, arranging suitable transportation, a colt fit for a king (as in Zech 9:9). As he rides in triumph into the city, the "multitude of the disciples" shout God's praises: "Blessed is the king who comes in the name of the Lord! Peace in heaven, and glory in the highest heaven!" (Luke 19:38). Although this acclamation recalls the angelic chorus after Jesus' birth (2:14), the relocation of peace from earth to heaven is striking. Divine visitation, with its offer of peace, will go unrecognized by Jerusalem. The Pharisees, in their final appearance in the Gospel, seek to silence the disciples' acclamation of Jesus as king (cf. 13:35). Then, delivering another prophetic oracle, Jesus laments the holy city's repudiation of God's visitation to grant peace, and foresees enemy forces surrounding the city (an image to which Jesus will return in 21:20–24). Israel's Messiah approaches his destiny, one that defies expectation—except his own, informed by his reading of Israel's Scriptures (9:22, 44; 17:25; 18:31–33; cf. 24:26–27, 44–46).

19:45–21:4. Jesus, Son of God, Among the Teachers in the Temple (Part Two). Jesus' culminating activity as teacher reprises his session with the teachers in the Temple as a youth (2:46–49). First, he reclaims the Temple for its intended purpose, expelling merchants from a sacred space that had been converted from a "house of prayer" to a "den of robbers" (drawing phrasing from Isa 56:7; Jer 7:11). Jesus then teaches each day in the Temple, his message driving a wedge between a receptive people and their leaders (including the priests who manage the Temple system), who want him dead. This power bloc sends a delegation to challenge Jesus' authority. He counters with a question: Was the prophet John's legitimation human or divine in origin? Realizing the trap Jesus has set (the same divide between receptive people and resistant elite resulted from John's ministry), the leaders confess their ignorance and Jesus refuses to answer their query.

He then tells the people a parable about a group of tenants who treat agents of their absentee landlord contemptuously and murder the owner's son, having taken designs on the land themselves. The allegorical cast of the parable is obvious: the owner of this vineyard (symbol of the nation, in its unjust practices, Isa 5:1–7) has a "beloved son" who is killed outside the vineyard. With this parable, Jesus interprets his rejection by leaders of his people and anticipates the divine judgment to follow. Acts 3–5 will begin to tell the story of this transfer of leadership over the vineyard (Israel) from one set of tenants (the Jerusalem elite) to another (the apostles). Even now, however, the powerful elite grasp the point. The parable chal-

lenges their authority, yet fear of the people prevents their moving against him, momentarily. Jesus places his rejection by the elite in scriptural context, picturing a stone rejected by builders as a cornerstone (tapping Isa 8:14–15). The Temple, whose stones will become a heap of ruins (Luke 21:5–6), must yield to a rejected stone that brings to ruin all who fall against it. So the crucified Messiah, bearer of salvation to God's people, remains a "sign opposed," resulting in the "falling and the rising of many in Israel" (2:34).

The elite priests and scribes next send "spies" to secure grounds for accusation of Jesus before the Roman governor. What better tack than to force Jesus to take a public stand on the unpopular obligation to pay taxes to Rome? Not to be outwitted, Jesus points to a coin sporting the image of the emperor. The conclusion seems unavoidable: "Pay to the emperor what belongs to the emperor [no basis for a charge of treason here], and to God what belongs to God [the claims of God trump any human authority]" (20:25, author's trans.; cf. Acts 5:29). Jesus' adversaries, still thwarted by the people, depart in silence.

Sadducees then ask Jesus about resurrection, a notion this elite priestly group does not affirm because the books of Moses lack explicit attestation (cf. Acts 23:6–10). The Sadducees ridicule resurrection belief through a *reductio ad absurdum*: In the resurrection life, who will be the husband of a woman married successively to seven brothers? Jesus' reply pictures marriage as a matter for this life, not the afterlife, and presents the message Moses heard at the burning bush—"God of Abraham ... Isaac, and ... Jacob"—in support of resurrection faith. God is God of the (perpetually) living (Luke 20:37–38). Scribes overhearing the exchange commend Jesus' answer, and the flurry of questions ends. However, Jesus has some barbs of his own to offer.

For Luke, David is Jesus' ancestor (1:32; cf. 2:4; 3:31), though his divine sonship is of greater import (1:32, 35; cf. 3:22; 9:35). Jesus now questions the tradition that the Messiah is "David's son" (20:41). If, according to Ps 110:1, King David called the Messiah "Lord," how can David's Lord—of superior status—be his son, lower in status? The argument is not about Davidic ancestry (which the narrative affirms) but Jesus' status as God's anointed ruler. It is through God's raising of Jesus from death that David's descendant comes to receive honor as Lord (asserted in Acts 2:29–36).

Jesus next cautions disciples (with "all the people" overhearing [Luke 20:45]) against conventional practices for seeking honor. Socially elite scribes who covet public reputation and construct a façade of piety while "devour[ing] widows' houses" win no approval from God (vv. 46–48). Jesus again presses his point about role reversal when he observes rich people placing their gifts into the Temple treasury, while a widow deposits two small coins. Her gift exceeds in value their much larger donations, the generosity of the poor outstripping that of the wealthy. Following the critique of 20:47 ("condemnation" for those who "devour widows' houses"), a widow's praise turns into Jesus' prophetic indictment of the Temple system's exploitation of the poor.

21:5–38. Words of Judgment and Hope for Disciples.
The Temple, site of Jesus' final public teaching, was impressive—and headed for ruin. Jesus presents a discourse about "last things," forecasting the destruction to befall Jerusalem and Temple, and summoning hearers to persevering trust in divine vindication.

Despite natural catastrophe and international strife, the end of history will delay, even if prophets announce its imminent arrival. An era of intense crisis will test faith but also afford opportunity for witness before religious and political powers, with assurance of divine guidance and protection (prophecy fulfilled in Acts). When Roman armies surround Jerusalem, the demise of city and Temple is imminent, and listeners should keep their distance. Gentile subjugation of the holy city will be temporary, but devastating. Finally, *after* Jerusalem's fall (which lies in the past [70 CE] for Luke's audience), cosmic portents will anticipate the glorious return of the Son of Man, which brings liberation for the faithful.

As the appearance of leaves on fig trees signals summer's approach, these dramatic events prefigure God's realm. Already present and, by anticipation, enacted in Jesus' ministry, God's reign will decisively transform the world—a basis for confident hope for Luke's audience. Even if the universe disappears, Jesus' word is reliable. He calls for enduring trust, vigilance, and faithful-

ness through time of crisis, until time itself runs out. The narrator follows this discourse about last things with the image of Jesus teaching the people each day in the Temple and resting each night on the Mount of Olives. Suspense continues to build; with enraptured people and enraged leaders, when will the prophet-Messiah who has predicted the Temple's destruction meet his destiny in the city where God's prophets perish (13:33–34)?

B. Ministry During the Passion (22:1–23:56)

Jesus has concluded his public teaching, but not before deepening the divide between people drawn to his message and the elite who reject his legitimacy as a divine agent. As Passover approaches, conflict intensifies and events move quickly toward the end Jesus has forecast.

22:1–38. A Final Passover Meal.
The Passover festival brought thousands of pilgrims to Jerusalem each spring. This year's Passover, memorializing God's exodus liberation of the people (Exod 12), will bring liberation—through the death of a first-born son (of God) who is himself the agent of deliverance. Elite priests and scribes, bested by Jesus in debate, gain an unlikely ally, an intimate associate of Jesus. Judas Iscariot strikes a deal with the Temple authorities to hand Jesus to them at a time when the sympathetic crowds are not present. Luke's explanation—"Satan entered into Judas" (22:3)—signals that the arch-enemy of God's purposes has renewed his fierce testing of Jesus' fidelity (cf. 4:13).

Jesus seizes the initiative, arranging a last meal with his disciples and delivering a farewell discourse that encourages and warns the disciples whom Jesus leaves behind. Jesus refrains from eating and drinking at this, his last meal, vowing to abstain until the banquet in God's realm. He offers bread and cup to the disciples, symbol of his body and life-blood, given for their benefit. Luke's words about bread and cup are distinctive, with repeating parallelism: eating (vv. 15–16)—cup (vv. 17–18)—bread (v. 19)—cup (v. 20). (This unusual pattern confused copyists, whose reworking of the text left its exact shape uncertain; some manuscripts omit all or part of vv. 19b–20, thus lacking the interpretation of the cup as "the new covenant in my blood," v. 20.) Meals in Jesus' ministry extended hospitality, especially to sinners and those of low status, and were characterized by joy. However, this is not another festive meal, nor one that enacts God's realm (cf. 14:15–24), but a somber leave-taking that enacts betrayal by a friend, whose identity remains hidden from the disciples, though not the reader (6:16; 22:3–6).

Having just heard that one of their number would betray Jesus, the disciples argue about who is greatest, as if Jesus had not repeatedly pictured God's household subverting conventional status-seeking. So he repeats the point: not the powerful are great but the youngest, those who serve— with Jesus himself the model to emulate.

Despite their failure to comprehend basic values of God's realm, the disciples win Jesus' commendation for their loyalty. He invites them to share in his rule over Israel; they will join him at festive meals in God's realm but also in his rule over the twelve tribes (a pledge that begins to be realized in Acts 3–5).

Jesus then singles out Simon Peter. Satan's malevolent designs on disciples notwithstanding, Jesus has prayed for Peter's perseverance in faith, yet he urges Peter to encourage the rest when he has "turned back," implying his failure, too. Peter protests that his commitment to Jesus will extend to prison and even death, bravado that earns a swift rebuke. Before dawn, Peter will three times have denied knowing his Lord. However, danger to life and loyalty awaits other disciples, too. For the peril that lies ahead, Jesus reverses his mission directive to travel light and rely on strangers' hospitality (cf. 9:3–4; 10:4–7). Now disciples should take purse and bag, and even purchase a sword, for Jesus must be "counted among the lawless" (22:37, echoing Isa 53:12). The two swords the disciples produce for inspection are "enough" (Luke 22:38); Jesus employs the sword as metaphor of the danger that is coming, not to advocate violent resistance.

22:39–53. Prayer, Testing, and Arrest. With crisis looming, Jesus retreats to the Mount of Olives and finds strength through prayer; the disciples, overwhelmed by grief, surrender to sleep rather than pray to escape "the time of trial" (vv. 40, 45–46; cf. 11:4). Despite earlier assertions of the inevitability of his suffering and death (9:22, 44; 17:25; 18:31–33; 22:22), Jesus petitions his "Father" to spare him the "cup" he must drink, but embraces God's will (v. 42). The

narrator depicts Jesus receiving an angel's support even as he continues to pray so intensely that his profuse sweat resembles drops of blood, a graphic display of anguish omitted in some manuscripts. Jesus faces death with courage but would have preferred life. Still, having drawn upon his customary resource (prayer), he is ready, unlike his sleepy followers, for what will happen next.

A crowd appears, led by Judas; ironically, the arrest will not, after all, occur in the absence of a "crowd" (v. 47; cf. 22:6). Before Judas can plant a kiss on his master's cheek, Jesus reframes this gesture of friendship as an act of betrayal. Unidentified members of the party accompanying Jesus brandish swords and one cuts off an ear of the high priest's slave. Jesus, though, halts the violence and (in a distinctively Lukan touch) heals the wounded man. The teacher who advocated love of enemies practices what he preached (6:27–36). Now addressing those enemies directly, he asks why they did not seize him while he taught in the Temple; readers know the answer: the power bloc feared the people (22:2). This is their moment, however; "darkness" (i.e., evil) rules—for now (v. 53*b*). Whatever else Luke may say about the Messiah's death as divinely purposed and prophetically scripted, it results from the decisions, and actions, of human agents who oppose the ways of God. They will not have the final word, however, as only this "hour" belongs to them.

22:54–71. Contrasting Witnesses: Peter Denies His Lord and Jesus Points to Divine Vindication. After Jesus is arrested and led to the high priest's residence, Luke's audience must wait to discover what will happen to him. First, the narrator follows Peter into the courtyard ("I am ready," he had vowed, "to go with you to prison and to death," v. 33). Three times, reacting to observers who link him to the arrested man, Peter denies connection to Jesus. Cascading events activate Peter's memory and bring him to remorse: on cue, the cock crows, and "[t]he Lord turned and looked at Peter" (v. 61). Realizing the enormity of his failure, Peter "went out and wept bitterly"— necessary prelude to his restoration. When Peter calls audiences to repentance in his sermons in Acts, he will speak from experience (Acts 2:38; 3:19; 5:31). Even sin of such shocking depth (cf. Luke 12:9) finds forgiveness from a God whose character is grace and mercy (6:36).

In contrast to Peter's failed testimony, Jesus, mocked and beaten, courageously testifies before an early morning council of elders. Their interrogation, garnering evidence for execution of Roman justice, probes whether Jesus claimed to be Messiah. He deflects the question but does speak of his imminent vindication, adapting imagery from Dan 7:13–14: "[F]rom now on the Son of Man will be seated at the right hand of the power of God" (Luke 22:69). This audacious claim prompts a follow-up query whether Jesus claimed to be Son of God. Jesus neither affirms nor denies the claim, putting its truth on his interrogators' lips, though, curiously, they condemn him for what they have heard "from his own lips" (v. 71). The outcome of the hearing is no surprise; the ruling elite were determined to have Jesus killed. The Roman agents of that death now step onto the stage.

23:1–25. Pilate and Herod Deal with an Inconvenient Truth. The Jewish leadership group brings Jesus before Pilate, whose cruelty has won notice (13:1). The Roman governor will draw the tetrarch Herod (Antipas) into the proceedings (23:6–7), and Herod's violent streak, too, is notorious (3:19–20; 9:9; 13:31). The proceedings hold a surprise, however, for Pilate repeatedly asserts that accusations against Jesus as a threat to Roman peace—corrupting the people, opposing payment of tax to Rome, and claiming to be king—lack any basis and attempts to release Jesus. Pilate sends the prisoner to Herod, hoping to sidestep a politically explosive situation (a vignette only Luke narrates among the canonical Gospels). Herod's soldiers mock the prisoner, but he returns a silent Jesus to Pilate, a gesture that the Roman governor interprets as recognition of the accused man's innocence and, improbably, helps patch serious differences between the two leaders. The irony is arresting; after encountering Jesus, even bitter foes are reconciled!

Present for the final session before Pilate are elite priests and other leaders, as well as "the people" (23:13). When Pilate announces his intention to have Jesus flogged and released, "they all" demand that Barabbas, a rebel jailed for murder, be released instead, and that Jesus be crucified. The scenario is repeated and Pilate relents, delivering Jesus to the death sentence "as they wished" (v. 25). The passion drama thus enacts the plot

of the parable of the throne claimant (19:12, 14); Jesus' own nation rejects its God-authorized ruler—not the last word about the people, but the basis for later appeals for repentance (Acts 2:23, 36, 38; 3:13–15, 17, 19; 5:30–31). The portrayal of Pilate is historically implausible; however, Luke is not bending history to defend Pilate but demonstrating that Jesus died a righteous man who did not merit death. God's suffering righteous one will die with courage and dignity that others fail to exhibit.

23:26–49. Crucifixion of God's Messiah. An undefined "they" lead Jesus to the execution site, forcing Simon of Cyrene to carry the cross "behind Jesus" (v. 26)—casting him in the role of disciple (9:23; 14:27), Jesus' own followers not being available for the part. In a scene unique to Luke, women mourners line the route to the cross and Jesus delivers an oracle that converts their lament for him into a warning of coming disaster for Jerusalem. Because conditions will soon be more combustible (when the city's judgment looms; the wood is now "green"), "[W]eep for yourselves and for your children" (23:28). Better to be childless, the destruction will be so devastating (cf. 19:27, 41–44; 21:20–24). Within a generation, Roman armies would impose this fate on Jerusalem (70 CE).

With two companions-in-crucifixion, Jesus is led to a site named "Skull." (Does the label come from the hill's shape or the executions carried out there?) The account is restrained, its horror left to the audience's imagination: "they crucified Jesus there with the criminals, one on his right and one on his left" (23:33). Not the details of crucifixion but Jesus' fidelity to his messianic vocation dominates, although the narrator shows soldiers gambling for his clothing and mocking him with sour wine, joining their voices to the chorus of ridicule led by the religious elite. Jesus dies as he lived: with integrity, saving sinners, forgiving enemies. He prays to his "Father," asking forgiveness for those who are taking his life (v. 34). (Many manuscripts lack this verse, likely because later copyists and their communities, embroiled in conflict with synagogues, were troubled by Jesus' petition for forgiveness.) So he remains true to his identity as Messiah and Son of God, not seeking to "save himself" (v. 35; cf. vv. 37, 39) but trusting in God and saving others instead. He even offers a repentant criminal an immediate place in Paradise, a benefaction exceeding the man's request to be remembered when Jesus became the king the placard above his head proclaimed him to be. Jesus goes to death doing what he has done throughout his ministry, saving the lost, modeling divine grace—king of the Jews, but only by way of a radically rewritten script for royal power.

The crucifixion scene has dramatic visual accompaniment; darkness descends from noon until 3:00 p.m. (imagery Amos 5:18–20 and Joel 2:31 associate with the "day of the Lord"), and a Temple curtain is torn (which curtain is unclear, but after Jesus' earlier indictment of the Temple system, this surely signifies judgment, 19:45–46). Jesus dies, a prayer on his lips, committing his spirit to his "Father." Reaction to his death is swift; a centurion brands him righteous (23:47; NRSV, "innocent"), another Roman voice attesting Jesus' death as unjust. And the crowds leave shaken and remorseful, while Jesus' friends, including the women who accompanied him from Galilee, observe the scene from a distance, ready to play the role of "witness" in Acts (e.g., 1:22; 2:32).

23:50–56. Burial of Jesus in Anticipation of God's Reign. Jesus' burial, together with the narrative of his birth and childhood, frames his life with symbols of Jewish piety: expectation of God's reign (cf. 2:25, 38) and fidelity to Torah (Sabbath observance). For the first time, readers learn that the Jerusalem council's action against Jesus was not unanimous; unable to effect justice then, Joseph of Arimathea honors Jesus with burial. The pattern of faithful Jewish life continues among Jesus' followers and sympathetic observers. But in the aftermath of the cross, what will come of their hopes for Israel's redemption? Unnamed women have taken note of the tomb where Jesus' body lies and prepared spices to perform burial rites; will the story's next turn prove Jesus right in his prophecy of divine vindication through resurrection (9:22; 18:33)?

C. Easter: Ministry of the Risen Jesus (24:1–53)

Moving from cruel death for Israel's Messiah and dashed hopes for the people's salvation to resurrection vindication and a Scripture-driven mandate to carry the message of forgiveness to the entire world, Luke's Easter story brings joyful closure to the account of Jesus' life and prepares for the narrative of Acts.

24:1–12. News Too Good to Trust?: Women Witness to Jesus' Resurrection. Early Sunday morning, a group of women (including Mary Magdalene, Joanna, and James's mother Mary) approach the tomb to complete burial rites for Jesus but discover the tomb empty. Two men wearing bright clothing (one, an "angel," appears in Matt 28:2, 5; a "young man" in Mark 16:5) announce that Jesus is alive and remind the women of Jesus' prophecy of his death and resurrection. The memory of the prediction has post-event precision lacking in the original phrasing (no mention of crucifixion or the agency of sinners in Luke 9:22, 44; 17:25; 18:31–33). The women disciples become heralds of the resurrection to "the eleven" and "all the rest" (Judas is no longer with them; cf. Acts 1:16–20, 25). The women's witness does not convince, although Peter inspects the tomb, with its discarded burial clothes. Only direct encounter with the risen Jesus will restore the disciples' shattered hopes.

24:13–49. Journey to Hope: Scripture Interpretation and Meal. The road to hope passes through the village of Emmaus, and then the few miles back to Jerusalem, where the Gospel ends and Acts will begin. Jesus leads the disciples from discouragement to faith, joining them at table, as he had so many times before, and interpreting his suffering and death as the fulfillment of scriptural promise. First Cleopas and an unnamed disciple (standing in for Luke's reader?) chronicle for Jesus—without recognizing him—the disastrous turn of events that had crushed their hope for Israel's redemption, though they also mention the women's news, too good to believe. He then provides a new lens for viewing Scripture, explaining that both Moses (law) and the prophets teach that the Messiah's route to glory passes through suffering and death. However, it is when they share a meal with Jesus, his words and gestures recalling the farewell Passover meal, that "their eyes [are] opened" and they realize who he is (Luke 24:30–31). They return to Jerusalem, only to discover that Peter, too, has met the risen Lord.

Jesus appears once more; the account emphasizes that he is no ephemeral spirit but the "real Jesus," flesh and bones, bearing the marks of suffering, and still one to enjoy a good meal. The risen

Lord is this same person—the divinely vindicated Messiah who lived, healed, taught, challenged the powers, and suffered death in disgrace. For Luke's readers, no less than for Jesus' first disciples, the story of Jesus generates massive cognitive dissonance between expectation and reality. A crucified Messiah, the experience of death-conquering resurrection life, the scandal of sin-erasing forgiveness: these are not the stuff of normal life, nor the things (at least the first two) one easily finds in the Jewish Scriptures. That is why a new reading lens—coming to perceive Scripture and experience anew in the light of the event of the cross and the message of Easter—must be supplied. That is why Jesus must teach this lesson, and teach it again and again. So he explains that Scripture pointed to the necessity of the Messiah's suffering, death, and resurrection, adding that Scripture's mandate (hence, God's will) calls for the message of "repentance and forgiveness of sins" to be declared "to all nations, beginning from Jerusalem" (vv. 44–47). Jesus charges his disciples with the task of "witness," but not until they receive divine empowerment. The stage is set, and the table of contents scripted, for Acts.

24:50–53. Closing the Book and Preparing for a Sequel Narrative. As Easter day draws to a close, Jesus blesses the disciples and is taken up to heaven—exalted to share in God's cosmic dominion. Luke's second book, re-telling the ascension in a way that commences, rather than closes, the story, locates the event forty days later (Acts 1:1–11). The Gospel narrative ends, as it began, with worship of God in the Jerusalem Temple. The notes of joy and praise, post-crucifixion, surpass the hope-filled praise of the book's opening chapters, though hopes have found fulfillment in unexpected ways. Luke closes, fittingly, with doxology to a God who counters cultural convention and defies human (even religious) expectation, but does so to bring life and liberation to God's people, and to the whole earth.

BIBLIOGRAPHY

R. A. Culpepper. "The Gospel of Luke." *NIB* (Nashville: Abingdon, 1995) 9:1–490; J. A. Darr. *On Character Building: The Reader and the Rhetoric of Characterization in Luke–Acts.* LCBI (Louisville: Westminster John Knox, 1992); J. A. Fitzmyer. *The Gospel according to Luke: A New Translation with Introduction and Commentary.* AB 28–28A. 2 vols. (Garden City, N.Y.: Doubleday, 1981–85); J. B. Green. *The Gospel of Luke.* NICNT (Grand Rapids: Eerdmans, 1997); _____. *The Theology of the Gospel of Luke.* NTT (Cambridge: Cambridge University Press, 1995); L. T. Johnson. *The Gospel of Luke.* SP 3 (Collegeville, Minn.: Liturgical, 1991); A.-J. Levine, ed. *A Feminist Companion to Luke.* Feminist Companion to the New Testament and Early Christian Writings 3 (London: Sheffield Academic Press, 2002); H. Moxnes. *Economy of the Kingdom: Social Conflict and Economic Relations in Luke's Gospel.* OBT (Minneapolis: Fortress, 1988); B. E. Reid. *Choosing the Better Part? Women in the Gospel of Luke* (Collegeville, Minn.: Liturgical, 1996); F. S. Spencer. *The Gospel of Luke and Acts of the Apostles.* IBT (Nashville: Abingdon, 2008); C. H. Talbert. *Reading Luke: A Literary and Theological Commentary.* Rev. ed. Reading the New Testament (Macon, Ga.: Smyth and Helwys, 2002); R. C. Tannehill. *Luke.* ANTC (Nashville: Abingdon, 1996).

JOHN

DOROTHY ANN LEE

OVERVIEW

The Gospel of John is, in some respects, the most difficult and mysterious of all the Gospels. Its meaning and message, as well as the circumstances of its composition, are not easily discerned and give rise to considerable disagreement. Yet, from the early Church onward, John's Gospel is widely regarded as one of the most profound spiritual texts within the Bible. In its religious and theological perspective, it stands alone in the New Testament (NT), offering a unique vision of Jesus Christ for the life of the believing community. John's Gospel does not offer a neutral account of Jesus' life and death but rather a theological reflection on the meaning of those events from the perspective of believing. It is written, in other words, "from faith to faith." Although there are important similarities to the other three Gospels (Synoptics), John's Gospel is distinctive. The stories he tells, his characters and characterization, his outline of the plot, his style of writing, and the theology that emerges, all have a characteristic Johannine stamp that has few parallels elsewhere.

John begins his story, not with the birth narratives as in Matthew and Luke, or the wilderness experience of the people of Israel, as in Mark but in the eternity before creation. There we witness the intimacy between the Logos (Word) and God, and the creative activity of the divine Logos in giving life and form to the world. The incarnation of the Logos, which is the high point of the opening verses, sets the narrative in motion. The evangelist reinforces his message through the witness of John the Baptist, two of whose disciples are first to gather around Jesus. The public ministry, which begins with the wedding at Cana and ends with the raising of Lazarus—both unique to John—demonstrates the "signs" and "works" of Jesus' ministry and manifests symbolically the glory of God revealed in him. Particularly important are the seven "signs," around which the first half of the Gospel turns.

The second half of the Gospel consists of the long farewell discourse, bounded on one side by the footwashing and on the other by the "high priestly" prayer of Jesus. These events take place in the intimate circle of Jesus' disciples at the Last Supper. The stress here is on Jesus' departure as beneficial for the disciples, associated with the gift of the Spirit and the love-command. With the passion narrative we move back to the public arena, in the arrest, the trial before Pilate, and the crucifixion, where the unnamed disciple and the mother of Jesus play key roles. The climax is the flow of blood and water from the side of the crucified Christ. The resurrection narratives, first in Jerusalem then Galilee, represent a move back to the intimate circle of discipleship, and Jesus renews his broken relations with the disciples, drawing them into Easter faith. With the giving of the Spirit, he commissions them for mission, pastoral leadership in the church, and witness in his name.

The Gospel of John is constructed around a series of "signs" and images, which the narrative unfolds, drawing out their symbolic significance and enticing the reader to share the evangelist's worldview. These great symbols center around two distinct yet interconnected themes: creation and incarnation. The first designates the beginning of the created order where God, through the divine Logos/Word, brings into being a world of beauty, light and truth. The second presupposes the tragic separation between God and creation, a separation that has disfigured the original goodness of the world. In both, God acts in self-giving, life-affirming love. In the second, God's gift is no less than God's own self, clad in the garb of creation. This is John's central theological affirmation, and it shapes the Gospel's religious vision from beginning to end. The self-revelation of God, in this Gospel, is through matter: through image, symbol, and metaphor, replaying the foundational theme of a deity disclosed in mortal flesh.

Perspective on Jesus. John's Gospel confirms from the beginning the identity of Jesus as the Word-made-flesh. To the Samaritan woman, Jesus discloses that his mission is to draw people to authentic worship of the Father (4:23). Toward the end of the Gospel, the author declares openly that his purpose in writing is to lead people to (deeper) faith and thus eternal life (20:31). The Gospel is concerned with truth (8:32; 14:6), but truth is understood personally, as well as objectively. To know the truth is not just about intellectual propositions—though it is at least that—but, more fundamentally, it constitutes a relationship of friendship, love, and obedience, a relationship grounded in the self-revelation of God.

As with the Synoptic Gospels, John is not to be read as a series of journalistic snap-shots of Jesus' life seen through the eyes of a neutral observer. John's Gospel emerges from a period of theological reflection, in which the author meditates on the significance of Jesus' life, death, and resurrection. Jesus is viewed through the lens of the resurrection, which permeates his speaking and acting throughout the Gospel. This is a Jesus interpreted through Christian eyes. Not just the earthly Jesus, therefore, but the fullness of the "real Jesus" of Christian faith pervades the Gospel: yes, the one who walked the earth, who lived and died but also the one who rose from the dead and who continues to indwell his people through the Spirit.

Relationship to Other Gospels. John differs significantly from the other Gospels. Mark's Gospel presents a short ministry in Galilee, followed by a single journey to Jerusalem, culminating in the cleansing of the Temple. In John, Jesus visits Judea and Jerusalem three times, cleansing the Temple near the beginning of his ministry on his first visit. Other events, familiar from the Synoptics, are absent, such as the institution of the Eucharist at the Last Supper. Jesus also speaks in a somewhat different manner in John, in long, self-revealing discourses based around central symbols rather than the short, succinct sayings and parables of the Synoptic tradition. And, inevitably, there are theological differences: a focus in John, for example, on the preexistent origins of Jesus, and emphasis on the fullness of life in the here and now. Yet it is important not to overstate these differences. Once the distinctiveness of the two traditions—Synoptic and Johannine—is acknowledged, there remains considerable overlap between them. This is apparent in the central characters, in key events, and in overall theological perspective.

Traditionally, the church has seen John as complementing the other evangelists. In the twentieth century, however, scholarship was more concerned to assert the independence of John and the gulf separating him from the Synoptics. In more recent years, there has developed increasing awareness of the complexity of the relationship between the Synoptic and Johannine traditions. While there is dispute over whether this is a direct or indirect relationship, there are unmistakeable signs of cross-fertilization between the two traditions. Indeed, given the close relationship between widely spread Christian communities in the first century, it is hard to imagine that John was unaware of the Gospel of Mark and unfamiliar with its contents. The Gospels quickly assumed an important place in the early church, and it is therefore possible that John knew also the Gospels of Matthew and Luke. Whatever view we take, John's place in the NT canon ensures that his voice speaks as an authentic expression of Christian faith, as important and legitimate as the Synoptic tradition. The point is strengthened if, as is possible, John assumes the Synoptic tradition and consciously builds on it, sometimes adapting, sometimes complementing, and at other times departing from it.

Author, Location, Dating. We have no direct evidence from the Gospel of its authorship, place or dating. The title, "according to John," tells us little, and the identity of the unnamed disciple is never disclosed within the Johannine text. Later in the Gospel, this character is referred to as "the disciple whom Jesus loved" (13:23–25; 19:26–27; 20:3–10; 21:7, 20–23), though elsewhere he is simply "the other disciple" (1:37–40; 18:15; 19:35). Many modern scholars conclude from this that the Gospel is more or less anonymous, the "John" referring to a later figure who edited the Gospel in its final form, and not necessarily the same as the unnamed disciple.

From the second century onward, the early church believed that the author was the Apostle John, son of Zebedee—though curiously the two "sons of Zebedee" only appear in one scene in the Gospel (21:2). Irenaeus (c. 130–c. 200) takes this view and traces his information back to Polycarp (c. 65–c. 155) who personally knew the apostles and other disciples of the earthly Jesus. But the early church also has a tradition of another John, ministering in the late first century, named "the Elder," a disciple of Jesus, and it is possible that the two Johns have been conflated. The Gospel concludes with an explicit identification of the unnamed ("beloved") disciple with the author and thus with the name John. There is no reason, moreover, to doubt that the "witness" language of the

Fourth Gospel reflects the stance of actual eyewitnesses, especially given the importance of eyewitness testimony in the ancient writing of history. If John the Elder wrote not only the Gospel but also the Johannine Epistles (2 John 1; 3 John 1), he can also be identified with the unnamed disciple, since it is possible that the Elder had known Jesus in his youth, though being outside the circle of the Twelve. The evidence for either person is plausible, though the possibility of later editorial work on the Gospel by a disciple of "John" cannot be ruled out and is, indeed, suggested by the closing verses of the Gospel.

A persistent tradition from the early church sees Ephesus as the place of composition. While this cannot be demonstrated from the text itself, it is likely that the Gospel originated in a Hellenistic city with a large Jewish population. On these grounds alone, Ephesus is a good guess; and the traditional association of both the apostle and the elder with Ephesus is strong. In many respects, Ephesus makes sense as the location for this Gospel, and there is no reason to doubt it: it had a vibrant Christian community, a large synagogue, and was a Greek-speaking Hellenistic city of considerable importance in the ancient world, culturally, religiously, and economically.

Internal evidence suggests a rather late date for its composition at the end the first century. The Gospel seems to reflect a context in which "Pharisees" could be interchanged with "Jews," a situation unlikely in the diversity and complexity of Judaism before the Jewish War (66–70 CE). Moreover, the conflict between Jesus and "the Jews" in the Gospel sets the Johannine community apart from the synagogue. While conflict was certainly part of Jesus' life and times, and that of the earliest church, it reached a new intensity in the period after the Jewish War, when the struggling Christian community found itself in competition with an equally struggling Judaism. A dating of around 95–100CE seems reasonable.

Structure. A common way of dividing the Gospel separates the Book of Signs (chs. 1:19–12:50) from the Book of Glory (chs. 13–20), with a Prologue (1:1–18) and an Epilogue (ch. 21). But this can be confusing, especially since glory is a major theme throughout the Gospel. Also the opening verses of the Gospel (1:1–18) and its concluding chapter (21:1–25), despite doubts raised by some scholars, both function as integral to the overall narrative. A more helpful organization is as follows:

OUTLINE

I. Prologue: Coming of John the Baptist and Jesus (1:1–18)

II. Jesus' Public Ministry (1:19–12:50)

    A. Gathering of the First Disciples 1:19–51
        1:19–34. Witness of John the Baptist
        1:35–51. Gathering of First Disciples

    B. Cana to Cana (2:1–4:54)
        2:1–12. First "Sign" at Cana:
            Wedding
        2:13–25. Cleansing of the Temple
        3:1–36. Jesus, Nicodemus,
            and John the Baptist
        4:1–42. Jesus and the Samaritan Woman
        4:43–54. Second "Sign" at Cana:
            Healing of the Official's Son

    C. Jesus and the Festivals of Judaism (5:1–10:42)
        5:1–47. Jesus and the Sabbath: The Son
        6:1–71. Jesus and the Passover:
            The Bread of Life
        7:1–52, 8:12–59. Jesus and
            Tabernacles: Water and Light
        9:1–41. Tabernacles: Healing
            of the Man Born Blind
        10:1–42. Jesus and Dedication:
            The Good Shepherd

    D. Climax of the Public Ministry: Resurrection and the "Hour" (11:1–12:50)
        11:1–12:11. The Raising of Lazarus
        12:12–19. Jesus' Entry into Jerusalem
        12:20–50. The Manifestation
            of the "Hour"

III. Jesus' Private Ministry: The Last Supper (13:1–17:26)

    A. Jesus Washes the Disciples' Feet (13:1–30)
        13:1–20. The Footwashing
        13:21–30. Revelation of the Betrayer

DETAILED ANALYSIS

I. Prologue: Coming of John the Baptist and Jesus (1:1–18)

The Prologue to John is arguably the most important passage in the whole Gospel. It func-tions as a musical overture, opening up the core symbols and central themes that provide the key to the Gospel's meaning at the outset. Unlike the characters in the ensuing narrative, we as readers know the truth about Jesus in a way they do not. Practically every section of the Gospel narrative can be headed with a phrase or verse or symbol from the Prologue, so well does it sum up the Gospel message.

Originally the Prologue may have been a hymn to the Logos, arising from the early Christian community. It has a poetic structure, and the language, though simple, has a grand, majestic tone. Yet, if so, the evangelist has adapted it to include not only the proclamation of Jesus' divine origins and identity but also the beginnings of the Gospel's plot: we encounter first the story of John the Baptist, then the narrative of Jesus the incarnate Word in his revelation of the Father.

The background to the idea of Logos derives from the Old Testament (OT) and intertestamental writings. In the first creation account, God's *word* speaks the world into being (Gen 1:1–2:4a). In the prophetic writings, God's life-giving *word* brings salvation and judgment to the people of Israel, in fulfillment of the covenant. In the wisdom writings of the OT and beyond, God's *word* is associated with Lady Wisdom who takes on a personalized status as the self-manifestation of God in creation and salvation: the hostess and nourisher who invites guests to share her food and drink. These ideas are Jewish, influenced also by Hellenistic ideas and imagery, including Greek (Stoic) notions of *logos* as the harmonious web of reason that holds all things in being. John's use of "Logos," thus provides an integrated picture of the source and ground of creation—that which gives rise to all created things and unites them, offering guidance and illumination to the created world.

John begins with the Logos in relationship to God and creation (1:1–5). The Logos (*logos*) has a complex relationship with God (*theos*): on the one hand, the Logos is "*with* God" in the sense of being "turned towards" or even face-to-face with God; on the other hand, the Logos also *is* God, sharing in the divine being, God's way of being present to the world, the sublime Utterance through which the world was made. In this sense, the Logos is portrayed as the agent of creation, the source of all life, a life that begins with the making of light

(Gen 1:3). The evangelist moves at once from the literal to the symbolic: this light, dawning at creation and shining through the world's history as a material, moral, and spiritual reality, can never be grasped (comprehended or overcome) by any force of darkness (1:5). This theme and this opposition are essential to the plot of the Gospel, where light does indeed appear to be quenched by darkness. Yet light is God's first and last word, as the Gospel will display in the history of the Logos.

The second section of the Prologue (1:6–13) outlines the response of faith to the dawning of the light, beginning with John the Baptist and concluding with the community of faith who believe his testimony. It may seem as if John the Baptist breaks into the poetic structure (1:6–8), but his role is a crucial one: he is the primary witness to the Logos, his testimony grounding the Prologue's exalted language in concrete reality—although the evangelist has not yet made the identification between the Logos and Jesus. In the following verses (1:9–13), John outlines the response of the world to the saving presence of the light. Note that John's theology here, though it refers to salvation, is nonetheless firmly grounded in creation. Those who reject the light ironically and tragically reject their own Creator and, by definition, their own identity (1:10–11). "His own" could refer specifically to the Jerusalem authorities in this Gospel who largely reject Jesus. But the evangelist refers to the world as a whole, which belongs to the Logos by right of creation. Yet the last word is not tragic: just as the light is not overwhelmed by the darkness, so creation is not lost to its Creator. Those who welcome the light rediscover their true identity, through faith, as "children of God" (1:12–13). Note that this is the first reference to "flesh" in John's Gospel, not negative and fallen but depicted here as ineffective. Flesh cannot bridge the gulf between Creator and creation; only God can.

We now reach the last and climactic section of the Prologue to which the previous two sections have been leading (1:14–18). The Logos is connected to creation not just as its Creator but through incarnation. So far the Prologue has maintained a distinction between "being," which signifies the divine realm, and "becoming," which is characteristic of creation. But now the gulf is crossed: that which *is* now *becomes*; Creator becomes creation. "Flesh" too now takes on a new quality:

this flesh achieves what ordinary human flesh could not. And now for the first time John speaks of "we": the believing community, those born of God, those who behold in the human flesh of the Logos the radiance of divine glory, "full of grace and truth" (1:14). This act of profound recognition is the meaning of salvation for the evangelist.

Glory is a vitally important concept in John's Gospel, though its meaning is not easy to pin down. It has strong tabernacle/temple overtones derived from the OT, the Temple in Jerusalem being the place where God's radiant, life-giving presence dwells for Israel; here the verb we translate as "live" (skēnoō) has the sense of "pitch one's tent," with its suggestion of the tabernacle in the exodus. There are implications also of Mt. Sinai and the giving of the Law, which is accompanied by the radiance of God's glory (Exod 34:29–35). In John's Gospel, glory evokes the life-giving, saving radiance of God, the divine presence with God's people in holiness, beauty, and love. That glory, for John, is now located in the "flesh" of the incarnate Logos.

And now, for the first time, the rather abstract language of "Logos" and "God" in the opening verses of the Prologue gives way before the vivid metaphorical language of "Father" and "Son," which is part of the core symbolism of the Gospel. The Logos is now revealed as the divinely human Son who stands face-to-face with the Father in intimate communion while sharing the same *being*; who enters the world and stands face-to-face with human beings, sharing their *becoming*. On this central theological tenet the Gospel hinges.

Once more we meet John the Baptist, bursting into the grandeur of the Prologue, and for the first time hear the words of his testimony: he witnesses to the one who is "First," a witness that will be repeated in the next section, binding the Prologue closely with the ensuing narrative (1:30). The Word-made-flesh is superlatively above and beyond the person of John the Baptist, as he is above everyone, because from the incarnate Logos comes the fullness of divine grace (1:16). He is even above Moses, though not over against him (1:17). The last verse of the Prologue (1:18) sums up its central message: the invisible, unseen God is made visible in the incarnation, disclosing the deepest intimacy between Father and Son, an intimacy into which believers are drawn. There is no more fit Revealer than this—the one who manifests divine glory through radical participation in mortal flesh.

II. Jesus' Public Ministry (1:19–12:50)

A. Gathering of the First Disciples (1:19–51)

1:19–34. Witness of John the Baptist. It is no surprise that Jesus' public ministry should begin with John the Baptist. The Prologue has already begun his witness, which now takes the form of a "trial" before members of the Jewish leadership. As in the Prologue John the Baptist witnesses to the preeminence of the Coming One, his baptism in water points symbolically to something greater. When Jesus himself appears—for the first time in the Gospel—it is the voice of John the Baptist we hear, testifying to him as "the Lamb of God who takes away the sin of the world" (1:29). John the Baptist then narrates the story of his own recognition of Jesus' identity, which he perceives as the result not of his own cognition but of divine revelation. Unlike the Synoptic Gospels, which narrate directly the story of Jesus' baptism by John the Baptist, the descent of the dove, and the divine voice, in John's Gospel the same story is narrated as a personal vision of John the Baptist. Jesus' own baptism in water is not told, though is perhaps assumed by the evangelist. What John the Baptist does bear witness to in this Gospel is the descent and abiding of the Spirit, confirming Jesus' identity as the Son of God.

The title, "Lamb of God" connects Jesus with the rich lamb symbolism of the OT. It suggests the Passover lamb, associated not so much with sin as with liberation and exodus. There are overtones also of the OT cult and the animals sacrificed as sin-offerings. The Suffering Servant who sacrifices himself vicariously for others, the very image of innocence and vulnerability, is also part of the symbolism. The story of the sacrifice of Isaac (Gen 22:1–14) may also form part of this association, where Abraham is called to sacrifice his beloved son—though the animal sacrificed in Isaac's stead is a ram. The symbolism can work at more than one level and suggest more than one meaning. At this point in the narrative, we do not know exactly what the title means, but its fuller significance will be disclosed on the cross, where Jesus dies as the true Passover lamb, the beloved Son sacrificed for sin. Note that John the Baptist speaks of "sin," not "sins," implying that beneath individual acts of wrongdoing lies a fundamental condition of alienation and darkness, which Jesus has come to eliminate. Indeed, as the incarnate Logos, he alone is capable of dealing definitively with "the world's sin."

1:35–51. Gathering of First Disciples. The testimony of John the Baptist bears immediate fruit. What follows is a witness chain beginning with John the Baptist, extending to his disciples, and moving on from them to others. The first to become disciples of Jesus are initially disciples of John the Baptist, and they approach Jesus on the basis of their master's testimony. The language of this preliminary encounter is evocative. Although they begin by following Jesus, it is his question that challenges them at the deepest level: "What are you looking for?" (1:38a). The evangelist uses the language of "abiding," a key concept in his understanding of discipleship, although it is somewhat masked by the English words "stay" and "remain" (1:38b–39). But abiding with Jesus is precisely what it means to be a disciple and involves a mutual recognition.

In the following verses the growing group of disciples, as they come in contact with Jesus, use a variety of titles to describe his identity—Rabbi, Messiah, the one about whom Moses in the law and the prophets wrote, Son of God, King of Israel—while Jesus, in turn, knows their identity before even they speak. Thus Simon is recognized and named Cephas (Peter, 1:42), and Nathanael is declared to be "an Israelite in whom there is no deceit" (1:47). The theme of Jesus' divine ability to see into the human heart is one that will continue throughout the Gospel.

Philip is the exception in the chain of witnesses; his summons comes from Jesus himself who calls him to follow (1:43). This small scene is closer to the Markan picture of the calling of the first four disciples (Mark 1:16–20) whom Jesus calls with startling authority and immediacy. Perhaps John shows here an awareness of the Synoptic tradition, even though he tells the story very differently. At the same time John emphasizes that, although the disciples bring each other to Jesus, the initiative lies with Jesus himself who draws them to his own self-revelation.

The climax of the chapter is reached with Nathanael who is amazed at Jesus' knowledge of his character and whereabouts, despite some initial scepticism. Jesus promises him the sight of far greater things, a statement that leads naturally into Jesus' public ministry. Yet Jesus concludes with what seems an odd claim, linked to yet another title that comes from the mouth of Jesus and appears to trump all the other titles used by the disciples. The promise of seeing angels ascending and descending on the Son of Man is not literally fulfilled in the narrative of the Gospel (1:51). Yet symbolically it is fulfilled throughout Jesus' ministry and in his exaltation on the cross. The reference to the ascent and descent of angels recalls Jacob's ladder (Gen 28:10–22), signifying the unexpected presence of God: "the house of God" ... "the gate of heaven" (Gen 28:17). As the Son of Man, who combines the divine glory of apocalyptic symbolism (Dan 7:13) with the mortal flesh of a human being (Ezekiel), the Johannine Jesus is himself the House of God and the Gate of Heaven. He brings to completion what is partially disclosed to Jacob, just as he does also with Moses, Abraham, and Isaiah. By the end of the chapter, the disciples are thus gathered around Jesus and have begun to discern, in an intensifying series of titles, who and what he is. All is ready for Jesus' public ministry to commence.

B. Cana to Cana (2:1–4:54)

2:1–12. First "Sign" at Cana: Wedding. The story of the wedding at Cana begins the first narrative cycle of the Gospel, a circular path from Galilee to Jerusalem to Galilee again, via Samaria. In each case, we encounter different responses to Jesus: Jew, Gentile, Samaritan. The overarching theme is the giving of new life in Jesus and the invitation to faith. At the same time—because Johannine narrative is spiral rather than strictly linear—the wedding at Cana also, in a sense, completes the faith-story of the disciples from ch. 1.

As the first miracle of the Gospel, the wedding at Cana (which does not appear in the Synoptic Gospels) plays a significant role. As the first of the Johannine "signs," this is a symbolic and theological narrative about the advent of the new through the incarnation and the relationship of the new to the old. The six stone jars of water represent Judaism and its ritual purifications, which are transformed by Jesus into the best wine: the new arises out of, yet surpasses, the old. In the OT and the Synoptic Gospels, marriage ceremonies are symbolic of the last days and the celebration of God's future reign. The imagery of the banquet suggests the sumptuousness of God's bounty, and the marriage signifies the perfection of union (covenant) between God and Israel. All this rich symbolism is operative here, mediated through the Johannine Jesus who brings the divine gift of eternal life radically into the present, in his own person.

Particularly difficult is the role of the mother of Jesus who is introduced without name or explanation (2:1). Like all narratives in this Gospel, the story of her encounter with Jesus is highly stylized and typically Johannine. While Jesus seems to distance himself from her initiative, he follows it nonetheless, as elsewhere in the Gospel when people approach him, since everything he does is primarily at the Father's initiative. More important, John introduces the theme of the "hour" (2:4), which points forward to the cross, Jesus' final act of glorification. The climax of the story makes this plain: the changing of water into wine is itself the revelation of divine glory (2:11), a glory derived from Judaism and now manifest in the flesh of Jesus. The mother of Jesus nurtures the faith of the disciples as she will nurture the Beloved Disciple at the crucifixion. What Jesus does at Cana, in other words, anticipates what he will do on the cross. Equally important, however, is her response (2:5), addressed as much to the disciples and the reader of the Gospel as to the attendants at the wedding. The mother of Jesus calls us to obey the word of the one who is himself the Word.

2:13–25. Cleansing of the Temple. The cleansing of the Temple also concerns the revelation of the new but with a more polemical note than the previous story. This narrative, familiar from the Synoptic Gospels as the prelude to the passion narrative, occurs in John at the beginning of Jesus' ministry and has a double focus. On the one hand, Jesus displays passionate "zeal" for the Temple (2:16; Ps 69:9), fulfilling OT expectations and showing a prophetic critique of all that might pollute the true worship of God. Note the typically Johannine use of "*my* Father's house," implying a unique relationship with God and a unique authority. At this level, the story is truly a "cleansing" of the Temple and its worship.

At the same time, the narrative also operates at a deeper level. In the ensuing conversation with the Jerusalem authorities, the Temple becomes a symbol of Jesus himself, and the prophecy of its destruction and rebuilding signifies his death and resurrection (2:18–21). Jesus is the true sanctuary, and the resurrection denotes the rebuilding of this incarnate "temple," destroyed by the authorities. Jesus, in other words, is the house in which/ whom the Father dwells. Thus by the end of the story, the Johannine Jesus has not only recovered the Temple for his Father, but has also claimed it as his own. The place of the Temple and Jesus' body are mysteriously fused, to be vindicated in the resurrection. In the first part, therefore, Jesus points to the Father, while in the second he points symbolically to himself. At both levels, it is only the later "remembering" of the disciples that confirms for them the true meaning of this event. Everything in this Gospel is thus seen through the lens of Easter, with the words of the Scriptures and the word of Jesus himself of equal stature (2:22).

The Johannine Jesus is reserved about the many who come to faith at Passover (2:23–25). For John, faith based on "signs"—on outward manifestations of power—can be, at best, superficial and, at worst, misleading. Real faith in this Gospel is perceiving the glory of God in the words and works, and person, of Jesus. Thus true faith involves seeing the inner meaning of the "signs," what they reveal about Jesus. At this point, Jesus will not entrust himself naively to those who profess trust in him (2:24–25),

3:1–21. Jesus and Nicodemus. The previous verses (2:23–25) have set the scene for Nicodemus' meeting with Jesus in Jerusalem: there is an ambiguity about his appearance, despite the sincerity of his opening greeting (3:2). Jesus at once moves to the heart of the matter in a solemn saying, summoning Nicodemus to be "born from above" (3:3), a saying then reiterated as "born of water and Spirit" (3:5). Nicodemus misunderstands, interpreting Jesus' imagery on a material level, as if Jesus were indeed speaking of literal birth (3:4). The word translated as "from above" (*anōthen*) can also mean "again," which is the way Nicodemus interprets it. Misunderstanding is common in this Gospel, and even necessary for growth in

faith; the challenge is to move beyond the material to the symbolic and spiritual. Here birth is employed as a metaphor for new life in Christ, a birth that can only be effected by the Spirit of God whose origins and operations are as mysterious as the wind (3:8). There are suggestions of baptism in this language, which itself represents rebirth into the kingdom of God (see 1:12–13). Note that this is one of the few occasions in the Gospel where John uses the term "kingdom," generally preferring the phrase "eternal life" to convey a similar meaning—although John places great stress on that life as a quality in the here-and-now.

The strange thing is that Nicodemus, while failing to grasp Jesus' words, now fades from the picture, and Jesus appears to address a wider audience—perhaps others like Nicodemus. The overall theme is entry into new life by faith, though the imagery shifts. First John makes it plain that the revelation comes from the Son of Man, who has descended from heaven in the incarnation and who will ascend in glory on the cross in order to give eternal life (3:13–15). For John, the bronze serpent in the wilderness, which healed those Israelites struck by plague, is a type of Christ whose death on the cross, in a similar paradox, gives healing and life (Num 21:4–9). All of this expresses God's radical love for the world that shows itself in the giving of the Son, even to death (3:16), a love that desires not condemnation and death but salvation and life (3:16–17). If there is condemnation, it is the free choosing of those who, like Nicodemus, are given the choice between light and darkness. In this sense, for John, final judgment has already come, anticipated in the human response to Jesus' offer of new birth. Here John develops the theme of light, introduced in the Prologue (1:4–5), imagery that is consonant with the symbolism of birth. By the end of the narrative, Nicodemus is left suspended between the light and the darkness, unable to choose the life Jesus offers. Yet his story, as we shall see later in the Gospel, is by no means finished.

3:22–36. Jesus and John the Baptist. The scene moves now from Jerusalem to the Judean countryside, where the focus shifts from one leader in Judaism to another, from Nicodemus to John the Baptist. The narrative presents two parallel but very different responses to the shining of the light. John the Baptist's ministry is continuing, we discover, as evident in his baptizing (note how the theme of baptism is closely allied to that of water throughout ch. 3). But John the Baptist's ministry is still directed at Jesus, as his testimony makes plain: with the advent of the new in Christ, John the Baptist is happy to retire, to give way as the lesser to the greater, just as the bridegroom's closest friend gives way before the bridegroom (3:28–30).

It is not easy to discern the speaker of the verses that follow (3:31–36). This is not uncommon in John where, in any case, Jesus and the evangelist speak the same language. It is possible that John has inserted the episode about John the Baptist into a discourse by Jesus, continuing on from 3:21. The Son bears witness to the Father, and the Father loves the Son: their relationship is one of intimacy and mutuality. Only by recognizing Jesus as the Son, and having faith in him, can true life be found. The bleak alternative is wrath, rejection, and death (3:36).

4:1–42. Jesus and the Samaritan Woman. The circle turns now from Judea to Galilee via Samaria. John sets up the narrative carefully, continuing the theme of water and baptism (4:1–2). Journeying with the disciples, Jesus is naturally weary by mid-day, the hottest part of the day, and sits beside Jacob's well while the disciples go to the village to buy food. When the Samaritan woman comes to draw water, Jesus at once engages her in conversation. While it is unusual for a woman to come alone to a well in the middle of the day, the narrative is again stylized: John is drawing a contrast between Nicodemus, the Jerusalem leader with name, rank, and education who comes by night, and the woman of Samaria, who without rank or status comes to Jesus in the full light of day.

Two factors are operative here: on the one hand, the woman belongs to a race despised by Jews, treated as Gentiles and seen as unclean; on the other hand, Jesus potentially loses honor and risks scandal by talking to such a woman in public. The woman expresses her surprise at Jesus' request for a drink, and John explains that Jews refuse to share eating and drinking vessels with "unclean" Samaritans. Yet the Johannine Jesus is indifferent to these conventions, using his own physical thirst as a way of pointing to the woman's deeper thirst (4:10). The dialogue turns on the phrase "living water" which has a double

meaning: at a literal level, it signifies flowing or spring water as opposed to the still water of the cistern, while at a Johannine level it is shorthand for "water of life," that is, eternal life. The woman, thinking on a material level, assumes the former meaning and points out the absurdity of Jesus' offer. How can he possibly be a water-giver? She introduces the figure of Jacob who, according to later Jewish tradition, originally dug the well so that the water flowed miraculously over the rim for seven days. But the Johannine Jesus is greater than Jacob, as he is greater than Moses, though standing in the same tradition: indeed Jacob, as water-giver, is a type of Christ himself. By the end of the scene, the woman is convinced that Jesus is offering a superior form of water so that she does indeed *ask* for the gift that Jesus offers, though her understanding is still limited (4:15).

The ensuing dialogue deepens the woman's understanding of the giver, the gift, and her own thirst. Jesus confronts her with the reality of her life—five husbands and one who is not her own husband—not so much to expose her guilt (after all, she may be the victim, given that women in the OT cannot initiate divorce) but to disclose her need for living water in the uncertainty and restlessness of her relationships (4:16–18). The woman begins to realize that Jesus is speaking about spiritual and religious realities and that he has prophetic power (4:19–20). Once again, she raises the distinction between Jew and Samaritan. Jesus' reply points to the centrality of worship in John's understanding, the role of the Spirit, and the desire of the Father to draw authentic worship to himself, thus outlining the purpose of Jesus' mission (4:21–28). The woman now recognizes that Jesus is speaking in messianic terms and refers to Samaritan expectations of a teaching Messiah (a *Ta'eb*) in the tradition of Moses; to this Jesus replies with the self-revealing "I am he, the one who is speaking to you" (4:26).

In face of the disciples' disapproval, it is not surprising that the woman departs, leaving behind her water jar, perhaps in token of her intention to return (4:27–28). Her words to the villagers express hyperbolically the conviction that Jesus has uncovered the truth of her life; they also raise the question of his identity; at once they set out to discover the truth for themselves (4:29–30). In this Gospel, Jesus as the Revealer reveals both his own identity and that of human beings: knowledge of the self and knowledge of God go hand-in-hand. The disciples have no real conception of what is happening and, as Jesus speaks metaphorically of the ripeness of the harvest, the Samaritans make their way toward him. The title, which serves as the climax of the story, "Savior of the world" (4:42), embodies the universalism of the Johannine message. Through the symbol of "living water," Jesus thus reveals himself as the one who offers universal salvation to all, regardless of race or gender. Though himself a Jew, the new life he offers is for all.

4:43–54. Second "Sign" at Cana: Healing of the Official's Son. The last episode in the "Cana to Cana" cycle concludes in Galilee where it began. The miraculous story of Jesus healing at a distance has distinct parallels with the wedding at Cana. In both there is a request for a miracle, and in both Jesus appears to spurn the one who requests it (4:48), underlining the evangelist's nervousness about faith based solely on "signs." In each case, however, the asker's faith shines forth in an exemplary way—though this time the Jewish mother of Jesus is replaced by the royal official, most likely a Gentile. Like her, the man believes "the word that Jesus spoke to him" and goes home in faith to be met on the way with the good news of his son's recovery (4:50–53). Both "signs" are numbered, emphasizing the connection between them. As with the wedding, the healing story is significant in its revelation of divine glory in the word of Jesus who is himself the Word. The cycle thus begins and ends with two extraordinary examples of faith in Jesus, the Savior not just of Jews but of the whole world.

C. Jesus and the Festivals of Judaism (5:1–10:42)

5:1–47. Jesus and the Sabbath: The Son. This story section of the Gospel centers on the festivals and rites of Judaism. Reference to these has already been present in the previous section, but now the feasts are given greater prominence, introduced by the unspecific "festival of the Jews" (5:1). In each case—Sabbath, Passover, Tabernacles, and Dedication—John presents Jesus as the one who gathers the feasts into himself, bringing them to fulfillment. At the same time, the controversy between Jesus and the Jerusalem authori-

ties intensifies, focussed on the significance of the festivals but with strong presentations of John's distinctive christology.

The story of John 5, the third "sign" in the Gospel, concerns the Sabbath. The fact that the healing of the disabled man takes place on a Sabbath is not revealed until later in the story (5:9b). Water is again part of the imagery, but John gives it no overt meaning. What the physical water of the pool cannot do in this case (5:7), Jesus is able to accomplish by word alone (5:8–9a). The indication of the Sabbath leads to conflict. The healed man seems to have no loyalty toward Jesus (unlike the man born blind in ch. 9) but betrays him to the authorities who are outraged at his breach of the Sabbath and who begin "persecuting" him (5:16). Jesus' warning to the man seems to imply a connection between his disability and his spiritual condition (5:14), but later in the Gospel John makes it clear that there is no necessary link between the two (9:2–3). The reference to sin is confined to one particular case, while the man's subsequent actions confirm Jesus' diagnosis.

The discourse that follows is profoundly revelatory of Jesus' identity and mission, and occurs in the context of sharp polemic. It expands on his preliminary self-defense: "My Father is still working, and I also am working" (5:17). This is a highly charged statement. The Judaism of the first century CE was aware of the theological problem of how God could rest on the Sabbath without creation grinding to a halt. They observed that God must, in some sense, continue to work, as evidenced in the fact that babies are born and people die on the Sabbath. Therefore, while still keeping the Sabbath, God is exempt in continuing to give life and to make judgment. This is precisely John's point here: Jesus is claiming to share the same divine exemption because he too is carrying out the uniquely divine task of giving life and judging. The story of the man's healing evidences both aspects of Jesus' ministry.

But why does Jesus, and Jesus alone, possess this godly exemption? For the simple reason that he is the divine Son (Logos) who dwells in intimate and loving union with the Father. Jesus as Son carries out the Father's work: he gives life, as the Father does, and exercises judgment as Son of Man. That life and that judgment are not only for the future but also realizable now—so much so that believers in the present can already be said to have "passed from death to life" (5:24). In Jesus' ministry, therefore, the Last Judgment is anticipated, a judgment and a life-giving based not on his own authority but that of the Father (5:25–29). John's conclusion is simple, therefore: the honor that is due the Father, as divine Life-giver and Judge, is due likewise to the Son (5:23).

Yet the Johannine Jesus does not testify to himself in making these extraordinary claims. John the Baptist has testified to him (5:32–35) but, even more so, the Father testifies to Jesus, and those who claim to know the Father must also recognize the Son (5:36–38). The Scriptures likewise testify to Jesus, including the preeminent figure of Moses, who stands as defense counsel for Jesus in his trial against the religious authorities—those who think they know the law but seek their own glory rather than the glory of God (5:39–47). Thus the Sabbath, for John, becomes a profound symbol of Jesus' identity and mission, revealing him as the Son who carries out the Father's work of giving life and judging. Both dimensions are present in the healing narrative and controversy of John 5.

6:1–71. Jesus and the Passover: The Bread of Life. Despite the geographical awkwardness, we now find Jesus suddenly in Galilee around the time of Passover. The imagery of this long and rather untidy narrative centers on the exodus: Moses, the manna, the paschal lamb, and the people of Israel journeying through the wilderness. John 6 contains two "signs," beginning with the multiplication of the loaves, familiar from the Synoptic tradition, yet with distinctly Johannine touches: the main disciples are Philip and Andrew, the loaves are barley loaves eaten by the very poor, and Jesus himself is both host and giver, distributing the food himself. The full Johannine meaning does not become apparent until the ensuing dialogue between Jesus and crowd, which is an extended commentary on the meaning of the feeding story.

That meaning begins to unfold in the crowd's response to the feeding: first they speculate as to Jesus' identity—the Moses-like prophet who is to come (6:14; see Deut 18:15, 18) and the king who feeds his people (6:14–15). Their attempt to crown him betrays both understanding and misunderstanding: Jesus is both prophet and king in this Gospel—though also far more, as the next, rather puzzling, scene indicates (6:16–21). Jesus' appearance on the lake is an epiphany, the second "sign" of this chapter and the fifth "sign" of the Gospel. It reveals Jesus' divine identity, manifest not just in the miracle of his walking on the water and the landing of the boat but in the self-disclosing, "It is I" (literally, "I am," 6:20).

The crowd seeking Jesus now find him and begin to explore the significance of the feeding. The dialogue works in typically Johannine style: misunderstanding leading to growing understanding, at least initially. Jesus makes a distinction between perishable food and the enduring "food" of eternal life (6:27), to which the miracle points, the only access to which is faith. The crowd begin to perceive the parallel with Moses who gave manna from heaven in the wilderness (6:31), but Jesus is quick to clarify their remaining misunderstanding: God is the giver of the manna, not Moses; the gift is not just a past event since God gives now in the present; the bread from heaven in the manna points to the true bread from heaven in Jesus; and the gift is not only life-giving for the Israelites but also for the world (6:32–33). Like the Samaritan woman (4:15), the crowd now asks for the gift and Jesus responds by revealing the full meaning of the feeding: he is himself the true bread come down from heaven on whom people must feed to gain eternal life (6:35). Jesus is both the giver and the gift.

This is the first of a series of metaphorical "I am" sayings in the Gospel, which reveal the identity of Jesus, just as the parables in the Synoptic Gospels reveal the kingdom of God. Tragically, however, Jesus' self-revelation in this case leads not to faith but rejection. The crowd cannot believe he is the bread from heaven and source of eternal life. They begin to "complain" (6:41)—a word that recalls the murmuring of the Israelites in the wilderness (Exod 16)—and cite Jesus' human identity as if it cancelled out his divine origins. Twice more Jesus repeats the "I am" saying (6:48, 51), drawing out the contrast with the manna in the wilderness, which had no power over death. The true manna, indeed, is Jesus' own flesh given "for the life of the world" (6:51).

This radical statement leads to open conflict (6:52), but Jesus, far from allaying his opponents' anxiety or soothing their repugnance, intensifies the metaphor of eating his flesh and drinking his blood. The evangelist draws on two traditions: first that of Lady Wisdom (Sophia), who as the nourisher is both the giver and the gift, the giver of food and the food itself, and second that of the paschal lamb, who is slaughtered and eaten at Passover in commemoration of the exodus. Yet this wealth of imagery also recalls vividly the Christian eucharist, where Jesus gives his flesh and blood to those who believe. This eucharistic self-giving comes through the cross, so that "giving" has a double sense: sacrificial death and table-fellowship. There are also overtones of breast-feeding, where the infant feeds from the maternal "flesh." The eucharist is here depicted as a relationship of "abiding," a mutual intimacy (6:57) where believers are drawn into the love of Father and Son.

Nonetheless, in the next section, the tragedy intensifies and many more abandon their discipleship (6:60–66). Jesus challenges them by drawing a distinction between the flesh he gives—which is life-giving—and human, material reality which, without the Spirit, is unable to bestow eternal life (6:63). Only the twelve are now left, and Peter speaks on their behalf in confirming his faith in the one who has "the words of eternal life" (6:68). Yet the tragic note does not end with the faith of these few disciples, for in their midst stands also the betrayer, Judas Iscariot (6:70). By the end of the narrative, then, through sign, festival, imagery, and dialogue, Jesus is revealed as the fulfiller of Passover, the true manna from heaven and lamb of God who gives himself in death and sacrament, and on whom believers must feed in order to find life.

7:1–52, 8:12–59. Jesus and Tabernacles: Water and Light.

The long Tabernacles discourse of the next two chapters, much of which consists of hostile dialogue between Jesus and the Jerusalem authorities, is not easy to follow. At first it seems disjointed, partly because readers do not always understand the rites of Tabernacles on which the dialogue and the imagery turn. It is also complicated by the story of the woman caught in adultery (7:53–8:11), which is not found in the oldest and best manuscripts. The Tabernacles discourse takes place in the Temple, in the context of Jesus' teaching, and surrounded by hostility both from his family (7:5) and from the crowds gathered to celebrate the Feast of Tabernacles. The debate focuses initially on Moses and the law, and the identity of Jesus as Messiah. Jesus does not answer in the terms of his opponents but speaks instead of his destiny, to return to the Father, which the crowd misunderstands. The authorities seek to arrest him, but Nicodemus defends Jesus and is abused for his pains (7:50–52).

In the midst of this conflict and uncertainty, Jesus reveals himself as the giver of living water, calling people to come and drink. Here John makes it explicit that water is symbolic of the Spirit. Yet water is also linked to the celebration of Tabernacles. One of the two main rites in the festival was the morning ritual of pouring water on the altar, first drawn from the Pool of Siloam. Thus by offering living water Jesus draws the festival to himself, revealing his giving of the Spirit as the promised gift of water flowing sumptuously from the Temple in the last days (Zech 14:8). Though English translations speak of water flowing from the believer's heart (7:38), the Greek is not as clear: the reference is probably, in the first place, to the flow of (blood and) water from the side of the crucified Christ (19:34) and only in a secondary sense the "spring of water gushing up to eternal life up" in the heart of the believer (4:14).

Later in the discourse Jesus alludes to the second great ritual of Tabernacles, the lighting of the great candelabra in the evenings so that the whole of the Temple was lit up. Using another "I am" saying, Jesus reveals himself as the light of the world (8:12), the one in whose light believers are illuminated. The claim gives rise to heightened hostility from the authorities; Jesus' claim parallels that of the Mosaic Law, which likewise enlightens the people of God (e.g. Ps 119:105). Jesus defends himself in relation to the Father, but the Jerusalem authorities fail to understand; ironically, only on the cross will his full identity be disclosed (8:28).

Not all those present at the festival, however, remain hostile to Jesus. Some come to believe, and Jesus encourages them to "continue in my word" (8:31), a word that will liberate them through knowledge of the truth. Yet the promise of freedom leads anew to hostility and wrath. How can the free children of Abraham need freedom? Jesus does not answer directly but points to himself as the Son, the only truly free member of the household. It is sin, not geneaology, that indicates one's true status, slave or free (8:34–36), and sin reveals itself, for John, in the rejection of Jesus and the rejection of the life he offers. The rest of the dialogue, as the polemic intensifies, focuses on Abraham as the father of faith and of true Judaism. The Johannine Jesus claims a status greater than Abraham, able to give life beyond that of Israel's leading ancestors. As with Moses and Jacob, Abraham too is on Jesus' side and "rejoiced that he would see my day" (8:56). The more Jesus reveals of himself, however, the more violently he is rejected: ironically, unbelief can be as revealing as faith. Finally, Jesus' claim climaxes in an ultimate statement of self-revelation: "before Abraham was, I am" (8:58). Here Jesus claims a divine status that derives from his identity as the Logos and Son before creation. His opponents, in face of this seeming blasphemy, attempt to execute him, but once again he escapes their violence (8:59; see 7:30, 32). Thus throughout the Tabernacles discourse, in dialogue and questioning, in hostility, aborted faith, and sudden violence, Jesus reveals himself as the giver of living water and light of the world, taking to himself the rites, metaphors, and inner meaning of the Feast of Tabernacles.

9:1–41. Tabernacles: Healing of the Man Born Blind.

The story of the man born blind, the sixth "sign" of Jesus' public ministry, belongs to John's development of Tabernacles imagery. John sets out the major terms of the narrative in the opening verses. The question of sin—for the man himself and for Jesus—will revolve around the Sabbath (9:14), while the imagery of light will dominate the plot (9:4–5). The light imagery is supplemented by that of water, since the man is told to wash in Siloam, with its Tabernacles overtones, which John interprets christologically (9:7). The man's sight is not *restored*; rather he is given *new* sight for the first time by the creative Word of God. Creation imagery is present in the way Jesus uses dust/clay to heal him (Gen 2:7).

A series of interrogations follow in which Jesus is paradoxically absent. First the man is questioned by his neighbors (9:8–12) and then by the Pharisees who are concerned about the breach of the Sabbath (9:13–17) and who cannot agree among themselves whether Jesus is a sinner. Even the man's parents are interrogated (9:18–23), confirming his natal blindness and demonstrating their terror of the authorities with the threat of excommunication (*aposynagōgos*, 9:22). The result is to throw the onus back on the man himself. This time, however, he engages the authorities with greater confidence and defiance (9:24–34). More and more he comes to side with Jesus, concluding that Jesus could not possibly be a sinner and must therefore have come "from God" (9:33).

The final, climactic scene sets out the basic reversal of the story. On the one hand, the man is sought out by Jesus and comes to full faith in him (9:35–38); this is the first time he actually *sees* Jesus in the narrative, though that "seeing" is both physical and spiritual. For the man himself, this is a tale of illumination where, even in Jesus' absence, he moves toward the light and recognizes Jesus as the Light of the world. The story would have been powerful in the early church, given Jesus' physical absence yet his continuing power to draw people to himself (see 12:32).

The story is equally about sin and judgment. The authorities move through the narrative from doubt to outright rejection, both of Jesus and of the man born blind, concluding that they are inextricably bound in sin (9:24, 34). Yet blindness of itself, says John, does not constitute sin. The problem with the Pharisees is their claim to sight and their self-delusion, condemning them to abide in sin (9:41).

10:1–42. Jesus and Dedication: The Good Shepherd.

While the imagery changes significantly in this chapter, the opening section also provides something of a commentary on the previous story. The figures of those who harm the sheep, as against the true shepherd recall the abuse the man born blind has suffered at the hands of the authorities. The opening verses set out the scenario (10:1–5). In the face of misunderstanding Jesus unfolds the imagery with the use of two "I am" sayings: the Gate of the sheepfold (10:7–10) and the Good Shepherd (10:11–18). In the first case, Jesus is the one—the only one—through whom access to life is possible. The gate gives the sheep access to security and protection at night, and pasture and nourishment in the day. So the Johannine Jesus gives abundant life to those who follow him, who belong to his flock (10:10). In the second case, the Good Shepherd imagery finds its background in the OT where the shepherd is used as an image for the king and leaders of Israel, just as the community of Israel is depicted as a flock of sheep (see Ps 23; Ezek 34). The background makes it clear that, for John, the symbolism points to Jesus' kingship and his authority over his flock, the people of God. Unlike the hired hand, the real shepherd has a real investment in the sheep.

At this point the imagery begins to stretch almost to breaking point (10:17–18). Unlike an ordinary shepherd, this shepherd is prepared to die for his sheep. Once more it becomes clear that Jesus gives life through death; he also possesses uniquely divine authority over life and death, including his own. He *lays down* his own life, and he also *takes it up* again. Unlike other NT statements of the resurrection, Jesus in this Gospel has the power and right to take back his own life, an authority that derives from the Father.

The discourse leads, predictably, to conflict with the authorities, so outrageous are Jesus' claims. The context is Dedication, the last festival in the cycle, a winter feast commemorating the liberation of God's people from their Syrian overlords and persecutors in the second century BCE (10:22). When challenged, the Johannine Jesus exposes the opponents who demonstrate by their behavior that they do not belong to the flock, and reiterates the basis of his authority and identity: "The Father and I are one" (10:30). So incendiary a statement serves only to irritate the authorities who accuse him of blasphemy. Yet what he has demonstrated in word and deed is the total *dedication* of his life to his God and Father. By the end of the cycle, Jesus has revealed himself as the fulfiller of the rites and rituals of Judaism, not discarding or overriding them but bringing them to fruition. For John, Jesus is the reality to which the OT symbols point, unfolding their true meaning.

D. Climax of the Public Ministry: Resurrection and the "Hour" (11:1–12:50)

11:1–12:11. The Raising of Lazarus. These chapters form the conclusion and climax of Jesus' public ministry; they also set in motion the passion and resurrection story. The hostility now reaches such a point that, instead of spontaneous attacks on Jesus, the authorities lay a careful plot against him, and Jesus enters Jerusalem with the knowledge that "the hour" of his glorification is at hand.

Although it is a little unclear where exactly this account ends, it seems to include the plot against Jesus and the anointing at Bethany, as well as the final attempt to kill Lazarus. This gives a circular, chiastic pattern to the narrative, the threat

to Lazarus' life forming the outer parameters (A and A', 11:1–16 and 12:9–11), Jesus' meeting with Martha paralleled by his anointing by Mary (B and B', 11:17–27 and 12:1–8), his meeting with Mary and the mourners the counterpart of the reaction to Jesus following the "sign" (C and C', 11:28–37 and 11:45–57) and the raising of Lazarus to life the center of the narrative (D, 11:38–44).

In the opening scene, the narrator sets out the main characters and their connection to Jesus, as well as Jesus' own response to the crisis. John's language for the relationship of Jesus to the Bethany family is that of discipleship: these are "friends" in the full, Johannine sense (see 15:15). Despite his closeness to the family, Jesus remains where he is for two days, having described Lazarus' illness as leading not "to death" but to the manifestation of glory (11:4, 6). The disciples misunderstand Jesus' reference to Lazarus being asleep (11:11), but the image illustrates the authority Jesus possesses: to raise his friend from the dead is no more difficult than rousing him from sleep (11:11–15). As Jesus departs, Thomas recalls the danger in his returning to Judea; the underlay of this story is the passion narrative.

The next two scenes take place before rather than after the miracle and draw out the meaning of the "sign," In the first of these, Martha's conversation with Jesus is of critical importance for the story as a whole (11:17–27). Though a "friend" of Jesus and therefore a disciple, Martha still does not understand the full implications of his identity. Despite some optimism, she assumes Lazarus is beyond hope and that resurrection is a future, postponed reality. But Jesus invites her to a new understanding in which resurrection is bound both to his own identity and to the present moment. This is centered on the "I am" saying, "I am the resurrection and the life" (11:25), which reveals that the life Jesus offers—the life he both gives and *is*—is a life that transcends death. For John, Christ's victory over death is already spelled out so that death is now, at most, a penultimate reality. The resurrection life of the last day can already be experienced in relationship to him. Martha accepts Jesus' self-revelation and, like Peter in the Synoptic Gospels, confidently declares her faith in Jesus as the Messiah (11:27)—though her later reservations at the tomb suggest that her faith is not yet complete (11:39). Jesus' subsequent meeting with Mary and the mourners shows again their lack of understanding (11:28–37); yet Mary's falling at Jesus' feet points forward to the anointing. His emotional response to their grief suggests not just his own very human grief and anger at death but also awareness of his approaching death.

The central scene is replete with symbolism. Lazarus now inhabits a domain that is beyond recall; no human voice can penetrate the walls of death. Yet Jesus' voice does precisely that, because he shares the Father's authority over life and death (see 5:25–26). Unafraid of the terrible stench of death, Jesus summons Lazarus into the light of life, bidding the bystanders unwrap the bonds of death and decay that entrap him (11:44). Revealed now as "the resurrection and the life," who prefigures the final resurrection of the dead and gives life in the now of human mortality, Jesus draws many of the mourners to faith in him (11:45–57). So enthusiastic is their response that the authorities, led by the high priest Caiaphas, plot to kill him, unwittingly serving not their own ends but God's, since Jesus will indeed "die for the nation" and for "the dispersed children of God" (11:49–52).

The banquet at Bethany expresses at one level the sisters' gratitude for the restoration of their brother. Mary's act of anointing parallels Martha's earlier confession of faith (11:27). Here Mary and Judas Iscariot stand in stark contrast as the true and the false disciple. The extravagance of Mary's action is an appropriate response to the costliness of what Jesus has done in bringing her brother back from the dead. In a deep sense, he has given his life for Lazarus, and Mary's act shows awareness of the death that will follow. For now, the beauty of the perfume, pervading the house, contrasts vividly with the stench at the open tomb, for this is a story—whether about Lazarus or about Jesus—whose last word is life. And yet, in the final scene, Lazarus' life is again threatened by the hostile authorities, who are out to destroy not only Jesus but also his friends (12:9–11).

12:12–19. Jesus' Entry into Jerusalem. The dual response to Jesus seen in the narrative of Lazarus is also present in the triumphal entry. Although this story is given less prominence than in Mark or Matthew, it is important for John that Jesus enters the city as its King, riding an animal of peace. Only later, remembering in the light of Easter, do the disciples perceive the significance of this event (12:16). In the meantime, many of the believing mourners testify to their faith, and the hostile authorities, in another unintentionally prophetic statement, exclaim in despair that "the world has gone after him!" (12:19).

12:20–50. The Manifestation of the "Hour." In the coming of the Greeks—probably Gentiles who are attracted to Judaism—Jesus at once recognizes the coming of his "hour," to which he has alluded several times throughout the Gospel (2:4; 7:30; 8:20). In each case it refers to the divinely appointed time of his death, which human beings try unsuccessfully to hasten. But now the presence of Gentiles who wish to "see" Jesus, to draw close to him in faith, is the trigger by which he recognizes the imminence of the passion. The coming of the Greeks signifies that "the world has gone after him," and that his gift of life has extended beyond Jewish borders to Gentiles, thus completing his public mission on earth. Jesus' response identifies the pattern of discipleship in the seed dying and rising (12:24), —the foundational pattern of his own life and death.

Jesus' distress is now apparent yet, unlike the Synoptics, it does not lead to his asking God to permit him to bypass the hour. He is so perfectly united to the Father that, in this Gospel, he does not struggle to obey the divine will; instead he prays for the Father's glorification and the Father responds in kind (27–28). In the Johannine cross, suffering, death, and evil are definitively overcome, provoking the final judgment and the giving of eternal life. Jesus' crucifixion is both literally and symbolically an exaltation, the revelation of who God is and what the incarnation means. The central symbol is that of Jesus raised high, his arms extended in love to embrace "all people" (or, possibly, "all things," 12:32) and to draw them to his light and life.

John concludes the public ministry with the hiding of the Light through unbelief, a tragic eventuality that Isaiah has already discerned having, like Abraham, seen Jesus' glory (12:38–41). Yet, as in the Prologue, the looming tragedy is not the last word; many do believe though fear of eviction by the authorities holds them back. Jesus' last words are a summons to faith: only in him and his revelation are salvation and life to be found, as well as freedom from judgment. All of Jesus' ministry thus far has been at the bidding, and with the authority, of the Father who has sent the Son to give life to the world.

III. Jesus' Private Ministry: The Last Supper (13:1–17:26)

In this major subdivision of the Gospel, Jesus turns from the public to the private world of his own disciples. Most of the material in these five chapters is uniquely Johannine and without extensive parallel in the Synoptic Gospels. The Farewell Discourse (13:31–16:33) contains material that is repetitious, and some have speculated that it originally circulated in two versions, both of which the evangelist has incorporated. Whatever its origins, these chapters in their present form are now largely integrated, thanks to the evangelist's careful editorial work, and despite some awkwardness in detail. Along with the events on either side—the footwashing and the prayer—which act as the frame, the whole forms a chiastic structure, with the vine symbolism at the center in the opposition of love and hate (15:1–16:4a). Jesus' departure acts as both the context and theme of the whole.

A. Jesus Washes the Disciples' Feet (13:1–30)

13:1–20. The Footwashing. The opening three sentences serve as a mini-prologue, outlining Jesus' destiny (just as the Prologue outlined his origins) and the implications for his disciples. The setting is just before Passover, the third Passover in John's Gospel, and John brings to it the festal associations of Jesus as the new temple, the Host at the table, the Lamb of God, and the true Bread from heaven. In John's Gospel, this is not a Passover meal as in the Synoptics. The arrival of the "hour," however, does signal the passion, which John interprets as Jesus' return to the Father. The main thrust of the first sentence is Jesus' love for his disciples, which is the motivation behind everything that is to follow in the second half of the Gospel (13:1c). Jesus' love for "his own" (see 1:11–13) extends "to the end" not just in terms of time—till the end of his life—but also in scope: his love for them is total, radical, complete. Though the betrayer is in the midst, ironically part of the intimate circle to which Jesus has turned (13:2), Jesus walks forward towards the passion in full knowledge of

what the Father has given him, and in obedience to his appointed destiny.

In this context Jesus performs the footwashing, an act that John outlines in careful, almost ritualized detail. Simon Peter's forceful reaction against it (13:4–8a) is both typical of his impetuous character and also gives the opportunity for Jesus to explain its necessity. His brief answer outlines its primary meaning: "unless I wash you, you have no share with me" (13:8). In the ancient world, footwashing was done for reasons of hygiene and hospitality, generally by a slave or other socially inferior person. It also had cultic significance, suggesting the ritual purity needed, for example, in entering the Temple. It is the latter meaning that has primacy here. The footwashing is fundamentally an act of ritual cleansing that enables the disciples to enter into full union with their Lord. Once Peter has grasped the point, he demands to be cleansed from head to toe. But Jesus explains that the disciples have already been cleansed and need only their feet washed, just as guests will bathe at home before a banquet and then have their feet washed on arrival—with the exception of Judas Iscariot, the betrayer (13:10–11). The footwashing, therefore, belongs in the context of the passion, signifying union with Jesus in his sacrificial death.

Yet John draws out a further meaning. Not only is the footwashing a symbol of cleansing and union with Christ, it is also symbolic of the love within the believing community (13:12–17). This kind of servant love is the love that Jesus has demonstrated for "his own" and is to be the basis of Christian love. Disciples are drawn into a community, not just with Jesus but also with one another. This will be an important theme in the Farewell Discourse: Jesus will be present to his people in their self-giving love for, and service of, one another. The circle of love that this creates has its origins in the Father (13:20).

13:21–30. Revelation of the Betrayer. For the second time in the Gospel, Jesus expresses his dismay and distress at the arrival of "the hour" (12:27; 13:21); this time, it is the intentions of the betrayer that prompt distress. Only now do the disciples become aware of what Jesus has been prophesying all along. This is also the first description of the unnamed disciple as "the disciple whom Jesus loved" (see 1:35–39). Note that he is "reclining next to" Jesus, holding the place of honor and intimacy at the banquet (13:23, 25), and he is therefore in a position to whisper to Jesus. John uses an expressive metaphor to describe the posture of this disciple: he is reclining next to Jesus' "heart" (literally, "bosom," *kolpos*, and "breast"," *stēthos*), occupying the place of the true disciple, just as Jesus is "close to the Father's heart" (*kolpos*, 1:18).

B. Farewell Discourse (13:31–16:33)

13:31–14:31. Jesus' Departure: The Way, the Paraclete, Love, and Peace. The current chapter division is unfortunately placed. The Farewell Discourse begins before ch. 14, and there is no gulf between 13:38 and 14:1. Jesus commences the discourse with the central motif of the passion, the mutual glorification of Father and Son. Just as Jesus will glorify God by revealing on the cross the full extent of the Father's life-giving love for the world (see 3:16), so God will glorify Jesus by lifting him up, through the cross (death, resurrection, and ascension), to return to the heavenly glory of the Father. In view of his imminent departure, Jesus gives his disciples the love command (13:33–35) as a sign of his presence and a sign to the world. What is "new" about this command is not the notion of love within the community, which belongs firmly within the Mosaic Law but rather the expression "just as I have loved you." The love of Jesus has been demonstrated ritually and symbolically in the footwashing and will be enacted on the cross.

Peter's desire to follow his Lord's path will prove illusory (13:36–38). Yet, for all the solemn warning, Jesus immediately goes on to comfort the disciples, faced with the pain of his departure and their own inability to follow as true servants of their Master (see 12:26; 13:16). This consolation is based in the temporary nature of their separation; Jesus' return to the Father means his preparation for a reunion with them, through the Father (14:1–3). Thomas and Philip take Jesus' language literally, failing to realize that Jesus is speaking symbolically and christologically. He is himself the true and life-giving Way to the Father who is the ultimate destination not just of Jesus but also the community of disciples (14:5–6); to see Jesus is to see the Father (14:8–9). That means that the access disciples have to Jesus—an access that will

continue, despite the separation—is access also to the Father.

It is difficult to know precisely how to interpret the language of Jesus' return throughout the Farewell Discourse. On the one hand, it suggests the idea of the *parousia*, Christ's future coming. At the same time, a very strong theology of the Spirit emerges in five distinctive passages throughout these chapters. In the first of these passages, the Spirit is named "the Advocate" (literally "Paraclete," *paraklētos*), who will *be* the presence of Jesus for the bereft and orphaned community (14:15–18). John's concept of the Spirit-Paraclete, confined to these chapters of the Gospel, is rich and complex, its range of meaning emerging throughout the discourse. While advocacy is part of that role, here in this context the idea of comfort dominates. As the Spirit of Jesus, sent from the Father, the Paraclete will bring consolation to the community. Note that John describes the Spirit as "another Advocate," implying that Jesus is the first and that his ministry will be paralleled by that of the abiding Spirit.

So is Jesus' coming a future event, at the end of history, or is it manifest in the imminent arrival of the Spirit-Paraclete? The answer is probably both. Though John gives considerable emphasis to the present moment, it is nonetheless an anticipation —of what God has promised for the future. The Spirit's presence guarantees the continuing love of Father and Son: to abide in that love means to hold to the love command, thus remaining within the divine circle of love (14:21). This love is not intended as a revelation to the "world"—and here John uses "world" in its most negative sense, as the realm of darkness that lies over against God— but is intended for the believing community, who are themselves the sign of Jesus' love for those outside. This leads into the second promise of the Advocate who, this time, has the role of Teacher and Reminder, making real and dynamic the teaching of the Johannine Jesus (14:26).

At this point, Jesus comes to the end of the first part of the discourse, underlining his departure with the gift of peace (*shalom*), the reiteration of his reassurance against anxiety and the promise of his return. Joy, not sorrow, is to be the appropriate response of the disciples in the face of Jesus' return to his beloved Father, who is the ground of his divinely human identity. That departure, via the cross, will bring about the radical overpowering of "the ruler of this world" (14:30). Though the light appears to be quenched, it cannot be overcome by the darkness (see 1:5); on the contrary, the darkness will be overcome by the light.

15:1–16:4a. Abiding-in-Love and the World's Hatred.

The Farewell Discourse now moves into more explicit symbolism, developing Jesus' words about love and union from the previous chapter (14:20–21). This section forms the chiastic center of chapters 13–17, with its key opposition between love and hate. The primary image is that of the vine, which becomes a kind of symbolic allegory of the relationship between Jesus, the Father and the believing community (15:1–11). As with the sheep and the sheepfold, the vine is an important symbol for Israel in the OT (see, e.g., Ps 80:8–13; Jer 2:21; Ezek. 17:6–8; Hos 10:1). In John the vine functions as a major symbol for the church, with the emphasis on the vital interdependence between vine, branches, and vine grower.

An important part of the viticulturalist's art is the pruning of branches to encourage new growth. This process involves both removing dead branches and cutting back those that remain. It is significant that John speaks literally of this pruning as a "cleansing," a purifying that takes place through the life-giving word of Jesus (15:2–3, 6). Pruning makes fruit-bearing possible, the maturation of the grapes for the vintage and the making of wine. Fruit most likely refers metaphorically to the exterior signs of love within the community, which enable believers to find abundant life and thrive in relation to one another.

Throughout the Gospel, John has used the concept of abiding to express his understanding of discipleship (see 1:38–39). Unfortunately, this theme is often obscured in English translation, which tends not to translate "abide" consistently but sometimes uses "stay" or "remain" (*menō*; see 1:38–39; 4:40; 9:41). Although John employs imagery of following to indicate discipleship, abiding is the more fundamental Johannine notion, articulating the intimacy, connection, and rest that lie at the core of faith. In the image of the vine, John brings the notion of abiding to prominence as the most apt metaphor to describe the mutuality and interdependence of divine love, and of the love between disciples and their Lord.

In the verses that follow, John develops the imagery of the vine in categories of love and friendship. Now friendship becomes the primary category of the relationship between Jesus and disciples rather than the master-slave paradigm (15:15). Yet this intimate friendship does not rule out the call to obedience (15:14, 17). Mutuality, rather than equality, is the nature of the union. Disciples are still called to obey their Lord but as free, adult children of the household, not infants or slaves. It is the mature obedience of those who have been invited into the circle of love and knowing (15:16). This friendship is profoundly christological: it is grounded in Christ's friendship for his own that shows itself most radically in his dying for them (15:13). Abiding with him on the vine draws disciples also into relationship with one another as intimate "friends," making complete the circle of love that originates with the Father. Although no explicit mention is made of the Spirit in these verses, the implications are present, carried over from the previous chapter. All that Jesus offers in his capacity as the Vine and true Lover of the disciples is sustained by the Paraclete who bridges perfectly the gap between the absent Lord and his future return.

The opposite of the love and friendship within the community of faith is the hatred and persecution of the world (15:18–16:4a). Here again John uses "world" in its most negative sense: not in reference to the material domain but the realm of death and darkness. The hatred of this realm is an inevitable concomitant of belonging to Christ; indeed, the world's hatred is really a hatred of Jesus himself—and ultimately hostility to the Father (15:20–23). Jesus' coming, in other words, has given rise to both illumination and judgment, a two-sided response that will continue in the disciples' experience in the world. In this context, the role of the Holy Spirit is forensic (15:26–27). In the third Paraclete passage, the Spirit is indeed the Advocate, who bears witness on the disciples' behalf, precisely in the context of the world's hatred. This promise gives strength and comfort to the community as it faces the inevitability of persecution (16:1–4a). Note that John's description of these tribulations comes, not from the pagan world but rather from within Judaism, with particular reference to exclusion from the synagogue (*aposynagōgos*, 16:2; see 9:22; 12:42). This reflects the struggle of the early post-70CE Christian community to establish itself over against the (also struggling) Jewish community, from whence it sprang. Once again, "remembering" plays an important role in the life of the believing community, a task that belongs rightly to the Paraclete (see 2:17, 22; 14:26).

16:4*b*–33. Jesus' Departure: The Paraclete, Joy, Love, and Peace. The third section of the Farewell Discourse provides a parallel with the first section, in its common themes of Jesus' departure, the coming of the Paraclete, the scattering of the disciples, and Jesus' gift of peace. Once again, while acknowledging the pain of Jesus' departure, John presents that departure as paradoxically of benefit to the community. Just as the Johannine Jesus speaks earlier of the Father being greater than himself (14:28), so now he describes the coming of the Paraclete as bringing greater advantage to the disciples (16:7). The role of the Spirit is again forensic in this fourth passage, but this time in prosecution against the world, convicting it of sin. The important point here is that the Advocate reveals that "the ruler of this world" stands already under judgment (16:11), a judgment effected through the cross.

In the fifth and last reference to the Paraclete in the Farewell Discourse, the Holy Spirit reveals the truth to the believing community: not a static view of truth but a dynamic, vibrant sense that implies the Spirit's continuing voice in the life of the church (16:13). This testimony to truth, which parallels Jesus' own ministry (see 8:32; 14:6), is authenticated by the Spirit's origins and purpose. Just as everything Jesus has said and done has been given him by the Father for the purpose of the Father's glorification, so everything to be said and done by the indwelling "Spirit of truth" will be given by the Son for the Son's glorification (16:13–15). In terminology developed in later centuries, John's understanding of God is trinitarian.

Turning now to the disciples, Jesus offers them consolation in view of his imminent demise. No less than modern readers of the Gospel are Jesus' disciples puzzled by his promise to return in "a little while" (16:16–19). Their bewilderment is resolved, however, not by direct answer (as is typical of the Johannine Jesus) but by the symbolic allegory of the woman who gives birth. In a mother's experience, as with disciples faced by the absence of Jesus, there is a paradoxical jux-taposition of pain and joy. The joy helps her to endure and leave behind the pain. Thus, within the framework of Jesus' imminent coming—both in the gift of the Spirit and in his own future return—the suffering of disciples is set within a wider perspective.

By the end of the Farewell Discourse, light has dawned on the disciples. They know now Jesus' true origins and destiny, they understand the temporal nature of the separation, and they comprehend the Father's love that embraces them (16:25–30). Jesus' last words to them are words of warning but mostly of consolation. Despite the persecution and the dispersion, despite their abandonment of Jesus, the disciples are held in his peace and victory, just as he is held in the Father's abiding presence (16:31–33). His conquest of death and darkness, paradoxically through the cross, will have the last word.

C. Jesus' Great Prayer (17:1–26)

Jesus' prayer forms the climax of this section of the Gospel, paralleling the footwashing in its focus on themes of love and unity. Technically, it indicates the conclusion of the fellowship meal (not a Passover meal in John) but also suggests farewell speeches of dying patriarchs in the OT who conclude their last utterances with prayer (see Gen 49; Deut 33; Josh 24). Traditionally, John 17 has been called the "high priestly prayer." Though John does not depict Jesus in high-priestly categories (as Hebrews does), Jesus, in this chapter, is engaging in intercession on behalf of his people. A more strictly Johannine title, however, is the "Prayer of the Departing Redeemer." A peculiar feature of John 17 is that elsewhere the Johannine Jesus seems to discount the need for intercessory prayer, so perfect is the unity of will between him and the Father (11:41–42; 12:27–28). Jesus' prayers, therefore, serve a wider function than strictly intercession: they point to the communion between Father and Son, and they draw the believing community—the objects of prayer—into Jesus' relationship with God.

17:1–5. Prayer for Glory. Jesus' great prayer is popularly read as a prayer for unity among Christians, but this is only a part of the story. Fundamentally it is a prayer for glorification, as the opening section indicates. Jesus reiterates his announcement of the "hour" (12:23; 13:1), and prays within the context of his passion for that mutual glorification that is its inner, Johannine meaning (17:1, 4–5). The opening verses are a summary of the mission of Jesus: at the heart of the revelation of glory is the gift of eternal life, found in intimate union with the Son and, through him, with the Father (17:2–3). The divine power that Jesus possesses and that authorizes him to bestow eternal life, is grounded in the Son's authority in creation, extending to all "flesh" and not just "all people" (*sarx,* 17:2) as the NRSV suggests .

From this it becomes clear that the whole prayer points in two directions at the same time. On the one hand, it points backwards to the beginning of the Gospel. The one who prays here is the Son who is "close to the Father's heart" (1:18), standing face-to-face with God as the eternal Word-made-flesh (1:1–2, 14). On the other hand, the prayer looks forward to the passion narrative to follow. The prayer is itself an act of glorification, and, in that sense, it both anticipates and enacts the passion. It illustrates that the deepest meaning of the cross in John's Gospel is the exaltation of the Son to the Father, an act of prayer and praise that draws creation into its boundless, life-giving embrace. What is played out here, on the historical plain, is the eternal self-offering of the Son to the Father and the Father's mutual love for the Son.

17:6–19. Prayer for the Disciples. Jesus turns now to his disciples and prays for them in the light of the impending separation. This part of the prayer acts as a kind of protective seal over the disciples, guarding them against the dangers of the world and emphasizing that the love they have already received from Jesus will not be taken from them. More fundamental than the intercessory level, however, is the notion of prayer as communion. In this sense, the disciples through the words and act of the prayer are drawn into the love and self-offering of the Son to the Father. Their place within the trinitarian circle of love is assured. Once again, though the Spirit is not named explicitly, it is precisely the role of the Paraclete to ensure and actualize that ongoing presence, despite the disjunction of Jesus' departure.

In these verses, the disciples are given the gift of the "name" to protect and inspire them (17:6, 11–13). In the OT, this refers to the divine name, the unspeakable and unpronounceable name of God. For John, by extension, the name is that of the Father, and the gift is given by Jesus himself who has such authority as, and only as, the Son. The disciples are protected also by the word that Jesus has given them, a radical self-giving that draws them like a magnet to holiness and truth (17:17–19). Yet this protection occurs within the world and not outside it. The disciples are not removed from danger and the power of the Evil One but rather protected in the Father's love and unity within the context of violence and persecution (17:15). These intercessions echo the petitions of the Lord's Prayer (Matt 6:9–13; Luke 11:2–4).

17:20–26. Prayer for Future Believers. The circle of intimacy between the Father and Son, which has widened (through the Spirit-Paraclete) to include Jesus' disciples, now widens even further: future believers are drawn into the orbit of the divine love and union. The focus of this last section is on the oneness of believers, which echoes and reflects the oneness within the divine being (17:20–21). This unity is part of the glory that Jesus renders to the Father and passes on to the believing community (17:22–23). John does not specify the nature of the unity among Christians. Rather, his focus is on its quality as a gift, an intrinsic part of the divine nature into which the Church is drawn. Therefore, "to know" signifies an intimate and life-giving relationship that draws creation into the trinitarian love at the heart of all things. As Son, Jesus draws believers into his own filiation, so that they too share in the intimacy of his union with the Father and become "children of God" (1:12–13). This relationship is the source and origin of eternal life, encapsulated in Jesus' prayer and enacted through the glory of his self-giving, life-giving death on the cross.

IV. Jesus' Death and Resurrection (18:1–21:25)

The Johannine passion and resurrection narratives are not a journalistic account of the crucifixion. They are also a highly stylized and symbolic portrayal of the meaning of that death for the believing community. This is not to say that the narratives lack historical basis but rather that they are so shaped as to draw readers to faith. The cross, in John, is a verbal or narrative icon, a profound meditation on the saving significance of the crucified and risen Christ. To gaze on this "icon" in faith is the Johannine understanding of salvation (19:27).

The narrative as a whole is bounded on either side by garden imagery: John refers explicitly to the arrest, burial, and first Easter appearance as taking place in a garden. In the OT the garden is a symbol of paradise, of Spring and new life, fecundity and harmony (Gen 2; Song of Songs). Symbolically, the garden is where creation begins and harmony founders, where, despite loss, hope remains of love flowering again in the promise of paradise restored. For John, this OT promise is fulfilled, paradoxically, in the brutality of the arrest and the mournful yet unexpectedly sumptuous burial. The imagery reaches its climax in the Easter garden where Mary Magdalene is reunited with her beloved Lord and commissioned to proclaim his resurrection to the disciples.

A. Jesus' Arrest and Trial (18:1–19:16a)

John 18 begins a new section of the Gospel. Jesus now moves from the private, intimate world of his disciples to the public arena and the hostility of his opponents. The irony is that one of the inner circle has treacherously bridged the divide between the two irreconcilable realms, between enemy and friend. To acknowledge this chapter as a new beginning, however, from a narrative point of view, should not obscure the way John writes, overlapping one story and one section with another. There is also a sense in which the passion commences much earlier in the narrative. Just as in Mark and Matthew the passion narrative begins with the anointing of Jesus' head, so the Johannine passion is foreshadowed by the washing/anointing of feet—Jesus' feet anointed by Mary of Bethany (11:1, 12:1–8) and the disciples' feet washed by Jesus (13:1–20), both of which prefigure the passion and resurrection, embodying Jesus' assent to his destiny.

18:1–11. Arrest in a Garden. The arrest itself is rather astonishing in John's account, carrying a touch of farce. The arresting party is ludicrously overblown for the seizure of one man and yet insignificant in view of his sublime identity. Judas leads a large contingent of Roman soldiers and Jewish police who bristle with weapons, lanterns, and torches to overpower the Light of the World. Yet when the soldiers approach Jesus, it is he who takes the initiative—"For whom are you looking?" (18:4, 7, author's trans.)—and his self-identifying, "I am he," which literally means "I am" (*ego eimi*), makes them fall to the ground, overcome by his majesty. John thus emphasizes that Jesus consents to what is occurring and never for a moment loses his identity; on the contrary, against adversity and enmity it shines the more brightly (see 1:5).

Jesus' concern is not for himself but "his own," those for whom he has just prayed (17:9–19). Loving them to the end (13:1), he ensures their safety above everything else. His request to those arresting him is authoritative (18:9). Although Peter's rash act of violence against the high priest's servant (named "Malchus" only in John, 18:10) is comprehensible in the circumstances, Jesus' rebuke indicates Peter's unwillingness to accept God's will—a will with which Jesus is in full accord (18:11)—as well as his folly in courting unnecessary danger.

18:12–27. Jesus and Peter at the High Priest's Court. The story of Peter's denial occurs, with variations, in all four Gospels (Mark 14:66–72; Matt 26:69–75; Luke 22:54–62). In each case, it is placed alongside, and contrasted with, Jesus' appearance before members of the Jerusalem hierarchy. In John, the contrast is also between the unnamed disciple (probably "the disciple whom Jesus loved"), who has access to the high priest's court, and Simon Peter, who does not. As at the Last Supper, the unnamed disciple takes precedence over Peter (13:23–25). Peter denies his Lord three times (18:17, 25–27a), thus fulfilling Jesus' prophecy and confirming his foreknowledge (13:37–38; 16:32; 18:27b). His desire to "follow" is not lacking, but his courage fails. At the end of the Gospel, Jesus prophesies that Peter will indeed follow him faithfully to death (21:18–19).

Jesus' trial before Annas is set within the story of Peter's denial. On either side, Peter is "standing and warming himself" in the wintry courtyard: outside in the cold, in company with Jesus' enemies (18:18, 25), denying all knowledge of Jesus. Peter's emphatic "I am not" contrasts with Jesus' earlier "I am" (18:5, 6, 8, 17, 25). By contrast, Jesus under questioning defends himself, protesting against the injustice that confronts him (18:20–23); there has been nothing covert or surreptitious about his teaching, as any witness could validate. By the end of the scene, the religious authorities seem at a loss and nothing is resolved. Jesus is handed over for questioning to Caiaphas, Annas' son-in-law (11:49–50), but nothing is said of its progress or outcome (18:24).

18:28–19:16a. The Trial before Pilate and Condemnation. The centerpiece of the Johannine trial narrative is the trial before Pilate, which occurs in seven scenes, with Pilate shuttling back and forth between his headquarters (the pretorium), where Jesus is, and outside, where the Jewish authorities are. Their fear of ritual defilement at Passover prevents their entering an unclean, Gentile edifice (18:28). In the first scene, outside the pretorium (18:29–32), Pilate tries to pin down the charge against Jesus, but the Jerusalem authorities want only to have him executed. John underlines that everything happens in fulfillment of either the Scriptures or, as now, the word of Jesus (18:32). The second scene, inside, is between Pilate and Jesus (18:33–38a). Again Pilate seeks to locate the charge against Jesus but again fails. Jesus does not answer his questions directly but describes his "kingdom" or "kingship" as not belonging to this world (*basileia*, 18:36). It is not unrelated to the world, but it does not use the methods of the world to establish itself. Its origins are "from above" and of a different quality from the world's understanding of power and authority. As King, Jesus embodies truth—and truth is what the trial is supposedly about. Yet Pilate answers with a shrug, as if the whole question were too difficult for him (18:38a) despite the fact that, as governor, he supposedly represents truth and justice.

The third scene (18:38b–40) makes it clear that Pilate is now convinced of Jesus' innocence. To appease the Jerusalem hierarchy, Pilate suggests releasing Barabbas, a "bandit" (a freedom-fighter or terrorist), while taunting them with the title "King of the Jews," underlining their subject status and increasing the enmity between them and Jesus. (John is, of course, writing after the Jewish War [66–70 CE], aware of the tragic consequences of the rebellion against Rome.) The fourth scene is the center of the chiasm (19:1–3). Jesus is taken before the Roman soldiers who flog him, dress him as a king, and ridicule him—the only mockery in John's account of the crucifixion. It represents Pilate's second attempt to release Jesus and to appease the Jewish authorities, yet it operates ironically to reveal Jesus' true iden-

tity. In the fifth scene (19:4–8), outside, Pilate presents the authorities with Jesus, mocked and bloody, taunting them with this derisive picture of their "kingship." Yet he remains convinced of Jesus' innocence (19:4, 6). His words of acclamation, "Here is the man!" (19:5) express both his contempt for the chief priests and his unwitting revelation of who Jesus really is, even in degrading circumstances. Demanding Jesus' crucifixion, the chief priests manifest their real objection to Jesus: his identity as Son of God (19:7). The title, with its overtones of Roman imperial status, fills Pilate with anxiety.

The sixth scene (19:5–11), inside the pretorium, has Jesus fall silent before Pilate, who threatens him with the power of Rome. But Jesus represents a far greater power, and only by permission of that power does Pilate have authority over him. The real culprit is not Pilate but "the one who handed me over" (19:11), most likely Judas Iscariot. In the final scene (19:12–15), Pilate makes a more determined effort to release Jesus. But just as he has played on the political sensitivities of the chief priests, so they in turn play on his. In effect, they question his loyalty to Rome: Pilate's release of Jesus would make him appear to support sedition against the Emperor. Pilate therefore reaches his decision and seats himself on the judge's bench (the Greek could also mean that he seats *Jesus* on the judge's bench!), where he condemns Jesus to death (19:16a). Even now, he cannot resist taunting the Temple authorities; they respond by swearing allegiance not to God but to Rome. Knowing the truth, Pilate denies it; despite their mutual enmity, the two groups collude in judicial murder.

B. Jesus' Crucifixion and Burial (19:16b–42)

19:16b–25a. The Inscription on the Cross and Seamless Robe. The crucifixion narrative consists of a series of symbols that draw out the meaning of the cross in John's understanding. Jesus, not Simon of Cyrene (Mark 15:21), carries his own cross-bar, emphasizing his divine control of events. Also, the inscription outlining the charge is more significant in John than in the Synoptics (Mark 15:26). While it signifies Pilate's determination, after having been outwitted, to score the last point off the religious authorities, it also speaks the ironic truth: Jesus is indeed the "King of the Jews," a kingship that is universal, as the three languages indicate (19:20).

The Roman soldiers, entitled to the remaining possessions of the condemned, divide his clothes but gamble for the seamless robe. In doing so, they fulfill the OT and also ironically and unintentionally confirm the divine unity, which Jesus represents and into which the believing community is drawn (19:23–24).

19:25b–27. The Mother of Jesus and the Beloved Disciple. One of the key symbols of the Johannine crucifixion is the relationship between the mother of Jesus and the unnamed disciple, which Jesus inaugurates. The difficulty here is knowing the limits of the symbolism. As Jesus has brothers in this Gospel (2:12; 7:3–5), provision for his aged mother is not the focus. More likely, Jesus' words to these two disciples are the sign of his love for "his own," as the language of "home" indicates (19:27b; see 17:11–12; 18:8), a love that will endure beyond the crucifixion. Yet the words do not include the others present (four women, paralleling the four soldiers), suggesting something unique about this relationship. The mother of Jesus and the Beloved Disciple are to be to each other as mother-son, symbolizing the intimate and familial bonds of the new community, born here from the death of Jesus. There are also overtones of Zion and Israel: John sees the ideal disciple placed under the care of mother-Zion, embodied by the mother of Jesus, a mothering that originates with Jesus himself and continues in the power of the Spirit-Paraclete (14:18; Isa 66:12–13). There is also an important link with the wedding at Cana, where the mother of Jesus is addressed likewise as "woman" in relation to the "hour" and where she nurtures the disciples' faith in Jesus (2:4–5). Some also see her as a type of Eve, the "mother of all living" (Gen 3:20), present at the undoing of the Fall. Whatever our view, the role of the mother of Jesus is brought to fulfillment in the advent of the "hour" and Jesus' glorification.

19:28–31. Jesus' Death. Jesus' thirst is also part of the Johannine symbolism, where once again the OT is fulfilled (19:28). At a literal level, Jesus' utterance, "I thirst," (author's trans.) signals the raging thirst associated with death. At a deeper level, by accepting the drink, Jesus indicates his passionate "thirst" for the will of God and readiness to drink the cup of suffering (4:34; 18:11). The sprig of hyssop—unlikely at a literal level, since it is a soft and yielding plant—belongs to the same symbolism: the link with Passover confirms Jesus as the paschal Lamb (whose sprinkled blood gave protection from the angel of death, Exod 12:22), and points to the purifying effects of his sacrificial death (Ps 51:7). Jesus' last utterance, "It is finished!" (19:30a), is a cry of triumph and achievement, neither the sense of abandonment of Mark's Jesus (Mark 15:34/par.) nor yet the quiet self-giving trust of Luke's (Luke 23:46). The Johannine Jesus has completed the Father's work in the world (17:4), revealing the divine glory in his mortal flesh, in both living and dying. His life's mission is accomplished. Note that Jesus gives up his own life at this point, emphasizing his authority over life and death (see 10:17–18). The ambiguous wording—"he gave up *his spirit*"—suggests also the Holy Spirit, donated by the crucified Jesus, a further symbol of the life that comes through Jesus' death (19:30b, *emphasis added*; see 7:39; 12:24).

19:31–37. The Piercing of Jesus' Side. The climax of the Johannine crucifixion occurs at this point, following the death of Jesus. John emphasizes once more the Passover connection: now is the hour at which the lambs are slaughtered in preparation for the Passover meal. Again we confront the religious scruples of the religious authorities, who fail to see before them the Lamb of God who takes away the world's sin (19:31; 1:29, 34). Unlike his fellow criminals, however, Jesus' legs are not broken: as OT prophecy makes clear, the paschal Lamb must be whole and its legs unbroken (19:33, 36; Exod 12:46). The piercing of Jesus' side by the soldier's lance—paralleling the centurion's declaration in the Synoptics (Mark 15:39/pars.)—acts at a literal level to ensure Jesus' death. Symbolically, however, it points to the life that issues from the death of Jesus, blood and water being sacramental symbols of life in this Gospel, associated with the Spirit (2:6–10; 3:5; 4:10–14; 6:53–56; 7:37–39; 13:3–5; 15:4–5). Paradoxically, the crucified Christ gives birth to the believing community, as attested by the faithful witness, the one "who saw this"—most probably the Beloved Disciple (19:35). Gazing on this extraordinary icon of life-through-death produces, in the viewer, either faith or judgment (19:37; Zech 12:10).

19:38–42. Jesus' Burial in a Garden. The Synoptic Gospels give Joseph of Arimathea the leading role in Jesus' burial (Mark 15:43–46), but, to this prominent disciple, John adds the figure of Nicodemus who now at last experiences his own "rebirth" through the death of Jesus (19:38–39*a*; 3:1–9). The secret sympathies of these two Jewish leaders are now unveiled. At considerable risk to themselves, they request of Pilate the body of a deceased criminal and bury him with sumptuous quantities of myrrh and aloes, as well as careful attention to the proper rites (19:39*b*–40). This is, indeed, a burial fit for a king. John notes the new tomb and the garden setting, preparing the reader for the new life that will unexpectedly appear in the Easter garden.

C. Jesus' Resurrection Appearances (20:1–21:25)

One of the main difficulties in John's resurrection narratives is the relationship between John 20 and John 21. After Jesus' appearance to Thomas, John seems to close off the whole Gospel with a summary statement that sets out his purpose (20:30–31), while John 21 gives the impression of a first appearance of the risen Christ. For some, this suggests that John 21 is a later addition or a kind of epilogue to the Gospel—perhaps even part of a second edition. However, despite the points of awkwardness (and John's narrative style often does not smooth things out), John 21 plays a significant role in the Johannine resurrection story, tying up a number of loose ends from the previous chapter. John 21 also has a number of connections with, and parallels to, the rest of the Gospel. Whatever its origins, in its present form it belongs as an integrated part of the Gospel and is a vital part of the Johannine narrative.

20:1–18. Appearance to Mary Magdalene. Mary Magdalene is first introduced into the Johannine narrative at the foot of the cross, where she stands alongside the other women and the Beloved Disciple (19:25). She now approaches the tomb in the predawn darkness (with no intention of anointing the body, unlike the "myrrh-bearing women" of Mark and Luke) and is dismayed to find the stone rolled away. She at once draws the wrong conclusion, that the body has been stolen, and runs to inform Peter and the other disciple—oddly enough, using the plural "we" to describe her findings (20:2). What follows is the strange and inconclusive story of the two disciples' visit to the tomb (20:3–9). There is a kind of competition

for precedence that takes place: the other disciple reaches the tomb first, yet allows Peter to enter first (20:4–6); Peter does not understand whereas the other seems to reach a level of faith, though what that level is the narrative does not disclose (20:8–9). The important point is that, as with the stone, so the grave clothes and the head cloth indicate that Jesus' body has not been stolen but, on the contrary, that Jesus has risen from the dead.

Mary has meanwhile returned to the tomb and the two disciples leave her there; not surprisingly, she begins to weep. Turning to the tomb, she sees not the grave clothes rolled up but two angels, seated at either end of the stone slab on which the body lay (20:12). This is a further sign of the resurrection, the position of the angels suggesting the cherubim on the mercy seat of the ark of the covenant (Exod 25:17–22; Heb 9:5). Their role is symbolic, for their only words to Mary are the question, "Why are you weeping?" (20:13). Despite her faith and love, Mary does not recognize the signs and, like other characters in the Fourth Gospel, misunderstands. Even when confronted by Jesus himself, her tears prevent her recognizing him, and she assumes he is the gardener. His naming of her, "Mary!," is enough: like one of the sheep she recognizes the voice of the Shepherd when he calls her name (20:16). Yet still there remains misunderstanding. Her embrace of him—possibly holding his feet (see Matt 28:9)—indicates that she assumes he will remain with her in flesh rather than through the Spirit; the problem here is not that she touches him but that she holds onto him. Jesus clarifies her misunderstanding and speaks of his impending ascension "to my Father and your Father, to my God and your God" (20:17). The language is carefully nuanced to show the commonality yet distinction between Jesus' relationship with the Father and that of disciples. Finally, Mary is commissioned with the message of the resurrection and proclaims the message to the other disciples: the first apostolic witness to the resurrection in this Gospel (20:18).

20:19–23. Appearance to the Disciples and Gift of the Spirit. John's account of the giving of the Spirit occurs on Easter evening and not fifty days later, as in Luke's reckoning (Acts 2:1–4), the fourth evangelist making clear the inextricable link between cross, resurrection, ascension, and sending of the Spirit. In John's Gospel, Jesus enters the locked room of the disciples' fears, offering them twice the gift of peace (20:19, 21). The fact that his body still bears the scars, although it is a risen body, maintains the vital continuity between the crucified Jesus and the risen Christ. But it is also profoundly iconic: for John, Jesus' wounds—and especially his wounded side—remain open to give life to the community of faith; believers always have access to that life-giving death. The disciples receive the Spirit—the breath of Jesus—and are commissioned with the authority to bring his forgiveness and reconciliation to the world (20:21, 23).

20:24–31. Appearance to Thomas and Summary of the Gospel. The story of Thomas' encounter with the risen Christ occurs, significantly, one week later: on the Sunday following Easter. Thomas at first refuses to believe, having been absent for the appearance of the risen Lord (for reasons the evangelist does not give). His refusal to believe does not necessarily suggest a more doubting disposition; rather, he demands access to the same evidence as the other disciples. His wish is granted when the risen Jesus again appears, with the greeting of peace, and offers Thomas sight and touch of his wounds (20:26–27). Thomas does not seem to avail himself of this invitation but rather responds with the highest confession of faith of any human being in this Gospel: "My Lord and my God!" (20:28). There are distinct echoes of the Prologue here: Thomas recognizes in the risen Jesus the incarnate Logos, the divine Son who stands face-to-face with God (1:1–18).

Jesus' response to Thomas is not so much a rebuke as an address to the readers of the Gospel. Though they lack the signs that Thomas demanded and are dependent on the testimony of Mary Magdalene and the others, they are no less blessed. Through the presence of the Spirit-Paraclete, their access to the risen Christ is as immediate and real. John concludes the first part of his resurrection story with a summary of Jesus' ministry, emphasizing that the purpose of the Gospel is to lead to faith in Jesus, and therefore to life itself. This is not a neutral account of Jesus but a story that arises from faith to faith, so that others too may have the same meeting with Christ and be drawn into the same union with the Father.

21:1–14. Appearance to Seven Disciples in Galilee. There is an abrupt change of scene in this narrative: from Jerusalem to Galilee, from those who have received their commission to those who still seem somewhat dispirited and lost. The list of seven disciples includes those mentioned in John 1, as well as the two sons of Zebedee, named here for the first time in the Gospel (21:2; 1:35–51). A similar story of a miraculous catch of fish, probably based on the same tradition, is found in Luke's Gospel, where it occurs at the beginning of Jesus' ministry (Luke 5:1–11). John's narrative contrasts the ineffective labor of the disciples in Jesus' absence with its astonishing power and effectiveness in his presence. The imagery is essentially about mission and ties in with the commission and gift of the Spirit in the previous chapter (20:21–23). Like the story of Mary Magdalene and the Emmaus story (20:16; Luke 24:13–33), the risen Christ is not at first recognized until he says or does something familiar, in this case conjuring up a large quantity of fish (21:6–7a). Once again, the characteristically Johannine parallelism between Peter and the unnamed disciple operates: the latter is the first to recognize Jesus, but Peter is first to jump into the sea and reach him (21:7b). Much speculation has gone into the symbolic number 153: it is possible that, for John, it suggests the universality and breadth of the church in its mission (21:11). On the shore Jesus provides the disciples with a meal of fish and bread, imagery that recalls both the miraculous feeding and the eucharist. Once again we meet the Jesus of John 6: the bread from heaven on whom the community feeds in order to find life.

21:15–19. Pastoral Role of Simon Peter. The conversation between Jesus and Peter is part of the same scene, reflecting in its imagery the context of the early church's mission. Much of this chapter is concerned with the ongoing life and leadership of the faith community. Using language that differs each time—to give stylistic variety and not for any difference in meaning—Jesus confronts Peter three times, in formal terms, with the question of his love for Jesus (21:15–17) and commissions him for his role in the community. However distressing, this dialogue reestablishes Peter after his three-fold denial of Jesus (18:17, 25–27), and confirms his leadership in the church: he is to shepherd the flock of the Good Shepherd (10:1–18). The prophecy of Peter's martyrdom further rehabilitates him and confirms his authority. He will surrender power over his own life, not just before his enemies but more fundamentally before the God whose will he obeys. This time Peter will follow Jesus faithfully to death, a death that like Jesus' own will glorify God (21:18–19).

21:20–25. Witness of the Author and Summary of the Gospel. The parallel between these two key disciples continues in the closing verses of the Gospel, taking us back to their presence at the beginning (1:35–42). Peter is concerned about the future of the other disciple, and the writer (probably a later editor) uses the opportunity to clear up misinformation about the latter's death (21:23). Peter's role is not to be inquisitive about the shape and form that the discipleship of others will take but to follow (21:19, 22). The last verses of the Gospel identify the Beloved Disciple as the witness and author of the Gospel, so that by the end, any hint of rivalry between the two disciples dissolves: each has his own role and place in the leadership of the church. The langue of witness here includes but is not confined to material eye-witness testimony: the unnamed disciple both sees and "sees," literarily and metaphorically. In the end John claims emphatic truth for his Gospel, even though it contains only a small portion of the Jesus story (21:25). This truth-claim confirms the divinely human identity of the Johannine Jesus and the divine origins of the church born from his death. For John, it is the risen Lord's abiding presence, through the Spirit-Paraclete, that guarantees its life, joy, love, unity, and peace.

BIBLIOGRAPHY

C. K. Barrett. *The Gospel According to St John.* 2nd ed. (London: SPCK, 1978); R. Bauckham and C. Mosser, eds. *The Gospel of John and Christian Theology* (Grand Rapids/Cambridge, UK: Eerdmans, 2008); R. E. Brown. *The Gospel According to John.* 2 vols. AB 29–29A (Garden City, N.Y.: Doubleday, 1966); R. A. Culpepper. *Anatomy of the Fourth Gospel: A Study in Literary Design* (Philadelphia: Fortress, 1983); C. H. Dodd. *The Interpretation of the Fourth Gospel* (Cambridge: Cambridge University Press, 1953); J. Elowsky, ed. *John 1–10, John 11–21.* 2 vols. Ancient Christian Commentary on Scripture. New Testament 4a, b (Downer's Grove: InterVarsity Press, 2006–2007);

C. Koester. *Symbolism in the Fourth Gospel: Meaning, Mystery, Community* (Minneapolis: Fortress, 1995); D. Lee. *Flesh and Glory: Symbol, Gender and Theology in the Gospel of John* (New York: Crossroad, 2002); F. J. Moloney. *The Gospel of John.* SP 4 (Collegeville, Minn.: The Liturgical Press, 1998); R. Schnackenburg. *The Gospel According to St John.* 3 vols. (Vols. 1–2, New York: Seabury, 1980; Vol 3, New York: Crossroad, 1982); S. M. Schneiders. *Written That You May Believe. Encountering Jesus in the Fourth Gospel* (New York: Crossroad, 1999); M. M. Thompson. *The God of the Gospel of John.* (Grand Rapids: Eerdmans, 2001).

ACTS

Joel B. Green

OVERVIEW

The Acts of the Apostles is the only narrative of its kind in the NT. Whereas the Gospels recount the significance of the advent, life, mission, death, and resurrection of Jesus, Acts picks up the story from the resurrection and ascension of Jesus and traces the development and mission of the early church. Like any historical narrative, Acts is selective in what it includes, so we would be mistaken to imagine that this book gives us "the history of the early church." Its focus is somewhat more narrow, oriented as it is around the missional agenda set forth by Jesus in 1:8: "you will be my witnesses in Jerusalem, in all Judea and Samaria, and to the ends of the earth." These words provide not so much the *outline* of Acts as the *mandate* that drives the narrative forward. Accordingly, Acts traces the story of the church through those who carry the good news from Jerusalem to Judea, Samaria, and the ends of the earth. Since the phrase "the ends of the earth" refers not only to places on the first-century Roman map (Ethiopia, for example) but also to the reach of God's salvation to include the Gentiles (see 13:46, citing Isa 49:6), much of Acts is devoted to the commission, mission, and witness of Paul and his companions, whom the Lord chose "to bring my name before Gentiles and kings and before the people of Israel" (Acts 9:15).

It is generally assumed that the Acts of the Apostles and the Gospel of Luke were written by the same person (compare Luke 1:1–4; Acts 1:1–2) and early tradition identifies that person as Luke. Neither of these NT books is "signed," however; they were originally anonymous documents. When the author refers to himself within the narrative (beginning in ch. 16, with references to "we"), he does so as a member of a group sometimes associated with Paul and not to himself as an individual by name. In fact, what we know about the author of Acts comes almost entirely from his own writing. For example, he is educated, probably urban, is at home in the Scriptures of Israel, and counts himself as a member of the "people of the Way"— that is, as a Christian. We have too little evidence to speak dogmatically of

the author otherwise; hence, in the commentary that follows, I will refer to the author of Acts as "Luke" as a matter of convenience.

If the Gospel of Luke and Acts were written by the same person and if Acts picks up the story at the ascension (the very place where the Gospel of Luke ends), this raises questions about their literary relationship. Do these two books comprise a single narrative? Is Acts a planned "sequel" to the Gospel? In the commentary that follows, it will be clear that I see Acts as the self-conscious continuation of Luke's Gospel, and that Luke has so constructed Acts as to reverberate with some of the emphases and patterns of the Gospel. This means that the mission of Jesus sets the contours and aims of the mission of those who follow him as his witnesses.

OUTLINE

I. The Preface (1:1–14)

II. Witnesses of the Resurrection in Jerusalem (1:15–6:7)

    A. The Lord Reconstitutes the Twelve (1:15–26)

    B. Jesus Receives and Pours Out God's Promise, the Holy Spirit (2:1–47)
        2:1–13. The Outpouring of the Holy Spirit
        2:14–41. Peter Testifies to Jesus' Enthronement
        2:42–47. The Daily Life of the Community of Believers

    C. Spirited Witness in Jerusalem (3:1–4:31)
        3:1–10. A Lame Beggar Enters the Temple, Restored
        3:11–4:4. Peter Addresses the Whole People
        4:5–22. Peter and John Under Inquiry
        4:23–31. God Powerfully Reconfirms His Mission

    D. Embodying the Resurrection Message in

DETAILED ANALYSIS

I. The Preface (1:1–14)

The author of any narrative is faced with the problem of a beginning: How far back in time must I go to make sense of the story? Luke simply ties Acts back into the Gospel of Luke with a preface that both recalls "volume one" and provides a transition into "volume two." He summarizes the Gospel of Luke in vv. 1–3 with reference to "what Jesus did and taught from the beginning," holding together in typical Lukan fashion both word and deed. What Jesus did he did "through the Spirit"—an apt description of the ministry of Jesus (see Luke 4:16–21) and anticipation of the central role the Spirit will play in Acts. Verse 3 looks forward to the role of Jesus' followers who bear witness to his resurrection (e.g., 1:8, 22) and sums up Jesus' message with the overarching description of "the kingdom of God." In the Gospel of Luke, the kingdom refers to the presence of God in the mission of Jesus to overturn competing authorities and to bring salvation in all of its fullness especially to those dwelling on the margins of society.

Verses 4–8 provide two representative scenes during the 40 days of post-resurrection fellowship between Jesus and his followers. Verses 4–5 center on what happened when Jesus had resumed table fellowship with the disciples. (The NRSV translates *synalizomenos* as "staying together," but "eating with" is far more likely.) Reaching back into the Gospel of Luke, Jesus anticipates the coming of the Holy Spirit (see Luke 3:16; 11:16; 24:49). John's baptism, so important for Luke and Acts, was a baptism of repentance—important but incomplete apart from the outpouring of the Spirit by Jesus. Jesus had spoken of the kingdom and promised the coming of the Spirit, so it is no surprise that his disciples wonder about the restoration of the kingdom to Israel (v. 6). After all, the coming of the Spirit was tied to the restoration of God's people from exile (see, e.g., Ezek 37; Joel 2:28–32). The second representative scene (vv. 6–8), then, provides Jesus the opportunity to direct the disciples' concern with restoration toward a mission-oriented program, setting Israel's hope within God's plan to include even Gentiles in God's saving work. Accordingly, 1:8 marks the rejection of a Jerusalem-centered map of God's purpose in favor of an orientation to the end of the earth—understood in Isaiah in terms of the coming of the good news of salvation to the Gentiles (see especially Isa 49:6, on which see Acts 13:47; also Isa 8:9; 45:22; 48:20; 62:10–11—all of which contain the Greek phrase used here, *heōs eschatou tēs gēs*).

The third scene is the climax of this preface to Acts, with the ascension of Jesus linking together Jesus' departure, the impending coming of the Spirit, and the anticipated return of Christ. Here is the literary and theological pivot point for the two-volume work: Jesus' ascension, recounted at the end of the Gospel (Luke 24:50–53) and again at the beginning of Acts (1:9–11). In terms of the literary form of Luke's account, Jesus' ascension is reminiscent of visions of enthronement. This, together with the repeated references to his going into heaven and his movement "up," underscore the significance of this event in terms of Jesus' exalted status. This is his exaltation into God's presence, at God's right hand (see Ps 110). Five times, Luke uses verbs of "seeing," again asserting the important role of the disciples as witnesses. As the narrative will clarify shortly, Jesus' ascension is not only the literary hinge between the Gospel and Acts but also the theological basis for the outpouring of the Spirit and the gift of salvation.

The preface closes with a summary statement (vv. 12–14). The community of believers includes both male disciples (only 11 names are given, preparing for Judas' replacement in 1:15–26) and women, with Mary explicitly named alongside the mention of Jesus' brothers.

II. Witnesses of the Resurrection in Jerusalem (1:15–6:7)

The first major section of Acts is bounded by two accounts in which the community of believers faces a problem within its own boundaries—in 1:15–26, the apostasy of Judas; and in 6:1–7, the integrity of the word embodied in an intercultural community. Between these two is a lengthy account of the church's early witness in Jerusalem—first sketching scenes of preparation (1:15–26) and empowerment (2:1–47), then alternating between reports of the interaction of Jesus' followers with those outside the community (in witness and/or persecution—3:1–4:31; 5:12–42) and accounts concerned with affairs within the community (with a focus on unity and distress—4:32–5:11; 6:1–7). Geographically, this section is localized in Jerusalem. Jesus had mandated that the disciples stay in Jerusalem until the outpouring of the Holy Spirit (1:4; cf. Luke 24:49), and this is exactly what they do (1:12–13). The landscape of these chapters is dotted with references to Jerusalem, the Jerusalem Temple, sites related to the Temple, and to Jewish leadership whose authority and identity is tied to the Temple. In this sense, the opening of Acts is reminiscent of Luke 1:5–2:52, the horizons of which are dominated by Jerusalem and the Temple. The centrality of Jerusalem and the Temple in Acts 1–6 includes some positive elements, including the use of the Temple precincts for prayer and instruction. At the same time, missionary sermons in this context consistently charge Jerusalem and its leadership with working at cross-purposes with God in rejecting and executing Jesus. Moreover,

hostility toward Jesus' followers, earlier predicted by Jesus (e.g., Luke 12:4–12; 21:12–19), is also central to the story. Given Jesus' directive in 1:8 ("in Jerusalem ... to the ends of the earth"), the early concentration of the narrative in Jerusalem is somewhat surprising. "From Jerusalem" (Luke 24:47) may necessitate bearing witness also in Jerusalem (Acts 1:8), but the Jerusalem believers nevertheless seem slow to depart the environs of the city. In fact, it requires the authorization of new leadership (6:1–7) and the witness of Stephen (6:8–8:3) to move the believers beyond the walls of the city, to Judea and Samaria (compare 1:8; 8:2).

Here, as elsewhere in Luke–Acts, the key figure is God, and we find evidence of God's aim and activity in references to the Scriptures (1:16, 20; 2:16–21, 25–28, 31, 35; 3:18, 22–25; et al.), in claims that God's aim was actualized in the life and mission of Jesus (2:22–24, 32; 3:13–15; et al.), and in the activity of the Holy Spirit (the promise of the Father—1:4; 2:33; cf. Luke 24:49). The opening section of Acts is thus a self-conscious continuation of the one story of God's dealings with God's people.

A. The Lord Reconstitutes the Twelve (1:15–26)

The replacement of Judas as one of the Twelve was necessary not simply because of his death, which is almost incidental to Luke's report. The problem, rather, was his defection (1:16, 25). Consistent with images of the kingdom, resurrection, and the coming of the Spirit—all intertwined with God's promise to restore Israel from its exile—is the need to reconstitute the Twelve. This would provide continuity not only with Jesus' mission in Luke's Gospel (e.g., 6:13) but also with Israel's twelve tribes (e.g., Gen 49; Exod 24:4). Throughout this scene, Luke highlights how God's plan was actualized—through references to divine necessity (*dei*, vv. 16, 21), to the Scriptures and their fulfillment (explicitly in v. 20, with reference to Pss 69:26; 109:8), to the work of the Spirit (v. 16), to prayer (vv. 24–25), and to the casting of lots (v. 26). (God had forbidden practices of magic among his people [e.g., Deut 10:11–13; 13; 1 Sam 28; 2 Kgs 21:6; 2 Chr 33:6], so the casting of lots was used to ascertain God's choice [e.g., Lev 16:18; Neh 11:1]. In this way, the intrusion of human desires could be bypassed in favor of ascertaining the divine will.) Thus, a replacement for Judas is chosen through a process involving the articulation of required qualifications, the nomination of two candidates, prayer, and the casting of lots. Later, when new leadership is needed, the process moves from articulating the required qualifications to the choice of leaders to prayer and laying on of hands (6:1–7); that is, the practice of casting lots disappears and is never again mentioned in the NT. Why this is so is never explained, though it might be imagined that the coming of the Holy Spirit to empower and guide God's people (Acts 2) rendered recourse to lot-casting unnecessary.

B. Jesus Receives and Pours out God's Promise, the Holy Spirit (2:1–47)

The outpouring of the Spirit is anticipated by John the Baptist (Luke 3:16) and Jesus (Luke 24:49; Acts 1:4, 8). The nature of this expectation is such that, apart from the Spirit's coming, the narrative must come to a standstill, since the witness of the apostles is contingent upon it. Looking forward, Acts 2 provides a pattern for progress in the mission. (See, e.g., 10:47; compare 11:17.) In this way, Acts 2 functions like Jesus' inaugural sermon in Luke 4:16–30—a scene that shares a number of parallels with the present account. For example, both are the first public event and first public sermon of Jesus and the apostles; the Spirit-anointing of Jesus and the Spirit-filling of his followers initiate their respective missionary activity; and these experiences of the Spirit are interpreted with reference to prophetic Scriptures (Isa 61:1–2/58:6; Joel 2:28–32).

"Pentecost" is shorthand for the festival celebrated on the fiftieth day after Passover, one of the three pilgrim festivals (see Exod 23:16; 34:22; Deut 16:10). Pentecost was the occasion for celebrating the harvest, and particularly for giving thanks to God for graciously bringing forth fruit from the land. This emphasis on the divine hand comports well with the Lukan narrative, the focus of which is Luke's portrait of God as the primary actor whose purpose directs these events.

2:1–13. The Outpouring of the Holy Spirit. For Luke's readers, this scene marks the baptism with the Spirit and fire predicted by John, the work of Jesus Christ, and the faithfulness of the Father who keeps his promise and responds graciously to the prayers of his people; serves as a manifestation of

the kingdom, the genesis of Israel's eschatological restoration; and announces the Spirit-empowered mission to all peoples (see Luke 3:15–17; 11:1–13; 24:44–49; Acts 1:4–8). For characters within the story, though, this scene is full of wonderment, leading to the all-important question, "What does this mean?" (v. 12), which sets the stage for Peter's speech, beginning in v. 14.

The phenomena Luke describes, both visual and auditory, are reminiscent of the theophany at Mount Sinai, when God gave the Ten Commandments (see Exod 19:16–19; Deut 4:11–12; Num 11:25). Old Testament allusions are also found in the combination of a list of nations (vv. 9–11) together with the emphasis on "other languages" in this scene, reminiscent of the interweaving of the Table of Nations with the story of the Tower of Babel in Gen 10–11. Since everyone gathered in Jerusalem on this extraordinary day would have spoken Greek, rendering unnecessary the disciples' speaking in other languages, this OT background becomes even more significant. Speaking in other languages was not needed in order for the disciples to be understood. Why, then, this speaking in tongues? Their doxology ("speaking about God's deeds of power," v. 11; compare Pss 106:2; 145:4, 12; Exod 15; Judg 5; 1 Sam 2), spoken in many languages, becomes a way by which God affirms the diversity of those gathered in a way that undermines Roman interests in creating a single people through subjugation. Any vision of the gathering of all people that denies the will of God for a diverse people scattered across the earth (Gen 1:28; 9:1; 19:32) is similarly denied. The unity of Jesus' followers, underscored at the beginning and end of the Pentecost story (2:1, 42–47), is not the consequence of the dissolution of multiple languages, nor of all social and national distinctives in the service of cultural uniformity. Instead, unity is the consequence of the activity of the Spirit who is poured out by Jesus and the shared identity of those baptized "in the name of Jesus Christ" (2:38).

2:14–41. Peter Testifies to Jesus' Enthronement. This is Peter's first public sermon in Acts, and as such can be compared with Jesus' first sermon in Luke's Gospel (4:16–30) and with Paul's (Acts 13:16–41). In each case, the contours of the speaker's mission and message are sketched, particularly in conversation with the Scriptures and, in the

case of Peter and Paul, in how the OT interprets Christ and the church's mission, and vice versa. The outpouring of the Spirit at Pentecost (2:1–13) had resulted in sneers and questions of meaning. These establish the need for Peter's speech, which has three pivot-points: (1) the phenomena witnessed in Jerusalem comprise nothing less than the outpouring of the Holy Spirit promised in Joel 2:28–32; (2) these phenomena, the Scriptures, and Jesus' followers together testify that Jesus is coregent with God (2:33); and (3) the outpouring of the Spirit marks the present as "the last days"—that is, the days of restoration promised by the prophet Joel, days that mark the offer of salvation to everyone and that call on everyone to respond with repentance and baptism. The result is Luke's emphasis on the saving significance of Jesus' exaltation to God's right hand, on the prophetic and missional character of the community of Jesus' followers, and the certainty that God has accomplished God's purpose not only in spite of but through those who opposed Jesus.

Careful readers of Luke's narrative will be familiar with the question raised by Peter's audience, "Brothers, what should we do?" (2:37), as similar questions have already been asked (Luke 3:10–14; 10:25; 18:18; compare Acts 16:30; 22:10). Peter's response combines repentance (a call to align oneself with God's purpose as this is understood through the life, death, and resurrection of Jesus) and baptism (understood as both the response of those who repent and a gift to those who are received into the community of believers). "Salvation" is represented by two of its central ingredients within Acts—namely, the forgiveness of sins and the gift of the Spirit. Both are oriented essentially to the life of the church, since forgiveness is the means by which people gain (or regain) entrance into the community of God's people and the Spirit generates the genuine experience of community among those who thus declare their allegiance to Jesus, Lord and Messiah.

2:42–47. The Daily Life of the Community of Believers. This summary statement provides a sense of what is typical of the community of believers generated and nurtured by the work of the Spirit poured out at Pentecost. Verse 42 is a kind of summary of the summary, developed in vv. 43–47, so that teaching is correlated with signs and wonders; fellowship is put on display in terms

of economic sharing; the breaking bread exhibits the unity of believers by focusing on hospitality; and prayer points to the habit of praising God. The language Luke uses, "all who believed … had all things in common" (v. 44), is reminiscent of Greco-Roman thought about ideal friendship, and has parallels among the Jewish sect known as the Essenes as well. In this way, the early church is represented as putting into practice the highest ideals. Selling all that one has was not a requirement, however, but was simply a natural outgrowth of the sense of fellowship shared by these followers of Christ. (See also 4:32–5:11.) The result is the ongoing numeric growth of the church—itself understood as the Lord's doing. Here, as often in Acts, the identity of "the Lord" is unclear. Is it the exalted Jesus; or is it the God who raised Jesus from the dead? Here, as often in Acts, this ambiguity may simply demonstrate how unnecessary it is to draw such a careful distinction.

C. Spirited Witness in Jerusalem (3:1–4:31)

This section has as its bookends two summaries of what is typical among these followers of Christ (2:42–47; 4:32–35); the section itself begins and ends with prayer (3:1; 4:23–31). Here begins the narrative of witness in earnest, as Luke relates how Peter, John, and others, empowered by the Holy Spirit, live out some of the specific practices Luke has just summarized (2:42–47). This includes, for example, the importance of signs and wonders, the name of Jesus, the teaching of the apostles, and prayer and praise. This series of four scenes is set in motion by the healing of a lame beggar; altogether, they provide a case study in the breadth of Luke's understanding of "salvation." Thus, salvation is human restoration (3:1–10, 16; 4:9–10), forgiveness (3:19), the end-time restoration of all things (3:20–21), the gift that enables people to align themselves with God's purpose (3:26), and the restoration of Israel (4:2).

3:1–10. A Lame Beggar Enters the Temple, Restored. Note the parallel in Luke 5:17–26. This represents one of many ways Luke provides parallels between Jesus and Jesus' spokespersons in Acts, including Peter, Paul, Stephen and others, and is one way Luke ties together his Gospel and Acts, as well as authorizes (or legitimizes) witnesses like Peter.

The setting is significant. Everything happens in the context of the Temple (3:1, 2, 3, 8, 10), that locus of God's presence whose architecture set up boundaries for those determined to be more or less pure or clean, from a religious perspective. The gate is at first a barrier (see Lev 21:16–18), then a point of entry. Three o'clock in the afternoon was a set time for prayer and evening sacrifices. Luke thus underscores the piety of these apostles. They encounter an apparently hopeless situation, a man born lame, completely dependent on almsgiving (e.g., Deut 15:7–11; Tob 4:5–11; Sir 17:22; Acts 10:2, 4, 31). However, within Luke's narrative, good news is for the lame (e.g., Luke 7:22; 14:13, 21; Acts 8:7).

Importantly, the lame man recognizes the ultimate source of his healing and restoration: he praises God (3:8–9). Peter and John thus bear witness to the efficacy of "calling on the name" (2:21; 3:6). Leaping (see Mic 2:13; Isa 35:6) epitomizes the age of salvation, symbolized in this instance by the healed man's entry into sacred space, the Temple, from which he had formerly been excluded.

3:11–4:4. Peter Addresses the Whole People.

The stage is thus set for Peter to invite those who witnessed the healing to reassess God's purpose and to respond accordingly. His speech is divided into two sections—the first indicating that this healing points to the status of Jesus in God's plan (3:11–16), the second drawing out the implications of this portrait of Christ and issuing in an urgent call to repent (3:17–26). In effect, Peter uses the people's amazement as an opportunity to interpret the past, present, and future work of God. Building on their shared witness of this man's restoration (3:12, 16), their shared ancestry and faith (3:12–13), Peter presses for a shared reconfiguration of life around God's agenda (3:19–26). The sermon pivots around 3:16, then, where Peter interprets this man's "perfect health" as a demonstration of the power of the name of Jesus, "the Holy and Righteous One," the "Author of life," God's glorified servant (3:13–15; Isa 52:13). Although Peter's audience had rejected Jesus (3:13–14), they now have the opportunity to repent because of their failure to comprehend the depth of God's plan. Peter's speech is centered on Christ, but it is profoundly theocentric: *God foretold* that the Messiah must suffer, the times of restoration, and even "these days" (3:18, 21, 24); *God fulfilled* God's plan (3:18); and *God made a covenant* (3:25; see Gen 12:3; 18:18; 22:18; 26:4). This portrait of God has come full circle: The God of Abraham, Isaac, and Jacob (3:13) made a promise to Abraham (3:25)—a promise now kept through the raising up of God's servant, Jesus; this is evidenced in the full health of this formerly lame man. Accordingly, the antidote to their ignorance is not simply new information about what God has done, but their reordering their lives in light of what God has done— that is, repentance.

The result of Peter's address is twofold: (1) an attempt to silence Peter and John through imprisonment and (2) growth of the faithful, from some 3,000 prior to this event (2:41) to "about 5,000" (4:4). Peter and John are arrested for two reasons: exercising influence among the people through their teaching and "proclaiming that in Jesus there is the resurrection of the dead" (Act 4:2). This last phrase is not simply a reference to Jesus' own resurrection, but also to its effects for the restoration of Israel, triumph over those hostile toward God's people, and the establishment of divine justice—for all of this is entailed in Israel's hope of "resurrection of the dead." That those most associated with the Temple are identified as those who place Peter and John in custody signals their very different interpretation of present events. Indeed, those whose powerful identity and status are most identified with present realities are least likely to welcome the promise of transformation and renewal.

4:5–22. Peter and John Under Inquiry.

Peter had already spoken to the question of what "power or piety" (3:12) was responsible for the healing of the crippled man; the rephrasing of the question in terms of the "power" or "name" maintains the focus on the basis of the healing, demonstrates the rulers' lack of awareness or support of Peter's earlier claim regarding the efficacy of the name of Jesus (3:16), and provides Peter with the opportunity to bear witness again to Jesus' resurrection and its saving effects.

Luke's account is a study in contrasts. The apostles are uneducated and ordinary, yet they speak with boldness as persons filled with the Spirit (see Luke 12:11–12). The Jerusalem council was the locus of moral and religious authority, yet their actions in rejecting Jesus were overturned by God's vindication of Jesus in raising him from the dead (see Ps 118:22). Jesus had been executed in humiliation, but the resurrection had signaled his exalted status as coregent with God. God is the source of salvation, but it is through the name of Jesus that salvation is available—as the presence of this man in good health testifies (4:10). How, then, can the Jerusalem council speak for God when it has worked so deliberately to counter God's plan? The rulers are caught in a vice, unable to counter Peter's witness to the "notable sign" represented by this healing, yet needing to save face with the people of Jerusalem. Their solution is to reassert their authority while also removing the threat of the apostles' influence.

4:23–31. God Powerfully Reconfirms His Mission. Twice warned not to bear witness to Jesus (4:18, 21), how will Jesus' followers respond? Jesus had earlier urged his followers, twice, to pray in the face of testing (Luke 22:40, 46), and this is precisely what they do now. The result is a prayer notable for its balance—the first half naming God as "Sovereign Lord" and centered on God's work in creation and in the anticipation of hostility toward God's Messiah, Jesus (4:24b–28; see Ps 2:2); the second half naming God as "Lord" and centered on the hostility encountered by Jesus' followers (vv. 29–30). In this way, a line is drawn from creation to David to Jesus to the early church, demonstrating the essential unity of God's purpose, even in the face of hostility. Importantly, the focus of the prayer is not on protecting the disciples from persecution, but on ensuring the ongoing witness to the good news. God's response to their prayer is as immediate as it is unmistakable. They pray for the gift of bold speech and for God to perform signs and wonders (4:29–30). Then, "when they had prayed, the place in which they were gathered together was shaken; and they were all filled with the Holy Spirit and spoke the word of God with boldness" (4:31). A stronger validation of the community of disciples is hard to imagine.

D. Embodying the Resurrection Message in the Community of Believers (4:32–5:11)

Luke's summary follows immediately on the heels of the prayer and outpouring of the Spirit narrated in 4:23–31. This shows that economic sharing is both the result of the Spirit's work and a characteristic of the community of believers filled

with the Spirit. Acts 4:32 serves as a heading for this section, with 4:33–35 indicating what is common among the believers, 4:36–37 providing a positive example of economic sharing, and 5:1–11 providing a negative example. The whole is held together by the repeated pattern: they had land, they sold land, they placed the proceeds at the apostles' feet (4:34b–35, 37; 5:1–2).

Verses 32–35 are remarkable for the way they correlate proclamation of the resurrection with care of the needy. The association of being raised up with hospitality and food is found elsewhere in Luke–Acts (e.g., Luke 4:38–39; 8:49–56; 15:11–32; 24:13–35; Acts 10:41). Economic sharing in this case is grounded in the formation of God's people in exodus (Deut 15:1–18); note how Luke's description in v. 34 borrows from Deut 15:4: "There will, however, be no one in need among you."

The examples of Barnabas on the one hand, Ananias and Sapphira on the other, are more easily understood when we grasp the relationship between economic sharing and social relations. Simply put, persons of the same kin group share everything, including possessions and, importantly in this context, the truth. Outsiders are under no such expectations, however, either with respect to possessions or the truth. Moreover, "to place 'x' at the feet of" is a gesture of submission (e.g., 1 Sam 25:24, 41; 2 Sam 22:39). Hence, Barnabas precisely recapitulates in his behavior what is characteristic of the community of the faithful. Ananias and Sapphira do not. It is not that they were required to do so (see 5:4), but rather that they conspired (5:2, 8, 9) to present themselves as exemplary insiders while behaving as outsiders (through withholding both possessions and the truth). In doing so, they aligned themselves with Satan, against God and God's people (5:3, 4, 9).

E. Signs and Wonders in Jerusalem (5:12–16)

Luke's summary continues to develop motifs mentioned earlier in 2:42–47. Here the focus is on the signs and wonders done by the apostles (see 2:43; 4:30). The effect of this report is twofold. First, the picture Luke presents is remarkably incongruous with the mandate Jesus had given his witnesses in 1:8. There, Jesus says that their work of bearing witness would move outward from Jerusalem to the end of the earth. Here, however, those from outside Jerusalem must bring those needing restoration into Jerusalem where they might be healed (that is, the motion is centripetal, moving inward, rather than centrifugal, moving outward). Why have the steps toward the wider mission not yet been taken? Second, these signs and wonders only exacerbate the problem the popularity of Peter and John had presented to the Jerusalem Council in 4:5–22. In a contest for social standing and the influence that comes through being held in high esteem, the apostles are gaining ground.

F. The Apostles on Trial (5:17–42)

The hostility between the apostles and the Jewish leadership reaches another highpoint. Having been instructed "not to speak or teach at all in the name of Jesus" (4:18), the apostles had nonetheless been engaged in public ministry (5:12–16), leading again to their arrest. The opposing sides are clearly drawn. "Through the hands of the apostles" (5:12, NRSV, "through the apostles") God performed signs and wonders, whereas the rulers "laid hands on the apostles" (5:18, NRSV, "arrested the apostles"). The Jerusalem rulers imprisoned the apostles so as to silence them, but an angel of the Lord released them from prison and directed them to "tell the people the whole message about this life" (5:20). That their escape from prison was God's doing is underscored by the subsequent discovery that the jail had remained securely locked. This leads to the bold assertion, "We must obey God rather than any human authority" (5:29), which emphasizes the central importance of the divine purpose not only to this scene but to Luke's narrative as a whole. Note that, according to Peter, God's Spirit is given to those who obey God, and the Spirit agrees with Peter's witness regarding Jesus' death, resurrection, and exaltation (5:32). This is a direct challenge to the legitimacy of the authority of the Jerusalem rulers; they claim to speak for God, but have been cast by Peter in the role of those who disobey God and therefore lack God's Spirit.

Peter's address before the Council borrows elements already well-established in Acts 2–4, including especially the identification of God as "God of our ancestors" (3:13; 5:30) and God's raising (2:24, 32; 3:15; 5:30) and exalting (2:33; 5:31; see 3:13) Jesus. In this case, however, Peter interprets Jesus' exaltation in redemptive terms: exalted as Leader and Savior, he is able to give repentance and forgiveness of sins (5:31). Here, the gift of repentance is designated for Israel; later the community of Jesus' followers in Jerusalem will recognize that this gift is given also to the Gentiles (11:18). Salvation is thus grounded in the exalted status of Christ.

Gamaliel plays a crucial if ironic role in the proceedings Luke recounts. Theudas and Judas the Galilean are also mentioned by the Jewish historian Josephus (*Ant.* 18 §23; 20 §§97–98; *J.W.* 2 §433), along with other leaders of Jewish prophetic movements. Gamaliel refers to them as examples of renewal movements that failed, drawing out the implication that, if the renewal movement represented by the apostles is of human origin, then it too will fail. The climax of Gamaliel's speech comes in 5:39: "but if it is of God, you will not be able to overthrow them—in that case you may even be found fighting against God!" As with Peter's speech, here is an affirmation of divine sovereignty (see 5:29). On this point, a leading Pharisee sides with the apostles; soon, another Pharisee will learn that fighting against the followers of Jesus is tantamount to fighting against the Lord (see 9:4).

Although Luke reports that the Council was persuaded by Gamaliel, they nevertheless take action against the apostles: flogging them and commanding again that they not speak in the name of Jesus (5:40). This is reminiscent both of Jesus' suffering (see Luke 23:16) and of Jesus' words anticipating the suffering of his followers (e.g., Luke 21). Their rejoicing in the face of suffering strikes a cord first sounded in the Sermon on the Plain (Luke 6:22–23).

G. A Shift in Leadership (6:1–7)

Given the twofold focus on hostility from outside the church and persistent unity within the church, this episode is surprising for its concern with disharmony among the believers. From within the biblical tradition that Luke embraces, to neglect widows at all is offensive (e.g., Exod 22:22; Deut 10:18; Luke 2:36–38; 4:25–26; 7:11–17; 20:45–21:4), for God is the "protector of widows" (Ps 68:5; cf. Ps 146:9). With his reference to "Hellenists" and "Hebrews," Luke apparently envisages two groups characterized by their dominant language, Greek and Aramaic, respectively.

The progression of the scene raises hard questions. Can one serve the word *and not care for widows*? Can one serve the word *and not serve at table*? These may appear to be practical issues, but for Luke they are profoundly theological. This is because Luke has already developed the language of "service" (*diakonia*) in terms that disallow different sorts of responsibilities. Is not Jesus himself one who serves at table (Luke 22:24–27; cf. 12:37)—in the sense of providing leadership in carrying out a mission that puts into practice the good news of God? Is not the apostolic task simply "service" (*diakonia*; Acts 1:17, 25; see also 20:45; 21:19)? Indeed, bearing witness to the resurrection cannot be divorced from caring for the needy (4:32–34). This line of interpretation is furthered by the choice of the Seven to engage in "service," for their "service" within Luke's narrative is manifestly not waiting on tables, but the "service" of preaching and evangelism (see 6:8–8:40). Accordingly, Luke narrates the succession of missional leadership from the apostles to Spirit-empowered witnesses like Stephen and Philip, who carry forward the missional directive of Jesus in 1:8.

III. Expansion from Jerusalem to Antioch (6:8–12:25)

Anticipated already in 1:8, Luke now relates the expansion of the mission beyond the walls of Jerusalem. The immediate cause of this expansion is the ministry and death of Stephen—his signs and wonders, his Spirit-enabled and wisdom-filled words, and his speech before the Jerusalem Council, leading to his death by stoning (6:8–8:3). The remaining material in this section of Luke's account traces two separate but related plot lines—the first, from Stephen's death to the activity of Philip, Paul, and Peter (8:4–11:18); and the second, from Stephen's death to the mission in Antioch and the persecution of the church in Jerusalem (11:19–12:25). As the first major section, 1:15–6:7, ended with the phrase, "the word of God continued to spread" (6:7), so Luke summarizes at the close of this section, "the word of God continued to advance and gain adherents" (12:24).

A. The Witness of Stephen (6:8–8:3)

Although Luke's account of Stephen's ministry, defense, and death is profound in its own right, it achieves much of its pathos and significance by the many points of contact between Stephen and Jesus. Stephen was rejected by the Jerusalem leadership, so it was all the more necessary to show Stephen's Christ-like character.

6:8–15. Stephen Provokes Opposition. Luke begins and ends with a character reference. In 6:8, Stephen is like the apostles, who are themselves like Jesus, in performing signs and wonders (2::22, 43; 5:12). In 6:15, "his face was like the face of an angel"—a phrase that gains its significance from the idea of the "face" as the external signpost of one's internal character (cf. Exod 34:35 Matt 17:2; 2 Cor 3:13; Rev 1:16; 10:1). Between these bookends is a record of the opposition Stephen attracted, first from his own people, the Hellenists (note, then, that the Hellenists were not a unified "party"), then from practically everyone (6:9, 12). The charges appear three times (6:11, 13, 14) and can be reduced to two: speech against the Temple and speech against the Mosaic law. These parallels show the close correlation between the Temple of God and the God of the Temple, and they demonstrate that what is at stake here is nothing less than the question of how best to practice faithfulness toward the God of Israel. Although the indictment brought against him assumes that he has spoken, Luke builds up the drama of his story by having Stephen accused and brought to trial before we hear anything he has to say.

7:1–53. Stephen Addresses the Council. Dramatically, Stephen's speech is significant because these are the first words we actually hear him utter. Theologically, their importance is heightened by the fact that Stephen is "a man full of faith and the Holy Spirit" (6:5), "full of grace and power" (6:8), whom Luke has characterized in language reminiscent not only of the apostles but of Jesus himself. His words are not his alone. This is crucial not only for understanding how Stephen responds to the high priest's question (7:1) by turning the charges against him back onto the Jerusalem leadership, but also for how his words demonstrate that the missional move away from Jerusalem is a legitimate extension of God's purpose. Stephen addresses both issues through the longstanding rhetorical move of recalling the story of Israel so as to recast it for his listeners. Like all storytelling, Stephen's is not an unbiased narration, but a legitimating one; it is a kind of "revealed" history, with the sacred story itself demanding the perspectives and practices associated with Jesus and his followers.

The perspective Stephen adopts at the outset is that of an "insider." He addresses his audience as though they were kin: "brothers and fathers" (7:2); then repeatedly uses first-person plural pronouns: "our" and "us" (7:2, 11, 12, 15, 17, 19, 38, 39, 44, 45). At the same time, and especially as the speech progresses, he distances himself from the Jerusalem council, referring to them as "you" and identifying them as opponents of God's agenda (7:4, 51, 52, 53).

Stephen's recounting of Israel's history is highly selective. He refers to Abraham, demonstrating that God is the primary actor in the story of Israel and reminding Luke's reader of the

Jesus–Stephen Parallels		
	Luke	Acts
Leadership understood as "service"	22:24–27	6:3–6
Full of Spirit	4:18–10	6:3, 5, 8, 10; 7:55
Signs and Wonders	(Acts 2:22)	6:8
Impossible to refute	21:15	6:10
Passion (confrontation, agitation, arrest, council)	22–23	6:10–12
Rejection by "his own"	4:16–30	6:9
Events at Death		
– Heavens opened	(compare 3:21)	7:55–56
– Son of Man ... at the right hand of God	22:69	7:55–56
– Out of city	(compare 4:29)	7:58
– Death cry	23:46	7:59
– Prayer at death	22:41	7:59–60
– Plea for forgiveness of executioners	23:34	7:60
– Report of death	23:46	7:60
– Burial by the righteous / devout	23:50–53	8:2
– Mourning	23:27, 48	8:2

earlier references to the actualization of God's promise to Abraham in the coming of Jesus (see Luke 1:5–2:52). Joseph appears as a precursor to Jesus, rejected by his own yet the agent of their deliverance. Moses is a precursor to Jesus, too. His birth fulfilled God's promise (7:17, 20), he grew in wisdom and power (7:22; see Luke 2:52), and he was sent by God as ruler and liberator (7:35; see 5:31). The pattern that develops focuses on the rejection of God's instruments—first Joseph (7:9–10), Moses (7:27–28, 39), and the prophets (7:52–53), then "the Righteous One" (that is, Jesus; see 7:52; 3:14). The speech actually does take into account the charges against Stephen regarding the law and the Temple. His detractors are the ones who have rejected the law, not him (7:53); and the building of the Temple is placed in a negative light—both by Stephen's reference to it as a "house made with human hands," by which he identifies the Temple with idolatry (compare, e.g., Ps 115:4; Acts 17:24–25), and by his reference to Isa 66:1–22. He thus undermines Jerusalem's claim to divine authorization as the center of Israel's worship and faith.

7:54–8:3. The Stoning of Stephen. Although Jesus was executed by means of crucifixion and Stephen through stoning, the parallels between their death-and-burial scenes are strong (see above, on 6:8–8:3). This positions Stephen with Jesus, "the Righteous One," as well as the prophets, Moses, and Joseph; their status before God was not canceled by their rejection by humans. Stephen's vision of the Son of Man standing at God's right hand is a strong vindication of Stephen and his message, since it identifies Stephen with Jesus' vindication, as well as displays God's residence in heaven rather than in the Temple (see 7:48–49).

Into this scene of Stephen's death, Luke introduces Saul. He is the only person named among those who reject Stephen and his status as a leader among those who resist Jesus' followers may be signaled by the fact that others laid their coats at his feet (7:58). Note the contrast in Luke's characterization: the devout bury Stephen, but Saul ravages the church. In a double irony, persecution leads to the actualization of the missionary portfolio Jesus had given the apostles in 1:8, yet the scattering involves everyone but the apostles who first received Jesus' commission.

B. The Proclamation of Philip (8:4–40)

Philip was introduced as a person "of good standing, full of the Spirit and of wisdom" in Acts 6:3 (see 6:5; 21:8–9). His "service" takes the form of missionary activity in Samaria and with an Ethiopian.

8:4–25. Philip in Samaria. "Proclaiming the Messiah" (v. 5) parallels "proclaiming the word" (v. 4), indicating that Philip's ministry is an illustration of the summary in 8:4. These two phrases also parallel the later expression, "proclaiming the good news about the kingdom of God and the name of Jesus Christ" (v. 12). This shows the close continuity between Philip and the words of Jesus and the apostles. In addition, Philip, like Jesus and the apostles, engages in a ministry accompanied by signs, exorcism, and healing (vv. 6–7). Similarly, the people of Samaria believe and are baptized (vv. 12–13), they "accepted the word" (v. 14), and, like the community of Christ-followers in Jerusalem, were "with one accord" (v. 6).

These points of similarity bring into sharp relief the anomalies of this episode: the location in Samaria, the interchange with Simon, and the delay in the outpouring of the Spirit among these new believers. The first may be the more remarkable, though it is also the easiest to miss. The Samaritans traced their ancestry back to Abraham, but rejected a Jerusalem-centered salvation history. The antipathy between Jews and Samaritans is represented already in Luke 9:53–53; 10:33–35; 17:11–19—texts that underscore both the inhospitality between the two groups and the Samaritans' status as "foreigners," but also portend their inclusion within God's redemptive plan (see Acts 1:8). Simon tracks with the Samaritans in terms of belief and baptism (vv. 12–13), but otherwise appears under a dark cloud; he seems to be engaged in a power encounter with these new missionaries. Indeed, Luke's account stresses both the power of the good news over the wiles of evil and the transition from "mighty power" to powerless in the case of Simon (note: in the end he must request others to pray for him, v. 24). Although we might be tempted to imagine that Peter and John dispense the Holy Spirit among the Samaritans in order to identify the Jerusalem church as a kind of headquarters, Acts gives no indication whatsoever that the Spirit can be withheld or given by human beings (compare 10:1–11:18!). Instead, Peter and

John witness the outpouring of the Spirit among the Samaritans in order that the apostles might see and participate in the work of God beyond Jerusalem, as the risen Jesus had directed (1:8).

8:26–40. Philip and an Ethiopian Eunuch. Like so many scenes in Acts, this one follows the simple movement from *problem* (vv. 26–31) to *resolution* (vv. 32–35) to *outcome* (vv. 36–40). The problem is twofold—the mixed status of the Ethiopian and the need for an interpreter. On the one hand, the Ethiopian has enviable status in his country, is able to travel, has a "chariot" (probably more of a wagon), has in his possession a scroll of Isaiah in Greek, and is literate. On the other hand, he is an outsider. From a Roman perspective, as an Ethiopian he inhabits the margins of the world; from a Jewish perspective, as a eunuch he is marginal to God's people (see Lev 21:20; Deut 23:1); and his dark skin only contributes to his "otherness." He is likely a Gentile. One's status is always determined in relation to a comparator group, and, in his characterization of the Ethiopian, Luke highlights both the Ethiopian's importance in his own world and his otherness in the world in which he now finds himself. The other need underscored in this account revolves around understanding the Scriptures and, particularly, resolving the question, To whom does Isaiah refer (see especially vv. 30, 31, 34)? The Scriptures are not self-interpreting, but require a hermeneut. Isaiah 52:13–53:12 is especially open to a variety of interpretations, since the text itself does not clarify the identity of the Lord's "servant." Identifying Jesus as the servant, Philip's interpretation ties the life of the Ethiopian into that of Jesus, so that the reversal Jesus experienced—from humiliation to being raised up by God—is good news for the Ethiopian too (see Isa 56:1–4).

Threading its way through this account is what may be its most important motif—namely, evidence of divine choreography: "an angel of the Lord said …" (v. 26), the pilgrimage of an Ethiopian to worship in Jerusalem (v. 27), the opportunistic meeting on a deserted road at midday (vv. 26–28), "The Spirit said …" (v. 29), the presence of water in the desert (v. 36), and Philip's disappearance (v. 39). Luke bathes this scene in testimony to divine intervention in order to show that the movement of the gospel to the "ends of the earth" (1:8) was (and is) divinely sanctioned.

C. The Choice of Saul as the Lord's Emissary to Gentiles and Jews (9:1–31)

This section of Luke's narrative is marked by repetition—repeated references to Saul's status as an enemy of Jesus' disciples (9:1–3, 13–14, 21, 26; see 7:58; 8:2–3), repeated references to the nature of Saul's encounter with the Lord (9:3–5, 13–14, 17, 27), and, thus, a heightened emphasis on the thoroughgoing transformation Saul has experienced (9:15–19, 20, 22, 23, 28–30). This transformation is dramatically realized in this: the one who breathed murder and threats against the Lord's disciples will now suffer for the sake of the Lord's name. The correlation of suffering and persecution with the extension of the mission was anticipated by Jesus (see, e.g., Luke 6:22; 10:16; 21) and experienced by the apostles (Acts 5:41); it will now be the lot of Saul (9:21, 23, 29*b*).

9:1–25. Saul Commissioned. Saul does not undergo "conversion" in the sense of leaving one religion to join another, but his "Damascus Road experience" remains a transformative experience. Note, for example, how the word "Lord" is used in vv. 1, 5; the one whom he identifies as Lord is none other than Jesus, the Lord of the disciples whom he has been persecuting.

Getting Ananias and Saul together is the outcome of divine orchestration. The commissioning of Ananias includes indications of his reluctance, providing opportunity for the Lord to emphasize the role he has chosen for Saul. In short, the directive Saul receives to go to both Jew and Gentile is grounded in divine initiative alone. Throughout the Lukan narrative "light" is related to the "enlightenment" of the good news (e.g., Luke 1:78–79; 2:1–20; 4:18–19; Acts 9:3, 7, 8, 9, 12, 16, 17, 18).

Two aspects of the Lord's commission to Saul (vv. 15–16) are *immediately* (*eutheōs*, v. 20) realized as Saul, (1) "empowered" by the Spirit (NRSV, "increasingly more powerful"; *endunamoō*, see Judg 6:34; 1 Chron 12:18), proclaims Jesus as Son of God and Messiah; and (2) is the object of a death plot.

9:26–31. Saul Speaks Boldly in Jerusalem. Saul escapes the plot against him in Damascus (vv. 23–25) only to find the door of hospitality closed to him among the disciples in Jerusalem. Their fear is consistent with his former hostility toward them (see 9:1–2, 13–14, 21, 26). Barnabas, introduced as an encourager in 4:36–37, now mediates on Saul's behalf. Speaking "boldly" is a cipher in Acts for Spirit-empowered speech (e.g., 2:29; 4:13, 29, 31), and so it functions here to authenticate Saul (vv. 27, 28). The phrase "the Jews" was used in vv. 22–23 to define a group in Damascus set against Saul and now, in Jerusalem, the phrase "the Hellenists" is used in the same way (v. 29). The hostility arrayed against Saul is an added authentication of his ministry (vv. 15–16).

The summary statement in v. 31 documents the ripple effect of Stephen's ministry and death (6:8–8:4)—the scattering and mission of witnesses like Philip (8:5–40) and the commission and proclamation of Saul (9:1–30). Persecution has led to peace and strengthening, living in the fear of the Lord and growth.

D. The Conversions of Peter, Cornelius, and the Jerusalem Church (9:32–11:18)

Peter has been largely absent from the narrative since ch. 5, though he and John are mentioned in connection with Philip's mission to Samaria (8:14, 20) and he would have been included in references to the apostles and disciples in 6:1–7; 9:26–27. Breaking into the story of Saul's commission and work, Peter is represented in this section of Acts as healer and preacher, but also as learner. His brush with issues of purity in 9:32–43 prepare him for his "conversion" in ch. 10, as he learns how far into conventional Jewish sensibilities the good news reaches.

9:32–43. Peter's Signs and Wonders Outside of Jerusalem.

Luke's last word about Peter was that he had returned to Jerusalem, so Luke's report of his going "here and there among the believers" (v. 32) raises questions about Peter's travels. It is remarkable, though, that Peter's journeying has apparently not been oriented toward evangelizing. His geographical movement to Lydda and then to Joppa sets the stage for the lengthy account involving Peter, Cornelius, and Cornelius' household in ch. 10. His movement can be plotted in another way, too—namely, in terms of purity: from a paralytic to a corpse, and from a corpse to the home of a tanner, this last location noted for its foul stench and the ritual uncleanness that would accompany the craft of working with the skins of dead animals (e.g., *m. Ketub* 7.10; *m. B. Bat.* 2.9).

This makes ironic Peter's later protests regarding his observance of Jewish practices regarding ritual purity (see 10:14).

The two healing stories stand in parallel, balancing the healing of a man and a woman, the presence of "saints" (vv. 32, 41), and commands "to get up" (vv. 34, 40). The term "holy" has been used of Jesus (3:14; 4:27, 30) and the Spirit (e.g., 9:31), so here and elsewhere in Acts identifies persons as Jesus' disciples (see 9:13; 26:10). Peter's "signs and wonders" (see 2:43; 4:30) occur within an already-established community of believers. Extensive detail accompanies the second of these two accounts, with its focus on Dorcas, whose benefaction on behalf of widows marks her as exemplary (compare 6:1–6!).

10:1–48. Complementary Visions, Complementary Conversions.

The importance of the episode Luke recounts in ch. 10 is underscored by its relative length and by its abbreviated repetition in 11:1–18; 15:7–9. Punctuating the whole scene is the variety of evidences of divine guidance—complementary visions and the timing of visions and travel in 10:1–16 and the autonomous work of the Spirit in 10:17–48, leading to the conclusion in 11:17–18: This must have been God's doing! Evidence of divine initiative throughout this scene is reminiscent of the work of God that threaded its way through the story of Philip's encounter with the Ethiopian. In both instances, it is clear that Luke wants to leave no doubt as to the divine source of these missional innovations.

The scene Luke paints is remarkable. Although neither a Jew nor a follower of Christ, but a God-fearer, Cornelius exhibits exemplary piety, his prayers are heard by God, and he is the recipient of an angelic visitation (10:1–6). (God-fearers are Gentiles who worship the God of Israel and who associate themselves with the life of the synagogue and certain aspects of Torah-observance, but have not fully converted to Judaism; see 10:2; 13:16, 26; see also, e.g., 16:14: "worshiper of God"; 17:17: "devout persons.") Although both a Jew and a follower of Christ—indeed, an apostle—Peter debates with the Lord (10:11–16) and struggles to understand what God is doing (10:17, 19, 21, 29) before finally recognizing, and proclaiming, that "God shows no partiality," that Jesus is "Lord of all" (10:34, 36). Thus, Luke portrays Peter as undergoing a "conversion" in the sense that he understands more fully and embraces more deeply the faith to which he is committed. Cornelius undergoes a "conversion" in the sense that he moves from his status as a God-fearer to that of a Christ-follower. God works in the lives of Cornelius and his household before Peter arrives and, quite apart from Peter's initiative, plan, or expectation, the Spirit intrudes into their exchange. Baptism is the church's recognition of and response to the prior gracious act of God.

11:1–18. Jerusalem's Acknowledgment of God's Work.

Although the conversion of Cornelius is often regarded as the conversion of the first Gentile in Acts, this honor actually belongs to the Ethiopian (8:26–40). However, that episode ended with the Ethiopian returning to his home and Philip's going on to Caesarea. This means that the account of the conversion of Cornelius and his household is the first report of a Gentile conversion to reach the ears of the disciples in Jerusalem. The concern registered by Jewish followers of Christ in Jerusalem is unrelated to the conversion or baptism of Gentiles per se, but instead to Peter's participating in Cornelius' hospitality. That is, the problem Luke confronts is not *whether* there is to be a Gentile mission but *its effects*. Peter's response to those who question his behavior is "to tell the story"—not "step by step," as the NRSV has it. Instead, Peter's telling is like Luke's literary achievement. Both are characterized by the adverb *kathexēs* (Luke 1:3; Acts 11:4), which suggests that theirs are "orderly" accounts, to be sure, but "ordered" according to a certain perspective or with a certain end in mind. A careful comparison of the first recounting in Acts 10 with Peter's report in 11:1–16 shows that Peter retells the story from his new vantage point, realizing that what has happened is nothing less than a divine gift. His account is "ordered" so as to force the decision either to embrace what has happened as God's work or to find oneself in opposition to God (11:17; compare 5:38–39).

What is the relevance of Peter's vision regarding food for the question of the Gentile mission? Since, from a Jewish perspective, a characteristic feature of Gentiles is their uncleanness, and since questions surrounding judgments regarding clean and unclean center on shared meals and hospitality, the leap in logic is not great. If God (rather than Peter—see 10:15, 28; 11:9, 12) is the arbiter

of what is clean or profane, if the Spirit unilaterally directs Peter "not to make a distinction between them and us" (11:12), if God cleanses the hearts of Gentiles (this will be made plain in 15:7–9), then it is appropriate not only for the good news to be extended to Gentiles but for Jewish Christians to be welcomed into the homes and at the table of Gentiles. After all, repentance for both Jew and Gentile is nothing other than a gift from God (see 3:26; 5:31; 11:18).

E. Christians in Antioch (11:19–30)

In 8:1, 4, Luke observed that the death of Stephen eventuated in the scattering of the church. With 8:5, he began to relate the story of Philip's mission, followed by the commission of Saul to both Jew and Gentile, and finally to the encounter with Cornelius and its aftermath. Now, with 11:19–20, he recalls the scattering of the church, but this time picks up the storyline from Stephen to Antioch, and particularly the formation of a predominately Gentile church at Antioch. Little fanfare accompanies the report at this juncture, as Luke has already prepared his readers for this turn of events leading to a Gentile mission and Gentile Christian community through the narrative running from 8:5–11:18. That storyline had been punctuated by evidences of divine initiative, divine direction, and divine authorization of just such a missional innovation. The one explicit note of this kind is Luke's testimony to divine support for and authorization of this Gentile-oriented mission: "the hand of the Lord was with them" (11:21). Here and in the immediate context, Luke ties the mission into the Lordship of Jesus (see the repetition of "Lord" in 10:20, 21, 23, 24). Like Peter's remark that Jesus Christ is "Lord of all" (10:36), so these references press political and religious boundaries, identifying Jesus as coregent with God and as the agent of God's saving benefaction, to be sure, but also identifying him as the one to whom all-embracing allegiance is due.

Barnabas, like some of the new believers, was a Cypriate (4:36; 11:19), so he might have seemed a natural choice as an agent of the Jerusalem church. More important, having been identified as an encourager when first introduced (4:36: *paraklēsis*), he now encourages (11:23: *parakaleō*; NRSV, "exhorts") these new believers. Apparently, they would have needed encouragement to faithfulness from someone like Barnabas. After all, to be called "Christians" would not have been at first a term of endearment, and it was not a name followers of Christ first adopted for themselves. It was a name given them by outsiders, probably in derision (see Acts 26:28; 1 Pet 4:16), however appropriate it might eventually seem (see Acts 5:16).

Verses 27–30 are interesting in three respects. First, they document the presence of a prophet within a people identified as a Spirit-endowed, prophetic community (see 2:17). Second, they show how the economic sharing characteristic of the early Jerusalem community of disciples (see 2:42–47; 4:32–35) might be mapped onto relationships among churches and not only within them. This is all the more important in this context, since the sharing of the Antioch church with the Jerusalem church was a sharing between Gentiles and Jews. Finally, reference to Claudius's rule (41–54 CE) is one of the few data given by which to date the progression of events in the early church.

F. Herodian Violence Against the Church (12:1–25)

Within a stretch of the book of Acts concerned with Antioch, Luke has placed this material related to Jerusalem. Acts 11:29–30 lead us out of Antioch, back to Jerusalem (12:1), while 12:25 and 13:1 return the narrative focus to Antioch. The collection of scenes in ch. 12 demonstrate that Herod's death is the consequence of his actions against the leaders of the church, while the placement of this material within Luke's presentation of the formation (11:19–30) and mission (13:1–3) of the church at Antioch shows that hostility against the church, even against its leaders, cannot stop the spread of the good news. In order to underscore his view that hostility from Rome's designated ruler against church leaders is not a denial of the status of those leaders or the church before God, Luke peppers his narrative with parallels between Jesus, James, and Peter. Data like these—together with the more explicit statements concerning Herod's actions and motivation in 12:1, 3a, 11—make it difficult to argue that Luke has a positive or even neutral view of Rome, even if he never sanctions open resistance against Rome (or its leaders). (The James in question is the brother of John—that is, the apostle James. James the brother of Jesus

seems already to have become a leader of the Jerusalem church in 12:17; see further, 15:13; 21:18.)

Luke's account of Peter's imprisonment and escape highlights elements of divine intervention on his behalf. Consider, for example, the measures taken to ensure that the prisoner is secure (12:6, 10), the appearance and guidance of an angel (12:7–10), Peter's lack of awareness of what was happening (12:9, 11), and the notation that the chains fell and the gates opened (that is, the exit was not forced by human efforts; 12:7, 10).

Another storyline is at work: prayers for the imprisoned Peter (12:5). Blending comic elements with reminiscences of the story of the discovery of the empty tomb of Jesus (see the chart, following), Luke sketches how Peter was finally able to gain entry to Mary's home to address the church. They are praying for him but seem not to anticipate that their prayers will be effective. Rhoda recognizes Peter, rejoices, and reports on his release, but others imagine that she has seen his ghost or, perhaps, his guardian angel (see Tob 5:22; Matt 18:10). Peter narrates his liberation in ways that may recall for us the exodus from Egypt (see already 12:3–4, 8; Exod 12:11) as well as Jesus' deliverance from death.

That Herod would return from Jerusalem to Caesarea is no surprise, since Caesarea was the provincial capital. The final installation to this sequence of scenes concerned with Herod (12:19–23) highlights his hubris. His title as "king" is repeated (12:1, 21) and this is matched with reference to his clothing (for the correlation of wealth, status, and clothing, see, e.g., Luke 16:19–21); he has the role of a patron who can give peace and on whom others depend (12:20); he is addressed as a god and does not deflect glory from himself to Israel's God (12:22–23). In this respect, he stands in sharp contrast to Peter, who has already twice declared himself to be no more than a human being when others assumed otherwise (3:12–13; 10:25–26). Herod's presumptuousness was already on display in his violent actions against the apostles James and Peter, and now it leads to his revolting demise (12:23).

Chapter 12, and with it the lengthy section of Acts beginning with 6:8, comes to a close with a summary statement (12:24–25). Read in relation to its immediate context, 12:24 marks the

Parallels: James, Peter, and Jesus		
Acts		Luke
12:1	Herod	23:6–17; Acts 4:27
12:3	Pleased the Jews	23:20, 23–25
12:3–4	Unleavened Bread / Passover	22:1–2
12:4	Before the People	23:4, 13
12:7	Angel	22:43–44; 24:4
12:4, 6	Security / Proof of Security	24:2
12:13–15	Women Believe and Rejoice / Others Doubt	24:1–12
(12:18–19)	Empty Tomb	24:2–3, 12
12:16–17	Departure	24:50–51

most startling of contrasts, between Herod and the word of God. Read in relation to the narrative unit it draws to a close, it demonstrates the fulfillment of Jesus' missional mandate in 1:8, even in the context of internal debates and hostility from Roman rule. Regarding 12:25, although the NRSV's rendering is possible, it makes no sense for Saul and Barnabas, having set out for Jerusalem in 11:29–30, now to return to Jerusalem. More likely the Greek text should be translated, "having completed their mission in Jerusalem, Barnabas and Saul returned [to Antioch]."

IV. Expansion from Antioch to Asia and Europe (13:1–19:20)

The commission Paul had received in Acts 9:15, "to bring my name before Gentiles ... and before the people of Israel," moves to center stage through these seven chapters, which center above all on Paul. Even if the initial order of names suggests the primacy of Barnabas in the partnership (11:30; 12:25; 13:1, 7), this order changes quickly (13:42, 43, 46, 50; 14:1) and, at the end of ch. 15, Paul and Barnabas go their separate ways, with Luke continuing his focus on Paul. Although mission among the Jews is never far from sight,

the drama surrounding Paul's mission revolves around what it means to include Gentiles among the people of God. The end of this section in 19:20 marks the third appearance of Luke's assurance, in this case a de facto commentary on Paul's mission, "So the word of the Lord grew mightily and prevailed" (see 6:7; 12:24).

A. The Expedition of Paul and Barnabas in the Province of Galatia (13:1–14:28)

Antioch emerges as a mission base from which Barnabas and Paul are sent. This, together with Luke's record of their economic partnership with the Jerusalem church (11:27–30) serves to legitimate this predominately Gentile congregation. Luke's fast-paced narration highlights a range of missionary activity (preaching, encouraging, evangelizing, strengthening, announcing, appointing, etc.). Response to the mission is divided, though not along easily determined lines. The surface impression one might get that Jews are hostile and Gentiles receptive to the good news (e.g., 13:45–48) is easily set aside, by both the positive response of some Jews (e.g., 13:43; 14:1) and hostility from Gentiles (e.g., 14:5–6). Nevertheless, the report Paul and Barnabas deliver to the church at Antioch reaches its climax as they share "how

[God] had opened a door of faith for the Gentiles" (14:27). In terms of the larger narrative, a primary purpose of chs. 13–14 is to set the stage for the Jerusalem Council in ch. 15.

13:1–3. Barnabas and Paul Commissioned.
Luke's account of the commissioning of Barnabas and Paul is tantalizingly brief. Apparently, Barnabas and Paul are so well-integrated into the church at Antioch that their names need not appear together in this list. We know that Barnabas and Paul are transplants into the church (11:22, 25–26). Both Simeon and Lucius are Africans, but when or how they found their way to Antioch is unknown. Perhaps with a note of irony, we find that a member of the court of Herod, the very ruler who met his demise due to presumptuous pride in ch. 12, is numbered among the "prophets and teachers" at Antioch. Importantly, the commissioning of two of their number is not the result of human initiative, whether that of the church or that of Barnabas and Paul themselves, but of God.

13:4–12. Contending in Cyprus.
Barnabas and Paul are sent by the Spirit (13:4), they proclaim the word of God (13:5, 7, 12), Paul is filled with the Holy Spirit (13:9), and he speaks as a prophet (13:10–11). Bar-Jesus is a magician and false prophet (13:6) who opposes Barnabas and Saul and tries to deceive Sergius Paulus (13:7); surprisingly, then, he is a Jew, who would have known the rejection of magic and the penalties related to false prophecy in the OT (e.g., Deut 10:11–13; 13; 18:9–14). Luke has thus sketched at the outset of this new stage of the mission a striking conflict between these agents of God's Spirit and this agent of evil (see the list of names Paul gives Bar-Jesus in 13:10!). The triumph of the divine word is realized in two steps—first, the prophetic judgment against Bar-Jesus; and second, the proconsul's faith (compare 8:4–25).

13:13–52. Preaching in Pisidian Antioch.
John Mark, whose role seems to have been a kind of assistant to Barnabas and Paul (13:5), departs—an event that Luke regarded as important enough to note but for which he provides no obvious motivation. That he leaves at this juncture in the narrative and returns to Jerusalem may signal his discomfort with the ascendency of Paul and his Gentile orientation. In any case, the real focus of these verses is Paul's address at the synagogue in Pisidian Antioch, his first and most lengthy address, which has its analogy in Peter's address at Pentecost (Acts 2:14–41) and Jesus' sermon at Nazareth (Luke 4:16–31). This speech is exemplary in that we can imagine this as the kind of thing Paul preached in synagogues more generally.

The argument Paul sets forth is a straightforward celebration of God's activity on behalf of God's people, which culminates in God's sending a savior, Jesus. God is identified as the subject of a series of verbs concerned with the election and guidance of Israel, so that the introduction of Jesus is continuous with God's efforts on their behalf. This, for Paul, is how to trace Israel's plot line, so that it leads unerringly, naturally, to Jesus. Jesus' role as Savior (see Luke 2:11; Acts 5:31) is connected to two claims regarding Jesus, both of which signify in him the restoration of Israel: Jesus' resurrection from the dead and the offer of forgiveness of sins. Salvation thus refers to the restoration of God's people, and this comports well with Paul's later insistence that his message concerns nothing but his belief in the hope of Israel (e.g., 26:6–7; 28:20).

In his speech, Paul devotes special attention to how in their hostility toward Jesus the Jerusalem leadership opposed God's plan. For the Paul known to us in his NT letters, this might have served as the backdrop for developing the saving significance of Jesus' crucifixion. Here in Acts, though, it is a precursor for the warning Paul issues at the end of his speech, with its implicit question, Will you embrace or reject the Savior whom God has brought to Israel? The outcome is mixed, with some Jewish and devout converts to Judaism following Paul and Barnabas, but others slandering them and rejecting their message. Paul's response echoes the words of Simeon over Jesus in Luke 2:29–32, with both citing Isa 49:6 as the basis for a mission to the Gentiles. Paul's words and behavior strike a note of apparent finality with respect to the offer of good news to the Jewish people; however, the pattern continues in Acts (see 17:1–2!): first to Jews, then to Gentiles. As in Luke's initial presentation of John the Baptist's proclamation (Luke 3:7–14), so now the first question is not whether one can claim Abraham as one's ancestor but how one responds to God's saving initiative.

14:1–7. The Reception of the Word of Grace in Iconium. The opening words, "the same thing," mark the episode at Pisidian Antioch as proto-typical for this phase of the mission: this kind of preaching in synagogues leads to divided responses. The language Luke uses is slippery, so careful reading is required. According to 13:4, "the Jews" are aligned against "the apostles," but this would refer to Jews who have rejected faith in Jesus (i.e., "unbelieving Jews," 13:2), since it is clear that a great number of "Jews" did become believers (13:1). Note that the "Greeks" who became believers did so in the synagogue, indicating that, despite the apparently obvious words of Paul in 13:46, he has not turned away from the Jews and toward the Gentiles, but is evangelizing God-fearers alongside Jews. Luke lays out the importance of signs and wonders in 14:3: they validate the divine origins of their message.

14:8–20. Good News in Lystra. In an account reminiscent of chs. 3–4, Luke shows how a healing (14:8–11; compare 3:1–10) sets the stage for procla-mation (14:12–18; compare 3:11–26), which leads to a response of resistance (14:19–20; compare 4:1–22). The parallels with the episode of healing are especially strong (located near a temple, a man lame from birth, intent looking, jumped up and walked), with both healing stories recalling Jesus' healing of a paralytic in Luke 5:17–26. This again helps to establish Paul's credentials. Greek mythol-ogy spoke of the importance of hospitality to the gods (Ovid, *Metamorphoses* 8 §§611–724), and the notion of gods taking the form of humans—and, thus of confusing humans for gods—was well-known in ancient literature. Separated from the people of Lystra by a language barrier (14:11), Paul and Barnabas are slow to respond (14:14), but when they do they contrast themselves with Herod (12:22–23), signaling their objections by tearing their clothes (compare Gen 37:29; Esth 4:1; Mark 14:63) and with words of denial.

Neither a synagogue nor Jews are mentioned in this encounter. Accordingly, rather than a rehearsal of Israel's history as preparation for the announcement of a savior (13:13–41), God's roles as creator and provider serve as witness (perhaps using the language of Exod 20:11; Ps 146:6). Christ is not mentioned at all, as these Gentiles are urged to turn from idolatry (that is, from inani-mate, worthless things—see, e.g., Ps 115:1–8) to the living God (compare 1 Thess 1:9–10). We must wait to learn that some responded with faith to Paul's proclamation (see 14:21–23; 16:1–2); here, the focus is on his lack of success in con-vincing the crowds that they were only human beings and then on persecution instigated by their Jewish opponents from other towns. (The persis-tence of this opposition is suggested by the fact that Antioch is about 100 miles from Lystra!)

14:21–28. Encouraging the Churches. With this textual unit we come full circle—having been sent from (13:1–3) and now returning to Antioch. Luke makes this connection explicit in 14:26, indicating that the material in chs. 13–14 must be read together. Luke summarizes the reports of Paul and Barnabas in two key ways. First, among new believers, they interpret the opposition they themselves faced during the mission and, presum-ably, that the new believers have encountered subsequently. This is not a denial of God's agenda, but the means by which God's purpose is actual-ized; what is more, by participating in the same sort of opposition that Jesus himself faced, believ-ers show themselves to have entered into God's saving rule. Second, whoever might imagine that the success of the mission is a consequence of the work of Paul and Barnabas would find themselves corrected, both by Luke's reminder that they had worked by means of God's grace (14:26) and their own report concerning "all that God had done with them" (14:27).

B. The Jerusalem Consultation and Its Aftermath (15:1–16:5)

The lengthy account of the mission of Paul and Barnabas can be summarized thus: "[God] opened a door of faith for the Gentiles" (14:27). What is cause of celebration for some (15:3) is the source of alarm for others (15:1, 5). In other words, the increasingly Gentile orientation of the mission of Paul and Barnabas provides the impetus for this more formal consideration of the place of the Gen-tiles among the people of God (compare 11:1–18).

15:1–5. Dissension and Debate. Luke's introduc-tion to the Jerusalem Consultation centers on the conversion of the Gentiles, with the lines between opposing perspectives sharply drawn. Twice, Paul and Barnabas report on the mission Luke has surveyed in chs. 13–14. Among the believers in regions outside of Jerusalem, these reports lead to joy (15:3), but some believers among the Pharisees resisted their testimony. It is not that the Pharisees knowingly resist God in this matter; after all, their claim is that circumcision and Torah observance are necessary according to God's plan (note the Greek term, *dei*, in 15:5). Earlier, with regard to the conversion of Cornelius and his household (11:1–18), the issue has been table fellowship and hospitality between Jewish and Gentile followers of Christ. Now, however, the issue runs deeper, to what is required for salvation itself (15:1). Here, as elsewhere, Luke's definition of salvation is bound up with the character of the people of God and, in particular, what it might mean to be included among that people.

15:6–18. Testimony and Deliberation. What follows is reminiscent of Peter and John's daring response to the Jewish Council in 4:20: "we cannot keep from speaking about what we have seen and heard"; the parallel is significant since in both instances the question is how best to discern and practice the will of God, and in both instances evidence of God's saving initiative invites renewed reflection on time-honored understandings of God's will.

Peter's testimony rehearses briefly the Cornelius-episode with which those gathered were already familiar (11:1–18), with primary emphasis placed on Peter's interpretation of the episode as *God's work*. (Notice how many verbs in Peter's speech have God as their subject.) Though he does not use the term "salvation," he does refer to the gift of the Holy Spirit, synecdoche for salvation in the Lukan narrative, and refers implicitly to the analogy provided by the Pentecostal outpouring of the Spirit (Acts 2) as the analogy for making sense of God's activity among Gentiles in Caesarea. Because there is "no distinction" (15:9; see 10:28–29; 11:12) between Jews and Gentiles in how people are included within the family of believers, then requiring circumcision and Torah-observance of Gentiles is a means of testing God's ability to save (*peiraz*, 15:10) rather than a divine necessity (15:5).

Since his audience has just learned of Barnabas and Paul's missionary activity among the Gentiles (chs. 13–14), Luke can summarize this part of the proceedings with a single sentence. By mentioning "signs and wonders," though, he draws atten-

tion to their work as *God's work through them* (see 14:3, 27).

It is unclear whether the "Simeon" to whom James refers in 15:14 is the "Simeon" of Luke 2:25–35 or the apostle "Simon Peter." If it is the former, then we are reminded of the blessing pronounced over the infant Jesus that he would be "a light for revelation to the Gentiles" (Luke 2:32; see Isa 42:6; 49:6). If it is the latter, then we are reminded of Peter's own testimony in 15:7–11, referring back to 10:1–11:18. Either way, a similar effect is achieved, leading to James' reading of Scripture and conclusion regarding the question at hand. Working with the LXX version of Amos 4:11–12, James concludes that God's agenda all along has been to include Gentiles among God's people. In this sense, the decision toward which the Jerusalem Consultation is moving does not abrogate scriptural instruction but recognizes a strong element of that instruction that had been downplayed or overlooked. Indeed, God has already made this clear, as in fact Luke has recounted in Acts 10–14.

15:19–29. Decision and the Letter. The decision James reaches, and which makes its way into the letter from the Jerusalem Consultation to Gentile believers, does not question the inclusion of Gentiles among God's people. Nor does it set up prerequisites for how Gentiles might thus be included. Instead, by naming four practices as outside the boundaries, it seeks to regulate the behavior of Gentile believers. As each of these practices is related to the practice of idolatry, the decree seems especially concerned with militating against the idolatry that would have been ubiquitous in the Gentile world (compare 14:15; 17:22–25; 1 Thess 1:9–10). The letter itself undermines the concerns about Gentiles expressed in 15:1, 5 (see especially 15:24) and provides solid affirmation of Barnabas and Paul, whose reputations as representatives of the faith might have been sullied by those who resisted their mission among the Gentiles (15:25–26).

15:30–35. Reception at Antioch. Luke's record of the harmony and rejoicing that accompanied the reception of the decisions made in Jerusalem suggest an interpretation of the Jerusalem Consultation as a necessary detour from the main path of missionary endeavor. It is surely important that the Jerusalemites, Judas and Silas, participated in

the building up of believers in Antioch, and were sent away in peace by the Antioch believers. But with a notation about the ministry of Paul and Barnabas at Antioch in 15:35, we have returned to their work among the disciples in Antioch prior to the interruption from certain Judeans (14:28; 15:1).

15:36–16:5. Paul and Timothy Strengthen the Churches. The purpose to which Paul sets himself is to backtrack through the territory covered in chs. 13–14 to review "how they are doing" (15:36). In the end, this is what Paul does, though with Timothy rather than with Barnabas. Although the immediate reason for the parting of the ways between Paul and Barnabas is clear enough—namely, their disagreement regarding John Mark (see 13:13)—the basis of that disagreement is unclear. The language of "desertion" (15:38) might suggest that Paul thought of John Mark as having forsaken the whole gospel, with its openness to Gentiles (the very issue on which the Jerusalem Consultation had just spoken!). Barnabas, on the other hand, appears in his customary role as mediator and encourager (a role he had played with Paul himself; see 9:26–27; 11:25–26). In any case, at this juncture Luke writes Barnabas and John Mark out of the story, following instead the work of Paul and his companions.

Although his legal status is uncertain, for Luke Timothy would be regarded among Jewish communities as a Jew. Note that the Jerusalem Consultation did nothing to mitigate for Jewish followers of Christ the requirements of Torah, with the result that Paul circumcised Timothy so as not to place in jeopardy the reception of the gospel.

Luke summarizes the results of their journey in two ways—first, by indicating the content of their message (16:4); and second, by indicating the thriving of the church. The two are cause and effect: embodying the gospel worked out in these multiethnic terms leads to health and growth.

C. Proclaiming the Good News in Macedonia (16:6–17:15)

Divine guidance moves Paul and his companions into Macedonia (16:6–10), where they remain until the travel summary in 17:14–15, which locates Paul now in Athens. This unit contains the first of the "we-passages" in Acts—that is, passages where the narration moves from third person

("they did such-and-such") to first person ("we did such-and-such") (see 16:10–17; 20:5–21:18; 27:1–28:16). The presence of the pronoun "we" has the immediate literary effect of inviting Luke's audience into active participation in the narrative, and contributes to the reliability of the narration. That it happens in only selected portions of the narrative shows that the narrator makes no claim to having been a constant companion of Paul, but an observer of Paul's mission nonetheless at some of its pivotal junctures.

16:6–10. The Call to Macedonia. A strong sense of divine guidance permeates this introduction to Paul's missional activity in Macadeconia, as does the affirmation of unwavering obedience to the divine voice (see "immediately" in 16:10). "Holy Spirit" and "Spirit of Jesus" (16:6, 7) are virtual equivalents, the latter reflecting Luke's view that Spirit is given by the exalted Jesus (2:33). Indeed, it was in the context of the Pentecostal outpouring of the Spirit that the eschatological promise of dreams and visions was rehearsed (2:17), and subsequently visions and dreams are used to advance the narrative (e.g., 9:10; 10:3, 10; 11:15).

16:11–15. The Baptism and Hospitality of Lydia. Luke devotes inordinate attention to identifying Philippi (16:12) and Lydia (16:14–15). This is strategic since it makes the first convert on European soil and in this Roman colony a woman—either divorced or widowed, a Gentile, the head of her own household. Later, Paul and his companions will be charged with "turning the world upside down" (17:6), but here we have already evidence of Roman conventions inverted. Apparently, Philippi has no significant Jewish presence, hence a gathering for prayer on the Sabbath (16:13). Luke highlights that Lydia's conversion was the Lord's doing (16:14), notes that the conversion of the head of the household signaled the conversion of the whole household (see 10:2, 48; 16:33), and ties the reception of the good news to the hospitable reception of its messengers. Indeed, her house seems to serve as a center for the mission (16:15, 40).

16:16–40. Imprisonment and Release in Philippi. Returning to a "place of prayer" (16:13, 16), Paul and his companions encounter another woman whose contrast with Lydia is sharply drawn. Rather than head of a household, this woman is enslaved to her masters as a prophet for business purposes. Her claims regarding Paul and his companions are met with rebuke in a way reminiscent of demonic claims regarding Jesus (e.g., Luke 4:34–35, 41). In the present case, this may be because her words can be heard by non-believers as affirmations of yet one more god among the gods, or because these missionaries do not need allies like this demonized woman. In any case, emphasis falls on the power of Jesus Christ.

Although the real concern of the owners is the loss of income they will experience on account of Paul's exorcizing the spirit of divination, their opposition is recast in terms of xenophobia and public disturbance. Like Peter before them (Acts 12), so Paul and Silas, cast into jail, are miraculously rescued from their secure imprisonment. Luke's story highlights the response of the jailer who is about to commit suicide when he himself is "saved." Here, Luke's readers can hear a double meaning: saved from the shame of having allowed his prisoners to escape and thus from his own execution (compare 12:19) versus saved in the sense of welcoming both the good news and its messengers into his home (on the jailer's question, see Luke 3:10–14; Acts 2:37).

17:1–9. Turning the World Upside Down in Thessalonica. Lest we imagine that the focus on Gentiles in the preceding material has marked a departure from a mission among the Jewish people, Luke reminds his audience that Paul's custom was to focus his work in the synagogue. The message centers on how to read the Scriptures so as to emphasize the Messiah's death and resurrection, which leads eventually to charges that Paul is leading the people astray. In all three respects, Paul is like Jesus, who habitually preached in the synagogue on the Sabbath (Luke 4:16–17), interpreted Israel's Scriptures in conformity with the divine plan regarding the suffering and resurrection of the Messiah (24:25–27, 44–46), and was indicted for leading the people astray (Luke 23:1–5). To what degree are these witnesses guilty of the charges brought against them? On the one hand, nothing in Luke's precis of their message militates against Rome or its conventions; on the other hand, by proclaiming Jesus as God's Messiah, they call into question all beliefs and practices that do not flow from embracing the reign of God. If Jesus is Lord of all, then all other allegiances are secondary.

17:10–15. The Word Welcomed in Beroea. With Paul and Silas' escape from Thessalonica, the pattern of proclamation in the synagogue is repeated. The difference is that the rabble-rousing of 17:5 is replaced with serious engagement with the Scriptures among the Beroeans—apparently among Jews and devout Gentiles (17:12). This underscores yet again the struggle within Judaism in the Second Temple period regarding how best to read the Scriptures, with Luke siding with these followers of Jesus in claiming that, read thoughtfully in light of God's purpose concerning God's Messiah, the Scriptures confirm the good news concerning Jesus.

D. Advancing the Good News in Athens (17:16–34)

As with the move into Lystra (14:8–20), so Paul's entry into Athens sets him and his message on the stage of Greco-Roman religion. Athens may have a synagogue (17:17), but the context of his proclamation of Jesus and his resurrection is Athenian idolatry (17:16, 23).

17:16–21. Paul Gains an Audience. Paul's exasperation (*paroxynō*, NRSV, "deeply distressed") at the city's idolatry leads to his engagement with the city's inhabitants in two arenas, the synagogue and the marketplace. We might think it strange that Paul argues about idol worship in the synagogue until we recall that idolatry is a pervasive issue in Israel's Scriptures, and life outside of Palestine was replete with enticement to participate in idol worship; it may also have been that Paul's arguments in the synagogue centered on the importance of Jewish testimony against the idolatry of the city. If Luke seems to present Paul as a "street preacher," it is worth recalling how common itinerant philosophers, as Paul must have seemed, would have been. Indeed, Luke has it that the marketplace provided the stage for interaction with representatives of two philosophical schools, Epicureans and Stoics. For Epicureans, the ideal life comprises never-ending, undisturbed happiness, free from anxiety, pain, and despair. Stoicism prioritized living in accord with human reason, with happiness not an affective response but a product of virtue. As to beliefs in the afterlife, for Epicureans, the soul was a substance of fine particles that dissipated at death; death, then, was annihilation. Stoics had no settled position on the afterlife, but would not have supported the idea of a "bodily resurrection." It is not at all clear that either of these groups understood Paul's proclamation, as they regard him as a mere babbler and apparently hear in his message a reference to two foreign deities: "Jesus" and "Resurrection."

17:22–31. Paul's Proclamation on the Areopagus. An altar to an "unknown god" was likely a safety precaution as the Athenians relied on gods known and unknown to secure their living and fortune. Paul's speech provides an essentially Jewish perspective on idols: it is wrong to locate God in a shrine (16:24; see 7:48); it is wrong to attempt to placate the living God who provides life (16:25); God is not a local god, unlike idols that are stationary and bound to a specific locale (17:26); and God has his own life, unlike idols, who are inanimate objects (see Ps 115:1–8). From a Greek perspective, Paul's critique raises a serious question, since wrong worship ought to lead to punishment from the gods. Thus, in 16:30–31, Paul explains why God has withheld judgment *and* explains why repentance is now the order of the day. (Recall that, in a city full of idols [17:16], turning away from idols to the Living God would have far-reaching social-religious consequences.) He puts forward the resurrection of the appointed judge both to certify that judgment will come and to mark the turning point in God-human relations.

17:32–34. The Response at Athens. In effect, Luke describes a range of three responses to Paul's resurrection message: (1) scoffing, presumably the response of Epicureans and those who shared their rejection of an afterlife, or who simply thought "resurrection" was a barbaric belief in "resuscitation of dead corpses"; (2) openness, presumably the response of Stoics and others like them who had a variety of views on the afterlife; and (3) coming to faith.

E. Proclamation and Persuasion in Corinth (18:1–17)

Luke provides in these textual units two points of contact with datable history—the expulsion under Claudius (49 CE) and the proconsulship of Gallio (51–52 CE).

Two central elements in the formation of a community in the ancient world were ethnic background and trade, so it is no surprise to see that, upon coming to Corinth, Paul identifies immedi-

ately with Priscilla and Aquilla, who were like him in so many ways: Jews, living away from their homes, and tentmakers. At the outset of his work at Corinth, Paul seems to have worked as a tentmaker Sunday through Friday (compare 20:34; 1 Cor 4:12; 9:1–23; 1 Thess 2:9) until Silas and Timothy arrived from Macedonia. Did his companions bring with them from Macedonia financial support (see Phil 4:15), allowing Paul then to occupy himself more fully with proclaiming God's word? In any case, as was Paul's habit (e.g., 17:2), we find Paul speaking to Jews and devout Gentiles in the synagogue, and then to Jews especially, testifying that Jesus was the Messiah. Jesus had preached in synagogues, too, but in Luke 13:10–17 he meets such opposition that, for the rest of Luke's Gospel, he never again enters a synagogue. Overall, Luke–Acts demonstrates the importance of the synagogue to the mission of Jesus and his followers, but also a move toward the household where there is greater receptivity to the good news. This is precisely what we find in this scene. Like 13:46–14:1, Paul's resolve to turn to the Gentiles in 18:6 has about it the note of finality but the very next scene has him in a synagogue (18:19).

Paul's vision (18:9–10) anticipates the heightened opposition he will face. When it does materialize, the charges against him (18:13) *could* be heard in terms of sedition, but, in his disinterest, Gallio hears only an intramural dispute among the Jews (18:14–15).

F. The Triumph of the Name of Jesus in Ephesus (18:18–19:20)

This is the final narrative unit devoted to Paul's mission in Acts. From 19:21 on, Paul will continue his journeys and proclaim the good news, but the focus will shift away from missionary proclamation more and more to a defense of the gospel in a series of judicial settings. This part of Luke's narrative closes with much that is familiar to us—e.g., Paul among believers in regions he has already visited, Paul preaching in synagogues, mixed responses to the good news. The storyline centers in Ephesus, capital of Asia, and it is in this city that Demetrius, a silversmith, observes that Paul had countered idolatry "not only in Ephesus but in almost the whole of Asia" (19:26). This speaks not only to Paul's faithfulness to Israel's God but also to the breadth of his influence as a proclaimer of the good news.

18:18–23. Interlude: Travel and Continuity. The crisscrossing of travels is hard to follow as Luke telescopes many miles and days into only a handful of verses. Paul's words in 18:21, "if God wills" (see Jas 4:15), place the whole journey under the canopy of the divine plan. This summary also contributes to Luke's portrait of Paul as a traveling witness, underscores his Jewish credentials (see 18:18, 19), introduces Ephesus—a center for church and mission in the paragraphs that follow—and locates Priscilla and Aquila in Ephesus during Paul's absence. Luke provides no details about the vow Paul makes, but what he does say parallels somewhat the Nazarite vow (Num 6:1–21).

18:24–28. Priscilla, Aquila, and Apollos. In the temporary absence of Paul, Priscilla and Aquila provide continuity with the larger narrative as well as instruction for Apollos. Apollos is an example of how John's baptism ought to lead someone to Jesus Christ and, thus, to the gift of the Spirit (see Luke 3:7–20). Accordingly, he has been instructed "in the Way of the Lord," his speech is alive with the Spirit (18:25; NRSV, "with burning enthusiasm"), he teaches accurately concerning Jesus, and he speaks with boldness (that is, as emboldened by the Spirit; compare, e.g., 4:31) in the synagogues. The role of Priscilla and Aquila (note that she is named first, suggesting her prominent teaching role) is to explain the Way of God "more accurately." Luke's summary of Apollos' message parallels that of Paul (18:28; see 17:3).

19:1–7. The Holy Spirit Comes upon Some Disciples of John. Although they are called "disciples," those whom Paul encounters upon his arrival in Ephesus are like Apollos only insofar as they know only the baptism of John. Otherwise, the Spirit is manifest in Apollos' speech, but they are ignorant concerning the Holy Spirit. Moreover, whereas Apollos is able to teach accurately concerning Jesus, Paul must instruct these "disciples" that John's baptism was to have moved them toward faith in Jesus. This suggests that, by "disciples," Luke has in mind "disciples of John" (see Luke 5:33; 7:18).

Remarkably, John's ministry took place in a region far removed from places like Ephesus, and decades earlier. That John is mentioned so often in Acts (1:5; 11:16; 13:25; 18:25; 19:3–4) reminds us of the widespread influence of his movement, and allows us to see how Luke puts John in his place as an important precursor (but only a precursor) to Jesus.

19:8–10. Arguing at Ephesus. The conflict between Paul and those among the Jews who resist him and his message reaches a new stage, with Paul not only departing the synagogue but "taking the disciples with him" (19:9). Such opposition notwithstanding, Paul and his message are clearly sanctioned by God: his speech is "bold" (that is, emboldened by the Spirit; see, e.g., 4:31), he argues "persuasively," his message concerns the kingdom of God, and his departure from the synagogue has the effect that "all the residents of Asia, both Jews and Greeks, heard the word of the Lord" (Act 19:10). Opposition fuels the spread of the mission.

19:11–20. Miracle and Magic. Luke provides three short vignettes, ostensibly to legitimate Paul as a worker of miracles, but actually to show that the name of the Lord Jesus is to be praised (see the repetition of the name in 16:13 [2×], 15, 17). First, Paul is described in ways analogous to the summary regarding Peter in 5:15; note, however, Luke's clear affirmation that these miracles were done *through* Paul *by* God (19:11–12). Second, some Jewish exorcists (compare Luke 11:19) attempt to use the name of the Lord Jesus but in the process we learn that they are not qualified to do so (as is Paul) since they do not name Jesus as Lord (19:13–16). The play on words in the Greek text adds to the humor of the episode: they call on Jesus the Lord (*kyrios*) but the evil spirit "lords it over" them (*kata-kyrieuō*, 19:16; NRSV, "mastered")! Finally, this leads to many becoming believers, exposing their magical practices and burning their books of magic (in spite of the fortune related to those practices), and the word of God not only grew but prevailed. This last point is a commentary not only on the power encounter Luke narrates, but also on his testimony that the spread of the mission has not been curtailed by the opposition it has encountered.

V. The Journeys of Paul, Missionary Prisoner (19:21–28:31)

Luke signals a major shift in the narrative of Acts, first, by the summary statement in 19:20 and, second, by the resolve that characterizes Paul's movement. The language of divine necessity will now move Paul forward toward Rome (compare 19:21; 20:16; 21:1–14). Along the way, Paul will fulfill his commission to "bring [the Lord's] name before Gentiles and kings and before the people of Israel (9:15); indeed, this last major section of Acts demonstrates Paul's allegiance to Jesus as he bears witness before rulers.

A. Paul Resolves to Travel to Jerusalem ... and Rome (19:21–22)

Paul's travel plans are not of his own invention. They are guided by the Spirit and reflect God's purpose. His resolve parallels that of Jesus as he begins his lengthy journey from Galilee to Jerusalem, and, like Jesus, he sends companions on ahead of him (compare Luke 9:51–52a).

B. Premonitions Concerning Paul's Arrival in Jerusalem (19:23–21:14)

What happens to persons in the Lukan narrative who embrace the divine will with radical resolve? Jesus and Stephen are case studies in the resistance God's spokespersons encounter. This section of Acts anticipates in both implicit and transparent ways the heightened hostility Paul will encounter too. Consider the furor arising in relation to temples made with human hands in Ephesus (19:24–27)—a flashback to Stephen's characterization of the Jerusalem Temple (7:48), likewise made with human hands; and a flash-forward to the indictment that will be brought against Paul in relation to the Temple (21:26–29). Paul's own words before the Ephesians are the best commentary on what to expect: "And now, as a captive to the Spirit, I am on my way to Jerusalem, not knowing what will happen to me there, except that the Holy Spirit testifies to me in every city that imprisonment and persecutions are waiting for me" (20:22–23).

19:23–41. Rioting in Ephesus. How best to read this narrative unit is suggested by its immediate aftermath in 20:1: Paul's departure from Ephesus; indeed, 20:17 has Paul address the elders of the Ephesian church from a location other than Ephesus. Although Paul and his companions escape this riot without being physically harmed, the opposition has grown to such an extent that the public mission in Ephesus seems to have been silenced.

On the one hand, there is much to commend the success of Paul's mission. Others participate in the mission (18:24–28), everyone hears the good news (19:10; compare 19:17), even his opponents admit the far-reaching influence of Paul and his message (19:26), and when Paul and his companions are faced with mob action, the town clerk intervenes and warns the crowds that they, not Paul, are acting outside of the law.

On the other hand, the opposition is rigorous, a consequence of the tentacles of Artemis worship that reach far into the social, religious, political, economic lives of this center of Artemis worship, Ephesus. The concern with prosperity and business sounded in 19:27 should not be reduced to simple greed. Rather, Demetrius speaks truthfully of how fully the temple and its worship are integrated into the whole of the city's life, so that Paul's message against idolatry (that is, against gods made with human hands) is a genuine threat to a way of life. What is more, the town clerk counters Paul's message by repeating the legend of Artemis—not (as Paul would have it) a statue made by human hands, but "the statue that fell from heaven" (19:35).

Luke thus demonstrates the inherently and inextricably social-political-economic-religious character of the good news, and thus the degree to which its opponents will go to keep the gospel from upsetting conventional life.

20:1–12. Resuscitation in Troas. The first half of this section is taken up with details of travel and companions, each of which is important in its own way. Travel, for example, is toward Jerusalem (see 19:21), and the route taken reflective both of the hostility Paul faced and the need to encourage the believers in the places of his ongoing mission. Luke names some of Paul's expanding entourage, themselves representative of the congregations he has founded. Those designated by the pronoun "we" had remained in Philippi in 16:40, and now they reappear to sail from Philippi to join Paul in Troas.

The story of Eutychus is often taken as humorous but its associations within the Lukan narrative actually commend it as a tragedy made good. Sleeping is precisely what disciples ought not to do (see especially Luke 22:39–46; compare Acts 20:28, 31), so Eutychus' having been overcome by sleep marks his inattentiveness to Paul's words, his lack of spiritual alertness. His resuscitation by Paul (compare 9:36–43) is a restoration of Eutychus to the faithful. Luke's portrait of the scene invites reflection, too, on the nature of believers gathered for worship and teaching: the first day of the week (that is, Sunday; compare 1 Cor 16:2), breaking bread (compare Acts 2:42), multiple lamps (light and sight are often related to the illumination of the gospel in the Lukan narrative), and an upper room (compare 1:13).

20:13–38. Farewell to the Ephesian Elders. This is the last Pauline speech before his captivity and it fits the well-known pattern of the "farewell discourse" found in biblical and other literature (compare, e.g., Luke 22:21–38). Thus, it provides a review of history (20:18–21), warnings about the future (20:22–24, 25, 29–30), appointment of successors (20:28), encouragement to follow teaching (20:31), blessings (20:32), and prayer for those left behind (20:36). Perhaps most interesting is Paul's characterization of himself in this address, which serves both to prepare Luke's readers to hear counter-charges against him in the chapters to follow and to provide an exemplar for faithful leadership. Others will distort the truth, but Paul proclaims the message of the kingdom and the whole purpose of God (which undoubtedly refers to the mission to Jew *and* Gentile); Paul is faithful with regard to money (compare Luke 16:14; 1 Tim 3:3; 6:10); and Paul's mission, including the opposition it attracts, reflects and serves the divine purpose (see especially 20:22, 24, 27). So, too, the ministry of these elders is given by God, to whose care Paul finally commends them.

21:1–14. Jerusalem Bound. Just as Luke had marked Jesus' growing proximity to Jerusalem with added detail concerning his travelogue (Luke 18–19), so now Luke provides startling detail about the progress Paul and his companions make en route to Jerusalem. Although many days and miles are covered in the span of only a few verses, the effect nonetheless is to slow down our reading of the narrative so as to gain a heightened sense of the solemnity with which Paul carries out the journey. Additionally, Luke's record of Paul's itinerary has the effect of drawing together what would otherwise be disparate communities of believers; of course, the bond that holds them together is the Lord, yet the evidence we have of this is the peripatetic mission of the Lord's witness, Paul.

Luke's attribution of direction to the Holy Spirit may give us pause. After all, it was "in the Spirit" that Paul resolved to go to Jerusalem (19:21), and it is the Spirit who says that Paul will be bound in Jerusalem and handed over to the Gentiles (20:11). How, then, can it be that disciples tell him "through the Spirit" not to go to Jerusalem (21:4)? This may be nothing more than an example of the apparent tension we find in 20:22–23—namely, Paul is a "captive to the Spirit" in his going to Jerusalem, but the same Spirit testifies that this journey will be one of imprisonment and persecution.

At the end of ch. 8, after his encounter with the Ethiopian, Philip had proclaimed the good news as he moved up the coast from Azotus to Caesarea. Tying off that loose thread, when Paul and his companions arrive in Caesarea they enjoy the hospitality of Philip ("one of the seven" [6:1–7], to differentiate him from Philip the apostle). Note that he is labeled as an "evangelist," a term that describes the actual work of sharing the good news in which he has been engaged in Acts; he is not a "deacon." His four daughters are "unmarried," probably a reference to their relative youth, and they are all prophets. Here in Caesarea, then, is the embodiment of the witnessing and prophetic community anticipated with the outpouring of the Spirit at Pentecost (see 2:17–21).

C. On Trial in Jerusalem (21:15–23:11)

This narrative section is focused on Jerusalem and includes Luke's account of Paul's journey from his arrival in Jerusalem in 21:15–17 to the Lord's promise in 23:11 that Paul would testify in Rome as well. Although he enjoys hospitality initially upon his entry in Jerusalem, Paul's Jerusalem experience is dominated by misunderstanding, accusation, and hostility—and, therefore, the opportunity to maintain allegiance to the whole purpose of God and to bear faithful witness.

21:15–36. Reception in Jerusalem. Although Paul's welcome in Jerusalem among the believers is warm, the situation soon turns critical (21:18–

26). James and the elders relate to Paul the presence in Jerusalem of "many thousands" of Jewish followers of Jesus who are zealous for the law, who have heard (and apparently believe) that Paul has taught Jews in the diaspora to forsake Moses. This is surprising for two reasons. First, Paul's report to James and the elders has focused on God's work among the Gentiles (21:19; compare 14:27; 15:3–4, 12). Second, never in Acts do we read of Paul's even hinting that Jewish followers of Jesus, much less that Jews in general, should forsake Moses. A comparison with the charges raised against Stephen (compare 6:11–14; 21:21) is suggestive on account of similar concerns with Torah, but also because of a key difference: Stephen was opposed by Jews in Jerusalem, but Paul is being challenged by Jewish followers of Jesus. The proposed solution comes as a directive: Paul is to pay for the shaving of the heads of four Jews who are under a vow. The identification of the vow (somehow related to a Nazirite vow [compare Num 6:1–21]?) is passed over in favor of the symbolism of Paul's prescribed act; he will be seen to be participating in a Jewish act of piety.

The irony, then, is that it is precisely Paul the observant Jew who stands accused (21:27–36). To be sure, the accusers are Jews from Asia (repeating a pattern of Paul's opponents following him from place to place to upset his ministry—e.g., 17:13). But this only presses the question, Where are James and the elders? Why do they not come to Paul's defense? Sounding another chord of irony, then, it is not the community of followers of Jesus in Jerusalem who come to Paul's rescue as a mob is formed, but Rome's representatives. Like Jesus before his passion, Paul is isolated from the disciples. And as with Jesus, so with Paul, the crowds shout, "Away with him!" (Luke 23:18; Acts 21:36).

21:37–22:29. Paul's Defense Before the Jewish People. The parallels with Jesus continue as Paul, like Jesus, is assumed to be a rabble-rouser (Luke 23:1–5; Acts 21:38). The tribune gives voice to Rome's real concern—namely, maintaining order and addressing any threat of insurrection. Paul's defense speech is directed not to Rome, though, but to the Jews in Jerusalem, and, indeed, to those Jewish followers of Jesus who had questioned his faithfulness as a Jew (see 21:21). Thus, in 22:1–5, he lines up, one after the other, an impressive list

of Jewish credentials. He claims kinship with his audience (22:1); he speaks Aramaic (21:40; 22:2; NRSV, "Hebrew"); he names himself a Jew, claims to have been reared in the center of the Jewish world, Jerusalem, recounts his strict education in Torah and its interpretation under Gamaliel (see 5:34), and bears witness to the zeal for God that he shares with those gathered (22:3); and he recalls his role in the service of the high priest and Jerusalem Council as a persecutor of followers of Jesus (22:4–5).

Even his report of his commission on the road to Damascus is saturated with demonstrations of Jewish faithfulness (22:6–16). He refers repeatedly to "the Lord," mentioning the name "Jesus" only because this was the name given to him in his vision. Ananias is presented not as a Christian but with transparent credentials as a devout Jew. Although Luke's readers know that the "him" and "his" to whom Paul refers is Jesus, Paul himself never makes this clear.

The climax of his speech comes in 22:17–21 as he recounts his vision in the Temple. Again, he refers to "him" and "the Lord," never mentioning Jesus. (The NRSV has added the name at 22:18.) He is in God's own house, holy space, when he receives a vision. He protests the message he receives from the Lord. In these ways it become irrefutable that his commission to go to the Gentiles was not self-imposed but came from the Lord himself.

Up to this point, the crowd had listened, apparently finding nothing of concern in Paul's speech. At this juncture, however, they break into his address with gestures and words of rejection. The parallel with Jesus' passion continues as they cry out for his execution (compare Luke 23:18; Acts 22:22).

The initial charges against Paul had been that he led people away from Torah and defiled the Temple (21:28). Rather than address these charges directly, Paul's defense had undermined the notion that he was anything but a faithful Jew. By the end of this part of the narrative, though, the real sticking point has been identified. Paul has made the case both that he can be a Jew *and* a follower of the Lord Jesus and that the Lord himself had shown Paul that followers of Jesus comprise a redirection of Israel's own history, a history that was now to include the Gentiles.

22:30–23:11. Paul's Defense Before the Jewish Council. Initiating the meeting as though he were in charge, Paul states credentials that call into question the whole string of events related to the opposition he has garnered in Jerusalem (23:1–5). He addresses the Council as "brothers," thus claiming "insider status" with these Jewish leaders (23:1, 5, 6); this could harken to his former role as persecutor on behalf of these leaders (see 7:58; 8:1). Second, he declares his "clear conscience before God." This may seem a strange assertion for one who has persecuted followers of Jesus, but it actually meshes well with Luke's biography of Paul. He has been zealous for God from first to last. To be sure, his experience on the road to Damascus has enhanced and transformed his understanding of what it might mean to align himself with God's purpose, but this only underscores the nature of his consistent commitment to serve (rather than work against) God's agenda. Drawing on imagery from Ezek 13:10–15, Paul associates the high priest with those who feign to speak on God's behalf but actually participate in unjust practices. In this, Paul calls into the question the legitimacy of this hearing.

Paul's subsequent claim to be a Pharisee "on trial concerning the hope of the resurrection of the dead" (23:6) functions at two levels (23:6–10). First, it comes across as a pragmatic move designed to throw the Jewish Council into turmoil—an effective strategy according to Luke's report. If Paul's rhetorical move seems to be a strategic manipulation of the Jewish Council, though, it remains true that his statement regarding the hope of the resurrection strikes at what he regards as the heart of faithful Judaism (see 24:15; 26:6–7; 28:20). This refers to the restoration of Israel by God—a restoration that, for Paul, signals the inclusion of the Gentiles—which has been set in motion by God's raising Jesus from the dead. Christology, the nature of salvation and God's people, and the end time thus come into focus in the one reference to the hope of the resurrection.

Paul's rescue from the Jewish Council by the Roman tribune leads that night to a vision, reminding us of how often Luke has recounted visions of assurance and divine direction (see 2:17–21; 16:9; 18:9–10; 22:17–18). The reach of Paul's witness is grounded in his commission (9:15), and now reiterated in this anticipation of the rest of the narrative of Acts (see also 19:21).

D. Custodial Journey to Caesarea (23:12–35)

Luke recounts the first stage of Paul's journey to Rome in remarkable detail. We have read before of Jewish plots against Paul (9:23–24; 20:3, 19), but only here do we have inside knowledge both of the plan and of its widespread support. Regarding the latter point, it is significant that the two groups before whom Paul has just spoken—the Jews in Jerusalem (21:37–22:29) and the Jewish Council (22:30–23:11)—are both involved (23:12, 14–15); Luke's report concerning the large number of actual conspirators and the death-vow they have taken only adds to the seriousness of the unfolding drama.

Even with this heightened devotion to detail, some points still are puzzling. Paul had a sister? A nephew? Luke passes over such matters, including why the tribune unquestioningly accepts the young man's report. Instead, we find that the tribune's name is Claudius, and that Claudius wrote a letter effectively transferring authority for Paul over to Felix, writing in such a way as to place himself in the most favorable light. (Compare 22:23–29 with 23:27!) Moreover, Claudius' letter serves to bear witness to Paul's innocence. From here to the end of Acts, Paul's innocence will be a constant refrain, reminiscent of the threefold statement of Jesus' innocence by Rome's representative in Luke 23:4, 14, 22.

E. Paul's Defense Before Felix (24:1–27)

Chapters 24–26 report Paul's making his defense before Rome's representatives, Governors Felix and Festus and King Agrippa. These allow Luke to sharpen the point of controversy between Paul and his detractors, and to show how, from a Roman perspective, Paul is innocent of all charges—and, accordingly, to raise the question why he continues to be imprisoned (see, e.g., 24:26–27; 25:9). Most important, this series of trials allow Paul the opportunity to maintain his allegiance to the Lord and to testify before Roman rulers (9:15).

Speeches in legal contexts like these typically unfolded in three parts: (1) an introduction designed to gain a favorable hearing, usually by

Jesus and Paul—On Trial		
Luke 23:1–25		Acts 25:1–26:32
23:1	Introduction	25:1
23:2–5	Hearing Before Roman Procurator	25:2–12
23:6–7	Introduction to Herodian Ruler	25:13–27
23:8–12	Hearing Before Herodian Ruler	26:1–23
23:13–23	Dialogue	26:24–29
23:24–25	Conclusion: Innocent … but	26:30–32

flattering the audience and presenting oneself in a positive light; (2) a statement of the facts designed to establish the question on which judgment is needed; and (3) reference to witnesses and testimony that prove the charge against the defendant is either true or false. In the material that follows, we see that Paul and his opponents disagree about the question on which judgment is needed. This is because, for Luke, to put Paul on trial is actually to place the gospel itself on trial.

24:1–9. Paul Accused. Although the high priest and some Jewish elders are present, they do not speak, apparently having procured the services of a professional orator to make the case against Paul on their behalf. Note the escalation of Paul's opposition, from mobs in 21:27 to a hired lawyer. Although Felix was generally regarded as a scoundrel, Tertullus proceeds to flatter the governor in the expected way. The charges against Paul boil down to his status as a public enemy (*loimos*; 24:5, NRSV, "pestilent fellow"), evidenced by his disturbing the peace (compare the charges against Jesus in 23:1–5), and, especially, profaning the Temple (see 21:27–29). His case is supported by the testimony of the Jews—presumably, that is, by Jews of such status as the high priest and elders mentioned in 24:1.

24:10–21. Paul's Defense. By way of contrast, Paul proceeds without the services of a professional lawyer and provides only what might be regarded as brief and ambiguous praise for the governor. His statement of the facts differs significantly, too. He repeats each stage of his defense:

(1) I went to worship in Jerusalem, not to cause trouble (24:11–12).

(2) Where is the proof (24:13)?

(3) In fact, I am a faithful Jew, holding to resurrection hope (24:14–16).

(1) I went to Jerusalem to bring alms and offer sacrifices in Jerusalem, and there was no disturbance when I did so (24:17–18).

(2) Where are my accusers (24:19–20)?

(3) The charge against me should be this, that I proclaim the resurrection (24:21).

Paul has thus countered Tertullus, first by disagreeing about the reason he is on trial, second by admitting to a charge (his belief in and proclamation of resurrection hope) that is outside of Roman legal concern. In effect, he has shifted the focus of controversy away from himself and onto the nature of Israel's faith—that is, onto the good news of God.

24:22–27. Felix Delays Judgment. Luke casts Felix initially in a neutral light, but this portrait quickly deteriorates. His decision to await the arrival of the tribune is understandable for someone concerned with civil order and removed from the events in question; moreover, the relative freedom Felix gives Paul in his imprisonment comports well with first-century practices, where the everyday maintenance of prisoners fell to friends and family rather than to the state. However, he rejects Paul's message when it turns to judgment, attempts to profit from Paul's situation, lets

Paul's case sit idle for two years, and, rather than dispense with the case, holds Paul's case over for decision by the new governor (24:25–27). This last (in)action suggests that Felix had no reason not to release Paul apart from his desire to curry favor from the Jews. Luke's portrait of Roman justice is thus a sullied one.

F. Paul's Defense Before Festus (25:1–27)

The narrative of Paul's trials before Festus and Agrippa in Acts 25–26 repeat familiar patterns from Luke's account of Jesus' trials before Pilate and Herod in Luke 23. The result is further legitimacy of Paul, not simply *in spite of* but *because of* the legal action taken against him.

25:1–12. Festus Favors the Jerusalem Leadership. Traveling to Jerusalem so quickly upon assuming the governorship of Judea may not be surprising given the reality that Festus' capital was Caesarea but the Jewish leadership was in Jerusalem. Ostensibly, then, he was seeking to establish a good relationship with Jerusalem. The issue of Paul is raised by the Jewish leadership and their request of a favor should be read within the elaborate web of social relationships in the ancient Mediterranean. It was one thing to be appointed governor, but quite another to rule; placing the Jewish leaders in his debt as they have suggested would be a firm step toward Festus' ability to rule over his people. Nevertheless, this encounter between the Roman and Jewish authorities (24:1–5) leaves us with the impression that Festus is nonprejudicial regarding Paul's case.

All of this changes once the governor returns to Caesarea. Having been prompted by the Jerusalem leaders, he has Paul brought before the seat of justice. Luke provides his audience with brief asides to let them know what is really going on in the ensuing encounter. The charges may be serious, but they cannot be proven (24:7). Festus may appear to be judicious, but in fact has joined his predecessor in seeing the disposition of Paul's case as a means of winning Jewish favor (23:27; 24:9). This leads to his suggestion that they take the case to Jerusalem. Paul's response is to deny all charges (compare 24:8 with 21:21; 24:5–6); to assert that the governor has stepped outside legal boundaries by suggesting a change of venue; and, indeed, having no hope of a fair hearing under

Festus, to appeal to be heard by the emperor himself.

25:13–22. Festus Confers with Agrippa. A comparison of the narrator's account of Festus' handling of Paul's case in 25:1–12 with Festus' version of what transpired is stunning. The narrator portrays Festus as anything but a paragon of fairness, but Festus presents himself as the quintessential Roman governor, having acted responsibly at every turn. Even so, Festus does sharpen the question of Paul's alleged wrongdoing, repeating to Agrippa only that the issue at stake had to do with the resurrection. Paul's consistent rhetoric has thus proven successful: it is not he himself that is on trial, but rather his belief in the resurrection (e.g., 23:6–10; 24:14–16, 19–21).

G. Paul's Defense Before Agrippa (25:23–26:32)

This is Paul's final defense speech, and the third and final account of his encounter with the risen Lord on the road to Damascus (9:1–25; 22:4–21; 26:9–23). What does Paul defend in this address? Note that no charges are named; Agrippa merely permits Paul "to speak for himself" (26:1). This gives Paul the opportunity to set the record straight simply by narrating what has happened. We are thus reminded that "narrative" is not just "story" but also "action"—shaping identity, legitimating beliefs and behavior, and demonstrating continuity with the past. Such aims as these characterize an address like Paul's, the character of which must thus be understood in apologetic terms. In the end, then, Paul's address is proclamation much in the same way that the author of Acts employs narrative to proclaim the good news.

25:23–26:1a. Preliminary Matters. The problem Festus faces is one of his own making: How can he prove that he is a good governor? Thus, he exaggerates the pressure he is under, declares Paul's innocence (a pronouncement of which there is no hint in Festus' earlier comments in 25:1–12), and, neglecting his own prejudicial behavior that resulted in Paul's appeal to Rome, claims that had Paul not done so he would be set free. With the stage set for Paul to speak, no charges have been stated; Paul has nothing to which he must respond.

26:1b–29. Paul Addresses Agrippa. Paul's introduction fulfills its expected role by preparing his audience, Agrippa, to hear him favorably. He lauds the king for his familiarity with "all the customs and controversies of the Jews" (26:3) as well as presents himself as a faithful Jew. In this way, he lays out the contours of his speech. What is on trial is not Paul's alleged rabble-rousing behavior, but rather the nature of Jewish belief regarding the hope of the resurrection. This does not render Paul and the gospel harmless from a Roman or political perspective, since the hope of the resurrection is shorthand for the restoration of God's people, Jew and Gentile; and the resurrection has as its corollaries a reordering of social and economic life and political allegiance to the Resurrected One, Jesus, who is "Lord of all."

Paul comes to the primary question in 26:6–8—namely, his definition of authentic Israel in terms of the promise around which they orient their lives. This promise is the resurrection of the dead. "Why is it thought incredible by any of you that God raises the dead?" (26:8)—this is the question around which the king's judgment turns. Paul has thus removed himself from the focus of this hearing, substituting in his place what is for him the center of the gospel, the resurrection of Jesus Christ. To anticipate the judgments that come in 26:24–32, Festus' response to Paul's question is that Paul has lost his mind. Agrippa sidesteps the pronouncement of judgment on the question Paul has posed, recognizing instead that the issue at hand is not the concern of Roman jurisprudence. According to its canons, Paul is innocent.

Paul's sketch of his encounter with the Lord on road to Damascus leads to the center of Paul's defense in 26:19–23, presented in an A–B–A' structure:

A (26:19–20). What Paul has done he has done in obedience to God. In terms that roughly parallel Jesus' missionary mandate in 1:8, Paul has proclaimed to Jews and Gentiles their need to repent.

    B (26:21). The action of the Jews against Paul was baseless. (After all, what he has done was in obedience to God [A] and was accomplished with God's help [A'].)

A' (26:22–23). What Paul has done, he has done with God's help. What is more, the

message he has proclaimed is grounded in Israel's own Scriptures.

Festus' outburst, "You are out of your mind!" is countered by Paul's claim to inspired, sober speech (26:24–25). The basis of Festus' interruption is not Paul's hysterical speech or babbling, but rather Paul's exposition of Scripture as witness to the death and resurrection of the Messiah. Lacking the conceptual categories to make sense of Paul's argument, Festus presumes that Paul is the one lacking in cognitive equipment. Agrippa, on the other hand, seems to have understood the evangelistic ramifications of Paul's address but sidesteps the issue. Belief in the prophets, belief in the resurrection of the dead as the restoration of Israel, belief that his being raised up marks Jesus as Lord, and belief that Jesus' resurrection invites people to align themselves with God's purpose through repentance—these are all interwoven in Paul's speech as Israel's hope. Hence, the final exchange between Paul and Agrippa underscores Paul's persuasive agenda; he is not so much defending himself as he is proclaiming the good news.

26:30–32. Paul's Innocence Reaffirmed. When measured against the interests of Roman law, Paul is innocent. On this, both Festus and Agrippa agree, with Agrippa making explicit what Festus had earlier implied (25:25–27), that Paul could have been set free except for his appeal to the emperor.

H. Custodial Journey to Rome (27:1–28:15)

These final two chapters of the narrative of Acts are analogous to the final defense of the gospel Paul has just made before Felix, Festus, and Agrippa in chs. 24–25. There could hardly be a more profound testimony to God's help than God's rescue of Paul and his shipmates from the storm at sea that left them swimming for their lives. And there could hardly be a stronger affirmation of God's directive and assurance to Paul that he would bear testimony to the gospel in Rome (see 19:21; 23:11) than his arrival in Rome as a witness.

27:1–44. Paul's Voyage and Shipwreck. Accounts of sea voyages and shipwrecks had a firm place in the literature of antiquity, where they often highlighted providential care. Lest we are tempted to imagine that this account is included for the sake of novel-like entertainment or merely to provide an informative travelogue, we should note the variety of ways in which ch. 27 witnesses to the overall Lukan message of salvation. First, the terminology of salvation dots the seascape of this story. Verbs for salvation appear in 27:20, 31, 43, 44 (NRSV, "brought safely") and the noun appears in 27:34 (NRSV, "to survive"). In addition, retrospectively Luke writes, "After we were saved ..." (28:1; NRSV, "reached safety"], and one of the natives of Malta observes of Paul that he was "saved from the sea" (28:4; NRSV, "escaped"). Although in Greek the language of "salvation" extends to notions of "rescue from danger," against the backdrop of the narrator's pervasive interest in salvation it is difficult not to read this chapter as an extension of that interest. This helps to underscore Luke's central concern that the agenda being served here is God's—and so this story highlights the lengths to which God will go to ensure that God's purpose is brought to fulfillment even against hurricane-level forces.

Second, the drama of Luke's narrative moves from a heightened emphasis on the danger of the journey to the declaration of divine promise, and from divine promise to divine deliverance. Note, e.g., how 27:1–12 underscores the difficulty of the journey: the winds were against them, they moved ahead with difficulty, they lost time, they were threatened by disastrous loss, etc. Acts 27:13–26 juxtaposes the desperate situation with hope: the winds achieved hurricane force, the ship was driven away from land, they had to strap the ship together, the ship was battered, they tossed their gear and cargo overboard, they were fearful, and darkness settled over them, so that "all hope of our being saved was at last abandoned (27:20); versus words of hope from Paul and his declaration that their safe arrival was woven into the divine plan (27:23–24a). And, indeed, it happened just as Paul had been told: the ship ran aground and was lost, but every person arrived on land safely (27:25, 41, 44).

Third, recalling that, for Luke, salvation is plotted as reversal of status and circumstances, it is instructive to read Luke's story in this light—e.g., movement from destruction at sea to safety at land, from darkness to daylight, from starvation to well-fed, and from discouragement to good courage (compare 27:20–26, 36; 28:15). All of this bears witness to the emphasis in ch. 27 on divine protection and deliverance.

28:1–15. Hospitality in Malta and Italy. If Acts 27 provided at times extraordinary detail of the voyage and shipwreck, Luke's narration of the three months (28:11) subsequent to the rescue of Paul and his fellow voyagers is far more sketchy. Undoubtedly, this is due to our proximity to the end of Acts, with Paul's long-anticipated arrival in Rome. Marking this interim period are two primary motifs, the first of which is hospitality (28:2, 7, 10, 14). The second is the identification of Paul as one through whom the power to heal is available. The snake incident on Malta may recall Jesus' words in Luke 10:19, that he had given his disciples "authority to tread on snakes and scorpions, and over all the power of the enemy," and promised that "nothing will hurt you." This kind of commentary comports well with the evidence of the divine hand in rescuing Paul and his fellow travelers in Acts 27 as well. For their part, the natives of Malta see the snake bite as a sign of divine judgment, the hand of Lady Justice (28:4; NRSV, "justice") identifying and punishing him as a murder. The motifs of healing and hospitality intertwine in 28:8–10, as Paul and the islanders engage in reciprocal relations: Publius provides hospitality and Paul healed Publius' father; Paul's work of healing extends to the rest of the island and the islanders repay him with gestures of honor and supplies.

I. Paul on Remand in Rome (28:16–31)

Although Paul is greeted by followers of Jesus (28:15), they appear incidental to the story. Since the form of his imprisonment was a kind of house arrest, we might assume that Paul received support from these believers throughout his time in Rome. However, Luke bypasses any discussion of how there came to be a church in Rome prior to Paul's arrival (see, however, 2:10) and the final paragraphs of his narrative are taken up with Paul's interactions with Jews in Rome rather than with Christians. Throughout this final section of Acts, the focus is twofold: the gospel, which concerns the kingdom of God and the Lord Jesus Christ (28:23, 31), and how Paul's audience responds to the gospel (28:24–28).

28:16–22. Paul Sets the Hope of Israel Before the Jewish Leaders. Paul's summary of how he came to Rome emphasizes first his fidelity as a Jew and second the heart of his message, "the hope of Israel" (28:20). The content of this hope is not developed in this context, but we know from chs. 24–25 that this hope concerns the resurrection of the dead. This is a claim about Israel, of course, but also about Jesus, since it is through his being raised up that he has been declared both Lord and Christ (2:36) and that God's promise for the restoration of Israel, including Jew and Gentile, is being actualized.

28:23-31. The Jews in Rome Divided; Paul's Unhindered Proclamation. Only with the passing of time does the shorthand, "hope of Israel," get developed, and then in terms of the kingdom of God and Jesus. As we have come to expect in Acts, the response to Paul's proclamation is divided: "Some were convinced ... while others refused to believe" (28:24). Paul interprets Jewish resistance with reference to the words of Isa 6:9–10, a text that has a long history of interpretation within Israel's life as a means of explaining Israel's recalcitrance. The message Paul draws from Isaiah is clear: even though the Jews in Rome say they want to hear Paul (28:22), he understands that many will not listen. The conclusion he reaches, that he will take his message to the Gentiles, might appear as the final rejection of the Jewish people. Three considerations militate against this impression, however. First, twice before Paul has made pronouncements of this kind, with strong notes of finality, only then to be found again proclaiming the good news in synagogues (see 13:46–47; 18:6–7). Second, 28:24 shows that some Jews hear and really receive the message. Third, the closing of Acts has Paul living in Rome *welcoming all* to his place of lodging. Here at the end, then, Paul's continued proclamation demonstrates that this proclamation is not silenced by opposition from any quarter and bears witness to the universal reach of the message he proclaims.

BIBLIOGRAPHY

K. L. Anderson. *"But God Raised Him from the Dead": The Theology of Jesus' Resurrection in Luke–Acts.* Paternoster Biblical Monographs (Milton Keynes: Paternoster, 2006); W. S. Campbell. *The "We" Passages in the Acts of the Apostles: The Narrator as Narrative Character.* Studies in Biblical Literature 14 (Atlanta: Society of Biblical Literature, 2007); R. J. Cassidy. *Society and Politics in the Acts of the Apostles* (Maryknoll, N.Y.: Orbis, 1987); B. R. Gaventa. *Acts.* ANTC (Nashville: Abingdon, 2003); L. T. Johnson. *The Acts of the Apostles.* SP (Collegeville, Minn.: Glazier, 1992); I. H. Marshall and D. Peterson, eds. *Witness to the Gospel: The Theology of Acts* (Grand Rapids: Eerdmans, 1998); F. S. Spencer. *Journeying through Acts: A Literary-Cultural Reading* (Peabody, Mass.: Hendrickson, 2004); M. Turner. *Power from on High: The Spirit in Israel's Restoration and Witness in Luke–Acts.* JPTSup 9 (Sheffield: Sheffield Academic Press, 1996).

ROMANS

CHARLES COUSAR

OVERVIEW

Romans stands first in the canonical presentation of the letters because it is the longest of Paul's letters, but it might well be placed first because of its theological profundity and historical significance. However much the letter reflects a specific situation in Paul's ministry, it also addresses deep and perennial issues of Christian experience and faith. Whether the topic is God's own righteousness, justification by faith, the atonement, the sanctifying work of the Spirit, eschatological hope, God's dealings with Jews and Gentiles, or Christian ethics, Paul's letter to the Romans is a resource and reference point.

The importance of Romans for Christian tradition is simply incalculable. Augustine famously took up Romans when he heard a divine voice commanding him to "Take and read," and the theological controversies that marked his career sent him repeatedly back to Romans. Martin Luther identified Rom 1:17 as the occasion for his insight about the gift of God's righteousness, and Calvin identified Romans as nothing less than the entry point for understanding all of Scripture. John Wesley's Aldersgate experience, where his heart was "strangely warmed," happened as a minister was reading aloud from the preface to Luther's commentary on Romans. Arguably, Karl Barth's commentary on Romans was the most generative and controversial theological text of the twentieth century. From across the theological and ecclesiastical spectrum, readers of Paul throughout the centuries would agree with Barth's observation that Romans always has something new to teach its audiences.

This history of influence itself may have contributed to the sense that Romans offers a summary statement of Paul's theology, that Romans is less situational than Paul's other letters. Yet the letter is scarcely an abstract summary of Christian doctrine; it is silent about the Lord's supper and refers to baptism only once (6:3–4) and it uses the word "church" only in the closing lines (16:1, 4–5, 16, 23). In addition, the nature of Paul's work, characterized by his urgent need to proclaim the gospel in new places (1 Cor 9:19–23; Rom 15:20–21)

and his concern about the flourishing of individual congregations, also makes it unlikely that he composed this letter as a dispassionate systematic reflection on the gospel. For these reasons, over the last several decades scholars have largely agreed that this letter, like Paul's other letters, addresses some particular situation, and considerable scholarly energy has been expended toward identifying Paul's reasons for writing to Rome and his reasons for writing this particular letter.

If it is relatively easy to agree that Romans is, like Paul's other letters, addressed to some particular situation, it is difficult to identify the exact contours of the situation. The difficulty has much to do with the fact that Paul had not yet been to Rome (1:10–13; 15:22–24). Here he writes to a community where he has not preached the gospel, so there is no appeal to their shared history (as in 1 Thess 1:2–2:16), no reference to previous instruction (as in 1 Thess 4:1–2), no direct reference to Paul's knowledge of their situation (as in Phil 4:3). From the greetings in ch. 16, however, it is apparent that Paul does know some people at Rome, and he greets them in quite affectionate terms: three are called "beloved," one couple is referred to as "kin" (or perhaps "compatriots"), one woman is described as "a mother to me," several are addressed as "brothers and sisters." Presumably, these are people he had met elsewhere, as is the case with Prisca and Aquila (see 1 Cor:16:19; Acts 18:1–3, 18, 26).

Some details about Paul's own situation are clear. First, Paul felt that his work in the Aegean region of Greece was completed (15:23). He then wanted to go to Rome and on from there to Spain, where he planned to carry out a new mission. Paul felt it critical to solicit support from the Roman church, perhaps even financial support (1:8–15; 15:22–32). Furthermore, Phoebe, who was about to leave from Cenchreae for Rome, and who was a good friend of Paul's, could be a trusted bearer of the letter, perhaps filling in gaps and responding to questions raised by the Roman church. She may have been a woman of means since she had served as "a benefactor of many and of myself as well" (16:2).

Before traveling to Rome or Spain, however, Paul faced an important and worrisome journey to Jerusalem. The predominantly Gentile churches Paul had founded throughout Macedonia and Achaia had collected an offering for the famine-stricken churches at Jerusalem (15:25–26), and it was Paul's job to deliver this gift to Jerusalem. But as he freely acknowledges (Rom 15:22–32), he was fearful of doing so for two reasons. First, given the tense political situation (the decade preceding the first revolt against Rome), he was perhaps afraid for his life. He admits to considerable anxiety (15:30–32). Many Jews would understandably be suspicious of Paul, a Jew who once persecuted the church and who now is known as the "apostle to the Gentiles."

Complicating matters further, Paul was uncertain whether the Jerusalem church would in fact accept the offering collected from the Gentiles. Some Jewish Christians may have encountered pressure from their kinfolk to avoid association with Gentile Christians. If they rejected the offering from the Gentile Christians, then Paul would have been devastated. To have the church splintered into Jewish and non-Jewish groups would have been crushing to Paul, who had fought so valiantly for a church where there was "neither Jew nor Greek." The gospel of which Paul is not ashamed and which he is eager to proclaim to those in Rome depends on a single message; the Lordship of Jesus Christ, in whom the righteousness of God is made known to all people, to the Jew first and also to the Greek.

Locating the situation in Paul's own ministry is far easier than learning anything about the situation of the Christians at Rome. Although the origins of Christianity at Rome are unknown, it seems likely that believers arriving in Rome would naturally have sought out the Jewish communities in the synagogues, where they would have encountered not only Jews but a number of Gentiles who were attracted to Jewish life and teaching. Writing in the second century, Suetonius reports in his *Life of Claudius* that in what would have been 49 CE the emperor Claudius expelled Jews from Rome due to the disturbances over Chrestus (probably a mistaken form of the Latin term for "Christ"). Given the size of the Jewish population, it seems likely that this reference has to do, not with the whole Jewish population, but with Jewish Chris-

tians whose preaching caused resistance and perhaps conflict in Jewish communities in the city. The same Jewish believers would have been allowed to return to Rome when Nero succeeded Claudius (in 53 BCE). If that is the case, then Christianity at Rome for several years may have been largely a Gentile phenomenon, and the return of Jewish Christians could have precipitated conflict between Jews who understood themselves as the rightful leaders of the communities and Gentile believers who had exercised leadership in the interval. This scenario helps to account for Paul's insistence on the priority of Jews (1:16; 2:9–10) and his fear of Gentile condescension (11:11–24), but it remains speculative and should be used with care.

OUTLINE

Most interpreters of Romans divide the letter into six major parts: 1:1–17; 1:18–4:25; 5–8, 9–11, 12:1–15:13, and 15:14–16:27. Though some have sought to place a major break between chs. 5 and 6, it is clear that the opening of ch. 5 contains themes that are developed throughout ch. 8. (In Romans, Paul has the habit of mentioning a problem, but then returning to deal with the problem in more detail at a later place in the letter.) Chapters 9–11 constitute a distinct unit dealing with the election by God of the Jews and of non-Jews. Chapters 12 and 13 then take up instructions for the lives of believers. These instructions are continued in 14:1–15:13, where Paul deals with conflicts having to do with diet and other religious observances and concludes with a plea for unity. The remainder of the letter (15:13–16:27) provides the conclusion, which includes comments about Paul's own plans and his greetings to people in Rome.

I. Introduction (1:1–17)

II. God's Righteousness Expounded (1:18–4:25)

    A. The Revelation of God's Wrath (1:18–3:20)

    B. The Revelation of God's Righteousness in Jesus Christ (3:21–31)

    C. God's Dealings with Abraham (4:1–25)

DETAILED ANALYSIS

I. Introduction (1:1–17)

The opening of Romans formally resembles Paul's other letters, beginning as it does with a salutation (1:1–7), followed by a prayer of thanksgiving (1:8–15), and a section commonly referred to as the theme of the letter (1:16–17, although the theme is only fully explained in 1:18–3:20 and then expanded upon throughout the letter).

Several features stand out in these opening lines. First is the length of the salutation. Presumably because this letter is Paul's first occasion for addressing the Romans, he offers a more extended identification of himself. He is a "servant" (literally, a "slave") of Jesus Christ, he is "an apostle," he is "set apart for the gospel of God" (v. 1). This reference to the gospel is unpacked in vv. 2–4, as Paul sets forth clearly the content of the gospel he preaches. Verse 2 connects the gospel with God's promises in Scripture, a comment that seems to anticipate the body of the letter, with its extensive engagement with Scripture. Several features of vv. 3–4 prompt scholars to conjecture that Paul is employing an early confession of some sort, possibly one already known to his Roman readers. Two parallel statements specify what is to be said about "his Son":

> "who was descended from David according to the flesh." (1:3)

> "who was declared Son of God with power according to the Spirit of holiness by resurrection from the dead." (1:4)

The first statement firmly connects Jesus to Israel by Davidic descent (cf. 9:5), and the second asserts that this particular son of David was established into the office of the Son of God on the basis of his being raised from the dead (see Acts 13:26–40).

With v. 5 Paul moves from a summary of the gospel's content to the mission generated by the gospel. It is from Jesus that "we" received "grace and apostleship" to bring about "obedience of faith among all the Gentiles" (1:5, NRSV). The REB unfortunately separates the phrase into two distinct results: "obedience and faith," whereas the NIV more correctly reads "the obedience that comes from faith," or "the obedience that consists in faith."

Verses 6–7 at last identify the recipients of the letter as those "called to belong to Jesus," "God's beloved in Rome," and "called to be saints." As elsewhere in Paul's letters (e.g., 1 Cor 1:2), it is not only the apostles who are called into service. Paul understands all believers to be such by virtue of God's calling to them.

The thanksgiving (vv. 8–15) acknowledges that the existence of the Roman churches is known throughout the world, and includes a typical statement about his constant prayers for them (v. 9; cf. e.g., 1 Thess 1:2–3). Also here Paul announces his long-standing desire to be in Rome and his hope that he is soon to be able to do so. Few details help readers to understand either why Paul wishes to be in Rome in particular or what circumstances have prevented his journey. He announces that he wants to "reap some harvest" there, which could mean either his hope for extending the gospel's message further into the populace of Rome, or it could refer to the support of Roman Christians for his planned mission to Spain (see 15:24, 28–29).

What is clear is Paul's sense of obligation to preach the gospel to all people. "To Greek and to barbarians" seems peculiar, given that he is writing to Rome rather than to a Greek city, but this phrase reflects the dominance of Greek culture. One way of dividing the human world was between those who would speak Greek and the "barbarians" who could not. All people, whether Greek-speaking or not, whether "wise" or "foolish" are intended to hear the gospel.

Verses 16–17, surely among the best known of all Paul's statements, constitute an announcement of the thesis of the letter. It begins with the claim that "I am not ashamed of the gospel" which is probably an example of litotes, a rhetorical use of understatement intended to affirm the positive side of a statement (as in Acts 20:12; 26:26). It could be rendered "I have complete confidence in the gospel." The gospel is "the power of God for salvation" (1:16). The gospel is not simply verbal, it actually consists of God's own power (cf. 1 Thess 1:4–5). Here Paul's apocalyptic perspective comes to the fore in that he writes about the gospel using the language of power (see below). Paul understands the tyranny under which human beings live and from which they needed to be freed (as he will make clear in chs. 5–7).

Having said in vv. 14–15 that his own preaching is for all people (Greeks and barbarian, wise and foolish), Paul reiterates that point here in a slightly different way. This saving power of God is available to "everyone who has faith," but it is to "the Jew first and also to the Greek." While Paul argues for the inclusion of the Gentiles among the people of God, he does not want the Gentiles to forget that there is a certain divine precedence in the order of things. Later in the letter, he speaks of the advantages of being a Jew (3:2), the promises to Abraham (4:13), and the gifts of God to Israel (9:4–5). He also reminds the Gentile readers,

who might be tempted to gloat over their status, that they are to "remember that it is not you that support the root, but the root that supports you" (Rom 11:18).

Verse 17 continues the announcement about the gospel with the claim that it reveals "the righteousness of God." This phrase appears often in Romans (1:17; 3:5, 21, 22, 25, 26; 10:3) and has been interpreted in at least three distinct ways. First, it has been thought of as denoting a moral attribute, a characteristic of God (as in the declaration that "Mother Teresa was a person of righteousness"), so that the gospel's role is to reveal knowledge about God's inherent goodness. A second interpretation imagines that the "righteousness of God" is language that finds its proper home in the courtroom, that the phrase denotes the favorable decision a defendant receives from a judge. Thus when Paul speaks of the "revelation of righteousness," he refers to the favorable verdict pronounced over the individual, declaring that the defendant's sins are forgiven. A third interpretation locates the "righteousness of God" in apocalyptic thinking and understands it as God's salvation-creating power that is at work in the world in the death and resurrection of Jesus Christ. This third interpretation involves both the subjective righteousness that belongs to God and its objective action in saving humankind, and it best accounts for the argument that unfolds in the chapters that follow. It is God's own righteousness, not in and of itself (as in moral righteousness) but in its action for human beings, indeed for the whole of the cosmos. The revelation of this righteousness is a cosmic event that stands at the beginning of a new era.

Paul concludes the introduction with the affirmation that God rectifies "through faith for faith; as it is written, 'The one who is righteous will live by faith'" (quoting Hab. 2:4; cf. Gal 3:11). But of whose faith does Paul speak here? Is this human faith that somehow of its own reveals God's righteousness? Or is it the faithfulness of God or of Jesus Christ? The Greek word *pistis* can bear either interpretation, either as human faith (in the sense of humanity's belief or trust in God) or as faithfulness (in the sense of God's own trustworthiness, God's reliability). The context emphasizes God's own action, and the chapters that follow underscore this point, making it likely that the revelation of God's righteousness "from faith to faith" means that "the saving promises of God are declared from the faithfulness of God in Christ to the responding faith of believers." God's revelation of righteousness comes through the divine faithfulness and not through human achievement.

II. God's Righteousness Expounded (1:18–4:25)

A. The Revelation of God's Wrath (1:18–3:20)

This first major section of the letter unpacks what Paul understands by the saving power of the gospel. He initially takes up the negative side of the argument by considering in stark and bold tones his diagnosis of the human situation (1:18–3:20). Having begun with a clear affirmation of the revealing of God's righteousness, Paul turns in 1:18 to the revealing of God's wrath. Because the notion of God's "wrath" conjures up images of an irrational and angry deity, some readers of Paul identify this divine wrath as impersonal, the natural consequences of human evil. But it is important to understand that God's "wrath" is indeed personal in the sense that it reflects God's refusal to accept humanity's distortion of the relationship between humanity and God, humanity's defiance of God.

Following the initial announcement about the revelation of God's wrath, Paul takes up "ungodliness and wickedness" in 1:18–32. Here he makes use of conventional Jewish stereotypes about Gentiles, who are regarded as ungodly because their religious practices involve many gods and who are sexually promiscuous (see, e.g., Wisdom of Solomon 13–14). Even if Gentiles have not received the same revelation of God as have Jews, Paul contends that God has nevertheless been made known to them so that their behavior is inexcusable. Importantly, the behavior Paul focuses on here is their refusal to honor God rightly and their distorted practices of crafting images of God (vv. 19–23). It is because of this initial rebellion against God that God "hands them over" (vv. 24, 26, 28) to their own desires. The description of same sex relations in vv. 26–28, along with the list of vices in vv. 29–31, is the result of the primal human sin of rejecting God.

Much controversy has focused on Paul's brief comments here about same sex relations. It is unlikely that Paul thought of homosexuality as a sexual orientation in the modern sense of an identity or a disposition; instead, he may well have in mind the sexual abuse of younger men by older ones (see 1 Cor 6:9) and the widespread conviction that relations between people of the same sex represented lust that was out of control (as in Dio Chrysostom, *Discourse* 7.151–52; Philo, *On Abraham* 133–36). Given the Old Testament's frequent association of idolatry and sexual immorality (e.g., Hos 1–4; Ezek 16; 23; Wis 14:12–31), it is not at all surprising that Paul places the two together here. Whatever readers conclude about these comments, it is important to study with equal seriousness the list included in vv. 29–31.

This indictment comes to a dramatic turning point at 2:1, where Paul shifts from the third person plural to the second person singular, now directly addressing his audience with "you." It is often claimed that Paul here is thinking of those Jews who condemn Gentile immorality without acknowledging their own, but it is not clear that the "you" addressed here is Jewish. What is clear is that the move from 1:32 to 2:1 is a rhetorical tool, by which those readers who imagine themselves exempt from the indictment (whether Jews or Gentiles) are caught in a trap. With this use of direct address, as often in Romans, Paul makes use of elements of the diatribe, a teaching strategy common among philosophical teachers.

On most any interpretation of the letter, Rom 2 is challenging. Here Paul speaks of God's kindness leading people to "repentance" (v. 4), a concept that is virtually absent from his other letters (see 2 Cor 7:9–10; 12:21). He also speaks of Gentiles who do "instinctively what the law requires" (2:14) although he will later say that the law's function is to reveal sin (3:20; 7:7). And he places stress on a final judgment of human beings based on their actions (2:6), although later he will contend that it is God's grace that saves (3:24; 5:21). There is no consensus about how this discussion functions in the larger argument, and some scholars conclude that Paul is simply inconsistent. Several things do emerge clearly: God's dealings with Jew and Gentile are impartial (v. 11); contrary to expectations, some Gentiles do what is good and some Jews do not.

Toward the end of ch. 2 Paul comes perilously close to denying any special status to Jews. A

Jew is not a person characterized by any external trait, such as circumcision; rather circumcision is something spiritual and not literal. One can speak only of an inward circumcision, a circumcision of the heart (see Deut 10:16). Given God's long and historic relationship with the Jews, Paul then has to face the question of whether the Jews have any advantage at all (3:1–5). Have their failures caused God to turn away from the Jews? Can God's promises to the Jews be trusted? And if God is so gracious as to overlook the sins of the Jews, then how can God judge the world? What about God's faithfulness (3:3), and God's righteousness or justice (3:5) and God's truthfulness (3:7)? Are these convictions about God called into question by God's failure to condemn the Jews? Paul's vehement response to these potential responses ("By no means!" vv. 4, 6) hints at his own convictions about God's faithfulness to Israel, convictions that will be articulated more fully in Rom 9–11. The problem is not that God is faithless but that human beings are.

With 3:9, Paul arrives at a pithy summary of his argument to this point: "all, both Jews and Greeks, are under the power of sin." Gentile sinfulness he takes as virtually self-evident, Jewish sinfulness he argues more cautiously, but the result is the same. Numerous attempts have been made to soften Paul's rhetoric, such as suggestions that he means that all people are prone to do what is wrong, or that Jews and Gentiles are equally capable of wrong-doing. But the compound citation of Scripture that follows, together with the argument offered in 5:12–19, suggests that Paul means what he says: all are under sin's power (cf. 11:32).

Paul reinforces 3:9 with an extended collection of quotations from Scripture in 3:10–18. It has been argued that Paul is drawing here on a preexisting text, but the collection seems to serve his argument well. Especially notable is the repetition of the phrase, "there is not (or 'no') one." No one is righteous (v. 10), no one seeks God (v. 11), no one shows kindness (v. 12), no one fears God (v. 18). The collection culminates with the solemn declaration of vv. 19–20, which reintroduces the role of the law (see earlier in 2:12–29): the law shows that all are silent before God.

B. The Revelation of God's Righteousness in Jesus Christ (3:21–31)

In 3:21–31, Paul turns away from his complex argument about the revelation of God's wrath (1:18) and returns to his initial statement about the revelation of God's righteousness (1:16–17). While repeating his conclusion that God's righteousness does not come through the law (that is, the law does not itself rectify people), Paul carefully reiterates the role of Scripture ("the law and the prophets") in witnessing to God's righteousness (3:21, and see 1:2). Both Jews and Gentiles have fallen short of the divine glory, but God has taken the initiative in the death of Jesus to remedy the human plight and to declare divine righteousness for all people.

God's initiative is repeatedly declared in these verses. It is God's grace that justifies (v. 24), God who puts forward Christ Jesus in the cross (v. 25), God who acts to make clear his own righteousness (vv. 25–26), and God who justifies humanity (v. 26). The reader who pays careful attention to Paul's emphasis on God's role will find this complex and important passage somewhat easier to grasp.

God's righteousness is "through faith in Jesus Christ," as the NRSV puts it, but a footnote indicates that the Greek can also be rendered as "through the faith of Jesus Christ." Literally, the phrase is *pistis Iēsou Christou*, "faith of Jesus Christ," and the Greek *pistis* can mean both "faith" in the sense of belief and "faithfulness" in the sense of reliability or trustworthiness. Generations of English translations reflect the presumption that what Paul means here and elsewhere is faith "in" Jesus Christ (Rom 3:22, 26; Gal 2:16 [twice], 20; 3:22; Phil 3:9), but in recent decades scholars have intensely debated whether Paul means that God's righteousness comes about through faith in Jesus Christ or whether it means that Jesus' own faithfulness brings about God's righteousness. Although some arguments from Greek grammar and usage are introduced, the question finally focuses on context, especially whether Paul seems to be pitting a human activity (fulfilling stipulations of the law) over against a divine activity (Christ's faithful obedience), or whether he is pitting one human activity (fulfilling the stipulations of the law) over against another human activity (believing). Particularly in 3:21–26 the phrase carries a "subjective" sense, designating the faithfulness of Christ to God, not a human's faith in God.

Paul further describes the righteousness of God in vv. 24–25, where he writes that God put Christ Jesus forward as a *hilastērion*. Discussions of this term often revolve around whether Paul refers to "propitiation," a means of warding off God's wrath, or to "expiation," a means of ridding the human being of guilt. Those two connotations, however, cannot be disentangled from one another. What is clear is that in the LXX the word *hilastērion* designates the cover over the top of the mercy-seat, where the high priest on the Day of Atonement sprinkled the blood of the bull, making intercession for his own sins and the sins of the people as a whole (e.g., Lev. 16:13–15). It is used similarly in Heb 9:5, the only other time the word appears in the NT. Following this usage, Jesus becomes the "mercy-seat," or, figuratively, he is the sacrifice that takes place there. This figurative usage of the term is found in 4 Maccabees, where *hilastērion* refers to the loyal Jewish mother and her seven sons who became martyrs at the time of the Hasmonean revolt (4 Macc 17:22; cf. 4 Macc 6:28–29).

It is tempting to make the exact connotations of this word pivotal to understanding the passage, but the difficulty with that strategy is that Paul nowhere else uses the word. In addition, while these verses are important for understanding Paul's interpretation of the death of Jesus, they are not his only statements on that subject. In 5:12–21, Paul will interpret the death of Jesus as the occasion in which human beings are incorporated in Jesus, as earlier they were incorporated in Adam. In 1 Cor 1:18 and 2 Cor 5:15–16, the death of Jesus becomes the point at which the corruption of human values and virtues is revealed.

The transition at v. 27 may seem abrupt, but it will be less so if readers have observed how emphatic in vv. 21–31 is Paul's insistence on God as the agent of righteousness. The question about boasting, then, is a question about whether it is God who justifies or whether human beings do so based on their keeping of the law. Paul's reintroduction of the law in vv. 27–28 prompts him in vv. 29–30 to return to his earlier discussion of Jews and Gentiles (see 2:9–16; 3:9), which then leads him to introduce Abraham.

C. God's Dealings with Abraham (4:1–25)

Since Abraham is the progenitor of the people and is the recipient of the sign of circumcision, Paul must deal with the figure of Abraham. This discussion, then, extends the comments made in 3:1–2 about the benefits that belong to Jews, and it also anticipates the longer discussion in Rom 9–11. Crucial to this discussion is Paul's interpretation of Gen 15:6, which he draws on in three slightly different ways (vv. 3, 9, 22) to underscore the fact that Abraham did not earn God's favor, but rather trusted in God. First, in vv. 3–5, he quotes Gen 15:6 as evidence that it was by faith that God puts the ungodly in a right relationship to himself and not by works. Here he elaborates with the analogy of work; workers are paid a wage that is due them for their labor. And in vv. 6–8, he introduces Ps 32:1–2 as evidence of God's gracious forgiveness. Second, in vv. 9–15 he takes note of the fact that Gen 15:6 mentions Abraham's faith prior to the time when, in Gen 17:9–14, circumcision is made essential for inclusion into the covenant people of God. Paul draws a conclusion from the order of the two stories: Abraham's experience of faith occurred before he was circumcised, and this makes Abraham the ancestor and model for non-Jews as well as for Jews (4:11*b*–12). And third, Gen 15:6 enters the discussion again as Paul emphasizes that Abraham grew strong in faith with regard to having a son, despite the barrenness of his aged wife Sarah and his own body that was "already as good as dead" (v. 19). He remained strong in faith, fully convinced that God was able to do what God had promised.

That this bit of exegetical interpretation is not simply of antiquarian interest becomes clear in v. 24, when Paul writes that the "reckoning" of righteousness was not just for the sake of Abraham but is "for ours also." Abraham is father of both the uncircumcised and the circumcised (vv. 11–12), those who believe in "Jesus our Lord" (v. 24).

III. "Boasting in our hope of sharing the glory of God" (5:1–8:39)

A. God's Justification of the Unrighteous in the Death of Jesus (5:1–21)

Romans 5:1–11 serves as a transitional unit into the second major section of the letter. "Therefore, since we are justified by faith" (5:1*a*) recapitulates the language of righteousness and justification in the previous section. Similarly, Paul also reiterates the language of boasting in vv. 2, 3, 11 (see 2:17, 23; 3:27; 4:2) and the nature of God's actions for the ungodly in v. 6 (see 4:5). But 5:1–11 also paves the way for movement into a new direction. After the beginning of ch. 5, there is no longer such emphasis on the language of "faith" or "believing" (see 1:12, 17; 3:3, 22, 25–31; 4:5, 9–16, 19–20), "the righteousness of God" (1:17; 3:5, 21, 22, 25, 26; 10:3), and "Jew" and "Greek" (see 1:16; 2:9–10; 3:9, 29) as the primary topics for consideration in chs. 5–8. Instead, these chapters emphasize the language of "hope" (5:2, 4–5; 8:20, 24; see 4:18), "life" (5:10, 17, 18, 21; 6:4, 22, 23; 7:10; 8:2, 6, 10, 38), "death" (5:10, 12, 14, 17, 21; 6:3–5, 9, 16, 21, 23; 7:5, 10, 13, 24; 8:2, 6, 38), the work of Adam and Christ (5:12–21), and attention to the role of the Spirit (see 5:5; 7:6; 8:1–17, 23, 26–27). Whereas OT texts were prominent in the first four chapters, only two citations (at 7:7 and 8:36) occur between 5:1 and 8:39. Furthermore, unlike the boasting referred to earlier (2:17, 23; 3:27; 4:2), here boasting is in God, which gives the section a doxological flavor (5:2, 11).

Two dimensions of 5:1–11 warrant special attention. First, at the beginning of the section, attention is directed to the future, as Paul writes that boasting is "in our hope of sharing the glory of God" (5:2b). "The glory of God," the very reality that humanity has lacked because of sin (3:23), becomes the object of hope, which for Paul is not mere wish but confident expectation (and see 8:18). This hope makes possible a positive attitude toward the sufferings of the present time. Rather than being the occasion for puzzlement or lament, afflictions are understood as the necessary part of the experience of grace. Then at the end of the section, in vv. 9–11, Paul returns to the theme of the future. In parallel rhetorical expressions ("much more surely") in vv. 9 and 10, readers are provided with a warrant not to fear the eschatological judgment but to "receive the abundance of grace and the free gift of righteousness" (5:17).

Second, Paul takes up again here the death of Jesus (as in 3:21–26), but he does so in a way that is striking. Jesus' death for the ungodly is an unparalleled event that occurs as a surprise (v. 6–8). There is no preparation for it, no contingency that makes it provisional, no call to repen-

tance to activate its results. It is a happening of unilateral and unconditional grace. The death of Christ for weak, ungodly sinners is both unanticipated and incomparable.

The "therefore" that introduces 5:12 connects the second half of the chapter closely to 5:1–11, as here Paul addresses the question as to how weak, ungodly sinners can have such confidence in their standing on the day of judgment. As Paul begins that explanation, however, he returns to the question of sin, this time introducing Adam with no reference at all to the involvement of Eve (cf. 2 Cor 11:3). The statement in 5:12 plays a significant role in the understanding of original sin that developed in Western Christianity, where the Vulgate's translation (the English equivalent of "in whom all sinned" instead of "because all sinned") suggested the possibility that sin is biologically transmitted. What Paul argues, based on Gen 3:3, 19, is that Adam's sin brought death into the world, and together they established controlling power over all humanity, power that is broken only in Jesus Christ.

In 5:15–21, Paul treats Adam and Christ less as individuals than as corporate figures; each of them includes in himself all of humanity. Each is the progenitor and prototype of all human beings. What distinguishes them is the result of their action; through the one person death spreads to all people; through the other person life comes to all (v. 18). But the one figure dominates the other. Obedience triumphs over disobedience; grace triumphs over sin; life triumphs over death.

The two-age scheme that has already been introduced in 5:1–11 is even more evident here. Adam and Christ personify the old and the new in strikingly antithetical ways. The act that each performs (disobedience and obedience) determines the destiny, not of a few, but of all people. Nothing is said to suggest that Christ's death made life potentially available to all people; nothing suggests that faith transforms the potentiality into reality. The language is quite comprehensive. In chapter six, Paul turns to the obligations that grasp those who do believe.

B. Death and Resurrection with Christ (6:1–7:6)

Paul's sweeping claims about how the obedient act of Jesus Christ brought about "justification and life for all" naturally prompts the accusation that he is advocating antinomianism. Already in 3:8 he has indicated that he is familiar with the accusation, and so he introduces it here directly: "Should we continue in sin in order that grace may abound?"(6:1).

Paul offers two responses to this fear that his understanding of the gospel is actually a provocation to moral chaos. First, he reminds his readers that they have been baptized into Christ's death. He makes similar statements about baptism in 1 Cor 12:13 and in Gal 3:27, although in both those cases the union with Christ is interpreted in the direction of unity of believers with one another. Here union with Christ in baptism marks, even more sharply than in those passages, union with Christ's own death. For Paul, baptism is no mere symbol or act of initiation; it is instead a realistic association between the human being and Jesus Christ in his death and burial. In addition, Christ's own resurrection is more than simply a resuscitation of life. "We know that Christ, being raised from the dead, will never die again; death no longer has dominion over him" (6:9). He leaves in his wake the broken power of death, the ultimate enemy, whose defeat signals the final triumph of God (see 1 Cor 15:24–28).

When Paul expounds on the association of believers with Christ in his baptism, he allows for what has come to be called an "eschatological reservation." Believers are united with Christ in his death and burial in the sacrament, but Paul carefully does not say that they have already been united with Christ's own resurrection; instead, they have "newness of life" as they await their resurrection with him (6:5, 8). For the present the newness of life to which believers are called is a cruciform life. In Christ the new age has come, but this old age has not yet gone, with the result that the age of sin continues to exist alongside the age of righteousness and life. While the ultimacy of sin's threat is removed, the struggle precipitated by the co-existence of the two ages remains. Thus readers are encouraged to live out of the new age and not out of the old, to present themselves as instruments of righteousness and not to let sin have dominion over their mortal bodies (6:12–13).

Using the images of slavery and freedom, the remainder of chapter six employs indicative verbs alongside imperative ones to declare lib-

eration from sin's clutches and at the same time to announce believers' accountability to God. Freedom from sin does not mean that human beings are free to do as they please. They are always slaves in one sense and free in another; the only question is whether the slavery is to God or to unrighteousness, whether the freedom is from righteousness or from sin. These two forms of freedom and enslavement are not equally balanced, of course, as vv. 21–23 make clear; slavery to sin brings death, and slavery to righteousness brings "sanctification," which in turn is God's gift of holiness to believers.

The brief section of Rom 7:1–6 provides Paul's second response to the charge that his understanding of the gospel results in libertinism. Here he uses an analogy that would be understandable to those familiar with Jewish law. A woman is bound by law to her husband and cannot simply take up an intimate relationship with another man while her husband is alive. The death of the husband creates a new situation for the widow. She is released from the binding marital code and is free to marry another husband. Likewise, the death of Christ brings freedom from the law and enables union with another—in this case with the risen Christ. The key is found in 7:6, where believers are declared to be "slaves not under the old written code, but in the new life of the Spirit." With these last words, Paul recalls 6:4 and also anticipates his important discussion of the Spirit in ch. 8.

C. The Law and Sin (7:7–25)

With the claim in 7:5 that the law itself arouses the sinful passions, Paul comes terribly close to saying that the law is sin. He has made other provocative remarks along the way that move in the same direction. The law brings "knowledge of sin" (3:20), "the law brings wrath," there is no "violation" without the law (4:15), the arrival of the law meant that "the trespass multiplied" (5:20). In 6:14 he came very close to equating law and sin with the statement that "sin will not have dominion over you since you are not under law but under grace."

At 7:7 Paul articulates the question of an imaginary interlocutor, "What then should we say? That the law is sin?" He replies to the question in 7:7 with his usual vehement response, "By no means!" But then Paul goes on in the remainder of the chapter to explain how it is that the law is "holy and just and good" (v. 12); but nevertheless, the law has become the tool of sin. In vv. 7–13, Paul draws on the specific prohibition of covetousness from the Decalogue (Exod 20:17; Deut 5:21) as he attempts to disentangle the role of the law from that of sin. The prohibition (i.e., the law) introduces knowledge of sin (v. 7), but then sin itself becomes active and multiplies covetousness. The arrival of the law provides the opportunity for sin, and sin itself is the agent producing death. Paul does not specify when it is that there was life without knowledge of the law. It may be that he has Adam in mind once again (as in 5:12–21), but the precise timing of this "event" is less important than the attempt Paul is making to arrive at his conclusion, "the law is holy." Verse 13 unpacks this conclusion: it is not the law in and of itself that bring death but sin's use of the law to increase its own power over human beings.

With vv. 14–25, Paul shifts from past to present tense and introduces the conflict between what one desires to do and what one actually does. Read in the wake of contemporary psychology, it is difficult to focus on anything except the tortured "I" who speaks here, but Paul's emphasis lies elsewhere. Verse 14 returns to the powerful assertion that "I" am "sold into slavery under sin" (cf. 6:16–23). In v. 17 and again in v. 20, Paul concludes from his analysis that "sin dwells within me." The situation is so dire that there are actually two "laws," God's own law which is a source of delight (v. 22), and "another law," the law controlled by sin itself (v. 23). Deliverance can come only though God's victory in Jesus Christ over the hideous power of sin, and it is the vision of this victory to which Paul will turn in ch. 8.

Paul's use of the first-person singular pronoun in this chapter has provoked controversy throughout the history of interpretation, with some readers convinced that Paul here refers to his pre-Christian experience and others equally convinced that he has in view his on-going Christian struggle. The difficulty with both of these views is that there is little evidence that Paul, either before or after his conversion, was afflicted by a guilty conscience (see esp. Phil 3:4b–16). In addition, 1 Cor 13 offers strong evidence that he can write in the first person without writing simply about

himself. (For these reasons, most scholars agree that the "I" in Rom 7 is a stylistic device rather than a reflection of Paul's own experience.)

D. The Spirit of Life in Christ Jesus (8:1–17)

With 8:1, Paul moves to take up the positive character of living in the Spirit, returning to elucidate the work of the Spirit he only touched on in 5:5 and 7:6. He opens with the declaration that there is "no condemnation for those who are in Christ Jesus," and then restates God's role in delivering humanity from sin. In this instance, however, Paul introduces the language of spirit and flesh with a series of contrasts between the mind as "set on things of the flesh" and life lived "according to the Spirit." This contrast between flesh and spirit (or Spirit; ancient manuscripts would not have distinguished between the two) has prompted many people to conclude that Paul has a negative attitude to the human body. Texts such as 1 Cor 6:15 ("Your bodies are members of Christ") and Rom 12:1 ("Present your bodies as a living sacrifice") strongly suggest otherwise. And Paul sometimes uses the term *sarx* ("flesh") in an entirely neutral way to refer to biological descent (as in Rom 1:3; 9:5). In Rom 8 (as in, e.g., 2 Cor 1:17; 5:16; 10:2–4; 11:18; Gal 5:17; 6:8), "flesh" has little to do with the human body in itself; it stands instead as a shorthand reference for a way of thinking, even a realm of existence. To think "the things of the flesh" is to be governed by a set of values that is no larger than oneself, while the "things of the Spirit" is a mindset that comes from the Spirit's own gift (vv. 9–11).

The contrast between the two groups, those who are "in the flesh" and those in whom the Spirit dwells, becomes especially stark in vv. 9–13. Nothing less than life and death are at stake here. Yet Paul does not linger over warnings but moves to the reassuring identification of "you" as God's children. God's children have been adopted, they cry out to God as their own father (v. 15), and they are even heirs with Christ himself (v. 17).

E. The Assurance of God's Love (8:18–39)

Being heirs along with Christ does not exempt believers from suffering, and in the second half of Rom 8 Paul returns to this point, already introduced in 5:3. Apparently the sufferings to which Paul alludes are the eschatological woes, which turn out to be the birthpangs of the new age. Here the dualism of the previous section of the argument yields to a concern for the whole of creation, since creation itself has been "subjected to futility" and longs for its own liberation and the future glory of God's children (vv. 19–21). Believers, because they have the "first fruits," join in this groaning, led by the Spirit to take their place in this earthly choir that gives forth unintelligible sounds of anguish. Even prayer is redefined in terms of "inarticulate groans " (8:26, NEB). Nevertheless, the Spirit works in the weaknesses of the believers and intercedes for them.

This leads Paul to claim that "all things work together for good for those who love God, who are called according to his purpose" (8:28). This tremendous affirmation includes God's intention to conform those who have been called "to the image of his Son" (v. 29). Again here Paul draws on familial language, identifying the Son of God as the "firstborn" of many brothers and sisters (v. 29). It is God who has predestined, called, justified and glorified. This powerful series of assertions returns Paul to the earlier topic of the "sufferings of the present time," and to his soaring insistence that no one and no thing can intercede between God and those whom God has chosen.

Paul's logic is clear: Recalling 4:25 and perhaps also the obedience of Abraham in Genesis 22, he asserts in 8:32 that the God who gave over his own Son will defend all children against any condemnation. In 8:36, Paul cites Ps 44:22, originally a cry of lament to God in the face of the assaults of Israel's enemies. In this context, the citation acknowledges the reality that God's faithful are always exposed to violent death, that tribulation is a mark of belonging to God. And yet none of these powers can separate believers from the love of God made known in Jesus Christ.

Finally Paul returns to the love of God, which he has already identified in 5:5–8 as the ultimate basis for hope. The gift of the Spirit stands in the gap between the present and the future and yet provides the ultimate basis for a confident hope. In 8:35 Paul asks whether anything can "separate us from the love of Christ," and decisively answers his own question in 8:38–39, "For I am convinced that neither death, nor life, nor angels, nor rulers, nor things present, nor things to come, nor powers, nor height, nor depth, nor anything else in all creation, will be able to separate us from the love of God in Christ Jesus our Lord."

IV. God's Election of Israel (9:1–11:36)

A. God's Word Has Not Failed (9:1–29)

The tone of the letter shifts dramatically at the beginning of ch. 9, as the triumphant rejoicing that nothing in all creation "will be able to separate us from the love of God in Christ Jesus our Lord" (8:39) gives way to lament and sorrow. What do those words of assurance mean for Jews who do not recognize Jesus as the Messiah of God? Put another way, who is included among the "us" who cannot be split off from God's love in Christ? Reminiscent of Moses' willingness to be cut off for the sake of worshipers of the golden calf (Exod 32:31–32), Paul offers himself in behalf of God's people.

Despite the shift in tone, Rom 9–11 does not introduce a new topic into the letter. From the very beginning, Paul has expounded his understanding of the gospel for the "Jew first and also the Greek" (1:16). Already in 3:1, he asks the pointed question whether there is any advantage to being a Jew. Does the Jew have any privilege that others do not also have? In answering in the affirmative, he declares that the Jew has the "oracles of God" (3:2). Returning to the question here at the beginning of chapter 9, he offers a longer list: they are recipients of God's adoption (cf. 8:15, 23), glory, covenants, the law, worship, the promises, and the patriarchs (vv. 4–5). Finally, as of most importance, it is from Israel that the Messiah comes "according to the flesh" (v. 5) that is, biologically. As the translation notes in the NRSV indicate, the final words of v. 5 are quite ambiguous, and it is debated whether Paul is affirming that the Messiah himself is God or whether he is following his reference to the Messiah with a blessing of God. What is clear is that this important section of the letter both begins (9:5) and ends (11:36) with an ascription of praise to God.

One possible interpretation of the anguish Paul reveals in vv. 1–5 is that he has concluded that there is no hope, that God's word has failed. But this conclusion he adamantly rejects in v. 6, which stands as the theme of the following three chapters. As he begins to explain how it is that the present rejection of Israel's Messiah does not mean that God's promises are at an end, Paul turns to the history of Israel in Scripture, and citations from and engagement with Scripture are dense in these chapters. First, he looks at the constituting of Israel, which has always come about by God's choosing or election. The promise made to Abraham was to Isaac and his descendants (vv. 7–9). Subsequently, God chose Jacob rather than Esau, doing so even before their births, before either of them had done anything good or bad (vv. 10–13). Even the role of Pharaoh was the result of God's choosing (v. 17). One of the striking things in this account is that Paul offers no critical remarks either about his own contemporaries or about the actions of Israel in the past (by contrast with Stephen in Acts 7:2–53). His point is not to criticize individual Israelites or even to identify the limits of Abraham's family but to insist that it is God who elects and God does so for God's own purposes.

This discussion leads into Paul's use of the familiar analogy of the potter and the clay (see, e.g., Isa 41:25; Jer 18:1–10; Wis 15:7; Sir 33:13; 1QS 11:22; 1QHa 1:21; 3:23–24; 4:29; 11:3; 12:26, 32; 18:12) which has led many readers of the text to take offense at the picture of an unfeeling, despotic God. Yet the point of the analogy is not the power of the potter to fashion a vessel, but the right (9:21) of the potter to determine the use of the vessel. The Greek of vv. 22–23 is exceedingly difficult, but these lines appear to be an elaboration on v. 21; God has indeed acted with mercy and with wrath, but God's actions have as their goal a glorious mercy, both for Jews and for Gentiles (v. 24). This section of the argument concludes with citations from Hosea and Isaiah. Stunningly, in vv. 25–26, Paul applies language drawn from Hos 1:10 and 2:23, texts that have to do with the restoring of Israel, to both Jews and Gentiles. He then, in vv. 27–29, draws on Isa 10:22–23 and Isa 1:9 to introduce the notion of Israel's remnant, to which he will return in 11:7–10. It is God who has elected Israel and God who will save. (It is important to understand that the qualifier "only" is added in v. 27 by the translators of the NRSV and does not appear in the Greek. Chapter 11 will suggest that there is a remnant, but this remnant is not the only object of God's salvation.)

B. God's Impartiality and Faithfulness (9:30–10:21)

As is clear already in 9:24, Paul is not concerned in these chapters exclusively with God's dealings with Israel, since God has now called Gentiles as well. The second stage in this discussion begins by observing an anomaly: Gentiles did not strive for righteousness and yet attained it, whereas the Jews who strived after righteousness did not achieve it. Most of the remainder of this section grapples to explain this situation of Jews, although 10:12–13 briefly refer to Gentiles as well. Paul begins by observing, in a compressed and elliptical fashion, that Gentiles attained righteousness through faith, whereas the Jews sought righteousness through law, which they did not succeed in fulfilling. They treated righteousness as if it were based on works. As a further explanation, Paul writes that Jews tripped over a "stumbling stone," which Paul illumines with a quotation that combines portions of Isa 28:16 and 8:14. Given the context, with its recent reference to the law, the "stumbling stone" has sometimes been identified with the law, but other early Christian texts draw on stone imagery to refer to Christ (e.g., Matt 21:42; Acts 4:11; 1 Pet 2:6–8), and the citation of Isa 28:16 again in 10:11 suggests that this is Paul's understanding in 9:33 as well. On either reading, it is noteworthy that the "I" who places the stumbing stone that causes Israel to trip is none other than Israel's own God.

Recalling 9:1–5, ch. 10 begins with a prayer for the salvation of Israel, reiterating that Israel has a zeal for God, but it is not enlightened. Paul is ascribing to Israel the same attitude that he himself had before coming to faith in Christ Jesus (cf. Gal 1:13–14; Phil 3:6; cf. Acts 22:3–5); like him, they were ignorant of the righteousness that God gives and were seeking to establish their own righteousness. Famously, it is at this point that Paul adds the statement that Christ is the *telos* of the law (v. 4). The NRSV translates *telos* as the "end" or "termination" of the law, which would entail a sharp difference between the law and the gospel. However, Paul has insisted that the law is holy, just, and good (7:12) and that it witnesses to the righteousness of God received through faith (3:21). And he has said that God acted in the death of Jesus Christ to fulfill "the just requirement of the law" (8:4), suggesting that the better translation is "goal" or "purpose." What Paul is affirming on this reading is that the law itself is about nothing else than Christ as the basis of righteousness for all believers. (Similarly, 1 Tim 1:5 says that "the aim [again: *telos*] of such instruction is love.")

In 10:6–8 Paul contrasts righteousness that comes from the law with righteousness that comes from faith and employs a midrashic commentary on Deut 30:12–14 to make his point. "The word of faith," which Paul has preached, is that Jesus is Lord (v. 9), and Jesus' lordship is impartial. Paul makes this point repeatedly in vv. 11–13, where he again quotes Isa 28:16 (as in 9:33), insists that there is no distinction between Jew and Gentile (as in 3:22–23), and further insists that there is one Lord for all (as in 3:30). Joel 2:32, which is crucial to the sermon of Peter in Acts 2:17–21, appears here as well: "Everyone who calls on the name of the Lord shall be saved" (v. 13).

The chain of questions in vv. 14–15 draw the connection between calling on the name and the preaching carried out by Christian missionaries. Yet Paul is quick in v. 17 to avoid the conclusion that faith comes about by his own work; it is the work of the "word of Christ." This section of the argument concludes by drawing on Ps 19:4; Deut 32:21; Isa 65:1–2; God's word has gone out, God has continually sought after Israel, and Israel remains disobedient (vv. 18–21). This dire diagnosis is not the final word, however, as becomes clear immediately at the beginning of ch. 11.

C. God's Electing Mercy (11:1–36)

Chapter 11 opens with the question that follows logically on ch. 10: "Has God rejected his people?" His adamantly negative response introduces an argument about the division within Israel, the divine use of that division for the salvation of Gentiles, and the extent of God's eschatological mercy to all people. Paul does this by first noting that he himself is an Israelite (as also in Phil 3:3:4*b*–6; 2 Cor 11:22), so God cannot have rejected all of Israel. Then he turns back to Israel's history once again in vv. 2–4, this time to the story of Elijah and the seven thousand who had not bowed their knees to Baal (1 Kgs 19; see esp. 19:10, 14, 18). Just as God preserved a remnant then, so God does now (and here the reference to a remnant in 9:27 comes again into focus). Once again, in

v. 6, Paul pauses to insist that this remnant is "by grace," not by anyone's achievement (as in 4:2–8; 9:11–16).

Verses 7–11 draw Paul's conclusions from his own experience and Israel's history: There is at present a division in Israel between the "elect" or the "remnant" and the "rest." In the context of what he has just said about himself and the time of Elijah, the "elect" refers to those Jews who believe Jesus to be the Messiah, those who have been called ("elected") by God into this role (as with the election earlier in 9:6–18). The "rest" refers to those Jews who do not believe Jesus to be the Messiah, those who have been "hardened" by God just as was Pharaoh (9:17). Paul reinforces this point by drawing on Deut 29:4, Isa 29:10, and Ps 69:22–23, texts that emphasize God's role in closing eyes and ears and in tricking the people (as in 9:33).

This emphatic statement about God's hardening of the "rest" provokes the question of v. 11: Is God's hardening of them permanent? And again the answer is "No," and beginning in v. 11*b* the remainder of the chapter endeavors to show that it is not only a remnant but "all" of Israel (v. 26) that God will save. First, vv. 11*b*–12 announce the logic: Through a strange and unanticipated inversion, Israel's salvation has come to the Gentiles, who in turn will make Israel jealous. In v. 13 Paul speaks directly to Gentile members of the house churches at Rome about his own work among the Gentiles. His hope is that the end result of that ministry is that it will contribute to God's salvation of Israel (vv. 13–14).

Paul amplifies his point with two images, the dough and the olive tree. The lump of dough offered as the first fruit (cf. 8:23) cannot be different in character from the loaf of which it is a part (v. 16; Num 15:17–21). As the "lump," the believing remnant of Israel signifies the whole loaf that lies in the future. Then Paul employs the image of the olive tree, first simply as a reiteration of the relationship between a lump of dough and the whole loaf: the same plant cannot have a root that is holy and produce branches that are not (v. 16). This image transforms in vv. 17–24 into a sharp warning against Gentile arrogance. Some of the branches of Israel have been broken off, and in their place wild olive shoots from among the Gentiles were grafted on. But this gives no right to the grafted branches to boast. The natural branches were broken off because of their unbelief, but the grafted branches remain a part of the tree only by virtue of the kindness of God. They cannot presume upon God's grace.

With v. 25 Paul moves toward his conclusion, which he terms a "mystery," a term with apocalyptic connotations (as in Dan 2:18-19, 27-30; 2 Esd 12:36-38) having to do with God's own plan (Rom 16:25; 1 Cor 2:1, 7; 15:51). Here he summarizes the argument he has been making in this chapter: God has accomplished the hardening of "part" of Israel (the "rest" of v. 7) while the Gentiles come in, and then "all Israel will be saved" (v. 26). He finds this mystery anticipated in the words of Isa 59:20-21 and 27:9 (although in altered form). Paul is rejecting at every point a rigid determinism that divides humankind into two groups, namely the "insider" and the "outsider," the "saved" and the "damned." While "part" of Israel is currently at enmity with God (see 5:10), Israel remains God's beloved.

Two verses provide the theological character of Paul's argument. First, God's faithfulness to Israel rests on the fact that "the gifts and calling of God are irrevocable" (11:29). It is not because Israel has demonstrated or will demonstrate such fidelity to God that God will decide to save Israel. Rather it is because God is steadfast and gracious concerning the gifts and calling. Second, the strange inversion rehearsed in 11:30-32 is possible because "God has imprisoned all (people) in disobedience so that he may be merciful to all" (11:32). The double use of the word "all" is intentional. For both Jews and Gentiles, all doors are closed tight, all windows are barred, so that only God can provide the salvation of all.

Romans 9-11 then ends as it began, with a doxology (see 9:5; 11:33-36), which is composed in part from OT citations (Isa 40:13 [LXX]; Job 41:11). God remains beyond human manipulation, and yet true faith and obedience and the hope of salvation depend on God who can be trusted. This is the God whom Paul praises at the conclusion of his argument.

V. Life in Christ (12:1–15:13)

The previous chapters have served to shape the identity of the house churches in Rome and to mold their understanding of themselves as Christian people. Readers are encouraged to think of themselves as people who belong to the new age inaugurated by God, people who have been redeemed by Christ, freed from the controlling power of sin, people who exist in the confidence that the promise-making God is also a promise-keeping God. Chapters 1–11 are often separated out from what follows and labeled as "theology," with the label "ethics" attached to 12:1–15:13. A more accurate term for this new section may be "embodying the gospel." For Paul, faithful thinking and faithful living are not to be distinguished, as they belong together. Here Paul speaks of "doing the will of God," but he does not prescribe a code or program of ethical action; neither does he explicitly invoke the teaching and example of Jesus.

A. "Be transformed by the renewal of your mind" (12:1–21)

At this critical point in the letter, when Paul has argued that Jews and Gentiles are both included in God's redemptive work, he begins his important admonitions with words about presentation of "your bodies" and "renewing of your minds" for discernment of God's will (vv. 1–2). The introductory "therefore" joins the practical appeal to what has just preceded it, namely, the electing mercy of God.

Several emphases stand out in these two verses, which may be thought of as the theme for all of 12:1–15:13. To begin with, they are addressed to a particular communal context, to the various members of the house churches in Rome. It is not an abstract ethic addressed to individuals. Paul never posits the ability of individuals to discern the divine will in the midst of the various complex decisions in which they are daily involved. The gospel that creates the community provides the context in which the demands are made for moral discussion and judgment. As he writes later in Rom 15:14, "You yourselves are full of goodness, filled with all knowledge, and able to instruct one another." Second, it is clear that Paul's understanding of the human embodiment of the gospel is eschatological. Readers are urged not to be conformed to this world (or better: "this age"), but to be transformed by the renewal of their mind. The Greek word translated in the

NRSV as "world" is *aiōn* rather than *kosmos*, and it refers to the inbreaking of God's new age into the present. Believers are called to set aside their conformity to the old age and to be renewed in their minds, which heretofore have been darkened and have produced only futility and senseless thoughts (Rom 1:21–22). A conventional way to put Paul's point is in terms of the integral relationship between the indicative and the imperative moods, between God's gift and God's demands, between the gospel itself and the faithful response it elicits. A third emphasis in Rom 12:1–2 is that Paul's comments embrace all of human life with metaphorical language. The mercies of God call for reordered lives that are offered as "a living sacrifice, holy, and acceptable to God." Further, such transformed selves are "your spiritual worship" (NRSV) or, as the KJV puts it, "your reasonable worship." Paul declares that such dedication of the entire self serves as the authentic worship appropriate to a reordered human life. A fourth emphasis in 12:1–2 is the critical role of discernment. The goal of transformation is "that you may discern what is the will of God" (v. 2). Paul does not attach "the will of God" to a specific pattern of behavior; instead, the phrase is a more general way of referring to the total claim God makes on believers. It must be repeatedly sought and tested in every new situation. Three qualities are specified in determining the will of God: the "good and acceptable and perfect." The gift of discernment enables the community to separate the important from the trivial, the genuine from the bogus, good from evil.

From announcing this important theme in 12:1–2, Paul turns at 12:3 to take up the marks of Christian community and the relationships of Christians with those beyond the community. The initial topic in vv. 3–8 concerns the crucial matter of self-evaluation, which can build up or undermine community life. Paul begins by urging his readers not to think more highly of themselves than they ought to think, but to think "with sober judgment," (v. 3) each person doing so according to faith's standards and not according to the world's standards. Paul draws attention to this admonition by employing the literary device of paranomasia (repetition of a root word); although obscured in English translation, four times in v. 3 he uses a form of the verb *phronein* ("to think or to regard")

This sobriety of self-judgment is essential for the proper activity of the church as the body of Christ. Drawing on the image of the community familiar from 1 Cor 12:4–31, he observes that members of the body do not all have the same function; instead, each one has a gift given by God that contributes to the well-being of the body. Each individual is to exercise his or her gift (prophecy, ministry, teaching, exhortation, giving, leadership, benevolence) in a way that is consistent with its source and in a fashion appropriate to its function for the body. Diversities are acknowledged, but they are radically subordinated to the norm of faith so that they lose their divisive power.

From 12:9–21 in staccato-like fashion Paul mentions the characteristics essential to the Christian experience. Love heads the list (v. 9), which is not surprising given that love often marks the embodiment of the gospel in Paul's letters (e.g., Rom 13:9–10; 1 Cor 13:1–13; Gal 5:22). Love is not for Paul an abstract ethical principle but is made specific in terms of the self-sacrifice of Christ, "who loved me and gave himself for me" (Gal 2:20). Paul declares that the only true love is that which is genuine (Rom 12:9) and free from dissimulation. With vv. 9*b*–13, he provides some indicators of what love looks like within the community of faith, as it energetically serves the Lord by serving the needs of those within the community.

In vv. 14–21, Paul takes up the challenge of dealing with hostility, especially with the temptation to take revenge. This section may well have in view hostility that comes from outside the Christian community, although vv. 15–16 probably reflect concerns for the community itself, and the conflicts Paul will address in 14:1–15:6 could also generate hostility inside the community. Not surprisingly, several of these statements have parallels elsewhere in early Jewish and Christian tradition (e.g., cf. v. 14 with Matt 5:44, Luke 6:28; v. 17 with Matt 5:38–39; 1 Pet 3:9; v. 19 with Prov 20:22; 24:20). And Paul explicitly references Deut 32:35 (v. 19) and Prov 25:21–22 (v. 20) to recall that God alone is judge (a claim to which he will return in 14:1–12) and to advocate generosity in response to hostility.

B. On Christian Obligations (13:1–14)

The passage that follows (13:1–7) has caused the church such grief through the years that it needs to be examined with great care. It has often been used as a biblical warrant to advocate for ecclesial support of oppressive governments such as Germany under the Third Reich and South Africa under apartheid, and there is every reason to expect that it may be called upon again elsewhere.

Because the passage begins somewhat abruptly and has no parallel in the other Pauline letters (although see 1 Tim 2:1–2; cf. 1 Pet 2:13–14), occasionally scholars suggest that it was added to Paul's original letter to Rome. There is, however, no early copy of the letter without these verses, which makes it likely that they were in fact part of the letter Paul sent. Because taxation plays an important role in this discussion (see vv. 6–7), it may be that the specific situation that prompts this discussion lies in that arena. Roman taxation could be abusive (hence the association in Gospel tradition between sinners and tax collectors; e.g., Matt 9:10–13; 11:19; Mark 2:15–17; Luke 5:30; 7:34), and the emperor Nero sought in 58 CE (shortly after the writing of this letter) to address widespread abuses in the system (see Tacitus, *Annals* 13.50). This situation could well mean that Paul hopes to discourage Roman Christians from withholding taxes and thereby putting themselves at risk for punishment; thus, he writes to provide specific directions rather than to offer a generalized statement on the nature of government.

To be sure, the notion that citizens owe the authorities an acknowledgment of their rightful place is not a novel proposal for a Jewish community. Both the OT and the literature of Hellenistic Judaism acknowledge the legitimate authority of various human rulers and call for obedience to such kings. At the same time, these texts recognize that the authority of God stands above and beyond human rulers, and the obligation owed to ruling powers is thereby limited (e.g., Jer 29:7; Prov 8:15–16; 24:21–22; Dan 2:21; Sir 17:17; Wis 6:1–11; *Letter of Aristeas* 196, 219, 224). In addition, the eschatological statements in 12:1–2 and especially in 13:11–14 serve to relativize current governmental structures and place the state in a penultimate position: Jesus, not Caesar, is Lord.

The initial imperative, "Let every person be subject to the governing authorities," (v. 1) demands that the readers take seriously the role of the magistrates in the sense of submitting to the order God has established. This is not the same thing as demanding unqualified obedience to those authorities. One might disobey the governing officials, if one thought their demands contrary to God's will (as, e.g., Acts 4:18–20; 5:29), and at the same time be exposed to their discipline and punishment. Civil rights leaders, who violated the segregationist laws and practices of the southern states and who went to jail for their actions, were disobedient to many local magistrates but they nevertheless continued to be subject to the authority of those same magistrates.

To the authorities, one gives what is due (v. 7), but that obligation stands in stunning contrast to the real obligation articulated again in v. 8, the obligation to love. Here Paul returns to his discussion of love begun in 12:9 and exhorts: "owe no one anything, except to love one another; for the one who loves another has fulfilled the law" (v. 8; NRSV). The Greek here is slightly ambiguous, so that v. 8b could possibly be translated, "the one who loves has fulfilled the other law." In this case, "the other law" would be the law Jesus gave to replace the Torah or perhaps the Mosaic law over against Roman civil law. There has been, however, no clear reference to "law" in the preceding sentences, and Paul does not elsewhere contrast Torah with Jesus' law or Roman law. Furthermore, Paul nowhere else uses the verb "love" absolutely (as in "the one who loves"), so that the NRSV is far preferable. Paul amplifies this comment in v. 9 by citing from the Decalogue (Exod 20:13–17; Deut 5:17–21), culminating in the admonition to love the neighbor (Lev 19:18; cf. Matt 5:43; 19:19). Fulfillment of the law involves not just loving someone other than oneself, or loving those who are comfortable and attractive, but loving each person whom God presents as neighbor.

Paul's language about fulfilling the law may seem surprising, given that much of what he has said about the law in earlier chapters is negative. The law gives sin its power by defining certain patterns of behavior as sinful and by a total inability to help people to accomplish what the law demands (e.g., 7:7–10). And yet Paul persists in declaring that "the law is holy, and the commandment is holy, just, and good" (7:12). And 8:4 anticipates that the "just requirement of the law" is fulfilled by those who walk in the Spirit of God. Here that "just requirement" takes on specificity and it can then be said, "love is the fulfilling of the law" (13:10*b*).

Paul concludes this initial discussion of the Christian life by returning in vv. 11–14 to the note of eschatological urgency with which he began (12:1–2). The metaphors of wakefulness (v. 11), daylight or light (vv. 12–13), and the putting on of new clothing ("armor"; v. 12) are common ways of depicting the radical change of life expected from those who are members of the Christian community. This change reflects their shared knowledge that "salvation" is at hand. In this context, "salvation" appears to be a shorthand reference to the return of Jesus, which Paul discusses more fully in 1 Thess 4:13–18 and in 1 Cor 15:12–58.

C. An Appeal for Harmony (14:1–15:6)

This lengthy section continues to address the transformation (12:1–2) brought about in Jesus Christ, but here Paul takes up a specific issue that causes tension. Some believers strictly observe certain regulations in the Mosaic law regarding dietary matters and "holy" days (including the Sabbath; see Exod 20:8–11; Deut 5:12–15); Paul refers to them as "the weak," presumably an epithet applied to them by others rather than a name they have given themselves. Other believers, those who presumably have given themselves the name "the strong," understand that the arrival of Jesus as God's Messiah has given them freedom to ignore such regulations. It may be that Paul takes up this question because of its currency in Corinth (see 1 Cor 8–10), and he is in Corinth as he writes to Rome (see Rom 16:1; Cenchreae is the seaport for Corinth). And there are some similarities, since in both texts Paul warns against individual freedoms that become hazardous for others (Rom 14:20–21; 1 Cor 8:9; 9:12), and in both texts he advocates actions that build up (1 Cor 8:1; Rom 14:19). However, in important respects the texts and probably the situations behind them differ. At Corinth, the food that proves controversial is food that has been offered to idols, such as was sold in the meat markets (see e.g., 1 Cor 8), and the debate revolves around the existence of other gods and around individual freedom, conscience, and

knowledge. At Rome, the debate revolves around the observance or non-observance of specific Jewish practices, and here questions of purity are at stake (14:14).

Whatever has given rise to the conflict at Rome, Paul's response is thoroughly theological. In vv. 1–12, he begins by insisting that neither side may judge or despise the other side because "God has welcomed them" (v. 3) Here he analogizes believers to household servants; all are servants in God's household and may not judge the servants of another (v. 4). All give thanks to the same Lord, whatever their dietary practices may be (vv. 5–6). All live and die in the presence of the same Lord (vv. 7–9). All will be judged by the same Lord (vv. 10–12). In support of this claim, Paul points to Isa 45:23 (and cf. Phil 2:10–11).

Although vv. 1–8 speak of believers as belonging to God who is Lord, in v. 9 he refers to Christ, whose death and resurrection mark him as "Lord of both the dead and the living." This seamless shift between references to God and to Jesus Christ may or may not be self-conscious, but it is among the features of NT writings that give rise to the church's later creedal formulations.

Apart from the use of the terminology of "strong" and "weak," vv. 1–12 are rather evenly balanced, in that Paul does not appear to favor either party in the dispute. With vv. 13–23, however, it becomes clear that he himself agrees with the so-called "strong"; nevertheless, it also becomes clear that his admonitions are largely intended for them rather than for the "weak." Nothing is unclean "in the Lord Jesus," that is, to those who have already been called into life in the new age inaugurated in Jesus Christ (v. 14), but it is nevertheless wrong to eat in a way that causes the weaker brothers or sisters to act against their own consciences.

In 15:1–6 Paul explicitly identifies himself with the strong and urges that they must "put up with" the weak. The translation "put up with" (v. 1) conjures up mere tolerance, but the Greek *bastazein* is closer to "carry" in the sense of "bearing with." As Paul explains what he means by this "putting up with," he returns to the language of building up, acting for the good of the neighbor. Christ himself is invoked as one who did not please himself, citing Ps 69:9, a prayer for deliverance on the part of the innocent person who is afflicted unjustly. Along with other early Christian writers, Paul saw this psalm as referring to Christ (cf. Ps 69:21*b* in Mark 14:36, John 19:28–29; Ps 69:4 in John 15:25). Scripture exists both "for our instruction" and as a source of hope (v. 4). Paul concludes with a prayer for the harmony of the community "in accordance with Christ Jesus" (v. 5).

D. Welcome to Jews and Gentiles (15:7–13)

With vv. 7–13, Paul returns to the language of "welcome" that introduced 14:1–15:6, but this section is more than a conclusion to that specific discussion. It also brings together several of the major concerns of the letter, constituting what a number of scholars regard as the climax of the entire argument. The opening admonition of 15:7 repeats that of 14:1: "Welcome." Here, however, the language of "strong" and "weak" has disappeared, as the dispute over dietary matters and the marking of holy days gives way to different terminology. The command to "welcome one another" in 15:7 does not now concern the "strong" and the "weak," but "the circumcised" and "the Gentiles." Each group is to "welcome" the other, accepting and respecting one another's differences, "just as Christ has welcomed you" (v. 7). In both cases, that welcome is for God's own glory; this is not hospitality for its own sake or simply to enhance the social life of a divided community.

With vv. 8–9*a* Paul succinctly describes Christ's "welcome." The Greek is complex and ambiguous, but Paul appears to be making parallel claims about Christ's welcome of both circumcised and Gentile. First, Christ became a "servant" (v. 8; *diakonos*; cf. 13:4; 16:1) of "the circumcised" (i.e., Jews), and he did so to confirm the promises (as in 4:13). Second, Christ also acted so that Gentiles might glorify God for God's mercy (see also 9:15–18, 23; 11:32). Paul underscores this claim about the way in which Christ has welcomed both Jew and Gentile with four quotations from Scripture (Ps 18:49; Deut 32:43; Ps 117:1; Isa 11:10), all of which specifically refer to the inclusion of the Gentiles among those who offer praise to God alongside Israel. The repetition of "and again" at the beginning of vv. 10, 11, and 12 dramatically reinforces the importance of Paul's expectation that Jew and Gentile together will offer praise to God. Paul draws this section to an end with a prayer-wish of hope (v. 13); it is God's power and

that of the Holy Spirit that brings about the shared praise of Jew and Gentile.

VI. Letter Closing (15:14–16:27)

A. The Romans and Paul's Mission (15:14–33)

Keenly aware that he has not yet been to Rome (1:10–15) and may have given offense, Paul reiterates in v. 14 his confidence about the health of the congregations, yet immediately in vv. 15–16 he appeals to his own vocation as a reason for his letter. Strikingly, v. 16 draws on liturgical language ("priestly service," "offering") to explain his vocation (cf. the use of liturgical language in 12:1–2). His service of the gospel concerns "the offering of the Gentiles" (v. 16), an ambiguous phrase that may refer to the Gentiles themselves as an offering or to the collection itself, which forms such an important part of Paul's own mission and is very much at the front of his thinking as he writes this letter (see vv. 25–33). Paul adds two remarks about his own work. In vv. 17–19, he is proud of what he has accomplished, although he also immediately asserts that his "boast" is in what God has done (as in 5:1–2 and also 1 Cor.1:31). And, turning to Isa 52:15, he specifies that the geographical extent of his work reflects his goal of preaching to those who have not yet heard the gospel (v. 21). The import of this comment emerges in what follows.

In vv. 22–33 Paul reflects on his plans for future travel. As he indicated at the beginning of the letter (1:10–13), he intends to travel to Rome. Now he adds that, after being in Rome, he wants to take the gospel to Spain (vv. 24, 28–29), and it appears that Paul seeks the support of the Roman congregations for his labor in Spain. But most immediately, Paul's work takes him to Jerusalem with a collection for the "poor among the saints" there (v. 26). This collection clearly occupies an important place in Paul's mission, as he refers to it also in Gal 2:10, 1 Cor 16:1–4, and at length in 2 Cor 8–9. Although he speaks about the collection in terms of human need (vv. 26–27), it is clear that Paul also understands this need in theological terms. The Gentile believers in Macedonia and Achaia have received "spiritual blessings" from Jewish believers and so are right to share in material goods (v. 27). More to the point, vv. 30–33 reveal Paul's deep concern that Jerusalem will reject the collection, as he calls for the Romans to pray that the collection will be acceptable and that he will be "rescued" in Jerusalem. Apparently, Paul fears that the unity of Jew and Gentile, a unity for which he has argued throughout the letter, will be rejected in Jerusalem.

Whether he was able to follow through with these plans remains unknown. Luke's account of Paul's arrest in Jerusalem seems to confirm that Paul was right to be apprehensive about his visit (Acts 21:27–36). Luke himself is curiously silent about the collection, although he may touch on it briefly in Acts 24:17.

B. Closing Greetings and Instructions (16:1–27)

The final chapter of Romans opens with a brief letter of recommendation for "our sister Phoebe" (vv. 1–2). Presumably she is the bearer of the letter and it is important for Paul that she be received with respectful hospitality by the congregations in Rome. Paul identifies her as a "deacon" (*diakonos*) of the church in Cenchreae, a harbor-town about seven miles east of Corinth. While the word "deacon" does not yet refer to a defined office in the church's life (as it apparently does in 1 Tim 3:8–13), there is at the very least the suggestion of some leadership role. That point is underscored when Paul refers to her as a "benefactor" (*prostatis*), a person of means who provides concrete support for Paul's mission (cf. Luke 8:1–3; Acts 16:14–15).

Verses 3–16 contain a lengthy list of greetings to twenty-four named individuals and a number of unnamed people associated with the named individuals (see vv. 5, 10–11, 13–15). Paul had not yet been to Rome, but he no doubt met many of these people while they were exiled from Rome and had taken up residence in Corinth and Ephesus (as is the case with Prisca and Aquila). It may be that he includes this lengthy list in order to secure a relationship with Rome and to gain a better hearing for his letter. The list itself includes many people who are otherwise unknown, but their names and Paul's brief comments about them still offer considerable insight into the makeup of early Christianity at Rome.

In Rome as elsewhere, early Christians did not worship in special buildings dedicated for that purpose but instead gathered in the homes of individuals (as in 1 Cor 16:19; Phlm 2; Acts 20:20). That practice is evident when Paul greets Prisca

and Aquila and "the church in their house" (v. 5), as well as in vv. 14–15 when he greets those "who are with them" in other households. In addition, the list may include at least one prominent household, that of Aristobulus (v. 10), perhaps a grandson of Herod the Great. And several of the names are among those often used for slaves or former slaves (e.g., Ampliatus, Hermes, Nereus).

Paul includes the names of several women, and his comments about them suggest their significant leadership in the house churches at Rome. To begin with, he greets Prisca (Priscilla) and Aquila, whom he identifies also as co-workers and who "risked their necks" on his account (vv. 3–4). Prisca and Aquila were expelled from Rome due to Claudius' decree and worked with Paul in Corinth (Acts 18:1–3). The husband and wife team then accompanied Paul to Ephesus (Acts 18:18, 24–26; see also 1 Cor 16:19) and now are back in Rome with their own house church (Rom 16:3–5). (This information from Romans, coupled with the information from Acts and Suetonius, is important in the reconstruction of the historical setting of Romans; see Introduction.) Paul lists Prisca before her husband (as also in Acts 18:18, 26; 2 Tim 4:19); given ancient practice, this suggests that she is a more prominent figure than he is, either socially (i.e., perhaps he is a freed slave) or ecclesially (i.e., she may have been the more important figure in Christian circles).

Prisca is not the only woman identified as working on behalf of the gospel. Paul employs similar language of Mary in v. 6, as well as Tryphaena, Tryphosa, and Persis in v. 12. Elsewhere he uses the same language to refer to his own apostolic labor (as in 1 Cor 15:10; Gal 4:11; Phil 2:16). Perhaps most revealing, in v. 7 he greets Andronicus and Junia, who were in prison alongside him and who are "prominent among the apostles." The NRSV footnote indicates that the female name "Junia" may in fact be accented as "Junias," the male version of the name. There is ample evidence, however, that the name "Junia" was often used among women whereas there is no evidence that the name "Junias" was ever used among men. Until at least the Middle Ages, Christian readers understood this person to be female, presumably another missionary couple like Prisca and Aquila. Whatever Paul's contested remarks elsewhere about women in worship may mean (see 1 Cor 11:2–16; 14:34–36), here he takes for granted the leadership of women in Roman congregations.

In vv. 17–20 Paul issues a warning to these friends that they keep an eye out for those who cause splits in the community and who smooth-talk their way into a position that is contrary to that which they have previously learned (cf. 2 Cor 11:12–15; Phil 3:18–19; Gal 5:11; 6:17; Rom 3:8). He then adds greetings from those who are with him and who may travel with him to Jerusalem (including Timothy, his often mentioned associate [e.g., Acts 16:1–2; 1 Cor 4:17; 1 Thess 3:2]; Lucius, perhaps the Lucius of Cyrene of Acts 13:1; Jason, possibly the Thessalonian host of Acts 17:5–9; and Sosipater, perhaps the Sopater of Beroea of Acts 20:4); the scribe Tertius to whom Paul has dictated the letter (v. 22); and finally, leading figures in the Corinthian community, namely Gaius, Erastus, and Quartus (v. 23).

It is not clear whether the doxological statement of vv. 25–27 is part of the original letter. In some ancient manuscripts of Romans it does not appear at all, and in some it is included after 14:12 or 15:33. Nevertheless, it provides a fitting conclusion to a letter in which praise of God plays a prominent role (e.g., 9:5; 11:33–36).

BIBLIOGRAPHY

K. Barth. *A Shorter Commentary on Romans with an Introductory Essay by Maico Michielin.* Maico M. Michielin, ed. (Burlington, Vt.: Ashgate, 2007); B. Byrne. *Romans.* SP 6 (Collegeville, Minn.: Liturgical Press, 1996); E. J. Epp. *Junia: The First Woman Apostle* (Minneapolis: Fortress Press, 2005); J. A. Fitzmyer. *Romans: A New Translation with Introduction and Commentary.* AB 33 (New York: Doubleday, 1993); K. Grieb. *The Story of Romans: A Narrative Defense of God's Righteousness* (Louisville: Westminster John Knox, 2002); R. Jewett. *Romans: A Commentary.* Hermeneia (Minneapolis: Fortress Press, 2007); L. T. Johnson. *Reading Romans: A Literary and Theological Commentary* (New York: Crossroad Publishing Co., 1997); E. Käsemann. *Commentary on Romans* (Grand Rapids: Eerdmans, 1980); L. E. Keck. *Romans.* ANTC (Nashville: Abingdon, 2005); P. Meyer. *The Word in This World.* NTL (Louisville: Westminster John Knox, 2004).

1 CORINTHIANS

Suzanne Watts Henderson

OVERVIEW

Written around 54 CE, Paul's first letter to Corinthian Christians plunges readers into a conversation well underway. The apostle has apparently spent considerable time with the community (1 Cor 2:1–5; 2 Cor 1:16–19; Acts 18:1–18), and the letter refers to various word-of-mouth reports about their conduct (1 Cor 1:11; 5:1; 11:18), as well as previous correspondence from both Paul (1 Cor 5:9) and the congregation itself (1 Cor 7:1). First Corinthians, then, presents Paul's side of a lively, on-going exchange about a range of topical concerns—from sexuality to meal practices to worship life—all of which he addresses in light of the "message about the cross" (1 Cor 1:18).

Social and historical factors at work in first-century Corinth shed important light on the matters that concern Paul in this letter. Reestablished as a Roman colony in 44 BCE, the city had emerged as a thriving melting pot where social mobility and economic opportunity fostered vigorous competition in the marketplace of goods, ideas, and even physical prowess. Within such a culture, the Corinthian Christians quite naturally found themselves divided along lines of apostolic loyalty (1:12), human erudition (1:26; 8:1), economic status (11:19–21), and religious expression (12–14). In response to such factionalism (1:10–11; 3:3), Paul challenges the Corinthian cultural value of self-promotion at every turn, advocating instead the kind of unity that results from imitating Christ's pattern of self-sacrifice (11:1).

Another cultural value that affected the Corinthian Christian community was the premium placed on freedom in that city, where a large number of freed slaves from throughout the Roman Empire had settled. Apparently, the Christian community embraced that notion of freedom and interpreted it, at least to some degree, as spiritual license for a wide range of moral and ethical behaviors that Paul challenges in the letter. Certainly, the sexual promiscuity they have tolerated—even boasted about (5:6)—reflects this notion of "freedom in Christ," but Paul argues just as vigorously against the kind of freedom that leads to eating idol meat to the det-riment of the "weak" (8:11). Such misconstrued liberty may indicate that the Corinthians affirmed the "already" of Christ's triumph over sin to the neglect of the "not yet" of Christ's decisive reign that Paul actively awaits.

Partly in response to this view, Paul attempts to situate the Corinthian Christians—including many former Gentiles—within the story of Israel, which for Paul culminates in the Christ event. Though scriptural citations are relatively sparse in this letter, Paul does invoke biblical testimony about God's wisdom (1:19; 2:9, 16; 3:19–20), the *Shema* (8:4) as reminder of God's oneness, Torah wilderness narratives of God's activity among the Israelites (whom he calls "our ancestors," 10:1–11), and prophetic expectations of eschatological hopes (15:54–55). In so doing, Paul casts the Corinthians' present experience of grace within the larger context of God's unfolding plan of salvation.

Even as he plants the Corinthians' faith story in the soil of Jewish scripture, Paul also freely deploys Corinthian idiom to convey the gospel message in familiar terms. He repeatedly quotes, and reinterprets, slogans that apparently reflect the wisdom and punditry of their culture (e.g., 6:12; 7:1; 8:1, 4, 8; 10:23). And he appropriates imagery drawn from cosmopolitan Corinth—from the workplace (3:10–15), sports (9:24–27), and political philosophy (12:12–31)—as he refracts the culture's self-serving, competitive values through the lens of the cross. Thus, Paul varies his means but not his gospel message in a manner consistent with his own apostolic strategy: "I have become all things to all people, that I might by all means save some" (9:22).

OUTLINE

B. Christ Crucified, the Wisdom of God (1:18–2:16)

C. Jealousy, Quarrels, and Factions (3:1–23)

D. Cruciform Apostleship (4:1–21)

III. Glorifying God in the Body (5:1–11:1)

A. Judging Immoral Behavior (5:1–6:20)

B. Promoting Morality in Marriage (7:1–40)

C. The Problem of Idol Food and Worship (8:1–11:1)

IV. Gathering as the Body of Christ (11:2–14:40)

A. Head Coverings (11:2–16)

B. Remembering the Lord's Death (11:17–34)

C. Spiritual Gifts Among the Members (12:1–31)

D. The "More Excellent Way" (13:1–13)

E. Spiritual Gifts in Worship (14:1–40)

V. Affirming the Resurrection Body (15:1–58)

A. Christ Raised (15:1–11)

B. Christ as the First Fruits (15:12–34)

C. Resurrection of the Spiritual Body (15:35–58)

VI. Closing (16:1–24)

A. Collection for the Saints (16:1–4)

B. Future Plans (16:5–12)

C. Exhortation and Greetings (16:13–24)

DETAILED ANALYSIS

I. Introduction (1:1–9)

A. Salutation (1:1–3)

In the letter's salutation, Paul attributes his apostleship not to his own credentials but to the divine will of the One who has called him. His co-writer Sosthenes (1:1) may be the Corinthian synagogue official mentioned in Acts 18:17; in any case, he appears only here in the Pauline corpus.

From the outset, Paul affirms God's sanctifying work among the Corinthians: they are both made "holy" (1:2; NRSV, "sanctified") in Christ and called "holy ones" (1:2; NRSV, "saints"; cf. Lev 19; Exod 19:5–6). Moreover, Paul binds them to "all those who in every place call on the name of our Lord Jesus Christ" (1:2).

B. Thanksgiving (1:4–9)

Paul continues his emphasis on God's activity among his audience by giving thanks "because of the grace of God that has been given you in Christ Jesus" (1:4). Already, Paul reminds the Corinthians that their status before God depends not on their own accomplishments, but rather on the free gift of God in Christ. In the claims that the Corinthians have been "enriched ... in speech and knowledge" (1:5) and are "not lacking in any spiritual gift" (1:7), Paul engages his audience on their own terms, telegraphing sources of the divisions he will address in the letter (e.g., 1:10–11; 3:3; 8:1). Here he identifies their riches with the grace of God and finds evidence of their spiritual abundance in the "testimony of Christ ... strengthened among you" (1:6). Their true wealth manifests itself not in their own aggrandizement but in the extent to which their lives bear witness to Christ.

Paul also introduces, at this early juncture, reminders of the eschatological nature of the gospel, reminding the Corinthians that they await the "revealing of our Lord Jesus Christ" (1:7) and the "day of our Lord Jesus Christ" (1:8). The thanksgiving concludes by affirming that, "God is faithful; by him you were called into the fellowship of his Son, Jesus Christ our Lord" (1:9). The term *fellowship* translates the Greek *koinōnia*, which implies not just social interaction but shared spiritual participation in the pattern of Christ's life, death, and resurrection (cf. 10:16). Though Paul casts these verses as thanksgiving, they also (though subtly) begin the task of critique that will characterize the letter.

II. Mending the Body (1:10–4:21)

This section features the first in a series of responses to reports—both written and oral—about the nature of the Corinthian Christians' life together. Here, "Chloe's people" have informed the apostle about divisions (1:11) that plague the community. Besides repeated and direct appeals for unity (1:10–17; 3:1–9), Paul recalls for the Corinthians the source of that unity, which is the apocalyptic "wisdom" of Christ's self-emptying death (1:18–2:16). And he models that pattern in his own apostleship (4:1–13), in turn enjoining the Corinthians to be "imitators of me" (4:16) so that they too might embody the foolish wisdom of the cross.

A. Quarrels and Factions (1:10–17)

Paul first addresses the problem of factionalism with a positive appeal for the Corinthians to "be in agreement" (1:10). Here as throughout the passage, Paul employs standard political idiom to promote cohesiveness among the community. Though the term *body* does not yet appear here, both the noun *schismata* (1:10; NRSV, "divisions"; see also 11:18; 12:25) and the participle *katērtismenoi* (1:10; NRSV, "be united") denote the restoration of a human body to its intended condition of wholeness.

The section also exposes the nature of the divisions that plague the community, as Paul quotes slogans that align individual believers with leaders in their midst. In light of the underlying image of the community as an integrated whole, Paul's reference to "each of you" (1:12) is striking. While it is probably not the case that the Corinthians belong to organized parties, Paul mentions allegiances to himself, to Apollos (see Acts 18:24–19:1; 1 Cor 3:4–6, 22; 4:6; 16:12), to Cephas (mentioned also in 3:22; 9:5; 15:5; cf. Gal 2:11–14), and even to Christ, in exclusive terms that subvert the gospel message. When Paul asks, "Has Christ been divided?" (1:13), he may imply two answers: a negative—since Christ has not been divided, neither should the Corinthians be—and a positive—as Christ's "body" on earth (see 12:1–9), their division has torn Christ himself asunder. In either case, their problem of social division matters precisely because they constitute the "body of Christ" in the world.

The rest of the passage militates against the notion that the one who baptizes new believers thereby wins their exclusive loyalty. Since Paul emphasizes *God's* redemptive work, he maintains that baptism, as the outcome of apostolic work, is of secondary concern to his primary calling: the proclamation of the gospel (1:17). With this claim, Paul subtly redirects attention from the matter of human authority to the heart of his message, which is the cross of Christ.

B. Christ Crucified: the Wisdom of God (1:18–2:16)

Having identified the problem of the Corinthians' factionalism, Paul begins to elaborate his "message about the cross" as the interpretive solution to that problem. The argument moves beyond theological musings toward the practical implications of this message for the Corinthian community. First, he stresses the motif of apocalyptic reversal entailed in God's wisdom, now personified in a crucified messiah (1:18–25). Second, he recalls for his audience the evidence of that reversal at work in their own call (1:26–31). Third, Paul sketches the contours of his own apostleship in a cruciform pattern (2:1–5). And finally, he draws attention to revelatory work of the spirit within the human sphere (2:6–16).

1:18–25. Paul begins this section by acknowledging sharply opposing responses to "the message about the cross" (1:18; *ho logos ho tou staurou*), and in turn highlighting the sacrificial nature of God's *logos*. The use of present participles (1:18: *those who are perishing; those who are being saved*) subtly recalibrates the Corinthians' eschatological timeframe, as he reminds the Corinthians that they still await the outcome of salvation (cf. 1:7–8). Further, both the citation from Isa 29:14 (1:19; the first on this letter's relatively short list of scriptural references) and the phrase "this age" frame the Corinthians' present existence within an apocalyptic scheme (cf. 10:24).

Paul devotes much of this section to the topic of wisdom. Summoning the "one who is wise," the "scribe," and the "debater of this age," Paul targets figures whose acclaim lies in the "wisdom of the world" (1:20). Their status as the educated elite, though, proves inadequate to the only goal that matters for Paul: the knowledge of God (1:20–21). Not only does human wisdom fail to grasp God's wisdom, but it also produces a pretense that construes the notion of a crucified messiah as "foolishness" and a "stumbling block." Only "those who are called" can perceive in Christ—that is, in his death—"the power of God and the wisdom of God" (1:24). Once again, Paul maintains that God has turned on end human notions of power and wisdom, replacing them with the divine foolishness and weakness that comprise the "message about the cross."

1:26–31. Paul now invites the Corinthians to reflect on the implications of God's wisdom for their own call (cf. 1:2). When he writes, "not many of you were wise by human standards, not many were powerful, not many were of noble birth" (1:26), Paul both tacitly acknowledges the elevated worldly status of *some* Corinthian Christians and underscores the subversive ways of a God who has chosen "what is foolish in the world to shame the wise ... what is weak in the world to shame the strong ... [and] what is low and despised in the world ... to reduce to nothing things that are" (1:27–28). To support the notion that this reversal of human power structures precludes boasting, Paul invokes the prophecy of Jeremiah: "Let the one who boasts, boast in the Lord" (Jer 9:24). "The Lord" probably refers to God (1:29), since Paul ascribes to God the Corinthians' "life in Christ Jesus" (1:30).

2:1–5. Paul correlates the logic of the cross with the method and content of his own proclamation. In Greek, the word order of 1 Cor 2:1 is reversed, stressing that it is "not according to lofty words or wisdom" that he came "proclaiming the mystery of God." Again, Paul challenges cherished cultural values such as polished rhetoric and conventional wisdom, which he believes are at odds with the wisdom of God (cf. 1:5, 17, 18; 21; 26).

For Paul, that wisdom consists in the one thing he claims to have known among the Corinthians, "Jesus Christ, and him crucified" (2:2), a claim as jarring, as one interpreter puts it, as "fried ice." For Paul, the notion of a crucified messiah is reflected in the cruciform shape of his apostolic mission. The language here is telling: by noting his own "weakness," "fear," and "trembling" (2:3), together with the failure of his "speech and proclamation" to be "persuasive" (2:4; NRSV, "plausible"), Paul carefully distinguishes between human resourcefulness and divine power. In Paul's witness, as in Christ's, God's power works most palpably in human weakness as it promotes faith that rests "not on human wisdom but on the power of God" (2:5).

Throughout the passage, Paul deliberately recalls his proclamation to the Corinthians in personal terms, addressing them directly in 2:1

("when I came to you"), 2:2 ("decided to know nothing among you"), 2:3 ("I came to you"), and 2:5 ("your faith"). Through such direct relational appeal, Paul submits his own apostolic witness—both in content and in delivery—as a pattern for them to emulate.

2:6–16. Having disclaimed any pretense to wise speech, Paul redefines wisdom in decidedly apocalyptic terms, denying that it belongs to "this age" or to the "rulers of this age" (2:6), while calling it "secret and hidden" yet "decreed before the ages" (2:7). The contrast implies that, in the gospel of a crucified Christ, the present evil age begins to yield to the new age of God (cf. 10:24), since "these things God has revealed (*apekalypsen*) to us through the Spirit" (2:10).

Paul presupposes an apocalyptic divide between the "spirit of the world" and the "Spirit ... from God" (2:12). Both divine and human realms are animated by s/Spirit, yet while the human spirit understands only human matters, God's Spirit discerns all things divine. Rather than through human acumen, it is through the Spirit of God that believers "understand the gifts bestowed on us by God" (2:12). Moreover, Paul differentiates his own Spirit-taught speech from speech taught by human wisdom (2:13). And he juxtaposes the human ruled by the psyche (*psychikos anthrōpos*; 2:14), who does not receive the "things of God's Spirit" (2:14; NRSV, "gifts of God's Spirit"), with the spiritual one (*pneumatikos*; 2:15), whose amenability to the "Spirit of God" makes it possible to understand or discern "all things" (*ta panta*; 2:15).

For Paul, Christ bridges the chasm between the human and divine realms, and in his closing reminder that "we have the mind of Christ" (2:16), he probably refers not just to himself and his apostolic co-workers, but also to his audience. Rhetorically, he appeals to their identity "in Christ," as those "taught by the Spirit" (2:13); thus, God has empowered them to discern divine wisdom as it turns on end the human wisdom so widely vaunted within their own social context.

C. Jealousy, Quarrels and Factions (3:1–23)

Having established the source of spiritual discernment, Paul returns to the pressing issue of division among the Corinthians by way of frontal attack: their factionalism, evident in "jealousy and quarreling" (3:3), reflects behavior shaped by "human inclinations" (3:3). Throughout the chapter, he employs workplace metaphors to recast apostolic leadership within the larger framework of God's redemptive purposes and thus to undermine one source of the community's divisiveness.

3:1–4. Paul diagnoses the Corinthians' spiritual condition by first recalling that he "could not speak to you as spiritual people, but rather as people of the flesh, as infants in Christ" (3:1). Notably, their orientation as *fleshly* does not preclude their being *in Christ*. To be sure, they remain dependent on others for nourishment, and Paul himself has assumed the role of nursing mother, who has given them milk because they were not—and still are not—ready for solid food (3:2; cf. 1 Thess 2:7).

As evidence of such fleshly orientation, Paul revisits the problem of division that began the letter (1:10), a division rooted, in this case, in alignment with particular apostolic leaders. Though the NRSV translates the term *zēlos* as "jealousy" (3:3), Paul's diagnosis here suggests a misplaced zeal, since the word often conveys fervent belief, and sometimes in a positive light (cf. 2 Cor 7:7, 11; 9:2; 11:2; Rom 10:2; Phil 3:6). Apparently, zeal becomes problematic precisely when it becomes divisive, particularly when Corinthian Christians direct their zeal toward their presumed leaders by claiming, "I belong to Apollos" or "I belong to Paul" (3:4; cf. 1:12). Such allegiances suggest that the Corinthians are "merely human" (3:4), a condition that contrasts sharply for Paul with the new life in Christ.

3:5–17. Through a series of three metaphors, Paul affirms the shared nature of the apostolic task, which is to promote God's redemptive agenda. First, he depicts both Apollos and himself as "servants" (*diakonoi*; 3:5) who labor for a mutual Lord, thus placing their respective authority squarely within the overarching authority of God. Invoking agricultural imagery to emphasize their role as workers in God's field, Paul goes so far as to claim (perhaps hyperbolically?) that neither the one who plants nor the one who waters "is anything, but only God who gives the growth" (3:7). Moreover, he underscores the "common purpose" (3:8) that he shares with Apollos, calling them "co-workers" (*synergoi*; 3:9) who toil in the same soil of God's field. The deliberate distinction between apostolic labor and its yield may offer a rare Pauline allusion to gospel traditions (see esp. Mark 4:1–30; cf. 7:10; 11:23–26).

Paul next uses the image of God's building (3:9b–15) to express the nature of the apostolic task. After reminding the Corinthians about God's calling grace (3:10; cf. 1:4; 15:10; Rom 1:5; 12:3; 15:15; Gal 1:15; 2:9), Paul portrays himself as a builder who has laid a foundation upon which others now build. His language holds in delicate tension both the shared nature of this building enterprise, based on a common foundation of Jesus Christ (3:11), and the respective choices of "each one" (3:10; NRSV, "each builder") involved in the building task. In the progression of materials selected—"gold, silver, precious stones, wood, hay, straw" (3:12)—Paul implies that some apostolic efforts may be more durable than others. Still, neither he nor the Corinthians will ultimately assess "what sort of work each has done" (3:13); judgment will come only with the eschatological "day" (3:13), when faulty construction will be destroyed and "the builder will suffer loss," yet "the builder will be saved ... through fire" (3:15). The final judgment itself functions not so much to condemn *people* as to disclose the true nature of their *work*, and thus to lead to their ultimate salvation (cf. 5:5).

Finally, Paul identifies the nature of God's building by depicting the Corinthians, collectively, as God's "temple" in whom "God's Spirit dwells" (3:16). The use of the plural pronoun you in these verses reflects Paul's communal concern. Further, despite his earlier discussion of the Corinthians' behavior as human rather than spiritual, he here reaffirms that the Spirit does reside in their midst (cf. 2:12). In the claim that God will destroy the "person" who destroys God's temple (3:17), the NRSV supplies a definite noun that is lacking in the Greek. Especially in light of the impulse for salvation discussed above (cf. 3:15), Paul may suggest the impending eradication of any corrupting *influence* (cf. 2 Cor 11:3) rather than the destruction of a *person* (false apostle?) per se.

3:18–23. Paul once again challenges the wisdom of "this age" and "of this world" by claiming it is "foolishness with God" (cf. 1:18–25). After an appeal to Israel's wisdom tradition (3:19–20; cf. Job 5:13 and Psalm 94:11), he offers this pointed exhortation: "Let no one boast with respect to human beings" (3:21; NRSV, "about human leaders"). The startling claim that "all things are yours" (3:21) once again reverses the power dynamics of the leader-servant relationship by maintaining that human leaders, along with "the world or life or death or the present or the future—all belong to you (pl.)" (3:22). Lest the Corinthians begin to invoke "lordship" for themselves, though, the apostle closes with a pointed reminder: "you (pl.) belong to Christ and Christ belongs to God" (3:23). Paul has taken the Corinthians' *individual* loyalty to apostolic *human* leaders (3:4) and refashioned it as a *collective* allegiance to *God*.

D. Cruciform Apostleship (4:1–21)

This chapter proceeds organically from earlier discussions about true apostleship, as Paul continues to root out division by addressing its flawed basis in the measuring of one apostle's work against another. Instead, he promotes a cruciform standard for apostleship that he will also apply to the Corinthians themselves.

4:1–7. Having insisted that everything "belongs to God" (3:23), Paul addresses the specific issue of judging. Though the Corinthians have apparently measured him against Apollos, he once again emphasizes what is common to them as "servants" and "stewards" of God's mysteries (cf. 3:9; 4:6). Noting the importance of apostolic faithfulness (4:2), Paul insists that it falls neither to the Corinthians nor to himself to discern the extent of that faithfulness, for it is "the Lord who judges" (4:5). Moreover, he corrects not just the Corinthians' judging tendencies but their timeframe as well, reminding them of decisive judgment that will yet occur when the Lord "comes" (4:5). Paul repeats here the positive outcome of that judging mentioned above: "each one will receive commendation from God" (4:5; cf. 3:15).

Paul reworks the Corinthians' schematic plans for apostolic assessment, since he has "applied (*meteschēmatisa*) these things to myself and to Apollos for your benefit" (4:6; NRSV, "to Apollos and myself"), thus confronting their adversarial pitting of "one against another" (4:6). His point is that they might "learn through us the meaning of the saying, 'nothing beyond what is written'" (4:6), a decidedly obscure reference that may refer back to Paul's earlier scriptural citations concerning boasting, or more broadly to his exhortation on the topic to this point in the letter. Whatever specific content he has in mind, one thing is clear: for Paul, "what is written" challenges the kind of puffing up that sets Corinthians, or their leaders, against each other.

A series of three rhetorical questions drives home Paul's message, though the first presents a translational challenge. According to the NRSV, Paul asks, "For who sees anything different in you?" (4:7a). Yet the Greek is far leaner: "For who distinguishes (*diakrinei*) you (sing.)?" Perhaps Paul implies that, since distinction among the Corinthians lies exclusively within God's purview, they overstep bounds of authority by forging distinctions among themselves. This reading makes clearer sense of the two questions that conclude the verse: "What do you have that you did not receive? And if you received it, why do you boast as if it were not a gift?" (4:7b–c) Together, these pointed queries indicate that boasting has no place among those whose status before God comes not through their own wisdom or resourcefulness but through the grace of God (see above, 1:4).

4:8–13. From such a scathing indictment of their boasting, Paul moves toward a distinction of his own, as he sharply contrasts the Corinthians' present status (4:8) with the status of "us apostles" (4:9). Three rhetorical questions drip with irony as they indict the Corinthians' pretense: "Do you already have all you want? Have you already become rich? Have you become kings apart from us?" (4:8; the NRSV presents the clauses as ironic statements). The underlying claims, with their accompanying hint of realized eschatology, drive a rhetorical wedge between the Corinthians' self-promotion and Paul's authentic, self-sacrificial pattern of apostleship.

The turning point of this passage comes as Paul reaffirms that "God has exhibited us apostles as last of all, as though sentenced to death" (4:9a), clearly aligning authentic apostleship with the plight of a crucified messiah. Moreover, it is this pattern of self-sacrifice, rather than the scheme of wealth and power embraced by some Corinthians, that constitutes the "theater" (*theatron*; 4:9b; NRSV, "spectacle") in which God's redemptive purposes have been performed for the world. As he sharply contrasts the apostles' condition (4:10;

"fools for the sake of Christ," "weak," "in disrepute") with the Corinthians' ("wise in Christ," "strong," "held in honor"), Paul caricatures the difference between God's wisdom and worldly acclaim. He drives home the point by emphasizing both the apostles' enduring deprival (4:11–12) and their self-denying response to mistreatment (4:12*b*–13*a*; cf. Luke 6:28; Rom 12:14).

A concluding statement about the apostolic role merits reflection: "We have become like the rubbish (*perikatharmata*) of the world, the dregs (*peripsēma*) of all things, to this very day" (4:13). Though these two Greek words are elsewhere unattested in the NT, and only scantly in the LXX, they share a loose association with purification that comes through unseemly sacrifice. Such graphic lexical choices, then, associate the perils of authentic apostleship with the scandalous, but sanctifying, ways of God's wisdom.

4:14–21. Paul concludes the first section of the letter with a strong relational appeal by casting his rebuke in thoroughly parental terms: "to admonish you as my beloved children" (4:14). As their "father" (4:15; cf. 3:2), he exhorts them to "be imitators of me" (4:16) and introduces his child Timothy, whom he will send "to remind you of my ways in Christ Jesus" (4:17). Lest the Corinthians infer Timothy's visit suggests that Paul parents from a distance, though, he adds quickly, "I will come to you soon, if the Lord wills" (4:19). He strikes a balance, too, between his preference to engage the Corinthians in a "spirit of gentleness" on the one hand and his willingness to wield an authoritarian "stick" (4:21) on the other. In any case, Paul's fundamental response to the Corinthians' divisiveness is to embody the "message about the cross" (1:18) as their ultimate source of unity.

III. Glorifying God in the Body (5:1–11:1)

Building on the foundation of his sustained appeal for unity, Paul shifts gears to address a wide-ranging list of practical concerns that arise out of reports, both oral and written, that he has received about the Corinthian Christians' conduct. Within these chapters, Paul continues to deploy the self-sacrificial logic of the cross as plumb line against which he assays the community's behavior, even as he urges his hearers to exercise the same kind of judgment among themselves. In each case, such discernment ultimately serves the larger purpose of promoting wholeness within the community, which in turn embodies God's saving impulse for the world.

A. Judging Immoral Behavior (5:1–6:20)

The first major section in this unit weaves together disparate concerns about the community's conduct, as Paul stakes out clear moral ground on sexual as well as legal matters. Taken together, the separate contingencies that provide the outline of this section indicate that, for Paul, the body matters; that is, as a community whose life is patterned after the apocalyptic reality of Christ crucified, the Corinthian Christians' practices ought to manifest God's glory in the world.

5:1–13. To detect in 1 Cor 5:1 the beginning of a second major section in the letter is not to deny that this opening verse flows naturally from the end of chapter four, where a parental Paul has threatened to bring a disciplining rod. Indeed, his rhetoric in the subsequent discussion does feature sharp verbal rebuke. Moreover, Paul continues to express concern over the arrogant posture at least some Corinthians strike toward objectionable conduct in their midst (5:2; cf. 4:18). In Paul's view, their problem lies not just in the sexual immorality itself (*porneia*; 5:1)—immorality that puts the Gentiles to shame—but, perhaps even more alarmingly, in their celebration of the offensive habit. While readers may be inclined to focus on the individual offenders and the egregiousness of their sin, Paul views the situation primarily through the lens of its impact on the community as body of Christ.

Several aspects of Paul's argumentation shift the weight of his judgment from the offender(s) to those who have accommodated the offense. In the first place, already in 1 Cor 5:2, Paul turns from the man sleeping with his father's wife to those who tolerate, or even celebrate, such licentious behavior. As he has before, Paul employs direct address to contrast the Corinthians' presumption with the response he deems more fitting: their mourning and removal of such sin from their midst (5:2).

Since they have failed to exercise that authority, Paul weighs in with a commanding judgment of his own. Despite his physical absence, he asserts that he is indeed "present in spirit" (5:3), probably referring both to his own spirit and to the

Spirit of God who serves as mediator (cf. 3:16). In any case, he offers a definitive rendering: "I have already pronounced judgment" (5:3). The ambiguous placement of the phrase, "in the name of the Lord Jesus Christ" (5:4), presents an exegetical challenge. Some interpreters, including the NRSV translators, read the phrase as an effort to enhance Paul's authority ("I have already pronounced judgment in the name of the Lord Jesus"). Others infer that the offender himself has predicated his sexual liberty on that same lordship ("the man who has done such a thing in the name of the Lord Jesus"). A third possibility has the phrase expressing the nature of the gathered community ("when you are assembled in the name of the Lord Jesus"). Though a clear resolution of the matter proves elusive, Paul's judgment stands squarely at the interface of the man's misdeeds and the community's response.

The ensuing instructions clearly illuminate Paul's communal concerns, since he anchors his command to "hand this man over to Satan for the destruction of the flesh" (5:5a), in the motivating clause that follows: "so that his spirit may be saved in the day of the Lord" (5:5b). While the NRSV supplies the possessive pronoun *his* to suggest that Paul focuses on the offender's salvation, a more accurate translation of the Greek ("*the* spirit") leaves the spirit's identity more obscure. In light of the passage's prevailing communal concerns—concerns which will be elaborated in the next three verses—it may be more prudent to place greater emphasis on the benefits (even "salvation") that accrue to the Corinthian body through the eradication of evil.

Paul next appeals to the story of Israel to depict the kind of salvation he has in view. Using the metaphor of bread to convey the deleterious effects of the "yeast" of sexual immorality on the batch of dough that is the Corinthian congregation, Paul maintains, "you really are unleavened" (5:7); by adding evocative Passover language ("paschal lamb," "sacrifice," "celebrate the festival"), he depicts both Christ and the Corinthians as active participants in Israel's sacramental story. In essence, Paul prods his hearers to recalibrate their moral compass so that it takes its bearings not from surrounding Gentile culture but from the landscape of Jewish scripture, which promotes

"sincerity and truth" rather than "malice and evil" (5:8).

Paul reiterates communal concerns as he clarifies previous instructions to the Corinthians about sexual immorality. Continuing with bread-baking imagery, he recalls what he wrote previously— "not to be mixed with sexually immoral persons" (5:9; NRSV, "be associated with")—before moving quickly to correct possible misunderstandings. Here, Paul broadens the question of morality to include not just sexual offense but also greed, idolatry, robbery, reviling, and drunkenness (5:10–11). In so doing, he seems to divert attention from a particularly salacious incident (i.e., sleeping with one's stepmother) toward the more pervasive patterns of self-satisfying human compulsions. Even as he emphasizes the need for judgment against the offender in question, he situates sexual immorality within a moral framework that likely indicts others within the community.

Even more significantly, Paul works to differentiate the respective jurisdictions of human and divine judging. Though earlier in the letter (4:1–5), Paul has denied the Corinthians the right to judge (him), citing instead the authority of God's eschatological judgment, here he reworks his position. With respect to behaviors in the community, Paul asks, "Is it not those inside that you are to judge?" (5:12), even as he insists, "God will judge those outside" (5:13). Such a shift in thinking reflects Paul's adaptive pastoral strategies. Without denying the decisive weight of God's end-time, universal judgment, he also keeps an eye on the meantime witness of the Corinthian community, a witness that is compromised to the extent that it tolerates, or even celebrates, self-indulgent conduct.

6:1–11. Though the topic at hand shifts from sexual licentiousness to legal disputes among believers, Paul offers further input on the Corinthians' own judgment. Whereas he has reiterated the call to judge immoral behavior within the community (5:12–13), now Paul charges them not to submit to the judgment of the *unrighteous* (*adikōn*; 6:1) but rather to resolve their disputes internally by deploying their own God-given judgment.

Paul's language telegraphs keen frustration with the Corinthians' glib accommodation to judgment by outsiders. Six times within this chapter (6:2, 3, 9, 15, 16, 19) he asks, almost in disbelief, "Do you not know ...?" (The question appears only eleven times in the Pauline corpus and nine times in this letter.) Likely, the phrasing is a play on words, intended as a subtle critique of the "knowledge" on which the Corinthians apparently pride themselves (cf. 1:5; 8:1; 13:2).

Paul's apocalyptic worldview construes creation in dualities. One group, those outside, are both "unrighteous" (6:1) and "unbelievers" (6:6) and thus lack the capacity to mete out God's judgment. On the other hand, the Corinthians are "holy ones" (6:2; NRSV, "saints"; cf. 1:2), who have been endowed with judgment. For Paul, the Corinthians' submission to judgment by outsiders is just as misguided as their rendering judgments *against* them would be (cf. 5:13). The two groups operate, in his view, under different jurisdictions, and he deems their legal decisions to be irreconcilable.

That is not to say, though, that Paul means to keep the spheres separate. Already, he has overtly denied any such impulse (5:10). And his consternation in this passage stems partly from the (negative) witness the Corinthian Christians' disputes reflect in the Gentile court of law. When he says it is "to your shame" (6:5) that he even broaches the topic, Paul implicitly includes the non-believing outsiders among those who notice the division within a congregation that should, according to the logic of the cross, be united. More than that, he calls the very existence of legal disputes "a defeat for you" (6:7). Where the Corinthians have the opportunity to be "wronged" or "defrauded" without seeking retribution, they apparently exercise injustices themselves, even among themselves (6:7; cf. 4:12–13). Though Paul does not make the point outright, the language here also hints at economic oppression by those in positions of power; such a dynamic of social stratification would only further fan the flames of Paul's ire (cf. 11:21–22).

The discussion about lawsuits concludes with a pointed reminder that the unrighteous "will not inherit the kingdom of God" (6:9). Though the section has begun with a clear distinction between outsiders (the "unrighteous") and insiders (the "saints"), here the lines of division are less clear. Paul has accused the Corinthians of injustice in the previous verse (6:8); now he employs

a traditional vice list to enumerate many of the behaviors that constitute such injustice. By casting the net of reproachful behavior far and wide, it surely ensnares some in his audience—and purposefully so.

Paul pulls back from the brink, though, attributing such conduct to the Corinthians only in hindsight: "this is what some of you used to be" (6:11). Using a series of aorist passive verbs, Paul indicates that now the Corinthians have been "washed," "sanctified," and "justified in the name of the Lord Jesus Christ and in the Spirit of our God" (6:11). That is, their standing before God comes wholly as the by-product of God's activity, not their own. Since God has claimed them, and decisively so, Paul implies that the Corinthians' behavior ought to comport with their standing as the "righteous."

6:12–20. As if aware of the dangers implicit in affirming such a status, Paul circles back to address the freedom that comes through both Christ and the Spirit. Probably he quotes a slogan the Corinthians themselves have uttered: "All things are lawful for me" (6:12*a*). Without denying the claim outright, he qualifies it: "not all things build up" (6:12*b*; NRSV, "are beneficial"; cf. 10:23; 12:7). His retort shifts the focus from the individual's prerogative to the impact one's personal conduct makes on others.

Paul's concern with bodily existence pervades the remaining verses in this chapter. Rooted in the Judaic notion of humanity's embodiment of the divine image (Gen 1:27), the notion that "body matters" finds fullest expression, for Paul, in Christ's bodily sacrifice. What is more, he reminds the Corinthians that their new life in Christ means that their "bodies are members of Christ" (6:15), implying their present bodily life continues to manifest Christ in the world. To participate in fornication (6:13, 18) or prostitution (6:15), according to Paul, is to engage in bodily sin that corrupts not just human flesh but the body, which is the "temple of the Holy Spirit" (6:19). Here the mystical and corporeal converge, and as a result, any claims to personal licentiousness fade from view.

B. Promoting Morality in Marriage (7:1–40)

Continuing his discussion of embodied existence, Paul responds in this chapter to specific queries the Corinthians have posed about sexual morality within the context of marriage.

7:1–16. The section opens with a slogan that the Corinthians have apparently quoted to Paul in their correspondence: "It is well for a man not to touch a woman" (7:1*b*). Though scholars disagree about whether the claim originated (1) with Paul, (2) with an ascetic contingent in the community, or (3) in the Corinthians' misinterpretation of Paul's teachings, he moves swiftly to clarify his positive position about sex within the marriage relationship. Probably still mulling the offenses addressed earlier, he maintains that "because of cases of sexual immorality" (7:2*a*), husbands and wives should exercise mutual sexual fulfillment.

Paul's view of sexuality in marriage is strikingly balanced in terms of gender roles, since the apostle crafts his recommendations so that they address not just the husband but the wife as well ("each man ... each woman," 7:2; "husband should give ... likewise the wife," 7:3; "wife does not have authority ... likewise the husband," 7:4). Especially in contrast with the cultural accommodation evident in later NT household codes (Eph 5:24; Col 3:18; 1 Pet 3:1, 6), this series of syntactical parallels expresses a degree of mutual authority and sexual prerogative that is unusual for its setting.

Though some interpreters believe that Paul calls marriage itself a "concession" (7:6)—as a lifestyle that is inferior to celibacy—the word "this" (*touto*) that opens the verse probably refers instead to the practice of mutual sexual denial "by agreement for a set time" (7:5). That is, he concedes sexless marriage, but only temporarily and under the right circumstances. Besides making better sense grammatically, this reading fits well with what follows, where Paul affirms not just celibacy but also the "particular gift from God" (7:7) that takes different, and implicitly equal, forms. Certainly he understands his celibacy as a gift, but so too does he affirm the gift of marriage, where sexuality as part of the God-given bodily existence finds pure expression.

As Paul turns to the matter of divorce, we find another rare allusion to the teachings of Jesus (cf. Mark 10:2–12; Matt 5:31–32, 19:3–9). Once again Paul promotes the marriage ideal while leaving room for the practical contingencies of real life. He first maintains that "the wife should not separate from her husband" (7:10), adding quickly that a divorced wife should remain unmarried or be reconciled to her husband (7:11). Some take this primary focus on women to reflect Paul's concern about Corinthian women who had taken their "freedom in Christ" to an extreme. Such a reconstruction, though, seems to overreach the evidence. More likely, Paul simply repeats his tendency (cf. 7:2–5) to vacillate between genders in this discussion of marriage between believing spouses.

Paul devotes even more attention to the durability of "mixed" marriages—between believers and non-believers—where he stakes out ethical ground that manifests the "message about the cross." Of greater importance than the institution of marriage per se, for Paul, are the human destinies affected through marriage. For believing husbands and wives married to willing unbelievers, Paul recommends remaining in marriage (7:12–13). The motivation he supplies has stumped interpreters: "for the unbelieving husband is made holy through his wife ..." and "wife, for all you know, you might save your husband" (7:14, 16). As some have noted, this contagion of holiness seems in tension with the letter's earlier suggestion that immorality is contagious (5:6). But there is here no indication of immorality on the part of the unbelieving spouse; once again, Paul underscores the witness that believers bear as members of the body of a self-sacrificing, reconciling messiah: "it is to peace that God has called you" (7:15).

7:17–40. The remainder of the chapter is sprinkled with allusive eschatological claims, which together establish the backdrop against which Paul forges all moral and ethical advice. While he has more to say in these verses about sex, marriage, and abstinence, the apostle grounds his instruction in his conviction about the impending salvation of Corinthian believers. Thus the recurring injunction to "remain as you are" (7:20; cf. 7:8, 11, 24, 40), that is, "in whatever condition you were called" (7:24), takes its cues from the impending eschatological "crisis" (7:26).

Paul's chief concern for the unmarried, widowed, divorced, and even the married, is that they live lives of "unhindered devotion to the Lord" (7:35) within the short span of eschatological time, since "the present form of this world is passing away" (7:31). Through his teaching, Paul promotes freedom from unnecessary anxieties on the one hand (7:32–34) and ardent extra-marital passion (7:36) on the other. As he has earlier in the chapter, Paul here advocates an ideal of unchanging social status, while demurring from any impulse "to put any restraint on you" (7:35).

In the midst of this discussion about marital status, Paul tackles two other matters that relate to the Corinthians' social status: circumcision and slavery. In the first instance, he denies both that circumcised believers should seek to undo their circumcision and that uncircumcised believers should seek circumcision (7:18). In either case, Paul views such concern with the foreskin, and the social status or embarrassment associated with it, as a distraction from the true calling of faith, which he identifies here as "obeying the commandments of God" (7:19).

Paul's directive to slaves proves more befuddling—to ancient as well as modern readers. The interpretive crux lies in the Greek phrase *mallon chrēsai* (7:21), an elliptical suggestion for slaves either (1) to remain enslaved even if freedom is possible ("it is better to use [your present circumstance]"; NRSV, "make use of your present condition [i.e., your slavery] now more than ever"), or (2) to seize the opportunity for freedom ("all the more, use [your freedom]"; NRSV note "avail yourself of the opportunity [to be freed]"). Despite the offense to contemporary readers' sensibilities, Paul probably intended that slaves, too, should "remain in the condition in which you were called" (7:20). Such a reading both coheres with the chapter's overarching bias against changing social status and makes better sense of the verse that follows, where Paul suggests that slaves experience a spiritual freedom in Christ, even when their social function remains in tact (7:22). Conversely, believers who are "free" in social terms are spiritual slaves to Christ. When Paul commands his hearers not to "become slaves of human masters" (7:23), he affirms the "slavery" of all believers to God and thus locates true power in that slavery, rather than in the human institution that was central to Roman society.

Paul devotes the rest of this section to casting decisions about marriage within his short-term eschatological landscape, in which "the appointed time has grown short" (7:29). The passage reflects his sustained attempt to balance the ideal, which is "unhindered devotion to the Lord" (7:35), with the realistic pull of human passion (7:36). Put simply, Paul writes that the unmarried man "who marries his fiancée does well [but] he who refrains from marriage will do better" (7:38). Applying the same standards to the widow, Paul writes, "in my judgment she is more blessed if she remains as she is" (7:40).

Paul's refusal to draw a line in the sand on the matter of marriage is telling. More important to the apostle than immutable injunctions to marry or not to marry is the concern that believers "be holy in body and spirit" (7:34) in light of the coming judgment. To the degree that marriage promotes anxieties "about the affairs of the world" (7:34), Paul finds it to detract from the proper concerns with "the affairs of the Lord" (7:32). But to the degree that, apart from marriage, the flames of passion rage, the freedom to marry safeguards bodily purity, which Paul views as critical to the end-time salvation that remains his overarching concern.

C. The Problem of Idol Food and Worship (8:1–11:1)

With the transitional phrase, "now concerning" (8:1; cf. 7:1), Paul shifts to the topic of idolatry, especially food sacrificed to idols. Yet once again, Paul will not prescribe strict regulation. Rather than fixed behavioral guidelines, he promotes his own pattern of self-sacrifice as the governing principle for the community's conduct. To the degree that they invoke "freedom" not to justify their own choices but to serve the interests of the weak in their midst, the Corinthians build one another up in the unity that Christ intends.

8:1–13. Paul uses two separate terms to introduce the topic at hand: *tōn eidōlothytōn* ("idol sacrifices"; 8:1) and *tēs brōseōs … tōn eidōlothytōn*, ("food of idol sacrifices"; 8:4). Though the NRSV translates the first expression as "food sacrificed to idols," the difference in the Greek indicates that, in 1 Cor 8:1–3, Paul broaches the topic of idolatry more broadly understood *before* turning to particular concerns about idol meat. In any case, the opening verse provides the ethical framework for the ensuing discussion: "knowledge puffs up, but love builds up" (8:1).

Apparently since they "know that, 'no idol in the world really exists'" (8:4), some Corinthians have justified either consuming food previously sacrificed to idols or participating in temple meals. Paul begins to address the issue by making a case for unity that is anchored in the oneness of God. As Paul contrasts the "many gods and many lords" (8:5) of Greek religious life with the central Jewish affirmation that "there is no God but one" (8:4; cf. Deut 6:4), he exposes the nature of idolatry even as he sets forth exclusive loyalty to "the one God, the Father ... and one Lord, Jesus Christ" (8:6) as the foundation of the social appeal that follows.

In Paul's view, ingestion of idol meat, or any food for that matter, is morally neutral: "Food will not bring us close to God" (8:8). Yet he evaluates the question at hand in light of the fundamental problem it exposes: the stratified nature of the Corinthian Christian community. Central to Paul's discussion of the eating of idol meat is his qualification of "this liberty of yours" (8:9), which may not be invoked so that it becomes a "stumbling block to the weak" (8:9). On the one hand, those with "knowledge" (8:1, 7, 11) rightly deny the existence of idols and thus divest the idol meat of any spiritual power; on the other hand, when such knowledge leads to their "eating in the temple of an idol" (8:10), it is to the detriment—even destruction (8:11)—of those whose weak "conscience" (8:7, 12) makes them susceptible to returning to idol worship (8:10). Thus he finds that, even if for them eating idol meat is a morally neutral activity, when viewed in light of its deleterious effect upon "your family" (8:12), the act becomes a "sin against Christ" (8:12; cf. Rom 14:15). The chapter concludes as Paul states his own willingness to forego eating meat "so that I may not cause one of them to fall" (8:13).

9:1–27. In the midst of his discussion of idolatry and idol foods, Paul presents an "apology" (*apologia*, 9:3; NRSV, "defense") for his own model of sacrificial servanthood as a template for the conduct of the Corinthians. Here the "message about the cross" (1:18) takes on embodied form in Paul's willingness to forsake personal prerogatives whenever they pose an "obstacle in the way of the gospel of Christ" (9:12).

Paul first aligns himself with those Corinthians whose "liberty" (*exousia*; 8:9) authorizes their eating of idol food: "Am I not free?" (9:1).

Through a series of rhetorical questions, Paul emphasizes his "right" (*exousian*; 9:4) to be accompanied by a believing wife (9:5) as well as to receive payment for his apostolic labors (9:4, 6–7). Moreover, he invokes the law of Moses, which he deems to be "written for our sake" (9:10), as clear sanction of the "rightful claim" (*exousias*; 9:12a) he has to "reap material benefits" (9:11) from the Corinthians themselves.

Despite mounting evidence for these rights of apostleship, "Nevertheless, we have not made use of this right (*exousia*), but we endure anything rather than put an obstacle in the way of the gospel" (9:12b). In essence, Paul sacrifices his established *rights* to the embodiment of the gospel. Indeed, Paul differentiates himself from those "employed in temple service [who] get their food from the temple" (9:13), even as he implicitly violates a command of the Lord "that those who proclaim the gospel should get their living by the gospel" (9:14). Once again, Paul refracts both Jewish religious practice and Jesus' authoritative teaching through his gospel lens: when established convention impairs his witness, he freely sets it aside.

Paul explains his own apostleship in subtly cruciform terms. Maintaining that he has "made no use of any of these [rights]" (9:15a), Paul adds emphatically, "I would rather die than that" (9:15b). That Paul here signals Jesus' own exemplary death seems evident when he claims that no one will "empty" (*kenōsei*, 9:15b; cf. Phil 2:5; NRSV, "deprive me of") his boast, which lies in his determination to "make full use of my rights (*exousia*) in the gospel" (9:18) by foregoing remunerative reward. Echoing the letter's earlier injunction to "let the one who boasts boast in the Lord" (1:31), Paul adopts the Lord's pattern of self-sacrifice as the means through which the gospel might take root in the world.

Paul's apocalyptic vision of eradicating socioreligious distinction is evident in the apostolic strategy he explains in 9:19–23. Framing his interaction with different groups in the context of his own self-denial, Paul begins, "though I am free with respect to all, I have made myself a slave to all" (9:19). His strategy toward Jews, those under the law, those outside the law, and the weak shares an underlying commitment to adopt each group's standing, in an effort to "win" its members (9:19, 20, 21, 22). The NRSV translates Paul's summary explanation this way: "I do it all for the sake of the gospel, *so that I may share in its blessings*" (9:23, emphasis added). Yet in the Greek, the motivational clause might better be translated "so that I might become a partner [in the gospel]." In other words, what motivates Paul's apostolic approach is his commitment to active participation (*synkoinōnos*) in the gospel by embodying it through his own self-sacrifice.

In the chapter's concluding verses, Paul engages his audience through metaphors drawn from Corinthian culture. Probably alluding to the Isthmian games held nearby every two years, Paul urges his hearers to "run in such a way that you may win" (9:24), even as he contrasts the prize of a "perishable wreath" worn by successful athletes with the "imperishable one" (9:25; cf. 15:42, 50, 53; Phil 4:1; 1 Thess 2:19) they might win. Notably Paul invokes the example of athletic, and perhaps philosophical, self-discipline ("I punish my body and enslave it," 9:27) as he acknowledges to the Corinthians the grueling demands of the life lived in service to the benefit of others.

10:1–22. Perhaps to counter some Corinthians' pretense to knowledge (cf. esp. 8:1, 4), Paul introduces the scriptural example of Israel's wilderness idolatry by insisting, "I do not want you *not to know*" (10:1; NRSV, "to be unaware"). Here he elaborates his earlier, more allusive appeal to the law of Moses (9:8), which he views as "written for our sake" (9:10), highlighting parallels between Israel's story and the Corinthians' circumstance: like Israel in the wilderness, the Corinthians have been set free by God's saving grace; like these spiritual forebears, they have been baptized (10:2), and like them, Paul's hearers enjoy a sacramental meal that signifies God's provision (10:3–4).

Paul turns rather abruptly from these positive points of contact to the doomful destiny of the Israelites: "God was not pleased with most of them, and they were struck down in the wilderness" (10:5). For Paul, these unfaithful Israelites serve as negative examples for the Corinthians, "so that we might not desire evil as they did" (10:6). Although idolatrous eating and drinking remain in view here (10:7), Paul addresses idolatrous behavior more broadly as well, noting the disastrous outcome for those who participated in sexual immorality (cf. Num 25:1–9). Paul both

establishes a spiritual continuity, through Christ, between the Corinthians and the wilderness story (10:3) and insists and that Israel's story need not—indeed, ought not—repeat itself in the activities of Corinthian Christians.

Even as Paul sketches an unfolding salvation history as backdrop, he believes that the Corinthians stand at a decisive apocalyptic moment, as those "on whom the ends of the ages have come" (10:11). While the present evil age, exemplified in Israel's idolatrous lapses, draws to a close, God's coming age, manifest in true worship of God, has begun to break through. Moreover, because of God's faithfulness, any present experience of testing also carries with it a "way out so that [they] may be able to endure" (10:13).

To support his instruction to "flee from the worship of idols" (10:14), Paul points to the mystical power associated with the Christian memorial meal. It is important to note that the cup of blessing and the bread shared by the Corinthian community entail their participation (*koinōnia*; 10:16) in Christ and, at the same time, their unity with one another, as the "many are one" (10:17). Likewise, Paul maintains that idol food is actually sacrificed not to idols but to demons, making the respective meals mutually exclusive: "You cannot partake of the table of the Lord and the table of demons" (10:21).

10:23–11:1. Paul's response to the question about eating meat from the marketplace—meat that may or may not have been ritually sacrificed to idols—is less clear. Avoiding categorical restriction on eating marketplace meat, Paul sets forth the same criteria he has affirmed throughout the letter: does the action benefit, or build up, the community (cf. 8:7–13)? The governing principle that emerges in this discussion is the "conscience" (*syneidēsin*; 10:25, 27, 28, 29; cf. 8:7, 10, 12), a word that seems to denote the awareness of whether or not the meat has been sacrificed to idols. As long as the believer remains ignorant about the meat's status as sacrificial, it is permissible, since "The earth and its fullness are the Lord's" (10:26). Once the believer knows that the food has indeed become idol meat, though, Paul advises, "do not eat it" (10: 28).

The questions that follow seem to contradict such straightforward advice: "For why should my liberty be subject to the judgment of someone else's conscience? If I partake with thankfulness, why should I be denounced because of that for which I give thanks?" (10:29*b*–30). The two dominant interpretive possibilities are as follows: (1) the questions somehow qualify the preceding verse; or (2) they come not from Paul but from an interlocutor whose views Paul counters. The coherence of the passage depends, to some degree, on the latter interpretation, which the final—and resounding—command to "give no offense to Jews or to Greeks or to the church of God" (10:32) clearly rebuts. In seeking not his "own advantage, but that of many" (10:33), Paul sets before the Corinthians the example of Christ crucified. The freedom they have received in Christ, then, entails the freedom to offer oneself in ways that build up the community (cf. 8:1). In this respect, Paul enjoins the Corinthians to "be imitators of me, as I am of Christ" (11:1).

IV. Gathering as the Body of Christ (11:2–14:40)

This section finds thematic coherence in its concern with matters related to the gathering of the Corinthian Christians. While Paul has previously addressed the conduct of believers as they operate within broader society, here he turns to behavior when they "come together" (11:17). Though the section presents a range of issues from head coverings to meal practices to spiritual gifts, Paul continues to promote the unity of the body of Christ.

A. Head Coverings (11:2–16)

Scholars are divided on their view of the literary integrity of 1 Cor 11:3–16. Not only do the verses articulate a gender hierarchy that many find inconsistent with other Pauline claims (cf. Gal 3:28), but their excision also leaves intact an unfolding discussion of eating and drinking that precedes and follows. As it stands in the text now, though, the passage introduces a new focus on issues that arise among the gathered community.

Paul broaches the topic of head coverings by first commending the Corinthians for their faithfulness to him and to the traditions he has "handed on" to them (11:2). The precise nature of those "traditions" remains unspecified in the verses that follow, which begin with the claim that "Christ is the head of every man, and the man is the head of the woman" (11:3; NRSV, "the husband is the head of his wife"). As the passage's catch word, *head* (*kephalē*) appears nine times in 1 Cor 11:2–26 and correlates appropriate head-coverings (including hairstyles) with appropriate authority: while a woman "should let her [head] be covered" (11:6; NRSV, "wear a veil"), "a man ought not to have his head covered" (11:7; NRSV, "veiled"). The theological warrant for such differentiation can be found in the creation story: "since [man] is the image and glory (NRSV, "reflection") of God; but woman is the glory (NRSV, "reflection") of man" (11:7). By employing the philosophers' strategy of appealing to "nature" (11:14) to support the distinction, Paul confirms that both Jewish and Greco-Roman convention undergird the practice.

Some interpreters believe that the verb *katalyptein* (11:5–7) refers to the binding of long hair, rather than the wearing of a veil, and suggest that Paul promotes a distinction, through hairstyle, between the Corinthian Christian women and (temple?) prostitutes. This reading finds support in the emphasis on male "headship" (11:3, 8–9), since the impulse here would be to domesticate (unattached) women, as well as in Paul's stance on gender interdependence: "in the Lord woman is not independent of man or man independent of woman" (11:11). Similarly, the odd recommendation that the woman who will not "cover herself … should cut off her hair" (11:6; NRSV, "veil herself") makes more sense in light of this translation.

At any rate, it is worth noting that the passage assumes rather than argues the point that women are praying in public settings (11:5). And the closing verse indicates that the Corinthians' head-related issues are particular to their own cultural context and do not warrant contentious debate (11:16), either within the original setting or outside of it. Together, these observations undermine the universal applicability of this passage, even if it is authentically Pauline and original to the letter.

B. Remembering the Lord's Death (11:17–34)

The remainder of 1 Cor 11 returns to the Corinthians' eating practices, which fail to reflect the logic of the cross. If 11:3–16 constitutes an interpolation, 11:17 follows the preceding commendation (11:2) with a sharp rebuke: "Now in the following instructions I do not commend you, because when you come together it is not for the better but for the worse." Paul addresses the situation by first diagnosing the problem of social stratification at shared meals (11:18–22), next recalling the cruciform solution to that problem (11:23–26), and finally warning the Corinthians of the dire consequences for not "discerning the body" (11:29) as they partake in the shared meal (11:27–34).

Though Paul has enjoined the Corinthians to "do everything for the glory of God" (10:31), he finds that their manner of eating and drinking as a gathered community reflects not that glory but the same divisions (11:18) he has argued against from the letter's outset (1:10–13). Paul denounces the Corinthians for gathering to share a meal that is not "a supper of the Lord" (*kyriakon deipnon*, 11:20). By translating the phrase as "the Lord's supper," the NRSV diminishes the rhetorical contrast that Paul depicts between a Lord-like supper, which patterned after Christ's self-sacrifice, and the Corinthians' habits of eating one's "own supper" (*idion deipnon*) in which "one goes hungry and another becomes drunk" (11:21). Though social custom may have afforded the wealthy a certain temporal priority, the division that concerns Paul has less to do with the timing of the meal than with the gaping chasm between those who lack enough food and those who gorge themselves.

Paul invokes traditional accounts of the Last Supper (11:23–26; cf. Matt 26:26–29; Mark 14:22–25; Luke 22:15–20) as narrative correction to the Corinthian meal practices he condemns. Though some have viewed these verses as digression from social to sacramental concerns, their content demonstrates the dynamic solution Paul once again promotes within this divided community. In the command to "do *this* in remembrance of me" (11:24), the demonstrative pronoun *touto* probably refers not just to the pro forma commemorative meal but also, and more critically, to the self-sacrificing dynamic of Jesus' death: "This is my body that is *for you*" (11:24). To the extent that the Corinthians eat their meals for themselves, rather than for others, they fail to "proclaim the death of the Lord" (11:26).

Lest the Corinthians fail to reflect the Lord's pattern of self-sacrifice, Paul offers a stern warning:

when the gathered community shares its meals "in an unworthy manner"—that is, *not* according to the "message about the cross"—judgment, even condemnation, will follow (11:27). Indeed, in Paul's estimation, judgment has already begun: "For this reason many of you are weak and ill, and some have died" (11:30). Whether he refers to external divine judgment upon some offenders or, more likely, to the more intrinsic consequences for the community of not providing sustenance and resources for those who are in need, Paul urges the community to "welcome one another" (11:33; NRSV, "wait for one another") when they gather, thus transforming a self-serving, stratifying meal to a self-sacrificial meal that embodies Christ's death.

C. Spiritual Gifts Among the Members (12:1–31)

Another source of stratification within the Corinthian community apparently concerns the wielding of spiritual gifts, particularly prophecy and ecstatic speech. Paul both affirms these powers while reminding the Corinthians of the vital function of *all* gifts, which provide the "manifestation of the Spirit for the common good" (12:7; cf. 6:12; 10:23)

12:1–11. Paul counters possible suspicion about Spirit-prompted speech by contrasting the "idols that could not speak" (12:2), which belong to the former Gentile life, with the Spirit of a living God, who does speak, albeit through believers. For Paul, evidence of God's Spirit comes straight from the message itself; wherever true confession is found ("'Jesus is Lord'"), there he discerns the activity the Holy Spirit (12:3).

Next, he expands the discussion by affirming varieties of gifts (12:4), services (12:5), and activities (12:6), all of which he attributes to the same Spirit (12:4), Lord (12:5), and God (12:6). Despite his dominant concern with the community as a whole, Paul enumerates a wide variety of ways in which the Spirit operates through individuals. For Paul, participation in the Christian community need neither elide distinction among its members, nor entail formulaic criteria for religious expression. The fact that prophecy and tongues appear last among listed items (cf. 12:28, 29–30; cf. Rom 12:6–8) may indicate that some Corinthians held them in higher esteem. In any case, the paradoxical nature of Paul's message about unity through diversity finds expression in the claim that "*all* these are activated by one and the same Spirit, who allots to each *one* individually just as the Spirit chooses" (12:11).

12:12–31. Earlier in the letter (6:15; 11:29), Paul has reminded the Corinthians of their intrinsic connection to the body of Christ. Here he adopts this metaphor, often used in Greco-Roman political discourse, to promote not just the countercultural notion of interdependence but also the power reversal evident in the "greater honor" that is given to the "inferior member" (12:24).

As starting point, Paul may allude to an early baptismal tradition: "in the one Spirit we were all baptized into one body—Jews or Greeks, slaves or free—and we were all made to drink of one Spirit" (12:13; cf. 10:3–4; Gal 3:27–28). Through their conversion from a Gentile past, the Corinthians' embodied existence has taken on a spiritual dimension that entails oneness, not division (cf. 3:1–5). Paul extends the metaphor to stress not just the interrelated nature of a body's members, but their utter lack of choice in the matter: the members can dissociate neither themselves (12:15–16) nor others (12:21) from the body, since "God arranged the members in the body, each one of them, as he chose" (12:18). This fits well with Paul's view of "gifts" discussed above (12:4–6); they are given by God at the discretion of the Spirit, not according to the whims, accomplishments, or even agency of the believers.

Also significant in Paul's use of the body metaphor is the claim that the "members of the body that seem to be weaker are indispensable, and those ... that we think less honorable we clothe with greater honor" (12:22–23). Rather than discrediting weakness, as the Corinthian culture would have, Paul invokes the needs of the weaker members as the basis for unity, since the members share the "same care for one another" (12:25).

Only after fleshing out the body metaphor in detailed fashion does Paul return to the list of roles that God has appointed among the members. Having affirmed mutuality among gifts, he presents the list of gifts progressively, beginning with apostleship—perhaps not surprisingly, Paul's own office (1:1)—and moving toward prophecy and teaching, then deeds of power and gifts of healing,

as well as assistance, leadership, and finally tongues (12:28). The sequence itself may reflect chronological development—with apostleship coming *first* and tongues being given only *later*—or a hierarchy of decreasing importance. In either case, such a list would diminish the significance of tongues, which the Corinthians may have prized as superior. For Paul, though, no spiritual gift can function in isolation; each gift becomes "greater" through its use for the building up of the community, which constitutes for Paul "a more excellent way" (12:31).

D. The "More Excellent Way" (13:1–13)

As the central chapter in Paul's sustained discussion about the spiritual gifts, 1 Cor 13 provides an interpretive key for the instructions that precede and follow. Both the hymnic nature of the passage and its lack of overtly theological claims lead some interpreters to infer that Paul quotes an earlier source to serve his rhetorical purposes. As presented, though, the chapter reiterates through lofty verse Paul's earlier imperative to "seek the advantage of the other" (10:24; cf. Phil 2:1–11), this time in the deployment of spiritual gifts.

Rather than a separate manifestation of the Spirit, the chapter's overarching concept of *love* (*agapē*; mentioned nine times in thirteen verses) indicates the disposition through which believers express the work of God's Spirit among them. In Paul's view, not only does Christian community entail interdependence among spiritual gifts (12:27), but those gifts lack authentication unless expressed through love. Apart from love, even those who possess the most powerful and impressive gifts are "nothing" (13:2).

At first, love appears as something the believer "has" (13:1, 2, 3), yet it assumes a life of its own in the chapter's central section, where love becomes the subject of a series of verbs (13:4–8). Though the connection between love and God is not explicit, claims found here parallel Paul's views about God and Christ elsewhere (cf. Rom 5:8; Phil 2:6–11). This love, which is neither boastful nor arrogant nor self-serving, fits well Paul's understanding of the self-emptying "message about the cross" (1:10).

Paul returns in 13:8*b* to specific gifts of prophecy, tongues, and knowledge, which are probably best understood as synecdoche for the wider range of gifts under discussion. Perhaps these three gifts have figured more prominently in the stratification of the community, and Paul wishes here to emphasize their fleeting nature in light of the coming "end." Invoking thoroughly eschatological language, especially in the claims that prophecy and knowledge will "come to an end" (13:8), Paul understands such gifts within the drama of impending apocalyptic reversal (cf. 1:28; 2:6; 15:24). Despite their present value for the building up of the community, such gifts belong to the realm in which "we know only in part (*ek merous*) and prophesy only in part" (13:9), echoing the earlier claim that, for now, individual Corinthians are "parts" (NRSV, "members") of the body of Christ (12:27). Once again, Paul reframes the crises of the community within the broader landscape of the coming end (*teleion*, 13:10). The present age is characterized by "enigmatic" vision (*ainigmati*, 13:12; NRSV, "we see in a mirror, dimly"), while the coming age will bring the kind of clarity in which "we will see face to face" and are "fully known" (13:12).

In the meantime, Paul reminds the Corinthians that "faith, hope, and love abide, these three" (13:13; cf. Gal 5:5–6; Col 1:4–5; 1 Thess 1:3, 5:8). Taken together, this familiar triad characterizes the new life in Christ for which the Corinthians have been gifted through the Spirit. Among them, Paul maintains, it is love that is the "greatest of these" (13:13).

E. Spiritual Gifts in Worship (14:1–40)

Paul's discussion of gifts mostly focuses in this chapter on the distinction between prophecy and tongues, as he combats spiritual elitism associated with the gift of tongues. The "building up" of the community (14:3, 4 [2×], 5, 12, 17, 26; cf. 3:9; 8:1, 10; 10:23)—together with its implicit witness to outsiders—serve as touchstone against which Paul evaluates the Corinthians' giftedness.

14:1–25. Without denying "tongues" as a spiritual gift (14:5), Paul qualifies its value to the community on several grounds. In the first place, such direct address to God is shrouded in mystery which "nobody understands" (14:2), so that "those who speak in a tongue build up themselves" (14:4). In Paul's view, the merits of such private devotion are limited "unless someone interprets, so that

the church may be built up" (14:5). To develop this notion, Paul draws on musical imagery, likening tongues to "lifeless instruments that produce sound, such as the flute or the harp" (14:7). The instruments themselves are vessels through which music is produced, but only through "distinct notes" (14:7)—that is, a discernable tone, rather than an "indistinct sound" (14:8). At issue is the relationship forged between the one producing the sound and the listener. Without an understanding of the sound, Paul maintains, "I will be a foreigner to the speaker and the speaker a foreigner to me" (14:11). Once again, Paul redirects attention from the form of the Corinthians' faith toward its reconciling, unifying social function.

A second drawback Paul associates with the gift of tongues stems from his conviction that worship involves the whole person—spirit, mind, and body together. Thus, he encourages the one who speaks in tongues to "pray for the power to interpret" (14:13), involving not just the spirit but also the mind (*pneuma, nous*) in both prayer and praise (14:15; cf. 1:10; 2:16). While Paul implicitly affirms the Corinthians' own preoccupation with knowledge (cf. 1:5; 8:1, 7, 10, 11; 12:8; 13:2, 8), which belongs to the realm of the mind, he judges its merit according to usefulness for the "building up" of others (14:17).

A third factor at work in this discussion about tongues concerns "outsiders" (14:16, 23, 24) or "unbelievers" (14:22–24), probably synonymous terms for onlookers who might assess the gospel message according to its expression within the gathered community. Elsewhere in the letter, Paul has alluded only obliquely to the effects of the Corinthian Christians' witness on those outside the congregation (6:1–8; 10:27–28), but here the evangelistic nature of their conduct is in clear view. First, he notes that an outsider cannot even add an "amen" to a prayer uttered in an unintelligible tongue (14:16). On the other hand, he notes that lucid prophecy might well lead to conversion: "After the secrets of the unbeliever's heart are disclosed, that person will bow down before God and worship him" (14:25). The gifts of tongues and prophecy, Paul maintains, should not hinder the gospel message for any who might enter the community.

What, then, does Paul mean when he claims, "Tongues, then, are a sign not for believers but for unbelievers, while prophecy is not for unbelievers but for believers" (14:22)? Though many interpreters, reading the claim in light of the preceding Isaianic quotation (14:21; Isa 28:11–12), find that tongues signal the condemnation of those outside, a more likely view is that, as a sign, tongues actually lead to—even point the way to—unbelief, while prophecy promotes belief. Regardless, Paul remains determined to fashion a community with permeable boundaries, a commitment that derives from his apocalyptic understanding that Christ's passion inaugurates not the division but the reconciliation of both insiders and outsiders.

14:26–40. The remainder of the chapter provides a framework for worship in which participants deploy a broad array of gifts, including "a hymn, a lesson, a revelation, a tongue, or an interpretation" (14:26). The section both reiterates the vital importance of interpreting tongues and promotes an orderly gathering, perhaps reflecting Paul's concern to differentiate Corinthian worship from other Greco-Roman religious practices characterized by ecstatic expression. The governing principle here lies in Paul's claim that "God is a God not of disorder but of peace" (14:32), so that the injunctions to silence (14:28, 30), together with the instructions for participants to speak "in turn" (14:27) and "one by one" (14: 31), promote a consistently peaceful gathering.

Modern interpreters generally take 14:34–35 (and sometimes v.36) as an early gloss, based on both extrinsic and intrinsic evidence. Though all known manuscripts include the verses, the Western tradition places them after 14:40, a discrepancy that is difficult to reconcile with a view of these instructions as original to Paul. Even more problematic for their authenticity are three internal difficulties: (1) the verses' digression from, even contradiction of, Paul's claims about the interdependence of spiritual gifts within the congregation; (2) their categorical prohibition of women's speech, which is at odds with the assumption, in 11:2–16, that women are indeed active as prayers and prophets in the gathered community; and (3) their authoritative appeal to "the law," which does not fit Paul's use of the term elsewhere (e.g., 9:8; 14:21) to introduces a specific text or to illustrate rather than to prescribe (but cf. Josephus, *Against Apion*, 2.200–201). Generally, those who do accept the verses as authentic

overlook their categorical rhetoric and maintain that they address particular Corinthian women whose disorderly conduct detracted from the community's worship life.

V. Affirming the Resurrection Body (15:1–58)

With the beginning of 1 Cor 15, Paul introduces a matter about which he has been entirely silent to this point in the letter: the resurrection of Christ. Consistently, he has promoted Christ's sacrificial death (2:2)—the "message about the cross" (1:18)—as the pattern believers are called to emulate (11:1). Here he expands that message, drawing into view Christ's resurrection from the dead, along with its implications for the coming resurrection of all who will be "made alive in Christ" (15:22). For Paul, the death and resurrection ultimately stand together as witness to God's decisive victory for all of creation.

A. Christ Raised (15:1–11)

Paul draws his hearers' attention back to the basics, as he recalls for them the "good news that I proclaimed to you" (15:1) as the foundation of their faith. Using transmission-of-tradition language (cf. 11:23), he repeats the gospel proclamation: "that Christ died for our sins in accordance with the scriptures, and that he was buried, and that he was raised on the third day in accordance with the scriptures" (15:3–4; cf. Rom 1:1–4). Even if the emphasis on scriptural fulfillment derives from the tradition's original setting within Jewish Christianity, it serves Paul's purposes well as he reads this mostly Gentile congregation into Israel's sacred story.

Besides restating such a creedal formula, Paul identifies in succession those to whom the risen Lord has appeared: Cephas (Peter; 1:12; cf. Luke 24:34), the twelve (Luke 24:36; John 20:19), more than five hundred brothers [and sisters] (Acts 2:1–42), James (Gal 1:19), all of the apostles, and finally Paul himself (15:5–7). While the list does not correspond exactly to the accounts in the Gospels or Acts—most notably leaving the women out of account—it does reflect their view that the risen Lord appeared to an ever-expanding group. The section ends with a self-denigrating digression on Paul's own experience of the crucified Christ (cf. Gal 1:15–16; Acts 9:3–6). Perhaps anticipating (or responding to) challenges to his "apostleship," Paul calls himself "one untimely born" (*ektrōmati*; 15:8), a term that in Jewish literature typically denotes a deplorable station in life. He continues the motif, acknowledging that he is "unfit to be called an apostle, because I persecuted the church of God" (15:9), yet he maintains that both God's grace and his own hard work through God's grace place him in the role of apostleship. Thus Paul both *identifies* with believers who have experienced the risen Lord and *distinguishes* himself from them, as one whose life story provides a powerful example of God's intervening grace.

B. Christ as the First Fruits (15:12–34)

Paul's claim that some say, "there is no resurrection of the dead" (15:12), has been read to designate a variety of views: (1) a Hellenistic notion of immortality without a body, which would fit the Corinthians' dualistic culture and make sense of Paul's concern with the "body" throughout the letter (cf. e.g. 6:19; 12:27); (2) a "realized eschatology" that posits that a spiritual resurrection has already taken place (cf. 4:8); (3) an Epicurean rejection of any afterlife (cf. 15:19, 32); or (4) a denial of the resurrection of corpses themselves, which might have seemed like base superstition. The immediate context itself suggests that Paul's main concern lies in affirming Christ's bodily resurrection as the preamble to the end-time resurrection of all (15:22; cf. Rom 8:11).

To nullify the "resurrection of the dead," Paul believes, is to deny the resurrection of Christ (15:13, 16) and, in turn, both the gospel proclamation itself (15:14) and the Corinthians' resulting faith (15:14, 17). In other words, without the general resurrection of the dead, the entire basis of believers' life in Christ comes crashing down. Underlying this claim is the (thoroughly Jewish) emphasis on resurrection not as an isolated individual's destiny but as the cosmic expression of God's decisive victory over death.

To make this point more explicit, Paul situates Christ's resurrection within the broader landscape of apocalyptic drama. Depicting Christ as the "first fruits" (15:20, 23; cf. Exod 23:19) and as a new "Adam" (15:22; cf. Rom 5:12–21), Paul elongates the timeframe of that drama in two directions: not only does Christ's story find its roots in "the beginning," but his resurrection also heralds the coming

"end." In his concern with the "order" (15:23) of the unfolding saga, Paul situates the Corinthians squarely within the temporary reign of Christ, who is subjecting all evil, and lastly death, before relinquishing ultimate power to the kingdom of God (15:24–28). Such a plotting of the eschatological timetable helps Paul explain the temporal delay between Christ's resurrection and the resurrection of "those who belong to Christ" (15:23), a delay that grows increasingly problematic in early Christianity.

Subverting the tendency to locate hope "for this life only" (15:19), Paul also mentions his own experience of bodily suffering. Consistent with his appeal for sacrificial living based in his own experience (4:9–13), he maintains, "I die every day" (15:31). His motivation comes from more than "merely human hopes" (15:32); thus he endures hardship and steers clear of self-indulgence (15:32), lest his long-term destiny fade from view. The "sober and right mind" (15:34) to which he calls the Corinthians counters the licentiousness that might naturally follow from the denial of coming resurrection.

C. Resurrection of the Spiritual Body (15:35–58)

Paul forges somewhat of a middle ground as he explains the nature of the resurrection he affirms. By distinguishing physical body (*sōma psychikon*, 15:44) or flesh (*sarx*, 15:39, 50: "flesh and blood"), which is perishable (15:53–54), from the spiritual body (*sōma pneumatikon*, 15:44), which is imperishable (15:53–54), he insists on the bodily nature of resurrection even as he denies the resuscitation of corpses.

Paul turns to the natural world to illustrate such a distinction. From agriculture, he borrows the example of seeds whose bodies differ from the grain they produce (15:38–39). Next, he differentiates diverse earthly bodies (humans, animals, birds, and fish) and heavenly bodies (sun, moon, stars), as well as the glory afforded them (15:39–41). Applying these observations to the question about the resurrection body seems for Paul to be a simple logical step. Sown in "dishonor" and "weakness," the perishable body will be raised in "glory" and "power" (15:43).

Paul returns to the Adam-Christ typology (see above, 15:22) to develop the succession from the physical to the spiritual body. While Adam, as a "man of dust" (15:47) serves as prototype for the physical body, Christ as last Adam functions as the "man of heaven" (15:48) who has become a life-giving spirit (15:45). Paul puts the contrast between the two types in this way: "Just as we have borne the image of the man of dust, we will also bear the image of the man of heaven" (15:49). While some textual variants read the clause's main verb as a cohortative ("let us bear ..."), the future tense reading better fits Paul's interest in the resurrection of the dead at Christ's coming.

To bring the matter to a close, Paul clarifies his position: "flesh and blood cannot inherit the kingdom of God" (15:50). How then will the dead be raised? Again invoking apocalyptic language, Paul calls the matter a "mystery" (15:51; cf. 2:1, 7; 4:1; 13:2; 14:2) and shifts his discourse from probative explanation to hymnic affirmation: "we will all be changed, in a moment, in the twinkling of an eye, at the last trumpet" (15:51–52). In that instant, the final defeat of evil will culminate in victory over death itself (15:26). As he does when he grapples with the mysteries of God elsewhere (cf. Rom 11:33–36), Paul concludes with a word of praise: "but thanks be to God, who gives us the victory through our Lord Jesus Christ" (15:57).

VI. Closing (16:1–24)

A. Collection for the Saints (16:1–4)

The cryptic allusion to the Jerusalem collection (cf. Gal 2:10; 2 Cor 8, 9) suggests the Corinthians' awareness of it, and its place near the letter's conclusion hints at its political ramifications. If Paul promotes the mending of factionalism within the Corinthian congregation, seeking monetary support for the mother church in Palestine displays his impulse toward reconciliation on a broader scale.

The delicate nature of the collection task is not lost on Paul, who promotes weekly contributions to the cause so that "collections need not be taken when I come" (16:2). (This verse contains the earliest known reference to "the first day of the week," which may already be recognized as a Christian Sabbath.) Paul does intend to shepherd the gift's delivery, when, after he arrives in Corinth, he will "send any whom you approve" (16:3) to Jerusalem and will accompany them "if

it seems advisable that I should go also" (16:4). By involving the Corinthians as both monetary participants and as human ambassadors in this collection, he promotes clear relational ties to the Jerusalem church.

B. Future Plans (16:5–12)

As the letter draws to a close, Paul announces a tentative itinerary. He has already disclosed plans to travel to Corinth "soon" (4:19); now he declares that he will visit "after passing through Macedonia" (16:5). More than simply providing a timetable, Paul presents his imminent return as evidence of his relational commitment to the Corinthian community, where he hopes "to spend some time with you, if the Lord permits" (16:7). He also notes a similar commitment to the church at Ephesus, where "a wide door for effective work has opened to me, and there are many adversaries" (16:9). For Paul, fruitful ministry does not entail the absence of conflict but seemingly its very presence.

For some reason, Paul apparently changed course and stopped briefly in Corinth between his trip to Ephesus and his tour of Macedonia, though he still meant to return to Corinth for a longer period before launching to Judea (2 Cor 1:16). From his report in 2 Corinthians, things did not go well. It was such a "painful visit" (2 Cor 2:1) that he decided to write a letter to give the embers of conflict a chance to die down before his return.

Paul also alerts the Corinthians to anticipated visits by his co-workers. Timothy has already been sent (see 4:17); anticipating potential conflict, Paul advises the Corinthians about their conduct toward his emissary "when Timothy comes" (16:10; NRSV, "if"). Since Apollos has been named earlier in the letter (1:12) as a leader around whom a (rival?) faction has rallied, Paul's explicit endorsement for Apollos's visit (16:12), whenever it occurs, promotes the unity he has fostered throughout the letter.

C. Exhortation and Greetings (16:13–24)

The apostle concludes with words of encouragement and personal greetings from other believers as well as himself. He frames the letter's ending section with eschatological reminders of the Lord's coming. The injunction to "keep alert, stand firm in your faith, be courageous, be strong" (16:13) summons the Corinthians to keen anticipation of the day of the Lord (cf. 1 Thess 5:6, 10) and reverberates in the citation of the Aramaic expression *maranatha* ("Our Lord, come," 16:22). The word may have been a catchword for the Corinthians, who otherwise would have known little Aramaic. Though it can be translated in the indicative ("our Lord has come"), the imperative better coheres with the letter's tendency to orient present Christian conduct toward the future reality of Christ's return (11:26; 15:28).

Within such an eschatological context, Paul draws attention to key relationships within the Pauline association of Gentile churches. Paul commends individual believers such as Stephanas (cf. 1:16), Fortunatus, and Achaicus, who have together served as intermediaries between the Corinthians and the apostle (16:15–18); he also delivers greetings from the "churches of Asia" and "Aquila and Prisca, together with the church in their house" (16:19; cf. Acts 18:1–3; Rom 16:3–5), as well as from "all the brothers and sisters" (16:20). Paul's ministry throughout the Mediterranean is vast, and he wants individual congregations to view their own ministry in this expansive light.

Though the letter has included sharp rebuke, Paul brings his personal greeting to a close with these words: "My love be with all of you in Christ Jesus" (16:24). Just as he has exhorted them to "let all that you do be done in love" (16:14), he offers himself as example (cf. 11:1). The phrase "in Christ Jesus" underscores the notion that the relationship forged between apostle and congregation is not merely social but intrinsically sacramental as well.

BIBLIOGRAPHY

G. Bray, ed. *Ancient Christian Commentary on Scripture VII: 1–2 Corinthians* (Downers Grove, Ill.: InterVarsity, 1999); T. Engberg-Pedersen. *Paul and the Stoics* (Louisville: Westminster John Knox, 2000); G. D. Fee. *The First Epistle to the Corinthians.* NICNT (Grand Rapids: Eerdmans, 1987); D. M. Hay, ed. *Pauline Theology, Volume 2: 1 & 2 Corinthians* (Minneapolis: Fortress, 1993); R. B. Hays. *First Corinthians.* Interpretation (Louisville: John Knox, 1997); D. B. Martin. *The Corinthian Body* (New Haven: Yale University Press, 1995); M. M. Mitchell. *Paul and the Rhetoric of Reconciliation: An Exegetical Investigation of the Language and Composition of 1 Corinthians* (Louisville: Westminster John Knox, 1992); G. Theissen. *The Social Setting of Pauline Christianity: Essays on Corinth* (Philadelphia: Fortress, 1982); A. C. Thiselton. *First Corinthians: A Shorter Exegetical and Pastoral Commentary* (Grand Rapids: Eerdmans, 2006); B. Witherington, III. *Conflict and Community in Corinth: A Socio-Rhetorical Commentary on 1 and 2 Corinthians* (Grand Rapids: Eerdmans, 1995).

2 CORINTHIANS

CRAIG S. KEENER

OVERVIEW

The major scholarly debate with regard to 2 Corinthians is its unity; this debate affects how we reconstruct the letter's situation. Some scholars believe that our current letter combines as many as six shorter letters or letter fragments; many others accept only the division between chs. 1–9 and chs. 10–13 (where the shift in thought is most abrupt). Because ancient writers, including Paul, often used digressions and framing devices, an increasing number of scholars also favor the letter's unity as it stands. Following the preference of contemporary literary criticism to read literary works as a whole when possible, we seek here especially to explain 2 Corinthians as a unity, while aware that many scholars construe the evidence differently in terms of sources, especially regarding the transition between 9:15 and 10:1.

In possible contrast to the earlier situation in 1 Corinthians, "opponents" are clear here (2:17; 3:1; 5:12; 10:12; 11:4, 12–14). That they were Jews (11:22) tells us little about them, since in this period most of Paul's allies and rivals alike were Jews. In contrast to the Jerusalem apostles, these Jewish rivals are apparently rhetorically proficient, a high value in Corinth (11:5–6).

Although the teachers' presence is most clear in chs. 10–13, their criticisms of Paul would explain why he must earlier emphasize his own apostleship in chs. 3–6, and why he is concerned that some are alienating the Corinthian believers from him (2:17–3:1; 5:20–6:1; 6:11–7:2). They may have also criticized his collection for the poor in Jerusalem; thus Paul addresses this collection (chs. 8–9, the heart of the letter) and greed (2:17; cf. 4:2) before confronting them at the end (12:14–18). His rivals may question his apostleship (3:1; 12:12) and refusal to accept pay (2:17; 11:7–9), whereas he rejects their criteria for commending themselves (5:12; 10:10–18). Although saving his direct criticism for the end of the letter, Paul is also preparing the Corinthians for it.

Because these rival teachers vie for the Corinthians' loyalty, Paul must quickly resolve any other conflicts between him and some Corinthians. Following rhetorical custom, Paul may reserve his more direct challenge to the rival teachers for the end. In the meantime, Paul's defense of his apostolic ministry reveals some deep working assumptions of this theology. His ministry is outwardly characterized by suffering but inwardly characterized by glory and power (2:14–7:1). As with the cross, only the true eyes of faith will discern its real nature. Paul's present experience of the eschatological Spirit (cf. e.g., 4:16–18; 5:5, 13; 12:1–4) provides him a window into reality that transcends earthly perspectives.

Paul's two defenses of his apostolic ministry (1:12–7:16; 10:1–13:10) frame the urgent issue of the collection—which his rival's criticisms risk hurting. Paul's extensive focus on the collection also reveals another important Pauline conviction: divine concern for the needy.

Throughout the letter, even where he challenges them most firmly (chs. 10–13), Paul's deep love for the Corinthian believers comes through. Paul threatens discipline, yet his reluctance to carry it out invites criticism. His protests are loving, and his tender affection for the believers in Corinth offers a model of pastoral theology.

Paul's letter probably did prove successful: later he did spend a few months with them (Acts 20:3, 6; Rom 15:26).

OUTLINE

I. Introduction (1:1–11)

II. Paul's Ministry to the Corinthians (1:12–7:16)

I. Introduction (1:1–11)

Letters opened by announcing the identity of the sender(s), then listed their addressees. Corinth was capital of the Roman province of Achaia. "Achaia" constituted much of Greece; at least forty settlements surrounded Corinth itself. A prosperous Roman colony in Greece, Corinth housed Roman citizens, Greek residents, and settlers from abroad. "Grace" (*charis*) sounded like the traditional Greek greeting (*chairein*), and "peace" was the standard Jewish greeting (already combined by some Jews; *2 Bar.* 78:2). Such phrases were equivalent to "God bless you," and invoked a deity for blessing (here including both the Father and Jesus as divine; 1:2).

The blessing of praise that Paul then uses (1:3–5) follows a traditional Jewish form (the *berakah*; e.g., Ps 72:18–19); for whatever reason, it substitutes here for Paul's usual thanksgiving

for his recipients. In 1:3–11, Paul praises God for comforting him and his coworkers in the face of sufferings, including potentially deadly perils in Ephesus (cf. 1 Cor 15:32). These sufferings and God's help become a theme running through most of 2 Corinthians, distinguishing Paul from his opponents. Paul also appeals to and reiterates the intimate relationship he has with the Corinthian believers.

II. Paul's Ministry to the Corinthians (1:12–7:16)

A. Dealing with the Corinthians (1:12–2:13)

1:12–22. Paul's Reliability. Various kinds of works in antiquity began with narratives summarizing the events that led to the work's writing. Before Paul dares confront the major issues with the false teachers, he must clear up a misunderstanding. The church was disappointed with Paul's failure to follow through on his visit, when they hoped to show him hospitality (1:15–16).

Greco-Roman culture despised fickleness and unreliability, so Paul reiterates his integrity (1:12, which may serve as a thesis statement for at least this part of the letter). He emphasizes his transparency (1:13), and later his "sincerity" (2:17) and "frankness" (3:12; 7:4). He and the Corinthians may affectionately boast in each other (1:14; 5:12). Paul's change of travel plans reflected no fickleness (1:17).

To some of Paul's critics, who suspected his dishonesty (12:16–18), Paul's change of plans reflected a more fundamental character flaw than a mere schedule conflict. If they could not trust Paul's promise to visit, why should they trust his apostolic message (an issue Paul must confront in 1:18–22 and more fully in 2:14–7:4)? Some probably also suspected Paul's motives regarding the collection, even as time to provide it was coming due (chs. 8–9).

Paul thus replies that his ministry is grounded in a God who is trustworthy regarding his promises (1:18–20); God confirmed that integrity by advancing them the Spirit as the down payment of future blessing (1:21–22).

1:23–2:11. Discipline and Forgiveness. Now Paul explains that the *real* reason he had delayed coming to Corinth (cf. 1:15–17) was to spare them

(1:23). Paul did not want to have to discipline them (2 Cor 2:1), hence confronted them in a letter first to test their obedience (2:9). His failure to carry through on promised threats to come administer discipline (cf. 1 Cor 4:18–21) would lead some of his critics to mock him for "meekly" confronting them by letters rather than in person (10:1–11).

Paul sent this "tearful letter" (2:4) with Titus, hoping to provoke them to repentance before his coming, lest he have to inflict discipline. Until Titus returned to him, however (shortly before the letter he is now writing, 2 Corinthians), Paul did not know the Corinthians' response (7:6–7). With Titus' return, Paul discovered that the Corinthians had repented, obeying the tearful letter (7:7–11).

The church had complied with his demand that they discipline the sin among them. Consequently, the man needing punishment had come to repentance, and they could now forgive him (2:5–11). (Scholars differ over whether the man in question is the same as the person mentioned in 1 Cor 5:1–5, as most church fathers thought, or a vocal critic of Paul, or both.) "Putting" someone "to the test" (2:9) was sometimes a sign of affection (cf. 8:8). What is most obvious here, as throughout 2 Corinthians, is Paul's pastoral affection for the Corinthians.

2:12–13. Paul's Anxiety over Titus. Ancient travel was precarious, and individuals hoping to rendezvous sometimes missed each other. Although Paul had much success in Troas (in northern Asia Minor), he feared how the Corinthians had responded to his letter, since Titus, whom he had sent to them, had not returned. So Paul crossed the Aegean into Macedonia (probably starting in Philippi), hoping to meet Titus on his way from Corinth (see 7:5–7, 13).

B. Paul and True Ministry (2:14–7:4)

2:14–17. Perspectives on God's Captive. Paul digresses so radically in 2:14–7:4 that some plausibly think this portion is a separate letter that has been accidentally inserted. Although that proposal would work well with electronic text or maybe misplaced pages (if they conveniently ended with sentences!), it makes less sense with the sort of documents available in the first century. This section cannot be the letter Paul sent with Titus (2:3–4), though it may draw from Paul's ruminations while waiting to hear their response.

Ancient speakers and writers sometimes digressed at length to build suspense and make a point (e.g., Pliny *N.H.* 28–32; Dio Chrysostom 36.1–7). If Paul is making such a rhetorical move, he is breaking off at the height of suspense and his love for the Corinthians (2:12–13) to begin his digression about his apostolic ministry.

Being led as captives in triumphal procession is not an image of honor to the captives: they were executed afterward. Paul portrays himself as one bound for death—like the crucified Jesus. To those without faith, such a state signified only death, but those with faith found life in it. Paul develops the theme further afterward: the mere letter brings death, but the Spirit brings life (3:6); true perception matters (5:7, 12, 16). God's servants appear to be dying on the outside, but in reality have eternal life (4:11–5:4).

God's servants' sufferings confirm their sincerity, contrasting them with those who simply do ministry for profit (2:17)—perhaps a backhanded warning against the opponents (cf. 5:12; 10:12; 11:13–14).

3:1–18. Glory of the Greater Covenant. Influential people often wrote "recommendation letters" to ask favors on behalf of those who depended on the writers (e.g., Cicero *Fam.* 13 passim). Although Paul rejects the need for formal letters of recommendation, he is forced at times to "recommend" himself again to the Corinthians, reminding them of what they should already know for themselves. Self-boasting was considered inappropriate unless people were forced to do it—as Paul felt he was by them (cf. 12:11).

Instead, the Corinthians' own faith constituted Christ's recommendation of Paul and his colleagues (3:2–3). People sometimes spoke of laws written in hearts (e.g., Plato *Gorg.* 784B; *Laws* 690B; Josephus *Ag. Ap.* 2.178), but in 3:3 and 6 Paul alludes specifically to Ezek 36:26–27 and Jer 31:31–34, both passages about Israel's end-time obedience. Ezekiel promised that God's people's hearts would no longer be "stony" (hard); instead, God's Spirit would make them obedient. Paul also contrasts God writing on hearts rather than (as at Sinai) on stone tablets (Exod 31:18); this contrast fits the promise of the new covenant that he mentions, in which God would write laws on hearts (Jer 31:31–34).

Paul was therefore confident in his ministry (2 Cor 3:4; cf. 3:12; 4:1; 5:6); it was God who made them "competent" (3:5–6, answering the question in 2:16, where the same term is translated, "sufficient"). In 3:6 Paul develops the new covenant image of 3:3, which implies moral transformation (Jer 31:31–34); mere letters written with ink (or in stone) can bring only the law's death sentence for violations, but the Spirit can inscribe believers' hearts so they can obey the law's principles (cf. 2 Cor 3:9; also Rom 8:2–4).

In 3:7–11, Paul develops the logical premise that the new covenant's glory must be greater than that of the old covenant under Moses; Paul develops the point by repetition, antithesis (contrasts), and "how much more" arguments, all readily recognizable to his contemporaries (e.g., *4 Ezra* 4:30; *m. Ab.* 1:5; *Sipre Deut.* 1.8.2–3). New covenant glory, unlike Moses', was permanent and greater—but is the glory of the Spirit *within* rather than without. Moses' revelation was incomplete, because no one could see God and live (Exod 33:20); the new covenant glory is complete and does not kill. It is a ministry producing righteousness (2 Cor 3:7), because the law is in the heart.

In 3:12–18, Paul contrasts the concealed (though visible) nature of Moses' glory with the public (though inward) nature of new covenant glory. The Greek version of Exod 34:29–30, 35 claims that Moses was "glorified"; but though the glory was only temporary, Moses had to hide it, since Israel could not bear it. Paul, by contrast, can speak frankly (openly) (2 Cor 3:12; cf. 2:17; 4:2, 13); his "transformation" did not injure his viewers. Without Christ, Moses' followers have only the old covenant, perceiving only the veiled measure of glory (3:13–16). Yet just as Moses removed the veil to talk with God, so one who turns to Christ sees the glory unveiled (3:14–16).

In Exod 33–34, Moses saw part of "the Lord's" glory; here, participants in the new covenant experience the Spirit (hence, "the Lord" of Exodus "is the Spirit," 2 Cor 3:17). Just as Moses was transformed by seeing part of God's glory, so are participants in the new covenant transformed progressively into God's glorious image as they behold God's glory (3:18). Perhaps the Corinthians questioned how much their characters had been transformed, but they could not question

the character of Paul, who had brought them the new covenant message (cf. 13:5–6). Many Greek thinkers believed that meditating on a deity's "pure," emotionless character made one like the deity (cf. e.g., Maximus of Tyre 11.9–12); many Jewish mystics sought visions of the divine (e.g., *b. Hag.* 14*b*, bar.). Paul is not interested in the passionless divinity of Platonic philosophy; rather, he believes that one meets God's glory in Jesus, God's purest image (4:4). Some Jewish thinkers conversant with Greek thought depicted divine Wisdom as a mirror revealing God's glory (Wis 7:26); but for Paul Wisdom is concrete in Jesus.

4:1–15. Glory in Weak Vessels. Despite opposition, Paul and his colleagues take courage (4:1), as elsewhere in the context (3:4, 12; 4:16). Philosophers emphasized such courage, but in contrast to them, the reason Paul offers for his courage is God's grace involved in his new covenant ministry (alluding back to ch. 3). His "open" presentation of truth (4:2) contrasts with Moses' veil (3:12–13); his persistent denial of "falsifying" God's message (4:2) may contrast with his opponents (cf. 2:17).

Just as a "veil" kept Israel from seeing God's glory (3:13–16), so now the good news was "veiled" from unbelievers (4:3). They could not see the gospel's glory because the god of this age had blinded them (4:4). Paul contrasts the situations in 4:4 and 4:6: the god of this age blinded unbelievers' minds, lest the light of Christ's glory shine in them, but the true God has shined the light of his glory in our hearts. In view of the contrast, most scholars think that "the god of this age" refers to the devil (some ancient interpreters thought of God, and others of the devil); cf. a false "god" in Phil 3:19.

Christ is God's "image" here (4:4, 6). Many Jews thought of divine Wisdom as God's "image" (see comment on 3:18); for Paul, such titles rightly belong to Christ. God made light shine in darkness in the first creation, and continues to do so in the new creation in Christ (4:6; cf. 5:17). (In addition to alluding to creation, Paul's wording alludes to the Greek version of Isa 9:1–2, which goes on to speak of the Messiah.)

Paul preached not himself but Christ (4:5); thus he was ready to acknowledge his own weakness alongside Christ's glory (4:7–11). As Paul earlier emphasized apostolic suffering (2:14–16) yet internal renewal by Christ's glory (3:6–18), so he does here. Archaeologists observe that Corinth manufactured many cheap pots, and such pots were easily discarded (cf. Ps 31:12; Jer 19:11). God's glory and power are hidden in outwardly weak vessels like Paul, so God may receive the honor (4:7).

Paul illustrates the contrast between his external weakness and the resurrection glory of Christ within him in 4:8–11. Here Paul follows an ancient literary form used by philosophers and others to validate their integrity: lists of sufferings (see also 6:3–10; 11:23–33; cf. 1 Cor 4:9–13; e.g., Maximus of Tyre 34.9; see most thoroughly Fitzgerald). Such lists reveal Paul's perseverance (11:23–33), but Paul especially underlines here God's power revealed in his weakness (4:7; cf. 12:9; 13:3–4). As a sharer in Christ's suffering, Paul also depends on resurrection power; he was being transformed into Christ's image (3:18).

Following Jesus' example, Paul was to suffer on behalf of the church (4:12, 15), ultimately for God's glory (4:15). Paul's allusion in 4:13 to Ps 116:10 may evoke the psalm's context of a righteous sufferer whom God has delivered. Corinthians understood the ancient civic practice (reflected in Seneca *Ben.* passim and many inscriptions) where benefactors contributed good to the public welfare, in turn receiving honor. Here God receives honor (4:15).

4:16–5:10. Future Hope for God's Servants. Paul is prepared to suffer in view of the resurrection life, which was already at work within him (4:8–11). His body suffered, but God kept renewing him (4:16–18; 5:5; cf. 1:9–10); this renewal constituted a foretaste of the ultimate resurrection even of his body and that of others (4:14; 5:1–4).

Suffering for Christ, Paul is inwardly renewed (4:16), i.e., conformed more to Christ's image (3:18; cf. Rom 12:2; Col 3:10). Present sufferings invited eternal glory to which the sufferings were barely comparable (4:17; cf. Rom 8:18). (Paul also knew—though the Corinthians might have not—that the Hebrew word for "glory" also meant "weight.") Greek thinkers often spoke of what was invisible and unchanging in the heavens as being eternal, in contrast to the visible, transitory matters on earth. Paul in 4:18 partly agrees, because he already, although in a hidden way,

shares Christ's resurrection life (4:7–11). Eventually his body will also share in the resurrection life (4:14; 5:1–4). Thus Paul does not agree with Greeks who viewed the body as merely the soul's prison or tomb (cf. even Philo *Alleg. Interp.*1.108). Nor does he believe, with some Greeks, that meditating on a "divine" entity in the heavens would liberate his soul from the body (cf. Seneca *Nat. Q.* 1. pref. 6, 11–13; Philo *Spec. Laws* 3.1); he was already united with Christ and now suffered with him, so he could be assured of resurrection life affecting every aspect of his person.

In 5:1–4 Paul is clear that his goal is not to be disembodied—"unclothed"—but rather to receive a permanent, heavenly sort of body. Some scholars think that Paul speaks of an intermediate body received at death in these verses, but it seems likely that he is simply countering the fear of disembodiment with the promise of future embodiment. Too much of his language echoes his earlier discussion of the resurrection body in 1 Cor 15 for this to be a coincidence (perishable vs. imperishable, 1 Cor 15:42, 50–53; earthly vs. heavenly, 15:49; the mortal clothed with what is not, 15:53–54).

He does not claim in 5:1 that we get the new body ("house") when our earthly body ("tent") dies; rather, we "have" it now, not because we are already resurrected, but because it belongs to us through the down payment of the Spirit (5:5). Thus, though Paul walks by faith and not yet sight (5:7), he trusts Christ's promise of this future body even while he shares Christ's sufferings.

Paul may depict the body as a "house" (5:1) because it is God's (1 Cor 6:19), and Jews expected God to make a new temple. Everyone would also understand his image of the body as "clothing" (5:2–4), since this was a common image of the day (e.g., Seneca *Ep. Lucil.* 66.3; Epictetus *Diatr.* 1.25.21). In contrast to Greeks who exercised naked (e.g., Diogenes *Ep.* 37) or Greek and Roman Gentiles who frequented Corinth's many public baths, most Jews felt that nakedness was shameful (e.g., *Jub.* 3:21–22; 1QS 7.12–14).

Philosophers often spoke of earthly passions as "weighing down" the soul, obstructing its ascent to the "pure" heavens ("burden" in 5:4 is a related term to "weigh down"; cf. 4:17). But Paul's response to the "burden" in 5:4 is "groaning," like birth pangs awaiting a new body (see Rom 8:23). The Spirit was a "pledge"—literally, a "down payment," a "first installment" on God's future promise (5:5). The Spirit's renewing him in the face of present obstacles reaffirmed the guarantee.

Ancient thinkers sometimes weighed whether it was better to live with suffering or to die (e.g., Cicero *Quint.* 1.3.1–2; Seneca *Ep. Lucil.* 58.36; *Dial.* 7.20.5). Paul's yearning was for a resurrection body more than for death, yet he valued even death (if God gave it) as rest from suffering, because he would be with the Lord undistracted (5:6–8). He could do this because of faith rather than sight (5:7)—depending on the eternal reality that is unseen (4:18).

What mattered from a genuinely eternal perspective was that his (and others') lives pleased the one who would judge them (5:9–10). This "fear of the Lord" (5:11) motivated Paul's preaching.

5:11–6:10. Faithful Ambassadors of Reconciliation. Because of their eternal perspective (4:16–5:10) that includes a view of the future judgment (5:10), God's servants stand in awe ("fear") of God, and hence must preach him (5:11). Paul thus claims to be Christ's agent with integrity—yet the Corinthians were not heeding him.

Paul emphasizes that he has left his heart open, and the Corinthians know it (5:11). His rivals boast merely in appearance, but the heart is what matters (5:12, using the language of 1 Sam 16:7). The term for "appearance" here (*prosōpon*) is the same used for "face" in 3:7, 13, where Moses received the veiled outward glory instead of (as in 3:18) the greater glory of the new covenant.

Paul explains that he is not boasting in himself (5:12, as in 3:1); apparently some Corinthians have complained about his previous defenses (see comment on 11:1). Paul is not boasting, he says, but giving them the opportunity to boast about him, as he does about them (1:14; 7:14; 9:2–3).

But even like Moses, Paul has greater freedom of heart with the Lord (5:13). Many "normal" people regarded being "beside oneself" in prophetic ecstasy or a philosophic worldview as madness (e.g., 2 Kgs 9:11; Diogenes Laertius 6.3.82), but prophets and philosophers often countered with the opposite perspective (e.g., Epictetus *Diatr.* 1.12.9; 1.21.4). Like Moses veiling himself in

public, Paul did not publicly boast of his private spiritual experiences, except when he needed to do so (12:2–4; cf. 1 Cor 14:18).

Not only wise fear (5:11), but also love (5:14) motivates the mission. Paul interprets the cross from the perspective of God's purpose, rather than the world's perspective of it as folly (cf. 2:15–16; 1 Cor 1:18–25); even regarding Christ, external, temporal perspectives are inadequate (5:16). Those who embrace Christ's death for them die to themselves and live for Christ in union with him (5:14–15). This is an internal transformation rather than outward appearance. Therefore, evaluation based on a "human point of view" (other translations: the "flesh") or appearance is useless and void (5:16). The proper basis for evaluation is not externals, but the eschatological life already at work within (5:17). Those with the down payment of the Spirit (5:5) have begun sharing Christ's resurrection life.

In view of all this, Paul, having been transformed as God's agent, appeals to the Corinthians to let this same "internal" and future gospel genuinely transform them (5:18–6:2). In ancient Mediterranean culture, true "reconciliation" or friendship with one required accepting the friend's friends and rejecting the friend's enemies (see Marshall). The Corinthians cannot be reconciled to God while rejecting God's agent and welcoming his rivals (cf. 6:14–16; Luke 10:16; Exod 16:8).

Paul and his coworkers have received the "ministry" and "message" of reconciliation (5:18–19) as "ambassadors" for Christ (5:20) and representatives of God's righteousness (5:21). (Paul would undoubtedly apply the principle to all believers who share the gospel with others.) The Corinthian Christians, by contrast, must now be reconciled to God (5:20), lest they have accepted his grace in vain (6:1)! Paul is seeking to seize their attention with dramatic language (cf. 1 Cor 6:9–11; Gal 5:4) to show the Corinthians that they must live consistently with their conversion. Jesus becoming "sin," though sinless (2 Cor 5:21), presumably involves his representative suffering for sin, perhaps combining Old Testament images of unblemished offerings with the scapegoat used to embody Israel's sin (Lev 1:3; 16:21–22).

Paul reiterates the invitation in 6:1, urging them not to "accept the grace of God in vain." Paul often uses such language to warn against failing to persevere in the faith (1 Cor 15:2; Gal 4:11; Phil 2:16). Paul underlines this invitation by appealing in 6:2 to Isa 49:8, showing that the time for salvation has come. The context in Isaiah includes the good news of God's reconciliation with God's people (Isa 52:7); Paul believes that Christ has inaugurated this time (2 Cor 5:18–19).

Paul returns to defending his ministry in 6:3–10, underlining its integrity with a list of sufferings that also should generate sympathy (ancients often appealed to rhetorical pathos; e.g., *Rhet. Alex.* 34, 1439b15–1440b3; Quintilian *Inst.* 6.2.20) from the Corinthians who know the sacrifices he has made for them. Contemporary orators produced lists like Paul's here, listing some elements sharing one parallel form, then others in another parallel form, and so forth (cf. e.g., lists in Seneca *Ep. Lucil.* 95.58; *Test. Jos.* 1:4–7). Paul lists nine sufferings (in Greek, each is prefaced by "in"; 6:4–5); eight virtues (6:6–7, also with "in"); and ten antitheses manifesting God's power in his weakness (6:7–10, three using the Greek *dia*, "through"; and seven using "as . . . and"). Lists of virtues (6:6–7) were common (cf. Gal 5:22–23; Phil 4:8), as vice lists were (cf. Rom 1:29–31; 1 Cor 5:10–11; 6:9–10; Gal 5:19–21). Like such orators, Paul also employs some oxymorons to shock his hearers into attention (cf. the philosopher Musonius Rufus 9, p. 74.10–12 Lutz).

While not "boasting" (3:1; 5:12), Paul will recount his sufferings; sages used lists of sufferings to demonstrate their integrity (see comment on 4:8–11). Although Paul labors to avoid giving people any opportunity to find fault with his ministry (6:3–4), people publicly humiliate (6:5) and slander (6:8) him (prison, beatings, and manual labor all exposed one to others' reproach). Yet the issue is not how those who perish view him, but how those with God's true perspective view him (cf. 2:15–16; 4:3–4; 5:12, 16). Living though dying (6:9, evoking Ps 118:17) in particular reiterates sharing Christ's sufferings yet also resurrection power (cf. 1:9–10; 4:10–17). His poverty (6:10) should allay any suspicions that he might abuse the collection (12:16–18; cf. chs. 8–9); it also reflects Jesus' example, who also became poor to enrich others (8:9).

6:11–7:4. Choose Paul over Belial. After defending his ministry's integrity at length (2:14–6:10),

Paul now turns to a rousing call to separation from what is evil (6:14–7:1), framed by an emotional appeal to embrace his ministry (6:11–13; 7:2–4). Writers and speakers would sometimes build their argument to an emotional climax, as Paul does here (in a more specialized form, cf. *Rhet. Her.* 4.34–35; Demetrius *Style* 5.270). Wronged leaders and lovers sometimes composed affectionate protests to emphasize the depth of their affection (e.g., Cicero *Att.* 1.5, 9, 12; 7.10; Fronto *Ad Verum Imp.* 1.3); although this passage does involve real conflict, it also exudes affection. Paul invites the Corinthians to make a choice; just as in the Roman partisan politics and system of alliances Corinth knew so well, they cannot maintain good terms with both Paul and his rivals. Being truly reconciled to God entails being reconciled with Christ's agent, Paul (2 Cor 5:20–6:2; 6:11–13), and rejecting paganizing "unbelievers" (6:14–16).

Paul's frank speech (6:11) is literally an "opened mouth," corresponding to his open heart in 6:11 and 13. This evokes his recent affirmations of his frank speech (cf. 3:12; 4:2; 5:12), which ancients associated with genuine friendship. Paul tells the Corinthians that they are the ones who have closed off the relationship, and that he desires reconciliation (6:12–13).

Because of the sudden shift in topic, many scholars argue that 6:14–7:1 is a later addition. But Paul often frames his digressions with parallel material (e.g., 1 Cor 6:1, 9; 11:2, 17; 12:31; 14:1), as here (6:11–13; 7:2–4). Moreover, it is the Corinthians' welcome of his rivals that has forced his preceding, impassioned defense in 2:14–6:10; now he demands that the Corinthians choose between them. If Paul elsewhere calls these rivals "Satan's ministers" (11:14–15), their association with Beliar and idols here (6:14–16) makes sense. The Corinthians must choose God's enlightenment or Satan's blinding (4:4–6), Christ's ambassadors (5:20) or Satan's (11:14–15).

The language of being "mismatched with unbelievers" (6:14) literally is "yoked with a different species" (cf. Deut 22:9–11); it may apply to Jews avoiding being associated with idolaters, and was also appropriate language for marital unions (Deut 7:3–4). Paul, however, may apply the principle to the Corinthians' affection for his rivals: Paul seeks to deliver them to Christ as virgins, while

Satan's ministers seek to corrupt them spiritually (2 Cor 11:2–4).

A series of rhetorical questions, like the stark antithesis Paul uses in them, would underline Paul's point rhetorically in 6:14–16 (cf. 1 Cor 9:1–13). "Belial" or "Beliar" (6:15) was a common name for Satan in this period (e.g., 1QM 13.11; 15.2–3; *Test. Reub.* 4:7). Qumran texts sometimes portray the chosen remnant as a temple, an image also used by many early Christians. As the temple set apart for God, the righteous could not contain idols (6:16). Because God was to dwell among them, in this temple (6:16), they had to separate themselves from anything that was unclean (6:17). In 6:16, Paul quotes Lev 26:11–12, a promise conditioned partly on avoiding idols (Lev 26:1, 3). In 6:17, Paul adapts the Greek version of Isa 52:11, involving the Levites who will bring back the temple vessels in the promised time of restoration (a restoration that has already spiritually begun; see 2 Cor 6:2). In 6:18, Paul may adapt different texts, but one is 2 Sam 7:14, which Christians and some others applied to the Messiah. Perhaps Paul uses this text because God's promises apply to Jesus' followers in him (2 Cor 1:20).

In view of such promises to those set apart for God, believers should confirm their holiness (being "set apart") by separating themselves from whatever defiles them (7:1). In the context of 2 Corinthians, this would mean separating themselves from the false teachers.

Finally Paul returns to his plea that they welcome him (7:2–4). After asking them to welcome him, Paul in 7:2 makes three denials of wrongdoing (each beginning in Greek with *oudena* [no one], such repetition reflecting the ancient rhetorical device *anaphora*—e.g., Cicero *Orator* 39.135; Fronto *Ad Antoninum Imp.* 2.6.1; *Ad Verum Imp.* 2.1.4), which may be meant to contrast him with the rivals. Willingness to die with someone (7:3) demonstrated the highest level of friendship in antiquity (e.g., Euripides *Orest.* 652, 1069–74, 1155; Chariton *Chaer.* 4.3.5; 7.1.7). "I often boast about you" (7:4, NRSV) might instead be translated, "I am being frank with you" (cf. 3:12, using the same word), an accepted sign of friendship in their culture.

C. Repentant Response to Paul's Letter (7:5–16)

At this point Paul resumes the narrative he was recounting at 2:13, before he digressed to defend his ministry (2:14–7:4). Some stylistic features show that Paul had not forgotten the intervening chapters: for example, he continues the first-person plural of 6:11–13 and 7:2–3 (contrast 2:12–13), and some language from 6:12; 7:2 and 4 may reappear here. But now that he has explained why the Corinthians *should* accept him, he gets on with the story of discovering that they *have* accepted him (at least regarding his previous demand).

Paul faces external conflicts in Macedonia (7:5); if this includes persecution (as in Asia, 1:8–10), it would fit earlier problems there (Acts 16:22–24; 17:5–13; Phil 1:28–30; 1 Thess 2:18; 3:4). But Paul's "fears within" (2 Cor 7:5) probably include his anxiety over how the Corinthians have responded to the letter he sent with Titus (2:13; for his anxiety for the churches, see 11:28; 1 Thess 2:17–3:5). Thus both Titus' safe arrival and his message about their loyalty to Paul encourage him (2 Cor 7:6–7).

While initially unhappy that his letter caused them pain, Paul recognizes that the pain had been necessary for their good (7:8). Grief is good if it produces repentance that leads to life rather than death (7:9–10; cf. the goal of Paul's ministry in 3:6). Ancient moral writers often portrayed themselves as physicians who had to inflict pain or to open wounds for the sake of healing (e.g., Diogenes *Ep.* 49; Diogenes Laertius 2.70; 6.1.4; 6.2.30). Ancient persuasion theorists recognized that when gentle admonition failed, speakers might need to use harsher reproof, inflicting shame, grief, fear (cf. 7:11) or other attitudes to produce repentance and change (Stowers, *Letter Writing* [1986], 133–34, notes parallels in Cicero and Plutarch).

The sixfold rhetorical repetition in 7:11 ("what …"; the Greek is still more emphatic) would appeal to an ancient audience. The list climaxes in their readiness to punish or (literally) "avenge," perhaps involving zeal to make up for what has been lost; Paul recalls that principle again in 10:6. Paul's real concern was less the offender (2:5–10), whom they did ultimately discipline, than that the Corinthians would recognize their relationship with Paul and obey him (7:12).

Paul returns to his joy at Titus' coming; they had received Titus and his mission warmly, thereby confirming their love for Paul (7:13–16). In this section Paul reiterates his confidence in the Corinthians (7:14, 16; cf. 7:4), but writers sometimes used such expressions to prepare hearers for a monetary (or other) request—to which Paul will turn in chs. 8–9. Paul is not embarrassed by his "boasting" to Titus (7:12), but he seems anxious about his boast about them regarding the collection (9:4). Their continuing zeal for Paul (7:7, 11) must express itself in maintaining their zeal for the collection as well (9:2). If the well-to-do Corinthian church neglects their promise to help the Jerusalem church, it could risk stalling the collection project as a whole (9:3–4).

III. Sacrificially Supporting the Saints (8:1–9:15)

A. Examples of Sacrificial Giving (8:1–15)

Although not as often as with regard to other divisions, some scholars argue that chs. 8–9 (or at least 9) are separate letters from 1–7. But the more complex argument must always bear the burden of proof, and it is usually easier to account for changes of subject in a single letter than to account for how different letters would be fused into one. Paul has had to deal with relational issues and his ministry before addressing the imminent collection more explicitly. His treatment of issues surrounding Titus' previous visit (7:5–15) leads naturally into those surrounding the next one (8:16–9:5). The collection would afford them opportunity to prove their zeal (7:7, 11; 9:2).

Chapters 8–9 may also prepare for Paul's responses to economic criticisms about him (11:7–12; 12:14–19) and of his agents (12:17–18). Not wanting to appear like a charlatan (2:17; 4:2), Paul has refused to accept the Corinthians' gifts (11:7–9; 12:16–18); he will accept gifts only for the Jerusalem church (9:12–13). (Like Jesus, Paul stressed care for the poor.) In 8–9, Paul manages to avoid speaking explicitly of "money," while using various synonyms common in business documents: e.g., "abundance" (8:2, 7, 14; 9:8, 12, sometimes used for "profit margins"); "grace" (NRSV, "privilege") or "generosity" (8:4, 6–7, 19); "case" (9:3); "undertaking" (9:4); "bountiful gift" (9:5); and "ministry" (*leitourgia*, 9:12). Paul

uses *diakonia* for both proclamation (3:3, 7–9; 4:1; 5:18; 6:3) and social ministry (8:19–20; 9:1, 12–13).

Probably before Paul and the Corinthians had a disagreement, Paul had boasted of the Corinthians' zeal to the Macedonians (8:24–9:2; for the reverse, see 8:1–8). Now, after the disagreement, he wants to be sure that the Corinthians will follow through on their commitment, or else both he and the Corinthians will be embarrassed when the Macedonian delegation arrives (9:3–4; cf. 8:11). Such an expression of concern is diplomatic—since Titus has already reported back to Paul, Paul undoubtedly knows that the Corinthians are not in fact ready. Thus he is sending Titus to them again (along with some colleagues), to ensure that everything is soon ready (8:6, 16–23; 9:5).

To further encourage Corinthian participation, Paul compares them with the Macedonians (the province to Achaia's northeast; 8:1–8, esp. 8:8). (He has also used the Corinthians' promises to spur the Macedonians, 9:1–5.) Leaders often played on cities' or regions' friendly rivalry to spur action (e.g., Xenophon *Cyr.* 2.1.22; 7.1.18). If the impoverished Macedonian Christians can give (8:1–5), how much more the prosperous Corinthians (8:6–8)? Philippi and Thessalonica had prosperity, but it had little effect on the poor, and Christians there had been persecuted. By contrast, Corinthian Christians are not suffering, and at least one even holds a civic position of some sort (Rom 16:23).

Giving "according to their means" (8:3) recalls Israel's example in Exod 35:24, although the language was also common for donations (language familiar from ancient business documents appears throughout the section). Ancients sometimes praised highly committed donors as giving "themselves" first (8:5; Danker, *II Corinthians*, 122, cites OGIS 339.19–20; SIG3 495.125); here the behavior imitates Jesus (8:9). Paul praises their spiritual gifts in a virtue list, inviting them to excel in this matter also (8:7).

The poor Macedonians give beyond their means (8:3), and Jesus, though rich in heavenly glory and power, went beyond even this (8:9; cf. Phil 2:5–8). Ancients praised generous benefactors, but no one expected them to impoverish themselves. Jesus made himself poor to enrich others, an example followed by Paul as well (2 Cor 6:10).

Paul reasons with them concerning what is "appropriate" (a term often used in ancient persuasive texts, 8:10); inscriptions also praised donors for "completing" as well as pledging (8:6, 10–11). Jewish sources recognized giving "according to what one has" (e.g., Tob 4:8, 16). Paul is not trying to make them poor, but to establish "equality," which was also to their own benefit; someday others might help them if they were needy (2 Cor 8:13–14). "Equality" was an ideal in ancient friendships, where it involved even quantitative equality (Plato *Laws* 8.837AB; Aristotle *N.E.* 8.7.3, 1158b). Whoever had more than enough should share with whoever had less, emulating the same principle exemplified in the manna: God provided just enough, so no one had too much or too little (8:15, citing Exod 16:18). While keeping the collection voluntary, Paul applies Jesus' teaching about possessions beyond individuals to churches in regions of the world. Churches benefiting from prosperous settings should partner with the churches of poorer nations and regions.

B. Two Delegations (8:16–9:5)

Now that Titus has returned with a good report of his relationship with the Corinthians, Paul is sending him back with a well-known brother (and perhaps others, 8:23). Paul is sending this delegation in advance to make sure that the Corinthian church will be ready before the Macedonian delegation arrives (9:3–5).

Having experienced Corinthian hospitality (7:13–15), Titus is eager to return (8:16–17). Paul writes "letters of recommendation" (cf. 3:1) for Titus (8:16–17, 23) and "the brother" (8:18–19, 22), although the latter case is unusual since recommendations (e.g., Cicero Fam. 13 passim) were not anonymous (though inscriptions do not always name delegates). Perhaps the unnamed delegate would risk persecution if a letter naming him were intercepted (though he traveled with the letter); no consensus exists as to why he remains anonymous.

To preclude scandal (8:20–21), the Macedonians and the Corinthians' own delegates, along with representatives of the other churches, ultimately would carry the collection to Jerusalem, verifying for each of the churches its appropriate delivery (1 Cor 16:3). Financial scandals were common (e.g., Josephus *Ant.* 18.81–84; *I. Eph.* 1a.17–19), and the mistrust of some (12:16–18) makes such precautions all the more essential (cf. "blame" in 8:20 with the same Greek term in 6:3). It is not Paul's honor here, but the Lord's own honor ("glory"), that is at stake (8:19, 23).

Titus is Paul's own representative, and the others represent the churches (8:23). The use of apostoloi for "messengers" may resemble a title for Diaspora bearers of the Jerusalem Temple tax (cf. Keith Nickle, *The Collection*). When ancient letters requested a proof of love (8:24), the request was normally meant affectionately (Fronto *Ep. Graecae* 6; *Ad M. Caes.* 3.2).

Many scholars divide ch. 9 from its preceding context, citing 9:1 as assuming that the collection has not been mentioned before. But ancient persuaders sometimes ironically raised a matter while claiming not to raise it (e.g., Phlm 19; *Rhet. Her.* 4.27.37; Cicero *Verr.* 2.4.52.116; 2.5.8.20–21), and the opening words of 9:1 in Greek are words that normally allude to preceding lines. In fact, a break between 8:24 and 9:1 is quite unlikely, since they belong to the same context. Paul is addressing the delegation in 8:16–23 and 9:3–5, digressing to remind the Corinthians of his trust in 9:1–2. In 9:1–5 he explains his boasting in 8:24; "brothers" in 9:3 depends on 8:16–24.

Paul is clearly anxious lest the Corinthians fail (9:4–5), but politely expresses confidence in 9:1–2; other ancient writers sometimes struggled to balance confidence and caution in such matters (e.g., Cicero *Fam.* 3.13). The advance delegation would ensure their readiness before the Macedonians came (9:3–5). The term translated "extortion" (*pleonexia*) in 9:5 might actually warn against the Corinthians accumulating beyond their needs (*pleonazō*), while others lack (8:15).

C. Harvesting Honor for God's Seed (9:6–15)

Reaping what one sowed was a standard agricultural principle (9:6, 9–10), often applied in moral settings (e.g., Prov 22:8; Hos 8:7) or to generosity and reciprocity. Paul's rhetorical structure in 9:6 (x ... y/x ... y) would appeal to ancient hearers. Their willing heart (9:7) recalls voluntary gifts in Exod 25:2; 35:5, 21–22, and "not reluctantly" recalls Deut 15:10 (LXX). Ancients praised honorable donors who gave "willingly" (cf. Musonius Rufus 19, p. 122.30 Lutz; Cicero *Fam.* 13.1.2). God's love for cheerful givers (9:7) recalls a Greek addition to Prov 22:8.

Paul reinforces the point in 9:8, by seven "p" words in one verse (five of them different forms of *pas*, "every"). The phrase translated "having enough" may mean, "having contentment with what one has," a common emphasis in ancient philosophy (e.g., Epictetus *Diatr.* 1.1.27; Marcus Aurelius 3.11.2).

In 9:9, Paul quotes Ps 112:9, where the righteous give to the poor, hence their righteousness endures. But Paul knows that God supplies for these righteous givers, and hence in 9:10 alludes to Isa 55:10 (God provides seed for the sower, i.e., for those who scatter in 9:9). Thus God would supply the Corinthians seed to sow, hence increase the harvest of their righteousness as they sowed generously (9:10).

Paul develops the principle in 9:11–15, and his argument would make sense to those steeped in ideas popular in Paul's day. Greek and Roman benefactors, or donors, gave gifts; recipients (often cities) reciprocated by giving the benefactors honor (see Seneca *Ben.* passim). In 9:11–15, however, the Corinthians' gifts do not earn them honor with the receivers (though they are objects of prayer) so much as the honor goes to God, the ultimate benefactor of all.

IV. Confronting the Rivals (10:1–13:10)

A. The Meek Writer's Competitors (10:1–18)

Although Paul nowhere else starts either a letter or a section with "and I" (NRSV, "I myself"), some think that 10:1 begins a new letter. This suggestion is likelier here than for any other proposed break in the letter, and may well be correct, but even here it remains open to debate. Writers could add addenda to letters, or add a second letter with the same messenger, if new reports came (though they usually specified this; e.g., Cicero *Fam.* 12.12.5; *Att.* 8.6).

Paul sometimes shifts suddenly in 2 Corinthians (8:1; 10:1), but he does this also in 1 Corinthians (5:1; 8:1; 12:1; 15:1). Whereas in Romans Paul shifts from theological argument to pastoral application at Rom 12:1, here he shifts from theological argument about true ministry to direct polemic at 2 Cor 10:1. If Paul sometimes sounds in tension with what he wrote earlier, Paul's rhetorical tightrope produces the identical effect even within sections: e.g., Paul both commends (4:2; 6:4) and does not commend (3:1; 5:12) himself. Rhetoric emphasized the value of shifting style and tone to keep a work more lively.

Although Paul has earlier noted his reconciliation with the Corinthians (2:6–11; 7:7–13), he views it as incomplete (5:20–6:2). Paul entreats them to receive him (6:12–13; 7:2), yet in a conciliatory way (7:3–4), as here (cf. 11:11; 12:14–15, 19; 13:7–8). Favoring unity with the rest of 2 Corinthians, Paul probably echoes earlier chapters here: testing them (2:9; 8:8; 13:6); speaking "before God in Christ" (2:17; 12:19); "craftiness" and "deceit" (4:2; 12:16); and especially talk of "boasting," "commendation," and "joy."

Paul's "meekness and gentleness" (10:1) was expressed in sending a corrective letter rather than first coming to impose harsh discipline (1:23–2:4). This kindness imitated Christ (10:1; cf. 8:9; Phil 2:8; Matt 11:29). They should have appreciated this, because people widely praised "meek" rulers, by which they simply meant "merciful" ones who used their power benevolently (Xenophon *Cyr.* 2.1.30; Tacitus *Hist.* 2.5).

But for Paul's critics (cf. 10:2), Paul was a *weak* leader (cf. 11:22), who threatened in letters but would not carry through in person (10:9–11). (This complaint may eventually force Paul to discipline them after all; 12:20–13:2.) They criticized him for acting by "human standards" (10:2), as if he had made his travel plans concerning them by "human standards" (1:17). Paul will soon demonstrate that it is his opponents who act by "human standards" (11:18)!

In reality Paul is strong, but expresses this strength not in harshness but in combating their false worldview (10:3–6). Ancient writers often used military imagery for battles against hostile passions or, as here, ideologies (10:4–5; cf. 2:14; 6:7; cf. Seneca *Ep. Lucil.* 109.8–9; 117.7, 28; Diogenes Laertius 6.1.13). Far from working by "human standards," Paul depends on God's power for this battle (10:4). Paul sought their complete obedience (10:6): although the Corinthians had begun to "obey" (2:9; 7:15) and "punish" or "avenge" their disobedience (7:11), it could not be complete so long as they welcomed Paul's rivals.

Paul fought their ideas, not the Corinthians themselves, because his authority was to "build" them up (10:8; 12:19; 13:10). The Corinthians themselves should have defended him against his rivals (3:1–2; 5:12; 12:11), but since they did not, Paul is forced to defend himself (10:8; see discussion of "boasting" at 11:1). His critics charge inconsistency (cf. 10:11): Paul was a strong writer but a weak speaker (10:9–10; cf. 11:6; 1 Cor 2:1–5). Greeks and Romans expected speakers to have not only good content but good delivery (e.g., gestures, appearance, dress, accent, voice tone), and evaluated them accordingly (e.g., Cicero *Brut.* 31.117; 55.203; 66.234; Pliny *Ep.* 2.3.9; 2.19.2–6). In this case, the Corinthians find Paul forceful in his letters but too "nice" in person (10:1, 11).

In 10:12–18, Paul turns the tables by attacking the very values by which his critics evaluate. Paul's rivals are commending themselves (10:12, 18) and boasting (11:12, 18), probably regarding worldly matters like status and impressive speech (5:12; 10:10–12; 11:6). Evaluation by means of comparison was a standard practice in schools used for speeches and literature (cf. Cicero *De or.* 3.14.52). One could compare oneself with others to exalt oneself (Cicero *Brut.* 93.321–22; *Pis.* 22.51), but some mocked those who simply exchanged compliments among their peers (cf. 10:12).

Paul ironically claims that he would not "dare" be so bold as his rivals (10:12; the same verb for "daring" in 10:2), though he will finally "dare" in 11:21 (the verb's only other appearance in this letter). (Paul's vague "certain persons" may have followed an ancient practice of refusing to honor some dishonorable adversaries by so much as naming them; e.g., Aeschines *Ctesiphon* 1; Dio Chrysostom 40.8–9; 47.20–23.)

To compare oneself with members of a class in which one obviously did not belong was considered unbridled, arrogant hubris (10:13–14). In reality, however, it is the rivals who are boasting outside their class! Boasting "beyond limits" (10:13) suggests that his rivals violate a major standard of Greek ethics (cf. Musonius Rufus 18B, p. 116.12 Lutz).

The "limits" here (10:13–15) probably especially reflect spheres of authority given by God.

Paul stayed within his God-given calling (cf. Rom 11:13; Gal 2:7–9), but his opponents did not. They lacked understanding (10:12), like the arrogant people Greeks complained about who did not "know themselves," i.e., their divinely appointed human limits (cf. Plutarch *E at Delphi* 2, *Mor.* 385D; *Oracles at Delphi* 29, *Mor.* 408E). Whereas Paul fathered the Corinthian church (1 Cor 4:15; cf. 2 Cor 12:14), his rivals boast in someone else's (Paul's) work (10:15). Paul does hope that, with the Corinthians' assistance, his own sphere will be expanded—but into new territory, not in claiming credit for another's work (10:16; Rom 15:18–21, 24, 28).

The only right way to boast is in the Lord (10:17). As in 1 Cor 1:26–31, Paul here refers to Jer 9:23–24. Divine commendation (2 Cor 10:18) was reserved for the judgment (5:10–12).

B. Compelled to Counter His Opponents' Folly (11:1–21a)

Paul trusts the Corinthians can "bear with" his foolishness (11:1), since they show this "courtesy" to his rivals (11:19). By underlining the foolishness of boasting even while reluctantly doing it, Paul exposes the folly of his rivals' behavior. Yet to meet their challenges, Paul must boast himself—though boasting in sufferings and weaknesses (11:23–33) changes the basis for status. He must answer fools according to their folly without being like them (Prov 26:4–5).

Ancient speakers found ways to make boasting seem less offensive, such as: denying they were boasting (3:1; 5:12); claiming that they were responding to charges (10:10); expressing concern for hearers (11:1–4); self-defense (11:5–6); countering others' arrogance (11:12); or noting its necessity (12:1) or that others compelled them to do it (12:11; see Plutarch, *Praising Oneself Inoffensively*, passim). Likewise, Paul must commend himself for their good (10:8) and within limits (10:13–17; 11:30; 12:5–6).

Like an ancient father (12:14; 1 Cor 4:15), Paul has arranged for the Corinthian church's betrothal (11:2)—here to Christ (cf. 1 Cor 6:15–17). Fathers were considered responsible to guard their daughters' virginity from immoral men (e.g., Deut 22:15–21; Sir 42:9–12). Paul thus feels the kind of jealousy God feels over God's people, whom God had married (e.g., Exod 20:5; 34:14).

Paul thus compares them with Eve, and the opponents, who are ministers of Satan, with the serpent and Satan (11:3, 13–15). In Gen 3:1–7, the serpent deceived Eve; Jewish tradition also claimed that Satan came disguised as an angel to seduce Eve (cf. 11:14; *L.A.E.* 9:1–2; *Apoc. Mos.* 17:1–2). How were these rivals preaching another Jesus (11:4)? Insofar as we can gather from the emphasis in Paul's response (11:23; cf. 2:14–6:10), they may play down Jesus' sufferings and the cost of following him, a message that could appeal in prosperous Corinth (as in the modern West).

Preparing for a more thorough comparison at 11:22–23, Paul insists that he is not inferior to these rivals (11:5). He mocks them as "super-apostles" (11:5; 12:11), elsewhere portraying such "super-" labels as arrogant (cf. *hyper-* prepositions in the Greek of 10:14, 16; 12:6–7). Although some scholars associate these with the Jerusalem apostles, most recognize that he refers instead to the rivals in Corinth (11:4; 12:11). These "apostles," unlike those in Jerusalem, could appeal to Greco-Roman speaking skills so as to compete with Paul (11:6). Whatever Paul's conflicts with some of the Jerusalem apostles were, he hardly would have denounced them as "false apostles" (11:13).

Claiming that he is "untrained in speech" (11:6) does not mean that he lacked even basic knowledge of rhetoric (the dominant advanced discipline in antiquity), or even that he was a poor speaker (even famous orators sometimes claimed to be unskilled compared to those who emphasized only rhetorical form; Dio Chrysostom 12.15; cf. Quintilian *Inst.* 4.1.8–11). As we have been pointing out, he contextualizes his message by using many Greco-Roman rhetorical devices. It does suggest that his rivals thought themselves better, and that Paul was unwilling to lay his emphasis on rhetoric. Just as philosophers criticized orators for valuing form over content (cf. Seneca Ep. Lucil. 20.2; 40.4; 86.16; 100.1), so Paul emphasizes his knowledge (11:6).

In 11:7–9, Paul responds to criticisms that he is a "volunteer," an "amateur," who took money from other churches but not from them. (Some similarly criticized Socrates as not accepting money because he was not worth any; Xenophon *Mem.* 1.6.12.) Corinthian money probably came with "strings attached"—they would treat Paul as their client or employee. Moreover, accepting support from any one Corinthian faction could expose him to the enmity of the other factions. At the same time, in their culture rejecting a gift constituted rejecting "friendship," preferring enmity (Cicero *Fam.* 14.3.1; Fronto *Ep. Graecae* 5). Thus Paul must explain in graphic, ironic language (e.g., "robbing" or "exploiting" churches) why he rejected their offer (probably in contrast to his rivals). Paul accepted Macedonian support for their good (11:9–11); if he boasted about the Macedonians (11:9–10), he had also boasted about the Corinthians (9:2).

Ancients accepted silencing others' arrogance as a justification for boasting (11:12); Paul warned that these boasters in others' labors were false apostles, Satan's ministers (11:13–15; on Satan as an "angel of light," see comment on 11:3–4). In 11:16–21, Paul again reinforces the foolishness of boasting (his rivals' behavior) and implicitly the foolishness of the Corinthians for welcoming this means of the opponents exploiting them. In 11:20, Paul stirs emotion with more rhetorical repetition (the Greek repeats "if someone" five times); he implies that their opponents (not his collection) exploit them financially (cf. 2:17; 11:7–9; 12:13–18).

C. Boasting as a Fool in His Sufferings (11:21*b*–33)

Paul boasts in both sufferings (11:22–33) and revelations (12:1–10). He did not "dare" to compare himself with his rivals in 10:12, but now he does (11:21*b*), and matches them point by point (a standard ancient persuasion technique; 11:22–23; cf. Menander *Rhetor* 2.3, 381.31–32; 386.10–13). (Paul probably uses the three groups in 11:22 interchangeably.) Ancients often provided boastful lists of their exploits and achievements (most famously Augustus' *Res Gestae*); Paul, however, lists not churches founded but sufferings. Ancients could use lists of sufferings to underline their integrity (see comment on 4:8–11); Paul also uses it to value the weakness through which God displays divine power (4:7, 10–11; 12:9; 13:4).

Paul's rivals cannot compete with him in sufferings for preaching Christ, with which Jesus associated his commission (e.g., Mark 8:34–38; Matt 10:24–25; Luke 10:16). Regardless of their rhetorical prowess or other bases for boasting, they do not sufficiently respect or reflect God's power in brokenness, and hence preach a different Christ (11:4).

Imprisonment and public beatings (11:23–25) were normally matters of public shame, but Paul boasts in sufferings for Christ. Refusing to renounce his membership in Israel, Paul faced synagogue beatings (11:24); much harsher were Gentile floggings with rods (11:25) and a stoning (11:25; cf. Acts 14:19). (Although Roman magistrates were not supposed to have Roman citizens flogged with rods, it did sometimes happen in the provinces, and could happen to Paul occasionally over the course of his ministry.) Expanding on Paul's journeys in 11:26, he uses eightfold repetition of "danger" to rhetorically intensify the point. The verse's climactic "false brothers and sisters" (11:26) fits the situation he now addresses (11:13). Paul's "anxiety" for churches (11:28–29) reflects a pattern the Corinthians had observed throughout Paul's letter to them.

Why does Paul add the account in 11:32–33 as an apparent afterthought? Probably Paul here offers one concrete example of danger in ministry. Romans boasted over the first soldier to scale an enemy wall; here Paul recounts his escape from a wall (though probably more as danger than as humiliation; cf. Josh 2:15; 1 Sam 19:12). The Nabatean ethnarch (not "governor," *pace* NRSV) need not mean that Aretas IV ruled Damascus (as many argue); the ethnarch may have been simply the leader of the Nabatean quarter there. (Jewish opposition in Acts 9:23–25 may help explain Nabatean opposition, especially if they acted in concert. Judeans and Nabateans had close ties in the region.)

D. Boasting as a Fool in Revelations (12:1–10)

On boasting, see comment at 11:1. After boasting in sufferings (11:23–33) Paul boasts in revelations (12:1), yet offers only one example (12:2–4) and emphasizes again his weakness, which compensates for revelations (12:7–9). Some Greeks sought visions (e.g., PGM 4.930–1114; 77.1–5); some Jews sought to see God's throne (e.g., *b. Hag.* 14b–15b). Paul does not claim to have solicited them, but only to have been "caught up" (12:2, 4; cf. Ezek 8:3; 1 En. 39:3; 52:1).

Since Paul is boasting in his visions (12:1), his anonymous visionary in 12:2–5 is presumably himself. One could call oneself "that person,"

and boast less offensively by transferring one's experience to another (while obviously speaking really of oneself). Jewish vision reports can be "in" (*1 En.* 39:3) or (more like Greeks) "outside" (*1 En.* 71:1–6) the body; for Paul, an experience outside the body might involve temporary death (5:6–8). Jewish texts promised a future "paradise" in Eden for the righteous (*4 Ezra* 7:36; 8:52; *2 Bar.* 51:11), and placed it in heaven for the present (*Test. Abr.* 20:14A; *3 Bar.* 4:6). (They differed on the number of heavens; "three" [as in *Test. Levi* 2–3] was one of the lowest estimates.)

Yet instead of recounting his vision's content, he declares that it is too sacred for telling (12:4)—thereby again underlining the folly of boasts. Some others spoke of divine secrets to be shared with only a few, or even too sublime to recount in words (Josephus *Ant.* 2.276; tos. *Hag.* 2:1; Iamblichus *Vit. Pyth.* 18.88; 34.247). When Paul does report the content of a revelation, it is the Lord's teaching of Christ's power in human weakness (12:9).

Scholars differ as to Paul's "thorn in the flesh" (12:7): temptation; a physical problem; or, as I think more likely (with many, including Chrysostom *Hom. 2 Cor.* 26.2–3), opposition. This opposition could include persecution (cf. 11:23–33; Paul elsewhere uses the term here for "torment" only in 1 Cor 4:11) and also Satan's other messengers (2 Cor 11:13–15). The expression alludes to an OT one used for God leaving Israel's enemies to test them (Num 33:55; Josh 23:13). Paul is ready to embrace any suffering for Christ if he may find there Christ's grace and power (12:10).

E. Summary and Final Appeal (12:11–18)

Paul summarizes (12:11, 13), cites his apostolic signs (12:12), reminds the Corinthians of how he has cared for them (12:13–15), and demands whether he or his colleagues had wronged them (12:15–18). (Speakers often appealed to hearers' emotions especially toward the climax [e.g., Demosthenes *Ep.* 2]; Paul does so here, although he has done so at other points as well.)

Whether or not his rivals claimed signs, Paul outclasses them (12:12). Although Acts offers more details, Paul's own letters attest that he believed that God provided miracles often as he evangelized (Rom 15:19). A sorer issue with the Corinthians, however, involved Paul's refusal to accept their support (see comment on 11:7–9), which comes up again here (12:13–14). Paul would not be their client; in fact, he is their patron and benefactor (12:14); parents were a sort of benefactor to their children (Seneca Ben. 3.11.2), and benefactors could receive only praise, not money, for their services (the latter made them an employee; cf. e.g., *Apollonius King of Tyre* 10). Like the greatest donors noted in antiquity, Paul gave even himself (12:15), following Jesus' example (8:9).

Paul asks the Corinthians, who earlier wanted Paul to depend on them, whether he or his colleagues have exploited them (12:16–18). If he would not exploit them for himself, would he do so for the needs of others? This climax of Paul's letter suggests the vulnerability of the collection at its heart (chs. 8–9). Because Paul has used language like "crafty" (12:16) earlier (in the Greek of 4:2; 11:3), and this is not his common language, he may be responding to his rivals' complaints against the collection.

Because Paul says that he "sent" Titus and the brother, many think that 2 Cor 10–13 must be a letter later than 8–9. This suggestion is plausible, yet "sent" could be an epistolary aorist, i.e., past tense only from the vantage point of when the Corinthians would be receiving the letter. (Paul in fact uses "epistolary aorists" in 8:18, 22, although the NRSV translates them as present there.) Those favoring separate letters also note that the "exploitation" question can sound more like an earlier visit.

F. Warning about Paul's Visit (12:19–13:10)

The affectionate parent (12:14) must now exercise discipline, but hates to do it. Paul had gently chosen to warn them by letter rather than by carrying out discipline in person (1:23–2:4). Because he did not carry out his "parental" threats, however (cf. 1 Cor 4:18–21), some critics charged him with talking menacingly in letters yet proving weak in person (2 Cor 10:8–10). Now Paul will carry out the discipline if he must (12:20–13:3)—though he again lovingly warns them, hoping to be able to avoid such harshness (13:10). The Corinthians repented regarding the offender (7:12), but despite Paul's diplomacy earlier in the letter, he must now confront the other issues he has reserved for his finale (as persuaders sometimes did).

Jesus embraced the epitome of human weakness in crucifixion and was raised by God's power; so Paul embraces whatever weakness God brings him, trusting God to compensate (13:4; cf. 12:5, 9–10). The Corinthians who wanted to evaluate Paul (cf. 11:5; 12:11) must now evaluate themselves (13:5). Was Christ in them, as he was in Paul (13:3–5), i.e., were they converted (cf. 5:18)? If so, they are proofs of his ministry (3:1–3). Paul's entire goal was for their good; although God could give authority to build up or tear down (Jer 1:10), Paul's ministry of grace (cf. 2 Cor 3:6) was especially to "build" them up (13:8–10; cf. 10:8).

V. Closing (13:11–14)

In 13:11, Paul summarizes his exhortations (including to unity). In 13:12, he sends greetings. Relatives and other persons who were close used light kisses (usually on the lips; e.g., *Jos. Asen.* 8:6), normally easily distinguishable from erotic kisses; members of the Christian family thus could express affection. (A letter writer could also ask a receiver to pass on the writer's kiss of greeting; e.g., Fronto *Ad M. Caes.* 1.8.7; 5.33 [48]; 5.42 [57].)

Finally, Paul closes with a blessing from Jesus, the Father, and the Holy Spirit (13:13; cf. Matt 28:19). Paul already recognized Jesus as divine Lord (cf. 1:2; 1 Cor 1:30; 8:6). Paul's blessing is a prayer for God to perform these works (such as love and fellowship) among them.

BIBLIOGRAPHY

F. W. Danker. *II Corinthians*. Augusburg Commentary on the NT (Minneapolis: Augsburg Publishing House, 1989); J. T. Fitzgerald. *Cracks in an Earthen Vessel: An Examination of the Catalogues of Hardships in the Corinthian Correspondence*. SBLDS 99 (Atlanta: Scholars Press, 1988); V. P. Furnish. *II Corinthians*. AB 32A (Garden City, N.Y.: Doubleday & Company, 1984); C. S. Keener. *1–2 Corinthians*. The New Cambridge Bible Commentary (Cambridge: Cambridge University Press, 2005); J. Lambrecht. *Second Corinthians*. SP 8 (Collegeville, Minn.: A Michael Glazier Book, The Liturgical Press, 1999); P. Marshall. *Enmity in Corinth: Social Conventions in Paul's Relations with the Corinthians*. WUNT 2, Reihe 23 (Tubingen: J. C. B. Mohr [Paul

Siebeck], 1987); F. J. Matera. *II Corinthians: A Commentary.* NTL (Louisville: Westminster John Knox Press, 2003); M. E. Thrall. *A Critical and Exegetical Commentary on the Second Epistle to the Corinthians.* 2 vols. (Edinburgh: T&T Clark, 1994, 2000); B. Witherington III. *Conflict and Community in Corinth: A Socio-Rhetorical Commentary on 1 and 2 Corinthians* (Grand Rapids: Eerdmans; Carlisle: Paternoster, 1995).

GALATIANS

Susan Eastman

OVERVIEW

The power of Paul's letter to the churches he founded in Galatia extends far beyond its original addressees. Its six chapters are polemical, emotionally charged, theologically packed, and rich in scriptural allusions. Paul argues for the singular staying power of God's unconditional grace in Christ Jesus, and against observance of the Mosaic law as a prerequisite for participation and sustenance in the Christian life. He passionately proclaims the enduring themes of grace, freedom, union with Christ, perseverance in the faith, and the life-giving fruits of the Spirit—all instigated and sustained by God's initiative in Christ.

Location and Date of the Letter. Both the destination and date of Galatians are uncertain. "Galatia" comprised all of Asia Minor, from the north, where ethnic Celts, called "Galatians," lived, to the Roman province of "Galatia" in the south. According to Acts, Paul founded churches in both regions: in the southern cities of Derba and Lystra on his first missionary journey (14:6–23), and in northern Galatia on his second and third journeys (Acts 16:1–6; 18:23). He wrote the letter shortly after his founding visit: either 48–49 CE if he wrote to churches in southern Galatia, or somewhere between 50 and 55 CE, if he wrote to churches in the north. His use of "Galatians" as an ethnic term (3:1) favors the latter destination and date.

Situation. Other Jewish Christian missionaries, perhaps representing the "circumcision party" in the Jerusalem church (2:12; cf., Acts 15:5), have come into Galatia, adding to Paul's teaching (2:6) by instructing his Gentile converts in the law of Moses. They teach that full membership in the people of God, and the powerful presence of the Holy Spirit, depend on keeping the "works of the law"—circumcision, food laws, and the liturgical calendar. That is, they teach that the Galatian Christians need to "live like Jews" (2:14). Not unreasonably, they view Gentile faith in Jesus, the Messiah, as entailing adherence to observance of the practices of Judaism. Paul, however, sees the imposition of law observance as a communally divisive subversion of the sufficiency of Christ. Here is the beginning of the parting of the ways between Judaism and Christianity.

In reconstructing the Galatian situation, two cautions are in order. First, Paul is very angry when he writes this letter, and we hear only his version of events. His descriptions of the other missionaries as coercive troublemakers who manipulate people by the threat of exclusion, and who themselves avoid persecution, probably differs significantly from their own self-understanding. Second, it is important not to confuse the issues posed by these teachers with Paul's own message. Their concern is how Gentile Christians can be Abraham's children and heirs. Paul insists that they already are children of Abraham, through Christ (3:29), and encourages them to stand fast in their reliance on Christ alone, rather than their own actions vis à vis the law.

OUTLINE

I. Salutation (1:1–5)

II. Trouble in Galatia (1:6–9)

III. The Authority of Paul's Gospel (1:10–2:21)

    A. Paul's Call and Ministry (1:10–2:10)

    B. Cephas in Antioch (2:11–14)

    C. The Sufficiency of Christ (2:15–21)

IV. Rectified by Faith, Heirs of the Promise (3:1–4:7)

    A. The Message of Faith and the Spirit (3:1–5)

    B. Sons and Heirs Through Faith (3:6–29)

    C. From Slavery to Freedom (4:1–7)

V. Return to Slavery (4:8–11)

VI. Motivational Appeals (4:12–5:12)

    A. Argument from Experience (4:12–20)

    B. Argument from Scripture (4:21–4:31)

    C. Warning Against Circumcision (5:1–12)

VII. Life in the New Community (5:13–6:10)

VIII. Conclusion (6:11–18)

DETAILED ANALYSIS

I. Salutation (1:1–5)

The salutation introduces key themes: the divine origin and hence authority of Paul's apostleship (1:11–12); the identity of God as father (3:26; 4:5–7), who through the resurrection of Jesus demonstrated life-giving power (3:22); the grace and peace that come through Christ (1:6, 15; 2:21; 6:16, 18); and liberation from the present evil age, accomplished by Christ's death on the cross. The phrase, "who gave himself for our sins," is an early creedal statement (2:20; 1 Cor. 15:3; cf. Rom. 4:25; 5:8, 15–19; 8:3, 32; 2 Cor 5:21; Matt 26:28; Titus 2:14; 1 Pet 2:24), which Paul quotes and distinctively interprets as deliverance from the enslaving and death-dealing powers that dominate life in this world (cf., 6:14–15). That is, our human predicament is not simply that we sin and need forgiveness, but rather that we are enslaved by the compulsion to sin and the dominion of death, and need liberation.

II. Trouble in Galatia (1:6–9)

Omitting his usual thanksgiving, Paul immediately launches into the situation that sparked his letter: the Galatians are defecting from his gospel ("good news") of the grace of Christ, and following some "troublemakers" who claim that their message is truly good news. "So quickly" (v. 6) indicates that little time has elapsed since Paul's visit. "The one who called you" (v. 6) is God (5:8; cf., Rom 8:30; 1 Cor 1:9; 1 Thess 2:12; 5:24), not Paul, who also is called by God (1:15; 1 Cor 1:1; Rom 1:1). At stake is the Galatians' adherence to the God of Jesus Christ, who calls human beings solely through grace, apart from the law (2:21; cf., Rom 3:21–26; 6:14).

III. The Authority of Paul's Gospel (1:10–2:21)

A. Paul's Call and Ministry (1:10–2:10)

The character of Paul's ministry (1:10), the divine origin of his calling (1:11–24), and the history of his dealings with the church in Jerusalem (2:1–14), all testify to the authenticity of his gospel.

Paul's gracious gospel might seem to tell people what they want to hear (1:10), but he contrasts such "people-pleasing" with his own calling as Christ's servant (literally "slave"), who indeed suffers for Christ (5:11; 6:17). What would appear to be easy—preaching grace—in fact stirs up violent opposition.

God is the initiator and guarantor of Paul's message, which is not a human teaching about God, but rather the direct apocalypse (vv. 12, 16; NRSV, "revelation") of Jesus Christ himself. More than a visual revelation, *apocalypse* signifies God's powerful intervention in human affairs, creating a "before" and an "after" (1:4) that is displayed in Paul's own life, as he now preaches the faith he once tried to destroy (1:24). Paul's description of his call echoes that of the prophets called from birth to proclaim good news to the Gentiles (cf. Isa 49:1–6; Jer 1:5). The divine interruption that changes his life also connects him to the purpose for which he was born.

"Arabia" probably refers to the ancient Nabatean kingdom southeast of Damascus. Paul's travel narrative first emphasizes his independence from the Jerusalem Church; he meets Cephas (Peter) and James the Lord's brother (2:9, 12; cf., Acts 15:13; 21:18) privately, as equals, in his first visit to Jerusalem (vv. 18–19). Subsequently, he demonstrates the ecclesial authorization of his ministry (2:1–10; cf., Acts 15:1–29). Despite the "false believers" (v. 4), whose infiltration of the Jerusalem meeting, and attempt to impose circumcision on Gentile converts, link them to the troublemakers in Galatia, the church leaders endorse Paul's circumcision-free mission to the Gentiles.

In all of Paul's letters, this is the only reference to Peter's Jewish mission (vv. 7–8) as distinct from Paul's Gentile mission. Whether either Peter or Paul abides fully by the Jerusalem agreement is unclear: Peter comes to the Gentile Christian church in Antioch and lives "like a Gentile" (2:12, 14), and apparently he baptizes Gentile converts in Corinth (1 Cor 1:12; 3:22; 9:5); Paul later boasts of receiving the synagogue discipline of thirty-nine lashes (2 Cor 11:24), implying that he continues to preach in synagogues.

B. Cephas in Antioch (2:11-14)

The Antioch congregation launched Paul's missionary travels to Galatia (Acts 11:19–26; 13:1–3), and it faced similar issues: intruders from the circumcision faction in the Jerusalem church are dividing the community into those who keep the Mosaic law and those who do not. The behavior of Cephas (Peter) illustrates the problem, and Paul's rebuke of "hypocrisy" indirectly addresses the Galatians as well.

C. The Sufficiency of Christ (2:15–21)

Three key concepts first appear in this dense passage. First is the phrase, "works of the law" (3:2, 5, 10). In the immediate situation it refers to practices of Mosaic law such as circumcision and food laws, but in the larger context it refers simply to human performance of the law's requirements (see Exod 18:20). Paul has "died" not simply to "works of the law," but to the law itself as the way to both righteousness (2:21) and the gift of the Holy Spirit (3:2–5).

Second are the terms, "to justify" and "justification." They are better translated as "to rectify" and "righteousness" (as in 3:6//Gen 15:6). To be rectified is to be freed from the power of sin that operates through both condemnation and compulsion. It is, as Paul's own life demonstrates, to be unmade and remade in union with Christ (2:19–20), by the power of the Spirit given freely through the message of faith (3:2). The verb, "justified," is in the passive voice, with God as the implied subject; if the law is what humans do (even when helped by the Spirit), justification is what God alone does to, for, and in human beings.

Third, the NRSV supplies "the faith of Jesus Christ" (2:16), and "the faith of the Son of God" (2:20) as alternative translations (cf. 3:22; Rom 3:22, 26; Phil 3:9). As the structure of 2:16 demonstrates, rectification is God's deed, enacted through Christ's faithful self-giving (2:21; cf., 1:4), which encompasses and guarantees human trust in Christ. Paul's emphasis on God's act rather than human decision liberates us from the self-absorption and paralysis of sin.

Paul then draws his conclusion, paraphrasing Ps. 143:2 (142:2 LXX): "no one will be justified" before God by works of the law. Because all are justified solely on the basis of Christ's faithful

death, the distinction between Jews and "Gentile sinners" dissolves in relationship to Christ. To rebuild it through insisting on the "works of the law" is to prove oneself a sinner, acting contrary to the work of Christ (vv. 18, 21).

IV. Rectified by Faith; Heirs of the Promise (3:1–4:7)

The powerful metaphor of inheritance dominates this section, as through Christ the Galatians already are heirs of the blessing promised to Abraham (3:14, 18, 22, 29; 4:7).

A. The Message of Faith and the Spirit (3:1–5)

Paul's initial preaching to the Galatians "publicly exhibited" Christ on the cross (3:1). He may be referring to his scars from persecution (4:4:13–14), which he interprets as marks of the crucified Jesus (6:17) who lives in him (2:20–21). The "works of the law" (vv. 2, 4) are paralleled with "the flesh" (v. 3), which denotes circumcision (6:12–13), merely human existence (2:20), and destructive passions (5:17–21) that war against the Spirit. In contrast, "the message of faith" (3:2, 5; NRSV, "believing what you heard") generates powerful miracles worked by the Spirit (3:4–5). Reminding his converts of that experience, Paul uses the word *paschē*, meaning, "to suffer" (3:4; NRSV, "experience"); suffering and the power of the Spirit often go together (Rom 5:3–5; 2 Cor 4:7–12; 12:9–10).

B. Sons and Heirs Through Faith (3:6–29)

The abrupt introduction of Abraham suggests that the Galatians have heard about him from the other missionaries, perhaps because Abraham was the first person to practice circumcision (Gen 17:10–14). Abraham and Sarah also were known as the father and mother of proselytes, and according to Jewish tradition they kept the Mosaic law even before it was given at Sinai (*Jub* 24:11; Sir 44:19–21). Paul, however, emphasizes Abraham's faith prior to circumcision (Gen 15:6), and the promise that the Gentiles will be blessed through him (3:8). Thus linking "faith" and blessing, he argues that all whose identity derives from faith share in Abraham's blessing (3:9, 14; see Rom 4:5). Almost every verse in the ensuing argument cites Scripture, which speaks and acts on God's behalf (3:22; 4:30).

By contrasting the theme of promise in Genesis with the theme of curse in relationship to the law in Deuteronomy and Leviticus, scripture grounds Paul's argument for the life-giving efficacy of faith, rather than law observance. Verses 9 and 10 are antithetically parallel: those who are "of faith" are blessed, while those who are "of works of the law" are under a curse. Paul gives two scriptural explanations for this "curse of the law." First, according to Deut 27:26; 28:58, a curse falls on all who fail to keep the law's requirements, just as, according to Lev 18:5: "whoever does them will live by them." Second, regardless of human obedience to the law, it is not the way to righteousness because it is not based on faith (v. 11; Hab 2:4). Habakkuk 2:4 (3:11; cf., Rom 1:17) thus governs Paul's interpretation of Deuteronomy and Leviticus (vv. 10, 12), by restating the principle of 2:21: Christ's death, not law, effects righteousness. Therefore, "the one who is righteous will live by faith." In Greek, "by faith" could modify either "will live" or "righteous," implying an interpretive choice between righteousness and life as the outcome of faith. This is a false choice, however, because righteousness is life (3:19–21), and to be rectified is to be made alive—by faith. In light of 2:16–21, this faith is in the first instance Christ's faithfulness; in light of 3:6–9, it is human trust in God. Paul's ambiguity thus leads us to speak of both Christ's faith and the human faith that it awakens. "The one who is righteous" may be a messianic reference to Christ.

Paul's reasoning depends on the logic of interchange: by suffering execution as a condemned law-breaker (Deut 21:22), Christ took our place in "becoming a curse for us" so that all people, including the Gentiles, might be blessed by receiving the Spirit (2 Cor 5:21; Rom 4:5; 8:3).

God's promise to Abraham is like a human will that cannot be annulled. The Greek word (diathēkē) can also be translated as "covenant," but "will" fits better as an "example from daily life" (3:15). Abraham's singular seed, Christ (3:16), is the heir through whom others share the inheritance (3:29). Just as Paul puts temporal brackets around his "former life in Judaism" in 1:12–17, now he brackets the Mosaic law: both Paul's and Abraham's "stories" begin with God's promissory call—for Paul, to preach to the Gentiles (1:16); for Abraham, to be a blessing to the Gentiles (3:8).

For both, the fulfillment of the promise is delayed by a period of time under the law (1:14; 3:17, 19–24), which is brought to an end by the advent of Christ (1:15–16; 3:24–25). Life under the law is a temporary arrangement that cannot annul God's promise (3:17).

"Why then the law?" Paul answers, "because of transgressions" (3:19). This enigmatic phrase could mean either "in order to provoke sin" (Rom 7:5–13), or "to restrain sin." In view of the law's restrictive function in 3:22–24, the latter seems more likely, yet perhaps the two meanings are not incompatible. Any parent knows that restraint often provokes the very action that it is meant to control.

Paul's point is that the law serves God's purposes by closing off all access to righteousness and life until the advent of Christ (3:22). Yet Paul's ambivalence towards the law is palpable: God gave the promise directly to Abraham's offspring, but the law was given indirectly through Moses (Lev 26:46; Num 36:13) and ordained through angels (Deut 33:2; Ps 68:17). In Jewish texts the presence of angelic hosts at Sinai is a sign of the law's glory, but in Paul's account it distances the law from God.

Furthermore, the law imprisons humanity "under sin" (3:22), like a pedagogue (NRSV, "disciplinarian"), a slave or freedman whose job was to restrain boys until they reached maturity (3:24–25). Most telling is the repeated preposition "under," which signifies "under the power of": "under a curse" (3:10); "under the power of sin" (3:22); "under the law" (3:23; 4:4, 5); "under a disciplinarian" (3:25); "under guardians and trustees" (4:2); "under (NRSV, "enslaved to") the elemental spirits" (4:3). Hence the law and sin function in tandem, the law restraining sin and yet unable to deliver humanity from its power. The implications of this insight are profound. We experience enslavement to sin in many ways, from corporate patterns of oppression to personal addictions, and it is tempting to prescribe a program of behavior as an antidote. Paul's answer to human bondage is not a program, but the powerful and gracious presence of Christ.

Again Paul uses the verb form of "apocalypse" (3:23; NRSV, "faith would be revealed") together with the verb, "to come," speaking interchangeably of the advent and apocalypse of Christ and of faith (3:23–25). Thus faith is not a general human attitude or attribute, but rather Christ himself, who is both its content and author, whose faithful self-giving in turn inaugurates human trust in God (Rom 8:3).

Baptism into union with Christ creates a new community in which the divisions of the old order no longer hold sway (3:27–28). In this community all are "sons of God" (v.26, NRSV, "children of God"), sharing Israel's special relationship to God (Exod 4:22; Jer 31:9; Hos 1:9–10; *Jub* 1:24–25). The words, as well as the imagery of changing clothes and "putting on Christ," may reflect an early baptismal rite (1 Cor 12:13; Rom 6.3; 13.14; Eph 4.24; Col 3.9–11). Just as name brand logos set people apart from one another in our culture, so in the first century clothing distinguished people's social class and status. Such distinctions are erased within the Christian community. The imagery draws on the OT: God is clothed with majesty (Pss 93:1; 104:1), God's priests are clothed with righteousness and salvation (Ps 132:9, 16), and Jerusalem will be clothed with the garments of salvation and the robe of righteousness (Isa 61:10).

C. From Slavery to Freedom (4:1–7)

Verses 1–7 develop the metaphor of the law as a pedagogue. Paul begins by depicting the change in status that automatically occurs when a minor child legally becomes an adult (vv. 1–3). But then he shifts to the metaphor of adoption, which implies a radical change from the status of a slave to that of a son (vv. 4–5). The point is the same: for adult heirs, enslavement to any overlords other than Christ is obsolete, and a return to such slavery via the works of the law signals regression to an infantile state. Perhaps Paul's opponents are promising the Galatians that law-observance will lead them to maturity (see 3:3), but Paul warns that it will have the opposite effect.

As in 3:13, in 4:5 Paul uses the word *exagorazō*, to redeem from slavery, to describe the effect of Christ's action. Again the key paradigm is that of a divine-human interchange initiated and sustained by Christ's participation in the human predicament. Christ was "born of a woman" into a cosmos divided by the law, so that we (both Jew and Gentile) might receive "adop-

tion as children." The experience of the promised Spirit (cf., 3:2–5, 14) who inspires us to call God "Abba! Father!" (Rom 8:15–17), is evidence of this new relationship.

V. Return to Slavery (4:8–11)

Paul restates the problem in Galatia: by observing the liturgical calendar, his converts are returning to their former slavery to "the elemental spirits" (4:3). These are the building blocks of the cosmos—earth, water, air, and fire—which in 4:8–9 are associated with "beings that by nature are not gods." Jews of Paul's day viewed pagan worship as veneration of the elemental spirits (*stoicheia* in Greek), but Paul here links Jewish religious observance itself with such veneration. Two observations will help us understand this radical claim by Paul. In Hellenistic thought the elements of the physical cosmos were divided into pairs of opposites (hot and cold, wet and dry). Similarly, in 3:28, Paul describes the social cosmos prior to Christ as consisting of pairs of opposites, and in 6:14–15 as constructed by the polarity between circumcised and uncircumcised humanity. Paul has died to this divided cosmos (2:19; 6:14–15), and the Galatians are in danger of returning to it as they seek to define themselves through works of the law. Such divisions belong to "the present evil age" from which Christ has redeemed them (1:4).

VI. Motivational Appeals (4:12–5:12)

A. Argument from Experience (4:12–20)

In an emotional appeal that is both personal in tone and cosmic in scope, Paul moves from discussion of Christian identity to matters of behavior. He bases the first imperative of the letter, "become as I am," on his own likeness with the Galatians (4:12). Here the pattern of interchange enacted by Christ's participation in the human condition acquires a personal face through the Galatians' own experience of Paul's intense investment in them. Christ's liberating power is mediated through vulnerable human interaction. Yet in what way did the Jewish Paul become like the Gentile Galatians, and how might they become like him? On one level, Paul became like a Gentile "sinner" by living outside the law (2:17–19). But on a deeper level, Paul and his converts become akin to each other only through Christ, because it is Christ, not the law or its absence, who is the foundation of their existence. Hence to become like Paul is to persevere in faith in Christ alone. This alone is the basis of unity in the church.

Apparently Paul first preached to the Galatians when he was recovering from some physical infirmity that put them "to the test" (vv. 13–14). We cannot know with certainty what this was. But surely Paul's body, scarred from being stoned and whipped (2 Cor 11:24–25), is Exhibit A of the crucified Lord whom he "publicly exhibits" when he preaches (3:1; 6:17). Such a picture of discipleship surely would test the Galatians' faith. Their warm reception of Paul is depicted colloquially by their willingness to tear out their eyes for him (4:15).

Whereas Paul became like the Gentile Galatians in a mutually reciprocal relationship, the circumcising missionaries require the Galatians to become like them—literally! By setting up circumcision as a prerequisite for fellowship, "they want to exclude you" (v. 17), acting like manipulative suitors who play "hard to get." Paul, however, yearns to be with his congregations, displaying a pastoral style that is extraordinarily vulnerable (v. 20). He employs the image of childbirth to depict his anguish (4:19). The metaphor of labor pains occurs frequently in the prophets, with Israel, Zion, the prophet, or God as the subject (e.g., Isa 13:8; 21:3; 45:10; Jer 4:31; 6:24; 8:21; 13:21). Sometimes it signifies the messianic birth pangs that signal the Day of the Lord (*1 En* 62:6; *4 Ezra* 4:42; Mark 13:8//Matt 24:8; Rom 8:22; 1 Thess 5:3; Rev 12:2). Here Paul's anguish melds with the labor pains of God's new creative act (6:15), for God, who in Isa 45:10 is both father and mother to Israel, is undoubtedly the power who brings to birth the community of the new creation through Paul's own apostolic labors. In Paul's labor, Christ who lives in him also labors (2:20). Thus when Christ is "formed" among them (the "you" is plural), their life also will display the presence of the self-giving Lord.

B. Argument from Scripture (4:21–31)

The witness of "the law" as revelatory narrative (4:21*b*) speaks directly to people who desire to be subject to "the law" as commandments (4:21*a*). In effect Paul says, "Let me tell you the story of Abraham's two sons (Gen 16–21); if the shoe fits, wear it." In Jewish traditions, Abraham is the first observer of the law, and Ishmael, not Isaac, is the source of the Gentiles (*Jub* 16:17–18). But by reading Abraham's story through the lens of Isa 54:1, Paul instead highlights the theme of divine promise and power. In Isa 54:1, the paradoxical motif of the "barren mother" depicts the miraculous restoration of Jerusalem, the mother city. This is a familiar motif in Jewish literature; later rabbis list Sarah, Rachel, Rebekah, Leah, Samson's mother, Hannah, and Zion as the "seven barren ones" (*Pesiq. Rab Kah.* 141), whose miraculous childbirth displays God's power despite human futility.

In Galatians, Hagar the slave and Sarah the free woman represent two ways of "begetting" converts: through the "flesh" and through the promise. As we have seen, *flesh* has many connotations; here it refers to circumcision in the flesh (6:13) as a missionary method. Hence the children of the slave woman, begotten into slavery, are those Gentiles who are being circumcised by Paul's opponents. The children of promise are those who come to faith and abide in it solely on the basis of Christ's faithfulness. In v. 30, "scripture" quotes Sarah's words to Abraham in Gen 21:10, which command him to cast out the slave woman Hagar and her son Ishmael. In this allegory addressed to those who want to be under the law (4:21), the quotation warns the circumcising missionaries and their followers of the destiny that awaits them if they persist in relying on works of the law, rather than on Christ alone (see 5:2). Paul balances this negative warning with the positive affirmation of their origin and destiny as "children of the free woman" (4:31).

C. Warning Against Circumcision (5:1–12)

The command to stand fast in freedom summarizes the preceding chapter and introduces what will follow: freedom from the yoke of slavery (5:1), for mutual love (5:13). "Yoke" designates the law, but "again" links it to the Gentile Galatians' former enslavement to pagan practices (4:8–10).

Paul solemnly warns the Gentile Christians against being circumcised, giving three reasons: they will be severed from Christ (vv. 2, 4); they will be obligated to keep the whole law (v. 3); they will revert to a social cosmos ordered by the distinction between circumcised and uncircumcised (v. 6). Never opposed to circumcision and law observance for Jewish Christians, Paul objects to law observance as a divisive prerequisite for Christian fellowship. Thus "faith working through love" (5:6) makes clear that Paul is not promoting immorality, but rather arguing against legalistic concerns that obstruct the love that truly fulfills the law (5:14), and constitutes obedience to the truth (5:7).

In the subsequent images of "running" and "yeast" (5:7–9), Paul attacks the opposing missionaries, who are getting the Galatians off the right path and spoiling the whole community. These are familiar sayings: life often is compared to a footrace in Greco-Roman society and in the early church (2:2; 1 Cor 9:24–27; Phil 3:14; 2 Tim 4:7; Acts 20:24); we talk about getting off track. Yeast represents the disproportionate effect of small things on larger matters, rather like our saying, "one bad apple spoils the whole lot" (1 Cor 5:6; Matt 13:33; Luke 13:21; Mark 8:15). And Paul's claim that he suffers persecution rather than preach circumcision (5:11) indirectly implies that his opponents do the opposite (6:11). At stake in this opposition between circumcision and the cross is solidarity with the crucified Christ, and confidence in the operation of God's sovereign grace. The circumcising missionaries are confusing and unsettling the Galatians, and Paul is not above wishing the knife would slip (v. 12)!

VII. Life in the New Community (5:13–6:10)

Having warned against enslavement under the works of the law, Paul now rehabilitates *slavery* and *law* in terms of mutual love (5:13–14), and *work* in terms of mutual burden-bearing (6:4). Verses 13–14 are thematic for Paul's ethics: "Do not use your freedom as a base of operations (NRSV, "opportunity") for the flesh (NRSV, "self-indulgence"), but through love become slaves to one another. For the whole law has been fulfilled (NRSV, "is summed up") in a single commandment, 'You shall love your neighbor as yourself.'" Here Paul quotes Lev 19:18 as a summary of the law (see Rom 13:8–10). *Base of operations* is military terminology anticipating the conflict between the flesh and the Spirit in vv. 16–17. The law *has been fulfilled* because Christ has enacted the perfect love it demands, so that through the Spirit

who unites believers to Christ, Christians also may serve one another in love rather than destroying one another through mutual acrimony.

Indeed, rather than fighting among themselves, the Galatians are to wage war against the destructive desires of the flesh (5:16–18). Their general in this war is the Spirit, who leads them to victory through grace that is more powerful than law (5:18; cf. Rom 6:14). *Flesh* signifies all practices that fracture the community, including works of the law as well as bodily passions. Thus the "works of the flesh" in vv. 19–21 parallel the "works of the law" in their divisive effects, including not only sexual immorality, but also "factions" such as those instigated by the circumcision mission (see 5:15, 26). The power that overcomes such negative influences is not preaching of the law in any form, but rather God's Spirit, given through the proclamation of Christ's faithfulness (3:2–5, 14; 4:6). In conflicts within the church today, Paul's pastoral wisdom guides us also to focus on Christ's faithfulness as the source of unity.

The "fruit of the Spirit" suggests the fecundity of the new age, when the Spirit of God is poured out and the earth is restored to fruitfulness (Joel 2:18–32; Isa 32:15–16). Recalling his own crucifixion with Christ (2:19; 6:14), Paul now tells the Galatians that they themselves "have crucified the flesh with its passions and desires" (5:24). The active verb emphasizes their agency, suggesting that in union with Christ they are empowered to resist the destructive impulses of the flesh and to enact the mutually up-building fruit of the Spirit.

One of those spiritual fruits is the restoration of people who have committed transgressions (6:1). To whom and about whom is Paul speaking? Based on 3:2–5 and 4:6, all Christians have received the Spirit and are thus addressed. Paul is not invoking a new division within the community between those who are Spirit-filled and those who are not; such distinctions would be anathema in this already fractured church. But there are people in need of restoration to fellowship, about whom Paul writes. In view of the letter as a whole, those who submit to the circumcision mission certainly fall within this category. The point is this: having warned that circumcision will sever the Gentile Christians from Christ, Paul still seeks their unity based on Christ alone.

The verb "to bear" appears in 6:2, 5 (NRSV, "carry") and 17 (NRSV, "carry"). Paradoxically, we must bear one another's burdens, and yet "all must carry their own loads" (v. 5). Paul's language suggests that we refrain from arrogant judgment and engage in mutual support, taking responsibility for our own actions while gently "bearing with" our neighbor's failings (see Matt 7:1–5). To do so is to bear the marks of Christ (6:17). "The law of Christ" (v. 2) is the law as accessed through Christ (5:14), and as displayed and enacted in Christ's sacrificial bearing of our sins, so that we also may bear with our neighbor's sins.

Verse 6 commands financial support for teachers (1 Cor 9:3–14; 2 Cor 11:7–11; Phil 4:10–11; 1 Thess 2:7–10), in a practical expression of the fellowship and mutual support that Paul enjoins in 6:2.

Paul's exhortations appear in the context of the final judgment, suggesting that carrying one's own load also implies one's individual responsibility before God. Then, as now, the maxim that "you reap what you sow" was common (v.7; cf. Job 4:8; Ps 126:5; Prov 22:8); here it echoes the imagery of the fruit of the Spirit (5:22–23). "If you sow to your own flesh, you will reap corruption," (v. 8) repeats the warning of 5:19–21 against the works of the flesh, as well as the warning against circumcision (5:4). The promise of eternal life motivates perseverance in loving service, especially to the "family of faith" (6:9–10). Such service is the ethical manifestation of the family system created and sustained by God's promissory faithfulness (4:27–28).

VIII. Conclusion (6:11–18)

As was common practice, Paul probably dictated the letter, but wrote the postscript in his own hand (v. 11; cf. Rom 16:22), in order to drive home his main point—the centrality of the cross and the new creation. The circumcising missionaries want to boast in their converts' circumcised flesh, and to avoid persecution (5:11). Paul boasts only in the cross, through which he has died to the old cosmos ordered and divided by the powers of the present evil age, including the distinction between those who are "in" (circumcised) and those who are "out" (6:14–15). Such divisions have no place in God's new creation. The contrast between circumcision and the cross has its basis in 2:21b: "if justification comes through the law, then Christ died for nothing."

Verse 16 is difficult to translate, and the NRSV nicely preserves the ambiguity of the Greek syntax. The first clause pronounces a conditional blessing of peace on all who follow the rule of the new creation, in a customized peace benediction typical of Paul's letters (cf. 2 Cor 13:11b; 1 Thess 5:23; Phil 4:9b). In 6:16b, however, the recipients of "mercy," and the identity of "the Israel of God," are unclear. The clause could continue the conditional blessing of peace in v. 16a. But because elsewhere in Paul's letters, "Israel" always refers to Jews, and "mercy" occurs primarily in reference to Israel (cf. Rom 9–11), it is equally plausible that Paul is praying for mercy on un-believing Israel. If so, then his vision of God's gracious rule extends beyond the confines of the immediate church, even in this letter so tightly focused on his beloved communities in Galatia.

The "marks of Jesus" probably denote Paul's scars from being stoned and whipped (2 Cor 11:23–30). The word for "marks" is *stigmata*, which could signify the brand of ownership burned into slaves' flesh. Antithetical to the identity marker of circumcision, Paul's scars show that he belongs to Christ, and thereby is under Christ's authority and protection. As Christ's slave, therefore, he commands, "let no one make trouble for me."

As in all his letters, Paul concludes as he began, with a blessing of the grace of Christ (6:18).

BIBLIOGRAPHY

J. M. G. Barclay. *Obeying the Truth: A Study of Paul's Ethics in Galatians.* SNTW (Edinburgh: T&T Clark, 1988); E. D. Burton. *A Critical and Exegetical Commentary on Galatians.* ICC (Edinburgh: T&T Clark, 1956); C. Cousar. *Galatians.* Interpretation (Atlanta: John Knox, 1982); S. Eastman. *Recovering Paul's Mother Tongue: Language and Theology in Galatians* (Grand Rapids: Eerdmans, 2007); R. B. Hays. "Galatians." *NIB* (Nashville: Abingdon, 2002) 11:181-348; R. Longenecker. *Galatians.* WBC 41 (Waco: Word, 1990); J. L. Martyn. *Galatians: A New Translation with Introduction and Commentary.* AB 33A (New York: Doubleday, 1997); S. K. Williams. *Galatians.* ANTC (Nashville: Abingdon, 1997).

EPHESIANS

Margaret Y. MacDonald

OVERVIEW

Ephesians has occupied a central place in the theology and spiritual life of Christians. Its majestic tone and liturgical influences have greatly contributed to its appeal in worship settings. The rich symbolism of Ephesians is especially powerful in articulating the identity of the church—always presented as the universal *ekklēsia*. Ephesians is, therefore, especially important for ecclesiology. Sharing a cosmological emphasis with Colossians, Ephesians is also promising for modern theological responses to crises of world significance such as environmental problems and the urgent need for peace.

But for all of its influence, Ephesians can prove to be frustrating. From a historical perspective, the work is difficult to pin down, and many commentators now argue that the work had more than one purpose. Unlike Colossians and the undisputed letters of Paul, there are no references to church meetings in the houses of believers. Even the usual troop of Paul's fellow workers is absent, with the exception of Tychicus (6:21–22). Although Ephesians does celebrate the unity of Jew and Gentile in 2:11–22, there is little evidence of the previous tensions, or of community conflicts of any kind. Even the identity of addressees cannot be determined with certainty for the words "in Ephesus" are missing from the greeting (1:1) in several important manuscripts and conclusive evidence for use of the superscription, "To the Ephesians," comes from the end of the second century CE. The only fact that can be recovered with any certainty about the recipients of the letter is that they were (predominantly?) Gentile (2:11–22; cf. 2:1–3; 4:17–19).

Although most scholars continue to associate the document with Asia Minor on account of its ethos, relationship to Colossians, and traditional association with Ephesus, some have argued that the gap in the address along with the universal tone point to more than one audience, and perhaps even to a circular letter (cf. 1 Pet 1:1; Rev 1:4). The majority of commentators today argue in favor of its epistolary genre, but some argue that it more closely resembles a liturgical piece, a sermon,

or even an "honorific decree" on account of the formal, public orientation of the work.

Theories concerning the pseudonymous nature of Ephesians have been based on a variety of historical and literary factors. With its reference to a church that is built on the foundation of the apostles and prophets, the work seems to look back to the past (2:19–20), offering a type of summary of Paul's thought for a new day. Its theological reflection (e.g., 5:21–33) seems best understood in light of the challenges of the latter decades of the first century CE when the death of the apostles and growing diversity of church teachings, including ascetic extremism, required new emphasis on the identity of the church. With respect to literary factors, the use of words and expressions not typically found in the undisputed Pauline epistles (see comments on 1:3–14), long sentences that bring together synonyms, and especially the parallels between Ephesians and other letters in the Pauline corpus (particularly Colossians, see comments on 6:21–24) have figured prominently in arguments concerning authorship. In modern scholarship, the majority view (e.g., Lincoln, MacDonald, Muddiman) is that the work was written in Paul's name by a close associate. But defenders of the traditional understanding of Paul as author continue to play an important role in the scholarly debate (e.g., Hoehner), and even the traditional understanding of the dependence of Ephesians upon Colossians does not go unquestioned (Best).

OUTLINE

I. Doctrinal Exposition (1:1–3:21)

    A. Greeting (1:1–2)

    B. Blessing (1:3–14)

    C. Thanksgiving and Prayer (1:15–23)

    D. God's Plan for the Universe: Believers Made Alive with Christ (2:1–10)

    E. The Unity of Jews and Gentiles: Peace Created by Christ (2:11–22)

F. The Role of Paul as Interpreter of the Divine Mystery (3:1–13)

G. Prayer and Doxology (3:14–21)

II. Ethical Exhortations (4:1–6:24)

A. Believers Should Lead a Life Worthy of Their Calling (4:1–16)

B. The Sons of Disobedience and the Children of Light (4:17–5:20)

C. The Household Code (5:21–6:9)

D. Call to Do Battle with Evil (6:10–20)

E. Personal Matters and Final Blessing (6:21–24)

DETAILED ANALYSIS

I. Doctrinal Exposition (1:1–3:21)

A. Greeting (1:1–2)

The opening phrase is identical to that found in Colossians and 2 Corinthians. Although the term apostle can sometimes refer simply to an emissary (literally, one who is sent), the special sense associated with being chosen by God for a mission (cf. Gal 1:12) is in view here as is made clear by the use of the expression "by the will of God." Ephesians is only one of two letters (the other is Romans) in the Pauline corpus that does not refer to a co-author such as Timothy (cf. Col 1:1). This lack of reference to a joint enterprise, coupled with the strong statement about Paul's identity, is in keeping with the emphasis on Paul's divine authority elsewhere.

Commentators who argue that Paul is the author of Ephesians usually view it as having been composed within the context of his imprisonment in Rome (cf. Acts 28:16–31), late in the apostle's career (the early 60s CE), near to the time of the composition of Colossians. For those who view the work as deutero-Pauline, an Asia Minor context in the latter decades of the first century is the usual explanation. The letter is addressed to the "saints" (tois hagiois; literally "holy ones"). This is a typical manner of referring to all believers in Pauline literature, and it is an expression that is found frequently in Ephesians (cf. 1:15, 18; 3:8; 4:12). Differences in the manuscript tradition

account for the fact that the phrase "in Ephesus" often appears in brackets in modern translations or as an alternate reading in the notes. Because the shorter reading is most likely the original (though grammatical difficulties remain), there have been many proposals as to the destination of the work (see Overview above).

The greeting referring to grace and peace is typical of Paul's letters and seems to combine Gentile and Jewish influences, in keeping with emphasis on the achieved unity of Jews and Gentiles in 2:11–22. The key Pauline term "grace" (charis) reflects the standard Greek salutation, "greetings" (chairein) and the traditional Jewish greeting, "peace" (shalom). Not only are both grace (1:6, 7; 2:5, 7, 8; 4:7, 29) and peace (2:14, 15, 17; 4:3; 6:15) central themes in the epistle, but these themes also create a link between the greeting and the closing.

B. Blessing (1:3–14)

The main body of Ephesians begins with a blessing similar to that found in the opening of 2 Corinthians (1:3–4) and 1 Peter (1:3–12). The background is the extended blessing or berakah that is found in the Old Testament (e.g., 1 Kgs 8:15, 56; Pss 41:13; 72:18, 19) and which also formed part of the Jewish worship of the day, as both the Dead Sea Scrolls (e.g., 1QS 11:15; 1QH 5:20) and Luke 1:68–79 demonstrate. Some have argued that Eph 1:3–14 is an early church hymn, but because its language has so many parallels with other Pauline texts, many have preferred the theory that the text is influenced more generally by worship forms.

This text contains many intriguing expressions and theological constructs. Ephesians 1:4, 6 introduce the central theme of love, which with the exception of 1:6 (and possibly 1:4), refers to human and not divine love in the epistle (cf. 1:15, 3:17; 4:2, 15, 16; 5:2, 25, 28, 33; 6:23, 24). The main focus, however, is on God's initiative (with Christ as God's agent), but the three members of the Trinity have a role to play in the text: God (vv.3–6), Christ (vv.7–12), the Holy Spirit (vv. 13–14). Ephesians 1:3 contains an expression not found elsewhere in the Pauline epistles: "the heavenly places" (literally, "the heavenlies"; ta epourania; cf. 1:20; 2:6; 3:10; 6:12), here indicating that believers already taste the invisible, heavenly world in Christ. It should be noted that the plural of the expression is in keeping with Hebrew thought and differs somewhat from the view of heaven that was later accepted in Christianity. The heavenly places are in the process of transformation in the new age; they contain evil forces that can still trouble the life of believers (cf. 3:10; 6:12), but they are also the domain of divine transcendence where Christ sits at God's right hand (1:20; 2:6).

Because of its focus on God's plan for the universe, Ephesians often makes use of concepts of election. Emphasis on God's design also shapes the use of the term "mystery" in this passage to refer to the revelation of God's will, the plan (*oikonomia*) for the fullness of time (1:9–10; cf. 3:3–10; 5:32; 6:19); in Ephesians the content of the mystery is often articulated with notable precision. The use of the term *oikonomia* (1:10; cf. 3:9) to refer to God's plan is unique to Ephesians. In Col 1:25 the term is best translated as stewardship and it is used in conjunction with Paul's apostolic commission (cf. 3:2); elsewhere in the NT it can refer to stewardship associated with the administration of a house or city (e.g., Rom 16:23). But here the term refers to God's direction of the cosmos and is employed in conjunction with another concept which plays a key role in the distinctive theological vision of both Colossians and Ephesians: "fullness" (*plērōma*; cf. 1:23; 3:19; 4:13). The term is used in both texts to stress the expansion and filling up of the universe with Christ. Such a theological vision is also central to reference to a summing of all things in Christ in 1:10. Down through the centuries the use of the term *anakephalaiōsasthai* ("summing up" or "gather together") has intrigued commentators (especially the Latin Fathers) with its image of the cosmic Christ who draws all things into himself (cf. Col 1:15–20).

Ephesians 1:12–14 offers the first example of the "you"/"we" contrast in the text which has traditionally been taken as an effort to distinguish between the (predominantly?) Gentile recipients of the letter (you) and the Jewish Christians associated with Paul (we) who first came to believe. But the contrast may represent a rhetorical strategy to draw the recipients into the discussion and may not offer reliable insight as to the nature of the audience. Increasingly, Jewish material is seen

as offering the most important intellectual background for Ephesians (allusions to Jewish Scripture and parallels with the Dead Sea Scrolls) and there is a general consensus that the document, whether by Paul or an associate, reflects Jewish-Christian authorship. But a growing appreciation of the Jewish presence in Asia Minor and the complexity of their position in Roman society (tolerated or persecuted to varying degrees) is leading to a tendency to leave open the very real possibility of the significant presence of Jewish Christians in the audience (see Muddiman; comments on 2:11–22).

C. Thanksgiving and Prayer (1:15–23)

This passage is closely related to the previous section, with the blessings experienced by the community (vv.1:13–14) providing a thematic link. Thanksgivings are associated with blessings in Jewish liturgical traditions and some of the language (e.g., references to glory) in both sections has a clear liturgical flavor. This thanksgiving offers a particularly long example of a typical feature of Pauline letters (cf. Col 1:3–4; Phlm 4–5), in keeping with Hellenistic letters whereby the author gives thanks to the gods for the health of the recipients. The emphasis on enlightenment and the description of possessing "a spirit of wisdom and revelation" (1:17–19) is especially distinctive and consistent with a broad interest in insight into the mystery of the divine will.

Angels have often been seen as important to understanding this text. Because of parallels with Dead Sea Scrolls (e.g., 1QS 11:7, 8), some have taken the reference to sharing "his glorious inheritance among the saints" (1:18) as a reference to sharing the lot of angels (cf. Col 1:12), which would mean a shift in meaning from Eph 1:15 where the saints clearly refers to believers (cf. 1:1; 2:19; 3:8). But such a shift would be in line with the emphasis on the heavenly ascent or enthronement of believers in Ephesians. Positive angelic powers are also sometimes in view with respect to the expression, "all rule and authority and power and dominion" (1:21)—a reference to spiritual powers subordinate to Christ. But it seems more likely that the "powers" are hostile spiritual beings (Eph 6:12; cf. 1 Cor 15:24–26). Magical practices may underlie the references to spiritual powers. Clinton Arnold has documented the widespread references to naming in the magical papyri; the recipients would have received a powerful message: Christ's name alone triumphs over the powers of evil.

The theological heart is the notion of Christ's exaltation in heavenly places (see notes on 1:3–14). This approach—highlighting God and Christ's power (see quotation of Ps 8:6 in 1:22)—responds to the menacing powers described above. Christ's authority over the church is also celebrated as God has "made him the head over all things for the church" (1:22). The church, referred to for the first time, is given a paramount role in God's plan for salvation (cf. 3:10, 21; 5:23–25, 27, 29, 32). As in Colossians, the church is explicitly equated with the body of Christ with Christ as the head (cf. 1:22–23; 5:23). The reference to "fullness" (see notes on 1:3–14) in 1:23 may refer back directly to Christ in v. 22, but is more likely a second symbol for the church. The notions of Christ, church, and the filling up of the universe are very closely linked. Although the present salvation of believers is stressed above all, Eph 1:21 offers a strong indication that the future remains important.

D. God's Plan for the Universe: Believers Made Alive with Christ (2:1–10)

While the previous section ends with a reference to the universal church (taken up again in 2:11–22), this passage returns to how God's plan for the universe is worked out through Christ. Offering a clear example of the "you-we" contrast found throughout Ephesians (see notes on 1:3–14), the author begins by describing the previous existence of believers as one of spiritual death caused by sin (cf. Rom 7:19–23). The present evil age is ruled by the devil, here described in 2:2 as "the ruler of the power of the air" (cf. John 12:31; 14:30; 16:11). Ephesians 2:3 reflects ancient cosmology, including the notion of the air as a type of intermediate realm between the earthly and heavenly realms that is subject to malevolent forces, including the devil (cf. Eph 6:12). Life without Christ is depicted in the most negative of terms, with descriptions of nonbelievers as "those who are disobedient" (literally, sons of disobedience) and "children of wrath." The reference to the "passions of our flesh" also is consistent with Jewish language, particularly characterizations of the Greco-Roman world as one of idolatry and sexual immorality (cf.

1 Thess 4:5). Interestingly, the word for desire in Eph 2:3 (*thelēma*) is the same as that used to refer to the will of God (cf. 1:1, 5, 9, 11); this passage describes a purely human orientation at odds with the will of God.

Just as Ephesians presents the past existence of believers in dire terms, so too it celebrates the grandeur of God's grace in the most exalted terms. The prominence of the theme of love in Ephesians (see notes on 1:3–14) is reflected in Eph 2:4, "out of the great love with which he loved us," but the emphasis continues to be on the major theological orientation of the opening passages: the initiative, mercy, and grace of God working through Christ. The strong contrast language is probably rooted in baptism where one is raised with Christ (2:1, 2:5–6). In line with Eph 1:20, Eph 2:6 is unreserved in describing the present situation of believers as sharing Christ's destiny, having been raised with Christ and seated with him in the heavenly places in Christ (see notes on 1:3–14). The Pauline expression "in Christ" occurs frequently in Ephesians in the locative sense, indicating the fact that believers are located in his body. Despite the emphasis on the present, the reference to the "ages to come" leaves an opening for a future manifestation of salvation.

The passage concludes with an intriguing expression of the faith-works contrast. Unlike the undisputed letters, there is no specific reference to the meaning of faith in Christ in relation to the works of the Jewish law. With some finding here an indication of deutero-Pauline authorship (the Pauline message for a new day), the works-law contrast is given a broad scope with a strong focus on God's sovereignty and the giftedness of salvation. In stating that believers are created for good works by God beforehand, the author essentially states that good works flow naturally from God's choosing to save us (see Eph 4:1–6:20).

E. The Unity of Jews and Gentiles: Peace Created by Christ (2:11–22)

The author clarifies the relationship between the (predominantly?) Gentile community and Israel. Yet the somewhat ambiguous use of labels, with metaphors that switch back and forth between announcing continuity with Israel (including the implicit equivalence between Israel and the church in 2:12) and projecting the church as a distinct entity (2:15), has led to puzzlement. With such a strong interest in the Jewish origins of church, there is a striking lack of interest in concrete relations with real Jews inside or outside the church. Recent research, however, has read this articulation of the nature of the church in light of an attempt to negotiate the boundaries of identity during a time when, depending on the circumstances, it might be valuable to be linked with the prestige of Israel or, in contrast, to be seen as a new entity in relation to the Jews. Given the significant population of Jews in both Ephesus and Asia Minor generally, there is good reason to suppose that Gentile members of the church had past and current association with the Jewish community and were sometimes labeled as Jews. If Ephesians comes from the time immediately following the destruction of the Jewish Temple in 70 CE, the complexity of the position of the Jews in the Roman Empire would be even more acute. Against prejudice, exclusion, and hostility, the author announces an achieved unity which creates a new entity where old patterns of nationhood, citizenship, and belonging are rendered irrelevant. This text includes politically-charged language with its reference to strangers, aliens, and citizens (Eph 2:12, 19). The four references to the term peace in Eph 2:14–18 include allusions to LXX Isa 57:19, but also to imperial propaganda for Roman rule. In contrast to the *Pax Romana*, the preaching of peace in Ephesians does not involve terror, intimidation, or military action; it is the peace that comes through the cross and belongs to the *ekklēsia*— the peace of Christ (cf. 6:15–16). In Eph 2:19–22, architectural, political/military, and familial concepts tied to the visible institutions of society are subverted by the image of the "holy temple" where believers become a dwelling place for God.

F. The Role of Paul as Interpreter of the Divine Mystery (3:1–13)

Although this section may appear at first glance to be a digression, it plays an important role in the transition between the doctrinal and ethical sections of the letter; it is Paul the revealer of the mystery of Christ (3:4) who has the indisputable authority to instruct believers to lead a life worthy of their calling (4:1). Beginning with a strong statement of Paul's authority as the imprisoned apostle, Paul is depicted both as literally in cap-

tivity (cf. 4:1), and also captive to Christ's power and control (cf. Col 1:23–29). At the same time, however, Eph 3:2 seems to suggest that Paul does not know the community very well: "for surely you have already heard of the commission of God's grace that was given me for you." The term for commission (*oikonomia*) is best translated elsewhere in Ephesians as "plan" (1:10, 3:9; see notes on 1:3–14), and here also it is closely tied to that concept to reinforce the notion that Paul's role is to bring God's plan to fruition. Paul is a communicator of the mystery that was made known to him by revelation, recalling themes in the earlier part of the letter (cf. 1:9–10; 1:18; see notes on previous sections). Most commentators today, in fact, take Paul's statement "as I wrote above in a few words"(3:3) as a reference to Eph 1:9–10 and 2:11–22, though it has sometimes been suggested that the phrase refers to Paul's earlier letters or even perhaps to Rom 16:25 (in support of the theory that Rom 16 was originally intended for Ephesus). Ephesians 3:4 presents Paul in an interesting way, as the interpreter of the mystery of Christ. A second reference to revelation in this passage (1:5; cf. 1:3) demonstrates that the source of revelation is the Spirit. Ephesians 3:6 expresses the content of the mystery (Gentiles have become fellow heirs ...) and constitutes perhaps the most concise expression of the Christian message in Ephesians.

Ephesians 3:7–12 tie many of the letter's themes directly to Paul's mission. Paul is a minister (*diakonos*, a word that came to designate the office of deacon)—a term used broadly in the ancient world to describe an agent of a high-ranking person (in this case, God). Ephesians 3:8 affirms Paul's identity as a redeemed persecutor (cf. 1 Cor 15:8–11; Phil 3:5–11). The point of his mission is to make all see the plan of the mystery hidden for ages in God (see 3:4, 9).But the following verses give one of the strongest indications of the importance of ecclesiology for Ephesians. Ephesians 3:9–10 announces the transition from the mystery made known to the select group of apostles and prophets (3:5) to the church and ultimately to the whole cosmos ("the rulers and authorities" are cosmic powers; on this expression and on "the heavenly places" see notes on Eph 1:3–14). It is through the church (the unified body of Jews and Gentiles) resulting from Paul's mission that the manifold wisdom of God is made known in accordance with God's eternal purposes. The final verse in this section, with its use of the term "therefore" (*dio*) and statement "I pray ...", provides a transition to the prayer in 3:14–21. The term for sufferings here (*thlipsis*, "affliction") is regularly used in the undisputed letters of Paul (e.g., Rom 5:3, 8:35; 2 Cor 1:4, 8) and in the parallel text of Col 1:24 is employed to describe the sufferings of Christ. The reference to glory here should not be taken as a glorification of suffering, but as a symbol and manifestation of the promise of salvation (cf. Rom 8:17–18).

G. Prayer and Doxology (3:14–21)

Taking up the thought that was interrupted at 3:1, this text links the prayer with the accomplished unity of Jew and Gentile (2:11–22). But the passage is also to be read in light of the previous section on Paul's authority as the instrument of God's plan to bring about this new creation. Homage is closely associated with prayer (cf. Rom 14:11; Phil 2:10). The description of the object of prayer in 3: 14–15 is especially interesting for its connections to other references to family/household in Ephesians. The word for Father (*patēr*) has a clear relationship to the word for family (*patria*). The expression, "the Father from whom every family ..." both recalls the description of the household of God in Eph 2:19 with its cosmic/spiritual dimensions, the entity joining Jew and Gentile together, and points forward to the ethical exhortations concerning families in 5:21–6:9. Thus, Eph 3:15 connects the earthly community to the heavenly community. "Every family in heaven," probably refers to the company of angels (perhaps good and hostile angelic beings—see notes on 1:15–23), but in keeping with Ephesians as a whole, we are reminded once again of God the Father's supreme authority over all.

The prayer, infused with liturgical expressions (e.g., "riches of his glory") in Eph 3:16–19 is for the most profound spiritual gifts, and is formulated in terms of three prayer requests ("I pray that" [3:16]; "I pray that" [3:18], "so that you" [3:19]). To be strengthened in one's inner being with "power through his Spirit" means that believers are shielded from cosmic powers (cf. 5:20; 6:10; see notes on 1:3–14). The "inner-self" and the "heart" in 3:16–17 are synonymous and in ancient thought represent the zone of commitment (often along

with eyes). Similarly, the indwelling of Christ corresponds to the strengthening that comes through the Spirit in 3:16. The central theme of love is juxtaposed with knowledge to make the point that to know the love of Christ surpasses any knowledge of a technical or academic kind (3:17–19). The third prayer request, "that you may be filled with all the fullness of God" is a request for union with God in the strongest possible terms (3:19). The passage culminates fittingly in a doxology proclaiming God's power (3:20–21). The fact that this is the only doxology in the NT containing both the phrase "in the church" and "in Christ Jesus" is especially noteworthy and is consistent with interest in the identity of the church. Doxologies in the NT typically make reference to eternity and end with Amen (cf. Rom 16:25–27; Phil 4:20).

II. Ethical Exhortations (4:1–6:24)

A. Believers Should Lead a Life Worthy of Their Calling (4:1–16)

This section constitutes the beginning of the second part of the epistle, the ethical exhortations. But there are clear linguistic links with the previous section, emphasizing an important theological point seen also in other Pauline letters: descriptions of the nature of salvation in the indicative lead to the imperatives of ethical exhortation. This is made especially clear by the use of the term "therefore" which relates this section to the celebration of God's power in the doxology of Eph 3:20–21. The same introductory term, "I beg you" (*parakalō*), is found in Rom 12:1 (NRSV, "I appeal to you"), and the self-designation of Paul as the prisoner in Eph 4:1 recalls 3:1 and 3:14.

This text is often cited as one of the most inspirational of the document. Along with Eph 2:11–22 and Eph 5:21–6:9, it plays a key role in weaving the theme of unity throughout the epistle. From the perspective of Ephesians, unity (closely associated with peace and love: 4:2–3, 15–16) is perhaps the most clearly visible product of God's interaction with the world, as believers come to "maturity, to the measure of the full stature of Christ" (4:13). Here the emphasis is on the unity of the Spirit that characterizes the life of the assembly (cf. 2:18). Frequent references to the body (4:4, 12, 15–16), the universal church governed by

Christ as its "head," strengthen this emphasis (see notes on 1:15–23).

The beautiful confession of unity in Eph 4:4–6 (including references to the persons of the Trinity) prepares the way for the treatment of the diversity of gifts and ministries that begins at v. 7 and continues to the end of the passage. The list of church leaders in Eph 4:11 seems to emphasize the teacher-preacher role: apostles and prophets as charismatic teachers of the early Christian movement are listed first (cf. Eph 2:20 and notes on 2:11–22). Evangelists (cf. Acts 21:8) and pastors (cf. Acts 20:28, a cognate verb occurs where "shepherding" is a task of the elders) are not mentioned in the undisputed letters of Paul. The importance of the role of teachers (cf. 1 Cor 12:28) is bolstered by the reference to false teaching in Eph 4:14.

Ephesians contains many allusions to Scripture, but only a few direct quotations. One of the most unusual is the citation of Ps 68:18 in Eph 4:8–9. The text may reflect points of contact with ancient rabbinic tradition that understood the psalm in terms of Moses ascending Mount Sinai. Therefore, Christ would be the new Moses who gives gifts (see especially Lincoln). There are also liturgical influences in this passage. The sustained, poetic repetition of "one" in Eph 4:4–6 and "all" in 4:6 suggests a liturgical context. Some have viewed the text as a self-contained hymn, but most view it as including liturgical echoes, especially of baptism (cf. 1 Cor 12:13; Col 3:15).

B. The Sons of Disobedience and the Children of Light (4:17–5:20)

This passage continues the emphasis on ethics begun at 4:1–16. In fact, the word "therefore" connects the two passages. Ephesians 4:17–5:20 is united by two common purposes: an effort to distance the way of life of believers from that of nonbelievers and determination to encourage unity among believers by means of adoption of ethical virtues and harmonious worship.

There is a strong dependence on tradition in this section, including reliance on Colossians (e.g. Eph 4:17–24 = Col 3:5–10), reworked material from the undisputed letters of Paul (e.g., Eph 4:17–19 = Rom 1:21–24), and great similarity to the language of the Qumran literature. With traditional influences brought together and sharpened by the author of Ephesians, the result is an uncom-

promising distinction between those outside the church and those inside (Eph 4:17–5:20). Comparison of Col 4:5 to Eph 5:15–16 makes this especially apparent, for Colossians leaves some opening for dialogue while Ephesians sets its call for walking wisely within the context of eschatological woes! In a society that was increasingly unfriendly to the early Christians, Ephesians is forthright about menacing evil and its ongoing threat. The stark contrasts of Ephesians do recall similar concepts from the Qumran literature, but the subsequent household code passage with its embracing of family life (Eph 5:21–6:9) makes it clear that Ephesians is not encouraging the kind of visible, physical measures to encourage segregation found among the Essenes.

While the uncompromising, categorical thinking of Ephesians may seem shocking to modern readers (and most see no place for it in Christian dialogue with the world), it is important to recognize that the first Christians were convinced that they now belonged to a perfected creation through Christ (4:20–24) and presented its alternative in the strongest possible terms. Moreover, many of the virtues and vices in this text continue to be viewed as having value for Christian life.

The recommendation of boldness in worship in Eph 5:18–20 should probably be read against an atmosphere where early Christians were being accused of disorderly, immoral behavior like other new cults. Worship for believers should be the opposite of drunkenness and debauchery. Instead, believers are to be filled with the Spirit. The picture is one of intimate worship where community members speak to one another with psalms, hymns, and spiritual songs (It is impossible to distinguish between these expressions, but songs, tongues, instrumental music, and psalms from the biblical psalter are all possible; an early Christian hymn is cited at 5:14).

C. The Household Code (5:21–6:9)

Commentators debate whether 5:21 is more closely connected with 4:17–5:20 or 5:22–6:9, but it is nevertheless clear that the 5:22–6:9 is a self-contained unit, the household code. This was a typical form of early Christian discourse (e.g., Col 3:18–4:1; 1 Pet 2:18–3:7), found in a theologically expanded form here, in comparison to Colossians. Although particular features of its structure seem to have evolved within early church circles, in general the exhortations concerning relations between familial pairs originated from Hellenistic discussions of household management. Many have viewed this reinforcement of the traditional arrangements of the family (including slavery) as rooted in the need for apologetic: the need to reassure outsiders that early church groups could live peaceably in society.

Feminist scholars, in particular, have noted the absence of such an explicitly hierarchical vision of family life from the undisputed letters of Paul and have highlighted the problematic nature of the language. It certainly requires sensitive interpretation in a modern context, with warnings against using metaphorical language to reinforce notions of male superiority (husbands are compared to Christ) in the face of female fallibility (wives are compared to the human church). Yet, many have identified some elements of the text with timeless value. For example, it offers one of the best illustrations of the two central and related themes of unity and love in the epistle. Because it is so heavily infused with theological reflection, this passage also offers some of the best illustrations of the fundamental link between doctrine and ethics in the work. Ultimately, it means that daily life, even when largely conventional, is filled with meaning for those who belong to the household of God (2:19) and are under the guidance of the Father from whom every family is named (3:14). The call to mutual submission in 5:21, and warnings against excessive severity and calls to love, warn fathers, masters, and husbands of their ultimate loyalty and accountability.

It is in the teaching on marriage where we find the most frequent allusions to Scripture, serving to anchor the theological message about the relationship between the human and the divine (Eph 5:26 [Ezek 16:9]; 5:28 [Lev 19:18]). A direct citation of Gen 2:24 is found in Eph 5:31, to speak not only about the nature of marriage but also to shed light on the mysterious relationship between Christ and the church (5:32). Mystery is a key concept in Ephesians associated with the revelation of the will of God (see notes on Eph 1:3–14).

A second direct citation of Scripture is found in Eph 6:2, the fourth commandment to honor parents (Exod 20:12; cf. Deut 5:16). Along with the parallel text in Colossians, Ephesians offers

arguably the earliest indisputable expression of the valuing of the parent-child relationship in the NT. The direct address to children demonstrates that they were present in the early church assembly. The reference to "the discipline and instruction of the Lord"(6:4) marks the beginning of an interest in the Christian socialization of children that extends into the period of the apostolic fathers (cf. 1 *Clem.* 21.6, 8; *Did,* 4.9; Pol., *Phil.* 4.2).

D. Call to Do Battle with Evil (6:10–20)

The term "finally" signals the conclusion of the ethical exhortation that began in 4:1. The text has been compared to segments of ancient addresses which sought to bring the work to conclusion and arouse the emotion of audiences (Lincoln). The speeches of generals before battle seem to offer particularly appropriate parallels, reminding soldiers of their superior strength and of their disdain for the enemy. Of course, the evil powers are spiritual agencies and not human authorities (6:12). But while they are not earthly enemies, these spiritual powers in Ephesians are understood as deeply affecting the society in which believers live (2:1–3). The dominion of the spiritual powers leads to moral decay and the only true protection is God's armor of ethical and spiritual virtues. The crowning touches of the armor are the helmet of salvation and the sword of the Spirit (6:17) which render the evil one powerless. The recipients of the epistle have been reassured that Christ's power transcends all spiritual forces and fills the universe. But this text offers an especially vivid example of the tension that characterizes the document as a whole between the victory already accomplished against evil (2:6) and the continuing threat of menacing powers. Like the speeches of generals before armed battles, it offers encouragement and strength in the face of suffering. This becomes especially evident in the shift from the image of the believer as armed soldier to the image of the suffering apostle in 6:18–20.

E. Personal Matters and Final Blessing (6:21–24)

The conclusion includes the only real reference to personal matters in the epistle, including the only individual named in Ephesians, Tychicus. He is consistently mentioned in the letters often considered deutero-Pauline (Col 4:7–8; 2 Tim 4:12; Tit 3:12) and, therefore, may have been associated with the final stages of Paul's ministry. In the Pastoral Epistles he is presented as the emissary to Ephesus. There is a very close literary relationship between Eph 6:21–24 and Col 4:7–8, and this has figured prominently in theories concerning the dependence of Ephesians upon Colossians and deutero-Pauline authorship.

The conclusion includes a final blessing and typical features of the endings of Paul's letters such as a wish for peace and bestowal of grace. "Peace" and "grace" (but in reverse order) are found in the initial greeting (1:2). The gifts of faith and love are also in keeping with previous teaching. In particular, love plays a key role in the ethics of the second half of the epistle; it is the means by which believers can emulate Christ (e.g., 5:2). The last phrase of Ephesians is subject to a variety of translations. The final expression, *en aphtharsia* (literally, "in immortality" or "in incorruptibility"), has often been understood as modifying "love" as in the NRSV, "undying love." But others hold that the expression modifies grace: "Grace be to all who love our Lord Jesus Christ in immortality" (author's trans.). This is consistent with the cosmic perspective of the epistle: a life with Christ (2:6) that grows into eternity.

BIBLIOGRAPHY

C. E. Arnold. *Ephesians, Power, and Magic: The Concept of Power in Ephesians in Light of its Historical Setting.* MSSNTS 63 (Cambridge: Cambridge University Press, 1989); E. Best. *Ephesians.* ICC (Edinburgh: T&T Clark, 1998); H. W. Hoehner. *Ephesians: An Exegetical Commentary* (Grand Rapids: Baker Academic, 2002); A. Lincoln. *Ephesians.* WBC 42 (Dallas: Word Books, 1990); M. Y. MacDonald. *Colossians and Ephesians.* SP 17 (Collegeville, Minn.: Liturgical Press, 2000); _____. "The Politics of Identity in Ephesians." JSNT (2004) 419–44; J. Muddiman. *The Epistle to the Ephesians.* BNTC (London and New York: Continuum, 2001); P. Perkins. *Ephesians.* ANTC (Nashville: Abingdon, 1997).

PHILIPPIANS

J. ROSS WAGNER

OVERVIEW

Locked in chains under Roman custody, the apostle Paul writes a letter full of joy, thanksgiving, and hope to a small group of believers residing in the Macedonian city of Philippi. By the first century CE, Philippi was the civic and economic center of a large, chiefly agrarian Roman colony. Though its population comprised Greeks, Romans, Thracians, and diverse foreigners, as a colony its public life was strongly oriented toward Rome. Its municipal government followed the Roman pattern; Romans held most of the important administrative offices; its official inscriptions appeared in Latin; and its citizens enjoyed Roman citizenship. The small Christian congregation in Philippi would have been surrounded by constant reminders of the power and glory of Rome, its emperor, and its gods.

Acts 16 recounts the founding of the Philippian church by Paul and his co-workers, including Timothy (cf. Phil 1:1; 2:19–23). Following the apostle's departure from the city, the community continued its partnership with Paul, sending emissaries to aid his mission in places such as Thessalonica and Corinth (Phil 4:15–18; 2 Cor 11:8–9). Paul and his coworkers appear to have returned to Philippi periodically (2 Cor 1:16; 2:13; 7:5; Acts 20:3; Phil 2:19–24). Though burdened with poverty, the Philippians further displayed their generous spirit through joyfully contributing to Paul's collection of relief funds for the Jerusalem church (2 Cor 8:1–5). The warmth and affection that pervade the letter reflect this long partnership in the work of the gospel.

The particular circumstances surrounding the writing of Philippians can be reconstructed only with difficulty. Complicating the endeavor is the possibility that our canonical Philippians is a composite of two or three originally separate letters. The arguments are complex but, on balance, the numerous connections of thought and language that run from the first chapter to the last—such as Paul's repeated call to adopt the "same mind" (1:27; 2:2; 3:15; 4:2) and his appeal throughout the letter to Christ's story (2:5–11) as moral paradigm—speak in favor of the unity of Philippians.

On this assumption, the occasion for the letter may be sketched as follows.

Paul is in chains awaiting a trial that may well result in his execution (1:19–20; 2:17, 23–24). The place and date of this imprisonment remain uncertain. The traditional setting is Rome (c. 60 CE or later), but strong cases have also be made for Ephesus (early-mid 50s, cf. 1 Cor 15:32; 2 Cor 11:23) and Caesarea (late 50s, cf. Acts 23:33–35). Hearing of Paul's imprisonment, the Philippians send an emissary, Epaphroditus, to encourage Paul and to care for his needs. But in carrying out his commission, Epaphroditus falls seriously ill and nearly dies. Upon his recovery, it is determined that he should return to Philippi (2:25–30). The letter that Paul sends with him expresses thanks to the Philippian congregation for their mission of mercy and offers news of his situation. More than this, however, Paul writes in order to continue his apostolic ministry among them by teaching, encouraging, and admonishing the congregation to pattern their common life after Christ's example of self-giving love. Through his letter, Paul seeks to further God's work in the community so that they may worthily embody the gospel of the Lord Jesus Christ in the midst of Roman Philippi.

OUTLINE

I. Address and Greeting (1:1–2)

II. Thanksgiving and Prayer (1:3–11)

III. Paul's Imprisonment and the Progress of the Gospel (1:12–26)

IV. The Philippians' Calling: Living as a Christ-Shaped Community (1:27–4:3)

    A. Thematic Exhortation: Live Your Common Life in a Manner Worthy of the Gospel (1:27–30)

    B. Exhortation: Adopt Among Yourselves the Mindset of Christ (2:1–5)

    C. Examples to Follow (2:5–3:21)

DETAILED ANALYSIS

I. Address and Greeting (1:1–2)

Paul's refashioning of the typical hellenistic letter opening—"A to B: Greetings"—emphasizes that God's actions in Christ determine the identities of author and recipients alike. Paul and Timothy write as "slaves (NRSV, 'servants') of Christ Jesus" (cf. Rom 1:1; 2 Cor 4:5; Gal 1:10), whose lives belong completely to their master and whose authority derives from his. They address the Philippians as "saints," members of a worldwide people (cf. 4:21–22) set apart in Christ Jesus as God's very own (cf. Exod 19:5–6). Paul greets them with a blessing, invoking "grace ... and peace" from God, the Father of them all, and from their common "master (NRSV, 'Lord') Jesus Christ." The reason for the special mention of "bishops and deacons," unique among Paul's letter openings, remains unclear. In any case, Paul addresses what follows to the community as a whole, as his repeated references to "all of you" attest (1:4, 7, 8).

II. Thanksgiving and Prayer (1:3–11)

Following his normal pattern, Paul introduces central themes of the letter in his opening thanks-giving and prayer. The clear note of joy struck here (1:4)—remarkable for a letter composed while in chains—resounds throughout the letter. Such joy arises, not from his circumstances or those of the Philippians, but from a deep-seated trust in the reliability of God, who is unfailingly working out God's good purposes for them all (1:6; cf. 2:12–13). A confident expectation of God's imminent triumph at "the day of Jesus Christ" (1:6; 10; 2:16) undergirds Paul's hopeful perspective as he eagerly looks forward to sharing in Christ's resurrection and vindication by God (cf. 2:16; 3:10–11; 3:20; 4:5).

The long partnership (*koinōnia*) between Paul and the Philippians, stretching from the apostle's founding visit to the present (1:5; 4:15–16), constitutes another major motif of the letter. Their participation in the proclamation, and now the defense, of the gospel is a sharing in God's grace (1:7), for it belongs to the good work God is accomplishing among them (1:6). Similarly, the spirit of mutual love in Christ that pervades Paul's thanksgiving comes to expression repeatedly in what follows. Paul prays that the Philippians' self-giving love, embodied most recently in the embassy of Epaphroditus (2:25–30), will "overflow more and more" (1:9). Shaped by "knowledge and full insight," this love will be able to determine "what really matters" (1:10, *ta diapheronta*; NRSV, "what is best"). Such discerning love, Paul will soon argue, represents the very mindset of Christ (2:5). Its outcome is "the harvest of righteousness that comes through Jesus Christ," and its goal "the glory and praise of God" (1:11; cf. 2:11; 4:20).

III. Paul's Imprisonment and the Progress of the Gospel (1:12–26)

As he reports on his circumstances, Paul addresses the Philippians in familial language (1:12, NRSV margin, "brothers"), reflecting the new social reality that God, their Father, has called into being in Christ. Rather than focus on the shame, deprivation, and affliction he himself is experiencing, Paul models for his brothers and sisters the Christ-shaped mindset that is able to discern "what really matters." He boldly asserts that, although he is bound with chains, what really matters is that the gospel is making progress (1:12). Because of his chains, the gospel has advanced right to the heart of Roman power (1:13).

Moreover, Paul's example has emboldened others in the community to speak God's word publicly without fear (1:14). Most do so out of love, desiring to labor alongside Paul, whom they recognize has been appointed by God "for the defense of the gospel" (1:16). Others, Paul believes, are motivated by selfish ambition, perhaps seeing an opportunity to increase their influence in the community at the apostle's expense while his activities are curtailed. Despite the pain of these personal rivalries, Paul chooses to rejoice. (Contrast his response in Gal 1:6–9, however, when he encounters those who preach "a different gospel.") What really matters are not Paul's own interests, but the interests of Christ that are being advanced as "Christ is proclaimed in every way, whether out of false motives or true" (1:18; cf. 2:4, 21).

A single-minded focus on "what is best" similarly shapes the apostle's reflections on his own uncertain fate. As he awaits trial on a capital charge, his chief concern is to continue to speak boldly (cf. 1:14) so that "Christ will be exalted now as always in [his] body, whether by life or by death" (1:20). Paul derives courage from his friends' prayers, and he relies on "the help of the Spirit of Jesus Christ." Like Job (Job 13:16–18), he trusts that his "deliverance," his vindication, rests firmly in God's hands (1:19; cf. 1:20, "not put to shame in any way"). The memorable phrase, "For to me, living is Christ and dying is gain," captures the heart of Paul's understanding of salvation. To live means sharing the fellowship of Christ's sufferings (cf. 3:10) by engaging in the "fruitful labor" of the gospel (1:22), while dying leads to the reward of life in Christ's very presence (1:23). Drawing on the economic language he will employ more extensively later (3:7–8), Paul acknowledges that he longs for the far greater "gain" that death promises. Yet, once again, he places others' interests above his own. Judging that it is "more necessary" for the Philippians that he remain alive, Paul looks ahead confidently to his release and to the "boasting" in Christ (cf. 1:20) that his reunion with them will occasion (1:24–26).

IV. The Philippians' Calling: Living as a Christ-Shaped Community (1:27–4:3)

Paul does not wait until he is safely back in Philippi, however, to resume his apostolic labor of advancing the community's "progress and joy

in faith." In this longest section of the letter, he urges the Philippians to shape their common life in accordance with the pattern of Christ's own self-giving love, and he parades before their eyes a series of exemplary figures who embody this cruciform pattern of life.

A. Thematic Exhortation: Live Your Common Life in a Manner Worthy of the Gospel (1:27–30)

The centrality of Paul's exhortation in 1:27 is underscored by the word which begins the sentence (both in Greek and in English)—"Only." Whether the apostle is present or absent, the community must maintain its focus on the one thing that really matters, namely, conducting their common life in a manner worthy of the gospel of Christ. It is difficult to capture the force of v. 27 in translation. The verb rendered by the NRSV, "live your life," *politeuesthe*, is related to the word "city" (*polis*), from which derives the English word "politics." Paul speaks here of their life as a community, conducted in public before a watching—and sometimes hostile (1:28)—society. The particular force of this word would not have been lost on Paul's hearers in Philippi, a city whose elites prided themselves on their status as citizens of a Roman colony. (It is conceivable that the Philippian church included citizens among its members, but there is no explicit evidence for this either within the letter itself or in the account of Paul's visit to Philippi in Acts 16.) The quality of their public, communal life is to be judged, not according to the standards of Roman society, but by its conformity to the new reality inaugurated by God's redemptive action in Christ and heralded by the gospel.

Just as concord represented a core value of the ancient city and of the various households and voluntary associations it comprised, so here Paul stresses the importance of unity—"in one spirit . . . with one mind"—for the sake of their communal witness to the faith of the gospel (1:27). Employing athletic imagery ("striving side by side," 1:27), he urges them to band together to "stand firm" in the "contest" (1:30; NRSV, "struggle") in which they are engaged.

Their opponents go unnamed. Evidence for a significant Jewish presence in the city in Paul's time is lacking (cf. Acts 16:13). Most likely these are Gentile neighbors who view this (predominantly Gentile) community's allegiance to the Jewish God and his crucified Messiah as a foreign and un-Roman manner of life. The small church constitutes a potential threat to public order and to the common welfare, which depends on the favor of the gods of the city and of the empire, as well as on the good will of the emperor (cf. Acts 16:20–21;17:6–7). Paul, however, offers his hearers an alternative narrative by which to interpret this conflict of cultures. God, in "graciously granting" them faith in Christ and partnership in the gospel (cf. 1:7), has also given them the grace, alongside Paul, of fellowship with Christ through sharing Christ's sufferings (1:29–30; cf. 3:10). And their steadfastness in suffering, which Paul likewise attributes to God's working among them (1:28; cf. 1:6), offers incontrovertible evidence that they will also share with Paul in Christ's vindication (1:28; cf. 1:19; 3:11).

B. Exhortation: Adopt Among Yourselves the Mindset of Christ (2:1–5)

In a carefully crafted appeal full of genuine warmth and pathos, the apostle reminds his hearers of the loving fellowship they enjoy by virtue of God's action among them through Christ and the Spirit (2:1). Heaping up expressions for concord ("same mind ... same love ... full accord ... one mind," 2:2), he implores them to "make [his] joy complete" by displaying their unity through loving, self-sacrificial service of one another. Anticipating his retelling of Christ's story in 2:6–8, Paul urges his listeners in "humility" (cf. 2:8) to "regard" (cf. 2:6) others' interests as more important than their own (2:3–4). He calls the Philippians to embody that particular unity which derives from adopting among themselves the "mind" displayed by Christ, a mindset that is already their own by virtue of the fact that God has united them together "in Christ" (2:5; together the NRSV text and margin capture well the—quite possibly intentional—ambiguity of Paul's wording). This mindset will shape their thoughts, affections, and actions in such a way that their lives will come to embody the pattern of self-giving love that characterized Jesus' life. It is this pattern that Paul's retelling of the story of Christ now vividly displays before their eyes.

C. Examples to Follow (2:5–3:21)

2:5–11. Christ the Paradigmatic Example. Although Paul transmits few sayings of Jesus, his depiction of Jesus' obedience to God through loving, humble service of others coheres at a fundamental level with the portraits of this figure painted by the four canonical Gospels. The poetic narration of Jesus' humiliation and exaltation in Phil 2:6–11, paralleled by more compact statements elsewhere in Paul's writings (e.g., Gal 2:20*b*; 2 Cor 5:14–15; 8:9), is widely thought to derive from an early Christian hymn. Whatever its origin, this narrative plays a central role in Philippians, for Jesus' story serves as the touchstone by which Paul evaluates the other exemplary figures in this letter.

Nearly every aspect of the background and interpretation of this so-called "Christ Hymn" continues to prompt lively scholarly debate. Yet the general plot-line of the story told here is clear. As one who existed in "the form of God," Christ did not exploit this "equality with God" for his own selfish advantage (2:6). Instead, he "emptied himself" for the sake of others (NIV, "made himself nothing") by voluntarily assuming "the form of a slave" (2:7). In "human likeness," he "humbled himself" by becoming "obedient to the point of death"—even to the extent of suffering the utterly shameful death of a slave on a Roman cross (2:8).

One crucial word—"therefore" (2:9)—signals the turning point of the story. Precisely on the basis of Jesus' obedient self-abasement for others, God has now "highly exalted" this "slave" by enthroning him as "master" (2:11; NRSV, "Lord"). The resurrection inverts human ideologies of honor and shame by publicly vindicating Jesus' life of loving obedience to God and self-sacrificing service to others. It thus implicitly calls into question any pretensions to "lordship" founded on conquest and domination. Living in a city that prided itself on its loyalty to the Roman Empire and its "Lord," Caesar, the risks of confessing Jesus as "Lord" would hardly have been lost on the Philippians.

But the implications of the Christ Hymn are more revolutionary still. In describing the universal homage paid to the exalted Jesus, vv. 10–11 draw on the language and imagery of Isa 45:23–25. This stunningly bold appropriation of Israel's Scriptures identifies the man Jesus with the one

God of Israel, who alone is worthy of worship. It finds a parallel in Paul's equally daring rewriting of the *Shema* (Deut 6:4: "The LORD is our God, the LORD alone") in 1 Cor 8:6 ("for us there is one God, the Father ... and one Lord, Jesus Christ"). By locating the story of Jesus within the story that determines the identity of the one God of Israel, Paul claims nothing less than this: that the loving self-donation of Jesus reveals what *God* is like in God's very being. For this reason, the universal acclamation, "Jesus Christ is Lord," serves the ultimate end of glorifying God the Father (2:11).

2:12–18. Exhortation: Work Out Your Salvation, for God Is Working Among You. Because the story of Jesus—indeed, the story of God—told in Phil 2:6–11 sets the pattern of life for Jesus' followers, the exhortations in 2:12–18 flow out of, and find their grounding in, this foundational narrative ("Therefore," 2:12). Just as Jesus was obedient to God (2:8), so the Philippians must continue to practice the obedience (2:12) that they have learned from Paul and consistently displayed in his presence (cf. 4:9). Paul deftly weaves together divine and human agency as he calls them to "work out" their own salvation (2:12) precisely because "it is God who is at work" among them (2:13). The Philippians' ongoing obedience, then, is itself the outworking of the prior and continuing activity of God, who is the one producing in them both "[their own] willing and [their own] working, for God's good pleasure" (2:13, author's translation).

In what follows, Paul fleshes out what it means for them to "work out" their salvation (2:14–16). To this end, he draws on two scriptural narratives—the wandering in the wilderness and the exile in Babylon—to help them envision their calling as God's people in Philippi. Paul's reference to "murmuring and arguing" (2:14) evokes images of the wilderness generation (see Exod 15:22–16:12; Ps 106:25; 1 Cor 10:10), while "children of God without blemish" (2:15) takes up and reverses the characterization of the Israelites in Moses' song (Deut 32:5; cf. Matt 17:17; Acts 2:40). By means of this allusive comparison of the Philippians to Israel in the desert, Paul gently reminds them of the dangers of unfaithfulness to God and exhorts them to a very different pattern of life in the midst of their own "crooked and perverse generation" (2:15; cf. Deut 32:5).

"Holding fast to the word of life" in this dark setting (2:16), the Philippians "shine like stars in the world" (2:15), just as Daniel and his compatriots faithfully bore witness to God in an alien land (cf. Dan 12:3*a* LXX: "those who have understanding will shine like the stars of heaven," author's translation). As the Philippians live their public, communal life in a manner worthy of the gospel, they commend the "message that brings life" (NRSV, "word of life") to those around them. "On the day of Christ," their faithful perseverance will be proof of God's working among them (cf. 1:6, 10) and the ground for Paul's "boast" that his labors on their behalf have not been in vain (2:16). Paul's reward for "running" and toiling in the gospel, his victor's "crown" (4:1), will be his joyful fellowship with the Philippians themselves in the presence of Christ.

Meanwhile, even as he faces the very real possibility of death as the immediate outcome of his tireless labors on their behalf, Paul rejoices over their lives of faithful obedience, which are a "sacrifice and offering" to God (note the language of worship also in 2:30; 3:3; 4:18). The stress in vv. 17–18 on the mutuality of their joy in one another represents yet another expression of the deep fellowship with the Philippians for which the apostle gives thanks throughout the letter.

2:19–30. Examples of Cruciform Living: Paul's Co-workers. Paul's letters commonly include information about the travel plans of the apostle and his co-workers. Philippians is no exception. Here, however, Paul's report concerning Timothy and Epaphroditus has the additional purpose of drawing the Philippians' attention to two people well known to them, whose lives embody the pattern of life that flows from the mindset of Christ.

Paul's characterization of Timothy recalls the Christ Hymn and its introduction. Just as the community is to strive for unity of mind ("with one mind," 1:27; "of one mind," 2:2), so Timothy is "likeminded" with Paul (2:20, KJV) in his deep concern for the Philippians' welfare as he works side by side with the apostle "like a son with a father" (2:22). Rather than seeking his own interests, Timothy serves "[the interests] of Jesus Christ" (2:21) by being "genuinely concerned for [the Philippians'] welfare" (2:20; cf. 2:4). Following Christ, who willingly made himself a slave (*doulos*, 2:7; see NRSV margin), Timothy—Christ's slave (*doulos*, 1:1; see NRSV margin)—has faithfully "served as a slave" (*douleuō*, 2:22, author's translation; NRSV, "served") alongside Paul.

Turning to Epaphroditus in vv. 25–30, Paul again draws on the Christ Hymn to portray a person whose life replicates the pattern of Christ's self-giving obedience. For the sake of "the work of Christ"—seeking Paul's welfare—Epaphroditus drew near "to the point of death" (2:30, author's translation; NRSV, "close to death"). It was God's mercy (2:27) that delivered Epaphroditus from death and spared Paul the sorrow of losing his "brother and co-worker and fellow soldier" (2:25). Epaphroditus functions as a particularly powerful example to the Philippians, for he is not an apostle, but one of them. His service as "minister" (*leitourgos*, 2:25) to Paul's need represents the "priestly ministry" (*leitourgia*, 2:30 author's translation; NRSV, "services") of the entire community, "all" of whom share together with Paul in the work of the gospel (1:4–5). Paul's instruction to "honor such people" implies that there will be other such exemplars of Christ's cruciform (cross-shaped) pattern of life among them (cf. 3:17; 4:3).

3:1–14. A Further Example of Cruciform Living: Paul's Own Story.

For some, the jarring transition between 3:1 and 3:2 reveals a seam created when a later compiler joined together two originally separate letters of Paul to Philippi. But the pairing of positive and negative examples is conventional in ancient moral instruction, and many scholars, impressed by the consistency of Paul's language and thought throughout the letter (see Introduction), attribute the abrupt shift to invective in 3:2 to Paul's rhetorical purposes and to the circumstances of his writing rather than to the clumsiness of a later editor.

Paul's argument flows more smoothly if his comment in 3:1 about writing "the same things" again as a "safeguard" refers to the sharp warning he immediately issues in 3:2 against "the dogs ... the evil workers ... those who mutilate the flesh." Vituperative language such as Paul employs here, while shocking to modern sensibilities, was a commonplace of ancient polemics, whether in political debates or in disputes between philosophical schools. Paul's probable target is rival missionaries who insisted that Gentile believers

in Christ submit to circumcision and take on at least some of the stipulations of the Jewish law (cf. Acts 15:1–5; Galatians). These opponents' abrupt appearance in the letter, and their just as sudden departure from it, suggests that they pose no immediate threat to the Philippian church. But hard experience in Galatia and Corinth has taught Paul the necessity of putting his congregations on guard against their eventual encounter with such traveling teachers. He does so by drawing a sharp contrast between zealous concern with outward manifestations of godliness such as physical circumcision—which by a play on words he dismisses as *kata-tomē*, "mutilation" (NRSV margin)—and inward devotion to God, for which he claims the term *peri-tomē*, "circumcision." Presupposing passages in Israel's Scriptures that speak of circumcision of the heart (Deut 10:16; 30:6; Jer 4:4), Paul identifies "the circumcision" as "we ... who worship in the Spirit of God" (3:3; cf. Gal 3:1–5; Rom 2:28–29). Their confidence rests solely "in Christ Jesus," and they refuse to rely on circumcision or any other mark of distinction that belongs only to "the flesh" to secure their right standing with God.

In 3:4–14, Paul offers himself as the paradigmatic example of what it means for one to "boast in Christ Jesus and put no confidence in the flesh" (3:3). The apostle's comparison of his past life with his present life in Christ has often been interpreted along anti-Jewish lines, but it is crucial to recognize that Paul nowhere renounces his Jewish heritage or disparages his past life as a Pharisee. Indeed, for his argument to work, these must represent real "gains," for only so does Paul's testimony to "the surpassing value" of Christ carry any rhetorical force.

Paul recounts his impeccable genealogy with evident pride: circumcised by parents who strictly observed the law of Moses, a descendant of Israel, a member of the tribe of Benjamin (a fact to which Paul also draws attention in Rom 11:1), a "Hebrew born of Hebrews" (3:5). This latter phrase probably refers to Jews who carefully preserved their ancestral traditions, including the Hebrew language, even in the Diaspora. Paul's identity as a Pharisee marks him as one who was deeply devoted to God and meticulous in observing God's commands. Following the pattern of national heroes such as Phinehas (Num 25:11; Sir 45:23; 1 Macc

2:26) and the Maccabean martyrs (1 Macc 2:27, 50), Paul demonstrated his "zeal" for the law by attempting to extirpate from Israel those he saw as blatantly violating God's covenant (3:6). With great confidence, he judges his former life to have been, in fact, "blameless" when measured by the law's standard of righteousness.

It is only in light of "the surpassing value of knowing Christ Jesus my Lord" that Paul now regards the very real "gains" of his past to register as "loss" (3:7–8). What is more, though Paul has lost everything for the sake of Christ, he considers these things to amount to nothing more than "rubbish" ("dung," KJV) in comparison with the immeasurable value of "gaining Christ." Paul has lost all confidence in his "own" righteousness based on his blameless fidelity to Israel's law (3:9). United to Christ by God's action ("found in him"), Paul has a righteousness—a right standing with God—that does not belong to him, but that comes from God *dia pistēs Christou*. Scholars debate whether this phrase in 3:9 should be translated "through faith in Christ" (NRSV text) or "through the faith of Christ" (NRSV margin). However, in view of Paul's emphasis in Philippians on the believing community's participation "in Christ" (see comment on 4:10) and his conviction that God's agency accompanies and interpenetrates human agency (see comment on 2:12–13), the difference may not be as great as is sometimes imagined. That is, for Paul, the response of faith and trust evoked by the gospel is itself "Christ-faith" (*pistis Christou*, author's translation), a participation in the faithful, trusting obedience of Christ, to whom they have been joined.

The treasure for the sake of which Paul has gladly lost all things is fellowship with Christ. His one passion is "to know Christ" and to share in Christ's resurrection life (3:10). In the present, this means experiencing the power of Christ's resurrection in paradoxical fashion—through sharing in Christ's sufferings. Paul pours himself out in service to others for Christ's sake (cf. 2:17), increasingly becoming like Christ in his self-giving death, so that he may also share in the resurrection from the dead, of which Christ is the first-fruits (3:11; cf. 1 Cor 15:20–23).

Paul takes pains to prevent misunderstanding at this point. Although fellowship with Christ is a present reality, he has not yet attained his goal or "been made perfect" (3:12, NRSV margin). But because Christ has already laid hold of him, he strives with the single-minded devotion of an athlete to lay hold of the prize to which God has called him: the immediate and unbroken fellowship with God in Christ that resurrection life will bring (3:13–14; cf. 1:23).

3:15–21. Call to Imitation with a Counterexample. Paul does not offer himself as a model of heroic virtue to which only a few may aspire. Rather, he asserts that all who are "mature" in faith will be led by God to share and maintain this same mindset (3:15–16). He calls his brothers and sisters in Philippi to unite in the task of imitating him, and he urges them to take careful note of those in their own midst who faithfully embody his example of a Christ-shaped pattern of life (3:17). Attention to such exemplars is crucial to the community's ability to live worthily, for they are surrounded by "many" whose manner of life is diametrically opposed to the pattern of obedient self-giving love displayed at the cross (3:18). These "enemies of the cross of Christ" indulge their own appetites and set their mind no higher than "earthly things" (3:19). In contrast, Paul and his hearers recognize that they are citizens of the heavenly *politeuma*, "commonwealth" (3:20, NRSV margin) ruled by God. It is from that realm that they await a "Savior" (a term the Roman emperors arrogated to themselves in order to legitimize their own allegedly beneficent tyranny). The crucified and exalted "Lord Jesus Christ" will return in person to deliver them. Those whose lives have been conformed to the pattern of Jesus' self-giving death will find their "humble bodies" transformed into the likeness of "his glorious [resurrection] body" (3:21; cf. NRSV margin). Christ's subjection of all things, expressed in scriptural terms (cf. Ps 8:6 and Ps 110:1), fulfills the divine purpose announced in Phil 2:10–11.

D. Specific Application: Restoring Unity Between Leaders (4:1–3)

With eyes fixed on the certainty of God's triumph, Paul reprises his opening exhortation (1:27), urging his beloved brothers and sisters to "stand firm" together (4:1; cf. 3:16). Here his call to unity has in view a very specific situation, the current lack of concord between two women who are apparently leaders in the congregation

(4:2–3). Paul's respect and affection for them both is evident. He addresses each one by name, commending them as his co-workers, beloved by God ("whose names are in the book of life"). He appeals to these women who have "struggled beside [him] in the work of the gospel" (cf. 1:27) to "be of the same mind in the Lord"—that is, to adopt toward one another the humble mindset of Christ that is oriented toward the other's interests. Paul calls on an unnamed companion to foster their reconciliation, for it is the community as a whole that is charged with living "in a manner worthy of the gospel of Christ" (1:27).

V. Final Exhortations: The Way of Joy and Peace (4:4–9)

Paul infuses his closing exhortations with the themes of joy and peace. Rejoicing is the fitting response of those who know the surpassing value of fellowship with Christ in life and in death (4:4). "The Lord is near" (4:5) may well carry a double meaning in this context: Sensible of the nearness of Christ's presence and confident of the nearness of his return (cf. 3:20), the Philippians are to conduct themselves with "gentleness" (NRSV; "moderation," KJV; "forbearance," RSV) toward "everyone" (4:5; cf. 2:15), even those who oppose them (1:28).

Though tempted to anxiety by their challenging circumstances, they are invited to pour out their needs before God in prayer with thanksgiving (4:6). As they do, God's peace will stand guard over their hearts and minds (4:7), enabling them to stand firm "in Christ Jesus" (cf. 4:1). Finally, Paul calls his brothers and sisters to a disciplined habit of mind that focuses on what is excellent and praiseworthy (4:8; cf. 1:10, "what is best") as well as to a consistent practice of the Christ-like pattern that they have seen displayed in Paul's own life (4:9). He reminds them that surrounding and undergirding their own strenuous efforts is the ongoing working of their gracious God (cf. 2:12–13; 1:6): "the God of peace will be with you" (4:9).

VI. Gratitude for the Philippians' Partnership in the Gospel (4:10–20)

Paul has occasionally been criticized for failing to show appropriate gratitude for the Philippians' gift. However, it is important to judge Paul's expression of thanks not by modern standards, but in accordance with ancient sensibilities. In his response to the Philippians' generosity, Paul draws on the language and conventions of friendship current in his day. Friendship was defined by moral philosophers as a relationship between self-sufficient equals. (Note, however, that Paul's own claim to be content is based not on self-sufficiency, but on the empowering presence of God [4:11–13].) It does not grow out of need, nor is it sustained by a relationship of reciprocal exchange. Rather, friends share a kinship of spirit in the pursuit of virtue. For this reason, the profuse expression of thanks for a gift—which was an obligatory feature of the relationship of a client to his patron—would have appeared completely out of place among friends.

Paul walks a thin line as he seeks to thank the Philippians for their generosity (4:10, 14, 15–16, 18) without giving the impression either that he is now under obligation to them or that he desires further gifts (4:11–13, 17, 19–20). Although Paul and the Philippians have a long history of sharing in material goods (4:15–16; cf. 2 Cor 11:8–9; 8:1–5), he resists being positioned as their dependent client, just as he refuses to assume the role of their patron. Instead, he seeks a genuine partnership with them in the work of the gospel, one that grows out of God's gracious working in their midst (cf. 1:3–8).

It is no accident, then, that as he expresses gratitude to the Philippian congregation, Paul very deliberately highlights the presence and activity of God at the center of their relationship. His joy at their recent demonstration of concern for him is joy "in the Lord" (4:10). Phrases like "in the Lord" and "in Christ" that repeatedly punctuate the letter (e.g., 1:1, 8, 26; 2:1, 5, 19, 24, 29; 3:1, 14; 4:1, 2, 4, 7, 19, 21) express Paul's fundamental conviction that their fellowship has its basis in God's having united them all to Christ, so that their partnership is a participation in Christ's own life. The apostle characterizes the ties that bind him to the Philippians as those of family rather than of "friendship" (a term which, like the word "friend," never appears in Paul's letters [cf. NRSV margin at 4:21]). Because God, "our Father," stands at the center of this relationship (4:20), the Philippians' service to Paul is ultimately "a fragrant offering, a sacrifice acceptable and pleasing to God" (4:18; cf.

2:17, 30). It is God, not Paul, who will repay them fully out of his superabundant "riches in glory in Christ Jesus" (4:19). And it is God who deservedly receives all the glory (4:20; cf. 2:11).

VII. Closing Greeting and Prayer (4:21–23)

As is typical for Greco-Roman letters, Philippians closes with an exchange of greetings. Even here Paul continues to pursue his apostolic mission of strengthening the Philippian congregation in faith. His reference both to the Philippians and to the "brothers [and sisters]" with him (4:21, NRSV margin) as "saints" reminds his hearers that their identity originates in God's calling (see comment on 1:1) and that membership in God's people extends far beyond their local community (4:21–22). He passes on greetings from "all the saints … especially those of the emperor's household," judging that this small, beleaguered community living in the midst of Roman Philippi will find it encouraging to learn that there are "saints" even among the vast network of slaves, freedmen, and other officials who make up the household of Lord Caesar (4:22). With words that echo his opening blessing, Paul's benediction commends them to the boundless grace of the one true Lord, Jesus Christ (4:23).

BIBLIOGRAPHY

K. Barth. *Epistle to the Philippians* (Louisville: Westminster John Knox, 2002); M. Bockmuehl. *The Epistle to the Philippians.* BNTC (London: A&C Black, 1998); C. B. Cousar. *Philippians and Philemon.* NTL (Louisville: Westminster John Knox, 2009); G. D. Fee. *Paul's Letter to the Philippians.* NICNT (Grand Rapids: Eerdmans, 1995); J. T. Fitzgerald, ed. *Friendship, Flattery, and Frankness of Speech: Studies on Friendship in the New Testament World.* NovTSup 82 (Leiden: Brill, 1996); S. E. Fowl. *Philippians.* Two Horizons New Testament Commentary (Grand Rapids: Eerdmans, 2005); P. Oakes. *Philippians: From People to Letter.* SNTSMS 110 (Cambridge: Cambridge University Press, 2001); M. Silva. *Philippians.* Baker Exegetical Commentary on the New Testament. 2nd ed. (Grand Rapids: Baker Academic, 2005); J. Reumann. *Philippians: A New Translation with Introduction and Commentary.* The Anchor Yale Bible 33B (New Haven: Yale University Press, 2008).

COLOSSIANS

Stephen Fowl

OVERVIEW

Paul (and Timothy) are the inscribed authors of this letter to a congregation located in the Lycus valley in the Roman province of Asia Minor. Although Paul did not found this congregation, Epaphras did (1:7), he feels a deep connection to the Colossians. It is clear that the Colossians and Paul manifest an abiding interest in each other's welfare.

Many contemporary scholars question whether Paul the apostle actually wrote this letter. There are some differences of style, tone, and theological emphasis between Colossians and those letters undisputedly written by Paul. We also know that followers of various ancient teachers sometimes wrote letters in the name of their teacher. This was not primarily with the aim of deceiving the readers, but in order to place their views in continuity with their master. How one judges this matter of authorship largely depends on how much diversity and continuity one thinks is possible for a single author. There is very little at stake here theologically either way. The letter is part of Scripture, and Christians engage it as Scripture.

If the letter is Pauline, then it was probably written in the early part of the 60s, not long before Paul's death. If it is not Pauline, then it was probably written by a disciple of Paul's in the time shortly after his death.

In addition to some close connections to Philemon, Colossians is most closely connected to Ephesians. Although some argue that there is literary dependence between these two letters (usually Ephesians being dependent on Colossians), there is actually very little evidence to sustain the claim that the two letters are literarily dependent on each other.

Some in the congregation appear to be advocating the view that the Colossians should supplement their faith in Christ (Paul calls the view "philosophy and empty deceit" in 2:8). In particular, these teachers argue that if the Colossians engage in a variety of ascetic practices (2:16–23), they can cultivate an ecstatic or mystical state whereby they might participate more directly in the worship of God; they might even participate in the angels' worship of God (2:18). These practices would appear to have a connection to Judaism, but many different groups in Paul's world thought that asceticism could lead to ecstatic visions and experiences.

Paul counters this teaching by asserting Christ's supremacy over all things. One can have no fuller experience of God than to be connected to Christ, "the image of the invisible God" (1:15). In every possible way Christ is superior to anything in the cosmos. Any way in which the cosmos is alienated from God is reconciled in Christ and nowhere else (1:15–20). Thus, because the Colossians have been bound to Christ through their baptism, there is nothing more they can or need to do in order to have the fullest possible knowledge and experience of God.

OUTLINE

DETAILED ANALYSIS

I. Salutation (1:1–2)

The senders are identified as Paul, "an apostle of Christ Jesus by the will of God," and Timothy the brother (cf. 2 Cor 1:1). An *apostle* is someone sent out, a person with a mission. The fact that Paul identifies himself as an apostle of "Jesus Christ by the will of God" indicates that Jesus Christ is the subject of Paul's mission and that God is the one who appointed Paul.

Timothy (cf. Acts 16:1–6) is identified as a brother in Christ. He is also mentioned at the beginning of Philippians. In Philippians, however, Paul goes on to speak in the first person singular. Here in Colossians, the first person plural is used, giving the sense that Timothy is not simply Paul's co-worker, but even a co-author of the epistle.

The Colossians are identified as "saints and faithful brothers and sisters in Christ." Just as the term *apostle* indicates someone who is set apart, the term *saints* also indicates the purpose for which the Colossians and all believers are set apart—sanctity or holiness. Of course, this is the same calling that God gives to Israel, "You shall be holy because I am holy" (Lev.19:2). Moreover, the believers in Colossae are identified as faithful, a characteristic not always noted in greetings to other Pauline churches (e.g. Galatia, Corinth). Finally, they are Paul's brothers and sisters in Christ. This recognizes that whatever else has and will pass between the Colossians and Paul, they are intimately bound to each other because

of Christ. Theirs is a three-way friendship. The greeting closes with Paul's standard wish of grace and peace.

II. Prayer for the Colossians (1:3–14)

A. Prayer for Faith, Hope, and Love (1:3–8)

As is typical in a Pauline letter, the greeting is followed by a prayer of thanksgiving. The prayer thanks God for the Colossians and reflects Paul's joys and concerns regarding the congregation. Paul's prayers for the Colossians invoke the three theological virtues of faith, which initiates and sustains their friendship with Christ, love, which guides the common life of the congregation, and hope, which directs them to their ultimate end in Christ. This is followed by a brief recounting of the Colossians' reception of the gospel through Epaphras, Paul's fellow slave and faithful minister in Christ.

B. Prayer for Knowledge and Wisdom (1:9–14)

Paul then moves to pray that God would fill the Colossians with knowledge and wisdom, so that the Colossians might be better able to "walk" in a manner worthy of the Lord. The three particular characteristics Paul prays for are strength, perseverance, and gratitude. In this way, Paul anticipates that growth in knowledge and wisdom will enable the Colossians to lead lives that more worthily reflect the nature of God's work among them. Paul characterizes this work as bringing the Colossians out of darkness and transferring them in the kingdom of Christ. The language here reflects a change of citizenship, and Paul expects the Colossians' affections and allegiances to reflect their new citizenship. Before developing this point, however, Paul moves to identify further the king in whose kingdom the Colossians now dwell.

III. Christ, King and Redeemer (1:15–20)

Rather than describe "the kingdom" of Christ as one might expect from 1:14, Paul describes the king in these verses. There was a period when it was common for scholars to call this passage an early Christian hymn (cf. 3:16), but there is little or no evidence here to support this claim. The passage poetically describes Christ relative to God, creation, and the church. All of these descriptions come into play when Paul combats the false teaching that seems to be attracting members of the congregation. At the same time, Paul does not defend this account of Christ in any way, assuming that the Colossians either know these things already or will find them uncontestable.

The passage begins by identifying Christ as "the image of the invisible God." Paul also speaks of Christ as the image of God in 2 Cor 4:4. In each of these cases Paul makes the point that Christ makes God manifest to humans in a way that would not otherwise be possible. Exodus 33:20 and Isa 6:5 both make the point that humans cannot gaze directly on the face of God. Thus, being the image of the invisible God would indicate that Christ uniquely, supremely, truly, and reliably manifests God to humans who could not otherwise see God. This notion will directly come into play as Paul addresses the false teaching that a connection to Christ needs to be supplemented by further spiritual experiences.

Paul elaborates on the nature of Christ's supremacy as the image of God by asserting Christ's primacy in creation because he is "first-born of all creation." This notion of primacy through temporal precedence is well attested in the NT (Rom 8:29; Heb 1:6; Rev 1:5) as well as the LXX (Ps. 88:28) and Philo (*De confusione linguarum* 147; *Legum allegoriae* 3.175; *De ebrietate* 31). Christ's primacy over creation stems from the fact that all things exist "in," "through," and "for" him. Christ provides creation with its unity, coherence, and *telos* or goal.

Paul then asserts Christ's supremacy in and for the church. He is the "head of the body" (v. 18). Both in creation and in the church, Christ, the image of the invisible God, reigns supreme.

The second half of this passage continues Paul's uncompromising assertion of Christ's supremacy over all by focusing on Christ's mission of reconciling all things to God. Paul's assertions assume that despite Christ's supremacy over creation, creation had become alienated from God and required reconciliation. Christ accomplishes the first stage of this reconciliation in his resurrection. This is what Paul means by claiming that Christ is the "firstborn from the dead." In defeating death, the most prevalent sign of creation's alienation from the creator, Christ enables all things to be recon-

ciled to God, "making peace through the blood of his cross" (v. 20).

By the end of this passage Paul has laid a firm foundation for his attack on the false teaching. Since Christ is preeminent over all things, since "all the fullness of God" (v. 19) dwells in him, there is nothing more the Colossians need to supplement their experience and life with God than to be connected to Christ.

IV. Being Connected to Christ Through Paul's Gospel (1:21–2:7)

A. The Colossians' Alienation from God (1:21–23)

In 1:18–20 Paul presumes a general story of creation's alienation from God. In these verses he offers a specific account of the Colossians' alienation prior to their reception of the gospel. Christ has overcome their estrangement from God, provided they remain steadfast in their faith in the gospel.

B. Paul's Calling (1:24–29)

Paul describes his calling in terms that support his claim to be an authoritative and reliable interpreter of the gospel. Paul is imprisoned (cf. 4:3) and he begins his discussion by noting that his sufferings are both an occasion for joy and "fill up what is lacking in Christ's afflictions." This formulation probably refers to a Jewish notion that Paul is participating in the "birthpangs of the Messiah," those tribulations that would usher in the messianic age (cf. Gal 4:19). Paul here wants to indicate that his sufferings have a purpose. They do not signify God's rejection of him. Rather, they testify to his full participation in God's drama of salvation. Indeed, Paul has been given a special role to play in this drama. God's surprising plan to bring about the salvation of the Gentiles through the crucifixion and resurrection of Jesus has been made known to Paul and the other apostles. It has fallen to Paul to make public this formerly hidden good news, and he devotes himself tirelessly to this task.

C. Paul's Hopes for the Colossians and Laodiceans (2:1–7)

After speaking of his efforts to proclaim the mystery of Christ in general terms, Paul now focuses on the churches in Colossae and Laodicea. Although he has not visited these churches himself, they are connected to him and he to them through their common commitment to the gospel. His desire for them is that they would be encouraged and united in love. This growth in love would lead them into a deeper knowledge of God's drama of salvation which reaches its climax in Christ. It is striking here that rather than increased knowledge leading to growth in love, Paul assumes that growth in love is prior to and necessary for growth in knowledge. As growth in love leads to a deeper knowledge of Christ, vv. 6–7 make it clear that such knowledge is to be directed to leading lives that are rooted and grounded in Christ (see also Rom12:1–2; Phil 1:9–11).

V. Confronting False Teaching (2:8–23)

A. Warning About Philosophy and Empty Deceit (2:8)

Everything Paul has said thus far indicates that the Colossians are more than willing to "walk" in a manner worthy of the gospel. This verse indicates that they may need instruction about what God's activity in Christ entails for their present situation. In 2:8 Paul addresses this by warning the Colossians not to let anyone capture them, take them off as booty. The metaphor here reflects a situation of battle where the Colossians themselves may be the prize that falls to the victor. If this is the case, then the weapons of the enemy are "philosophy and empty deceit" which is "according to human tradition [and] ... the elemental spirits of the universe." The terms used here are very general and offer outside readers very little information about the nature of the teaching Paul warns against.

Many scholars take the term "elemental spirits of the universe" [Gk.: *stoicheia tou kosmou*] to be a reference to demonic forces that were thought to control aspects of human existence. These would be the principalities and powers mentioned in 1:16. The Greek term can just as easily refer to worldly rules and regulations. The problem is that the Greek term *stoicheia* is quite elastic and can refer to a wide range of things. In such a situation the immediate context in which the term appears must be determinative. In the case of Colossians one must look, then, at 2:8 and 2:20 where the same phrase occurs.

In 2:20 it is quite clear that the *stoicheia tou kosmou* are closely connected to the rules and regulations mentioned in 2:21–22. It is also clear, however, that Paul refers to the *stoicheia* as if they were personal forces. In Romans Paul refers to the Torah as both a set of commandments and as something personified, either as a spiritual force on its own or as a something controlled by a demonic force such as Sin (cf. 5:12–21; 7:7–13). It is sometimes hard to disentangle these two things and it is not always clear that one has to. Given the similar contextual factors in Colossians, one might say that the *stoicheia* can be a set of rules and regulations and that these can function either as representatives or tools of demonic forces to frustrate believers. This would indicate that the teaching Paul warns about in 2:8 is tied to observing special rules and regulations that might seem to enhance one's following of Christ but are ultimately of human origin and will frustrate one's life in Christ.

B. Fullness in Christ Through Baptism (2:9–15)

Having warned against being captivated by false teaching that is according to human tradition and not according to Christ, Paul describes the Colossians' life in Christ in ways that both echo 1:15–20 and directly address the false teaching threatening the Colossians.

All of God's fullness dwells in Christ, and because the Colossians have been joined to Christ in baptism they, too, participate in that fullness. There is nothing more they can do to add to this fullness. The Colossians do not need whatever "fullness" the false teaching offers. No spiritual power, hostile or otherwise, can stand between the Colossians and the fullness of God because in Christ they participate in the one in whom all God's fullness dwells. No further rules and regulations can enliven their experience of God. Although at one point the Colossians were dead and alienated from God, they have now been made alive in Christ, the one who triumphs over death.

The connection between circumcision and baptism in this passage indicates that the false teachers may have advocated that baptized Gentile believers needed to further their life in Christ by becoming circumcised. In any case, this is one of the few places where Paul speaks about baptism.

He treats it as the analog to circumcision in that it brings people fully into a covenant relationship with Christ.

C. Practices of the False Teaching (2:16–23)

This is the passage that reveals the most about the practices which the false teachers advocate for the Colossians. In the light of previous passage's emphasis that the fullness of God is only found through participation in Christ, one can infer that these practices aimed to deepen or enhance the Colossians' experience of God. We also know that there were both Jewish and pagan groups that advocated various ascetical practices as a means to attaining mystical visions and ecstatic experiences. Further, one can easily imagine that relatively new believers would be attracted to claims of enhanced spiritual experiences through observance of various ascetical disciplines as a supplement to their faith in Christ. Here in this passage we learn of some of those practices. The teachers seem to advocate the observance of certain festivals and days devoted to God, along with ascetical practices related to food and drink. These same terms describe Israel's distinctive practices (cf. Hos 2:11; Ezek 45:17; 1 Chr 23:31; *Letter of Aristeas* 141–43). Whatever validity such observances may have had in the past, now in the light of Christ they can add nothing to the Colossians' experience.

As this passage continues it appears that the aim of the practices mentioned in 2:16 is to cultivate a form of self-abasement, leading to an ecstatic state in which one might mystically enter into the heavenly realms and either observe or participate in angelic worship (2:18). Although we know little about the specific details involved in the Colossian false teaching, we do know that both pagan and Jewish groups thought that through specific practices and initiatory rites one could incrementally advance in one's knowledge of divine things.

If the Colossians assent to this way of thinking they will not be advancing in Christ. Rather, they will be abandoning Christ, the head who animates and sustains the church, leading it to true growth in God. What makes this false teaching so pernicious is that it aims at something good, but misperceives the true nature of this good and seeks to achieve this good in misguided ways. Ultimately, it cannot lead the Colossians into a deeper knowledge and experience of God. Rather, it will frustrate and undermine their life in Christ.

As Paul wraps up this part of the argument he reminds the Colossians that becoming a Christian involves dying with Christ to any and all forces that—no matter how well intentioned—keep people alienated from God. Thus, ch. 2 ends with a sustained call to resist any continued allure held by the promises of the false teachers and to hold fast to Christ. As ch. 3 begins, Paul focuses on how one should live in the light of being raised with Christ.

VI. Seeking Christ/Living in Christ (3:1–4:6)

A. Raised with Christ (3:1–4)

The false teaching pursues access into the heavenly realms through self abasement. Paul here tells the Colossians that they have been raised with Christ who is already in the heavenly realms. When Christ is revealed in his final glory, they too will be revealed with him. Hence, they should focus their attention on heavenly matters rather than earthly matters, where Paul has repeatedly located the concerns and practices of the false teaching.

B. Avoiding Vices (3:5–11)

Seeking the things above will involve transformation, just not the type of self-abasement that the false teachers advocate. Instead the Colossians are to "put to death" those habits and practices that alienate them from God and each other. The vices in 3:5*b* (fornication, impurity, passion, evil desire, and greed) reflect people's overweening desire to grab what is not theirs. In this light, it is not surprising that the final vice, "greed," is characterized as idolatry. This is because idolatry is, at its root, a turning of one's love and attention away from God and toward something or someone else. The second list (anger, wrath, malice, slander, abusive language, and lying, in vv. 8–9) reflect habits and practices that distort one's relationships with others. Paul speaks of these as garments that are to be cast off; the Colossians are to clothe themselves with a new self. As Paul goes on to describe this new self, it becomes clear that it is actually the self God originally intended for humans at their creation and that God is renewing in humanity.

As God intended things at the outset, there are no racial, ethnic, linguistic, status, or economic divisions separating people from one another. In Christ they are harmoniously united and perfected.

C. Cultivating Virtue (3:12–17)

In this light, Paul goes on to speak of putting on a new set of clothes. This image is used to convey an admonition to cultivate a set of virtues. These virtues all require the presence of others in order to be displayed. They are relational virtues. Moreover, when there is a failure of virtue, the Colossians are encouraged to forgive each other as God has forgiven them. These virtues and indeed the common life of the Colossian congregation are bound together by love. In addition,, the Colossians are told to let the word of Christ dwell in them, which will enable them to instruct one another wisely and to worship with gratitude.

D. Relations in the Household (3:18–4:1)

After Paul has advocated the cultivation and practice of a variety of virtues, all held together by love, he quickly moves to discuss the three sets of relationships that made up a typical Greco-Roman household: husbands/wives, parents/children, and master/slave. Discussions of household management were quite common in Greco-Roman writing going back at least as far as Aristotle. Jewish writers such as Philo and Josephus also touched on this subject. Although this passage will make modern readers very uncomfortable, there is no way of knowing how the Colossians received this advice. For all of its traditional trappings, there are several points that stand out here.

First, husbands are admonished to love their wives and not to treat them harshly. In addition, fathers are not to provoke their children. These may in some ways modify the sense of absolute control that the father/husband held over the household. The vast majority of the commands in this passage address masters and slaves. Having noted in 3:11 that in Christ the slave/free distinction is dissolved, Paul reminds both slaves and masters that they are both slaves of Christ. (The NRSV does not render the Greek of 3:25 as strongly as it ought in this case.) At the same time, Paul recognizes that slavery in the Greco-Roman world was not going away. Given the large proportion of slaves in this world, it would have been inevitable

that masters and slaves both would have found themselves within the body of Christ.

E. Final Instructions (4:2–6)

Paul adds a final set of instructions here. The first focuses on prayer. His brief remarks indicate that he feels it is a great blessing to be able to offer prayers to God. Recognition of this should generate thanksgiving in believers. In addition, Paul reveals that although he is in prison, he hopes to continue to "declare the mystery of Christ." Paul's final admonitions about wisdom and speech indicate that he hopes that the Colossians themselves will be able to participate in declaring the mystery of Christ.

VII. Farewell and Final Greetings (4:7–18)

As is typical, Paul concludes with a list of greetings and tidbits of information about various characters. There is a remarkable diversity in this group, including: Jews and Gentiles, a physician (Luke), a slave (Onesimus, cf. Philemon), a woman of sufficient wealth to be able to host a gathering in her home (Nympha). It is interesting to note that in Acts 15:36–40 a disagreement over Mark's role leads Paul and Barnabas to part ways. Here he is mentioned as one of Paul's companions. Many of the same people mentioned here also appear in the list of greetings in Phlm 23–24. It is also clear that there is a relatively close relationship between the churches in Colossae and Laodicea. (The two towns were about 10 miles apart.) Paul has written to each church and they are to share their epistles. These greetings indicate the rich network of relationships that helped to sustain Paul in his work. Even though he begins his letter by noting that he is an apostle, a particular individual with a specific mission, he cannot fulfill his charge without numerous co-workers, friends, and supporters.

BIBLIOGRAPHY

A. Lincoln and A. J. M. Wedderburn. *Theology of the Later Pauline Letters* (Cambridge: Cambridge University Press, 1993); P. O'Brien. *Colossians and Philemon.* WBC 44 (Waco, Tex.: Word, 1982); M. M. Thompson. *Colossians and Philemon.* Two Horizons New Testament Commentary (Grand Rapids: Eerdmans, 2005).

1 THESSALONIANS

SZE-KAR WAN

OVERVIEW

Widely regarded as the earliest of Paul's letters, 1 Thessalonians is free of controversies over the law or polemics against his opponents that characterize the apostle's later writings. The letter is distinguished by its irenic spirit and warmth towards the recipients. Paul's praise for the Thessalonians is so effusive that it takes little imagination to categorize this as a "friendly letter," a standard type in ancient epistolography. But the positive tone cannot mask an anxiety over some unspecified persecution the young converts are facing, persecution that may or may not have been also responsible for Paul's own hasty retreat from the city almost immediately after he founded the congregation. In the meantime, deaths of some members unsettled the community and might have caused them to rethink their belief in the Lord's coming. Thus, while Paul is concerned about the perception that he has abandoned the Thessalonians at this critical time, he is equally concerned that the Thessalonians not lose hope in the final revelation of Christ. His personal integrity, the authenticity of his message, and the cohesion and ongoing vitality of the new congregation have all become one and the same issue.

After dispatching Timothy to Thessalonica to strengthen the community and upon receiving favorable news from him (see 3:1–6), Paul writes this letter, declaring his profound love for the community in an effort to draw the Thessalonians closer to him in spite of his absence. He exhorts the congregation to maintain unity in the face of afflictions from without, and he counsels them to console one another about the deaths of members without losing hope in the Lord's coming. Paul also takes the opportunity to answer a number of queries raised by the congregation.

OUTLINE

I. Prescript (1:1)

II. Thanksgiving (1:2–3:13)

A. Prayer (1:2–10)

B. Paul's Sincerity and Purity of Motives (2:1–12)

C. Encouraging the Congregation Under Persecution (2:13–16)

D. Paul's Desire to Visit the Thessalonians (2:17–3:13)

III. Exhortations (4:1–5:22)

A. Warnings Against Sexual Immorality (4:3–8)

B. Concerning Life in the Community (4:9–12)

C. Concerning Those Who Are Asleep (4:13–18)

D. Concerning the Imminence of the Parousia (5:1–11)

E. General Parenesis (5:12–22)

IV. Postscript (5:23–28)

DETAILED ANALYSIS

I. Prescript (1:1)

Paul introduces himself without the usual title "apostle" (contrast to Rom 1:1; 1 Cor 1:1; 2 Cor 1:1; Gal 1:1). The only other self-designation comparable in simplicity is that of Philippians (1:1), which like 1 Thessalonians is a friendly letter overflowing with warmth and praise for the addressees.

II. Thanksgiving (1:2–3:13)

A standard feature in ancient letter writing and in most of the undisputed letters of Paul, the thanksgiving in 1 Thessalonians is unique in its unusual length. In fact, this section is so long that it may well be considered the main body of the letter. Some take the thrice-repeated thanksgiving (1:2; 2:13; 3:9) to indicate multiple letters, but the narrative flow of the entire section does not support that theory.

A. Prayer (1:2–10)

The thanksgiving prayer proper conforms to the usual Pauline form and function. The opening is standard: "We always give thanks to God for all of you and mention you in our prayers, constantly" (1:2; cf. Rom 1:8; 1 Cor 1:4; Phil 1:3; Phlm 4). It announces, as is Paul's custom, major themes of the letter: the Thessalonians' conversion (1:4–5, 9), Paul's past labor in their midst (1:5, 9), persecution (1:6), and apocalyptic urgency (1:10).

That the Thessalonians were Gentile converts is clear, since they "turned to God from idols, to serve a living and true God" (1:9). Though used sparingly by Paul, *to turn* (*epistrephein*) was a technical term for Gentile conversion to Judaism (e.g., LXX Ps 21:28; Isa 19:22; Jer 18:8, 11; Tob 14:6) and was adopted by the Jesus movement (e.g., Acts 3:19; 9:35; 14:15). "To serve (*douleuein*, literally "to be a slave") a living and true God" means complete surrender to God as a slave to a master. Here and elsewhere, Paul conceives of conversion not so much as liberation but as switching allegiance to a different master, from mute idols to "a living and true God" (see, e.g., Rom 6:6, 12–23; 7:25; 12:11; 14:18; 16:18; Gal 4:8).

Paul reminds the Thessalonians of their conversion for the purpose of binding them closely to himself despite his absence. He praises his hearers for their "work of faith and labor of love and steadfastness of hope in our Lord Jesus Christ" (1:3), but makes clear that all this finds its basis in God's prior love and election; the Thessalonians are "beloved by God" and have been chosen by God (1:4). Verse 5 could be taken as proof of election, as the NRSV translation ("because") might suggest, but more likely it explains how God's election took place—by the preaching of the gospel "not in word only, but also in power and in the Holy Spirit." Paul claims that his initial founding visit was the instrument by which God elected the Thessalonians, Gentiles heretofore being outside the covenant.

Giving his own preaching such a prominent role might seem egotistic, but Paul is adopting the rhetorical strategy of popular philosophers who boasted perfect congruence between words and deeds as basis for confidence in their message. Persuasiveness of the message depended on the authenticity of the messenger. In using this argument, however, Paul also turns it upside down.

When Paul boasts of his "full conviction" (1:5), he contrasts his words not to his personal deeds but to the power of the Holy Spirit. Then and only then could the Thessalonians discover what sort of person Paul turned out to be. For Paul, authenticity of the message proves the credibility of the messenger, and that was the warrant for imitating him. Ultimately, Paul hastens to add, the Thessalonians were in reality imitating the Lord (1:6).

Paul has reason to fear for the viability of his relationship with the Thessalonian community. He left the city soon after he established the congregation, and it is now experiencing persecution (2:14; 3:3). To encourage them to stand firm, Paul reminds them of persecution at the time of their conversion (1:6) and informs them of his own before and after his visit (2:2; 3:7). Imitation means more than just mimicking the teacher; it means also sharing his paradigmatic suffering. He alludes to all this in the apocalyptic climax of the prayer, encouraging his new converts to wait for "Jesus, who rescues [note present tense] us from the wrath that is coming" (1:10). Despite the warm tone and praises elaborated on the Thessalonians, therefore, Paul is concerned about the current state of the young congregation, and he is anxious to re-establish relationship with them.

B. Paul's Sincerity and Purity of Motives (2:1–12)

The spotlight that started shifting from the addressees to Paul in the thanksgiving prayer is now trained squarely on Paul. He begins, "You yourselves know" (2:1). The formula is repeated numerously times in this letter (see also 1:5; 2:2, 5, 11; 3:3, 4; 4:2, 4; 5:2; also 2:9, "you remember"; 2:10, "you are witnesses") not only to stress the open honesty with which Paul conducted himself among the Thessalonians but especially to underscore the shared knowledge that establishes a common bond between them. This bond lays a foundation for a friendly persuasion in the remainder of the thanksgiving and especially in the exhortations. He reminds them again of the manner in which he first gained entrance to them (2:1; cf. 1:9) despite the shameful treatment he had received in Philippi (2:2). But that made the Thessalonians' imitation of Paul that much more moving and significant, for they themselves received the gospel "in spite of persecution" (1:5).

In addition, the relationship is also founded on personal integrity. Paul claims purity of his motives (2:3, 5), sincerity of his words (2:5), and upright and blameless conduct (2:10), in the manner of popular philosophers. But just as before, his self-claims only appear excessive; they are ultimately dependent on God, who alone forms the basis for self-regards and confidence. He maintains that he performed his arduous tasks to please God, not mortals (2:4, 6).

In an effort to bind the Thessalonians to himself, Paul uses a number of familial metaphors. He compares himself to a nurse "tenderly caring for her own children" (2:7). Gentleness of the wet nurse was a well-known trope in Roman literature, but Paul amplifies it by twining it with *thalpein* ("*to warm*"), evoking the image of a mother bird warming her eggs. *Her own children*, as opposed to children under her professional care, emphatically underscores her tenderness. Paul also compares himself to a father (2:11), this time as a moral authority and instructor, "urging and encouraging you and pleading that you lead a life worthy of God" (2:12).

C. Encouraging the Congregation under Persecution (2:13–16)

From professed sincere motives and personal integrity, attention is now returned to the young congregation, which finds itself under some unspecified siege and is in need of encouragement. Paul begins his encouragement the same way he begins the letter, with another thanksgiving prayer that is formally and thematically similar to the first one: "We also constantly give thanks to God" (2:13; cf. 1:2). Why? A thanksgiving, especially in a friendly, paraenetic letter like 1 Thessalonians, highlights the strengths of the recipients as cause for gratitude, thus setting up a common ground for exhortation, even instruction. The Thessalonians had accepted the word of God (2:13), but amidst persecution: "For you, brothers and sisters, became imitators of the churches of God in Christ Jesus that are in Judea, for you suffered the same things from your own compatriots as they did from the Jews" (2:14). All three themes—reception of the word of God, persecution, and imitation—are already adumbrated in the first thanksgiving prayer (1:6). But whereas in the first instance imitation appears to be an act

of volition, here it is involuntary. Whether they chose it or not, the sufferings of the Thessalonians have rendered them imitators of the Judean churches. Their choice is to endure the persecution, but in so doing they have followed the path of their fellow believers in Judea. Their conscious emulation of Paul has strengthened them to be in solidarity with other sufferers.

The harsh judgment against the "Jews" in 2:14–16 has led some to judge the passage to be a later interpolation. But many difficulties can be resolved by recognizing that *Ioudaioi* (2:14) means literally "Judeans." Since the comparison is between the Thessalonians' persecutions by their fellow citizens and those suffered by the Judean communities in the hands of their kinsfolk, the word should perhaps be translated literally. References to killing the prophets and opposition to the Gentile mission (cf. Gal 1:13, 23) all point in the same direction. Paul's strong condemnation is leveled not against all ethnic Jews but against only the inhabitants of Judea. In the same vein, *eis telos* (2:16) means literally "*until the end*" so that the final, eschatological judgment should be read: "God's wrath has come upon them continually until the end" (2:16).

D. Paul's Desire to Visit the Thessalonians (2:17–3:13)

Paul continues to cultivate his relationship with the Thessalonians, this time by sharing his deep yearning to be with them in spite of physical separation. He does so by reversing a familiar kinship metaphor: "We were made orphans by being separated from you—in person, not in heart" (2:17a). To say one is present in spirit but absent in body was a standard epistolary device to exhort the recipients to live as thought the writer were present. It was especially effective when the writer, such as a teacher or a father, enjoyed a higher status than the recipients. Paul uses this convention to make his presence felt (Funk coins the term "apostolic parousia" to describe the phenomenon), but instead of calling his children (cf. 2:7, 11) orphans, as one would expect, he calls himself orphaned by the separation. The effect is not only deep pathos, as conveyed by "we longed with great eagerness to see you face to face. For we wanted to come to you—certainly I, Paul, wanted to again and again" (2:17b–18). It is also pastoral and paraenetic. Pastoral, because in expressing his dire need to be reunited with the Thessalonians, Paul lets them know that he empathizes with their desolation, for he himself is bereft of them as they are of him. Paraenetic, because the Thessalonians must now fulfill what is lacking in Paul by being blameless until the end: "For what is our hope or joy or crown of boasting before our Lord Jesus at his coming? Is it not you? Yes, you are our glory and joy!" (2:19–20; cf. 3:13; 5:13).

The travelogue in 3:1–10 explains the events that led to the writing of the letter (cf. Acts 17:1–9, 15; 18:1. In his anxiety for the congregation, Paul dispatches Timothy from Athens to Thessalonica "to strengthen and encourage" the children he left behind (3:1–2, 5), so that they might not be shaken by "these persecutions" (3:3). That Paul has actual events in mind, and not just emotional distress, seems clear from his specific references both here and in 2:14, even if the nature of the actual persecutions is far from clear. Paul might well fear that these afflictions could cause his young converts to lose hope for the last day, which is why he is at pains to remind them of the coming of the Lord (2:19; 3:13; 4:15; 5:23). Paul's praises the Thessalonians for their faith, love, and hope (1:3), but Timothy's report mentions only of their faith and love, not hope (3:6). Even though the news is good, therefore, hope for the final rescue (1:10) might be waning. The conclusion of the travelogue introduces the occasion for writing the letter: "Night and day we pray most earnestly that we may see you face to face and restore (literally, "to mend" or "fulfill") whatever is lacking in your faith" (3:10). Paul even makes his living conditioned on the Thessalonians' perseverance: "We now live if you continue to stand firm in the Lord" (3:8). His children must now take responsibility for the well-being of their father.

A concluding prayer (3:11–13) to the thanksgiving recapitulates Paul's deep yearning to be reunited with the Thessalonians and to hold fast "in holiness that [they] may be blameless before our God and Father at the coming of our Lord Jesus with all his saints" (3:12).

III. Exhortations (4:1–5:22)

The exhortations are introduced by a recapitulation of the urgent theme of holding firm to the formal instructions the Thessalonians had received from Paul (4:1–2). *Paralambanein* ("to receive," 4:1; NRSV, "to learn") was a technical term for accepting and learning formal tradition, and *parangelia* ("announcement, military command, precept," 4:2; NRSV, "instructions") referred to a precise message conveyed by one party to another. Paul uses these terms to remind the Thessalonians what they already know: "you received from us how you ought to live" (4:1, author's trans.) and "you know what precepts we gave you" (4:2, author's trans.). Since the integrity of the teacher and his love for his students are no longer in doubt, the authenticity of these instructions can be taken in good faith. Moreover, these reminders serve the same function as the formula "as you know": namely, they establish a bond between Paul and the congregation based on common traditions and behaviors.

A. Warnings Against Sexual Immorality (4:3–8)

These warnings are likewise set in a framework of reminders. Toward the conclusion of this subsection, Paul warns that "the Lord is an avenger in all these things"—referring to the list of injunctions of 4:3*b*–6*a*—but adds, "just as we have already told you beforehand and solemnly warned you" (4:6*b*).

That all the warnings in this section are against sexual immorality is indicated in 4:3: "Abstain from fornication." The meaning of *skeuos* in 4:4 is uncertain. It can mean the male genital and thus synecdochically *body*, hence the translation, "Each one of you know how to control your own body in holiness and honor" (NRSV). Because of its literal meaning *vessel*, the word can also refer euphemistically to a woman engaged in sexual activities. Thus, an alternative is: "Each of you learn how to acquire your own wife in holiness and honor." "Lustful passion" (4:5) was the Stoic moralists' standard pet peeve, since they judged passion irrational. But given Paul's characterization of Gentiles as not knowing God (4:5), it is likely a part of standard Greek-speaking Jewish polemics against Gentiles in general (e.g., *Testimony of Joseph* 7:8; cf. also Rom 1:24, 26; Col 3:5). The language of exploitation (literally, "do not trespass or covet") in 4:6 also fits the overall theme of sexual immorality, since Greek moralists have compared committing adultery to stripping the man of his prized possession, his wife.

B. Concerning Life in the Community (4:9–12)

That this and the next two topics are introduced by "concerning" suggests that the Thessalonians had raised them with Paul through Timothy (as in 1 Cor 7:1). The two topics covered therein—brotherly love, on which Paul commends them for loving all throughout Macedonia (4:9–10), and working diligently with their hands, a reminder that harks back to an earlier command (*parangellein*, 4:11; NRSV, "directed," cf. the noun *parangelia* used in 4:2)—appear to have little to do with each other until we notice that they are set in the context of a community. Its self-conscious distinction from outsiders ("behave properly toward outsiders," 4:12) points to a close-knit community with clear boundaries marking insiders from outsiders. Its love-ethos, which earns profuse praise from Paul and from other Jesus-communities (cf. 1:8–9), combined with Paul's injunction that members of this community must perform manual labor (cf. 2:9), possibly indicates some form of communal sharing that takes care of poorer members within the community. Whatever they do, Paul affirms it. He urges them "to do so more and more" (4:10), and "to mind [their] own affairs" (lit. "to do their own things," 4:11), which is to say affairs proper to the community. But he also warns them of freeloaders, who could threaten the stability of the community and who, Paul demands, must be willing to "work with [their] hands" (4:11).

C. Concerning Those Who Are Asleep (4:13–18)

The discussion of the end time in 4:13–5:11 is the longest and most detailed among Paul's letters. In the first half, 4:13–18, Paul deals with the Thessalonians' grief over those who have "fallen asleep" [author's trans.], specifically what will happen to those still alive at the coming of Christ. In the second half, 5:1–11, he warns against the suddenness as well as the imminence of the Lord's coming. While these issues are certainly theological, the ultimate motive for introducing them is pastoral: both halves end with the consolation, "Encourage one another " (4:18; 5:11).

The issue has to do with deaths in the community after Paul's departure. Paul had obviously instructed the Thessalonians of the Parousia (1:10; 2:19; 3:13; 4:15; 5:23), with many details drawn from Jewish apocalyptic imagery ("For the Lord himself, with a cry of command, with the archangel's call and with the sound of God's trumpet, will descend from heaven," 4:16; cf. e.g., Dan 7). The catalyst was the question raised by the Thessalonians: How will those who have fallen asleep before the Son comes be rescued? (1:10). That this topic is introduced differently from the others, "We do not want you to be uninformed" (4:13), indicates the novelty of the question.

Paul's answer is summarized in v. 14, "Since we believe that Jesus died and rose again, even so, through Jesus, God will bring with him those who have died" (lit., "fallen asleep"). In this passage, Paul consistently calls the dead "those who have fallen asleep" (4:13, 14, 15; 4:16 the only exception), because they will be awakened. He draws his support from a seldomly used warrant, "the word of the Lord" (4:15), which could refer to a Synoptic-like tradition or a direct prophetic word. The content of the words is summarized in v. 15 and expanded in vv. 16–17: Those who have fallen asleep will be raised first at the Parousia, followed by those still alive being "caught up in the clouds together with [the dead in Christ] to meet the Lord in the air; and so we will be with the Lord forever" (4:17).

D. Concerning the Imminence of the Parousia (5:1–11)

Paul continues his discussion of the Parousia under the heading of the "times and seasons" of the Parousia (5:1). It is evidently an old teaching, "for you yourselves know very well (lit., "precisely") that the day of the Lord will come like a thief in the night" (5:2) or "as labor pains come upon a pregnant woman" (5:3). The "Day of the Lord" is a biblical idea that the Almighty will wage war of retribution against the impious (e.g., Isa 13:6; Jer 46:10; Ezek 13:5; Joel 2:1, 11; Amos 5:18, 20). Paul uses it as a synonym for the Parousia, but stresses its salvific outcome for the elect instead (1 Cor 1:8; 5:5; 2 Cor 1:14; Phil 1:10; 2:16). Thus, Paul exhorts his hearers, "God has destined us not for wrath but for obtaining salvation through our Lord Jesus Christ, who died for us, so that whether we are awake or asleep we may live with him" (5:9–10; cf. 1:10). The precondition is that as "children of light" who "belong to the day" (5:5, 8), believers must stay vigilant and sober, "[putting] on the breastplate of faith and love, and for a helmet the hope of salvation" (5:8). The imminent arrival of the Lord requires that combatants stay ever alert and maintain their ethical urgency.

The warlike language about children of light and children of darkness was also used by the Essenes, who withdrew themselves from what they regarded as defiled Jerusalem in order to keep themselves pure and ready for the day of the Lord. Though there is no evidence that Paul had direct contact with them, the sectarian tendency in 1 Thessalonians is comparable. In 4:12, Paul calls attention to outsiders to encourage mutual responsibility between members of the same love-community. In 4:13, he makes a sharp distinction between the believers and "the rest" (*hoi loipoi*, NRSV, "others") of humanity who have no hope. In 5:5–7, he consigns the same outsiders, "the rest" of the world who fall asleep and are drunk, to the night and darkness. Some commentators, perhaps influenced by later Christian apocalypses and 5:20–22, think those who espouse "Peace and security" (5:3) are false prophets. But the saying was a standard slogan of Roman political propaganda designed to boast the superiority of *Pax Romana*. It therefore cannot be discounted that Paul here mobilizes dualistic symbols of apocalypticism to resist pressure, if not outright persecutions (2:14), from Thessalonian society at large. The difference between the Thessalonian congregation and the Essene sectarians, however, is that Paul never suggests total withdrawal from society. It is still important to him that his Jesus-followers make a good impression on outsiders (4:12).

E. General Parenesis (5:12–22)

These general admonitions begin with a series of imperatives on life in the community (5:12–15) before branching off into a loose collection of aphorisms (5:16–22). Paul counsels respect for leaders of the community because of their labor (5:13). The exhortations, "[to] be at peace among yourselves" (5:13), "to admonish the idlers, encourage the fainthearted, help the weak, be patient with all of them," (5:14), and not "[to repay] evil for evil, but always seek to do good to one another and to all" (5:15), might seem unrelated unless we recognize that they are all issued against "the disorderly people" (*ataktoi*; lit., "out of ranks,"

5:14; NRSV, "idlers"). In 4:11 idle freeloaders take advantage of communal sharing and thereby threaten the order of the love-community; the only remedy is to work with their hands. Thus the appeals of 5:14–15 are all made with such internal relations in mind.

IV. Postscript (5:23–28)

Paul ends the letter with his customary prayer, in which he repeats the theme of being blameless at the Parousia (5:23–24), a request for prayer (5:25), greeting to all (5:26), and a final benediction (5:28). It also includes a "solemn command" (*enorkizein*; lit., "to swear") that the letter be read out loud to the congregation (5:27). In spite of the literary quality of the letter, therefore, it is the oral performance of it that is meant to be a substitute for the absent apostle.

BIBLIOGRAPHY

F. F. Bruce. *1 & 2 Thessalonians.* WBC 45 (Waco: Word, 1982); K. Donfried. *Paul, Thessalonica, and Early Christianity* (Grand Rapids: Eerdmans, 2002); R. Funk. "Apostolic *Parousia*: Form and Significance." *Christian History and Interpretation.* W. Farmer et al, eds. (Cambridge: Cambridge University Press, 1967); V. P. Furnish. *I Thessalonians and II Thessalonians* (Nashville: Abingdon, 2007); H. Koester. "I Thessalonians: Experiment in Christian Writing." *Continuity and Discontinuity in Church History. Essays Presented to George Huntston Williams on the Occasion of his 65th Birthday.* F. F. Church and T. George, eds. (Leiden: Brill, 1979); _____. "Imperial Ideology and Paul's Eschatology in 1 Thessalonians." *Paul and Empire.* R. A. Horsley, ed. (Harrisburg: Trinity Press International, 1997); R. Jewett. *The Thessalonian Correspondence: Pauline Rhetoric and Millenarian Piety* (Philadelphia: Fortress, 1986); A. Malherbe. *The Letters to the Thessalonians.* AB 32B (New York: Doubleday, 2000); _____. *Paul and the Popular Philosophers* (Minneapolis: Fortress, 1989); A. Smith. "'Unmasking the Powers': Toward a Postcolonial Analysis of 1 Thessalonians." *Paul and the Roman Imperial Order.* R. A. Horsley, ed. (Harrisburg: Trinity Press International, 2004).

2 THESSALONIANS

SZE-KAR WAN

OVERVIEW

The interpretation of 2 Thessalonians cannot be separated from the question of authorship; that is, did the apostle Paul actually write this letter. The major reason for questioning the attribution to Paul is that 2 Thessalonians so closely resembles 1 Thessalonians in structure and content. Both letters, for example, have multiple thanksgivings (2 Thess 1:3 and 2:13; cf. 1 Thess 1:3 and 2:13), whereas there is never more than one in all other undisputed letters of Paul. Both close the thanksgiving with a benediction (2 Thess 2:16–17; cf. 1 Thess 3:11–13), immediately followed by "finally" (2 Thess 3:1; cf. 1 Thess 4:1). The prescripts and postscripts of the two letters are nearly identical (prescript, 2 Thess 1:1–2; cf. 1 Thess 1:1; postscript, 2 Thess 3:16, 18; cf. 1 Thess 5:23, 28). Yet, in spite of the similarities between the two letters, there are differences. The tone of 2 Thessalonians is far less personal than 1 Thessalonians. The author does not call for imitation of himself, apart from his example of working for a living so as not to burden the community (3:7–8). Otherwise he displays little of the pathos that characterizes 1 Thessalonians, or the anxiety to maintain his personal bond with his recipients. Instead, the letter is full of warnings and commands (e.g., 3:6, 10, etc.), all set in an apocalyptic context of judgment against unbelievers (e.g., 2:12; 3:2). The end time as envisioned in 2 Thessalonians also appears different from that of the earlier letter. Whereas in 1 Thessalonians the Parousia is said to be coming like a thief in the night (1 Thess 5:2), 2 Thessalonians appears to envision several stages leading to the final revelation of Christ (2 Thess 3:12).

Second Thessalonians might well reflect a later period in the life of the congregation, when persecution, already prevalent at the writing of 1 Thessalonians, grows in intensity and scope.

If so, the main purpose of 2 Thessalonians is not so different from that of 1 Thessalonians. It was written to console a congregation in crisis. Sufferings have created desolation, which combined with an insidious teaching that the day of the Lord had already arrived, fostered a sense of hopelessness (2:2). The underlying problem was not "realized eschatology," but a lack of vigilant expectation for the coming of the Lord, which the present sufferings heralded. The hearers would know if they could interpret the signs. The imminence of the end is thus used in a pastoral letter of consolation. Meanwhile, the social structure of communal sharing practiced by the congregation was threatened by some refusing to work for the good of the community. Concerned, our author adds instructions to correct the situation.

OUTLINE

I. Prescript (1:1–2)

II. Thanksgiving Prayer (1:3–12)

    A. Praise for the Thessalonians' Faith and Love (1:3–4)

    B. Judgment Against Those Who Inflict Sufferings (1:5–10)

    C. Prayer That the Thessalonians Be Worthy of Call (1:11–12)

III. Warnings About the Parousia (2:1–12)

    A. Warning Against Thinking the Parousia Has Already Come (2:1–2)

    B. The Lawless One Must Be Revealed First (2:3–5)

    C. The Restrainer Keeps the Lawless One from Being Revealed (2:6–7)

    D. At the Revelation of the Lawless One, He Will Be Destroyed (2:8–10)

    E. All Who Do Not Believe In the Truth Will Be Destroyed (2:11–12)

IV. Second Thanksgiving Prayer (2:13–17)

    A. Thanksgiving for God's Having Chosen the Thessalonians (2:13–14)

    B. Stand Firm and Hold Fast to Traditions (2:15–17)

DETAILED ANALYSIS

I. Prescript (1:1–2)

The author introduces himself simply as "Paul" (1:1), much like 1 Thessalonians 1:1, and except for an additional phrase ("from God our Father and the Lord Jesus Christ"), the peace (1:2) is identical as well.

II. Thanksgiving Prayer (1:3–12)

The thanksgiving prayer, as is the custom in Pauline letters, announces the major themes to be pursued in the body. It begins conventionally with praise of the hearers' faith and love for one another (1:3), which garners them fame beyond themselves despite persecutions and afflictions (1:4). Hope, however, which plays a prominent part in the thanksgiving of 1 Thessalonians (cf. 1 Thess 1:3), is not mentioned.

The rumor that "the day of the Lord is already here" is causing alarm (2:2), and hope is evidently its first victim.

The next section, 1:5–10, reads like a parenthesis. Its tone changes abruptly from praise to somber warning, but is at heart consolatory, which is the main focus of the letter. How "evidence of the righteous judgment of God" (1:5a) is related to the preceding is unclear; perhaps it introduces a new discussion on how God's judgment will be carried out in the end time and how the discussion is "intended to make you worthy of the kingdom of God" (1:5b). The reprobates, whom the author describes as not knowing God and not obeying the gospel (1:8), and who inflict suffering on the Thessalonians, will be condemned to "eternal destruction, separated from the presence of the Lord and from the glory of his might" (1:9). Description of the end time in 2 Thessalonians is no less colorful than that of 1 Thess 4:16–17: "The Lord Jesus [will be] revealed from heaven with his mighty angels

(lit., "messengers of his power")" (1:7), and when he comes in glory (1:9b) he will be "glorified by his saints" (1:10). Ultimately, though, the main purpose of the thanksgiving prayer is to console the Thessalonians undergoing persecution, for the day of the Lord is a double-edged sword, as is clear from the prophets (e.g., Amos 5:18, 20). While the just God repays with affliction those who mete out affliction, God will also repay the afflicted with relief (1:6–7a). The flip side of condemnation is deliverance.

There is remarkably little that the author asks the hearers to do throughout the prayer, and in that respect the main theme of the thanksgiving and therefore the letter is not paraenesis but consolation and encouragement. Even the concluding prayer asks that God would make the hearers worthy of the call (1:11). The verse does not mean some kind of metamorphosis that might transform the Thessalonians into worthy subjects. The Greek verb used here means *to count as worthy;* it is up to God to count someone as worthy, just as it is God who "[fulfills] by his power every good resolve (lit., *every delight in goodness*) and work of faith" (1:11).

III. Warnings About the Parousia (2:1–12)

This section of 2 Thessalonians has often been characterized as the author's countering a "realized eschatology" by postulating stages of development leading to the end (see Overview). But in Jewish apocalyptic literature, the device of dividing world history into periods has a pastoral function: namely, to exhort the readers to hold on until the end, because the current sufferings represent but a temporary stage toward the inexorable glorious consummation that has been foreordained by God and prophesied by the ancients long ago. The value of periodization is not its supposed predictive power but its assertion that God is in charge of world events, not the current pretenders who are perpetrating atrocities and arrogating to themselves the title of the supreme God. That is the main purpose of the apocalypse in 2 Thessalonians, as is also the case of 1 Thess 4:13–5:11, where Paul tries to console the Thessalonians because of those who have died before the coming of the Lord. In fact, both passages presuppose the imminence of the Parousia. While 1 Thessalonians details how the dead will be raised at the Parousia, 2 Thessalonians exhorts his hearers to hold fast, for the current sufferings are not final.

The section begins with a warning against a rumor that "the day of the Lord is already here" (2:2b). That the author has to distinguish sharply his own view from those who purportedly came "either by spirit or by word or by letter, as though from us" (2:2a) suggests that the erroneous view was the result of misinterpreting Paul or an earlier letter, possibly the canonical 1 Thessalonians. A passage like 1 Thess 1:10 ("to wait for his Son from heaven, whom he raised from the dead—Jesus, who rescues us from the wrath that is coming"), which describes Jesus's rescue operation as a present reality (note present tense of *rescues*), could well lend itself to such an interpretation.

The author introduces a mysterious figure he calls "the lawless one ... the one destined for destruction" (2:3). He is said to arrogate to himself the place of God, even to set himself up as a supreme object of worship: "He opposes and exalts himself above every so-called god or object of worship, so that he takes his seat in the temple of God, declaring himself to be God" (2:4). The only reason that the lawless one has not been revealed is that an equally mysterious figure, simply referred to as "the one who now restrains," imposes some unspecified restraint on him (2:7; cf. 2:6). The identity of the lawless one remains unknown and probably unknowable, but three observations should be made. First, to attribute all the woes to an arch-villain has been a standard trope in apocalyptic tradition since Dan 7 and the Maccabean Revolt. In all cases the leading figure fighting on the side of Satan is a powerful ruler declaring war on God's elect. Second, the reminder to the Thessalonians of Paul's teachings, "Do you not remember that I told you these things when I was still with you?" (1:5), regardless of the authorship of the letter, is a self-conscious attempt to link up with the historical Paul. While the function of such reminder in 1 Thessalonians was to establish and strengthen a personal bond between Paul and his audience based on common afflictions, here the appeal takes the place of the fictive sage of old, again a standard literary figure in Jewish apocalyptic writings, who has already foretold the mystery that is unfolding now, the end time. Third, even though the "revelation" of the lawless one still is to take place in the future,

his lethal effects are felt now, "for the mystery of lawlessness is already at work" (1:7). In all likelihood, this is a reference to the current afflictions the Thessalonians are suffering, which Paul had predicted and which are now coming to pass. The audience might even be given to understand that what they are going through now is the very same persecution that drove Paul and his companions from the city (cf. 1 Thess 2:2). To call the present suffering a "mystery" is to interpret it in an apocalyptic setting, and "revelation" in this connection refers to the apocalyptic disclosure of the lawless one as the enemy of God's elect.

The final revelation of the lawless one will spell his destruction, however, for it will coincide with Christ's Parousia, according to the author's apocalyptic reckoning: "The Lord Jesus will destroy [him] with the breath (lit., "spirit") of his mouth, annihilating him by the manifestation of his coming" (2:8). Before that, though, God gives them up to lies and unrighteousness, sending to them "a mighty work of delusion" (2:11; NRSV, "powerful delusion") so that they will continue to believe in lies and to delight in unrighteousness (2:11–12). A similar sentiment is expressed in Rom 1:18–32.

IV. Second Thanksgiving Prayer (2:13–17)

A second thanksgiving following the first (1:3–12) resembles the two thanksgivings of 1 Thessalonians (1:2–10 and 2:13). A prayer concludes the second thanksgiving in 2 Thessalonians (2:16–17) just as it does in the first letter (1 Thess 3:11–13). In 1 Thessalonians, the second thanksgiving returns to the theme of imitation introduced in the first and turns it into encouragement for the Thessalonians to withstand persecution (1 Thess 2:14–16), a theme that is also touched on in the first thanksgiving. In 2 Thessalonians, however, the two thanksgivings do not correspond in this same way. The second thanksgiving uses the election of God as a basis for exhorting the audience to hold onto "traditions that you were taught by us, either by word of mouth or by our letter" (2:15). Here the author introduces the paraenesis that occupies the rest of the letter.

Elsewhere Paul uses *tradition* (*paradosis*) carefully, reserving it for a stable, technical body of knowledge, to be passed on from one to another. In 1 Cor 11:2, the term refers to the tradition of the Lord's Supper. In Gal 1:14, it means the teachings of the sages in Judaism. The verb *paradidonai* has a broader range of meanings, but among them is *to hand down a tradition*. So, in 1 Cor 11:2, Paul *handed down* the words of institution to his congregation. In 1 Cor 15:3, he *handed down* the teaching on the death and resurrection of Jesus, as well as his resurrection appearances, which he is careful to say did not originate with him but he received in the same way the Corinthians did, by careful transmission. In no case does he call his own words "tradition," as he does twice in 2 Thessalonians (2:15 and 3:6). This use of the language of tradition for Paul's own words may represent a later stage in the Thessalonian congregation, where Paul's earlier letters have taken on the appearance of authoritative writings.

V. Paraenesis (3:1–15)

The exhortations begin with two prayer requests, first for the continual success of the gospel (3:1), the second for the safety of the missionaries in their evangelization efforts (3:2). The intimate relationship between these two requests is made clear in the explanatory sentence, "not everyone has faith" (3:2b). The requests effectively divide the world between those who have faith and those who do not, and it is the latter who are called "perverse and evil." In keeping with the apocalyptic warnings of ch. 2, the underlying perspective is apocalyptic dualism, good versus evil. In such a world dangers remain, but the author continues with a prayer that the Lord will safeguard the Thessalonians and keep them from this evil age (3:3).

The paraenesis proper (3:6–12) is framed by two personal notes designed to appeal to Paul's apostolic authority. The first (3:4–5) stresses positively the confidence with which the author has in the Thessalonians that they will do what he commands (3:4), a command that sounds more like a threat in light of his proposed visit (3:5). The resort to command is repeated later in 3:6, 10, 12. The seriousness of the command is reinforced by another personal note that closes the paraenesis, this time appealing to the letter of Paul which must have attained a status of authority by now (3:13–15).

The paraensis raises two issues that appear on surface unrelated to each other, disorderliness

(3:6, 7, 11) and idleness (3:8, 10, 11, 12), but the intertwined discussion of the two, sometimes in the same sentence (see 3:7b–8, 11), would suggest that they are but two aspects of the same problem. The situation presupposed in this discussion might well be some form of communal sharing that sought to provide for those who were less well off or could not fend for themselves. Such an organization could open itself to abuse, however, by freeloaders taking advantage of the community's generosity. Their refusal to work could threaten the core values of the community and tear at the fabric of its structure. It is unclear how this problem is related to the community's apocalyptic outlook.

The problem was severe enough to warrant a command (3:6, 12). The new command reinforces an old one, "If anyone does not wish to work, let the person not eat" (3:10, author's trans.). Apparently this command was part of Paul's instructions during his initial visit. This stricture refers to assistance of needy members in the form of a meal. It also means that the community is in a position to dictate who could or could not receive such assistance, reflecting an organizational structure based on material sharing and pooling of common resources. The criterion for who could benefit from the communal largesse is not that everyone must work for a living regardless of ability. Instead, only those who do not wish to work would be ostracized and forbidden to participate in communal sharing, for such behavior constitutes disorderliness, and those who abuse the system thus must be separated in order to ensure the continual vitality of communal living (3:6). In this context, *tradition* must refer to what Paul taught the Thessalonians (3:10).

VI. Postscript (3:16–18)

Other than the usual blessing of peace and grace (3:16, 18), which are identical to their counterparts in 1 Thessalonians (5:23, 28), the postscript is distinguished by its absence of Paul's warm greeting with a holy kiss or his instruction to have the letter be read out loud to the congregation (cf. 1 Thess 5:26–27). Instead, the author calls attention to an autograph signature to assure his audience of its authenticity. Such insistence seems out of place and assumes the recipients would read the letter rather than hear it performed orally.

BIBLIOGRAPHY

F. F. Bruce. *1 & 2 Thessalonians.* WBC 45 (Waco: Word, 1982); K. Donfried. *Paul, Thessalonica, and Early Christianity* (Grand Rapids: Eerdmans, 2002); V. P. Furnish. *I Thessalonians and II Thessalonians* (Nashville: Abingdon, 2007); R. Jewett. *The Thessalonian Correspondence: Pauline Rhetoric and Millenarian Piety* (Philadelphia: Fortress, 1986); A. Malherbe. *The Letters to the Thessalonians.* AB 32B (New York: Doubleday, 2000).

1–2 TIMOTHY

Matthew Skinner

OVERVIEW

The two Letters to Timothy along with the Letter to Titus form a distinct collection within the NT. These three books address two of the Apostle Paul's prominent associates to guide them in organizing Christian communities in ways that reflect right doctrine and confront challenges brought by rival teachers. The letters offer moral exhortation rooted in theological assertions, insisting that adherence to sound teaching manifests itself through a quality of personal conduct and social organization that was widely valued and also promoted by moral-philosophical traditions of the wider Greco-Roman world.

For almost 300 years Bible scholars have referred to 1–2 Timothy and Titus as the Pastoral Epistles in recognition that these letters' main purpose is to provide instruction about Christian leadership. To understand the nature and significance of this instruction, it is necessary to consider the literary character of the Pastorals and the circumstances they address. Although the letters bear Paul's name, a strong majority of scholars finds much evidence in them to suggest they come from a later time and a different author. Their basic terminology and theological emphases differ greatly from the content of other Pauline letters whose authorship is not disputed. Their ethical outlook and concerns about false teachings appear to reflect circumstances that arose after Paul's death. Written likely within a decade of the year 100 CE by an unknown author to unknown audiences, the Pastorals stage a literary communication between Paul's legacy and later beneficiaries of his ministry. These letters demonstrate their commitment to perpetuating Paul's ministry and teaching by adapting the Pauline tradition and calling it into service in new ways to equip churches facing new challenges and opportunities. They eschew conduct and ideas that outsiders could regard as antisocial, and they promote a vision of Christianity that exists relatively harmoniously with the wider society's values.

First Timothy shares much with Titus, for both books offer instruction about community organization and proper lifestyle. They say little about the specific duties of overseers (from a term that later Christians would equate with the office of bishops), wives, older or respected men (later equated with elders or presbyters), widows, helpers (deacons), and slaves. Rather, the author prescribes qualifications for these people, moral standards that square well with virtues promoted in other Greco-Roman writings concerning the proper ordering of society. In that ancient context, households were the primary social and economic units, headed usually by a man and composed of extended family, slaves, and various clients. First Timothy and Titus conceive of the church as "the household of God" (1 Tim 3:15), which, like any other household in that particular culture, depended upon an established ordering of its members and their roles if it was to thrive, attract repute, and contribute positively to those around it. "Household management" in the church is not merely for show; it manifests the "godliness" (*eusebeia*) at the heart of the faith that Paul's successors inherited and preserve through their teaching. In the Pastorals' semantics, such "godliness" carries the sense of *loyalty*—loyalty to God and adherence to God's purposes. Virtuous and godly lives, therefore, express God's gracious intention to bring salvation to all (Titus 2:11–13).

Second Timothy likewise praises the godliness that corresponds to sound teaching and commends good works, but its focus falls less on church order and more on the faithfulness Paul exemplified in his ministry. Written in the voice of one expecting death (4:6–8), it resembles testamentary literature, in which a revered figure gives final, sometimes quite personal instructions and warnings to followers (cf. 1 Kgs 2:1–9; Acts 20:18–35). The letter depicts Paul as an archetypal model of endurance and faithfulness, qualities commended to Timothy as he continues the apostle's ministry while dealing with rival teachers whose radicalism threatens to cause offense and alienate the church from its wider society.

The Pastorals occasionally cite rich material from Christian hymns or liturgies, and yet their most vital theological contribution may not come from their specific assertions about God, the gospel, or faithful living. Instead, their greatest theological value emerges from observing how they *do theology* by drawing upon the figure of Paul to equip churches that are moving into new circumstances and challenges. The Pastorals take received traditions and recast them in different language with new emphases so as to shape both the witness that Christian faith can offer and the self-understanding of Christian communities within a particular cultural setting. In doing so, these writings imply that Christianity never stands detached from culture but must continually and creatively draw from the societal constructs and norms it encounters as it endeavors to embody the message of God's salvation in ways that people will find relevant and meaningful.

OUTLINE

First Timothy

I. Salutation (1:1–2)

II. God's Ordering of Things and the Need for Instruction (1:3–20)

III. Instructions Concerning Worship (2:1–3:1*a*)

IV. Instructions Concerning Church Leaders (3:1*b*–13)

V. The Nature of the Church and the Threats It Faces (3:14–4:5)

VI. Instructions Concerning Timothy's Leadership (4:6–16)

VII. Instructions Concerning Church Organization (5:1–6:2*a*)

VIII. Commands to Stand Firm amid Conflict (6:2*b*–19)

IX. Concluding Instructions (6:20–21)

Second Timothy

I. Salutation (1:1–2)

II. Thanksgiving and Reminder (1:3–7)

III. Exhortations to Remain Faithful (1:8–2:13)

IV. Warnings about Those Who Oppose the Truth (2:14–3:9)

    A. The Rival Teachers (2:14–21)

    B. The Need for Patience and Gentleness (2:22–26)

    C. The Moral Bankruptcy of False Teachers (3:1–9)

V. A Charge to Persevere and Proclaim (3:10–4:8)

VI. Concluding Instructions and Greetings (4:9–22)

DETAILED ANALYSIS

FIRST TIMOTHY

Timothy, the letter's addressee, was perhaps the best known of Paul's partners. The book of Acts and several of Paul's letters mention his cooperation with Paul, and some of those letters name him as their coauthor (e.g., 2 Corinthians, Philippians, 1 Thessalonians, Philemon). By addressing a known emissary of Paul, both this letter and Second Timothy strengthen their claim to be a reliable expression of the Pauline tradition, for as the apostle's "loyal child" Timothy functions as a conduit for the authority associated with Paul's personal and theological legacy.

1:3–20. The letter restates Timothy's role in Ephesus: to instruct people and correct contrary doctrines, thereby displaying love. Authentic teaching corresponds to the way God would have things ordered, in keeping with God's role as Savior (see 1:1; 2:3–4; 4:10). The word in v. 4 translated by the NRSV as "training" refers rather to God's "household management" (*oikonomia*). False teachers do not conform to God's gospel, as demonstrated in their profane, disorderly behavior. Regarding their connection to the Christian faith, because they abandon conscience, they exist as if desolated and cut off by a shipwreck.

2:1–3:1a. This section begins with exhortation concerning prayer, including prayers for governing authorities. Such petitions for the well-being of all society do not promote accommodation or loyalty to the Roman Empire merely to insure the church's security (although that is part of it); in 2:3–6 the justification for these prayers cites liturgical language to declare God's authority over the world. Thus the author asserts that "a quiet and peaceable life," a life that corresponds to society's conventional understanding of "godliness and dignity," manages to express God's desire for the salvation of all the world.

Focus on prayer resumes in 2:8, but then the author turns to women's adornment and commands that women remain silent in public worship. Concern for respectable order, as construed according to particular expectations in ancient culture, underlie these verses. Much of what the letter says about women mirrors misgivings expressed by Greco-Roman moralists. Virtuous women were expected to be modest and submissive to their husbands. Also common were suspicions that falsehoods easily ensnare women, an assumption that governs the interpretation of Adam and Eve's story in 2:13–14. By restricting women's roles in worship to conform with certain patriarchal norms about households, the author perhaps tries to curb the influence of women who had been influenced by rival teachers (see 2 Tim 3:6–7) and thus to prevent the specific Christian communities he has in view from appearing scandalous to outsiders. An affirmation of women's salvation, underscored by the author as a reliable "saying," concludes this section, again associating salvation with traditionally prescribed roles and ethical virtues.

3:1b–13. Instructions about overseers (bishops) and helpers (deacons) describe not their functions but the qualifications of those who would assume these leadership roles. Nothing about the expectations concerning these men, their wives, and their children is uniquely Christian. Greco-Roman moralists commended essentially the same practical virtues for military commanders and heads of households. Overseers seem to have possessed significant authority in the congrega-

tions (see also Titus 1:7–9), for v. 5 compares their management over households to their administration of the church. Honorable leaders who keep God's household (see 3:15) in proper order give outsiders no cause to take offense, which appears to be a primary rationale behind the prescribed qualifications.

3:14–4:5. As they bring about a pause in the series of instructions to Timothy, these verses offer keys to the letter's purpose. First, in 3:14–16, statements about the church and God provide theological justification for all the exhortations. The church as God's "household" (*oikos*) draws upon the notion that families or households reflected Roman society as a whole. The Pastorals depict the church as an embodiment of the society God intends, one made possible only by the salvation God provides, and therefore they regard prized social values as capable of modeling God's design for the world. In the context of 1 Tim 2–3, this theological premise explains why women, overseers, and helpers should manifest orderly and honorable virtues. A quotation from a Christian hymn reiterates that part of "the mystery of our religion (*eusebeia*)" is that it brings heaven and earth into relationship, for the revealing of Jesus results not only in his heavenly glory but also in proclamation and belief among all "throughout the world."

Next, 4:1–5 asserts that certain people threaten the church's ability to live in conformity with the teaching it has been given, making the letter's instructions to Timothy all the more necessary. Rival teachers, described as having renounced the doctrines ("the faith") Timothy must promote, advocate ascetic life-styles. In response, the author strongly confirms the goodness of creation, indicating that perhaps these teachers characterized salvation in terms of escape from or renunciation of the material world—ideas that conflict with Jesus' having been "revealed in flesh" (3:16) and that may have made the church appear socially subversive.

4:6–16. Instructions to Timothy flow from the previous verses' refutation of rival teachings, emphasizing the importance of his leadership in the struggle against divergent ideas. Timothy's role revolves around teaching the tenets of "the faith" that has nourished him thus far. The author apparently assumes readers know these doctrines, for the letter does not delineate them. Paul's connection to "sound teaching" authenticates the teaching, and it coheres with the Scriptures read in public worship (cf. 2 Tim 3:16–17). Timothy's persistence in contending for this teaching involves living an exemplary life. Once again the letter claims that right doctrine aligns with right behavior and that both express the truth that God is Savior (see also Titus 2:11–13).

5:1–6:2a. The string of instructions to Timothy continues, now focusing on various groups within the Christian community. Standard exhortations in 5:1–2 reinforce the familial identity of the church. Discussion of "widows who are really widows" in 5:3–16 refers to women who require support from the wider community of believers because they have no husbands or families to care for them. Only certain aged widows who will not remarry and who display esteemed virtues qualify to be included on a roster. The roster probably identifies the people to whom a church provides material support, although some interpreters think it could indicate an exclusive cadre of older unmarried women who served churches in a formal, recognized way. In any case, the remarks in 5:13–15 betray deep suspicion about women's behavior, probably in response to the influence rival teachings have had (see 2 Tim 3:6–7). Instructions about older men in 5:17–22 refer to those among them who provide leadership through preaching and teaching, distinguished as elders or presbyters. Finally, and in keeping with cultural norms, slaves must honor those whom they serve. All these exhortations apply to the organization of the churches that comprise the letter's intended ancient audience; they reiterate the household character of Christian communities, affirm the need for leadership that maintains the desired organization of those communities, and ensure that vulnerable members receive care. The author expects the communities' good works and upstanding morality to prevent God's name from being dishonored (5:7, 14, 25; 6:1), in keeping with God's salvific intentions for the world.

6:2b–19. Verse 6:2b points backward to preceding instructions while also transitioning into what follows, which contrasts Timothy's conduct with the depravity that accompanies contrary doctrines. In keeping with much contemporary Greco-Roman moral discourse, the Pastorals frequently turn polemical, opposing rival teachings by impugning the character of those who teach them. In this case, dissenters stray from "godliness" and adherence to a particular moral order; desire for riches and willingness to exploit godliness for personal gain are among the causes of their waywardness (see 2 Tim 3:1–5). To guard against their damage, Timothy must stand firm in good conduct and fulfill the commission or "commandment" laid upon him as a leader in ministry until the coming intervention or "manifestation" (*epiphaneia*) of Jesus Christ, whose glory is extolled with liturgical language in vv. 15–16.

Having spoken sharply about the greed of rival teachers, the letter returns to riches in vv. 17–19 so as not to paint all the wealthy with a single brushstroke. Just as leaders must not be enslaved to money (see 3:3, 8), any who possess wealth must not let it displace God but should attend to good works and generosity. Wealthy persons clearly belonged to churches when the letter was composed. These verses strike a balance between a caution toward riches' power to corrupt and an acknowledgement that wealth allows for generosity that can promote the good works that mark authentic Christian living.

6:20–21. The concluding words to Timothy recapitulate the letter's perspectives. In his role as teacher and manager of God's household he is to "guard the deposit" (v. 20a, author's trans.; see also 2 Tim 1:12, 14). He must vigilantly preserve and propagate a doctrinal, ethical, and pastoral inheritance, summed up as "the faith." This inheritance, anchored in Paul's legacy, has itself been fashioned by the letter's author to render a vision of Christian existence that conforms to the structures, language, and norms of a particular culture. As it contends for believers to embody God's salvation, First Timothy provides an innovative attempt at adapting Christian theology and conduct to certain circumstances, even if the letter's addressee is not himself encouraged to take similarly creative steps toward re-adapting the tradition when those circumstances change.

Second Timothy

1:1–2. On the address to Timothy, see the comments on 1 Tim 1:1–2, above.

1:3–7. These opening verses set a tone that resounds throughout the letter, urging Timothy to persist in faith and exercise bold leadership. His faith has deep, sure roots in his family; it is part of who he is (see 3:14–15). The primary exhortation speaks of rekindling (literally, it tells Timothy to persist in "fanning into flame again") a spiritual gift of ministry and thereby suggests that the substance of the whole letter is nothing new. Timothy's ministry perpetuates a received tradition of doctrine and practical instruction, and thus the letter uses the figure of Timothy to transmit that tradition in the authority of the Apostle Paul. When the letter exhorts Timothy to continue faithfully in what has been bequeathed to him, it implies that readers uphold and abide by that illustrious Pauline tradition when they themselves heed the exhortations.

1:8–2:13. The first set of exhortations in this section, in 1:8–14, derive from Paul's experiences and call Timothy to emulate the apostle. The letter describes Paul as imprisoned (see also 1:16; 2:9; 4:16), which meant suffering and shame for him. Timothy remains faithful if he suffers for the gospel as Paul did, by holding to the teaching received from Paul, thereby guarding the "good treasure" (or, "good deposit"; see comments on 1 Tim 6:20–21, above). Contending for the gospel Paul preached and suffering are not separate things but two sides of a single coin (see 3:10–12). Suffering, despite its attendant shame, cannot discredit the gospel, for the gospel both acknowledges and minimizes the reality of suffering as it declares the power of God to bring life from death (1:8*b*–10). This power demonstrates God's grace, something that was always part of God's salvific plan even "before the ages began" and was made known or "revealed" (*phaneroō*) through the "appearing" (*epiphaneia*) of Christ Jesus in the flesh.

Other people's deeds provide negative and positive illustrations of faithfulness in 1:15–18. Those who turned from Paul turned from the gospel and the shame they feared. By contrast, Onesiphorus remained faithful, even though remaining loyal to an imprisoned friend could have brought him great dishonor in that society.

Another set of exhortations to Timothy concludes this passage, beginning in 2:1–7. The notion of power or strength from 1:7–8 reappears

in 2:1. Also, just as 1:13–14 told Timothy to guard Pauline teaching, he should entrust others to teach the same (2:2). Talk of suffering, introduced in 1:8, resumes in 2:3. The examples of soldiers, athletes, and farmers emphasize the single-minded devotion, discipline, labor, and expectation of reward that characterize the leadership Timothy must exercise through his suffering. Theological realities justify all these exhortations. The imperative to "remember Jesus Christ" (2:8) gives strength for enduring hardship; Christ, "raised from the dead," demonstrates that God's word cannot be confined. The author likely quotes from an early Christian hymn in 2:11*b*–13 to reiterate that perseverance is a hallmark of Christian living and ministry, because the gospel is a movement from death to life and nothing can sever Christ's faithfulness toward believers.

2:14–3:9. Attention shifts toward those Timothy should instruct, although exhortations still address his responsibilities as they warn about the influence of those who teach rival doctrines. The "them" in 2:14 may recall "the elect" mentioned in 2:10, indicating all believers, or it may go back to the leaders identified as "faithful people" in 2:2. "Wrangling over words" refers to verbal battles or quarrels, presumably concerning doctrine (see 1 Tim 1:3-5; 6:4; Titus 3:9). The leadership envisioned here does not host discussions, it only explains "the word of truth" (2:15). The author warns about the disruptive effect of false teachings, assuming that readers already know their substance. Just the mention of some who claim "that the resurrection has already taken place" provides a glimpse into a specific contrary doctrine. That vague statement offers little more than the suggestion that other teachers do not focus on a resurrection to come. They instead advocate a kind of spiritual existence in the present time, perhaps an ascetic lifestyle (see 1 Tim 4:3–5). In 2:20–21, attention returns to Timothy's calling and the idea of his presenting himself for God's service (cf. 2:15). The metaphor of utensils in a great house encourages him to strive to be useful to God, for he and all he teaches will be available for honorable purposes and good works if they are not contaminated by the profane teachings and destructive behaviors of rival teachers.

The next part of this section, 2:22–26, urges Timothy to live virtuously and again warns against quarrelling. A new emphasis appears when the author calls for humble "gentleness" in correcting opponents. A refusal to engage in debates over doctrine, therefore, neither requires nor permits a refusal to engage opponents. The one who serves the Lord displays patience with adversaries, specifically because they may yet repent, for God's salvation is never out of reach (see 1 Tim 2:4; Titus 2:11–13). Even opponents of the truth might eventually come to do God's will (following the NRSV's footnote on the translation of 2:26).

False teachings' capacity to harm nevertheless remains great, as 3:1–9 emphasizes through warnings about moral decline in "the last days." These comments do not predict future events but discredit false teachers by linking them to excessive moral depravity. This brand of polemic and the rattling off of vices in 3:2–5 are common in the Pastoral Epistles and other literature from their time (see also 1 Tim 6:2b–5). Surely the specific opponents in the author's crosshairs were not utter antisocial degenerates; the point is that their teachings, which cloak themselves in a guise of godliness, are actually corrupt and therefore hypocritical. They evidence a flawed understanding, which necessarily leads to disorder and danger (cf. comments on corrupted minds and consciences in 1 Tim 1:19; cf. 4:1–2; 6:5; Titus 1:15–16). If, as the Pastorals regularly insist, godly living is made possible by God's salvation as comprehended by adherence to sound doctrine, then false teachers prove the inverse through teachings that go hand in hand with aberrant conduct. To confirm this, the author mentions those who prey on women, whom cultural stereotypes considered easily manipulated by passions and falsehood. Apparently these teachers had converted some female believers to their views, creating situations in which women were violating the social norms that the Pastorals elsewhere go to great lengths to reinforce as appropriate for Christian living (see 1 Tim 2:8–3:1a; 5:13–15; Titus 2:3–5). False teachers foolishly oppose God's servants just like Jannes and Jambres, names traditionally associated with the Egyptian magicians who appear anonymously in Exod 7–9.

3:10–4:8. In this climactic section the letter returns to issuing Timothy exhortations that stem from the experiences and example of the Apostle Paul, similar to the material in 1:8–2:13. As Paul ministered and endured persecutions, he manifested the virtues consistent with sound doctrine (3:10–11a); Timothy is to do the same. Deceivers and deception will continue to pose threats, but Timothy must persist in the truth he has been taught. Exactly *what* he has been taught is not discussed; the focus falls on the people (the pronoun *whom* in 3:14 is plural, indicating Paul and other progenitors of Timothy's faith) who have taught him and on how long he has known these things (3:14–15). In this regard, the letter delivers motivation, not explanation. It grounds confidence in the legacy and certitude of this faith, not necessarily in theological proofs. "The sacred writings," namely Jewish Scriptures, are a source of Timothy's theological instruction, for they make him and others "wise for salvation" (3:15, NIV) and thereby equip them for the training and living that correspond to God's salvation.

The future, specifically Christ's return as judge, motivates the charges in 4:1–5. Paul's ministry becomes Timothy's ministry. Like the apostle, Timothy must proclaim, teach, endure suffering, and be an evangelist. Paul's impending death casts these instructions as perhaps his final words to his successor in God's service (4:6–7). Paul's fidelity ensured that "the crown of righteousness" awaited him as his reward (4:8). Still, this crown remained the Lord's to give. Paul did not earn it, but his faithful service buttressed his confidence, just as it can for Timothy and anyone else who eagerly awaits the next manifestation or "appearing" (*epiphaneia*) of the Lord (see also 1:10; 4:1; 1 Tim 6:14; Titus 2:11–13). Paul emerges as a model for readers to emulate in every dimension: his faithfulness, his conduct, his adherence to sound teaching, his suffering, his endurance, and his expectation of future reward.

4:9–22. Specific commands to Timothy enhance the letter's ability to stage a communication from the apostle to his delegate. Writings composed in the name of a dead and revered figure sometimes included such realistic details, and yet the blessing to a plural "you" in v. 22b, duplicating 1 Tim 6:21b, may acknowledge that the Pastorals were really addressed to a community. The mention of many who abandoned Paul provides an opportunity to reprise the confidence with which the letter began (see 1:5–7, 12b). Although people forsook or opposed Paul, he remained confident in the

Lord's care (vv. 17–18). Their turning from him may represent their turning from God, but Paul's endurance remained exemplary.

BIBLIOGRAPHY

J. M. Bassler. *1 Timothy, 2 Timothy, Titus.* ANTC (Nashville: Abingdon, 1996); R. F. Collins. *1 & 2 Timothy and Titus: A Commentary.* NTL (Louisville: Westminster John Knox, 2002); B. Fiore. *The Pastoral Epistles: First Timothy, Second Timothy, Titus.* SP 12 (Collegeville, Minn.: Liturgical, 2007); F. Young. *The Theology of the Pastoral Letters.* New Testament Theology (Cambridge: Cambridge University Press, 1994).

TITUS
MATTHEW SKINNER

OVERVIEW

The vocabulary, style, subject matter, and theological outlook of Titus reveal its close connections to 1–2 Timothy. The common features of these three books invite interpreters to consider them as a collection, and so they are widely known as the Pastoral Epistles. For more on their background and content, see the overview of 1–2 Timothy in this commentary.

Titus appears last in the canonical ordering of the Pastorals because it is the shortest of the three. No one knows when it was composed in relation to its companion letters, but the presence of an extended theological rationale for Paul's apostleship in 1:1–3 may indicate that it preceded the Letters to Timothy, which have much shorter and less formal salutations, or that it performed an introductory function for the trio. Although Titus shares much with 1 Timothy, especially in its concerns about internal dissension and its exhortations regarding community organization and the value of good works, the two letters do not duplicate one another. Titus mentions neither widows nor helpers (deacons), and its comments about the Holy Spirit and baptism (3:4–7) root its instructions in theological themes that are absent from 1 Timothy.

OUTLINE

I. Salutation (1:1–4)

II. Organization That Preserves Sound Doctrine (1:5–16)

III. Exhortations to Promote God's Doctrine and Good Works (2:1–14)

IV. Behavior That Manifests God's Salvation (2:15–3:8a)

V. Commands to End Internal Conflicts (3:8b–11)

VI. Concluding Instructions and Greetings (3:12–15)

DETAILED ANALYSIS

I. Salutation (1:1–4)

The salutation describes the theological thrust of Paul's apostleship, making use of several of the Pastoral Epistles' most prominent theological topics: faith, knowledge, truth, godliness, and a proclamation that centers on God's identity as Savior and reveals God's word. Titus, the letter's addressee and a Gentile, was one of Paul's associates. He accompanied Paul and Barnabas to Jerusalem (Gal 2:1) and served as Paul's envoy among the Corinthians (2 Cor 7:13–15; 8:16–24; 12:18). By addressing a known emissary of Paul, the letter strengthens its claim to be a valid expression of the Pauline tradition as it delivers exhortations backed by the authority of Paul's apostleship, transmitted via Paul's delegates, and now to be heeded by its readers.

II. Organization That Preserves Sound Doctrine (1:5–16)

1:5–16. This letter includes no words of thanksgiving but immediately instructs Paul's associate about administering congregations on the island of Crete. No other New Testament writing refers to Christian ministry occurring on Crete, but by the time of this letter's composition there appear to be believers in multiple towns.

These verses first instruct Titus about appointing older men (elders or presbyters) and overseers (bishops) to positions of leadership (vv. 5–9) and then explain that such people play important roles in silencing those who teach contrary doctrines that disrupt households and are tantamount to denying God (vv. 10–16). Any formal distinction between the mature (not necessarily elderly) men who lead and overseers, if there is one, remains vague; the focus falls on their similar qualifications (see also 1 Tim 3:1b–7), virtues that confirm their ability to manage their own households honorably and with authority. Their stable management stands in sharp contrast to the rival teachers' proclivity for "upending whole households" (v. 11, author's trans.; see 2 Tim 2:18). An overseer must adhere to received doctrine ("teaching") to fulfill his role as a teacher who refutes rebellious ideas.

Other than brief references to "circumcision" and "Jewish myths" (see also 3:9), the author gives few clues about the substance of contrary teachings, preferring instead to vilify those who teach them with a slur about Cretans and disparaging remarks about their character.

III. Exhortations to Promote God's Doctrine and Good Works (2:1–14)

2:1–14. The letter shifts to tell Titus to encourage groups of Christians to live in ways that accord with sound doctrine. The moral exhortations of vv. 2–10 call for orderly living and, like the qualifications for leaders given in 1:6–8, align well with recognized Greco-Roman ideals pertaining to the hierarchical structure of households and the roles of their members. The arrangement of this section of the letter has pivotal significance, for the practical exhortations are followed and explained by words about salvation in vv. 11–14. Honorable behavior and "good deeds" are not the totality of Christian faith. The commended virtues serve as "an ornament to the doctrine of God our Savior"; reputable living becomes possible through the salvation God gives and is the appropriate way of life between the time when God's saving grace "appeared" or made itself known (*epiphainō*) in Christ (v. 11) and the coming "manifestation" (*epiphaneia*) of Christ in glory (v. 13).

IV. Behavior That Manifests God's Salvation (2:15–3:8*a*)

2:15–3:8*a*. Resembling the previous section, exhortations about believers' conduct again precede an explanation of their theological basis. Christians should live peacefully and honorably by submitting to civil authorities. They must shun quarrels, because mistreatment of others characterizes life apart from Christ. For when God "appeared" (*epiphainō*) and revealed salvation through Christ (3:4), it was an expression of "goodness and loving kindness," which believers now embody through their charitable and irreproachable behavior toward others. The rich statements in 3:4–7 appear to be taken from a hymn or another liturgical formula. The author approves their claims with the comment, "The saying is sure."

V. Commands to End Internal Conflicts (3:8*b*–11)

3:8*b*–11. These verses connect closely to the previous section, with v. 8*b* resuming the instruction that Titus call people to "good works" (cf. 3:1). The author exhorts against debating over issues raised by rival teachers or divisive people (see 1 Tim 1:4; 6:4; 2 Tim 2:23). The courtesy toward others commended in 3:2 gives way in 3:9–11 to unyielding resistance of any dissension that arises within the community. Titus should not entertain theological discussions but teach and maintain traditions bequeathed to him. In this instruction the letter assumes the patent validity of theological traditions associated with Paul's legacy rather than delineating or contending anew for them.

VI. Concluding Instructions and Greetings (3:12–15)

3:12–15. Specific commands to Titus enhance the sense of the letter as communication between Paul and his envoy on Crete. Realistic details like these were sometimes included in writings composed in the name of a dead and revered figure, and yet the concluding blessing to "all of you" in the plural may acknowledge that the letter was really addressed to a community. A final reference to good works underscores the Pastorals' insistence that Christians' lives promote well-being, manifest virtues, and so express the basic conviction that God brings salvation to all.

BIBLIOGRAPHY

J. M. Bassler. *1 Timothy, 2 Timothy, Titus.* ANTC (Nashville: Abingdon, 1996); R. F. Collins. *1 & 2 Timothy and Titus: A Commentary.* NTL (Louisville: Westminster John Knox, 2002); B. Fiore. *The Pastoral Epistles: First Timothy, Second Timothy, Titus.* SP 12 (Collegeville, Minn.: Liturgical, 2007); F. Young. *The Theology of the Pastoral Letters.* New Testament Theology (Cambridge: Cambridge University Press, 1994).

PHILEMON

EMERSON POWERY

OVERVIEW

Although the letter to Philemon contains only 25 verses and 335 words, through it readers see the rhetorical skill of Paul, the negotiation between church leaders, the network of house churches, and the social world of slavery in first-century Christianity. The letter also raises numerous difficult questions, including: (1) How does Onesimus meet Paul? Is Onesimus an escaped slave seeking Paul's assistance, or is he sent to assist Paul during his confinement? (2) If Onesimus has run away, does he do so because of the the general provocation of "slavery" in first-century Rome, or does Onesimus have other tensions with his owner? (3) What does Paul expect of Philemon—Onesimus's freedom or simply acceptance back into the household *without* any legal penalty? (4) Does the letter primarily wrestle with the condemnation and possible death of one human being or does it address the entire slave system?

The Greco-Roman world held firm laws on slavery. The enslaved were property, thereby subject to all Roman laws related to ownership. Slaves had no civil rights within Roman society. Although laws were in place to check the most flagrant abuse of slaves, the Roman government rarely intervened in the rights of owners over their property. Indeed, there were severe laws against those who interfered with this part of the social order. Assisting runaway slaves was illegal. Once recaptured, escaped slaves normally received severe punishment, even death. The head of a household, as Philemon apparently was (vv. 1–2), could legally execute returned slaves.

Slavery was also an ancient Israelite practice. What Paul would have heard, when the Scriptures were read in the synagogues, may not have challenged directly what he would have heard in Roman courts. Neither would it have coincided precisely with the slave system of his day. Despite Israel's exodus from Egypt, slavery was allowed. But it was considered punishment for foreign captives whom Israelites could buy and bequeath to their heirs (Lev 25:44–46). The enslavement of fellow Hebrews, however, should last for a 6-year period only (Deut 15:13–15). Finally, most relevant to Paul's letter, an escaped slave should *not* be returned to his/her master (Deut 23:15). Philo, a Jewish contemporary of Paul, interprets Deut 23 as if the fugitive should not be returned to a *cruel* master and implies that the enslaved could be sold to someone else (cf. *On the Virtues* 24.124). In another treatise, *On the Contemplative Life*, Philo knows of some Essenes who viewed slavery as against nature (9.70–71; cf. Josephus, *Jewish Antiquities* 18.21; but cf. *Damascus Document* XI.12; XII.10–11). Yet Paul does not cite Deut 23:15, and he may not have sensed the tension between these two viewpoints, the Roman world and its laws *and* the story of ancient Israel. Nevertheless, it is hard to imagine that he was not aware of it, given his comments in 1 Cor 7:20–24.

In Philemon, a brief letter to one prominent Christian and the members of this household community, Paul writes from under house arrest (vv. 1, 9, 10, 13, 23) in the early 60s of the Common Era with a plea and a request. Paul's appeal here, in this subtle protest, is based on love.

OUTLINE

I. Introduction (1–7)

    A. Greetings (1–3)

    B. Thanksgiving (4–7)

II. Body of the Letter (8–21)

    A. Preface to the Appeal (8–9)

    B. The Decision, Appeal, and Mixed Emotions (10–13)

    C. Mixed Emotions and Potential Expectation (14–16)

    D. Do What Is Right (17–21)

III. Conclusion (22–25)

    A. A Rhetorical Transition (22)

    B. Final Greetings (23–24)

    C. Closing Benediction (25)

DETAILED ANALYSIS

I. Introduction (1–7)

A. Greetings (vv. 1–3)

Paul's opening identification of himself as a "prisoner of Christ Jesus" is unique among the Pauline letters, although he writes other letters from a prison cell (e.g., Philippians). More often, he employs the designation "servant of Christ Jesus" (Phil 1:1; cf. Rom 1:1) or "apostle of Christ Jesus" (e.g., Rom 1:1; 1 Cor 1:1; 2 Cor 1:1; Gal 1:1).

This self-description initiates a common motif throughout the letter. This "prisoner of Christ Jesus" (1:1) is the "prisoner" making the appeal (1:9) while "in his chains" (1:10, author's trans.) during his "imprisonment for the gospel" (1:13). Paul's own sacrifice on behalf of others should not go unnoticed, especially as he seeks a "benefit" from Philemon (v. 20).

Other features of this opening should be mentioned briefly. (1) Paul's "brother" and partner, Timothy, appears often in Paul's letters (e.g., 2 Cor 1:1; Phil 1:1; 1 Thess: 1:1; cf. Col 1:1; 2 Thess 1:1). (2) Recognizing Philemon as a "fellow worker" creates an *inclusio* with the end of the letter (v. 24). (3) This is the only Pauline letter addressed to a female leader, Apphia "our sister," in the early Christian communities. Some scholars suggest that she may be Philemon's wife or sister, for which there is no evidence here; if not, she still bears part of the responsibility for the outcome of the enslaved in this household church. (4) Addressing the "church in your house" reminds readers of the (semi-)public nature of these documents. The social interaction of this house church in Phrygia would affect Philemon's decision.

B. Thanksgiving (4–7)

The thanksgiving offers words of affirmation and encouragement. First, Paul remembers fellow believers in his prayers (v. 4; cf. Rom 1:8–15; Phil 1:3–11; 1 Thess 1:2–10; cf. Col 1:3–14). Second, he recognizes the "love and faith" the addressees share for others in the mission (v. 5; cf. Rom 1:8–15; 1 Thess 1:2–10; cf. 2 Thess 1:3–12). Here, Philemon is singled out for his reputation in the wider, nascent Christian movement. But the idea that Paul *himself* has been excited (i.e., "received much joy") and comforted (v. 7) because of Philemon's actions toward the "saints" is distinctive. Some scholars argue that v. 7 indicates that the Colossian church sent Onesimus to Paul. Paul hopes, in the construction of this letter, to convince Philemon to "refresh my heart in Christ" (v. 20) once again even as he has previously.

II. Body of the Letter (8–21)

A. Preface to the Appeal (8–9)

Prior to addressing the primary concern of this short letter, Paul offers prefatory remarks that combine "boldness in Christ" with love. He also reinforces his appeal by his status as an "elderly person" (*prebytēs*) and a "prisoner of Christ Jesus." His status as "prisoner" is repeated throughout (vv. 1, 9, 10, 13, 23) and, in first-century culture, maturity commanded respect.

B. The Decision, Appeal, and Mixed Emotions (10–13)

Finally, Paul raises the issue of contention. Significantly, Paul turns to familial language in order to introduce Onesimus as his own child. This "birth" suggests a new beginning for Onesimus, perhaps to his conversion. In addition, Paul describes Onesimus as "my own heart" (v. 12, using *splanchna*, a term that refers literally to a person's "inward parts" or "bowels." Just as "the hearts (*splanchna*) of the saints have been refreshed" by Philemon (v. 7), so Paul wishes for his heart (*splanchna*) to be refreshed (v. 20), an emotion that is entangled with the person of Onesimus (v. 12).

Verse 11 prompts questions about how Onesimus has become "useful" to Paul? Apparently, he is providing some service for Paul during his imprisonment (v. 13). Through wordplay, Paul describes Onesimus as "useful" (*euchrēston*), not "useless" (*achrēston*). [These terms play off of the name "Onesimus," which also means "useful" or "beneficial."] It is not clear how Onesimus was "useless" to Philemon, perhaps due to what may have been owed (cf. v. 18) due to his absence from Philemon's household. But Paul is apparently troubled. So, against the dictates of the Torah (cf. Deut 23:15) but in line with Roman mores, Paul has already dispatched Onesimus back to the house church in Colossae.

C. Mixed Emotions and Potential Expectation (14–16)

Paul's anguish seems sincere. He wants Philemon to act on his own accord, that is, "voluntarily" (cf. 2 Cor 9:7). So, Paul offers a compelling suggestion: Philemon should accept Onesimus back "no longer as a slave but more than a slave, a beloved brother." It is unclear whether Paul seeks Onesimus' freedom, his acceptance, or something more countercultural.

Paul also uses "brother" language for Timothy (v. 1) and for Philemon (v. 20), as Onesimus' *spiritual* status has changed, as he has become committed to Paul's message of the gospel (vv. 10, 11, 13; cf. Col 4:9). May the theological, familial language indicate something more about his *social* status as well? In Paul's egalitarian words, Onesimus should be considered a brother "in the Lord" *and* "in the flesh" (v. 16). Can Philemon treat Onesimus as a "brother … in the flesh" without altering their own social relationship?

D. Do What Is Right (17–21)

Paul shifts to a series of conditional clauses, establishing the "conditions" for Philemon's decision. First, and perhaps most importantly, Paul considers himself to have a special relationship with Philemon, what he calls a "partner" (*koinōnos*), a term he uses elsewhere for his close relationship with Titus (2 Cor 8:23) and for some Corinthian believers (2 Cor 1:7). The Greek implies that Philemon considers Paul to be his "partner." For Paul, however, this relationship may be at stake if Onesimus is not accepted. Paul claims that he would not have written had he not been persuaded before he wrote. In fact, Paul claims to have written this letter "in my own hand" (v. 19), an emphasis uncommon in the traditional Pauline letters (cf. Gal 6:11). Of course, this is part of the apostle's attempt to influence the decision of his addressee from a remote distance. Paul's partnership with Philemon is dependent on Philemon's treatment of Onesimus. In reality, the whole household church is watching!

The second conditional clause (v. 18) provides the only possible hint that Onesimus may have committed wrongdoing. Paul's conditional state-

ment implies that Onesimus may have committed an injustice or, more likely, owes Philemon something. If Onesimus actually stole something from Philemon, which the passage does *not* say, it may have been the funds to travel safely to Paul! In any case, Paul suggests that charges should be applied to his own account, an account that already has a surplus from Philemon's debt (v. 19). Paul does not request forgiveness for what Onesimus owes, but promises reparations!

Finally, Paul's switch to the optative mood ("let me have this benefit"; *onaimēn*), the Greek mood furthest removed from reality, indicates Paul's awareness that he cannot control Philemon's actions. It is his "wish" and his "polite request" that Philemon would do what Paul considers to be the right thing to do and, despite the force of his language elsewhere (e.g., "knowing that you will do even more than I say" in v. 21), Paul's use of the optative here betrays how tenuous this situation is.

III. Conclusion (22–25)

The closing provides a rhetorical "bridge" for Paul's argument: his upcoming plans to visit the Phrygian household church (v. 22). Given Paul's imprisonment, it is unclear whether he actually intends a visit or whether this is a strategy for discovering Philemon's decision. Only the addressees, who know Paul's prison status, would know the truth of this sentiment.

As with other letters, Paul sends greetings from "fellow workers" (i.e., Mark, Aristarchus, Demas, and Luke), singling out his "fellow prisoner," Epaphras who believers in this region probably know (cf. Col 1:7; 4:12). The other names are also grouped together elsewhere in the NT (e.g., Col 4:10–14; 2 Tim 4:10–11).

Paul's customary final word and blessing ends the letter (v. 25) and the need for "grace" is not perfunctory for the situation at hand.

Whatever interpreters may think about this short and poignant letter, one fact remains. Paul is *not* indifferent to Onesimus' plight. He uses his vast rhetorical skill to secure a release for his fellow believer in Christ. Why Paul returns Onesimus at all remains unanswerable. His "love" appeal may be one reason. And many readers have wished for a more forceful argument. The ambiguity of his request, and the circumstances surrounding this situation, has led to misunderstanding and misuse of this document in the history of its interpretation. African Americans, for example, have borne the brunt of misinterpretations in the United States. Nevertheless, Paul's expectations are high that Philemon would do "even more" than asked. Paul allows Philemon to act on his own accord in light of the weight of the gospel and in the company of other believers in the household.

BIBLIOGRAPHY

A. Callahan. *Embassy of Onesimus: The Letter of Paul to Philemon* (Valley Forge, Pa.: Trinity Press International, 1997); C. H. Felder. "Philemon." *NIB* (Nashville, Tenn.: Abingdon Press, 2005) 11:883–905; C. Frilingos. "For My Child, Onesimus: Paul and Domestic Power in Philemon." *JBL* 119 (2000) 91–104; J. A. Fitzmyer. *The Letter to Philemon: A New Translation with Introduction and Commentary.* AB 34C (New York: Doubleday, 2000); J. Glancy. *Slavery in Early Christianity* (New York: Oxford University Press, 2002); L. A. Lewis. "Philemon." *True to Our Native Land: An African American New Testament Commentary* (Minneapolis: Fortress Press 2007); C. Martin. "The Eyes Have It: Slaves in the Communities of Christ-Believers." *Christian Origins: A People's History of Christianity* 1 (Minneapolis, Minn.: Fortress, 2005). O. Patterson. *Slavery and Social Death: A Comparative Study* (Cambridge, Mass.: Harvard University Press, 1982); N. Peterson. *Rediscovering Paul: Philemon and the Sociology of Paul's Narrative World* (Minneapolis, Minn.: Fortress, 1985); S. Winter. "Paul's Letter to Philemon." *NTS* 33 (1987) 1–15.

HEBREWS

Daniel J. Harrington

OVERVIEW

What is customarily called the Letter to the Hebrews is a sermon in written form for Christians (most likely of Jewish origin). This "word of exhortation" (13:22) may have been written anywhere between 60 and 100 CE. Its literary style and theological conceptuality are very different from those in Paul's letters. It may well have addressed discouraged Jewish Christians at Rome around Nero's time (13:24). For early evidence of the use of Hebrews, see *1 Clement*, which is traditionally associated with the church at Rome and dated around 100 CE. But other scenarios are possible.

Hebrews interweaves biblical exposition and exhortation. The author has some familiarity with Platonic philosophical concepts, and is quite adept at writing in a sophisticated Greek style and at employing Greco-Roman rhetorical techniques. He is also familiar with the OT and skilled in using Jewish methods of biblical interpretation. But most of all he is a Christian preacher who uses all his learning and persuasive powers in the service of the gospel. The goal of the exposition that follows is to help readers today to follow the work's rich but often difficult train of thought, and to appreciate better its profound significance for Christian theology.

The main topic of Hebrews is the saving significance of Jesus' death and resurrection (the paschal mystery). Its starting point is the early Christian confession that "Christ died for our sins in accordance with the scriptures" (1 Cor 15:3). It portrays Jesus' death as the perfect sacrifice for sins. And since Jesus went willingly to his death, it presents him as the great high priest who offered himself as the perfect sacrifice (7:27).

The focus of Hebrews is not the earthly or historical Jesus. The author never cites a saying of Jesus found elsewhere in the Jesus tradition, and never mentions specific healings or other miraculous actions done by Jesus. Nevertheless, Hebrews does provide some information about Jesus while developing a theological argument about Jesus as the perfect sacrifice for sins and the great high priest.

In presenting Jesus as the great high priest the author admits the problem that Jesus did not come from the tribe of Levi but rather "was descended from Judah, and in connection with that tribe Moses said nothing about priests" (7:14). Therefore he constructs in Heb 7 a complex scriptural argument to the effect that Jesus represents another priesthood "according to the order of Melchizedek" (Ps 110:4) that is older and better than the levitical priesthood.

While stressing Jesus' identity as the Son of God, the author of Hebrews also insists on Jesus' humanity. In 2:5–9 he interprets Ps 8:4–6 and its mention of "the son of man" to refer not to humankind in general but rather to the humanity or incarnation of Jesus. And in 2:14–18 he insists that Jesus shared our "flesh and blood," and because of his full humanity he "did not come to help angels, but the descendants of Abraham" (2:16). Jesus' humanity is viewed as a necessary condition for carrying out his mission "to make an effective sacrifice of atonement for the sins of the people" (2:17, author's trans.).

OUTLINE

DETAILED ANALYSIS

I. Jesus the Son of God

1:1–4. Prologue. In one long sentence the author introduces the major characters, motifs, and themes. The use of several words beginning with the letter "p" (alliteration) helps attract the hearer's attention. All the clauses are attached in various ways to the main clause in 1:2 ("in these last days he has spoken to us by a Son"). The periodic sentence establishes at the outset the author's command of Greek grammar, style, and rhetoric.

The series of contrasts in 1:1–2a—"long ago" versus "in these last days," "our ancestors" versus "us," and "by the prophets" versus "by a Son"—highlights the climactic and definitive character of God's self-revelation through Jesus. The dynamic here is similar to that of John 1:1–18 where Jesus is celebrated as the Word of God. The fact that God is the speaker in both cases establishes God as the point of continuity between the old and the new ways of divine revelation.

The description of the Son as "heir of all things" in 1:2b alludes to the royal Ps 2—one of the author's favorite biblical texts—and identifies him as the Messiah (see Ps 2:8, "I will make the nations your heritage"). The statement that through the Son, God "created the worlds" evokes the figure of personified Wisdom as present at the creation of the world (Prov 8:22–31).

Jesus' identity as the Wisdom of God is further developed in 1:3a where there are striking parallels with (or perhaps direct influences from) Wis 7:25–26: "a pure emanation of the glory of the Almighty ... a reflection of eternal light."

Here Jesus is said to be what Wisdom is and to do what Wisdom does. He reflects God's glory, is the imprint or "character" of God's being, and sustains the world by his word. These attributes and functions point to Jesus as not simply Wisdom personified but rather as a divine figure in his own right.

The major theme of Hebrews is Jesus' death as the perfect (in the sense of truly effective) sacrifice for sins in contrast to the ineffective material sacrifices offered annually on the Day of Atonement by levitical priests (see Lev 16:30). According to 1:3b, Jesus brought about genuine purification from sins through his death on the cross and was therefore exalted (in his resurrection and ascension) to God's right hand, which is a messianic image taken from Ps 110:1 (LXX 109:1), which is another of the author's favorite biblical texts.

Much of Hebrews is concerned with proving the superiority of Christ to the angels, Moses, Joshua, and so on. That motif is introduced in 1:4, which also leads into the first comparison (with the angels) that follows in 1:5–14. The name that Christ "inherited" is that of "the Son" (of God)—an echo of two terms used previously in 1:2.

1:5–14. Superior to Angels. The first comparison consists of seven biblical quotations arranged in three pairs (1:5; 1:6–7; 1:8–12) plus a single text (1:13). The use of biblical texts to make an argument (known as a *catena* or *florilegium*) assumes that the texts are authoritative and probative. Examples can be found among the Qumran scrolls and in the NT (e.g., Rom 3:10–18). It is not certain that there was a cult of angels or an angel Christology that needed to be combated. The author's main concern is to show the Son's qualitative superiority to angels on the basis of Scripture.

In the first pair of OT texts (Ps 2:7 and 2 Sam 7:14) the author assumes that God is the speaker and is addressing Christ. Both OT texts were associated originally with the Davidic Messiah, the first as part of the coronation ritual, and the second as an element in Nathan's prophecy to David. In both cases the Messiah is called "my Son," something God never calls an angel (though angels collectively are sometimes called "sons of God").

In the second pair (Deut 32:43/Ps 97 [LXX 96]:7 and Ps 104[LXX 103]:4) the assumption is that the third-person singular pronouns ("he, his, him") refer not to God but to the Son. In the first text the angels are said to worship the Son, thus admitting his superiority to them. The second text identifies angels as servants of the Son and so creatures who are inferior to him.

In the third pair (Ps 45 [LXX 44]:7–8 and Ps 102 [LXX 101]:26–28) the assumption is that the one addressed is the Son and that he is properly called "God" and "Lord." Originally part of a royal wedding song, Ps 45:7–8 affirms that the Son as the anointed one (Messiah/Christ) presides over a righteous and eternal kingdom. Ps 102:26–28 contrasts the eternity of Christ with the corruption that happens to material goods like clothing, and proclaims him to be the same forever (see 13:8). These texts suggest that as God and Lord the Son is qualitatively superior to angels.

The final text (Ps 110 [LXX 109]:1), already alluded to in 1:3*b*, is (like Ps 2) taken from the coronation ceremony and is here understood as addressed to the Son. As the argument of Hebrews unfolds, Jesus' passion, death, resurrection, and ascension will be interpreted as moments in his exaltation to God's right hand. In 1:14 the author concludes that angels are merely servants of God and their mission is to help humans "inherit salvation."

2:1–9. Superior Salvation. Good preachers combine biblical interpretation and personal application. The exhortation in 2:1–4 begins with a call to pay greater attention to the teachings of Scripture with three first-person plural verbs ("we"), culminating in a warning not to "drift away." The image is that of the ship failing to come to shore into its harbor and thus floating away aimlessly. For Christ as a "a sure and steadfast anchor of the soul," see Heb 6:19.

The seriousness with which the salvation offered under the new covenant is to be taken is indicated by a comparison with the old (Sinai) covenant. The reasoning here is from the lesser to the greater (as is common in both Greco-Roman and rabbinic rhetoric). The Sinai covenant, which is said to have been given "through angels" (see Acts 7:53; Gal 3:19), specified punishments for the infractions of it (2:2). If that covenant was

binding and taken seriously, how much more seriously should the new covenant through Christ (2:3*a*) with its even greater promise of salvation be taken.

The nature of this covenant and the salvation associated with it are specified further in 2:3*b*–4. It takes its starting point from Jesus' proclamation of God's kingdom. It has been given witness by Jesus' first followers and transmitted to the next generation. And it is carried on in church life through "signs and wonders" and the exercise of the charisms. The trinitarian dimension of this superior salvation is brought out by mentions of "the Lord" (Jesus) as well as "God" and the "Holy Spirit." Such a great act of salvation on God's part deserves even greater attention than the exodus from Egypt under Moses.

How this great act of salvation came about is explained with a christological interpretation of Ps 8:4–6 in 2:5–9. Psalm 8 celebrates the dignity of humans (literally "man" and "son of man") as only a little less than that of angels. The author of Hebrews finds in "man" and "son of man" the person of Jesus. Whereas care of this world or age was assigned to angels (Dan 10:20–21; 12:1), the world or age to come (which has already begun with Christ) is now subordinated or subjected to the risen Christ. In his incarnation and especially in his passion and death, Jesus was made lower than the angels "for a little while." But now since his resurrection, he is "crowned with glory and honor" (see Phil 2:6–11). Although his present dominion over all creation may not yet be visible to all, it is nonetheless real. Moreover, all humans can now participate in the benefits of his vicarious suffering and death, and so come to right relationship with God (justification) through him.

2:10–18. The Son's Solidarity with Humans. What is called "fitting" in 2:10 is a basic theme in Hebrews: In bringing humans to divine glory, God the creator and sustainer of the universe has sent his Son to be our forerunner or "pioneer" (*archēgos*) through his passion, death, and resurrection. The Son is "perfect" (*teleios*) in the sense of having achieved the intended goal or end (*telos*) of his mission. To do so, the Son became one of us and shared our humanity even to the point of suffering and death.

The basis of the solidarity between the one who sanctifies (Christ) and those who are sanctified (humans) is the fatherhood of God (2:11). Christ's solidarity with humans is demonstrated in 2:12–13 with more OT quotations in which Christ is assumed to be the speaker. According to Ps 22 (LXX 21):22 Christ proclaims God's name to his fellow humans and praises God in their assembly. According to Isa 8:17 and 18, Christ first professes his trust in God and then identifies himself as being in solidarity with his brothers and sisters. As the pioneer of our salvation, Christ has gone through what we go through (suffering and death) and so can bring us closer to our common Father. Thus he functions as the perfect mediator between God and humans.

Why did God become human? This is a famous question in Christian theological history (*Cur Deus homo?*). The answer given in 2:14–15 is that in this way God could free humans from the (cosmic-apocalyptic) power of death and from the (psychological) fear of death. By sharing fully in our human weakness and undergoing the physical death that awaits us all, Christ overcame and defeated the forces that had enslaved humans. According to 2:16, Christ did this not to help angels (who do not die) but rather to help humans (who do die). The descendants of Abraham include not only the people of Israel but also those who share Abraham's faith in God's promises (Gal 3; Rom 4).

In 2:17 the author introduces the two central christological images of Hebrews: Christ is the "merciful and faithful high priest" who willingly offered himself as the perfect sacrifice for our sins. To do so, he became one of us. The idea of suffering as a test or discipline is common in the Bible and elsewhere. In the case of Christ the Son of God who became human for us, the test (2:18) revealed what kind of Son of God he is (see Matt 4:1–11 and Luke 4:1–13) and enabled him as the merciful and faithful high priest in order to help other humans persevere during their testings.

3:1–6. Superior to Moses. The comparison with Moses is designed not to denigrate Moses but rather to affirm the qualitative superiority of the Son in his status and role. Both are distinguished for their fidelity to God. But Moses was faithful as a servant in God's household (the people of God), whereas Christ is faithful as the Son of God who presides over God's household. Just as in ancient households the firstborn son outranked every servant, so Christ the Son outranks Moses the servant in the economy of salvation.

The author's direct address to the hearers in 3:1 as "holy partners in a heavenly calling" reminds them of their solidarity with God's Son. The christological titles of "apostle" and "high priest," which appear only in the Hebrews in the NT, recall from 2:10–18 why the hearers can now approach God with confidence and pride (3:6).

The comparion developed in 3:2–6 takes its starting point from Num 12:7 with its description of Moses as the servant who was "faithful in all God's house." Here God's house is a metaphor for the people of God. The comparison proceeds on the levels of the house (3:3–4) and status within the household (3:5–6). With regard to the house, the builder who designs and constructs the house deserves and gets more honor than the house itself. The house is the reflection of the builder's good planning and execution. Here the comparison assumes the Son's divine status and role in creation (1:2, 10–12). With regard to their persons, Moses was faithful in the house as a servant of God and fulfilled his role as prophet and mediator on behalf of God's people. But Christ the Son was "over" the household in the sense that he exercised a directive and authoritative role within and for the people of God.

In 3:6*b* the author reminds his hearers that "we are his house," that is, the people of God. But he also warns them that this dignity is provisional upon their holding firm in faith and hope. The boldness and boasting that undergird their hope reside in the Son who is their pioneer, apostle, and high priest. The warning prepares for the exposition of Ps 95 that follows.

3:7–19. The Wandering People of God. Good preachers use examples. As a way of underlining the provisional character of his hearers' identity as the people of God, the author cites the negative example of the exodus generation (see Exod 17:1–7 and Num 14:22–23). He introduces the quotation of Ps 95 (LXX 94):7–11 as emanating from the Holy Spirit (see 10:15; cf. 2:6). The text of Ps 95:7–11 consists of a call to hear God's voice "today," a warning not to repeat the behavior of the exodus generation at Meribah ("rebellion") and Massah ("testing"), and a reminder of God's anger at their disobedience and his oath that they would not enter his "rest" (*katapausis*).

Good preachers actualize and apply Scripture to the needs of their congregations. Here the author's application begins and ends in 3:12 and 3:19 with the verb *blepō* ("take care ... we see"). In 3:12–13 he urges the hearers to avoid the unbelief and sinfulness displayed by the exodus generation. The term "today" connects the example of the exodus generation cited in David's psalm to the situation of early Christians tempted to give up their new found faith in Christ. The process of actualization is possible because God's word is "living and active" (4:12). The applicability of this text is underscored in 3:14–15 by a reminder of the provisional character of the hearers' identity as God's people and a repetition of Ps 95:7–8.

Good preachers often use rhetorical questions to get their points across. In 3:16–19 the author develops the application of the biblical passage to his hearers' situation with three series of rhetorical questions and their answers. The first series (3:16) identifies the rebels as the exodus generation. The second series (3:17) identifies the exodus generation as the object of God's anger. The third series (3:18–19) identifies the exodus generation as the object of God's oath that they would not enter his "rest." It also explains why they failed to do so. It was because of their disobedience and unbelief (see Num 14:22–23). But it leaves still unexplained what exactly is meant now by "rest."

4:1–13. God's Sabbath Rest. The author clarifies the meaning of "rest" by a combination of biblical exposition and exhortation. He shows that the real Sabbath rest is eternal life with God, and that it demands faith and obedience on the part of those who seek to enter it. As a good preacher the author includes himself among those being addressed ("let us," 4:1, 11). While the promise of entering God's rest remains open, it demands an appropriate response. Again in 4:2 the exodus generation provides the negative example to be avoided by Christians. There was nothing wrong with the promise and the message given to them. But because they did not respond with faith and obedience, they failed to enter the "rest" that God had prepared for them.

In 4:3–5 the author argues that this "rest" was not merely the land of Canaan. He prefaces his quotation of Ps 95:11 with a reminder that those who believe and obey can and do enter God's rest. And after it, he suggests that "rest" must refer to something connected with God's work at "the foundation of the world." This leads into the quotation of Gen 2:2 ("and God rested on the seventh day from all his works") and to the author's use of the ancient Jewish exegetical practice of interpreting one difficult biblical verse by another verse containing the same word or idea. In Gen 2:2 "rest" refers to God's own eternal life, and so the deeper or spiritual sense of Ps 95:11 must be the same.

In 4:6–8 the apparent tension or contradiction between "rest" in Ps 95:11 (the land of Canaan) and "rest" in Gen 2:2 (God's eternal life) is resolved by appeal to Ps 95:7 with its emphasis on "today." The eternal Sabbath rest promised by God remains open today to all who hear God's voice and act upon it. In Jewish circles in NT times David was regarded as the author of the Psalms (see Mark 12:35–37). But David lived long after Joshua led the remnants of the exodus generation into the promised land. The name "Jesus" is a variant of "Joshua" ("the Lord saves"), and in the author's logic Jesus of Nazareth has done what Joshua the son of Nun could not do, that is, lead God's people into eternal life ("rest") with God. And so with his emphasis on "today" David (writing in the promised land) reminds God's people that God's rest remains a possibility for them provided that they respond with faith and obedience in the present ("today").

In other words, "a sabbath rest still remains for the people of God" (4:9). The promise of rest demands a decision and an appropriate response now. Entering this rest will mean entering the kind of rest that God has enjoyed from the time of creation as described in Gen 2:2. The biblical exposition is capped off in 4:11 by an exhortation ("let us") to do whatever is necessary to enter God's perfect rest.

The reflection on the "word of God" in 4:12 serves as an interlude and a bridge between the first two major parts of Hebrews. It explains why Scripture and its interpretation are so important in Hebrews, and identifies Scripture as one way in which God communicates with humankind. While referring most obviously to Scripture (which for the author and his first hearers was the OT), it also points toward Jesus as the Word and Wisdom of God (Heb 1:1–4; John 1:1–18; Col 1:15–20) as the definitive revealer and revelation of God.

The reason why the author (and people of all generations) can engage in the actualization and application of Scripture is precisely because it is not a dead letter left over from the ancient past but rather remains the living and active word of God able like a two-edged sword to penetrate the deepest mysteries of God and human existence.

In 4:13 "before him" seems to refer back to God in the phrase "word of God" in 4:12. As a good preacher the author often tempers his most positive messages with reminders of the divine judgment to which we all must submit. Having laid before his hearers the possibility of eternal "rest" with God and having challenged them to respond positively with faith and obedience, he now warns them that they must render an account before the divine judge who will reward or punish them on the basis of their response.

II. Jesus the High Priest (4:14–10:18)

4:14–5:10. The Great High Priest. Whereas the first part of Hebrews focused on Jesus as the Son of God, the central section (4:14–10:18) emphasizes his identity as the great high priest. Since Jesus belonged to the tribe of Judah rather than to the priestly tribe of Levi, he could not have functioned as a Jewish priest during his lifetime. Fully aware of this fact (see 7:14), the author must explain how Jesus could ever be called a "great high priest."

In the first explanation (4:14–16), the author alternates between theological statements and exhortations. Just as on the Day of Atonement according to Lev 16 the Jewish high priest passed through the curtain separating the Holy of Holies from the rest of the Temple complex, so Jesus the Son of God has passed through the heavens (in his resurrection and ascension) into the heavenly temple. The first exhortation (4:14b) encourages the hearers to persevere in their profession of Christian faith. Then he notes that just as the Jewish high priest as a weak human could sympathize with those for whom he offered sacrifices on the Day of Atonement, so Jesus as fully human knew human weakness and had been thoroughly tested (though without sinning) to the point of offering himself as the perfect sacrifice for sins.

The second exhortation (4:16) urges the hearers to approach God not with fear but rather with confidence in full expectation of receiving mercy and divine favor.

In the longer discussion of Jesus' high priesthood in 5:1–10, the author focuses on the themes of mediatorship, solidarity, and divine appointment. He first predicates in 5:1–4 three characteristics of "every high priest" and then in 5:5–10 shows in reverse order how Christ fulfills each of them. In offering sacrifices for sins "every high priest" serves as a mediator between God and humans (5:1), is able to sympathize and deal gently with sinners because he too is a sinner and offers sacrifice not only for others but also for himself in solidarity with them (5:2–3), and must be called and approved by God just as Aaron (Moses' brother) was (5:4).

Then in 5:5–10 the author shows how Jesus met these three criteria. That he was called and appointed by God to be a great high priest is deduced from the combination of Ps 2:7 and Ps 110 (LXX 109):4 in which God is understood to be the addressing Jesus and designating him as both Son and high priest (5:5–6). Next in 5:7–8 Christ's solidarity with other humans is established with reference to his suffering and death. His plea to be saved from death (in Gethsemane?) was indeed heard in his being raised from the dead. Despite his divine sonship he showed himself obedient to his Father's will and in solidarity with humans through his sufferings. Finally, according to 5:9–10, by fulfilling his mission to bring about right relationship between God and humans he proved himself to be the effective mediator needed to make the hope for "eternal salvation" possible for all humans The allusion to Ps 110:4 ("a high priest according to the order of Melchizedek") foreshadows the full explanation of Christ's non-Levitical priesthood in Heb 7.

5:11–6:12. Call to Spiritual Renewal. Between identifying Jesus as the great high priest and explaining the priesthood of Melchizedek, the author places a long exhortation (see 10:19–39). It consists of a rebuke, a warning, and a word of encouragement.

The rebuke (5:11–6:3) begins with an admission that the priesthood of Christ is hard to explain. But in 5:12 the author blames his hearers for their spiritual immaturity as shown in their failure to grasp the "oracles of God," which are most likely those OT passages that point toward and find their fulfillment in Christ (see 6:1). While by now they ought to be teachers, they remain in their spiritual infancy like small children still being fed with milk rather than with solid food. In 5:13–14 he elaborates his distinction between the spiritually immature ("unskilled in the word of righteousness") and the mature ("trained by practice to distinguish good from evil"). For the author as well as other NT writers, Christian spirituality involves both doctrine and practice. The rebuke is softened in 6:1–3 by the resumption of first-person plural language ("let us"). The author urges his hearers to move forward from the basics of Christian life toward greater spiritual maturity. His list of basics includes repentance and conversion, rites of initiation, and belief in resurrection and final judgment. But he realizes the no progress is possible without God's help.

The warning in 6:4–8 is directed against apostasy. In the strongest terms ("it is impossible") the author contends that there will be no restoration for those who have adopted Chrisianity and then reject it. Such persons are saying that Jesus' passion and death had no effect. The act of apostasy nullifies the confession that Christ died for our sins. For further harsh words about apostasy, see Heb 10:26–29 and 12:17. The point is driven home by the comparison in 6:7–8 between good soil that produces an abundant crop and receives God's blessing, and bad soil that produces only thorns and thistles and deserves to be burned up. For a more extensive treatment of the problem of postbaptismal sin in the mid-second century church at Rome, see *Shepherd of Hermas*, in which the solution is to allow one act of repentance after baptism but no more than that (see *Mand.* 4.3.1–7; *Sim.* 8.8.2–5).

Recognizing the severity of his teaching in the exhortation thus far, the author in 6:9–12 consoles his hearers by addressing them as "beloved" for the first and only time, and by offering them words of encouragement and hope. He expresses confidence that they will attain to "the things that belong to salvation" on the basis of God's justice and their good works, especially the love that they have shown to other Christians ("the saints"). The reason why he has been exhorting them is so that they may attain what they hope for, that is, eternal life with God. While not withdrawing his charge of spiritual sluggishness, he urges them to display even greater faith and patience in order to "inherit the promises."

6:13–20. God's Promise and Oath. In Gen 12:1–3 God promised to make Abraham into a great nation, and in Gen 15:5–6 he repeated the promise to make Abraham's descendants as numerous as the stars in the sky. In Gen 22:16–18, after Abraham had proved his obedience to God's word by his willingness to sacrifice Isaac, God reiterated the promise, "I will surely bless you and multiply you." There the promise is prefaced with an oath: "By myself I have sworn, says the Lord." By his patient waiting Abraham eventually received the promise of many descendants through Isaac (who is a type of Christ).

The combination of God's promise and oath in Gen 22:16–18 leads the author into a reflection in Heb 6:16–18 on the nature of oaths (see also 7:20–22). People usually swear by someone greater than themselves, and often close off arguments or debates with oaths ("I swear to God"). Since no one is greater than God, God can only swear by himself ("by myself I have sworn"). The two "unchangeable things" are God's promise and God's oath. In the context of Hebrews, the heirs of the promise are Christians as the people of God descended from Abraham ("we"). They now can obtain what Abraham was looking for—"a better country, that is, a heavenly one" (11:16).

In 6:19–20 the author returns to the pivotal role played by Jesus in fulfilling God's promise. His role is described with images from three different contexts: nautical ("anchor of the soul"), military ("forerunner, pioneer, scout"), and cultic ("high priest"). The third image sets the stage for identifying Jesus as a priest according to the order of Melchizedek.

7:1–28. Jesus' Superior Priesthood. Besides Ps 110 (LXX 109):4, Melchizedek is mentioned in Gen 14:17–20 in the context of Abraham's victory over a coalition of kings. In their encounter Melchizedek blesses Abraham, and Abraham gives him one tenth of the spoils (a tithe). The name "Melchizedek" can be translated "king of righteousness" or "righteous king," and "Salem" (which is probably a form of Jerusalem) is connected with the Hebrew word for "peace." In 7:3 the author notes that in Gen 14 Melchizedek appears out of nowhere and soon disappears. The absence of his genealogy and of any notice of his further activities makes Melchizedek into a type of Christ who existed before creation (1:2) and now lives forever.

In 7:4–10 the author focuses on two elements in Gen 14:17–20: Abraham gave a tithe to Melchizedek, and Melchizedek blessed Abraham. We expect that an inferior figure might give a tithe to a superior person. By giving a tithe to Melchizedek, Abraham in effect acknowledged his superiority. Likewise, we expect that a superior person might bless an inferior one. By accepting Melchizedek's blessing, Abraham again acknowledged his own inferiority to him. What made this case even more significant for the author was that Abraham was the great-grandfather of Levi, the son of Jacob from whom Jewish levitical priests derived their identity as priests. The author imagines that Levi was somehow already present in "the loins of his ancestor," and thus Levi also acknowledged the superiority of the priesthood of Melchizedek.

In 7:11–19 the author tries to show that Jesus belonged to this older and better priesthood of Melchizedek. He shifts back to the only other OT text about Melchizedek (Ps 110:4) and interprets it as pointing toward the eternal and therefore superior priesthood of Christ. He argues that if perfection (access to God) were possible through the levitical priesthood, there would have been no mention of another priesthood (that of Melchizedek) in the Bible. He admits in 7:13–14 that Jesus could not have functioned as a levitical priest according to the OT law because he belonged to the tribe of Judah and not to the tribe of Levi. By what right then can he speak of Jesus as the great high priest? The chief point of likeness between Melchizedek and Jesus is their eternity (7:3). What made Christ "a priest forever according to the order of Melchizedek" was his resurrection and exaltation ("through the power of an indestructible life," 7:16). Whereas the sacrifices offered by the levitical priests could not produce right relationship with God, Jesus' self-offering has given humans a "better hope" in approaching God (see 4:14–16).

Having established that Christ belongs to the older and better priesthood of Melchizedek, the author in 7:20–25 contends that Christ's priesthood is superior to the levitical priesthood in other respects. Since Ps 110:4 is prefaced by another divine oath ("the Lord has sworn," see 6:13–20), the promise attached to this priesthood is founded on the "better covenant" established through Jesus (see 6:13–20). Moreover, although there had been many levitical priests and all died, the risen Christ lives forever. And so his priesthood is permanent, and he can at any time exercise his priestly ministry to "save those who approach God through him" (7:25). The comparison concludes in 7:26–28 with a list of Christ's attributes as the great high priest ("holy, blameless, undefiled ...") and a contrast with the levitical priests who every day offered material sacrifices for their own sins and those of the people. In 7:27 the author expresses the major thesis of his whole sermon: "this he [Christ] did once for all when he offered himself." In other words, Christ is both the offering and the priest, that is, the perfect sacrifice for sins and the great high priest who offered that sacrifice. In 7:28 the author observes that whereas under the Mosaic law a succession of weak men were appointed high priests, God has sworn an oath (see 7:20–22) that the Son (the risen Jesus) should be the one great high priest forever.

8:1–13. Minister of the New Covenant. After a summary of ch. 7 ("we have such a high priest"), the author describes the risen Christ in terms of Ps 110 (LXX 109):1 ("Sit at my right hand") and defines his present occupation as "minister in the sanctuary and true tent." The Greek word *leitourgos* refers to a public benefactor who provides at his own expense some event, entertainment, monument, or service for the local populace. The benefaction provided by Christ—access to "the throne of grace" (4:16)—is the greatest one of all.

The author imagines the heavenly realm as containing the ideal sanctuary that provided the blueprint for the tabernacle in the wilderness and the Temple. What sounds like a Platonic idea is given a biblical basis in 8:5 by the quotation of Exod 25:40. Although Jesus could not have functioned as a levitical priest in the earthly tabernacle, he now exercises his priestly service (*leitourgia*) in the "true tent" in the heavenly realm. The earthly tabernacle (and the Temple) was merely a "sketch and shadow of the heavenly one" (8:5). Through his death and resurrection Jesus now fulfills his priestly role as "mediator of a better covenant" that is based on "better promises" than those on which the Sinai covenant was founded.

Reference to a "better covenant" leads into the longest sustained OT quotation (Jer 31:31–34) in the NT. The author's main point (8:7) is that talk about a "new" covenant suggests that there was something wrong with the old one. Moreover, since God is the speaker in Jer 31:31–34 ("says the Lord"), it is God who found fault with the Sinai covenant. The author uses the OT quotation to bolster his idea of a new and better covenant enacted by Christ, and his contention that the Sinai covenant failed to achieve its desired effect (right relationship with God) because the people failed to observe it properly. By contrast, the new covenant comes directly from God (cf. 2:2) and is interior in the sense that it is written on the hearts and minds of God's people in Christ. Moreover, this new covenant can bring about genuine forgiveness of sins through the mercy of God.

In a concluding comment on the OT "new covenant" text, the author in 8:13 declares that the first (Sinai) covenant is now "obsolete." Then he qualifies that judgment by noting that the first covenant is "growing old" and "will soon disappear." In other words, it still exists, and when and how it will disappear is not made clear. Will it be with the destruction of the Second Temple (as with Jeremiah's prophecy about the First Temple) or with the full coming of God's kingdom (as with Paul's hope in Rom 11:25–32)? At any rate, the author's qualification pulls him back from full-scale supersessionism (declaring the Sinai covenant absolutely null and void), though among the NT writings Hebrews does come closest to supersessionism.

9:1–10. The Earthly Sanctuary. In preparation for treating the perfect sacrifice of Christ, the author describes the earthly sanctuary (first the tabernacle or tent of meeting, and then the Jerusalem Temple) at which sacrifices were offered daily and especially on the Day of Atonement. The description is based mainly on Exod 25–26 and Lev 16. He begins and ends by referring to the "regulations" of the old covenant under which that worship was carried out.

After noting the Holy Place (which he calls the outer tent) and its furnishings in 9:2, he focuses in 9:3–5 on the Holy of Holies (the inner tent) and its furnishings. According to the ritual described in Lev 16, the high priest once a year, on the Day of Atonement, entered the Holy of Holies and sprinkled blood on the "mercy seat" in order to "wipe away" (the basic meaning of the Hebrew verb *kipper*) his own sins and those of the people. In 9:8–10 the author asserts that this ritual was at best a symbol that fit the present (now past) age. Nevertheless, these material rituals (especially sprinkling the blood of sacrificial animals) were incapable of really cleansing the consciences of worshipers. They were only provisional until the new age inaugurated by Jesus' life, death, and resurrection took effect.

9:11–22. The Blood of Christ. In the biblical world (and in many places today) blood is a symbol of life rather than death, and is regarded as an agent of purification rather than defilement. Here the author reflects on the power of Christ's blood to take away sins and to inaugurate the new covenant. In 9:11–14 he contrasts the sacrifices of the high priest on the Day of Atonement and the sacrifice of Christ on Good Friday. The sacrifice of Christ was set in the heavenly tabernacle made by God, involved his own precious blood rather than animal blood, and had the effect of obtaining eternal redemption. Whereas the blood of the animals offered in sacrifice at the tabernacle (and the Temple) pertained to the realm of the flesh (the material), the blood of Christ shed in his passion and death as part of the perfect sacrifice offered to God through the Holy Spirit is able to purify the interior spirit ("conscience") of persons and enable them to worship the living God.

In 9:15–22 the author shows how the blood of Christ inaugurated the new covenant. According to 9:15, the sacrificial death of Christ made possible redemption from the transgressions committed under the old covenant and opened up the possibility of eternal life under the new covenant. To explain why Christ had to die, the author in 9:16–17 plays on the double meaning of the Greek word *diathēkē* as "last will" and "covenant." Just as a last will and testament does not take effect until the person dies, so the new covenant did not take effect until Christ died. In 9:18–21 he goes on to remind the readers that when the old or first covenant was inaugurated, Moses sprinkled blood on the sacred vessels and on the people (Exod 24:3–8). Finally in 9:22 he clinches the argument by alluding to Lev 17:11 ("life ... is in the blood") and by insisting that there is no forgiveness of sins without the shedding of (Christ's) blood.

9:23–28. The Priestly Work of Christ. In the author's Platonic worldview spiritual realities are better than material things. According to 9:23–24, the rituals of the Day of Atonement and the earthly sanctuary were mere "sketches" of Jesus' perfect self-sacrifice for sins and the heavenly sanctuary that he has entered. His sacrifice was "perfect" (*teleios*) in the sense that it achieved its goal or end (*telos*). Whereas the Jewish high priest entered the earthly sanctuary every year with animal blood, Christ has entered the heavenly sanctuary once for all with his own blood and removed sin by the sacrifice of himself (9:25–26). His priestly action marked the end of "this age" and the beginning of "the age to come." Yet his priesthood has not ended. In the present time he appears before God on our behalf as a mediator, and in the future he "will appear a second time" to save those who are awaiting him. The priesthood of Christ involves purifying us from past sins, mediating for us in the present, and delivering us in the future.

10:1–18. Christ's One Perfect Sacrifice. At the end of the central section of Hebrews the author restates several of his main points. In 10:1–14 he asserts that the OT law was a "shadow" of better (spiritual) realities, and that its material sacrifices could never achieve what Christ's offering of himself did. The very fact that the old covenant stipulated that its sacrifices had to be offered year after year indicated that they never achieved the goal of bringing humankind into right relationship with God. In a kind of *reductio ad absurdum* the author in 10:4 observes that "it is impossible for the blood of bulls and goats to take away sins."

In 10:5–10 he uses Ps 40:6–8 to underscore the superiority of Christ's sacrifice to the material sacriifces offered by the OT priests. He assumes that Christ is the speaker in the psalm, and that at the incarnation he recited the words of Ps 40 according to which the sacrifice of his body would replace the material sacrifices offered in the sanctuary. The author argues that the sacrifices of the first covenant have been superseded by the one perfect sacrifice of Christ. It was perfect in the sense of having reached its goals of the forgiveness of sins, right relationship with God, and eternal life with God. This sacrifice was in accord with God's will, brought about sanctification for humans, and took place in "the body of Jesus Christ once for all" (10:10).

Once again in 10:11–14 the author contrasts the repeated sacrifices made by the levitical priests with the single, effective sacrifice made by Christ and his subsequent exaltation at God's right hand in fulfillment of Ps 110 (LXX 109):1. In 10:15–17 he comes back to Jer 31:31–34 (see 8:8–12) with its themes of the new covenant, written by God on the hearts and minds of humans, and bringing about the forgiveness of sins. With 10:18 he proclaims Christ's one perfect sacrifice as the only remedy for sin and thus the end of the material sacrifices offered under the old covenant. This means that all Christian discourse about sacrifice and priesthood must take its starting point from the one perfect sacrifice offered by Christ the great high priest (as in Hebrews), and not from the OT legislation about sacrifices and the levitical priesthood (as in the Torah).

III. Implications for Christian Life (10:19–13:25)

10:19–39. Exhortation to Persevere. The structure of this long exhortation is similar to the one in 5:11–6:12. It consists of an appeal (10:19–25), a warning (10:26–31), and a word of encouragement and hope (10:32–39). In this section and those that follow the author draws out some implications of the divine sonship and the priesthood of Christ for Christian life.

As a good preacher the author begins his appeal (10:19–25) by recalling and building on the two great themes of the preceding section: Christ's sacrifice that made access to God possible, and Christ as the great high priest now presiding over the world. The three appeals in 10:22–25 ("let us") concern faith, hope, and love, respectively, and are based on what Christ has done in the past, what he promises to do in the future, and what should go on in the present within the Christian community. The suggestion that some have been absenting themselves from the community assemblies recalls the rebuke about their spiritual sluggishness in 5:11–6:12.

The warning in 10:26–31 (see 6:4–8) concerns postbaptismal sin in general and apostasy in particular. Since the OT sacrifices have been superseded and since the apostate has effectively spurned Christ's one perfect sacrifice for sins (10:29), there can be no remedy for this sin. If sins of idolatry and blasphemy merited the death penalty in the Mosaic law on the testimony of two or three witnesses (Deut 17:6), how much more will the penalty be for those who sin against God, the Son, and the Holy Spirit (10:28–29; see 2:1–4). In 10:30–31 the author drives home the seriousness of the warning by quoting Deut 32:35–36 ("Vengeance is mine") about divine vengeance and then issuing the dire statement, "It is a fearful thing to fall into the hands of the living God."

In 10:32–39 (see 6:9–12), the author closes his exhortation with some words of encouragement and hope. He first reminds the hearers in 10:32–34 how well in the past they have endured persecution, abuse, and loss of material possessions, since they knew that they "possessed something better and more lasting." Then in 10:35–38 he urges confidence and patience in the hope of receiving the reward of eternal life with God. With a combination of Isa 26:20 and Hab 2:4 he reminds them that Christ ("the one who is coming") will come soon and will reward the righteous who have lived by faith. Finally in 10:39 he associates himself with his hearers again ("we") as people who have faith and can expect to be saved when Christ returns.

11:1–40. Examples of Faith. The mention of faith in 10:39 leads into a catalogue of models of persevering faith from the OT. Similar lists of heroes appear in Sir 44–49 and Wis 10:1–11:4. As a good preacher the author develops a rhythm and intensity by introducing the examples with the expression "by faith" (the literary figure known as anaphora)

The famous definition of faith in 11:1 poses problems of translation and interpretation. That faith involves "things hoped for" and "things not seen" is clear enough. The problem comes with the Greek words *hypostasis* and *elenchos*, and whether they should be translated subjectively ("assurance ... conviction") as in the NRSV, or objectively ("realization ... evidence") as in the NAB (Revised). Of course, faith always has both subjective and objective elements, and it is often

hard to separate the two. The examples that follow are intended to illustrate the programatic statement in 11:1–2. The first set of examples (11:3–7) are taken from Gen 1–11: creation, God's acceptance of Abel's offerings, the assumption of Enoch into heaven, and the rescue of Noah from the flood. The author's comment in 11:6 insists that faith is necessary in order to please God, approach God, and be rewarded by God.

The second set of heroes of faith (11:8–22) includes figures mentioned in Gen 12–50. The focus is Abraham who by faith set out from his homeland, believed that he and Sarah would conceive a child in their old age, and was willing to sacrifice his son Isaac at God's command. However, Abraham never attained what he really wanted, which was to be in his true homeland in the city of God (11:10, 14). Thus he and the other early heroes of faith remained "strangers and foreigners on the earth" (11:13). Why Abraham was willing to sacrifice Isaac (Gen 22) is explained in 11:19 as due to his belief that God can raise the dead to life. The patriarchs Isaac, Jacob, and Joseph are praised in 11:20–22 for their willingness to look into the future and to trust that God would bless and guide his people.

The third set of heroes (11:23–31) includes Moses and other figures from the exodus generation. Faith guided and strengthened Moses in his infancy, in identifying with his own people, in willingness to leave Egypt, in observance of the first Passover, and in passing through the Red Sea. By the faith of Joshua and his people the walls of Jericho came down, and by faith Rahab the prostitute sheltered Joshua and Caleb who had been sent to spy out the land of Canaan. According to 11:26, the abuse that Moses suffered along with his fellow Israelites was in some way related to and prefigured the sufferings of Christ.

Good preachers know when to move on, and so in 11:32 the author begins to wind down his catalogue of OT examples of faith by asking, "And what more should I say?" After listing more heroes from Gideon to Samuel and the prophets, in 11:33–34 he gives examples of the triumphs that these and other heroes have experienced, and then in 11:35–38 he provides examples of the sufferings endured by women and men of faith. The references to resurrection in 11:35 most likely allude to 2 Maccabees (especially ch. 7), and help to explain why the martyrs could endure such terrible trials (see 11:19). They like Abraham were "strangers and foreigners on the earth" (11:13), in search of their heavenly homeland. Despite the admiration that the author has for all these OT heroes of faith, he contends that they did not obtain what has now been made available for "us" through Christ: forgiveness of sins, right relationship with God, and eternal life with God (11:39–40).

12:1–17. Another Call to Persevere. Throughout Hebrews there have been hints about persecution and abuse from outside the community and about discouragement and even apostasy within the community. As he nears the end of his long sermon, the author addresses these problems even more directly. He exhorts his hearers to "run with perseverance the race that is set before us" (12:1). He points to the OT heroes of faith listed in ch. 11 as a "cloud of witnesses" and to Christ as the "pioneer and perfecter of our faith" (12:2). He focuses on Christ's willingness to endure the shame of the cross in order to enter into glory at God's right hand (Ps 110:1). In 12:3–4 he points to Christ as an example of persevering faith that receives its rewards from God, and reminds his hearers that they have not yet suffered to the point of "shedding your blood" (martyrdom).

Having placed before his hearers the example of Christ and other examples of persevering faith, the author in 12:5–13 urges them to look upon their present sufferings as a divine discipline designed to strengthen them and prepare them to share in God's own holiness (12:10). In 12:5–6 he quotes Prov 3:11–12 to the effect that "the Lord disciplines those whom he loves," and in 12:7–11 he applies it to the present situation of the hearers. Just as good parents discipline their children, so God is disciplining them through the present sufferings. Just as the benefits of good parental discipline are great for children, how much greater will be the benefits from the discipline now being administered by God.

With allusions to Isa 35:3 and Prov 4:26 the author challenges his hearers in 12:12–13 to pull themselves together and get back on the road that leads to God. In 12:14–15 he urges them to pursue peace and holiness, and to avoid divisions (the "root of bitterness," Deut 29:18). And in 12:16–17

he brings up again the troublesome matter of apostasy (see 6:4–8 and 10:26–31) by pointing to the negative example of Esau who sold his birthright and was unable to get it back again (Gen 25:29–34; 27:30–45).

12:18–29. Call to Heavenly Worship. The author first contrasts worship under the old covenant symbolized by Mount Sinai (12:18–21) and worship under the new covenant symbolized by Mount Zion understood as the heavenly Jerusalem (12:22–24). The experience of God at Mount Sinai is described with features found mainly in Exod 19 but is presented in such a way as to inspire terror rather than awe. It even terrified Moses (Deut 9:19). By contrast the experience of God in the heavenly Jerusalem is called a "festal gathering" (12:22) and includes angels, the righteous dead, and the martyrs, God ("the judge of all"), and Jesus ("the mediator of a new covenant").

This contrast leads in 12:25–29 to a warning to heed "the one who is speaking" (God) on the grounds that if those who lived under the old covenant were punished severely for their failings, how much more those who live under the new covenant will suffer for their sins. At Mount Sinai God shook the earth, and in Hag 2:6 God promised to shake not only the earth but also the heavens "yet once more." Using his Platonist lens, the author distinguishes between the "shaken" (created, material things) and the unshakable kingdom (heaven). Since Christians already live in the unshakable kingdom symbolized by the New Jerusalem, they can already participate in the heavenly worship. However, they must always approach God "with reverence and love" since "our God is a consuming fire" (Deut 4:24; Isa 33:14).

13:1–19. Call to Community Life. In the present Christians still live on earth and find their identity in the Christian community. In 13:1–6 the author sets forth a general principle ("let mutual love continue") and gives advice about hospitality, compassion, chastity, and avoiding greed. By quoting Ps 118 (LXX 117):6 he affirms that with God as "my helper" there is no reason to fear.

In 13:7–19 instructions about attitudes toward past and present community leaders (13:7–9, 17–19) bracket reflections on community worship (13:10–16). The leaders mentioned in 13:7 may include not only those who evangelized the community but also OT heroes of faith as well as the apostles and Jesus. The description of Jesus in 13:8 ("the same yesterday and today and forever") sounds formulaic, but it also neatly summarizes the author's own understanding of him. The "regulations" about food most likely refer to the Jewish food laws and sacrifices, but may allude to the dispute at Rome between the "weak" and the "strong" (Rom 14:1–15:13). If so, the author clearly sided with the strong.

The instruction concerning worship in 13:10–16 covers many topics. The altar mentioned in 13:10 refers to the "altar" in the heavenly sanctuary at which Christ the great high priest now presides as opposed to the altar on earth where the levitical priests preside. In 13:11–12 the author alludes again to rituals carried out on the Day of Atonement (Lev 16) to explain why Jesus suffered outside the city gate, and once more contrasts the effects of animal sacrifices and of the one perfect sacrifice of Christ. Using this imagery in 13:13–14, the author urges his hearers to share in the abuse and shame that Christ suffered so that they may also share in his heavenly glory in "the city that is to come." Meanwhile, according to 13:15–16, the proper worship for Christians is "a sacrifice of praise to God," consisting of professions of faith, good works, and sharing possessions. These are the earthly sacrifices that "are pleasing to God."

The leaders mentioned in 13:17–19 include the current leaders of the hearer's community as well as the author himself. He urges their obedience to and cooperation with the former, and asks for prayers and good thoughts for himself until he meets them again in person.

13:20–25. Final Prayer and Greetings. The prayer in 13:20–21 asks that the "God of peace" may make the recipients able to do God's will and what pleases God. While the references to Jesus' resurrection and to his "blood of the eternal covenant" recall major themes in Hebrews, the identification of him as "the great shepherd of the sheep" is not (see John 10:11 and 1 Pet 5:4). The prayer concludes with a doxology.

In 13:22 the author describes his work as a "word of exhortation" (usually interpreted to mean a sermon), and characterizes it (somewhat disingenuously) as "brief." The mention of Timothy in 13:23 is the only link with Paul. The author may have known and worked with Timothy. Or perhaps the notice was added by a later scribe to establish a connection with Paul. The greeting from "those from Italy" in 13:24 can be interpreted to mean Christians who were originally from Italy but now resided elsewhere and were addressing other Christians in Italy (perhaps Rome). But it can also be read in the opposite way, that is, as referring to Christians in Italy who were greeting others somewhere outside of Italy. The final blessing in 13:25 ("Grace be with all of you"), while formulaic (see Titus 3:15), expresses well the author's own theological conviction that Jesus' life, death, and resurrection are the ultimate manifestation of God's favor toward humankind.

BIBLIOGRAPHY

H. W. Attridge. *The Epistle to the Hebrews.* Hermeneia (Philadelphia: Fortress, 1989); F. B. Craddock. "The Letter to the Hebrews." *NIB* (Nashville: Abingdon, 1998) 12:1–174; D. J. Harrington. *What Are They Saying About the Letter to the Hebrews?* (New York: Paulist, 2005); L. T. Johnson. *Hebrews: A Commentary.* NTL (Louisville: Westminster John Knox, 2006); E. Käsemann. *The Wandering People of God: An Investigation of the Letter to the Hebrews* (Minneapolis: Augsburg, 1984); C. R. Koester. *Hebrews: A New Translation with Introduction and Commentary.* AB 36 (New York: Doubleday, 2001); W. L. Lane. *Hebrews 1–8; Hebrews 9–13.* WBC 47A-B. (Dallas: Word Books, 1991); B. Lindars. *The Theology of the Letter to the Hebrews* (Cambridge: Cambridge University Press, 1991); T. G. Long. *Hebrews.* Interpretation (Louisville: Westminster John Knox, 1997); A. J. Mitchell. *Hebrews.* SP 13. (Collegeville, Minn.: Liturgical Press, 2007); V. C. Pfitzner. *Hebrews.* ANTC (Nashville: Abingdon, 1997); A. Vanhoye. *Structure and Message of the Epistle to the Hebrews* (Rome: Editrice Pontificio Istituto Biblico, 1989).

JAMES
ROBERT W. WALL

OVERVIEW

No scholarly consensus has been reached on any detail of this letter's point of origin, in large part because its hortatory idiom and lack of specific background information make it difficult to pin down a particular provenance and date. The Jewish character of James and its measured use of Hellenistic literary conventions (e.g., paraenesis, diatribe) have led some to suggest "the twelve tribes in the Dispersion" (1:1) is the actual address of a Jewish Christian community living somewhere outside Palestine. The absence of any mention of circumcision suggests a date prior to Paul's Gentile mission. This evidence coupled with images from first-century Palestine has led to the conclusion that the letter's author (or source) is likely James, the Lord's brother and leader of the Jerusalem church, whose exhortation—perhaps to dislocated former congregants living outside of Palestine—is an exercise of his pastoral office.

When considering the book's correspondence with the ideas and language of a Pauline canon already in circulation, however, others place James in a post-Pauline era when the earlier controversies of the Gentile mission were replaced by other conflicts between Pauline and non-Pauline Christianities. In this case, the letter's address may recall a Jewish (i.e., non-Pauline) Christianity represented by the figure and teaching of the venerated James the Just.

Theological considerations may prompt a shift of interest altogether from the letter's origins to its subsequent reception as the first of seven Catholic Epistles. This interpretive angle considers the role of James within the final redaction of the NT and privileges the ecclesial context of the letter. Whatever circumstances occasioned the composition of each Catholic Epistle, their subsequent formation into a discrete and coherent collection sometime during the fourth century was in some sense a response to the church's use (or misuse!) of its extant Pauline canon (cf. 2 Pet 3:15–16). This fresh combination of Catholic and Pauline letter collections provides the church with a more "apostolic" conception of Christian existence, and James' repeated insistence upon a practiced "faith that works" reminds the faith community that a professed "faith without works" forged by a myopic reading of Paul alone is an insufficient condition for maintaining a community's covenant relationship with God.

The Pauline index of the Jerusalem "Pillars" (Gal 2:9) finally frames the relationship between the two epistolary collections, Pauline and Pillars, aptly introduced by Jas 2:22 (author's trans.): "faith [in Christ=Pauline] is made complete by works [like Christ=Pillars]." This conception of Christian existence is the principal characteristic of friendship with God (Jas 2:23). For James, whenever the gospel is distorted by the appropriation of one to the exclusion of the other—whether as a faith without works or works without faith—the community's friendship with God is seriously threatened.

OUTLINE

I. Greetings (1:1)

II. Introduction: The Nature and Source of the Community's Wisdom (1:2–21)

III. An Essay on the Wisdom of "Quick Listening" (1:22–2:26)

IV. An Essay on the Wisdom of "Slow Speaking" (3:1–18)

V. An Essay on the Wisdom of "Slowing Anger" (4:1–5:6)

VI. Conclusion: The Future of the Wise Community (5:7–20)

DETAILED ANALYSIS

I. Greetings (1:1)

James follows the form of most Hellenistic letters by beginning with an author's salutation of the audience. The attribution of James recalls two earlier traditions that help to contextualize the reading of this letter: Paul mentions the story of Jesus' appearance to James on Easter (1 Cor 15:7; cf. Jas 2:1) and Acts portrays him as the leader of the Jewish church (Acts 15:13–21; 21:18–26; cf. Gal 2:11–12). His pastoral concern is aimed at the corporate effect of saving grace embodied in a congregation's purity practices (cf. Acts 15:20, 29; 21:25; cf. Jas 1:26–27); and his only appearances in Acts are to resolve intramural conflicts provoked by his church's misunderstanding of Paul's mission (cf. Acts 15:1–21; 21:21–26; cf. Jas 2:14–26).

The letter's recipients are greeted as "twelve tribes in the Dispersion." This address is symbolic of a religious location in which "twelve tribes" are believers whose spiritual "dispersion" (*diaspora*) within a hostile world unsettles their faith and tests their allegiance to God. James proffers wisdom that will help secure this community's embattled faith.

II. Introduction: The Nature and Source of the Community's Wisdom (1:2–21)

The main body of James is introduced by a powerful vision of Christian existence. Central to this vision is the believer's routine experience of "trials of any kind" (1:2), which tests a faith in God (1:3) but to which thoughtful believers respond with "nothing but joy." This response is possible when trials are "considered" against the horizon of a coming age when human existence will be "mature and complete, lacking in nothing" (1:4b). Restated as a beatitude, God promises to bless those who "endure temptation" with "the crown of life" (cf. Rev. 2:10) as reward for their devotion to God (1:12).

But hardship also occasions a theodicy that tests the devotion of immature believers who are "unstable in every way" (1:8). "Trials" (1:2) and "temptation" (1:12) translate the same Greek word, *peirasmos*, so that James is connecting suffering with the potential of spiritual failure. According to James, hardship can produce either a steady allegiance to God or it can "give birth to sin" and "death" (1:14–15). Although demonic impulses (cf. 3:15; 4:5, 7) and external factors (cf. 2:2–7; 5:1–6) may tempt the believer to failure, James stresses the individual's responsibility to

make wise choices since the inward "desire" is "one's own" (1:14) to control.

But the believer enjoys heavenly support in controlling his self-centered desire. When God is trusted as generous and impartial (1:5), God is petitioned for the necessary wisdom or knowhow one may lack to pass the spiritual tests that trials occasion. Rather than doubting God's goodness (1:6–8) or being deceived by the belief that God is responsible for one's misfortune (1:16), the knowing response is to petition "the Father of lights with whom there is no variation" (1:17b) for wisdom; and God will invariably respond with "generous acts of giving, with every perfect (*teleios*) gift" (1:17a). The perfect gift is "the word of truth" (1:18) because it is God-given and because it supplies the wisdom necessary for a life that is "mature (*teleios*) and complete" (1:4).

The stated content of "the word of truth" is a stock synthesis of proverbial wisdom—"let everyone be quick to listen, slow to speak, slow to anger" (1:19b); but the primary role of the letter's main body is to provide the reader with a fresh and elaborate commentary of this "implanted word that has the power to save your souls" (1:21).

III. An Essay on the Wisdom of "Quick Listening" (1:22–2:26)

The letter's main body consists of three essays that comment on the nature of a wise response that passes the test of faith. The sequence of these essays is determined by the proverbial triad of 1:19: accordingly, the first essay concerns the wisdom of "quick listening." Simply put, to listen quickly means to obey the "perfect law, the law of liberty" promptly (1:22–25), which commands the merciful treatment of the poor neighbor (1:26–2:7). "The distress of orphans and widows" (1:27) is a biblical metaphor for society's most vulnerable members, and their presence in a congregation occasions a spiritual test that requires a fresh application of heavenly wisdom. To care for poor and powerless is the hallmark of God's covenant-keeping people (cf. Exod 22:22; Deut. 24:17–21; Ps. 146:9; Isa. 1:17; Jer. 5:28; Acts 2:45; 4:32–35; 6:1–7; 9:36–42), and to abandon them risks God's displeasure (cf. 2:12–13).

Two case studies of "quick listening" are mentioned. The first concerns the community's leaders who discriminate against the poor in favor of the rich, giving the rich the best seats in the house while seating the poor "at my feet" (2:2–4). These practices are foolish in an assembly of the "glorious Lord Jesus Christ" (2:1), who exemplifies God's preferential option for the poor (cf. Luke 14:7–14). The second case studies discrimination in the civil-law court to draw a damning analogy between the community's leaders and the very rich they foolishly privilege who "drag you into court ... and blaspheme the excellent name" of Jesus (2:6–7; cf. Luke 18:1–8).

Two congregations are differently appraised by God (1:23–27, author's trans.). Those who "hear the word but are not doers" and so delude themselves since what they profess but fail to enact is worthless to God (v. 26; cf. 1:22–23; 2:15–16). Rather the "pure and undefiled" religion is approved by God because of what it does: it cares for its own poor without being contaminated "by the world" (1:27).

The word that is heard is "the perfect (*teleios*; cf. 1:4, 17) law, the law of liberty" (1:25). While this law is "perfect" because its source is divine (cf. Ps 18:7 LXX), the prior uses of *perfect* in Jas 1:4, 17 forge a still thicker meaning of perfection that relates the law to the congregation's moral practices. "Perfect" signifies the goal of Christian existence, formed in faithful reception of God's gifts (1:17–18) and in response to spiritual tests (1:3–4). A "perfect law," then, is a "word of truth" that "saves your souls"; the wise response is to obey such a law and live. Moreover, this phrase trades upon Torah's Jubilee legislation: the "law of liberty" concerns "the year of liberty" (Lev 25:8–24), which became important especially during the Second Temple period for fashioning a sociological model of God's coming kingdom (cf. Luke 4:16–21; Jas 2:5). The promise of future blessing introduced in 1:12 is here repeated to link enduring temptation/trials with the wisdom of law keeping.

The economic practices of the "glorious Lord Jesus Christ" (2:1) establish the criterion by which God measures the community's treatment of its poor (cf. 2:12–13). While the Lord's used here alerts the reader to the letter's Easter ethos, more significant is the question related to the reader's faithfulness: better translated, "do you have the faith of our Lord Jesus Christ?" This phrase recalls the similar phrase used by Paul in which "the faith of Jesus Christ" (cf. Rom 3:22; Gal 3:22, author's trans.) is a subjective genitive of the crucified Christ's faithfulness that secures the world's salvation from sin. James 2:1 is aimed differently: it concerns Christ's ministry to the poor in obedience to the "royal law" (2:8) rather than Christ's death on the cross.

The reception of the wisdom of quick listening is profusely illustrated by both positive and negative example. God's appraisal that "you do well if you really do the royal law" (2:8) contrasts sharply with the "senseless person" who supposes that "you do well" by merely professing orthodox faith (2:19–20) but without a complement of works (2:14–17).

Besides the example of Jesus, two other biblical figures, Abraham and Rahab, are mentioned as wise exemplars of caring for the poor in their distress. Their cases are introduced by the common-sense assertion that profession does not save. For example, if the pious benediction, "go in peace," is given to the hungry and naked without also feeding and clothing them, nothing redemptive happens either for the poor or for the community (cf. 2:14–17). The believer who claims to have the faith of Jesus apart from doing his will is no different from the shuddering demon who does the same (cf. 2:18–20).

The final example combines patriarch Abraham (2:21–24) and prostitute Rahab (2:25) to make a universally valid claim: a profession of "faith without works is also dead" (2:26). According to rabbinic tradition, Isaac's binding is Abraham's final exam. Whether he passes or fails his spiritual test secures the promises God makes regarding Israel's destiny. According to James, Abraham is befriended by God because his faith is "brought to completion by the works" (v. 22).

Rahab's story (cf. Josh 2:1–15) makes this same point by what it does and does not mention. Hardly another biblical figure offers a more impressive profession of faith than does Rahab (cf. Josh 2:8–11); yet James does not mention it. Only her hospitable and courageous actions toward "the messengers" are noted. The rhetorical effect is to impress upon the reader that the wise believer understands that God befriends people on the basis of their merciful "works and not by faith alone" (2:24).

IV. An Essay on the Wisdom of "Slow Speaking" (3:1–18)

The wisdom of "slow speaking" is directed at those who aspire to become teachers (3:1). The letter has already noted that even believers sometimes lack the wisdom necessary to control the inward desires that incline them toward doubt and sin (1:5–6, 7–8, 13–15). That is, "all of us make many mistakes" (3:2). This realism is deepened by the bracing awareness that God will judge believers on the basis of what they say and do (1:12; 2:12–13).

To slow down what one says is not a matter of better diction; it concerns the careful choice of words the teacher uses. The difficulty of controlling what is said is illustrated by three examples from everyday life with increasing tension. The teacher controls the tongue (= speech) much like the rider controls the bit to guide the movement of a horse (3:3) or the pilot controls the rudder to maneuver a ship through strong winds to safe harbor (3:4–5a). The teacher's failure to control the tongue is likened to the "small fire" (lit. "spark") that can destroy a great forest (3:5b–6a).

James applies the problem of a teacher's careless speech with damning effect (3:6): careless speech is a "world of iniquity (that) stains the whole body" (cf. 1:27) and directs the community's destiny—its "cycle of nature"—away from God's reign toward a future "inflamed by *Gehenna*" (author's trans.; cf. Mark 9:45, 47; 1 Enoch 26–27). *Gehenna* is the Hellenized form of Hinnom, a valley on the south side of Jerusalem used as a garbage dump. Over time this site became an important metaphor for evil and even envisaged as a possible location for the final defeat of those who have sinned against God. No doubt this is the subtext of James' use in v.6.

The more positive application of talking the walk is framed by the practical question: "who is wise and understanding among you?" (3:13). The question alludes to the instruction of Moses for Israel to search for "wise and understanding" leaders to broker disputes that might threaten the tribal confederacy (cf. Deut 1:12–13). The readers of this letter, faced with their own search for congregational leaders/teachers, are guided by a sharply worded contrast between two different kinds of wisdom with very different outcomes.

The wise and understanding teacher has a skill set that is not learned from experience or education; rather its source is a "wisdom from above" (3:17; cf. 1:17–18). Unlike the foolish teacher whose selfish character (cf. v. 14, 16a) is formed by a wisdom that "does not come down from above, but is ... devilish" (v.15) and whose résumé chronicles "disorder and wickedness of every kind" (v. 16b), the wise and understanding teacher is formed by "the wisdom from above" and mediates "a harvest of righteousness ... sown in peace" (v. 18).

The catalogue of virtues in v. 17, which characterizes the peace-making speech of the wise and understanding teacher, has many parallels in antiquity. Even though consisting of universally upheld virtues, such lists are carefully fitted into their writings to perform particular roles for their audiences. The Pauline letters, for example, include similar lists of virtue that characterize those in Christ (Gal 5:22–23). Central to Pauline anthropology is the profile of a new creature whose existence is the effect of divine grace made possible by the faithfulness of Christ and mediated by his life-giving Spirit. The anthropology of James assumes that believers must take responsibility for their destiny with God by making wise choices that resist doubt or their desire for worldly evils.

V. An Essay on the Wisdom of "Slowing Anger" (4:1–5:6)

Anger toward others stems from an inward desire for material pleasure and threatens the community's internal life (4:1–3). This text uses images of strife both military ("conflicts" and "war") and interpersonal ("disputes" and "murder") to characterize its seriousness. The experience of being poor can provoke the impulse to covet the worldly goods of others (4:4–5), which tests the believer's friendship with a God who resists the arrogant and exalts the pious poor (4:6–12; cf. 2:5). To slow down anger requires one to resist "friendship with the world" (4:4; cf. 1:27; 3:6) and submit to God. James conforms to teaching found in other Jewish texts that human nature contains two competing "spirits" or *yetsrim*—one inclined toward evil, the other toward good: to engage the one is to resist the other (4:7).

In response to this spiritual reality, v. 5 is better translated to pose a pair of rhetorical questions that expect a negative answer: "Or do you think Scripture says foolish things? Does the spirit that God made to dwell within us incline us intensely toward envy?" The wisdom of Scripture rather discloses that the promise of divine exaltation (vv. 6, 10) is aimed at a congregation that worships God by purifying its heart (vv. 7–9). The sanctified sinner no longer covets the goods of others but is a doer of God's law (4:11–12) that forbids coveting his neighbor's possessions.

The opening invocation, "Come now" (4:13*a*; 5:1*a*), links together two examples of friendship with the world to illustrate how a passion for things can subvert the believer's devotion to God and relations with others. The first example is the arrogant merchant (4:13–17) whose single-minded pursuit of financial profit takes him "to such and such a town" to "[do] business" (rather than God's law; cf. v. 15) and "[make] money" (rather than receive God's grace; cf. v. 6). The shift of pronoun to "you" (v. 14) suggests this merchant typifies the kind of arrogance opposed by God (v. 6). They are functional atheists who plan their lives as though God does not exist (cf. vv. 14, 16) instead of making choices that please God (cf. vv. 15, 17).

The related illustration is of the rich farmer whose practices embody the foolishness of those who choose friendship with the world rather than with God and so "wail for the miseries that are coming" (5:1). The choice against God rests on two catastrophic mistakes. The first is a misappraisal of the long-term worth of material goods: they do not endure but riches" rot, "clothes are moth-eaten ... gold and silver" rust (5:2–3; cf. Matt 6:19–21). The second is a faulty assessment of theodicy and God's sense of justice: their luxurious lifestyle, purchased at the expense of workers who are mistreated and underpaid, is the hard evidence of guilt that will be used against them in the heavenly court case convened by "the Lord of hosts" (v. 4). In a vivid reminder of the coming "great reversal," their death sentence will be carried out in "the last days" (v. 3) as a "day of slaughter" (v. 5).

The antecedent of James' curious reference to the murder of a single "righteous one" in v. 6 is much debated. In Christian tradition, the phrase fulfills the promise of the Isaianic servant whose suffering on behalf of the world is marked by his "righteousness" before God (Isa 53:11; cf. Luke 23:47). In a letter that emphasizes God's vindication of the pious poor and indictment of the rich (cf. 1:9–11; 2:2–7; 4:4–6), however, the metaphor more likely functions as a metonym of poor laborers who are starving for lack of food, either because of neglect (especially during famine) or juridical injustice (cf. 2:6–7). If the intended readers are believers whose marginal existence is characterized by these kinds of financial trials, then they might rightly hope—and so make their choices—for a future of reversed fortune, when the last will be first and the first last.

VI. Conclusion: The Future of the Wise Community (5:7–20)

The letter's conclusion recalls important catchwords from the letter's opening to form an *inclusio* that frames the three wisdom essays between. But this repetition is more than a retrospective on what has already been written; it supplies the principal motivation for following the letter's exhortation to make wise choices when faith is tested by tribulation: the coming triumph of the Lord is near (5:7–9). God's epic battle against and eventual victory over the evil forces that provoke human suffering is among Scripture's principal responses to the problem of suffering. The farmer's experience waiting for "the early and the late rains" (5:7) to water the crops to harvest exemplifies the kind of intelligent patience that awaits God's ultimate victory. This exhortation is made more urgent by the pointed assertion that the Lord's *parousia* is imminent (v. 8)—"see, the Judge is standing at the doors" (v. 9).

The exhortation not to engage in "[grumbling] against one another so that you may not be judged" (v. 9) recalls the story of Job (v. 11) who endured to the end despite his complaining friends. James places him among the prophets who suffered with patient confidence when they "spoke in the name of the Lord" (v. 10; cf. Luke 11:47–54). The background for this exemplary Job is the LXX, followed by the *Testament of Job*, which unlike his portrait in the Hebrew Bible links his famous patience with his merciful treatment of the poor and it to his eventual restoration by a "compassionate and merciful" God (*T. Job* 51–53; v. 11; cf. Jas 1:26–2:26). To care for the poor without complaint is to deal with life wisely.

This exhortation for patience is complemented by another to pray for healing (5:13–16a). Patience and prayerfulness are the twin dispositions of an apocalyptic worldview, which views Christian existence before the Lord's arrival through the lens of suffering and powerlessness. The opening imperative to pray for the lacking wisdom (cf. 1:5–6), which when "implanted" and acted upon is able to "save the soul" (1:21), is here recast as "the prayer of faith will save the sick" (v. 15). The elders are summoned because they "implant" the saving word in the community's life and so now lead in a liturgy of healing that "prays over (the sick)" and "[anoints] them with oil" (v. 14). The olive oil administrated "in the name of the Lord" can either be understood as medicinal or, more likely in a worship practice, as invocative of the powerful presence of the risen Lord who "will raise them up" (v. 15; cf. Mark 6:13; 9:38; Acts 3:6, 16)—whether at the end of the age or in physical healing is uncertain (cf. Acts 3:19–21). The logical connection between the healing of sick and the forgiving of sinner is thematic of the gospel tradition (vv. 15b–16a; cf. Matt 6:12).

The earlier uses of "righteous/-ness" in James suggest the "prayer of the righteous" (5:16) is "powerful and effective" because it coheres with God's pattern of salvation (cf. 2:23–24; 3:18). According to Jewish and Jesus traditions, the prophetic exemplar of effective prayer is Elijah (5:16b–18), whose words on Mt. Carmel produced rain because they aligned with God's words for Israel (cf. 1 Kgs 18; Sir 48:1–11; Luke 4:25). That is, prayer offered by the righteous for healing or forgiveness is a practice of wisdom because it produces "powerful and effective" results.

The final verses of James (5:19–20) form a benedictory that enlists readers for a mission to "save the sinner's soul from death" (cf. 1:21). These sinners are lapsed believers who have "[wandered] from the truth" of God's word (cf. 1:18, 21). Without this sacred compass, doubt and inward desire "[give] birth to sin" and sin, death (1:14–15). The practice of the wisdom of James, then, concludes on these final words of hope: the repentance and restoration of those believers who have failed their test of faith is mediated by the community made wise for salvation by the instruction of this letter (cf. 2 Tim 3:15).

BIBLIOGRAPHY

R. J. Bauckham. *James* (London: Routledge, 1999); P. H. Davids. *Commentary on James.* NIGTC (Grand Rapids: Eerdmans, 1982); P. J. Hartin. *James.* SP (Collegeville, Minn.: Liturgical Press, 2003); L. T. Johnson. *The Letter of James.* AB 37A (New York: Doubleday, 1995); R. W. Wall. *Community of the Wise: The Letter of James.* NTC (New York: Continuum, 1997).

1–2 PETER

M. Eugene Boring

1 Peter

Overview

This letter is attributed to Peter, one of the earliest disciples of Jesus (Mark 1:16–20; John 1:35–42), who became the principal leader of the earliest Jewish Christian community in Jerusalem and advocate of Jewish Christianity (cf. Gal 2:11–14). Peter later came to Rome, where he continued his apostolic ministry, which he finally sealed with a martyr's death (*1 Clement* 5–6; Ignatius *Romans* 4:3; cf. John 21:18–19). In Rome, the ministry of the Apostle Peter continued among disciples influenced by him and in a stream of tradition emanating from him.

Paul, advocate of Gentile Christianity, had also come to Rome and had been martyred there (*1 Clement* 5–6; 2 Tim 4:7–17; Acts 20:25, 36–38; 28:30–31). In the next generation, the church in the capital of the empire found itself the heir of both Paul and Peter, and the custodian of the traditions associated with each. While the traditions represented by Paul and Peter were different, they were not mutually exclusive alternatives, and were not seen as such by the Roman church, which in the latter part of the first century began to see itself as supporter of and teacher to other struggling churches outside Rome.

First Peter represents this Roman combination of Petrine and Pauline tradition expressed in a letter encouraging churches in five provinces of Asia Minor who are facing a hostile social situation. The letter includes and interprets a considerable amount of earlier Christian tradition, including materials used in teaching and liturgy. It is not, however, a baptismal sermon modified into the letter form. This view, popular in the last century, has now been generally rejected. Like the Pauline letters, it was intended for reading in the worship services of the congregations, not for private study. Like other early Christian letters, it functions not so much by directly teaching doctrine and offering specific instructions, but by projecting a narrative world that stretches from creation to eschaton, a grand story of which the God revealed in Christ is author, and which will have a worthy conclusion

at the final revelation of Jesus Christ. First Peter is thus preeminently a message of hope, encouraging its readers to understand themselves as called to follow the example of Christ in the context of a hostile world that misunderstands them, and to hold fast to their faith until the end. Although written in the name of the beloved apostle, 1 Peter was most likely not written by Peter himself (who was killed ca. 64 CE), but by one of his disciples in Rome, about 90 CE This conclusion is widely accepted in current scholarship for the following reasons. (1) The letter lacks the kind of material one would anticipate from an eyewitness, such as sayings of Jesus that would be relevant to the author's purpose. (2) Instead, the letter reflects much of the language and thought of the Pauline letters, and, like Paul, appeals to the OT (cited consistently in the LXX Greek translation) rather than sayings and deeds of Jesus. (3) *Paul's* companions are associated with *Peter* (Silvanus = Silas; Mark, 5:12–13). (4) The letter is written in sophisticated Greek, some of the best in the NT, not likely to have been written by a Galilean fisherman. (5) There are indications of a late date such as "Babylon" as a designation for Rome, which became current only after 70 CE. (6) Except for the first word, the letter makes no claim to authorship by an apostle, but specifically indicates that the letter was written by an elder (5:1).

Writing in the name of one's authoritative teacher in order to extend his teaching into a new situation was a common and respected practice in the ancient world. That 1 Peter was not written directly by Simon Peter does not impinge on its status as Holy Scripture, but acknowledging its pseudonymous authorship is an aid to understanding the text in its own terms.

Outline

I. Salutation (1:1–2)

II. Thanksgiving (1:3–12)

III. Body of the Letter (1:13–5:11)

A. The New Identity as the Elect and Holy People of God (1:13–2:10)

B. Christian Existence and Conduct in the Given Structures of Society (2:11–3:12)

C. Responsible Suffering in the Face of Hostility (3:13–5:11)

IV. Conclusion of the Letter (5:12–14)

DETAILED ANALYSIS

I. Salutation (1:1–2)

1:1. Apostle means "authorized representative." By attributing the letter to Peter, the author expresses the claim that the letter represents the apostolic faith. Pontus, Galatia, Cappadocia, Asia, and Bithynia were five Roman provinces comprising most of modern Turkey. The *elect* is the characteristic biblical designation of Israel as the chosen people of God (e.g. Deut 7:6; 10:15; 14:2; 1 Chron 16:13; Ps 105:6). Likewise, "exiles of the Dispersion" reflects the terminology used in the OT and Jewish tradition for the scattered people of Israel who live as Jews throughout the world, often in a hostile environment. The term designates "sojourners" or "resident aliens," people living in a land where they are more than tourists but do not have the rights of citizens ("transients," "undocumented migrant workers"; cf. Gen 23:4; Ps 39:12; Heb 11:13). The words are not meant literally, but express the outsider status in their own country which they now experience because of their Christian faith. The contrast is not between earthly life and their true heavenly homeland, but refers to their marginal social status in this world.

1:2. The readers are chosen because God the Father has destined them, has sanctified them through the Spirit, and set them apart for obedience to Jesus Christ. Sprinkling with blood reflects the language of the OT covenant (cf. Exod. 24:3–8). The readers are addressed as members of this (renewed) covenant, now sealed with the blood of Christ (Mark 14:24; 1 Cor 11:25; Heb 9:20; 10:29; 13:20).

II. Thanksgiving (1:3–12)

The salutation of Hellenistic letters was usually followed by a brief thanksgiving section that typi-

cally began with ""I thank God" (as e.g. Rom 1:8; 1 Cor 1:4), but could also begin with familiar synagogue form of prayer, "Blessed be God …" (2 Cor 1:3; cf. Eph 1:3).

1:3. The language of new birth continues to emphasize the divine initiative—people do not choose to be born, but are given life as a gift. The believer receives a new life of hope through the resurrection of Jesus Christ encountered by the word of God in Christian preaching (1:12, 23). For 1 Peter the Christian life has an essential future dimension. *Hope* in biblical perspective refers to that which is real, but not yet—the certain future victory of God. Hope plays an even more decisive role than "faith" for this author, and can serve as the one word that sums up the meaning of the Christian life as such (e.g. 1:3; 3:5, 15). This hope has to do with the inheritance God has already kept in heaven for believers, but the picture here is not of going up to heaven to receive it, but going forward in history to receive it in the last time (1:5) when Christ is revealed (1:7).

1:6. The trials are not the ordinary difficulties of everyday life, but the harassment and discrimination the readers suffer on account of their faith. The joy here described is not a superficial "feel good," but is a deep, inexpressible joy permeated by the presence and glory of God.

1:8. The contrast is not between author and readers, as though the author had seen Jesus but the readers had not, but is a statement about the Christian life as such. Christians, including the author, love, trust, and obey Christ on the basis of the faith that has come to them by Christian preaching and the power of the Holy Spirit (1:12).

1:9. In the biblical understanding, soul is not a part of the person, immortal or otherwise, but is a way of talking about the whole person (cf. 1:22; 2:25; 3:20; 4:19; in which the same Greek word is used).

1:10–11. Since they believed that the Christ had come and that the eschatological age had begun, early Christians reread their Bible in the light of this conviction, and found many texts they believed spoke directly of Christ and the church. The early Christian community rightly saw that the biblical prophecies had a future orientation, pointing to a later time when the ultimate plan of

God would be revealed. The readers were regarded suspiciously by their neighbors, who thought of them as belonging to a new cult. The author assures them that they have been incorporated into the plan of God of which the ancient prophets spoke, a plan that embraces all history from creation to the final revelation of Christ.

III. Body of the Letter (1:13–5:11)

A. The New Identity as the Elect and Holy People of God (1:13–2:10)

1:13. The flowing garments worn in the ancient Near East were tightened about the waist and hips in preparing for work. "Roll up your mental sleeves and get ready for hard thinking" is the modern equivalent. The ancient Israelites ate the first Passover "[with] their loins girded" (Exod 12:11; cf. Luke 12:35). The author throughout applies to Gentile converts the whole exodus experience of Israel: former slaves are freed by the mighty act of God, are redeemed by the blood of the lamb, have been made participants in the divine covenant within which they have pledged their obedience, and are presently underway through a series of testings and harassments toward their promised inheritance, en route becoming a holy people and royal priesthood. As Israel in the wilderness longed for the fleshpots of Egypt, Christians are now tempted to long for their former social life.

1:15. Holiness is the quality of being separate from the ordinary. It belongs first of all to God, the Holy One, the Wholly Other, the Creator who is different from everything created (Isa 6:1–5). God's people are holy because God has called them to live a distinctive life within the world as witnesses to God's mighty acts (2:9). The author applies Lev 19:2, originally spoken to Israel, directly to his Christian readers.

1:17–19. Since the readers, as newborn children of God, now invoke God as father, they must live differently from the way they have been conditioned to live by the cultural traditions inherited from their ancestors (lit. "fathers").

1:19. The imagery is from Exod 12:1–28. The Passover lamb was not a sacrifice for sins, but the means of deliverance from death and slavery. The *ransom* of Jesus' blood does not here deliver us from the guilt of sin, but from the old way of life, continuing the exodus imagery that forms much of the metaphorical framework for this section.

1:22. The love called for by the author should not be sentimentalized or romanticized. When outsiders said, "See how they love one another," they did not intend a compliment, but were expressing the resentment and suspicion of those who loved each other but disdained outsiders and had been charged with "hatred for the human race" (cf. Tacitus, *Annals* 15.44; Tertullian, *Apology* 39). First Peter specifically resists yielding to the temptation to show love only to insiders.

2:1–3. The family imagery continues. The newborn babes of the Christian family are to mature as they are nourished by the word of God that generated faith in them (cf. (Deut 8:3; Matt 4:4). They are to put away those attitudes and behavior that destroy community: malice, deceit, hypocrisy, envy, slander. They now belong to the household of faith, and their ethic cannot be individualistic and privatistic.

2:4–10. The metaphor now changes from household to the house itself. Making use of a collection of three "stone" texts that had already become traditional, the author understands the rejected-but-vindicated stone to be both Christ and the Christians (Isa 8:14; 28:16; Hos 1:6–9). Christian lives are paralleled to the life of Christ. He was and is rejected by the world in general (not just by the Jewish leaders); in him the Christian readers of 1 Peter recognize their own experience of being rejected by pagan society. Christ was vindicated; the rejected stone turned out to be the chief cornerstone. Christian readers will be vindicated at the eschaton.

The imagery expands still further, as additional biblical descriptions of Israel are applied to the Christian community. The readers are addressed as a "holy priesthood" or "royal priesthood" (2:5, 9). The point is that the Christian community as a whole plays the role of the continuing people of God in history, which includes being a priestly community on behalf of the world. Like the Israel of the Bible and history, the church as the people of God is called into being not for its own sake, but as an expression of the divine mission to the world, and is itself charged with a mission. The gift becomes a responsibility.

B. Christian Existence and Conduct in the Given Structures of Society (2:11–3:12)

For many modern Christians, this section is the most difficult part of the letter to take seriously. It gives instructions for Christians who live their lives in the established social structures of another time and place. It is neither a protest against Rome and the cultural standards of the time, nor simply a call to conform. The distinctiveness the author calls for is a nuanced, discriminating countercultural conformity. Codes of household duties had been developed in the Hellenistic world to represent what an orderly society should be. Hellenistic Jews and Christians in the Pauline tradition had already adapted these traditional codes as a means of teaching Jewish and Christian ethics (cf. Eph 5:22–6:9; Col 3:18–4:1; 1 Tim 2–3; 5:1–6:3; Titus 2:1–10). The author of 1 Peter is not formulating new rules, but joining a discussion and adapting a tradition. Household slaves in non-Christian households and wives married to non-Christian husbands are taken as examples illustrating the attitudes and behavior to which all Christians in such a society are called. The slaves and women here addressed have already made a courageous decision to join a despised foreign cult that is not the religion of their non-Christian masters and husbands. That is, they have already shown that they are not merely submissive. This makes them a model for the church as a whole. Mission, not submission, is the focus of this text. The challenge is to remove a false stumbling block, so that people may decide for or against the truth of the Christian message without being put off by [their perception of] the cultural forms associated with it. To be good citizens subordinate to the civil authorities is to silence the objections of outsiders, i.e. it is in the service of the Christian mission (2:15).

3:1–7. In the same way as all Christians, including husbands and young people, wives are to fit into the existing social order as part of the Christian mission (see on 2:13). Women are directly addressed as responsible members of the community. Like all Christians (3:16), they are to offer their witness to the faith through gentleness and meekness. Their new-found freedom does not mean that they may now dress in what would have been a countercultural manner that calls attention to themselves. For women of another culture in later generations to adopt these instructions as

normative rules would make them stand out from expected social conventions—the precise opposite of their intention. Likewise, Christian husbands are not simply to accept the dominant role assigned to them by first-century society, but are to show consideration and honor to their wives as co-heirs of the gift of (Christian) life received from God. Husbands are to relate to their wives not merely in terms of cultural expectations, but according to knowledge, i.e. as those who understand the Christian faith as articulated in 1:3–2:25.

3:8–12. Just as the unit began in 2:11–12 with general instructions to the whole Christian community, so it concludes by addressing all Christians. Jesus had suffered unjustly and had taught non-retaliation (Matt 5:44/Luke 6:28). While aware of Jesus' example (2:21), the author typically does not quote Jesus to support his point, but the Scripture (Ps 34:13–17).

C. Responsible Suffering in the Face of Hostility 3:13–5:11

3:13–17. Christian conduct is not a strategy for success. Christians are to respond to misunderstanding and abuse not only by patient suffering, but also with a coherent explanation of the meaning of the Christian faith to outsiders who misunderstand.

3:18–22. The ethical conduct to which Christians are called is grounded not on the basis of logic, general principles, or common sense, but christologically. How to understand the details of this obscure passage continues to be debated, but the main point is clear: the Christ who endured unjust suffering has triumphed completely over all the hostile forces of the universe, so Christians can endure unjust suffering in the assurance of sharing this ultimate victory. These verses probably include part of an ancient Christian hymn familiar to the readers then, but now lost. Such hymns celebrated the cosmic victory of Christ (cf. Phil 2:5–11; Col 1:15–20; 1 Tim 3:16). "Spirits in prison" probably refers to the rebellious transcendent beings (also called "angels," "demons" and "sons of God") who corrupted the human race and were imprisoned in the nether world awaiting eschatological judgment (cf. Gen 6:1–4; *1 Enoch* 10:4–6; 1 Cor 6:3; 2 Pet 2:4; Jude 6). It is not clear whether the proclamation Christ made to them after his death communicated doom or salvation. As the waters of the flood separated Noah and his family from the old world, so baptism separates Christians from their old life. As only a few in Noah's time were delivered, so the minority status of Christians in society does not mean they are rejected by God. That angels, authorities, and powers are finally subject to Christ (3:22) may point to their final redemption (cf. Eph 1:9–10, 19–22; Phil 2:9–11; Col 1:19–20).

4:1–2. The preceding line of thought continues: the sinless Christ (2:22) suffered to bring the reign of sin to an end. Christians too have finished with sin, since they participate in Christ's suffering and death because they are baptized, and their own sufferings are part and parcel of the Christ-event that is now their own story. They can never return to their old way of life.

4:6. This text has traditionally been interpreted in relation to the "spirits in prison" of 3:19, but there is probably no connection. The dead to whom the gospel was preached are deceased members of the Christian community. From the perspective of this world, their death was a judgment, i.e. they died like everyone else, despite their Christian faith. But their death was not the end; they are vindicated in the transcendent spiritual world.

4:7–8. Like much of early Christianity, the author believes that with the advent of Jesus the end of history had come, and that Christ's final manifestation would occur in the near future. This faith encouraged loving care for other people, especially those of the Christian community.

4:10. Each member of the community has received a gift. There is a variety of gifts, and the gifts are not for individual self-aggrandizement but for strengthening the Christian community as a whole (Rom 12:4–8; 1 Cor 12:4–31).

The name *Christian* is found in the NT only here and Acts 11:26; 26:28. Though the name later became a badge of honor, it was originally a demeaning term, "Christ-lackeys," and those who designated themselves by this name suffered ostracism and worse. The Christian response to unjust suffering is not sullen resignation but actively doing good, in the glad confidence that their lives are in the hands of the faithful Creator.

5:1–5. Speaking in the first person for the first time since the opening greeting, the author presents himself as a presbyter (elder) in the Roman church, who writes with apostolic authority (cf. Overview; on elders, see Acts 11:29–30; 14:23; 20:17–38; 1 Tim 5:17–25; Titus 1:5–9; Jas 5:13). The author does not claim to have been present at the crucifixion. Rather, he is presenting his testimony to the meaning of the cross, as all Christians are called to do. The churches addressed are led by elders who, like the author, participate in the apostolic authority, but all are subordinate to Christ the chief shepherd (5:5).5:9 The little house churches scattered throughout Asia Minor are members of the one church, a world-wide community of faith.

IV. Conclusion of the Letter (5:12–14)

Silvanus is the same as Silas (cf. 1 Thess. 1:1; 2 Cor. 1:19; Acts 15:22 and often in Acts). "Through Silvanus" does not mean he is co-author or secretary in the composition of the letter, but that he was active in delivering it (cf. Acts 15:22–23). This [unjust suffering for the sake of Christ] is the true grace of God: see on 2:19–20.

5:13. In 70 CE the Romans had destroyed the second Temple just as the Babylonians had destroyed the first in 586 BCE. After 70 CE, Rome was thus sometimes called "Babylon." "My son Mark" is not literal, but refers to Mark as Peter's convert and younger coworker, as Paul had referred to himself as "father" of Onesimus and Timothy (Phlm 10; 1 Cor 4:17; cf. 1 Tim 1:18; 2 Tim 1:2). Both Silvanus/Silas and Mark had been associated with Paul (1 Thess. 1:1; Phlm. 24). Their association with Peter is here a signal of the later combination of Petrine and Pauline traditions in Rome (cf. Overview).

2 PETER

OVERVIEW

Second Peter combines two literary genres, the letter and the testament. Beginning with the conventional letter framework adopted and adapted from Paul, the body of the composition has the typical form and content of the "farewell speech" or testament known in both traditional Judaism and early Christianity.

In this letter an early Christian teacher of the first half of the second century writes in Peter's name, giving instruction to the church struggling to consolidate its faith in the face of false teaching and disappointed hopes. On the writing of letters in Peter's name, see the overview of 1 Peter. Second Peter stands in this same tradition, reflecting later developments in the circle of Peter's disciples that continued his teaching. Compelling evidence indicates that the letter was not written by Peter himself: (1) The letter has excellent command of Greek language and rhetoric, tending toward a grandiose style. (2) Theological concepts represent an integration of traditional Christian faith and Greek philosophical terminology unlikely for a Galilean fisherman. (3) Second Peter uses the Letter of Jude as a primary source, reflected throughout and incorporated almost bodily into the author's argument (compare especially the wording of Jude 3–18 and 2 Pet 2:1–3:4). (4) The church of the second and third centuries was hardly aware of the letter, and many churches did not accept it as canonical after the fourth or fifth century. (5) The letter reflects evidence of a date long past the lifetime of Simon Peter, including 3:2, which looks back on the time of the early prophets and apostles, 3:4, which reflects the viewpoint of a later generation, and 3:15–16, which indicates Paul's letters have already been collected, circulated, and regarded as Scripture.

OUTLINE

I. Salutation (1:1–2)

II. Thematic Summary: God's Blessings and the Believers' Response (1:3–11)

III. Body of the Letter: Peter's Testament, Responding in Advance to the False Teachers (1:12–3:13)

IV. Concluding Exhortation and Doxology (3:14–18)

DETAILED ANALYSIS

I. Salutation (1:1–2)

In the opening words, an authoritative apostolic voice from the past addresses readers of a later generation. Using the Jewish form of his name (cf. Acts 15:14), *Simeon* speaks as one who was a companion of Jesus and rooted in the earliest church, declaring that the readers of a later generation share the same faith. Here, as in Jude 3, *faith* refers not only to the personal trust with which one believes, but to the content of the faith itself. Those who come after the first generation do not have a hand-me-down, second-hand faith, but one that is equal to that of the first generation.

II. Thematic Summary: God's Acts and the Believers' Response (1:3–11)

1:3–4. God has acted in the past not only in the saving Christ-event, but by calling the readers into the community of faith. God will act in the future—this is the implication of "his precious and very great promises" that are denied by the false teachers. Living one's life on the line between God's act in Christ and the final coming of God's kingdom has ethical consequences. For the author, this weaving together of faith and life is crucial. Bad ethics results from bad theology; good theology must produce ethical living.

1:5–11. This combination of faith and ethics is immediately illustrated by adapting a Hellenistic list of virtues to represent the distinctive substance of the Christian life. Typically, such lists began with *knowledge*, and right understanding was considered the basis for the good life. In contrast, Peter begins with *faith*, which here refers not to the content of what is believed, but personal trust in the God revealed in Christ. The conventional Hellenistic virtues follow, but the whole is flavored by Christian content. The list that begins with faith concludes with love, expressed by the word (*agapē*). While this term itself can be used in a variety of ways, in early Christianity it developed a distinctive meaning and was often used to express the unselfish love of God made effective in the church as love for others (e.g. John 13:35; Rom 5:5). The author again emphasizes that such living is based on and is the expression of their *call and election* received in the past, and their confident hope of the *eternal kingdom* that will appear at the return of Christ. Those who do not live this way—the author has the false teachers and their disciples in mind—have forgotten their past and denied their future.

III. Body of the Letter: Peter's Testament, Responding in Advance to the False Teachers (1:12–3:13)

1:12–15. Here the author makes the testamentary character of his writing explicit. The tradition that Jesus informed Simon Peter of his impending martyr's death is also found in John 21:18–19. Although the author himself is reinterpreting the traditional faith into new categories, he presents his interpretation as only reminding the readers of what they already know, i.e. their inherited traditional faith, which does not become something new by being reinterpreted in new language and concepts.

1:16-21. The author does not charge his opponents with propagating such myths (contrast 1 Tim 1:4; 4:7; 2 Tim 4:4; Titus 1:14). The false teachers charge traditional Christians who affirm the eschatological parousia with believing myths, fabricated to manipulate immature people. The author responds that the basis of faith is not mythology spun out of speculative imagination, but authentic apostolic testimony of actual events (16–18) and the prophetic word of Scripture (19–21). Since the event described "on the holy mountain" is similar to the Transfiguration scene portrayed in the Synoptic Gospels (Matt 17:1–8; Mark 9:2–8; Luke 9:28–36), this text has traditionally been understood as "Peter's" claim to have been present at the transfiguration. So understood, it is difficult to see the connection between this claim and the following references to the prophetic word of Scripture being confirmed. It is more likely that the author's line of thought is as follows. He and other traditional Christian teachers appealed to the Scriptures to support their view of the eschatological parousia of Christ. The false teachers dispute this interpretation of Scripture. The author responds that this interpretation is not merely a matter of private, idiosyncratic interpretation, but is confirmed by a revelatory experience that revealed Jesus as God's Son enthroned in heavenly glory, the one who will come as eschatological judge and savior. The church may be assured of seeing the glory of Christ in the future, because the glory of the exalted Christ has already been seen in the past. In this reading "Peter" is not appealing to a pre-Easter transfiguration, but to a post-Easter prophetic revelation that confirms his reading of the prophetic Scriptures (cf. Matt 28:18–20; 1 Thess 4:15–17). Neither Scripture nor interpretation is a matter of arbitrary human will, but divine prophetic revelation.

2:1–22. This extensive central section is an attack on the false teachers, responding to their objections and charging them with defective theology, rejection of proper authority, and personal immorality. The author relies heavily on Jude, adapting the earlier material by making some significant changes: (1) He adjusts the chronology to conform to that of biblical narrative. Jude's triad Israel / sinful angels / Sodom and Gomorrah becomes sinful angels / Noah / Lot, in the order found in Gen 6–19. (2) He includes positive examples of God's deliverance (Noah, Lot) contrasting with the negative examples of God's judgment. (3) He omits Jude's citations from non-canonical literature (*1 Enoch*, *Testament of Moses*), basing his argument entirely on material considered biblical. The point of all this is not to convert the false teachers, who are not addressed, but to warn the unsuspecting churches of the dire threat in their midst.

3:1–13. Broad streams of first-generation Christianity had expected Christ to return soon to complete his saving work by establishing God's justice and bringing in the kingdom of God (e.g. Matt 10:23; 16:28; Mark 9:1). The false teachers of the author's own time argue that the whole idea of Christ's second coming was false and should be abandoned, adducing three main arguments: (1) Since Jesus did not return within the expected time, history has shown it to be a false expectation. (2) The constancy and consistency of the world order, that continues to function as it always had done, shows that history will continue without divine intervention—hence there is no final judgment to be feared. (3) In any case, Christ has set us free from the law, we will not be called to account, so judgment is unnecessary.

The author understands this view to promote moral laxity and opposes it by appealing to the constancy of God's act as seen in Scripture. The biblical pattern of creation, judgment, and re-creation will be repeated at the end. The delay of the parousia does not mean it will not happen. Appealing to Ps 90:4, the author argues that as a (human) day is a thousand years for God, and a thousand (human) years is one day for God, so God's promises are not constrained by human conceptions of time. The "delay" from the human perspective is in reality an expression of the patience of God who wants all people to repent and gives them more time. The author's ultimate conviction is that the parousia is certain, whenever it may come, because it is not a matter of human speculation but of God's promise.

IV. Concluding Exhortation and Doxology (3:14–18)

3:14–16. The writings of Paul had apparently been exploited by the false teachers, who interpreted Paul's emphasis on Christian freedom and the presence of salvation to mean there would be no future judgment. The author reclaims Paul for emerging mainstream catholic Christianity. This affirmation of *Pauline* Christianity by "Peter" is an extension of the unifying theology of 1 Peter.

3:17–18. The brief concluding doxology emphasizes remaining steadfast in the traditional faith until the return of Christ, the *day of eternity*.

BIBLIOGRAPHY

R. J. Bauckham. *Jude, 2 Peter*. WBC 50 (Waco, Tex.: Word, 1983); M. E. Boring. *1 Peter*. ANTC (Nashville: Abingdon, 1999); A. Chester and R. P. Martin. *The Theology of the Letters of James, Peter, and Jude*. NTT (Cambridge: Cambridge University Press, 1994).

1, 2, 3 JOHN

GEORGE PARSENIOS

OVERVIEW

Pauline scholars often claim that reading Paul's letters is like reading someone else's mail. For, while inclusion in the biblical canon means that Paul's letters are now addressed to all believers, each letter was first addressed to first-century believers. We are reading their mail. First, Second, and Third John push this historical distance one step further. They are not only the mail of someone else, but of someone whose identity is cloaked in mystery. They provide only a few enigmatic details about both senders and recipients. Second and Third John, for instance, are the shortest writings in the New Testament, and identify their sender by the cryptic title "the Elder." Second John is sent to the equally enigmatic "Elect Lady and her children." And, even though 3 John helpfully tells the name of its recipient (Gaius), and refers to a conflict with a certain Diotrephes, the very brevity of the letter makes it unclear precisely what this conflict is. As for 1 John, it is much longer than the other two, and contains an elaborate polemic against beliefs that it opposes. But it mentions nothing about who sent it, to whom it was sent, and who specifically is committing the wrongs it seeks to correct. The circumstances that produced 1–3 John, then, are not immediately obvious.

A related problem arises regarding authorship. Since antiquity, people have wondered whether all three writings come from the same pen. Among those who reject common authorship, the most frequent assumption is that the author of 1 John, who is anonymous, is different from the Elder, who wrote 2 and 3 John. The evidence of the letters themselves, however, strongly suggests a common origin. Second John provides the adhesive that unites the trio. For, on the one hand, 2 John addresses more briefly the same theological errors that occupied 1 John, and, on the other hand, it shares the same author (the Elder) with 3 John. Because 1 John and 3 John are thus connected to 2 John, they are also connected to one another. A common language and style across all three letters, with appropriate levels of variation, also points to common authorship.

In addition to debating how they relate to one another, interpreters also question the relationship of 1–3 John to the Gospel of John. Among early Christian interpreters, 1 John was early attributed to the same author as the Gospel, while 2 and 3 John were only later accepted as his. Similarities in language, thought, and style, however, make some connection with the Fourth Gospel all but certain for all three. Less certain is the precise nature of that connection. Were 1–3 John written before, during, or after the composition of the Gospel? Were they all written at the same time? The evidence is not conclusive. A persistent assumption has been that the three letters reflect the later controversies of the community that produced the Fourth Gospel, and so are written after it, but are still products of the Johannine school. This will be the perspective adopted here. If 1–3 John follow the Gospel of John, which is dated to around 90, they can be hypothetically dated to somewhere between 100 and 110.

This does not mean, however, that the connections between 1–3 John and the Gospel of John are straightforward. Indeed, ideas from the Fourth Gospel often appear in the letters in an altered form, as when the letters apply to the Father things that the Fourth Gospel applies to Jesus. In the Gospel of John, for instance, Christians abide in Jesus (15:4–10, etc.), but in 1 John they abide in God (2:5–6, etc.). Likewise, the Gospel of John places the command to love one another in the mouth of Jesus (13:34, etc.), but 2 John ascribes the love command to God (4–6). The significance of these variations will be discussed in the commentary.

OUTLINE

I. 1 John

    A. Prologue (1:1–4)

    B. The Message Is "Light" (1:5–3:10)

    C. The Message Is "Love" (3:11–5:12)

    D. Epilogue (5:13–21)

DETAILED ANALYSIS

I. 1 John

A. Prologue (1:1–4)

First John does not open as ancient letters typically did by naming its sender and recipient. It begins with a prologue that resembles in various ways the prologue to the Gospel of John (1:1–18). Both prologues employ key Johannine terms such as *testify*, *life*, *Father*, *Son*. Further, while the Fourth Gospel opens (1:1) by speaking of the word (*logos*) that was in the beginning (*archē*), 1 John discusses the word that was from the beginning. The respective meanings of "beginning" and "word" are different, however. In the Gospel, Jesus is the Word who existed in the beginning, where beginning has an eternal, cosmic sense. In 1 John, by contrast, the word is not Jesus, but the proclaimed word that the disciples preached from the beginning, meaning the beginning of their earthly ministry. The same key terms are used, therefore, but very differently. What explains this similarity in difference? It likely reflects a conflict over the proper interpretation of the Johannine tradition. By opening with such elaborate allusions to the Fourth Gospel, 1 John claims that it represents the proper extension of the Johannine tradition, and argues against former members of its community who separated themselves (2:19) and distorted this tradition. The ensuing argument against these opponents does not develop in clear, linear fashion, however, but cycles back and forth over several issues that can be conveniently summarized under the headings of christology and ethics.

B. The Message Is "Light" (1:5–3:10)

To divide 1 John into coherent units is difficult due to its repetitive structure. R. Brown, however, helpfully observes that the phrase "This is the message (*angelia*)" at 1:5 and 3:11 divides the letter into two parts. Beginning at 1:5, the argument focuses mostly, though not exclusively, on ethics. At 3:11 the argument turns for the most part, though again not exclusively, to christology.

The first section, then, opens at 1:5. The claim that God is light (1:5) is an ethical claim that describes neither an attribute of God nor his nature, but tells us what God *does*. A little further on we read that to walk in the light is to love one another (2:9–11), and God is later even defined as love (4:8, 16). Therefore, although the debate in this letter seems to be one centered on beliefs, light is not here connected to the clarity of true belief but to the purity of correct practice, to the call to love one another. This is what it means to say that God is light.

The section from 1:5–2:2 contains six clauses that begin with "if" and then define a particular condition as true or false. The notion of truth here has the typical Johannine sense of "reality." What is true is what is real, and two things especially are affirmed here as real. The first is human sin (1:8, 10, 2:1), and the second is that sins are forgiven through Jesus, the atoning sacrifice for sins (2:2). Both are real, and to deny one is to deny the other. For, if human beings have no sin, then Jesus need not have been an atoning sacrifice for sin.

Since he was such a sacrifice, however, and so has changed the human situation, the next section (2:3–11) emphasizes the reality of new life in Christ. It claims that "the darkness is passing away and the true light is already shining," (2:8). To walk in this light, believers must put aside the darkness of hatred and show love for one another. Verses 2:12–17 develop an important Johannine theme (John 15) that love for God and for one another is possible only for those who do not love the world (2:15).

Christology appears explicitly for the first time in 2:18–27, as does the term "antichrist," which in the entire New Testament appears only in 1–3 John (2:18, 22; 4:3; 2 John 7). The connection between christology and the antichrist is not accidental, and recurs throughout 1–3 John. In 2:22–

23, the antichrist is one who "denies the Father and the Son," and a similar christological concern accompanies every reference to the antichrist (see also 4:3; 2 John 7). This explains why 2:18 quickly shifts from *the* antichrist to *many* antichrists. The many opponents who hold a false christology are all antichrists. What they believe is not clear, though. What does it mean, after all, to "[deny] the Father and the Son?" (2:22). Interpreters disagree. In the Gospel of John, Jesus' opponents saw him only as a human being, not the divine Son or the Messiah. Because Jesus was persecuted for making himself equal to God (John 5:18), the Fourth Gospel defends the divinity of Jesus. Does the same christological problem arise here, with some believers denying that Jesus is the Messiah? That is highly unlikely, since they are part of the community that wrote the Fourth Gospel and so surely accept its message. The current passage is too cryptic to conclude anything absolutely. Later verses (4:1–6) provide more clues.

First John 2:28–3:10 emphasizes that those who abide in God do not sin, which seems to contradict the emphasis on human sin in 1:5–2:2. But there may be no contradiction. It is possible that the opponents insisted on human sinlessness when they rejected 1 John's christology. To combat this teaching, 1 John first underscored the reality of human sin (1:5–2:2). But 1 John also emphasizes that Jesus achieved the forgiveness of sins. In light of this new circumstance, 1 John now urges believers to transform their lives in order to reflect their new life, with special emphasis on the need to love one another (3:10).

C. The Message Is "Love" (3:11–5:12)

Verse 3:11 opens the second half of the letter by repeating the phrase "this is the message" from 1:5, and here the "message" is to love one another. The greater emphasis in the first half of 1 John was on ethics, with some concern for christology. In the latter half, the greater concern is on christology, but without ignoring ethics. Indeed, 3:11–18 actually emphasize the ethic of the love command, and the need to love "not in word or speech, but in truth and action" (3:18). First John 3:19–24 include a dual commandment that weds christology and the love command: "And this is his commandment, that we should believe in the name of his Son Jesus Christ and love one another" (3:23).

The command regarding belief in Jesus will dominate verses 4:1–6, while the command to love one another occupies 4:7–18.

The issue of true belief occupies 4:1–6 and recalls the earlier mention of christology (2:18–22). When 4:2 insists that "Jesus Christ has come in the flesh," it tells us more about the opponents' beliefs we heard in ch. 2. The problem in 1 John seems to be the opposite of that in the Fourth Gospel. Where the Gospel of John affirmed Jesus' divinity against those who considered him only a human, 1 John affirms Jesus' humanity against those who see him as only divine. The opponents seem to have overemphasized Jesus' divinity to such a degree that his humanity, his work in the flesh, is considered irrelevant for salvation. Those who "[deny] that Jesus is the Christ" (2:22), therefore, might accept that the divine Word entered the world in Jesus, but they deny that the earthly Jesus performed any act necessary for salvation. Later groups called Docetists also devalued human flesh, refusing to believe that the divine Word saved humanity through the flesh. The English term *docetic* comes from the Greek word *dokein*, "to appear," suggesting that the divine Word only appeared to take on human flesh and suffer pain and crucifixion, but did not do so in reality. Some seed of docetism seems to characterize the opponents in 1 John. Against them, 1 John insists that it is precisely Jesus' work in the flesh, especially his atoning death, which is required for the remission of sins and human salvation (2:1–2). That the divine Word took on humanity, real humanity, is necessary for him to renew humanity.

Precisely since humanity is new in Christ, new possibilities are available in human relations. To explain this, 4:7–18 develops the latter part of the commandment in 3:23, to love one another. Love among believers imitates God's love reflected in the sending of the Son in human flesh (4:9–11), since the purpose of this sending was a loving act of sacrifice. To affirm that Christ acted out of sacrificial love requires believers to imitate this sacrifice in their interactions with one another. But, even more, God's love that was manifest in the sending of the Son is continued wherever believers love one another. Christology and ethics, then, are not separate concerns, but variously connected.

D. Epilogue (5:13–21)

Verse 5:13 draws 1 John to a close as it explains, "I write these things to you who believe in the name of the Son of God, so that you may know that you have eternal life." This statement connects 1 John to the Fourth Gospel by echoing what many believe was the original epilogue of the Gospel: "But these are written so that you may come to believe that Jesus is the Messiah, the Son of God, and that through believing you may have life in his name" (20:31). As in the prologue, therefore, allusions to the Fourth Gospel emphasize that 1 John presents the true extension of the Johannine tradition. This may explain why 1 John closes with the obscure and dire warning to avoid idols (5:21). How does this conclude the preceding argument? If idols are taken as false gods, the admonition may refer to the false beliefs of those who seceded from the community and no longer know the true God. To end with this negative tone, however, differs from the optimistic ending of the Fourth Gospel (21:25). The ominous conclusion of 1 John reflects the severity of the rift it addresses and the immediacy of the issues at stake.

II. 2 John

A. Greeting (1-3)

Like a standard ancient letter, 2 John begins by announcing that it is sent from the Elder to "the Elect Lady and her children." The term Elder (*presbyteros*) is a common leadership title in the early church (Acts 14:23, etc.). Some speculate that the Lady and her children are actual people, but these names surely symbolize a church (the Lady) and its members (her children).

B. Body (4–12)

By adhering to the standard letter form, 2 John differs from 1 John. In its content, however, it closely resembles 1 John. Verses 4–6 repeat and stress the command to love one another, while vv. 7–9 defend the reality of Jesus' coming in the flesh (cf. 1 John 4:2). Why was 2 John written if it seems only to summarize 1 John? Theories abound. One possibility is that both documents combat the same teaching at the same time in different places.

Further, 2 John not only refutes its opponents but urges that they not be permitted "into the house" (10) which means the church. For, showing false teachers hospitality supports their teaching (11). The connection between the Elder's authority and hospitality are even more important in 3 John.

C. Farewell (13)

Second John closes with an echo of its beginning, by saying, "The children of your elect sister send you their greetings," referring symbolically this time to the Elder's church and its members.

III. 3 John

A. Greeting (1–2)

Like 2 John, 3 John fits the formal criteria and typical brevity of ancient letters. It is the shortest New Testament document, and the only one not to mention the names Jesus or Christ, though it employs Johannine terminology like *love*, *truth* and *testify*. It is a letter of recommendation from the Elder to Gaius, on behalf of Demetrius (12). Recommendation letters were a formal convention between friends in antiquity, being sent to one friend in support of another for various reasons.

B. Body (3–15)

The letter commends Gaius for showing hospitality to strangers, suggesting that he provides material support to Christian missionaries (5–8). The crux of 3 John is the conflict with Diotrephes, who refuses such hospitality to the Elder's envoys (9–10). The verb *epidechesthai* is often translated differently in vv. 9 and 10. In 9, it is rendered as "recognize authority," while in 10, it is translated "receive." The change is unjustified, however, and in both cases *epidechesthai* should mean "receive." In v. 9, therefore, Diotrephes does not receive the Elder's letter, and in v. 10, he does not receive the Elder's envoys. Some interpreters associate Diotrephes with the christological conflict in 1 and 2 John, but 3 John makes no such connections, avoiding theological concerns altogether.

C. Farewell (15)

The connection between recommendation letters and the conventions of ancient friendship makes it interesting that 3 John closes by sending greetings from the "friends" (15). The term *friend* evokes also the typical language of the Fourth Gospel (John 15).

Although 3 John appears unconnected to the theological conflicts in 1 and 2 John, a theological bond connects all three works. 3 John works out in practical terms what 1 and 2 John address more abstractly. 1 and 2 John connect the love command to correct christology, while 3 John associates the spread of true teaching with hospitality among believers. By supporting traveling missionaries, Gaius actualizes the connection between love for others and the preservation of the truth. Thus, a common theological emphasis is clear throughout 1–3 John

BIBLIOGRAPHY

C. C. Black. "1, 2, & 3 John." *NIB* (Nashville: Abingdon, 1998) 12:363–470; R. E. Brown. *The Epistles of John.* AB 30 (Garden City, N.Y.: Doubleday, 1982); J. Lieu. *The Theology of the Johannine Epistles.* New Testament Theology (Cambridge: Cambridge University Press, 1991); D. Rensberger. *1 John, 2 John, 3 John.* ANTC (Nashville: Abingdon, 1997).

JUDE

Steven Kraftchick

OVERVIEW

Because of its brevity, oblique style, and harshness of tone, Jude presents interpretive challenges. In its few verses one finds references to ancient traditions (vv. 6, 9, 14–15), an apostolic prophecy (vv. 17–18), and a mysterious set of false teachers (e.g. vv. 4, 12–13, 16, 19). This is a letter not penned in the calm of theological reflection, but as an intervention to protect the "common salvation" from forces that would destroy it.

Most pointedly Jude wanted to reveal the error of those who displayed an arrogant disrespect for God (vv. 4, 6, 7, 10, 11, 15) and the ethical consequences of their false beliefs. In this writer's calculus, purity is related directly to fidelity: right belief results in godly obedience while false belief necessarily manifests itself in acts of immorality. Thus Jude writes to warn against the danger of self-delusion, especially of confusing the church's status as one of privilege rather than responsibility. Because the narrow difference between faithfulness and infidelity is easily missed, Jude calls the church to a life of self-scrutiny, which requires a diligent pursuit of truth and obedience (cf. vv. 4, 20–23).

The problems cited in the letter were typical of the early Gentile church, and the characterization of the "intruding" teachers is created from stock religious polemic, making the dating of the letter difficult. The author purports to be the brother of Jesus (v. 1), which would mean a date sometime between 50–70 CE. If "Jude" is a pseudonym, then the exhortations to contend for the "faith" as received (v. 3) and "to remember the apostolic predictions" about the end times (v. 17) point to a second or third generation church community and a later date. Since Jude was a source for 2 Peter (see 2 Peter 2:1–6; 10a–18), an upper limit for composition would be 100 CE.

OUTLINE

I. Greeting and Prescript (1–2)

II. The Letter's Themes (vv. 3–4)

III. Three Examples of Disobedience (5–7)

IV. Disobedience of the Intruders (8)

IV. Obedient Archangel Michael Contrasted to the Arrogant Intruders (9–10)

VI. Three Examples of Disobedience (11)

VII. The Moral Identity of the Intruders Exposed (12–13)

VII. Prophetic Judgments of the Disobedient (14–19)

VIII. Exhortation to Faithfulness (20–23)

IX. Concluding Doxology (24–25)

DETAILED ANALYSIS

The author calls himself "Jude, the brother of James" (v. 1), a reference to "Lord's brother" (Mark 6:3), who was a leader of the Jerusalem church. The letter begins with a conventional salutation and a wish for peace (vv. 1–2) among those God has called, but the tone shifts abruptly in v. 3 when the author urgently states the reasons for writing: to contend for the truth in thought and action. Although Jude desired to write about "our common salvation," he found it necessary to redirect his letter and initiate a "contention for the faith" (v. 3, author's trans.). It had come to his attention that false teachers were threatening the existence of the congregation by denying "the authority of God and Christ" (v. 4, author's trans.), and so wishing to warn his audience but fearing that they would not perceive the danger these teachers posed, the author changed his letter from one of exhortation to warning in order to reveal the false nature of the intruding teachers' belief and behavior. This is done in the starkest and most acerbic of terms. Throughout the letter Jude presents the opponents as immoral deceivers bent on destroying the truth. They are described not simply as present but as "intruders" (v. 4) who are polluting the community's worship (v. 12). They do not just hold alternative understandings of the gospel, but they "defile the flesh" (v. 8), "slander whatever they do not understand" (v. 10), and follow their own ungodly desires (vv. 15, 16, 18). They are devoid of substance, "waterless clouds," "trees without fruit," and "wandering stars" (vv. 12–13) who delude themselves with specious references to spirituality (v. 19). The author further isolates the opposition by the strategic use of impersonal pronouns ("these/these people," vv. 8, 10, 11, 12, 14, 16, 19), which results in their objectification as a malevolent and insidious influence that sates itself at the expense of the community's health and wholeness (vv. 12, 19). In contrast, the audience is referred to warmly as those "who are beloved" or "loved by God" (vv. 1, 3, 17, 20, 21). As such they have been given a status maintained by God's grace (v. 24) and sustained in their willing acceptance of responsible care for God's people and purpose (vv. 20–23). The implication of the author's portrayals is obvious: he hopes that once the congregation recognizes the true nature of the teachers and remembers its own identity, it will understand the threat posed by the intruders and expunge them from its midst.

The author gives substance to his depictions of the intruders with three examples of disobedience drawn from Israel's past (vv. 5–7). Comparing the intruders to those who murmured in the wilderness (Num 14:1–35), the angels who mated with humans (Gen 6: 1–4, cf. *1 Enoch* 6–19), and the Sodomites who attempted to rape angelic messengers (Gen 19:4–11), Jude reveals the base nature of the false teachers (v. 8). This is contrasted with the faithful allegiance demonstrated by the archangel Michael when he disputed the devil's claim to Moses' corpse (*Testament of Moses*). A second set of examples compares the teachers to Cain, Balaam, and Korah (v. 11), archetypes of those who defy the ordinances of God. The argument concludes with references to the prophetic witness of Enoch (vv. 14–16; cf. *1 Enoch* 1:9) and the original apostles (vv. 17–19), both of whom anticipated the apostasy the false teachers represent. The author thus presents a cohesive argument against the intruders, revealing the nature of their disobedience and its consequences both in present forms of immorality (vv. 8, 11, 18) and future judgment (vv. 14–15). The letter draws to a close with an exhortation to his audience to persist in their own faithfulness (vv. 20–23; see v. 3) and to trust in God who will deliver them from the present trial and evils intrinsic in this world (vv. 24–25).

BIBLIOGRAPHY

D. J. Harrington and D. Senior. *1 Peter, Jude and 2 Peter.* SP 15 (Collegeville, Minn.: Liturgical Press, 2003); R. J. Bauckham. *Jude, 2 Peter.* WBC 50 (Waco: Word Books, 1983); S. J. Kraftchick. *Jude/2 Peter.* ANTC (Nashville: Abingdon Press, 2002).

THE REVELATION TO JOHN

Judith L. Kovacs

Overview

"Hallelujah! the kingdom of this world is become, the kingdom of our Lord, and of his Christ, and He shall reign forever and ever." These words, set to glorious music in Handel's *Messiah*, have inspired generations of Christians. Many who sing them would be surprised to learn that they come from the Revelation to John (19:16; 11:15), a book better known for its visions of world cataclysm than for its promise of a perfect world centered on worship of the divine creator. For many readers the essence of the book is the three plague sequences of the seven seals, trumpets, and bowls. Interpretations of the book in music and art, however, remind us that these images of destruction are framed by scenes of divine order, peace, and blessing (Rev 4–5; 21–22) and punctuated by stirring hymns and scenes of worship.

Historical Context. As is the case with many other biblical books, we know nothing about the author or the addressees of Revelation except for what we can infer from the book itself, namely that the author was an early Christian prophet named John, who experienced visions on Patmos (1:9), an island off the western coast of Asia Minor (modern Turkey). According to a tradition that goes back to church fathers in the second century, John is the son of Zebedee, one of the twelve closest followers of Jesus, who also composed the Gospel and Letters of John. This attribution seems unlikely, among other reasons because the son of Zebedee, a fisherman from Galilee (Mark 1:19), is unlikely to have written a book in Greek. Also the author never calls himself an "apostle," and when he speaks of the "twelve apostles" as the foundation of the New Jerusualem (21:14) he suggests no connection with himself. Further, there are marked differences in style and theological emphasis between Revelation and John's Gospel.

The prophet John addresses his book to seven Christian communities in cities on or near the western coast of Asia Minor: Ephesus and Smyrna on the coast, to the east of Patmos, and the other five in the interior (1:4, 14; chs. 2–3). If John was an itinerant prophet, the order of the messages may reflect his circuit, running north from Ephesus to Smyrna and Pergamum, then heading south through Thyatira, Sardis, and Philadelphia to Laodicea. From early times the book has been thought to date from the late first century, in the latter part of the rule of the emperor Domitian (81–96), and this receives support from internal evidence (see on 17:1–6).

John addresses his readers: "I, John, your brother who share with you in Jesus the persecution and the kingdom and the patient endurance." (1:1, author's trans.) Based on this verse as well as scattered references to persecution (e.g. 2:13; 17:6), it has often been assumed that Revelation is a martyr text whose main concern is to offer consolation to a persecuted church, but there is actually little evidence of extensive persecution of Christians in the first century. More likely is that John expects increased persecution in the near future. The book's message is not, however, confined to exhortations to passive endurance or comfort in the face of persecution. John also writes to alert Christians to a less obvious danger, the threat to their faith posed by normal life in the Roman Empire and the ideology that supports it. He challenges his audience to active resistance, not in the form of armed revolt, but as courageous witness to Christ, the "Lamb that was slain." Underlying the concrete realities of daily life, the book argues, is a life-and-death struggle between God and Satan; and the Roman Empire, the power that dominates political, social, and economic life, is on the side of Satan. John challenges his audience to witness to the sovereignty of God and Christ and refuse to participate in any activity that is in opposition to Christ, which might include not only obvious affronts such as offering divine honors to the emperor but also the more everyday activities such as participating in trade associations that have a connection to pagan gods. (See on Rev 13 and 17).

Biblical Context. John's Revelation is unusual in its style and literary genre (see on 1:1), but there is much that connects its teaching to the rest of the Bible. In every chapter, John's visions are informed by the traditions and images of the OT. Understanding this background provides a richer appreciation of the book's message and the resonance of its symbols. Three parts of the tradition are particularly important:

(1) The exodus from Egypt. First is the exodus, his most important salvific event in the OT, which brought the people of Israel into being as a covenant people. The rescue from slavery in Egypt is narrated in Exodus 3–15, recalled again and again in the OT, and celebrated by Jews throughout the centuries in the festival of Passover. According to Exod, Pharaoh's decision to let the Israelite slaves go is brought about by means of ten plagues visited on the Egyptians. The book of Revelation also teaches that redemption—in this case eschatological redemption—will be preceded by suffering inflicted on the enemies of God (see on 6:1–17; 8:2–9:21;16:1–21). A key event in the exodus, the crossing of a great sea (Exod 14), is celebrated in the "song of Moses" (Exod 15). In Revelation God's triumph over his enemies is celebrated in the "song of Moses . . . and of the Lamb" (15:3–4), sung by his victorious people who stand by a "sea of glass" in heaven. Also reminiscent of the exodus is the dominant christological title, "the Lamb," which recalls the festival of the Passover in Exod 12, when Israelites were commanded to sacrifice of the Passover lamb. The exodus from Egypt is followed by the giving of the Law of Moses on Mount Sinai (Exod 20–Deut 34), preceded by a theophany in which God's presence is signaled by thunder, lightning, smoke, earthquake, and trumpet blast (Exod 19). Revelation uses similar imagery is to describe the awesome nature of God's presence (Rev 4:5; 8:1–5; 15:5–8).

(2) The Davidic monarchy and the Temple in Jerusalem. Revelation also presupposes OT traditions about the Davidic monarchy and the Temple in Jerusalem. Only three kings ruled over all of the twelve tribes of Israel—Saul, David, and Solomon—but this period of their rule (ca. 1020–922 BCE) had enormous influence on Israelite religion and politics. David, the greatest king Israel ever had, conquered the city of Jerusalem and made it his capital, the center of a strong state whose boundaries were the largest Israel ever achieved. In later centuries, people looked back to the time of David as the golden age; and when Israel was weaker, prophets expressed their hope for a better future by looking for a "messiah," i.e. an "anointed one," who would be like David, a strong political and religious leader. Revelation,

like all NT books, expresses the belief that Jesus Christ is the expected "messiah, son of David," come to rescue his people (5:5; 22:16). Echoing the royal Ps 2, which speaks of the Davidic king's triumph over the enemies of Israel, Revelation presents Jesus as the "lion of the tribe of Judah"(cf. Gen 49:9) who through his death has "conquered" (5:5) and who will return to complete his victory over the "kings of the earth" (12:5,10; 19:15).

Closely associated with the Davidic monarchy is the Temple in Jerusalem. Built by David's son Solomon, it became the center of Israelite worship and a powerful symbol of the special presence of God with his chosen people. The exaltation of Jerusalem and its Temple on Mount Zion, is evident in many strands of the OT, for example in the Psalms: "Great is the Lord and greatly to be praised/in the city of our God. / His holy mountain . . . / is the joy of all the earth, / Mount Zion" (Ps 48:1; cf. Ps 84:1). While only one passage in Revelation (11:1–3) speaks of the Temple in Jerusalem (which was destroyed by the Romans in 70 CE), imagery from the Jerusalem Temple pervades the scenes of worship in the heavenly temple that punctuate John's narrative (Rev 4:1–5:13: 8:1–5; 11:19; 15:5–8).

(3) Prophetic traditions. John refers to his book as prophecy (1:3; 10:17; 22:19), and the influence of the OT prophets is evident throughout the book. Central to the message of the OT prophets is the proclamation of God's judgment and redemption, as it is revealed in the history of Israel. These themes are also prominent in Revelation, which announces that the time of God's final judgment is at hand (11:18; 16:7; 19:2; 20:11–15) and offers in the plague sequences a vivid portrayal of God's judgment on the wicked. John celebrates the redemption of a new people for God through Jesus Christ (1:5–6; 5:9–10), and he looks forward to the completion of this work of salvation in the New Jerusalem (21:1–22:7), where death will be no more and God will dwell with his "peoples" (21:3)

From the OT prophets, John inherited a rich tradition of symbols. Prophets such as Hosea, Jeremiah, and Ezekiel spoke of the intimate relation between God and his covenant people by comparing it to a marriage, in which Israel played the part of the wife. In prophetic poetry Israel appears variously: as beloved wife, expressing

God's special love for her, and also as adulteress and whore, symbolizing her lack of faithfulness to the covenant (Hos 1–3; Jer 2–3; Ezek 23). Another common feature of prophetic symbolism is the personification of the capital cities of Israel and her enemies (e.g. Babylon) as women whose varying status symbolizes the fate of the people (Ezek 23; Isa 54; 60; Jer 50–51). Revelation employs both types of symbolism when it portrays Babylon (a code name for Rome) as a great whore (Rev 17–18) and Jerusalem as the bride of the Lamb (Rev 19–21). Another prominent image in Revelation, the beast from the sea (Rev 13), reflects an ancient tradition of portraying the chief enemy of God as a sea monster (e.g. Dan 7; Job 41; Isa 27:1; 51:9–11). By using ancient imagery to depict the situation of Christians in the first century CE, John ties the church's story to the long history of the people of God.

Literary Techniques. John tells us his book is based on visions experienced on the island of Patmos; this connects his work with other vision accounts in the NT (see, e.g., 2 Cor 12:1–4; Matt 3:16–17, Acts 7:54–56; 9:1–9). But features of the book such as asides to the reader (13:18) and cross references suggest that when John turned his recollections of what was shown to him into a book, he made use of a number of literary techniques to organize and interpret his material. These include the following:

(1) First is the use of the number *seven* as an organizing principle, for example the seven messages to the churches in Rev 2–3 and the three series of seven plagues in Rev 6–9 and 15–16. In the ancient Mediterranean world seven appears frequently as a symbol of completion or perfection.

(2) Second is the deliberate repetition of themes and images. This presents a challenge for interpreters who try to read the book as a blueprint for eschatological events that will follow one after another exactly as depicted. Take, for example, the picture of the last battle, the final act in the conflict of the armies of God with the forces of evil. In the popular imagination this is often referred to as the battle of Armageddon, a name that derives from the sixth bowl vision of in 16:12–16, which pictures the marshalling of armies "for the great day of God the Almighty." The seventh bowl vision (16:17–20) goes on to describe the destruction of Babylon and the fall of

the cities of the nations. One might think that the book has reached its climax and that the description of the New Jerusalem would follow. But the next chapter envisions a still standing city/lady of Babylon riding on the beast and predicts that the Lamb will make war on the beast (17:14). Another picture of the last battle follows in 19:11–21 when Christ returns as a rider on a white horse to "judge and make war," with a coda in 20:1–9 when the dragon (Satan) is imprisoned only to be released and defeated again.

A more obvious example of repetition is the portrayal of divine judgment through three separate series of seven plagues each. The book is more profitably read not as a blueprint of end time events but as a poetic work that appeals to the emotions as well as the mind, moving and instructing the reader through the heaping up of vivid images.

(3) Another literary technique is the use of interludes that separate two sections that belong together. For example, between the sixth seal (6:12–17) and the seventh (8:1–6) John inserts a vision of the 144,000 who are sealed by the Lamb, a scene of calm and triumph in the midst of the dramatic unfolding of the plagues. Similarly, between the sixth and seventh trumpets (9:13–20; 11: 15–19) John has inserted a description of John's commission to "prophesy again" (10:1–11) and a narrative of two mysterious witnesses (11:1–14), both of which portray the situation of Christians in the present. This technique of interweaving connects different blocks of material and also gives particular emphasis to the interludes and to the penultimate member of the interrupted series.

(4) A fourth technique is the juxtaposition of heavenly and earthly scenes. In ch. 12, for example, the story of the woman clothed with the sun (12:1–6; 13–17) is interrupted by a vision of a heavenly battle in which the archangel Michael defeats the great dragon (Satan). The events are interconnected: Satan is cast out of heaven and the battle spreads to earth as the dragon pursues the woman and her messianic child. A central claim of Revelation is that for true understanding of what is going on in the present, an *apocalypse*, a revelation of heavenly truth, is required. This is also illustrated in chs. 2–6. Chapters 2–3, the messages to churches, portray the present situation of Christians in seven churches in ancient Asia Minor; then in 4:1 the scene suddenly shifts

as John see a door open in heaven. Taken up, he gets a glimpse of what is really real (4:1–5:13). Then, with the opening of the seven seals (6:1–13), John's vision returns to earth, as God's plans for the consummation of human history begin to unfold.

Central Themes. The juxtaposition of heavenly and earthly scenes is more than a literary technique. it is also provides a clue to the central message of the book. When John goes through the door into heaven (4:1), what he learns is the nature of the other level of reality that underlies and is at the heart of what happens on earth. In the sights and sounds of the divine throne room he glimpses the sure reality of God's kingship over all, acknowledged by countless heavenly powers who bow in adoration before him. The three plague sequences, which describe God's righteous judgment on human sin, are framed by Rev 4–5 on the one hand and Rev 21–22 on the other. The plotline of the book goes from the present situation when God's rule is celebrated in heaven but hidden on earth—where it is obscured by the activity of Satan and the weakness of God's earthly witnesses—to a "new heaven and a new earth" (21:1), where God's kingship is universally recognized.

A second theme, in counterpoint to the first, creates narrative tension: the revelation or "unmasking" of the true nature of the reality faced by Christians in the present time, viz. the potent nature of evil powers on earth. Seeing this requires revelation—heavenly insight—for the powers of evil are deceptive and seductive (Rev 12:9; 13:14; 17:1–5; 18:23). Apparent virtues, such as acting as good citizens of the Roman Empire, might actually involve service of Satan. The powers of evil are involved in a life-or-death struggle with the Lamb. The challenge addressed to the seven churches is to take sides: to recognize that in the concrete events of their daily lives the eschatological battle has begun and to have the courage to enroll in the winning side, the army of the Lamb, whatever the cost.

Related to both these themes is a third, encapsulated in two scenes at the end of the book. In 19:9–10 and 22:8–9 John, overwhelmed by all he has seen and heard, prostrates himself before the angel who has mediated his revelation, only to be admonished: "You must not do that! ...

Worship God!" John's apocalypse is an invitation to worship the only true God and a strong warning against false worship (see especially 13:3–17; 9:20; 14:9–11 16:2; 19:20). The reward for those who are victorious in the battle against evil is not only the absence of sorrow, trouble, and death (21:4) but also the joy of worshiping God: "But the throne of God and of the Lamb will be in [the city], and his servants will worship him; they will see his face" (22:3–4).

OUTLINE

DETAILED ANALYSIS

"The revelation of Jesus Christ which God gave him to show his servants what must soon take place" (1:1). The best known parts of Revelation are the eschatological events signaled in v. 1 by "what soon must take place": the scenes of judgment and redemption that begin with the seven seals in ch. 6 and conclude with the glorious picture of the New Jerusalem in chs. 21–22. But these chapters are to be read in the context the first five chapters, which provide important clues for understanding the message of this eschatological scenario. These chapters identify the book's author, its intended recipients, and its purpose.

I. Introduction (1:1–20)

1:1–3. Prologue. The first word of the book, "revelation" or "apocalypse" (Gk.: *apokalypsis*), indicates the origin and authority of what follows. This is the only time "apocalypse" is used in the book. The original meaning of the word is not, as in common English usage, the cataclysmic end of the world, but an "unveiling"; a means to insight into the past, present, and future; an alternative vision to the normal perception of reality. John's book has provided the name for a literary genre represented by Jewish apocalypses written in the last centuries BCE and in first century CE, including Dan 7–12, the *Apocalypse of Abraham*, the *Apocalypse of Moses*, *1 Enoch*, and 2 Esd (= 4. Ezra), as well other Jewish and early Christian works. Characteristics of this genre include: a two-level view of reality in which heavenly and earthly events are closely linked, a narrative framework within which the secrets of heaven and God's eschatological purposes are revealed, cosmic dualism, description of ascents to heaven and the final battle between the armies of God and Satan, elaborate images and symbols, and the mediation of revelation through angels. John also calls his book a prophecy (1:3; cf. 10:11; 22:19). Although he does not quote directly from prophetic books, the influence of earlier prophetic traditions is evident throughout the book (see Overview, Biblical Context).

1:4–8. Salutation. John's opening greeting to the seven churches contains a three-fold description of Jesus Christ as "the faithful witness, the firstborn of the dead, and the ruler of the kings of the earth," celebrating his sacrificial death, his resurrection from the dead, and his kingly power. The first two titles recall Paul's summary of the gospel as proclamation of the saving events of Jesus' death on the cross and his resurrection (1 Cor 15:3–7). The word translated "witness," *martys*, later took on technical meaning of "martyr," one who dies for a cause. *Testify* and *testimony* in 1:2 are from the same Greek root, and witnessing is an important theme throughout Revelation. The third title, "ruler of the kings of the earth," indicates Christ's future role as universal ruler and judge. Revelation is much concerned with kingship and kingdom. It celebrates the kingship of God and Christ the Lamb, presently acknowledged by the hosts of heaven (4:1–5) and soon to be clearly established over all the earth (19:11–22:5). In 1:6 the addresses of the book are described as God's "kingdom."

The reference in 1:1 to "what must soon take place" is given more specific content in 1:7, which speaks of Christ's "coming with the clouds," the first of several allusions to Dan 7. The salutation concludes with a direct address from God the Father: " 'I am the Alpha and the Omega', says the Lord God, who is and who was and who is to come, the Almighty" (1:8). The first and last letters of the Greek alphabet, used to designate God's all-encompassing power, are repeated in

another word of God at the end of the book (21:6), and in 22:13 Christ uses them of himself. From early on Alpha and Omega appear frequently in Christian art. Although Revelation does not call Jesus "God," as does John 1:1, its use of the same epithets for God the Father and Christ expresses a high Christology. The phrase "who is and who was and who is to come" (cf. 4:8; 11:17; 16:5), recalls the revelation of God's name to Moses at the burning bush as "I am who I am," alternately translated as "I will be what I will be" (Exod 3:14). God is in control of the world from beginning to end.

1:9–11. Author and Setting. The divine revelation is doubly mediated, through an angel (1:1) and the prophet John. John tells us little about himself, saying only that he was on the island of Patmos "because of the word of God" and that he shares "the persecution and the kingdom and the patient endurance" (1:9). The author is an otherwise unknown early Christian prophet (1:3), perhaps an itinerant prophet who traveled among the seven churches mentioned in Rev 2–3 (see Overview, Historical Context).

Artists such as the Limbourg Brothers and Hieronmyous Bosch present John in exile on a tiny island, attended by an eagle. Ever since Irenaeus, bishop of Lyons in the late second century, interpreted the four living creatures in 4:7 as symbols of the four Evangelists, the eagle has been associated with the apostle John in Christian art (with the lion standing for Mark, the ox for Luke, and a man or angel for Matthew). John says that he was on Patmos for the sake of the "testimony of Jesus" (1.9); this is often interpreted to mean that he was exiled because of his preaching. John says he has experienced suffering for his Christian activity, using two terms that will be repeated in subsequent chapters, "persecution" (cf. 2.9, 10, 22; see on 7:14) and "patient endurance" (cf. 2.2, 3, 19; 3:10; 13:10; 14:12), but he gives no details of his situation. His vision takes place on the Lord's Day (1:10), probably a reference to Sunday (see 1 Cor 16:2).

1:12–16. Vision of the Son of Man. Martin Luther initially relegated Revelation to a subordinate place within the NT canon, saying "Christ is not taught or known in it." This judgment is hard to square with the wealth of christological description in this opening vision and the prominence of

Christ the Lamb in the rest of the book (and in fact Luther modified his view in later editions of his NT, after he recognized the book's usefulness for anti-Catholic polemic). Both the vision of 1:12–20 and the christological epithets in the preceding verses present Christ as a powerful, awe-inspiring figure, who deserves honor equal to that of God the creator.

Christ is portrayed as a "one like a Son of Man," a title for the expected eschatological judge and sovereign based on Dan 7:13–14 and used in all four gospels to refer to Christ's role at the end time (Mark 14:62 par.; John 5:27; cf. Rev 14:14). Between seven lampstands (explained in 1:20 as the heavenly counterparts of the seven churches) Christ appears in majestic form, with brilliant face, eyes like fire, and a deafening voice. In his hair like white wool he resembles God the "Ancient of days" in Dan 7:9. The two-edged sword issuing from his mouth (cf. 2:12, 16; 19:15, 21) is a warning of divine judgment.

The seven lampstands of 1:12 recall the menorahs that burn before God in the Jerusalem Temple (Exod 27:20–21)—the first of many examples of temple imagery in Revelation. Worship is seen as communion with heaven, in which the earthly saints join with the heavenly hosts in lauding God. The book's frequent mixing of past and present may reflect a liturgical sense of time, in which different times are inextricably linked.

1:17–20. Christ Commissions John. John's response of fright, a common motif in prophetic call visions (Isa 6:5; Ezek 1:28), prompts a word of reassurance. Christ proclaims that he is alive forever; he is the "first and the last" who holds the keys of Death and Hades. He commissions John to write "what you have seen, what is, and what is to take place after this." In addition to giving a glimpse of eschatological events, John's book is to unveil the true nature of present reality.

II. Messages to the Seven Churches (2:1–3:22)

In chs. 2–3 the heavenly Christ addresses individual messages to seven churches in Asia Minor. Speaking in the Spirit, he addresses them through their angelic counterparts, who resemble the angels in charge of nations or individuals in Jewish texts (Deut 32:8 LXX; Dan 10:13; 12:1; *Jubilees*

15:31–2; *1 Enoch* 89: 59–62; cf. Matt 18:10). The messages provide important clues about the book's purpose. A reader who focuses only on the plague sequences in chs. 6–9 and 15 could assume that the book's only concern is to reassure Christians that God will wreak vengeance on their enemies. The seven messages make clear, however, that the book's warnings of God's impending judgment are in the first instance directed to a Christian audience.

The messages can be understood as modeled on letters or edicts. The letter was an important vehicle for early Christian teaching; 21 of the 27 books of the NT are called letters, and the letters of Paul and his followers were particularly influential. In their structure the seven messages resemble the edicts of ancient kings and emperors. All have a common form, including: (1) an address to the angel of each church, (2) a description of Christ as sender, (3) words of praise and/or blame, and (4) promises to "the one who conquers."

There are no criticisms in the messages to Smyrna (2:8–11) and Philadelphia (3:7–13), only praise and warnings of trials to come. The message to the church in Laodicea (3:14–22), on the other hand, consists entirely of criticism and a call to repent. In the other four messages praise is mixed with blame. While study of the culture and topography of the seven cities suggests John's familiarity with the situations of the various communities, much of the criticism and commendation is in very general terms. This has facilitated an interpretation, popular through the ages, that the seven churches typify the church as a whole. (Another popular interpretation has been to see them as symbols of the different epochs of church history or world history). More specific clues to the situation in the churches are given in the warnings against false teachers and references to suffering for the faith. Christ praises Christians who have patiently endured such trials and predicts that more trials will follow.

The seven messages look back to the opening vision of Christ as the glorious Son of Man and anticipate the themes of judgment and apocalyptic battle that figure prominently in the rest of the Apocalypse. Christ promises to subdue his followers' enemies at Philadelphia (3:9) but also to exercise judgment upon unfaithful Christians (3:19). He will "make war ... with the sword of my mouth" on those Christians in Pergamum who follow the teaching of the Nicolaitans (2:16) and punish Jezebel and her followers in Thyatira (2:22–23 cf. 3:16). The reference to the devil who will attack Christians in Smyrna (2:10) prepares for descriptions of the last battle between the forces of God and Satan in chs. 12–20, as do the promises to "the one who conquers" that conclude each of the seven messages (2:7, 11, 17, 26; 3:5, 12, 21).

2:1–7. To the Church in Ephesus. Ephesus was the largest city of the Roman province of Asia, and Paul was active there (1 Cor 15:32; Acts 18:19–28; 19:1; 20:16–17). This message, like the other six, begins with a christological epithet. Most of these echo ch. 1, especially the vision of the glorious Son of Man. Christ describes himself as: (1) one who holds seven stars and walks among the lampstands (to Ephesus in 2:1, cf. 1:13, 16); (2) "the first and the last, who was dead and came to life" (to Smyrna in 2:8, cf. 1:17–18); (3) holder of the "two-edged sword" (to Pergamum in 2:12 cf. 1:16); (4) as possessing "eyes like a flame" and feet of "burnished bronze" (to Thyatira in 2:18, cf. 1:14–15); (5) holding seven stars and seven spirits (to Sardis in 3:1; cf. 1:4, 16, 20); (6) is "the holy one, the true one who has the key of David / who opens and no one will shut, / who shuts and no one opens" (to Philadelphia in 3:7; cf. the keys of Death and Hades" in 1:18); (7) "the Amen, the faithful and true witness, the origin of God's creation" (to Laodicea in 3:14, cf. 1.17: "I am the first and the last"). Christians at Ephesus are praised for resisting "false teachers" and Nicolaitans, about whom we have no specific information (2:6; cf. 2:16).

2:8–11. To the Church in Smyrna. While several of the messages refer to suffering for the faith in a general way, the messages to Smyrna and Philadelphia speak more specifically of slander at the hands of the "synagogue of Satan" (2.9; 3.9), probably a reference to Jews bringing charges against Christians before Roman authorities. An example of such a case is narrated in Acts 18:12–17, which tells of Jews in Corinth bringing charges against Paul. Christ warns Christians in Smyrna that they will soon be tested by having to endure ten days in prison, and he exhorts them to be faithful unto death (2:10). Official, widespread persecution of Christians began only a century and half after the

book of Revelation was written, under the emperor Decius. The experiences of persecution referred to in Revelation were of a sporadic and local nature, and one should not overemphasize the role that actual persecution played in the genesis of the book. The persecution of Christians is more something anticipated than already experienced.

2:12–17. To the Church in Pergamum. Pergamum was a large and prosperous city, whose native Attalid rulers built a splendid acropolis intended to rival that of Athens. Its temple of Augustus and Roma, built in 29 BCE, was an important center of the imperial cult. This may be the reference of "Satan's throne" (2:13); another possibility is that it refers to the magnificent altar of Zeus, built around 190 BCE and now occupying a large room in the Pergamum museum in Berlin. The message to Pergamum contains the book's only reference to a specific Christian who has died for the faith, a man named Antipas who, like Christ in 1:5, is called a faithful "witness" (*martyr*).

Several letters speak of false teachers, who are variously identified as "apostles" (2:2), Nicolaitans (2:6, 15), Balaam (2:14) and Jezebel (2:19–23), but John says little about their teachings, except that both Balaam and Jezebel persuade people to "eat food sacrificed to idols and to practice fornication" (2:14, 20). Both teachers are referred to by a pseudonym that associates them with figures from the OT. Numbers 22–24 presents Balaam positively as a pagan seer who refuses the command of a Moabite king to curse Israel, but in Num 31:8, 16 he is put to death for causing the Israelites to commit idolatry at Peor. An account of this idolatry was given in Num 25 immediately following the Balaam story. Several other biblical texts present Balaam in a negative light (Deut 23:4–5; Josh 13:22; Neh 13:2 ; 2 Pet 2:15–16; Jude 11).

2:18–29. To the Church in Thyatira. Christ castigates Christians in Thyatira for tolerating a prophet he calls "Jezebel," giving her the name of a villain from the OT. Jezebel was the Canaanite wife of Ahab, king of Israel in the eighth century BCE, who became a symbol of idolatry because she persuaded Ahab to sanction the worship of other gods besides the God of Israel (1 Kgs 18–19; 2 Kgs 9). By calling the teachers in Pergamum and Thyatira "Balaam" and "Jezebel" Christ warns first-century Christians that they face dangers similar to those of their Israelite ancestors. It is likely that "fornication" refers not to sexual sins but rather to the worship of other gods, following the usage of OT prophets, who describe Israel's idolatry as "whoring after other gods" (see, e.g., Jer 2; Hos 2). Christ gives stern warning against any compromise with the dominant Greco-Roman religious cult. The phrase "food sacrificed to idols" (2:20; cf. 2:14) suggests that certain teachers active in the churches at Thyatira and Pergamum were encouraging a more relaxed attitude. We know from Acts 15 and 1 Cor 8 and 10 that it was a matter of debate among early Christians whether they could eat meat from animals slaughtered in pagan rituals, much of which was sold in the ordinary markets. According to Acts 15:20, 29, an early meeting of Christian leaders in Jerusalem forbade eating such meat, but Paul says that there is nothing intrinsically wrong with this as long as it does not involve the intent to worship of pagan gods (1 Cor 8:4–8; 10:23–27).

3:1–6. To the Church in Sardis.
Members of the church at Sardis are exhorted to "wake up!" and repent. As in all the other messages, those who "conquer"—that is who play their part in the eschatological battle against Satan—are promised blessings. As the christological epithets in the messages relate back to the opening vision of ch. 1, so these promises at the end of the messages anticipate themes from later visions of the last battle, the resurrection of the dead, and the New Jerusalem in 19:11–22:5. These promises include: (1) eating from the tree of life (2:7, cf. 22:2); (2) not being harmed by the second death (2:11, cf. 20:14; 21:8); (3) hidden manna and a white stone (2:17); (4) ruling with a rod of iron (2:27; used of Christ in 12:5) and the morning star (2:28, used of Christ in 22:16); (5) white robes (3:5; 6:11; 7:9, 13; 19:14) and a name written in the book of life (3:5; cf. 20:15: 21:27; 13:8: 17:8); (6) becoming a pillar in the temple of God (3:12); (7) possessing God's name (3:12, cf. 22:4; 14:1) and the name of the New Jerusalem that comes down out of heaven (cf. 21:2); (8) a place on Christ's throne (3:21; cf. 20:4).

3:7–13. To the Church in Philadelphia.
Although Christ has no words of blame for Christians at Philadelphia, he warns of the "hour of trial that is coming on the whole world" (3:10). Here and elsewhere in the book—most notably in the three plague sequences of chs. 6–9 and 16—is reflected a tradition common in Jewish apocalypses, the "messianic woes," that is a time of great suffering expected right before the advent of the kingdom of God (see on Rev 6). Christ identifies himself as the one who holds the "key of David" (3:7), a symbol of his messianic power.

3:14–22. To the Church in Laodicea.
The description of this church as neither hot nor cold but "lukewarm" has found much resonance, as interpreters through the ages have seen therein a reference to their own context. The Christians in Laodicea are exhorted to "buy" gold and white robes (both of which symbolize purity) and salve for their eyes. The last item is an example of how the messages reflect local realities; the medical school at Laodicea was known for its eye ointment. Verse 19 makes clear that the judgment of which Revelation speaks applies to Christians as well as outsiders: "I reprove and discipline those whom I love." The immediate relevance of the warnings and promises in the seven messages is highlighted in Christ's proclamation in 3:20: "Listen! I am standing at the door, knocking; if you hear my voice and open the door, I will come in to you and eat with you, and you with me."

III. God's Kingship Acknowledged in Heaven (4:1–5:14)

4:1–7. The Heavenly Throne Room.
After the messages to the seven churches, which ground the book in a concrete situation, there is an abrupt shift of scene in 4:1. John sees a door opening into heaven and hears a voice instructing him to come up to see "what soon must take place" (author's trans.). This signals the book's central message: that behind ordinary human experience there is a something higher and deeper, and this is what ultimately matters. What John sees and hears in this chapter is not the timetable of eschatological events but the supreme reality that underlies past, present, and future: the glory of God the creator. The message that there are two distinct but closely connected levels of reality—earthly and heavenly—is something John's book shares with other apocalypses. Their claim is that a privileged glimpse of the higher level is required in order to understand ordinary experience, for example the experience of Jews troubled by the Romans' destruction of the Temple in Jerusalem in 70 CE (the situation the concerns the seer in 2 Esdras) or

the challenges faced by seven fledgling churches in Asia Minor.

Interest in visions of God and God's throne is a central component of Jewish mysticism, from the return from exile in Babylon down to the Hasidic movements in our own day. In several Jewish apocalypses (e.g. *1 Enoch* 14, *Apocalypse of Abraham* 11–18) an ascent to heaven is followed by a vision of God dependent on Ezek 1 and Isa 6. Short of the eschaton, describing God's throne is a way of talking about what cannot be fully seen or expressed. In the eighth century BCE Isaiah receives his prophetic commission during a vision of God enthroned in the holy of holies of the Jerusalem Temple (Isa 6:1–13), where the wings of two enormous creatures called *cherubim* covered the ark of the covenant and formed the symbolic throne of God (1 Kgs 6:23–28; 8:6–7; 2 Kgs 19:15). Ezekiel, living in exile in Babylon in the sixth century BCE describes in detail his vision of the divine throne, which appears as a fiery chariot, and of the four "living creatures"— half human and half animal—on whose wings the throne is carried (Ezek 1:1–28). He describes the divine figure seated on the throne with great reserve: "something that seemed like a human form"; fire, lightning, amber, and a splendid rainbow symbolize God's awe-inspiring presence (Ezek. 1:26–28).

In Revelation, as in the Jewish apocalypses to which it is akin, much of the symbolism is traditional, adapted from prophetic books and earlier apocalypses. This is evident in Rev 4, where many of the images from Ezek 1 reappear: the glory of God is symbolized by precious stones, flashes of fire, lightning, and thunder, and his majestic throne is surrounded by a rainbow, a crystal sea and four "living creatures." In Ezek 1 each of the living creatures has four faces, which resemble a human being, a lion, an ox, and an eagle respectively; in John's vision each of the four creatures resembles one of these four. The transformation of Ezekiel's image continues in later Christian tradition; ever since the church father Irenaeus interpreted the human being, lion, ox, and eagle as symbols of the four Evangelists (*Against the Heresies* 3.11.8), these images have been used in Christian art to represent Matthew, Mark, Luke and John, respectively.

Features of John's vision not paralleled in Ezek 1 are the seven flaming torches, identified as the seven spirits of God (cf. 1:4), and twenty-four elders dressed in white and wearing golden crowns. While it is not clear what these beings represent—possibly heavenly counterparts of the twelve tribes of Israel and the twelve apostles—they have captured Christian imagination, appearing for example on the portals of medieval cathedrals, along with the four living creatures.

4:8–11. Worship of God by the Heavenly Host. In v. 8 visual imagery gives way to sounds, as the living creatures initiate an unending song of praise, the first of many hymns that punctuate the book's visions: "Holy holy, holy, / the Lord God the Almighty; / who was and is and is to come." The triple *sanctus*, which first appears on the lips of seraphim in Isaiah's Temple vision (Isa 6:3), has echoed through the centuries in Christian liturgy and hymns. The sound is magnified as the twenty-four elders join in the praise of God as creator, prostrating themselves before the throne and casting down their crowns.

5:1–7. The Lamb Appears to Open the Scroll. Although Revelation owes much to the conventions and imagery of Jewish apocalyptic, ch. 5 makes clear that this is a Christian book. Continuing the vision of God's heavenly throne room, it portrays the "one seated on the throne" holding a scroll. Written on both sides and sealed with seven seals, it symbolizes God's plans for the *eschaton*, the consummation of world history. A search in heaven and earth finds no one worthy to open the scroll, which leads the prophet John to weep bitterly. One of the twenty-four elders consoles him: "See the Lion of tribe of Judah, the Root of David, has conquered, so that he can open the scroll and its seven seals." This description encapsulates a christological claim made throughout the NT: that Jesus came as the messiah ("anointed one") from the line of David (see, e.g. Matt 1:1; Luke 1:26–33; Rom 1:3; Acts 2:30–32). "Lion of Judah" is a messianic title that goes back to Gen 49:8–12, where the patriarch Jacob prophesies that a "lion" will arise from the tribe of Judah (from which king David came), triumph over his enemies, and rule his brothers; the "root of David" (cf. 22:16) echoes other messianic prophecies (Isa 11:1, 10; Jer 23:5).

Verse 6 introduces the christological title that will dominate the rest of Revelation: the Lamb of

God. He has conquered not, as expected for the Davidic messiah, by military conquest (see e.g. Ps 2) , but through his faithful death, a sacrifice that ransomed and redeemed a people coming from every tribe and nation (5:9). This title is less common in the NT, being reflected outside of Revelation only in John 1:29, 36 and 1 Pet 1:19 (in both texts a different Greek word for "lamb" is used) and 1 Cor 5:7, where Paul says: "Christ our Passover is sacrificed for us." The latter text suggests that the title has its background in the sacrifice of the Passover lamb (Exod 12); it may also recall the twice daily sacrifice of a lamb in the Temple in Jerusalem (Exod 29:38–42; Josephus, *Antiquities* 3.237–247). In Acts 8:32 Jesus is identified as the "lamb silent before its shearer" of Isa 53, a passage that became important in later Christian interpretation of Christ's death. The Lamb John sees has seven horns and seven eyes (5:6), the eyes suggesting his omniscience and the horns the power he will exhibit as the book unfolds.

The awkwardness the juxtaposition of "Lion" and "Lamb" points to the unique eschatological reality to which John bears witness. Experience of Christ as Lamb has affected normal apocalyptic conventions, and hitherto accepted patterns of discourse are shattered along with the understanding of the course of history. As John looks on, the Lamb appears before the divine throne and receives the scroll from God. The divine plan for the eschaton, begun in the life, death, and resurrection of Christ, is about to be brought to completion.

5:8-14. Worship of the Lamb. The significance of the appearing of the Lamb is made clear through a series of hymns, as an ever-widening chorus celebrates his power and wisdom. The living creatures join the twenty-four elders, carrying bowls of incense that symbolize the prayers of Christians and praising his sacrificial death that has ransomed a people for God and made them a kingdom and a priesthood (cf. 1:5–6). They are joined by an enormous company of 10,000 times 10,000 angels, who sing: "Worthy is the Lamb that was slaughtered/to receive power and wealth and wisdom and might/and honor and glory and blessing!" The sound becomes deafening as all earthly creatures join the heavenly song. The narrative that follows will be punctuated with visions of the divine throne room (7:9–17: 8:1–5; 11:15–19; 14:2–3; 15;2–8: 19:1–10; 21:3–8), a reminder that the kingship of God and of the Lamb is fully established in heaven and soon to be established over all who dwell on earth.

IV. First Cycle of Seven Plagues (6:1–17; 8:1-6)

Chapter 6 begins one of three sequences of seven plagues each (seals, 6:1–17; 8:1–2, trumpets, 8:2–9:21; 11:15–19, and bowls,16:1–21). These ordered, enumerated pronouncements of woe on an unrepentant world reflect a widespread Jewish and early Christian tradition of "messianic woes," which predicts disaster preceding the time of bliss (Dan 12:1; Mark 13, Matt 24; Luke 21; Rom 8:22). In two apocalyptic texts roughly contemporary with the Apocalypse, 2 Esdras 5:1–12 and the *Apocalypse of Baruch* 25–7, there is a fixed quota of "messianic woes" (see also *Jubilees* 23:31). The term *apocalyptic* is often associated with such catastrophes.

The second and third plague cycles also draw on the biblical accounts of the exodus. According to Exod 7–10 Pharaoh's decision to release the Israelite slaves is brought about by means of ten plagues visited on the Egyptians. Revelation also teaches that redemption—in this case eschatological redemption—will be preceded by suffering afflicted on the enemies of God.

The plague cycles are the part of Revelation that tends to call forth the strongest emotional reactions, whether of fear or revulsion. The graphic description of the plagues of the end time raises difficult theological questions. John follows OT prophets in proclaiming God's justice as well as his mercy. God's wrath—his righteous anger that leads to acts of judgment—is a prominent theme in the OT, and it also runs through the NT (see, e.g., Matt 25; Rom 1:16; 2:1–10), though this is often overlooked because of the NT emphasis on God's mercy and love. The Bible as a whole teaches that a holy, just, and loving God cannot forever tolerate human unfaithfulness and injustice. Revelation particularly emphasizes God's opposition to the injustice present in social and political systems as well as individual lives. For this reason it has spoken especially to oppressed groups, such as African-American slaves or South Africans living under apartheid. John's warnings of impending judgment, like those of the prophets, imply a hope that the working out of God's righteous anger will be averted if people repent (9:20–21; 16:9–11); this message is especially emphasized in the messages to the seven churches (2:5, 14–16, 20–23; 3:1–3, 16–19).

6:1–8. Seals 1–4: The Four Horsemen. The first verse of ch. 6, like 4:1, emphasizes the link between heaven and earth: earthly trials are unleashed by two figures from the heavenly throne room; the Lamb opens the first seal, and one of the four living creatures calls forth a rider with a bow, who is told to ride out and conquer. This pattern is repeated in the next three seals, as the three other living creatures call forth riders who bring war, famine, and death to the earth. These four visions may be inspired by the four of horses of Zech 1:8 and 6:1–3, who execute God's judgment over the earth. The description of the fourth horseman in Rev 6:8 summarizes the consequences of all four: a quarter of the earth is to suffer death and famine, a combination familiar from prophetic sources (Jer 14:12; 15:2; 21:7; Ezek 5:12–15; 14:21; 33:27). The vision of the four horsemen unleashed one after the other has particular dramatic power, and it has had considerable influence on popular imagination, inspiring many songs, book titles, and works of art (e.g. the famous woodcut Albrecht Dürer made in 1511).

6:9–11. Seal 5: Cry of the Martyrs. The opening of the fifth seal produces a very different scene. John sees the altar of incense in the heavenly temple, a counterpart to the altar of incense in the earthly tabernacle (Exod 30:1–10). Under it are the souls of those who have died because of their testimony to Christ (on witness cf. 1:2; 11:1–13; 12:11; 20:4). Their martyrdom is presented as a cultic sacrifice (cf. 2 Tim 4:6 and Phil 2:17). Echoing the language of the Psalms, the souls cry out, asking God "how long?" before he will vindicate them (cf. Ps 79:5; 2 Esd 4:35). The divine response offers both comfort and challenge. The martyrs are told to rest and are given a white garment, symbolizing their purity and their standing in heaven (cf. 4:4; 3:4–6; 7:13). But Christian readers are presented with a challenge. Following a Jewish apocalyptic tradition that God has foreordained a fixed number of martyrs (cf. 2 Esd 4:35–38; 2:36; 2 Bar 30:2) the souls are told that their final reward must wait until this

number is fulfilled. John sees the world's persecution of Christians as just beginning; his prophecy does not offer Christians easy comfort but calls them to courageous witness, no matter what the cost. The martyrs' cry will find a fuller answer at the end of the book: 19:1–8 announces that the blood of God's servants has been avenged in the destruction of the whore of Babylon, and Christian martyrs receive a special reward in the millennial kingdom (20:4–6).

6:12–17. Seal 6: Cosmic Upheaval. While the first four seals bring about disorder in human society, the sixth seal unleashes cosmic catastrophes: there is a great earthquake, the sun is darkened, the moon becomes like blood, and stars fall from the sky, all images used in prophetic oracles of judgment (Isa 13:10; 38:19; 50:3; Joel 2:10). The sky is rolled up (cf. Isa 34:4), a preview of its later transformation into a "new heaven" (21:1). According to Mark 13:24–31 (cf. Matt 24:29–35; Luke 21:25–33), Jesus predicts similar phenomena before the coming of the Son of Man to gather his elect, as signs that end is near (cf. 2 Esd 5:1–12).

These cosmic signs prompt a reaction of utter terror. The rich and powerful, along with slaves and free men, seek hiding places in caves and mountains, fearing the "great day" of the wrath of God. From the time of the prophets the "day of the Lord" and similar phrases (e.g. Rev 16:14: "the great day of God the Almighty"; 1 Cor 3:13: "the day") are used in the OT and NT to designate the time of God's judgment, either within history (e.g. Amos 5:18–20: judgment on Israel; Jer 50:27–31: judgment of Babylon; Isa 24:21: judgment of "the kings of the earth"; Ezek 38:17–23, judgment of the mythic enemy of Israel, Gog of Magog), or at history's end (e.g. 1 Cor 1:8; 3:13; 5:5; 1 Thess 5:2; 2 Thess 2:2; 2 Peter 3:10). African-American spirituals such as "My Lord, What a Mornin' " use images from the plague sequences, such as falling stars and darkening of sun and moon (6:12), falling rocks (cf. 6:16; 8:8), fire from heaven (8:5, cf. 20:9) and trumpets (8:2–9:20; 11:15–19) to describe the dramatic end of the present situation.

V. Interlude: Sealing of the Elect (7:1–17)

7:1–8. Sealing of the 144,000. This chapter is the first example of a phenomenon that recurs several times in Revelation: the interruption of a sequence at a point just before its completion (cf.

10:10–11:14). The rush of eschatological events unleashed by the opening of the first six seals is interrupted by a two-part vision of the assembly of the people of God. This vision, together with its counterpart in Rev 14, has its roots in prophetic texts that predict an assembly of the dispersed Israelites in Zion (Isa 2; Mic 4; Ezek 37:12; cf., Deut. 30:3-5; 2 Esd 13).

The opening of the seventh seal is postponed for a different kind of seal: a mark placed on the forehead of faithful believers to identify them as God's own, as the Hebrews at the time of the exodus were protected from the plagues on the Egyptians by means of a mark of blood on their doorposts (Exod 12:21–27). This sealing closely mirrors a vision of the prophet Ezekiel set in Jerusalem shortly before the Babylonian exile. As God's executioners are about to punish those whose idolatrous practices have polluted the Temple, Ezekiel beholds a figure sent to mark the foreheads of those who refuse to participate in idolatry (Ezek 9). In Rev 7 the angels in charge of the four winds are about to punish recalcitrant humanity; this recalls Jer 49:36, where God promises to deliver punishment by unleashing winds from the four quarters of heaven.

The four angels are told to wait by a fifth angel who appears from the "rising of the sun" to seal the elect. The sealing suggests a signet ring used to guarantee a person's identity; there may also be a secondary allusion to baptism, which several NT texts call "the seal" (1 Cor 9:2 2 Cor 1:22; Eph 1:13; cf. Eph 4:30). This seal that marks the faithful is mentioned several times in what follows (9:4; 14:1; 22:4), and it has its opposite number in the mark on the forehead and right hand that identifies those who follow the "beast from the sea," the arrogant enemy of God (13:16–17; 14:9;16:2; 19:20; 20:4).

This vision of the 144,000 expresses the continuity of the church as the true Israel with God's chosen people of the OT (cf. Rom 9:6–7; 11:17–21; Gal 6:16; cf. Jas 1:1). The symbolic number, a multiple of twelve, suggests the twelve tribes of Israel, as the list in 7:5–8 confirms. Possibly this group refers to Jews or Jewish Christians, while the countless multitude "from all tribes and peoples and languages" in 7:9–17 symbolizes Gentile Christians. More likely is that the first group refers to Christians who are faithful to the point of mar-

tyrdom and the second, larger group symbolizes all faithful Christians including the martyrs. The identification of the 144,000 as martyrs is suggested by another description in 14:1–5, where they are said to "follow the Lamb wherever he goes"; they are called "first fruits," an OT image for a sacrificial offering (Exod 23:19: Deut 26:2; Jer 2:3; cf. Rom 16:5) Although there is no evidence of widespread persecution of Christians at the end of the first century, Revelation issues a repeated call to be faithful onto death (cf. 2:13; 6:9–10; 11:7–14; 20:4–6).

7:9–17. The Multitude from Every Nation. While the sealing of the 144,000 takes place on earth, the second vision of ch. 7 is located in the heavenly throne room (cf. 4:1–5:13), where the throng of the faithful "from every nation" who have survived the "great ordeal" (*thlipsis*, 7:14) stand before the throne of God, in the company of angels, elders, and living creatures, and sing praises to God and to the Lamb, echoing the hymns of 5:11–13. This is a proleptic vision of the blessed reward of all those who will triumph with God in the eschatological battle, an anticipation of the New Jerusalem described in Rev 21–22. If the first vision of Rev 7 implies the continuity of the church with Israel, the second expresses the universality of its mission.

Elsewhere in the NT *thlipsis* (used in Rev 1:9; 2:9, 10, 22), which can also be translated "tribulation," describes the suffering that is to come immediately before the fulfillment of God's saving purposes (see, e.g. 1 Cor 7:26; Col. 1:24). Those who survive this "tribulation" are said to have "washed their robes ... in the blood of the Lamb" (7:14), probably a reference to the redemptive effects of Christ's death (cf. 1:5; 5:6–9; cf. Heb 9 on the cleansing effect of Christ's blood). They are promised great reward, but this does not mean they will be spared from all suffering, contrary to the claims of some interpreters of Revelation who insist that true Christians will not experience one moment of the "tribulation" because they will be snatched up to heaven before the plagues of the end time are unleashed. This idea of the "rapture," an important theme in many other popular interpretations of Revelation, goes back to the teaching of nineteenth-century English clergyman John Nelson Darby, which was popularized in *The Scofield Reference Bible*. (Belief in a "rapture," a theme not found in Revelation, is based on 1 Thess 4:13–17, where Paul speaks of the second coming of Christ). In Rev 7 the 144,000 are marked with the Lamb's seal not in order to be "raptured" but for faithful witness, even onto death; and the multitude of Christians from the nations must come through the "great ordeal."

The chapter concludes with a moving picture of the life of the faithful will experience at the consummation (7:15–17). The specific promises of freedom from hunger and thirst, protection from scorching sun, and abundant water echo words uttered to the exiles in Babylon by the prophet, Deutero-Isaiah (Isa 49:10) and anticipate the description of the New Jerusalem in Rev 21:1–22:5. Their greatest blessing will be the direct presence of God and of the Lamb. The awesome figure on the throne, adored by the heavenly hosts (4:1–11), is also the one who will "wipe every tear from their eyes" (cf. 21:4 and Isa 25:8).

VI. Second Cycle of Seven Plagues (8:1–9:21; 11:15–19)

8:1–6. Seal 7 and Distribution of 7 Trumpets. The seven trumpets are preceded by a vision of heavenly worship. Once again we glimpse the heavenly throne-room (cf. 4:1–5:13), a reminder that what happens on earth has its origins with God. This paragraph joins together the first two plague sequences. After the interlude of the sealing of the 144,000, the Lamb opens the seventh seal, which leads to a half-hour of silence in heaven, after which seven angels are entrusted with trumpets. The eschatological silence is reminiscent of several OT texts (Ps 46:10; 62:1; Zech 2:13; cf. *Letter of Aristeas* 95). In 2 Esd 7:30 the universe returns to silence after the upheavals of the last things.

The sounding of the trumpet has a long history within the Bible: it is a sign of crisis, marking decisive moments in the nation's life (Lev 25:9) and also signaling the judgment of God (Joel 2:1). In Matt 24:31, 1 Thess 4:16, and 1 Cor 15:52 it forms part of the eschatological scene when Jesus returns to gather the elect.

8:7–13. Trumpets 1–4. The seven trumpet visions of Rev 8–9 and the seven bowl visions of Rev 16 are largely repetitions of the seven seals in Rev 6; all three cycles describe the same eschato-

logical scenario, the "messianic woes" that according to Jewish tradition would precede God's final redemption of his chosen people. One difference of the second and third plague sequences from the seven seals is that their consequences are even more severe. While the seals affect a quarter of the earth (6:8), the trumpets affect a third (8:7; 9, 10, 11, 12; 9:18) and the effects of the bowls have no limit (16:3). A further difference from the seal cycle is that trumpet and bowl visions use imagery from the ten plagues by which God delivered the Israelites from slavery in Egypt. Three of the first four trumpets call forth plagues reminiscent of those in Egypt: the first brings hail, fire, and blood that destroy vegetation (cf. the seventh plague of Exod 9:13–25); the second resembles the first Egyptian plague, as water in the sea is turned to blood (cf. Exod 7:14–25); the darkening of sun, moon and stars brought by the fourth trumpet recalls the darkness of the ninth Egyptian plague (Exod 10:21–28). The third trumpet causes a blazing star called "wormwood" to fall into rivers and springs, making them bitter. This has no parallel in Exodus, but it recalls Jer 23:15: "I am feeding this people with wormwood, and giving them poisonous water to drink" (cf. Prov 5:4 on the bitterness of wormwood). Also without parallel in Exodus is the burning mountain called forth by the second trumpet.

Over the centuries, some readers have understood the twenty-one plagues of the seal, trumpet, and bowl cycles as describing a literal, chronological sequence of end time events (one contemporary example is the popular *Left Behind* series of novels). This reading is made difficult by obvious discrepancies in the narrative; for example, the sixth seal implies that all the stars fall from heaven (6:13), but they are still in place in 8:12 when the fourth trumpet blows, causing a third of them to be darkened. The visions are better read as evocative rather than predictive of a literal sequence of events. They use images from the OT and Jewish tradition to make real to the reader the seriousness of human injustice and impiety and the certainty that God will judge them; his holiness cannot tolerate human evil forever.

9:1–12. Trumpet 5. The introduction to the last three trumpet blasts in 8:13 as three woes suggests that their consequences will be particularly disastrous. When the fifth trumpet is blown, John sees a star fall from heaven with a key to the "bottomless pit" (or "abyss"), the temporary abode of demons (cf. 9:11; 11:7; 17:8; 20:1–3). From the pit comes a swarm of terrifying locusts, reminiscent of the eighth plague visited on the Egyptians (Exod 10:1–20) and also of Joel 1:1–2:11. Joel describes a loathsome attack by swarms of locusts, an image to express how God will execute judgment by handing Israel over to its enemies. Like the locusts in Joel 2:4–9, the frightening creatures in John's vision look like "horses equipped for battle" (9:7). The demon who is the locusts' king is called *Abaddon*, the destroyer (9:11, from the Hebrew meaning "place of destruction"; cf. Job 26:6; Prov 15:11), and also *Apollon*, from the Greek word for "destroy," perhaps also playing on the name of the Greek god Apollo

The locusts are allowed to torture humans for five months, and the suffering they inflict will be so great that their victims will long for death. Protected from their attack, however, are those who have the "seal of God" on their foreheads, an allusion to the sealing of the 144,000 in 7:1–8.

9:13–21. Trumpet 6. The sounding of the sixth trumpet brings the second great woe, and John sees the Euphrates River, the boundary between the Roman and Parthian empires. A voice from the heavenly altar of incense (cf. 6:9–11 and 8:3–5) orders the release of four angels bound there, who become an immense army, 200 million strong, whose horses do even more damage than the locusts. They kill a third of humanity by breathing fire, smoke, and sulfur out of their mouths and stinging with their tails.

The chapter concludes in 9:20–21 with a reminder of the purpose of the plagues: they are God's judgment on human idolatry and the sins of murder, sorcery, fornication, and theft, a judgment that should lead to repentance. But those who experience the plagues do not repent (cf. 16:9, 11, 21; 11:13), repeating Pharaoh's "hardness of heart" (Exod 7:13, 22: 8:15). In the letters to the churches, however, Christ holds out hope for repentance (2:5 21; 3:19).

VII. Interlude: The Situation on Earth (10:1–11:19)

10:1–11. The Little Scroll: John's Second Prophetic Commission. In the first two plague sequences, the action is interrupted after the penultimate number, creating a sense of dramatic tension and giving emphasis to the material inserted. Depicted in 10:1–11:14 are John's renewed prophetic commission and the story of two mysterious witnesses. This time John is told not only to write and see as in 1:10–11 but also to prophesy to nations, peoples, and languages (10:11). Allusions to the commission of Jeremiah (Jer 1:10) and Ezekiel's eating the scroll (Ezek 3:1–10) connect John's vocation with that of the OT prophets.

As in 5:2, revelation is given through a "mighty angel." The appearance of this angel is magnificent, underscoring the importance of his revelation. Like the Son of Man (Christ) he appears in a cloud and has a face shining like the sun (cf. 14:14; 1:12–16). With a rainbow over his head (cf. the rainbow surrounding the throne of God in 4:3), he takes a stance with one foot on sea and the other on land, indicating that his revelation is valid for all of creation. His legs "like pillars of fire" are reminiscent of the "pillar of fire" in which God was present with the Israelites in Exod 13:21.

The "little scroll" open in the angel's hand recalls but is not the same as the scroll that was opened by the Lamb in Rev 5; both concern God's plans for the end time. Like the OT prophet Ezekiel, John is commanded to eat the scroll, symbolizing his acceptance of his prophetic commission (10:8–11) and providing an authentication of the prophecies that will follow in the rest of the book. Up to this point John has been a witness to the revelation unfolding before his eyes and ears; now he is commanded to participate in it. John finds that the scroll tastes sweet at first, but then bitter. Like the prophets of the OT, he is to deliver a message of judgment and redemption; before God establishes his kingdom in all the world, humanity must experience God's righteous judgment over all idolatry and injustice. As Paul says in Rom 1:16–18, God's salvation and his wrath are revealed at the same time.

John's encounter with the mighty angel is interrupted by a mysterious revelation from heaven, as the angel's shout, loud as a lion's roar, is drowned out by something even more deafening: seven thunders followed by a voice from heaven (10:3–7). This voice tells John to "seal up" the message of the seven thunders and declares that the mystery of God that was revealed to the prophets will be fulfilled with no delay, when the seventh trumpet is blown.

11:1–2. Measuring the Temple. Revelation is full of imagery of the heavenly temple, but this is the only passage that speaks of the earthly Temple in Jerusalem. The motif of measuring the temple comes from the OT prophets. During the Babylonian exile Ezekiel saw a vision of a superhuman figure measuring the various parts of the Jerusalem Temple (Ezek 40:1–42:20); this image of restoration is repeated in Zech 2:1–5. In Revelation John is told to measure not only the temple and the altar but also those who worship there, suggesting the preservation of those who are faithful to God (cf. 7:3–8); but this does not preclude their suffering, as we see from the rest of ch. 11. The picture of hostile forces trampling the Jerusalem Temple to the very threshold of the holy place suggests the siege of Jerusalem in 70 CE (recorded in Josephus' *Jewish War*), when Roman legionaries drew ever closer to the Temple precincts. Either John's visionary imagination was suffused by the searing impact of this event, or, as early historical scholars suggested, he made use of a Jewish oracle from the days before the fall of Jerusalem, when Zealots took refuge in the sanctuary and were inspired by a prophet who promised deliverance (Josephus, *War* vi.122; 285–7; cf. Luke 21:24).

11:3–14. The Two Witnesses. Bearing faithful witness is an important theme in Revelation, which summons Christians to follow in the footsteps of Christ, the "faithful witness" (1:5, 9; 2:13; 3:8–11; 6:9; 12:11, 17; 19:10; 20:4; 22:16, 20). Christ urges the members of the seven churches to be fearless in testimony, in their lives as well as their words. Chapter 11 makes clear the cost of Christian witness. It presents two witnesses, who prophesy for 1260 days—a symbolic number used in Daniel and elsewhere in Revelation (12:6; cf. Dan 7:25; 12:7) to represent a predetermined, limited time. They perform incredible miracles, but after the appointed time is over they are killed by a beast that ascends from the "bottomless pit." Their bodies are exposed in the streets of Jerusalem, and all peoples of the earth celebrate the removal of the witnesses and their disturbing prophecies.

Images from the OT color the picture of the witnesses. They are compared to two olive trees, a symbol in Zech 4: 3, 14 for God's "anointed ones":

Zerubbabel, the Davidic heir, and Joshua, the high priest, who were involved in efforts to restore the Temple after the Babylonian Exile. In their power to perform miracles the witnesses resemble Moses and Elijah. Like Moses, they turn water into blood (cf. Exod 7:14–25); like Elijah, who could control rain (1 Kgs 17:1; 18:1), they have power to "shut the sky" (11:6).

In the messages in Rev 2–3, Christ promises great things to "those who conquer." In ch. 11 we begin to see what this means, as we are introduced to the main earthly adversary with whom Christ and his followers have to contend, the beast (11:7) that will be the focus of attention in 13:1–10 and 17:8. In later interpretations of Revelation this beast is often referred to as the "antichrist." His power is indeed great, and he wins the first skirmish, killing the witnesses and brutally exposing their bodies in the streets of Jerusalem (here called "Sodom" and "Egypt"), the city where their Lord was crucified. But this is not the last word; after the time appointed by God (11:11, "three and a half days"), God acts both to redeem and judge: the witnesses are brought back to life and snatched up to heaven; a great earthquake strikes the city, killing 7,000 of its inhabitants and bringing the rest to worship God – a rare account of divine punishments leading people to repentance (contrast 9:20–21).

11:15–19. Trumpet 7: A Hymn of Victory. With the blowing of the seventh trumpet the scene shifts back to the heavenly throne room, where voices sing: "The kingdom of the world has/ become the kingdom of our Lord/and of his Messiah,/and he will reign forever"—a text well known from its setting in the "Hallelujah Chorus" from Handel's *Messiah*. The twenty-four elders join the chorus, announcing that the time for judgment and reward has arrived. The time has come for God's kingship—celebrated in heaven in the hymns of Rev 4–5—to be acknowledged by all on earth. This message is reinforced by a dramatic vision of the heavenly temple opened to reveal the ark of the covenant – the heavenly counterpart of the inner sanctum of the Jerusalem Temple. God's awesome presence is indicated in lightning, thunder, earthquake, and hail.

VIII. The Combatants in the Final Battle (12:1–14:20)

12:1–6. The Woman Clothed with the Sun and Her Child. The abrupt announcement of "a great portent in heaven" begins a series of visions in which the main combatants in the eschatological battle are introduced more clearly. In a complex of visions that have affinities with the popular culture of the ancient Mediterranean world and roots in early Christian mythology, John sees a woman clothed with the sun pursued by the dragon, followed by war in heaven between the archangel Michael and Satan. The woman clothed with the sun exemplifies the multivalence of Revelation's symbols. Many different interpretations have been suggested, no one of which accounts for all the details of her depiction. Similarities with various figures—including the Egyptian queen of heaven, Isis, who wore a crown of stars, and Leto, who in Greek myth was pursued by the dragon Python when she was about to give birth to the Greek god Apollo—suggest that this image would have resonated with John's audience.

The child the women bears is the Messiah, who is destined to rule the nations "with a rod of iron," an allusion to the royal Ps 2:8–9 (also cited in 2:26–27; 19:15). For this reason the woman is sometimes interpreted as the people Israel, from whom the Messiah came. In the earliest Christian interpretations (e.g. Hippolytus, *Antichrist* 61) she was understood as a symbol of the church, who "bears" the Messiah by teaching the nations about him. More influential has been her identification as the Virgin Mary, mother of the Messiah; and this vision has influenced the development of doctrine and iconography concerning her: the moon under the woman's feet and stars in her crown appear frequently in artistic portrayals of Mary. Compared with the rest of Revelation this passage is unusually prominent in Christian lectionaries because of its Marian connections and its association with the feast of Michael and all angels. After the pope's approval of the doctrine of the Immaculate Conception of Mary in 1476, it became one of the proper scriptural readings for the corresponding feast.

The great red dragon, who reappears in 13:2–13 and 16:13, is identified as Satan in 20:2. The dragon attacks the woman as she is about to give birth to the Messiah. In this preliminary skirmish God protects both the son, who is snatched up to heaven, and the woman, who is given a safe haven in the wilderness. Her story is interrupted by a scene of the heavenly battlefront, to be continued in 12:13–17.

12:7–9. The Great Dragon Defeated by the Angel Michael. This chapter exemplifies especially clearly the two-level drama that is characteristic of apocalyptic writings, as heavenly and earthly events are juxtaposed and closely related to each other. The great battle between the forces of God and the army of Satan—a theme hinted at in the calls to "conquer" in Rev 2–3—is now given fuller description, in both its heavenly and earthly aspects. The war in heaven and Satan's expulsion are both familiar themes in Jewish and early Christian sources. The *War Scroll* (1QM) from the Dead Sea Scrolls describes elaborate preparations for a final battle in which spiritual and human forces join (cf. Dan 10:10–21). In John's vision the human side of the battle involves prophecy, endurance, and witness, rather than force of arms (12:11).

The struggle with suprahuman powers is an important theme in early Christian writings (1 Cor 2:6–8; Eph 6:11–17). Particularly close parallels to our passage are Luke 10:13-15 and John 12:31: "Now is the judgment of this world; now the ruler of the world will be driven out"; the story of the temptation of Jesus by Satan (Matt 4:1–11 par.) belongs to the same theological complex.

12:10–12. Hymn Celebrating Victory in Heaven. The hymn of victory expresses the close connection of the two levels of the battlefront, in heaven and on earth. The victory achieved by the faithful death of Christ the Lamb, celebrated in the hymn of 5:9–13, is here connected with the ancient story of Michael's victory in heaven and also with the witness of Christian believers in the present time. Like the hymn in 11:15, it anticipates the arrival of God's kingdom. Battle imagery gives way to language of the courtroom as Satan is called the "accuser," a reminder of his role in Job 1:9–11.

12:13–17. The Dragon Attacks the Woman. Expelled from heaven, the dragon wreaks havoc on earth, once again attacking the woman and then "making war" on the rest of her children, i.e. Christians who "hold the testimony of Jesus" (cf. 11:7). The story of the woman's escape to the wilderness (cf. 12:6) is repeated, but this time she flies on the wings of a great eagle, a detail that connects her story to that of the Israelites preserved in the wilderness after the exodus. Arriving at Mount Sinai, they are told by God: "You have seen what I did to the Egyptians, and how I bore you on eagles' wings and brought you to myself" (Exod 19:4).

12:18–13:10. The Beast from the Sea. John pictures the dragon taking his stand beside the sea, where he gives his power to a beast arising from the sea, his chief earthly minion. This beast, who first appeared in 11:7 emerging from the abyss to make war on the two witnesses, is now described more fully. Like many other symbols in Revelation, the beast is a traditional image, shared with other biblical and apocalyptic books. The influence of Dan 7, seen already in John's call vision in 1:9–20 and in 11:7, is particularly evident here. In Dan 7:1–8 four beasts that arise from the sea represent four kingdoms and serve as a kind of philosophy of history, explaining the necessity of a pre-ordained succession of world empires before the arrival of the kingdom of God. In Revelation, features of Daniel's four beasts are combined in a single beast with multiple heads.

The beast, like the woman clothed with the sun, has more than one level of meaning. It evokes Dan 7 and also the ancient myth of cosmic combat, a story told in many forms, for example the Babylonian creation story, the *Enuma Elish*, the Canaanite tale of the victory of the chief god, Baal, over Yam (= the Sea), and the story of Leto attacked by the serpent Python. In these stories, which express the triumph of order over chaos and life over death, the enemy of the divine order is often portrayed as a dragon or a sea monster. In the *Enuma Elish*, for example, the god Marduk becomes king of the gods by defeating a sea monster called Tiamat. Traces of this ancient story are evident in prophetic and poetic texts in the OT, most notably in the depiction of God's power over the terrifying sea monster Leviathan in Job 41 (cf. Job 3:8; 7:12; 26:12–13; Ps 74:13–14; 89:9–10; Isa 27:1; 51:9–11); and it informs descriptions of the last battle between God and the forces of evil in apocalyptic texts, including Dan 7. In a startling example of political protest, the ancient image of the sea monster now serves to describe the domi-

nant power of John's day, the Roman Empire and the emperors who rule it.

Specifically the beast evokes the emperor Nero (who ruled 54–68), the first emperor to order persecution of Christians. Blaming Christians for a great fire in Rome in 64 CE, he had Christians set alight as human torches. Although his persecution was short and limited to the city of Rome, it had a lasting effect on Christian consciousness, and Nero became a prime symbol of evil power. Nero also lived on in the memory of his Roman supporters, but in a positive way. After he was forced by political opponents to commit suicide, many of his followers believed he would return and restore their fortunes, giving rise to the myth of *Nero redivivus*, that is "Nero alive again." In Jewish and Christian texts this myth is turned on its head: Nero the expected hero becomes Nero the chief adversary of God in the end time (*Sibylline Oracles 3* 24:119–124, 138–39; 5:137–52, 362). There is an allusion to this tradition in Rev 13:3: "One of its heads seemed to have received a death-blow, but its mortal wound had been healed" (cf. 13:14:"the beast that was wounded by the sword and yet lived"; 17:8).

The association of the beast from the sea with Nero is strengthened by 13:18: "Let him who has understanding reckon the number of the beast, for it is a human number; its number is 666" (author's trans.). Over the centuries there have been thousands of different interpretations of this verse, but Nero is the most likely referent. This is an example of an ancient practice called *gematria*, the symbolic interpretation of numbers. In Hebrew, Greek, and Latin, where there are no separate numbers, letters are used to indicate numbers, with a=1, b=2, etc. If you add up the numerical equivalents of the name "Nero Caesar" in Hebrew you get 666. Perhaps this example of *gematria* based on Hebrew was preserved in the Greek-speaking churches of Asia Minor; several features of Revelation, including its odd, Semitic Greek, suggest that the author was a Jewish Christian from Palestine. On another level, the beast may also symbolize the emperor Domitian, during whose reign (81–96) Revelation was probably written (see on 13:11–18 and 17:1–6).

13:11–18. The Beast from the Land. A second beast appears from the land to enforce worship of the beast from the sea. Here again John uses traditional imagery to represent contemporary reality. In Job 40–41 the sea monster Leviathan is joined by a beast called Behemoth, who dwells on the earth (a tradition echoed in *1 Enoch* 60.7–10, 24 and 2 Esd 6.47–52). Together the two beasts represent the forces of evil and chaos defeated by God at the beginning of creation. John's description of the beast from the land as performing signs and wonders and deceiving the people is also reminiscent of the false prophet of Deut. 13:1–5. This second beast probably symbolizes the local priesthood of the Roman imperial cult, or perhaps the local authorities in Asia Minor who encouraged worship of the emperor in order to curry favor. In Rome itself a number of emperors, beginning with Augustus, were worshiped as divine (*divus*) after their death; according to the Roman author Pliny (*Pan.* 52.1, 7) the emperor Domitian went further and demanded sacrifices to himself during his lifetime. In the Eastern provinces such as Asia Minor worship of the living emperor was more common. For example, in 89–90 a temple called the "temple of the *Sebastoi* [revered ones]" was dedicated to Domitian.

Interpreters of Revelation often refer to the beast from the sea as the *antichrist*, a word used in 1 John 2:18, 22; 4:3 and 2 John 7 for an earthly representative of Satan. Although the word does not occur in Revelation, it is an apt description of this beast, who is the opposite number and chief earthly opponent to Christ. He is also a counterfeit Christ, who has a "mortal wound" (13:3) that mimics the crucifixion of the Lamb (13:8; 5:6). This was given graphic illustration in a fresco entitled "The Preaching of the Antichrist" painted by Luca Signorelli around 1501 in the San Brizio Chapel of the cathedral in Orvieto, Italy; here the *antichrist* has features traditionally used to depict Christ. In Rev 13:8 the beast mimics Christ in receiving worship from the "whole world," but this is false worship, not the true worship of God and the Lamb celebrated throughout the book of Revelation.

14:1–5. The Lamb and the 144,000. Once again John sees 144,000 people who have God's name on their foreheads (cf. 7:3). Now they stand with the Lamb on Mount Zion, the Temple mountain in Jerusalem (cf. 2 Esd 13, where the savior figure assembles a throng on a mountain). In 14:2 the scene shifts to the heavenly throne room (cf. 4:1–

5:14), and John hears a thundering chorus as the 144,000 join the heavenly hosts in a "new song." The 144,000 are described as "virgins," which suggests the traditions of holy war in the OT; abstaining from sexual relations was required as preparation for battle (Deut 23:9–14; 1 Sam 21:5; 2 Sam 11:9–13; *1QM* 7:3–9; *11QTemp* 58:17–19; cf. Exod 19:15, where sexual relations are to be avoided before approaching the holy mountain of Sinai). That the 144,000 represent Christian martyrs is suggested by their description as "first fruits" (an image from the OT for a sacrificial offering; Exod 23:19: Deut 26:2; Jer 2:3; cf. Rom 16:5), who follow the Lamb "wherever he goes."

14:6–13. Messages of Three Angels. With the loud singing in his ears, John looks up and sees three angels flying in mid-heaven, and attention shifts from the faithful followers of the Lamb to the unrepentant worshipers of the beast. The first angel proclaims an "eternal gospel," a call to all people to worship God. Like 7:9–17, this call "to every nation and tribe and language and people" expresses the universal scope of the Christian mission. The next two angels pronounce judgment. Those who fail to repent of their false worship and turn to the true God will drink the "wine of God's wrath" (an image for divine judgment in Jer 25:15–17) and experience eternal torment (cf. 20:10). The second angel proclaims: "Fallen is Babylon"—the first reference to Babylon, used in Revelation as in other apocalypses as a code name for Rome, whose destruction will be described more fully in Rev 17–18. As in 11:11–15, the conclusion of the eschatological events is anticipated. The stark contrast this chapter draws between followers of the Lamb and those marked by the beast resembles the two-way doctrine in early Christian texts such as *Didache* 1–3 and the *Epistle of Barnabas* 18–20. Now is the time for a decision.

14:14–20. Harvest of the Son of Man. The chapter concludes with images that anticipate the last judgment that will be narrated in 20:11–15. Judgment is portrayed through the traditional image of a harvest (cf. Hos 6:11; Matt 3:12; 9:37; 13:30, 39). John sees "one like the Son of Man" seated on a cloud, wearing a golden crown and carrying a sickle (cf. 1:12–16). The title is based on Dan 7:13–14, where it describes an angelic figure installed as universal ruler; it is used often for Jesus in the Gospels, which expect his second coming seated on the clouds and accompanied by angels (Mark 8:38; 13:26–27; 14:62; cf. Rev 1:7 where it is said of Christ: "he is coming with the clouds").

The "one like the Son of Man" is told to reap by an angel who emerges from the heavenly temple, symbolizing that the judgment is ordered by God. His sickle recalls the description of God's judgment on the nations in Joel 3, which includes the oracle: "Put in the sickle, / for the harvest is ripe. / Go in, tread, / for the wine press is full. / The vats overflow, / for their wickedness is great" (Joel 3:13). John sees two harvest scenes: a grain harvest in 14:15–16 and a harvest of grapes in 14:17–20. The first harvest may depict the gathering of the elect; according to Mark 13:26–27 the Son of Man and his angels will gather his elect "from the four winds" (cf. the harvest image in John 4:33–38). The grape harvest symbolizes the negative side of divine judgment; the vivid imagery of treading the "wine press of the wrath of God" recalls a frightening depiction in Isa 63 of God's coming to redeem Israel by wreaking judgment on the nations, his garments red with the juice of grapes.

IX. Third Cycle of Seven Plagues (15:1–16:21)

15:1–4. Preparation in Heaven: The Song of Moses.
Chapter 15 sets the stage for the third plague sequence, which will unfold in ch. 16. John sees a heavenly portent, seven angels who will unleash the seven last plagues. As in 4:2–5 he sees God's heavenly throne room, with its "sea of glass" and four living creatures. Beside the heavenly sea stand "those who had conquered the beast and its image and the number of its name"—a description that looks back to 13:5–18, where "conquering" indicates worshiping God alone, no matter what the costs, and refusing to be complicit in the idolatrous worship demanded by Rome.

The sea of glass recalls the miraculous crossing of the great sea in Exod 14. The song Moses and the Israelites sang after seeing their pursuers drowned in the sea (Exod 15) is recast as the "song of Moses ... and the Lamb": "Great and amazing are your deeds, / Lord God the Almighty! / Just and true are your ways .... / All nations will come / and worship before you, / for your judgments

have been revealed" (15:3–4). In contrast to 13:3, where the "whole earth" worships the beast, this text expresses an optimistic view of the success of the Christian witness to God (cf. 21:24–25; 22:2), a counterpoint to the many images of God's judgment on an unrepentant world.

15:5–8. Seven Bowls Prepared in the Heavenly Temple.
Next John sees "the temple of the tent of witness" being opened (cf. 11:19), which reflects the view that there is a heavenly model for the tabernacle in the wilderness (cf. Exod 25:9; Heb 8:2; 9:11). Tabernacle/Temple imagery continues in the seven golden bowls full of God's wrath that one of the living creatures hands over to the angels, which suggest the vessels of the tabernacle and the Jerusalem Temple (Exod 27:3). God's awesome power and glory is evident as the Temple fills with smoke; his holiness cannot forever endure the evil and injustice that reigns on earth.

16:1–11. Bowls 1–5 Poured out on Earth.
Chapter 16 contains the third series of plagues, all of which describe the messianic woes, the trials of the *eschaton*. While there is much here that repeats the earlier plagues, this sequence is introduced as the "last plagues" (15:1, cf. 16:17) indicating finality. The bowl sequence, like the seven trumpets, contains much imagery from the Egyptian plagues. When the first bowl is poured out, those who worship the beast (13:4–8) experience painful sores, paralleling the sixth plague in Egypt (Exod 9:8–12; cf. 7:14–25). The emptying of the next two bowls causes sea and rivers to turn to blood, recalling the first plague when Moses turned the Nile and all the waters of Egypt to blood (Exod 7:14–25). When the angel empties the fourth bowl over the sun, it scorches people with intense heat; the fifth bowl, poured over the throne of the beast, brings darkness over his whole kingdom, similar to the ninth Egyptian plague (Exod 10:21–28).

The plagues are punctuated by commentary. After the first three bowls an angel sings a doxology that interprets them as God's judgment on an unjust world: "You are just, O Holy One, who are and were, / for you have judged these things; / because they shed the blood of saints and prophets." Descriptions of the fourth and fifth plagues include judgment of those affected for their failure to repent.

16:12–16. Bowl 6: Armageddon. John again sees the Euphrates River (cf. 9:14), the boundary between the Roman and Parthian empires; now it is dried up so that the Parthians and their allies can cross and attack, a common Roman fear. The dragon and the two beasts of Rev 12–13 reappear. From their mouths come forth evil demons in the form of frogs who assemble kings from the whole world for the last battle in the "great day of God the Almighty" (see on 6:17). A direct address of Christ to the reader warns that this day is near: "See I am coming like a thief" (16:13, cf. 3:3 and 22:7).

The frogs recall the second plague in Exodus (8:1–15). That the demons issue from the mouths of a dragon and beasts may imply a war of words in which Roman propaganda extolling the universal sovereignty of emperor and empire competes with Christian claims for God and his Messiah (cf. 13:11–14). The kings of the world assemble at Armageddon (NRSV, "Harmagedon"), a transliteration of a Hebrew word that means the mount of Meggido, the site of many important battles in the history of Israel, a name deeply rooted in Jewish hope and fears (see Judg 5:19; 2 Kgs 23:29–30; 2 Chr 35:22–24; Zech 12:11). The word *Armageddon* pervades popular imagination about global cataclysm. The site of Israel's victory over Canaanite kings and of king Josiah's defeat has become an image of the ultimate conflict. In popular interpretation, the battle scene described here is the end of the story, but the narrative of Revelation continues for six more chapters, and the theme of the last battle will be repeated several times (17:12–16; 18:8–10; 19:11–16; 20:7–9).

16:17–21. Bowl 7: Babylon Destroyed. With the emptying of the seventh bowl, John hears a voice from the heavenly temple saying "It is done!"—a proleptic statement of the end (cf. 21:6). There follows a powerful earthquake, accompanied by lightning, rumbling, and thunder, signs of divine power and holiness evident in the theophany at Mount Sinai (Exod 19:16) and in descriptions of God's heavenly throne in 4:5 and 11:19. These bring about the destruction of Babylon/Rome (announced in 14:8), which is split in three parts, and the fall of the "cities of the nations." The awe-inspiring character of the divine appearance for judgment is further underlined as mountains and islands flee (cf. Ps 97:5; Ezek 38:20; Isa 40:3–4).

The last plague concludes with the fall of hail, echoing the seventh Egyptian plague of thunder and hail (Exod 9:13–35) as well as the "heavy hail" brought on by the seventh trumpet (11:19). Here, at the climax of the twenty-one plague visions, the punishment is magnified so that each hailstone weighs 100 pounds.

X. The Whore of Babylon and Her Destruction (17:1–19:10)

17:1–6. Vision of the Whore of Babylon. John is carried away in the Spirit to the wilderness, where he beholds an arresting sight: a sumptuously clad woman who holds a golden cup "full of abominations" and seduces the "kings of the earth" to fornicate with her. The personification of a great city opposed to the ways of God as a wayward woman is common in the prophets (e.g. Jerusalem and Samaria in Ezek 23, Tyre and Sidon in Isa 23; Babylon in Jer 51). The whore of Babylon symbolizes the city of Rome and the seductive power of the Roman Empire with its ideology of might and prosperity. In Revelation as in the OT, fornication is a metaphor for idolatrous worship of other gods and also for putting trust in earthly political powers instead of the true God (cf. Hos 1–3; Jer 2–3). The whore is intoxicated by her power, including the power to claim political and religious allegiance and to persecute those who do not comply. She is drunk with the blood of saints, i.e. Christian martyrs (cf. 6:9–10). Her attire in luxurious fabrics and precious jewels symbolizes the attraction of earthly power in general, and Rome in particular—a vivid contrast to with two other symbolic women in Revelation, the women clothed with the sun in Rev 12 and the pure bride of the Lamb in 19:7–8; 21:2–27.

17:7–17. Explanation of the Vision. The extraordinary vision of Babylon enthroned on the beast includes a feature that is unusual in John's apocalypse. While the book of Daniel is full of explanations of its dreams and visions, John's images usually remain without interpretation. Revelation 17 offers a notable exception (cf. 1:20; 4:5; 13:18). We are told that she represents the "great city that rules over the kings of the earth" (17:18; cf. 17:15) and that the heads of the beast she rides are seven mountains (17:9), suggesting the seven hills of Rome. Facilitating this personification of Rome was the practice of worshiping Rome as a goddess

(*Dea Roma*), to whom temples were dedicated. John follows Jewish apocalyptic tradition in using "Babylon" as a code name for Rome (17:5; cf.2 Esd 4:2.28–31; 16:44, 46; *2 Apocalypse of Baruch* 10:2; *Sibylline Oracles* 5:143, 159), an association suggested by the Roman destruction of the Temple in Jerusalem in 70 CE, which recalled the Babylonian destruction of the first Temple in 586 BCE.

Chapter 17 is closely linked with the depiction of arrogant powers in rebellion against God in Rev 13. The scarlet beast on which the whore rides has seven heads and ten horns and is full of "blasphemous names," like the beast from the sea in 13:1 (which in turn plays on Dan 7:7, 20, 24). The heads of the beast are given a second interpretation as seven kings: "five of whom have fallen, one is, and the other has not yet come, and when he comes, he must remain only a little while" (17:9–10, author's trans.). Ancient Jewish writers engaged in similar allusive reference to Roman emperors (e.g., *Sibylline Oracles* 5:12). The sixth king (the one who "is") must be the emperor during whose rule John writes—probably Domitian, though there is no agreement on how to match up the six "kings" to whom John refers with the list of the Roman emperors. Perhaps seven is used only as a general symbol of a complete sequence. In the beast who "was, and is not, and is about to ascend from the bottomless pit" (17:8; cf. 17:11: who is "an eighth but it belongs to the seven"), there is another allusion to the myth of *Nero redivivus* (see on 12:18–13:11). This description parodies the praise of God as the one "who was and is and is to come" in 4:8 (cf. 1:4, 8).

The ten horns of the beast are explained as ten kings (cf. Dan 7:24), mirroring the practice of Roman generals of enlisting client kings in the eastern provinces. The ten kings join the beast in "making war" on the Lamb; the battle described here is the same eschatological battle narrated in 19:11–21, and prepared for in 9:13–19 and 16:12–16. Such repetitions tell against interpretation of Revelation as giving a literal blueprint of end time events that will follow one another in a strict chronological sequence. As in 19:16 the victorious Lamb is called "Lord of lords and King of kings," a title used for God in Dan 2:37, *1 Enoch* 9:4, and 1 Tim 6:15.

18:1–3. An Angel Celebrates the Fall of Babylon.
God's judgment on Rome/Babylon is made vivid by being portrayed from several points of view. First a resplendent angel announces "Fallen is Babylon the great"; as in 11:15 and 14:8 present and future are intertwined. John's critique of Rome/Babylon follows a common prophetic form, and it parallels in many specific points Jeremiah's predictions of judgment on Babylon (Jer 51) and Ezekiel's lament over the city of Tyre (Ezek 27–8). The chapter echoes many prophetic texts and contains several word-for-word quotations, e.g. 18:2: "fallen, fallen is Babylon" (Isa 21:9) and 18:4: "Come out of her!" (Jer 51:45). The critique of Rome has religious, political, and economic dimensions. Babylon is cursed as the dwelling place of foul animals and demons (cf. Isa 13:21–22; Jer 51:37); she has seduced nations and kings to give her their primary loyalty, thus committing "fornication" against the only true God.

18:4–8. Call to Come out of Babylon.
A voice from heaven makes clear the point of this chapter for the Christian audience. Echoing words of the OT prophets, it commands them: "Come out from her," i.e. do not participate in her sins. Lady Babylon (Rome) is mocked for her love of luxury and her arrogance. Her fall will come suddenly, as she is overtaken by pestilence, mourning, famine, and fire; and she will be paid double for all her misdeeds.

18:9–20. Kings, Merchants, and Sailors Lament Babylon's Fall.
In contrast to Jer 51, which describes Babylon being destroyed by enemy armies, Rev 18 does not describe Rome's destruction directly but instead reports what three groups of onlookers see and feel as they behold the destruction from afar, rather as the chorus in a Greek tragedy comments on the play's action. The dirge for Babylon/Rome is spoken in three parts by kings of the earth, merchants, and sailors. The kings, seeing Babylon burn, are awe-struck by the swiftness of her judgment. The lament of the merchants contains a detailed list of the luxury goods they carry for Rome (cf. the lament for Tyre in Ezek 27). Rome is judged not only for her arrogance and love of luxury but also for her injustice: the list of precious cargo ends with "human lives"—a condemnation of slavery. John's voice is heard, calling on heaven and "saints and apostles and prophets" to rejoice (18:20). The cry for justice by the souls of the martyrs (6:9–11) has been answered; God has given them justice against Rome.

18:21–24. Angel Predicts Fall of Babylon. The prophets of the OT delivered their message through prophetic actions as well as words. Jeremiah orders the bearer of his oracles of judgment against Babylon to tie them to a stone and throw them into the Euphrates River, symbolizing the total demise of the city (Jer 51:63–64). A similar symbolic action concludes Rev 18: a mighty angel throws an immense millstone into the sea, foretelling the total destruction of Rome.

19:1–10. Hallelujah!: A Hymn Celebrates the Coming of the Kingdom of God. Throughout the book, John's accounts of his visions are punctuated by hymns that celebrate the power and glory of God and the Lamb, and their triumph over the powers of evil (4:8, 11; 5:9–13; 7:10-12; 11:15–18; 12:10–12; 15:3–4; cf. 16:5–7 and 21:3–4). The last of these songs in 19:1–8 celebrates God's judgment of the whore of Babylon, which has avenged the blood of God's servants. This echoes the hymn in 11:18 that rejoices that the time has come "for destroying those who destroy the earth." God's judgment is part of his salvific action, which is praised as just: "Salvation and glory and power to our God, for his judgments are true and just"—a point emphasized also in earlier songs (15:3; 16:5–7).

This hymn has four strophes: the first two are sung by a "great multitude" in heaven (cf. 7:9), after which the twenty-four elders and four living creatures of 4:4–11 join the chorus. In the last strophe, a multitude again sings, now in deafening tones: "Hallelujah!/For the Lord our God/the Almighty reigns." The coming of the kingdom of God is a major theme in the teaching of Jesus (see, e.g., Mark 1:14–15). In Matt 6:10 Jesus teaches his followers to pray: "Your kingdom come./Your will be done,/on earth as it is in heaven" (cf. Luke 11:2). The movement of Revelation is from the present situation, when the kingship of God and of Christ the Lamb is acknowledged by all the hosts of heaven (4:1–5:13) to the final visions of the New Jerusalem, the ideal state of affairs when God's kingly rule is fully established in all the earth, and death and evil are no more. This final state, anticipated in the hymnic praises of 11:15–16; 12:10, and here in 19:6, is about to be realized by the return of the Lamb of God, his final defeat of the powers of evil, and his marriage to his pure bride, the antithesis to the whore of Babylon.

An angel instructs John to write: "Blessed are those who are invited to the marriage supper of the Lamb." John prostrates himself before the heavenly messenger, only to be rebuked and told: "Worship God!" (19:9–10) These two words encapsulate the message of the book (see on 22:6–9).

XI. The Completion of God's Kingdom (19:11–22:7)

19:11–16. The Second Coming of Christ as the Rider on a White Horse. In 4:1 John saw a door open up into heaven, and now in 19:11 he sees the heaven opened, and the last act of the eschatological drama begins. Like many other NT books, Revelation understands Christian existence as poised between the two advents of Christ, his first coming as Jesus of Nazareth to live and die for the sake of humanity, and his second coming in glory to complete God's redemption of the world through a final victory over the forces of evil. Many NT texts speak of the *parousia*, the second coming of Christ (e.g., Matt 25:31–46; Mark 13:4, 24–27; Luke 19:11; 21:27; Acts 1:8–11; 1 Pet 1:5–7; 5:4; 1 John 2:28–3:3). Saint Paul eagerly anticipates Christ's return, when all the dead will be raised and Christ will complete his victory over the enemies of God and deliver the kingdom over to God the Father (1 Cor 16:22, 15:22–28, 50–56; cf. 1 Thess 4:13–17; Rom 13:11). In Revelation the visions of judgment are framed by references to Christ's first coming, as the Lamb that was slain in Rev 5, and this vision of his second coming to judge and "make war" in 19:11–16.

The description of Christ as rider is full of messianic images and titles of honor. It echoes biblical passages where God is portrayed as divine warrior (e. g. Exod 15:3; Isa 59:17–19) and recalls John's vision of Christ as "one like the Son of Man" who has eyes "like a flame of fire" and a sword issuing from his mouth (1:12–20; cf. 14:4–20). The sword in his mouth to smite the nations parallels messianic prophecies like Isa 11:4: "With righteousness he shall judge the poor . . . he shall strike the earth with the rod of his mouth" (cf. 2 Esd 13:9–11; *Psalms of Solomon* 17:24; 2 Thess 2:8). These passages suggest that judgment comes by the power of the word of God rather than through force of arms. His rule with the "rod of iron" is based on a description of God's "messiah" in Ps 2:8–9 (cf. Rev

12:5). In the NT Christ is called *Logos*, or "Word of God" only here and in John 1:1 and 1 John 1:1. "King of Kings" (cf. 17:14) was used as an honorific for Persian rulers (see Ezra 7:12); elsewhere in Jewish and early Christian literature it refers to God the creator (Dan 4:37; *1 Enoch* 9:2; 1 Tim 6:15). The robe dipped in blood connects the rider to the slain Lamb of Rev 5. That it also refers to the enemies' blood is suggested by Isa 63:1–6, where the divine warrior wears garments stained red from treading the winepress of his wrath. The heavenly armies that accompany the rider may also have a double reference to angelic hosts and human beings who follow the Lamb.

19:17–21. The Last Battle: Defeat of the Two Beasts. Christ comes to judge and to make war (19:11). God's final judgment on all that resists his righteous rule is at hand. This is described in 19:17–20:10 with battle imagery; a picture of the Last Judgment follows in 20:11–15. Imagery of war conveys the seriousness of the threat posed by human and superhuman evil powers. First introduced in the calls to Christians to "conquer" in Rev 2–3 and running through the book (9:7; 12:3–13; 13:7; 14:17; 16:12–16; 17:12–14), it climaxes in Rev 19–20 with the declaration of final victory over the beast, the "false prophet"(cf. 16:13; 13:11) and the "kings of the earth." The grisly feast of birds called to consume the flesh of the "kings of the earth" is a macabre twist on the "messianic banquet" that in Jewish and NT texts expresses the joy of the *eschaton* (e.g. Isa. 25:6–8; 55:1–2; 65:13–14; Matt 8:11; Luke 13:29; 14:15; 22:16, 29–30; cf. the "wedding feast of the Lamb" in Rev 19:9, author's trans.). The text closely parallels Ezek 39:4, 17–20, where God promises to hand over the mythic enemy of Israel, Gog of Magog, to the birds of prey. When the beast and the false prophet are confined to the "lake of fire," God's victory over his human enemies is complete. The picture of eternal punishment of those who resist God up to the end reinforces the book's repeated calls to repentance. Though the time of the last battle is near, there is still time to repent and turn to God (22:12–21).

20:1–6. The Millennium: Satan Imprisoned While the Martyrs Rule for 1,000 Years. After the rider's victory over all human enemies, the reader awaits the final victory over Satan. But first there is a surprising detour, lasting for 1,000 years, when Satan is locked into a pit so that he cannot deceive "the nations," and the martyrs are resurrected and reign together with Christ. The expectation of an earthly kingdom was common in Jewish eschatology and was also typical of Christian hope in the second century (e.g. in Justin, Irenaeus, Tertullian, the Montanists), though no other text speaks of a "millennium," i.e. a 1,000-year kingdom. There are hints of God's reign on earth elsewhere in the NT (Mark 14:25; 1 Cor 6:9; 15:25), but with no mention of a specific time period. Papias of Hierapolis (early second century) recalled a saying of Jesus that the creation would return to and exceed the perfection of the original creation (cited in Irenaeus, *Against the Heresies* 5.33.3–4). The two-stage eschatology in Rev 20–21, in which an intermediate this-worldly messianic period precedes the further eschatological events of resurrection, judgment, and descent of the New Jerusalem, has parallels in the Jewish works *Apocalypse of Baruch* and 2 Esdras. There was considerable debate about this subject in the early centuries of the church, with influential theologians such as Origen and Augustine disputing the belief that there would be a literal earthly kingdom.

In Revelation the millennial rule of the martyrs provides them with a special reward, an answer to the souls of those slain for their testimony in 6:9–11, who cry out for vengeance. Although description of the millennium takes up only three verses (20:4–6), this special feature of the book's eschatology has been very influential in later interpretations of the book, especially among those who understand Revelation as providing a blueprint for the *eschaton*. The words *millennial*, *millenarian*, and *chiliastic*, which are based on the Latin or Greek words for "one thousand," are used in a variety of ways, often to refer more generally to an expectation of an earthly kingdom without any specific reference to its length. *Chiliastic* is used to describe the earliest phase of Christian hope when an earthly kingdom of God was earnestly expected. In the sociology of religion, *millenarian* designates groups that expect a radical change in history and an earthly reign of the saints or the down-trodden. *Millennialism* takes several forms. *Premillennialism*, which has been very popular among American evangelicals in the 20th and 21st centuries (e.g., Hal Lindsey, Jerry Falwell, and the *Left Behind* series) holds that Christ's second coming will take place *before* the messianic reign on earth. This is often associated with a cataclysmic eschatology that envisages a divine invasion of history in a period of "tribulation" (see on 7:9–17). *Postmillennialism* holds that Christ's appearance will take place only *after* the millennium, a view often linked with evolutionary views of history inexorably moving towards its eschatological goal. This view was popular in early America. Christopher Columbus wrote in his journal of his vocation to find on earth the "new heaven and the new earth" of which John spoke in 21:1. The Boston minister Cotton Mather (d. 1638) expected that the New Jerusalem would be centered in New England. The term *amillennialism* refers to those who reject the idea of a future messianic reign on earth, either because they believe that 20:4–6 refers to what has already happened in the cross and resurrection of Christ or in the emergence of the church, or because they understand the passage in a purely symbolic sense. Augustine's interpretation of the millennial kingdom as time of the church is an influential example of the former. He held that the binding of Satan (20:1–3) happened in the first coming of Christ and is repeated whenever men and women are converted to the Christian faith (*City of God* xx.7–8). This interpretation, which drew on NT texts such as John 5:24–25 that emphasize the "already" rather than the "not yet" of God's eschatological action (cf. Mark 1:15; Luke 17:21; 3:19, Rom 3:21), became the standard interpretation in the early Middle Ages. Much of Christian eschatology can be called "amillenialist," and in many interpretations of Revelation the millennial kingdom of 20:4–6 is conflated with the description of the New Jerusalem of 21:1–22:5.

20:7–10. Satan Released and Defeated. At the end of the thousand years Satan is released and proceeds to "deceive" a multitude from the "nations," described as Gog and Magog in dependence on Ezek 38–39 (see on 19:17–21). With their attack on the saints in the "beloved city" (Jerusalem), the really last battle is engaged. Fire from heaven destroys the devil's army, and he is thrown into the "lake of fire" to experience eternal torment.

20:11–15. The Last Judgment. There follows the "second resurrection" when all the dead join the martyrs raised in the "first resurrection" (20:5), and all are judged according to their works (cf. Matt 25:31–46; Rom 2:5–11). The theme of judgment pervades biblical books from Noah's flood in Gen 6–8, through repeated predictions of judgment on a recalcitrant people in the books of Kings and prophets to the Gospels, Paul, and the Apocalypse. In the OT most judgment texts are not strictly-speaking eschatological. However severe the prophetic predictions, they usually envision continued life on earth after the divine judgment is executed in history (e.g. by delivering his people over to foreign powers such as Babylon), not a final assize after which there would be no future on earth. The idea of a last judgment for all at once appears relatively late in Jewish history, in Daniel 12:1 and 7:9–10 (second century BCE) and in the earliest parts of the Enochic corpus, e.g. *1 Enoch* 10 (probably third century BCE). As in Dan 12:1, judgment in Revelation is preceded by the resurrection; the judgment scene in Revelation is particularly close to that of Dan 7:9–10 with its heavenly courtroom and books opened for scrutiny (for heavenly books see also *1 Enoch* 81 and *Testament of Abraham*, Rec A 12). In the NT the theme of judgment appears frequently, but there are only a few descriptions of a final tribunal (Matt 25:31–45; cf. John 5:28–29). Paul looks forward to a personal assize (Rom 2:3–10; 14:10; 2 Cor 5:14) and also one in which the saints will judge the world (1 Cor 6:9).

21:1–8. The New Jerusalem: Establishment of God's Kingdom. In 21:1–22:7 the visions of God's righteous judgment on sinful humanity give way to a moving picture of what human life will be like when God's rule, celebrated in heaven in 4:1–5:14, is fully established also among the creatures of earth. Chapter 21 draws together themes from the rest of the book: as in 1:8 God proclaims himself "Alpha and Omega"; reference to one who conquers (21:7) takes up promises that conclude the messages to the seven churches (2:7, 11, 17, 26; 3:5, 12, 21). The radical nature of the transformation that establishes God's kingdom is expressed in language from the last chapters of Isaiah (65:17; 66:2): John sees a "new heaven and a new earth," and God declares that he is "making all things new." The statement that "the sea was no more" (21:1), read in the context of the ancient myth of cosmic combat (see on 12:18–13:6), is a powerful statement of the absolute sovereignty of God. While texts such as the Babylonian *Enuma Elish* and Job 41 recount God's defeat of the fearsome sea monster, the symbol of evil and chaos, here the hostile sea is entirely obliterated.

Next John sees the New Jerusalem coming down from heaven; that there is a Jerusalem above is alluded to briefly in Gal 4:26 and Heb 12:22 (cf. Phil 3:20). A voice coming from the heavenly throne describes the ideal state of affairs at the end time when God is truly worshiped by all in his holy city. "They will be his peoples," the voice promises, both echoing and expanding the covenant promise made to Israel by God, who proclaimed at Mount Sinai "You shall be my treasured possession out of all the peoples" (Exod 19:5; cf. Ezek 37:27–28). The message of Revelation is intended for all peoples (cf. 14:6; 15:3–4). Mourning and pain, and death itself will be abolished (cf. 1 Cor 15:26, where Paul says that at his second coming, Christ will conquer death, the "last enemy"). Promises given to the 144,000 servants of God in 7:15–17 are extended to all the inhabitants of the New Jerusalem: they will drink from the springs of the "water of life," and God himself will "wipe every tear from their eyes" (cf. Isa 25:8, author's trans.).

After this intimate and inspiring promise of divine presence and blessing, readers are reminded that they must make a choice. For only the second time in Revelation, God speaks directly in 21:5–8, declaring that the promised blessings are for those who "conquer"—that is Christians who side with the Lamb in the eschatological battle against the forces of evil. Those who prove to be cowardly and faithless will share the "lake of fire" with murderers and other grave sinners.

21:9–27. Description of the City. The New Jerusalem, symbol of the culmination of God's gracious plans for humanity, announced in 21:2, is described in 21:9–22:7. Jerusalem is a place—the promised abode for those who "conquer"—and also a people, the bride of Christ (mentioned in 19:7–9; cf. 2 Cor 11:2 and Eph 5:25–33, which describes the church as the bride of Christ). OT prophets had compared the intimate relation between God and his covenant people Israel to a marriage, in which Israel played the part of the wife. In prophetic poetry female images—beloved wife, adulteress, barren woman, widow—express the varying status of the covenant people, depending on her degree of faithfulness to her marriage vows (see, e.g., Hos 1–3; Jer 2–3; Ezek 23; Jer 50–51). For example, during the Babylonian Exile, the prophet Deutero-Isaiah portrays Jerusalem as a barren and forsaken wife who will be taken back by her divine husband and become the mother of many children (Isa 54; 60). Details of John's vision echo these prophetic texts: Jerusalem will be built with precious stones (21:11, 18–21, cf. Isa 54:11–12); the Gentiles will stream into her, bringing tribute through gates that are always open (21:24–26 cf. Isa 60:5–13).

As God is opposed by Satan and the Lamb has a negative counterpart in the beast from the Sea (the *antichrist*), so the New Jerusalem is contrasted to lady Babylon/Rome. The detailed description of the beauty of the city, which far surpasses the superficial beauty of the whore of Babylon (17:1–6) serves as a powerful counterweight to the attractions of Rome. Like the holy of holies of the Jerusalem Temple, the city is described as a perfect cube (21:15–16; cf. 1 Kgs 6:20). Hyperbolic description indicates that the glory of God's final kingdom is beyond imagination: the city is of immense size, fifteen hundred miles square. It is of pure gold; the foundations of its walls are made up of every precious stone imaginable, and an immense pearl forms each of the twelve gates.

Similar descriptions are found in the description of the renewed Jerusalem and its Temple in Ezek 40–48 and the *Temple Scroll* found in Cave 11 at Qumran. The main point of Ezekiel's vision is the return of the glory of the Lord to the Temple in Jerusalem, which would be rebuilt after the Exile (Ezek. 43:3–5). Similarly, in Revelation the divine glory previously located in heaven now returns to a transformed earth. The throne of God which John glimpsed in heaven (4:1–5:14; cf. 7:9–17: 8:1–5; 11:15–19; 15:2–8; 19:1–6), is now found on earth. The New Jerusalem of Revelation differs from its precedents in the presence of the Lamb (21:9, 22), and also in the absence of a temple.

22:1–7. The City as Paradise. An angel brings John further revelation about the city where the throne of God and the Lamb will be found, now in terms reminiscent of the garden of paradise in Gen 2–3, with its rivers (Gen 2:10–14) and "tree of life" (Gen 2:9). In the Christian Bible, the last chapters of Revelation offer a fitting conclusion to the story of God's dealing with humanity that began in Genesis: the end recapitulates and surpasses the beginning, with its new creation of heaven and earth (21:1) and a park-like city reminiscent of the garden of Eden, where God "walked" with the first human beings (Gen 3:8). Absent is the serpent of Gen 3: "nothing accursed will be found" (22:3; cf. 21:27; cf. Gen 3:14). The description also recalls the renewed temple of Ezekiel's vision, from which water will gush out, bringing great fertility (Ezek 47:1–12). The "tree of life" found "on either side of the river" whose leaves will heal the nations (22:2) resembles the many trees of Ezek 47:12 whose "fruit will be for food, and their leaves for healing." Echoing the prophecy of a renewed Jerusalem in Isa 60, the angel tells John that in the New Jerusalem the brilliance of divine glory will be such that there will be no need for lamps or even the sun (22:5); God will be its light and the Lamb its lamp (21:23–24; cf. Isa 60:1–3; 19–20).

The picture climaxes in 22:4, which promises that the inhabitants of the New Jerusalem "will see his face." Much of Jewish tradition holds that no human being can see God's face and live (e.g. Exod 33:12–23); the Gospel of John says that "No one has ever seen God" (1:18). The only other reference in Revelation to God's face says that heaven and earth flee before it (20:11). In the vision of Rev 4 John does not see God but only glimpses his glory, which he compares to precious jewels and flashes of lightning. In the beatitudes Jesus promises: "Blessed are the pure in heart for they will see God" (Matt 5:8), and Saint Paul presents seeing "face to face" as the ultimate hope (1 Cor 13:12). This is what awaits those who are faithful witnesses to Christ: the direct enjoyment of God, their creator.

XII. Epilogue (22:8–21)

A concluding word of the revealing angel relates back to 1:1–3, authenticating John's revelation and setting him in the line of inspired prophets. Christ himself then speaks, declaring "See I am coming soon!" and pronouncing a blessing on all who keep the words of John's prophecy. John addresses the reader: "I, John, am the one who heard and saw these things" (cf. 1:4, 9). In a scene that closely resembles the one in 19:9–10, the prophet, overawed by all he has seen and heard, falls down in homage before the angel and is once again admonished: "Worship God!" (22:9 cf. 19:10). This theme, introduced at the very beginning of the book (1:5–6), is portrayed vividly in 4:1–5:14 where John sees the hosts of heaven falling down in adoration before God and the Lamb. The scenes of judgment that make up so much of this book are framed by this picture of heavenly worship, on the one hand, and the vision of the New Jerusalem (21:1-22:5) on the other. As the heavenly hosts are even now falling in adoration before God, so will he be worshiped by all humanity in the New Jerusalem (cf. 15:3–5). As writers of hymns and spirituals and composers such as Handel have realized, John's Apocalypse provides not only the command to worship but also words for carrying it out, in its many hymns of praise: "Holy, Holy, Holy,/the Lord God the Almighty" (4:8); "Worthy is the Lamb that was slaughtered,/to receive power and wealth and wisdom and might" (5:12); "Hallelujah!/For the Lord our God,/the Almighty reigns" (19:6; cf. 4:11; 5:9–13; 7:10, 12; 11:15–18; 12:10–12; 15:3–4; 16:4–7; 19:1–8; 16; 21:3–5).

The final verses in 22:12–21 offer testimonies about the importance of the book, warnings to all who alter or fail to heed its words, blessings, and invitations. Blessings reinforce images from the book's visions: those who "wash their robes" (cf. 7:14) are promised food from the "tree of life" (cf. 22:2; 2:7), drink from the "water of life" (cf. 7:17; 22:1), and the right to enter the city by its gates (cf. 21:21, 25–26). The Apocalypse began with an appearance of the awe-inspiring "one like the Son of Man" (1:12–16), followed by his words to the seven churches (2:1–3:22). Here at the end, John again hears words of Christ, who declares himself David's heir and the "bright morning star" and claims for himself a title earlier given to God: "I am the Alpha and the Omega, the first and the last, the beginning and the end" (22:13, cf. 1:8; 21:6). The book ends on a note of eager expectation: a thrice-repeated command to "Come!" invites all to partake of the blessings John's visions promise. Repeating his earlier words (1:3, 7–8; cf. 2:16; 3:11) Christ promises to come soon, and John responds: "Amen. Come, Lord Jesus!"

BIBLIOGRAPHY

D. Aune. *Revelation*. 3 vol. WBC 52A–C (Dallas: Word, 1997–98); R. Bauckham. *The Theology of the Book of Revelation* (Cambridge: Cambridge University Press, 1993); A. Y.

Collins. *Crisis and Catharsis: The Power of the Apocalypse* (Philadelphia: Westminster, 1984); J. Kovacs and C. Rowland. *Revelation.* Blackwell Bible Commentaries (Oxford: Blackwell, 2004); F. Murphy. *Fallen is Babylon: The Revelation to John* (Harrisburg, Penn.: Trinity, 1998); B. Rossing. *The Rapture Exposed* (Boulder: Westview, 2004); C. Rowland. "Revelation." *NIB* (Nashville: Abingdon, 1994) 12:503–743; F. Van der Meer. *Apocalypse: Visions from the Book of Revelation in Western Art* (London: Thames and Hudson, 1978).

HOW THE BIBLE WAS CREATED

David L. Petersen

The object of this commentary, the Christian Bible, is the result of a long and complicated process of growth. Portions of the OT (e.g., Judg 5) probably date to the Early Iron Age, prior to the time that David ruled Israel. The most recently completed literature (e.g., 1 John) in the New Testament stems from ca. 100 CE.

The literature that emerged in this one-thousand-year period reflects a number of differing perspectives. Some were designed to testify to momentous events in the life of the religious community, whether poetic versions of God's victories on Israel's behalf (Exod 15) or prose accounts concerning the arrival of the Holy Spirit among early Christians (Acts 2). Both Testaments preserve accounts created to narrate the lives of pivotal individuals, e.g., Moses and David in the OT, Jesus and Paul in the NT. Such accounts include a "biographic" component—where possible constructing accounts of births and/or deaths—but the literature includes far more than that, namely, the torah presented by Moses and the numerous sayings of Jesus. Biblical authors attended both to individuals and to the communities of which they were a part.

This literature emerged in diverse ways. Some literature may be readily traced to an identifiable individual—a Micah who uttered the oracles preserved in the book known by his name or a Paul who composed lengthy letters such as the book of Romans. (Letters or, more generally, communications within the religious community, e.g., Jer 29 and the NT epistolary literature, are prominent in the Bible.) Other literature is anonymous. No one knows for certain who wrote either the book of Ruth or the Gospel known as Matthew. Nonetheless, there can be little doubt than each book was composed by one individual. Other literature, also anonymous, emerged from the community's life, such as worship. For example, Psalms (100 or 150) are made up of traditional and oft-repeated phrases. Similarly, the hymn preserved in Col 1:15–20 was available for use by the author of this putative letter. The community itself is best understood as the author of these hymns.

Once emergent biblical literature was at hand, editors/redactors arranged and often supplemented it. Someone ordered the Psalter and divided it into five books, no doubt mirroring the five books of the Torah. Someone else placed the sayings of Jesus in a meaningful sequence. Such individuals also created additions to the literature they inherited, e.g., Hosea 14:9 and Mark 16:9–20. These unnamed contributors were responsible for the shape of the Christian Bible.

Religious communities preserved particular forms of the Christian Bible. Early Christians used the Greek Old Testament (LXX), which includes a form of the book of Jeremiah that is one eighth shorter than that in the Hebrew Bible. The shorter form of Jeremiah is still used by the Orthodox churches. As a result, one must recognize that there are multiple versions of the Christian Bible, the differences reflecting the needs and practices of particular religious communities.

CANON OF THE OLD TESTAMENT

EILEEN M. SCHULLER

The phrase "Canon of the Old Testament" depends upon concepts and vocabulary adopted by the Christian church from the fourth century CE. *Canon* designates the list of those books that are considered to be inspired, sacred, and authoritative, and, hence, that make up the Bible. These books constitute a norm or a standard (the basic sense of the Greek word *kanon* is "a reed/measure") for the definition of both what is to be believed (faith) and what is to be done (action). The language of *canon* per se was not traditionally used in Judaism, though other terminology such as "the holy writings" and "books that make the hands unclean" designated a body of literature of special sacredness and authority.

In its strictest sense, canonicity concerns the decision of what books are to be included and what books are to be excluded so as to result in the formation of a fixed corpus. In the early Christian world, the development of the idea of canon was probably influenced by changes in the ways in which texts were written. The codex (a book with pages) came to be the standard format for writing the Bible, in contrast to earlier collections of loose scrolls, each containing one or more works. With a codex, it was immediately obvious what was "in" or between the covers. The scope of the term *canon* was sometimes expanded to include the ordering of the individual books. Though it has sometimes been assumed that the establishment of canon also involved the identification of a specific text of a given book, the decision about canonicity was in fact usually limited to a book per se, without specifying a specific textual form. For example, the book of Jeremiah was judged canonical, whether in its longer Hebrew form or its shorter edition preserved in Greek translation in the Septuagint. Many other matters are closely related to issues of canonicity, such as the authority of a particular biblical book, the establishment of its authenticity (i.e., who really wrote it), and the language of inspiration ("inspired by God" 1 Tim 3:16).

There are different Old Testament canons: the Jewish Canon, the Protestant Canon, the Roman Catholic Canon, and the various canons of the Orthodox churches. This variety is not surprising since a canon is intrinsically linked to a community and to the authority of that community to make decisions about what will define its identity. Such decisions represent the "process of canonization."

One may examine this process by looking at the final stage and then moving to the question of when and how these lists were compiled. Judaism has a canon of twenty-four books, divided into three sections: the Law/*Torah* (five books of Moses, the Pentateuch); eight books of Prophets/*Nevi'im* (Joshua, Judges, 1–2 Samuel [one book], 1–2 Kings [one book], Isaiah, Jeremiah, Ezekiel, and the Twelve Minor Prophets [considered as a single book]); eleven books of Writings/*Ketuvim* (Psalms, Proverbs, Job, Song of Songs, Ruth Lamentations Ecclesiastes, Esther, Daniel, Ezra-Nehemiah [one book], 1–2 Chronicles [one book]). The order of this third section is that of the talmudic lists (*b. B. Bat* 14b–15a) though in many Masoretic manuscripts (e.g., the Leningrad Codex) the order can vary, with Chronicles coming first. The rabbis used the acyronom *Tanak (Torah – Nevi'im – Kebuvim)* to designate their scripture. The Protestant canon, as defined at the time of the Reformation, contains the same books as the Jewish canon, but counted as thirty-nine (for example, each of the Minor Prophets is counted separately). The Roman Catholic Canon, as defined by the Council of Trent in 1546, contains these books plus seven more (Tobit, Judith, 1–2 Maccabees, Wisdom Ecclesiasticus (also called Sirach), and Baruch, as well as Additions to Daniel and Esther). The canon of the various Orthodox churches has been less clearly defined but regularly includes additional books such as 1 Esdras, Prayer of Manasseh, 3 and 4 Maccabees, and Esdras. In the various Christian canons, the books are divided into four sections that come in the order: Pentateuch, the Historical Books, the Wisdom Books, and the Prophets, i.e., in an order different from that of the *Tanak*. In the Christian church, it is the Old Testament canon followed by the New Testament canon that makes up the Bible (*Biblica*, "the books").

Scholars are now challenging and revising many of the traditional assumptions about the development of the canon.

The traditional view, articulated in the Middle Ages, was that, in the post-exilic period, Ezra and "Men of the Great Assembly" had already assembled a collection of twenty-four books that were then divided into three parts. In the nineteenth century, a number of scholars (such as Heinrich Graetz, Frants Buhl, Herbert Edward Ryle) formulated what came to be the standard hypothesis. They theorized that the canon emerged in three distinct historical stages: (1) the Law/Torah was in place circa 400 BCE, as is suggested by Ezra bringing back "the law of your God" from Babylon (Ezra 7:14), a book that was apparently read and accepted by the community in Jerusalem (Neh 8). (2) The Prophets were fixed by approximately 200 BCE as attested by Ben Sira especially in his "Praise of Famous Men." Sirach 9–44 clearly knows most of the prophets and the collection of the twelve minor prophets. Moreover, in the Prologue of Ben Sira (written in 132 BCE), his grandson writes that "many great teachings have been given to us through the law and the prophets and the others that followed them" (vv. 1–2, 7–10, 23–25). (3) The third section (Writings) was fixed at the end of the first century CE at the so-called "Council of Yavneh" (*Jamnia* in Greek), an assembly of learned sages that was supposedly held at a coastal city that had became the center of Jewish learning after the destruction of Jerusalem in 70 CE. At that time, the sages debated the status of certain disputed books (Ecclesiastes, Song of Songs) and made decisions about what belonged in the canon. This theory explained certain puzzling features of the Bible (for example, Daniel, though containing prophetic-like words, appears in the Writings. It could not have been placed with the Prophets, since that collection had been "closed" prior to the time that Daniel was written.)

Beginning in the 1960s, a number of scholars (e.g., Jack Lewis, Peter Schäfer, G. Stremburg) reexamined the rabbinic materials related to Yavneh and concluded that there is little evidence to support the aforementioned theory. The picture of a council of sages drawing up a list and making decisions about what to include and exclude was largely a retrojection from how later Christian church councils worked. Whatever discussions went on at Yahveh were concerned only with limited questions about a few specific books that were already accepted, even though debate about these books continued for a long time. Then, in the 1970s, various scholars (especially Albert Sundberg) reexamined the evidence for the claim that there had existed an alternate, more expansive "Alexandrian canon" that had been fixed by Diaspora Judaism and then taken over by the Greek-speaking Christian church. Sundberg demonstrated that there is no evidence that such an Alexandrian canon existed and hence it was not passed on to the Christian church as the basis for the fourth and fifth century CE Christian codices (Vaticanus, Sinaiticus).

But if a "Council of Yavneh" was not the defining moment, when can one begin to talk of a "canon"? Certain scholars, (e.g., Sid Z. Leiman, Roger Beckwith) have attempted to push the fixing of set lists of books back to the second century BCE, making central such texts as 2 Mac 2:14, "Judas also collected all the books that had been lost on account of the war that had come upon us." But such a view reads far too much into an isolated statement, and there is much evidence that simply does not fit with such an early dating for the lists of biblical books.

With the discovery of the Dead Sea Scrolls (1948–1956) and their subsequent publication, scholars now have literature that provides a window on what were the authoritative texts for at least one group of Jews in the Second Temple period. These documents reveal a much more complicated picture than the older paradigm presented. Many scholars contend that to use the language of "Bible, biblical" during the Second Temple period is inappropriate. There is no evidence for a set list of "books of the Bible" during this time. Nonetheless, it is clear that some books were authoritative and used for teaching and interpretation. As a result, one can speak about a developing concept of scriptures, if not yet Bible. In the Scrolls and in the New Testament, the formula "Moses and the prophets," often clearly refers to written texts—the books of Moses and the prophets—and these are cited as authorities for teaching and legal regulations, "as God said through xxx," "as it is written in xxx." Clearly Moses and the Prophets are the two primary canonical categories (so the Prologue to Ben Sira quoted above); and there is sometimes a third category of "David" or "Psalms" (cf. Luke 24:44, "everything written about me in the law of Moses, the prophets, and the Psalms") but the contents of this third category is much less clear during this period.

The Scrolls present clues about the importance and stature of individual biblical books. One might infer that Genesis, Deuteronomy, and Isaiah—with fifteen, twenty-nine, and twenty one copies, respectively—had a somewhat different status or at least played a different role than books like Proverbs or Chronicles, of which only one or two copies are preserved. In addition, commentaries were being written on the Torah and many of the prophetic books, not only to explain problematic passages (e.g., the *Commentary on Genesis*, 4Q252) but more frequently to indicate how these words from the past have ongoing relevance and, when properly interpreted, are actually addressing the contemporary community (e.g., *Peshar Habakkuk*, 1QpHab). It is especially significant that there are also at least eleven copies of 1 Enoch and fifteen or sixteen copies of Jubilees (more copies than of many "biblical" books), and these are taken up in later works, e.g., the Damascus Document quotes Jubilees (CD 16:2–4) and the Letter of Jude cites 1 Enoch as a source of authority (Jude 14–15). A book such as the *Temple Scroll*, which is formulated in the first person as the very words of God, may have functioned as authoritative scripture for this particular group of Jews, whose scrolls were preserved at Qumran, but it may not have had similar stature among other groups like the Pharisees.

The Dead Sea Scrolls demonstrate that there was not yet a uniform and standardized textual form for many or even most important books. Both long and short books of Jeremiah, for instance, seemed to have been read and quoted; the same is true for different editions of the books of Samuel. For the book of Psalms, there were different collections in circulation, some closer to what became the standard Masoretic collection of 150 psalms, others with some different contents and ordering, suggesting that at least the final third of the Psalter was not yet standardized. For the Pentateuch, it is sometimes very difficult to know whether a particular manuscript would have been considered simply another version of the text or whether is was now something different, a commentary on or "rewriting" of Scripture. Clearly there was a developing sense of a "sacred scripture," but the definitive canon was still not in place.

The earliest evidence concerning the enumeration of biblical books—though not an actual list— comes from two Jewish sources, both circa 90–100 CE. In *Contra Apionem* 1.34-43, Josephus claims that there are twenty-two "justly accredited books"—the same number as the 22 letters of the Hebrew alphabet. According to Josephus, antiquity of composition was a prime consideration for inclusion in this list; all these books were written in the time from "from Moses until Artaxerxes," the time of "the exact succession of the prophets. " In addition, Josephus included four books that "contain hymns to God and precepts for the conduct of human life." The author of 4 Ezra (2 Esdras)14:45–46 knows ninety-four sacred books, but he distinguished between "the twenty-four books" that all have access to, in contrast to "the seventy that were written last" and reserved for "the wise." Fourth Ezra probably had much the same corpus in mind as Josephus, but they were arranged and enumerated differently.

In the decades after the destruction of the Temple, the process of defining what books were to be considered authoritative for the Jewish community continued. Some books were excluded, e.g., *1 Enoch*, *4 Ezra*, *Jubilees*, though the reasons for such decisions are not self-evident. These reasons may have included the language in which a book was written; no books written in languages other than Hebrew (though portions of Ezra-Nehemiah and Daniel are written in Aramaic) were included. No books containing revelations to figures other than Moses (for instance, Enoch) were included. In addition, there was apparently minimal interest in books filled with apocalyptic speculations and in books promoting a solar calendar (rather than the lunar calendar of the rabbis). The Babylonian Talmud (*b. B. Bat* 14b–15a) includes one of the earliest lists of biblical books. The early Christian community was going through much the same process in the first centuries of the Common Era. The major Christian codices (Sinaiticus, Vaticanus, Alexandrinus) did not share exactly the same combinations or orderings of books. The letter of Melito of Sardis gave one of the earliest lists (though Esther is omitted) and the *Festal Letter* of Athanasius of Alexandria (367 CE) used the language of "the books included in the canon and handed down and credited as divine." In the late fourth century, Jerome distinguished between those books that were accepted by the Jews and those that were not, calling the latter "apocrypha"or "deuterocanonical" (that is, a "second" list). Other church fathers, especially Augustine, advocated an expanded canon; and his view prevailed. At the time of the Reformation, debates about what books to include in the canon came to the fore for a variety of reasons, including renewed attention to reading the Bible in Hebrew and debates over doctrinal issues, some of which were justified on the basis of texts in books not in the shorter canon (e.g., 2 Macc 12:46 ,"it is a holy and wholesome thought to pray for the dead"). In the end, Luther and the Anglican church adopted the shorter "Hebrew" canon, although they urged the publication of the Apocrypha in a separate section of the Bible. The German Bible of 1534 states, "these books are not held to be equal to the sacred scriptures, yet are useful and good for reading." And the Anglican "Thirty-Nine Articles of Religion" (1563) says that the books of the Apocrypha are to be read "for example of life and instruction of manners" though "not for the establishment of doctrine." Churches that followed the Reformed tradition of Geneva gave no status to the Apocrypha, and these books were not printed with the Bible. It was in this context that the Council of Trent (1546) for the first time made a definitive conciliar list of books, including seven not present in the Hebrew Bible (Tobit, Judith, 1–2 Maccabees, Wisdom, Sirach, and Baruch) that are to be accepted as "sacred and canonical ... in their entirety and with all their parts" (Session 4, Decree 1). In recent years, many editions of the Bible, especially those published for scholarly use, have included a full selection of Apocryphal books (not only those accepted at Trent, but others used by various Orthodox churches), usually printing these as a separate section.

In addition to seeking a better understanding of the processes by means of which the OT canon developed, there has recently been renewed interest in thinking theologically about canon. For a religious community that has a canon, no one book can be read in isolation; one portion of the canon must be read as a part of a larger whole. For example, precisely because the reward–punishment dynamic of Proverbs is read in conjunction with the radical questioning of Job, both are read quite differently than if only one of those texts were in the canon. Canon assumes a foundational and underlying unity, even as it highlights and allows for theological diversity. For Christians, the Old Testament is always read with the New Testament, and concomitantly the New Testament is always read with the Old Testament. In recent discussion, much attention has been devoted to the formative stages of the process—the movement from communal, epic literature to authoritative texts and then to a set list of canonical books. Yet the closure of canon is not the final word. A religious community that has a canon must engage in ongoing interpretation of it; in that sense the fixing of canon is a starting point as much as it is an end point.

BIBLIOGRAPHY

R. Beckwith. *The Old Testament Canon of the New Testament Church* (Grand Rapids: Eerdmans, 1985); S. Leiman. *The Canonization of the Hebrew Scriptures: The Talmudic and Midrashic Evidence* (Hamden, Conn.: Archon Books, 1976); L. Martin MacDonald. *The Biblical Canon: Its Origin, Transmission and Authority* (Peabody, Mass.: Hendrickson, 1995, 3rd edition); L. M. MacDonald and J. Sanders. *The Canon Debate* (Peabody, Mass.: Hendrickson, 2002); J. Sanders. *Canon and Community: A Guide to Canonical Criticism* (Philadelphia: Fortress, 1984); A. C. Sundberg. *The Old Testament of the Early Church* (Cambridge, Mass.: Harvard University Press, 1964).

CANON OF THE NEW TESTAMENT

SHANE BERG

The New Testament canon refers to the collection of ancient Christian documents recognized in varying ways as authoritative and normative by most Christian traditions. The term *canon* derives from a Greek word that means "rule" (i.e., a tool for measurement), and by extension "standard" or "norm," and in the ancient church originally connoted a list of approved writings. The term eventually came also to refer to the normative status of such approved writings for Christian life and faith.

I. THE EMERGENCE OF THE CANON OF THE NEW TESTAMENT IN THE ANCIENT CHURCH

The earliest core of the New Testament canon comprises the Pauline letters, the four Gospels, and Acts. The letters of Paul began to be compiled not long after his death, though such collections went beyond the letters typically regarded by modern scholars as being from Paul's own hand (Romans, 1–2 Corinthians, Galatians, Philippians, 1 Thessalonians, and Philemon) to include the pseudepigraphic Ephesians, Colossians, 2 Thessalonians, 1–2 Timothy, Titus, and sometimes also the anonymous Epistle to the Hebrews. References in the writings of Clement of Rome and Ignatius of Antioch clearly indicate that such Pauline letter collections were in circulation by the early second century CE. The earliest attested manuscript evidence for the Pauline letter collection is P46, a papyrus codex dating roughly to the beginning of the third century CE that originally contained ten epistles arranged according to length (Romans, Hebrews, 1–2 Corinthians, Ephesians, Galatians, Philippians, Colossians, 1–2 Thessalonians).

By the end of the second century CE, the four Gospels (Matthew, Mark, Luke, and John) were circulating together, at least in the West, as is attested by Irenaeus in his creative apology for the fourfold Gospel in *Adversus Haereses* (3.11.8). Tertullian, writing in north Africa at the beginning of the third century, also clearly regards Matthew, Mark, Luke, and John as the exclusively authoritative Gospels for Christians. In the Greek-speaking East, however, other Gospels seem to have flourished alongside Matthew, Mark, Luke, and John well into the third century CE. The papyrus codex P45, dating to the first half of the third century CE, is the earliest manuscript witness to a collection of the four Gospels (it includes Acts as well).

The Acts of the Apostles was written by the same author as the Gospel of Luke and clearly intended as a literary complement to it. Acts was nonetheless separated from Luke at an early stage of transmission and had a textual history independent from it for more than two centuries. The Catholic Epistles—so called because they do not address specific communities or congregations and thus are "catholic," or universal—came together as a collection much more slowly than the Pauline Epistles or the Gospels. 1 Peter and 1 John were known in the second to fourth centuries CE, but their status is unclear. Even more murky is the standing of 2 Peter, Jude, 2–3 John, and James. Their circulation seems to have been limited to particular local areas until the fourth century, when Eusebius characterizes them as widely-known but of disputed status as authoritative Christian literature (*Ecclesiastical History* 3.25.3).

The Apocalypse of John, also known as Revelation, has a colorful history in the ancient church. It is widely attested from the second century CE onward, but its status as authoritative wavered due to disputes about its appropriate interpretation. Despite some dissenters, Revelation was generally accepted in the West by the third century CE. Disagreements continued late into the fourth century in the East, however; and even after it acquired authoritative standing, its interpretation was a frequent source of contention.

An important snapshot of the emerging canon is provided by Eusebius, bishop of Caesarea, in his *Ecclesiastical History* (c. 325 CE). He assigns books to one of three categories based on their status in the Christian communities with which he was familiar.

The first category comprises the universally recognized books, and Eusebius places here the four Gospels, the Acts of the Apostles, the Pauline epistles, 1 Peter, and 1 John. The second category contains books whose status is disputed, and here he lists James, Jude, 2 Peter, and 2–3 John. The final category is that of spurious books, in which he puts the Acts of Paul, the Shepherd of Hermas, the Epistle of Barnabas, and the Didache. Eusebius lists Revelation under both the recognized and the spurious books, indicating both times the uncertainty of its inclusion. He also notes that some regard the Epistle to the Hebrews as spurious.

A variety of canon lists is attested in the fourth and fifth centuries CE. Athanasius' *Festal Letter* of 367 CE is the first known time that the canon is defined as the 27 books that comprise the contemporary Christian canon. While the boundaries of the canon were not definitively set at this point, especially in the East, its overall shape changed little in the ensuing debates about particular books in the following two centuries.

The great parchment codices of the fourth and fifth centuries CE are the earliest extant manuscript witnesses to an entire canon of the New Testament. Sinaiticus and Vaticanus are typically dated to the fourth century CE, while codices Alexandrinus and Ephraemi belong to the fifth century CE. All five of these codices contain the 27 books of the traditional New Testament canon, but they contain a few additional works as well, such as the Epistle of Barnabas and the Shepherd of Hermas (Sinaiticus) and 1–2 Clement (Alexandrinus).

II. THEOLOGICAL DISCUSSIONS ABOUT THE CANON OF THE NEW TESTAMENT IN THE ANCIENT CHURCH

Older scholarship tended to emphasize the significance of conflict as the definitive factor in the emergence of a canon of the New Testament in ancient Christianity. The threat posed by Marcion and his unique canon (the Gospel of Luke and select Pauline letters, all heavily edited) in the second century CE, for example, was regarded as a major impetus for the formation of a canon among orthodox Christians. The Montanist and Gnostic movements of the second and third centuries CE were similarly considered significant catalysts for the definition of a canon of the New Testament.

While there is little doubt that such conflicts exerted some influence on the emerging canon, their impact has been exaggerated by those who view ancient Christianity as a struggle between a proto-orthodox church and various heretical groups. Locating the development of the canon of the New Testament against this sort of historical narrative falls short in two ways. First, the historical narrative itself is flawed insofar as its portrait of an embattled orthodox church is anachronistic and grossly oversimplifies the fluid and complex landscape of Christianity in the second, third, and fourth centuries CE. Second, emphasizing the role of conflict in the formation of the canon of the New Testament ignores the fact that early Christian theological discussions do not themselves typically highlight the role of conflict. They rather tend to provide positive reasons for the inclusion of books in the canon.

Leaders in the ancient church articulate several positive criteria by which the canonical status of a book is to be judged. Though these criteria are not constant and vary widely in their interpretation and application, they nonetheless are broadly attested. One key marker of a book's status within the canon was its coherence with apostolic teaching as summarized in the "rule of faith," a narrative summary of core Christian beliefs. Another was a book's "catholicity," by which was meant the relevance of its content for the wider church rather than for a limited community. Finally, a book that had been profitably read over a long sweep of time by a large number of Christian communities of faith was often regarded as canonical, and it is reasonable to suggest that such traditional use of a book was the most influential factor in the ultimate shape of the canon of the New Testament.

The 27 books that came to comprise the canon of the New Testament by the end of late antiquity remain authoritative to the present day for Protestant, Roman Catholic, and Orthodox Christians.

BIBLIOGRAPHY

J. Barr. *Holy Scripture: Canon, Authority, Criticism* (Philadelphia: Westminster, 1983); H. Von Campenhausen. *The Formation of the Christian Bible* (Philadelphia: Fortress, 1972); H. Gamble. *Books and Readers in the Early Church: A History of Early Christian Texts* (New Haven: Yale, 1995); L. McDonald. *The Biblical Canon: Its Origin, Transmission, and Authority* (Peabody, Mass.: Hendrickson, 2007); B. Metzger. *The Canon of the New Testament: Its Origin, Development, and Significance* (Oxford and New York: Oxford, 1987).

HEBREW NARRATIVE

Tod Linafelt

Approximately 3000 years ago, there emerged in ancient Israel a new form of storytelling: extended prose narrative. There are, to be sure, extended narratives from the ancient world that predate biblical narrative, including the justly famous *Epic of Gilgamesh* and the less well-known but more closely related Ugaritic (or Canaanite) narratives. But these are in *verse*, or poetic, form, and bear more clearly the markings of oral composition. However, with the earliest Hebrew biblical narratives, one can see the effects of the transition to writing, including a more flexible *prose* form of storytelling, where composition is not bound to the strict rhythms of the poetic line. Moreover, the author of a literary text, unlike the singer of an orally composed tale, can work at a more leisurely pace, can stop writing and return to the work, and can edit at will. The resulting long narrative form—found for example in the books of Genesis and of Samuel—displays many of the literary techniques that will come to mark both history-writing and the novel: a third-person narrator who is removed from the plot and whose presence is less strongly felt by a reader than the traditional oral storyteller's presence is felt by an audience; the ability to track changes undergone by characters over the course of a lifetime and by families or nations over several generations; and the presence of allusion, of ambiguity, and of irony. Later biblical authors, working out of this tradition of written, prose narrative, will produce a shorter form—represented by the books of Ruth and Esther—in which the complexities of plot and character are condensed to the length of a short story. And in the late books of Ezra and Nehemiah one finds, unusually for the Bible, a first-person narrator (e.g., Ezra 8:15–34; Neh 13).

Perhaps the most distinctive characteristic of biblical Hebrew narrative is its rigorous economy of style. That is, biblical narrative evinces a drastically stripped-down manner of storytelling, making use of a fairly limited vocabulary and tending to avoid metaphors and other sorts of figurative language. Indeed, biblical narrative tends to avoid description of any sort, metaphorical or otherwise. What do Adam and Eve look like? Abraham? Sarah? Moses? Readers do not know. Occasionally a certain quality is ascribed to some person or object: readers are told that Eve perceives that the tree of knowledge is "a delight to the eyes" (Gen 3:6), and likewise we are told that Joseph is "handsome and good-looking" (Gen 39:6). But, as a rule, such minimal notations are given only when necessary to introduce some element that is important to the development of the plot. In the present cases, the attractiveness of the tree of knowledge leads, of course, to the eating of its fruit, and Joseph's attractiveness leads, in the next verse, to the sexual aggression of Potiphar's wife and thus indirectly to Joseph's imprisonment. But even here, readers are not told what it is that makes the fruit attractive or just what physical qualities make Joseph so handsome.

Beyond a lack of physical description in the biblical stories, descriptions of personal qualities are largely absent. Characterization in biblical narrative, in other words, is rarely explicit, but rather must be teased out of the narrative based on what characters do and what they say. One learns Jacob is cunning and deceptive, for example, not because readers are told so but because they see him trick his brother, his father, and his brother-in-law Laban, and they hear him lie to them. As a rule, it is the actions and the dialogue of the characters that leads the readers' judgments about them, rather than explicit commentary or moral evaluation on the part of the narrator. By not directly revealing the qualities of character of the actors in the narrative, the narrator puts the onus of interpretation on the readers, who must work out on their own—albeit with hints given—what they think of these characters.

Beyond the question of what characters might look like or what sort of people they might be, readers may best see the complexity of this mode of characterization when it comes to the inner lives of the characters. Biblical narrators rarely report what a character might be thinking or feeling at any given moment. What are Eve and Adam thinking when they reach for the fruit from the tree of the knowledge of good and evil in the garden of Eden? What is God thinking in forbidding that fruit? (Despite Christianity's long tradition of original sin, the answer to neither of these questions is immediately clear, and both prove quite interestingly complex if taken seriously.) What goes through Abraham's mind when God demands, in Gen 22, that he sacrifice his son Isaac? (The inner calm of absolute faith? Perhaps. But perhaps also anger, disbelief, or even disgust—with God for demanding such a sacrifice, or with himself for failing to protest.) What is going through Aaron's mind when his two sons are burned alive with fire from God (Lev 10)? (The narrator reports only that "Aaron was silent." Does this indicate mute acceptance? Crippling grief? A barely controlled anger? Pure shock?) As these representative examples show, biblical narrative exploits to great effect a genuine inner life and a complex, private subjectivity. Biblical narrative is, then, essentially "realistic" in its portrayal of human characters, since in real life people do not have direct access to the complicated inner lives of those they encounter, learning to rely instead on hints they receive about what people are really thinking or feeling, and basing their sense of what sort of people they are on what they do and what they say, on actions and dialogue.

One way, at least, in which biblical narrative is not entirely realistic is the sometimes jarring concreteness with which God is imagined as active in the world: God shows up at the tent of Sarah and Abraham to promise them offspring (Gen 18); God destroys Pharaoh's army at the Red Sea (Exod 14); God inscribes with God's own hand the tablets of the covenant at Sinai (Exod 34:1); and in the final, poignant scene of the Torah, God buries Moses after allowing him a vision of the promised land that he is not finally to enter (Deut 34:1–8). But if the Hebrew literary imagination is relentlessly concrete in its workings, including its imaginings of God, it is not without subtlety. In fact, divine agency and human agency are imagined in these narratives as being bound together in such a way that neither is autonomous or effective in and of itself. And so, God announces to Rebekah (Gen 25) that the elder of her twins (Esau) will serve the younger (Jacob), but two chapters later, when the time has come to deliver the blessing to the proper son, God has apparently left the matter to Rebekah to work out, which she does with great effectiveness. In Gen 50, Joseph may declare to the brothers who, thirteen chapters and many years earlier had sold him into slavery, that "even though you intended to do harm to me, God intended it for good," but the story also makes clear that it is largely his own wits and talent, rather than any supernatural intervention, that allow him to survive and prosper in Egypt. And in the exodus story, we learn that God claims responsibility for "hardening" Pharaoh's heart so that he refuses to allow Israel to leave (Exod. 7:3; 14:4); but Pharaoh is said by the narrator to have hardened *his own* heart (8:15, 32). Still other times a passive voice is used, so that Pharaoh's heart "was hardened" or "became hard" (7:14; 8:15; 9:7), thereby leaving the agency behind the hardening unclear. This ambiguity allows the narrative to retain a sense of God's sovereign activity in history, while at the same time affirming the moral culpability of Pharaoh, whose repeated promise of freedom is never fulfilled and thus represents rather realistically the psychology of tyranny. Logically, readers may want to know, which was it? Did God harden Pharaoh's heart, or did Pharaoh harden his own heart? But the story refuses to come down on one answer or another, giving us a "both/and" that reflects a pronounced trend in biblical narrative to render not only the inner lives of both humans and God, but creation and history itself, as unfathomably complex and finally unresolvable.

BIBLIOGRAPHY

R. Alter. *The Art of Biblical Narrative* (New York: Basic, 1981); E. Auerbach. "Odysseus' Scar." *Mimesis: The Representation of Reality in Western Literature* (Princeton: Princeton University Press, 1953) 3–23; J. P. Fokkelman. *Reading Biblical Narrative* (Louisville: Westminster John Knox, 2005); E. Greenstein. "On the Genesis of Biblical Prose Narrative." *Prooftexts* (1988) 347–63; D. M. Gunn and D. N. Fewell. *Narrative in the Hebrew Bible* (Oxford: Oxford University Press, 1993); R. Kawashima, *Biblical Narrative and the Death of the Rhapsode* (Bloomington: Indiana University Press, 2004); M. Sternberg. *The Poetics of Biblical Narrative: Ideological Literature and the Drama of Reading* (Bloomington: Indiana University Press, 1987).

LEGAL LITERATURE

James W. Watts

The Old Testament collects almost all laws in the Pentateuch/Torah. Here ancient Near Eastern traditions and genres of legal, ritual, and wisdom literature are mixed together in collections of laws to reflect the divine identity of the law-giver. Normative applications of this prescriptive literature were initially based on the Pentateuch's status as Temple law, and only later extended to other aspects of ancient Jewish life.

The laws of the Old Testament appear in several distinct collections. Both Exodus and Deuteronomy present the Decalogue as a separate unit (Exod 20:2–17; Deut 5:6–21) and give it priority before the larger collections that follow it. Exodus continues with three chapters of instructions and regulations ("the Covenant Code," Exod 20:22–23:33). Its contents resemble but do not match the much larger collection of laws in Deut 12–26 and to a lesser degree the stipulations of Lev 17–27. The latter collection is usually called "the Holiness Code" because of the refrain, "You shall be holy as I, the LORD your God, am holy" (19:2, 20:7, etc.). Other materials in the Pentateuch may also count as legal literature, depending on how one defines "law." Scholars often label the instructions for offerings and rituals in Lev 1–7 and 11–16 as "the Priestly Code." Related materials are scattered through Numbers (18–19, 28–30, 35–36). The instructions for building the tabernacle and for ordaining the priests (Exod 25–31; cf. Exod 35–40; Lev 8–10) share many similarities in style and content with the Priestly Code, but are not usually included in it. Counting inclusively, however, laws and instructions make up more than half the contents of the Pentateuch.

That explains the Jewish name for this collection, the Torah. The word, *torah*, may be translated as "law" or "instruction" (see "Torah," *NIDB*). That term appears in the Pentateuch to designate individual provisions ("This is the *torah* of the guilt offering," Lev 7:1; author's trans.) and to function as a summary term for the entire divine revelation ("This is the *torah* that Moses set before the Israelites," Deut 4:44, author's trans.). The latter usage led to its application to the Pentateuch as a whole. The designation of the five books as the Torah, however, does not just reflect the preponderance of legal material in that literature. It also refers the fact that law appears almost exclusively *here* in the Hebrew Bible. The only exception is Ezek 40–48, which also presents itself as "the law of the Temple" (43:12). Like the Pentateuch, these chapters depict God delivering law through the vision of a priest-prophet, but Ezekiel instead of Moses. Other biblical books contain many genres of literature, but no law. Despite the fact that they narrate stories about many kings, they never depict kings issuing laws. The Old Testament portrays almost all of Israel's laws as having come from God through Moses. Though the Pentateuch's legal collections were written at different times, mostly long after Moses, the biblical writers nevertheless retrojected them back into the period just after the exodus from Egypt. For these writers, all Israel's laws were presented to Israel by Moses.

The diverse legal collections of the Pentateuch show clear indications of deriving from a tradition of legal literature rooted originally in Mesopotamia. Archeologists have uncovered legal collections by Sumerians and Babylonians dating from the late third and early second millenniums BCE. These traditions of criminal and civil laws influenced the later codes of the Assyrians and the Hittites, as well as biblical law. For example, the law of the goring ox appears in almost all of the collections (e.g., Exod 21:28–32). Though each presents a variant on the regulation about how to compensate for damage inflicted by an ox, they contain enough similarities to confirm that they are the products of a continuous tradition of legal thought.

Biblical legal collections, however, distinguish themselves from this tradition in two major respects. Their contents mix ritual regulations and moral exhortations among the civil and criminal laws, something unprecedented in the Mesopotamian legal collections. Of course Sumerian, Babylonian, Assyrian, and Hittite literatures contain many ritual and exhortatory texts, but they do not include that kind of material with their legal collections. The Pentateuch stands out for combining genres of ritual instruction and of wisdom teachings with legal traditions. That the Pentateuch's legal literature appears within a

---

953

story that credits all of it to God is its other major distinguishing feature. Many other ancient legal collections also appear between narrative introductions praising the law-givers' achievements and concluding sanctions promising blessings on those who preserve the laws and curses on those who do not (cf. Lev 26; Deut 27–31). While Mesopotamian legal collections sometimes credit a god with inspiring the sense of justice behind a particular text, however, they give the credit for formulating the laws themselves to a king (e.g. Hammurabi). The Pentateuch, by contrast, has no room in its story for an Israelite king (though Deut 17:14–20 makes brief provision for the possibility of a future king). Instead, Yahweh God of Israel takes the role of king, defending Israel against its enemies (Exod 6–13) and issuing its laws. Because the royal lawgiver is also divine, however, the Torah shows as much concern for ritual regulations (frequently credited to divine revelation in the ancient Near East) and moral exhortation (often attributed to divine wisdom if not inspiration) as for criminal and civil laws.

It would be easy to assume that the Bible owes its normative authority to the fact that the Torah contains so much legal literature. Yet legal collections do not seem to have played normative roles in ancient Mesopotamia. None of the many documents from law courts that have survived cite written laws or legal collections, nor do ancient courts seem to have conformed to written laws in any other ways. Court procedures were governed by oral custom. Written collections of law seem rather to have been the product of an academic tradition of legal reflection, which was occasionally employed as propaganda by kings like Hammurabi to legitimize themselves as just and, therefore, legitimate rulers.

Ritual texts, on the other hand, were frequently cited to justify the ritual practices of temples and kings. In Egypt, lector priests displayed the scrolls publicly that mandated the proper performance of various rites. Mesopotamian kings would search for old foundation texts to tell them the architectural plans for restoring ruined temples. Hittite kings cited old texts to revive abandoned rituals in hopes of warding off plagues and famines. The first written documents to have been used as normative guides for practice seem to have been ritual texts.

That was also the case in Israel. The accounts of Israel's history after settlement in the land (Joshua, Judges, Samuel, Kings, and even Chronicles) do not depict the Torah, or any written law, being explicitly cited very often except by the narrators of these accounts. When a "book of the Torah" does finally appear in the narratives late in the Judean monarchy and again after the Babylonian Exile, it is mainly used by Josiah and Ezra to persuade the people of Judea to engage in ritual reforms, especially to revive proper observance of the pilgrimage festivals, Passover and Sukkot (Tabernacles). The stories imply a lack of attention to written Torah in Israel's previous history by noting that these festivals had not been observed correctly, or perhaps observed at all, since the time of the Judges (2 Kgs 23:22; Neh 8:17).

Thus Torah first wielded normative authority over ritual affairs. During the Persian period, it was recognized as Temple law in Jerusalem. Only later in the Second Temple period, as the ritual requirements of Temple worship were gradually extended to other places and aspects of Jewish life, did written law come to be applied directly to criminal procedures (Sus 62). During the same period of time (the last half of the first millennium BCE), other Mediterranean cultures (e.g., Athens, Gortyn, Rome) also employed public inscriptions and written law collections more frequently to promulgate and revise ritual, civil, and criminal laws.

The Pentateuch anticipates this development in its literary portrayal of Moses. Though only the messenger of the divine law-giver in Exodus, Leviticus, and Numbers, he emerges in Deuteronomy as the authoritative reinterpreter of divine law for a new generation. The Deuteronomic laws in Moses' voice claim continuity with God's law from Sinai even as they revise and modify many of its provisions. Thus the Pentateuch not only promulgates divine law as normative for Israel, it also models the continuous interpretation and revision necessary to keep any law relevant over time.

BIBLIOGRAPHY

F. Crüsemann. *The Torah: Theology and Social History of Old Testament Law.* A. W. Mahnke, trans. (Edinburgh: T&T Clark, 1996); G. N. Knoppers and B. M. Levinson, eds. *The Pentateuch as Torah: New Models for Understanding its Promulgation and Acceptance* (Winona Lake, Ind.: Eisenbrauns, 2007); M. LeFebvre. *Collections, Codes, and Torah: the Re-characterization of Israel's Written Law.* LHBOTS 451 (New York: T&T Clark, 2006); B. M. Levinson, ed. *Theory and Method in Biblical and Cuneiform Law: Revision, Interpolation and Development.* JSOTSup 181 (Sheffield: Sheffield Academic Press, 1994); J. W. Watts. *Reading Law: The Rhetorical Shaping of the Pentateuch.* The Biblical Seminar 59 (Sheffield: Sheffield Academic Press, 1999); _____. "Ritual Legitimacy and Scriptural Authority." *JBL* 124/3 (2005): 401–17.

PROPHETIC LITERATURE

Robert R. Wilson

The prophetic literature of the OT developed from the work of prophets, who were active in Israel throughout the biblical period. Stories about their activities sometimes appear in the narrative literature of the OT, particularly in the books of Samuel, Kings, Jonah, and Jeremiah, while collections of their words appear in the books to which the names of individual prophets have been attached. However, the process that led from prophetic deeds and words to the final form of the prophetic literature was complex and involved the behavior of the prophets themselves, as well as the reactions and interpretations of the people who heard them, collected their stories and sayings, wrote them down, and finally edited them in their present form. A full appreciation of the prophetic literature, therefore, requires some understanding of the nature of prophecy itself, as well as some insights into the general processes by which prophetic materials reached their final written form.

PROPHECY AND THE OT PROPHETS

The phenomenon of prophecy is known outside of ancient Israel and is particularly well attested in Mesopotamia, with a few examples coming from Canaan. In general, ancient Near Eastern prophecy involved deities transmitting messages through human intermediaries, who bore various titles and who thought about their responsibilities in various ways. In biblical Israel, the prophets claimed to have received their revelations from God, either through the agency of dreams and visions or, more commonly, by means of divine words spoken directly to the prophet. Once the divine messages were received, they were delivered to audiences in a number of different social settings.

All prophetic speeches involved claims of divine revelation, claims that could not easily be tested by the people listening to the prophets. The problem of the authentication of the prophets' words was particularly difficult when prophetic messages conflicted with each other. In such cases the audience seems to have relied on various means of testing prophetic claims (e.g., Deut 13:1–5; 18:21–22; 1 Kgs 22; Jer 28). However, false prophecy always remained a danger, and, in the end, some hearers believed a particular prophet's words and some did not. Those who believed sometimes became the prophet's supporters and may have helped to collect and preserve the prophet's words.

The contents of Israel's prophetic messages were highly variable. The prophets usually addressed a specific audience, so they often spoke to a contemporary situation. On other occasions, they spoke about events in the future, although those future events were sometimes contingent on actions taken or not taken by the audience at the time the prophecies were delivered. Similarly, addresses to the present and predictions about the future occasionally involved the past, so past, present, and future references could appear in the same prophetic oracles. The OT prophets often spoke of social and religious change, which was necessary to avoid a future disaster. At other times, however, they advocated preserving current conditions.

ORAL AND WRITTEN PROPHECY

Scholars generally agree that the OT prophets originally delivered their oracles in oral form. The oracles were usually brief and poetic, marked by short, parallel, or echoing lines and the use of vivid imagery. The prophets often prefaced their messages with a "messenger formula" ("thus says the Lord"), in order to indicate the source of the revelation and to give it added authority (e.g., Amos 1–2). Prophets employed a number of different literary genres and drew language from a variety of social settings. Legal language from the courts, laments and words of woe from experiences of disaster, hymns from worship settings, songs from public gatherings, curses, threats, warnings, announcements of judgment, and promises of a brighter future all found their way into the prophets' oracles. Prose materials were used as well, and the prophets sometimes described visions that they had seen (e.g., Amos 7–9) or symbolic actions that they were to perform (e.g., Jer 19).

The process by which the prophets' oral oracles were collected and preserved in writing is not fully understood. Scholars usually assume that the prophets' supporters remembered and collected the oral sayings and eventually wrote them down or paid scribes to record them (Isa 8:16–18). The prophet Jeremiah is said to have dictated a collection of his oracles to a scribe and later to have added materials to the original collection (Jer 36). There were at least two reasons for wanting to record the prophets' words in writing. First, when the prophets spoke about future events there was often no way to determine the truth of their words except to wait for the future to unfold. In such cases, the written record could be used to test the accuracy of what the prophets had predicted. However, a second factor was sometimes involved as well. At least in some cases prophecies that had already been fulfilled were thought to be still applicable to new situations, so the written record could be used for the benefit of future communities experiencing circumstances similar to those of the original audience (e.g., Isa 7–11).

In addition to preserving the words of the prophets, the prophets' supporters may have also been responsible for collecting stories of prophetic activities, and these stories too may have eventually been written down. It is important to note, however, that the writing down of oral material did not necessarily mean the end of oral prophecy. Rather, prophets seem to have continued to deliver oral oracles even after earlier prophecies had been recorded in writing.

Although much of the OT's prophetic literature originated in oral form, some prophets may have themselves created written works. This phenomenon seems to have begun about the time of the exile, perhaps because the dispersion of Israelites at that time made the circulation of oral materials unusually difficult. Scholars have suggested that books such as Ezekiel, the latter portions of Isaiah, the narrative material in Jeremiah, and most of the post-exilic prophetic books did not go through an oral stage but were originally created in written form.

The Growth of the Prophetic Literature

With the advent of written oracle collections and written prophetic narratives, a new phase began in the development of the prophetic writings. As long as oral prophecies were still being delivered, the collecting and shaping of prophetic materials presumably remained in the hands of the prophets themselves and in the hands of the prophets' supporters. However, once the transition to written prophecy began to take place, a new influence in the growth of the prophetic literature began to emerge. Even with the relatively simple Hebrew alphabet, the production of lengthy written texts required specialized literary and scholarly skills, and, as a result, about the time of the exile trained scribes began to play an increasingly important role in the shaping of prophetic texts.

The degree to which the scribes influenced the contents as well as the shape of prophetic texts is uncertain. It is possible that some prophets such as Ezekiel were scribes themselves and therefore capable of shaping their own prophetic writings. Others, such as Jeremiah, may have hired scribes and then dictated the contents of their prophetic writings. However, it is also likely that in many cases the scribes who produced or copied oracle collections also felt free to edit their contents. This editorial activity occurred in different ways with different prophetic works, but it seems to have been in full flower by the beginning of the post-exilic period.

The extent of scribal editorial shaping remains a matter of scholarly dispute, but there is general agreement on the likely sorts of literary developments that took place. Oracles were organized according to various literary principles, sometimes according to literary form (Amos), sometimes according to contents (Hos 12–14), and sometimes according to chronological sequence (Ezekiel). Superscriptions were added to oracle collections in order to situate them in particular historical and social contexts. Many of the prophetic stories were placed in the so-called historical books (Samuel, Kings, Chronicles), although some stories were integrated into prophetic books (Isaiah, Jeremiah). Collections of oracles were updated to take into account later events such as the exile and the subsequent return to the land of Israel. There is some evidence for scribal interpretive activity involving the recognition of apparently related prophetic texts and the addition of interpretive comments. Finally, some of the smaller prophetic collections, known today as the Minor Prophets, were organized loosely into a unit, perhaps in stages, with smaller collections eventually giving rise to a larger one.

At the end of this period of scribal activity, the prophetic writings were fixed in their present form. Although prophets continued to appear in Israel, their words no longer had authority for the whole biblical community, and new prophetic revelation came through the process of interpreting the earlier prophetic writings. Through this interpretive process, the ancient prophetic materials continued to speak to new communities and historical contexts.

BIBLIOGRAPHY

J. Blenkinsopp. *A History of Prophecy in Israel.* Rev. and enlarged ed. (Louisville:Westminster John Knox, 1996); D. L. Petersen. *The Prophetic Literature: An Introduction* (Louisville: Westminster John Knox, 2002); P. L. Redditt. *Introduction to the Prophets* (Grand Rapids: Eerdmans, 2008); R. R. Wilson. *Prophecy and Society in Ancient Israel* (Philadelphia: Fortress, 1980).

HEBREW POETRY

BRENT A. STRAWN

Poetry in any language is hard to describe. Samuel Taylor Coleridge's (1772–1834) definition remains memorable: "poetry,—the best words in their best order." In the case of Hebrew poetry, "the best words" typically include: (1) the *presence* of rare terms not found extensively in prose, and (2) the *absence* of many "prosaic" elements like relative pronouns, definite articles, even the conjunction. "The best order" in Hebrew poetry means that the syntax is more varied than it is in comparable prose texts.

These characteristics indicate that Hebrew poetry is like poetry in other literature: it is terse, compressed language with unusual diction that renders it evocative and simultaneously more difficult to interpret. The concision of poetic language is, ironically, what makes it dense. This density causes the reader to slow down and pay attention not only to the *what* of the language, but also to its *how*. Poetry is and becomes *atypical* speech—elevated language that, in and by means of its elevation, speaks of significant topics in arrestingly profound ways. Poetry can also speak of the mundane, of course, but in so doing, poetry invests the normal with the *super*-normal meaning.

Other types of literature—excellent prose, for instance—have many of the same characteristics. Poetry is not, therefore, completely unlike other literature. This is especially true for Hebrew verse, which apparently lacks the hallmark of poetry as classically known and defined—namely, meter. While some scholars still look for meter in Hebrew prosody, most now admit that the verse present in the Old Testament is too varied to permit talk of a metric system. Meter, if present, that is, is *not* a dominant or regular characteristic of Hebrew poetry. This should not be misunderstood, however, as suggesting that Hebrew poetry and prose are basically identical. While one may need to reckon with a continuum of shared features (Kugel), most scholars agree that poetry is to be differentiated from prose by its comparatively denser use of images and tropes and the way in which these are structured into recurrent patterns. Another distinctive feature of Hebrew poetry is what has come to be called "parallelism." This is the way two (a bicolon) or three (a tricolon) lines of poetry are related to one another. Ever since Lowth's groundbreaking study of parallelism in the mid-eighteenth century, it has been common to treat parallelism as fundamentally of three types: synonymous, in which the two lines say the same thing; antithetical, in which they say the opposite; and synthetic, which designates those lines that do not fit either of the first two categories. These three types of parallelism (along with Wilson's alternative nomenclature) can be illustrated by virtually any example of Hebrew poetry:

Synonymous (or *affirming*):
I called to the LORD out of my distress,
and he answered me;
out of the belly of Sheol I cried,
and you heard my voice. (Jonah 2:2)

Antithetical (or *opposing*):
Hear, my child, your father's instruction
and do not reject your mother's teaching. (Prov 1:8)

Synthetic (or *advancing*):
He has broken down his booth like a garden,
he has destroyed his tabernacle;
the LORD has abolished in Zion
festival and Sabbath,
and in his fierce indignation has spurned
king and priest. (Lam 2:6)

Nonetheless, Lowth's typology has outlived its usefulness. Synthetic parallelism, in particular, is particularly suspicious (and specious) due to its "catch-all" nature. Close attention to almost any example of synonymous or antithetical parallelism reveals problems with these categories as well. In Prov 1:8, for example, the "father's instruction" and "mother's teaching" are hardly opposed. Similarly, in Jonah 2:2, "distress" is not coterminous with Sheol throughout the Bible, nor is one's self always the same as one's

959

voice. Perhaps more significantly, there is an identifiable *progression of thought* from the first line to the second, marked by the shift from third person ("*he* answered me") to second person discourse ("*you* heard my voice").

Paradoxically, then, parallelism is both more complex and more simple than Lowth's three categories would permit. It is more complex because parallelism can be exceedingly complicated, e.g., a semantically "antithetical" construction may be stated in a grammatically "synonymous" structure. It is more simple since the two (or three) lines of a Hebrew verse are typically related in terms of their seconding (Kugel) or intensifying nature (Alter). This seconding or dynamic movement between lines is evident in the progression in Jon 2:2, in the shift from father to mother in Prov 1:8, and in the specification of the Lord's targets in Lam 2:6. In each case, this parallelistic seconding or dynamism is predicated on similarity/repetition (a hallmark of all poetry). Difference, that is, is also present, giving the lines their cumulative sense, their forward movement. That being granted, difference should *not* be (overly) emphasized at the expense of sameness. It is the nature of Hebrew parallelism to traffic in both qualities.

The same is true for the imagistic language found in Hebrew poetry. This too tends to function by means of comparison. Nowhere is this truer than in the case of figurative language par excellence: the metaphor. Metaphors both compare and contrast—they make connections even while dissimilarities remain evident. Yahweh can be likened to a lion (Hos 13:7, 8*b*), for example, but not solely a lion, also a bear or other wild animal (13:8*a*, 8*c*). That demonstrates, among other things, that Yahweh is *not* a lion or a bear—at least not exactly—despite the straightforward sense of the metaphor. All images function in this manner: speaking of one thing in terms of another, emphasizing both similarity and distinctiveness.

It should come as no surprise that imagistic language and metaphor, on the one hand, and parallelism, on the other, share this quality of similarity and difference. Poetry in no small measure is an attempt to speak of one something in terms of another something—speaking in ways that are recognizable but at the same time different than usually or otherwise known. Poetic similarity and difference is manifested linguistically, especially in word-pictures and various poetic forms or structures, which for Hebrew includes, but is not restricted to, parallelism. Key words, repetition, allusion, personification, rhythm, word/sound play, imagery, metaphor, acrostic design, inclusios, and refrains are all important. In brief, poetry creates an alternative world. It is "not just a set of techniques for saying impressively what could be said otherwise. Rather, it is a particular way of imagining the world" (Alter, 151). All literature does this—at least to some degree—but poetry does it in a way distinct from and more powerfully than prose, most especially by its terseness, which does not answer every question, and by its metaphorical nature, which invites every kind of question. In these ways, poetry makes a seminal contribution to the Old Testament, a third of which is poetic. This richly poetic Old Testament, in turn, is of signal importance to the Christian canon given the marked lack of things poetic in the New Testament. Without poetry and the poetic imagination, theology and Scripture becomes prosaic in the worst sense of the term. With poetry, along with its concomitant gifts of imagery and metaphor, imagination and evocation, theology and Scripture become an alternative world—a place imagined and figured by psalmist, sage, and prophet, ready to be inhabited by those of us living in a flatter, less colorful, and a-theistic landscape.

BIBLIOGRAPHY

L. A. Schökel. *A Manual of Hebrew Poetics.* SubBi 11 (Rome: Pontifical Biblical Institute, 2000); R. Alter. *The Art of Biblical Poetry* (New York: Basic, 1985); A. Berlin. *The Dynamics of Biblical Parallelism* (Bloomington: Indiana University Press, 1985); M. Kinzie, *A Poet's Guide to Poetry* (Chicago: University of Chicago Press, 1999); J. L. Kugel. *The Idea of Biblical Poetry: Parallelism and Its History* (New Haven: Yale University Press, 1981); R. Lowth. *Lectures on the Sacred Poetry of the Hebrews.* 4th ed. G. Gregory, trans. (London: Tomas Tegg, 1839 [orig: 1753]); M. Oliver. *A Poetry Handbook* (San Diego: Harcourt, 1994); D. L. Petersen and K. H. Richards. *Interpreting Hebrew Poetry.* GBS (Minneapolis: Fortress, 1992); A. Preminger and T. V. F. Brogan, eds. *The New Princeton Encyclopedia of Poetry and Poetics* (Princeton: Princeton University Press, 1993); G. H. Wilson. *Psalms, Vol. 1.* NIVAC (Grand Rapids, Mich.: Zondervan, 2002).

WISDOM LITERATURE

Harold C. Washington

The wisdom literature of the OT includes Proverbs, Job, and Ecclesiastes (Qoheleth); and in the Apocrypha or deuterocanonical books, Sirach (Ecclesiasticus), and the Wisdom of Solomon. In these writings, Wisdom (*khokhmah*), is the rare attainment of intelligence, sound judgment, ethical conduct, humility, and the distinctive piety named in the motto of the book of Proverbs: "The fear of the Lord is the beginning of wisdom" (Prov 9:10; cf. 1:7, 29; 14:27; 19:23; Eccl 12:13; Job 28:28; Sir 1:11–30). The wisdom literature teaches readers how to live well and faithfully; it also tests the limits of human understanding. Wisdom is a divine attribute, evident in creation. Wisdom is also the hard-won result of long experience, learning, and critical reflection. Although wisdom can be taught, ultimately it is a gift from God.

The basic unit of the wisdom literature is the proverb, a short saying (*mashal*), typically consisting of two, parallel poetic lines. Major collections of proverbs are found in Prov 10:1–22:16; 25–29; and individual proverbs appear frequently in Ecclesiastes and Sirach. The instruction form comprises longer units of second person address: from father to son, or teacher to student. Such instructions appear chiefly in Prov 1–9, 22:17–24:22. The dialogue or disputation on divine justice characterizes the book of Job, where it is combined with lawsuit language and the lament form of the psalms. Pseudo-autobiography appears in Prov 4:3–9; 24:30–34; Eccl 1:12–2:26; Sir 33:16–18; 51:13–22; and Wis 7:1–8:21. The Hellenistic genre of philosophical exhortation is found in the Wisdom of Solomon. Other literary forms, e.g., the numerical saying, allegory, and riddle, appear less frequently in wisdom literature.

Biblical wisdom literature belongs to a broader tradition found in ancient Egyptian and Mesopotamian writings. The Egyptian instruction genre spans from the Old Kingdom period (third millennium BCE) into the Ptolemaic era. Typically set in a royal milieu or in the ranks of officialdom, Egyptian instruction commends just conduct, prudent speech, receptiveness to learning, and other topics familiar in the instruction of Proverbs. The Egyptian *Instruction of Amenemope* (ca. 1100 BCE) is noteworthy for its influence on the book of Proverbs, especially in the "Words of the Wise" (Prov 22:17–24:22). Several Egyptian texts extol, like Sirach, the elevated position of the scribe or sage. Other writings invite comparison with Job and Ecclesiastes in their struggle with the inequities of human existence and the question of life's value in the face of death. From Mesopotamia there are numerous collections of proverbs as well as instruction from the third millennium BCE onwards. Several works anticipate Job's theme of the righteous sufferer: a Sumerian text, *A Man and His God*; and Akkadian writings including *I Will Praise the Lord of Wisdom*, also known as the *Babylonian Job*; and the *Babylonian Theodicy* (ca. 1000 BCE). The sixth century BCE Aramaic book of Ahiqar contains sayings similar to those of Proverbs, though set within a narrative frame.

The biblical wisdom books are relatively late compositions. Proverbs and Ecclesiastes were likely composed in the Persian or the Hellenistic period, fifth to third centuries BCE, presumably in Jerusalem. Job, also of Judean provenance, might have been written as much as a century earlier. Sirach wrote his work in Jerusalem, ca. 180 BCE. A half-century later in Alexandria, his grandson translated the book from the original Hebrew into Greek. The Wisdom of Solomon was composed in Greek by a Hellenistic Alexandrian Jew in the first century BCE.

The Hebrew wisdom tradition likely originated with the folk wisdom of the earliest Israelite villages and families. From time immemorial, children received their elders' wisdom in proverbial form, and adults invoked traditional sayings for amusement and persuasion. The wisdom books, however, are the product of an intellectual elite with the luxury of education, expensive writing equipment, and time for literary pursuits. Consequently the wisdom literature at times reflects an upper-class perspective (e.g., Prov 14:20; 17:8; Eccl 5:8, 13–16). In the pre-exilic period, these privileged scribes and scholars were likely attached to the royal court and administrative offices. There is no evidence of institutional schools for the training of this select professional class. Instead, individual education probably occurred through apprenticeship. Apart from the royal administration, however, there could also have been some urban elite families with the means to sustain literary cultivation. Perhaps these households preserved the Hebrew wisdom tradition after the monarchy ended with the destruction of Jerusalem in 587 BCE.

In the post-exilic period, sages and teachers independent of the royal court and Temple produced the biblical wisdom literature. In this era Proverbs appears to have been directed toward the education of young Judean men preparing for adult responsibilities. Ecclesiastes is described as a sage and a teacher of traditional wisdom forms, though radical in his approach (e.g., 12:9–12). In the second century BCE, Sirach celebrates the honored role of the scribe, who studies wisdom, torah, and prophecy (i.e., the whole of scripture; 38:24–39:11); and he invites the uneducated to his school ("house of instruction;" 51:23).

Major OT themes such as the promises to the ancestors, the Exodus-Sinai tradition, the Davidic monarchy, and Temple worship are markedly absent from Proverbs, Job, and Ecclesiastes, though they appear to some extent in the later wisdom books (cf. Sir 35:1–12; 44:1–50:24; Wis 11:1–19:21). Rather than viewing God as Israel's redeemer and covenant partner, wisdom literature centers upon God as Creator. Wisdom is found not in divine revelation, but from recognizing the divinely established moral order of creation. The sages observe the benefits of living in accord with this divine order and the detriments of violating it. These may be conceived as inherent relations between acts and their consequences (Prov 26:27), or as instances of divine retribution and reward (e.g., Prov 16:5, 7). Righteous living results in well-being, prosperity, and long life; wickedness leads to suffering, deprivation, and early death. The way of the wise and righteous is characterized by qualities such as integrity, diligence, insight, self-restraint, prudent speech, and generosity; that of the foolish and wicked by dishonesty, indolence, thoughtlessness, gluttony, rash speech, and meanness.

This neatly two-sided perspective sets the terms for instruction and character formation in Proverbs (e.g., Prov 4:10–27), but it runs afoul of the reality that, sometimes, the wicked prosper and the righteous suffer. The moral discourse of wisdom, therefore, is subject to challenge and critique. The sages are keenly aware of the limitations of human understanding and the inscrutability of God's ways. Proverbs is far from a collection of immediately applicable teachings; the book raises as many questions as it answers. The sages recognize that things are not always what they seem (17:28), and that the proverbs are beneficial only when accompanied by insight (26:7, 9). Many sayings stand in tension with others, and some appear to contradict each other (e.g., 26:4–5). The proverbs therefore are context-sensitive, within the book and in their relevance to life; they are multivalent and not to be applied mechanically. Job presses the question of innocent suffering to its limits, and in doing so, profoundly complicates the moral scheme of righteous and wicked. Ecclesiastes observes the futility of the human urge to secure one's life or to understand God's providence. Nonetheless the book commends enjoying life and work, living in the fear of the Lord.

In Prov 1–9, divine wisdom is vividly personified as a woman. Like a prophet, she cries out dire warnings; she beckons her followers with the language of love; and in the manner of a grand hostess, invites the unwise to a life-giving banquet. Divine wisdom is more precious than silver or gold. She is present with God at creation, taking delight in the world and in humanity. In Sir 24, divine wisdom comes forth from the mouth of God, covering the earth like mist. She traverses the heavens, seeks a dwelling place on earth and, at God's command, lodges with Israel in Jerusalem. Ultimately wisdom is identified with Torah, "the book of the covenant of the Most High God" (Sir 24:23). Wisdom of Solomon conceives divine wisdom as a breath of God's power, an emanation of glory, reflection of eternal light, and perfect image of divine goodness (7:25–26).

Other early Jewish writings with affinities to the wisdom literature include Tobit, whose last testament resembles the instruction genre (4:1–19) and Baruch, which heightens Sirach's identification of wisdom with Torah (3:9–4:4). There are several wisdom writings among the Qumran texts. The Mishnaic treatise Pirqe Abot (Sayings of the Fathers) and subsequent rabbinic writings carry on the traditions of the sages. Likewise in the NT there are important strands of wisdom thought. Jesus appears in the synoptic Gospels as a wisdom teacher; a Wisdom Christology is especially evident in Matthew (e.g., Matt 11:28–30; cf. Sir 51:23–27). The Prologue to the Gospel of John adapts the motif of personified wisdom, conceiving Christ as the preexistent Word (*logos*), with God and through whom God created the world. Paul refers to Christ as the wisdom of God (1 Cor 1:24), and the hymn of Col 1:15–20 is also based on the figure of divine wisdom. Finally, the Epistle of James contains many wisdom themes.

BIBLIOGRAPHY

R. J. Clifford. *The Wisdom Literature.* IBT (Nashville: Abingdon, 1998); J. L. Crenshaw. *Old Testament Wisdom: An Introduction.* Rev. and enlarged ed. (Louisville: Westminster John Knox, 1998); R. E. Murphy. *The Tree of Life: An Exploration of Biblical Wisdom Literature.* 2nd ed. (Grand Rapids: Eerdmans, 1996); K. M. O'Connor. *The Wisdom Literature.* MBS (Collegeville, Minn.: Michael Glazier, 1993).

APOCALYPTIC LITERATURE

CAROL A. NEWSOM

The terms *apocalypse* and *apocalyptic* derive from the Greek *apokalypsis*, meaning "revelation." The earliest use of the term to refer to a literary work comes from the opening line of the book of Revelation, "The *apokalypsis* of Jesus Christ." Indeed, this book is sometimes referred to simply as "the Apocalypse." Even though many other Jewish and Christian works of similar genre do not use this term for themselves, scholars commonly refer to them as apocalypses and to the worldview characteristic of these works as apocalyptic.

I. LITERARY GENRE AND WORLDVIEW

A widely used definition of the genre apocalypse takes it to be a writing with a narrative framework in which a revelation is mediated to a human by an otherworldly being. The content of the revelation concerns a transcendent reality that has a temporal dimension, insofar as it is concerned with eschatological salvation, and a spatial dimension, insofar as it refers to a supernatural world. Apocalypses vary considerably from one another, but can be roughly grouped into two types, depending on which dimension of transcendent reality is more prominent. In historical apocalypses the seer frequently receives symbolic visions that disclose the course of history over a long period, culminating in an eschatological climax in which evil is defeated by divine forces. The other type features an otherworldly journey in which the seer is shown the mysteries of the cosmos and of heaven itself. These otherworldly apocalypses may also be concerned with the eschatological climax of history or may focus more on personal eschatology, that is, the fate of individual souls after death. Apocalypses also incorporate a variety of other genres within themselves (e.g., exhortations, dialogues, midrashic narratives), giving them a diverse character.

With the exception of the book of Revelation, whose actual author, John of Patmos, is named, apocalypses are typically pseudepigraphic. That is to say, they are attributed to important figures from the past (e.g., Adam, Enoch, Abraham, Moses, Ezra). Early Christian apocalypses were also written in the names of Peter and Paul. These attributions were not intended to deceive but represented the author's conviction that he wrote in the tradition of these figures and so could claim their authority for his work. Apocalypses also construct a sense of authority for their claims through their vivid, often highly visual descriptions of heavenly scenes or the content of mysterious visions. The reader thus shares in the experience of the seer. Although many apocalypses are simply literary creations, it is likely that religious practices designed to encourage ecstatic experiences were also part of the apocalyptic phenomenon.

Many of the beliefs and assumptions common in apocalypses (e.g., interest in supernatural realities, concern for personal and cosmic eschatological fates, a dualistic struggle between good and evil) were widely shared in the Hellenistic and Roman eras. Thus it is not surprising to find these ideas in many other types of literature besides apocalypses. They are prominent in the letters of Paul, in the Synoptic Gospels, and in various types of literature from the Dead Sea Scrolls. Thus the category of apocalyptic literature is broader than just the literary genre of apocalypse.

II. ORIGINS OF APOCALYPTIC LITERATURE

Apocalyptic literature emerges at a time of rich cultural mixing in the late Persian and Hellenistic periods, and it is not surprising that the scribes responsible for its development appropriated elements from a variety of foreign cultures, combining them with native Israelite traditions. In *1 Enoch* the biblical patriarch (Gen 5:18–24) incorporates traits of the legendary Mesopotamian sage from before the flood, Enmeduranki. The interest in astronomical phenomenon also reflects Babylonian intellectual interests, while the section of *1 Enoch* known as the *Book of the Watchers* engages Greek myths and traditions of cosmic geography. The figure of Daniel is represented as someone learned in the language and literature of the Chaldeans (i.e., Babylonians), and there are elements of Persian historiography in the eschatological dream in ch. 2. The Mesopotamian tradition of literary prophecies, in which pseudo-predictions of past events are followed by a genuine attempt to predict a coming event, has probably influenced the similar phenomenon in Jewish historical apocalypses. Although Persian traditions are notoriously difficult to date, elements of cosmic dualism, belief in resurrection, periodization of history, and traditions of heavenly journeys bear striking resemblance to early Jewish apocalyptic ideas. The influence of Persian dualism is virtually certain for the *Two Spirits Treatise* in the Qumran *Community Rule*.

Authors of apocalyptic literature also made creative use of older Israelite traditions. Ancient mythic motifs concerning God's combat with the chaotic sea are alluded to in Daniel, *4 Ezra*, and Revelation; and the representation of the "Ancient of Days" and the "Son of Man" in Daniel 7 bears a striking resemblance to the imagery of the Canaanite gods El and Baal, already appropriated for Yahweh in Israelite religion. Apocalyptic authors also made use of biblical traditions concerning the divine council (cf. 1 Kgs 22:19–22; Ps 82:1) to speculate on the nature of the heavenly world, and invoked the prophetic "Day of Yahweh" as they envisioned eschatological events. Liturgical traditions from the Temple clearly influenced apocalyptic notions of heavenly praise (cf. *Songs of the Sabbath Sacrifice* from Qumran; Rev. 4–5). Above all, the prophetic vision of the divine Glory in Ezek 1 and the symbolic visions of Zech 1–6 were models for envisioning the divine presence and the apocalyptic seer's reception of hidden knowledge. This lively appropriation and transformation of both traditional and foreign religious and historiographical traditions made apocalyptic literature a highly creative form of religious literature that flourished for centuries and served to address a variety of changing social circumstances.

III. Development of Apocalyptic Literature in Judaism

Although apocalyptic is often referred to as "crisis literature," that is something of a misconception. The earliest Enochic traditions and many later apocalypses featuring otherworldly journeys (e.g., The *Similitudes* in *1 Enoch*, *2 Enoch*, *3 Baruch*) seem largely interested in the mysteries of the heavenly world and the workings of the cosmos. Nevertheless, even in many of these apocalypses, there is a sense that something is out of joint in the cosmos that will require an ultimate judgment of God to put right. In some texts (e.g., the *Book of the Watchers* in *1 Enoch*, *4 Ezra*, the Qumran *Two Spirits Treatise*) there is an explicit concern to explain the origin of evil and its ultimate defeat. In significant measure, the sense of something wrong with the world reflects the experience of Israel as subject to a succession of harsh imperial powers. Apocalyptic literature reaffirms the sovereignty of God over the whole cosmos and God's eventual defeat of both supernatural and human enemies of Israel and of the righteous.

Apocalyptic's preoccupation with these issues made it well suited to engage acute political crises. Thus several apocalypses (Daniel 7–12, the Enochic *Apocalypse of Weeks* and *Animal Apocalypse*, the original version of the *Testament of Moses*) were all composed as responses to the persecutions of Antiochus IV Epiphanes in 167 BCE and the Maccabean revolt. Yet they differed from one another in their understanding of the appropriate stance to take, the Enoch traditions embracing militancy, the Daniel apocalypses urging insight into God's plan, and the *Testament of Moses* endorsing martyrdom. Following the Maccabean revolt, apocalyptic literature continued to be influential. Although the Qumran community did not compose apocalypses, they were influenced by them and created new literary genres and even a form of communal life that was deeply informed by apocalyptic perspectives. Whether there were other apocalyptic social movements at this time is difficult to tell, although both Daniel and the Enoch literature suggest some sense of a social group that identified with these figures.

The crisis of the Jewish revolt against Rome (65–70 CE) and the destruction of the Temple evoked another outpouring of apocalyptic literature, most notably *4 Ezra*, *2 Baruch*, the *Apocalypse of Abraham*. In these works there is less a sense of a group or movement and more of an individual writer attempting to use the resources of apocalypse to make sense out of an unbelievable tragedy. At least from the early first century CE on, apocalyptic speculations had fueled messianic hopes, and such hopes also attached to Bar Kochba, the leader of the last revolt against Rome (132–135 CE). The devastating consequences of his defeat did much to discredit apocalyptic ideas within Judaism, and it subsequently played a more limited role in Jewish religious experience. Except for the book of Daniel, none of the Jewish apocalypses composed between the third century BCE and the second century CE was preserved in Jewish circles.

IV. Development of Apocalyptic Literature in Early Christianity

Christianity emerged in an environment in which apocalyptic ideas were widespread and influential. Although a few scholars have argued that Jesus was primarily a wisdom teacher who was relatively uninfluenced by apocalyptic ideas, most think that he, like John the Baptist, shared many of the eschatological expectations that characterized apocalyptic theology at that time. Certainly the early Christian writings reflect the imprint of the apocalyptic. Paul claims to have experienced a heavenly journey and to have had visions (2 Cor 12:1–7) and often speaks of the enmity of Satan (1 Thess 2:18). He understood the resurrection of Jesus to be the first act of the eschatological drama that will soon be fulfilled (1 Cor 15:15–28; 1 Thess 4:13–18). The Synoptic Gospels clearly incorporate apocalyptic ideas and motifs. In each, Jesus is presented as giving an apocalyptic discourse (Mark 13; Matthew 24–25; Luke 21) in which he describes the events of the end time, which is to occur soon. Matthew, for example, describes the eschatological coming of the Son of Man with an angelic host and the final judgment (Matt 25:31–46).

The only actual apocalypse in the New Testament is the book of Revelation, composed in western Asia Minor in the late first century during the reign of Domitian. As in similar Jewish writings, the resources of apocalyptic imagery are used to resist the claims of imperial power, which is represented as part of Satan's dominion. In a heavenly journey that takes him to the divine throne room (Rev 4), John is made privy to the contents of the sealed scroll that contains the events of the end times, including the defeat of Satan and the beasts who are his servants (the Roman empire), the triumph of Christ, resurrection, the final judgment, and the descent to earth of the new Jerusalem.

The Christian experience of marginalization and persecution during the second and third centuries made apocalyptic literature, with its vivid narratives of hope, judgments of the wicked, and divine triumph over evil, a significant religious resource. Many of the Jewish apocalypses were preserved only in Christian circles, sometimes being edited to include specifically Christian beliefs (e.g., the *Ascension of Isaiah*). In addition, new Christian apocalypses, such as the *Shepherd of Hermas* and the *Apocalypse of Peter* were composed. With the change in status of Christianity that resulted from Constantine's edicts in the early fourth century CE, the importance of the apocalyptic as resistance literature receded. Despite the ambivalence of many Christian theologians, apocalyptic ideas have remained an important element of Christian religious culture and have periodically experienced a revival of popularity.

BIBLIOGRAPHY

J. H. Charlesworth, ed. *The Old Testament Pseudepigrapha.* 2 vols. (Garden City, N.Y.: Doubleday, 1983–1985); A. Y. Collins, *Cosmology and Eschatology in Jewish and Christian Apocalypticism* (Leiden/ Boston: Brill, 2000); J. J. Collins, *The Apocalyptic Imagination: An Introduction to Jewish Apocalyptic Literature.* 2nd ed. (Grand Rapids: Eerdmans, 1998); A. Y. Reed, *Fallen Angels and the History of Judaism and Christianity: The Reception of Enochic Literature* (New York: Cambridge University Press, 2005); C. Rowland, *The Open Heaven: A Study of Apocalyptic in Judaism and Early Christianity* (New York: Crossroad, 1982).

NARRATIVES OF THE NEW TESTAMENT

Susan R. Garrett

The narratives of the NT consist of the Gospels, Acts, and brief sections of other writings (e.g., Gal 1:13-2:14). A *narrative* is a type of writing in which a narrator recounts a story centering on characters' actions, speech, and relationships. The events in a narrative follow a *plot*, meaning that they are causally related and move through some kind of tension or problem to resolution. In all narratives, the narrator relates events from a particular *point of view*, which is conveyed through the narrator's selection and rhetorical presentation of all aspects of the story world. Point of view may be expressed through direct address (Luke 1:1–4), the voices of characters in the story (Mark 8:17), portrayal of characters' emotions and motivations (Luke 23:8), and various other details of plotting and characterization.

CHANGING QUESTIONS IN STUDY OF THE NT NARRATIVES

Since the Enlightenment, debate has raged on how best to understand the narratives of the NT. As scholarly opinions about the nature of the documents have shifted, so have the questions put to them— and hence also meanings assigned to them.

A. What Really Happened?

One persistent line of inquiry has aimed to ferret out what really happened in the ministries of Jesus and his followers. The premise of this *quest for the historical Jesus* (and also of study of the early church) has been a conviction that the NT narratives are not unbiased accounts but have been shaped by the mythic sensibilities and apologetic concerns of the earliest believers. Since it first began in the eighteenth century, the quest has been through many phases and has given rise to convictions about the Gospels and Acts that have in turn shaped subsequent study. For example, the search for the most reliable foundation for Jesus research led to the discrediting of the Gospel of John as a historical source because it was, supposedly, much later and more influenced by Hellenistic thought than the Synoptic Gospels. This supposition has, however, come under intense scrutiny and dispute. Meanwhile, the status of the Gospel of Mark rose in the nineteenth century as scholars concurred that it was the earliest of the Gospels and therefore closest in proximity to the events it recounts. Today many scholars agree that Mark is the earliest of the Gospels, but insist that it, like the others, incorporates post-Easter perspectives into its portrayal of Jesus and the disciples.

B. How Were the Traditions Preserved, and Why?

Another line of inquiry has pertained to oral traditions about Jesus and his followers. Known as *form criticism*, this method of inquiry dates back to the early twentieth century and was influenced by studies of folklore and its transmission. Form critics noted that within the Synoptic Gospels it is possible to identify discrete units of tradition, which they termed *pericopes*. They divided these pericopes into various categories, such as *miracle stories* and *controversy dialogues* (different researchers offered different classifications). Form critics argued that the traditions circulated orally during the decades between the crucifixion of Jesus and the composition of the Gospels, and were shaped by their transmitters to accomplish various functions within the religious lives of communities of faith. In form criticism, the focus was not on what really happened in the depicted events but on the lives of these early Christian communities. Form critics' assumption that the communities controlled the shape and content of the traditions—and the corollary that minimized the evangelists' authorial role—would be disputed in following decades. But the attention to the form and social function of specific traditions (not just Gospel stories but also stories in Acts, and speeches, epistles, and sections of epistles) would continue, with effort devoted to understanding these traditions in light of literary and rhetorical forms current in the first century.

C. What Did the Evangelists Believe?

Yet another line of inquiry has focused on the work and thought of the evangelists. In the 1950s, some scholars had begun to notice that Matthew and Luke each adapted their source material from Mark and from another presumed shared source (dubbed *Q*) in consistent ways. This observation suggested that the evangelists weren't mindless collectors of oral traditions as form critics had alleged, but creative authors with distinct viewpoints. Known as *redaction criticism*, this method of inquiry endeavored to lay bare the evangelists' respective theologies by paying special attention to differences in Luke and Matthew over against Mark and the original form of Q with respect to word choice, additions and modifications, and the ordering of traditions. Redaction critics applied their analytical skills also to texts whose sources are no longer extant, including Mark, John, and Acts. They did this by postulating an earliest form of traditions within these works, based on such data as the respective authors' typical vocabulary and stylistic habits and the existence of literary seams (places where distinct traditions had apparently been joined together).

Though it is still enlightening to compare the Gospels' parallel traditions, researchers have identified shortcomings in the redaction critical approach. *Composition critics* argued that because redaction critics focused on literary differences among the Gospels, their summaries of the evangelists' theologies highlighted their distinctive emphases but neglected their many shared convictions. Only by attending also to what the evangelists took over without change from their sources can a full portrait of each one's theology be painted. *Narrative critics* rejected the effort to mine the Gospels and Acts for theologies assumed to precede and transcend the narratives. Rather, the meaning of a given narrative can scarcely be separated from the structural details of the narrative itself. Influenced by literary critical methods popular in the mid-twentieth century, narrative critics engaged in close readings of the Gospels and Acts, paying special attention to aspects of their form such as plot, point of view, character development, and the use of irony and various other rhetorical techniques. They tended to view the narratives as theologically cohesive works that effectively conveyed meanings intended by their respective authors. (Luke and Acts were treated as a two-volume work reflecting a single authorial perspective.) But from the late 1980s on, scholars influenced by *postmodern* and *deconstructionist* literary critical methods have questioned the supposed thematic integrity of the NT narratives. Might this unity not reside chiefly in the eye of the beholder? Highlighting the fissures, tensions, and outright contradictions in the narratives, deconstructive critics have also questioned the supposed transparency of authorial intention as well as its sufficiency. Authors are themselves partially governed by cultural and other factors of which they are imperfectly aware, and never exercise perfect mastery over the meaning of their own writings. Meanings that are implicit in their words but that they themselves never considered will be evident to readers of different backgrounds or generations.

D. What Role Does the Reader Play?

Taking cues from literary critics, in the late 1970s some biblical scholars began to shift away from the discipline's longstanding emphasis on the authors of the NT narratives and to emphasize the role of their readers (or hearers). Readers are, after all, partners with authors in negotiating the meaning of texts. Some reader-oriented critics have focused on describing the way a first-time, "naïve" reader (i.e., one without substantial knowledge of depicted events) would encounter and make sense of the documents. Thus, whereas an experienced Christian would discern Eucharistic allusions in the accounts of the loaves and fishes, a first-time reader would not—but might hark back to the feeding miracles when coming to the account of the Eucharist itself. Other reader-oriented critics have tried to estimate how historical audiences would have responded to the narratives. What ancient cultural knowledge and specific knowledge of Jesus traditions might a Gospel's readers have possessed, and how would that knowledge have inclined them to interpret the story? Are they likely to have known the Exodus story of manna in the wilderness, for example, and if so, how might their knowledge of that earlier narrative have affected their reading of the miraculous feeding accounts? Still other reader-oriented critics have explored ways in which the cultural context and life experience of the modern reader affect the interpretation of the NT narratives. Thus, an African-American reader might interpret the depictions of master-servant relationships in the

Gospels and Acts (e.g., Matt 21:33–41; Acts 16:16–19) differently than would a reader of another cultural heritage, insisting that such depictions are not innocuous but potentially dangerous because they seem to validate such oppressive relationships (even portraying them as normative for the relationship between humans and God: see Matt 18:23–35).

CONCLUSION

The great variety of interpretive approaches to the NT narratives in recent centuries—and the multiplicity of outcomes of these approaches—is instructive for interpreters today. The lesson to be learned concerns the incredible complexity of the task of interpretation. As in premodern times so also today, readers' cultural and rhetorical assumptions and the questions they ask play a large role in the meanings that they take away from the NT narratives. Some readings will be more historically sensitive, and therefore more congruent with meanings intended by the evangelists or perceived by the first readers of the narratives. But even first-century readers had to make interpretive decisions as they read through the NT narratives, and disagreed about where interpretive crossroads were to be found and how best to traverse them. There is not nor has there ever been one "correct" interpretation of each of the NT narratives; rather, there are many possible interpretations, each of which responds to the interests, assumptions, and questions of a particular interpretive community. It is against the norms of such communities—norms that may be informed by Scripture or theological tradition as much as by academic standards—that the legitimacy of a given reading is to be measured.

BIBLIOGRAPHY

A. K. M. Adam. *Faithful Interpretation: Reading the Bible in a Postmodern World* (Minneapolis: Fortress Press, 2006); S. D. Moore. *Literary Criticism and the Gospels: The Theoretical Challenge* (New Haven: Yale University Press, 1989); M. A. Powell. *Fortress Introduction to the Gospels* (Minneapolis: Augsburg Fortress Press, 1997); C. Tuckett. *Reading the New Testament: Methods of Interpretation* (Philadelphia: Fortress Press, 1987).

LETTERS

DAVID DOWNS

Much of the story of the early Christian movement is a story told in letters. Though less frequent today in an age of email, faxes, and cell phones, correspondence through the sending of letters is perhaps as old as the written word itself. In the Greco-Roman world of the first century, letters facilitated communication between parties separated by distance. Of the twenty-seven documents that make up the canon of the NT, twenty-one are letters. These include thirteen letters ascribed to the Apostle Paul, the anonymous letter to the Hebrews, James, 1–2 Peter, 1–3 John, and Jude. Letters are also embedded in other NT writings, such as those found in Acts 15:23–29; 23:25–30; and Rev 2:1–3:21.

How Were Letters Written?

Modern (particularly Western) notions of letter writing typically involve images of a solitary figure sitting at a desk with pen and paper. In Rembrandt's classic painting "The Apostle Paul" (ca. 1657), for example, Paul the letter-writer is depicted in just such a fashion: alone and deep in thought in a dark room, Paul leans forward at his desk, his quill pen resting in his right hand, sheaves of blank paper spread across a wooden table. This image does not correspond with what is known about the composition of letters in the ancient world, however.

Letter writing in the Greco-Roman world was anything but an isolated endeavor. First, ancient letters were frequently transcribed by secretaries. In a context where, by some estimates, only around 10 percent of the population was literate, dictation to scribes was necessary for the vast majority of those who wished to send a letter. Scores of official letters and legal documents, for example, are punctuated with a formulaic clause indicating that the letter was composed by a scribe: "I [name of scribe] have written for [sender] because he/she does not know letters" (cf. P. Oxy. II 275.41–43). Yet secretaries were also employed even by the literate. In Rom 16:22, for instance, a scribe named Tertius identifies himself as "the writer of this letter" and sends his greetings to the church in Rome. Paul was clearly the author of Romans (Rom 1:1–7), yet Tertius was involved in the production of the epistle as the secretary who transcribed it (cf. Gal 6:11). It might be helpful to think of the function of secretaries in terms of a continuum from mere transcribers of dictated words to contributors in the process of composition to freely-empowered composers of epistles.

Second, the concept of the authors of NT letters as isolated figures is challenged by the fact that these letters were communal products. On the one hand, most of the letters attributed to Paul contain references to co-senders in the greeting, including Sosthenes (1 Cor 1:1), Timothy (2 Cor 1:1; Phil 1:1; Col 1:1; 1 Thess 1:1; 2 Thess 1:1; Phlm 1:1), Silvanus (1 Thess 1:1; 2 Thess 1:1), and "all the members of God's family who are with me" (Gal 1:2; cf. 1 Pet 5:12; Jude 1:1). Although the exact role played by these co-senders in composition is debated, their presence in the greetings indicates that Paul was not alone when writing to his churches and that he had some assistance in crafting his missives. On the other hand, the NT letters themselves were, for the most part, documents addressed to communities and not individuals. The instructions in Col 4:16 suggest that letters were to be read aloud in church and then perhaps shared with other congregations. Even letters ostensibly addressed to individuals typically assume community involvement. Philemon is an epistle written from Paul to his beloved friend and co-worker, yet also named in the address are Apphia, Archippus, and the church that meets in Philemon's house (Phlm 1–2). Indeed, the persuasive rhetoric that Paul employs to challenge Philemon is made more effective by the public nature of the document, for the community is implicitly invited to gauge Philemon's response. Even 1 Timothy, 2 Timothy, and Titus, often called the "Pastoral Epistles" because they are the only Pauline letters addressed to individuals and not churches, conclude with wishes that God's grace be with "you" in the plural (1 Tim 6:21; 2 Tim 4:22; Titus 3:15). 3 John, written from an anonymous "elder" to an individual named Gaius is the exception to this communal emphasis among the NT letters, yet even that text ends with an exchange of greetings among other anonymous "friends" (15).

How Were Letters Sent?

In the 1ˢᵗ century, there was a well-organized postal system for the official correspondence of the Roman Empire. Private citizens had to rely on other methods for conveying letters, however. Those with greater wealth could employ carriers or commission slaves; those with lesser means often relied on merchants, friends, and even strangers who happened to be traveling to the same locale as the letter. The early Christian communities frequently used individuals and envoys associated with the churches in order to transmit correspondence (Rom 16:1–2; Col 4:7–8; 1 Pet 5:12). Upon arrival, these carriers might read the letter aloud to the congregation (1 Thess 5:27) and they could provide additional information from and about the sender (1 Cor 1:11; Eph 6:21–22). It appears that the apostle Paul sometimes sent letters when communication via the written word would be more effective (or less controversial) than a personal visit (cf. 2 Cor 2:1–4; 7:5–16).

What Were the Types of Letters?

There were many varieties of letters in antiquity, and it is not possible to provide a simple system of classification for the assortment of types. Literary theorists in the classical world struggled with this problem of categorization. One ancient text (probably designed as a handbook for scribes) identifies and provides examples of twenty-one different types of letters based on their purpose. Letters are classified as friendly, commendatory, blaming, consoling, allegorical, thankful, etc. (Pseudo-Demetrius, *Epistolary Types*). In the early part of the 20ᵗʰ century, scholars often drew a distinction between "letters" (i.e., nonliterary, common, private) and "epistles" (i.e., literary, artistic, public). To some extent the division of nonliterary and literary letters holds true. For example, a short, occasional letter from a Roman solider to his father in Egypt requesting news from home (BGU II 423) reads quite differently from, say, the philosophical missives from the hand of the elite Roman statesman Seneca to his wealthy friend Lucilius. Yet any sharp distinction fails to recognize that nonliterary (including diplomatic) and literary letters often overlap in both form and function. Although NT letters are sometimes classified as nonliterary because of their occasional nature, they contain many of the sophisticated rhetorical devices seen in literary texts.

In spite of the difficulty of classifying letters according to function or literary style, it is possible to speak broadly of the form of ancient letters. Just as modern letters follow a relatively fixed format (i.e., opening: "Dear John"; closing: "Sincerely Yours"), so also letters in the Greco-Roman world regularly adhered to a standard pattern of organization. A brief look at a 3ʳᵈ-cent. CE Greek letter from Egypt illustrates this form (*P.Mich.* 8.513):

Chairemon to Serapion.	*Sender and Addressee*
Greetings.	*Salutation*
Before all else I pray that you are well and I make your obeisance before the Lord Sarapis daily.	*Thanksgiving or Prayer*
I want you to know that you have sent me no word from the day that I came to Alexandria. If then you love me, do not neglect to write to me.	*Body of Letter*
I greet Sarapis and her children. Pasoxis the carpenter greets you and your children ... and his wife ...	*Closing Salutation*
[*Opposite side*] Deliver to Sarapion from Chairemon	

The NT letters tend to employ this same basic structure, although often with some elaboration, particularly of the salutation and thanksgiving. For example, the typical Hellenistic salutation "greetings" is often replaced in NT letters with some variation of the phrase "grace and peace [from God our Father and the Lord Jesus Christ]" (cf. Rom 1:7; 1 Cor 1:3; 1 Cor 1:2; Gal 1:3; Eph 1:2; Phil 1:2; Col 1:2; 1 Thess 1:1; 2 Thess 1:2; 1 Tim 1:2; 2 Tim 1:2; Titus 1:4; Phlm 3; 1 Pet 1:2; 2 Pet 1:2; 2 John 1:3; Rev 1:4). Similarly, the thanksgiving section in NT letters is frequently developed in a sophisticated manner that anticipates major themes developed elsewhere in the epistle (see e.g., 1 Cor 1:4–9). That is not to say that all NT letters adhere to this standard format; deviations from the conventional structure are also telling. Galatians, for instance, contains an extended letter opening (1:1–5) yet lacks a thanksgiving section, features closely related to the rhetorical context of that epistle. The opening of Hebrews does not conform to the customary letter form, which has led to suggestions that the document is not a letter but a Jewish-Christian homily. Yet the closing benediction (13:20–21) and postscript (13:22–25) do seem to place Hebrews within the genre of Greco-Roman letter.

Conclusion

It is often said that reading NT letters is like reading other people's mail. This is partly true. Since letters in the NT address particular historical and rhetorical contexts, they represent one side—or one moment—of an ongoing conversation. Thus, the task of reading these letters calls for careful consideration of the contexts in which they were produced.

Yet certain early Christian letters were included in the canon of the NT, located in this canon after the Gospels and the Acts of the Apostles but before the Apocalypse of John. This placement too provides a context for reading the letters. The Pauline writings are positioned first among the letters and organized in order of descending length. Presumably they follow Acts because of the important role that Paul plays in the second half of that narrative. Hebrews, which was initially associated with Paul but now no longer is comes next, followed by the so-called "Catholic Epistles," named for their allegedly universal appeal. These "Catholic Epistles" include James, 1–2 Peter, 1–3 John, and Jude, a grouping that may be based on the order of the names of the apostles mentioned in Gal 2:9, with Jude coming last since Jude is not mentioned in that passage. The fact that these early Christian letters are placed in the canon of the NT also means that they are not strictly "other people's mail." In addition, they are documents that belong to the communities that canonized them as Scripture.

BIBLIOGRAPHY

H-J. Klauck. *Ancient Letters and the New Testament: A Guide to Context and Exegesis* (Waco, Tex.: Baylor University Press, 2006); E. R. Richards. *Paul and First-Century Letter Writing: Secretaries, Composition and Collection* (Downers Grove, Ill.: InterVarsity, 2004); S. K. Stowers. *Letter Writing in Greco-Roman Antiquity* (Philadelphia: Westminster, 1986); J. L. White. *Light from Ancient Letters* (Philadelphia: Fortress, 1986).

CULTURES OF THE ANCIENT NEAR EAST

Joel LeMon

Introduction: The Bible as an Ancient Near Eastern Text

Until the early nineteenth century, the Old Testament was the single most important cultural relic from the ancient Near East. Other artifacts had endured through the centuries, including pyramids, obelisks, colossi, ziggurats, mummies. And while these testified to humanity's long and complicated history in the Near East, the writing that appeared on these artifacts was largely indecipherable. Thus the objects and the cultures that produced them were shrouded in mystery. Only the Bible could be read; so it provided the clearest source of data about the cultures of the ancient Near East. And since the Bible alone seemed to speak straightforwardly about its own historical and cultural context, the Bible was, in a sense, its own best interpreter.

This situation began to change, however, when scholars deciphered the ancient scripts of Mesopotamia (cuneiform) and Egypt (hieroglyphs) in the early and mid-1800s. Modern readers began to hear voices from long-silent cultures. Standing alongside biblical texts were ancient stories of heroes and gods, accounts of creation and the flood, laws, prayers, and historical annals. Today, the Bible is no longer the lens through which the ancient Near East is viewed. In fact, the very opposite is the case. Now the ancient Near East serves as the dominant lens through which scholars view the Bible.

Material Culture of the Ancient Near East

One could define culture quite simply as the particular set of beliefs and behaviors that characterize a group of people. When one cannot observe the behaviors of such a group firsthand, one must rely on archaeological artifacts to formulate a picture of the society. Scholars refer to these physical remains as *material culture*, a category that includes (but is not limited to) tools, pottery, architecture, writing, and art. Of these, the literary artifacts of the ancient Near East have received the most intense scrutiny, especially the so-called "Ancient Near Eastern parallels" to biblical texts.

Comparison with ancient Near Eastern texts has illumined every major category of biblical literature. Prayers to various gods and goddess have revealed standard forms of addressing deities—forms such as laments and hymns of praise that also appear in the Bible. Annals of Mesopotamian and Egyptian kings have provided a better understanding of the nature, accuracy, and rhetorical features of comparable biblical histories. Cuneiform law codes have enabled scholars to classify and date various legal materials in the Bible. Divination texts have shown how the activities of biblical prophets reflect practices of ancient diviners, even as they remained quite unique within that cultural landscape. From covenants to love poetry, literature from the ancient Near East has enabled fruitful interpretation of biblical texts.

Of all the so-called "parallel" texts, the ancient Near Eastern creation stories may well be the most compelling. Creation myths provide a deep sounding about a culture's conception of itself, how it understands the various relationships among gods, the cosmos, humans, and all other forms of life. Further, cultures often seek to work out critical issues such as the nature of sin, suffering, power, sex, and justice in those accounts. They have thus proven to be some of the most important texts for comparative analysis. What follows, then, is a brief survey of creation mythology in the Ancient Near East and an account of the significance of these texts for interpreting biblical creation accounts.

A Case Study: Creation Accounts in the Ancient Near East

Sumerian civilization, which thrived in southern Mesopotamia during most of the third millennium BCE, produced some of the earliest Near Eastern creation accounts. One of them, the story of *Enki and Ninmah* (*COS* 1.159) recounts how Enki, the god of subterranean waters, creates humans to relieve the burden of lesser gods who were hard at work digging channels for water in the newly created earth. Enki forms these humans out of lumps of clay (cf. Gen 2:7; 3:14), which are then placed in the womb of his mother Nammu. The clay figures come to life when Nammu gives birth to them, and she sets them

973

promptly to work. Another Sumerian text, known as *KAR 4* (see Clifford 1994, 49–51), describes the origin of the world rather differently. This account begins with the creation of the world, seen as a process of separating heaven and earth (cf. Gen 1:6–7), after which a divine council convenes and determines to slay two gods. From their blood, the council decides to create humans. As in the story of Enki and Ninmah, the humans are then set to work cultivating and irrigating the earth (cf. Gen 2:15; 3:23). One other Sumerian creation account deserves mention, the *Song of the Hoe* (*COS* 1.157). It describes the god Enlil creating the world by wielding a hoe, a tool used for brick-making among many other things. After he sets the cosmos in order with his hoe, Enlil uses it to bring humans up from the ground (cf. Gen 2:7) as one would scoop up mud for making bricks. Once created, humans take up their own hoes to commence constructing temples for the gods.

Sumerian culture had a palpable impact on later Mesopotamian ones. By the middle of the second millennium BCE, Semitic-speaking people came to prominence in both Northern and Southern Mesopotamia, known as Assyria and Babylonia, respectively. Their common language of Akkadian drew its writing system from the Sumerians. Moreover, themes and figures in Akkadian literature reflect Sumerian influence. For example, the *Atrahasis Epic* (*COS* 1.130) begins with a description of a class of lesser gods complaining about all their hard work. In response, Enki and the mother goddess create humans by mixing clay with the flesh and blood of a slaughtered god. As humans take up the drudgery of the gods, they multiply rapidly and create an unbearable din. The earth-god Enlil is so vexed by the humans that he sends a series of plagues and, ultimately, a flood to wipe out humans. Only Atrahasis, having been forewarned of the coming deluge, escapes the waters by building a large boat (cf., generally, the creation and flood story of Gen 2–11).

An equally dramatic Akkadian account of creation is found in the *Enuma Elish* (*COS* 1.111), a text that also shows the influence of Sumerian myth. In this text, the creation of the world is the result of a violent conflict between the gods. Its critical moment occurs when the Babylonian god Marduk slays Tiamat, the goddess of the chaotic primordial waters, and splits her body in two. He elevates one half of her corpse to be the heavens and stretches out the other half as the foundation of the earth (cf. Gen 1:1–8). Through the eye sockets of the slain Tiamat flow the great rivers, the Tigris and Euphrates (cf. Gen 2:14). As the new head of the Babylonian pantheon, Marduk continues his creative work by ordering his father Ea to fashion humans out of the blood of Tiamat's slain partner. In the *Enuma Elish*, like the earlier Sumerian and Akkadian myths, humans assume the heavy labor that was formerly imposed upon the lesser gods.

As in Mesopotamia, the literary traditions of ancient Egypt spanned thousands of years and preserved multiple creation myths. Three of these accounts—from the important cities of Heliopolis, Memphis, and Hermopolis—illustrate how certain common themes and motifs reappear in various forms. The Heliopolis creation account (*ANET*, 3) is the most ancient. It describes how the god Atum emerged from the primordial waters as a mound of earth. His appearance in this form recalls the mounds that emerge teeming with life when the yearly Nile floods recede. Atum alone sets creation in motion when he produces, through his own bodily fluids, the god of air, Shu, and the goddess of moisture, Tefnut. Shu and Tefnut then produce two more gods: Geb, the earth god, and the sky goddess Nut, whose body is the dome of the heavens (fig. 1, cf. Gen 1:6–8). These gods, who embody the essential cosmic elements, are part of the Ennead—a family of nine primary gods. This Ennead appears in the Memphis tradition as well (*COS* 1.15), though there it was Ptah who ultimately created these gods and the cosmos that they represent. His creativity is described not through emitting bodily fluids but through a twofold work. First he plans in his heart to create the world and then he speaks the world into existence (cf. Gen 1:3). The tradition at Hermopolis presents yet another variation of the creation myth (*COS* 1.16), here with Amun as the primary actor and source of all created things. The god of hiddenness and obscurity, Amun initiates a mysterious process of evolution through which everything else ultimately emerges. In this tradition, he is the one associated with the primordial mound that first rises from the waters of chaos.

Comparing these texts with each other and with the biblical material yields important insights. First, it is clear from this survey that even within one culture multiple creation myths could exist side by side for long periods of time. Many modern readers find this phenomenon odd—especially given current "creation vs. evolution" debates—though, in fact, the Bible itself exhibits this very tendency to confirm and record the numerous creation accounts that typically coexisted within a single ancient Near Eastern culture. The varying descriptions of creation in Gen 1:1–2:4*a* and Gen 2:4*b*–11:9 serve as the parade example of how different ideas about origins can coexist even within Israel.

Second, readers encounter ancient Near Eastern creation accounts in diverse literary genres. These include epics, songs, hymns, funerary texts, and monumental inscriptions. It is difficult to establish a single theology of creation in a given Near Eastern culture not only because of the various, divergent creation accounts within that culture but also because they appear in so many genres.

Determining an Israelite theology of creation is similarly difficult because Israel likewise described creation through diverse genres. Accounts of the origins of the world exist not only in the narratives of Genesis but also in prophetic literature, psalms, and wisdom texts. For example, at critical points within Second Isaiah, the reader encounters poetry in which the divine voice describes the works of creation (see Isa 40:12–31; 44:24–45:25; 51:12–16). Likewise, in the book of Job, God issues an account of creation in the context of a wisdom discourse (Job 38:4–39:30). Job too reflects upon God's creative work in his speeches, wherein he describes creation as God's act of conquering the chaotic waters, personified as Rahab, the sea serpent (Job 9:5–13; 26:5–14). This motif of cosmic combat appears in the Psalms as well (e.g., Ps 74:12–17) and clearly resonates with other ancient Near Eastern creation accounts, especially Marduk's battle with Tiamat in the *Enuma Elish* and Baal's conflict with the sea god Yamm in the Ugaritic *Baal Cycle* (*COS* 1.86). In the Psalms, these cosmogonic activities are routinely conflated with God's saving works during the exodus at the Re(e)d Sea (e.g., Pss 77:11–20; 89:5–18; 114:1–8; cf. Isa 51:9–10). In doing so, the psalmist modifies and reframes ancient Near Eastern creation traditions, binding them with the story of the exodus into one cosmic and creative event.

This observation leads to a third important insight about the ancient Near Eastern creation accounts. Ancient Near Eastern cultures borrowed heavily from one another. In many cases they shared names and functions of deities, details of plot, motifs, and themes. As a result, it should be no surprise that the biblical creation accounts have numerous commonalities with ancient Near Eastern myths. For example, the Sumerian theme of gods creating humans to work on their behalf persists both in later Babylonian and Assyrian creation accounts. This theme also appears in modified form in Genesis, as God appoints the human to tend the garden of Eden (Gen 2:15) and later to toil in the earth to produce food (Gen 3:17–19). Likewise, the idea that humans are fashioned from the blood of gods or clay or from both appears in virtually all Mesopotamian accounts. A version of this idea occurs too in the Genesis accounts, in which humans are created not from the stuff of gods (i.e., their blood) but in the image of God (Gen 1:26–27) and from the dust of the ground (Gen 2:7). Also, the Egyptian idea that creation commenced by Ptah's divine fiat resonates strongly in Gen 1:1–2:3 with its emphasis on God's creative word. Finally, the notion that creation was the outcome of a divine conflict between a warrior god and a sea god(dess) is broadly shared throughout the ancient Near East. It likely originated in Syria, then migrated into both Akkadian and Canaanite literature, and ultimately into the biblical text itself (e.g., Ps 74:12–17, see above).

These texts illustrate that when borrowing exists, the ideas are not simply adopted and applied indiscriminately in new literary and cultural contexts. Rather, adaptation and appropriation always obtain. It is clear then that the biblical authors did not simply copy ancient Near Eastern literary prototypes, but modified them to suit their own theological agendas. The same is true, of course, for other ancient Near Eastern cultures.

Reconsidering Ancient Near Eastern "Parallels"

When one begins to grasp the extent of the cultural interchange that these texts exhibit, it is worth asking whether in fact one should refer to them as ancient Near Eastern "parallels" at all. Parallel lines, after all, never intersect. The fact that these lines are completely independent of one another classifies them as parallel. Yet, as this survey of creation myths shows, *intersection* and *mutual interdependence* are the very hallmarks of ancient Near Eastern literary works.

It is more accurate then to speak of these Near Eastern creation accounts as exhibiting various degrees of congruency with one another. That is to say, the different Egyptian creation accounts, while not identical, share a high degree of congruency with one another. In contrast, the Heliopolis creation account shows relatively less congruity with the *Enuma Elish* or Gen 1:1–2:4*a*. That granted, there are nevertheless congruent elements between the Egyptian and other texts, such as the idea that creation is an act of separating heavens from earth, or that the chaotic primordial waters existed prior to the creative act. When such areas of congruity appear across cultures, we can inquire how and why these emerged. It is possible that the situation arose: (1) through a direct borrowing and adaptation of another culture's ideas; (2) through a process of mediated borrowing by which a third culture transmits various elements of an idea; or (3) through independent but nevertheless similar ideas endemic to more than one culture.

Ancient Near Eastern Iconography

Ancient art, or *iconography*, is another element of material culture that has proved helpful in understanding the cultures of the ancient Near East and their relationship to the Bible. By comparing ancient Near Eastern iconography and biblical texts, scholars have identified various levels of congruency between literary images in the Bible and pictorial material from the ancient Near East. Three crucial areas deserve mention.

1. *Vivid literary imagery* is a common feature in the Bible's poetry and prose. These compelling images often seem odd. For instance, the modern reader might wonder what it means for the lover in the Song of Songs to say, "your eyes are doves" (Song 4:1). Study of ancient Near Eastern iconography includes numerous scenes in which doves fly from the outstretched arms of goddesses as messengers of the deity (fig. 2). When aware of these ancient visual images, the modern reader can better understand the significance of the literary image—like the doves coming from a goddess, the look from the woman's eyes expresses a message of love.

2. The value of ancient iconography for biblical studies is not limited to unlocking native and now opaque literary images, however. Iconography serves as a *critical resource for historical reconstruction*. The "Siege of Lachish," a massive wall relief found at Sennacherib's palace in Nineveh (near the modern city of Mosul, Iraq), provides a well-known example. The relief shows the Neo-Assyrian army's brutal and effective campaign against the Judean town of Lachish (fig. 3). The Bible also describes this event, along with its immediate political implications for King Hezekiah (2 Kgs 18:13–18; 2 Chr 32:9). Both the biblical texts and the congruent Neo-Assyrian iconography provide different, yet mutually illuminating perspectives on the political and military events that occurred at Lachish in 701 BCE.

3. Iconography also serves an equally important role in *understanding religious history*. Gods and goddesses are common subjects for ancient artists in virtually every period and location throughout the ancient Near East. Thus, representations of gods, shrines, altars, and temples—and the way these representations changed over time—provide crucial data. These artifacts show how religious systems interacted and developed over the course of thousands of years and how the theological ideas and ritual practices in Israel relate to these larger movements.

Conclusion: When an Ancient Near Eastern Text Is Scripture

Situating Scripture within the ancient Near Eastern world can have the effect of archaizing the text, making it seemingly inaccessible for readers in the twenty-first century.

Yet the Christian tradition has consistently recognized the Bible's antiquity. Indeed, its antiquity has often been seen as substantiating its authoritative position. The designation *Scripture* underscores the Christian belief that the Bible speaks beyond its ancient context into our own. Seen in this light, it is not only helpful but critical to understand the differences between our culture and the cultures that gave rise to the Bible. Indeed, much harm has been done by those who have read the Bible as if it were written just yesterday, just around the corner, and just for them. Realizing the ancient Near Eastern context of the Bible provides a helpful corrective for such myopic readings.

In light of the material culture of the ancient Near East, modern interpreters of the Bible as Scripture must work within a constant tension. On the one hand, they are aware that given its antiquity the Bible requires interpretation. On the other hand, they realize that being a *faithful* interpreter requires a certain recognition—that the same Spirit that inspired the writing, editing, and transmission of the text is active in each successive interpretation, including their own. Evidence of this activity may be found in the remarkable and undeniable fact that modern communities of faith continue to be deeply shaped by this ancient text—that the Bible really can and does speak from its ancient Near Eastern context to our own.

BIBLIOGRAPHY

R. J. Clifford. *Creation Accounts in the Ancient Near East and the Bible.* CBQMS 26 (Washington, D.C.: Catholic Biblical Association, 1994); B. R. Foster. *Before the Muses: An Anthology of Akkadian Literature.* 3rd ed. (Bethesda, Md.: CDL Press, 2005); W. W. Hallo, ed. *The Context of Scripture.* 3 vols. (Leiden: Brill, 1997); O. Keel. *The Song of Songs.* F. J. Gaiser, trans. CC (Minneapolis: Fortress Press, 1994); _____. *The Symbolism of the Biblical World: Ancient Near Eastern Iconography and the Book of Psalms.* T J. Hallett, trans. (New York: Crossroads, 1985); O. Keel and C. Uehlinger. *Gods, Goddesses, and Images of God in Ancient Israel* (Minneapolis: Fortress, 1998); A. Kuhrt. *The Ancient Near East, c. 3000–330 BC.* 2 vols. Routledge History of the Ancient World (London: Routledge, 1995); M. Lichtheim. *Ancient Egyptian Literature: A Book of Readings.* 3 vols. (Berkeley: University of California Press, 1973–1980); J. B. Pritchard. *The Ancient Near East in Pictures Relating to the Old Testament.* 2nd ed. with suppl. (Princeton: Princeton University Press, 1969); _____. *Ancient Near Eastern Texts Relating to the Old Testament.* 3rd ed. (Princeton: Princeton University Press, 1969); K. L. Sparks. *Ancient Near Eastern Texts for the Study of the Hebrew Bible: A Guide to the Background Literature* (Peabody, Mass.: Hendrickson, 2005); C. Uehlinger. "Clio in a World of Pictures—Another Look at the Lachish Reliefs from Sennacherib's Southwest Palace at Nineveh." *"Like a Bird in a Cage": The Invasion of Sennacherib in 701* BCE. L. L. Grabbe, ed. (London: Sheffield Academic Press, 2003) 221–305.

Fig. 1. An Egyptian cosmography with Shu, the god of dry air supporting his daughter Nut, the sky god, while his son Geb, the earth god reclines below. (After Othmar Keel, *The Symbolism of the Biblical World: Ancient Near Eastern Iconography and the Book of Psalms* [translated by Timothy J. Hallett; Eisenbrauns, 1997], fig. 27.)

Fig. 2. Middle Syrian Cylinder Seal. (Taken from *Gods, Goddesses and Images of God in Ancient Israel* by Othmar Keel and Christoph Uehlinger, copyright © 1998 Augsburg Fortress. Used by Permission.)

Fig. 3. Siege of Lachish. Stone panel from the South-West Palace of Sennacherib, Nineveh, 700–681 BCE. (Courtesy of the Institute of Archaeology, Tel Aviv University.)

CULTURE OF EARLY JUDAISM

Amy-Jill Levine

From ca. 538 BCE, when Judeans exiled to Babylon returned to what became known as the Persian province of Yehud, to 135 CE, when Rome destroyed Jerusalem, Jews were, in general, indistinguishable from Gentiles and Samaritans in terms of physical features, dress, and use of local languages. Nor was Jewish life static: each imperial shift—Babylonian, Persian, Ptolemaic-Greek, Seleucid-Greek, Hasmonean autonomy, Roman—and each neighborhood setting from Jerusalem to the far reaches of the Diaspora influenced its traditions and practices, texts and beliefs.

Scholars no longer speak of "Late Judaism" with its negative connotations of ossified post-exilic legalism. Preferred terms include Early Judaism, Middle Judaism, and Second Temple Judaism. In some cases the Greek term *ioudaios* should be translated "Judean" to signal an ethnic group from a particular area; in other cases, "Jew"—with its emphasis on belief and practice—is the more appropriate translation. "Judaism" (2 Macc 2:21; 8:1; 14:38; Gal 1:13—14) refers to the way of life, and it has religious, cultural, and geographical connotations. To complicate the articulation of Jewish/Judean identity: Judeans could reject "Judaism" in the sense of practice and belief (see, e.g., 3 Macc 1:3; Philo, *On the Virtues* 182; *On the Life of Moses* 1.31). Conversely, Gentiles could adopt Judaism's beliefs and practices.

To understand Early Jewish culture, the best scholars can do is sketch parameters using, with caution, all available sources: the Scriptures of Israel (broadly defined), Dead Sea Scrolls, Josephus and Philo, the Deuterocanonical and Pseudepigraphal literature, Greek and Roman reports, the New Testament, early Rabbinic texts and targums, archaeology, macrosociological studies and cross-cultural models, and so on. To address Early Judaism in a Bible commentary means focusing on materials that Bible, and especially New Testament, readers need to know to understand the texts. Given this consideration together with the limitations of word count, the following ten general categories offer helpful parameters.

First, Jews claimed an ancestry from Abraham, with whom their God had established an eternal covenant. Converts were welcome (e.g., Achior the Ammonite [Jdt 14:10]; Nicolaus [Acts 6:5]; the royal house of Adiabene [Josephus, *Antiquities* 20:2]; proselytes [Philo, *Virtues* 182]). Jews generally did not seek converts, for they did not believe Gentiles needed to be Jewish in order to be in a right relation with God. Some promoted the concept of seven Noachide commandments (establishing just courts, prohibiting idolatry, blasphemy, murder, theft, sexual immorality, and eating the limb of a living animal) for Gentiles; these appear in inchoate form as early as the third-century *Jubilees* 7:20–28.

Second, Jews worshiped the God of Israel, whom they regarded as having made covenants with Noah, Abraham, and David, as well as with the people Israel through the hand of Moses at Mt. Sinai. This God became present in the lives of Israel via the holy spirit (*ruach ha-kodesh*), the Word (*logos, memre*), and Wisdom (*Chochma/Sophia*). The *Shekinah*, the feminine manifestation of the divine, has its origins in later texts (e.g., Sanhedrin 39*a*, Berachot 6a, Megillah 29*a*). Jews generally understood God to be a loving provider—their "father" or "abba"—rather than a distant judge.

Third, they related to the ancestral land of Israel, seen as promised to Abraham (Gen 12:7; 13:15–17, etc.); specific borders changed as did the empires. Galilee returned to Jewish rule under the Hasmoneans, and all evidence indicates the population's full investment in Torah and Temple (*Antiquities* 20:118; Luke 13:1). Diaspora Jews maintained their connection to the land by participating in the pilgrimage festivals of Sukkot (Booths, Tabernacles), Pesach (Passover), and Shavuot (Weeks, Pentecost).

Fourth, the Torah, their sacred book, contained the commandments of their God along with their history. Some Jews, such as Sadducees, held only the Torah as sacred; most had a broader canon including the Prophetic writings (*Nevi'im*) and Psalms. By the late first century CE, most of the Writings (*Ketuvim*) were included. Some Jews included in their canons *1 Enoch*; others 1 and 2 Maccabees, and so on. Jews heard their Scriptures in Greek, in Hebrew, or through Aramaic paraphrase (*Targumim*). Some read literally, others allegorically; interpretations were as varied as the Jews who held them.

979

These texts represented both a connection to the past and the influences of the present. By writing their story, Israel created an ethnic/national identity with its own ancestry, history, practices, and role in the divine plan. The books that were in use by the end of the first century CE constituted a canon that is close to the Jewish canon of today. They offered historical narrative, ethnic claims, specific legal teachings, and broad theological views: thus they offered a coherent identity and a breadth of theological views.

Fifth, the Torah mandated specific practices that in the aggregate served as identity markers, including male circumcision, Sabbath observance, dietary restrictions with a particular avoidance of pork, and the eschewal of idolatry. Jews needed to determine the extent to which they would participate in Greek and Roman culture (e.g., arts, philosophy, gymnasium education, politics, avoidance of circumcision); the responses were as varied as the possibilities. Some Jews saw themselves as different from Gentiles in that they regarded Gentiles as participating in idolatry and sexual immorality. Conversely, Jewish/Gentile intermarriage was not unknown.

Mark 7.3–5 refers to "the tradition of the elders," and Josephus (*Antiquities* 13.297) describes the Pharisees as following "observances handed down by their fathers" (see *m. Avot* 1.1). Some of the 613 commandments (*Makkot* 23*b*, *Yevamot* 47*b*) take precedence over others (see, e.g., 1 Macc 2.35–41 on fighting on the Sabbath). Most Jews would have celebrated a healing on the Sabbath (see Luke 13:16–17) and all would likely have agreed that saving a life overrides other commandments. Such interpretations contributed to the formation and maintenance of groups such as Pharisaic schools, Sadducees, Essenes, and the Jesus movement as well as engaged individual thinkers, such as Philo.

Commandments concerning ritual purity refer generally to temporary, unavoidable conditions (e.g., menstruation, ejaculation, childbirth). They are unrelated to sin. Sickness, unless caused by leprosy or manifested by genital discharge, does not convey impurity. Purity concerns focus on matters of life and death, with a corpse being the most defiling. However, burying corpses was a mitzvah (see Tobit 1:16–20; Josephus, *Against Apion* 2.30.211; *m. Nazir* 7:1; Luke 10:31–32 depicts the failure of the priest and Levite to do what was *expected*). Regaining a state of purity typically involved a period of waiting and immersion in water.

By the Herodian period, purity had become a strong marker of Jewish life. In Galilee, the absence of pig bones and graven images, as well as the extensive presence of stone vessels (see John 2:6) and *miqva'ot* [ritual baths] show increased concern for purity. Purity was a means of sanctifying the body, resisting assimilation, proclaiming identity, and reinforcing community boundaries. Gentiles also engaged in practices of ritual purity, usually associated with visiting temples.

Sixth, Jews had a relationship to the Jerusalem Temple, an enormous complex of approximately 169,000 square feet that could accommodate almost half a million pilgrims. It was designed, like most temples in antiquity, to reflect increasing degrees of sanctity, from the outer court of the Gentiles to the court of the Jewish women, then of Jewish men, then of the priests. At the center was the Holy of Holies. The Temple was the place of pilgrimage, prayer, teaching, sacrifice, and national identity.

In 152 BCE, the Hasmonean ruler Jonathan arranged with his Seleucid allies to be appointed high priest, and the priesthood stayed in the family until Herod's rule. Herod appointed successors from minor families; when Rome took control of Judea in 6 CE, it took control of the priesthood as well. High priest and Roman governor worked together, and by maintaining control of the priestly vestments, the governor controlled Temple festivals. When in 41 Caligula attempted to place his statue in the Temple, "tens of thousands of Jews with their wives and children" told the Syrian governor that they would not fight, but they would rather die than violate their laws (*Antiquities* 18:264; see *War* 2.197; Philo, Embassy to Gaius). The Temple also served as national bank. Roman governors raided the treasury for public works projects. At the end of the First Revolt, Rome transformed the half-shekel/two denarii Temple tax (*Antiquities* 14:110–114; Matt 17:24) into the *Fiscus Judaicus*, the "Jew tax," to be paid by all Jews for the upkeep of the temple of Jupiter in Rome (*War* 7.218).

Popular support for the Temple did not always translate into support for its administration. The Dead Sea Scrolls posit an alternative eschatological temple (11QTemple; 4QFlor 1.1–12; *1 Enoch* 89–90). Josephus (*War* 6.300–305) mentions a Jesus ben Ananias who in 62 began, like Jeremiah and Jesus of Nazareth, to predict the destruction of the Temple. In 67, Zealots replaced the high priest, appointed by Agrippa II, with a priest chosen by lot. Bar Cochba put images of the Temple on his coinage.

Seventh, Jews gathered in "synagogues" (Greek for, appropriately, "gather together") for Torah reading, worship, and general social, political, and educational activities (see Josephus, *Against Apion* 2.175; Luke 4:16–17; Acts 13:14–15). This regularized reading of Scripture in synagogues appears to have been a uniquely Jewish practice. Synagogues were not run by Pharisees but by "synagogue leaders" (Mark 5:22–38; Luke 8:49; 13.14; Acts 13:15; 18:8, 17), a capacity in which both women and men served. Synagogues did not restrict women to balconies (most synagogues are single-story buildings), and there is no evidence women were hidden behind screens or relegated to separate rooms. Synagogues welcomed Gentile affiliates.

The first-century Greek "Theodotus inscription" found in Jerusalem, records that Theodotus, a priest, a "leader of the synagogue," (*archisynagos*) and the son of a synagogue leader, built the synagogue "for the reading of Torah and for teaching the commandments" and as lodging for strangers. Although John 9:22; 12:42; 16:2 mention synagogue expulsion, early Jewish sources do not record this practice. To the contrary, synagogue discipline consisted of physical sanctions (Matt 10:17; 2 Cor 11:24).

The eighth consideration turns to family life. The *Ketubah* (marriage contract) secured the marriage and protected wives financially in case of divorce. Early Jewish culture offered several opinions on divorce, from prohibition (Mark 10:11; 1 Cor 7:11) to gradations of cause, to the most trivial reason (similar to the system available to Roman citizens; see *m. Gittin* 9.3, 10). Celibacy was rare but not unknown (e.g., *War* 2.120, 160; Philo, *On the Contemplative Life* 68; Matt 19:12; Rev 14:4).

Jewish women conformed to the same gender roles as their Gentile sisters within homosocial Roman society. They had freedom of travel, appeared in public spaces including synagogues, law courts, the market, and the Jerusalem Temple. They had access to their own funds, owned homes, ran businesses, and served as patrons as well as clients. No law prohibited their conversing with men, or men with them. They were not ostracized during menstruation or after childbirth.

Ninth, there was a diversity of messianic and soteriological thought. Not all Jews expected a messiah or held eschatological hopes. Some awaited a prophet like Moses (cf. Deut18:15), a military figure, a priest, Enoch, Elijah, the "son of Man" (cf. Dan 7; *1 Enoch* 37–71) or the angel Michael. The messiah of the *Psalms of Solomon* (ca. 63 BCE) combines the roles of king, judge, and shepherd. Most but not all expected a messianic figure of Davidic descent, and most messianic views were not militaristic. Many anticipated a messianic age marked by the ingathering of the exiles, peace, universal worship of the God of Israel, and a general resurrection. Some were apocalyptic visionaries with a sense of an imminent eschaton; some expected, and even hoped, that the world would continue. Jews did not, in general, follow Torah in order to *earn* divine love or other-wordly salvation (see *m. Avot* 1.3; John 11:24; *m. Sanhedrin* 10); these qualities were inherent in the covenant.

Finally, tenth, Jewish life was so sufficient, robust and diverse that some scholars prefer to speak of early "Judaisms." Different schools of thought, such as Pharisees and Sadducees, provide only small indication of this diversity; most Jews did not fall into any of these categories. Claims that the "council of Jamnia" (Yavneh) ca. 90 established the canon, mandated synagogue policy and liturgy, and created a normative Judaism grossly overstate the evidence. Jews generally claimed a common ancestry and history, set of practices and texts, theology, relation to land and Temple, and synagogue communities. Within these parameters, they were able to accommodate various beliefs and practices, adapt to changing rule, and survive national disasters without losing their identity.

BIBLIOGRAPHY

B. Chilton, H. C. Kee, A-J. Levine, E. M. Meyers, J. Rogerson, and A. J. Saldarini. *The Cambridge Companion to the Bible, 2d edition; Part Two: Jewish Responses to Greek and Roman Cultures, 322 BCE to 200 CE* (Cambridge: Cambridge University Press, 2007); S. Cohen, J.D. *The Beginnings of Jewishness: Boundaries, Varieties, Uncertainties* (Berkeley: University of California Press, 1999); M. Goodman. *Judaism in the Roman World: Collected Essays* (Leiden/Boston: Brill, 2007); E. S. Gruen. *Diaspora: Jews Amidst Greeks and Romans* (Cambridge, Mass.: Harvard University Press, 2002); A-J. Levine and M. Brettler, eds. *The Jewish Annotated New Testament* (New York: Oxford University Press, 2011 [forthcoming]); _____, D. C. Allison Jr. and J. D. Crossan, eds. *The Historical Jesus in Context.* Princeton Readings in Religion (Princeton, N.J.: Princeton University Press, 2006); G. W. E. Nickelsburg. *Jewish Literature between the Bible and the Mishnah: A Historical and Literary Introduction.* 2nd ed. (Minneapolis: Fortress Press, 2005); J. VanderKam. *An Introduction to Early Judaism* (Grand Rapids: Eerdmans, 2001).

CULTURES OF THE GRECO-ROMAN WORLD

John T. Fitzgerald

The Greco-Roman world requires careful analysis because of its daunting complexity. The following brief survey will focus on its political history, its cultural interactions, its religions, and its education, rhetoric, and philosophy.

POLITICAL HISTORY

The Persians were the major power in the ancient Mediterranean world for some two centuries (539–331 BCE), but their domination was brought to an end by Alexander of Macedon (356–323) when he decisively defeated them at Gaugamela (in modern Iraq) in 331. With Judea (332) and Egypt (332–331) already under his control, Alexander turned his attention eastward, going through Iran and Afghanistan, and proceeding into India. In the words of one Jewish author, Alexander thus "advanced to the ends of the earth" (1 Macc 1:3). Along the way he founded at least six cities, including Alexandria in Egypt and Kandahar in Afghanistan. The latter's connection with the Macedonian is reflected in "al-Iskandar," the Arabic name for Alexander.

When Alexander died in 323, his vast empire began to fall apart, and his generals and their descendants began jockeying among themselves for power. What emerged from these power struggles were ultimately three major Hellenistic kingdoms whose founders traced their origins to Alexander and thus are known as his "Successors" (*Diadochoi*). These were the Antigonid kingdom centered in Macedonia, the Ptolemaic kingdom centered in Egypt, and the Seleucid kingdom centered in Syria. In addition to these three successor kingdoms, there were other Hellenistic kingdoms that attained considerable distinction. Of these, the two most prominent were the Attalid kingdom centered at Pergamum, which had an excellent library and developed the use of parchment as a material for writing, and the rulers of the island of Rhodes, which, with its five harbors, became the major Hellenistic clearing house for commercial traffic between the East and the West.

For the history of early Judaism during the Second Temple period, the most important of these Hellenistic kingdoms were the Ptolemaic and the Seleucid, which fought six Syrian Wars over the control of Coele-Syria (lower Syria, including Judea) during the third and second centuries. The Ptolemies were in effective control of the region from 301 to 198, during which time Alexandria not only emerged as the greatest city of the Mediterranean world but also became a major center of Diaspora Judaism. It was here that the Old Testament began to be translated into Greek, a project that culminated in the version known as the Septuagint. The Ptolemies lost control of Coele-Syria during the Fifth Syrian War (202–195) when the Seleucid king Antiochus III (the Great) defeated them. In an effort to foster Jewish support for his regime, he granted various rights and privileges to Jerusalem and its Temple. One of his sons, Antiochus IV Epiphanes, endeavored to incorporate Egypt into his realm during the Sixth Syrian War (170–168), but failed when Rome intervened and issued an ultimatum forcing him to withdraw. It was at this point that Antiochus IV revoked the rights granted by his father to the Judeans, prompting the revolt led by Judas the Maccabee and his brothers. This revolt led ultimately to the establishment of an independent Jewish state led by the descendants of Judas' family.

All of the Hellenistic kingdoms, including that of the Maccabees, were eventually to lose their independence as Rome rose to power. Rome's expansion into, and ultimate control of, the Mediterranean world is a remarkable story. At the beginning of the Hellenistic Age in 336 (when Alexander became king of Macedon), Rome was a small city-state in central Italy. By its end in 31, when Octavian (Augustus) defeated Marc Antony and Cleopatra VII at Actium and proceeded to incorporate Ptolemaic Egypt into the Roman realm, it had conquered or absorbed all of the Hellenistic kingdoms and become the world's undisputed superpower. During those three centuries it had first gained control of central Italy by defeating the Samnites, and then proceeded to conquer the Italian peninsula (Magna Graecia). Next, by defeating Carthage in the course of three Punic Wars (262–241, 218–201, 149–146), Rome established control of the western Mediterranean, and it began its expansion eastward by engaging in four Macedonian Wars (214–205, 200–196, 171–167, 150–148). The last of these wars resulted in the establishment of Macedonia as a Roman province in 148, with Thessalonica as its capital. The subsequent Achaean War (146–145) brought the razing of Corinth in 146 and the partial dissolution of the Achaean Confederacy, functionally ending Achaia's political independence. When Attalus III, the last king of Pergamum, bequeathed his kingdom to Rome in 133, he was only recognizing political and military reality. Three wars against Mithridates VI (89–85, 83–81, 73–63), the Hellenistic king of Pontus (1 Pet 1:1), solidified Roman control of Asia Minor, setting the stage for the end of both the Seleucid and the Maccabean kingdoms, and the establishment of Syria as a Roman province in 63. Octavian's victory at Actium in 31 ended the Ptolemaic kingdom and marked the beginning of the Roman Empire. By that point, Herod the Great had already become one of Rome's client kings, having been declared king of the Jews by the Roman senate in 40 and having won his kingdom by 37. Ten years later, in 27 BCE, the Roman senate bestowed on Octavian the title of "Augustus." That same year Achaia was established as a Roman province, with Corinth (having been refounded as a Roman colony by Julius Caesar in 44) as its capital. Two years later (in 25 BCE), the Roman province of Galatia was formed. The pattern begun during the waning years of the Republic and the early years of the Empire continued for centuries. Rome controlled the ancient Mediterranean world through its provinces and its client kings, sending Romans to the provinces to serve as proconsuls (such as Gallio, Acts 18:12), legates (such as Quirinius, Luke 2:2), prefects or procurators (such as Pontius Pilate [Matt 27:11], Felix [Acts 23:24], and Festus [Acts 24:27]), and other administrators, or appointing non-Romans as client kings (such as Herod Agrippa I [Acts 12:1] and Aretas IV [2 Cor 11:32]).

Augustus (31 BCE–14 CE) and his four immediate successors (Tiberius, 14–37 CE; Gaius Caligula, 37–41; Claudius, 41–54; and Nero, 54–68) were related by birth, adoption, or marriage, and comprise what is known as the Julio-Claudian Dynasty. Following a period of civil conflict (68–69), the Flavian Dynasty arose, which consisted of Vespasian (69–79) and his two sons, Titus (79–81) and Domitian (81–96). It was followed by a long period during which each emperor adopted his successor: Nerva (96–98), Trajan (98–117), Hadrian (117–138), and Antoninus Pius (138–161), who was the first ruler of the Antonine Dynasty (138–192). He was followed by Marcus Aurelius (161–180), Lucius Verus (161–169), and Commodus (177–192). Politically and economically, the first two centuries of the Empire were its strongest, with declines in both areas becoming manifest in the late second century.

CULTURAL INTERACTION

Alexander's campaigns set the stage for much greater cultural interaction during the subsequent centuries. He did not initiate this interaction, which was already underway, but rather accelerated the pace at which it transpired. Among the texts found at Kandahar, for instance, is a third-century bilingual Buddhist inscription (*SEG* 20.326), written in Greek and Aramaic, of the Mauryan king Ashoka (ca. 268–232). Without Alexander's campaigns and the cities that he founded—his most important cultural legacy—such a text is inconceivable. The term that is most often used to describe this cultural interaction is "Hellenization," which is especially used with reference to the Hellenistic Age, that is, the period from 336 to 31 BCE. The term itself has been used both positively (to refer to the diffusion and triumph of Hellenic values) and negatively (to condemn cultural imperialism and the ruthless imposition of Greek practices on resistant Eastern populations). It is best used neutrally to describe an interactive process by which Greek customs, ideas, institutions, practices, and terms spread into non-Greek regions and, to varying degrees, were not only appropriated by some indigenous individuals and groups but also resisted and rejected by others. The adoption or adaptation of Greek culture was usually selective rather than comprehensive. Those who learned the Greek language and adopted some aspects of Greek culture did not necessarily embrace all aspects of that culture. Given this selectivity, Greek culture did not replace local, indigenous culture but either became amalgamated with it or existed alongside it. Local customs during the Hellenistic Age continued not only to exist but also, in many cases, to thrive. The same is true of most Eastern languages; although Greek became the lingua franca of the Mediterranean world, local languages continued to be spoken (e.g., Acts 14:11), and translations both from Greek and into Greek were routinely made. The same selectivity is seen in buildings. For example, whereas temples to Greek deities are well attested for cities such as Gadara (Matt 8:28), which Meleager (fl. ca. 100 BCE) called "an Attic fatherland among Syrians" (*Anth. Pal.* 7.417), there is no evidence for theaters anywhere in Hellenistic Syria or Palestine. Depending on the time and place, the degree of Hellenization was sometimes significant, at other times superficial. In general, Hellenistic influence is discernible in cities rather than in villages, and among the social elite rather than the lower classes. Except in rare circumstances, the adoption or rejection of Hellenism was voluntary, and there was never any prolonged systematic attempt on the part of the Greeks to impose their culture on others. When compulsory measures were applied and traditional indigenous practices banned, these steps were typically taken with the support of many local inhabitants. Even in the case of Antiochus IV Epiphanes, who prohibited any practice that made the Jewish people distinctive, the author of 1 Maccabees makes clear that the initiative for Hellenization came from members of the Jewish community (1:11–15) and that even the oppressive measures had the support of many Jews (1:43, 52). In short, Hellenistic cultural interaction led to social, cultural, and religious changes, some of which enjoyed broad support and others which were fiercely resisted.

Rome's rise to power brought no significant cultural change to the eastern Mediterranean. Although individual Romans in the East regularly spoke Latin and sometimes used Latin for their monumental inscriptions (as Pontius Pilate, for example, did at Caesarea Maritima for a dedication to Tiberius), Rome itself made no attempt to Latinize its provinces in the East. The Greek language remained the lingua franca of the eastern Mediterranean, and Greek became increasingly used at Rome. Indeed, Paul's letter to the Christ-believers at Rome was written in Greek, and Greek remained the primary language of the Christian community at Rome for many years. Many natives of the East traveled to Rome or became residents of the city, and numerous Romans had extensive contact with Greece and the East. Cicero, for example, was a student in both Rhodes and Athens, and served as proconsul of Cilicia, the province where the Apostle Paul was born (Acts 22:3). Moreover, some Roman emperors were philhellenes, such as Hadrian, whose journey to the Roman East in 129–131 CE brought Hellenistic influence to an unprecedented new apex in Syria-Palestine. Yet it also had disastrous consequences. His plan to rebuild Jerusalem as a Roman colony (Aelia Capitolina), complete with shrines to the major deities of the region as well as a temple to Jupiter Capitolinus, was one of the factors that led to the Bar Kokhba revolt of 132–135.

RELIGION

Religion took diverse forms in the Greco-Roman world, including civic cults, healing cults, hero cults, mystery religions, private associations, and ruler cults. It was practiced in cities and in the country, in homes and at shrines, by priests and prophets, and publicized with festivals and processions. There was continuity with the past as well as a host of new options for religious expression. Traditional Greek religion, which centered on the worship of the gods depicted by archaic writers such as Homer and Hesiod, was a continuing religious option, with temples built and worship offered to deities such as Zeus and Hermes (Acts 14:12). One key difference, however, was that the peoples of the Greco-Roman world tended to identify the gods and goddesses of the Greek pantheon with their non-Greek counterparts. For example, instead of regarding Zeus and the Roman god Jupiter as two different gods, they equated them. Similarly, Hermes was identified with Mercury, Hera with Juno, Poseidon with Neptune, and Aphrodite with Venus. The same kinds of identifications were made with the gods of other peoples, including the Jews, with Yahweh equated with Olympian Zeus (2 Macc 6:2). Such crosscultural identifications reflected the syncretistic principle of polyonymy, that "the gods have one nature but many names" (Maximus of Tyre, *Or.* 39.5).

Greco-Roman religions were polytheistic and non-exclusive, so that the worship of one deity did not exclude the worship of another. To insist on the worship of just one god to the total exclusion of others, as did both Judaism and Christianity, struck many people as being narrow-minded, intolerant, and disdainful of most of the divine world. The salient feature of divinity was widely regarded as power—an idea still reflected in the modern use of "omnipotent" as an epithet for God—so that it was thought that it was only prudent to acknowledge that reality. One did not have to love the gods, but it was foolish to ignore their power, which could be used to harm the religiously negligent. In a sense, Greco-Roman religion was essentially concerned with the management of divine power, seeking to ensure it was used to one's benefit rather than detriment. A Greek word used to designate this attitude was *deisidaimonia*, "fear of/reverence for divinity." It entailed taking precautions against needlessly offending the gods, and the Athenians' erection of an altar to "an unknown god" was interpreted as a display of such religiosity (Acts 17:22–23). Philosophers, on the other hand, tended to regard this fearfulness as superstitious cowardice, and the Pauline emphasis on love for God and confident boldness in approaching the divine (Eph 3:12) was the antithesis of *deisidaimonia*.

We also know that many pagans' understanding of the divine world was quite similar to that of Jews and Christians, prompting some scholars to speak of "pagan monotheism." Pagan monotheists may have worshiped a multiplicity of gods, but they tended to think in terms of one supreme deity whose power was conveyed through lesser divinities, such as minor gods, angels, or other supramundane mediators. This pagan monotheism, which arose independently of Judaism and prior to Christianity, is evident, for example, in the widespread cult of "The Greatest God" (*Theos Hypsistos*), which was especially popular in Asia Minor and is attested as early as the second century BCE. This pagan tendency toward a monotheistic conception of the divine, along which a henotheistic penchant to pay homage to a particular deity, means that it is fundamentally misleading to make a simplistic contrast between "pagan polytheism" and "Jewish and Christian monotheism." The Apostle Paul himself acknowledged the existence of "many gods and many lords" yet did not view that as a contradiction of his monotheistic understanding of God (1 Cor 8:5–6). Like Augustine centuries later (*City of God* 9.23), what he denied was the ultimate divine status of such beings, not their existence.

Worship typically took three principal forms: prayers, votive offerings (gifts offered in fulfillment of a vow), and sacrifices, with both animals and vegetables offered. Of these, sacrifice merits emphasis because it was so widespread and central to many Greco-Roman religions. Within this context, the fact that the early Christians, while using the language of sacrifice (e.g., in regard to the death of Jesus), did not practice animal sacrifice was conspicuous. This absence of sacrifice, which was tantamount to a modern religion not praying, was one of the aspects of Christianity that its religious neighbors found baffling.

EDUCATION, RHETORIC, AND PHILOSOPHY

Greco-Roman education, though fluid and varied, generally involved three stages: primary, secondary, and tertiary, with a diminishing number of individuals advancing to the second and third stages. The standard curriculum developed early in the Hellenistic Age, not long after Alexander's campaigns, and always gave emphasis to physical education. Elementary students, who were usually escorted to and from school by a custodian (*paidagōgos*, Gal 3:24), learned simple arithmetic, how to copy and read aloud simple texts, and how to write. Already at this initial stage students were introduced to such forms as gnomes and chreiai (anecdotes). The liberal arts (grammar, literature, mathematics, music, etc.) were the focus of the secondary stage, with a core curriculum that included Homer and Euripides as well as an extended curriculum that exposed students to Menander (quoted in 1 Cor 15:33) and some rhetoric. Basic instruction in the writing of letters was taught at this stage, and the "preliminary exercises" (*progymnasmata*), which were designed as transitional exercises that prepared students for more difficult and sophisticated rhetorical exercises, were increasingly introduced into the secondary curriculum during the late Roman Republic and early Empire, though some students did not learn them until the third stage of education.

Tertiary education involved a choice between philosophy and rhetoric, with the vast majority of students opting for the latter. The goal of rhetoric was the acquisition of the art of persuasive eloquence, an indispensible skill whatever one's profession or role in civic life and administration. That entailed knowledge of the various parts of a speech, skill in developing arguments and proofs, expertise in the rhetorical methods involved in composing and delivering speeches, and mastery of three basic types of speeches: the forensic speech, designed for courtroom accusations and apologies relating to past actions; the deliberative speech, aimed at persuading or dissuading the undertaking of future endeavors; and the epideictic speech, devoted to the bestowal of praise and blame in the present. Epistolary theory was also a concern of tertiary education, where attention was given to enhancing literary style and to developing skill in how to write different kinds of letters, such as thank-you notes for gifts received or services rendered, congratulatory letters for accomplishments and awards, notes of condolence on occasions of death and disappointment, requests, paraenetic letters of moral exhortation, letters of recommendation, and words of advice.

Various philosophical schools developed during the Hellenistic Age, with the four major sects being Platonism, Aristotelianism, Stoicism, and Epicureanism. Others included the Cynics, the Neopythagoreans, the Skeptics, and various eclectics. At the beginning of the period, Athens was the unquestioned center of philosophy, and any serious student went there to study. Toward the end of the second century BCE that began to change, in part because of the expansion of Roman power into the eastern Mediterranean and the growing interest of Romans in philosophy. Influential philosophers began to leave Athens and teach elsewhere, such as Panaetius (d. 109 BCE), who lectured in his native Rhodes and was a frequent visitor to Rome. When the Roman general Sulla sacked a considerable portion of Athens during the First Mithridatic War (89–85 BCE), it precipitated a major exodus of philosophers, their schools damaged or destroyed. This had two major consequences. The first was the radical decentralization of philosophy, with schools now established all across the Mediterranean world and influential philosophers active in various places. Posidonius of Apamea in Syria (ca. 135–51 BCE), for example, the most important Stoic of the first century BCE, taught at Rhodes and was never head of the Stoic school in Athens. Similarly, the Epicurean philosopher Philodemus (ca. 110–40 BCE), who was born in Gadara of Syria and studied in Athens, made Italy his base of operations. There were, of course, philosophers still in Athens in the first century CE (Acts 17:18), yet Athenian supremacy in philosophy was over. The second major consequence was a corollary of the first. Philosophical education increasingly involved instruction in the doctrines of all the philosophical schools, not just those of the particular sect with which one was affiliated, along with the exegetical study of the various "classic" texts of philosophy. Editions of, and commentaries on, key texts now began to appear, and histories of philosophy began to be written. The canonization and exegetical study of the Old and New Testament thus took place within a cultural context in which philosophers were similarly engaged in discussions about what the founding fathers had written and taught.

BIBLIOGRAPHY

P. Athanassiadi and M. Frede, eds. *Pagan Monotheism in Late Antiquity* (Oxford: Clarendon, 1999); M. Beard, J. North, and S. Price. *Religions of Rome*. 2 vols. (Cambridge: Cambridge University Press, 1998); P. Green. *Alexander to Actium* (Berkeley: University of California Press, 1990); H.-J. Klauck. *The Religious Context of Early Christianity* (Edinburgh: T&T Clark, 2000); A. A. Long and D. N. Sedley. *The Hellenistic Philosophers*. 2 vols. (Cambridge: Cambridge University Press, 1987); T. G. Parkin and A. J. Pomeroy. *Roman Social History* (London: Routledge, 2007); M. Sartre. *The Middle East Under Rome* (Cambridge: Harvard University Press, 2005); D. Sedley. "Philodemus and the Decentralisation of Philosophy." *Cronache Ercolanesi* 33 (2003) 31–41; Y. L. Too, ed. *Education in Greek and Roman Antiquity* (Leiden: Brill, 2001).

BIBLE AND SPIRITUALITY

Richard Valantasis

Spirituality—the practices that reflect, influence, and sustain the interior religious life of a person or community that in turn flows outward into exterior activities—has always connected deeply with the Bible for Jews and Christians because the core of Jewish and Christian religious life emerges from a sustained reflection on Scripture. Spirituality may be described as both corporate and personal.

PUBLIC PRAYER

All biblical interpretation takes place in a social context so that corporate spiritual formation emerges from interpretative strategies by individuals and groups in community. In the most general sense, the corporate spiritual reading and interpretation of the Bible represents a discursive practice, a meditative and philological exploration of the meaning of biblical texts perceived to be hidden or inherent in the words, narratives, personalities, events, and experiences expressed in the text. The earliest years of rabbinic Judaism and formative Christianity, when the books of the Bible began to be organized into the canonical texts read today, witness to this discursive practice. The rabbis debated the interpretation of Scripture and engaged with other rabbis with differing interpretations. Their students recorded these discursive studies of the meaning of the Bible and eventually enshrined them around the biblical text in the Talmud, the Jewish books that compiled the various oral teachings of the rabbis. In contemporary Judaism this discursive practice is called "learning" and it constitutes the primary contemporary spiritual practice for the majority of Jews. Early Christians also engaged in this discursive practice for the development of their spirituality. Christian scholars, theologians, bishops, and educators produced commentaries and sermons engaging the various levels of the text, searching out its hidden and spiritual meanings in a process of allegorical reading (reading for "other" moral or spiritual understandings). The central role of the mind as a medium of connection to the divine mind of God founds the spirituality of these discursive practices.

Communities of faith regularly read biblical texts as part of their worship, often reading through entire books of the Bible over the course of a liturgical season. The liturgical reading of texts achieves a number of spiritual goals: it founds the community in its sacred narrative and books; it connects contemporary understandings of God to those of the ancients who produced the Scriptures; it provides a window into the ways in which God has been perceived in previous generations; and in some cases it constitutes a set of rules for the regulation of community behavior and beliefs. Some communities, both Christian and Jewish, gather daily to read the Scriptures, to sing hymns (often including the Psalms), and to pray as part of the regular expression and development of their spirituality. Most communities also gather on their holy day (Saturday for Jews, Sunday for Christians) to read Scripture, hear an exposition of the text and apply that exposition to the daily lives of the people and the community, and to pray as a means of renewing their identity as a spiritual group by expressing and developing their particular spiritual perspective. But it is not only religious communities that use the Scriptures as a way of articulating their identity. Often the Bible is used to establish the spiritual and religious identity of a nation, as when the Supreme Court invokes biblical precedents for its decisions, or when a politician refers to a biblical text to support a political position.

Worship most always includes hymnody as a primary expression of spirituality because hymns often paraphrase, reference, metaphorize, or in some other way invoke biblical texts. The Psalms of David in particular have formed the heart of Christian and Jewish worship, not only in their direct recitation and chanting but also in their versified forms in hymns. And virtually every other book of the Bible has become part of a hymn text. Christmas hymns explore the riches of the story of Jesus' birth, and there are hymns to guide the spiritual life of the seeker through the exodus, the mission of Jesus and his followers, the transfiguration on Mount Tabor, the passion and death, and the resurrection of Jesus. Hymns make the biblical narratives accessible to the imagination, emotions, and intellect of seekers, and provide a rich medium of spiritual formation for individuals and communities. The Bible has provided ample resources throughout the ages for operas, oratorios, anthems, and other musical pieces.

Iconography and art also advance the experiential dynamic of reading Scripture and worship. For centuries, artists have made renditions of biblical stories that may be found in many art museums around the world. Moreover, it is now commonplace to find the architecture of religious buildings adorned with biblical stories, motifs, iconography, and art. These renditions frequently reflect the spirituality and theology of the age from which they come, and provide not only a window into the spiritual experience of the artist and the artist's audience but also a way of reading how they read the Bible, how they applied biblical texts to the understanding of their own lives. The standard iconography of an Eastern Orthodox Church presents the history of salvation in pictorial form on the interior walls of the church. Beginning with Adam and Eve and the creation at the west entrance to the church, the icons follow the life of the Christian Old Testament until the birth of Jesus, which is represented in a number of forms in the east sanctuary. Then from the sanctuary, it proceeds with the New Testament stories leading to the Last Judgment in the west entrance opposite the creation. In an Eastern Orthodox Church, one not only reads the Bible but also enters it and lives in it during the various worship services. The Bible also has influenced other arts that enhance the religious life of individuals and communities: plays, poems, television documentaries, films, popular music, advertising, novels and short stories, and Internet sites. These continual references to the biblical text indicate the way that the Bible has become a part of the spiritual and cultural fabric of modern society. The Bible forms an integral part of communal formation, both religious and secular.

PRIVATE PRAYER

Personal spirituality also employs the Bible as an important resource. In addition to the spiritual benefit accrued to the individuals who participate in the corporate settings, some specific personal spiritual practices have become prominent.

Ignatian

The Bible plays an important part in personal meditative practices. In its most general description, the meditator actively applies the imagination to a biblical story in order to experience the biblical event by stepping into it. Ignatian meditation, for example, begins with a "composition of place" in which the meditator visualizes every minute detail of the story as it is written, and then begins to imagine the sights, smells, conversations, emotions, thoughts, and reactions of the context and the characters in the story. The meditator thus becomes not only a spectator but also a participant in the story. Many variations of this Ignatian method exist in both individual and group settings, where a leader will guide the meditator through the complexities and intricacies of a biblical story. The goal in this sort of meditation is to bring the biblical story to life in the imagination and to break down the perceived distance between the reader of the biblical text and the text itself.

Mantra

Another very basic form of meditation is the biblical verse mantra. Taking a short verse or phrase from the Scriptures, the person repeats the phrase slowly and deliberately for a period of time, sometimes regulating the breathing in order to quiet the body and focus the mind. Many Eastern Orthodox Christians, for example, use the phrase "God, be merciful to me, a sinner" (Luke 18:13) as such a mantra, repeating it fifty or a hundred or a thousand times in a slow sequence. Frequently Western Catholic Christians will use phrases from the psalms such as "God, make speed to save me" (Ps 70:1; Catholic Bible 69:1). The use of such scriptural mantras enables the meditators to inscribe the Scriptures onto their mind and body.

Memorization

Related to mantra meditation is simple memorization of biblical verses. This practice, with its deep monastic roots, frees the person from dependence upon the written word in order to make the biblical text a living and vital part of the meditator's life. Through memorization, the body (specifically the eyes and hands) is released from the physical work of reading in order to concentrate attention on the spiritual, mental, or oral assimilation of the verse, which may even take place in the dark or in places where books hinder.

Scripture may also be used as a spiritual talisman, as a verbal or written object to ward off evil forces and to sanctify a space for spiritual activity to occur. The Jewish mezuzzah contains written portions of the Torah that observant Jews hang on every door of their houses in order to remind them of their obligation and joy of faithful living as well as to ward off any evil that might intrude. For Christians, Bible verses have been used since early Christianity to ward off the deadly vices or sins (pride, envy, gluttony, lust, anger, greed, sloth, and sometimes listlessness) in a process of using scriptural verses as a means of changing the psychological dynamics of a person from a temptation to evil activities toward the embracing of virtuous and godly ones. Even some modern Bibles contain pages of references for people to use when, for example, they are depressed, troubled, frustrated, angered, or weary. As a talisman, the Scripture verses intervene in a negative psychological dynamic or simply remind the person of trusted spiritual realities.

The talisman also seems related when Scripture functions as an instrument for the reformation of character. The reader searches out the Scriptures for clues about ways of living a spiritual life satisfying at once to God and to the person. Over years of personal spiritual work and memorization, the seeker changes to reflect the biblical principles that have emerged. In the tradition such biblical metaphors as restoring humans to the "image" and "likeness" of God (Gen 1 and 2) and "holiness" articulate the goal of such reformation.

Biblical spirituality also plays a major role in kataphatic and apophatic theology. Kataphatic theology is the theology that assembles the names and attributes of God by reading and meditating on the Scriptures. For example, because of the creation story in Genesis, God is Creator, the One who names all things good, the Good itself. Because of the exodus, God is Light, Pillar, Savior. Based on John 6, the Bread of Life Discourse, God is Bread, Life, Manna from heaven, and Eternal Life. These attributes help the seeker to discover the reality of God and to perceive God's nature as it is manifest in Scripture. Scripture comes to life as a place for encountering the divine names that then feed the mind, soul, and body of the seeker. Apophatic theology strips away the scriptural divine names to come to a knowledge of God that is beyond human discourse and comprehension in a post-discursive union with God.

Lectio divina ("divine reading") is the Western Christian counterpart to the Eastern kataphatic and apophatic tradition and constitutes the most common use of the Bible in personal corporate spiritual formation today. This reading begins with a slow, methodical, meditative reading of the text with the mind and heart attuned to the way God is speaking through it. This reading leads to meditation upon the text in which the personal life of the reader begins to blend with the text. Lectio divina ends in prayer, a conversation with God aimed toward the consecration of the reader, and contemplation, a resting in the divine presence.

BIBLIOGRAPHY

M. Cox. *A Handbook of Christian Spirituality* (San Francisco: Harper Collins, 1985); P. Sheldrake. *Brief History of Spirituality* (Oxford: Blackwells, 2007).

THE BIBLE IN THE LIFE OF THE CHURCH

BEVERLY ROBERTS GAVENTA

Any discussion of the place of the Bible in the church's life threatens to dissolve into the problem of chicken and egg, since there is no Bible without the life of the church and no church exists without the Bible. The earliest generations of Christians continued to turn to Jewish Scriptures (Christian Old Testament) for instruction and understanding. And their developing need to give expression to their convictions about Jesus Christ gave rise to the writing, the communal use, and the collection of Christian texts into what is known as the New Testament. To be sure, today the Bible is of broad interest in the academy and beyond because of its deep influence on Western history and culture, but that interest exists because of the church's relationship to the Bible, not apart from it.

If the Bible emerged from the life of the church, it is also true that the church draws its life from the Bible's testimony to God. That testimony shapes the church in a variety of ways, although given the vast diversity within the churches, any description of those ways is at best partial. Perhaps the most obvious place of the Bible in the church's life is in worship, since the reading and interpretation of the Bible is a hallmark of virtually all forms of corporate Christian worship. The precedents for this practice derive from the Bible itself, which depicts Ezra reading and interpreting "the book of the law of Moses" at a religious ceremony (Neh 8:1–8) and Jesus reading and interpreting Scripture in the synagogue (Luke 4:16–30; see also Acts 13:13–43). Paul closes his earliest letter with a strong admonition that the letter be read aloud when the entire community is gathered together (1 Thess 5:27), underscoring the notion that the practice of reading Christian texts together is an ancient one.

The Bible also plays a significant role in the teaching ministry of the church. Contemporary distinctions between teaching and preaching would have been lost on early generations; the two activities were linked together (as in Acts 28:31) and there would have been no separation between worship life and educational program. The Bible's own testimony to the necessity of education is as ancient as the instruction that Israel should teach God's commandments to every generation (see Deut 11:18–21; also 5:31; 31:9–13).

In ways that shift across denominational lines, the Bible shapes the church's very self-understanding. That may mean particular forms of ecclesiology, ranging from an emphasis on the priesthood of all believers (as in 1 Pet 2:9) to the centrality of Peter and his successors (as in Matt 16:18–29 and Acts 6:1–6). It also means particular forms of service, ranging from civil disobedience (Acts 5:29) to peacemaking (Matt 5:9) to the provision of food and other necessities (e.g., Acts 2:44–45, 6:1–6) to acts of healing (James 5:13–18). Although Christians of goodwill disagree about the exact character of the Bible's witness, they share a commitment to take that witness seriously.

BIBLIOGRAPHY

Ellen F. Davis and Richard B. Hays. *The Art of Reading Scripture* (Grand Rapids, Mich.: Eerdmans, 2003); John Webster. *Holy Scripture: A Dogmatic Sketch* (Cambridge: Cambridge University Press, 2003).

LECTIONARIES

David L. Bartlett

Overview

A lectionary is a list of Scripture readings assigned for use in the worship of the synagogue or the church. Though lectionaries have been used in some communities for centuries, the twentieth century saw a growth in interdenominational use of lectionaries for worship and preaching. In response to a revived interest in the Bible at the Second Vatican Council the Roman Catholic Church published its "Order of Readings at Mass" (The Common Lectionary) in 1969. In 1992 the North American Consultation on Common Texts published the Revised Common Lectionary, a revision of the Catholic lectionary for official use in Episcopal, Presbyterian, United Methodist, Reformed, Lutheran, and Disciples of Christ denominations. Many local congregations of other denominations also use a lectionary on a fairly regular basis.

The History of Lectionaries

According to Luke 4:16 Jesus stands up in the synagogue at Nazareth and reads the text handed to him from Isaiah 61, presumably the text assigned for that particular Sabbath. Acts 15:21 does not indicate that there was a list of assigned verses for synagogue worship but does indicate that the books of Moses were read aloud on every Sabbath. Acts 13:15 suggests that the weekly readings included texts both from the Torah and from the Prophets. The Mishnah, a codification of Jewish legal interpretation from the third century CE, indicates that Sabbath worship was to include readings both from the Law and from the Prophets.

Though there is no evidence of commonly used lectionaries in the early church, there is evidence that particular preachers had their own collections of readings that they used as the basis for their sermons. Ambrose of Milan directed that at each worship service the Prophets should be read, and then the Epistle, and finally the Gospel. From studying Augustine's sermons scholars can discover the series of readings he used in leading worship at Hippo. In Augustine's use of biblical texts it also becomes clear that particular readings are associated with particular feasts of the church.

By the sixth century in the Western Church there were lists of readings called the Comes, which were wrongly attributed to Jerome but which did have widespread use beyond the worship of any single congregation. Up until the tenth century a number of lists of assigned readings appeared. With the publication of the Missal in the tenth century CE the lectionary texts were incorporated into the Missal itself until the publication of the Common Lectionary in 1969.

In the Eastern Church we have lectionaries of the Greek readings of the Epistle and Gospel lessons going back to the early Middle Ages. The lectionaries were organized around the Gospel lessons, and the Gospel lessons were often coordinated to feasts of the Christian year—texts on baptism for the Baptism of the Lord, for example.

The Church of England published a lectionary in 1871, and the Episcopal Church in the United States did so shortly thereafter.

The twentieth century revival of interest in the Lectionary began with the "Constitution on the Liturgy" of Vatican II with its concern that the riches of Scripture—OT and New—should be provided more fully for Catholic congregants over a set cycle of years. From this directive followed the Common Lectionary of 1969. Shortly thereafter many North American Protestant congregations came together to produce the Revised Common Lectionary, a first proposal in 1983 and the finished work in 1992.

Principles

The Revised Common Lectionary provides a three-year cycle of readings for use in Christian worship. Each year focuses on one of the three Synoptic Gospels (Matthew in Year A; Mark in Year B; Luke in

Year C.) On the whole the Lectionary assigns the texts in the same order as they are found in the Bible itself, but there are exceptions dictated by the liturgical calendar. For instance the Advent readings always include eschatological material from chapters later in the Gospel than the "next" chapters in canonical order. (Year A of Advent goes from Matt 14 to Matt 3 to Matt 11 to Matt 1). Most, but not all, of the Synoptic Gospels are included as is a goodly portion of the Gospel of John, especially during the Sundays after Easter in every cycle.

In the Roman Catholic Common Lectionary the assigned OT texts for each Sunday (almost) always have a kind of typological relationship to the NT text; that is, for Christians the OT text can be read in conversation with the Gospel text, either as a kind of foreshadowing or as a promise whose fulfillment is found in the Gospels. Those who designed the Revised Common Lectionary were concerned that the typological constraint limited both the range and the meaning of OT texts that could be read. Therefore in the season from Pentecost to Advent (so-called "Ordinary Time") the Revised Common Lectionary is more apt to go through one OT book at a time, in a kind of continuous reading. For instance in year B the Sundays immediately after Pentecost provide the opportunity to go through 1 and 2 Samuel at some leisure, and over a period of almost three months.

For the sake of those churches that want to maintain the close thematic connection between OT and Gospel texts a second set of OT readings is given for those weeks between Pentecost and Advent. So while one set of lections in Year B is going through 1 and 2 Samuel in order, the other set of OT lections is drawn from Genesis, Ezekiel, Job, the Wisdom of Solomon, Amos, Jeremiah, 1 and 2 Kings, Exodus, and Proverbs.

The Revised Common Lectionary also assigns an Epistle reading for each Sunday. These readings draw for several weeks from one epistle and follow the order of that epistle. The lectionary is not designed with the assumption that the epistle text will have any particular thematic connection with the Gospel text for that Sunday. During the Sundays after Easter, texts from Acts are often substituted for the OT readings.

The Psalms are assigned with an eye more to prayer than to preaching. Psalms are chosen because of the rich possibility they provide for penitence and praise, and no particular attention is paid to the way in which their content may relate to the content of the Gospel texts. (This does not mean that the psalm cannot provide an appropriate text for a sermon in its own right.)

The use of the lectionary in worship represents a juxtaposition between the content of the Christian story and its replication in time. That is, the lectionary balances attention to the Bible with attention to the liturgical year. Historically it seems that the lectionaries were first used in conjunction with the great festivals of the church, and the richness of lectionary preaching and liturgy is most evident in those seasons like Christmas, Easter, and Pentecost where calendar and text reinforce and illumine one another.

Advantages and Disadvantages of Preaching from the Lectionary

The very juxtaposition of calendar and content can enrich both Christian preaching and worship. Furthermore the use of the lectionary has the following clear advantages.

The use of the lectionary can broaden the range of texts that the preacher preaches and the congregation hears. The lectionary provides a protection against the tendency of preachers to recycle favorite texts and favorite themes week after week and helps to ensure that, for instance, justice and mercy will be balanced not only among the attributes of God but among the sermons preached to honor God.

The use of the lectionary also allows the congregation to participate in the life of the church universal. For lectionary-based congregations, worship provides the opportunity not just to gather around a common table but around a common set of texts. Less crucially, the use of a common lectionary provides for lectionary study groups among preachers from diverse denominations as they prepare their diverse sermons based in the same assigned texts.

On the other hand, the lectionary is highly selective. The Gospel of John is seriously underrepresented. No Gospel, not even any Epistle—except for the conveniently brief Philemon—is present in its entirety. Even the decision about which verses to include and which to omit from a particular pericope sometimes seems arbitrary and oddly anti-canonical.

The list of four lessons sometimes tempts the preacher to use the sermon as an opportunity to determine what it is that these four texts all have in common. Apart from a reference to the God of Abraham, Sarah, Jesus, and Paul the answer is sometimes precious little.

Many preachers complain that devotion to the lectionary prevents attention to the pressing needs of the congregation. No doubt from time to time this is true. More often the lectionary—like the church it is intended to serve—puts the pressing needs of the congregation in the larger framework of the liturgical year and the scriptural promises.

BIBLIOGRAPHY

J. W. Aageson. "Early Jewish Lectionaries." *Anchor Bible Dictionary* (Doubleday: New York, 1992) 4:270–271; P. C. Bower, ed. *Handbook for the Revised Common Lectionary* (Louisville: Westminster John Knox, 1996); F. West. *Scripture and Memory: The Ecumenical Hermeneutic of the Three-Year Lectionaries* (Collegeville, Minn.: Liturgical Press, 1997).

PREACHING THE BIBLE

Thomas G. Long

Christian preaching, from its very beginning, was the proclamation of good news "in accordance with the scriptures" (1 Cor 15:3*b*). Patterned in large measure on the ways that synagogue preaching brought Scripture to bear on events in the present, early Christian preaching announced the events that constituted the core of the gospel—the life, death, and resurrection of Jesus Christ—in relation to the images, themes, promises, and prophecies of the OT. Luke's description of Jesus' conversation with the two followers on the road to Emmaus almost surely expresses a concise definition of early Christian preaching: "Then beginning with Moses and all the prophets, [Jesus] interpreted to them the things about himself in all the scriptures" (Luke 24:27).

The essential movements of Christian preaching from the outset, then, were in two directions. The sermon both beckoned the hearers *into* the Scriptures as attentive listeners and *out* into the world as faithful disciples. We can see these two movements reflected in Justin Martyr's second-century description of a typical Christian worship service:

> And on the day called Sunday, all who live in cities or in the country gather together
> to one place, and the memoirs of the apostles or the writings of the prophets are read,
> as long as time permits; then, when the reader has ceased, the president verbally
> instructs, and exhorts to the imitation of these good things.

Notice that both the OT ("the prophets") and what will eventually become the NT ("the memoirs of the apostles") are read. The hearers are drawn into the readings in order that, through the sermon by the presider, the Scripture may become a pattern for the Christian life ("the imitation of these good things").

BIBLICAL PREACHING AND THE ACT OF INTERPRETATION

Christian preaching is biblical preaching. While not all Christian sermons are biblical in the strict sense of being acts of interpretation based on particular biblical texts, even those sermons that are called "topical," that is, sermons based on some general theme or issue or theological concept, if they are Christian sermons, are finally grounded in biblical understanding. There is room, of course, for the Trinity Sunday sermon that begins by exploring a doctrine or a pastoral care sermon that examines the experience of grief or a prophetic sermon that engages a political development from the front page of the newspaper. But normative Christian preaching—normative both in the sense of being the *norm*, the standard by which all preaching is measured, and the *normal* and customary practice—involves sermons that are explicit expressions of biblical texts. In this sense, Christian preaching is a continuation of Jesus' inaugural sermon in the synagogue at Nazareth, in which he read a passage from the prophet Isaiah and then proclaimed, "Today this scripture has been fulfilled in your hearing" (Luke 4:21).

In order to preach biblically, preachers must first be exegetes, interpreters of biblical texts. This is a matter of prayer, freedom, and method. First, biblical interpretation is a matter of prayer because it is not finally the words of the text we wish to hear and repeat but the voice of God speaking in and through the Bible. All faithful preachers do exegesis on their knees, pleading prayerfully, "Speak to me that I may speak."

Good exegesis is also a matter of freedom, freedom for the text and freedom for the interpreter. Theologian Klaus Berger has argued that exegesis and application (of the sort that occurs in preaching) are obviously connected but that they should also be seen as separate activities for the sake of these freedoms. If the looming needs of the preacher become too dominant, if the preacher simply "uses" the text to get up next Sunday's sermon, then the freedom of the text is curtailed. It cannot interrupt the preacher's agenda by raising concerns not anticipated by the preacher. On the other hand, if the text is allowed to dominate the conversation completely, the freedom of the interpreter to raise questions and issues never envisioned by the text in its original setting is eliminated. Effective biblical interpretation is like a good conversation between two friends: each person in the dialogue is, in some sense, an independent agent and worthy of respect. If one of the partners does all of the talking or narrowly sets the agenda, the conversation will ultimately be unsatisfying. But if the interchange proceeds in freedom, each making a contribution and each attending to the other, then the conversation between them creates something new, fresh, and unexpected.

Finally, interpreting biblical texts for preaching involves specific methods and techniques. Preachers do not go to biblical texts as naïve readers or as blank tablets; they go with strategies of reading. If two people are standing on the side of a high mountain road at a scenic overlook and suddenly one of them cries out to the other, "Look!" it is not immediately clear exactly what the other is supposed to do. "Look where? Look at what?" they will probably respond. Just so, preachers as biblical interpreters need to approach biblical texts knowing where to look, how to look, and what they are looking for. In order to answer those questions, preachers have employed, throughout the history of the church, a variety of methods of biblical interpretation. At one point, the method of allegorical interpretation, that is, seeking to find the deeper, symbolic and spiritual meanings of texts, was in vogue. At another point, typological interpretation, seeing past events in Scripture as patterns or types of events in the future, was in fashion. In other eras, "plain sense" interpretation of texts or theological interpretations were the methods of choice. A number of forces determine a preacher's preferred method of interpretation: theological perspective, education, ecclesial tradition, and others.

It is tempting to say that these methods of biblical hermeneutics are developed in the academic laboratory by biblical scholars and then borrowed and employed by the practitioners, by preachers, but this would be misleading in two ways. First, for most of the history of the church, there was no such division of labor. Biblical scholars were preachers and preachers were the biblical scholars of the church. For example, Augustine wrote one of the first scholarly treatises on biblical interpretation for preaching (*On Christian Doctrine*), but he wrote it while serving as pastor of a congregation and preaching almost every day. Second, even when contemporary biblical scholars, serving in the academy, write books and articles about biblical interpretation, the best of them never take their eye off of the practices of the faithful community. They develop and refine critical methods for engagement with Scripture not to silence the voice of the preacher but to give it clarity, truthfulness, and strength.

THE METHODS OF BIBLICAL INTERPRETATION

It is a feature of contemporary church life that preachers have available not just one or two approaches to biblical interpretation but a quiver full of methods and strategies. Textual criticism, form criticism, redaction criticism, canonical criticism, sociological criticism, literary criticism, narrative criticism, feminist and liberationist criticism are but a few of the entrees on the cafeteria line of biblical hermeneutics. Most preachers have found value in all of these methods, and rather than settling in to one well-worn approach the biblical texts, it is better if these many methods are viewed as tools in a surgeon's bag. The preacher can select the best set of tools depending upon the task at hand.

For example, imagine that a preacher is developing a sermon on Mark 10:13–16, the story of the day when people were bringing their children to Jesus to have him touch them, only to be rebuked by the disciples. It would be helpful for the preacher to pull several hermeneutical tools out of the "surgeon's bag." Form and literary criticism would reveal that this is a pronouncement story and that the center of attention in the story is in Jesus' statement, "Let the little children come to me; do not stop them; for it is to such as these that the kingdom of God belongs. Truly I tell you, whoever does not receive the kingdom of God as a little child will never enter it." Sociological criticism would give another perspective, making it clear that the children in this story are not the cute "Gerber babies" that modern readers tend to see, but persons of low social standing, many of whom would not live to see age six and who are utterly dependent upon their parents, especially their fathers, for every scrap of life's resources. Historical criticism would uncover the fact that this story was important to the early church because they were struggling, in quite practical ways, with the role of children in the community.

In broad terms, preachers can use the multiple methods of biblical interpretation to explore *behind* the text, *under* the text, and *in front of* the text. To look *behind* the text is to examine the social, cultural, and historical conditions out of which the text comes. For instance, some of the rather harsh "woe to you!" language that Jesus directs against the scribes and Pharisees in the Gospel of Matthew has sometimes been misinterpreted in ways that pit Christianity against Judaism and has led to sermons that have, at least in an unconscious way, the tint of anti-Semitism. This language is clarified, perhaps even softened, in light of the fact that, historically, Matthew was addressing a young and fragile Jewish Christian community, which was in a tense yes-and-no relationship with its former community of faith, the synagogue. The text is not the language of non-Jews denouncing Jews. Everybody involved is Jewish, and the language reflects the stresses and strains of an urgent intramural debate over how God intends for the heritage and promise of Judaism to be carried forward.

To probe *under* the text is to examine the text's form and structure, to crawl around under the chassis and to see how the gears and pulleys of the text are assembled to make it work. For example, exploring under the text of Mark 5:21–43 discloses what some biblical scholars have named the "sandwich technique": Mark tells one story, in this case the story of the synagogue leader Jairus and his gravely ill daughter, but before he finishes this first story he interrupts it by inserting, like sandwich filling between two slices of bread, a second narrative, here the account of the woman suffering from hemorrhages for twelve years. This is not an accidental technique but a very sophisticated way to invite the reader to interpret the two stories simultaneously.

One place this simultaneous reading is quite strong is at the seam between story #2 and the ending portion of story #1. Story #2 ends with Jesus saying to the ill woman, "Daughter, your faith has made you well; go in peace, and be healed of your disease" (5:34). Notice, however, how the next verse reads, "*While he was still speaking*, some people came from the leader's house to say, 'Your daughter is dead'" (5:35, emphasis added). In other words, the sandwich technique in the text has created here a stereophonic effect. The two statements—"Daughter, your faith has made you well" and "Your daughter is dead"—are meant to be heard at one and the same time. The way the text is structured has, in effect, placed before us simultaneously two theological views of the world, one with the power of the gospel and one without it.

To explore the world *in front of* the text is to ask what possibilities for the preacher, and for those who will hear the sermon, the text opens up. Take, for example, the parable of the widow and the judge in Luke 18:1–8. It is important, of course, to do the homework of inquiring behind this text and under this text, to see the parabolic structure of the story and to realize both the importance of and the struggle with prayer, the theme of the story, to Luke and to Luke's community historically. Finally, though, the preacher must stand in that middle space between the text and the preacher's own situation. This parable moves to create the insight that if a widow who has no power or standing can finally wrangle justice from a judge who has no honor, how much more will God's "chosen ones" receive what they need when they cry out to God for justice. In front of this text, then, is a reassurance about prayer, but not only about prayer. In front of the text is a world in which the faithful are God's "chosen ones" and are in a relationship of deep trust with God. This opens up insights not only about prayer but about many other things, such as taking risks in faith, being hopeful in a world of injustice, and the eternal worth of self and others.

BIBLIOGRAPHY

J. Barton. *The Nature of Biblical Criticism* (Louisville: Westminster John Knox, 2007); Y. Brilioth. *A Brief History of Preaching* (Philadelphia: Fortress, 1965); T. G. Long. *Preaching and the Literary Forms of the Bible* (Minneapolis: Forstress, 1989); B. K. Lundblad. *Marking Time: Preaching Biblical Stories in Present Tense* (Nashville: Abingdon Press, 2007).

TEACHING THE BIBLE

GORDON S. MIKOSKI

The cornerstone of Christian education through the ages has been the teaching of Scripture. The task of teaching the Bible is both lofty and difficult. Teaching the Bible involves important decisions about aims, characteristics of learners, roles and responsibilities of the teacher, shape of the curriculum, and appropriate methods of engagement with learners.

Aims. In the long history of teaching the Bible, many different, often overlapping, aims have been pursued: religious conversion, edification and guidance of the church, prophetic critique and correction of society, cultural literacy, and mystical insight. While the ends of teaching the Bible can in some sense only be determined in relation both to larger theological or philosophical questions and to the complexities of social location, most Christian communities tend to agree with Augustine that the purpose of teaching the Bible is love. Most centrally, this means bringing into bold relief the amazing and tireless love of God for the human family through the ages, culminating in the life, teachings, death, resurrection, and ascension of Jesus. Metaphorically stated, teaching the Bible is akin to the preaching of John the Baptist: it points authoritatively beyond itself to the living Word of God, Jesus Christ (John 5:39-40). As the aim of teaching the Bible, love also means hearing and heeding the call to respond to God's love through grateful obedience and love for God, love for one's fellow human beings, and loving care for all of creation. For Christian communities and individuals, the purpose of teaching and studying the Bible can never function as an end in and of itself; teaching the Bible always points to reconciliation and transformation in the direction of the reign of God.

Learners. Teaching the Bible also involves deep attentiveness to the character, needs, capacities, and social contexts of the learners. Students of the Bible come in all shapes, sizes, ages, ability levels, and cultural backgrounds. Teaching the Bible necessarily involves interaction between the multidimensionality of the text and the multidimensionality of those who encounter the text in particular situations. For example, how one teaches the Bible to three year olds in an American upper-middle-class, white, suburban, mainline Protestant church school setting on a Sunday morning differs considerably from the way one might teach the Bible with older women in an impoverished, inner-city Pentecostal setting in Central America during a midweek prayer meeting. Teaching the Bible entails knowing the learning profiles, needs, capacities, and life situations of those who seek to learn from its contents. Basic principles of developmental psychology and educational sociology need to be combined with personal knowledge of particular learners in order to maximize the effectiveness of teaching the Bible. Recent research in the interdisciplinary sciences of learning and social constructions of meaning can greatly enrich an understanding of those who seek to learn from the Bible.

Teachers. Christian communities teach the Bible through the ethos they foster in their pattern of life together. That is, the life of a church—and subgroups within it—make up a significant part of what curriculum theorist Eliot Eisner calls the "implicit curriculum." Individual learners learn to make meaning out of what they encounter in the Bible partly as a result of what they experience in the social air that they breathe. Parents and other primary caregivers in the home, along with occasions for intentional instruction in the church, provide ways for learners to learn the "explicit curriculum" of biblical instruction. This means that parents, primary caregivers, volunteer teachers and youth group leaders, and peers teach the Bible. Theologically trained pastors and church educators play a particularly important role as catalysts for learning and as knowledgeable resources about the Bible. There are also countless, subtle ways that the larger societal context in which learners live teaches important lessons about the Bible and its message.

At the deepest level, the Holy Spirit serves as the primary and most effective teacher of the Bible. Christian communities through the ages have consistently maintained that divine illumination is required to understand the Bible and to grasp its central message for one's life and times. While many teachers and scholars in the humanities have rightly held that a basic knowledge of the Bible is available to unaided reason and that such knowledge is a necessary component of a well-rounded cultural education, Christian churches through the ages have and do affirm the necessity of divine pedagogy. Ideally, those who teach the Bible combine the best tools of textual, literary, historical, and theological scholarship with the practices of prayer, dialogical discernment, and openness to the subtle work of the Holy Spirit.

Curriculum. According to John Chrysostom, one of the greatest teachers of the early church, studying the Bible always involves three levels: a depiction of a some key revelatory event, figure, or teaching that has significance beyond its original facticity; engagement with what the writer of the biblical text thought about the subject matter; and a confrontation with the culture and life situation of the contemporary reader. Chrysostom made clear that teaching the Bible is never simply about the book and its contents; it is always and necessarily also about the context, needs, problems, and frameworks of meaning of the reading community or individual. Given this complexity, what specifically ought teachers of the Bible to teach?

To draw again briefly from Augustine, one can say that the central content involved in teaching the Bible is God's love for human beings and the call of God to human beings to love God, neighbor, and creation. To be sure, the central theme of love can be parsed and nuanced in a myriad of ways. Still, each part of the Bible needs to be taught with an awareness of this central theme.

There are many ways to structure the content of biblical teaching. Curricula and programs have been developed that lead learners on a journey of discovery through the Bible as a whole. Other curricular approaches mesh with the three-year Common Lectionary. Curricular approaches that emphasize particular genres of biblical literature or individual books are readily available or can be improvised. Key themes or particularly pithy or difficult passages can also serve as organizing principles for study of the Bible. Still other options highlight the importance of gaining a working knowledge about the historical, cultural, linguistic, and religious backgrounds of biblical literature.

Methods. In section four of his book *On Christian Doctrine*, Augustine emphasizes the crucial importance of finding the appropriate register for biblical teaching and preaching. The methods employed must be informed by a clear sense of the aims, capacities and contexts of the learners, the role and responsibilities of the teacher, and the shape of the curriculum. However, several other principles should be included. For instance, learning activities should be selected that allow for the active engagement of the learners with the subject matter. A variety of modes of encounter with the subject matter also tends to result in effective and durable learning. Methods of interaction between learners and the relevant subject matter should reflect sensitivity to the learning preferences, cultural norms, and interests of the learners. The methods used must reflect and reinforce the curricular content being purveyed.

Several methods for Bible study have proven effective over time. For example, a whole family of methods for studying the Bible situate study within the larger context of prayer or worship, as in the *Lectio Divina* approach. Other groupings of methods highlight the integration of the arts (music, drama, visual expression, multimedia, and creative writing). Many methods of teaching the Bible share family resemblances in that they emphasize the importance of small group interaction, spiritual care, personal disclosure, and empathy. Yet another collection of methods stresses the importance of the use of literary, historical, and comparative tools for analysis of the text.

BIBLIOGRAPHY

Augustine. *On Christian Teaching [De Doctrina Christiana]* (New York: Oxford, 1999); K. Barth. *Church Dogmatics 1/1, The Doctrine of the Word of God* (Edinburgh: T&T Clark, 1975); W. Brueggemann. *The Creative Word: Canon as a Model for Biblical Education* (Philadelphia: Fortress, 1982); J. Calvin. *Institutes of the Christian Religion.* LCC 20–21 (Philadelphia: Westminster, 1960); E. Eisner. *The Educational Imagination: On the Design and Evaluation of School Programs* (Upper Saddle River, N.J.: Merrill Prentice Hall, 2002); H. Gardner. *Frames of Mind: The Theory of Multiple Intelligences* (New York: Basic Books, 2004); H. R. Lang and D. N. Evans. *Models, Strategies, and Methods for Effective Teaching* (Boston: Pearson, 2006); A. C. Orstien and F. P. Hunkins. *Curriculum: Foundations, Principles, and Issues* (Boston: Pearson, 2004); J. Pelikan. *Whose Bible is it? A History of the Scriptures through the Ages* (New York: Viking, 2005); R. K. Sawyer, ed. *The Cambridge Handbook of the Learning Sciences* (New York: Cambridge, 2006).

CHRONOLOGIES

Old Testament Chronology

*Because of the fragmentary nature of available literary
and archaeological sources, dates are approximate.*

? Creation

? Flood

2000–1500 BCE? The Patriarchs (Abraham, Isaac, Jacob, Joseph)

1300 BCE? The Exodus from Egypt

1200–1020? The Judges

1020–1000 BCE? King Saul

1000–960 BCE? King David

960–930 BCE? King Solomon

930–922 BCE? Division of the Kingdom

Kings of Judah	Kings of Israel
Rehoboam 922–915	922–901 Jeroboam I
Abijam 915–913	
Asa 913–873	
	901–900 Nadab
	900–877 Baasha
	877–876 Elah
	876 Zimr
	876–872 Tibni [†*]
	876–869 Omri
Jehoshpaphat 873–849 [†]	
	869–850 Ahab
Jehoram 849–843	850–849 Ahaziah
Ahaziah 843–842	843–815 Jehu
Athaliah 842–837	
Jehoash 837–800	
	815–802 Jehoahaz
Amaziah 800–783	802–786 Joash
	786–746 Jeroboam II [*]
Azariah/Uzziah 783–742 [†]	
	746–745 Zechariah
	745 Shallum
	745–737 Menahme
Jotham 742–735 [†]	
	737–736 Pekahiah
Ahaz 735–715 [†]	736–732 Pekah

† Date range includes coregency years.   * Rival rule.

Kings of Judah (cont.)

Hezekiah 715–687

Manasseh 687–642

Amon 642–640

Josiah 640–609

Jehoahaz 609

Jehoiakim 609–598

Jehoiachin 598–587

Zedekiah 587

Kings of Israel (cont.)

732–24 Hoshea

722 BCE Fall of Samaria (the Northern Kingdom) to Assyria

597 BCE First deportation of Judah

587 BCE Fall of Judah (the Southern Kingdom) to Babylonia. Second deportation of Judah.

538–539 BCE Cyrus, King of Persia, decrees that the Jews may return to Judah and rebuild the Temple. The Jews return under the direction of Sheshbazzar.

520 BCE Zerubbael, the new governor of the Persian province Yehud (formerly central Judah) attempts to rebuild the Temple. Local opposition thwarts these efforts.

516/515 BCE By decree of Darius I, work continues on the Temple, which is completed and dedicated.

458 BCE With a commission from Artaxerexes I, Ezra goes to Jerusalem to establish pentateuchal law as the law in the province of Judea and to regulate temple worship, (Some scholars date this event and all of Ezra's ministry to 398 BCE and after).

457/458 BCE Ezra reads the law publicly and launches a formal inquiry into mixed marriages.

445 BCE Artaxerxes I appoints Nehemiah governor of Judah.

445–433 BCE Nehemiah serves as governor of Judah, rebuilds Jerusalem's city walls, and enlarges the city's population.

433? BCE or later Nehemiah returns to Judah and initiates various religious reforms.

Hellenistic, Maccabean, and Roman Era Chronology

*Because of the fragmentary nature of available literary
and archaeological sources, many of the dates are approximate.*

332 BCE Alexander the Great conquers Palestine.

301 BCE After Alexander's death in 323, Palestine eventually falls under the control of Ptolemy I Soter.

301–198 BCE Palestine ruled from Egypt by the Ptolemaic dynasty.

198 BCE The Seleucids, from Damascus, defeat the Ptolemies at the Battle of Panium and take control of Palestine.

167 BCE The Seleucid ruler Antiochus IV Epiphanes uses repression to stop political infighting in Jerusalem. Torah scrolls are burned, circumcision is forbidden, the Sabbath is outlawed, participation in Greek religious festivals is forced, Jews are forced to eat pork, the Jerusalem Temple is devoted to Zeus Olympios and other gods.

167 BCE The priest Mattathias and his sons, known as the Maccabees, revolt against Seleucid repression.

165 BCE Following the death of Mattathias, his son Judas Maccabeus assumes leadership of the revolt, defeats the Seleucid forces, and reoccupies and cleanses the Temple.

164 BCE Judas opens negotiations with Roman ambassadors, thus initiating Rome's involvement in the affairs of Judah.

161 BCE Upon Judas's death, Jonathan Maccabeus continues the resistance against the Seleucids and becomes effective ruler of Judea.

143–135 BCE The last surviving son of the Maccabees, Simon, becomes high priest and effective ruler of Judea.

143–37 BCE In the midst of internal political infighting and wars with the Seleucids and other surrounding states, the Hasmoneans (the later name for the Maccabean Dynasty) take control of Palestine, and Judah becomes an independent state.

63 BCE Political unrest and opposition to Hasmonean rule results in the Roman general Pompey's being invited to intervene. Pompey takes Jerusalem.

37 BCE The Hasmoneans retain nominal rule until the Romans execute Aristobulus (Antigonus Mattathias).

40 BCE Rome elevates Herod the Great (son of an official in the local Roman government) to kingship.

37 BCE Herod the Great begins to rule.

New Testament Chronology

Because of the fragmentary nature of available literary
and archaeological sources, many of the dates are approximate.

4 BCE Jesus born? Herod the Great dies.

28–33 CE Jesus' one-year ministry within this period?

30 CE? Jesus' crucifixion, death, and resurrection.

40 CE? Paul's conversion/call on the road to Damascus (Acts 8; 2 Cor 11:32).

41–44 CE Herod Agrippa I rules Judea; apostles persecuted (Acts 12); James executed.

44 CE Herod Agrippa I dies (Acts 12:20-23).

51–53 CE Paul in Corinth.

63–64 CE? Paul's execution in Rome?

66 CE First Jewish Revolt begins.

70 CE Jerusalem destroyed.

95 CE Domitian emperor of Rome; localized persecutions in Asia Minor. John of Patmos writes Revelation?

112 CE Trajan emperor of Rome; localized persecutions in Asia Minor under Pliny the Younger.

CHRONOLOGIES

Roman Emperors	Political Leader in Galilee	Political Leader in Judea
Augustus 31 BCE–14 CE	Herod the Great 37–4 BCE	Archelaus 4 BCE–6 CE
Tiberius 14–37 CE	Herod Antipas 4 BCE–40 CE	Roman procurators 6–41 CE
		—Pontius Pilate in office 26–36 CE
Caligula 37–41 CE	Agrippa I 40–44 CE	Agrippa I 41–44 CE
Claudius 41–54 CE		Roman procuarators, 44–66 CE
Nero 54–68 CE	Agrippa II 54–93 CE	—Felix in office 52–60 CE (Acts 24)
		—Festus in office 61–62 CE (Acts 25–26)
Galba, Otho, Vitellius 68–69 CE		
Vespasian 69–79 CE		
Titus 79–81 CE		
Domitian 81–96 CE		
Nerva 96–98 CE		
Trajan 98–117 CE		

MEASURES AND MONEY

Gordon B. Duncan

Calculations of biblical measures are at best approximate. For convenience the equivalents in the tables given here have been chosen as round numbers. Though obviously not exact, they lie within the limits indicated by the varying data.

Table 1. Lengths

Unit	Relation to Cubit	Approximate Equivalent
finger	÷24	.75 in. / 1.9 cm
handbreadth	÷6	3 in. / 7.6 cm
span	÷2	9 in. / 22.8 cm
cubit		1.5 ft. / .46 m

Table 2. Dry Volumes

Unit	Relation to Ephah	Approximate Equivalent
kab	÷18	.89 qt. / .84 L
omer	÷10	1.6 qt. / 1.5 L
seah	÷3	.67 pk. / 5.9 L
ephah		.5 bu. / 17.6 L
lethech	×5	2.5 bu. / 88 L
homer	×10	5 bu. / 176.1 L
cor	×10	5 bu. / 176.1 L

Table 3. Liquid Volumes

Unit	Relation to Bath	Approximate Equivalent
log	÷72	.56 pt. / .26 L
hin	÷6	3.33 qt. / 3.15 L
bath		5 gal. / 18.9 L
cor	×10	50 gal. / 189.2 L

Table 4. Weights, Sanctuary Standard

Unit	Relation to Shekel	Approximate Equivalent
gerah	÷20	.017 oz. / .48 g
beka	÷2	.17 oz. / 4.8 g
shekel		.33 oz. / 9.35 g
mina	×60	1.25 lb. / .56 kg
talent	×3,000	62.5 lb. / 28.3 kg

Table 5. Weights, Commercial Standard

Unit	Relation to Shekel	Approximate Equivalent
gerah	÷24	.017 oz. / .48 g
beka	÷2	.2 oz. / 5.7 g
pim	÷1.5	.267 oz. / 7.6 g
shekel		.4 oz. / 11.3 g
mina	×50	1.25 lb. / .56 kg
talent	×2,500	62.5 lb. / 28.3 kg

Lengths and Areas

The measure of length most often mentioned in the Bible is the **cubit**, which originated as the distance from elbow to tip of middle finger. The **span**, originally the distance between the tips of thumb and little finger of the outstretched hand, came to be considered half a cubit. In the vision of the restored temple in Ezek. 40:1-48 the dimensions are given in cubits described as a handbreadth longer than usual (40:5; 43:13). Probably this represents a return to a standard known or at least believed to have been in use when Solomon's temple was built (cf. II Chr. 3:3).

In the NT **fathom** translates a Greek measure based on the distance between fingertips of the outstretched arms, ca. 6 feet. It was used for land as well as water. **Mile** in Matt. 5:41 is probably the Roman mile of 1,000 paces (double steps), standardized at ca. 58 inches each, or a total of ca. 1,618 yards. Elsewhere in the NRSV miles are conversions into modern terms of Greek distances in stadia, the stadion being 400 cubits, ca. 200 yards. Similarly **hundred yards** (John 21:8) is a conversion of 200 cubits.

A **sabbath day's journey** was the distance one could travel from home on the sabbath without violating the injunction of Exod. 16:29. Most evidence indicates it was 2,000 cubits, ca. 1,000 yards (cf. Josh. 3:4). **Day's journey** was not a standardized distance.

Area, when not indicated by dimensions in cubits, was measured by the "yoke," translated **acre**—i.e. the land a yoke of oxen could plow in a day, perhaps ca. 0.6 acre like the corresponding Roman term—or else by the amount of grain needed to seed the plot (cf. Lev. 27:16; 1 Kings 18:32).

Volumes

The derivation of the name **homer** shows that originally it was an assload of grain, which would be carried in a large sack (cf. Gen. 42:27). No doubt the quantity became standardized along the trade routes, and at various places local smaller measures came to be adjusted to convenient fractions of this major unit. The series in Table 2 may represent a combination of 2 or more systems that developed in this way.

Measure is the regular NRSV translation for seah (Gen. 18:6; Ruth 3:15, 17; 1 Sam. 25:18; 1 Kings 18:32; 2 Kings 7:1, 16, 18; Matt. 13:33; Luke 13:21; see footnotes). It is also occasionally the translation for ephah (Deut. 25:14-1 5; Prov. 20:10; Mic. 6:10), bath (Luke 16:6), and cor (Luke 16:7).

Weights and Weighed Money

Most references to weights in the OT concern precious metals used as money. Until the introduction of coins into Palestine during the Persian period pieces of gold, silver, and bronze used in exchange had to be valued by weighing in balances.

All the biblical data about relationships among weights are found in connection with the **shekel of the sanctuary**, specified repeatedly in the P legislation (e.g. Exod. 30:13-14; Lev. 5:15; Num. 3:47-48) as the standard for offerings, esp. the contribution of a half shekel, or **beka** (Exod. 38:24-26), required yearly of each adult male. In several of the passages the sanctuary shekel is defined as containing 20 **gerahs**, evidently in distinction from a shekel containing another number, probably that referred to elsewhere in P (Gen 23:16) as "according to the weights current among the merchants," i.e. the commercial standard. Calculation from the figures in Exod 38:24-26 shows that there were 3,000 sanctuary shekels in a **talent**. Ezekiel 45:12 states the relation of the sanctuary shekel to the **mina**.

The repeated insistence of the P legislation on the sanctuary standard might suggest that it was heavier than the commercial standard, and this has often been assumed. On the other hand the reference in Neh 10:32 to the yearly temple contribution as a 3rd of a shekel, presumably commercial, implies otherwise. If the same amount as half a sanctuary shekel is intended, the commercial shekel would be heavier by a ratio of 3 to 2. Other evidence, however, suggests a lesser difference. In Babylonia the shekel contained 24 gerahs, a relation that may well have been customary in Palestine also. Evidence indicates that the Canaanites counted 50 shekels to the mina and 50 minas to the talent, and thus it is likely that by the Palestinian commercial standard there were 2,500 shekels in a talent. If so, 2,500 24-gerah shekels by the commercial standard would make a talent of the same weight as the 3,000 20-gerah shekels by the sanctuary standard indicated in Exod. 38:24-26. Probably, therefore, the sanctuary standard differed from the commercial by having a shekel a 6th lighter. No doubt the name "beka"—derived from a root meaning "split"—was used for a half of either shekel.

Tables 4 and 5 display the assumed relations and equivalents of the OT weights according to the sanctuary and commercial standards as explained above. The **pim** is included on the basis of excavated weights so inscribed. No example has been found, however, of the **qesitah** (Gen 33:19; Josh 24:32; Job 42:11; see NRSV footnotes) and its value and relations are unknown.

In the NT weights are specified only in John 12:3; 19:39, where **pound** probably means the Roman pound of ca. 11.5 oz., and Rev 16:21, where a **hundred pounds** is a translation of "talent." Elsewhere in the NT both "pound" and "talent" refer to sums of money (see below).

Coined Money

Coins seem to have been invented in Asia Minor or Greece in the seventh century BCE, and some of them soon found their way into Palestine, as revealed by excavations. The first coins officially used there, however, were the Persian gold **darics** issued by Darius the Great (522–486). Sums in darics appear in Ezra–Nehemiah; a reference to them in the time of David (1 Chr 29:7) is of course an anachronism. The Persians also issued silver **shekels**, valued at 20 to the daric, which weighed only half a shekel by the Palestinian commercial standard. Whether a tax of 40 shekels which Nehemiah mentions (5:15) refers to these coins or to weighed silver is uncertain.

Alexander the Great introduced Greek **drachmas** throughout the Near East. In the Greek monetary system, which had developed in Asia Minor under Babylonian influence, the terms **mina** and **talent** were used for larger sums, mina meaning 100 drachmas and talent 60 minas, so that a talent was 6,000 drachmas. Since the drachmas issued by the Ptolemies in Egypt in the third century approached the weight of half a sanctuary shekel, the LXX translators in some of the passages translated "shekel of the sanctuary" as "didrachma," i.e. 2-drachma coin. For "gerah" they used "obol," the smallest Greek silver coin, which was actually a sixth of a drachma rather than a tenth.

Later the drachma was devalued so that a talent became 100 minas or 10,000 drachmas, while silver shekels minted in the Phoenician coastal cities of Tyre and Sidon followed a heavier standard than that of Table 5. Thus in NT times the shekel was equated with the tetradrachma, i.e. 4-drachma coin. In the NRSV of Matt 17:24 **temple tax** is an interpretation of the lit. "didrachma," and coin in v. 27 stands for "stater," here meaning a tetradrachma. The lost coin in Luke 15:8-9 is a drachma, and the **pounds** in the parable of Luke 19:11-27 represent minas. The payment to Judas, lit. "thirty of silver" (Matt 26:15), means 30 shekels as in the corresponding Hebrew phrase in Zech 11:12. Since the Jews first minted shekels during their revolt against Rome in 66–70 CE, the coins given Judas would have to be Phoenician shekels or else tetradrachmas counted as shekels.

The money most often mentioned in the NT is the **denarius**, a Roman silver coin bearing the likeness and title of the emperor (Matt 22:20; Mark 12:16; Luke 20:24). Though slightly lighter than a drachma, it was valued more highly because officially required for paying taxes (cf. Matt 22:19). The implication that a denarius was a normal day's wage for a field laborer (Matt 20:2; cf. Tobit 5:15, where a drachma is the daily wage for a guide and bodyguard on a long journey) provides a basis for judging the actual value of money in ancient times. Perhaps the suggestion that 200 denarii would buy a minimum meal for 5,000 (Mark 6:37, 44) gives a clue to its purchasing power.

Penny as a price for sparrows (Matt 10:29; Luke 12:6) refers to the assarion, a bronze coin issued by local rulers as an approximate equivalent for the official Roman bronze as, which was valued at a sixteenth of a denarius. Elsewhere (Matt 5:26; Mark 12:42) "penny" stands for the quadrans, the smallest Roman bronze coin, worth a fourth of an as. The smallest Greek bronze coin, the lepton, is represented by the **two copper coins** contributed by a poor widow, which together are said to equal a quadrans (Mark 12:42).

INDEX

A

Aaron, 38-43, 50-52, 57, 63-65, 70, 78, 83, 85-86, 90, 92-97, 106, 119, 221, 268, 497, 565, 577-578, 625, 886, 952

Aaronic priesthood, 86-89, 101, 158, 242, 245, 249-250, 341-342, 537

Abaddon, 358, 929

Abba, 674, 829

Abednego, 586

Abel, 1, 5-7, 10, 16, 22-23, 25, 30, 32, 148, 212, 891

Abiathar, 190, 198, 200, 209-210, 216-217, 426

Abigail, 189, 198-199, 203, 210

Abihu, 50, 65, 249

Abimelech, Canaanite king, 18-19, 22, 24

Abimelech, son of Gideon, 162, 171-172, 174, 207, 319

Abiram, 83, 94-95, 102, 120, 624

Abishag, 216-217

Abishai, 199, 203, 207, 210-211, 213

Abner, 199, 201-204, 210-211, 213

Abraham, 36, 44, 52, 72, 79-80, 117, 119, 133, 147, 150, 160, 173, 175, 233, 241, 254, 276, 320, 323, 338-339, 410-411, 414, 431, 453, 462, 494, 537, 549, 551, 574, 577, 587, 626, 632, 671, 680-682, 685, 700, 702-703, 714-715, 720-721, 723, 741, 746, 752, 771-772, 774, 778-779, 825, 827-828, 830, 881, 884, 887-888, 891, 896, 951-952, 964, 979, 994, 1000 (occurs 192x in Genesis)

Abram (Abi-ram), 2, 10-15, 25, 146, 553

Absalom, 201, 203-204, 208-211, 310

Acco, 154

Achan, 143-144, 150-152, 159, 241

Achish, 197, 199-200, 319

Achor, 151

Acrostic, 308, 312, 316, 319-320, 340, 342, 349, 351, 366, 451, 454, 518-519, 579, 960

Acts of the Apostles, 33, 37, 151, 159, 340, 359, 415, 487, 490, 500, 502, 633, 635, 640-641, 654, 656, 659, 661-663, 667, 670-672, 674-675, 677-680, 682-683, 685-692, 696-697, 701-708, 732, **735-767**, 770-771, 779-780, 783, 786-790, 805, 808-809, 816, 822, 825-827, 831, 834, 839, 842, 844-847, 852, 856, 858, 860, 868-869, 883, 895, 899-900, 904-905, 911, 917, 922-925, 937, 943, 948, 967-970, 972, 979, 981, 984-987, 991-993, 1002-1003 (occurs 102x in the Acts of the Apostles)

Acts of Paul, 949

Adam, 4-7, 9-10, 32, 100, 241, 300, 562, 571, 578, 684-685, 774-775,

Adam (city), 148, 496

Additions to Esther, 552, 555, 557, 590, 620

Admah, 498

Adonijah, 203, 216-217

Adoption, 77, 248, 379, 644, 778, 829, 839, 984-985

Adultery, 72, 74, 87, 109, 129-130, 179, 201, 207-208, 297, 300, 323, 354, 419, 429, 445, 495, 564, 570, 589-590, 632, 636, 649, 668, 720, 860

B

INDEX

C

D

H

K

L

M

N

O

P

Q

R

S

T

W

X

Y

Z